THE PERENNIAL DICTIONARY of WORLD RELIGIONS

The Perennial Dictionary of World Religions

Keith Crim
General Editor

Roger A. Bullard
Larry D. Shinn
Associate Editors

1817
Harper & Row, Publishers, San Francisco
New York, Grand Rapids, Philadelphia, St. Louis
London, Singapore, Sydney, Tokyo, Toronto

FIRST HARPER & ROW PAPERBACK EDITION PUBLISHED IN 1989. REPRINTED BY ARRANGEMENT WITH ABINGDON PRESS.

Originally published as *Abingdon Dictionary of Living Religions.*

Interior Design by Nancy G. Johnstone

Library of Congress Cataloging-in-Publication Data

Dictionary of world religions / Keith Crim, general editor ; Roger A. Bullard, Larry D. Shinn, associate editors. — 1st Harper & Row pbk. ed.

p. cm.

Reprint. Originally published under title: Abingdon dictionary of living religions. Nashville, Tenn. : Abingdon, 1981.

ISBN 0-687-00409-5

ISBN 0-06-061613-X (pbk.)

1. Religions—Dictionaries. I. Crim, Keith R. II. Bullard, Roger Aubrey. III. Shinn, Larry D., 1942- . IV. Title: Abingdon dictionary of living religions.

BL31.A24 1989

291'.03—dc19 89-45260

CIP

89 90 91 92 93 RRD 10 9 8 7 6 5 4 3 2 1

C O N T R I B U T O R S

Charles J. Adams, Professor and Director, Institute of Islamic Studies, McGill University: *'Abdul-Bahā; Bāb; Bahā'ī; Bahā'Ullāh; Shoghi Effendi*

Roy C. Amore, Associate Professor, Department of Religious Studies, University of Windsor: *Āsavas; Dāna; Dhammapada; Dukkha; Eightfold Path; Fable; Fate; Four Noble Truths; Jātaka; Kilēsa; Mahābodhi Society; Nirodha; Pūña; Sakka; Sārnāth; Sīla; Taṇhā; Vipassanā*

Phillip H. Ashby, William H. Danforth Professor of Religion, Emeritus, Princeton University: *Hinduism*

William S. Babcock, Associate Professor of Church History, Perkins School of Theology: *Art and Architecture, Christian; Cathedral; Cross; Icon*

George Baker, Managing Principal, Baker & Associates, San Francisco: *Buddhism in America*

James S. Bare, Education Specialist, Control Data Corporation: *Apsaras; Aryan; Atman; Bāṇa; Bhāsa; Cakra; Dāsa; Dhruva; Dravidian; Ghee; Iṣṭa Devatā; Kali Yuga; Karma-Yoga; Kaśyapa; Kurukṣetra; Mārga; Nālandā; Nāstika; Pāṇḍava; Rūpa; Sarvodaya; Smārtas; Smṛti; Śrī; Śruti; Śuṅga; Sūrdās; Sūtra; Tat Tvam Asi; Thug; Vaikuṇṭha; Yakṣa; Yantra; Yogi*

Leonard Emmanuel Barrett, Professor of Religion and Culture, Temple University: *Rastafarian Movement*

Patricia Lyons Basu, Assistant Professor, Department of Social Sciences, Elizabeth City State University: *Akbar; Aurangzīb; Bodhi; Kabīr; Khajurāho; Konārak; Tagore*

Agehananda Bharati, Professor of Anthropology, Syracuse University: *Kuṇḍalinī; Tantrism*

Kalman P. Bland, Associate Professor of Religion (Jewish Studies), Duke Univesity: *Abravanel, Isaac; Baal Shem Tov; Caro, Joseph; Dibbuk; En Sof; Gematria; Gilgul; Golem; Hasidism; Jacob ben Meir Tam; Judah ha-Levi; Kabbala; Kimḥi, David; Kuzari; Lilith; Lubavicher Movement; Luria, Isaac; Maggid; Maggid of Mazeritz; Merkabah Mysticism; Mishneh Torah; Moses ben Maimon; Moses ben Naḥman; Naḥman of Bratslav; Rebbe; Saadiah ben Joseph; Sabbatai Zvi; Sefer Bahir; Shulhan Aruch; Simeon bar Yohai; Solomon ben Gabirol; Solomon ben Isaac; Wandering Jew; Zaddik; Zohar*

H. Lawrence Bond, I. G. Greer Professor of History, Appalachian State University: *Antony of Padua; Babylonian Captivity of the Church; Becket, Thomas à; Bede, the Venerable; Boniface VIII; Crusades; Great Schism; Gregory I; Gregory VII; Hospitalers; Innocent III; Joan of Arc; Leo I; Leo X; Nicholas I; Nicholas of Cusa; Patrick, St.; Templars; Wenceslas*

Noah S. Brannen, International Christian University, Tokyo: *Hōza; Ikeda, Daisaku; Kōmeito; Makiguchi Tsunesaburo; Mappō; Naganuma, Myōkyō; Nichiren; Nichiren Buddhism; Niwano, Nikkyo; Risshō Kōseikai; Sōka Gakkai; Taisekiji*

R. C. Briggs, Emeritus Professor, New Testament Interpretation, Interdenominational Theological Center, Atlanta: *Angels; Antichrist; Apocalyptic; Apostle; Eschatology; Heaven and Hell; Justification by Faith; Logos; Paul; Satan*

Roger A. Bullard, Professor of Religion and Philosophy, Atlantic Christian College: *Abraham; Basil the Great; Elijah; Footwashing; Gabriel; Great Schism; Hagia Sophia; John the Baptist; Livingstone; Schweitzer*

Kenelm Burridge, Professor of Anthropology, University of British Columbia: *Oceanic Tribal Religions*

Eamon R. Carroll, O. Carm., Professor of Theology, Loyola University of Chicago: *Annunciation; Assumption of Mary; Ave Maria; Immaculate Conception; Magnificat; Mary; Virgin Birth*

JAMES P. CARSE, Associate Professor of Religion, New York University: *Death; Evil*

JOHN ROSS CARTER, Associate Professor of Philosophy and Religion, Director of Chapel House and of the Fund for the Study of the Great Religions of the World, Colgate University: *Bodhisattva; Kṣhitigarba; Maitreya; Mañjuśrī*

KENNETH K. S. CH'EN, Emeritus Professor of Oriental Languages, University of California, Los Angeles: *Buddhism*

IRA CHERNUS, Associate Professor of Religious Studies, University of Colorado: *Aggadah; Chumash; Haggadah; Masoretes; Midrash; Pirke Aboth; Targum*

FRED W. CLOTHEY, Associate Professor and Chairman, Department of Religious Studies, University of Pittsburgh: *Kāpālika; Kārttikeya; Murukaṉ; Nāyaṉār; Pilgrimage; Ritual; Skanda*

EARLE JEROME COLEMAN, Associate Professor of Philosophy and Religious Studies, Virginia Commonwealth University: *Abrupt Doctrine; Absolute; Being and Nonbeing; Dharmakāya; Ideation; Mahāyāna; Mandala; Mantrayāna; Monism; Nirmānakāya; Revelation and Manifestation; Sambhogakāya; Triple Body; Vairocana; Vajrayāna; Vasubandhu; Vehicle; Yogācāra*

JOHN E. COLLINS, Associate Professor of Religion, Wake Forest University: *Aurobindo; Sāvitrī*

PAUL B. COURTRIGHT, Assistant Professor, Department of Religious Studies, University of North Carolina at Greensboro: *Ashram; Āśrama; Brahmacārin; Gaṇeśa; Gṛhastha; Mīrābāī; Nāmdev; Sannyāsin; Vānaprastha*

JULIA R. CRIM, Freelance Writer, New York City: *Art and Architecture, Buddhist; Congregationalism; Episcopacy; New Testament; Old Testament; Theosophy*

KEITH CRIM, Professor of Philosophy and Religious Studies, Virginia Commonwealth University: *Agnosticism; Ainu Religion; Anthroposophy; Aramaic; Cargo Cult; Children of God; Christ; Dengyō Daishi; Deuterocanonicals; Divine Light Mission; Established Church; Fátima, Our Lady of; Free Church; Gurdjieff; Halo; Immortality; Jen; Kōbō Daishi; Korean Religion; Li; Lohan; Lucifer; Meiji; Moon, Sun Myung; Necromancy; Passion; Presbyter; Presbyterianism; Preta; Ritsu; Roshi; Ryobu Shintō; Shōtoku; Steiner, Rudolf; Subud; Sunni; Tuṣita Heaven; Unification Church; Wu Wei*

WALTER T. DAVIS, JR., Executive Director, Atlantans for International Education and Associate Professor, Sociology of Religion, Interdenominational Theological Center, Atlanta: *Christianity in Africa; Kimbanguism*

DONALD G. DAWE, Professor of Theology, Union Theological Seminary in Virginia: *Bardo Thodöl; Bön; Buddhism, Tibetan; Dalai Lama; Lama; Oṃ Maṇipadme Hūm; Padma-Sambhava; Panchen Lama; Prayer Wheel; Salvation*

FREDERICK MATHEWSON DENNY, Associate Professor of Religious Studies, University of Colorado: *Adhān; Apostasy in Islam; Circumcision (Islam); Food Proscriptions, Muslim; Hospitality in Islam; Jihād; Kalām; Khuṭba; Kufr; Marriage and Divorce in Islam; Mu'tazila; Pillars of Islam; Prayer in Islam; Purdah; Purification; Sajjāda; Shirk; Tajwīd; Turban; Wahhābīya; Zakāt*

WALTER B. DENNY, Associate Professor of Art History, University of Massachusetts at Amherst: *Art and Architecture, Islamic; Azhār Mosque; Dome of the Rock; Mosque; al-Quds*

CORNELIA DIMMITT, Associate Professor of Theology, Georgetown University: *Yuga*

EDWARD C. DIMOCK, JR., Distinguished Service Professor, Department of South Asian Languages and Civilizations, The University of Chicago: *Caitanya; Gītā Govinda; Gopī; Jayadeva; Kīrtana; Rādhā; Vaiṣṇavism*

RICHARD HENRY DRUMMOND, Professor of Ecumenical Mission and History of Religions, University of Dubuque Theological Seminary: *Ajātasattu; Ārāḍa Kālāma; Bodhgayā; Buddha, Life of Gautama; Devadatta; Gautama; Kapilavastu; Kusinārā; Lumbinī; Makkhali-Gosāla; Māra; Māyā, Mother of Buddha; Moggallāna; Rajagṛha; Śākyamuni; Sāriputta; Siddhārtha; Suddhodana; Tathāgata; Udraka Rāmaputra; Vaiśālī*

DONALD F. DURNBAUGH, Professor of Church History, Bethany Theological Seminary: *Amish; Boehme, Jakob; Brethren, Church of the; Brethren of the Common Life; Mennonites; Moravians; Pietism; Spener, Philipp*

H. BYRON EARHART, Professor of Religion, Western Michigan University: *Butsudan; Fuji, Mt.; Hachiman; Isé; Izanagi and Izanami; Japanese Religion; Jikaku Daishi; Jimmu Tennō; Kamakura; Nembutsu; Pure Land; Pure Land Sects; Shingon; Shinran; Shintō; Tea Ceremony; Yamabushi*

DIANA L. ECK, Assistant Professor of Hindu Religion, Department of Sanskrit and Indian Studies, Harvard University: *Ganges; Hindu Sacred Cities; Hindu Sacred Rivers*

CLIFFORD W. EDWARDS, Associate Professor of Philosophy and Religious Studies, Virginia Commonwealth University: *Amaterasu; Bodhidharma; Buddha, General Concepts of; Bushidō; Chi-tsang; Chih-i; Daibutsu; Daimoku; Dharmadhātu; Diamond Cutter; Dōgen; Fa-hsiang; Haiku; Hakuin Ekaku; Horyu-ji; Hsüan-tsang; Hui-neng; Ichijitsu; Kōan; K'uei-chi; Lotus Posture; Pagoda; Satori; Seng-chao; Suzuki, D.T.; Tao-sheng; Tathatā; Tendai; Zazen; Zen*

ROBERT S. ELLWOOD, JR., Bishop James W. Bashford Professor of Oriental Studies, School of Religion, University of Southern California: *Black Mass; Christadelphians; Demons, Demonology; Freemasonry; Jehovah's Witnesses; Rosicrucians; Satanism; Scientology; Spiritualism; Swedenborgianism*

MELVIN B. ENDY, JR., Associate Dean of the College and Associate Professor of Religion, Hamilton College: *Fox, George; Friends, Society of; Oneida Community; Penn, William; Shakers*

LESTER FAGEN, Graduate Student, The Jewish Theological Seminary of America: *Baeck, Leo; Buber, Martin; Cohen, Hermann; Heschel, Abraham; Kaplan, Mordecai; Mendelssohn, Moses; Musar Movement; Rosenzweig, Franz; Schechter, Solomon; Wise, Isaac*

NANCY E. AUER FALK, Professor of Religion, Western Michigan University: *Women, Status and Role in Religion*

LOUIS C. FARON, Professor of Anthropology, State University of New York at Stony Brook: *South American Tribal Religion*

JOHN Y. FENTON, Associate Professor, Department of Religion, Emory University: *Bible; Founders, Religious; Scriptures, Sacred*

MICHAEL FISHBANE, Associate Professor of Biblical Studies, S. Lane Chair in Jewish History and Social Ethics, Brandeis University: *Judaism*

EVA FLEISCHNER, Professor of Religion, Montclair State College: *Anti-Semitism; Badge, Jewish; Blood Libel; B'nai B'rith; Crystal Night; Ghetto; Holocaust; Profanation of the Host; Protocols of the Elders of Zion; Yad Vashem*

KENDALL W. FOLKERT, Associate Professor of Religion, Central Michigan University: *Ādinātha; Ājīvika; Cārvāka; Digambara; Jainism; Jīva; Kaivalya; Mahāvīra; Śvetāmbara; Tīrthaṅkara*

KENNETH J. FOREMAN, JR., Professor of Church History, Reformed Theological Seminary, Jackson, Mississippi: *Christianity in Asia*

SAM D. GILL, Associate Professor of Religious Studies, Arizona State University: *Shamanism; Time*

WILLIAM ALBERT GRAHAM, Associate Professor of Islamic Religion, Harvard University: *Bukhārī; Burdah; Ḥadīth; Ijmā'; Mawlid; Muslim ibn al-Ḥajjāj; Qur'ān; Shafā'a; Sharia; 'Ulamā'*

ROWAN A. GREER, Associate Professor of Anglican Studies, Yale Divinity School: *Agnus Dei; Alleluia; Amen; Ave Verum Corpus; Benedictus Qui Venit; Breviary; Credo; Dies Irae; Divine Office; Dominus Vobiscum; Doxology; Gloria in Excelsis; Gloria Patri; Hosanna; IHS; Kyrie Eleison; Lectionary; Litany; Liturgy, Christian; Lord's Prayer; Mass; Miserere Nobis; Missal; Nunc Dimittis; Offertory; Requiem; Sanctus; Sursum Corda; Te Deum*

ROBERT C. GREGG, Associate Professor, Patristics and Medieval Church History, Duke Divinity School: *Apostolic Succession; Arianism; Athanasius; Church Fathers; Docetism; Holy Spirit; Homoousion; Mandeans; Manicheism; Marcion; Origen; Orthodoxy and Heresy; Pelagianism; Trinity*

DENNIS E. GROH, Professor of the History of Christianity and Director, The Center for the Study of Eastern Mediterranean Religion and Culture, Garrett-Evangelical Theological Seminary: *Apostasy; Apostolic Fathers; Augustine; Christology; Councils of the Church; Donatism; Filioque; Gnosticism; Iconoclastic Controversy; Jerome; Monophysitism; Montanism; Nestorianism; Nicaea, Council of*

RITA M. GROSS, Associate Professor of Philosophy and Religious Studies, University of Wisconsin, Eau Claire: *Feminine Dimensions of the Sacred*

JOSEPH GUTMANN, Professor of Art History, Wayne State University: *Art and Architecture, Jewish*

THOMAS O. HALL, JR., Professor and Chairman, Department of Philosophy and Religious Studies, Virginia Commonwealth University: *Ascension of Christ; Atonement; Communion of the Saints; Dispensation; Incarnation; Predestination; Rapture; Redemption; Repentance; Second Coming; Sin, Christian and Jewish; Sin, Original; Sin, Unforgivable; Sins, Seven Deadly; Virtues, Seven; Zion*

RICHARD L. HARRISON, JR., Associate Professor of Church History, Lexington Theological Seminary: *Albigenses; Anabaptists; Bezer; Bucer; Campbell, Alexander; Christian Churches (Disciples of Christ); Huss; Lollards; Savonarola; Tyndale; Waldenses; Wycliffe; Zwingli*

NORVIN J. HEIN, Professor of Comparative Religion and Director of Graduate Studies, Department of Religious Studies, Yale University: *Avatar; Līlā; Mathurā; Rāmcaritmānas; Tulsī Dās*

JAMES HELFER, Department of Religion, Wesleyan University: *Āraṇyaka; Avidyā; Brahmā; Brahma Sūtras; Brahman; Kṣatra; Upaniṣads; Vidyā; Yājñavalkya*

JAMES HENNESEY, S.J., Professor of the History of Christianity, Boston College: *Aggiornamento; Anathema; Antipope; Bull; Canon Law; Dispensation; Ex Cathedra; Excommunication; Imprimatur; Index Librorum Prohibitorum; Infallibility; John XXIII; Leo XIII; Loisy, Alfred; Modernism; Papacy; Roman Catholicism; Vatican Councils*

LOUIS A. HIEB, Head Special Collections Librarian, The University of Arizona Library: *Native American Tribal Religion*

ALF HILTEBEITEL, Associate Professor, Department of Religion, George Washington University: *Bharata; Bhīma; Bhīṣma; Damayantī; Dhṛtarāṣṭra; Draupadī; Droṇa; Duryodhana; Karṇa; Mahābhārata; Nārada; Yudhiṣṭhira*

FREDERICK H. G. HOLCK, Academic Vice-President, North Carolina Wesleyan College: *Asceticism*

THOMAS J. HOPKINS, Professor of Religious Studies, Franklin and Marshall College: *Bhakti Hinduism; Nārāyaṇa; Prasāda; Pūjā; Vishnu*

D. DENNIS HUDSON, Professor, Department of Religion, Smith College: *Āḻvār; Arjuna; Bhagavad Gītā; Mīnākṣī*

LEON HURVITZ, Professor, Department of Asian Studies, University of British Columbia: *Meru, Mt.; Lotus Sūtra*

DOROTHY IRVIN, Assistant Professor, College of St. Catherine: *Ezra; Jehovah; Kethubim; Nebi'im; Sheol; Tanak*

RAPHAEL ISRAELI, Lecturer in Chinese History and Islamic Civilization, Hebrew University, Jerusalem: *Islam in China*

DONALD R. JACOBS, Executive Director, Mennonite Christian Leadership Foundation: *Conversion*

CLIFFORD REIS JONES, Visiting Associate Professor of Asian Drama, Department of Drama and Theatre, University of Hawaii at Manoa: *Art and Architecture, Hindu; Ellorā; Taj Mahal*

MARK JUERGENSMEYER, Associate Professor of Religious Studies, the Graduate Theological Union and the University of California, Berkeley; Co-Director; Berkeley/Harvard Cooperative Program in Comparative Religion: *Hare Krishna; Hinduism in America; Transcendental Meditation*

LEANDER E. KECK, Dean and Winkley Professor of Biblical Theology, Yale Divinity School: *Apocrypha; Beatitudes; Gospel; Jesus; Kingdom of God; Resurrection; Sermon on the Mount*

MENACHEM MARC KELLNER, Senior Lecturer, Department of Jewish Thought, University of Haifa: *Eretz Israel; Haskalah; Marranos; Messiah; Orthodox Judaism; Reform Judaism*

VESELIN KESICH, Professor of New Testament, St. Vladimir's Orthodox Theological Seminary; Faculty Member, Comparative Religion, Sarah Lawrence College: *Armenian Church; Athos, Mt.; Constantine; Coptic Church; Dukhobors; Ethiopic Church; Greek Orthodox Church; Jacobite Church; Maronite Churches; Old Believers; Old Catholics; Orthodox Churches; Russian Orthodox Church; Uniat Churches*

CHARLES F. KEYES, Professor of Anthropology and International Studies; University of Washington: *Hinduism in Southeast Asia; Southeast Asian Tribal Religion*

CHRISTOPHER R. KING, Assistant Professor of Communication Studies, University of Windsor: *Bharatanāṭyam; Hindī; Kālidāsa; Kathak; Kathākali; Kauṭilya; Mudrā*

WINSTON KING, International Student House, Kyoto: *Anatta; Anicca; Mahāsatipaṭṭhāna Sutta; Meditation, Buddhist*

DAVID R. KINSLEY, Associate Professor of Religious Studies, McMaster University: *Durgā; Goddess (India); Kālī; Lakṣmī; Pārvatī; Pṛthivī; Śakti; Sarasvatī; Satī*

DAVID M. KNIPE, Professor, Department of South Asian Studies, University of Wisconsin: *Aditi; Agni; Agnihotra; Ājur Veda; Āśvins; Brāhmaṇa; Bṛhaspati; Indra; Mitra; Pitṛ; Prajāpati; Rāhu; Rig Veda; Ṛta; Rudra; Sacrifice; Sāma Veda; Soma; Śrāddha; Sūrya; Varuṇa; Vāyu; Veda; Vedic Hinduism; Viśvakarman; Yajña; Yajur Veda; Yūpa*

ROBERT KOLB, Assistant Professor, Concordia College, Saint Paul: *Luther; Lutheran Churches; Reformation, Protestant*

KOSUKE KOYAMA, Professor of Ecumenics and World Christianity, Union Theological Seminary, New

York: *Kagawa; Little Flock Movement; Missions, Christian; Mukyōkai; Nee, Watchman; Ricci; Uchimura*

Whalen Lai, Assistant Professor, Program in Religious Studies, University of California, Davis: *Icchantika; Nara Buddhism*

Gerald James Larson, Professor of History of Religions, University of California, Santa Barbara: *Ahaṃkāra; Āsana; Dhyāna; Guṇa; Haṭha Yoga; Īśvara; Patañjali; Prakṛti; Prāṇayāma; Puruṣa; Siddhi; Yoga*

Bruce B. Lawrence, Professor of Religion, Duke University: *'Abbāsids; 'Abd al-Qādir Bedil; 'Abd al-Qādir Jilāni; Afghānī, Jamāl ad-Dīn; Aḥmad al-Badawī; Aḥmadiyya; Bisṭāmī; Charms and Amulets; Dervish; Dhikr; Dhu'l-Nūn Miṣrī; Dreams and Visions; Faqīr; Firdausī; al-Ghazzālī; Ḥāfiz Shīrāzī; al-Ḥallāj; Hejaz; Hira, Mt.; Ibn 'Arabī; Ibn Ḥazm; Ibn Rushd; Idris; Islam; Islam in South Asia; Junayd; Khālid; Khiḍr; Lāt; al-Māturīdī; Miracles; Mir'āj; Muhammad 'Abdūh; Muslim; Nabi; Nafs; Persian; Rūḥ; Rūmī, Jalāl ad-Dīn; Ṣaḥāba; Satan; Ṣawm; Shahāda; Shahīd; Shaikh; Sin, Muslim Concept; Sufism; Ṭarīqa; Tasbīh; Tawḥīd; Umayyads; Umma; 'Urs; Walī; Waqf; Wird*

John H. Leith, Pemberton Professor of Theology, Union Theological Seminary in Virginia: *Apostles' Creed; Arminius; Athanasian Creed; Augsburg Confession; Calvin; Catechism; Chalcedonian Definition; Covenanters; Creeds and Confessions; Edict of Nantes; Helvetic Confessions; Huguenots; Knox, John; Nicene Creed; Reformed Churches; Theology, Contemporary Christian; Thirty-nine Articles; Westminster Confession*

Miriam Lindsey Levering, Assistant Professor of Religion and East Asian Studies, Oberlin College: *Amida; Avalokiteśvara; Ch'i; Eight Immortals; Hsi Wang Mu; Millenarian Movements; T'ai-Chi; Taoism, Religious; Wu-hsing*

Aaron Lichtenstein, Author, Baltimore, Maryland: *Calendar, Jewish; Torah*

James M. Lindholm, Assistant Professor of Tamil, The University of Chicago: *Tamil*

Charles Howard Lippy, Associate Professor of History and Religion, Clemson University: *Book of Mormon; Latter-day Saints; Smith, Joseph*

Alexander Lipski, Professor of History and Religious Studies, California State University, Long Beach: *Ārya Samāj; Brāhmo Samāj; Dayānanda; Radhakrishnan; Ram Mohan Roy; Reform Movements in India; Vivekānanda*

David Little, Professor of Religion, University of Virginia: *Ethics*

Beatrice St. Laurent-Lockwood, Ph.D. Candidate in Islamic Art, Harvard University: *Minaret*

J. Bruce Long, Director, Blaisdell Institute for the Advanced Study of World Cultures and Religions, Claremont: *Asura; Astrology; Bhagavān; Daṇḍa; Deva; Gandharva; Hiraṇyakaśipu; Manu; Manu, Laws of; Śaiva Siddhānta; Śaivism; Trimūrti; Yama*

William C. McCormick, Professor of Anthropology and Linguistics, University of Calgary: *Lingāyat*

James P. McDermott, Associate Professor, Department of Religious Studies, Canisius College: *Abhidhamma Piṭaka; Ānanda; Brahmavihāras; Buddhaghosa; Dīgha Nikāya; Dīpavaṃsa; Karma; Karuṇā; Mahā-Parinibbāna Sutta; Mahāvaṃsa; Mahāvastu; Mettā; Milindapañha; Nikāyas; Pātimokkha; Prajñā; Prajñapāramitā Sūtras; Sutta Piṭaka; Tripiṭaka; Vinaya Piṭaka; Visuddhimagga*

Hugh T. McElrath, Professor of Church Music, Southern Baptist Theological Seminary: *Bay Psalm Book; Gospel Songs; Gregorian Chant; Music, in Christianity; Sacred Harp*

H. Neill McFarland, Professor of History of Religions, Perkins School of Theology: *Deguchi Nao; Hōtoku Movement; Kawate Bunjiro; Konkō-kyō; Nakayama Miki; Ōmoto; PL Kyōdan; Reiyūkai; Seichō no Ie; Sekai Kyūsei-kyō; Shingaku; Taniguchi Masaharu; Tenchi Kane no Kami; Tenri-kyō; Toritsugi*

H. Newton Maloney, Professor, Graduate School of Psychology, Fuller Theological Seminary: *Religious Experience*

Bernard Martin, Abba Hillel Silver Professor of Jewish Studies, Case Western Reserve University: *Amidah; Ark; Bar Mitzvah; Circumcision; Kiddush; Kiddush ha-Shem; Magen David; Matzah; Menorah; Mezuzah; Minyan; Mitzvah; Mohel; Piyyut; Rabbi; Shema; Shofar; Tallith; Tefillin; Yarmulka; Yeshivah*

Martin E. Marty, Fairfax M. Cone Distinguished Service Professor, The University of Chicago, and Associate Editor of The Christian Century: *Christianity; Protestantism*

Eric M. Meyers, Professor of Religion; Director of the Graduate Program in Religion and of the Center for Judaic Studies, Duke University: *Akiba; Antiochus Epiphanes; Bar Kochba; Diaspora; Essenes; Gamaliel; Hillel; Jamnia; Johanan ben Zakkai; Judah ha-Nasi; Maccabees; Meir; Pharisees; Philo; Sadducees; Samaritans; Sanhedrin; Shammai; Synagogue; Zealots*

Glenn Thomas Miller, Associate Professor of Church History, Southeastern Baptist Theological Seminary:

Baptist Churches; Creationism; Dispensationalism; Edwards, Jonathan; Evangelicals; Finney, Charles G.; Fundamentalism; Graham, Billy; Great Awakening; Henry, Matthew; Millenarianism; Moody, Dwight L.; Mott, John R.; Pilgrim Fathers; Plymouth Brethren; Revivalism; Scofield, C. I.; Sunday Schools; Williams, Roger; YMCA; YWCA

ROBERT N. MINOR, Assistant Professor of Religious Studies (Asian Religions), University of Kansas: *Cow, Symbolism and Veneration; Kubera; Nāga; Śeṣa*

VASUDHA NARAYANAN, Assistant Professor, Department of Religious Studies, DePaul University: *Tamil*

WALTER G. NEEVEL, JR., Associate Professor of Philosophy and Religious Studies; Coordinator, Comparative Study of Religion Program, University of Wisconsin, Milwaukee: *Āgama; Gāyatrī Mantra; Mantra; Nimbārka; Oṃ; Pañcarātra; Rāmānuja; Teṅgalai; Vaḍagalai; Vallabha; Viśiṣṭa Advaita; Yāmuna*

J. ROBERT NELSON, Professor of Systematic Theology, Boston University: *Church; Ecumenical Movement; Methodist Churches; National Council of Churches; Perfection, Christian; Wesley, John*

GORDON DARNELL NEWBY, Associate Professor of History, North Carolina State University: *Abū Bakr; Abū Lahab; Abū Ṭālib; 'Ā'isha; Allah; Anṣār; Arabic; Bilāl ibn Rabāh; Burāq; Caliph; Eschatology; Fātiḥa; Fāṭima; Fiqh; Hanafites; Ibn Ḥanbal; Ibn Isḥāq; Ibn Taymīyya; Ismā'īl; Jinn; Khadīja; Malā'ika; Malik ibn Anas; Maryam; Muhammad; People of the Book; Qiṣās; Quraish; Rasūl; al-Shāfi'ī; Sunna; Sura; Time of Ignorance; 'Umar; Waḥy*

FRANCIS OAKLEY, Professor of History and Dean of the Faculty, Williams College: *Abelard; Albertus Magnus; Anselm; Auto-da-Fe; Bonaventure; Duns Scotus; Francis Xavier; Ignatius of Loyola; Inquisition; Jansenism; Peter Lombard; Reformation, Catholic; Scholasticism; Thomas Aquinas; Trent, Council of; Vincent de Paul; William of Occam*

DANIEL WM. O'CONNOR, Charles A. Dana Professor and Chairman of the Department of Religious Studies and Classical Languages, St. Lawrence University: *Bethlehem; Catacombs; Gethsemane; Golgotha; Holy Sepulchre; Jerusalem; Mount of Olives; Nazareth; Peter; Rome; Sinai; United Church of Christ*

MARY EILEEN ODELL, Assistant Professor of Anthropology, Virginia Commonwealth University: *Ancestor Veneration*

WENDY DONIGER O'FLAHERTY, Professor of History of Religions in the Divinity School; the Committee on Social Thought, and the Department of South Asian Languages and Civilizations, The University of Chicago: *Kailāsa; Liṅga; Naṭarāja; Paśupati; Shiva; Yoni*

CARL OLSON, Assistant Professor, Southern Illinois University, Carbondale: *Gupta Dynasty; Mauryan Dynasty; Sacred Thread; Twice Born*

DOUGLAS F. OTTATI, Instructor of Theology, Union Theological Seminary in Virginia: *Atheism; Barth; Bultmann; Death of God Theology; Kierkegaard; Küng; Liberation Theology; Neo-Orthodoxy; Niebuhr, H. Richard; Niebuhr, Reinhold; Pannenberg; Rahner; Schillebeeckx; Social Gospel; Teilhard de Chardin; Tillich*

DANIEL L. OVERMYER, Associate Professor, Department of Asian Studies, University of British Columbia: *Chinese Popular Religion; Feng-shui; Household Gods; White Lotus Society*

DENNIS E. OWEN, Assistant Professor of Religion, University of Florida: *Magic; Voodoo; Witchcraft*

WILLARD GURDON OXTOBY, Professor of Religious Studies and Director of the Centre for Religious Studies, University of Toronto: *Avesta; Fire Temple; Gabar; Parsis; Towers of Silence; Zoroastrians*

W. PACHOW, Professor of Asian Religions and Buddhist Studies, University of Iowa: *Anāgāmin; Arhant; Bhavacakra; Paṭiccasamuppāda; Sakadāgāmin; Sotāppana*

HARRY B. PARTIN, Associate Professor of History of Religions, Duke University: *Ash'arī; Hajj; Hijra; Jahannam; Janna; Ka'ba; Madrasa; Mecca; Medina; Qiblah; Ramadan; 'Umra; 'Uthmān; Wuḍū'; Zamzam*

WILLIAM O. PAULSELL, Dean and Professor of Historical Theology, Lexington Theological Seminary: *Antony of Egypt; Bernard of Clairvaux; Desert Fathers; Francis of Assisi; Francis of Sales; Imitation of Christ; Pachomius; Prayer in Christianity; Simeon Stylites; Theologica Germanica*

JAMES LOWE PEACOCK III, Professor of Anthropology, University of North Carolina at Chapel Hill: *Islam in Southeast Asia*

HANS H. PENNER, John Phillips Professor of Religion and Dean of the Faculty, Dartmouth College: *Garuḍa; Haṃsa; Nandi; Purāṇas; Religion, Study of: Vāhana*

KARL H. POTTER, Professor of Philosophy and Chairman, South Asian Studies, University of

Washington: *Advaita; Darśana; Dvaita; Madhva; Śaṃkara; Vedānta*

Charles S. Prebish, Associate Professor, Department of Religious Studies, Pennsylvania State University: *Buddhist Councils; Buddhist Sectarianism; Hīnayāna; Theravāda*

Walter H. Principe, C.S.B., Professor, Pontifical Institute of Medieval Studies and Professor, University of Toronto Graduate Centre for Medieval Studies and Graduate Centre for Religious Studies: *Augustinians; Beguines; Benedictines; Capuchins; Carmelites; Carthusians; Celestines; Cistercians; Dominicans; Flagellants; Franciscans; Jesuits; Mendicant Friars; Religious Orders; Trappists; Ursulines*

Jill Raitt, Associate Professor of Historical Theology, Duke Divinity School: *Borromeo; Contarini; Curia; Erasmus; Melanchthon; Pole, Reginald*

Velcheru Narayana Rao, Department of South Asian Studies, University of Wisconsin: *Agastya; Bāli; Hanumān; Lakṣmaṇa; Rāma; Rāmāyaṇa; Sanskrit; Sītā; Vālmīki*

Frank E. Reynolds, Professor of History of Religion and Buddhist Studies, and Chairman of the Committee on Southern Asian Studies, The University of Chicago: *Aśoka; Buddhism in Southeast Asia*

Russell E. Richey, Associate Professor of Church History, The Graduate and Theological Schools, Drew University: *Deism; Socinianism; Unitarian Universalist Association*

Mac Linscott Ricketts, Chairman, Department of Religion and Philosophy, Louisburg College: *Androgyny; Dance, Sacred; Trickster*

Max Gray Rogers, Professor of Old Testament, Southeastern Baptist Theological Seminary: *Covenant; Moses; Ten Commandments; Yahweh*

Minor L. Rogers, Associate Professor of Religion, Washington and Lee University: *Hōnen; Kami; Kami no Michi; Kamidana; Kojiki; Nihon Shoki; Torii*

Max Roth, Rabbi, The Park Synagogue, Cleveland, Ohio: *Cantor; Music in Judaism*

Abdulaziz Abdulhussein Sachedina, Assistant Professor, Department of Religious Studies, University of Virginia: *Agha Khan; Ahl-i Ḥaqq; Ali; Assassins; Ayatollah; Bohorās; Druzes; Fatimid; al-Ḥasan; al-Ḥusayn; Ibn Sīnā; Ikwān al-Ṣafā; Imam; Imāmiyya; Ismāʿīliyya; Karbala; Khārijites; Khōjās; Mahdi; Mashhad; Mufti; Mujtahid; Mullah; Qarmaṭians; Sabʿiyya; Sayyid; Sharif; Shiʿa; Zaydiyya; Ziyāra*

David J. Schnall, Associate Professor of Public Administration; Director, The Institute for Public Studies, Long Island University, Post Center: *Ashkenazim; Balfour Declaration; Falasha Jews; Hannukah; Hebrew; Herzl, Theodor; Kaddish; Kol Nidre; Kosher; Ladino; Passover; Purim; Rosh ha-Shanah; Sabbath; Seder; Selihot; Sephardim; Shalom; Shavout; Simhat Torah; Sukkot; Yahrzeit; Yiddish; Yizkor; Yom Kippur; Zionism*

Allan M. Schwartzbaum, Associate Professor, Department of Sociology and Anthropology, Virginia Commonwealth University: *Ancestor Veneration*

Yehuda Shamir, Associate Professor of Religion, University of Miami: *Amoraim; Baraita; Benedictions; Gemara; Great Synagogue; Halakah; Mekhilta; Mishnah; Prayer, Jewish; Responsa; Siddur; Talmud; Tannaim; Tisha be'Av; Tosefta; Western Wall*

Ishwar C. Sharma, Department of Philosophy, Cleveland State University: *Sat; Śramaṇa; Svayaṃvara; Tapas*

Massey Hamilton Shepherd, Jr., Hodges Professor of Liturgics, The Church Divinity School of the Pacific: *Anglican Churches; Book of Common Prayer; Canterbury; Martyrs, Christian; Puritans; Taylor, Jeremy; Westminster Abbey*

Larry Dwight Shinn, Associate Professor of Religion, Oberlin College: *Auroville; Balarāma; Bhāgavata Purāṇa; Bhaktivedānta Swami; Brahmin; Dharmaśāstras; Gandhi; Hiraṇyagarbha; Hoysāḷa; Jagannātha; Kaṃsa; Krishna; Myth; Puruṣa; Rāja; Saṃhitā; Saṃskāra; Śāstra; Satyāgraha; Swami; Tīrtha; Vṛndāvana*

George H. Shriver, Professor of History, Georgia Southern College: *Booth, William; Christian Science; Salvation Army; Seventh-Day Adventism*

Seymour Siegel, Ralph Simon Professor of Ethics and Theology, The Jewish Theological Seminary of America: *Conservative Judaism; Hirsch, Samuel R.*

Khushwant Singh, Editor, Hindustan Times, New Delhi: *Ādi Granth; Gobind Singh; Golden Temple; Gurmukhi; Japji; Khālsā; Nām; Nānak; Rādhā Soāmī Satsang; Śabad; Satguru; Sikhism*

Bardwell L. Smith, Chairman, Department of Religion and Professor of Asian Studies, Carleton College: *Ajaṇṭā; Bhikkhu; Gandhāra; Saṅgha; Stūpa; Triratna; Uposatha*

Frederick J. Streng, Professor of History of Religions, Southern Methodist University: *Mādhyamika; Mudrā; Nāgārjuna; Śūnyatā*

H. Patrick Sullivan, Dean of the College and Professor of Religion, Vassar College: *Harappā; Indus Valley Civilization; Mohenjo-daro*

Donald K. Swearer, Professor of Religion, Swarthmore College: *Anāthapiṇḍika; Āvāsa; Buddhism, Lay; Monasticism; Mysticism; Vihāra*

Harold Vinson Synan, Assistant General Superintendent, Pentecostal Holiness Church: *Baptism in the Holy Spirit; Charismatic Movement; Faith Healing; Glossolalia; Pentecostal Churches; Snake Handling*

Charles R. Taber, Professor of World Mission, Emmanuel School of Religion, Johnson City, Tennessee: *Animism; Food, Religious Attitudes Toward; Life Cycle Rites; Mana; Reincarnation; Soul, Spirit; Taboo; Totem*

Thomas J. Talley, Professor of Liturgics, The General Theological Seminary: *Absolution; Advent; All Saints Day; All Souls Day; Ash Wednesday; Baptism; Calendar, Christian; Candlemas; Christmas; Churching of Women; Colors, Liturgical; Confession; Confirmation; Consubstantiation; Corpus Christi; Easter; Ember Days; Epiphany; Eucharist; Godparents; Good Friday; Holy Week; Holy Years; Host; Lent; Maundy Thursday; Ordination; Palm Sunday; Pentecost; Sacraments; Sunday; Transubstantiation; Trinity Sunday; Unction*

Rodney L. Taylor, Associate Professor, University of Colorado: *Analects; Chu Hsi; Confucianism; Confucius; Doctrine of the Mean; Filial Piety; Great Learning; Mandate of Heaven; Mencius; Wang Yang-ming*

Christoph von Fürer-Haimendorf, Professor Emeritus of Asian Anthropology, University of London: *Caste; Harijan; Kṣatriya; South Asian Tribal Religions; Śūdra; Vaiśya*

Chrysogonus Waddell O.C.S.O., Professor of Theology and Liturgy, Choirmaster, Abbey of Gethsemani, Trappist, Kentucky: *Beatification; Canonization; Celibacy; Crucifix; Dead, Prayers for; Genuflexion; Holy Water; Indulgences; Kiss of Peace; Latin; Limbo; Lourdes; Madonna; Mar Thoma Church; Pieta; Purgatory; Relics; Rosary; Sacred Heart; Saint Peter's Basilica; Saints, Veneration of; Shroud of Turin; Sign of the Cross; Stations of the Cross; Stigmata; Taizé; Vatican City*

John W. Waters, Associate Professor of Old Testament, The Interdenominational Theological Center, Atlanta: *Black Religions in the United States; King, Martin Luther, Jr.; Muhammad, Elijah*

Keith Watkins, Professor of Worship, Christian Theological Seminary: *Abbot; Acolyte; Anticlericalism; Archbishop; Archdeacon; Bishop; Brother; Cardinal; Catholicos; Clergy, Christian; Curate; Deacon; Diocese; Elder; Father; Friar; Metropolitan; Monsigneur; Nun; Parish; Patriarch; Prelate; Priest; Primate; Prior; See; Sister; Vicar*

G. R. Welbon, Associate Professor, Department of Religious Studies, University of Pennsylvania: *Ahiṃsā; Dharma; Nirvana; Samādhi; Samsara; Skandha*

Charles S. J. White, Professor of Philosophy and Religion, The American University: *Ācārya; Guru; Hindu Holy Persons; Krishnamurti; Meher Bābā; Rāmakrishna; Ramana Maharshi; Rishi; Sādhu; Satya Sai Bābā*

D. Jerry White, Assistant Professor of English, Central Missouri State University: *Blake; Bunyan; Dante; Grail, Holy; Lewis, C. S.; Milton*

James D. Whitehead, Consultant, Center for Pastoral and Social Ministry, University of Notre Dame; Associate Faculty of the Graduate School, Loyola University of Chicago: *Kumārajīva; Vimalakīrti*

Glenn E. Yocum, Associate Professor of Religion, Whittier College: *Aiyaṉār; Appar; Artha; Hindu Aims of Life; Kāma; Kāma Sūtras; Māṇikkavācakar; Māriyammaṉ; Māyā; Mokṣa; Nammāḻvār*

David C. Yu, Professor of History of Religion and Chairman, Department of Philosophy and Religion, Colorado Women's College: *Alchemy; Chuang Tzu; I Ching; Lao Tzu; Taoism, Philosophical; Yin and Yang*

Grover A. Zinn, Professor of Religion, Oberlin College: *Eckhart, Meister; Hesychasm; Hugh of St. Victor; John of the Cross; Monasticism; Mysticism, Christian; Pseudo-Dionysius; Teresa of Avila*

Evan M. Zuesse, Department of Religion, Case Western Reserve University: *African Traditional Religion; Divination; Initiation*

EDITOR'S PREFACE

The *Perennial Dictionary of World Religions* is designed to provide an authoritative guide to the historical development, beliefs, and practices of the sometimes bewildering array of religions in today's world. The practical need for such a work has never been greater. As contacts with adherents of other religions increase in frequency and in intensity, there is both the possiblility of greater mutual understanding and the danger of greater friction. A work of this sort cannot create good will, but it can provide the information necessary for sympathetic appreciation of those things that are of supreme value to our neighbors.

School teachers and college professors whose disciplines require some familiarity with religion will profit much from both the general and specialized entries. In additon, the student of religion at both the graduate and undergraduate level will find the dictionary a helpful and increasingly indispensable companion.

It is also the hope of the editors that members of churches, synagogues, and other religious organizations will find the dictionary useful in a variety of ways. Discussions among differing religious groups are doomed to flounder unless they have accurate information about each other, and adult, youth, and mission study programs can be enriched by the fuller knowledge of the religious beliefs and practices of the areas they are studying.

Last but not least, men and women with business contacts in other nations, members of the armed forces stationed abroad, and anyone who has contacts with overseas students in American colleges and universities or with new immigrants to our shores will find many occasions for turning to this dictionary.

From the outset it was the aim of the editors to avoid special pleading and partisan statements and to leave to the reader the decision about the truth claims of religious traditions and the utility of their practical expressions. Most writers are members of faculties of religion or religious studies at colleges and universities; others are adherents of the religion about which they wrote. Contributions from other disciplines, such as history, sociology, and anthropology, add to the scope of this work. The overarching concern has been to present each topic with sensitivity to the various approaches and interpretations applicable in each case, and contributors were chosen with this in mind. Some of them are well-known, established scholars; others are younger and have published less widely.

The dictionary deals only with "living" religions, that is, religions practiced in the present day. Thus the great religions of the Ancient Near East and the pre-Christian religions of Europe are excluded. Treating the living religions in their historical development, however, required the discussion of movements (e.g., GNOSTICISM) that are no longer practiced today, and sects (e.g., QARMATIANS) that have no adherents.

In the selection of topics to be discussed and the type of information to be provided, the editors had in mind a primary readership in North America. What would these readers want to know, and how much prior knowledge could be assumed? Even this geographical limitation includes a wide variety of readers. The much discussed but poorly defined general reader will find most of the material in the dictionary accessible, but some articles will be primarily of interest to the specialist.

THE PLAN OF THE DICTIONARY

Each major religious tradition (and some minor ones) has an extended article devoted to it. By turning to such comprehensive articles as ISLAM, BUDDHISM, CHRISTIANITY, or HINDUISM, the reader will find a discussion of that religion's history from its origins, of the major sects and movements that have arisen, major beliefs, and other significant topics. Because of the distinctive nature of each religion, the comprehensive articles do not follow a uniform outline.

A system of cross references directs the reader to other articles that give additional information on related topics. Thus it is possible to move from one of the comprehensive articles to a great variety of specialized articles, or to begin with a specific topic and follow it up with further study of related material. In each article the first time that the title of another article is mentioned, it is printed in small capitals (e.g. DHARMA; VISHNU; TALMUD). Because of the sentence structure a cross reference may appear in slightly different form from the title of the article to which it refers (e.g. TANTRIC is a cross reference to TANTRISM and GNOSTIC to GNOSTICISM). Where there might be confusion if the cross reference were included in the text, or where it is more indirectly related to the text, it is given in the form *see* MIRACLES IN ISLAM.

Wherever religions have spread to new geographical regions through migration or missionary activity, it is necessary to consider regional developments in articles such as CHRISTIANITY IN AFRICA; ISLAM IN SOUTH ASIA. In the Far East religious developments have resulted in a mixture of traditional elements with major religions. It seemed appropriate therefore to deal with religion in Japan and Korea in special articles. Many traditional (or tribal) religions have assumed new importance or have been studied extensively by modern scholars. Accordingly, there are articles on SOUTH AMERICAN TRIBAL RELIGIONS; AFRICAN TRADITIONAL RELIGION, and on religions in other parts of the world.

Various topics of importance do not fit into the framework of any one religion and are best studied across traditions. Articles are included on such topics as EVIL; TIME; SACRIFICE; MYSTICISM: WITCHCRAFT. As an aid to the comprehensive study of different traditions, selected articles are grouped in categories in the front of the the dictionary, pp. xv-xvi.

If an entry falls within one or more of the religious traditions dealt with in comprehensive articles an abbreviation within parentheses identifies the tradition, e.g. (B & H), (I), (Ja). Where appropriate, a further abbreviation identifies the language from which the term is derived, e.g. (Heb.), (Chin.), (Skt.).

NON-ENGLISH TERMS

Entries come from many languages. Where the term or proper name is not in general English usage, or where there may be uncertainty about pronunciation, the most widely accepted pronunciation is indicated, using sounds that are standard in English. This means that various phonemes in other languages can only be approximated, but for a general work of this nature the gain in simplicity outweighs the loss to the specialist, who already knows how to pronounce the term.

A related problem is the orthography of words transliterated from one system of writing to another. Where a term has been accepted in English and can be found in *Webster's Third International Dictionary,* the spelling used there has been adopted, e.g. SAYYID; AVATAR; GHEE. For transliterations of Chinese words, the Wade-Giles system has been retained, since it is used by most works listed in the bibliographies. Every effort has been made to achieve uniformity in transliteration, especially in the use of diacritical marks, but scholars are not always agreed. In Tamil studies scholars are working toward the establishment of a new system.

There is also a side variety of preference as to whether to translate a term into its closest natural English equivalent or to retain it in transliterated form. In most cases the preference of the writer was followed. Etymologies are indicated where relevant, and for most entries a literal translation of the non-English term is supplied.

MAPS AND ILLUSTRATIONS

In the body of the text there are a few sketch maps illustrating the articles they accompany. For the most significant religious sites a series of color maps has been specially prepared for this dictionary. They represent no one historical period, but give the location of important cities, shrines, rivers, mountains, and regions which are referred to in articles. Other geographical features are included as helps in locating the religious sites in reference to better-known modern sites.

A particular problem is presented by the art and architecture of the various religions. Paintings, statues, and buidings reveal much about a religion, and both reflect and mold religious thought. Yet this topic alone would have called for several volumes. Accordingly, articles were commissionsed that would discuss the interplay of faith and art, emphasizing major lines of development. Photographs were selected to accompany specific articles. Bibliographies point the reader to further resources. While there are no comprehensive articles on literature, there are specific articles on some significant writers.

TEXTS AND CHARTS

The texts of some of the more important creeds, prayers, and mantras have been given in full. A special table lists selected Buddhist terms in Sanskrit (or Pali), Chinese characters, and Chinese, Japanese, and Korean pronunciations of those characters, showing both the discontinuity in the transition from Indic languages to Chinese, and the continuity among these three languages that use the Chinese system of writing.

For all articles dealing with Islam, Professor Bruce Lawrence of the Department of Religion, Duke University, served as special consultant. We are indebted to him for selecting the entries for inclusion, for suggesting writers on Islamic subjects, and for writing many of the central articles.

All the editors have benefited from the careful work of Jean Hager, Special Projects Editor of Abingdon Press. Her precision and her creative imagination were of great help at every step of the way, especially in the selection of the illustrations. My editorial assistant, Martin R. Crim, helped with details of the editorial process and with the solution of problems of English style and usage.

KEITH CRIM
GENERAL EDITOR

A SELECTED GUIDE TO KEY ENTRIES

In addition to the major entry for each religion, the following articles, chosen from many others in each tradition, should be consulted by anyone seeking a comprehensive understanding of the tradition.

BUDDHISM

Ahiṃsā
Amida
Anatta
Anicca
Arhant
Art and Architecture
Bardo Thodöl
Bhikkhu
Bodhisattva
Buddha, General Concepts of
Buddha, Life of Gautama
Buddhism, Lay
Buddhism in Southeast Asia
Buddhism, Tibetan
Buddhist Sectarianism
Dhammapada
Dharma
Eightfold Path
Four Noble Truths
Karma
Lohan
Lotus Sūtra
Mādhyamika
Mahāyāna
Mandala
Mantra
Māyā
Meditation, Buddhist
Nara Buddhism
Nichiren Buddhism
Nirvana
Pali Canon
Pure Land Sects
Samsara
Saṅgha
Satori
Stūpa
Śūnyatā
Tantrism
Tapas
Tendai
Theravāda
Triple Body
Vihāra
Zen

CHRISTIANITY

Art and Architecture
Bible
Calendar
Charismatic Movement
Christianity in Africa
Christianity in Asia
Christology
Church
Clergy
Councils of the Church
Creeds and Confessions
Jesus
Liturgy
Mary
Missions
Music, in Christianity
Mysticism, Christian
Orthodox Churches
Paul
Prayer, Christian
Protestantism
Reformation, Catholic
Reformation, Protestant
Religious Orders
Revivalism
Roman Catholicism
Sacraments
Scholasticism
Theology, Contemporary Christian
Trinity

HINDUISM

Ahiṃsā
Art and Architecture
Avatar
Bhagavān
Bhagavad Gītā
Bhakti Hinduism
Brahman
Caste
Cow, Symbolism and Veneration
Darśana
Dharma
Goddess (India)
Hindu Holy Persons
Hindu Sacred Cities
Hinduism in Southeast Asia
Karma
Krishna
Liṅgāyat
Mahābhārata
Mandala
Mantra
Māyā

HINDUISM (Cont.)

ISLAM

JUDAISM

REGIONAL TRADITIONS

CROSS TRADITIONAL ARTICLES

ABBREVIATIONS

A—Aṅguttara Nikāya
AB—Aitareya Brāhmaṇa
AHC—Annaurium Historiae Conciliorum
Arab.—Arabic
Aram.—Aramaic
AU—Aitareya Upaniṣad
AV—Atharva Veda

B—Buddhism
Ba—Bahā'ī
BĀU—Bṛhadāraṇyaka Upaniṣad
BEFEO—Bulletin de l'école française d'extrême Orient
Bh.G—Bhagavad Gītā
Bh.P—Bhāgavata Purāṇa

ca.—around
Ch—Christianity
Chin.—Chinese
Con—Confucianism
CU—Chāndogya Upaniṣad

ed.—editor, edition
EI—Encyclopedia of Islam, ed. Gibb and Kramers (1960)
EJ—Encyclopedia Judaica (1971)
ET—English translation

f.—feminine

Gr.—Greek

H—Hinduism
Heb.—Hebrew
HR—History of Religions

I—Islam
IDB—Interpreter's Dictionary of the Bible
IDBS—Interpreter's Dictionary of the Bible Supplementary Volume
IU—Īśa Upaniṣad

Ja—Jainism
JAAR—Journal of the American Academy of Religion
JAOS—Journal of the American Oriental Society
Jap.—Japanese
JAS—Journal of Asian Studies
JE—Jewish Encyclopedia
JNES—Journal of Near Eastern Studies
JQR—Jewish Quarterly Review
JRAS—Journal of the Royal Asiatic Society
JTS—Journal of Theological Studies
Ju—Judaism

Kath. U—Kaṭha Upaniṣad
KJV—King James Version of the Bible
Kor.—Korean
KU—Kena Upaniṣad

Lat.—Latin
lit.—literally

M—Majjhima Nikāya
Mait. U—Maitrāyaṇi Upaniṣad
Mbh—Mahābhārata
MU—Muṇḍaka Upaniṣad
MW—Muslim World

NT—New Testament

OT—Old Testament

Per.—Persian
Pkt.—Prākrit

Rām.—Rāmayāṇa
rpr.—reprinted
RV—Rig Veda

S—Sikhism
ŚB—Śatapatha Brāhmaṇa

S.B.B.—Sacred Books of the Buddhists
S.B.E.—Sacred Books of the East
SEI—*Shorter Encyclopedia of Islam,* ed. Gibb and Kramers (1953)
Sh—Shintō
Skt.—Sanskrit
ŚP—Śiva Purāṇa
SV—Sama Veda
Śvet. U—Śvetāśvatara Upaniṣad

T—Taoism
TĀ-Taittirīya Āraṇyaka
TDNT—*Theological Dictionary of the New Testament*
trans.—translator, translated
TU—Taittirīya Upaniṣad
TWNT—*Theologisches Wörterbuch zum Neuen Testament*

U—Upaniṣad

VP—Vishnu Purāṇa

YS—Yogasūtra
YSB—Yogasūtrabhāṣya
YV—Yajur Veda

Z—Zoroastrianism
ZDMG—*Zeitschrift der deutschen morgenländischen Gesellschaft*
ZRG—*Zeitschrift für Religions- und Geistesgeschichte*

Abbreviations of biblical books are those used by the Revised Standard Version (RSV).

PRONUNCIATION TABLE

ă act, bat
ā able, cape
â air, dare
ä art, calm

b back, rub
ch chief, beach
d do, bed

ĕ ebb, set
ē equal, bee

f fit, puff
g give, beg
h hit, hear

ĭ if, big
ī ice, bite

j just, edge
k kept, make
l low, all

m my, him
n now, on
ng sing, England

ŏ box, hot
ō over, no
ô order, ball
oi oil, joy
oo book, put
o͞o ooze, rule
ou out, loud

p page, stop
r read, cry

s see, miss
sh shoe, push
t ten, bit

ŭ up, love
ū use, cute
û urge, burn

v voice, live
w west, away
y yes, young
z zeal, lazy, those
zh vision, measure

ə occurs only in unaccented syllables and indictates the sound of
a *in* alone
e *in* system
i *in* easily
o *in* gallop
u *in* circus

A

'ABBĀSIDS ăb bä´ səds (I). Muslim dynasty (750-1258) who succeeded the Umayyads. All the rulers of this family line were descendants of Muhammad, and it was through Muhammad ibn Alī, great-grandson of al-'Abbās, the Prophet's uncle, that they laid claim to the Caliphate. They shifted the capital city from Damascus to Baghdad, with the result that during their long reign a Persian-Iraqi clientele *(mawālī)* became ascendant at court and Islam was transformed from a Mediterranean into an Asian empire. The cultural achievements of the 'Abbāsids in literature, philosophy, science, art, architecture, and music were as diverse as they were splendid, but the emergence of sectarian dissent (Fatimid Shi'ites in Egypt) and ethnic autonomy (Seljuk Turks in Central Asia) weakened the effective power of the caliph long before the Mongols sacked Baghdad in 1258. *See* Islam §4a.

Bibliography. P. Hitti, *History of the Arabs,* 7th ed. (1960), pp. 288-489.

B. Lawrence

ABBOT (Ch—Aram.; lit. "father"). The head of an independent monastic community, usually called an abbey. The abbot is ordinarily elected for life by members of the community, and exercises religious and temporal superintendency over that group.

K. Watkins

'ABD-AL-QĀDIR BEDIL ăb´ dăl kä´ dēr bē dĭl´ (I; 1644-1721). Major Indo-Persian poet, comparable in output and influence to Rūmī. Born in Patna, Bihar, India, he was educated in traditional Islamic studies before coming to Delhi in 1665. There he met an ecstatic Sufi saint who changed the course of his life. After disconsolate wanderings, Bedil married and settled down in Delhi, where he began to write the verse for which he has become famous throughout Central Asia. He evolved a new, highly obtuse style of poetry, at once mystical and rational, beguiling and incomprehensible.

Bibliography. A. Ghani, *Life and Works of Abdul Qadir Bedil* (1960).

B. Lawrence

'ABD-AL-QĀDIR JILĀNI ăb´ dăl kä´ dēr jē lä´ nē (I; 1077-1166). Sufi mystic of legendary fame. Born in Jilan, Iraq, he was trained in Hanbalite law at Baghdad (*see* Ibn Ḥanbal). Around 1100 a Sufi teacher inspired him to pursue the mystical path. After twenty-five years as a desert recluse, he reappeared in Baghdad in 1127 to become one of the most popular preachers and teachers that Islam has ever known. He established a school (Madrasa) and inspired an order (Ṭarīqa) that eventually set up branches in every Muslim country.

Bibliography. D. S. Margoliouth, "Contribution to the Biography of 'Abd-al-Qadir of Jilan," *JRAS* (1907), 267-310; J. S. Trimingham, *The Sufi Orders in Islam* (1971).

B. Lawrence

'ABDUL-BAHĀ ăb dŭl bä hä´ (Ba; 1844-1920—Arab. & Per.; lit. "Servant of the Glory"). The eldest son of Bahā' Ullāh, his father's successor as head of the Bahā'ī community, and official interpreter of Bahā' Ullāh's teachings. He was chiefly responsible for the spread of Bahā'ī to Europe and America.

C. J. Adams

ABELARD, PETER (Ch; 1079-1142). Philosopher, theologian, poet, and monk. After a turbulent life, which included his seduction of Héloise, niece of one of the canons of Notre Dame in Paris, and his subsequent castration and disgrace, he died at the monastery of Cluny. His *Sic et non,* brought together contradictory texts from the Scriptures and church fathers. *See* Scholasticism §2.

F. Oakley

ABHIDHAMMA PIṬAKA ŭb hĭ dhäm´ mŭ pĭ´ tŭ kŭ (B—Pali; lit. "Basket of Higher Subleties of the Doctrine" [*abhi*—"higher" + *dhṛ*—"to hold"; *piṭ*—"assemble"]) **ABHIDHARMA PIṬAKA** (B—Skt.). The third and historically the latest of the three "baskets" or collections of the Pali Canon. A number of other Buddhist sects had their own Abhidharma collections, the most notable exception being the Great Community (Mahāsāṅghikas), the forerunners of Mahāyāna. In addition to the Pali Abhidhamma, the most important of the collections still in existence is the Abhidharma Piṭaka of the Sarvāstivādins. The original Sanskrit texts exist today only in fragments. *See* BUDDHIST SECTARIANISM.

1. **Nature and approach.** The Abhidhamma literature is based mainly on the doctrinal content of the discourses (SUTTA PIṬAKA) but is distinctive in its scholastic treatment. Ideas are presented in outline without illustrative material. The language is technical; and little attempt is made to connect the abstract matter with everyday existence. No mention is made of individuals or concrete events. Abhidhamma is thus a reworking of materials from the discourses and monastic discipline in a schematic form, but not a systematic treatment of Buddhist philosophy. Its first characteristic is analysis of the full range of doctrines and terms, with special emphasis on consciousness.

A second characteristic is the investigation of the relationships between things *(dhammas; see* DHARMA). Two types of relations exist: (a) causal relations of the type "Y happens because of X," and (b) a system of correlations, such as "X as a condition, object, etc. relates itself to Y."

The intent of the work is to organize knowledge out of a concern for its function in liberating humanity from the bonds of passion and suffering. Though its content is not of popular interest, the work is highly honored in Theravāda countries, especially Burma.

2. **Pali Abhidhamma works.** The Theravāda Abhidhamma Piṭaka consists of seven works: (a) Dhammasaṅgani, or Enumeration of Phenomena, an analysis of mental and bodily factors. It is a kind of Buddhist manual of psychological ethics. (b) Vibhaṅga, or Book of Treatises. Something of a supplement to the Dhammasaṅgaṇi, it concerns such matters as the aggregates of existence, foundations of mindfulness, and factors of enlightenment. (c) Dhātukatthā, or Discussion of Elements, a classification of the elements of reality. (d) Puggalapaññati, or Designation of Human Types. It classifies types of personality according to their ethical characteristics. (e) Kathāvatthu, or Points of Controversy, a polemical treatise refuting the views of schismatic groups of monks of the third century B.C. It is attributed to the monk Moggaliputta Tissa, chairman of the third great Buddhist Council. (f) Yamaka, or Book of Pairs, in some ways similar to a thesaurus. (g) Paṭṭhāna, or Book of Casual Relations, a massive work concerned with causality.

3. **Sanskrit Abhidharma of Sarvāstivāda.** This also has seven works: (a) Jñānaprasṭhāna, or Method of Knowledge, dating from the second century B.C. (b) Saṅgītiparayāya, a commentary on a discourse where the Buddha's teachings are summarized in order to forestall possible schism. (c) Dhātukāya, a synopsis of the elements of existence. (d) Vijñānakāya, or Synopsis of Consciousness, a polemic concerning the controversial idea of the self. (e) Prakaraṇapāda, a collection of explanatory verses. (f) Dharmaskandha, a collection of discourses on the steps to perfection. (g) Prajñapti Śāstra, or Treatise on Communication, which is basically concerned with cosmology.

Bibliography. Nyanatiloka, *Guide Through the Abhidhamma-Pitika* (1957); C. S. Prebish, ed., *Buddhism: A Modern Perspective* (1975), 59-64.
J. P. MCDERMOTT

ABLUTION (I). *See* WUDŪ'.

ABRAHAM (Ju, Ch & I). Biblical patriarch, known as the ancestor of the Hebrews through his son Isaac and of the Arabs through his son Ishmael (ISMĀ'ĪL). In Gen. 12 Abraham obeyed God's call to leave his home in Ur and lead a life of wandering, believing God's promise that he would be the father of many peoples and that a land (thus, the Promised Land) would be theirs. His willingness to sacrifice his son Isaac (Gen. 22) is seen as the supreme test of his faith. In the QUR'ĀN it is Ismā'īl who was to be sacrificed.

God's acceptance of Abraham's faith and obedience as righteousness (Gen. 15:6) becomes in the NT an exegetical basis for PAUL'S doctrine of JUSTIFICATION BY FAITH (Gal. 3:6-9; Rom. 4:13-25) and the Christian interpretation of the CHURCH as the new Israel.

In the Qur'ān, God revealed the true religion to Abraham, who was thus the first MUSLIM (Sura 3:67). Along with his son Ismā'īl he constructed the KA'BA.
R. BULLARD

ABRAVANEL, ISAAC ä brä vä nĕl′ ē′ säk (Ju; 1437–1508). Diplomat, financier, biblical commentator, and philosopher. His major biblical commentaries, written in Hebrew and in classical scholastic style, focused on the historical and prophetic books of the Hebrew BIBLE. Three of his works are devoted to messianic themes; they were profoundly influential in shaping the APOCALYPTIC mood and literature of the next two centuries. His many philosophic works include a commentary on MOSES BEN MAIMON'S *Guide for the Perplexed.* Throughout his writings CHRISTIANITY is subjected to careful scrutiny and criticism. His theological posture was conservative, and he rejected the excesses of rationalism and naturalism. For Abravanel, revelation and its truths are superior to all other forms of knowledge.
K. P. BLAND

ABRUPT DOCTRINE. Ch'an (ZEN) Buddhist view according to which enlightenment is to be achieved suddenly rather than gradually. While Shen-hsiu (605-706), representing the Northern School of Ch'an, taught that enlightenment was to be attained by degrees, HUI-NENG (638-713) established the Southern School which preached the doctrine of immediate enlightenment.
E. J. COLEMAN

ABSOLUTE. The infinite, perfect, ultimate reality which is the metaphysical ground or source of all beings. Although frequently identified with a personal God as in the Judeo-Christian tradition, the absolute has also been interpreted as the suprapersonal

Buddhist Śūnyatā, Hegelian cosmic mind, and Hindu Brahman. E. G. Coleman

ABSOLUTION (Ch). A liturgical formula for conferral of pardon or assurance of forgiveness to the penitent as an act of the Church grounded on the mercy of God and the authority of Christ. Earlier used to mean release from penitential discipline, the term was also used for the final release (commendation) of a body at funerals. T. J. Talley

ABŪ BAKR ä′ bo͞o bä′ kər (I; d.634). The first Caliph or political successor to Muhammad and father of Muhammad's wife 'Ā'isha. He is said to have been three years younger than Muhammad, but little is known of his life until his conversion. He was apparently a merchant of modest means and an expert in Arab genealogy. An early convert to Islam (in some traditions the first outside of Muhammad's immediate family), he was a staunch supporter of Muhammad. When Muhammad reported the Night Journey (*see* Muhammad § 4), Abū Bakr was one of the few to believe immediately, thus earning the epithet aṣ-Ṣiddīq, "The Witnesser to the Truth." He was chosen by Muhammad to accompany him on the Hijra, a position of honor and potential danger. As Muhammad's primary adviser he accompanied him on most of the major military expeditions, but did not have a separate military command. He was designated to lead the pilgrimage (Hajj) in the ninth year and led the public Prayer during Muhammad's last illness. His short two-year caliphate was spent in the Islamicization of Arabia and starting the Wars of Conquest. He was buried next to Muhammad, and his simple, pious life became legendary among later pietist writers. G. D. Newby

ABŪ ḤANĪFA ä′ bo͞o hä nē′ fä (I). *See* Hanafites.

ABŪ LAHAB ä′ bo͞o lä′ həb (I—Arab.; lit. "the possessor of the flame"). Nickname of 'Abd al-'Uzza ibn 'Abd al-Muṭṭalib, an uncle and strong opponent of Muhammad. He and his wife are condemned to hell (Jahannam) by the Qur'ān (Sura 111) for their treatment of Muhammad and the Muslims.
G. D. Newby

ABŪ ṬĀLIB ä′ bo͞o tä′lĭb (I). 'Abd Manāf ibn 'Abd al-Muṭṭalib, known as Abū Ṭālib; Muhammad's uncle and protector and head of the Hāshimite clan after the death of Muhammad's grandfather. While it seems certain that he did not convert to Islam, he remained a loyal supporter of his nephew and protected him against the Meccan persecutions, even at the expense of having to lead his clan into confinement during an economic boycott. He died three years before the Hijra. As the father of Ali, he is held in higher regard by the Shi'ites than by the Sunnites.
G. D. Newby

ĀCĀRYA ä chär′ yŭ (H & Ja—Skt.; lit. "knowing or teaching the rules" [*ācāra*—"conduct, ordinance, precept"]). Persons with both liturgical and intellectual functions. As preceptors they ensure proper performance of rituals and give the final initiation to disciples. Furthermore, they molded the philosophical tradition of Vedānta through their debates on the nature of Brahman, Atman, Jīva, and Māyā. Especially among the Vaiṣṇavas (followers of Vishnu) the chosen deities of the *ācāryas* became the focus of the cult in the sects that they founded.
C. S. J. White

ACOLYTE ă′kō lĭt (Ch—Gr.; lit. "follower"). A person who performs certain duties in worship, such as preparing bread and wine and lighting and carrying candles; used to describe both those ordained to a lesser ministerial office and lay persons, including children and youth. K. Watkins

ADHĀN ə thän′ (I—Arab.; lit. "announcement"). The Islamic call to prayer, uttered immediately before each of the five daily prayers by the muezzin, or crier. Instituted by Muhammad in the early Medinan period as a unique way of calling the Muslims to worship, distinguishing them from the Christians (who used a bell or wood clapper) and the Jews (who blew a horn). Bilāl ibn Rabāh was the first muezzin.

The *adhān* is chanted in a loud voice from atop a Mosque or Minaret, or from within if necessary, by any mature, ritually pure, male Muslim. There are professionals, too, who have traditionally often been blind (partly because one who occupies a high vantage point should not be able to see into private quarters). The caller faces the Qiblah with his hands raised to his ears. Nowadays a public address system is often used.

During the *adhān* the hearers should repeat it as it proceeds, except for lines four and five, which are

ADHĀN

Allāhu akbar.
Ashhadu an lā ilāha illallāh.
Ashhadu anna Muhammadan rasūl Allāh.
Ḥayya 'alā 'ṣ-ṣalāt.
Ḥayya 'alā 'l-falāḥ.
(Ḥayya 'alā khayri 'l-amal.)
(Aṣ-ṣalātu khayrun min an-nawm.)
Allāhu akbar.
Lā ilāha illallāh.

God is most great! (4 times)
I testify that there is no god but God. (2 times)
I testify that Muhammad is the Messenger of God. (2 times)
Come to prayer. (2 times)
Come to salvation. (2 times)
(Come to the best work. [Shi'ite])
(Prayer is better than sleep. [2 times, at the dawn prayer])
God is most great! (2 times)
There is no god but God. (once for Sunnis, twice for Shi'ites)

replaced by *Lā ḥawla wa lā quwwata illā billāh*—"There is no power and no strength save in God."

Bibliography. Al-Baghawī, *Mishkāt al-Maṣābīḥ,* ET J. Robson (1965), I, 133-40; M. A. Rauf, *Islam: Creed and Worship* (1974), pp. 69-71, an authoritative manual of ritual.

F. M. Denny

ĀDI-BUDDHA ä´ dē bood´ hŭ (B). *See* Buddha, General Concepts of §4b.

ĀDI GRANTH ä´ dē grŭnt (S). The sacred scripture of the Sikhs; traditionally referred to as the Granth Sahib ("Book of the Lord"). The prefix Ādi ("first") is affixed to distinguish it from the Dasam ("tenth") Granth, a compilation made by the tenth Guru, Gobind Singh. While the Dasam Granth is treated with reverence, only the Ādi Granth is accorded scriptural status and regarded as the "living" embodiment of all the ten gurus.

1. **Editions.** The Ādi Granth was compiled by the fifth guru, Arjun, who dictated it to his disciple Bhai Gurdas. It was completed in August A.D. 1604 and formally installed in the Harimandir (*see* Golden Temple) in Amritsar with Bhai Buddha (1518-1631) as the first *granthī* (scripture reader).

Several copies of Guru Arjun's compilation were made for use of the communities scattered over Northern India, and in the process extraneous matter was incorporated into them. According to Sikh tradition, Guru Gobind Singh prepared an authentic version in which he incorporated hymns composed by his father, the ninth guru, Tegh Bahadur. The original edition edited by Guru Gobind was lost, and three copies made of that edition are slightly different from each other.

2. **Contributors.** There are almost six thousand hymns in the Ādi Granth, consisting of the compositions of the first five gurus, the ninth guru, Tegh Bahadur, writings from Bhakti Hinduism and from Sufism as well as a few compositions of bards attached to the courts of the earlier gurus. The single largest contribution (over two thousand hymns) is from the pen of Guru Arjun.

The earliest parts are the hymns of Jai Dev (twelfth century A.D.) and the last those of Guru Tegh Bahadur (seventeenth century). Since the hymns were taken from the writings of Hindus and Muslims living at different times and in different regions, there is a wide range of dialects, nomenclature, and style. However most of the compositions are in Sant Bhāsā, a Punjabi dialect used extensively for composing religious verse and not difficult to comprehend. Except for the Japji, composed by Nānak, all the remaining hymns are divided into thirty-one *ragas* or musical modes.

3. **Uses.** The Ādi Granth is the central object of worship in every Sikh *gurdwārā* (temple). It is draped in silks and placed on a cot under an awning. Offerings of money, flowers, or food are made to it, as it is regarded as "the true Emperor."

The Ādi Granth is formally opened every morning and put to rest in the evening. On special occasions there is nonstop recitation *(akhand pāth)* by a relay of readers, which takes two days and nights. A seven-day *(saptāh pāth)* reading during daytime is also common. Sikh children are usually named after the first letter on a page opened at random. Sikh marriages are performed by the couple going round the Ādi Granth four times to the chanting of hymns.

Bibliography. S. Singh, *The Seekers Path* (1959); S. S. Kohli, *A Critical Study of the Adi Granth* (1961).

K. Singh

ĀDINĀTHA ä´ dē nä´ thŭ (Ja—Skt.; lit. "chief lord," "primary deity" [*ādi*—"first, primeval, primary"; *nātha*—"refuge, lord, master"]). 1. Title and proper name often given to Ṛṣabha, the first Jaina Tīrthaṅkara, particularly in connection with Jinasena's (ninth century A.D.) *Ādipurāṇa* ("Account of the Beginnings"). This Jaina version of the history of the cosmos portrays Ṛṣabha as the creator of the Caste system and of human culture in general. 2. The name of a famous and still active Jaina temple on Mt. Abu, one of the great Jaina pilgrimage and temple centers.

K. W. Folkert

ADITI ŭ´ dĭ tē (H—Skt.; lit. "not tied" [*a*—"not" + *diti*—"bound"]). The "Infinite," the "Boundless Expanse," a primordial goddess of Vedic Hinduism, mother of the gods and particularly mother of the Ādityas, a class of sovereign deities. She is the limitless sky, but also the earth as well, and a cow who provides milk for the gods. As she is "bondless" she is invoked to free her devotees from distress and evil. Her sons, the Ādityas, six, seven, eight, or twelve in number, include Varuṇa as paramount, Mitra, Aryaman, Dakṣa, and others. In post-Vedic mythology Dakṣa is her father, not her son, and Vishnu as a dwarf and Vivasvat as the sun are among the twelve Ādityas, often linked to the twelve solar months.

Bibliography. A. A. Macdonell, *Vedic Mythology* (1897).

D. M. Knipe

ADVAITA ŭd vī´ tŭ (H—Skt.; lit. "nondualism"). The type of Vedānta which denies the reality of difference, holding that the only reality is the one distinctionless Brahman. The most important figure in this tradition is Śaṃkara. It is the most widely known of the Hindu philosophical systems; indeed, so prominent is it that it is sometimes taken to be the only Vedānta, or even the only kind of Indian philosophy.

Advaita is to be contrasted with other Vedāntic systems through its unique hypothesis of a projective ignorance (Avidyā or Māyā) which causes the world of manifold distinctions to appear to us in accordance with our karmic residues. It emphasizes the path of knowledge rather than action or devotion as the key to liberation. *See* Vedānta §2 and bibliog.

K. H. Potter

ADVENT (Ch). A preparatory period before CHRISTMAS. Originating in Gaul in the fourth century as a fast of three weeks, it was extended to six weeks. Similar fasts are observed in the Eastern ORTHODOX CHURCHES today. The present Western Advent of four weeks focuses on expectation of the age of the MESSIAH. *See* CALENDAR, CHRISTIAN. T. J. TALLEY

AFGHĀNĪ, JAMĀL al-DĪN ăf gä′ nē jə mäl′ əl dēn′ (I; 1839–1897). Muslim reformer, apologist, and anti-colonialist. He spent his formative years in Afghanistan before traveling extensively throughout the Muslim world and Europe. From 1871 to 1879 he taught and wrote in Cairo, spurring unrest against the British, which was forcefully put down in 1882. Twice, in 1886 and 1889, the Qajar Shah of Iran invited him to Tehran. Each time the two men fell out, the second time over the Shah's 1890 tobacco concession to the British. During the 1890s he settled in Istanbul, where Sultan ʻAbd al-Ḥamīd II used him to promulgate pan-Islamic ideals. Their friendship cooled, especially after Jamāl al-Dīn's alleged complicity in the 1896 assassination of the Shah.

Jamāl al-Dīn Afghānī was most effective as a pamphleteer, journalist, orator, and revolutionary activist. The development of philosophical bases for Islamic modernism was left to his most illustrious pupil from the Cairo period, MUHAMMAD ʻABDŪH.

Bibliography. *EI* II, 416-19; C. C. Adams, *Islam and Modernism in Egypt* (1933); A. Hourani, *Arabic Thought in the Liberal Age, 1798-1939* (1962); N. R. Keddie, *An Islamic Response to Imperialism: Political and Religious Writings of Sayyid Jamāl ad-dīn al-Afghānī* (1968). B. LAWRENCE

AFRICAN TRADITIONAL RELIGION. Those sub-Saharan African religions which do not clearly belong to the major world religions may be termed traditional religions. They are diffused throughout their societies, and their personnel, cultus, and values are hard to separate from general social institutions. Consequently there is hardly any distinction between sacred and profane dimensions of life.

1. **The nature of African religion.** Indigenous African religions might be termed "traditional" rather than "tribal." African societies often number in the millions, and one society may include several "tribes," particularly in the urbanized cultures of West Africa. Within the extraordinary range of traditional cultures can be found hunting-and-gathering bands (now rare) in which there is little or no "tribal" concept, and also elaborate urbanized empires where the term "tribal" does not apply.

The vast majority of sub-Saharan Africans dwell in village communities and are sustained by hoe ("shifting," or "slash-and-burn") agriculture, often supplemented by hunting and (especially in east, central, and southern Africa) cattle-herding. The culture-history of Africa is complicated not only by the widely varying ecological environments (rain forest, savannah, highland plateau, etc.), but also by

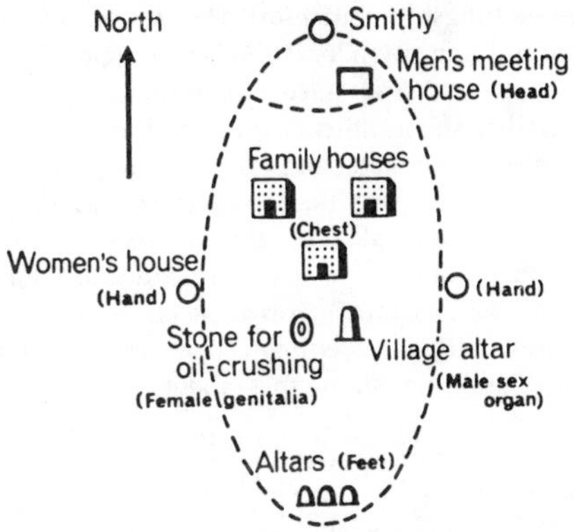

Diagram of village

From M. Griaule, *Conversations with Ogotemmeli;* courtesy the International African Institute

The layout of Dogon villages centers on the creative union of male and female in God.

different historical and social contexts, such as migrations, trade influences, military conquests, and missionary activity. The extent of social differentiation has been a major factor in religious development, since more differentiated societies have tended to develop priestly elites, complex mediumistic cults, many-layered initiatory mysteries, and intricate mythical-philosophical systems.

In general, the rain-forest cultures may be distinguished from those of the more open savannah lands. The former tend to be protected from outside influences, more isolated, and therefore more archaic. Hunting bands still survive in the Congo forest, and the Pygmy reverence for water serpents and leopards as forms of the Master of animals can also be found among the forest Bantu who live in isolated farming-hunting villages. Cults restricted to initiates and usually centering on masked forest spirits, including the royal leopard, are found throughout the rain forest from Sierra Leone to eastern Zaire. Elders in such cults generally exercise juridical powers over the rest of their society, and success in the hunt is thought even by farmers to assure fertility for their wives and the village fields.

In the rolling savannah, however, ancient local traditions have tended to be swallowed up or strongly influenced by the appearance of vast empires and the rise of far-flung trade. In the West African Sudan in particular, ancient Mediterranean, Hellenistic, and Muslim influences have affected sub-Saharan cultures, as is shown even today by themes in esoteric initiatory myths, divination practices, and widely diffused traits of divine kingship.

Less varied than West African cultures are those of the Bantu peoples of central, southern, and eastern Africa who formed kingdoms south of the Congo forest and spread into the highlands from Angola in the west to Mozambique in the east and from Rhodesia north to Buganda. There are some instances of divine kingship, but most cultures center on the village and clan, with local chiefs and regional priests serving the ancestral culture hero or fertility spirit. The fertility spirit, chief of the ancestors, dwells in a local river pool or lake, and often assumes the form of a serpent. It governs both human and agricultural fertility. Present also in the rainbow, it is the intermediary of God, or is even regarded as a form of God and assures rain in response to sacrifices.

African religions tend not to be concerned with personal salvation or dogmas about God. They are instead *religions of structure,* in which self-realization arises through participation in the socio-cosmic web of relationships first laid down by God and the primal beings. God and the spirits are primarily worshiped because they, together with man, maintain the divinely established order. Life's goal is to maintain the transcendental structures which sustain normality, not to escape them or view them as evil, profane, or illusory. As in Judaism, holiness is sanctified normality; the divine is realized through everyday life.

2. **The ultimate sources of reality.** Genuine reverence for a Supreme Being is part of almost all African religions, despite considerable variation even within the same culture in how this reverence is expressed.

The cattle-herding Nilotic peoples of Sudan and Uganda (the Nuer, Dinka, Shilluk, etc.) are especially remarkable for intensity of devotion to God. It is customary to offer brief morning prayers (in some areas also evening prayers), in which God is thanked for the gift of another day of life, and his help is invoked for the day's tasks. Impromptu prayers are usual before any special activity such as a hunt or trading voyage is begun. The heavens are God's particular dwelling place, from which he looks down on the "black ants" who humbly worship him. Doubt of God's existence is inconceivable to such a people as the Nuer. As Evans-Pritchard remarks in a classic study of Nuer religion, the Nuer "faith" in God must be understood in the Hebraic sense of total existential "trust" rather than in the Hellenistic and later Christian sense of cognitive "belief."

The Nuer envision a pyramid of spiritual forces governing the world, flowing from and finally expressing one God and affecting specific localities, clans, streams, trees, or even magical charms. Each force may be separately invoked, but all are merely "refractions" of God, not independent entities. Some Nilotic peoples conclude logically and tolerantly that every cultural group has its own distinct culture hero sent by God specifically to sustain and direct it. The Shilluk, for example, say that they have Nyikang (the archetypal hero who continues to dwell in each divine king), Europeans have Christ, Muslim Arabs, Muhammad—all equally from God and equally sacred.

The image of a pyramid of forces may describe many African religions, but the image should be variously understood. For some cultures, the nearer forces take on distinct individuality and separate existence, and are likened to ministers serving a great chief (e.g., Zulu, Shona, Ila, Luba, Goura, Ashanti, and Yoruba). Proper reverence to God dictates that one approach him through his servants, perhaps referring to him only in the third person, or (most deferentially) not at all. Or we may be told that God has delegated his powers entirely to his spirits, and retired from any direct involvement in the petty afairs of earth-folk (e.g. Nyoro, Ganda and Soga of Uganda, and Thonga of Tanzania). Another frequently encountered justification for lack of direct worship of God is that God is so good he would never inflict bad luck or illness on anyone, so to avoid these misfortunes one must appeal directly to the undependable or hostile lesser spirits who, when honored in worship, desist from harming mankind, and even aid the devotee. The extreme development of this tendency elevates the intermediary spirits to the

Musée de l'Homme

Dogon dance mask used in rites to expel the souls of the recently dead status of demi-gods or gods, as among the forest kingdoms of the West African coastal regions (from Ghana to Nigeria) and amongst the Buganda of Uganda (in East Africa). In these complex societies (the Fon of Dahomey and the Yoruba of Nigeria are truly urban), we have imposing polytheistic systems. The Fon say that Mawu-Lisa, the androgynous Creator, is parent of all the gods. Most often she is referred to simply as Mawu, the Mother of the universe. She gave the gods their particular spheres, some the sky, others the earth and wilderness, still others the sea, streams and rain. Each group is autonomous, yet they replicate each other in their inner hierarchies to a large degree, with Mawu-Lisa often identified by the priests of each cult with the major deity of their own pantheon. In the case of the very similar religion of the Yoruba, E. Bolaji Idowu suggests that the façade of many gods merely masks an intense conviction that one God alone rules all things, acting through various modes.

The ANDROGYNY of Mawu-Lisa is not exceptional. In many central and west Sudanic cultures, in the West African coastal kingdoms, and in other formerly imperial societies, we often find esoteric philosophies which insist that God and all reality are androgynous, generated out of the interaction of female and male modes throughout the universe. Among the matrilineal "Voltaic" cultures of northern Ghana, and in some eastern Nigeria cultures, God is visualized as female, perhaps celestial or perhaps dwelling in the underworld and identical with the Mother Earth widely worshiped in these areas.

In many east, central, and southern African religions we find prophets inspired directly by God. They may be priestly "rain-makers" with their own shrines, or people "called" by God at times of crisis to alert the people to God's anger at misdeeds and to proclaim a new order. Jewish or Muslim influences may have helped shape some of these prophet cults. The Meru of Kenya, for example, betray clearly Jewish motifs (*see* Bernardi).

However intense the belief in God, the reality of this sensory world remains in the foreground as the miracle to be explained and sustained. God, the ancestors, the spirits of local streams and hills—all participate in a universal web of spiritual interchange to maintain fertility and the health of all beings. This pragmatic orientation of African religions expresses a profound spiritual assurance of the goodness of life.

It is very rare to encounter real secularism. A number of societies in western Tanzania, victims of centuries of Arab slave raids and wars, local tyrants, epidemics, rapid social change, colonial pressures, and the rise of intensive long-distance trading, are the apparent exceptions (not only agriculturalists like the Fipa and Nyika, but even hunters like the Hazda, seem affected). Here God and even the spirits are too weak and remote to affect life (*see* R. Willis).

A seemingly paradoxical but widespread theme in African religions is that God shows his active benevolence by remaining in heaven and permitting everyday life to continue without intervention. If God comes too near, sickness, madness, or death is likely. Throughout East Africa those struck by lightning are thought to be chosen and touched by God. Shrines are generally erected to the victim's spirit, which has become an intermediary to God. Such divine activity is greatly feared, and lightning storms are times of widespread repentance and prayers begging God to go away.

This is perhaps why direct prayers and cultic worship by the entire populace are to be expected above all at times of great catastrophe and upheaval, for these transformations are both evidence of God's near approach and proof of the inability of all lesser spirits to control the divine order.

It is evident, then, that the deepest focus of African religion is on the underlying divinely sustained normative order. An extreme instance of this is the bwami cult of the Lega of eastern Zaire described by Biebuyck. The bwami society is one form of the "leopard societies" (*see* §1 above). Like many other cultures with such cults, the Lega have no supreme chief or king, but keep order through the initiatic cult itself (they call bwami their "king"). Arguments between feuding villages are arbitrated by regional bwami elders, who are held to embody the universalistic peace-loving attributes of the earth itself. To rise high in bwami, one must learn to transcend the transient passions of local village affairs, and the elders form a trans-village community, dedicated to the maintenance of the cosmos. Although the cult dramatizes the divine order, its rituals include no prayers to God or spirits, no sacrifice of any sort, and no cultivation of ecstatic states. Bwami does not justify itself by any elaborate myths. It simply consists of the repetition in song and dramatic dance of thousands of outwardly commonplace proverbs. Every elevation in rank requires the memorization of hundreds of new proverbs, together with their associated songs and dances. The individual proverbs may refer to the patience of the elephant or the useless jabbering of monkeys, but all of them together communicate to the initiate an entire symbolic world, a vision of wisdom and ethical norms whose elements are the stuff of everyday life. Enactment of bwami norms realizes (in the sense of "making real") the eternal truth at the heart of things. Because bwami celebrates eternity in the midst of time, its initiates are certain of immortality. No worship of ancestors is necessary because every celebration regenerates them by regenerating reality itself. So to drive illness, sterility, bad hunting, or death from a village, it is enough for initiates to gather and rehearse their songs and dramatized proverbs.

3. The concept of the self. One of the most vivid demonstrations of the importance of relationships in African religions is the universal African belief that numerous "souls" constitute a person. Each soul is the inward extension of a particular sphere of nature or society that shapes the self. The way to spiritual (and also physical) health lies not in extricating the self from its ties to the world and the flesh, but rather in harmonizing it with the environment. Since the African world is above all social, social relationships are essential to spiritual equilibrium. The various ancestors who inhabit the self as "souls" or guardians, and even the blood, flesh, and bones which were supplied by one's mother and father (and still resonate to the feelings of their ancestors and relatives), demand proper respect. One must therefore be loyal and generous with living family members, and offer regular sacrifices to the ancestral shades, to be at peace inwardly and flourish outwardly. Each person is really a multitude. Ignoring obligations to others really disrupts oneself, causing illness, bad luck, and even death. Frequently the core of medical ideology is propitiating offended spirits who demand that one's dependence on them be acknowledged fully and publicly. An irritated spirit will often possess a person in trance to communicate its desire to another member of the same family for more recognition or for moral reform. The ancestors are disturbed if their descendants argue among themselves or are not sharing the family wealth properly.

According to a survey of African soul-concepts by J. V. Taylor, a basic tripartite division can be detected in the bewildering variety of souls. The "life-soul" contains the vital forces, the "individual-soul" determines the personality and conscious will, and the "transcendental-soul" determines the destiny which is linked directly to God. The life-soul pulses in the blood and is often derived from the mother and her ancestors; passionate desire, anger, or even depression express its workings. The individual-soul (located in the bones, semen, etc.) is often linked with patrilineal ancestors, and governs the character; strong or weak charisma is due to this soul. The first two souls are fused to each other and to the body by the transcendental-soul which comes from God. Thus to be in harmony, each person must honor both parents and all relatives, and fulfill all traditional norms of loyalty and responsibility. While the life-soul generally remains in the body throughout the lifetime, the individual-soul often wanders in dreams and can be displaced by a more powerful soul or spirit in possession trance, or kidnapped by a witch. If the soul is not restored to the body, death will ensue. After death, the life-soul is usually thought to fade away, the individual-soul joins the ancestors, while the transcendental destiny-soul returns to God. It is remarkable how often we find that the name for God is the same as the name for the destiny-soul. The Ruanda call God Imana, and personal luck is also *imana* (shrines can be established to one's personal *imana*). They also say that all *imana* are really Imana, for God is one. Similar beliefs are common among the Nilotic peoples (where the term is generally Jok or *jok*). There is a band of cultures spanning a thousand miles from eastern Nigeria westward through the coastal forest which use basically the same term (*si, so, chi,* etc.) both for God and the destiny-soul. Shrines to one's personal destiny are common in these societies, constituting a kind of direct personal cult to God. Generally the destiny term for God implies an impersonal concept, while the proper name which may also be used to address God directly implies a more personal deity. Thus the Fon call God Mawu in a personal context, but Se when referring to her as Universal Spirit (each person has his or her own *se,* or destiny-soul).

Of course, the rigid application of these ideas would result in oversystematization. In fact the destiny-soul may be lacking, or there may be several life-souls (perhaps one in the shadow—taboos on stepping on the shadow are common in Africa), or each major organ may have its own soul. Furthermore, a person's name is very widely believed to carry spiritual power. In any case, the self is more than one can consciously control. One's life is to a very significant degree out of one's hands. Thus if one does heroic or repugnant acts, these may be explained as due to particular souls. Personal responsibility is therefore to a degree diluted. For, example, the divine or sacral king found in many traditional African cultures generally was thought to derive his divinity from the soul of the culture hero which "possessed" him. Since all of life is ranged in a hierarchy of souls and powers, possession cults are a natural way of acknowledging and propitiating the powers directing one's life.

4. The life-cycle and sex roles. Since each person is a totality of selves, true individuality and strong character can only come from the progressive integration of roles and responsibilities, not by isolation from society. The rituals that accompany the major stages of maturation illustrate the widening circles of the self and its increasing definition. The baby in many African societies is welcomed with modest rituals, involving the nuclear family and perhaps primarily the mother and child. A preliminary secret name may be divined for the child, derived from the ancestor who has been discovered to be the guardian of its life. But if it dies, a full funeral is usually not held. (*See* Life Cycle Rites.)

Initiation at puberty joins the individual with his entire generation, enabling him to become an adult and a full family member. Marriage and the events of later years add further to the self, embracing more and more persons and intimately affecting their lives. Parents live on in their children, and the homage of slaves or other dependents also increases the spiritual power and "selfhood" of a person. An elder or ancestor, no longer personally involved in the striving and ambitions of youth, can act for the welfare of all his descendants and dependents, who now ideally form a great multitude. Thus the funeral of an elder is (in contrast to that of an infant) a community event, with many attending even from other villages and regions.

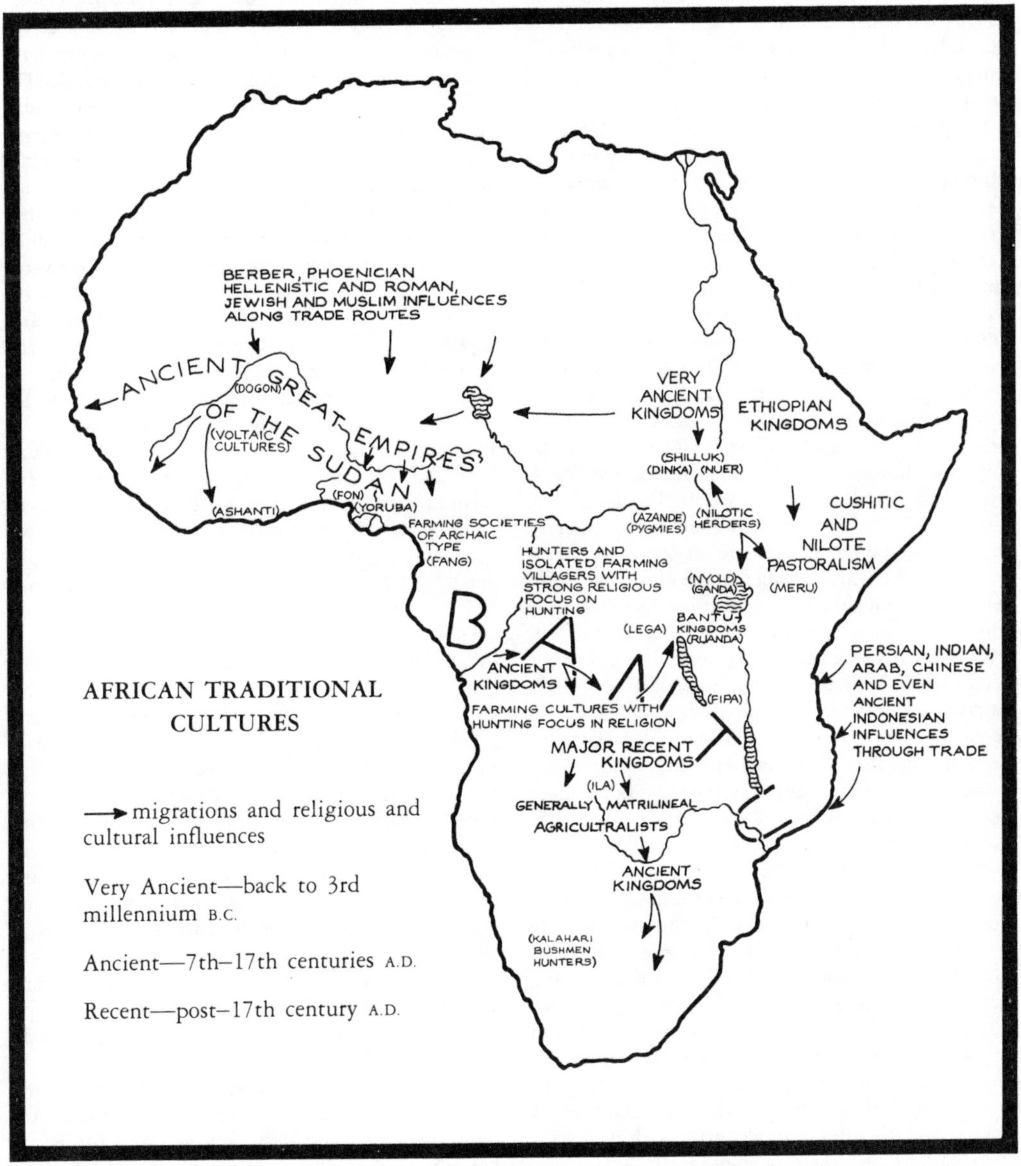

AFRICAN TRADITIONAL CULTURES

⟶ migrations and religious and cultural influences

Very Ancient—back to 3rd millennium B.C.

Ancient—7th–17th centuries A.D.

Recent—post–17th century A.D.

The ancestor continues the elder's role, but now with single-hearted devotion to family norms. African religions tend to be past-oriented; the ancestors must be propitiated, or their mystical curse or spiritual possession of descendants will cause illness, madness, or death. But harmony with the ancestors will bring crop fertility, many children, health, and prosperity. Since the ancestors oversee fertility, the harvest ceremonies are the special time to acknowledge their presence. During the New Year's harvest festivals in traditional West African towns and cities sacrifices are made to the dead, food is piled up before shrines, and alcoholic beverages fermented from the recently harvested grains are drunk, sexual liberties and wild behavior are permitted, and the entire world seems to be going through a general reversal of norms. In the land of the dead, according to traditional Ashanti conceptions, all the activities of the living continue, but in reverse. Abnormal behavior at the harvest, especially when it involves fertility themes, therefore merely acknowledges the presence of the ancestral dead. It is the time of carnival, when the spirits of the wild and of night take over the day, and normal behavior is actually forbidden. A striking characteristic of these festivals (lesser analogues of which are common throughout Africa not only at times of harvest, but also at other ritual occasions) is the lampooning of chiefs, priests, and other high-status figures. At such time, all persons are equal and all status is leveled or even reversed. All this is to assure the vital contact with the spiritual world so necessary for renewed life and fertility in the coming year.

No person, it follows, is free of dependency on others. Moreover, the chief result of harmonious submission to divine norms is fertility and enhanced life. These are fundamental African values, affecting decisively the self-image of both men and women. Men, for example, sometimes could expect to attain almost life-and-death powers over their own family (wife, children, and grandchildren), but they also remain dependent on their dependents: i.e., the more persons who are subject to you, the greater your spiritual power. If some defect or die, your power is correspondingly weakened. Men must also exhibit complete loyalty to clan elders, village chiefs, the king, and the ancestors. Power in the male sphere is generally political, but with a spiritual undertone. A village chief is often believed to maintain his position through magical arts, defending his people and their fields against envious witches (some of whom might well be rival chiefs). His own health and fertility have a direct effect on the fertility of the villagers and their fields while his wife may be explicitly likened to the "land" which he keeps fecund. Therefore the chief's main wife is often in effect the priestess of the Earth. There are many variations on the basic symbolic complex, but they all assume that human sexuality contains a great cosmic mystery which plays itself out on every level of reality.

The power of women is more spiritual than political, but that does not mean that it is any less real for Africans. In many African societies, especially those in which women participate actively in agricultural work and so control something of the product, women have independent economic and even political power. But in all societies religious ideas guide the basic attitude of respect for and even fear of women's sacral energies. This is often expressed as fear of "pollution" in menstruation and childbirth. In some societies it is thought that men can even be "unmanned" by coming into contact with women at this time. As with men, women ideally have as the goal of their lives to be submissive to the divine norms and the hierarchy of souls and spirits, and to seek greater fertility and enhancement of life. This generally means, however, that they should be submissive not only to their elders and relatives, but also to their husbands. Men's contribution to the common goals may be culturally explicit and under conscious control (political authority, initiatic wisdom, etc.), but that of women is natural, mysterious, beyond male control, and even to a degree beyond their own, and therefore more dangerous. Since much of African religion is oriented to fertility, it is possible to suggest that the feminine is at the center of religious concern. Sometimes the men seek to gain control over female fertility by linking their own activities to it (thus hunting peoples and even agriculturalists of the Congo forest believe that the hunt controls the fertility of women: much game caught means many children will be born). The ancestor cult is very much concerned with such control, and the festivals also center on this theme. Nevertheless, a woman who refusing to cooperate with men remains infertile, or rejects her traditional roles, or even "bewitches" her children so that they die, is assumed to be a witch. As such, she is allied with the sterile wilderness against the cultivated fertile fields, with the animals of the forest against the hunters, etc. Like the fertile wife, she possesses mysterious and even involuntary powers over life and death, but in her case they are turned to evil.

5. Witchcraft and sorcery. There is in fact a tendency to associate women with WITCHCRAFT, which involves natural and often involuntary powers to harm, and men with sorcery, which requires learned techniques of manipulating medicines and charms to work evil. Nevertheless, in most cultures even sorcerers are thought to have some link to witchcraft, and witches may also use medicines. Both witches and sorcerers, in addition, are usually isolated figures, such as old, lonely people living at the edge of the village or alone in the bush, the unusually ugly or beautiful, the woman who is sterile while her co-wives are not, or even the man whose exceptional good fortune has separated him from others and made him a target for their envy and suspicion. Witches and sorcerers are thought to be in rebellion against the divine order, rejecting the normal invigorating interchange of life forces and seeking to center all things on themselves. They like therefore to render men impotent and women sterile; they destroy infants and seeds in the ground. Anyone in process of transformation (such as initiates, pregnant women, the sick, or even the newly dead) is particularly vulnerable, for witches love to abort creative change, turning its energies to their own advantage. Thus the newly dead might be devoured in ghoulish feasts, or dug up from the grave and forced into zombie servitude, in this way being prevented from becoming ancestors. If the divine order consists of harmonious structure, witchery is dedicated to anti-structure and demonic, petty, self-centered meaninglessness.

Yet precisely the rejection of transcendental norms that defines witchcraft also gives it a larger meaning within the divine order. As Evans-Pritchard first showed for the Azande, witchcraft offers a logical explanation for all events that go wrong. There is no chance in a universe inhabited by witches; there is the benevolent divine order, and there is demonism. Peculiar unlucky coincidences or personal disasters are attributed to mystical hatreds or personal jealousies.

6. Possession and divination. African religions place an unusually positive emphasis on possession trance. Such trance states have been no less significant among Mediterranean and European cultures, but there they are generally viewed as demonic, anti-social, or pathological, and only in a few cases as due to positive spirituality (Bourguignon). In contrast to this predominantly exorcistic Western approach, the African attitude stresses integration and healing in connection with spirit possession. For example, "cults of affliction" (Victor Turner) are common throughout eastern and central Africa, and illness or mental disturbance is explained by spirit affliction. When a shrine is set up to the spirit and it is allowed to possess the victim openly, the illness is cured. In modern times cults to "European" spirits have sprung up in many areas, as Bantu peoples have sought to come to terms with colonial dislocation and stress. Possessed mediums in such cults might insist on European dress, take up European postures and mannerisms, sip tea, etc. The compensatory nature of such cults is obvious, but since the spirits generally act to reaffirm the social norms of the community they also strengthen traditional society. Sheila Walker has distinguished three major types of African possession cults. In some, the medium behaves in a wild or largely idiosyncratic fashion, under the influence of a minor or even previously unknown spirit (here personal pathology is uppermost). In others that are much more common in Africa the medium's behavior is more stereotyped, often as the result of training during a long initiation. Here the spirit is a significant one in the culture (generally an ancestor), and is anxious to support traditional norms. The third and rarest type of cult, of which the Fon of Dahomey are the chief example, is predominantly controlled by cultural and normative considerations. Mediums are chosen not on the basis of personal predisposition, but essentially arbitrarily, for the sake of cultic communication with the major spirits controlling the universe. Trance states are not deep, and the medium's behavior is stereotyped.

Possession cults would appear to imply a sense that the socially defined ego-self is trapped by social hierarchies and roles; the only way the transcendental experience of divinity is possible is through submission to other, more powerful and freer selves, who can break through the social self and take control. Such cults are in fact much more likely in densely populated, hierarchically stratified societies, which are common in Africa. Hunting peoples, who live in egalitarian bands, seldom have possession cults, although shamanism (in which the ego-self retains conscious awareness and even control in trance) is quite common.

Possession trance is frequently a part of divination in Africa. Generally divination is used to find out the inner meaning of events which have already occurred, for example, what spirits are making the family children fall ill. Two basic types of divination can be distinguished: (1) the most common folk variety, which makes use of spirit possession either of human mediums or of animals or even objects to find the answer to questions; and (2) the highly philosophical systems of divination which make use of a complex classification of all reality to obtain a "reading" of events. The latter apparently generally stems historically from esoteric circles of diviners at royal courts.

The constant recourse to divination at every point of doubt or choice does not imply a fatalistic outlook. On the contrary, it merely underlines the general African sense that every moment involves transcendental forces in delicate equilibrium, many of which are more powerful than humble human beings. The basic impulse is a religious sense of finitude and dependency on the otherness of life. When the forces affecting one's life are known, they can be invoked and propitiated, and bad luck can almost always be changed by sacrifice to the spirits that caused it.

7. **Modernization and change.** In the past few centuries, traditional African religions have been retreating before the united onslaught of Christianity, colonial and national social transformation, and Islam. But traditional religions are far from dead. It has been estimated that in 1971 there were in Africa about 75 million Christians, 140 million Muslims, and 120 million adherents of traditional religions. The full dimensions of the influence of traditional religions, however, cannot be appreciated by such figures, for many Christians and Muslims understand their own religions in distinctively African ways which derive from traditional values. (*See* CHRISTIANITY IN AFRICA §3; ISLAM §5.) At the same time the traditional religions have shown surprising resilience in adjusting to the new realities of urban life and nationalism.

It has been suggested, for example, that the strong tendency toward monotheism and egalitarian sociopolitical philosophies that is found in Africa today partly expresses a traditional response to the experience of radical crisis. Modernization breaks down social boundaries, just as formerly earthquakes and epidemics did. The African response has always been to appeal directly to the Supreme Being when all intermediary powers (and the restricted spheres they govern) are shattered. During such crises, as ritualized in New Year's ceremonies or at the death of chiefs and divine kings, social divisions are done away with and all stand equal before God. This terrifying (and not merely unifying) crisis has often become permanent under modern pressures; it resists ritual resolutions and seeks formal expression in Christian, Muslim, or even Marxist terminology. Of the perhaps 6,000 new religious movements that have arisen in the past half-century most attempt to find structure and meaning in the new realities by predicting the overthrow of all oppressive institutions, and the restoration of true community directly under God. Such movements have become a major focus of modern research in African religions.

Another traditional African emphasis that has not been lost in the transition to Christianity or Islam is the tacit belief that the locus of spiritual life and power lies in this world. Otherworldly, ascetic types of spirituality have little attraction for Africans. Religion remains very much a social enterprise, not a quest for personal salvation or private states of consciousness. Most of the new religions mentioned above have been oriented to healing, opposition to witchcraft, and an enhanced sense of life's holiness. Many of the new movements reflect the African interest in proverbs and in the rhetorical arts, weaving African and Western ritual symbols together sermonically and in everyday experience with astonishing sophistication. Possession trance is another traditional feature retained in these movements.

In sum, traditional practices continue to thrive in African towns and cities, even apart from their influence on the new religions, on Islam, and on Christianity. Witchcraft beliefs, for example, often seem to flourish in the threatening world of urban change. Traditional modes of healing are maintained along with modern medicine; e.g., doctors often report that many of their less Westernized patients seek out traditional healers after leaving the hospital, combining the practical efficacy of Western medicine with the spiritual healing that only harmony with the past and with the ancestors can evoke. The traditional African view of the self is continued in recourse to spirit shrines and mediums to enhance personal persuasiveness, business success, or health. Furthermore, there is increasing evidence that some form of ancestor reverence and cult is often maintained in the midst of industrialization. Even highly educated Africans may insist that there is a mysterious dimension to life that is missed by Western empiricism, but is more truly understood and dealt with by traditional wisdom.

Bibliography. For general introductions, B. Ray, *African Religions* (1976); B. Davidson, *The African Genius* (1969); J. Mbiti, *African Religions and Philosophy* (1969); M. Douglas, *Purity and Danger* (1966) and *Natural Symbols* (1960); J. V. Taylor, *The Primal Vision* (1963); R. Willis, *Man and Beast* (1970); and E. Zuesse, *Ritual Cosmos* (1979), each with bibliographies.

On views of God, E. W. Smith, ed., *African Ideas of God* (3rd ed., 1966), and A. Shorter, *Prayer in the Religious Traditions of Africa* (1975). On possession cults, J. Middleton and J. Beattie, eds., *Spirit Mediumship and Society in Africa* (1969); E. Bourguignon, ed., *Religion, Altered States of Consciousness and Social Change* (1973); and S. Walker, *Ceremonial Spirit Possession and Mediumship in Africa and Afro-America* (1972). On "prophetism," B. Bernardi, *The Mugwe: A Failing Prophet* (1959). On witchcraft, J. Middleton and E. H. Winter, eds., *Witchcraft and Sorcery in East Africa* (1963), or for a general survey, L. Mair, *Witchcraft* (1969). For new religious movements, a basic source is H. W. Turner, *Bibliography of New Religious Movements in Primal Societies*, Vol. 1: *Black Africa* (1977).

For a detailed listing of titles on African religions, see P. E. Ofori, *Black African Traditional Religions and Philosophy: A Select Bibliographic Survey of the Sources from Earliest Times to 1974* (1975). Some of the classic studies in the anthropology of religion that have emerged from African studies include: E. E. Evans-Pritchard, *Nuer Religion* (1940) and *Witchcraft, Oracles and Magic among the Azande* (1937); G. Lienhardt, *Divinity and Experience: The Religion of the Dinka* (1961); J. Middleton, *Lugbara Religion* (1960). A highly influential student of Evans-Pritchard is V. W. Turner, whose *Forest of Symbols* (1967), *Drums of Affliction* (1968), and *Revelation and Divination in Ndembu Ritual* (1975), all deal with the ritual symbolisms of the Ndembu of Zambia and are required reading for Africanists. D. Biebuyck, *Lega Culture* (1973), is an important study of the bwami cult. The French school of ethnology has made some extraordinary studies of esoteric myths and philosophies, such as M. Griaule, *Conversations with Ogotemmêli* (1948); M. Griaule and G. Dieterlen, *Le Renard Pâle* (1965); and G. Calame-Griaule, *Ethnologie et langage* (1966), all dealing with the Dogon of Mali; J. P. Lebeuf, *L'habitation des Fali* (1961), on house design and village layout among a Cameroons people. A recent development is studies of African religions by Africans such as E. Bolaji Idowu's *Olódùmarè: God in Yoruba Belief* (1963). For brief but outstanding essays on specific religions from various areas of Africa, see D. Forde, ed., *African Worlds* (1954).

E. M. Zuesse

ĀGAMA ä´ gŭ mŭ (B, H & Ja—Skt.; lit. "tradition, received teachings" [*ā-gam*—"to come"]). Generally, in Indian religions, a tradition's sacred scripture or body of teachings, handed down by an unbroken line of teachers. In Jainism it is, together with the term *Siddhānta* ("established teachings"), the most general designation for the canonical texts, while in Buddhism it is employed most distinctively for those portions of the Sanskrit canon (preserved in Chinese translation) that correspond to the Pali Nikāyas (*see* Pali Canon §4). Within Hindu religion it designates primarily a class of post-Vedic sectarian Sanskrit scriptures, basically ritualistic in character and believed to have been revealed by one of the personal deities, Vishnu, Shiva, or the Goddess (*see* Śakti).

While the terms Tantra (*see* Tantrism) and Saṃhitā are often used synonymously with Āgama, in some contexts it is convenient to employ them to distinguish the three major Hindu streams of Āgamic or Tantric religion. Thus Āgama can be used for Śaiva texts devoted to Shiva and forming the scriptural basis for such traditions as Śaiva Siddhānta, the Liṅgāyats, and Kashmir Śaivism; Saṃhitā for Vaiṣṇava ones dedicated to Vishnu, such as the Pañcarātra works utilized by the Śri Vaiṣṇavas and others; and Tantra for the Śākta texts governing the worship of the Goddess or Śakti.

These sectarian scriptures and traditions become increasingly influential throughout the first millennium A.D., with the earliest extant Āgamas generally being placed in the fifth century, although some would date them several centuries later. In the general historical development of Hindu religion, the Āgamas as a class of scriptures follow upon the classes of Śruti (the eternal Vedic revelation) and Smṛti (Vedic traditional literature of human authorship). They continue the emphasis on Bhakti or popular devotional worship of personal deities found in such *smṛti* texts as the Purāṇas. Seen as new revelations for the present age or Kali Yuga, they are held equal in authority to the *śruti* or Veda, both being based upon the faultless consciousness of the Godhead. Their rise coincides with the growth in importance of temples housing divine images, and the Āgamas are essentially the ritual texts that govern the worship (Pūjā) and other devotional practices *(sādhanā)* associated with these temples and centering on the realization of the various gods and goddesses enshrined in them.

While differing in many particulars, the Āgamas represent a definite genre of literature. Theoretically, an Āgama should have four sections dealing respectively with 1) "knowledge" (Vidyā) of the Godhead and its relation to the manifest universe; 2) "meditative discipline" (Yoga) or techniques for concentration on the divine images or forms, especially by means of Mantras or sacred formulas; 3) "action" *(kriyā)* such as the building of temples and the making and consecrating of images; and 4) "conduct" *(caryā)* or rules for daily worship and festivals, social behavior, etc. While most of the Āgamas do not in fact conform to this pattern, they are united by their practical concern with the external ritual worship of divine images in temples and home shrines and the techniques for internal "mental worship" and realization of the divine forms.

Bibliography. J. Gonda, *Medieval Religious Literature in Sanskrit* (1977): J. A. B. van Buitenen, ed. and trans., *Yāmuna's Āgama Prāmāṇyam* (1971). W. G. Neevel

AGASTYA ŭ gŭs′ tyŭ (H—Skt.). Sage who is reputed to have civilized the south of India. In the Rāmāyaṇa of Vālmīki, Rāma visits his hermitage and receives instruction from him. It is said that Agastya was born out of a waterpot and that he was short in stature. He was sent by the gods to control the pride of the Vindhya mountains in the south, which were growing higher and higher in competition with the northern Mount Meru and obstructing the movements of the sun and moon. Agastya crossed the Vindhyas on his journey to the south, and the mountains prostrated themselves before him in respect. The sage commanded the mountains to stay in that position until he returned, but he settled in the south and never passed that way again. The Rāmāyaṇa has a story which narrates how Agastya killed the two cannibal demons, Vātāpi and Ilvala. The demons would invite Brahmin sages for dinner, and Vātāpi would become a ram whom Ilvala would cook and feed to the Brahmins. After the dinner, Ilvala would call his brother, who would resume his demon form and burst out of the Brahmin's belly. Agastya was also invited by the brothers and was fed the ram's meat, but, unlike the other Brahmins, he was strong enough to digest it. He then killed Ilvala as well, thus making the southern part of India safe for Brahmins. V. N. Rao

AGGADAH, HAGGADAH äg gä dä′ (Ju—Aram. & Heb.; lit. "telling"). Portions of rabbinic literature dealing with any subject other than Halakah (law). Prominent themes include theological and ethical teachings (often in Midrash form), descriptions of eschatological reward, wisdom sayings, folk tales, liturgical matters, stories about rabbis, etc. No unanimity was sought by the rabbis in the realm of aggadah, and therefore no aggadah is considered binding.

Bibliography. L. Ginzberg, *Legends of the Jews* (1909-1938); G. F. Moore, *Judaism* (1927); E. E. Urbach, *The Sages, Their Opinions and Beliefs* (1975). I. Chernus

AGGIORNAMENTO ä jŏr′ nä mĕnt′ ō (Ch—Italian; lit. "updating"). Used to describe processes begun in Roman Catholicism by Pope John XXIII, who said on June 5, 1960 that Vatican Council II should update church legislation and practice and that theology should become dynamic and concrete so as to cope with problems of the modern world.
J. Hennesey

AGGREGATE (B). *See* Anatta; Skandha.

AGHA KHAN ä′ gä kän (I—Turkish; "chief, master, lord"). The hereditary title of the head of the Nizārite sect of the Ismā'īliyya; originally bestowed on Hasan Ali Shāh by a ruler of the Qājar dynasty of Iran, Fath Ali Shāh (d. 1834), who also appointed him governor of Kirman. When the dynasty weakened, the Agha Khan lost his governorship and went to live in Maḥallāt, the most important post-Mogul Ismaili center in Iran, and a Sufi stronghold. After his death in Bombay in 1881, he was succeeded by his son Agha Ali Shāh, who died in 1885, succeeded in turn by his eight-year-old son Sulṭān Muhammad. This Agha Khan visited India and east Africa from time to time to meet with his followers, and established himself in Europe during his journeys there. The present Agha Khan IV, Karīm, counted by the Nizārites as their forty-ninth Imam, succeeded his grandfather in 1957. From headquarters in Paris he continues to provide both temporal and spiritual guidance to his followers.
A. A. Sachedina

AGNI ŭg′ nē (H & B—Skt.; "fire" or the deity of fire [*ag*—"to drive"; cognate, Latin *ignis*]). The fire god of Vedic Hinduism, praised in some two hundred hymns of the Rig Veda, and after Indra the most important of Vedic deities. The hearth for domestic sacrifices, the fire in lightning, the sun, waters, and plants—all are Agni, celebrated for his multiple births. The mystical numbers three, five, and seven are associated with him. He is generated anew each morning from the kindling sticks on earth, and he is born in the atmospheric waters and in the highest heaven, from which he is acquired as a gift to humans from the gods. His triadic births make him at home in the three levels of the universe—earth, midspace, and heaven—and his sacrificial structure is correspondingly threefold, in a cooking fire, a defensive fire, and an offering fire that make up the Vedic householder's three-fire system. He is described as "lord of the house" *(gṛhapati),* a father, an honored guest. As *jātavedas,* "knower of beings," he is omniscient; as *vaiśvānara,* "he who belongs to all men"; as *kravyād,* the cremation fire who devours corpses.

In the BRĀHMAṆAS, particularly the Śatapatha Brāhmaṇa, there is revealed the fivefold character of Agni. In the great *agnicayana,* the piling of the fire altar in a year-long ritual, the search for, collecting, and assembly of Agni in five layers is a cosmogonic operation recovering all of the dispersed elements of space and time. Here Agni is linked with PURUṢA-PRAJĀPATI. As the first sacrificer, Agni is designated oblation-bearer *(havya-vāhana)* and is thus a messenger between humans and gods. He functions also in all the priestly roles—invoker, executive, supervisor, and chaplain—and is a sage and seer as well.

Agni also has sevenfold physical characteristics—seven tongues and seven arms or rays. His brightness is much discussed, his burning head faces in all directions, and he is butter-backed, flame-haired, tawny. In the Rig Veda he is associated with numerous animals; in post-Vedic mythology he is often represented by a goat.

Bibliography. A. A. Macdonell, *Vedic Mythology* (1897); D. M. Knipe, *In the Image of Fire* (1975).

D. M. KNIPE

AGNIHOTRA ŭg nē hō´ trŭ (H—Skt.; lit. "oblation to AGNI"). In VEDIC HINDUISM an obligatory offering consisting of cow's milk—or sometimes cooked rice or barley, curds, or clarified butter (*see* GHEE)—performed every morning and evening by a TWICE BORN householder throughout his life. The offering *(homa)* is made into the fire immediately after MANTRAS are recited for sunrise and sunset.

D. M. KNIPE

AGNOSTICISM ăg nŏs´ tə sĭz əm (Gr.; lit. "nonknowledge"). The view that it is impossible for the human mind to know either that there is a god or that there is no god. Because the limits of the mind may not be the limits of the real, agnosticism does not necessarily imply ATHEISM.

K. CRIM

AGNUS DEI. äg´ noos *or* än´ yoos dā´ ē (Ch—Lat.; lit. "O Lamb of God"). Liturgical adaptation of John 1:29 borrowed from the Eastern LITURGY and introduced into the Latin MASS in the seventh century. By the eleventh century it was repeated three times with "grant us peace" instead of "have mercy upon us" as the third response.

R. A. GREER

AHAṂKĀRA ŭ hŭng kä´ rŭ (H—Skt.; lit. "I-maker, ego, self-awareness, conception of individuality" [from *aham,* "I," plus *kāra,* "maker"]). The principle of "ego" or personal identity in classical SĀṂKHYA philosophy.

G. J. LARSON

AHIṂSĀ ŭ hĭm´ sä (H, B, & Ja—Skt. & Pali; lit. "noninjury; absence of a desire to kill" [*hiṃs*—"injure, kill" + negative prefix *a*]). Not harming or wishing to harm any being; cornerstone of traditional Indian ethics (often called the highest DHARMA) and especially prominent in JAINA doctrine and the activities and teachings of Mohandas GANDHI.

Ahiṃsā is one of many negative (or passive) expressions employed traditionally in India to emphasize specific, positive (or active) significations not explicit in simple, affirmative "equivalents." Thus, although on the surface it suggests only an "absence" and recommends nothing beyond abstention or, perhaps, general passivity, *ahiṃsā* is considered to be the essence of compassion and humane nature (*see* KARUṆĀ; METTĀ). As such, it informs BHIKKHUS, YOGINS, and social activists about principles of conduct and urges them to positive practices that may include vegetarianism and cow-protection. (*See* COW, SYMBOLISM AND VENERATION.)

First attested in AŚOKA'S inscriptions (third century B.C.), *ahiṃsā* has been a major force in the history of ideas in India, and in recent decades, because of Gandhi's achievement, throughout the world.

1. The word *"ahiṃsā."* *Hiṃs,* the verbal root from which *ahiṃsā* is derived, is usually considered to be a desiderative of *han,* "strike, hurt, kill," that is, an expression of the wish to do what is specified by the primary root. Hence, *ahiṃsā* can mean *"not desiring* to kill" rather than simply "not killing," and one of its traditional definitions is *anabhidroha,* "absence of malice." Like KARMA, a concept it is closely linked with, *ahiṃsā* has been differently understood from tradition to tradition, and its exact meaning in any context will depend on the degree to which intention or volition is stressed. (*See §3 below.*)

2. Source of *ahiṃsā.* Sacrifice (YAJÑA) is central to VEDIC religion, and animal offerings are important in sacrifice. Further, Vedic texts sanction meat-eating. Since certain historically distinctive features of *ahiṃsā* are not found in the VEDA, many scholars assign its introduction to "extra-Vedic" movements—to Jainism and BUDDHISM in particular. Though plausible, this view is incomplete and necessarily remains somewhat conjectural. More probably, the rich nuances and implications of the word were forged in the various encounters of Vedic and non-Vedic thought.

Vedic sacrifice affirms and revivifies the ordered set of relationships in which humans, gods, and other beings participate. One one level, sacrificial offerings are conduits facilitating communication between men and gods. Beyond that, they are microcosms, symbols of a vast network of kinetic, relational values. Sacrificial "victims" are not simply killed or destroyed. They are transformed and revealed in ritual. Through them reality is confirmed. *Ahiṃsā* is frequently and rightly understood to emphasize the unity of life, and in this sense is present in every Vedic sacrifice.

But Vedic sacrifice has also been viewed differently and less charitably. To some it was wrong-headed spectacle and senseless slaughter. This, of course, was neither a matter of squeamishness nor of any appreciably enhanced awareness of economic values. Instead, it was the protest of those who either did not comprehend Vedic paradigms or rejected them. For them, *ahiṃsā* was a renunciation of the Veda's sense of an extended society in favor of a search for individual realization. Here *ahiṃsā* condemns particular acts and the entire world view on which they are based. And within Vedic tradition a contemplative few were increasingly heard to declare that sacrifice was meaningful only if you knew what you were doing—indeed, that knowing was tantamount to doing. When the word *ahiṃsā* first appears in Vedic literature (Chāndogya Upaniṣad III.17.4), it is in connection with describing the entire life of an individual as the equivalent of a "sacrifice." In this metaphor "ascetic restraint, liberality, personal rectitude, *ahiṃsā,* and truthfulness" are the "payments" to the sacrificial priests.

3. ***Ahiṃsā* in several traditions.** *Ahiṃsā* is so important for Jainas that it may be said to imply all Jaina values. The core of Jaina YOGA is *cāritra,* "good conduct," or *ahiṃsā* made explicit. The "minor vows" of Jaina lay persons and the ascetics' "great vows" hinge on *ahiṃsā*. Householders must not kill any animals. Their other vows—such as limiting the geographical area of their activities, refusing to eat certain vegetables and fruits, not recommending agriculture as a profession, not producing farm implements, and so forth—stem from *ahiṃsā*. Jaina ascetics must be even more assiduous. They are required to exercise the greatest care to avoid being in any way a cause of any kind of injury to any being. Pushed to its "logical" conclusion, this can mean refraining from any action whatsoever.

For Jainas, *ahiṃsā* is understood in the strictest possible sense. There are no pardonable lapses of conduct; ignorance, accident, and "good intentions" cannot count as excuses. The fact of injury—intended or not—is all-important, and one's duty is to prevent injury. The perspective is austere but should not be taken as simplistic or mechanistic.

Buddhists, too, accord *ahiṃsā* a central place in their ethics. To become a lay Buddhist, a person affirms the "Three Jewels" (TRIRATNA) and then vows to adhere to five precepts *(pañcaśīla),* the first of which is "not taking life." It applies to all life forms, but Buddhist literature analyzes the notion of "killing" very closely. Five conditions must be present: a living being; the knowledge or awareness that a living being is present; an intention to kill; an act of killing; and a death. If a *single* condition is missing, there is no killing properly so-called. That is, the moral precept against taking life has not been violated. This should not be thought to be an instance of sophistry. It emphasizes, rather, the fundamental Buddhist understanding that perceivable acts are manifestations of volitions, and thus it is one's intentions which determine the "fruits" (karma) of thought or actions.

Buddhist *bhikkhus* ("priests"), like Jaina ascetics, subscribe to a more demanding code than their lay counterparts. However, the stress on intention is enhanced and not superseded. Through discipline based on the EIGHTFOLD PATH the *bhikkhu* attains mastery of "self." Right intention will be a consequence, and because of it destruction of life becomes inconceivable.

Buddhist and Jaina interpretations of *ahiṃsā* clearly are not identical. Withdrawal, disengagement, and a scrupulously severe restriction of physical activity are especially obvious in the Jaina view. By contrast, the Buddhist attitude seems more dynamic, and the allied positive virtues of compassion and universal friendliness appear more conspicuous. Still, a profound respect for life permeates both traditions, and the expression of *ahiṃsā* in both may often be the same.

Hindus of different schools and backgrounds also hold *ahiṃsā* in high esteem. The yogin begins the journey to enlightenment (SAMĀDHI) by perfecting his conduct through restraints, of which the first is *ahiṃsā* (*see* YOGA). The great gods of BHAKTI HINDUISM are believed to love and aid all beings; their devotees strive to emulate that model. In devotional ceremony (PŪJĀ) flowers and fruits and vegetables are offered and shared. Here, the cow is not sacrificed but serves as a symbol of earth and its sustenance.

4. **Contradictions?** *Ahiṃsā,* though extremely important, has never been a universal standard in India, and in fact it is a subject of conflicting discussions in many texts until the medieval period. A first objection calls attention to the fact that, through the centuries, warfare has been no less common in India than elsewhere. Of course, an ideal's imperfect realization in practice is not uniquely an Indian problem. A related question asks: If *ahiṃsā* is the "highest dharma," why is it the KṢATRIYA'S dharma to fight? It is first to be remembered that dharma is not only "law" in general; it is also personal obligation tied to individual circumstance and status. Thus, it is dharmic for some to fight but not for others. And though force is part of the warrior-administrator's dharma, there is a widely celebrated ideal of the *cakravartin,* the great ruler whose administrative "force" is dharma itself. Furthermore, at least from the time of the BHAGAVAD GĪTĀ much attention has focused on the need to abide by dharma without thought of personal gain or loss. Warriors should fight because their dharma requires it. However, if they fight in anger, their action is not dharma. So, to do one's duty and to fight "without malice" is to respect an important dimension of *ahiṃsā's* meaning.

5. **Gandhi, *ahiṃsā,* and SATYĀGRAHA.** Through Mohandas Gandhi, *ahiṃsā* became part of an international vocabulary in the twentieth century. In one form or another, this question has been frequently asked: Was *ahiṃsā* for Gandhi the "traditional Indian" ideal or some modification of it? To answer this question one must consider that Gandhi was born

and raised in an environment in which Vaiṣṇava Hindu, Jaina, and Muslim teachings and values met, competed, and mingled. A late-comer to the serious study of his traditional background, he read and was strongly impressed by Leo Tolstoy's works before he knew the Indian classics. He also acknowleged that he had been influenced by the Bible, John Ruskin, and Henry David Thoreau. Although it has been said that Gandhi was a "pluralist"—even an eclectic—drawing inspiration from disparate sources and then fabricating an intensely personal philosophical position, that in itself would not set him apart from many other Indians in any century.

Gandhi was known and revered as *Mahātma,* a "great soul," a saint, a Guru, and that is the most significant consideration of all. In him his followers saw living truth, tradition embodied. His role was typical of India's great teachers and exemplars who have breathed life into traditional values. To live *ahiṃsā* is a more critical issue than to debate its historical origins, according to Gandhi.

No doubt Gandhi's *ahiṃsā* has its distinctive features. For example, "positively inviting injury . . . as a form of resisting evil" was, according to some, a Gandhian extension of *ahiṃsā's* meaning. Yet that attitude is shown in the Buddhist Jātakas, and the supposedly idiosyncratic aspects of Gandhi's interpretation of *ahiṃsā* do not make it a hybrid, even if the arena of its application is new. That, however, is a tribute to Gandhi's genius and a fitting commentary on the persisting liveliness, the complex of meanings, and the potential of this idea of "noninjury."

Bibliography. W. W. Brown, *Man in the Universe* (1966), pp. 43-67; on Gandhi, S. Ray, ed., *Gandhi, India and the World* (1970).

G. R. Welbon

AHL-I ḤAQQ äl ē häk´ (I—Pers.; lit. "people of truth") **AHL-I SILSILA** äl ē sĭl sĭl ä´ (I—Per.; lit. "people of chain"). Followers of a syncretistic religion with principal centers in western Iran. Extremist Shi'ite elements connect the sect with the 'Ali-Ilahi sect of the Shi'a, although Ali ibn Abī Ṭālib is not their principal figure. They do not appear to be directly connected with Ismā'īliyya, because they always speak of the twelve Imams. Their religious system is based on additional sections of the Qur'ān.

They have adopted such Sufi rites as Dhikr, gathering and distribution of food, and brotherly union. The religion has a popular, pietistic outlet in hagiographical legends, which have been collected in *Kitab-i Saranjam* in Persian.

They also believe in seven successive manifestations of the divinity, continuing until the advent of the "Master of the Age" (*ṣāḥib al-zamān),* who will fulfill the desires of the followers (*see* Mahdi).

A. A. Sachedina

AḤMAD al-BADAWĪ äh´ mäd ăl bă dă wē´ (I; *ca.* 1200-1276). The most renowned Sufi saint of Egypt and founder of an order (Ṭarīqa) known as the Badawiyya. Born in Fez, Morocco, of a Sayyid family, he made the pilgrimage (Hajj) to Arabia and later visited Iraq before a vision impelled him to travel to Tanta in Egypt, where he remained till his death. His behavior was both ascetic and eccentric: he ate little, sometimes fasting for forty days; during one period he might remain completely silent, at another time he might scream continuously. From the roof of his house he was said to have gazed directly at the sun till his eyes became red blotches. Throughout the night he would stay awake, reciting the Qur'ān. He also worked numerous Miracles, and elicited both absolute loyalty and fierce hostility from many Egyptians during his lifetime.

Despite a meager literary testament, Aḥmad gained enormous posthumous fame due to the powers associated with his tomb. No less than three well-attended celebrations of the anniversary of the saint's death (*see* Mawlid; 'Urs) take place in different parts of Egypt. Numerous accounts have been written of the miracles resulting from that hallowed event.

Bibliography. E. W. Lane, *An Account of the Manners and Customs of the Modern Egyptians* (1836; rpr. 1954), pp. 246-49; E. Littmann, ed. and trans., *Ahmed il-Bedawī, ein Leid auf den ägyptischen Nationalheiligen* (1950).

B. Lawrence

AḤMADIYYA äh mə dē´ yə (I). Contemporary messianic movement originating in South Asia. Its founder, Ghulām Aḥmad Qādiyānī (d. 1908), was a Punjabi Muslim who attempted to regenerate Islam in the face of challenges from the British raj, Protestant Christianity, and revitalized Hinduism. His visions led him to believe that he was an agent of the apocalypse, at once the Mahdi and the Messiah whom Muslims expected at the end of time. In 1889, by accepting his first disciples, Ghulām Aḥmad launched the movement named after him. It grew rapidly during his lifetime and continued to grow after his death. But his successor, Nur ad-dīn, was not able to prevent the outbreak of factionalism among the Aḥmadiyya. In 1914 a split, due as much to personal antagonisms as doctrinal differences, evolved between the Qādiyānī and Lāhorī branches of the movement, and persists to the present day. The Lāhorīs have been consistent apologists for a progressive, modernist Islam, defending their faith against propaganda attacks from other religions, while the Qādiyānīs, by insisting on the uniqueness of Ghulām Aḥmad as a prophet, have been engaged in a rearguard polemical debate with other Muslims. Neither faction associates or communicates with the other, but both are zealously missionary in outlook and organization, accounting for the diffusion of Aḥmadī communities throughout the Western world, Africa, and Asia.

The prolific writings of Ghulām Aḥmad (numbering over eighty, many of them lengthy books) reveal him to have been both a reformer and a traditionalist. He inveighed against a militant interpretation of

JIHĀD (holy war) and yet upheld the validity of polygamy and PURDAH (veiling or seclusion of women). He criticized many of the Traditions (*see* ḤADĪTH) ascribed to MUHAMMAD, while at the same time accepting the QUR'ĀN as an error-free document of divine inspiration, not one word of which could be abrogated or superseded. What evoked continuing controversy was Ghulām Aḥmad's identification of himself as a prophet *after* Muhammad, thus appearing to contradict normative Muslim teaching that Muhammad was the last divine emissary, "the seal of the prophets" (*see* NABI). Stressing the affinity between himself and JESUS as prophets (both opposed foreign rule, perfunctory religion, and the use of violence), Ghulām Aḥmad argued that his own prophethood was only partial, reviving the law of Muhammad just as Jesus had revived the law of MOSES. Neither he nor Jesus was sent to bring new laws; they merely completed, by updating and restoring, the law in their respective prophetic cycles.

Representatives of orthodox Islam, especially the learned functionaries or 'ULAMĀ', never accepted Ghulām Aḥmad's arguments, and his community suffered increasing difficulties after the formation of Pakistan in 1947. Many of the Aḥmadīs had migrated from Qadiyan in North India to Rabwah in Pakistan after 1947, only to find that they were the objects of repeated hate campaigns (in 1949, 1952, 1953, and 1974). At last in 1974, agitation against the Aḥmadīs led to an amendment to the constitution of Pakistan, declaring that followers of Ghulām Aḥmad were a non-Muslim minority and were debarred from holding public office.

Bibliography. *The Review of Religions* (published by the Lāhorī branch of the Aḥmadiyya, 1902-); H. A. Walter, *The Ahmadiya Movement* (1918); H. J. Fisher, *Ahmadiyyah* (1963); J. Robson, "The Ahmadis," in A. J. Arberry, ed., *Religion in the Middle East* (1969), pp. 344-62; S. Lavan, *The Ahmadiyah Movement* (1974).
B. LAWRENCE

AHRIMAN äh´ rē mŭn. *See* ZOROASTRIANS §3.

AHURA MAZDA ä hoor´ ŭ mäz´ dŭ. *See* ZOROASTRIANS §3.

AINU RELIGION ī´ nōō. The Ainu people, are the aboriginal inhabitants of Japan who were, from about the seventh century A.D., gradually driven northward by the Japanese. By the MEIJI era (late nineteenth century) they were found only in the northernmost of the main islands of the Japanese archipelago, Hokkaido. Since that time the tendency has been for them to be assimilated by the dominant Japanese culture.

1. **Central elements.** *a) Ramat,* usually translated as "soul" or "spirit," is indestructable and pervades everything. It varies greatly in amount and concentration from object to object and can shift from place to place, but the total amount of *ramat* is never diminished. When humans, animals, or plants die, *ramat* leaves them, and weapons and utensils that are buried with the dead are ceremonially broken, so that the *ramat* may go with the deceased. *Ramat* may also leave the body of a person who is asleep or unconscious.

b) Kamui are a numerous class of deities and lesser spirits. Some are remote from human affairs, some are accessible and trustworthy, some are in the form of animals (e.g., bears, wolves, foxes), some are mischievous and malicious.

c) Inau are solid sticks of wood that resemble batons. Since living wood contains *ramat* from the great soul of Shiramba Kamui, Upholder of the World, it is the most effective material for protection against evil and for the promotion of welfare. The willow is the most effective for making *inau* for good *kamui. Inau* vary in length from eight inches to about two feet, and are made in various forms. Munro provided photographs of the major types. Most of his examples have been carefully whittled from one end so that numerous thin shavings remain attached to the stick and bush out in a thick curly mass or hang down in various patterns. At celebrations *inau* are arranged in rows outside the sacred east window of the home.

2. **Household worship.** The typical Ainu house consists of one large room with a high ceiling over the rectangular open fire pit or hearth in the center. The roof is high enough to be beyond reach of sparks and to let the smoke escape at either end of the ridge. Since the Ainu have no temples, the house serves as the place for worship of the *kamui.*

The most trusted and revered deity is Kamui Fuchi, the "Supreme Ancestress," or the deity of the hearth. No other *kamui* can be approached unless preliminary prayers are addressed to her. The hearth, over which she keeps watch, is the central and sacred spot of an Ainu home. It is also the entrance to the world of the dead. The hearth fire is never extinguished but each night it is covered with ashes, and Kamui Fuchi is believed to retire to rest. All food at any ceremony is hers and is placed near the hearth before being distributed to guests. She also protects against evil spirits, but as judge she withdraws this protection to punish wrongdoers.

3. **Sacrificial practices.** Traditionally, animals were ceremonially butchered, prayers were made to their skulls, and their spirits were sent off with respect so that they would return again in physical form. The bear was the most revered animal, and bear cubs were captured and reared in cages until reaching the proper size for sacrifice. A bowman shot one or two pointed bamboo arrows that killed the bear, freeing its *ramat.* The sacred blood was caught and drunk reverently, and the head was placed near the sacred east window as chief guest of the feast that followed.

Bibliography. N. G. Munro, *Ainu Creed and Cult* (1962).
K. CRIM

'Ā'ISHA ä´ ī shə (I; *ca.* 614-678). Daughter of ABŪ BAKR and third wife of MUHAMMAD; born in MECCA and married to Muhammad shortly after the HIJRA. When she went to live in an apartment in Muhammad's house, she took her toys and games; this childhood innocence, combined with her charm and beauty, made her Muhammad's favorite. She was the leader in the harem, but her relations with Muhammad were marked by an incident in which she was accused of infidelity. Her innocence was proved by the Qur'ān (Sura 24:11-20), but ALI IBN ABĪ ṬĀLIB was among those who advised Muhammad to send her back to her father to avoid even the hint of impropriety, thus earning 'Ā'isha's undying enmity. She was always loyal to Muhammad and to her father, and seems to have played no role in politics until the caliphate of 'UTHMĀN, whom she opposed on moral grounds. She was not implicated in 'Uthmān's death, being in Mecca at the time, but she may have been there organizing her own party, for shortly after the murder she was found in Basra with an army of a thousand, including Talḥa and Zubayr, who were, while claiming to seek vengeance for 'Uthmān, also opposing the caliphate of Ali. Her forces were defeated in December, 656, but she was well treated and lived until July, 678. She is the source of many ḤADĪTH (traditions).

Bibliography. N. Abbott, *Aishah, the Beloved of Muhammad* (1942).

G. D. NEWBY

AIYAṈĀR ī yŭn är (H—Tamil). Tutelary village deity popular in South India. Unlike the typical goddess who protects South Indian villages he receives only pure, vegetarian offerings. His connection with Brahmanical Hinduism is seen in the myth which regards him as the offspring of Mohinī (VISHNU in female guise) and SHIVA.

G. E. YOCUM

AJAṆṬĀ ä jŭn´ tä (B). A complex of thirty rock-cut cave dwellings (VIHĀRAS) and worship halls (Skt. *caityagṛhas*) about 88 km. from Aurangabad in Western India. A site of major significance for both the history of Buddhist art and social and religious history, Ajaṇṭā was among the most important of over fifty such Buddhist monastic communities, with more than one thousand caves, which grew and flourished between the second century B.C. and the sixth or seventh century A.D. These communities were located principally on the Deccan plateau—its trap rock being ideally suited for excavation—and frequently near trade routes connecting commerical centers. (*See* ELLORĀ.)

At Ajaṇṭā are found the remains of two phases: the early or HĪNAYĀNA period (*ca.* second century B.C.—second century A.D.), coinciding roughly with the Śātavāhana rule in this region; and the MAHĀYĀNA period (early or mid-fifth to late sixth or early seventh century A.D.), corresponding in the first portion with the reign of the Vākāṭakas, a dynasty which earlier had been linked by marriage with the imperial GUPTAS of Northern India. The extent of the Mahāyāna period at Ajaṇṭā remains a subject of debate among scholars, some finding evidence for the end of new architectural activity, sculpture and wall painting in the fifth century, while others see continuance of this activity for another century or more. The Hīnayāna and Mahāyāna phases were separated by a period of transition (*ca.* A.D. 200-450), following the collapse of the Śātavāhana kingdom. Continued patronage for artistic activity was apparently unavailable, but we have no knowledge about life at Ajaṇṭā during these two centuries.

From an artistic and religious standpoint both the continuity and the disjunction between these two phases are striking. While it was not uncommon in Indian Buddhist history for Hīnayāna and Mahāyāna monks to reside concurrently in the same monastic complex, the artistic evidence at Ajaṇṭā points basically to successive phases. Early motifs, based upon the reluctance to portray the Buddha directly (devotional emphasis was directed more toward the STŪPA and its circumambulation), are transmuted by the Mahāyāna vision of the Buddha and his influence. Countless images of the BUDDHA, of BODHISATTVA figures, and of divine, human, animal, and floral motifs, orchestrated in adoration of the mysterious peace and power sensed in this new vision, abound. The architectural changes, together with the accompanying sculpture and wall paintings, provide clear evidence of an artistic and religious vigor which expanded the perception of Buddhist insight, incorporating earlier canonical practices and teachings.

Besides its intrinsic value as an artistic site, Ajaṇṭā confronts the student of Buddhist history with a number of important questions which, by the comparative study of other sites within India, call for further research. These include the relationship between monks and the laity, the complex process of religious and artistic assimilation and synthesis, the mutual influences of various regional styles and motifs, and a more detailed examination of Hīnayāna life and practice in the face of an expanding Mahāyaña tradition.

Bibliography. J. Burgess, *Report on the Buddhist Cave Temples and their Inscriptions, Archaeological Survey of Western India,* Vol. IV (1964); V. Dehejia, *Early Buddhist Rock Temples* (1972); J. Ferguson and J. Burgess, *Cave Temples of India* (1880); A. Ghosh, ed., *Ajanta Murals* (1967); D. Mitra, *Ajanta* (3rd ed., 1964); M. Singh, *Ajanta: Ajanta Painting of the Sacred and the Secular* (1965); W. Spink, *Ajanta to Ellora* (1967); S. Weiner, *Ajaṇṭā: Its Place in Buddhist Art* (1977); G. Yazdani, *Ajanta,* 4 vols. (1931-55).

B. L. SMITH

AJĀTASATTU ä jät´ ŭ sŭt´ tú (B—Pali) **AJĀTAŚATRU** ä jät´ ŭ shŭt´ rū (B—Skt.). The son and murderer of King Bimbisāra of Magadha, who was one of the Buddha's chief patrons. Ajātasattu, while respectful of the BUDDHA, evidently gave special support to DEVADATTA. Nonetheless, Ajātasattu was among those who requested relics of the Buddha after his death (Vinaya Piṭaka, Cullavagga VII, 1-5).

R. H. DRUMMOND

ĀJĪVIKAS ä jē′ vī käs (H, B & Ja—Skt.; lit. "one who practices a [certain mode of] livelihood"(?), perhaps originally used with sarcastic intent [*ājīva*—"livelihood, profession"]) **ĀJĪVAKAS** ä jē′ vä käs (Skt. variant). An ascetic movement in India (sixth century B.C. to fourteenth century A.D.) which was noted for its strict determinism. Its leader/founder was named Maskarin Gośāla; he was a contemporary of the BUDDHA, and at one time a colleague of MAHĀVĪRA, the JAINA teacher/founder.

1. **Early developments.** The only extant accounts of the early history of the Ājīvikas are Buddhist and Jaina texts which refer to Maskarin Gośāla (MAKKHALI-GOSĀLA in Pali; Gośāla Maṅkhaliputta in Jaina Prākrit texts) and his followers. There is some inscriptional and other incidental evidence for the later history of the movement. The Ājīvikas, like the Buddhists and Jainas, appear to have coalesced out of the myriad groups of ascetics (ŚRAMAṆA) found in India in the sixth century B.C. The details of Maskarin Gośāla's life are not known. He is said to have been of humble birth and to have left his household in order to take up the career of an ascetic. The date commonly assigned to his death is *ca.* 485 B.C.

No systematic record of his ascetic and teaching career exists. Jaina accounts portray him as having been at one time a companion of Mahāvīra, and the most important source for Gośāla's life, the Jaina Bhagavatī Sūtra, states that Gośāla was a disciple of Mahāvīra. It is more likely that similarities in ascetic practice led them into a temporary relationship. In any case, they spent some period of time living and teaching together until a dispute or series of disagreements led them to separate. Thereafter Gośāla and his followers centered their activities around the city of Srāvastī. No single leader or group of leaders is recorded as having replaced Gośāla after his death, but the movement retained its cohesiveness to such an extent that Buddhist texts often appear to regard the Ājīvikas as more serious religious rivals than the Jainas.

2. **Practice and doctrine.** The ascetic practices of the Ājīvikas are not always distinguishable from those of the larger mass of ascetics of the time of Gośāla. By all accounts the Ājīvikas practiced ascetic nudity, renounced all possessions, begged all sustenance, and engaged in rigorous penances, including long and difficult fasts. There is some evidence that they developed a unique, and perhaps physically deforming, initiation into their order; and they may have made ritual use of chanting and dancing. The Ājīvikas do not appear to have been so insistent on nudity, restrictive diet, and physical penance as the Jainas (at least in part) later came to be, nor so moderate with respect to such matters as the Buddhists. (*See* JAINISM.)

In matters of doctrine, it is less difficult to assign a particular position to the Ājīvikas. They are noted for holding a rigidly deterministic view of the destiny of the individual and a cosmology stressing an unchangeable orderliness in the universe. These doctrines, along with matters of discipline and practice, were, according to Jaina sources, contained in a set of texts now lost. The earlier movement appears to have had ten books of scripture, eight of these forming one text known as the Mahāṇimitta, and two others known as Maggas. The later Ājīvika tradition in South India is said in the *Nīlakeci* (a Jaina Tamil poem) to have had a sacred text known as the Oṇpatu-katir ("The Nine Rays").

Ājīvika determinism held that *niyati,* "fate" or "destiny," governed all things. SAMSARA (the endless round of birth, death, and rebirth) and KARMA (the effect of past and present deeds on one's present and future existences) were both interpreted within a deterministic framework. According to the Ājīvikas, each individual soul must simply live out a path of countless rebirths through countless aeons, a path determined by "destiny," whose operative mechanisms are karma and samsara. Human effort cannot affect the slightest change in a soul's predetermined path. Salvation is to be attained only by bearing patiently the long progression of lives through samsara. Asceticism itself is therefore seen as a result of *niyati;* the penances and deprivations of the naked mendicant are simply his fate, not a means of hastening release.

Niyati is likewise the governing principle of the physical universe. The Ājīvikas were atheists in that they posited no deity as creator, prime mover, or final resting place of the cosmos. The sum total of the material in the universe was held to be eternal and to remain constant, while the workings of *niyati* led to its being formed into entities which change or pass away into new entities. The universe thus moves in its own stately pace, all things folding and unfolding according to destiny.

3. **Later history.** As noted, the Ājīvikas remained active and visible after the death of Maskarin Gośāla. Epigraphic evidence and imperial donations of cave-monasteries to the Ājīvikas indicate numerical and geographical expansion in the period of the MAURYAN DYNASTY (third century B.C.). Thereafter, however, the Ājīvikas apparently became steadily less in number and influence in Northern India, dying out by the early GUPTA era (fourth century A.D.).

In the South, in eastern Mysore and the Tamil country, the Ājīvikas remained active for another millennium. Their teachings underwent change, perhaps due to the assimilation of doctrines from other movements. Their cosmology de-emphasized *niyati* and replaced it with a notion of a static universe in which perceived change is illusory. Gośāla was viewed by at least some of these later Ājīvikas as a manifestation of an ineffable cosmic principle.

In sum, the Dravidian Ājīvikas began to develop ideas that may have led to their assimilation into other movements; or they may have simply fallen into such disfavor that the movement eventually disintegrated. In any case, by the end of the fourteenth century A.D., they had passed from the scene.

Bibliography. A. L. Basham, *History and Doctrines of the Ājīvikas,* (1951), an absolutely indispensable source, with an excellent bibliography. K. W. FOLKERT

ĀJUR VEDA ä´ jûr vä´ dü (H). *See* YAJUR VEDA.

AKBAR äk´ bär (I; 1542-1605). Emperor of North India. Of all the Mogul rulers of India, only Akbar is remembered with fondness by present-day Hindus, for whom his name has become synonymous with religious tolerance. From the standpoint of ISLAM, however, Akbar is often pictured as a heretic, intent upon destroying the "true faith" in the interests of political expediency. Deeply moved by several intense mystical experiences, Akbar established a Hall of Worship where, every Thursday, Muslims of various sects would debate points of theology. In 1582 he apparently gave up his attempts to reform Islam from within and founded a new religion, the Dīn Ilahī ("Divine Faith"), an eclectic faith aimed more at synthesizing Indian and Mogul culture than at preaching a new path to the Divine. Seasonal vegetarianism was encouraged and killing cows was punishable by death. Special taxes against Hindus were lifted and many were appointed to administrative positions in Akbar's government. No new mosques were allowed to be built; the study of Arabic and Muslim law was discouraged; no male could bear the revered name of Muhammad. Akbar found fault with all dogmas; hence, on his deathbed he would not allow sectarian prayers of any kind to be said for him. Akbar and his Dīn Ilahī thus passed into history as intriguing curiosities—a Muslim with Hindu sympathies and a religion with no stated creed. *See* ISLAM IN SOUTH ASIA §3.

Bibliography. M. L. R. Choudhury, *The Din-I-Ilahi or The Religion of Akbar* (1952). P. L. BASU

AKIBA ä kē´ bä (Ju; d. *ca.* A.D 137). Rabbi, scholar, and teacher, Akiba ben Joseph was one of the most venerated sages of the period of the formation of the TALMUD. He left an indelible imprint on the earliest codes of Jewish life, the MISHNAH and TOSEFTA, as well as the Talmud and later codes.

Although Akiba never held formal office at JAMNIA, his debates with Eliezer ben Hyrcanus won him the respect of the whole academy there. Taking over a method of scriptural interpretation from his master, Nahum of Gimzo, he based his entire juristic program upon words and phrases, many of which earlier followers of HILLEL had considered unimportant.

As a proponent of egalitarian principles and opposed to patrician ways, he was involved in political events. When Emperor Hadrian (A.D. 130) took restrictive measures against the Jewish population, Akiba became a major supporter of the claims of BAR KOCHBA to be the MESSIAH. Carrying on his teaching throughout the war of rebellion against Rome (A.D. 132-35), Akiba was eventually imprisoned and martyred at Caesarea.

Bibliography. L. Finkelstein, *Akiba, Scholar, Saint and Martyr* (1936). E. M. MEYERS

ALAYAVIJÑĀNA ü lü yü vīj nyä´ nü (B—Skt.; lit. "storehouse-consciousness"). In the YOGĀCĀRA school, a storehouse of karmic impressions or "seeds" (*see* KARMA), which ripen into thinking, whereby each believes that it is a self. These individuations in turn produce new karmic seeds in an ongoing cycle of rebirths. *See* SAMSARA. K. CRIM

ALBERTUS MAGNUS (Ch; 1193 or 1206/7—1280). DOMINICAN friar; philosopher, natural scientist, and theologian, known as Magnus, "the Great"; CANONIZED in 1931. F. OAKLEY

ALBIGENSES ăl´ bə jĕn´ sēz (Ch). A medieval sect named after the southern French town of Albi; they were also called "Cathari." They rejected orthodox Christianity and held the dualist position that all matter is evil. A CRUSADE begun under INNOCENT III virtually eliminated them by 1250. *See* MANICHEISM. R. L. HARRISON

ALCHEMY. The art of attaining longevity or physical immortality through the use of an elixir of base metals that have been transformed into gold or gold-like substances. The laboratory process is always buttressed by a cosmological or metaphysical system which constitutes the "theory" of alchemy. While the adept believes that the transmutation process has an empirical basis, he also views the entire operation as a ritual impregnated with spiritual and symbolic meaning. One aspect of this is the relation between the *materia prima,* symbolized by the base metals in the heated vessel, and the life of the adept, which undergoes a spiritual transformation. While the above definition refers primarily to the alchemy in traditional China, with some qualifications it is also applicable to Hellenistic alchemy and that of Medieval Europe.

1. **Alchemy in China.** In earliest times the minerals underneath the earth were regarded as sacred, and miners, smelters, and smiths enjoyed a near divine status in their societies. The transmutation of metals was believed to affect their spiritual transmutation toward some higher planes (purification, rejuvenation, immortality). The LAO TZU likens creation of the cosmos to the making of tools with a bellows, and in the CHUANG TZU the Creator is depicted as a divine smith.

a) External alchemy (wai-tan). The belief that physical immortality was possible arose in China in the eighth century B.C., and the making of elixirs through chemical processes probably began in the Warring States period (403-222 B.C.). By 133 B.C. there was recorded evidence about the "making of gold" as an elixir for attaining immortality on earth. It was the religious Taoists (*see* TAOISM, RELIGIOUS) who appropriated this ancient belief and pursued the art of alchemy. The fact that ancient China did not have a belief in the immortality of the soul compelled Taoists to seek for an alternative in physical immortality on earth or in some natural realm.

The Taoist alchemists developed a system of complex cosmological ideas for the interpretation of the chemical process, based on the doctrine of YIN AND YANG, the theory of the five agents (wood, fire, earth, metal, and water), and the idea of the eight trigrams, derived from the I CHING. These cosmological ideas were used to explain the chemical process; hence, for example, yang is a symbol of mercury and yin a symbol of lead. And the fusing of mercury and lead in the crucible resulted in the production of the alloyed gold. Thus the making of the elixir is analogous to the cosmic union of the yin and yang. The alchemists used the trigrams and hexagrams as symbols for both the progressive stages of the chemical process and the spiritual transformation within the body. Thus "furnace" can refer either to the laboratory apparatus or to the body of the adept. This alchemical theory is presented in the *Ts'an-t'un-ch'i* ("The Kinship of the Three": i.e., the alchemical operations, Taoist theories, the system of the *I Ching*), attributed to Wei Po-yang and composed about A.D. 142. It represents the collective effort of a long alchemical tradition.

The second important book of alchemy is the *Pao-p'u-tzu* ("The Philosopher Embracing Simplicity"), composed by Ko Hung (A.D. 284-343). The author provides a great number of alchemical recipes inherited from his teacher. These recipes give primacy to arsenic and mercury compounds for the making of the alloy which has the appearance of gold. Prior to entering the laboratory, which should be on a mountain, the adept must undergo fasting, worship, and the observation of moral discipline and dietary rules. Also, the practice of breath circulation speeds up the alchemical process. The taking of elixirs would result in preserving the corpse of the adept, and from such a well-preserved corpse a metamorphosis will take place like that of the butterfly emerging from the chrysalis. The new body continues to have the same personal identity as the old.

Another important work is the *Tan-ching yao-chueh* ("Essential Formulas from the Alchemical Classics"), written by Sun Ssu-mo (581-682), a Taoist physician. Its author had personally experimented with many of the recipes included, and recounts his laboratory experience. A majority of his recipes are aimed at curing diseases or promoting longevity rather than gaining immortality.

The external alchemy movement began to recede in the Sung dynasty (960-1279), partly due to the influence of Buddhism, which promised rebirths in the hereafter, and partly due to the rise of Neo-Confucianism, which was opposed to the doctrine of physical immortality and critical of the practice of alchemy. But external alchemy did not disappear completely, and over one hundred works on it are included in the Taoist canon.

b) Internal alchemy (nei-tan). Breathing exercises were used to produce an internal elixir called the "immortal embryo." Once the adept realizes the elixir (produced through the combination of "pure breath," "spirit," and "seminal essence") within the body, he becomes immortal, even though his body will perish. Internal alchemy used the same vocabulary as external alchemy, but used it to refer to the numerous centers or organs within the body. Internal alchemy has two parallel planes: at the physiological level it refers to the circuits of breath control, and at the symbolic level it refers to the adept as a miniature cosmos.

Internal alchemy developed in the Sung (960-1279) and Ming (1368-1644) dynasties as a metaphor of external alchemy, and eventually replaced it. It is still practiced by Taoists today, both laity and priests, as a religious ritual and for therapeutic purposes.

2. Alchemy in Europe. *a) Hellenistic alchemy.* European alchemy had its origin in the city of Alexandria, in the era immediately before and after the time of Christ. The Greek alchemical writings, discovered by the Arabs in the late seventh or early eighth century A.D., show interest in the transmutation of base metals. Pseudo-Democritus in the first century A.D. believed that the base metals contain "seed" of regeneration which could be brought about through the process of heating and moistening. Mary the Jewess in the second century invented an apparatus called *kerokakis,* a covered vessel in which compounds of metals were transmuted under the influence of vapors. Zosimus in the third century believed that the spiritual quality of gold could be attained through the evaporation of vapors. The Alexandrian alchemists also developed a syncretic philosophy which included Gnostic cosmology, Hermetic theology, and the Aristotelian view of substances; the latter refers to the perfectibility of matter through the transmutatory process. But due to their strong belief in divine illumination and in the doctrine of redemption, both of which presuppose a transcendent source of salvation, the Hellenistic alchemists did not develop a doctrine of physical immortality. For them immortality meant an everlasting spiritual life in the hereafter.

b) Medieval alchemy. According to Needham, the Arabs were responsible for bringing Chinese alchemy to the West, as they had earlier brought Hellenistic alchemy. European alchemists continued to learn from the Arabs regarding the theoretical and technical aspects of alchemy until the thirteenth century, by which time European alchemists were making alloyed gold and silver as elixirs. Roger Bacon (*ca.* 1214—*ca.* 1294), who had a full knowledge of contemporary alchemy, wrote that there was a medicine which was able to take off so much of the corruptibility of the body that human life may be prolonged for centuries. Paracelsus, a leading sixteenth century alchemist-physician, held that there are natural elixirs within the body that could be utilized for human longevity. European alchemy was mainly concerned with longevity rather than immortality on earth, because its metaphysical basis in Christian theology promises immortality in the hereafter. The base metals became a symbol of Christ's death and regeneration, and the alchemical process became inevitably a ritual assurance of eternal life.

Bibliography. M. Caron and S. Hutin, *The Alchemists* (1961), a summary survey of European alchemy; M. Eliade, *The Forge and the Crucible* (1962), origins of alchemy and alchemy in Europe, India, and China; W. Ganzenmüller, *Die Alchemie im Mittelalter* (1938); J. Needham, *Science and Civilisation in China,* Vol. 5, pt. 2 (1974), a critical study of Chinese alchemy and comparisons with Europe, India, and Middle East; N. Sivin, *Preliminary Studies in Chinese Alchemy* (1966), an annotated translation of the alchemical work *Tan-ching yao-chueh* and a critical survey of the history of Chinese alchemy; F. S. Taylor, "A Survey of Greek Alchemy," *Journal of Hellenic Studies,* 50 (1930), 109-39.

D. C. YU

ALI IBN ABĪ ṬĀLIB ä lē´ ïb´ən ä bē´ tä lēb´ (I; A.D. 597–661—Arab.; lit. son of Abī Ṭālib). Cousin and son-in-law of MUHAMMAD; fourth CALIPH of the Sunnites; first IMAM of the Shi'ites. He was about ten when he embraced Islam, and is considered the first Muslim after KHADĪJA, Muhammad's wife. He grew up in Muhammad's household, and on the night of the HIJRA he occupied the Prophet's bed, in order to facilitate the latter's emigration to MEDINA. Some months later he married Muhammad's daughter FAṬIMA, and of their marriage were born ḤASAN and ḤUSAYN. During the Prophet's lifetime Ali took part in almost all the expeditions; one exception was Tabūk, during which he had the command at Medina. His bravery as standard-bearer and sometimes commander of these expeditions has become legendary.

After Muhammad's death a dispute arose between Ali and other companions of the Prophet on the question of succession. This dispute divided the Muslims into two major factions: those sympathetic to Ali's claim, known as the SHI'A (partisans) of Ali; and those who accepted the caliphates of ABŪ BAKR, 'UMAR, and 'UTHMĀN with Ali as the fourth caliph. Ali had inherited events which he could not avert as a caliph. A KHĀRIJITE struck Ali in the mosque of Kūfa with a sword, and he died two days later at the age of sixty-three. His burial place at al-Najaf, some miles from Kūfa, where his MASHHAD subsequently arose, became an important site for the Shi'ite pilgrimage and center for the TWELVER Shi'ite learning.

The personality of Ali is difficult to assess. While his stature as a distinguished judge, pious believer, and ardent warrior for Islam is unquestioned, the Shi'ite concept of Ali alongside God and the Prophet as a pivot of religious belief is rejected by Sunnites.

A. A. SACHEDINA

ALID ä lïd´ (I). *See* SAYYID.

ALL SAINTS DAY (Ch). A festival honoring all Christian SAINTS, known and unknown, universally observed in the Western church on November 1 since the ninth century. The eve (All Hallows Eve, or Halloween) is popularly observed with childrens' pranks. Eastern ORTHODOX CHURCHES observe All Saints on the Sunday after PENTECOST.

T. J. TALLEY

ALL SOULS DAY (Ch). The commemoration of the souls of all the faithful departed on the day following the feast of ALL SAINTS. Its observance was ordered in all monasteries of the Cluniac congregation of BENEDICTINES by Odilo of Cluny in A.D. 988 and spread to the rest of the Western church from that time.

T. J. TALLEY

A. A. Sachedina

Courtyard of the Kūfa Mosque, showing area where Ali was assassinated

ALLAH əl läh′ (I—Arab.; lit. "God"). The name for God among Muslims and other Arabic-speaking monotheists.

1. **Allah before Islam.** The name Allah is found in numerous inscriptions of the pre-Islamic period in both North and South Arabic. It is of uncertain etymology, some deriving it from a contraction of the definite article *al-* and the normal word for deity, *'ilāh,* and thus related to the Northwest Semitic *'el ('elōh),* meaning "god." Many Western scholars see an ultimate foreign origin for this formation in the Aramaic *ĕlāhā*. None of these explanations account for the occurrence of an emphatic pronunciation of the doubled *lām* (the letter *l*) in some dialects. Commentaries on the QUR'ĀN add little to our understanding of the origins of the name.

Allah was a central figure in the pre-Islamic pantheon, but he seems not to have been worshiped as the chief deity. The Qur'ān (Sura 53:19-20) mentions three deities who were apparently thought to be daughters of Allah: Manāt, al-Lāt, and al-'Uzza, who were widely venerated. This notion parallels the position of Baal in the Northwest Semitic pantheon (Gordon). The Meccans regarded Allah as the creator and possibly the controller of the weather, functions appropriate to the head of a pantheon (*see* Sura 13:16; 29:61, 63; 31:25; 43:9-19). JINN were also thought to be related to Allah (Sura 37:158) and to associate with him in his activities (Sura 6:100). We cannot ascertain to what degree concepts of God derived from JUDAISM and CHRISTIANITY had penetrated the pre-Islamic view of Allah, but we do know of several individuals who abandoned paganism in favor of the monotheistic worship of Allah. They were called *Ḥanīfs*, a term also applied to the patriarch ABRAHAM, and were clearly influenced by Jewish and Christian doctrines, as is seen in the career of Waraqa ibn Nawfal, the cousin to MUHAMMAD's first wife, KHADĪJA. When the idea of Allah as universal and transcendent was introduced by Islam, the pre-Islamic Arabs are represented as aware of this notion, although rejecting it.

2. **Muhammad's view of Allah.** One of the earliest public statements about Muhammad's view of Allah is found in Sura 112: "Say: He is Allah, the One, Allah the eternally Besought of all; He begetteth not nor was begotten. And there is none comparable to Him." (Pickthall trans.) "Allah, the One," is the Allah of Judaism and Christianity, and "Allah the eternally Besought of all," or, in an alternate translation, "Allah with the divine staff," is the Allah of pre-Islamic paganism. Muhammad rejected any definition that associated anything with Allah. The creedal statement, "There is no deity except Allah," said by millions of Muslims several times daily, is the essential condensation of the Qur'ānic view. Allah was for Muhammad the only reality, the Truth, the Creator, the Sustainer, the Possessor, the Destroyer, the Redeemer, who has all power and might. Allah is the Seer, the Knower, the Hearer, the Wise. These epithets, or "names" as they are often called in Islam, are found throughout the Qur'ān as seeming definitions, though it would appear that in defining God Muhammad was more concerned as a prophet than as a theologian. Some ninety-nine descriptions, not all derived directly from the Qur'ān, are known in later Islam as the "ninety-nine beautiful names of Allah." They present difficulties for systematic theologians who see excessive anthropomorphism in such ideas as Allah's hearing or seeing, but Muhammad accepted these notions without question.

Human relationships to Allah are subservient and contractual. People are God's servants. All that they have is from God, and their obligations are to him (Sura 23:60 *et passim*). In the Qur'ān God is seen as above his creation, directing it by his will. He guides whom he wills and leads into error whom he wills (Sura 13:27; 74:31), sealing the hearts of the sinners (Sura 7:99-100). He is also the giver (Sura 3:8) and the provider (Sura 51:58). Humans are obligated to recognize this fundamental dependent relationship but are saved from arbitrary acts by God's promise that whoever acts in accordance with the precepts of Islam will be properly rewarded. People owe Allah gratitude, worship, and right conduct. To be ungrateful is to be an unbeliever. The Qur'ān is filled with commercial terminology describing personal relationships to Allah, and the notion of Islam itself, as a kind of peace deriving from the certitude of divine reward and punishment, is contrasted with the noncontractual uncertainty of paganism, in which the individual is subject to the whim and caprice of numerous deities whom it is impossible to please or appease.

3. **Allah in later Islam.** While the view of God in the Qur'ān is expressed in metaphor and contrasting opposites, the tendency in tradition and systematic theology is toward a logical, consistent understanding. As Islam expanded outside Arabia, coming within its first century to control the ancient intellectual centers around the Mediterranean, the necessity arose of presenting a coherent picture of Islam to potential converts in terms with which they were familiar, namely the Judeo-Christian modifications of the Hellenistic philosophical heritage. During the first Islamic century the extreme positions were represented by the KHĀRIJITES on the one hand and the Murji'ites on the other. The extremely puritanical Khārijites stressed God's nature as judge, holding that anyone who had committed a mortal sin was no longer a Muslim. The Murji'ites, on the other hand, stressed God's freedom to reward or punish whom he willed, postponing judgment until the Day of Judgment. These movements, while chiefly political in character, were important in their contribution to increased systematic discussion about the nature of God. When the CALIPHS, chiefly beginning with the 'ABBĀSIDS, began to patronize the translation of Greek philosophical works into Arabic,

first from Syriac and then directly from Greek, definitions of such aspects of God as his unity were subjected to strict logical definition. Among the MU'TAZILITES, for example, who themselves are supported by the early 'Abbāsids, there is absolute denial of the existence of any attribute of Allah separate from his essence. The ninety-nine "names," regarded as attributes, are deprived of any real meaning. God is held to be without a hand, a tongue for his speech, or an eye for his sight, since these would both limit him in space and be coeternal with him. This stance set the Mu'tazilites against the strict Traditionists *(Ahl al-Ḥadīth),* who were regarded as anthropomorphists for their strict and literal interpretation of the Qur'ān, and set the arguments for those who would employ philosophy as theology. God was held not to be in any place, not to be perceived by the senses or compelled to act justly toward his creatures, and as entirely different from the created world.

Following the initial reaction to the Hellenistic philosophical heritage, compromisers appeared whose teachings attempted to harmonize the God of revealed monotheism with the requirements of the new "science." One of the most influential was Abu'l-Ḥasan Alī ASH'ARĪ (873-935), who used the arguments of the Mu'tazilites to defend orthodoxy. The other SUNNITE theological school is from Abū Manṣūr Muḥammad al-MĀTURĪDĪ (d.944). Among the SHI'ITES, particularly the ISMĀ'ĪLIYYA, God was understood in Neoplatonic terms that emphasize his ineffable mystery, his absolute unity, and his absolute transcendence.

Modern discussions continue to exhibit a range and diversity comparable to earlier periods. Some commentators have attempted to define God in terms of atomic theory or the principles of thermodynamics, while others have preserved or revived literalist or fundamentalist views of God based on a methodology of Qur'ānic interpretation not unlike that employed by the Traditionist opponents of the Mu'tazilites.

Bibliography. For references to specific thinkers and commentators, see J. D. Pearson, *Index Islamicus* (1962–), and W. M. Watt, *Islamic Philosophy and Theology* (1962). Also see M. Abduh, *Theology of Unity* (1957); T. Andrae, *Mohamed* (1960); J. Baljon, *Modern Muslim Koran Interpretation* (1961); R. Bell, *Origin of Islam in its Christian Environment* (1926); T. Fahd, *Panthéon de l'arabie centrale à la vielle de l'hégire* (1968); M. Fakhry, *History of Islamic Philosophy* (1970); H. Gätje, *Qur'ān and its Exegesis,* A. Welch, trans. (1971); L. Gardet, "Allah," *EI;* I. Goldziher, *Richtungen der islamischen Koranauslegung* (1920) and *Muslim Studies,* 2 vols., S. Stern, trans. (1967-71); C. H. Gordon, "Daughters of Baal and Allah," *MW,* 33 (1943), 50-51; T. Izutsu, *God and Man in the Koran* (1964); G. Levi della Vida, "Pre-Islamic Arabia," in N. Faris, ed., *Arab Heritage* (1944); D. B. Macdonald, *Development of Muslim Theology* (1903); T. O'Shaughnessy, *Koranic Concept of the Word of God* (1948); G. Ryckmans, "Les religions arabes preislamiques," *L'histoire générale des religions* (1960); J. Sweetman, *Islam and Christian Theology* (1947); A. Tritton, *Muslim Theology* (1947); W. M. Watt, *Free Will and Predestination in Early Islam* (1948); J. Wellhausen, *Reste arabischen Heidenthums,* 3rd ed. (1961); A. J. Wensinck, *Muslim Creed* (1932); F. V. Winnett and W. L. Reed, *Ancient Records from North Arabia* (1970); F. V. Winnett, "Allah before Islam," *MW,* 28 (1938), 239-48, and "Daughters of Allah," *MW,* 30 (1940), 113-30.

G. D. NEWBY

ALLĀHĀBĀD äl lä' hä bäd. *See* HINDU SACRED CITIES.

ALLELUIA (Ch—Heb.; "praise God"). Liturgical acclamation in the psalms. Associated with EASTER in the early church, it came to be used in the response following the Epistle in the Latin MASS. Western usage excludes the Alleluia from the penitential season before Easter. R. A. GREER

ALMS TAX (I). *See* ZAKĀT.

ĀḺVĀR äl' vär (H—Tamil; lit. "one who is immersed" [*āl*—"to dive," "be immersed"]). Any one of twelve poet-saints of South India (*ca.* A.D. 650-940) noted for spiritual immersion in the divine qualities of VISHNU through overwhelming devotion (BHAKTI) to him in his various forms (*see* AVATAR), and for expression of their experience in 4,000 TAMIL verses of intense feeling and immediacy. The ŚRĪ VAIṢṆAVA sect regards the Āḻvārs as incarnate portions of the divine being and their Tamil verses as a vernacular form of VEDA (*see* ŚRUTI), equal in status and content to its SANSKRIT form but in contrast accessible to all devotees regardless of CASTE.

1. **History and poetry.** Historical information about the Āḻvārs derives primarily from their poems. They emerged in the southern *bhakti* movement which included devotees of SHIVA (*see* NĀYAṈĀRS), but as BHĀGAVATAS were devoted exclusively to Vishnu as primal origin of all gods. They developed Bhāgavata devotion, drawing upon older Tamil traditions of Vishnu worship, upon the Sanskrit lore of the Epics (*see* RĀMĀYAṆA, MAHĀBHĀRATA, BHAGAVAD GĪTĀ) and the Harivaṃśa and Vishnu Purāṇa (*see* PURĀṆA), and probably upon the liturgies of temple worship (*see* ĀGAMA, TANTRISM, PAÑCARĀTRA, PŪJĀ) instituted in numerous southern temples (e.g. at Tirupati, Kāñcī and Śrīraṅgam).

Tradition identifies the Āḻvārs with specific regions of the South, though their poems indicate pilgrimages to widely dispersed Hindu sacred places. The earliest three Āḻvārs, unnamed in their own poetry, are remembered as Poykayār, Pūtam, and Pēy (*ca.* 650-700) from the east coast Pallava region centered at Kāñcī. Each wrote a single poem of one hundred stanzas. The west coast was represented by Kulacēkara (*ca.* 800), who called himself conqueror of the Pāṇḍyans and Chōḻas and who in his 105 verses gave special attention to the major temples (Śrīraṅgam and Tirupati) of the Chōḻa and Pallava regions. Two Āḻvārs from the ancient Chōḻa region also gave special attention to the Lord at Śrīraṅgam. Toṇṭaraṭippoṭi (*ca.* 825) wrote two poems totaling fifty-five verses, one to be used for awakening the Lord in the morning ritual service, and Tirupāṉ (700?-850?) wrote a single unsigned ten-verse poem describing the immaculate beauty of the Lord's iconic form.

The most prolific of the Āḻvārs lived during the dynastic conflicts between the Pallavas at Kāñcī, the renascent Chōḻas at Tanjore, and the Pāṇḍyans at Madurai, and called himself "Kaliyan, ruler of Maṅkai," a region near Tanjore. Also called Tirumaṅkai (800-870), he composed 1,227 verses, often using the heroic and erotic themes of earlier bardic poetry transposed into praise of Vishnu's cosmic conquests and into the expression of his own burning anguish of separation from his beloved Lord. His militant *bhakti* perhaps reflects his own involvement in the dynastic conflicts of his region. An unsigned composer of two poems in 216 verses is also associated with the Tanjore region and is remembered as Tirumālicaippirāṉ (*ca.* 850).

The remaining Āḻvārs lived during the ninth and early tenth centuries in the region of Pāṇḍyan rule at Madurai (*see* MĪNĀKṢĪ). Viṭṭucittaṉ wrote 473 verses expressing special fondness for KRISHNA as a child, refining the devotional technique of writing as a participant in Krishna's life, e.g. as Krishna's cowherd mother responding to his mischievous acts. He is remembered as Periyāḻvār, "the great devotee." His daughter Kōtai wrote two works in 173 verses, both of refined erotic passion focused on Krishna as an adolescent. In one she writes as a GOPĪ starting out with others to awaken him and ending up in his inner chamber offering him unlimited service forever. In another she dreams of her own marriage to him. Such intense and vigorously expressed love for Krishna gave her the popular name Āṇṭāḷ, "she who rules [the Lord]." Ardent devotion and intellectual depth were combined best by Āḻvār Māṟan or Caṭakōpaṉ (*ca.* 880-930). His 1,296 verses comprise four works and infuse passionate longing for the Lord with the metaphysics of VEDĀNTA. Śrī Vaiṣṇavas regard them as the most authoritative poems of all, each work said to express the essence of one of the four VEDAS, and remember him by the title given by the Lord, NAMMĀḺVĀR, "our own devotee." The final poet-saint was Madurakavi, remembered for a single poem of eleven verses in praise of Nammāḻvār.

2. Sectarian developments. Officially there are only ten Āḻvārs, for Āṇṭāḷ is excluded as a woman and Madurakavi as lauder of Nammāḻvār and not of the Lord, but the verses of all twelve form the sacred text, *The Four Thousand Divine Verses (Nālāyira-divya-prapantam)* edited in the tenth century by Nāthamuṉi, the first sectarian teacher (see ĀCĀRYA). Entire poems or select verses are used in daily worship in Śrī Vaiṣṇava homes and temples, in periodic festivals, and in theological inquiry. Oral and written commentary on the verses by *ācāryas* has continued from Nāthamuṉi to the present, producing literature in Sanskrit and Tamil but most importantly in the hybrid of the two called Maṇipravāḷa. The Āḻvārs themselves are models of devotion. Their hagiography first appeared in *The Adventures of the Divine Sages*, a Sanskrit work by Garuḍavāhaṇa Paṇḍita, probably of the twelfth century, and was elaborated in the following century in *The Splendor of the Succession of Teachers in Six Thousand Granthas (Āṟāyirappaṭi-guru-paramparā-prapāvam)*, a Maṇipravāḷa work by Piṉpa-ḻakiya Perumāḷ Jīyar. This hagiography may have some historical value, but its symbolic and didactic nature is primary; the Āḻvārs were born at the end of the previous era (YUGA) or the beginning of the present one; each was an avatar of one of Vishnu's royal accessories, such as his conch, disk, bow, mace, the Goddess Earth, etc.; two Āḻvārs merged with the image of the Lord at Śrīraṅgam; collectively the twelve saints represent the spread of socio-ritual strata from BRAHMIN to untouchable; and individually each life portrays the transcendent Vishnu's intimate interaction with his earthly but devoted servants.

Bibliography. K. V. Zvelebil, *Tamil Literature: A History of Indian Literature*, X, Fasc.1, ed. Jan Gonda (1974); A. Govindāchārya, *The Holy Lives of the Āzhvārs or the Drāvida Saints* (1902); J. S. M. Hooper, *Hymns of the Āḻvārs* (1929).

D. HUDSON

AMATERASU ä mä tē rä´ soo (Sh—Jap.; lit. "Heavenly-Shining-Deity"). Sun goddess associated with the imperial sword, jewels, and mirror, revered at the national shrine at ISÉ; KAMI through whose grandson, Ninigi-no-Mikoto, the legitimacy of the imperial line of Japan was established.

The KOJIKI and NIHON SHOKI recount Amaterasu's creation through a primal act of purification (*see* IZANAGI AND IZANAMI), her angry retreat to a rock cave when provoked by her brother, Susa-no-wo, reappearance in response to an ecstatic dance, and her sending Ninigi-no-Mikoto to rule on earth.

Recent Japanese scholarship indicates matriarchal and shamanistic influences and the possible elevation of the *ohirume* ("handmaid") of a male sun kami to account for the goddess Amaterasu. The cave episode has been interpreted as reflecting an annual imperial *chinkonsai*, a court ritual reviving the spirit of the emperor through the dance of a female SHAMAN.

C. W. EDWARDS

AMEN (Ju & Ch—Heb.; "so be it"). Found in Scripture to signify assent (Deut. 27:15 ff), "amen" has been used since antiquity in Judaism as a response to a prayer or blessing given by another. As early as Justin Martyr (*ca.* 155) it was used liturgically among Christians for the assent of the people at the end of the Eucharistic prayer, and since the ninth century for the conclusion of any prayer. In many churches it is used as a spontaneous response to remarks in a sermon.

R. A. GREER

AMIDA ä´ mē dä (B—Jap.), **AMITĀBHA** ä mē tä´ bä, **AMITĀYUS** ä mē tä´yoos (B—Skt.; Amitābha, lit. "infinite light"; Amitāyus, lit. "infinite life"). A

BUDDHA extensively worshiped in Central Asian, East Asian, and TIBETAN BUDDHISM; lord of the Western Paradise (PURE LAND). (*See* BUDDHA, GENERAL CONCEPTS OF.)

1. **The story of Amida Buddha and his Pure Land.** For Far Eastern Buddhists the most important traditions about Amida were of his decision many millions of ages ago to become a BODHISATTVA and purify a land (a realm of direct influence) which, when he became a Buddha, would be his Buddha-land. According to the version of this story found in the *Larger Sukhāvatī-vyuha* an immeasurably long time ago a king, upon hearing the preaching of a Buddha, decided to give up his kingdom and become a monk, taking the name Dharmakara. Dharmakara studied and practiced under the Buddha named Lokeśvararaja. Conceiving the desire to found a Buddha-land, he asked his teacher to manifest for him hundreds of thousands of Buddha-lands so that he might study the particular perfection of each. After seeing these Buddha-lands, he was absorbed in meditation for a period of five *kalpas* (cycles of time). When he rose from meditation, he had decided to integrate all the excellences he had observed in one land of purity and happiness. He vowed that unless forty-eight conditions governing the nature of his land and the means and universality of access to it were fulfilled, he did not wish to attain the highest enlightenment (i.e., Buddhahood). He also vowed to devote himself for innumerable *kalpas* to the practice of good deeds in order to accumulate the merits needed to make possible the fulfillment of his vows. Ten *kalpas* ago Dharmakara became the Buddha Amida. He is now residing in his land called Sukhāvatī, (Pure Land), where it is possible for him, by virtue of his incalculable merit, to enable all to be reborn.

2. **Descriptions of Amida.** The Amitāyur-Vipaśyana Sūtra *(Discourse Concerning Meditation on Amitāyus)* describes the Pure Land, the bodily form and posture of the Buddha Amitāyus (in East Asia, considered identical to Amitābha), his attendant bodhisattvas AVALOKITEŚVARA and Mahāsthāmaprāpta, and many other details. From these descriptions Buddhists have been able to imagine (and depict in painting, poetry, and sculpture) the appearances of the Pure Land and its presiding Buddha. Amida's figure is said to be of yellowish gold color, seated on a lotus, emitting golden rays. His body is of unimaginable height and brightness, his eyes are like the water of the four great seas, with iris and pupil clearly distinct. He is surrounded by an immense aureole (*see* HALO), larger than thousands of millions of worlds, in which there are hundreds of thousands of Buddhas. He has 84,000 "marks," each of which has 84,000 materialized virtues. Each virtue emits 84,000 rays of light, illumining the ten directions. The sūtra tells us that the body of Amida is such that the mental power of an unenlightened person cannot imagine it. Despite this, Amida vowed that any person who tried to imagine him should succeed; to this end, although he can appear as large as space, he

Courtesy the Powers Collection; photo by O. E. Nelson

Seated Amitābha; wood and laquer statue from Japan (*ca.* A.D. 800); hands are held in the traditional gesture of teaching

also appears in forms only eight or sixteen feet high. He is chiefly depicted as sitting on his lotus seat while teaching, but the Amitāyur-Vipaśyana Sūtra also describes him as descending to welcome beings to his land.

Buddhists differ on what kind of manifestation of eternal Buddhahood they believe Amida to be. TENDAI Buddhists regard him as a provisional manifestation of the eternal ŚĀKYAMUNI. Buddhists of the PURE LAND SECTS regard him as the fundamental DHARMAKĀYA itself.

3. **The Pure Land.** The Sukhāvatī or Pure Land is described as rich, fertile, and filled with gods and men, but not with beings from the other realms of existence: animals, ghosts (PRETA), or denizens of hells. Women are reborn there as men. It is filled with gem-trees, jeweled palaces and terraces, strings of bells, lotus lakes, golden sand, and showers of flower petals. Swans, curlews, and peacocks give concerts, and scented rivers give forth music. All of the sounds heard in the Pure Land induce a constant remembrance of the TRIRATNA: Buddha, DHARMA, and SAṄGHA. There is neither bodily nor mental pain, and the sources of happiness are innumerable. Beings may remain in the Pure Land until they reach NIRVANA.

4. **How to merit birth in the Pure Land.** Persons who believe in and understand the Buddha's teaching, practice the precepts, do not indulge in evil conduct, and have developed a compassionate mind, deep faith, sincerity, and determination to be reborn in the Pure Land are assured birth there. But the sūtras teach that even a person who violates lay or

monastic precepts, steals property of the *saṅgha,* claims position in the dharma pretentiously, or commits other kinds of evils can be reborn there if he at the moment of death meets a benefactor who teaches him to call on Amida's name, or to think of Amida, for ten moments continuously. SHINRAN argued that faith in Amida's vow can overcome the karmic fruits of all offenses without exception.

5. **Amitābha in Tibet.** In Tibet, unlike East Asia, Amitāyus and Amitābha are considered names of two different Buddhas. Amitābha is particularly important, not as a savior figure, but as one of the five primordial, self-born Dhyāni Buddhas; Avalokiteśvara is his manifestation in active, bodhisattva form. Tibetans ritually recognize, for example, that the sacred MANTRA of Avalokiteśvara, OṂ MAṆIPADME HŪṂ, derives primordially from Amitābha. Amitābha's symbol is the begging bowl, his mount the peacock, his color is red, his posture that of meditation (dhyāna-MUDRĀ), his element water, his sacred symbol "ba" or "ah," his direction the west. Amitāyus is represented iconographically with the pot containing the water of immortality *(kalasa).*

M. LEVERING

AMIDAH ä mē´ dä (Ju—Heb.; lit. "standing"). The prayer which serves as the chief element of all prescribed daily Jewish services. Among the ASHKENAZIM, it is commonly known as the *Shemoneh-Esreh* ("Eighteen") because of the eighteen benedictions of which it originally consisted. The BENEDICTIONS of the Amidah appear to have evolved during the last decades of the Second Temple. Shortly after the destruction of the Temple (A.D. 70), the Amidah was finally "edited" by Rabban Gamaliel II and his associates. On weekdays the Amidah consists of nineteen benedictions; on the SABBATH and festivals, there are only seven benedictions, except in the additional service of ROSH HA-SHANAH when there are nine. By Talmudic prescription the Amidah is to be recited in a standing position, as its name indicates, and the worshiper is to face JERUSALEM.

The traditional nineteen benedictions consist largely of petitions. Several are for universal human needs such as wisdom and understanding, forgiveness of sins, the healing of the sick, and acceptance of prayer. The others reflect the national hopes of the Jewish people for the redemption of Israel, the ingathering of the exiles, the building of Jerusalem, and the restoration of the Davidic dynasty.

Bibliography. I. Abrahams, *A Companion to the Authorized Daily Prayerbook,* rev. ed. (1922), pp. 55-71; A. Z. Idelsohn, *Jewish Liturgy and its Development* (1932), pp. 92-110.

B. MARTIN

AMIDAH

O Lord, open Thou my lips and my mouth shall declare Thy praise.

Praised art Thou, O Lord our God and God of our fathers, God of Abraham, God of Isaac, and God of Jacob, mighty, revered and exalted God. Thou bestowest lovingkindness and possessest all things. Mindful of the patriarchs' love for Thee, Thou wilt in Thy love bring a redeemer to their children's children for the sake of Thy name.

O King, Thou Helper, Redeemer and Shield, be Thou praised, O Lord, Shield of Abraham.

Thou, O Lord, art mighty forever. Thou callest the dead to immortal life for Thou art mighty in deliverance.

Thou sustainest the living with lovingkindness, and in great mercy callest the departed to everlasting life. Thou upholdest the falling, healest the sick, settest free those in bondage, and keepest faith with those that sleep in the dust. Who is like unto Thee, Almighty King, who decreest death and life and bringest forth salvation?

Faithful art Thou to grant eternal life to the departed. Blessed art Thou, O Lord, who callest the dead to life everlasting.

Holy art Thou and holy is Thy name and unto Thee holy beings render praise daily. Blessed art Thou, O Lord, the holy God.

Sabbath and Festival Prayer Book (1946)

The first three benedictions of the Amidah, given here, are common for all services, as are the final three. There are additions to and variations on the benedictions for certain special occasions (Sabbath and holidays).

AMISH (Ch). A strict MENNONITE branch of Swiss ANABAPTISTS now found primarily in North America. In 1693 Jakob Ammann (1644?-1725?), Mennonite elder near Berne, began to enforce church discipline rigidly. He insisted that excommunicated members be shunned, even in domestic and marital relations. When other elders did not agree, Ammann proceeded to excommunicate them. Other issues involved prescribed costumes, footwashing, and attendance at non-Mennonite church services.

The Ammann-led faction found adherents among Mennonites in Alsace and South Germany as well as in Switzerland, Holland, and Russia. The focus shifted to North America, beginning with migration to Eastern Pennsylvania in the 1720s. Today the Amish are concentrated in Ohio, Pennsylvania, and Indiana—in that order. They have 112 settlements in twenty states, Ontario, Honduras, and Paraguay.

The Old Order Amish have grown to 75,000 (1977), despite predictions that a counter-culture so different could not avoid absorption by society. Their growth is almost entirely due to the large size of their families.

For the Amish, the church is a voluntary brotherhood of obedient Christians, following the narrow way of the NT, aided by mutual admonition and support. Their major emphases are scriptural literalness; practicing the Sermon on the Mount; mutual aid (symbolized by the famous barn-raisings for brethren in distress); rejecting worldly ways of dress, amusement, and comfort to live in "plain" garb of hooks-and-eyes and broadbrims, caped dresses and bonnets; nonresistance, refusing military service while paying legitimate taxes. They permit elementary education, preferably with teachers of their faith, but reject higher schools (causing legal problems in several states). The U.S. government waives Social Security taxes, as Amish refuse on principle to accept benefits from the program.

They are a clannish people, living in clusters of twenty to thirty families, with a bishop, ministers, and deacons providing spiritual and practical guidance. Leaders serve for life without compensation. Amish meet alternately for services in their sparsely furnished but shiningly clean homes; they use horse-driven buggies; as recreation from their hard work, they enjoy singing, farm-lot games, and auctions. The high cost of farm land and the onslaught of mass tourism are driving some of them from Lancaster County, Pennsylvania, where their families have resided continuously since the colonial period.

About every generation there is a schism from the Old Order Amish, as voices are raised for liberalization. The most important division is the Beachy Amish (1927), with perhaps 5,000 members. Amish leaving individually tend to join one of the Mennonite churches.

Bibliography. J. A. Hostetler, *Amish Society* (1963); J. A. Hostetler and G. E. Huntington, *Children in Amish Society* (1971); J. B. Mast, ed., *The Letters of the Amish Division* (1950).

D. F. Durnbaugh

AMORAIM ă mō rä´ ēm (Ju). Sages and teachers of Gemara, expounding on the Mishnah and other teachings of the Tannaim from the compilation of the Mishnah (*ca.* A.D. 200) to the completion of the Jersualem and Babylonian Talmuds (*ca.* A.D. 450 and 500). They developed Halakah and Aggadah.

Y. Shamir

AMRITSAR ăm rĭt sär (S). *See* Golden Temple.

ANABAPTISTS (Ch—Gr.; lit. "rebaptizers"). A term applied broadly to a number of sixteenth century religious groups that regarded infant baptism as invalid and required those who had received it to be "rebaptized." The movement has also been called the "Radical Reformation" and "Left Wing of the Reformation." The presence of revolutionaries among them marked all radicals as potentially dangerous to the state, and gave impetus to the persecution of Anabaptists by Lutheran, Reformed, and Roman Catholic authorities.

While there is no one set of accepted Anabaptist beliefs, most would affirm the following: (1) believer's baptism, i.e. baptism of adults; (2) restitution of the primitive, NT church, with only true believers as members; (3) discipleship, obedience to strict moral precepts; (4) pacifism; (5) separation of church and state; (6) autonomy of each congregation. During the early decades, the indwelling of the Holy Spirit was their primary authority, but in recent centuries the Bible, usually interpreted literally, has become the chief guide for belief and practice. Some, most notably the Hutterites (founded by Jacob Hutter, d. 1536), practiced a form of communal living. The Mennonites, founded by Menno Simons (1494?-1561), are the largest surviving Anabaptist group.

Because of their sectarian nature, and especially their advocacy of pacifism and of a strict separation of church and state, Anabaptist groups have continued to suffer displacement and persecution well into the twentieth century. *See* Reformation, Protestant; Luther, Martin; Zwingli, Ulrich.

Bibliography. C. J. Dyck, ed. *The Mennonite Encyclopedia*, 4 vols. (1955-59); G. H. Williams, *The Radical Reformation* (1962).

R. L. Harrison

ANĀGĀMIN än ä gä´ mĭn (B—Pali; lit. "non-returner"). The third of the four fruitions in Theravāda sanctity. When a disciple destroys the five fetters (belief in a soul, belief in rituals, doubts, sensuality, and malevolence), he will not return to this world but will reside in heaven. From there he becomes an Arhant (*see* Sotāpanna; Sakadāgāmin).

W. Pachow

ANALECTS (Con—Chin.; *lun-yü* loon yo͞o; lit. "discourses"). The reputed sayings and conversations of Confucius, compiled a century or more after his death. In the second century B.C. there were three extant versions, of which only the Lu version has survived. The Analects is the most informative source on the life and teachings of Confucius. In it the major tenets of Confucian teaching emerge: the central role of "humanity" or "humaneness" (Jen); the gentleman *(chün-tzu)* as the paradigm of sagely virtue; the centrality of the doctrine of the rectification of names *(cheng-ming),* and the ultimate source of authority, *T'ien* or Heaven. In many passages, however, the full meaning is only hinted at, and later Confucian tradition attempted to articulate the meaning more completely. The Analects has exercised extraordinary influence upon the peoples and cultures of East Asia, occupying a central place in the literature of China since the official establishment of Confucianism during the Han dynasty (second century B.C.). After Chu Hsi included the Analects among the basic Confucian classics, the Four Books, it became the pillar of the Chinese educational system and the civil service examination system as well as a source of personal moral learning and self-cultivation.

Bibliography. W. T. Chan, *A Source Book in Chinese Philosophy* (1963), ch. 2, a translation of selected passages; W. T. deBary, *Sources of Chinese Tradition* (1960), ch. 2; A. Waley, *The Analects of Confucius* (1938), a clear, scholarly translation of the complete work; K. Shigeki, *Confucius* (1956).

R. L. Taylor

ĀNANDA ä nŭn´ dŭ (B & H—Pali & Skt.; lit. "bliss" [*ā-nand*—"to rejoice"]). 1. In Buddhism, a cousin and leading disciple of the Buddha. Significant for his contribution to the founding of the order of nuns, and for the role which tradition assigns him in the settling of the PALI CANON. For the last twenty-five years of his master's life, Ānanda (d. *ca.* 462 B.C.) served as his personal attendant and living repository of his teachings.

a) Argues for nuns. Having been widowed, the Buddha's foster mother, Mahāpajāpatī, sought permission to enter the monastic order. The Buddha refused her three times, whereupon Mahāpajāpatī shaved her head and with a group of other women followed after him. Finding them crying, Ānanda personally took their case to the Buddha. Getting the Buddha to admit that women are capable of enlightenment, he finally convinced the Buddha to ordain them as nuns, with the proviso that they submit to eight strict rules not required of the monks. Even then the Buddha warned that admission of women would greatly shorten the existence of the monastic order.

b) Monastic administration. As the Buddha's death approached, Ānanda was concerned with the orderly transition from the Buddha's personal leadership and requested that the Buddha appoint a successor. Noting that he had never thought of the community as dependent on him, the Buddha refused. He indicated that they needed no other support than their own effort, guided by what he had taught. In response to Ānanda's continued concern, he then spelled out four ways of recognizing authoritative teachings. Shortly after the Buddha's death, in a conversation with the Prime Minister of Magadha, Ānanda outlined the authoritative principles for the administration of the order. Basic is the absence of centralized power and authority, coupled with the respect paid to all worthy monks.

c) Role in settling scripture. Within months of the Buddha's death, his fully enlightened disciples under the leadership of Mahākassapa assembled at RĀJAGṚHA to recite and agree upon the words of the Buddha. Ānanda finally became enlightened on the eve of this first Council. Because of his close association with the master and faultless memory of his words, Ānanda was invited to recite the Buddha's discourses. Tradition considers this recital the first step in settling the Collection of Discourses (SUTTA PIṬAKA). Many of the canonical discourses begin with the phrase: "Thus have I heard . . ." The "I" here is taken to refer to Ānanda, who is also considered the author of a collection of verses in the canonical Theragāthā (Verses of the Elders). At the first Council Ānanda was censured for a number of past faults, among them his failure to request the Buddha to live longer, and his efforts to persuade the Buddha to create an order of nuns. Though Ānanda did not consider these deeds faults, he confessed out of respect for his fellow monks.

d) Death and cult. Tradition places Ānanda's death the year before that of King Ajātasattu of Magadha. The Chinese pilgrim Fa-hsien claims that it took place while Ānanda was fording a river between two kingdoms, and that his relics were split between the two and enshrined. The figure of Ānanda became ritually important in Sri Lanka during the reign of Sena II (A.D. 851-55). Sena performed a ceremony in which the image of Ānanda was carried through the streets to overcome an epidemic. (*See* BUDDHIST COUNCILS; MAHĀ-PARINIBBĀNA SUTTA.)

2. In Hinduism, bliss or pure joy. In the UPANIṢADS and especially in the VEDĀNTA philosophy, *ānanda* is important as an essential characteristic of BRAHMAN, the Absolute. In later Vedānta it became common practice to refer to Brahman in terms of three such characteristics, using the formula "sac-cid-ānanda" (being, consciousness, bliss). These are not considered attributes of Brahman, being rather its peculiar essence. The description of Brahman as bliss summarizes its character as "beyond hunger and thirst, beyond sorrow and illusion, beyond old age and death" (BĀU 3. 5. 1). The origin of the doctrine of Brahman as bliss is probably to be found in BĀU 4.3.19-33. There it is suggested that in the state of sleep we attain a temporary union with Brahman in which the subject/object split is overcome. Since in such sleep all suffering is also overcome, the same state is described as the highest bliss.

In Hindu devotional cults, bliss is understood at times as a divine characteristic, and at others as a goal of the devotee's devotion (BHAKTI).

Bibliography. P. Deussen, *The Philosophy of the Upanishads* (1906), pp. 126-31, 140-46; D. R. Kinsley, *The Sword and the Flute* (1975), pp. 66-72. J. P. MCDERMOTT

ANANTA än än´ tä (H). *See* ŚEṢA; NĀGA.

ANĀTHAPIṆḌIKA ä nät´ ŭ pĭn dī´ kŭ (B). A banker of Śrāvastī who exemplified generosity to the BUDDHA and his followers. Meeting the Buddha in Rājagṛha during the first year after the Buddha's enlightenment, Anāthapiṇḍika invited him to spend the monsoon rains retreat (*see* ĀVĀSA) at Śrāvastī. For this occasion Anāthapiṇḍika constructed the Jetavana "pleasure grove."

Frequently mentioned in the PALI CANON, JĀTAKAS, and commentaries, Anāthapiṇḍika's great generosity reduced him to poverty; however, Sakka (INDRA) restored his wealth. Anāthapiṇḍika's generosity provided the occasion for several sermons preached by the Buddha, and this devoted layman represented the views of the Buddha in a debate with a group of wandering mendicants. D. K. SWEARER

ANATHEMA ə nă´ thə mə (Ch—Gr.; lit. "accused," "separated," "set aside"). In biblical use "something loathsome" (Rom. 9:3; Gal. 1:9). Used by Christians from NICAEA to VATICAN COUNCIL I to indicate a ban or curse by church authority, a condemnation of a doctrine, or that the contrary of a statement is defined as doctrine. J. HENNESEY

ANATTA ŭn ä´ tä (B—Pali; lit. "no self") **ANATMAN** ŭn ät´ mŭn (H & B—Skt.). *Anatta* is one of the most important terms and central doctrines in THERAVĀDA Buddhism. It is one of the three inherent and basic qualities of time-space existence in the Theravāda view, the other two being ANICCA (impermanence) and DUKKHA (dis-ease or suffering).

1. **Historical origin.** As its negative form indicates, *anatta* is a denial—a denial of the Brahmanical-Hindu belief in selfhood (Atman). Rightly or wrongly, early Buddhism understood the ATMAN as an unchanging, undying, essentially perfect spiritual essence or being that resided within the body, somewhat as described in the Bhagavad Gītā: "It is not born, nor does it ever die: Nor having come into being, will it ever cease to be. This ancient one is unborn, eternal, everlasting and is not killed when the body is killed. Swords cut it not, fire burns it not, water wets it not and wind dries it not. It is eternal, omnipresent, established and immovable." (II.20, 23-24) Another related factor was the Brahmanical view that human salvation was not so much an alteration of the human being, certainly not of the Atman, as it was the discovery of the identity of the Atman with the supreme BRAHMAN, the eternal, all-inclusive, distinctionless essence of the universe.

The Buddhist view, encapsulated in the *anatta* doctrine, was the precise reverse of this. It perceived the essential nature of the universe to be change, impermanence, and insubstantiality *(anicca).*

2. **Two modes of *anatta* analysis.** The *anatta* doctrine applies most specifically to the human individual. One mode of demonstrating a human being to be "soulless" is the cross-sectional analysis of an individual employed in the famous chariot analogy of *The Questions of King Milinda* (MILINDAPAÑHA). At the end of a long discussion, the monk Nāgasena and King Milinda come to the conclusion that just as the term "chariot" is only a way of naming a collection of particular items, so too is the term for "human being." Human being signifies only a loosely joined set of physical body-parts; or more inclusively, five temporarily connected "heaps" (SKANDHAS) which are a form, sensation, perception, the predispositions, and consciousness. "Form" refers to bodily form primarily, and "predispositions" to the KARMA inherited from past lives.

The Milinda passage, as well as many others in the PALI CANON, categorically denies that there is any enduring *atta*-like ego to be found in the empirical analysis of a person, either as a core of the supposed "self," or as one of its constituent elements, or as the totality of body-mind. There are thoughts, feelings, and bodily activities, but no thinker, feeler, or actor. The "thinker" *is* the thought, the "feeler" *is* the feeling, the "actor" *is* the action—nothing more.

The same lack of an integral self is revealed in a longitudinal-temporal analysis. Thoughts, feelings, and the body itself are in constant flux. Their nature, content, and qualities vary from moment to moment. They arise in response to stimuli, persist for a fraction of a second, and vanish. What is taken for enduring personal identity is only the repeated perception of the similarity of successive feelings and thoughts.

3. **Religious implications.** Contrary to Brahmanical conceptions of salvation as the realization of the self's unchangingness through seemingly changing experiences, Pali Theravāda Buddhism maintains that salvation results from the full, existential awareness that there is *no* "self." If anyone cherishes body, mind, feeling-state and the like as a "self," as "himself," and thinks them to be real and enduring entities, the result is an egoism and a deep attachment to his own continuing existence. This produces selfishness and makes release into NIRVANA impossible. Final deliverance from rebirth can occur only when the delusion of selfhood is utterly destroyed.

Because of the extremes to which *anatta* logic was carried, MAHĀYĀNA Buddhism to some extent reestablished selfhood in its doctrines of the ALAYAVIJÑĀNA (storehouse consciousness) as a kind of enduring subconscious, and of the Buddha nature as a kind of *true* selfhood found in every man. Yet even here there remains the sense of the empirical self's unreality and the necessity for a nonindividualized awarenes in achieving salvation.

Bibliography. H. C. Warren, *Buddhism in Translations,* (1962), Ch. II. esp. pp. 129-34; W. L. King, *In the Hope of Nibbana* (1964), pp. 1-68. W. L. KING

ANBIYĀ ăn bē yä´ (I). *See* NABI.

ANCESTOR VENERATION. The ritual homage and placation of the spirits of the dead by their living descendants. Its ideology holds that ancestors are dependent upon such attention for sustenance and often for continued existence. They are also concerned with the fortunes of members of their kin group and may intervene, for good or for evil, in the affairs of the living. The needs and desires of people are not felt to change at death, and descendants provide for satisfaction of these needs by ritual offerings. Ancestors are pleased by dutiful attention and angered by neglect, attitudes which are reflected in their treatment of the living.

1. **Origins.** Systems of ancestor veneration are best known from Africa, China, Taiwan, and Japan. In all cases ancestral cults are embedded in broader religious systems. DIVINATION is invoked in both Africa and Asia to assess the disposition of ancestors (Fortes 1967, Goody). In Africa offended ancestors cease to protect inattentive descendants from WITCHCRAFT and witches may serve as agents of ancestral punishment. Ancestor veneration in Asia is syncretically entwined with BUDDHISM, CONFUCIANISM, SHINTŌ, and folk religious practices.

Radin has suggested that ancestor veneration may have emerged from the worship of guardian spirits, an idea which receives support from Asian data. In China, for example, ancestor veneration developed as putative ancestors of tribes and clans were converted to domestic guardians when the family eclipsed the clan as the central unit of social and political organization in the Chou period (1111-249 B.C.). At this time entreaties for aid were gradually redirected from tribal spirits toward deceased members of one's own lineage.

The increased structural importance of the family is reflected by Confucian teachings which placed the family at the center of the ethical system. Thus the seal of FILIAL PIETY and moral duty was stamped on the original concept of ancestors as guardian spirits. Confucian teaching imparted to East Asian ancestor veneration a particular focus on the involvement of the living. CONFUCIUS himself placed emphasis not on the spirits but on the emotions created in the living by respectful remembrance of ancestral spirits. The involvement of ancestral spirits with divination, witchcraft, and MAGIC, so conspicuous in African systems, forms only a minor element in Asian ancestor veneration.

The emergence of ancestor veneration in East Asia was linked to the spread of Buddhism and TAOISM, and from this common influence comes the uniformity of ancestral representation throughout the area. Within the elaborate code of Buddhist and Taoist iconography gods multiplied rapidly. (*See* ART AND ARCHITECTURE, BUDDHIST.) Ancestors retained their sacred character, but images became the exclusive reserve of the deities, and small wooden tablets were used to represent the ancestors, becoming more formal and conventional over time. In the absence of a tradition of written records in Africa the origins of ancestor veneration remain obscure. However, the role of ancestors as mnemonics in the complex oral histories of many African peoples suggests that ancestral cults developed in concert with the political emergence of the tribes themselves.

2. Ritual practices. Ancestor veneration involves presentation of food, drink, and other favored objects at ancestral shrines. (*See* FOOD, RELIGIOUS ATTITUDES TOWARD.) Objects such as wooden tablets in Asia and carved sticks or stools in Africa serve as representations of the ancestors but are not considered permanent residences of ancestral spirits. As ancestors exist in spirit, they are not thought to require human form. Material representations serve rather as foci through which ancestors and descendants may communicate through ritual offerings.

Ritual activity directed toward ancestors may occur either publicly, involving an entire lineage, or privately at the level of the household or individual. The latter rituals are conducted in the ancestral hall or domestic shrine housing ancestral representations and are most often oriented toward the recent and remembered dead. These rituals include daily commemoration of the group of household ancestors and private occasions such as appeals to one or more ancestors in cases of fortune or misfortune or anniversaries of recent deaths. Responsibility for these rituals is nominally accorded to the head of the household who, in Africa, is the only one who can directly approach the ancestor. He acts as intermediary for those within and without the lineage who wish to offer sacrifice to particular deceased individuals (Fortes 1967, Goody). In some cases this responsibility may be delegated. Thus in Japan daily ritual may be performed by a spouse of the domestic head or by some other relative on a regular basis (Smith). Annual circulation of lineage ritual responsibilities among the component households of the lineage has been reported from Taiwan (Ahern).

Public ritual occurs at a temple or other sacred place and frequently addresses the ancestors, recent and remote, as a group. Ancestral sacrifices associated with the agricultural cycle in Africa and the Japanese Festival of the Dead are examples of this type of observance. These ceremonies are performed by a lineage head on behalf of a wide group of kinsmen from multiple households.

Thus, as the ancestors become less personal because of genealogic distance, the form of encounter with them becomes less intimate. At the intimate end of the continuum the worshiper experiences a sense of personal involvement with the ancestors and feels that they notice and care about him. As the ancestors become more remote, their influence on local affairs lessens and the performance of ritual takes on the character of an official duty. Public rituals are often linked to other religious systems, such as Buddhism in Japan and earth cults in Africa, and serve to integrate the fragmented cult of the ancestors into the religious practice of the community as a whole.

3. The nature of ancestorhood. The syncretism of Buddhism and ancestor veneration poses a logical dilemma in that the survival of ancestral spirits is inconsistent with the doctrine of REINCARNATION. This issue was avoided, if not resolved, by Buddhist injunctions that prayers should be chanted for the well-being of the departed, a ritual practice which has come to form an important element in funerary and commemorative rites for the recent dead in East Asia.

Another issue is the distinction between recently departed forebears and the remote dead. Death itself does not confer ancestorhood, and as long as living memory remains, the deceased cannot be merged with the group of ancestors. The passage from deceased to ancestor involves a ritual socialization of the soul parallel to that of the child and of approximately equal length. In Africa the deceased exists as a personality only until replaced at the death of his successor, and in Asia this is the case until at a specified period after death (23-33 years) his memorial tablet is moved from the domestic shrine to the Buddhist temple. In the latter case this transition is made in stages over the years and is marked by cumulative rituals that mirror the maturation of the living. Thus, human existence consists of two parallel cycles. The first occurs in the individual's natal family and, if successfully completed, creates the conditions—marriage and parenthood—necessary to embark on the second, which begins at death. An unsuccessful rite of passage at any level precludes the movement of the individual to full ancestorhood. (*See* LIFE CYCLE RITES.)

4. **Functions of ancestor veneration.** Two areas of functional significance can be distinguished. Ancestor veneration has a fundamental role in the psychological adjustment of the living to the facts of life and death, and it serves in some sense to maintain and reinforce important principles of social organization.

a) Psychological adjustment. Ancestor veneration provides a religious solution for the psychological problem of individual mortality. In societies with a strong unilineal descent principle, the brevity of a single human life is counteracted by the permanence of the lineage. Through the practice of venerating lineage ancestors, the individual can hope for continued existence as an ancestor as long as there are living descendants to conduct rituals. This dependence of ancestors on the living for survival explains in part the acute anxiety focused on continuation of the line. A termination of the descent line would result in extinction of the corporate group and all its members, causing the individual to confront a total death. In this context veneration of the ancestors is a prelude to affiliation with them. As all ancestors, actual and potential, have a strong interest in the continuity of the line, and as such continuity is dependent on successful marriage and child-bearing among the living, it is entirely reasonable to request ancestral intervention for the good of the corporate group.

Ancestor veneration is not destroyed by lack of living memory. In fact, seldom are the actual identities of the majority of ancestors known to the living. The moral authority and influence of the remote dead are sustained by the descent structure and belief system built around the functional roles of the departed. Beyond living memory the ancestors merge to form a spiritual whole, although the conception of a possible anonymous but specific founder of the kin group remains.

Ancestor veneration is intimately involved in the grief process. The transition from death to full ancestorhood occurs through funeral and commemorative rituals which may extend for many years from the time of death. The needs of the deceased are felt to be greatest immediately after death, a time at which social and psychological difficulties are apt to be greatest among the surviving family members. Rituals involved in conferring ancestorhood allow this severance of ties to occur gradually and in an established way and make provision for periodic return visits of the deceased, analogous to those a bride makes to her natal home. Thus, these rituals maintain a link to the departed and provide an antidote to the loneliness and isolation brought about by physical death.

b) Reinforcement of social organization. Ancestor veneration has an important role in preserving the continuity of the social order in spite of the death of individuals. Because ancestorhood is a status in a unilineal descent system, the reciprocal obligations between the living and the dead tend to be confined to the lineage. However, the presence of both absolute and conditional obligation to the deceased extends religious activity beyond the boundary of the lineage and reflects the full complexity of social relationships. Descent alone creates an absolute obligation, and designated members of each lineage are compelled to give homage to their parents and senior members of their line, but examination of actual behavior reveals a diversity of conditional obligation which transcends descent.

Among the strong patrilineal Tallensi, for example, individuals express a sense of ritual obligation to the patrilineage of their mother (Fortes, 1967). Scrutiny of associated tablets on domestic altars in China and Japan reveals the commemoration of individuals who are not, strictly speaking, members of the descent group (R. J. Smith). These anomalies reflect the fact that, in life and death, people have a range of obligations to those who have contributed to their welfare, regardless of descent. In particular, it is essential to include in the system benefactors who might not otherwise be worshiped because they have left no living descendants. The absolute obligation of the corporate descent group to the ancestors arises from a concern for the welfare of the lineage as a whole, but the extension of worship to other individuals reflects the full scope of human relations. Also, in this manner, ancestor veneration preserves a chronicle of what is unique in the history of individual lineages as well as a record of what is typical.

5. **Theoretical explanations** proposed for ancestor veneration fall roughly into three overlapping categories: psychological, economic, and sociological.

a) Psychological theories usually hold that ancestor veneration acts as a means for coping with strong human feelings toward mortality or recurrent conflicts among the living. A classic statement on the subject is that of Frazer, who believes that fear of the dead is a major religious motivation for all "savage" and "barbarian" peoples. The primary goal of cults of the dead, of which ancestor veneration is one case, is to eliminate the dead from the sphere of the living. Failing this, however, people endeavor to render them harmless by ritual propitiation. Ancestor veneration has been assigned an important role in the maintenance of filial piety, essential in view of the built-in contradiction between the role of sons as valued offspring and their role as heirs with a material interest in the demise of their fathers (Fortes 1970). Wallace, while speaking of sacrifice to the dead generally, suggests that such religious practices may serve to alleviate the guilt which arises from the inevitable failure of offspring to act perfectly toward their parents during life.

b) Economic theories suggest that ancestor veneration serves to validate the rights of heirs in the family estate. In a study of the Lo Daaga of Northwest

Ghana, Goody concludes that sacrifices are offered to ancestors because their continued interest in property after death entitles them to a share in the fortunes of the lineage. Failure to provide this payment to the forefathers results in misfortune—normally illness or death—to the living members of the kin group. Ahern, in a study of Chinese ancestor worship, suggests that the transfer of an inheritance is the only guarantee of veneration after death.

c) Sociological theories of ancestor veneration view such customs as a means for maintaining the continuity of the social order in spite of the death of individuals. Edward Tylor, one of the earliest writers on comparative religion, states that veneration of the ancestors represented an extension of paternal authority beyond life, a view which was supported by W. R. Smith. Radin sees ancestor veneration as a developmental stage in which the guardian spirits of TOTEMISM become the property of the clan, and one which gives rise to theocracy through the apotheosis of royal ancestors. In an extension of the psychological argument Fortes maintains that the filial piety arising from ancestor veneration is essential to the continuity of jural authority in unilineal societies. Similar to this idea is Radcliffe-Brown's notion that ancestral cults define and maintain the unilineal descent group.

Ancestors occupy a position between the spirits and the living, and in some sense belong to both realms. Their concern is directed toward the living, but they are able to interact with the spirit world. At the same time, they move in an inner circle far removed from gods. In this sense, the form of ancestor veneration supports the Durkheimian view of religion as a projection of mortal relationships into the world beyond life. The close relationship between departed ancestors and their living kinsmen reflects the intimate group of family members and relatives (Hsu). Gods are likely to be seen as neutral and distant and mirror attitudes to political and social structures which lie beyond the circle of the family. The living head of the lineage serves his kinsmen by mediating between them and the external officials. After death he serves in the same capacity as an ancestor, acting as a link between his descendants and the spirit world.

See AFRICAN TRADITIONAL RELIGION §§3, 4; SOUTHEAST ASIAN TRIBAL RELIGION §1; SOUTH ASIAN TRIBAL RELIGION §4; for Hinduism *see* PITṚ; ŚRĀDDHA.

Bibliography. E. M. Ahern, *The Cult of the Dead in a Chinese Valley* (1973); W. T. Chan, "Religions of China," in *The Great Asian Religions* (1969); M. L. Cohen, *House United, House Divided* (1976); E. Durkheim, *The Elementary Forms of the Religious life* (1915); M. Fortes, *The Web of Kinship Among the Tallensi* (1967), and "Pietas in Ancestor Worship," in *Time and Social Structure* (1970); R. Fortune, *Manus Religion* (1935); J. G. Frazer, *The Fear of the Dead in Primitive Religion* (1933); M. Freedman, *Lineage Organization in Southeastern China* (1958); J. Goody, *Death, Property and the Ancestors* (1962); F. L. K. Hsu, *Americans and Chinese* (1970); A. L. Kroeber, *Anthropology* (1923); C. Lévi-Strauss, *Totemism* (1963); B. Laufer, "Development of Ancestral Images in China," in W. A. Lessa and E. Z. Vogt, eds, *Reader In Comparative Religion* (1965), pp. 445-50; R. H. Lowie, *Primitive Religion* (1924); R. R. Marett, *Faith, Hope, and Charity in Primitive Religion* (1932); A. R. Radcliffe-Brown, *Structure and Function in Primitive Society* (1952); P. Radin, *Primitive Religion: Its Nature and Origin* (1937); R. J. Smith, *Ancestor Worship in Contemporary Japan* (1974); W. R. Smith, *Lectures in the Religion of the Semites*, 3rd ed. (1927); E. Tylor, *Primitive Culture*, 7th ed. (1924); A. F. C. Wallace, *Religion: An Anthropological View* (1966).

M. ODELL and A. M. SCHWARTZBAUM

ANDROGYNY ăn drăj′ ə nē (Gr.; lit. *andro*, "man," *gyno*, "woman"). The state of possessing characteristics of both sexes in one body. A synonymous term, hermaphroditism, derived from the name of a Greek god (Hermaphroditus) who was androgynous, is used more commonly for bisexual organisms occurring in nature, whereas androgyny is reserved for mythical occurrences of bisexuality.

1. **Major interpretations.** The most extensive study of androgyny in mythology and religion was made by Hermann Baumann of the German Culture History School. He found bisexual gods and other myth-beings in societies of archaic cultivators on all continents and in the South Pacific and Indonesia, as well as in higher cultures such as those of the ancient Germans, Egyptians, Babylonians, Chinese, Iranians, Greeks, and Aztecs, and in GNOSTICISM and European ALCHEMY. In his view mythical androgyny is an attempt to overcome the sexual antagonism which arises when patriarchies come into conflict with matriarchal systems. Furthermore, in Baumann's view, the symbol of androgyny often encompasses all bipolarities. R. Pettazzoni agrees, since he finds mythical androgyny especially in tribal groups which have divided into moieties.

For M. Eliade the androgyne is one of numerous symbols of the coincidence of opposites, all of which signify dissatisfaction with the human condition and the desire to transcend life's dualisms in order to attain a state of perfect wholeness. The androgynous creator-god or first human being signifies a conception of perfection at the beginning of the world, while rituals in which one sex symbolically appropriates characteristics of the opposite sex denote human longing to be "whole" and "complete." In a similar way, Carl Jung explains androgyny in psychoanalytic terms as representing the uniting of the divided halves of the psyche—the conscious mind and the unconscious—which he terms the "individuation process."

2. **Ritual androgyny in tribal societies.** Examples of androgynous divine beings are rare or absent in mythologies of hunting and gathering peoples, though male (and occasionally female) creators who produce offspring without the aid of a partner of the opposite sex may perhaps be classed as androgynes. Rather than myths, what we find here are rituals which apparently symbolize the androgynization of the participants.

The celebrated subincision rite of certain Central Australian tribes may be explained as a means of giving

Cleveland Museum of Art, purchase from the J. H. Wade Fund

Androgynous Shiva (half Shiva, half Pārvatī)

the males a symbolic vagina. Likewise, the symbolic transformation of boys into "women" (and vice versa) by means of transvestism during initiation is documented for certain African tribes (Masai, Nandi, Nuba, and Sotho) and for tribes of New Guinea and the Torres Strait. Eliade proposes that the religious meaning of this ritual androgyny is that the novice has a better chance of achieving a particular mode of being if he has first symbolically become a totality.

3. **Androgynous tribal deities.** Beginning with the archaic agriculturalists, explicit androgyny occurs in myth and ritual. The Ngaju Dyak (*see* Schärer) and certain other tribes in this region believe in a bisexual god, the Hornbill-Watersnake, symbol of the Upperworld and Underworld conceived as a unity. In all major myths and rites the two deities appear as one unit. Male mediums or priest-shamans *(basir)* of the godhead become in effect hermaphrodites, dressing and behaving like women. As mediators between the two regions, heaven (masculine) and earth (feminine), they must be bisexual.

Some of the Naga tribes of Assam have a supreme being who is regarded by many tribespeople as bisexual. Gawang, for example, is basically a sky god, but his name means "Earth-Sky" and he is invoked to give children, a function of goddesses. *See* South Asian Tribal Religions §2.

In West Africa androgyny is a motif in the mythology of several tribes. Mawu-Lisa is the female-male supreme deity of the Fon. Mawu (f.) is the moon, Lisa the sun, and yet they are thought of and spoken of as a united entity. The Dogon and Bambara peoples of the western Sudan have an elaborate mythology as recorded by Griaule and Dieterlen. The creator, Amma, intended to create only androgynous, "twin" beings. The egg in which his first creations, two bisexual twins (Nommo), are generated is a female projection of himself. The male half of one of the Nommo, for obscure reasons, bursts out of the egg too soon, leaving his female half behind; this act introduces disorder and evil into the cosmos. Humans are descended from the other Nommo which behaved properly and out of whose placenta four androgynous couples were made. Consequently, according to Dogon belief, each child at birth is given a bisexual soul to compensate for not being a "twin" (androgyne). But since children must grow to be either male or female adults, at puberty their nondominant soul is severed from their bodies by circumcision or excision. Yet even after this initiation rite, a "shadow" of the lost soul is said to remain. It is difficult to imagine a clearer expression of nostalgia for androgynous wholeness. *See* African Traditional Religion.

Judging by the above examples, it appears that androgynous creators result from the fusion of two originally independent deities, a sky-father and an earth-mother. In numerous mythologies, the sky and earth are in close embrace and have to be separated forcibly before creation can proceed. Such deities are but one step removed from true androgyny. Both types probably arise out of a conjunction of matriarchal and patriarchal cultures. Thus, as C. Long observes, the myths serve to reconcile antagonisms between the sacred power peculiar to each sex.

4. **Hinduism and Buddhism.** In the Rig Veda the heaven-earth couple, Dyaus-Pṛthivī, must be separated by Indra. The frequent invoking of Father Dyaus in the feminine gender (*see* Kramerisch) shows that he and the mother were probably conceived as an androgyne. Aditi and Dakṣa, who are said to have given birth to each other, are evidently bisexual. Agni is called a bull-cow and Prajāpati, Lord of Creatures, is an androgyne who divides himself, producing *Vāc,* speech (f.), for purposes of procreation. Puruṣa, similarly, "desired a second. He became as large as a man and woman in close embrace. He caused himself to fall in two. . . ." (BĀU 1.4.3-ff.). The cosmogonic egg which, in other texts, splits to become heaven and earth, reveals Brahmā, who likewise projects a female counterpart.

In the later Purāṇas Rudra-Shiva appears as the divine androgyne, the right half male, the left female, sprung, according to some accounts, from Brahmā. The feminine half of Shiva, called Śivā, Śakti, Pārvatī, etc., is in many ways simply a female reflex of the god. Whether depicted as a loving couple, as Liṅga and Yoni conjoined, or in hermaphrodite form as Ardhanārīśvara, "the Lord whose half is woman," Shiva and his spouse are really one. Their union is not truly sexual, since procreation is not its purpose. Rather, the couple symbolizes the union of the polarities that exist in the cosmos.

In TANTRISM, both Buddhist and Hindu, the realization of the union of these opposites is sought through ritual and meditation. The YOGI who awakens the sleeping KUṆḌALINĪ (f.) and raises her to union with the male principle at the top of the head realizes androgyny within. The *yab-yum* (father-mother) icons of Tibetan and Nepalese Buddhism are further symbolizations of the union of opposites sought by all Tantrics: a state in which "male" and "female" permanently "copulate." *See* BUDDHISM, TIBETAN.

5. Antiquity. A number of Greek gods and goddesses engendered offspring asexually, and examples of androgynous representations of Zeus, Aphrodite, Venus, Dionysus, and others, have been found, although their significance is not well known. M. Delcourt believes these androgynous deities, as well as ritual androgyny, were intended to enhance fertility.

Plato (*Symposium* 189D-ff.) related a "myth" of the first humans as spherical, bisexual beings whom Zeus sliced in two, and Orphism taught that the world came ultimately from a cosmic egg, a symbol of unity, hence androgyny. From these beginnings, via Philo, the Neoplatonists, and the Hermetic tradition, the idea of human perfection as a unity of all opposites, especially of the sexes, was passed on to reappear among other places in GNOSTICISM.

6. Judaism. YAHWEH in the OT appears as a sexless god who creates asexually, by fabrication or by speech. Once the OT metaphorically imputes motherhood to God: he is "the Rock who bore you" (Deut. 32:18); elsewhere Yahweh is referred to in masculine images. It is not evident that the Yahwist meant to imply androgyny in the case of Adam at his creation, though in effect he was indeed a hermaphrodite. Some Greek versions of Gen. 1:27 evidently read, "male and female he created *him,*" lending support for theories of Adam's androgyny in Hellenistic Judaism and later. According to several midrashim, Adam and Eve were created as one being, back to back or laterally, and were split apart by God. The ideal of the androgynous primeval man and of paired male-female emanations of God appeared in some medieval versions of KABBALA.

7. Gnosticism. Androgynous beings abound in the texts of Gnosticism, where in general they represent a condition superior to the sexually separate state of man in this world. The offspring of the original One are all androgynous beings who reproduce asexually. In some systems the "fall" is due to the desire of Sophia to create apart from her male half: i.e., she breaks the perfection of androgyny. Yet even her offspring, Yaldabaoth (the Demiurge), is sometimes said to be androgynous (e.g., Hypostasis of the Archons). Basing themselves on Gen. 1:27 and 2:21-24, several Gnostic accounts state that Adam was created an androgyne: this was the teaching of the Naassenes, for example. The Valentinian Gospel of Philip (68) states: "When Eve was still in Adam death did not exist. When she was separated from him death came into being. If he again becomes complete and attains his former self, death will be no more."

Androgyny in Gnosticism reflects not only a longing for wholeness, but also a loathing for sexuality by which imperfect human life is perpetuated. Actual sex relations are eschewed, being replaced by a spiritual *hieros gamos* which reestablishes an original bisexual—actually asexual—existence.

8. The alternate reality tradition in the West. Hermeticism, Neoplatonism, Gnosticism, and other undercurrents have persisted in the West, perpetuating, among other ideas, that of androgyny as the image of perfection. ALCHEMY, studied by Eliade and Jung, was a quest not only for gold, but more importantly for human perfection and wholeness.

The longing to overcome sexuality and duality, de Cusa's *coincidentia oppositorum,* can be traced in the centuries since the Renaissance in such figures as JAKOB BOEHME (salvation as restoration of Adamic androgyny), the German Romantics, Emanuel Swedenborg (God is androgynous; marriage in heaven as androgyny; *see* SWEDENBORGIANISM), Goethe, and Balzac (*Séraphita*). The Androgyne appears in Tarot cards as another name for the Fool.

Eliade sees the symbol of the androgyne as having become debased in late nineteenth century literature and its meaning as a religious symbol largely lost. The theology of the UNIFICATION CHURCH, however, represents God as a single male-female being (probably from the Chinese YIN AND YANG concept); marriage "centered on God" reproduces in effect God's dual unity on earth. In CHRISTIAN SCIENCE God, who is "spirit," is addressed in prayer as Father-Mother. Some advocates of women's equality have attempted to introduce this form of address into mainline churches, and the popularity of "unisex" clothing in the 1970s may indicate the desire of some to return to a whole, androgynous condition. *See* FEMININE DIMENSIONS OF THE SACRED.

Bibliography. H. Baumann, *Das doppelte Geschlecht* (1955); M. Delcourt, *Hermaphroditea: Recherches sur l'être double promoteur de la fertilité dans le monde classique* (1966); M. Eliade, *Mephistopheles and the Androgyne* (1965), ch. 2; C. G. Jung, "The Psychology of Transference," *The Practice of Psychotherapy, Complete Works,* XIV (1966), *ibid., Psychology and Alchemy,* XII (1968); *ibid., Mysterium Coniunctionis, ibid,* XIV (1970); R. Pettazzoni, *The All-Knowing God* (1956); H. Schärer, *Ngaju Religion* (1963); M. Griaule, *Conversations with Ogotemmâli* (1965); G. Dieterlen, *Le Renard Pâle* (1963); Charles H. Long, *Alpha: The Myths of Creation* (1963); S. Kramerisch, "The Indian Goddess," *HR,* XIV (1975); James M. Robinson, ed., *The Nag Hammadi Library in English* (1977).

M. L. RICKETTS

ANGELS (Gr. *aggelos;* lit. "messenger"). Superterrestrial beings who mediate the divine presence on earth either as agents of revelation or as executors of the divine will. The motif represents one form of witness to divine activity in the realm of human experience. Other terms—DEMONS, spirits, etc.—

express the same idea. "Angel" testifies to benevolent divine activity in terms of popular religious mentality within the pattern of the contemporary world view. The term appears frequently in the vocabulary of ZOROASTRIANISM, JUDAISM, CHRISTIANITY, and ISLAM (*see* MALĀ'IKA).

1. **History of the concept.** "Angel" appears in Greek literature as early as Homer. In primitive Greek thought the term referred both to a personal agent and to an impersonal force. Subsequently it was used primarily of a personal agent in a religious or secular role.

Angels play only a restricted role in the Israelite tradition prior to the time of the Babylonian exile. The Israelite experience in exile, however, affected the concept in two respects: it stimulated the development of strict monotheism—a perspective which led to the concept of angels as mediators—and it provided access to Iranian and Babylonian terminology and cosmology to express the concept of angels. Although the development of the doctrine of angels in Jewish thought was not uniform, a full-orbed angelology is evident in specific areas of Jewish literature, particularly in nonbiblical material. Angels play an important role in APOCALPYTIC thought as revealers of esoteric information. Scattered references to angels appear in rabbinic writings but their role is carefully circumscribed. Most modern Jewish interpreters understand references to angels as poetic symbolism or as obsolete remains of an earlier cosmology.

Christians adopted Jewish beliefs about angels, but the doctrine of the HOLY SPIRIT set definite limits to the development of Christian angelology. Angels are frequently mentioned in the NT, (Luke 1-2; I Thess. 4:16; Rev. 16:1-17, etc.), but tendencies toward angel worship were subjected to a sharp critique (Col. 2:8-10). PSEUDO-DIONYSIUS (sixth century A.D.) developed a heavenly hierarchy from seraphim at the top to archangels and angels at the bottom. Most popular ideas about angels stem from him, not the Bible. European religious art also reflects his influence, though classical *putti* were the inspiration for "cherubs."

2. **Angels in modern thought.** Various attempts have been made to restate Jewish-Christian angelology. Psychoanalysis points to structures of personality that are analogous to the tripartite structure of the universe assumed by angelology. In some circles belief in angels is supported by appeal to the literal meaning of the scripture or to earlier teachings of the church. However, since the Copernican revolution they are commonly understood as elements of an obsolete cosmology.

Bibliography. J. Michl, *et al.,* "Engel," *Reallexikon für Antike und Christentum* IV (1959), 59-322; D. W. Boussett & H. Gressmann, *Die Religion des Judentums* (1966), pp. 330-31; G. F. Moore, *Judaism,* I (1946), 401-14.

R. C. BRIGGS

ANGKOR än´ kōr. *See* HINDUISM IN SOUTHEAST ASIA §1.

ANGLICAN CHURCHES (Ch). A worldwide fellowship of national or regional, self-governing churches in full intercommunion with one another. Their union is neither juridical nor confessional, but expresses a common loyalty to an inheritance of doctrine, discipline, and worship that stems from the sixteenth-century reformation of the Church of England. Historically, these churches developed with the expansion of British dominions overseas, beginning in the seventeenth century, and with planned missionary activity in non-English-speaking lands and cultures since the early nineteenth century. The term "Anglican" was first used *ca.* 1851.

The ethos of Anglican church life is one of comprehension: the Bible as the final source of doctrine "necessary to salvation," and acceptance of the Apostles' and Nicene Creeds, but with considerable latitude in interpretation; a prescribed liturgy in various recensions of the BOOK OF COMMON PRAYER; the ancient, ordained, ministerial orders of bishops, priests, and deacons, maintained in APOSTOLIC SUCCESSION; and, less definable, respect for church tradition, reason, and personal religious experience. Anglican theology is biblical and pastoral, not dogmatic in expression; its ethical teaching is applied according to general principles rather than rigid rules.

Anglican churches are constitutionally governed by legislative synods, both diocesan and national, that include bishops, priests, and lay persons. Diocesan synods elect their own bishops, except in England, where their selection is by the sovereign. Primatial archbishops and presiding bishops, except in the United States and Canada, are also diocesan bishops.

Since 1867, at approximately ten-year intervals, the Archbishop of Canterbury invites the Anglican bishops for consultations in the Lambeth Conference. Their resolutions and reports are influential but not binding. A small Anglican Consultative Council of representative bishops, priests, and lay persons meets every two or three years for cooperative planning and missionary strategy. A full-time secretary general assists coordination and intercommunication.

Anglican churches take an active part in the ECUMENICAL MOVEMENT, in the World Council of Churches, and in national and local interdenominational councils. Many are engaged in negotiations for reunion with Protestant churches. Relations with the Eastern churches are friendly. In 1967 official dialogue was inaugurated with the Roman Catholic Church. Anglican dioceses have joined the United Churches of South India (1947), North India, and Pakistan (1970), and will shortly do so in Sri Lanka. There are concordats of intercommunion with the Old Catholics, the Philippine Independent Church, the Mar Thoma Church (India), the Lusitanian Church (Portugal), and the Spanish Reformed Episcopal

Church; and between the Church of England and the Lutheran Churches of Sweden and Finland.

As of 1978 there were 405 dioceses with about 46 million members in 24 autonomous churches—in the British Isles, the Americas, Asia, the South Pacific, the Middle East, Africa, and the Indian Ocean; two regional councils (East Asia and South America); and a few extraprovincial dioceses.

See APOSTLES' CREED; ARCHBISHOP; BISHOP; CANTERBURY; DEACON; DIOCESE; NICENE CREED; OLD CATHOLICS; PRIEST; PRIMATE; REFORMATION, PROTESTANT.

Bibliography. J. W. C. Wand, *Anglicanism in History and Today* (1961); H. G. G. Herklots, *Frontiers of the Church* (1961); S. F. Bayne, Jr., *An Anglican Turning Point* (1964); S. Neill, *Anglicanism* (4rd ed., 1978). M. H. SHEPHERD, JR.

AṄGUTTARA NIKĀYA än´ gōō tär ä nĭ kī´ yŭ (B). *See* NIKĀYAS.

ANICCA ŭ nē´ chŭ (B—Pali; lit. "not enduring") **ANITYA** ŭ nēt´ yŭ (H & B—Skt.). Impermanence, one of the three basic and inherent characteristics of all existence in time and space, along with "no self-nature" (ANATTA) and "suffering" (DUKKHA). As in the case of *anatta,* here too Buddhism is at odds with the Brahminical-Hindu tradition of the genuine reality of spiritual and material substance.

1. **Basic meaning.** From its beginning Buddhism has held that a direct, unbiased observation of our human experience will reveal that there are no enduring entities. Even on the level of ordinary observation we can see the change of seasons, the birth and death of plants, animals, and human beings, as well as sweeping historical and geological alterations. A more intensive observation will show that the human being, both physical and mental, as well as the objects of direct human experience, are only changing processes, in flux at every moment.

2. **Forms and related doctrines.** Some Buddhist schools of thought, e.g. the Sarvāstivādins, developed this doctrine into a theory of radical momentariness. They said that physical reality consists of an infinitesimally rapid pulsation of sense stimuli, which appear in units of such split-second length that they do not truly "exist," i.e. endure, at all and that even faster thought impulses respond to them. But rapid as these thought-pulses are, the physical reality-pulse to which thought responds has ceased before even a percept (conscious image), let alone a concept (such as "red"), has arisen. Thus "reality" is always one step ahead of conscious experience, whose images and concepts pretend to report it. The doctrine of dependent co-origination (PAṬICCASAMUPPĀDA) interlocks and supports that of *anicca.* Dependent co-origination specifies the compound nature of everything—physical objects, selves, concepts. A "tree" or a "man," for example, is constituted by a set of factors in temporary association. This temporary association of elements *is* the object, and it "causes" the object or being to "exist." There is no substance which carries over from cause to effect, only a changing proportion of elements. Hence, objects and beings are *anatta,* empty of self-reality.

3. **Religious significance.** This sense of impermanence has much the same importance as *anatta.* Persons should not attach themselves emotionally or intellectually to the substantial, changing entities of experience as though they were real, whether they are objects, persons, feelings, or thoughts. To do so is ignorantly to bind oneself to the misery of rebirth. To become aware of the impermanence of all that exists in time and space, including oneself, is a step toward enlightenment.

See MAHĀSATIPAṬṬHĀNA SUTTA; DHARMA; BUDDHIST SECTARIANISM and their bibliogs. W. L. KING

ANIMISM. The belief that all of reality is pervaded or inhabited by spirits or souls; the belief that all of reality is in some sense animate. (*See* SOUL, SPIRIT.)

The term, which was introduced by Tylor, is often used imprecisely for the religions of all the small, isolated, technologically simple, preliterate societies of the world—the societies which are sometimes pejoratively and inaccurately called "primitive." Some form of animism is a characteristic feature, often an important one, of such religions, but it is also found in some of the so-called "higher" ones.

1. **History of the term.** When Tylor introduced the term he used it to designate what he conceived to be the earliest form of religion devised by human beings as they emerged into humanity from their prehuman origins. Thus, "primitive" had its true etymological meaning. In Tylor's scheme, animism was successively replaced by polytheism and then by monotheism. These successive forms of religion he judged to have corresponded to and been appropriate for more developed, technologically and structurally more complex societies. Tylor therefore saw causal relations between the evolution of religion and the processes of cultural evolution in technology and social structure. This was in keeping with the dominant question in anthropology at the time, the question of the origins and evolution of cultural forms.

Tylor's explanation for the emergence of animism was surprisingly rationalist, considering that he assigned it to early hominids for whose intellect he and his contemporaries had scant respect. He postulated that as early human beings speculated rationally about their experiences and observations involving dreams, fainting and death, they concluded that there must be an inner part of human and other beings and objects that was in principle separable from the material manifestation or body of each. This "explained" how a person could at the same time be inert on a bed or in a grave and also wandering about doing all kinds of things. It was the separation of this inner being from the body which caused the inertness of sleep, fainting, and death. By analogous logic, Tylor claimed, people arrived at the notion that all entities, and in fact all of reality, was equally possessed of an inner being which Tylor called a "soul" (Lat. *anima*).

Tylor thought the soul was, in its most primitive form, a quite crude and material concept. It was later that more advanced people refined the concept into the notion of true "spirit." This was an intermediate stage on the way to what later was to become polytheism, as various kinds of nature spirits (and in some cases ancestor spirits) were promoted to genuine divine status. (*See* ANCESTOR VENERATION.)

Contemporary students of the religions of simpler societies most often accept only part of Tylor's construct. They admit that belief in soul-spirit is an almost universal dimension of such religions, and they admit that such beliefs were probably very ancient, predating any of the so-called "higher" religions. In general, however, anthropologists today reject the more rigidly evolutionary aspects of Tylor's theory, at least in the deterministic sense which he attributed to it.

Our knowledge of truly prehistoric religions is at best inferential. Evidence comes from three directions: the circumstantial evidence of archaeological finds, which requires interpretation about which there is often room for disagreement; the evidence of the contemporary religions of societies whose technological, structural traits are apparently similar to those of prehistory; and the earliest recorded mythologies, which clearly point back to still earlier preliterate beliefs. In general, the convergence of these types of evidence supports the idea that prehistoric religion was in some important respects like the religions of contemporary simple societies. But it must also be added that these differ widely among themselves, so that the evidence only establishes broad limits within which conjectures are more or less plausible.

2. Dimensions of contemporary animism. Animists are seldom ontological dualists. They usually believe that soul-spirit is the inner face of matter, not a separate kind of reality. It may be linked or equated with the breath, the blood, the shadow or image, the name, or some other dimension of a living thing. It may be localized, or it may pervade the body. Its function, whether it is simple or complex, is to animate the body; in addition, it may be assigned the function of constituting the individual personality, and also other psychological roles.

Patrilineal societies often argue that the soul comes from the father; matrilineal societies, that it comes from the mother. There are ambilineal societies which say that one part of the person comes from father, another from mother. And there are also societies which believe that a child is the REINCARNATION of an ancestor. The soul-spirit may begin in a particular body at, before, or after birth.

Any gain in soul (or life force, vitality) contributes to health and well-being; this whole process is often referred to by the verb "to live"; conversely, any diminishment of soul, whether through illness, adversity, witchcraft or sorcery, etc. (these are not mutually exclusive), is referred to by the verb "to die," which is only the logical conclusion of the process.

Most animistic societies believe in the survival of the soul after death, whether as a ghost, an ancestor, or in some other form. It is often believed that the soul of an evil person becomes an evil spirit, continuing to work mischief among the living.

Just as human beings have soul-spirit, so do all other things; there are thus nature spirits of all kinds. And in addition, there are often ethically defined spirits, whether good or evil. These can be very numerous, and exist in highly specialized orders, causing a variety of good and bad effects in human experience. But the popular image in the West according to which "primitive" peoples are ridden by constant terror of evil spirits fits only a small number of cases. Most people can call upon good spirits or protective magic to help them against evil spirits; or they are protected by good conduct and the good offices of ancestors. Truly gloomy world views in this area are found, apparently, chiefly in societies which have been subjected to massive forced change imposed from without, so that people feel helpless.

It can be documented from many cases that animism is in no way incompatible with belief, sometimes well developed, in a supreme being, who is usually thought to be the creator and to be good and benevolent. *See* REINCARNATION; TOTEM.

Bibliography. E. Durkheim, *The Elementary Forms of the Religious Life* (1915); E. E. Evans-Pritchard, *Theories of Primitive Religion* (1965); E. A. Nida and W. A. Smalley, *Introducing Animism* (1959); P. Radin, *Primitive Religion* (1937); E. B. Tylor, *Primitive Culture* (1871). C. R. TABER

ANNUNCIATION (Ch). The announcement of the ANGEL Gabriel to the Virgin MARY (Luke 1:26-38), as God invites her to become mother of the MESSIAH by the power of the HOLY SPIRIT. Annual feast is celebrated March 25. A considerable homiletic literature has grown up around this theme, and it continues to exercise great appeal in music and art.

E. R. CARROLL

ANṢĀR ān sär′ (I—Arab.; lit. "helpers"). Name given the Arabs of MEDINA from the tribes of Aws and Khazraj who converted to Islam and assisted MUHAMMAD and his followers at the time of and after the HIJRA. While the term can be derived from a regular singular meaning "one who assists," it was likely influenced by Sura 61:14 of the QUR'ĀN, in which there is a play on the word "helpers" and the word for Christians, *naṣārā*. The title came to designate those who descended from Medinese stock as opposed to the Meccans, who were called *muhājirūn* (lit. "ones who made the Hijra"). The *anṣār* are mentioned twice in the Qur'ān, along with the *muhājirūn,* and are promised a reward in Paradise (Sura 9:100, 117).

From the "Constitution of Medina," preserved in IBN ISHĀQ's *Sīra,* we see that most of the *anṣār* were parties to that early agreement with Muhammad to make him first among equals in the city. It is unclear to what extent they participated in the earliest raids, but they were well represented at the Battle of Badr, and thereafter constituted the major support for Muhammad.

At Muhammad's death, the *anṣār* attempted to form a party to select one of their own as CALIPH, but were frustrated by the *muhājirūn.* As a group they declined in influence, partly because of the survival of pre-Islamic rivalries, the *anṣār* deriving from the South Arabs and the Meccans from the North, according to popular genealogies, and partly because they opposed the caliphate of 'UTHMĀN and, later, the UMAYYADS. Many were supporters of ALI's cause and supported the 'ABBĀSIDS. Medina, rather than MECCA, became the chief Arabian center for learning, even after the capital of Islamic government was removed from Arabia, and the *anṣār* and their descendants became patrons of many famous non-Arab Muslims.

Bibliography. Ibn Ishāq, *Life of Muhammad,* A. Guillaume, trans. (1955); L. Caetani, *Annali dell'Islām* (1905-26); W. M. Watt, *Muhammad at Medina* (1956); M. Shaban, *Islamic History A.D. 600-750* (1971). G. D. NEWBY

ANSELM (Ch; *ca.* 1033-1109). ARCHBISHOP of CANTERBURY; perhaps the most distinguished of the early scholastic theologians and philosophers. Remembered for his *Cur Deus Homo* (1098) on the theology of the ATONEMENT and the *Monologion* and *Proslogion* (1078-79) on the proofs for the existence of God. *See* SCHOLASTICISM §1. F. OAKLEY

ANTHROPOSOPHY ăn thrə pŏs′ ə fī (Ch—Gr.; lit. "knowledge of mankind"). An occult movement begun in the late nineteenth century by RUDOLF STEINER; its greatest influence has been in German-speaking countries.

Alarmed by the dominance of materialistic thought, Steiner sought to develop a view of reality based on direct perception of the spirit world. He drew on the writings of J. W. von Goethe and Hindu concepts popularized by THEOSOPHY, and taught that the self-conscious human ego is an immortal self whose home is the spirit world. The self continues to develop its nature (KARMA) through a series of reincarnations. Under the influence of the demons AHRIMAN and LUCIFER, mankind had steadily descended into materialism throughout successive epochs until the time of Christ, who initiated an ascent to spirituality.

The belief that the human body has three physical centers, one each for willing, feeling, and thinking, led Steiner to formulate theories of education, especially for mentally handicapped children, in an effort to reverse the karmic effects of their previous lives.

Bibliography. J. Hembeben, ed., *Rudolf Steiner in Selbstzeugnissen und Bilddokumenten* (1963); A. P. Shepherd, *A Scientist of the Invisible* (1954). K. CRIM

ANTICHRIST (Ch). A mythological figure, the concept and terminology of which were appropriated from Iranian and Jewish APOCALYPTIC sources. He is to appear at the close of history to challenge CHRIST (I John 2:18, 22; 4:3; II John 7). Christians have identified persecutors and apostates as manifestations of the Antichrist. R. C. BRIGGS

ANTICLERICALISM (Ch). Opposition to the influence of clergy in secular affairs; resistance to the domination of the church through its ordained and professional leaders. K. WATKINS

ANTIOCHUS IV EPIPHANES ăn tī′ ə kŭs ə pĭf′ ə nēs. Seleucid king of Syria from 175-163 B.C., during whose reign the MACCABEAN uprising occurred. An admirer of Rome, he embarked upon a vigorous policy of forced Hellenization. His restrictive measures and defilement of the JERUSALEM Temple led to outright rebellion of the Jews, to all of whom his title *Theos Epiphanes* ("God Manifest") was blasphemous. E. M. MEYERS

ANTIPOPE. Person who claims or exercises the office of the PAPACY (bishop of Rome) illegitimately. The term dates from the twelfth century. The official Roman list counts thirty-seven, from Hippolytus (died *ca.* 235) to Felix V, who abdicated in 1449. Reasons for the existence of an antipope vary from usurpation to genuine confusion over who was the legitimate bishop of Rome. J. HENNESEY

ANTI-SEMITISM. A nineteenth century term which has come to denote general prejudice toward Jews throughout history. A distinction is sometimes made between anti-JUDAISM (general anti-Jewish prejudice) and anti-Semitism (prejudice based on race), first elaborated in the nineteenth century. The term is used here for both types of prejudice.

1. Ancient world. In the ancient world we find many manifestations of anti-Semitism, due in part to the Jews' refusal to mix with other peoples. Already in Palestine there was friction between Jews and Gentiles, which increased under Greek domination of Palestine. The Hellenistic rulers saw Jews as an obstacle to the spread of Greek culture, while Jews, on the other hand, fought Greek influence as a threat to their religion.

Jewish separateness contrasted strongly with general practices in the ancient world and often caused Jews to be looked upon askance, giving rise to libels which were to reappear with slight variations throughout history, as late as the twentieth century. It was alleged that the Jews are a strange, leprous people, who have no right to the land they claim.

Under Roman domination the centrality of emperor worship exacerbated hostilities and made Jews vulnerable to the charge of treason. Nonetheless their situation in the Roman Empire was tolerable. Jews enjoyed freedom of movement and played a role in economic life, and their religious customs were safeguarded by order of the emperor. During the first century B.C. friction increased, particularly in Alexandria and Syria. Although the laws protecting Jews remained in force, earlier stereotypes and libels reappeared, and were propagated by some of Rome's leading writers (e.g., Horace, Martial, Tacitus, and Juvenal).

2. **Early Christian era.** CHRISTIANITY began as one among several Jewish sects. Its founder, JESUS, was a Jew, as were his followers. The first Christians combined belief in Jesus as the MESSIAH with adherence to Jewish law. Already in those early years, however, the seeds of future conflict were sown because the young CHURCH saw itself as the new community of Israel in which God had fulfilled his promises through the coming of Jesus as the Christ (Messiah). It took over the Jewish scriptures as its own, reinterpreting them in the light of belief in Christ. Jews for a time tolerated the new sect, but soon came to view Christians as heretics and a threat to Judaism.

The incipient hostility was exacerbated by two factors. The first was the coming into the church of Gentiles in ever larger numbers. This led by the middle of the first century to the debate as to whether or not Gentile converts to Christianity must accept Jewish law (TORAH). At a council in Jerusalem PAUL, a PHARISEE by birth who had become a zealous Christian, was the spokesman for those who maintained that faith in Christ alone sufficed and that Gentiles were not subject to Torah. His view prevailed, opening wide the door to the influx of non-Jews into the church. By the late first century Jewish Christians had become a small minority.

The second event was the Roman war of A.D. 66-70 and the destruction of JERUSALEM. During the siege the Christian community of Jerusalem left the city, interpreting the impending disaster as divine punishment visited upon the Jews for their rejection of Jesus and as fulfillment of his prophecy. Christianity thereby severed its destiny from that of Judaism. Henceforth the two religions went their separate ways, in growing mutual hostility. Jewish Christians were expelled from SYNAGOGUES, while Christians looked upon Jews as obdurate in their refusal to recognize Christ, hence punished by God, with no land of their own, doomed to wander homeless over the face of the earth for all time. The Christian scriptures (NEW TESTAMENT), edited for the most part in their final form after A.D. 70, reflect this hostility: cf. John's largely pejorative use of the term "Jews," the whitewashing of Pilate and the Romans in the crucifixion accounts, and the text in Matthew's Gospel, "And all the people answered, 'His blood be on us and our children' " (27:25). By the mid-second century the charge of deicide (murder of God) had been added to other accusations.

The early church's hostility toward Judaism may be seen in part as resulting from its effort to find its own identity. Since the church saw itself as the new Israel, superseding the old and inheriting its privileges, the continued existence of Judaism confronted it with the problem of having to explain this existence. It did so in purely negative terms, seeing Jewish survival as a symbol of rejection of God and a warning to the world. This teaching, to which Jules Isaac in the twentieth century was to give the name "Teaching of Contempt," was further elaborated in the preaching and writings of the fourth century church fathers, among whom John Chrysostom stands out for his extreme vituperation of the Jews. The Teaching of Contempt was now full-blown, and is being laid to rest only fifteen hundred years later (cf. §7 below).

With Christianity's new status as official religion of the Roman Empire in A.D. 321 Christian theological claims began to be translated into legislation. Jews now forfeited many of their ancient rights, were forbidden to intermarry with Christians, and were excluded from the mainstream of the socio-economic order.

3. **Middle Ages.** In a society permeated by Christianity in every aspect of its life Jews were inevitably perceived as outsiders. Yet there is evidence, particularly in the early Middle Ages, of friendly contact between Christians and Jews, even of a certain attraction of Judaism for Christians. The picture is complex. While church COUNCILS from the twelfth centuy onward enacted discriminatory legislation against Jews (*see* BADGE), individual bishops and popes frequently tried to protect them against popular outbreaks. The first and most devastating of these occurred in 1096, during the first CRUSADE, when the crusaders on their way through France and Germany massacred thousands of Jews. Other outbreaks followed in the thirteenth and fourteenth centuries. Economic factors contributed to anti-Semitism at a time when European commerce began to flourish. Usury (money lending at interest) was considered sinful by the medieval church, hence forbidden to Christians. Since it was, however, essential to economic growth, Jews, who stood outside Christian society, were encouraged to engage in usury, which frequently drew popular hatred upon them. Ancient anti-Jewish legends now reappeared in Christian versions (*see* BLOOD LIBEL; PROFANATION OF THE HOST). In the fourteenth century Jews were made the scapegoats for the Black Death, which was said to have been caused by their poisoning of wells. In 1215 the Fourth Lateran Council legislated special clothing for Jews to segregate them from the rest of the population. This heightened the popular belief that Jews were different, evil, and possessed attributes of the devil. Medieval iconography typically depicts Jews with tails and horns and a variety of repulsive

features, some of which were to reappear in the Nazi era (*see* HOLOCAUST).

During the thirteenth century Jews were expelled from England, and were the object of massacres in France and Germany. They found refuge in Poland in the late Middle Ages. In Spain they enjoyed peace and prosperity for centuries under the Muslims, until Islamic rule came to an end and they were expelled by Ferdinand and Isabella in 1492. Frequently the objects of forced conversion, baptized Jews in Spain (also called "New Christians" or MARRANOS) became easy targets for the INQUISITION.

4. **Reformation.** Although CALVIN and the PURITANS tended to esteem Jews, LUTHER'S anti-Semitism matched that of the church fathers. His opposition of grace and faith to law and works led him to see Jews as the embodiment of all that is alien to God. In 1543, shortly before his death, he wrote a tract, *Against the Jews and their Lies,* which outlined a program of practical measures for expelling Jews from society and included burning their synagogues. Hitler was to use part of this tract during the Holocaust.

5. **Enlightenment and emancipation.** In the measure in which Christianity lost much of its hold on Western society the Jews' lot improved markedly. Intellectual leaders of the Enlightenment such as Lessing and Montesquieu were sympathetically disposed toward Jews, stressing their dignity and humanity, even making them the embodiment of their own humanitarian ideals (cf. Lessing's *Nathan the Wise*). In daily reality, however, ancient stereotypes tended to persist, fostered by intense anti-Semitism of other figures of the Enlightenment such as Voltaire and Diderot, who despised Judaism as much as Christianity. Even those who sought to rehabilitate the Jews did so on the basis of their humanity rather than their Jewishness, as is evident from the 1791 declaration of French revolutionaries: "To the man, everything, to the Jew, nothing." Whatever the motives, however, Jews were at long last free to enter universities, the professions, and military service. A new era of freedom seemed to have dawned for them.

6. **Nineteenth and twentieth centuries.** The promise was to be realized only partially. Despite their new participation in the mainstream of Western society, Jews were still often looked upon as different, a fact which caused many, particularly in Germany, to convert to Christianity in the hope of obtaining full acceptance by their fellow citizens. At the popular level and in many clerical circles religious anti-Judaism persisted, even gaining in intensity in the late nineteenth century in France. The anti-Semitic campaign waged there by Edouard Drumont led to the celebrated Dreyfus Affair. THEODOR HERZL'S chance presence at Dreyfus' first trial in Paris awakened in him the conviction that even in modern Europe Jews were not safe from anti-Semitism, and made of Herzl the father of political ZIONISM. The nineteenth century also saw the birth of a new variety of anti-Semitism, based on racial rather than religious roots. Its two chief theoreticians were Count Gobineau and Houston Stewart Chamberlain. The latter, as Wagner's son-in-law, became highly influential in Germany. It was there that the term "anti-Semitism" was invented by Wilhelm Marr in 1879.

Even the new waves of anti-Semitism, however, did not prepare the world for what was to be the most devastating outbreak of anti-Semitism in all of Western history. This was reserved for the twentieth century. Germany's economic and political collapse after World War I made the country ripe for Hitler's vicious anti-Semitic propaganda. The "stab in the back" theory portrayed the Jews as responsible for Germany's misfortunes, providing a convenient scapegoat. It was Hitler's opportunity to realize his dream of ridding Germany—and eventually Europe—of Jews once and for all (*see* HOLOCAUST). Nazism, while in many ways the antithesis and enemy of Christianity, was able to build its "final solution" on the ancient Christian anti-Semitism of the West.

7. **After World War II.** The marked decrease in anti-Semitism in the West since World War II is in large measure the result of the Holocaust. Worldwide sympathy for the survivors of Hitler's slaughter played an important role in the establishment of a Jewish homeland in 1948. The existence of the State of Israel, however, has led to manifestations of anti-Semitism in the New Left, and to new anti-Jewish feeling in Arab countries, a part of the world where, during the Middle Ages, Jews had fared far better than under Christianity. Nonetheless efforts to eliminate anti-Semitism continue to make progress. The change is perhaps greatest in the churches, both Protestant and Catholic, which not only publicly condemn the Teaching of Contempt today, but seek to replace many of its traditional features with a positive understanding of Judaism as a living and rich religious tradition. One of the last remaining strongholds of anti-Semitism is the Soviet Union, whose three million Jews suffer discrimination and often persecution. The vehement anti-Semitism of czarist Russia has reappeared in new forms under the Russian communist regimes.

Bibliography. M. Hay, *Thy Brother's Blood* (1975); J. W. Parkes, *Anti-Semitism: A New Analysis* (1964); L. Poliakov, *The Aryan Myth: A History of Racist and Nationalist Ideas in Europe* (1977), *The History of Anti-Semitism,* 2 vols. (1974); R. Ruether, *Faith and Fratricide* (1975); M. Simon, *Verus Israel* (1964); J. Trachtenberg, *The Devil and the Jews* (1943).

E. FLEISCHNER

ANTONY OF EGYPT (Ch; *ca.* 250-356). Early Christian hermit. At age twenty he gave away his wealth and became a desert solitary. He visited Alexandria twice to encourage potential martyrs and oppose ARIANS. His life was popularized by ATHANASIUS' biography which included vivid accounts of spiritual combat. *See* DESERT FATHERS.

W. O. PAULSELL

ANTONY OF PADUA päd′ oo ä (Ch; 1195-1231). FRANCISCAN FRIAR and the order's first official professor of theology. Born and educated in Portugal, Antony later achieved renown for his conversion of heretics in France and northern Italy and for his preaching at Padua, where he came to be venerated as a wonder-worker and patron saint.

H. L. BOND

APOCALYPTIC (Ju & Ch). (1) A religious world view oriented to eschatology; (2) a genre of literature that articulates this world view. Some primary characteristics are cosmic dualism, focus on transcendence, and a deterministic, pessimistic view of history. Apocalyptic literature makes extensive use of symbolism, emphasizes ecstatic experience as the realm of revelation, and identifies superhuman beings—angels and demons—as agents of a cosmic conflict. This literature is normally pseudonymous. It arose in Jewish circles about 150 B.C. and flourished in the succeeding three or four centuries.

1. **Jewish apocalyptic.** Jewish apocalyptic thought is the result of an extended process that derived material from both Jewish (wisdom, prophecy) and non-Jewish (Babylonian, Persian) sources. The syncretistic nature of the material frustrates efforts to demonstrate a direct continuity with any single religious or cultural heritage. This distinctive vision of reality emerged in Jewish thought in the crucible of suffering inaugurated by the Babylonian captivity (587 B.C.) and stressed that God's intervention will consummate the process of history and inaugurate his reign. This expectation appears in the book of Daniel, as well as in the nonbiblical works of Ethiopic Enoch, the Testaments of the Twelve Patriarchs, the Sibyllene Oracles, etc. Apocalypticism existed largely, if not exclusively, outside orthodox rabbinic thought.

2. **Christian apocalyptic.** Although Christianity made no original contribution to apocalyptic, it originated in circles imbued with the apocalyptic mentality. John the Baptist, JESUS, the primitive Christian community (including PAUL), all reflect the apocalyptic perspective. In addition certain characteristic Christian concepts—the new age, the parousia, Son of Man, etc.—are derived from apocalyptic concepts. However, because early Christianity identified God's eschatological act with a person active in recent history—Jesus—it was not possible to appropriate the total Jewish apocalyptic scheme of events. Accordingly, only a single Christian apocalyptic work, the Apocalypse of John (the book of Revelation), appears in the NT. Elements of apocalyptic thought and symbolism do appear in fragments of other NT writings (I Thess. 4:13–5:2; Jude, vs. 9: Mark 13, etc.)

Elements of this apocalyptic heritage have persisted throughout Christian history. In general, however, ecclesiastical structures and formal theology have relegated apocalyptic thought to a peripheral role in the total life of the church. Some notable exceptions may be noted in MONTANISM (second century), Thomas Münzter (fifteenth century), and certain contemporary sectarian groups (SEVENTH DAY ADVENTISTS, LATTER-DAY SAINTS, and JEHOVAH'S WITNESSES).

Bibliography. E. Hennecke and W. Schneemelcher, "Apocalypses and Related Subjects," *New Testment Apocrypha* II (1965), 579-803; D. S. Russell, *The Method and Message of Jewish Apocalyptic* (1969).

R. C. BRIGGS

APOCRYPHA (Ju & Ch). The fourteen books and parts of books included in the Greek version of the OLD TESTAMENT and which come into the Roman Catholic OT by way of the Latin Vulgate, but which were excluded from the Protestant Bible (therefore "apocrypha" [from Gr. "hidden away"]). Modern Roman Catholics generally call this literature "deuterocanonical." Strictly speaking, there is no NT Apocrypha, but the phrase is often applied to certain early Christian writings not in the NT.

L. E. KECK

APOSTASY (Ch). The abandonment of or departure from God, or defection from one's CHURCH or monastery. As an abandonment of God (cf. II Chr. 29:19), usually under pressure from pagan authorities (cf. I Macc. 2:15), apostasy was considered a cardinal sin by early Christian authors (cf. Tertullian, *On Modesty* 19) and held a prominent place in debates about the scope of the church's powers to remit sins.

D. E. GROH

APOSTASY IN ISLAM. *Irtidād* (ĭr tĭ däd′) and *ridda* (rĭd′ də) are the technical Arabic terms and an apostate is a *murtadd* (mər′tad; lit. "one who turns the back"). In the QUR'ĀN God's punishment for *irtidād* is only in the afterlife (Sura 16:106 ff.; 3:86 ff.; 2:217), although one who repents, not having become confirmed in apostasy, will be saved.

In the Prophetic Traditions, apostasy is punishable by death, a view which is upheld and detailed in both the SUNNITE and SHI'ITE law books. However, the offender is usually granted an opportunity to recant. Only adult, sane, male apostates who have acted freely are to be executed (traditionally by the sword). Women are either imprisoned until they recant (HANAFITES and Shi'ites) or are executed (MALIKITES, SHĀFI'ITES and HANBALITES).

The death penalty is rarely carried out today, but there remains a powerful sense of outrage among Muslims when one of their number forsakes the community.

Bibliography. Muhammad Ali, *The Religion of Islam* (n.d.), pp. 591-99; S. M. Zwemer, *The Law of Apostasy in Islam* (1924); Burhān al-Dīn 'Alī, *The Hedaya,* ET C. Hamilton (1791), II, 227.

F. M. DENNY

APOSTLE (Ch & I). The instrument or agent through which the will of the sender of a message is expressed; the agent or messenger of revelation. MUHAMMAD was called the apostle (RASŪL) of God.

According to the Synoptic GOSPELS, JESUS commissioned twelve disciples (Mark 3:14-19) with authority to act in his behalf (cf. Matt. 28:16-20). However, Paul claimed the title as an equal with the twelve (Gal. 1:1-2). The NT also refers to other persons as apostles: Matthias (Acts 1:26); Barnabas (Acts 14:14); Andronicus and Junias (Rom. 16:7); Epaphroditus (Phil. 2:25); unnamed persons (II Cor. 8:23).

Critical investigation has raised problems concerning the connotation of the term in early Christian history (cf. Gal. 1–2 with Acts 1:21-22). The evidence implies an extended development—related to the issue of authority—from the role of missionary (Pauline era) to officially accredited representatives appointed by Jesus (Synoptic concept: Mark 3:14). Apostolic Succession claims that the authority which Jesus bestowed upon the twelve is exercised in perpetuity by divinely appointed successors. This belief has played an important role in the history of the church, particularly in the self-understanding of Roman Catholicism.

Bibliography. K. Rengstorf, "Apostolos," *TDNT*, I, 407-44; W. Schmithals, *The Office of Apostle in the Early Church* (1969).

R. C. Briggs

APOSTLES' CREED (Ch). The most widely used creed in the Western Church. Legend has it composed by the Apostles, but in fact it is based upon a baptismal creed in use in Rome in the third century. It was given its present form late in the sixth or seventh century in southwest France. *See* Creeds and Confessions §2.

J. H. Leith

APOSTLES' CREED

I believe in God the Father Almighty, Maker of heaven and earth:

And in Jesus Christ his only Son our Lord: Who was conceived by the Holy Ghost, Born of the Virgin Mary: Suffered under Pontius Pilate, Was crucified, dead, and buried: He descended into hell; The third day he rose again from the dead: He ascended into heaven, And sitteth on the right hand of God the Father Almighty: From thence he shall come to judge the quick and the dead.

I believe in the Holy Ghost: The holy Catholic Church; The Communion of Saints: The Forgiveness of sins: The Resurrection of the body: And the Life everlasting. Amen.

Book of Common Prayer (1928)

APOSTOLIC FATHERS (Ch). A diverse group of eight Greek writers of the late first and early second centuries who were presumed to have been in contact with the Apostles or their immediate disciples. In the seventeenth century the category included Clement of Rome, Ignatius of Antioch, Barnabas, Polycarp, and Hermas. Subsequently, Papias of Hieropolis, the Epistle to Diognetus (an apologetic writing of unknown authorship), and the Didache (oldest manual of church order yet recovered) were included.

Clement of Rome's name was attached to a First and Second Epistle. The latter is now recognized as being a homily of unknown authorship, the former as a letter from the church at Rome to the church at Corinth. Modern scholars credit Ignatius with authorship of only his seven letters in their shorter recension. Polycarp of Smyrna (d. 156) has left only one document, consisting of one, or possibly two letters to the Philippians; but an account of his martyrdom, included in collections of the Apostolic Fathers, survives. Papias' writing (*ca.* 130) survives only in fragments.

Although varying in form, style, and interests, the Apostolic Fathers represent our earliest extensive catholic sources of the postapostolic age, apart from the NT. The Shepherd of Hermas, 1 Clement, and Barnabas were regarded by some ancient writers as scripture, or very near to it.

Bibliography. R. M. Grant, *The Apostolic Fathers, A New Translation and Commentary*, Vol. I (1964); J. Lawson, *A Theological and Historical Introduction to the Apostolic Fathers* (1961); J. Quasten, *Patrology*, I (1962), 29-105.

D. E. Groh

APOSTOLIC SUCCESSION (Ch). The teaching, developed in Christianity's early centuries, that authority of church leaders derived from and was guaranteed by their historical connection and continuity (through successive ordinations) with the Apostles. This succession is claimed today by Roman Catholicism, Orthodox Churches, Anglicans, and others.

As associates and envoys of Jesus, the apostles commanded special honor in NT times, and subsequent generations regarded the apostolic age as harmonious and unerring in belief, especially when contrasted with disruptions which beset later eras. Around A.D. 95 Clement of Rome based his plea for resolution of a struggle for leadership in the Corinthian church on the divine and model order by which Christ's ministry was extended through the apostles and their appointees (1 Clem. 41 ff.). Confronted in the late second century by Gnostic Christian groups claiming possession of truths restricted to Jesus' inner circle (and preserved in secrecy by the apostles), Irenaeus and Tertullian asserted that apostolic traditions concerning Christ were not esoteric but public, having been committed to the guardianship of Bishops instituted by the apostles and, in turn, to their successors.

The idea of apostolic succession, in various forms, has recurred in later Christian epochs—notably during the Reformation, when Catholic and Protestant thinkers exchanged charges of innovation, and in modern times, when it has been a problem in the Ecumenical Movement.

Bibliography. A. Ehrhardt, *The Apostolic Succession* (1953); T. G. Jalland, *The Church and the Papacy* (1944).

R. C. Gregg

APPAR äp pär (H—Tamil; lit. "father"). A Tamil poet-devotee of the god Shiva; one of the sixty-three Nāyaṉārs. He flourished in the early seventh century. His 312 extant hymns form the fourth through sixth books of the *Tēvāram*, a collection of devotional lyrics still in use. He is especially revered as exemplifying the role of a humble servant of the god.

G. E. Yocum

APSARAS ŭp sä´rŭs, **APSARĀ** ŭp sä´rä (H—Skt.; lit. "moving in water"). Any of a large number of celestial nymphs said to reside in INDRA's heaven. Originally supposed to be personifications of water-permeated clouds and mists, the *apsarases* more commonly appear as voluptuous and willing partners to both gods and men. In numerous stories they are sent to earth by the gods in order to test the resolve of would-be holy men. J. BARE

ARABIC LANGUAGE. A Semitic language generally classified as South Semitic, though exhibiting features common to North Semitic, possibly through long contact with ARAMAIC and HEBREW. The oldest inscriptions in Arabic script are from the early fourth century A.D., although most extant pre-Islamic inscriptions date from the early sixth century. The script was probably formed in the vicinity of Hira by Christian missionaries for writing a dialect different from that of the QUR'ĀN, which is called Classical or Literary Arabic. The literary language, in a modified form, is the written language of the Arab countries today, standing beside numerous dialects, and it is the religious and liturgical language for Muslims around the world.

From the earliest indications, mostly involving Islamic poetry, speakers of Arabic have traditionally learned two related dialects: their tribal or regional vernacular and a literary dialect called Classical Arabic, which exhibits many archaic features, including full grammatical inflexion and a root-pattern vocabulary system, to a higher degree than in any other Semitic language. Classical Arabic seems always to have been an artificial language used mainly for poetry, religious texts, and intertribal communications. With the rise of Islam, it became the dominant dialect because the Qur'ān was expressed in it. It did not, however, eliminate dialects; native speakers continued to use two language levels, the vernacular for speaking and everyday commerce, and Classical Arabic for writing, religion, etc.

In many instances the dialects of pre-Islamic Arabia constitute the basis for the modern regional dialects of the Arab countries, partly because the invading Muslim forces maintained their tribal groups. Jews and Christians had their own dialects of Arabic, which received written expression in the scripts associated with their confessions; Judeo-Arabic is written in Hebrew characters, Garshūnī in Syriac script, and Maltese in Roman. These dialects have extensive literatures but do not reflect Classical Arabic.

Classical Arabic, because of the model of the Qur'ān, retained preeminence as the standard for written expression, but, with the conversion of non-Arabs to Islam, it was often relegated to the status of an academic language. A highly modified form, sometimes called Middle Arabic, became the official language of the courts. New vocabulary entered the language through the vernacular dialects and Middle Arabic before being accepted into Classical Arabic, thus repeating the pre-Islamic process.

Classical Arabic enjoys wide currency today and is little changed from the language of earliest Islam. This is one of the factors which contribute to a sense of unity among Muslims, whose mother tongues include widely different dialects and languages.

Bibliography. M. Bateson, *Arabic Language Handbook* (1967); J. Fück, *Arabiya* (1950); C. Rabin, *Ancient West-Arabian* (1951); A. Jeffery, *Foreign Vocabulary of the Qur'ān* (1938); G. Newby, "Observations About an Early Judaeo-Arabic," *JQR,* LXI (1971), 212-21; N. Abbott, *Rise of the North Arabic Script and its Qur'ānic Development* (1939); for bibliog. see "Arabiyya," *EI.* G. D. NEWBY

ĀRĀḌA KĀLĀMA ä rä´ dŭ kä´ lä mŭ. A religious teacher of VAIŚĀLĪ. After leaving his family Gautama visited Kālāma and evidently participated briefly in a form of religious training under his leadership and the leadership of UDRAKA RĀMAPUTRA.

R. H. DRUMMOND

ARAMAIC LANGUAGE (Ch & Ju). A general name for a group of Semitic dialects closely related to HEBREW. "Official Aramaic" served as the *lingua franca* of the Neo-Babylonian Empire (625-539 B.C.) and the Achaemenian Persian Empire (538-330 B.C.). Parts of the OT books of Ezra and Daniel are in Aramaic, and it was probably the native language of JESUS. Some of his sayings are preserved in Aramaic, e.g. Mark 5:41; 15:34. The GEMARA is in Aramaic, as are parts of contemporary Jewish liturgy, notably the Mourner's KADDISH, portions of the HAGGADAH, and folk songs sung at PASSOVER. K. CRIM

ĀRAṆYAKAS ä rŭn´ yŭ kŭs (H—Skt.; lit. "relating to the forest" [*araṇya*]). The Āraṇyakas are *śrauta* ("revealed") texts attached to the RIG and YAJUR VEDAS which deal with the symbolic and allegorical meanings of VEDIC ritual and were intended for those who had taken the vow of a VĀNAPRASTHA or "forest dweller." Traditionally, they were thought to have been formulated to enable those who could no longer perform the rituals and sacrifices to meditate upon and interiorize their meaning, or were viewed as particularly dangerous or esoteric texts safe only for those outside the normal structures of society. This traditional view has long been questioned by modern scholars who do not see any marked distinction between the content of the Āraṇyakas and that of the earlier BRĀHMAṆAS or the later UPANIṢADS.

Deussen's suggestion that the traditional designation of certain texts as Āraṇyakas was made in order to make the Vedic corpus consonant with the ĀŚRAMA doctrine (with four "levels" in each) remains a plausible hypothesis. Chronologically and conceptually, the traditional ordering of Vedic texts is: Vedas, Brāhmaṇas, Āraṇyakas, Upaniṣads. However, the SĀMA VEDA and the ATHARVA VEDA have no Āraṇyakas, while those of the other SAMHITĀS ("collections") vary widely in relation to their respective Brāhmaṇas and Upaniṣads. For example, the Taittirīya Āraṇyaka is supplementary to the Taittirīya Brāhmaṇa with books

VII-IX forming the Taittirīya Upaniṣad, and the Bṛhad Āraṇyaka is the fourteenth book of the Śatapatha Brāhmaṇa and is an Upaniṣad. The origins of the so-called Āraṇyakas and their interrelations with earlier and later texts lead to the conclusion that their traditional distinction in form, content, and purpose is probably artificial.

Bibliography. P. Deussen, *Philosophy of the Upanishads* (rpr. 1966).

J. HELFER

ARCHBISHOP (Ch). The title used in some churches to designate a BISHOP who presides over a major province or region; designation of bishops of equivalent honorary rank. K. WATKINS

ARCHDEACON (Ch). The title used in some churches to designate high ranking assistants of bishops, with duties that often include administration of properties, supervision of ecclesiastical districts, and adjudication of ecclesiastical disputes. *See* DEACON. K. WATKINS

ARHANT är′ hänt (B—Pali; lit. "the worthy" [*arh*— "to deserve, to be worthy"]) **ARHAT** är′ hät, **ARAHANT** är ä hänt′, **ARHAN** är′ hän (B—Skt. variants). A person who has achieved the highest stage of perfection in THERAVĀDA BUDDHISM.

In pre-Buddhist India the god Agni, kings, and priests are called *arhant,* because they occupy distinguished positions and are worthy to receive gifts and respect. This honorific title may be rendered "Right Honorable" (Rig Veda, II,3,3). In the sixth century B.C. any religious mendicant who practiced self-mortification or behaved strangely such as "creeping on all fours, or sprawling on the ground, taking food . . . with his mouth only" was regarded an *arhant.* Such was the case with Kora, the naked ascetic who was admired by Sunakkhatta, a rebellious disciple of the BUDDHA. As in many other instances the Buddhists borrowed this term and gave it a new connotation.

1. The Buddhist definitions. (a) An *arhant* is a person who has reached the end of the EIGHTFOLD PATH, gained the insight into the true nature of phenomena and the knowledge of emancipation, destroyed rebirth, lived the higher life and done what had to be done (*The Dialogues,* pt. III, p. 4; II, p. 169). This means an *arhant* is a saintly sage who has realized the absolute truth and is no longer subjected to the wheel of becoming (BHAVACAKRA). (b) Among the *arhants* GAUTAMA BUDDHA was most eminent. He was the pathfinder, the others were merely followers. Further, among his ten epithets *arhan* and *sammasaṃbuddha* (the fully enlightened Buddha) are placed side by side and are synonymous. This was his exclusive privilege, as no reference was made to other *arhants* as Buddhas. (c) Five following criteria are used to verify that one is an *arhant*: an *arhant* is not attracted to, nor repelled by, things seen, heard, sensed, or cognized, and his mind is free, open, and unaffected; he understands the true nature of the five aggregates of grasping (i.e., the attachment to physical form, sensation, perception, predisposition, and consciousness), namely, they originated dependently; he has no notions of "I," "mine," or "self" in relation to the six elements *(dhātu)*; he has no attachment to the internal and external sense spheres; he knows the doctrine of causation (PAṬICCASAMUPPĀDA). If a disciple can claim achievement of all five criteria, he may be declared to be an *arhant* (Majjhima Nikāya, III, 29-37). (d) An *arhant* possesses the threefold superknowledge, namely, knowledge of his own previous births, knowledge of the rebirths of other persons, and knowledge concerning the final cessation of mental intoxicants (ĀSAVA). (e) Attempting to trace the etymology of *arhant,* the Majjhima Nikāya (I, 280) states that it is associated with *araka* ("remote"), because all sinful deeds are remote *(araka)* from such a person. In addition, he is described as having destroyed the spokes *(ara)* of the wheel of samsara. These interpretations appear to be far-fetched. The Arhant-Vagga of the DHAMMAPADA (No. 90) has this to say of an *arhant:*

There is no anguish for him who has
Ended his journey, and is freed from
All grief, is emancipated in every way,
And has destroyed all ties.

This may sum up the attainment of an *arhant* based on the Theravāda tradition. However, Mahādeva of the Mahāsāṅghika sect held the view that an *arhant* did possess the five imperfections: "Tempted by others, ignorance, doubts, indirect realization and the Path appearing through utterance" (*Taishō,* 27, pp. 510c-512a).

2. Who may become an *arhant?* It is stated in the Therigātha and MILINDAPAÑHA that monks, nuns, and lay devotees are all able to achieve spiritual perfection and become an *arhant.* However, according to tradition, when a lay disciple becomes an *arhant* he should immediately enter the order the same day; otherwise he would die. This may be a later speculation, as it cannot be found in the PALI CANON. The process that finally leads to becoming an *arhant* requires prior attainment of the first three stages of stream-entrant (SOTĀPANNA), a once-returner (SAKADĀGĀMIN), and a non-returner (ANĀGĀMIN). Each stage further loosens the bonds of SAMSARA. The *arhant* alone is fully free.

3. Bodhisattva vs. *arhant.* Based on the foregoing considerations, an *arhant* was understood to be the embodiment of purity, virtue, morality, and true wisdom. Yet when the ultra-altruistic ideals of a BODHISATTVA became popular, the *arhant* came to be regarded as selfish, with no concern for others. This seems unfair, because the Buddha and his disciples spent their entire lives spreading the message of equality, compassion, morality, and spiritual cultivation. The instruction given to Sigāla concerning social ethics is ample evidence of their deep concern for society and the welfare of the people (*The Dialogues,* pt. III, pp. 173–84). *See* LOHAN.

Bibliography. T. W. Rhys Davids, trans., *The Dialogues of the Buddha* (1959), pt. III, pp. 173-84; and *The Questions of King Milinda,* (1894), pt. II, p. 96; J. Takakusu, *et al.*, eds., *Taishō Daizōkyō* (1957), 27, pp. 510-12; U. Dhammajoti, trans., *The Dhammapada* (1943), ch. 7.
W. PACHOW

ARIANISM âr´ ē ən ĭsm (Ch). Condemned as heresy at councils of NICAEA (325) and Constantinople (381); doctrine and movement originated by the Alexandrian priest Arius (d. 336), who maintained that the Son was both "creature" and "God," different in essence from the Father but related to him by "participation" and by "adoption"—i.e., as a creature elevated through obedience to the paternal will. Stressing the dissimilar essences of the persons, Arians believed in a TRINITY in which Son and HOLY SPIRIT were subordinate to the unbegotten Father.
R. C. GREGG

ARYA-SATYA är´ yă sŭt´ yŭ (B). *See* FOUR NOBLE TRUTHS.

ARJUNA är´ jū nä (H—Skt.; lit. "white, clear"). Third of the five PĀṆḌAVA brothers, noted for his pure character; Arjuna's bowmanship and friendship with Lord KRISHNA brought Pāṇḍava success in the MAHĀBHĀRATA war. This left-handed archer, like his brothers, was more than human, having been fathered by INDRA. From Indra and other gods he received a chariot with HANUMĀN as emblem, the bow Gāṇḍīva, two inexhaustible quivers, and the conch Devadatta, and from SHIVA the magical *pāśupata* weapon for countering missiles. He trained five years in Indra's court in weaponry, music, and dance and conquered the gods' enemies. In the Bhārata war his charioteer was Krishna, the two being forms of an ancient divine pair, Nara and NĀRĀYAṆA. But Arjuna was also human: he won princess DRAUPADĪ by his archery, and though her favorite, shared her as wife with his brothers. She bore him a son, Śrutakarman. Krishna's sister Subhadrā, whom he abducted and married, bore him a son, Abhimanyu. When the Bhārata war began, his compassion led him to refuse to fight, but he was roused to action by Krishna (*see* BHAGAVAD GĪTĀ), and fought with skill, some deceit, and rage. Thirty-six years later he performed Krishna's funeral and was himself the third Pāṇḍava to die due to pride in his own heroism (*see* KARMA). Parīkṣit, Arjuna's grandson by Abhimanyu, assumed the throne and began the present KALI YUGA.

Bibliography. J. A. B. van Buitenen, trans. *The Mahābhārata,* (1973-); C.V. Narasimhan, *The Mahabharata* (1965); V. Mani, *Puraṇic Encyclopaedia* (1975).
D. HUDSON

ARK (OF THE TORAH) (Ju). The chest or closet in the SYNAGOGUE that serves as the repository of the scrolls of the TORAH. The ark is the major architectural element in the synagogue and traditionally is built into the "eastern" wall, i.e., the wall facing toward JERUSALEM.

Bibliography. C. Roth, *Jewish Art* (1961).
B. MARTIN

ARMENIAN CHURCH (Ch). Native MONOPHYSITE church of the Armenians. According to tradition the church was founded by the apostles Thaddaeus and Bartholomew. Gregory the Illuminator converted and baptized King Tiridates (*ca.* 238-314), was consecrated at Caesarea in Cappadocia, and was appointed primate or CATHOLICOS of the church. Armenia was the first established Christian state. Gregory's son Aristakes succeeded him, establishing for a time a hereditary primacy. In the fourth century the church became independent from Caesarea, and St. Mesrob (*ca.* 345-440) created the Armenian alphabet. In the next century the BIBLE was translated into Armenian. In 491 an Armenian council rejected the formulation of the Council of Chalcedon. (*See* CHALCEDONIAN DEFINITION.) Throughout their turbulent history, Armenians have lived under the domination of Arabs, Turks, Russians, and others.

The church accepts the dogmas of the first three ecumenical COUNCILS. It is the only Eastern church to use unleavened bread in the EUCHARIST. It celebrates the LITURGY of St. Basil, keeps the Julian calendar, and observes the nativity of Christ as part of EPIPHANY on January 6. The Supreme Catholicos resides in Etchmiadzin, in Soviet Armenia, where about a third of the world's approximately 3½ million Armenians now live. Around 125,000 live in North America.

Bibliography. A. S. Atiya, *A History of Eastern Christianity* (1968), pp. 303-56.
V. KESICH

ARMINIUS, JACOBUS är mĭn´ ĭ ŭs (Ch; *ca.* 1559-1609). Dutch REFORMED theologian, sponsored for the ministry by the church in Amsterdam and one of the first students to enroll at the University of Leiden. His advanced education was in Geneva under tutelage of BEZA and at Basel under Grynaeus. He was also influenced by Peter Ramus. He was a pastor in Amsterdam from 1588 until he became professor of theology at Leiden in 1603.

The Dutch Reformed Church had difficulty synthesizing the indigenous reforming tradition with the international Calvinism of the period, especially the theology of Beza. The conflict between these two traditions came to a focus in Arminius' teaching on PREDESTINATION. Arminius insisted that human will toward the good is not only wounded but also "imprisoned, destroyed and lost." Response to the divine call is the work of grace. Yet Arminius insisted upon the cooperation of the human will. He based predestination upon the faith of the elect. Arminius did not solve the problem of divine grace and human freedom, but he did maintain an emphasis on the freedom and integrity of the will over against hyper-Calvinism. Arminius remained a member of the Dutch Reformed Church and continued to recommend CALVIN'S writings, including the *Institutes,* though he added they should be read with discrimination.

The controversies that Arminius precipitated were dealt with at the Synod of Dort (1619), which rejected his positions along with those of his more radical opponents.

Bibliography. C. Bangs, *Arminius* (1971).

J. H. Leith

ART AND ARCHITECTURE, BUDDHIST. The Buddhist arts arose from the need for a tangible focus for devotion and worship, and are chiefly drawn from popular beliefs rather than from scholarly traditions. The artistic forms used for this purpose were taken from indigenous traditions, and as artisans adapted old forms to the new religion, non-Buddhist gods came into Buddhism.

Each sect has its distinctive styles and types of art. Hīnayāna focuses primarily on Jātaka Tales and episodes from the life of the Buddha. Mahāyāna added to these the icon for veneration. Esoteric Buddhism contributed intricate Mandalas and a number of many-armed deities. Pure Land Sects and Zen have created their own iconographies.

Indian Buddhist art and architecture are the source of that of other Buddhist countries, but the Indian prototypes were always modified by native traditions and preferences.

1. **Architecture.** *a) India.* The earliest Buddhist structures were temporary huts for use in the rainy season; they were round, built of wood and thatch, and roofed by branches curved into a dome. The first rock-cut sanctuaries, cut during the Mauryan dynasty, were, in imitation, circular and domed. Toward the end of the first century B.C. Buddhists began to build *caitya* halls, sanctuaries with barrel-vaulted nave with a semicircular end in which is placed a Stūpa or, later, an image. The nave is flanked by aisles for circumambulation. The façade was elaborated first in wood (e.g. Bhaja, or Cave X at Ajaṇṭā), and later in stone, with decorative motifs and figures of the Buddhist pantheon.

In Hīnayāna *caitya* halls (e.g. at Bhaja), the *stūpa* is the most important element. In Mahāyāna examples (e.g. cave XIX at Ajaṇṭā) the *stūpa* has an image carved into it, or is totally replaced by an image.

The Vihāra is the monastic dormitory, a rectangular hall surrounded by individual cells. Sanctuaries were included at first by using the center back cell to house a *stūpa,* later by enlarging this chamber and adding an antechamber. The caves were decorated with wall paintings and reliefs.

In the Gupta Dynasty (*ca.* A.D. 320-540) the first permanent free-standing *caitya* halls were built. Some kept the floor plan of the rock-cut halls; others are rectangular sanctuaries entered through a columned porch, with a *sikhara* (spire) above the end containing the *stūpa* or image. Both these types were also used for Hindu temples.

Although Buddhism virtually disappeared from the rest of India in the seventh century, it survived in Bengal until the Mongol invasions of the twelfth century. The architecture of this period is characterized by towers, such as the "fairy towers" at the university of Nālandā which enchanted the Chinese pilgrim Hsüan-tsang. At Paharapur, dating from the late seventh or early eighth century, a stepped pyramid in the shape of a maltese cross recreated the world mountain. It is a three dimensional Mandala which the pilgrim walks around and climbs, and in so doing experiences the cosmic order.

b) Ceylon and Southeast Asia. Ceylon was closely attached to Indian Buddhist culture, and remained primarily Hīnayāna; thus, the *stūpa* is of paramount importance. The temples were modeled on the *vihāra* form, rectangular columned halls with the entrance on a long side. Particularly notable is a nine-storied monastery at Anurādhapura, built of wood and decorated with precious materials. Monks closer to enlightenment were housed in the higher stories.

The greatest products of Southeast Asian Buddhist architecture are pyramidal temples recreating the world mountain. These can be complex structures connected by stairs and terraces, or small stepped pyramids with a shrine inside the bottom level. In Cambodia, the Bayon at Angkor Thom, from the early thirteenth century, is carved with intricate reliefs. It is later than the famous Hindu world-mountain temples of Angkor.

Borobudur, Java, possesses perhaps the most

Courtesy of the Smithsonian Institution, Freer Gallery of Art, Washington, D. C.

Painting of a seated Lohan *(arhant);* Japanese silk panel attributed to Ryozen (late 14th century)

Nelson Gallery—Atkins Museum, Kansas City, Missouri (Nelson Fund)

The bodhisattva Avalokiteśvara, or Kuan-yin; statue of polychromed wood (Chinese, 12th-13th century)

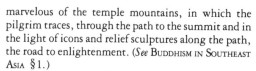

Reproduced by courtesy of the Trustees of the Bristish Museum

Bodhisattva, Gandhāra style

marvelous of the temple mountains, in which the pilgrim traces, through the path to the summit and in the light of icons and relief sculptures along the path, the road to enlightenment. (*See* BUDDHISM IN SOUTHEAST ASIA §1.)

c) Central Asia and the Far East. As traders and pilgrims crossed the deserts of Central Asia, there developed in the oases an eclectic art with influences from GANDHĀRA in western India, MATHURĀ, on the Yamunā River, TANTRISM, China, and Iran. Miran, on the southern trade route in western India, is the earliest of these (late third or early fourth century A.D.). The best accounts of these fascinating sites are still to be found in the works of Sir Aurel Stein, who pioneered explorations in Central Asia.

The trade routes joined at Tun-huang in the far west of China, where a remarkable series of caves was carved out and filled with wall paintings and painted banners, between the late fifth century and the early eighth century. Here one can see a Chinese Buddhist style of painting being worked out.

The Chinese excavated cave temples in western China, but most of China did not have suitable terrain for such temples, and so indigenous secular forms were adapted to temple architecture. Like palaces, temples consist of a group of rectangular pavilions generally one or two stories high, arranged on axes in a courtyard surrounded by a wall. They are usually of wood, their tile roofs supported by a system of columns and brackets. The buildings typically include an assembly hall, a relic shrine, a library, housing for the monks or nuns, and one or two PAGODAS. The temple complex points south, and is entered through a great south gate.

Esoteric temples, built on mountains, tend to follow the natural terrain rather than the axial symmetry of mainline Buddhism. Zen temples place great emphasis on the garden as a focus for meditation. (*See* illustrations for HORYU-JI; KOREAN RELIGION; ZEN.)

2. Sculpture. *a) India and Southern Asia.* Our knowledge of Buddhist sculpture begins with the MAURYAN DYNASTY, when King AŚOKA erected pillars with edicts on the DHARMA carved on their bases and symbolic sculpture on their capitals.

In the Sunga period (second-first century B.C.) *stūpas* were elaborated with relief sculptures on the stone railings and gateways that surrounded the *stūpa.* The popular subjects were deities, fertility figures, Jātaka tales, and stories from the life of the Buddha. The scenes are arranged in tight patterns, giving a rich effect much loved in Indian decoration. *Caitya* halls were also embellished with sculpture.

As Mahāyāna Buddhism developed, devotional icons began to supersede narrative sculpture. There are two seminal styles of icons, both developed under the Kushan dynasty (first-third centuries A.D.). The first arose in Gandhāra and the second in Mathurā.

In Gandhāra the Kushans sponsored an art which joined provincial Hellenistic style with Buddhist iconography. The elegant figures wear full robes cascading in more or less classical folds over smooth bodies. The oval faces have classical noses, half-closed eyes, and remote expressions.

Mathurā developed a Buddhist sculpture based on ancient Indian traditions. The fleshy, rounded figures wear minimal drapery. The forms are simple, the presentation of the figures straightforward. Often the Buddha's robe is over one shoulder only.

The classical age of Indian sculpture is the Gupta Dynasty, the synthesis and culmination of these earlier styles and direct model for later Buddhist art in Southeast Asia and the Far East.

Gupta sculpture took its inspiration from Mathurān style, but transmuted its rather stocky figures and robust curves into slender figures and simplified the anatomical representations. As the period went on, there was an increasing sway to the figures, and often there are ridges derived from Gandhāran folds in the drapery. Icons of the Buddha followed certain formulas to show his divine nature: perfect serenity and thirty-two (some not always present) signs, among them the *usnisa,* a protuberance on the top of his head, snail-shell curls of hair (not a Gandhāran feature), and the *urna,* or third eye, in the forehead. There is a HALO or mandorla behind him. His hand gestures (MUDRĀS) represent different aspects of his nature and events in his life. He is seated in the LOTUS POSTURE or standing, and his feet are bare. He usually wears the monastic robe, but in late Indian icons he may wear jewels as signs of his transcendent nature. BODHISATTVAS are dressed in princely clothes and embellished with ropes of jewels, elaborate hair, and halo.

In Bengal, after the close of the Buddhist period in the rest of India, Gupta style was continued, adapted to esoteric Buddhism, and hardened toward the dry, sharp-featured, heavily decorated styles of Nepal and Tibet. (*See* BUDDHISM, TIBETAN.)

The Gupta style of sculpture was imitated in Southeast Asia, where each country subtly adapted Gupta types to its own sensibilities and racial types, and created works both distinctive and beautiful.

b) China. Chinese Buddhist sculpture begins in the three kingdoms–six dynasties period (A.D. 220-581), and a number of vigorous and distinctive schools quickly grew up under the patronage of the different states. Artists were at this time working with both a foreign iconography and a foreign style, but they soon transformed their prototypes with their love of linear definition of form and of abstract patterning, and their disregard of anatomy. These characteristics unite Chinese sculpture, whether the figures are short and chunky or slender, free-standing or relief.

In the T'ang dynasty (618-907) figures acquired a soft fleshiness of both body and face which continues to modern times.

Popular themes for sculpture, and for painting as well, are the LOTUS SŪTRA, triads of Buddhas or of a

K. Crim

Main building of Kŭmsan-sa Buddhist Temple, Korea

Buddha flanked by bodhisattvas, Kuan-yin (AVALOKITEŚVARA), sometimes with multiple heads, and from the tenth century, portrait statues of LOHANS. Pure Land Buddhism employed images of AMIDA singly or in his paradise.

c) Korea and Japan. Whereas the Chinese sculpture is linear, with attention directed to the decorative patterns made by edges of robes, jewlery, and facial features, both Korean sculpture and its derivative, Japanese sculpture, have a finely tuned sensitivity to volumes: the swelling and diminishing of an arm, for example, or the egg shape of a head. In Korean sculpture beauty is sought in smooth, only slightly modulated forms. The Japanese found pleasure in this style and also in exaggerated musculature, as in their guardian figures.

3. **Monumental sculpture.** On his pilgrimage to India Hsüan-tsang visited two colossal Buddha images at Bāmiyān in north-central Afghanistan. The older one dates from the second or third century A.D. and stands 120 feet high; the second, from about two hundred years later, is 175 feet. The statues and the niches in which they stand were carved from a sandstone cliff. Only a rough approximation of the body and head was actually cut from the cliff; the folds of the drapery were modeled in mud mixed with chopped straw, with a coating of lime plaster that served as a base for polychroming and gilding. Here the Buddha was portrayed as more than the simple teacher; he is lord of the world. These first colossi influenced the rock-cut colossi at Yünkang and Lungmen in China, giant Korean statues, such as that of MAITREYA near Nonsan, and the DAIBUTSU statues in Japan. (*See* illustration for KOREAN RELIGION.)

4. **Painting.** *a) India.* As painting is more perishable than stone sculpture, less is known of early Buddhist painting. Gandhāran wall painting, inspired like its sculpture from Hellenistic art, is known from such sites as Miran in Turkestan (late third century). At Ajaṇṭā painting began at least in

Courtesy the Cleveland Museum of Art

The Second Coming of the Fifth Patriarch; section of a handscroll by Yin-t'o-lo (Yuan dynasty, ca. mid-14th century)

the first century B.C., and was well-developed by the third century, but the greatest examples are late fifth century, including the painting of the bodhisattva Avalokiteśvara as Padmapāṇi ("He who holds the Lotus") from Cave I. Here is an art both sensuous and poetic, peopled by swaying figures with sweet, gracious faces.

b) The Far East. Buddhist painting in the Far East, from the art of the Tun-huang caves on, was separated (with the exception of Zen painting) from the monochrome calligraphic style for which the Orient is most famous. Instead, it is usually heavily colored with blue, green, and red, and sometimes gold and silver, and the colors are contained by fine black outline.

Zen (Ch'an) painting is radically different. It employs the monochromatic freely brushed technique of the scholar painters, rather than the craftsman's carefully pretty colors. It creates an impression of spontaneity, or irrationality, in order to embody the Zen concept of enlightenment. Compared to the other calligraphic styles, this style was considered completely unrestrained by rules. Beginning in China in the eighth century, Zen painting was practiced with great zest in Japan as well.

Bibliography. B. Rowland, *The Art and Architecture of India* (1967); L. Sickman and A. Soper, *The Art and Architecture of China* (1971); A. Soper and R. Paine, *The Art and Architecture of Japan* (1955); A. Coomaraswamy, *History of Indian and Indonesian Art* (1927, rpr. 1965), outdated in some particulars but important for its philosophy, and *Elements of Buddhist Iconography* (1935); J. Rosenfield, ed., *Japanese Arts Library,* a multivolume history written by Japanese scholars, presently being published in English; M. Sullivan, *Arts of China* (1973), and *The Cave Temples of Maichishan* (1969); P. Mus, *Barabudur* (1935); S. Weiner, *Ajanta: Its Place in Buddhist Art* (1977); J. Harle, *Gupta Sculpture* (1974); A. Stein, *Ancient Khotan,* 2 vols. (1907), *Serindia,* 5 vols. (1921), and *Innermost Asia,* 4 vols. (1928).

J. Crim

ART AND ARCHITECTURE, CHRISTIAN. Christian art encompasses the full array of visual images which Christians have associated with their religion. It includes not only great achievements of religious art, but also images of little artistic merit. Similarly Christian architecture covers the entire range of structural forms, from the most accomplished to the most ordinary, which Christians have used to house their worship and to provide for their communal activities. Considered together, the varieties of Christian art and architecture may be conceived as a complex vocabulary of images and

J. M. Ward

Christ and the twelve apostles; bas-relief from the Monastery of Santo Domingo de Silos, Spain (12th-13th century)

forms which has served both to express and to sustain the shared imagination of the Christian community at the different stages and in the varied traditions of its history.

It is important to note that Christian art cannot be defined in terms of a specific style or a particular view of art's religious significance. Individual styles have dominated various periods or traditions in Christian history, but no one style is uniquely characteristic of Christian art or architecture as a whole. Nor has Christianity consistently maintained a single understanding of the religious role of the visual image. Christian attitudes toward the arts have ranged from uncompromising rejection to the most intimate incorporation of imagery into the church's devotional life. In the one case, visual images have been associated with idolatry; in the other, they have been treated as vehicles of the holy. Neither view, however, can be identified as the typically Christian outlook.

It is noteworthy too that Christian art cannot be defined with reference to specifically Christian subject matter. Scripture and the lives of the SAINTS have undoubtedly provided the chief content of Christian imagery. But Christians have also borrowed imagery from non-Christian sources and have occasionally employed abstract, virtually imageless, motifs such as appear in the ornamentation of certain early medieval manuscripts or in some twentieth century art. Christian art and architecture cannot, then, be reduced to simple unities of content, style, or religious import. They can, however, be read as the visible expressions of the changing moods and tones of the church's visual imagination.

1. Christian imagery. Christian art began, apparently not earlier than the third century, with a limited stock of images deployed in a narrow range of contexts. It embraced funerary art, represented by paintings in the CATACOMBS (underground cemeteries, chiefly in ROME) and by carvings on Christian sarcophagi, and baptismal art, represented by the wall paintings in a room used as a baptistery in a Christian building in ancient Dura-Europos, a Roman border town on the Euphrates river. The imagery contains motifs borrowed from the pagan environment (especially "the good shepherd," a common symbol of philanthropy which could be applied to CHRIST) and scenes from the Jewish scriptures, e.g., Jonah, Daniel in the lions' den (Dan. 6), the three Hebrews in the fiery furnace (Dan. 3). Only a very few NT images appear, e.g., the raising of Lazarus (John 11:38-44), the healing of the paralytic (Mark 2:1-12). Rarely is there any suggestion of a sequence or cycle of images; most often the scenes appear in isolation or in apparently random conjunction. The images were, it seems, more or less interchangeable, each evoking the same associations as the others and each portraying God's special care for the believer.

After CONSTANTINE (d. 337) made Christianity the favored religion in the Roman empire, both the content of Christian imagery and the range of its use expanded rapidly. To the initial vocabulary of images were added newly prominent scenes from the OT, e.g., the sacrifice of Isaac (Gen. 22:1-19) and further miracles from the NT, e.g., the healing of a blind man (John 9:1-12). New themes mingled with the motif of divine care as incipient image-cycles began to develop: scenes of Christ's birth and BAPTISM, images of Christ's PASSION (although rarely the crucifixion itself) and RESURRECTION, "portraits" displaying Christ's majesty, episodes from the lives of the apostles and the saints. This expanded and more individualized imagery circulated widely, often on portable objects. It appeared on liturgical and domestic implements and on personal jewelry. Scenes associated with specific holy places were imprinted on the souvenir flasks *(ampullae)* bought by pilgrims in the holy land. As late as the ninth century, a recognizably similar range of images decorated the shafts of high CROSSES at monastic sites in Ireland. This was the visual *lingua franca,* the shared visualization of biblical history and Christian belief, in patristic and early medieval Christianity. Elements of this imagery are still alive in the ICONS widely used since antiquity in ORTHODOX CHURCHES.

Specifically liturgical settings were especially important in the elaboration of Christian imagery after Constantine. Under the influence of the public art used to portray the emperor and his court, there emerged, in the churches of the period, highly developed image programs which defined the visual setting for Christian worship. The mosaics of San Vitale, a sixth century church in Ravenna, provide a striking example. Images appropriate to the EUCHARIST adorn the chancel and culminate in the commanding figure of Christ, situated in the semi-dome of the apse and exercising visual control over the entire liturgical space. Christ is portrayed as divine ruler, the cosmic counterpart of the earthly emperor. It is an image of power, authority, control; and it remained the church's dominant visualization of Christ well into the medieval period. A twentieth century attempt to recapture something of its effect, also in a liturgical setting, can be seen in the Graham Sutherland tapestry in Coventry Cathedral in England.

Also important for the development of Christian imagery was the illuminated manuscript. The flat pages of the codex, used by Christians in preference to the scroll, opened the way for ambitious programs of scriptural illustration. The earliest surviving Christian illuminated codices come from the fifth century; and they, with those that followed, show how images were recast to fit specific texts, how new images emerged for episodes not previously represented in Christian art, and how image sequences were elaborated to achieve a narrative or storytelling art. The special characteristics of textual illustration kept manuscript imagery from circulating readily in other contexts, where the relation between text and image was less close-knit. But there was always some interchange between contexts, and it is not surprising that scenes from a sixth century Genesis manuscript, for example, were reproduced in the thirteenth century mosaics of St. Mark's in Venice.

In a variety of contexts, then, Christianity devised a lively visual imagery with which to imagine and portray the great themes and episodes of its religion. Despite regional variations the imagery was widely shared, linking Christians in common patterns of visual imagination. The imagery was not, of course, unchanging. New images were added, old ones dropped; enduring images were treated in divergent styles; images were selected and arranged in different patterns for different purposes. Such variations reveal changes not only in Christian art but also in Christian religious sensibility. The stiff-figured creation of Adam in the Moutier-Grandval Bible (ninth century) and Michelangelo's creation of Adam in the Sistine Chapel (sixteenth century) reflect utterly different visions of God and man, despite their common themes. Similarly the emergence, in the medieval period, of dramatic images of the crucified Christ indicates a new religious apprehension of his human suffering and its redemptive import (*see* CRUCIFIX). The crucifixion panel of Grünewald's famous Isenheim altarpiece (southern Alsace, sixteenth century) is far removed, both visually and religiously, from the earlier mosaics of Christ as divine ruler.

W. S. Babcock

Irish high cross; Muiredach's cross, Monasterboice, Co. Louth (10th century)

Photo by Nicholas Servian FIIP, Woodmansterne Ltd.

High altar and tapestry by Graham Sutherland, Coventry Cathedral

Since the sixteenth century Christianity's common imagery and shared imagination have undergone a process of gradual dissolution. Several factors have contributed to the process. Some branches of PROTESTANTISM, in breaking with the visual imagination of medieval Christianity, showed strong antagonism to the visual arts and bequeathed that hostility to large segments of the Christian community. In addition the arts have increasingly come to constitute a distinct cultural sphere, functioning in its own right and separating the artist's treatment of Christian images from the Christian community at large. Especially important has been the role of competing imageries—most recently, the broadly disseminated imageries of cinema and television—which have captured the imagination more vividly than current forms of Christian art. Christian art has not been impoverished by this process (note, e.g., the works of Georges Rouault); but the relation of the art to the church's communal imagination has become tenuous and diluted. The imagery no longer provides a shared visual context for the faith and practice of the believer; and twentieth century efforts to achieve a new convergence of Christian imagery and Christian community (e.g., Coventry Cathedral) have so far had only local and partial success.

2. **Christian architecture.** The interior space most frequently employed for Christian worship has been a rectangular hall given a longitudinal axis by locating the center of liturgical action at one end of the rectangle (*see* LITURGY, CHRISTIAN). The dimensions and proportions of the hall have varied widely, as have the architectural style of the building and the interior disposition of the enclosed space. Consequently, different churches provide different visual contexts for worship and evoke different responses from those who use them. It is not true, of course, that Christians have used only rectangular interiors to house their worship or that the liturgy dictates a single, uniform ground-plan for the buildings that enclose it. From an early date to the present Christians have also employed a central plan (square, circle, octagon, etc.). The earliest use of this plan is often associated with *martyria* (i.e., memorial churches at sites connected with the life of Christ or of a saint) or baptisteries; but it was clearly used for congregational churches as well. Yet the rectangular plan, in one version or another, is a persistent feature of church architecture; and consideration of selected variations on that plan will show how architectural forms define visual settings for liturgical practice and, in this way, serve to express and sustain the visual imagination of the Christian community.

The architecture of any building is limited by the characteristics of the building materials, the construction techniques known to the builders, and the available financial resources. The evidence for pre-Constantinian Christian architecture is scanty. Under imperial patronage, however, the church commanded financial resources sufficient to make accessible both the materials and the techniques of the empire's public architecture. Under these circumstances the church adapted the secular basilica (a large hall serving judicial, commercial, or governmental purposes) to its own use. In its Christian version the basilica had a rectangular plan with the interior space divided longitudinally, into side aisles and a central nave, by colonnades which supported either galleries on the upper level or a clerestory rising above the roofs of the aisles to provide, with its windows, additional light for the interior. At one end was a semicircular apse which might either project beyond or be incorporated within the dimensions of the rectangle itself. The apse held the BISHOP's chair *(cathedra)* or throne, from which he preached to the congregation; and in front of the apse was placed the altar, surmounted by a canopy *(ciborium),* which defined the liturgical focus of the building for the celebration of the eucharist. This liturgical area, reserved for the CLERGY, was enclosed by chancel barriers extending outward from the apse and across in front of the altar.

The exterior approach to the building was frequently defined by a colonnaded forecourt (the atrium) and then a narthex through which one passed to the doors of the church itself. But the lines of the building were often obscured by a jumble of smaller structures contiguous with or attached to the basilica; and the dimensions of the architectural shell, although sometimes impressive, often produced a squat appearance. Thus the chief visual effects were interior rather than exterior. They were created by the use of multicolored marble, decorative pavements, sumptuous liturgical furnishings, and especially, after the fourth century, by the colors and imagery of mosaics. As a setting for worship, then, the basilica was a relatively plain architectural vehicle for its interior decor. It was more the ornament than the architecture that gave the building its specifically liturgical character.

Liturgical space is treated quite differently in the great Gothic CATHEDRALS of medieval Europe. Evidences of the rectangular hall remain, but the plan of these churches is cruciform: the nave representing the shaft, the transepts the arms, and the choir or chancel the upper part of the cross. In effect, the church was divided into two distinct areas, the nave and the choir, with the transepts and crossing marking the line of division. The aisled nave, itself rectangular, was the portion of the church open to the laity; the choir, also rectangular, was reserved for the often extensive body of the cathedral clergy. It was lined with choir stalls along either side and culminated in the high altar at the east end. Encircling the choir was the ambulatory, which opened into small chapels against the outside walls of the building. Additional chapels were located in the transepts and in the side aisles of the nave; and the choir itself was closed off from the nave by a chancel screen. As the disposition of the interior space makes clear, the medieval cathedral was no longer focused on a single liturgical

The Dumbarton Oaks Collection

The Crucifixion depicted on a Palestinian lead ampulla, or flask (5th-6th century)

center. The liturgically unified area is the choir, while the remaining space has been dissolved into a number of liturgical subcenters. (*See* ilustration for CATHEDRAL.)

At the same time the role of interior ornamentation has diminished and that of the structure itself expanded in defining the visual setting for worship. Several features of Gothic architecture are noteworthy here. Most obvious, perhaps, is the sheer height of the building; the vertical dimension overwhelms the horizontal. Also important is the way in which the weight and thickness of the masonry are disguised so as to give the interior an almost delicate appearance. The decor is defined by the lines and proportions of the structural members (vaults, ribs, arcades, etc.) rather than the ornamental covering of the walls; and the walls themselves, since they bear relatively little weight, are partially dissolved by the extensive use of windows in stained glass. The combined effect is a liturgical setting delineated by the soaring height of

G. L. Carr

Notre Dame de Ronchamp, France, Le Corbusier, architect (20th century)

the building and by the linear patterns of an architecture no longer dominated by heavy masses and solid surfaces.

The differences between the early basilica and the Gothic cathedral are not merely differences in construction techniques and architectural skills. The two kinds of churches also represent different delineations of the liturgical space in which Christian worship transpires. A more complete catalogue of church architecture would include a wide variety of additional styles: the domed churches of Byzantine Christianity, for example, or the meetinghouses of colonial New England, or the experimental churches of the twentieth century. Because so many of these churches are variations on a rectangular plan, they too can be viewed as alternative articulations of liturgical space, dictated as much by conceptions of what is visually appropriate to worship as by the physical requirements of the liturgy itself. In this sense the church's architecture as well as its imagery can be seen as an expression of its visual imagination and its religious sensitivity in the various phases and traditions of Christian history.

3. Conclusion. At times (e.g, the ICONOCLASTIC CONTROVERSY, the PROTESTANT REFORMATION) Christians have shown deep distrust of visual imagery, thus displaying affinities with Jewish and Islamic rejection of figural art. But this view has not triumphed; such attempts to exclude the visual image are perhaps better interpreted as ways of disavowing particular versions of the church's visual imagination than as rejections of imagery altogether. More often Christianity has justified its visual images for their pedagogical value or even as vehicles of divine presence. Even without the justifying theories, however, the church's visual arts have clearly functioned, and perhaps still function, to express and sustain the shared imagination of the believing community and thus have served as one of the bonds holding the community together.

Bibliography. E. Newton and W. Neil, *2000 Years of Christian Art* (1966); J. Dillenberger, *Style and Content in Christian Art* (1965); G. Schiller, *Iconography of Christian Art*, 5 vols. (1971-), only 2 vols. of the ET published so far; J. Rykwert, *Church Building* (1966); J. White, *Protestant Worship and Church Architecture* (1964), excellent bibliography; A. Grabar, *Early Christian Art* (1969) and *The Golden Age of Justinian* (1967); C. Morey, *Medieval Art* (1942); E. Male, *Religious Art from the Twelfth to the Eighteenth Century* (1949); P.and L. Murray, *The Art of the Renaissance* (1963); O. Benesch, *The Art of the Renaissance in Northern Europe* (1945; rpr. 1965); W. Wilson, *Modern Christian Art* (1965); H. Davies and H. Davies, *Sacred Art in a Secular Century* (1978); D. Diringer, *The Illuminated Book*, 2nd ed. rev. (1967); K. Weitzmann, *Late Antique and Early Christian Book Illumination* (1977); R. Krautheimer, *Early Christian and Byzantine Architecture* (1965); C. Mango, *Byzantine Architecture* (1976); O. von Simson, *The Gothic Cathedral*, 2nd ed. rev. (1962); M. Donnelly, *The New England Meeting Houses of the Seventeenth Century* (1968); B. Spence, *Phoenix at Coventry* (1962); P. Hammond, *Liturgy and Architecture* (1960).
W. S. BABCOCK

ART AND ARCHITECTURE, HINDU. Two major concepts are keys to the function of the arts in the Indian religious traditions. The first is that art forms can be used singly or in combination to induce an ideal transcendent state called *rasānanda* (lit. "blissful essence"), often regarded as the aesthetic counterpart to the spiritual state of SAMĀDHI (enlightenment and bliss). The second concept is that buildings and rituals are oriented to sacred space (location, directional bearings, etc.).

1. **The combination of the arts.** In striving for the goal of *rasānanda* the most powerful and evocative forms of the arts are to be found in their combinations. This is illustrated in the Viṣṇudharmottara Purāṇa (*ca.* fifth century A.D.). In a dialogue with a sage (III, 2.1-12), a king says that he desires to learn the canon of sculpture. He is told that he must first understand the theory of painting and, before that, dance and drama. When he agrees to this, the sage further insists that the king shall begin his study with literature, then music and song, for without a knowledge of all the arts their effect in space and time cannot be fully understood nor their purpose achieved.

L. D. Shinn

Exterior view of the porch, portico, worship hall, and image spire of the Lakṣmaṇa (Vishnu) Temple at Khajurā

The statement that the principles governing painting are related to those governing dance or drama is illustrated by the way in which artists represent volume and arrange figures in space, and also by the use in painting of attitudes, gestures, styles, and dramatic expressions developed by the actor-dancer's art (*see* MUDRĀ). The use in drama of themes from Epic and PURĀNIC literature involves not only prose but poetry. Drama involves also the use of systems of measurement, the full range of the dynamics of rhythmical structures, and tonal, temporal, and spatial relationships, both visual and aural. Then, in turn, the subject matter and the technical vocabulary of the theater inform the arts of painting and sculpture. Moreover, the concepts of time and interval, measurement and perception of space, lead to the construction and embellishment of architecture. Therefore, the ideal artistic expression combines a series of reflections and counter-reflections of all the arts. The relative intensity of tone and interval in a musical "mode" (*rāga*) suggests the relationships of the spectrum of color and its relative tonal range and intensities. Both, when cultivated, heighten the perception of the psychological effects of color, sound, and form in emotional terms, both abstract and thematic. Each has its potential counterpart in the other, and each reacts with the other. Therefore, when they are combined, they become a more powerful instrument of aesthetic communication.

The visual and aural styles of expression of India's arts have continually changed through time, though acknowledging an evolving canonical order, identity, and purpose. From the art styles of the Maurya (*see* MAURYAN DYNASTY) and Śuṅga in the North and the Sātavāhana and Pallava in the South, the transformation and synthesis of the arts have been continuous, at times slowly changing, at other times abruptly evolving new forms and expressions. Elements of the Greco-Achaemenid art and, later, the Greco-Roman influences were absorbed in the early period, and reached their apogee under the influence of the GUPTA DYNASTY (fourth to sixth century A.D.). During this period concepts of philosophy, literature, and the arts were further developed and their synthesis was textually codified. The later rich proliferation of regional styles and schools of postclassical art and architectural theory depended greatly upon the classic models achieved during the time of the Gupta Empire. Though there were earlier contacts with the rest of Asia, the exportation of Indian culture, religion, philosophy, literature, architecture, and art stems largely from this period and continued until about the thirteenth century.

L. D. Shinn

This temple carving on the Kudal Aligarh Temple in Madurai, South India, depicts the defeat of the serpent Kāliya by Krishna

L. D. Shinn

Gaja-Lakṣmī ("elephant-attended Lakṣmī") symbolizes prosperity and is often found above temple entrances. Shown here is the Aligarh Temple near Madurai, South India

2. **Orientation of sacred space.** Architecture is obviously the ideal art for the demonstration of the principles of orientation because it combines the technical tools of mathematics and geometry with the ancient sciences of astronomy and astrology, constituting the practical means by which symbol and form can be expressed in space. Basic to this expression are the several canonical systems of iconometry and formal iconography which govern the measured organization, form, and techniques of sculpture and painting, as well as the final realization of the ideal temple structure.

The path of the sun from east to west is fundamental to both religious and domestic architecture and constitutes the major axis of orientation in architecture, art, and ritual. Astronomy, astrology, and both solar and lunar time determine the measurement systems of sacred and domestic architecture and the interval and performance of ritual. Sacred space is conceived both vertically and horizontally, and is projected as the square, the circle, the ten directions (the four quarters and their intermediate points, plus the two polarities of the underworld and the heavens). Concentric rings of deified powers govern intervening space. Enshrined at the center is the supreme and pure creative principle, symbolized by one's chosen deity (e.g. VISHNU or SHIVA) or by BRAHMĀ (the Creator); then come zones of deities successively diminishing in power to the outermost and lowest realm of the demons and ultimate disorder. The symbolic analogies between the imagined order of the abstract cosmos and the image of the perceived world and its order are almost limitless. At the center of the ideal political state was the *cakravartin,* the world ruler, who controlled all within the wheel of the earth's horizon, a reflection of divine order. The canonical construction of a temple conceived in abstract terms was a reflection of the body of the cosmos from its inception to the final consecration of all its symbolic, aesthetic, and functional structures, a focal point of mediation between man and the infinite.

3. **Theory expressed in temple architecture.** Beyond the more subtle meaning of the abstract symbolism built into the sacred plan and construction of architecture, the arts in the service of traditional religion employed the full range of sensual perception—visual, aural, and tactile—to express the world view of its ruling hierarchy, whether Hindu, Buddhist, or Jaina. No matter which individual sectarian view was expressed, the basic concepts governing the technique, function, and purpose of the arts and architecture were similar. Ultimately the orientation and patterning of sacred space as well as the function of the arts in religion have didactic significance at several levels: a communication process is taking place. This is one of the principal orderly and integrated systems for the celebration and communication of Hinduism's values and ethos.

a) Materials. In the earliest periods temples were built of wood, brick, and plaster, and were largely of an ephemeral nature. If the donor was of sufficient importance and the wealth to be expended on the particular structure great enough, stone and metal were also used. Even precious metals and jewels might be used in the overlay of doors and pillars. Gilt metal–tiled roofs are known from early literature, and examples exist today. Temples also were hewn in solid rock in the form of cave shrines, in which the details of structural architecture were reproduced but without function (*see* ELLORĀ; AJANṬĀ). By the Gupta period, wholly free-standing temples were constructed of stone. In the medieval period immense complexes of temples such as those of KONĀRAK, KHAJURĀHO, MĪNĀKṢĪ and Tanjore were constructed. The building technology evolved in terms of great blocks of stone, producing massive effects like sculpted mountains soaring into space. The functional details of wooden architecture were superimposed upon these masses of stone as surface decoration.

Again, underlying concepts reveal themselves. SANSKRIT texts list according to quality and permanence the materials used for the construction of sacred objects, from earth or clay through wood to the finest stone and metals, to be used for the construction of the LIṄGA, the phallic emblem of Shiva. Such a range of materials found use also in the production of figural sculpture. Stone is prescribed as the most permanent of building materials, and permanence, longevity, and immortality were as central to the expression of Hinduism as was the idea of purity. To perform VEDIC sacrifice, or to construct a great temple, was to gain immortality for the patron. A complete reversal of this idea occurred in the later medieval period when the BHAKTI ecstatics declared that only the human body of the devotee was the proper temple of God and that all else was illusion.

b) Functions. The temple complex, particularly from the medieval period to the present, has served Hindu society as a spiritual and cultural focus. In earlier periods its function was also that of a school of higher learning, an economic resource, a landowner and patron, a refuge, and, in times of strife, often a fortified citadel. In addition to being a center of formal rites and religious ritual, it could also be a focus of individual, personal devotion. The temple as the focus of all the major art forms—architecture, sculpture, painting, and the ancillary arts—was the environment within which literature and poetry were recited, sung, danced, and acted to the accompaniment of music. A large group of professionals was maintained for the performance of these arts as well as for the ritual and administrative functions of the temple. The counterpart of the temple in the temporal sphere was the royal court with its extensive patronage of the arts. Indeed, the principal patron of the temple was most often the local ruler, who was also the protector of the temple, the spiritual source that legitimized his temporal power. Ideally he was the royal servant of the deity, charged with maintaining an equilibrium between divine and temporal power for the prosperity of his people. The fine arts and architecture were as much an integral expression of this power as were the arts and sciences which served politics and war.

Bibliography. H. Goetz, *India: Five Thousand Years of Indian Art* (1959); S. Kramrisch, *The Hindu Temple,* 2 vols. (1976), Vol. II, pp. 437-42, gives extensive listings of Sanskrit source materials on the theory and practice of Hindu art and architecture; S. Kramrisch, ed. and trans., *The Vishṇudharmottara, Part III: A Treatise on Indian Painting and Image-Making,* rev. ed. (1928); T. A. Gopinath Rao, *Elements of Hindu Iconography,* 4 vols (1914); B. Rowland, *The Art and Architecture of India: Buddhist, Hindu, Jain* (1970). C. R. JONES

ART AND ARCHITECTURE, ISLAMIC.

1. Origins. ISLAM originated in a culture in which circumstances of geography, economy, and historical inheritance had not favored the development of a strong tradition in the visual arts. The ARABIC LANGUAGE itself, best exemplified in the towering poetry of the QUR'ĀN, was the preeminent art form of the early Muslims. The precipitous expansion of

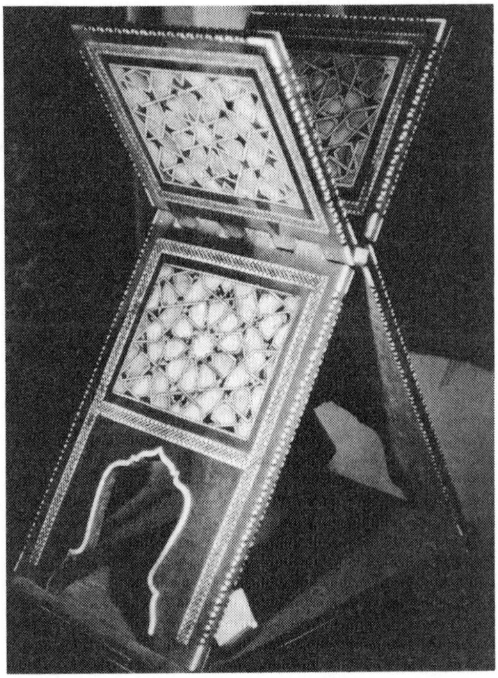

W. Denny

Wooden rahle, or Qur'ān stand, inlaid with mother-of-pearl (Ottoman, 17th century)

Islam brought the Arabs, with their puritanical and iconoclastic religion, into contact with the cultures of Syria, Iran, and Egypt, all of which were rich in painting, sculpture, and the decorative arts. The reaction of the Muslim Arabs to this new and almost bewildering artistic environment was complex and even self-contradictory. The emerging pattern of Islamic kingship under the UMAYYADS led to the expropriation of established artistic symbols of royalty, resulting in the building of elaborate palaces such as Khirbat al-Mafjār, near the Jordan River one mile north of Jericho. This palace included luxurious Roman baths and sculptural decoration. We also find in early Islam the use of those silk textiles and gold vessels so rigorously proscribed by MUHAMMAD and his early followers. At the same time, the Islamic religion itself was forced into a sort of competition with the surviving artifacts of the religions of conquered areas, which led to the building or Islamic refurbishing of religious buildings of large scale and splendid decoration, such as the DOME OF THE ROCK in JERUSALEM or the Great Mosque of Damascus. The syncretism of early Islamic art blended elements of absorbed artistic traditions with Arabic calligraphy and the new Islamic functional imperatives. Gradually, the whole began to assume more importance than the sum of its parts, as the process of formation of an Islamic style in art progressed. The development of a major architectural genre, the MOSQUE, provided one impetus to the emergence of an Islamic artistic tradition; another was the need to adapt inherited traditions that had elaborate iconography to a theology which proscribed human or animal images. These pressures eventually resulted in the development of a complex decorative repertory suitable at once for architectural decoration and for other artistic genres. The art of Arabic calligraphy was combined with various vegetal and geometric elements, collectively known as the arabesque, which in succeeding centuries formed the nucleus of the Islamic decorative style in virtually all Islamic lands.

2. The classical age. The reign of the ʿAbbāsids constitutes in many ways the classical age of Islamic civilization, the direct evidence of whose artistic legacy has through time and conquest largely disappeared. Of the art of Baghdad in its heyday we know relatively little, but excavations at Samarra have uncovered a diverse range of building revetments, iconic paintings, ceramics, and other artistic remains which point to important artistic activity. The great surviving monuments of the ʿAbbāsid period exist largely in the geographic periphery. The great Mosque of Qayrawān in Tunisia and the Great Mosque of Cordoba, built under the rump Umayyad regime in Spain, blend reused classical elements into a bold new synthesis: the Arab mosque with its columned *riwāqs* or loggias around a courtyard, a closed hypostyle prayer hall on the *qiblah* or Mecca side, and a domed *mihrāb* or prayer niche on the main axis. In early medieval Iran preexisting Sasanian iconographic traditions were incorporated into a complex silk textile art, and under the Samanids, Iranian and Islamic traditions blended in a bourgeois Islamic art which paralleled the art of mosque and court. The heterodox Fatimid rule in Egypt fostered an artistic tradition of great vitality and variety. Four centuries after the Hijra the geographic, ethnic, and cultural diversity reflected in Islamic art was nonetheless incorporated into a broad Islamic artistic style reaching from the Indus to the Guadalquivir.

3. Genres in Islamic art. *a) Calligraphy.* Calligraphy, illumination, and bookbinding were arts sanctified by the fundamentalist approach to the Qur'ān, by the traditional reverence for learning in Islamic culture, and by the generally negative attitude of the theologians of Islam toward the representation of human or animal forms in art. The early Kufic calligraphy, at once the most fundamental and compelling of Islamic art forms, developed through the monumental building inscriptions of medieval times into complex local forms and variants. The codification of six basic styles of cursive script in the tenth century by Ibn Muqla led to a system of rules which, in combination with a shared sense of the propriety of use of various script styles, did much to further stylistic unity in Islamic art.

b) Figural art. In sharp contrast to the abstract nature of calligraphy and the arabesque was a countervailing Islamic tradition of representation of human and animal forms, associated with the secular sphere and drawing upon traditions of royal imagery rooted in Byzantine, Sasanian, and Central Asian

W. Denny

Mosque lamp in enameled glass, from Egypt or Syria (Mamluk, 14th century)

W. Denny

Ivory casket made in Cordoba for Prince al-Mughira (Umayyad, 10th century) cultures. The earliest paintings and sculptures which have come down to us are the almost overwhelmingly vulgar decorations of the palaces of parvenu Umayyad princes. It can be safely said that, from the point of view of surviving art works at least, the distinctive aspects of the Islamic figural style emerged in the intimate arts of ivory carving, manuscript illustration, and ceramic decoration; in the latter medium, especially, court figural styles rapidly diffused into the art of middle classes. The uneasy coexistence of figural art and orthodox theology, complete with elaborate casuistry when needed, provides a sort of cyclical tension throughout the history of Islamic art as artistic "liberalism" and religious "conservatism" traded places in ascendancy. Figural art achieves its most important place in manuscript illustration and other media providing relatively intimate theaters for viewing art of dubious theological merit.

From the earliest important surviving Islamic miniatures from Mesopotamia, with their themes of kingly patronage coexisting with practical, scientific illustrations on the one hand and bourgeois fables and tales such as al-Hariri's *Maqamat* on the other, the tradition of Islamic painting developed on two levels, court painting and provincial painting. The great court ateliers of later Islam, especially those of Iran, Turkey, and India, produced a series of brilliantly illustrated manuscripts, often executed by artists of considerable reputation (Junayd, Behzād, Sulṭan-Muhammad, Reẓa), which influenced each other from generation to generation in complex ways. From the miniature paintings executed in thirteenth century Baghdad, a tradition developed through the Il-Khanid court of Tabriz, continued by Jalayrids and then Timurids throughout the fifteenth century, finally branching into the three great Islamic painting schools of the sixteenth and seventeenth centuries in the Ottoman, Safavid, and Mogul empires. Parallel to this court style were various provincial schools of painting, often reflecting in the palest of fashions the tastes of the major metropolitan centers. In the early sixteenth century the court style of Herat and the provincial Turkmen style of western Iran fused in Tabriz under Shah Ismā'īl into the splendid early Safavid figural style, which then influenced the formation of Mogul and Ottoman court styles by mixing with other provincial traditions. Common themes given richness by a diversity of geographic styles and the recognizable attributes and eccentricities of individual artists then led on to the complex traditions of the sixteenth and seventeenth century Islamic courts. (*See* Plate IIb.) The arts of the book were the seminal arts of these times; from calligraphy, illumination, bookbinding, and miniature painting grew styles which then directly influenced metalwork, ceramics, carving in precious materials, textiles, carpets, and the decoration of architecture itself.

c) Architecture. Architecture, as the visual setting in which the other arts were nurtured in early Islamic art, developed as a complex set of responses to environmental, political, symbolic, and liturgical needs in Islam. The two major forms of the Islamic prayer hall, the multicolumned Arab mosque and the Iranian mosque with its central court and *iwān* recesses, developed and mutated in various complex ways, both as mosques proper and through their reflections in secular and social-service architecture. The early sprawling courtyard mosques of Islam, typified by the great urban mosques of Kūfa, Damascus, Samarra, Qayrawān, Cordoba, and that of Ibn Tulūn in Cairo, gradually developed variations in response to the conditions brought about by increased urban population density. In Cairo, for example, the mosque and its educational cousin the *madrasa* developed asymmetrical forms of great originality in response to complex urban freehold patterns and the haphazard network of urban streets and alleys. The Iranian mosque turned from brick to stone in Anatolia, while the harsher climate of Asia Minor gradually almost eliminated the open courtyard, substituting for it vaulted and domed spaces. The forms codified in mosques were adapted to other functions: the *madrasa* or institution of higher learning, the *zawiya* or convent, the *'imāret* or various charitable institutions for the dispensation of food, medical care, water, or learning—all took their architectural forms from the mosque and adapted them to other functional purposes. Secular buildings, from the urban dwellings of Cairo with their *qa'a* or reception halls echoing both the *madrasa* and the Roman atrium, to the great *ribāts, fundūqs* and *khāns* which provided secure sojourn for merchant travelers and their goods, also partook of the general styles and structures of mosques, adding secular elements of many kinds. Religious buildings were maintained by WAQF endowment trusts, administered under religious auspices and supposedly secure from political interference; the maintenance and ultimately the survival of many an Islamic building depended therefore on the solidity and the administration of its endowment.

Islamic architecture, especially that undertaken by great princes, was often closely allied with developments in what we now call civil engineering. The complex hydraulic systems which supplied water to endowed public fountains in many Islamic cities, and the often awesome Islamic accomplishments in the realm of military architecture, demonstrate the ability to organize gigantic projects efficiently and to use forms and structures in original and unprecedented ways. The Islamic genius for building is often not only a triumph of visual effect, but a triumph over materials, the physical environment, and the restrictions of economics as well.

d) Court and ceremonial art. The architectural setting of the Islamic palace and the Islamic urban milieu provided a backdrop for the ceremonial arts of Islam, those examples of conspicuous consumption destined to be seen by wider or narrower audiences according to the social and political motivations which led to their creation. Sometimes these art forms were quite ephemeral, such as the objects of paper, confectionary sugar, and wood lath used in various festivals. Other forms have endured. The splendid Islamic weaponry, a high art in virtually all Islamic lands, combined advanced technology in tempering and forging with the arts of carving, chasing, and damascening, producing in the great royal examples stunning visual creations whose efficient and deadly *raison d'être* was almost forgotten. Another ceremonial art attaining great prominence in Islam was weaving. The linen, cotton, and silk textiles of court looms, with their imagery of royalty, their monumental inscriptions, and their brilliant colors, were but the conspicuous edge of the economically important textile industry. Along with weaponry, court robes were the ultimate symbols of status in Islamic societies, and systems of sumptuary laws and conventions often gave them added social importance. Textiles were also incorporated into the flags, banners, and pennons used in Islamic ceremonies.

The portable and public nature of ceremonial weapons and textiles carried the symbols and splendor of the court to the broader society, whether through the great urban parades of the Fatimids through Cairo or in the awesome panoply of the Ottoman armies on the march. The knotted rug, one of the most characteristic and important of all Islamic art forms, although originating in Turkic tribal traditions where articles woven in this technique were used for a variety of symbolic and utilitarian purposes, was adapted in the Islamic court to the designs and symbology of the arts of the book and architectural decoration. The court carpet, whether in the permanent architecture of palaces or in the portable architecture of tents and tent pavilions, was a setting for royal audiences and other activities, while carpets using court-derived designs then became the standard form of decoration for the floors of mosques in many Islamic lands.

The small luxury objects of Islamic courts, including carved works in ivory, crystal, and jade, as well as objects of cast and inlaid metal, jewelry, and glass, were more intimate still. The carved ivories of Cordoba and Fatimid Cairo, the brilliant inlaid metalwork of East Persia, Mesopotamia, and Egypt, and the carved jade of Timurid Iran and Mogul India, rarely went before the public eye. Artisanship of royal quality did appear in royal gifts to mosques, such as the famous Ayyūbid and Mamluk enameled-glass lamps, or the carved wooden mosque furniture which throughout the Islamic world formed one of the most brilliant sculptural creations of Islamic art.

e) Pottery. The one Islamic art form surviving in more examples and in more bewildering variety than any other is that of decorated ceramics. Pottery was an art form available to all social classes, while often utilizing the forms and symbols found in more expensive court works of art. The calligraphic slip-painted pottery of the Samanids bore homely maxims urging thrift, piety, and good wishes, while

W. Denny

Wooden pulpit, Mosque of Lala Pasha, Kayseri, Turkey (Seljuk, 13th-14th century)

excavations at Samarra have uncovered ninth century attempts at imitations of imported Chinese T'ang pottery. The figural decorations of lustre-painted Fatimid wares reflected the broad spectrum of everyday life in that society, while under the Seljuks the Iranian potters of Kashān and other centers developed a range of techniques unequaled in history. In later Islamic times the brightly painted Turkish polychrome wares were exported to Europe in great quantities.

W. Denny

The Jami Masjid, Delhi (Mogul, 17th century)

4. **Scholarship.** The study of Islamic art is a comparatively recent phenomenon. Although long admired and frequently imitated in the West, the various artistic genres favored by Islamic peoples presented complex problems of technique, epigraphy, and documentation, which together with the traditional anonymity of most Islamic artists served as impediments to serious study. This situation has changed over the last five decades, and new scholarship is at last pulling aside the veil of obscurity which covered many Islamic artistic achievements in the past.

See illustrations for MOSQUE; MINARET; TĀJ MAHAL.

Bibliography. O. Grabar, *The Formation of Islamic Art* (1973); T. W. Arnold, *Painting in Islam* (1928); J. D. Hoag, *Islamic Architecture* (1977); R. Ettinghausen, *From Byzantium to Sasanian Iran and the Islamic World* (1972); J. Sourdel-Thomine and B. Spuler, *Die Kunst des Islam* (1973); an extensive bibliography of Islamic art is K. A. C. Creswell, *A Bibliography of the Architecture, Arts and Crafts of Islam* (1961) and its *Supplement* (1973).
W. DENNY

ART AND ARCHITECTURE, JEWISH. 1. Definition. The earliest reference to "Jewish art" appeared in an article by Rabbi David Kaufmann in 1878; prior to that time the possibility of Jewish art had been denied for spiritual and metaphysical reasons. ORTHODOX JUDAISM rejected artistic endeavors on the basis of the restriction against images imposed by the Second Commandment ("You shall not make for yourself a graven image," Exod. 20:4*a*) and elaborated in the SHULHAN ARUCH. And many secular thinkers followed Hegelian metaphysical speculation, which declared that the Jewish *Volksgeist* (national spirit) had deprived Jews of the development of any artistic talent; it was claimed that "paganism sees its god, Judaism hears him."

Recent archaeological discoveries and scholarly research, as well as the prominence of Jews among the foremost twentieth century artists, now render incontestable the existence of art among Jews. Scholars, however, still debate whether Jewish art is to be defined in functional, ethnic, or national terms. No one of these designations provides an adequate definition covering all relevant aspects of the subject. Jewish history, unlike that of other continuous entities, developed and evolved primarily within multiple societies, cultures, and civilizations. For this reason, a critical inquiry into all known artistic remains reveals no monochromatic, readily isolated thread of uniquely Jewish art, but a multicolored one woven into the very fabric of Jewish involvement in non-Jewish society. Something so distinctly Jewish as the Temple of Solomon turns out, on examination, to be an integral part of ancient Near Eastern art; similarly, the art of the SYNAGOGUE is not *sui generis*, but grows out of Greco-Roman art, while the art in medieval Hebrew manuscripts is inseparably linked to medieval Christian and Islamic art. The style and decoration of Jewish art has always been rooted in and adapted from the dominant contemporary non-Jewish society. Yet, until the nineteenth century the art of the Jews was an integral part of the specific Jewish community which produced or commissioned it. It expressed a distinctive Jewish life and tradition, reflecting the collective thought, feeling, and symbolism of many diverse communities. Until the nineteenth century there is warrant for using the term "Jewish art" in a religio-communal sense.

2. **The Second Commandment.** Some believe that a rigid iconoclasm has always prevailed in Judaism, and fail to understand that the Jewish interpretation of the Second Commandment cannot be viewed as unchanging. Rather, as each Jewish society had to cope with the biblical view of art according to sharply differing needs, new interpretations of the Second Commandment were developed. Thus the biblical injunction against art has meant something different to each novel historical context. To mention but a few examples, first century Palestinian Jewry cited the Second Commandment when they refused to place a statue of the Roman emperor Caligula in the Jerusalem Temple. However, in third century Babylonia no such objection was raised against the statue of a king installed in the synagogue of Nehardea. Similarly, while the fifteenth century German-Jewish scholar Jakob Mölln strenuously objected to using beautifully decorated prayerbooks handed him for synagogal devotions, Profiat Duran, a contemporary Spanish-Jewish scholar, claimed that "the contemplation and study of pleasing forms, beautiful images and drawings broadens and stimulates the mind" (*Ma'aseh Efod*, 19). The very book of Exodus, which contains the Second Commandment, elevated Bezalel, the desert artist, to unparalleled heights. Furthermore, it should be realized that dogmatic proclamations of religious leaders in any specific social context are frequently not in harmony with the practices prevalent among large segments of their followers.

3. **The biblical period.** Art discovered from the biblical period consists largely of pottery, ivory plaques, small statuettes, and architecture. While the Temple of Solomon was undoubtedly a significant artistic endeavor, its remains are unfortunately buried under the Temple Mount in Jerusalem, and our only information about it is restricted to its description in I Kings.

4. **The Roman-Byzantine period.** The most revolutionary discovery of Jewish art to date is without doubt the cycle of biblical paintings found in the Dura-Europos synagogue, dated A.D. 244-45. These paintings have seriously challenged the accepted historiography of the period. They reopen, as well, an older debate about whether the origins of Christian art may be rooted in an antecedent, but now lost, Jewish art. Of the three figured bands of paintings that cover the four sides of the synagogue, roughly 60 percent has been preserved. Little agreement exists as to the identification of individual panels, although they deal with such familiar biblical figures as Abraham, Isaac, Jacob, MOSES, Aaron,

Courtesy Hebrew Union College, Cincinnati

Torah shield, silver with gilt overlay and precious stones; Germany (19th century)

Samuel, Elijah, Ezekiel, David, Solomon, Mordecai, and Esther. In addition, scholars have noted legendary details in many scenes that can only be understood by reference to AGGADAH and the MIDRASH. There is no accord on the meaning of the entire cycle. Most scholars, with the exception of Goodenough, agree that any explanation of the paintings must be rooted in contemporary rabbinic Judaism; Goodenough insists that these paintings reflect a mystic Hellenistic Judaism. Gutmann has recently proposed that they are the earliest forerunners of the great programmatic painting cycles, based on the Bible and extrabiblical literature, which appear in fifth century Christian art. It is doubtful that the Dura paintings are based on lost illustrated Jewish manuscripts; most likely they are based on cartoons or pattern books. The Dura paintings are the earliest Jewish biblical scenes found to date, since the so-called first century A.D. "Judgment of Solomon" fresco from Pompeii may not be biblical at all, and the third century Roman plate showing King David dancing is a modern forgery. Mosaic pavements have been found in ruins of synagogues in Palestine, Greece, and North Africa dated to the fourth to sixth centuries. Three main elements are sometimes found: (a) a biblical scene dealing with a theme of salvation; (b) a zodiacal cycle which encloses the sun god Helios; (c) a depiction of the Torah ARK flanked by the MENORAH and other symbols of the Jewish holidays.

Of the many CATACOMBS in Rome, the catacombs of Vigna Randanini on Via Appia and that of Villa Torlonia on Via Nomentana are important for Jewish art; Jewish symbols and ornamentation cover the third-fourth century catacombs. At Beth-Shearim in Galilee a significant catacomb complex dating from the late second–fourth century has been discovered; especially noteworthy is Catacomb 20 with its sarcophagi decorated with human figures and ornamental designs.

5. The Middle Ages. No illuminated Hebrew manuscripts are extant from the Roman, Byzantine, or Sasanian Empires. The earliest comes from Tiberias, Palestine, dated A.D. 895. Known as the Moshe ben Asher Codex, it contains only the books of the Prophets. This, together with other Bibles, was

American Jewish Archives, Hebrew Union College—Jewish Institute of Religion

Beth Sholom Synagogue, Philadelphia, Frank Lloyd Wright, architect

probably made for the KARAITES, a schismatic Jewish movement from the 'ABBĀSID East. The geometric, abstract ornamentation in these manuscripts shows many features in common with contemporary QUR'ĀN manuscripts. From seventeenth century Persia we have illuminated Hebrew manuscripts with figural miniatures; they illustrate biblical epics, such as those written by the fourteenth century Persian-Jewish poet Maulana Shahin. Hebrew manuscripts from the Islamic East and the Christian West adapted the contemporary stylistic and decorative elements of those cultures, but differ from them in several respects. Eschatological, liturgical, and ceremonial scenes summarize the distinct Jewish spiritual experience; the depiction of God is scrupulously avoided, with a hand or rays usually indicating the presence of the Almighty. Since Hebrew script uses no capital letters, the dominance of the initial letter, common in Latin Christian manuscripts, is rarely found; instead, there are panels for initial words.

American Jewish Archives, Hebrew Union College—Jewish Institute of Religion

Interior of the Touri Synagogue, Newport, Rhode Island

Another distinctive feature is the decorative use of micrography (minute script) for the annotations of the MASORETES which appeared in Muslim Hebrew manuscripts and continued to be featured in Hebrew manuscripts in Europe. The most beautiful manuscripts come from Europe and date from the thirteenth to the fifteenth century A.D. An important type introduced in Christian Spain was the HAGGADAH intended for the home SEDER during PASSOVER. This private liturgical codex had illustrations of the ritual and textual aspects of the Haggadah. It was prefaced by full-page miniatures illustrating events primarily from the book of Exodus (a feature undoubtedly patterned on contemporary Latin Psalters, which also contained pictorial OT prefaces). The most significant illuminated manuscripts in ASHKENAZI communities were of the *maḥzor*—a book containing the complete prayers and PIYYUTIM for the seven special sabbaths and all the holidays. Many of the *maḥzorim* come from southern Germany and the Rhineland. From Renaissance Italy come splendid manuscripts of Hebrew legal works and philosophical and secular texts in Hebrew translation. Painted by some of the leading Renaissance artists, they were probably made for Jewish loan bankers.

The extant ceremonial objects used during synagogue services and in the celebration of the Jewish life cycle and holidays date primarily from the seventeenth and eighteenth centuries. Few have survived from the Middle Ages; one, a pair of *rimmonim* (headpieces) for TORAH scrolls can be securely attributed to fifteenth century Sicily.

6. The Synagogue. Just as the classical basilica served as a model for Byzantine synagogues, so the structural and stylistic forms current in Christian Europe were adapted for European synagogues—although with modifications in keeping with the requirements of Jewish worship and with certain restraints imposed by the society in which the Jewish minority resided. The most important features of the synagogue were the pulpit (variously called *almemor, bimah,* or *tevah*), where the scripture was read, and the Torah ark (called *aron* or *hekhal*) on the eastern wall facing Jerusalem. The ark housed the Torah scrolls, and in front of it the prescribed liturgical prayers were recited. The spatial relationship between the pulpit and the ark, from which the basic liturgical components, reading of scripture and recitation of prayers, are performed, varied from age to age. Sometimes both features were given equal prominence; sometimes one was dominant over the other.

Bibliography. E. R. Goodenough, *Jewish Symbols in the Greco-Roman Period* (1953-1968); J. Gutmann, ed., *The Temple of Solomon: Archaeological Fact and Mediaeval Tradition in Christian, Islamic and Jewish Art* (1976), and *The Image and the Word: Confrontations in Judaism, Christianity and Islam* (1977), *The Dura-Europos Synagogue: A Re-Evaluation (1932-1972)* (1973), *The Synagogue: Studies in Origins, Archaeology and Architecture* (1975), *No Graven Images: Studies in Art and the Hebrew Bible* (1971), *Hebrew Manuscript Painting* (1978), *Beauty in Holiness: Studies in Jewish Customs and Ceremonial Art* (1970),

Jewish Ceremonial Art (2nd ed. 1968); R. Wischnitzer, *The Architecture of the European Synagogue* (1964).

J. GUTMANN

ARTHA är′ tŭ (H—Skt.; lit. "object, wealth, property"). Material gain, one of the four *puruṣārthas* or HINDU AIMS OF LIFE. *Artha* encompasses both economic and political activity. The best known classical Hindu text on *artha* is KAUṬILYA's Arthaśāstra.

G. E. YOCUM

ARTHAŚĀSTRA är′ tŭ shä′ strŭ (H—Skt.). An authoritative text on ancient Indian politics and law. Parts of it probably antedate the DHARMAŚĀSTRAS, from which it differs chiefly in its more secular outlook. Its reputed author is KAUṬILYA, and its chief concern is to increase the prosperity (ARTHA) of the state through a wide variety of means, notably war.

C. R. KING

ĀRYA SAMĀJ är′ yŭ sŭ mäj′ (H—Skt.; lit. "noble society"). A society founded by Swami DAYĀNANDA in 1875 to reform Indian society on the basis of the traditional VEDAS. Its conservative efforts to regain Hindu converts from ISLAM caused some inter-religious tensions. Although favoring social and religious reform, it defended cow protection and some Vedic rituals. It continues to have a large following in Northern India. *See* REFORM MOVEMENTS IN INDIA §3.

A. LIPSKI

ARYAN är′ yŭn (H—Skt. [*ārya*—"noble"]). A powerful group of Indo-European-speaking people who spread through Iran and Northern India in the first half of the second millenium B.C. Aryan is also the name given to the group of languages descended from the one spoken by this group, the modern representatives of which include Farsi, Hindī, Urdu, Bengali, Marathi, Gujerati, and others.

1. **Split into two groups.** After the Aryans had settled in Iran for several centuries, a major cultural split occurred around 1500 B.C., resulting in the migration of a large subgroup through Afghanistan into India. The Zoroastrian AVESTA and Hindu RIG VEDA are the earliest respective testimonies of this linguistic and religious split, and since there is evidence that some of the Rig Veda was composed in Iran, it is probable that the subcultures were already quite divergent even before the migration.

2. **Cultural traits.** The picture of the Aryans which emerges from the Rig Veda is that of a semi-nomadic, militaristic people, organized into tribes and, within the tribes, classes. Though technologically advanced, their economic system remained primitive. The poetry fashioned by their priests as the body of the Rig Veda was most likely passed on only through oral transmission.

3. **The Aryans in India.** As the migratory branch moved into India, it defeated and later assimilated the native population, which was probably composed in large part of DRAVIDIAN peoples. It now seems clear that the process of mutual assimilation proceeded more rapidly than was once believed. Scholars have shown that Dravidian linguistically influenced the earliest stratum of the Rig Veda, and there is evidence that, even during the Vedic period, influential non-Aryans were being admitted into the higher castes. Thus from an early period, in India at least, the term *ārya* began to lose its original racial connotations in favor of class- and caste-oriented ones.

Modern Hinduism is an especially interesting product of Aryan and Dravidian mutual assimilation. The Aryans arrived in India with a pantheon of deities and a body of ritual closely related to that of their Persian cousins. Within a comparatively short time, some of the most important among the original Vedic deities had been nearly forgotten, and most of the remainder had had their characters completely revamped through the admixture of attributes belonging to their more or less similar indigenous counterparts.

The long-held view of the Aryans as the bearers of culture to the primitive and ignorant natives of India has had thus to be significantly revised. It is truer to say that the Aryans had profound effects upon the native culture of India, but that the native culture proved in the long run to be both absorbent and enduring.

Bibliography. A. L. Basham, *The Wonder that Was India* (1954), pp. 29-44.

J. BARE

ĀSANA ä′ sŭ nŭ (H—Skt.; lit. "sitting, sitting down" [*ās*—"to sit quietly, abide, remain"]). The third "limb" (*aṅga*) of the "eight-limbed" YOGA of PATAÑJALI, referring to the appropriate and comfortable bodily postures requisite for the practice of Yoga. Patañjali's Yogasūtra (II.29, II.46) prescribes only that posture should be "steady" (*sthira*) and "comfortable" (*sukha*), suggesting, in other words, that the purpose of this practice is simply to discover a posture for the body that enables the YOGIN to meditate for long periods of time free from bodily distractions. The most common posture is the well-known LOTUS POSTURE (*padmāsana*) in which the yogin's two feet are placed on the two (opposite) thighs, the chin lightly touches the chest, the eyes are partly closed, and the hands and arms rest comfortably on the knees. In other traditions of Yoga (for example, in HAṬHA YOGA), emphasis is placed on more complicated and painful postures in the belief that unusual postures may be conducive to physical health. Some later Yoga texts refer to as many as eighty-four different postures, four of which are usually mentioned as being the most important: (i) *padmāsana*, described above; (ii) *siddhāsana*, "perfect posture," with the left heel placed near the anus, the right heel just above in the region of the genitals, the chin on the chest, and an overall erect sitting position; (iii) *siṃhāsana*, "lion's posture," with the heels crossed under the rectum or genital region, the hands with the fingers extended resting on the extended knees, an erect sitting posture (on the heels) with the mouth open, tongue extended, and eyes focused on the tip of the nose; and (iv) *bhadrāsana,* "splendid posture," with the heels crossed as in *siṃhāsana* but with arms crossed behind the back and grasping the toes of the feet, the chin firmly on the chest, and the eyes focused on the tip of the nose.

G. J. Larson

ĀSAVA ä´ sŭ vŭ (B—Pali) **ĀŚRAVA** ä´ shrŭ vŭ (B & Ja—Skt.; lit. "discharges" [*śru*—"flow"]). Certain mental defilements that keep the mind spiritually ignorant and corrupt. The term may have originally referred to intoxicating liquids which flow from plants and to discharges from sores. Its most common meaning in Buddhism is as a metaphoric reference to three or four mental corruptions that must be eliminated if one is to become a saint (Arhant). No single English synonym exists, hence, translations of the term have included: "intoxicants, cankers, sores, outflows, influxes, and fetters."

The Buddhist list of four *āsavas* includes "sensuality" (Kāma), attachment to "existence" *(bhava),* reliance upon "speculative views" *(diṭṭhi),* and spiritual "ignorance" *(avijjā).* Passages listing only three omit speculative views. Various means for destroying the *āsavas* are mentioned, including insight meditation (Vipassanā) and realization of the Four Noble Truths.

Jainism, having arisen out of the same milieu as Buddhism, employs the term *āśrava* (Skt.) to refer to the inflow of karmic matter which causes misery. For the soul to achieve its ultimate goal of liberation from Samsara, such *āśrava* must be eliminated.

Bibliography. T. H. Perera, *The Four Cankers* (Bodhi Leaves no. B.35, 1967); "The Cankers," *The Book of the Gradual Sayings,* E. M. Hare, trans. (1961), III, 276-78.

R. C. Amore

ASCENSION OF CHRIST (Ch). In the NT, Christ's visible post-resurrection ascent into Heaven, occurring near either Bethany (Luke 24:50-51) or the Mount of Olives (Acts 1:9-13). Theologians who hold heaven to be a condition, not a place, nevertheless stressed the theological significance of the ascension accounts.

T. O. Hall, Jr.

ASCETICISM (Gr. *askesis;* lit. "exercise" [*askein,* "to train or practice," especially in gymnastics or athletics]). The practice of extreme self-denial as a means of religious discipline.

As early as the Orphic-Pythagorean cults (late sixth century B.C.) *askesis* assumed a religious significance in reference to the purification of the immortal soul for its release from a mortal body. This was accomplished by dietary restrictions, Celibacy, and other physical and mental austerities. This religious form of ascetic discipline was grounded, as in countless similar manifestations in the history of religion, in a belief in the dualism of matter and spirit.

There are many ascetic traditions, with differing philosophical and religious bases and a variety of purposes. In some traditions austerities are performed to please the deity or to atone for the violation of divine commandments. In others there is the monastic life of poverty, chastity, and obedience for the love of God and for the service of one's fellowman. Yet there are also traditions in which self-mortification and austerities are practiced with the goal of generating enormous powers of destruction to be used in acts of revenge.

1. **Types of asceticism.** *a) sporadic and periodic self-discipline,* of either predominantly physical or mental nature, for the sake of purification. Such austerities are often used as preparation for a crucial event, or simply as an expression of humility or dedication to a deity. This category includes the Israelite practice of fasting on the annual Day of Atonement for the expiation of sins (*see* Yom Kippur), or the temporary fast of King David, who hoped to save his son's life by humbling himself before Yahweh (II Sam. 12:16-20). Occasional fasting in the context of worship was also common among early Christians (Acts 14:23). Preparatory asceticism is illustrated by the forty-day seclusion and fast of Christ prior to embarking on his ministry (Matt. 4:2) and since the fourth century by the forty days of penance during Lent in preparation for Easter. In Islam the lunar month of Ramadan, with its twenty-eight days of fasting and sexual continence during daylight, became a period of self-discipline and expression of faith. In Buddhism it is meritorious for a layman periodically to enter the monastic life, commonly during the twelve-week monsoon season, for meditation and spiritual advancement (*see* Buddhism, Lay). In the Jaina tradition the conclusion of each year is observed with a penitential fast. The Hindu Laws of Manu developed a whole system of sporadic penance as a means of purification. In this context fasting is often prescribed to atone for violating rules of conduct. A fast of three days and nights will remove the guilt of stealing grass, wood, food, etc., whereas the contamination from consuming liquor can be neutralized by drinking boiling cow's urine until death occurs. The severity of the transgression normally determines the length and intensity of the penance.

Most Life Cycle Rites include temporary ascetic exercises. It is a common phenomenon among North American Indians for a novice to fast for four days and undergo various forms of self-discipline before he is ready for initiation into adult society. (*See* Native American Tribal Religion.) In the secular sphere, especially in modern times, the therapeutic value of fasting and reducing diets, often combined with yogic-style exercises, has led to the adoption of periodic pseudo-ascetic life-styles.

Although physical acts prevail in this category, mental expressions of asceticism, such as study of the

VEDAS and repentance for the removal of mortal sins or recitation of the entire QUR'ĀN during Ramadan, often go along with physical austerities.

b) Prolonged and continuous types of asceticism presuppose religio-philosophical views and social developments which allow elaborate ascetic systems to evolve. They are found mainly in those religions that allow a dualistic world view, such as Hinduism, Jainism, Manicheism, and others. The most diversified forms of asceticism developed in India. Early in its history Hinduism established prolonged and continuous periods of self-discipline and mortification as part of the quest for perfection. Members of the upper three castes (BRAHMINS, KṢATRIYAS, VAIŚYAS) were expected to divide their lives into four stages (ĀŚRAMA) with well-defined obligations. The first stage entered upon by way of initiation (*upanayana*) was that of a student of the Vedas (BRAHMACĀRIN), who had to observe *brahmacarya* (chastity), self-control, restricted diet, and absolute obedience to his GURU (teacher), ideally for twelve years or longer. This phase was followed by the stage of a householder (GṚHASTHA), whose life was still to reflect the Hindu ideal of self-discipline and moderation in all his activities. After an indefinite number of years, when he had seen his hair turn white, his skin wrinkle, and his grandchildren born, the householder became a forest dweller (VĀNAPRASTHA) to prepare for a life of total renunciation. His disengagement from society, property, and comfort, his sexual abstinence and fasting, and his meditating on the liberating sacred knowledge of the ĀRAṆYAKAS and the UPANIṢADS then enabled him to enter the final stage of life as an ascetic (SANNYĀSIN), in which he intensified his asceticism to such a degree that this last step was considered the same as dying. The philosophical basis for renunciation was the belief that the phenomenal world in all its manifestations is illusory (MĀYĀ) and an obstacle to acquiring union with true reality.

In JAINISM, the religion of asceticism *par excellence*, the "ideal" life for both lay people and monks, who differ from each other only in degree, was an existence of continuous observation of ascetic vows. The conviction that only moral and passionless behavior and uninterrupted self-mortification can purify the soul from the contaminating karma-matter and thus lead to liberation is grounded in the teaching that it is the physical weight of KARMA which prevents the soul from rising to heaven.

The radical dualism of MANICHEISM, with its opposing principles of spirit-matter, good-evil, light-darkness, knowledge(gnosis)-ignorance, throws each disciple, for an entire lifetime, into the power struggle between the opposites, armed with only one effective weapon: an all-inclusive asceticism, which will lead eventually into the Paradise of Light.

The Christian tradition, too, besides its seasonal observances, knows perpetual vows of celibacy, obedience, and poverty in the institution of MONASTICISM. However, unlike Hinduism, Christianity ascribes reality and goodness to the material world and therefore maintains only a conditional negation toward the objects of renunciation (Hengstenberg).

Some primitive societies require of their SHAMANS continuous dietary and sexual abstinence in order to acquire magic powers or preserve ritual purity for their dealings with supernatural forces.

2. Forms of asceticism. *a) Age, sex, and identity of ascetics.* Although in the majority of cases the ascetic is a male, middle-aged or older, the history of religion can point to many instances in which males and females of any age were engaged in occasional or continuous acts of ascetic self-discipline for a variety of reasons. The great third century Christian thinker ORIGEN began with youthful enthusiasm a life of self-mortification as a "God-pleasing sacrifice," while ANTHONY OF EGYPT (250-356), despite his early start, became the epitome of the aged ascetic. The beautiful Jaina Princess Mallinathā, the only female TĪRTHAṄKARA, maintained celibacy and fasting throughout her life for liberation's sake, whereas the Hindu Princess Ambā of Banāras underwent severe castigation for many years to acquire superhuman powers for the purpose of taking revenge on her deadly enemy, Prince Bhīṣma. In many traditions widows, irrespective of age, were often expected to live the rest of their lives in mourning and renunciation, either by entering a convent (as in Christianity and Jainism) or by withdrawing from society (Hinduism; *see* SATI §2). It is not only human beings who utilize the power of asceticism. In ancient Hindu literature, where the efficacy of self-mortification (TAPAS) was understood as universally applicable, gods and demons also applied it for their own advantage. For example, the gods PRAJĀPATI and BRAHMĀ increased their creative powers by practicing asceticism for an extended period, and the demon Tāraka frightened the Vedic pantheon through the heat aroused by ascetic fervor.

b) The appearance of ascetics may differ considerably. Both in ancient Christianity and early Islam barefoot or sandal-clad penitents wore woolen or haircloth garments, as can be seen from John the Baptist's "garment of camel's hair" (Matt. 3:4) or from the Islamic cloak of wool (*ṣūf*) after which the mystical movement of SUFISM is named. In medieval and modern Christianity the style and color of monastic habits differed according to the order. It was not uncommon for fervent ascetics to expose their bodies directly to haircloth, intensifying the contact by means of belts or chains. Besides carrying a begging bowl, monastic orders in Hinduism, Jainism, and Buddhism have generally worn white or saffron-yellow robes of cotton. A dispute about clothing among Jaina monks resulted in an ongoing division between the moderate "white-robed" (SVETĀMBARAS) and the very strict and naked "space-clad" (DIGAMBARAS). Following their ancient leader MAHĀVĪRA, both sects carry in addition a soft broomlike utensil for removing insects from the path and a small cloth before the mouth to prevent them from being

Henrich Zimmer, *The Art of Indian Asia: Its Mythology and Transformations*, ed. Joseph Campbell. Bollingen Series XXXIX. Vol. 2, copyright © 1955, 1960 by Princeton University Press. Reproduced by permission, plate 65.

The Fasting Buddha

swallowed. In Western Christianity and in Eastern religions most organized monks with established rules wear their hair short, shaven, or tonsured, and occasionally are bearded, while anchoritic ascetics, such as Sannyāsins, YOGINS, or itinerant SĀDHUS, often express their independent status by individualized hairstyles and garments.

c) Location of ascetic activities. Although there is unlimited variety of locations for practicing asceticism, the best suited are those that offer privacy and protection from disturbing worldly influences. In both Oriental and Occidental asceticism the most common places throughout history have been monasteries, whether in isolated areas such as deserts, islands, mountains, forests, and valleys, or compounds within cities. Outstanding examples are the Tibetan fortresslike monasteries of Lhasa, the impressive monastic compound in Bangkok, the BENEDICTINE archabbey of Monte Cassino, or the theocratic republic of Mt. ATHOS. Within some of these structures, especially in Christian monasticism, can be found cloistered areas or individual cells where ascetics, mainly nuns, live entirely secluded from outside contact while leading a contemplative life. Some orders, such as the Benedictine, also require of their members at the time of their profession the "vow of stability," implying a lifelong relationship with the local monastery, while others, such as Jaina ascetics, are expected to wander about from place to place to prevent attachments of any kind, their mobility being restricted only during the monsoon season when the ground is covered with insects and worms. Occasionally very unusual places of isolation serve for the practice of mortification, such as graveyards, caves, and cremation grounds. Some early Christian hermits of the Eastern church disciplined themselves by living on top of pillars. Saint Alipius Stylites stood for over half a century on top of a column, attracting imitators and admirers. In Indian tradition (MAHĀBHĀRATA), ascetic champions such as Viśvāmitra or Saubhari resided in water for long periods.

d) Manifestations of ascetic behavior may reach from simple forms of abstinence to acts of self-torture and mutilation. The most common phenomenon of self-discipline is quantitative and qualitative *fasting.* Its apotropaic function can be recognized in most primitive taboo systems. As the consumption of certain foods or eating on certain occasions can cause defilement or threaten life, partial or total abstention will not only prevent this but may even increase one's powers. Thus it was customary in China to observe nocturnal fasts during mourning periods to protect the living from demonic attacks. Shamans and medicine men, on the other hand, utilize fasting as an invigorating preparation for their functions.

Mild forms of fasting are the preparatory EUCHARISTIC fast one hour prior to receiving Holy Communion according to Roman Catholic practice, or the abstention from meat, milk products, and eggs during specific days and seasons. Severer expressions are found among the early Christian desert monks of Eygpt who continually restricted their diet to bread, salt, and water. The legendary King Viśvāmitra, who "lived on air alone for a thousand years" to subdue his carnal desires, and the suicidal fast in Jainism may serve as examples of extreme forms of asceticism. The altruistic dimension of fasting can be recognized in those cases where the purpose of abstention is self-control and freeing oneself for service to the divine or fellowmen.

Celibacy is another common expression of ascetic behavior. It may be motivated by a variety of factors, from the magical to the religio-ethical. In many primitive societies only celibate medicine men are believed to generate or remain in possession of magic powers. Effectiveness in ceremonial functions required virginity, as in the Roman cult of Vesta. The idea of ritual impurity caused by sexual intercourse can be inferred from the OT requirement of temporary sexual continence (I Sam. 21:4). In such dualistic systems as Pythagoreanism and Jainism, permanent abstinence is an essential ingredient in the endeavor to achieve eternal salvation for the soul. Jainism, in its negative view of sexuality, even went so far as to see in sex and women "the root of all miseries."

The most radical expression of celibacy is mutilation. Origen emasculated himself early in life "for the kingdom of heaven's sake," as did the Skoptsy, the Russian sect of castrates. The religio-ethical aspect of sexual continence is reflected in the dedication of one's life to the divine and to mankind. This ideal was pursued by Mahātma GANDHI, who advocated total abstinence and self-control of the senses (*brahmacarya*) by sacrificing marital love for the sake of Universal Love. Voluntary sexual continence in the NT (I Cor. 7:25-31) and priestly celibacy in Roman Catholicism reveal a similar dedication.

Although *silence* in the context of religion is not always an ascetic expression, its practice, nevertheless, is a common form of self-discipline in Eastern and Western religious traditions. It can be a spiritual exercise by a mystic preparing for enlightenment, as in the case of BODHIDHARMA, who is said to have meditated for nine years facing a stone wall. Wherever there are mystical movements, true ascetic silence, which implies both outward quietness and freedom from disquieting thoughts and emotions, is found. In Indian religions silence manifested itself early as an ascetic discipline; in Christian monasticism it was probably introduced by Benedict of Nursia and became a distinctive characteristic of TRAPPIST and CARTHUSIAN monks and of the seventeenth-century Quietists as well as the HESYCHASTIC mystics of Oriental Christianity.

Asceticism may involve *self-denial* for the sake of others in addition to redemptive benefits for one's self. This is expressed by the Sanskrit term AHIMSĀ, meaning not only the virtue of "noninjury" to living beings as practiced to various degrees in Hinduism, Jainism, and Buddhism, but also, consequently, abstention from meat consumption and from any activities which might inflict pain on others. In modern times Gandhi extended its meaning to "universal love" which requires the sacrifice of total dedication, including voluntary poverty.

Extreme forms of asceticism include self-torture, self-mutilation, and the more exotic expressions of *tapas* in some Indian traditions. These acts serve as penances and self-humiliation, as parts of mourning rituals, as preparation for tribal initiation, as magic practices for generating superhuman powers, or as means of liberation. The flagellation of Christ inspired many medieval penitents and ascetics of monastic orders to imitate his suffering by disciplining their bodies with spiked leather straps, chains, or thorny whips. An impressive case of self-mutilation is claimed in the Mahābhārata (I.201.9), where two ascetic brothers "threw portions of their flesh into a flame," to the chagrin of the frightened gods. A Christian penitent, performing a similar act, buried small pieces of his flesh in the ground (Gretser). Indian literature depicts numerous examples of extended yogic breath-holding (PRĀNAYĀMA), lacerating, and maiming postures, or the five-fire-penance, in which the ascetic exposes himself to intense heat of the sun in addition to sitting in the midst of four surrounding fires. Although most of these radical forms are phenomena of the past, some of the more moderate expressions can still be found in contemporary religious life.

Bibliography. M. G. Bhagat, *Ancient Indian Asceticism* (1976); O. Chadwick, ed., *Western Asceticism* (1958); M. Eliade, *Rites and Symbols of Initiation* (1958); H. E. Hengstenberg, *Christliche Askese* (1948); Arthur Vööbus, *History of Asceticism in the Syrian Orient*, Vols. I & II (1958); J. Gretser, *De Spontanea Disciplinarum Seu Flagellorum*, Vol. I (1743).

F. H. HOLCK

ASH WEDNESDAY (Ch). The first day of LENT in the Western church. The beginning of penance on this day included sprinkling of ashes on the heads of penitents in ninth century Gaul, a custom which became general by the end of the eleventh century. *See* CALENDAR, CHRISTIAN.

T. J. TALLEY

ASH'ARĪ, ABU' L-ḤASAN ALĪ ä shä´ rē ä bool hä sän´ ä lē´ (I; b. A.D. 873). Muslim theologian, founder of orthodox scholasticism (see KALĀM), noted for his use of reason to support revelation and his intellectual defense of Sunnite (*see* SUNNI) religious beliefs.

He began by supporting the rationalist methods and positions of the MU'TAZILA school, but about A.D. 912 abandoned that school in favor of Hanbalite (*see* IBN ḤANBAL) interpretations of Sunnite belief.

Against the Mu'tazilites he held that the QUR'ĀN is eternal and uncreated, not created. Further, he argued that the anthropomorphic expressions in the Qur'ān referring to ALLAH should not be interpreted as metaphors but accepted *bi-lā kayf* ("without asking how"). Most importantly, al-Ash'arī originated the concept of "acquisition" *(kasb)* with which he opposed the Mu'tazilite doctrine of human free will. He argued that Allah creates all the acts of humans but that they "acquire" these acts, thereby becoming responsible for them without creating them. This formula preserved divine determination and sole creatorhood, while making humans responsible and thereby liable to judgment.

Bibliography. R. McCarthy, *The theology of al-Ash'arī* (1953).

H. B. PARTIN

ASHKENAZIM ăsh kĕ nă zĭm´ (Ju—Heb.; lit. "Germans"). Jews whose ancestry lay in North, Central, or Eastern Europe, as distinct from SEPHARDIM of Spain and North Africa. In the BIBLE, Ashkenaz refers to Armenia (Gen. 10:3), but the term came to be associated with Germany in medieval rabbinic literature.

Scholars disagree about Ashkenazic origins. The prevailing theory is that Mediterranean Jews were invited by Charlemagne to settle Germanic territories (*ca.* 800), and a steady emigration followed. These gradually moved eastward to Poland, particularly after LUTHER'S efforts to expel Jews from the Germanic states. By 1600 Poland became world Jewry's primary population center. Immigration to the United States in the nineteenth and twentieth centuries transformed it into an Ashkenazic center despite its early communities of Spanish Jews.

Ashkenazic distinctiveness is cultural rather than geographic. Medieval Ashkenazim were less secular than Sephardim, holding TALMUDIC learning superior to philosophic speculation. Their greatest intellectual figures were Talmudists of little secular learning; their mysticism lacked the abstraction of Sephardic KABBALISM, emphasizing magical incantations and pronouncements instead. Ashkenazic communities prided themselves on an ideological willingness to undergo martyrdom, particularly during the CRUSADES and the seventeenth century Cossack uprisings, criticizing those who accepted BAPTISM rather than die for the faith. (*See* ANTI-SEMITISM.)

Liturgically, the Ashkenazic rite differs from its Sephardic counterpart in text and sequence, though uniformity was maintained with respect to basic law. Linguistically, Ashkenazim adopted YIDDISH. These differences of culture, language, and custom often bred intergroup rivalry which occasionally inhibited cooperation on external matters. Modern frictions are visible in Israel, where political and economic leadership is Ashkenazic though a majority of the population is Sephardic.

European Jews were commonly isolated in physical and social GHETTOES, but barriers began to fall in the seventeenth and eighteenth centuries as increased economic interaction led to greater social and cultural exchange. Gentile governments furthered the process, granting civil and political rights to Jews in the nineteenth century. Social and religious acculturation became the symbol of emancipation, with religious reform and even conversion common. Nevertheless, the charge persisted that Ashkenazic Jewry constituted an alien element within the European body politic. Widespread Anti-Semitism in nineteenth century Europe stimulated emigration to the United States and the birth of ZIONISM. The HOLOCAUST virtually eliminated the Jewish communities of Europe; survivors today live primarily in North America, Israel, and the U.S.S.R. Smaller settlements are found in South America, Britain, Scandinavia, Australia, and South Africa.

Bibliography. S. Dobnow, *History of the Jews in Russia and Poland* (1916-1920); A. Marx and M. L. Margolis, *History of the Jewish People* (1928); H. Sachar, *Course of Modern Jewish History* (1963).
D. J. SCHNALL and S. BAYME

ASHRAM äsh´ rŭm (H—*see* ĀŚRAMA). In classical India, a remote hermitage of an ascetic or teacher established as a center for religious study and practice. These habitations tended to include small huts for the Hindu ascetic or teacher—and often student disciples—along with some provisions for keeping a few domestic animals. In such locations the sage would carry on an austere and disciplined life of meditation, study, and instruction. In Hindu mythology such habitations are frequently depicted in utopian terms as places where wisdom and DHARMA flourished. Kings were enjoined to protect these hermitages from harm by demons and other evildoers.

In modern India the ashram has served as a retreat center for religious and political figures. GANDHI'S ashram at Wardha in western India, for example, was his spiritual retreat and political headquarters. More recently, Hindu teachers who have brought Hinduism to Europe and America have established ashrams, frequently in rural areas, as centers for meditation and religious teaching. (*See* HINDUISM IN AMERICA.)

P. COURTRIGHT

AŚOKA ä shō´ kŭ (B). King Aśoka was a major figure both in the political history of India and in the history of Buddhism. From the political point of view he made his mark by extending the great MAURYAN empire founded by his grandfather, Chandragupta Maurya (who ruled from *ca.* 321 to *ca.* 298 B.C.), and by successfully governing that empire for a period of more than thirty-five years (*ca.* 269 to *ca.* 232 B.C.). From the Buddhist perspective he made his distinctive contribution by adopting the DHARMA (the norm for religious morality) as the legitimating and guiding principle of his rule, and by giving special support to the Buddhist cause.

1. **The historical Aśoka.** The most important sources for any attempt to understand the historical career and activities of Aśoka are a fascinating series of edicts which he himself had inscribed on various pillars, rocks, and cave walls widely distributed throughout his empire. Though these edicts were obviously instruments of royal governance and propaganda, they provide important information concerning the development of his personality, as well as crucial insights into the policies which he pursued.

During the early years of Aśoka's reign he continued the Mauryan military tradition by mounting a major campaign against the Kalinga kingdom, which had previously remained independent. However, soon after this expedition had been successfully completed (and the natural limits of the empire's geographical expansion had been reached), Aśoka came under the influence of Buddhism. Publicly announcing his repentance for the sufferings his military expeditions had caused, he became a lay Buddhist.

According to his various edicts he renounced violence as a policy of state; he prohibited the sacrifice of animals; he adopted a policy of toleration and support of all traditions that he considered to be conducive to true religion and morality; he enjoined administrative officials to be concerned for the welfare of the people; he appointed a number of special "dharma ministers" to guard the public morality and to see to it that proper services were provided; and he initiated an extensive program of public works that included support of hospitals for men and animals, the construction of rest houses along highways, and the digging of wells in convenient locations.

Moreover the edicts show that Aśoka took a special interest in Buddhism and gave significant support and guidance to Buddhist institutions. He engaged in pilgrimages to sacred Buddhist sites; he built or refurbished a number of Buddhist STŪPAS (commemorative burial mounds); he worked to maintain proper teaching and unity in the Buddhist monastic community; and he encouraged the spread of Buddhism to new areas both within his empire and beyond its boundaries.

2. The legends of Aśoka. As the Buddhist tradition developed in India and other parts of Asia, the memory of King Aśoka came to play a very significant role. Throughout the Buddhist world Aśoka was recognized as the greatest of Buddhist kings, and the accounts of his activities were enthusiastically embellished. For example, he was credited with fabulous acts of piety including the simultaneous construction of 84,000 *stūpas* spread throughout India. Moreover the legends concerning his great acts of merit provided a model for Buddhist kings in various parts of Asia. The Aśokan tradition of royally sponsored meritorious activity was particularly strong in the traditional THERAVĀDA kingdoms of Sri Lanka and Southeast Asia. In addition, contemporary Sinhalese and Southeast Asian leaders such as S. W. R. D. Bandaranaike and U Nu have appealed to the Aśokan paradigm as a legitimating basis for their own efforts to establish welfare states based on Buddhist ideals and support.

Bibliography. On the historical Aśoka, B. Gokhale, *Asoka Maurya,* Twayne's Rulers and Statesmen of the World Series No. 3 (1966); R. Mookerji *Asoka* (1962). For traditional Buddhist literature featuring Aśoka, J. Przyluski, *The Legend of the Emperor Asoka in Indian and Chinese Texts* (1967). On the role of the Aśokan model, B. Smith, ed., *Two Wheels of Dhamma: Essays in the Theravada Tradition in India and Ceylon,* AAR Studies in Religion (1972); and E. Sarkisyanz, *Buddhist Background of the Burmese Revolution* (1965).

F. E. REYNOLDS

ĀŚRAMA äsh′ rŭ mŭ (H—Skt.; lit. "a stage in which one exerts oneself" [*śram*—"to exert"]). Any of the stages in the life of a Hindu of TWICE BORN status. According to the DHARMAŚĀSTRAS there are four stages: 1) student (BRAHMACĀRIN), 2) householder (GṚHASTHA), 3) forest-dweller (VĀNAPRASTHA), and 4) renouncer (SANNYĀSIN).

From the time of the UPANIṢADS (*ca.* 700 B.C.) the Hindu tradition has recognized a multiplicity of religious and moral goals. As one text put it, "There are three branches of duty [DHARMA]. Sacrifice, study of the Vedas, alms-giving—that is the first. Austerity [TAPAS], indeed is the second. A student of sacred knowledge [*brahmacārin*], dwelling in the house of a teacher, settling himself permanently in the house of a teacher, is the third. All these become possessors of meritorious worlds" (CU 2.23). A high-caste Hindu male understood himself to be born into the world with three debts: to the ancestors he owed sons who would continue to honor them with praise and food in the death rites (ŚRĀDDHA); to the gods he owed sacrifice; and to the sages he owed chastity. A similar formulation of human religious goals appears in the Dharmaśāstras. Here human life comes under the rule of four aims: pleasure *(kāma),* profit *(artha),* duty *(dharma),* and release *(mokṣa)* (*see* HINDU AIMS OF LIFE).

The obvious difficulty the Hindu tradition faced with these various goals or debts was that they were fundamentally in conflict with one another. Sacrifice to the gods, producing sons to care for the ancestors, and the pursuits of pleasure and profit all required that one play an active role in the worlds of marriage, society, and economy. Yet in order to attain what came to be regarded as the more significant religious goal, that of release (MOKṢA) from the bonds of KARMA and rebirth, one had to renounce attachment to pleasure, family, wealth, and position in society. The dichotomy between affirming the world as the legitimate realm of religious action and denying the validity of that same world as a precondition for religious fulfillment lies at the heart of the Hindu tradition. As Dumont has pointed out, this dichotomy takes institutional form in the traditions of CASTE and renunciation. Within caste society one lives in a complex network of social and ritual relationships, obligations to the gods, ancestors, and persons past and present. In the institution of renunciation one lives apart from society—as an individual—and pursues the more radical religious goal of release from desire for wealth, pleasure, sociality, and even life itself.

One attempt to overcome this dichotomy between the religion of caste and the religion of solitude is the Hindu tradition's formulation of *āśramas* or stages of life. It represented an effort, no doubt more an ideal than a lived reality, to integrate these conflicting goals into a single framework which would accord legitimacy to each goal while preserving the integrity of the system as a whole. It was not a question of whether one lived in the world producing sons and offering sacrifice or left the world of human and divine relations in the pursuit of ecstatic autonomy, but when and in what contexts it was appropriate to take up each goal in its proper turn. According to the theory of *āśrama* one passed through four stages of life, paying one's debts, as it were, as one went along.

After the years of childhood were completed a young man was initiated into the first *āśrama,* that of the *brahmacārin* or student. In the rite of initiation, called *upanayana* (*see* TWICE BORN), the young man was given over to his teacher (ĀCĀRYA) for a period of years, during which time he was obliged to remain chaste, study the VEDAS, and live a life of poverty and service to his teacher. When his instruction was completed the young man could return to his family and prepare himself for the second *āśrama.*

Upon the performance of the rite of marriage a young man entered the stage of the householder (*gṛhastha*). During this stage he maintained the sacred fires, produced sons, provided for the welfare of his family and ancestors, and took his proper place in society. The Dharmaśāstras stress that the householder is the foundation of the four *āśramas* because without his maintenance of the ritual and moral structure of the universe, all the other stages would be impossible.

At the point in his life when his own sons have reached maturity, the Hindu male is enjoined to enter the third stage, that of the forest-dweller (*vānaprastha*). During this stage he should continue to keep the sacred fires, but live in increasing simplicity and nonattachment. He should study the Vedas and withdraw himself from his desires. His wife may accompany him, but they should remain chaste.

When he has reached the point of sufficient nonattachment he should embrace the final stage, that of the renouncer (*sannyāsin*). In this stage he should live alone, homeless, nameless, and without possessions. He should abandon keeping all fires for cooking and sacrifice. He should practice noninjury (AHIMSĀ) and seek to achieve a condition of desirelessness within himself.

Women were not specifically included within the *āśrama* system. The Dharmaśāstras regarded marriage as an initiation comparable to that of the student stage for males. Service to the husband and performance of household duties, including keeping the domestic ritual fire, were regarded as the appropriate dharma for women. While renunciation among women was not unknown, it was never incorporated into any system of obligatory stages as it was for men.

Bibliography. L. Dumont, "World Renunciation in Indian Religions," *Contributions to Indian Sociology,* IV (1960), 33-62; P. V. Kane, *History of Dharmaśāstra,* Vol. II (rpr. 1974).

P. COURTRIGHT

ASSASSINS (I). The name given in medieval times by Europeans to the followers of the Nizārī branch of the ISMĀ'ĪLIYYA sect of SHI'ISM (*see* AGHA KHAN). It was used first in Syria, and then extended to include the Persian branch of the sect. The origin of the appellation can be traced back to the Arabic *hashīsh,* a name for Indian hemp (*cannabis sativa*). The name was carried to Europe by the CRUSADERS, who were confronted by members of this sect (*hashīshiyya*) in the hill fortresses of Syria. The term eventually passed into various European languages in the form "assassin." The meaning of the word has gone through changes reflecting the deep impact Syrian Assassins made on the imagination of Europe. At first it was a general name for the mysterious sect in Syria and other Islamic lands; then following Marco Polo's description of the gardens of paradise belonging to the "Old Man of the Mountains," whose devoted followers were ready to carry out his command to get rid of their opponents by assassination, "assassin" became a common noun meaning "murderer."

Though it has been widely believed that Nizārī leaders made secret use of *hashīsh* to give their emissaries a foretaste of the delights of paradise that awaited them on the completion of their missions of murder, this is not supported by the sources, even when the name *hashīshiyya* is used of the Nizārīs. The term was, in all probability, applied to the Ismailis, who were despised as a minority and thus associated with the prevailing vices of the time.

The history of Assassins or the Nizārīs begins with Ḥasan-i Sabbāḥ, who seized the key fortress of Alamut, south of the Caspian, in A.D. 1090. Between then and 1256 there were eight rulers of Alamut who as the IMAMS of the Ismailis played an important role in the new "summons to truth." Their downfall in Iran and in Syria was effected by the Mongols in 1256 and 1258, and the Mamluk Sultan Baybars dealt the Assassins of Syria a final blow in 1272. (For the present-day community of Assassins *see* KHŌJĀS.)

Bibliography. S. de Sacy, "Mémoires sur la dynastie des Assassins et sur l'origine de leur nom," in *Mémoires de l'Institut Royal,* IV(1818), 1-85; M. G. S. Hodgson, *The Order of Assassins* (1955); B. Lewis, *The Assassins* (1968).

A. A. SACHEDINA

ASSUMPTION OF MARY (Ch). The teaching in ROMAN CATHOLICISM that the Virgin MARY, mother of JESUS, was united body and soul with CHRIST in glory after her life on earth. Belief in this anticipation for Mary of the general resurrection is postbiblical. The first references to the assumption approved by the church occur in the sixth century, for a feast of August 15 which had been known earlier as the "memory of Mary," for Mary's "passing" (*transitus*) or "dormition" (falling asleep).

ORTHODOX CHURCHES kept the feast with splendor, as seen in the seventh and eighth century sermons of Andrew of Crete, John of Damascus, and Germanus of Constantinople. It became a great feast in western Europe also, as the English Lady Day in Harvest. The PROTESTANT REFORMATION rejected the doctrine as nonbiblical. In 1950 Pope Pius XII defined the assumption as DOGMA.

Bibliography. D. Flanagan, "Eschatology and the Assumption," *Concilium,* XLI (1969); K. Rahner, "The Interpretation of the Dogma of the Assumption," *Theological Investigations,* I (1961).

E. R. CARROLL

ASTROLOGY. The art, science, or pseudo-science of deciphering the influence which cosmic forces radiating from celestial bodies have on any part of the universe, but especially on the life of humans. The enterprise assumes a sympathetic and causal relationship between celestial and terrestrial phenomena, more particularly between the orderly movement of the heavenly bodies (stars and moon particularly) and the progression of human events. Its antiquity makes astrology one of the oldest systems of human learning. In ancient times it was recognized as the "queen of the sciences" and the chief means of divining the course of future events (*see* DIVINATION). It originated in ancient Babylonia, spread from there to Greece, Rome, and

Egypt, then to Iran and India, and from there to Central Asia, Tibet, China, Korea, and Japan. It flourished in Europe in the fourteenth and fifteenth centuries and declined from the sixteenth century on with the advent of modern science, only to experience a limited renaissance in twentieth century Western popular culture.

The field of astrology can be divided into three subdivisions: 1) "natural," the reading of celestial *omina* or astrology in the strict sense; 2) "genethliacal," or horoscope charting of the nativity of persons by reading the position of the constellations at the moment of birth or conception; and 3) "judicial," the study of the influence of the stars on human destiny. In ancient times astrological readings were viewed as a means of forecasting the occurrence of famines, epidemics, floods, war, good or bad harvests, and especially the welfare of the king and his household.

1. **Origins in Babylonia.** Our knowledge of the development of horoscopic astrology in Mesopotamia is scanty in contrast to the abundance of evidence from Hellenistic Egypt and the Roman and Byzantine periods. In Mesopotamia astrology was regarded as the most typical form of divination. But the casting of horoscopes developed rather late in its history (*ca.* fifth century B.C.). Celestial bodies were considered to be both deities and personified numbers. There was no application of horoscopic or omenic readings for individual clients; all forecasts were directed exclusively toward the welfare of the community and especially the king and the royal family, on whose well-being the whole cosmos depended. In addition, Babylonian astrology was based almost entirely on the observation of single astral events, or constellations, and the frequent deviations from normal patterns. It never bothered to seek geometric explanations of stellar or planetary motions and was quite content with determining the position of a given constellation at a given moment. Therefore it was satisified with an *Ephemerides* (an almanac listing the changing positions of celestial bodies on a daily basis). Two advances during the Seleucid period (*ca.* 410 B.C.) stand out: 1) the division of the ecliptic (the orbit of the sun around the earth) into twelve zones of 30° each, and 2) the development of lunar calculation and the planetary tables.

The distinctive features of Babylonian astrology include the understanding that the heavens contained the "mansions" of the three principal gods who govern the "celestial paths," which were the three belts running along the celestial equator (Anu), the Tropic of Cancer (Enlil), and the Tropic of Capricorn (Ea). The movements of the celestial bodies were believed to represent the will of the gods, and thus by reading the signals of celestial phenomena the course of future events could be foreseen. The picture of astral events was viewed as the celestial counterpart of the arena of human affairs. This correlation of the "microcosm" and the "macrocosm" was represented by dividing the surface of the moon into four sectors representing the four great countries and the cardinal points of the Babylonian world: Elam, Akkad, Amuru, and Subartu. Babylonian astrologers attributed greater importance to the relative brightness of a star than to its position in the sky. A pale star was regarded as a minor influence and a bright star a strong influence on the course of human events. Readings of stars and planets were determined by tracing the movements of the moon, with special regard for lunar eclipses. The time of observation was important for each of the four countries, and attention was given to circumstances attendant upon the position or brightness of a given star, including such meteorological phenomena as the configuration of clouds, the number of claps of thunder, the presence of a halo around the moon, etc.

The ideological basis of Babylonian astrology is the belief in the divine governance of the universe. The stars were considered to be "writing in heaven," and their pathways a pictographic language expressive of the nature of heaven and the will of the gods. The regular movement of the stars and constellations indicated that the heavens existed under the influence of strict natural law. Accordingly, all celestial and terrestrial realms were the result not of fortuitous occurrences but of the will of the gods. Each of the planets was identified with a particular deity in the Babylonian pantheon. Jupiter was paired with Marduk, Venus with the goddess Ishtar, Saturn with Ninib, Mercury with Nebo, and Mars with Nergal. The movements of the five planets were regarded as signs of the will of the five primary deities, just as the sun represented the god Shamash and the moon, Sin. Numerous factors in Babylonian culture influenced this identification. *a) Mythological ideas:* Marduk, chief deity in the pantheon and identified with various heavenly bodies, was quite naturally placed in the role of Sun-god, the supreme source of light and warmth. *b) Alterations in the socio-religious system:* the gradual increase in the popularity of sun worship contributed directly to the decline in the importance of the moon in both religious and astronomical spheres. *c) Agricultural needs:* the necessity of defining measured segments of time in order to identify the proper times for planting, harvesting, etc., led the Babylonians to identify a god as ruler over each of the months. Thus, the ideas and values within the religious and scientific spheres constantly reacted upon one another through an association of ideas; the two enterprises were often scarcely distinguished and often unambiguously identified.

The development of techniques for observing astral phenomena, defining the configuration of their movements, and interpreting the times and degrees of their deviations from normal patterns in Assyro-Babylonian culture provided the basis for Greco-Roman and Egyptian astrology and for many of the principles in European astrology up until the sixteenth century. Despite its mathematical inaccuracies, the Babylonian discovery that terrestrial events are influenced by the movements of celestial bodies represents an important step toward the development of a concept of natural law. In this sense, then, astrological prophecies were the precursors of scientific prediction.

2. **Greco-Roman astrology.** Although astrology began to mature in Babylonia by the end of the fifth century B.C., it did not have significant impact on Greek, Roman, and Egyptian culture until the middle of the fourth century B.C. The Greeks and Egyptians developed both astrology and astronomy far beyond the level achieved by the Babylonians, and the meshing of the two disciplines seems to be perpetuated almost until the rise of modern science in the sixteenth century. The practical rules for casting the horoscope were conceived in Babylonia but were not provided a theoretical basis until Ptolemy's *Tetrabiblos*. The idea that each day of the week was influenced by a planet is of Babylonian origin, but the actual correlation of the seven planets (Saturn, Jupiter, Mars, Sun, Venus, Mercury, and the Moon, in that order) with particular hours of the day was a Hellenistic innovation.

Hipparchus (*ca.* 130 B.C.) is credited with discovering the procession of the equinoxes and thereby laying the foundation for the development of horoscopy as we know it today. The attempts to chart the destiny of the individual by casting his horoscope on the basis of the position of the stars, the times of their heliacal risings and settings, and their relations with each other are the most significant contributions of the Greeks to astrology. So accurate are the predictions based upon the Greek models that this Greco-Roman system was passed on to the Arabic thinkers, to the KABBALA in Judaism, and to Christians with almost no major revision required until the beginning of the modern scientific era. The Greeks enlarged further upon the astrological system inherited from the Babylonians by associating it with almost every science and pseudo-science then known: medicine, alchemy, botany, mineralogy, and anatomy. In an ever-widening association of ideas, the various planets and other astral bodies were identified with the color appropriate to their visual features or symbolic characteristics. In the Ptolemaic system Saturn was associated with gray, Mars with red, Jupiter with white, and, because of its ever-changing nature, Mercury with whatever color was appropriate to the circumstance. Additional symbolic value was assigned to each of the planets by identifying each with a particular metal (the sun with gold, the moon with silver, etc.), with stones, plants, and animals.

It is from the Greeks that we derive the fully developed zodiac, marked by its twelve "stations" or "mansions" of 30° each and a particular animal linked with each of the twelve zones. Saturn was identified with a goat, Jupiter with a centaur, Mars with a horned ram, the Sun with a lion, Venus with a bull, Mercury with a maiden holding a stalk of grain, and the Moon with a crab. By adhering to this principle of symbolic pairing of astral bodies with entities in the natural world, a multi-tiered language of representational value was created for the purpose of forecasting future events.

Because of the centrality of the individual human being in Greco-Roman astrology and the idea of the mystical identity between the microcosmic sphere of human life and the macrocosmic sphere of the life of the universe, Greek astrologers identified the planets with various parts of the body: Saturn with the limbs, Jupiter with the feet, Mars with the head, the Sun with the flanks, Venus with the buttocks, Mercury with the bladder, and the moon with the breast. The zodiac was thus regarded as a prototype of the human body, and the fate of the individual was determined by defining the planet in ascendancy at the time of birth and its relationship to the corresponding zodiacal signs.

Toward the end of the second century A.D. there occurred a general rise in the popularity of astral religion, and with it a general decline of interest in the strictly mathematical and scientific aspects of astrology. Irrational and anti-rational ideas swept the Greco-Roman world like a storm, due, in large part, to a widespread adherence to a variety of mystery and mystical cults (viz., those dedicated to Dionysos, Cybele, Isis, Baal, and various solar gods). Other contributory factors were the spread of thaumaturgical practices, the influence of the GNOSTIC movement, and the resurgence of the hermetic tradition supposedly based on the writings of Hermes Trismegistos. Astrological practices received added impetus from the Stoics, who viewed the astrological system as confirmation of the unity of the Platonic universe.

3. **Indian astrology.** There are no astrological references to be found in any of the VEDIC, BUDDHIST, or JAINA texts before the beginning of the Christian era. It was only under the influence of Greek thought that horoscopic astrology made its appearance in India and developed largely along the lines established in Greco-Roman literature. The creative period in the development of Indian astronomy was the Greco-Bactrian period after the Alexandrian invasion of northwest India. The texts of this period were composed in an Aramaic script (modified to conform to Indian linguistic requirements) known as Karosthī. Greek astrological ideas appeared first in Buddhist texts and were transmitted from there to Central Asia, Tibet, China, Korea, and Japan.

The earliest known SANSKRIT text is the *Gargasaṃhitā* of the first century A.D. Other texts of authoritative stature to appear subsequently are: *Bṛhatsaṃhitā* by Varāhamihira (*ca.* 550), in which the order of the *nakṣatras* (or lunar mansions) is defined; *Bhadrabāhu-saṃhitā,* a Jaina text of the tenth century; *Pariśiṣṭas* or "Supplements" of the ATHARVA VEDA (tenth-eleventh centuries); and *Tājika* of the thirteenth century. The most significant body of literature in Indian astrology is the *Pañca-siddhānta,* "Five Solutions" (sixth century), of which the only extant text is the *Sūrya Siddhānta* ("Solution of the Sun") also attributed to Varāhamihira. It contains materials pertaining to a variety of astronomical topics: e.g. temporal metrics, sine-tables, equinoxes and solstices, planetary motions, heliac risings and settings of the stars, cosmography, and lastly calendrical computations. The most prominent contribution of Indian astrologers to the enterprise of astrology is the concept of the *nakṣatra.* This term originally referred to constellations in general. Later it designated the "mansions" or "stations" through which the moon passes as the sun moves along the twelve signs of the zodiac. There are either twenty-two or twenty-eight *nakṣatras* in each month, depending on the principle of calculation. Like the planets, they are influential in determining the fate of the individual. Every horoscope contains reference to the *nakṣatra* under which one was born and each male child is given a secret name linked to the *nakṣatra* through which the moon was passing at the hour of birth.

4. **Arabic astronomy.** The technical Arabic term *'ilm ahḳam al-nudjūm,* "the science (or art) of the degrees of the stars," connotes both astrology and astronomy. No clear distinction was made between the two disciplines until the nineteenth century. In keeping with the Aristotelian school of thought, astrology was regarded by Muslim writers as one of the seven or nine branches of the "natural sciences," along with medicine, physiognomy, alchemy, and the interpretation of dreams. The Arabic system manifests many of the same features and techniques of horoscopic reading as the Hellenistic and Indian models.

Among the most critical influences operating in astrological prediction are the particular nature and movements of the celestial bodies; mythical places in heaven that influence the effects of a star with which they stand in special relation; the horizon and the meridian together with their intersection with the ecliptic defining the four pivotal points of the zodiac; the relative positions of the planets in relation to the sun, moon, and earth; and the geographical location of the astrologer and his client. There are three principal systems of horoscopic reading: 1) *interrogationes,* questions regarding a lost object, the optimum time to plant a crop, etc.; 2) *electiones,* the determination of the auspicious moment for undertaking a particular task; and 3) "genethliacal casting," determining the destiny of the individual by reconstructing the configuration of the constellations at the moment of birth or conception.

The astrological aspects of Arabic astronomy were greatly admired in the Holy Roman Empire, inspired by the works of Ibn Abī'l Rijāl and Abū Ma'shar. Arabic astronomy is derived from a diverse array of sources: the Greek masters (Ptolemy being the most important), Pahlavī and Indian texts, and the oral traditions of Mesopotamia, Syria, and Egypt. While drawing extensively on all these sources, the Muslim astrologers developed effective experimental methods based on careful observations and meticulous mathematical calculations. Their writings served as the guide of medieval Christian writers following the rediscovery of the writings of Aristotle in the twelfth century.

5. **Medieval Christian and modern European astrology.** Astronomy was one of the branches of knowledge of the *quadrivium* (arithmetic, music, geometry, and astronomy) but it was also used for the "practical" purposes of horoscopy. Greek astrological knowledge was revived only with the translations of Arabic astrological and astronomical treatises in Spain during the twelfth and thirteenth centuries. A renaissance of interest in astrology occurred in western Europe in the fifteenth and sixteenth centuries in conjunction with the revival of Neoplatonism and Hermeticism. In the writings of Paracelsus (1493-1541) the ideas and techniques of physiognomy, astrology, alchemy, and other disciplines were amalgamated to form a single, complex system.

Astrology lost its remaining rational and scientific underpinning and its acceptance among the intelligentsia in Europe with the advent of the new cosmology of Copernicus (1473-1543), Galileo (1563-1642), and Kepler (1571-1630) and the discovery that the earth itself is a planet like all other planets, subject to astrophysical laws that leave no room for the influence of stellar forces on the fate of humans.

6. **Astrology in modern times.** The development of Newtonian physics completed the dismembering of the superstructure of astrology begun by the nominalistic and rationalistic philosophies of the late Middle Ages and the sixteenth century. Astrology in all its forms has been rejected by most educated persons in the West, who have exchanged it for a largely undefined belief in the capacity of economic and historical forces (Marx), of natural selection and the survival of the fittest (Darwin), of the dark and often uncontrollable forces of the subconscious (Freud), or of human decisions (Sartre). Nonetheless, there has been a widespread popular following of daily astrological charts in the mass media (particularly magazines and newspapers), and many persons in the middle class visit the horoscopic reader on a regular or occasional basis in hopes of gaining some knowledge of the future. Still, for many this custom is little more than a leisure activity on a par with gardening and tennis. Despite the popular appeal of astrology in modern times, the enterprise has little or no theoretical basis commensurate with the principles of modern science.

Although the ideas and values identified with astrology have significant impact throughout the world today, there are few comprehensive scholarly studies of the status of astrological practices in contemporary religion and culture, and even these studies focus primarily on small, tertiary cultures. Investigation of the role of astrology in the major religions of the world is greatly to be desired.

Bibliography. General: R. Eisler, *The Royal Art of Astrology* (1947); L. Thorndike, *A History of Magic and Experimental*

Sciences (1923-41). Assyrio-Babylonian and Greco-Roman: F. Cumont, *Astrology and Religion among the Greeks and Romans* (1912, 1960); M. Jastrow, *The Religion of Babylonia and Assyria* (1911); H. Lewy, *Chaldean Oracles and Thaurgy* (1956). Greco-Roman: M. Nilsson, *The Rise of Astrology in the Hellenistic Age* (1943). Indian: A. L. Basham, *The Wonder That Was India* (1959); P. V. Kane, *History of Dharmaśāstra,* Vol. V, pt. 1 (1962); D. Pingree, *Census of the Exact Sciences in Sanskrit* (1970-). Islamic: E.S. Kennedy and D. Pingree, *The Astrological History of Māshā'allāh* (1971); C. A. Nallino, articles in the *Encyclopaedia of Islam* and *Encyclopaedia of Religion and Ethics*. Judeo-Christian: J. Seznec, *The Survival of the Pagan Gods* (1953); F. Yates, *Giordano Bruno and the Hermetic Tradition* (1964). Modern: L. Macniece, *Astrology* (1964); O. S. Rachleff, *Sky Diamonds: The New Astrology,* (1976).

J. B. Long

ASURA ŭ sû´rŭ (H & B—Skt.; lit. "antigod, demon" [*asu*—"the breath"; *a-sura*—"anti-god"]). A spiritual, incorporeal, or divine being; a "living power" or "Sacred Presence," either benign or malevolent.

In early Vedic texts, *asura* designated a god and was applied to numerous deities (e.g., Varuṇa, Agni, Mitra, Indra). In later books, the term attained the opposite meaning of demon or anti-god. The Dāsyus (slaves) noted in Vedic texts, aboriginals conquered by the Aryans and reduced to servitude, are sometimes called *asuras*. Some identify the *asuras* with the aboriginal Kolarian peoples of Choṭa Nāgpur region who are still known as Asur. *Asuras* are often called *Daityas* and *Dānavas,* terms derived from names of the two groups of demons, *Diti* ("boundary") and *Danu* ("limit," "restraint"). Both groups sprang from the same father, Kaśyapa, making them half-brothers. Like their parents, the demons are the spiritual personifications of "boundary" or "constriction" and are the demonic forces who are in perpetual conflict with the gods over possession of world sovereignty or the elixir of immortality (*amṛta* or Soma; cf. Gr. *ambrosia*). The Brāhmaṇas credit Prajāpati with their creation from his abdomen or lower breath. Elsewhere, they are created from drops of water which the Creator accidentally spilled. The chief of the *asuras* is *Vṛtra,* the cosmic dragon or serpent abiding in the waters of chaos, who engages in battle with Indra and, finally, loses. In the Epics and Purāṇas, Indra relinquishes his role as chief opponent of the demons to Rāma and Krishna.

The line of demarcation between gods and demons is blurred. They both share numerous divine powers, have the same lineage and are physically indistinguishable. Both groups are morally ambivalent. For example, in the myth of the "Churning of the Ocean" (Mahābhārata I.15-17; Rāmāyaṇa I.45), the demons initially obtain the elixir when one of their number, Rāhu ("the seizer" who seizes the sun and moon in eclipses), assumes the guise of a god and drinks it, but then loses it as the result of a deceitful trick of Vishnu in the form of a seductive female, Mohinī ("the enchantress"). This myth illustrates the fact that the gods and demons may be opposed functionally, but appear identical in essence. Functionally, the gods are associated with the sky, light, life, and with the creatures of the aerial regions; the demons are associated with the earth or underworld, darkness, death, and the creatures of the subterranean realms (e.g., the serpent). *See* Demons, Demonology.

Bibliography. A. K. Coomaraswamy, "Angels and Titans. An Essay in Vedic Ontology," *JAOS*, LV (1935), 373-419, and "The Darker Side of the Dawn," *Smithsonian Miscellaneous Collections,* 94 (1935); J. B. Long, "Life out of Death: A Structural Analysis of the Myth of the 'Churning of the Ocean of Milk,' " in *Hinduism. New Essays in the History of Religions* (1976), pp. 171-207; W. D. O'Flaherty, *The Origins of Evil in Hindu Mythology* (1976). J. B. Long

AŚVINS ŭsh´ vĭns (H—Skt.; lit. "the two horsemen" [from *aśva,* "horse"]). Celestial charioteers who are youthful, beautiful, and amiable twin deities in Vedic Hinduism. As sons of the sky, appearing in the early dawn in their horse-drawn (sometimes bird-drawn) golden chariot, they are auspicious, benign, "friendly" (*nāsatya,* their earlier name, occurs also in the Avesta), and "wondrous" *(dasra).* They are connected with the fertility of herds, crops, and humans, and often are associated with honey and Soma. They are rescuers and healers of the afflicted and as an auspicious pair are invoked in marriage rites. In the Rig Veda the Aśvins are mentioned more often than any deities except Indra, Agni, and Soma. The Aśvins are an inseparable unit in the Vedas, but are individualized with the epithets Nāsatya and Dasra in post-Vedic literature. In the Mahābhārata they are the fathers of the twin heroes, Nakula and Sahadeva.

Bibliography. A. A. Macdonell, *Vedic Mythology* (1897).

D. M. Knipe

ATHANASIAN CREED ăth ə nā´ zhən (Ch). Probably composed sometime between 440 and 542 in the vicinity of the monastery at Lerins. Of uncertain authorship, it is a masterful statement of Augustinian theology in its affirmation of the Trinity and the doctrine of the person of Jesus Christ, but its greatness is obscured by its dogmatism. *See* Creeds and Confessions §2.

Bibliography. J. N. D. Kelly, *The Athanasian Creed* (1964).

J. H. Leith

ATHANASIUS ă thăn ā´ shŭs (Ch; *ca.* 295-373). Bishop of Alexandria from 328 to 373, championing, in polemical writings and in his vigorous public life, the doctrine of the council of Nicaea (325); a zealous, uncompromising foe of the Arians and the schismatic Meletians. Athanasius' fortunes as a leader were subject to the pacification policies and theological sympathies of the Emperor Constantine and his successors, who banished him on five occasions (totaling seventeen years). During exiles in Italy and Gaul, Athanasius rallied support for the Nicene cause and reported to Western Christians the heroics of the ascetic Desert Fathers of Egypt.

Most of Athansius' literary energy, like his ecclesiastical career, was devoted to attacking Arian teaching. His *Letters concerning the Holy Spirit* (to Serapion) argue the divinity of the HOLY SPIRIT of the TRINITY against "spirit-fighters" of the latter part of the fourth century. Especially influential among Athanasian works are the apologetic treatise *On the Incarnation of the Word* (the companion volume to *Against the Pagans*), with its argument that the divine Word's assumption of flesh makes possible the deification of mortals, and the *Life of Antony,* which recounts the faith and feats of the Egyptian hermit who quickly came to symbolize Christian rigorism and self-denial.

Bibliography. F. L. Cross, *The Study of Athanasius* (1945).

R. C. GREGG

ATHARVA VEDA ŭt hŭr´ vŭ vā´ dŭ (H—Skt.; lit. "knowledge of the Atharvans" [*atharvan;* a class of fire priests]). One of the four primary texts of VEDIC HINDUISM, a collection (SAMHITĀ) of 731 hymns in twenty books; composed at the close of the second or early in the first millennium B.C. Two recensions survive. Unlike the other three *saṃhitās,* the Atharva Veda includes elements of popular religion and medicine—spells, charms, incantations, and remedies. *See* VEDA.

D. M. KNIPE

ATHEISM. Denial of the existence of god. Broadly conceived, it indicates the denial of any principle or being as worthy of divinity. Specific meanings vary widely in accordance with the conception of god that is denied.

In a Christian context, for example, god has specifiable characteristics and atheism may signify the denial of the god who has these characteristics. Indeed, the affirmation of a deity deficient in one or more of these characteristics, or the affirmation of a god whose traits contradict those of the god of JESUS CHRIST, may also entail the denial of divine reality as Christians understand it. This accounts for the fact that persons who affirm the existence of some god or gods, e.g., Jews, Muslims, Hindus, and various philosophers, have sometimes been referred to as atheists in Christian literature.

Regardless of how one conceives of god, it is arguable that some religions are atheistic. BUDDHISM affirms that nonbeing or NIRVANA is the goal of all temporal effort. Does nonbeing qualify as an existent deity? TAOISM includes a view of the world and prescriptions for behavior, but no affirmation of an existing god.

Some theologians distinguish theoretical from practical atheism. On this view a professed believer might for all practical purposes deny the reality of some god(s) in the way he lives, while a professed atheist might similarly affirm the reality of some god(s) in the way he lives.

D. F. OTTATI

ATHOS, MT. ā´ thäs (Ch). Independent monastic republic, the main spiritual center of the ORTHODOX CHURCHES, located on a peninsula in northeast Greece. It was founded by St. Athanasius of Trebizond *ca.* 960. There are presently about three thousand monks, grouped into twenty ruling monasteries, seventeen of which are Greek. The Russians, Serbians, and Bulgarians each have one. There are several forms of monastic life: community, semi-heremitic, and idiorrhythmic (one in which a monk follows his own way). Women are not allowed to enter. Its monasteries are rich in ancient manuscripts and ICONS. Mt. Athos is under the jurisdiction of the Ecumenical Patriarch of Constantinople.

V. KESICH

Wide World Photos

Monks of the Vatopedion Monastery, Mt. Athos, in front of the religious murals decorating their walls

ATMAN ät´mŭn (H—Skt.; lit. "breath, self, soul"). That part of a living being which is eternal and beyond physical description. According to VEDĀNTA philosophy, the Atman is of the same nature as the Universal Soul (BRAHMAN), and as such seeks union with it in mystical liberation (MOKṢA).

J. BARE

ATONEMENT (Ch). The death of JESUS Christ—though not in isolation from his life, teachings, and RESURRECTION—by which sinful humans can be reconciled with God.

1. **Theories of atonement.** *a) The classic theory.* Also known as the patristic, dramatic, Eastern, or Greek theory, and, because the main idea is that of victory over SIN and the Devil, *Christus Victor.* For the first thousand years of Christian history the major emphasis was upon Christ's victory achieved through giving a ransom to the devil. Jesus voluntarily gave

his life as a ransom for humanity, but because of his resurrection the Devil could not hold him.

b) Satisfaction theory. Advocated by ANSELM (d. A.D. 1109), Archbishop of Canterbury, in a monumental work, *Cur Deus Homo?* this theory holds that human sin has dishonored an infinite God to whom reparation or satisfaction is due. Since finite man cannot pay an infinite debt, God became man in Christ and satisfied the debt.

c) Demonstrative theories. Peter ABELARD (d. A.D. 1142) saw the death of Christ as a picture of God's love, which in turn elicits human repentance and love. Among modern theologians who held this view were Schleiermacher, Ritschl, and Bushnell. (*See* THEOLOGY, CONTEMPORARY CHRISTIAN.)

d) Penal substitution theory. This view that Christ's death was to propitiate God by bearing the penalty for man's sin was advocated by CALVIN and has been adopted by some moderns, e.g., Charles Hodge, A. H. Strong, L. Berkhof. This view is rooted in the interpretation of the OT SACRIFICE as substitutionary.

e) Identification theory. This theory is based on an interpretation of the OT sacrificial system which sees the basic idea in sacrifice as identification rather than substitution. The laying of hands on the sacrificial animal did not transfer guilt or sin but rather identified the worshiper with the unblemished sacrifice. The atonement becomes efficacious when through faith the individual identifies himself with Christ's sacrificial death.

2. **Extent of the atonement.** There has been major debate whether the effects of the atonement were limited to those specially chosen by God or were to extend to all humanity. *See* PREDESTINATION.

Bibliography. G. Aulen, *Christus Victor* (1969); Anslem, *Why God Became Man* (ET 1969); D. Baillie, *God Was in Christ* (1948), pp. 157-202; E. Brunner, *The Mediator* (1942); R. Culpepper, *Interpreting the Atonement* (1966); V. Taylor, *The Atonement in New Testament Teaching* (1941).

T. O. HALL, JR.

ATONEMENT, DAY OF (Ju). *See* YOM KIPPUR.

AUGSBURG CONFESSION (Ch). The most influential of Lutheran confessions, due to its historical significance and intrinsic merit. Prepared by PHILIP MELANCHTHON for presentation to Charles V at the Diet of Augsburg, 1530, it was designed to establish the integrity of PROTESTANTISM and to justify correction of abuses in the church. Its tone is moderate and conservative. *See* CREEDS AND CONFESSIONS §5.

J. H. LEITH

AUGUSTINE OF HIPPO (Ch; 354-430). Aurelius Augustinus, North African bishop of Hippo Regius (modern Bône, Algeria); the most influential theologian of late antiquity. His voluminous writings have influenced theologians to the present day.

1. **Early life.** Augustine's mother, Monica, was a devout Christian; his father, Patricius, was a pagan, bent on giving his son a good education and career. Augustine's spiritual autobiography, *The Confessions,* details his struggle with these options—beginning with his public pursuit of a career as a teacher of rhetoric and his private pilgrimage through MANICHEISM and Platonism—culminating in his conversion to a monastic variety of Christianity in 386.

2. **Thought.** Augustine has been portrayed as a Christian philosopher, committed to the exposition of human life's true end, faith in and understanding of God as immaterial Highest Good. But just as important to his entire thought was the process of how one is to arrive at final salvation, defined as eternal life in, and with, God. Here there was a crucial shift of emphasis over the course of life—from an emphasis on *faith* (believing assent in God's promises), to *will* (intending what God intends for a person), to perfect *love* (which delights and freely rejoices in God).

By the time of *The Confessions* (401), a decade after his conversion, he had abandoned his belief that reasoning faith would bring him to possess the vision of God in this life and had become concerned with the problem of human inability to will single-mindedly what God wills (*Conf.* 8.5.10 and 22). Also the contemporary DONATIST controversy forced Augustine to distinguish sharply between an external means of grace (e.g. SACRAMENT of BAPTISM) and its internal effect on the heart for salvation (e.g. *On Baptism* 2-4).

By the early anti-PELAGIAN treatises (412) Augustine distinguished between *believing,* which lies within human power, and *loving,* which God must initiate and effect (*On the Spirit and the Letter* 58). Later, he equated *will* and *love* and insisted that salvation lay entirely in God's hidden election of those to whom God freely gives the gift of love (*On Grace and Free Will* 45 [23]; *see* PREDESTINATION). Thus the City of God in its perfected state is constituted by love of God and one another in God.

This shift of emphasis can be seen in Augustine's treatment of infants, who in the earlier writings (*Conf.* 1.7.11) symbolized the destructive quality of human volition, but in the late period are signs of God's free and unmerited choosing of some for salvation (*On Grace and Free Will* 44 [22]).

Bibliography. P. Brown, *Augustine of Hippo* (1967); J. Burnaby, *Amor Dei: A Study of the Religion of St. Augustine* (1938); R. A. Markus, *Saeculum: History and Society in the Theology of St. Augustine* (1970); R. J. O'Connell, *St. Augustine's Early Theory of Man, A.D. 386-391* (1968).

D. E. GROH

AUGUSTINIANS ô gəs tĭn′ yənz (Ch). The Order of St. Augustine (OSA) or Austin Friars, Roman Catholic MENDICANT FRIARS, became a RELIGIOUS ORDER by unions (1244, 1256) of hermit groups using the Rule of St Augustine. In the early seventeenth century two branches arose: Augustinian Recollects (OAR) and Discalced (Barefoot) Augustinians (OAD). There are also communities of Augustinian nuns.

W. H. PRINCIPE

AURANGZĪB ō räng′ zēb (I; 1618-1707). Muslim emperor of North India who is usually perceived as completely opposed in temperament to his great-grandfather, AKBAR. If Akbar's reign is characterized by the word "tolerance," then Aurangzīb's is summed up in "persecution."

Aurangzīb observed the precepts of ISLAM faithfully. He lived in the palace almost as if he were an ascetic and, like his great-grandfather, turned to a largely vegetarian diet. A strict legalist, he could not condone the "idolatry" of his Hindu subjects. Ironically, his fanatical dedication to Islam did more to hamper the spread of that faith than did Akbar's alleged apostasy. Under Aurangzīb, Hindu Indians once again resisted their foreign rulers. Within Islam bitterness developed between those who were doggedly determined to follow the militaristic rules of the QUR'ĀN and those inclined to the spreading of faith in ALLAH by example and preaching. Aurangzīb's reign marked the beginning of the end for the Mogul empire. His narrow vision of justice and his grim determination to unite his subjects by force finally shattered the fragile foundations of peaceful cooperation which Akbar had sought to establish.

Bibliography. S. Lane-Poole, *Aurangzīb and the Decay of the Mughal Empire* (1901). P. L. BASU

AUROBINDO ôr ō bĭn′ dō (H; 1872-1950). Śrī Aurobindo Ghose was a product of the union of East and West. He was born in Calcutta of Indian parents, but his father, a surgeon in the Civil Medical Service, became convinced of the inferiority of Indian culture and determined that his own son would know only the values and traditions of the West. Aurobindo entered a French school at Darjeeling when he was five, and then was sent to England when he was seven. In England he studied first under private tutors, then at St. Paul's in London, and finally at Cambridge, where he won a number of awards and scholarships for his outstanding academic achievements. Having completed his studies, Aurobindo returned to India at the age of twenty and began a career in teaching and academic administration at Baroda College (in contemporary Gujarat State). During this period he first began reading the classical works of the Indian tradition, teaching himself Sanskrit and other Indian languages in the process. Soon he was completely captured by the Indian spirit, and became not only an advocate of Indian culture and tradition, but also a militant rebel in the early Indian nationalist movement. He moved back to his native Bengal and traveled widely, making speeches in favor of nationalism and seeking recruits for the battle against the British. His political activity culminated in 1908 when he was imprisoned for a year on a charge of sedition.

While he was in prison, the focus of Aurobindo's life changed radically. He began an intensive study of the BHAGAVAD GĪTĀ and took up the practice of yoga as the first step in a spiritual pilgrimage which was to consume him for the rest of his life. When he was released from prison, he left British India, forsaking all political activity, and went to the French controlled enclave of Pondicherry in South India. Here he devoted himself completely to study, writing, the practice of YOGA, and, during the first years, to the administration of his ASHRAM, which soon attracted followers from all over India. By the time of his death in 1950, Aurobindo's reputation as a poet, philosopher, and spiritual leader was well established, and his ashram had grown to a large complex of buildings housing hundreds of his disciples.

From the time of his retirement to Pondicherry, Aurobindo began writing on a variety of subjects, and his collected works now fill twelve large volumes. Of these, perhaps the most important to an understanding of his spiritual teaching is his epic SĀVITRĪ. This exceptional poem of over 24,000 lines, which on the surface may appear to be merely a poetic expansion of an ancient Indian story, is the literary record of Aurobindo's own spiritual experiences and insights. It is a record of the events of his inner life which were the direct result of forty years of intense spiritual discipline. In *Sāvitrī* the spiritual growth of the individual soul, which parallels the cosmic evolution of consciousness, is described in detail: each level of accomplishment is portrayed in vivid imagery rich with multidimensioned symbolic meaning. The progress of the soul is carefully followed through the worlds of matter, life, and mind, and finally through the sphere of supermind to the realm of pure spirit. One might expect the narrative to end when this divine world has been reached, for at this point the soul has been freed from all bondage; but with Aurobindo this is not the case. Having reached the pinnacle, the soul must turn and descend the ladder of consciousness, carrying the insights of the higher realms to the lower worlds, so that they too might be fully awakened to spiritual truth and reality. This transformation of the spheres of matter, life, and mind by the descent of the spirit from above was the goal of Aurobindo's yoga. He fully believed that this transformation, which he refers to as the "descent of the Supermind" and "the supramental manifestation upon earth," would take place during his life and would be the beginning of the complete spiritualization of the world. Thus, for Aurobindo, *Sāvitrī* was neither an epic poem nor a personal diary; it was rather a book of inspiration, a manual of spiritual revolution.

In *The Life Divine,* his most important philosophical work, Aurobindo offers an intellectual explanation of his understanding of reality—past, present, and future. He points out how the spiritual progress of the individual is related to and significantly involved in the process of cosmic evolution. At the present time it is clear that life has evolved out of matter and that mind has evolved out of life; but, as Aurobindo explains in *The Life Divine,* the process of evolution is not yet complete: a fourth stage of evolution, the arising of spirit out of mind, is now beginning to be manifest in human existence; and it is the purpose of the human race to facilitate the advance toward this final goal of evolution. Man is unique in that he alone stands between matter, life, and mind below and spirit above; he must do all he can to accomplish the integral union of these realms. In the struggle to accomplish this cosmic task he is not alone, for the spirit is always available as a resource for inspiration, direction, and energy. Without this constant activity of the spirit, evolution could not have happened, and the final goal could never be reached. As earth and man reach up to spirit through evolution, and at this point in human history through the practice of spiritual discipline, spirit, through its emissary, the Supermind, is reaching down to earth and man. According to Aurobindo, this process will soon be fulfilled and will culminate in the transformation of matter, life, and mind into spirit and the establishing of the "Life Divine" on earth. The duty of man at this auspicious time is to prepare himself through spiritual discipline, a technique which Aurobindo describes in detail in his *Essays on the Gītā* and *The Synthesis of Yoga,* so that he might receive the supramental descent.

Bibliography. Aurobindo, *Sāvitrī* (1954), and *The Life Divine* (1965); R. A. McDermott, ed., *Six Pillars* (1974).

J. COLLINS

AUROVILLE ôr′ ō vĭl (lit. "City of Dawn"). A utopian city five miles north of Pondicherry along the Coromandel coast of South India, established by a French disciple of the Hindu sage AUROBINDO.

1. **Background.** Auroville is intended to be an experimental application of the teachings of Aurobindo which claim: (1) that all humanity is evolving progressively toward a new consciousness which will reflect an innate divinity (ŚAKTI); (2) that both consciousness (mind) and matter (body) are caught up in this progression toward divinization ("descent of the Supermind"); and (3) that this process can be hastened by spiritually alert working in the world ("integral YOGA").

Mira Richard (called "the Mother" by disciples), Aurobindo's favorite disciple and the head of his ASHRAM from 1922 until her death in 1974, had a vision in 1956 of "a place where all human beings of goodwill . . . could live freely as citizens of the world, obeying one single authority, that of supreme truth." When Auroville was established in 1968, its charter claimed: (1) Auroville belongs to all people who are willing to strive toward Divine consciousness; (2) it will be a place of unending education (spiritual and technological); (3) it will build on the past but intends to hasten the evolution of humankind; and (4) it will be an experiment focused upon "a living embodiment of an actual Human Unity."

2. **A concrete dream.** Auroville is being built on three thousand acres of arid, red land overlooking the Bay of Bengal. The spiritual though not geographic center of the city is the Matrimandir ("House of the Mother"), a concrete dome structure that rises nearly one hundred feet in the air on the highest elevation in the city. The Matrimandir was to have been the central point of a MANDALA-like city with four zones: residential, industrial, cultural, and international. Beyond the central city of 50,000 (projected) exists a "green belt" of agricultural and horticultural activity. The goal of social harmony does not repudiate individuality; rather, unity is to be a product of autonomous seekers achieving a level of common inner spiritual direction which would create "unity in diversity."

3. **The existing city.** Work on the Matrimandir has been extended over more than eight years by a lack of funds, building materials, and sufficient work force. Given the Mother's encouragement of individual autonomy, instead of four surrounding zones of activity, there are more than twenty near autonomous communities housing the nearly four hundred residents of Auroville, and each community has some blend of functions (residential, educational, industrial, etc.). Many of the communities were given names by the Mother like "Hope," "Aspiration," and "Promise," and the population of Auroville includes Indian, American, French, and German nationals.

The goal of building a creative, unifying community which influences surrounding peoples is to some extent realized in settlements such as Udavi (TAMIL for "Help"), where an incense factory, schools, and a deep well provide jobs, education, and self-help opportunities for nearby Tamil villagers. However, the ideal of a city of a human unity which reflects the Divine is still remote.

Bibliography. *Auroville—The First Six Years: 1968-1974* (1974).

L. D. SHINN

AUSTRALIAN TRIBAL RELIGIONS. *See* OCEANIC TRIBAL RELIGIONS.

AUTO-DA-FÉ out′ ō də fā′ (Ch—Portuguese; lit. "act of faith"). The set of solemn public ceremonies (procession, MASS, sermon), especially in Spain and Portugal from the late fifteenth to the early nineteenth centuries, linked with the publication of sentences pronounced on convicted heretics by the INQUISITION.

F. OAKLEY

AVALOKITEŚVARA ä və lō′ kĭ tĕsh vä′ rə (B—Skt; lit., "looking-on lord" [*avalokita,* "looking on," and *īśvara,* "lord"]). A BODHISATTVA whose infinite compassion for suffering beings causes him to be always available to teach and to rescue them from danger. Loved throughout the MAHĀYĀNA Buddhist world, Avalokiteśvara more than any other bodhisattva exemplifies the infinite compassion of the enlightened mind and is widely thought of as a feminine being (*see* §5). He/she realizes the ideal of all Mahāyāna Buddhists who vow to postpone freedom from suffering and delusion (i.e., Buddhahood) until they can save all other beings from suffering as well.

1. **The name Avalokiteśvara.** In Sanskrit, Avalokiteśvara might mean "the lord who looks in every direction," or "the lord of what is seen" (that is, the created world). One scholar suggests that Avalokiteśvara originated as the personification of the wise and compassionate glance *(avalokana)* which the future Śākyamuni Buddha cast from the Tuṣita Heaven upon the suffering world before entering it. Others suggest that the name means "observer of sounds, or voices," and point to Avalokiteśvara's compassionate response to any being in danger who calls upon him. Still others suggest that the term originally meant "the shining lord," the one who illumines the world. Whatever the original meaning, translations into Central and East Asian languages show that Buddhists have understood the name to refer to Avalokiteśvara's compassionate gaze. In Tibet, Avalokiteśvara is known as sPyan-ras gzigs ("with a pitying look"), and in Mongolia as Nidü-ber üjegči ("he who looks with the eyes"). In China he/she is known as Kuan-yin ("regarder of sounds," i.e., the voices of the suffering), as Kuan-shih-yin ("regarder of sounds of the world"), or as Kuan-tzu-tsai ("one who truly sees, and, transcending, is free in the existent"). In Japanese the Chinese names are pronounced as Kannon and as Kanseon. Likewise in Korea he/she is known as Kwanŭm and Kwanseiŭm. Among Avalokiteśvara's other names are Padmapāṇi ("lotus-bearer") and Lokeśvara ("Lord of the world"), the name invariably used for him in Indochina and Thailand. In Sri Lanka he is known as Nātha-deva.

2. **Avalokiteśvara in Indian Buddhism.** Sūtras, paintings, and statues show that Avalokiteśvara was widely revered in India from the third to the seventh century A.D. His virtues and powers are recounted in more than eighty sūtras. Among the earliest and most influential are the Saddharmapuṇḍarīkasūtra (the Lotus Sūtra) and the long and short Sukhāvatīvyūha Sūtra (Sūtra of the Land of Bliss, or Pure Land). In the former he appears in many guises to teach those who are destined to learn from a certain kind of being, and he rescues those who call upon or think upon him in any kind of danger. In the latter he appears as one of the two chief assistants (with Mahāsthāmaprāpta) of the Buddha Amitābha (*see* Amida) in the latter's Buddha-world, the Pure Land. These early sūtras show that he has great compassion for all beings, preaches the Dharma, destroys false views and passions, frees beings from suffering, and brings them to the joy of unconditional safety. Another sūtra portrays his journeys into the worlds of the dead to save those who are there. In later texts he is shown as "emperor of the magician kings," having supreme power in that he possesses the all-powerful six-syllable formula (Mantra), Oṃ maṇipadme Hūṃ. In still other texts we find Avalokiteśvara as both the creator of this world and the macrocosm itself.

3. **Tibet and Central Asia.** In the seventh century Avalokiteśvara was introduced into Tibet, where he quickly became the most popular Buddhist figure. There he is understood, following an Indian tradition, as the manifestation in bodhisattva form of the active compassion of the eternal Dhyāni Buddha Amitābha, whose figure is depicted in the headdress. (*See* Buddha, General Concepts of.) Avalokiteśvara protects this world in the interval between the departure of the historical Buddha, Śākyamuni, and the coming of the next Buddha to appear in this world, Maitreya. He is the creator of our world, and the protector of Tibet in particular. Tārā is his consort, and he is reincarnated in each Dalai Lama, the temporal ruler of the theocratic kingdom. (*See* Buddhism, Tibetan.)

4. **East Asia.** A number of the Indian sūtras in which Avalokiteśvara figures prominently were popular in China and Japan from very early times. In the Prajñāpāramitā Hṛdaya ("Heart") Sūtra *(Hsin Ching),* a very popular text in China and Japan, Avalokiteśvara, the speaker, enters into deep Samādhi and describes the highest wisdom about the relation of the phenomenal and ultimate realms. In the Śūraṅgama Sūtra, Avalokiteśvara, as paradigm of one on the path to Buddhahood, describes the process by which he entered into *samādhi.* The twenty-fifth chapter of the Lotus Sūtra, perhaps originally an independent text, has enjoyed wide circulation as the Avalokiteśvara Sūtra *(Kuan-yin Ching).* The sūtra teaches that if one thinks of Avalokiteśvara, fire ceases to burn, swords fall to pieces, enemies become kindhearted, bonds are loosened, spells revert to whence they came, beasts flee, and snakes lose their poison. Chinese and Japanese commentators have seen the meaning of this text on two levels. On one level, the infinite compassion of Kuan-yin is able to save beings from suffering and dangers by awakening them to their own enlightened mind. On another, more popular, level, the text's description of Avalokiteśvara's miraculous intervention on behalf of those who call upon him stands as myth, conveying belief in the bodhisattva's miraculous power to rescue and teach.

In China, Korea, and Japan, as in Tibet, the powerful assistance of Avalokiteśvara can be invoked by single-mindedly reciting certain mantras. The most popular is (in its Chinese version) *na-mu chiu-k'u chiu-nan ta-tzu ta-pei Kuan-shih-yin p'u-sa,* "homage to the one who saves from sufferings and disasters, the greatly compassionate greatly pitying bodhisattva Avalokiteśvara."

The Pure Land schools in China and Japan emphasize Avalokiteśvara's role as assistant to Amitābha in welcoming beings to the Pure Land and in ruling and teaching there. In Pure Land temples an image of Avalokiteśvara is often enshrined to the left of Amitābha, and in paintings Kuan-yin is frequently shown welcoming souls at death into the Pure Land.

5. **Avalokiteśvara as feminine.** In China, Korea, and Japan Kuan-yin has been thought of as a feminine bodhisattva. This concept, which suggests that the compassion of the enlightened bodhisattva is

like that of mother, sister, friend, and queen, can be traced to the fifth century in China, but it was not until the twelfth century that feminine representations came to predominate. Some hold that the change has roots in Indian Buddhist sūtras. One view widely held in the Buddhist world is that an advanced bodhisattva has transcended distinctions of gender, so that the combination in the original icons of Avalokiteśvara of flowing drapery, soft body contours, and a visible moustache is meant to suggest transcendence of sexual identity, not masculinity. Further, early sūtras state that Avalokiteśvara can take feminine form to teach, and the Lotus Sūtra and other scriptures establish Avalokiteśvara as the fulfiller of all wishes and the giver of children. Others hold that from at least the twelfth century Chinese worshipers of Kuan-yin have seen in the bodhisattva qualities associated with aspects of other feminine divine figures, such as HSI WANG MU, or the legendary self-sacrificing princess Miao-shan, or Tārā, the white-robed consort of Avalokiteśvara in Tibet. Others point out that a particular manifestation known as Cundī-Avalokiteśvara, "mother of seven kotis (*ca.* ten millions) of Buddhas," was known in China from the seventh century, and may have influenced the concept of Kuan-yin as feminine. None of these theories completely explains the development of this unique feminine bodhisattva, nor takes away from the fact that the Buddha's compassion and powerful aid are appropriately symbolized in feminine form. Kuan-yin's feminine representations are in perfect accord with the intimate feeling of trust and love that Chinese, Japanese, and Koreans have for the radiant, gracious, serene, and powerful bodhisattva of compassion. (*See* illustration, ART AND ARCHITECTURE, BUDDHIST.)

6. **Iconographic representations.** The earliest Indian pictorial representations of Avalokiteśvara (fifth to eighth centuries) at AJAṆṬĀ and Aurangebad show him saving beings from distress, as do contemporary early paintings at Tun-huang in China. In Indian and Tibetan writings there are two kinds of descriptions of Avalokiteśvara's manifest physical forms. The first are fantastic, unimaginable; meditation on these will bring about trance and union with the bodhisattva by confounding the imagination and rational processes. The second are precise descriptions intended as instructions for those who construct his image either in the mind or in sculpture and MANDALA painting. Here the purpose is to enable the meditator to unite with the bodhisattva by first successfully imagining his form with its symbolic meanings. Forms taken by Avalokiteśvara appropriate for meditation are quite various: one Nepalese text describes 108 distinct manifestations, while groups of 31 or 32 are common. In India, Tibet, and Nepal he is frequently depicted as Avalokiteśvara-Padmāpaṇi (lotus-bearer), wearing princely ornaments and holding a lotus blossom. As Avalokiteśvara-Siṃhanāda ("with the voice of a lion") he is depicted seated on a roaring lion, carrying a sword rising out of a lotus and a trident entwined with a snake; in this form he is invoked to cure disease. Often he is shown seated on a lotus throne in a "sportive" posture *(lalitasana),* apparently taking his ease. Another form shows him with from two to twelve arms (usually six), usually seated, holding the *cintramani* (wish-fulfilling jewel) and wheel, which symbolize his great capacity for saving beings. Two other popular forms that originate in esoteric Buddhism are Ekādaśamukha ("eleven-headed"), able to look in all directions to save creatures, and "thousand-armed," with an eye in each hand. These symbolize the power of the enlightened mind to see and respond to the different needs of all beings simultaneously, because, having moved beyond the distinction of "I" and "other," such a mind encompasses all things and moves freely without distraction. Other popular forms of Avalokiteśvara include Cundī-Avalokiteśvara (*see* §5) and the "horse-head" Avalokiteśvara, shown with a fierce face and a horse's head in the headdress (probably related to the Tibetan protector of horses, Hayagriva). All of these representations became popular in China and Japan from the eighth century A.D.

In the Avataṃsaka Sūtra and elsewhere we find descriptions of Avalokiteśvara's residence, the mountain Potalaka, which can be reached from this world. Some descriptions place it in the ocean southwest of India and Sri Lanka; the Chinese monk-pilgrim HSÜAN-TSANG mentions it as a mountain near Mt. Malaya. Potalaka is described as a rocky mountain, extremely difficult to reach. Avalokiteśvara's residence is on the top of the mountain on the shore of a lake, from which a river flows into the sea.

7. **Kuan-yin in popular religion.** More than any other Buddhist figure, Kuan-yin (Kannon) has entered fully into the religious imagination not only of Buddhists, but of all Japanese, Chinese, and Koreans. She is enshrined not only in almost all Buddhist temples, but also in most temples of TAOISM and CHINESE POPULAR RELIGION. She figures in many vernacular stories and novels (e.g., the Chinese novel *Journey to the West,* also translated as *Monkey*), funerals, popular rituals and festivals (e.g., in Taoist *p'u-tu* rites for general salvation of those souls reborn in hells). She is the first bodhisattva to whom lay people turn in time of trouble, and whom they seek to worship in gratitude for blessings.

Bibliography. M. T. Mallmann, *Introduction a l'étude d'Avalokiteçvara* (1948); G. Tucci, *Tibetan Painted Scrolls* (1949), and "Buddhist Notes I: A Propos Avalokiteśvara," *Mélanges Chinoises et Bouddiques,* XLVIII (1960), 173-219; C. N. Tay, "Kuan-yin: The Cult of Half Asia," *HR,* XVI (1976), 144-77; for a popular treatment, see J. Blofeld, *Bodhisattva of Compassion* (1978).
M. LEVERING

ĀVĀSA ä vä´ sü (H & B—Skt. & Pali; lit. "dwelling, residence"). In the Buddhist tradition a single monastic dwelling for one monk, or huts for a small group of monks located within established, preferably natural, boundaries. Originally a shelter during the three-month monsoon rains retreat *(vassa), āvāsa* refers to a specific monastic community rather than the ideal SAṄGHA ("Saṅgha of the Four Quarters"). Hence, the *āvāsa* was a locus of collective monastic meetings and the congregational precept-confessional (UPOSATHA). Monks at an *āvāsa* held goods in common, as evidenced by the equal distribution of robes presented by the laity after the rains retreat. *Āvāsas* constructed by monks themselves were distinguished from *ārāmas* ("pleasure gardens"), property donated by a lay person for the monks' use (later, *ārāma* came to denote a large monastery). *Āvāsa* referring to a collectivity was also distinguished from a VIHĀRA, which originally denoted a single dwelling. Later the term *vihāra* assumed the much broader meaning of "monastery." Likewise, *āvāsa* finally came to refer to a center of monastic resident activity and a separate ecclesiastical district rather than a temporary shelter. *See* MONASTICISM.

D. K. SWEARER

AVATAR, AVATĀRA ä´ vŭ tär (H—Skt.; lit. "a descent" [*ava-tṝ,* "to descend into"]). A human or animal identity assumed by a deity, especially VISHNU, when entering into a career on earth. The conception is not found in the VEDAS or UPANIṢADS. It is expressed first in the BHAGAVAD GĪTĀ 4.1-8, where KRISHNA confides that he has been born into the world again and again in evil times to revive true doctrine, to destroy the wicked, and to restore righteousness. The unnamed "descents" suggested here developed in the later Epics and PURĀṆAS into a widely accepted list of ten: The Fish *(Matsya)* Avatar saved MANU, the Hindu Noah, from a universal flood. The Tortoise *(Kūrma)* helped the gods obtain the nectar of immortality. The Boar *(Varāha)* raised up the drowning earth when it had sunk beneath the sea. The Man-Lion *(Narasiṃha)* saved the devotee Prahlāda from persecution. The Dwarf *(Vāmana)* in three great strides reclaimed the world from the demon Bali. Rāma-with-the-Ax *(Paraśurāma)* destroyed the KṢATRIYAS and restored the due authority of the BRAHMINS. RĀMA rescued his kidnapped wife and destroyed the demon RĀVANA. Krishna rid the world of evil king KAṂSA. The BUDDHA preserved the purity of the Vedic rites by diverting unfit humans into a new religion. At the end of our age, Kalki Avatar will unseat barbarian kings and restore the happy priestly order. This lore of divine descents counterbalanced a Hindu stress on the remoteness of the Supreme Being and sustained faith in a moral order and divine support.

In this list substitutions are common. Some delete Krishna, saying he is not an avatar of Vishnu but the Supreme Being himself. Many new avatars were added in the course of centuries. The BHĀGAVATA PURĀṆA names twenty-two but adds that the avatars are numberless. Most Hindus honor all avatars but for personal worship select their favorite.

The birth of an avatar does not occur by the usual compulsion of past KARMA, but by the deity's free and gracious choice. RĀMĀNUJA speaks of God's purpose to make his unfathomable nature accessible to the minds of his worshipers. Bengal VAIṢṆAVAS see the activity of avatars as the sportive divine self-expression (LĪLĀ), and the assisting of humanity as only the spontaneous by-product of God's enjoyment.

An original belief in the corporeality of avatars gave way before the anti-materialist feeling of later Hinduism. The ŚRI VAIṢṆAVAS believe the bodies of avatars to consist of *śuddha-sattva,* the "pure essence" of which the forms of heavenly beings are made. The Bengal Vaiṣṇavas hold that God descends to earth unchanged, his eternal form assuming only the appearance of an earthly body. The ADVAITA school understands avatars to be unreal projections, useful for provisional instruction only. These repudiations of the fleshliness of avatars make it improper now to call them incarnations.

Modern values have brought some significant alterations in avatar thought. A general distaste for mythological and miraculous elements in religion has all but terminated the worship of the animal avatars, and the entire concept of avatar was rejected by the BRĀHMO SAMĀJ and the ĀRYA SAMĀJ. But the strong moral teaching of the Bhagavad Gītā and the RĀMĀYAṆA has brought to the cults of Rāma and of Krishna the devotion of millions. In another development the use of the term "avatar" has become broader through the Bhāgavata Purāṇa's recognition that human beings can become avatars through the charismatic entry into them of the divine spirit. This view has allowed the title to be extended to powerful modern religious leaders (e.g., Mahatma GANDHI, SATYA SAI BĀBĀ, A. C. BHAKTIVEDANTA, etc.), and to such world figures as JESUS and MUHAMMAD.

Bibliography. G. Parrinder, *Avatar and Incarnation* (1970); S. L. Katre, "Avataras of God," *Allahabad University Studies,* X (1933), 37-130; H. Jacobi, "Incarnation (Indian)," *Encyclopedia of Religion and Ethics,* VII, 193-97.

N. J. HEIN

AVE MARIA ä´ vā mä rē´ ə (Ch—Lat.; lit. "Hail, Mary"). A common Catholic prayer to MARY, the

AVE MARIA

Ave Maria, gratia plena,
Dominus tecum.
Benedicta tu in mulieribus,
et benedictus fructus ventris tui, Jesus.
Sancta Maria, mater Dei,
ora pro nobis peccatoribus,
nunc, et in hora mortis nostrae.
Amen.

Hail Mary, full of grace!
The Lord is with thee.
Blessed art thou among women,
and blessed is the fruit of thy womb, Jesus.
Holy Mary, Mother of God,
Pray for us sinners,
now, and at the hour of our death.
Amen.

mother of Jesus, often set to music. The first part is based on the Annunciation and the words of Elizabeth (Luke 1:28, 42). The second part, "Holy Mary . . . pray for us sinners," evolved gradually, and took on fixed form by A.D. 1500. E. R. Carroll

AVE VERUM CORPUS ä´ vā vā´room kôr´ poos (Ch—Lat.; "Hail, true body"). First words of an anonymous fourteenth century Eucharistic hymn originally used during the silent canon of the medieval Latin Mass and later used at the Eucharistic devotion called Benediction (from the sixteenth century). R. A. Greer

AVERROES ăv ə rō´ ēz (I). *See* Ibn Rushd.

AVESTA ä vĕs´ tə (Z—Pahlavi *apastak;* lit., "basic text"). The scripture or principal sacred books of the Zoroastrians, written in an old Iranian language which is called Avestan because the Avesta is practically its only surviving example. The contents of the Avesta are largely hymns, prayers, and liturgical invocations; indeed, the recitation of portions of the Avesta constitutes one of the principal ceremonial activities of Zoroastrian priests. The Avesta also contains, in a part called the Vendīdād or Vidēvdāt (Avestan—"law against demons"), a code of the principal instructions for Zoroastrian ritual and moral practice.

1. **Composition.** The principal divisions of the Avesta are: Yasna, Visparad, Vendīdād, Yashts, and Khorda Avesta. Of these the last, whose name means "Shorter Avesta," is essentially an anthology of extracts from the others; it serves as a sort of prayerbook and is the portion of the Avesta most commonly circulated among Zoroastrians who are not practicing priests.

Of the Avestan material the five hymns known as the Gāthās ("songs") differ from the remainder by being in a different dialect, more archaic in its linguistic features and thus either older or from a different region of Iran. Found in the Yasna, these hymns reflect a distinctively personal address to God and are generally agreed by both ancient tradition and modern scholarship to be our closest record of the words of the prophet Zoroaster. They focus on the demand for righteousness, on the reward of the righteous at the end of this age, and on the sovereignty of Ahura Mazda as God. Later theologians in the Zoroastrian tradition often based their thought on interpretations of the prophet's teaching as contained in the Gāthās.

The rest of the Avesta, while linguistically less archaic, reflects religious conceptions and practices that can be argued to antedate the prophet's teaching. There are, for example, *yashts* (hymns) to various deities or spirits, some known to us also from the Vedic hymns of India, and their tone is far more ritual than moral. Yet in much of the Avesta these hymns are presented as quotations from the prophet Zoroaster. One explanation of this attribution is that the old Indo-Iranian polytheistic tradition was later given the prophet's name by way of introduction after his teachings had become influential.

2. **History.** The text of the Avesta has undergone a long period of transmission. In its present form it appears to be the result of editorial activity under the Sasanian dynasty in Iran (third to seventh centuries A.D.), under which Zoroastrianism was established as the state religion. The script adopted for Avestan resembles that used for Pahlavi, the Iranian language then current. According to one Pahlavi tradition, what survives is not all that once existed; two official copies of a fuller version of the Avesta, written in gold ink on ox-hide parchment and kept by the Achaemenid Persian kings at their capital, reportedly were destroyed when Alexander the Great conquered Persepolis in 331 B.C.

Europeans were unaware of the Avesta until the seventeenth century when, with the growth of trade with India, manuscript copies began to reach England. The first modern translation was made by A. H. Anquetil du Perron. In 1755 he made the acquaintance of Parsis in Surat, on the coast north of Bombay, where he paid a priest to teach him to read the Avestan texts. Their translation and interpretation subsequently paralleled and drew support from European study of the earliest Sanskrit literature, to which the Avesta is linguistically related. The name Zend-Avesta, used by nineteenth century European writers, is an erroneous conflation of the name Avesta, "basic text," with the term *zand,* "commentary."

Bibliography. O. Klíma, "Avesta" in J. Rypka, ed., *History of Iranian Literature* (1968), pp. 3-65; S. Insler, *The Gāthās of Zarathustra* (1976); J. Darmesteter and L. H. Mills, trans., *The Zend-Avesta (Sacred Books of the East,* Vols. 4, 23, 31) (1880-87).
W. G. Oxtoby

AVICEBRON ăv ĭ sē brôn´ (Ju). *See* Solomon ben Gabirol.

AVICENNA ăv ə sĕn´ ə (I). *See* Ibn Sīnā.

AVIDYĀ ŭ vĭd´ yä (H—Skt.; lit. "not-knowledge"). Ignorance, the ground and object of spiritual delusion, the human condition.

1. **Vedic period.** In the early *śrauta* (*see* Śruti) literature *avidyā* was merely the absence of knowledge *(vidyā)* preventing one from fulfilling the religious, ethical, and moral obligations prescribed by authority and tradition. For example, ignorance regarding the burial rites could result in an unpropitious rebirth for the deceased (BĀU I. 5.17). Overcoming *avidyā* was of particular concern to Brahmins, since precise knowledge of the Vedas was essential to their role in perpetuating and revitalizing the cosmos and society by performing and supervising the rites, as well as to their livelihood (cf. CU I.10). The necessity of knowledge in fulfilling the prescribed rites is

typically expressed as, "If, without knowing this, one performs the *agnihotra,* it would be like removing the burning coals and pouring the offering on mere ashes" (CU V.24.1).

2. **Upaniṣadic period.** Although *avidyā* is a minor speculative problem in the UPANIṢADS, the rare references to it provide important authority for later orthodox views, particularly those of ADVAITA VEDĀNTA. Certain Upaniṣadic passages state the view that *avidyā* was not merely the lack of requisite knowledge, but a state of being that clouds human minds and prevents their release. Such persons, "living immersed in *avidyā,* wise in their own estimation, believing themselves learned, are but fools walking a crooked path, the blind led by the blind" (Kaṭh. U I.2.4.) Immersed in *avidyā,* unaware of their ignorance, these are like dreamers (BĀU IV.3.20) who merely imagine their aims accomplished, when in reality each unknowing act plunges them further into bondage and SAMSARA. In order to avoid the effects of *avidyā,* it is necessary to distinguish it from *vidyā*: "He who knows *vidyā* and *avidyā* together crosses over death with *avidyā* and attains immortality with *vidyā*" (ĪU IX; Mait. U VII. 9). This view, while recognizing that *avidyā* is incomplete in itself and does not directly result in MOKṢA, insists upon its value and its correlation with *vidyā* in the attainment of immortality. The following statement locates both in the nature of the supreme being. "Hidden in the infinite imperishable Brahman are both *vidyā* and *avidyā. Avidyā* is perishable; *vidyā* is immortal; and he who controls both transcends them" (Śvet. U V.1).

3. **Śaṃkara.** The post-Vedic period completed the evolution of *avidyā* from a mere absence of knowledge regarding edifying social and religious behavior to a ubiquitous, negative, and cosmic power of spiritual and intellectual delusion. ŚAMKARA, the eighth century A.D. exponent of Advaita Vedānta, declared all forms of knowledge predicated upon distinctions (between subject and object, humans and the world, ATMAN and BRAHMAN, etc.) to be *avidyā* and illusory. In short, all alleged knowledge *(vidyā)* that does not result in union with Brahman was, spiritually, nonsense and nonknowledge, or *avidyā.* In this view, the basis of human knowing was ignorance, the object of knowledge was ignorance, and the result was mere illusion.

Śaṃkara's characterization of the human condition as one arising from, grounded in, and tending toward *avidyā* ignited metaphysical and theological discussions and traditions that were of significance within Vedānta, but had little perceptible impact on Hindu spirituality. With the exception of Baladeva (*ca.* A.D. 1750) none of the major figures following Śaṃkara accepted his elitist contention that *vidyā* alone was a sufficient cause of release.

J. HELFER

AYATOLLAH ä yä tōl′ lä (I—Arab.; lit. "Sign of God"). Among the SHI'ITES, a jurist (MUJTAHID) who is regarded by his followers as the most learned person of the age, whose righteousness and piety are well established, and whose knowledge of Islamic jurisprudence enables him to make independent judgments. The full title is *ayatollah 'uẓmā* ("the supreme"). He is backed by the authority of the infallible Shi'ite IMAM, and his legal rulings are made accessible to his followers throughout the world.

A. A. SACHEDINA

ĀYURVEDA ä′ yo͞or vā′ dŭ (H & B—Skt.; lit. "knowledge of life" [*āyus*—"life" + *veda*—"knowledge"]). An ancient and still flourishing system of medicine closely related to the development of VEDIC HINDUISM, YOGA, Hindu religious thought in general, and BUDDHISM. The classical manuals of *āyurveda* are those of Caraka (the Caraka-saṃhitā, *ca.* first century A.D.) and Suśruta (the Suśruta-saṃhitā, *ca.* fourth century A.D.), but first millennium B.C. antecedents in Vedic texts, particularly in the ATHARVA VEDA and the Kauśika Sūtra, are evident. Basic to traditional Indian medicine are certain micro-macrocosmic correspondences. The human body, like the cosmos itself, is composed of five elements—earth, water, fire, air, and ether. Combinations of these produce the three vital humors *(doṣas)* of the body—wind *(vāyu),* bile *(pitta),* and phlegm *(kapha* or *śleṣman).* Each humor is related to one of the three universal qualities (GUṆAS) and each is itself fivefold, with specific locations and functions in the body for each constituent.

Proper balance and separation of the three humors is necessary; imbalance or mixing results in disorder and disease. According to Suśruta the seven ingredients of the body are chyle, blood, flesh, fat, bone, marrow, and semen, developing in that order from digested food in the metabolic cycle. Ancient Indian medicine was particularly advanced in such techniques as lithotomy, plastic surgery, bone-setting, caesarean operation, and dietetic therapy, and in its extensive pharmacopoeia (Suśruta utilized 760 medicinal plants). Today *āyurvedic* physicians treat a large percentage of India's population, particularly in rural areas where modern physicians are scarce, and departments of *āyurveda* are maintained in traditional Hindu universities.

Bibliography. J. Filliozat, *The Classical Doctrine of Indian Medicine* (ET 1964).

D. M. KNIPE

AẒHĀR MOSQUE äz här′ (Arab.; lit. "brilliant"). Founded in Cairo under the FATIMID dynasty in the eleventh century, the MOSQUE al-Aẓhār has come to occupy a place of special prominence in the Islamic world, not as a house of worship but as a center of Islamic learning. Originally a focal point for Ismaili doctrines (*see* ISMĀ'ĪLIYYA), the mosque regained prominence as an influential SUNNI or orthodox center under the Mamluk dynasty (1250-1517), and today enjoys university status in the Egyptian Arab Republic. Its most important role in the Islamic world is as a training center for teachers, who come from many Islamic countries to study in Cairo and return to their native lands as instructors of the Islamic religion and the ARABIC LANGUAGE.

Al-Aẓhār's traditional prominence is due in large part to its central location in metropolitan Cairo, to the vast size of its buildings and its WAQF endowments, and to its survival as the only bastion of traditional Arabic Islamic learning during the many centuries of Ottoman domination of Egypt. Much of the present-day physical arrangement of the Aẓhār buildings dates from major eighteenth century reconstructions during the Ottoman period. Al-Aẓhār's virtual monopoly on religious studies in Egypt, coupled with its resistance to nationalistic reforms, led from the eighteenth century onward to its emergence as a major intellectual center of traditional Islam, while its rector, the Shaikh al-Aẓhār, assumed great prominence in the world of Sunni Islam, which increased with the abolishing of the caliphate by Ataturk in 1923.

Students at the Aẓhār mosque were organized into national groups much as were the students in the cosmopolitan medieval European universities. Rivalries among student groups were often intense; the MALIKITE, SHAF'ITE, and HANAFITE groups have been the strongest factions in recent times. Reforms instituted under khedival and later under royal and republican regimes have to some extent altered the structure, if not the fundamental directions, of al-Aẓhār. Over the past century the reforming impulse has largely originated from without as attempts have been made by various Egyptian governments to bring the somewhat anomalous status of the autonomous Aẓhār faculties into some relationship with the organizational structures of the various Egyptian state universities. These reforms have included the institution of formal examinations, uniform standards for admission, and a trilevel structuring of the al-Aẓhār University into primary, secondary, and upper divisions.

The resistance of al-Aẓhār to reform has led to a paradoxical situation: its prestige in Egypt has suffered because its graduates have found difficulty in finding positions upon graduation, while its conservativism and devotion to traditional Islamic values have increased its standing among devout Muslims in other Islamic lands. Today al-Aẓhār is still the primary training center for IMAMS in the Islamic world, and its influence as a major missionary force for Islam all over the world attests to the continued importance of its traditional approach to Islamic learning. *See* MADRASA.

Bibliography. J. Jomier, "Al-Azhar," *EI;* I. Salama, *L'enseignement islamique en Egypte* (1939).

W. DENNY

B

BAAL SHEM TOV bôl shĕm tōv (Ju; 1700-1760—Heb.; lit. "master of the Good Name" or "good master of the Name"; yields acronym "Besht"). The popular name for Israel ben Eliezer, founder of Eastern European HASIDISM. The details of his life and teachings must be extracted from traditional biographies and disciples' reports that mix fact with legend according to the Hasidic idealization of the personality and deeds of its leaders.

He was born in Poland and orphaned at an early age. After serving for a time as a minor functionary in a SYNAGOGUE, where one of his jobs was to accompany children back and forth to school, he retired to the Carpathian mountains with his second wife, living in relative seclusion, working at menial jobs, and spending much time with nature. Later he and his wife operated an inn. When he turned thirty-six, Israel revealed himself as a charismatic miracle healer, a *Baal Shem*, who cured people by writing amulets using the mystico-magical names of God. He attracted a circle of devoted disciples that included scholars, preachers, and rabbis. The biographies abound with stories of the Besht's many travels, his exorcisms, miraculous cures, ecstatic visions, ransoming of captives, his encounters with all types of people, and his intense experiences at PRAYER.

The Besht's teaching emphasized the uplifting of fallen spirits. He was opposed to self-recrimination or melancholy and to any practice or mood that fostered them. According to the Lurianic KABBALA, all reality was composed of a captive spark of God's divinity whose redemption or liberation depends on the individual's deeds. The Besht's psychological and personal understanding of these doctrines of God's presence in all things, and the elevation of these sparks within and by the individual, characterize all later Hasidic elaborations of his ideas. To recognize God's reality within all things meant seeing things from God's perspective, rather than from the ordinary, human point of view. This is the achievement of the true ZADDIK, the Hasidic master.

As God descends into the concrete forms of life, so too the zaddik joins in perpetual communion with God, descends to the ordinary, to the everyday, and to the people, and as God's agent lifts the everyday, even the profane, into the redemptive aura of holiness. This doctrine was personified by the example of the Besht.

After his death his disciples transformed his life and teaching into a pietistic and enthusiastic religious movement.

Bibliography. D. Ben-Amos and J. R. Mintz, eds., *In Praise of the Baal Shem Tov* (1970).
K. P. BLAND

BĀB bäb (Ba—Arab. & Per.; lit. "Gateway"). The title claimed by Sayyid Ali Muhammad of Shiraz (1819/20-1850), founder of the new religion of the BĀBĪS (*see* BAHĀ'Ī §1). His religion had a strong eschatological focus upon a future figure called "He Whom God Shall Manifest," later taken by Bahā'īs to mean BAHĀ' ULLĀH; it also rejected many of the teachings of the Islamic SHARIA and developed a distinctive metaphysic of its own. The Bāb and his followers were severely persecuted by the Persian authorities, and he himself was imprisoned and then executed in 1850. His principal teachings are contained in the two *Bayān* (one each in ARABIC and Persian).
C. J. ADAMS

BABYLONIAN CAPTIVITY OF THE CHURCH (Ch). A pejorative phrase, coined by the Italian humanist Petrarch to characterize the period when the PAPACY was located at Avignon in southern France from 1309 to 1377. The metaphor is based on the captivity of the ancient Israelites in Babylon (586-538 B.C.). *See* GREAT SCHISM.
H. L. BOND

BADGE, JEWISH. A distinctive mark to set off Jews from the rest of the population. To be worn on clothing under force of law, it varied in shape, size, and color. The first records of special Jewish dress date from the Fourth Lateran Council (1215). Abrogated at the end of the eighteenth century, the badge was reintroduced by the Nazis (*see* HOLOCAUST).
E. FLEISCHNER

BAECK, LEO bĕk (Ju; 1873-1956). German RABBI, philosopher, and historian of religion. In *The Essence of Judaism* (1936) he stresses the dialectical relationship between mystery and command. Influenced by HERMANN COHEN, he maintained that piety and ritual functioned in the service of ethics. During the HOLOCAUST he was imprisoned in Theresienstadt.

L. FAGEN

BAHĀ'Ī bä hä´ ī (Arab. & Per.; lit. "glory [of God]"). The faith founded by Mīrzā Ḥusayn Ali, known as BAHĀ' ULLĀH ("The Glory of God") in Iran in the mid-nineteenth century. It spread to Europe, America, and elsewhere under the successors of Bahā' Ullāh; the main tenets are the unity of all religions and the unity of all humankind. Its principal center is located in Haifa, Israel, near the graves of Bahā' Ullāh and his predecessor, the BĀB.

1. **History.** Bahā'ī is the outgrowth of a movement known as Bābism inaugurated by Mīrzā Ali Muhammad (1819-50) of Shiraz, an important city in southern Iran. In 1844 this young man, who was a direct descendant of the prophet MUHAMMAD, proclaimed himself to be the Bāb (lit. "gate" or "door"). The concept of the Bāb owes its origin to the doctrines of the Twelver SHI'A sect of Islam (*see* IMĀMIYYA), who believe that the twelfth in the series of their imams (divinely appointed leaders), who disappeared from human view, is still alive and is to come again at the end of time as the Imam Mahdī ("rightly guided imam") to initiate an era of justice and peace. During the early part of the twelfth Imam's occultation he maintained communication with his followers through a series of chief disciples who bore the title Bāb, signifying that they were the channels for contact with the hidden divinely appointed spiritual leader. In the early nineteenth century an Iranian Shi'ite sect called the Shaykhīs revived the notion of the awaited imam and sent representatives all over Iran to search for him. Mīrzā Ali Muhammad was a Shaykhī, as were his earliest and most important followers. By proclaiming himself the Bāb, he set himself up as the forerunner of one who was to come after him, "He Whom God Shall Manifest," identified by the Bahā'īs as Bahā' Ullāh. The claims of the Bāb for himself evolved far beyond the notion of a "forerunner" for another; in time he taught that he himself was the expected imam, the very "Point" of a new revelation. In Shi'ite Iran this proclamation had political as well as religious implications, and as a result there was much persecution of the Bābīs, as the Bāb's followers were known.

Following his proclamation, the Bāb quickly gathered disciples and began to seek converts throughout Iran. Eighteen of the closest of the disciples, called by the Bāb "The Letters of the Living," have a special importance for Bābī history and thought. With the success of the new movement came opposition from the authorities and the clergy; the opposition increased greatly following a convention in 1848 in Khurasan, where the Bābīs declared their secession from ISLAM and the abrogation of its sacred law. After a series of uprisings that resulted in massacres of Bābīs and widespread persecution, the Bāb himself was put to death by a firing squad in Tabriz in July of 1850, having spent much of the previous six years in prison. The persecution, however, took on a new sharpness after an attempt in 1852 on the life of Nāṣir al-Dīn Shāh by two Bābīs enraged by the persecution. This led to more massacres and to the exile from Iran of the leading surviving Bābī figures, among them Bahā' Ullāh and his half brother, Mīrzā Yaḥyā, also known as Ṣubḥ-i Azal ("The Dawn of Eternity").

Bahā' Ullāh, often called "The Blessed Perfection" by his followers, the son of a nobleman and minister at the court of the Qājār Dynasty, was born in Tehran in November, 1817. He had no formal education but showed an early inclination toward religion. He was one of the earliest disciples of the Bāb, though he never met him personally, and he suffered all the hardships to which the Bābīs were subjected.

While in prison in 1852 as a victim of the fierce persecution of that time, Bahā' Ullāh had a mystical experience in which he detected the first indication of his prophetic mission. The following year he went into exile in Iraq. There, in 1863 in a garden on the outskirts of Baghdad called the Garden of Riḍwān, he declared to a small group of followers that he was "He Whom God Shall Manifest," the figure predicted by the Bāb. Soon afterward he was banished to Istanbul and then to Adrianople, where he remained for five years and began publicly to proclaim his mission. The Adrianople period is marked by a series of letters which Bahā' Ullāh sent to various world rulers and also by the appearance of factionalism in the emigré Bābī community. A split between the majority who accepted Bahā' Ullāh's claims and a minority who followed his brother, Ṣubḥ-i Azal, as the Bāb's legitimate successor led to friction and violence and provided the grounds for the banishment of one faction to Acre and the other to Cyprus. The fundamental cause of the division was Bahā' Ullāh's conviction that he represented an entirely new divine dispensation, a universal religion, that went beyond the narrowly Shi'ite associations of Bābism.

The latter part of Bahā' Ullāh's life was lived out in Palestine in Acre and vicinity as a more or less strictly guarded prisoner. The most important of his many works were composed during this time, and the organization and propaganda of the community were slowly nurtured. Upon his death, after some controversy, leadership of the community passed to one of his two sons, known as 'ABDUL-BAHĀ ("The Servant of Bahā"), who had been designated in his father's will as the "Center of the Covenant," the "Model of Bahā'ī Life," and as his successor.

The spread of Bahā'ī beyond the Middle East was largely the work of 'Abdul-Bahā, who had shared in

Bahā' Ullāh's travels and tribulations. When he was released from prison by the Turks in 1908, he set out on a series of missionary journeys which took him to Egypt, Europe, and America, in each of which he established branches of the community. Propagation of the Bahā'ī faith in America had actually begun around 1892 through the efforts of Ibrāhīm George Khayrullāh, a Lebanese convert and immigrant, and from 1898 onward there were Bahā'ī pilgrims to Acre from the United States. Today the United States is the principal stronghold of the faith outside Iran, though there are Bahā'ī communities in more than two hundred countries. 'Abdul-Bahā also performed the important function of interpreting his father's teachings to the community, and he is chiefly responsible for the elaboration of Bahā'ī doctrine as it is known in the Western world.

After the death of 'Abdul-Bahā in 1920 the leadership was assumed by his grandson, SHOGHI EFFENDI Rabbani, who had been designated in the will of his predecessor as "Guardian of the Cause of God." Much of the work of consolidating the worldwide community, of creating its characteristic institutions, of establishing the central administrative headquarters in Haifa, and of translating the works of Bahā' Ullāh was done by Shoghi Effendi or under his direction. Throughout most of his career as leader Shoghi Effendi lived in Haifa, where he died in 1957.

2. **Beliefs.** The Bahā'ī faith is largely practical in its orientation, giving much greater attention to ethical and social teachings than to theological speculation or metaphysics. It differs in this way from Bābism. There is also a distinct difference between Bahā'ī in Iran, where it retains more of its original flavor, and Bahā'ī in the Western world, where the social and ethical emphasis is stronger. Bahā'ī does, however, have certain doctrines laid down in the teachings of the founder and his successors. Bahā'īs hold that God in himself is a completely unknowable essence who, however, mainfests himself in a number of ways. One of the principal ways is the creation of the world itself, which, together with traditional Islamic philosophers, the Bahā'īs think of as an eternal process, since it has always been and always will be the nature of God to manifest himself. For religious purposes, however, the special manifestation or theophany of God in the prophets is of more importance. There has been a series of these theophanies beginning with Adam, the first prophet, and continuing through the life of Jewish prophets, JESUS, and Muhammad, who in turn has been succeeded and superseded by Bahā' Ullāh. For the Bahā'īs the Bāb was only a forerunner, whose importance disappeared with the advent of "He Whom God Shall Manifest" (i.e., Bahā' Ullāh), and they give correspondingly little attention to his writings and teachings. Each prophet in the series foretold the coming of his successor, and each new manifestation was invariably scorned and rejected by most followers of his predecessor. There is also a place in Bahā'ī theology for other great religious, though nonprophetic, figures such as the BUDDHA. Each prophet or founder represents a divine dispensation appropriate for the time in which he appeared; thus the history of religions shows a progressive evolution toward an ever higher realization of the divine truth. While all religions have been at one in teaching the same truth, Bahā'ī is nonetheless held superior to others because it is the latest of the divine dispensations, the abrogator of preceding dispensations, the initiator of a new cycle of prophecy to replace that which came to an end with the Bāb, and the religion most suitable for this scientific age. Bahā'ī belief also includes the possibility of other prophets still to come in the distant future. Indeed, there can be no end to this process, no final revelation, and no last prophet. The very heart of Bahā'ī piety, however, is devotion to the person of Bahā' Ullāh, who is looked upon as himself divine in the sense that he reflects the divine nature and attributes in himself as a theophany. Other Bahā'ī beliefs include immortality, which is spiritual in nature, though they give little attention to the details of the hereafter and consider HEAVEN AND HELL to be only symbols of man's progress or lack of progress in the spiritual realm.

3. **Scriptures.** The Bahā'īs look upon all the writings of the founder and his successors as revelations and, therefore, as SCRIPTURES. Most are in PERSIAN, though there are writings in ARABIC and some in English (from Shoghi Effendi) as well. The most important of this considerable body of material are the *Kitāb al-Aqdas* ("The Most Holy Book"), which gives the fullest account of the laws and ordinances instituted by Bahā' Ullāh, the *Kitāb-i Īqān* ("The Book of Certitude"), *Haft Wādī* ("The Seven Valleys"), and *al-Kalimat al-Maknūnah* ("The Hidden Words"). The great Persian writing of the Bāb, the *Bayān* ("Statement or Explanation") is considered to have been superseded by the revelations of Bahā' Ullāh, as have the previous scriptures.

4. **Social teachings.** Bahā'ī teachings have as their goal the improvement of the conditions of human life. The most fundamental is the belief in the unity of the human race. Consequently, Bahā'ī rejects all racial, political, or other prejudice and insists upon equal rights for the sexes. Strongly pacifist in its orientation, Bahā'ī envisages world peace as one of its goals and urges its followers not to do military service. The faith is especially insistent on the elimination of religious prejudice because of its teaching that all religions constitute a vast unity, progressively unfolding a single truth. There is also much concern for the state of the poor and the oppressed; both poverty and great wealth should be eliminated and resources shared among all. The ultimate social goal is a kind of world government in which the principles of equality and justice will prevail. To this end Bahā'ī advocates the use of an

international language and the establishment of an international tribunal.

5. **Organization.** Bahā'īs are organized into a multi-tiered administrative system with local spiritual councils and national spiritual assemblies, chosen by election, and culminating in a universal spiritual assembly known as the Universal House of Justice. This body has administrative, judicial, and legislative functions, and has the right to frame new rules for situations not provided for in the teachings of the founder. Instruction and interpretation of doctrine for the community are provided by the "Guardian of the Cause of God," a hereditary post in the line of descent of Bahā' Ullāh. The Guardian is assisted by a group of "Hands of the Cause of God" whom he appoints. The administrative structure of the Bahā'ī community serves as the model for the world order toward which Bahā'ī ultimately aims. There are no priests, though the community builds temples in various places, one of the most important being in Wilmette, Illinois, beside Lake Michigan.

Bibliography. Besides the writings of Bahā'Ullāh see J. E. Esselmont, *Baháulláh and the New Era* (1923).

C. J. ADAMS

BAHĀ' ULLĀH bä hä´ ül läh´ (Ba; 1817-1892—Arab. & Per.; lit. "Glory of God"). Religious name of Mīrzā Ḥusayn Ali Nūrī, founder of Bahā'ī, known to his followers as "The Blessed Beauty" or "The Ancient Beauty." Bahā' Ullāh was among the earliest converts to the movement known as Bābism, and in 1863 he proclaimed himself "He Whom God Shall Manifest"as foretold by the BĀB. His declaration produced a schism in the Babī community and led to intrigue and violence. Bahā' Ullāh was the victim of persecution and banishment several times during his life. In 1863 he was banished to Adrianople, and then in 1868 to Acre in Palestine, where he ended his days a lightly guarded prisoner.

Bahā' Ullāh claimed to be the founder of a new universal religion which superseded that of the Bāb, who had, in his turn, superseded the prophets before him. He is believed by Bahā'īs to be a theophany, a mirror wherein the nature of the unknowable God is faithfully reflected. His numerous writings, therefore, are considered to be revelations. His most important book, *Kitāb al-Aqdas* ("The Most Holy Book"), contains detailed instructions for Bahā'ī life.

Bibliography. Shoghi Effendi, *God Passes By* (1945).

C. J. ADAMS

BAHIR bä hēr´ (Ju). *See* SEFER BAHIR.

BALARĀMA bäl ŭ rä´ mŭ (H—Skt.; lit. "strong-armed RĀMA"). Born as the elder brother of KRISHNA, Balarāma was said to be the incarnation of the serpent ŚESA upon which VISHNU reclines in the cosmic ocean. His divine origin was evidenced in his death, when, according to Purāṇic traditions, a serpent issued from his mouth.

L. D. SHINN

BALFOUR DECLARATION (Ju). Popular title for the statement of British sympathy for the establishment of a Jewish homeland in Palestine. These intentions were communicated by Foreign Secretary Arthur Balfour to Lord Rothschild on November 2, 1917. Balfour, a former Prime Minister, had previously displayed support for the Zionist cause.

With the entry of the Turks, proprietors of Palestine, on the side of the Central Powers in World War I, many envisioned a mutual confluence of Zionist and English aims. The Zionists saw in Britain a power able to help create the desired homeland. The British, aside from some desire to facilitate such a creation, viewed support for the Zionist cause as a means of strengthening their foothold in the Mid-East and enlisting American Jewish support for the war effort.

The Balfour Declaration by no means represented unequivocal support for the Zionist cause. It favored a Jewish national home, providing "nothing shall be done which may prejudice the civil and religious rights of existing non-Jewish communities in Palestine." Further, the Sykes-Picot Treaty of 1916 and other British statements were at variance with its very spirit and exhibited British intentions to maintain a stronghold in Palestine or support the creation of an Arab state. *See* HERZL, THEODOR; ZIONISM.

Bibliography. W. Lacqueur, *A History of Zionism* (1972); H. Sachar, *The History of Israel* (1976); L. Stein, *The Balfour Declaration* (1961).

D. J. SCHNALL

BĀLI bä´ lē (also known as **VĀLI** vä´ lē). Monkey king of Kiśkindhā. His story is narrated in the RĀMĀYAṆA. While Bāli was away from the kingdom fighting the demon Māyāvi, his younger brother Sugrīva usurped the throne. Bāli returned and banished his brother, who took refuge on Mt. Ṛsyamūka. Sugrīva made an alliance with RĀMA, and while Bāli and Sugrīva were fighting, Rāma killed Bāli by shooting an arrow from behind a tree.

V. N. RAO

BĀṆA bä´ nŭ (H). Revered as the greatest writer of SANSKRIT prose, Bāṇa, or Bāṇabhaṭṭa, was a protégé of the Buddhist emperor Harṣa (A.D. 606-47). His two major works, both incomplete, are the *Harṣacarita,* a historical epic based on the life of his patron, and the *Kādambarī,* an involved prose romance.

J. BARE

BANĀRAS bŭ när´ ŭs. *See* HINDU SACRED CITIES.

BAPTISM (Ch). A ritual washing for initiation; the sign of remission of sin and spiritual rebirth through symbolic (sacramental) participation in Christ's death, burial, and RESURRECTION.

1. **Background to Christian baptism.** Purificatory washings were common in JUDAISM, and one use in particular, i.e., the initiation of proselytes, is thought

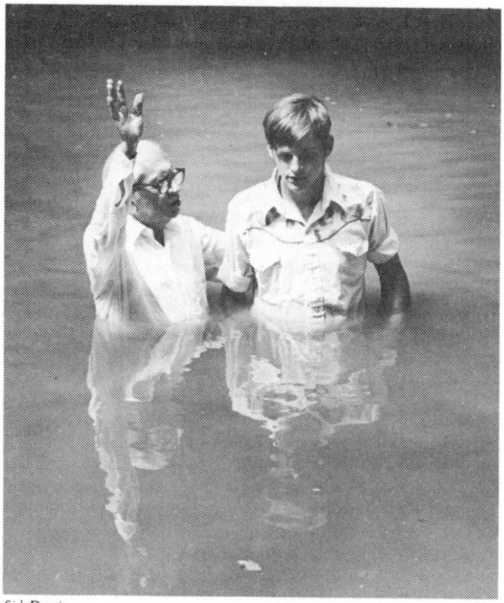

Sid Dorris

Traditional creek baptizing, Hollis Chapel General Baptist Church, Tennessee

by many to lie behind the baptism administered by JOHN THE BAPTIST. His baptism, however, called Jews as well as Gentiles to repentance and baptism for the remission of sins, an ethical dimension not found in ritual purification as such. It is in the context of his baptism by John that the NT places the beginning of the public ministry of JESUS (Mark 1:2-11 and parallels).

2. **Baptism in the New Testament.** While the NT makes some reference to baptism during the ministry of Jesus (John 3:22-23; 4:1-2), it is from PENTECOST that it is clearly the rite of initiation into the Christian community (Acts 2:38, 41). For PAUL baptism is a washing away of sin (I Cor. 6:11), a personal union with Christ (Gal. 3:27), and a salvation event in which one dies and rises with Christ (Rom. 6:1-11). The Gospel of John presents Jesus as saying that one can enter the kingdom of God only if he is "born of water and the Spirit" (John 3:5). Some have seen this reference to the Spirit as pointing to a related but distinct initiatory act such as the laying on of hands in Acts 8:14-17, but most writers see the action of the HOLY SPIRIT in baptism itself.

3. **Early Christian initiation.** In the third century in Syria there was an anointing before baptism, while in North Africa baptism was followed by anointing and the imposition of the hand. In *The Apostolic Tradition* (commonly taken to reflect the usage of ROME, *ca.* 215) there is an exorcistic anointing before baptism, an anointing with "oil of thanksgiving" after baptism, and still another anointing with the same oil, accompanied by the imposition of the BISHOP'S hand, before the assembled congregation. This last action is frequently understood to be the seed of the separate act of "confirmation" in the Western church. In Eastern ORTHODOX CHURCHES baptism is followed by chrismation, anointing with a perfumed oil analogous to the oil of thanksgiving.

4. **Baptism and profession of faith.** All such anointings were discarded by the churches of the PROTESTANT REFORMATION, though many retained a rite of CONFIRMATION as later ratification of vows made at infant baptism. The NT makes no clear reference to infant baptism, and whether infants were baptized in the primitive church remains in dispute. Tertullian opposed the practice, but others in the third century seem to take it for granted. Certainly adult baptism was the norm for the early church, and it was this which the process of instruction presupposed. This process (catechesis) frequently lasted three years or more, ending with solemn baptism at EASTER. Although immersion seems to have been most common in the patristic age, baptism by pouring is recognized as early as the Didache (early second century). Some today (e.g., BAPTISTS) insist on baptism by immersion and only upon profession of faith.

Bibliography. W. F. Flemington, *The New Testament Doctrine of Baptism* (1964); R. Schnackenburg, *Baptism in the Thought of St. Paul.* T. J. TALLEY

BAPTISM IN THE HOLY SPIRIT (Ch). The promise of Jesus, realized on the day of PENTECOST when 120 disciples "were all filled with the Holy Spirit, and began to speak in other tongues, as the Spirit gave them utterance" (Acts 2:4; cf. Acts 8:17; 10:45-46; 19:6).

Twentieth century PENTECOSTAL CHURCHES see baptism in the Holy Spirit as an experience subsequent to conversion, with the "initial evidence" of speaking in tongues (GLOSSOLALIA). The CHARISMATIC MOVEMENT in the traditional churches tends to define the experience as a "release of the Spirit" that one had already received at water baptism. H. V. SYNAN

BAPTIST CHURCHES (Ch). Descendants of the spiritual ferment of seventeenth century English PURITANISM. Characteristically, Baptists believe in the authority of the BIBLE, the right of private interpretation (soul liberty), the BAPTISM of adults only, a regenerate church membership, and the separation of church and state.

Baptists originated in two separate movements: General and Particular, names derived from their theories of atonement. General Baptists believe in a universal or general atonement in which Christ died for all, while Particular Baptists believe in the limited or "particular" death of Christ for believers only.

John Smyth (*ca.* 1554-1612), who gathered a congregation in Gainsborough, England and moved it to Amsterdam in 1608 to find religious liberty, is generally regarded as the first English Baptist. It was while his congregation was in Holland, however, that the practice of baptizing only adults began. Thomas Helwys (*ca.* 1550-1616), one of the members of this church, became disenchanted with the direction that the Amsterdam congregation was taking—particularly its association with continental ANABAPTISTS—and returned to England, where he founded the first Baptist church in that country.

Particular Baptists began in 1638 when a small group left the separatist congregation founded by Henry Jacobs (1562-1624) over the issue of baptism. The practice of baptism by immersion seems to have been instituted shortly after the group was formed.

In the United States some Massachusetts settlers had Baptist leanings. Henry Dunster (1609-59), the first President of Harvard, was among them. ROGER WILLIAMS is usually given credit for establishing the first Baptist church in the New World at Providence, Rhode Island in 1639. The center of Baptist life in the colonial period, however, was in Philadelphia, where a strong "association" of churches was centered.

During the GREAT AWAKENING, many CONGREGATIONALISTS left the established churches of New England and joined separatist churches. In time, many of these congregations became Baptist, giving the denomination a distinct bias toward REVIVALISM.

In the early part of the nineteenth century Baptists became committed to the missionary movement and began to establish regional and national organizations (conventions) to coordinate activities involving more than one congregation. The strongest of these, the Triennial Convention, divided in 1844-45, leaving white Baptists separated into a northern and a southern group.

Following the Civil War, the number of black Baptist churches increased rapidly. Although the seeds of this expansion antedate the war, the primary reason for this growth was the appeal of Baptist principles to men and women who had recently won their freedom. Black Baptist churches were free to conduct their own affairs without interference from the white society around them. (*See* BLACK RELIGIONS IN THE UNITED STATES §1a.)

Today, although Baptists are strongest in the United States, there are Baptist churches in 122 countries. The major American Baptist organizations are the Southern Baptist Convention; the American Baptist Churches in the U.S.A. (earlier Northern Baptist Convention); the National Baptist Convention in the USA, and the National Baptist Convention of America.

Bibliography. R. Torbet, *A History of the Baptists* (1963).

G. MILLER

BAR KOCHBA bär kōk′ bä (Ju—Aram.; lit. "son of the star"). Claimant to the title of MESSIAH, who led the Jewish nation in a second revolt against Rome (A.D. 132-35). Bar Kochba was supported by Jews from all over the Roman Empire, including the great rabbi AKIBA. An independent Jewish state was proclaimed, and coinage issued. The revolt, concentrated in Judea and the coastal plain, was finally crushed by overwhelming Roman military force, and JERUSALEM was destroyed. Letters found in recent excavations of rebel-occupied caves in the Judean desert confirm the strong religious convictions of the rebels.

Bibliography. Y. Yadin, *Bar-Kokhba* (1971).

E. M. MEYERS

BAR (BAT) MITZVAH bär (bät) mĭtz′ vä (Ju—Heb.; lit. "son [daughter] of the commandment," i.e., one obliged to fulfill the commandments of the TORAH). The term denotes (1) arrival at religious and legal maturity and (2) the occasion on which this status is formally assumed and celebrated. Talmudic law designated the age of religious and legal responsibility for boys as thirteen years plus one day, and for girls twelve plus one day. Although the term appears in the TALMUD to designate one who is obliged to observe the law (*Baba Metzia* 96a), its modern use does not appear before the fifteenth century. No references to a special celebration for a girl, the bat mitzvah, is found before the nineteenth century, and this ceremony is observed far less frequently than bar mitzvah.

The central element in the celebration is the calling up of the boy or girl to read the Torah in the SYNAGOGUE, usually on the first SABBATH after his or her thirteenth birthday. He or she reads or chants the prescribed BENEDICTIONS, as well as (in most cases) the concluding part of the Pentateuch reading and the prophetic lesson.

The chief ritual obligation traditionally imposed on a boy reaching the age of bar mitzvah is to put on the TEFILLIN for the daily morning service.

Bibliography. H. Schauss, *The Lifetime of a Jew* (1950); C. Roth, in A. I. Katsh, ed., *Bar Mitzvah* (1955), pp. 15-22.

B. MARTIN

American Jewish Archives, Hebrew Union College—Jewish Institute of Religion

A bar mitzvah celebrant reads the Torah as his father and the rabbi look on.

BARAITA bə rī´ tä (Ju—Aram.; lit. "outside"). 1. A statement of one of the TANNAIM; 2. a collection of such statements, as in the TOSEFTA; 3. the other literature of the Tannaim not in the MISHNAH of JUDAH HA-NASI.

Y. SHAMIR

BARDO THODÖL bär´ dō tō dəl´ (B—Tibetan; *Bar Do,* "between state"; *THos gRol,* "liberation through hearing"). A text of TIBETAN BUDDHISM, more commonly known as "The Tibetan Book of the Dead." The concern of the book is the liberation of a person during the period from the time of death until he or she enters another incarnation. This is the *bardo,* or "intermediate state." The book contains instructions for those attending the dying person, characterizations of the intermediate or *bardo* plane of existence, and the means for seeking salvation, "the great liberation by hearing" *(thodöl),* while in the *bardo.* It has served not only as a ritual text for Buddhist practice in Tibet but also as a philosophical and psychological source for students of the Tantric traditions. (*See* TANTRISM.)

1. **Texts and translations.** Traditionally it is believed that the Bardo Thodöl was composed by PADMA-SAMBHAVA and written down by his wife Yeshe Tsogyal. It is counted as one of the hidden or buried texts that was brought to light by Karma-Lingpa in the fourteenth century. It is also counted as a text of the Nyingmapa sect, founded by Padma-Sambhava, although variant texts are said to exist among other sects, including a Mongolian version. The Tibetan text on which recent translations are based was prepared by E. Kalsang in 1969 from a variety of manuscripts that had come through the Trungpa lineage of the Kargyupa sect. Translators have usually introduced changes from variant handwritten or block printed texts.

For some time Western interpretation of the Bardo Thodöl was dominated by the English translation of Dawa-Samdup and Evans-Wentz, which was itself retranslated into French and German. The effect was to view the text as an example of a universal GNOSTICISM or THEOSOPHY, or as a symbolic psychological text, as did Carl Jung. There is a modernizing tendency, even among some of the refugee interpreters, such as Chögyam Trungpa, that overlooks the magical-ritualistic aspects of the text in the interest of psychological interpretation.

2. **The context of the Bardo Thodöl.** *a) Death ceremonies.* The Bardo Thodöl is to be used in rituals at the time of death and for up to forty-nine days afterward, at the end of which, it is believed, the person enters a new incarnation. A LAMA or YOGIN is summoned at the approach of death. He is seated near the head of the dying person, and the lamenting relatives are dismissed. In the silence he addresses the dying person with chants to effect "the ejection of the consciousness" from the body and direct it to the Western Paradise of Amitābha (*see* AMIDA). If this is successful, then the *bardo* existence is avoided completely. While watching for the final signs of death, the officient reads to the person instructions from the Bardo Thodöl for obtaining liberation. This reading continues after death, with the corpse tied in a sitting position. After four days, disposal is usually made of the corpse. After the funeral a lama returns to the home of the deceased for up to seven weeks to read the Bardo Thodöl to an effigy or picture of the dead person. The length and complexity of these after-death rituals vary greatly, with few extending for the whole forty-nine days.

b) The terma *tradition.* These death rites, which are the setting for the Bardo Thodöl in Tibetan life, are probably pre-Buddhist with their origins in the SHAMANISM of BÖN. However, the work as a whole embodies a sophisticated Buddhist philosophy and psychology that go far beyond its origins in shamanistic rituals. The belief that this text is one of the *termas,* or "hidden texts," indicates an inner development as later traditions came to be related to earlier ones by redaction. The idea of a text disappearing and then being miraculously rediscovered suggests points at which later ethical, philosophical, and psychological ideas were grafted onto an earlier ritualistic tradition. Internal evidence shows signs of a tension between the devotees of an intellectual, ethical, meditative tradition, and the illiterate, the boorish, or ethically careless who seek salvation by magical rituals.

3. **The structure of the Bardo.** The forty-nine days of *bardo* existence are divided into three unequal periods.

a) The *Chikhai Bardo,* the state of a person at the moment of death, may extend up to four days, depending on how long it takes the consciousness to be separated from the body. If a person has good KARMA, has been properly instructed, is given to meditation, and is assisted properly by a lama at the moment of death, he may attain immediate salvation by union with the DHARMAKĀYA along the "Great Straight Upward Path." This first *bardo* is one of luminosity in which the great light of reality overwhelms the dying person. Unfortunately, few reach liberation at this point. But for those who were properly instructed, it is possible to perceive the unity between the luminosity of their own minds, symbolized by the female Buddha *Samantabhadri,* and the luminosity of the ultimate voidness of all reality, symbolized by the male Buddha *Samantabhadra.*

b) The *Chönyid Bardo* is entered by all who do not reach liberation along the "Great Straight Upward Path." It lasts fourteen days, during which the person is confronted with brilliant visions of the peaceful and wrathful deities. The attending lama gives the deceased instruction on how to be freed of either the allurement or terror of these gods and thus to obtain the tranquillity of mind needed for liberation. The vivid characterizations of the deities have repeatedly been given powerful expression in the Tibetan *tankas* (paintings on silk).

The peaceful and wrathful deities are not separate beings sent to help or hinder the salvation of the deceased, nor do they represent some higher order of reality in which a person believes. Rather the deities are projections of the karmic forces binding the mind of the deceased. As they now appear in this externalized form, these deities still have the capacity of all karma to bind the mind and prevent liberation. As the deities appear, the deceased must be prepared to recognize their true nature. So the attending lama admonishes the person to give up all desire and fear, remember the TRIRATNA, and "recognize whatever appears as my projection and know it to be a vision in the *bardo*. . . . I will not fear the peaceful and wrathful [deities], my own projections."

c) The *Sidpa Bardo* extends for about three weeks. In this stage the chances for liberation are slight. The luminosity of the first two stages of the *bardo* has now faded into a gray twilight. At this stage a person is drawn again toward SAMSARA and ultimately enters a womb to be born once more. The deceased comes before the Lord of Death to have his good and evil deeds counted out before him. Yet no matter what terrors are inspired at the thought of impending judgment, the deceased may realize that even the Lord of Death is only an appearance of his own karma. Failing this insight, he receives a vision of the six worlds of samsara into which he may be born. One last strategem remains to prevent birth. It is a series of meditations "to close the door of the womb." The person in the third stage of *bardo* is increasingly drawn to watching couples having sexual intercourse. But if by meditation he is able to see the man and woman as the male and female aspects of the Buddha, he may find in their union a means for preventing entry into a womb. One thin thread of hope is left. The person may at the last moment gain the needed insight and in revulsion from samsara be given special rebirth into the PURE LAND or Western Paradise.

4. **Philosophy and psychology of the Bardo Thodöl.** One meaning of *bardo* is immediately evident in the text: it is the forty-nine-day period between death and rebirth in which a person may reach liberation. Yet the text also makes it clear that the *bardo* is immanent in all of life. The word means "gap" or "interval of suspension" and refers to a time of uncertainty. Its usual translations as "after-death state" or "intermediate state" limit its meaning to characterizations of some supposed form of life after death. But *bardo* also means "state of uncertainty" and, as such, may characterize all existence in samsara. This opens the way to the psychological interpretation of the text in which the appearances, particularly in the second stage of *bardo*, are viewed as symbolic expressions of paranoia, guilt, fear, and uncertainty. The words spoken by the lama are the means for resolving these experiences that occur in all of life, not simply a resource given to the dead in their struggle with rebirth. The psychological interpretations of the *bardo*, however, distort the text when they are used in a modernizing apologetic fashion to play down its use in the ritual life of Tibetan Buddhism.

As encounter is made in the second stage of *bardo* with the peaceable and wrathful deities, their true meaning is found to be that they are projections of the karmic forces that have left their indelible imprint on the mind. These deities are not beings on some higher than human plane of existence but externalizations of the self. In this teaching the Tibetans anticipated by centuries the analysis of the gods as psychological projections made by Feuerbach and Freud. In secular Western thought awareness of psychological projection as the source of supernatural being has served to demythologize demons, goblins, angels, and saints and rob them of their power. The Bardo Thodöl, however, speaks of the deities as "projections" but never as "mere projections." The deities are present and must be dealt with religiously by means of prayers, rites, and incantations, not just by intellectual insight. The intellectual may well wander back into samsara, while the unlettered follower of the rituals and prayers may find salvation. The doctrine of projection in the Bardo Thodöl does not say that there is really nothing there and thus nothing to fear. Rather it identifies what is there, the self confronted with itself, and provides a means of overcoming it.

Bibliography. The Tibetan text: Karma-glin-pa, *A Collection of Rediscovered Texts From the Gter-ma of Karma-glin-pa, Including the Bardo Thos-sgrol* (1969); W. Y. Evans-Wentz, *The Tibetan Book of the Dead* (1927); F. Fremantle and C. Trungpa, *The Tibetan Book of the Dead* (1975); D. I. Lauf, *Secret Doctrine of the Tibetan Book of the Dead* (1977). D. G. DAWE

BARTH, KARL bärt (Ch; 1886–1968). Swiss Protestant theologian; prime mover in NEO-ORTHODOXY and active in the struggle against Nazism. He stressed the infinite difference between God and humanity and revelation and reason, and centered his theology on the divine word made known through JESUS Christ; the Christian life demands obedience to God's commands which, while known in each situation, are ordinarily consistent with the BIBLE. *See* THEOLOGY, CONTEMPORARY CHRISTIAN §3.

D. F. OTTATI

BASIL THE GREAT bā´ zĭl (Ch; *ca.* 330-379). Cappadocian theologian and monk, whose contribution to the controversies over the TRINITY (Father and Son are of one substance: HOMOOUSIOS) helped defeat ARIANISM at the council of Constantinople, 381-82. He composed a monastic rule which has ordered the life of MONASTICISM in the ORTHODOX CHURCHES ever since. R. BULLARD

BASMALA bäs´ mə lə (I). *See* QUR'ĀN §1.

BAY PSALM BOOK (Ch). Popular designation for the first collection of metrical versions of the psalms (with a much longer title) to be published in the North American colonies (Cambridge, Mass., 1640). The work of several New England clergymen, it went through over 50 editions; no other English psalter achieved such popularity. H. McElrath

BEATIFICATION (Ch). The papal decree permitting public veneration of a deceased person reputed for holiness. It is, generally, only for a particular region or religious order. The beatified person has the title of "Blessed," and the beatification process must precede Canonization. Before the seventeenth century, bishops could authorize the local cult of deceased Christians for their own diocese. *See* Saints, Veneration of. C. Waddell

BEATITUDES (Ch). The opening of the Sermon on the Mount, consisting of a series of congratulatory exclamations: "How blessed!" or "How fortunate!" In the OT, "blessed is the one who . . . " is a common formula extolling virtues, thus teaching morality. The Beatitudes in Matthew follow the OT form, but in Luke 6, closer to Jesus' own formulation, they address the hearer, "Blessed are you poor," etc.
L. E. Keck

BEAUTIFUL NAMES OF GOD (I). *See* Allah.

BECKET, THOMAS à (Ch; *ca.* 1118-1170). Archbishop of Canterbury and English Martyr. Named royal chancellor and then primate of the English church by King Henry II, Becket became involved in a bitter controversy with the king over ecclesiastical liberties and jurisdiction. Following a supposed reconciliation, Becket was slain before his altar at Canterbury, which became one of the most popular centers for Pilgrimage in the Middle Ages.
H. L. Bond

BEDE bēd (Ch; *ca.* 673-735). Monk of the monastery of Jarrow, theologian, and only Englishman named "Doctor of the Church." An outstanding example of Christian scholarship and piety in Anglo-Saxon England, Bede, named "venerable" by the Synod of Aachen (836), is considered the "father of English history." Born in the kingdom of Northumbria, he accompanied the abbot Ceolfrid to Jarrow at the time of its foundation (*ca.* 682). Using its considerable monastic library, he spent the rest of his life there teaching, preaching, and writing. His career marked the end of the great era of early English Christianity and the beginning of the assimilation of northern culture within Western Christian thought. He provided an inspiration for the scholars of the Carolingian Renaissance and became the first Anglo-Saxon scholar to have wide influence. His writings, especially his scriptural commentaries, were widely circulated throughout the Middle Ages. His most significant work was his *Ecclesiastical History*, which traces English church history from the time of Caesar to A.D. 731. He also composed texts on grammar and metrics, a chronological tract on the calculation of Easter, a scientific treatise on natural history, a history of the abbots of his monastery, and a life of the abbot Cuthbert in verse and prose.

Bibliography. A. H. Thompson, *Bede: His Life, Times, and Writings* (1935); P. H. Blair, *The World of Bede* (1970).
H. L. Bond

BEGUINES bē gēnz′ (Ch). Groups of devout women dating from the twelfth century who lived without vows or special rule in convents or in a *beguinage* (individual cottages inside an enclosure), active in the Low Countries, France, and Germany. Their decline (late Middle Ages) was partly owing to some being accused of unorthodoxy or immorality. *See* Religious Orders. W. H. Principe

BEING AND NONBEING. Broadly speaking, what applies to everything that there is and what applies to nothing that there is. The distinction between these two primary categories is sometimes expressed in terms of existence as opposed to nonexistence or in terms of the real as contrasted with the unreal. *Ca.* 600 B.C. Parmenides insisted that to speak of nonbeing was to utter nonsense, because everything which can be conceived of or enunciated logically belongs to the domain of being. Describing being as one, eternal, and unchanging, he relegated all apparent plurality and change to the status of illusion. Plato complicated the issue by discussing the ontological mode of becoming. For him, "being" pertained to unchanging, immaterial forms or ideas, and "becoming" applied to the ever-changing physical objects of sense perception. Finally, Plato stated that his supreme form, the Form of the Good, was "beyond being." As the cause of all being, this highest form was necessarily elevated over its effects. Nonbeing could now be construed as either the nonexistent or the ultimate metaphysical reality.

Augustine of Hippo, profoundly influenced by Neoplatonism, assigned a moral dimension to the categories of being and nonbeing. As a Christian, he believed that all of God's creation was good, leaving no room whatever for evil in the realm of being. Instead, Augustine considered evil to be a privation, lack, or absence of the good. In short, he regarded evil as nonbeing, rather than as a species of being produced by God and for which God could be held responsible. Karl Barth held a similar view.

In Taoism, Buddhism, and Hinduism, the supreme reality is often characterized as nonbeing. Nonbeing, in such contexts, does not refer to absolute nonexistence, but to the ground of all being. Negative terminology is used in order to distinguish between the prior, spiritual reality which serves as origin and all particular beings which proceed from this source. Because Taoists regard the Tao as ineffable and because all beings can be named or described, it follows that the indescribable Tao is nonbeing (*wu*). Here nonbeing is not the opposite of being but that pristine being which exists before all differentiations and multiplicities appear. Therefore, Tao is also referred to as *p'o,* or the "uncarved block" which precedes the emergence of the myriad things. Since all the objects of this world proceed from being, being itself must proceed from some source which is not being and which is accordingly called nonbeing.

In Mahāyāna Buddhism ultimate reality is often identified with ŚŪNYATĀ (the void, emptiness, or nothingness); it is empty of all distinctions, and is nothing in the sense of being no particular thing but that which gives rise to all things. Finally, in Hinduism the expression "neti, neti" ("not this, not this") is a reminder that BRAHMAN as ultimate reality is not to be confused with this or that particular being, for as all-inclusive, Brahman is far more than any limited manifestation. Hence, it is not surprising that Brahman was sometimes identified as nonbeing.

E. J. COLEMAN

BENEDICTINES bĕn ə dĭk´ tənz (Ch). Roman Catholic monks following the rule and spirit of St. Benedict (d. *ca.* 547), noted for moderate ASCETICISM, vowed stability in one monastery for life, worship united with work both manual and mental. They were leaders in Christianizing western Europe and furthering culture. The ABBOT, spiritual father of the monks, has full authority. Although in recent centuries kindred monasteries have joined in congregations, each monastery remains autonomous. The Order of St. Benedict (OSB) is a loose confederation, with no juridical ties, of these congregations. Benedictine nuns follow the rule and spirit of St. Benedict. *See* RELIGIOUS ORDERS.

W. H. PRINCIPE

BENEDICTIONS (Ju & Ch). Recitations of praise to God. They have an important place in Jewish piety and have been a part of Christian worship since the early church.

In the Bible, "Blessed be the Lord," in the third person is common (Gen. 24:27; Exod. 18:10). The Dead Sea Scrolls use the second person, "Blessed art Thou, O Lord, who hast given unto man the insight of knowledge, to understand thy wonders." It is now a long-standing practice to begin a prayer *"Barūkh attah Adonai,"* "Blessed art Thou, O Lord" (cf. Ps. 119:12; I Chr. 29:10), followed by "our God, King of the Universe" (introduced in protest against the Roman emperor's cult in the second century A.D.). The prayer continues in the third person (e.g., "who hast sanctified us by his commandments and commanded us on the washing of the hands"). Long formulas repeat "Blessed art Thou, O Lord" at the end. In a series of praises the opening formula appears only in the first.

Rabban Gamaliel II sanctioned the Eighteen Benedictions (*see* AMIDAH) as the core of daily prayer (late first century A.D.). Rabbi MEIR deemed it a duty to recite one hundred benedictions daily. MOSES BEN MAIMON points out in his MISHNEH TORAH that there are benedictions said before the enjoyment of food, for performance of a religious duty, and as grace after a meal.

Christian worship, both Catholic and Protestant, makes frequent use of benedictions and other prayers of blessing, especially in the EUCHARIST and at the conclusion of worship.

Bibliography. A. Z. Idelsohn, *Jewish Liturgy and its Development* (1967); S. Zeitlin, "The Tefillah, the Shemoneh Esreh," *JQR,* LIV (1964), 208-49; C. Westermann, *Blessing* (1978).

Y. SHAMIR

REPRESENTATIVE JEWISH BENEDICTIONS

Before eating bread
Blessed art Thou, O Lord, our God, King of the Universe, who brings forth bread from the earth.

Before drinking wine
Blessed art Thou, O Lord, our God, King of the Universe, creator of the fruit of the vine.

On seeing the rainbow
Blessed art Thou, O Lord, our God, King of the Universe, who remembers the covenant, is faithful to his covenant, and keeps his promise.

Before putting on the prayer shawl
Blessed art Thou, O Lord, our God, King of the Universe, who hast sanctified us through his commandments, and hast commanded us to wrap ourselves in the fringed garment.

BENEDICTUS QUI VENIT bĕ nĕ dĭk´toos kwē vĕ´ nĭt (Ch—Lat.; "Blessed is he who comes"). First words of the acclamation of Jesus by the crowds on PALM SUNDAY (Matt. 21:9; cf. Ps. 118:25f.); appended to the SANCTUS in the Gallic LITURGY by the sixth century, when it is mentioned by Caesarius of Arles.

R. A. GREER

BERNARD OF CLAIRVAUX clăr vō´ (Ch; 1090–1153). Mystic and leader in the CISTERCIAN monastic reform. The son of French nobility, he entered the monastery of Citeaux, which had been founded in 1098 to observe strictly the Rule of St. Benedict. In 1115 he established a daughter house at Clairvaux, where he served as abbot until his death. The Cistercian movement grew rapidly under his leadership.

His activities outside the cloister included resolving a papal schism between Innocent II, with whom he sided, and Anacletus; engaging in controversy with ABELARD, whose rational approach to religion he disliked; and preaching the Second CRUSADE. He corresponded extensively with kings, princes, popes, and bishops. Canonized in 1174, he was proclaimed a Doctor of the Church in 1830.

His best known work is eighty-six sermons on the Song of Solomon, treating it as an allegory of the mystical life in which Christ is the bridegroom and the Christian the bride.

Bernard felt that the highest achievement of

monastic life was the union of the soul with God through love. *See* MONASTICISM; TRAPPISTS.

Bibliograhy. J. Leclercq edited the critical edition of Bernard's works, *S. Bernardi Opera*, beginning in 1957; an English edition, *The Works of Bernard of Clairvaux*, was begun in 1970; E. Gilson, *The Mystical Theology of Saint Bernard* (1940); W. Williams, *Saint Bernard of Clairvaux* (1952).

W. O. PAULSELL

BESHT bĕsht (Ju). *See* BAAL SHEM TOV.

BETHLEHEM bĕth′ lĭ hĕm. A village in Judah, about eight km. SSW of JERUSALEM. Primarily renowned as the birthplace of JESUS (Matt. 2; cf. Mic. 5:2). In the modern town is the Church of the Nativity, first built by Constantine (*ca.* A.D. 330) and refurbished by Justinian (*ca.* A.D. 550). Excavations beneath the basilica reveal occupation in the Iron Age and in the first century A.D.

D. W. O'CONNOR

BEZA, THEODORE bē′ zä (Ch; 1519-1605). French-born Protestant theologian and Calvin's successor as leader of the Genevan Reformation. He provided French Protestants a theological basis for resistance to political authority during the Wars of Religion (1560-98). Doctrinally, he expanded upon Calvin's concepts of predestination and church discipline.

Bibliography. J. Raitt, *The Eucharistic Theology of Theodore Beza* (1972).

R. L. HARRISON

BHAGAVAD GĪTĀ bŭ′ gŭ vŭd gē′tŭ (H—Skt.; lit., "song of the glorious one" [*bhaj*—"to distribute, share in (wealth, glory)"; *gai*—"to sing, recite, relate"]; *see* BHAGAVĀN). Sanskrit poem relating a dialogue between Lord KRISHNA and ARJUNA consisting of seven hundred two-line stanzas in eighteen chapters (23-40) of book six of the Hindu Epic MAHĀBHĀRATA; as part of the Epic classified as fallible "recollection" (SMṚTI) but as Krishna's exposition of the nature of reality treated as infallible "revelation" (ŚRUTI) and called an UPANIṢAD; a succinct summary of dominant themes in Hindu theology and a classic in world literature of devotion and mysticism.

1. **Setting.** The occasion for the Gītā is the battle between the PĀNDAVAS and their cousins the Kauravas on the Kuru Field near modern New Delhi at the close of the previous YUGA. Krishna, an AVATAR of the godhead known as the Supreme Person *(paramapuruṣa)*, the Supreme Self *(paramātman)*, or just the "Glorious One" (Bhagavān), serves as charioteer for his close friend Arjuna, chief hero of the epic. Events in the battle are reported to the blind Kaurava king DHṚTARĀṢTRA by a messenger and the Gītā is his report of the battle's beginning when Arjuna, standing in his chariot, surveyed the enemy, dropped his bow, and refused to fight, and Krishna, acting in the charioteer's role as advisor, responded.

2. **Content.** The poem's opening words, "On the Field of Dharma, on the Kuru Field," suggest the theme of Krishna's response regarding the correct knowledge of and action in accord with the "true order" of reality (*see* DHARMA). Arjuna's refusal to fight is motivated by compassion and grief, as he argues that killing his enemies will destroy the family, the heart of Vedic (*see* VEDIC HINDUISM) society, and bring ruin to all and that he would rather be slain unarmed by his evil cousins, the Kauravas, and preserve the family than slay them righteously and destroy that for which he fights. Krishna dissolves this truly human dilemma in a gradual shift of Arjuna's perspective from his "old fashioned" Vedic view based on family law and rites of sacrifice (YAJÑA), which is affirmed but removed to a subordinate position in a larger whole. The immediate problem, argues Krishna, is Arjuna's misperception (AVIDYĀ) of himself as a unitary and autonomous individual when in fact he is binary—an acting psychosomatic sheath "woven" out of Matter (PRAKṚTI) by his own actions in previous lives (KARMA) and a true Self (ATMAN) of eternal consciousness which neither acts nor is acted upon. This binary analysis extends to the whole of reality, manifest and unmanifest, composed on one hand of innumerable selves and of being and on the other of matter, unified however, in Krishna the Supreme Person. Hence matter, being, and selves are forms of Krishna himself which he both acts through and transcends. Most importantly, as Supreme Person, Krishna Bhagavān responds with love and grace *(prasāda)* to those embodied selves who, like Arjuna, love him most dearly, and his grace frees all his devotees from the never ending "play" of SAMSARA (*see* MOKṢA; LĪLĀ). Krishna makes it clear that for Arjuna it is not a question of not fighting—because his warrior's nature and the Lord's own activity will cause him to fight despite his resolve—it is a question of the attitude with which he will fight: namely, motivated by desire to gain his own personal ends, or by love and devotion (BHAKTI) to the Glorious One thereby offering him all his acts as sacrifices, unconcerned with their consequences (familial or otherwise). With Arjuna clear in mind and roused to act, the Gītā ends. This richly conceived poem, concrete in imagery yet suggestively ambiguous, is so grand in metaphysical vision that for over two thousand years it has elicited a sense of sacred mystery and meaning in lives of millions of Hindus who regard the battle as both history and metaphor and Arjuna's dilemma as their own.

3. **History.** Judging from parallel references and structures the Gītā was part of the Mahābhārata's earlier versions, probably *ca.* 400-100 B.C., and arose as the response of Vedic culture of the western Gangetic plain to non-Vedic ascetic traditions (*see* ŚRAMAṆA, BUDDHISM, JAINISM) from the eastern region of Magadha. In the opening chapters ascetic renunciation of society is reinterpreted using categories of SĀṂKHYA YOGA to affirm it while renouncing all egocentrical desire as motivation in acting; one should act according to established DHARMA for the

good of the whole. Other chapters add Upaniṣadic teachings and devotion to the Supreme Person as Krishna, and thus the text is often summarized as teaching three disciplines (yogas): action or karma-yoga (chaps. 1-6), knowledge or jñāna-yoga (chaps. 7-12), and devotion or bhakti-yoga (chaps. 13-18). Clearly a theistic text, it probably originated among early sectarian BHĀGAVATAS who identified the Vṛṣṇi hero Krishna with gods NĀRĀYAṆA and VISHṆU, and for them it has remained important down to the present (*see* PAÑCARĀTRA). In nonsectarian Hindu theology (*see* DARŚANA) the Gītā serves along with the Upaniṣads and BRAHMĀ SŪTRAS as one of three textual bases for VEDĀNTA, receiving its earliest surviving commentary from ŚAṂKARA (eighth century A.D.), who understood it as teaching the ultimate nonduality of reality (advaita); RĀMĀNUJA (eleventh century) and MADHVA (thirteenth), among others, countered with commentaries and theologies more consistent with the text itself (*see* VIŚIṢṬA ADVAITA, DVAITA). Modern Indian nationalists have seen in it a call and guide for political and social action, notably Swami VIVEKĀNANDA, B. G. Tilak, M. K. GANDHI, Vinoba Bhāve, and AUROBINDO Ghose; neo-Vedāntins use it widely, stressing its teachings on action and knowledge more often than devotion (*see* RADHAKRISHNAN, S.).

Bibliography. R. C. Zaehner, trans., *The Bhagavad-Gītā* (1968), thorough analysis within its intellectual context; E. Deutsch, trans., *The Bhagavad Gītā* (1968); V. S. Sukthankar, *On the Meaning of the Mahabharata* (1957).

D. HUDSON

BHAGAVĀN bŭg´ ŭ vän (H & B—Skt.; lit. "possessing fortune or wealth, fortunate, blessed, holy"). A reverential title for those gods and men who are believed to possess great material and spiritual wealth. The term is used in speaking of or addressing spiritual masters, ascetics, saints, or gods but is reserved particularly for the invocation of the second member of the Hindu triad, VISHṆU. The original meaning of the word is "that one who possesses his [proper] share," and refers to a person who is entitled to a full share in tribal property. When used in referring to a divine being, it often indicates the belief that gods are superintendents over the bounties of the world and distribute to each creature his or its due portion.

As early as the time of the Epics (*ca.* second century B.C.—second century A.D.) Vishnu was worshiped under the name Vāsudeva-KRISHṆA and was invoked as "Bhagavān." The devotees of this deity called themselves BHĀGAVATAS, "worshipers of Bhagavān," the "Lord of [all] shares" or the "Bountiful Lord." Bhagavān is a fitting title for that "High God" in the Hindu pantheon who is the divine agent of preservation, according to the TRIMŪRTI concept, and who, as an expression of his boundless goodwill toward the universe, invigorates, nurtures, and directs the lives of all creatures.

In Indian village society the term *Bhagwān* is used in addressing God, or more properly "the Great God." The villagers believe that *Bhagwān* sets forth an individual's destiny even before birth and unswervingly guides each person to that predetermined end throughout his lifetime. *Bhagwān* is the remote, impersonal, and absolute supreme divinity who creates the universe and then departs into the realm of quiet blissfulness. He rarely appears in the myths and legends of the tribal people. He is regarded as the cause of almost every event or situation of any importance and is believed to be beyond human control. He (or, more accurately, "It") lives in the "highest heaven" beyond the influence of human prayers and rites. Nonetheless, considerable time, energy and wealth are expended in attempting to cultivate his pleasure and to quell his wrath by means of prayers, offerings, and sacred festivals. He is the embodiment of Fate or Destiny *(bhāga)* by virtue of the fact that he distributes to all creatures their proper portion *(bhāga)* of the world's goods and withholds goods from those who are undeserving of rewards because of their sinful deeds.

The study of Indian folklore indicates that *Bhagwān* appears in the guise of both SHIVA and Vishnu indiscriminantly. Nonetheless, he is always and everywhere the supreme creator, preserver, destroyer, and overlord of the universe, seen as the limitless store of wisdom and goodness.

Bibliography. W. J. Culshaw, *Tribal Heritage: A Study of the Santals* (1949); S. K. De, *Early History of the Vaiṣnava Faith and Movement in Bengal* (1942, 1961); V. Elwin, *Myths of Middle India* (1949); C. von Fürer-Haimendorf, *The Aboriginal Tribes of Hyderabad* (1943-48); S. Jaiswal, *The Origin and Development of Vaiṣṇavism* (1967).

J. B. LONG

BHĀGAVATA bŭg ŭ vŭ´ tŭ (H—Skt.: lit.: "one who belongs to Bhagavat"). The term used from the time of the MAHĀBHĀRATA to designate the worshipers of Nārāyaṇa-Vishnu (also called Vāsudeva-Krishna). Hence, a Bhāgavata is one who follows, belongs to, and adores Bhagavat or BHAGAVĀN. Under this title VISHṆU is revered as the chief among the Hindu gods; i.e., the only divinity worthy of highest devotion.

The derivation of the name is as clear as the origins of the cult are obscure. The word is derived from *bhaj,* "to divide, allot, distribute, share with, or partake of" and is related to *bhāga,* "wealth, share or portion." The term by which this deity is most frequently addressed is derived from *bhaga-vat,* "possessed of material wealth." The term was originally applied to both gods and men who were believed to be wealthy or to control the distribution of wealth.

There is widespread belief that the Bhāgavata cult is non-Vedic (and perhaps pre-Vedic) in origin. The name NĀRĀYAṆA (another title of Vishnu) may be traceable to the INDUS VALLEY CIVILIZATION, and some of his features are reminiscent of the Sumerian god *Ea* or *Enki* who, like Nārāyaṇa, sleeps on or in the cosmic waters. The cult of Nārāyaṇa is also closely associated with asceticism and with the austere practices of wandering ascetics, a fact that also suggests a non-Vedic origin of his tradition. In all likelihood, this cult had developed into a highly complicated and syncretized religion, with a rich mingling of Vedic and non-Vedic elements, by the time of the GUPTA DYNASTY (fourth-sixth century A.D.).

The Bhāgavatas make an initial appearance in the Mahābhārata *(Śānti-parvan)* and are mentioned with increasing frequency in the PURĀṆAS until they burst into full bloom in the BHĀGAVATA PURĀṆA (*ca.* tenth century).

According to Jaiswal, the Bhāgavatas should be distinguished from the PAÑCARĀTRAS, the latter community being the other primary segment of the VAIṢṆAVA sect from the time of the Epics. The main difference between the two sects is that the Bhāgavatas were devotees of Nārāyaṇa and adopted the claims of the Brahminical social order, while the Pañcarātras were indifferent to that order and perhaps antagonistic toward it. The Bhāgavatas enjoyed the support of the ruling classes and they, in turn, supported the CASTE system. So popular was this cult by the second century B.C. that even the Greek ambassador and author of the famous Besnagar inscription, Heliodorus, identified himself as a Bhāgavata.

Bibliography. R. G. Bhandarkar, *Vaiṣṇavism, Śaivism and Minor Religious Systems* (1929); S. K. De, *Early History of the Vaiṣṇava Faith and Movement in Bengal* (1942, 1961); S. Jaiswal, *The Origin and Development of Vaiṣṇavism* (1967).

J. B. LONG

BHĀGAVATA PURĀṆA bäg ŭ vät´ ŭ pŭ rän´ ä (H). A later PURĀṆA (*ca.* tenth century A.D.) which extols the might and mercy of VISHNU, especially in his descent as the AVATAR KRISHNA. Building upon earlier warrior-Krishna traditions from the BHAGAVAD GĪTĀ and Harivaṃśa, the tenth canto or book of this Purāṇa tells a composite story of the cowherd Krishna and his later exploits as an adviser to the PĀṆḌAVA brothers. This Purāṇa remains a central source for Krishna devotionalism. L. D. SHINN

BHAJANA bŭj ŭ nŭ (H). Southern form of North Indian KĪRTANA.

BHAKTI HINDUISM bŭk´ tē (H—Skt.; lit. "devotion"). The complex popular Hinduism of later times as distinguished from the priestly VEDIC Hinduism of the ARYANS. In contrast to the Vedic emphasis on sacrificial rituals and transcendental knowledge, Bhakti Hinduism centers around devotion to personal deities and includes a variety of popular and non-Vedic practices. Images and image worship, home shrines and temples, poet-saints and holy men, devotional songs and dances, religious dramas, festivals, and PILGRIMAGE are all interwoven with elements of Vedic thought and practice in the variegated fabric of Bhakti Hinduism. Most of the characteristic features of Hinduism from the early centuries A.D. onward are associated with this synthesis of popular and priestly religion.

1. The beginnings of Bhakti Hinduism. The popular origins of Bhakti Hinduism are relatively obscure. The INDUS VALLEY CIVILIZATION had a developed religious system before the Aryans entered India around 1500 B.C., but we know little about its survival in the ensuing Vedic period. For the next thousand years our data on Indian religion come mainly from texts produced by Vedic priests who had little interest in popular religious practices. By the second century B.C., however, the Vedic tradition had been gradually weakened by the decline of the old Aryan kingdoms. The invasion by Alexander in 326 B.C. had opened India to outside contacts, and the Mauryan emperor AŚOKA (*ca.* 272-232 B.C.) had given official support to the Buddhist cause. At that point, from a variety of sources, we begin to get glimpses of the popular religions which emerged in Bhakti Hinduism.

The non-Vedic Buddhist movement provides some of the earliest evidence of popular religious practices, especially in the several centuries after Aśoka. Aśoka himself performed pilgrimage to Buddhist sacred places and erected commemorative columns at these sites. In his campaign to promote Buddhism, he also supported the construction of numerous STŪPAS (burial mounds for Buddhist relics) throughout northern India. Sculpture from the first century B.C. indicates that *stūpas* by that time were an important object of worship along with the BODHI tree, the scene of the Buddha's enlightenment. Numerous relief carvings from this period show *stūpas* and *bodhi* trees enclosed in railings and surrounded by crowds of devotees offering gifts and garlands of flowers in worship. Even more striking is the sculptural evidence at the same sites of the worship of fertility gods and goddesses (*yakṣas* and *yakṣīs*) who had no place in official Buddhist religion but were obviously important to the pilgrims who visited these sacred centers.

The first direct references to Hindu worship are consistent with this Buddhist evidence. Second century B.C. inscriptions from northern and western India record the building of a stone-walled enclosure for the worship (PŪJĀ) of Lord Vāsudeva and the erection of a stone column in honor of the same deity by a Bactrian Greek who refers to himself as a BHĀGAVATA or devotee of the Lord. The practices seem clearly parallel to Buddhist practice and indicate a common pattern in the emerging non-Vedic religions.

Foreign support of popular gods is evident from the images of deities on coins issued by the Bactrian Greek rulers of northwest India in the second and first centuries B.C. and the Kushān rulers of northern India in the first three centuries A.D. Most of the gods on their coins are foreign, but particularly in the Kushān period there are also many Hindu deities. The warrior god SKANDA-KĀRTTIKEYA appears frequently with a variety of forms and names, but even more numerous are the figures of SHIVA standing with his trident spear accompanied often by his bull and, on a few coins, paired with a goddess identified as Umā. Shiva's popularity is further confirmed by a Kushān sculpture of the second century A.D. which shows two Kushān nobles worshiping a LINGA, undoubtedly by then a standard representation of Shiva.

Vāsudeva and Shiva appear from this archaeological evidence to be the most important of the emerging Hindu deities, a fact confirmed by later developments in which Vāsudeva was merged with KRISHNA and identified with the Vedic god VISHNU, while Shiva was merged with the Vedic RUDRA. Late Vedic texts of the fifth to second centuries B.C. indicate also the growing importance of Vishnu and Shiva, but the context is not yet that of popular religion. Vedic religion remained sacrificial and aniconic and was dominated by elitist priestly standards, while popular religion was devotional and iconic and open to participation even by foreigners. Only when the two were merged do we have Bhakti Hinduism. The earliest indication of such a merger is found in the BHAGAVAD GĪTĀ.

2. Bhakti Hinduism in the Mahābhārata. The Bhagavad Gītā, which was added to the much larger MAHĀBHĀRATA epic some time before A.D. 200, reflects the major popular religious movements and at the same time preserves the continuity of the Vedic tradition. The Gītā gives a central place to theistic devotion as the preferred means of salvation and argues that devotion, properly understood, is the fulfillment of social duty, UPANISADIC knowledge, and Vedic ritual obligations. Not everyone can be a priest or learned seer, but everyone can know the Lord through devotion and can perform his duties as a form of devotion to him. This, according to the Gītā, is the true meaning of sacrifice, not the offering of Vedic sacrifices for worldly gain. Whatever one has to offer, if given in devotion, is sufficient: "a leaf, a flower, fruit, or a sip of water—that offering of a pure-souled person who offers with devotion I will accept" (Bh G 9.26).

Pūjā, the offering of gifts and services to the deity or to an image of the deity, is effectively validated by this position. Elsewhere in the Mahābhārata, other practices receive similar sanction. The performance of pilgrimage to sacred places, long established at the popular level, is especially praised as a meritorious activity. One explicit passage explains that "a poor man cannot rise to the sacrifices, for they require many implements and a great variety of ingredients. . . . But hear to what injunction even the poor can rise. . . . This is the highest mystery of the seers—the holy visitation of sacred fords, which even surpasses the sacrifices" (Mbh 3.80. 35-40).

Pilgrimage thus emerged as a major religious practice accessible, like *pūjā,* to people at all social levels. These and other forms of Bhakti Hinduism could either complement or replace the more elitist Vedic ritual practices. Performed in the Gītā's devotional spirit of action without desire for its fruits, they could be seen as an even higher form of religious practice. The key is devotion *(bhakti),* which can transform the humblest religious practice into a sacrifice equal to Vedic rituals. Based on this premise, Bhakti Hinduism revised the pattern of Indian religious life.

3. The deities of Bhakti Hinduism. Devotion necessarily involves a personal rather than impersonal conception of the divine (*see* BRAHMAN). The rise of devotional Hinduism thus went hand in hand with an increased acceptance of personal gods and goddesses within the Hindu mainstream. Vishnu and Shiva, with both Vedic and popular connections, became the main focal points of Hindu theism, which tended to grow by association of other deities with these two central figures. Paralleling this development was a similar development of goddesses, both as wives and consorts of the gods and as independent deities in their own right. All of these deities were eventually represented by images with clearly defined iconographic forms to express their special qualities, giving Bhakti Hinduism both a rich and varied texture and a high degree of uniformity.

Shiva was the first of the Hindu deities with a clear set of personal characteristics. His primary identity was that of a YOGIN dwelling on Mount KAILĀSA, his snow-clad mountain in the Himalayas. This essentially non-Vedic figure was merged with the Vedic Rudra, a deity noted for both benevolence and violent activity. Shiva retained this ambivalence, and two main images of Shiva combine the complementary qualities of detachment and activity. The most common image is the *liṅga,* a representation of the eternally erect phallus, which symbolizes both Shiva's generative potency and his yogic powers of self-control. The other main image is Shiva as NAṬARĀJA, Lord of Dance, displaying his manifold powers of creation and destruction while remaining blissfully detached. Both retain the tension between unity and diversity, creation and destruction, which is so characteristic of this complex deity.

Vishnu combines a range of qualities and characteristics by appearing in the world in a series of incarnations (AVATARS). One such incarnation is Krishna, the divine teacher in the Bhagavad Gītā, who is worshiped also as an infant and young cowherd sporting with his friends and lovers in Vṛndāvana, his childhood home on the banks of the Jumna River. Another incarnation is RĀMA, hero of the Rāmāyaṇa, who epitomizes the virtues of self-denial and dedication to duty as a model king ruling and ruled by the highest ethical standards. Vishnu is worshiped in other forms as well, but the incarnations as Krishna and Rāma were the most important and fully developed personalities for Bhakti Hinduism. Images were developed to portray the various roles and powers of these gods, with iconographic details drawn from the stories. Rāma with his bow, defeating the demon-king Rāvaṇa; the flute-playing Krishna dancing with the cowherd maidens or subduing the serpent-demon Kāliya—these and other episodes were depicted in sculpture and painting, praised in poetry and song, acted out in dance-dramas or miracle plays, and used as the focal images for a wide range of devotional styles.

Although Shiva and Vishnu were the main unifying deities in Bhakti Hinduism, various female deities also were important in the emergence of popular religion into the Hindu mainstream. The term *devī* ("goddess") is used as a generic name for these female figures, but their separate identities persist, and their roles have been distinctively different (*see* GODDESS [INDIA]). They can be classified to some extent, however, on the basis of their origins and special functions: goddesses who manifest mainly life-supporting qualities, and goddesses who manifest qualities of destructiveness.

The prototypes of the life-supporting goddesses are the *yakṣīs*, or fertility goddesses, who appear on the post-Mauryan Buddhist monuments, invariably portrayed as wide-hipped and full-breasted females standing near and sometimes embracing the trunk of a flowering or fruit-laden tree. The Hindu goddess LAKṢMĪ or Śrī, bestower of wealth and prosperity, appears on coins and sculptural reliefs as early as the first century A.D. in the form of a *yakṣī*-like female on a lotus with two flanking elephants. Gaṅgā, the personification of the GANGES River, appears soon after as a *yakṣī* figure with lotuses and water symbols in place of the *yakṣī's* tree, a pattern followed also in representations of Yamunā, the personified Jumna River. All of these lotus-symbol goddesses represent qualities consistent with those of the *yakṣīs* as supporters of the life process. It is Lakṣmī, however, who in later Hinduism combined their collective qualities as the goddess of bounty and good fortune and was chosen as patron goddess of the GUPTA emperors in the fourth century A.D.

An equally important goddess with very different origins is Umā or PĀRVATĪ. In contrast to the early independent career of Lakṣmī, Umā is regularly mentioned as Shiva's wife in the Mahābhārata and was already paired with Shiva on Kushān coins of the second century A.D. The marriage of Shiva and Pārvatī was the basis for a later family unit which included the warrior god Skanda-Kārttikeya and the elephant-headed god GAṆEŚA as sons of Shiva and Pārvatī, linking these originally separate gods with the expanding Śaivite religious system. Pārvatī was also seen as an expression of ŚAKTI ("power"), the female principle of energy and activity which united with the detached yogic Shiva to form an eternal cosmic pair.

Goddesses could also be violent and untamed, and Śakti could be destructive as well as creative and life-supporting. This is acknowledged throughout India at the folk or village level in the worship of many goddesses with malign qualities and associations such as Manasā, the goddess of snakes, and Śītalā, the goddess of smallpox, but most such goddesses have remained important only in a limited area. Two goddesses with terrifying malevolent qualities, however, DURGĀ and KĀLĪ, entered into the Hindu mainstream to rival even Vishnu and Shiva in importance.

Durgā is mentioned in the Mahābhārata, but her place in Bhakti Hinduism was established by the *Devī Māhātmya*, a hymn to her powers and exploits which was written several centuries later. According to this account, Durgā was created to subdue the great demon Mahisha, who had taken the form of a water buffalo. Produced from the combined energies of the gods, Durgā destroyed the demon and won back the world for gods and men. Kālī is also first described at length in the *Devī Māhātmya* where, in a later battle against the demons, her dreadful form springs forth from Durgā's anger-darkened brow. Gaunt, black, with gaping mouth and lolling tongue, adorned with a garland of human heads and wielding as weapons a sword and noose, Kālī gleefully slays the demons and drinks their blood. Though sometimes paired with Shiva, both terrifying goddesses have been worshiped independently—Durgā as Protector and Kālī as Mother of the World.

4. The institutions of Bhakti Hinduism. Bhakti Hinduism emerged alongside two established religious systems, Buddhism and Brahmanical religion, both of which had long-established institutional structures. The new devotional theism had widespread popular appeal, but equivalent institutions were developed only after it was merged with Brahmanical religion to form Bhakti Hinduism and received the support of kings as well as commoners. The rationale for this merger had already been worked out in the Bhagavad Gītā, but the needed royal patronage came only with the rise of the Gupta Empire (A.D. 320-540). At that point, both priestly and royal support came to fruition in the two most significant institutions of Bhakti Hinduism: the PURĀṆIC scriptures and the Hindu temple (*see* ART AND ARCHITECTURE, HINDU).

The earliest scriptures of Bhakti Hinduism were the two great Epics, the Mahābhārata and Rāmāyaṇa, both of which were greatly expanded in their later versions by the addition of theistic myths and teachings. The format of the Epics made continuing expansion awkward, however, and another class of texts known as Purāṇas was used as the vehicle for devotional theistic writings after the third century A.D. Existing Purāṇas were transformed by the addition of new material, and new Purāṇas were written to meet the needs of various groups.

Despite their blend of Brahmanical and popular concerns, the primary topics of the Purāṇas are clearly those of popular religion: myths of the major Hindu deities, sectarian theistic doctrines, devotion, *pūjā*, pilgrimage, festivals, holy places, and the establishment and support of temples. These are related wherever possible, however, to Brahminical standards and practices, and an effort is made to preserve the authority of Brahmin priests. The result is both an increase in status for popular religion and an extension of Brahmanical authority, a classic exchange of mutual benefits seen also in the support of devotional theism by Gupta rulers.

When the Guptas came to power in the fourth century, both Brahmanical authority and the power of native kings had been weakened by centuries of Buddhist expansion and foreign rule. The Guptas reversed this pattern by supporting not only traditional Brahmanical religion but also Bhakti Hinduism, especially worship of Vishnu. They identified themselves as the human counterparts of Vishnu on earth in the role of world protectors and as partners with the goddess Lakṣmī, divine personification of wealth, prosperity, and good fortune, who represented the qualities which the king should provide for his kingdom. They also gave their support to an extensive program of building and endowing temples which brought royal wealth and popular worship together for the first time to produce the earliest Hindu temples in stone.

Temple building became a standard activity of kings throughout India and eventually replaced the performance of Vedic fire sacrifices as a means of expressing royal power and ensuring the stability of the kingdom. Donations were also made for continuing performance of rituals and services, and temples became major centers of wealth. Eventually, as the Purāṇas reduced the importance of the Vedas, so temples reduced the prestige and power of traditional Vedic priests, whose role in Bhakti Hinduism was limited largely to household rites and family rituals.

5. **The continuity of Bhakti Hinduism.** Once Bhakti Hinduism was established, it remained the dominant factor in Indian religious life. Its main characteristics have never changed substantially from those laid down in the Purāṇas, although new developments have added to its richness and complexity. Sectarian traditions have been formed around most of the major deities, with distinctive forms of worship and religious practice backed up by sectarian texts. New devotional movements have periodically arisen to revitalize these traditions, stimulated most often by saints and poets who have expressed their devotional fervor in the languages and images of the common people, tapping again and again the rich sources from which Bhakti Hinduism first emerged. The list of these saints is endless, but their ranks include the Vaiṣṇavite ĀLVĀRS and Śaivite NĀYAṆĀRS of the Tamil region; Jnānadev, Tukārām, and other Vaiṣṇavite poet-saints of Maharashtra; KABĪR and TULSĪ DĀS, Rāma devotees in the Hindi region of north India; MĪRĀBĀĪ, the female devotee of Krishna from Rajputana; the Krishna devotee CAITAṆYA in Bengal; and the Śaivite reformer Basavanna in Karṇataka. These and many others have sparked new movements and integrated whole regions by the force of their devotion. RĀMAKRISHNA, the nineteenth century Bengal saint and devotee of Kālī, and A.C. BHAKTIVEDANTA, founder of a contemporary international movement of devotion to Krishna, are evidence that the spark has not died out.

Bibliography. Primary texts: *The Bhagavad Gītā,* trans. E. Deutsch (1968); *The Mahābhārata,* trans. J. A. B. van Buitenen (1973-). Secondary sources: R. G. Bhandarkar, *Vaiṣṇavism, Śaivism and Minor Religious Systems* (1965); S. Bhattacharji, *The Indian Theogony* (1970); S. Chattopadhyāya, *The Evolution of Theistic Sects in Ancient India* (1962); J. Gonda, *Viṣṇuism and Śivaism* (1970); T. J. Hopkins, *The Hindu Religious Tradition* (1971); D. R. Kinsley, *The Sword and the Flute: Kālī and Kṛṣṇa* (1977); W. D. O'Flaherty, *Hindu Myths* (1975); C. Dimmit and J. A. B. van Buitenen, *Classical Hindu Mythology* (1978).

T. J. HOPKINS

BHAKTIVEDANTA SWAMI, A. C. bŭk´ tĭ vū dän´ tä swä´ mē (H; 1896-1977). The GURU and founder of the International Society for Krishna Consciousness (HARE KRISHNA MOVEMENT) who was born as Abhay Charan De in Calcutta, educated in English, philosophy, and economics, and was a successful executive with a chemical company. Though initiated into the VAIṢṆAVA BHAKTI faith in 1922, De did not take the vows of renunciation (SANNYĀSIN) until 1959. He was nearly seventy when he came to the United States in 1965 to begin his missionary preaching of the KRISHNA faith, which led to the founding of the Hare Krishna movement. L. D. SHINN

BHARATA bŭr´ ŭ tŭ (H—Skt.). In the MAHĀBHĀRATA, one of the ancestors of the Epic's heroes. Bharata's name provides one of the eponyms for the Lunar Dynasty and the one used in the Epic's title, which means "the great [story] of the descendants of Bharata." He is credited with spreading the dynasty's fame. His story is never told at length and is treated most fully as a subplot in the more famous tale concerning his parents. King Duḥṣanta, intending to visit the hermit Kanva in the forest, finds instead the RISHI's adopted daughter Śakuntalā and charms her into a quick Gandharva marriage in which lovers may wed in secret (*see* GANDHARVA). She bargains for their offspring to be the heir apparent. The child is born after three years gestation. By age six he is of disproportionate size and fetters wild animals around the hermitage, earning the name Sarvadamana, "tamer of everything." One account indicates that he did this to excess, until his mother stopped him. Kanva declares that the boy is ready to be installed as Duḥṣanta's heir-apparent, and Śakuntalā brings him before his father. At first Duḥṣanta refuses to acknowledge son or wife, but a heavenly voice declares the son is his. He accepts them, and at the heavenly voice's command he gives the boy the name Bharata, confirming that his mother bore him (from the root *bhṛ*) and that Duḥṣanta should support him (*bhṛ*) as well. Bharata becomes a *cakravartin,* an emperor who "turns the wheel" of DHARMA (duty), and is noted for his conquests, sacrifices, and virtue. A. HILTEBEITEL

BHARATA-NĀṬYAM bŭ rŭ tŭ nät´ yŭm (H—Skt.; lit. "drama of Bharata" [*bhṛt*—"to hold, maintain"; *naṭ*—"to act, dance"]). A religious dance form of South India, accompanied by voice, drum, instrumental music, and a chanter, and including both pure dance and interpretative dance based on devotional, philosophical, and love songs.

Bharata-Nāṭyam, like other major dance forms of India, traces many of its elements to the Nāṭya Śāstra (*ca.* 100 B.C.–A.D. 100), a comprehensive work on dramaturgy by the legendary sage Bharata Muni. It assumed its present form sometime in the seventeenth century, although it underwent a significant reformation at the hands of a famous quartet of musician-composer-choreographer brothers around the turn of the nineteenth century. Its traditional patronage came from the temples and courts of South India, and its almost exclusively female performers from hereditary CASTES of court and temple dancers. The accompanying music falls within the classical Karnatic (South Indian) system.

The usual Bharata-Nāṭyam performance is solo and divided into six sections of varying length. The chanter guides the pure dance sections by reciting rhythmic syllables to which the drum beats and the steps of the dancer must correspond exactly. The interpretative sections use a complex technique of hand gestures (MUDRĀS) combined with highly stylized facial expressions and dance movements to interpret sung texts from the GĪTĀ GOVINDA, the PURĀṆAS, the RĀMĀYAṆA, and the MAHĀBHĀRATA. *See* KATHAK; KATHĀKALI.

Bibliography. C. R. Jones, "India's Dance and Dance-Drama," *Chapters in Indian Civilization* (1970).

C. R. KING

BHĀSA bhä´ sŭ (H). One of the earliest of the known SANSKRIT dramatists, Bhāsa probably wrote during the fourth century A.D. or earlier. Before the rediscovery and subsequent publication in 1912 of thirteen plays attributed to him, including the beautiful *Svapna-vāsavadatta,* little was known of Bhāsa's work.

J. BARE

BHAVACAKRA bŭ vä chŭk´ rŭ (B—Skt.; lit. "the wheel of becoming") **BHAVACAKKA** bŭ vä chŭk´ kŭ (B—Pali). Based on the formula of dependent origination (PAṬICCASAMUPPĀDA), the Buddhist concept of repeated births might be described in a linear fashion. However, Buddhist commentators like Buddhaghosa expressed the idea of a rebirth in circular terms as a wheel of becoming. This analogy for the birth process involves the theory of KARMA and its retribution. According to one text, the Divyāvadāna, the Buddha directed the drawing of a five-spoked wheel placing the five possible rebirth destinations *(gati)*—namely, in hells, animals, ghosts, gods, and men—between each spoke. The three sections of the wheel—the spokes, nave, and rim—represented the five destinations, the three evil dispositions, and the twelve causal links respectively. Gods and men occupy the highest positions on the wheel. However, later paintings of *bhavacakra* found in AJAṆṬĀ caves and Tibetan monasteries have six spokes. The additional one represents the ASURAS (titans). The main features are similar to early tradition, except for the detailed pictures, illustrating the twelve links of dependent origination. For instance, "ignorance" is represented by a blind man and so forth. Thus, the *bhavacakra* represents the endlessness of existences in various destinations until one achieves ultimate emancipation from the "wheel of becoming."

Bibliography. E. B. Cowell, ed., *Divyāvadāna* (1866), p. 300.

W. PACHOW

BHIKKHU bĭk´ kōō (B—Pali) **BHIKṢU** bĭk´ shōō (B—Skt.). A fully ordained Buddhist monk. The office represented both a continuation of world renunciation *(sannyāsa)* and an important modification of it at many points. To begin with, the life of the wandering almsman (Skt. *parivrājaka;* Pali *paribbājaka*) or recluse (Skt. ŚRAMAṆA; Pali *samaṇa*) rapidly became a corporate life within Buddhism, and with this came the trend toward permanency (*see* SAṄGHA). Despite sectarian developments the *bhikkhu-saṅgha* remained a cohesive force. Also, unlike many forms of renunciation, the life of the *bhikkhu* or *bhikkhuṇi* (nun) was more typically related to the life of the laity, even though those who left home and normal social life lived in monasteries (VIHĀRAS).

The ritual of going forth was called *pabbajjā* and represented the act of admission to the order of novices (Pali *sāmaṇeras*). In the earliest days this act was often accompanied by the ordination proper, *upasampadā*. These two rites rapidly became distinguished, however, and, depending upon the age of the candidate, separated by several years, since ordination was restricted to those who had reached the age of twenty. The regulation of monastic life took canonical form in the VINAYA PIṬAKA, with continuing interpretation in the commentary literature. (*See* SAṄGHA.)

D. K. Swearer

A Buddhist *bhikkhu* on his early morning begging rounds

In addition to the search for enlightenment, the role of *bhikkhus* especially has been to serve as a model for lay men and women (Pali *upāsaka* and *upāsikā*), to be an expositor of the dhamma (Dharma), and in various ways to exercise influence upon leadership for promoting the social order itself. At the same time, a more strict life was maintained by those who lived apart from the *vihāra* in forest hermitages.

B. L. Smith

BHĪMA bē´ mŭ (H—Skt.). Bhīma is the second oldest Pāṇḍava brother in the Mahābhārata. His father, the wind god Vāyu, imparts to him great speed and strength: at birth his mother Kuntī drops him on a mountain which shatters into a hundred pieces. Born on the same day is Duryodhana. Some have seen in their antagonism a continuation of an Indo-Iranian mythological dualism. Bhīma grows apace with an appetite that earns him the name Vṛkodara, "wolf-belly." He withstands several attempts by Duryodhana to kill him. Both are trained to use the mace by Krishna's brother Balarāma.

Bhīma is the quickest to anger of the Paṇḍavas, but most of his outrage smolders until the great war described in the Mahābhārata. His greatest griefs result from insults to Draupadī at the dice match, and much of his activity is motivated by her. It is Bhīma who rises to her defense and vows to slay her tormentors: Duryodhana by breaking his thigh, Duḥśāsana by drinking his blood. During their year in disguise Bhīma protects Draupadī when Kīcaka tries to seduce her. Elsewhere Bhīma shows his attentiveness by scaling Himalayan peaks and fighting Yakṣas to bring Draupadī flowers she had requested.

Bhīma briefly has another wife, the Rākṣasī Hiḍimbā. She bears him the son Ghaṭotkaca, who helps the Pāṇḍavas in the war. During the war, Bhīma's main activity consists in fulfilling his vow to kill the hundred Kauravas, lastly Duryodhana, whom he fells, at Krishna's prompting, with an illegal mace blow to the thigh.

A. Hiltebeitel

BHĪṢMA bēsh´ mŭ (H—Skt.). A great Mahābhārata hero, Bhīṣma is the oldest son of Śaṃtanu, a Lunar Dynasty king, and the river Ganges. He is the incarnation of Dyaus, "sky." Though born with the names Gaṅgeya ("son of Ganges") and Devavrata ("divine vow"), his name Bhīṣma ("terrible") describes the nature of his vow: to satisfy his father's wish for more sons and a second wife, Bhīṣma promised never to rival his half-brothers for the throne, and to become a celibate, thus producing no rival offspring. In gratitude Śaṃtanu gave him the boon of deciding the moment of his death.

To the Kauravas and Pāṇḍavas, Bhīṣma is the "grandfather." With Droṇa, he is an elder statesman and weapons connoisseur. Duty-bound to fight for Duryodhana in the war, he marshals the Kaurava army through the first ten days of battle. The Pāṇḍavas cannot win while he fights, and when Krishna spurs Arjuna against him, a celebrated episode results. Ready to break his own noncombatant vow, Krishna strides toward Bhīṣma wielding his discus. Recognizing Krishna as God, Bhīṣma is overjoyed to die at his hands, but Arjuna tackles Krishna to make him keep his word. Bhīṣma soon tells the Pāṇḍavas of another vow: he would never fight one who, in a previous birth, was a woman. The Pāṇḍavas use this information to defeat him, and Bhīṣma falls filled with arrows. He postpones death until the sun enters its northern course, and while he lies on the battlefield he discourses at length to the war's survivors on matters of virtue and salvation.

A. Hiltebeitel

BIBLE (Ch & Ju—Gr. *biblia,* collection of writings or scrolls; pl. of *biblion,* book). With "the," the sacred scriptures of the Christian tradition or of the Jewish tradition; any sacred scripture short enough to be bound together in one volume; and loosely, the sacred oral or written tradition of any people.

1. **Contents and canonization.** Jewish tradition regards the Hebrew scriptures as the revealed "Word of God" and the teaching of the way of obedience to God for his people, Israel. Primary authority is ascribed to the Torah (teaching, law, way), secondary authority to the Nebi'im (Prophets), and tertiary authority to the collection known as Kethubim (Writings). The first two divisions of the Hebrew scriptures probably arrived at their present form by the late fourth century B.C., but the content of the Writings remained fluid until the end of the first century A.D. The Greek translation of the Hebrew scriptures (Septuagint), made for the Jewish community in Alexandria about the second century B.C., contained additional writings that were eventually excluded by the Jewish tradition, but were included as part of the Old Testament by the Greek-speaking primitive Christian church. According to Jewish tradition, prophecy ceased about 400 B.C. so that there could be no new scriptures after that time. Christians maintained, on the contrary, that prophecy continued and that the writings that eventually became the New Testament were also divinely inspired.

The Septuagint text of the Old Testament was standard in the Christian church until the Reformation, when most Protestant churches restricted the Old Testament to the Hebrew Bible. The Hebrew Bible is divided into twenty-four books comprehensively called "Tanak" (an acrostic for the three major divisions of scripture). The thirty-nine books of the Protestant Old Testament are the result of dividing books classed together in the Hebrew Bible. The order of books also varies. The excluded writings were called by Protestants "Apocrypha" ("hidden," "secret") and were judged to be edifying but not scriptural. Roman Catholics regard these books as Deuterocanonical scripture, while the Eastern

ORTHODOX CHURCHES include them in the Old Testament canon ("norm," "measure").

For the Christian traditions, JESUS the CHRIST is the "Word of God" who is revealed in the Christian writings that are regarded as a "New" Testament or COVENANT with the new people of God, the CHURCH. The coming of the Christ is also understood to be the inner meaning and fulfillment of the Hebrew scriptures now characterized by Christians as the Old Testament. The significance of the Hebrew Bible as Tanak and as Old Testament is thus widely divergent.

Faced with a variety of heresies and "late" revelations, the Christian churches worked out a definitive list of New Testament books by a complex process completed by the fourth century A.D. Writings included were affirmed to be of apostolic inspiration (and thus prior to the end of the first century A.D.), to express true doctrine, and to have been used widely in the church. A variety of other writings were excluded. The New Testament of the Orthodox, Catholic, and Protestant traditions contains twenty-seven books including four GOSPELS, Acts, twenty-one apostolic letters, and Revelation. The ETHIOPIC CHURCH has a larger collection while the Syrian-NESTORIAN Church has a smaller one.

2. **The Bible in the religious community.** The influence of the Hebrew Bible is felt not only through Jewish tradition, but it is also the indispensable historical, cultural, and ideational framework for the New Testament and the Christian tradition. The biblical outlook permeates Western history and culture.

a) Judaism. The Torah is affirmed to be the revelation of God to his people. The Hebrew scriptures set the giving of the Torah, the formation of Israel as the people in covenant with God, the acquisition of the promised land, and the history of the Kingdom of Israel in the context of the creation and of universal human history. The commandments of the Torah as interpreted and applied to changing conditions through oral tradition (collected in writing as TALMUD) are believed to be the revealed norm of obedience to the covenant and are intended to hallow the total existence of the individual and the community. Ethical and devotional observance is as much a concern of the individual and of the family as it is of the community gathered in the synagogue for the SABBATH or for festivals of the liturgical year. SYNAGOGUE worship is focused upon and largely consists of scripture or derivations from the scriptures. The Torah and the Prophets are read and expounded. Selections from the Writings are read as appropriate on festival days. The SHEMA and the BENEDICTIONS are biblical. Psalms are read and sung, and both individual and corporate prayers are derived from biblical texts. The psalms, which run the entire spectrum of religious emotions, form the basic prayerbook.

b) Christianity. The Bible is regarded by the Christian tradition as the apostolic book teaching the truth about God, the Christ, the human condition, and salvation, and it thus is a regulative principle of Christian life, the life of the church, and theology. The Bible is continued as not only a written text but also a living oral tradition in reading and in worship. Broadly speaking, the sources of religious truth are scripture, tradition, reason, and inspiration by the Holy Spirit. The official norm of many Protestant denominations is "scripture alone," but in practice the biblical text can be interpreted for the faith only in the context of tradition within the community of the faithful. Different Christian traditions often emphasize special books of the New Testament, such as the letters of Paul or Revelation, as the "essence" by which the remainder of the Bible is to be interpreted.

How the "Word of God" is in the Bible is a matter of considerable divergence among different types of Protestants. Liberal Christian theologians tend to treat the Bible as a history of stages of progress in human ideals and divine-human inspiration moving from relatively primitive notions toward ethical idealism. Fundamentalists tend to believe the written word to be the inerrant truth of God's revelation, not only on matters of faith and doctrine, but also with regard to natural facts such as the process by which the physical world and human beings evolved. NEO-ORTHODOXY distinguishes between the written words of the Bible, the words preached, and the words that may become the "Word of God" for the hearer when inspired by the Holy Spirit. The Roman Catholic tradition has generally maintained the authoritative truth of the scriptural word, but it distinguishes three senses of scripture besides the literal, and, in addition, interprets scripture in context of ecclesiastical oral tradition. Modern historical-literary criticism of the Bible aims at recovering the original meaning of the texts for their authors in their life-contexts. Insofar as the need of the church is to recover what the biblical texts meant at the time they were spoken or written, historical criticism may be seen as an indispensable aid to the church's interpretive task.

The Christian church took over its basic liturgical forms from Jewish synagogue worship. The extended use of the Bible in worship is apparent in the Catholic and Orthodox liturgical quotations and paraphrases in the AMEN, ALLELULIA, HOSANNA, KYRIE ELEISON, GLORIA PATRI, the Peace, the LORD'S PRAYER, Benedictions, and the EUCHARIST. Scripture readings for the day are determined by a lectionary. Psalms are read and sung, and hymns are frequently derived from psalms. Catholic and Orthodox liturgies are oriented toward the Eucharist, but Protestant worship often separates instruction from the Eucharist (Lord's Supper) and centers worship on the biblical word read and preached.

3. **The Bible and other religious traditions.** The Bible began to spread worldwide in the sixteenth century A.D and is now translated wholly or partially

into over fifteen hundred languages. The Bible has occasioned varying degrees of admiration, relative recognition, and incorporation among adherents of other religious traditions, but in general the Bible, like other scriptures, is sacred in its own traditional character only for people of the faith. The QUR'ĀN urges belief in both the Hebrew Bible and the New Testament as books revealed to prophets before the revelation to MUHAMMAD, the Apostle of God and the Seal of the Prophets. But both the Torah and the Gospels are regarded as corrupted in their present form, and whatever in these earlier revelations disagrees with the Qur'ān is abrogated by the Qur'ān. The Qur'ān retells many stories found in the Hebrew Bible and in the New Testament Gospels. No doubt the majority of Muslims acquire their knowledge of the Bible solely from the Qur'ān. Nevertheless, throughout Islamic history many Muslims have studied the Bible and several novelized lives of Jesus have been published in the twentieth century, especially in Egypt.

Outside Islam the New Testament is generally better known than the Hebrew Bible. Educated Hindus have often been impressed with New Testament ideals and with the character of Jesus. Their "formal" recognition of Jesus as one of many AVATARS (descents of the divine) makes an openness to the New Testament possible by negating its claim to uniqueness and by subordinating its message to the "higher truth" in the Hindu Way. The manner of Jesus' death is distasteful to many Buddhists, and the symbolic eating of his flesh and drinking of his blood is seen by some Buddhists as violent and repelling. Other Buddhists have found much to admire in the teachings of Jesus; theological dialogue between Christians and Buddhists occurs; and even THERAVĀDA Buddhists have at times affirmed that they believe in something like the Christian God. The New Testament is generally treated with respect at a distance except by aggressive movements such as the Japanese SŌKA GAKKAI.

See also SCRIPTURES, SACRED.

Bibliography. F. F. Bruce and E. G. Rupp, *Holy Book and Holy Tradition* (1968); L. Bouyer, *The Meaning of Sacred Scripture* (1958); J. Neusner, *The Way of Torah* (1970); L. E. Keck, *The Bible in the Pulpit* (1978); E. G. Parrinder, *Jesus in the Qur'an* (1965).

J. Y. FENTON

BILĀL IBN RABĀH bə läl′ ib′ən rə bäh′ (I; d. *ca.* 641). A manumitted slave of Abyssinian origin whose early interest in Islam and stentorian voice won him his freedom and the honor of being the first person to hold the position of *muezzin,* calling the Muslims to PRAYER. After being purchased and freed by ABŪ BAKR, he lived in Abū Bakr's house, made the HIJRA with MUHAMMAD, and accompanied Muhammad on his campaigns. He was one of only five non-Arabs to receive stipends from the pay register drawn up by the caliph 'UMAR I. He died at the age of sixty at Damascus after having participated in the Wars of the Conquest. Especially honored among Black Muslims. *See* BLACK RELIGIONS IN THE UNITED STATES §5.

G. D. NEWBY

BIMBISĀRA bĭm bĭ sär′ ä (B). *See* RĀJAGṚHA.

BISHOP (Ch—Gr. [*episkopos*—lit. "overseer"]). Often used in nonbiblical Greek and in Greek-speaking Judaism, the word from which "bishop" is derived occurs only five times in the NT, once referring to Christ (I Pet. 2:25) and the other times referring to church leaders (Acts 20:28; Phil. 1:1; I Tim. 3:2; and Tit. 1:7). It may be, as Acts 20:28 and Tit. 1:5-7 imply, that "bishop" and "elder" were different titles for the same office or function, but by the second century the office of bishop had become the more prominent in the church's organization.

In the Roman Catholic and Orthodox churches bishops serve as chief pastors in their regions, responsible for the character and conduct of worship and preaching, spiritual discipline, and temporal affairs. They ordain priests to the ministry and supervise their work. Some Protestant churches assign the bishop's functions to delegated assemblies of ministers and representatives of congregations; some assign them to superintendents or local pastors. In other Protestant churches bishops continue to exercise liturgical, pastoral, and administrative oversight.

Recent ecumenical statements on ministry and church union continue the office and title of bishop—as a sign of continuity and unity, as pastor among pastors, and as leader of the church in worship and mission. The tendency is to accept the office on constitutional grounds, leaving open the theological definition of its nature. *See* CLERGY, CHRISTIAN; APOSTOLIC SUCCESSION.

Bibliography. Herman W. Beyer, in *Theological Dictionary of the NT,* ed. G. Kittel, II (1964), 599-622; J. M. Urtasum, *What Is a Bishop* (1962); K. Rahner, *Bishops: Their Status and Function* (1964).

K. WATKINS

BIṢṬĀMĪ, ABŪ YAZĪD bĭs tä mē′ ä bo͞o′ yă zēd′ (I; d. A.D. 874). The prototype of the ecstatic SUFI, renowned for his paradoxical utterances. Little is known of his life. His hometown, Bistam, was in northwestern Iran and his spiritual master was Abū 'Alī Sindī, possibly from Sind in present-day Pakistan. This has given rise to speculation about possible Hindu influences on his spiritual formation.

What distinguishes Abū Yazīd among early Sufis is his renunciation of renunciation. "How can one give up God?" he asked. In his yearning to find God alone, he was continually frustrated, and yet he never ceased to yearn. His legendary quest has been condensed in numerous anecdotes and aphorisms, of which the most famous is *Subḥānī* "Glory be to Me!" Like *Ānā'l-Haqq* ("I am Truth!") of AL-ḤALLĀJ, it defies explanation, and perhaps for that reason both phrases echo through the writings of later Persian Sufis.

Bibliography. H. Ritter, "Die Aussprüche des Bāyezīd Bistāmī," in *Westöstliche Abhandlungne, Rudolf Tschudi Zum Siebzigsten Geburstag*, F. Meier, ed. (1954); A. Schimmel, *Mystical Dimensions of Islam* (1975), pp. 47-51.

B. Lawrence

BLACK MASS. A rite attributed to European and American Satanists. It is referred to in accounts from the fourteenth century on, and is prominent in the lore of Satanism in France in the age of Louis XIV and in the late nineteenth century occult revival. The ceremony is a parody of the Roman Catholic Mass, performed in honor of Satan. The altar may be the body of a nude woman, the chalice may be a turnip, and various obscenities are involved. The rites may be performed in a variety of ways, all of which represent the Prince of Darkness as a deity parallel to the Judeo-Christian God. R. S. Ellwood

BLACK MUSLIMS. *See* Black Religions in the United States §5.

BLACK RELIGIONS IN THE UNITED STATES. Most blacks who claim any religious preference are Christians. Although there is an increasing number of black Roman Catholics and a few black members of the Eastern Orthodox Church, the vast majority of blacks are Protestants, primarily Baptists (about nine million) and Methodists (about three million). There are also adherents of Buddhism, Islam, Judaism, and other non-Christian religions.

The degree to which black Christians today have retained some African religious heritage is debatable, although the element of Voodoo is of definite African origin. Members of the Yoruba Temple, a black nationalist sect based in New York, claim to follow the practices of ancient African Yoruba religion. Outside of Sheldon, S. C., is the Yoruba village of Oyo-Tunji, a community established by priests of the Orisha-Voodoo Cult. Witchcraft, voodoo, sorcery, and various pseudo-Yoruban rituals are practiced. Elements of Obeah worship can be found in various forms in Louisiana and South Carolina. In such locations there is a strong belief in "conjuration," most often referred to as "root working." (*See* African Traditional Religion.)

During the 1960s, many black religious leaders sought to demonstrate an African heritage by introducing African folkways into worship services. African chants and ornamentations were used, members dressed in traditional African attire, and in several instances churches painted their images of Jesus black. These changes did not prove to be widespread or enduring.

1. **Origins of the black church.** In colonial America efforts were made to Christianize black slaves, but these efforts were resisted by whites who feared that Christianization would lead to emancipation. In spite of opposition, however, blacks were indoctrinated, sometimes by force, into the Christian faith. These new converts fused their African religious heritage with their new religion, producing a syncretistic faith which gave rise during slavery to the institution known as the "invisible church."

In the decades following the Revolutionary War the cause of "freedom" led numerous whites to consider the plight of slaves. Congregationalists (now United Church of Christ), Presbyterians, and members of the Society of Friends were actively engaged in efforts to manumit slaves. Some blacks became Presbyterians prior to the Civil War but were kept in segregated presbyteries. After the war blacks were incorporated into the major Presbyterian groups. The United Church of Christ has had a consistent, but limited, appeal to educated blacks. Few have been attracted to the Society of Friends.

a) Baptists. Since Baptists did not require formal education for the ministry and allowed for the autonomy of local congregations, many blacks formed Baptist churches from the time of the Revolution on. Although slave insurrections led by black Baptist ministers resulted in restrictions on Baptists in the South, the movement flourished among free Northern blacks. After the Civil War its growth throughout the U.S. was phenomenal.

Racism, growing race consciousness, and splits within local congregations gave rise to separate black Baptist organizations. During the 1880s the National Baptist Convention of America (NBCA) was organized (1956 membership, 2,668,799). Two decades later, a dispute over control of property and publications led to a split. The larger body adopted the name the National Baptist Convention, U.S.A., Inc. (NBUSA; 1958 membership 5,500,000); the smaller group retained the original title.

The NBUSA has remained the largest black religious association in America, but internal problems and failure to respond directly to the civil rights issues of the 1950s precipitated the withdrawal of a sizeable number of congregations. In 1961 the Progressive National Baptist Convention, Inc. (PNBC) was organized (1967 membership 521,692).

The NBUSA and the PNBC differ on educational, political, and social issues, though, with the NBCA, all agree on basic Baptist theology and polity. Many churches maintain an affiliation with a predominantely white convention, usually the American Baptist.

The National Primitive Baptist Convention of the U.S.A. has over 600 congregations located mostly in the South (1975 membership 250,000). Their worship, theology, and concept of missions are distinctly different from that of other Baptist bodies.

b) Methodists. Racism in St. George's Methodist Episcopal Church in Philadelphia gave rise to an independent black Methodist movement. In 1787 Richard Allen, Absalom Jones, and several other black parishioners were virtually dragged from their knees as they prayed in St. George's. Refusing to suffer such indignity, Allen and Jones left St. George's and started their own society. Allen, however, favored the Methodist model of church organization, and Jones, that of the Protestant Episcopal Church. Jones subsequently organized the St. Thomas African Protestant Episcopal Church in Philadelphia. Richard Allen, along with the majority of blacks who left St. George's, organized the Bethel African Methodist Episcopal Church (AME) of Philadelphia. The movement spread to other cities, and in 1816 representatives from various AME churches established the church as an independent denomination (1951 membership 1,166,301). Allen was elected its first bishop and a book of discipline was adopted.

The desire among free Northern blacks for their own churches led in 1796 to a secession from the M.E. Church. This group, with the blessings of Bishop Francis Asbury, secured a charter in 1801. In 1821, a number of black M.E. churches in the New York City area, along with black churches with similar polity, met and organized the AME Zion Church (1973 membership 1,024,974). Its first bishop, James Varick, was elected in 1822.

The Methodist Episcopal (M.E.) Church split over the slave issue in 1844. The southern branch continued its affiliation with blacks until 1870, when the black members withdrew and organized the Christian (originally "Colored") Methodist Episcopal Church (1965 membership 466,718).

Numerous black congregations remained with the M.E. Church. When the M.E. Churches North and South merged in 1939, the M.E. Church, North agreed to a separate jurisdiction for black congregations still in the M.E. Church. Known as the Central Jurisdiction, it existed as a separate entity until the formation of the United Methodist Church in 1968.

c) Holiness and Pentecostalism. PENTECOSTALISM, frequently developing out of Baptist and Methodist traditions, has had an increasing influence. Though there were black Pentecostals prior to 1900, two twentieth century personalities are prominent in the growth of Pentecostalism among blacks: W. J. Seymore, credited with the Apostolic Faith movement (1975 membership 4,100), and C. H. Mason of the Church of God in Christ (1965 membership 425,000).

2. The black minister. *a) Education, status, and tradition.* The control which blacks have had over their own churches, the economic strength of the combined membership, and the general lack of interest by whites in black religion are some of the factors which have contributed to the prominence of the black minister as speaker for the race. The ministry has been an honorable profession open to men barred from others. In the nineteenth century Nat Turner, Denmark Vesey, Henry H. Garnet, Henry M. Turner—all ministers—championed the rights of blacks in America. Twentieth century figures include: Adam Clayton Powell, Jr., Calvin B. Marshall, MARTIN LUTHER KING, JR., Jesse Jackson, and Andrew Young. These have been articulate, biblically versed men who could enunciate effectively the doctrinal beliefs of blacks and provide hope.

Standards for the ministry are few. Emphasis is placed on the experience of being "called" by God, and ORDINATION is a simple formality. The vast majority of black ministers have no formal theological training, though many have attended Bible schools or similar institutions. A large number are not high school graduates.

Black ministers in the predominantly white Christian denominations tend to be better educated, since Presbyterians, Episcopalians, Roman Catholics, and the United Church of Christ have higher educational standards for the ministry than do the traditional black bodies. Black ministers within these bodies serve almost exclusively black congregations.

There is a trend among the well-established black congregations toward demanding a better educated ministry. Often the demand does not include seminary, since many blacks believe seminaries do more harm than good. However, attendance at predominantly black seminaries continues to increase.

b) The minister as social activist. Until the mid-1950s, black religions were only marginally involved in civic and social issues. Involvement amounted to continuous support of the NAACP and lethargic support of the Urban League. Occasionally an isolated black minister would speak out on social ills, but black theology was dominated by concerns with the afterlife. It was the development of student protest and the black power movements of the 1950s and 60s which forced ministers to speak to the issue of civil rights.

Jim Crowism in the South was the first thing attacked by black students. Sit-ins and boycotts became common. In retaliation, whites bombed black churches; attacked, beat, and sometimes killed demonstrators; and had others fired from jobs. Many black ministers denounced the action of the demonstrators, but others seized the opportunity to participate in civil disobedience. By the time of the massive civil riots of 1967, hundreds of black ministers across the country from every denomination and the Nation of Islam had become involved, leading to the passage of the various U.S. civil rights acts between 1964 and 1968. Martin Luther King, Jr., through his Southern Christian Leadership Conference (SCLC), is given much credit for challenging the *status quo.* Such leaders as Stokely Carmichael, Jim Blake, and James Farmer were instrumental in getting black ministers and black people involved in the struggle through civic organizations and the church.

3. Black religious music. *a) Negro spirituals.* Black religious music in America originated in slave days, when the Negro spiritual, a fusion of African heritage and Christian faith, was created. Spirituals developed as a means by which blacks could give free expression to their grief over physical oppression and their joyous hope of deliverance. The language of the spirituals, for the most part, is biblical, though the texts are often disguised. This music is not always sad; examples abound of happy, soul-stirring spirituals. Many of this latter type tend to be otherworldly, e.g., "In That Great Gettin' Up Mornin'."

The Negro spirituals are indicative of the pervasiveness of religion in black life, but they had other functions. Some relate historical events from the lives of blacks; others are protest songs. Although the spiritual has a proud heritage, it does not occupy a prominent role in contemporary black religion.

b) Gospel and other music. The religious music of black folk, until the Depression era, consisted of "line singing," gospel songs (now called "white"), regular Protestant hymns ("The Gospel Pearl" had wide circulation), and spirituals. Thomas A. Dorsey added to these types through his arrangements and compositions for choirs and soloists.

Gospel music, rooted in a fusion of jazz and blues, pervades most of contemporary black worship. It tends to be an upbeat music and highly emotional, with highly ornamented recitatives and imaginative instrumentation, both with an improvised quality. Gospel music can be dramatic and moving. In it the individual has a personal relationship with the words and the rhythmic drive. Contemporary choirs use a large range of instrumental accompaniment: electric organ, piano, horns, drums, etc. Choirs stage performances with music carefully chosen to elicit an audience response at the desired time. This music parallels what is current among the black "pop" generation, leading some of its critics to call it licentious.

4. **Religion in the cities.** *a) Urban migration and the Catholic Church.* In the twentieth century there was massive migration of blacks to urban centers after each world war. In the second migration blacks moved into many areas inhabited by low-income white Catholics. The more economically secure blacks sought admission for their children in parochial schools; the destitute sought handouts at the missions. The church responded positively to black migrants if they converted to Catholicism. In 1965 there were about 766,000 black Catholic parishioners.

b) Storefront churches. "Storefront churches," housed in converted stores, theaters, and houses, began as a Northern black phenomenon in response to the failure of the major denominations to accommodate the urban migrant. They are now found nationally along decaying business thoroughfares. Invariably, they are of the Baptist, Pentecostal/Holiness, or Spiritual persuasions. Some congregations, outgrowing the original storefront, move into a former white church or synagogue, or build a new edifice. For the most part, the storefront maintains the character of rural black religion.

c) Cults and sects. The frustration of urban living, the failure of the established churches to address realistically black socio-economic and spiritual needs, and the emergence of the storefronts, combined to produce an environment in which cults and sects could develop.

i. *The African Orthodox Church.* Beginning in 1916 Marcus Garvey's Universal Negro Improvement Association (UNIA), with emphasis on the political, religious, recreational, cultural, and economic aspects of black life, attracted wide support. With the assistance of G. A. McGuire, an Episcopal priest, Garvey established the African Orthodox Church in 1920. This group has taught since its inception that God is made in the image of man, and that black people should visualize a black God. The church provided an early example of a Black Christ and a Black MADONNA and Child and had international ties, especially with African Christian groups. In 1974 its members numbered 40,000.

ii. *Faith healers.* The Father Divine Peace Mission originated during the Depression era in New York. Father Divine moved his mission in 1932 from Long Island to Harlem, where he found terrible hopelessness among the blacks. Divine persuaded his followers that he could relieve them of their physical as well as emotional illnesses. His followers pledged to pay just debts and to refrain from stealing, drinking, smoking, vulgarity, gambling, playing numbers, racism, and any form of hatred, greed, bigotry, selfishness, or lust. They were encouraged to engage in business for themselves. The cult gained many followers, both black and white, all over the country. It became popular because of its concern with feeding and clothing its followers at little or no expense to them.

Bishop Charles Emmanuel Grace founded the United House of Prayer for All People. "Sweet Daddy Grace" and money were at the center of this cult. When Daddy Grace died in 1960, he had amassed a fortune and had churches and followers in most major cities. The cult continues with United Houses of Prayer in many urban centers, though, like Father Divine's Peace Mission, its influence has diminished.

iii. *Black Jewish groups.* Racism and other factors turned many blacks away from Christianity to non-Christian groups. From 1915 on, several black Jewish congregations came into existence in Washington, Philadelphia, New York, and other northern cities. The earliest such group however, was the Church of God and Saints of Christ, founded in 1896 in Lawrence, Kansas, by William S. Crowdy (1959 membership 38,217). Crowdy taught that blacks are descendants of the lost tribes of Israel. The cult observes the OT sabbath and feast days and uses Hebrew names for the months of the year.

Prophet F. S. Cherry established the Church of God (Black Jews) in Philadelphia. Cherry taught that the true Jews are black and that Jesus was black. His followers were required to read the Christian BIBLE and the TALMUD.

The largest congregation of black Jews is the

Commandment Keepers Congregation of the Living God, sometimes referred to as the Royal Order of Ethiopian Hebrews, the Sons and Daughters of Culture, Inc. Founded in 1919 by Rabbi Wentworth D. Mathew in Harlem, this sect follows the teachings of Orthodox Judaism, contending that blacks in America are really Ethiopian Hebrews or FALASHAS stripped of their heritage. They teach that blacks are the lost sheep of the House of Israel, and that absolute holiness is possible through the Law. The doctrines of KABBALA are prominent among them.

iv. *The Black Christian Nationalist Church.* The Black Christian Nationalist Church (BCN), founded in Detroit by Albert B. Cleage, is a black nationalist sect affirming the divinity of Jesus. It has adopted many principles of a black economic revolution similar to those utilized by the Nation of Islam in the West.

Central to the BCN is the concept that Jesus was a black revolutionary messiah. He belonged to an underground movement interested in the separation and liberation of the black Nation of Israel from Roman control. His message has been corrupted by the teachings of Paul and the theologians of white, Western civilization. The BCN stresses the importance of the black church to black liberation. It calls for black unity, such unity being dictated by the principles of the BCN. There is a de-emphasis of individualism in favor of communal life, which it teaches is essential to the survival of black people.

5. The Nation of Islam in the West. The Nation of Islam, the Black Muslims, began in Detroit during the Depression. Its founder, W. D. Fard, gathered followers from among the poverty-stricken blacks of Detroit and organized the Detroit Temple. Fard's teachings included "the deceptive character of the white man and the glorious history of the black race." Illiterate followers were taught to read so that they could read for themselves the history of their great race. Fard wrote two manuals which are now the basic documents for the movement: *The Secret Ritual of the Nation of Islam* and *Teaching for the Lost Found Nation of Islam in a Mathematical Way*. Fard established the ritual and worship of the temple and founded the University of Islam to provide elementary and secondary education. The Fruit of Islam, a paramilitary organization for men, was established to deal with unbelievers. Members were taught military tactics, including the use of weapons.

As the movement developed, Fard established a hierarchy under a minister of Islam, ELIJAH MUHAMMAD. Upon Fard's disappearance in June 1934, Elijah Muhammad ran into difficulty with the moderate element of the movement which gained control of the Detroit Temple. He moved to Chicago and took charge of Temple No. 2. There he began to reshape the movement and to make it more militant. Through the teachings of Elijah Muhammad, Fard was identified with ALLAH, which made it possible for prayer and sacrifice to be made to him. Muhammad assumed the titles "Prophet" and "Messenger of Allah."

Under Elijah Muhammad the movement gained international prominence. Mosques were started in most major cities of the U.S. Schools, apartment complexes, stores, and farms owned by the Nation of Islam came to be commonplace. The publication *Muhammad Speaks*, now the *Balalian News*, came to be read by Americans of all races.

The Muslims have had phenomenal success with converting convicts, criminals, and dope users. An excellent example of this transformation is the life of Malcolm Little, better known as Malcolm X. There is a strict morality among the Muslims. A devout member prays five times daily. Before prayer, the proper ablution must be made. Cleanliness of body and spirit is essential. Dietary laws are rigidly enforced, fasting is encouraged, and tobacco and alcohol are forbidden. There is a strict sexual code.

Traditionally, the Nation of Islam has taught that Christianity is a white religion and that it is a disgrace for blacks to call themselves Christians. Central to the traditional teachings are: (a) the black man has a manifest destiny; (b) whites are the personification of evil, a hindrance to black freedom and moral development; (c) the original man was black; (d) there is a divinity in blackness; and (e) the white race was created by a black scientist (Yakub) who had rebelled against Allah.

Upon the death of Elijah Muhammad in February 1975, his son Wallace D. Muhammad assumed the spiritual leadership of the movement and took the title of IMAM. The most significant of the changes he introduced involves the attitude toward whites, who are now permitted to become members. Under this leader the movement assumed the title "The World Community of al-Islam in the West."

6. Black theology. For the most part this movement has reflected socio-political conditions. The denial of opportunities for work and education has led to a theology which incorporates nationalism and Pan-Africanism. This was reinforced by the teachings of Garvey, Noble Drew Ali (founder of the Moorish Science Temple, Newark, N. J., about 1913), the Muslims, and others who stressed the unity of black people. The faith healers have taken the black experience of oppression and turned it into a theology of hope. By teaching immediate access to God and God's imminent presence they help many to cope with their physical and mental restrictions. This leads, all too often, to the belief that religion, through the faith healer, will make everything all right. In contrast, many black theologians stress the mission of blacks to the worldwide Christian community. Some see blacks in the OT "suffering-servant" motif—a collective interpretation of the Servant Songs in Isaiah 42-53; others believe the black race is the "liberating messiah" of Western Christendom. This latter concept draws heavily on the LIBERATION THEOLOGY which has developed out of the Latin American church. A third avenue suggests that the only legitimate role for the black race is assimilation; black folk religion will cease to function once black people have been assimilated by Western culture. This view conflicts with the black nationalist stress on the need for racial unity as a basis for direct action.

Bibliography. M. J. Adler, ed., *The Negro in American History* (1969); H. Brotz, *The Black Jews of Harlem* (1970); A. B. Cleage, *Black Messiah* (1969), *Black Christian Nationalism* (1972); Consultation on the Negro in the Christian Ministry, *Toward a Better Ministry* (1966); H. Courlander, *Negro Folk Music USA* (1963); W. E. B. DuBois, *Souls of Black Folk* (1903); A. H. Fauset, *Black Gods of the Metropolis* (1944); E. F. Frazier, *The Negro Church in America* (1963); R. F. Johnston, *The Development of Negro Religion* (1954); R. J. Jones, *A Comparative Study of Religious Cult Behavior among Negroes* (1939); A. Locke, *The Negro and his Music* (1936); B. E. Mays and J. W. Nicholson, *The Negro's Church* (1933); H. A. Ploski and W. Marr, eds., *The Negro Almanac*, 3rd. rev. ed. (1976); P. I. Rose, ed., *Americans from Africa* (1970); J. Washington, *Black Religion* (1964); G. S. Wilmore, *Black Religion and Black Radicalism* (1973); C. G. Woodson, *History of the Negro Church* (1921); J. W. Work, *American Negro Songs and Spirituals* (1940).

J. W. Waters

BLAKE, WILLIAM (Ch; 1757-1827). English poet and artist. Born in London, he was studying drawing by age ten, and in 1772 was apprenticed as an engraver. But poetry also attracted the young Blake, and in 1783 friends published his *Poetical Sketches*, including poems from as early as 1768. In many of his later works Blake united his creative talents in "illuminated printing," integrating text and illustration. His works, which have earned for him such labels as mystic, visionary, prophet, myth-maker, social critic, philosopher, genius, and lunatic were largely ignored or considered unintelligible during his lifetime. Among his works are *There Is No Natural Religion* and *All Religions Are One* (1788), two early aphoristic works; *Songs of Innocence* (1789) and *Songs of Experience* (1794), companion collections of deceptively simple lyric poems; *The Book of Thel* (1789); *The Marriage of Heaven and Hell* (1793); *America* (1793); *The Book of Urizen* (1794); *The Four Zoas* (*ca.* 1804); *The Everlasting Gospel* (*ca.* 1818), Blake's most extensive statement on Jesus; *Jerusalem* (*ca.* 1820); and *Illustrations of the Book of Job* (1826).

Bibliography. J. G. Davies, *The Theology of William Blake* (1948); R. L. Grimes, *The Divine Imagination: William Blake's Major Prophetic Visions* (1972). D. J. White

BLOOD LIBEL (Ju). The accusation of murdering members of another religion, especially children, to obtain blood for one's rituals, has been brought against various religious miniority groups in the course of history. It was developed most fully and with devastating consequences in medieval Europe against Jews (even though blood sacrifices were expressly forbidden in Judaism). A mixture of superstitions, popular belief, and deliberate lies, the libel is based on a view of Jews as murderous, hating Gentiles, especially Christians (*see* Anti-Semitism). The motif of torturing and murdering Christian children in mockery of Jesus' passion is found throughout the twelfth and thirteenth centuries, and appears in Chaucer's *Prioress' Tale*. At times it is combined with the drinking of blood by Jews for medicinal purposes.

Although emperors and popes generally condemned the blood libel as false and inhuman, it persisted in the popular imagination into modern times, particularly in Eastern Europe. Numerous blood libel charges are found in Russia, one of the best-known of which, the Beilis case, occurred as late as 1911. The Nazis revived the ancient propaganda. For more than eight hundred years the blood libel fed passionate hatred of Jews, often leading to their torture, expulsion, and murder.

Bibliography. M. Samuel, *Blood Accusation* (1966).

E. Fleischner

BLOOD VENGEANCE (I). *See* Qiṣās.

B'NAI B'RITH bə nā′ bə rīth′ (Ju—Heb.; lit. "sons of the covenant"). The Anti-Defamation League of B'nai B'rith (ADL) is the world's largest Jewish service organization, founded in 1913 by Samuel Livingston, a Chicago attorney, to fight Anti-Semitism and discrimination of any kind. Through education, legislation, and the media, the ADL has played an important role in safeguarding America's democratic institutions. Its interreligious department is actively engaged in the Ecumenical Movement. The ADL today has twenty-eight regional offices and its own publications. E. Fleischner

BODHGAYĀ bōd gī′ yä. A town in the central part of the modern Indian state of Bihar. Gautama the Buddha experienced enlightenment in a garden-like spot named Uruvelā not far from Bodhgayā *ca.* 530 B.C. It is here he is said to have preached his famous Fire Sermon. R. H. Drummond

BODHI bō′ dhē (B—Skt; lit. "enlightenment" [*budh*—"to be awake"]). 1. Unlike the state of Nirvana, which surpasses the ability of human language to describe, the *bodhi* experience of Gautama Buddha has a specific content which can be transmitted to others. It is better described as a perfect clarity of mind rather than a spiritual state.

According to the Theravāda tradition, during the night Gautama sat in deep meditation he experienced a wider vision of his own existence and derived from that vision a blueprint for the religious life. During the first part of the night Gautama remembered each of his past lives. During the second part he came to an understanding of causality, i.e., he grasped the nature of Samsara. Finally, in the third part, he synthesized his experience in a logical diagnosis of the human condition and a prescription for putting an end to suffering (the FOUR NOBLE TRUTHS).

Bodhi, both the experience and its content, forms the core of Buddhist ritual and teaching. Meditation with "zestful ease" is the method par excellence of realizing the wisdom the *bodhi* experience affords. Following the noble EIGHTFOLD PATH is the way of putting the supreme wisdom into practice. The strong Buddhist emphasis on orthopraxy (correct practice) over orthodoxy (correct belief) stems from the nature of Gautama's *bodhi* experience which invites others to "come and see" rather than to "come and believe." Whereas the attainment of Nirvana is difficult if not impossible to describe, the experience of *bodhi* is more easily grasped and duplicated.

2. **Bodhi tree.** The tree under which the Buddha was enlightened, *Ficus religiosa* (peepul or bo-tree), is an Asiatic fig that begins life as an epiphyte and may attain a height of one hundred feet. It branches indefinitely (like the banyan tree) and has thick prop roots that support the extended branches. Its fruits are a purplish black, about a quarter of inch in diameter, and are a favorite food of birds. A tree plays a significant role at two points in Gautama's life. According to one late tradition, his first experience in meditation was as a boy when he slipped naturally into a trance while seated under a rose-apple tree. At the age of thirty-five, then, having abandoned the ascetic life, Gautama recalled that first experience in meditation and again sought refuge under a tree to compose his mind and await enlightenment. The tree which sheltered him throughout that night became known as the Bodhi tree, or tree of enlightenment, and the place BODHGAYĀ, or place of enlightenment.

When King AŚOKA of India sent his daughter to Sri Lanka as a Buddhist missionary, she took with her a branch of the famous Bodhi tree. The branch took root in Sri Lanka, as did the new religion, and the tree in Anurādhapura is said to be an offspring of the original in Bodhgayā.

Bibliography. W. L. King, *In the Hope of Nibbana* (1964); M. Eliade, "Vegetation: Rites and Symbols of Regeneration," *Patterns in Comparative Religion* (1968).

P. L. BASU

BODHIDHARMA bō dē dûr′ mŭ (B—Skt.; *ca.* A.D. 470-543) **P'U-T'I-TA-MO** pōō tē dä′ mō (B—Chin.) **DARUMA** dä′ roo mä (B—Jap.). Reputed twenty-eighth Indian patriarch and first patriarch of China in the Ch'an (ZEN) tradition; semi-legendary founder of Ch'an.

1. **The problem.** Early records describe Indian and Chinese meditation masters before Bodhidharma's time. Why has Zen tradition focused on this shadowy figure as its founder? Most early references to him are so obviously legendary that some scholars question his historicity, and accurate description of his life and teachings may well be impossible.

2. **The legend.** Terse references to Bodhidharma in sixth and seventh century texts suggest his arrival

The Metropolitan Museum of Art, gift of Mrs. Winthrop W. Aldrich, Mrs. Arnold Whitridge, and Mrs. Sheldon Whitehouse, 1963

Porcelain figure of Bodhidharma, late Ming Dynasty (14th-17th centuries)

in South China during the Liu Sung Dynasty (420-79) and his presence in the Northern Wei kingdom about 520. The later *Record of the Transmission of the Lamp* (by Tao-yüan in 1004) sets Bodhidharma's arrival in Canton at 520 (or 526) and describes an interview with Emperor Wu in which Bodhidharma declares the emperor's temple-building and sūtra-copying to be of "no merit whatever" and the "holy doctrine" to be "vast emptiness, with nothing in it to be called holy." He is described as sitting in contemplation before a wall at Shao-lin-ssŭ monastery for nine years, and accepting Hui-K'ê as disciple only after the latter proved his sincerity by cutting off his arm. Further legendary accretions describe Bodhidharma crossing the Yangtze on a reed, and appearing in Central Asia after his death and burial in China.

3. **Thought and significance.** Most scholars agree that the "Six Treatises of Bodhidharma" are spurious, though some hold that a brief text entitled "Two Entrances and Four Acts" indicates his teachings agree with the Mahāyāna VIMALIKĪRTI and Nirvana SŪTRAS. All that is essential to Zen was attributed to Bodhidharma, as in this T'ang Dynasty stanza credited to him:

Special transmission outside scripture;
No dependence on words or letters;
Direct pointing at the soul of man;
Seeing into one's own nature and attaining
  Buddhahood.

4. **Art and culture.** Black ink paintings of Bodhidharma emphasizing his fierce eyes became a

standard subject in Zen painting, and Japanese "Daruma-dolls" are a traditional gift for persons who have attained some goal through perserverance. The martial arts likewise look to Bodhidharma, tracing Shao-lin boxing to his physical training for monks.

Bibliography. See bibliog. for ZEN. C. W. EDWARDS

BODHISATTVA bō dī sät´ və (B—Skt.; lit. "a being [*sattva*] for enlightenment [*bodhi*]") **BODHISATTA** bō dī sät´ tə (B—Pali). A being who undertakes a quest for enlightenment (BODHI). This meaning is found in all strands of the Buddhist tradition in the past and at present and occurs in the earliest strata of extant Buddhist texts, where it is used by the Buddha to refer to himself prior to the attainment of enlightenment. In rather early passages the term was used to designate the former Buddhas while they were still in their quest for enlightenment (*see* JĀTAKA), and also to designate the next Buddha, MAITREYA. In MAHĀYĀNA the bodhisattva postpones his final complete enlightenment and attainment of NIRVĀNA in order to aid all other beings in their quest for enlightenment.

The belief that a bodhisattva is destined for full enlightenment, as was Gautama, is communicated through Buddhist art, especially by those artists who depicted bodhisattvas in royal attire and characteristic poses suggestive of wealth and leisure, recalling the princely life of the Buddha prior to his going forth from home in search of enlightenment. (*See* BUDDHA, LIFE OF GAUTAMA; ART AND ARCHITECTURE, BUDDHIST.)

1. **Three modes of religious quest.** In holding that former Buddhas were bodhisattvas prior to their enlightenment and that the next Buddha is to be understood as a bodhisattva at present, Buddhists established the way of a bodhisattva as a mode of questing for full enlightenment (*samyaksambodhi*). Also rather early in the tradition there was a category of silent sages known as Pratyeka Buddhas, solitary Buddhas, those who attained enlightenment on their own, who chose not to teach or to form a group of disciples. (*See* BUDDHA, GENERAL CONCEPTS OF.) This way of a Pratyeka Buddha was established as one mode of questing for enlightenment. However, the earliest strata of the Buddhist canonical tradition represent the way of an ARHANT, "a worthy one" (worthy because of attaining salvific insight into DHARMA by fulfilling the disciple's career) as the standard mode for the religious quest. (*See also* LOHAN.)

Within the THERAVĀDA tradition, the path of the *arhant* is the ideal model for religious aspiration. With the rise of the Mahāyāna movement the bodhisattva path became preeminently the ideal model, and this to such extent that one might interpret Mahāyāna as primarily the *bodhisattvayāna*, the bodhisattva's VEHICLE.

2. **Development of the bodhisattva ideal.** Fundamental elements of diverse historical origin and of different chronological strata that have come together into a formulation of the bodhisattva doctrine within the Mahāyāna are (1) having the proper disposition, (2) developing the thought of enlightenment (*bodhicitta*), (3) prediction, (4) engaging in a bodhisattva career replete with wisdom and means, (5) performing six model perfections (*pāramitā:* later formally structured as ten, yet the first six continue to be those most stressed), and (6) coursing through stages (*bhūmi*) of the career. On the whole, the bodhisattva doctrine as presented in the PALI CANON corresponds with this basic structure, but differs in detail, emphasis, and focus; in Theravāda the bodhisattva career is a legitimate alternative, while in Mahāyāna it is the ideal.

Courtesy of the Smithsonian Institution, Freer Gallery of Art, Washington, D. C.

Marble bodhisattva from China (6th century A.D.)

One Theravāda source (Sutta-Nipāta Commentary: Being Paramatthajotika II, II.486) says that a bodhisattva is "a being characterized by awakening, a being worthy to go to full enlightenment," a definition to which Mahāyāna would readily ascribe. Another Theravāda source (Sāratthappakāsinī, the commentary on the Saṃyutta Nikāya, II. 21) says: "Here bodhi means knowledge. A being [*satta*] for the purpose of bodhi [*bodhiyā*]. One possessing knowledge, possessing wisdom, one learned is what is meant. This being, learned from the time of his resolution, not a blind fool, is a bodhisatta. Or, just as a lotus, that has risen from water, firm, that has attained fullness will naturally be awakened by the warmth of the sun's rays and is called an 'awakened lotus,' so because of the gaining of the prediction in the presence of the Buddhas, having naturally fulfilled the perfections without interruption, he will awaken; and so a bodhisatta is a being characterized by awakening. He proceeds wishing for that *bodhi,* which is reckoned as the knowledge of the four paths and so 'a being attached to *bodhi*' is a bodhisatta."

In the Mahāyāna, the quest is for enlightenment, in terms of "emptiness" (ŚŪNYATĀ), a penetration into the way things are, into "suchness" (TATHATĀ) or "thusness," which is simultaneously expressed as the unobscured manifestation of fundamental "Buddha-nature." The bodhisattva postpones his final complete enlightenment and attainment of Nirvana for the sake of all beings, who, through his wisdom *(prajñā)* and compassion *(karuṇā),* are to be aided in their religious quest by his teaching, life, example, or direct agency.

3. **Becoming a bodhisattva.** In the preliminary stages leading to the arising of the thought of enlightenment *(bodhicitta),* one demonstrates the proper disposition, whether innate or acquired, for undertaking the quest for enlightenment. The poet Sāntideva (early eighth century A.D.) in his *Bodhicaryāvatāra* shows how acts of devotion can complement meditative practice and intensify an aspiration for enlightenment without engendering or sustaining a sense of self-gain. This demonstrates the standard Mahāyāna notion that emptiness (śūnyatā), either as goal of a religious quest for understanding or when holistically realized, is expressed through human behavior in acts of compassion.

When the thought of enlightenment *(bodhicitta)* arises, it marks a total orientation of heart and mind (represented by *citta*) toward enlightenment *(bodhi).* With this total commitment, one becomes a bodhisattva, a being for the purpose of enlightenment. The bodhisattva then makes his ardent wish or great vow. These vows vary from text to text, from century to century, but one of the best known, and one that communicates well the commitment to and scope of the bodhisattva's adventure, is

Living beings are countless—
  I vow to save them all.
Passions are inextinguishable—
  I vow to extinguish them all.
Dharma-truths are measureless—
  I vow to master them all.
The Buddha-way is unexcelled—
  I vow to attain it.

According to a basic formulation of the bodhisattva doctrine, the vow is made in the presence of one believed to be a "living Buddha," who makes a prediction of the bodhisattva's future attainment of enlightenment. Failing this, the vow is expressed in the presence of another on the bodhisattva career or, while in meditation, in the presence of all Buddhas and bodhisattvas.

The bodhisattva enters his career, a path replete with wisdom *(prajñā,* i.e., penetrative insight into emptiness) and means *(upāya,* perseverance in the path and outreach to others). Great effort is placed on developing to completion the perfections *(pāramitā)* of giving, virtue, forbearance, striving, and meditation, in the process of developing and complementing wisdom.

4. **The career of the bodhisattva** has been structured into ten stages *(bhūmi),* and occasionally the "six perfections" are combined with four others to harmonize with these ten stages. The titles and descriptions of these stages differ from text to text. A standard interpretation of the stages is given in the Sūtra Concerning the Ten Stages (Daśabhūmika Sūtra), where they are called (1) "joyful," (2) "spotless," (3) "luminous," (4) "radiant," (5) "hard-to-conquer," (6) "face-to-face," (7) "going far," (8) "immovable," (9) "stage of the good," and (10) "cloud of dharma."

The formulation of the elaborate doctrine of the bodhisattva career is packed with detail and pervaded with devotion by schoolmen and poets. It represents a way of personal discipline consonant with a world view that enables one to eradicate what is detrimental in oneself by cultivating the well-being of others in the quest for enlightenment.

5. **Bodhisattva and arhant.** Within Mahāyāna sources the career of the bodhisattva is set over against (partly for polemical purposes but primarily for didactic purposes) the career of an *arhant,* called "disciple" *(śrāvaka*—"hearer"), and the point is made in some Buddhist sources and numerous Western studies that the way of the *arhant* is "selfish," lacking in the compassion manifest in the career of the bodhisattva. The *arhant* is seen as seeking his own release, while the bodhisattva is committed to assist all beings in their realization of release.

Early in the Mahāyāna movement a profound interpretation of Buddhist teaching was affirmed: that the whirl of existence (SAMSARA) and Nirvana are not opposed to each other, but are the same, that both are, indeed that everything is, emptiness (śūnyatā), that there is a fundamental "thusness" or "suchness" that constitutes Buddha-nature, and that this is absolute reality. In light of this insight, the bodhisattva has no conception of Nirvana over against samsara. Within the older discernment the way of the *arhant* led to the attainment of final Nirvana, which, when attained, is synonymous with final transcendence. Within their respective world views the modes of religious quest could not be formulated otherwise. For the *arhant,* to remain in samsara is to continue to be bound; for the bodhisattva, to seek Nirvana apart from samsara is to misunderstand. Both modes have, within their separate strands of the Buddhist tradition, provided models of religious living that communicate, with remarkable fidelity, qualities of life to be discerned in the life of the Buddha, in living in accordance with dharma.

6. **Celestial bodhisattvas.** Also forming a part of the bodhisattva doctrine within Mahāyāna is the presence of great bodhisattvas *(mahāsattvas).* These beings have progressed far in the way of a bodhisattva, are worthy of devotion, are capable of rendering aid, are able to provide assistance in the worshiper's own development, and are suitable objects for meditation. Buddhist Mahāyāna literature heralds these great beings: MAITREYA, MAÑJUŚRĪ, AVALOKITEŚVARA, KSHITIGARBA, Mahāsthāmaprāpta, Samantabhadra, and many others.

Bibliography. H. Dayal, *The Bodhisattva Doctrine in Buddhist Sanskrit Literature* (1932, rpr. 1970); H. R. Robinson and W. L. Johnson, *The Buddhist Religion.* 2nd ed. (1977), pp. 96-107.

J. R. CARTER

BOEHME, JAKOB bû´ mə (Ch; 1575-1624). German lay theologian and mystic. A shoemaker in Görlitz, Silesia, he described his visions in the book *Aurora* (1612). He was denounced by Lutheran clergy but his many theosophical writings found a wide readership, and deeply influenced the Romantics and philosophers from Schelling to Heidegger. *See* THEOSOPHY D. F. DURNBAUGH

BOHORĀS bō hō´ räs **BOHRĀS** or **BUHRAH** (I—Gujarati; lit. "trader," "merchant" [*vohorvu*—"to trade"].) Muslim community in western India whose members, for the most part, belong to the ISMĀ'ĪLIYYA sect of SHI'ISM and recognize al-Must'ali (1094-1101) as IMAM and successor to his father al-Mustanṣir, the FATIMID, against the claims of his brother Nizār. Nizār's adherents are represented in India by the KHŌJĀS. *(See also* ASSASSINS.) The name implies the Hindu origin of the earliest converts to this sect. There are also SUNNI and even Hindu Bohorās. The Bohorās keep their religious books secret, but their works on law were well known, because the IMĀMIYYA have had access to their *Da'ā'im al-islām* from early times.

Bibliography. T. Lokhandwalla, "A Muslim Community in Gujarat," *Studia Islamica* (1955) pp. 117-35; Abbas H. al-Ḥamadānī, *The Ismā'īlī Da'wa in Northern India* (1956).

A. A. SACHEDINA

BÖN bən. The ancient, pre-Buddhist religion of Tibet and the traditions and practices that have persisted from it down to the present. The meaning of the name remains obscure but probably refers to the conjuring of gods by magic formulas. The practitioners of this religion refer to themselves as *Bön-Po.* Bön is found in the more isolated and culturally backward parts of northern and western Tibet, although originally its extent was much greater. It originally embraced a loose aggregate of animistic-shamanistic practices of various tribal cults which coexisted and combined syncretistically. After the mission of PADMA-SAMBHAVA in the mid-eighth century A.D. Buddhism emerged as dominant. Yet Bön continued to exist, partly in opposition to and partly in cooperation with Buddhism. (*See* ANIMISM; SHAMANISM.)

The Bön-Po believe in a King of Heaven who is surrounded by heavenly beings, one of whose sons became the first king of Tibet. At that time the heavenly beings had direct access to earth by a ladder. Gri-grum, the eighth king, while the victim of a black magic attack, cut the ladder to heaven, and access to the King of Heaven was ended. Severing the link with the King of Heaven rendered him irrelevant to human life. Only a few magicians and priests could ever hope to grasp the "spirit rope" and ascend to the highest heaven. Now salvation is in gaining control over the spiritual beings who affect human life. These are divided into the *lHa,* "gods" or good, and *aDre,* "goblins" or evil. They are rooted in nature and reflect the capricious and violent forces of nature that render life in Tibet precarious.

The central figure in Bön iconography is the blue-robed *gSHen Rabs,* "the man of the lineage of the Bön shaman," reputed founder of the Bön religion. He is not a BODHISATTVA but one possessed of power to control the spiritual beings and, as such, is the archetype of all Bön shamans *(gSHen).* The shaman-priest practices magic to control gods and demons, heal the sick, control the elements, tell fortunes, and destroy enemies by maledictions. The *gSHen* carries a knife and could offer bloody sacrifices of animals and human beings, although this practice has largely been abandoned under Buddhist opposition. In these rites the *gSHen* enters a trance and is possessed by either the *lHa* (god or gods) or the *aDre* (goblins) who bestow extraordinary powers.

Prayers in Bön and Buddhism share many verbal forms and rhythmic chants. Although they share some shrine sites, the Bön make the circumambulation in a counter-clockwise direction and the Buddhist in a clockwise direction. Buddhists give to Bön-Po the status of *Nang Ba* (within ones), although often with a measure of condescension. However, at times the superior power of a *gSHen* is recognized by Buddhists who utilize him in difficult exorcisms or in burial rituals.

Bibliography. H. Hoffman, *The Religions of Tibet* (1961); R. B. Ekvall, *Religious Observances in Tibet* (1964); D. Snellgrove, *The Nine Ways of B'on* (1967).

D. G. DAWE

BONAVENTURE bŏn â vĕn´ tūr (Ch; 1221-1274). FRANCISCAN mystical theologian whose short work, the *Itinerarium mentis ad Deum,* has enjoyed an enduring readership through the centuries; CANONIZED in 1482. *See* SCHOLASTICISM §2. F. OAKLEY

BONIFACE VIII bŏn´ ĭ fās (Ch; *ca.* 1235-1303). Pope from 1294 and vigorous advocate of papal absolutism. He challenged the rising national monarchies in Europe, and his failures marked the triumph of lay over ecclesiastical power. Boniface's PAPACY was dominated by conflicts that grew out of his efforts to restate the most extreme claims of his predecessors. Attempting to establish an independent papal diplomacy, he took as his major objectives the pacification of Europe and the liberation of the Holy Land from the Turks. Bold claims and successive defeats, however, marked his reign from the start. His most significant failure was his inability to stop the war between England and France by depriving them of their main financial resources, taxation of the clergy. This led to the fierce antagonism between Boniface and Philip IV of France, resulting in Boniface's humiliation and eventual death. Boniface accused Philip of abusing his powers and subverting the church; subsequently, in his bull *Unam Sanctam* (1302), he claimed full jurisdiction over all temporal rulers. At the first States General (1302) Philip presented countercharges against him. Before Boniface could announce the king's excommunication, forces led by William Nogaret and Sciarra Colonna seized the town of Anagni and captured the pope. Although quickly freed, Boniface never recovered from the experience and died soon afterward.

Bibliography. C. T. Wood, *Philip the Fair and Boniface VIII: State vs. Papacy* (1967). H. L. BOND

BOOK OF CHANGES (Con). *See* I CHING.

BOOK OF COMMON PRAYER (Ch). The official liturgy of the ANGLICAN CHURCHES, in various recensions according to the use of each church. With the Bible and a hymnal, it contains all forms and texts required for corporate worship and ministration of the sacraments: the calendar of the church year, with tables of scriptural lessons; daily offices of morning and evening prayer, with additional prayers and litany; the rites of Holy Communion (or EUCHARIST), baptism, confirmation, marriage, thanksgiving after childbirth, ministry to the sick, and burial. Bound with it are the Psalms and the Ordinal for conferring ministerial orders of deacons, priests, and bishops, and appendices that may contain forms for special occasions, family prayers, and the THIRTY-NINE ARTICLES OF RELIGION.

The Book was a product of the English Reformation in the reign of Edward VI and was largely the work of Thomas Cranmer, Archbishop of Canterbury. The first Book of 1549, imposed (as were its successors) by an Act of Uniformity, was a moderate revision in a felicitous English style of medieval Latin services, with borrowings from ancient Greek and Gallican liturgies and Lutheran sources. The second Book of 1552 showed stronger Protestant sympathies by reducing prescribed ceremonies and restructuring both the form and doctrine of the Holy Communion. Suppressed by Queen Mary in 1553, the second Book was restored by Elizabeth I in 1559 with some modifications.

The enforcement of the Book by Elizabeth and the early Stuarts provoked Puritan groups to antagonism against its "read prayers" and nonbiblical elements. This, combined with political and economic grievances, led to Parliament's abolition of the Prayer Book and episcopacy (1645) and the monarchy (1649). With the accession of Charles II the Prayer Book was restored in 1662, but many dissidents rejected its moderate revision. The Episcopal Church of Scotland, disestablished in 1689, reshaped its Eucharist after the 1549 model; its consecration prayer was adopted in the first American Prayer Book of 1789.

Social changes, advances in liturgical studies, and internal controversies about ritual, led to overall revisions in the early twentieth century. Although the English proposed Prayer Books of 1928-29 were rejected by Parliament, revised Books were adopted in Scotland, Ireland, Canada, and the United States. After World War II most Anglican Churches took up revision again in both inter-Anglican and ecumenical contexts of exchange, with experiments in contemporary English, wider choices of texts, and agreements reached regarding common structures of the Eucharist, initiatory rites of baptism and confirmation, ordination rites, and the church year. *See* LITURGY; PURITANS.

Bibliography. Sources and texts 1549-1662: F. E. Brightman, *The English Rite*, 2 vols. (1921); recent eucharistic rites: B. Wigan, *The Liturgy in English* (2nd ed., 1964); C. O. Buchanan, *Modern Anglican Liturgies 1958-1968* (1968) and *Further Anglican Liturgies 1968-1975* (1975); history and rationale: M. H. Shepherd, Jr., *The Oxford American Prayer Book Commentary* (1950); G. J. Cuming, *A History of Anglican Liturgy* (1969); H. Davies, *Worship and Theology in England*, 5 vols. (1961-75). M. H. SHEPHERD, JR.

BOOK OF THE DEAD, TIBETAN (B). *See* BARDO THODÖL.

BOOK OF MORMON (Ch). Sacred text of the LATTER-DAY SAINTS or Mormons, who accept it as the accurate history of America's earliest inhabitants, beginning with the Jaredites, who are reported to have left from the Tower of Babel and crossed to America in windowed barges. The Jaredites' story is brief, for they extinguished themselves in internecine wars.

The text primarily concerns the Lamanites, ancestors of the American Indians, and their fraternal foes, the Nephites. Both are presumed descendants of a "lost tribe" of Israel who arrived around the time of the Babylonian Exile. At first, both possessed the divine revelation which brought salvation. The text tells of an American post-resurrection appearance of Christ to establish proper religious order and confirm religious truth. America thus became the promised land where the millennial kingdom of Christ would be established.

In time, the Lamanites became apostate and attacked the faithful Nephites. Of the Nephites, only

Mormon, who wrote the text on golden plates, and his son, Moroni, survived. Moroni buried the plates on the hill Cumorah, near Palmyra, New York, in A.D. 438.

In 1822 JOSEPH SMITH claimed to have uncovered the plates, written in reformed Egyptian hieroglyphics, following a vision of Moroni. With a curtain separating them, Smith dictated a translation to a copyist. Smith's wife was the first copyist, but three others assisted before the Book of Mormon was published in 1830.

The Book of Mormon has long engendered controversy. One question concerns its authorship. Since Smith declared that an angel removed the plates, no one else has seen them except in ecstatic visions. Detractors have noted parallels between the Book of Mormon and the purported manuscript of an unpublished novel by Solomon Spaulding. Some attribute authorship to Sidney Rigdon, a zealous early convert to the Mormon way. But little in the text itself requires ascription of authorship to any other than Smith.

More important are the structure of the Book of Mormon and its relation to the religious scene of Smith's day. The work is modeled on the first six books of the OT in its emphasis on history and inclusion of numerous pronouncements and guidelines for believers. Many of these concern issues, such as believers' baptism by immersion, which were controversial in the nineteenth century. In language, the English text echoes the King James Version of the BIBLE and borrows some 27,000 words directly from it. Grammatical errors abound. These factors have led scholars to assume that the work at least came from the hand of someone familiar with the King James Version and conversant with nineteenth century religious issues, if not from Smith himself.

Within the tradition the Book of Mormon joins Smith's *Doctrine and Covenants* and the *Pearl of Great Price*, which contains the *Book of Abraham* and the *Book of Moses*, as sacred texts supplementary to the Bible.

Bibliography. G. Arbaugh, *Revelation in Mormonism* (1932).

C. H. LIPPY

BOOTH, WILLIAM (Ch; 1829-1912). The founder of the SALVATION ARMY. He broke with the Methodist New Connection in 1861 to become an itinerant preacher, and in 1865 founded a group which evolved into the Salvation Army in 1878. As its first general he led this international organization until his death. G. H. SHRIVER

BOOTHS, FEAST OF (Ju). *See* SUKKOT.

BORROMEO, CHARLES CARDINAL bōr´ rō mâ´ ō (Ch; 1538-1584). Papal Secretary of State to his uncle Pius IV; helped prepare Session III of the Council of TRENT and implemented its reform decrees as Archbishop of Milan; founder of the Confraternity of Christian Doctrine. Paul V CANONIZED him in 1610. *See* REFORMATION, CATHOLIC. J. RAITT

BRAHMĀ brä´ mä (H—Skt.; lit. "swelling, growth, tumescence, expansion" [*bṛh*—"to be thick, grow great or strong, increase"]). A personification of BRAHMAN (holy power) in its creative aspect (to be distinguished from Brāhmaṇaspati, a personification of the sacerdotal aspect of *brahman*); the creator god in the TRIMŪRTI.

1. Origins. In the Śatapatha Brāhmaṇa it is said that Brahmā arose when fire and the priesthood were joined together, i.e., from the sacrifice. Although not a historical answer to the question of Brahmā's origins, this is suggestive, since Brahmā's origins are intimately connected to the sacrifice. Like the primordial man, PURUṢA, "though mortal, he created the immortals" and his highest creation was "that he created the gods who are superior to him" (BĀU I.4.6).

Brahmā is most prominent in the BRĀHMAṆAS and UPANIṢADS of the YAJUR VEDA, where he gradually replaces PRAJĀPATI as the creator (just as Prajāpati had earlier replaced Puruṣa as the divine sacrifice). One text declares: "Brahmā arose as first among the gods, the maker of the universe, the protector of the world (MU I.1.1). Brahmā's world *(loka)* is said to be the highest bliss, free from evil, impurity, and doubt; a world from which there is no return; one of unlimited freedom (characteristics identical to those attributed to the attainment of the supreme Brahman).

2. Source of knowledge. The most striking of Brahmā's qualities are his affinity for knowledge and his authority as a teacher of gods and men. All the lists of renowned teachers in the Śatapatha Brāhmaṇa and the Bṛhadāraṇyaka Upaniṣad attribute the origins of knowledge and wisdom to him. The Śvetāśvatara Upaniṣad (V. 6) states: "That which is hidden in the Upaniṣads which are hidden in the VEDAS, Brahmā knows as the holy womb of the Vedas." In the Subāla Upaniṣad he is the divine principle of understanding *(buddhi)*; and in the Muṇḍaka Upaniṣad he is credited with teaching Atharvan "the knowledge of Brahman, the foundation of all knowledges" (I.1.1).

3. Transitional god. Brahmā shows a marked transition from Vedism to BHAKTI HINDUISM. The seminal changes during this period are: a) the rise of devotional theism; and b) the transformation of *brahman* from the holy power immanent in the sacrifices to BRAHMAN, the supreme spirit and focus of orthodox theological and philosophical speculation. In the former, Brahmā's role is decidedly secondary to those of VISHNU and SHIVA, although he does figure in the *trimūrti* doctrine of the SMṚTI literature as a creator god with four heads who rides a swan (HAṂSA) as his vehicle (VĀHANA).

The major change during the *bhakti* period is the evolution of Brahman; and in this Brahmā assumes a role crucial to the rise of the medieval speculative systems, particularly VEDĀNTA. In this process

Brahmā assumes, with Īśvara, the Lord, the guise of the supreme spirit as it is made manifest in the world of men, in the realm of "the many." In the Taittirīya Upaniṣad (I. 1. 1) one finds: "Hail to Brahmā! You are the visible Brahman. I shall speak of you, the perceptible Brahman." In a series of Upaniṣadic passages, the distinction is made between the higher and lower Brahman, between the unmanifest and the manifest, the formless *(nirguṇa)* and the formed *(saguṇa)*, the unheard and the heard, the timeless and the temporal, the immortal and the mortal. Although in the Upaniṣads these two forms of Brahman are usually viewed as two aspects of one reality, ADVAITA Vedānta used the distinction between Brahmā and Brahman as the basis of the doctrine of *saguṇabrahman* (Brahman with qualities) and *nirguṇabrahman* (Brahman without qualities) and condemened the former to the realm of illusion and nonbeing.

J. HELFER

BRAHMA SŪTRAS brä′ mŭ so͞o′ trŭs (H—Skt.) A series of incomplete aphorisms attributed to Bādarāyaṇa (*ca.* 200 B.C.—A.D. 200) comprising the SŪTRAS of Uttaramīmāṃsā or VEDĀNTA; more accurately called the Vedānta Sūtras.

Among the Sūtras of the orthodox DARŚANAS, those of Bādarāyaṇa (which are probably the most recent) stand out as esoteric to the point of being unintelligible. It has often been noted that they are meaningless unless interpolated and interpreted by an authoritative gloss and commentary *(bhāṣya)* from within the same tradition, the earliest of which is that of ŚAṂKARA, the eighth century scholiast and dogmatic theologian of ADVAITA Vedānta. His *bhāṣya* is also thought to incorporate the earliest extant (and "complete") text of the Sūtras, and therefore every interpretation of the Brahma Sūtras must take into account the fact that the earliest intelligible text is that interpolated by Śaṃkara. For example: the second Sūtra (I.2) is "from which the origin of this" (Thibaut, p. 15). Śaṃkara interpolates thus: "[Brahman is that] from which the origin [i.e., the origin, subsistence and dissolution] of this [world proceed]."

It is worth noting that the other eminent commentator, RĀMĀNUJA, interpolates and interprets these Sūtras quite differently. Therefore, since the Sūtras are unintelligible without a commentary, their meaning must be restricted to the views of the commentator. Since the earliest extant commentary was written no earlier than five centuries after the Sūtras, serious questions must be raised regarding the integrity of Śaṃkara's claim that he and Bādarāyaṇa stand within a common tradition arising from the UPANIṢADS. In fact, their only historical meaning and value is the fact that they became the authoritative Sūtras of the Vedānta 500 to 800 years after their composition.

Bibliography. G. Thibaut, *Vedānta-Sūtras*, SBE vols. 34, 38 (rpr. 1962).

J. HELFER

BRAHMACĀRIN brŭ mŭ chär′ īn (H—Skt.; lit. "wandering about in Brahman"). A student; the first of the four stages of life (ĀŚRAMA). When a young Hindu man of high CASTE reached the age of eight to twelve, he was initiated into the stage of the student through the rite of *upanayana* (*see* TWICE BORN). He was given over to his teacher (ĀCĀRYA) for instruction in the sacred tradition for a period of years. He was to serve his teacher unquestioningly, remain chaste, and live a life of poverty.

P. COURTRIGHT

BRAHMAN brŭ′ mŭn (H—Skt.; lit. "a swelling, expansion or growth" [*bṛh*—"to become great, swell, expand"]). Holy power; the power of sacrifice and prayer; creative power; the supreme spirit of the VEDĀNTA.

1. **Vedic period.** In the earlier texts of the VEDAS, *brahman* ("prayer"—often hypostatized as Brāhmaṇaspati or Bṛhaspati, the lord of prayer) is the inherent potency of the sacrifices. Essentially the power manifest in all aspects of the ritual (which is the locus of power in the Vedic cult), it is also seen as the vital force present in all manifestations of power: natural, human, and divine. It is said that PRAJĀPATI, the lord of creatures, "first created the sacrifice; and, after creating the sacrifice, he created *brahman*" (AB VII. 9); that *brahman* was the holy power with which the gods, who were created mortal, became immortal (ŚB II. 2.3.6); and with which, in the form of speech or prayer, they overcame the demons (*ibid.* I.5.4.6). In itself amorphous, *brahman* is present in the sacrifice, the three Vedas, AGNI (fire), SOMA, the altar or *vedi*, the sacrificial formulas, the metal and wooden implements, the officiating priests, the sacrificer, the sacrificial post and fuel, the sacrificial animal, etc. It invigorates terrestrial, atmospheric, and celestial bodies and is the vital force of the gods.

Like MANA, an analogous phenomenon, *brahman* is surrounded by taboos due to its holy, powerful, and therefore dangerous nature. It can be evoked and approached only in ritually controlled and sanctified circumstances and then only by those whose office, knowledge, or purity protects them from injury. Those who are ignorant of *brahman* or are impure (e.g., ŚŪDRAS and women) approach the holy power at the risk of injury or even death, and may participate in its radiant power only indirectly. For those sanctified by knowledge or status, its uses range from the magical (invoking it to destroy those whom one hates or to increase one's material wealth) to the mystical (achieving union with the cosmic power itself).

In the early Vedic texts which cite *brahman* most often, particularly the BRĀHMAṆAS of the YAJUR VEDA, the dominant deity is Prajāpati. Compared to him, *brahman* is a ubiquitous if vague power infrequently noted or invoked. In the later portions of these same texts, however, there is strong evidence of the gradual ascendency of *brahman* over the anthropomorphic lord of creatures, and many of Prajāpati's attributes (particularly the more holistic and abstract) devolve upon *brahman*.

2. **Upaniṣadic period.** In the Brāhmaṇas, Prajāpati incorporates within himself most opposites; he is formed and formless, temporal and eternal, distinct and indistinct, male and female, heard and unheard, seen and unseen, mortal and immortal. *Brahman* gained the ascendency over Prajāpati in the early UPANIṢADS and was transformed from the magical and religious potency of sacrifice and manifest power into Brahman, the supreme spirit that is the coalescence of all power and the focus of all knowledge. This is illustrated in the Bṛhadāraṇyaka Upaniṣad: "Truly, there are two modes of Brahman, the formed and the formless, the mortal and the immortal, the stable and the unstable, the this and the that" (II.3.1).

As Brahman gained hegemony over Prajāpati and all other Vedic deities except VISHNU and SHIVA, other changes took place. There was an intensified focus on the interior or psychological meaning of ritual (cf. CU VIII.5); a concern to grasp the universal spiritual essence (ATMAN) of man (cf. BĀU II.4 and CU VI); an increase in the use of yogic techniques and meditation (Mait. U IV.4); and, generally, a concern with the unity of the universe and the acquisition of spiritually potent knowledge (VIDYĀ). In short, although theistic devotionalism took new forms in ŚAIVISM and VAIṢṆAVISM, the philosophical efforts of an orthodox spiritual elite continued the quest for epistemological certainty and ontological truth. This quest centered upon Brahman and upon the Atman (believed to provide direct and unequivocal access to knowledge of Brahman).

There is no systematic treatment of the concept of Brahman until the medieval period (seventh-eighth century A.D.), but all the major facets of a doctrine of Brahman are either prefigured in or found in the Upaniṣads. While rarely condemning ritual action outright, and often insisting on the relevance of certain essential rites to attaining knowledge of Brahman, the Upaniṣads generally recognize knowledge *(vidyā)*, asceticism *(tapas)*, or meditation *(dhyāna)* as superior means.

Brahman is manifested differently to persons of different capacities, but it is also seen as the sole principle of unity in the cosmos. Brahman is the source of all beings, " the thread by which this world, the other world, and all beings are held together" (BĀU III.7.1.); "the great [one] hidden in all creatures" (Śvet. U III.7); "the inner controller" (BĀU III.7); and that within which name and form exist (CU VIII.14). It is said that knowledge *(vidyā)* of this one thing, as the Atman, leads to omniscience; that "one who knows the highest Brahman, becomes Brahman" (MU III.2.9).

The tendency toward the interiorization of holy power among the spiritual elite is seen in the relation between Brahman and the Atman. Epistemologically, the Atman is that "by which the unhearable becomes heard, the unperceivable perceived, and the unknowable known" (CU VI.1.3). In its qualities and powers, the Atman is a readily experienced entity and most similar to Brahman. For example, the Atman is the knower, Brahman is knowledge; the Atman is the experienced source of bliss, Brahman is bliss; the Atman is man's being in the world, Brahman is being as such. For the Upaniṣadic spiritual elite, release (MOKSA) from the world (SAMSARA) could best be attained "by knowledge, ascetic discipline or meditation" (Mait. U IV.4) that led to union with Brahman.

3. **Vedānta.** The earliest extant attempts to expound a doctrine of Brahman are the Vedānta Sūtras of Bādarāyaṇa (*see* BRAHMA SŪTRAS) and Gauḍapāda's gloss on the brief Māṇḍūkya Upaniṣad. Their incompleteness and obscurity, however, necessitates turning to ŚAMKARA'S commentaries on these writings and the Upaniṣads for the earliest systematic exposition. Armed with the dogmatics of ADVAITA Vedānta, Śaṃkara concentrated on the passages attributing the unity of the cosmos to Brahman, particularly those that did so paradoxically (e.g., formed and formless, mortal and immortal, temporal and eternal). He taught that there were two distinct and ultimately unrelated Brahmans—one with qualities *(saguṇa)* and one without qualities *(nirguṇa)*.

Saguṇa Brahman (or Īśvara, the Lord), while not unreal in the strict sense (like "a barren woman's son"), was merely a pseudo-real entity, a divine form with anthropomorphic qualities, controlling a cosmos immersed in transcience, ignorance (AVIDYĀ), and illusion (MĀYĀ)—in short, a mere pietistic necessity for the benighted. Nirguṇa Brahman was, for Śaṃkara, the sole reality. Knowledge or mystical experience of this absolute Brahman utterly eradicated all prior knowledge, resulted in the immediate and total cessation of all distinctions (e.g., between the self and others) and all ignorance, and brought freedom from samsara.

Later Vedānta (e.g., RĀMĀNUJA and MADHVA) and Hindu theism ignored or denied the value and revelance of a supreme spirit so utterly at odds with human experience, and affirmed a Brahman not unlike Prajāpati—a Brahman who was the active agent and knower of all cosmic processes, in whom all opposites were made harmonious, who was the source and goal of all excellence, the Lord. *See* SHIVA; VISHNU; BRAHMĀ; TRIMŪRTI.

J. HELFER

BRĀHMAṆAS brähʹ mŭ nŭs (H—Skt.; lit. "explanations" of *bráhman* [neuter], the "sacred word"). Extensive ritual and theological discourses in Vedic literature were developed in the early centuries of the first millennium B.C. by specific schools as commentaries on the earliest Vedic texts, the SAMHITĀS ("collections"). Each of the four VEDAS acquired such Brāhmaṇas as commentaries: for the RIG VEDA the Aitareya and Kauṣītaki (or Śāṅkhāyana); for the YAJUR VEDA, the Kāṭhaka, Taittirīya, and Śatapatha; for the

Sāma Veda, the Pañcaviṃśa (or Tāṇḍyamahā) and its appendix, the Ṣaḍviṃśa, and Jaiminīya (or Talavakāra); and for the Atharva Veda, the Gopatha. Not all Vedic schools generated independent Brāhmaṇas. The Maitrāyaṇīya school of the Black (Kṛṣṇa) Yajur Veda retained its prose "explanations" within the *saṃhitā* material itself.

While the *saṃhitās* are mostly in verse, the Brāhmaṇas are India's oldest prose documents, produced approximately from the tenth to seventh century B.C. Their focus, the sacrificial system, places them at the heart of Vedic Hinduism, subsequent to the poetic mythology of the Rig Veda and prior to the speculation of the Upanisads and the emergence of classical Hindu theism. Central to all these "explanations" of *bráhman* (i.e. the eternal word) is the doctrine of correspondences: the sacrifice is an elaborate system of homologies between all the components of the universe, and the ritualist or sacrificer is "one who knows" and thereby controls ritually such cosmic equivalences. In addition to directions for all the sacrifices (often abbreviated, presuming foreknowledge), discussions of their priorities and results, exegesis of the Mantras, and speculations on the correspondences, the Brāhmaṇas contain some mythological material, usually concerned with the origins of rites. Considered to be the most important of all Brāhmaṇas is that of the "100 Paths," the Śatapatha, 100 discourses surviving in two recensions. *See* Vedic Hinduism.

Bibliography. J. Gonda, *Vedic Literature* (1975), pp. 339-422. D. M. Knipe

BRAHMAVIHĀRAS brŭ´ mū vĭ hä´ rŭs (B—Pali; lit. "abodes of Brahma"). The universal positive virtues or divine attitudes stressed by the Buddha: (a) loving kindness (Mettā), (b) compassion (Karuṇā), (c) sympathetic joy *(muditā)*, and (d) equanimity *(upekkhā)*. They have been variously described as sublime states of mental development, boundless states, and blessed dispositions. Cultivation of the *Brahmavihāras*, which were familiar in Indian thought even before the time of the Buddha, is believed to lead to the freeing of the mind.

Their classic formulation is found in the Tevijja Sutta, part of the canonical collection of longer discourses (*see* Pali Canon §4). The Path of Purification (Visuddhimagga) gives a detailed exposition of the *Brahmavihāras*, recommending them as subjects for meditation.

Mettā, sometimes translated as "friendship," is a selfless, universal, all-expansive love. *Karuṇā* is compassion for all living beings in their suffering, with no sense of superiority over them. *Muditā* is an altruistic joy in the success or welfare of others. Finally, *upekkhā* is an attitude of seeing things without partiality, calmly and with an even mind.

Bibliography. W. L. King, *In the Hope of Nibbana* (1964), pp. 149-65. J. P. McDermott

Courtesy Kenneth Morgan and the Hazen Foundation

This retired Brahmin still performs daily religious ceremonies for families who pay him for his services.

BRAHMIN brä´ mĭn (H—Skt.). The words *brāhmaṇa* and *brahman* are used in Hindu contexts to refer to certain prayers, literature, conceptions of reality, and a socio-religious group ("priests"). To avoid some confusion regarding the multiple meanings of these Sanskrit terms, a common scholarly practice utilizes the anglicized spelling "brahmin" to refer to priests and their Caste to distinguish them from the absolute reality Brahman. L. D. Shinn

BRĀHMO SAMĀJ brä´ mō sŭ mäj´ (H—Skt.; lit. "theistic society"). A society founded in 1828 by Ram Mohan Roy. It was dedicated to the propagation of monotheism and the elimination of social abuses in India. It chiefly attracted westernized Indian intellectuals. After undergoing two schisms it declined toward the end of the nineteenth century. *See* Reform Movements in India §2. A. Lipski

BRETHREN, CHURCH OF THE (Ch). A church founded in Germany in 1708 uniting the influences of Pietism and the Anabaptists. They baptize adults by immersion, earning them the nicknames "dunkers" and "dunkards." They also practice as church ordinances the love feast (footwashing, fellowship meal, Eucharist), anointing, and laying on of hands.

Brethren migrated to America from 1719 to 1733. After the Revolution they moved westward, pioneering in Kentucky, Ohio, Indiana, and Illinois. Though they reached the west coast in 1850, Brethren population has concentrated in Pennsylvania, Virginia, Ohio, and Indiana.

Brethren tend to be conservative in life-style but liberal in social outlook. They have traditionally rejected military service, and are active in relief, rehabilitation, and disaster reconstruction.

Church government combines CONGREGATIONALISM and PRESBYTERIANISM, with an annual delegated conference as final authority. Former mission churches in China, Nigeria, India, and Ecuador have joined indigenous bodies; fraternal workers are still sent to the last three. Brethren cooperate with ecumenical movements on all levels.

Smaller groups stemming from the Brethren are: Old German Baptist Brethren (1881), Brethren Church (1883), Dunkard Brethren (1926), and Grace Brethren (1939). Together the Brethren number about 243,000 members in North America.

Bibliography. D. F. Durnbaugh, ed., *The Church of the Brethren Past and Present* (1971).

D. F. DURNBAUGH

BRETHREN OF THE COMMON LIFE (Ch). A semi-monastic order which was founded in Holland and flourished from the late fourteenth through the seventeenth centuries. It was known for schools, literary productivity, and deep piety. The IMITATION OF CHRIST, a classic devotional manual, emerged from Brethren circles. D. F. DURNBAUGH

BREVIARY (Ch). From the eleventh century the book containing the entire DIVINE OFFICE of the Western church. The daily hours, which include psalms, lessons, hymns, and prayers, are the seven day hours (lauds, prime, terce, sext, none, vespers, and compline) and the night office (matins). Seasonal variations require the division of the office, usually into four parts. Offices for the SAINTS, the dead (*see* DEAD, PRAYERS FOR), and special occasions are included.

The offices of the breviary derive from ancient Christian practice. The EASTER Vigil set a precedent for the structure of the ancient offices, which consisted largely of psalms and Scripture lessons. ORIGEN (d. 254) argues from Scripture that prayer should be made at least three times a day (Dan. 6:13), morning, evening, and night. In the fourth century under the impact of the monastic movement and the Jerusalem church it became common to have nocturnal offices (later vespers, matins, and lauds) and day offices (later terce, sext, and none). Further development took place in the monasteries. Under the influence of Ambrose (d. 397) and Benedict (d. *ca.* 550) hymns were added to the offices.

The Rule of St. Benedict (*ca.* 540) gradually established the normal Western method of reciting the offices, but it was not until 1568 after TRENT that Pope Pius V issued the *Breviarium Romanum* in the interest of reform and uniformity. Similar reforms were made by later popes, and in 1971 following the Second VATICAN COUNCIL Pope Paul VI issued a completely new breviary.

Bibliography. P. Batiffol, *Histoire du bréviaire romain* (1893; ET 1898); J. A. Jungmann, *Brevierstudien* (1958).

R. A. GREER

BṚHASPATI brĭ´ hŭs pŭ´ tē (H & B—Skt.; lit. "lord of prayer" [*bṛh*—"prayer, devotion" + *pati*—"master, lord"]). Also called Brahmaṇaspati, the chaplain and sacrificer for the gods in VEDIC HINDUISM. Often associated with AGNI or INDRA in the RIG VEDA, he is in post-Vedic literature a god of wisdom and poetry, GURU of the gods, and is known as the planet Jupiter and husband of Tārā, a star.

D. M. KNIPE

BROTHER (Ch). Male member of a religious community such as a monastery; often used of monks who are not ordained to distinguish them from those who are; a mode of address in some Protestant churches, used of ministers and laity.

K. WATKINS

BUBER, MARTIN bo͞o´ bər (Ju; 1878-1965). Jewish religious thinker and Zionist heavily influenced by HASIDISM. In *I and Thou* (1927) he viewed interpersonal relations in terms of two dialectical modalities: the reciprocal I-Thou relation and the exploitative I-It relation. *See* JUDAISM §6d.

L. FAGEN

BUCER [also **BUTZER**], **MARTIN** bo͞o´ tsər (Ch; 1491-1551). Protestant reformer of Strasbourg. Much of Bucer's career centered on efforts to unify Lutherans and Zwinglians. He had a profound impact on Calvin, particularly in regard to ecclesiastical discipline, and also influenced the liturgical reformation of the Anglican Church.

R. L. HARRISON

BUDDHA, GENERAL CONCEPTS OF. 1. Śākyamuni as Buddha. The term "buddha" is participle of the Sanskrit verbal root *budh,* "to awaken," and is employed as a title, "The Awakened One" or "Enlightened One." The primary application of this title has been to SIDDHĀRTHA GAUTAMA, sage of the Śākya tribe ("Śākyamuni"), a human being who attained enlightenment, founded an order, and spent his life teaching the DHARMA.

2. Previous Buddhas. Early orthodoxy seems to have focused upon Śākyamuni Buddha as a human distinguished from others only in that he was "producer of the unproduced path" while disciples were "endowed with it afterward." But great veneration was given Gautama even during his lifetime, pilgrimage sites relating to his life may have had his own deathbed sanction, and speculation soon began regarding his many extraordinary preparatory births (JĀTAKA) as BODHISATTVA (Buddha-to-be) in the form of animal, god, and human. This growing interest in past lives led to speculation regarding Buddhas previous to Śākyamuni. Stories accumulated concerning seven, twenty-four, and even a thousand Buddhas (TATHĀGATAS, "Thus-Come-Ones"), carrying the dharma from one world-age to another. Through the symbolism of seven STŪPAS and BODHI trees carved stonework at the ancient *stūpas* of Sāñchī and Bhārhut represents a set of seven Tathāgatas, with Śākyamuni as the last. At GANDHĀRA, MATHURĀ, and AJANṬĀ, the seven Buddhas are represented in human form.

3. Speculation regarding the Buddha's nature. Different emphases regarding the nature of the Buddha distinguished one sect from another in early Buddhism (*see* BUDDHIST SECTARIANISM). The Lokottaravadin school's legendary account of the Buddha's life, the *Mahāvastu*, presented Gautama as a superhuman miracle worker, while the *Lalitavistara*, associated with the Sarvāstivādins, described Gautama's life as the "sport" or "play" (LĪLĀ) of the transcendent Buddha. Speculation of the Mahāsāṅghikas prepared the way for the elaborate doctrines of the Mahāyāna. In the Mahāyāna sūtra called the *Lotus of the Good Law* (*see* LOTUS SŪTRA), Buddha was presented as transcendent savior, available in many forms in spiritual realms where conditions were perfect for humans to come to enlightenment, and visiting earth in various physical guises to bring the dharma to lost humanity.

4. Mahāyāna teachings. The popular appeal of the MAHĀYĀNA owes much to its elaborate doctrines regarding the Buddha. The ARHANT, who was intent upon his own salvation, and the Pratyeka Buddhas, private Buddhas who attained full enlightenment but did not proclaim it to others, were devalued, and Mahāyāna preached the ideal of the bodhisattva ("Enlightenment-being") and the availability to the faithful of Buddhas with saving power.

a) Eternal Buddhas and bodhisattvas. While one might meet Buddhas and bodhisattvas on earth in human form, great emphasis was placed upon eternal Buddhas and bodhisattvas who existed in spiritual realms and offered their merits, protection, and help toward enlightenment to all who were devoted to them through acts of merit, simple prayers, or meditation. Some sources viewed these eternal ones as attributes or ideas reflecting the Absolute or Buddha nature, while other sources viewed them as saints who gradually accumulated merit and finally achieved transcendent status. In either case, Buddhism seems to have incorporated elements of the Indian system of gods and heavens, and responded to the popularity of BHAKTI HINDUISM, personal devotion to savior deities.

Chief among the eternal bodhisattvas was AVALOKITEŚVARA, a personification of compassion, sometimes appearing in a trinity with the eternal Buddha Amitāyus (*see* AMIDA) and the bodhisattva Mahāsthāmaprāpta. Other popular bodhisattvas include MAÑJUŚRĪ, personification of wisdom, and MAITREYA, who is to descend from the TUṢITA HEAVEN to become the next earthly Buddha. Often little distinction can be found between these bodhisattvas and the eternal Buddhas. Among the eternal Buddhas, "innumerable as the sands of the GANGES," were Akṣobhya (The Imperturbable), and Amitābha (Eternal Light) or Amitāyus (Eternal Life), central to the PURE LAND sūtras. Each of these many eternal Buddhas presided over a "Buddha-field," or mystical realm of influence which believers might attain by devotion to the Buddha's name (*see* NEMBUTSU) or meditation upon the Buddha's perfections. In such a spiritual kingdom the faithful might mature to enlightenment under the Buddha's guidance.

b) Three bodies of the Buddha. Later Mahāyāna elaborated a TRIPLE BODY doctrine to help explain the sometimes confusing elements of its teachings. A single DHARMAKĀYA (Truth-body) is the unity behind all manifestations of the Buddha. Impersonally, the *Dharmakāya* might be spoken of as the Absolute, Suchness (TATHATĀ) or Emptiness (ŚŪNYATĀ), though some schools, including TANTRISM, spoke more personally of Ādi-Buddha (Primordial Buddha) or Mahābuddha (Great Buddha). The *Dharmakāya* manifests itself in spiritual realms as SAMBHOGAKĀYA, the "Reward" or "Enjoyment" body, as in the eternal Buddhas invisible to the senses but experienced by the faithful as Amida, VAIROCANA, or countless other Buddhas. The *Sambhogakāya* finally becomes visible to the ordinary senses in the earthly form of Gautama and other earthly Buddhas (NIRMĀṆAKĀYA).

c) Arrangements of Buddhas. Eternal Buddhas were later arranged in specific patterns (*see* MANDALA). Amitābha, Akṣobhya, Vairocana ("Sun-like"), Ratnasambhava ("Jewel-born"), and Amoghasiddhi ("Unfailing Power") are regularly depicted together as the Five Celestial Buddhas, and each can be associated with a particular earthly Buddha and a transcendent bodhisattva as aid. Thus Amitābha is related to Gautama the earthly Buddha and Avalokiteśvara the bodhisattva, while Amoghasiddhi is related to Maitreya and the bodhisattva Viśvapāṇi. The Tibetan VAJRAYĀNA describes Ādi-Buddha as emanating five Dhyāni (meditation) Buddhas, who in turn emanate Dhyāni bodhisattvas, each of whom was represented on earth by a human embodiment or Manushi Buddha. Thus the human Buddha Gautama was Manushi Buddha of the Dhyāni bodhisattva of this age, Avalokiteśvara. The entire pattern, embellished with Tārās as female consorts, provides the cosmic symbolism and structure for meditative discipline in Tantric Buddhism.

Bibliography. E. Conze, *Buddhism: Its Essence and Development* (1951); H. Schumann, *Buddhism* (1973).

C. W. EDWARDS

BUDDHA, LIFE OF GAUTAMA gou´ tū mū (B—Skt.; *ca.* 560–480 B.C.) GOTAMA gô tä´ mä (B—Pali). Siddhārtha Gautama, who came to be called the Buddha ("the Enlightened"), was the founder of BUDDHISM. He was born in KAPILAVASTU, which lay in a fertile, irrigated plain of modern Nepal near the Indian border. His time was one of intense intellectual and spiritual ferment especially in this region of the Indian subcontinent.

1. **Problems of sources.** The older Pali or Sanskrit texts of Buddhism contain only incidental or fragmentary references to events in the life of the Buddha. His earliest monastic followers stressed his humanness, but the developing community increasingly came to see his life as divinely archetypal, i.e. as a mode of spiritual manifestation. One result of these changing attitudes was the appearance of "lives of the Buddha."

The first instance of a formal "biography" is the Sanskrit *Buddhacarita* of Aśvaghoṣa, composed probably toward the end of the first century A.D. From about the same period stems the largely legendary work *Lalitavistara* (The Pleasurable Biography). More important for its later influence is the *Nidāna-Kathā*, written by the great Ceylonese scholastic BUDDHAGHOSA in the fifth century A.D. Even the earliest Pali texts of which copies have survived were written in Ceylon as late as 89-77 B.C. Thus the "biographies" are both late in origin and replete with legendary and mythical material, and the oldest canonical texts are the products of a long process of oral transmission that evidently included some revision and much addition.

As a result, various degrees of skepticism regarding the life and teaching of the Buddha have emerged in the scholarly community, even to the extent of dismissing the life of the historic Buddha as a solar myth. Heinrich Zimmer contended that not a single word of the recorded teaching can be ascribed with unqualified certainty to Gautama himself. This statement cannot be specifically denied; but it does not represent the present state of Buddhist studies. There is in fact wide agreement that certain main lines of the teaching derive from the Buddha. There is a consistent thread which runs through this material and strongly intimates a primary source. Therefore, by careful study of the texts and the history of the times, we are able to give a coherent account of the life of Gautama the Buddha and his teachings.

2. **The life of the Buddha.** Siddhārtha Gautama was born into the KSATRIYA (warrior) caste as the first son of the rāja of Kapilavastu. His education was most likely in accord with the standards of a martial aristocracy. The portrayals of magnificence and luxury in the later biographies probably represent the authors' wish to heighten the contrast with his later sacrificial renunciation.

The PALI CANON texts say that Siddhārtha married at the age of sixteen or seventeen while other sources state that he had several wives and concubines. According to the Pali texts, his wife, Yosōdharā, bore him a son, who was given the name Rahula ("Hindrance"). At the age of twenty-nine, Siddhārtha was driven by an inner compulsion to leave the princely life for the homeless religious life. In the context of his own time and place, the decision was neither an isolated one nor out of keeping with an important segment of contemporary religious ideas.

Siddhārtha is said to have visited LUMBINĪ Park in Kapilavastu over a succession of days. Here he beheld a decrepit old man, a diseased man, a dead man, and a religious ascetic. The last, in spite of his few possessions, is described in one account as "carefully and decently clad," apparently happy and possessing spiritual victory. This tale vividly portrays the frailty and impermanence inherent in all forms of phenomenal existence and of the possibility of a solution in the life of a monk. According to early texts Gautama's reflection on the causes of his renunciation include his shame and disgust at the pathetic situation of others even though, as a human being, he was destined to meet the same fate (Aṅguttara Nikāya I, 145).

Gautama left his home to travel south and eastward toward the cultural centers of the Ganges river basin. The texts record the grief and resentment of Yośōdharā at her husband's departure, although she was of course not left without care. Gautama visited certain prominent teachers, notably ĀRĀḌA KĀLĀMA of Vaiśālī and UDRAKA RĀMAPUTRA of Magadha, under whom he practiced religious exercises for a time. He was not satisfied, however, to become a permanent disciple of any of them.

Gautama then began a regimen of meditation, with increasingly severe ascetic practices. One text describes in exaggerated fashion the effect of his fasting as, when he touched the skin of his belly, he felt his backbone and when he stroked his limbs with his hand, the hair fell off. In the course of this regimen Gautama acquired five disciples, evidently attracted by his sincerity and the heroic style of his austerities. But while his ascetic life enabled him to achieve a certain measure of self-control, it gave him neither inner peace nor spiritual enlightenment.

The Majjhima Nikāya (I, 240-47) reports that Gautama's experience of the futility of the method of extreme asceticism led him to look for a better way. He recalled how in his youth he had meditated without austerities and had experienced mental self-control, insight, and even rapturous awareness. He decided to try this method again as a better way to his goal of enlightenment and happiness transcending sensory pleasures. Gautama neither at this time nor later divorced meditation from strenuous moral and intellectual discipline, but his turning at this point was away from harsh austerities to a "Middle Way."

According to the traditional accounts, Gautama found a suitable spot under a large tree, and as he meditated the experience came to him that was ever afterward to be known as the Enlightenment. He had become the Buddha. The nature of this event was such as to make personal experience a primal element in the entire Buddhist tradition.

Major texts (Dīgha Nikāya XXII, Majjhima Nikāya I, 4) describe in detail the several stages of consciousness which the Buddha experienced at this time, although the earlier poems of the Sutta Nipāta make no reference to the first four stages. Apart from later scholastic formulations, however, the experience was evidently profound and sweeping in its range.

There is little information in the texts which suggests development or maturation of the thought of the Buddha in his later life. In the reports of the first sermon after his Enlightenment we find a relatively full statement of his teaching in the form of the FOUR NOBLE TRUTHS, including the Noble EIGHTFOLD PATH as descriptive of the ethical conduct proper to the "Middle Way." This sermon was addressed to his former disciples, the five ascetics who had left him in disgust after his decision to turn to this way of moderation. They were now converted and became the nucleus of what came to be the community (SANGHA) of Buddhist monks. A related order of nuns was formed later.

The Buddha evidently had remarkable success from the beginning in winning followers, both monastic and lay. According to one traditional account, at a relatively early period the Buddha gave his initial directive to the monks to enter upon what was in principle a universal mission. They were to go out singly (later, by two or in larger groups) and teach the DHARMA, which is "lovely at the beginning, lovely in the middle, lovely at the ending" (Vinaya Piṭaka, Mahāvagga I, 11, 1).

The monks were received and ordained perhaps with a fixed formula from a very early period. In the texts, however, we find instances of the Buddha's calling and receiving men into the order with the simple phrase, "Come, O monk." In contrast to the UPANISADIC tradition, Buddhist monastics understood their commitment to the homeless life as involving lifelong mendicant poverty and chastity. Their life-style was meditative, mendicant, and missionary.

The monastics were under one head, the Buddha, who was their teacher and spiritual guide. Throughout his life he remained the final court of appeal in all disputes of doctrine or discipline, but he disavowed the role of leader in a formal sense and exacted no vow of obedience to himself. The "leader" and refuge of all was dharma as experientially known in the life of each individual.

For the remainder of the Buddha's long life, he and his disciples wandered throughout the larger Ganges river basin, proclaiming his teaching to whoever would hear. The three months of the rainy season were usually spent in fixed abodes, which soon came to include donated grounds and buildings. During the rest of the year they traveled from place to place, meditating in the early morning, begging their nourishment at noon, teaching the "many folk" and taking their rest in the shade of trees.

It was on just such a missionary journey that the Buddha died, after a short illness, at the age of eighty. Among his final words was the admonition to his disciples not to depend on him but on dharma and themselves. His very last words were "Decay is inherent in all component things. Work out your own salvation with diligence" (Dīgha Nikāya II, 99-101, 156).

A modern Thai painting depicting the Buddha near death by fasting while being attended by five disciples

3. **The teaching of the Buddha.** There is good evidence in relatively early texts that a primary and abiding element of the inner life of the Buddha was friendship or intimacy with the "lovely" (*kalyāṇa*). We note that friendship with the lovely was the forerunner or prior condition for both the beginning and the sustained practice of the ethical life that leads to the goal and is also its fruit. On one occasion the Buddha is recorded as saying that the holy life he taught "consists in friendship, in association, in intimacy with what is lovely." The primary event of liberation was possible "because of my friendship with what is lovely" (Saṃyutta Nikāya V, 29-35; V, 2).

The "lovely" for the Buddha was primarily dharma. NIRVANA, as both spiritual condition and "realm," was supremely the goal of primitive Buddhism. It denoted serene peace, the extinguishing of the fires of self-centered desire and attachment, realizable in this world and at death. But dharma emerged in the teaching of the Buddha with a dynamic meaning beyond that of traditional Indian perception. It was particularly the cosmic force that "makes for righteousness," not to be identified with phenomenal existence in part or whole, yet at work and available within it. Consequently, dharma was always understood as connoting specific ethical qualities, especially those cited in the Noble Eightfold Path. Above all, however, dharma was "the lovely," and a dependent relationship with it was the basis for both the beginning and the continuation of the religious life.

Basic to both the Buddha's personal experience and teaching was the theme of liberation, which meant an abiding freedom from selfish desires and attachments, from self-centered malice and despair. Initially, however, it meant delivery from the causal chain (PATICCASAMUPPĀDA) of rebirth. This was a claim of no slight significance, for it meant liberation from one's *saṃskāras*—the predispositions or habitual tendencies of character which were believed to condition the present state of sentient beings as the result of past actions.

The basic explication of the Buddha's insights came to be formulated as the Four Noble Truths. These truths state the universal fact of suffering, the cause of suffering, the overcoming of suffering, and the way of overcoming suffering or the Noble Eightfold Path. The term "suffering" in this formulation meant pain of mind and feeling as well as of body and included grief, anxiety, frustration, and despair. In this understanding a sense of the transitoriness (ANICCA) of all phenomenal existence loomed large.

The cause of suffering was seen as thirst, craving, or inordinate desire for anything that is not worthy of such desire. The Buddha did not totally deny value to the persons and things of phenomenal existence, but he did affirm that they lack ultimate value and dependability. Only Nirvana as the goal and dharma as the way are worthy of aspiration.

The Buddha evidently perceived inordinate desire for lesser values as both mistaken and morally wrong. The evil, however, lay more in selfishness and pride than in intellectual misapprehension, and the cure was inextricably linked with the ethical life. Cessation of craving did not mean cessation of relationships with the persons and things of this world, only of the kind of relationships by which we are infatuated. The ethical goal was friendliness (METTĀ) and compassion (KARUṆA) toward all living beings, and it was these two attitudes which permeated the Eightfold Path.

Bibliography. A. Bareau, *Bouddha* (1962); R. H. Drummond, *Gautama the Buddha* (1974); H. Nakamura, *Gōtama Buddha* (1978); H. Oldenberg, *Buddha* (1961); R. H. Robinson, *The Buddhist Religion* (1970); E. J. Thomas, *The Life of the Buddha* (3rd rev. ed., 1949). R. H. DRUMMOND

BUDDHAGHOSA bood´ dŭ gō´ sŭ (B—Pali; lit. "voice of the Buddha"). Fourth to fifth century A.D. author of numerous commentaries on Buddhist scripture and the authoritative Path of Purification (VISUDDHIMAGGA); the greatest scholar of post-canonical THERAVĀDA Buddhism.

Our major source concerning his life is the Sinhalese chronicle, the Cūlavaṃsa (*see* MAHĀVAṂSA). A fifteenth century collection of legends about the man, the Buddhaghosupatti, is less reliable.

Though the chronicles say he was born into a Hindu priestly caste in north India, some modern scholars assert that he came from the south. Having converted to Buddhism, he went to Sri Lanka where he mastered Buddhist doctrine. To show he was qualified to translate the Sinhalese commentaries on the canon into Pali, Buddhaghosa wrote his masterpiece, the Visuddhimagga. He also wrote commentaries on the Monastic Discipline and the principal collections of canonical discourses, and commentaries on other texts are also attributed to him. Because of his vast knowledge and eloquent language, he became known as "the voice of the Buddha."

Bibliography. B.C. Law, *Buddhaghosa*, rev. ed., 1946; Ñyānamoli, trans., *The Path of Purification* (1964).

J. P. MCDERMOTT

BUDDHISM.

1. History
2. Theravāda Buddhism
3. Mahāyāna teachings
4. Mahāyaña schools in China
5. Tantrism
6. Monastic community
7. Literature
8. Rituals and ceremonies
9. Present trends
Bibliography

1. **History.** *a) Origin.* Buddhism was founded by an Indian prince, SIDDHĀRTHA, also known as ŚĀKYAMUNI, the son of the ruler of a small state in what is now Nepal. He is said to have lived during the years 560-480 B.C. Tradition has it that at the age of twenty-nine he left the household life to seek a solution to the problem of suffering. At age thirty-five through meditation he found the solution, became enlightened, and henceforth became known as the BUDDHA, or the enlightened one.

After this momentous event the Buddha spent the next forty-five years of his life wandering up and down the Ganges Valley, preaching his message to ascetic and lay persons alike. For this long period of his life no connected account exists, with the only indication of his travels being the names of cities and towns mentioned in the scriptural discourses. The cities most often mentioned were the capitals of the important states of the period. At age eighty he died.

b) Early growth. In the first centuries after his death the religion founded by the Buddha was centered in the eastern reaches of the Ganges Valley. In the middle of the third century B.C. the great Indian monarch AŚOKA, after bringing most of India under his rule, embraced Buddhism and began an extensive campaign to spread the religion. He sent his son Mahinda and his daughter Sanghamitta to Ceylon to introduce and propagate the religion. From Ceylon and India, Buddhist monks in later centuries carried the message of the Buddha to Burma, Thailand, and Indo-China. In the opposite direction the religion spread northwestward to GANDHĀRA and Kashmir. To manifest his zeal, Aśoka embarked on a religious tour in which he visited the sacred places connected with the life of the Buddha. He had the teachings of the Master inscribed on rocks and pillars, many of which have been deciphered, furnishing us with valuable information about his reign and his activities on behalf of Buddhism. Due mainly to Aśoka's efforts, Buddhism burst out of its narrow confines in eastern India to take its place in the mainstream of world culture.

c) Expansion. i. Ceylon (Sri Lanka). After its introduction into Ceylon, Buddhism developed rapidly to become the state religion of the island, resulting in the practice that only a Buddhist could become king. Fa-hsien, a Chinese monk who visited Ceylon during the early years of the fifth century A.D., wrote that there were sixty thousand monks in the island, and that the king always had enough food prepared to feed five thousand monks at one sitting. Of the numerous monasteries in the land the most famous was the Mahāvihāra ("Great Monastery") in the capital Anurādhapura, which, besides being the center of Buddhist learning, also preserved the legitimate line of monastic ordination going back to the founder of the religion.

ii. Burma. Burmese traditions state that Buddhism was introduced into what is now Burma during the reign of Aśoka, but there is no clear evidence prior to the fifth century A.D. Epigraphic evidence from that century contains the well-known Buddhist formula, "The dharma of which the origin and cause has been preached by the Buddha, their cessation has also been spoken by the Great Sage" (Vinaya 1.40), and portions of the canon that were found in 1926 point to the presence of a THERAVĀDA community in South Burma. In later centuries, TANTRIC Buddhism infiltrated northern Burma. In the middle of the eleventh century, King Anawrahta of northern Burma united the country by conquering the south. He carried back to the north as booty some sets of the Theravāda canon, and Theravāda Buddhism came to replace the Tantric brand that had been in vogue. These events mark a significant turn in Burmese history, and ever since that time Burma has been the land which has preserved Theravāda Buddhism in its purest form.

iii. Thailand. Buddhist influence from Lower Burma had early infiltrated what is now Thailand, and when King Anawrahta adoped Theravāda Buddhism, he invaded northern Thailand and introduced his newly acquired religion there. Thus when the Thai people entered the region during the twelfth and thirteenth centuries from southwestern China, they found the religion already well established in the area. They made it their state religion when they formed the Thai kingdom in 1238. To this day Buddhism has remained the dominant force in the life of the Thai people.

iv. Indo-China. It is reasonable to assume that sometime during the first century A.D. Buddhism had arrived in this region via the sea route. By the end of the second century there was already in existence a flourishing Buddhist community in the Tonkin area, as attested by a Chinese convert who was in the area at that time. He recorded that the Buddhist monks shaved their heads, wore saffron-colored robes, and ate but once a day. Because Indo-China was under the cultural influence of the Chinese, the form of Buddhism that came to dominate there was affiliated with the MAHĀYĀNA tradition, with the Ch'an School of Chinese Buddhism being the dominant force.

v. China. As a result of the impetus given by King Aśoka, Buddhism had become well established in northwestern India during the two centuries before the Christian era. From that area the religion was carried across the mountains into such regions in Central Asia as Parthia, Sogdiana, Khotan, and Kucha. (*See* Central Asia Map.) Sometime during the first century A.D. Buddhist monks, probably in the company of merchants, made the hazardous journey from northwestern India and Central Asia across the trackless deserts to reach the populous Chinese Empire. In succeeding centuries a steady exchange was maintained, with Chinese pilgrims such as HSÜAN-TSANG going to India to study their religion at first hand and to bring back the sacred texts, and Indian and Central Asiatic monks going to China to assist in the translation of the texts into Chinese. By the seventh century the religion reached its apogee, claiming as converts all elements of Chinese society—the imperial household, the nobility, the great and wealthy families, and the common people. Scattered all over China were monasteries large and small, and associated with the monasteries were vigorous and influential schools of Buddhism founded by creative Chinese monks. Beginning with the ninth century, however, the religion began to decline, but while it was enjoying its heyday, Japanese monks went to China in large numbers to learn all that the Chinese had to offer, after which they returned to Japan to propagate the faith.

vi. Korea. When Buddhism was introduced from China in the third century A.D., Korea was divided into three kingdoms. The government of Koguryo in the north built the first Buddhist temples in 375. Paekche in the southwest sent missionaries to Japan, but it was Silla in the southeastern part of the peninsula that saw the greatest flourishing of the faith. Silla unified the country in the late seventh century and ushered in a golden age of Buddhist art and literature that lasted throughout the Koryŏ Dynasty (935-1392). During the Yi Dynasty (1392-1910) Buddhism experienced a steady decline. (*See* KOREAN RELIGION.)

vii. Japan. Buddhism was transmitted to Japan in the beginning by Korean missionaries. The first official transmission took place in 538 when a Korean prince dispatched Buddhist monks to the Japanese court carrying Buddhist texts, images, and banners. Initially the religion gained a mixed reception among the Japanese, with the military clansmen opposed to any innovation while government officials seemed willing to accept new ideas. The issue was resolved in 593 when Prince SHŌTOKU assumed the regency of the empire and came out in active support of the newly introduced religion. Under his leadership Buddhist philosophy began to be studied, monasteries constructed, monastic institutions established, and music and rituals cultivated. (*See* NARA BUDDHISM.) In succeeding centuries, especially during the Heian (794-1185) and KAMAKURA (1185-1333) periods, spurred by numerous contacts with Chinese monks, the religion developed into the dominant faith of Japan, with a variety of schools which shaped the national character of the Japanese.

viii. Tibet. Though Tibet is closer to the cradle of Buddhism than China or Japan, it was not until the early years of the seventh century that the religion was introduced there. The Tibetans connect this event with the marriage of the Tibetan king with a Nepalese princess, who brought with her to Tibet several images of the Buddha. At first Buddhism faced the determined opposition of the Tibetan nobility, who allied themselves with the practitioners of the native BÖN faith, a form of SHAMANISM. The religion was able to overcome such opposition and to flourish, largely through the leadership of the Indian monks PADMA-SAMBHAVA, who arrived in Tibet in 747, and Atisha, who laid the firm foundation for the later growth of the religion after his arrival in 1042. Thereafter, huge and powerful monasteries sprang up, presided over by abbots who held not only religious but also temporal powers. In the ensuing struggle for supremacy among these monasteries, one school, the Yellow Sect, whose leader was the DALAI LAMA, finally emerged triumphant to assume spiritual and temporal powers over all of Tibet. This situation lasted until the middle of the twentieth century when the armies of the People's Republic of China occupied the country. (*See* TIBETAN BUDDHISM.)

2. Theravāda Buddhism. *a) Karma and rebirth.* The Indians at the time of the Buddha were already a highly sophisticated people with well-developed ideas of religion, deities, and the meaning and purpose of life. Two of the important ideas developed by the Indians were taken over by the Buddha and incorporated into his system. These were the doctrines of KARMA ("fruits of actions") and SAMSARA ("rebirth"), according to which a living being will be reborn endlessly in the ceaseless cycle of existence in accordance with his karma. Karma results from acts or deeds as well as the intentions behind those deeds, and represents the "fruits" arising from those thoughts and actions. Every deed or thought produces karma which may be good or evil. According to the karma of the past, a living being will undergo

James Ware

Temple of Ten Thousand Buddhas, Sha Tin, Hong Kong. Statues from the Taoist hall illustrate the syncretism often seen in popular Buddhist temples.

repeated rebirths and assume a different form in each rebirth. In Buddhism there are five states of existences, the good states of deity and humanity and the evil states of animal, hungry ghost (PRETA), and denizen of hell. Though rebirth as a human is not the highest state, it is the most desirable, because it is only humans who can achieve salvation and NIRVANA. However, rebirth as a human is most difficult to achieve, even more difficult than for a turtle which comes to the surface of the ocean once in a century to push its head through the hole in a log floating aimlessly on the surface.

As long as the individual is revolving in the five modes of existence, he is motivated by cravings for power, material wealth, sensual pleasures, and continued existence to perform deeds that generate karma. However, the Buddhist insists that this does not result in a fatalistic scheme of life. We are heirs of our previous existences with all the potentialities of the long past within us, but we are also the creators of our future before us. This is where our intentions come in. It is within our power to develop good intentions, leading to the performance of meritorious deeds which will result in rebirth in a good state of existence, or to practice the religious discipline prescribed by the Buddha for breaking the bonds of rebirth.

b) Eightfold path. The core of the Buddhist discipline is directed toward the eradication of cravings, which may be achieved by the practice of the noble EIGHTFOLD PATH. This eightfold path may be divided into three categories: moral conduct (right speech, right action, right livelihood); mental discipline (right effort, right mindfulness, right concentration); intuitive wisdom (right views, right intentions).

i. Moral conduct is summarized as not to commit any evil, to do good, and to purify one's mind. Any act that is harmful to oneself and to another is considered an evil act whose fruits would be suffering. Evil is not looked upon as transgression of some divine law but as originating in the minds and deeds of man.

ii. Mental discipline has for its object the control of the mind. There is a Buddhist proverb which says that there is not enough leather to cover the whole earth to make it smooth, but put on leather shoes and the whole earth will be smooth. In the same way we cannot destroy all the external objects which impinge upon the senses from all sides to give rise to passions, greed, and covetousness, but we can control the mind so that it will not make the mistake of regarding unpleasant, impure, and impermanent things as pleasant, pure, and permanent. After a rigorous period of mental discipline, the individual is able not only to control his mind but also to empty it of all contents, so that the mind remains perfectly tranquil and serene.

iii. Intuitive wisdom. The Buddha once declared that mental discipline will lead one to intuitive wisdom, or the seeing of things as they really are. The last two parts of the eightfold path, right views and right intentions, lead to this goal.

To take the right view of things is to hold to the truths that all existence is suffering (Dukkha), all existence is impermanent (Anicca), and there is no permanent self or soul (Anatta). In his first discourse the Buddha emphasized that birth is suffering, old age is suffering, death is suffering, the five modes of existence are suffering. To illustrate the universality of suffering, the Buddha once told the story of a woman who asked him to restore to life her dead child. The Master said he would do so if the woman could find a family which had never suffered the grief of death. Filled with hope the woman went out, but she soon discovered that every family she visited had experienced such suffering. She then decided to give up her quest and to become a follower of the Buddha. This universal suffering is brought about by craving for continual existence, sensual pleasures, fame, and power. Such cravings give rise to deeds that generate karma which in turn leads to further rebirth.

The second fundamental truth, that all existence is impermanent *(anicca),* was stressed by the Buddha just before he died when he said, "Subject to decay are all compounded things." For the Buddhist everything is a becoming, which is the middle path between the two extremes of materialism (everything is) and nihilism (everything is not). Life therefore is never static but is always in a flux. We become something else every moment in our life.

Besides suffering and impermanence, the third fundamental truth proclaimed by the Theravādins is that there is no permanent self or soul *(anatta).* The Upanisads taught that the true self of man is the universal self, and that as soon as one realizes this unity, one becomes emancipated. The Buddha surveyed the world and found mankind attached to this self or soul, thinking it to be something eternal and permanent. Such a belief in the permanence of a self was held by the Buddha to be a pernicious error, as it gives rise to attachment, attachment leads to egoism, egoism begets craving for existence, fame, pleasure, and fortune, and this binds the individual to further rebirth and suffering. To counteract this belief, the Buddha taught that there is no permanent self or soul in an individual, that an individual is only a combination of the five aggregates (Skandhas), matter, sensation, perception, predisposition, and consciousness, every one of which is constantly arising and disappearing. At every moment in our life, we are a temporary combination of these five aggregates, or the sum total of what we are, see, hear, taste, smell, touch, or think. When we realize that the self is only a stream of perishing physical and psychical phenomena, then we eradicate our selfish desires and interests, and we abandon our egoistic pursuit of sensual pleasure and personal gain.

If we are only a momentary conglomeration of the five aggregates, then who is reborn, who stores up karma and reaps its rewards? To answer such questions, the Buddha taught that at death the five aggregates which constitute the living being disintegrate. However, the karma which that living being had accumulated in the past does not perish but must bear fruit in the rebirth of a new living being which is not the same as the former living being but which is not different either, as the new living being has inherited the karma of the previous one. Moreover, the early records say that the Buddha also taught that a living being is not only a conglomeration of the five aggregates but also a series of states, a lifestream connecting the different rebirths, each one originating in dependence upon the previous state. To illustrate this idea of the stream of life, the Buddha often referred to the example of the river, which appears to maintain one constant form, though the water of the river at any one point is always changing. He also noted that when a flame is transmitted from one candle to another, the light is one and the same, for there is no interruption, but the two candles are not the same. In the scriptures there is the story of a girl who was betrothed to a man when she was young but who married another man when she became of age. The first man claimed that the girl belonged to him, while the second man claimed that the grown woman whom he married was not the same person as the young girl. When the two men brought the dispute to the Buddha for settlement, the Buddha decided in favor of the first man, because even though the grown woman was not the same as the young one, she was not different either, as the two belonged to the same lifestream and the former sprang up from the latter. By such examples, the Buddha sought to impress upon his followers the idea that even though two successive combinations of the five aggregates may not be the same, there is continuity between the two because of the operation of karma.

Right views in the eyes of the Buddhist embrace not only the truths of suffering, impermanence, and no permanent self, but also a correct understanding of the chain of causation (PAṬICCASAMUPPĀDA), or the formula of dependent origination. It appears that the Buddha enunciated this formula to emphasize the truth that events follow one another in regular sequence and not just by chance or by the arbitrary will of a divine agent. In the scripture the formula is usually stated as follows: "I will teach you the doctrine, when this exists, that exists; with the arising of that, this arises; when this does not exist, that does not exist, with the cessation of that, this ceases." (Majjhima Nikāya 3.63) The formula conveys the idea that no phenonemon in the universe is isolated and without cause but is linked with every other phenomenon. The chain itself consists of twelve factors: ignorance, predisposition, consciousness, name and form, six sense organs, contact, sensation, craving, grasping, becoming, birth, old age and death. It is expressed in the following manner: when ignorance arises, predisposition arises; when predisposition arises, consciousness arises; when birth arises, old age and death arise. Stated in another manner, when ignorance ceases, then all the following members of the chain will also cease and there will be no more birth, old age, and death.

c) Nirvana. By adhering strenuously to the regimen of moral conduct, mental discipline, and intuitive wisdom, which may stretch over numerous rebirths, the individual hopes to eradicate the craving that is the generating force behind all karma and repeated rebirth, and when he realizes this goal, he achieves emancipation or NIRVANA.

The word "nirvana" has the meaning of extinguishing or covering up, as in the extinguishing of a lamp or fire. In his famous Fire Sermon the Buddha preached that the whole world was inflamed by the fires of lust, hatred, and delusion, and that only in Nirvana were these fires extinguished. In the Buddhist scriptures one will find reference to two kinds of Nirvana, Nirvana with a residue and Nirvana without a residue. The former appears to be the Nirvana achieved by the ARHANT here and now or by the Buddha under the bodhi tree when he was thirty-five years of age. The five aggregates are still present, although the cravings that lead to continued rebirth are extinguished. Nirvana without a residue refers to the state achieved by the *arhant* or the Buddha after death, and in the sacred literature this state is distinguished from the former by the designation *parinirvana*.

Nirvana with a residue is often characterized by negative terms, extinction of cravings, eradication of all lust, hatred, and delusion, annihilation of the false idea of self, unconditioned. However the Buddha also referred to it in positive terms as one of peace and serenity, perfect tranquillity, passionlessness, purity, and supreme bliss and happiness. As for Nirvana without a residue, the Buddha maintained a discreet silence. This silence is brought out forcefully in a discourse in which a monk named Malunkya asked the Buddha a series of questions, one of which was whether the saint does or does not exist after death. The monk said that he had not received a satisfactory answer to this question, and called upon the Buddha to admit that he did not know if he could not provide such an answer. The Buddha, however, refused to answer the question directly. Instead he replied that the question had nothing to do with the fundamentals of the religion and did not tend to the absence of passions conducive to Nirvana. Anyone who attempts to answer such a question would become confused and hopelessly lost in a metaphysical jungle from which he could not extricate himself.

By his silence the Buddha refused to discuss the final and ultimate Nirvana with limited and finite words; to do so would serve only to delimit and circumscribe the final reality, which he said was profound, indescribable, and incomprehensible.

d) Development of Theravāda doctrine. This aspect of Buddhism described in the foregoing is called THERAVĀDA Buddhism, Doctrine of the Elders. It is essentially a discipline which an individual practices in order to achieve salvation for himself by himself. The merit that he accumulates as he lives the religious life is applicable only to himself and cannot be transferred to others. In Theravāda Buddhism the individual who achieves this goal of salvation is called the *arhant*. Only a monk can achieve *arhantship*. Because this goal of *arhantship* is attainable only by the few who have the stamina and will power to live the strenuous religious life, this aspect of Buddhism is sometimes called HĪNAYĀNA, or Lesser Vehicle, by its critics.

During the years immediately after the death of the Buddha the living memory of the Master served as a unifying force that prevented doctrinal controversy from arising within the community of monks. With the passage of time, however, dissensions arose. For their strict adherence to the letter of the teachings, the Theravāda monks were criticized as being too conservative and literal-minded. The *arhant* ideal with its emphasis on self-improvement and personal salvation was also criticized as being too narrow and individualistic, and as not being in consonance with the truth of *anatta* or nonself, since the *arhant* was still thinking in terms of a dualism, his own self and the other. Records tell about BUDDHIST COUNCILS, one of which was held a hundred years after the death of the Buddha to decide on the differences of opinion held between what might be called the conservative and liberal wings of the monastic community. Out of this council arose a school, the Mahāsāṅghika, or Great Assembly, which developed ideas that played an important role in the formation of the second aspect of Buddhism, the MAHĀYĀNA, or Great Vehicle. It is called great because it conveys many to salvation.

3. **Mahāyāna teachings.** In this new aspect of Buddhism one of the most important doctrines is that every sentient being possesses the Buddha nature and is therefore capable of becoming a Buddha. This is in contrast to the Theravāda teaching that there can be only one Buddha in an aeon and that enlightenment is reserved for the elite few.

a) Faith. If the goal of Buddhahood is open to all, then the path to the goal must be made easier, and this is what the Mahāyāna did. Instead of the strenuous ascetic discipline of the Theravāda, the Mahāyāna emphasized faith and devotion to the Buddha and love and compassion for all living beings. According to the LOTUS SŪTRA, anyone who has heard the Master's teachings, who worshiped an image of the Buddha, or who made a STŪPA of sand or mud, would become enlightened. Followers of the Amitābha cult were told that anyone who has faith in the Buddha Amitābha, and who manifests that faith by repeating the formula *namo Amitābha* (I pay homage to Amitābha), would be reborn in the paradise presided over by that Buddha. (*See* AMIDA; PURE LAND; NEMBUTSU.)

Such an emphasis on faith and devotion is indeed a development of far-reaching consequence. Whereas in Theravāda the stress was on self-reliance and self-emancipation, now the Amitābha cult emphasized the saving grace of Amitābha, an external force. This was probably due to the Mahāyāna belief that a loving and compassionate Buddha would not restrict the effects of his meritorious karma to himself but would transfer such merits to all mankind.

b) Concept of the Buddha. The concept of the Buddha also underwent an important change. In early Buddhism the Buddha was looked upon as a human teacher who lived and taught just as any other human teacher. In Mahāyāna Buddhism there developed the idea of an eternal Buddha who embodies the absolute truth. For example, the Lotus Sūtra teaches that the Buddha has lived since beginningless time and will live for countless ages in the future. However, in order to reveal his message to mankind, this eternal Buddha manifests himself from time to time as an earthly Buddha to live and work among man. Śākyamuni the son of MĀYĀ was just one of these earthly appearances, a phantom apparition created by the eternal Buddha. Such a concept enables the Mahāyāna to develop the notion of countless Buddha-worlds, each one presided over by its own Buddha. It also enables the Mahāyāna to claim that any teacher or founder of a religion was but another manifestation of this eternal Buddha. (*See* BUDDHA, GENERAL CONCEPTS OF.)

c) Bodhisattva. Instead of the cold and passionless *arhant*, the Mahāyāna ideal is the BODHISATTVA, a being already enlightened but who delays his final entry into Nirvana until he has carried out his vow to save every sentient being from this world of misery. Mahāyāna doctrine claims that the bodhisattva through his spiritual advancement has accumulated a vast store of merits which he now gladly transfers to less fortunate beings, so that these also might enjoy the rewards of these accumulated merits. The chief virtues of the bodhisattva are perfect wisdom and universal compassion manifested by complete self-sacrifice. He is usually considered to be the personification of some particular traits of the Buddha. The bodhisattva MAÑJUŚRĪ is the personification of the wisdom of the Buddha; AVALOKITEŚVARA, of his compassion.

d) Emptiness. According to the Theravāda teaching of dependent origination, all phenomena are conditioned; that is, they come into existence as a result of causes and conditions. Phenomena are said to be compositions of constituent elements or *dharmas* (see DHARMA §5c). For example, an individual is analyzed as a composition of the five elements (SKANDHAS), matter, sensation, perception, predisposition, and consciousness. According to the theory of momentary existence, each element comes into existence for a brief moment and then disappears. However, the *dharmas* follow one another as cause and effect and they are held together by the law of dependent origination to give the impression of a stable world. The important thing to remember is that the Hīnayāna claims these elements are real in that they exist, even though for the briefest moment.

The earliest Mahāyāna sūtras, known as the Wisdom Sūtras, which probably date back to the beginning of the Christian era, attacked this viewpoint that the *dharmas* are real and exist for a moment. Instead they propounded the idea that the *dharmas* are empty and void, because they have to depend on causes and conditions for their existence. Take away the causes and conditions and the *dharmas* do not exist. They do not possess their own self-nature, they are empty of their own being, hence they are said to be empty or void (*śūnya*). This is one of the great truths propounded by the Mahāyāna, that ŚŪNYATĀ, emptiness, is the mark of all the *dharmas*. Anyone who realizes this truth may be said to have achieved wisdom.

e) Nirvana. In Hīnayāna there are two planes, the phenomenal plane where misery and karma prevail, and the Nirvana plane where misery and karma cease. The Hīnayānist believes that by eradicating misery and karma he would realize Nirvana. The Mahāyānist claims that all this is mere fancy. To him, Nirvana requires no eradication of phenomenal existence, for all phenomena are empty and void to begin with. Not only so, but Nirvana is also empty and void, for the Buddha had already declared that Nirvana is beyond all discriminations, particularities, and predication. Based on the thesis that emptiness is the mark of both phenomena and Nirvana, the Mahāyānist came to the conclusion that the phenomenal world is Nirvana and Nirvana is the phenomenal world. Therefore, the Mahāyānist argues that the ignorant Hīnayānist is deluded when he thinks that the phenomenal world exists and that Nirvana is the end of it. The moment the individual ceases to think in terms of a dualism and realizes that the phenomenal world and Nirvana are identical, and that undifferentiated emptiness is the absolute truth, he is enlightened and realizes the Buddha nature within himself. This is the Nirvana of the Mahāyānist.

f) Mādhyamika School. The doctrine of emptiness stressed in the Wisdom Sūtras was picked up and elaborated in greater details by NĀGĀRJUNA, the famous Mahāyāna philosopher who lived during the second century A.D. and who founded the MĀDHYAMIKA School, or the School of the Middle Path. Using the Hīnayāna formula of dependent origination as the starting point of his system, he contended that what is produced by causes does not exist by and of itself, and he came up with his own formula of the eightfold negation; nothing comes into being, nor does anything disappear. Nothing is eternal nor has anything an end. Nothing is identical or differentiated, nothing moves hither nor does anything move thither. By applying this formula as his weapon with merciless logic, he set out to explain the truth of the doctrine of emptiness. He took whatever viewpoint was necessary to refute his opponents. In his mind, the gravest weakness of his opponents was that they adhered to a system, for a system is always open to the criticism that it is inconsistent and contradictory. To avoid being exposed to such criticism, Nāgārjuna did not hold to any system. However, when he denied a thesis, he insisted that he could not be charged with holding the opposite viewpoint, for as he put it, our words are not policemen.

The best source for Nāgārjuna's thought is the *Mādhyamika-kārikā* ("Stanzas on the Middle Path"), consisting of twenty-seven chapters, each one dealing with a specific topic such as causality, motion, fire, and fuel, Nirvana, etc.

Nāgārjuna not only proclaims that all is *śūnya,* or empty, but that the principle of śūnyatā is also empty. He willingly destroys the principle itself, all for the sake of salvation. If he did not do so, then the principle of śūnyatā would become an object of attachment, and this would be an impediment to salvation. This is Nāgārjuna's absolute emptiness, total nonattachment.

g) Vijñānavāda (Yogācāra) School. This Mahāyāna school was established by the brothers Asaṅga and VASUBANDHU, who probably lived during the fourth century A.D. In an earlier Hīnayāna school the view had been advanced that we do not have a direct perception of the external world, but only mental representations that lead us to infer the existence of that world. Asaṅga and Vasubandhu now claimed that there is no need to talk about an external world; accepting the doctrine of emptiness, they contended that it exists only in the mind of the perceiver. Therefore, the fundamental tenet of this school is "all this world is ideation only."

4. **Mahāyāna schools in China.** *a) T'ien-t'ai.* The Mahāyāna teachings of emptiness, nonduality, ideation only, and the presence of the Buddha nature in every sentient being were transmitted to Tibet, China, Korea, and Japan in later centuries to play significant roles in the religious and philosophical life of those countries. In China, the T'ien-t'ai (Jap. TENDAI) School used the Chinese concepts of substance and function *(t'i-yung)* to explain the identity of absolute and phenomenon. In its substance, the absolute is one and undifferentiated, but in its function it is diverse and particular. Despite this diversity, all phenomena are integrated in the absolute. As the T'ien-t'ai masters put it, all the Buddhas may be present in one grain of sand. Phenomenal life is not denied but affirmed as part of the absolute, as the life of the layman is also the life of the Buddha.

b) Hua-yen. In the Hua-yen (Jap. Kegon) School the terms used to denote absolute and phenomena are *li* and *shih,* and the Hua-yen masters resorted to clever instructional methods to impart the truth of the mutual interpenetration between *li* and *shih* and between *shih* and *shih.* The universality of life is thus affirmed, as we are all sons of the Buddha and possess the Buddha-nature within us. (*See* NARA BUDDHISM §3.)

c) Ch'an (Zen). Whereas the Hua-yen School sought to emphasize the potential within all persons by an elaborate philosophical framework, the Ch'an (ZEN) School resorted to the simple and more direct method of meditation to realize the Buddha nature within. The Ch'an masters contended that such efforts as reciting the sūtras, worshiping images of the Buddhas and bodhisattvas, and the performance of rituals are all external paraphernalia and have nothing to do with the essence of the religion. They argued that the essence of Buddhism was the inner experience of realizing the Buddha nature within us, and the way to do this was the practice of meditation, which was the method used by the Buddha to achieve enlightenment. In this insistence on meditation and nonreliance on reciting and studying the sūtras, the Ch'an School represented what is sometimes called the Chinese revolt against Indian verbalism and scholasticism. This same Ch'an after its introduction into Japan was to play a major role in the religious, social, artistic, literary, and material life of the Japanese.

d) Pure Land. Finally, the element of faith associated with Amida Buddha became a major factor in China, Korea, and Japan through the establishment of the PURE LAND SECTS in those countries. Promising an easy path to rebirth in the Western Paradise, these schools became enormously popular among the laity. In one of the Pure Land SECTS in Japan, the Jōdo-Shin, its followers believe that the saving grace of Amida is so absolute that it can erase whatever evil one may commit, even that of marrying and begetting children. This is indeed a far cry from the strict monastic vows of Theravāda Buddhism.

5. **Tantrism.** Besides the Hīnayāna and the Mahāyāna, there is a third Buddhist vehicle called

CHINESE, JAPANESE, AND KOREAN EQUIVALENTS OF SELECTED BUDDHIST TERMS

This table gives an introductory overview of the results of adapting Buddhist terminology to the Chinese language and system of writing, and the varying pronunciation of the terms in three languages that use that system. Some terms and proper names were transliterated into Chinese approximations of the Sanskrit pronunciation (e.g. *arhant; bhikkhu; dhyāna*); others were translated into Chinese terms deemed the closest natural equivalents in meaning (e.g. *dharma; samsara; mantra*). The written form then remained the same for all dialects of Chinese and for the Japanese and Korean languages, which borrowed the system of writing and adapted the pronunciation to their own sound structure. Thus Buddha became *Fo, Butsu,* and *Pul,* respectively. The Japanese also read the character as if it were a purely Japanese term, *Hotoke.* The system was further complicated by the development of new terms for which there is no Sanskrit original (e.g. *Tendai* and *Dainichi*). The use of small capitals for a term in this table constitutes a cross reference to an article in the dictionary.

		Romanized Pronunciation		
Sanskrit (Pali)	Chinese	Chinese	Japanese	Korean
Buddhas, Bodhisattvas				
Amitābha	阿彌陀	Omit'o	AMIDA	Amit'a
AVALOKITEŚVARA	觀音	Kuan-yin	Kannon	Kwan-um
Baisajyaguru	藥師	Yao-shuai	Yakushi	Yaksa
BODHISATTVA	菩薩	P'u-sa	Bosatsu	Posal
BUDDHA	佛	Fo	Butsu (Hotoke)	Pul
KṢHITIGARBHA	地藏	Ti-tsang	Jizō	Chijang
MAITREYA	彌勒佛	Mile-fo	Miroku	Mirŭk
MAÑJUŚRĪ	文殊尸利	Wen-shu-shih-li	Monju(shiri)	Munsusiri
ŚĀKYAMUNI	釋迦牟尼	Shih-chia-mou-ni	Shaka, Shakuson	Sŏkkamoni
TATHĀGATA	如來	Ju-lai	Nyorai	Yorae
VAIROCANA	毗盧遮那	P'i-lu-che-na	Birushana	Pirojana
———	大日	———	Dainichi	———
Doctrine, Philosophy, General				
ARHANT	阿羅漢	Alohan, LOHAN	Arakan	Arahan, Nahan
AVIDYĀ	無明	Wu-ming	Mumyō	Mumyŏng
BHIKKHU	比丘	Pi-ch'iu	Biku	Pigu
BODHI	菩提覺悟	P'u-t'i Chüeh, Wu	Bodai, Kaku, SATORI	Pojei, Kak, O
DHARMA	法	Fa	Hō	Pŏp
DHARMADHĀTU	法界	Fa-chieh	Hokkai	Pŏpkye
DUKKHA	苦	K'u	Ku	Ko
JÑĀNA	智	Chih	Chi	Chi
KARMA	因緣	Yin-yüan	Innen	Inyon
KARUṆĀ	悲	Pei	Hi	Pi
KILĒSA	煩惱	Fan-nao	Bonnō	Pŏnnoi
MANDALA	曼多羅	Man-ta-lo	Mandara	Mandara
MANTRA	呪	Chou	Ju	Chu
MOKṢA	解脫	Chieh-t'o	Gedatsu	Haet'al
MUDRĀ	印相	Yin-hsiang	In-zō	Insang
NIRVANA	涅槃	Nieh-p'an	Nehan	Yŏlban

Doctrine, Philosophy, General *(continued)*				
PRAJÑĀ	慧 智慧	Hui, Chih-hui	E, Chie	Hei, Chihei
SAMSARA	輪迴	Lun-hui	Rinne	Yunhoi
SAṄGHA	僧伽	Seng-chia	Sōgya	Sŭngga
SKANDHAS	五蘊	Wu-yün	Goun	Oon
ŚŪNYATĀ	空	K'ung	Kū	Kong
Trikāya	三身	San-shen	Sanshin	Samsin
DHARMAKĀYA	法身	Fa-shen	Hosshin	Pŏpsin
SAMBHOGAKĀYA	報身	Pao-shen	Hōjin	Posin
NIRMĀṆAKĀYA	應身	Ying-shen	Ōjin	Ŭngsin
Schools, Sects				
HĪNAYĀNA	小乘	Hsiao-ch'eng	Shōjō	Sosŭng
MAHĀYĀNA	大乘	Ta-ch'eng	Daijō	Taesŭng
Abhidharma-Kosa	俱舍	Chü-she	Kusha	Kusa
Avatamsaka	華嚴	Hua-yen	KEGON	Hwaŏm
Dharma-Laksana	法相	Fa-hsiang	HOSSŌ	Pŏpsang
DHYĀNA	禪	Ch'an	ZEN	Sŏn
MĀDHYAMIKA	三論	San-lun	SANRON	Samnon
Mantra	真言	Chen-yen	SHINGON	Chinŏn
Satyasiddhi	成實	Ch'eng-shih	JŌJITSU	Sŏngsil
Sukhāvati	浄土	Ch'ing-t'u	JŌDO	Ch'ŏngt'o
THERAVĀDA	上座部	Shang-tso-pu	Jōzabu	Sangjwabu
VINAYA	律	Lü	RITSU	Yul
YOGĀCĀRA	瑜伽	Yü-chia	Yuga	Yuga
———	天台	T'ien-t'ai	TENDAI	Ch'ŏnt'ae
Sacred Writings				
ĀGAMA	阿含	Ahan	Agon	Agam
DHAMMAPADA	法句經	Fa-ku-ching	Hokkugyō	Pŏpgugyŏng
DHARMAŚĀSTRA	經論	Ching-lun	Kyōron	Kyŏngnon
JĀTAKA	本生	Pen-sheng	Honjō	Ponsaeng
PRAJÑĀPĀRAMITĀ	般若波羅蜜經	Panjo-polomi-ching	Hannya-haramitsukyo	Panya-paramil-kyŏng
Saddharmapuṇḍarīka (LOTUS SŪTRA)	妙法蓮華經	Miaofa-lienhua-ching	Myōhōrengekyō	Myobŏpyŏnhwa-kyŏng
TRIPIṬAKA	三藏	San-ts'ang	Sanzō	Samjang
VINAYA PIṬAKA	律藏	Lü-ts'ang	Ritsuzō	Yuljang
SUTTA PIṬAKA	經藏	Ching-ts'ang	Kyōzō	Kyŏngjang
ABHIDHAMMA PIṬAKA	論藏	Lun-ts'ang	Ronzō	Nonjang
Vajra Sūtra (DIAMOND)	金剛經	Chin-kang-ching	Konggōkyō	Kŭmgangkyŏng

Table compiled by John O. Barksdale and Keith Crim. Calligraphy by John C. Kang.

TANTRISM, also called Tantrayāna because it is based on a body of esoteric literature called Tantras, and Mantrayāna because of its emphasis on MANTRAS or mystic syllables. Tantrism differs from the other two aspects through its emphasis on sacramental action. Instead of stressing such concepts as faith or wisdom it relies on a consecration consisting of actions of the body, speech, and mind. The human body is not deprecated but is valued as the instrument through which actions are performed to achieve salvation. Such actions entail complicated rituals that require oral instruction under a recognized master, and such instructions are given only to those who are properly qualified.

a) Mantras and mudrās. One type of sacramental action consists of the recital of mantras. A mantra is usually a string of syllables with or without meaning. When pronounced correctly, it can generate enormous powers for good or evil. An example of an auspicious mantra is the one favored by the Tibetans, OM MAṆIPADME HŪM (O the jewel in the lotus), the repeated utterance of which is believed to result in a favorable state of rebirth or salvation. Another type of action is the MUDRĀ, ritual gestures of the body, hands, or fingers. It is thought that the devotee can get in touch with a deity by performing the special gestures associated with that deity.

b) Mandala. Initiation into the MANDALA represents the final step in the consecration process. A mandala is a mystic circle or cosmogram in which the Tantric deities are represented in their visible forms or by symbols. It may be painted on a piece of paper or cloth, or drawn on the ground. For the initiation ceremonies, the mandala is usually drawn on the ground to delimit it from its profane surroundings. The initiation ceremonies consist of baptism by water, wearing of the diadem, placing the sacred band on the shoulder, touching with the bell and thunderbolt, taking a secret name, and receiving the bell and thunderbolt from the master. For those who are considered spiritually ready, the initiation ceremonies may include erotic-yogic practices which are interpreted as a symbol of the drama of cosmic evolution. It is this idea that is responsible for the creation of the *yab yum* (father-mother) image in Tibetan icongraphy, in which the Buddhas are locked in embrace with their consorts. In such images the Buddhas represent compassion, their female consorts wisdom. Just as enlightenment in Mahāyāna Buddhism results from the union of compassion and wisdom, so the union of the *yab yum* figures represents the great bliss or Nirvana.

Tantrists believe their way is superior to Hīnayāna and Mahāyāna because it does not require the long road that the Mahāyāna bodhisattva or the Hīnayāna *arhant* has to travel, but allows them to achieve salvation within a single lifespan.

Tantric Buddhism was introduced into Tibet by Padma-Sambhava (*see above* §1c). In the eighth century this aspect of Buddhism also flourished in China, and from there it was introduced into Japan during the early years of the ninth century. In China and Japan its practitioners concentrated on mantras and ritual gestures.

6. Monastic community. *a) Monks.* The Buddhist SAṄGHA or monastic community comprises monks, nuns, and male and female novices, but the emphasis here will be on monks, since they constitute the most important element of the community and the ordination of nuns is no longer valid in Sri Lanka, Burma, and Thailand. The English word "monk" is the common translation of the technical term BHIKKHU or *bhikṣu,* meaning one who subsists on alms. To be eligible for monkhood, the individual must be at least twenty years of age, free from certain physical and occupational impediments, and have undergone a period of tutelage as a novice under a senior monk. If the individual is eligible, then he is presented by his tutor, who asks the assembly of monks three times if it will accept him. There must be a quorum of at least ten ordained monks for this ceremony. If there is no negative response, the novice is accepted. After the completion of the ceremony, the monk takes up residence in a monastery and patterns his life after the precepts contained in that part of the canon called the Vinaya or Rules of Discipline. Such precepts include the vow to abstain from unchastity, murder, stealing, exaggeration of one's miraculous powers, lies, intoxicating liquor, perfumes or unguents, handling money, etc. He is to devote all his time and energy to the pursuit of the religious life in the hope of attaining salvation and to spreading the teachings of the Master to the devoted laity.

b) Fortnightly assembly. The purity of the *Saṅgha* is achieved by the observance of the UPOSATHA, or fortnightly ceremony, held on the days of the new and full moon. All the monks residing in a monastery must attend. The presiding monk recites each of the rules of the monastic code, followed by a pause to allow for the confession by any monk who had violated that rule. After the confession comes the punishment. The nature of the punishment is determined by the type of offense committed. For major offenses such as unchastity, murder, theft, and exaggeration of one's miraculous powers, the penalty is expulsion from the order. For misconduct toward women, other monks, and the laity, the penalty is temporary expulsion from the order, and for minor offenses such as lying, committing nuisances in public places, or drinking intoxicating liquor, the penalty is merely confession.

c) Secular functions. Monks also perform such secular duties as being schoolmasters of the youth and advisors to rulers. Through the ages the monasteries operated schools to give religious as well as secular education, and it has been only within the last century or so that the state has taken over the educational function. Being the best educated group in their societies, monks were often called upon to serve as advisors to the ruling classes, to the extent that at times these political clerics were more powerful than the occupants of the throne. Within the last century, monks have been in the forefront of the struggles for nationalism and independence in such countries as Sri Lanka and Burma.

d) Laity. For the laity, whose main duty is to provide alms for the monks, the goal is not Nirvana but rebirth in one of the Buddhist heavens or a better rebirth in the next state of existence. (*See* BUDDHISM, LAY).

e) Changes. In Theravādin countries, entry into the *Saṅgha* was an individual affair, to be determined by the individual or his family. In China during many periods of history, however, the state played an important role in determining who should enter the *Saṅgha* and how. The imperial authorities fixed the number of ordinations that might be permitted annually, supervised the examinations to determine who would be eligible, and issued ordination certificates to the successful candidates. A more drastic modification occurred in Japan, where the preachers of the Jōdo-Shin School may marry and rear families.

7. **Literature.** *a) The Pali Canon.* The sacred languages of Buddhism are Pali and Sanskrit. Pali is the language of the Theravādin canon, while Sanskrit is the language of Mahāyāna scriptures.

The Pali Canon consists of three parts or "baskets," the VINAYA PIṬAKA, or Book of Discipline, SUTTA PIṬAKA, or the discourses of the Buddha, and ABHIDHAMMA PIṬAKA, or the higher subtleties of the law (*see* TRIPIṬAKA).

The Book of Discipline contains not only the precepts that govern the conduct of monks, but also a rich and informative body of materials relating to social, economic, and religious conditions in India during the formative years of Buddhism.

In the Pali Canon the Suttas are divided into five collections: Long Discourses, Middle Length Discourses, Kindred Sayings, Gradual Sayings, and Minor Anthologies. The first two collections are the most valuable and useful, for the Suttas in them discuss the whole gamut of Buddhist doctrines in the most detailed fashion.

The third basket, Abhidhamma, is not for the laity but for the learned monks whose interests lie in the subtle metaphysical problems raised in the Suttas. Analysis and classification of phenomena are the chief preoccupation of the seven items in this collection.

None of the contents of the Pali Canon can be dated with any certainty. The only safe statement is that they were compiled over a number of centuries from the fourth century down to the first century B.C., when the canon was reduced to writing. Nor are any of the compilers known, with the exception of Tissa Moggaliputta, who is said to have compiled the Kathāvatthu (Points of Controversies), one of the works in the Abhidhamma. (*See* PALI CANON.)

b) Mahāyāna literature. There is really no Mahāyāna canon, only a collection of separate texts written in SANSKRIT. Many of these Sanskrit originals are no longer extant, but before they were lost they were translated into Chinese and Tibetan and are now preserved in those languages. The Tibetan translations are most faithful to the Sanskrit original, and for this reason are very valuable for comparative textual studies and for the restoration of lost portions of the original Sanskrit texts. On the other hand, the Chinese versions are not really translations but free renditions of the meaning of the original texts.

Mahāyāna literature is characterized by diversity, extravagant imagination, colorful personalities, and inordinate repetitions. One of the most influential texts, the Heart Sūtra, consists of only about seven hundred Chinese characters, while the Garland Sūtra, basic text of the Hua-yen School in China and Japan, consists of eighty chapters. The collection of Wisdom Sūtras in Chinese fills three volumes of the standard edition of the Chinese Tripiṭaka, each volume consisting of about a thousand pages. Some texts stress one theme, as the Wisdom Sūtras which emphasize the doctrine of emptiness. Others cover a wider scenerio, as the LOTUS SŪTRA which elaborates on such themes as the eternal Buddha, universal salvation, and the bodhisattva. In the VIMALAKĪRTI Sūtra, the layman Vimalakīrti is presented in such forceful and clear-cut fashion that he became a model for the educated Chinese to emulate. As for the extravagant imagination, one finds constant references to myriads of Buddha worlds, as numerous as the tiny specks of dust in the four continents, each one presided over by its own Buddha. Each Buddha is surrounded by bodhisattvas as numerous as the sands of the Ganges. The lifespan of each Buddha is calculated to be hundreds of thousands of myriads of years.

As in the case of the Pali Canon, no definite date or author can be ascribed to many of the Mahāyāna scriptures. Very likely the composition of such texts as the Lotus Sūtra spanned a number of centuries, with portions being added from time to time. In view of the late appearance of the Mahāyāna literature, the Hīnayāna followers charged that they are not the words of the Buddha and hence are not canonical. In replying to this charge, the Mahāyāna follower claims that the Buddha preached the Hīnayāna sūtras first to those who were ignorant and unlearned, but to the wise and learned he preached the Mahāyāna doctrines, which were transmitted orally by the elite disciples from generation to generation until they finally appeared in writing as the Mahāyāna scriptures.

8. **Rituals and ceremonies.** *a) Ritual actions.* In all Buddhist ceremonies there are certain basic ritual actions that are performed by the worshiper. First, there are the offerings, usually in the form of flowers, food, water, or candles. Second, there is what is commonly called motor behavior, such as bowing before the image of the Buddha, an act of reverence that consists of the worshiper touching the ground three times with his forehead. Another is removing

one's shoes or sandals when entering the place of worship. Finally, there is the verbal behavior, such as the uttering of devotions, charms, or spells.

b) Objects of worship. The most common object of ritual worship is the Buddha image. Next in importance is the STŪPA, originally a funerary mound containing the relics of the Buddha, and as such, the outward and visual symbol of the Master. Because there is only a limited number of relics of the Buddha, some *stūpas* merely contain the relics of famous monks. However, in Buddhist countries of Southeast Asia, especially Burma, *stūpas* do not need to contain any relics; they are constructed by their donors primarily to acquire merits. Another object is the BODHI tree under which the Buddha achieved enlightenment. Finally, there are the teeth of the Buddha, scattered all over Asia, with the most famous one kept in Kandy, Sri Lanka.

c) Crisis rituals. The above may be termed expressive rituals, as the worshiper performs them to express his emotions or attitudes toward certain objects of the religion. Another category may be labeled crisis rituals, performed by the Buddhist during certain critical moments in life, such as illness, accidents, natural calamities, snakebites, or banditry. In order to guard against such happenings, Buddhists have evolved magic rituals for their own protection. The most common is the recital of certain chapters or verses taken from the canon. The portions which are recited are called *parittas*. The *Khanda-paritta* is said to have been composed by the Buddha himself as a protection against snakebites, a most common danger in South and Southeast Asian countries. Chanting of the *Ratana-paritta* is said to be efficacious against sickness, wild beasts, pestilence, and natural calamities, while the *Mora-paritta* is recited to guard against the temptations of beautiful women. Buddhists believe that protective rituals are effective because they are endowed with the powers of the Buddha, but such powers are generated only if the worshiper is a faithful devotee.

d) Calendrical ceremonies. i. Daily ceremonies. Bowing and making offerings before the Buddha image are usually performed as part of larger ceremonies, the most common of which are the calendrical rites, so called because they may be divided into a daily, monthly, or annual cycle.

The daily cycle consists mainly of the private devotions performed morning and evening by the faithful worshiper before the family shrine, which invariably consists of an image of the Buddha and a vase to hold floral offerings. The ceremonies include the offering of flowers, the lighting of candles, and the recitation of such expressions as the formula of the TRIRATNA (I take refuge in the BUDDHA, I take refuge in the DHARMA, I take refuge in the SAṄGHA), and the five cardinal precepts (not to kill, steal, tell lies, commit adultery, or drink intoxicating liquor). The devotee also asks for certain boons, e.g., rebirth in a good state of existence, avoidance of misfortunes, and freedom from personal defects. Public devotions are also performed daily in the village chapel, consisting of the presentation of flowers, recitation of the five precepts, and invocations to the Buddha.

ii. Monthly ceremonies. The most important is the observance of the *uposatha*, held on the days of the new and full moon. Lay participation is optional, but laymen often take part because of their desire to acquire merits.

iii. Annual ceremonies. The first festival in the annual cycle is the Buddha Day, occurring at the full moon in May and commemorating the birth, attainment of enlightenment, and death of the Buddha. In the past, this festival was celebrated in India and China by a procession of images of the Buddha. Next is the observance of the rainy season from July to October. Due to the presence of the monsoon rains in South and Southeast Asia, monks cannot travel and so they remain within their monasteries to carry on their studies and meditation. Even in countries which are not affected by the monsoons, such as China, Korea, and Japan, monks still observe the rainy season. At the end of the season in October the *kathina* ceremony, the offering of robes to the monks, is observed by the royalty, nobility, and commoner alike.

For the Buddhists in China, Korea, and Japan, there is the *Ullambana* or All-Souls' Feast celebrated on the fifteenth day of the seventh lunar month. This festival is based on the legend concerning one of the chief disciples of the Buddha, MOGGALLĀNA, who descended to the deepest of Buddhist hells to search for his mother, reborn there because of her avariciousness and deceit. To rescue her from her sufferings, the Buddha suggested that Moggallāna and the community of monks make a united donation of food, clothing, and wealth, not only on behalf of Moggallāna's mother, but also for the sake of all departed ancestors. This was accordingly done and the mother rescued. Because of its identification with the Chinese virtue of FILIAL PIETY, the All-Souls' Feast became probably the most popular annual Buddhist festival in China. This popularity was carried over into Japan, where the *urabon* celebrations included dances and the lighting of lamps which were set adrift on rivers or lakes.

In Kandy, Sri Lanka, there is also the annual celebration of the Tooth Festival in August. According to tradition, a tooth of the Buddha was taken to Ceylon from India in the fourth century A.D. and has been regarded as an auspicious symbol to be honored with an annual procession of elephants. Probably the earliest mention of this procession was by the Chinese monk Fa-hsien, who witnessed it in the capital, Anurādhapura, *ca.* A.D. 413. Even today the celebration of the festival in Kandy lasts for ten days, with the procession being led by a huge gaily decorated elephant carrying the sacred tooth as it wends its way through the streets of the city.

9. **Present trends.** At present, with China and Tibet under the control of the People's Republic of

China, Buddhism is no longer a living force in those countries. The *Saṅgha* has been decimated and the monasteries converted to museum pieces. Elsewhere, the religion is still the living faith of the people of Sri Lanka, Burma, Thailand, Taiwan, Korea, and Japan.

Present trends include participation in the political process, involvement in social welfare programs, popularity of meditation, secular education for monks, and emphasis on the scientific nature of Buddhism.

One of the most significant trends in recent times is the increasing participation of the Buddhist clergy in the political life of the country. Sri Lankan and Burmese monks were among the most vocal and active advocates of nationalism and independence against their colonial rulers in the past, and after independence they have continued their participation in the political process. Sri Lankan monks have formed political parties, joined united fronts, supported political candidates, and staged political campaigns. In Japan, Sōka Gakkai, a lay Buddhist organization, has its own political party, the Kōmeitō, which has staged successful political campaigns in local and national elections.

In one of his discourses the Buddha indicated that in order to eradicate poverty and crime, the ruler must improve the economic conditions of his country by providing for the growth of agriculture and business and assuring that adequate wages are paid to workers. With these teachings in mind, the *Saṅgha* in Sri Lanka and Thailand has embarked on various projects aimed at community development and rural uplift. Centers have been established to train monks who would devote their lives to the improvement in rural areas, and farmers' associations have been organized dedicated to the same end. Buddhist leaders now contend that monks should no longer confine themselves to their monasteries but should go out and work for the spiritual and material welfare of the people.

One of the means advocated to improve social conditions is the practice of meditation. Through meditation, the individual Buddhist can achieve the kind of self-control and selflessness that will lead to greater commitment for the common good. This belief has led to the establishment of meditation centers in Colombo, Rangoon, and Bangkok.

It would seem that if Buddhism is to play an increasing role in the political and social life of its people, then the education of the Buddhist monk must assume a more secular dimension. Such a trend has indeed developed. Monks are broadening their education by studying in Buddhist universities established in Sri Lanka and Thailand. The Mahāchulalongkorn University in Thailand has a Faculty of Humanities and Social Welfare which offers instruction in hygiene, politics, sociology, law, art and archaeology, geography, and history.

In its competition with other world religions such as Christianity and Islam for the attention of the modern world, Buddhism claims that it deserves special consideration because its approach and teachings are compatible with those of modern science. A number of Buddhist leaders have repeatedly stressed that Buddhism is scientific because it has no notion of an absolute deity, an immortal soul, or a first cause, and because all its teachings are based on universal laws. In its methodology, Buddhism is said to be experimental in that the Buddha called upon his followers not to accept his teachings merely because he taught them, but that they should first test them to see if they were efficacious. Moreover, the Buddhist apologists also claim that such Buddhist teachings as the doctrine of non-self, universal flux, and the cyclic theory of evolution are all scientific in nature, and that therefore Buddhism is indeed a religion suitable for modern humanity. *See* Buddhism in America; Buddhism in Southeast Asia; Art and Architecture, Buddhist; Buddhist Sectarianism; Mahābodhi Society.

Bibliography. M. Winternitz, *A History of Indian Literature*, II (1933); K. Chen, *Buddhism, the Light of Asia* (1978); R. Robinson, *The Buddhist Religion*, 3rd ed. (1981); M. Spiro, *Buddhism and Society* (1970); Walpola Rahula, *What the Buddha Taught* (1959) and *The Heritage of the Bhikkhu* (1974); E. J. Thomas, *The History of Buddhist Thought* (1951); D. Swearer, *Buddhism in Transition* (1970). K. K. S. Chen

BUDDHISM IN AMERICA. In speaking of Buddhists in America a distinction has to be drawn between Buddhists of Asian birth or descent for whom Buddhism is a natal and family religion, and Buddhists of American birth for whom Buddhism is an adopted religion. The Buddhism of Asians in America is strongest among first-generation immigrants and is, therefore, to be found most often among the recent arrivals from Korea, Japan, China, Vietnam, Thailand, Burma, Cambodia, and Sri Lanka. In contrast, the Buddhism of Western converts does not follow generational lines. In keeping with the spirit of the Indian tradition of searching for a spiritual master, Western Buddhist followers are apt to change groups, sometimes leaving one Buddhist tradition to join a group in another. Western Buddhist groups in America are usually quite small, many having only five or ten members who regularly attend meditation or chanting sessions. Many of these groups meet in the private residence of one of the members, who may serve as a coordinator but usually not as a meditation teacher. Only exceptional groups have the funds and energy to support an organizational staff, a separate building, and a resident teacher. For example, according to a 1978 survey, there were in California sixty-eight groups, and of these perhaps only a dozen had their own buildings and a membership of fifty persons or more.

1. **History.** The first intentional reflection on Buddhist values and ideas by American intellectuals occurred in the writings of the New England transcendentalists in the 1830s. During the next

half-century, as America's political, economic, and philosophical horizons moved steadily westward (Commodore Perry landed in Japan in 1854), interest was aroused by Indian and East Asian literature and religions. In 1875 the Theosophical Society was founded in New York in order "to promote the study of Aryan and other Eastern literatures, religions, and sciences." (*See* THEOSOPHY.) In 1880 two of the leading members of the society, Colonel Henry Olcott, an American, and Madame H. P. Blavatsky, a Russian emigré, journeyed to Sri Lanka and subsequently became highly influential in the revival of Buddhism in what was at that time a British colony. In 1893, at the World Parliament of Religions in Chicago, there were several Buddhists. One was Anagarika Dharmapala, a monk who had met Colonel Olcott in Sri Lanka; another was Soyen Shaku, a Japanese Rinzai ZEN master. Later, in the wake of the Parliament, Paul Carus, who had attended the Buddhist program, invited D.T. SUZUKI, a disciple of Soyen Shaku, to serve as an editor for Open Court Publishing; and it was principally through the writings and lecturers of Suzuki that Euro-Americans came to learn about Buddhism.

Recent Western interest in Buddhism has appeared in two forms: as a new academic discipline creating a new generation of "Buddhologists," and as a new spiritual discipline led by a new generation of Buddhist "masters" who made their appearance on the American religious scene in the 1960s and 70s. Persons in the first group are often fascinated by Buddhist theories (e.g., FOUR NOBLE TRUTHS and ŚŪNYATĀ), while persons in the second group are interested less in Buddhist belief systems and more in religious practice. Because of the dogmatic way in which Buddhist meditational practice is usually taught, and because of the radical social and philosophical implications of participation in meditation groups, adoption of Buddhism and dissent from mainline American values have often gone hand in hand. Thus the meditators of the 1970s were often the former social and political activists of the 1960s. For them the reform movements of the 60s suffered from the inner, psychological violence that gave rise to social protests.

In the Asian-American communities (chiefly along the Pacific Coast), Buddhism was the natal religion of the majority of the immigrants. In 1898 the Young Men's Buddhist Association (YMBA) was organized in San Francisco; and in 1899, with the arrival of the first official Jōdo Shin-shū missionaries from Japan (*see* PURE LAND SECTS), the North American Buddhist Mission (NABM) was founded. In 1944, following the imprisonment of the Japanese population of the West Coast, the NABM changed its name to Buddhist Churches of America (BCA). The BCA has served the Japanese-American community as a medium in which Japanese social and cultural values may be preserved and in which adaptation to the American culture may be expressed. In this way the BCA has served, paradoxically, both as a constraint and as a catalyst to acculturation.

2. **Forms and structures.** In Asia, Buddhism exists on two essential planes, the monastic and the lay. In America, Buddhism has taken on analogous forms as well as distinct indigenous social forms and organizations. In Asia the contemplative Buddhism of the monastery is, for the most part, a world apart from that of the devotional Buddhism of the village. In America it is in the Asian and Asian-American Buddhist communities that the traditional gap still exists. In such communities the resident Asian monk (where there is one) lives in one world, that of the scholar, translator, or meditator, while the ceremonially minded Buddhist congregation lives in another, that of the extended family embedded in ancestral traditions and rituals. The monk and the lay community, as in Asia, have a formal, mutually sustaining relationship.

The situation is quite different in the new, non-Asian Buddhist groups in America. In such lay groups the social structure of the local "Zen Center" is organized in a manner echoing that of the Buddhist monastery of Asia. In some instances (e.g., that of the Gold Mountain Monastery of San Francisco) the monastic atmosphere is a replica of that of a Chinese monastery, and all social and personal aspects of life, dress, diet, daily schedule—even the posture for sleep (a sitting position)—are formally regulated. The monastic atmosphere tends to prevail even in Buddhist centers with American teachers. Examples here include the San Francisco Zen Center and the Rochester Zen Center in New York. In these groups only a small percentage of the participants are formally ordained as monks or nuns, yet the atmosphere tends toward that of the monastery and emphasis is given to the cultivation of teaching relationships between members of the group. Members of such groups tend to behave toward each other as if they were monks. The result is that the distinction between monk and layperson, which is central to Asian Buddhism, is of only nominal importance in the non-Asian groups in the United States and Canada.

In several ways the sociological picture of American Buddhism is analogous to Buddhist patterns in Asia. What is striking on the American scene is the ethnic polarization that exists in Buddhist, "village-like" communities. The corresponding phenomenon in Asia is the ethnic, national, and ethno-sectarian compartmentalization of Buddhism. In Asia there has been little ecumenical contact across national and denominational lines, and in America this situation has continued. For example, Korean and Japanese Buddhist immigrants to America have little contact as Buddhists, and in Carmel Valley, California, there is both a Korean-style Zen temple and a Japanese-style Zen monastery with resident Western followers, but proximity has not fathered interdenominational dialogue. However, while Buddhist society in Asia (and in Asian communities in America) traditionally has been organized along hierarchical, patriarchical, and androcentric lines, in many Western groups this pattern has been altered. There are, for example, women who are "DHARMA teachers" as well as staff officials, and there is at least one woman, Jiyu Kennett, who is a ROSHI (a Japanese term for Zen master). Within a given monastic community in Asia as well as within a given Western, meditation-oriented group in America there are career roles for administrators, scholars, translators, and painters, as well as for temple curators and priests. Very rarely does a person come to be regarded as a "master" in any of these Buddhist vocational fields, and, of those persons, fewer still are known for being spiritual teachers. In America the direction and tone of a given group will typically reflect the particular monastic specialization that an Asian-born or Asian-trained master acquired in Asia. Therefore, a monk trained as a scholar-translator, such as Master Hsüan Hua, abbot of Gold Mountain Monastery in San Francisco, will train his Western followers to be translators of the Buddhist canon.

Dr. Thich Thien-An is an example of the teacher-monk. He was a monk for fifteen years in a monastery in Hue, Vietnam. He then studied Buddhist and Oriental philosophy in Tokyo from 1954 to 1962. Afterward, he was a teacher and scholar of Zen Buddhism at the University of Saigon and at Van Hanh (Buddhist) University. In 1966, as the American military effort in his country intensified, he moved to the University of California at Los Angeles to serve as a visiting professor of Oriental languages. In 1970 he established the International Buddhist Meditation Center in Los Angeles as a nonsectarian center for Buddhist meditational practice. In 1973 he founded what became after four years the University of Oriental Studies in Los Angeles. He has published about ten books in three languages, including *Buddhism and Zen in Vietnam* (1975). His career in America as a Buddhist teacher, scholar, and educational innovator illustrates the vision and energy of a number of Asian and Western Buddhist leaders, prominent among whom are Richard Baker, Jiyu Kennett, Philip Kapleau, Hsüan Hua, and Tarthang Tulku.

3. **Perspectives.** The phenomenon of Buddhism in America may be understood from three independent perspectives: the history of Buddhism, American studies, and cultural criticism (including theological and social-scientific analyses of religion).

Viewed from the perspective of the history of Buddhism, the appearance of Buddhism in America is accounted for differently by believers and nonbelievers. For a Buddhist the spreading of the Buddhist dharma, or teachings, is a tenuous, fragile process which requires great effort, but for a nonbeliever the same spreading is to be seen as a process of cultural diffusion. Both views are alike, however, in viewing American Buddhism as a product of the transmission or spreading of a classical Asian religion to other culture areas. The arrival of Buddhism in America is, from this perspective, only the most recent stage in a missionary process that began 2,500 years ago in India, and a new development which must be evaluated in the context of established Buddhist norms and practices.

Viewed from the perspective of American studies, Buddhism appears as a minor phenomenon in the history of American religious traditions. First, Buddhism appears as the predominant religious affiliation of Asian immigrants, from the 1840s to the present. Second, it appears as the "heir" to one branch of theosophy, from the 1890s forward (as illustrated in the life of Beatrice Lane Suzuki, a Theosophist who married the famous Zen teacher D. T. Suzuki). Third, interest in Buddhism appears as an important component in the "Beat," "Zen Catholicism," and "countercultural" movements that occurred partially in consequence of the war with Japan and the later Korean and Vietnam wars. Finally, Buddhism appeared in the 1970s as a new force and focus in American higher education. Not only were new courses on Buddhism offered in numerous colleges, seminaries, and universities, but such courses were offered in a large number of new, residential centers for Buddhist education (of which the Naropa Institute in Boulder, Colorado, and the Nyingma Institute in Berkeley, California, are two prominent examples).

Viewed from the perspective of cultural criticism broadly conceived, Buddhism in America is both an object of inquiry and a method of investigation. Furthermore, American-nurtured Buddhism has offered its own critique of the culture of the West in general, and of America in particular.

The history of the Buddhist critique begins with non-Buddhists who were disenchanted with the status of religion in the West. Two books illustrative of this trend are: *The Supreme Doctrine,* by Hubert Benoit, an essay on the Buddhist statement of the nature and process of spiritual life, which appeared as early as 1951, and *Zen Catholicism,* by Dom Aelrod Graham, a suggestive examination of areas common to the Buddhist and Catholic traditions which received wide attention upon its publication in 1963. In addition, an interest in Buddhism appeared as an important visionary component of the "Beat," LSD, and "countercultural" movements of the period; and the Buddhist-oriented writings of Jack Kerouac, Gary Snyder, Alan Watts, and, later, Philip Kapleau, served for many readers as the starting point of a new approach, first to philosophy and then to religion.

Three contemporary books written by Tibetan LAMAS are examples of the new Buddhist critique by Buddhists living in America: *Cutting Through Spiritual Materialism* by Chögyam Trungpa (1973), *Time, Space, and Knowledge* by Tarthang Tulku (1977), and *The Life of Milarepa,* translated by Lobsang P. Lhalungpa (1977). In these works, and others like them, the purpose is not so much to expound the doctrines of Buddhism as it is to offer a new statement of the nature and causes of spiritual restlessness of the modern person in the West and the relevance of the Buddhist solution.

With the arrival of Asian Buddhist masters the Buddhist message and criticism sometimes assumed rather esoteric or apologetic forms. For instance, one critique of American society would remedy the spiritual plight of the modern rationalist by freeing a person from what is perceived to be a hopelessly entangled knot of rationalization. Quite different routes toward the realization of this purpose are being taken by the great variety of foreign-born Buddhist teachers in America. An example is Seung Seon Sa Nim, a colorful Korean monk whose playful, idiosyncratic teaching style may be seen in the seemingly flippant title of his sermons, or "dharma talks": *Dropping Ashes on the Buddha* (1975). For him, "academic Zen"—the Zen of Buddhologists, philosophers, and translators—is like candy: good for a taste, but in excess harmful to the digestion. In consequence he shuns canonical and psychological terms and instead sprinkles his lectures with KŌAN-like neologisms: "I-my-me-mind," "don't-know mind," and "only-go-straight mind." In this way, by his constantly changing his terminology, his followers are prevented from taking a "doctrinal" approach to his teaching. Eventually his followers may come to see that Zen is "before thought" and that true religion exists beyond doctrines and creeds.

Buddhist groups have also come under criticism: on the one side by classical Buddhist scholars like Charles Prebish, who have said that some groups have tended toward heterodoxy and syncretism, in some cases becoming unrecognizable as Buddhist; and on the other side by American social historians and critics like Peter Marin, who have seen in Buddhist groups a tendency toward narcissim and social irresponsibility. Marin's major criticism is directed against the moral passivity of Western followers who, in their relations with their Tibetan master, showed little capacity for independent ethical thought or action. Other critics have commented on the elitist and ethnocentric tendencies that are found in the behavior and mindset of Buddhist followers, Asian and Western, whose veneration for the aesthetic criteria, ritual, and mystique of a given Asian strain serves as a socio-economic screen that filters out possible participation by ethnic minorities, for example, Blacks and Chicanos, whose presence is virtually nonexistent. The members of the new Buddhist groups are typically white, middle-class (often Jewish) professionals and preprofessionals.

4. **Prognosis.** An overall assesssment of the significance and life expectancy of the new Euro-American Buddhist groups in America should be made with reference to the religious or nonreligious traditions from which the members are recruited. For example, the rise of American Buddhist groups made up of former Jews and Christians may be understood in at least two ways: as representative of the supposed decline in the vitality or relevance of traditional forms of religiosity (in which a move from Judaism or Christianity to Buddhism may be seen as a critique of the abandoned traditions); and, paradoxically, as an indication of the durability of native Judeo-Christian attitudes and values as observed in the egalitarian ethos of Buddhist groups in America where the Zen master is apt to be treated more as a special friend than as a master. If this type of egalitarianism is traced back to its origins in the Judeo-Christian idea of the equality of all persons before God, then the egalitarian quality of the new Buddhist groups in America (contrary to their Asian monastic counterparts) may be seen as one manifestation of the Judeo-Christian ideal. Thus, the vitality of Buddhism in America may well depend upon its adaptability to and adoption of certain values and structures of Western spirituality.

Bibliography. No comprehensive study of the forms of Asian and Western Buddhism in America exists, nor are there studies of the American experiences of most of the Buddhist immigrant groups. An important exception is T. Kashima's *Buddhism in America* (1977), a sociological study of Japanese groups. Valuable essays on Zen are found in J. Needleman, *The New Religions* (1970); L. Nordstrom, *Namu Dai Bosa: The Transmission of Zen Buddhism to the West* (1977); and R. Ellwood, *Alternative Altars* (1979). H. Cox's *Turning East* (1977) is largely oriented toward Tibetan groups, but contains references to other Buddhist and "Eastern" groups as well. Comparative and interpretive material is found in E. M. Layman's *Buddhism in America* (1976) and C. Prebish's *American Buddhism* (1979). For P. Marin's critique see "Spiritual Obedience," *Harper's*, Feb., 1979. Buddhism as a "new religion" is treated from several perspectives in J. Needleman and G. Baker, eds., *Understanding the New Religions* (1978). G. BAKER

BUDDHISM, LAY. Buddhism has conventionally been understood in the West primarily as a monastic religion. Although in comparison with CHRISTIANITY, Buddhism, especially in its THERAVĀDA form, is singularly monastic in orientation, the role of the lay person should not be neglected. Indeed, the term SAṄGHA, usually translated as "monastic order," actually refers, in its most general usage, to four categories of people: monks, nuns, laymen, and laywomen. An examination of some of the Pali terms used to designate lay persons will serve to indicate the nature or place of the laity within the Buddhist tradition: (1) *Upāsaka/upāsikā,* layman/laywoman, is derived from *upāsati,* meaning to sit near, attend, serve. The lay person serves the monk (BHIKKHU) by providing for his material needs. (2) *Gahaṭṭha* (Skt., *gṛhastha*) is the Pali term for householder. It denotes the fact that lay persons, unlike the mendicant monk, live in a home or settled dwelling. (3) *Saddha* (Skt., *śrāddha),* faith, suggests that the Buddhist lay person is defined by faith in the TRIRATNA or Triple Gem (BUDDHA, DHARMA, SAṄGHA). (4) *Dāyaka* means one who gives, bestows, or provides. The function designated by the *dāyaka* is, there-

Courtesy Thailand Tourist Organization

Offering food to the monks

fore, that of one who attends to the needs of the monastic order. The composite picture derived from these terms depicts the Buddhist lay person as a householder who demonstrates his faith in the Buddha and the monkhood by providing for the material needs of the monastic community.

1. **The lay Buddhist ideal.** The above characterization of a Buddhist lay person emphasizes the supportive role of the laity in relationship to the monastic order. In their own right, however, lay persons are expected to exemplify the highest ideals of the Buddha's teachings. In the first instance, these are ethical. The good Buddhist is expected to follow the Five Precepts, the most widely known ethical code of Buddhism, and the Ten Principles of Good Conduct: to refrain from taking life, from stealing, from sexual misconduct, from falsehoods, from sarcastic provocations, from vulgar speech, and from meaningless and nonsense talk; to destroy covetousness, restrain feelings of resentment or revenge, and to follow the path of dharma. In addition to these ethical principles the Buddhist lay person is expected to be a responsible actor within the social fabric of family and community. In the Theravāda tradition these responsibilities are outlined in the *Sigālovāda Suttanta*. It exhorts children to support their parents and be worthy of their family heritage; instructs parents to restrain their children from vice and train them in a profession; admonishes teachers to love and train their pupils, and pupils to serve their teachers; and further describes the duties of husband and wife, clansman and friends, master and servant. The virtues and duties of rulers are a subject of much discussion in the Buddhist texts. Above all they should govern with righteousness and compassion as a RĀJA (king) of dharma (truth). In this regard the great Indian ruler AŚOKA (third century B.C.) came to symbolize the paradigm of the just Buddhist king.

The virtues of the ideal Buddhist lay person are both various and demanding. They are popularly exemplified in the *paramitā* or "moral perfections" of both the Theravāda and MAHĀYĀNA traditions. In the Theravāda the ten most highly regarded virtues are hypostasized in ten stories of previous lives of the Buddha *(dāsa-jātaka)* which often serve as topics for ethical instruction and exhortation. The ten virtues are: giving, virtue, renunciation, wisdom, energy, forbearance, truth, resolute determination, friendliness, and equanimity. In the Mahāyāna tradition either six or ten *paramitā* are associated with the BODHISATTVA concept (giving, virtue, forebearance, energy, meditation, wisdom).

The ideal Buddhist lay person, however, is more than a responsible citizen and an embodiment of moral virtues, as exemplary as this role may be. The laity are often depicted as full of insight and wisdom, of equal spiritual capacity to the monkhood. Stories depicting exceptional lay persons call into question an unduly sharp split between the two estates of the broader community *(Saṅgha)*. Such a distinction has been more often applied to the Theravāda than the Mahāyāna. Yet, even Theravāda sources depict the lay person as one who is filled with the qualities of faith, moral virtue, sacrifical concern, and wisdom of mind and body, a list that could apply equally well to the monk. King Milinda or Menander, who ruled the Indo-Greek state of Bactria in the latter part of the second century B.C., stands out as a Buddhist lay person whose wisdom exceeds that of all the monks of his day with the exception of Nāgasena (*see* MILINDAPAÑHA).

In the Mahāyāna tradition the most famous layman is undoubtably VIMALAKĪRTI, celebrated in the Vimalakīrtinirdésa Sūtra. He helped the poor, followed the moral principles, was patient and devoted, serene and wise. Although married and with children, Vimalakīrti was diligent in his practice of pure living. He was a householder but not attached to his possessions; wore jewels and ornaments but adorned his body with spiritual characteristics; ate and drank like others but tasted the flavor of meditation. He upheld the dharma and taught it to young and old, and was revered by all who met him.

2. **Relationship to the monastic order.** The interrelationship between the laity and the monastic order has various facets and permutations, including the laity in its role as *dāyaka* or provider for the order's material well-being, the lay person as ritual actor, and the laity as active reformer.

Traditionally, the role assumed by the laity in relationship to the monastic order was that of "provider" *(dāyaka.)* The monk as *bhikkhu* (almsman) necessarily had to rely on the householder community for his material well-being. Although in time, especially in East Asia, monasteries (VIHĀRAS) became large landholders with monks cultivating the land, the ideal of the laity as the support for the monastic community remained. Today in Theravāda countries like Thailand and Burma the laity can be seen either bringing food to the monasteries early in the morning or, more typically, giving food to the monks as they pass by on their morning alms rounds. Most major religious celebrations are opportunities for lay persons to present gifts to the order, and it is thought exceptionally meritorious to fund or build a new monastery. Why is the *dāyaka* role so revered? The monastic status being a highly revered one but without means of self-support leads logically to the central significance of lay provision for the monastic order. Moreover, supporting the monastic order earns merit (PUÑÑA) for the giver, which in the metaphysics of Theravāda Buddhism favorably affects a person's balance of KARMA and future rebirths. Hence, the relationship between lay person as *dāyaka* and the monk functions reciprocally; providing for the material well-being of the monastic order brings both material and spiritual rewards to the laity. It is rather like a material and spiritual symbiotic relationship.

In Buddhist ceremonies the monk plays the primary priestly and mediatorial roles ranging from giving a congregation moral instruction at the beginning of a worship service to saying prayers on behalf of deceased ancestors. However, lay persons also have ritual roles which relate to the monastic order. Not infrequently, a lay person will be the chief officiant during parts of Buddhist ceremonies which reflect non-Buddhist, e.g. Brahmanical, magical-animistic, elements. Furthermore, in gift-giving or meriting-making ceremonies, a lay officiant will not only lead the congregation as a master of ceremonies but will act as a mediator between the monastic order and the laity. In these situations a hierarchy of power is established among the Buddha represented by his image, the monks who chant the Buddha's teachings, the lay leader representing the congregation, and, finally, the laity as a body. In such instances both monk and lay leader act as mediators of the power of the Buddha, on the one hand, and the laity on the other. Such ritual relationships serve to symbolize the importance of the laity in relationship to but as distinct from the monastic order.

Finally, since the purity of the order has been both symbolically and practically associated with general political harmony and peace in the land, political leaders have often sought to reform and/or stabilize the monkhood. King Aśoka, for example, is associated with the third Buddhist council which, in the eyes of the Theravāda tradition, established the orthodoxy of the Theravāda. (*See* BUDDHIST COUNCILS.) In Burma the tradition of political rulers integrating the monastic order ranges from Anuruddha, the great thirteenth century ruler of Pagan, to U Nu in the twentieth century. Other examples could be taken from Sri Lanka, Thailand, Tibet, China, and Japan. In such situations lay authority may even appear to supersede monastic authority, as for example in modern Thailand, where the king formally appoints the head of the monastic order.

What is the status of the laity in relationship to the monastic order? Is the monk superior because he has more obviously embarked on a path to a higher goal? In one sense the answer to the latter question is quite clearly yes. Buddhist texts make abundantly clear the necessity of the monastic life for serious study of the Buddha's dhamma (truth) and the pursuit of meditative disciplines. Although these highly valued endeavors are more difficult for the laity, one finds that throughout Buddhist history they have practiced them. Furthermore, when we consider the high regard given to Buddhist rulers and the authority they have exercised over the monastic order, the significant ritual role played by certain lay persons in relationship to the monkhood, and even the place of lay benefactor *(dāyaka),* we have a much better idea of why the early Buddhist concept of *Saṅgha* (community) included not only the monkhood but the laity as well.

3. Modern movements. If one accepts the premise that the laity has had a status different from but no less important than the monkhood, the role of the Buddhist laity has not been substantially altered in the modern period. Certainly it has assumed new forms; furthermore, the social and political disruption caused by Western colonialism has both freed the lay person to act in new ways and has even necessitated that he do so for the well-being, if not the survival, of Buddhism. New areas of lay activity include their role in Buddhist revitalizations, social services, and community development.

Toward the end of the colonial period, i.e. during the second half of the nineteenth century and the first half of the twentieth, a revitalization of Buddhism took place in many parts of Asia. Much of its stimulus and leadership came from the laity. In China lay persons organized Buddhist clubs for instruction in Buddhist teachings and for both social and charitable purposes. For example, during the 1921 famine a Buddhist Relief Association was established which collected sufficient funds to send several tons of food and thousands of items of clothing to five drought-stricken provinces in North China. In Ceylon (Sri Lanka) the American theosophist Henry Steel Olcott worked with Buddhist monks and lay persons to secure passage of the Buddhist Temporalities Bill for monastery properties, the organization of the Buddhist Theosophical Society, the establishment of the Buddhist Educational Fund, the opening of Buddhist schools and charitable institutions, and the recognition of Vesak (celebrating the Buddha's birth, enlightenment, and final Nirvana) as an official holiday. (*See* THEOSOPHY.) An even more important contribution to the revitalization of Buddhism in Sri Lanka was made by Don David Hewavitarne, better known as the Anagārika Dharmapala. He was the founder of the world famous MAHĀBODHI SOCIETY and worked to raise funds for the restoration of the most venerated and ancient Buddhist shrines of India. He was a powerful and influential champion of Ceylon's national and religious struggle for independence and liberty, and abetted the Buddhist temperance movement and the Ceylon Social Reform Society of 1905. The Buddhist revival in Ceylon reached a major turning point in 1956 with the election of S. W. R. D. Bandaranaike, who explicitly pledged to promote the cause of Buddhism.

In Burma, Bandaranaike's counterpart was U Nu, prime minister from 1948 to 1962. He made Buddhism the cornerstone of his political program, espousing a Buddhist socialism based on the theory that a national community could be built only if individual members are able to overcome their own acquisitive self-interests. Like the Buddhist kings of old he attempted to unify and purify the monastic order. He created a Buddhist Sasana Council to propagate Buddhism and supervise monks, appointed a minister of religious affairs, and ordered government departments to dismiss civil servants thirty minutes early if they wished to meditate. From 1954-65 he sponsored an ecumenical Buddhist council to revise the Theravāda canon and spent considerable sums to restore Buddhist monuments in Burma.

In Japan, the Sōka Gakkai an aggressive lay movement of Nichiren-Shō-shū Buddhism, has become one of that country's largest voluntary organizations. Since 1962 its political party, the Kōmeitō, or Clean Government Party, has been the third largest party in the Upper House of the Japanese Diet. Sōka Gakkai espouses a Buddhist socialism interpreted in terms of the Middle Way of Buddhism.

The lay contribution to Buddhist revitalization in Asia has not been dominated exclusively by political leaders of national prominence. As in China in the 1920s new Buddhist lay organizations such as the YMBA (Young Men's Buddhist Association) have been created in Sri Lanka and Burma. Various lay groups dedicated to various forms of social service have developed. In Sri Lanka the Vinaya Vardena Society formed in 1932 has worked to reform the monastic *Saṅgha*, and an organization like the Sarvodaya Shramadana is working to help the people build a new society from the village up, based on a Gandhian philosophy which incorporates the "Buddha-Aśoka" tradition. Lay-dominated Buddhist social service organizations also appeared in Vietnam and Thailand. Such lay organizations may be organized on a national level, although more traditionally they are local in nature. In Thailand, for example, lay temple committees are increasingly concerned with projects that entail both social utility and service to the monastic community. In Japan many of the new religions are basically lay movements with a strong social service orientation. Risshō Kōseikai, founded in 1938, has been characterized as a society of lay persons dedicated to the perfection of their character through following the teachings of the Buddha. Although in the Nichiren tradition, it is less militant than Sōka Gakkai. One of the basic principles of the Risshō Kōseikai is the bodhisattva ideal of helping others.

A specific form of Buddhist social services has been cooperation between the *Saṅgha* and government agencies in the area of community development. In Thailand, especially in politically sensitive areas bordering Laos and Cambodia, teams of monks and government personnel have been trained to instruct villagers in numerous aspects of development ranging from the construction of sanitary toilets to psychological aspects of effective village leadership. Such projects reflect the changing patterns of society and, in turn, the changing patterns of relationship between Buddhist monk and Buddhist laity, a relationship which has been one of mutual benefit throughout the entire history of Buddhism.

Bibliography. T. W. Rhys David, trans., *The Questions of King Milinda,* Pt. I (1963); C. Luk, ed. and trans., *The Vimalakirti Nirdesa Sutra* (1972); D. K. Swearer, *Buddhism in Transition* (1969), pp. 55-62; H. Welch, *The Practice of Chinese Buddhism 1900-1952* (1967), pp. 377-82.

D. K. Swearer

BUDDHISM IN SOUTHEAST ASIA. Buddhism has enjoyed a very long and eventful history in Southeast Asia, both in the Indonesian archipelago and on the mainland. Because of the fragmented geography of the region and the paucity of documents, its history is complex and difficult to trace. Nevertheless it is clear that the development of Southeast Asian Buddhism has occurred in two distinct though overlapping phases. The early development (extending from the introduction of the tradition sometime after the third century B.C. until the beginning of the thirteenth century A.D.) was characterized by its intimate association with a process of Indianization in most of Southeast Asia, and also with a process of Sinicization in north Vietnam. The later development (extending from the early centuries of the first millennium A.D. to the present) has been characterized by the revival and dominance of Theravāda Buddhism in Burma, Thailand, Laos, and Cambodia, by the geographical expansion of Mahāyāna influence in Vietnam, and by the immigration of Chinese Buddhists into virtually every Southeast Asian country.

1. The period of Indianization. It is difficult to trace the process of Indianization and Buddhization in Southeast Asia. Maritime contacts between various areas of the Indian subcontinent and Southeast Asia were very ancient, and there are indications that Buddhist missionaries may have come into the Mon country in southern Burma and/or central Thailand as early as the third century B.C. By the early centuries of the Christian era both archaeological evidence and the testimony of Chinese historical texts confirm the existence of several well-traveled land and sea routes from India across Southeast Asia to southern China. They attest to the emergence, along these trade routes, of a number of kingdoms organized on the Indian model, both on the mainland and in the Indonesian islands. And they clearly suggest that in many of these kingdoms the late HĪNAYĀNA or early Mahāyāna form of Buddhism was the dominant religious tradition.

Throughout the first millennium A.D. the trade routes from India through Southeast Asia continued to operate, and developments in India continued to exert a powerful influence. During the first half of the period much of the area was dominated by the kingdom of Funan, which had its center at the strategic tip of the Indochina peninsula; and then, as Funan declined, a number of important successors appeared on the scene—among them Champa in central Vietnam, Chenla and then Angkor in Cambodia, the Sailendra and Sri Vijaya kingdoms in the Indonesian islands and Malay peninsula, and the kingdoms of Dvaravati, Srisketra, and Pagan in Thailand and Burma. Generally speaking the religious changes that occurred in Funan and the later kingdoms followed the basic pattern that was evident during the same time span in India. The growing importance of Hindu theism was reflected in the gradual rise in the relative importance of Hindu deities and traditions. The transformations that took place within Indian Buddhism—including the growing importance of the later Mahāyāna and VAJRAYĀNA versions of the teaching and cult, the successive emergence of the Gupta and Pala styles of Buddhist art, and the tendencies toward Hindu/Buddhist syncretism—were reflected in the similar changes that took place in the Buddhist communities in Southeast Asia. But it should also be noted that there were significant variations in the developments that took place in different areas. For example, the northern area of Vietnam remained within the Chinese Empire during most of this period and was strongly influenced by Chinese forms of Buddhism including Ch'an (ZEN); in the Indonesian, Malayan, and Cambodian areas Mahāyāna, Vajrayāna, and syncretistic tendencies were particularly strong; and in the Mon and Burmese kingdoms of Dvaravati, Srisketra, and later Pagan the older Hīnayāna tradition (in both its Sanskrit and Pali forms) continued to play a very significant and in some cases even dominant role.

Though it is clear that there were a number of important centers of Buddhist scholarship in Southeast Asia throughout the period of Indianization, there is little evidence concerning significant texts that may have been produced or doctrinal contributions that may have been made. On the other hand there is a plethora of archaeological evidence that displays the architectural and artistic creativity that was generated by the building activities sponsored by Buddhist kings. For example, the Javanese STŪPA built at Borobudur around A.D. 800 and the Bayon temple built at Angkor Thom in the late twelfth or early thirteenth century rank among the most

magnificent of all expressions of Buddhist piety and aesthetic excellence. Moreover, both these monuments represent a synthesis of Buddhism with distinctively Southeast Asian religious, cultural, and political traditions. In each case they express the coalescence of Indian Buddhism with indigenous mountain and royal cults; and in each case they are replete with magnificent bas-reliefs that utilize Indian artistic forms but at the same time depict a wide variety of aspects of indigenous Southeast Asian life.

The Javanese *stūpa* at Borobudur was built by a king of the Sailendra dynasty as a funerary monument through which he sought to confirm his own attainment of Buddhahood. The monument is built over a natural hill, with a series of stone terraces leading up to a culminating central *stūpa* in which the remains of the deceased monarch were probably deposited. The whole assemblage serves as a representation of the late Mahāyāna/Vajrayāna cosmos with all its various levels and its extensive pantheon of BUDDHAS and BODHISATTVAS. The construction is such that the devotee, by climbing some four miles around and up the richly decorated terraces (the more than two thousand bas-reliefs along these terraces depict many kinds of scenes including incidents from the previous lives of the Buddha, incidents from the Buddha's final life as ŚĀKYAMUNI, and illustrations of the famous Mahāyāna account of the pilgrim Sudhana's quest for enlightenment), makes his way through the various levels of worldly existence until, at the very top, he breaks out into the open area which is occupied by the central *stūpa* containing the royal remains. In so doing he gains a vision of the ultimate Buddhist goal of NIRVANA or release.

The great pyramid temple of Bayon, on the other hand, was constructed to serve as the symbolic and cultic heart of the last of the great royal cities of the Angkor kingdom of Cambodia. The monument included a central pyramid structure that was forty-five meters in height. It included an inner courtyard containing sixteen small sanctuaries bounded by galleries that extended 70 meters in width and 80 meters in length and were covered with magnificent bas-reliefs. And it also included an outer courtyard bounded by similarly decorated galleries that extended 140 meters in width and 160 meters in length. The tower of the central pyramid was, according to a late thirteenth century report by a Chinese visitor, covered with gold; and the whole assemblage was given a unique and awesome appearance by approximately forty-nine different towers that arose from the galleries, each bearing the four faces of the deity to whom the temple was dedicated. After extensive research and numerous debates, it has now become well established that the monument was essentially Buddhist in character. Moreover it has become clear that it was devoted to the great bodhisattva AVALOKITEŚVARA (Lokevara), and that the central cult of the temple was the veneration of an image representing King Jayavarman VII as a *Buddha-rāja* or Buddha-king. In addition scholars now generally agree that the four faces on the towers represented Jayavarman VII as *Buddha-rāja* in his role as the supreme authority in the various provinces or administrative centers that were incorporated in the Angkor empire.

In retrospect it is clear that the building of Angkor Thom came at the very end of the period of Indianization and represented the last flowering of the classical type of Southeast Asian civilization. In Indonesia and Malaya the older kingdoms with their established forms of Hindu/Buddhist syncretism continued to hold sway for another two centuries, but then collapsed under the increasing pressure of Islamic religion and culture. In the other Indianized areas on the mainland the power of the two great classically oriented kingdoms of Pagan and Angkor was decimated by the intruding Mongols on the one hand, and by the rising power of the Tai peoples on the other. At the same time the classical form of Chinese Buddhism that had continued to be the dominant religious force in northern and north central Vietnam during the reign of the indigenous Li dynasty (1009-1225) gradually lost ground in the face of the growing influence and prestige of Neo-Confucianism. (*See* CONFUCIANISM §3.)

2. From the twelfth to the twentieth centuries. The religious effects of the demise of the Indianized kingdoms and cultures that occurred in the early centuries of the second millennium A.D. were quite different in various regions. For example, in Indonesia and Malaya the collapse of the old order resulted in the virtual elimination of Buddhism as an effective religious and cultural force. To be sure, a fascinating version of Hindu/Buddhist syncretism was preserved on the beautiful but isolated island of Bali. And during the twentieth century this remaining classical enclave, along with the Buddhism brought by the large number of Chinese who have migrated into the area, have been the focal points for a small but significant revival. However, Buddhists remain a tiny minority group in Indonesia; and in Singapore and Malaya, Buddhism has a following only among the more conservative segments of the Chinese immigrant population.

In contrast to this situation, Buddhism in the other areas of the mainland proved to be much more resilient. In the heartland region from western Burma to the western segment of south Vietnam the collapse of the old order was accompanied by the rise to prominence of another form of Buddhism—a reformed Sinhalese version of the Theravāda tradition. And in Vietnam the Mahāyāna form of Buddhism was able to persist as a significant component of Vietnamese religious and cultural life.

In the heartland area, early hints of the different kind of development that was to take place were already apparent at the time of the rise of the last of the great Indianized kingdoms in Pagan (founded *ca.* 1044). This kingdom was established by an ethnic group (the main body of Burmese) that had not previously been a major factor in Southeast Asian political life; and what is more, the early Burmese kings of Pagan chose to give special encouragement to an indigenous Southeast Asian form of Theravāda Buddhism. However, the real beginnings of the transformation to a new political and religious order appeared in the last half of the twelfth century and were associated with three closely related events: (*a*) a major change from the literary use of the Indianized written language the early kings of Pagan had borrowed from the Mon, to the use of Burmese as the primary vehicle of communication for the elite as well as the masses (*ca.* 1157); (*b*) the importation of the newly reformed Theravāda tradition of Sri Lanka to Southeast Asia by a group of monks and novices (according to later accounts the mission returned to southern Burma *ca.* 1190); (*c*) King Narapathisitthu's (ruled 1173-1210) formal recognition and support of the newly imported Sinhalese sect, thus legitimating its status and fostering its spread.

During the centuries that followed, the new political and religious order in mainland Southeast

Asia gradually took form. In Burma the Pagan kingdom came to an end in 1287, and from that time forward the Burmese had to share political hegemony not only with the Mon, but also with a Tai group known as the Shan. In Thailand and Laos the northern areas came under the domination of Tai groups known as the Yuan, who founded the kingdom of Chiengmai (*ca.* 1296), and the Lao, who established the kingdom of Luang Prabang (*ca.* 1353). In the central Menam basin still another Tai group known as the Siamese or Thai established the kingdoms of Sukothai (*ca.* 1228) and Ayuddhia (*ca.* 1315). Soon thereafter a series of Thai invasions forced the evacuation of the old imperial center of Angkor (*ca.* 1431) and reduced subsequent Cambodian kingdoms to a status that hovered between minimal independence and vassalage. Moreover the political changes that occurred were closely intertwined with the spread of the newly imported Sinhalese version of Theravāda Buddhism. Though the previously established forms of the Theravāda tradition (as well as certain well entrenched Sanskritic elements) continued to exert a significant influence, the Sinhalese version of Theravāda teaching and practice became accepted as the paradigm of orthodoxy throughout the entire area.

Once established, the Sinhalese Theravāda tradition (hereafter referred to simply as the Theravāda tradition) demonstrated a remarkable tenacity and adaptability. In the many shifting premodern kingdoms in Burma, Thailand, Laos, and Cambodia the main Theravāda monasteries served as the centers of elite intellectual and artistic activity. In so doing they contributed both to the development of the Buddhist tradition itself and to the enrichment of the various local cultures. For example, the Burmese monastic centers made a number of significant refinements in Theravāda ABHIDHAMMA philosophy, and those in Thailand played a key role in generating important new styles of art and architecture. Theravāda cosmological conceptions and cultic practices, supplemented by the ritual and administrative activities of the BRAHMIN priests, served to legitimate the power of the kings and to maintain a sense of political and moral community. In addition, Theravāda teachings, rituals, and institutions became primary factors in the life of the ordinary villages, where they came to coexist and to interact with various elements of popular Brahminism and a wide range of indigenous spirit cults.

In the modern period the Theravāda tradition has given still further evidence of its tenacity and adaptability. In each of the four Theravāda countries that have emerged as contemporary nation-states a variety of monastic and lay leaders have encouraged reform movements that have helped to maintain the support of a significant portion of the more modernized elite; and in addition they have had considerable success in identifying the Theravāda tradition with the anti-colonial and nationalist aspirations of the people as a whole. Recent developments in these four countries have been diverse. In Thailand, where there has been a relatively high degree of political stability and a great deal of cooperation between the government and religious institutions, the Theravāda tradition has continued to prosper and to perform a variety of very significant religious and social functions. In Burma, where the political situation has been far less stable and the relationship between the government and religious institutions far more uneven and ambivalent, the traditional Theravāda teachings and institutions have been less dynamic and innovative, but have nevertheless managed to hold their own. In Laos and Cambodia the internal warfare of the 1960s and early 1970s seriously disrupted the traditional patterns of religious practice and organization; and since the Communist takeovers in 1975 the government policy toward Buddhism has ranged from relatively mild pressures for an ideological and social transformation (primarily in Laos) to violent destructiveness (primarily in Cambodia).

A very different kind of development has taken place in Vietnam. Although Vietnamese Buddhism was never able to regain the preeminent position that it had held during the eleventh through the thirteenth centuries, it nevertheless remained a significant factor in Vietnamese life and spread, along with the Vietnamese themselves, southward along the coast into the Mekong Delta. During the remainder of the premodern period Ch'an and PURE LAND influences emanating from China continued to make an impact on the Vietnamese Buddhist tradition. At the same time, Buddhism was incorporated into a distinctively Vietnamese religious synthesis that included elements of CONFUCIANISM and TAOISM as well as indigenous ancestor worship and spirit cults. At the state level the large monasteries were kept under strict state control and performed important ritual functions related to the monarchy. In addition, most of the villages had a local pagoda or *stūpa* where Buddhist divinities similar to those in the Chinese Buddhist pantheon were venerated, and where Buddhist festivals such as the annual festival for the dead were held.

Since the early nineteenth century, Vietnamese Buddhists have been successively confronted by the challenge of Western colonialism, by the successes of Roman Catholic missionary activity, by the rise of "new religions" that have combined Western and indigenous elements, and, more recently, by political instability and the subsequent establishment of a Communist government. In the early phases of the colonial era, Vietnamese Buddhists were put completely on the defensive, and the continued existence of the tradition seemed to be in doubt. However, beginning in the early 1930s a Buddhist reform movement was initiated; modern study programs were established; and in the southern part of the country a new interest in Theravāda doctrine and practice was generated (thus making Vietnam the one country where significant Mahāyāna and Theravāda groups were active in the same ethnic community). Unfortunately these reform activities were seriously disrupted by the incessant warfare that engulfed Vietnam during the decades immediately following World War II. In the period since the Communist takeover, first in the north (1954) and then in the south (1975), reliable information concerning the direction and fate of Buddhism has been difficult to obtain.

Contemporary Buddhism in Southeast Asia is a complex and diversified phenomenon. The Theravāda branch of the tradition continues to hold sway and to exert an important social influence in the more conservative mainland areas of Burma and Thailand. Theravāda and Mahāyāna Buddhism continue to exist under varying degrees of pressure in the newly communized countries of Indochina. Popular Chinese forms of Mahāyāna continue to be practiced in the Chinese immigrant communities that are established in urban centers throughout the entire area. And in Indonesia a modest Buddhist revival is continuing to develop.

Bibliography. D. G. E. Hall, *History of Southeast Asia* (3rd ed., 1968); C. Keyes, *The Golden Peninsula: Culture and Adaptation in Mainland Southeast Asia* (1977); B. Smith, *Religion and Political Legitimation in Thailand, Laos and Burma* (1978); M. Spiro, *Buddhism and Society: A Great Tradition and Its Burmese Vicissitudes* (1970); S. Tambiah, *World Conqueror and World Renouncer: A Study of Buddhism and Polity in Thailand against a Historical Background* (1976) and *Buddhism and Spirit Cults in Northeastern Thailand* (1970); Tran van Giap; "Le Bouddhisme en Annam: Des origines au XIIIe siècle," *Bulletin de l'École Français Extrême Orient*, XXXII (1932), 191-268; H. Dumoulin and J. C. Maraldo, eds., *The Cultural, Political and Religious Significance of Buddhism in the Modern World* (1976).

F. E. Reynolds

BUDDHISM, TIBETAN. The Tantric form of Mahāyāna Buddhism, sometimes called "Lamaism," that has been the dominant religion of Tibet from the eighth century A.D. until the 1950s. The state of Buddhism in Tibet under the People's Republic of China remains uncertain. However, among Tibetan refugees and a growing circle of Europeans and Americans, Tibetan Buddhism has been cultivated in a widening circle of influence.

Tibetan Buddhism is founded on the Four Noble Truths of Gautama Buddha. It seeks the ultimate release of all sentient beings from the suffering of the endless cycle of reincarnations (Samsara). Enlightenment is found through Bodhisattvas, who although they are liberated themselves forego Nirvana to bring the message of salvation to others. These bodhisattvas are not only found in great saints from the past but have contemporary expression in lamas who are themselves incarnations of the power of enlightenment. Salvation is in the confluence of the way of compassion and the way of knowledge. Ultimately the mind is able to know that the gods and Demons by which it is beset are only projections of itself and the Karma that binds it. From this follows full awareness of the voidness (Śūnyatā) of the world and the self which is Nirvana.

The ways in which humans may reach the saving enlightenment range from the most highly intellectual meditation to the utilization of magic formulas and cultic devotions. Standing in the Tantric tradition, Tibetan Buddhism seeks to utilize not only the capacities of mind but also the physical and emotional vitalities which are not to be crushed but channeled by discipline into the search for salvation. Because the Tibetan Dharma is complex, it has been seen on the one hand as the most sophisticated philosophy and psychology and on the other as a mélange of superstitions and magic.

1. The establishment of Buddhism. *a) Early history.* Although there is a legend of a miniature Stūpa and some Buddhist writing appearing miraculously during the reign of an earlier king, there is no historical evidence of Buddhism coming to Tibet before the reign of Srong-bStan sGam-Po (A.D. 620-649). The indigenous religion of Tibet was an animistic Shamanism called Bön. (*See* Animism.) It was able to resist the early spread of Buddhism and continued to exist even after Buddhism became dominant.

King Srong-bStan married Chinese and Nepalese princesses, both of whom were Buddhist and who hoped to civilize and convert the Tibetans. The king sent the scholar Sambhota to India for Buddhist books that were translated into the newly established written language of Tibet. Although the king built some temples and shrines for the images brought by his wives, Buddhist influence was limited and its future remained uncertain because of the strong influence of Bön. Yet the epoch-making importance of Srong-bStan and his wives in introducing Buddhism is enshrined in Tibetan iconography that pictures him as an incarnation of Avalokiteśvara and his two wives as incarnations of Tārā.

By the eighth century opposition to Buddhism grew not only among the politically threatened Tibetan aristocracy but also among critics of the eroticized Buddhism that was being propagated. It was said that the demons of Tibet were greatly angered by the coming of the new religion. Buddhism could spread only if these demons were overcome by a powerful master. So Padma-Sambhava was summoned.

b) Padma-Sambhava. This strange holy man and sorcerer arrived in Tibet in A.D. 747 from India, where he had trained in Tantrism. He left his mark on Tibetan Buddhism in such a basic way that he is celebrated as a second Buddha. It is impossible to reconstruct his history out of the highly mythological sources. There is even debate over the exact nature of his influence. Traditionally he is pictured as the author of profound religious texts, while others look

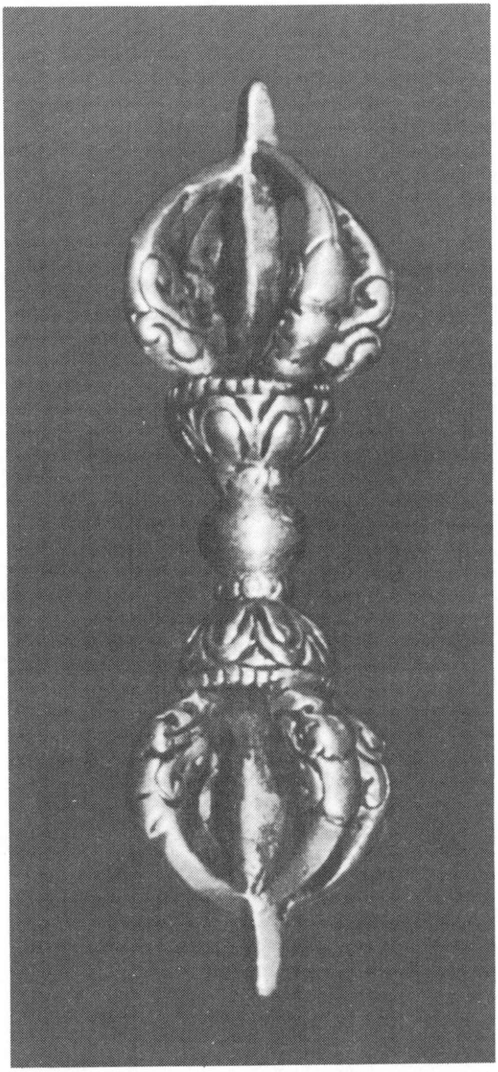

Left: the ghaṇṭâ ritual bell, used in all rituals and initiations. The ghaṇṭâ and vajra are handed together to new initiates or ordained monks. Right: the five horns of the vajra symbolize the order of the five Tathāgatas who form the principal mandala of Vajrayāna

upon him as little more than a kind of public relations man. Legend describes how he triumphed over the evil spirits of Tibet and converted them into protective deities in the Buddhist pantheon through contests of magic. What lies behind these legends is a complex religious syncretism between the indigenous religion and VAJRAYĀNA Buddhism of India out of which the distinctive Buddhism of Tibet emerged.

Padma-Sambhava also brought about the building of the first monastery in Tibet, the famous *bSam-yas*, completed in 787. The establishment of monasteries and orders of monks gave the Buddhism of Tibet the institutional structure and ritual focus it needed to survive.

c) Indian Background. The native religion of Tibet and the Tantric Buddhism of India in the seventh and eighth centuries had much in common that made a creative relationship between them possible. Since the emergence of Mahāyāna, Buddhist traditions broadened not only in their philosophical scope but also in their utilization of gods and rituals from many sources. Philosophically, Tibetan Buddhism looks back to NĀGĀRJUNA, teacher of the MĀDHYAMIKA or the system of "the Middle Way."

The path to salvation in early Buddhism was one of moral discipline and intellectual discernment. But in Mahāyāna the stern struggle for personal perfection (the ARHANT ideal) was replaced by the bodhisattva, or "being of enlightenment." Devotion to the bodhisattvas and participation in the cult surrounding them provided a path to salvation. By the seventh century still another element had been added to Buddhism from Indian Tantrism—the Vajrayāna (Skt., lit. "Diamond Vehicle"; Tibetan *Dor-Je*) way of salvation. The Vajrayāna introduced male and female deities, whose union was the triumph over the duality characteristic of samsara. It also taught the efficacy of magic formulas to give initiates sudden enlightenment along "the direct path" to Nirvana.

d) The reform movements. In the complex syncretism by which Padma-Sambhava and his followers gained dominance in Tibet, the ethical and intellectual heritage of the older Buddhism was not lost. Over the centuries the translation and commentaries on religious texts resulted in a vast literature. By the fifteenth century the *Kanjur,* the authoritative words of Buddha, filled one hundred large volumes, while the *Tanjur,* the collection of translations and commentaries, consisted of 225 volumes.

Tension between the ethical-intellectual and the magical-ritualistic elements in the tradition has been the source of the reform movements that have characterized the growth of Tibetan religious life. In the fourteenth and fifteenth centuries a reformation disciplined a corrupt priesthood and established the Dalai Lama as the spiritual and temporal head of Tibet.

2. The lama. Tibetan Buddhism is centered in its monasteries and sustained by a large number of monks. Estimates claim that at times those in religious orders equaled one fifth of the population. Monks not only provided ritual and intellectual leadership to the religious life but also served as teachers, doctors, landowners, and civil servants. Tibetan monks are sometimes referred to as "lamas," although strictly speaking the term should be used only of "emanation body" (Tibetan *sPrul sKu)* monks who are reincarnations of a bodhisattva. The lamas are leaders of the monastic hierarchy chosen by "hubilganic succession"; i.e., after the death of a leading lama oracles are consulted and search made for a child in whom the lama is to be reincarnated. If the child is able to identify correctly objects belonging to his predecessor, his selection is verified, and he is trained for his leadership role. The succession of lamas provides an orderly means of governance for the community and a living voice for tradition. The lamas are a contemporary physical manifestation of the saving power of enlightenment.

3. The sects. There are four major orders:

a) The Nyingmapa, the "ancient ones," or the "Red Hat" order, so called because of the distinctive head wear that differentiates them from the later reform group that wears yellow hats. The Nyingmapa trace their lineage back to Padma-Sambhava.

b) The Kargyupa is a school of oral tradition in which the secret mystical traditions are passed on from teacher to pupil by word of mouth. It was founded by Marpa in the eleventh century and looks back to the great Indian teacher Naropa.

c) The Saskyapa, founded in the eleventh century and named for its chief monastery, wielded great political power at one time and was the first to establish the idea of a priestly monarchy.

d) The Gelugpa, the "merit system ones," or so-called "Yellow Hats," was founded in the fifteenth century as an outgrowth of the reform movement of Tsong-Kha-Pa. This reform order is headed by the present Dalai Lama, the latest in a line who ruled Tibet from the seventeenth century until 1959.

4. Interpreting the religion of Tibet. Few religious traditions have roused such passionate interest as those of Tibet. Only recently has a balanced understanding of Tibetan Buddhism started to emerge from a number of approaches.

a) Travelers and anthropologists. Since Alexander Csoma de Körös, in the first half of the last century, travelers and anthropologists have made the Tibetan language and civilization known. They were able to observe the concrete functioning of Tibetan Buddhism, its rites and institutional forms, and not simply its religious texts. Their reports were often pejorative, such as those of Austine Waddell, who saw so much as only magical and deceptive, or more admiring, such as those of Alexandria David-Neal. Robert Ekvall and others were able to give more balanced anthropological presentation of Tibetan religion as it existed before 1951.

b) Theosophists and students of mysticism. Tibetan Buddhism was introduced to Western intellectual

Reprinted by special arrangement with Shambhala Publications, Inc., 1123 Spruce St., Boulder CO 80302. From *Tibetan Sacred Art* by Detlef Ingo Lauf. Copyright 1976 by Shambhala Publications, Inc.

Lamas of the Gelugpa sect, wearing the raiment and crowns of the five Buddhas

life earlier in this century by W. Y. Evans-Wentz and others as an expression of a universal GNOSTICISM or THEOSOPHY in continuity with Egyptian, Hellenistic, Christian, and other forms of MYSTICISM. While their reading of the texts was often markedly nonhistorical, they did help to elucidate the complex heritage of Tibetan Buddhism and to provide a needed corrective to the cultural imperialism of scholars who reduced Tibetan traditions to insignificance.

c) Comparative linguists and historians of religion. Much scholarly interest has centered on the translations of Buddhist Sanskrit texts into Tibetan. The accuracy with which many of these had been made opened the possibility of using them as a means of reconstructing the originals that had been lost with the collapse of Indian Buddhism. But as Guenther rightly objected, this approach obscures the creativity of the Tibetan teachers in reinterpreting and expanding on the traditions they had received. Through the work of Hoffman and a number of other scholars, the history of Tibetan religion and its texts are being given careful exposition.

d) Philosophers and psychologists. Carl Jung was one of the first to recognize the important psychological insights of Tibetan Buddhist texts with his exposition of the BARDO THODÖL and its teaching on the nature of psychological projection. Since the coming of Tibetan refugee teachers to the West, including the Dalai Lama, the philosophical and psychological interpretation of Tibetan texts and training in meditative techniques have been carried on by Chögyam Trungpa, Tarthang Tulku, Geshe Wangyal, and American and European scholars. They seek to explore the unique ways in which Tibetan Buddhism illumines human life and the search for meaning. In the translations of Francesca Fremantle, Jeffrey Hopkins, and others, Tibetan writings are becoming part of a world literature through which the contemporary religious search is being carried forward. While this approach has marked a great gain in relevance for the tradition, it is open to modernist misunderstandings because it is separated from the full liturgical and communal life within which the texts first took shape.

5. The future of Tibetan Buddhism. The secularization of the country by the Chinese has resulted in destruction of monasteries, the forced laicizing of monks, and the persecution of believers. Programs of education and youth groups based on Communist ideology have been used to win the younger generation of Tibetans. Yet it would be impossible to conclude that so deep and pervasive a tradition has been completely eradicated. Into the mid-1970s, the Dalai Lama expressed hopes for a return to Tibet to meet the religious needs of the people. But no matter what the secret life of Buddhism in Tibet may be today, its public life is centered in the refugee community that seeks to preserve and reinterpret its religion in the modern world.

See also PRAYER WHEEL; VAIROCANA.

Bibliography. L. A. Waddell, *Tibetan Buddhism* (1895); H. Hoffman, *The Religions of Tibet* (1961); H. V. Guenther, *Tibetan Buddhism in Western Perspective* (1977); A. David-Neal, *Magic and Mystery in Tibet* (1933); P. P. Karan, *The Changing Face of Tibet* (1976); R. B. Ekvall, *Religious Observances in Tibet* (1964).

D. G. DAWE

BUDDHIST COUNCILS. Following Buddha's death (around 483 B.C.), the Buddhist community or SANGHA was in a quandary because Buddha had not appointed a successor who could resolve difficulties and clarify fine points of doctrine and discipline. The community held a council in the rainy season immediately following the leader's demise, and this council became the model for adjudicating major points of controversy. There have been four traditional councils in the history of Indian Buddhism: at Rājagṛha in 483 B.C., at Vaiśālī in 383 B.C., at Pāṭaliputra under the reign of King AŚOKA, and in Kashmir (or Gandhara) under the reign of King Kaniṣka. There is also evidence that another council, not cited in the various Buddhist canons, was held sometime between the council of Vaiśālī and the one in Aśoka's reign.

1. Sources of council literature. For the first two recorded councils the major source of information is the Skandhaka portion of the Vinaya Piṭakas of the various Buddhist schools. For the supposed council held between the Vaiśālī council and Aśoka's council, we refer primarily to the Samayabhedoparacanacakra of Vasumitra, the Nikāyabhedavibhaṅgavyākhyāna of Bhavya, the Abhidharmamahāvibhāṣā-śāstra, and the Śāriputraparipṛcchā-sūtra; for information on Aśoka's council, the Pali Vinaya and its commentary (the Samantapāsādikā) as well as the Dīpavaṃsa, and Mahābodhivaṃsa; finally, for information on Kaniṣka's council, the works of Vasumitra and historical fragments in other Sarvāstivādin texts.

2. The first council (at Rājagṛha). In King Bimbisāra's capital city, five hundred enlightened monks (ARHANTS) gathered together under the presidency of KAŚYAPA (or in some sources Ājñāta Kauṇḍinya) to recite the DHARMA (doctrine) and Vinaya (discipline). Buddha's chief servant (and cousin), ĀNANDA, recited all the various sermons preached by Buddha, and these were collected into the canonical literature known as the SUTTA PIṬAKA or "basket of discourses." Upāli, another leading disciple, recounted all the disciplinary regulations, which were gathered together into the VINAYA PIṬAKA or "basket of disciplinary regulations." The council closed with its attendant monks agreeing that they had preserved the totality of Buddha's teachings intact. Later scholarship has questioned this latter point as well as the historicity of the entire event.

3. The second council (at Vaiśālī). A century later, another council was convened at Vaiśālī at the insistence of a wandering monk named Yaśas who reported he had seen ten illicit practices among a group of monks known as the *vṛjiputraka bhikṣus*. Under the presidency of a monk named Revata, the ten points were debated by seven hundred monks, resulting in the condemnation of the items and reaffirmation of proper discipline.

4. **The intervening council.** This council, mentioned only in noncanonical sources, is surmised by the majority of scholars to mark the true beginning of the Buddhist sectarian movement. According to Bareau it was held in 137 A.N. (i.e., after Buddha's NIRVANA) under the reign of Mahāpadma Nanda, and separated the Sthaviras and Mahāsāṅghikas, primarily due to doctrinal innovation and disciplinary laxity on the part of the Mahāsāṅghikas. This thesis has recently been challenged by Nattier and Prebish, arguing that both the date and cause of separation are inexact. *(See* BUDDHIST SECTARIANISM.)

5. **The third council (at Pāṭaliputra).** As a response to alleged heretics entering the Buddhist community, King Aśoka convened a council during the seventeenth year of his reign (around 252 B.C.). Under the direction of a famous monk, Moggaliputta Tissa, one thousand monks reaffirmed Buddhist orthodoxy and expelled the exponents of heretical views.

6. **The fourth council (at Kashmir or Gandhara).** Late in the first century A.D., King Kaniṣka, at the advice of a Sarvāstivādin master named Pārśva, held a fourth Buddhist council. Said to have been attended by 499 famous Buddhists, it was directed by Vasumitra with assistance from Aśvaghoṣa, thus indicating that both Hīnayānists and Mahāyānists were in attendance. A new Vinaya was established, and the debates held were recorded in the Abhidharmamahāvibhāṣā-śāstra.

Bibliography. A Bareau, *Les premiers conciles bouddhiques* (1955). C. S. Prebish, "A Review of Scholarship on the Buddhist Councils," *JAS* XXXIII, 2 (1974), 239-54.

C. S. PREBISH

BUDDHIST SECTARIANISM. Sometime during the second century following BUDDHA's death, Buddhism was beset by a sectarian movement, and in the next 500 years approximately thirty sects proliferated. It was originally thought that the first sectarian division occurred as a result of the second great council at Vaiśālī (*see* BUDDHIST COUNCILS). This theory held until 1946, when M. Hofinger demonstrated that no canonical records of the Vaiśālī council indicated any trace of the supposed schism.

By around 200 B.C., a movement began in Buddhism which offered a new literature known as Prajñāpāramitā or "perfection of wisdom," a new Buddhology, a redefinition of the goal of Buddhism (as well as a new path to that goal), a radical new approach to the question of reality, and an attempt to provide a more expansive role to the laity. This new movement referred to itself as MAHĀYĀNA or "great vehicle," while branding the earlier Buddhist sects, which included primarily the Sthaviras, Mahāsāṅghikas, Pudgalavādins, and Theravādins as HĪNAYĀNA or "lesser vehicle."

1. **Sources of sectarian literature.** It is necessary to sift through the records and texts of each individual group, for each offers its own variants of Buddhist sectarian history. The most informative Theravādin source is the DĪPAVAṂSA. From the Sarvāstivādin tradition, we can consult Vasumitra's Samayabhedoparacanacakra, the Abhidharmamahāvibhāṣā-śāstra, and the first tradition recorded in Bhavya's Nikāyabhedavibhaṅgavyākhyāna. The Pudgalavādin group (namely the Saṃmitīyas) is represented in the third tradition of Bhavya's above mentioned text, while the Mahāsāṅghika tradition is embodied in the second tradition of Bhavya's text as well as the Śāriputraparipṛcchā-sūtra. For the Mahāyāna sectarian movement, there are a host of SŪTRAS and ŚĀSTRAS composed during the initial 500 years of Mahāyānist history.

2. **Causes of the initial schism.** The chief cause in the rise of Buddhist sectarianism was the death of the founder. Since no new leader had been appointed, the infant community suffered from a distinct lack of leadership. This dilemma was compounded by the geographical expansion of Buddhism, with individual communities appearing throughout India, not only fostering divisions by adapting to local customs, but also lacking communication with one another.

It was initially surmised that the first great schism in Buddhism, separating the previously unified community into the rival sects known as Sthaviras and Mahāsāṅghikas, resulted from disciplinary laxity on the part of the future Mahāsāṅghikas. Other scholars then argued that the schism resulted from doctrinal innovations on the part of the latter, most notably in five innocuous theses regarding the status of the saint (ARHANT) propounded by a monk named Mahādeva. More recently, however, Bareau has concluded that both disciplinary laxity and doctrinal innovation are to blame. He further notes that this split occurred in 137 A.N. (after the Buddha's NIRVANA), as the outcome of a noncanonical council held in Pāṭaliputra during the reign of Mahāpadma Nanda. This latter thesis was challenged in 1977 by Nattier and Prebish who, utilizing the same sources as Bareau, conclude that the schism occurred in 116 A.N. (during the reign of Kālāśoka) and was not due to Mahāsāṅghika disciplinary laxity or doctrinal innovation, but to expansion of the canon by the future Sthaviras. They further designate Mahādeva as belonging to a period one generation later, thus negating his role in the event.

3. **Hīnayāna sects and their theories.** The Mahāsāṅghikas offered primarily new Buddhology, a new path to enlightenment, the beginnings of Buddhist devotionalism, and a generally liberal viewpoint. In contrast, the Sthaviras were conservative in all respects. The Mahāsāṅghikas divided in-

ternally in the course of time into several subsects, the doctrines of which foreshadow to some extent the rise of Mahāyāna. From the Sthaviras, the first sects appear to be the Pudgalavādin group (around 280 B.C.) who posited an entity called the pudgala (lit. "person") that not only experienced Nirvana, but also transmigrated (not unlike the Hindu ATMAN). Although popular, they were considered quasi-heretical by more orthodox Buddhists. During AŚOKA's council (around 250 B.C.) the Sthaviras spawned the Sarvāstivādins and the Vibhajyavādins. The Sarvāstivādins migrated to northwest India, becoming sophisticated scholastics, known for their theory that "everything exists," and for their careful analysis of Buddhist philosophy. The Vibhajyavādins, in turn, gave rise to the Theravādin (*see* THERAVĀDA) and Mahīśāsaka schools in the second century B.C. Other major groups spawned by the Sthavira tradition include the Sautrāntikas and Dharmaguptakas.

4. **Mahāyāna sects.** From the Mahāyāna movement three major sectarian traditions emerged. First, the PURE LAND sect, that grew out of the devotional tradition noted in the larger and smaller Sukhāvatīvyūha-sūtras. This sect believed that through devotion and faith it was possible to gain rebirth in the Pure Land of Amitābha Buddha (*see* AMIDA) from which the attainment of complete Buddhahood was more readily possible. This school has been most influential in China, Korea, and Japan, and prospers today. Second, there is the MĀDHYAMIKA sect, organized (*ca.* 250 A.D.) around the great philosopher NĀGĀRJUNA, and taking its name (lit. "middle path") from his most famous text. Promoting the notion of emptiness (ŚŪNYATĀ), Nāgārjuna argued vigorously against abstruse philosophizing, and emphasized the direct experience of the world as it is. After enjoying brief popularity in China and Japan, the school died out, but had a lasting impact on all the Mahāyāna meditational traditions, particularly ZEN and SHINGON. Finally, there is the YOGĀCĀRA school, organized by the brothers Asaṅga and VASUBANDHU, and offering an innovative theory of consciousness. This school also had much influence on Chinese and Japanese Buddhism, while enjoying a rather short history in its Indian homeland.

Bibliography. A. Bareau, *Les sectes bouddhiques du petit véhicule* (1955); N. Dutt, *Buddhist Sects in India* (1970); J. J. Nattier and C. S. Prebish, "Mahāsāṁghika Origins: The Beginnings of Buddhist Sectarianism," *HR*, XVI (1977), 237-72.

C. S. PREBISH

al-BUKHĀRĪ, MUHAMMAD IBN ISMĀ'ĪL āl bo͞o khä´ rē mo͞o häm´ mäd ĭb´ ən ĭs mā ēl´ (I; 810-870). Muslim scholar born in Bukhara; best known and revered for his encyclopedic collection of HADĪTH, *al-Jāmiʿ al-Ṣaḥīḥ* ("The Authentic Collection"). Often viewed popularly in Islam and until recently in modern scholarship as the first to assemble a comprehensive, critically selected, topically arranged corpus of the most reliable *ḥadīth*, Bukhārī must now be seen as one whose work followed and was based upon previous written collections. This does not diminish, however, his book's importance among Muslims as, along with the *Ṣaḥīḥ* of MUSLIM IBN AL-ḤAJJĀJ, the most respected source for reports of Muhammad's normative words and actions.

Bibliography. I. Goldziher, *Muh. Studien*, II (1890), 234-45 [ET 1971, pp. 216-26]; M. Z. Siddiqi, *Ḥadīth Literature* (1961), pp. 88-97.

W. A. GRAHAM

BULL (Ch—Lat. [*bulla*—"bubble"]). Leaden seal used to authenticate royal and papal documents. Since the thirteenth century the word has been used to designate the documents themselves—e.g., Emperor Charles IV's "Golden Bull" (1356)—especially papal documents having to do with appointment of BISHOPS, CANONIZATION of saints, and definitions of doctrine.

J. HENNESEY

BULTMANN, RUDOLF bo͞olt´ män (Ch; 1884–1976). German biblical scholar who related historical studies to theology. He attempted to get behind myths in scripture to the existential picture they present of God, self, and the world ("demythologization"). His interpretation of Christian life as "radical obedience" meant listening and responding to God's urgent demands in and through the present situation. *See* THEOLOGY, CONTEMPORARY CHRISTIAN §3.

D. F. OTTATI

BUNYAN, JOHN (Ch; 1628-1688). English writer and preacher. Born in Elstow, Bedfordshire, John Bunyan was the son of a poor Anglican brazier. Though he received little formal education, he read much in chivalric adventure tales and Puritan tracts. In 1653, Bunyan joined the separatist church of Bedford. Here he employed his elocutionary skills as a lay preacher, a role which stirred criticism from some university-educated clergy. After the Restoration, Bunyan's refusal to cease preaching led twice to imprisonment, but he continued writing and preaching until his death. Among his nearly sixty books are *The Doctrine of the Law and Grace Unfolded* (1659), a treatise on his Calvinistic theology; *Grace Abounding to the Chief of Sinners* (1666), his spiritual autobiography; *The Pilgrim's Progress* (1678, 1684), Bunyan's allegorical pilgrimage of the Christian soul; *The Life and Death of Mr. Badman* (1680), a morally inverted sequel to *The Pilgrim's Progress;* and *The Holy War* (1682), an allegorical treatment of spiritual conflict.

Bibliography. R. L. Greaves, *John Bunyan* (1969); U. M. Kaufmann, *The Pilgrim's Progress and Traditions in Puritan Meditation* (1966).

D. J. WHITE

BURĀQ bo͞o räk´ (I—Arab.; lit. "lightning"). The heavenly mount upon which MUHAMMAD is supposed to have ridden on his night journey (Mi'rāj) from Mecca to Jerusalem and then through the seven heavens; also Abraham's mount in post-Qur'ānic legend. Usually depicted as a mare with a woman's head and a peacock's tail. G. D. Newby

BURDAH bo͞or´ dä (I—Arab.; a woolen cloak used at night as a blanket). 1. The mantle of Muhammad, which he gave the poet Ka'b ibn Zuhayr as reward for a poem. Bought by the first Umayyad caliph and preserved as a symbol of the caliphate until Mongols burned it in 1258. The Ottomans later claimed it was still extant and in their possession. It is preserved as such today in Istanbul.

2. Also the popular name of the beloved panegyric poem on Muhammad by al-Būṣīrī (d. 1294), probably the most widely known poem in Arabic and a favorite for recitation on all occasions, especially the Mawlid of Muhammad.

Bibliography. R. Bassett, *EI*,[2] I, 1314-15; trans. of Būṣīrī's poem by A. Jeffrey, *Reader on Islam* (1962), pp. 605-20. W. A. Graham

BURIAL CUSTOMS. *See* Death.

BUSHIDŌ boo shē dō´ (Sh—Jap.; lit. "military-warrior-way"). The social code of the military class developed from the Kamakura period (1185-1333) and systematized during the Tokugawa (1600-1867), especially in the writings of Yamaga Sokō (1622-85) on the warrior's creed *(bukyō)* and way of the samurai *(shidō)*.

Bushidō developed as the life-and-death bond committing the households of military retainers to their *daimyo*-lords on the feudal fiefs of Japan. It bears resemblance to the European code of chivalry, though the love of nature replaces romantic respect for women. During the long Tokugawa peace, Bushidō further developed to encourage the samurai's maintenance of military discipline while pursuing the arts of peace, engaging in civil service, and providing moral example for the populace. The Five Relationships of Confucius, Zen's fearlessness and serenity, and Shintō's aesthetic devotion to things Japanese were idealized in stories of samurai heroes. Armed with all virtues, the warrior held one sword to battle worthy enemies and another to commit ritual suicide *(seppuku)* if honor required. The spirit of Bushidō passed through the samurai class to become the moral ideal of ordinary Japanese citizens, and continues in the fusion of spirituality and martial arts, corporate ideals of discipline, respect, and loyalty in Japanese culture today.

Bibliography. M. Anesaki, *History of Japanese Religion* (1963); I. Nitobe, *Bushido*, (1907); K. Singer, *Mirror, Sword and Jewel* (1973). C. W. Edwards

BUTSUDAN boo tsoo dän´ (B—Jap.; "Buddha-altar"). An altar for enshrining Buddhist statues within Buddhist temples, sometimes in the form of a niche or alcove, sometimes in the form of an encased box with a door; as a popular term it refers to the household shrine, which contains one or more small Buddhist statues or pictures but whose major religious significance is the enshrining of memorial tablets of family ancestors. It is usually a black wood cabinet with double doors, which are opened when memorial services are held.

H. B. Earhart

C

CABBALA (Ju). *See* KABBALA.

CAITANYA chī tŭn´ yŭ (H—Skt.; 1486–1533). The revivalist and most outstanding religious leader of the VAIṢṆAVA sect in eastern India. He was born on the night of an eclipse of the moon in the month of Phalgun (February-March), in the town of Navadvīpa, in the district of Nadia, about seventy miles to the north of present-day Calcutta. It was a town famous as a center of scholarship, especially of the Navya-Nyāya school of philosophy. His father was BRAHMIN by caste, and had migrated to Navadvīpa from a village in eastern Bengal.

The facts of his life are difficult to discern, since his many biographers seek to stress their religious view that he was an AVATAR of KRISHNA. It seems that his early life was not atypical for a Brahmin boy of his time. He studied SANSKRIT grammar, and after his father's death, he opened a Sanskrit school of his own. When he was twenty-two years old, he went to the city of Gaya to celebrate his father's funeral obsequies. On the way he met and took initiation at the hands of an ascetic named Īśvara Purī. He was nominally a member of a monistic order of ascetics, but he returned to Navadvīpa to propagate a dualistic religion of love for the Lord Krishna. He remained about two years more in Navadvīpa, holding KĪRTANA, ecstatic dancing and singing of the names and praises of Krishna, in the courtyard of his elderly friend and neighbor Śrīvāsa.

At the end of two years he decided to complete his ascetic vows, which required that he leave home. At his mother's tearful request, he agreed to go to live in Purī, near the great temple of JAGANNĀTHA, a place more accessible to Bengal than VṚNDĀVANA, the place of his beloved Krishna, where he originally intended to go.

After only a few days in Purī, he started on a two-year pilgrimage which took him down the eastern coast of southern India, to Cape Cormorin, up the west coast to Maharashtra, and across central India back to Purī. There he stayed until his death, except for one journey to Bengal and one to Vṛndāvana in north central India. Each year pilgrims from Bengal visited him. The manner of his death is uncertain. Some traditions say he was absorbed into the great image of Jagannātha (he being identical with that god), others that he drowned in the sea, and one claims that he injured his foot during his ecstatic dancing and died from an infection of the wound. It is clear that during the last several years of his life he was more and more absorbed in his love for Krishna, and increasingly withdrawn from the world of humans.

It was this absorption that facilitated the theological interpretation of Caitanya as Krishna and RĀDHĀ in one body—having the full divinity of Krishna, and the love and longing that Rādhā felt for her divine Lord. This view inspired a religious movement of BHAKTI HINDUISM, which swept over eastern India in the century or so following his death, and which is a vital force in the religious life of the country today.

Bibliography. S. K. De, *An Early History of the Vaiṣṇava Faith and Movement in Bengal* (1961).

E. C. DIMOCK, JR.

CAKRA chŭk´ rŭ (H & B—Skt.; lit. "wheel") **CAKKA** chŭk´ kŭ (B—Pali). In HINDUISM the wheel represents solar or cosmic energy, spherical space, and the cycle of time. In BUDDHISM it became the symbol of the religion itself, as the *Dharma-cakra* or Wheel of the Law. As a religio-political term, *cakravartin* refers to a "wheel-turner," that is, a "world ruler"—like AŚOKA—whose character and power upholds social and cosmic law (DHARMA) and order. J. BARE

CALENDAR, CHRISTIAN. The earliest Christians arranged the week in a pattern which allowed for common worship on a given day and, somewhat later, for weekly fast days. In the course of time they came to celebrate two annual cycles of fast and feast and a cycle of saints' days.

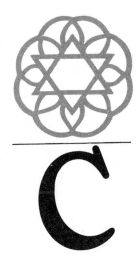

1. Lent to Pentecost. By the end of the first century the celebration of the Jewish PASSOVER (Gr. *pascha*) had taken on a distinctive quality for Christians, the Day of Preparation being observed as a

fast commemorating the death of JESUS. This Christian observance of Passover marks the beginning of the Christian shaping of the year. In the second century this observance came into conflict with the older tradition of celebrating the RESURRECTION on the first day of each week so that, outside Asia, the fast occupied the one or two days before the SUNDAY following Passover and the fast was broken only on Sunday (EASTER). By the first half of the third century these two days of strict fast had been extended to six days. In the fourth century we find a fast of forty days (LENT) prior to this Christian pascha. This longer fast is frequently associated with Jesus' fast of forty days after his baptism in the Jordan River (Mark 1 and parallels), and Coptic sources suggest that it may originally have been observed apart from the one week paschal fast (HOLY WEEK). In the fourth century, however, the longer fast absorbed the paschal fast to make a total of six weeks of fasting or, alternatively, it was prefixed to that one week to give a total fast of seven weeks. The paschal season was celebrated for fifty days following Easter and ended on the day of PENTECOST, which in the fourth century became itself a feast honoring the outpouring of the HOLY SPIRIT on the CHURCH (Acts 2). By the end of that century the ASCENSION OF CHRIST was celebrated on the fortieth day after Easter. The dates of this cycle are moveable, depending on the date of Easter.

2. **The Christmas cycle.** A second group of festivals developed around pagan celebrations of the winter solstice. The earliest of these was the feast now known as EPIPHANY (January 6, an ancient Egyptian date for the solstice). In Egypt this celebrated the BAPTISM of Jesus, but in Jerusalem his nativity. Elsewhere both themes were combined, but at Rome the feast was not kept at all until later. There the birthday of the Invincible Sun, established by Aurelian on December 25 in the third century, was Christianized as the feast of Jesus' nativity *ca.* 336. This festival was promulgated in the ORTHODOX CHURCHES, and its adoption there can be traced in the later fourth century, a development which allowed the Epiphany to focus entirely on the baptism in Jordan. Still, when the January 6 feast was adopted at Rome it did not bring that theme, but was observed as a doublet of the nativity, celebrating the adoration of the magi at BETHLEHEM. In France from the fourth century there was a preparatory fast before Epiphany (and later Christmas). It was extended from an original three weeks to six by the sixth century. This is the ADVENT season, now observed in the West for only four weeks before Christmas (although Milan still observes six weeks).

3. **The sanctoral cycle.** In addition to this temporal cycle there is the sanctoral cycle, festivals commemorating particular SAINTS, most commonly on the dates of their deaths. Originally local commemorations were made of local MARTYRS or BISHOPS, but movement of populations brought broader dissemination of these local festivals. In an early list of such commemorations at ROME (A.D. 354) two North African feasts are added to the list of local martyrs. While early sanctoral lists included only martyrs and bishops, in time all memorably holy persons might be so commemorated. A process of CANONIZATION developed to control growth of the calendar and afford a measure of uniformity. Apart from the death dates of the saints, feasts stem also from the anniversaries of the translation and reburial of their remains or anniversaries of the dedication of churches. More recent are feasts which simply focus attention on a theological idea (e.g., TRINITY SUNDAY, CORPUS CHRISTI).

4. **Recent calendar reform.** Reform in the present century has sought to restore the primitive importance of each Sunday as a feast of Christ and to restore and preserve the integrity of the temporal cycle. The sanctoral cycle has been simplified for ROMAN CATHOLICS, enriched for ANGLICANS and LUTHERANS, and rendered more flexible and sensitive to local concerns.

Bibliography. N. M. Denis-Boulet, *The Christian Calendar* (1960); A. A. McArthur, *The Evolution of the Christian Year* (1953); A. Nocent, *The Liturgical Year,* 4 vols. (1977).

T. J. TALLEY

CALENDAR, JEWISH. In JUDAISM years are numbered from a traditional reckoning of the year of creation; hence 1981 is the year 5741 *anno mundi.*

The Jewish calendar is based on a 354-day year of twelve lunar months, each of which begins with the new moon. To bring the lunar year into harmony with the solar year of 365¼ days, a thirteenth month (Adar II) is inserted into seven of every nineteen years. This calendar is credited to Hillel II (mid-fourth century A.D.).

The present-day New Year falls in the autumn in the biblical seventh month, Tishri. The names of the months were adopted from the Babylonians after 586 B.C., and in the Bible are found only in such late books as Nehemiah; earlier books simply number the months, sometimes adding descriptive names. The first day of a month was celebrated in accordance with Num. 28:11, with the first two days sometimes celebrated (I Sam. 20:34). The months are:

Tishri	Sept./Oct.
Heshvan	Oct./Nov.
Kislev	Nov./Dec.
Tevet	Dec./Jan.
Shevat	Jan./Feb.
Adar	Feb./Mar.
Adar II	Added every 3rd, 6th, 8th, 11th, 14th, 17th, and 19th year of a 19-year cycle
Nisan	Mar./Apr.
Iyyar	Apr./May
Sivan	May/June
Tammuz	June/July
Av	July/Aug.
Elul	Aug./Sept.

The year begins Tishri 1 (Rosh ha-Shanah). The festival prayerbook *(maḥzor)* calls this the "Day of Remembrance," on which the ram's horn (Shofar) is sounded. One line of tradition has it that the day commemorates the creation of man, and that people pass before God for a year's allotment of life and prosperity. Ten days of penitence (the Days of Awe) follow, leading up to Tishri 10, Yom Kippur (the Day of Atonement),

Tishri 15 begins the longest festival, Sukkot (Booths), also called Feast of Tabernacles (Lev. 23:33 ff.). The annual reading of the Torah is joyfully completed on the eighth day of the feast, called Simhat Torah (Joy in the Torah). In the Diaspora this falls on the ninth day, Tishri 23.

On Kislev 24, Hannukah (Dedication) begins. Celebrated for eight days with the lighting of lamps, it recalls the rededication of the Temple and the nation under the Maccabees about 165 B.C. On Adar 14 falls Purim, commemorating the events described in the book of Esther.

Passover, lasting seven days (eight in the diaspora), begins during the first of the biblical months, on Nisan 15. Also called the Festival of Matzah and the Holiday of our Freedom, it is explained during the Seder meals from Haggadah booklets, with biblical and Midrashic accounts of the exodus from Egypt.

During the seven-week span from Passover to Shavuot the nights are counted off (Lev. 15:15). Called the "Counting of the Omer," it signifies the progress from Passover's freedom to the responsibility of Torah. Shavuot, the anniversary of the giving of the Ten Commandments, is celebrated on Sivan 6 (*see* Pentecost).

On the thirty-third day of the Counting of the Omer falls *Lag BaOmer,* commemorating several happy historical events. On this occasion Oriental Jews in Israel take their three-year-old boys to Safed for an initiating haircut. It is celebrated out of doors, in great measure, by the remaining communities.

Tammuz 17 is a fast day memorializing the seizure of Jerusalem by Babylon and by Rome. It begins a three-week mourning period climaxed by the fast Tishah be'Av, which memorializes the burning of the Temples. (Tishri 3 and Tevet 10 are also fast days recalling these losses; cf. Zech. 8:19).

The last month is Elul, during which the shofar is blown daily, a reminder that a new year and its Days of Awe approach.

Sabbath occurs every seven days, and supersedes all calendar holidays when in conflict. Each day begins at nightfall, but holidays and most calendar events begin as soon as the sun has passed the horizon.

A. Lichtenstein

CALIPH, KHALĪFA kə lē′ fə (I—Arab.; lit. "successor, follower"). The temporal successor to the prophet Muhammad who, in theory at least, succeeded to all his authority except that of prophethood. The term *khalīfa* is normally restricted to the Sunnite branch of Islam; the concept of a successor to Muhammad is also found among the Shi'ites, but is generally referred to by the term Imam. The word appears in both the singular and the plural in the Qur'ān but not as a technical term. In the singular it refers to Adam (Sura 2:30), where it seems to mean that Adam will have power over the earth. It also refers to David: "O David! Lo! We have set thee as a viceroy *(khalīfa)* in the earth; therefore judge aright between mankind" (Sura 38:27, Pickthall trans.) where there is a judicial function implied. It is not at all clear that the Qur'ān can be seen as the source for the institution of the office of the caliphate except after the fact. Indeed, the first successor, Abū Bakr, most likely did not use the term, and it was not until the second caliph, 'Umar I, that it regularly alternated with the title Commander of the Faithful. In the meaning "vice-regent," it was used as "Vice-regent of Allah" *(khalīfat Allah)* alongside "Vice-regent of the Prophet" *(khalīfat rasūl Allah)*, implying divine sanction for the authority.

The theoretical foundation came later than the institution of the office, and, to some extent, as a justification of what had occurred. This stipulated that the caliph had to come from the tribe of Quraish, be male, and receive complete obedience from the faithful; in the eyes of many theorists, to rebel against the caliph was to rebel against God. 'Alī ibn Muhammad al-Māwardi (974-1058) adds that the caliph should be over the age of majority, of good character, and free of defect, should possess talents and abilities in government and law, and, contrary to historical reality, be elected. This last point had to be cleverly argued in the face of the hereditary nature of first the Umayyad and then the 'Abbāsid dynasties. Other jurists, however, did not hold to the doctrine of election, but held that even a usurper should be obeyed if it were in the interest of the Muslim state. Finally, a view that formed the basis of Ottoman law is represented in a tradition which asserts that the caliphate ended with the reign of the fourth caliph, Ali.

The Khārijites held the position that the caliph could be anyone, Arab or no, free or slave, and that the Muslim society could function with a civil government not headed by a caliph. Their position is most directly opposite the legitimist doctrines developed among the Shi'ites.

The history of the caliphate is, until the thirteenth century, the history of the main portion of the Islamic world. The first caliph, Abū Bakr, started his term of office as a part-time ruler, tending to his own commercial interests for his income, until the pressure of rebellion and conquest required his full attention. The first four caliphs, often called "Rightly Guided," adhered closely to the Arabian custom of the ruler as first among equals, but with the accession of the Umayyads and the expansion of Islam outside Arabia, the caliphal court took on more elaborate trappings, and the caliph became increasingly a despot removed from the people. The early function of leading the faithful in prayer was abandoned under the Umayyads as a regular obligation, but the community still was expected to include the caliph in the congregational prayers, omission of which was usually a signal for rebellion. With the rise of the 'Abbāsids, after A.D. 750, the caliph became the patron of religious scholars, and the state was more Islamicized at the expense of the Arabic cultural elements. With the growth of the bureaucracy, the caliph lost effective control to administrators. The last years of the caliphate saw the caliph under the control of temporal rulers, often called sultans, who held the caliph hostage to ensure his blessing on the regime. In 1258, when the Mongols captured Baghdad, the last 'Abbāsid caliph was killed. Numerous attempts to revive the caliphate met with only regional and ephemeral success.

Bibliography. A. J. Wensinck, *Concordance de la tradition musulmane* (1943); A. v. Kremer, *Geschichte der herrschenden Ideen des Islams* (1868); T. W. Arnold, *Caliphate* (1924); W. Muir, *Caliphate* (1925), caution is in order toward some conclusions; J. Sauvaget, *Introduction to the History of the Muslim East,* C. Cahen, ed. and trans. (1965). G. D. NEWBY

CALL TO PRAYER (I). *See* ADHĀN.

CALVARY (Ch). *See* GOLGOTHA.

CALVIN, JOHN (Ch; 1509-1564). French Reformer, churchman, and theologian who led in the consolidation of the REFORMATION in Geneva. Born in Noyon in Picardy, the son of bourgeois parents, he was first trained at Paris for an ecclesiastical career. He studied law at Bourges and Orleans and then became a humanist scholar studying under the Royal Lecturers at Paris and publishing his first book as a commentary on Seneca's work on clemency. Christian humanism, LUTHER'S writings, and Calvin's own experience of the BIBLE as the Word of God contributed to his break with ROMAN CATHOLICISM sometime before he gave up his benefices at Noyon on May 4, 1534.

Events now forced him to leave France. Intending to spend his life in scholarship, he published the first edition of the *Institutes of the Christian Religion* in 1536. William Farel, the reformer of Geneva, found Calvin passing through Geneva and demanded under the threat of the damnation of God that Calvin should help him in the reformation of the church. A struggle over the independence of the CHURCH from the state resulted in the city council's sending Calvin and Farel into exile in 1538. Most of the next three years were spent as pastor of the French church in Strasbourg, writing a commentary on Romans, revising the *Institutes,* devising a Reformed LITURGY, and attending the ecumenical meetings with the Roman Catholics at Regensburg, Frankfort, Hagenau, and Worms. In 1541 the council persuaded Calvin to return to Geneva. He was in constant struggle with the council in regard to the nature of the Reformation and the independence of the church, but from 1555 until his death in 1564 Calvin had a firm hold on the leadership of the church. He was given citizenship in the city in 1559, and in the same year an academy, a long cherished dream of Calvin's, was established. Geneva became a model of Protestantism, and Calvin's leadership of Reformed Protestantism generally was an important factor in resisting the pressures of the CATHOLIC REFORMATION.

Calvin can best be described as a churchman. Better than any other reformer, he combined in his person the functions of scholar, biblical exegete, theologian, preacher, and pastor. He wrote the most influential statement of Protestant faith, *The Institutes of the Christian Religion.* He reformed worship. He initiated and sponsored the preparation of the Genevan Psalter. He reorganized the church, and his church ordinances became one of his most influential writings. His commentaries and sermons qualify him as one of the great interpreters of church history. His vision of the Christian community and his leadership in the transformation of Geneva guarantee his place in political and social history. His letters, eleven volumes of them in the *Corpus Reformatorum,* reveal the range of his pastoral concern and of his leadership of the Reformed wing of Protestantism. *See* REFORMED CHURCHES.

Bibliography. F. Wendel, *Calvin, the Origins and Development of His Religious Thought* (1963); T. H. L. Parker, *John Calvin: A Biography* (1975). J. H. LEITH

CAMPBELL, ALEXANDER (Ch; 1788-1866). One of the founders of the CHRISTIAN CHURCHES (DISCIPLES OF CHRIST). Campbell was influenced by the rationalism of John Locke. He abhorred the sectarianism of frontier religion and joined his father, Thomas, in calling for a union of all Christians on the basis of a restoration of NT Christianity. However, the tension between union and restoration was never resolved, and has been a major cause of division among his followers. In 1840, to ensure an educated ministry, he established Bethany College in what is now West Virginia.

Bibliography. R. Humbert, ed., *A Compend of Alexander Campbell's Theology* (1961). R. L. HARRISON

CANDLEMAS (Ch). A feast on February 2 celebrating the presentation of JESUS in the Temple on the fortieth day after his birth (Luke 2:22-39) in accordance with the Law (Lev. 12). Observed with a candlelight procession at ROME from the seventh century, it became the occasion for the blessing of candles in the Western church. Kept on February 14 by ARMENIANS. T. J. TALLEY

CANON LAW (Ch—Gr.; lit. "rule, norm, measure"). Law which regulates the internal operation of an ecclesiastical society. It deals with the members of the society and their roles, property, organizations, worship, sacraments, legal processes, and penal laws. An early set of rules for Christian living is found in the late third century *Didascalia Apostolorum (Teaching of the Apostles)*. Church councils in both Eastern and Western churches enacted "canons," and the Council of NICAEA termed church laws the "ecclesiastical canon." Emperor Justinian's sixth century codification of civil law influenced church practice. The ninth century "False Decretals" were fabricated to lend a veneer of antiquity to norms already widely accepted. Pope Gregory VII's late eleventh century *Dictatus Papae (Papal Axioms)* strongly asserted the role of law and of the pope as lawmaker in the church (*see* PAPACY). The twelfth century Camaldolese monk Gratian is called the "father of canon law." His *Decretum*, a collection of canonical texts with commentary, together with five later collections form the fundamental *Corpus Juris Canonici (Body of Canon Law)* of the Western church. The first official collection of canon law was published in 1209 by Pope INNOCENT III. ROMAN CATHOLIC canon law has been gathered in 2,414 canons in the *Codex Juris Canonici (Code of Canon Law)* of 1918. Since 1963 a revision of the *Code* ordered by Pope JOHN XXIII has been under way. Eastern ORTHODOX Christians honor the early canonical collections, and the several churches have collections of synodal legislation. Systematization of a Western-style canon law for Eastern churches united with Rome was begun in 1930. The law of ANGLICAN CHURCHES is based, with some changes, on pre-Reformation canon law, together with subsequent acts of the conventions of CANTERBURY and York, the British Parliament, and, since 1919, the Church of England assembly. Supreme legislative competence in the Episcopal Church in the United States has rested since 1789 with the general convention. J. HENNESEY

CANONIZATION (Ch; Roman Catholic and Orthodox). The definitive act by which a deceased individual is inscribed in the catalog of saints. Based on the authentification of the practice of heroic virtue during life and of miracles after death, the decree of canonization has since the twelfth century been reserved to papal authority in ROMAN CATHOLICISM. In the ORTHODOX CHURCHES, canonization depends on the synod of bishops. C. WADDELL

CANTERBURY (Ch). Chief primatial SEE since 601 of the Church of England, whose ARCHBISHOP ranks first among the bishops of the ANGLICAN CHURCHES. The present CATHEDRAL, built between 1100 and 1498 in several architectural styles, is a worldwide focus of pilgrimage. *See* ART AND ARCHITECTURE, CHRISTIAN.

Bibliography. R. Church, *Portrait of Canterbury* (rev. ed., 1968); S. Rousham, *Canterbury, The Story of a Cathedral* (1975).
M. H. SHEPHERD, JR.

CANTOR kăn′ tər (Ju—Lat.; lit. "singer"; Heb. *hazzan*). The cleric who leads the synagogue service by virtue of his expertise in Hebrew liturgical chant. In Reform Judaism this may be a woman. *See* MUSIC, IN JUDAISM. M. ROTH

CAPUCHINS kăp′ o͞o shĭns (Ch). The Friars Minor Capuchin (OFMCap), FRANCISCANS named for their special capuche or hood, arose in the sixteenth century from reforms by Matteo de Bascio and others. In 1608 Pope Paul V separated them from the other two Franciscan branches. Zeal and rapid growth made them leaders in the CATHOLIC REFORMATION and missions. *See* RELIGIOUS ORDERS.
W. H. PRINCIPE

CARDINAL (Ch). An ecclesiastical official of the Roman Catholic Church, appointed by the pope and second only to the pope in rank and dignity. The holders of this title constitute the pope's council. *See* PAPACY. K. WATKINS

CARGO CULTS. MILLENARIAN MOVEMENTS in New Guinea and Melanesia that began in the late nineteenth century and reached their peak in the 1930s and 40s. In reaction to the frequent arrival of overseas cargo for the Europeans, Americans, and Japanese, natives foresaw an end to this era of foreign domination by a cataclysm, followed by an era in which material wealth would come to them as cargo from their ancestors. *See* ANCESTOR VENERATION.
K. CRIM

CARMELITES cär′ mə līts (Ch). Roman Catholic RELIGIOUS ORDERS originating from hermits on Mt. Carmel, Palestine, organized in Europe (thirteenth century) as MENDICANT FRIARS, joined (fifteenth century) by cloistered nuns as the Carmelite Second Order. Reforms in sixteenth century Spain separated Discalced (Barefoot) Carmelite friars, nuns (OCD) from the Ancient Observance (OC). Carmelites stress contemplative MYSTICISM. Several active sisterhoods are Third Order Carmelites. W. H. PRINCIPE

CARO, JOSEPH kä′ rō yō săf′ (Ju; 1488-1575). One of the central and universally recognized authorities in rabbinic law and author of the legal compendium the SHULHAN ARUCH. A mystic as well, he records in his diary, *Maggid Mesharim*, the nightly revelations he received from a heavenly figure embodying the MISHNAH. K. P. BLAND

CARTHUSIANS cär tho͞o′ zhəns (Ch.) Roman Catholic religious order of contemplative monks started (1084) by St. Bruno in the French Alps. The monks pray, work, eat, and sleep in solitary huts, coming together only for community worship and one weekly conversation period. *See* RELIGIOUS ORDERS.
W. H. PRINCIPE

CĀRVĀKA chär′ vä kä (H—Skt.; lit. "sweet-voiced," "agreeable speaker"). The materialist school (DARŚANA) of Hindu religious philosophy; often also called the Lokāyata *darśana* ("Lokāyata" may mean "[the views] held by the common people"; its etymology is uncertain). The origin of the name Cārvāka is unclear, and it may have been a nickname for the school.

Historical evidence for an actual school called the Cārvāka is extremely slim. No independent primary source belonging to such a school has been found. The evidence that does exist consists of accounts of the Cārvākas in the writings of other schools. Therefore, the teachings of the Cārvākas must be pieced together from sources hostile to them. This process yields a picture of a *darśana* whose primary tenets are: (1) that valid knowledge is attainable only through direct perception; (2) that there is no enduring soul or spiritual essence in the person, nor any deity; and (3) that the attainment of pleasure and the avoidance of pain are the chief goals in human life. Since these views are directly antithetical to basic positions in Hindu philosophy, it is possible that Cārvāka was a foil contrived by other schools to establish their own positions.

Bibliography. M. Hiriyanna, *Outlines of Indian Philosophy* (1932); S. Dasgupta, *A History of Indian Philosophy*, Supplement to Vol. I (1940). K. W. Folkert

CASTE. A term applied to social groups in India which rank in a hierarchic order and within which there is a minimum of social mobility. The word "caste" first appeared as a term *(casta)* by which the Portuguese travelers of the fifteenth century referred to the divisions of Indian society. Although some modern sociologists speak of "caste-like" categories with reference to the rigid sections of societies divided along lines of color, race, or class, caste in the narrow sense of the term is a phenomenon confined to Indian civilization. Indian languages lack any word precisely corresponding to "caste," which includes what Indians refer to as *varṇa* (color) and *jāti* (birth group).

Unlike the classes of Western societies and the racial elements of such societies as those of the United States or South Africa, the Indian castes have their roots in a system of ideas which claims religious sanction for hierarchical social ordering of people as an essential part of the Hindu world view. The underlying assumption of caste is the idea that persons are born with different intellectual and spiritual qualities and capabilities which result largely from their actions (Karma) in previous existences. Membership in a caste is seen as a birth-given condition which remains unchangeable during a lifetime, though merit or demerit acquired in one life determines one's status in a future rebirth. The idea of reincarnation (Samsara) is inseparable from the ideological foundations of the caste system.

1. **Ancient India.** In ancient India the present complex social order consisting of innumerable castes and subcastes had not yet developed, but the basic structure was already evident. The sacred Vedic hymns present a division of humanity into four categories or estates, the *varṇas* (lit. "colors"). Though this fourfold division was to become the framework for the rank-order of castes, it was different from the caste system of contemporary India. The *varṇa* order consisted of four descending ranks: Brahmins (priests), Kṣatriyas (warriors and rulers), Vaiśyas (merchants and husbandmen), and Śūdras (menial artisans, laborers, and servants). A creation myth contained in a Vedic hymn ascribes this division of humanity to the very beginning of the present world age. Puruṣa, an original divine being whose immense body filled the whole universe, was sacrificed by the gods in such a manner that the parts of the body transformed themselves into the various elements of the creation: his mouth turned into the first Brahmin, his arms into Kṣatriya warriors, his thighs into Vaiśyas, and his feet into Śūdras.

In Vedic times there was still some mobility between these four categories, and marriages between Brahmins and Kṣatriyas were not unusual. The members of the three higher ranks were described as Twice Born, because young males of these groups underwent an initiation rite regarded as a second birth, which admitted them to the religious life and imposed on them the obligation to observe all the taboos prescribed for adults. The Śūdras, the lowest order, were excluded from most ritual activities and were not allowed to study the sacred Vedic texts.

2. **The classical age.** The system of *varṇa* was codified in one of the earliest Indian law books, the Laws of Manu, the mythical first ancestor and originator of the social order. The final formulation of this code is probably not older than the second century A.D., but incorporated rules specifying the functions of the four *varṇas* which must have prevailed in much earlier times.

Manu's codification coincided with a hardening of the divisions of Hindu society. The mobility between the *varṇas* declined, though it persists even now in some outlying areas such as the highlands of the Himalayan kingdom of Nepal. The differentiation in the rights and duties of the members of the four estates became more pronounced. Manu decreed that all actions should be judged according to the status of the doer, and males of high castes were not only granted many privileges but were also burdened with many obligations and restrictions. From them a higher standard of behavior was expected than from those of low birth, and persons of high status guilty of certain offences were to be punished more severely than persons of lower rank who had committed identical crimes.

The Laws of Manu also determined the relations between Brahmins and Kṣatriyas, priests and rulers. Whereas in ancient times Indian princes had the right to perform religious functions, Kṣatriyas were essentially deprived of all their religious prerogatives, and were subordinated to the spiritual power of Brahmin priests. But the supremacy of the Brahmin's spiritual power was never expressed in the political sphere, and in this the Kṣatriyas ruled supreme.

3. **Caste in contemporary India.** The fourfold, hierarchically ranked *varṇa* system extended over the whole of India, and provided a model for the structure of Hindu society. From about 300 B.C. onward, numerous "castes" or *jāti* (lit. "birth groups") developed within the *varṇa* framework. *Jāti* were social groups whose members married only among themselves, and endogamy remains one of the most characteristic features of the modern and complex *jāti* or caste system. Each caste is a closed group with distinctive customs and ritual practices, strict dietary rules, and occupational preferences. From birth the individual is provided with a fixed social and religious milieu from which no vicissitude of fate can remove him unless he violates the rules of his caste to such a degree that he is either temporarily or permanently excommunicated or "outcasted." Most castes are subdivided, and it is within the local subcaste that a man or woman finds most social contacts.

While each caste and subcaste is a largely self-contained unit, there is a pronounced interdependence of castes, which render each other numerous services in both the religious and economic spheres. For instance, Brahmins act as family priests for all individuals belonging to the "twice born" castes, while members of many lower castes (e.g. potters) have priestly roles in the ritual practices of a village community. Because of the occupational specialization of castes in traditional Indian society no one group could dispense with the services of the other social groups. Modernization and industrialization have recently undermined this interdependence of occupational castes.

Basic to the caste system is the belief in the unequal degree of ritual purity attaching to the various groups. Hindus hold that certain types of contact, such as eating with a member of a lower caste or even accepting water from his hands, defiles a person of higher status, and the avoidance of such polluting contacts and the maintenance of ritual purity is a constant preoccupation with Indians of high caste. There is in addition the underlying belief that impurity prevails over purity. While the purity of persons of high caste is diminished by contact with members of the lower groups, the latter do not enhance their purity if they are touched by a high-caste person. Conformity to every detail of the rules which regulate the conduct of caste members is considered the supreme virtue in a Hindu. A violation of the rules, even if committed accidentally, may result in dire consequences. Thus a Brahmin who unknowingly partakes of food cooked by a person of low status loses his ritual purity and with it his own caste status.

The right manner in which a person should approach any problem of conduct is determined by the DHARMA or duties of his caste. He cannot choose freely, for he belongs to a group, a family *(jāti)*, a guild, or a sect, and he must in all his actions behave in a way consistent with the dharma that is appropriate to his role as a caste member. Hindu society sees the individual not so much as an independent agent guided in his conduct by the promptings of his own conscience, but as a member of a tightly organized community whose actions affect not only his own status but also that of those closest to him. Therefore, an individual's wrong conduct can cause a chain reaction to innocent members of his household or kinsmen and friends, who eat food from his "polluted" hands.

Because the pollution which results from certain offenses against caste rules is automatic and contagious, no group can afford to permit freedom to the individual in the regulation of his life. Caste members are therefore critical of deviations from the narrow path of orthodox behavior on the part of other individuals in the group, and even close kinsmen will disown a family member who has lost status by close contact with a person of lower caste. Given the different duties attendant on one's birth rank, actions permissible for members of one caste are wrong for those of another, and instead of a universally applicable moral code there are as many different standards of behavior as there are castes.

4. **Outcastes (untouchables).** The lowest castes, including artisans that do polluting work such as tanning, leather working, and scavenging, are everywhere regarded as "untouchable," and bodily contact with them pollutes members of clean castes. Today these untouchables are known by the euphemism HARIJAN (lit. "children of God"), but though public discrimination against them is now illegal, they still form an underprivileged class, which in many parts of India comprises a large percentage of the population. Most Hindus take the hierarchy of castes, and hence also the low status of Harijans, for granted and consider it part of a world order closely integrated with orthodox Hindu religion.

Religious reformers through the ages have attempted to abolish immutable caste distinctions, but they have had no lasting effect. Likewise sects which preached the equality of all persons usually ended up as closed groups similar to castes—and are now regarded as such by the rest of Hindu society. However, although the caste system has made for a static and conservative Indian society, it has at the same time facilitated the incorporation into Hinduism of various races and nationalities, each of which has retained many of its social and religious practices.

In recent years the religious aspects of the system have somewhat receded into the background, while at the same time castes have gained in importance as political pressure groups, whose cohesion and strength are rooted in the traditional solidarity of their members. Despite official attempts to create an egalitarian society in which caste privileges have no legally recognized place, castes persist as distinct social units in Indian society. As groups which dominate social life castes inevitably influence their members' economic and political attitudes. There has been a power shift in recent times from the castes of highest ritual and educational status to those which are economically and politically prominent in a given region. The chief beneficiaries of the new order are non-Brahmin castes, not necessarily of "twice born" status, which have become the new dominant castes through large landholdings. These new elite groups are usually conservative, as it is in their interest to impede as far as possible the rise of such low castes as the numerically strong but economically weak Harijans.

Even measures designed to bring about equality of opportunities tend to perpetuate the caste system. Groups which have been classified as "backward" and enjoy such privileges as reserved seats in the legislatures and a quota of posts in government service are naturally reluctant to forgo these benefits and are in the process of becoming a new politically influential class. In contemporary India caste solidarity affects political relations more than ever, and democracy in India operates at present through a careful balancing of different caste interests.

Bibliography. J. H. Hutton, *Caste in India* (1946); D. G. Mandelbaum, *Society in India,* 2 vols. (1970), contains an extensive bibliography; A. C. Mayer, *Caste and Kinship in Central India* (1960); M. N. Srinivas, *Caste in Modern India* (1962).

C. von Fürer-Haimendorf

CATACOMBS (etymology obscure; probably derived from Gr. *kata kumba*—"near the place of or in the shape of a cup"). In the Roman Republic the term referred to subterranean excavations in soft rock for the burial of the dead. In the later Christian period large labyrinths of galleries, three to four feet wide, were dug with connecting chambers going off at various angles. In Christian catacombs the graves *(loculi)* were parallel to the galleries, while in pagan areas the *loculi* were set at right angles. As one gallery was filled, the floor would be excavated and so on until as many as seven stories were dug. The catacombs in Rome extend for several hundred miles, containing thousands of *loculi,* each of which contained one to four bodies. Sarcophagi were very rare. The graves were closed with painted marble slabs placed along the walls of the galleries. These paintings provide some of the earliest examples of Christian art.

Celebrations in pagan areas took place at a given grave on the day of burial and the anniversary of death. Because of the relative sanctity and privacy of the catacombs eucharistic services were held there on the anniversaries of the Martyrs. Shafts were dug for air and light to facilitate these celebrations, which continued to be observed for several centuries. The major period of catacombs may be dated to the third and fourth centuries. By the time of Jerome (ca. 360) burial was not common, and when Alaric sacked Rome in A.D. 410 interment in the catacombs had virtually ceased. As time went by, their existence was forgotten until they were rediscovered in 1578. They have been excavated and thoroughly studied by such early scholars as Antonio Bosio (d. 1629), and in modern times by G. B. de Rossi, O. Marrucchi, P. Styger, and E. Kirschbaum.

While there are catacombs in or near a number of ancient cities in Egypt, Malta, Lebanon, Sicily, and Palestine, the most famous and most important are to be found in the vicinity of Rome. The most noteworthy are Sts. Callistus, Praetextatus, and Sebastian on the Via Appia; St. Domitilla on the Via Ardeatina; and St. Agnes on the Via Nomentana. At least six Jewish catacombs have been found at Rome; they resemble the Christian, except that they lack the large rooms for public meetings.

Until recently some scholars mistakenly believed that the Catacombs of San Sebastiano marked the place of burial of Peter and Paul. After a half century of investigation, it seems reasonable to suppose that a cult of these two apostles did exist there *ca.* A.D. 260 and perhaps as early as A.D. 200, but no convincing evidence has been advanced that the apostles were originally buried there or that their bones were transferred there after earlier burial elsewhere.

Bibliography. H. Leclerq in *Dictionnaire d'archéologie chrétienne et de liturgie,* Vol. II, pt. 2 (1910), cols. 2376-2486 with bibliog., cols. 2447-50; P. Styger, *Die römischen Katakomben* (1933); L. Hertling, E. Kirschbaum, eds., *Le catacombe romane e i loro martiri* (1949).

D. W. O'Connor

CATECHISM kăt′ ə kĭz əm (Ch). A manual for Christian instruction, either in question and answer form or treatise form. Catechesis, the more general term, refers to the art of expounding and communicating the faith.

Catechetical instruction for adults was common in the ancient church. Augustine (354-430) wrote on the method and substance of catechetical instruction, pointing out the advantage of the question and answer method as well as dealing with the psychological factors involved. Prior to the Reformation there were numerous manuals of instruction concentrating on the Creeds, the Ten Commandments, the Prayers, the Sacraments, the mortal Sins, and the rudiments of household piety.

The Protestant Reformation emphasized catechetical instruction, especially for the young. Martin Luther's Small Catechism of 1529 is a classic example of the question and answer method. Calvin's Catechism (1541) and the Heidelberg Catechism (1563) are the most influential among the Reformed. The English Puritans were prolific writers of catechisms, debating with much vigor catechetical methods and forms.

Roman Catholic catechisms include those of Canisius (1556), Bellarmine (1598), and the Catechism of the Council of TRENT (1566).

No contemporary catechism has the influence that older catechisms exercised in the church. Examples of contemporary catechisms are *The Draft Catechism of the Church of Scotland* (1954) and *A New Catechism, Catholic Faith for Adults* (1966) of the Dutch Roman Catholic Church. Protestant and Roman Catholic scholars in Europe produced *The Common Catechism* (1973), written in treatise form.

J. H. LEITH

CATHEDRAL (Ch—Gr.; *kathedra,* "seat"). The church in which a BISHOP has his official seat; thus the principal church in a DIOCESE. From medieval times, the typical Western cathedral has followed a floor plan in the shape of a CROSS, in which nave, transepts, and choir are the main elements. *See* ART AND ARCHITECTURE, CHRISTIAN. W. S. BABCOCK

CATHOLICOS kă thŏl′ ĭ kəs (Ch). The title given to the highest ranking ecclesiastical official in some of the ORTHODOX CHURCHES. K. WATKINS

CAUSATION (B). *See* PATICCASAMUPPĀDA.

CELESTINES sĕl′ ĕs tēnz (Ch). Name given to (1) a branch of BENEDICTINES founded (thirteenth century) by Peter of Morrone, later Pope Celestine V, and noted for severity of life, and (2) a group of radical FRANCISCAN Spirituals who received special protection from Celestine V but who were distinct from Benedictine Celestines. Neither group exists today. *See* RELIGIOUS ORDERS. W. H. PRINCIPE

CELIBACY. The state of life without marriage, undertaken for spiritual or religious ideals; in a more restricted Christian context, the state of abstinence from marriage "for the sake of the kingdom of heaven"; and in a still more restricted sense (chiefly ROMAN CATHOLICISM and Eastern ORTHODOXY), the canonical state of renunciation of marriage freely accepted as a means of total consecration to God's service in the clerical state.

1. **Non-Christian religions and Old Testament.** For pagan antiquity and primitive religious cultures in general, the whole area of sexuality risks exposure to numinous or demonic powers. Abstinence from sexual activity means (negatively) a distancing from the demonic and (positively) an ascetic discipline directed toward the intensification of spiritual strength and communion with higher beings through liberation from the corporeal. Celibacy accordingly is found chiefly in religions with an institutional priesthood and special consecrated persons, e.g., Vestal virgins, or in religions which stress the ascetic and mystical, e.g., BUDDHISM. Religions which deny the demonic or the possibility of communion with the divine also tend to reject

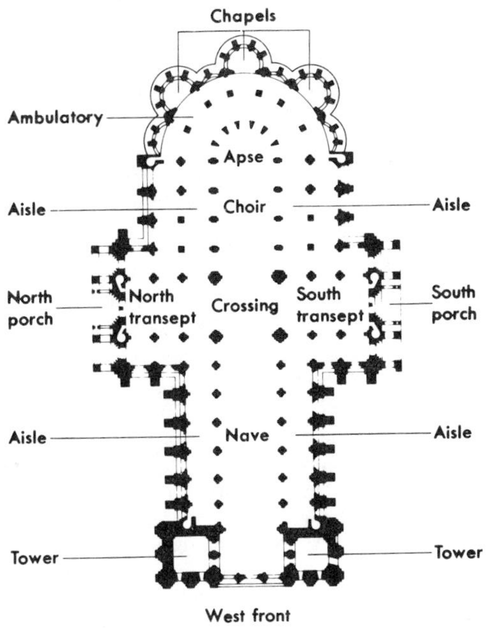

Floor plan of a typical medieval cathedral

celibacy, e.g., ISLAM, Jōdo Buddhism (*see* PURE LAND SECTS). The widely verifiable practice of temporary continence as a form of purification with view to worship should not be confused with the permanent life of celibacy. In the OT, virginity, though desirable for the nonmarried, was impermanent in the light of the obligation of marriage for all.

2. Christianity. The Christian foundation of celibacy rests chiefly on the demands of radical discipleship (renunciation of family ties "for the sake of the kingdom": Mark 10:29; Luke 18:29) and on the greater freedom of the unmarried for the service of God and of the church (I Cor. 7:32-34). For the early church, however, celibacy remained an individual gift ("Who is able to receive this, let him receive it," Matt. 19:12), and marriage was in no way incompatible with ecclesiastical office. Many BISHOPS, PRIESTS, and DEACONS opted for celibacy, but in spite of sporadic attempts to render clerical celibacy compulsory, it was not general throughout the patristic period. But by the seventh century the present Eastern practice had already crystallized: unmarried bishops; priests and deacons married, but only if marriage precedes ORDINATION. In the West reforming efforts of popes and councils succeeded in rendering clerical celibacy obligatory; and from the time of Pope GREGORY VII (d. 1085) onward, reception of holy orders was held to include an implicit vow of celibacy. While the PROTESTANT REFORMATION abolished mandatory celibacy as being of merely human institution, the CATHOLIC REFORMATION renewed emphasis on the medieval practice while explicitly recognizing it as an ecclesiastical institution, and therefore subject to possible change. The post–VATICAN COUNCIL II norms for the permanent diaconate provide for married deacons (1967). Mandatory celibacy for priests is among the most hotly contested current issues in the Roman Catholic Church. *See* ASCETICISM; CLERGY; TAIZÉ.

Bibliography. H. C. Lea, *History of Sacerdotal Celibacy in the Christian Church,* 2 vols. (1907); P. Delhoy, "Celibacy," *New Catholic Encyclopedia,* II (1967), 366-74; Paul VI, *Encyclical Letter on Priestly Celibacy {Sacerdotalis celibatus}* (1967).

C. WADDELL

CHALCEDONIAN DEFINITION kăl sə dō´ nē ən (Ch). The formulation of the Council of Chalcedon, 451, affirming that JESUS Christ is one person in two natures, divine and human, which cannot be confused, changed, separated, or divided. It drew on the resources of the theologians of Antioch, Alexandria, and Rome, condemning the heresies of Arius, Apollinarius, Nestorius, and Eutyches. *See* CREEDS AND CONFESSIONS §2.

J. H. LEITH

CH'AN chän (B). Chinese name for ZEN.

CHANDRA GUPTA II chän´ drŭ go͞op´ tŭ. *See* GUPTA DYNASTY.

CHARISMATIC MOVEMENT (Ch). A movement within the traditional Christian denominations which emphasizes the gifts of the HOLY SPIRIT. Beginning in the major PROTESTANT denominations about 1960, the movement reached ROMAN CATHOLIC churches in 1966. By the end of the 1970s the "renewal," as it is called, had entered every major Christian denomination.

The charismatic movement represents the spread of Pentecostalism into the "mainline" churches. The PENTECOSTAL CHURCHES began in 1901 as an outgrowth of the emphasis on CHRISTIAN PERFECTION in the METHODIST CHURCHES. Basic theological premises laid down by JOHN WESLEY and John Fletcher led Methodists to seek a "second blessing" of "entire sanctification" through the BAPTISM IN THE HOLY SPIRIT. Added to this teaching was the "restoration" theme of such English groups as the PLYMOUTH BRETHREN, who looked forward to a restoration of supernatural signs of spiritual power to herald the SECOND COMING of Christ.

The Pentecostal movement in America took up this theme under the leadership of Charles Parham and W. J. Seymour, who taught that baptism in the Holy Spirit was always accompanied with speaking in tongues as the "initial evidence." (*See* GLOSSOLALIA.) Those who experienced this attestation to their baptism were excommunicated from their churches and in time established flourishing Pentecostal denominations around the world.

After World War II the rapid growth of these bodies attracted the attention of the Christian world. Leading Pentecostal figures such as evangelist Oral Roberts, ecumenist David duPlessis, and lay leader Demos Shakarian (founder of the Full Gospel Businessmen) created a better reception for Pentecostalism in the traditional churches. Many pastors who experienced glossolalia during these years either were excommunicated from their churches or kept their charismatic activities secret from their superiors.

The first minister to make a public issue of his Pentecostal experience was Dennis Bennett, pastor of St. Marks Episcopal Church in Van Nuys, California. In 1960 Bennett spoke in tongues in a private prayer meeting. When he reported it to his congregation, the church divided. Bennett resigned his pastorate and moved to an inner city parish in Seattle, where he was permitted to promote Pentecostalism while remaining an Episcopal priest.

In the wake of Bennett's experience, hundreds of ministers of various denominations gave public support to the movement. These new tongue-speakers were dubbed "neo-Pentecostals."

Suddenly neo-Pentecostalism became a *cause célèbre* among many Protestants, and formed a theological counter-culture to the liberal theologies that had dominated the major Protestant denominations for decades. Surprisingly, the movement attracted intellectuals and theologians of the sacramental churches. By 1963 speaking in tongues broke out among students and faculty at Yale University.

Observers noted that the new Pentecostals did not fall into trances but seemed in control as they chanted their Hebrew-like glossolalic phrases.

Reaction to the neo-Pentecostals was mixed. Some Episcopalians saw it as a sign of hope for the future of the church, while Bishop James A. Pike of California denounced it as a case of "heresy in embryo." Other Protestant churches initiated studies of the movement that continued into the 1970s.

In 1966 the first Catholic Pentecostal prayer meeting was held in Pittsburgh, Pennsylvania. In a weekend retreat at Duquesne University, two theology professors, Ralph Keifer and Billy Story, led about twenty students and professors into a Pentecostal experience which involved glossolalia.

In the months that followed, the movement swept through the Catholic student populations at the University of Michigan and the University of Notre Dame. The Catholic Pentecostal movement gained its early leaders, mostly young lay people, in this first sweep into the Catholic heartland of America.

The Ann Arbor group soon became the largest and most influential center for the Catholic movement. There an ecumenical community was founded called the "Word of God," which became a model for other communitarian experiments across the nation. Ann Arbor leaders also produced a periodical entitled *New Covenant,* which served as a central clearinghouse of information about the movement. New songs were written and published for the hundreds of prayer groups that began to spring up in America and in other countries. Notre Dame became the chief conference place for the Catholics who flocked to the movement in phenomenal numbers.

As more Catholics and Protestants joined the burgeoning neo-Pentecostal movement, theologians began to reflect on its theology and ecclesiology. By 1970 the movement was being called "the charismatic renewal," and the people themselves "charismatics." The word "renewal" was used to show that the purpose of the movement was to renew the existing churches rather than to establish new denominations.

A basic Catholic charismatic theological approach was worked out by 1972 by Kilian McDonnell, Edward O'Connor, and Donald Gelpi, and it was followed closely by leaders in the Presbyterian, Episcopal, and Lutheran sectors of the renewal.

In this view, glossolalia was not necessarily the only "initial evidence" of receiving the baptism in the Holy Spirit, although it would be viewed as a normal and expected occurrence. One might later "yield to the gift of tongues," or never speak in tongues at all. Tongues was only one of many gifts which might be received. Even with an apparent de-emphasis on glossolalia, charismatics tended to use tongues as a "prayer language" and "sing in tongues" more than their Pentecostal predecessors. Baptism in the Holy Spirit was also viewed as essentially a part of the "rites of initiation" which included BAPTISM, CONFIRMATION, and EUCHARIST. What charismatics received in their Pentecostal experience was a "release of the Spirit" which had already been given at baptism. The ensuing charisms (spiritual gifts) were thus an "actualization" of graces already received.

Given this understanding of the charismatic experience, the Roman Catholic bishops in the United States accorded the movement cautious approval in 1969 and directed that it be "allowed to develop in the church." Noting that those in the renewal experienced a deeper taste for prayer, praise, the gifts of the Spirit, and a desire to read Scripture, Pope Paul VI in 1973 gave his blessings to the movement. Later in a charismatic mass in ST. PETER'S in ROME (1975) Pope Paul encouraged the charismatics to "share" the joy of the Holy Spirit with everyone.

One reason for the papal blessing was the participation of Cardinal Leon Joseph Suenens of Belgium in the leadership of the movement. As the ranking Catholic charismatic prelate in the world, Suenens did much to add respectability and strength to the movement among both Protestants and Catholics.

Bibliography. D. J. Bennett, *Nine O'clock in the Morning* (1970); K. McDonnell, *Charismatic Renewal and the Churches* (1976); E. D. O'Connor, *The Pentecostal Movement in the Catholic Church* (1971); R. Quebedeaux, *The New Charismatics* (1975).

H. V. SYNAN

CHARMS AND AMULETS (I). Sanctioned by the ḤADĪTH, charms and amulets became an integral part of Islamic popular belief and were sought by rich and poor, the educated and the illiterate. Some are used to protect against the evil eye, to prevent loss of property or virility, or to ensure a safe journey. Others are designed to counter the effects of bodily afflictions, both low-level (tumors, fevers, sores) and potentially fatal (plague, cholera, epilepsy). Normally the charm contains a passage from the QUR'ĀN, an invocation to the Almighty, or both.

Bibliography. C. Elgood, *"Tibb ul-nabbi (sic)* or Medicine of the Prophet," *Osiris,* XIV (1962), 33-192.

B. LAWRENCE

CHASIDISM hă′ sĭd ĭsm (Ju). *See* HASIDISM.

CHEN-YEN jən yən′ (B). Chinese name for SHINGON.

CH'ENG-SHIH chəng′ shar. *See* NARA BUDDHISM §3b.

CHI-TSANG jē′ dzäng (B—Chin.; 549-623). Systematizer of the teachings of the MĀDHYAMIKA or San-lun ("Three Treatise") School of Mahāyāna BUDDHISM, author of the *Ehr-ti chang* ("Treatise on Two Levels of Truth") and *San-lun hsüan-i* ("Profound Meaning of the Three Treatises").

Born of a Parthian father and Chinese mother, Chi-tsang studied under Fa-lang, and became an advocate of NĀGĀRJUNA's Middle Path of Eightfold

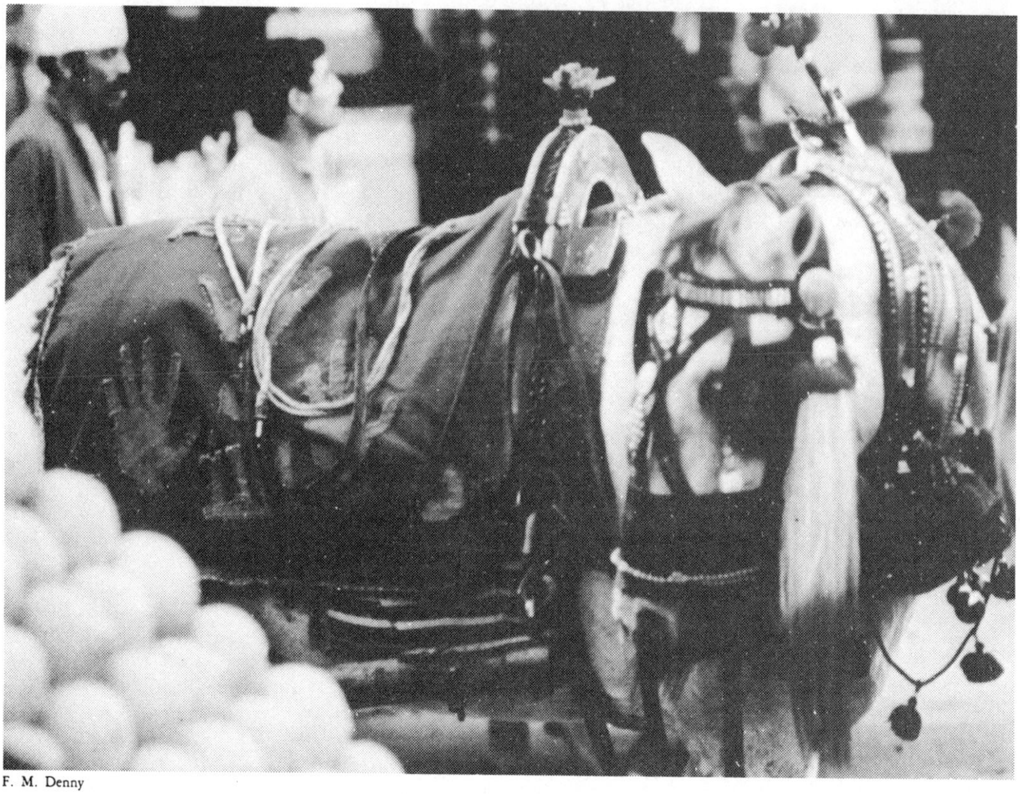

F. M. Denny

Horse with amulet blanket, the bazaar, Cairo. The "hands of Fāṭima" on the blanket fend off evil. *See* CHARMS AND AMULETS.

Negations which arrives at a level of truth beyond being and nonbeing called emptiness (ŚŪNYATĀ). The designation K'ung tsung ("Emptiness School") is therefore sometimes given. C. W. EDWARDS

CH'I chē (T & Con—Chin.; lit. "breath, vapor"). One of the fundamental substances of the cosmos. In living things the *ch'i* circulates to ensure vitality and strength. (*See* TAOISM, RELIGIOUS.) In Neo-Confucian thought, it signifies the "material force" that contrasts with "principle" *(li)*. *See* CONFUCIANISM §3.
M. LEVERING

CH'ING-T'U chĭng tōō´ (B). *See* PURE LAND.

CHIH-I jər ē´ or **CHIH-K'AI** jər kī´ (B—Chin.; 538-597). Founder and organizer of the T'ien-t'ai (Jap. TENDAI) School of Buddhism on T'ien-t'ai Shan ("Heavenly Terrace Mountain") in Chekiang, China.

Orphaned by a military massacre in 554, Chih-i turned to the monastic life, became a disciple of Hui-ssŭ, and attained SAMĀDHI while reading the LOTUS SŪTRA. He formulated a comprehensive system which arranged the confusing variety of Buddhist SŪTRAS into "Five Periods and Eight Teachings," culminating in the Lotus Sūtra as the apex of the Buddha's teachings.

Bibliography. L. Hurvitz, "Chih-i," *Mélanges Chinois et Bouddhiques,* 12 (1962). C. W. EDWARDS

CHILDREN OF GOD (Ch). A FUNDAMENTALIST movement among young people, with emphasis on imminent judgment and communal living. Founded in the late 1960s by David Berg (Moses David).

Bibliography. R. M. Enroth *et al., The Jesus People* (1972).
K. CRIM

CHINESE POPULAR RELIGION. The earliest historical sources note a variety of religious practices and beliefs, including ANCESTOR VENERATION, fertility cults, sacrifices to spirits of sacred objects and places, belief in ghosts, exorcism, DIVINATION, and the activities of spirit-mediums. By the Sung dynasty (A.D. 960-1279), these traditions had blended together with Buddhist ideas of KARMA and purgatory and Taoist charms and methods of ritual renewal to form the beginnings of modern popular religion. This complex aggregate can be defined by its location in the midst of ordinary social life, its pantheon of personified deities, its demonology and associated semi-dualistic world view, and its characteristic specialists and rituals.

Though there are many interrelationships, popular religion can be distinguished from monastic BUD-

DHISM, priestly TAOISM, philosophic CONFUCIANISM, and the official state cult. It is not possible, however, to define it along lines of geography, social class, or literacy, because at least from the Sung dynasty it has been practiced in both village and city by members of all classes, whether or not they are literate. Popular religion continues to survive in Taiwan, Hong Kong, and Chinese communities overseas, but it has largely died out in the People's Republic.

1. **Social setting.** The social setting of popular religion is first of all the family, village and urban marketplace. Its base is ancestor veneration and the cult of HOUSEHOLD GODS centered on the family altar. Through the regular offering of incense, food, and prayers this family cult provides ethical sanctions for everyday life and a sense of intimate divine concern for every significant place and activity. The veneration of ancestors in particular provides the context from which deified human beings become new gods for the popular pantheon.

Beyond the household, the ancestral cult is practiced in clan temples, which are associated with a variety of social, educational, and economic activities of the clan. Each neighborhood in the city or the countryside is loosely divided into jurisdictions of local gods *(t'u-ti kung)* responsible for the fertility and well-being of their respective areas. Shrines for local gods are maintained by each neighborhood family in rotation. The same geographical principle of organization applies to village temples and, beyond them, to temples of city gods in larger towns. These city gods are responsible for the whole county or market-area in which they are located. A geographically based popular cult can extend beyond the city temple through connections with pilgrimage centers and through associations elsewhere of those from a whole district or province.

James Ware

Tao Sin Temple, Kowloon, Hong Kong, basically Taoist, is surrounded by fortune telling and divining booths. This one uses phrenology and palm readings as well as divination slips.

James Ware

Earth gods *(t'u ti)* are one of the oldest types of patron deities, usually limited in influence to a field or other small area.

The social context of popular religion also involves a variety of voluntary associations such as shops, trades, secret societies, and religious sects. Membership cuts across family lines, and in the past sometimes extended through the whole country and beyond. Their deities are patron saints of particular activities and saviors of more or less universal scope.

People of different classes and educational levels participate in all of these social groups and their cults. The great majority of scholars and officials in the traditional period practiced various types of divination, worshiped personified deities, believed in omens, and on occasion even exorcised demons through the power of orthodox texts and moral character. Numerous emperors in different dynasties invited popular spirit-mediums, diviners, and spirit-writers to perform at court.

In practice, Chinese popular religion can first be defined by what a reasonably orthodox scholar/official would *not* do. He would not participate in rituals involving spirit possession, trance, or other ecstatic emotional activity. (However, some officials did participate in spirit-writing sessions, involving literacy.) In addition, a well-educated official would not join a sect centered on a mother goddess or espousing a radical MILLENARIAN mythology. Nor could he become an active devotee of a local cult based on the deification of a homeless ghost.

Confucian, Taoist, and Buddhist intellectuals had firm concepts of heresy, and what they attack as heresy usually corresponds roughly with what we would call popular religion: personified, emotional, immediate, concrete, available to all. The minimum demarcation of Chinese popular religion comes from within the culture itself. In the modern period a further definitional split has developed: that between a Westernized elite and those who maintain the old popular traditions. Even here, however, overlap occurs.

2. **Deities.** The characteristic gods of Chinese popular religion are human beings deified over time by increasing recognition of their efficacy and status. They are deities with a history of triumph over difficulties, who specialize in offering to their devotees the powers and virtues exemplified in that history. As such, they can be distinguished from symbols of natural forces in the state religion, such as mountains, rivers, and YIN AND YANG, and from the astral deities of Taoism. Popular deities are also different from Taoist immortals and from Buddhist BUDDHAS and BODHISATTVAS, none of which are believed to be related to society in the same intimate way. Popular deities, having once been human, owe their status to veneration by the living and to the practical blessings they confer. Thus, they are involved in a reciprocal relationship which constrains them to respond, unlike the more transcendent Buddhas and immortals who, it is believed, attained their status through their own insight and power.

In traditional China it was believed that at birth each person was allocated a certain amount of vital energy which was to last through his or her predestined span. If one died before his time in a violent or unjust way, some of this unused energy might remain to propel his spirit. Because of this, spirits of such persons were believed to be potentially dangerous in their search for fulfillment or revenge. Perhaps first as a means of placation, shrines were sometimes erected in honor of a restless spirit, called a *yu-ying kung*, "gentleman who responds" (to petitions). Most such shrines remained obscure, but some *yu-ying kung* were believed to perform miracles of healing, etc., particularly if they were associated with a spirit-medium. Thus, their cults grew, their fame spread, and eventually they came to be regarded as gods, with their ghostly past forgotten. So began the careers of such well known deities as Ma-tsu, goddess of fisherman, at first the soul of a pious girl who died before marriage. In other cases the venerated spirit was that of a famous person such as Kuan Yü, a great war hero of the third century A.D. who soon after his death came to be worshiped as a symbol of courage and loyalty.

The gods of popular religion were organized in a great celestial bureaucracy presided over by Yü-huang Shang-ti, the Jade Emperor. Beneath him is a pantheon of deities in charge of ministries such as Thunder and Wind, Fire, Epidemics, etc. Beneath these ministries in turn are gods of particular functions such as healing and bringing children, or of localities, such as the city god, and deities of neighborhoods and households. Though this pantheon was systematized in Taoist texts, at the popular level many of its details are ignored. The Jade Emperor is a symbol of moral order and divine power, who can send envoys to reward or punish, and to whom local deities make regular reports. In popular texts he is said once to have become so enraged at man's avarice and cruelty that he decided to destroy the world. At the pleading of subordinate deities and bodhisattvas, however, he relented, and permitted them to descend with a new message of salvation. So he sits on his throne, receiving little direct worship, but providing the ultimate sanction for goodness.

Popular deities owe much to older celestial hierarchies in China going back to Shang-ti, the "Emperor on High" of the Shang (1751-1112 B.C.) and Chou (1111-249 B.C.) periods. This hierarchical principle is further elaborated in Taoist texts. Buddhism contributed the ideal of the compassionate bodhisattva who descends to save others. The government contributed as well through granting official status and promotions to emerging deities with wide popular appeal. Popular deities combine all these factors with the attraction of eminent persons worshiped in image form.

3. **Demonology and world view.** Many of the gods, symbols of order, are equipped with weapons and troops. Such force is necessary because beneath the gods is a vast array of DEMONS, hostile influences which bring disorder, suffering, and death. Though ultimately subject to divine command, these demons are most unruly, and often can be subdued only through repeated invocation and strenuous ritual action. It is in such ritual exorcism that the struggle between gods and demons is most starkly presented. This struggle in turn implies a semi-dualistic world view, in which hostile forces abound, but hope for restored order persists through faith in the hierarchy of power.

For Chinese philosophy the world is produced through the harmonious interaction of abstract modes of energy such as yin and yang and the five agents (wood, fire, earth, metal, and water). The wise man seeks to understand and conform with these forces. At the popular level such forces are personified and given dramatic roles. In the process, modes of power once considered complementary have come to be perceived as potentially or actively hostile toward each other. In such a richly mythological context, one's task is not so much to conform with the natural order of things as to seek allies in a struggle against malevolent forces.

Demons or *kuei* are portrayed as monstrous, misshapen figures which can take the form of animals or human beings. The damage they cause ranges from epidemics and floods to the seduction of unwary travelers by *kuei* in female form, a seduction which leads to death through loss of vital breath. These creatures can attack singly or in panic-causing hordes and disperse only in daylight, or because they are exorcised.

Most *kuei* are the spirits of the restless dead who died unjustly, or whose bodies are not properly cared for. As such they are placated through offerings, spirit marriages, or relocation of graves. Other demons represent the essence of natural forces such as rocks or mountains which can be perceived as hostile. Still others might be destructive imps ordered by the gods to bring retribution to individuals or communities. *Kuei* are everywhere, in houses, along roads, in fields, mountains, and forests. Some, particularly spirits of the dead, may be based in purgatory, from which they emerge occasionally to seek redress.

The practice of popular religion is very much involved with rituals of exorcism and renewal, both for individuals and communities. These rituals provide a sense of drama which both reflects the struggles of everyday life and gives support to those involved in them.

4. **Leadership and specialists.** There are three different types of leadership in Chinese popular religion—hereditary, selected, and charismatic—though of course in any given situation these types can be mixed. Hereditary leaders include the fathers and mothers of families who carry out ancestor worship in the clan temple and household, and sect and secret society leaders who inherit their positions. Village temples, on the other hand, tend to be led by a village elder selected by lot, on a rotating basis. Charismatic leaders include spirit-mediums, spirit-writers, magicians, and healers, all of whom are defined by the recognition of their ability to bring divine power and wisdom directly to bear on human problems.

The charismatic leaders are specialists trained in the arts of healing disease or summoning spirits. They are employed by families or communities to deal with particular needs, or assist in rituals of renewal. If they are particularly successful, they gather a clientele which can become a new sect, perhaps centered on the specialists' tutelary god.

There are other types of popular specialists as well, such as fortune tellers and geomancers to select sites for graves and buildings (*see* FENG-SHUI). In addition, Taoist priests and Buddhist monks are brought into popular religion as ritualists, in roles different from those they play in their orthodox communities.

5. **Rituals.** The rituals of popular religion are basically offerings of incense and food to the gods, both in reverence and in hope of favorable response to prayers. The gods are believed to partake of the essence of these offerings, after which the food that is sacrificed may be eaten by the devotees to their health and well-being. Thus, the model for ritual is the communal meal which establishes mutual obligation and support. The deity residing in its temple and the ancestral spirit in its tablet on the household altar are treated as guests at such a meal.

Different types of offerings are presented in different situations. In the home incense may be offered daily before the ancestral tablet, with food and even a whole meal added on festival days. Popular deities are offered incense on every visit, and cooked meat, vegetables, rice, and dumplings at festivals, and perhaps on the first and fifteenth of the lunar month as well. Ghosts of the dead are presented with uncooked food at their gravesites, or at places they are believed to haunt.

These offerings are presented in accord with a cycle of annual festivals marking each turn of the year, beginning with the most important, the New Year festival. The birthdays of temple gods are celebrated with offerings, processions, special rituals, and the performance of popular operas to entertain both gods and men. In addition, at intervals usually calculated in units of seven years, local communities might sponsor ceremonies of community renewal *(chiao)* involving several days of elaborate food offerings, rituals by Taoist priests, and operas.

There is also a variety of occasional rituals performed to meet special needs for both individuals and communities: masses for the spirits of the dead in purgatory, carried out by Buddhist monks or lay reciters, exorcism of disease-bringing demons, séances by spirit-mediums, etc. In addition, spirit-writing, which is widespread among all classes, involves elaborate rituals of bowing, offering, invocation, petition, and transcription.

All these different kinds of ritual are intended to facilitate communication between gods and men, and bring recognition and blessings to both.

6. **Values and ethics.** The chief values in Chinese popular religion are health, a full lifespan, prosperity, family harmony, continuation of the family line, and protection from calamity. For the more pious these values include a quick passage through purgatory, followed by a good rebirth on earth, or direct admittance to AMIDA Buddha's paradise in the west, the PURE LAND. That is to say, popular values for the most part are pragmatic, this-worldly, and social.

The ethical principles through which one can attain these values are FILIAL PIETY, reciprocal consideration, loyalty to family and friends, honesty, frugality, industriousness, and piety. These principles are derived both from Confucianism and Buddhism and from the necessities of peasant life.

It is generally believed that after death one aspect of the soul goes to purgatory, there to be punished for its sins according to the principle of karmic retribution. There are ten courts in purgatory, each presided over by a judge who fits the suffering to the crime. Passage through purgatory can be ameliorated through the transfer of merit money by Buddhist rituals. When its guilt has been purged, the soul advances to the tenth court, where the form of its next existence is decided.

Particularly in popular sects of Buddhist origin it is believed that members can go directly to paradise. However, this may involve a more strict regimen than is true for popular religion in general, including a vegetarian diet, meditation, and the study of scriptures. *See* WHITE LOTUS SOCIETY.

Bibliography. E. M. Ahern, *The Cult of the Dead in a Chinese Village* (1973); P. C. Baity, *Religion in a Chinese Town* (1975); C. B. Day, *Chinese Peasant Cults* (1940); W. Eberhard, *Guilt and Sin in Traditional China* (1967); J. J. M. de Groot, *The Religious System of China,* 6 vols. (1892-1910); H. Maspero, "The Mythology of Modern China," J. Hackin *et al.*, eds., *Asiatic Mythology* (n.d.), pp. 252-384; L. G. Thompson, *Chinese Religion: An Introduction,* 2nd ed. (1975); C. K. Yang, *Religion in Chinese Society* (1967). D. L. OVERMYER

CHRIST krīst (Ch—Gr; lit. "the anointed one" [*chriō*—"to rub on, anoint"]). The title given to JESUS in the NT, indicating that his followers regarded him as the MESSIAH whom God had promised in the OT. It soon came to be used as a personal name for Jesus. K. CRIM

CHRISTADELPHIANS (Ch). Denomination founded by John Thomas (1805–71). Emigrating from England to New York as a young man, Thomas first joined the followers of Thomas and ALEXANDER CAMPBELL, founders of the CHRISTIAN CHURCH (DISCIPLES OF CHRIST). He broke with them over his affirmation of the necessity of baptismal immersion and his rejection of the immortality of the soul, believing that the Bible teaches only the resurrection of the dead. He established an independent following, which took the name Christadelphians ("Brethren of Christ") when, during the Civil War, their opposition to military service necessitated denominational identity.

The Bible is the only Christadelphian creed. Believers stress the application of biblical prophecy to contemporary events. They reject the Trinity and the doctrine of a pre-existent Christ who took human form, saying that Jesus is the son of God, not God the Son. They are strongly MILLENARIAN, and believe that the wicked are annihilated.

The basic unit is the local congregation, called an ecclesia. There is no paid ministry, and the groups usually meet in homes or rented halls. Its early appeal was largely to the working-class, but it is now more broadly based. In the 1970s there were about 20,000 Christadelphians in the U.S., and about the same number in Great Britain. Ecclesias are also found in other British Commonwealth countries and Germany.

Bibliography. B. R. Wilson, *Sects and Society* (1961).
R. S. ELLWOOD

CHRISTIAN CHURCHES (Disciples of Christ). A Protestant church group which originated on the American frontier during the early nineteenth century.

Foremost among the founders were Barton Stone and ALEXANDER CAMPBELL, Presbyterians who reacted against sectarian frontier religion and urged a union of all Christians founded upon a restoration of NT Christianity. They advocated adult baptism by immersion, weekly observance of the Lord's Supper, and autonomy of the local congregation.

During the second half of the nineteenth century disputes erupted, and by 1906 a separately recognized group called Churches of Christ had emerged, distinctive in their rejection of the use of musical instruments in worship. They are conservative, interpreting the NT as the source of all that is permissible for worship and belief. They also believe that there is no biblical justification for organizations beyond the local congregation. (Beginning in 1849, a number of national organizations for Sunday schools and foreign missions had been formed.)

Another division began during the early twentieth century, generally along conservative/progressive lines but with the significant new issues of open membership (accepting as members those who had not been immersed as adults), modern approaches to biblical interpretation, and ecumenical activities. The progressive wing has formed the Christian Church (Disciples of Christ).

Bibliography. L. McAllister and W. E. Tucker, *Journey in Faith* (1975). R. L. HARRISON

CHRISTIAN SCIENCE. Religious movement native to the U.S.

1. **History.** The Church of Christ (Scientist) was founded by MARY BAKER EDDY (1821–1910), a semi-invalid for much of her early life, who believed she had been healed after a severe injury in 1866. For the previous four years she had been learning from Phineas P. Quimby, who allegedly effected amazing cures without medicine. One of the most heated controversies surrounding Mrs. Eddy is the relationship between her teachings and those of Quimby. Was she indebted to him or vice versa? "Outside" accounts generally accept the former position, and "inside" accounts always adopt the latter. Quimby died in 1866 and later in that year Mrs. Eddy had her healing experience, which she subsequently described as the discovery of Christian Science. From this moment on she dedicated her life to an emphasis on the healing aspect of Christianity. In 1875 she completed the first edition of *Science and Health with Key to the Scriptures*. On August 23, 1879, the Church of Christ (Scientist) was incorporated and given a charter. The headquarters was to be in Boston, and the stated purpose was "to commemorate the word and works of our Master, which should reinstate primitive Christianity and its lost element of healing." Mrs. Eddy became the pastor of the revered Mother Church and wrote the *Manual of the Mother Church,*

which continues to govern the now worldwide movement. On December 3, 1910, Mrs. Eddy "passed on," having taught that there is no death. Control of the church was left with a self-perpetuating board of directors, its first members appointed by Mrs. Eddy.

2. **Practice.** Christian Science is highly centralized. Mrs. Eddy's control remains for perpetuity through *Science and Health* and the *Manual.* Though Mrs. Eddy at first preached in the services, she stipulated that the Bible and *Science and Health* would be pastor of all the Christian Science services. Thus no sermon is preached. Prescribed portions of the Bible and *Science and Health* are read by the second and first readers, respectively. (Since *Science and Health* is keyed to the King James Version, this is tne only version read in services. Privately, members may read other translations.) Hymns are sung from the official hymnal and silent as well as audible prayers are offered. It is expected that each branch church will operate a reading room where one may borrow, buy, or read literature such as the *Christian Science Monitor, Christian Science Journal*, and *Christian Science Sentinel.* The office closest to pastor is that of practitioner, filled by a man or woman who has received special education in Christian Science and devotes full time to healing. At Wednesday services in the churches members testify concerning their healings.

3. **Beliefs.** The doctrines of Christian Science are often confusing to the outsider and require careful study. The basic premise is that God is divine Mind, the "divine Principle of all that really is." Mind and Spirit are eternal and real; matter is an illusion subject to decay and dissolution. Since evil has to do with matter, evil is unreal—an illusion. An often-quoted paragraph from Mrs. Eddy is appropriate: "All reality is in God and His creation, harmonious and eternal. That which He creates is good, and He makes all that is made. Therefore the only reality of sin, sickness, or death is the awful fact that unrealities seem real to human, erring belief, until God strips off their disguise. They are not true, because they are not of God." It is obvious that Christian Science does not ignore what it considers to be unreal, but it does attempt to overcome this error by prayer and spiritual development. This results, in Mrs. Eddy's teaching, in health, happiness, and holiness. "Healing" then is not actually "miraculous"; it is divinely natural. Heaven is harmony and spirituality; hell is the reign of mortal, carnal belief. The divinity of Jesus Christ is accepted but not his deification; when Christian Science speaks of the Trinity, it does not mean three persons but rather the unity of Father, Son, and Holy Spirit. No sacraments are celebrated.

Bibliography. N. Beasley, *The Cross and the Crown,* (1952); C. S. Braden, *Christian Science Today* (1958); D. John, *The Christian Science Way of Life* (1962). G. H. Shriver

CHRISTIANITY. The religion of those who believe in and follow Jesus Christ. Numbering almost one billion members, it is the largest of the world religions and is represented in most areas of the globe.

1. History
2. Scripture and teachings
3. Social institutions
4. Major branches
5. Ethics and customs
6. Rituals and worship
7. Festivals and seasons
8. Arts and architecture
9. Current issues and trends
   Bibliography

1. **History.** Christianity developed when a group of Jews two thousand years ago gathered around the rabbi Jesus of Nazareth. After they had seen him executed, they regathered to proclaim that he had risen from the dead. The fact that he was a Rabbi and that they were Jews has colored most of Christian life and history.

As Jews, the Christians were monotheists; that is, they believed that there was only one God. For them this God was the Lord of Israel in whom Jews believed, and they certified their own faith in this Lord by taking over and continuing many aspects of Jewish belief. Their early gatherings were on the soil of Israel, especially in Jerusalem and Galilee. At first they met in the Synagogues, and then carried over many features of synagogue worship into their own worship. The sacred scriptures of Israel, which they later called the Old Testament, became charter documents of the transformed faith. With very few exceptions, Christians ever since have seen the Hebrew Scriptures to be the Word of God or a witness to the Word of God alongside the documents of Christian beginnings called the New Testament.

Jesus of Nazareth, who was born about 4 B.C.—the curious date results from later calendar revision—recognized a call to a special mission almost thirty years later. For about three years he exercised this ministry entirely in the land of Israel, though the earliest records envision that faith in him was intended to be proclaimed in all the world. Some of these records, called Gospels, tell of his challenge to the existing religious authorities. They report his crucifixion as a result of conflict with Jewish leadership and under Roman powers who then dominated Israel. While the reasons for his sentencing are not wholly clear in those records, Christians soon began to claim that his death was an act of sacrifice and love for them. Somehow through it they were made right with the God of Israel whom Jesus called *Abba* or Father. When they experienced his Resurrection from the dead they proclaimed that God had thus put his seal on the sacrifice of Christ and, because of it, promised victory over death and the enemies of their soul.

Weeks after the resurrection they gathered for the festival of Pentecost in Jerusalem. Special signs of the power of God, the Holy Spirit, then came to them, and they became a defined new body, soon to be called "the CHURCH," or "called out" people. From this event Christians began to move beyond Israel, first through Jews of the DIASPORA or dispersion. Thanks chiefly to the ministry of the convert Saul, who became PAUL the APOSTLE, they converted Gentiles throughout Asia Minor and in parts of Europe. These apostles preached that Jesus was the promised MESSIAH or Christ, the anointed one of Israel who was being rejected by most Jews. This roused antagonism; soon Christians distanced themselves from their parent faith. After the destruction of Jerusalem by the Romans in A.D. 70 the breach between the two peoples became formal and permanent. In later centuries few Jews ever converted to Christianity, and the two faiths became rivals. As Christians outnumbered Jews and came to dominance, the normal relationship of the two was one of repression and often persecution by Christians. (*See* ANTI-SEMITISM.) Anti-Jewish Christians at their worst put Jews to death for refusing to accept Jesus as the Christ; at their best they segregated Jews in GHETTOS. In recent times repentant Christians have tried to overcome the separation not by seeking to merge the two faiths but by reappropriating neglected Jewish elements in Christianity and by affirming the integrity of Jewish faith.

As a largely Gentile faith Christianity also came into conflict with the Roman Empire. Romans were tolerant of the myriad sects and cults that flourished in the early Christian centuries, and would likely have overlooked this new group that appeared to be one more Jewish sect. However, Christians refused the minimal act of commitment to the emperor, which would have called for them to offer him a kind of religious respect. As a fast-growing and often apparently subversive cult with suspicious rites, Christianity soon became a target of persecutions by emperors from the time of Nero (d. A.D 68) into the fourth century. Many believers were harassed and some were martyred (*see* MARTYRS, CHRISTIAN), but their oppression only led to more growth. During the first three centuries after Christ, though they retained the scriptures of Israel, Christians began to adopt Greek ways of thinking and speaking. Their own NT was written in a vernacular form of Greek. They also adopted Roman ways of governing and acting.

The conversion of the emperor CONSTANTINE and a number of his official acts, culminating in the Edict of Milan in A.D. 313, was a turning point for Christians. Their faith became established as the formal religion of the Romar Empire. An edict of the emperor Theodosius in A.D. 380 went further: now the once persecuted Christians became the persecutors who allowed no other faith on the soil of the empire. This policy, with many variants, lasted almost everywhere that Christians were dominant until the late eighteenth century in America, after which time the civil and religious spheres began to be separated.

From the fourth century on then, the church tied its fate to the destiny of the Roman Empire. Now called Catholic, which implied that it was worldwide in scope and that it reached into all aspects of life, its head was the Roman pope. But as the fortunes of Rome declined and the power of empire moved eastward to Constantinople, Christianity became increasingly divided into western and eastern forms. The thought patterns and styles of governance of the two forms began to differ; the two led separate histories and formed differing civil allegiances. After centuries of such drift, a split occurred in 1054 between the eastern and western churches. The east usually is called Eastern ORTHODOX and the west ROMAN CATHOLIC. Although in the twentieth century new cordiality has appeared across east-west lines, the breach remains.

During the centuries between 380 and 1054 Christians continued two major forms of activity. The first of these was missionary. (*See* MISSIONS, CHRISTIAN.) In the fifth century PATRICK was credited with saving Ireland. Sometimes kings experienced CONVERSION and carried their people with them into the fold. The baptism of King Clovis in 496 led to the conversion of the Franks, on soil that became France. After 597 England turned Christian under the influence of Augustine of Canterbury. In the eighth century Boniface was an instrument for the conversion of Germany. In the East, Cyril and Methodius carried on converting activities in the ninth century, as the Slavs came to faith. Russia entered the Christian orbit in the tenth century, rising to such prominence that eventually Moscow came to call itself "the Third Rome." (*See* RUSSIAN ORTHODOX CHURCH.)

The other activity that influenced all later Christian life was the development of statements of faith in a sequence of ecumenical church COUNCILS. (*See* CREEDS AND CONFESSIONS.) At these events BISHOPS gathered, often in the company of the emperor and civil officials, to debate and formulate teachings. While the first of these councils was held at Jerusalem in Paul's lifetime, the larger assemblages began at NICAEA in 325. Constantine himself presided at that gathering, at which the church fathers concentrated on the issue of Jesus' divine sonship. In 381 the church had to face up to conflicts between Rome and "New Rome" at Constantinople. Typical of subsequent councils was one held at Chalcedon in 451; its major achievement was a statement that conceptually held together the divine and human natures of Jesus Christ. (*See* CHALCEDONIAN DEFINITION.)

While Christians had control of their own destiny as missionaries and creedmakers, they were threatened from without by the rise of a rival faith, ISLAM, after the seventh century. The prophet MUHAMMAD proclaimed himself the newest bearer of the divine message and the successor to both Jewish prophets and Jesus himself. At first Christians underestimated the new faith, but they made no more mistakes of that order after the invasion of the Iberian peninsula. The victory by Charles Martel over Arab invaders at Poitiers, or Tours, in France in 732 represented the beginning of Islamic setbacks in Europe. For eight more centuries, however, Catholics had to remain wary of Muslim advances from the southeast toward Vienna. Much of Eastern Christendom came under Muslim dominance, and remains so to the present.

In the eyes of many, the Middle Ages were the classic period of Western Catholicism. The pope was the peer of the emperor, the bishops were at the side of princes, the church became a major landholder. Many men and women entered RELIGIOUS ORDERS as monks and nuns. (*See* MONASTICISM.) From their monastic houses where they had kept learning and piety alive during the "Dark Ages" (sixth through tenth centuries), they engaged in reform and new intellectual endeavors. From the Muslim enemy they appropriated the thought of the Greek philosopher Aristotle and used it to develop the theology of SCHOLASTICISM. This synthesis of faith and reason has supported Catholic thought for seven centuries since the death of the greatest scholastic, THOMAS AQUINAS (d. 1274).

The Middle Ages saw the building of the European CATHEDRALS, the expression of art in the service of the church, and various new endeavors to spread good works. Most notable among these were the efforts of monks like FRANCIS OF ASSISI (d. 1226), who founded the FRANCISCAN Order. Through these centuries there was also a flowering of CHRISTIAN MYSTICISM, as gifted religious geniuses tried to achieve spiritual union with God.

The Catholic synthesis was not to go unchallenged, however. The supremacy of the pope was called into question in the fifteenth century, when a new school of philosophers questioned the assumptions of Thomas Aquinas and new church councils began to claim authority alongside that of the pope. Beginning around 1517 through the activities of the German monk MARTIN LUTHER, western Europe churned with efforts at reform. Building on reform attempts by the councils and the individual heroism of the Czech JOHN HUSS, the Englishman JOHN WYCLIFFE, and other pioneers, the reformers of the sixteenth century came into conflict with Rome and formed separate Protestant churches across northwest Europe. (*See* PROTESTANTISM.) Under King Henry VIII the Church of England refused to obey the pope and became independent. Scotland, the Netherlands, much of Switzerland, all of Scandinavia, many territories in Germany, and large factions in France followed the Protestant lead. Mediterranean Christians remained Catholic, however, and the Eastern church largely ignored the disputes and schisms. (*See* REFORMATION, PROTESTANT; REFORMATION, CATHOLIC.)

Many reasons lay behind the Reformation. While Catholics were busy reforming their own church (later Catholic historians have admitted that moral corruption and abuses were widespread), most Protestants contended that they were interested in reexamining more than morals. They repudiated the authority of the pope, advanced the cause of the BIBLE as the sole authority, and gave new stress to the idea that God rescues men and women through grace and mercy, as a gift, and not because of human achievement. (*See* SALVATION.) The rising nationalism of northern European nations also played a part in the decision of churches there to separate from Rome. From the sixteenth to the twentieth century the pattern of divisions increased, though in modern times the ECUMENICAL MOVEMENT has begun to bring churches into concord and unity.

The story of the Christian church in the past three or four centuries has been one of advance through missions into all the world, of mixed responses to nationalism and modern totalitarianisms, and of setbacks in the face of competing ideologies. The Renaissance of the sixteenth century and the Enlightenment of the eighteenth put a premium on the autonomous human individual. With the rise of science, older explanations of nature no longer sufficed. Some philosophical movements announced "the DEATH OF GOD" and others found talk about God to be meaningless. To some analysts the whole process appeared to be secularization, the turning from transcendent or divine orders to simply mundane concerns. To others the word "modernization" better described events, since modernization meant that Christianity was not being removed but relocated. Christians were still free to act in matters that dealt with personal and family life, with leisure activities and residentially based concerns. But it was harder for them to act in the ever more powerful social and corporate worlds of modern politics, industry, and letters.

Despite these new hazards, and despite the frustration of Christian missions in huge portions of the world like China, the decline of religious practice in the old heartland of Europe, and ongoing divisions in their ranks, late in the twentieth century there were more Christians than ever before. The century saw signs of vitality in the ecumenical movement, in agencies for Christian service, in revivals of theology and lay activity, and in growth in some parts of the world, most notably in Africa. (*See* CHRISTIANITY IN AFRICA; CHRISTIANITY IN ASIA.)

2. **Scripture and teachings.** Christians look to the BIBLE for inspiration, substantiating the Muslim designation of Christians as PEOPLE OF THE BOOK. Most of them consider the Old and New Testaments to be divinely inspired documents, in which God speaks. Some Protestants tend to identify the Bible with the Word of God and to see it as inerrant. (*See* EVANGELICALS; FUNDAMENTALISM.) Moderate Protestants and most Catholics quote the Scriptures to the effect that Jesus is the Word of God, and that the Bible is a witness to that Word. While these see the Bible as the chief if not only source and norm for church teaching, they believe that it is authoritative only as a guide to faith and salvation. Most Christians own a Bible or at least the NT for their personal use. Preaching usually takes the form of a contemporary comment on biblical stories and teachings.

In recent centuries scholars have applied tools of literary and historical analysis to the Bible. They find multiple authorship for many books listed under one author, such as the prophecy of Isaiah. They do not believe that many of the people whose names head NT writings—John, PETER, and the like—did in fact produce them, and they point to inconsistencies in texts and treatments of events. To conservatives such biblical criticism looks destructive of authority and faith. Christian critics, on the other hand, argue that their work only enhances the true meaning of the Bible, helping readers learn more about the original intention and context of the writers.

Through the centuries Christians have come to cherish postbiblical authors and have turned to them as authorities. Thus the creeds, for which no one claims divine authorship, may serve as guidelines when CLERGY are ordained to their office and take their vows. Christians tend to show great respect for the fathers of the early church, most notably AUGUSTINE, who in his theology outlined a charter for Christendom. Protestant groups look back on the writings of their founders as having special weight. The written legacy of saints, devotional leaders, and thoughtful philosophers command respect. Catholics and Orthodox Christians particularly tend to grant high status to tradition as an authority alongside the Bible. But all these receive a different kind of attention from that accorded the Bible. When twentieth century Christians, divided by denominations, cultures, and outlooks, began to meet each other in ecumenical conversation, they often found that the Bible alone provided their common language.

It is possible to distill certain core teachings from the Bible and the creeds. Christians are theists; they believe that behind the visible processes of the world there is a divine being or person. They are monotheists in insisting that this originator and preserver of creation is one Lord. Theirs is a biblical faith because they say that this one Lord is the Lord of Israel. They are Christian because they see this Lord as the Father of the divine and human figure of Jesus Christ. Most of them are trinitarian because they recognize that this one God is a divine unity of the Father, the Son, and the Holy Spirit who calls together and guides the church. (*See* TRINITY.)

Christians believe that humans are fallen and are in need of rescue. While God has guided them by giving them his law, they despair of becoming acceptable to him through following it. The creeds assert that God took on human form in Jesus, who humbled himself by dying as a criminal on behalf of others. God vindicated him by raising him from the dead. People who come to him in faith receive the gift of grace that enables them to serve God and to live in peace with him and with each other. Most creeds conclude with belief in a life to come. Christians claim that God is the Lord of history and that history will have an end, with either a literal or figurative SECOND COMING of Jesus Christ.

3. Social institutions. Because of its worldwide character and its internal divisions, it is hard to speak of Christian institutions and administration in an inclusive sense. Virtually all Christians consider themselves to be members of a single CHURCH. Some of them have regarded their own organization as having a monopoly on Christian truth. Thus Roman Catholicism has taught that "outside the church there is no salvation." Many members have taken "church" there to mean the company of those who are obedient to Rome. Eastern Orthodoxy claims that its tradition is the distinctive and true perpetuator of Christ's original church. Many small Protestant groups believe that they alone are faithful to the norms of the first Christian generation. But even among those who make such claims most persistently, there has also usually been some sort of faith that an "invisible" church exists. That church is made up of true believers who belong to church bodies that do not have all their truth to themselves. The modern ecumenical movement has helped to moderate all exclusive claims, stimulate a general appreciation for the integrity of many other Christian churches, and encourage a belief that a fuller expression of the single Church lies ahead.

This whole or universal Church is broken into many parts. Thus in the modern world not only East versus West or Protestant versus Catholic schisms determine the outlines of the Church. There are hundreds of "denominations" or separated churches. (Sometimes the more withdrawn and intense of these are called "sects.") But denominationalism is not the only pattern. Christian church bodies are usually divided into regional units. In Catholic, Orthodox, ANGLICAN, and some Protestant bodies these are called dioceses and are under the rule of a bishop. Many churches employ patterns of governance such as synods, councils, or conventions. These determine matters relatively democratically. Smaller than dioceses are local parishes or congregations, which have become the standard small units for Christian life. At the head of most of these is a priest or a specially called minister.

Most Christian groups divide their ranks into CLERGY and laity. The clergy have special tasks, though they are not always regarded as being especially holy or as having a higher status than laity in God's sight. Ordinarily theirs are the main tasks of presiding over the rites and SACRAMENTS, doing most of the proclaiming or preaching of the Word, and undertaking many kinds of administration. In most Catholic bodies (Roman, Orthodox, Anglican), the priesthood, which was restricted only to men, is a special order. ORDINATION confers extraordinary divine powers, even if those who hold them are fallible and even corrupt.

At the summit of the Catholic half of Christianity is the bishop of Rome, the pontiff or pope who, according to tradition, is a successor to Jesus' apostle Peter. Final authority rests with him, though since the Second VATICAN COUNCIL (1962-65) he is to share it collegially with bishops. In the First Vatican Council the bishops declared that when speaking officially in matters of faith and morals and when making a special claim, he is infallible. INFALLIBILITY, however, has been invoked only once since the council and applied only once to declarations from before 1870. In Catholicism a College of Cardinals, made up of highly placed bishops, serves as electors of the pope. (*See* PAPACY.)

The Catholic churches believe that all bishops are in APOSTOLIC SUCCESSION, that an unbroken line of ordainers have assured continuity in the church since the first generation. Many Protestants are ruled by bishops or presidents who possess extensive authority but for whom no such claims are made. Many Christians also perpetuate the biblical offices of PRESBYTERS, or lay elders, and DEACONS, who share in spiritual and administrative tasks. For most believers the representative and most accessible leaders are the parish clergy, some of whom in modern Protestantism and in some sectors of Anglicanism may be women. In Protestant churches the congregations may call these clergy to serve them. In some Protestant traditions the congregation has been the highest authority not only in the calling of leadership but in every other respect as well.

Christian polities draw their names from the kind of jurisdictions they favor. Those that have bishops are called episcopal, after the Greek word for bishop. Those that make the most of presbyters and lay leadership and often gather in synods are presbyterian. Where the local church is autonomous, they are called congregational. It must be said that the demands of bureaucratic life in the modern church have tended to make the polities appear more and more like each other, despite differences over their theoretical meaning and rationales.

Through the centuries Christians have devised many instruments for carrying on their work. Among these are the RELIGIOUS ORDERS in Catholicism, the monastic groups like the JESUITS, FRANCISCANS, DOMINICANS, and BENEDICTINES. They tend to specialize in one or another form of service, be it teaching, hospital work, or prayerful contemplation. In the modern world Christians band together in voluntary associations, many of them lay-controlled agencies for promoting missions or engaging in acts of charity. Christians claim much of the credit for pioneering in the development of hospitals, nursing agencies, universities, and other educational institutions.

4. Major branches. The three fundamental Christian divisions are ROMAN CATHOLIC, with over 550 million members, ORTHODOX, with about 85 million, and PROTESTANT with 320 million. The largest Protestant element, the LUTHERAN CHURCHES, are 70 million strong, chiefly in northern Europe and North America. The ANGLICAN Communion, with about 40 million adherents, is strong in England and North America, but thanks to missionary efforts during the imperial period it is represented as widely as any Protestant group. BAPTISTS, strongest in the United States but growing rapidly in the developing nations, are congregational in organization. Similar in polity is the CHRISTIAN CHURCH (DISCIPLES OF CHRIST), an attempt by nineteenth century Americans to reproduce primitive Christian simplicity. METHODIST CHURCHES, heirs of a renewal in the eighteenth century Church of England, have spread from England and America into many mission territories. Presbyterians, REFORMED, and Congregational Churches, many of them shaped by reformer JOHN CALVIN, have had great impact on English and American life. In some nations, like Canada, a "United Church" has grown up as an effort to unite some of these bodies.

The Protestant world has been fertile in production of new churches. Most Christians regard the healing-minded Church of Christ, Scientist (*see* CHRISTIAN SCIENCE) and the Mormons (Church of Jesus Christ of LATTER-DAY SAINTS) to be unorthodox spin-offs. They totally reject the JEHOVAH'S WITNESSES, a third nineteenth century American group, even as Jehovah's Witnesses reject all of them. Needless to say, Christian Scientists and Mormons consider themselves to be the true embodiments of Christianity.

More conventional are the PENTECOSTAL CHURCHES, vibrant and fast-growing modern bodies that try to reproduce the fervor and some practices that fell into neglect after early Christian times. Chief among these is GLOSSOLALIA or "speaking in tongues." The SOCIETY OF FRIENDS, or Quakers, born of radical English Protestantism, stresses the "inner light"; they are well known as pacifists. SEVENTH-DAY ADVENTISTS, who expect the imminent return of Christ, are distinctive because they worship on the sabbath, or Saturday. They see the choice of Sunday by other Christians to be an illegitimate departure. The SALVATION ARMY is known for its fervor and its urban humanitarianism. At the far left of Protestantism is the UNITARIAN UNIVERSALIST ASSOCIATION, which rejects most Christian orthodoxy and does not believe in the divinity of Christ.

While the vast majoriy of Protestants belong to these named groups, hundreds of variations among and beyond them are the despair of those who try to enumerate Protestant groups.

5. Ethics and customs. Living as they have in many cultures, Christians have developed a bewildering variety of ethical patterns and habits. At the heart of all their efforts is the idea that they should be responsive to the divine law, as they read and hear it in the Scriptures. But most of them do not believe that it is possible to obey the whole law of God and thus please the Holy One. As Christians they believe that Jesus, far from coming to destroy the Law (*see* TORAH), fulfilled it, and kept it perfectly on their behalf. While remaining responsible to God, Christians thus claim a new basis for ethics in Christ.

The core of this moral response is centered in the idea of love, a term that appears with astonishing frequency in the NT. This love, called *agape,* is spontaneous, unmotivated by anything it finds attractive in its object, the kind of love that God showed sinful humans. Now they are to show it to others who may not be worthy of it: those in need, the sick, the lonely. The NT directed Christians to show this love chiefly to each other, to the "household of faith." But there as elsewhere Christians were taught to let the love of God control them, to live sacrificially for others.

Through the centuries Christian influence has been strongly supportive of the family, which it sees to be established by God. Children are taught to be obedient to parents. Until recently much familial teaching stressed the authority of the male and the submissiveness of the female, but twentieth century Christianity has spawned numerous feminist impulses. These lead believers back to biblical sources that stress companionship, not dominance. Within the family, Christians have called for restriction of genital activity to marital partners, but have often clouded marital sex itself with negative connotations.

More problematic have been Christian attitudes to the state. One element of the tradition, deriving from Romans 13, asks believers to be obedient to higher authorities. Response to this has turned many Christians into passive citizens who submit even to evil rule. As is the case with most religions, Christianity in practice tends to endorse the *status quo,* to side with conservatives, and to bless the cannon in "just wars." But there is also a contrasting element, drawing on the prophetic tradition and calling Christians to utter judgment on all human achievement, including the state and the political order.

Christians have experimented with many economic patterns, from the communalism described as a transient experience in the biblical book of Acts, through various millennial or utopian communities, to modern individualism. Much of the impetus for modern capitalism has come from European and American Christian ethical resources. These call for careful stewardship of resources, unwillingness to waste time or opportunity, and a sense that Christians should live out their divine calling in the mundane world. While sociologist Max Weber spoke of this as the Protestant Ethic, other Christians in the industrializing nations have also lived on the basis of it. The resultant capitalist order does not go without challenge, however, particularly by Christians in developing nations, where some sort of socialism seems to them to have more potential for achieving economic justice.

Various Christian groups issue precise guidelines for behavior and custom, but these differ so much that it is hard to generalize about them. Thus for centuries Roman Catholics refrained from eating meat on Friday. Some sects like the AMISH and the MENNONITE urge extremely simple ways of living upon their largely rural memberships. Many Protestant groups forbid the use of intoxicating liquors or stimulants. Seventh-Day Adventists and others are vegetarians. In general Christians have taught restraint in earthly enjoyments; they are to shun mere worldliness and sensual pleasures. At the same time, they are to find and express joy in simple and harmless delights.

6. **Rituals and worship.** The two fundamental and most widespread Christian devotional activities are gathering for common worship and practicing private prayer. In the earliest church most believers changed the day of main worship from Saturday to SUNDAY. They were to come together to celebrate weekly the resurrection of Jesus from the dead and to face the beginning of the week in a kind of "festival of light" on Sunday. Those who neglected to worship were marginal members; they occasioned great concern among the faithful. If believers were, as they claimed, members of the single Body of Christ, they had to know each other and come into his presence in worship.

Like other religions, Christianity developed and still celebrates a variety of rites. At Sunday worship there is normally a homily or sermon; a presiding cleric or, on occasion, a lay person pronounces words of judgment or encouragement based on the Bible. From the beginning, Christians have been singers, and have welcomed the music of choirs. (*See* MUSIC, IN CHRISTIANITY.) Worship allows for expressions of common concern, for intercessory prayer, and the giving of gifts. The overwhelming majority of Christians, especially in Catholic traditions, see the sacred meal as the climax of worship on Sundays and feast days. This meal, which goes by the name of the EUCHARIST, the Mass, Holy Communion, or the Lord's Supper, derives from and memorializes a last meal Jesus shared with his disciples. Held in the Jewish PASSOVER season, the meal from the first season carried connotations of the sacrifice he made of his life. The Gospel accounts also pictured it as a foretaste of a heavenly banquet, a feast to enjoy. But Christians have associated it with many other ideas that come from biblical sources; it is a remembrance, an act of dedication, a sign of communion; a mark of thanksgiving, as believers eat bread and drink wine. While its meal has inspired as much argument as it has devotion, at heart Christianity believes that in a special way Jesus Christ is present in the rite.

The Lord's Supper is called a sacrament, which means a divinely instituted act that uses visible means along with the sacred word to effect grace. The other sacrament enjoyed by all Christians except the Friends is BAPTISM. This is a washing or immersion which uses water as a mark of entrance into the divine kingdom, initiation into the church, sealing of the covenant with God, or for the forgiving of sins. Baptist bodies insist that baptism wait until believers can come to active faith and express it for themselves. Most other Christians baptize infants who cannot consciously participate in the rite. Many of these bodies follow baptism with a CONFIRMATION of faith in later years and, in the case of adult converts, expect a conscious expression of faith to be associated with baptism.

Most Protestants engage in other sacred acts but do not join Catholics in speaking of them as sacraments. Among these are marriage, ordination, PENANCE or confession and forgiveness, and the use of oils at the time of death (*see* UNCTION). The Catholic tradition has tended to stress that sacraments work *ex opere operato,* which means that they work their effects by the mere act. This idea struck Protestant critics as too magical or mechanical, and they have accented instead the faith people bring to sacramental life. Some groups, notably Baptists, prefer to call even baptism and the Lord's Supper "ordinances" rather than "sacraments."

Christians are expected to worship also when they are not gathered in public. The characteristic form of such devotion is private prayer. (*See* PRAYER, CHRISTIAN.) In prayer the believer mentally or verbally converses with the unseen divine power, and God somehow hears and acts, though not always in the sought-after ways. For some Christians such prayer is vivid and highly personal; and their interpretations of divine responses are precise and confident. Other believers express a more generalized sense that their prayer teaches them to conform to the divine will, that somehow they become part of the activity of a God who is Lord of all time but who may not necessarily intervene in supernatural ways in daily life. The difference shows up particularly in the matter of healing. One school of thought tends to minimize the role of technical medicine and to expect miracles that lead to organic healing. (*See* FAITH HEALING.) The other calls upon attitudes of response that bring about a sense of assurance that God is active, that medicine operates under divine auspices, and that one's spiritual outlook on the body plays a part in healing.

Intimate prayer is common in the Christian home at bedtime and when people arise, and often at mealtimes, but there are no set hours which all must follow as there are in Islam. Many individuals and families also engage in daily Bible reading. Christians have often nurtured meditation and silence as ways to communicate with God.

7. **Festivals and seasons.** Every sabbath for sabbatarian Christians and every Sunday for the majority are the basic festivals. But just as these days heighten the weeks, so there are other annually commemorated events. Common consent sees greatest importance in three festivals. The first of these is CHRISTMAS, observed on December 25 in the West and twelve days later by most eastern Christians. No one knows in what season Jesus was born, but the December-January date evidently rose to displace old pagan winter rites. Next is the cluster of events that move through GOOD FRIDAY, the day of Jesus' death, to the climactic EASTER, which celebrates his rising again. The early Christians kept a vigil through the night before Easter and performed baptisms during it. At sunrise they observed his resurrection. The date of Easter varies each year, falling on the Sunday following the first full moon after the vernal equinox. Fifty days after Easter is PENTECOST or Whitsunday, an event that recalls the coming of the Holy Spirit at the birth of the church.

Just as there are festive days, so there are especially serious seasons. The four weeks before Christmas make up the season of ADVENT and the six weeks before Easter are the time of LENT. Many Christians have used these periods for fasting, repentance, serious reflection, and preparation for festive joy. In addition to these, Christians observe numerous saints' days to recall the

J. M. Ward

Christianity's central symbol, a cross, this one in front of the monastery of San Agustín, Acolman, Mexico (16th century). The "hands" on the horizontal bar and the skull at the base are pre-Columbian motifs.

lives of exemplary and often martyred Christians of the past. (*See* SAINTS, VENERATION OF; MARTYRS, CHRISTIAN.) In general, Catholic Christianity has made most of these, and it has also enhanced sacred festivals with folk rites of a more secular character. Protestants originally were more austere and shunned festivals because they saw secular and even pagan associations in them. Through the years, however, there has been an increasing understanding of the ritual character of human existence, and Protestants are more observant of annual festivities. (*See* CALENDAR, CHRISTIAN.)

8. **Arts and architecture.** As Jews, the early Christians carried over a reluctance to portray the deity in images, fearing that this might lead to idolatry. But soon they were decorating their gathering places and burial sites with symbolic representations of Jesus and biblical scenes. From these simple beginnings there issued a most impressive lineage of sacred art. From the ancient world come mosaics, while the Eastern church was especially creative in producing ICONS, sacred painted images of Jesus, his mother MARY, and the saints. The house of worship—the basilica of the East and the church or cathedral of the West—allowed the imperial church to be lavish in its visible devotion. For

J. M. Ward

An example of present-day Christian architecture: the Church of St. Augustine, Isleta Pueblo, New Mexico.

centuries most art was devoted to Christian themes, though beginning in the Renaissance even the popes, collectors of art, began to welcome pagan themes. In the modern world Christian art continues, but it is seen chiefly in the sanctuaries.

Even Christians who were wary of icons and images have tended to encourage singing. In modern centuries most of the great Western composers have written masses or motets devoted to church motifs. Johann Sebastian Bach, Wolfgang Amadeus Mozart, and Ludwig van Beethoven head the list, which has continued down to Igor Stravinsky, Leonard Bernstein, and François Poulenc. Similarly much of the literature of the West has been inspired by Christian themes. Dante and Milton wrote epics on such bases, but modern poets like T. S. Eliot and W. H. Auden and novelists like Graham Greene and Walker Percy keep alive the lore of Christianity in the literary world. (*See* Art and Architecture, Christian; Music, in Christianity.)

9. **Current issues and trends.** The first issue for Christians, as it is for every social group including the most sacrificial, is survival. While Christians believe that they should give of themselves for the sake of others, most of them believe that they should not spend the church out of existence. They must devote some resources to the continuation and expansion of the faith.

Especially since the loss of privilege when imperial Christianity ended and church and state were separated, believers have been conscious of their precarious condition—even though they number a billion members. Since no single racial, ethnic, or national bond naturally unites believers, and since many are driven away in totalitarian regimes while others drift away in the conditions of freedom, the senior generation must always act to make up for losses. Some groups are especially aggressive and missionary as they set out to gain the uncommitted to membership, the marginal to nuclear participation, and sometimes, it must be said, the "misplaced" Christians into groups they consider to be more faithful.

While evangelism therefore preoccupies many sectors of the church, for others the chief agenda item is ecumenism, the effort to see unity in the churches. They reason that a divided church is a contradiction of the biblical assertion that there is one Lord, one faith, and one baptism. Such Christians have participated in activities to bring into being councils, federations, mergers, and at the very least new conciliation between still separated groups.

Another set of Christians, whether primarily missionary or ecumenical in outlook, contends that both concerns are too "churchy," too introverted and selfish. The church should live for the sake of the world, should take risks in the social order. In prosperous societies this may mean taking unpopular stands concerning the use of natural resources. In racially divided cultures Christians would work for the dignity of all and reconciliations based on justice. Such Christians also work for peace, and seek to combat hunger and poverty by working for systemic change and justice, even if their activity inconveniences vested interests.

Others see the current Christian problem to be a crisis of meaning. They hear the claim that God is dead, eclipsed, or silent, and see how many spheres of life no longer relate to Christian faith. Because millions ignore the claims and the promises of the church, they want to formulate new systems of meaning based on the old revelation.

In all four instances, Christians tend to argue their case on the basis of the Bible, the recall of the first Christian generation, and the traditions that have grown out of them, relating their efforts to the central figure of Jesus Christ.

Bibliography. R. Bainton, *Christendom,* 2 vols. (1966); K. S. Latourette, *A History of Christianity* (1953), and *A History of the Expansion of Christianity,* 7 vols. (1971); B. A. Gerrish, ed., *The Faith of Christendom: A Source Book of Creeds and Confessions* (1963); J. Pelikan, *The Christian Tradition,* 5 vols. (1971-); H. Küng, *The Church* (1967); E. Troeltsch, *The Social Teachings of the Christian Churches* (1956); H. Chadwick, *The Early Church* (1967); R. M. Grant, *Augustus to Constantine: The Thrust of the Christian Movement into the Roman World* (1970); J. N. D. Kelly, *Early Christian Doctrines* (1968); R. W. Southern, *Western Society and the Church in the Middle Ages* (1970); O. Chadwick, *The Reformation* (1964); J. N. Nichols, *History of Christianity, 1650-1950* (1956); G. R. Cragg, *The Church and the Age of Reason* (1960); A. R. Vidler, *The Church in an Age of Revolution* (1961).

M. E. Marty

CHRISTIANITY IN AFRICA. In 1976 two significant events occurred in the life of the Christian church in Africa. The Association of Third World Theologians was inaugurated in Dar es Salaam, and the All Africa Conference of Churches, comprising 114 member churches from 33 African countries, met in Alexandria and issued a contemporary African Confession of Faith. These events are symbolic of the growing maturity and self-reliance of the churches founded during the nineteenth and twentieth centuries by missionaries from abroad. (*See* Missions, Christian.)

All emerging peoples discover the necessity of rewriting history from their own perspective. The Association of Third World Theologians has called for a new methodology in the writing of church history in Africa, since "missionary history"—the story of the planting and growth of the church from the perspective of the expatriate agents—is now regarded as a special literary genre, a hagiography of yesterday which neglects the larger processes of socio-religious change.

The Confession of Alexandria represents a growing African consensus in regard to the past, as a foundation for the contemporary challenges facing the churches in Africa during the next several decades.

From THE CONFESSION OF ALEXANDRIA

The Christian Community in Africa gives praise to God for His revelation through Jesus Christ, His Son and His constant presence among His people through the Holy Spirit.

As members of Christ's Church in Africa today, we have become conscious of the fact that we are inheritors of a rich tradition.

Our current concern with issues related to:
—economic justice
—the total liberation of men and women from every form of oppression and exploitation, and
—peace in Africa

as well as our contemporary search for authentic responses to Christ as Lord over the whole of our lives have led us to a deeper understanding of the heritage delivered to us by the Fathers of the Early Church in North Africa.

Our commitment to the struggle for human liberation is one of the ways we confess our faith in an Incarnate God, who loved us so much that He came among us in our own human form, suffered, was crucified for our redemption and was raised for our justification. Such undeserved grace evokes a response of love and joy that we are seeking to express and to share in language, modes of spirituality, liturgical forms, patterns of mission and structures of organization that belong uniquely to our own cultural context.

All Africa Conference of Churches, 1976

1. **Phenomenal growth.** For the past fifty years the churches in Africa have been growing faster than on any other continent. This was not always the case. Prior to the European "scramble for Africa" in the last two decades of the nineteenth century, missionary efforts produced meager numerical results. The Coptic Church in Egypt and the Ethiopic Church, the fruits of early Christianity in North Africa, had managed to survive over the centuries in the midst of Islamic expansion, but Western missionary incursions met with limited success. The sixteenth and seventeenth century Portuguese attempt to evangelize Central Africa presents a scenario that was repeated frequently during the early part of the nineteenth century in sub-Saharan Africa. After an initial period of hospitality and tolerance during which a number of Africans were converted, including members of the royal family, the local people gradually discovered the traumatic impact on their culture of Christianity and Western trade, including a heavy trade in slaves. A clash was inevitable. In the sixteenth and seventeenth centuries and until the imposition of colonial rule, this clash resulted in the falling apart of missionary work. With

the advent of colonial power, it was tribal culture that succumbed.

Statistics illustrate this story. In 1875, after several decades of missionary activity, there were fewer than half a million Christians in sub-Saharan Africa. Most of these were freed slaves or misfits and rejects from traditional society who found comfort and release in tiny Christian communities and mission stations. By 1925 their number had swelled to five million or 3 percent of the total population.

2. **The Cross and the sword.** This tenfold increase in numbers from 1875 to 1925 can only be explained by the establishment of Western colonial rule around the turn of the century. As early as the mid-nineteenth century DAVID LIVINGSTONE had envisioned the need for an alliance of Western business, government, and the church to eradicate the slave trade and bring the blessings of "commerce, civilization, and Christianity" to the African continent. A popular aphorism expresses the widespread resentment of Africans today: "First came the traders, then the missionaries, and finally the soldiers."

Christianity served as the social ideology which both justified colonial rule and explained its success. Once colonial rule had been established, Christianity provided attractive new solutions for personal problems, a new religious community which socialized its members into the colonial context, and an avenue for upward mobility in the modern urban sector of society. The seeds of growth which had been planted in the nineteenth and early twentieth centuries—the translation of the BIBLE into almost every major African language, the creation of ecclesiastical structures, the training of an African CLERGY, and the construction of hundreds of hospitals and thousands of schools all over the vast continent—had just begun to bear fruit in the 1920s. By 1980 there were about 100 million Christians in sub-Saharan Africa with an annual growth rate of more than 5 percent, or twice the growth rate of the population. This means that Christians now number between 40 and 45 percent of the total population of this area.

The fastest growing churches are called "African Independent Churches" because their origins lie within Africa rather than outside. These churches now account for 10 to 15 percent of all Christians south of the Sahara and must be seen in part as a product of the ambiguous colonial alliance of cross and sword. On the one hand are those Independent Churches with nationalist origins which separated from mission churches because the foreign missionary personnel resisted the relinquishing of power to African leadership. These churches retain many characteristics of missionary Christianity.

More numerous, on the other hand, are those Independent Churches which resulted from prophetic visions on the part of extraordinary African personalities. (*See* KIMBANGUISM.) These churches, which number well over six thousand, are closer to the traditional African world view and the daily spiritual needs of the masses than are the Mission Churches. Their emphasis on FAITH HEALING, ecstatic PRAYER, indigenous liturgical practices, and traditional forms of leadership and organization give them a more African flavor than the Westernized bureaucratic Mission Churches. Although most Mission Churches have now successfully completed the process of ecclesiastical decolonization in leadership, the task of contextualization—theological, organizational, and liturgical—still lies ahead.

3. **Authenticity.** This task of contextualization is referred to as the search for authenticity. The impetus for this search on the part of Mission Churches derives from at least three sources: competition with the Independent Churches, hostility from cultural nationalists and social revolutionaries, and the personal needs of their own members. The dynamism of the Independent Churches attracts members not only from the non-Christian population but from the Mission Churches as well. Cultural nationalists attack not only the racism and ethnocentrism implicit in the "civilizing mission" but also the universalist claims of the Christian message itself. Both the resurgence of African traditional religious cults and the widespread skepticism of the educated elite reflect the suspicion that Christianity may be a white man's religion incapable of authentic incarnation in African soil.

Theological schools and university departments of religious studies have responded to cultural nationalism by inaugurating programs in the study of AFRICAN TRADITIONAL RELIGION and by the development of a growing body of "African theology" which interprets traditional religions as forms of natural revelation preparatory to the Christian gospel. This emphasis on the continuity of traditional and Christian world views has led to numerous empirical studies of African religions and a much more positive evaluation of Africa's religious heritage than was possible while the churches were under the spell of a colonial mentality. It has also served to correct many of the European ethnocentric and racist views of African culture.

The influence of social revolutionaries far outweighs their numbers. They rightly point out that political independence involved the transfer of power from Europeans to Africans without any fundamental change in the exploitative structures of society or the religious ideology which supports those neo-colonial structures. What is needed, they insist, is not merely a change of the guard, but new economic and political institutions that are neither traditional nor colonial.

The Christian search for authenticity seeks to combine the views of the cultural nationalists and the social revolutionaries. It attempts to incorporate the African heritage critically, and to adapt both this heritage and missionary Christianity to the needs of the future. The relative emphasis on the past or the future depends in large measure upon the local context. In West Africa, where powerful hierarchical traditional societies are still intact, the churches tend to place more stress on tradition. In South Africa, where the political and economic structures of *apartheid* are blatantly oppressive, theologians place less stress on the values of the tradition and more on the need for radical transformation not only of society but of the traditional and Christian heritage as well.

The Independent Churches are not immune to the pressure for authenticity. While they are much closer to traditional African culture than the Mission Churches, many of these groups have already traversed the common path from sect to church and are now most effective vehicles for individual social mobility among the lower social strata, both urban and rural. Thus far their role in society has been more adaptative than transformational. For these churches authenticity requires a more relevant involvement in social transformation.

4. **Christianity and Islam.** Outside observers sometimes depict a competitive struggle in Africa between Christianity and ISLAM. It is true that competition for scarce opportunities (education, jobs, services) does exist in those countries like Nigeria where large Christian and Muslim populations live in contiguous regions or side by side within the same region. But the competition is more secular and political than religious. Although about 25 percent of Black Africa is Muslim—the figure is 42 percent for all of Africa—numerically Islam is expanding only at the rate of population growth, about 2.7 percent annually. Christianity, with a growth rate almost double this figure, is still the predominant "modernizing" religion. This may change in the decades ahead as Muslims cast off conservative Islamic practices and demand a larger role in social change.

In many parts of East and West Africa, the Christian-Muslim dialogue takes place within extended families. This day-to-day interaction is complemented by an increased study of the two religions at both the secondary and university levels, thus defusing some of the conflicts which could arise from lack of information or distorted views of either religion.

5. **Church and state.** The close alliance of the Christian churches with colonial regimes has given way to two predominant types of post-independence patterns, both of which disestablish the churches from their hegemonic positions. These are the promotion of religious pluralism, in which Christianity is only one among many religions, none of which receives official preferential status or treatment; and the replacement of Christianity by a quasi-religious ideology such as "Mobutism" (for President Mobutu) in Zaire, or Marxism in a growing number of nations such as Guinea, Congo, Benin, Angola, Mozambique, and Ethiopia. In most countries religious freedom is not put in jeopardy, but the public role of Christianity is eclipsed. For these countries the pluralism of the purely secular state has insufficient moral force to mobilize the masses for social change, and the inherited form of Christianity is regarded as inadequate because of its individualism and middle-class bias.

This trend toward disestablishment was inevitable, for the Christian churches represented a virtual *imperium in imperio* at the time of political independence in the 1960s. The churches administered 90 percent of all schools, the vast majority of all hospitals and clinics, and a predominant proportion of community development programs throughout sub-Saharan Africa. Not only are the churches more firmly rooted in local communities; they enjoy greater loyalty and respect than do most government officials. Therefore, the government take-over of the educational and health care systems from which the churches derived much of their prestige was predictable. From the perspective of national governments the churches' near monopoly in these areas represented not only an unfair religious advantage for the predominant churches, but also a source of interreligious division and national disunity.

This process of disestablishment is still moving forward in most countries. The reaction of the churches has been mixed. In a few instances the churches have welcomed this process as the shedding of a burden which frees them to devote their energies to new forms of ministry and innovative models of service. In most cases the churches have protested government take-overs, but in vain. A few articulate Christian statesmen interpret this trend as vital to the future health of the Christian churches, because now that the churches are freed from official ties with the state they are more likely to exercise a critical and prophetic role in public affairs. This includes the analysis and evaluation of political programs, public policies, and national development plans, as well as the constant championing of the needs of the most neglected and oppressed sectors of the population. It is a natural role for the churches, for the attractiveness of Christianity in the future will depend not on schools and hospitals, but on the churches' degree of solidarity with the peoples' needs. A number of Christian leaders have lost their lives because they dared to exercise this prophetic role under repressive conditions.

6. **Southern Africa.** This part of the continent, which has experienced the strongest Western impact, illustrates the above trends in their sharpest form. As in other parts of the continent the colonizing powers erected a "modern" sector on top of the traditional societies. The struggle for political independence in Black Africa during the 1950s and 1960s was motivated by a desire to open up access to the modern sector for all Africans. However, in South Africa, in Namibia, and until recently in Zimbabwe, the white settler population has successfully blocked the aspirations of the black majority by erecting a racist system which reserves all political and economic opportunity for the whites. In South Africa the Dutch Reformed Church (*see* REFORMED CHURCHES) justifies this policy of "separate development" *(apartheid)* with a racist theology. For the other churches in South Africa, the struggle against this system of white racism has overshadowed almost every other issue.

Pressure for change has come both from within South Africa and Namibia (which is still controlled by South Africa) and from without. The World Council of Churches' Programme to Combat Racism has given significant moral and material assistance to liberation movements in Angola, Mozambique, and Zimbabwe. This has served to legitimize these independence struggles to the outside world, and demonstrate to the local peoples that the churches are committed to the struggle for fundamental change. As the circle of surrounding independent countries has tightened, greater pressure has been exerted on South Africa, thus reinforcing the internal pressures of the churches and other allied groups. The South African government has reacted with even more repressive measures, making it all the more likely that basic change, when it does finally come, will be massive and violent.

At the same time, more fundamental economic issues are being raised by Christians. From the very beginning Christianity has appealed to Africans in large part because of its promise of a better life now on this earth. Economic improvement has been central to the African definition of "the abundant life." Christianity provided a ready ladder for personal social advancement of the elite during the colonial period. Now the question is being raised whether the inherited capitalist system can deliver a more abundant life to everyone. The leadership of Tanzania, Angola, Mozambique, and Zimbabwe believes that some form of socialism is necessary if the masses are ever to be mobilized for a more equitable pattern of economic advancement; and the continued role of multinational corporations in supporting the white regime in South Africa lends credence to the view that international capitalism is inimical to African interests.

The churches in southern Africa are not alienated from these struggles for fundamental political and economic transformation as they have been on other continents during earlier periods of history. Instead, the churches of southern Africa are participating fully in the larger movement to bring about new societies. This is in keeping with the historical role which the churches have played from the beginning of the modern missionary movement in Africa.

Bibliography. J. F. Ajayi, *Christian Missions in Nigeria 1841-1891* (1965); K. Appiah-Kubi and S. Torres, eds., *African Theology en Route* (1979); E. A. Ayandele, *The Missionary Impact on Modern Nigeria* (1966); C. G. Baeta, ed., *Christianity in Tropical Africa* (1968); A. A. Boesak, *Farewell to Innocence* (1977); C. P. Groves, *The Planting of Christianity in Africa*, 4 vols. (1948-58); E. B. Idowu, *African Traditional Religion* (1973); B. Moore, ed., *The Challenge of Black Theology in South Africa* (1974); J. Peel, *Aladura: A Religious Movement Among the Yoruba* (1968); A. Shorter, *African Culture and the Christian Church* (1973); S. Torres and V. Fabella, eds., *The Emergent Gospel* (1978); F. Welbourne and B. Ogot, *A Place to Feel at Home* (1966).

W. T. Davis, Jr.

CHRISTIANITY IN ASIA. At the beginning of the 1980s Christianity outside the Indian subcontinent was flourishing, languishing, insignificant, or suppressed, usually in consequence of two unrelated factors: 1) the method followed by those who laid the foundations for Christianity in the given area or country, and 2) the policy of the government presently controlling that area or country.

1. **Factors in church strength.** Generally speaking, the strongest Christian churches and movements were flourishing where their founders had required self-government, self-propagation, and self-support as a matter of course from the beginning. As a result, the Methodist tribal churches of the remote Yunnanese highlands in mainland China and their counterpart Presbyterian tribal churches in the mountains of Taiwan, the Presbyterian churches of Korea, and the great Dutch Reformed tribal churches in the Batak fastnesses of Indonesia were overwhelmingly the strongest religious communities and influences of their respective areas.

Yet where the government was using the powers of a modern state to reduce the leadership of organized Christian churches to spokesmen of the ruling party, as in most of mainland China—or had moved to stamp out the organized church and all individual Christians, as in North Korea, or permitted it no entry, as in the Islamic Maldive archipelago or in communist-controlled Tibet and Outer Mongolia—Christianity had become insignificant or else had been suppressed or precluded entirely.

2. **Areas of strong churches.** Although in nearly every country around the rim of Asia an identifiable Christianity could be found, only in the islands of the sea, in the Philippines, in Papua New Guinea, and in South Korea was it the obvious and pervasive religion of the land.

In the Philippines a long-established Roman Catholicism continued to command the allegiance of a majority of the population and to set the tone of society, with parallels to Latin America at a number of points. In the islands the results of the evangelization of earlier generations, largely carried out by islanders themselves, had not been attacked by industrial or academic revolution in the general society or in its leadership.

In Papua New Guinea mass movements of tribe after remote tribe were under way into a Christianity which was enthusiastic, dramatically different from traditional tribal religion, and, since new, elementary in the extreme.

In South Korea the most vigorous and dynamic churches in the modern world, having survived decades of Japanese oppression (1910-45) and two waves of communist suppression, were systematically and enthusiastically carrying out the Christianization of the remaining 80 percent of the Korean people and were planning to make Korea the mission center for the whole world. (*See* Korean Religion §§5, 6.)

3. **Japan.** In Japan, on the other hand, which had adopted Western ways on a vast scale but where the methods employed for Christian outreach had twice failed to capitalize on Japanese openness (Meiji era and

post–World War II), Christianity remained largely an intellectualized, urban concern of scarcely more than one percent of the population, with half of the one percent holding aloof from any church connection (*see* MUKYŌKAI). Foreign domination of the major Christian denominations—reflected in the insistence by the old-line American churches that their Japanese counterparts remain in the union church (Kyodan) established by the Japanese government at the time of World War II, and in the fact that less than 40 percent of the salaries of Japanese pastors came in 1979 from the offerings of Japanese congregations—was continuing to contribute to the stagnation of Japanese Christianity as compared with the growth of vigorous new Buddhist movements in Japan. (*See* JAPANESE RELIGION §4.)

4. **In Burma,** where evangelism has been a mark of the Christian church, just as isolation has been since 1945 a mark of Burmese national policy, Christian Kachin tribesmen are severely persecuted, and much of the other tribal evangelism curtailed or severely limited by military edict. Yet individual Christians are prominent in local, regional, and national government, and the churches have been reporting growth of 3 percent or more each year. Of about 1 million Christians in a population of 28 million, a little over half are BAPTISTS and a little over a quarter are Roman Catholics. Most are members of tribal rather than Burmese ethnic groups.

5. **In Thailand,** whose Christian roots go back to 1555 and which has seen Roman Catholic Christianity at work continuously since 1662 and Protestants since 1816, less than one half of one per cent of the nation's people are Christian and less than one tenth of one per cent are Protestant. But radio broadcasting and literature have begun to carry a wide range of evangelistic appeals, and the tiny Christian constituency has been reinforced by large influxes of new missionaries following the closing of China in 1949. Today what had been confined to largely moribund Roman Catholic and Presbyterian ("Church of Christ in Thailand") forms of Christianity has begun to reach out geographically to fifty hitherto untouched provinces, reawakened by genuine spiritual revivals, which have in many cases transformed nominal Christians.

6. **In Cambodia, Laos, and Vietnam,** Christian life continues in spite of enormous losses through death and expulsion. Never large, and in Vietnam principally Roman Catholic except among some mountain tribes, the Christian churches of this area have seen most of their villages wiped out and from some to most to all of their people killed or forced to flee.

7. **Singapore,** three quarters Chinese in population, by the early 1980s was perhaps 10 percent Christian on a population base of eighteen million. Ninety-seven percent of the Christians are Chinese, among whom some are enormously wealthy and some are devoted to a persistent and wide-ranging evangelism. Malaysia, by contrast, has had relatively little Christian work, and its Christian community is small indeed. Persecution by the Muslim majority contributes to the high dropout rate among new Malaysian Christians.

8. **Brunei,** a Malay nation as early as the year 600, is surrounded by Borneo Iban tribesmen, 20 percent of whom were Christian by the early 1980s. It is ruled by a Muslim sultan who permits existing Christian groups (about 3.5 percent of the population) to meet but bans new missionaries.

9. **Indonesia,** fifth largest nation in the world (over 120 million and growing rapidly), is officially over 80 percent Muslim, but there is continued, spectacular growth of the 10 percent Christian minority. The Batak churches in northern Sumatra total over a million members; some have undergone deep spiritual revival and doubled their membership in two or three years. Contemporary people's movements among small, tough, remote tribes have brought results such as the conversion of more than 65 percent of the population of the Irian Barat area. Yet the explosive growth of industrial and urban areas and the apathy of many third- and fourth-generation Indonesian Christians are typical of the challenges which are only now beginning to be faced by Indonesian Christian leaders and churches.

10. **Mainland China** offers few statistics and conflicting reports of its remaining Christians. Many individuals, now mostly old, have remained faithful. Pastors, now almost all elderly, have been forced out of Christian work with only a handful of exceptions, and replacements are not provided for in the system. A handful of organized congregations exist by sufferance, and only where the government feels the need for a church to show foreign visitors. The continuing existence of underground Christian groups and congregations is testified to by persistent rumor and occasional refugee report.

11. **In Hong Kong** some 12 percent of the population of over 5 million was Christian by the early 1980s. Roman Catholics are slightly over half, Protestants slightly under, with their ANGLICAN, Baptist, CONGREGATIONAL, LUTHERAN, and Presbyterian forms increasingly paralleled by indigenous Chinese churches and more recently arrived PENTECOSTAL and other Protestant groups. Numerous Protestant independent relief and evangelistic agencies base their Asia operations in Hong Kong, and work there as well. Audiovisual resources are outstanding, and relief of suffering and need has a high priority.

12. **In Taiwan** the Christian community has grown since 1945 from 30,000 to more than 700,000, numbering more than 4 percent of the population. The most recent growth has been in the mountain tribes and in the indigenous Chinese denominations such as the Pentecostal True Jesus church and Wang Ming-Tao's Little Flock; the traditional Roman Catholic and Presbyterian bodies have leveled off and tended to remain as they were after their postwar spurt in growth.

Bibliography. For bibliographical data *see* D. E. Hoke ed., *The Church in Asia* (1975), the most comprehensive collection of first-hand studies of the history, statistics, temper, and state of Christianity in Asia. K. J. FOREMAN, JR.

CHRISTMAS (Ch). The festival commemorating the birth of JESUS at BETHLEHEM, observed on December 25 (except by Armenians). A festival on this date, associated with the winter solstice, was established by the Emperor Aurelian in the third century A.D. By A.D. 336 the festival had been Christianized to refer to Christ, "the Sun of Righteousness," and stood at the beginning of the liturgical year at Rome. The Chronograph of 354 begins its list of MARTYRS' feasts with this day. Earlier the nativity was celebrated by the Eastern church on January 6, often united to the celebration of Jesus' BAPTISM. The ARMENIAN CHURCH still celebrates this unitive festival of the birth and baptism on January 6. In JERUSALEM the birth alone was celebrated on the later date in the fifth century, but by that time the December feast had been adopted elsewhere in the East. Speculation on the birth date of Jesus is as old as Clement of Alexandria (he suggested May 20), but the actual date remains unknown. The Roman date fell within a season of rejoicing initiated with Saturnalia on December 17, and that same merriment continued to characterize the Christian feast. Its popularity at Rome is indicated by the celebration of three masses there, the most recently established of them, the "Midnight Mass," having proved especially popular in the Western church. English PURITANS sought to curtail Christmas festivity by an act of parliament in 1644, but the popularity of the feast returned after the Commonwealth and continues to the present. (*See* CALENDAR, CHRISTIAN.)

Bibliography. A. A. McArthur, *The Evolution of the Christian Year* (1953). T. J. TALLEY

CHRISTOLOGY (Ch). In a narrow sense, the study of the relation of the divine and human elements (or natures) in JESUS Christ; in a wider sense, the problem of the relation between the redeemer and God (on the one hand) and the redeemer and the redeemed (on the other) expressed anthropologically in the person of the Christ. Because the early church assumed that Christ should himself model the SALVATION he was to bring about for others, Christological doctrines frequently involved, implicitly or explicitly, doctrines of God and salvation.

1. **Early formulations.** The earliest Christological formulas were little more than titles such as "Lord" expressing Jesus' significance for salvation. More developed formulations could encapsulate, often hymnically, confessions of this significance that were fundamentally different in Christological conception (cf. John 1:1-5 and Phil. 2:5*b*-11). In the second century such differences became fundamentally differing ways of formulating the nature of Christ.

a) Anti-docetic Christology. Both GNOSTIC and radically ascetic Christian groups had tended either to deny that the redeemer had a physical body or to downplay its importance. Ignatius of Antioch, as well as the main LOGOS Christologians, opposed this docetic Christology by stressing the crucial importance of Christ's double lineage (from God and from human parentage) and the reality of Christ's flesh as seen in his suffering, death, and resurrection.

b) Logos Christology. The "Logos" Christologians portrayed the redeemer as the Logos (word: both reason and revelation) of God, who became incarnate for human salvation. The idea of the preexistence of the redeemer, already present in a number of NT Christologies, received renewed stress, as theologians linked this preexistent one metaphysically to God the Creator and expanded with more precision his role in the work of creation.

The basic movement of Logos Christology was a descent of the preexistent Logos of God and subsequent enfleshment, so that the redeemer represented in his person both unchanging divinity and redeemable humanity. This descending redeemer could elevate humanity to divinely intended perfection by sharing fully in human suffering.

c) Spirit Christologies. The high Christologies of both the NT and the Logos Christologians had identified the preexistent redeemer figure with the Christ, the Son of God. But the fundamental deity of the second century and the prime agent in salvation was the HOLY SPIRIT. This meant that in certain Christologies the Spirit was the one who preexisted and acted in redemption by "adopting" persons as children of God.

More sophisticated writers like ORIGEN created an elaborate scheme of salvation that combined elements of Logos Christology (which emphasized the *descent* of divinity to the world) and adoptionist Christology (which emphasized the progress and *ascent* of righteous humanity to divine status). As late as 268, Paul of Samosata was condemned by the council of Antioch for teaching a Christology which denied preexistence to the Son (but not the Spirit) and which envisioned him as an obedient messenger, adopted and raised to divine sonship by the Spirit.

2. **The Nicene Era** (*ca.* 318-381). What divided advocates of the Christology of the COUNCIL OF NICAEA from their opponents was the question of whether Christ was the uniquely divine Word of God or was a preexistent creature created and chosen by God, on the basis of foreseen obedience, to be the willing pioneer and prototype of salvation (*see* ARIANISM). ATHANASIUS of Alexandria, leading Nicene exponent for some forty years, emphasized the descent of the Logos (fully equal in essential nature to God, though slightly subordinate in rank), who brought his divine essence into contact with material flesh to redeem creation. His Arian opponents suspected him of promulgating the old Gnostic Christology, for it seemed to them that salvation required obedience to

the will of God, and not a divine substance brought into contact with human flesh, a suggestion they considered heretical.

That Athanasius crossed the line into such heresy is doubtful, but his true intellectual successor was the heretic Apollinaris of Laodicea (*ca.* 310-*ca.* 390). His anthropology eliminated a rational mind (and hence ignorance and wrong choice) from the Christ and replaced it with the Logos of God; this would ensure a victorious redeemer who could not lose the battle with rebellious and sinful flesh and thus could guarantee the truth and stability of human salvation.

Supporters of the Nicene Christology such as Gregory of Nazianzus (d. 390) redressed anti-Arian and Apollinarian tendencies in an overzealous orthodoxy and returned to Christological formulas that saw the mediator as the truly divine Logos of God and yet allowed for will and mind common to the mediator's nature and to the Father.

3. **The Christological settlement** (381-451). By the fifth century Christological thinking had crystallized into two patterns of thinking, represented by Alexandria and Antioch. Cyril of Alexandria (d. 444) continued the Athanasian concern to emphasize the unity of the divine Logos and the flesh in the incarnation, so that the descent and victory of the divine nature in the incarnation received the greatest stress. The opposing Antiochenes, such as Theodore of Mopsuestia (d. 428) and Nestorious (d. *ca.* 450), continued to stress the necessity of cooperation between the divine and human for salvation and, therefore, in the person of Christ. The ascent and progress in obedience of a discernably cooperating human will, responding to the divine initiative, was crucial to the Antiochenes, regardless of what kind of natural union between divine and human natures was envisioned.

Nestorius, bishop of Constantinople, objected to referring to MARY as "Mother of God" (Gr. *theotokos*), a favorite Cyrilian term, suspecting that it led to pagan notions of a mother giving birth to a god and thus of mixing the divine and human natures. Cyril favored the term, and also a Christology that emphasized the Logos as the dominant reality in the united person of the redeemer. He suspected Nestorius' "two-natures" Christology of compromising the certitude of the divine victory over fallen humanity by introducing notions of a cooperative relationship or consenting union between divine and human natures in the incarnation.

The Council of Chalcedon (451) rejected the extremes of both schools, insisting upon a Christology in which divine and human elements were united. But the CHALCEDONIAN DEFINITION prescribed a union in which the distinct and discrete elements of both natures were united in the single agent of salvation, Jesus Christ. Although the settlement ultimately pleased neither side, it provided a way to bring the Eastern church's Christology into conformity with the West, and the Western churches have accepted the formula to the present day.

Bibliography. A. Grillmeier, *Christ in Christian Tradition,* 2nd ed. (ET 1975); R. C. Gregg and D. E. Groh, *Early Arianism—A View of Salvation* (1980); R. A. Norris, *Manhood and Christ* (1963).

D. E. GROH

CHU HSI jū shē (Con—Chin; 1130-1200.) **SHU SHI** shū shē (Con—Jap.). Philosopher whose interpretation of CONFUCIANISM dominated Chinese, Korean, and Japanese thought for centuries. He was responsible for the systematization and culmination of the "School of Principle" *(Li-hsüeh)* or "Ch'eng-Chu School" of Neo-Confucianism, and for establishing the authority of the Four Books: ANALECTS, MENCIUS, GREAT LEARNING, and DOCTRINE OF THE MEAN.

R. L. TAYLOR

CHUANG TZU jwäng´ dzə (T—Chin.; lit. "Master Chuang"). The most important book, next to the LAO TZU, in TAOISM. Its author (or authors) not only was acquainted with the major contemporary schools of philosophy but was also a trained dialectician. Although he used his dialectics to repudiate the doctrines of the rival schools, his purpose was not nihilistic but was to prepare the ground for understanding ultimate reality (Tao or the Way). The author appears to be constantly arguing with himself, proposing various alternatives for the solution of metaphysical problems (e.g., is reality a dream?). He discusses these alternatives in order to show that the Tao cannot be understood intellectually or rationally. Because it is ineffable it can only be understood through intuition.

In several passages (chs. 2, 6) of the Chuang Tzu the creator (Tao) is called the "Great Clod" *(Ta-kuai),* probably an allusion to the archaic creation myth of Chaos (*Hun-tun,* ch. 7). The book also uses the same metaphor of "clod" to designate the ontological state of an enlightened person (chs. 7, 33), referring to his primitive nature or ignorance.

The Chuang Tzu differs from the Lao Tzu by being nonpolitical; it was composed for the spiritual well-being of the intellectual elite and taught that freedom requires liberation from knowledge or words. It also differs from the Lao Tzu by avoiding the contradiction between purposiveness and nonpurposiveness in regard to human conduct; it holds consistently that nonpurposiveness is preferable.

The Chuang Tzu presents a way of life that complements CONFUCIANISM, by offering consolation and quiet to Confucian officials during their off-duty hours as an escape from their otherwise highly controlled, rationalistic, and public life.

1. **Style and structure of the book.** The Chuang Tzu was written in a highly imaginative and, occasionally, lyrical style. Although it is prose, it soars into poetry in many of the passages which describe the mystic union with the Tao. It contains

many anecdotes, tales of divinities and immortals with supernatural or magical power, and myths and legends about ancient China. These were narrated either to illustrate some philosophical principle or to stretch one's imagination and arouse curiosity. The Chuang Tzu uses many paradoxical expressions and mixes pathos with humor in its descriptions of human predicaments. The "profane" and the "sublime" are often blended. In this regard, its style parallels the literature of ZEN Buddhism.

The present Chuang Tzu, following the edited version with commentary by Kuo Hsiang (d. A.D. 312), is divided into thirty-three sections, arranged in three groups. The first seven sections are called "inner chapters," the next fifteen, "outer chapters," and the last eleven, "miscellaneous chapters." The "inner chapters," reflecting a distinct style and a homogenous quality, contain the central ideas of the book. The rest of the work, with some notable exceptions, appears to be imitations or elaborations of the "inner chapters."

Some passages in the Chuang Tzu are obscure and textually corrupt. Fortunately, these passages are not crucial for understanding the principal ideas.

2. Authorship and date. The *Records of the Historian (Shih-chi)* attributes authorship of the book to the man Chuang Tzu (369-286 B.C.?), whose personal name was Chou. He was a contemporary of kings Hui of Liang (370-319 B.C.) and Hsüan of Ch'i (319-301 B.C.). His native home was Meng (present-day Honan) in the state of Sung, a fief of the descendants of the Shang dynasty. The Sung people were known by their contemporaries as being "backward" and adhering to the religious beliefs and practices of their ancestors. This may account for Chuang Tzu's familiarity with ancient tales and folk beliefs. Fung Yu-lan believes that Chuang Tzu probably was a native of the state of Ch'u in Central China, home of Chinese SHAMANISM, because the religious beliefs and rituals alluded to in the Chuang Tzu reflect archaic shamanism.

Because of our scanty knowledge of the man Chuang Tzu, it is impossible to identify him as the historical author of the book. Based upon internal evidence and the language of the work, modern scholars generally agree that the principal part of the Chuang Tzu was written about the same time as the Lao Tzu, between 350 and 275 B.C., but most of the "outer chapters" and the "miscellaneous chapters" were written near the end of the Warring States period (403-222 B.C.) or the beginning of the Former Han (206 B.C.—A.D. 8). Chuang Tzu represents a different school of Taoism from that of the Lao Tzu, and contains a distinct tradition embracing several generations of philosophical reflection. By the time of political disunion (A.D. 265-589) this school became popular and was connected with the school of Lao Tzu, resulting in the combined designation of "Lao-chuang"—the philosophy of Lao Tzu and Chuang Tzu.

3. Ideas of the book. *a) Tao as the transformation of things.* (*See* TAOISM, PHILOSOPHICAL §2.)

b) Distinction between the meaning of Tao and words. Chuang Tzu believed that there is a distinction between the meaning *(i)* of Tao and the words (*yen*) used to describe it. The meaning of Tao is a whole which cannot be divided into parts. But words, being finite and conditioned, can only give meaning to the parts; they may be able to point to the whole but they can never be identical to it. Indeed, knowledge (words) can be an obstacle to understanding Tao. For Chuang Tzu, the meaning of Tao can only be apprehended through intuition which comprehends the whole. Thus the Tao and words belong to two different orders of understanding; one refers to the ultimate meaning and the other to conventional knowledge. The difference between these two is like the difference between footprints and the shoes which created the prints (ch. 14).

c) Natural equality of things. Because the Tao functions and is present in all things in accordance with its own law and because things are transformed into one another in cycles, there is no special center in the universe. Unlike the Confucianists, Chuang Tzu does not view humanity as a special creation. He believes that everything is endowed with a certain natural capacity, and insofar as it lives according to its natural capacity, it is just as good as any other thing. Thus the morning mushroom which lives only a day is equal to P'eng Tsu (the Chinese Methuselah), who lived for several hundred years. The quail that can fly only a few feet is equal to the big roc that can fly for many hundreds of miles (ch. 1). It can be seen that the equality of things is predicated upon their natural capacities. But because people begin to accumulate knowledge and build a civilization, they feel that they are superior to nature; therefore they become separated from it. Moreover, knowledge engenders desires and ambitions; therefore competition and contention ensue, resulting in great inequality among individuals. Chuang Tzu criticizes Confucianism because its emphasis upon knowledge and morality necessarily entails a man-centered world of inequality. This is also the reason why Chuang Tzu advocates the discarding of knowledge and the abandonment of morality; he wants people to return to their original equality.

d) Nonpurposiveness as a way of life. A dominant idea in Chuang Tzu is that the highest attainment must be accomplished nonpurposively. Conversely, one cannot consciously attain the highest. The logic of this paradox is that whatever is purposively entertained involves words or names which are finite and conditioned. But Tao is infinite and unconditioned; one must transcend words or names in order to understand it. Expressions such as "mindless" *(wu-hsin),* "thoughtless" *(wu-szu),* or "forgetting" *(wang)* in Chuang Tzu's language refer to this basic notion. It is necessary to give up preconceptions and particular thoughts about the Tao in order to be one with it. This nonpurposive attainment is the meaning of freedom, which Chuang Tzu called "spontaneity" *(tzu-jan)* or "no-action" (Wu Wei).

e) The image of a journey. Chuang Tzu refers to numerous incidents of cosmic travel by birds, animals, sages, immortals, or gods who "journey," "roam," or "fly" through the sky. It is impossible to say with certainty whether he views these tales metaphorically or literally. It is most likely that they are symbolic references to freedom or the mental attitude of a liberated person. In archaic Chinese shamanism a prevalent feature was the ritual of "magical flight" in which the shaman-poet imagines himself flying. The recurrence of these tales might be viewed as Chuang Tzu's unconscious desire to reenact the archaic shamanic ritual which later reappears in Religious Taoism and Chinese Popular Religion.

Bibliography. W. T. Chan, trans., *A Source Book in Chinese Philosophy* (1963), pp. 177-210; H. G. Creel, "The Great Clod," in *What Is Taoism?* (1970), pp. 25-36; Y. L. Fung, *A History of Chinese Philosophy*, I (1952), 221-45; D. Bodde, trans., *Chuang Tzu* (1968), seven "inner chapters" based on the commentary by Kuo Hsiang; A. C. Graham, "Chuang Tzu's Essay on Seeing Things as Equal," *HR*, IX (1969-70), 137-59; N. J. Girardot, "Returning to the Beginning and the Arts of Mr. Hun-tun in the *Chuang Tzu*," *Journal of Chinese Philosophy*, V (1978), 21-69; B. Watson, trans., *The Complete Works of Chuang Tzu* (1968). D. C. Yu

CHUMASH hoo´ mäsh (Ju—Heb.; lit. "one-fifth"). The Five Books of Moses, also called Pentateuch or Torah. The term probably referred originally to any one of the five books. I. Chernus

CHURCH (Gr. *kuriakon;* lit. "belonging to the Lord"). The Christian community considered in four ways: (a) the universal body of all who profess faith in Jesus Christ; (b) a particular communion, confession, or denomination of Christians; (c) the institutional form of any such communion; (d) a building used for Christian worship. Throughout history many sects or denominations have arisen. Sociologically, it is difficult to call all of these various manifestations *the* church. Yet by intention and belief, all hold that there is only one church of Christ, however divided.

1. **Biblical pattern.** Christians believe that the church originates in God's plan for salvation, in continuity with ancient Israel (Gal. 6:16; I Pet. 2:9-10). They see the history of Israel as God's Covenant with his chosen people as he teaches them divine law, promises them Salvation from sin, and sustains them by hope in the coming of the Messiah and the new age of righteousness (Acts 7; Heb. 11).

Jesus' community of disciples was the nucleus of a reconstituted Israel centered on a new understanding of the covenant. It is questionable whether Jesus "founded" the church as a new institution. (*See* Founders, Religious.) The interpretation of Jesus' saying to Peter, "On this rock I will build my church" (Matt. 16:18), is much disputed. It is clear, however, that the disciples devoted themselves to forming Christian communities, both Jewish and Gentile, and that Peter had a preeminent role. They saw the church as continuing Jesus' divine mission to form redemptive communities of the people of God among all nations.

The primary purpose of the church was, and remains, witness or Mission. The Apostles who succeeded Jesus preached a gospel of forgiveness and hope. Their words were backed by acts of compassion, justice, and self-sacrifice. This mission was empowered by the Holy Spirit, poured out at Pentecost and ever after to be given to the church (Acts 1:6-8).

The communal life of the church was characterized ideally by mutual love, worship, and common ownership of property (Acts 2:42-47; 4:32-35). Continuing to eat together as the disciples had done with Jesus, Christians developed the sacramental, or eucharistic, meal which was the focal point of worship and common life (*see* Eucharist; Liturgy). The still plastic organizational structure of this society was based on gifts and tasks. Each gift (Gr. *charisma*) of the Spirit enabled a man or woman to strengthen the church through preaching, teaching, healing, interpreting ecstasies, or administering. Every church member was called a "priest" and "saint" as each lived a life of faithfulness to God's will known in Christ. Some indispensable functions in the community developed into distinct offices: Deacons for service; Elders, or presbyters, for teaching, governing, and leading worship; and Bishops for overseeing. After the second century these became orders of ministry (I Cor. 12:12-31; Eph. 4:4-16; *see* Clergy, Christian).

The difference between the church and other religious communities and societies which worship, teach high ideals, and propagate beliefs lies in the concept of the church as the body of Christ. It is the historical form of existence of the risen Christ: Christ living in the human community, the members incorporated into Christ (Col. 1:12-29; Rom. 12:4-18).

Such exalted biblical doctrines seem remote from the utterly mundane, human aspects of the churches as they are known. Therefore, some have posited an "invisible church" as the body of Christ and a "visible church" as its earthly counterpart. But this encourages a retreat into unreality and illusion. The "real" church is at once visible and invisible, both the Communion of Saints and the company of forgiven sinners. It resembles its Lord, who was both God's Word incarnate and the humiliated suffering servant. The church fits precisely in this pattern of paradox, essential to the Christian doctrine of salvation.

2. **Diverse churches.** Diverse and distinctive forms have evolved from the original biblical insights on the definition of the church. The Orthodox Churches adhere strictly to a hierarchical structure of priestly and episcopal ministry, the ancient liturgies and Creeds, dogmas and rules of the seven ecumenical Councils (called the Holy Tradition). The several

Orthodox Churches are self-governing. ROMAN CATHOLICISM shares this allegiance to the tradition and the hierarchy, but with the chief difference of a unified governance and teaching authority under the primacy of the Bishop of Rome as pope. ANGLICAN CHURCHES continue the traditions of Western Catholicism, maintaining the historic episcopate as indispensable to continuity and unity. These churches, however, are much influenced by the theology of the REFORMATION, which saw the church as a congregation of the faithful where the Word is purely preached and the sacraments rightly administered (MARTIN LUTHER). LUTHERAN CHURCHES allow flexibility in ministry and polity; REFORMED CHURCHES hold that a pattern of ministry of presbyters, or elders, is required by the NT. Emphasizing the gathered community, or free fellowship of the Spirit, and rejecting a hierarchical order of ministry are the UNITED CHURCH OF CHRIST, BAPTISTS, CHRISTIAN CHURCHES (DISCIPLES OF CHRIST), PENTECOSTALS, FRIENDS, and other groups. METHODISTS have much in common with the worship and episcopal ministry of Anglicanism, but are closer to other Protestants in beliefs and ethos.

Bibliography. A. Dulles, *Models of the Church* (1974); J. R. Nelson, *The Realm of Redemption* (1964); H. Küng, *The Church* (1967).

J. R. NELSON

CHURCH OF CHRIST. *See* CHRISTIAN CHURCHES (DISCIPLES OF CHRIST).

CHURCH OF ENGLAND (Ch). *See* ANGLICAN CHURCHES.

CHURCH FATHERS (Ch). Early ecclesiastical writers (to the eighth century) adjudged orthodox. By the fourth century theologians had begun to appeal to doctrinal authority of the "church fathers" (Eusebius, *Against Marcellus* 1.4) and the "fathers of Nicaea" (Basil, *Epistles* 52). Modern study of these writers is called "patristics" or "patrology."

R. C. GREGG

CHURCHING OF WOMEN (Ch). The act of thanksgiving by a woman after childbirth, derived from Jewish purification (Lev. 12:6). Formerly on the fortieth day after birth, it is now part of the rite of infant BAPTISM in ROMAN CATHOLICISM. Since GREGORY I it has been treated as a thanksgiving rather than release from ritual impurity. T. J. TALLEY

CIRCUMCISION. 1. In Judaism. Surgical removal of the foreskin of a male Jewish infant or of a male convert to JUDAISM. Genesis 17:10-12 presents circumcision as a divine injunction laid on Abraham and his descendants and serving as a sign in the flesh of the covenant (Heb. *berit*) between God and Israel. Circumcision came to be called *berit milah*, "the covenant of circumcision" or the "covenant of our father Abraham." The ceremony is often called *beris*, the YIDDISH pronunciation of *berit*.

The operation is to take place on the eighth day after birth, even if that day falls on a SABBATH or the Day of Atonement (YOM KIPPUR), unless there are medical reasons to warrant postponement. Circumcision may be entirely omitted only if two previous children of the family have died as a direct result of the operation, e.g., in cases of hemophilia.

Legally, the duty of circumcision is incumbent on the father, but in traditional Judaism he usually delegates it to a trained circumciser, called a MOHEL. Surgeons are used in Reform. During the course of the ceremony the child is given his Hebrew name. Generally the ceremony is concluded by a festive banquet at which hymns are sung.

Bibliography. N. Gottlieb, *A Jewish Child Is Born* (1960); H. Schauss, *The Lifetime of a Jew* (1950).

B. MARTIN

2. In Islam. Known as *khitān* ("circumcision"), *ṭahāra* ("purity"), and *sunnat* ("custom"; esp. Indonesia); universally observed although not required by the QUR'ĀN. Variously performed from seven days after birth until puberty, as well as for adult male converts. Female circumcision—clitoridectomy—is also practiced in some regions (e.g. Arabia, the Nile Valley). Although not a prominent topic in Islamic law, the popular religious consciousness attaches great importance to circumcision.

Male circumcision is often surrounded with elaborate ceremony, while the female type has little, if any. In regions where boys are circumcised toward the age of puberty, the event often accompanies a ceremony recognizing the attainment of proficiency in reciting the Qur'ān. The two events constitute a powerful rite of passage into manhood. But the most important religious idea connected with circumcision is expressed by the euphemism *ṭahāra*, "purity," for all Islamic ritual begins with PURIFICATION.

Bibliography. E. W. Lane, *Manners and Customs of the Modern Egyptians* (rpr. 1954), pp. 58-60, 512-15; Haji Mohtar bin H. Md. Dom, *Traditions and Taboos* (1979), pp. 35-43, provides vivid detail of Malaysian practices; O. F. A. Meinardus, *Christian Egypt: Faith and Life* (1970), esp. pp. 325-32, which deal with Islamic female circumcision.

F. M. DENNY

CISTERCIANS sĭs tûr´ shənz (Ch). Monks of two Roman Catholic RELIGIOUS ORDERS—Cistercians of the Common Observance (Sacred Order of Cistercians: SOCist) and Cisterican of the Stricter Observance (OCSO: TRAPPISTS)—originating from reforms of BENEDICTINE monasticism begun in 1098 at Citeaux (*Cistercium*) and furthered by BERNARD OF CLAIRVAUX. Large numbers accepted their monastic ideal of strict poverty, ASCETICISM, manual labor; like-minded women formed convents of Cistercian nuns. Later decline led to reform movements from the sixteenth century on, finally to division into two branches.

Today the Common Observance tends to be more active, the Stricter Observance more contemplative.

W. H. Principe

CLERGY, CHRISTIAN. The ordained leadership of the Christian church. The word is derived from the Greek *kleros,* an object used in casting lots, such as those used by the OT priests (Deut. 18:1ff.), or those used in the selection of a successor to Judas Iscariot (Acts 1:17, 25-26). The word can also refer to an allotted portion, hence its use in I Pet. 5:3 of persons assigned to the care of elders.

1. **Origins.** The early church was influenced by both the traditions of leadership in Judaism and the general patterns of organization in Greco-Roman culture. Although the NT often refers to people exercising leadership, either because of spiritual gifts or because of offices held, no single pattern of organization can be discerned from available evidence. Lists of leaders and positions of leadership are given, which, though similar, are not identical (I Cor. 12:27-30; Rom. 12:4-8; Eph. 4:6-12). Titles include prophet, teacher, elder, deacon, overseer. The church seems to have established early a group of ministries which it assigned to qualified persons. In the first decades the apostles exercised unique functions because of their relationship to Jesus and their part in the founding of the church. Persons in other offices sometimes assisted them and came to be responsible for much of the work the apostles had previously done.

By the end of the first century, the most clearly defined office was that of the Bishop, or overseer, of a local gathering of the faithful; he was responsible for worship and the care of the poor. Closely related to the bishop, and soon associated with him in the pastoral care of the congregation, was a second office, that of Elder. Some NT passages indicate that the office of elder was similar to that in Jewish organization. Acts 20:17, 28 uses both terms to describe leaders in the Ephesian church, implying a closer identification of elder and bishop than does I Tim. 3-4, which shows them as distinct offices. It may be that elder and bishop refer to essentially the same development, the former arising in congregations with primarily Jewish antecedents and the latter in those with primarily Hellenistic associations.

Another movement toward definition of church leadership in the NT involved the office of Deacon (from Greek *diakonos,* servant, attendant, or minister). Deacons also seem to have been associated with the work of bishops (Phil. 1:1; I Tim 3:1ff.).

2. **Emergence of a hierarchy.** By the end of the first century, Christians were using the term "sacrifice" to describe the eucharistic Liturgy, and the term Priest to refer to the officiant at the eucharistic sacrifice. Gradually the title "priest" came to be used in place of "elder." Ordained leadership was thus consolidated into three offices—bishop, priest, and deacon—which together were responsible for transmitting the faith, presiding at worship, maintaining discipline in the congregation, administering its affairs, and caring for its people. The bishops' responsibilities were concentrated in fairly compact territories, but as the church expanded their work became less personal ministry and more superintendence of the priests, who were assigned responsibility in local parishes. Priests presided at worship, exercised pastoral care, and generally saw to the affairs of the congregation. Deacons were assistants, usually assigned to bishops, but also available to help the priests.

A distinction arose between the secular clergy, who worked in the world *(saeculum)* and the regular clergy, who lived under a rule *(regula),* usually in communities. (*See* Monasticism.)

The threefold ministry was present in Eastern and Western churches, though with variations in terminology, organization, and policies with respect to matters such as marriage of priests (forbidden in the West, allowed in the East except for bishops). Just as Roman Catholicism and Eastern Orthodoxy developed distinctive modes of spirituality and conduct, so their respective orders of ministry, while parallel in structure, are distinct from one another in ethos.

3. **Protestant clergy.** The Protestant Reformation had as one goal the reshaping of the ministry. Reformers emphasized the priestly responsibility of all Christians and the servanthood of the ordained leadership. They softened traditional distinctions between priest and bishop, some groups abolishing the office of bishop. The title "priest" was suppressed, and the titles "pastor," "minister," and "preacher" came to be used. Ministers were allowed to marry and in other ways live according to lay patterns.

European patterns of ministry were transmitted to other parts of the world, gradually changing in the process. In North America, where indigenous cultures were supplanted by modifications of European culture, ecclesiastical systems have remained close to their Old World counterparts, whether Protestant or Catholic. Even in North America, however, these patterns have been modified by the frontier and its populist mentality, by the voluntaristic character of church membership, and by denominationalism.

In the younger churches of Africa, Asia, and Latin America, indigenous cultures have survived. Consequently, traditional patterns of ministry have been greatly influenced by continuing strains drawn from pre-missionary structures of community life. *See* Christianity in Africa; Christianity in Asia.

4. **Current practice.** Virtually all church bodies use specially trained, publicly authorized, salaried leaders, usually ordained, the most numerous and ordinarily most influential being those assigned to local congregations. Whether known as minister, priest, or pastor, they are responsible for administration, leadership in mission, and for leading congregational life and worship. They share work and authority with lay leaders. Structures for supervision

and sacramental leadership exist above the congregational level in some groups, but often with relatively modest power and responsibility. Current theories describing church leadership tend to draw from secular disciplines such as sociology, and less from theology or philosophy than formerly.

Ecumenical discussions dealing with ministry often lead to a consensus at a theological level, but tend to break down at the level of practical organization, the place of the episcopal office being a major barrier. Recently a new dimension has been added to ideas of Christian ministry by the ordination of women to offices formerly held only by men.

Bibliography. H. W. Beyer in *Theological Dictionary of the NT*, G. Kittel, ed., II (1964), 81-93, 599-622; H. R. Niebuhr and D. D. Williams, eds., *The Ministry in Historical Perspective* (1956); R. E. Osborn, *In Christ's Place* (1967); B. Cooke, *Ministry to Word and Sacraments* (1976). K. WATKINS

COHEN, HERMANN (Ju; 1842-1918). German Jewish philosopher, founder of the Marburg school of Neo-Kantianism. Although he initially held religion to be merely a precursor to the ideals of ethics, he later granted it an independent position within philosophy. His thought significantly influenced REFORM JUDAISM. *See* JUDAISM §6d. L. FAGEN

COLORS, LITURGICAL (Ch). The color of vestments and altar hangings seems to have been subject to no particular systematic regulation prior to the twelfth century, although individual colors are mentioned without limitation to certain feasts. INNOCENT III (1198-1216) describes the Roman pattern of his day: white for feasts, red for MARTYRS, black (or violet) for penitential seasons, and green for other times. In time, black was limited to GOOD FRIDAY and funerals, and violet was used in penitential seasons. Throughout the Middle Ages, however, the color schemes varied widely from place to place, often employing many other colors or hues than these. In the REFORMATION most Protestants discontinued such use of color, but some have resumed it in the twentieth century. The reforms following the Council of TRENT standardized the Roman system outlined above. It is this Roman scheme that has achieved popularity in most Western churches in this century. Recent reform of the Roman MISSAL has introduced some change. White is now indicated for feasts of Christ (except of his Passion), of the Virgin MARY, of SAINTS not martyrs, and for certain feasts of APOSTLES. Red is worn on days associated with Christ's Passion, with martyrs, and with the HOLY SPIRIT. Violet is assigned for ADVENT and LENT and is allowed for funerals unless black is preferred. Green is worn in neutral seasons when no other color is prescribed. The General Instruction of the Roman Missal (no. 309) also provides that "on special occasions more noble vestments may be used, even if not of the color of the day." In the U.S., white may be substituted for black or violet at Roman Catholic masses for the dead.

T. J. TALLEY

COMMUNION, HOLY (Ch). *See* EUCHARIST.

COMMUNION OF SAINTS (Ch—Lat. *communio sanctorum*). An article of the APOSTLES' CREED now appearing immediately after and thought by some to be in apposition to the phrase "holy catholic church."

The words first appeared in the creed in the fifth century, though the phrase can be traced back as early as the Council of Nimes (A.D. 394), where its usage denoted participation in holy things, i.e., SACRAMENTS. In slightly later usage it meant communion (fellowship) with holy persons. The ambiguity of *sanctorum,* whether masculine or neuter, makes it impossible to determine which was the original intended meaning. Though used in the first sense by Abelard and Aquinas, the second has predominated. There is general agreement that the fellowship includes all living Christians, but some have maintained it includes the deceased (including OT believers) and angels.

Bibliography. W. Barclay, *The Apostles' Creed for Everyone* (1967), pp. 291-99; A. C. McGiffert, *The Apostles' Creed* (1902), pp. 200-204; F. J. Badcock, "Sanctorum Communio as an Article in The Creed," *JTS,* XXI, (1928) 106-26.

T. O. HALL, JR.

COMPANIONS OF THE PROPHET (I). *See* ṢAḤĀBA.

CONFESSION (Ch). (1) An affirmation of faith; applied to doctrinal statements and the communities professing them and to the faith of MARTYRS. (*See* CREEDS AND CONFESSIONS.) (2) The act of admitting sin and the liturgical forms in which the admission is cast. In ROMAN CATHOLICISM confession is made to a priest as part of the SACRAMENT of penance.

T. J. TALLEY

CONFIRMATION 1. (Ch). An anointing or imposition of hands relating to the HOLY SPIRIT'S indwelling in the baptized. Originally part of the rite of BAPTISM, from the sixteenth century it became a later ratification of vows by those baptized in infancy. It is often identified with the anointing immediately after baptism in the Eastern church. (*See* SACRAMENTS.)

T. J. TALLEY

2. (Ju). A graduation ceremony or exercise, usually at the end of the ninth or tenth grade, from formal religious education. Initiated in the last half of the nineteenth century by REFORM JUDAISM, it was adopted by many CONSERVATIVE congregations. In most synagogues it is observed on SHAVUOT.

CONFUCIANISM kŭn fyōō´ shŭn ĭsm. The system of social, political, ethical, and religious thought based on the teachings of CONFUCIUS and his successors. This designation is Western in origin. In Chinese the tradition is termed *ju chia* (roo jyä) or "School of the Literati," i.e. scholars and teachers of the ancient literature, especially the Five Classics, which according to tradition were edited by Confucius: Book of Poetry *(Shih Ching)*, 305 poems of the early Chou Dynasty (1111-249 B.C.); Book of Rites *(Li Ching)*, three major works on ritual, including discussions of the philosophical meaning of ritual; Book of History *(Shu Ching)*, a collection of documents from the time of the legendary Emperor Yao (third millennium B.C.) to the early Chou; Spring and Autumn Annals *(Ch'un Ch'iu)*, the events of Confucius' home state of Lu from 722 to 481 B.C.; and the Book of Changes (I CHING).

1. **Classical Confucianism.** In the several centuries that followed the death of Confucius four major statements of Confucian perspective emerge and constitute what might be called Classical Confucianism: MENCIUS, GREAT LEARNING, DOCTRINE OF THE MEAN, and Hsün Tzu.

a) Mencius held that man's nature is originally good, and that man's task is to develop the inherent goodness through a balance of effort and spontaneity, eventually realizing the commonality of man's nature with the nature of Heaven. He is often called the representative of the idealistic wing of Classical Confucianism for his faith in the human potential for goodness.

b) The Great Learning. This work formulates a method of bringing peace to the world by personal moral cultivation. It stresses the need for exhaustive effort in learning and so stands nearer to Hsün Tzu than to Mencius.

c) Doctrine of the Mean. Unlike the Great Learning this work stresses the metaphysical nature of human potentiality. It recognizes the manifestation of man's genuine or sincere nature (a nature shared with Heaven) as man's fulfillment. In this respect it has much in common with Mencius.

d) Hsün Tzu. The third great teacher of the Confucian school, Hsün Tzu (*ca.* 298–*ca.* 238 B.C.) lived during the final years of the Chou dynasty and may have seen the unification of the empire under the Ch'in in 221 B.C. To Hsün Tzu faith in the original goodness of human nature seemed naïve. Human nature was not good but evil, and man and society needed controls in the form of laws and rites (LI). Hsün Tzu is often described as the realist of the Confucian tradition because of his views of human nature, his attempt to refute old beliefs including even the active role of Heaven in history, and for his refusal to venerate sages of the past. He shared with the tradition, however, the belief in the perfectability of man through learning, in the necessity of righteouness *(i)* and humanity (JEN), and in the supreme value of education. In many respects Hsün Tzu and Mencius are not in as great opposition to each other as might appear. If Hsün Tzu is concerned to refute a philosophical position, it is that of TAOISM, which he regarded as a threat to civilization, because it denied what the Confucians deemed the essential humanism of man. Hsün Tzu had greater influence through the Han dynasty than did Mencius, the Great Learning, or the Doctrine of the Mean, and he has been called the father of Han dynasty Confucianism.

2. **Han Confucianism.** During the Han dynasty (206 B.C.—A.D. 220), Confucianism was officially established as state orthodoxy, a Confucian canon developed, and there are the beginnings of a cult of Confucius which eventually led to the establishment of the Confucian temple.

a) State orthodoxy. The Confucian classics came to be regarded as the basis for individual learning as well as preparation for government service, and the Confucian scholars were responsible for the codification of rituals for official sacrifices. Tung Chung-shu (*ca.* 179—*ca.* 104 B.C.), one of the major philosophers of the Han dynasty, recommended the exclusive establishment of Confucianism. A university was opened in 124 B.C. to train young scholars in the Confucian classics as preparation for a life of government service. The position as state orthodoxy was maintained with few periods of eclipse until the twentieth century.

b) The Confucian canon. During the Han dynasty scholars devoted much effort to history, lexicography, and the editing of ancient texts. There were issues of authenticity of texts, particularly because of the burning of the books by the first emperor of the Ch'in dynasty (221-206 B.C.). Many texts existed in two versions which represented significant philosophical differences. The so-called New Text versions had much in common with Tung Chung-shu's interpretation of Confucianism, employing YIN AND YANG theory, interest in omens, and an attempt to attribute hagiographic features to Confucius' life. The Old Text versions remained free of such tendencies. Various commissions were appointed by the emperor to edit, annotate, and adjudicate variant versions. Eventually an orthodox interpretation of the five Confucian Classics was established, and they, together with the ANALECTS, were engraved in stone.

c) The cult of Confucius. A cult of Confucius as the patron of scholars preceded the official establishment of Confucianism, but when Confucianism became state orthodoxy, the cult emerged as part of the state religion. The literati offered sacrifice to Confucius, and such sacrifice was included among the state sacrifices performed by the emperor. During the Han dynasty writings that attempted to deify Confucius were judged apocryphal, and Confucius remained, even within the context of a cult and eventual temple, a human teacher venerated for his wisdom.

3. **Neo-Confucianism.** The term Neo-Confucianism was coined to designate the movement marked by the revival, growth, and unfolding of the Confucian tradition from the Sung dynasty (960-1279) to the present day. Two major schools exist: the School of Principle (Li-hsüeh), or the Ch'eng-Chu School,

named for Ch'eng I (1033-1107) and Chu Hsi (1130-1200), the great teachers of the school during the Sung dynasty, and the School of Mind (Hsin-hsüeh), whose major proponent is Wang Yang-ming (1472-1529) of the Ming dynasty (1368-1644). The term Neo-Confucianism suggests a significant break from tradition, i.e., the incorporation into Confucianism of elements of Buddhism and Taoism, particularly in the area of metaphysics and forms of mental discipline. There is no doubt that there was such influence, particularly of Buddhism, but it may be measured more in terms of a model for the religious life than a metaphysical framework.

a) A return to virtue. The Neo-Confucians—and their precursors during the T'ang dynasty (618-907)—insisted upon a return to the fundamental ethical teachings of the tradition. According to the Confucians both Buddhism and Taoism lacked ethical foundations and as such were of little use to man or society. Han Yü (768-824) asserted the fundamental superiority of Confucianism over Buddhism; others attempted to reinstate Confucian principles by restructuring or even rebuilding society, something frequently discussed at the beginning of the Sung dynasty and a characteristic of Neo-Confucianism as late as the nineteenth century. With the inevitable failure of massive institutional change, the focus of such attempts became interiorized, however, with stress upon realizing the ethical teachings within the family setting and ultimately within the individual himself.

b) Priority of man. Humanism is as characteristic of Neo-Confucianism as it is of Confucianism, and within the context of Neo-Confucianism it became an argument against both Buddhism and Taoism. Buddhism with its ultimate relativity of all human values and Taoism with its sense of the indifference of the universe to man were seen as untenable. The Neo-Confucians strongly reassert the importance of man and his values, presupposing the goodness of man's nature and the correspondence of the ethical nature of man to that of the universe.

c) Rationalism. In countering the Buddhist emphasis on emptiness (Śūnyatā), Neo-Confucianism extolled the virtue of rationalism, a term not excluding faith or intuition, but simply emphasizing the "principle" *(li)* inherent in the universe and man's ability to comprehend and understand it. This underlying principle was primarily ethical in character. A rational investigation of principle was more characteristic of the School of Principle than the School of Mind, but the latter still held to the fundamental principle underlying the universe and accessible to human understanding.

d) A sense of history. The study of history is a way of understanding the ethical values of the early teachings as well as the institutions that exemplify those values. Human history itself is seen as an exemplar of value and moral order and as a guide to understanding principle. This suggests the need for book-learning, and a broad program of study and investigation was viewed as the method of learning. The School of Mind focused the method of study far more upon one's own innate nature and the intuitive grasp of its inherent goodness.

e) Ming and Ch'ing developments. Because of the excessive focus upon study and rational investigation during the Sung period, in the Ming dynasty (1368-1644) both the School of Principle and the School of Mind emphasized more the interior search for principle than the external intellectual investigation. Thus for the School of Mind the focus is upon an intuitive grasp of the principle of one's mind in the midst of activity, demonstrating what Wang Yang-ming regarded as the unity of knowledge and action. For the School of Principle the interior experience of the self, often accompanied by meditation and expressed autobiographically, became the avenue of knowing, a mode of living characterizing a personal orthodoxy as well as the state orthodoxy. During the Ch'ing period (1644-1912) Confucian scholars were suggesting a return to the basics of Confucius himself, away from the speculative tendencies of Sung and Ming Neo-Confucianism. In the late nineteenth century K'ang Yu-wei (1858-1927), following a long-standing precedent, suggested institutional reform based on a Confucian model, but under the impact of Western technology and philosophy that model was rejected.

4. Social institutions. *a) Propriety: individual, family, and state.* For Confucianism, state, family, and individual are not separated from each other any more than all three are separated from the ways of Heaven. To this extent social institutions mirror the fundamental teachings of the tradition. The text that epitomizes the integration of state, family, individual, and Heaven is the Great Learning. Rites or propriety *(li)* serve as the cement of society as well as the family and reflect often in formal ways the humanism *(jen)* of the Confucian experience. Filial Piety *(hsiao)* suggests the fundamental importance of the proper relation of children and parents. Classical Confucianism, as well as Neo-Confucianism, stresses the ideal of sageliness within and kingliness without, suggesting the intimate relation of the social institutions to the individual's inner experience of the fundamental teachings.

b) Worship in a Confucian context. Worship activities in Confucianism include traditional rites *(li)* as well as sacrifice at individual, family, and state levels. The gentleman *(chün-tzu)* understands that the benefits of rites and sacrifice consist in the perfection of man's moral nature, while the common man believes he is serving the spirits. This is exemplified in Ancestor Veneration, which, for the gentleman, is a means of showing respect as well as grief for the departed and, through the performance of such rites, the emulation of virtuous ways. For the common person it is the maintenance of the life of the ancestral spirits. The religious dimension is found in the attitude of reverence *(ching),* which suggests the sacredness of all acts of worship as models of Heaven's norms.

c) Sacrifice to Confucius and the Confucian temple. The first mention of a cult of Confucius is during the Han dynasty, the period in which Confucianism was established as official state orthodoxy. In A.D. 59, Emperor Han Ming Ti recognized Confucius as patron of scholars and ordered that sacrifice should be offered to him. Sacrifice was carried out by the emperor himself, indicating the inclusion of Confucianism into the official state religion. Sacrifice itself resembles a solemn banquet given in honor of the venerated figures and serves as an occasion, from the Confucian perspective, for instilling reverence and propriety among men rather than the propitiation of spirits. Strict attention is paid to the ritual preparation and offering of selected dishes including ox, pig, sheep, as well as assorted viands and wine.

During the T'ang dynasty, a period noted for the resurgence of interest in the Confucian tradition, temples to Confucius were constructed throughout the country. From the T'ang dynasty to the twentieth century they perpetuated the cult of Confucius as a component of the state religion.

The temple in itself is a memorial hall. None of the figures are regarded as deified, but famous Confucians from throughout history are venerated. The main temple contains tablets of Confucius, his four closest disciples, and several additional groupings of Confucian scholars. Sacrifice is held twice a year, mid-spring and mid-autumn, and performed by Confucian literati. The scholars represented in the temple are not a static group. Different periods of history have seen the inclusion or exclusion of particular figures, and there appears to be a correlation between those venerated in the temple and the orthodoxy of a given period.

5. Modern developments. The twentieth century has seen significant changes in the outward authority of the Confucian tradition. In 1905 the imperial examination system, the system whose source was the official Neo-Confucian orthodoxy, was abolished, ending the status of the Confucian tradition and the Neo-Confucian orthodoxy as the avenue of access to government service. Sacrifice to Confucius in the Confucian temple terminated in 1928 and thereafter Confucianism ceased to be an official religion. However, Confucianism as a significant component in the make-up of Chinese and other East Asian cultures or even more significantly as an individual ethico-religious world view is far from extinct. The attack on Confucius in the People's Republic and the veneration of the Confucian tradition by Nationalist China are indications of its vitality.

Bibliography. General works: W. T. Chan, *A Source Book in Chinese Philosophy* (1963); W. T. deBary, ed., *Sources of Chinese Tradition* (1960); L. G. Thompson, *Chinese Religion: An Introduction* (1975). Classical Confucianism: D. Munro, *The Concept of Man in Early China* (1969); A. Verwilghen, *Mencius: The Man and His Ideas* (1967); D. C. Lau, *Mencius* (1970); E. R. Hughes, *The Great Learning and the Mean in Action* (1943); Tu Wei-ming, *Centrality and Commonality: An Essay on Chung-yung* (1976); H. H. Dubs, *Hsüntze* (1927); B. Watson, *Hsün Tzu: Basic Writings* (1963). Neo-Confucianism: W. T. deBary, "Some Common Tendencies in Neo-Confucianism," D. S. Nivison and A. F. Wright, eds., *Confucianism in Action* (1959), pp. 25-49, a systematic summation of the salient features of Neo-Confucianism; A. C. Graham, *Two Chinese Philosophers: Ch'eng Ming-tao and Ch'eng Yi-ch'uan;* (1958); W. T. Chan, trans., *Reflections on Things at Hand (1967);* W. T. deBary, ed., *Self and Society in Ming Thought* (1970) and *The Unfolding of Neo-Confucianism* (1975); J. Ching, *To Acquire Wisdom: The Way of Wang Yang-ming* (1976); Tu Wei-ming, *Neo-Confucian Thought in Action* (1976); W. T. Chan, trans., *Instructions for Practical Living* (1963); R. L. Taylor, *The Cultivation of Sagehood as a Religious Goal in Neo-Confucianism* (1978); A. F. Wright and D. Twitchett, eds., *Confucian Personalities* (1962); A. F. Wright, ed., *The Confucian Persuasion* (1960). Confucian temple: J. K. Shryock, *The Origin and Development of the State Cult of Confucius* (1932). Modern developments: W. T. Chan, *Religious Trends in Modern China* (1953); T. A. Metzger, *Escape from Predicament: Neo-Confucianism and China's Evolving Political Culture* (1977).

R. L. Taylor

CONFUCIUS kən fyo͞o´ shəs; Latinized form of K'UNG FU-TZU koong fo͞o´ tzə; lit. "Great Master K'ung" (Chin.; 551-479 B.C.). Philosopher and teacher who created one of the major ethico-religious and social-political traditions of China, Vietnam, Korea, and Japan.

1. The life of Confucius. The most authentic sources for the life and teachings of Confucius are the Analects and the Mencius, but the writings of opposing schools of philosophy also give information which became part of the tradition. Mo Tzu, for example, attacked Confucian teachings, while Chuang Tzu mocked Confucius, suggesting that in the end he became a Taoist. The philosophical writings attributed to Confucius or his immediate circle of disciples, such as the commentaries to the I Ching or chapters in the *Book of Rites (Li Chi),* represent later philosophical thought. The *Tso Chuan* commentary to the Spring and Autumn Annals *(Ch'un Ch'iu)* gives little information on Confucius' life, focusing instead on his supernatural abilities. The *Kuo Yü,* which includes a history of the state of Lu, gives only isolated incidents and emphasizes Confucius' supernatural powers, while the *K'ung Tzu Chia Yü* contains even more hagiographic features. It is not surprising then that when Ssu-ma Ch'ien (*ca.* 145-85 B.C.) wrote in his Historical Records the first biography of Confucius it differed little from previous accounts. He portrayed Confucius as possessing supernatural powers, as a member of the aristocracy, and as a seeker of Taoism.

Confucius was born in the small feudal state of Lu, located in present-day Shantung. His family name was K'ung, his personal name Ch'iu. His family was of the nobility, but lowly in rank. When Confucius was young, his father died, and the family appears to have struggled with poverty, Confucius providing for his own education. In his early adult years he may have held various minor posts in the state of Lu. According to tradition he eventually became a high official in Lu around the age of fifty, but he soon recognized the disinterest of his superiors in his policies, quit, and wandered from state to state with the hope of initiating political and social reforms. After some thirteen years he returned to Lu to teach and, according to tradition, edit the Confucian classics. (*See* CONFUCIANISM.) His following is said to have grown to some three thousand disciples of whom seventy-two were considered close to the Master.

2. Teachings. Confucius was witness to the political disintegration of the feudal order, an era characterized by the hegemony of various states and almost constant internecine warfare. His solution to the conditions of his day was a return to the ways of virtue neglected since the sage emperors of antiquity.

a) "Humaneness" (JEN). To bring order and peace to the world, man ought to return to "humaneness" *(jen),* a word also translated as "humanity," "benevolence," or most literally as "man-to-man-ness." "Humaneness" covers a number of specific virtues in the Analects, notably "reciprocity" *(shu),* described by Confucius as not doing to others what you would not have them do to you (Analects V, 11; XV, 23). To the rulers of the day the teachings offered little of practical value, and Confucius himself did not argue them on utilitarian grounds as would the Mohists after him. For Confucius virtue stood as its own reward, and the mark of the man of humanity was to remain unsoured even though his merits were unrecognized by others (I, 1). The humane man has no concern for what is profitable or utilitarian; he stands on virtue alone. Confucius believed that only in such a manner could peace and order come to the various states and eventually to all under Heaven *(T'ien-hsia),* and in the end man's ways would accord with those of Heaven. He appealed to a fundamental humanism and the rationality of man and his universe.

b) Heaven and history. The study of history was central to man's understanding of himself and the ways of Heaven. Heaven acted in history, and through the study of the traditions, literature, rites, and music of the past a template of action in accordance with the ways of Heaven would reveal itself. Particular points in history were exemplary for virtue. For Confucius the legendary sage emperors Yao and Shun as well as the founders of the Chou dynasty (1111-249 B.C.), Kings Wen and Wu, and the Duke of Chou, were paradigms of such virtue. Early Chou society, perhaps more than any other period, epitomized virtuous rule.

c) Rites and music. The rites and the music of the early Chou period became for Confucius symbols of the virtue possessed by the rulers and in turn the virtue manifest throughout society. Confucius condemned the rites and the music of his own day, not because he abhorred incorrect performance, but rather because, lacking inherent virtue, rites and music had become an empty shell. Confucius asked whether rites mean nothing more than jade and silk, and music nothing more than bells and drums (XVII, 11). To violate rites and music is to violate the virtuous ways of man and Heaven.

d) The rectification of names (cheng-ming). That rites and music ought to fully manifest their potential, that is, that they ought to correspond to all that their names respectively imply, illustrates a prominent concept in Confucian thought called the "rectification of names." When asked what would be the first act undertaken if he were given a state to rule, Confucius replied he would rectify names (XIII, 3). The king should act as a king, the subject act as a subject; the father act as a father, and the son act as a son (XII, 11). The significance of the concept goes beyond the mere correct use of language and the need for name and reality to correspond; it implies the recognition of man's virtuous nature. Thus a king to be a king must act as a king, that is, he must act in virtuous ways. In turn, rites and music must correspond to what they in fact are, the outward manifestations of the virtuous natures of man and Heaven.

e) The gentleman (chün-tzu). Confucius' teachings were directed toward the gentleman, the man who never lost sight of virtue regardless of hardships endured (I, 1) and who always found fault with his own shortcomings rather than blaming others (XV, 20). The term was thus a designation of character rather than birth. Prior to Confucius it had signified a member of the aristocracy, but Confucius accepted as a disciple anyone who had enthusiasm for learning. The importance of learning and respect for the learned became hallmarks of the Confucian school, and it is perhaps fitting that Confucius' birthday is celebrated as Teacher's Day (August 27).

3. Religious dimension. The use of the term "humanism" precludes for some the religious dimension, while for others it only redefines the religious potential. When asked about death, Confucius replied that he knew nothing of life, how could he know about death (XI, 11). When asked about spirits he stated that one should respect them but keep them at a distance (VI, 20). Both passages emphasize the focus upon man and life and as such substantiate the essentially humanist stance. On the other hand, Confucius in an autobiographical note illustrates a life whose goal is accord with the ways of Heaven (II, 4). Heaven and man from the Confucian view are not fundamentally separate, and man living in accord with his virtuous nature is man in relation to Heaven, the key to understanding the Confucian religious life.

Bibliography. General works: *See* CONFUCIANISM. Life and teachings of Confucius: A. Waley, *The Analects of Confucius* (1938); K. Shigeki, *Confucius* (1959); D. H. Smith, *Confucius* (1973); H. G. Creel, *Confucius and the Chinese Way* (1960); H. Fingarette, *Confucius: The Secular as Sacred* (1972).

R. L. TAYLOR

CONGREGATIONALISM (Ch). The form of church governance in which each local congregation is autonomous. The Congregational Church was a prominent denomination in New England from the early seventeenth century until its inclusion in the UNITED CHURCH OF CHRIST. BAPTISTS, CHRISTIAN CHURCHES (DISCIPLES OF CHRIST), and many other churches are congregational. J. R. CRIM

CONSERVATIVE JUDAISM. The centrist movement within contemporary Judaism; initiated by Zecharias Frankel (1801-75), chief rabbi of Dresden and later head of the Breslau Theological Seminary in Germany. He called it positive-historical Judaism, stressing that Judaism should remain true to its traditional character and make changes slowly and without radically modifying the practice of Jewish faith. In the United States, SOLOMON SCHECHTER (1850-1915), head of the Jewish Theological Seminary of America, was the central figure in promoting Conservative Judaism. His thought was based on the idea of "catholic Israel" as the determinant factor in the ongoing life of Judaism.

Conservative Judaism is, at present, the largest of the three main groupings in American Judaism and has established branches in Israel and Latin America. The movement's center is the Jewish Theological Seminary in New York City, where rabbis are trained and where intellectual and scholarly foundations of the movement are established. The rabbinic group, called the Rabbinical Assembly, numbers more than one thousand members. The synagogues are organized in the United Synagogue, which includes almost one thousand congregations. The movement also includes the Women's League for Conservative Judaism and various youth groups. In addition, a journal, *Conservative Judaism,* is published.

The worship services of the movement are characterized by family pews, a modernized liturgy, which includes English, and the inclusion of women in the ritual life of the congregation.

Bibliography. R. Gordis, *Understanding Conservative Judaism* (1978); I. Klein, *A Guide to Jewish Religious Practice* (1979); S. Schechter, *Studies in Judaism* (1961); S. Siegel, *Conservative Judaism and Jewish Law* (1977). S. SIEGEL

CONSTANTINE I or "the Great" (Ch; *ca.* 288-337). First Roman emperor to embrace Christianity. After the death of his father in 306, Constantine was acclaimed in Britain as the Emperor of the West. To secure his position he fought his rival Maxentius, who had established himself in Rome and Italy. On the eve of the battle of the Milvian Bridge in 312, he saw in a dream a cross of light with the inscription "In this sign you will conquer." He ascribed his ensuing victory to the Christian God. In the Edict of Milan (313) he and Licinius, the Eastern emperor, gave favored status to the Christian church.

In 323 Constantine defeated Licinius, becoming the ruler of the entire Roman Empire. He established a new capital, called New Rome or Constantinople, on the site of the Greek city of Byzantium. Although committed to the Christian cause, he postponed BAPTISM until on his deathbed, fearing that he would sin after baptism.

Constantine needed the undivided church as a unifying factor in the empire. To combat DONATISM he convened a synod of bishops in Arles (314), and when the Donatists refused to accept its decision, he persecuted them.

With the rise of the ARIAN controversy in the East, Constantine summoned the first ecumenical COUNCIL of bishops in NICAEA (325) and presided over it.

Bibliography. A. Schmemann, *Historical Road of Eastern Orthodoxy* (1963). V. KESICH

CONSUBSTANTIATION (Ch). The doctrine that the substance of Christ's body and blood is present with that of bread and wine in the EUCHARIST. Although Martin LUTHER did not use the term, it is associated with his teaching; he used the analogy of fire present in a red-hot iron. *See* TRANSUBSTANTIATION.
T. J. TALLEY

CONTARINI, GASPARO CARDINAL kōn´ tä rē´ nē (Ch; 1483-1542). Born into Venetian nobility, Contarini was created a lay cardinal in 1535 and led the group that in 1537 presented to Pope Paul III proposals for reforming the church. He was papal legate to the Roman Catholic–Protestant Regensburg Colloquy (1541). Both LUTHER and Rome repudiated the agreements reached there. *See* REFORMATION, CATHOLIC. J. RAITT

CONVERSION. The term "conversion" is given a variety of definitions by the world's religions. In some, such as CHRISTIANITY and ISLAM, it is a dominant theme, while in HINDUISM and many folk or traditional religions it is seldom used. When it is employed, it denotes the deliberate abandonment of one way of life or one religious system in favor of another.

1. Conversion as climactic or gradual. Religious literature describes two major types of conversion: climactic and gradual or progressive. Climactic conversion is normally an adult phenomenon because it entails a deliberate decision which has psychic, sociological, and religious consequences. It implies a more or less instantaneous espousal of a particular religious system. The second is a more gradual process of change which is produced through pedagogical or nurturing processes. The outcome of both is similar.

Climactic conversions happen at almost any time in life, while gradual conversions coincide with the normal maturation process, and passing through puberty and becoming converted are experienced at approximately the same time. (*See* LIFE CYCLE RITES.)

In JUDAISM the word is only used to describe the way a person who was born a non-Jew becomes a Jew. It is synonymous with becoming a proselyte. Likewise many folk religions do not normally use the term "convert," even though they do find it necessary to lead youth into cultural conformity, a "conversion" type of experience. In folk religions it is assumed by the community that every person born in that community is an integral part of that society; therefore the neophyte must simply accept what is already there. In some Christian denominations on the other hand, especially in some PROTESTANT churches, even children of believing parents are to be converted in order to be full members.

Within each religious tradition doctrinal positions emerge which define the nature of conversion. Those who hold to the doctrine of total depravity of humanity usually stress radical conversion, while those who have a greater trust in the potential of the human spirit may interpret conversion more in terms of development, nurture, training, and maturation. However, in each case the religious system assumes the need for some orientation away from the life of unbelief to the life of belief.

If the conversion is from one religious system to another, usually some rite or series of rites is employed to both announce the transition and to give psychic reinforcement to the individual's conversion experience. These rites include BAPTISM, CIRCUMCISION, ritual cleansing, PILGRIMAGE, or some similar rite. It is possible to determine whether a person is "converted" or not by observing whether he has undergone the transition rites and whether he subscribes to the appropriate TABOO systems.

2. **Conversion as intracultural or intercultural.** Another, perhaps more helpful, way to view conversion and its consequences is to examine it against the backdrop of culture. It becomes evident that conversions are either intracultural or intercultural.

Intracultural conversions occur when a person, having been born into a particular religious tradition, can be converted from being a nonbeliever and therefore a nonparticipant in that religious system to being a believer in it. If this is the case, the convert moves from a stance of noncompliance and nonparticipation in the normal religious routines of the community to active, committed involvement.

Even though persons are born into a particular religious system and are therefore expected to subscribe to the group's belief patterns, it can be observed that societies recognize in human beings tendencies toward anti-religious and anti-social behavior. Therefore societies prescribe the rites of passage through which a novice must go in order to attain a state of compliance with the mores, taboos, and value system of the folk religion—to become adult, so to speak. The traditional religions of Bantu Africa, for example, provide illustrations of sometimes elaborate puberty rituals through which each generation passes. Rebirth is reenacted in these rites which result in the production of committed novices, each, it is hoped, prepared to shoulder full responsibility as an adult in the community. (*See* AFRICAN TRADITIONAL RELIGION.) These puberty rituals normally commence with the onset of puberty and culminate in the birth of the first child (in some instances the first male child). It is during that period of human awakening and maturation that society can exert its most telling influence upon persons. Upon completion of the conversion process the individuals are expected to exemplify the normal time-honored participation in the values, rites, and taboos of the folk religion. This type of conversion is intracultural, is not a result of proselytism, and does not entail a radical change in world view.

On the other hand, when intercultural conversion takes place, there is normally a radical departure from the local culture's cosmological understandings. The conversion process becomes complicated, because the convert is faced with a cultural readjustment in a direction away from his traditional world view. This process is exemplified wherever evangelists of one culture call persons of a radically different culture to conversion. The efforts of modern Western Christian MISSIONS around the world typify this process.

3. **Conversion and cosmological reorientation.** Intracultural and intercultural conversion differ in both process and consequence. When conversion is intracultural, no significant reorganization of one's own world view is required. A person's cosmology and metaphysics remain virtually unchanged, because his conversion is simply a sociological movement within a culture.

When, however, a person who has been reared in one culture converts to belief in a religion whose origins are in a radically different culture, significant changes often occur in his world view which place very heavy demands upon him. This may result in cultural alienation.

One solution to the problem of cultural alienation is for a convert simply to enter into the rites and symbols of the new religion without making any significant adjustments in his world view. This is a common approach, and in such a case the new faith is held precariously. History shows that this type of conversion is difficult to sustain.

In the history of Christian missions, conversions which endure do not follow upon enforced change. Conversions which simply adopt some alternate rites and ceremonies but are not marked by a reorientation of cosmological reality likewise do not endure. Christianity requires the injection of JESUS Christ into the cosmology as the power preeminent among all other powers. If this does not happen, reversion to pre-Christian cosmologies usually follows.

4. **Conversion and relationship to culture.** The phenomenon of conversion is of increasing concern to missiologists, especially with reference to the nature of conversion from one religion to another. The issue

is complicated by a variety of factors, including the expectations which the believing community has for the convert.

There are normally three distinct stages through which individuals and communities move as they are converted as a result of transcultural missions. The initial stage is marked by a rejection of the preconversion world and a movement toward the sociological and cosmological orientation of the culture of the missionary or evangelist. During this stage marks of conversion include a preference for the exotic and a rejection of traditional views. In the second stage, the Christian community, which has by then taken on some aspects of a distinct subculture, reviews its relationship with the culture which it has left and seeks to realign itself vis-à-vis that culture in such a way as to convince the dominant culture that it is in cultural solidarity with it. A third stage follows, in which a more even-handed position is taken, and some aspects of the dominant culture are accepted, while others are rejected. Each stage places its own peculiar expectations upon the converts.

See Religious Experience.

Bibliography. J. A. Loewen, "Socialization and Conversion in the Ongoing Church," *Practical Anthropology*, XVI (1969), 10-11; E. A. Nida, *Message and Mission* (1960); J. Stott and R. T. Coote, eds., *Gospel and Culture* (1979); A. R. Tippett, "Conversion as a Dynamic Process in Christian Mission," *Missiology*, V (1977), 203-21. D. R. Jacobs

COPTIC CHURCH (Ch—*Copt.* "Egyptian"). Native Monophysite church of Egypt. With the rejection of the Council of Chalcedon (451) for theological and political reasons, it separated from the Orthodox Church. By 457 a Monophysite was Patriarch of Alexandria. Since the Arab conquest of Egypt of 642, the church has been under Muslim domination. During severe persecutions in the tenth and eleventh centuries, many churches were destroyed and great numbers of Christians converted to Islam. Throughout its long and uncertain history this church has preserved its ancient faith and tradition. Christian Monasticism began in Egypt, and has been kept alive there without interruption. At present there is a revival of monastic life as educated men and women enter monasteries.

The head of this hierarchical church, "Pope of Alexandria and Patriarch of the See of St. Mark," has had his seat in Cairo since the eleventh century. The church language is Coptic, which is no longer used in modern Egypt. They use the Liturgy of St. Basil most commonly, during which they address many prayers to "the Nile, the fish and things living." In our century discoveries of the rich tradition of Coptic religious art have attracted worldwide attention.

Coptic Christians occupy professional positions, as doctors, lawyers, and social workers, far out of proportion to their numbers. Worldwide, there are about three million Copts, including fourteen churches in the United States with 30,000 members.

Bibliography. A. S. Atiya, *A History of Eastern Christianity* (1968), pp. 11-145. V. Kesich

CORPUS CHRISTI (Ch). A festival of Roman Catholicism honoring the Holy Eucharist on the Thursday after Trinity Sunday, but today often kept on the following Sunday. First promoted by Juliana of Liège (*ca.* 1230), the feast was promulgated by Urban IV in 1264 and became universal in the Western church in the following century.

T. J. Talley

COSMOLOGY. *See* individual articles on the major traditions.

COUNCILS OF THE CHURCH (Ch). In the wider sense, any regularly assembled meeting of Clergy and laity called together to discuss and decide upon ecclesiastical doctrine, administration and discipline, and Liturgy. In the more technical sense, those assemblies of Bishops and their decisions regulating Christian life and practice. Councils can be considered normative for Christians either for reasons of their formative influence on subsequent Christian groupings or because of the formal adherence of major Christian groupings to their decisions (*see* § 2 *below*). The former, even though sometimes regional in membership and outlook, have historical importance and are usually referred to simply as "councils." The latter, holding sway because of their more universal position at the time or their subsequent ratification by major Christian bodies, are usually designated "general" or "ecumenical." Viewed more abstractly as a structure for decision-making, the councils of the church constituted the adjudicatory forum for achieving ecclesiastical agreement.

1. Terminology. *Council* (Lat. *concilium*) in the West and *synod* (Gr. *synodos*) in the East are equivalent terms in ecclesiastical sources for designating a decision-making ecclesiastical assembly. After the Council of Nicaea (325), Western sources also employed *synod* to designate such an assembly. In nonecclesiastical usage the terms designate a religious association (cf. Josephus, *Antiquities* 14.235; Tertullian, *Apology* 13). These terms as found in the old Latin and Greek Bibles do not refer to a church council, which did not appear as an ecclesiastical form until the late second century (*see* §3a). The first contemporary attestations to the practice of gathering clergy for a council come at the beginning of the third century from Tertullian (*On Fasting* 13.6) in the West (referring to a Greek practice) and from the mid-third century from Dionysius of Alexandria (in Eusebius, *Ecclesiastical History* VII.7.5) in the East.

2. Types and membership. Before the fourth century councils were constituted by bishops (Cyprian, *Epistle* 73.1; Eusebius, *EH* VII.5.5) of a local, provincial, or regional area. Lower clergy and frequently laity attended (cf. Eusebius, *EH* VI.33.3; Cyprian, *Ep.* 19.2), although decision-making seems to have belonged to the bishops (Cyprian, *Ep.* 73.1). Emperor CONSTANTINE inaugurated the practice of summoning the bishops to a council, the so-called "imperial" council. From 325 on, there are numerous examples of imperially summoned regional councils, as well as a new type designated as "ecumenical" or "general," whose decisions were binding on Christians and were enforced by civil authorities.

3. **History.** *a) The formative period (ca. 180-251).* Despite the later church's view that the so-called Apostolic Council (Acts 15) was both a council and ecumenical, the first councils were probably those held (*ca.* 180) in Asia Minor over MONTANISM. In the late second and early third centuries other councils were held in various Eastern and Western regions, as occasion demanded, over such disputed questions as the proper day of the week for the celebration of Easter (e.g. Eusebius, *EH* V.23.2), the testing of doctrinal tenets of particular individuals (e.g. Beryllus in Arabia: Eusebius, *EH* VI.33.3), and the rebaptism of persons baptized initially by sectarian or schismatic groups (e.g. Cyprian, *Ep.* 73.3). But it was the general persecutions of the mid-third century and their aftermath which entrenched the council of bishops as a major structural force in ecclesiastical decision-making.

b) Emergence of conciliar decision-making (251-312). Councils were held in North Africa, Rome, and Alexandria to deal with such issues as readmittance of Christians who lapsed under persecution, status of schismatic churches and their SACRAMENTS (especially BAPTISM), and disputed episcopal elections (particularly in Rome and North Africa).

The writings of Bishop Cyprian of Carthage (d. 258) describe the African regional councils. Bishops assembled under his presidency, as he was bishop of the largest city of the area, and acted in collegial consort in decisions. The Montanist Tertullian had claimed that the totality of the universal church could be present in a spiritual practice performed by a regional gathering (*On Fasting* 13.6; cf. *Against Praxeas* 24.5 for *representatio*). Cyprian claimed the full participation of each individual bishop in the apostolic authority of PETER (*On the Unity* 4). This guaranteed the sovereign collegiality of the assembled bishops and gave Cyprian a basis to disagree with Stephen of Rome over the question of rebaptism. The consensus of the African bishops (Seventh Council of Carthage, 256) was against the practice of the Church of Rome and showed the emerging problem of regional councils. The practice of voting on issues in a given region and then informing other areas of decisions, a practice begun long before Cyprian (Eusebius, *EH* V.23.1) and continued long afterward (Alexander of Alexandria, *Letter to Alexander*), would work for unanimity only if regional differences did not involve cardinal matters.

It would take the "imperial" Synod of Arles (314) to resolve the difference between Rome and Africa on this particular question, but the coming together of major Eastern bishops at the Council of Antioch (268) to condemn Paul of Samosata may be seen as a universalizing trend begun by the churches even before the great councils of the fourth century. It was, however, the advent of Constantine that regularized this process and gave a new legal authority to the decisions of such councils, as well as a new solemnity, best represented by the application of the adjective "holy" to councils beginning with the Synod of Ancyra (314).

c) Conciliar regulation and ecumenical councils (312-451). The need for transregional uniformity and for a means of enforcing the decisions of a given council were accentuated by DONATISM in the West and ARIANISM in the East, calling forth the first imperially summoned councils in the West (313-18) and the first ecumenical council in the East (Nicaea). Their decisions were to be binding on all signators and on all Christians of the empire.

At Nicaea, Canons IV and V made an important step forward in regularizing councils. Canon IV codified guidelines for the election of a bishop by all the bishops in a province with the long-established right of ratification given to the METROPOLITAN, the bishop of the leading city of the province. Canon V tried to provide for ratification of an excommunication in one province by other provinces (after due examination of the facts of the case) in councils which were to meet in every province twice annually.

So difficult was it to build consensus for the Creed of Nicaea in the years after the council, and so abused was the practice of producing compromise creeds throughout the fourth century, that subsequent ecumenical councils were reluctant to produce a creedal statement, preferring rather to affirm their adherence to "the faith" of Nicaea (cf. Gregory of Nazianzus, *Ep.* 102). The ecumenical Council of Chalcedon (451) tried to take this stance, but under imperial pressure had to write a creed. In fact, this, the fourth ecumenical council, is the first witness that the ecumenical Council of Constantinople (381) wrote a creed. Most scholars today think that the Creed of Constantinople, recited today in Christian churches under the name "Nicene Creed," was not composed by that council. Its acceptance at Chalcedon, however, made it the ecumenical statement of the church's doctrine of the TRINITY. (*See* CREEDS AND CONFESSIONS §2.)

4. **Positions on the authority of councils.** While PROTESTANTISM usually recognizes the authority of only the first four ecumenical councils, both the GREEK ORTHODOX and ROMAN CATHOLIC churches jointly recognize seven: Nicaea (325), Constantinople (381), Ephesus (431), Chalcedon (451), Constantinople (553), Constantinople (680), and Nicaea (787). The Roman tradition went on to designate an eighth ecumenical council (Constantinople, 869-70) and then to pursue its own separate conciliar enumeration and history.

Councils in the medieval West were subordinated to and ratified by the PAPACY; but the increasing imperialization of a schism-ridden papacy and centralization of the CURIA led, in the late fourteenth and early fifteenth centuries, to developing notions of conciliarism, in which councils were seen as representing the total authority of the church to which even the pope was subject. After a series of early defeats, Pope Eugene IV (1431-47) succeeded in moderating conciliar activity and subordinating it to papal authority.

With MARTIN LUTHER (*On the Councils and the Churches,* 1539) the main Protestant position arose: both popes and councils were to be subject to the authority of scripture, for what makes a council authoritative in its teaching is its "apostolic" character. Where the councils rendered judgment in accordance with scripture (as did the first four ecumenical councils) they are "apostolic" and authoritative in their teaching.

Bibliography. F. Dvornik, *The Ecumenical Councils* (1961); J. A. Fisher, "Angebliche Synoden des 2. Jahrhunderts," *AHC,* IX (1977), 241-58 and "Die ersten Synoden," in W. Brandmüller, ed., *Synodale Structuren* (1977), pp. 27-60; C. J. Hefele, *A History of the Christian Councils,* Vol. I, 2nd ed. rev. (1872); G. Kretschmar, "The Councils of the Ancient Church," in H. J. Margull, ed., *The Councils of the Church* (1966), pp. 1-81; H. Küng, *Structures of the Church* (1964); A. Lumpe, "Zur Geschichte des Wortes *synodos* in der antiken christlichen Gräzitat," *AHC,* VI (1974), 40-53 and "Zur Geschichte der Wörter *Concilium* und *Synodus* in der antiken christlichen Latinität," *AHC,* II (1970), 1-21; H. Marot, "Conciles anténicéens et conciles oecuméniques," in *Concile et les conciles* (1960), pp. 19-43 (for gradual growth to Nicaea rather than its discontinuity with the past).

D. E. GROH

COVENANT (Ju & Ch). An agreement between parties of equal or unequal rank which could be initiated by either party. As is normative for all contracts, covenants carried stipulations, whether explicitly stated or not, which are accepted by both parties. Ancient Near Eastern treaty forms have been compared with covenants in the OT, where the term is used for Israel's covenants with YAHWEH, especially as established with MOSES on SINAI. Other covenants were made with Noah (Gen. 9:9-17), ABRAHAM (Gen. 15:18-21), and David (II Sam. 23:5). The Deuteronomic Reformation (II Kings 23:1-27) marked a renewal of the covenant concept as the unique bond between Israel and Yahweh.

The concept of a New Covenant (Jer. 31:31-34) became a basic metaphor for the relationship of JESUS to the CHURCH (Heb. 8:8-13; 12:24), and is used as an alternative for NEW TESTAMENT in many English versions of the Bible. In the REFORMED CHURCHES covenant has been a frequent symbol for the renewal of the church.

M. G. ROGERS

COVENANTERS (Ch). PRESBYTERIANS in Scotland were frequently called Covenanters from the sixteenth century on because of their proclivity to support their convictions by signing covenants, the most notable of which (1638) resisted the effort to impose a service book and Episcopal polity. After the restoration in 1660 the title was applied to the most determined resisters to EPISCOPACY, many of whom suffered death for their cause. *See* REFORMED CHURCHES.

J. H. LEITH

COW, SYMBOLISM AND VENERATION (H). In India the cow is a symbol of divine benevolence and, hence, an animal to be protected and revered. Its products are "gifts" often used for spiritual cleansing. According to W. N. Brown, the sanctity of the cow is the result of five factors: its importance for Vedic sacrifice; its figurative usage in Vedic literature which later was taken literally; prohibitions against killing a BRAHMIN's cow; the doctrine of "noninjury" (AHIṂSĀ); and association of the cow with the mother-goddess. To this should be added the importance of the cow for the sustenance of human life and the symbol of cow protection as an affirmation of religious solidarity against Muslim invaders.

Though the bull is not protected as is the cow in modern India, seals from the INDUS VALLEY CIVILIZATION depict bulls as objects of veneration. In the VEDAS both the bull and the cow are at times called *aghnya,* "not to be killed." The epithet is used as an appositive to *dhenu,* "milk cow," or in contexts which refer to its ability to give milk or to reproduce. This indicates that the cow was not to be slain because of its economic or reproductive value. In the RIG VEDA cattle represent wealth and are sought in prayer to the gods, yet they are important sacrificial items as are their products.

The cow was regularly used as food, especially when entertaining guests. Pāṇini (Sūtra III. 4.73) called a guest *goghna,* "one for whom a cow is slain." YĀJÑAVALKYA, Vedic sage and metaphysician, declared, "I for one eat it [beef], provided that it is tender." (ŚB III.1.2.21). In the Bṛhadāranyaka Upaniṣad eating beef is part of a prescription for vigorous offspring, and in the later SŪTRA literature the eating of meat is taken for granted, but restrictions are placed upon the manner of killing the animal.

The Vedas use the cow figuratively and symbolically. The gods are called "cow-born," *gojatah.* The cosmic waters are regularly referred to as cows, e.g., they are said to come forth like lowing cows in RV I.23.2. The goddess ADITI is called a cow and the earthly cow is addressed as Aditi. The cow also symbolizes the earth, heaven, and speech.

Four hymns of the ATHARVA VEDA are entirely devoted to securing protection for the possessions of the Brahmin, especially his cow. To injure the cow of the Brahmin is said to be equal to injury of the Brahmin himself (5.18-19; 12.4-5).

In the fourth century BUDDHISTS and JAINAS emphasized the doctrine of *ahiṃsā,* "noninjury," which was less important in Vedic literature. This doctrine did not single out the cow as its object, but was meant to protect all living things. Both the PALI CANON and the Epic literature, however, indicate a chasm between the ideal and popular practice. Butchers *(goghataka,* "sellers of beef ") are mentioned as well as hunters and trappers. Indian rulers as late as the twelfth century A.D. still were attempting to enforce a ban on meat eating (e.g. the Jaina king Kumarapala of Gujarat, 1142-1172). On the other hand, the MAHĀBHĀRATA warns that the killer of a cow will be reborn in hell for as many years as there are hairs on its body (13.74.4). The Manu Dharmaśāstra (*see* MANU, LAWS OF) is inconsistent, including cow-slaughter in a list of crimes (11.60), but allowing the eating of "consecrated flesh" (5.27-42). The ARTHAŚĀSTRA likewise protects the cow in 2.26 and 3.10, but also speaks of cattle "fit only for the supply of meat" in 2.19.

The cow becomes a symbol of the sacred in the Epic literature. It is especially sacred to SHIVA, whose vehicle is NANDI the bull. VISHNU's heaven is called the "world of cows," *goloka,* and cow dung is viewed as a symbol of his discus. Kāmadhenu, a cow associated with the Vedic god INDRA, symbolizes the cow as mother, the provider of needs. She was produced at the churning of the primordial ocean by the gods and now grants all human desires.

The sanctity of the cow increased even more in the PURĀṆAS and it gained there the stature it has today. The cow is said to be created on the same day as the god BRAHMĀ and cow-slaughter is equal to killing a Brahmin. The Bhāgavata Purāṇa (1.16-17) notes that lack of reverence for the cow is one of the symptoms of the final age (KALI YUGA) and emphasizes the cow as a part of the life of the god KRISHNA, a cowherd. Vishnu Purāṇa 1.13 proclaims that the cow was given to provide vegetation for the earth.

Between A.D. 800-1200 *ahiṃsā* became a more central element of Indian ethics and the cow was singled out as its symbol. Writings after 1500 show consistent reverence for the cow and the proscription of meat eating. With the Muslim invasions, cow protection became a symbol of indigenous religion against the invaders' sacrificial use of the animal. Shivaji (1627-1680), the Maharashtran hero and leader, asserted that it, CASTE, and protection of the Brahmin are essential doctrines.

The modern period has witnessed an ongoing struggle between those who cherish the symbol and those who would emphasize economic issues. GANDHI claimed, "Cow protection is the gift of Hinduism to the world," because the cow represents the indissoluable bond between the human and the subhuman and an example of complete giving for others. A directive of the Indian Constitution (no. 48) attempts a compromise, condemning cow-slaughter but recommending the use of breeding techniques.

All that comes forth from the cow is held sacred as a gift of the great Mother to humankind, especially the *pañcagavya,* five products of the cow: milk, GHEE (clarified butter), curds, dung, and urine. These are used separately or in a mixture for purification from defilement caused by breaking caste or ritual taboos. They may be ingested for personal purification or used by the housewife, to cleanse her kitchen, or the priest, to purify the place of ritual. Even dust from the hoofprint of the cow may be used in medicine.

Actual cultic worship of the cow takes place today primarily on one day of the year—*Gopastami,* the "cow holiday," when she is treated as an image of a god. In the temple courtyard she is bathed, decorated, and given offerings of flowers, moistened wheat, incense, etc., in the hope that she will continue her blessings.

Bibliography. W. N. Brown, "The Sanctity of the Cow in Hinduism," *The Economic Weekly* (Bombay), XVI (February, 1964), 244-55; A. Heston, *et al.*, "An Approach to the Sacred Cow of India," *Current Anthropology,* XII (1971), 191-201; T. Magul, "Present-Day Worship of the Cow in India," *Numen,* XV (1968), 63-80. R. N. MINOR

CRAVING (B). *See* TAṆHĀ.

CREATIONISM (Ch). The belief that the first two chapters of the BIBLE must be interpreted as a history of the origin of the world. Creationists are opposed to the teaching of evolution in public schools, insisting that evolution is only one of the possible interpretations of the origins of life.

Creationism became an issue in the United States after the publication of Charles Darwin's *The Origin of Species* in 1859. After a period of examination, many Christians decided that the new scientific theory did not contradict Christian doctrine and proposed a reconciliation between science and theology. Henry Ward Beecher (1813-87), popular pastor of Brooklyn's Plymouth CONGREGATIONAL Church, was a leader in this reconciliation. Most liberal ministers and theologians came to take a similar position before World War I.

Other Christians were not as sure of the new science. Charles Hodge (1797-1878), a professor at Princeton Seminary and influential PRESBYTERIAN theologian, put the argument against Darwinism in its strongest terms in his *What is Darwinism?* (1874). The problem, Hodge maintained, was that the theory did not contain a sufficiently convincing explanation of how one species evolved into another.

Unfortunately, Hodge's high road of scholarly debate was not the only critical response to evolution. Many popular evangelists attempted to deal with the new doctrine by subjecting it—and its adherents—to ridicule. The new teaching was accused of furthering immorality, destroying human dignity, and being without factual foundation.

After World War I many Americans believed that the nation was in deep danger and were willing to listen to those who offered easy solutions. The creationists began to make gains in their attempts to ban evolution from the public schools, and in some states, including Tennessee, Oklahoma, and Florida, laws were passed prohibiting the new biology. In addition, public opinion was able to secure the dismissal of some faculty members from both state and private schools. The 1925 trial of John Scopes, a Tennessee high school biology instructor, marked the high point of the creationist campaign. The trial, in which William Jennings Bryan (1860-1925) argued against evolution and Clarence Darrow (1857-1938) for it, was treated as a farce by the pro-evolutionist press. In the 1970s supporters of creationism mounted a new campaign to have it taught in the nation's schools.

Bibliography. R. Ginger, *Six Days or Forever: Tennessee vs. John Thomas Scopes* (1958). G. MILLER

CREDO krā´ dō (Ch—Lat.; "I believe"). First words of the NICENE CREED as used in the Latin MASS. The use of a creed in the EUCHARIST began in Constantinople (sixth century) and spread widely. Introduced by Charlemagne at his court, it soon became common throughout the West. R. A. GREER

CREEDS AND CONFESSIONS (Ch). Christian creeds have their roots in the theological tradition of ancient Israel, which was unified by its historical credos and declaratory affirmations of faith. The need for creeds and confessions arises from two basic facts: (1) the nature of the human mind, which has the capacity for reflection, and (2) the nature of the faith itself. "Faith seeks understanding (intelligibility)" (ANSELM).

1. **The Bible.** Precise, fixed creeds did not appear until the third or fourth century of the CHURCH'S history, but the process that culminated in them had its beginning in the historical credos (Deut. 26:5-9; 6:21-25) and the declaratory affirmations of the OT (Deut. 6:4-5; I Kings 18:39). In the preaching, singing, praying, witnessing of the NT church the Christian faith became increasingly fixed in creedlike formulas (e.g., I Cor. 15:3-7; Phil. 2:6-11; Matt. 28:18-20; Rom. 10:9). Some credal statements are simple Christological affirmations of the lordship of JESUS Christ (Mark 8:29; I Tim. 3:16; Rom. 10:9). Others are two-article formulas confessing both God and Christ (I Cor. 8:6). Three-article statements affirming Father, Son, and HOLY SPIRIT (Matt. 28:19; II Cor. 13:13) also appear in the NT.

2. **The ecumenical creeds.** The consolidation of the faith of the Christian community into precise, stereotyped, formal summaries of the faith continued in the early church. Some of these formulas appeared in theological writings such as the letters of Ignatius (*ca.* 107), *Epistula Apostolorum* (Dialogues of Jesus with His Disciples after the Resurrection [*ca.* 150]), *The Witness of Justin Martyr* (*ca.* 165), *The Profession of the Presbyters of Smyrna* (*ca.* 180), and the Balyzah Papyrus (*ca.*200 or later). Along with these short summary statements there also developed long, more diffused rules of faith that served as guides for preaching and teaching, which may be found in multiple forms in the writings of Irenaeus, Tertullian, and ORIGEN.

The church needed creeds and confessions for numerous purposes: the teaching ministry of the church and catechetical instruction (*see* CATECHISM), a hermeneutical guide for interpreting scripture, an antidote to heresy, and a witness to the world. The church also needed creeds preeminently for worship and in particular for BAPTISM. Baptism in the name of the Father, Son, and Holy Spirit was the occasion for the development of an interrogatory creed on a trinitarian framework. (*See* TRINITY.) Hippolytus gives us the text of such a creed that was in use in Rome about 215.

> Do you believe in God the Father All Governing (*pantokratora*)?
>
> Do you believe in Christ Jesus, the Son of God, Who was begotten by the Holy Spirit from the Virgin Mary, Who was crucified under Pontius Pilate, and died (and was buried) and rose the third day living from the dead, and ascended into the heavens, and sat down on the right hand of the Father, and will come to judge the living and the dead?
>
> Do you believe in the Holy Spirit, in the holy Church, and (in the resurrection of the body [*sarkos*])?

Catechetical classes needed a declaratory creed which was traditioned (authoritatively delivered) to the catechumen at a point in classes and then was rendered back by the catechumen. Such a creed, very similar to the interrogatory creed of Hippolytus, was in use in ROME in the third century. This old Roman Symbol became the mother creed for declaratory creeds in churches in the West.

The APOSTLES' CREED, according to legend written by the apostles, is a daughter creed of the Roman Symbol, first appearing in southwest France sometime in the late sixth or seventh century. Its present text is first found in the *De singulis libris canonicis scarapsus* of Priminius, which is dated between 710 and 724. This creed, which owed much to Rome, became the common creed of the Frankish empire and was finally adopted in Rome. It became the most universal creed in the West, but it was not known in the Eastern Churches.

The NICENE CREED is the first creed to have synodical authority. It was promulgated by the Council of NICAEA (325) in response to the teaching of an Alexandrian PRESBYTER named Arius concerning the deity of Jesus Christ. The church had always spoken of Jesus as God, but it had never defined in what precise sense it meant that Jesus was God. Christians had spoken of Jesus as Lord, Savior, the Word, Son of God, Son of Man, prophet, priest. All of these titles refer to the activity of Jesus Christ and to his relation to his disciples, to his meaning or value for them.

Arius changed the question. He did not ask how Jesus is related to us and what he means for us. He asked the prior question, Who is Jesus Christ? Is he really God? Or is he a creature? Arius himself was willing to say that Jesus was the noblest of all creation but still a creature. The church at the Council of Nicaea declared that in Jesus Christ, God himself is present insofar as God can be embodied in and expressed through a human life. The council took an Eastern creed and inserted into it four phrases about Jesus Christ that ruled ARIANISM out. These phrases were (1) from the being of the father, (2) true God from true God, (3) begotten not made, and (4) from the same essence (HOMOOUSION) as the Father. The last phrase was the crucial affirmation, and every creed that included this phrase was regarded as Nicene. The decision of the Council of Nicaea was vigorously debated for fifty years, but it was reaffirmed at the Council of Constantinople in 381. The creed which was associated with this council, and which was similar to the one at Nicaea in 325, became the Nicene Creed of the church's liturgy. It is the most universal Christian creed, and it is the most important because it deals with the fundamental Christian affirmation and it rejects the most serious Christian heresy.

The Nicene Creed made it necessary for the church to define the doctrine of the person of Jesus Christ and the doctrine of the Trinity. Having said that Jesus was truly God, it had also to deal with the basic Christian conviction that Jesus was truly man. After a series of attempts by theologians and councils to deal with the divine and the human in the person of Jesus Christ, the Council of Chalcedon in 451 declared that Jesus Christ is truly God and truly man in one person, one acting subject. The mystery of the divine self and the mystery of the human self united in Jesus Christ can neither be confused, changed, separated, or divided. Chalcedon, which was truly catholic in utilizing the theological resources of Antioch, Alexandria, and Rome, did not solve the problem, but it set the boundaries in which an affirmation about the person of Jesus Christ must take place. (*See* CHALCEDONIAN DEFINITION.)

The doctrine of the Trinity did not receive such full-scale conciliar treatment. The deity of Christ was affirmed at Nicaea and the deity of the Holy Spirit at the Council of Constantinople in 381. The ATHANASIAN CREED, written between 440 and 542 under the influence of Augustinian theology, gives full expression to this doctrine along with the doctrine of the person of Christ. Its dogmatism and its anathemas upon those who do not accept its teachings have obscured its theological significance.

3. **Creeds of Eastern Christendom.** The Nicene Creed, which was a revision of a creed of an Eastern church, is the most notable Eastern creed. It is also universally accepted. Among the later doctrinal statements of the Eastern ORTHODOX CHURCHES are the Orthodox Confession of Peter Mogilas (1643), the Answers of Jeremiah (Patriarch of Constantinople) to Lutheran theologians (1576), the confession prepared by Metrophanes Critopulus to explain Eastern Orthodoxy to Protestants (1625), and the Russian Catechisms, especially the Longer Catechism of Philaret (1839). A confession appearing under the name of Cyril Lucar (1629), Patriarch of Constantinople, was sympathetic to Protestantism and was repudiated by the majority of Orthodox. The Confession of Dositheus, approved by the Synod of Jerusalem in 1672, in opposition to the Protestant sympathies of the previous documents is more representative of the Eastern Church.

4. **Roman Catholicism.** The canons and the decrees of the Council of TRENT (1545-63) were formulated in the context of the Protestant REFORMATION. They also narrowed many of the options that were open to Christians in the fluid theology of medieval Catholicism. The Creed of the Council of Trent (1564) is a short summary of the lengthier document. The Council of Trent fixed the shape of modern Roman Catholicism. There have been other notable pronouncements of doctrine such as the Dogma of the IMMACULATE CONCEPTION (1854), the Dogma of Papal INFALLIBILITY (1870), and the Dogma of the ASSUMPTION of the Virgin Mary (1950), in addition to numerous papal encyclicals of great importance. The whole shape of Roman Catholicism received new interpretation in the work of the Second VATICAN COUNCIL (1962-65).

5. **Protestantism.** Protestants were prolific writers of confessions. Some early Protestant confessions were brief and precise statements of fundamental commitments in the form of theses, such as MARTIN LUTHER'S Ninety-Five Theses (1517) or the Ten Conclusions of Berne (1528). In general, Protestant confessions reaffirmed the theology of the ancient catholic church, in particular the doctrine of the person of Jesus Christ and the Trinity. They also sought to explicate in a comprehensive and systematic way the faith of the church with an emphasis upon Protestant doctrines of SALVATION, church, and SACRAMENTS.

The Lutheran confessions, the AUGSBURG CONFESSION (1530), the Apology of the Augsburg Confession (1531), the Smalcald Articles (1537), Treatise on the Power and Primacy of the Pope (1537), the Small Catechism of Dr. Martin Luther (1529), and the Large Catechism of Dr. Martin Luther (1529), were written by Martin Luther and PHILIP MELANCHTHON. These were incorporated in a *Book of Concord* (1580) which also included the *Formula of Concord* dealing with disputes as to Luther's authentic teaching.

Calvinist and Reformed Protestants emphasized the occasional nature of confessions and wrote them most prolifically. Among the most important were the Gallican Confession (1559), the Scots Confession (1560), and the Second HELVETIC (1566). Protestant scholasticism stated the faith with a precision, logical coherence, and comprehension not found in the earlier documents. The WESTMINSTER CONFESSION (1647), the Canons of Dort (1619), and the Helvetic

Consensus Formula (1675) were important statements of Reformed Protestantism.

The THIRTY-NINE ARTICLES of the Church of England (1563) combined Calvinist and Lutheran influences as well as the indigenous English tradition with that of the Catholic tradition. At the other extreme of the Reformation were the radical reformers among whose more important confessional statements are the Schleitheim Articles (1527) and the Dordrecht Confession of 1632.

6. **Contemporary confessions.** The creed-making process never ends, and numerous confessions have been written in the modern period. The German church struggle during the Nazi period gave rise to one of the most notable of modern confessions, the Barmen Declaration (1934), which affirmed the lordship of Jesus Christ in the church. The emergence of the church in nonwestern countries has also led to efforts to state Christian faith in the idiom of nonwestern traditions. The Creed of the Batak Church (Great Synod of the Huria Kristen Batak Protestant Church of Indonesia) is an example.

Creeds and confessions suggest authority as well as witness and testimony, but it is difficult to define precisely their authority. Church courts have declared their authority and within limits this authority holds. In the long run the authority of creeds inheres in their ability to command the approval of the commonsense wisdom of the Christian community.

Bibliography. J. N. D. Kelly, *Early Christian Creeds,* 3rd ed. (1972); P. Schaff, *Creeds of Christendom,* 6th ed. (1931); J. H. Leith, *Creeds of the Churches,* rev. ed. (1973).

J. H. LEITH

CROSS (Ch). Ancient and widespread religious symbol, often of solar or cosmic significance, but especially identified with CHRISTIANITY, where it represents the redemptive import of JESUS' death as God's victory over sin and mortality. It is the principal Christian symbol.

Verbal references to the cross abound from earliest Christian times, but visual representations became frequent only after CONSTANTINE (d. 337) extended imperial favor to the church. A story from the later fourth century that the "true cross" on which Christ was crucified was found in JERUSALEM during Constantine's reign furthered this development. Initially the cross was portrayed chiefly as an emblem of victory associated more with Christ's transfiguration or resurrection than with his death. In contrast, medieval and later portrayals in the form of the CRUCIFIX—i.e., Christ on the cross—vividly represent his human suffering as the measure of God's care for humankind. The cross functions, then, as a symbol of both divine love and divine triumph. *See* SIGN OF THE CROSS.

Bibliography. N. Laliberte and E. West, *History of the Cross* (1960).

W. S. BABCOCK

CRUCIFIX (Ch). A cross bearing an image of the crucified Christ. Early Christians saw the cross as a symbol of triumph, but avoided any realistic representation of Christ crucified. The earliest known crucifixes (sixth century) show Christ the Victor reigning from the Tree, where he stands crowned and robed in royal splendor. By the twelfth and thirteenth centuries, devotion to the PASSION of Christ found expression in crucifixes which stressed Christ's suffering. Common in the West as the main figure of the rood-screen or reredos, the crucifix became a central object on the altar itself only in the fifteenth century; the trend in Roman Catholic churches since 1969 has been to move the crucifix to a position behind, beside, or above the altar.

C. WADDELL

CRUSADES (Ch—Lat. *cruciata;* lit. "a marking with the cross," i.e. the insignia worn by crusaders, *crucesignati,* who took vows and wore a cross of scarlet wool on their shoulders). The armed PILGRIMAGES and military expeditions undertaken by European Christians from the eleventh through the fifteenth centuries to recover the Holy Land from the Muslims and to assist in the defense of the Byzantine Empire. By the thirteenth century the term was broadened to include wars sanctioned by the PAPACY against those it declared to be the enemies of Christ; consequently, "crusade" also designated certain papal BULLS which authorized expeditions against non-Christians (e.g. Muslims in Spain or the Slavs), heretics (e.g. the ALBIGENSES), or political opponents (e.g. the Hohenstaufen emperors) and which provided the crusaders with plenary INDULGENCE, the remission of punishment due to sin. Following the fall of JERUSALEM (1070) and the loss of Asia Minor with the battle of Manzikert (1071), the Byzantine emperor Michael VII asked assistance from Pope GREGORY VII, who planned but could not actually launch an expedition to rescue the empire and the HOLY SEPULCHRE. At the council of Piacenza (March, 1095), Emperor Alexius II Comnenus also asked for mercenaries, and Pope Urban II at the council of Clermont (November, 1095) responded by calling the first of successive crusades to the East.

The specific crusading expeditions occurred from 1095 to 1464. The first (1096-99) included the Peasants' Crusade and later the main forces commanded by a papal legate and French and Norman barons. Antioch and Jerusalem were captured. Thereafter a series of four crusader states were established: Antioch, Tripoli, Jerusalem, and Edessa. The second (1147-49), the Crusade of Kings, and third (1189-92) reacted to the Muslim resurgence under Saladin, but both failed to recapture Edessa or Jerusalem.The infamous fourth crusade (1202-4) took Constantinople from the Byzantines and established a Latin empire (1204-61) in Greek lands. The Children's Crusade of 1212 ended with the loss of thousands of French and German children. The fifth

(1218-21) attacked Egypt but failed to hold the important city of Damietta. The sixth (1228-29), led by Frederick II of Germany, though opposed by INNOCENT III, gained control of NAZARETH, BETHLEHEM, and Jerusalem, along with access to the sea, by peaceful negotiation. The seventh (1248-54) failed to recapture Jerusalem, which had fallen to Muslim mercenaries (1244). With the fall of Acre (1291) Latin rule in the Holy Land collapsed. Crusading ventures afterward mainly attempted to curb Ottoman Turkish expansion. When Constantinople fell in 1453 and Pius II was unable to initiate a further campaign before his death in 1464, the crusading movement came to an end.

Though they failed to achieve their primary objectives, the eastern crusades served to accelerate existing tendencies such as the growth of trade and towns; the undermining of feudalism; the widening of geographical horizons; advances in military technology; and a livelier exchange of art and culture. They also produced a vast literature and a countermovement in the form of the FRANCISCAN crusade to convert not by arms but through the preaching of the GOSPEL.

Bibliography. S. Runciman, *A History of the Crusades* (1951-54).

H. L. BOND

CRYSTAL NIGHT (*Kristallnacht,* "Night of the Broken Glass"). Nazi attack on Jews throughout Germany and Austria, November 9-10, 1938, in which some 800 Jewish shops and 191 synagogues were destroyed, and 30,000 Jews were sent to concentration camps. The attack was a reprisal for the assassination in Paris of a minor German official by Herschel Grynszpan. *See* HOLOCAUST.

E. FLEISCHNER

CURATE kū′ rĭt (Ch—Lat. [*curatus*—lit. "one charged with care of souls"]). Once a title given to any pastor or minister; now ordinarily applied to an assistant or deputy of a parish minister, most commonly in ROMAN CATHOLICISM and ANGLICAN CHURCHES.

K. WATKINS

CURIA, ROMAN kūr′ ĭ ä (Ch). The agency of the pontifical government of the ROMAN CATHOLIC Church. All members and activities of the Curia are subject to the Pope, who appoints the heads, usually cardinals, of the curial offices: the Congregations, pontifical Courts, special Offices, and Commissions.

J. RAITT

D

DAIBUTSU dī´ boo tsoo (B—Jap.; lit. "great Buddha"). Gigantic gilt-bronze statue of the Sun Buddha (Vairocana) commissioned by Emperor Shomu in A.D. 743 for Todaiji, the national center for worship at Nara. 53 feet high and weighing 452 tons, the statue was sponsored through popular donations, marking the democratization of Buddhism in Japan. Also refers to the giant statue of Amida at Kamakura.

C. W. Edwards

DAIMOKU dī mō´ koo (B—Jap.; lit. "sacred title"). Sacred formula chanted by Nichiren Buddhists; the invocation *Namū-myō-hō-renge-kyō,* "Adoration to the Sūtra of the Lotus of the Wonderful Law" (Lotus Sūtra). The Japanese monk Nichiren (1222-82) concentrated all Buddhist truth in this invocation and inscribed it on a tablet, the *Gohonzon.*

C. W. Edwards

DAINICHI dī´ nē chē (B). Japanese name of Vairocana.

DAKHMA däk´ mə (Z). *See* Towers of Silence.

DALAI LAMA dä´ lī lä´ mə (B—Tibetan, from Mongolian *ta-le;* lit. "ocean," suggesting "breadth" or "depth" of wisdom, and Tibetan *bla-ma,* "superior one," the title applied to those believed to be the reincarnation of a Bodhisattva). The title of the successive heads of the dominant Gelugpa order of Tibetan Buddhism who were the spiritual and temporal rulers of Tibet until the occupation of Tibet by the People's Republic of China in 1959.

The dominance of the Dalai Lama was an outgrowth of a reformed movement started by TSong-KHa-Pa (1357-1419), who established the Gelugpa or "Yellow Hat" sect of monks. In 1438 dGe-Dun-Grub-Pa, who is reckoned as the first Dalai Lama, established a monastery at Tashilhunpo. His successor became abbot of the monastery of Drepung, near Lhasa, which became the principal seat of the Dalai Lama. The actual name "Dalai Lama" was first applied to the third in this succession, rGyal-Ba bSod-Nams rGya Mteho (1543-88), by the Mongol leader Altan Khan, when he and his followers became converts to Buddhism. Ties with the Mongolians were strengthened when the fourth Dalai Lama was found incarnate in a grandson of Altan Khan. This stirred the fears of the Chinese, who intervened to counter the growing influence of the Dalai Lama.

The fifth Dalai Lama, Ngag-dBang bLo-bZang rGya-mTsho (1617-82), is the symbol of Tibetan nationalism, who with Mongol help extended the temporal rule of the Gelugpas over all Tibet. He built the great winter palace of the Potala in Lhasa that has long stood as a symbol of the nation. On the basis of some *terma* (ancient hidden texts) miraculously discovered in his reign, the preeminence of the Dalai Lama was established as a Reincarnation of Avalokiteśvara.

The fourteenth Dalai Lama, bsTan-dZin rGya-mTsho, was born in Kumbum, Tsinghai Province, China, of Tibetan parents on June 6, 1935. The party searching for a successor to the thirteenth Dalai Lama was guided by oracles and omens in selecting the next incarnation. Positive identification was made when the child, without prompting, selected objects having belonged to the previous Dalai Lama. He was confirmed by the state oracle as the fourteenth Dalai Lama and consecrated on February 22, 1940, although actual rule was maintained by regents. After the Sino-Tibetan treaty of 1951 he tried to work within the framework of Chinese power, despite their efforts to use the Panchen Lama to undermine his influence. With the revolt of 1959, the Dalai Lama was forced to flee to India, where he now works to preserve the cultural and religious heritage of Tibet from his center in Dharamsala, Himachal Pradesh.

Bibliography. P. P. Karan, *The Changing Face of Tibet* (1976); H. Hoffman, *The Religions of Tibet* (1961); T. Gyatsho, *The Opening of the Wisdom Eye* (1971), *The Buddhism of Tibet and the Key to the Middle Way* (1975), and *My Land and My People* (1964).

D. G. Dawe

DAMAYANTĪ dŭ mŭ yän´ tē (H—Skt.). Damayantī is the heroine of the *Nalopākhyānam* or "Story of Nala," which is recited in the Mahābhārata to console Yudhiṣṭhira about suffering caused by gambling. Perhaps originally a regional folktale of northwest India, the story is prized for its graceful Sanskrit, attention to human motivations, wit, and lack of theologization. But it was probably adapted to Mahābhārata themes. Damayantī and Nala, never having met, conceive a "love of the unseen" for each other. She chooses him at her "self-choice" marriage ceremony over four gods who impersonate him to trick her. She then becomes a typical "chaste wife": her loyalty unquestioned but tested, and a motive force behind her husband and their story's plot.

Kali and Dvāpara, Yuga and dice demons, resent Damayantī's choice of Nala and conspire to separate them. Kali possesses Nala, Dvāpara enters the dice, and Nala gambles everything away to his brother. But he refuses to stake Damayantī (unlike Yudhiṣṭhira with Draupadī), and the pair go to the forest where Nala, still possessed, leaves her. After various adventures, both assume disguises, Damayantī as a low caste chambermaid (Draupadī's disguise). Damayantī's father finally recovers her, and she cleverly tracks down Nala. Having learned the secret of dice from a repentant Kali, Nala now stakes Damayantī and recovers his kingdom. A. Hiltebeitel

DĀNA dä´ nŭ (B—Skt. & Pali; lit. "giving, a gift" [*dā*—"to give, to share"]). Any gift or act of generosity, but especially gifts such as alms made to members of the Saṅgha or to the whole *saṅgha.* The perfection of *dāna* was one of the spiritual pursuits of the Buddha during his Bodhisattva career, as exemplified in many Jātaka stories.

The Buddhist canon says that generosity brings rewards such as long life, good appearance, happiness, and strength, according to one list; and affection, good friends, good reputation, self-confidence, and rebirth in heaven according to another. *Dāna* heads the list of three kinds of meritorious activities, the others being morality and meditation.

It is customary for Buddhist families to invite several monks to their homes for a ritual *dāna* on such occasions as the building of a house, the imminent birth of a baby, a serious illness, the arrangement of a marriage, an imminent death, or a memorial for a deceased relative. The rituals vary with the occasion, but usually include chanting of special texts and always include *dāna,* gifts of food and perhaps cloth for robes. Just as the laity provide material gifts to the monks, the monks reciprocate by giving "spiritual gifts." *See* Puñña §3.

Bibliography. *The Book of Gradual Sayings* (1961, 1962), II. 71-77; III. 31-34. R. C. Amore

DANCE, SACRED. Dance may be defined as a succession of patterned, rhythmic movements of the body, expressive of a range of emotions, especially joy. Dance is *sacred* when it serves to express emotions deemed to be religious and/or when it is a part of a religious ritual.

M. L. Ricketts

Shiva and Pārvatī dance together in this Tantric statue from Nepal.

1. **The universality of dance.** Probably no society has existed in which dancing, unless prohibited, was not practiced, and among preliterate peoples virtually all activities, especially religious rituals, are accompanied by dancing. So ubiquitous is dancing in tribal societies that anthropologists frequently refer to religious ceremonial complexes as "dances" even though other ritual acts are involved (e.g., the Ghost Dance and the Sun Dance in Native American Tribal Religion).

Among more "advanced" peoples, dancing tends to be divorced from worship and to become on the one hand an art practiced professionally for entertainment, and on the other hand folk or social dancing. Between sacred and secular dancing are the dance dramas of ancient Greece (the chorus), contemporary India (Bharata-Nāṭyam, Kathākali, Kathak, and Manipuri), Southeast Asia and Indonesia (based especially on the Rāmāyaṇa epic), the Himalayan region (*see* Buddhism, Tibetan), China, and Japan (Nō, Kabuki). Among the major religions of the world, Hinduism, Shintō, and Confucianism have retained the dance; in Judaism it survives tangentially; and it has been opposed by orthodox Buddhism, Christianity, and Islam.

2. **Studies of sacred dance.** Surprisingly, historians of religion and theologians have written very

little on the subject of sacred dance. Oesterley compared dance in Israelite cult with dances in other cultures. Sachs and Sorell mention sacred dance in their general surveys, but have little to say about it. While several proponents of the use of dance in modern Christian worship have written essays in justification of their innovations, no major theologian has broached the subject.

Van der Leeuw shows that the dance is the original "art" out of which the others evolve. In the beginning dance and religion were united—indeed, almost equated—but this unity too was broken. Van der Leeuw denies that animal "dances" are comparable to human dance, since the former are instinctual while the latter is a cultural creation. As such, the dance may express any of the three basic ways humankind has dealt with nature: mastery (magic), submission (ecstasy), and objectivity (art, science, contemplation). Dances imitative of animals and all pantomime dances are ways humans have sought to appropriate the powers of other beings. In ecstatic dancing humans lose themselves and become one with the dance or the god. In the third type, the man or woman dances in mystical contemplation of God as the Great Dancer.

3. **Classification of sacred dances.** On the one hand the meaning of dance seems obvious: it expresses and reinforces emotion. On the other hand the subject seems too vast and complex for generalization. Nevertheless, some classification and generalization beyond that of van der Leeuw appears both possible and necessary.

a) To stimulate and express emotion. It may be assumed that many dances of this type arose spontaneously as individuals or groups were seized by strong emotion. New dances are continually being introduced into some tribal societies by this means (e.g., American Indian tribes which have a "vision quest"). The motivating emotion might be fear or awe (as a result of a dream, vision, shamanistic flight, peyote, Holy Spirit, etc.); or it might be joy and gratitude (for a successful hunt, harvest, act of war, birth, forgiveness of sin); or sorrow, rage, terror (over a death, famine, epidemic, eclipse, defeat). The list of emotions that have been "danced" religiously could be extended and illustrated indefinitely.

Once dances have been created they may become part of a group's "liturgical repertoire," and when an individual or the group wishes to express an emotion, the appropriate dance will be danced. As is true of any ritual, dance is not only a means of expressing emotion, but also of intensifying it and even evoking it. It is not necessary that all persons dance: often the majority only watch or else participate by providing rhythmic accompaniment.

b) To experience ecstasy or divine possession. Many dances, such as those of shamans entering into trance or seeking to be possessed or "ridden" by spirits, aim at more than ordinary emotional exhilaration. Dancing in these instances results either in a trance or in a state of consciousness radically altered and reoriented. The Dionysian maenads and devotees of Cybele, the DERVISHES, Taoist exorcists, female shamans of Burma who become "wives" of the *nats,* and the Cannibal Society dancers of the Kwakiutl Indians are further examples of this type. (*See* TAOISM, RELIGIOUS; SHAMANISM.)

To a certain extent all dancers are "possessed" and have become "other persons," moving in a trance. The paint, masks, and costumes, as well as the gestures, enable the dancer to assume a new identity. But not all achieve the heightened state of frenzy required of the shaman or the medium.

c) To obtain some object external of the dance. The aim here is "magico-religious." Included in this type are pantomime dances acting out the tracking and killing of game (hunting and gathering peoples), fertility dances (agriculturalists), war dances, dances to heal by exorcising evil spirits, and rain dances (for which the Pueblo tribes are famous). Some of these types seem indicated in cave paintings from Paleolithic Europe and North Africa.

d) To instruct. Here the dance becomes dramatic, being the portrayal of a story (MYTH, sacred legend) in rhythmic gesture. Creation, the emergence of humans from the earth (Pueblos), the wanderings of tribal ancestors (Australians), and modern presentations of biblical narratives in dance-dramas in churches are examples. The semireligious dance-dramas of India and elsewhere still serve their ancient function of instructing the young and the unlettered in the sacred traditions, although they also may provide "entertainment." To tell a story in any form is a powerful means of touching the imagination, but to do it through the beauty of dance enhances the power of narrative to the utmost.

e) To entertain the gods. When human beings appreciate the value of dance as entertainment, they may begin to offer it as entertainment for the gods. To be sure, all dances "entertain" and "amuse"; some—such as those of the sacred clowns of the Pueblos—are intentionally humorous and are no less "religious" for that. But when dance is severed from cult and religious festival and its function is merely to amuse, it has ceased to be sacred dance. This has happened to much of the sacred dancing of India. Once performed in the temples by devoted girls *(devidāsīs),* dancing became secularized, due partly to the demands of the Mogul rulers, and the girls became outcastes.

In China, troupes of professional actors traditionally danced their "ballet-operas" ostensibly for the god's delight, and hence they performed in temple courtyards. The KOJIKI, Japan's ancient chronicle, states that when the Sun Goddess AMATERASU hid in a cave, one of the lesser goddesses performed a ludicrous and lascivious dance which made all the KAMI laugh, and Amaterasu, curious, reappeared. This dance is held to be the origin of the Kagura, the sacred Shintō dance, which is thus seen as entertainment for the *kami.*

4. **Dancing gods.** Many dances of "primitives" are held to be imitations of mythical divine dances.

Such, for instance, is the phallic dance of Legba, the Fon TRICKSTER of Dahomey. Similarly, the Dogon dancers in part imitate the first dance of the Jackal, but in part they also imitate the whole world order as danced in the beginning. The Hopi and Zuni kachinas are dancing deities. The gods of some Hellenistic mysteries, above all Dionysus, danced.

The Gnostic group, probably Valentinians, that produced the Acts of John represented Jesus and the disciples dancing after the Last Supper, in imitation of the heavenly beings in the eightfold Godhead. (*See* GNOSTICISM.) Lucian, Roman poet of approximately the same time, wrote of the dance of the heavenly bodies that came into being at creation, a notion traceable to Plato. This fancy of the dancing heavenly bodies or beings becomes in orthodox Christianity the idea of dancing angels. To the latter was added in the Middle Ages the *dance macabre,* the ritually enacted dance of the personified figure of Death.

The divine dancers par excellence are found in Hinduism. In the VEDAS, gods did not dance, though King INDRA was entertained by dancing heavenly nymphs, the Apsarases. But SHIVA and his female counterpart PĀRVATĪ or Kālī of later Hinduism are worshiped as dancers. As NAṬARĀJA, King of Dancers, Shiva is the patron of dancers and archetypal dancer of the 108 *tāṇḍava* dances. Pārvatī dances all the graceful, feminine dances. By his dancing, Shiva creates, sustains, destroys, brings beings to birth, and saves them from MĀYĀ. Both Shiva and the Bengal goddess Kālī are dancers in the burial grounds. In the Tantric iconography of Nepal, Shiva and Pārvatī often are represented dancing together, sometimes even while copulating. This last form resembles Tantric Buddhist icons of Śamvara and his spouse who dance in sexual embrace inside a MANDALA of dancing *dakinīs* (females).

KRISHNA is famed for his dancing, especially with the GOPĪS, of whom Rādhā is his favorite. Worshipers are to make themselves "female" that they may "dance" as Krishna's partner. Under the influence of CAITANYA'S BHAKTI tradition, dancing in praise of and in mystical union with Krishna has become widespread. In India such dances are done mostly by troupes of trained performers, but in some locales a new form of worship in which all devotees dance with the Lord is becoming popular (*see* Singer). In America and elsewhere the HARE KRISHNA people offer joyous dances as part of their regular worship.

5. The dance in Judaism and Christianity. Dancing is mentioned only occasionally in the OT, but in such ways as to show it was a regular feature of festivals, requiring no particular comment. The dancing at the sea (Exod. 15:20), David's dance before the ark (II Sam. 6:14), and references in the Psalms (149,150) are most noteworthy. Processions supplanted dances in rituals, but folk dances have continued in Judaism, especially in connection with weddings. Fervent and even ecstatic dancing is practiced in Hasidic communities. (*See* HASIDISM.)

There is evidence of dancing in Christian worship from the third century onward, but by the latter part of the fourth century objections were being raised to it because of excesses and unholy associations. Church councils, bishops, and popes condemned dancing in the church in every century from the fourth to the eighteenth, but dancing continued to be popular, especially in the Middle Ages. Most dances were expressions of joy and adoration in connection with festivals. Some involved the whole congregation, but more often a choir performed. The Reformation and the Council of Trent effectively halted almost all sacred dancing in churches in the West. Exceptions are the church of Seville, Spain, where, with special papal permission, altar boys *(los seises)* dance before the altar thrice yearly; the SHAKERS of the nineteenth century; and some Pentecostals (*see* PENTECOSTAL CHURCHES) of today who sometimes dance spontaneously in worship.

Proponents of so-called "modern dance" seek to restore sacred dance to the churches. Dance dramas and liturgies have been created and presented in American Protestant and Catholic churches. The Sacred Dance Guild, formed in 1955 to promote dance in worship, includes Catholics, Jews, and members of many Protestant denominations. In the 1960s the song "Lord of the Dance," by Sydney Carter, which was inspired by Shaker example, was popular with young Christians.

Bibliography. C. Sachs, *World History of the Dance* (1937); W. Sorell, *The Dance through the Ages* (1967); W. O. E. Oesterley, *The Sacred Dance, a Study in Comparative Folklore* (1923); J. Huizinga, *Homo Ludens* (1949); A. E. Jensen, *Myth and Cult among Primitive Peoples* (1963); G. van der Leeuw, *Sacred and Profane Beauty* (1963); E. L. Backman, *Religious Dance in the Church and Popular Medicine* (1952); M. F. Taylor, *A Time to Dance* (1967); D. Adams, *Congregational Dancing in Christian Worship* (1971); A. Coomaraswamy, *The Dance of Shiva* (2nd ed., 1957); R. Singh and R. Massey, *Indian Dances: Their History and Growth* (1967); M. Singer, "The Rādhā-Krishna *Bhajanas* of Madras City," *HR,* II (1963); F. Berk, *The Chasidic Dance* (1975); F. G. Speck and L. Broom, *Cherokee Dance and Drama* (1951); R. Bunzel, "Zuni Katchinas," *47th Annual Report of the Bureau of American Ethnology* (1932).

M. L. RICKETTS

DANDA dŭn´ dŭ (H—Skt.; lit. "stick, staff, rod, club"; "coercion," "punishment"). Staff given at investiture of the SACRED THREAD; emblem of religious and political authority; a magical instrument, as well as an emblem of high rank and dignity. In Hindu polity, as the symbol of authority and punishment, the *daṇḍa* is one of the chief modes of statecraft. It is the active, applicatory arm of the universal law of right or cosmic order (DHARMA). It is also the student's staff, which he carries as a symbol of his chastity and commitment to the renunciation of all diversionary pleasures.

J. B. LONG

DANTE ALIGHIERI dăn´ tē ä´ lē gyâ´ rē (Ch; 1265-1321). Italian poet, born in Florence. His first major work was *Vita Nuova* (1292-94), an autobiographical work extolling the glorious Beatrice, an early love, who had died in 1290. Dante's entrance into political life in 1295 eventually led to his exile from Florence in 1301. Though he never returned, he remained active in public affairs until his death. After the death of Beatrice, Dante began a period of intense study in classical and medieval authors. Between 1304 and 1318, he wrote *Convivio (The Banquet),* a feast of knowledge intended to justify his turning from Beatrice to philosophy, and *Monarchia,* his political ideal for church and state. Dante's masterpiece, the *Commedia (The Divine Comedy),* was composed between 1307 and 1321. An allegory of Dante's own spiritual journey, the poem is made up of three books—"Inferno," "Purgatorio," and "Paradiso." Guided first by Virgil and then by Beatrice, the poet tours the regions from the depths of hell to the empyrean, where he is granted visions of God.

Bibliography. E. Gilson, *Dante and Philosophy* (1949); C. H. Grandgent, *Companion to The Divine Comedy,* C. S. Singleton, ed. (1975).

D. J. White

DĀR al-ḤARB; DĀR al-ISLĀM där əl härb′; där əl ĭs läm′. *See* Islam; Jihād.

DARBYITES där′ bē īts (Ch). *See* Plymouth Brethren.

DARŚANA där′ shū nū (H—Skt.; lit. "seeing" [*dṛś*—"to see"]). Any Indian philosophical view, or system or school espousing that view. A philosophical system in classical Indian parlance characteristically sets forth a world view consistent with and explanatory of the possibility of gaining liberation (Moksa) from the cycle of rebirth (Samsara). The prime exception to this is Cārvāka, or Lokāyata "materialism," frequently termed a philosophical system, but which rejects the possibility of liberation.

All Indian systems accept the traditional theory of Karma, according to which one's acts produce residues whose fruits, in the forms of experiences, must be lived out in subsequent lives. Normally, this experiencing will be accompanied by further acts with further results, and so the endless cycle of rebirth is engendered. However, the mechanical operation of karma usually functions in a context in which the agent is ignorant of the real nature of things, in particular of himself. This ignorance is a persistent causal factor, and by its removal the operation of the karmic mechanism can be stopped. The stoppage is called liberation or release *(mokṣa).*

Many systems recommend Yoga of some form as the method of attaining liberation. It is often said that there are three kinds of yoga or discipline: (1) the discipline of *karmayoga,* unattached action, which may be ritually prescribed actions or, as in the Bhagavad Gītā, action without concern for its fruits; (2) the discipline of *jñānayoga,* knowledge, which involves understanding the nature of the world and particularly of oneself (or, in Buddhism, the realization that there is no persisting self); (3) the discipline of *bhaktiyoga,* devotion, in which the seeker surrenders to God. Sometimes Patañjali's Yoga is added as a fourth, or *rājayoga.*

Philosophers differ between and even within schools about the relative emphasis to be placed on these various yogas or disciplines. These differences are correlated with differences among schools and philosophers about the nature of the universe in such a way that each account makes it appropriate to emphasize certain disciplines over others. This leads the philosophers to develop extensive metaphysical systems to justify their recommendations about a particular path. They also speculate at length over what sources of knowledge there are which can provide them, and us, with an understanding of the truth about all these things. This leads to special attention to the nature of good arguments, so that they become experts in logic. In this manner Indian philosophy comes to cover many of the topics associated with philosophy in the Western world.

Although medieval and recent expositions sometimes count the Indian philosophical systems as six in number, such lists have not always mentioned the same six. Furthermore, many lists include Buddhist and Jaina philosophies as well as Hindu.

A popular account mentions six Hindu systems, viz., Nyāya-Vaiśeṣika, Sāṃkhya, Yoga, Pūrva-mīmāṃsā (*see* Mīmāṃsa), and Vedānta. To these should be added the Grammarian or Vyākaraṇa philosophy propounded notably by Bhartṛhari (sixth century) in his *Vākyapadīya,* as well as various sectarian philosophies of Śaivism and Vaiṣṇavism (Śaiva Siddhānta, Caitanya, Pañcarātra); but there are others equally important, such as Kashmir Śaivism and Vīraśaivism, the philosophy of the Liṅgāyats.

Buddhist and Jaina philosophers of the first millennium A.D. engaged in extensive polemics with Hindu philosophers, and both sides learned much from the confrontations. Among the major systems of Buddhist thought were a number of types of Abhidharma or Hīnayāna (*see* Buddist Sectarianism). Among Mahāyāna schools two stand out: the Mādhyamika system propounded by Nāgārjuna (150-250 A.D.), and the Vijñānavāda or Yogācāra system. This latter system is said to have at least two branches, one pioneered by Asaṅga (310-90 A.D.) which emphasized meditation, and the logical school of Dignāga (fifth century) and Dharmakīrti (seventh century), which rivalled the Nyāya system in its detailed analyses of logical and epistemological matters.

Jaina philosophy also developed a logical tradition, and although the philosophical terminology which it developed differed systematically from that used by Hindu and Buddhist logicians, all the logical schools were aware of each other and offered frequent criticisms of one another. A considerable literature of Jaina philosophy is extant, and provides us with many important clues for our understanding of the views not only of the Jainas themselves but also of their rivals. Among the most important Jaina philosophers are Umāsvāti (fifth century?), author of the *Tattvārthasūtras;* Haribhadra Sūri (eighth century), who wrote many treatises on Jaina yoga and philosophy; Hemacandra (1088-1172), an influential scholar and litterateur; and Yaśovijaya (1624-88), a prolific giant among more recent writers.

Bibliography. K. H. Potter, ed., *Bibliography of Indian Philosophies* (1970), with periodic supplements published in the *Journal of Indian Philosophy*, provides a comprehensive survey of materials on Indian philosophy; S. N. Dasgupta, *History of Indian Philosophy*, 5 vols. (1922-1955); S. Radhakrishnan and C. Moore, eds., *A Source Book in Indian Philosophy* (1957); K. H. Potter, *Presuppositions of India's Philosophies* (1963).

K. H. POTTER

DARUMA dä´ roo mä (B). See BODHIDHARMA.

DĀSA dä´ sŭ (H—Skt.; lit. "slave, barbarian, fiend"). The name given by the ARYANS to a large group of people encountered and subjected by them while sweeping into India. It is still a matter of controversy whether the word *dāsa* was applied generally to all the conquered peoples or to only one particular subgroup. *See* DRAVIDIAN. J. BARE

DAYĀNANDA dī ä nŭn´ dŭ (H; 1824-1883). A BRAHMIN from Gujarat, Dayānanda had a traditional Hindu education almost untouched by Western influence. He became a SANNYĀSIN, studying the VEDAS under a traditional GURU, who convinced him that the Vedas contained all essential truth. Later Dayānanda utilized the Vedas to prove that they contained principles for social reform and even the discoveries of modern science. In 1875 he founded the ĀRYA SAMĀJ. He vigorously endorsed such reforms as emancipation of women and eradication of caste bias. His polemics against Moslems and Christians raised the self-confidence of Hindus. *See* REFORM MOVEMENTS IN INDIA § 3.

Bibliography. H. B. Sarda, *Life of Dayānanda Saraswati* (1946). A. LIPSKI

DEACON (Ch—Gr.; *diakonos;* lit. "one who executes the commands of another"). The church gave this title to persons who acted on its behalf, probably in caring for the poor and in the general administration of congregations. The "deacons" appointed in Acts 6:1-6, however, include individuals later involved in evangelism. Women could be deacons, as Rom. 16:1 indicates. Deacons are associated with bishops in Phil. 1:1 and I Tim. 3:1-12.

When the church stabilized its patterns of leadership, the office of deacon became the first in the threefold ministry of deacon, PRIEST, and BISHOP; deacons served primarily as assistants to bishops. Churches with episcopal government still continue this pattern of ministry. The office has become more limited, however, and often means little more than the first step toward ordination. In other churches deacons are lay officers. *See* CLERGY, CHRISTIAN.

K. WATKINS

DEAD, PRAYERS FOR THE (Ch). The earliest evidence of Christians praying for their departed is found in second century tomb epitaphs and catacomb inscriptions. The practice, however, may be traced back to the Judeo-Christian tradition implicit in II Macc. 12:39-45, where prayer and sacrifice are offered for the sins of Jews slain on the field of battle. II Tim. 1:18 ("May the Lord grant him [Onesiphorus] to find mercy from the Lord on that Day") has sometimes been understood as a NT reference to prayer for the departed, since the context of the passage suggests that Onesiphorus is dead. As early as 211 Tertullian refers to anniversary days of the Christian departed as to an immemorial custom; and from that time onward evidence of prayer for the dead as well as for the living is abundant, especially in connection with the EUCHARIST. Protestant churches rejected this practice at the time of the REFORMATION, but present-day practice in the Eastern Othodox and Roman Catholic Churches (memorial of the departed at every Eucharist, anniversary celebrations, special prayers and eucharistic formularies) continues the early Christian belief and practice. Theologians understand intercession for the departed in connection with the doctrine of PURGATORY, as a consequence of the reality of the COMMUNION OF SAINTS, and as a manifestation of our mutual interdependence within the saving plan of God's love and mercy.

Bibliography. J. H. Wright, "Prayers for the Dead," *New Catholic Encyclopedia* (1967), IV, 671-73.

C. WADDELL

DEATH (H, B, Ju, Ch). The major religious traditions have developed their approaches to death around differing basic conceptions of human mortality. In the East, HINDUISM and BUDDHISM offer separate views of death and its meaning, and therefore distinct intellectual and ritual attempts to integrate the fact of death into a comprehensive understanding of life. In the West three major ways of conceiving death have developed in Platonism, JUDAISM, and CHRISTIANITY.

1. **Hinduism.** In the VEDAS, the oldest literature of the Hindu tradition, little attention is given to death as such. The life-affirming authors (RISHIS) of the Vedas seem to stress delaying the occurrence of death. They speak only vaguely of surviving death, have no developed concept of soul, and fear most what they refer to as the "redeath" or "second death" that occurs after the death of the body.

The UPANISADS, the collection of highly reflective teachings meant to be an interpretation of the Vedas, were written by sages whose view of life is far more negative than that of their Vedic predecessors. They give prominence to ATMAN, the eternal soul that dwells within but has no personal characteristics.

Atman is the birthless, deathless reality that is at once the inmost being of each person and the inmost being of all that exists. "Concealed in the heart of all beings," one of the sages declares, "is the Atman; smaller than the smallest atom, greater than the vast spaces" (Kaṭha Upaniṣad 2.20). In its most inclusive sense Atman is identical to BRAHMAN, or that which is truly real behind the tangible universe (MĀYĀ) that only appears to be real.

Death, in this setting, cannot therefore be a reality. Atman can neither come to an end nor have a beginning. In the BHAGAVAD GĪTĀ, a work written slightly later than the major Upaniṣads, the god KRISHNA addresses Prince ARJUNA, who is grieving over the anticipated loss of many friends and relatives in a coming battle: "The truly wise mourn neither for the living or the dead. There never was a time when I did not exist, nor you, nor any of these kings. Nor is there any future in which we shall cease to be" (II. 11, 12). What is born and subsequently dies is not the real, but an illusory self. This illusory self is a creation of, and totally subject to, the contingent world. It is therefore carried along by the causal laws of the world according to which all things are endlessly being transformed. For this reason the feared redeath of the Vedas now becomes a dreaded rebirth. This is the doctrine of reincarnation (SAMSARA), in which the unliberated soul is carried forward by its own habitual deeds and their effect (KARMA) into successive births and deaths.

It is the highest spiritual goal of early Hinduism to be freed from what Krishna describes for Prince Arjuna as "the terrible wheel of death and rebirth." Their desire was not to achieve an immortality of the soul, but to eliminate all the false modes of existence. This means wiping away all those ways of existing in which the "I" is in the center. "I-ness" and "mine-ness" represent a kind of selfhood that has concrete being in the world. Insofar as we are such beings we shall be caught in the repeated causal cycles of rebirth, passing from one death to another like the caterpillar that reaches the end of a blade of grass and immediately extends itself toward the next.

It is because persons have misunderstood the nature of self and world that they attach themselves to it. According to the Upaniṣads, they can remove themselves from the "terrible wheel" only by the acquisition of true knowledge. This cannot, however, be a knowledge of objects, since it is this sort of knowledge that snares one in illusion. It is rather an experiential knowledge that eliminates the distinction between subject and object, for only then can one be complete in oneself, detached from the world, free to be united to the deathless, birthless Atman/Brahman. "Whoever knows Brahman," another Upaniṣadist exclaims, "becomes Brahman" (Muṇḍaka Upaniṣad 3.2.9).

The method by which this liberating knowledge is acquired is identified in the Upaniṣads as YOGA. A spiritual discipline of great subtlety and variety, yoga is only briefly described in the Upaniṣads, but in time develops a tradition of its own. Its most definitive treatment in classical Hinduism is in the philosophy of PATAÑJALI, who described yoga as the successive attainment of eight levels of increasing spiritual perfection. The highest stage is known to Hindus as SAMĀDHI, a mode of existence in which one can neither be born nor die. Yoga is sometimes referred to as the "medicine of immortality," though what is meant by this term is not the possession of an immortal soul. *Samādhi* is viewed either as an isolation of the eternal self (PURUṢA) or as the union of Atman and Brahman in which all traces of personhood have been erased. It is a state often compared to a deep, dreamless sleep from which one could never be awakened.

Upaniṣadic thought probably constitutes the most important philosophical tradition in Hinduism, but popular religious practice has come to center on a great accumulation of divinities, each with its own notion of divine grace which ensures escape from rebirth and union with one's chosen deity. (*See* BHAKTI HINDUISM; ŚRĀDDHA.) While devotional Hinduism appears to have little in common with the lofty abstractions of the Upaniṣads, one can nonetheless discern that ubiquitous Hindu desire not to continue after death in an ego-bound new birth.

2. Buddhism. The understanding of death distinctive to Theravāda Buddhism takes its shape from an insight that came to the BUDDHA on the occasion of his enlightenment. He saw first that all existence stands under the power of suffering (DUKKHA), and that suffering is caused not by something that happens to one, but by one's own craving. The Buddha also came to see that all things exist by way of "dependent origination" (*see* PAṬICCASAMUPPĀDA). That is, nothing can bring itself to existence; it must have its origin in something else. All things are caused. Nothing is permanent. Everything will pass away.

Human existence is therefore under the power of death as well as suffering. There is no aspect of one's personal being that can escape causation and avoid oblivion. The Buddha's analysis of this condition includes the understanding that human suffering comes precisely from our resistance to this radical impermanence. What we most deeply crave is to be exempt from the causal nature of things. We desire to remain forever the same, never to change, much less to die. The cure he proposed for this spiritual distress was to cease struggling against our impermanence and to yield to it.

Classical Hindu sages taught union with the changeless, birthless Atman as the way of overcoming death. By sharp contrast, traditional Buddhists have taught the achievement of *anātman* (ANATTA), nonself, as the highest spiritual attainment. Yielding completely to the causal flux wipes away all possibility of timeless selfhood and permits one to focus on the middle path which eliminates suffering.

There are serious difficulties lying in the way of reaching this goal. One is our deep mental habit of thinking of ourselves as permanent beings. "All that we are is the result of what we have thought," begins the first chapter of the DHAMMAPADA; "it is founded on our thoughts, it is made up of our thoughts. If a man speaks or acts with an evil thought, pain follows him, as the wheel follows the foot of the ox that draws the wagon." (I. 1, trans. I. Babbitt.) This verse reveals what Buddhists regard as the "primacy of mind." The mind is dangerous because it can lead us into spiritually destructive fictions, one of the most powerful of which is that death can be avoided by making life permanent, that is, by having a deathless, changeless soul.

If we are to be released from these painful falsehoods, we must use mind to free us from mind. Buddhists have developed a variety of strategies for doing so. The Buddha is reported in ancient texts to have cured his followers' desire to seize eternal truths by his use of the "fourfold denial." When asked, for example, whether the saints will continue to exist after death, he typically replied: A saint exists after death; a saint does not exist after death; a saint both exists and does not exist after death; a saint neither exists nor does not exist after death. The purpose of this response is not simply to avoid answering a difficult question, but to shock his followers into seeing that neither the question nor the answer is important to spiritual enlightenment.

In other words, the classical Buddhist view of death is that it is an unavoidable feature of existence and it can cause anguish only when one attempts, in whatever way, to elude it, even if it is by way of mental speculation on the nature of death or of an eternal soul.

One of the most striking methods of bringing this point to mind occurs in some of the monastic disciplines in which monks are compelled to sit silently in the presence of a corpse in varying stages of decay (*see* MAHĀSATIPAṬṬHĀNA SUTTA). The object of this practice is not simply to develop a proper attitude toward death, but to use decay and death to develop a proper way of existing. Death, one is to learn after meditating for long periods of time on a corpse, is nothing in itself; and if death is nothing in itself, neither is life.

Death therefore serves a function quite like that of the ZEN Buddhists' KŌAN, a meaningless expression (such as "the sound of one hand clapping") on which one meditates so intensely that the mind is emptied of all its other contents. This is a method of rendering the mind incapable of that kind of speculation that will lead one back to suffering. When death is dealt with as a kōan, all things, including life and death, will be viewed as *śūnya*, or empty, having no permanence whatsoever (*see* ŚŪNYATĀ). This elimination of all craving for the changeless is what Buddhists call NIRVANA, or extinction, the achievement of *anātman*, or nonself.

3. Platonism. One of the prevailing views of death in the Western world has its most decisive origin in the philosophy of Plato. In an early dialogue, the *Phaedo*, which purports to be a conversation between Socrates and his friends on the day of his execution, Plato cites Socrates' reasons for believing the soul to be immortal.

Socrates' belief in the immortality of the soul rests chiefly on the nature of knowledge. As he shows his friends, knowledge is composed of ideas, and ideas can neither come from things nor consist of things. If the horse is beautiful, there is nothing in the horse itself that constitutes its beauty. Beauty can be perceived in the horse only if there is an idea of beauty already existing in the soul. Now the horse will perish, the marble of a beautiful statue will turn to dust, but the idea of beauty, like all ideas, will endure forever.

If ideas cannot change, they can neither come into existence nor pass away. Moreover, since they reside in the soul, it must follow that the soul is also changeless. Socrates draws several conclusions from this view of the soul. The first is that the soul is altogether separate from the body. While the body suffers ceaseless alteration, the soul suffers none at all. Neither the birth of the body, nor its death, can have the merest effect on the soul.

A second conclusion is that the soul not only survives death, it exists before birth. Indeed, each soul has dwelt in innumerable bodies, it has seen all things, and as a result has "knowledge of everything." This has the effect of making the soul virtually equivalent to God. Plato frequently refers to the soul as "divine."

A third conclusion follows: inasmuch as the soul is located temporarily in the body, its vision of the truth can be obscured. It can mistakenly come to understand itself as a body. This leads to the fear of change and death with which most persons are afflicted. True philosophers, Socrates tells his friends, never fear death. On the contrary, they make dying their profession. They attempt through the discipline of philosophy to get the body out of the way in order that they might "contemplate things by themselves with the soul itself." Plato is not urging suicide, but arguing that the soul, already separate from the body, can, with proper training, see that it is capable of knowing the truth and is therefore deathless.

Still another conclusion indicates even more vividly the importance of philosophy to Plato. If the soul cannot distinguish itself from the body, it will be reborn into another body, and may even pass into such diminuitive creatures as ants, bees, and wasps, making its rescue from the bondage of ignorance exceedingly difficult. It is the task of philosophy, therefore, not simply to inform one of the truth, but to free the soul to its own eternal existence.

In this latter respect Plato virtually raises the role of philosophy to that of religion. While it is true that in succeeding centuries Platonism came to have a quasi-religious status, the most important consequences of Plato's theory of immortality lie in the influence it has exerted on the major religious traditions of the West, most notably Judaism and Christianity, even though both originate with an understanding of death that has nothing in common with Platonism.

4. **Judaism.** The distinctive Jewish understanding of death can already be discerned in one of the creation narratives in Genesis (2:4–3:24). God commanded the man he had made, Adam, not to eat of the Tree of the Knowledge of Good and Evil, though he could eat freely of the Tree of Life. Later when the temptations of the serpent had led both Adam and his mate, Eve, to eat of the forbidden tree, God drove the pair from the garden. Their punishment consisted of pain in childbirth, the burden of toil for their well-being, and death.

It is true that death is a punishment according to this account, but it is also the case that it comes with a considerable compensation—a knowledge of good and evil, that is, the power and responsibility to make decisions that have a future consequence. Previous to the fall of the first pair, life in the garden was little different from that of the innocent animals that dwelt there with them. Adam and Eve lost their immortality, but acquired consciousness instead. God drove them out of paradise into death, but also into history.

The essential relation of death to history characterizes all subsequent understanding of death in Jewish tradition. In that portion of the history of Israel found in the BIBLE, God never rescues his people *from* history, but always *for* history. There is nothing in this literature resembling Plato's confident expectation of the soul's survival of death. God's promise to Abraham, for example, is not that he will reward Abraham's faithfulness with immortality, but will grant him descendants as great in number as the "dust of the earth" (Gen. 13:16).

Although the dead are lamented, and although the sufferings of this existence can lead Job to cry out, "I loathe life" (Job 7:16), it is nonetheless clear that God's design for the people of Israel is not to save them from death, but to save them from their enemies in order that their history might continue. God led Israel out of Egyptian bondage to a promised land that would give history renewed meaning, and not to a deathless kingdom that would resemble the Garden of Eden.

In all of this there is no hint of the soul's survival after death. It is true that the Bible frequently speaks of SHEOL, a place to which the dead go. But Sheol is neither a heaven nor a hell; it is a vague region where the person gradually slides into oblivion. Nothing happens there. There is not even any possibility of relating to God in that place. It is not truly an after*life;* it is rather an after*death*.

Following the biblical period, however, Jews began increasingly to regard the soul as immortal. Occasionally the soul's survival is described in terms of resurrection rather than immortality as such; that is, an act of God in which all the dead are raised and brought to a final judgment. This is a prominent theme in the TALMUD, even though there is only one biblical passage in which both the wicked and the righteous will be raised to face the Judge—Dan. 12:2 ff.

More often, in the Talmud and in later Jewish thought, there is an unmistakable Platonic influence on the way the soul is conceived. Rabbi Leona Modena (1571–1648), for example, admits it is "frightening" that "we fail to find in all the words of Moses a single indication pointing to man's spiritual immortality after his physical death," but he nonetheless insists that reason compels us to believe the soul continues.

Many Jews, though not all, have continued to believe either that God will resurrect the dead after a period of time or that the soul is already deathless. However, Jewish funeral customs point back to the older conception that God does not save us, as individuals, from death, but saves Israel for history, regardless of death.

This can be seen in the customs still practiced. The respect paid to the body of the deceased by the ritual cleansing and strong resistance to both embalming and autopsy indicate that a person is not, as for Plato, a separable soul that takes flight at the moment the body expires. Other customs reflect the power and loss of death for the mourners. Those closest to the deceased are, for the seven days following death, a period known as *shiva,* forbidden to engage in work, to bathe, to put on shoes, to have marital intercourse, to read the TORAH, or to have their hair cut. These demands of the law have the effect of asking the mourners to behave as if they were themselves dead. They point to the solidarity of one's physical existence with one's family and friends, as well as with one's religious community.

Jewish law allows for an immediate reaction of inconsolable grief; then, during the period of *shiva,* requires a moderation in one's bereavement, saying that whoever grieves too much grieves for something other than the death of a loved one. This is in the spirit of returning mourners to the gradual resumption of normal life. Following *shiva* there is a period of reduced mourning lasting one month. By the end of the year one is asked to set aside all expressions of grief except for a yearly remembrance of the day of death.

In sum, while Jewish thinkers have largely found space for a Platonic theory of immortality, Jewish funeral customs have preserved the more ancient belief in the inseparability of the body and the soul, and a sense of the indispensable importance of history.

5. **Christianity.** From the sayings attributed to JESUS in the Synoptic Gospels (Matthew, Mark, Luke), we can infer that he thought there was a place where one goes after death, for he refers to an "outer darkness" where the wicked will be punished. Although such remarks are both rare and vague, it is clear that Jesus has in mind something more definite than the Sheol referred to in the Torah and Prophets. Whether he believes there is another place where the righteous go is less obvious. On one occasion he declares that when the dead are raised they will be like angels in heaven. He not only fails to explain what it means to be "like" angels, but adds, as a warning

against such speculation, that God "is not the God of the dead, but of the living" (Mark 12:25 ff.).

The Synoptic Gospels show Jesus generally to be unconcerned with the question of death as such. In the major collection of his teachings, the Sermon on the Mount, there is not one reference to death. It was apparently a matter of little interest to his disciples as well, for we find them asking no questions concerning the survival of the soul after death, in contrast to the disciples of the Buddha. Jesus does often refer to his own impending death and resurrection, but this is usually related to the appearance of the Son of Man "who will repay every man for what he has done" (Matt. 24:29 ff.). The theme in these passages is one of judgment. There is no promise of a general RESURRECTION in which the righteous will be raised with Jesus in glory.

The absence of any interest in a general resurrection, much less a theory of immortality, is most conspicuous in the resurrection narratives themselves. In the several stories of Jesus' appearance to his disciples and friends after the crucifixion he is not reported to have made the merest reference to the resurrection of anyone beside himself. The Synoptic Gospels do not deny that such will occur; they rather offer a Jesus who seems utterly concerned with the living, and content to "leave the dead to bury the dead" (Matt. 8:22).

In the Gospel of John we have a somewhat different picture of Jesus. As in the other Gospels he does not speak of death directly, or speculate on the soul's survival, but he does declare a union of himself with believers by which they will share in his resurrection: "I am the resurrection and the life; he who believes in me, though he die, yet shall he live" (11:25).

This implies that survival of death is not because the soul, as Plato had taught, is inherently deathless. Eternal life is available only to the faithful who will be raised with Jesus. In the letters of PAUL the resurrection theme is yet stronger. Paul's references to a future resurrection are much more explicit: "Lo! I tell you a mystery. We shall not all sleep, but we shall all be changed, in a moment, in the twinkling of an eye, at the last trumpet" (I Cor. 15:51-52).

Paul adds a theme essentially missing elsewhere in the NT: in faith, the resurrection that is to occur in the future is already a present reality. If by faith we carry the death of Jesus in our bodies, it follows that his life will also be manifested in us: "If any one is in Christ, he is a new creation; the old has passed away, behold, the new has come" (II Cor. 5:17).

Paul is most explicit on the fact that the new life we have from Christ overcomes the death we have from Adam. All major Christian traditions follow Paul in citing Adam's original sin as the source of death. But it is a sin each person has subsequently repeated; death is therefore as much the result of our own sinfulness as it is Adam's. The importance of this doctrine to Christians is that, first, death is to be understood not as a matter of fate, but a consequence of one's own doing, and, second, it is serious enough that one cannot undo death without the saving action of God in Christ. In the Platonic conception, by contrast, divine salvation from death would be superfluous since the soul is by nature unable to die.

In spite of the fact that Christians have stressed the dependence of the faithful on God for their salvation from death, the Platonic theory of immortality has had wide influence on Christian thought after the biblical period. The great third century thinker, ORIGEN, actually adopted the complete Platonic teaching that the soul both survives the death of the body and exists before its birth, and added the further belief that in time all souls would be saved by God. Both views were declared heretical at the Council of Constantinople in 553. AUGUSTINE, in the fourth century, was troubled by the discrepancy between Plato's teaching and the biblical view that sin is punished by death, and proposed a "second death" in which one is "never dead, but endlessly dying."

In popular belief there are elaborate dwelling places for the saved and the damned. The major Christian theologians, however, have resisted preoccupation with life after death, and have placed emphasis on the eternal life that is available now, through faith. Twentieth century theologians have widely interpreted the Christian tradition to hold a view that absolute birth and absolute death stand at the beginning and the end of every human life, quite like the creation and the consummation stand at the beginning and end of human history. The ultimate destiny of each person therefore lies entirely in the hands of God, and while Christians have always held to the promise of a resurrection, precisely how it will occur and in what the resurrection life will consist is as mysterious to present believers as it was to the disciples of Jesus.

Bibliography. F. Hock, ed., *Death and Eastern Thought* (1974), a study of the beliefs and practices concerning death, chiefly in Buddhism and Hinduism; J. Riemer, ed., *Jewish Reflections on Death* (1975); W. Marxsen, *The Resurrection of Jesus of Nazareth* (1970), a study of the resurrection narratives in the New Testament; J. Pelikan, *The Shape of Death* (1961), a survey of the views of death in early Christian thinkers.

J. CARSE

DEATH OF GOD THEOLOGY (Ch). Theological movement of the 1960s which claimed that meaningful talk about God is impossible for two reasons: modern people require empirical evidence, and the idea of a benevolent ruler of the world is morally repugnant in light of such events as the HOLOCAUST. *See* THEOLOGY, CONTEMPORARY CHRISTIAN §4a.

D. F. OTTATI

DEDICATION, FEAST OF (Ju). *See* HANUKKAH.

DEGUCHI NAO dĕ goo´ chē nä´ ō (Sh—Jap.; 1836-1918). A seer of peasant origin, who along with her adopted son Deguchi Onisaburo (1871-1948) founded ŌMOTO. Born near Kyoto to poor parents, she was married at age twenty to Deguchi Masagoro. After an unhappy marriage and the birth of eleven children, she was widowed and destitute at age fifty-two. Three children had died in infancy; two daughters became insane; two sons ran away. Seeking respite in religion, she became a member (later a teacher) of Konkō-kyō.

In 1892 Nao was possessed by the deity Ushitora no Konjin (cf. Tenchi Kane no Kami). Thereafter her behavior became so erratic that her family, thinking her insane, confined her in a room. There she began to receive oracles and, upon divine command (though she was illiterate), to record them, using a nail to scratch crude characters of the *hiragana* syllabary. Supplied with writing materials, she continued to record these messages for the remaining twenty-seven years of her life.

Through this miracle of automatic writing Nao began to amass a following. Claiming only to be a prophet, she looked toward the coming of a savior. She left Konkō-kyō in 1897 and in 1898 met Ueda Kisaburo, who believed himself led to her by divine direction. In 1900 she recognized him as the promised savior. Ueda married Nao's daughter and was adopted into the family as Deguchi Onisaburo, becoming the interpreter of Nao's oracles and the principal shaper of Ōmoto.

H. N. McFarland

DEIFICATION. *See* Perfection, Christian; Orthodox Churches §6.

DEISM (Ch). The Enlightenment endeavor to purify Christianity; rid religion of all that was not rational, natural, and moral; and develop a natural religion. An international movement, Deism reflected local religious, philosophical, and social expressions of the Enlightenment. In England, it was critically concerned with the origins of religion, but positive in moral and religious affirmation; in France it was anti-Catholic, shading into skepticism, atheism, and materialism; in Germany it was championed alongside rationalist metaphysics and historical criticism; in America, it embraced a revolutionary creed. Deist thinkers were intellectually diverse but committed to reasonable religion and critique of orthodox doctrines, rituals, practices, hierarchies, enthusiasms, and mysteries. Acknowledged in this rational, natural religion were the existence of God, the necessity of worship and morality, and rewards and punishments in a future state.

Though indebted to various European cultural developments, Deism was particularly an early eighteenth century English affair. Important literary productions included John Locke's *Reasonableness of Christianity* (1695), John Toland's *Christianity not Mysterious* (1696), and Matthew Tindal's *Christianity as Old as Creation* (1730). Typical was the latter's pursuit of the primitive, natural, superstitionless religion, identified with that of Jesus.

Bibliography. P. Gay, *The Enlightenment* (1966) and *Deism: An Anthology* (1968); H. F. May, *The Enlightenment in America* (1976).

R. E. Richey

DEMONS, DEMONOLOGY (Gr; *daimōn*—"a spirit").Originally simply a spirit, especially one which, like Socrates' famous *daimōn,* influenced the personality and work of a particular person. Although the word was originally morally ambiguous, it has come to refer only to personal spiritual entities which work evil. Beings of this sort can be found in the traditional forms of virtually all religions, although their nature and role differ considerably in the mythologies of monotheistic, dualistic, and polytheistic religious systems.

Belief in demons or devils is clearly related to the problem of Evil. However naïve some examples of demon belief may seem, they can only be understood rightly as attempts to deal with perhaps the most intractable of all problems of religious philosophy, one which has baffled sage and simpleton alike—explaining the presence of evil in a world whose ultimate origin or meaning appears to be other than evil. To posit—and experience—personal malevolent entities set loose in the world to work ill is not a complete answer to the problem and is not usually seen as such by the sophisticated, but it serves to interpret many concrete instances of evil, such as sickness or disaster. A doctrine of demonic powers in a religion also establishes certain motifs for dealing with the problem of evil that may be carried into theology as well as reflected in popular belief, for demonism suggests such abstract principles as that evil is embodied in personality, and aligned to will, yet also, at least in part, extraneous to humanity so that it is something humankind suffers as well as perpetrates. It suggests finally that evil is a force of cosmic dimensions, whose defeat is beyond human power alone and requires divine activity on a large scale.

1. Tribal religion. In tribal religions most spiritual entities are generally not thought of as absolutely good or bad, but rather benevolent or malevolent according to situation. The spirit of a mountain or an ancestral ghost will be benign if well propitiated but dangerously angry if offended or neglected. The spirit world can also be manipulated by Witchcraft, which in many places is a common explanation of ill-fortune. In some societies mythic and supernatural evil has a much greater place than in others; some observers have seen a striking correlation between it and the relative prevalence of aggression and anxiety.

Nonetheless, certain common figures in the primitive mythic cosmos have roles especially suggestive of demonism and doubtless deeply influenced the emergence of developed demonologies. Ghosts, especially those of offended ancestors, abandoned infants, or of persons ill-used, are often greatly feared. They are said to punish transgressors, and are frequently represented in ceremonials by fearsome masks.

Mythologies often contain congenitally fierce gods, such as Tu in the Polynesian story. When the divine children of the first parents, heaven and earth, debated whether to kill the progenitors who were suffocating their offspring between their immense bodies or merely push them apart, Tu wished the parents dead—but did not prevail. The TRICKSTER, like the Polynesian Maui, the Germanic Loki, or the Native American Coyote, has demonic overtones in his rebellion against heaven and delight in cruel jokes, yet enigmatically is also beloved as culture hero and comedian. Finally, one often finds a guardian of the Underworld or the Land of the Dead who has demonic features.

2. **Hinduism.** The ambivalent origin of most demonic figures is vividly demonstrated in HINDUISM. The ASURAS, who play the role of powerful malevolent beings in later mythology, were gods in earliest VEDIC HINDUISM; an example is VARUNA, a sovereign deity parallel to the Iranian Ahura (*asura)* Mazda. But with the rise of new generations of Aryan deities in India, represented first by INDRA and then VISHNU, the race of *asuras* became demons who fought against them—not the last time the gods of one era were transmuted into the devils of another. In the VEDAS connected with Indra, the *asuras* were powerful in darkness, but the morning sacrifices strengthened Indra and his band of followers, the Maruts, to overcome them again.

The demons of India could acquire great power by the same means as HINDU HOLY PERSONS—austerities. Through the forces engendered by ASCETICISM, they could compel the gods themselves, especially BRAHMĀ, to do their will. Like the Western devil, the *asuras* could be clever theologians, but in myth after myth the gods outwit them, or win by their own austerities and prayers. Finally the *asuras* were weakened when deprived of *amṛta*, the nectar which gave the gods strength. Their final defeat was at the hands of the great AVATARS of Vishnu, especially KRISHNA, who even in infancy exercised an infinite divine potency against which the *asuras* were helpless. Now, in enfeebled state, most of them dwell in Patala beneath the ocean.

Another class of Hindu evils beings, the *rākṣasas,* are more demonic in the strict sense; rather than cosmic opponents of the gods they are entities who attack humans to possess them and drive them mad, or to cause petty misery. RĀVAṆA, the adversary of RĀMA in the great epic the RĀMĀYAṆA, was a *rākṣasa.*

It should also be noted that the terrifying aspect of some deities accounted ultimately good, such as KĀLĪ, DURGĀ, and even SHIVA, appears to be a projection of the same dark vision which creates the demonic. Its appearance in these gods communicates that what appears good and evil is ultimately absorbed in the mystery of being itself, and signifies the nondualist resolution of the problem of evil toward which intellectual Hinduism has generally moved.

3. **Buddhism.** In its demonology, BUDDHISM can be considered in close conjunction with Hinduism. MĀRA, who according to traditional lives of the BUDDHA tempted the Awakened One on the night of his enlightenment, was said to be an *asura*—by some even a DEVA or lower deity—who was jealous of the power being acquired by a human, for a Buddha is greater than *devas* or *asuras,* and is teacher of gods and men. While Buddhism has no place for a cosmological dualism of personal spiritual entities, it took over from Hinduism demonological folklore and the concept of six lokas, or places of reincarnation, including the realm of the *asuras* and hells equipped with tormenting demons.

Just as certain great Hindu gods can show ambivalence between benign and fearsome aspects, so do many Buddhist deities, especially in the VAJRAYĀNA Buddhism of Tibet and adjacent regions (*see* TIBETAN BUDDHISM). Some of these fierce yet enlightened entities, familiar to readers of the Tibetan Book of the Dead, are borrowed from Hinduism, some are indigenous, and some are cosmic Buddhas who by manifesting all aspects of reality personify the adamantine essence of nondualism. They also show that the human drives which give rise to the demonic, while brought under tutelage by Buddhas, have not been exhausted. (*See* BARDO THODÖL.)

4. **Chinese and Japanese religion.** Demonology is no part of the great metaphysical and cosmological systems of CONFUCIANISM, TAOISM, SHINTŌ, or the Buddhism of China and Japan. Their dualisms, whether YIN AND YANG or the Buddhist conditioned reality versus NIRVANA, have no important mythologies involving demons and would be much misunderstood if put in such terms. However, in folk religion evil spirits, including demonic figures from India brought in with popular Buddhism, have had an immense role. These have included river and lake spirits who cause drownings, unwholesome mountain-haunters, and the ghosts of ill-treated ancestors or officials seeking vengeance and sending epidemic or catastrophe. (*See* JAPANESE RELIGION; CHINESE POPULAR RELIGION; PRETA.)

5. **The Ancient Near East and Europe.** In examining the demonologies of ancient Egypt, Mesopotamia, Persia, and Greece, we find ourselves moving closer to the dualistic world of traditional JUDAISM, CHRISTIANITY, and ISLAM, and also to cultures whose influence on the demon concepts of those great monotheistic faiths can clearly be perceived.

In ancient Egypt the gods and goddesses were generally not thought of as absolutely good or evil, though some may have had greater tendencies one way or the other. The demonological pattern in Mesopotamia and Canaan, where hosts of good and evil spirits were identified, was closer to the Judeo-Christian-Islamic world and undoubtedly affected it. Evil spirits were said to cause all sorts of ill: bad luck, toothache, drought. Dualism was suggested not only by the phalanxes of evil spirits, but also by the creation myth with its battle of gods against chaos, and the Tammuz-Baal cult.

Dualism reached its most explicit expression in the ZOROASTRIANISM of neighboring Persia. There the universe was a battleground between the high god, Ahura Mazda, and the hosts of darkness led by Angra Mainyu or Ahriman. The forces of evil were now more consolidated and personalized into a single will opposed to a divine will than ever before, a move marking out the future of demonology. Certain of Ahriman's host, such as Aeshma Daeva (Asmodeus), who became king of demons in the TALMUD, even moved into Western demonology with their original Persian epithets.

In Greece, another culture which had an incalculable impact on the West, the sense of evil was more diffuse. As we have seen, the *daimōn* was originally a guiding spirit. However, the underworld of Dis or Hades to which Persephone went foreshadows the later abode of SATAN and his demons, and Pan, with his horns and hoofs, certainly affected the popular conception of the Christian devil.

6. **Judaism.** In early Hebrew religion, as in the early strata of other faiths, personal forces of good and evil were not radically polarized. When he first appears, the divine adversary Satan is a member of the heavenly court whose function is to present an opposing point of view to God, like a public prosecutor—the role he has in the book of Job. Other early demonic figures, probably much influenced by Mesopotamian and Canaanite prototypes, include Leviathan and Rahab representing chaos, LILITH the female night demon, and Azazel, the scapegoat who becomes demon of the wilderness.

During the sixth century B.C. and after, probably under Persian influence, Jewish thought became much more dualistic. Satan appears as the eternal adversary of God, who had tempted Eve in the Garden of Eden, who even now seeks to thwart the divine will, and who has an army of demonic assistants. During the Hellenistic period this strand of Judaism, finally expressed in GNOSTICISM and Christianity, reached its peak. Thus the NT takes for granted that the world is infested by a host of demons causing sickness, madness, and other ills under the leadership of Satan, Lucifer, or Beelzebub, the "Prince of this World." But while much of Jewish demonology's wealth of speculation and legend was carried over into Christian and occult lore, demonology receded in importance in the mainstream rabbinical Judaism of the diaspora, and is now little regarded in Jewish thought and life. However, in the Middle Ages and Renaissance demonology continued to exercise a certain fascination for both Jews and Christians: kabbalistic thinkers devised a demonic counter to the sephiroth of the tree of light, and tales of great Jewish magicians who for good or ill had dealings with demons were common. Such familiarity was attributed, along with *grimoires* or magical texts, to Jews from King Solomon to the fifteenth century Abramelin the Mage. Demonology also persists in Jewish folklore regarding DIBBUKS or evil spirits, and GOLEMS or artificial humans created by sorcery. (*See* KABBALA.)

7. **Christianity.** Classical Christianity adopted the highly dualistic and demon-filled perspective of the Gospels and of Hellenistic Judaism, a view inclined to give Satan and his minions very wide sway indeed—the entire kingdom of evil, plus practical charge of this fallen world, even though the latter was originally created good by God. This was not as great a realm, to be sure, as that awarded the house of darkness in the quasi-Christian "heresies" of Gnosticism and MANICHEISM, wherein the Lord of Light is an Unknown God represented only in Jesus Christ, and even the God of the OT, who made the material world, and the planetary prison-keepers of Earth are fallen beings with no love for humankind.

Normative Christianity did not reach such extremes, although the covert influence of Gnosticism and Manicheism on it is not to be underestimated. It maintained the identity of the OT Creator and Lawgiver with the Father of Jesus Christ, and the original goodness of the creation. But it developed an elaborate cosmic scenario, familiar to readers of DANTE and MILTON, attributing evil both to human will and to human entanglement in the cosmic rebellion of Satan and his angels. Cast out from heaven, the devil and his hosts landed at the center of Earth, the hell prepared for them. They tempted Adam and Eve, and now strive to ensnare other humans on the surface of Earth, and those whom they win join them forever below as miserable prisoners, under God's righteous judgment.

Between the fifteenth and seventeenth centuries Christian demonology reached its peak of social influence and elaboration. It was the era of the notorious witch trials, and the temper of the times called for ornate doctrines of demons, detailing their hierarchies, invocation and exorcism, pacts with humans, and methods of operating. The leading lords of malevolence, such as Beelzebub, Asmodeus, Ronwe, Xaphan, and Mammon, were described and portrayed in their grotesque shapes, and the salacious activities of *incubi* and *succubi* studied. Rumors of SATANISM and BLACK MASSES were rife. While most of the names and concepts have a long medieval history and often can be traced back to Hellenistic and even Babylonian sources, it was in the tumultuous, spiritually anxious dawn of modernity that, paradoxically, they had their greatest play. But while demonological doctrines have never disappeared from orthodox Christian chuches, and have enjoyed occasional revivals in the popular Christian imagination, demons have never again had the hold on Western culture that they had before the Age of Reason.

8. **Islam.** The demonology of Islam is closely related to that of Judaism and Christianity. Opposed

to Allah, "The God," is Iblīs or Shaiṭān, created by God out of fire. He disobeyed God by refusing to do obeisance to Adam. He is the chief of the JINN (genies), spirits often mentioned in the QUR'ĀN and popular Islamic lore who, while not always malicious, are generally ill-disposed to humans and seek to lead them astray. But Iblīs is also lord of the shaiṭāns, "satans," genuine devils who aid him in his rebellion. There is much popular and quasi-theological teaching about the jinns and shaiṭāns, their orders and eschatological role, but though their reality must be affirmed by the orthodox, most of this teaching is peripheral to the central concerns of Islam.

9. **Modern interpretations of demonology.** Interest in demons is far from dead in the modern world, and indeed has had something of a revival in the twentieth century, though the understanding of the persistent nightmare of the human race they represent has varied immensely. Conservative theologians, as well as lay writers such as Denis de Rougemont, have continued to argue for the existence of personal demonic powers at work in the world, pointing to such phenomena of our age as the rise of the hellish Nazi regime. The Protestant theologian PAUL TILLICH shifted emphasis from "demon" to the adjective "demonic," using it to refer not just to supernatural personal entities, but to any force which absolutizes that which is less than the ultimate and thus creates division and chaos. The psychoanalysis of Sigmund Freud and the analytic psychology of Carl Jung has taken the demons of art and legend seriously, but has seen them essentially as projections of the buried fears and repressions of the psyche. Finally, the modern interest in occultism and hallucinogenic drug experience has called forth demons in yet another way, for their kindred appears not uncommonly in the visions of that new magic. Demons, who have been with humankind through all our known existence in one form or another, have yet to take lasting flight.

Bibliography. J. Boyd, *Satan and Mara* (1975); R. Cavendish, *The Black Arts* (1976); G. Davidson, *Dictionary of Angels* (1967); E. Langton, *Essentials of Demonology* (1949); E. Maple, *The Domain of Devils* (1966); W. O'Flaherty, *The Origin of Evil in Hindu Mythology* (1976); P. Ricoeur, *The Symbolism of Evil* (1967); D. de Rougemont, *The Devil's Share* (1944); J. B. Russell, *The Devil: Perceptions of Evil from Antiquity to Primitive Christianity* (1977).

R. S. ELLWOOD

DENGYŌ DAISHI dĕn gyō dī shē (B; 766-822 [lit. "great teacher Dengyō"]). Posthumus title of Saichō, Japanese Buddhist monk and scholar who studied T'ien T'ai (TENDAI), mystical doctrines, and other teachings in China and systematized the Tendai school in Japan.

K. CRIM

DERVISH dĕr´ vīsh (I—Per.; lit. "poor"). A member of a SUFI order (ṬARĪQA), specifically a mendicant or beggar. Paradoxically the true beggar is one who does not beg at all but relies completely on God for the fulfillment of every material and spiritual need. In the Sufi classification of mendicancy, one kind of beggar goes from door to door, publicly asking for alms; the other sits in his corner, hypocritically giving the impression even to himself that he is busy with God, but secretly he moves from door to door.

The term "dervish" was also applied to a group of nonaffiliated, itinerant Sufis, sometimes known as Malamatis or Qalandars or Hyderis. In the company of others they would engage in bizarre, deliberately offensive behavior, but because they claimed total reliance on God, they were often tolerated, and even rewarded, by domiciled, organizational Sufis.

"Dervish" entered the English language from association with the "Whirling Dervishes," a name derived from the frenzied yet orderly dance which they performed during musical assemblies. The real name of this group is the Mawlāwīs, since they were members of the order loyal to the Mawlānā, JALĀL AD-DĪN RŪMĪ.

Bibliography. J. P. Brown, *The Dervishes* (1868); M. Molé, "La danse extatique en Islam," *Sources orientales,* VI (1963), 229-79.

B. LAWRENCE

DESERT FATHERS (Ch). In the last decades of the third century some Christians, despairing of the worldliness of the church, left the cities of Egypt and lived as hermits in the desert. Moved by the words of Jesus that perfection required one to sell possessions, give to the poor, and follow Christ, they lived in caves, huts, or brick cells, out of sight of each other but sometimes coming together for EUCHARIST and instruction. Their lives were characterized by chastity, poverty, and sometimes a highly competitive ASCETICISM which included fasting, going without sleep, and standing for long periods of time.

They supported themselves by weaving palm leaves into mats and baskets as well as tending small gardens. Severe physical deprivation was seen as a spiritual discipline, but their lives exhibited remarkable humility and diplomacy.

The mid-fourth to the mid-fifth centuries constituted the golden age. Thousands of people moved to the desert, and older monks complained about the loss of solitude. Gradually, small communities formed where the life was directed by an older, experienced monk. The next development was cenobite or communal MONASTICISM where people lived under a rule in obedience to an abbot. *See* ANTONY OF EGYPT.

Bibliography. H. Waddell, *The Desert Fathers* (1936); B. Ward, *The Sayings of the Desert Fathers* (1975).

W. O. PAULSELL

DESIRE (B). *See* TANHĀ.

DEUTEROCANONICAL (Ch). Having a status secondary to that of the fully canonical books of the

BIBLE; designation preferred by the ROMAN CATHOLIC CHURCH for the OT APOCRYPHA. K. CRIM

DEVA dĕ´ vŭ (H & B—Skt.; lit. "a shining being" [*div*—"to shine, gleam"]) **Deus** dĕ´ ŭs (Gr.) **Daeva** dī´ vŭ (Per.). A *deva* is a shining or dazzling being, composed of light or resident of the realm of light and, as such, an embodiment and source of light, warmth, and life.The term sometimes refers to a demonic power and is also applied to human beings of high excellence (e.g., kings, teachers, holy men). In Iran the term originally referred to a god but after the reforms of Zoroaster, to a demon. In India, the process was the reverse. The plural refers to the entire company of gods, *viśva-devas* ("all the gods"), as a class of deities to whom sacrifice is offered.

The *devas* are regarded throughout the Hindu tradition as high, exalted, mighty, powerful, immortal, protectors of mankind, drinkers of SOMA, by and large free from malice and treachery, and reservoirs of benevolence whose devotees approach them for such boons as progeny, wealth, power, strength, military victory, glory, fertility, and general well-being.

All hymns and sacrificial oblations of food and drink belong uniquely to the *devas*. "Even as men must eat [food], so the gods must eat," states one early text. The "sustenance" derived from the offerings enables the gods to lengthen or shorten the lifespan of creatures, to grant or withhold rain and other types of fertility, and to provide all the potencies necessary to the effective operation of the cosmos. The gods are strong and powerful (especially in battle) and are often imagined to be celestial soldiers. In this guise, the gods ride on a vehicle (animal, bird, or chariot) or are carried by another being.

Significantly, the *devas* are the half-brothers of the ASURAS (demons), with whom they are locked into an eternal and indissoluble conflict. See DEMONS, DEMONOLOGY; VEDIC HINDUISM.

Bibliography. C. Dimmitt and J. A. B. van Buitenen, *Classical Hindu Mythology* (1978); J. Gonda, "The Concept of a Personal God in Ancient Indian Religious Thought," *Studia Missionalia*. XVII (1968), 111-36, rpr. in *Selected Studies* (1975); C. W. J. van der Linden, *The Concept of Deva in the Vedic Age* (1955). *See* bibliog. for ASURA. J. B. LONG

DEVADATTA dĕ vŭ dät´ tŭ (B). A cousin of Gautama the BUDDHA who became one of his monastic disciples, only later to become an archenemy. Various texts agree in reporting that he had developed what we now call psychic powers (SIDDHIS). He was evidently a man of commanding presence and considerable leadership qualities, as well as of no little spiritual maturity. These qualities were such as to impress Prince AJĀTASATTU, the son and murderer of King Bimbisāra of Magadha. Bimbisāra during the latter part of his lifetime was one of the chief patrons of the Buddha and his monastic order.

Prince Ajātasattu's generous patronage of Devadatta, according to an account which may contain reconstructions from after the event, apparently turned the latter's head. As a result of this change of mind, he personally requested of the elderly Buddha permission to lead the order and was refused. After this refusal he is said to have resorted to various attempts to murder the Buddha. The latter was able to thwart these attempts by his psychic powers, but he was evidently saddened by Devadatta's hostility and by the schism that he was able to effect, the first in the history of the order. As a result of this schism a sect arose which was to last for many centuries.

The hostility of Devadatta was evidently confined to the latter period of the Buddha's life. The evidence is strong that, in earlier years, Devadatta had enjoyed great respect among the chief monastic disciples and lay followers of the Buddha, and that his own religious practice included relatively severe austerities (Vinaya Piṭaka, Cullavagga VII, 1-5).

Bibliography. *See* bibliog. for BUDDHA, LIFE OF GAUTAMA.
R. H. DRUMMOND

DEVIL. *See* DEMONS, DEMONOLOGY; SATAN.

DHAMMA dŭm´ mŭ (B & H). *See* DHARMA.

DHAMMAPADA dŭm´ mŭ pä´ dŭ (B—Pali) **DHARMAPADA** där´ mŭ pä´ dŭ (B—Skt.). A book of the Buddhist canon containing verses covering nearly every facet of Buddhist teaching (DHARMA).

1. **Setting.** The Indian spiritual masters of BUDDHA's era were expected to sum up their teachings in memory verses called *gāthās*. It was the Buddha's habit to conclude a sermon with such a verse, or verses, and these were preserved and included in the earliest books of BUDDHISM. Later, an anonymous Buddhist made a collection of his or her favorite verses under the title Dhammapada, "Teaching-verses."

2. **Texts.** Four recensions are extant or partially extant in Indian languages: the Dhammapada of the THERAVĀDA sect in the Pali language, complete with 26 chapters and 423 verses; the Dharmapada of a Northern sect (Dharmaguptaka?) in the Gāndhāri language, with most of the 26 chapters extant; the Udānavarga, an expansion of the Dharmapada composed by Dharmatrāta of the Sarvāstivāda sect in the first century after Christ, with nearly a thousand verses, now partially extant in Sanskrit and complete in Chinese and Tibetan; the Dharmapada of the Mahāsāṅghika sect, with only two chapters extant; plus several Chinese and Tibetan translations from Indian language recensions. (*See* BUDDHIST SECTARIANISM.) It may be assumed from the extant versions that virtually every sect of early Buddhism had a recension of the Dhammapada as part of its collection of teachings, and that the original Dhammapada contained approximately 350 verses loosely arranged topically into 26 chapters.

3. **Content.** There is no plot line or logical sequence of the verses of the Dhammapada because they are collected from other places in the Buddhist PALI CANON, mostly from the Suttas, the JĀTAKAS, and the Sutta-nipāta. For this reason, the order of the chapters and the arrangement of the verses within chapters varies greatly among the recensions. The appeal of the verses lies in their simplicity and their poetic power to relate the Buddhist teaching to everyday life, as may be seen in the following examples from the Pali Dhammapada as translated by Piyadassi Thera.

The Dhammapada begins with two verses that go to the heart of the KARMA doctrine: "All [evil mental] states have mind as their fore-runner, mind is their chief, and they are mind-made. If one speaks or acts with a polluted mind, then suffering follows one even as the wheel follows the hoof of the draught-ox. All [good mental] states have mind as their fore-runner, mind is their chief, and they are mind-made. If one speaks or acts with a pure mind, then happiness follows one as one's shadow that never departs."

The verse best known by Theravāda Buddhists is no. 183: "The giving up of all evil, the cultivation of all that is good, cleansing of one's mind, this is the teaching of the Buddhas." Many other verses also encourage the doing of good rather than evil; for example, "Irrigators lead the water; fletchers fashion the shaft; carpenters carve the wood; the wise discipline themselves" (no. 80). Or, "Though one conquers in battle a thousand times a thousand men, yet he is the greatest conqueror who conquers himself" (no. 103).

Many verses make comparisons between humans and animals or nature. For example, "Take delight in mindfulness, mind your mind, draw yourself out of the mire [of passions] as would an elephant sunk in mud" (no. 327). And, "As a solid rock is not shaken by the wind, even so the wise remain unshaken amidst blame and praise," or "As a deep lake is limpid and calm, so do wise men become calm on hearing the Dhamma, the teaching" (nos. 81-82).

Another important type of verse makes the point that the (Buddhist) monks who have brought their passions under control and purified their minds are the true religious elite, the true "Brāhmaṇas" (BRAHMIN priests): "He who does no evil through body, speech and mind, he who is restrained in these three respects—him I call a brāhmaṇa" (no. 391).

Numerous verses deal with the ethic of nonviolence (AHIṂSĀ) that is at the heart of Buddhist practice. For example, "Conquer the angry man by love; conquer the ill-natured man by goodness; conquer the miser with generosity; conquer the liar with truth" (no. 223). And, "Happily, indeed, we live without hate among the hateful, among men who hate let us live without hatred" (no. 197). The emphasis is upon the power of love to overcome hatred: "Hatred is never appeased through hatred in this world; by love alone does it appease. This is an ancient Law" (no. 5).

Most Dhammapada verses are applicable to both lay and ordained Buddhists, but others, such as the following from the chapter entitled "The BHIKKHU," exhort monks and nuns to be diligent in their efforts of discipline and self-control. "Restraint of the body is good. Restraint of speech is good. Restraint of the mind is good. Restraint everywhere (i.e. in the eye, ear, etc.) is good. The bhikkhu restrained everywhere is freed from all suffering" (no. 361). Or, "O bhikkhu, do censure yourself; do examine yourself. Self-guarded and mindful, O bhikkhu, you will live happily" (no. 379).

Finally, the Dhammapada includes verses on the ultimate goal of the Buddhist path. For instance, "The bhikkhu who abides in loving-kindness, who takes delight in the Teaching of the Buddha, attains the Happy Haven of Peace [NIRVANA] which is the calming of conditioned things" (no. 368). And, "To the bhikkhu who has entered an empty abode, whose mind is calmed, and who sees with insight the Dhamma [truth], there comes supreme joy transcending that of men" (no. 373).

4. **Commentary.** As is the case with most other texts of the Buddhist canon, there exists a commentary on the Dhammapada, written in approximately A.D. 450. It consists primarily of stories that have only a loose connection with the Dhammapada verse(s) under consideration. The commentary is most concerned with the encouragement of meritorious behavior among the readers. The stories tell of the rewards that come from good behavior and vice versa. The commentary also assumes that the Buddha knew what would happen before it happened, to a much greater extent than is assumed in the earlier Buddhist writings. Many of the commentary stories reflect a well-established, prosperous SAṄGHA, which also distinguishes them from earlier, canonical stories.

5. **Role.** The Dhammapada verses have played an important role in Buddhism in every century. The book is a favorite among lay Buddhists, who find it possible to commit at least some of its verses to memory (*see* BUDDHISM, LAY). The verses sum up the doctrine and spiritual path of Buddhism in a manner that is simple yet not simplistic. Because the verses offer such an effective entrance point into Buddhist teaching, they are used in the education of Buddhist youth and in winning converts among non-Buddhists.

Bibliography. There are many good English translations of the Pali Dhammapada, including I. Babbitt, *The Dhammapada* (1936); S. Radhakrishnan, *The Dhammapada* (1950); and Piyadassi Thera, *Dhammapada: Sayings of the Buddha* (1974). The commentary has been translated by E. Burlingame as *Buddhist Legends* (1921). W. W. Rockhill, *Udānavarga* (1892), a translation from Tibetan. J. Brough, ed., *The Gāndhārī Dharmapada*, a good critical edition of the text.

R. C. AMORE

DHARMA där´ mŭ (H, B, & Ja—Skt.; lit. "that which is established; law" [*dhṛ*—"support, bear"]) **DHAMMA** dŭm´mŭ (B—Pali). Righteousness or duty; "law" in the broadest sense, including natural order as well as the details of human propriety and personal, ethical norms.

No other term in traditional Indian religious thought is more important, more complex in the variety of its technical usages from system to system, and therefore more difficult to translate simply than dharma. In its most embracing sense, it describes proper order and defines and enjoins the principles of conduct that maintain it. Especially for Hindus and Buddhists dharma is, then, often equivalent to what is commonly meant by "religion."

1. **Dharma in early Vedic literature.** Alone or in composition the word "dharma" (*dharman* as a noun) appears more than 130 times in the RIG VEDA. Occasionally it signifies an agent: "supporter, sustainer." More frequently it seems to mean "(religious) prescription or ritual." In some instances its meaning apparently is broader: "regulation or code of conduct." Dharma is also linked to three other key terms: ṚTA (cosmic "order"), *satya* ("truth"), and *vrata* ("vow").

Fundamental in Vedic religious thought is belief in the need for human and divine interaction to maintain a universal commonweal. Sacrifice (YAJÑA) is occasion and instrument for reaffirming and renewing the cosmos. The universal order that is refreshed through sacrifice is *ṛta*. In the literature's earliest strata, the god VARUṆA is celebrated as the guardian of *ṛta*. He and MITRA also oversee all human promises, agreements, and contracts. Guaranteed by Varuṇa, *ṛta* is upheld by faithful performances. (Two forms related to *ṛta* are *ṛtu* ["a fixed time for any act," and especially the "time appointed for sacrifice"] and *ṛtvij* ["sacrificing at the correct time; a sacrificial officiant or priest"]).

Satya ("in accordance with reality; truth") and *ṛta* are allied; indeed, say the hymns, *ṛta* is *satya*. *Vrata* (lit., "a vow") is any solemn pledge to perform some signficant act. Therefore, *ṛta, satya,* and *vrata* reinforce one another, each isolating and emphasizing an aspect of cosmic reciprocity.

Dharma originally may have specified the activity—itself the outcome of true vows—that supports order *(ṛta)*. Over time, that order was denoted more and more frequently by dharma alone. An important reason for dharma's coming to be the preferred term was the enhanced role of sacrifice. Instrumental in sustaining order, sacrifice was increasingly viewed as the origin, structure, and animating force of the universe. The place of the gods declined. *Ṛta* was succeeded by dharma. The idea of cosmos remained intact, but the responsibility was shifted.

Rig Veda 10.90, the best-known cosmogonic account in the Vedic hymns, asserts that a PURUṢA (lit., "man") was sacrificed by the gods and that cosmos resulted. Each part of the cosmic man-offering became a part of the natural or social universe. For example, its eye became the sun. And the four classes (*see* CASTE) constituting paradigmatic human society rose from its face, arms, thighs, and feet respectively. "Gods offered sacrifice with the offering; these were the first appearances of *dharma*" (RV 10.90.16).

Subsequent texts confirm and elaborate upon that view. Dharma is manifested through action, and it appears both in particulars and their relationships. In the most embracing sense, dharma (ordering) is the network of individual dharmas (duties). Dharma as the ordering of proper behavior and its outcome is not fixed for all time. Rather, it exists because it is and ought to be reaffirmed at all times. The essential metaphor is organic; better, it is human. *Puruṣa,* "man," is universal "substance" and also the formal, functional behavioral model.

Conduct, then, is dharma's crucial focus, and human conduct is the theme of the extensive literature issuing from traditional Hindu reflection on human obligations. This literature—DHARMAŚĀSTRA, "science of dharma"—is undergirded by a metaphysics; but its contents are understandable also in moral and legal terms as prescriptions, regulations, and statements of customs and norms in societal context.

2. **Dharmaśāstra: sources and characteristics.** Vedic literature is ŚRUTI (that which is "heard"); hence, it is understood to be revealed and self-validating. SMṚTI (that which is "remembered") is tradition and is authoritative insofar as it does not conflict with (and therefore can be justified by) *śruti*. Dharmaśāstra literature is *smṛti par excellence*. While the surviving texts in this body of learning share general perspectives and many common assumptions, each has emerged within specific circumstances and represents the positions of an individual "school" at a particular time.

Dharmaśāstra begins in the Kalpa Sūtras, "statements on (sacrificial or ceremonial) duties," which are the most important of the six ancillary disciplines essential for correct ritual performances that are known collectively as *Vedāṅgas* ("Limbs of the Vedas"). Kalpa Sūtras are technical manuals theoretically divided into two major parts: a section on major sacrifical rituals (Śrauta Sūtras, "statements pertaining to *śruti*") and one prescribing right actions for men at every stage of their lives in the home and the world at large (Smārta Sūtras, "statements relating to *smṛti;* the rules of tradition"). Smārta Sūtras ideally are subdivided into Gṛhya Sūtras and Dharma Sūtras—respectively, rules dealing with householders' obligations (daily domestic rituals, ceremonies at critical life stages [SAṂSKĀRA], etc.) and rules concerning personal duty and status in society.

Complete Kalpa Sūtras are rare, and distinctions between the sections of Smārta Sūtras are blurred in many surviving texts. Still Dharma Sūtras—whether extant as discrete works or incorporated in broader Kalpa Sūtra divisions—are the bases of Dharmaśāstra and are generically called "the *smṛtis*." Grounded on these *smṛtis,* the considerable Dharmaśāstra literature is fundamentally exegetical. It is commentary, at some times restricted to elaboration and clarification and, at others, focused on reconciling variant traditional or customary norms.

The subjects dealt with in Dharmaśāstra range over all aspects of life. Civil and criminal law are treated in detail. But the domain of Dharmaśāstra is broader. Much of the material in this encyclopedic corpus can be subsumed under *varṇāśramadharma,* "duty for social class and stage of life." (*See* ĀŚRAMA.)

3. **Varṇāśramadharma.** One's own dharma *(svadharma)* is that set of duties appropriate to one's place in society and time of life. The ideal society comprises four groups or classes *(varṇa):* priests (BRĀHMAṆAS/BRAHMINS), warrior-administrators (KṢATRIYAS), "the people" (artisans *et al.;* VAIŚYAS), and servants (ŚŪDRAS). (Though CASTE is often loosely employed as an equivalent of *varṇa* [lit., "color"], it better translates *jāti* or "birth." The many *jāti* groups are regularly accounted for in Dharmaśāstra as the result of sexual misconduct and a mixing of *varṇas.*)

With only minor variations, Dharmaśāstra texts agree on the principal duties, the core dharma, for each *varṇa.* The *Manusmṛti* (LAWS OF MANU) is representative: Brahmins teach and study the Veda, sacrifice for their own benefit and for others, give and accept alms; Kṣatriyas protect the people, bestow gifts, offer sacrifices, study the Veda, and should abstain from attachment to sensual pleasures; Vaiśyas tend cattle, bestow gifts, offer sacrifices, study the Veda, trade, lend money, and cultivate land; and Śūdras live only to serve the other three *varṇas.* (*See The Laws of Manu,* G. Bühler, trans., p. 24.)

Dharma is both class-specific and time-specific, a matter of when as well as where. Dharma involves *timing,* and what is required of any individual depends on his stage of life *(āśrama)*—a personal time reckoned not so much by physical age as by ritually achieved status—and on the great time period (YUGA) in which he lives.

Traditionally, the first three *varṇas* were called *dvija* or TWICE BORN, first as natural offspring and second as initiates into Vedic study. (Quite early, *dvija,* however, becomes practically synonymous with Brahmin.) To be initiated into Vedic lore is to enter a dharmic life of four stages. First is *brahmacarya,* the period of celibate studentship. *Gṛhastha* or the stage of householdership follows, during which domestic fire is tended (and all rites centering on it are performed), a man marries and fathers children, and all societal duties are honored. *Vānaprastha,* "the forest life," succeeds *gṛhastha.* Signaled variously (by seeing one's grandson or a gray hair, for example), *vānaprastha* is the period of retirement from society, and it is usually said that an individual withdraws with his wife and the household fire. *Saṃnyāsa,* "renunciation," is the final stage. In it, all attachments are abandoned. Wife and fire are left behind, and the person pursues the spiritual life utterly alone. (*See* SANNYĀSIN.)

Human lives are organized and cosmicized by life-stage duties *(āśrama-dharma).* But this scheme is not without tension. Not all Dharmaśāstra texts insist that one pass through all *āśramas.* For example, the *Āpastambhadharmasūtras* sanction a short-circuit, declaring that one may proceed from studentship to the renouncing, ascetic stage. And it is otherwise apparent that dharma has different nuances for householders, who participate fully in society, and for renunciants, who divest themselves of social roles and responsibilities. The latter seek release (MOKṢA) from the very order that dharma signifies for the man-in-society.

4. **Dharma and the goals of life.** Generally, classical Hindu tradition locates four legitimate goals of human life: (1) pleasure (aesthetic, sexual, etc.), (2) material success, (3) righteousness, and (4) liberation—respectively *kāma, artha, dharma,* and *mokṣa.* These are the *puruṣārthas,* "aims of man." Again, however, a certain tension is manifest. The first three goals constitute a triad differing in kind from the fourth. They are dharmic and cosmic, encapsulating in themselves the ideals of life-in-the-world. *Mokṣa* is radically different and there is evidence that it was not originally part of the *puruṣārtha* scheme. As householdership is not a necessary precursor or precondition of renunciation, so *kāma, artha,* and *dharma* do not entail *mokṣa.* (*See* HINDU AIMS OF LIFE.)

Although Indian religious systems regularly insist that moral conduct is the beginning and continuing support of any quest for release, dharma clearly becomes problematic if it is considered to be preliminary rather than ultimate. Vedic ritual and speculation reveal an intense desire to comprehend, affirm, and participate in order. Dharma emerged as the principal term used to express what order is and how it ought to be sustained. Pervading physical and social space and time, dharma is the right order of rightly ordered constituents, and it links individual lives with cosmic process and with all generations.

When the natural order itself came to be viewed darkly as a confinement (SAMSARA) from which individuals sought release, dharma necessarily submitted to new interpretations. Dharma and *mokṣa,* world affirmation and world rejection, are fundamentally opposed, and to accommodate both in a single system is to relativize one or the other. Through time, many solutions have been put forth to resolve the conflict between dharma and *mokṣa.* In some, an effort to subordinate *mokṣa* is apparent, stressing that dharma is self-transcending or, better, that there is *nothing* beyond dharma. (*See,* e.g., the BHAGAVAD GĪTĀ.) In others, dharma is seen only as an essential means to a goal that lies beyond it. Still other thinkers—most notably ŚAṂKARA—have proposed that knowledge *(jñāna)* is the only access to *mokṣa* and thereby have relegated dharma, right action (KARMA), and the world itself (samsara) to a realm not merely subordinate but ultimately false and illusory.

5. **Dharma in Buddhism.** Much that is true of the Hindu understanding of dharma holds equally for the Buddhist view. Certainly dharma (Pali, *dhamma*) occupies a place of no less importance in Buddhist thought, and with justification dharma has been called the central conception of Buddhism. Its meanings in Buddhism are several, and Buddhists themselves have not always agreed about its exact sense in a given context. There are three general constellations of meaning, each of which relates intimately to and is elucidated by the others.

a) Buddhadharma. The BUDDHA's teaching is dharma. It is about truth. It is true. And it is itself truth. The Buddha's discourses are dharma and so are the texts (*see* PALI CANON) that record them. Dharma from this perspective, then, is teaching, doctrine, scripture, authority. It should be noted also that *Buddhadharma—saddharma* ("true or fine teaching")—is distinguishable from the Buddha's person in this understanding. That is, according to the formula of the TRIRATNA ("Three Jewels"), a Buddhist seeks refuge in the Buddha, the dharma, and the community (SAṄGHA). This emphasizes that the truth of teaching is independent of the teacher. Early Buddhist tradition records the Buddha's declaration that one who had seen the dharma had seen him. Presumably such an idea—initially stressing the importance of the teaching—is one source of the DHARMAKĀYA, "dharma-body," notion well-developed in MAHĀYĀNA Buddhology and metaphysics.

b) Morality. For Buddhists, dharma also means duty, proper conduct, and morality in general. Here their usage seems especially close to that of the Hindus. But there is a difference: As morality and righteousness, dharma in Buddhism is universal, and *varṇa* or social class is irrelevant to it. The Buddhists' social environment is the *Saṅgha,* a community without classes. Certain conduct demanded of monks (BHIKKHUS) is not required of lay persons *(upāsaka),* yet both the renunciant and the lay "assemblies" in the *Saṅgha* accept dharma as a single, absolute standard of right behavior.

Dharma in the sense of righteousness pervades SĪLA, the correct, disciplined conduct indispensable for attaining NIRVANA. Both as doctrine and as the moral and practical dimensions of doctrine, dharma is seen by many Buddhists (particularly the THERAVĀDINS) as an instrument that should not be mistaken for the goal to which it leads. In the Buddha's famous simile, dharma is like a raft that carries a person across the water from danger to safety. When the other shore is reached, the "raft" should not be borne about on that person's shoulders.

c) Reality. The Buddha's teaching and the virtuous conduct prescribed by it are dharma because they accord with and are sustained by reality, the "way things are" in fact. Hence, reality is dharma or, put somewhat differently, all realities are *dharmas.* The ontological and cosmological meanings of dharma in Buddhism are several, but they all cohere in a general dharma theory accepted by all Buddhist schools.

Buddhism is grounded on a systematic analysis of reality that discloses the inadequacies and error of casual, common-sense attitudes. This analysis reveals that there are no "selves"—that is, no abiding entities. Rather, reality is a dynamic set of unanalyzable, undefinable elements. These irreducible ultimates are *dharmas,* the objectively real factors or events behind appearances, including persons (*see* SKANDHAS).

Broadly, then, dharma is the reality of conditioned, composite things and the regulating law of their mutual dependence (PAṬICCASAMUPPĀDA). Indeed, dharma is the transcendentally and absolutely real; so Nirvana is the supreme, unconditioned dharma. In short, dharma encompasses everything—absolute and relative, good and evil, here and there.

6. **Dharma according to the Jainas.** The Jainas employ the terms *dharma* and *adharma* in two quite distinct senses, one unique in traditional Indian thought. Dharma may refer simply to the accepted teachings of the Jinas; and, in that context, adharma would mean immorality, error, or anything contrary to those teachings. Ontologically, however, dharma and adharma are held to be real constituents of the universe. In this context, dharma is an all-pervasive, immaterial factor that could be called the "principle" or "condition" of movement. Intrinsically active, the self or JĪVA requires an environment in which motion is possible just as a fish needs water in order to swim, and dharma is that necessary environment.

Perfect rest is the Jainas' goal, and *mokṣa* requires transcending the circumstances making activity possible. Beyond this world there is no dharma, hence no movement. But there *is* adharma, the condition of nonmovement or inertia that permits liberated selves to remain at rest. Thus, adharma is not merely dharma's absence but an ontologically real, positive, and pervasive factor.

7. **Summary.** Underlying the many technical meanings of dharma are certain common understandings. Dharma is morality: the network of human rights and obligations constituting and guaranteeing social order. And dharma is universal order: the network of right relationships between cosmic or natural factors. Human and cosmic aspects of dharma complement—even require and complete—one another. What is beyond dharma? Nothing? Chaos? Release from strictures and deliverance from relative to absolute personal freedom? In these questions are the seeds of the dharma-*mokṣa* controversy so important in the history of ideas in India.

Bibliography. On dharma in Hindu tradition, P. V. Kane, *History of Dharmaśāstra* (1930-62); W. O'Flaherty and J. D. M. Derrett, *The Concept of Duty in South Asia* (1978). For dharma in Buddhism, E. Conze, *Buddhist Thought in India* (1962), pp. 92-116 and *passim;* T. Stcherbatsky, *The Central Conception of Buddhism and the Meaning of the Word "Dharma"* (1923; rpr. 1956).

G. R. WELBON

DHARMADHĀTU där mä dā´ tū (B—Skt.; lit. "truth-realm"). Spiritual realm in contrast but not separate from Lokadhātu (realm of particulars); luminous universe of unimpeded mutual interpenetration of particularity and universality as described in the final chapter of the Avataṃsaka Sūtra; basic to the Mahāyānist Hua-yen School (Kegon); *see* NARA BUDDHISM §3. C. W. EDWARDS

DHARMAKĀYA där mə kä´ yə (B—Skt.; lit. "body of dharma or truth"). One of the three aspects which together constitute the Mahāyāna Buddhist conception of TRIPLE BODY (*Trikāya*). The *Dharmakāya* refers to the Buddha as the absolute, formless, ineffable reality which underlies all phenomena.
E. J. COLEMAN

DHARMAŚĀSTRA dhär mŭ shä´ strŭ (H—Skt.; lit. "teachings on the law [dharma]"). Early in Indian religious literary history, proper social and religious conduct was identified as an area of religious instruction alongside discussion of proper ritual conduct. Interpretations of the VEDAS often included sections devoted to one's domestic and CASTE duties (DHARMAS) and paved the way for separate didactic texts (ŚĀSTRAS) which developed such concerns. These texts were called Dharmaśāstras, or "explications of dharma," and the most influential of these was the *Mānava-dharmaśāstra* (*see* MANU, LAWS OF).

Bibliography. P. V. Kane, *History of the Dharmaśāstra* (1930-62). L. D. SHINN

DHIKR thĭ´ kər (I—Arab., lit. "remembrance"). Prolonged repetition of certain words or formulas in praise of God, one of the most distinctive and characteristic SUFI activities. *Dhikr* may be done individually or corporately, silently or aloud. The scriptural passage most frequently cited to legitimate all forms of *dhikr* is QUR'ĀN 33:41: "O believers, remember God oft and give him glory at the dawn and in the evening." Not only do Sufi brotherhoods use *dhikr* to supplement canonical PRAYERS *(ṣalāt),* they are often distinguished by the *dhikr* which the founder or major leader has prescribed for his followers.

By its nature *dhikr* is linked to prayer litanies (WIRD) and also to musical assemblies. For orders such as the Mawlāwiyya or Whirling DERVISHES *dhikr* and song with instrumental accompaniment are supplemented, just as their effect is heightened, by the performance of ritual DANCE; the dance on such occasions becomes a rhythmic expression of silent *dhikr.* B. LAWRENCE

DHṚTARĀṢṬRA drĭ tŭ räsh´ trŭ (H—Skt.). In the MAHĀBHĀRATA, Dhṛtarāṣṭra is the father of the hundred Kauravas. Since he was born blind and thus prevented from ruling, the kingship falls to his younger brother Pāṇḍu, putative father of the PĀṆḌAVAS. His blindness seems to represent destiny (Bhaga, a god of destiny, is also blind). After PĀṆḌU'S death, he is the regent who arbitrates the claims of the Kauravas and Pāṇḍavas to sovereignty. Ideally neutral, he vacillates, favors DURYODHANA, and ever laments destiny's course. But he has the "divine eye," with which at times he recognizes destiny's true course and KRISHNA'S divinity. A. HILTEBEITEL

DHRUVA drōō´ vŭ (H—Skt.). Mythological grandson of MANU Svāyambhuva and son of Uttānapāda, Dhruva renounced his claim to the throne of his father and, though a KṢATRIYA, joined a society of RISHIS. By successfully resisting the attempts of Indra to distract him from his penances (TAPAS), he won the respect of VISHNU, and was raised to the heavens as the pole-star.
J. BARE

DHU'L-NŪN MIṢRĪ thool´ nōōn mīts rē´ (I; 796-859—Arab.; lit. "the Egyptian man of the fish"). Ninth century Egyptian SUFI master. Imprisoned by the MU'TAZILITES during their brief rule, he was later set free and acquired fame for his penetrating scholarship in several fields, including philosophy and alchemy. His status as an exemplary Sufi was secured by numerous anecdotes ascribed to him. He composed lucid Arabic poetry and prayers of unsurpassed beauty. Whether or not he originated the doctrinal views which later Sufis attributed to him, he seems to have been fond of intimating the kernel of mystical truth through opposite yet complementary concepts, e.g., knowledge and insight, fear and shame, and God's beauty and wrath, which together comprise perfection.

Bibliography. A. Schimmel, *Mystical Dimensions of Islam* (1975), pp. 42-47. B. LAWRENCE

DHYĀNA dī ä´ nŭ (H—Skt.; lit. "thought, reflection, meditation" [*dhyā*—"to think of, imagine, contemplate, meditate on"]). The seventh "limb" *(aṅga)* of the "eight-limbed" YOGA of PATAÑJALI, referring to the even flow of awareness that the YOGIN attains vis-à-vis a particular object or focus in meditation. The term *dhyāna* also appears in BUDDHIST texts (in the Skt. form *dhyāna* or its Pali equivalent, *jhāna*) and frequently is used as a general term for "meditation." The Chinese word *Ch'an* and the Japanese word ZEN are East Asian variants of the Sanskrit word *dhyāna.*

In Patañjali's technical usage, *dhyāna* is a second component in the threefold practice of *saṃyama* or "complete restraining" (*see* YOGA § 3c). The yogin first practices attaining "one-pointedness" *(ekāgratā),* or "fixing" *(dhāraṇā)* of awareness or attention on an object of meditation. Such "fixing" has three dimensions: (i) the "subject," or *grahītṛ;* (ii) the "object," or *grāhya;* and (iii) the intentional act of awareness that relates the subject and object, or *grahaṇa.* "Fixing," or *dhāraṇā,* is the experiential realization of these three dimensions in the context of meditation. "Meditation" itself, or *dhyāna*, is the focusing of the yogin's awareness on the intentional act of awareness itself (*grahaṇa*) in the presence of the "subject" and the "object." The yogin strives to prolong and become engrossed in this even flow of awareness. Theoretically, at a certain point the yogin will become so engrossed in this even flow that the threefold dimensions (namely, subject, object, and intentional flow) will begin to dissolve. When this occurs the yogin passes from *dhyāna* to SAMĀDHI, in which the usual distinctions of ordinary awareness are no longer relevant (*see* YOGA § 3d). The yogin has then passed beyond all conventional manifestations of awareness and has reached the ground or presupposition of awareness itself (or pure *citta*).

G. J. LARSON

DHYĀNI BUDDHA dyä´ nē boo´ dŭ. *See* BUDDHA, GENERAL CONCEPTS OF §4c.

DIAMOND CUTTER (Vajracchedikā Prajñāpāramitā) vŭj´ rŭ chä´ dĭ kä prŭj ngä pär rŭ´ mĭ tä (B—Skt.; lit. "perfection of wisdom that cuts like a diamond [or thunderbolt]"). SŪTRA belonging to the Prajñāpāramitā literature of the MAHĀYĀNA. Probably originating in fourth century India, this sūtra presents a sermon on the career of the BODHISATTVA as preached by the Buddha to Subhuti. C. W. EDWARDS

DIASPORA dī äs´ pô rä (Ju). The "dispersion" of the Jews outside the land of Israel, which dates back to the sixth century B.C. The main centers of the ancient diaspora were Egypt, Babylonia, Greece, Asia Minor, and Italy. For many Jews the modern state of Israel constitutes the fulfillment of a dream and represents an end to the diaspora. E. M. MEYERS

DIBBUK dĭb bûk´ (Ju—Heb.; lit. "attached"). A DEMON or disembodied soul that possesses the living body of another person and which must be expelled by exorcism. This folkloristic belief, found in many traditions, was combined with Jewish mystical views concerning transmigration of souls (*see* GILGUL). When the *dibbuk* was the restless soul of a dead person, its wandering in the world in search of a body was understood to be punishment for its sins. The possession itself was also understood to be the result of some sin in the person whom the *dibbuk* seized.

K. P. BLAND

DIES IRAE dē´ äs ē´ rä (Ch—Lat.; "day of wrath" [cf. Zeph. 1:15]). First words of a thirteenth century hymn used as the sequence following the Epistle at the REQUIEM MASS in the West. R. A. GREER

DIETARY LAW (Ju). *See* KOSHER.

DIGAMBARA dĭg ŭm bä´ rä (Ja—Skt.; lit. "sky-clad"). One of the two major monastic traditions in JAINISM. The name refers to the requirement that monks renounce all possessions, including all clothing, and live completely naked, i.e., "dressed [only] in the four directions [of the compass]." The ŚVETĀMBARA tradition permits the wearing of simple white garments. K. W. FOLKERT

DĪGHA NIKĀYA dēg´ hŭ nĭ kī´ yŭ (B—Pali; lit. "collection of long discourses"). The first collection of discourses in the "Sayings" Section (SUTTA PIṬAKA) of the sacred scriptures (PALI CANON) of THERAVĀDA BUDDHISM; corresponds to the Dīrgha Āgama in the Buddhist Sanskrit traditions. It consists of thirty-four generally longer discourses divided into three "books," or sections:

1. **Section of Ethical Rules.** A number of these discourses are centrally concerned with ethics; others enumerate and refute the false views of rival sects and teachers.

2. **The Great Section.** The discourses of the second "book" are "great" both in terms of their length and their importance. Two of these, the Great Discourse on the Final Decease (MAHĀ-PARINIBBĀNA SUTTA) and the Great Discourse on Foundations of Mindfulness (MAHĀSATIPAṬṬHĀNA SUTTA), have especial significance in their own right as independent books.

3. **The Pāthika Section,** that is, the Section of Discourses with the Pāthika as the first, includes two important discourses which have also been published as separate books: (a) the Sīgalovāda, a code for lay disciples, and (b) the Āṭānatiyā, a protective charm. These are especially popular among lay people.

Bibliography. T. W. and C. A. F. Rhys Davids, trans., *Dialogues of the Buddha*, S.B.B. vols. II-IV (1899, 1910, 1921).

J. P. MCDERMOTT

DIOCESE dī´ō sēs (Ch). The name given in some churches to the geographical district over which a BISHOP exercises supervision and pastoral care; corresponds to the "conference" in some other churches that also use the office of bishop, e.g., The United Methodist Church. K. WATKINS

DĪPAVAṂSA dē´ pŭ vän´ sŭ (B—Pali; lit. "Island Chronicle"). The oldest extant chronicle of Sri Lanka (Ceylon) in Pali. It presents the tradition of the introduction of Buddhism to Sri Lanka by the Buddha, and recounts its development through the end of the reign of Mahāsena (A.D. 325-52). Probably compiled in the late fourth or early fifth century, much of its material seems derived from the earlier Sinhalese Aṭṭhakathā. The Dīpavaṃsa's rough style and apparent lack of narrative plan suggest a mixed collection of verses by unskilled writers rather than a homogeneous work. *See* MAHĀVAṂSA.

Bibliography. H. Oldenberg, ed. and trans., *The Dīpavaṃsa* (1879).

J. P. MCDERMOTT

DISCIPLES OF CHRIST. *See* CHRISTIAN CHURCHES (DISCIPLES OF CHRIST).

DISPENSATION (Ch). 1. In ROMAN CATHOLICISM and some other traditions, an act by which a legitimate authority withdraws from the power of a church law a case which would normally be subject to it. The law is left intact, and the case is acknowledged to come under it, but exception is made because of particular needs. Dispensations can be granted only by the one who issued the law, his delegate, or his lawful successor. J. HENNESEY

2. In PROTESTANTISM, a period of time during which God deals in a distinctive manner with all or part of mankind. Dispensationalists (who are often premillenarian) claim scriptural basis for seven such ages—the dispensations of innocence (Adamic), conscience, human government, promise, law, grace, and the Kingdom (millennium). Some claim that many early church fathers were dispensationalists. *See* DISPENSATIONALISM. T. O. HALL

DISPENSATIONALISM (Ch). An eschatological doctrine, popular in FUNDAMENTALISM, that stresses the SECOND COMING of Christ in the immediate future. Dispensationalism received its name from its view of history as divided into seven periods, or "dispensations": 1) the age of innocence or Eden before the fall; 2) the age of conscience, after the expulsion from the garden; 3) the age of human government, or the COVENANT with Noah; 4) the age of promise, or the covenant with ABRAHAM; 5) the age of the law, or the covenant with MOSES; 6) the age of grace, or the covenant established through Christ; and 7) the millennial reign of Christ. Each period ends with man's disobedience of God and rejection of God's offer of grace. Dispensationalists believe that between the sixth and the seventh periods Christ will call his followers to meet him in the air in the RAPTURE. (*See* MILLENARIANISM.)

Dispensationalism originated in the theological work of John N. Darby (1800-1882), a former priest of the Church of Ireland and early leader of the PLYMOUTH BRETHREN. His ideas spread rapidly outside the boundaries of his sect. DWIGHT L. MOODY (1837-99), one of the leading evangelists of the nineteenth century, was the best known early convert to this position.

C. I. SCOFIELD, a Congregational minister and educator, put the dispensationalist position into its classic form in his notes in the *Scofield Reference Bible* (1909), which has been very influential among conservatives. Bible schools, especially Moody Bible Institute in Chicago, have trained many ministers in the dispensationalist system and helped to establish it as one of the most popular theologies in America. G. MILLER

DIVINATION. Methods of discovering the personal, human significance of future or present events. To a degree, science itself (despite its present disinterest in the unique or personal) has been a form of divination, especially in its origins. Current interest in ASTROLOGY and the I CHING (even by well-educated persons) shows that the personal aspects of "deciphering" reality remain a profound concern today. Divination is religious in that it gives meaning to unique, personal events within an all-encompassing transcendental reality. Thus to view divination as "magic" is to ignore its deep implications for the view of the self, others, and reality.

1. **Basic forms.** A preliminary classification may be made on the basis of the means used to obtain insight: dreams (oneiromancy), hunches and presentiments, involuntary body actions such as sneezes or twitches, ordeals, mediumistic possession, consulting the dead (necromancy), observations of animal behavior (augury, e.g., flight of birds) or manner of dying and form of internal organs (haruspicy), mechanical manipulations (casting lots, tossing coins), "reading" natural phenomena (astrology, etc.), and miscellaneous (*see* Rose, cited by Collins in bibliog.). More penetrating is the dual classification made by Plato (*Phaedrus* 244 and *Timaeus* 72) and many after him, distinguishing ecstatic from nonecstatic types.

But emotional states are unpredictable and sometimes ambiguous. More significant is the indigenous *meaning* given divination, as being caused by spirit manipulation ("possession" divination), by the operation of impersonal laws expressing a coherent divine order ("wisdom" divination), or arising from the immediate context ("intuitive" divination). Possession may not only be used as a theory to explain the full oracular trance, but may also "explain" hunches, the flight of birds, or the movements of a ouija board, while "wisdom" divination may teach the necessary macrocosm-microcosm correlations between heavenly and temporal events and bodily states (as in palmistry, Chinese body divination, etc.; *see* Lessa), or may culminate in such elaborate forms as Babylonian ASTROLOGY, the Muslim *hati* system, the Chinese I Ching, or the West African *Ifa-Fa-Eba* systems. "Intuitive" divination or "insight" generally features the heightened consciousness and guesses of the diviner; for example, the Shona of Zimbabwe esteem their *hombahomba* diviners because they can spontaneously tell the names, family connections, and problems of strangers who come from far off for help. But, showing how forms may be mixed together, the *hombahomba* precedes his intuitive guesses with the casting of *hakata* dice (a form of "wisdom" divination), after which, in one case, the diviner became possessed.

a) Wisdom divination. Intuitive divination is perhaps the elementary form out of which by various interpretations the other two developed, and we seldom find it much stressed (although its distribution, as hunches or presentiments, is universal). We can notice a tendency for folk practice to stress possession theories and experiences of divination, while complex wisdom divination generally stems from priestly or intellectual elites serving central institutions and seeking to maintain the cosmos, often from royal court circles. Thus in China the I Ching developed in courtly circles and was further elaborated by mandarin officials; the complicated swarm of spirits and gods in folk religion are not recognized in this very abstract classic. But peasants continued to consult mediums, to cast lots, or even select I Ching symbols through a spirit-guided bird who pecked at printed cards. Even reference to the I Ching by the folk, in short, expressed a typical "possession" view of reality as arbitrary, spirit-controlled, and personal, while to Confucian literati the classic communicated a sense of elemental, impersonal reality undergoing constant, well-regulated flux, a typical "wisdom" perspective. Interestingly, as Chinese society became more complex and literacy diffused widely (especially from the Ming dynasty on), the I Ching began to be used for strictly individual and personal reasons and no longer for official matters alone. Control over it was no longer centralized, and, as in the contemporary West, this text served as a quiet, intellectualistic protest against general social structures and scientific cosmology on behalf of the individual self.

A history similar to the I Ching was traced by Babylonian astrology. Furthermore, astrology continues to serve as a protest against everyday social roles and relationships. Today it appeals especially to people who feel oppressed or on the fringes: e.g. those of the "counter-culture," women, the lower and lower-middle class, etc. To these devotees astrology offers an exotic alternative identity which links them immediately to an invisible universe and a cosmic family. Social restrictions are symbolically negated, personal deficiencies now become cosmic patterns outside personal fault, and the center of the self is bound to transcendental harmonies. Like the Hermetics and the politically disenfranchised in Hellenistic and Roman times (*see* Cramer), devotees of astrology today protest nonviolently and intellectualistically against their felt lack of authentic social identity, ignoring the fact that the zodiac "houses" and their stellar correlates are now literally two thousand years out of congruence, making the system obsolete in its own terms.

b) Possession divination. Satisfactory cross-cultural studies of possession divination not involving mediumship have not yet been made, but there are indications that such methods are typical in SHAMANISM, and imply a view of reality as mysterious, arbitrary, and governed by personal powers whose messages may be given to strong egos. One study (*see* Bourguignon, *Possession,* p. 47) suggests that hunting-fishing cultures (where we usually find shamanism) generally depend on short-term risks and personal initiative where individuals must be self-reliant and self-sufficient. These societies do not have mediumistic trance; rather, shamans preserve their lucidity in ecstasy. The world may be filled with spirits, but survival requires alertness and powerful personalities.

Agricultural societies, however, train their children for compliance, reliability, and patience; cultivating crops needs long-term cooperation by many people, and social harmony is at a premium. Here mediumistic trance can be expected: individual power is enhanced (or extra-social identity expressed) by total abdication and self-effacement before the spirits. Other studies show that possession trance is most common in societies having slaves and two or more hereditary classes (e.g., commoners and nobility), and dense populations over 100,000—societies, we may add, where life is constantly involved with people and in unequal personal conflicts, making relative deprivation a constant experience. Less advantaged groups (women, the poor, etc.) are typically more drawn to possession trance than others (*see* Lewis); but in such cultures, the spirits that speak through the mediums usually divine for group health, prosperity and norms or at least provide a needed authoritative voice for the weak and ignored: social harmony is sustained in mediumship (*see* Beattie and Middleton). Mediumship thus expresses a view of the world as beyond personal control but governed by personal powers who can only be cajoled by total submission. Possession divination indicates that the immediate social context and even the social identity is felt to be insufficient, and so it too is a form of muted protest, like wisdom divination, but of an ecstatic sort.

When the entire social structure as such is felt to be insufficient, and the cosmos and its governing powers hostile to the self, mediumistic ecstasy tends to express itself in APOCALYPTIC predictions where the muted protest becomes explicit and radical, forming the basis for new MILLENARIAN MOVEMENTS. Wisdom divination, with its stress on rationality and integration, does not have such extreme consequences as the more passionate, power-oriented possession divination. In fact, as we have seen, wisdom divination often criticizes implicitly the passionate folk world of possession divination, much as traditional theology in Christianity has been suspicious of charismatic movements.

2. Sacrificial motifs. The "protest" dimension of divination could also be called "spiritual distancing." Precisely because divination is directed to specific human problems and actual suffering, but subsumes them and the immediate world of the ego under transcendental imperatives, it is religious. This transcendental orientation (like that of all religion) has two forms: orientation to a transcendental structure undergirding all events (wisdom divination) or orientation to a transcendental self (possession divination). Whatever the form, however, sacrificial rites and symbolisms shape procedures. Almost all African divination, for example, ends in SACRIFICE to the spirits named in the consultation, and many rites also begin with sacrifice. A client among the Fon (Dahomey, West Africa) must not only bring preliminary gifts to the diviner, but must also make offerings to Legba, the wanton TRICKSTER gate-keeper. Some Fon even say that Legba likes to stir up trouble so that he can get sacrifices. Legba may be said to stand for divine chance, the intrusion of mystery into orderly life. Certainly Fon know that bad luck, suffering, illness, and death all indicate the active presence of transcendental beings who demand explicit recognition and humble placation. So after learning in the divinatory session the name and complaints of the troublesome spirit, the client must end by offering up the prescribed sacrifices to it publicly (*see* Bascom). Very often the act of divination is simply a sacrificial rite: from the entrails of the victim the answer is discovered (haruspicy, common among East African pastoralists, the peoples of Borneo, the ancient Greeks and Romans, in fact worldwide), or the last movements of the victim give the answer (among the ancient Gauls, Strabo tells us, a human sacrificial victim was often killed by a sword-stroke in the back; the future was told from the way he fell, the nature of his convulsions, and the flow of the blood). It is interesting that in the Ifa and related systems of divination (Yoruba, also the Fon, of Nigeria-Dahomey), the divining apparatus must be "activated" by the novice diviner by sacrifices; the "basket divination" so highly esteemed in central and southern Africa (Turner) uses animal bones obtained from sacrificial victims, and the basket contents must also be drenched in the blood of a victim before they "speak" truly. The origins of the I Ching are sacrificial (both mythically and historically), and it is interesting that our first evidence of Chinese writing comes from "oracle bone" inscriptions of the Shang dynasty (1751-1112 B.C.): notations on the shells of sacrificed tortoises, relating to divinatory sessions. In many Congo cultures simply the fact that an animal has been accepted by the divine (ultimately by God) as a sacrifice constitutes the most common form of divination: chickens are fed a poison which kills in half the cases and leaves the victim unaffected in the others. If the chicken dies, God and the spirits have given an affirmative answer to the question posed.

But in a deeper sense the logic of all kinds of divination is sacrificial, since they all center on an act of transformation in which one's existence is offered up to the divine in order to receive it back renewed and restructured in accordance with the divine will. Only this can explain why we so often find that mediumistic initiations symbolize the novice as a sacrificial offering to the spirits or gods who now possess him or her.

3. Anthropological aspects. G. K. Park has suggested that divination, whether mediumistic or not, assists in decision-making precisely by removing the decision from contesting parties and bestowing on it an exterior, superior legitimacy, not only through its spiritual source but also through the convincing ritual drama. "Spiritual distancing," as it has been called, evidently works to allay anxiety and make effective social coordination possible; moreover, by ending the client's anxiety, concentrating his attention, and giving moral value to the solution, more effective action or cure of "spirit-caused" illness is facilitated. O. K. Moore has even argued that the scapulimancy performed on deer shoulder blades by the Naskapi Labrador Indians aids them in effective hunting by removing the question from the personal arena and "randomizing" the hunt. Following the essentially random configurations of cracks in the heated bone, hunters do not "overhunt" a particular area and are actually more likely therefore to find game. But even if the divinatory "reading" is not random, but is affected by the situation of the participants, the final decision is given an authority lacking any merely human opinion. For example, most wisdom divination merely gives generalities to clients: the Ifa system produces proverbs, specific myths, and ritual prescriptions; the I Ching offers cryptic poetic images, etc. The client must "discover" the practical meaning by applying it to his or her situation, but this does not lessen the sense of divine instruction. Doubt is now allayed; order is discerned in previously random events; debated issues and social tensions are resolved. By offering a transcendental, seemingly irrelevant symbol or proverb, in fact, the diviner may force the client to think through his situation from a wholly new perspective, and actually see a satisfactory solution to it. For example, astrology may sometimes "work" in this way. In decision-making, however, what is crucial for a person or a group is often not the "correctness" of the solution but the coherency of the group and the general acceptance of authority. From an anthropological perspective, often the "real" problem that brings a client to a diviner is that his group is torn by conflict and cannot achieve harmony by itself. History is filled with examples of kings legitimating their conquests or decisions by giving divinatory confirmation; possibly the most celebrated case is CONSTANTINE the Great's use of dream divination to justify his Parthian wars and to proclaim Christianity the official religion of the Roman Empire.

4. Divination in Western religions. Passing references throughout this discussion have indicated the presence of many forms of divination in the West. However, here we have something of a paradox, since both in JUDAISM and in CHRISTIANITY a scriptural basis can be found to reject divination, and while many sages and saints in both traditions have advocated and made use of divination, as diverse as astrology and dream divination, others, especially in modern times, have derided such methods.

In Judaism the ambivalence goes back to the TORAH and the TALMUD. Dream divination was used by Joseph in Egypt and later at local shrines in ancient Israel; the "Urim and Thummim" of the high priest were used to cast lots down to the time of King David, and certainly the great prophets divined the future through the power of God in them. Yet all appeals to local spirits of nature and of the dead were repeatedly condemned as denying God as the one source of all events (Deut. 18:10, 33:8; Judg. 18:5 ff; I Sam. 14, etc.): true divination is through God alone. Meditation on his word or wisdom (Torah) produced elaborate wisdom divination by Talmudic times, crystalizing in the *Sefer Yetsirah;* "prophetic" visions were also cultivated, leading to an extensive apocalyptic literature in the Second Temple period and a less extremist MERKABAH MYSTICISM thereafter. Water-gazing is reported in the Talmud, and astrology was accepted by many authorities throughout the Middle Ages, despite MOSES BEN MAIMON'S influential attack on it. In general, influences from surrounding cultures are the chief cause for folk divination in medieval Judaism and the rabbinical attitude was often sharply critical of them. The KABBALA, however, developed its own forms of body divination, basing this on the "divine image" idea and the belief that all things mutually influence each other, i.e., a wisdom divination. Mystics like Abraham Abulafia also sought prophetic visions, while on the folk level souls of the dead sometimes seized unfortunate persons and had to be exorcised. While these souls or DIBBUKS were not ruled by Satan nor were fully demonic (unlike demonic possession in medieval Christianity), they were sometimes malicious. The source for such beliefs can be traced through Hellenistic and Persian practices back to ancient Babylonia.

Christianity sharpened the dichotomy between good and bad divination into a full-fledged war between CHRIST and SATAN. The modern theological argument that Christianity is anti-magic chiefly bases itself on the identification of divination, etc., with the Satanic varieties condemned in the NEW TESTAMENT and thereafter. Astrological signs were accepted when they involved a new star over BETHLEHEM; dream divination by Joseph or Pilate's wife, casting lots, or ecstatic divination are all accepted in the NT (Matt. 1:20; 2:2, 12; 27:19; Acts 1:26; 10:10, etc.), except when they are done by non-Christian cult leaders like Simon Magus, or other "sorcerers" (Acts 8:9; 13:6; 16:16, etc.). Appeals to the dead, dream divination, lots, and a multitude of other methods are reported in use in the early Christian centuries by monks as well as common folk, while the Synod of Laodicia (*ca.* A.D. 343-81) "outlawed" divination. A major effort in the early church had to be exerted to bring schismatic CHARISMATIC MOVEMENTS, with their "prophetic" visions and apocalyptic forecasts, under control—a suppression all the more necessary in that Christianity itself began in the same way. The centrality of Christ, and by the early Middle Ages also of the Virgin MARY and the saints, tended to make divination by any other sources "Satanic." Astrology, however, despite criticism of it by some highly educated church leaders in the late Roman Empire, finally came to be universally accepted as part of the workings of a unified cosmos. This attitude continued unchallenged in Europe until the Renaissance renewed acquaintance with classical rationalistic objections. The interest in divination even in later Protestant circles, however, can be seen in the very widespread custom of obtaining divinatory answers by opening the Bible at random.

Bibliography. General articles are in Hastings' *Encyclopaedia of Religion and Ethics,* IV: 775-830; W. A. Lessa and E. Z. Vogt, eds., *Reader in Comparative Religion,* 2nd ed. (1965). Also see: J. Collins, *Primitive Religion* (1978); W. Abimbola, *Ifa* (1976); W. Bascom, *Ifa Divination* (1969); J. Beattie and J. Middleton, eds., *Spirit Mediumship and Society in Africa* (1969); E. E. Evans-Pritchard, *Witchcraft, Oracles and Magic Among the Azande* (1937); V. W. Turner, *Revelation and Divination in Ndembu Ritual* (1975); E. Bourguignon, *Possession* (1976); ed., *Religion, Altered States of Consciousness and Social Change* (1973); I. M. Lewis, *Ecstatic Religion* (1971); W. A. Lessa, *Chinese Body Divination* (1968); H. Wilhelm, *Change: Eight Lectures on the I Ching* (1960), and *Heaven, Earth and Man in the Book of Changes* (1977); F. H. Cramer, *Astrology in Roman Law and Politics* (1954); H. W. Park, *The Delphic Oracle,* 2 vols. (1956), and *Oracles of Zeus* (1966). A superb general history concentrating on Europe up to the early modern period, but beginning with two volumes on antiquity, is L. Thorndike, *History of Magic and Experimental Science,* 8 vols. (1944).

E. M. ZUESSE

DIVINE LIGHT MISSION. The American organization of the GURU Maharaj Ji (b. 1958). His followers consider him an embodiment of God, and the essential fact of life is their relationship to him. During the early 1970s he attracted extensive media coverage in the United States, but disputes with members of his family weakened his influence.

K. CRIM

DIVINE OFFICE (Ch). The daily prayers of the Western church contained in the BREVIARY and recited by monastics and priests; also used of non-Eucharistic services such as morning and evening prayer in the BOOK OF COMMON PRAYER. R. A. GREER

DIVORCE IN ISLAM. *See* MARRIAGE AND DIVORCE IN ISLAM.

DOCETISM dō´ sĕt ĭsm (Ch—Gr.; from *dŏkein*—"to seem, to appear"). The belief, in Gnostic Christian circles (*see* GNOSTICISM), that JESUS Christ had no fleshly existence, but visited the world in human "semblance" without being corrupted by materiality.

R. C. GREGG

DOCTRINE OF THE MEAN (Con—Chin.; *chung-yung;* lit. "centrality and normality"). Originally a chapter of the Confucian classic *The Book of Rites (Li Chi);* from an early date it received special attention because of its religious and philosophical subtlety. Authorship has been ascribed to Tzu Ssu, Confucius' grandson, but modern critical scholarship places it as late as the early Han dynasty (second century B.C.) and generally regards it as a collection of sayings from the Confucian school. The text is, however, a consistent statement revealing the depth of the Confucian ethico-religious point of view. CHU HSI placed it last in his basic collection of Confucian texts, the Four Books, as an indication of its profundity.

The terms "centrality" *(chung)* and "normality" *(yung)* suggest the meeting ground of the ways of man and Heaven. To manifest "genuineness" *(ch'eng)* is to fulfill the potential unity of one's human nature with Heaven, a unity that is the central feature of the Confucian religious life.

Bibliography. Tu Wei-ming, *Centrality and Commonality: An Essay on Chung-yung* (1976), argues for the hermeneutical unity and the religious profundity of the *chung-yung*, suggesting a new level of research on the text.

R. L. TAYLOR

DŌGEN dō´ gĕn (B—Jap.; 1200-1253). The most creative figure in Japanese ZEN, founder of the Japanese Sōtō school, and author of the *Shōbōgenzō* ("Treasury of Knowledge of True Law").

Born to court nobility, Dōgen lost father and mother by age seven, and was ordained a TENDAI monk by age thirteen. In 1223 he set out with his teacher, Myōzen, for China. He studied there with Ju-ching, and received the seal of enlightenment and succession to the Ts'ao-tung (Sōtō) school of Zen. He returned to Japan in 1227, and in 1236 established Kōshōhōrinji, the first independent Zen temple in Japan.

Dōgen was critical of sectarianism, and stressed the simplicity and daily labor which prevail in monastic life to this day. While venerating the entire Buddhist tradition, he simplified Buddhism to the practice of ZAZEN, which he identified with enlightenment itself.

Bibliography. Y. Yokei, *Zen Master Dōgen* (1976); R. Masunaga, *A Primer of Sōtō Zen* (1971).

C. W. EDWARDS

DOGMA (Ch—Gr.; lit. "that which seems true" [*dokeō*—"to think, imagine"]). In ROMAN CATHOLICISM a doctrine accepted as a truth revealed by God, appealing to the present faith of the church, rooted in the BIBLE, supported by tradition, and consonant with other Catholic doctrines.

E. R. CARROLL

DOME OF THE ROCK (I). The Dome of the Rock *(Qubbat al-Sakhra)* is one of the most venerable of Islamic shrines. Built atop the Temple Mount in JERUSALEM, on the purported site of Solomon's temple, the great wooden dome on a drum set inside a double octagonal ambulatory marks the place where, according to Islamic tradition, the Prophet MUHAMMAD touched the earth on his mystical journey of the MI'RĀJ, which took him from the realms of hell to the throne of God. As the third most venerated shrine of the Islamic world (after the sacred mosque of MECCA and the tomb of Muhammad in MEDINA) the Dome of the Rock's position is a major complication in the political status of a city holy to Christians, Muslims, and Jews. In addition to its symbolic and religious significance, the Dome of the Rock is one of the oldest and most important artistic monuments of Islamic civilization, in whose structure and decorations can be seen the first steps in the formation of Islamic art.

The original shrine was built under CALIPH 'Abd al-Malik ibn Marwān of the UMAYYAD dynasty between the years 688 and 691, in an enclosure known as the Ḥarām al-Sharīf, which also contains the MOSQUE al-Aqsa. The annular plan of the Dome of the Rock has been shown by Creswell to relate closely to earlier church plans in the Near East, but the practical implications of the structure are political as well as artistic. The tension between the Umayyads and a rival caliphate in the HEJAZ has led to the speculation that the *sakhra*, or holy rock itself, was put forward by the Umayyads as a pilgrimage center in direct competition with Mecca and Medina. (*See* HAJJ.) The ambulatories therefore served to facilitate the *tawāf* or ceremonial circumambulation which was an essential part of the Islamic pilgrimage ritual. A second stimulus for building the structure, which also explains its size, scale, and richness of decoration, was a competition with the monuments of conquered CHRISTIANITY. The Arab Muslims, without a strong architectural tradition, were stimulated by the importance and beauty of Christian monuments in Syria and Palestine to give architectural and decorative form to a countervailing political statement in the form of a major religious monument. Thus while the plan and decoration of the building owe much to central-plan churches of Syria, the Dome of the Rock was erected specifically in competition with the shrine of the HOLY SEPULCHRE, the major Christian shrine in Jerusalem.

The building proper consists of a timber dome approximately 20.5 meters in diameter, today covered with gold-anodized aluminum, set on a drum which rests on four rectangular pillars, with three slender round columns between each two pillars, forming a circle around the rock itself. Around this central circle is an octagon delimited by eight large pillars, each alternating with two columns, with the roofed space between octagon and circle forming an inner ambulatory. The octagonal outer wall of the building encloses the entire structure, creating a second ambulatory. The exterior walls are approximately 12 meters high including a parapet, and each side of the building is approximately equal in length to the diameter of the dome. The spaces of the two ambulatories are covered by a wooden roof sheathed today with sheets of lead, and both the exterior and interior of the building are extensively decorated, the latter with mosaics which show a synthesis of Byzantine technique and Sasanian vegetal forms.

The Dome of the Rock and other structures within the Ḥarām al-Sharīf have undergone extensive changes over time, as the result of shifting political events in Jerusalem. In 1548 the building was extensively redecorated under the patronage of the Ottoman Sultan Süleimān I, and the exterior was covered with ceramic tiles and a roof of lead sheeting. Damage to the structure in 1948 led to the extensive restoration of the exterior and the addition of gold-anodized aluminum sheathing to the dome. Many of the precious objects donated to the shrine in past times have now been dispersed into various museums throughout the world. *See* ART AND ARCHITECTURE, ISLAMIC.

Bibliography. K. A. C. Creswell, *Early Muslim Architecture* I, (1969); O. Grabar, *The Formation of Islamic Art* (1973).

W. DENNY

DOMINICANS dō mĭn′ ə kənz (Ch). Roman Catholic Religious Order of MENDICANT FRIARS, officially titled Order of Friars Preachers (OP), commonly called Dominicans because founded (1216) for promoting Catholic faith by St. Dominic (Domingo de Guzmán). Adapting the Rule of St. AUGUSTINE in an unusually democratic way, Dominicans have stressed contemplation, study, preaching, teaching, missions; among their leading theologians are THOMAS AQUINAS, ALBERTUS MAGNUS, and ECKHART. The First Order of friars was soon joined by the Second Order of contemplative nuns. Tertiaries, Third Order members, live the Dominican spirit individually or in numerous active congregations of Dominican sisters. *See* RELIGIOUS ORDERS. W. H. PRINCIPE

DOMINUS VOBISCUM dō′ mĭ noos vō bēs′ koom (Ch—Lat.; "The Lord be with you"). Liturgical salutation preceding the collect, the announcement of the Gospel, the SURSUM CORDA, and the dismissal in the Latin MASS. It derives from biblical salutations such as Ruth 2:4; the response ("and with thy spirit") finds echoes in II Tim. 4:22, Philem. 25, Gal. 6:18, and Phil. 4:23. R. A. GREER

DONATISM dŏn′ ə tĭs əm (Ch). A schismatic North African movement (early fourth–mid-seventh centuries A.D.) stressing the purity of the CLERGY as the guarantee of valid SACRAMENTS, opposing cooperation with secular authorities, and emphasizing MARTYR ideals. Named after an early leader of the group (Donatus). *See* AUGUSTINE §2. D. E. GROH

DOXOLOGY (Ch). An ascription of praise to God, often in trinitarian form. The GLORIA IN EXCELSIS and the GLORIA PATRI are known as the Greater and the Little Doxologies. The word is also commonly used to refer to T. Ken's (1637-1711) verses, beginning "Praise God from whom all blessings flow."

R. A. GREER

DRAUPADĪ drô′ pŭ dē (H—Skt.). Draupadī, the leading heroine in the MAHĀBHĀRATA, was born from the altar of a sacrificial fire. A heavenly voice announces that she will cause the death of the warrior caste. She is an incarnation of Śrī, goddess of prosperity and sovereignty. Draupadī's favor symbolizes sovereignty throughout the Epic.

Modern scholarship depicts Draupadī's marriage to the five PĀṆḌAVA brothers as symbolic, and not a reminiscence of non-Aryan tribal polyandry. When the Pāṇḍavas bring her home, they tell their mother they come with "alms" *(bhikṣā),* literally, "what one desires to share." The mother replies with an irreversible command: "share it (her) all equally." At the dice match, YUDHIṢṬHIRA only reluctantly bets Draupadī as the last stake. When he loses, she is dragged into the gambling hall menstruating and wearing a single garment. She keeps her wits and asks a subtle question: if Yudhiṣṭhira bet himself before her, was his staking her legal? This appeal to a technicality leads to the match's nullification and a rethrow which results in the Pāṇḍavas and Draupadī's exile. The humiliation of Draupadī is the Epic's pivotal scene. DURYODHANA crudely bares his thigh, inviting her to sit there; Duḥśāsana (second oldest Kaurava) says she must now "share" herself with the Kauravas and tries to disrobe her, being foiled only by the miraculous appearance of additional saris to cover her; and KARṆA calls her a "slave." The Pāṇḍavas and Draupadī respond with vows that can only result in the destruction of the Kauravas and the warrior caste. Draupadī's destructive side seems to prefigure such goddesses as DURGĀ and KĀLĪ.

A. HILTEBEITEL

DRAVIDIAN drŭ vĭd′ ĭ ŭn (H—Skt. [*drāviḍa*—"Tamil"]). A family of languages spoken throughout Southern India, the main modern representatives of which are TAMIL, Kannada, Telugu, and Malayalam. By extension, the term also refers to the peoples speaking these languages.

Before the ARYAN invasion of India around 1500 B.C., the homeland of the proto-Dravidians included Northwest India, and it appears probable that the INDUS VALLEY CIVILIZATION is attributable to them. Their original homeland is still a matter of some controversy, however. Theories have been advanced connecting the Dravidian languages with Finno-Ugrian, with Asianic and Basque, and with Elamite, with the weight of evidence seeming to favor Elamite. This, along with supporting archaeological and anthropological evidence, points to a Palaeo-Mediterranean place of origin. If this is correct, the Dravidians would seem to have entered India from the northwest, just as the Aryans were to do centuries later.

Once popularly imagined as backward aborigines before the Aryans arrived on the scene to enlighten them, the Dravidians (if from the Indus Valley) were culturally more advanced than their conquerors. Town planning, architecture, art, navigation, agriculture, food preparation, and dress are only some of the fields in which they made definitive contributions to Indian culture. Many of their deities and religious ideas were taken over by the Aryans, and modern devotional (BHAKTI) Hinduism, though deriving its form from the Aryans, may be in content predominantly a Dravidian bequest.

Bibliography. D. W. McAlpin, "Toward Proto-Elamo-Dravidian," *Language*, 50 (1974), 89-101; S. V. Visvanatha, *Racial Synthesis in Hindu Culture* (1928). J. BARE

DREAMS AND VISIONS IN ISLAM. An integral part of Muslim belief, they are carefully distinguished from the apparitions and divinations of pre-Islamic Arab sorcerers. In the QUR'ĀN they occur in connection with biblical prophets, viz., Joseph (Sura 12:4, 101) and ABRAHAM (Sura 37:105). MUHAMMAD received his first revelation (Sura 96:1-5) and became convinced of his vocation in a dream. The night journey and ascension (MI'RĀJ) are often interpreted as a two-part vision. The Islamic call to prayer (ADHĀN) is derived from a dream.

Particularly important is the validation that dreams or visions impart to momentous transitional events in the life of an individual. Muhammad's decision to reconquer MECCA, for instance, was confirmed by a vision (Sura 48:27). Dramatic dream confrontations caused the conversion to Islam of pagan rulers in realms as distant from Arabia as West Africa and Southeast Asia. The nocturnal appearance of a SUFI master or the mysterious KHIDR often led a pious Muslim to leave home and family in order to follow the Path (ṬARĪQA). Outstanding Persian poets, such as Jāmī and FIRDAUSĪ, were inspired by dreams, while major mystical writings, e.g., IBN 'ARABĪ's *Fuṣūṣ al-ḥikam* and *Futūḥāt al-makkīya,* originated from dreamlike visions.

It was possible for JINN and Shaiṭān (SATAN) to offer diabolic inspiration through dreams, but the nocturnal visitation of Muhammad himself to a respected person was accepted as firm fact. It could settle a doctrinal or legal dispute, lead to recovery from illness, and, above all, assure entrance into Paradise at death. In the late medieval period many Islamic scholars were preoccupied with understanding the world of images *('ālam al-mithāl),* defined as a visionary realm intermediate between the spiritual and physical world. The optimal experience for them, as for devout Muslims of all ages, was the vision of God Almighty, whether anticipated in anthropomorphic or, more often, luminous form.

Bibliography. S. Digby, "Dreams and Reminscences of Dattu Sarvani," *The Indian Economic and Social History Review*, II (1965), 52-80; G. E. von Grunebaum and R. Callois, eds., *The Dream and Human Societies* (1966), pp. 3-21, 351-429; N. Levtzion, ed., *Conversion to Islam* (1979), pp. 129-58, 217-35. B. LAWRENCE

DROṆA drō´ nŭ (H—Skt.). In the MAHĀBHĀRATA, Droṇa is born when the RISHI Bharadvāja, performing a SOMA sacrifice, ejaculates at seeing the skirt fall from the nymph Ghṛtacī and puts his sperm in a *droṇa* (wooden vessel used in connection with the soma sacrifice). Droṇa is thus connected from birth with sacrifice; he also incarnates BṚHASPATI, priest of the gods. As a BRAHMIN youth, Droṇa befriends the KṢATRIYA prince Drupada (whose name means sacrifical stake), but when Drupada becomes king of Pāñcāla, he says friendship between warriors and priests cannot last. Droṇa is incensed, and, having already learned weaponry from the Kṣatriya-Brahmin Paraśurāma, he gains revenge by training the Kauravas and PĀṆḌAVAS in arms and demanding as GURU's fee the conquest of Drupada. Droṇa, a Brahmin, thus comes to rule Pāñcāla's northern half, and Drupada, left with the poorer south, seeks revenge by a sacrifice that gives birth to Dhṛṣṭadyumna and DRAUPADĪ. The former is an incarnation of the fire god AGNI.

Droṇa and his son Aśvatthāman become allies of DURYODHANA in the epic war. Droṇa becomes the second marshal of the Kuru army in the *Droṇaparvan* section of the epic, during which most of the kings die. This seems to reflect Droṇa's role as a priest in the "sacrifice of battle." Droṇa is finally killed through the Pāṇḍavas' most famous misdeed. YUDHIṢṬHIRA, at KRISHNA's bidding, tells Droṇa that an elephant named Aśvatthāman has been slain, but whispers the word elephant. Droṇa, hearing only the reference to his son, drops his weapons and Dhṛṣṭadyumna beheads him. A. HILTEBEITEL

DRUZES drōō´ zəz (I). A Syrian people professing a faith derived from the ISMĀ'ĪLIYYA sect of SHI'ISM. The name comes from al-Darazī (d. 1019), a non-Arab leader of the movement, which originated in the last years of the reign of al-Ḥākim, CALIPH of the FATIMID dynasty of Egypt (996-1021). In the Ismaili religious hierarchy al-Ḥākim was regarded as the infallible IMAM and was also an absolute monarch, exercising spiritual supremacy as possessor of the "active intellect," transmitted by the divine will through a divinely ordained family. Al-Ḥākim, an eccentric ruler in the exercise of his authority as both temporal and spiritual head of the Ismailis, seems to have wished to be regarded as an incarnation of divinity. Out of the resulting confusion over his claims, which greatly weakened the Fatimid establishment, the Druze movement arose in 1017. Ḥamza ibn Ali, a Persian, was responsible for establishing al-Ḥākim's standing among the Druzes as the embodiment of the ultimate One who created the first cosmic principle, the intellect. The Ḥākim cult in this sense became the worship of the One alone, manifested in al-Ḥākim. From this belief comes the appellation *muwaḥḥidūn* ("unitarians"), which the Druze apply to themselves. Ḥamza's teaching was founded on extremist Ismailism in its descriptions of the spiritual hierarchy which embodies cosmic principles. According to Ḥamza, there were five great cosmic ranks, each embodied in a human leader: the intellect, which was Ḥamza; the universal soul, Ismā'īl ibn Muḥammad al-Tamīmī; the word, Muḥammad ibn Wahb al-Qurashī; the preceder, Salāma ibn 'Abd al-Wahhāb; and the follower, Bahā' al-Dīn al-Muqtanā. Below these were a number of missionaries and preachers embodying cosmic effort, and subordinate to them were the ordinary believers. In opposition to these cosmic ranks were a series of false ones, also created by the One, al-Ḥākim, and these embodied the evil side of the cosmos. The latter will be abandoned by al-Ḥākim in the Last Days, when the messianic culmination of the era will be marked by the establishment of the worship of the One, revealed in al-Ḥākim. The Druzes await the return of both al-Ḥākim and Ḥamza, who are believed to be in "occultation," like that of the Imamite twelfth imam. (*See* Mahdi; Imāmiyya.) During the occultation of Ḥamza, al-Muqtanā became the link between Ḥamza and his followers, and it was under him that Druze orthodoxy was established. In A.D. 1033 al-Muqtanā also went into occultation, a state corresponding to the "complete" occultation of the Imamites. From then on the Druzes became a closed community, keeping their religious doctrines secret. Those who know the system are known as "the wise"; the others in the community are the "ignorant." The wise alone take part in the religious services on Thursday evening, although the ignorant may be admitted to the least secret of these services.

Bibliography. The fundamental work is S. de Sacy, *Exposé de la réligion des Druzes* (1838). A valuable outline of the Druze religion is given in the article "Druzes" in *EI*. by M. G. S. Hodgson. A. A. Sachedina

DU'A' dōō´ə. *See* Prayer in Islam.

DUALISM. A conception of the universe which postulates two irreducible ultimate principles, in mutual opposition and nearly evenly matched. In Western philosophy the term refers to a distinction between spirit (or mind) and matter (or the world); describing Indian speculation, the term has been used of the distinction between the individual self or soul and the world-soul. These dualities can be called timeless, but "dualism" in Near Eastern religious history refers to mythological narratives. A Zoroastrian account, found in the *Bundahishn* in late antiquity, pits God (Ahura Mazda) against the devil (Angra Mainyu) in an ethical struggle, in which the physical world is the scene but is morally neutral; earlier Zoroastrian texts and modern Zoroastrian piety do not, however, give the evil spirit equal status with the good. W. G. Oxtoby

DUKHOBORS dōō´ kə bôrz (Ch). Pacifist Russian sect which appeared in the mid-eighteenth century near Kharkov, later moving to the Caucasus. They called themselves the "People of God" or true Christians, but their opponents gave them the name *dukhobor* ("spirit-wrestlers"), those who fight the Holy Spirit. They accepted the name but gave it a new meaning: those who fight with the Spirit dwelling in each person. They rejected doctrines such as the Incarnation and the Trinity, believing that each generation has its own mortal Christ, a moral teacher. The only symbols of their faith are bread, salt, and a water jug kept on the table in the center of their meeting place. They are agrarian and hold property in common.

Dukhobors are particularly known for their defiance of the state's right to interfere in their lives with military service, taxation, education, and censuses; this brought them many persecutions. One militant group of 7,400 were helped by Leo Tolstoy to emigrate to Canada in 1898-99.

It is estimated that there are about 50,000 members throughout the world, of which 20,000 are in Canada and 11,000 in the Soviet Union. Their distrust of outsiders and officials leads them to conceal membership figures and to defy the social norms and customs of the larger society. V. Kesich

DUKKHA dook´ kŭ (B—Pali; lit. "unpleasant, dis-ease") **DUHKHA** doo´ kŭ (B—Skt.). The bodily and mental suffering that characterizes human existence from the moment of birth to the moment of death. In Buddhist thought *dukkha*, "suffering," is an important concept that constitutes one of the three characteristics of existence and the first of the Four Noble Truths.

Buddhist commentators speak of a threefold and a fourfold classification of *dukkha*. The threefold classification includes 1) suffering from pain: that is, consciously experienced mental or physical suffering; 2) suffering from the aggregates (Skandha): that is, suffering traceable back to the unsatisfactoriness of the composite, ever-changing nature of one's psycho-physical makeup; and 3) suffering from change: that is, suffering inherent in even pleasant things due to their inevitable decline. Of these three dimensions of suffering, the first two are emphasized in the use of *dukkha* as the first of the four noble truths, and the third is especially relevant to the occurrence of *dukkha*, along with impermanence (Anicca) and no-soul (Anatta), among the three characteristics of human existence.

The fourfold classification of *dukkha* includes 1) unmanifested suffering, in which the pain and its cause are not apparent; 2) manifested suffering, in which one is aware of the pain and its cause; 3) indirect suffering, which refers to experiences that contain the seeds of later suffering; and 4) direct suffering, which refers to experiences immediately associated with suffering. R. C. Amore

DUNKARDS (Ch). *See* Brethren, Church of the.

DUNS SCOTUS, JOHN dūns scō´ tŭs (Ch; *ca.* 1266-1308). Franciscan philosopher and theologian who attempted to create a new synthesis of Christian belief with Greek and Arab philosophy, with greater emphasis on the liberty of God and the role of will in God and man. *See* SCHOLASTICISM §2.

F. OAKLEY

DURGĀ dūr´ gä (H—Skt.; lit. "the inaccessible one"). A Hindu goddess. Famous as a demon slayer and worshiped as the queen of the cosmos; rides a lion and is sometimes associated with the god SHIVA. *See* GODDESS (INDIA) §3.

D. R. KINSLEY

DURYODHANA dûr yōd´ hŭ nŭ (H—Skt.). In the MAHĀBHĀRATA, Duryodhana leads the hundred Kaurava brothers against their cousins, the five PĀṆḌAVAS. Inauspicious omens attend his birth and prompt his father DHṚTARĀṢṬRA's advisors to recommend that he be abandoned; but the blind father refuses. Duryodhana incarnates the demon Kali (the ASURA of the KALI YUGA) and the Kauravas are said to be incarnate RĀKṢASAS. Pride and jealousy of his cousins are the vices which consume him; but courage, loyalty in friendship, and an apparently benevolent reign are traits which inspired a late nineteenth century "inversion theory" that he was the Epic's original hero.

Duryodhana undertakes early efforts to kill the Pāṇḍavas, then defeats them at dice and forces their exile. After the exile he refuses to honor the agreement to return their half of the kingdom. War follows and ends with his arch rival BHĪMA killing him in a mace duel. At KRISHNA's prompting, Bhīma illegally deals a low and fatal blow to the thigh. This avenges Duryodhana's most villainous act: the baring of his thigh to Draupadī to invite her to sit thereon after the Pāṇḍavas had gambled her away in the dice match.

A. HILTEBEITEL

DVAITA dvī´ tŭ (H—Skt.; lit. "dualism"). That type of VEDĀNTA philosophy pioneered by MADHVA. It emphasizes the absolute distinctions between God, man, and world, as well as the plurality of things in the world, thus standing diametrically opposed to ADVAITA.

Bibliography. *See* bibliog. for VEDĀNTA; MADHVA.

K. H. POTTER

DVIJA dvī´ jŭ (H). *See* TWICE BORN.

E

EASTER (Ch). The annual festival celebrating the Resurrection of Jesus from the dead.

1. **The primitive pascha.** The earliest Christians kept every Sunday as celebration of the resurrection, but from around the end of the first century there appeared as well an annual observance of Christ's death and resurrection called *pascha*. This term is the Greek word for Passover, though some early writers sought to derive it from the Greek verb *paschein,* to suffer. This primitive observance was actually the anniversary (14 Nisan, according to the Jewish lunar calendar) of Jesus' crucifixion on the day of Preparation for the Passover, the date of the crucifixion given by the Fourth Gospel (*see* Calendar, Jewish). This date could fall on any day of the week. In the primitive observance the day was kept as a fast day, concluding in the evening with a eucharistic meal which celebrated the resurrection. This came into conflict with the weekly celebration of the resurrection on Sunday, and a controversy developed between those who insisted that the paschal fast be ended only on a Sunday and those who observed only 14 Nisan (called Quartodecimans from the Latin for "fourteen"). This and other controversies over the date of Easter continued until the Council of Nicaea in A.D. 325. There the date for the feast was set as the Sunday following the first full moon after the vernal equinox. The date of the feast is still defined in that way, but various factors (the Gregorian reform of the calendar in the sixteenth century and periodic adjustments of the nineteen-year lunar cycle in the West) have caused divergence between the computation of the date in the Eastern Orthodox Churches and in the West, though these coincide from time to time.

2. **The paschal vigil.** Characteristic of the Easter observance from the beginning has been an extended vigil during the night from Saturday to Sunday. The *Epistula Apostolorum* (*ca.* 150) speaks of such a watch until cockcrow. From the early fifth century at Jerusalem comes the first detailed account of the liturgical content of this vigil: twelve readings from the OT, each followed by a period of prayer, during which time Baptism was administered by the Bishop in the baptistry. At the end of the vigil readings the newly baptized were led by the bishop into the assembly and the Eucharist was begun. To this outline (OT readings and prayer, baptism and eucharist) later development in the West added only an initial ceremony of light: the blessing of a new fire, the lighting of the paschal candle (symbol of the risen Christ), and the singing of *Exultet,* a praise poem which weaves together the themes of the exodus and the resurrection.

3. **The paschal fast.** Integral to the celebration is the fast on the preceding Friday and Saturday *(biduana)* and the ceremonies which later extended to the preceding Thursday as well. These days *(triduum sacrum)* form a unified complex running from the Last Supper to the celebration of the resurrection as climax to Holy Week.

4. **The paschal rejoicing.** From the outset Easter was celebrated for the fifty days until Pentecost (the fiftieth day), and the Council of Nicaea forbade fasting or kneeling in worship during that period. Recent reforms have reemphasized the keeping of Easter as the "Great Sunday," the fifty days being approximately one seventh of the year. *See* Calendar, Christian.

T. J. Talley

EASTERN ORTHODOX CHURCHES (Ch). *See* Orthodox Churches.

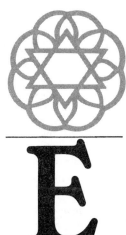

ECKHART, MEISTER ĕk′ härt mī′ stər (Ch; 1260-1327). Dominican friar; one of the great Christian mystics. He stressed the need to strip the mind of all active thought and images, emptying it for the mystical experience which he describes as the birth of the Eternal Word in the soul. For Eckhart God is "intellect," and only secondarily "being," and is accessible through the human intellect, which is nondiscursive and differs from both the senses and the rational consciousness. Beyond God, the Trinity is the "desert" of the Godhead which is unknowable, silent, and unified, but is experienced by the mystic. Eckhart studied at Paris and occupied positions of responsibility in the Dominican Order. He preached regularly in German to friars and nuns. His ideas were suspect during his lifetime and twenty-eight propositions from his writings were condemned. His influence continued in the group known as "Rhineland mystics" (Tauler, Suso, Ruysbroeck). Otto has compared his ideas to those of ŚAṂKARA.

Bibliography. R. B. Blakney, trans., *Meister Eckhart,* (1941); R. Otto, *Mysticism East and West* (1932); J. M. Clark, *Meister Eckhart* (1957); C. F. Kelly, *Meister Eckhart and Divine Knowledge* (1977); D. E. Linge, "Mysticism, Poverty and Reason in the Thought of Meister Eckhart," *JAAR,* XLVI (1978), 465-88.

G. A. ZINN

ECUMENICAL MOVEMENT (Ch—Gr. *oikoumenē;* lit. "the whole inhabited world"). A movement to express the wholeness of the Christian faith as held by diverse churches in pursuit of a common worldwide mission.

1. **Origins.** The movement gained momentum in the early twentieth century with three purposes: (a) healing the historical divisions of the churches, thus stimulating renewal in faith and worship; (b) struggling by social and political means to secure freedom, mutual aid, justice, and peace; (c) extending the mission of the gospel to all spheres of society.

These purposes were advanced by three ecumenical organizations, which were the products of voluntary initiatives in the nineteenth century: (a) the Universal Conference on Life and Work, which enlisted church resources for human well-being; (b) the World Conference on Faith and Order, which focused on church union and internal renewal; (c) the International Missionary Council, which coordinated agencies and societies devoted to world MISSION. Most PROTESTANT and ORTHODOX CHURCHES cooperated in the first two; only Protestants in the third. ROMAN CATHOLICISM and some Protestant groups remained apart, though often invited.

The movement was also advanced by local and national councils of churches, national Christian councils, YMCA and YWCA, student movements, peace organizations, and the denominational federations. The many efforts being made by denominations to achieve unions were adding to the movement.

2. **World Council of Churches.** The major institutional consequence was the inauguration in 1948 of the World Council of Churches. This united the organizations concerned with Faith and Order with those concentrating on Life and Work, and in 1961 the International Missionary Council joined also. Now comprising 288 member churches, the World Council of Churches, based in Geneva, Switzerland, carries on numerous functions for the furtherance of Christian unity and the churches' influence on society. It also engages in programs of dialogue with people of other faiths and ideologies.

3. **Catholic participation.** Since 1965 the Roman Catholic Church has been actively related to world and national councils, though not as a member church. The Second VATICAN COUNCIL urged all Catholics to develop a spirit of ecumenical understanding and love. This opened the way for many bilateral conversations with other Christian bodies, exploring ways to mutual recognition and practical expressions of unity.

4. **Church unions.** The visible unity of the church remains the focal point of ecumenism. Negotiations between denominations have led to more than fifty church unions. These involve for the most part Presbyterians, Methodists, and Congregationalists, with Anglicans participating in India and Pakistan. Unions have taken place in Canada, Great Britain, Japan, Australia, the Philippines, Zaire, and the United States.

Bibliography. R. Rouse and S. C. Neill, eds., *A History of the Ecumenical Movement* (1954) is the standard work up to its date; N. Goodall, *Ecumenical Progress* (1972).

J. R. NELSON

EDDY, MARY BAKER (Ch; 1821-1910). Founder of CHRISTIAN SCIENCE.

EDICT OF NANTES nänt (Ch). A promulgation of Henry IV of France in 1598, granting toleration to REFORMED Christians (HUGUENOTS) but far less than full freedom of worship and assembly; nonetheless a milestone on the road to a free church in a free society. It was revoked by Louis XIV in 1685, leading to an exodus of Huguenots from France.

J. H. LEITH

EDWARDS, JONATHAN (Ch; 1703-1758). American philosopher, revivalist, and theologian. During the 1730s his congregation was the center of a major revival which affected the other churches in the Connecticut Valley. His account of this revival, *A Faithful Narrative of the Surprising Work of God* (1737), helped to inspire the GREAT AWAKENING that swept the American colonies in the next decade. He was a missionary to the Indians and served as president of The College of New Jersey (now Princeton University) for a short time before his death.

Edwards' theology was a skillful combination of PURITAN orthodoxy, the new science of Newton and Locke, and his own observation of human life. At its base was a philosophy of experience that emphasized the role of the emotions as the ground of human behavior. Thus religion, by changing the emotional composition of humanity, could redirect history toward its final goal in the Kingdom of God.

Bibliography. P. Miller, *Jonathan Edwards* (1949).

G. MILLER

EIGHT IMMORTALS (T). A commonly depicted group of Taoist immortals. The eight usually include Chung-li Ch'uan, whose emblem is a fan; Chang Kuo-lao, whose emblem is a drum; Lü Tung-pin, who carries a sword; Ts'ao Kuo-chiu, whose emblem is a pair of castanets and who is dressed in official robes and court headdress; Li T'ieh-kuai ("Iron-crutch Li"), who is represented as a beggar leaning on an iron crutch, and whose emblem is the pilgrim's gourd; Han Hsiang-tzu, nephew of the famous scholar Han Yü, whose emblem is the flute; Lan Ts'ai-ho, whose emblem is the flower basket; and Ho Hsien-ku, a woman, whose emblem is the lotus and sometimes a bamboo ladle. *See* TAOISM, RELIGIOUS §5.

M. LEVERING

EIGHTFOLD PATH (B). The last of the FOUR NOBLE TRUTHS, the practical discipline with eight parts taught by the Buddha as a way from ignorance to knowledge, from suffering to NIRVANA.

The idea of comparing a spiritual discipline to a road, way, or path was not original with the BUDDHA. The spiritual masters of old India were expected to lay down a practical means to enlightenment, a path through SAMSARA to liberation. Distinctive of BUDDHISM is the teaching of a *middle* path with *eight* parts.

1. **Setting.** The Eightfold Path was originally taught by the Buddha in his famous first sermon delivered in the deer park at SĀRNĀTH, near modern Banāras. There the newly enlightened one outlined a middle way to Nirvana. He told the five ascetics who constituted his first disciples that they should follow a path between two extremes. On the one hand they should not lead a worldly life of sensual indulgence, for such a life is low, base, unworthy, and harmful. On the other hand they should avoid the opposite extreme of self-mortification, of extreme asceticism (TAPAS), as practiced by many spiritual questers of the day.

The Buddha had himself practiced asceticism to the extreme for six years, before nearly dying. Now, he spoke with the authority of one who had found Nirvana, and from that perspective he argued that extreme asceticism is painful, unworthy, and unprofitable. His own success had come after he had ceased his severe fasting and begun to take food in moderation, so he taught that the middle way was the proper, productive path toward liberation.

Having established that the extremes were to be avoided, the Buddha outlined his insights concerning the nature of reality in the form of FOUR NOBLE TRUTHS. The first truth was that human existence is characterized by *suffering,* by mental and physical distress (DUKKHA). The second truth was that the underlying cause of such suffering is the world-centered *craving* (TAṆHĀ) which inevitably binds persons to an impermanent, decaying world. The third truth was that it would be possible to bring about the *cessation* (NIRODHA) of suffering if craving itself could be stopped. The fourth truth was the *path* leading to the cessation of suffering by this method, and this path consisted of eight practical parts.

2. **Parts.** The eight parts of the path are not progressive stages to be undertaken successively, so their order is not as important as the nature of the parts themselves.

a) Right understanding or right views. This refers to holding a correct view of the nature of reality. Buddhism stresses the importance of experiencing the nature of reality for oneself, so right understanding is not to be seen as a matter of accepting a body of orthodox dogma. However, there is a specified content to Buddhist teachings and therefore there are certain insights that the disciple is expected to develop. For example, correct understanding involves gaining a deep realization of the four noble truths themselves.

Besides right understanding of the four truths, there is a lower level of right understanding, which concerns KARMA. Disciples should understand that they are the owners of their good and bad moral actions (karma), and they should further understand the workings of karma; for example, that giving (DĀNA) and offerings produce good karma, that taking care of one's aged parents brings good karma, and so on.

b) Right thought. This is understood to mean thoughts free from sensuous desire, from ill-will, and from cruelty. Often the meaning of right thought is said to embrace thoughts of renunciation, thoughts devoid of malice, and nonviolent (AHIṂSĀ) thoughts. Renunciation here means the renouncing of striving for gratification of the five senses, of the whole body, or of the mind. It means the state of mind that is devoid of greed. Thoughts devoid of malice refer to a state of mind characterized by lovingkindness, goodwill, and benevolence rather than by hatred, ill-will, and aversion. Nonviolent thoughts mean that feelings of gentleness and compassion toward humans and animals have replaced cruelty and unconcern.

c) Right speech, which includes the following four categories. One's speech should not be false in any sense of the word. One should not be the bearer of any tales that might lead to the breakdown of friendships or other problems. One should also abstain from harsh speech, which includes words delivered in anger, abusive words, vulgar, "animal-like" speech, or slurs against someone's family, race, occupation, etc. Finally, one is to avoid useless chatter, whether one's own (e.g. gossip) or others' (e.g. public entertainment that has no educational or spiritual value).

d) Right action. While there are numerous wrong actions to be avoided and right ones to be followed, three categories of actions to be avoided are usually specified under this heading. First, one should refrain from killing *(ahiṃsā)* any living creature. (Buddhist laymen are not enjoined to adhere to this law very strictly with regard to small animals such as insects, but monks ideally practice nonviolence as far as humanly possible.) Second, one should refrain from all forms of stealing. Third, one must avoid wrong conduct in matters of bodily pleasures (especially wrong sexual practices), intoxicants, and gambling. Wrong sexual practices include adultery, rape, incest, intercourse with a juvenile, and the like. For monks and nuns, who are under a rule of celibacy, all forms of sexual contact are forbidden.

e) Right livelihood is closely related to right action. It forbids four types of behavior. The disciple may not earn a living by any conduct that is contrary to the spirit of right speech and right action. This means that occupations that involve killing, such as hunting or fishing, are to be avoided. (Plowing is accepted reluctantly, for it involves unintentional killing of creatures in the soil.) The second improper means of livelihood (applying mainly to monks and nuns) is engaging in any form of commerce or performing any service for hire. Instead the ordained Buddhists are to live on alms, or (in some Buddhist countries) food they have grown themselves. The third type of wrong means of livelihood also applies mainly to ordained Buddhists, who are not allowed to practice any form of trickery, magical display, or other gimmick intended to gain food or gifts. This has been an important rule, for it has tended to keep Buddhist monks from engaging in displays of magical powers and from boasting about their accomplishments in meditation or wisdom. The prohibition against earning a living by such means as palmistry or astrology is the fourth rule.

f) Right effort refers especially to efforts made with regard to karma. The disciple strives to avoid the generation of any new unwholesome actions and their effects; that is, any bad karma. With regard to actions that are karmically good, the disciple makes an effort to develop wholesome features of the past and to cultivate wholesome states of mind in the present. These right efforts at purifying the mind are summarized under four terms: *avoiding* and *overcoming* unwholesome states of mind while *developing* and *maintaining* wholesome ones.

g) Right mindfulness is especially important. It is the heart of Buddhist meditation, known as *satī* (Pali) or *smṛti* (Skt.). In contrast to the practice of YOGA, in which the mind is stilled, in the practice of this meditation the disciples become more alert, more aware or mindful of themselves. In canonical passages such as the MAHĀSATIPAṬṬHĀNA SUTTA, mindfulness of four sets of objects is urged. First is contemplation of the body, typically begun by practicing mindfulness of breathing; that is, fixing one's attention upon one's own breathing, thinking "now I am breathing out" and "now I am breathing in." In this manner all the body parts and functions are considered until awareness of the body's transiency is fully experienced. One extreme of this contemplation, which is a corrective to personal vanity and attachment to one's own body, is the disciples' consideration of corpses in various states of decay and dismemberment. The skillful monk will be mindful when he sits, walks, stands, or sleeps.

The second classification is the contemplation of feelings, which involves becoming aware of one's own feelings, of how they originated and of how they will subside.

Third is the contemplation of the mind and its activity, which involves an awareness of the moments of consciousness. Here the disciples realize the nature and products of a greedy mind, a hateful mind, etc.

Fourth is the contemplation of mental objects. These mental objects include the "five hindrances" (lust, anger, sloth, restlessness, and doubt), the five aspects of psychosomatic existence (material nature and four mental factors), the nature of sensing, the seven factors of enlightenment (mindfulness, investigation of doctrine, energy, enthusiasm, tranquillity, concentration, and equanimity), and the four noble truths.

In these four contemplations and their many facets, the disciples aim to become more aware of the nature of all reality, especially of their own mental and physical constitutions.

h) Right concentration (SAMĀDHI). The essence of concentration is a unification of the mind, a "one-pointedness." The Buddha taught that the four contemplations of right mindfulness are the marks of concentration, and the four aspects of right effort are prerequisite to concentration. Thus, right effort and mindfulness work together to develop right concentration, and the reverse is true as well.

There are various meditation-objects recommended for the cultivation of right concentration. Contemplation should be focused upon ten positive objects (four colors, four elements, space, and light), ten kinds of corpses, the parts of the body, one's breathing, and the three divine virtues (lovingkindness, compassion, and sympathetic joy). The practice of concentration upon some or all of these twenty-five subjects should lead to one-pointedness of mind and, it is hoped, to Nirvana.

3. Three instructions. Within Buddhist thought the question arises as to how the eight parts of the path correspond to the three instructions; namely, the instructions in morality, concentration, and wisdom. The THERAVĀDA tradition understood *morality* (SĪLA) to include right speech, action and livelihood; *concentration* (SAMĀDHI) to include right effort, mindfulness and concentration; and *wisdom* (PRAJÑĀ) to include right understanding and thought. Progress on the parts of the path are interconnected, yet perfect morality is usually achieved before concentration techniques are fully effectual, and wisdom clearly depends fully upon success on the two previous levels. Thus, although right understanding is listed first and in a lesser form is prerequisite to the other seven, the perfection of undertanding is the final and highest achievement. With this in mind, some MAHĀYĀNA schools of Buddhism emphasized the perfection of wisdom in their versions of the path to enlightenment.

Bibliography. "The Foundation of the Kingdom of the Norm," *The Book of the Kindred Sayings* (1965), V. 356-65, the Theravāda version of the Buddha's first sermon, giving the noble eightfold path; Buddhaghosa, *The Path of Purity* (1971), a classical commentary on the three instructions of the path; L. Sayadaw, *The Noble Eightfold Path and its Factors Explained,* Wheel Publication no. 245-47 (1977), a modern Burmese Buddhist's commentary; P. Thera, *The Buddha's Ancient Path* (1964), a modern Sri Lankan's commentary.

R. C. AMORE

EIGHTEEN BENEDICTIONS (Ju). *See* AMIDAH.

ELDER (Ch). A title of respect and of office in the church. In the Jerusalem church of the NT, following Jewish custom, elders (PRESBYTERS) served as the governing council of the congregation (Acts 21:18) and, with the apostles, as a ruling council for the whole church (Acts 15).

In I Tim. 5:1-2, the term seems to refer primarily to age, but in other places (e.g., Acts 20:28; Jas. 5:14; and I Tim. 5:17-22), the primary reference seems to be to office. Elder and BISHOP are described in similar ways in the NT, but by the early second century the office of bishop can clearly be seen as organizationally superior to that of elder.

Responsibility for pastoral oversight of local groups of Christians was assigned to elders—increasingly one person in a place rather than several, as seems to have been the case in the NT. Their work was to preside over worship, care for the pastoral needs of the congregation, and share in the governing of the church.

The title "elder" continues in use. The METHODIST tradition maintains two levels of ministerial authority, deacon and elder. The latter is fully authorized to serve as minister in the churches. In other traditions the title denotes local church officials who exercise spiritual leadership but are not part of the clergy. For example, in Presbyterian churches and those of the CHRISTIAN CHURCHES (DISCIPLES OF CHRIST) and Churches of Christ elders are selected and in some cases ordained to office. They share with pastors in the care of the congregation, the ordering of worship, and the administration of the Lord's Supper. *See* CLERGY, CHRISTIAN.

K. WATKINS

ELIJAH (Ju, Ch & I). Ninth century B.C. Israelite prophet, assumed bodily into heaven (II Kings 2). In Jewish ESCHATOLOGY he is to be the forerunner of the MESSIAH (Mal. 3:1; 4:5), and as such is identified in the NT with JOHN THE BAPTIST. In Judaism he is the unseen guest for whom a cup of wine is poured at the PASSOVER SEDER, and at the CIRCUMCISION ceremony, where a chair is reserved for him. In the QUR'ĀN (Sura 37:123-32) he is remembered as a prophet sent to turn his people from Baal worship to monotheism (*see* KHIDR).

R. BULLARD

ELLORĀ ĕl lōr´ ä (B, H & Ja). Ancient religious site near the city of Aurangabad in the state of Maharashtra, India. The cave-temples and monasteries at Ellorā herald the last phase of rock-cut architecture in India. The shrines here were literally carved into the rock hillsides for monks and lay devotees of BUDDHISM, HINDUISM, and JAINISM. The series of Buddhist excavations date from mid-fifth to mid-sixth century and comprise series of monastery complexes consisting of assembly halls and shrines with cells to accommodate resident monks. The most outstanding monument in the Hindu group is the Kailāsanātha Temple, which is an excavated replica of the free-standing structural Pallava temple at Kāñcīpuram in South India. It was begun and consecrated under the patronage of the Rāṣṭrakūṭa ruler Krishnarāja I (757-783) and enlarged by later kings of that dynasty. The final group of excavated temples at Ellorā are those of the Jainas, begun about 800. The Jaina excavations as well as other additions at Ellorā appear to have been terminated by the early tenth century. *See also* AJANṬĀ.

Bibliography. P. Brown, *Indian Architecture: Buddhist and Hindu* (n.d.), pp. 71-74, 86-92.

C. R. JONES

EMBER DAYS (Ch). Seasonal fasts observed in the Western church on the Wednesday, Friday, and Saturday following the first Sunday of LENT, PENTECOST, September 14, and December 13. Since the late fifth century they have been favored as times for ordination. While still observed by many ANGLICANS, they have virtually disappeared from the Roman MISSAL of Paul VI.

T. J. TALLEY

EMPTINESS (B). *See* ŚŪNYATĀ.

EN SOF ān sōf´ (Ju—Heb.; lit. "without end," "infinite"). In KABBALA a term for God in himself, the ultimately transcendent and hidden reality of God beyond logical definition or intuitive comprehension, as opposed to God as he is known through the *sefirot* (*see* SEFIR BAHIR §1) and active in creation, revelation, and redemption. Like the Neoplatonic notion of the One, *En Sof* suggests a thoroughly apersonal conception of God. It is often referred to as the "cause of causes," "root of all roots," or "will of all wills." The question of the relationship between *En Sof* and the *sefirot* involves the processes, either creation or emanation, which comprise the connection between God and the universe.

K. P. BLAND

ENLIGHTENMENT (B). *See* NIRVANA; SAMĀDHI; SATORI.

EPIPHANY (Ch). The feast of the Manifestation of Christ on January 6. Its theme is the BAPTISM OF JESUS in the Eastern church, but in the West it commemorates the visit of the magi. The ARMENIAN CHURCH celebrates both the birth and baptism of Jesus on this day. Other themes associated with the feast have been the miracle at the wedding at Cana and the transfiguration. *See* CHRISTMAS.

T. J. TALLEY

EPISCOPACY (Ch—Lat. *episcopus*). Church governance by BISHOPS; used by the ROMAN CATHOLIC, Eastern ORTHODOX, ANGLICAN, METHODIST, and some other churches.

J. R. CRIM

EPISCOPAL CHURCH (Ch). *See* ANGLICAN CHURCHES.

ERASMUS, DESIDERIUS (ROTERODAMUS) ē răz´ məs dĕs ĭ dĕr´ ĭ əs (Ch; 1467?–1536). Born in Gouda, the Netherlands. Schooled by the Brothers of Common Life at Deventer, Erasmus became an Augustinian canon in 1486 or 1487 and was ordained a priest in 1492. In 1495 he entered the Collège de Montaigu in Paris, but most influential upon his future work was his stay at Oxford in 1499. There he met the biblical humanist John Colet, who persuaded him to devote himself to biblical and patristic studies. Erasmus' most important biblical work is his 1516 edition of the NEW TESTAMENT. His most popular works, however, are *Praise of Folly,* written in the home of his friend Thomas More, and *Colloquies.* His religious thought is best captured in *Enchiridion militis Christiani* (Handbook of a Christian Soldier), which praises a life of true piety and love as opposed to scholastic argumentation and exterior religious practices. Erasmus hoped to reform Christendom through high-minded dedication to truth and morality summed up in his term *philosophia Christi* (philosophy of Christ). He argued for free will in *De libero arbitrio* against LUTHER'S doctrine of the bondage of the will. Although he stood with the reformers against many Roman practices, he protested that he was a loyal Roman Catholic. He died in Basel, Switzerland, and was buried in the Basel Cathedral. Erasmus is best known as a Christian humanist whose sharp wit and prodigious productivity influenced every scholar of his day.

Bibliography. D. Erasmus, *Christian Humanism and the Reformation: Selected Writings,* ed. J. C. Olin (1956); R. H. Bainton, *Erasmus of Christendom* (1969). J. RAITT

ERETZ ISRAEL ĕ´ rĕts yĭs´ rä ĕl (Ju—Heb.; lit. "land of Israel"). Biblical name of the land of the Israelites and of the Northern Kingdom. In postbiblical times, the accepted designation of the homeland of the Jews, promised them by God and ultimately to be redeemed by the MESSIAH. It is the modern Hebrew equivalent of Palestine.

M. M. KELLNER

ESCHATOLOGY ĕs kə tŏl´ ə jē. The understanding of the essential nature of existence in terms of its goal or destiny. Eschatology constitutes one element in practically all religious and philosophical systems of thought. At the same time, the concept contains an element of ambiguity: it may refer to the realm of the absolute (the philosophical "ground of existence"), or it may point to the events that mark the goal of the historical process. In the former instance eschatology is expressed as a series of REINCARNATIONS which culminate in absorption into Being itself (HINDUISM). In the latter case eschatology relates to a historical process that encompasses humanity or even all creation (JUDAISM and CHRISTIANITY). The primary subjects in Jewish and Christian eschatology are death, RESURRECTION, judgment, HEAVEN AND HELL, etc. Eschatology is a theological concept and is to be distinguished from a prognosis of the future based upon the laws of scientific causation.

1. **Judaism.** The basis for Jewish eschatology is found in God's choice of the nation as his instrument for achieving his purposes. The expectation of the MESSIAH who is to establish God's rule in the earth expresses Israel's early hope (Ps. 2; Isa. 11:6-9). Beginning in the second century B.C. APOCALYPTIC thinkers pointed to the pre-existent agent who would effect God's purposes at the end of history. This emphasis upon transcendence both supplemented and supplanted earlier messianic hopes (Dan.; Isa. 24-27; I Enoch). Apocalyptic eschatology existed largely, if not entirely, outside rabbinic Judaism.

2. **Christianity.** Primitive Christians understood themselves as the eschatological community envisaged in Israel. However, by identifying JESUS as God's eschatological agent, they set definite limits upon the use of traditional Jewish apocalyptic systems. Although the Messiah had already come, they anticipated his imminent return to consummate the process he had begun (Mark 13:1-26, etc.). Hellenistic Christianity focused on the contemporary reign of the Exalted One (Col. 1:9-20).

Christian theology has generally treated eschatology as a distinct subject which relates primarily to life after death. Consequently the issue has frequently become the primary concern of sectarian movements outside the mainstream of Christian thought. During the twentieth century eschatology has again come to occupy a place of importance in Christian theology. Since the time of Johannes Weiss (1863-1914) and ALBERT SCHWEITZER (1875-1965) it has been understood as an integral element of the Christian confession itself.

Classical Christian art found in the themes provided by eschatology a rich source of inspiration. Subsequent to the conclusion of World War II, reflection on the horrors of Nazi savagery (*see* HOLOCAUST) has revived interest in eschatological speculation, often in the context of the scientific mentality.

Bibliography. H. Berkhof, *Well-Founded Hope* (1969); H. A. Guy, *The New Testament Doctrine of Last Things* (1948).

R. C. BRIGGS

3. **Islam.** The central theme is the Day of Judgment, which will be the end of the historical process, the termination of the existence of the earth, and the time for judging the behavior of all of ALLAH'S creatures (both humans and JINN) and assigning each individual to either reward for correct behavior in paradise (JANNA) or punishment for incorrect behavior in hell (JAHANNAM).

In both Muslim and Western dating of the passages

of the QUR'ĀN, the theme of the Last Day, Day of Judgment, also called "the Hour," is present from the earliest period of MUHAMMAD'S mission. Throughout the early portions of the Qur'ān there are vivid pictures of the final catastrophe, but when one sees these signs it will be too late, for no one knows when the Hour will come except Allah (cf. Sura 7:187). All who are then alive and all who had been alive will be brought to the judgment place (cf. Sura 36:81), be given a record of their deeds (Sura 18:50) at the blast of a trumpet, and will be assigned to either hell or paradise (Sura 78:17ff.). This resurrection will be both of the spirit and the body (Sura 75), and the rewards and punishments are described throughout the Qur'ān in graphic physical as well as spiritual terms.

Post-Qur'ānic exegesis elaborates on the themes in the Qur'ān, supplementing them with material derived from Jewish and Christian eschatology, popular in the first Islamic century and a half. The Qur'ānic word for hell *(jahannam)* is ultimately derived from the Hebrew *gē-hinnom* (Josh. 15:8), but it is not clear through what source the word entered Arabic. The notion of hell is indistinct in the Qur'ān, but later writers describe it as a place of punishment (cf. AL-GHAZZĀLĪ) or as a place with different levels of punishment. Similarly, paradise, also called the Garden, is described as a lush garden under which rivers flow and in which the faithful are rewarded with fruit, ease, sexual partners, and wine, the last forbidden them in this life. The most important of all the rewards, though, is the beatific vision. The notion that one could see Allah caused problems for those speculative theologians employing Greek logical categories, particularly the MU'TAZILITES, who denied this possibility so as not to limit Allah in space or time. There has been much speculation about the so-called "maidens" of Paradise, usually called "houris" in English (Arab. *ḥūr,* evidently the plural of *ḥawrā',* "a white one," often described with reference to the eyes, possibly "cow-eyed"). These creatures are described in Suras 2:25; 3:15; 4:57; 55:72; 56:22 and in the commentaries as women of great beauty, perpetual virgins, pure, made of precious herbs and perfumes, and of two varieties, one for men and one for the believing jinn. The commentator al-Bayḍāwī regards them as merely metaphors for the heavenly rewards.

Gog and Magog appear in the Qur'ān (Sura 18:95 ff. and 21:96) as agents of the final hour. Following themes found in versions of the Alexander Romance, Gog and Magog are thought to be presently walled up behind a barrier constructed by Alexander the Great. Near the last hour, however, they will break forth, lay waste to the earth, assault heaven, and be destroyed by Allah. Only the faithful will be saved. In some versions Gog and Magog will be led by the ANTICHRIST. This eschatological topos has parallels in Jewish and Christian literature, and as early as aṭ-Ṭabarī (d. 923) Gog and Magog were associated with peoples at the northeastern extremities of Islam, usually the Turkic peoples.

Parallel to the concept of Gog, Magog, and the Antichrist is the belief in the messianic MAHDI. In SUNNITE Islam, the notion of the eschatological Mahdi is less strong than among SHI'ITES. There is, for example, no mention of the Mahdi in the two great compendia of ḤADĪTH, but in the popular religion the figure of a destroyer of evil and restorer of correct worship has always been prominent. Sometimes that figure is identified with JESUS, but usually Jesus' role is only that of killing the Antichrist, with the Mahdi as the chief eschatological figure. This popular notion has been used several times in Islamic history to rally public support behind political pretenders who have assumed the name for their temporal ends.

Bibliography. Commentaries on the Qur'ān: aṭ-Ṭabarī and al-Bayḍāwī; A. J. Wensinck, *Concordance de la tradition musulmane* (1933-). See also H. A. R. Gibb, *Mohammedanism* (1949); A. J. Wensinck, *The Muslim Creed* (1932); E. Cerulli, *Il Libro della Scala* (1949); B. Carra de Vaux, *Fragments d'eschatologie musulmane* (1895); E. Berthels, "Die paradiesischen Jungfrauen (Ḥūrīs) im Islam," *Islamica,* I (1928), 263 ff.; D. B. Macdonald, *Religious Attitude and Life in Islam* (1912); articles in J. D. Pearson, *Index Islamicus* (1958-).

G. D. NEWBY

ESSENES ĕs´ sēns (Ju; etymology unknown). The identity of this sect of ancient Palestine remains in doubt; however, prevailing opinion relates the Essenes to descendants of the early Hasidim (pietists) of the Maccabean era.

Described extensively by Josephus, PHILO, and Pliny the Elder, the Essenes appear to be the same group pictured in the Dead Sea Scrolls. These were produced by a Jewish sect living on the western shore of the Dead Sea and in distinct groups within Judea, who were dissatisfied with the Hasmonean leadership and believed it had corrupted and usurped the high priesthood. Many theories have been offered to identify the precise time when the Essenes withdrew from society, but archaeological excavations at Khirbet Qumran support a date in the middle of the second century B.C. The Essenes flourished there until A.D. 70 (with a hiatus after the 31 B.C. earthquake), living as an APOCALYPTIC community awaiting the final battle between the forces of good and evil.

Their writings provide a clear picture of their unusual monastic behavior: practicing extreme ritual purity, mostly disdaining marriage, sharing work and belongings, holding riches in contempt, and practicing a religious system to rival Jerusalem's. Their biblical commentaries *(pesharim)* attempt to authenticate their status as the elect priestly community of God. Especially interesting are the Essene belief in several MESSIAHS, use of the solar calendar instead of the lunar, belief that bodies were corruptible, and belief in their ability to foretell the future.

The Essene library of biblical manuscripts has

revolutionized the study of the text of the Hebrew BIBLE. The unique social structure of their community and unusual beliefs have shown a greater variety in first century Judaism than previously known, and this has contributed to a new understanding of many aspects of the NT.

Bibliography. F. M. Cross, *The Ancient Library of Qumran* (1961); A. Dupont-Sommer, *The Essene Writings from Qumran* (1961); G. Vermes, *The Dead Sea Scrolls* (1978).

E. M. MEYERS

ESTABLISHED CHURCH (Ch). Any church recognized by civil law as the official religion of a country or region; in England the ANGLICAN CHURCH, and in Scotland, the Church of Scotland (PRESBYTERIAN). In some European countries the ROMAN CATHOLIC CHURCH has a privileged relation with the civil government, as does the GREEK ORTHODOX CHURCH in Greece. K. CRIM

ETHICS, TYPES AND THEORIES. The word *ethics* has many meanings. It can refer to the study of standards of conduct and practical judgments, and is thus equivalent to moral philosophy and moral theology. It can also refer to the system or code of conduct of a particular philosopher, religious thinker, religious group, profession, etc., as in Kant's ethics, CALVIN'S ethics, Buddhist ethics, or legal ethics. Moreover, ethics overlaps, but is not synonymous with, *morals* and *morality*. The term "Calvin's morals" is not equivalent to "Calvin's ethics," but seems rather to convey something about Calvin's personal standards of conduct and perhaps about his behavior. "Calvin's ethics" refers more precisely to his systematic thinking regarding what proper behavior is.

For our purposes, however, ethics can refer to two things. It can refer to the "first-order" sets of judgments, standards, principles, and rules of conduct (actual and ideal) of a given individual or group, whether the group be professional, national, or religious. This is close to our general use of the term *morality,* as well as of the terms *ethical code* and *moral code.* In present-day usage, morals would be a subset of first-order ethics, with a shading toward the judgments, standards, principles, and rules of sexual conduct, and of conduct concerning basic honesty and fidelity. Even this is not fixed. In phrases like "the manners and morals of . . . ," morals simply means general customs or habits.

In the next place, ethics can refer to "second-order" reflection on these first-order judgments, etc. This sort of reflection is synonymous with moral philosophy and moral theology. When, for example, the ethics of Christians or Buddhists are subjected to critical study and systematic analysis, we have ethics in this second sense. This article is an example of second-order ethics, insofar as it seeks to classify and reflect systematically on some examples of first-order ethics, especially as held by religious people.

1. **Types of ethical reflection.** A central feature of making first-order ethical judgments about everyday problems is the practice of giving reasons to justify those judgments. Such reasons, whether religious or not, appear to fall into two major patterns or types.

a) "Ends" ethics. Reasons of the first type give special prominence to the *ends* for which proposed acts are undertaken. (This type is called an "ends-oriented" or "teleological" ethical theory.) On this view the intended result of an act justifies the means. In the contemporary literature of Christian ethics, Joseph Fletcher exemplifies this sort of ethical theory.

Fletcher explicitly adopts a utilitarian standard of ethical justification: "the greatest happiness for the greatest number." As a Christian he interprets that standard in the light of the notion of Christian love or *agapē,* so that his basic reason for recommending any particular act is "Always seek the greatest amount of neighbor welfare for the largest number of neighbors possible." In Fletcher's terms, this standard is the basis for what he calls an "agapeic calculus."

Fletcher illustrates how his agapeic calculus works with the following examples: i) A physician, faced with a decision between saving a mother of three or a skid row drunk, when he cannot save both, will decide to save the mother, because he will thereby serve the welfare of more neighbors. ii) Following World War II a German woman, incarcerated by the Russians, was justified in committing adultery with a guard so that she might become pregnant and consequently be discharged from prison and restored to her husband and children. Ethical rules ought to be broken if, as in this case, the happiness of the greater number of neighbors is increased. iii) "On a vast scale of 'agapeic calculus' President Truman made his decision about the A-bombs on Hiroshima and Nagasaki." In Fletcher's view, a certain means of action (namely the direct taking of innocent life) would appear to be justified as long as that act prevents the death of a greater number of neighbors. iv) One should likely favor abortion, not only for the sake of the mother's physical and mental health, but also for her self-respect or happiness or simply because "no unwanted or unintended baby should ever be born." The mother's welfare outweighs that of the fetus.

b) "Duty" ethics. Reasons of the second type of ethical justification give prominence to certain features of actions that are considered determinative of the proper thing to do, regardless of the consequences. (This type is called a "duty-oriented" or "deontological" ethical theory.) Among contemporary Christian moral theologians, Paul Ramsey in part exemplifies this view. In numerous books and articles he has taken sharp issue with the ends-oriented beliefs of Fletcher and others.

One such fixed restriction on Christian action, Ramsey believes, is the principle of nonmaleficence. According to this principle, one may never deliberately and voluntarily cause direct injury to an innocent person in order to accomplish some greater good. To act in that way is to treat persons as dispensable, as "means" to other ends. This is the primary danger of all ends-oriented positions, Ramsey believes.

For example, Truman's decision to use the atomic bomb against the civilian populations of Hiroshima and Nagasaki in order "to shorten the war" and save more lives was, to Ramsey, simply a way of deliberately and voluntarily causing direct injury to innocent persons, something that is, on the principle of nonmaleficence, ethically repugnant.

Ramsey is no pacifist. He believes that armed conflict can be justified out of regard for protecting the innocent neighbor. But in such conditions only military personnel and targets ought deliberately and directly to be attacked. Even though some collateral civilian damage may result from such an operation, it occurs only indirectly and inadvertently.

A second example of Ramsey's attempt to apply a duty-oriented ethic to current problems comes from the field of nuclear policy. Consistent with his condemnation of Truman's decision, Ramsey argues that any present policy that targets cities (and thus civilians), and that intends under some circumstances to bomb those cities, is in violation of the principle of nonmaleficence. He advocates targeting only military installations, and contends that the collateral civilian damage caused by bombing those installations would not have been deliberately intended and is thus blameless.

In cases where life-and-death choices must be made (as in Fletcher's example of the mother and the skid row drunk), Ramsey is inclined to make the selection on a random basis in order to avoid computing the relative value of various individual lives, as Fletcher does. Ramsey thereby protects, he believes, the equal dignity of all human beings.

Ramsey's generally conservative position on abortion is a further application of the principle of nonmaleficence. He considers abortion to be wrong unless it is performed as an unavoidable means for saving the life of the mother. Fletcher's rule that "no unwanted and unintended baby should ever be born" would, for Ramsey, be a clear example of treating one human being (the fetus) as dispensable in relation to the "greater good" of the parents or family.

In describing the differences between Fletcher and Ramsey, the ends-oriented versus the duty-oriented approach, we have been analyzing and comparing two versions of what is called *normative ethical theory* (an examination of the basic norms used to justify first-order ethical judgments). It would be a mistake to conclude that these are anything more than two examples of many possible expressions of ethical reasoning, even though Fletcher and Ramsey happen to represent patterns of thought that, in one version or another, are widely prevalent in both secular and religious ethics.

c) "Responsibility" ethics. H. RICHARD NIEBUHR, the American moral theologian, contended that aside from the ends-oriented and duty-oriented approaches there is a third pattern of ethical reasoning, characterized by the notion "responsibility." If the ends-oriented position attends primarily to goals and ideals, and the duty-oriented approach to restrictions and requirements (duties and obligations), the "responsible self," as Niebuhr termed it, attends to what is the *most fitting* thing to do in a given set of circumstances, by responding appropriately to "what is going on." This is to be done, apparently, more by developing desirable character traits or virtues, which enable one properly to interpret or discern the best thing to do, than by committing oneself, like Fletcher and Ramsey, to an explicit rational decision method. Since this approach emphasizes inner disposition more than the method of reaching a decision, it is harder to generalize about it in reference to everyday practical problems than was the case with Fletcher and Ramsey. Still, Niebuhr's "third way" has had important and continuing influence on contemporary Protestant moral theologians like James Gustafson and Stanley Hauerwas.

2. Basic ethical terminology. *a) The nature of the "good" and the "right."* When Fletcher, Ramsey, and Niebuhr dispute among themselves, or with representatives of other religious or nonreligious ethical beliefs, as to which position is superior, they will be disputing over several different sorts of considerations. First, they will be arguing over the *meaning* of the basic terms of ethical reasoning: "good/bad," "right/wrong," "duty," "obligation," etc. Fletcher's understanding of "neighbor welfare" as the highest ethical good may be quite different from a Buddhist's or Confucian's idea of the highest good. All three might have an ends-oriented ethical theory, but they might differ over what the proper end of human action is.

For example, in the THERAVĀDA BUDDHIST tradition, a benevolent act is more worthy the more spiritually advanced the recipient is (referred to as "the doctrine of the suitable recipient"). This is true because the end of proper action is, finally, spiritual advancement and fulfillment. One suspects that Fletcher's view of a suitable recipient would be rather different, as would Ramsey's and Niebuhr's views.

Again, a crucial point of difference between the ethical beliefs of a "secularist" philosopher like Jeremy Bentham and those of Fletcher, both of whom share an ends-oriented theory, concerns the meaning of the proper end of action. Whatever specific content Fletcher's notion of *agapē* may have, it does not seem equivalent to Bentham's pleasure principle, according to which good action maximizes the balance of bodily pleasure over pain for the greatest number of persons.

b) Religion and ethical knowledge. The difference between Fletcher and Bentham regarding the goal of ethical behavior illustrates an additional consideration that is relevant to the dispute about the meaning of basic terms in various ethical positions. As Fletcher advances a "religious" ethic and Bentham does not, it will be necessary for each to clarify just what is religious and what is not about a given position, and exactly what difference a religious conception of proper action makes. The same point, of course, applies to all versions of religious ethics.

The matter of what is and what is not religious about ethical belief is a central problem for most religious traditions, including Western Christianity. In the Christian case, for example, it is typically assumed that human beings have some ethical competence apart from special religious insight or direction. This is an important assumption. Without it individuals could not be held ethically accountable unless they were Christian believers in good standing. This same assumption is typically made in other religious traditions as well.

Still, the difference that religious belief is supposed to make to ethical activity varies within the Christian tradition and among religious traditions. Fletcher, for one, is explicit about the relevance of Christian conviction to ethical behavior; namely, Christian ethics is different from any other rationale motivationally but not normatively. In this claim Fletcher is following the British moral philosopher Stephen Toulmin, who states that ethics provides reasons for choosing the "right" course, while religion provides the emotive impetus. In this view the basic problem with ethical behavior is not knowing what is right, but being able to do it. Religion solves that problem.

Other Christians, like the Swiss theologian KARL BARTH and the American theologian Paul Lehmann, appear to believe that religious revelation supplies direct moral knowledge of "God's command," knowledge that is not available to the unbeliever. The Dutch theologian Hendrik Kraemer holds a somewhat different version of this position. For him Christianity, and only Christianity, yields a duty-oriented ethic, an ethic which Kraemer believes to be exclusively legitimate: "All ethics in the world, except the Christian ethic, are some form of eudaemonism [ends-oriented ethic]."

Still others, like H. Richard Niebuhr and Gustafson, seem to hold that religious belief provides a special ethical sensitivity, or way of apprehending or intuiting the right thing to do in given situations.

A fourth position, which seems to be that of Paul Ramsey and certain traditional Protestant and Roman Catholic "natural-law thinkers," refers to two kinds of moral knowledge. One is natural and available to human reason without benefit of religious revelation, and the other is, so to speak, privileged and therefore accessible only to religiously inspired individuals.

3. **The validity of ethical assertions.** In addition to clarifying and explicating the meaning of basic ethical terms, including the distinction and relations between ethical or moral beliefs and religious beliefs, there is the problem of *how one knows* that a particular interpretation of ethical terms is true, or that a particular normative theory is correct. (Generally, this is the epistemological problem in ethics.)

Insofar as religious ethical positions affirm the possibility of "natural" moral knowledge, or moral knowledge independent of special religous insight, then it will be necesssary to join hands with one or another nonreligious theory of knowledge. One might, with Ramsey and H. Richard Niebuhr, embrace an intuitionist theory of knowledge, such as that proposed by the British philosophers W. D. Ross and A. C. Ewing. According to that view, there are certain basic moral truths (keeping promises, returning kindnesses, abhorring cruelty) that one "just knows."

Or one might, with Fletcher, adopt a pragmatic theory of knowledge. This involves identifying certain basic and unavoidable "human interests or needs," and contending that ethical knowledge consists in discovering optimally efficient ways to satisfy those interests. The pragmatic and intuitionist theories of knowledge are, of course, only two possible examples.

Religious ethicists must take responsibility for showing not only how they know the truth of nonreligious ethical beliefs (to the extent they accept them), but also how they know the truth of religious beliefs. Here it is necessary to defend some notion of religious REVELATION, enlightenment, or intuition above and beyond the natural access to knowledge that nonbelievers have, or that believers innately have as humans beings. The traditional discussions of philosophy of religion and theological apologetics become relevant at this point.

Bibliography. K. Barth, *Against the Stream* (1954); J. Bentham, *An Introduction to the Principles of Morals and Legislation* (1789); A. C. Ewing, *Ethics* (1953); J. Fletcher, *Situation Ethics* (1966); W. K. Frankena, *Ethics* (1973), and *Perspectives on Morality* (1976); J. Gustafson, *Protestant and Roman Catholic Ethics* (1978), and *Theology and Christian Ethics* (1974); R. M. Hare, *Essays on Moral Concepts* (1972); S. Hauerwas, *Vision and Virtue* (1974); W. D. Hudson, *Modern Moral Philosophy* (1970); H. Kraemer, *The Christian Message in a Non-Christian World* (1938); P. Lehmann, *Ethics in a Christian Context* (1963); D. Little and S. Twiss, *Comparative Religious Ethics* (1978); H. R. Niebuhr, *The Responsible Self* (1963); P. Ramsey, *Deeds and Rules in Christian Ethics* (1967); W. D. Ross, *The Right and the Good* (1930); S. Toulmin, *An Examination of the Place of Reason in Ethics* (1950); G. Outka and J. Reeder, eds., *Religion and Morality* (1973).

D. LITTLE

ETHIOPIC CHURCH (Ch). Indigenous church in Ethiopia, until recently the ESTABLISHED CHURCH. In the fourth century Frumentius brought the gospel to Ethiopia and was appointed head or *Abuna* of the church by ATHANASIUS, Bishop of Alexandria (328-373). The *Abuna* was appointed by the Coptic Church of Egypt before 1959, when a native Ethiopian first became patriarch.

After the Council of Chalcedon (451) the church became MONOPHYSITE, following the COPTIC Church.

Isolated from the outside world by ISLAM, it had little contact with Europe from the seventh to the thirteenth centuries. Catholic and then Protestant missionaries encountered Ethiopic Christians but had little success in converting them.

In matters of faith the church has followed the Coptic Church, but has retained certain unique traditions. Some are due to Jewish influence, such as the distinction between clean and unclean food, observation of SABBATH on Saturday, and the practice of CIRCUMCISION.

Until the fall of Emperor Haile Selassie (1974) this hierarchical church was involved with all aspects of political and family life. A quarter of the male Christian population performed some priestly function. Services are conducted in Ge'ez, an ancient language not spoken in modern Ethiopia. Priests administer the SACRAMENTS. Lay helpers *(dabtaras)* chant, read, and teach in the schools. Large tracts of land were set aside for churches and monasteries. It has been estimated that until recently there were 20,000 churches in Ethiopia.

Bibliography. A. S. Atiya, *A History of Eastern Christianity* (1968), pp. 146-66. V. KESICH

EUCHARIST (Ch). The most widely accepted title for the central act of Christian worship, the ritual meal of bread and wine as sign of unity in and with CHRIST. Other titles are the Lord's Supper, Holy Communion, Divine Liturgy, and the MASS. The NT gives four accounts of its institution by Christ on the night before his crucifixion, one by PAUL (I Cor. 11) and three in the Synoptic Gospels (Matt. 26; Mark 14; Luke 22), these latter identifying the meal as the PASSOVER. The thanksgiving (Gr. *eucharistia*) over the final "cup of blessing" gave its name to the rite after the church discontinued celebration of the meal around the end of the first century. The resulting purely ritual meal of only bread and wine centered in a PRAYER of thanksgiving which, by the third century, included a paraphrase of the scriptural institution narrative in which JESUS identified the bread with his body and the cup with his blood ("of the covenant" in Matt. and Mark). Virtually all traditional eucharistic prayers follow this narrative with a formula in which the gifts are offered to God as memorial (Gr. *anamnēsis*) of Christ's death and RESURRECTION. From as early as the third century this oblation formula made explicit the sacrificial understanding of the eucharist already evident in earlier documents (e.g., Didache 14).

This notion of eucharistic sacrifice received much development in following centuries and eventually posed complex questions regarding the relationships between the eucharist and the total sufficiency of Christ's sacrifice on Calvary, questions which led the reformers of the sixteenth century to reject the notion of eucharistic sacrifice entirely. They emphasized rather the act of communion as the means by which the faithful receive the benefits of Christ's sacrifice and are spiritually fed by union with him, though they differed widely in their understanding of this communion. LUTHER held that Christ's body and blood are really present in the bread and wine after their consecration, ZWINGLI saw the rite as only a symbolic act of remembrance involving no change at all in the elements, and others (CALVIN, BUCER, *et al.*) found positions intermediate between these two. All the reformers opposed the current ROMAN CATHOLIC doctrine of TRANSUBSTANTIATION, introduced at the Fourth Lateran Council in 1215 and more precisely defined at the Council of TRENT in 1551. This doctrine, according to which the gifts at their consecration cease to be bread and wine in all but appearance and become Christ's body and blood, was the outcome of a growing eucharistic realism since the ninth century, given more subtle expression by appeal to the philosophical categories of Aristotle. More recent Roman Catholic theology has seen a withdrawal from the Aristotelian presuppositions of SCHOLASTICISM and theologians today often speak of "transignification" or "transfinalization" to describe the effect of eucharistic consecration. Biblical and liturgical studies also have engendered considerable ecumenical rapprochement in regard to both the question of eucharistic sacrifice and that of communion with Christ in the eucharist. *See* SACRAMENTS; CONSUBSTANTIATION.

Bibliography. D. Stone, *A History of the Doctrine of the Holy Eucharist,* 2 vols. (1909); Y. Brilioth, *Eucharistic Faith and Practice, Evangelical and Catholic* (1930); E. Schillebeeckx, *The Eucharist* (1968). T. J. TALLEY

EVANGELICALS (Ch). The term "evangelical" has a long history. In the REFORMATION era it described the adherents of the AUGSBURG CONFESSION in contrast to ROMAN CATHOLICISM or REFORMED CHURCHES. It still retains that meaning in Europe and appears in the official names of many LUTHERAN CHURCHES.

In the eighteenth century the term came to be applied to those who favored a PROTESTANT Church of England (*see* ANGLICAN CHURCHES) and to their supporters among the Nonconformists. English evangelicals tended to stress the importance of the BIBLE, the right of private interpretation, the need for saving faith, high standards of personal morality, and the vicarious atonement.

Early eighteenth century British evangelicalism was led by such people as George Whitefield (1714-70) and Selina, Countess of Huntingdon (1707-91). However, in the latter part of the century leadership passed to the Clapham circle, which included such socially prominent individuals as Charles Grant (1746-1832), William Wilberforce (1759-1833), Lord Teignmouth (1751-1834), and Henry Thorton (1760-1815). This group was deeply involved in the struggle against slavery. In 1807 they secured an act abolishing the slave trade, and in 1833 a general emancipation act capped their efforts.

In nineteenth century America the term "evangelical" was applied to those churches which used techniques of REVIVALISM. These churches were believed to have more in common with each other than with other denominations, and their leaders hoped that an evangelical united front could help make America a Christian nation. In 1838 Samuel Schmucker, professor at Gettysburg Theological Seminary, published his *Fraternal Appeal to the American Churches* in which he argued for a federation of American churches.

In 1846 opponents of the Anglo-Catholic movement in England formed a cooperative venture, the Evangelical Alliance. The Alliance affirmed a nine-point statement of faith that included the inspiration of the Bible, the vicarious ATONEMENT, the TRINITY, and the fall and depravity of man. Seventy-five American clergymen participated in this meeting, and in 1867 an American Evangelical Alliance was formed.

The sense of unity that had been developing among evangelicals in the early part of the century was broken by the impact of Darwinism, higher criticism, and industrialization. Members of the evangelical churches developed different responses to these problems, and the classical evangelical movement split into liberal, conservative, and SOCIAL GOSPEL parties. Although the term "evangelical" did not disappear from American church life, it was used less frequently as other language became more descriptive of ecclesiastical alignments.

In the 1940s a new evangelical movement began to form as American FUNDAMENTALISM developed a progressive wing that was more open to the world and church tradition than the older movement. Carl F. H. Henry, a Baptist clergyman and educator, signaled the beginning of this neo-evangelicalism with the publication of his *Uneasy Conscience of Modern Fundamentalism* (1947). E. J. Carnell (1919-67) was the early theologian of this new type of conservative faith.

At the same time that fundamentalist theology was maturing, conservative churches in America entered into a period of growth that is still continuing. The strength of the evangelical movement in the local churches in turn contributed to a strengthening of extracongregational institutions. Such evangelical seminaries as Gordon-Conwell, Fuller, and Trinity now have firmly established reputations as well as growing student bodies.

By 1970 the new evangelical movement had become a major force in American Protestantism. Neo-evangelicals were the fastest growing religious group in the United States. Not only were the local churches continuing to grow, but the intellectual movement associated with Henry and Carnell was showing considerable vigor. A new generation of conservative theologians, led by such thinkers as Donald Bloesch, Richard Lovelace, and David Wells, has taken up the theological task with much promise.

Bibliography. R. Quebedeaux, *The Young Evangelicals* (1974); D. Bloesch and R. Webber, *The Orthodox Evangelicals* (1978); R. Nash, *The New Evangelicalism* (1963); J. Barr, *Fundamentalism* (1977); D. F. Wells and I. D. Woodbridge, *The Evangelicals* (1975).

G. MILLER

EVANGELISM. *See* MISSIONS, CHRISTIAN; REVIVALISM.

EVIL. The term evil can be applied either to acts or to conditions. The problem of evil, as it is addressed in religious and intellectual traditions, is almost always located in conditions, or in the evil that persons suffer, rather than in acts, or the evil that persons do. Although Kant said the only evil thing is an evil will, it is still the case that if the study of evil were limited to the actions of the will, those evils, common to experience, that result from actions taken in the highest motivation would be neglected.

All major theories of evil presuppose that persons have free and proper desires which may not be fulfilled because their fulfillment depends on other agencies. In other words, evil is a condition in which what one most deeply desires is denied by a power over which one has no control.

Most theories of evil contain an implied solution to the problem they describe. Surprisingly rare are those theories which find evil to be ineradicable, without any solution whatsoever. In the world's major religious and intellectual traditions there are at least five ways in which the problem of evil has been dealt with: the denial of human freedom, the overcoming of desire, the unification of all agency, the final victory of one agent over the others, and the acceptance of an ineradicable dualism of good and evil.

1. **The denial of human freedom.** The essence of this approach to the problem of evil lies in the view that human desire does not originate in freedom, but is a caused phenomenon. In antiquity Epicureanism is the most typical expression of this view, and in the modern world it is found in those schools of psychology, sociology, and the natural sciences which persist in accounting for human behavior in exclusively causal terms.

If human desire is a caused phenomenon, like all other events, then it cannot be said to be one's own. According to this view, the felt desire for long life, or happiness in love, or a productive vocation, is in reality only an expression of one's social and/or genetic background, and not a true desire. An early death and romantic or professional failure are therefore not evils as such but are to be understood only as the lawful outcome of a caused sequence of events in which no independent agency is involved. It is a serious mistake to credit such misfortune to a malevolent source or to one's own moral failures, or even to believe it could have been averted by proper behavior.

Although both Epicureans and modern scientific theorists have placed great emphasis on the necessity with which events occur, they both also give some importance to the phenomenon of chance. Epicurus speculated that the atoms which compose all existing things have the curious quality of unpredictably "swerving" from their path, causing a variability to appear in physical events. For this reason, any beast can always identify its own offspring, however rigorously the process of birth might follow natural law, by the minute variations that make it unique among countless other newborn. For this reason also the dishonest person can be prosperous, and the honest remain in want. Modern physical theory also allows for a degree of unpredictability in the movement of electrons, thus introducing a factor of chance into every otherwise lawfully caused sequence.

But chance is not freedom. While one person's fortune may be greater than another's, neither that person nor any other agent can be held responsible for the disparity. It is strictly accidental. On the basis of this view of evil the Epicureans counseled careful moderation of desire and an attitude of indifference toward the outcome of all human events. While modern scientific theory does not offer counsel of this sort, it echoes the Epicureans in its "value-free" attitude toward all events and its consequent obliviousness to evil.

2. The elimination of desire. This strategy is found in such disparate traditions as BUDDHISM, Stoicism, and existentialism. What each of them shares with the others is the conviction that evil begins with desire and that desire originates in one's own freedom.

The BUDDHA'S enlightenment is said to have come with the realization that all suffering comes from craving, and that we shall cease to suffer only when we cease to crave (*see* FOUR NOBLE TRUTHS). In substance, craving is the attempt to have what we do not and cannot possess, and to be what we are not and cannot be. It is to be attached to a world which is marked by suffering (DUKKHA) and transiency (ANICCA), and results in acts which simply bear more life-sustaining fruits (KARMA).

Since such craving is exclusively one's own, it is only through one's own free act that it can be eliminated. This is apparent in the fact that Buddhism has its origin in the unaided meditation of a perfectly human monk, who appealed to no deities in his struggle to overcome suffering, nor urged others to do so. But this is not to say that craving can be easily overcome. Even the desire to stop craving is merely another manifestation of it. The persistence of suffering, and therefore of evil, is expressed in Buddhism through the doctrine of karma, or the powerful influence of the past on the present.

The prominence of karma as an explanation of evil, particularly in early Buddhist literature, appears consistent with the radical freedom implied in the unaided enlightenment of the Buddha himself, for it suggests that its origin lies in each individual's past decisions and actions and that evil is therefore something we create for ourselves.

The extinction of desire, or NIRVANA, means the thorough elimination of all selfhood and any sense of an independent mind or will that can remain unchanged while all else changes. It is a yielding of selfhood to endless change. In this way, and only in this way, can evil be overcome.

The Stoics, although living in very different philosophical and cultural circumstances, also conceived evil as the consequence of willfully resisting the inevitable course of events. The Stoics urged *apatheia,* or an absence of personal interest, in their relations to others and to the world. Their indifference to personal suffering is illustrated in the casual way in which prominent Stoics are reported to have committed suicide. And their disregard for the evils of social inequality is evident in the fact that one of the most famous of Stoics, Epictetus, was a Roman slave, while another, Marcus Aurelius, was a Roman emperor.

Existentialists generally hold the view that suffering arises out of one's own free desire to exist as someone or something else. While the existentialists only rarely speak of evil as such, it is clear that what evil there is could only be found at the personal, and not the social, level, and can be traced to no cause outside the free choice of each existing person. Kierkegaard exalted the category of "subjectivity," or perhaps more accurately, "subject-ness," by which he meant the mode of existence in which one is the subject of one's own actions and never the object of the actions of any other person. This leaves no space for excuses, or for blaming any other agency for one's misfortunes.

Friedrich Nietzsche (1844-1900) declared that both good and evil are not realities in the world but creations of the individual will. Moreover, they are creations which arise from the will's denial of its own freedom and the desire to find external reasons for acting as we do. Good and evil are, therefore, not impingements on the freedom of the individual but inventions by which one attempts to conceal that freedom. A pure act of will, therefore, takes one, in Nietzsche's famous phrase, "beyond good and evil." The sheer spontaneity of the will in this sense, as Nietzsche himself acknowledged, bears a striking resemblance to Buddhist thought.

3. The unification of all agency. Probably the most common conception of evil and the corresponding mode of eliminating it arise from the belief that there is a single agency harmoniously organizing the universe as a whole. Forms of this belief can be found most strikingly in the VEDĀNTA tradition of Hinduism, and in the West in Plato, Plotinus, and Leibniz. The heart of this view is that the experience of evil derives from an incomplete vision of the whole universe or the whole of being.

Vedāntist Hindus, from the time of the UPANIṢADS to the present, have argued that there is only one reality, BRAHMAN, and the perception of anything else as truly real is only illusory. This does not mean, of course, that what is experienced as evil does not really happen; on the contrary, it is really happening, but we have only misunderstood it when we regard it as evil. The reason for this misunderstanding is our inability to see the single, unified reality in the midst of the great plurality of isolated things. What is experienced as evil, therefore, is only experienced as a part of the whole or as a conflict of wills, while in truth the whole is complete and in perfect agreement with itself, thus making true evil impossible.

The dualism implicit in the earlier dialogues of Plato suggests that evil is to be associated only with material things which are finite and subject to causal necessity. The realm of ideas is described as something removed and unaffected by matter. Since one's relation to this eternal realm is always by way of knowledge, Plato took the position that to know the good was to do it. Evil derives then from ignorance or blindness. What one cannot see is that only the ideas are real, the material world changeable and passing. Evil is therefore the result of identifying the sensory world of things as the only true world. The later work of Plato, particularly the *Timaeus,* establishes a much more certain continuity between the ideal and the material. Evil now is not merely a conflict between temporal existence and the eternal realm of ideas, but is rather the failure of the part to see its connection with the whole. Persons are not evil when they simply yield to the flesh, but only when they assume that their partial vision of the whole is truly the whole.

This unified conception of being is much more consistently developd by Plotinus, who composed his philosophy in Rome during the chaotic second century A.D. Plotinus envisioned a sequence of continuous levels of being, beginning with the plurality and darkness of mere matter and ending in the nameless "One," understood as the source of all things. Plotinus' vision of the One is extraordinary in its perfection. The One is so completely one that it can have no other. It cannot have a name because that would distinguish it from others; neither can it act, or even be aware of itself.

This exalted doctrine also leaves no possibility of saying that the One creates, and raises a dilemma as to the way in which the many can be related to it. Plotinus' solution to this dilemma is offered in the form of a famous metaphor: the One does not create, he declared; it *emanates,* quite as the sun radiates light and heat, or as an eternal spring issues its pure waters into the multitude of lakes and streams. At the highest level of emanation, closest to the One, is mind, or that level where ideas and forms originate. Below mind is soul, the active principle by which the forms are joined to matter at the lowest level. Evil, in this scheme, cannot be found either in the One or in mind, and not at the higher levels of soul, but only where the darkness of matter has reached upward into the light, obscuring the clear vision of individual human souls, causing them to look away from their fundamental unity with each other in the Universal Soul, and therewith their unity in the One.

According to this influential conception evil is not to be understood as an active principle in which an independent force struggles with the Good, but rather as a mere absence of Good. Evil is not a form of being, in short, but a form of nonbeing. (*See* BEING AND NONBEING.) To suggest that evil possesses its own agency is to fracture Plotinus' sublime MONISM and to compromise the perfection of the One.

A serious difficulty arises here in Plotinian thought, a difficulty characteristic of all similar conceptions of evil. In his proposal that evil is properly to be regarded as the absence of being, Plotinus has offered what subsequent thinkers refer to as a theory of "metaphysical evil." According to this theory evil is constituted by the nature of things, and does not represent the expression of a contrary will. Evil is inevitable, Plotinus argues, in the nether reaches of emanation of the One where the light dims and finally yields to the darkness. Numerous thinkers after Plotinus have argued that simply because the world is finite, and because things are subject to chance, evil is inevitable.

The difficulty here is that in addition to metaphysical evil Plotinus wants to include what comes to be known as "moral evil." That is, it is not sufficient to ascribe all evil to natural or accidental causes, as it is clear that evil can also be found in the actions of individual persons. But moral evil is meaningless unless it is grounded in the freedom of the individual, and if the person is truly free, then the pure monism of the One is damaged, and the universe is governed by a plurality of discordant agencies.

Later philosophers and religious thinkers, drawn to Plotinus' conception of evil as the absence of being, were never able to reconcile the conflict between metaphysical and moral evil. Perhaps the most important attempt to do so occurs in the 1710 essay of Leibniz on "theodicy," or the problem of justifying God's creation of a world that contains evil. Leibniz argued that this is the best of all the possible worlds that God could have created, because the evil that occurs here, while often vexatious, is necessary to the full expression of good, quite as bitterness causes us to appreciate sweetness.

Leibniz' examples suggest that he had a limited familiarity with the actual suffering of the world. Philosophically, he also left himself exposed to the attack of such philosophers as Hume, who argued that it is impossible to suppose we could ever have a knowledge of the whole sufficient to make such claims. From our limited point of view it is just as reasonable to assume that this universe was created by an infant deity who, having done such a clumsy job of it, went on to fashion better ones. In sum, the Plotinian conception must either admit moral evil into its system, along with a plurality of wills, or admit to intellectual ignorance concerning the necessity of metaphysical evil.

4. The final victory of a single agent. None of the major theistic religions of the West—Judaism, Christianity, and Islam—has had the least difficulty in including moral evil in its view of human affairs. While it is true that all three religions have occasionally allowed for the existence of an independent satanic force, rivaling the unexceptional goodness of the Creator, it is still the case that evil is more commonly traced to the free inclination of the sinner.

AUGUSTINE, for example, although deeply affected by the Plotinian philosophy, clearly enunciated a voluntarist source of evil. Although SATAN tempts Eve into violating God's commandment, and even deceives her, he does not in fact force her to eat the forbidden fruit. Even if he did, there would remain the question of Satan's own will, for he was after all one of the sons of God and doubtless created good. Augustine is clear in his rejection of the Platonic theory that to know the good is to do it, for Satan certainly knew what the good was.

Parallel views are held in Judaism and Islam. But difficulties arise with this conception as well. The problem of theodicy occurs in all three traditions, for one must account for the possibility of a plurality of evil wills, all in conflict with the supreme will of the creator. While there are attempts in each religion to explain the presence of evil in a manner similar to that of Leibniz, the most fundamental conception is quite different. Evil is seen as a force in direct opposition to God, whether it is found in individual wills or personified in the devil, requiring God to engage in a battle to subdue it. Mythological themes found in ancient Iranian religions portray the good divinity as a warrior god subduing his foes. Even in the deeply dualist ZOROASTRIANISM there is a compelling belief in the ultimate victory of the good over evil. In Judaism, Christianity, and Islam these mythological motifs have the result of portraying human history itself as the field in which the battle is waged. The end of history coincides with the inevitable victory of God over the forces of evil.

5. **The acceptance of ineradicable dualism.** It is significant that all the previous conceptions of evil include in themselves the method of its elimination. In each case this is achieved either by the denial of freedom altogether or by the denial of an irreconcilably conflicting plurality of free agencies. Two important instances can be cited of thinkers whose views of freedom led them to a belief in the permanent and active existence of both good and evil. Jakob BOEHME, seventeenth century visionary, insisted that since God himself was perfectly free, good and evil were equally possible—even for God. Neither one can be thought superior to the other. Boehme is a solitary figure in religious history, having only an indirect influence on other thinkers. His most important heir is the English poet and seer, WILLIAM BLAKE, who sustained Boehme's vision of a reality endlessly torn by the irreconcilable contraries of good and evil.

In his *Religion within the Limits of Reason Alone,* Kant argued that a person cannot be morally responsible unless free, and if free cannot have an irresistible inclination toward either good or evil. Both must be possible at all times. This means that there can be no way of eliminating either. Therefore, he concluded, there must be a "radical evil" that can never be expunged from human existence. However, Kant sharply curbed the power of evil by arguing further that there is an inherent rationality in each human mind, and that it is altogether rational to do the good and avoid evil.

Bibliography. Curatorium of the C. G. Jung Institute, *Evil* (1967), a useful collection of mythological and psychological studies; B. A. G. Fuller, *The Problem of Evil in Plotinus* (1912); J. Hick, *Evil and the God of Love* (1966), a comprehensive theodicy with particular reference to Christianity; G. W. Leibniz, *Theodicy,* E. M. Huggard, trans. (1952), the classical attempt to justify God's creation of evil; H. J. McCloskey, *God and Evil* (1974), a philosopher's attempt to show the difficulty in all theodicy; W. O'Flaherty, *Origins of Evil in Hindu Mythology* (1976); R. Taylor, *Good and Evil* (1970), a vigorous presentation of a distinctive understanding of these terms.

J. CARSE

EX CATHEDRA ĕx kə thē′ drə (Ch—Lat.; lit. "from the chair" [symbol of bishops' and professors' teaching authority]). The First VATICAN COUNCIL declared that the pope speaks *ex cathedra* "when in discharge of the office of pastor and teacher of all Christians, by virtue of his supreme apostolic authority, he defines a doctrine regarding faith or morals to be held by the universal church, by the divine assistance promised to him in blessed PETER." *See* INFALLIBILITY; PAPACY.

J. HENNESEY

EXCOMMUNICATION (Ch). Exclusion of a baptized person from Christian fellowship, particularly the EUCHARIST. It presupposes a serious offense against God and is remedial in intention: to bring the sinner back to righteousness. Excommunications under CANON LAW in ROMAN CATHOLICISM may be automatic or pronounced by judicial sentence.

J. HENNESEY

EXTINCTION (B). *See* LOTUS SŪTRA §2; NIRVANA.

EZRA ĕz′ rə (Ju & Ch—Heb.; "[Yahweh] helps" ['*zr*—"to help"]). 1. Name of scribe "learned in the law (TORAH) of MOSES" (Ezra 7:6) and active in restoring religious observances in JERUSALEM (*ca.* 458 B.C.) after the Babylonian captivity; traditional founder of the GREAT SYNAGOGUE and renowned figure in the development of Judaism.

2. Book of the OT forming a continuum with Nehemiah; records the activities of the exiles returning from Babylon, as well as the building of the second Temple and the fortification of Jerusalem.

D. IRVIN

F

FA-HSIANG fä shē äng′ (B—Chin.; lit. "dharma characteristics"). Classical school of Chinese Buddhism founded by Hsüan-tsang on the teachings of Indian Yogācāra Idealism; also known as *Wei-shih tsung* ("Consciousness-Only school").

The Mahāyāna metaphysics of the Indian scholar Asaṅga had provided the basis for the Chinese She-lun school. Hsüan-tsang, the famous seventh century Chinese pilgrim to India, replaced the She-lun with the Fa-hsiang based on the development of Asaṅga's thought by Vasubandhu and Dharmapāla. Hsüan-tsang's *Ch'eng-wei-shih lun* ("Treatise on the Establishment of the Consciousness-Only Doctrine") describes the external world as the creation of consciousness. Eight consciousnesses are described, including manas (self-conscious mind) and ālaya (storehouse consciousness). Seed-impressions of the ālaya, when disturbed by manas, produce the illusion of ego and external objects. Through Prajñā (perfect wisdom), manas can be enlightened and one can attain the third level of knowledge, suchness or Ultimate Reality (*see* Tathatā).

The Fa-hsiang school flourished during the middle of the T'ang Dynasty, but faded in the persecution of 845. Too abstract to compete with Ch'an (Zen) and Pure Land Buddhism, it nevertheless contributed to Ch'an's emphasis on "mind." *See* Nara Buddhism §3d.

C. W. Edwards

FABLE. A fictional narrative personifying nonhuman characters and carrying moral implications.

Fables are told to entertain and to instruct in practical morality. They are made entertaining by attributing human personality traits to animals, trees, or even inanimate objects. The instruction is achieved by constructing the narrative in such a way that a moral lesson may be drawn, either by a character in the story or by the reader. For example, in Aesop's parable of the fox and the crow, the point is made that the crow was tricked into dropping the cheese because in his vanity he was taken in by the fox's flattery, whereas the fox got the cheese because of his cunning. The reader learns with the crow that vanity should be avoided.

The morality of fables is usually practical and seldom theological. Fables often celebrate such qualities as cunning, wit, common sense, and resistance to flattery rather than religious piety or theological insight.

Throughout their history, fables have played upon the social conflict between the weak and the powerful, with the weak typically triumphing by wit or virtue. Weak animals find means to achieve their goals, while powerful animals are rendered hapless and helpless. For this reason some stories about the triumph of a humble person over a powerful adversary are sometimes also classed as fables and found alongside animal fables in some collections.

1. **Classical collections.** *a) Greek.* The Greek tradition is surely older than Aesop (sixth century B.C.), as evidenced by the occurrence of at least one fable in the work of Hesiod, but Aesop was such a master of the art form that his name soon became almost synonymous with it. There are few available facts about his life; the tradition that he was a slave goes back to Herodotus. Although it is not known how many he actually wrote, later Greek and Latin collections owe a great debt to his fables.

b) Latin. The most important Latin collection of fables was authored by Phaedrus, who is said to have been a liberated slave of the household of Caesar Augustus. Many of his poems are retellings of Aesop's stories, but others seem to be original. Both Phaedrus and Babrius (second century A.D.) expanded on the scope of the fable by sometimes employing it in political satire. Their Latin collections were the most readily available ones in medieval Europe, usually in the form of the Romulus collection, a Latin prose collection that dates back at least to the tenth century.

c) Sanskrit. Contemporary with the Aesop fables was an important oral fable tradition from India, known in its later written form as the *Pañcatantra* (the "Five Books"). As suggested by the name, this collection consisted of five divisions of animal fables that were loosely tied together by an overarching narrative framework.

The *Pañcatantra* mothered two other very important fable collections. One is the collection associated in Western recensions with the name Pilpay (or Bidpai) and known as *Kalilah and Dimnah*. This collection has been translated into nearly all European languages, coming to the West through a Persian translation. The fables of Pilpay differ from those of Aesop in that the narratives are longer and more complex. The main animals in them have well developed characters and exhibit great piety. The characters' piety is incidental to the plot, and it has been noted that the nature of the piety varies greatly from translation to translation, as the collection passed through the hands of Persian, Greek-Christian, and other redactors.

The second important offspring of the *Pañcatantra* is the *Hitopadeśa*. This Indian collection dates from the ninth century A.D. or later and derives about three-fourths of its stories from the *Pañcatantra*. It too has been translated into various Indian and non-Indian languages, with the first English translation appearing in 1787.

The frame story tells of a wise teacher who undertakes to teach practical knowledge to a king's three dull sons. To accomplish this in only six months, he employs stories that teach a ruler's obligations and prudence in friendship, power, and wealth. The first two divisions of the *Hitopadeśa* deal with the winning and losing of friends, and the last two with war and peace. The fables' good characters do exhibit many of the high ideals of India (hospitality, generosity to BRAHMINS, and marital fidelity), but the real morals of the stories deal more with diplomacy than with spirituality. For instance, the moral that introduces one story reads, "Fraud may achieve what force would never try: The Jackal killed the Elephant thereby."

2. Trickster cycles. A common animal story known as a TRICKSTER tale may be seen as a type of animal fable. In these stories some animal accomplishes its ends by trickery, and several stories often go together to form a trickster cycle.

a) Plains Indians. Most of the Plains Indian tribes possessed a cycle of stories about a coyote who accomplished many things by his cunning and trickery. For example, in one story he managed to steal the sun from its former residence and placed it in the sky where it benefits all. A trickster's goals are often lofty, but his means are not.

b) African. A spider named Anansi is the trickster in a cycle of stories widespread in traditional Africa south of the Sahara, especially in West Africa. In these stories the spider again and again tricks the creator god, gaining from him, for example, a knowledge of his powerful stories. In another story the spider arranges to have the sun, the creator's youngest son, made king rather than two older brothers. He is also widely known in the Caribbean.

3. Religious adaptations. *a) Buddhist.* Fables have probably played a greater role in Buddhism than in any other living religion. This is because so many fables were incorporated into the JĀTAKA, a canonical collection of stories about the past lives of GAUTAMA BUDDHA. Most of the over five hundred Jātaka stories of the PALI CANON tell of previous human lives of the Buddha, but in other stories the Buddha was reborn as an animal, and many of these stories are Buddhist adaptations of fables. In keeping with his lofty mission, the BODHISATTVA—one who has taken a vow to become a Buddha—is usually identified in the animal stories as the king of the lions, cobras, etc. The animal of the story typically exemplifies important Buddhist values, such as generosity, self-sacrifice, or nonviolence. For example, according to one story the bodhisattva was once born as a rabbit who gave his life for the sake of a starving hunter by throwing himself into the hunter's campfire. The rabbit's act shows great self-sacrifice, and the fact that he killed himself spared the hunter the defilement (bad KARMA) associated with killing. Other animals display courage, truthfulness, cunning, and wisdom.

Buddhist temples are typically filled with paintings of scenes from Buddhist stories, including the Jātakas, and so the fables have earned themselves a lasting role in Buddhism.

b) Hebrew. An important Hebrew collection is that of Natronai ha-Nakdan, who wrote *Fox Fables* around A.D. 1200. He drew upon numerous earlier collections, including one written in English a few years earlier by Marie de France, the Aesop tradition as represented in the Romulus and Avianus collections, and very likely a collection that had its origins in the *Pañcatantra*. He wrote in biblical Hebrew, with many biblical citations, in a rhymed prose style. His title reflects the popularity in the twelfth century of the cunning fox Renart (Reynard) and his dealings with a dim-witted wolf.

The author abhorred the English morality of his day and wrote fables in hopes of strengthening the weak against their rich oppressors. The author narrates his story, adapted from whatever source, and then states the moral and applies it to specific life situations. He typically cites a biblical verse that makes a similar point. This procedure makes the fables apply rather specifically to the circumstances of poor Hebrews living in an England characterized by oppression and class conflict. The author refers to the conflict between rich and poor, however, and not specifically between Jew and Gentile. His most biting criticism is of the crown, for he begins with the depravity of rulers.

The *Fox Fables* is perhaps the most explicit of all fable collections in applying the morals of fables to actual life, and in reflecting its social environment.

c) Christian. The most famous Christian fabler is the Frenchman Jean de la Fontaine, who wrote twelve books of fables between 1668 and 1694. His fables were not meant primarily for children, as they came to be employed, but for adult connoisseurs of the fable. Often drawing upon previous collections such as that of Phaedrus, La Fontaine wrote in flowing French verse that earned him the title "The Fabler." He understood his fables to reveal the foibles of humanity through fiction. For example, his talking animals exhibited the very human characteristics of vanity, pride, social pretension, and bravado.

La Fontaine contrasted *fable* poetry, which revealed the baser side of human nature, with *epic* poetry, with its celebration of man's heroic nature.

In spite of La Fontaine's intention of writing for adults, his fables, as well as those of the Greek and Latin fablers, have often been used over the centuries as school readers in Europe. Christian educators evidently were pleased with the practical morals taught in such fables.

4. **Conclusion.** Fables are used by most, if not all, living religions. The stories are usually about animals that have to some extent taken on human traits, especially that of talking. The motif of personifying animals permits the fabler to draw morals, implicitly or explicitly, about human relations. Fables owe their widespread appeal to their ability to entertain, but their success in communicating moral values accounts for their role in religion.

In the Western world the height of the fable's popularity was reached in the eighteenth century, with a gradual decline in interest ever since. Yet it may be that the cartoon medium, with its personification of animals and its preoccupation with power struggles, cunning, and the failure of evil intent, represents a revival of the fable in a new form.

Bibliography. E. Arnold, trans., *The Book of Good Counsels; from the Sanskrit of the Hitopadesa* (1896); K. Doderer, *Fabeln: Formen, Figuren, Lehren* (1970); F. Duke, trans., *The Best Fables of La Fontaine* (1965); F. Edgerton, "The Hindu Beast Fable and the Story of its Travels," *University of Pennsylvania University Lectures, 1915-16* (1916), pp. 359-79; M. Guiton, *La Fontaine: Poet and Counterpoet* (1961); M. Hadas, *Fables of a Jewish Aesop: Translated from the Fox Fables of Berechiah ha-Nakdan* (1967); J. Jacobs, ed., *History of the Aesopic Fable* (1889, rpr. 1970); T. Noel, *Theories of the Fable in the Eighteenth Century* (1975); L. Sternbach, *The Hitopadesa and its Sources*, American Oriental Series, Vol. 44 (1960), and *The Fables of Pilpay* (1872); H-Y. Yang and G. Yang, trans., *Ancient Chinese Fables* (1957).

R. C. Amore

FAITH HEALING (Ch). The practice of faith healing has its roots in the ministry of Jesus and the apostles and has enjoyed a revival among Christians in the twentieth century. Biblical warrant is found in Mark 16:18, where Christ promised his followers that "they will lay their hands on the sick; and they will recover." In I Cor. 12:9 healing is listed as one of the gifts of the Holy Spirit, while in James 5:14 the elders are instructed to pray for the sick while "anointing" them with oil in "the name of the Lord."

Faith healing has been practiced to some degree throughout the history of the church, although the tendency has been to view miracles of healing as confined to the apostolic age.

A revival of interest in healing began in the late nineteenth century among some English and American evangelicals. In England the followers of J. N. Darby and Edward Irving taught that a restoration of the gifts of the Spirit would include divine healing for the body (*see* Plymouth Brethren). In America, A. J. Gordon and A. B. Simpson taught healing for the body "as in the atonement" citing Isa. 53:4-5 for evidence. This teaching became a feature of the Keswick Conventions in England after 1875. The American Holiness Movement also adopted divine healing as an extension of the belief in the entire santification of the body.

By 1885 faith healing had become so popular that a Divine Healing Conference was held in London. Outstanding practitioners of the era included Andrew Murray of South Africa, J. A. Dowie of Australia, and Mary Woodworth-Etter of the United States.

Dowie's healing campaigns in America in 1889-90 resulted in the formation of the American Divine Healing Association in San Francisco in 1890. Later, Dowie built near Chicago a community called "Zion City" where the sick could come for prayer.

When the Pentecostal movement began in Topeka, Kansas, in 1901, its leader, C. F. Parham, was already widely known as a faith healer. After the Azusa Street meeting of 1906 under W. J. Seymour, the Pentecostal Churches practically preempted the teaching and practice of faith healing in the public mind.

The twentieth century has seen a procession of faith-healing evangelists who have gained widespread attention and support. In the 1930s Aimee Semple McPherson captured the public imagination and founded a new denomination,"The International Church of the Foursquare Gospel," based on her healing ministry. In the 1950s Oral Roberts, a Pentecostal Holiness minister (later Methodist) from Tulsa, Oklahoma, gained a wide following through his tent crusades and national television ministry. In the 1960s Roberts founded Oral Roberts University in Tulsa to propagate his ministry, and in the 1970s began the massive "City of Faith" medical school and hospital to demonstrate the compatibility between faith healing and medical science.

In the 1960s and 70s the Charismatic Movement in the mainline churches emphasized faith healing, especially through the Order of St. Luke in the Episcopal Church, and in the ministry of Katherine Kuhlman, whose followers were largely from the traditional churches. A parallel development occurred among Roman Catholics. The popularity of the grotto in Lourdes, France, and other sacred sites proved that interest in faith healing knew no denominational bounds. Despite criticism by the press and some branches of medicine, it was apparent that faith healing in answer to prayer continued to have appeal to Christians in the twentieth century.

Bibliography. J. Harrell, *All Things Are Possible* (1975); M. T. Kelsey, *Healing and Christianity* (1973).

H. V. Synan

FALASHA JEWS fä lä′ shə (Ju—Ethiopian; lit. "stranger"). An Ethiopian sect whose tradition derives its descent from the union of Solomon and the Queen of Sheba (I Kings 10:1-13). The community bases its religious beliefs on the Bible and certain Apocryphal sources, accepting little of post-biblical Judaism, though rabbinic traditions are found in their literature. Falasha credentials were upheld by Israel's chief rabbis in 1975.

Falasha ritual revolves about the *mesgid,* or house of worship, which is divided between priestly and public sections. Prayer and Torah reading are performed in the Ge'ez language, a classical Ethiopian dialect. Festival observance follows scriptural dicta closely and includes Sabbath ritual, a Rosh ha-Shanah celebration and Yom Kippur fast, and a Passover sacrifice. It is estimated that there are between twenty and thirty thousand Falasha presently in Ethiopia, though official repression has made a more precise count impossible.

Bibliography. W. Leslau, *The Falasha Anthology* (1951).

D. J. Schnall

FAMILY RELATIONSHIPS. *See* Life Cycle Rites.

FAQĪR fä kēr′ (I—Arab.; lit. "poor"). Poverty was commended by both the Qur'ān (Sura 35:16) and the Ḥadīth, according to which Muhammad said, "Poverty is my pride." Most often applied to Sufis, it has two levels of meaning: 1) it may characterize the material impoverishment voluntarily sought by most Sufi adepts; and 2) it may connote every virtue which the seeker of the way to God embraces, for only by making oneself poor, i.e., by ceasing to be self-centered, can one become the channel for God's grace and the obedient lover of the Divine Beloved. It is in this latter sense that one Sufi author has used a catena of ninety-four qualities to describe the true *faqīr.* (*See* Dervish.)

Bibliography. A. Schimmel, *Mystical Dimensions of Islam* (1975), pp. 120-24.

B. Lawrence

FASTS. *See* Asceticism §§1a, 2d; Lent (Ch); Ṣawm (I); Yom Kippur (Ju).

FATE. That which has been decreed or predetermined for someone, especially the major events of one's life, including the time and manner of death; hence, one's "destiny." Also, the agency or agencies which determine a person's destiny.

The history of religion reveals that humans of every time and place have been largely unsatisfied with only rational and physical explanation for serious illnesses, misfortunes, and premature deaths. The universal question in time of trouble seems to be, "Why me?" Partly in their search for an underlying cause for the disasters which seem to fall upon all persons regardless of seeming justification, humans have postulated seemingly capricious, supernatural causes—i.e., fate.

Physical causes of fateful occurrences (i.e., the bite of a poisonous snake or the blow of an enemy) are not discounted, but are thought to be secondary to the underlying supernatural causes. Our knowledge of prehistoric expressions of religion is too sketchy to permit a reconstruction of the rise of supernatural explanations for fortunate or unfortunate events, but it may be noted that in the distant past of many races and cultures there is a strong belief that dramatic changes in fortune reflect "that which has been allotted or decreed." The Greek *moira,* Arabic *maniyah,* and Latin *fatum* (Eng., fate) refer to that which has been decreed or allotted, and the Sanskrit *daivam* similarly refers to that which comes from the divine (the sky, the gods).

A distinction is sometimes made between fate as something predetermined by an impersonal supernatural force and that which is willed by a god or goddess. This distinction is important to theologians concerned with attributing to a particular divine personage only that which is traditionally claimed and not what is imputed by those who, having suffered misfortune (e.g. a child dies), look for a transcendent cause (e.g., "God took him from us").

A further distinction may be made between the belief that one's fate is sealed at or before birth and that it is fixed annually, usually at the beginning of the new year. On the one hand, Astrology asserts that the pattern of the stars at the time of birth fixes one's destiny. Other forms of Divination presuppose that the permanent destiny that has been allotted is discernible from, for example, one's palm print or skull shape. On the other hand, the belief that one's fate is set annually is encountered in such cultures as that of the Ibo (Nigeria), who believe that fate bundles are prepared annually for humans, and that the bundle one gets is determined by the blind selection of one's guardian spirit.

1. Greek thought. It is probably true that fate (*moira*) played a larger role in Greek thought than in any other ancient or modern society. The Indo-Aryan ancestors of the Greeks long before had told of three women (*morae*) who sat at the foot of the tree at the center of the world and spun the fates of humans. These women were probably the prototype of the Greek conception of the fates as old women who spin human destinies.

Homer speaks of fate in the singular. In his writing fate is an impersonal power that often seems functionally interchangeable with the gods, but elsewhere it seems to transcend even the gods and include them under its control.

After Homer the references are most often to the three fates, along the lines of the three spinners of

Aryan mythology. Their names are Clotho ("The Spinner"), Lachesis ("The Dispenser of Lots"), and Atropos ("The Unalterable"). The first goddess spins each human "thread" (fate), the second dispenses it, and the third cuts it off. Fate is a central concept in the Greek tragedies, as may be seen in Sophocles' story of Oedipus. In all Sophocles' tragedies, oracles play an important role in communicating a human's fate. This reflects the basic meaning of fate as "that decreed."

The justice of the gods operates in the long run, and is not the kind of justice that calls for frequent intervention in history, according to the Greek tragedies. The hero's character and also chance play a role, without a doubt, but the main events, especially those surrounding the hero's death, are unalterably predetermined by fate, as Oedipus discovered.

2. **Hinduism.** As was the case with the Greeks, Hindus often spoke of time *(kalā)* itself as akin to—or at least as the bringer of—destiny or fate. One traditional term for fate in Hinduism is *daivam* (lit. "from the gods"). Thus, *daivam* as "the divine" took on the meaning of "that which is ordained by some supernatural power." The nature of the supernatural power(s) is not usually specified.

A more common, and certainly more famous, explanation for human success or tragedy is the Hindu concept of Karma (i.e., one reaps what one sows). Unusual occurrences in a person's life may be explained as the consequence of moral actions from earlier in this life or from a previous life. This near mechanistic and impersonal explanation for human destiny justifies why a great evil or good is happening to a particular person without reference to fate *(daivam)*.

It is possible in Bhakti Hinduism to attribute great fortune or calamity to the influence of a particular god or goddess. The sectarian god (e.g, Shiva, Vishnu, or Kālī) not only can dictate the events of a devotee's life (even altering predetermined karma) but fully controls access to the highest heaven as well (e.g., *see* Śaiva Siddhānta).

The above three explanations of good and evil coexist in Hindu thought, but not without some confusion and overlap. It is possible in many cases, for example, for the same person who has experienced a bad turn of fortune to simply say, "It is my karma," "It is fate," or even, "It is the will of Shiva."

Instances of the various explanations for fortuitous or evil events may be found in all or nearly all of the sacred texts of Hinduism, including the Vedas, the Upaniṣads, the Epics and the Purāṇas. For example, in the Bhagavad Gītā the god Vishnu is incarnated as a man, Krishna, who has taken upon himself the task of driving the chariot of Arjuna, a general. When Arjuna loses his will to fight just before the battle, Krishna encourages him to rise up and fight according to his duty as a warrior (Kṣatriya). However, are the outcome of the battle and Arjuna's eventual role in it fated? It is said that the five factors of causation include fate (18:14-15), and the men of the opposing army are predestined to die (18:61-62). But a following verse (18:63) suggests that at least some degree of free will is operative. The reader of the Bhagavad Gītā is left with the impression that the will of the god Vishnu and the past karma of the individuals involved combine to predestine the events that transpire in the Gītā, and in the whole of the Mahābhārata of which it is a part.

In popular Hinduism the fate *(daivam)* explanation for evil has been nearly as important as the karmic explanation. This is especially so among some of the Tamils of South India, who traditionally have believed that one's fate is fixed before birth and written invisibly on his or her forehead. This head-writing may be discernible by a skilled fortune teller, but never by oneself.

In general, most Hindus believe that many of the major events of life, such as one's birth status, overall health, marriage partner, number and sex of offspring, and time of death are fixed before birth, either by fate, by one's past action, or both. Some Hindus believe that it is possible that an accident or a supernatural being might cause a premature death, or that taking refuge in certain holy places and deities might alter one's destiny. Divination, especially by astrology, plays an important role in revealing one's fate, thus making fate more manageable.

3. **China.** As early as Neolithic times the Chinese heated ox bones to divine the future. Later the aristocracy of the Shang period (1751-1112 B.C.) employed professional diviners to prepare and inscribe questions upon bones and turtle shells in order to divine the outcome of such matters as wars and pregnancies, or to predict the weather. It is not clear exactly what supernatural force(s) was thought to have done the decreeing, but the Chinese of this ancient period typically appealed to an ancestor for help in giving the correct answer to the question. (*See* I Ching.)

Confucius' teachings reflect a belief that the decree of heaven (T'ien) is very important in determining one's life. The task of the sage is to discern heaven's decree and harmonize his life with whatever is decreed. Likewise, fate *(ming)* played an important role in traditional Chinese politics, for it was believed that a particular dynasty ruled only because it enjoyed the Mandate of Heaven. Heaven—here conceived almost as a god—had the freedom to withdraw its mandate from evil emperors and dynasties, however, in which case the people had a right to revolt and establish on the throne someone heaven had chosen. (*See also* Chinese Popular Religion.)

4. **Judaism.** There is little evidence in the Torah for the belief that the major events of an individual's life were fated, in the Greek sense of the term. There is abundant evidence, on the other hand, of the belief that the major events in the life of the people of Israel were predetermined by God. Acting as Lord of history and judge, God governs the powers of nature, as

expressed in Psalm 148, which declares that all waters, all weather, mountains, fruit trees, and so forth are ordained by God. Foreign armies punish Israel's offenses or are overthrown by Israel according to God's will, not according to fate. For example, in Amos 3:6 God asks if an evil such as a foreign conquest can befall a city except by his will.

There is evidence that many important decisions were made by casting lots, which were thought to reflect not chance but the will of God (Prov. 16:33). Or it was thought that God himself was the actual caster of the lots (Isa. 34:17). This divination expresses the belief that the outcome of events is determined, but in typical Hebrew fashion the determiner is God and not fate.

In the rabbinic period the belief arose that God had foreknowledge of the major events of one's life, such as the choice of a marriage partner and the length of life. The RABBIS insisted, however, that such divine foreknowledge did not amount to fatalism or the loss of free will.

The three heavenly books in which are inscribed at the autumnal New Year the destinies of the evildoers, the pious, and those in between constitute a record of what individuals have done and the corresponding retributions, and are not books of future fate after the fashion of Ibo fate-bundles.

5. Islam. The concept of fate *(maniyah)* that plays an important role in ISLAM is traceable back to ARABIC poetry before the time of MUHAMMAD.

a) early Arabic poetry. Maniyah (from *mny,* "to count, measure out, assign") and related words for fate appear frequently in Arabic poetry before Muhammad, typically in the context of death. The poet may be referring to someone who died in battle, through an accident, or of disease, but in each case the real underlying cause is said to be that the death was determined.

Closely related to the concepts of fate and destiny is that of decree (*qadar* and *qada*), which may be used to mean "that which has been decreed," in the sense of destined. It is difficult to determine to what extent the decreeing agent was thought to be a god, as opposed to an impersonal force. The high God, ALLAH, was (prior to Islam) closely associated with fate, but the poets were not especially religious and so did not emphasize the connection between destiny and divinity, thus leaving the impression that they believed in fate rather than divine determination.

b) Qur'ān. The situation is quite different in the QUR'ĀN, which ascribes destiny to the will of Allah and not to impersonal fate. For example, the Qur'ān speaks of the assigned time when the world as we know it will come to an end, but God is the assigner. There is also a suggestion (e.g. 3:139) that the day of one's death is predetermined, but by God rather than blind fate.

All the activities of humans and animals are said in the Qur'ān (e.g., 10:62) to be written in a heavenly book, with the implication that the date of any particular person's death is written therein.

c) Ḥadīth. Great emphasis upon Allah's decree is found in the collections of ḤADĪTH, "Traditions." The *ḥadīth* take the position that a belief that God ordains all that happens to one, both good and evil, is an essential part of the faith. Some of the traditions specify that during the embryonic period an angel writes down God's dictation as to the individual's future state of happiness, lifespan, sex, and means of livelihood. This record is then kept by the angels and nothing can be added or omitted.

d) Theology. Muslim theologians were divided on the issues of free will and determinism. Those who favored determinism did so because they followed the Qur'ānic tradition of ascribing all things to God's destiny. Different schools of theology were especially concerned with other doctrines derived from the Qur'ān such as the call to decision for obedience to God and the belief that God was always just in his judgments. Given these concerns they tended to minimize the role of divine destiny in favor of personal choice. In doing so, such theologians greatly softened the Muslim doctrine of God as the decreer of fate or destiny. The doctrine was strengthened, however, by those SUFI mystics who sought to practice, and write poems about, an attitude of total surrender to what God had decreed. On the other hand, SHI'ITE Islam, with its belief that the legitimate caliphate had been tragically rejected by the SUNNI majority, modified the notion of God's decree via an appreciation of the tragic suffering of the innocent in history.

Despite the variations, the general Islamic stance has been that many or all events are determined by God, but not in such a way as to undermine human freedom completely. (*See* KALĀM.)

6. Conclusion. The belief that major events are decreed or fated appears to make life more bearable in that it enables the believer to affirm the underlying rationality of the universe in the face of apparent irregularities and injustices. In strongly theistic religions such as Islam the concept of fate often becomes subordinate to that of divine PREDESTINATION, whereas in the religions of India fate has been juxtaposed with the concepts of an impersonal karma and a personal god's will.

There are instances of such a strong belief in fate that the term "fatalism" has been applied, as in the case of Islam, for example. Yet within these traditions it is argued that free will exists, and more importantly, people do attempt to avoid evil occurrences in their lives. Fate is often an explanation given after the fact; for example, after efforts to prevent death have failed. The otherwise inexplicable event may be fitted into a perspective or meaning by saying, "It was decreed."

Bibliography. S. M. Cahn, *Fate, Logic and Time* (1967); W. C.Greene, *Moira: Fate, Good, and Evil in Greek Thought* (1944);

Y. Kaufmann, *The Religion of Israel: From Its Beginnings to the Babylonian Exile* (1967), especially pp. 73-74; P. M. Kolenda, "Religious Anxiety and Hindu Fate," *Religion in South Asia*, E. B. Harper, ed. (1964), pp. 71-81; J. S. Martin, *Ragnarok: An Investigation into Old Norse Concepts of the Fate of the Gods*, Melbourne Monographs in Germanic Studies, vol. 3 (1972); W. O'Flaherty, *The Origins of Evil in Hindu Mythology* (1975); H. Ringgren, "Studies in Arabian Fatalism," *Uppsala Universitets Arsskritt* (1955) 2, 1-225, and *Fatalistic Beliefs in Religion, Folklore, and Literature* (1967); M. M. Watt, *Free Will and Predestination in Early Islam* (1948).

R. C. Amore

FATHER (Ch). Title applied to God in the Bible and Christian theology, referring primarily to God as first person of the Trinity; also applied to some of the Christian writers in the early centuries of the church; in some churches a title given to Priests, and also used in direct address.

K. Watkins

FĀTIḤA fä′ tĭ hə (I—Arab.; lit. "opening" [*fātiḥat al-kitāb*, "opening of the Scripture"]). The opening chapter (Sura) of the Qur'ān, containing seven verses, recited several times in each *ṣalāt* (*see* Prayer in Islam), so at least seventeen times a day. It is referred to in Sura 15:87, under one interpretation, as the "seven repeated ones," and as the "Mother of Scripture" in Sura 3:7; 13:39; and 43:4. It was probably not included in some of the earliest collections of the Qur'ān, but nevertheless appears to have had early liturgical use. Many commentaries assert that it has prophylactic and therapeutic value. Muslim tradition is not agreed on dating it, some asserting that it was revealed twice, once in Mecca and once in Medina.

G. D. Newby

FĀṬIMA fä′ tĭ mə (I; *ca.* 605–*ca.* 633). Daughter of Muhammad by his first wife, Khadīja; wife of the fourth caliph, Ali. Little is known of her life, most sources reflecting later tendential biases. She was the mother of two sons, Ḥasan and Ḥusayn, born about five years after the Hijra. She is mentioned as having accompanied her father on only two expeditions, the one to take Mecca in year eight and the Farewell Pilgrimage in year ten. She lived only a year after her father's death and was completely opposed to the caliphate of Abū Bakr.

While Sunnite Ḥadīth collections mention Fāṭima only rarely, the Shi'ites regard her as a paradigm for womanhood, a devoted daughter and a perfect wife. The Fatimids take their name from her. Later Sunnite literature reflects this same hagiographic tendency and becomes increasingly sympathetic to her.

Bibliography. aṭ-Ṭabarī, *Ta'rīkh;* Ibn Sa'd, *aṭ-Ṭabaqāt al-Kabīr*, IIIi, 11-16, VIII, 11-19 (1917); H. Lammens, *Fatima et les filles de Mahomet* (1912); Ibn Isḥāq, *Life of Muhammad*, A. Guillaume, trans. (1955), pp. 286, 398, 551, 683; for the treatment of the legendary Fāṭima, "Fāṭima," *EI*.

G. D. Newby

FÁTIMA, OUR LADY OF fä tē′ mä (Ch). Shrine in central Portugal marking the site of six apparitions of the Virgin Mary from May 13 to October 13, 1917. The reports of three shepherd children, aged 8, 9, and 10, that they had seen the figure of a lady "brighter than the sun," attracted crowds of increasing size, but only the children could see her. At the last apparition the sun seemed to tremble, rotate, and dance over the heads of the crowd. In 1930 the bishop of Leira authorized the cult of Our Lady of Fátima. Between 1928 and 1953 a basilica with a lofty tower was built on the site. In 1951 over a million people visited it to mark the closing of a Holy Year.

K. Crim

FATIMID fä tē′ mĭd (I). Ismaili dynasty (A.D. 909-1171) which ruled in North Africa and later in Egypt after the decline of 'Abbāsid power. The dynasty, which takes it name from Fāṭima, the daughter of Muhammad, or perhaps from al-Ḥusayn's daughter Fāṭima, was founded by a certain 'Ubayd Allah (d. 933), who claimed to be the Mahdi, the expected messianic leader from among the descendants of al-Ḥusayn.

Fāṭima played a distinctly esoteric role in Ismā'īliyya, linking the Fatimid caliphs to Shi'ite esotericism. This created a dynamic social and intellectual movement that led to the establishment of the Fatimids as a Shi'ite caliphate under a legitimate "Commander of the Faithful," and providing a position of leadership for the entire Islamic world.

Bibliography. W. Ivanow, *Ismaili Traditions Concerning the Rise of the Fatimids* (1942), and *The Alleged Founder of Ismailism* (1940).

A. A. Sachedina

FEMININE DIMENSIONS OF THE SACRED. Throughout the history of religion the sacred has been conceptualized in remarkably diverse ways, almost always with an indication of gender. Sacred entities, whether they are anthropomorphic deities or non-anthropomorphic cosmic forces and philosophical principles, are usually thought of as either female or male, or a combination of both female and male. Among these options, the image of a feminine dimension of the sacred, though unfamiliar to many Westerners, is common. Feminine names, attributes, and activities have been assigned to aspects of nature, cosmic forces, or deities in most of the world's religions and in all historical periods, though they are somewhat rarer in the three Western monotheistic religions (Judaism, Christianity, Islam).

1. **General historical considerations.** Most scholars have concluded that humankind's earliest religious conceptions the world over included significant attention to a feminine sacred principle. Archaeological sites from India to Western Europe yield numerous female figures, often with exaggerated sexual characteristics. The earliest figures occur in

sites from the Gravettian-Aurignacian cultures of the upper Paleolithic, which may go back as far as 25,000 or 30,000 B.C., and which flourished for 10,000 years. Cultures of the proto-Neolithic (9000 to 7000 B.C.) yield similar statues which are usually interpreted as representations of the Mother Goddess. Neolithic sites, especially Catal Hüyük, one of the earliest known cities (Anatolia, 6500 B.C. onward), clearly indicate the presence of an important goddess cult. With the emergence of writing in the fourth millennium B.C., written records as well as material artifacts give evidence that feminine attributes were attached to the sacred in the religious outlook of all the original centers of Western civilization—Mesopotamia, Egypt, and Crete.

The meaning of this early feminine sacred presence is difficult to determine, since most of the evidence consists of material artifacts rather than written texts. It is also difficult to determine the relationship of the goddess to any male sacred beings. Most scholars think that the early cult of female sacred beings was concerned with fertility, growth, and life in general, including rebirth and renewal after death. Consequently the mystery and wonder of the birth-giving female was one of the primary images of the sacred. Some speculate that the goddess reigned supreme in the beginning of human history, before the male role in fertility was known, with the cult of a young male god, the son-lover of the goddess, being introduced when the male role came to be understood. Later this image was replaced by that of a more egalitarian couple. Only at the last stage of a long development do we find a pantheon dominated by male gods or a religion devoted to a single male deity. Whether or not this is the exact sequence, it is clear that there was a general development away from feminine symbolism of a sacred presence and toward symbolism of the sacred that drew much more heavily on male imagery.

The historical and social processes that resulted in more male-centered images and concepts of the sacred are not clearly understood. One possibility is that the shifts to more complex techniques of agriculture and to more intensive urbanization fostered male dominance, both socially and in religious conceptions. Another is that the growing cult of a male sacred principle was linked to the triumph of invading, semi-nomadic, less civilized, warlike, and highly patriarchal populations who worshiped a male deity, either as head of the pantheon or as the sole deity. The latter circumstance was important in the history of both major sources of Western civilization, Greek and Hebrew civilizations, as well as in the history of the Indian tradition. The Indo-ARYANS, who originated somewhere in the central Eurasian landmass, invaded both Greece and India in successive waves beginning in the late third millennium B.C. (*See* INDUS VALLEY CIVILIZATION.) In India the result was a relative suppression of the goddess for many centuries followed by a very strong resurgence of cults of the goddess in later BHAKTI HINDUISM. Eventually Hindu goddesses again became as important as they had been in prehistoric India. In Greece the result was an uneasy compromise between the male deities of the Aryan invaders and the strong female deities of the indigenous populations. Zeus may have reigned supreme in theory, but the Eleusinian mysteries, dedicated to the goddess Demeter and her daughter Persephone, were extremely popular in fact. There was a major revival of goddess religion in the late pre-Christian centuries throughout the Greco-Roman world, and only with the triumph of Christianity were the last temples to the goddess closed about A.D. 500.

In many ways Hebrew religion was much more decisive to the eclipse of a feminine dimension of the sacred in Western religions. The monotheistic god worshiped by the Hebrews and bequeathed to Western religions usually is thought of as male rather than androgynous or neuter. The developments of biblical theology seem to involve not only monotheism replacing polytheism, and history replacing nature as the realm of divine activity, but also the male deity replacing the female. Many scholars have failed to take note of this last dimension. However, even in biblical religions, the eclipse was not total at any point.

2. The feminine sacred in world religions. It is useful to keep in mind three generalizations. First, feminine imagery of the sacred is a primordial and basic religious response found in the earliest known cultures, and found almost universally. Like most symbols of the transcendent, it has a foundation in basic human experience. Second, though most traditions at some point display a tendency toward predominantly male-centered images of the sacred, there is usually some resurgence of feminine imagery in the later history of that same tradition. Third, though there are exceptions, the strongest feminine imagery tends to be found in "folk" levels of a tradition rather than at the more elite levels. Thus art and mythology, rather than formal theology, tend to be the best sources for feminine imagery of the sacred, even though these sources are often overlooked by scholars of religion.

a. Tribal religions. Since most of the tribal religions found throughout the world recognize multiple sacred beings and are concerned with fertility and well-being—obvious concerns of female sacred beings—it is not surprising that some feminine dimension of the sacred is recognized in most tribal traditions. However, the importance and significance of feminine sacred beings varies greatly among the traditions. For example, in aboriginal Australia, some groups have major myth and ritual cycles dedicated to female totemic ancestors while other groups are primarily oriented to male ancestors. (*See* OCEANIC TRIBAL RELIGIONS §3.) In Africa one commonly finds an androgynous, distant Supreme Being and numerous more active male deities and ancestors. However, female deities and ancestors are also important in many groups. (*See* African Traditional Religion §2.) Among native American traditions, a sense of the earth as Sacred Mother—not quite an anthropomorphic deity but a sacred force—is common. Changing Woman, of the Navajo, and Sedna, the Eskimo Mistress of Animals, are well-known examples of female sacred beings. (*See* Native American Tribal Religion.)

b. Far Eastern religions. In Chinese religions cosmic forces rather than deities are the most significant representations of the sacred in the religious outlook of the more elite classes. Tao, the most basic, overarching, and primordial of these forces, is often described in feminine terms, as the "Mother of all things" and as the "Mysterious Female." One who follows Tao is advised to play the female part, to be soft and yielding and, thereby, to become invulnerable. (*See* Lao Tzu; Taoism, Philosophical.) The operation of Tao is often understood as the interaction of Yin and Yang, complementary, noncompeting opposites that are imaged as female and male among other primary attributes. (*See* I Ching.) In Chinese Popular Religion deities, including numerous female deities, are important. Generally, they are embodiments of mercy and grant boons of all kinds to their faithful followers. In Japanese Religion, Amaterasu, the important sun-Kami, the founder and patron of the Japanese nation and one of the most important figures in Japanese mythology, is likewise feminine. (*See* Shintō.) It is also important to note that in Far Eastern Buddhism the Bodhisattva Kuan-yin (Jap. Kannon) was popularly known as the Goddess of Mercy, despite her Indian antecedents as the male Avalokiteśvara.

c. Religions of the ancient world. The high religions of the ancient world are among the classic sources of goddess tradition. Everywhere one finds strong feminine sacred beings, especially in earlier periods. Isis, Hathor, and Nut in Egypt, Inanna-Ishtar in Mesopotamia, Anat in Palestine, the goddesses of Crete, and Demeter, Athena, and Artemis in Greece are a few of the more important and better known goddesses of the ancient world. In late antiquity the religion of Isis became extremely popular throughout the Greco-Roman world. Her religion was only one of a number of religions devoted to female sacred beings that swept westward in the same waves of religious activity that eventually produced Christianity. These goddesses are almost impossible to characterize briefly since they were involved with every important human concern from fertility to salvation.

d. Western monotheistic religions. Judaism, Christianity, and Islam have less overt feminine imagery of deity than any other major religions. There is controversy about whether the concept of deity prevalent in these religions contains any hint of sexuality at all. Many contend that part of God's transcendence is that he is beyond sexuality entirely. On the other hand, masculine pronouns and metaphors like "Father," "King," and "Judge" abound, while there is an absence of feminine pronouns and metaphors like "Mother" or "Queen." But in less overt ways one does find a significant feminine dimension in concepts of the sacred, even in these religions. There is some feminine imagery of God in the Hebrew scriptures, (e.g. Isa. 42:14; 49:15) and later Judaism speaks of the Shekina, the indwelling feminine presence of God. The theology of mystical Judaism or Kabbala is quite thorough in its reintroduction of a feminine dimension to images of deity. Christianity shares the same heritage of cryptic scriptural references to a feminine dimension of God combined with an overtly masculine set of basic metaphors. From that base it developed imagery of the Holy Spirit as feminine, common to the Eastern Orthodox Churches, and occasionally some imagery of a feminine Christ in mystical traditions. Much more accessible to the average Christian throughout history and even to the present day is the veneration of the Virgin Mary, often the most revered and loved figure in the religion. It is hard to explain the immense popularity of Mary as anything but a resurgence of a feminine dimension of the sacred. Islam, on the other hand, seems almost invulnerable to any sense of a feminine dimension to the sacred. The Qur'ān and the theological tradition specifically denounce goddess worship. Only rarely in mystical Islam does the male seeker imagine the divine as feminine.

e. Indian religions. Hinduism presents the most developed example of feminine dimensions of the sacred in the contemporary world. In theistic sects of Hinduism, feminine images of deity are as numerous, popular, and well-developed as male aspects of deity. They are worshiped and portrayed alone or with their husbands-consorts. Kālī, Durgā, Sarasvatī, Lakṣmī, Śakti, Gaṅgā, and Pārvatī are some of the most important goddesses. (*See* Goddess [India].) As is always the case in traditions with well-developed imagery of feminine dimensions of the sacred, these goddesses cannot be easily summarized because they are so involved in every facet of human life and longing. Though Theravāda Buddhism is nontheistic, Mahāyāna and Vajrayāna (Tantric) forms of Buddhism do know sacred beings of various types, and female sacred beings re-emerge. Prajñāpāramitā, the personification of transcendent wisdom and "Mother of all Buddhas," and Tārā, "She Who Helps One Cross Over," are important in Mahāyāna Buddhism. Furthermore, Tantric Buddhism is famous for its attention to feminine principles.

3. Meanings of feminine dimensions of the sacred. It is difficult to generalize about so much material from so many times and places, but the topic is important because scholarship has often either simply ignored the overwhelming mass of data regarding feminine dimensions of the sacred or interpreted it negatively.

Four interpretive generalizations can be made. First, goddess religions are in general this-worldly and life-and-world affirming. The goddess gives birth to all things and nurtures them. Intimacy and joyful participation in life are major themes. Basic life processes, especially birth and sexuality as well as all aspects of the human, embodied condition, are affirmed. Second, though it may seem paradoxical at first, female sacred beings are also intimately connected with death. The Hindu goddess Kālī is the best-known example of this theme. In her imagery, as with many other goddesses, there is realistic and graphic emphasis on death. However, rather than being some kind of morbid fixation, the goddess' connection with death is part of the general affirmation of embodiment and life. The limits of the life process are accepted without embellishment. The first two generalizations, when combined, mean that goddess traditions provide an immanent sacred power which is less alienated from basic cosmic and bodily realities than is characteristic of religions without strong feminine traditions.

Third, while connections with birth, motherhood, and sexuality are prominent in goddess imagery, female sacred beings are by no means confined to maternity or materiality, but are involved in a broad range of cultural activities and culturally valued goals. Thus, Athena, clad in full armor, guards the city of Athens, one of a number of warrior-goddesses found in various religions. In Hinduism, the goddess Durgā defeats in single combat the demon who had overwhelmed the male deities, and Sarasvatī promotes the arts and education. As for religions that promote liberation from worldly concerns, Mary and Kālī, in very different ways, show devotees the path to release, and in some forms of Buddhism, Prajñāpāramitā, transcendent wisdom, is mother of all Buddhas because she is the goal of spiritual discipline.

The final generalization concerns the relationship between a symbol system involving feminine dimensions of the sacred and the social system that gives rise to the symbols. Do goddesses reflect some sort of feminine dominance? Do societies that worship a goddess allow women more independence, respect, and power than societies that are not oriented toward a goddess? Or are female sacred beings some further device to limit women to prescribed roles and then glorify those roles? Such questions have intrigued scholars for at least a century, with hypotheses covering the entire gamut of opinions from the hypothesis that feminine dimensions of the sacred are evidence for some sort of matriarchy to the hypothesis that goddesses are creations of male imagination unconsciously, or perhaps consciously, designed to keep women within a limited sphere. The most reasonable hypothesis seems to be that a symbolism of a feminine dimension of the sacred does not necessarily indicate political or economic dominance or independence of women. (*See* WOMEN, STATUS AND ROLE.) However, significant attention to feminine dimensions of the sacred does always indicate a veneration for the feminine principle, especially as it connotes continuity and nurturing of ordinary human life.

4. **Contemporary developments.** In traditional religious symbol systems, there seems to be no diminution of attention to feminine dimensions of the sacred. The most significant contemporary development is a strong resurgence of such interest in some segments of Judaism and Christianity. At present, both those who wish to remain within Judeo-Christian traditions and those who consider themselves representatives of a post-Judeo-Christian outlook are interested in feminine imagery of the sacred. Much of the energy involved in this revaluation of Christian and Jewish symbols undoubtedly derives from secular liberation ideologies. Since changes in symbol systems are usually correlated with changes in socio-economic patterns, it remains to be seen whether this renewed interest will take root in Western religious consciousness and whether there will be repercussions from this development in other religions.

Bibliography. Sources on this topic are scattered and incomplete. There is no general survey. For prehistory, see R. Levy, *The Gate of Horn* (1948). For a survey of the ancient world, see E. O. James, *The Cult of the Mother Goddess* (1959). P. Trible's *God and the Rhetoric of Sexuality* (1978) discusses changing images of god and goddess in ancient Israel as does R. Patai's *The Hebrew Goddess* (1967). Among numerous books on Mary, R. Ruether's *Mary, the Feminine Face of the Church* (1977) is most aware of Mary as a feminine dimension of the sacred. There is no reliable survey of Indian goddesses but for an excellent study of Kālī, see D. Kinsley, *The Sword and the Flute* (1975). C. M. Chen's "Tao as the Great Mother and the Influence of Motherly Love in the Shaping of Chinese Philosophy," *HR,* XIV (1974), 51-63, and J. Blofield's *Bodhisattva of Compassion* (1978) can be consulted for aspects of Far Eastern tradition. For the best interpretation of the goddess as evidence of women's status and power, see M. Stone, *When God Was a Woman* (1976), and for examples of re-emergence of goddess tradition in the Western context, see C. Christ and J. Plaskow, *Womanspirit Rising* (1979). R. M. GROSS

FENG-SHUI fūng shwē (Chin.; lit. "wind and water"). The traditional Chinese art of locating graves, buildings, and cities in auspicious places, where there is a concentration of the vital energy of earth and sky. The presence or absence of such energy is revealed by the geographical configuration of hills, streams, vegetation, and directions. For feng-shui the earth is alive, with conduits just beneath the surface for the flow of cosmic power. If a grave is located at the conjunction of such conduits, this power will cause the bones of the dead to radiate beneficial influences on their descendants. For dwellings and cities, the benefits of a good location are directly available to their inhabitants.

Feng-shui theory is a variation of traditional Chinese cosmology, and as such it holds that features of the landscape manifest either YIN or YANG modes of energy, and can be classified according to the "Five Agents" (wood, fire, earth, metal, and water). These agents or phases can be understood as either producing or attacking one another. In an ideal site these forces are balanced with a slight preponderance of yang energy, and the agents are mutually supportive. However, the value accorded to earthly elements varies with the influence upon them of the stars and planets, as determined by the feng-shui practitioner. Feng-shui thus involves ASTROLOGY as well as mystic geography. A good grave site is typically located midway down the slope of a mountain, facing south, protected on the north and west, overlooking a body of water. This water stops the flow of vital energy from the mountainside and concentrates it in front of the grave. The site should be in an area of abundant vegetation, free of strong winds, with dry soil, and with meandering streams on either side. The mountain itself should be at the end of a connected series of ranges. A good site should also be beautiful and cause one standing by it to feel a sense of comfort and well-being. A deficient site can be strengthened by the addition of artificial mounds, pools, walls, etc., and even the best location must be recognized and used before it can produce results.

Feng-shui has no relationship to deities except through the petitioning of local gods for permission to use sites under their control. Though in theory it operates without ethical considerations, in practice its specialists stress that good results will come only to the moral and compassionate. In some popular conceptions its efficacy is believed to be due to the fact that a good site makes the ancestors content, and thus more willing to bless their descendants.

Feng-shui seems to have been first developed in the Han dynasty (206 B.C.—220 A.D.), though there are references in earlier sources to choosing a site for a city by divination, to water as the "blood and breath of the earth" flowing as through veins, and to guilt incurred by cutting such veins during the construction of the "Great Wall." The earliest extant feng-shui texts are attributed to famous diviners of the third and fourth centuries A.D. From that time numerous feng-shui books and local traditions continued to be produced on into the twentieth century, where they still appear in Taiwan. By the T'ang dynasty (618-907 A.D.) a geomantic compass came into use as aid to properly aligning graves and buildings.

Bibliography. J. Needham, *Science and Civilisation in China*, II (1956), 359-63; IV (1962), 239-45, 293-97; Hong-key Yoon, *Geomantic Relationships Between Culture and Nature in Korea* (1976).

D. L. OVERMYER

FESTIVALS. *See* RITUAL §4c; individual articles on the major traditions.

FILIAL PIETY (Con—Chin. *hsiao*; lit. "respect for parents"). One of the central virtues of the Confucian tradition, characterizing in part the gentleman *(chün-tzu)* who has perfected his moral nature. The DOCTRINE OF THE MEAN (19) characterizes the filial son as one who is able to continue the will and transmit the work of the father. According to the ANALECTS (II, 7), if filial piety were nothing more than caring for the parents' physical needs, man would not differ from animals. In the *Classic of Filial Piety (Hsiao Ching)* filial piety is described as the root of all other virtues and is seen as the paradigm of sagely conduct.

R. L. TAYLOR

FILIOQUE fē lē ō´ kwē (Ch—Lat.; lit. "and [from] the son"). A phrase inserted in the eighth century into the Western text of the Creed of the Council of Constantinople (381), describing the procession of the HOLY SPIRIT from the Father "and the Son." (*See* NICENE CREED.) The phrase seemed to Eastern Christians to compromise the Father's role as sole source of deity and was a major theological factor in the schism between Western and Eastern Churches in 1054.

D. E. GROH

FINNEY, CHARLES GRANDISON (Ch; 1792-1875). American PRESBYTERIAN evangelist; president of Oberlin College (1851-66). Finney won national acclaim through his successful revivals in upstate New York. He introduced such "new measures" as week-long evangelistic meetings and the "anxious bench," special seating for the almost-saved. In his theology, he stressed the importance of the human will. *See* REVIVALISM §4.

G. MILLER

FIQH fīk (I—Arab.; lit. "knowledge, understanding, skill"). In the field of law, the application of QUR'ĀN and its associated disciplines, of ḤADĪTH and its associated disciplines, of precedent, and of independent judgment to the broad spectrum of legal matters. It is a concept of law which covers all aspects of human activity. Legal theory generally holds that *fiqh* has four sources: ALLAH'S revelation in the Qur'ān, the SUNNA of MUHAMMAD, analogic reasoning, and consensus (IJMĀ').

Traditional Islamic views of the history of jurisprudence hold that there is an unbroken chain of legal practice from the time of Muhammad to the beginning of the personal schools of law in the end of the first and the beginning of the second Islamic centuries. These traditions hold that Muhammad established the practice of interpreting the Qur'ān and setting modes of behavior in response to queries or circumstances. The practice was continued by the Companions (ṢAḤĀBA) of Muhammad after his death, using the recollections of his actions and sayings transmitted in the form of *ḥadīth*. Because they were held to be consonant with Muhammad's divinely inspired behavior and with Allah's command (the Qur'ān), actions so derived were regarded as incumbent on the believing community.

From a historical perspective, it can be seen that Islamic jurisprudence came into being at the end of the first Islamic century when pious groups began to form a theocratic state based on Islamic principles to replace the essentially secular Arab state which had ruled in the name of Islam. In the three major administrative centers, Syria, Iraq, and MEDINA, groups or schools developed whose ideal was to regulate all human conduct under one divine law. The early schools reflected procedures derived mainly from local custom, supplemented by the discretionary opinion of those who acted as judges. The judgments were modified by Qur'ān and traditions from Muhammad and the Companions only insofar as they were admitted by the individual rendering the decision. By the process of comparing, accepting, or rejecting UMAYYAD administrative practices to the developing Islamic ideals, both *fiqh* and SHARIA were developed, the second rising from the first. The early schools reflected regional customs in spite of a common approach. The parallels between Islamic legal practice and that of Roman and Jewish law can be traced in part to this early period.

In the second Islamic century controversies arose between the schools of Islamic law and the Traditionists, in which the Traditionists insisted that *fiqh* must be based on *ḥadīth* from Muhammad. The triumph of this demand forced a profound change not only in law but in almost all other areas of Islamic learning, producing the "science" of *ḥadīth,* reassessments of Muhammad's biography, biographical lists and dictionaries, new types of Qur'ān commentaries, and the rejection of any detectable Jewish and Christian intellectual influences. The most famous literary jurists of this early period are Abū Ḥanīfa (d. 767, *see* HANAFITES), Abū Yūsuf (d. 798), ash-Shaybānī (d. 805), and MALIK IBN ANAS (d. 795). By far the most important, however, was AL-SHĀFI'Ī (d. 820) who, while deriving from the Medinan school, used the arguments of the Traditionists in his *Rasāla,* the first work on the roots of jurisprudence. He raised the status of the *sunna* of Muhammad to a primary position as a paradigm for correct behavior and as a means of interpreting the Qur'ān, rejected discretionary opinion and substituted analogic reasoning *(qiyās),* and argued for the infallibility of consensus *(ijmā').* Of his Traditionist disciples, Aḥmad IBN ḤANBAL (d. 855) rejected even analogic reasoning in jurisprudence, preferring weak traditions to strong reasoning.

By the middle of the third Islamic century the influence of these metropolitan schools had given way to schools formed around the methods of individual masters, e.g. the Malikites (*see* MALIK IBN ANAS) of Medina and the Hanafites of Kūfa. In subsequent centuries numerous short-lived schools were formed around the legal thinking of particular individuals, but after the eighth century only four have been commonly accepted in Sunnite Islam: the Malikites, the Shafi'ites, the Hanafites, and the Hanbalites, all of which are regarded as equally valid interpretations of jurisprudence. By the fourth Islamic century a general consensus was reached that all legal activity could only be interpretive, since the early masters had exhausted the possibilities of independent reasoning. Aside from the consideration of theoretical issues which would not change the accepted fundamentals of law, the jurist (MUFTI) could issue legal decisions which relate the law to new situations on a piecemeal basis. This restricting led to the formation of parallel secular courts of administration, often merely police courts, relegating *fiqh* and sharia to areas of personal conduct and family matters.

SHI'ITES differ in their concept of the roots of *fiqh* primarily through the doctrines of the IMAM and through the reliance on traditions from Muhammad derived through the family of ALI, but, in fact, the content of the body of tradition on which the law is based and the practical effects of the application of the law are not greater than the differences among the several SUNNITE schools, a situation to be accounted for, in part, by the catholicity of Islam and by the interaction of historical forces. In both branches of Islam the jurisprudential method has led to an emphasis on orthodoxy of practice. Only in modern times with the development of nationalism and the replacement of sharia by Western-style codes has *fiqh* been repudiated. *See* ISLAM §4e.

Bibliography. For a general overview see J. Schacht, *Origins of Muhammadan Jurisprudence* (1959) and *Introduction to Islamic Law* (1964), with bibliog. For a modernist view which tries to place *fiqh* in a broad perspective, see M. G. S. Hodgson, *Venture of Islam* (1974), particularly I, 315-58. See also N. J. Coulson, *History of Islamic Law* (1964), with bibliog.

G. D. NEWBY

FIRDAUSĪ, ABU'L-QĀSIM fər dou´ sē ä bool´ kä´ səm (I; *ca.* 940-1020). Iranian poet. His tragic life underscores his lyrical brilliance and monumental achievement as author of the *Shāhnāma* (The Book of Kings)—a *mathnavī* (*see* PERSIAN LANGUAGE) in approximately 50,000 distichs. Its idiomatic Persian minimizes not only non-Iranian themes and people but also non-Iranian, specifically Arabic, words. The *Shāhnāma* extols the importance of kingship as the most lofty status to which heros could aspire.

Bibliography. J. Rypka, *History of Iranian Literature* (1968), pp. 154-66; M. G. S. Hodgson, *The Venture of Islam,* II (1974), 154-59.

B. LAWRENCE

FIRE TEMPLE (Z). A building in which a sacred fire, the central symbol of divine presence and focus of ZOROASTRIAN worship, is kept constantly burning. Known among the PARSIS of India as an *agiāri* (Skt. AGNI "fire" and *āri* "place"), a fire temple has within its inner hall, often behind open grillwork, a stone base supporting a metal urn, which may be as large as one meter or more in height and diameter. There, on a bed of ash, burns the sacred fire, which is fed with wood by the priest at five times of prayer through the day and evening.

Congregational worship is not a regular feature of

Zoroastrian ritual; rather, the individual layman wishing prayers to be said for himself or others may at any time bring to the entrance of the inner enclosure an offering, especially of costly and sweet-smelling sandalwood, which the officiating priest will add to the fire. All continuous Zoroastrian fires are in India, Iran, and Pakistan, with the exception of one remaining in Zanzibar. Overseas Zoroastrian communities have generally not been able to afford to maintain fires around the clock. In India, entrance to fire temples is restricted to Parsis.

Zoroastrian fires are of three grades: the *ātesh dādgāh,* or "fire of the appointed place [for ceremonies for the dead]," maintained either in the home or in the fire temple; the *ātesh adarān,* or "fire of fires," constituted by bringing together from various sources four ceremonially ignited fires; and the *ātesh Behrām,* "fire of [the guardian] Varahrān," consecrated through a most elaborate ceremonial combination of fires from sixteen sources. There are nine *ātesh Behrām* fires in the world: one in Iran and eight in western India. Of them the oldest and holiest is at Udvada, 175 kilometers north of Bombay, which though relocated several times has according to tradition been maintained for over eleven centuries.

W. G. Oxtoby

FLAGELLANTS flă´ jə lənts (Ch). Those practicing public whipping as penance or Asceticism. Organized bodies of flagellants appeared in the thirteenth century. Later, some such groups were approved by church authorities, but many were forbidden by civil and church leaders owing to their morbidity, disorderliness, and heretical tendencies. Some still exist in Spanish America. W. H. Principe

FOOD PROSCRIPTIONS, MUSLIM. The Qur'ān expressly forbids the use of the following substances for food (Sura 2:173): anything which dies of itself (interpreted to include all animals, except fish and locusts, not expressly killed for food); blood; pork; and any food over which any but God's name has been invoked. In cases of dire necessity, any of the above may be consumed. The Ḥadīth further proscribe four-footed predators with canine teeth, birds of prey with talons, domestic asses, mules, ravens, and bustards. The law books extend the list still further. Permitted *(ḥalāl)* creatures must be slaughtered properly (*see* Sacrifice), with complete draining of the blood and invoking God's name.

The Qur'ān also prohibits the drinking of wine (Sura 5:93) and the *ḥadīth* extend this to include all intoxicants, although there is considerable hair-splitting among the jurists on this latter issue.

In addition to food proscriptions, the *ḥadīth* and law books contain detailed regulations on the means, manners, and contexts of food and beverage consumption, ranging from questions of simple etiquette to matters of serious defilement.

See also Kosher; Food, Religious Attitudes Toward.

Bibliography. Maulana Muhammad Ali, *The Religion of Islam* (1936), pp. 727-40, an authoritative compendium of Islamic beliefs and practices, used widely by English-speaking Muslims.

F. M. Denny

FOOD, RELIGIOUS ATTITUDES TOWARD. The search for or the production of food, and its distribution and consumption, are basic to human existence and therefore to human culture. Until recent decades these activities occupied the bulk of human time and energy, and represented the most consistent and effective human impact on the material universe. They were also at the foundation of human economic and social systems. It is axiomatic that such a pervasive and fundamental matter should almost universally be vested with multidimensional religious significance. The nature of the religious involvement will, of course, vary according to the character of the Power Beyond that is invoked and its relationship to the sources of food.

1. Religious dimensions of the obtaining of food. *a) Overcoming difficulties.* The difficulties and uncertainties of the obtaining of food are everywhere proverbial. For hunters and gatherers, the unreliability from year to year of the supplies of plant food, the elusiveness of game, and the hazards of the chase; for pastoralists, the dangers of beasts of prey, disease, and infertility; for agriculturalists, the problems of weather and vermin—all make the supply of food, and therefore life itself, rather precarious. In simple societies the odds in favor of human beings are not always high. In such situations hunter and fisherman, farmer and shepherd, readily call upon powers beyond them to improve the odds.

The powers involved may be simply impersonal, in which case Magic will be invoked: spells, incantations, Ritual, the use of charms and amulets, and so on. The farmer or his agent may imitate rain to bring rain; the herdsman may attempt to influence the outcome of the breeding of his herds and flocks (Gen. 30:25-43); the hunter may invest his weapons with potency and himself with invulnerability. If the powers are ancestors, they must be placated, promised a share in the good results, and so on. Many agricultural peoples worship spirits or divinities of the earth (Mother Earth) or of the agricultural process (e.g. the Greek Demeter). In such cases these must be invoked in prayer, ritual, and offering. The earth must be treated with proper care and respect during the preparation of the fields. Rituals involving fertility spirits and divinities belong here. Frequently, there are also spirits or divinities of the rain which must be induced to favor the quest for food.

b) Thanksgiving. The other side of the picture is the widespread use of rituals of thanksgiving when the quest has been successful. Hunters give a feast and make offerings of choice parts of the game, along with verbal and ritual expressions of gratitude and joy. Pastoral people may offer the choice of the flocks and herds, e.g. the firstborn (Deut. 15:19-22). Agricultural peoples almost always have festivals of harvest and thanksgiving at which they express gratitude and fulfill the vows made earlier and give offerings of their produce.

2. **Socio-religious attitudes.** *a) Marks of status.* To the extent that the existence or status of a group or person is believed to have religious sanction, the sanction is marked in various ways. Not infrequently, the marking involves peculiarities in the use or nonuse of food. This can apply to a whole people, as evidenced by the Jewish laws governing what is KOSHER (Lev. 11), which serve along with other signs to emphasize the distinctiveness of Israel. Or it can apply to some people only, as when priests and other religious functionaries have special food privileges or TABOOS (e.g. the use of sacrificial animals as food for priests, Lev. 7:1-10; the Nazirite taboos, Judg. 13:4, 5, *passim*). (*See* FOOD PROSCRIPTIONS, MUSLIM.)

b) Food for ancestors. Peoples that practice the cult of ancestors often give them food and drink on a regular basis, or on the occasion of special efforts to propitiate them or invoke their aid. Altars and rituals for this purpose are ubiquitous and in frequent use.

c) Ritual participation. In many societies eating a part of a human being, either literally or symbolically, is practiced in order to participate in that person's life, or to endow oneself with some particular virtue for which that person was noted: strength, courage, wisdom, etc. This type of cannibalism was usually infrequent and was just as far removed from everyday eating for nourishment as the Christian EUCHARIST, itself a rite of participation in the life and virtues of Jesus Christ. In a few societies that practice ANCESTOR VENERATION, the dead are consumed so that the living can share in unbroken continuity the life that is traceable back to the first ancestor. (*See* TOTEM.)

d) Feasting and belonging. In almost all societies, eating together is a sign of belonging; enemies do not eat together; or if they do, they cease to be enemies, as when treaties are solemnized by the sharing of food. This symbolism may take on a religious character when it is the ancestors, the spirits, or the gods who are feasting with humans. This is also a part of the signification of the Christian Eucharist.

3. **Offerings and sacrifices.** In addition to the offerings and sacrifices mentioned above, food offerings, especially slaughtered animals, are frequently involved in two more kinds of religious pursuits, in which they are conceived of as a feast for spirits or gods.

a) Propitiation and atonement. Here the supplicant seeks to gain the favor of the ancestor, spirit, or divinity by making a gift, which may or may not take on moral-ethical dimensions as an atonement for sin.

b) Peace. This seems to be different from the previous sacrifice in that generally good relations are assumed to obtain, so that there is a certain element of gratuitousness in the offering; but it seems to be intended to cement and express the connection from the point of view of the supplicant.

4. **Fasting.** Abstention from food and/or drink, whether total or partial, is a frequent accompaniment of other religious activities. (*See* RAMADAN.) One may as a penitent refrain from eating and drinking as one sign of humility and repentance. Or one may as a supplicant underline the importance and urgency of a prayer by denying oneself the usual necessities of life. Or, finally, one may seek mystical union with the divine by renouncing such attachments to the earth and matter as are signaled by eating. (*See* ASCETICISM.)

C. R. TABER

FOOTWASHING (Ch). A ceremony practiced by many Christian groups, by some in imitation of JESUS' washing his disciples' feet before the Last Supper (John 13:1-15), and by others in obedience to the command of John 13:14. It is an optional part of the MAUNDY THURSDAY observance in the ROMAN CATHOLIC, ANGLICAN, and ORTHODOX traditions, where the priest (or abbot of a monastery) washes the feet of a select number of those present. In Rome it is customary for the pope to wash the feet of twelve paupers.

The practice was taken up by some ANABAPTIST groups during the PROTESTANT REFORMATION, but here it was a required accompaniment to the Lord's Supper (*see* EUCHARIST), and all communicants participated as both agents and recipients, with the sexes separated. Footwashing is continued by some groups of Anabaptist heritage, such as the MENNONITES. It is also found in the worship of the Churches of God, Free Will BAPTISTS, SEVENTH-DAY ADVENTISTS, BRETHREN, and a wide variety of other Protestant bodies.

R. BULLARD

FOUNDERS, RELIGIOUS. 1. Definition. Persons regarded by religious traditions as their initial human organizers and leaders and their continuing primary human authorities on religious matters; hence, persons whose devotional biographies (hagiographies) proclaim the founders' normative significance as persons uniquely related to transcendent reality, as ideal models of the religious life, and as mediators of human transformation.

Three categories of religious founders may be distinguished with respect to the historical verifiability of the roles ascribed to them by their traditions. (1) Those founders whose biographies can be historically reconstructed and whose actual lives agree at least broadly with the roles and functions ascribed to them by their traditions. For major religious traditions, these include Mani (third century A.D.) for Manicheism, and MUHAMMAD (seventh century A.D.) for ISLAM. (2) Those founders whose historical biographies can be reconstructed only in bare outline, whose ascribed roles and functions develop in their later traditions to a great degree (even though they may broadly derive from the founder's spirit and inspiration). Included are MOSES (thirteenth century B.C.) for the Hebrew tradition; JESUS (first century A.D.) for the CHRISTIAN tradition; SIDDHĀRTHA GAUTAMA the

BUDDHA (sixth to fifth century B.C.) for the BUDDHIST tradition; Zoroaster, Zarāthustra (sixth to fifth century B.C.) for the ZOROASTRIAN tradition; MAHĀVĪRA (sixth to fifth century B.C.) for the JAINA tradition; and NĀNAK (fifteenth to sixteenth century A.D.) for the SIKH tradition. (3) Those founders whose roles in their traditions have a tenuous historical basis, and are the result more of the transposition of their life stories into ideal types that meet needs and express aspirations of their followers than a reflection of the actual careers of concrete, historical persons. These are CONFUCIUS (sixth to fifth century B.C.), whose reconstructable biography is quite discrepant from his function in Confucian tradition; LAO TZU, who was more probably a composite ideal sage than an actual individual; and KRISHNA, who is a composite and diverse symbol associated with a variety of possibly historical individuals.

2. Symbolic biographies of founders. *a) The biographical process.* Autobiographical references in the QUR'ĀN give a far more reliable and more complete historical account of Muhammad than is available for any of the other religious founders. The facts of the biographies of other founders are reconstructable only in general outline and character. The earliest strata of the biographical materials are concerned with what was most important for the first generations of followers, e.g., with the enlightenment and public teaching of the Buddha, with the preaching and PASSION of Jesus, and with the revelation of the mature Krishna of the MAHĀBHĀRATA and the BHAGAVAD GĪTĀ. Early sayings attributed to the founders tend to emphasize typical rather than verbatim reports, and the narratives provide settings in which the theological image of the founders takes precedence over the details. The earliest oral traditions associated with both Jesus and the Buddha consisted of short pronouncements, parables, debates, and miracle stories. The early biographers joined these self-contained units together in easily remembered forms (such as chains of related metaphors, BEATITUDES, prophecy sayings, institutional rules, and dialogues) and provided the subject matter with narrative occasions. The resulting story is typically episodic rather than chronologically continuous.

The developing biographies of founders often exhibit a self-conscious theological intent not only to fill out what was previously unknown about the founder, but also to give narrative form to his salvific significance. The biographies also find precedents in the founder's teaching, behavior, and travels for later developments in the tradition. Some additions to the story are no doubt exaggerations, interesting inventions, or misattributions. Other additions expand upon the supernormal or miraculous power of the founder if these powers are consonant with the founder's image in the tradition. The resuscitation of a dead man in the NT Gospel of John, for example, prefigures Jesus' own resurrection by showing his power over life and death. Other stories such as Siddhārtha's encounters with sick, old, and dead men and Jesus' temptation by the devil project psychological or spiritual experience into external dramatic encounters. In general, a developing hagiographical tradition represents a symbolic unfolding of different aspects of the founder's significance for his tradition. In the founder's life and mission it is claimed that a transcendent reality is present or revealed.

Developing hagiographies are also conditioned by cultural and cross-cultural notions of the "Great Man," the "Holy Man," or the "Divine Man." The major phases in the lives of Gautama and Mahāvīra and the stylized accounts of their predecessors are in close parallel. The predecessors of Mahāvīra and Krishna in some cases share the same names. The future destinies of the founders are predicted before or at the birth of Jesus, Krishna, Mahāvīra, and Gautama. The circumstances of conception, gestation, and birth are supernormal in various ways for Zoroaster, Jesus, Mahāvīra, Gautama, and Krishna, and natural signs (e.g., earthquakes) and miraculous phenomena (e.g., angels' singing) often accompany the birth. Mahāvīra and Krishna are each transposed from the womb of his original mother to the womb of another mother. Krishna, Jesus, and Moses are associated with double birthplaces and with different socio-ethnic groups. Krishna, Mahāvīra, Gautama, and Jesus are provided with royal genealogies. Holy men recognize Gautama and Jesus as future saviors in childhood. The slaughter of other male children born at the same time as the future founder by a wicked ruler is recounted for Krishna, Jesus, and Moses. Evil demons recognize Krishna, Gautama, and Jesus as the future savior.

b) History, myth, and saving story. The symbolic biographies of religious founders are important not *merely* to the degree that they are factual. The mytho-historical form of the saving stories is designed to communicate and to evoke the significance of the founder's revelation in the persons who hear it. Telling the story witnesses to the meaning of the person and his message for the faithful; it expresses the foundation of belief, behavior, and belonging within the religious tradition. Therefore, symbolic biography proclaims, celebrates, and embodies the founder and his way. It teaches, commands, enlightens, and reveals the transformation of human existence. The story is true or is accepted as true of the human condition and of the way to salvation or liberation. Elaborations of the story develop the existential possibilities inherent in the tradition. The founder's significance lives on in the tradition in its new creative embodiments—not only in oral or written story, but also in art, architecture, theater, dance, and in ritual and festival reenactment.

3. Roles and functions of religious founders. *a) Authority.* Cross-cultural description of the religious founder as one type of important religious leader has been significantly aided by the research of Gerardus Van der Leeuw. While every religious experience is, in a certain sense, a beginning, Van der Leeuw emphasized the especially intense degree of the experience of the religious founder. The divine power to which the founder witnesses is such that it has visible, large-scale historical effects. It arouses similar subsequent religious experiences for large numbers of other persons, both among his immediate followers and for a considerable historical period in the tradition that claims his inspiration. The founder functions as prophet, teacher, theologian, and reformer, and he becomes an exemplary model of the revelatory ideal that he mediates for his followers. Wach emphasized the imperative inherent in the founder's experience to find expression in thought structures, practice, and organizational forms. As a sociologist of religion, Wach particularly stressed the religious founder's charisma, the unique gift he had that led subsequent followers to adhere both to his person and to his message.

The founder's religious experience and charisma are elements contributing to his authority, and he reveals the truth and the way with an authority from beyond himself. The vocational form of the founder's authority varies from that of the prophet (Muhammad) to whom the truth is revealed by God, to AVATARS (Krishna) and the incarnation (Jesus) who embody the transcendent, to the wise men or sages (Lao Tzu or Confucius) who are illumined by the truth. While there is some difference in emphasis among the founders as emissaries of new teaching as opposed to their being exemplars of the ideal they proclaim, tradition asserts and appropriates the authority embodied in their lives and behavior as well as in their messages. Both oral and written tradition passed on by leaders of the tradition transmit the founder's practice, insight, or spirituality as normative for subsequent generations. Authority is sometimes viewed as a personal quality of individual leaders, gurus, or spiritual masters. At other times authority is embodied primarily in institutions or scriptures (e.g. TORAH or Qur'ān). Buddhist Sūtras begin, "Thus have I heard . . . ," thus deriving teaching, practice, and institutions from the words of the Buddha and his close followers. Orthodox Christianity is authorized in the life and teaching of Jesus and his apostles. Christian connotations of "founder" have led some Westerners to refer mistakenly to Islam as "Mohammedanism." But for Islam as for Judaism, God is the founder, the authority, and the focus of the story, including the story of the founder. Moses and Muhammad are venerated as prophets or messengers but, unlike Krishna and Jesus, they are not worshiped.

In all of the religious traditions there is a certain tension between the primordial character of the truth that is eternally true and the validation of truth by its specific revelation. The Qur'ān, for example, is a recitation from the "Mother of the Book," the eternal Book with ALLAH, although Muhammad is also the "Seal of the Prophets." Each of the founders reveals something new and thus is a reformer, but he is at the same time reannouncing or reenacting an ancient, primordial truth. Moses proclaims the commandments of the God of Abraham, Isaac, and Jacob; Gautama and Mahāvīra bring the truth of this age previously brought by a succession of Buddhas and TĪRTHAṄKARAS (crossing-makers); Krishna brings the "secret" previously revealed but lost; and Jesus is the LOGOS of God present at the creation and yet personally embodied in a specific human form. What appears to be innovation is depicted as reform, the recovery of the original way or truth. And even if there is expectation of a future founder-like figure (AVATAR, MESSIAH, MAITREYA, the MAHDI), or a recognized succession of spiritual leadership, the founder retains his status as the central authoritative figure of the tradition—as long as this age lasts.

b) Relation to transcendent reality. Theologically speaking, the authority of the religious founders lies in the unique character of their relations to a sacred Reality or a God. The richness and depth of the figures of the founders are larger than any single designation or title ascribed to them by their traditions. The founders reveal the transcendent through a certain hiddenness or mystery so that there is something unsayable or unfathomable about how they embody the human ideal. The character of this relationship varies from the founder's being "beyond gods and men" (Gautama), to his being divine (Krishna, Jesus), to his being "chosen" or "closer to God" (Moses, Muhammad, Zoroaster), to his having been "wiser" than other men (Confucius) or more "attuned" to the Way (Lao Tzu). In many cases the beginning of their vocations is marked by a "call" or "illumination" experience of great intensity. In other cases (Krishna, Jesus), the absence of such watershed experiences appears to underline their direct relation to the transcendent from their birth or even before.

Mahāvīra is the omniscient, venerable great hero, the conqueror of suffering and passion. Gautama is the awakened, enlightened teacher of truth. Later tradition understood Gautama as a human descent from or a manifestation of absolute reality (DHARMAKĀYA). Muhammad is the Seal of the Prophets, the friend and apostle of God, the human messenger who recites the Word of God. Moses is the chief of the prophets and the father of prophets through whom was mediated the covenant, law, and cult of the Torah. He was the "man of God" who spoke to God face to face. Zoroaster was the holy prophet who preached the truth, calling for moral earnestness in thought, word, and deed. He was the friend of truth and God's friend. Confucius was a social and political teacher, a religious man (but not a religious leader in the usual sense) who is later acclaimed as the supreme sage of the Confucian tradition. Krishna is God descended to the human stage in divine play; the divine being both veiled and revealed in his human form. Jesus the Christ is the human and divine Word of God who brought salvation in the nearness and presence of God; who died and rose again, ascended to heaven, and is the spirit of his body, the church. Lao Tzu was the miraculous sage empowered by the Tao, the source and course of the universe.

c) Exemplary models. The religious founders exhibit and proclaim a new image of the human being personified in their sacred biographies. True religious life becomes in many respects an imitation, reenactment, or participation in these saving symbols of human faith. The life of the prophet is for SUNNI Islam a spiritual guide to true submission (Islam). For the SUFI tradition Muhammad's legendary ascent to heaven (MI'RĀJ) becomes a model for the soul's ascent to God. Imitation of Christ is a frequent Christian theme. Krishna's play (LĪLĀ) is both joined and imitated by his devotees. The Buddha ideal is approached by the ARHANT. The enlightenment of the BODHISATTVA reveals the Buddha nature within.

d) Mediators. The founders are depicted as human beings with limitations and some vulnerability. But they are also set apart, and they tend to occupy a structural position between a sacred reality and the human sphere. Their missions are not merely the product of previous history but are, in some sense, the inbreaking of transcendent power. The mediating function of founders is frequently evidenced in liturgy. Buddhists take refuge in the Buddha as well as in his teaching and in the monastic community. After his confession of the unity of God, the Muslim acknowledges Muhammad as the apostle (RASŪL) of God. The Christian prays and worships through the Christ and in his name. Repeating Krishna's name is the practice of the presence of God. Moses, however, is not mentioned in the Passover HAGGADAH, and is of only minor importance in the psalms and the early prophets. Moses and Muhammad are mediators only in a secondary sense. Closer to God than other men, they are models of the ideal of true worship.

e) Deliverers. Most and perhaps all of the major religious traditions detect something fundamentally wrong with the human condition that needs to be set right. The founders bring deliverance from this "out-of-joint" situation. They are the channels through which human beings may be delivered from meaninglessness or evil. They institute the way human life should be transformed to achieve its true purpose. Through the founders, meaning is provided, a way through pain and suffering is demonstrated, sleepers are awakened, broken relationships are restored, obedience is commanded and made possible, true human society is revealed, and death is mitigated.

f) Leaders. The Muslim calendar begins, not with the revelation of the Qur'ān to Muhammad, but with the foundation of the Islamic state in MEDINA. Islam is ideally the submission of all of life to the will of Allah. Thus Muhammad was political leader and legislator as well as prophet, especially while he was in Medina. The leadership traditionally ascribed to Moses also extended over the entire community in all respects, social and political as well as specifically religious. The social, political, and institutional impact of other religious founders was typically more indirect, being mediated through their traditions and in the course of their development. To Mahāvīra and the Buddha are ascribed the institution of regulations and ritual for both the monastic and lay communities. The authority for the foundation of the Sikh *khālsā panth* (community of the pure) is traced ultimately back to Nānak. Confucius and MENCIUS (the "Second Sage" of the Confucian tradition) provided the principles of government and society that at least to some degree became embodied in Chinese government, civil service, and family structure.

4. Renewal of the saving story. The lives of the religious founders have been continually expanded, developed, appropriated, and reinterpreted as later generations in the traditions seek the founders' meaning for their own times. New contexts provoke the discovery of new facets of their power and relevance. In the last twenty-five years, for example, new saving stories have developed of Jesus as the leader, as the liberator, and as the mediator of a Black theology for the racially oppressed. Gautama Buddha has been demythologized as a philosophical teacher, as a therapist, and as a near-Marxist social reformer. Muhammad has also been rediscovered as the reforming force leading to a still-to-be-achieved ideal Islamic society.

Bibliography. G. Van der Leeuw, *Religion in Essence and Manifestation* (1938); F. E. Reynolds and D. Capps, eds., *The Biographical Process* (1976); G. Parrinder, *Avatar and Incarnation* (1970); G. Widengren, "Prolegomena: The Value of Source Criticism as Illustrated by the Biographical Dates of the Great Founders," in C. J. Bleeker and Widengren, *Historia Religionum,* II (1971), 1-22; J. Wach, *Sociology of Religion* (1962), pp. 331-74.

J. Y. FENTON

FOUR NOBLE TRUTHS (B). Four interconnected insights into human existence that summarize Buddhist teaching and practice.

1. Setting. The four noble truths were, according to tradition, formulated by the Buddha as a means of instructing five students of asceticism who comprised his first audience and who became his first disciples. The BUDDHA's four truths were quite different from those espoused in the ancient VEDAS of the ARYAN priests (BRAHMINS), but he nonetheless called them *āryan* truths. In so doing he dismissed the racial and social connotations Vedic authors attached to *ārya* and gave the term an ethical interpretation of "noble" or "fine." The great commentator BUDDHAGHOSA gives other reasons for the term *noble* here, explaining that the four truths are called noble because they are taught by noble ones, such as the Buddha; because realizing these four truths leads to a state of nobleness; and because they are true.

Later in his teaching career the Buddha similarly gave new ethical interpretations to other Vedic concepts such as "knower of the three Vedas" and

"BRAHMAN/Brahmin." Thus, the Buddha's teachings altered what was meant by *truth* and *knowledge* in the orthodox interpretations of the Brahmins to conform with the tradition of meditating sages. Consequently, the Buddha was most commonly known in his day and in early Buddhism as the "Sage of the Śākyan Clan" (ŚĀKYAMUNI).

2. **Medical formula.** The Buddha is said to have formulated his insights, gained from meditation, in a fourfold form suggestive of a medical formula, and for this reason he was also revered under the titles "Peerless Physician" and "Supreme Surgeon." The first of the four truths is said to name the *symptom;* in this case, suffering. The second truth is comparable to a *diagnosis,* the third to a *prognosis,* and the fourth to a *prescription* designed to cure the symptom.

The medical formula is not intended for a particular disease, however, but for all dis-ease; so the four truths apply to all human existence and express all Buddhist wisdom. As SĀRIPUTTA, a leading disciple of the Buddha, expressed it: just as an elephant's footprint can contain all other kinds of footprints, so the four noble truths encompass all other truths (Middle Length Sayings 28).

3. **Suffering.** The first truth is the truth of suffering (DUKKHA). The Buddha explained that birth is suffering, aging is suffering, death is suffering; sorrow, lamentation, pain, grief, and despair are suffering. He summarized his point by saying that all five mental and physical components of the person (the five SKANDHAS) are subject to suffering (*see* ANATTA).

The meaning of the first truth is that human existence is characterized by unsatisfactoriness, dis-ease—which is the meaning of the word *dukkha.* This is not to deny that humans do enjoy many moments of happiness and many satisfactions, but rather to point out that even pleasant experiences and relationships lead to suffering due to their transitory nature. Humans suffer physically when they are too hot or too cold, when they are being born, when they are sick, when they become ill, and when they eventually become senile and then die. They suffer mentally when they are forced by circumstances to be with someone or something they dislike, or when they are separated by death or other reasons from someone or something that they are attached to. Hence, all worldly attachments, whether temporarily pleasant or painful, eventually lead to suffering and rebirth.

4. **Cause.** The second noble truth is that suffering is caused by craving (TANHĀ). The Buddha taught the five ascetics that craving is the origin of suffering, for craving, together with lust and greed, keeps the person oriented toward transitory existence rather than NIRVANA. Such craving may be of three types, the Buddha continued. It may be craving for sensual pleasures (and the avoidance of displeasures), craving for existence itself, or craving for nonexistence. The person who craves for existence commits the Eternalist heresy and the one who craves for nonexistence is an Annihilationist, according to the Buddhist tradition.

With the senses and the mind itself deeply rooted in desire for what is pleasant, ironically, humans are led into more and more suffering.

5. **Cessation.** The third noble truth is that the cessation of suffering (*dukkha*-NIRODHA) is possible. The realization of this truth involves a further insight into the nature of causation. It has been seen in the second truth that craving is the cause of suffering, and here in the third truth one is to realize that craving itself could be eliminated, and without the continuing support of craving, suffering would soon cease.

In the words ascribed to the Buddha, the noble truth of the extinction of suffering foresees the complete fading away, the giving up, the detachment from craving—which amounts to liberation. Elsewhere, the Buddha said that the exhaustion of craving is Nirvana.

6. **Path.** The fourth truth is the EIGHTFOLD PATH leading to the extinction of suffering. The eight parts of the path are not to be taken up successively, like rungs of a ladder, but are to be co-practiced. The eight parts embrace the whole of Buddhist practice, it is said, although they make no direct reference to such cultic practices as veneration of the Buddha, the BODHI tree, and the STŪPA. To put the matter another way, the Eightfold Path is principally a way to Nirvana rather than a path of merit leading to rebirth in heaven.

7. **Analogies.** There are a number of pedagogical analogies used by Buddhist teachers and commentators to assist in understanding how the four truths are related to one another. One is the analogy of a disease already mentioned. Another is that the truth of suffering is like a burden; the truth of origin is like the bearing of the burden; the truth of cessation is like the putting down of the burden; and the path is like the way to put down the burden. Or, the four may be compared to a danger, the root of the danger, freedom from danger, and the means to that freedom.

8. **Realization.** The four noble truths are thought of as being deep and difficult to comprehend. The Buddha once asked his disciple ĀNANDA which was easier for a skillful archer, to shoot several arrows through a small hole or to split a hair one hundred times. When he agreed that splitting a hair would be the more difficult, the Buddha remarked that it is even more difficult to penetrate with understanding the four noble truths. He concluded by urging his disciple, who was not yet enlightened, to make a great effort to fathom the four noble truths (*Kindred Sayings,* V. 381-82).

The realization of the four noble truths is typically the result of insight-meditation (*see* MAHĀSATIPAṬṬĀNA SUTTA). Consequently it has traditionally been a goal of monks more than of lay Buddhists, who have often been content with acts of merit and lesser levels of understanding of the four noble truths. For this reason, the four noble truths do not play a large role in LAY BUDDHISM and its worship, but they do figure in sermons and especially in meditation.

Bibliography. "The Foundation of the Kingdom of the Norm," *The Book of the Kindred Sayings* (1965), V. 356-65, a primary resource; A. J. Bahm, *Philosophy of the Buddha* (1969), an interpretive approach by a Western scholar; Buddhaghosa, *The Path of Purity,* P. M. Tin, trans. (1971), pp. 585 ff., the most important Theravāda Buddhist commentator's description of the four noble truths and the path; V. V. Gunaratne, *The Significance of the Four Noble Truths,* Wheel Publication no. 123 (1968); Piyadassi Thera, *The Buddha's Ancient Path* (1964), an exposition of the four noble truths by a Sinhalese bhikkhu; R. Story, *The Four Noble Truths,* Wheel Publication no. 34/35 (1968).

R. C. AMORE

FOUR STAGES OF LIFE (H). *See* ĀŚRAMA.

FOX, GEORGE (Ch; 1624-1691). A practical mystic who was the major founder and early leader of the SOCIETY OF FRIENDS; known as a great preacher, controversialist, and writer.

Bibliography. *Journal*, ed. J. Nickalls (1952).

M. ENDY

FRANCIS OF ASSISI (Ch; 1182-1226). Founder of the Friars Minor (OFM). Imprisonment during war and serious illness led the young Francis to a serious reflection about life. A journey to Rome, where he dressed as a beggar, and a vision of Christ telling him to rebuild the church resulted in conversion. He married "Lady Poverty," worked among lepers, and rebuilt churches. His example of apostolic poverty attracted disciples, and INNOCENT III granted verbal approval to the new order in 1209. The FRIARS preached and worked among the poor, making a strong impression when the church was being criticized for its wealth.

When Francis returned from a visit to the Near East in 1219-20, he found that the order had compromised his ideals, particularly that of poverty. Practical necessity required a revision of his rule, and the order was divided into liberal, moderate, and conservative wings.

According to FRANCISCAN tradition, Francis lived the rest of his life in solitude and poor health, receiving the STIGMATA, the wounds of Christ, on his body in 1224. His simplicity, charity, and love of nature have made him one of the most popular saints. He was canonized less than two years after his death.

Bibliography. B. Fahy, trans., *The Writings of St. Francis* (1963); L. Cunningham, *Saint Francis of Assisi* (1976); *The Little Flowers of Saint Francis* was produced a century after his death to support the ideals of the conservatives in the order.

W. O. PAULSELL

FRANCIS OF SALES (Ch; 1567-1622). Mystic and leader in the CATHOLIC REFORMATION in French-speaking lands. Ordained in 1593, he began missionary work in Chablais, Savoy, where he debated Calvinists and won converts to Catholicism. In 1620 he was made Bishop of Geneva.

His best known writing is his *Introduction to the Devout Life* (1608). Its five parts treat the desire for a devout life, prayer and the sacraments, the practice of virtue, temptation, and exercises for spiritual renewal. In 1616 he published *On the Love of God.* With Jeanne de Chantal, he founded the order of the Visitation nuns. He was canonized in 1665, declared a Doctor of the Church in 1877, and in 1923 proclaimed patron saint of writers.

Bibliography. R. Kleinman, *Saint Francois de Sales and the Protestants* (1962).

W. O. PAULSELL

FRANCIS XAVIER zā´ vĭ ər (Ch; 1506-1552). Spanish JESUIT missionary to India, Sri Lanka, Malaya, and Japan; canonized in 1622. With IGNATIUS OF LOYOLA, he was a founding member of the Jesuits in 1534.

F. OAKLEY

FRANCISCANS frăn sĭs´ kənz (Ch). MENDICANT FRIARS of three Roman Catholic RELIGIOUS ORDERS originating from St. FRANCIS OF ASSISI and his joyful gospel ideals of poverty, brotherhood, prayer, preaching, and peace. The Friars Minor (OFM), Friars Minor Conventual (OFMConv), and Friars Minor CAPUCHIN (OFMCap) divided over practice of Francis' ideals. Their ministry is mainly preaching, missions, and parish service, but also scholarship and teaching. Poor Clares are women in the Second Order of St. Francis. Laity follow Franciscan ideals individually as members of the Third Order. Some men among these united as the Third Order Regular of St. Francis (TOR); its rule is followed by many active Franciscan sisterhoods who are Third Order members.

W. H. PRINCIPE

FREE CHURCH (Ch). Any denomination free from government control or support, in contrast to an ESTABLISHED CHURCH. In England, BAPTISTS, CONGREGATIONALISTS, PRESBYTERIANS, and others are free churches, and in Scotland several groups that left the Church of Scotland have been so designated.

K. CRIM

FREEMASONRY (Ch). The common designation of secret fraternal orders and related groups descended from medieval guilds of stonemasons. In the seventeenth and eighteenth centuries these guilds were joined by persons who were not "operating" masons, but interested in their "speculative" side—the teachings inculcated by the guilds' impressive rituals. That movement was stimulated by the formation of the Grand Lodge of England in 1717.

In the eighteenth century Masonic lodges were popular among freethinkers, deists, and political progressives, and did much to disseminate such ideas, as well as the teachings of SWEDENBORGIANISM and ROSICRUCIANISM. The rituals are influenced by the symbols of medieval and renaissance occultism, while their content is of a deistic and ethical character. The Roman Catholic Church and a few Protestant bodies have traditionally been opposed to Freemasonry.

In the 1970s there were nearly six million Freemasons worldwide, of whom four million were in the U.S. and one million in Great Britain. In the English-speaking world Freemasonry is now relatively nonideological, and for many members as much social as spiritual. In Latin countries, however, it retains a strongly anti-clerical and rationalistic character.

Bibliography. J. Katz, *Jews and Freemasons in Europe 1725-1939* (1970); N. Mackenzie, ed., *Secret Societies* (1971); F. Pilk, *et al.*, *Pocket History of Freemasonry* (1969).

R. S. ELLWOOD

FRIAR (Ch— Lat. "brother"). A member of one of the four Roman Catholic monastic orders that have been supported by alms (FRANCISCANS, DOMINICANS, CARMELITES, and AUGUSTINIANS); occasionally used of monks in other orders. K. WATKINS

FRIENDS, SOCIETY OF (Ch). A form of radical Christianity that arose in England during the splintering of PURITANISM in the 1650s; it is marked especially by its belief in the divine light of Christ in all people, its meditative form of worship or group MYSTICISM in reliance on the Holy Spirit, and its humanitarian social witness. Known also as Quakerism, the Society of Friends can be understood as either a radical form of PROTESTANTISM or as a third form of Western Christianity, relying on the inner light as its main authority, instead of the Roman Catholic and Protestant reliance, respectively, on church and scripture. Some Friends, because of the belief in the universality of the inner light and Quaker opposition to creeds, see themselves as mediators between Christianity and other religions or as being identifiable more by a style of living than by beliefs.

1. **History.** The Society of Friends crystallized in England in the early 1650s out of the experiences of Seekers, General BAPTISTS, Ranters, and others who began experiencing a new dispensation of the Spirit. GEORGE FOX was the preeminent leader of the new movement. It was marked by the belief that the divine light within all people brought true religion by enabling one to experience a radical rebirth and to cultivate a style of living that culminated in perfect obedience to God. It included such distinctive elements as plain speech and dress and refusal to pay tithes, take oaths, use pagan names for days and months, and engage in worldly courtesies such as doffing one's hat. Although persecuted until 1689, the English Quakers continued to grow and to establish Quaker meetings in many parts of the world, especially in the British colonies in America, where WILLIAM PENN's "holy experiment" was especially notable.

Their eschatological hopes for transforming the world having waned by 1700, the Friends began to withdraw from "the world" and to stress their distinctive attributes. The Puritan heritage of the movement, however, made it susceptible to influences from PIETISM later in the eighteenth century and led some Friends to regain their Protestant moorings. The resultant clashes between those, such as Elias Hicks and John Wilbur, who emphasized the uniqueness of Quakerism, and more evangelical Friends, such as J. J. Gurney and later revivalists and even FUNDAMENTALISTS, led to diversity and division in England and America in the nineteenth and early twentieth centuries. A variety of forces, including the American Friends Service Committee founded by Rufus Jones in 1917, produced a unification process in the twentieth century. The major groups in the United States today are the Friends United Meeting (moderately evangelical; 66,000), Friends General Conference (liberal; 26,000), and the Evangelical Friends Alliance (extremely evangelical and fundamentalist; 26,000). Of the nearly 200,000 Friends in the world in 1978, 121,000 were in the United States, 20,000 in Great Britain, 45,000 in Africa (F.U.M. converts), and 6,000 in Latin America (E.F.A. converts).

2. **Beliefs and practices.** The central Quaker conviction is that the saving knowledge and power of God are present as divine influences in all human beings through what is variously called the inner light, the light of the eternal Christ within, or "that of God." This belief has inevitably produced distinctive approaches to, and often de-emphasis on, the historic Christian doctrines of the TRINITY, the person and work of Christ, bondage to sin, and the uniqueness of Christianity. Although some evangelical Friends have "pastoral meetings" and Quakers rely on recorded ministers, clerks, ELDERS, and DEACONS, they have no ordained ministers and do not celebrate the SACRAMENTS. Belief in "that of God" in every person is also responsible for the distinctive form of Friends' worship, and accounts for their general confidence in working for the kingdom of God in the world and their specific emphases on peace, relief of suffering, abolition of slavery, and prison reform. In governance as in worship, the Friends rely on the guidance of the inner light working through any individual and bringing the whole group to a consensus. Although largely congregational in operation, the Society has a hierachy of administrative units including monthly, quarterly, and yearly meetings as well as associations linking various yearly meetings.

Bibliography. H. Brinton, *Friends for Three Hundred Years* (1952); the journals of George Fox (ed. J. Nickalls, 1952) and John Woolman (ed. P. Moulton, 1971). M. ENDY

FUJI, MOUNT fōō′ jē. A cone-shaped dormant volcano 12,388 feet (3,776 m) above sea level, the highest mountain in Japan, located about seventy-

Fogg Art Museum, Harvard University, loan from the Kimiko and John Powers Collection

Mount Fuji, Japanese silk hanging scroll (Nagasawa Rosetsu, 18th century)

five miles southwest of Tokyo. From ancient times its aesthetic beauty and sacred character have been extolled in poetry and acted out in ritual. It has erupted frequently in recorded history, most recently in 1707.

Although it is sometimes known in the West as "Fujiyama," the correct Japanese name is Fujisan. This confusion arose because the names of Japanese mountains contain a Chinese character that may be pronounced in either of two ways: *yama* or *san*. Some mountains are called *yama,* the Japanese word for mountain, and others are called *san,* the Japanese pronunciation of the Chinese loan word for mountain.

The eighth century anthology of poetry, the *Man'yoshu,* contains poems celebrating the mountain's beauty. Ascent of Fuji is recorded in a ninth century account, and through medieval times Buddhists visited the mountain; also the mountain ascetics known as YAMABUSHI climbed Fuji as part of their religious austerities. Konohana-sakuyahime is considered the goddess of Mount Fuji, and there is a tradition of an early SHINTŌ shrine constructed for her. But the opening of climbing routes probably dates from the fifteenth century, due to the efforts of *yamabushi.* In the seventeenth century pilgrimage associations called *kō,* made up of laymen, began to climb the mountain in considerable numbers. Women were barred from climbing beyond the first station until after the MEIJI Restoration of 1868.

The religious character of Mount Fuji is not unique, but should be understood in terms of the Japanese heritage of "mountain religion" *(sangaku shinkō),* the widespread veneration of Japanese mountains. Nature is highly regarded in Japan, and mountains are seen in various sacred aspects: as bridges to the other world for humans, a means of descent for divinities (KAMI), as sources of water and fertility. Pilgrims who climb Mount Fuji observe the practices of their particular sect. Traditionally pilgrims have worn a white robe (white for purity), used straw sandals, and carried the pilgrim's staff. If possible, they arrive at the summit at sunrise to greet the rising sun, and then visit the Shintō shrine at the summit. Probably they have already stopped at one of the Shintō shrines around the base of the mountain. The ascent and descent are possible in two days, with an overnight stay in one of the many mountain huts built for pilgrims.

There is now a road, with bus service partway up the mountain. A large number of secular tourists climb the mountain during July or August. Mount Fuji and its immediate environs are a national park, since this is a remarkable site for the study of nature.

H. B. EARHART

FUNDAMENTALISM (Ch). A term originally applied to opponents of liberal PROTESTANTISM. The name originated with the publication of a series of tracts, *The Fundamentals* (1910-13), a widely distributed defense of the conservative position.

The roots of fundamentalism, however, antedate these pamphlets. After the Civil War, American Christians had to deal with the issues raised by Darwin, higher criticism of the BIBLE, and industrialization. These issues placed stress on the fabric of American evangelicalism, and pastors as well as theologians took different views of their significance. Liberals saw them as providing an opportunity for a major revision of belief, while conservatives feared that they might erode the historic Christian faith.

Two nineteenth century movements helped some conservatives come to terms with the modern world: DISPENSATIONALISM and the Princeton theology. Dispensationalism combined a literal interpretation of the Bible and a resultant rejection of evolution and higher criticism with a view of SALVATION that was largely otherworldly. It represented a retreat on the part of evangelical Christians from the social issues of the day.

The Princeton theology originated at Princeton Theological Seminary, which had been founded to protect historic PREBYTERIANISM from DEISM and REVIVALISM. The school sought to defend the WESTMINSTER CONFESSION and the related CATECHISMS as a true expression of biblical faith.

In the latter part of the nineteenth century, partially under the leadership of B. B. Warfield (1851-1921), Princeton and its graduates became committed to the defense of orthodoxy against biblical criticism. Under its leadership, the Presbyterian Church in the U.S.A. issued the Portland Declaration, which affirmed five points as necessary to Christian faith: the verbal inspiration of the Bible, the VIRGIN BIRTH, the substitutionary doctrine of the ATONEMENT, the miracles of JESUS, and the physical character of the RESURRECTION. This position was reaffirmed in 1893, 1894, 1899, and 1910. As a result of this addition to the standards, professors Charles A. Briggs and Henry P. Smith were tried and convicted of heresy.

Characteristic of Princeton orthodoxy was its insistence that only the original manuscripts of the Bible were without error. There was, however, a need for textual criticism, since later copies of the text contained errors.

In the 1920s, fundamentalists and liberals engaged in a classic confrontation. In the midst of a religious decline, conservatives believed that liberals were gaining control of the most influential pulpits and denominational offices. The conflict was most bitter in the Presbyterian Church, where Harry Emerson Fosdick, a popular visiting minister at the First Presbyterian Church in New York City, became the symbol of the dispute. Northern BAPTISTS were also divided. The result of the dispute in that denomination was the loss of many churches, the formation of new conventions (national organizations), and a continuing bitterness in Baptist affairs.

In the popular mind the drive for laws prohibiting the teaching of evolution in the public schools was the center of the fundamentalist movement. The 1925 trial of John Scopes in Tennessee for teaching evolution was the climax of this aspect of the movement. (*See* CREATIONISM.)

During the 30s and 40s, the fundamentalist movement largely disappeared from public view and spent its time building its own institutions. In the late 1940s, it emerged from this self-imposed isolation to begin playing a major role in church affairs. *See* EVANGELICALS. G. MILLER

G

GABAR gä´ bär, **GAUR** gōr (Z—Per. [Arab. *kāfir*—"unbeliever"]). A derogatory term used until modern times, particularly by Muslims, to denote a member of the Zoroastrian community of Iran. Such a person would refer to himself as *zartoshtī,* "Zoroastrian," or *behdīn,* "of the Good Religion." The Zoroastrians of Iran, numbering fewer than thirty thousand by even the most generous estimates, constitute only about one-tenth of one percent of Iran's population and therefore only a tiny remnant of what was the national religion of that land before Islam. For centuries they survived in villages in central Iran; in modern times many have migrated to the nearby cities of Yazd and Kirman and from there to Tehran, the capital, where half the Iranian Zoroastrians now live.

Bibliography. M. Boyce, *A Persian Stronghold of Zoroastrianism* (1977).

W. G. Oxtoby

GABRIEL gä´ brē əl (Ju, Ch & I). In the Bible, an Angel who appears to Daniel (Dan. 8:16; 9:21) and, as the angel of the Annunciation, to the father of John the Baptist and to Mary (Luke 1:11-38). Christian tradition makes him the archangel whose trumpet signals the Last Judgment (I Thess. 4:16). In Islam, Gabriel (Jibrīl) is the angel who revealed the Qur'ān to Muhammad.

R. Bullard

GAMALIEL THE ELDER gə māl´ yəl (Ju). Grandson of Hillel, Gamaliel lived in the first half of the first century A.D. According to Acts 22:3 Paul was among his students. He was responsible for a number of legal reforms, especially those having to do with women's rights (Gittin 4:2-3).

E. M. Meyers

GAṆAPATI gän ä pät´ ē (H). *See* Gaṇeśa.

GANDHĀRA gŭn där´ ŭ. A region in the area of what is now northwest Pakistan and northeast Afghanistan, and a composite style of art (first century B.C.—sixth century A.D.) named after that region. Located on the trade routes connecting the Mediterranean and Persian world with India, Central Asia, and China, Gandhāra was noteworthy for the manner in which it produced art forms whose motifs were to a large degree Buddhist but whose stylistic origins were predominantly classical Greek and Roman, with Iranian and Central Asian features often present.

From the standpoint of Buddhist art one of Gandhāra's striking contributions was the development of anthropomorphic imagery of the Buddha. Drawing its inspiration from the Śākyamuni legends more than from the Jātaka stories of the Buddha's earlier lives, it evolved not only Buddha images but sculptural forms of Bodhisattvas along with a host of human and divine figures paying homage to the Buddha. The Gandhāra style, with its distinct classical references and its multitude of images both in stone and stucco, may be contrasted with the Mathurā style of Indian Buddhist sculpture which was evolving at the same time in the eastern sector of the Kushan empire and which matured under Gupta influences beginning in the fourth century A.D. These two styles include the earliest known representations of Buddha images and have been extensively compared for their very different portrayals. Among the many other aspects of Gandhāran Buddhist art is its more vertical development of the Stūpa, seen by some to be a foreshadowing of the Pagodas found soon afterwards in East Asia. *See* Art and Architecture, Buddhist.

Bibliography. M. Bussagli, "Gandhara," *Encyclopedia of World Art,* Vol. VI; M. Hallade, *Gandharan Art of North India* (1968), and *The Gandhara Style* (1968); J. Marshall, *The Buddhist Art of Gandhāra* (1960); A. K. Narain, *The Indo-Greeks* (1957); H. Zimmer, *The Art of Indian Asia,* 2 vols. (1955).

B. L. Smith

GANDHARVA gŭn där´ vŭ (H—Skt.; lit. "imbibers of song," hence, "musician"). As a single personage, a demigod or semi-divine being who dwells in the aerial region; as a generic class of beings, celestial musicians who live in the ocean as subjects of VARUṆA, the Lord of the Deep. *Gandharvas* are half-man, half-bird creatures who are renowned for guarding the sacred beverage (SOMA), which they stole from the gods. Among their extraordinary powers is a knowledge of all celestial secrets, sovereignty over the powers of fecundation in the waters, and the ability to control the hearts of women. As an extention of their erotic natures, they are invoked at all marriage ceremonies, and the form of marriage based on mutual consent (i.e., a love match) is named for them.

The Rig Veda knows only one *gandharva,* Viśvavasu, the father of YAMA and Yamī, who protects the soma and presents it to the gods. According to later tradition, the *gandharvas* were born from the nose of BRAHMĀ and drink of the essence of the goddess of speech *(vāc),* whence their epithet, "Imbibers of Song." The wild, intoxicated, long-haired *Munis* are said to travel by the way of the APSARAS, *gandharvas,* and deer, and these same characters are described as lustful, charming, and highly spirited. They are believed to cause ecstatic states of mind and possession by evil spirits. Because of their guardianship over soma, they are invoked as physicians who possess the antidote to all human afflictions.

In the Epics and PURĀṆAS, *gandharvas* are a special class of semi-divine beings, 6,000 in number, who dwell in INDRA's paradise. They are often employed by the gods to seduce saints and ascetics when the latter threaten to surpass the power of the gods through their severe penances. Like YAKṢAS, whom they resemble in many ways, the *gandharvas* are ambivalent creatures, at once the cause of all forms of possession and mental derangement and the ever-reliable protectors against the attacks of malevolent spirits.

J. B. LONG

GANDHI, MOHANDAS KARAMCHAND

gän´ dē mō hŭn´ däs kä´ rŭm chänd (H; 1869-1948). Twentieth-century Indian leader known as the *Mahatma* (lit. "great souled") because of his social, political, and religious activity. Although Gandhi was world famous for his role in India's independence movement, millions of dispossessed Indians whom he named HARIJANS ("children of God") knew him simply as their friend and "beloved Father" *(bapuji).*

1. **Life.** Born in the western Indian seaside town of Porbandar, Gandhi was the youngest of four children of the politician Karamchand and his deeply religious wife, Putlibai. His early years reflected the traditional yet advantaged life of one born into the privileged Bania CASTE. His arranged marriage at age thirteen to the attractive Kasturbai set the stage for the most influential event of his youth. One night Gandhi left his father's sickbed to enjoy love-making with his wife only to be interrupted by a servant who said that his father had just died. Gandhi later said that this traumatic experience served as an impetus for his emphasis on ascetic self-restraint (TAPAS).

Mohandas K. Gandhi

Gandhi studied law in England (1888-91) but seemed more excited by encounters with THEOSOPHISTS, CHRISTIANS (especially JESUS' SERMON ON THE MOUNT), and his own religion's BHAGAVAD GĪTĀ. Upon his return to India he tried to follow a legal career in Porbandar but was both uncomfortable and ineffectual. When a MUSLIM firm asked him to represent them in South Africa for a year, Gandhi accepted.

One of his first cases in South Africa required Gandhi to travel to Pretoria. Though dressed as an English barrister and holding a first-class ticket, he was ordered to leave the first-class compartment and retire to the baggage car, due to a white man's complaint about riding with a "colored man." When Gandhi refused he was thrown off the train. Shivering throughout the cold night in the hill station of Maritzburg, Gandhi vowed to fight against racial prejudice in South Africa. For the next twenty-one years (1893-1914), he devoted much of his time, money, and talents to perfecting the spiritual and political technique he called SATYĀGRAHA (lit., "truth force").

Upon his return to India in 1915, Gandhi immediately threw his considerable talents into India's struggle for political independence. Though at first he tried to reconcile both British and Indian interests, a massacre in Amritsar at Jallianwalla Bagh in 1919 galvanized Gandhi's growing opposition to *any* British role in India's future. His opposition took the forms of *satyāgraha* techniques such as writing for periodicals (e.g., *Young India* and *Harijan*), fasts (e.g., Ahmedabad Mill fast of 1918 and the

Hindu-Muslim fast of 1947), and noncooperation campaigns (e.g., the Salt March of 1930).

Throughout Gandhi's long struggle for Indian self-rule, he was as concerned with the personal growth of the *satyāgrahi* ("truth-seeker") as with the ultimate goal of political independence. Ironically, it was precisely Gandhi's efforts through a fast, speeches, and compromises to heal Hindu-Muslim antagonisms during 1947 that led to his death at the hands of a Hindu extremist.

2. Thought. Upon the assumptions of *satyā* (truth), AHIṂSĀ (noninjury) and TAPAS (self-restraint) Gandhi built his plan of practical action or *satyāgraha*. Derived from a SANSKRIT root *sat*, which literally means "being" or "reality," *satyā* refers not just to veracity of speech but more generally to a way of living. Since Absolute or Transcendent Truth (later equated with "God" by Gandhi) cannot be fully known, humans can live or act out only relative truths. Therefore, while *satyāgraha* campaigns always focused upon a goal (e.g., better wages and working conditions for Ahmedabad mill workers), the content of such a relative truth was not unalterable for Gandhi. On the other hand, the "force of truth" depends upon the assumption that each person has an innate "center" reflecting Absolute Truth.

For Gandhi, Absolute Truth is characterized by *ahiṃsā*. Moving beyond some traditional, negative interpretations of it as the absence of harm or injury, Gandhi asserted a positive notion of *ahiṃsā* as "the largest love" or "fullest compassion." A life based upon Truth and marked by *ahiṃsā* requires self-sacrifice and active compassion for others, not merely an absence of harming. Thus to awaken the Truth that lies dormant in an opponent may require accepting physical and mental abuse oneself. Here the age-old Indian concept of self-denying austerity was used by Gandhi, who asserted that true "self-rule" *(swarāj)* is first self-control and a disciplined will, and only then economic and/or political self-determination.

To act nonviolently is not merely to withhold angry actions from a superior foe (like a frightened mouse before a hungry cat), but to act with the force *(graha)* of truth *(satyā)* honed by compassion and self-restraint. For Gandhi the means is "the ends in the making." Therefore, hatred is far more dangerous to the one who hates than to the one who is hated. A successful violent revolution will be haunted by its means of accomplishment. For Gandhi, Absolute Truth is necessarily marked by nonviolence and self-giving.

3. Legacy. Gandhi's life and thought led in his day to a SARVODAYA (lit., "giving to all") land-sharing movement led by Vinobe Bhave, and in the 1970s to a similar Buddhist relief movement by the same name in Sri Lanka. The civil rights movement in America was given nonviolent impetus by Gandhi through MARTIN LUTHER KING, JR., though it was couched in Christian categories and symbols. Furthermore, the first non-Congress Party to rule since India's independence (i.e., the Janata Party) used Gandhian economic and political platforms for its appeal and was headed by Marorji Desai, a long-time *satyāgrahi*. Yet the real legacy Gandhi left in such symbols as the spinning wheel (a symbol of total "self-rule") was a model of a simple and self-sacrificing life which is often ignored in favor of the political strategies and techniques of *satyāgraha*.

Bibliography. M. K. Gandhi, *An Autobiography or My Experiments with Truth* (1927), and *My Religion*, B. Kamarappa, ed. (1955); R. Iyer, *The Moral and Political Thought of Mahatma Gandhi* (1978); J. Bondurant, *Conquest of Violence* (1965); L. Fischer, *The Life of Mahatma Gandhi* (1950).

L. D. SHINN

GAṆEŚA gŭ nēsh´ ŭ (H). Elephant-faced son of SHIVA and PĀRVATĪ, who is worshiped as the overcomer of obstacles at the beginnings of rites or other undertakings.

Gaṇeśa, whose name means lord *(īśa)* of the group *(gaṇa)* of Shiva's attendants, is also known by other names: Gaṇapati (leader of the group), Vināyaka (obstacle-remover), Lamdodara (pot-bellied one), Gajānana (elephant-headed one), and Piḷḷiyār (son). There are no explicit references to Gaṇeśa as an elephant-headed deity in the RIG VEDA, although there is one brief MANTRA to him in the White YAJUR VEDA (23.30). His full entry into the world of Hindu myth and worship comes during and after the GUPTA period (*ca.* A.D. 320).

Myths of Gaṇeśa appear in most of the major PURĀṆAS regardless of their sectarian affiliations and revolve around three themes: his birth, his beheading

P. Courtright

Gaṇeśa

and restoration, and his placing and removing obstacles.

Gaṇeśa's birth takes place, according to most variants, when Pārvatī desired to have a son, but Shiva refused to conceive one with her or was absent altogether. She therefore scrubbed the surface of her body, and out of the material from the scrubbing she fashioned a small child. She commanded life to come into the child and took him as her son. In some variants of the myth the child is created with the head of an elephant, but in most he receives his head from Shiva after some tribulation.

Gaṇeśa's beheading occurs when, on instruction from Pārvatī, he denies Shiva entry into her private quarters. Shiva, who does not know Gaṇeśa's identity as Pārvatī's son, becomes angry and in the battle that follows cuts off Gaṇeśa's head. In other versions of the story Paraśurāma attempts to gain entrance into Shiva and Pārvatī's bedchamber and beheads Gaṇeśa, who guards the doorway to prevent him, or Gaṇeśa loses his head as the result of a cursed glance by Śani (Saturn) when Pārvatī displays her new child to the assembly of the gods. In each case, Gaṇeśa's headless condition provokes Pārvatī's rage to the point that she threatens to destroy the universe and all the gods unless the head of her son is restored. Shiva dispatches his attendants to find the first suitable head and bring it to him. They return with the head of an elephant, by some accounts the head of INDRA's elephant, Airāvata, and Shiva restores the child. He then adopts him as his own son and gives him charge over all his attendants. He instructs the gods to worship Gaṇeśa at the beginning of all rites and undertakings in order to avoid calamity and achieve success.

The stories of Gaṇeśa as the one who places obstacles probably come from his association with a class of demons *(vināyakas)* which were originally thought to bring calamities of all sorts unless they were propitiated with rites and offerings. In one myth Gaṇeśa creates difficulties for the pious devotees of Shiva when the heavens were becoming overcrowded with good people. Gaṇeśa also curses the king of Banāres, Divodāsa, and causes the city to be emptied so that Shiva and Pārvatī might make it their home.

More commonly, however, Gaṇeśa is regarded as the remover of obstacles and the upholder of righteousness (DHARMA). According to a myth regarding the composition of the epic MAHĀBHĀRATA, Gaṇeśa agreed to serve as the scribe to the sage Vyāsa, but on the condition that his pen never cease writing. As he wrote down the bard's poetic recitation he "knit the knots close together," thus making the text difficult to read. Many other myths tell of Gaṇeśa's assistance in removing obstacles in less ambivalent terms. A number of stories recount how, at the requests of the gods, Gaṇeśa saved the universe from the rule of the evil demon Traipura.

Shrines and temples to Gaṇeśa can be found all over India and his image appears throughout Buddhist Asia as a Buddhist deity. Frequently an image of Gaṇeśa can be found at the doorway to temples of other gods. His threshold position at the doorway enables worshipers to do homage to him first as they enter the temple compound, thus making any later ritual gestures free from obstacle. Although he is worshiped by all Hindus in his role as obstacle-remover, a small sect of devotees, the Gāṇapatyas, who are found most frequently in the southern and western parts of India, regard him as the embodied form of the divine PURUṢA or BRAHMAN.

Near the end of the monsoon season an annual festival to Gaṇeśa is widely celebrated, particularly in western India. This festival, Gaṇeśa Caturthī ("Gaṇeśa's Fourth"—because it falls on the fourth day of the first half of the Hindu month of Bhādrapad), is observed by installing a clay image of Gaṇeśa in the home and worshiping it for ten days. At the end of that period the images are carried in procession to a nearby river or well, where they are immersed.

At the end of the last century, the militant Hindu nationalist Bāḷ Gaṇgadhār Ṭiḷak transformed the Gaṇeśa festival into an occasion for rallying mass support among Hindus against British policies, specifically a bill which stipulated the minimal age for marriages. The festival became a time for recitation of traditional stories, singing of devotional songs, and making revivalistic political speeches.

Over the past seventy years Gaṇeśa's popularity has increased markedly, perhaps because of his associations with overcoming obstacles, whether they be foreign rule, religious divisions, or economic and technological backwardness. As modernization has moved forward in this century Gaṇeśa's fortunes have increased, and his image and personality have shown themselves to be compatible with social and economic change.

Bibliography. A. Getty, *Gaṇeśa: A Monograph on the Elephant-Faced God* (1936).

P. COURTRIGHT

GAṄGĀ gän´ gŭ (H). *See* GANGES.

GANGES gän´ jēz (H—Skt. *Gaṅgā*). The greatest of India's sacred rivers, known to Hindus as a goddess

D. M. Knipe

A man performing śrāddha offerings for his deceased parents in the Ganges River

and mother. In English the goddess is always called Gaṅgā. The Ganges is seen as a celestial river, originating from the merciful foot of Vishnu and flowing across the heavens before falling to earth. King Bhagīratha instigated the goddess' famous "descent" (*avatarana*, female AVATAR) in order to bring life to the ashes of his ancestors. She fell first upon the head of SHIVA, and from there descended to earth. She has thus become goddess-consort of Shiva, a liquid form of his divine energy or ŚAKTI, often depicted as a water nymph in Shiva's hair. For Hindus the Ganges is life-giving and purifying and is ritually invoked into all sacral waters. *See* HINDU SACRED RIVERS.

D. L. ECK

GAONIM gă ō nēm´ (sing. Gaon). (Ju). Heads of academies in Babylonia, from A.D. 589 to mid-eleventh century. Through their RESPONSA they united the Jews under the authority of the TALMUD. The term was also used as a title of honor and is still applied to outstanding scholars.

Y. SHAMIR

GARUḌA gŭ rū´ dŭ (H—Skt.). A mythical bird whose name means "devourer"; an eagle-like bird.

Garuḍa is VISHNU's mount (VĀHANA) and the emblem of his flagstaff. The birth and deeds of this famous mythical bird are told in the MAHĀBHĀRATA. Breaking the shell of his egg, he immediately grew to his giant size and flew into the atmosphere. The gods, awed at his brilliance, sing his praise. Garuḍa eventually kills the great snakes who are protecting the elixir of immortality (*amṛta*, SOMA) and steals the elixir from the snakes and gods, who in a previous battle had taken it from the demons (ASURAS).

Flying upward with the elixir he encounters Vishnu and requests two boons: that he, Garuḍa, will always be above Vishnu, and that without drinking the elixir he will never age or die. Vishnu grants the wish. In return Garuḍa grants Vishnu a boon. Vishnu requests that Garuḍa become his mount. The request is granted. Garuḍa is neither a god nor an *asura;* he mediates between them and remains the "enemy of snakes." He carries all the worlds, all that moves and stands, on the quill of one of his feathers. In Hindu iconography Garuḍa is often portrayed with Vishnu and sometimes as a part-bird and part-man.

Bibliography. J. Gonda, *Aspects of Early Visnuism* (1954); J.A.B. van Buitenen, ed. and trans., *The Mahābhārata,* (1973); *see* bibliog. *for* VĀHANA.

H. H. PENNER

L.D. Shinn

The Garuḍa figure guards the entrance to the Nārāyaṇa (Vishnu) Temple in Patan, Nepal

GĀTHĀ gä´ tä (Z). *See* AVESTA.

GAUTAMA gou´ tŭ mŭ (B—Skt.) **GOTAMA** gō tä´ mŭ (B—Pali). The family or clan name of Siddhārtha Gautama, who became the BUDDHA. Gautama is a name of a BRAHMIN caste group, although Siddhārtha's family is traditionally included among the KṢATRIYA or warrior caste (Jātaka I, 49). As the family name Gautama suggests, the Buddha's family was either of ARYAN origin or, if not, had become at some earlier time participants in Vedic-Aryan civilization.

R. H. DRUMMOND

GĀYATRĪ MANTRA gä´ yŭt rē mŭn´ trŭ (H—Skt.). The properly transmitted and recited Vedic verse (RIG VEDA 3.62.10) or MANTRA composed in the archaic Gāyatrī meter and evocative of the illuminating, inspiring, and purifying radiance of the divinity of the sun, SŪRYA or Savitṛ (the "Stimulator"). Its reception from the mouth of a qualified teacher in the Vedic initiation ritual generates the second birth qualifying one for study of the VEDA, the knowledge that leads from darkness into light. TWICE BORN Hindus, especially BRAHMINS, are enjoined to recite it daily in "twilight" (*saṃdhyā*) ritual meditations at dawn and sunset.

Bibliography. J. Gonda, "The Indian Mantra," *Oriens,* XVI (1963), 284-94. On its translation see also V. Bandhu, "The Gāyatrī," *Research Bulletin of the University of the Panjab,* XIII. iv (1954).

W. G. NEEVEL

GĀYATRĪ MANTRA

tat savitur vareṇyam
bhargo devasya dhīmahi
dhiyo yo naḥ pracodayāt

Let us celebrate the lovely brilliance
of the deity Savitṛ (the Sun);
May it inspire and purify our visions
and hymns of praise.

Rig Veda 3.62.10 (trans. by W. G. Neevel)

GEMARA gə mä´ rə (Ju—Aram.; lit. "study," "memorization," "tradition," or "completion"). (1) The Babylonian and Jerusalem TALMUDS, and more specifically (2) the discussions of the AMORAIM on the MISHNAH (edited *ca.* A.D. 200), which represent creativity of the academies of Palestine up to A.D. 450 and Babylonia up to A.D. 500, dedicated mainly to the HALAKAH.
Y. SHAMIR

GEMATRIA gē mät´ rĭ ə (Ju—Heb.; lit. "numerical value" [Gr. *gēometría*]). The assignment of numerical value to letters, words, or phrases according to a variety of different schemes. It is found in rabbinic literature as a hermeneutical device for the AGGADIC interpretation of scripture and is a device favored by Jewish mystics, especially in medieval German HASIDISM. An identical numerical value for different words is understood to indicate a substantive identity between the objects they name; e.g., nature *(hātevā)* and God *(elohim)* both equal eighty-six.
K. P. BLAND

GENUFLEXION (Ch). A ceremonial reverence consisting of a momentary kneeling on the right knee. Practiced chiefly in Roman Catholicism and Anglicanism, genuflexion began superseding the traditional profound bow in the late fifteenth century. Long series of repeated genuflexions were popular in medieval devotions and ascetic practices.
C. WADDELL

GETHSEMANE gĕth sĕm´ ə nĭ. Site on the MOUNT OF OLIVES across the Kidron Valley from JERUSALEM, where Jesus prayed (Matt. 26:36; Mark 14:32) before his betrayal by Judas. The exact location is uncertain. Excavations have revealed remains of a fourth century A.D. church beneath the Church of All Nations.
D. W. O'CONNOR

al-GHAZZĀLĪ, ABŪ ḤĀMID ăl gâz zä´ lē ä bōō´ hä´ məd (I; 1058-1111). Jurist, theologian, and mystic; a major figure in the intellectual life of medieval ISLAM. As a jurist he defended the integrity of the SUNNI creed, and was especially concerned to show its superiority to the system of the Nizārī Ismailis, a SHI'ITE sectarian group whose speculations attracted and challenged him. As a scholastic theologian he inherited the Neoplatonic philosophical categories introduced into Islam through Arabic translations from Greek, popularized by the rationalist, free-thinking MU'TAZILA movement and elaborated by the Turkish metaphysician al-Fārābī (d. 950) and his Persian successor, IBN SĪNĀ (Avicenna; d. 1037). Ghazzālī reworked the dialectical categories of earlier Muslim theologians such as AL-ASH'ARĪ (d. 935) and his own teacher, al-Juwaynī (d. 1085), but it was as a mystic that he attained his greatest fame and effected his most lasting influence. In the autobiographical *al-Munqidh min al-ḍalāl* (The Deliverer from Error) he describes how his intense pursuit of truth led him to investigate all academic disciplines available to an educated medieval Muslim. None, including SUFISM, satisfied him because, as he discovered, truth was gained only through immediate experience. Oral instruction and the study of Sufism were no substitute for walking in the Way. After agonizing self-examination, Ghazzālī resigned his teaching post at the prestigious Baghdad Niẓamiyya MADRASA (college). For more than ten years he remained outside public life, opting for solitary reflection interrupted only by consultations with "men of the heart," i.e., Sufis. Yet Ghazzālī did not merely meditate, he also wrote. The resulting spiritual diary was a formidable book, one that surpassed all his previous literary productions in scope and insight: the *Iḥyā 'ulūm ad-dīn* (The Bringing to Life of the Sciences of Religion). It is a survey of the entire range of Muslim theological, philosophical, devotional, and sectarian thought in the early medieval period. Its mystical fervor is cloaked in a tight schematic garb, worthy of the former professor. The *Iḥyā* is divided into two parts, each of which has two quarters, the first two dealing with external devotional acts; the last two with matters of the heart, corresponding to the most common Sufi dyad, the outer *(Ẓāhir)* and the inner *(Bāṭin)*. Each of the quarters, in turn, has ten books, for a total of forty books, a number whose symbolic reference to the forty-day retreat of Sufis was not lost on Ghazzālī's contemporaries. The *Iḥyā,* despite its length of over one thousand pages, was widely read and quoted in ARABIC. Ghazzālī himself rendered it into a PERSIAN abridgment entitled *Kīmiyā-yi sa'ādat* (The Elixir of Happiness). Other adaptations, translations, and commentaries appeared throughout the medieval, and even into the modern, period.

Abū Ḥāmid has sometimes been compared unfavorably with his younger brother, Aḥmad, a Sufi SHAIKH and consummate poet. Both men opened up new directions for the future course of Muslim spirituality, but to date the prolific and scholarly Abū Ḥāmid has attracted the attention of Western orientalists far more than the ecstatic but terse Aḥmad.

Bibliography. W. M. Watt, *The Faith and Practice of al-Ghazzali* (1953), and *Muslim Intellectual; A Study of al-Ghazzali* (1963); M. G. S. Hodgson, *The Venture of Islam,* II (1974), 180-92; M. Molé, *Les mystiques musulmans* (1965), pp. 91-97; H. Lazarus-Yafeh, *Studies in al-Ghazali* (1975).
B. LAWRENCE

GHEE, GHĪ gē (H—Hindī) **GHṚTA** ghrĭ´tŭ (H—Skt.; lit. "sprinkled" [*ghṛ*—"to sprinkle"]). Clarified butter, i.e., butter that has been brought to the boiling point, had the impurities skimmed off, and then allowed to cool. Ghee is important as an offering in Hindu ritual, often being "sprinkled" by the priest upon the sacred fire.
J. BARE

GHETTO (Ju). Although there are instances of Jews living in seclusion in the ancient world, the term is first found in sixteenth century Venice, used for that part of the city where Jews were forced to live. It was soon used of other segregated Jewish quarters—voluntary as well as enforced—throughout the West. The ghetto was almost unknown in Muslim countries. Today the word refers more generally to homogeneous settlements of non-Jews as well, such as blacks in U.S. cities.

The ghetto disappeared in Europe in the early nineteenth century but was revived in 1939 by the Nazis, who established nearly 1,000 ghettos in Eastern Europe. Unlike medieval times, these ghettos were never intended as permanent residential quarters, but were way stations to death camps (*see* HOLOCAUST). The concentration of Jews in specified areas facilitated their deportations. Despite extreme conditions of overcrowding, malnutrition, and disease, the ghettos developed elaborate social and educational structures of self-help. Each ghetto was administered by a German-appointed Jewish Council, whose members were held responsible for carrying out Nazi orders. Despite genuine efforts to alleviate suffering they ultimately served the death machinery. There are instances of armed resistance in many ghettos (e.g. Lodz, Kovno, Bialystok), the best-known of which is the Warsaw Ghetto uprising of April-May, 1943. All the ghettos were eventually liquidated as part of the "final solution."

Bibliography. R. Hilberg, *The Destruction of the European Jews* (1961); E. Ringelblum, *Notes from the Warsaw Ghetto* (1958, 1974).
E. FLEISCHNER

GHĪ gē (H). *See* GHEE.

GHOST, HOLY (Ch). *See* HOLY SPIRIT.

GHOST, HUNGRY (B). *See* PRETA.

GHOSTS. *See* SOUL, SPIRIT.

GILGUL gĭl gool′ (Ju—Heb.; lit. "wave"). The technical term for REINCARNATION or transmigration of souls. Jewish philosophy unequivocally repudiated it, but from its first literary appearance in the SEFER BAHIR it became a central doctrine in Jewish MYSTICISM. It is almost always understood to be an opportunity for souls to perfect themselves and to undo the sins of earlier lives.
K. P. BLAND

GĪTĀ GOVINDA (of Jayadeva) gē′ tŭ gō vĭn′ dŭ (H—Skt.). "The Love Song of the Dark Lord," as it has recently been called by Miller, is a late classical SANSKRIT poem, probably of the twelfth century A.D. It consists of a series of twenty-four interrelated lyric poems on the theme of the love between RĀDHĀ and KRISHNA: their early union, their separation from one another, and the joy of their reunion. Although the poetry is carefully wrought, rich, and earthy in its conception and imagery, later interpreters have considered it an allegory of the relationship of love between the devotee and God, much as has been done with the biblical Song of Songs. There are indications, moreover, that the author, JAYADEVA, intended this, for throughout the text he states that the human love he is praising has its echoes in the cosmos.

The twenty-four songs of the text were meant to be sung. Each of them is characterized by a musical mode, a *rāga,* and each by a refrain, or *dhruvapada,* which has echoes from song to song, thus serving as a unifying device for the whole poem. Prominent also is the elaborate *alaṃkāra* or prosodic device—end rhyme, alliteration, punning, and general verbal exuberance. Though all had been used in Sanskrit poetry previous to Jayadeva, their elaboration in his work, plus an examination of his metrics, have led some scholars to speculate that his poetic sources may lie within the non-Sanskritic Apabharaṃśa tradition.

The mood of the poem is the erotic, explored by Jayadeva in both of its manifestations—the lovers in union and the lovers in separation. It begins with an invocation of the ten incarnations of the divine Krishna, proceeds to examine the various facets of the pain of the lovers in separation, and culminates with the union of the lovers in the forest in springtime. An interesting and effective device the poet uses is that of the friend who goes between the lovers to describe to the one the passion of the other. These descriptive passages allow the reader to witness the divine love from a third, more objective point of view, and the result is the total involvement of the audience with the poem and with the love of the divine pair.

The poem is the culmination of the tradition of erotic poetry in Sanskrit, and the prototype of all erotic religious poetry to follow. The Bengali VAIṢṆAVA tradition in particular followed it, and it became not only the paradigmatic statement of the divine love between Rādhā and Krishna and of the proper love of the worshiper for God, but the model of a whole school of devotional aesthetics. *See* BHAGAVAD GĪTĀ; BHAKTI HINDUISM; CAITANYA; GOPĪ; KĪRTANA.

Bibliography. B. S. Miller, *The Love Song of the Dark Lord* (1977).
E. C. DIMOCK, JR.

GLORIA IN EXCELSIS glō′ rē ə ĭn ĕks tsĕl′ sēs *or* ĕks chĕl′ sēs (Ch—Lat.; "Glory to God on high"). First words of the Greater DOXOLOGY, one of the ancient "private psalms" of the church and an elaboration of the angelic song at the nativity (Luke 2:14). Used at morning prayers in the Eastern churches from the fourth century, by the sixth century it was used on special occasions in the Latin MASS and is now a regular part of festal EUCHARISTS in the West.
R. A. GREER

GLORIA PATRI glō′ rē ə pät′ rē (Ch—Lat.; "Glory to the Father"). First words of the Little DOXOLOGY, derived from biblical doxologies and reworked according to trinitarian formulas. By the fourth century it was employed as a conclusion to the psalms in liturgical use. The Western form, with the conclusion "as it was in the begining, etc.," is first mentioned explicitly in the sixth century.

R. A. Greer

GLOSSOLALIA gläs ə lā′ lyə (Ch). The utterance of speech or language-like words and phrases which are unknown to the speaker, usually in a context of profound religious experience. Although known primarily as a Christian phenomenon, glossolalia was prevalent in the ancient Greek mystery cults and has been reported in various tribal religions down to modern times. Non-Christian glossolalia has usually been associated with ecstatic trances and altered states of consciousness.

Christian glossolalia first appeared on the day of Pentecost, when the entire church spoke in tongues "as the Spirit gave them utterance" (Acts 2:4). The phenomenon appeared whenever the church reached new classes of converts, i.e., as at the "Jewish Pentecost" (Acts 2); the "Roman Pentecost" (Acts 10); and the "Greek Pentecost" (Acts 19). Glossolalia always occurred in conjunction with the reception of the Holy Spirit or in the operation of the gifts of the Spirit.

The church at Corinth became known for an exaggerated use of glossolalia in its worship services. Paul regulated but did not forbid tongues in the normal life of the church (I Cor. 12-14).

In the second century a new outbreak of glossolalia occurred in the Montanist heresy. It recurred among the French Protestant Camisards and in Catholic Jansenism in the seventeenth and eighteenth centuries. Nineteenth century outbreaks were reported among the Shakers and Latter-day Saints in the U. S. and among the followers of Presbyterian pastor Edward Irving in London.

The twentieth century has seen a vast increase of glossolalia among Christians around the world, not only in the Pentecostal Churches, but in traditional Protestant churches, Roman Catholicism, and the Orthodox Churches. (*See* Charismatic Movement.)

Three distinct types of miraculous claims have been made: (1) *glossolalia*—speaking in a language unknown to the speaker or the hearers (without interpretation), e.g., the church at Corinth; (2) *xenoglossolalia*—speaking in a known foreign language unknown to the speaker but known to the hearers, e.g., the disciples on the day of Pentecost; (3) *heteroglossolalia*—speaking in a language known to the speaker while the audience hears in their own language, e.g., Francis Xavier.

Early scientific studies of glossolalia tended to view the practice in terms of personality disorders or economic and social deprivations. With the appearance of glossolalia among well-educated and wealthy members of traditional churches, these theories were largely abandoned.

Bibliography. W. J. Samarin, *Tongues of Men and Angels* (1972); J. L. Sherrill, *They Speak with Other Tongues* (1964).

H. V. Synan

GNOSTICISM näs′ tə sĭz′ əm. A mixed and diverse group of thinkers, ideas, and treatises which became a force in the second century A.D. and continued to exert an important influence on ancient religion into the fourth century. While the most recent scholarship has tended to emphasize pagan and Jewish, as well as Christian, forms of Gnosticism (beginning in the first century), the major Gnostic impact was made on the doctrine and structures of the Christian church in the second and early third centuries. Its critics, both Christian and pagan, seem to have regarded it primarily as a Christian heresy.

In addition to numerous scattered groups, two main schools of systematic Gnostic thought seem to have existed in the second century—the Basilideans and the Valentinians, the latter divided into Eastern and Western branches. In addition, Marcion, a radical exegete of Paul tinged with Gnostic assumptions, founded a group and made the first attempt to create a closed "canon" of the NT. Marcion and the Western Valentinians appear to have been the most feared by catholic theologians.

Until recently, our knowledge of Gnostic thought was almost exclusively dependent upon the reports of its critics (e.g., Irenaeus, Hippolytus, Tertullian, Origen, Plotinus); but a cache of documents found at Nag Hammadi in Egypt in 1945 has provided originals of some treatises alluded to by those critics and has enabled scholars to see how much more widespread and diverse Gnosticism was than previously imagined. At the heart of the Gnostic concern was the revelation of the hidden *Gnosis* (Gr. "knowledge"), the possession of which would free one from the fragmentary and illusory (or evil) material world (bodily existence) and teach one about the origins of the spiritual world to which the Gnostic belonged by nature. Radical discontinuity between appearance and reality; between bodily, literal perception (both experiential and exegetical) and spiritual insight (the inner perception); between historical existence (frequently expressed as being under the sway of an alien secondary god, creator of the phenomenal world and/or God of the OT) and spiritual existence (belonging to the eternal reality or "fullness" of the high God and/or God of the NT)—these were the linchpins of various Gnostic systems. These presuppositions were at once the explanation of how the rift between appearance and reality occurred and the prescription for return from appearance into reality. The best recent work on the Valentinian Gnostics (Pagels) has stressed this soteriological aim and clarified their complicated principles and presuppositions.

Reaction to Gnostic concerns exerted a formative influence on the shape and content of Christian doctrine, views of tradition, NT canon, and ecclesiastical structure. The continuing contribution of Gnosticism in its psychological aspects can be seen in the writings of C. G. Jung.

Bibliography. H. Jonas, *The Gnostic Religion,* 2nd ed. rev. (1963); E. Pagels, *The Johannine Gospel in Gnostic Exegesis* (1973), *The Gnostic Paul* (1975), and *The Gnostic Gospels* (1979); J. M. Robinson, ed., *The Nag Hammadi Library in English* (1977).

D. E. Groh

GOBIND SINGH gō´ bĭnd sĭng (S; 1666-1708). The tenth and last of the Sikh gurus; born in Patna, the only child of Guru Tegh Bahadur. He was nine years old when, following the execution of his father, he was proclaimed Guru of the Sikhs. He spent his adolescence and youth in the foothills of the Himalaya Mountains, studying, composing poetry, hunting, and training his followers in martial exercises. He built a chain of fortresses: Anandgarh, Keshgarh, Lohgarh, and Fategarh. He was married twice and his two wives bore him four sons: Ajit Singh, Jujhar Singh, Zoravar Singh, and Fateh Singh.

1. **Militant Sikhism.** In April 1699 Gobind summoned his followers to Anandpur and baptized them into a new military fraternity called the Khālsā or "the pure." Sikh chronicles maintain that upward of 20,000 men were baptized that day. Thereafter many peasant communities joined the Khālsā. The eruption of the militant bands brought the guru into conflict with neighboring hill chieftains. Finally, the Mogul armies attacked the guru's fortresses. In these encounters two of his elder sons were killed and the younger boys, aged nine and seven, were taken prisoner and executed. The guru and a small band escaped and sought refuge in the Punjab jungle.

In the struggle for power after the death of the Mogul Emperor Aurangzīb, Guru Gobind Singh lent support to the eldest son, Bahadur Shah, and paid him a formal visit at Agra. He accompanied Bahadur Shah on his campaign against his brother, who had sought refuge in the Deccan. On October 7, 1708, at Nanded on the banks of the river Godavari the guru was assassinated by two Muslim servants.

2. **Literary developments.** Guru Gobind Singh is credited with editing the final recension of the Ādi Granth. By Gobind's decree, he was to be the final living guru, with the Ādi Granth serving as the teacher henceforth. His own compositions were compiled by a follower, Mani Singh, in a volume popularly known as the Dasam Granth (book of the tenth guru).

The authenticity of the writings in the Dasam Granth has been questioned. It consists of eighteen separate books in four different languages—Braj, Hindī, Persian, and Punjabi. A large section is devoted to themes from Hindu mythology, and some of it is outspokenly erotic. Most scholars now believe that since the guru was a patron of poets—fifty-two are said to have been in his court in Anandpur—many of these compositions are from their pens. Some works can, however, be clearly identified as the guru's works. Extracts from these compositions are currently used in Sikh prayer and ritual, particularly the *pahul* (baptismal) ceremony.

Bibliography. G. C. Narang, *Transformation of Sikhism or How the Sikhs Became a Political Power,* 5th ed. (1963); J. S. Grewal and S. S. Bal, *Guru Gobind Singh: A Biographical Study* (1967).

K. Singh

GOD. For Christianity *see* Trinity. For Islam *see* Allah; Tawḥīd. *See* Judaism esp. §§ 1, 2 and Yahweh. *See* Hinduism esp. §§ 2, 6e, 8 and Shiva; Vishnu; Goddess (India). *See also* Buddha, General Concepts of; Kami (Sh); Nam (S); African Traditional Religion §2; South American Tribal Religion; South Asian Tribal Religion §2; Southeast Asian Tribal Religion §1.

GODDESS (INDIA). Goddesses have been revered in India from ancient times to the present. Archaeological evidence from the Indus Valley Civilization and from earlier village cultures indicates that feminine deities were widely worshiped from around 2500 B.C. The earliest religious text in India, the Rig Veda (*ca.* 1400 B.C.), also mentions a variety of goddesses worshiped by the Indo-Aryans. However, in the literary traditions of India goddesses remained subordinate to male deities, usually as their wives or consorts, until the end of the Epic period (A.D. 400). Goddesses only began to rival male deities in Sanskrit literature around the sixth century A.D. At that time several goddesses began to appear prominently as world protectors, saviors, and creators of the cosmic order. Furthermore, there appeared a being known primarily as the Great Goddess (Mahādevī), who subsumed within herself all manifestations of the divine feminine and revealed all the Hindu characteristics of supreme divinity. Today hundreds of local goddesses are known and dominate the religious life of the majority of Hindus, especially of lower castes and in the villages in all regions of India.

1. **Goddesses in ancient India.** Little is known concerning the goddesses worshiped in the Indus Valley Civilization and the village cultures surrounding it. From the many seals and figurines discovered, however, it seems clear that goddesses were central to the religion of this ancient civilization in Northwest India and that they had something to do with agriculture, fertility, and vegetative life generally. Although many goddesses appeared in Vedic literature, it is clear that male deities dominated Vedic religion and continued to dominate Indian religions until a late date.

Pṛthivī is the goddess associated with the earth. In

most of the hymns addressed to her she is paired with Dyaus Pitā, Father Sky. As a couple these deities are called the parents of all the gods. Dyaus fertilizes Pṛthivī with rain, and she produces all forms of life. Pṛthivī is especially extolled for her breadth and stability. She supports humans and all other life, and is praised as a nourishing, fertile presence who provides wealth and abundance.

Uṣas is associated with the dawn and is described as a lovely maiden. As the regularly recurring dawn that banishes darkness she is said to stir all men to activity, to impel life on its way, and thus she is associated with the vital aspects of reality in general. She is also said to hunt skillfully and eventually to wear down all living things because she is associated with time, the endlessly recurring rise of the sun. Uṣas has a twin sister, Rātrī, the goddess Night, and together they measure out time. Although Rātrī is usually described as beautiful and benign, she is sometimes feared, and Uṣas at times is praised for dispelling her fearful sister.

Descriptions of Sarasvatī make it clear that the Vedic poets have a river by that name in mind when they sing her praises. She is praised for her might and fertility and is petitioned to grant her worshipers wealth, long life, and sons, as are most Vedic deities. In later literature Sarasvatī becomes associated with the goddess Vāc, and in later Hinduism she becomes the goddess of wisdom and education. In India today her annual festival is particularly observed by school children.

Vāc is the goddess who reveals herself in speech. As such she lends intelligibility to human life and enables men to differentiate between friend and foe. She inspires religious seers in their visionary quests and embodies the truths of their visions in poetic hymns. In this sense she is the ground of perceived truth, and that truth itself. Vāc is particularly significant because she indicates the centrality of sound as the essence of creation in the early Hindu tradition.

The most prominent feature of Aditi is her motherhood. She is the mother of the Ādityas, a group of seven powerful gods, and usually is asked to guard her devotees and provide them with wealth. Her name means "the unbound one," and she is often asked to free her worshiper from various bonds. In later Vedic literature she becomes synonymous with Pṛthivī and in later Hinduism becomes insignificant.

In Vedic sources most of the important male deities are said to have wives, and minor goddesses are associated with the forest, abundance, progeny, and sacrifice. Nearly all these goddesses are benign and provide wealth and long life. The exception is the goddess Nirṛti, who is associated with everything inauspicious and whose blessing is realized only in her absence.

2. The Epic period (400 B.C.—A.D. 400). By the time of the great Hindu Epics, the Mahābhārata and Rāmāyaṇa, of the goddesses known to Vedic religion only Pṛthivī and Sarasvatī persist as significant deities. The most important goddesses of the Epic period are Pārvatī, Lakṣmī, and Sītā. Also of significance are certain groups of goddesses such as the *mātṛkās* ("the mothers") and classes of female beings such as the *yakṣinīs,* Apsaras, and *rakṣasīs.*

It is not until the time of the Epics that we find Pārvatī occupying a central place in the Hindu pantheon. She continues as one of the most important Hindu goddesses to this day. Her role as Shiva's consort and her association with mountains, particularly the Himalayas, dominate her mythology. The name Pārvatī means "daughter of the mountain," and in Hindu mythology she is said to be the daughter of Himavat, the Himalayas personified, and his wife Menā. She undertakes severe austerities to win Shiva for her husband and succeeds in distracting him from his yogic meditation. The two are then married. Many myths delight in describing their married bliss. They dwell on Mount Kailāsa in the Himalayas and indulge in erotic dalliance or play dice. Eventually they produce two children, Kārttika, the general of the gods, and Gaṇeśa, the elephant-headed god, both of whom become deities of considerable popularity in medieval Hinduism. In general, Pārvatī plays the role in Hindu myths of domesticator of the ascetic god Shiva. She dotes on her husband and involves him in the important affairs of protecting and maintaining the world. As his partner in his cosmic dance, she balances the destructive tendencies of some aspects of his dance (*see* Naṭarāja). Compared to her often wild husband, Pārvatī is described as patient, protective of the world, and supportive of domestic life and, as such, provides a model for Hindu women.

The goddess Lakṣmī, also known as Śrī ("good fortune"), is mentioned in pre-Epic literature, and a long hymn to her is found in a late appendix to the Rig Veda. However, she only assumes a central role in Hindu mythology in the Epic period. She has continued as a popular Hindu goddess to this day. In the Epics Lakṣmī is especially associated with wealth, prosperity, and kingly power. She represents good luck. Where Lakṣmī is present, kings and commoners both prosper. Where she is absent, bad luck (*alakṣmī,* sometimes personified as her sister) rules. In the Mahābhārata Lakṣmī is associated with several male gods, the most important of whom are Indra and Vishnu. Lakṣmī is sometimes described as fickle, bestowing and withdrawing her favors unpredictably. In later Hindu literature, however, she is invariably Vishnu's wife and serves him dutifully. Vishnu is portrayed as a heavenly king who lives in a heavenly court, Vaikuṇṭha. It is appropriate, therefore, that Lakṣmī should be his wife, representing as she does kingly power and prosperity. As Vishnu's wife, Lakṣmī is typically portrayed in iconography as massaging her Lord's feet while he rests on the cosmic serpent Śeṣa. In most respects Lakṣmī, like Pārvatī, is a model wife. She is sometimes said to act as an intermediary between Vishnu and his devotees.

Today in India Lakṣmī is worshiped especially by merchants and is petitioned to grant wealth and success. Her annual festival, Lakṣmī Pūjā, is held in the autumn, and people of all castes take part in it to seek her blessing.

Vishnu is often shown with a second wife, Bhūdevī, the goddess Earth. Bhūdevī is actually Pṛthivī, and again it is appropriate that she becomes associated with Vishnu, as he is the protector par excellence of the earth. It is to relieve the burden of Earth that he descends from time to time in his various incarnations or AVATARS.

In the Epics Sarasvatī has become associated with the god BRAHMĀ as his consort. She has lost nearly all connection with the River Sarasvatī and is usually praised as a goddess of inspiration and wisdom.

Sītā, whose name means "furrow," is the daughter of Earth and the heroine of the Rāmāyaṇa. As the wife of the hero, RĀMA, she shares all his misfortunes without complaint and has come to be the most popular model of a faithful Hindu wife. In the Rāmāyaṇa, Rāma is an incarnation of Vishnu. In later Hinduism, however, Rāma assumes a position of supreme divinity among his devotees, and by association Sītā is also elevated to divinity and is adored as a goddess by Rāma's devotees. DRAUPADĪ, the wife of the five heroes of the Mahābhārata, has also come to be worshiped as a goddess, primarily in South India.

The presence of various groups of female beings in the Epics probably indicates the beginning of a process whereby the Sanskrit tradition, dominated by an elitist BRAHMIN group, recognized the presence and the importance of a great many local and regional goddesses who had been worshiped for centuries by most of the Indian population. Early Buddhist sculpture depicts various female beings, and it is likely that the *yakṣinīs, apsaras, rakṣasīs,* and *mātṛkās* mentioned in the Epics were no newcomers to the Indian religious tradition.

Yakṣinīs (masc. YAKṢA) are primarily deities of the forest and are associated with trees and vegetation. It has been suggested that the earliest form of temple worship was in honor of *yakṣas* and *yakṣinīs,* who are generally associated with particular sacred locales. *Apsaras* are primarily famous for their dancing and inhabit the heavens of all major Hindu deities. The *rakṣasīs* (masc. *rakṣasa*) are demons who haunt thick forests and cremation grounds. They are flesh eaters and are almost always hostile to humans.

The *mātṛkās,* or "mothers," are referred to several times in the Mahābhārata. Their number varies from several hundred to six or seven. They are often said to have malign habits, including a fondness for harassing children. They are sometimes said to live in uncivilized and inaccessible areas and to speak foreign tongues. Although tamed by certain gods in the Mahābhārata, they are generally demonic in appearance and habit. The *mātṛkās* probably represent various local, non-Brahminic goddesses who were worshiped with blood offerings, were associated with childhood diseases, and indeed appeared foreign to the redactors of the Mahābhārata. In later Sanskrit mythology and Hindu iconography the number of mothers is usually seven, and although their characteristics are somewhat softened, they are typically said to get drunk on blood and to dance out of control, threatening the stability of the world.

In the Epics various goddesses are associated with prominent geographical features of the Indian subcontinent. The most famous of these is the goddess Gaṅgā, the GANGES River personified. Many other sacred places are personified as goddesses, and this remains true today.

By the Epic period, then, goddesses had become increasingly important in the Hindu tradition. However, there is no evidence in literary sources up through the end of this period that goddesses had assumed preeminent positions in the pantheon. Various goddesses may well have dominated local worship at this time, but this is difficult to prove on the basis of the literary and iconographic evidence.

3. The medieval period (*ca.* A.D. 600-1850). In the medieval period the goddesses Pāravtī, Lakṣmī, Sarasvatī, Bhūdevī, and others known earlier in the tradition continue to be important. Several goddesses who were barely mentioned in the Epic period, however, come to dominate worship of the divine feminine in Hindu literature and iconography. These are the goddesses DURGĀ, KĀLĪ, and RĀDHĀ. It is during this period, too, that a being known by a great variety of names, but most popularly known as the Mahādevī, the Great Goddess, becomes widely known.

Durgā is famous for slaying the buffalo demon, Mahiṣāsura. When the various male gods were unable to defeat this cosmic menace, they pooled their splendor and created Durgā, a beautiful and mighty battle queen, who handily defeated the demon. This goddess is also known for her defeat of the demons Śumbha and Niśumbha. While Durgā is sometimes associated with Shiva, and is said to be his wife in Śaivite literature, she is essentially an independent goddess and is declared by her devotees to be the highest manifestation of deity. In many respects she is similar in function to the great male gods. In her mythology she assumes their role as the leader of the gods in the endless struggle between the gods and demons, and like Vishnu she is said to descend to the world from time to time to defeat various demons. Durgā is particularly popular in Bengal, and the most festive celebration in Bengal is Durgā Pūjā, an autumn festival at which Durgā is worshiped and her exploits celebrated. At the festival animal sacrifices are made to her, and it is well known that she is pleased by blood offerings. The festival is also associated with agriculture. Her festival takes place at the harvest season, and it seems clear that she is identified with the growth and fertility of the crops. The blood offered to her in worship is probably believed to reinvigorate the earth, from which so much vitality has been reaped by man during the harvest of his crops.

Kālī is also pleased by blood and in her myths is typically described as becoming intoxicated by drinking the blood of her victims on the battlefield. Kālī, whose name means the "black one," is nearly always described as having a terrible appearance. Her hair is disheveled, her fangs sharp, her breasts pendulous, her stomach shrunken, and her demeanor fierce. She is usually said to be naked except for a garland of severed heads and a girdle of severed arms. Her habits are equally fearsome. Her favorite dwelling place is the cremation ground, where she is often pictured seated on a corpse, and she has been associated for centuries with thieves and is infamous for having been the patron goddess of the THUGS. She has been widely worshiped throughout India but, like Durgā, is most popular today in Bengal. She is often associated with Durgā and Pārvatī in mythology, usually appearing as the personified wrath of these goddesses. Like Durgā she is often said to be Shiva's wife, but unlike Pārvatī, for example, she rarely plays the role of model wife. Instead she dominates Shiva or incites him to frenzied, destructive acts. The worship of Kālī is nearly always accompanied by animal sacrifices, her thirst for blood being seemingly unquenchable.

The most common iconographic image of Kālī shows her standing on or dancing upon Shiva. This image is usually interpreted as expressing the nature of reality as a combination of stasis (the prone, motionless Shiva) and activity, or the personified might of the divine (ŚAKTI). In the active role Kālī expresses the creative aspects of the divine as they manifest themselves in nature *(prakṛti)* and ego-centered existence, or nescience (MĀYĀ). As Śakti Kālī expresses this aspect of the divine as out of control and perhaps dangerous. As such, she must be confronted and overcome in the yogic process of spiritual fulfillment.

It is at a more exoteric level, however, that Kālī is worshiped by the majority of her devotees, who typically address her as Mother. Despite her terrible appearance and her thirst for blood, her devotees approach her for protection, fertility, and prosperity. The logic of her worship at the popular level seems to be that if she is given blood, which she is daily at some of her temples, she will be renourished sufficiently to continue to give unstintingly to her devotees. Reality as expressed by Kālī would seem to be similar to an organism which, although it gives birth continually, must periodically be renourished for the process to continue. In this respect she reveals dramatically the truth that metabolism itself necessitates death, that life must feed on death.

The goddess Rādhā is the consort of the god KRISHNA. She is not widely known until the twelfth century A.D., when she appears as the heroine of JAYADEVA'S GĪTĀ GOVINDA. She is described in early accounts as the wife of another man, so her affair with Krishna is clearly illicit and as such is taken as a metaphor of the divine-human relationship. The affair disregards social norms if necessary and is dangerous, painful, and totally absorbing. In later VAIṢṆAVA-Krishna texts such as the Brahmavaivarta Purāṇa, Rādhā has achieved the position of divine creator. As Krishna's embodied power, *śakti,* she is said to represent PRAKṚTI, the material, natural order, and in eternal dalliance with Krishna she is said to create, preserve, and destroy the universe. In popular devotion, however, Rādhā is important primarily as the embodiment of the ideal devotee of Krishna. Her passion for Lord Krishna overcomes all obstacles, disregards propriety if necessary, and is extremely intimate. Such should one's devotion to Krishna be.

The appearance of the Great Goddess in the early medieval period indicates a growing acceptance on the part of the Sanskrit tradition of the divine feminine and is clear evidence that for millions of Hindus the highest expression of the divine is female. The Great Goddess is not a completely new creation. The portraits we find of her, for example in the *Devī-māhātmya, Saundaryalaharī,* and *Devī-bhāgavata Purāṇa,* clearly draw upon well-known goddess traditions. The Great Goddess, for example, is frequently called by names that associate her with Pārvatī, Lakṣmī, Sarasvatī, Durgā, Kālī, and the *mātṛkās*. In fact, an essential theological point in these texts is that all manifestations of the divine feminine are simply parts of her. Some texts even say that wherever there is a woman, there the Great Goddess resides. As a result, the Great Goddess' characteristics are diverse, complex, and vary from text to text. Generally, however, she is described as the queen of the cosmos, the creator of the great male gods, and is said to appear in various forms as certain tasks arise to be accomplished for the welfare of the world. She is also typically described as having benign and ferocious manifestations. Among her most famous ferocious forms are: Kālī, Chinnamastā ("the severed-headed one"), and Cāmuṇḍā. Among her most famous benign manifestations are: Lakṣmī, Sarasvatī, Pārvatī, and Annapūrṇā ("the one filled with good," who came to rescue the world during a severe drought by making rain with her tears). Some late texts say that the Great Goddess has ten great appearances (the *daśamahāvidyās*), which seem to be patterned on Vishnu's ten incarnations (avatars). The Mahādevī is sometimes said to be Shiva's wife, but most texts celebrating her insist that she is essentially independent and transcends all male gods. In nearly every respect she is said to possess the characteristics of supreme divinity, is often identified with BRAHMAN (the Absolute), and is said to be formless *(nirguṇa)* in her ultimate essence. In her creative role she is identified with *śakti* (divine might personified), *prakṛti* (the natural order), and *māyā* (embodied existence).

4. The modern period (A.D. 1850 to the present). Today in India there are shrines or temples to local goddesses in nearly every village, and it is quite likely that these goddesses have been worshiped from ancient times and have dominated the religious life of a great many Hindus. The names of these goddesses vary from village to village and from region to region, but they are usually associated with immediate concerns such as disease, prosperity, and fertility. Although villagers will often associate these goddesses with a goddess of the Sanskrit tradition, or with the Great Goddess herself, it is clear that most of these goddesses have distinctive local or regional histories and characteristics.

Of the hundreds of local goddesses worshiped today in India, two of the best known are Manasā and Sītalā. Manasā is primarily associated with snakes, and her blessing is sought to avoid the tragic consequences of snake bite. There is a long Bengali poem concerning her attempts to gain the worship of Shiva's devotees. This poem probably indicates the process whereby a local goddess (in this case a Bengali goddess) sought recognition in the wider Sanskrit tradition. Sītalā is worshiped throughout India and clearly represents characteristics of numerous local goddesses associated with disease. She is at once the cause of smallpox and the means by which it is cured. In her wrath she waxes hot and oppresses her victims with fever. She is especially revered at those times of year associated with smallpox.

One of the most popular goddesses of South India is MĀRIYAMMAṈ. She is almost always associated with a specific village or hamlet, primarily as a protectress of that area. Her images are of a diverse nature and vary from elaborate, anthropomorphic images usually found in temples to small painted rocks, decorated poles, or pots of water. Whatever form she may take, her worship usually dominates local religious life. In contrast, the great gods Shiva and Vishnu, although often housed in splendid temples, are only occasionally worshiped by the lower castes. Māriyammaṉ, like local goddesses throughout India, is truly a people's deity. She is almost always worshiped for pragmatic reasons. She is appealed to during epidemics and natural disasters, but especially by women who seek to have children. She is associated with disease, especially smallpox, as both its cure and its cause, and her worship typically involves pouring water over her image or symbol to cool her anger, which manifests itself as heat and fever. Unlike the great gods Shiva and Vishnu, who usually must be worshiped in their temples by specially trained BRAHMINS, Māriyammaṉ's priests are taken from low castes, and people from the lowest castes are welcome to worship at her temples. While Māriyammaṉ may be identified by some Hindus with goddesses of the Sanskrit pantheon, her association with local geography, concerns, and history are what imbue her worship with its intensity and popularity.

The Indian struggle for independence, during which fervent devotion to the motherland was generated among Hindus, gave rise to the cult of a new "goddess," Mother India (Bharat Mā). In some respects this cult is not entirely new. Since the time of the Mahābhārata various prominent geographical features of the Indian subcontinent have been worshiped as important goddesses. The imperial GUPTAS (third through sixth centuries A.D.) seem consciously to have cast themselves in the role of protectors of Bhūdevī, whom they equated with the Indian subcontinent. And the famous myth of SATĪ tells of her dismembered body falling to earth (namely India) in various places and sacralizing those places as centers of goddess worship. The modern cult of Bharat Mā, however, is a clearer, more self-conscious expression of reverence for the Indian subcontinent itself. So although this goddess is depicted in anthropomorphic forms at times, in most of her temples the object of worship is a relief map of India. The cult, then, has had clear political overtones and is an inextricable mix of religion and politics.

5. Buddhism and Jainism. BUDDHISM and JAINISM also revere a great many goddesses, many of whom are the same goddesses honored in Hinduism, but they include in their pantheon several goddesses distinctive to their particular traditions. The goddess PRAJÑĀ ("wisdom") in Buddhism, for example, who is said to be the mother of all the Buddhas, is clearly a peculiarly Buddhist deity and is primarily a personification of redemptive knowledge as described in Buddhist texts. As in Hinduism, the various BUDDHAS and BODHISATTVAS are often shown with consorts, or *Śaktis,* and it seems clear that many goddesses and female spirits were worshiped, especially by lay persons, in both Buddhism and Jainism for material prosperity and fertility.

See FEMININE DIMENSIONS OF THE SACRED.

Bibliography. N. N. Bhattacharyya, *History of Śākta Religion* (1974); S. B. Dasgupta, "Evolution of Mother Worship," *Aspects of Indian Religious Thought* (1957), pp. 42-106; E. A. Payne, *The Śāktas* (1933).

D. R. KINSLEY

GODPARENTS (Ch). Sponsors at the BAPTISM of infants who make the baptismal promises in the name of the child and promise on their own part to see to the nurture of the child in Christian faith and to participate in that nurture by prayer and example.

T. J. TALLEY

GOLDEN TEMPLE (S). The most sacred shrine of the Sikhs in Amritsar, northern India. Known as the Harimandir (Temple of God), it is built of marble, topped by gilded copper domes, and stands in the middle of a pool of water. Access is by a bridge. It has a rich display of semi-precious stones and frescoes. According to the district gazetteer, Ram Das, the fourth guru of the Sikhs, acquired the land in A.D. 1577 by grant from Emperor AKBAR, by making a cash payment to the local landowners. Ram Das had a pond dug and moved with his family and disciples to the site. The town came to be known after him as Ramdās Purā. Ram Dās' son, Arjun, had the temple built in the middle of this pond. According to Sikh tradition, he invited the Muslim saint Mian Mir of Lahore to lay the foundation stone. Unlike northern Hindu temples, which are built on a platform, Arjun's temple was one level lower than the surrounding land. Also unlike Hindu temples, which have only one entrance, the Harimandir was open on all four sides. These features were meant to emphasize that in a Sikh temple the lowly and oppressed had to go lower for worship and its doors were open to all four CASTES of Hindus. Guru Arjun installed the ĀDI GRANTH (sacred scriptures) in the Harimandir in A.D. 1604. He also persuaded merchants to set up business and renamed the town Amritsar—the Pool of Nectar. The Harimandir was blown up by Afghan invaders more than once. It was finally built in its present form by Maharajah Ranjit Singh (1780-1839).

Facing the Harimandir is the *akāl takht* (Throne of the Timeless God) built by Arjun's son Hargobind. This became the seat of authority where Sikh leaders assembled to pass *gurumattā* (resolutions) and issued *hakumnāmāh* (ordinances) to the community. Weapons used by the later gurus are on display at the *akāl takht*. Also within the confines of the temple walls are a museum of Sikh relics, a picture gallery depicting incidents in Sikh history, and an archive of manuscript copies of the Ādi Granth.

K. SINGH

GOLEM gō´ lĕm (Ju—Heb.; lit. "amorphous mass"). A legendary human-like figure created through incantations and secret formulas. In early Jewish mystical circles the creation of the *golem* was a contemplative, ecstatic achievement. The basis for the act is found in the TALMUD (Sanhedrin 65) as interpreted in the light of early cosmogonic-magical texts. By the fifteenth century the legend was understood to mean the creation of an actual, physical being, usually without the powers of speech.

K. P. BLAND

GOLGOTHA gŏl´gə thə (Ch—Aram.; "skull," also called Calvary from Lat. *calva*—"scalp"). The hill near JERUSALEM where Jesus was crucified. It was outside the city walls (John 19:20) and near the place of burial, but the exact location is uncertain. Most scholars prefer the site within the Church of the HOLY SEPULCHRE.

D. W. O'CONNOR

GOOD FRIDAY (Ch). The commemoration of JESUS' crucifixion on the Friday before EASTER; observed with fasting in many places since the second century. A LITURGY developed at JERUSALEM in the fourth century focused on the veneration of the wood of the cross and liturgical readings during the hours from twelve to three P.M.

T. J. TALLEY

GOPĪ gō´ pē (H—Skt.; lit. "cow-keeper," hence, "female cowherd"). The *gopīs* are the cowherd girls and women, inhabitants of the place called VṚNDĀVANA, who, in the cycle of KRISHNA myths, are in love with him. Some are married, some unmarried, but taken collectively they represent the notion common in VAIṢṆAVA religious doctrine that it is necessary to flout social custom for the love of God. In the early texts they are left rather undifferentiated, but in later stories take on names and other characteristics. Eight of them are friends of RĀDHĀ, and assist Rādhā and Krishna in their tryst.

E. C. DIMOCK, JR.

GOSPEL (Ch—Gr.; *euangelion* = Lat. *evangelium* [lit. "proclaimed good news"]). (1) an oral message; (2) the generic name for an account of Jesus' words and deeds. Although the plural is found in Greek literature, in Christian texts, where the term became central, only the singular is found; this reflects the conviction that there is only one decisive piece of good news—that concerning the religious significance of JESUS. Apparently Paul introduced *euangelion* into Christian usage, though possibly Jesus used the verb, "to announce good news." In Christian usage the gospel was an oral message.

"Gospel" as a written account of Jesus is a secondary development. The NT contains four Gospels (Matthew, Mark, Luke, John); the first three are commonly called "Synoptic" because of their similar structure and content. The extent to which the Gospels resemble ancient biographies and aretalogies (stories celebrating the virtues and exploits of a hero) is disputed, though there is agreement that the Gospels are not biographies in the modern sense.

There are no non-Christian Gospels; all Gospels portray Jesus from a particular Christian standpoint. They are all either anonymous, as in the NT (the names are traditional ascriptions), or pseudonymous.

The Synoptic Gospels compile reports and sayings of Jesus. Originally these circulated independently in Christian communities which used these traditions in teaching, preaching, and worship. Moreover, these communities apparently did not distinguish sharply between reports of what Jesus had said during his lifetime and what the resurrected Jesus was believed to be saying through prophets. Consequently, historical critics distinguish genuine from nongenuine sayings.

The writers of the Synoptic Gospels apparently used collections of sayings and stories, some of which were written. Majority opinion holds that Matthew and Luke are based on Mark (*ca.* A.D. 70) and on a collection of Jesus' sayings (labeled "Q"), as well as traditions peculiar to each writer's circle. A vigorous minority opinion, however, denies that Q ever existed, and insists that Luke use Matthew and that Mark is an extract from both.

The Gospel of John apparently represents an

independent tradition, which developed in a distinctive Christian community. John's portrayal of Jesus is quite different from that of the Synoptics, as is its vocabulary and style. Probably all the NT Gospels were written before the end of the first century A.D.

By the end of the third century A.D. Christians had produced many more gospels. The noncanonical books are quite diverse in literary form and content.

Bibliography. E. Hennecke and W. Schneemelcher, *New Testament Apocrypha.* 2 vols. (1963, 1965), translations, introductions, bibliographies; C. H. Talbert, *What Is a Gospel?* (1977); W. R. Farmer, *The Synoptic Problem* (1964), claims that Mark is the last of the Synoptics; F. C. Grant, *The Gospels* (1957), Mark is the first of the Synoptics; R. E. Brown, *The Gospel According to John.* 2 vols (1966, 1970), Vol. 1 has good discussion of major questions. L. E. KECK

GOSPEL SONGS (Ch). A generic term for religious songs composed for purposes of evangelism. Specifically, it refers to a form that originated during the nineteenth century revivals in the U.S. and was made popular by P. P. Bliss (1838-76), Ira D. Sankey (1840-1908), and others. In a wide variety of styles, it lives on in the worship of EVANGELICALS.

H. MCELRATH

GRAHAM, WILLIAM FRANKLIN "BILLY" (Ch; 1918-). American evangelist, noted for his successful use of large-scale evangelism. Following his 1949 revival in Los Angeles, he became known nationally as a leading conservative. He has been an innovator in the use of modern communications, especially television, to spread the GOSPEL.

G. MILLER

GRAIL, HOLY (Ch). Object of quest in Arthurian legend. The myth of the Holy Grail has received extensive and varied artistic development. Its origin, the subject of continuing debate, has been surmised to lie in fertility rites of ancient Greece, Celtic legend, and Christian liturgy. The term "Grail" is associated with a number of objects, including the dish from which Christ ate the paschal lamb at the Last Supper, the chalice from which he drank, the container in which Joseph of Arimathea collected Christ's blood (generally one of the vessels from the Last Supper), a talismanic stone similar in properties to the philosophers' stone of alchemy, and the spear which pierced Christ's side. In the legend, Joseph of Arimathea is said to have brought the Grail to England, where it is protected by his descendants, the Fisher Kings. A knight sets out to find the elusive castle of the Fisher King and thus to end the suffering of this ill or wounded king and his distressed realm. The quest becomes a spiritual journey in search of true chivalry, Christian love. Having flourished during the late twelfth and early thirteenth centuries, the legend reappeared in works such as Malory's *Morte D'Arthur,* Tennyson's *Idylls of the King,* Wagner's opera *Parsifal,* and Eliot's "The Waste Land."

Bibliography. A. C. L. Brown, *The Origin of the Grail Legend* (1943); E. Jung and M.-L. von Franz, *The Grail Legend,* (1971); R. S. Loomis, *The Grail: From Celtic Myth to Christian Symbol* (1963); M. J. C. Reid, *The Arthurian Legend* (1938); J. L. Weston, *From Ritual to Romance* (1920). D. J. WHITE

GRANTH-SAHIB grūnt sä hēb (S). *See* ĀDI GRANTH.

GREAT AWAKENING (Ch). A series of revivals in British North America between 1720 and 1750. George Whitefield (1714-70), a British evangelist, was the center of various movements which took different forms in different regions and denominations. The revivals were highly controversial and resulted in serious divisions in the PRESBYTERIAN and CONGREGATIONAL Churches (*see* REVIVALISM).

Bibliography. E. S. Gausted, *The Great Awakening in New England* (1957). G. MILLER

GREAT LEARNING (Con—Chin.; *ta-hsüeh* dä shwē). Originally a chapter of the Confucian classic *The Book of Rites (Li Chi).* Authorship has been variously ascribed to Tzu Ssu, CONFUCIUS' grandson, to Tseng Tzu, one of Confucius' disciples, or to one of Tseng Tzu's pupils, though critical modern scholarship now places it as late as the end of the Han dynasty (third century A.D.). CHU HSI (1130-1200) placed it first in his grouping of basic Confucian writings called the Four Books, as representing the general principles of the Confucian teaching.

The text is addressed to rulers as a guide to bringing order to the world, but the self-cultivation of the ruler and that of the individual do not differ, and the text suggests the fundamental Confucian belief that order in society will result only from the proper moral cultivation of the individual. The program outlined in the Great Learning involves eight steps; the last three concern societal order and the first five refer to the cultivation of the individual. The eight steps suggest the essential continuity of the moral order of Heaven and human nature and thus the relation and balance of individual self-cultivation and moral order in society.

Bibliography. E. R. Hughes. *The Great Learning and the Mean in Action* (1942). R. L. TAYLOR

GREAT SCHISM, THE (Ch). 1. "Eastern." The division of the church into East and West, marking the beginning of the ROMAN CATHOLIC and ORTHODOX CHURCHES as distinct entities. Differences go back to the time of CONSTANTINE, centering on matters such as CELIBACY, use of ICONS, the FILIOQUE phrase, and especially the power of the PAPACY. In 1054 an impasse was reached in which the pope and the Eastern patriarch excommunicated each other, from which time the schism is customarily dated. Attempts were made to heal the breach, but the CRUSADES exacerbated feelings, and the schism was accepted as fact after the Turks took Constantinople in 1453. In 1965 Pope Paul VI and Patriarch Athenagoras rescinded the actions of 1054.

R. BULLARD

2. "Western." The division of medieval Roman Catholicism into first two and then three papal allegiances from 1378 to 1417. The phenomenon of several popes each claiming legitimacy and each with his own college of CARDINALS partly resulted from tensions created by the Avignonese PAPACY. Gregory IX died shortly after he returned the papal office from Avignon to ROME. The college of cardinals, apparently under strong pressure to elect an Italian pope, chose Urban VI on April 8, 1378. After a series of bitter disputes with the new pontiff, the cardinals withdrew to Anagni, where they declared Urban's election invalid. In September they elected a second pope, Clement VIII, a cousin to the French king. Clement returned to Avignon while Urban assembled a new set of cardinals in Rome. For nearly forty years there were two lines of popes, producing a grave constitutional crisis within the church. RELIGIOUS ORDERS, dioceses, and lay authorities aligned themselves behind one or other of the rival pontiffs. Finally, in 1408, a majority of cardinals from the two allegiances summoned a general council at Pisa. The united cardinals declared both popes schismatics and elected a third pope, Alexander V. The emperor-elect, Sigismund, forced the calling of a new council, which met at Constance (1414-18). It formally ended the schism with the election of Martin V in 1417. *See* BABYLONIAN CAPTIVITY OF THE CHURCH.

Bibliography. W. Ullmann, *Origins of the Great Schism* (1948); J. H. Smith *The Great Schism* (1970).

H. L. BOND

GREAT SYNAGOGUE or Great Assembly (Ju). Judean legislative and administrative council in the Persian period (538-331 B.C.). Traditionally a body of 120 (or 85) religious leaders, whose origin is attributed to EZRA the Scribe in the fifth century B.C. In the MISHNAH, PIRKE ABOTH, they are presented as responsible for justice, education, and legislative measures to preserve the TORAH. Y. SHAMIR

GREAT VEHICLE (B). *See* MAHĀYĀNA.

GREEK ORTHODOX CHURCH (Ch). The self-governing national state church of modern Greece.

1. **History.** The beginning of the church goes back to the missionary work of PAUL. Acts and Paul's letters to the churches in Philippi, Thessalonica, and Corinth picture the life and the problems of these earliest Christian communities on Greek soil.

After Christianity became the religion of the empire under CONSTANTINE, the churches of Greece remained mainly under the jurisdiction of the Patriarch of Constantinople, sharing the same destiny until the nineteenth century.

The church of the empire expanded into the missionary field. Here the greatest achievement of the Greek church was the conversion of the Slavs by two brothers from Thessalonica, Cyril (d. 869) and Methodius (d. 885), "the apostles to the Slavs."

Theological differences, reinforced by different languages, cultural attitudes, and political rivalry, contributed to the split with the ROMAN CATHOLIC CHURCH. Despite the GREAT SCHISM in 1054, the relations between these two churches continued until the CRUSADES, particularly the Fourth, when a Latin kingdom was established in the East (1204-61).

After the conquest of Constantinople by the Turks in 1493, the church lived for more than three centuries under Turkish rule, and it was considered a crime to convert a Muslim to Christianity. The PATRIARCH of Constantinople was both the spiritual and civil political leader of all Greek Christians under Turkish domination. Whatever their national origin, Christians were regarded as members of a single nation *(millet)*, and the Patriarch performed the role of *millet-bashi*, the head of this nation. This system was beneficial for the Turks, who could hold him responsible for the activities of the people. It also enabled the Greeks to survive as a distinct nation, but periods of relative peace alternated with oppression. The church was identified with the national aspirations of the people and took an active part in the wars of independence in the 1820s

2. **Modern situation.** The Greek Church became self-governing in 1833, but continues united in faith and sacraments with other Eastern ORTHODOX CHURCHES. It is ruled by the Holy Synod, with the Archbishop of "Athens and all Greece" presiding, and contains more than eight million members.

Several religious associations are currently engaged in theological and spiritual revival. The best known is the brotherhood of theologians, or *Zoē*, organized in 1907. These celibate priests and unmarried laymen live a semi-monastic life without permanent vows; the members are free to leave the brotherhood at any time. (*See* MONASTICISM.)

The Greek Church in North and South America has more than a million members, and is under the jurisdiction of the Ecumenical Patriarchate in Istanbul.

Bibliography. P. Hammond, *The Waters of Marah* (1956).

V. KESICH

GREGORIAN CHANT (Ch). The traditional liturgical song literature of ROMAN CATHOLICISM, named after Pope GREGORY I, who is thought to have developed it. Known also as plainsong, it is unisonous, in free rhythm, and completely subservient to its liturgical texts. H. MCELRATH

GREGORY I, THE GREAT (Ch; *ca.* 540-604). Pope from 590; last of the four great Latin "Doctors of the Church" and founder of the medieval PAPACY.

Gregory moved quickly and independently to consolidate the papal power of ROME and to secure the city against invasion. He negotiated an arrangement with the Lombards against future attacks and assumed temporal as well as spiritual jurisdiction over the civil government. He organized and effectively administered the vast papal patrimony and used its revenues to assist the needy, to ransom captives, and to finance peace, as well as to administer church affairs. He vigorously upheld the supremacy and universal jurisdiction of the Roman SEE in both East and West and rebuked the PATRIARCH of Constantinople for his presumptuous self-designation as "universal patriarch." Preferring the title "servant of the servants of God," he worked to strengthen the church in Spain, Gaul, and Northern Italy and promoted the conversion of England by commissioning Augustine, later of Canterbury, and about forty other missionaries for that purpose. Because he influenced major liturgical changes and encouraged the development of liturgical music, the Gregorian Sacramentary and the GREGORIAN CHANT, though of later derivation, came to be associated with his name.

Bibliography. F. H. Dudden, *Gregory the Great* (1905); P. Batiffol, *Saint Gregory the Great* (1929).

H. L. BOND

GREGORY VII (Ch; *ca.* 1023-1085). Pope from 1073. Important transitional figure from the early to the late medieval PAPACY, renowned for his efforts to centralize the papal government in ROME by restricting the power of the BISHOPS, reforming the CLERGY, and forbidding the granting of church offices by laymen (lay investiture). Gregory was elected pope by acclamation of the Roman people with a later ratification by the CARDINALS, contrary to the procedures of the papal election decree of 1059. The validity of his election, however, was not disputed until after 1076. He initiated a sweeping reform program at the Lenten synods of 1074-75, calling for a moral revival of the church and forbidding simony and clerical marriage. In 1075 he forbade lay investiture and threatened the Emperor Henry IV of Germany with EXCOMMUNICATION. At Worms (1076) Henry had Greogry denounced as a false pope and deposed. Gregory then excommunicated the emperor, forgiving him only after he presented himself as a penitent at Canossa (1077). The struggle over investiture soon worsened, and at the synod of Brixen (1080) Henry brought about the election of an antipope, Clement III. Henry invaded Italy, and Gregory's cardinals deserted him, forcing him into exile in Salerno, where he died. His use of CANON LAW and his definition of a Christian social order under papal jurisdiction continued to influence church history throughout the Middle Ages.

Bibliography. W. Ullmann, *The Growth of Papal Government in the Middle Ages* (1962). H. L. BOND

GṚHASTHA grĭ hŭs´ thŭ (H—Skt.; lit. "standing in the home"). Householder, the second of the four stages of life (ĀŚRAMA). Upon entering into marriage a Hindu male entered the stage of "householder." It was his duty to maintain the sacred fires, offer worship to the ancestors, produce sons, and provide for the welfare of his family and community.

P. COURTRIGHT

GUṆA gū´ nä (H—Skt.; lit. "thread, cord, strand, quality, attribute, secondary characteristic"). A secondary or constituent dimension of nature (PRAKṚTI) in classical SĀṂKHYA and YOGA philosophy. The term *guṇa* generally means quality or attribute in Indian philosophy, but Sāṃkhya and Yoga construe it in its older sense as "cord," "strand," or "constituent." For these schools *guṇa* is never a quality or attribute of nature, but constitutes its very essence. Nature *(prakṛti)* is then to be understood as something "primary" or "principal," and *guṇa* as "secondary," in the sense that a cloth is primarily cloth, but secondarily an interweaving of threads.

In classical Sāṃkhya and Yoga there are three *guṇas: sattva* (intelligibility or brightness); *rajas* (activity or passion); and *tamas* (dullness or inertia).

G. J. LARSON

GUPTA DYNASTY go͞op´ tŭ (*ca.* A.D. 320-540). The first true empire in India after the MAURYAN DYNASTY. Because of significant developments in grammar, mathematics, astronomy, astrology, literature, philosophy, and religion, this period has often been called the classical age of India.

The dynasty was founded by Chandra Gupta I (*ca.* 320-35), who by his marriage to Kumāradevī, a Lichchavi princess, became ruler of most of Bihār and portions of Bengal and Awadh. His son Samudra Gupta (*ca.* 335-76), who was a poet and musician, expanded the kingdom, and Chandra Gupta II (*ca.* 376-415), another patron of literature and the arts, secured the western border of India, giving the dynasty control over most of northern India. The dynasty, however, never ruled territory equal to the total extent of the Mauryan empire. During the reigns of Kumāra Gupta (*ca.* 415-54) and Skanda Gupta (*ca.* 454-67), the dynasty was threatened by the Hūnas, who eventually gained control over northern, and parts of central, India. Around A.D. 540 the empire fragmented into small kingdoms.

During this period much popular worship was directed to the images of the Jaina saints and the Buddha. The MAHĀYĀNA schools were driving out the HĪNAYĀNA schools by capturing the imagination of the people with their assertion that anyone could become a BODHISATTVA (enlightened being). Chinese pilgrims testify to the worship of AVALOKITEŚVARA, MAÑJUŚRĪ, and Tārā, and the veneration of STŪPAS. In addition, the Jaina Canon was arranged at the second Council of Valabhī (*ca.* 512 or 525), and there were important literary activities among the Buddhist sects. These included the writings of Buddhaghosa, the brothers Asanga and Vasubandhu, and the logician Dignāga. Nonetheless, these heterodox religious movements lost considerable popular support to sectarian Hinduism.

In the Gupta period, the Hindu sects devoted to Shiva and Vishnu often received royal patronage, whereas the Buddhists did not. The dynasty identified itself particularly with Vishnu by adopting the bird Garuda, a vehicle of Vishnu, as its royal emblem, using the boar Avatar as a symbol of royal power, and by referring to themselves on coins as worshipers of Vishnu.

The Guptas also continued to practice the ancient Vedic religion. Samudra Gupta revived the Aśvamedha (horse sacrifice), and the Vedas continued to be viewed as the infallible, sacred, and eternal revelation. However, the powerful appeal of the ancient texts, rites, and deities was losing out to the newer devotional faiths. (*See* Bhakti Hinduism.)

Another important development was the emergence of Śakti cults, which were based on indigenous beliefs and exhibited Tantric influence. Consequently the consorts of the major theistic gods gained in importance. Lakṣmī, the wife of Vishnu, appears on many dynastic coins. The expectation is raised that the king will embody her qualities of beauty, prosperity, and good fortune. An androgynous form of Shiva is found on one Gupta seal.

Bibliography. R. Thapar, *A History of India* (1966), I, 136-66; R. C. Majumdar, ed., *History and Culture of the Indian People,* vol. III (1954). C. Olson

GURDJIEFF, GEORGES IVANOVITCH goor′ jə ĕf (1872-1949). Founder of the Institute for the Harmonious Development of Man in Fontainebleau, France, where, through calisthenics and music he helped his followers to higher planes of consciousness. He claimed to base his teachings on those of a "hidden brotherhood" in Central Asia. The Gurdjieff Foundation of New York continues his work, though now his writings are the focus of mystic contemplation and philosophical speculation. K. Crim

GURMUKHI gûr mo͞ok′ hē (S). The thirty-five-letter alphabet in which the sacred scripture of the Sikhs, Ādi Granth, was written. Various conjectures have been made about its origin, of which the most commonly accepted is that it is an adaptation of *landé,* a script used by the trading community of northern India. It is believed that the second guru, Angad (1504-1552), took the thirty-five letters of the acrostic composed by Nānak as the basis for the new alphabet and gave it the name *gurmukhi*—"from the mouth of the Guru." Some scholars maintain that the alphabet is much older than Nānak and was known as *painti,* "thirty-five," and was derived from Brahmi letters which were in use in the time of Emperor Aśoka (third century B.C.).

The *gurmukhi* alphabet was employed by the gurus and later Sikh writers but used sparingly by Punjabi Hindus, who preferred the Sanskrit *devanāgarī,* or Muslims, who used the Arabic alphabet. After partition of the Punjab (1947), Sikh-dominated governments of the Indian Punjab were able to make the teaching of the Punjabi language in *gurmukhi* script compulsory in all primary schools in the state. K. Singh

GURU go͞o ro͞o (H—Skt.; lit. "heavy, weighty"). The gurus of Hinduism have played all of the roles of the teacher. Among the fighting Castes the guru was renowned for skill in the implements of warfare or hunting. On the other hand he or she may have been the preceptor in a caste that specialized in music or dance. In popular Hinduism today the term is often applied to a man or woman acknowledged to be in deep union or communion with deity. This individual may teach a particular technique for god-realization and/or be worshiped as god-incarnate. *See* Hindu Holy Persons §1b. C. S. J. White

H

HACHIMAN hä chē män´ (Sh & B—Jap.). One of the most important deities in Japan, formally considered the god of war and enshrined at numerous SHINTŌ shrines throughout the country. Hachiman's complex interrelationship of Shintō and Buddhist elements set a precedent for the linking of Japanese KAMI (divinities) and Buddhist deities.

The first Hachiman shrine was at Usa on the island of Kyushu. Hachiman rose to greater national importance when the deity was consulted through oracle, with favorable results, for the casting of the Great Buddha at the central temple, Tōdaiji, in NARA during the eighth century. Subsequently Hachiman received from an emperor the title *daibosatsu* (great BODHISATTVA), and Buddhist interpretations of Hachiman and his religious significance are many. According to Shintō interpretations Hachiman actually represents three deities: Emperor Ōjin, Empress Jingū, and the deity known as Hime-gami. In Shintō the deity is known as Hachimanjin (*jin* is another reading of the character for kami); with the MEIJI Restoration of 1868 and the government policy of separating Shintō and Buddhism, it was ordered that the *daibosatsu* title of Hachiman be replaced with the term *jin* (Hachimanjin), but popular faith in Hachiman appears to be little affected by such official changes.

H. B. EARHART

ḤADĪTH hä dēth´ (I—Arab.; lit. "talk, speech, narrative; news" [*ḥ-d-th*—"to speak; to be new"]). A narrative, or "tradition," usually short, which reports what MUHAMMAD said, did, approved (or disapproved), or was like in appearance or character. *Ḥadīth* (pl., *aḥādīth*) refers not only to a single tradition, but as a collective noun also to the entire corpus of tradition preserved and recorded by Muslims. Technically, the term applies to the unit composed of the *matn,* or text, of the report and the *isnād* (also *sanad*), or supporting "chain"*(silsilah)* of transmitters through which the text has been handed down from the Prophet's time to that of the latest transmitter. Among Muslims generally, and especially among SUNNIS, the *ḥadīth* has served together with the QUR'ĀN as the major source of authoritative guidance for human affairs, both in more narrowly "legal" issues and in all other aspects of communal and personal life. If the function of the Qur'ān in Muslim life can be likened to that of Christ in Christian life, one Islamic analogy for the Christian NT would be the *ḥadīth.* Historical information, legal precedents, exhortations to piety, rules for personal hygiene and ritual action, and stories about God, his angels, his prophets, and the Last Day—all make the *ḥadīth* the detailed supplement and guide to the Qur'ānic message upon which Islamic ideas and institutions, faith and society, have been founded and elaborated for fourteen centuries.

1. Origins and development. With Muhammad's death, active revelatory and prophetic guidance ceased. The only recourse for interpretation of the vision of human life and community that had created the Muslim UMMA was now to the Qur'ānic "recitations" and the remembered words and actions of Muhammad. It is thus logical that traditions were early sought after, collected, and passed on (as well as sometimes invented or altered for pious or impious purposes) within the community, and that they came to serve as the vehicle of the SUNNA, as surrogate for Muhammad, in much the way that the Qur'ān as book served as surrogate for active revelation after the Prophet's death. Similarly, where the CALIPHS became the temporal "successors" to Muhammad, those Muslims who dedicated themselves to conserving the *ḥadīth* alongside the Qur'ān became the spiritual "successors" of the Prophet (*see* 'ULAMĀ'). The first 150 years of Islam (to *ca.* 767) saw ever-increasing attention devoted to preservation of the extra-Qur'ānic heritage of Muhammad and the early Medinan *umma,* which in practice meant the preservation of *ḥadīth.* Although the first half of this period is hard to reconstruct in detail, great progress is now being made in tracing evidence of continuous written transmission of tradition back to the end of the first century, something which many earlier scholars held to be impossible. Now it seems certain that written records went hand-in-hand with oral reports, and by the mid-second century of Islam both the use of the *isnād* and the evaluation and collection of *ḥadīth* reports were well established. The "journey in search of knowledge" had become a respected institution by which the disparate centers of learning in the Islamic empire were bound together in the cultivation of *ḥadīth* and associated scholarship.

2. **Major collections.** It is, however, only with the third Islamic (ninth A.D.) century that the "comprehensive" collections of tradition make their appearance. Some of these compilations have been so widely relied upon by later Islam that they can be called in some sense "standard." Sunnis have at least nine and SHI'ITES three. The major Sunni works are the "six books" of BUKHĀRĪ, MUSLIM IBN AL-ḤAJJĀJ, Abū Dāwūd (d. 888), Tirmidhī (d. 892), Nasā'ī (d. 915), and Ibn Mājah (d. 886)—or, as sixth in the view of some, Dārimī (d. 869), or (in North Africa) even MALIK IBN ANAS (d. 795). The *Musnad* of IBN ḤANBAL (d. 855) is also of major importance, although not considered as rigorous in its criteria for selection as the others. Among Shi'ites, where many *ḥadīths* are traced back to ALI and the IMAMS (especially Ja'far al-Ṣādiq), the most revered collection is *al-Kāfī* of al-Kulīnī (d. 939); also important are those of al-Qummī (d. 991) and al-Ṭūsī (d. *ca.* 1067).

3. **Criticism.** Traditional Muslim scholarship devoted massive energy to the study and criticism of *ḥadīth*. Concern for the probity of the transmitters in the *isnād* was a major stimulus to stunning achievements in biographical lexicography: careful evaluation of individual transmitters in each generation after Muhammad, and complex classification of *isnāds* and *ḥadīths* according to their qualities and defects. Although such interests, especially the biographical ones, date from at least as early as the second Islamic century, it was only two hundred years later that the formal "sciences of tradition" (*'ulūm al-ḥadīth)* in these areas began to receive full scholastic elaboration by Rāmahurmuzī (d. 971), al-Ḥākim al-Naysabūrī (d. 1014), al-Khaṭīb al-Baghdādī (d. 1012), and others.

4. **Place in Islam.** It is hard to overemphasize the role of *ḥadīth* in Muslim life and history. As a literary form, the *isnād-matn* unit became the fundamental element in the major genres of Islamic writing. Biography, history, scriptural exegesis, mystical exposition, theological argument, and legal disquisition all consist substantially of, or are interlaced with, discrete reports in *ḥadīth* format. After the Qur'ān, the *ḥadīth* is the basic source for "proof texts" in Islamic writing. Theologically, the *ḥadīth* is held to be divinely inspired, albeit according to sense rather than word-for-word like the Qur'ān. There are even some words of God reported by Muhammad in the *ḥadīth*, although such a "divine saying" *(ḥadīth qudsī)* has no special status above that of a normal "prophetic tradition" *(ḥadīth nabawī)*. Only the Qur'ān has higher authoritative status than the *ḥadīth;* yet since it can only be interpreted by reference to the *ḥadīth*, there is functional validity to the *ḥadīth* reported by Dārimī: "The *sunna* is arbiter of the Qur'ān, not the Qur'ān of the *sunna*."

Bibliography. I. Goldziher, *Muhammedanise Studien* II (1890 [ET 1971]), 1-274; M. Z. Siddiqi, *Ḥadīth Literature* (1961); J. Robson, *EI* ²; III, 23-29; F. Sezgin, *Geschichte des arabischen Schrifttums, I* (1967); N. Abbott, *Studies in Arabic Literary Papyri*, II (1967), 1-83; R. Paret, in *Tschudi Festschrift* (1954), pp. 147-53; J. Fück, in *ZDMG*, XCIII (1939), 1-32; M. M. Azmi, *Studies in Early Hadith Literature* (1968); J. van Ess, *Zwischen Ḥadīt und Theologie* (1975); W. A. Graham, *Divine Word and Prophetic Word in Early Islam* (1977); J. Schacht, *Origins of Muhammadan Jurisprudence* (1975).

W. A. GRAHAM

ḤĀFIZ SHĪRĀZĪ hä fiz shē rä´ zē (I; 1326-1390). The supreme lyricist in the classical PERSIAN LANGUAGE. He lived his whole life in his native Shiraz, except for a brief interlude in the early 1370s. Though he was poor in his youth, a brilliant academic record won him a position of influence and wealth at the royal court in Shiraz. Due to the intrigue of hostile courtiers, royal favor was withdrawn, and only in the final years of his life, under a different patron, was he restored to his former position.

Ḥāfiz excels not only in selection of lyrical phrases but also in juxtaposition of metaphors that maximize the ambiguity of his dominant theme: love (bodily and spiritual, profane and sacred, terrestrial and celestial) absorbs the attention of man and draws him to the height, which can quickly become the depth, of emotional, aesthetic, and mystical experience. *See* ISLAM, §4f.

Bibliography. J. Rypka, *History of Iranian Literature* (1968), pp. 263-71; R. M. Rehder, "The Unity of the Ghazals of Hafiz," *Der Islam* 51/1 (1974), 55-96.

B. LAWRENCE

HAGGADAH häg gä dä´ (Ju—Heb.; lit. "telling").

1. The liturgy for the PASSOVER SEDER meal, centered around the story of the Exodus. It includes relevant biblical verses and much MIDRASH upon them, as well as BENEDICTIONS over the food, psalms, hymns, traditional prayers, and instructions for the conduct of the ritual. The Haggadah is a miscellany of many diverse elements, the product of spontaneous organic development rather than a definitive edition or redaction. While much of its basic content seems to date from the time of the TANNAIM or earlier, it contains material from every phase of Jewish history and continues to be a central focus for liturgical innovation and creativity today.

2. Alternate Anglicized spelling of AGGADAH.

Bibliography. T. H. Gaster, *Passover* (1949); P. Goodman, *The Passover Anthology* (1961); N. N. Glatzer, *The Passover Haggadah* (1969).

I. CHERNUS

HAGIA SOPHIA hä´ gyə sō fē´ ə (Ch & I). The most important ancient church building surviving. At Constantinople (Istanbul) the present structure, a domed basilica, dates from 537. It was converted to a MOSQUE in 1453, and its Christian art work destroyed or covered. Four MINARETS at the corners were added at different times. A masterpiece of Byzantine architecture, it has been a museum since 1935, with much of its original mosaic work uncovered.

R. BULLARD

HAIKU hī´ koo (B—Jap.). Japanese poem in a single breath reflecting an immediate experience of a moment in nature; generally in seventeen sound-units arranged in lines of 5, 7, 5. Traditionally the haiku has shown close kinship with Japanese religious sensibilities, has been the art of wandering poet-priests, and has expressed a ZEN awareness of the eternal in the temporal.

1. **Origin and development.** Earliest Japanese literature beginning with the KOJIKI included poetry. The oldest regular poetic form was the *tanka* (or *waka*) in 5 lines of 5, 7, 5, 7, 7 *ji-on* ("sound-units"). As increasingly complex rules for writing *tanka* made it the property of the aristocracy, *renga* ("linked-verse") became a popular pursuit open to all. Gatherings of samurai or merchants would cooperate in the game of linking 5, 7, 5 and 7, 7 sound-unit lines to create a chain-poem with as many as 1,000 links. The aristocracy began to claim even the *renga,* but commoners retained a *haikkai* ("comic," "playful") style *renga* that resisted aristocratic formalisms. Through the creativity of a few great writers, *haikkai* came to represent an entire movement in literature open to the masses and emphasizing profundity in simplicity. Some *haikkai* poets so developed the *hokku,* or opening link of a *renga,* that *hokku* began to be collected apart from the links that followed. About 1890 the poet Shiki advocated the use of the term "haiku" for these independent *hokku* in the *haikkai* style, and the term "haiku" has prevailed ever since.

2. **Haiku and Zen.** The origin and development of the haiku and of Zen had much in common. Both were democratizations resisting aristocratic encroachment, both turned from scholasticism and formalism to direct experience and the unpretentious, and both utilized purposeful brevity and a focus on nature. It was inevitable that the "way of haiku" and the "way of Zen" would meet. This is exactly what happened in the work of Matsuo Bashō (1644-94). Bashō revolutionized the art with his crow haiku, which embodied such qualities of the Zen arts as *sabi* ("loneliness"), *wabi* ("poverty"), and *yūgen* ("mystery"):

On a withered branch
A crow flaps down and settles
This autumn evening.

After studying with the Zen monk Butchō, Bashō wrote the most famous of all haiku, relating the timeless and the momentary in Zen fashion:

An age-old pond—
A frog suddenly leaps out
Splashing water.

The artist-poet Buson (1715-83) refined the *haiga,* a combination of haiku and ink-painting, while Issa (1762-1826) and Shiki (1867-1902) brought the haiku to the high level of popularity it enjoys to this day.

Bibliography. H. Henderson, *An Introduction to Haiku* (1958); K. Yasuda, *The Japanese Haiku* (1957); D. Keene, *World Within Walls* (1976); G. Brower, *Haiku in Western Languages: An Annotated Bibliography* (1972).

C. W. EDWARDS

HAJJ häj (I). The annual PILGRIMAGE to MECCA; one of the five PILLARS OF ISLAM. Hajji is the honorific title given each Muslim who has performed the pilgrimage. The QUR'ĀN (Sura 3:90-92) enjoins on every Muslim, male and female, the obligation to journey to Mecca at least once during one's lifetime to visit the KA'BA and other sacred sites near Mecca and there to perform prescribed religious rites.

1. **Pre-Islamic origin.** The custom of journeying to a sacred place to perform religious rites was familiar in pre-Islamic Arabia, as generally among the Semitic peoples. Moreover, the sacred places in and near Mecca which Muslim pilgrims visit as well as many of the rites performed are pre-Islamic in origin. The pre-Islamic elements, however, were transformed in the course of their incorporation into Islam so as to make them appropriate to its monotheistic orientation.

2. **Muhammad's hajj.** Muhammad's "farewell pilgrimage," performed several months before his death in A.D. 632, is believed by Muslims to provide the model for their own performances. Its paradigmatic character, the injunctions of the Qur'ān, and mythical episodes in a sacred history centering mostly on Abraham provide the principal means by which the hajj has assumed its Islamic character.

3. **Meccan rites.** While a Muslim may visit Mecca at any time, the hajj may be performed only during the twelfth (lunar) month. The hajj begins with the pilgrim's departure from home after settling his affairs and praying for God's protection on the journey and a safe return. Before entering the sacred territory which surrounds Mecca, the pilgrim performs a rite of sacralization *(ihrām),* which includes the donning of a simple white garment worn by all pilgrims, regardless of status. At this point one becomes subject to certain prohibitions, including sexual relations. After arriving in Mecca the pilgrim goes to the Ka'ba to perform the circumambulation *(tawāf)* of arrival, consisting of seven circuits of the Ka'ba, beginning at the corner containing the sacred black stone, which one kisses or touches, after the example of MUHAMMAD. Appropriate prayers are uttered during the circuits. Then the pilgrim goes to the nearby *maqām Ibrāhīm* ("station of Abraham") where he prays before (but not to) the stone said miraculously to have retained the footprint of Abraham, builder of the Ka'ba at ALLAH'S command. Next the pilgrim goes to the well of Zamzam and

Aramco World Magazine, photo by S. M. Amin

The courtyard of the Great Mosque, Mecca. Pilgrims surround the Ka'ba.

drinks from it, before leaving the great mosque. Then follows the ritual of running *(sa'y)* seven times between two "hills," as-Safā and al-Marwa, now enclosed in a long passageway. This re-enacts the activity of Hagar. Abandoned here with her son Ishmael by Abraham at the command of God, she ran back and forth, calling for aid and searching for water. These acts at or near the Ka'ba form the preliminaries of the hajj but may be performed at any time, whether as part of the hajj or not. Together they constitute the 'Umra, sometimes referred to as "the little pilgrimage," although it is not in fact a pilgrimage.

4. **Rites at Arafat and Minā.** The hajj proper begins on the eighth day of the pilgrimage month when the pilgrims make their way toward Arafat, some dozen miles east of Mecca. There on the following day the pilgrims "stand" before Allah from noon until sunset, praying for divine forgiveness and acceptance. This simple event *(wuqūf)* is both the climax and the *sine qua non* of the hajj, and seems to have eschatological overtones as an anticipation and rehearsal of the final judgment.

At sunset the pilgrims hasten back along the road toward Mecca. They spend the night at Muzdalifa and the following day proceed to Minā, collecting on the way pebbles with which to "stone the devil," represented by pillars at three places in Minā. The justification for this action is the story of the devil's tempting Abraham to disobey the divine command to sacrifice his son Ishmael in this place (not Isaac, as in Gen. 22:1-19). By throwing stones at the devil as Abraham did, the pilgrims express their own resistance to temptation.

The same mythical narrative provides the justification and model for the pilgrims' performance of an animal sacrifice at Minā, inasmuch as the story concludes with Allah's provision of a sacrificial animal in the place of the son.

5. **Conclusion of the hajj.** After the animal sacrifice the pilgrim performs a sacrifice of his hair. A man's head is shaved; women have a lock clipped. This is among other things an act of desacralization, for the pilgrim may now change from the pilgrimage garment and is freed from most of the restrictions of the *ihrām* state. There follow three days of feasting and celebration in which Muslims throughout the world join through the celebration of *al-'īd al-kabīr* ("The Great Festival").

On returning to Mecca the pilgrim again visits the Ka'ba. Before departing the city he performs a "circumambulation of farewell." Although it is not required, some pilgrims go north to the city of Medina to visit the Mosque of the Prophet, which contains the tomb of Muhammad.

6. **Significance of the hajj.** In making the pilgrimage the Muslim becomes personally present at the center of his world, toward which he has directed his face daily in the performance of the prayers (*see* Qiblah). Further, it is a place exclusive to Muslims; non-Muslims are not knowingly permitted to enter the sacred territory.

While the number of pilgrims varies annually, in recent years it has approached a million, coming from even the most distant parts of the Islamic world. The hajj is not only a response to the divine command and an expression of the essential equality of all Muslims before Allah but also a means to unity and solidarity among Muslims.

Bibliography. G. von Grunebaum, *Muhammadan Festivals* (1951); A. Kamal, *The Sacred Journey* (1961); D. Long, *The Hajj Today* (1979). H. B. Partin

HAKUIN EKAKU hä koo ĭn´ ĕ kä´ koo (B—Jap.; 1685-1768). Rinzai Zen Buddhist priest. Hakuin pursued the monastic life from age fifteen and had a series of deepening enlightenment experiences. In 1716 he moved into Shoinji, the dilapidated temple near his birthplace, and served as religious advisor to feudal lords, peasants, and an increasing number of monks.

Hakuin revived the moribund Zen of his day through a rigorous course of Kōan exercise that has determined the nature of Rinzai Zen to this day. His detailed descriptions of his own enlightenment experiences, his Zen painting and calligraphy, and his use of popular songs and stories to teach Buddhism mark him as unique in the history of Zen.

Bibliography. P. B. Yampolsky, *The Zen Master Hakuin: Selected Writings* (1971). C. W. Edwards

HALAKAH hä lä´ käh (Ju—Heb. & Aram.; lit. "path" [from *hlk,* "to walk"]). 1. The legal system of Judaism. 2. The legal part of the Talmud. 3. An individual legal decision.

The Pharisees taught that both the written and the oral Law were given to Moses on Mt. Sinai. However, there was probably a long development even in the Pentateuch. The Holiness Code (Lev. 17-26), the Deuteronomist, and the Priestly Law come from different periods. The Sadducees and the Qumran Sect had other rules, but the Pharisee tradition became normative for rabbinic Judaism, although later opposed by the Karaites.

The Great Synagogue prepared "a fence" (additional preventive measures) for the Torah, and in the Mishnah and the Talmud halakah was established according to majority rule, aided by traditional rules of hermeneutics. In case of doubt, the stringent view was accepted with regard to a rule from Torah, unlike the practice in the case of a rabbinical injunction (Babylonian Talmud, *Beẓah* 3b). Customs and the words of the *soferim* (scribe-scholars) are other sources of law. Commentaries, Responsa, and codes were based on the authority of halakhists.

Orthodox Jews believe in a God-given law *(Torah min ha-shamayim),* including all 613 commandments (*see* Mitzvah) regulating life. The Reform movement holds only to the moral laws as eternally binding. Conservative Judaism sees the halakah as a developing organism, yet also inspired.

Bibliography. G. F. Moore, *Judaism in the First Centuries of the Christian Era,* 3 vols. (1927-30), on law and morals; C. Tchernowitz, *Toledot ha-Halakha,* 4 vols. (1934-50), on the history of oral Law; M. Kadushin, *The Rabbinic Mind* (3rd ed., 1972), on the value concepts expressed in halakah, with bibliog. Y. Shamir

al-ḤALLĀJ, ḤUSAYN IBN MANṢŪR ăl hă läj´ hōō sĭn´ ĭb´ ən măn tsōōr´ (I; A.D. 858-922). The most famous and controversial Sufi figure in medieval Islam. Born in Fars, a cotton-carder *(ḥallāj)* by trade, he pursued the mystical path under two spiritual masters, one of whom, Junayd, was lauded for his "sobriety." Ḥallāj, however, has been viewed as the exemplar of "intoxication," since he once declared: *"Ānā'l-Haqq"* ("I am Truth!"). Since "Truth" is one of the names of God, this was considered blasphemy. He traveled widely, performing the pilgrimage (Hajj) three times, and making numerous enemies as well as friends in Muslim communities of Central and Southern Asia.

A book of poetry and one of anecdotes are among the numerous writings ascribed to al-Ḥallāj. He never tired of talking about the relationship of love between man and God. It entails endless suffering, but it also brings a strange kind of joy, known only to the devotee.

Ḥallāj became the first Sufi martyr (Shahīd) when he was executed by dismemberment, and his corpse was crucified (or hanged) and burned. Each act of his degradation has become a topic for his subsequent exaltation among Sufi poets, including Jalāl ad-Dīn Rūmī.

Bibliography. L. Massignon, *La passion d'Al-Ḥosayn ibn Manṣour Al-Ḥallāj* (1922); M. Molé, *Les mystiques musulmans* (1965), pp. 68-72; A. Schimmel, *Mystical Dimensions of Islam* (1975), pp. 62-77. B. Lawrence

HALO (Ch & B; Gr. *halōs*) 1. In Christian art a symbol placed around the head of a person considered holy or divine. A triangular halo is used exclusively for the Trinity, especially God the Father. To portray Christ, the Virgin Mary, and saints a circular halo is used, and for living persons, a square halo. Christ or the Virgin may also be entirely surrounded by an aureole or nimbus, a framework of rays of light, also called "mandorla" because of its almond shape.

2. In Buddhist painting and sculpture the heads of Buddhas, Bodhisattvas, and Arhants are often surrounded by circular halos, many of which contain floral or geometric designs. The typical aureole begins slightly above the bottom of the figure, curves upward to a point, and is filled with stylized flames and, in some cases, with Buddha figures.

K. Crim

HAṂSA hŭm´ sŭ (H—Skt.). A mythical bird, a goose or gander; also translated as swan.

Haṃsa is the most exalted of all mythical birds and animals in Hinduism. He is the vehicle (Vāhana) or mount of the creator god Brahmā. We usually associate Brahmā with the lotus *(padma)* on which he is seated as he creates the cardinal points and worlds, but in Hindu iconography he is also portrayed as seated on or standing near Haṃsa. The mythical metaphors of lotus and gander have a common

Reproduced through the courtesy of the Michigan-Princeton-Alexandria Expedition to Mount Sinai

Christ enthroned (*ca.* 7th century); icon showing halo and nimbus

significance; neither is bound, rooted or fixed to the waters upon which they float. Haṃsa, the mythical gander, is both aquatic and atmospheric, capable of floating on the waters and flying through the air. He is not bound by water or atmosphere. The symbolic meaning of Haṃsa is quite complex. We cannot simply translate the physical properties of a gander into the meaning of the mythical bird Haṃsa. The gander's flight from north to south to north may symbolize Brahmā's mediation between life and death: south in Hindu cosmology always signifies the land of the ancestors (Pitṛs). In the Upaniṣads, Haṃsa is usually related to Brahmā and is identified as the soul which wanders to and fro in this world and the next, or, as the immortal self (Atman). In the Mahābhārata, Brahmā appears as "the golden gander" in this famous discourse with the Sādhyas, the "perfected sages."

Bibliography. *See* Vāhana. H. H. Penner

HANAFITES hă´ nă fīts (I). School of Islamic law (*see* Fiqh) named after Abū Ḥanīfa (d. 767). It originated in Iraq and was the school adopted by the 'Abbāsid Caliphs. It gained popularity in Transoxania, Khurasan, Afghanistan, India, and China. In the Mediterranean it became the school of the Ottoman empire, and is the one generally recognized in its former provinces. Its method can be characterized as more formal and literalist than some other schools, although it allows greater use of legal strategems to circumvent positive provisions of the law.

While the school took its name from the Kūfan jurist Abū Ḥanīfa, credit for its foundation is generally given to two of his pupils, Abū Yūsuf Ya'qūb (d. 798), author of a treatise on the tax of non-Muslims, and his better known contemporary Muhammad ibn al-Ḥasan al-Shaybānī (d. 805), who wrote a treatise central to the foundation of the school, *The Book of Roots,* and two works with the designations *The Small Collection* and *The Large Collection.* Since there is often disagreement among Abū Ḥanīfa, Abū Yūsuf, and al-Shaybānī, the school is less uniform and coherent in its doctrine than other schools. During the period of controversy between the old legal schools and the Traditionists in the second and third Islamic centuries, the school was attacked for its use of the discretionary opinion of individual jurists, but in fact it is only slightly more tolerant on this point than the extreme Hanbalites, who prefer traditions to juristic reasoning (*see* Ibn Ḥanbal).

The Hanafite school used legal strategems to circumvent the positive precepts of laws governing such things as interest on loans. While interest is forbidden, it could be effected by use of the double sale in which the lender would buy the collateral, for an agreed price, and the borrower contracted to repurchase the collateral at a future date for a higher price, the difference between the two prices representing the interest. In line with this use of strategems, the Hanafites are more formalistic than either the Hanbalites or the Malikites (*see* Malik ibn Anas) and do not inquire into the motives of the individual, concentrating instead on the external act. The Malikites accuse the Hanafites of permitting legal means to achieve illegal ends. The Hanafites would not inquire into the motives of contracting, consummating, and ending the marriage of a woman to a third party in order to allow remarriage to a former husband after divorce, taking the act as evidence of having fulfilled the requirements of the law.

In modern times Hanafite principles have influenced family law by their incorporation into the codes of several of the former Ottoman provinces, e.g. Turkey and Egypt, although, because of the adoption of Western style codes, these cannot still be said to belong to the Hanafite school.

Bibliography. *See* Fiqh. G. D. Newby

HANBALITES hăn´ bă līts (I). *See* Ibn Ḥanbal.

HANUKKAH hă nū kăh´ (Ju—Heb.; lit. "dedication" as of a public building). A minor festival celebrated on the twenty-fifth of Kislev (December), during which there are no restrictions on labor or food preparation. Lights are kindled for each of the successive eight days of the festival on a special candelabrum called a *hanukiah.* In addition, special prayers are used to commemorate the day.

The origins of Hanukkah are post-biblical and are recorded mainly in rabbinic literature and such contemporary sources as the books of the Maccabees and Josephus. It dates to the Hellenist oppressions under Antiochus Epiphanes (*ca.* 168 B.C.), who decreed that images were to be worshiped in the Jerusalem Temple. A revolt, led by Judas Maccabee and his brothers of the priestly Hasmonean family, ejected the Hellenists from the city after three years of battle.

Several traditions surround the eight-day celebration and the kindling of lights. The most popular tells that upon entering the Temple, the Judeans found that the supply of oil used for lighting its gold candelabrum was defiled. Only one vial with an unbroken seal could be found. Though sufficent for only one day, the oil miraculously fueled the candelabrum for eight days, enough time to prepare a fresh supply and rededicate the Temple. Other customs include eating potato pancakes and jelly doughnuts, betting on the spins of a four-sided top, and offering coins to young children.

Bibliography. E. Bickerman, *From Ezra to the Last of the Maccabees* (1962).

D. J. Schnall

HANUMĀN hŭn´ o͞o män (H—Skt.). The monkey god, one of the principal characters of the Rāmāyana. His mother Añjanā was married to Kesari, but Vāyu the wind god, overcome by her beauty, made love to her. Their child Hanumān was strong and had the power to fly faster than any bird. When he was a child he flew into the sky to eat the sun, which he thought was a fruit. To stop him Indra hit him on the jaw. The wind god was angered by this act and took Hanumān into a cave to shelter him. But when the wind god disappeared, people in the world were no longer able to breathe. At the request of the gods, Brahmā went into the cave and healed Hanumān's wounds. Because of this incident which left his jaw permanently swollen, the child was known as Hanumān (lit. "one who has a big jaw"). Brahmā also gave him the power to assume any form at will, while the other gods gave him many additional powers, including eloquence of expression.

Hanumān plays a dominant role in the fifth book of the Rāmāyaṇa. He is the chief minister of Sugrīva (*see* Bāli), who later helps him to make friends with Rāma. He crosses the ocean to Sri Lanka, conveys Rāma's message to Sītā, and in various other ways plays the role of Rāma's chief servant. (*See* Plate IVb.)

The Rāma devotees consider Hanumān to be the model of devotion to god. Folk belief attributes to Hanumān the power to protect his devotees from the influence of evil spirits.

V. N. Rao

HAOMA hō´ mä. Zoroastrian name for Soma.

HARA här´ ŭ (H). A common epithet for Shiva.

HARAPPĀ. hŭ räp´ pä The culture type-site of the Indus Valley Civilization. Situated along the Ravi, the now dry tributary of the Indus River in northern Pakistan, Harappā flourished as a center, if not a capital of the civilization. About three and a half miles in circuit, it exhibits the high level of city planning and the cultural uniformity known throughout the civilization. Although devastated by plundering in the nineteenth century to provide ballast for a railway line, the remains of Harappā provide clear evidence of the city's having been a prosperous settlement.

H. P. Sullivan

HARE KRISHNA MOVEMENT hä´ rē krĭsh´ nŭ (H). A Hindu movement in North America based on ecstatic devotion to Lord Krishna. The founder, A. C. Bhaktivedanta Swami (Abhay Charan De, 1896-1977), had completed a successful career as a businessman in Bengal before embarking for America as a Hindu missionary in 1965. Establishing himself in Los Angeles, the Swami taught a form of Hinduism with which Americans had previously been unfamiliar: Vaiṣṇava Bhakti. This follows the teachings of a medieval Indian saint, Caitanya, and advocates the frequent chanting of the names of Vishnu and his incarnations. Swami Bhaktivedanta's organization, the International Society for Krishna Consciousness (popularly known as the Hare Krishna Movement), is

BST Photos

Devotees chant the Hare Krishna mantra.

largely Western in membership, but its followers adopt Indian names and the saffron clothing and shaven heads of Indian holy men. Their temples are replicas of those in India, centering on the worship of the images of deities. Some of the followers are from humble social origins and had been drug users before their conversions. Some of the devotees are serious students of Indian religion, and through their publishing firm in Los Angeles, Bhaktivedanta Book Trust, distribute scholarly and interpretive works on the writings of Caitanya and translations of the classical Krishna devotional literature. (*See* Hinduism in America.)

M. Juergensmeyer

HARE KRISHNA MANTRA

hare kṛṣṇa, hare kṛṣṇa,
kṛṣṇa, hare hare,
hare rāma, hare rāma,
rāma, rāma, hare hare.

hä´rä krish´nū
hä´rä rä´mū

Beloved Krishna, beloved Krishna,
Krishna, Kirshna, Lord, Lord,
Beloved Rama, beloved Rama,
Rama, Rama, Lord, Lord.
Literal trans.

O all-attractive, all-pleasing Lord,
O energy of the Lord, please
engage me in your devotional service.
Hare Krishna Movement trans.

HAREM (I). *See* PURDAH.

HARI här´ ē (H). A common epithet for VISHNU.

HARIJAN här´ ĭ jŭn (H—Skt.; lit. "children of god"). A euphemism coined by Mahatma GANDHI to refer to the untouchables of India. Inherently polluting to members of other Hindu castes, the Harijans stand outside the fourfold CASTE structure of Indian society. Yet Harijans comprise about 15 percent of the Indian population and number nearly 80 million spread over all parts of the country. Harijans have always been economically depressed, and the most despised forms of work, such as scavenging, the removal and skinning of dead animals, tanning and all types of leather work, are their traditional occupations. Until recently Harijans were—and often still are—forbidden to draw water from wells used by clean castes, and were subject to many other social restrictions. In South India they were until recently denied access to public roads in the vicinity of Hindu temples. In 1955 the Indian parliament passed an act forbidding any public discrimination against Harijans. The Constitution also gave the Harijans, officially described as "Scheduled Castes," the right to reserved seats in the legislatures and to a quota of posts in the public services.

Although untouchability is now illegal and a few educated Harijans have risen to high positions in their professions and in politics, the condition of the majority of Harijans living in rural areas has not changed appreciably. The persisting social gap between Harijans and "clean" castes is often emphasized by the separation of their settlements from those of the other castes, on the assumption that any bodily contact pollutes members of "clean" castes. For a number of reasons, traditional attitudes toward Harijans have been difficult to modify by legislation alone. The idea of pollution has deep roots in the Hindu beliefs in inherited inequalities. Such ideas have been reinforced by the vested interests of the upper castes in such matters as wages and agricultural employment. To escape from the prejudicial attitudes of Hindus many Harijans have adopted Christianity or Buddhism, whose egalitarian principles appeal to the underprivileged.

C. VON FÜRER-HAIMENDORF

al-ḤASAN IBN ALI IBN ABĪ ṬĀLIB ăl hă săn´ ĭb´ən ă lē´ ĭb´ən ă bē´tä lēb´ (I; *ca.* 624-669). Eldest son of ALI and FĀTIMA, the daughter of MUHAMMAD. After his father's assassination in 661 he was proclaimed CALIPH, but after about six months he reached an agreement with the first UMAYYAD caliph, Mu'awiya, and retired with wealth to MEDINA. According to most SHI'ITES he is the rightful successor to Ali, and thus the second IMAM, although there seems to have been, at least until his death, a faction of Shi'ites who refused to recognize him as imam because he renounced the caliphate.

A.A. SACHEDINA

HĀSHIM hä´ shĭm (I). Great-grandfather of the prophet MUHAMMAD and eponymous ancestor of the Hashimites, the clan to which the Prophet belonged. They were one of the less powerful clans of the QURAISH tribe.

K. CRIM

HASIDISM, CHASIDISM hă´ sĭd ĭsm (Ju—Heb. *hasīd;* lit. "pietist"). Two socio-religious movements in medieval and modern Jewish history, with mystical ideology.

1. **German Hasidism.** This movement emerged in the Rhineland valley in the wake of the massacre of the Jews during the CRUSADES. Its abundant exegetical, legal, and moralistic literature is marked by an ascetic piety emphasizing self-effacing forms of penance, a profound commitment to the punctilious observance of Jewish law and ethics, and a theology of divine immanence or panentheism made up of elements drawn from the philosophic tradition, earlier stages of Jewish MYSTICISM and speculation, and rabbinic theology. Scholars have also discovered the influence of Christian monastic ideals in these writings. Inspired by the awesome example of mass martyrdom during the Crusades, German Hasidism found ordinary piety and common religiosity to be inadequate expressions of human potential for heroic action in fulfilling God's will.

2. **Eastern European Hasidism.** In the eighteenth century a second pietistic popular movement arose in Eastern Europe, where conditions were ripe for a new style of Jewish existence. In 1648 a Ukranian uprising against Poland brought with it widespread massacre of the Jewish population. Eighteen years later came first the elation and then the sudden, bitter disappointment caused by the messianic career and apostasy of SABBATAI ZVI. The progressive turmoil within Jewish life was exacerbated by the continuing upheavals in Poland itself. Even the best intentioned rabbinic leadership struggled in

vain to preserve Jewish morale against the impossible circumstances of physical suffering and economic deterioration in an unstable, declining Poland. Modernity was beginning to unravel the patterns of adjustment that characterized Jewish life throughout the medieval period.

Hasidism drew upon the mystical tradition which, since the sixteenth century, had struck deep roots in Polish and Russian Jewry. ASCETICISM and KABBALA, as well as theology and activity derived from Sabbatai Zvi, permeated every level of society. The mystical ideals of communion with God and the hope for ultimate redemption were living realities for these Jews. Familiarity with an already developed ethical literature that translated theosophical speculations into norms of personal behavior and attitude was widespread. Hasidism repudiated asceticism, defused a messianism that called for a change in historical circumstances, and taught that true redemption was to be found in the internal religious spirit of each individual. Hasidism, like other mystically informed religions, is founded on the principle that reality as seen by our eyes cannot be changed, therefore change the eyes which see reality.

This movement was born in the 1730s when the BAAL SHEM Tov attracted to himself a select circle of preachers, scholars, mystics, and Jewish functionaries, who spread his ideals of spiritual renewal. In Slavic Europe, the domain to which its growth was largely restricted, it attracted many followers by virtue of its leaders, who were recognized as being in the most intimate connection with God, but who lived among the people and cared for their needs.

It was a vigorous, powerful, and highly original movement, but by the middle of the nineteenth century it began to stagnate for internal reasons—i.e., institutionalization of charisma—and for external reasons—i.e., persistent rabbinic opposition and the growing forces of Jewish secularism. The Hasidic world of Eastern Europe was destroyed during Hitler's genocidal war against the Jews. Out of the remnants of the HOLOCAUST the Hasidic movement is recovering its strength in ERETZ ISRAEL and in America. It is staunchly orthodox and is characterized by its refusal to accommodate to modernity.

3. **Characteristic doctrines.** As must be expected from a popular movement that is organized in distinct groups, is led by an unusual number of highly original charismatic leaders, and is informed by the complex variety in mystical and rabbinic theology, Hasidic doctrines defy definition. Though its daily life has always been rigorously governed by rabbinic law, its ideational content displays a wide spectrum of theological positions: from theism to acosmism; from mysticism to existentialism; from theocentricism to humanism; from affirmation of the world to denial of the world; from ZIONISM to anti-Zionism; from sober intellectualism to exuberant emotionalism. Often a perplexing combination of all these polarities is found in a single REBBE, or master.

There is also a bewildering variety of literary expressions. Hasidic writings contain theoretical expositions by diverse masters with differing points of view, as well as an abundance of less explicit homiletic materials, legendary biographies of the masters, parables, tales, and stories. Many believe that the Hasidic spirit is best expressed in the rich tradition of melodies, most of which are sung without words.

Scholars are agreed, however, that the two foci of Hasidic thought are the notions of *devekut,* or communion with God's presence in all things, and the nature of the ZADDIK, or Hasidic master. Inspired by the example of his zaddik, each Hasid strives to sanctify the everyday. *See also* LUBAVITCHER MOVEMENT.

Bibliography. M. Buber, *Tales of the Hasidim* (1947-48), *Hasidism and Modern Man* (1958), and *Origin and Meaning of Hasidism* (1960); L. Jacobs, *Hasidic Prayer* (1972); J. Langer, *Nine Gates to the Chasidic Mysteries* (1961); L. I. Newman, *Hasidic Anthology* (1934).

K. P. BLAND

HASKALAH häs kä´ lä (Ju—Heb.; lit. "enlightenment"). Movement in late eighteenth century Judaism, originating in Germany with MOSES MENDELSSOHN and his circle. By promoting secular education among the Jews the movement sought to accelerate Jewish acculturation and thus speed emancipation.

Bibliography. J. Katz, *Tradition and Crisis* (1961).

M. M. KELLNER

HAṬHA YOGA hä´ tŭ yō´ gŭ (H—Skt.; lit. "exertion, violence, force" [*haṭh*—"to treat with violence, oppress"]). A type of YOGA practice that emerged from the ninth through the twelfth centuries A.D (and thus well after the classical Yoga of PATAÑJALI), emphasizing a program of rigorous physical culture and claiming to be a preparatory discipline for doing classical or Rāja Yoga. The expression Haṭha Yoga, or the "discipline of exertion," is also said to mean "sun" *(ha)* and "moon" *(ṭha)* "discipline" in which "sun" refers to *prāṇa* (or the "breath" that circulates from the chest to the nose and mouth) and "moon" refers to *apāna* (or the "breath" that circulates from the abdominal region to the feet). This discipline is, thus, one of coordinating and controlling all of the life forces in the body. Haṭha Yoga presupposes an ancient theory of spiritual physiology which describes various bodily veins or channels *(nāḍī)* and "centers" or foci of energy *(cakra)* within the body (running from the base of the spine to the top of the head and usually said to be six or seven in number). The discipline is designed to awaken and make available to the YOGIN an inherent but usually dormant energy (ŚAKTI, which is sometimes symbolized as "serpent power" or KUṆḌALINĪ).

G. J. LARSON

HAZZAN hä zän´ (Ju). *See* CANTOR.

HEAVEN and HELL. Originally cosmological terms that identified regions of the universe but which also came to function as vehicles of religious thought. The ideas expressed by these terms are integral to practically all religions, both ancient and modern. Variations among the systems reflect the cosmological and religious perspectives of their respective understanding of the world and human existence. In most religions heaven and hell came to express eschatological ideas related to final states of existence, whether of blessedness (heaven) or curse (hell).

1. **Heaven.** In ancient Near Eastern thought "heaven" identified a region of the observable universe, which pointed beyond itself to the realm of transcendence (divinity). According to Homer, Zeus dwells on Mount Olympus. The OT refers to heaven as God's abode (I Kings 8:30) from which he exercises his sovereign rule (Ps. 29:20) and to which he finally welcomes the faithful righteous (Ps.73:24-25).

The NT reflects the perspectives of first-century Hellenistic Jewish thought, modified in some cases by syncretistic contemporary ideas. Heaven is God's creation (Mark 13:33) in which he resides (Heb. 4:24). Jesus ascended into heaven (Acts 1:9, cf. however, Eph. 4:9) from which he will return (I Thess. 4:16). Since God inhabits heaven, the term also refers to the final blessedness of the faithful.

2. **Hell.** Hell, like heaven, designates a region of the cosmos. In Near Eastern thought the departed dead (shades, spirits, etc.) populated SHEOL (Gr. *hades*; Ps. 80:49). Later Jewish thought refers to sheol as the temporary abode of the righteous who are awaiting final judgment (Ps. 16:10), but the wicked are confined there forever (Slavonic Apocalypse of Enoch 10).

The NT appropriated Jewish concepts and terminology, i.e., hades is the temporary abode of the dead (Rev. 20:3) and *geenna* is the final place of punishment for the wicked (Matt. 18:18). Christian concepts of heaven and hell are brought to poignant expression in the art and literature of the medieval church and the Renaissance, sometimes in grotesque materialistic terms (Michelangelo, *The Last Judgment;* Tintoretto, *The Glory of Paradise;* DANTE, *The Divine Comedy;* etc.).

Outside the Judeo-Christian tradition other symbols describe the conditions of the departed dead. BUDDHISM refers to stages in the afterlife (seven hells and twenty-six heavens). Islamic literature enumerates seven heavens and seven hells (*see* JANNA; JAHANNAM). Modern Christians generally conceive of heaven as the condition of blessedness and personal fulfillment and hell as the absence of these blessings, i.e., as deprivation, deterioration, and degradation and suffering. *See* ESCHATOLOGY; IMMORTALITY.

Bibliography. J. Jeremias, "Hades," *TDNT* I, 146-49; H. Traub, "Ouranos," *TDNT* V, 497-536.

R. C. BRIGGS

HEBREW LANGUAGE (Ju). The language in which most scriptural, rabbinic, and classical Jewish literature is written, and the official language of the State of Israel. Like other Semitic tongues it is written right to left, generally utilizing consonants only, of which there are twenty-two. Current usage is traced to the Tiberias system devised in the eighth century A.D. Variations developed between ASHKENAZIM and SEPHARDIM, Yemenite and Babylonian Jews remaining closest to the original. Israeli Hebrew has borrowed from both traditions, but is closest to Sephardic usage.

Hebrew was the spoken language of the Israelites during most of the scriptural period, competing with ARAMAIC—a Phoenician dialect—at its close. The latter ultimately gained preeminence, becoming the language of commerce and much of the TALMUD. Jews adapted vernacular languages to Hebrew script during the Middle Ages, relegating Hebrew to prayer, ritual, and religious literature, and studying its grammar for purposes of biblical exegesis. (*See* LADINO; YIDDISH.)

Hebrew experienced a renaissance during the eighteenth century HASKALAH, or enlightenment. Initiated first in Western, later in Eastern, Europe, this movement undertook a renewal of Hebrew as a secular tongue. At the end of the nineteenth century with the rise of ZIONISM, Hebrew assumed nationalist importance, though few actually spoke it. A prominent figure in this development was Eliezer Ben-Yehuda, editor of an extensive Hebrew dictionary and founder of the Hebrew Language Council in 1890.

Contemporary Hebrew is spoken in many parts of the world as a secondary language related to Jewish identity and has served as a rallying point for persecuted Jews. In Israel it has adapted "Americanisms" in its syntax and vocabulary, in place of older Hebrew usages.

Bibliography. E. Horowitz, *How the Hebrew Language Grew* (1967); M. Waxman, *A History of Jewish Literature,* 2nd ed. (1938).

D. J. SCHNALL

HEGIRA hĭ jī´ rə (I). *See* HIJRA.

HEJAZ hə jăz´ (I—Arab. Ḥijāz). The northern Arabian highland area along the east coast of the Red Sea, extending from just south of MECCA to the north of MEDINA, over two hundred miles away. The coastal city of Jidda is the port of entry for pilgrims coming by air or sea for the HAJJ. B. LAWRENCE

HELL, ISLAMIC CONCEPT OF. *See* JAHANNAM.

HELVETIC CONFESSIONS hĕl vē´ tĭc (Ch). The First Helvetic Confession (1536) was written by Swiss Reformers to bring about union between the LUTHERANS and the Swiss. The Second Helvetic Confession, written in 1561 as the personal confession of Heinrich Bullinger, ZWINGLI'S successor in Zurich, was made public in 1566 and became a widely accepted confession of REFORMED CHURCHES. Moderate in tone and catholic in outlook, it related Christian theology to Christian experience. *See* CREEDS AND CONFESSIONS §5. J. H. LEITH

HENRY, MATTHEW (Ch; 1662-1714). English nonconformist minister and biblical scholar. Although Henry had originally planned to study law he decided to follow his father in the ministry and served as the PRESBYTERIAN pastor in Chester from 1687 to 1712. He is best known for *Exposition of the Old and New Testaments* (1708-10), a series of commentaries still popular among conservatives.

G. MILLER

HERESY (Ch). *See* ORTHODOXY AND HERESY.

HERZL, THEODOR hĕrts´ əl (Ju; 1860-1904). The father of political ZIONISM by virtue of his founding the World Zionist Organization and his writings, particularly *Der Judenstaat.* Born in Budapest, Herzl moved to Vienna in 1878, where he received a doctorate in law. From 1891 to 1895 he was Paris correspondent for the *Neue Freie Presse* of Vienna. There his concern for the condition of European Jews was increased by the virulent ANTI-SEMITISM of the mobs at the expulsion of Alfred Dreyfus from the French army January 5, 1895. Herzl abandoned an early scheme for conversion to CHRISTIANITY as a solution to the Jewish problem and chose territorial resettlement as the alternative.

Herzl petitioned Jewish philanthropists, and met with political leaders from Britain, Turkey, and Austria-Hungary. He conceded that a Jewish homeland might be founded in Palestine, Argentina, or Uganda. Some Jewish notables questioned the wisdom of a homeland and some Zionists would have only Palestine.

Herzl convened the first Zionist Congress in Basel, August 29-31, 1897. He chaired it and five subsequent congresses, leading to the establishment of the World Zionist Organization. His early death kept him from seeing his plans to fruition.

Bibliography. *See* ZIONISM. D. J. SCHNALL

HESCHEL, ABRAHAM JOSHUA hĕ´ shəl (Ju; 1907-1972). Jewish theologian, who taught at Hebrew Union College in Cincinnati (1940-45) and at the Jewish Theological Seminary of America (1945-72). His major scholarly works are in the areas of prophecy, medieval Jewish philosophy, KABBALA, and HASIDISM. *See* JUDAISM §6f. L. FAGEN

HESYCHASM hĕs´ ə kă zəm (Ch—Gr.; lit. "quiet"). Method of contemplation which became popular among monks of MT. ATHOS in the thirteenth and fourteenth centuries. It involved physical discipline (breathing, posture) and repetition of the Jesus Prayer (*see* MYSTICISM, CHRISTIAN §1) as a way to achieve interior quietness, leading to the possibility of the vision of the light of God's uncreated energies, identified with the light of Jesus' transfiguration. The method owed much to Symeon of Studion, the "New Theologian" (949-1022), and was given theological justification by Gregory Palamas (1296-1359). After much controversy it was received in 1351 as official doctrine of the GREEK ORTHODOX CHURCH and opponents were excommunicated.

Bibliography. V. Lossky, *The Mystical Theology of the Eastern Church* (1957). G. A. ZINN

HIGH HOLY DAYS (Ju). *See* ROSH HA-SHANAH; YOM KIPPUR.

HIJRA hĭj´ rə (I). The migration of MUHAMMAD from MECCA, the city of his birth, to MEDINA, marking the beginning of the Islamic era. It has been latinized as hegira.

Hijra is often mistranslated as "flight." The Arabic verb from which it is derived does not mean "to flee" but rather "to break off relations, emigrate." The event marked Muhammad's break with the Meccans and his establishment of relations with Medina.

Muhammad is said to have arrived in Medina on September 24, A.D. 622. However, the Muslim calendar does not begin with this date, as is sometimes mistakenly said, but with the first day of the first (lunar) month (Muharram) of the Arabian year in which the hijra occurred. This day corresponded with July 16, A.D. 622. Islamic years and dates are indicated by the abbreviation A.H. *(Anno Hegirae).*

Bibliography. *See* HAJJ. H. B. PARTIN

HILLEL THE ELDER hĭ lăl´ (Ju). Contemporary of Herod the Great (73-4 B.C.) and probably born in Babylonia; commenced his rabbinic ministry *ca.* 40 B.C. His rabbinic cohort SHAMMAI shares to some extent his central leadership of the SANHEDRIN (30 B.C.—A.D. 10?), but it is Hillel more than any other PHARISEE except JOHANAN BEN ZAKKAI who shaped the early course of classical Judaism.

Probably a student of ESSENE thought for a short while, Hillel was early attracted to the brotherhoods of the Pharisaic movement. He championed MIDRASH exegesis—biblical interpretation used to justify the Oral Law.

His commitment to the poor endeared him to the common people and his preaching of social justice won him respect and admiration. His social reforms, especially enactment of the *prosbul,* designed to protect creditors, did much to correct the societal and economic abuses which emerged during Herod's reign and after the great earthquake of 31 B.C.

It was his emphasis on living out the HASIDIC ideal, inherited from the early MACCABEAN pietists, however, which enabled him to transform the world of Judaism. With tremendous emphasis on TORAH study and ritual purity, Hillel elevated the life of the mind to an exalted place in Jewish life, as a means for reexperiencing God's word to his people.

Although skeptical of power politics, Hillel urged his fellows to stay in society and transform it. No aspect of life was seen as irrelevant but was given significance by the law. His memorable advice to proselytes best summarizes his teaching: "What is hateful to you do not do to your neighbor: that is the whole of Torah; the rest is commentary; go study" (Shabbat 31a).

Bibliography. N. N. Glazter, *Hillel the Elder: The Emergence of Classical Judaism* (1956). E. M. MEYERS

HĪNAYĀNA hī nü yä′ nü (B—Skt.; lit. "small vehicle, lesser vehicle"). The pejorative name applied to all the early schools of Buddhism by an emergent, radical group (*ca.* 200 B.C.) which referred to itself as MAHĀYĀNA (lit. "large vehicle, greater vehicle"). Hīnayāna thus became a general designation for the two major early schools of Buddhism, the Sthaviras and Mahāsāṅghikas, and their subschools (including the Theravādins). Although traditionally there were eighteen schools cited in this category, in actuality there were many more, most of which died out early. *See* BUDDHISM §2. C. S. PREBISH

HINDĪ hīn′ dē (H & S—Per.; lit. "of India" [*hind*—"India" from Skt. *sindhu*—"the Indus river"]). The official language of the Republic of India and a religious and literary language of North India including several important dialects.

Hindī and its dialects bear a relationship to SANSKRIT like that of the Romance languages to Latin. They developed from Sanskrit, share a common script with it (the Devanagari), and derive much of their vocabulary from it. Much of Hindī literature has been inspired by Sanskrit literature, and both spoken and written Hindī serve to transmit the sacred Sanskrit texts of HINDUISM to the Hindu masses of North India.

The most important literary dialects of Hindī from the fifteenth century well into the nineteenth were Brajbhāṣā and Avadhī. Both served to express BHAKTI HINDUISM, the former centering around the life of KRISHNA, the latter around that of RĀMA. The most famous Hindī poet, TULSĪ DĀS, wrote his RĀMCARITMĀNAS, an Avadhī version of the Sanskrit RĀMĀYAṆA, in the sixteenth century. Another famous Hindī poet of the same century, MĪRĀBĀĪ, wrote many devotional lyrics in praise of Krishna. The ĀDI GRANTH, the sacred book of SIKHISM, includes works by KABĪR and other Hindī poet-saints.

From the latter half of the nineteenth century to the present, the most important dialect of Hindī in both secular and religious terms has been Khaṛī Bolī. DAYĀNANDA, founder of the ĀRYA SAMĀJ, used it to propagate his doctrines. During the same period a massive Hindī movement with pronounced pro-Hindu and anti-Muslim overtones, centered in Banāras and Allāhābād, resulted in Khaṛī Bolī Hindī becoming the official language of India. Simultaneously the number of Hindī publications, many religious, increased dramatically.

Bibliography. R. A. Dwivedi, *A Critical Survey of Hindi Literature* (1966). C. R. KING

HINDU AIMS OF LIFE (PURUṢĀRTHAS) pū ro͞osh är′ täs (H—Skt.; lit. "human objects, aims, goals" [*puruṣa*—"person, man"; *artha*—"object, purpose"]). The classical Hindu tradition categorized the goals of human existence under four headings: right conduct (DHARMA); material gain (ARTHA); pleasure, understood primarily as sexual love (KĀMA); and spiritual liberation (MOKṢA). Along with the ethical ideal which emphasized that proper conduct varies according to an individual's inherited social position *(varṇa)* and stage of life (ĀŚRAMA), the *puruṣārtha* classification became a convenient way of stating the salient features of the Hindu householder's way of life as understood by its Brahmin promulgators. Generally speaking, these aims of life represent the aspirations of TWICE-BORN Hindu males.

The major primary sources for statements about the Hindu aims of life are the Hindu śāstras, especially the legal treatises (DHARMAŚĀSTRAS), and the two great Hindu Epics, the MAHĀBHĀRATA and the RĀMĀYAṆA. The early strata of these texts know of only three goals of human existence, called *trivarga* ("three categories"), which are identical to the first three aims of life (e.g., Manu Smṛti 2:224). Of the three dharma is usually accorded primacy, and indeed when only three aims of life are mentioned, dharma seems to connote some of what was later subsumed under the category *mokṣa*. Dharma in this sense is both proper moral and social conduct, and also the way, the norm, of what is usually labeled "religion." When *mokṣa* is added as a fourth aim of life, the meaning of dharma is restricted mainly to the area of social and moral order. The tendency to categorize all proper human activity under the rubrics of dharma, *artha*, and kāma even appears in some of the early regional vernacular literature of India. The most notable example of this is the *Tirukkuṟaḷ* ("The Sacred Kuṟaḷ") by Tiruvaḷḷuvar, a TAMIL collection (*ca.* fifth century A.D.) of gnomic verse which treats moral, political, and erotic concerns in a nonsectarian and nontheological manner.

The full-blown, fourfold *puruṣārtha* scheme reflects the classical Hindu integration of world-affirmative, householder-oriented values prominent in early Vedic thought with the ascetic tendencies which are more pronounced in the UPANISADS and the major "heterodox" movements of BUDDHISM and JAINISM. Dharma, *artha*, and kāma, as the first three *puruṣārthas*, are especially appropriate to the life of a householder, who must fulfill social obligations, pursue material gain, and enjoy sexual pleasure, if human life and human society are to continue. Spiritual liberation is added as the fourth and culminating goal, the supreme aim of human existence.

Dharma encompasses all the duties and rules of conduct in the ideal society. Each person's behavior should properly reflect the role one is required to play given one's social position and stage of life. To live in complete accord with one's dharma is thus to cease to be a unique individual and to become a perfect mirror of the natural order of things. Dharma also includes ritual duties. The LAWS OF MANU is the best known Hindu text on dharma.

Artha signifies material gain, but this concept includes not simply commerce and economics but also the whole range of activities encompassed by statecraft, diplomacy, administration, and the exercise of power. The acquisition of wealth is thus recognized as necessary for the maintenance of the family, of society, indeed of life itself.

Kāma complements *artha* since both goals are most appropriate to the householder stage of life. While kāma includes within its scope all sensual pleasures, its primary reference is to sexual love. Thus, according to classical Hindu ideas, eros is not deemed vulgar or shameful, a force merely to be repressed or sublimated, but rather when properly regulated kāma is seen to be one of the principal goals of human existence and worthy of a "handbook" entitled the KĀMA SŪTRA.

Finally, spiritual release or *mokṣa* completes the range of legitimate human aspirations. However, *mokṣa* is a goal which is clearly separable from the other three; for it signifies the release of the human self (ATMAN) from the cycle of birth and death (SAMSARA), that is, from the ordinary world, which is the sphere for attaining the first three aims of life. Nevertheless, a person should not strive for *mokṣa* until he has fulfilled the other *puruṣārthas*. *Mokṣa* is thus a goal sought and attained by relatively few Hindus, though ideally the goal of all at some distant point, no matter how many lifetimes in the future. *Mokṣa* as a human aim is often correlated with the final stage of life, that of the SANNYĀSIN or complete renouncer of the world.

Bibliography. W. T. de Bary, ed., *Sources of Indian Tradition* (1958), I, 206-361; P. V. Kane, *History of Dharmaśāstra* (1930–62), II, 2–11; III, 8–10, 239–241; V, 1510–11, 1626–32; Tiruvaḷḷuvar, *The Sacred Kural*, trans. H. A. Popely (1958).

G. E. YOCUM

HINDU HOLY PERSONS. Mircea Eliade's thesis that *to be* religiously means to undergo a *change in mode of being* implies that persons evidencing a unique holiness and sanctity are recognized in acts and dispositions distinct from general human behavior. Thus the "holy person" of HINDUISM is the man or woman who by birth or individual achievement has special access to the divine power which he/she may manipulate or transmit to produce miracles or psychic wonders. The Hindu holy person must also give evidence of extraordinary communion with or absorption in a god or goddess or the Absolute Reality (BRAHMAN). The varieties and modes of "holiness" in Hinduism are presented below according to general "types" occurring in all ages and in terms of the historical development of those types.

1. Vedic and early Hindu typology. The first literary documents of Hinduism, the hymns of the RIG VEDA, are attributed to holy men or seers called RISHIS who heard the revelation (ŚRUTI) and, as the supreme spiritual personages of their time, composed the hymns attesting to the power and glory of the gods. Since scholars assume that the core of the Rig Veda predates the ARYAN entry into India (*ca.* 1800 B.C.) it is likely contemporary with the so-called Proto-SHIVA of the INDUS VALLEY CIVILIZATION. The Proto-Shiva is an "indigenous" iconic representation possibly of an archaic, ascetic holy man with attributes of divinity. This image was found incised on a seal datable before 2000 B.C. The development of the notion of "holy person" in early India thus has at least two aspects, one the increasingly anthropomorphic presentation of the great heavenly beings of the supraphysical world whose myths, starting with the Rig Veda, work out a particular thesis of the nature of the gods, and the second the "divinization" of actual persons under various modes and modalities.

a) The ascetic (*see* ASCETICISM; ŚRAMAṆA). A recurring subject with origins in the Vedic literature is that of the male or female who through TAPAS, i.e., ascetic practices, acquires a superabundance of power. As long as the ascetic retains control of himself/herself, and, particularly, remains sexually charged, this energy will accumulate and can raise the individual's power to the level of that of the gods. Typical physical traits of the Vedic ascetic included wearing soiled garments, going naked, having long matted hair, and being unresponsive to one's own sexual arousal.

b) The guru. Analogous to ascetic power is the power of knowledge in the GURU, who has a skill, perhaps of a practical sort, but who is more likely to be renowned because he is knowledgeable about God. One source of the guru's authority was the ritual knowledge required of the various BRĀHMAṆA orders performing the Vedic sacrifices. The priestly power of manipulating the divine through ritual means was gradually redirected toward mental discipline and higher levels of concentration until certain individuals, through mystical experience, could claim to know the fundamental reality beyond the manifested worlds.

c) The avatar. The separation between God and humans is bridged further when the Indian religious mind envisages the descent (AVATAR) of the god VISHNU. Ten avatars or "descent forms" (including a fish, a man-lion, and several human forms) are presented in the Vishnu Purāṇa and elsewhere. Although it is true that even the anthropomorphic incarnations (e.g., RĀMA and KRISHNA) are difficult to establish on a historical basis, from the time of MAHĀVĪRA of the JAINAS and GAUTAMA of the BUDDHISTS (*ca.* 600 B.C.) it is credible that historical persons did achieve for their followers the level of full "divine" meaning. Also related to the avatar concept, the subsequent growth of the temple cults of various deities (ritually "made alive" in their often anthropomorphic images) sensitized Hindus to perceive God in living human beings.

2. The process of myth. In dealing with the Hindu view of anthropomorphization and divinization, contemporary scholars have exercised ingenuity in grappling with the hidden structure and meaning of Hindu mythology. As myths relate to the Hindu holy person there may seem to be conflict with the orthodox social theory propounding four stages of life (ĀŚRAMA). The second, third, and fourth stages appear to offer antagonistic ends. The second or householder stage requires full involvement in the world, including child-begetting, while the third, the forest dweller, and the fourth, the SANNYĀSIN, assume sexual renunciation.

How does such social theory fit with the myths of SHIVA and VISHNU that show the supreme models of anthropomorphized divinity engaged in sexual relations with wives and lovers? Moreover the cult and praxis of the majority of the ŚAIVA and VAIṢṆAVA sects demand *vairāgya,* or renunciation, to rise beyond the gross physical world to some state of communion or union with deity. This paradox is alleged to become acute in the case of the full ascetic model with its insistence on complete sexual restraint. One school of thought holds that the great variety and confusion in restatement of erotic/ascetic themes in the myths show that the "mythic imagination" struggles futilely to resolve the paradox and that such futility may even be a general characteristic of Hindu myth.

The issue is indeed complex and cannot be entirely resolved, but the myths are only one aspect of the matter. Ritual act and ascetic teaching and practice need focus only on certain themes of the anthropomorphic role of divine models. The ultimate arena of resolution, as well as the working out of the "paradox" of the divine-human or human-divine relationship (not by any means exclusively confined to Hinduism), is interior or mystical. Mythic statement is one of the avenues toward mystical experience but not the only one. It is simplistic and tautologous to blame myths for the paradox of ascetic-sexual tension. The problem is not artificial. The hypothesis underlying most Hindu views is that the demands of one's own sexuality can be transcended: partially on the path of the spiritual aspirant; fully for the God-realized person. (For other positions on this question *see bibliog.*).

3. **Classical Hindu typology.** In the succeeding period of Indian religious history, additional genres of spirituality tended toward the creation of distinctive classes of adepts.

a) The yogi. Sāṃkhya-yoga teaching (*see* YOGA) had an immanent/transcendent view of the individual PURUṢA (soul), which is the final category of the spiritual quest. The self-realized yogi or yogini (f.) was the equivalent of "God." In later Hinduism the metaphysical categories of Sāṃkhya-yoga were reinterpreted to fit widely divergent religious or philosophical systems, but the underlying idea of the self-realized individual persisted.

b) The jñānī. Almost at the opposite pole from Sāṃkhya-yoga was the proposition of UPANIṢADIC origin, rationalized by the monist ŚAṂKARA. According to this theory, at the higher stages of spiritual realization the world perceived by the senses dissolves before the one universal Spirit (BRAHMAN). The way to the realization of that Spirit is through the psychological process of *viveka* or discrimination. This path (*jñāna* yoga) was said to require such mental exertion that it was not a real possibility for most people. Yet, up until modern times there have been individuals esteemed for their absorption in Brahman and accorded divine honors.

c) The siddhas. The base of the paranormal, miracle-working aspect of the holy person is found in the TANTRIC tradition of SIDDHIS, powers acquired through ritual, *tapas,* or other means, which are capable of being employed for good or ill. The belief that certain individuals, *siddhas,* have these powers is widespread in the Hindu world as is the positing of a line of masters who can initiate disciples into arcane experiences or transmit their powers to them. In India's past the Tantric masters and schools are obscure, partly because Tantric teachings were secret or stated in special "twilight" language *(Saṃdhyā-bhāṣā);* however, aspects of Tantric practice, particularly the use of sound, in the teaching of the MANTRA, an initiatory word or phrase repeated in meditation, were generally accepted as useful for the preparation of individuals for union or communion with God.

4. **Śaivism, Vaiṣṇavism, and medieval trends.** As we move forward in time we become more aware of the conservative character of Hinduism. There is, however, a change in mood that arises from the underlying structure and contributes to creating new forms; for example, the late classical and medieval mood of Hinduism which gave itself up more and more to devotion or *bhakti* (*see* BHAKTI HINDUISM).

a) Śaivism. The main *bhakti* movement began in South India. There in the Tamil language is the first poetry of devotion to Shiva. The poets of ŚAIVA SIDDHĀNTA, recognized as saints, do not incarnate God (*pati*—Lord) but rather show how the creature *(paśu)* can overcome the bonds *(pāśá)* of separation or illusion that keep him/her from union with God. In the *Periya-purāṇam* of the *Tirumurai* (the canonical works of Southern Śaivism) we find the life stories of the sixty-three Śaiva saints (NĀYAṈĀRS). These, according to the Śaiva Siddhānta, pursue their relationship with God through the modes of (1) *caryā,* the path of the servant; *(2) kriyā,* the path of the son who regards God as his father; (3) *yoga,* in which the devotee regards God as his friend; (4) *jñāna,* the path of final union.

In *bhakti,* the ecstatic lover of God who communicates his/her feeling in poetry can arouse analogous feelings in a wide audience of readers or listeners. The classic ŚĀSTRAS ("sciences") of literary criticism demand that poetry induce this "distanced" mode of participation. When linked to the religious life, it gives the poet-saint almost the function of the dramatic actor whose gestures evoke a response in the inner state of the "observer." Therefore, the "plot" of the poet-saint's life with its high points giving rise to ecstatic utterance is incorporated into the tradition and even into the forms of worship of the deity.

b) Vaiṣṇavism. The followers of Vishnu felt less constraint to declare that certain great devotees of God could incarnate Vishnu himself. Thus it is mainly Vaiṣṇavism that projects the idea in popular Hinduism today that God repeatedly descends into the world as an avatar.

In South India are found the origins of Vaiṣṇava *bhakti.* There the ĀḺVĀRS of ŚRĪ VAIṢṆAVISM (A.D. 700-900) composed poetry on what Mahadevan *(see bibliog.)* calls "Bridal Mysticism," in reference to the erotic imagery employed to relate the ecstatic experience of the Āḻvārs. For them the Lord alone is male and the devotees all are female. Yet, these poet-saints incarnate the Lord's aspects or his accouterments (such as conch, discus, mace, lotus, or *Kaustubha* jewel).

The Vaiṣṇava *bhakti* movement spread across India but, apart from its Tamil origins, seems to have reached its literary climax in such regions as Maharashtra, Braj Bhūmi (a part of modern-day Uttar Pradesh near Delhi), and Bengal. As in the South the poet-saints of the North communicated in the spoken language of the people. To summarize a complex development, the main new types of holy persons in the late classical (A.D. 1000-1200) and medieval periods (A.D. 1200-1800) are the following:

i. The philosopher-saint. This type arose as a counter-balance to the Śaṃkara school of Vedānta. The Vaiṣṇava philosophers (*see* ĀCĀRYA), influenced by *bhakti,* defended the continuing relationship between the soul and God (Vishnu) but disagreed among themselves as to the correct way of defining that relationship. Such variations were incorporated into their respective sects that included priestly/ascetic hierarchies and differences in theology and cultic ritual.

ii. "Realized" poet-saints or avatars. Vernacular mystical poems of high literary value, composed and sung mainly under the inspiration of love for Vishnu or one of his male or female forms such as Krishna, Rāma or RĀDHĀ, are collected into "scriptures" for new sects. The poets themselves were sometimes worshiped in iconic or symbolic form together with the deities whom they idealized through their verses. Jñāneshvar, Eknāth, and Tukarām were poets of this type in Maharashtra.

iii. Dynastic hierarchies. Several of the medieval saints were married, and their charisma was continued through their descendants, who in some instances were regarded as partial or complete avatars, especially of Krishna. It is noteworthy that such "hereditary sanctity" did not necessarily require poetic or ecstatic gifts in its later possessors, since the literary/ritual cult, deriving from the founder, was the source of their charisma. Śrī Hit Harivaṃś of the *Rādhāvallabha Sampradāy* founded such a line.

iv. Individualistic ecstatics. The memories of certain devotees, such as MĪRĀBĀĪ and Raskhān, were preserved solely in relation to their poetry which survived in the oral and written tradition without giving rise to sectarianism.

v. Syncretism and iconoclasm. Through several saints of the Middle Ages, Muslim and Hindu themes are woven together. In their cult, scriptural devotion replaces idol worship almost completely, even though the founders of such sects may be very highly revered. The sects founded by KABĪR, the SIKH gurus beginning with NĀNAK, and the Rajasthani saint Prānnāth are of this type.

5. The modern period. The holy persons in Hinduism since the beginning of the nineteenth century synthesize the typologies of the past while also possessing new features.

a) Saints as principal deities. In this period the "mood" of Hinduism as a whole shifts more and more toward the saints, gurus, and avatars. Some religious leaders came to be regarded as the complete embodiment of all previous divinities. Śrī RĀMAKRISHNA of Bengal is the archetype in this development, but most well-known saints of contemporary India would tend toward this extreme position. Miracles and psychic wonders are alleged in profusion from these "God-realized" individuals.

b) Western religions and westernization. The influence of Western religions upon Hinduism becomes more pronounced in that the gurus, saints, and avatars know parts of the NEW TESTAMENT and QUR'ĀN and contribute to the adaptation of Hinduism to the Western model under the rubric of *sanātana dharma* or eternal religion. Some of the avatars, such as Rāmakrishna, declare themselves to be the reembodiment of JESUS Christ. The holy persons respond positively and negatively to the introduction of Western cultural values—including the scientific outlook. Some spiritual teachers redefine Hindu values to make them more "reasonable" to the modern person. Some teachers (*see* DAYĀNANDA) adopt an aggressive, condemnatory attitude toward Western values and attempt at the same time to restore Hinduism to the pristine state of its ancient glory.

c) Politics and society. Certain saints and gurus initiate political or social transformation and espouse humanitarian causes in an unprecedented manner. Such leaders as GANDHI and Vinoba Bhave set a standard that has influenced the public role of other contemporary saintly figures.

d) Modern methodologies. Contemporary holy persons use mass communication media and are elevated to celebrity status. Such elements contribute to the influx into India of numerous foreign disciples and the travel abroad of gurus and saints to meet a demand for enlightenment or self-realization, concepts that appeal to the "experience" (as contrasted with theoretical or philosophical) orientation of many modern persons, young and old alike.

Bibliography. W. D. O'Flaherty, *Asceticism and Eroticism in the Mythology of Śiva* (1973); T. M. P. Mahadevan, *Ten Saints of India* (1961); C. S. J. White, "Swāmi Muktānanda and the Enlightenment through Śakti-Pāt," *HR,* XIII (1972), for developmental character of a saint's life, and "Structure and the History of Religions: Some Bhakti Examples," *HR,* XVIII

(1978), for transformational roles of holy persons; P. Brent, *Godmen of India* (1972), personal reactions to a variety of holy persons in Hinduism today.

C. S. J. WHITE

HINDU SACRED CITIES. 1. The multiplicity of India's sacred places. The many deities, paths, and sectarian movements in the Hindu tradition have produced many sacred cities and centers. However, there is no ready way to speak of a "sacred city" in the Sanskrit tradition. Such places of PILGRIMAGE are called *tīrthas* (crossings or fords), *dhāmas* (abodes), *kṣetras* (fields), or *pīṭhas* (seats) of the divine. Some of these are cities; others are hilltop shrines, Himalayan caves, or river confluences. There are thousands of such sites—of local, regional, or all-India significance, of sectarian or trans-sectarian importance.

Tīrtha is the most common word for these places, and *tīrtha-yātrā* (pilgrimage) is one of the most popular forms of Hindu religious life. Many of India's great *tīrthas* were literally fords on the banks of her great rivers. Now as places of pilgrimage they are fords in a spiritual sense as well; i.e., places where the "other shore" is more clearly visible and more readily accessible. Some are places famous for their natural beauty; some are known for the spiritual power of the many sages and ascetics who gather there. Many are places where the image of the deity is acclaimed as *svayambhū* ("self-born"), not established by human hands but revealed by the divine.

Tīrthas are often associated with particular events of myth or legend such as the stories of the RĀMĀYAṆA or the MAHĀBHĀRATA, the episodes of the lifetime of KRISHNA, the mighty deeds of SHIVA or the goddess Devī. The vast variety of Hindu myths is inseparably interwoven with the sacred geography of India's holy places. A few of them are the great cities, such as Vārāṇasī (Banāras), which have centered and disseminated Hindu culture through their traditions of pilgrimage and teaching. Most of them, however, are the countless towns, groves, and hilltops which have, in a sense, incarnated Hindu culture, engraving in the geography of India the many stories of its gods and sages, yogis and devotees.

2. Groupings of sacred places. Among those *tīrthas* known throughout India are the "Seven Cities" *(saptapurī)*: Vārāṇsī, Ayodhyā, Mathurā, Hardvār, Kāñcī, Ujjain, and Dvārakā. In addition, there are the four divine "abodes" *(dhāmas)* situated at the directional compass points of India: Krishna's city of Purī in the east; Shiva's LIṄGA at Rāmeśvaram in the south; Krishna's capital of Dvārakā in the west; and VISHNU's temple of Badarīnāth, high in the Himalayas in the north. In visiting these four "abodes," pilgrims circumambulate the entire land of India. The wholeness and unity of the motherland is also suggested by the many *pīṭhas* or "seats" of the goddess, each of which corresponds to part of her body. Other groups of sacred places include the twelve *jyotirliṅgas* ("*liṅgas* of light") of the Śaivas; the 108 *divyadeśas* ("divine places") of the Śrī VAIṢṆAVAS; and the six centers of the South Indian cult of MURUKAṆ.

3. The city of Vārāṇasī. Vārāṇasī (Banāras) is widely acknowledged to be the greatest of India's *tīrthas*. To Hindus it is known more commonly as Kāśī, the "Luminous," the "City of Light." A consideration of this one place and its praises gives access to an understanding of other cities and *tīrthas* which shall be mentioned more briefly below.

Like many of India's sacred sites, this was the ancient abode of indigenous deities called YAKṢAS and NĀGAS, both beneficent and fearsome, who inhabited its many groves and pools. As the birthplace of the TĪRTHAṄKARA Pārśvanātha in the eighth century B.C., it became significant to the JAINAS. Later, it was in the groves of SĀRNĀTH in Kāśī that the BUDDHA preached his first sermon. For 1500 years the city was a Buddhist monastic center as well as a Hindu center of learning and pilgrimage. Through the centuries Vārāṇasī has accumulated layer upon layer of tradition, and in this respect it resembles JERUSALEM, MECCA, and many other sacred cities whose significance is far more ancient than any of the particular traditions of sanctity associated with them.

Vārāṇasī is the city of Shiva. Among its many names is Avimukta, the "Never-Forsaken" of Shiva, who has made this place his permanent dwelling. Even in the time of the universal periodic dissolution *(pralaya)* this city is said to be raised high upon Shiva's trident, out of the reach of the waters of destruction. The foremost of Vārāṇasī's Shiva temples is Viśvanātha, the "Lord of All." Shiva temples are so abundant in the city, however, that there is said to be a *liṅga,* the aniconic symbol of the supreme Shiva, at virtually every step. From another perspective, it is said that the entire circular sacred zone of Kāśī is one great *liṅga* of light—the shaft of brilliance which, in the Purāṇic myth, burst through the earth in the presence of BRAHMĀ and Vishnu and pierced the highest heavens. This city-*liṅga* is circumambulated by pilgrims along the famous Pañcakrośī Road, a circuit of some twenty-five miles which takes five days to complete.

The river GANGES is also important to the city's sanctity. Bathing in the Ganges followed by *darśana* (the "sight") of Viśvanātha constitutes the heart of Kāśī pilgrimage. According to the tradition, however, the city was already there long before the Ganges fell to earth from heaven. When the river arrived and skirted the city, Kāśī became doubly powerful. (*See* HINDU SACRED RIVERS.)

Kāśī is famous throughout India as the city of MOKṢA (liberation) for all who die there. People come during the last years or the last days of their lives. There Shiva is said to whisper the *tāraka* MANTRA, the enlightening words of the "crossing," into the ear of the dying. For them Kāśī is the final *tīrtha* which ferries them across the river of SAMSARA (the round of birth and death) never to return. Many pilgrims come to Kāśī to place the ashes of the dead in the Ganges or to perform the ŚRĀDDHA death rites for departed ancestors. Although all seven cities are said to bestow liberation, it is said in Kāśī that the other six cities secure for one a final rebirth in Kāśī, whence liberation is attained.

As a "sacred" city, Kāśī combines two kinds of sacredness. First, it gathers together everything that is auspicious and is therefore called *sukhada,* "bestower of blessings." This one city is a microcosm of all of India's sacred geography. All the seven cities and four abodes, all the mountains and rivers, all the gods and *tīrthas* are present in the various pools, temples, and groves of the city's own topography. Second, Kāśī not only intensifies the whole auspicious world, it also stands apart from the world, transcending the cycles of time which bring repeated creation and destruction, and is lifted on Shiva's trident out of the world of ordinary space. As a transcendent place, Kāśī is *mokṣada,* "bestower of liberation."

4. **The seven cities.** Vārāṇasī is one of the seven cities, and the nature of its sacred space is more elaborately articulated than the others which are named below. Each, however, has its own praises and its own field of faithful pilgrims.

a) Ayodhyā, located on the Sarayū River in north India, is the ancient capital of Lord RĀMA of the Epic RĀMĀYAṆA. Although no longer a city, the quiet town of Ayodhyā is still a popular place of pilgrimage, filled with temples and sites which link the pilgrim to the golden kingdom of Rāma. Pilgrims flock to Ayodhyā especially during the spring month of Caitra on Rāmanavamī, the birthday of Rāma.

b) Mathurā, on the Yamunā River in north India, is the birthplace of Lord Krishna. While the city today is a great Hindu center, it is clear that in ancient times it was a place of religious activity for the Buddhists and Jainas as well. In the early centuries A.D., Mathurā was the site of a flourishing Buddhist community of monks and laity whose artisans produced some of the earliest images of the Buddha. Excavations have also uncovered a considerable Jaina presence. As the Krishna sectarian movement rose to prominence in medieval times, many sites of Krishna's life were identified by the faithful. Particularly was this true during the sixteenth century when CAITANYA's disciples, the Gosvāmīs, settled at nearby Vrindāvan (VṚNDĀVANA), the scene of Krishna's childhood and youth. Today, Mathurā, Vrindāvan, and the surrounding countryside of Braj are filled with temples, shrines, pools, and groves where the particular events of Krishna's life are remembered. Pilgrims come expecially during the monsoon month preceding Janmāṣṭamī, the birthday of Krishna, to witness the many *līlās* ("plays") of Krishna's life.

c) Hardvār, located at the foot of the Himalayas where the Ganges River leaves the mountains and enters the plains of north India, is sometimes called Gaṅgādvārā, the "Gate of the Gaṅgā." It is said that when Bhagīratha brought the Ganges into India he stopped here, worshiped Lord Brahmā, and was granted a boon: that Brahmā, Vishnu, and Shiva would all reside here. Today it is called the "Gate of Hara (Shiva)" by ŚAIVAS and the "Gate of Hari (Vishnu)" by VAIṢṆAVAS. Here pilgrims bathe in the Ganges at the place called the "Footstep of the Lord," where part of the fast-moving river has been diverted into a bathing area for the safety of the bathers. A short distance upstream from Hardvār is Rishikesh, with its many riverside ASHRAM retreats.

d) Kāñcī or *Kāñcīpuram,* located in Madras State in south India, was once a center for Buddhists and Jainas as well as Hindus. Today it is divided into Shiva Kāñcī and Vishnu Kāñcī, each with its own nucleus of temples. Shiva Kāñcī, claiming the sanctity of Kāśī, has its own Kāśī Viśvanātha (cf. Banāras) temple as well as its famous Ekāmreśvara temple. It is also the most famous south Indian "seat" of the goddess: Kāmakoṭī *pīṭha,* which has long been the headquarters of one of India's foremost ascetic orders.

e) Ujjain is also known by the name Avantikā, the "Victorious," and was once the capital of the ancient kingdom of Mālwā in central India. In the third century B.C. it was still an important capital, ruled by the vice-regent Aśoka. From that time to the present Ujjain has retained its prominence as a political, commercial, and religious center. Its great Shiva *liṅga,* Mahākāla, is one of the twelve *liṅgas* of light.

f) Dvārakā, located in western India on the coast of the Kathiawar peninsula, is one of the four "abodes" as well as one of the seven cities. It was in Dvārakā that Krishna lived and ruled as king in his later years. Although it is doubtful that the Dvārakā of ancient times is the one now known, this city with its Dvārakādhīśa temple is of great importance for worshipers of Krishna today. Its Nāgeśa temple is also said to be one of the twelve *liṅgas* of light.

5. **Other *tirthas*.** a) *Sites of the goddess.* All the seven cities are also *pīṭhas* of the goddess. There is Viśālākṣī in Kāśī and Harasiddhi Devī in Ujjain, for example. Among the many other *pīṭhas* in India are the great KĀLĪ at Kālī Ghāṭ in Calcutta and the famous Kāmākṣā near Gauhāṭī in Assām.

b) Sites of Krishna. Purī on the eastern seacoast in Orissa, one of the four *dhāmas,* is the site of the enormous temple complex of Krishna JAGANNĀTHA. In this cultic center both indigenous and Brahmanical traditions are present, and the temple rituals incorporate both Vaiṣṇava and Śāktā elements. The distinctive wooden images of Krishna along with his brother Balarāma and sister Subhadrā are pulled in procession in a huge chariot during the yearly *rathayātrā* festival in the summer month of Āṣāḍha. While Purī attracts pilgrims on an all-India and trans-sectarian basis, Nāthdvārā in Rājasthān, the residence of Krishna as Śrīnātha, is primarily important to the VALLABHA tradition of Vaiṣṇavas. The town of Paṇdharpūr in Maharashtra, where Krishna is present as Lord Viṭhobā, is important for Vārkarī Vaiṣṇavas and for all people of Maharashtra.

c) South Indian sites. In addition to Kāñcī, south India is famous for Rāmeśvaram on the southern coast of Madras State, where the Shiva *liṅga* is said to have been established by Rāma before launching his campaign to Laṅkā to retrieve the kidnapped SĪTĀ. Pilgrims from afar visit Rāmeśvaram, one of the four "abodes," often bringing Ganges water to sprinkle the *liṅga* and returning to the Ganges with sands from Rāmeśvaram. Madurai in Madras State is the site of the temple of the goddess MĪNĀKṢĪ and her consort Shiva Sundareśvara. The city is of great interest for its MANDALA layout, the central temple being surrounded by concentric rectangular streets used for the procession of the deities during various yearly festivals. The Śrī Vaiṣṇava site of Śrīraṅgam on an island in the Kāverī River has a similar layout. Tirupatī in Andhra Pradesh is one of the most popular south Indian *tīrthas*, attracting hundreds of thousands of pilgrims annually. Above the town of Tirupatī is the "Sacred Hill" of Tirumalai, where sits the temple of Śri Veṅkaṭeśvara. The image of Veṅkaṭeśvara, seen today as Vishnu, has at times been claimed by Śaivas, Śāktas (*see* ŚAKTI), and worshipers of SKANDA as their own. For those who come to fulfill a vow and enlist the aid of the Lord, the offering of the hair at one of the numerous "hair-offering" centers, followed by a bath in the Puṣkariṇī tank, precedes the *darśana* ("viewing") of the deity.

d) North Indian sites. The ancient city of Prayāg (now Allāhābād), called the Tītharāja ("King of Tīrthas"), is sometimes included among the seven cities. It is located where three sacred rivers meet: the Ganges, the Yamunā, and the mythical Sarasvatī (*see* HINDU SACRED RIVERS). Bathing at the confluence, called the Triveṇī, is a triple blessing and death here, as at Vārāṇasī, is said to bring liberation. The Kumbhamelā, the greatest of all India's *melās* (pilgrimage-fairs), takes place here every twelve years, attracting millions of holy men and pilgrims. No other single event of Indian pilgrimage is as impressive or important. Smaller Kumbhamelās take place every six years as well and are held at three additional sites: Hardvār, Ujjain, and Nāsik. The four places are said to have been consecrated by four drops of the nectar of immortality which spilled from the *kumbha* (pot) when the gods whisked it away to heaven. Gayā, on the bank of the Phalgu River in Bihār, has a very specialized role as a *tīrtha:* the performance of *śrāddha* rites for the dead. Although *śrāddha* in Prayāg, Vārāṇasī, and other places is a customary part of pilgrimage, *śrāddha* in Gayā is the sole purpose of pilgrimage and is said to relieve one of all further monthly and yearly ritual obligations to the ancestors. *See* PILGRIMAGE.

Bibliography. All of the eighteen Sanskrit Purāṇas celebrate the various *tīrthas*, their myths and pilgrimages. In addition, the Vana Parva of the MAHĀBHĀRATA contains a long section on *tīrthas*. The most helpful secondary sources include P. V. Kane, *History of Dharmaśāstra*, IV (2nd ed., 1973), 552-827, which describes various *tīrthas* drawing upon Epic and Purāṇic sources; H. J. Dave, *Immortal India*, 4 vols. (1957-1961), which contains chapters on dozens of *tīrthas;* A. Bharati, "Pilgrimage Sites and Indian Civilization," in J. W. Elder, ed., *Chapters in Indian Civilization*, (1970), pp. 85-126, which lists and comments on many *tīrthas* region by region; and S. M. Bhardwaj, *Hindu Places of Pilgrimage in India* (1973), which is a socio-geographical study of *tīrthas* with a very good introduction.

D. L. ECK

HINDU SACRED RIVERS. 1. The rivers of ancient India. Hindus have long praised India's great rivers as divine and life-giving to both the land and the people of India. The ancient INDUS VALLEY CIVILIZATION was a river culture, and in the surviving ruins of MOHENJO-DARO a great cermonial tank suggests the significance of cleansing waters in the ritual life of its people. The later VEDIC literature of the ARYAN invaders contains several river hymns in praise of the river goddesses. In one prominent Vedic myth, INDRA slays the great serpent Vṛtra, coiled around the vault of heaven, releasing the nectar waters to run upon the earth. In short, both the indigenous people of India and the Aryans shared traditions associated with the life-powers of water, and ritual bathing, whether in the great rivers or in waters near at hand, has long been central in the HINDU tradition.

The Vedic hymns repeatedly mention seven mother-rivers: the Sindhu (Indus), the Sarasvatī, and the five rivers of the Punjab. All seven were in northwest India. As the Aryans moved farther south, the GANGES (Gaṅgā) is mentioned among the great rivers (RV X.75). The preeminence of the Sindhu and Sarasvatī gradually yields to that of the Ganges. According to tradition, the Sarasvatī, flowing from the Himalayas, disappeared into the north Indian desert. Many of the powers and myths of the mysterious Sarasvatī seem to have been transferred to the Ganges.

2. Heavenly waters. India's sacred rivers, called "goddess-waters" and "mother-streams," are said to flow with the nectar of immortality, *amṛta*. The rivers are sometimes imaged as mother cows, released by Indra from the heavenly enclosure, running out upon the earth laden with milk for their young. In any case, the waters are divine in origin. The earthly rivers have their counterpart in the heavenly waters. In the Epics and PURĀṆAS, the myth of the descent of the river Ganges from heaven repeats the theme of the life-giving release of the heavenly waters.

3. The Ganges and the seven rivers. There are seven rivers held to be most sacred in India today. The great Ganges, while one of those seven, is also called the "sevenfold" Ganges, the source and prototype of all sacred waters. In descending to earth, the Ganges is said to have split into seven streams, three flowing east, three west, and the Bhagirathī—India's Ganges—flowing south. Thus, it is more than a single river. Others are homologized to it in India, such as the Kāverī, the "Ganges of the South," and the countless streams which become "Ganges" for those who dwell nearby.

The other rivers held to be among the sacred seven are the Sindhu, Sarasvatī, Yamunā, Narmadā, Godāvarī, and Kāverī. The ancient Sindhu and the mythical Sarasvatī have been mentioned above. The Yamunā rises to the west of the source of the Ganges in the Himalayas. The two river sources, Gaṅgotrī and Yamunotrī, are popular places of Himalayan PILGRIMAGE. The Yamunā, flowing through the north Indian plains, passes the sacred city of Mathurā and joins the Ganges and the Sarasvatī at Prayāg (Allāhābād), one of India's greatest bathing sites. (*See* HINDU SACRED CITIES.)

The Narmadā, rising south of the Vindhya mountains, flows west across central India. Its waters are said to issue from the body of Shiva, and its source is the powerful *tīrtha* (sacred crossing) called Amarakaṇṭaka. From the river bed of the Narmadā the famous smooth stones called *bāṇa liṅgas* are taken for use as symbols of Shiva in temples throughout India.

Further south is the Godāvarī, rising in western India at the *tīrtha* of Tryambaka, the site of one of Shiva's twelve *liṅgas* of light near the city of Nāsik. The Godāvarī, which flows eastward, is sometimes called "Gaṅgā" (Ganges) and sometimes "Gautamī" after the ancient sage Gautama who is said to have diverted the Ganges to this place.

The Kāverī in Mysore and Madras State is called the "Ganges of the South," brought from the north in the water pot of the legendary sage Agastya. Along its course is the famous VAIṢṆAVA island sanctuary of Śrīraṅgam and the great *tīrtha* of Chidambaram.

4. The river as a sacred crossing. For Hindus, the river is a powerful symbol of the flow of this life of birth and death called SAMSARA. Along the river banks are the *tīrthas,* the sacred "fords" that take one across to the "other shore." The river is not only that to be crossed, however. It is also the *means* of crossing; i.e., sacred rivers are themselves *tīrthas*. Having descended *(avataraṇa)* from on high, they become the means of ascent *(taraṇa)*, staircases to heaven.

Bibliography. Rig Veda I.32; II.12; IV.28: X.43,64, 75; Rāmāyaṇa, Bāla Kāṇḍa 38-44, contains the myth of the Gaṅgā's descent; P. V. Kane, *History of Dharmaśāstra,* Vol. IV (2nd ed., 1973) on the various rivers; H. J. Dave, *Immortal India,* Vol. IV (1961), is devoted to India's rivers; S. G. Darian, *The Ganges in Myth and History* (1978). D. L. ECK

HINDUISM hĭn´ do͞o ĭsm ([*hindū*—Persian; lit. the people and culture of the Indus River region; hence, synonym for "Indian"]). The variety of religious beliefs and practices making up the major religious tradition of the Indian subcontinent.

Hinduism had its primary beginnings in two distinct sources dating from sometime in the third millennium B.C. to the middle or late second millennium B.C. The first is the INDUS VALLEY CIVILIZATION associated with the cities of HARAPPĀ and MOHENJO-DARO. Excavations of these well-planned and extensive cities prove the existence of a highly developed system of life before the appearance of what is usually regarded as the primary source of Hinduism, the ARYANS and their oral scriptures, the VEDAS. Since that time Indian religion has gone through various periods of change that were slowly to create a consciousness of the distinct religion we now know as Hinduism.

1. Indus Valley Civilization
2. Vedic religion
3. Brāhmaṇic religion
4. Divergent movements
5. Development of the conception of orthodoxy
6. The rise of Hinduism
7. Classical Hinduism
8. Popular theism
9. Religious reaction to Islam
10. Modern Hinduism
11. Religious life and social responsibilities
12. Current trends
Bibliography

1. Indus Valley Civilization. Scholarly interpretations of the Indus Valley or Harappān Civilization are at best hazardous, since the small number of known inscriptions are as yet undeciphered and the exact nature of the function of many of the structures in the cities is unknown. Small pieces of terra cotta and stone sculpture have been found that deal primarily with animals, with emphasis upon the male, while representations of humans concentrate upon the female. Also, there are soapstone seals that are primarily concerned with and skillfully reproduce animals and in some cases give an emphasis to trees, while the human representations tend to be elementary. There are, however, many female figurines specially dressed and in various dancing poses. These, along with hundreds of doughnut and phallic shaped stones, clearly indicate a strong interest in fertility, and have led some scholars to claim a Mother Goddess cult for the Indus Valley peoples. These finds, together with the obvious architectural emphasis upon water baths, drainage, and personal cleanliness, have been interpreted by scholars to indicate that Harappān religion concentrated upon natural powers and the essential role of water in cleansing human beings in order that they might approach and/or be in proper relationship with the powers resident in natural phenomena. As yet there is no knowledge of a system of thought, oral tradition, or myth that supported any cult. We are left simply with the conjecture that there was an awareness of powers different from, opposed to, or superior to, humans. By the time of the coming of the Aryans to Northwest India sometime in the second millennium B.C. Harappān civilization was decaying or had disappeared, but the basic religious emphasis upon animals, trees, water, and fertility as related to superhuman powers was to continue as a submerged but not inconsequential element in the emerging thought and cult that in varied forms constitute what is later known as Hinduism.

2. Vedic religion. The second early source of Indian religion, and that which was to give it much of its formal cultic structure, myth, and intellectual expression, was the religious beliefs and practices of the Aryan peoples who invaded Northwest India. These tribes were a part of the great migrations that spread to the shores of the Atlantic in the West and to Central and South Asia in the East. This broad wandering and subsequent settling down of tribes having to some degree cognate societal, linguistic, and religious traditions was to provide in India and adjacent areas to the West a common broad core of religious myth and related deities.

The religion of the Aryans is known to us through hymns brought together in collections known as the VEDAS. For a long period after its origin, Vedic literature was oral rather than written. Indeed, down to modern times the orthodox Hindu has been highly concerned with the accuracy of the text and has emphasized an oral mnemonic approach in order to establish textual accuracy and to ascertain and absorb the truths the literature embodies. The SANSKRIT word *veda* denotes knowledge and the Vedic literature in time came to be understood as the divinely revealed word or knowledge which contains the truth of all existence and of all time. The four major collections contain verses of praise—RIG (Ṛg); sacrificial formulas to be used by priests—YAJUR; verses or chants for priests at the time of sacrifices—SĀMA; and a later collection primarily concentrating upon spells and magical means of obtaining human desires in this world—ATHARVA.

The religion revealed by the Vedas is primarily one of sacrifice to the many gods who are conceived as powers in the heavens, in the atmosphere, in the earth and, perhaps, also as divine counterparts to the priests, rulers, and masses of humanity. The structure of nature, the functions of the gods, and the ordering of human society are understood to be in a divinely ordained configuration in which each is in some fashion dependent upon the others. This proper structure of existence, ṚTA, is right order, it is truth. There is a uniformity and a symmetry to all of existence, and this *ṛta* is not only strengthened, it is maintained, by human society's strict observance of the proper sacrifices. As a result VEDIC religion was highly sacrificial in nature, while at the same time its emphasis upon the material aspects of existence gave it a "this worldly" physical exuberance. Ritual observance by the society and its members assured a materially happy life as part of the great cosmic order, *ṛta*.

3. Brāhmaṇic religion. *a) Sacrifice.* As part of the Vedic literature the Brāhmaṇas or priestly commentaries upon the Vedic verses served as guides for the priests by giving elaborate instructions for the proper performance of the sacrifices. Given the fundamental conviction of Aryan society that the sacrifices are absolutely necessary, and that they must be done constantly in a recurring time pattern so that the order of the universe and society will be maintained, the BRĀHMAṆA texts and the priests who knew them came to hold a near-divine status in Vedic-Brāhmaṇic society.

While it is difficult to be precise in dating specific periods in Indian history, by around the beginning of the first millennium B.C. a fundamental aspect of Brāhmaṇic Hinduism developed, namely, an emphasis upon a correct relationship between human society and divine powers and the central role of the priests (*brāhmaṇas*) as especially endowed guides in the conduct of the cultic ritual necessary for the attainment and continuation of that relationship. The many and varied Vedic deities waxed and waned as their importance to maintenance of cosmic order and human well-being was espoused or denigrated by schools or groups of priests. The essential matter, and one continuing in importance in traditional orthodox Brāhmaṇic Hinduism, was the role of society and the individual in maintaining the cosmic *ṛta*. And as a later and somewhat broader concept known as DHARMA came to replace the notion of *ṛta*, the conviction that all of human activity has a proper (that is, a cosmological, ontological, divine) pattern to follow became a fixed ideal in the development of Indian religious thought and practice.

In addition to this cultic sacrificial emphasis with its stress upon the "correct," the "proper," and *ṛta*, there was during the early centuries of the first millennium B.C. a discernible development of a concern for knowledge of the divine structure and man's relationship to it. The centrality of the sacrifice had demanded a highly trained group of priests (*see* BRAHMINS) to follow and interpret the Vedas and the Brāhmaṇas. Now certain individuals with the necessary turn of mind and intellectual endowments began to search for the knowledge hidden within the Vedas and the sacrifice. The meaning of the sacrifice came to be more important than its actual performance, and there developed a mental performance of the sacrifice in which the individual attained for himself the power of the sacrifice in an even greater degree than the priests who performed it but did not know its essence.

The Rig Veda had in certain hymns referred to TAPAS or "heat" as a basic element of power in creation. *Tapas* had come to be a possession of the priest and the sacrifice he performed as a creative force in sustaining the cosmos. Now the individual who performed the sacrifice within himself, and who could do so only because of his knowledge of its essence, was in the possession of a unique *tapas*, the heat that is at the foundation of all being. As aids in the development of such knowledge there came into existence a body of literature as appendices to the Brāhmaṇas, the ĀRAṆYAKAS or "Forest Books," so named because they were used by groups or individuals in quiet retreats in the forest. While there had been forerunners of philosophical speculation and query in the Vedas, it is in the Āraṇyakas that the stage is set for the later flowering of Indian-Hindu philosophy and theology.

These early sources for and developments of Indian religion in the general period of 1000-800 B.C. combined to establish as essential elements within emerging Hinduism the Aryan-Vedic-Brāhmaṇic sacrifical emphasis with its stress upon the cult. This was joined with a less well documented factor, which nevertheless was obviously active: that is, pre-Aryan indigenous awe of and sacrifice to the many powers obvious in nature and the requirement of ritual cleanliness in approaching these powers as they are manifested in animals, vegetation, rivers, and the like. In addition, the growing tendency toward speculation upon the knowledge inherent in the Vedas, as in the instance of the Āraṇyakas, was slowly and firmly establishing certain central concepts as fundamental truths of cosmic and empirical existence. Thus there were three elements: sacrifice, primarily to the great gods or powers of the universe; worship and dread of the many smaller but no less intimidating natural powers encountered in daily life; and a conviction that intellectual reflection upon Vedic truth can endow humans with the *tapas* that enables them to rise above human limitations. Each of these elements in one way or another was to continue as a central factor in the development of Indian religion as over the centuries it became what at a much later time could properly be designated as Hinduism.

b) Religious thought. During the early centuries of the first millennium B.C. certain powerful ideas about human life and fate became central to the developing Indian religious mind-set and came to govern all Indian-Hindu religious speculation and belief. As essential themes upon which Indian philosophy and theology rest, they played major roles in the formulation of Hinduism and BUDDHISM, as well as serving to inform the thought of two other Indian religions of consequence, JAINISM and SIKHISM. For Hinduism they are philosophical-theological givens or dogma; for the other religions, a rejection of one or more of the particular themes may be a specific dogma serving to differentiate that religion from Hinduism. As a result, these beliefs served primarily as positive or negative foci around which Indian religious thought evolved.

The primary concepts are those of rebirth-redeath and KARMA-SAMSARA. Briefly stated, these themes teach that individual souls exist from beginningless time, passing on from one form of existence to another in a continuous rebirth-redeath. The conditions or circumstances of each new form of existence are determined by the merit or demerit of the actions (karma) that have taken place in previous forms of existence.

As a result of this perception of the human situation, religious thinkers came to see life as being at worst an inescapable experience, frustrating in its unending struggles and defeats, and at best a meaningless repetition of pleasure and pain, with pain always coming in the form of death at the end of an existence that was not actually at an end but only beginning again. A revealing word in this regard is the frequently used *punarmṛtyu,* meaning "repeated dying," for it suggests that not only is there a focus on rebirth, but the consequence of birth, namely death, is what is to be feared.

Birth and its resultant death are inevitable consequences of the karma or actions of men. When something is done, a chain of actions or reactions inevitably flows from the initial deed. Thus the human being and those around him or her are caught in a never ending chain of causation. Once a person exists as human—that is, as a physical being in the empirical dimension—it is of the very nature of his condition that he will be forced to act, and by acting he is caught in the cycle of karma. Whatever he does will have a consequence.

Further, this process of rebirth-redeath is not limited to humans. It is of the inherent nature of existence itself. All being is in such flux, is in a process of developing and withering away only to develop and go through the same cycle again and again. This is the concept of samsara, the cyclical process that applies to the cosmos and all entities within the cosmos. Samsara, literally "wandering," is the frustrating, meaningless, unending process that confronts everything that exists.

From about the eighth century B.C. onward the primary development within Indian religious thought was the attempt to come to terms with the human and cosmic situation believed to exist as a result of the samsaric fact of existence. While the emphasis upon the sacrifice and an awareness of the need to be in proper relationship with the gods both high and low did not diminish, the new central and enduring aspect of Indian religion was a growing philosophical, theological, and meditative activity. This process not only served as a basis for religious thought specifically associated with later Hinduism; it also furnished much of the categories of thought, both positively and negatively, for such other expressions of Indian religion as Buddhism and Jainism.

The literature associated with this development, the UPANIṢADS, appeared before 500 B.C. and continued to be produced until about A.D. 200. While there are a great many Upaniṣads, traditional Hindu orthodoxy usually lists 108 and considered perhaps 12 or 13 of them to be of primary significance. The word Upaniṣad suggests the sitting near a teacher and receiving hidden truth. In a fashion similar to the Brāhmaṇas, which were commentaries on the Vedas, and the Āraṇyaka commentaries on the Brāhmaṇas, the Upaniṣads served as appendage commentaries to the Āraṇyakas.

At the center of the thought of the Upaniṣads is the conviction that the Vedas are ŚRUTI, that which is heard. They had been revealed directly to ancient wise men (RISHI) and therefore they contain absolute truth. Passages in the Brāhmaṇas ascribe this divine origin to the Vedas, and the Upaniṣads repeat the theme. The Ultimate, the Divine, has revealed truth to humans through the Vedas, and it is knowledge of this truth that is the goal of the Upaniṣads.

Earlier scriptures had expressed the conviction that there is a unity which is behind, and which pervades, all of the multiplicity present in the physical world. This unity and order *(ṛta)* is even behind and above the various gods (DEVAS). The Upaniṣads go further in asserting more specifically that there is a consciousness at work in the creation and maintenance of the world of being. This consciousness, BRAHMAN, is the continuing power that pervades and upholds the total structure of the universe. Of special importance for Indian religious thought, this Brahman is not to be confused with any of the deities of the Vedas, for even these *devas* are dependent upon Brahman. The gods possess their power and have their place in the structure of things as a result of the inital power of Brahman.

In their attempt to fathom the nature of Brahman the Upaniṣadic thinkers were conscious of the mysteriousness and unknowability of the Brahman. Convinced that Brahman pervades all of existence and that it is greater than any individual part of the whole of existence, they developed a highly refined system of thought in which Brahman is said to be this thing and that thing until all possible material physical aspects of existence are mentioned. Though Brahman is to be found in particular phenomenal objects, it must be understood as transcending all of them since phenomenal substance is not Brahman, but is, rather, only a habitation of Brahman. Thus it is that all particular aspects of existence must be considered as referring back to a single source, the One that lies underneath, within, and beyond all existence, namely Brahman.

Very early in the development of the thought associated with the Upaniṣads, Brahman was conceived as being ATMAN, a term meaning "self" in common usage but which came more and more to mean the essential or inner self of man. Therefore, if it is correct to use the terms Brahman and Atman interchangeably, then it is proper to say that Self is the source of all existent things, all vital energies, worlds, deities, all beings. Brahman, Self, Atman, is "the Real of the real." It is the ultimate essence that constitutes the foundation or core upon which the apparent rests. That which appears to be real is real only in a secondary fashion. The true reality of that which appears to be real is *the Reality* that is Brahman, and not the empirical objects themselves. Thus it is that the Brahman is related to all that is at the same time it is held to be beyond all that is.

It is at this point that descriptions which utilize series of negations to characterize Brahman come to their highest expression. That which is ultimately unknowable must be given predicates in order to be conceived, yet every predicate that can be stated about Brahman must at the same time be denied, because Brahman is not to be limited to any fact of empirical existence. The supreme statement of this approach to the understanding of the Ultimate is *neti, neti*—"not this, not that!" No matter what might in a sense be legitimately said concerning the nature of Brahman, it must be followed with the statement that this is not ultimately so. The positive statement that is necessary in order to probe into the unfathomable must be followed by a negation in order that the depth and richness of the unfathomable are preserved.

Within the Upaniṣads, however, there was also the growth of a conception of Brahman as being somehow manifest in the human person. And it was in this that the ground was laid for the later VEDĀNTA ("end of the Veda" or highest teachings of the Veda) understanding of the nature of persons. If a person could come to a correct knowledge, i.e. a suprarational predicateless knowledge, of his ultimate self he would come as close to a comprehension of the Brahman as is possible for human rationality and intuition.

As we have noted, Atman (Self) had come to be used in reference to Brahman, and it was also in common usage a reference to the intrinsic human self (as opposed to the ego or personality). In the developing dialectic of the Upaniṣads, Atman came to be reserved in most cases to indicate the inmost essence within a person, while Brahman was set apart to suggest the ultimate essence of the universe. However, some of the Upaniṣadic literature was emphatic in declaring that the two are one and the same. From this we get a fundamental theme of one major type of Hindu religious-philosophical thought, namely, Atman equals Brahman, Brahman equals Atman, "That art thou" *(tat tvam asi).*

Some of the Upaniṣadic thinkers reasoned that the inmost Self of a person, the Atman, lies deep within. They sought to strip away each successive cover until they arrived at the final essence (Atman) completely separated from the physical and psychical elements which appear on the surface to constitute that person. Later Hindu thinkers were to give various interpretations to the nature of this human self (Atman) and its relationship to the ultimate Self (Brahman). In any case, whether there is an absolute identity between them—*tat tvam asi*—or a close relationship, Upaniṣadic speculation upon the revealed truth *(śruti)* present in the Vedas laid a firm philosophical-theological foundation for subsequent intellectual formulations of Hinduism, as well as serving as a usually covert platform for much of the popular Hinduism of the Indian people.

The primary factor behind and within Upaniṣadic speculation was the concern to overcome the human situation that results from the karma-samsaric limitation with its inevitable rebirth and redeath. Is there no escape, no release from the endless wandering of the self throughout endless time? And, if there is a release, is it a momentary and brief interlude before beginning the cycle again, or is there a state of nonempirical being beyond human understanding, where the wandering that is the essential characteristic of samsaric being is forever brought to an end?

The concept of permanent release—MOKṢA—first attains prominence in the Upaniṣads. Since, however, there was no absolute uniformity on the subject, later commentators and philosophic schools were to develop various interpretations concerning *mokṣa* and the Upaniṣadic teachings about the release of the self from samsaric existence. It is of paramount importance to note, however, that Indian religious thought from the time of the Upaniṣads and even before has had *mokṣa*, release from this samsaric universe, as a fundamental and ultimate goal.

4. **Divergent movements.** Adequate understanding of Indian religious history and of the development of Hinduism must take into account that during and following the period discussed above, there were a number of developments in religious thought and practice that deviated greatly from the Vedic-Brāhmaṇical patterns. Each of them in its own way exerted influence upon Indian history and upon emerging Hinduism. Primary among these developments were that of the ĀJĪVIKAS, the Jainas, and the Buddhists. They all made their appearance in or around the sixth century B.C. and in one way or another protested against the sacrifical system of the Brāhmaṇas as being of no aid in enabling humans to overcome the basic samsaric limitations of existence.

a) Ājīvikas. The Ājīvikas accepted the fundamental Indian concept of rebirth-redeath and, therefore, samsara, but denied the doctrine of karma. The universe and everything within it were predetermined by a cosmic principle, destiny *(Niyati),* they held; there is nothing a person can do to change his or her present or future condition. There is no such thing as good or bad karma that will influence the future life or lives. Everything will follow its predetermined destiny and cease when that destiny so determines. Even the extreme asceticism and nakedness that was the hallmark of the Ājīvikas was for them a predetermined condition unrelated to any attempt on their part to obtain rewards or a better state in a future existence. The place of extreme asceticism and also of some cynicism in Indian religious practice and thought, while certainly not solely traceable to the impact of the Ājīvikas, finds much of its source and strength in this movement and its continuation over many centuries.

b) Jainism. Associated with the teaching of a non-Brahmin prince, Vardhamāna, later known as MAHĀVĪRA (Great Hero), Jainism explicitly rejected the sacrifice and gods central to Brāhmaṇism. Firmly believing in rebirth-redeath and maintaining an absolute and extreme doctine of karma, Jainism taught that there is no way of overcoming karma except by the cessation of karma itself. There is a spark or element of life (JĪVA) in all material entities that now have their present form because of the karma that has gathered around them. The only way by which the *jīva* can free itself from accumulated karma and the karma that increases daily by the mere fact of living is by an asceticism that removes the person from the very acts that create karma. Jainism thus encouraged a religious ascetic life of the individual, withdrawn from all the normal cares and occupations of life. It also gave a place to lay persons who, while not yet ready for such a difficult life, could follow certain occupations and lead a life of noninjury (AHIṂSĀ) and so prepare themselves for the more strenuous ascetic life in a future birth. When the accumulated karma of the past and that of the present life were erased, then the freed *jīva* would be in its proper state of inactive bliss. No sacrifices to the gods are helpful, for there are no gods. Every person must rely upon himself. "Man! Thou art thine own friend. Why wishest thou for a friend beyond thyself?"

Jainism had periods of great strength and royal patronage in various areas of India, and continues today as the religion of a small but influential number of Indians. As a result of that early strength and continued presence, it has had considerable influence on the structure and thought of Hinduism.

c) Buddhism. The most significant non-Brāhmaṇical religious movement of this period and of all Indian religious history was that associated with the religious experience of SIDDHĀRTHA GAUTAMA. Like Vardamāna, a member of the ruling class rather than a priest, Prince Siddhārtha rejected Brāhmaṇic sacrifice and the authority of the Vedas in favor of a personal search and self-reliance to free the individual from the bondage of samsara. The traditional account of Siddhārtha's own search and his attainment of enlightenment whereby he became the BUDDHA, the Enlightened One freed from samsara, together with the thought and activities of the Ājīvikas and Jainas, is indicative of the variety of indigenous religious thought and practice present in India from the middle of the first millennium B.C. on through many succeeding centuries. Buddhism accepted certain fundamental themes of Brāhmaṇism. Rebirth-redeath and karma and samsara are central in the Buddha's search and in his answers to the predicament of humanity. However, he radically rejected the concepts of Brahman and Atman, and the prevalent hierarchical and sacrificial structure of society so central to Vedic Brāhmaṇism. These differences and the rapid acceptance of his views by many Indians over the next few centuries served to increase the awareness on the subcontinent that there were in existence different religions, or better stated, different understandings of life with sharply expressed beliefs and ways of living.

As a result, nascent Hinduism was confronted with powerful forces that not only challenged some of its intellectual and cultic bases but also succeeded in gaining the support of important rulers and segments of society. However, one of the central characteristics of Indian religion has been the acceptance of diversity within a broader unity. Intellectual formulations of religious concepts and variety in cultic practice have not generally been considered to be matters that exclude individuals or groups from the larger whole. Because of this, the direct influence of groups such as the Ājīvikas, Jainas, Buddhists, and others that were to come later have been more subtle and less disrupting than might have been expected.

5. Development of the conception of orthodoxy. *a) Śruti.* There were two basic factors in the growing conception of orthodoxy within Indian religion as it becomes what we later designate as Hinduism. One factor is *śruti* (*see* §3 b). As it became apparent that some systems of thought rejected the *śruti* doctrine (the divine revelation of truth through the Vedas) while others upheld it, there developed a more marked consciousness of distinctions between the systems. Those that accepted *śruti* were *āstika* (believing), while those that rejected it were *nāstika* (unbelieving). Down into modern times this has been one of the central factors in the orthodox definition of Hinduism. Despite the fact that certain systems of thought expressed the "belief" feebly, if at all, as long as they did not accentuate their "disbelief" they were able to maintain their *āstika* status. The Ājīvikas, Jainas, and Buddhists were soon seen to be clearly *nāstika*.

b) Varṇa. The second factor in the increasing awareness of what is proper religiously or, stated negatively, what places a group outside Vedic Brāhmaṇism, was related to the Brāhmaṇic conception of the ideal society and membership within that society. It is important to distinguish between the Vedic fourfold *varṇa* classification of groups within the society and the later, and most certainly less rigid, caste (*jāti*) system. Here we are concerned with the Vedic *varṇa* structure. *Varṇa* means "color," and the *varṇa* system is believed to have much of its original reason for being as a result of the Aryan attempt to keep its "nobility" segregated from the "lower," indigenous peoples of India as the Aryans settled in the country.

The *varṇa* groupings, Brahmin (priest), Kṣatriya (warrior), Vaiśya (peasant), and Śūdra (serf), were held by Brāhmaṇism to be the proper social groups in society as correlates of the divine structure of the universe and of the sacrifice. One text claims the cosmic person (Puruṣa) was the source of the *varṇa* groupings of human society. Indeed, in the great cosmic sacrifice these groups with their resulting status were created from various parts of the *Puruṣa* (RV X.90.11-14). *See* Caste.

The divergent groups directly attacked the Brāhmaṇic source for knowledge of truth, the Vedas, and the sacrifical system inherent to the Vedic understanding of existence, and rejected the *varṇa* structure of society considered by Brāhmaṇism to be cosmically ordained. In so doing they played an important role in giving self-identity to the religious thought and practice that was to become what we know as Hinduism.

6. The rise of Hinduism. In addition to the foregoing elements of Vedic Brāhmaṇism, and the less discernible pre-Aryan non-Vedic beliefs and cults that were a part of Indian religion, other components that also were to be primary aspects of Hinduism appeared in the following period.

a) Sūtras and Śāstras. 500 to 200 B.C. is frequently referred to as the Sūtra period, a time when various texts or Sūtras were written as instructions concerning the sacrifices and the Brāhmaṇas upon which the sacrifices were based. In addition, the Sūtras concerned themselves with religious acts or ceremonies in the household, and some were primarily guides for human conduct. Along with the Sūtras another form of much the same material appeared in what are known as Śāstras (instructions). Their topics included matters of personal human conduct, and they also expanded their concern to problems of law and statecraft, thereby giving standards of dharma or propriety in all spheres of human conduct (*see* Manu, Laws of). Through their teaching Hinduism gained a second source of authority to be added to the *śruti* of the earlier Vedic literature. The Sūtras and Śāstras are Smṛti (remembered). They have great authority, but are usually deemed secondary to the Vedas, since they lack the quality of direct revelation.

b) The Epics. During the same general period other types of literature appeared in the basic form that they have maintained in succeeding centuries. The Epics, the Mahābhārata and the Rāmāyaṇa, with their accounts of the exploits of gods in human form living and fighting on earth for the establishment of the good (dharma) and the destruction of evil, have served throughout Hindu history to assure the Hindu that the gods act on behalf of humans and their divinely ordained society. Furthermore, the Epics have been primary sources along with the later Purāṇas for the inculcation of ideals for the proper behavior of the individual in whatever station of life he or she may be. Also they have as central figures in the dramas two of the important deities or Avatars (descents of the divine) of later Hinduism, Rāma and Krishna (Kṛṣṇa). A section of the Mahābhārata, the Bhagavad Gītā, was to serve as one of the great scriptures of Hinduism, a source of doctrinal teaching, ethical injunction, and religious devotion.

c) Purāṇas. Along with the Epics a further primary vehicle for the religious beliefs and worship of the masses of the Hindu people is the literature known as the Purāṇas ("Antiquities"). The eighteen principal Purāṇas and the innumerable local or regional Purāṇas found throughout India and usually associated with local temples tell of the exploits of the gods or of a particular god to whom the temple is dedicated. They describe the creation and dissolution of the world, and in manifold ways bring to the Hindu a sense of the presence of the divine in past and present history as well as assuring the believer that the future course of the universe will follow a preordained divine or dharmic pattern. Here again, as in the

Epics, the divine in manifold forms is brought close to the individual and his community. Loving or wrathful, male or female, in human or some other form, the gods and godesses are portrayed as struggling for the good against the evil and the suffering that unceasingly buffet humankind. Of special significance is the emphasis on the devotion *(bhakti)* to the gods that it is necessary for the devout believer to practice. The divine elements of the universe serve men and women, and the human way of serving the gods is by performing sacrifices and living according to the requirements of one's *varṇa*, the Sūtras, and the Śāstras. Further, the Purāṇic teaching in a dramatic way established a firm ground for the place of personal devotion and self-giving to the gods by the individual person. Together with the Bhagavad Gītā, the Purāṇas were to serve as essential supports for the rise of devotional Hinduism in subsequent centuries.

d) Yoga. An additional practice or teaching of great significance for Hinduism that becomes clearly distinguishable in the post-Upaniṣadic period is that of YOGA ("yoke, discipline"), which was obviously of ancient origin when it began to appear as a distinct school. Three factors were important: the notion of power to be gained by meditation and asceticism which was at the heart of much of the teaching of the Āraṇyakas; the Upaniṣadic distinction between intrinsic self and material person; and the increasing emphasis upon the ability of the ultimate self to control the body. These prepared the way for the wide acceptance of yoga in Indian religion. Its classic statement within Hinduism is associated with PATAÑJALI, who is generally thought to have lived in the first centuries A.D.

At the heart of yoga is the conviction that *mokṣa* requires the individual to be detached from the samsaric world. It is obvious that the first step in attaining such release is the controlling of the body's actions by the essential self of the individual. Further, the discipline necessary for such a strenuous effort is of such intricacy and magnitude that one cannot act alone. An accomplished teacher (GURU) is essential to guide the seeker as he or she leaves the familiar ties of human society and overcomes the demands of the body.

All the indigenous Indian religions have had a place for schools of yoga with varying techniques. For classical Hinduism a primary contribution of Patañjali was his utilization of a school of philosophic thought (SĀṂKHYA) which made a sharp distinction between matter (PRAKṚTI) and spirit *(puruṣa)*. Spirit is absolutely distinct from matter and its samsaric condition, and by proper discipline a person can obtain *mokṣa* and its nonsamsaric freedom.

e) Bhakti. A further major element is devotion *(bhakti)* to a personal god (*see* BHAKTI HINDUISM). Here also the origins of such devotion are discernible early in Indian religious history and become clearly expressed in the centuries following the emergence of Jainism and Buddhism. The deities identified with Vedic Brāhmaṇism and those of the popular, less structured religion of Indian society were generally ignored in Upaniṣadic thought. Also, noted above, the ultimate Divine, Brahman, was held by Upaniṣadic thinkers to be without qualities *(nirguṇa)* and therefore is beyond human thought and unapproachable in a personal devotional manner. Nevertheless during the later Upaniṣadic period and especially in the Epics and Purāṇas certain gods were at times held to be supreme over others, or were thought to be closer to and more involved with individuals and human society.

Two factors are of special importance here. First, some of the Upaniṣads, despite their emphasis upon the Brahman without qualities, did refer to the Brahman in a personalized manner as the cause of existence and the ground or source of the human self. In this sense, then, Brahman is with qualities *(saguṇa)* and as such is in some degree knowable and approachable by human beings. Over time various deities were identified with this supreme "with qualities" Brahman. In one of the later Upaniṣads, the Śvetāśvatara, a direct connection is made between the personal *saguṇa* Brahman and the Vedic god RUDRA, later known as Rudra-Shiva and today as SHIVA. The foundation was thus laid for the development of a place for theistic devotional worship within the Vedic-Brāhmaṇic tradition.

Secondly, the Epics and Purāṇas are first and foremost accounts of the great adventures of beings whose very nature is obviously that of divinity. Sometimes in human form, sometimes not, these beings exhibit in one way or another a gracious and loving concern toward humankind and the maintenance of truth (dharma). The literature itself asserts that these beings are *the* ultimate Divine now descended to earth for specific purpose. As the Avatar Krishna (descent of the Lord VISHNU) says in the Bhagavad Gītā IV.8: "For the protection of the good, for the destruction of the wicked, and for the establishment of righteousness, I come into being from age to age."

The end result of this personalization of the impersonal Brahman of the Upaniṣadic philosopher-theologians was the firm establishment within Hinduism of a place for a personal devotional theism of an intense and persuasive quality. Hinduism was now equipped to meet the diverse religious desires and inclinations of the great majority of the Indian people. It is argued by some scholars that Buddhism finally became a minor though not uninfluential factor in India due to the widespread appeal of Bhakti Hinduism.

7. Classical Hinduism. *a) Philosophical schools.* Distinctions between various schools of thought and practice within Indian religion were only gradually seen to be of such magnitude that they constituted separate "religions" (*see* §4). During the Sūtra period in the late centuries B.C. and the early centuries A.D. the

Indian philosphical traditions which in one manner or another allied themselves with the Vedas began the process of systematizing their beliefs. As a result there was a growing consciousness of the particularities of the various traditions. The Sūtras themselves were shorthand enigmatic "threads" or aphorisms containing the thought of particular schools. Given the brevity of the Sūtras there was a growing necessity for authoritative interpretations and commentaries that would establish more clearly and firmly the specific positions of the various systems of thought.

The early centuries of the first millennium A.D. witnessed a systematization of philosophical-theological thought into what are known as the Six Schools of Hindu Philosophy. In some instances the classical formulations of the schools came centuries later. Each of the schools was recognized as being equally valid as a guide to *mokṣa* and classified as *āstika* (orthodox) in contradistinction to the *nāstika* (heterodox) teachings of Jainism and Buddhism. Paired together into three groups, the six were: NYĀYA and Vaiśeṣika; SĀṂKHYA and YOGA; and MĪMĀṂSĀ and VEDĀNTA. Individually they were concerned with various items such as logic, epistemology, physics, the evolution of matter, etc. All, however, were held to be a DARŚANA, "a looking at" the truth.

b) Vedānta. It is Vedānta that has served preeminently as the theological expression of Hindu religion. The emphasis of its paired school, Mīmāṃsā, that the Vedas are eternal and authoritative, provided a claim for revealed knowledge and was central to the theological assumptions and structures of succeeding Vedānta thinkers. The primary source for the different schools of thought within Vedānta is the Brahmā (also called the Vedānta) Sūtra composed by Bādarāyaṇa sometime in the later Sūtra period. Three Vedānta systems in particular have been central to Hindu theological thought.

i. Śaṃkara. ŚAṂKARA (*ca.* A.D. 800) claimed that his teaching was based only upon the Vedas and is, therefore, the stating of ultimate truth in human terms. His first step was to prove the existence of the self and thereby uphold the Upaniṣadic base for an entity within the human being that is related in some manner with the ultimate person, Brahman. Further, this human self, the Atman, is independent of the physical body and the mental or psychic aspects of the human being. The fundamental error made by persons is the identification of the self with the body and/or the mind. This false transference of the self to something that it is not leads to ignorance (AVIDYĀ), and it is the source of the problems of all humans. And it is from this ignorance that rebirth-redeath arise. Samsara and the pains of this world are the result of ignorance.

A primary root of this ignorance is the confusion of the empirical with the ultimately Real. Individuals seek to know that which exists rather than that which is above, below, and within existence, the Brahman. Knowledge of Brahman will destroy ignorance, "the seed of the entire process of rebirth." Humans are confronted through the senses with external manifestations of the Real, but these manifestations must not be confused with the Real. A person must consider the phenomenal world real for the purposes of his own physical existence, but this reality must not be confused with ultimate Reality, which, unlike the world, is independent, enduring, and unchanging. The Real is the Brahman that is beyond causality and is without limitation; the empirical world experienced through the sense and mental capacities obviously does not possess these qualities.

The world of such experience is MĀYĀ, a changing process resulting from the creative power or play of Brahman. Its permanency and value is illusory; it is not real. As long as a person keeps his attachments to the realm of *māyā*, a dimension of changing form with qualities, the qualityless Brahman will be unknown. The Vedas contain the knowledge *(jñāna)* necessary to overcome the ignorance within the arena of *māyā*. *Mokṣa* is available to those who are spiritually disciplined and able to plunge themselves with full intensity into meditation upon the Upaniṣadic texts. This is the way of individuals who have renounced the world (SANNYĀSIN) and are prepared to follow the discipline (yoga) or path *(mārga)* of knowledge. The knowledge gained is a knowledge of the identification of the human self with the ultimate Self, of the Atman with the Brahman, an absolute nondualism (ADVAITA) that for Śaṃkara is the central and ultimate teaching of the Upaniṣads.

ii. Rāmānuja. RĀMĀNUJA, a Vedāntist thinker in the eleventh century, emphasized the reality of the world, the individual self, and the Brahman. Brahman is viewed as primary, and both the world of existence and the individual selves of men depend upon the Brahman. The self comes from Brahman, but it remains a separate, distinct, though dependent entity. This view is called a qualified nondualism (VIŚIṢTA ADVAITA) in that the unified Brahman is manifesting itself both as selves and as matter. For Rāmānuja *mokṣa* is to be obtained by the knowledge of Brahman that results from meditation, devotion, and the necessary addition of the divine grace of the Brahman "with qualities" that responds to that devotion. And the condition of release from samsara is one of a separate, eternal, blissful relationship between the liberated self and the personified Brahman.

iii. Madhva. The thirteenth century thinker MADHVA gives an eternal permanency to Brahman, human selves, and the world, thereby espousing a strict dualism (DVAITA). Though permanent, selves and the world are not equal to the Brahman and are dependent upon it. In extending Rāmānuja's thought, Madhva emphasizes the role of the Brahman in controlling the world and all selves. Greatly influenced by the BHĀGAVATA PURĀṆA, which recounts the adventures of Krishna as an avatar of the great god

Vishnu, Madhva argues that Vishnu and Brahman are one. Thus devotion to Krishna as the descent of Vishnu to earth is devotion to Vishnu or Brahman. Vishnu releases humans from samsara by his grace, selecting those who lead pure lives for a state of bliss close to him; individuals who are neither pure nor totally evil are predestined to a hell whose primary condition is essentially one of great remoteness from Vishnu.

Thus it was that the Vedānta laid the basic foundation for Hindu religious thought and devotion. Claiming their positions to be the end or aim of the Vedas, despite the variety of thought and the disagreements between them, the theologians of Vedānta maintained the *śruti* of the Vedas, the existence of the Ultimate (Brahman), and the presence in humans of a self either identical with, or possessing an actual or potentially close relationship to, the Brahman. *Mokṣa* is possible from the limitations of samsara and its inevitable rebirth-redeath. The human condition when freed from samsara is one of blissful relationship or identity with the Divine.

During the centuries when the more formal theological statements of Vedānta were in the process of formulation, a threefold conception of the way to *mokṣa* became firmly established in the Hindu religious mind. Long a part of Indian religious thought and practice, these paths or disciplines were supported in varying degree by different facets of Vedāntic thought and thereby obtained a recognized status as essential aspects of Hinduism. The way of action (karma) or deeds, in which the individual by performing the proper cultic sacrifices and social responsibilities of his station in life fulfilled his dharma, was to a large extent a continuation of the Vedic-Brāhmaṇic tradition. The way of knowledge *(jñāna)*, involving a withdrawal from the usual human and social activities and requiring a discipline of the body and mind in the endeavor to ascertain the true self, received its intellectual structure primarily from the thought of Śaṃkara. The way of devotion *(bhakti)*, with its concentration upon self-giving love and adoration to a personal Lord, was supported by the theological systems of Vedāntist thinkers such as Rāmānuja and Madhva. And while individual Hindus might emphasize one path to the neglect of the others, in general practice the pious Hindu would have a place for some aspects of all three paths in his or her personal life.

8. Popular theism. Despite many varieties of thought and action, the essential features of the Hinduism of the great majority of the Indian people for the past one thousand or more years are associated with the path of devotion. *Bhakti mārga* centers upon the worship of the "Adorable One" (BHAGAVĀN), who may be given any one of a great variety of names taken from the many Hindu names of the gods or avatars. A further aspect of such worship is associated with adoration of female manifestations of the divine, the ŚAKTI or divine consorts of the male gods; goddesses who possess creative power and are active in the affairs of the mundane world (*see* GODDESS [INDIA]).

The *bhakti* expression of Hinduism concentrates primarily on the worship of some aspect of the great gods Vishnu (VAIṢṆAVISM) or Shiva (ŚAIVISM). The literary or scriptural base for *bhakti* is the Purāṇic literature and the Epics, especially the Bhagavad Gītā portion of the Mahābhārata. The Purāṇas in particular have served as vehicles for the popular understanding of the gods and their activities in relationship to each other and to man. By means of the dance, drama, and storytelling, the great all-India Purāṇic accounts of the gods, goddesses, and the divine wonders in the universe have been made known to the vast majority of Hindus. In addition, there are regional Purāṇas associated with local temples and holy places that are readily accessible to worshipers in their own locality. A local deity, or name for a god, is frequently understood to be identical with either Vishnu or Shiva, a *Śakti*, or an avatar. Thus the great gods of Hinduism are localized for popular worship and made the objects of intense devotion. *Mokṣa* is available to men and women as a result of the gracious love bestowed by the Adorable One to those who adore God in whatever form is most meaningful to them.

The intellectual and devotional structure and leadership of the various theistic movements within Hinduism from the time of Rāmānuja onward was provided by a series of remarkable individuals who by their own religious experience and intense devotion influenced great numbers of followers. Among them, Rāmānanda (1400-1470) spoke to the people in their local language rather than the Sanskrit that was traditionally used in religious discourse, objected to caste distinctions among worshipers, and preached the message of the love of Vishnu for mankind as seen in Vishnu's avatar Rāma; Rāma is god. CAITANYA (1486-1533) carried his message of intense love of god to all castes, and taught that Vishnu's avatar Krishna is to be worshiped; Krishna is god.

Others expressing their intense devotion to the Adorable One through the medium of non-Sanskrit vernacular poetry inspired great masses of Hindus to emulate their adoration of god. Earlier in South India, poet-saints, including some from the lower castes and women, and within both the Śaivite (NĀYAṆĀRS) and Vaiṣṇavite (ĀLVĀRS) traditions, had expressed such devotion in the Tamil language. Much later, TULSĪ DĀS (1532-1623) wrote in Hindī the epic poem RĀMCARITMĀNAS (The Sacred Lake of the Deeds of Rāma) based on the great Epic Rāmāyaṇa. His work came to serve as a primary source for the drama and song that is central in the *bhakti* worship of Rāma in North India.

9. Religious reaction to Islam. ISLAM began to make its way into India proper in the eleventh century as Muslim invaders from Afghanistan began their forays into North India. By the middle of the thirteenth century firm Muslim rule was established in the North, and at the height of the Mogul empire in the seventeenth century Muslim political power extended over the whole of the subcontinent with the exception of the extreme South. It was natural that some Indians would convert to Islam, but the great majority of Hindus remained within the Hindu tradition, frequently expressing their faith through a rigid Brāhmaṇical orthodoxy.

However, there were those individuals who while Hindu in origin adopted certain of the basic teachings of Islam as part of their own religious thought and worship. Primary among these was KABĪR (1440-1518), a poet and holy man from the northern holy city of Banāras, a follower of Rāmānanda and devotee of Rāma. Kabīr's Vedāntic belief in one God by whatever name and his fervent *bhakti* devotionalism led him to proclaim himself and all persons to be children of both Rāma and ALLAH. As children of the one God they are not to be separated by social caste distinctions, nor should they be bound by the dogmatic traditions of either Hinduism or Islam. The image worship of the Hindus and the literal worship of the QUR'ĀN by Muslims were only trappings that had become substitutes for the worship of the one true God.

A major tenet of Kabīr's teaching was the role of the spiritual teacher or guru in the individual's spiritual progress, an ancient tradition within Indian religion. Kabīr's emphasis on the importance of a human spiritual adviser reinvigorated this concept and laid the foundation for a number of subsequent Hindu religious groups, who under a charismatic guru would blend into their Hinduism some Muslim beliefs and/or practices.

The primary example of this is NĀNAK (1469-1539) and the religion that resulted from his teachings, SIKHISM. Nānak's teaching concentrated upon the worship of one God, the "True Name," to whom the many Hindu gods, he maintained, bear witness. Accepting the doctrines of karma and *mokṣa,* he attacked the distinctions of caste and the worship of images, while retaining a place for many of the personal and family religious ceremonies (SAMSKĀRAS) that were at the heart of Hindu piety. Ultimately rejected by Hindu orthodoxy and Muslim dogma, Nānak and his disciples (Sikhs) became a distinct religious group and for a brief time established a separate political entity in northwest India in order to escape military and religious persecutions.

10. Modern Hinduism. The life and work of RAM MOHAN ROY (1772-1833) and the REFORM MOVEMENTS IN INDIA begun by him and others in the nineteenth century brought a new perspective and type of leadership to some levels of Hinduism. Roy's BRĀHMO SAMĀJ, the ĀRYA SAMĀJ of DAYĀNANDA, the Ramakrishna Mission based on the teachings of RĀMAKRISHNA and organized by Swami VIVEKĀNANDA, and other groups of less renown marked the beginning of a self-conscious effort by some Hindus to meet the particular challenges and opportunities of the nineteenth and twentieth centuries. The impact of Western culture, of non-Asian political and economic control, and more recently of the worldwide process of modernization—all combined to bring a ferment to Hinduism unlike anything experienced before. For the most part, however, this experience was limited to the more educated groups within Hinduism, and as a result its full impact is still difficult to assess.

During the present century those Hindu intellectuals who have endeavored to express their religious beliefs and live their lives in consonance with modern thought and science have found guidance in the writings and examples of AUROBINDO Ghose (1872-1950) and Sarvepalli RADHAKRISHNAN (1888-1975). Aurobindo, while giving a place to human reason and modern science, maintained that the ultimate truth of existence can only be attained from the mystic vision that arises from a life of devout meditation. Radhakrishnan, a brilliant philosopher and statesman, who through his many writings brought the richness of Indian philosophy and the depths of the Hindu religious quest to the attention of many Westerners, at the same time clarified Hinduism and made it more meaningful for many of his fellow Hindus.

In the second quarter of the twentieth century the life and activities of M. K. GANDHI (1869-1948) caught the attention of the world and fostered an interest in India and Hinduism. A devoutly religious, though unorthodox, person, he gave many Hindus an ideal of service to humanity and devotion to the divine, the impact of which upon future Hinduism remains to be seen.

Nevertheless, despite the work of these men and others, "modern" Hinduism is largely traditional BHAKTI HINDUISM, a way of living and thinking in accord with the Indian and specifically Hindu apprehension of the divine element of existence. The frame of mind that results from this perception of the divine, whether conscious or not, is one that holds life to be an ongoing portion of a larger cosmic whole, a totality of being in a rhythmic pattern in which the present momentary person is in a process of becoming more than he or she has been before. For the intellectual this can be stated in language and forms commensurate with philosophical integrity and modern scientific thought. As for the peasant, the laborer, and the nonintellectual in general, their basic wisdom within the rich confines of the tradition they know primarily through the Purāṇas and Epics gives them an equally vivid sense of the divine and its presence here and now. The devout Hindu of every level of education and social status finds meaning in his or her close relationship with the divine being(s) made vividly present in the home shrine, the village temple, and the great temples and holy places of India.

Contemporary Hinduism has no one expression nor is it a mere syncretism of all previous religious expressions. Hinduism includes the near-naked ascetic wandering from one Hindu sacred place to another as well as the insurance executive dressed in a Western suit who performs his own private Pūjā in his home each morning and evening. Hinduism can be seen in the pan-Indian festivals which include all social and religious groups as well as in the life-cycle rites available only to the upper castes and controlled by the traditional Brahmin priesthood. Myriads of gods and goddesses attract devotion in rituals as varied as the bloody sacrifice of a goat to the silent meditation of the *bhakti* yogin. All of this, and much more, is included under the umbrella of contemporary Hindu practice.

There are, of course, those Hindus for whom religion is less important, a periodic matter rather than a constant, vibrant, informing factor in their lives. Yet even these individuals have a sense of the religious life of which they are a part and the social responsibilities that are theirs because they live and have their reason for being within the divine structure of existence that is central to the Hindu perception of the universe.

11. **Religious life and social responsibilities.** The religious life of the Hindu people for many centuries has been based upon the various structures noted above, §§6, 7, 8. The Purāṇic teachings about the gods and their avatars, together with special devotion to and adoration of a particular manifestation of the divine, are central to the daily and periodical religious activities of the devout person. To be a Hindu is to be aware of the responsibilities of true devotion. The strong emphasis of Vedic times on the necessity of sacrifice (Yajña) has over the centuries been superseded by the honoring (*pūjā*) of the god or gods. This honoring or worship has the purpose of giving satisfaction to deity in much the same manner as did the sacrifice of Vedic religion. From the human standpoint Hinduism insists that proper attention to worship is essential as a discipline in bringing the individual person into a proper relationship with deity.

There is a great variety of worship forms and activities within Hinduism. This is the result of many factors, primary among which are the caste of the worshiper, the religious sect to which the individual belongs, the traditional religious practices of the particular region of the country, the specific time or purpose of the act of worship, and whether the *pūjā* is performed within the home, at the temple, or at the time of a religious festival. The degree of piety of the individual involved will also lead to differences in practice and intensity of worship. However, underlying the diversity there is a unity of scriptural claim and social structure that gives a commonality to Hindu worship wherever it is performed.

a) Caste and dharma. There has been much debate in recent years concerning the place and role of the Caste *(jāti)* system within Hindu religion. There can be no doubt of the central significance of caste within Indian society. The debate, however, is related to the disabilities which caste status places upon those who are not members of the higher castes, and whether those restrictions are sanctioned by the Hindu religion itself. Religious leaders and reformers have sometimes sought to eliminate caste within their own religious groups and have maintained that in the worship of God it is not caste that establishes superiority or quality, but sincerity of intent and intensity of devotion. Nevertheless, certain features associated with caste are important in relation to the worship and responsibilities of the religious person.

A paramount distinction between groups within the caste system is that between the "Twice Born" castes and those that are not twice born. The twice born castes fall within the upper three groups of the *varṇa* classification: Brahmin, Kṣatriya, and Vaiśya. They are born twice due to the sacrament of initiation with its investiture of the Sacred Thread *(upanayana)* whereby the males are theoretically if not actually initiated into the study of the Vedas. For most of the twice born castes marriage is traditionally considered to be the female sacrament of initiation.

The fourth *varṇa* classification, the Śūdra, is composed of the many castes that are not entitled to Vedic study and the wisdom that accrues from such familiarity with *śruti*, and whose religious duties and potentialities are consequently less. This has been the view of orthodox Hinduism for centuries, and it is only in recent times that there has been any discernible change.

The religious responsibility that falls upon the individual on the basis of caste is an individual dharma, a law, a weight, a responsibility that the person must carry, since failure to do so involves a karmic liability that must be avoided. To fulfill one's dharmic duty is to be true to one's parents and ancestors; it is to take one's rightful place within the universal scheme of things. And by so doing the individual demonstrates devotion to God and also satisfies his or her own spiritual needs.

b) Home worship. Worship in the home is for the orthodox Hindu preeminently the opportunity to fulfill the five daily obligations of the twice born individual: to make offerings to the gods, to the rishis or wise men who heard the Vedas, to one's forefathers who have given one life, to animals, and to guests. In the case of the last two offerings, the animal is most frequently the cow, which is considered the mother of the world, while the offering to guests is symbolized by giving food to a priest or giving food or aid to the poor. (*See* Cow, Symbolism and Veneration.)

Each of these activities has a specific time of day for its performance, beginning early in the morning and continuing until evening. Physical and ritual purity for the person and the image of the deity are strict requirements for the orthodox believer. They are obtained by the proper following of age-old religious instructions, which guide the worshiper to propriety in bathing, eating and fasting, the clothing of the body, physical posture, and the specific acts of the worship itself.

Whether the believing Hindu is orthodox or not, or whether he or she is twice born, in some form or other worship in the home is a paramount part of daily life. Hindu worship is especially individual in nature and is to be carried on in the closest of individual relationships, that of the family. The family home with its image or shrine is at the heart of the continuing Hindu cult and its vitality.

c) Temples, pilgrimages, and communal worship. Hindu temples and shrines are understood by the devout to be the residence of the particular god, or the locality where that deity has manifested itself in some peculiar and powerful manner. Except for the smaller shrines, they are usually surrounded by a wall, contain a courtyard and tank of water, and at their heart have a comparatively small sacred room where the main image of the deity is kept.

The image is treated with great respect and care, and in the daily ceremonies that are carried out by temple priests it is served as a great king or queen would be. Different priests have specific functions to perform, and a well-managed temple accentuates the analogy to the court of powerful royalty. Since sounds are believed by Hindus to be particularly powerful in sustaining the world and in pleasing the deities, a MANTRA (a single syllable, a Vedic verse of many syllables, or the name of the god) may be repeated in a murmuring tone *(japa)* over and over by the priests.

The great temples of India and renowned regional temples and shrines are centers of PILGRIMAGE throughout the year. At times of great festivals celebrating some particular activity associated with the deity of the temple, they are crowded with pilgrims. At such times, the pilgrims make offerings to the deity, fulfilling a vow they had made when seeking a boon, and are, perhaps, desiring the great religious satisfaction of "seeing" and being "seen" *(darsána)* by the divine being. While at the temple the worshiper may seek the aid of a temple priest in having a prayer made to or a boon granted by the deity. Above all, attendance at the temple is a time of joyous celebration and the expression of devotion and need. It is not an occasion for congregational worship as it often is in the Western world.

However, there is in Hinduism a type of communal worship that is primarily associated with *bhakti* sects. It includes group praying and singing of praises to the deity, perhaps accompanied by other cultic acts. Such prayer groups and devotional singing (KĪRTANA) traditionally have been the activity of worshipers gathered around an ecstatic charismatic leader such as Caitanya (*see above* §8). Today throughout India there is a growth of locally organized community groups meeting periodically in the homes of participants for such prayers and devotional singing.

12. Current trends. India and Hinduism during the past one hundred years have been confronted by Westernization and modernization. Indian economics, education, politics, and societal expectations have

P. Courtright

Clay images carried through the streets on the tenth day of the annual festival to Gaṇeśa

undergone profound changes, though at the same time the style of life of the great majority of the Indian people remains much as it was for their ancestors.

The same is true for the religion of the Indian people. Hindu intellectuals and those whose occupations have brought them into close association with the processes of modernization have adapted to a style of life and thinking radically different from that of their forebears. But to expect or to forecast startling changes of thought or practice within Hinduism in the foreseeable future would be to ignore the facts of Indian religious life as well as to assume that the devout Hindu feels there is need for such change. There are, however, some discernible trends that suggest both a continuation and a strengthening of Hinduism now and in the future.

a) Religious thought. The present-day Hindu philosopher-theologians who express themselves in the modern mode are to a noticeable degree the inheritors of the reform tradition associated with the work of Ram Mohan Roy, and the renaissance of pride in Hindu thought expressed by such vastly different men as Vivekānanda, Aurobindo, and Radhakrishnan. Expressing their understanding of the human situation in contemporary, and frequently Western, philosophical and scientific categories, such thinkers are finding further evidence which to their minds validates the beliefs central to the Vedāntic tradition.

b) Religious practice. In the realm of cultic practice much continues as it has over the centuries. Two important trends, however, are evident. One is within the popular theistic *bhakti* movements, many of which had their origins some five hundred years ago (*see above* §8). The new feature here is the use of modern means of communication and organization. Traditional enthusiasm and piety are gaining wider influence through the use of techniques identified with modernization (*see* Singer).

The second trend is associated with the temples, ancient and modern, that are central features of the Indian landscape. Great temples that are centers of pilgrimages from all over India, and local temples that are visited more frequently by neighboring populations, now use the printing press, modern electronics, and other technological means to make themselves and their Purāṇic traditions known and meaningful to the Hindu people.

c) Hinduism outside India. Recent decades have witnessed the spread of Hindu sectarian groups throughout the world among non-Indian peoples. This is a decidedly new feature, and from the perspective of orthodox Hinduism is highly suspect. Nevertheless, if the trend continues it will be of significant aid in bringing traditional Hindu themes and values to the attention of the modern world. Together with an increasing interest in India and Asia on the part of the people of the Western world, the active claim by Hindu groups that their religion is of relevance to all humans everywhere suggests that the religion that evolved through some three thousand years or more on the Indian subcontinent can face the present and future with confidence (*see* HINDUISM IN AMERICA).

Bibliography. A. L. Basham, *The Wonder That Was India* (1963); M. Eliade, *Yoga* (1969); T. J. Hopkins, *The Hindu Religious Tradition* (1971); K. W. Morgan, ed., *The Religion of the Hindus* (1953); S. Radhakrishnan and C. A. Moore, eds., *A Source Book in Indian Philosophy* (1957); M. Singer, ed., *Krishna: Myths, Rites and Attitudes* (1966); T. W. Organ, *Hinduism* (1974); C. Dimmitt and J. A. B. van Buitenen, *Classical Hindu Mythology* (1978); M. Singer, *Traditional India: Structure and Change* (1959).

P. H. ASHBY

HINDUISM IN AMERICA. The Hindu ideas, practices, and teachers that have gained currency in America comprise something of an intercultural phenomenon, related to both American and South Asian contexts but the sole product of neither. Only certain aspects of Hinduism have been appropriated by Americans. Philosophic and mystical teachings and the fellowship of religious movements have had wider appeal in America than Hindu concepts of ritual and familial duties or Hindu customary practices and divine mythologies (*see* HINDUISM). Since Hindu spiritual and social values are closely linked with India's distinctive cultures and traditions, Hinduism in America might be regarded as an anomaly. Yet Hindu influences have made an impact on America's religious consciousness from the early nineteenth century to the present.

1. **History.** New England transcendentalism provided the first significant entrance of Hindu concepts into American religious thought. Ralph Waldo Emerson (1803-82) employed the ideas of BRAHMAN and KARMA in his writings, and the first American books to widely disseminate Hindu ideas were written by transcendentalists in the 1840s: e.g., James Freeman Clarke's *Ten Great Religions* and Samuel Johnson's *The Religion of Asia.* Like transcendentalism itself, however, these early evidences of Hindu thought remained only in literary images and philosophical ideas.

Later in the century the increase in Christian missionary activity produced some excellent ethnographic and interpretive studies of Hinduism, but the popular reports from the mission field tended to exaggerate what were viewed as the barbarous customs and idolatrous beliefs of the Hindus. In the late nineteenth century the writings of Friedrich Max Müller and other European Orientalists did much to dispel these images and revive an American interest in Hinduism. A personal, mystical Hinduism was discovered by the Theosophical Society (*see* THEOSOPHY).

In 1893, in Chicago, the history of Hinduism in America entered a new phase with the dazzling performance of Swami Vivekānanda at the World Parliament of Religions. The very idea of convening such a parliament was an indication of the liberal religious spirit of America at the time. Vivekānanda presented an image of Hinduism which fit the new mood and forever dashed the exaggerated images reported by the Christian missionaries. Vivekānanda's Hinduism was VEDĀNTIC, nontheistic, morally respectable, philosophically interesting, and above all rational. Vivekānanda's Ramakrishna Mission (named after his well-known teacher) and his Vedanta Societies, established in 1897, grew rapidly in both India and America; they appealed to an educated and liberal following, including the philosopher and writer Aldous Huxley.

The immigration of South Asians to America in the first decades of this century increased the number of Indian Hindus in America, but the immigrants did not make a significant contribution to the spread of Hindu ideas. The Indian immigrants remained culturally isolated, except for a small number who joined the Vedanta Society, finding it an acceptable compromise between an American church and their own religious heritage. However, many of the approximately ten thousand South Asian immigrants were not Hindus; even though many Americans persisted in calling them that, they were in fact SIKHS. The first Sikh temple (also called a *gurdwārā*) was established in Stockton, California, in 1912, and much later other Sikh temples were built in El Centro and Marysville, California, and more recently in most of the major American cities on both the East and West coasts.

Vivekānanda and his Vedanta Societies set the major pattern for the development of Hinduism in twentieth century America. Like Vivekānanda, many other vibrant and charismatic Hindu religious figures have come to America, reversing the flow of missionary activity from that of the nineteenth century; and many established societies and centers on Western shores. At the same time, the availability of quick and inexpensive global transportation made it possible for Americans to go to the East, and there some of them joined Hindu movements which became international. In turn, local chapters of these centers became established in America. The major growth of these movements in America has been during the turbulent postwar years of the 1920s, the 1940s, and especially the 1970s, America's years of complex crises and exploration on both personal and cultural levels.

2. **Internationalization of Hinduism.** Perhaps the greatest stimulus for the growth of Hinduism in America came from India itself. There the presence of British officials, Christian missionaries, and Western education encouraged new currents within early twentieth century Hinduism which were defensive of Hindu tradition, but presented that tradition in modern terms. This made Hindu ideas accessible to the West, and Western followers often were sought as verifications of the universal appeal of Hindu truths.

Śrī Aurobindo Ghose developed a highly imaginative and evolutionary system of integral Yoga which appealed as much to Westerners as to Indians. While imprisoned by the British, Aurobindo underwent a dramatic spiritual conversion in 1909, and thereafter established a religious center in Pondicherry, South India. His most faithful disciple and successor after his death was a French woman, Mira Richard, known as "the Mother," who established an international utopian city in South India, Auroville. The city has received support from agencies of the United Nations, Germany and India.

Another Hindu movement which early developed an international following was the Rādhā Soāmī Satsaṅg. Unlike Aurobindo's elaborate system, the teachings of the Rādhā Soāmī line of masters, established in Agra in 1861, were more consistent with the Yoga of the universal sound current *(surat shabd yoga)* and the devotion to Rādhā Soāmī masters *(gur-bhakti)* closely echoed medieval esoteric Hindu teachings. The novelty of Rādhā Soāmī came in the establishment of an industrial city at Dayalbagh, near Agra, and the creation of an international center by a branch of the movement at Beas, in the Indian state of Punjab. The movement first attracted Western followers in the late nineteenth century from among British officers stationed in India. In 1910 chapters of the movement were established in the United States. The American growth accelerated after the power to initiate new members was granted by proxy to the Beas master's representative in California. The followers of the Ruhani Satsaṅg movement, which was established by Kirpal Singh (b. 1894), a disciple of one of the Rādhā Soāmī masters, are predominantly Western and its American center is in Franklin, New Hampshire.

The explosion of new religious movements in India after its independence in 1947 resulted in a proliferation of American auxiliary movements. One of India's most popular faith healers and prophets, Satya Sai Bābā (b. 1926 as Satya Narayan), has achieved an American following through his international organization, Spiritual Advancement of the Individual Foundation, Inc. Perhaps better known in the West is Meher Bābā who, like Satya Sai Bābā, proclaimed himself an Avatar ("descent" of God). Meher Bābā was born a Parsi, but his teachings reflect Hindu as well as Islamic Sufi ideas. There are Meher Bābā organizations throughout the United States, such as the Meher center located at Myrtle Beach, South Carolina.

One of India's most controversial new movements, Ananda Marg, which emphasized social service (Karma-Yoga) as well as meditation techniques, has had one of the largest Western followings. After the movement founded a political party in Bihar and allegedly attempted to kill government officials, the Indian government arrested its leader, Ānandamūrti, who himself was indicted (and acquited) for the murder of two disgruntled disciples. Subsequently the movement fragmented, lost most of its mass appeal, and has become little more than a radical, if not fanatical, sect. Another controversial Guru in India, Bhagwan Rajneesh (b. 1931), is also predominantly supported by Americans and other Westerners. Rajneesh mixes psychological insights with traditional Hindu teachings; that, along with his open-minded attitude toward changing morality, accounts for both his American supporters and his Indian skeptics.

3. **Hindu missionaries to America.** Many of the most visible of the new Hindu movements were made in America. They appear to be similar to the American auxiliaries of India's new movements, but unlike them they have little or no organizational ties to India. In most cases they were established by lone Indian religious figures who came to America for that purpose, though devotees and successors are usually American. Thus, these are American religious movements even though their teachings—and in some cases their physical appearances—are traditionally Hindu. The following are some better-known examples of these missionaries and their movements.

a) Paramahansa Yogananda (Self-Realization Fellowship). The first Hindu missionary to settle in America was Yogānanda (Mukunda Lal Ghosh, 1893-1952), a Bengali who, like Swami Vivekānanda, came to America to attend a conference—the

International Congress of Religious Liberals in Boston, in 1920—and stayed to establish his own organization. Unlike Vivekānanda, however, Yogānanda remained in the West, establishing a center at Los Angeles and achieving wide recognition through his published memoirs, *Autobiography of a Yogi*. Although he taught the basic philosophy of the classical YOGA SŪTRAS and the technique of *kriyā-yoga* ("applied" or "practical" yoga), his "Churches of All Religions" have many of the characteristics of Christian fellowships and Sunday morning services.

b) Maharishi Mahesh Yogi (see TRANSCENDENTAL MEDITATION*).*

c) Maharaj-ji (Divine Light Mission). The so-called "boy guru," Maharaj-ji (b. 1958), came from a line of spiritual masters who taught at the holy city of Hardvār. After the death of his father, the widely respected Hans-ji Maharaj, his mother ("Mata-ji") sent the boy off on a series of world tours, commencing in 1970. His teachings were related to those of the Rādhā Soāmī movement with emphases on the divine experience of pure energy, the fellowship of believers, and complete devotion to the guru. The movement had a large and enthusiastic, albeit short-lived, following in America, which dissipated after the boy guru and his mother disagreed over his life-style and romantic interests in an American devotee. The mother returned to India, establishing her own movement, while the boy guru and his new wife remained in America.

d) Bhaktivedanta Swami A. C. (see HARE KRISHNA MOVEMENT*).*

e) Yogi Bhajan (3HO/Sikh Dharma Brotherhood). When Yogi Bhajan (b. Harbhajan Singh Puri, 1929) first came to America in 1969 from his native Punjab, where he had been an office worker, his teachings were those of the Hindu KUṆḌALINĪ Yoga and HAṬHA YOGA traditions. His American followers were organized into religious communes which Yogi Bhajan called the "Happy/Healthy/Holy Organization" (3HO). In the 1970s the emphasis shifted toward the teachings of the Sikh tradition of the Punjab, and the movement became known as the Sikh Dharma Brotherhood. Like the Sikhs in the Punjab, Yogi Bhajan's "American Sikhs" do not cut their hair; they wear white turbans and white Indian clothes, and adopt Punjabi names. The movement has been centered in California, but has branches throughout the United States.

f) Others. Most of the other Hindu missionaries to America have been similar to Yogānanda and the Maharishi. Their teachings usually have been Vedāntic, they have advocated various Yoga techniques, and their American tours have been sufficiently frequent to maintain their busy American religious organizations. Swami Vishnu-Devānanda (b. 1927) has set up an organization with Yoga camps and centers, which he calls True World Order; it is based on a similar large movement, the Divine Life Society, established by his famous teacher Swami Śivānanda in the Indian holy city of Rishikesh. Another disciple of Swami Śivānanda, Swami Satchidānanda, established a center in Connecticut; he calls his combination of Yoga practices "integral Yoga" (as did Śrī Aurobindo), and an institute with that name was established in 1966. Swami Muktananda (b. 1908) teaches Siddha Yoga and travels between his Indian center in Ganeshpuri and his American center in Oakland. Śrī Chinmoy (b. 1931) has devoted himself to Western tours and writing books aimed at Western audiences since 1964; he teaches a combination of Yoga techniques.

4. American Hinduism. It was perhaps inevitable that Hindu missionary activity in America would produce an indigenous American Hinduism. Theosophy may have been the precursor of recent movements lead by Bābā Rām Dās (born as Gordon Alpert) who, along with Timothy Leary, was once a professor of psychology at Harvard, and Bubba Free John (b. Franklin Jones, 1939), who founded the Dawn Horse Community in California and freely borrows from the teachings of Hindu masters. One of Yogānanda's disciples, Swami Kriyānanda (b. Donald Walters, 1926), broke from the Self-Realization Fellowship and established a separate commune, the Ānanda Community, in the California foothills of the Sierra mountains.

5. Influence on American religion. Elements of Hinduism pervade the new religious movements in America, especially those with eclectic teachings, such as Arica, the MSIA movement lead by Dr. John-Roger Hinkins, and the commune headed by Stephen Gaskin. The teachings of the Eckankar movement founded by Paul Twitchell are largely those of Rādhā Soāmī. In addition to the new religious movements, Hindu mysticism and meditation practices have contributed to a revival of interest in spirituality, charismatic gifts of the spirit, and spiritual exercises among mainstream American Protestant, Roman Catholic, and Jewish communities.

Metaphysical and idealistic ideas from modern Hinduism have come into American thought through the works of Rabindranath TAGORE and Sarvepalli RADHAKRISHNAN, who wrote as much for international audiences as they did for educated Indians. A profound vision of Hindu social ethics came from the life and teachings of Mohandas Karamchand GANDHI, who was a major influence on the pacifist thought of the civil rights leader MARTIN LUTHER KING, JR., the Christian pacifist and activist A.J. Muste, and the folksinger and activist Joan Baez.

6. Impact in India. The extraordinary American interest in Hinduism has alternately amused and impressed Indians, who have utilized Hare Krishna devotees as comic relief in Hindi movies, but who also regard Swami Vivekānanda's success at the 1893 parliament in Chicago as an indication of Hinduism's entry into the modern world. There also has been a phenomenon—which an American scholar, Agehananda Bharati (himself a Hindu convert), calls "the pizza effect"—in which Hindu ideas and teachers that receive recognition in America thereafter become more greatly appreciated in India. Gandhi learned much about Hinduism from Theosophists while studying in London (1888-91), and the popular Hindu teacher Jiddu KRISHNAMURTI was tutored by the Theosophists. The Hare Krishna movement has become established in India at the Krishna pilgrimage center, Vrindāvan, where American devotees attempt to convert Indians to the movement. At the central shrine of the Sikhs, in Amritsar, Punjab, pictures of American Sikhs are proudly displayed, and they have named Yogi Bhajan the representative of Sikh Dharma in the Western Hemisphere. Thus American Hindu movements, although products of their separate Indian and American contexts, at times build lively links between them.

Bibliography. R. S. Ellwood, Jr., *Religious and Spiritual Groups in Modern America* (1973); M. H. Harper, *Gurus, Swamis, and Avataras: Spiritual Masters and Their American Disciples* (1972); J. S. Judah, *Hare Krishna and the Countercuture* (1974); J. Needleman, *The New Religions* (1970); J.P. Rao Rayapati, *Early American Interest in Vedanta* (1973).

M. JUERGENSMEYER

HINDUISM IN SOUTHEAST ASIA. A catalog of SANSKRIT texts or of deities with Hindu names found in Southeast Asia would reveal that many religions in this region carry the impress of Indian influence. Yet these religions as they are actually practiced are almost without exception not direct transplants of Indian HINDUISM. Rather, from the time some two millennia ago when Indian civilization first began to be transmitted to Southeast Asia until the present, Hindu religious motifs have been adapted to carry practical meanings different from those with which they have been associated in India.

The first major adaptation of Hindu religion in Southeast Asia came during the period from the ninth to the fourteenth centuries when the "Indianized" civilizations of Southeast Asia held sway. Subsequently, Hindu religious elements were molded into a new syncretism with Islam in Java (see ISLAM IN SOUTHEAST ASIA) and were accorded a supporting role in the world views of BUDDHISM in mainland Southeast Asian socieities. While Hinduistic practices are still followed among a small number of Chams, in southern Vietnam and Cambodia, only among the Balinese in Indonesia did a distinctive Southeast Asian Hinduism remain and develop. During the nineteenth century migrants from India, many from Hindu backgrounds, began to settle in large numbers in several Southeast Asian states. Yet their Hinduism also underwent significant change as they adapted their religious practices to life in their new homes.

1. **Indianized civilizations in Southeast Asia.** Indian influences began to manifest themselves in Southeast Asia from about the turn of the Christian era. As they were carried from the entrepôt ports of the region to the seats of local chiefs, they were molded together with local cultures to create new ideological foundations for a number of emerging states. By the ninth century a number of these states had begun to achieve dominance over their local regions. The eleventh and twelfth centuries saw the climax of Indianized civlizations with Angkor in Cambodia, Champa in southern Vietnam, Pagan in Burma, and Majapahit in Java. These civilizations were Indianized not because they had been created or peopled by natives from the Indian subcontinent—significant Indian migrations to Southeast Asia did not occur until the nineteenth century—but because their culture, art, architecture, and patterns of sociopolitical action had been formulated with reference to the thought of India.

The rulers of the Indianized states, together with their religious advisers who were at times BRAHMINS from India or descendants of such Brahmins, promoted beliefs in Hindu as well as Buddhist deities and cosmologies in their efforts to establish themselves as god-kings *(deva-rāja)* or Buddha-kings *(buddha-rāja)*. In their capitals, these rulers attempted to create in architecture a microcosm of an Indian-conceived sacred cosmos.

At Angkor the divinity of the ruler was believed to reside in a LIṄGA, a phallic representation of SHIVA, which was situated in a pyramidical replica of MT. MERU located at the center of a cosmologically oriented city. But the king at Angkor was by no means always seen as Shiva. King Suryavarman II (1113-50) built the well-known Angkor Wat as a shrine to VISHNU, a Vishnu identified with the king himself. Jayavarman VII (1181–*ca.* 1218) had his portrait assimilated to that of the BODHISATTVA Lokeśvara in the four-faced images of the Bayon, the central monument of Jayavarman's city, Angkor Thom. On Java the great eleventh century ruler, Airlanga (1016-49), claimed, as did his successors, to be an incarnation of Vishnu; yet inscriptions attest to the fact that in the old Javanese civilization Śaivite Hinduism and MAHĀYĀNA Buddhism also flourished and received royal support. At Pagan, the capital of the first major Burmese civilization, Buddhism, both Mahāyāna and THERAVĀDA, was manifestly the dominant religion. Still the great Pagan king Kyanzittha (1084-1113) claimed in his inscriptions not only to be a bodhisattva, a *cakravartin* ("world ruler"), and a "lord abounding in merit," but also to be an AVATAR of Vishnu.

During the thirteenth to fifteenth centuries the religious syncretisms which included Hinduism as a component came under serious challenge both as a consequence of almost continuous political upheaval and also because of the propagation of Islam in insular and peninsular Southeast Asia and of orthodox Theravāda Buddhism on the mainland. Hinduism did not, however, entirely disappear from Southeast Asia following the collapse of the Indianized civilizations. It remained a vestigial element among the court customs of some of the successor states in the region; it assumed a distinctive place in the popular religions of the Islamic Javanese in Indonesia and the Buddhist peoples of the mainland; and it survived and developed into a unique religious tradition on the island of Bali.

2. Hinduism and Javanese religious syncretism. The spread of Islam throughout insular and peninsular Southeast Asia might have been expected to have effected the disappearance of Hinduism from the religious traditions of the societies in these regions. In practice this occurred only in those coastal societies which maintained intensive and continuous contacts with Islamic societies outside Southeast Asia. Elsewhere, and particularly in Java, a new religious syncretism emerged.

The religious syncretism of Java in which an older Hindu-Javanese tradition has been combined with a newer Islamic tradition carries a distinctive name, *abangan*. The *abangan* syncretism has two modes of expression. Among the peasantry, both Hindu and Islamic beliefs are subordinated to a quest for harmony with all forces, human and supernatural, indigenous and foreign-derived, through a ritual feast called *slametan*. For the elite of Javanese society, the *prijaji*, the quest for harmony has taken more Hinduized forms, including the practice of Hindu-derived mysticism. Yet whichever mode the *abangan* tradition takes, it is contrasted with the *santri* tradition, found in Java and elsewhere in Indonesia, whose practitioners stress adherence to orthodox Muslim beliefs.

The rulers of the inland Javanese kingdoms such as Mataram, which emerged in the seventeenth century, no longer claimed, as their predecessors had, to be incarnations of Hindu deities. They were Muslim rulers, sultans. Yet these same sultans continued to order their capitals and their realms with reference to Hindu cosmological ideas right up to the time when the Dutch took control of the island in the eighteenth century. Subsequently the Hinduism of the Javanese tradition was perpetuated by the bureaucratic elite who first served under the Dutch and then in the new republic which gained independence after World War II.

Since colonial times this elite—the *prijaji*—has included not only those who claim descent from the semi-mythical royal families of Java but also others who have succeeded in finding employment in government service. *Prijaji* see themselves as inheritors of a KṢATRIYA (warrior, ruler) status in a system in which the peasantry can be equated with ŚŪDRAS (servants) and the *santri*, who are usually employed in commercial occupations, with VAIŚYAS. However, this system is not truly comparable to the Indian *varṇa* (CASTE) system because, most importantly, there are no recognizable Brahmins in the Javanese system. Without Brahmins there are no rituals performed by Brahmins nor instruction and interpretation of texts by Brahmins. Without Brahmins the Hindu component of Javanese religion is communicated primarily through the medium of the *wayang*, or shadow play performances, in which stories are derived primarily from the great Indian Epics, the MAHĀBHĀRATA and the RĀMĀYAṆA.

The *wayang* tradition is known to all Javanese, but it is the *prijaji* who have stressed the values of this tradition as particularly appropriate for their own ways of acting. The *prijaji* seek to speak and act in ways which are *alus*, "refined," rather than *kasar*, "coarse." Further, they seek to maintain themselves in harmony *(tjotjog)* with their external surroundings and in their internal states. The search for inner harmony is often pursued through following the instruction of a teacher (GURU) who interprets Hindu texts or commentaries on such texts.

3. Court and folk Brahminism in Theravāda Buddhist societies. While Brahmins disappeared from Java after the introduction of Islam and subsequent colonialization by the Dutch, a small number of Brahmins continued to exist at the courts of the Buddhist rulers of Thailand and Cambodia; indeed in Thailand today there still remains a small coterie of court Brahmins. But the court Brahmins of Thailand (like those which existed until recently in Cambodia) are but a shadow of the Indian prototype. Those in Thailand who carry the title of Brahmin are native Thai whose long-forgotten Indian ancestors married with local Thai women. They are not members of a larger caste grouping in Thai society, but are functionaries of the court. Before they are Brahmins they are Buddhists, and must have spent time as Buddhist novices before being initiated into their ritual roles as Brahmins. Moreover, their own private religion is Buddhism. Their knowledge of the Sanskrit texts which they use in their court rituals is sufficient only for reading the letters; it does not extend to comprehension of the content. They perform both VAIṢṆAVA and ŚAIVA rituals, the difference between those being accorded no particular significance.

While court Brahminism may have had true religious import in premodern Thailand or Cambodia, since at least the middle of the nineteenth century, when Western influences and Buddhist reforms began to make themselves felt, this tradition has become but an elaborate set of ritual forms which carries little meaning for those who perform or witness them.

Just as court Brahminism in Thailand is subordinate to Buddhism, so is folk Brahminism. Characteristic of folk Brahminism is belief in Indian-derived deities (*thēwadā* in Thai) and in a vital essence *(khwan)* which is secured to the body by invoking the deities and situating oneself with reference to a cosmic order based, in part, on Indian ideas. However, folk Brahminism does not constitute a distinct integrated world view for the Thai, or for the Lao who also share it; rather it is subordinated to and articulated within an overarching Theravādin world view.

In northeastern Thailand and in Laos there are practitioners who perform rituals associated with folk Brahministic beliefs who carry the title *phām,* a term derived from Sanskrit *brāhmaṇa.* But these *phām,* like their counterparts in court centers, do not constitute a caste, and their status is acquired through learning rather than fixed by birth as in India. Moreover, they have learned their practice as a consequence of having been members of the Buddhist SAṄGHA. In short, these *phām* can perform their roles in folk Brahminism only because they are first and foremost good Buddhists.

The Hinduism which has been perpetuated in both the folk and court Brahminism of the Buddhist societies of Southeast Asia does not, as does the *wayang* tradition in Java, constitute a distinctive component in a religious syncretism. Rather, its significance derives entirely from providing residual meanings in a system which is based fundamentally on orthodox Theravāda Buddhism. In Java, on the other hand, without the Hinduism of the *wayang* tradition, the Javanese world view would have to be something radically different—something, perhaps, more like that advocated by orthodox Islamic *santri.* By the same token, the Hindu element of Javanese religion is clearly conditioned by the Islamic component which also belongs to the syncretism.

4. **Balinese Hinduism.** Although Balinese religion shares some of the history of Javanese religion, it is sharply differentiated by a lack of Islamic elements. On Bali a distinctive Indonesian type of Hinduism has developed. Balinese call their religion *āgama Hindu-Bali,* meaning Hindu-Balinese religion; they also call it *āgama tīrtha*, meaning "religion of the water," thus indicating the central importance of the consecrated water prepared by Brahmin priests *(pedanda)* for all major rituals.

Although the history of early Indian influences in Bali is still very hazy, it is known that between the tenth and fourteenth centuries there were significant connections with the Indianized states of Java. In the fifteenth and early sixteenth centuries the last great Indianized civilization of Majapahit declined and finally collapsed, and a new civilization which drew upon Islam began to emerge in Java, while Hindu-Javanese culture found a refuge on Bali. In many of the descriptions of Balinese religion it is made to seem as though the Balinese tradition represents a freezing of Hindu-Javanese culture of the fifteenth century. Yet such a picture leaves a distorted impression, for Balinese religion actually continued to evolve during the subsequent centuries, even during the long period of relative isolation which finally ended with the Dutch conquest at the turn of the twentieth century. Most important of the changes was the diffusion of the Hinduized tradition from the court and the officials (the equivalent of the Javanese *prijaji*) to the general populace. As Balinese Hinduism became a true popular religion, the typically Hindu-Balinese patterns of accentuated etiquette and focus upon the Indian Epics in *gamelan* music, dramatic performances, dance, and ritual observances were adopted by the populace in general.

The highly distinctive character of the Hindu-Balinese tradition was also formulated with reference to the contrasting traditions of surrounding peoples; notably with reference to that of the upland Bali Aga on the island itself and even more importantly in contradistinction to the Islam of the Javanese and the peoples of other neighboring islands. Balinese themselves point to their death customs, and particularly to the practice of cremation, as the characteristic features of their Hinduism in contrast to the death customs of the upland people or of the Muslims.

The lavish, immensely expensive, and highly ornate cremations on Bali are believed to ensure that the souls of the dead will be reborn. However, unlike orthodox Hindus, Balinese believe that the soul will be reborn into his or her ancestral line. Thus, when Balinese sponsor cremations, they fulfill responsibilities not only to the ancestors but also to their descendants.

Perhaps the most dramatic formulation of the "steady state system," as Balinese religion has been characterized, is to be found in the ritual struggle between the witch Rangda, the personification of evil and suffering, and the clown-like dragon Barong, who encapsulates all the strengths and weaknesses of humankind. The ritual drama, during which many of the participants fall into trance, as they also do in other rituals as well, ends in stalemate between these two opposed forces. So too in the eternal cosmic conflict between the ultimate verities there will never be a final resolution.

In their ritual actions, and even in their everyday secular actions, Balinese seek to orient themselves to and harmonize themselves with the various manifestations of a dualistic cosmic order. These expressions include rituals at a bewildering number of temples. Superficially temple rituals appear comparable to BHAKTI cults in India, but a closer examination reveals that the gods worshiped at the temples are mostly nameless and that the rites are performed with far greater concern for their form than for their content.

Also seen as a manifestation of a cosmic order is the system of sanctification of social inequality. Basic to this system is a stratification of title holders, called *warna* (from Sanskrit *varṇa*), which is predicated upon a basic distinction recognized in the Indian caste system between the TWICE BORN of the three upper groups (in Bali called the *triwangsa*)—Brahmins, Kṣatriyas, and Vaiśyas—and the lower group, the Śūdras. However, lacking from Bali are the rigid rules of ritual purity associated with caste in India. In Bali, for example, there are few restrictions on sharing food between members of different *warna.* Nonetheless, each title-holding group in Bali has a ranking along a hierarchy of cultural prestige, and members of such groups seek to perpetuate their positions by marrying primarily within the same group.

The peculiarities of Balinese Hinduism are a consequence of the tradition having developed totally within an Indonesian context for many centuries. Only in recent decades have Balinese begun to look directly to India for new interpretations of the tradition to which they adhere. The inspiration which Indian thought has brought to Bali appears, however, unlikely to lead to a reconstruction of the tradition in Indian Hindu terms. Rather, the reformist Parisada movement in Bali appears to be creating, in part with regard to contemporary Indian thought, a more rationalized religion, but one which is still distinctively Indonesian.

5. **Overseas Indian Hinduism.** Orthodox Hinduism was brought to Southeast Asia by Indian migrants who began to settle in the region in significant numbers in the nineteenth century. Most of the hundreds of thousands of migrants settled in the British colonial dependencies of Burma and Malaya, but a few pushed into other countries and formed small communities in Thailand, Indochina, and Indonesia. Many migrants did not remain, but spent only a few years in the region before returning to India. In Burma, thousands of migrants and their descendants who had thought of that country as their home left or were forced out after the change in government in 1962. Still, overseas Indians remain as an element in the ethnic mosaic of the region, and particularly in Burma where they constitute 2 to 3 percent of the population and in Malaysia where they make up about 11 percent of the total.

Most of these Indian migrants came from peasant backgrounds. The communities which they formed in the region—communities which included not only Hindus but also Muslims and Sikhs—had fewer religious specialists than did the communities from which they had come. These overseas communities also lacked the familial and local foci of religious and secular action which had existed in India. New ties were formed which cut across the religious, linguistic, caste, and cultural groupings that exist in India. As a consequence the Hinduism of those Hindu Indians in Southeast Asia cannot be assumed to be simply a transplanted replica of the Hinduism found in India itself.

To date little attention has been given to the religion practiced by Indians in Southeast Asia. What little has been written suggests that practitioners are quite eclectic in their worship of various Hindu deities, the choice being determined more by propinquity to a particular shrine than to any cultic affiliation. For example, a film made at a shrine at the Batu Caves near Kuala Lumpur in Malaysia depicting an annual festival in honor of Murukaṉ, a son of Shiva, shows thousands of devotees, by no means all Tamil Hindus (the people who brought the festival of *Tai pūcam* to Malaysia). Indian gurus (only some of them Brahmins) have attracted followers in some parts of Southeast Asia from among non-Indians as well as from Indian communities. In such ways Hinduism thus remains a vital, if minor, element in the religious life of Southeast Asians.

Bibliography. S. Amarstratnam, *Indian Festivals in Malaya* (1966), one of the few studies of Hindu religious practice in overseas Indian communities in Southeast Asia; B. R. O'G. Anderson, *Mythology and Tolerance of the Javanese* (1965), a good source on the *wayang* tradition of Java, *Bali, Studies in Life, Thought, Ritual* (1960), and *Bali, Further Studies in Life, Thought, Ritual (1969)*; G. Bateson, "Bali: The Value System of a Steady State," in *Social Structure: Essays Presented to A. R. Radcliffe-Brown*, Meyer Fortes, ed. (1949), pp. 35-53; J. Belo, *Bali: Rangda and Barong* (1949), *Bali: Temple Festival* (1953), *Trance in Bali* (1960), and *Traditional Balinese Culture* (1970), among the best accounts of Balinese religious practice; J. A. Boon, *The Anthropological Romance of Bali, 1597-1972* (1977), a good introduction to the Western literature on and interpretations of Balinese religion; L. P. Briggs, *The Ancient Khmer Empire* (1951), excellent account of Angkor; G. Coedes, *Angkor: An Introduction* (1963), and *The Indianized States of Southeast Asia* (1968), excellent study of the process and results of Indianization in Southeast Asia to the fifteenth century; C. Geertz, *The Religion of Java* (1960), contains excellent detailed analyses of *abangan* and *prijaji* traditions on Java, and *Person, Time, and Conduct in Bali* (1966); J. Gonda, *Sanskrit in Indonesia* (1973); R. Hatley, "The Overseas Indian in Southeast Asia: Burma, Malaysia, and Singapore," in *Man, State, and Society in Contemporary Southeast Asia*, R. O. Tilman, ed. (1969), pp. 450-66, a general overview; R. Heine-Geldern, *Conceptions of State and Kingship in Southeast Asia* (1956), source of the idea of capitals of Indianized states being constructed as microcosms of an Indian-conceived macrocosm; C. Hooykaas, *Agama Tirtha: Five Studies in Hindu-Balinese Religion* (1964), *Religion in Bali* (1973), and *Cosmogony and Creation in Balinese Tradition* (1974); A. T. Kirsch, "Complexity in the Thai Religious System: An Interpretation," *JAS*, XXXVI (1977), 241-66; G. H. Luce, *Old Burma—Early Pagan* (1969-1970), best detailed study of Pagan civilization; U. Mahjani, *The Role of Indian Minorities in Burma and Malaya* (1960); R. C. Majumdar, *Hindu Colonies in the Far East* (1963); P. Mus, *India Seen from the East: Indian and Indigenous Cults in Champa* (1975), excellent study of early Indianization; T. Pigeaud, *Java in the Fourteenth Century: A Study in Cultural History* (1960-63), best detailed study of Indianized civilization in Java; H. B. Sarkar, *Indian Influences on the Literature of Java and Bali* (1934); S. J. Tambiah, *Buddhism and the Spirit Cults in North-East Thailand* (1970), contains good descriptive analysis of folk Brahminism; H. G. Q. Wales, *Siamese State Ceremonies* (1931), best source on court Brahminism in Thailand.

C. F. Keyes

HIRA, MOUNT hĭ rä´. A mountain in the environs of Mecca, to the northeast of the city. Muhammad is said to have received here his first revelation (Wahy) from Allah around A.D. 610, probably the passage in the Qur'ān 96:1-5.

B. Lawrence

HIRAṆYAGARBHA hĭr ŭn´ yŭ gär´ bä (H—Skt.; lit. "golden womb"). A name of Brahmā, the creator god in Hinduism, and of a cosmic "egg." According to the Laws of Manu, the formless Brahman planted a "seed" in the chaotic, cosmic waters. This seed became a golden egg *(hiraṇyagarbha)* from which Brahmā and all creation then issued. The whole material cosmos, therefore, was contained in this primordial egg.

L. D. Shinn

HIRAṆYAKAŚIPU hĭr ŭn yŭ kä´ shĭ pū (H—Skt.; lit. "having golden garments"). A demon who was the father of Prahlāda. He obtained from SHIVA the boon of universal rulership and later tried to prevent his son Prahlāda from worshiping VISHNU. The demon had been granted the boon of invulnerability against attacks by man or beast, inside or outside his dwelling, by day or by night. At the behest of the gods, Vishnu assumed the form of a man-lion and slew him at the entrance to his house at twilight. Thereby he was killed neither by man nor beast, but by a man-beast; neither indoors nor outdoors, but on the threshold; neither by day nor by night, but at dusk. J. B. LONG

HIRSCH, SAMSON RAPHAEL (Ju; 1808-1888). Founder of modern ORTHODOX JUDAISM. As RABBI in Frankfurt-am-Main he developed the idea of strict orthodoxy in religion combined with secular training. His main works were *The Nineteen Letters on Judaism* (1836) and an original German translation of the Bible. *See* JUDAISM §6b. S. SIEGEL

HOLOCAUST (Ju). In Hebrew *Sho'ah* (whirlwind) and *Churban* (catastrophe). The systematic slaughter of 6,000,000 Jews by the Nazis, 1933-45. Originally found in the Bible to designate a sacrifice totally consumed by fire, the term has taken on a symbolic meaning since World War II. The Nazi word *Endlösung* (final solution) expresses the goal of this greatest of all mass murders in Western history: to settle the "Jewish problem" once and for all.

1. **Prelude.** ANTI-SEMITISM, with its roots in nineteenth century Europe, reached a new intensity under the Nazis, fanned by carefully planned propaganda against the Jews, who were made the scapegoat for Germany's defeat in World War I. A stream of books, pamphlets, and periodicals depicted Jews as parasites, vermin, the cause of all misfortune. As early as 1920 Hitler said that "it is our duty to arouse, whip up, incite in our people the instinctive repugnance toward the Jews." The ground had been prepared by centuries of anti-Semitism in the West.

2. **First phase** (1933-39). In a series of laws, chief among them the 1935 Nuremberg Laws, Jews were defined, publicly identified, excluded from professions, and deprived of citizenship and all legal recourse. Their passports were stamped with "J," and beginning in 1939 they had to wear a clearly visible BADGE whenever they appeared in public. While the only major pogrom of this period was the CRYSTAL NIGHT, life for Jews in Germany and Austria (annexed in 1938) was rapidly becoming intolerable. Emigration was still possible at this time, but difficult. The Conference of Evian-les-Bains called by Roosevelt in July, 1938 to discuss help to the refugees was a failure and sealed the fate of millions of European Jews.

3. **Second phase.** The outbreak of World War II in September, 1939 made further emigration impossible. If Germany and its occupied territories were to be made *judenrein* (cleansed of Jews), extermination was the only way. The full weight of technology was harnessed to achieve the "final solution." GHETTOS were established throughout eastern Europe, and deportations through the vast railroad system got under way. The mass shootings on the Eastern front by *Einsatzgruppen* (mobile killing units) were followed by the construction of death camps (among the best known are Auschwitz, Buchenwald, Bergen-Belsen, Maidanek, Treblinka). In the largest of these, Auschwitz-Birkenau, 10,000 Jews were gassed per day and their bodies cremated. By the end of the war European Jewry had been largely wiped out.

Although most of the facts were known to the Allied governments and the Vatican, no serious attempt was made to stop the slaughter. There were heroic efforts on the part of some non-Jews to save Jews, but these could not stop the process of death.

4. **Aftermath.** The majority of survivors emigrated to Palestine (still a British mandate) and the U.S. The Nuremberg War Crimes Trials attempted to bring to justice the major war criminals (Hitler, Goering, Goebbels, and Himmler had committed suicide at the war's end), but many escaped and are living abroad and in Germany thirty-five years later. The Eichmann trial in Jerusalem in 1961 aroused worldwide attention. The memory of the Holocaust has deeply traumatized Jewish experience, while the rest of the world seeks today to come to grips with its share in the catastrophe through silence and apathy. The West German postwar government has attempted to make "reparations" by paying large sums to survivors and the State of Israel. The annual observance of the Holocaust on *Yom Hashoa,* 27 Nisan (April-May) has become a new element in Jewish liturgy and is also being observed by many Christians.

Bibliography. R. Hilberg, *The Destruction of the European Jews* (1961), p. 790; N. Levin, *The Holocaust* (1968, 1973) p. 768; *Encyclopedia Judaica,* Vol. 8, "The Holocaust"; all the fictional writings of Elie Wiesel. E. FLEISCHNER

HOLY GHOST (Ch). *See* HOLY SPIRIT.

HOLY SEPULCHRE. The traditional site of the burial of Jesus; it lay 100 to 150 meters outside the city walls of JERUSALEM. CONSTANTINE built a church on the site *ca.* A.D. 336. The present church dates from 1810. The latest restorations were begun in 1960 by the Greek Orthodox, Roman Catholic, and Armenian churches. D. W. O'CONNOR

HOLY SPIRIT (Ch). Conceived by earliest Christian thinkers as the empowering presence of God and the particular endowment of the CHURCH; regarded, since important theological formulations of the fourth century, as God, the third person of the TRINITY, distinct from, but consubstantial and co-eternal with, the Father and the Son.

Early Christian writers built upon OT conceptions of the Spirit of God as the power present in Israel's leaders, seers and heroes, as the mode of God's action in creation (Gen. 1:2), covenant renewal (Ezek. 11:19 ff.), judgment (Isa. 32:15), and eschatological hallowing (Joel 2:28-29). The Spirit is portrayed in the GOSPELS as active in the conception, BAPTISM, temptation, and mighty works of JESUS (Luke 1:35; Mark 1:10-12; Matt. 12:28), and is announced as the "Counselor," or "Paraclete," who is to be with and in believers after Christ's return to his Father (John 14:15, 26; 15:26). Important to the author of Acts is the role of the Holy Spirit in equipping the church for proclamation of the "mighty works of God" (Acts 2), and in specific tasks and deliberations of the apostles (8:15 ff.; 15:28). Paul speaks of the "Spirit of Christ" (Rom. 8:9) and apparently equates the believers' condition of being "in Christ" with being "in the Spirit" (Gal. 5:5-6), contrasting the latter to life "in the flesh" (Rom. 8:9). The Spirit is also the source of gifts which give life to the church and its mission (I Cor. 12), and an intercessor with God the Father (Rom. 8:26 ff.).

Despite attempts to elaborate on NT triadic language found, for example, in Matt. 28:19, the role and character of the Holy Spirit was only imprecisely defined in the second century. One of the writings of the APOSTOLIC FATHERS depicts the Spirit as one of God's two Sons (Hermas, *Similtude* 5.4-6), and Justin Martyr does not make clear the relation in which the Spirit, or "Spirit of prophecy," stands to the Word of God and to the ANGELS (*Apology* 6, 33 ff.).

Conceptions of the Holy Spirit were sharpened by both ecclesiological and doctrinal conflicts. The claims of the second century Phrygian prophet Montanus (*ca.* 157) to be the instrument of new disclosures of the Spirit compelled writers like Hippolytus (*Refutation of All Heresies* 8.12) to attend to closer descriptions of the Holy Spirit's work; Cyprian (*ca.* 250-258) and AUGUSTINE of Hippo countered the rigorist schismatic parties (Novatians and DONATISTS) who argued that the Holy Spirit could not be present in communities tainted by apostasy in times of persecution. The most significant doctrinal dispute centered on the denial by Pneumatomachians ("Spirit-fighters") of the plenary deity of the Holy Spirit, whom they suggested was a preeminent angel. In arguments emphasizing both equality of the three persons of the Trinity and the evidence of the effective power of the Holy Spirit in baptism and sanctification, BASIL of Caesarea (*On the Holy Spirit*) and Gregory of Nazianzus (*Oration* 31) provided the foundations of the assertion in the creed of Constantinople (381) that the Spirit is "worshiped and glorified together with the Father and the Son." (*See* NICENE CREED.)

In contrast to Constantinople's teaching that the Holy Spirit proceeds from the Father, Western Christendom has maintained (since the third council of Toledo in 589) that the Holy Spirit proceeds from both the Father and the Son (*see* FILIOQUE).

Bibliography. H. B. Swete, *The Holy Spirit in the Ancient Church* (1912); J. N. D. Kelly, *Early Christian Doctrines*, 2nd ed. (1960); H. Cunliffe-Jones, ed., *A History of Christian Doctrine* (1978).

R. C. GREGG

HOLY WATER (Ch). Water blessed for religious purposes and used in rites of purification and blessing. Traceable to the fourth century in the East and the fifth century in the West, the use of holy water often serves as a reminder of BAPTISM. Since at least Norman times (tenth century), holy water stoups have been placed at the entrance to Catholic churches.

C. WADDELL

HOLY WEEK (Ch). The week preceding EASTER. An earlier fast on Friday and Saturday was extended to the six days of this week by the middle of the third century. The liturgies of this most solemn week in the Christian year contain elements of great antiquity focused on the PASSION of Christ. *See* PALM SUNDAY; MAUNDY THURSDAY; GOOD FRIDAY; CALENDAR, CHRISTIAN.

T. J. TALLEY

HOLY YEARS (Ch). In ROMAN CATHOLICISM years in which the pope grants "Jubilee" indulgences to pilgrims to ROME, under certain conditions. Inaugurated by BONIFACE VIII in 1300, Holy Years were intended to be observed each century, but the interval was gradually shortened to twenty-five years by 1470, and that interval is still observed.

T. J. TALLEY

HOMOOUSION hō mō o͞oz´ ē ən (Ch—Gr.; lit. "of the same substance"). Celebrated and contested term employed (notably in the NICENE CREED of 325) by orthodox opponents of Arius (*see* ARIANISM) to assert that Jesus Christ was "one-in-essence" or "consubstantial" with the Father. It underlined orthodoxy's insistence that the Son was co-equal and co-eternal with the Father, and thus fully divine in a way requisite to his work as savior. Later (at Chalcedon in 451) the term was used in a parallel manner to state that Christ shared full humanity with persons. *See* TRINITY.

R. C. GREGG

HŌNEN hō´ nĕn (B—Jap.; 1133-1212). Eminent priest, also known as Genkū, who founded the Jōdo (PURE LAND) sect. Hōnen studied at the great TENDAI center at Mt. Hiei before retiring to a nearby hermitage. At age forty-three he began to make known his discovery that the NEMBUTSU ("calling the name of AMIDA Budda") provides the only path to salvation in the latter age of DHARMA (MAPPŌ). In 1186 he set down his ideas in a work which classifies all Buddhist teachings into two paths, the one based on disciplined self-effort (study of doctrine, ritual activity) and the other based on simple devotion to Amida expressed through reciting the Nembutsu. His choice of the latter path and the popularity of his teachings led to his banishment from Kyoto in 1207 for four years. Hōnen's thought provides the starting point for his disciple SHINRAN's Shin Buddhist teachings. M. L. ROGERS

HORYU-JI hō ryū´ jē (B—Jap.; lit. "law-flourishing-temple"). The oldest existing Buddhist temple of Japan, a temple complex of the seventh century A.D. on twenty-five acres at Ikaruga, Nara Prefecture; a repository of Japan's national treasures of early Buddhist art, including the world's oldest wooden buildings, earliest oil paintings, and some of the most perfectly preserved bronze and wooden sculpture of the Orient.

1. **Background of the Buddhist temple.** The earliest Buddhist monks of India were wanderers who often spent the rainy season in retreat at some donated grove at a *caitya,* or sacred spot. As the monks became more settled the Buddhist temple complex developed around a BODHI tree, representing the enlightenment, a STŪPA (PAGODA) containing relics, representing the BUDDHA'S entering NIRVANA, and a large wooden hall for preaching and reciting texts, perhaps representing the palace of the gods within which the Buddha is said to have preached. As Buddhism moved north and east, this plan was significantly influenced by the plan of the Chinese palace, and later by the Korean art of building temples with wood. Both Chinese and Korean artisans entered Japan in the sixth and seventh centuries, and their contributions were combined with native Japanese elements. The Horyu-ji is viewed by many as the culmination of the best of these traditions in a single temple complex standing today. Because of the destruction of most early Buddhist temples and accompanying art in China and Korea, many features of Horyu-ji are cited as the best preserved examples of early Buddhist temple art in the entire Orient.

2. **History of Horyu-ji.** Prince SHŌTOKU, the "father of Japanese Buddhism," chose the region south of Nara as the site for his palace in 601, and had a temple, the original Horyu-ji, built west of the palace in 607. Named *Horyu-Gakumonju,* "Horyu Temple of Learning," it was intended as a center of Buddhist monastic training, academic and artistic activities for the Empire.

The original Horyu-ji was struck by lightning and burned in 670, and the *Sai-in,* "West Precinct," of the present Horyu-ji was built before the end of the seventh century just west of the original site. The national capital was moved to Nara in 710, and Horyu-ji was showered with imperial donations of art as well as lands to provide regular tribute. Priest Gyoshin saw to the addition of a *To-in,* "East Precinct," on the old site of the palace of Prince Shōtoku. Over the centuries new buildings were added, and a few buildings were lost to fire.

3. **Temple plan.** There is a history of controversy regarding the precise date of the present Horyu-ji and the origin of its ground plan. It is believed to be the one major temple complex representing the earliest period of Japanese Buddhist temple architecture, the

From Minoru Ooka, *Temples of Nara and Their Art*

Aerial view of the West Precinct, Horyu-ji

Asuka period (555-646), and its plan may witness to creative experimentation in Japan with the Chinese and Korean temple plans of that era.

The oldest portion of Horyu-ji, the West Precinct, consists of a rectangular compound formed by a covered colonnade 300 feet by 200 feet. The long south side of this cloister contains an impressive two-level Middle Gate *(chūmon)* whose two openings are protected by wooden guardian kings *(Nīo)*. Upon passing through the Middle Gate, one views a Golden Hall *(Kondō)* to the right (east) and a five-storied pagoda *(gojūnoto)* to the left (west) dominating the enclosed compound. Through the space between these two buildings, one can view the lecture hall *(Kōdō)* built into the northern side of the colonnade. Although from time to time smaller buildings were added to Horyu-ji and to other temples, the rectangular colonnade and the four basic structures noted above became the essential elements of a Buddhist temple.

The buildings, superb examples of carpentry as an art form, are fitted together without nails, and the *irimoya* (gabled and hipped) multiple roofs are covered with gray clay tiles in Buddhist fashion. The Golden Hall houses the chief image, a trinity, the central figure of which is Śākyamuni Buddha. The pagoda, representing the Buddhist universe, holds the sacred relics. The dominant horizontal lines of the temple complex are broken by the vertical of the pagoda (twice the height of the main hall), and the whole is combined in an informal balance representative of the best of the developing Japanese aesthetic.

4. Temple treasures. From the days of Prince Shōtoku, art treasures were lavished on Horyu-ji. The chief treasure is the bronze image in the main hall, which depicts Śākyamuni and two attendant Boddhisattvas. Completed in 623 by master sculptor Tori Busshi, grandson of a Chinese immigrant, it is the only large, high quality bronze work of its sort in a perfect state of preservation in the Orient.

Horyu-ji likewise houses some of the most valuable paintings of Eastern art. The paintings of Buddha-lands on the walls of the main hall, though badly damaged in a 1949 fire, have been judged "the finest achievement in Mahāyāna painting," and the Buddhist scenes painted in a mixture of lacquer and oil paint on Horyu-ji's Tamamushi shrine may be the only authentic Asuka paintings in existence, and perhaps the earliest oil paintings in the world.

Numerous other pieces of sculpture, metal work, painting, and textiles are housed in Horyu-ji's modern Treasure Hall, making the temple one of the world's chief repositories of Buddhist art.

Bibliography. J. E. Kidder, Jr., *Japanese Temples* (1964); S. Mizuno, *Asuka Buddhist Art: Horyuji* (1974).

C. W. Edwards

HOSANNA (Ch & Ju—Heb.; "Save, we beseech thee"). The crowd's acclamation of Jesus on Palm Sunday (Matt. 21:9,15; Mark 11:9-10; John 12:13), an adaptation of Ps. 118:25. As early as the Didache (*ca.* 100) it was used liturgically and has become a fixed part of the Benedictus Qui Venit (*see* Mass). For usage in Judaism *see* Prayer, Jewish §3; Sukkot.

R. A. Greer

HOSPITALERS (Ch). The Knights Hospitalers of the Hospital of St. John of Jerusalem, known after 1310 as the Knights of Rhodes and after 1530 as the Knights of Malta. Originally founded at Jerusalem (*ca.* 1070) to care for those on Pilgrimages or Crusades, the order became militarized and, with the Knights Templars, furnished the Kingdom of Jerusalem with a permanent armed force.

H. L. Bond

HOSPITALITY IN ISLAM. Hospitality to strangers is enjoined in both the Qur'ān and the Ḥadīth. In the former, Abraham and Lot are paradigms of the generous and loyal host (Sura 11:69-73, 78; 15:51, 68; 54:37). True piety *(birr)* includes spending of one's own substance, out of love for God, for relations, orphans, the poor, the wayfarer, and those who request it (Sura 2:177). Muhammad is reported to have said: "He who believes in God and the last day should honor his guest. Provisions for the road are what will serve for a day and a night; hospitality extends for three days" (*Mishkāt,* XX, 1). Moreover, the guest may take what he is entitled to, even if it is not offered.

The great Qur'ān commentator al-Zamakhsharī (d. 1143) chose hospitality as the theme for his epitaph: "Almighty God! here, in the bosom of the earth, I have become thy guest; and the rights of the guest are acknowledged by every generous host. As a gift of hospitality, bestow on me the pardon of my sins; the gift is great, but great is thy hospitality" (Ibn Khallikān, III, 327).

Bibliography. *Mishkāt al-Maṣābīḥ* of al-Baghawi, J. Robson, trans., III (1965-66), 898-902; Ibn Khallikān, *Biographical Dictionary,* De Slane, trans., III (1868), 327.

F. M. Denny

HOSSŌ hô sō´. *See* Nara Buddhism §3.

HOST (Ch). The bread of the Eucharist, especially the large unleavened wafer for the communion of the celebrant. The term is derived from Latin *hostia,* "victim," a sacrificial term in classical usage which occurs frequently in the eucharistic prayer in reference to the gifts of bread and wine.

T. J. Talley

HŌTOKU MOVEMENT hō´ tō koo (Jap.; lit. "repayment of blessings" movement). A religious and ethical movement founded by the "peasant sage" Ninomiya Sontoku (1787-1856) for the benefit of the peasantry. An eclectic teaching—a "pill," as Ninomiya described it, composed two parts of Shintō and one part each of Confucianism and Buddhism—it was perhaps more importantly a practical application of ethical principles to the solution of rural economic problems.

The basic theory is implied in the name of the movement. Since the life of each generation is made possible only through the devotion and labors of its forebears, it is the duty of each generation to repay its blessings and pass them on, through hard work, frugality, and human kindness. By this means gratitude is rendered to "heaven, earth, and man" and a capacity for concerted action leading to prosperity is generated.

Not only a teacher but also a man of action, Ninomiya developed and implemented plans for the restoration of neglected farm land and villages and for the improvement of agricultural production. In so doing he took exception to the passive attitudes toward nature which he associated with Buddhism and Confucianism and advocated instead actions that make nature as productive as possible.

One of Ninomiya's disciples, Fukuzumi Masae, organized the Hotokusha (lit. "society for repayment of blessings"), which still functions throughout Japan in spreading the teaching and work of the master.

Bibliography. R. N. Bellah, *Tokugawa Religion* (1957); R. Tsunoda, ed., *Sources of the Japanese Tradition* (1958).

H. N. McFarland

HOURI hoo´ rē (I). *See* Eschatology §3.

HOUSEHOLD GODS (CHINA). The family was the primary ceremonial group in traditional China, and the ancestors and household gods were the center of its ritual life. This is still the case in rural Taiwan and Hong Kong, and in Chinese communities elsewhere. Chinese Popular Religion was organized in levels of jurisdiction, from gods of empire and province through those of county, village, and neighborhood. Household gods represented the most specific and intimate level of authority, connected to the larger pantheon through a system of regular reports to superiors. In addition, some household gods might be more powerful deities from a local temple or sect, present in the form of small images or brightly colored pictures. In this case their connection with the larger divine world could be further symbolized through having in the household incense burner ashes from that of the village temple. The ashes were renewed annually on the god's birthday.

Household gods symbolized sacred power, orientation, and ethical principles in the midst of everyday life. People turned to them for protection from misfortune and for the blessings of family harmony, wealth, and fertility. As observers of family behavior these deities provided sanctions for proper conduct.

The center of family worship was a household altar in the main room of the house, facing the front door, on which were located the tablets of more recent ancestors and tablets or small images representing deities. Hanging above this altar might be a large scroll picture of the Buddhist savior Kuan-yin (Avalokiteśvara) with written inscriptions on either side assuring the continued support of ancestors and Buddhas. Local customs differed, but the altar might hold a tablet in honor of heaven and earth, the emperor, ancestors and teachers, and images of Kuan Kung (a god of loyalty and martial courage), a village temple god, or a local agricultural spirit.

The most important household deity was the Stove God, whose picture was enshrined above the great earthen range in the kitchen. As an official appointed by the celestial court he was responsible for family behavior, which he reported once a month to the local city god, and at the end of each year to the supreme deity of the popular pantheon, the Jade Emperor.

Homage was also paid to various other gods, who were represented at the appropriate spot by paper pictures. Rituals for these deities could include daily offerings of incense before the household altar and similar offerings to the Stove God on the first and fifteenth of the lunar month. Food and wine were presented on festival days, and a feast for the Stove God just before his annual departure to the Jade Emperor's court on the twenty-fourth of the twelfth month. Incense was offered to the Goddess of the Privy by women and girls on the fifteenth of the first month, and a few times a year to the Lord and Lady of the Bed. Offerings to other spirits varied with local custom. In general, however, every significant aspect of the home was personified and given due ritual attention.

Bibliography. *See* Chinese Popular Religion.

D. L. Overmyer

HOUSEHOLDER (H). *See* Gṛhastra.

HOYŚĀḺA hoi´ shä lä (H). A dynasty in Mysore region from the eleventh to fourteenth centuries, notable for its military prowess and religious patronage. Its legendary founder was Śāḻa, whose act of heroism in killing a tiger *(hoy)* to save a Jaina ascetic gave his ruling house its name of "tiger killer." Hoyśāḻan kings who converted to Śaivism or Vaiṣṇavism built and supported major temples in Halebīd, Belūr, and Somnāthpur. The design of the Hoyśāḻan temples is unlike either traditional northern or southern temple styles. Each Hoyśāḻan temple is built upon a raised, star-shaped platform with tiers of intricately carved animals, humans, and designs decorating the exterior walls of the central four-walled structure built on the platform. Notable also is the absence of the vertical, pyramid-shaped spire *(śikara)* commonly associated with Hindu temples.

L. D. Shinn

HŌZA hō´ zä (B—Jap.; lit. "circle of the law/Dharma"). Counseling circle where about twelve persons sit, Japanese fashion, on the floor. It is both a place where members practice mutual concern for their spiritual and physical needs, and an organizational unit of Risshō Kōseikai. N. S. Brannen

HSI WANG MU shē wäng´ mōō (T—Chin.; lit. "Royal Mother of the West"). Important female immortal, popular at least since the former Han Dynasty (206 B.C.—A.D. 9); believed to live in the Western land of the immortals in the K'un-lun mountains. Wives pray to her for children. *See* TAOISM, RELIGIOUS §5.

M. LEVERING

HSÜAN-TSANG shū än´dzäng (B—Chin.; 596-664). T'ang Dynasty monk who described his pilgrimage to India in a travel journal, collector and translator of Indian MAHĀYANA texts, and founder of the FA-HSIANG or *Wei-shih* ("Consciousness-Only") school of Buddhism.

Hsüan-tsang entered a PURE LAND monastery at age thirteen, and from 618 devoted himself to the study of Buddhist texts and doctrines in Ch'ang-an, Ch'eng-tu, and other centers of learning. Troubled by inconsistencies in Chinese Buddhist doctrine, he became convinced of the need for study in India, and traveled there by stealth when permission for his pilgrimage was denied by the Chinese Court.

The journal describing his travels to India provides a valuable historical record for conditions in Central Asia and India in the seventh century. Almost murdered by his guide, lost in the desert, befriended by rulers who admired his learning, he made his way to Kashmir, was captured by bandits on the Ganges, visited Banāres and other sacred sites, and studied Buddhist philosophy and Sanskrit at NĀLANDĀ. His renown in India led even Harsha, emperor of India, to receive him and hear his great learning. With an escort and 520 cases containing Buddhist objects and texts, he returned to Ch'ang-an in 645 and was received with great honor.

Under imperial patronage, Hsüan-tsang spent the rest of his life translating 75 of the Buddhist texts he had collected in India. Many were YOGĀCĀRA works which provided the basis for his *Ch'eng-wei-shih lun* ("Treatise on the Establishment of the Consciousness-Only Doctrine") and for the Fa-hsiang school he founded.

Bibliography. S. Beal, *Life of Hsüan-tsang* (1911).

C. W. EDWARDS

HUA-YEN hwä yĕn´. *See* NARA BUDDHISM §3.

HUGH OF ST. VICTOR (Ch; d. 1141). Regular canon of the Abbey of St. Victor, Paris. He stressed history in biblical exegesis, wrote theological and mystical works, and introduced ideas from PSEUDO-DIONYSIUS into CHRISTIAN MYSTICISM and theology.

Bibliography. Hugh of St. Victor, *Selected Spiritual Writings* (1957).

G. A. ZINN

HUGUENOT hū´ gə nät (Ch). A name of uncertain origin applied to the REFORMED French PROTESTANTS. The Reformed movement in France had roots in the French humanism of Jacques Lefèvre and Guillaume Briçonnet, and in the writings of MARTIN LUTHER. It received leadership from the reformation that took place in French-speaking Switzerland, especially Geneva, largely under the guidance of French exiles William Farel, JOHN CALVIN, and THEODORE BEZA. A Reformed congregation existed in Paris in 1555, and in 1559 a national church was organized along the lines of PRESBYTERIAN polity with local, district, provincial, and national courts or councils and with a confession of faith to which John Calvin contributed.

The Reformed were an influential minority, but the king had no reason to espouse their cause in the light of the close relationship which existed between the church and the government. After 1560 the Protestants became revolutionaries engaging in a political power struggle to gain recognition, aligning themselves with the Bourbons, who had Protestant commitments, against the Guises, who believed the security of France required maintenance of the ROMAN CATHOLIC faith. The Wars of Religion ensued, and the conflict was violent with atrocities on both sides. The Massacre of St. Barthlomew's Day on August 23, 1572, decimated the Protestant leadership. Henry IV, who became heir to the throne in 1594, secured the crown by converting to Roman Catholicism. In 1598 he granted the EDICT OF NANTES that provided limited toleration for the Reformed, who probably numbered 10 percent of the population at that time.

The Edict was revoked by Louis XIV in 1685, leading to a great exodus, estimated as more than 300,000, of Huguenots from France. A later edict gave freedom to the Protestants in 1787.

J. H. LEITH

HUI-NENG hwē´ nĕng (B—Chin.; 638-713) **YENO** yē´ nō (B—Jap.) Accepted by tradition as sixth Chinese patriarch of CH'AN (ZEN) Buddhism; author of the influential T'an-ching (Platform Sūtra); credited with transforming Indian meditative Buddhism to Chinese Ch'an.

Hui-neng is depicted as a poor southern youth who journeyed to the Yellow Plum Monastery of Hung-jen, the fifth patriarch, and was accepted as a mere kitchen worker. Though an illiterate layman, his enlightenment verse won in contest over that of Hung-jen's chief disciple, Shen-hsiu. The fifth patriarch secretly acknowledged Hui-neng as heir and sent him south for his own safety. In the north, Shen-hsiu was publicly accepted as sixth patriarch, beginning the split of Ch'an into rival northern and southern schools.

A disciple of Hui-neng, Shen-hui, apparently created much of the Hui-neng legend to oppose the citified scholasticism of northern Ch'an with the rustic and experiential Ch'an of the southern provinces. In Hui-neng's name, southern Ch'an preached sudden enlightenment and the identity of meditation (DHYĀNA) and wisdom *(prajñā),* opposing quietistic meditation and the study of sūtras. Masters of the T'ang era accepted Hiu-neng as legitimate

Sixth Patriarch, determining the nature of Ch'an (Zen) to this day.

Bibliography. P. B. Yampolsky, *The Platform Sutra of the Sixth Patriarch* (1967). C. W. EDWARDS

al-ḤUSAYN IBN ALI IBN ABĪ ṬĀLIB ăl hoo sān' ĭb' ən ă lē' ĭb' ən ă bē' tä lēb' (I; 625-680). Second son of ALI and FĀṬIMA, the daughter of MUHAMMAD; born in MEDINA. The fame of al-Ḥusayn is based on his martyrdom at KARBALA on the tenth day of Muharram, the first month of the Islamic year (Oct. 10, 680). In response to an invitation to assume leadership of the early SHI'ITES, the followers of his late father, Ḥusayn started to Kūfa in Iraq with his harem and a small escort of relatives and supporters. Yazīd I, the second CALIPH of the UMAYYAD dynasty, sent the governor of Kūfa with a detachment of cavalry to stop Ḥusayn's advance. The two forces met at Karbala, and after a final summons to Ḥusayn to surrender, the Umayyad force attacked and overwhelmed the fierce resistance. Some sources state that Ḥusayn killed many of the attackers. He finally fell wounded, and Sinān ibn Anas ibn 'Amr al-Nakha'ī struck him again and then beheaded him. His corpse was stripped naked and trampled by horses. After the Umayyad troops left, it was buried on the spot. His head was taken to Kūfa and then to Damascus; several sites dispute the honor of being the place where his head was buried. Only one of Ḥusayn's sons survived, a young boy who lay sick at the time of the battle. From him all the numerous line of Ḥusayn's offspring are descended.

In both SUNNITE and Shi'ite traditions Ḥusayn has been regarded as a man of piety, idealism, nobility of character, and ascetic detachment. He upheld an ideal of Islamic social and political life which he saw violated in Umayyad rule. The drama of Karbala has had a remarkable history in the folklore, literature, art, and piety of the Shi'ite community, and is commemorated annually. A. A. SACHEDINA

HUSS, JOHN (Ch; 1372 or 1373-1415). A teacher at the University of Prague and a priest, Huss was influenced both by JOHN WYCLIFFE and a native Czech reform movement. His powerful preaching led to his being recognized as the leader of the reform party in Bohemia. He based theology and church structure on the Bible and taught that the true church is the assembly of the predestined, with Christ, not the pope, the head of the church. His greatest emphasis was on a moral reformation of both church and society.

Because of the political turmoil of the era, Huss was able for a time to preach with relative impunity. However, he was eventually excommunicated and called to appear at the Council of Constance, where, in spite of assurances of safe conduct, he was condemned and executed. (*See* COUNCILS OF THE CHURCH.) News of his death resulted in a revolution in Bohemia, where he was regarded as a martyr. The successful Hussites soon divided into two factions, the more extreme Taborites and the Utraquists (the name is derived from the practice of offering both cup and loaf to the laity in the EUCHARIST). A civil war allowed the Utraquists to negotiate a settlement through which the Bohemian church was once again in communion with Rome, while retaining the right to administer the cup to laity. The Hussite heritage left Bohemia receptive to the Protestant Reformation, and succeeding generations of Czech Protestants have understood themselves as rooted in the work of Huss. *See* REFORMATION, PROTESTANT; MORAVIANS.

Bibliography. M. Spinka, *John Hus* (1968).

R. L. HARRISON

I

IBLĪS ĭb lēs (I). *See* Satan §3.

IBN 'ARABĪ, MUḤYĪ 'D-DĪN ĭb′ ən ä rä bē′ moo yēd′ dēn (I; 1165-1240). The most celebrated and prolific of Sufi theorists. Born at Murcia, Spain, he lived and studied in Seville before setting out to visit the eastern parts of the Muslim world *ca.* 1200. Eventually, after many travels, including the Hajj, he settled in Damascus, where he died. A mosque built over his tomb is still much frequented by visitors and pilgrims.

Though he founded no order (Ṭarīqa) Ibn 'Arabī influenced speculative Sufi thought more profoundly than any other thinker. He left a list of his own literary output, totaling 270 works, 176 of which deal with Sufism. Two of the 176 have received special attention: *The Meccan Revelations,* because it is partially autobiographical and otherwise sets forth much of interest about famous Sufis as well as the central teachings of Sufism, and *The Wisdom of the Prophets,* in which each of the 27 major prophets (*see* Nabi) is allotted an individual chapter that describes not him but the approach to unity (Tawḥīd) characteristic of him. Revealed to Ibn 'Arabī in a single night at age sixty-five, *The Wisdom of the Prophets* is a brilliant, insightful book without parallel in Sufi history.

Ibn 'Arabī's thought, at once radical and comprehensive, scriptural and mystical, inspired defenders and detractors, sparking a debate over "Unity of Being" and "Unity of Witness" that relates to the fundamental question: How does one feel, think, act, and pray as a Muslim?

Bibliography. S. H. Nasr, *Three Muslim Sages* (1964); M. Molé, *Les mystiques musulmans* (1965), pp. 100-105; Ibn 'Arabī, *The Wisdom of the Prophets,* T. Burckhardt and A. Culme-Seymour, trans. (1975).

B. Lawrence

IBN ḤANBAL ĭb′ ən hän′ bäl (I; 780-855). Aḥmad ibn Muhammad ibn Ḥanbal, founder of the Hanbalite school of Islamic law.

A student of al-Shāfi'ī and widely traveled, as was the custom for students of traditional learning, Ibn Ḥanbal was in strong sympathy with the Traditionists and adamantly opposed to speculative theology, particularly that of the Mu'tazilites. Under the 'Abbāsid caliphs, when Mu'tazilism became the state confession, Ibn Ḥanbal was persecuted, flogged, and imprisoned because of his adherence to Traditionist positions. Only with the return of the state to orthodoxy under al-Mutawakkil was he saved from further persecution, by which time he had a wide reputation as a staunch defender of the faith. His most famous work, the *Musnad,* compiled by his son 'Abdullāh, is really a work on Ḥadīth more than a treatise on Fiqh, as are most of his other writings, and some have not regarded him as an authority on *fiqh,* notably the historian and Qur'ān commentator Muhammad ibn Jarīr aṭ-Ṭabarī (d. 923). However, his views on jurisprudence are quite clearly set forth in the form of opinions on disputed points of law. At his death in Baghdad, he was given elaborate burial, and his tomb became the object of veneration, despite his opposition to such veneration.

Ibn Ḥanbal's Traditionist stance has marked the character of the Islamic legal school named after him. He rejected judicial discretionary opinion and even the more restrictive analogic reasoning, preferring to base law on the Qur'ān and the Sunna. For this reason Hanbalites have a tendency to prefer weak traditions to any form of judicial reasoning. This preoccupation with tradition has led to one of the best analyses of *ḥadīth,* by Ibn Abū Ḥātim (854-938). The school adopted a strong moral approach to law and was consequently opposed to the strategems of the Hanafites. On the question of consensus (Ijmā') the Hanbalites rejected the notion that it was possible to obtain agreement among all the qualified jurists, and the famous Hanbalite jurist Ibn Taymīyya (1263-1328) reserved the theoretical right of a type of independent judgment *(ijtihād)* which had been discarded by the other schools on the basis of consensus. The seeming conservative nature of this school has led, because of its emphasis on Qur'ān and tradition, to a greater degree of individual responsibility in contractual obligations, including Marriage, and allows greater freedom to women than the other schools. The Hanbalite school did not enjoy dominance in any particular geographic area, although its influence was pervasive, until its adoption by the WAHHĀBĪS.

Bibliography. See FIQH. G. D. NEWBY

IBN ḤAZM, ABŪ MUḤAMMAD ĭb′ ən hă′ zĕm ä bōō′ moo häm′ məd (I; 994-1064). Major intellectual figure of eleventh century Muslim Spain. A native of Cordova, he was renowned for his analysis of language, logical precision, psychological and moral insight, and social cynicism. He made distinctive contributions as a poet, historian of religions, philosopher, theologian, and jurist. The school of law which he espoused, the Ẓāhirī, was a minority tradition in Andalusia, where MALIKITE jurists prevailed. To bolster the legitimacy of the Ẓāhirī viewpoint, Ibn Ḥazm tried to redefine FIQH only on the basis of the QUR'ĀN and ḤADĪTH (prophetic traditions), rejecting the enormous spate of legal decisions derived from consensus (IJMĀ') and individual interpretation *(ijtihād)*. His *Kitāb al-fiṣal wa'l-niḥal* is a brilliant, painstakingly accurate summation of different viewpoints, though the ideas of some opponents are occasionally dismissed with a disdain bordering on mockery.

Ibn Ḥazm sparked both admiration and abuse after his death. Among his admirers was the noted Sufi theorist, IBN 'ARABĪ. B. LAWRENCE

IBN ISḤĀQ ĭb′ ən ĭs häq′ (I; *ca.* 704—*ca.* 767). Muhammad ibn Isḥāq ibn Yasār, author of the first complete biography *(sīra)* of MUHAMMAD; born in MEDINA into a non-Arab Muslim family of Traditionists. (*See* SUNNA; ḤADĪTH.) He collected traditions, stories, and poems about Muhammad from many sources and, though renowned for his knowledge, came into conflict with more conservative authorities. In Baghdad under the patronage of the 'ABBĀSID CALIPH al-Manṣūr, he wrote the biography as a school text for the prince al-Mahdī. The work was modeled on the Bible, the history of the world from creation to Muhammad comprising the "OT" portion, and the life of Muhammad comprising the "NT." The work portrays Muhammad as the new ABRAHAM, MOSES, Jacob, and particularly JESUS, among others, although it is reasonably historical for Muhammad's Medinan career. Abridged by Ibn Hishām (d. 834), it became the most popular biography of Muhammad in the Muslim world.

Bibliography. J. Fück, *Muḥammad b. Isḥāq* (1925); Ibn Ishaq, *Life of Muhammad,* A. Guillaume; trans. (1955); G. Newby, "An Example of Coptic Literary Influence on the Sīrah of Ibn Isḥāq," *JNES,* XXXI (1972), 22-8, and "Abraha and Sennacherib . . ." *JAOS,* XCIV (1974), 431-37.
G. D. NEWBY

IBN RUSHD ĭb′ ən roo′ shəd (I; 1126-1198). Outstanding Hispano-Arab astronomer, theologian, philosopher, and physician; known in the West as Averroes. Of noble birth, he spent all his life in Andalusia (Muslim Spain), serving as courtier and judge in addition to writing treatises and extensive commentaries on a wide variety of traditional subjects. In philosophy he attacked both IBN SĪNĀ's and al-GHAZZĀLĪ's solutions to major problems. His most notable achievement was a commentary on Aristotle's *Metaphysics,* unmatched in its faithfulness to the original text. Many of his writings have been preserved in LATIN and HEBREW as well as ARABIC.
B. LAWRENCE

IBN SĪNĀ ĭb′ən sē′nä **AVICENNA** äv ə sĕn′ ə (I; 980-1037). The most renowned and influential philosopher of medieval ISLAM, who united philosophy with the study of nature. He was born near Bukhara, then the capital of the Persian Sāmānid dynasty. His father belonged to the ISMĀ'ĪLIYYA, but he himself did not find this sect intellectually stimulating. Endowed with extraordinary intelligence and intellectual independence, he was largely self-taught and by the age of eighteen had mastered all the then known sciences. The last years of his life were spent in Isfahan as physician to the prince, during which time he made astronomical investigations. Over a hundred of his works have survived: philosophy, science, and religious, linguistic, and literary matters. They are not the product of a man who lived in books, since most of his energies were taken up with the day-to-day affairs of state.

Bibliography. Ibn al-Qifṭī, *The Life of Ibn Sīnā,* trans. W. E. Gohlman (1903; ET 1974). A. A. SACHEDINA

IBN TAYMĪYYA ĭb′ ən tī mē′ yə (I; 1263-1328). Taqī ad-Dīn Aḥmad ibn Taymīyya, Hanbalite jurist (*see* IBN ḤANBAL). He was born in Harran, but owing to the Mongol invasion was raised in Damascus, where he succeeded his father as professor of Hanbalite law in 1282. He taught QUR'ĀN, ḤADĪTH, law, and theology, and was a staunch anthropomorphist. In 1299, while in Egypt on his return from a pilgrimage (HAJJ), he got in trouble with the Shafi'ite populace and was imprisoned for a time. His polemics against other scholars earned him few friends, and much of his adult life was spent in prison.

Opposed to what he interpreted as innovation, and having essentially rejected consensus (IJMĀ'), he also rejected customs which were not based on either Qur'ān or prophetic SUNNA, such as the veneration of saints (WALĪ). He was equally opposed to speculative theology and philosophy, claiming that it led to unbelief, and wrote a number of treatises against the practices of other schools, e.g., the use of legal strategems by the HANAFITES. He rejected allegorical and symbolic interpretation of the Qur'ān and professed to follow a path of submission to the words of ALLAH and to leave his mystery to him. He regarded an Islamic state as necessary to implement the law and impose discipline on Muslims. Although his influence waned with the rise of the Ottomans, it was revived by WAHHĀBI interest in his writings.

Bibliography. H. Laoust, "Ibn Taymiyya," *EI* (1971); N. J. Coulson, *History of Islamic Law* (1964).

G. D. NEWBY

I CHING ē jĭng´ (Con—Chin.; lit. "book of changes"). One of the five classic texts of CONFUCIANISM. The book is based on the ancient practice of DIVINATION and is used to the present day as a text for divining the wisest course of action. It assumes that human destiny depends upon cosmic order, which is in constant change; therefore human situations must be continuously modified and human behavior adjusted to meet the changes in nature.

The book deals with eight "trigrams" composed of solid and broken lines (*see* illustration) and sixty-four hexagrams, each composed of two trigrams, in all the possible combinations. These are cosmic symbols depicting the patterns of changes in nature, society, and individual humans. The unbroken lines represent the yang or male principle and the broken lines the yin or female (*see* YIN AND YANG). With the exception of the first two of the trigrams and hexagrams, all contain both unbroken and broken lines.

The I Ching trigrams; the yin-yang symbol is in the middle

1. Composition and date. The book contains many fragments of myths and rituals of archaic China. It began as a manual of oracles but was later expanded to include proverbs, folk wisdom, historical and legendary allusions, and the cosmological theories of yin yang and the five agents or elements (wood, fire, earth, metal, and water). Its oldest stratum was probably in existence as early as the twelfth century B.C. and other strata were gradually added. It was completed in its present form by a Confucian editor in the first century A.D. Thus the book evolved over a period of at least a thousand years.

2. Contents. *a) The trigrams and the hexagrams (kua).* The trigrams were attributed to Fu Hsi, one of the legendary cosmogonic figures. The sixty-four hexagrams were ascribed to King Wen (reigned 1191-1122 B.C.), father of the founder of the Chou dynasty. Although tradition views the trigrams as antedating the hexagrams, there is no convincing evidence that this is so.

b) Judgments (t'uan). Each hexagram is accompanied by a short paragraph expressing how a given action would entail good fortune or misfortune. These judgments also were attributed to King Wen.

c) Images (hsiang). Each hexagram is also accompanied by a pithy paragraph describing an idea, a situation, or an archetype as conveyed by the symbols it contains. Thus each paragraph or image serves as an appropriate pattern of action. These images were also ascribed to King Wen.

d) Appended judgments (hsi-tz'u). Appended to each hexagram is an explanation containing six units, each describing the meaning of a corresponding line in the hexagram. These are attributed to Duke Chou (d. 1094 B.C.) and constitute the principal part of the book. Lines are explained from the bottom to the top. The descriptions are abstruse and pertain to the appropriateness or inappropriateness of action. For example, regarding the first hexagram *Ch'ien:* the Creative, its bottom line is described as: "Nine (the numerical value assigned to a solid line) at the beginning means: /Hidden dragon./ Do not act." The top line is described as: "Nine at the top means: /Arrogant dragon will have cause to repent./" Since all the lines are nines, it means: "There appears a flight of dragons without heads,/ Good fortune." The six lines indicate a pattern of changes in nature and society and advise action or inaction in a given situation. The explanation of an individual line is called *yao;* thus each Appended Judgment consists of six *yao*.

e) Ten Wings (Shih-yi). The above items constitute the canonical part of the book, which was known to CONFUCIUS (551-479 B.C.). The Ten Wings refer to the various commentaries on the canon. They were attributed to Confucius, although most of them were composed by his school after his death.

i. T'uan-chuan (Commentaries on the Judgments). First and second wings; fuller explanations of the Judgments.

ii. Hsiang-chuan (Commentaries on the Images). Third and fourth wings; each commentary begins with the interpretation of the opposite meanings of the two trigrams in the hexagram and concludes with the synthesis of the two contrasted meanings as expressing the ideal behavior recommended by the hexagram.

iii. Hsi-tz'u chuan (Commentaries on the Appended Judgments). Fifth and sixth wings; these consist of 1) a collection of metaphysical essays dealing essentially with the cycles of the opposite poles in nature and man (heaven and earth, firm and yielding, light and darkness, etc.); and 2) a compilation of fragmentary comments on the individual lines in the Appended Judgments.

iv. Wen Yen (Commentaries on the Words of the Canon). Seventh wing; fragments of comments on the first two hexagrams: *Ch'ien* (Creative) and *K'un* (Receptive). They consist of four commentaries on the Creative, describing its four attributes as corresponding to the Confucian virtues (humanity, rightousness, propriety, wisdom), and one commentary on the Receptive.

v. Shuo Kua (Discussion on the Trigrams). Eighth wing; a collection of essays of considerable antiquity on the symbolic meaning of the eight trigrams. They initiated the tradition of matching each trigram with a member of the nuclear family: 1) *Ch'ien,* the Creative, Father; 2) *K'un,* the Receptive, Mother; 3) *Chen,* the Arousing, Eldest Son; 4) *Sun,* the Gentle, Eldest Daughter; 5) *K'an,* the Abysmal, Second Son; 6) *Li,* the Clinging, Second Daughter; 7) *Ken,* Keeping Still, Third Son; 8) *Tui,* the Joyous, Third Daughter.

vi. Hsü Kua (Sequence of the Hexagrams). Ninth wing; brief explanations of the names of the hexagrams as symbolizing the cycles of changes from one pole to its opposite.

vii. Tsa Kua (Miscellaneous Notes on the Hexagrams). Tenth wing; one-line sentences interpreting the names of the hexagrams or anticipating the outcomes that these names may entail. They seem to be based on the interpretations of the sequence of the hexagrams.

3. Principal features. *a) Cyclical view of changes.* Changes are viewed in terms of cycles which consist of opposite movements (e.g., expansion and contraction, rise and fall). When one pole is reached, the movement invariably reverts to the opposite pole. This principle was used to explain the ebb and flow in nature, society, and individuals. One's basic attitude should be to accept this cosmic order and to be a part of it. Under this conception of change the opposite poles are complementary and the ideal way is to accept both the high and the low poles. The LAO TZU, however, teaches that there is a way to avoid this reciprocity—at least for the individual's own life—by choosing to abide by the low (soft) pole. The high invariably declines, but the low does not necessarily ascend to the high if one is determined to remain lowly.

b) The hexagrams as archetypes. The hexagrams embody the universal patterns or situations that lie beneath the collective consciousness of man, and correspond to the archetypes of present-day thought. The different strata of explanations and commentaries are various attempts to interpret the meanings of these archetypes. Because archetypes lie in the unconscious, their interpretation generally requires the use of a symbolic and esoteric language in order to express what the ordinary language cannot. This may be why the book often uses the world of nature, animals, plants, and human beings as symbols or metaphors to communicate ideas that cannot be stated conceptually or as propositions.

c) The process of divination. The classic method of divining with the *Book of Changes* is to manipulate stalks of the yarrow plant *(achillea millefolium)* so as to arrive at a number from six to nine, which indicates the nature of the bottom line of a hexagram as either yin or yang. Six indicates yin, seven, "old" yang, eight, "old" yin, and nine, yang. The process is repeated until all six lines are identified, and the resulting hexagram and the commentaries on it are studied to determine the appropriateness of the action contemplated. Any "old" yin line or "old" yang line is then replaced by its opposite. This produces a different hexagram, which is then studied for its answer to the question. *See* CONFUCIANISM; TAOISM, PHILOSOPHICAL; TAOISM, RELIGIOUS.

Bibliography. W. T. Chan, *A Source Book in Chinese Philosophy* (1963), pp. 262-70; Y. L. Fung, *A History of Chinese Philosophy,* D. Bodde, trans. (1953), II, 88-123; *The I Ching, or Book of Changes,* ET by C. Baynes from German trans. of R. Wilhelm, 2 vols. (1950); J. Needham, *Science and Civilization in China,* II (1971), 304-45; L. K. Tong, "The Concept of Time in Whitehead and the *I Ching,*" *Journal of Chinese Philosophy,* I (1974), 373-93; H. Wilhelm, *Change, Eight Lectures on the I Ching,* C. Baynes, trans. (1960); C. Baynes, *Heaven, Earth, and Man in the Book of Changes* (1977).

D. C. YU

ICCHANTIKA ĭ chăn tē´ kə (B—Skt.; etymology unclear). A being lacking Buddha-nature and thus incapable of enlightenment. The term first appears in the Nirvana Sūtra (Mahāparinirvāṇa Sūtra) along with the opposing idea of "universal Buddha-nature." The Hindu idea of CASTE may have influenced the concept. In the early chapters of the sūtra, the icchantika is condemned to eternal ignorance, but the last section says "even the icchantika has Buddha-nature." The latter doctrine was discovered by TAO-SHENG (*ca.* 360-434) and became normative in Far Eastern Buddhism. The dissenting tradition that kept to the earlier understanding of icchantika was condemned. However, the Laṅkāvatāra Sūtra offers a positive interpretation: the BODHISATTVA may, for the sake of sentient beings in SAMSARA, voluntarily renounce his "seed of enlightenment" and become an icchantika.

W. LAI

ICHI JITSU ĭ´ chĭ jĭt´ soo (B & Sh—Jap.; lit. "one reality"). Affirmation of the LOTUS SŪTRA that all Buddhas are "one reality," applied in TENDAI circles to identify native KAMI as local appearances of Buddhist divinities. Ichi Jitsu Shintō or Sanno Shintō is similar to the RYOBU SHINTŌ developed in SHINGON Buddhism.

C. W. EDWARDS

ICON (Ch—Gr.; lit. "image, likeness"). A religious image, usually painted on flat panels of wood or

Reproduced through the courtesy of the Michigan-Princeton-Alexandria Expedition to Mount Sinai

Virgin and Christ Child between two saints (probably 6th century)

canvas, composed according to traditional canons of style and subject, which is venerated in ORTHODOX CHURCHES in both public worship and private devotion. The style is generally frontal, hieratic, and addressed to the viewer; subjects include CHRIST (*see* illustration for HALO), the Virgin MARY, angels, saints, and selected biblical scenes. One well-known icon type is that of Christ "not made with hands" (Gr. *acheiropoietos*), believed to be a direct impress of Christ's face rather than the product of human skill.

Icons are understood as vehicles for the presence of their subjects. Miraculous interventions have often been attributed to them. During the ICONOCLASTIC CONTROVERSY, however, the second Council of Nicaea (787) decreed that the icon is not itself an object of "worship" (reserved for God alone) but of "veneration." In the classic statement of Basil (d. 379), bishop of Caesarea, "the honor paid to the image passes over to the original."

Bibliography. L. Ouspensky and V. Lossky, *The Meaning of Icons* (1952); K. Weitzmann *et al.*, *A Treasury of Icons* (1966); D. and T. T. Rice, *Icons and Their History* (1974).

W. S. BABCOCK

ICONOCLASTIC CONTROVERSY (Ch; 727-787; 815-843). A movement, led by Byzantine emperors of these periods and their ecclesiastical supporters, which prohibited the veneration of religious images (ICONS) of Christ and the saints and ordered the destruction of such images on the grounds that their veneration was idolatrous. The controversy brought to a head a long period of uneasiness about this practice, but iconoclasm ultimately did not prevail. (*See* ART AND ARCHITECTURE, CHRISTIAN §3.)

D. E. GROH

IDDHI ĭd′ hē (H). *See* SIDDHI.

IDEATION (B). A term referring to mind, consciousness, or thought and a key concept in the idealistic Hossō (mere ideation) school of NARA BUDDHISM. According to this movement, nothing exists apart from the mind or mental activity. Hossō drew directly from the YOGĀCĀRA (mind only) Buddhism of VASUBANDHU. E. J. COLEMAN

IDRĪS, HERMES ĭd rēs′, hĕr′ mēz (I). Idrīs is a nonbiblical figure mentioned twice in the QUR'ĀN (Sura 19:57-58, 21:85-86). He has been identified both with the biblical prophet Enoch and with Hermes of alchemical and astrological fame. Hermes, in turn, was sometimes linked to Idrīs/Enoch by pseudo-scientific medieval Muslim commentators, sometimes to a person who allegedly appeared in Babylonia after the flood and revived the study of talismanic and other esoteric sciences before migrating to Egypt. Idrīs/Hermes sparked the imagination of numerous Muslim writers and, through them, some early Renaissance scholars.

Bibliography. M. Plessner, "Hirmis," *EI*, III, 463-65; G. Vajda, "Idrīs," *EI*, III, 1030-31. B. LAWRENCE

IGNATIUS OF LOYOLA loi ō′ lâ (Ch; 1491-1556). Founder of the JESUITS and first general of that order; CANONIZED in 1622. Born into a noble family at Loyola in the Spanish province of Guipúzcoa.

In the course of a military career, Ignatius sustained severe leg wounds in 1521. During a prolonged convalescence, he was influenced by reading Ludolph of Saxony's *Vita Christi* and the lives of the saints and underwent a dramatic CONVERSION experience. This led him to devote himself to the spiritual life with a fervor as great as that which had distinguished his military career.

After a year of mortification and prayer in retreat at Manresa, he embarked on the spiritual quest that took him first to ROME and JERUSALEM and then to a protracted period of study (Latin, philosophy, theology) at Barcelona, Alcalá, Salamanca, and Paris (1524-35). At Paris in 1534, together with FRANCIS XAVIER and others, he vowed himself to a life of poverty, chastity, and apostolic labor. In 1540 the new society received papal approval as the Society of Jesus. In the following year, having completed the *Spiritual Exercises* summing up the spiritual insights gained at Manresa, Ignatius became the order's first general. In his *Constitutions* for the order he eliminated much that had been traditional to the monastic life and placed his central stress on obedience, above all, to the pope. *See* PAPACY.

Bibliography. P. Dudon, *St. Ignatius of Loyola* (1949); J. Brodrick, *Saint Ignatius Loyola: The Pilgrim Years* (1956).

F. OAKLEY

IHS (Ch). Latin monogram for "Jesus" formed from the Greek abbreviation found in NT manuscripts. Greek *eta* (H) was later misunderstood as Latin H, and the letters explained as standing for *I*esus *h*ominum *S*alvator (Jesus, Savior of men) or *I*n *h*oc *s*igno [vinces] (In this sign you will conquer).

R. A. GREER

IJMĀʻ ĭj mä′ (I—Arab.; lit. "settling, resolving; agreement, concurrence"). Term used in Islamic languages for the "consensus" of the UMMA about any issue, especially any God-given norm (*ḥukm)* for human life. In SUNNI legal theory, *ijmāʻ* is the third "source" of authority (*see* FIQH), after QUR'ĀN and SUNNA, for decision on any question. Specifically, it is held to represent the consensual judgment of the qualified scholar-legists ('ULAMĀ') of the community. *Ijmāʻ* both ratifies Islamic customary practice—which theoretically follows the sunna—and effectively creates it, where an unprecedented issue arises. However, conservative interpretation restricts *ijmāʻ* to the "consensus" formed by the early *umma* in its practice and thus sharply curtails creative interpretation (*ijtihād)*—a restrictive concept of *ijmāʻ* that modernists like Muhammad 'Abduh and Kemal Faruki have rejected for an ongoing *ijmāʻ* that changes with circumstances. The SHI'ITE reliance on the IMAM'S guidance of course obviates the need for such an *ijmāʻ* "doctrine," whether conservatively or liberally interpreted.

Bibliography. M. Bernand, "Idjmāʻ," *EI* 2; N. Coulson, *A History of Islamic Law* (1964), pp. 75-85; G. Hourani, "The Basis of Authority of Consensus in Sunnite Islam," *Studia Islamica,* XXI (1964), 13-60.

W. A. GRAHAM

IKEDA, DAISAKU ē kā′ dä dī′ sä koo (B—Jap.; 1928-). Born in Ōmori, Tokyo, the fifth son of a seaweed merchant. While working in the Niigata Iron Works, he met and married Kaneko, the daughter of the vice-chairman of SŌKA GAKKAI'S Board of Directors. He served under Sōka Gakkai's second president, Toda, as an executive in the youth department and was personally selected by Toda to succeed him. Ikeda served as its third president from 1960 until his resignation in 1979.

Ikeda continued Toda's emphasis on organization, publication, and growth, and added to these his personal attraction for youth and his interest in overseas mission. His publications include a biography of Toda, talks with Arnold Toynbee on religion, and commentaries on the sacred writings of Nichiren Shō-shū. *See* NICHIREN BUDDHISM §3.

N. S. BRANNEN

IKHWĀN al-ṢAFĀ ĭk wän′ äl sä fä′ (I—Arab.; lit. "brethren of purity"). A secret philosophical-religious society which arose in the tenth century at Basra, in Iraq. They were associated with the Bāṭinī Ismailis, who had engaged in secret political propaganda since the death of their IMAM, Ismā'īl ibn Ja'far al-Ṣādiq, in A.D. 760. (*See* ISMĀ'ĪLIYYA.) The Brethren injected into this propaganda a new scientific and philosophical spirit and dedicated themselves to enlightening and spiritually purifying themselves. They propagated their ideas in various parts of the Islamic empire and produced fifty-two philosophical epistles and a compendium of their teachings.

A. A. SACHEDINA

IMAM ĭ mäm′ (I—Arab.; lit. "he who stands before"). 1. In SHI'ITE Islam, a spiritual leader whose authority is derived directly from the Prophet MUHAMMAD through a line of succession through ALI and his descendants. He alone is endowed with the power of interpreting Islamic truth in the age in which he lives. He is regarded as infallible and as possessing the light of God which attracts people to him. There is an imam in every age, but he may be concealed, because God is enraged at those who have threatened the safety of the imam. In the IMĀMIYYA branch of Shi'ism the twelfth imam is expected to return as the MAHDI and institute a just Islamic society.

2. In SUNNITE Islam, the leader of worship in the MOSQUE, who stands in front of the assembled believers to ensure unison in the movements of the prayers; also a jurist who is consulted in matters of SHARIA. Sunnis also accord the title to such prominent figures as Ali, an imam of the Shi'ites.

A. A. SACHEDINA

IMĀMIYYA ĭ mäm ē′ yä (I—Arab.; lit. "followers of the imam") **ITHNA 'ASHARIYYA** ĭth′ nä ä shä rē′ yä (I—Arab.; lit. "twelvers," i.e. followers of the twelve imams). Imāmiyya is a general designation of those SHI'ITES who believe in the necessity of the office of IMAM, the infallibility of the imam, and his being designated to the office by his predecessor *(naṣṣ)*. It refers in particular to the "Twelvers."

1. **Basic beliefs.** Imamite authors, in their exposition of the Shi'ite creed, divide the principles of religion into five tenets: *a)* the affirmation of the unity of God; *b)* belief in the justice of God; *c)* belief in prophecy; *d)* belief in the imamate; *e)* belief in the Day of Judgment. In four of these principles, *a, b, c,* and *e,* Imamites share common ground with the SUNNITES, although there are differences in details. Sunnites, however, do not consider the fourth principle a fundamental of religion, while the Shi'ites make it their cardinal principle.

2. **The succession of imams.** The Shi'ites regard their imams as designated by God through MUHAMMAD his Prophet, in accordance with the testament revealed to the Prophet, which announces the names of those who would succeed him. The testament also carried instruction for each imam to follow. Thus the first three imams, ALI (d. 661), al-ḤASAN (d. 669), and al-ḤUSAYN (d. 680), chose to resist the UMAYYAD rule; while the next eight imams, Ali ibn al-Ḥusayn (d. *ca.* 712), Muḥammad al-Bāqir (d. 731), Ja'far al-Ṣādiq (d. 765), Mūsā al-Kāẓim (d. 799), Ali al-Riḍā (d. 818), Muḥammad al-Jawād (d. 835), Ali al-Hādī (d. 868), and al-Ḥasan al-'Askarī (d. 874) chose political quietism until the rising of the twelfth imam, Muhammad al-Mahdī, who went into "complete occultation" in A.D. 940, in compliance with the instruction in the testament.

3. **Functions of the imams.** The special mark of the imam, as it was known to the later Imamites, was infallibility. Whereas Sunnite theologians considered infallibility to be a peculiar quality of the Prophet, Shi'ite theologians contended that since the imamate was intended as the continuation of the Prophet's mission, the community needed an infallible leader. The difference between the two creeds became marked when the Shi'ite imam was asserted to have possessed the light of God, which was passed on to him by the Prophet.

The prophetic heritage of the imam guarantees the survival of religion in his person. He alone is endowed with the power of interpreting religion at different times. As a result, a person who dies without acknowledging his imam dies a death of ignorance. This means there is an imam in every age, whether manifest or concealed, who calls people to the way of God. But there are times when the world can be without a manifest imam; this is so when God is enraged at the people who have threatened the safety of the imam and who are unable to see the imam who is in occultation although he sees them. Occultation is a state chosen by God for the imam who is in danger of being slain by his enemies. Thus the twelfth imam, al-Mahdī, went into occultation and will continue to live in this state for as long as God deems it necessary. Then God will command him to reappear and take control of the world, in order to restore justice and equity. During this period of concealment the imam is not completely cut off from his followers but has spokesmen, in the person of learned jurists (MUJTAHIDS) who can act on his behalf and guide the Shi'ites in religious, social, and political matters. (*See* MAHDI.)

4. **Expressions of piety.** Imamite piety, although differing little from Sunnite piety in its adherence to the SHARIA, developed its own sharia. Imamites depended on the QUR'ĀN as well as ḤADĪTH for validating religious injunctions, but they looked to the SUNNA of the imams in addition to that of the Prophet. Yet except for the special place given to the reports of the imams, their *hadīth* were often almost identical with those of the Sunnites. However, their piety included the devotion of the imams as expressed in the annual commemoration of the *ta'ziya*—the wrongs committed against the household of the Prophet, especially the murder of al-Ḥusayn—and the visit (ZIYĀRA) to the tombs (MASHHADS) of all the imams, believed to have suffered at the hands of oppressive Sunnite caliphs. The other marks of Shi'ite piety include dissimulation of one's true opinion as part of the religious duty, in order not to arouse animosity of other Muslims, and the payment of the "fifth," a tax intended for pious purposes and particularly for the descendants of the Prophet.

Bibliography. Muḥammad ibn Muḥammad al-Nu'mān al-Mufīd, *al-Fuṣūl al-mukhtāra min al-'uyūn wa al-maḥāsin* (1962); 'Aḍad al-dīn al-Ījī, *Sharḥ al-mawāqif* (1907), 3:261 ff; Muhammad ibn Ya'qūb al-Rāzī al-Kulaynī, *al-Uṣūl min al-kāfī* (1972); Muḥammad ibn 'Alī ibn Bābūya, *A Shi'ite Creed* (1942); A. A. Sachedina, "*Al-Khums:* the Fifth in the Imamite Legal System," *JNES*, XXXIX (1980), 275-89.

A. A. SACHEDINA

IMITATION OF CHRIST (Ch). A late medieval devotional book. It was a product of a mystical movement associated with the BRETHREN OF THE COMMON LIFE in the Rhineland and the Netherlands that stressed a simple inward piety of prayer and withdrawal from the world. Traditionally attributed to Thomas à Kempis, a monk of Mount St. Agnes near Zwolle, its authorship is debated. Early manuscripts lack an autograph. Some scholars believe that Thomas edited the works of others or that the book was written by earlier spiritual writers.

The *Imitation* is divided into four books. The first contains brief chapters on the spiritual life. Books Two and Three treat the interior life of the Christian. The final book is on the MASS.

Opening with an admonition to imitate the life of Christ, the *Imitation* suggests regarding oneself as a stranger and pilgrim, whose true home is heaven. While not anti-intellectual, the *Imitation* says that all knowledge of value is related to salvation. The two most important kinds of knowledge are "illuminations from above" and "a humble knowledge of oneself" which comes from inward examination.

A dominant theme of the *Imitation* is contempt for the world. The Christian should live in seclusion searching for God. To love Jesus is the highest good, and meditation on the life of Christ brings peace and confidence. Self-denial and adversity are ways to a deeper awareness of God.

Bibliography. A. Hyma, *The Christian Renaissance* (1925); R. R. Post, *The Modern Devotion* (1968).

W. O. PAULSELL

IMMACULATE CONCEPTION (Ch). The doctrine that God by his grace kept the Virgin MARY free of original sin from the first instant of her existence as a human person, in anticipation of the saving work of JESUS. Mary's freedom from original sin, hence "immaculate," occurred at her coming into being as the child of two human parents (by legend Joachim and Anne), hence, "conception," or, better, "passive conception." It should not be confused with the completely different doctrine of the VIRGIN BIRTH, that is, the virginal conception of Jesus.

By the fifth century the sense of Mary's holiness as part of her vocation to be the mother of Christ suggested a freedom from original sin as well as personal sin. Yet for centuries the position that original sin was inescapable for all human beings who come into existence in the normal way of marriage inhibited general acceptance of the immaculate conception. Clarification of original sin as a "spiritual lack" removed this obstacle. Finally came the suggestion of DUNS SCOTUS (d. 1308) that Mary was beneficiary of a "preservative" redemption, even more indebted to the Savior than is the rest of humanity. This put her clearly in the redemptive order, and answered the difficulty of many great theologians, even THOMAS AQUINAS (d. 1274).

The Feast of the Immaculate Conception, December 8, was first celebrated in the eighth century, spread gradually, and from the fifteenth century had Roman approval. In 1854 Pius IX declared the doctrine a revealed truth, binding on Catholics (*see* DOGMA).

Bibliography. E. D. O'Connor, ed., *The Dogma of the Immaculate Conception: History and Significance* (1958); K. Rahner, "The Immaculate Conception," *Theological Investigations.* I (1961).

E. R. CARROLL

IMMORTALITY. The belief that the soul or other center of consciousness of humans (and in some traditions, of other beings as well) survives death and lives again in this world or another world. In no religion can belief in immortality be properly understood in isolation from that religion's ethos and world view.

In systems that hold some form of philosophical MONISM, sentient beings are immortal because they consist of the same basic stuff as ultimate reality, or the ABSOLUTE, which by definition is eternal. In HINDUISM the individual ATMAN, or self, is the same as Atman in general, and Atman is identical with BRAHMAN. BUDDHISM denies that there is a self (*see* ANATTA), but holds that a finite personality structure, multifaceted and laden with KARMA, passes through a series of births and deaths. For Buddhism, Hinduism, and JAINISM the phenomenal world is ultimately empty (*see* ŚŪNYATĀ), but sentient beings are tied to it in a round of rebirths or SAMSARA. The search for escape from samsara is directed toward liberation—MOKṢA in Hinduism and Jainism and NIRVANA in Buddhism. This escape implies the termination of individual existence. MAHĀYĀNA Buddhism developed a belief in various heavens and hells, where beings dwell between births (*see* TUSITA HEAVEN) or from which they can enter Nirvana (*see* AMIDA; PURE LAND). TIBETAN BUDDHISM seeks to guide the dying individual through the intermediate BARDO state to a favorable rebirth.

CHINESE POPULAR RELIGION includes a belief in ghosts of the dead (*see* PRETA) and rituals for placating them. It has continued to coexist with RELIGIOUS TAOISM, which sought to discover an elixir of immortality, Buddhism with its concern for life in other realms, and ANCESTOR VENERATION, in which departed ancestors continue to influence the living.

JAPANESE RELIGION holds out to the individual the hope of achieving immortality by becoming KAMI at death.

Belief in SOUL, SPIRIT, variously defined, is normative in JUDAISM, CHRISTIANITY, and ISLAM. Souls of the dead are thought to continue to exist in PURGATORY, or in heaven or hell. (*See* HEAVEN AND HELL.) The physical body shares in immortality through a RESURRECTION. (For Islam *see* JAHANNAM; JANNA; NAFS; RŪḤ.)

REINCARNATION, taught in a variety of forms in many cultures, assumes that the self survives death, but after a series of rebirths it may or may not cease to exist.

K. CRIM

IMPERMANENCE (B). *See* ANICCA.

IMPRIMATUR ĭm prĭ mä´ tŭr (Ch—Lat.; lit. "let it be printed"). A statement that a manuscript has been cleared for publication. Formerly both civil and religious, now in practice restricted to ROMAN CATHOLICISM. The *nihil obstat* ("no objection") by an appointed expert reader is his judgment that the manuscript contains nothing contrary to faith or morals. Members of RELIGIOUS ORDERS must have permission to publish from their superiors. A local bishop normally gives the *imprimatur*. Since 1975 it is required for editions of Scripture, devotional, liturgical, catechetical, and other basic religious textbooks.

J. HENNESEY

INCARNATION (Ch—Lat. *incarnatio;* lit. "being flesh"). The unique event in which the LOGOS of God—his revelational, creative, redemptive activity—assumed human form with all essential human characteristics in JESUS of Nazareth. Generally the Logos has been identified with the second person of the TRINITY.

Although the term "incarnation" is not found in the NT, the concept is found in John 1:14, "And the word became flesh." Further scriptural support has been deduced from Heb. 1:1-4; Phil. 2:5-11; II Cor. 5:19.

Christianity has historically maintained that Jesus possessed two natures—the human and the divine—inextricably bound in one personality without violence to either nature. Many heresies have challenged this doctrine. These include ARIANISM, which held Jesus to be a demigod; DOCETISM, which so emphasized Jesus' divinity as to vitiate his humanity, even denying the actuality of his body; and NES-

TORIANISM, Ebionism, and adoptionism, which depreciated the meaning of his deity. (*See* CHRISTOLOGY.)

The incarnation is considered concurrently the highest revelation of God's character and man at his noblest and best. It is generally viewed as integral to the ATONEMENT. *See* REVELATION AND MANIFESTATION.

Bibliography. D. Baillie, *God Was in Christ* (1948); F. Ferrier, *What Is the Incarnation?* (1962); J. Hick, ed., *The Myth of God Incarnate* (1977); G. Parrinder, *Avatar and Incarnation* (1970); B. Skard, *The Incarnation* (1960).

T. O. HALL, JR.

INDEX LIBRORUM PROHIBITORUM ĭn´ dĕx lĭ brō´ rūm prō hĭb ĭ tōr´ ŭm (Ch—Lat.; lit. "list of forbidden books"). A list of books, the reading and selling of which was forbidden to ROMAN CATHOLICS under pain of EXCOMMUNICATION, first published in 1559. A special department in papal government supervised it after 1571. In 1917 supervision was transferred to the Congregation of the Holy Office (formerly the Inquisition), and since 1966 the *Index* is no longer operative. J. HENNESEY

INDIANS, AMERICAN. *See* NATIVE AMERICAN TRIBAL RELIGION.

INDRA ĭn´ drū (H, Ja & B—Skt.; etymology uncertain). A warrior deity, god of the atmosphere or midspace between heaven and earth, the most important god in VEDIC HINDUISM, celebrated in more than 250 hymns of the RIG VEDA, where he is a conqueror of demons and of the forts of enemies of the ARYANS. Patron of the warrior class, Indra is a powerful, gigantic, bearded, hard-drinking, chariot-driving fighter who wields a thunderbolt weapon *(vajra)*. Of all the gods only Indra undergoes physical birth, and only he commits crimes against the three classes of society. His most famous exploit is the destruction of the cloud-demon Vṛtra (variously *ahi*, the serpent) who withholds the creation waters and light; for this cosmogonic conquest, which periodically releases fecundating waters, Indra is designated Vṛtrahan, "slayer of Vṛtra." A Proto-Indo-European background is suggested by the resemblances in physical description and mythical episodes between Indra and Thor of Scandinavian mythology. Likewise, later Indo-Iranian mythology provided a model with the victory god Verethraghna in the AVESTA. In India a conflation of the Avestan deity (cf. Vedic Vṛtrahan) with Indra may have resulted in the specification of *vṛtra* ("resistance") as a monsoon-withholding demon periodically slain by heroic Indra's thunder-weapon.

Indra's great strength—as well as his drunken boasting—increases under SOMA intoxication. He is "the bounteous" *(maghavan)*, possessing a hundred powers, and he becomes king of the gods, surpassing even VARUNA, by virtue of his self-rule *(svarāj)* and physical might. Among his victories are the theft of the soma plant, with the aid of an eagle, from the highest heaven and the release of cows imprisoned in a cave by demons. The Maruts, sons of RUDRA, are his allies in battle and he is also linked with AGNI (sometimes his twin brother) and the divine twins, the AŚVINS. Indrāṇī is his wife. In post-Vedic mythology and iconography, including that of JAINISM and BUDDHISM, Indra retains his role as chief of the gods, although in Hinduism he is subordinate to VISHNU and SHIVA. In the MAHĀBHĀRATA, where he is associated with the eastern quarter and rides the white elephant Airāvata, he is the father of the warrior ARJUNA. His seduction of Ahalyā, wife of the sage Gautama, results in a terrible curse against him. And since Vṛtra is in later accounts regarded a BRAHMIN, Indra is also guilty of brahminicide.

Bibliography. A. A. Macdonell, *Vedic Mythology* (1897); Georges Dumézil, *The Destiny of the Warrior* (1970).

D. M. KNIPE

INDULGENCES (Ch). Originally, the remission of a public penance imposed by the church for a certain period of time (hence the now obsolete terminology of an indulgence of so many days or years), but more recently understood in terms of a remission through the prayer of the church of temporal punishment due to sin. The practice of indulgence grants arose in the eleventh century. In time the carrying out of specific good works was introduced as a condition for gaining indulgences: support of charitable institutions, alms giving, PILGRIMAGES, participation in CRUSADES. Despite attempts at regulation from the time of the Fourth Lateran Council (1215) onward, abuses connected with trafficking in indulgences grew rife, and were an immediate cause of the REFORMATION. When disciplinary measures enacted by the Council of TRENT remained ineffective, Pope Pius V abrogated in 1567 all indulgence grants connected with monetary contributions or the equivalent. In the Apostolic Constitution *The Doctrine of Indulgences* (January 1, 1967) and in the new *Handbook of Indulgences* (June 29, 1968) quantitative expressions of earlier times are rejected, and emphasis is placed on the church's prayer for the repentant sinner and on the personal dispositions of the faithful in their works of piety. C. WADDELL

INDUS VALLEY CIVILIZATION. A civilization which arose in the lower Indus River Valley (of what is present-day Pakistan) sometime after 2500 B.C. Also called the Harappan Civilization (*see* HARAPPĀ) it achieved a geographical distribution of nearly half a million square miles, extending over almost all the area of Pakistan and into India eastward to near Delhi and southward into Gujurat.

1. Origins and end. The precise origins of the Indus Valley Civilization are not known, but there is increasing evidence that village communities of Baluchistan provided the cultural context for the generation of the attitudes and technologies which were to develop into an urban culture on the alluvial plains of the Indus. A relationship between the Indus

Civilization and Sumerian Civilization which arose a thousand years earlier is problematic, but it may be reasonably assumed that development of the Baluchistan cultures was stimulated by influences from Mesopotamia. What was required for the emergence of urban culture—and what the Indus Valley provided—were natural resources, fertile soil, and abundant water.

The end of the civilization is as enigmatic as its beginning. Speculations range from natural calamities to invasions by foreigners. The archaeological evidence is inconclusive, and probably a number of factors, human and natural, contributed to the civilization's extinction. Clearly it did not die out all at once but in phases, just as it began. Perhaps around 1750 B.C. organized life in major cities, Harappā and MOHENJO-DARO, ended after a period of decline due to growing population and decreasing food production. Elsewhere the civilization died out at a somewhat later date, also after a period of deterioration. Certainly by 1500 B.C. the major sites were extinct, although enclaves of the culture may have persisted well beyond that time.

2. **Characteristics.** Of the approximately 150 known sites of the civilization only about a half dozen are truly cities. Of these Mohenjo-daro and Harappā in particular stand out for their size and the diversity of their material remains. They exhibit a remarkable uniformity of culture, especially in town planning, found throughout the civilization's geographical expanse and its many centuries of existence. The settlements were laid out with an artificial mound or "citadel" on the west and the town itself on the east. The citadels, with their imposing buildings, were probably the administrative and religious centers of the communities. The residential and commercial quarters of the town were established on a grid plan of wide streets and intersecting lanes. Fired bricks and wood were the common building materials. Construction was very well designed and executed, with particular attention paid to sanitation. The overall impression conveyed by the remains of the civilization is of an urban culture of a highly sophisticated yet pragmatic sort, carefully planned, possibly centrally administered, and conforming rigidly to unchanging tradition.

3. **Artifacts.** The most intriguing and potentially informative, but as of now the most frustrating, artifacts of the civilization are its seals, upon which are written inscriptions in a thus far undeciphered script. Generally cut from steatite and measuring ¾ and 1¼ inches, the seals also bear intaglio (relief) designs of considerable artistic quality. Represented are animals of various sorts, both real and imaginary, and occasionally human figures, but these lack the aesthetic fineness of the animal depictions. Although some promising steps have been taken toward an understanding of the script, until a convincing decipherment has been achieved, the purposes of the seals will not be known. At the present time it is supposed that they had multiple uses—commercial, administrative, religious, and personal. Clearly many of the seals bear depictions of a cultic and ritual sort and seem important to an understanding of the religious life of the civilization.

Other artifacts include numerous terra cotta figurines, usually of females, crudely fashioned, naked to the waist, often with elaborate headdresses, necklaces, bangles, and other ornaments. It is possible that these figurines were children's playthings, but, given their number and stylization, it is more likely that they were votive representations of a goddess.

4. **Religious life.** Since the discovery of the Indus Civilization in 1921, investigators have been impressed with its strongly religious character. Although no buildings have been definitely identified as temples or shrines, it is probable that some of the structures on the citadels had a religious function. Certainly the cemeteries at Harappā and elsewhere indicate a developed religious attitude toward death. Bodies were positioned north-south and were accompanied by personal ornaments, funerary furniture, and pottery which probably contained food. This suggests a religious belief which demanded the ritual preparation and burial of the dead.

But it is chiefly the seals and figurines which provide evidence of religious life. Among the seal depictions with an apparently religious character those of a tree deity are especially prominent. In at least two cases they are adored by ministrants and receive animal sacrifice. Another representation of note is that of a figure seated crossed-leg upon a platform or throne, its hands resting on its knees. On two seals the figure wears a buffalo-horn headdress, many bracelets and necklaces. On one seal it is surrounded by animals and on another, this time without headdress, it is worshiped by kneeling suppliants which flank it and behind whom rise great hooded cobras. Sir John Marshall, one of the first investigators, saw this figure as the prototype of the classical Hindu god SHIVA. The posture of the figure suggested Shiva's traditional designation as the "Great YOGI," while the company of animals seemed to point to Shiva's identity as "Lord of the Animals." Supporting his identification of "proto-Shiva" Marshall found what may be small stone phalli, the phallus being an important iconographic representation of Shiva. The chief difficulty with Marshall's interpretation is that it reads into the Indus materials an iconography and mythology which did not fully develop until at least a thousand years after the termination of the civilization.

Any interpretation of the religious life of the Indus Valley Civilization, or of other aspects of its culture, will be at best conjectural until a convincing decipherment of the script is achieved, if then. However, given the seal depictions of the supposed tree divinity and the abundant female figurines, it can be surmised that the religious life of the civilization

Seal of a horned god from the Indus Valley civilization

centered around a fertility cult—probably that of the Great Goddess in her form as the earth mother and "mistress of the animals" of the sort known elsewhere in archaic civilizations.

Bibliography. B. and F. R. Allchin, *The Birth of Indian Civilization* (1968); W. A. Fairservis, Jr., *The Roots of Ancient India* (1971); J. Marshall, *Mohenjo-daro and the Indus Civilization* (1931); A. Parpola, "Tasks, Methods and Results in the Study of the Indus Script," *Journal of the Royal Asiatic Society*, No. 2 (1975), 179-209; H. P. Sullivan, "A Re-examination of the Religion of the Indus Civilization," *HR*, IV (1964), 115-25; M. Wheeler, *The Indus Civilization* (3rd ed., 1968).

H. P. Sullivan

INFALLIBILITY (Ch). 1. The inability to err in teaching revealed truth, claimed by the Roman Catholic church in Vatican Councils I and II to belong to the church by the will of Christ (Luke 22:32; John 16:13) and applicable in clearly specified circumstances to certain judgments of (1) the pope, speaking Ex Cathedra and (2) the body of bishops in communion with one another and with him, either dispersed throughout the world or gathered in ecumenical council. The object of an infallible definition must be a doctrine of faith or morals proposed absolutely and definitively to be held by the whole church. *See* Papacy.

2. *See* Bible; Fundamentalism.

J. Hennesey

INITIATION. The ritualization of spiritual or social transformation; through it, outsiders are inducted into both a sacred society and a cosmos.

1. **Types of initiation.** In native religions initiation is chiefly of three varieties: (1) *generational* rites transforming adolescents into adults (cross-culturally, males are initiated in groups, females in milder rites with one or a few novices), (2) *specialized "secret" societies* rites (medicine cults of Plains Indians, masked societies of the forest peoples of West Africa, mediumistic cults of the Yoruba of Nigeria, etc.), and (3) *individualized ecstatic* rites (vision quest of American Indians, Shamanism of Siberians, etc.). Initiation in folk religions, however, generally creates a deepening of commonly shared spirituality, while in more differentiated cultures it often presents alternative spiritualities: novices enter new universes or self-consciously separate "cults" or subgroups within the civilization. The initiation is then a "conversion" ritual. The spiritual fragmentation of complex cultures also permits sharply individualistic initiation experiences, especially when the intense ecstatic transformation becomes the main content of religion per se (as in many mystical and meditational cults). Generational initiation is, however, also important in the central religious institutions of complex societies, and offers deeper commitment to and insight into commonly shared values (e.g., Confirmation in Christianity, the Bar Mitzvah of Judaism, "capping" in Confucianism, and laying on of the Sacred Thread in Hinduism). Thus all varieties of initiation persist in more distinct form in complex civilizations, even in such secularized versions as "boot camp," or fraternity hazing.

2. **Theories of initiation.** Theories "explaining" initiation generally focus on generational rites in folk religions. Freudian theory supposes initiation to be a sadomasochistic climax to father-son Oedipal conflict, dramatically producing adult sexuality and culture through a fusion of violence or death fantasies and incestuous desires to displace paternal authority. Death and rebirth symbolisms are certainly important in all types of initiation, as are pain, suffering, and sexual taboos. Jungians agree on the centrality of mythic "archetypes" as novices recapitulate the quest of identity of the culture hero or god, and thus achieve their own cultural selfhood. Time is momentarily abolished, and novices dwell in the ancestral primal age, i.e., in their own "collective unconscious" or racial memory. This descent into the dream-stuff is the psychological experience of death leading to heroic rebirth.

Cognitive theories reveal a remarkably uniform psychological dynamic, which we may call "stripping" (*see* Sargent). In general, initiation induces a radical reorientation of consciousness, by removing from it all its customary supports and forcing dependence on externally manipulated information for any stable sense of reality. The initiate is physically isolated from his or her familiar environment, is subjected to forcible alteration of the body image (nudity or uniforms, restricted movements, mutilation), has ego-identity destroyed (enforced passivity or activity only in groups, sharp criticism of all independent views, etc.), and is prevented from employing clear, rational thought (sensory deprivation or overload through sleep and food reduction, ordeals, torture, etc.). The meanings offered by authorities therefore give the only stable basis on which to rebuild world view and identity.

Sociological theories stress the value of initiation in clarifying and legitimating new social roles. Initiation is a "rite of passage" from one identity to another, and is often performed "outside" society (in the bush, etc.) in the "nonsocial sacred" realm, so as to facilitate reentry on a totally different social level. To underline this "nonsocial" aspect, social boundaries are broken down and abnormal behavior enforced. But the authority of leaders is stressed, and in fact norms do structure initiation. Recent studies (*see* Koch) show that dramatic, violent generational initiation occurs in cultures where men must act collectively (in feuds, hunting, etc.) but where boys are relegated to their mothers, even sleeping with them past infancy and developing feminine identity. Hence, drastic initiation creates a male self-image, but adult males still have ambivalent, macho "protest masculinity" and fear of female "magic." We may conclude that ambivalent identities combined with sharply distinguished social roles and groupings produce dramatically harsh initiation.

Spiritually, the significance of initiation lies in the *recentering* of the self in the divine order and in the transcendental other. One "dies" to the banal, egoistic self and is "reborn" filled with wonder at a new universe oriented by sacrality. The "wisdom" offered by initiation really consists of this profound reorientation, and very many initiation rites include no elaborate philosophical instruction (e.g., many Bantu cults, Hellenistic "mystery" religions). When one simply enacts the rituals and their myths one dwells in the divine presence, one becomes the first ancestors and knows the self from their perspective. One becomes more than just an individual. Intellectual instruction, when added to this, is often to justify the creation of an "elite" distinct from profane folk, or is required by the growing complexity and disharmony of culture. We can note, in fact, a tendency for the most intellectualized forms of initiation to express the most dualistic, gnostic types of religion, but such varieties are quite atypical.

Bibliography. Psychological orientation: B. Bettelheim, *Symbolic Wounds* (1962); E. Neumann, *Origins and History of Consciousness* (1970); and J. Halifax, *Shamanic Voices* (1979). Sociological and sociopsychological: A. van Gennep, *The Rites of Passage* (1960); K.-F. Koch "Sociogenic and Psychogenic Models in Anthropology: The Functions of Jalé Initiation," *Man*, n. s., IX (Sept., 1974), 397-422; A. I. Richards, *Chisungu: A Girl's Initiation Ceremony* (1957); W. E. H. Stanner, *On Aboriginal Religion* (1960); V. W. Turner, *Forest of Symbols* (1967) and *The Ritual Process* (1969). Cognitive: W. Sargent, *Battle For the Mind* (1971). Phenomenological, religious perspective: C. Bleeker, ed., *Initiation* (1965); M. Eliade, *Rites and Symbols of Initiation* (1965). E. M. ZUESSE

INJĪL ĭn jēl′ (I—Arab.; Gr. *evangelion*—"gospel"). *See* PEOPLE OF THE BOOK.

INNOCENT III (Ch; *ca.* 1160-1216). Pope from 1198. One of the most powerful popes in the Middle Ages, the first to use the title "Vicar of Christ," whose leadership raised the PAPACY to the zenith of its medieval authority. Innocent centralized the administrative, financial, and political powers of the church under his aegis and restored papal prestige in ROME and throughout Italy. He compelled Philip Augustus of France to reach a marital reconciliation and by placing England under the interdict forced John of England to approve Stephen Langton as ARCHBISHOP of CANTERBURY (1213). Initially he promoted the Fourth CRUSADE, but opposed it when the crusaders seized Constantinople (1204). He centralized the INQUISITION at Rome and directed attacks against heresy, including a crusade against the ALBIGENSES in southern France (1208). He limited the founding of new RELIGIOUS ORDERS though he actively supported the DOMINICANS, the FRANCISCANS, and the Trinitarians. He established a sound financial administration by instituting new sources of revenue such as a tax on CLERGY; he reformed the papal CURIA and the papal chancery courts and made vigorous use of cardinal legates to oversee diocesan affairs. In 1209-10 he issued a compilation of his most important decretals, the first officially published body of CANON LAW. The high point in his papacy was the convocation of the Fourth Lateran Council (1215). Its seventy decrees defined the essence of Roman Catholic faith and practice for centuries.

Bibliography. L. E. Elliott-Binns, *Innocent III* (1931); C. E. Smith, *Innocent III, Church Defender* (1951).

H. L. BOND

INQUISITION (Ch). Permanent ecclesiastical tribunal established by Pope Gregory IX in 1231 to search out and prosecute suspected heretics; staffed largely by members of the DOMINICAN and FRANCISCAN orders. The Spanish Inquisition was in some measure a distinct organism, established in 1479 by the Spanish monarchs and subject to their control.

F. OAKLEY

'ĪSĀ ē sä (I—Arab.; Gr. *Iesus*—Jesus). *See* PEOPLE OF THE BOOK.

ISÉ SHRINE ē′ sā (Sh—Jap.). The shrine of the imperial ancestress AMATERASU (the Sun Goddess), regarded as the most sacred shrine compound in Japan. In Japan the shrine is called *Ise no Jingū*. The pre–World War II term, *Ise Daijingū*, is usually translated as the "Grand Shrine of Isé." This is the only shrine to have the rank of *Daijingū*.

In mythological accounts, the imperial family was directly descended from Amaterasu; therefore the emperor was considered a kind of manifest KAMI (divinity), and in the earliest times Amaterasu was worshiped within the imperial palace. But according to the eighth century chronicle NIHON SHOKI Emperor

The main sanctuary of the Isé Shrine from the northwest

Sūjin (traditional reign dates 97-30 B.C.) feared the power of Amaterasu and another goddess, Toyouke Ōmikami, also enshrined in the palace, and had them entrusted to a princess for worship in another village. However, the next emperor, Suinin (traditional reign dates 29 B.C.—A.D. 70) entrusted the worship of Amaterasu to another princess, who sought out an ideal place for a shrine; Amaterasu instructed her that Isé was the place she wished to be enshrined, and the Nihon Shoki records that this is where Amaterasu first descended from heaven. From that time the Grand Shrine of Isé has grown into the largest and most revered of all SHINTŌ shrines.

The Isé Shrine is situated in the contemporary Mie Prefecture, within the Shima Peninsula of Honshū. The vast shrine compound by the Isuzu River amid evergreen woods is of great natural beauty itself; added to this is the distinctive architecture of Isé, with unpainted wood buildings on raised pillars and covered with thatched roofs. The design may hark back to South Pacific antecedents, but contemporary international architects have praised the simplicity of lines and natural elegance of these buildings as being some of the best ever produced in Japan. Among the many shrines within the compound the most important is the *Naikū* (lit. "inner shrine"), where Amaterasu is enshrined, and the *Gekū* (lit. "outer shrine"), where Toyouke Ōmikami is enshrined.

Traditionally imperial princesses were entrusted with supervision of worship at the Isé Shrine, but the emperor also participated periodically as a kind of chief priest of the imperial family and indirectly of the Japanese nation.

In medieval times veneration for the Isé Shrine was expressed in popular pilgrimages to the site, and protective talismans and almanacs were distributed to the people. One of the distinctive rites of the Isé Shrine is the rebuilding of the main sanctuary, which formally should take place every twenty years. The old shrine is dismantled, and the new shrine is built at an alternate site. The first site is then used again for the next rebuilding. The considerable cost involved in this rebuilding was in prewar times subsidized in part with state funds (supplementing individual donations). After 1945, when separation of state and religion was enacted, the state was not allowed to contribute money. There has been a continuing debate about the status of the Isé Shrine, whether it is part of the imperial family's religious tradition and therefore the personal prerogative of the emperor, or a national tradition serving the state and entitled to state funds. Although the matter has not been settled, the emperor still pays visits to the Isé Shrine, and some politicians have resumed the prewar practice of making important announcements there.

H. B. Earhart

ISLAM ĭs läm′ (Arab.; lit. "surrender"). A religious polity of global scope, embracing some eight hundred million adherents, chiefly in Africa and Asia (*see* Umma). To understand all aspects of Islam, both historical and contemporary, demands an approach that is at once interdisciplinary and multicultural. Ethnic, linguistic, economic, and military factors, however, will be less emphasized here than the social, literary, and religious factors that have shaped Islamic culture from its beginnings.

1. Theological overview
2. Historical overview
3. The early period (to A.D. 750)
   a. The Arabian setting
   b. The life of Muhammad
   c. Muhammad's earliest successors
   d. The Umayyads
   e. Developments in Muslim thought
4. The middle period (750-1500)
   a. New developments
   b. The rise of the Shi'ites
   c. Regional dynasties
   d. The Mongol conquests
   e. The rise of the schools of law
   f. Theology and mysticism
5. The modern period (1500 to the present)
   a. The great Muslim dynasties
   b. The decline of the Muslim empires
   c. Modern forces of change

Bibliography

F. M. Denny

Boy reciting the Qur'ān

1. **Theological overview.** In its religious structure Islam is both ethnic and confessional. Because it had its beginnings in the Arabian Peninsula and has always retained a decisive Arab component, Islam is an ethnic religion, comparable to Judaism and Hinduism, which also espouse a universal teaching but channel it through one restricted group of people. The Islamic accent on Arab tribal origins is comparable to the Jewish emphasis on the twelve tribes of Israel or the Hindu elevation of the four Aryan Castes to a quasi-divine status. Important in each case are ascriptive identity markings, characteristic of numerous other primitive societies with a strongly territorial and tribal outlook.

For Islam, Arabic has become even more sacrosanct in its canonical form than Hebrew for Jews or Sanskrit for Hindus, since it is the language of the Qur'ān, the scripture which sets forth a series of divine revelations given to the prophet Muhammad through an angel during the latter part of his life, *ca.* A.D. 610 to 632. Though it might seem obvious that God would choose Arabic to communicate with an Arab prophet, the choice of Arabic has meaning for all Muslims, even non-Arabs. For it was not merely the content of the Qur'ān, but its expression in Arabic that embodied the full measure of divine revelation. Muslims have never sanctioned the translation of the Qur'ān into a language other than Arabic; it can be "interpreted" or "paraphrased," as it has been in countless Oriental and Western languages, including English, but the Qur'ān can never be authentically translated. Instead, the "Arabicity of the Qur'ān" remains a doctrine in Islam, reinforcing the ethnic Arab character of the core of Muslim belief and ritual.

Yet Islam is also a confessional religion, less similar to Judaism or Hinduism than to BUDDHISM and CHRISTIANITY, both of which are universal not only in doctrine (as are Judaism and Hinduism) but also in missionary outreach. As a missionary faith, Islam encourages converts because the absolute truth it espouses can theoretically be recognized and embraced by any perceptive human being. The creed of Islam (SHAHĀDA) is as simple as the Christian affirmation of the TRINITY or the Buddhist testimony to the TRIRATNA (Three Jewels). To become a Muslim one has only to declare in sincerity, and preferably in the presence of a person already professing Islam, "I testify that there is no god but God, and that Muhammad is the Prophet of God." The first part of this creed presupposes a cosmology that includes an invisible as well as a visible world. The invisible world may be called heaven or hell (*see* ESCHATOLOGY §3), just as this world is called earth, and creatures, whether angels (*see* MALĀ'IKA) or demons (*see* JINN), inhabit that world, in the same way that humans and other animal life populate this one. The cosmology also postulates that a purposeful force has created both worlds, that it governs, guides and ultimately judges them as well. Because that force is all-powerful rather than competitive with others or compromised by their existence, it is singular (God; *see* ALLAH) not plural (gods). In effect, the first part of the Muslim creed is a dialectically rigorous rejection of polytheism in favor of monotheism. It underlies the pivotal Muslim doctrine of divine unity (TAWḤĪD), and has historical antecedents in both Judaism and Christianity.

The transcendent oneness which Islam isolates as the root motivating force of the universe is only knowable through human mediaries, men who have been set apart to fill a special function within their community in a given generation. These are the prophets (*see* NABI), and the second part of the Muslim creed specifies Muhammad as one of their number. He is God's messenger (RASŪL) to the Arabs, as MOSES was to the Jews, JESUS to the Christians, and Zoroaster to the ZOROASTRIANS. Underlying the cosmology of the first part of the creed, which is universalist and acknowledged by all monotheistic faiths, is a concept of prophecy which is particularist and, by demanding recognition of Muhammad as God's prophet, becomes unacceptable to non-Muslims. Though Muhammad disavowed any divine status for himself, opting for a role closer to that of Moses than to that of Jesus, he did function as an anchor tying the monotheism of the Qur'ān to Arab tribes and the Arabic language through his own personal authority as the latest and, in Muslim doctrine, the last of the prophets. The limits of his personal authority became a divisive issue. The majority SUNNIS subordinate his prophetic role to the content of the revelation, while the SHI'ITES extol his role as progenitor of a new spiritual autocracy.

The basic creed becomes the key to seeing how

F. M. Denny

Qur'ān seller's stand, Cairo

Islam functions in both a complementary and adversary relationship to antecedent monotheistic faiths. Like Christianity, it has a kerygmatic or confessional tone, perceiving its message ("there is no god but God") as demanding a response from all peoples in all generations. Like Judaism, it has an indissoluble ethnic focus (of the Arab people, the Arabic language, and, above all, the Arab prophet). None of the teachings of prophets who preceded Muhammad are denied. From Adam and ABRAHAM to Solomon and Jesus, the biblical (and even extrabiblical) prophets are affirmed, many of their actions and utterances being lauded in the pages of the Qur'ān. But since Muhammad, the Arab prophet, is also the last prophet, the revelations communicated through him supersede, even as they mark the culmination of, all earlier SCRIPTURES. The authority of both Jewish and Christian scripture is subordinated to the content of Muslim revelation; the former serve as a theological, not merely a chronological, preamble to Islam.

The social position of Jews and Christians under Muslim rule directly mirrored the theological valuation of their scriptural sources: they were protected but second-class citizens. Contrary to popular belief, they were not faced with the choice of Islam or the sword (*see* JIHĀD). In the abode of Islam (*dār al-Islām*), they were accepted as PEOPLE OF THE BOOK. Though required to pay a steep tax for their

F. M. Denny

Seller of religious objects, Cairo. The leaves are held as a magical defense against the evil of the camera.

rights as citizens, they were permitted to occupy public buildings, perform age-old liturgies, and continue the religious education of their young. Jews, Christians, and Zoroastrians, while considered inferior to Muslims, were nonetheless superior to polytheists and unbelievers.

The requirements of Muslim belief and ritual underscore the ambivalent relationship of Islam to its monotheistic forebears. The *shahāda* is the first of five PILLARS OF ISLAM. It leads naturally into the daily cycle of PRAYER, since it is assumed that whoever acknowledges the one God will pray to him, following the example of Muhammad. The orientation for prayer (QIBLAH) was at first JERUSALEM, a city sacred to Jews and Christians as well as Muslims, but following the rejection of Muhammad's prophetic status by the Jews of MEDINA *ca.* A.D. 622, it was permanently shifted to MECCA. Mecca, and by extension Arabia, has therefore been the geographic focus for the daily devotional life of Muslims since the inception of Islam. Its centrality is supported by a third pillar of Islam: the canonical pilgrimage (HAJJ). Unlike ritual prayer *(ṣalāt),* the hajj is an occasional rather than a daily requirement. Yet it is incumbent on each able-bodied male Muslim to undertake the arduous and often expensive journey to Mecca and Medina at least once during his lifetime. Further differentiating Muslims are the other two pillars, fasting (ṢAWM) and alms-giving (ZAKĀT). Each of these disciplines was observed, and its value acknowledged, by both Jews and Christians before the rise of Islam. One can even trace early Islamic tithing practices to Jewish and Christian antecedents. But the Muslim observance of almsgiving was linked to the particular needs of Muhammad's community, even as the period prescribed for fasting during the month of RAMADAN was legitimated with reference to the calling of Muhammad as the last prophet.

Islam has more in common with Judaism and Christianity than with any other major religious tradition. Yet Islam has charted an independent course, one that emphasizes negligence more than sin as the fundamental human condition and corporate guidance rather than individual salvation as the prescriptive divine intent. The only valid history of Islam, therefore, concerns the shaping and reshaping of the Muslim community.

2. Historical overview. When the record of Islamic peoples is examined, many of even the most comprehensive points have to be qualified with respect to the group, the place, and, above all, the period being discussed. It is extraordinarily delicate and difficult to set forth guidelines about chronology that do not themselves contain a prejudgment about the events described. Unfortunately, the chronology developed by M. G. S. Hodgson *(see bibliog.)* is too minutely refined and too unwieldy to be used here. This article will give equal weight to three periods: 1) the earliest period, from A.D. 610, the time of Muhammad's first revelation, to 750, the fall of the UMAYYAD Caliphate; 2) the middle period, from 750, with the rise of the ʿABBĀSIDS, to 1500, a *terminus ad quem* for the regional diffusion of post-ʿAbbāsid times; and 3) the modern period, from 1500 on, marked by two major developments, (i) the emergence of three mutually competitive yet flexible and enduring Muslim empires, the Ottomans, the Safavids and the Moguls, coupled with (ii) the introduction of mercantile and military forces from Europe, later accelerating into a process of colonialization and westernization, the legacy of which still determines the political profile and social dynamic of most Muslim nations.

Muslim scholars have a tendency, too readily emulated by Western scholars, to focus on biography as the *sine qua non* for assessing major trends and locating pivotal moments in Muslim history. The decisions of major rulers, the battles of major warriors, or the writings of major thinkers are valuable points of documentation in describing the historic past of a civilization which places great stress on temporal achievements and their literary record. Yet it is all too easy to assume that biographical sketches, or dates linked to great men, can fully explain the history of an entity remote in time and purpose for the Christian or Western experience. Despite its diversity, Western civilization shares a common perception of the world and the human role in it. Structures, relationships, and values determine much of our corporate identity. They may be expressed through people but transcend any one person or generation. To offset a personalist bias in our understanding of Islamic society, the second part of this article will focus on some recurrent themes of Muslim religious life, especially tensions or paradoxes, that elucidate the distinctive character of Islam in a way that biographical sketches cannot.

3. **The early period** (to A.D. 750). *a) The Arabian setting.* Contrary to widespread belief, the Arabian Peninsula in the late sixth and early seventh centuries A.D. was not an unsophisticated cultural backwater, but was in contact with the surrounding Byzantine, Sasanian, and Abyssinian empires. Commerce within and beyond the peninsula played a decisive role in the structure of urban society and the practice of religion. Muhammad himself was married to a rich widow whose business he successfully managed prior to his call to prophesy. Merchants visiting Mecca sought the blessings of the idols in the KA'BA shrine, whose revenue was managed by prosperous Meccan families. The conflicts of the nomadic tribes of interior Arabia were not simply internecine and localized feuds; several decades before Muhammad two frontier confederations of South Arabian origin, the Ghasanids and the Lakhmids, had become vassals or client states in North Arabia of the Byzantines and Sasanians, respectively. Throughout the sixth century the two groups contended with each other, and this protracted rivalry formed a bridge between interior Arabia and the adjacent powers.

Moreover, the religion of pre-Islamic Arabia was varied and reflected external influence. The beliefs and rituals of the pagan Arabs are scarcely known from any literary source except heavily biased Islamic chronicles or tribal odes compiled during the Muslim era. This period, referred to as *jāhiliyya* (TIME OF IGNORANCE), in contrast to the full light of Qur'ānic revelation, may have produced religious dispositions no more profound than "elementary polydaemonism, with elements of fetishism and animalism," as F. Gabrieli has conjectured, but the pre-Islamic pagan Arabs could not have remained unaffected by the sizable Jewish and Christian communities in their midst. Jews, for instance, had migrated to Arabia at the beginning of the DIASPORA; their presence in the urban and oasis settlements of Yemen and the HEJAZ is well attested from numerous Qur'ānic passages. Christians, coming as NESTORIAN and MONOPHYSITE missionaries, seeking a haven from the long arm of Roman orthodoxy, penetrated even the interior spaces of the Arabian desert, converting tribal confederations such as the Ghasanids and Lakhmids, together with numerous smaller tribes. Symbols of an active, proselytizing Christian presence, e.g., the solitary hermit, are evident in Arab poetry of the *jāhiliyya* period.

Clearly, Arabia before the rise of Islam was exposed to monotheism as well as to tribal polytheism. It was the singular genius of Muhammad to understand the currents of thought and the social realities of his time, preponderantly tribal and animistic, before mobilizing alliances and interests under a consistent yet flexible monotheism. The prophet of Islam was a statesman and administrator with the same zeal, skill, and ultimate success that he demonstrated as a prophet and charismatic preacher. If the situation was ripe for the man, the man made the most of the situation.

b) The life of Muhammad. The rise of Muhammad ibn 'Abdallah was marked with peril and near failure at every turn. He was orphaned soon after his birth (*ca.* A.D. 570) and adopted into a minor branch of the Quraish tribe of Mecca. His uncle, ABŪ ṬĀLIB, reared him in dire poverty. How he first joined the commercial ventures emanating from his native city is not clear, but he profited from association with, and later marriage to, a rich widow named KHADĪJA. At the age of forty, after many intervals of protracted meditation in caves near Mecca, Muhammad felt compelled to proclaim the absolute unity of God and to denounce idolatry, including the profitable rituals at the Ka'ba shrine of Mecca. Initially his appeal met with only a lukewarm response. As local opposition to his preaching increased, he sought an opportunity to move elsewhere. Five years after his first revelation, he sent some of his followers to Ethiopia, allegedly for their own safety but perhaps also to prepare for his own migration there. In 622, however, some disputing groups in Yathrib (later renamed Medina) requested Muhammad to adjudicate their rival property claims. Almost killed by the Meccans before he escaped and made his way to Medina (*see* HIJRA), Muhammad gradually gathered a loyal constituency at Medina. He averted near catastrophes on the battlefield, where his former townsmen, in alliance with client tribes, sought to destroy him. By 630 he was able to return to Mecca as the victorious leader of a new religio-political movement. At the time of his death two years later, Islam had extended its authority over much of the peninsula, largely through pacts of personal loyalty sworn by tribal leaders to Muhammad.

At the core of this extraordinary transition from a tribal to a confessional polity was the dictation, in an intermittent sequence, of divine directives to Muhammad, the Qur'ān, establishing day-to-day policies as well as providing long-term ethical, legal, and doctrinal patterns for the community of his followers.

c) Muhammad's earliest successors. When Muhammad died in 632, he had appointed no one to succeed him as leader of the Muslim community. Despite numerous marriages, he had fathered no son who reached maturity. Islam might have dissolved except for the line of able successors (*see* CALPIH) who were elected by Muhammad's companions (*see* ṢAHĀBA) to fill his role as religious and political leader of the nascent Muslim community. Four Meccans—ABŪ BAKR, 'UMAR, 'UTHMĀN, and ALI—ruled for nearly thirty years, from 632 to 661, and have become known as the patriarchal or righteous caliphs (*rashīdūn*). During their rule, fraught though it was with tensions, conflicts, and recurrent acts of violence, even against the caliphs themselves (three of them were assassinated), Arab armies, fighting under the banner of Islam, conquered a vast, diverse geographic area extending from North Africa to the frontier of India. Whether the first wave of Islamic expansion is seen as the result of a fervent, universalist, proselytizing religious movement, or as a military conquest fueled by economic needs and political ambitions, the scope of the conquest itself must be kept in mind. The area conquered during the first decades of Islam was equal in size to the Arabian peninsula, itself larger than the portion of the United States east of the Mississippi River. Within a generation after the Prophet's death, Muslim armies had come to control an area at least as large as the continental United States minus California. This expanse included the former territories of two major civilizations, the Byzantine and the Sasanian. No amount of analysis can explain that phenomenal achievement; it stuns the mind and stands as one of the most enduring accomplishments of Islam.

A further aspect of the initial Islamic expansion deserves special attention. Not only was it achieved through a series of land assaults by bedouin tribesmen, but it was dependent on the governmental apparatus of the Sasanians far more than that of the Byzantines or any other non-Arab group. With the collapse of Sasanian power after the critical battle of Nihawand (642), Muslim Arabs obtained a base of operations in portions of present-day Iran and Iraq from which they were able to extend their rule over much of the Middle East. The emerging profile of the new Islamic polity was Persian as well as Arab, and the continuous cross-fertilization of the two traditions—in society and culture as well as religion—was such that Hodgson opted to describe the entire region from the Nile to the Oxus rivers as characteristically Irano-Semitic. The interaction of the two cultures began with the initial Muslim conquests, when the traditions as well as the territories of the Sasanian Empire were grafted into *dār al-Islām*. For this reason it is often difficult to separate Arab and non-Arab elements in Islamic civilization. For instance, tribesmen from several parts of Arabia migrated northward from the mid-seventh century A.D., joining the victorious armies and settling in the former Sasanian lands. But the pre-Islamic inhabitants of these lands, usually known as *mawālī* or clients if they converted to Islam, often became Arabicized by linking themselves to one of the Arab tribes. They also learned Arabic and adopted Arab customs, while suppressing other, non-Arab, values. Yet the Arabs did not regard the *mawālī* as full partners in the Islamic enterprise; that cleavage between Islam as a universalist tradition and Arab tribalism as an ethnically determined system persisted through the early period (up to 750), and has remained a source of tension, with fluctuating intensity, through the entire span of Islamic history.

It would be natural to assume that in the early period the Arabs as Muslims would have welcomed the *mawālī* as equal partners in *dār al-Islām*. They did not. The Arabs, though Muslims, were still Arabs, and their re-ranking as Arabs was effected in detail by the second caliph, 'Umar (634-644), in a *dīvān*, or register, he compiled for determining booty distribution after each conquest.

By its comprehensive and precise character the *dīvān* assured the ascendancy of Arabism in the new Islamic polity. The social, and also the ritual, scale was hierarchically, centrally Arab. Moreover, the corporate structure of the Islamic *umma* remained dependent on allegiance to the person at its head. 'Umar made many remarkable decisions that determined the subsequent course of Islamic history. He affirmed the corporate nature of the nascent Muslim community by adding the title "commander of the faithful" to the title "successor" adopted by Abū Bakr (632-634). He also changed the dating system so that years were counted from the date of Muhammad's emigration (hijra) from Mecca to Medina in 622. This calendar was computed on a lunar rather than solar cycle, in effect countervening agricultural seasons while stressing the timeless quality of Islamic ritual observances.

'Umar's personal zeal for modest dress and strict piety qualified him as an exemplar of the Muslim ideals he wished to propagate as head of state. He may have transcended Arab tribalism but he did not disavow it; he recast the nature of Arab loyalties without eliminating them.

At 'Umar's death in 644, a group of senior Companions to the Prophet elected a third Meccan, 'Uthmān Ibn 'Affān, to be his successor and the leader of the Muslim community. He proved a skilled military tactician and a forthright administrator, but he had two shortcomings, one distinctly Muslim, the other distinctly Arab: 1) though a father-in-law to Muhammad, he was from a group of Meccans who were late in accepting Muhammad's prophetic mission; and 2) he did not act to avenge the death of the man who murdered his predecessor. After 'Umar had been killed, 'Umar's son had taken the law into his own hands by killing the accused, a Persian general. A group of the Prophet's companions, including his cousin and son-in-law Ali, had demanded revenge against 'Umar's son, but 'Uthmān did not accede to their request and so alienated them.

Throughout the twelve years of 'Uthmān's reign, the party of Ali grew as a focal point for discontent, and groups within the Arab armies of Iraq and Egypt saw Ali as a symbol for the redress of grievances they harbored against 'Uthmān and his principal advisers, most of whom, like the caliph himself, came from the wealthy patrician families of Mecca which, in contrast to the loyal "helper" families of Medina (*see* ANṢĀR), had not supported Muhammad until 630, when he returned victorious to Mecca.

In 656 'Uthmān was murdered by Egyptian dissidents. Ali was acknowledged by most Medinans and many Meccans as the next caliph. Ali, too, had his detractors, however, among whom was Muhammad's favorite wife, 'Ā'ISHA. He made Kūfa, the provincial capital of lower Iraq, his capital, and successfully established caliphal rule from there. But the governor of Syria, Mu'āwiya, never acknowledged Ali's claim to the caliphate, and was calling for revenge on behalf of the murdered 'Uthmān, his cousin. By 657 a large-scale encounter between Mu'āwiya and the followers of Ali took place at Siffin. Ali was on the verge of defeating Mu'āwiya's forces when he was lured into accepting arbitration. Some of Ali's soldiers, becoming angered at this, deserted his standard and formed a separatist movement known as the KHĀRIJITES. The results of arbitration went against Ali, who rejected them and took to the battlefield again, seeking to pummel Mu'āwiya into acceptance of his caliphate. But Mu'āwiya had gained ground among those Arabs who took sides (many Muslims remained neutral). In 661, before a decisive battle could be fought, Ali was murdered by a Khārijite zealot.

d) The Umayyads. Mu'āwiya was subsequently acclaimed caliph in all the provinces of *dār al-Islām,* reigning in that capacity from 661 to 680 and beginning the second, or Umayyad, dynasty. Ali's influence nonetheless persisted and even increased after his death. The group which had supported him and his family in Kūfa continued to resent and to resist Umayyad power, which was based in a rival province, Syria, and in a lesser branch of Muhammad's family (Mu'āwiya could only claim to be a brother-in-law of the Prophet, and had no significant role in the formative period of Islam). This group, known as the *shī'at al 'Ali,* or the party of Ali, became the precursors of that dissenting body of Muslims known as the SHI'A or Shi'ites. While it represented the tensions of an intra-Arab dynastic struggle, it also extended to the *mawālī,* non-Arab Muslims, many of whom resented their continued exclusion from the top administrative posts of the empire under the Umayyads. The anti-Umayyad uprising of al-Mukhtar in Kūfa (685-687), for instance, was aided by the participation of disgruntled *mawālī,* and it was from this time on, according to Watt, that Shi'ism was linked with the political grievances and aspirations of non-Arab Muslims. At the same time, the defeat of Ali and his murder by another Muslim became a symbolic event underscoring the power of Arab factionalism within Islam. The tension between the role of the caliph as leader of the whole Muslim community and as a member of a particular tribal or regional group conflicting with other tribal or regional groups within Islam was never resolved.

Mu'āwiya was probably a much more fair-minded advocate of Islamic unity than subsequent histories (much of them anti-Umayyad) have suggested. But his son and successor, Yazīd (680-683), was unable to control the numerous forces which had to be shrewdly balanced to govern the still expanding *dār al-Islām.* In establishing his rule, Yazīd had to put down a rebellion by Medinan Muslim families who had encouraged ḤUSAYN, Ali's younger son and Muhammad's grandson (through Ali's wife, FĀṬIMA), to lay claim to the caliphate. Ḥusayn, with a small band of his followers, was killed at KARBALA in 680, an event which, like the earlier death of Ali, became memorialized in Shi'ite circles by its annual recitation and reenactment.

At the death of Yazīd there was no worthy successor in his immediate family, and it was only after a further period of disturbance, which included the occupancy of the caliphate by a non-Umayyad, that a second cousin of Mu'āwiya, 'Abd al-Malik (692-705), took office. 'Abd al-Malik has been justly acclaimed as the third most notable and influential sovereign of the early Muslim *umma* (after 'Umar and Mu'āwiya). He established his rule and that of his successors on the principle of *jamā'a,* or Muslim group solidarity, over against Arab tribal factionalism. Yet he faced a dilemma which was not resolved until after the fall of his dynasty: beyond the ideals expounded in the Qur'ān, the text of which had been fixed from the reign of 'Uthmān, there was no adequate basis for defining and applying Islamic solidarity apart from Arab customs, some of which presupposed and were even consciously modeled on age-old Arab tribal conflicts.

e) Developments in Muslim thought. There were legal, ascetic, and philosophical movements at work in later Umayyad times. None of them, however, adequately interpreted the nature of Islamic corporate identity. The creed of Abū Ḥanīfa (d. 767), ascribed to this period, does emphasize the importance of knowing God and publicly professing faith in him, but it was probably not widely accepted before 750 (*see* HANAFITES). What had to emerge to provide a genuine basis for solidarity was a scriptural authority complementary to the Qur'ān but more specific in detail, avowedly Arab in content yet also Islamic in tone. This norm began to emerge only toward the end of the Umayyad dynasty from among that group of pious Muslims known as Qur'ān reciters (*see* TAJWĪD). Trained to intone the scriptural core of Islamic faith on ritual, public occasions, they also circulated among themselves reports about what the Prophet and his companions had said or done that would be relevant for those attempting to lead a fully pious Islamic life. Such reports (*see* ḤADĪTH), each with a text and a verifiable line of transmitters, became the basis for constructing the biography of Muhammad. Some provided background detail for the occasions on which passages in the Qur'ān had been revealed to him; others described the Prophet's reaction to skirmishes and battles in which he had participated. *Ḥadīth* were, therefore, supplementary to the Qur'ān in detail and complementary to it in authority. Yet they were not immediately evaluated, arranged, and compiled as independent books of particular importance for Islamic jurisprudence (FIQH). By 750, their potential for defining Muslim corporate and private modes of conduct was still unrealized. Extraordinary fluidity in range of material and scope of interpretation continued to characterize legal, doctrinal, ascetic, and philosophical issues to the end of the Umayyad period.

4. The middle period (750-1500). *a) New developments.* The second major phase of Islamic history begins with the fall of the Umayyad caliphate and the ascendancy of the 'Abbāsids. Yet 750 portends a change in the nature of the Islamic community that goes far beyond chronological shifts or dynastic turnovers. The locus of power remained in the cities of the Fertile Crescent, but while the Umayyad capital had been Damascus in Syria, the 'Abbāsids chose a new site near the former Sasanian capital of Ctesiphon in lower Iraq, and constructed on the banks of the Tigris a magnificent urban complex which they named Baghdad. With the shift from Damascus to Baghdad Islam's center of gravity moved perceptibly eastward, to the edges of the former Sasanian Empire. Persians came to have an increasingly important role in administrative and military functions, and influence on the social and literary styles of the 'Abbāsid capital. Beginning in the early ninth century, Turks were also brought to Baghdad as trained bodyguards, auguring the *mamlūk* or slave soldiery who later became powerful regional rulers in the dynasties of Egypt (1250-1517) and India (1205-1526).

The basic nature of the caliphate also changed, as the capital and other urban courts became ethnically pluralistic and the authority of the caliph tended to be absolutized. An ascending hierarchy of functionaries served at his will alone. The caliph ceased to be first among equals, as had been the case, at least in theory, during earlier periods. Under the 'Abbāsids caliphal succession became an increasingly bitter struggle, with the spoils of a wealthy imperial court going to the winners. Extravagant patronage became the most obvious demonstration of the caliph's authority; each 'Abbāsid tried to exceed his predecessor in the dazzling splendors—both architectural and literary—which he produced in Baghdad. Hārūn ar-Rashīd (reigned 786-809) stands out for the profusion of litterateurs, grammarians, prosodists, and translators whom he sponsored, and his son and eventual successor, Ma'mūn (reigned 813-833), showed keen interest in having scientific and philosophical texts rendered from Greek and Syraic into Arabic.

Among those who had been excluded from power under the Umayyads and who worked diligently for the transition from Umayyad to 'Abbāsid rule were the *mawālī*, *dhimmis* and Shi'ites. The first group, consisting of non-Arab Muslims, became less intent on connecting themselves with Arab tribal names and were publicly accorded fairer treatment under the 'Abbāsids. The danger in their new freedom, however, is illustrated by the Barmakids, a Persian family of Central Asian Buddhist stock, who rose to the top of the 'Abbāsid bureaucracy under Hārūn ar-Rashīd, only to arouse the jealousy and suspicion of the caliph. All their prominent males were executed or imprisoned. *Dhimmis,* or protected people, on the other hand, continued to enjoy general favor, in part because their major festivals still reflected the seasonal fluctuation abandoned in Islam since the lunar calendar was introduced by 'Umar. In the major cities *dhimmis* retained or could acquire positions of leadership; in the villages they tended to be deprived of leadership roles. Actual circumstances varied enormously from region to region. The Christian Coptic Church in Egypt, Zoroastrians in Iran, Jews in the commercial centers of the Maghrib and Andalusia—all existed throughout the middle period, and make it difficult to generalize about the "protected people" of medieval Islam. Their status was secondary to that of Muslims but their lives were not devoid of religious freedom or occupational opportunity.

b) The rise of the Shi'ites. The Shi'ites were not content with secondary status. Because they were Muslims and linked to the purest Islamic stock, i.e., the Prophet's family, they considered themselves the natural elite. Unable to realize their objective of political leadership under the early 'Abbāsids they became a dissident community, undeniably legitimate but creedally fragmented. Their common strength was loyalty to the memory of two dead heroes: the fourth caliph, Ali, and his son Ḥusayn. In the register of 'Umar it is already evident that the wives and family of Muhammad were to be accorded special respect by other Muslims. Even those Muslims who had opposed Ali or were neutral during his struggle with Mu'āwiya were inclined to esteem him. He was related to the Prophet both by blood and by marriage; many *ḥadīth* stressed the close personal relationship between Ali and Muhammad; and he was the father of Ḥusayn, Muhammad's ill-fated grandson. (The Prophet's only other grandson, Ḥusayn's older brother, Ḥasan, was also murdered, but because he had already compromised himself with the hated Mu'āwiya, his significance for Shi'ites has always been minor in comparison to that of Ḥusayn.) From an early date, those who favored Ali equated his death and Ḥusayn's with the death of early martyrs (*see* Shahīd) who had been killed on the battlefield fighting to defend or to extend the borders of the Islamic empire. They were entitled to immediate access to the divine presence, without the waiting interval before Judgment Day that faced ordinary believers at death. Special ritual significance was attached to the occasion of Ali's death, and even more to the tenth of Muḥarram, the anniversary of Ḥusayn's death, which has become the peak day on the Shi'ite liturgical calendar, marked especially at the Iraqi pilgrimage sites of Najaf (Ali's tomb) and Karbala (Ḥusayn's shrine) but also at other devotional centers throughout the Islamic world where there are Shi'ites (*see* Mashhad, Ziyāra). Theologically, Ali, together with all his descendants through Ḥusayn, was reputed to have a special proximity to God, and to be blessed with a knowledge of him unavailable to others (*see* SAYYID).

The consequences of such ascriptive loyalty, cumulatively nurtured by those lacking in political power but certain of their right to its exercise, are evident. The first three successors to Muhammad were impugned or reviled. The worst of the three, of course, was 'Uthmān, the first Umayyad ruler. He, along with all the Umayyad caliphs, was roundly condemned. In time criticism extended to the first two patriarchal caliphs, Abū Bakr and 'Umar, since, according to the Shi'ites, they, like 'Uthmān, had usurped the role reserved for Ali alone. One might say in retrospect that the entire line of reasoning applied by Ali's followers to the early period of Islamic history (with consequences for both the middle and the modern periods) had its genesis in Muhammad's fateful failure to appoint a successor openly acknowledged by the senior members of his community, including his relatives.

Politically, the consequences of Shi'ite belief were twofold: 1) perpetual hostility to all existing forms of government and 2) constant vigilance for a descendant of Ali, who might be advocated as caliph. During the eighth and ninth centuries the Shi'ite community split into two branches, both professing absolute loyalty to a succession of IMAMS, inspired descendants of Ali through Ḥusayn. They differed in the number of imams succeeding Ali. The smaller group, the Seveners, stopped the line of succession at the seventh imam, Ismā'īl (*see* ISMĀ'ĪLIYYA). The dominant group, the Twelvers (*see* IMĀMIYYA), continued the line of imams as far as the twelfth, Muhammad al-Mahdī. Both groups, as well as other Shi'ite sects (e.g., *see* ZAYDIYYA), held that the last in the line of imams did not die but went into hiding. All governments, including the SUNNI caliphate, will topple at the apocalyptic moment when, by divine design, the hidden imam will come out of hiding, reveal his true identity as the MAHDI or "guided one," and restore Islam to its pristine purity.

The political explosiveness of Shi'ite messianism was revealed during the early 'Abbāsid period. At the accession of the caliph Manṣūr (754-775), a group of Shi'ites backed a relative of Ali's older son, Ḥasan, as caliph. They rallied dissident forces on his behalf in the religious heartland of Arabia, the Hejaz. The Umayyads defeated this coalition, but Shi'ism continued to evolve more and more fantastic end-of-the-world schemes that reached a kind of mythical completeness by the end of the ninth century. In the tenth century a Sevener Shi'ite group, the FATIMIDS, succeeded in gaining power in Egypt, and ruled there from 969 to 1171. In the same period, though for a shorter time (945-1031), a group of Twelver Shi'ites known as the Buyids exercised effective political control in Baghdad while retaining the nominal Sunni caliph.

c) Regional dynasties. The Buyids and Fatimids were only two of numerous regional dynastic elites that appeared from the mid-tenth century on. Among others were the Arab Hamdānids of Syria, the rump Umayyad Caliphate of Andalusia (Muslim Spain), and the Persian Samānids of Transoxiana. Three Turkish absolutist dynasties, the Ghaznavids, the Karakhānids, and the Seljuks, vied with one another and the Samānids for control of Transoxiana, Khurasan, and Western Iran, with the Seljuks ultimately dominating. These regional dynasts reduced the authority of the 'Abbāsid caliph in Baghdad. The Shi'ite influence, represented by the Buyids and Fatimids, had reached its zenith by the end of the eleventh century, and with the ascendancy of the Seljuk Turks in the early twelfth century the central Islamic lands returned to the fold of Sunni loyalism. The Seljuks themselves, however, soon divided into independent principalities, further diffusing political power in the Fertile Crescent. Thus the CRUSADERS were confronted not by the Seljuks but by the Ayyūbid Egyptians under Saladin (d. 1193) and his successors.

d) The Mongol conquests. The major question of the middle period, still unanswered and perhaps unanswerable, is that of the influence upon Islam of the vast destruction wrought by the Mongol hordes beginning in the early thirteenth century and continuing for the next century and a half. In rapidity and scope of territorial conquest the Mongol eruptions resembled the early expansion of Islam. However, there were two initial, and finally determinative, differences between the two groups. The Arabs had a universalist ethos which they sought, however imperfectly, to transplant in conquered lands; the Mongols reigned through the terror of nomadic tribal power. The Arabs were attracted to city life and trade; the Mongols, at least at first, hated both. In time, the Mongols did learn to patronize the arts and sciences in mercantile urban centers. They rebuilt destroyed cities or, as in the case of Samarkand, founded new ones. They encouraged agriculture, commerce, and scholarship on an unprecedented scale. Indeed, the Mongols, though military absolutists, marshaled agrarian resources to sustain a court life of such brilliance that all Islam benefited from the nomad-urban symbiosis which they forged.

e) The rise of the schools of law. The genesis of the Islam inherited, transmitted, and elaborated by the Mongols lay in juridical developments of the early 'Abbāsid period. The critical, recurrent issue, still unresolved at the end of the Umayyad dynasty, had been to define the Islamic community *(umma)* and its solidarity. Scholars of the eighth and ninth centuries had realized that the community could only be based on the directives of the Qur'ān supplemented by sayings of the Prophet and then applied to the lives of believers. The system they evolved set forth a tacit as well as an explicit code of behavior; comprehensive yet elastic, it became the law (*see* SHARIA). Within this framework advocates of Islamic mysticism (*see* SUFISM) and theology (*see* KALĀM) later expounded their interpretations of normative thought, belief, and action. "Without the *sharia* there is no Islam," according to a popular dictum. Islam has sometimes been viewed as a community of people bound together by their common acceptance of, and adherence to, minute legal prescriptions. The precepts of Islam had always been based on Qur'ānic passages and the *sunna*, or conduct of Muhammad, that was to serve as an example. But from the mid-eighth century on, they, together with all aspects of the *sharia*, were particularized with further reference to the consensus (IJMĀ') of a particular group of Muslim scholars or the independent decision *(ijtihād)* of a single jurist. Scholars, jurists, and other legal functionaries came to comprise a class known as the 'ULAMĀ'. They were the guardians of the *sharia*, but how they applied its provisions depended on the nature of decisions which had been rendered within the school of law of which they were the custodial agents.

When a question arose concerning the *ḥadīth*, the MUJTAHID served as the investigating judge, and on the basis of his enquiry a subordinate judge *(faqīh)* would weigh the applicability of the ruling to the ordinary Muslim. The *faqīh* could consult his colleagues in order to reach a consensus of opinion on the matter, and this opinion became part of the *sharia*. A MUFTI, or advisory judge, could then deliver to a petitioner a legal decree on the matter, but it was the *qadi*, or court judge, who decided whether or not to assess a penalty for failure to conform to that part of the *sharia*. From early 'Abbāsid times, the *qadi* was a useful officer of the state, though his politicization raised a new and persistent problem. What if the wishes of the caliph or local Muslim ruler clashed with the most honorable and accurate reading of the law?

That problem was never solved, and the emergence of four overlapping but distinct schools of law further indicates how the *sharia* became an extension of geopolitical interests. The HANAFITE school, originating from Abū Ḥanīfa, became accepted in Turkey, the Fertile Crescent, Afghanistan, and the Asian subcontinent. The Malikites, named after MALIK IBN ANAS (d. 795), were dominant in Upper Egypt, the Maghrib, and much of western Africa, while the Shāfi'ites, followers of the most systematic and influential theorist, AL-SHĀFI'Ī (d. 820), extended their sway over northern Egypt, eastern Africa, southern Arabia, and the Asian archipelago. The Hanbalite school, by far the most extreme in its precepts, was the most limited in its geographical scope. Deriving from the deeply pious, fervently ascetical *ḥadīth*-collector, Aḥmad IBN ḤANBAL (d. 855), it achieved dominance only in parts of the Arabian Peninsula and isolated pockets of the Fertile Crescent.

After the endeavors of these pioneering jurists, the *ḥadīth* were compiled into numerous books, of which six became especially authoritatve. The efforts of men such as AL-BUKHĀRĪ and MUSLIM IBN AL-ḤAJJĀJ reinforced the legacy of the jurists and made it appear that the *sharia*, through persistent study, could be fully learned and comprehensively applied. *Ḥadīth* became the key to the *sharia*. According to al-Shāfi'ī, *ḥadīth* were necessary to complement but also to interpret the Qur'ān, with the result that Sunni Islam came to rest on a twofold scriptural authority. By the end of the tenth century, the desire for scriptural legitimation, abetted by the rapid growth of sectarian movements, regional dynasties, and philosophical speculations, produced a series of efforts to close the gate of interpretation *(ijtihād)* and to rely on compliance with time-sanctioned models for conduct (*see* SUNNA). The *'ulamā'*, who generally promoted such efforts, were themselves subjected to further institutionalization in the eleventh century when MADRASAS proliferated as the principal institutions for Islamic religious education. The *'ulamā'* staffed the *madrasas*, and there taught both new converts and successive generations of established Muslim families the full array of traditional Islamic sciences. But the *'ulamā'* were not disinterested teachers; they were increasingly manipulated by the military leaders and notables, whether at caliphal or provincial courts, who founded the *madrasas* and funded their staffs. It may be deduced that the concept of an independent Muslim judiciary, to the limited extent that it was ever feasible, died with the phenomenal, rapid growth of the *madrasa* network.

Little room was left for the incorporation of local custom, especially important to Persian and Turkish ethnic groups, who did not become widely Islamized beyond the major cities until the eleventh and twelfth centuries. The *madrasa* curriculum, with the *'ulamā'* as its instructors, underscored Arabization as the bedrock of Islamic identity. Not only was it necessary for a Muslim to learn the Arabic of the Qur'ān and *ḥadīth* (which varied considerably from the colloquial Arabic spoken even in the medieval period), but one had also to identify with the norms of seventh century Arabian society since, as the context for Muhammad's thought, belief, and conduct, they were the ideal for every generation and every segment of Muslim society.

The Shi'ites did not cooperate with, or participate in, this system. They belonged to none of the four schools of law, nor did they accept the Sunni *ḥadīth* as authoritative compilations of Muhammad's dicta. Yet they did develop a parallel structure of community life and religious education, with their own schools of law and *ḥadīth* compendia, and with MULLAHS, rather than the *'ulamā'*, as instructors.

It was, therefore, Islam as expressed in *sharia*, taught in the *madrasa*, defined by jurists, refined by traditionists, and promulgated by the *'ulamā'*, which established a pattern of community consciousness for Sunni Islam that survived up to and beyond the Mongol incursions. Mongol rulers, in fact, helped to freeze the form of Sunni Islam which they adopted, for it was during the fifteenth century, toward the end of the Mongol period, that dynastic law (which had been applied *de facto* in some pre-Mongol Islamic states) became welded to the *sharia*. Not only was the law acknowledged to be a final, unchanging code, but it was to be administered by the exemplary ruler, himself the repository of truth and the authority of last resort. The *'ulamā'*, despite their scholarly credentials, served at the ruler's will and as his functionaries.

f) Theology and mysticism. Yet even before the Mongols succeeded in molding the *sharia* to their own absolutist aims as military monarchs, it had provoked two reactions of wide influence throughout the middle, and into the modern, period of Muslim history. One of these served to elaborate the eternal, logical character of the *sharia;* the other to stress the adaptable, personal, localized aspect of Islam. The first reaction was most evident among elite urban scholars who, having been acquainted with the categories (and often also the writings) of Greek philosophy, engaged in theological discourse *(kalām).* The second reaction occurred among widely different segments of Islamic society, elite as well as nonelite, rural as well as urban, often non-Arab, i.e., Persian and Turkish, Muslims who, after conversion, still retained a strong sense of ethnic, linguistic, and regional identity and hence a preference for local custom *('ādah).* Their aspirations were often channeled through the movement known as SUFISM.

Mysticism, theology, and law in Islam were not mutually exclusive. All three presupposed the *sharia;* they differed in how to interpret and apply its precepts to Muslim society. The task of the theologian was to justify Islam on two fronts: 1) as the fulfillment of monotheistic faith, which was initiated by pre-Islamic prophets from Adam through Jesus, and which culminated in Muhammad, and 2) as the perfect cosmology, ontology, epistemology, completing but also transcending Platonic and Aristotelian categories. The collective endeavors of quasi-rationalists (*see* MU'TAZILA) inspired, then provoked, the first Islamic theologians, ASH'ARĪ (d. 935) and AL-MĀTURĪDĪ (d. 944), both of whom disowned the conclusions of philosophy while using its analytical methods to bolster their own faith claims. Popular philosophical movements, such as the IKHWĀN AL-ṢAFĀ, enjoyed sporadic success, while theological discourse itself aroused suspicion among many of the *'ulamā'*. Even the acclaim of encyclopedic and incisive Muslim philosophers, such as IBN SĪNĀ (d. 1037) and IBN RUSHD (d. 1198), was blunted by the anti-philosophical polemic which prevailed in *madrasa* and *sharia*.

The mystic was not removed from the intricacies of theology and law. Typically theological speculations and juridical pronouncements came from the same person who was also a practitioner of mystical exercises, or at least sympathetic to an interiorized definition of Islamic piety. The usual example of such a multi-disciplinary intellectual and spiritual giant is AL-GHAZZĀLĪ (d. 1111). His contributions to the Islamic society of his day may have been exaggerated for a variety of reasons, not the least of which was his stature as a bilingual (Persian and Arabic) advocate of Sunni Islam in a pluralistic society embracing non-Arabs as well as Arabs. Yet Ghazzālī's fearless quest for the truth was extraordinary by any canon of human judgment.

Because he stands at a pivotal point in Muslim history, Ghazzālī is often credited with initiating two major developments in Islamic mysticism (Sufism). These developments actually reflect changes in Muslim society rather than the direct impact of one man, and they have persisted through the Mongol period into the modern period. One is the elaboration of theoretical or theosophical Sufism in both prose and verse, dramatized by the literary legacy of the Andalusian IBN 'ARABĪ (d. 1240) and the Anatolian JALĀL AD-DĪN RŪMĪ (d. 1273). Another is the emergence of mystical brotherhoods, known as ṬARĪQAS or *silsilas,* which became vehicles both for personalizing Islam and for incorporating local customs into Muslim ritual. The brotherhoods acted as institutional extensions of Sufi theory; their masters, often called SHAIKHS, may or may not have introduced Islam into those regions of the world (such as interior Africa and the Indonesian archipelago) where many Muslim communities ascribe their origins to itinerant saints, and yet the role that Sufi charismatic leaders performed in facilitating the acceptance of Sunni Islam (and the concomitant exclusion or minimalization of Shi'ite Islam) is undeniable.

Sufism also provided a spur to literary activities. Even in the case of a major Persian poet such as ḤĀFIZ (d. 1390), who was not affiliated with a hospice or attached to a shaikh, the imagery of mystical Islam added a heightened tone of ambiguity and allurement to his verse. Many poets, both Persian and Arab, from the middle period of Islamic history were directly linked to and inspired by organized Sufi brotherhoods. Nor did the Mongol devastations bring to an end the literary productivity of medieval Muslim poets. Ḥāfiz, one of the greatest Persian poets, lived during the period of Mongol hegemony. Jāmi (d. 1492) lived in its aftermath, as did the foremost Chagatay (Eastern Turkish) lyricist, 'Ali Shēr Nawā'i (d. 1501). Achievements within other intellectual traditions, especially astronomy and historiography, and the flourishing visual arts (Persian miniatures, splendid gardens, MOSQUES, mausoleums, and palaces) all attest to the enduring vitality of Islamic civilization under the Mongols. (*See* ART AND ARCHITECTURE, ISLAMIC.)

5. The modern period (1500 to the present). This period of Islamic history is shaped in part by the Mongol legacy but even more by the introduction of a new, equally powerful force of destruction and change, European colonialism.

a) The great Muslim dynasties. From the early sixteenth to the early eighteenth century, the Muslim world was dominated by three extensive and powerful military patronage states, all reflecting the peculiarly Mongol marriage of dynastic law to the *sharia*. The Ottomans controlled, in addition to their Anatolian homeland, the Balkans as far as Vienna, most of the Middle East, and the northernmost stretch of Africa, from Egypt to Algeria. The Safavids ruled an area that comprises present-day Iran and a portion of neighboring Afghanistan and Pakistan. The Moguls expanded the Muslim presence in South Asia to include, by the end of the seventeenth century, almost all the Indian subcontinent and the portions of present-day Afghanistan and Pakistan not claimed by the Safavids. Nor were the Ottomans, Safavids, and Moguls the only Muslim dynasties of the later or modern period. A group known as the Özbegs, succeeding the Mongols, exercised almost exclusive control over the Syr-Oxus river basins in Central Asia, while Morocco in the far West and Indonesia in the far East also witnessed the emergence of significant Muslim ruling elites.

Perhaps one of the most remarkable developments of Islam took place in sub-Saharan Africa. Muslim loyalties became established there through a gradual process of cultural penetration that proceeded at different rates in the west, in central Africa, and along the Indian Ocean coast. As early as the eleventh century Islam had been represented in west Africa by foreign Muslim residents. Gradually it had gained local support, until it succeeded in reforming indigenous customs at will. Later, in the eighteenth and nineteenth centuries, strong Muslim states were able to resist the European colonial powers. Along the east coast of Africa, Islam had come to dominate the port cities by as early as the twelfth century. Zanzibar and Mogadishu were initial centers of influence, and the distinctive Swahili culture developed out of the amalgam of diverse populations and languages. In the interior, Muslim societies had been threatened by the Ethiopian Christians, by turbulent nomads, and, beginning in the fifteenth century, by the Portuguese. Early Sufi influences were pervasive; subsequently they were modified by the Wahhābīya and by the development of indigenous cultures. In modern times the sheer demographic growth of African Islam (see Umma) has been astounding. For the remainder of the twentieth century Isalm will clearly continue to evolve as a major religious and cultural force in the savannah belt that extends across the continent between desert and forest.

Yet it is impossible to appreciate the character of twentieth century Islam, in Africa or elsewhere, without an awareness of the nature of the three major sixteenth and seventeenth century empires. Ottomans, Safavids, and Moguls controlled different geographic areas, represented different constituencies, and advanced different creedal emphases, but they were all Muslim and they shared many important features. Each established a court life of stupefying grandeur, impressive even to European travelers. Each patronized art, architecture, literature, miniature painting, and religious institutions on a lavish scale that was never matched by subsequent Muslim rulers. Each state also weathered political and religious dissidence within its borders during the period of ascendancy. In the eighteenth century all three began to decline, though at varying points and with disparate outcomes.

The Ottoman was not only the earliest of the three empires to emerge (in 1299); it also survived the longest (until 1919). It expanded from an obscure thirteenth century kingdom in northwest Anatolia to embrace by 1500 the heartland of the former Byzantine empire and its capital, Constantinople. The height of its glory was attained under Selīm the Grim (ruled 1512-20) and Süleimān the Magnificent (ruled 1520-66). The armies of these sultans conquered Egypt, Syria, Iraq, the coastlands of North Africa and the Red Sea, the island of Rhodes, and the Balkans as far as the Hungarian plain. Twice the Ottomans laid siege to Vienna (1529 and 1683), but they were unable to operate effectively at such a distance from their Anatolian base.

The Ottomans were staunch proponents of Sunni Islam, though theirs was a modified form not fully welcomed by their Arab subjects. It is not surprising, therefore, that the stiffest internal resistance to Ottoman hegemony came from Arabia. Southwest Yemen asserted its independence from Constantinople (Istanbul) in 1635; the Arab rulers of the holy cities, Mecca and Medina, while acknowledging Ottoman suzerainty, were beholden to Cairo rather than Istanbul. The bedouin of interior Arabia maintained their independence throughout the Ottoman period and in the middle of the eighteenth century gave birth to a powerful spiritual movement, which some have compared in force and influence to the rise of Islam itself, the Wahhābīya. The movement's puritanical asceticism became a threat to the Ottoman sultan when the Wahhābīs took control of Mecca and Medina in the early nineteenth century. A swift, punitive action undertaken by Muhammad ʿAli, the Ottoman viceroy in Egypt, broke the power of the Wahhābīs in 1818. Their influence was confined to the interior of Arabia for the next few decades, but they once again erupted in the mid-nineteenth century and again during the first decades of the twentieth. From their origins they were allied with the Saudi royal house and thus have controlled events in post-Ottoman Arabia.

Though their territories were less extensive than the Ottomans, the Safavids were a major force in determining the mood and course of Islam. Not only did they usher in one of the peak periods in Persian culture and spur the development of an almost obsessively bureaucractic state. They also nurtured the first full-scale Muslim polity that espoused Twelver Shiʿism (Imāmiyya). There was a curious irony in this development, which has contemporary parallels. Despite the fact that the imperial government identified with the Shi'ite cause (which necessarily meant stifling expressions of Sunni loyalism among religious functionaries, landed aristocracy, and mystics), its own legitimacy was thrown into question by the fact that institutional Shi'ism, so long an oppositional movement, had developed its own authorities apart from any government. The Shi'ite *'ulamā'* or mullahs claimed that only the most learned and pious among them were fully qualified to interpret the law as mujtahids, because they alone were in touch with the Hidden Imam. The Safavid monarch also claimed to be a spokesman for the Hidden Imam, and during the period of Safavid ascendancy his claim was upheld, at least publicly. With the decline of Safavid fortunes in the seventeenth century, however, the Shi'ite mullahs reasserted their position that the only qualified interpreter of the law, who was also a direct recipient of guidance from the Hidden Imam, was some learned and pious member of their own group, chosen by the entire group to serve as its spokesman. Safavid Shi'ism, therefore, made an inadvertent but essential contribution to the contemporary Iranian spirituality by exalting the Shi'ite concept of Imam and linking it exclusively to a member of the religious classes.

The Mogul empire, like the Safavid, was more restricted in territory and wielded less nearly absolute power than the Ottoman. It did, however, witness a unique blend of Islamic and indigenous values in the person of the greatest Mogul ruler, AKBAR (reigned 1556-1605; *see* ISLAM IN SOUTH ASIA). Too often the syncretistic nature of Akbar's religious beliefs have been stressed, with resulting lack of attention to his strength as an administrative genius and persuasive codifier of dynastic law. In that sense, Akbar is most aptly compared to the foremost Ottoman sultan, Süleimān, and the great Safavid monarch, Shah 'Abbās (1587-1629). It is perhaps because of their creating an enduring legal system that each of these rulers was revered as an exemplary emperor during his lifetime, and subsequently, when their empires began to decline, that their reigns were recalled with greatest nostalgia.

b) The decline of the Muslim empires. The decline of the Ottoman, Safavid, and Mogul empires and the Muslim world in general began in the eighteenth century. This decline cannot be easily or uniformly charted. It is easy to say, as many have, that internal factors, such as prolonged inflation, military conservatism, and political corruption, made the Ottoman downfall inevitable. The blunt fact is that the Ottomans survived a long time, despite their repeated confrontations with an assertive and militarily superior European enemy. The Ottoman navy was destroyed at Lepanto in 1571, their army was decimated at Zenta in 1698, resulting in the Treaty of Karlowitz (1699), and yet they were still fighting and winning wars in the eighteenth century. It was only the Treaty of Kuchuk Kaynarja (1774) which "shattered the Ottoman image of themselves as a vigorous, revitalized, invincible empire" (Lewis, p. 284).

The downfall of the Moguls and Safavids, like that of the Ottomans, can be tied to particular historical events. But in each case downfall was also the result of underlying shifts in the worldwide balance of economic and military power. During the eighteenth and nineteenth centuries the industrial age in Western Europe caused spectacular change in commodity production, communication systems, and military efficiency. Since European production depended on a simultaneous and accelerated acquisition of new customers and sources of raw material, market economies expanded and colonial empires were launched. Commercial necessity, more than political aggrandizement, military chauvinism, or missionary zeal, led to the rapid formation of British, French, Portuguese, Spanish, Italian, and Dutch empires in remote corners of the world. Many of these marketing regions were Islamic. The Dutch, for instance, carved out a sphere of influence in non-Muslim South Africa, as well as in Indonesia, which by this time was Muslim (*see* ISLAM IN SOUTHEAST ASIA). For Islamic peoples the gradual perception of an aggressive, dominating colonial presence in their lands was a threat at several levels. 1) It meant a loss of economic and military power by Muslim ruling elites whose longevity had seemed to reinforce the view that *dār al-Islām* enjoyed worldwide political hegemony. Though they had often been bitter rivals, the Safavids, Moguls, and Ottomans had fought one another as Muslim powers. 2) The rise of Europe augured a weakening of faith in a bedrock tenet of the Muslim world view, that history was the continuous, progressive affirmation of the truth of Islam. The Ottoman historian Naīma relied on the social analyses of a fourteenth century North African, Ibn Khaldūn, to persuade his countrymen that history has an ebb and flow, that the temporary reversals suffered by Ottoman arms would be followed by eventual victory. The eighteenth century North Indian theologian, Shah Wali Allah, interpreted the external decline of Mogul fortunes as an incentive, indeed a catalyst, to the internal toughening of the Muslim spirit both within and beyond India. 3) European colonialism brought a direct confrontation with another universalist missionary faith. The long history of Islamic interaction with Christianity dates back to the Prophet Muhammad, encompasses the early period of Muslim expansion and extends through the Crusades. But in each encounter Islam was victorious. Beginning in the eighteenth century, however, the Christian missionaries who circulated through various parts of the Muslim world in the wake of their commercially minded countrymen represented a superior civilization and polity. The enormity of that challenge was unprecedentd.

c) Modern forces of change. Hodgson, among others, has argued that the resurgence of Europe affected only some elements of traditional Muslim societies, namely, the literate, economically prosperous, militarily dominant, politically powerful elite. These elite, though at first resisting colonialism, later accommodated themselves to it. The bulk of Muslims remained untouched by the European presence in their homelands. Till the end of the nineteenth century major changes in the public sphere were evident only in communications, health care, and education. The twentieth century, however, brought two further technological changes that have affected all Muslims: the discovery and production of oil, a resource vital to European industrial growth, and the development of the airplane and automobile. Added to these has been the unexpected, rapid population growth, due to reduced infant mortality rates and increased life expectancy. Perhaps most important of all the twentieth century European imports, especially for the fragmenting affect it has wrought on the Muslim world view, has been nationalism.

It is an error of most studies on contemporary Islam that they focus on religious responses to the challenge of modernization or westernization. It is important to determine why particular Muslim leaders opt to return to a pure Islam (Qaddafi of Libya, Khomeini of Iran) or to reject their Islamic past in large part (Ataturk of Turkey), or to accommodate Islam to Western technology and institutions (Bourgiba of Tunisia, Sadat of Egypt). But it cannot be ignored that in every case Muslim leaders are coming to terms with Western civilization, science, technology, and power in the guise of the most Western of all institutions, nationalism. Following World War I, there was strong sentiment in support of the pan-Islamic movement, which had particular appeal to Muslim constituencies in certain regions, such as North India, but which had also a universal urgency because it represented a distinctly Muslim resistance to nationalism. By the peace settlement of Versailles and other post–World War I conferences, some Arab kingdoms, such as Saudi Arabia and Yemen, were granted outright independence as national entities, while others, ironically comprising the most sophisticated and culturally advanced Muslim populations of the Middle East—i.e., Palestine, Lebanon, Iraq, Syria, Egypt, and Iran—were carved into spheres of influence under of League of Nations mandates. Ostensibly the British, French, and Spanish mandates were created to protect the rights of the disputing ethnic and religious groups within their purview, but they also allowed the dominant European nations to divide the spoils of the Allied victory. Nationalist movements, some predating World War I, spread throughout the Muslim world as a protest against the colonial presence. Their leaders were the educated and politically powerful urban elite, but they also succeeded in mobilizing the masses to support their cause. Not all were caught up in the tide of nationalism, however, and a few spiritually perceptive, fervently anti-colonial Muslims rallied behind the pan-Islamic movement as the last opportunity to reclaim their own identity under a political structure that was Islamic rather than Western in both inspiration and form. Their endeavors failed. The caliphate, which had been the symbolic focus of the movement, was abolished by the new secular ruler of Turkey, Kemal Ataturk, in 1924. The burr of ZIONISM, the conflict between rival Muslim factions, and the constant reminder of Western political, military, and economic superiority all detracted from the appeal of the pan-Islamic movement. During the hectic interwar years a few Muslim countries gained independence as nation-states, while others continued the bitter struggle, until by the mid-1950s only British colonies in the Arabian peninsula, together with French and Spanish mandates in North Africa, remained under direct foreign rule.

However, this long struggle, which occupies much of the twentieth century history of Islamic peoples not only in the Middle East but also in Africa and Asia, is based on a self-contradictory premise. Islam, from its origin, has been a religious polity. A Muslim, unlike a Jew or a Christian, cannot readily separate his spiritual from his national identity. As the *sharia* makes clear, in tone as well as content, the basic vocabulary of Islamic life is at once religious and political. Church (i.e., mosque) and state are not separable; they are complementary expressions of the same, single reality: that Islam applies to all spheres of life. Hence, nationalism, even Muslim nationalism, will continue to elicit tensions and pose paradoxes that will continue to riddle Muslim public behavior and private faith.

It would be wrong to underestimate the resilience of Islam. Amid staggering perplexities there persist genuine aspirations for a confident, progressive worldwide Muslim community, one which would uphold the traditions of the past while adapting to forces of change. The future of Islam may well lie not with national political leaders but with the local custodians of the *sharia,* the *'ulamā'*.

See BLACK RELIGIONS IN THE UNITED STATES § 5; ISLAM IN CHINA.

Bibliography. General: K. Cragg, *The House of Islam* (1969); C. J. Adams, "Islām," in C. J. Adams, ed., *A Reader's Guide to the Great Religions* (1977); J. Hayes, ed., *The Genius of Arab Civilization* (1975); H. A. R. Gibb, *Mohammedanism* (1949); M. G. S. Hodgson, *The Venture of Islam,* 3 vols. (1974); P. M. Holt *et al., The Cambridge History of Islam,* 2 vols. (1970); A. Jeffrey, ed., *A Reader on Islam* (1962); B. Lewis, *The Arabs in History* (1950); B. Lewis, ed., *Islam and the Arab World* (1976); S. H. Nasr, *Ideals and Realities of Islam* (1966); F E. Peters, *Allah's Commonwealth* (1973); F. Rahman, *Islam* (1966); R. M. Savory, ed., *Introduction to Islamic Civilisation* (1976); J. Schacht and C. E. Bosworth, eds., *The Legacy of Islam* (1974).

Early Period: A. J. Arberry, *The Koran Interpreted* (1955); B. Ahmad, *Muhammad and the Jews* (1979); T. Andrae, *Mohammed, the Man and His Faith* (1960); R. Bell, *The Origin of Islam in its Christian Environment* (1926); F. Gabrieli, *Muhammad and the*

Conquest (1968); O. Grabar, *The Formation of Islamic Art* (1973); G. E. von Grunebaum, *Classical Islam* (1970); M. A. Shaban, *Islamic History*, I (1971); C. C. Torrey, *The Jewish Foundation of Islam* (1933); W. M. Watt, *Muhammad: Prophet and Statesman* (1961), and *Bell's Introduction to the Qur'ān* (1970).

Middle Period: V. V. Barthold, *Four Studies on the History of Central Asia*, 3 vols. (1956-62); J. A. Boyle, *The Cambridge History of Iran*, V (1968); G. E. von Grunebaum, *Medieval Islam* (1953); F. Rosenthal, *The Classical Heritage in Islam* (1975); J. Schacht, *An Introduction to Islamic Law* (1964); A. Schimmel, *Mystical Dimensions of Islam* (1975); M. A. Shaban, *Islamic History*, II (1976); J. S. Trimingham, *The Sufi Orders in Islam* (1973).

Modern Period: A. Bennigsen and P. Lemercier-Quelquejay, *Islam in the Soviet Union* (1967); D. Eickelman, *Moroccan Islam* (1976); C. Geertz, *The Religion of Java* (1960); H. A. R. Gibb, *Modern Trends in Islam* (1947); G. E. von Grunebaum, *Modern Islam* (1962); N. R. Keddie, ed., *Scholars, Saints and Sufis* (1972); E. W. Lane, *Manners and Customs of the Modern Egyptians* (1836); B. Lawrence, ed., *The Rose and the Rock* (1979); P. Mansfield, *The Arabs* (1976); W. C. Smith, *Islam in Modern History* (1952); J. S. Trimingham, *Islam in Ethiopia* (1952) and *A History of Islam in West Africa* (1962).

B. LAWRENCE

ISLAM IN AMERICA. *See* BLACK RELIGIONS IN THE UNITED STATES §5.

ISLAM IN CHINA. 1. The obscurity of Chinese Islam. The Muslims of China, who now number some thirty million people, constitute one of the largest yet least known communities in the Islamic world. There are several reasons for their obscurity.

a) The influence the Muslims have in China is almost insignificant, because they constitute such a small part of the huge population of that country.

b) Muslims in China have always lived on the far periphery of the Islamic world.

c) China has been governed by basically totalitarian, highly centralized regimes which never legitimized minority or heterodox ideologies and organizations. This was true of the dominant Confucianism in traditional China and of communism in contemporary China. The short period of Republican China (1911-49) was an exception.

d) China has been isolated to a great extent, both spiritually and geographically, from the rest of the world. Therefore, except for short periods of free contact, such as the Yüan Dynasty (1279-1368) and the Republic, during which Chinese Muslims could openly relate to the Muslim world, Chinese Islam has remained virtually isolated.

2. The development of Islam in China. Islam made very modest beginnings under the T'ang Dynasty (618-907), when Muslim merchants settled in some of China's coastal cities, the best-known of which is Zaytun (Chüan-chou). They gained virtual extraterritorial privileges and were permitted to practice their faith (or, from the Chinese viewpoint, were restricted to their separate quarters), and kept aloof from the rest of the population. This situation continued, and under the Yüan Dynasty even improved. The Yüan (Mongol) rulers employed some of the local and "imported" Muslims as bureaucrats to help impose their rule over the Chinese. It was apparently during this time that Chinese Islam expanded all over the Empire, including remote provinces such as Yünnan and Kansu, where Muslims now constitute a high proportion of the population. Under the Ming Dynasty (1368-1644), which reverted to isolation and the predominance of Confucian values, Islam was again relegated to the fringes and had to adopt a low profile to survive. However, the Muslim minority grew steadily, from the few thousand settlers who came via the sea route in the eighth century, through a massive migration via the land routes of Central Asia in the thirteenth and fourteenth centuries, to a sizable and cohesive group which numbered in the millions by Ming times. The community was well enough organized to sustain its membership in times of hardship and was so closely united by the Islamic faith as to ensure the continued loyalty of its adherents. Its ranks grew as Muslims married Chinese women and purchased Chinese children, whom they raised as Muslims.

Throughout its history Chinese Islam remained organizationally fragmented. Each community elected its own religious leader, or IMAM (*A-hong* in Chinese). Whenever a Muslim community was large enough, there would be several congregations centered around their mosques, but no organization was available or permissible on the national level. Under the Ch'ing (1644-1911), itself a foreign (Manchu) dynasty, the nineteenth century brought inner unrest and foreign aggression. The Muslim minority, like other groups in China, took part in a series of rebellions in Northwestern and Southwestern China. However, unlike such rebel groups as the Taipings, who aspired to replace the central government in Peking, the Muslims, being outside the Confucian order, were content to secede from it. These uprisings also had an inner dynamic of their own, for during the nineteenth century a revivalist movement swept Chinese Islam as a result of impulses for change which apparently originated in Arabian Wahhābism (*see* WAHHĀBĪYA) and spread throughout the Islamic world, including territories adjacent to China, such as India and Burma. The revolts were also linked with the rise of the "New Sect" in Chinese Islam, an offshoot of Central Asian Naqshbandi SUFISM. These militant elements stood in opposition to the "Old Sect," the normative Islam of the Hanafi school which predominated in China (*see* HANAFITES).

3. The modern period. The Republic of China (1911-49) recognized the Muslims as one of the five major components of the Chinese people. However, when the loose and chaotic government of that era was replaced by the centralized and authoritarian regime of the People's Republic, there was a reversal to the traditional concept of the state. Although minority groups were recognized and several autonomous regions were established, a decisive course of

Sinicization and population transfers has been pursued, with the ultimate aim of assimilating the Muslims and all other minorities.

Unlike the other institutional religions of China, which have all but disappeared, Islam is still practiced by many. The government is lenient to them out of political considerations, particularly in view of China's relations to Islamic countries in the Middle East and the Third World. Moreover, the Muslim minority has proved too tough and too proud to subdue. In the 1950s, when the "Hundred Flowers" bloomed in China and people were allowed to speak out, some Muslim pockets throughout the country again proclaimed their identification with Arabia and with the Arabic language.

The People's Republic has certainly taken its toll upon the Muslim population, inasmuch as Muslim youth are educated as party cadres, and Muslim notables are induced and even compelled to serve the regime. This policy is likely to succeed in regions where the Muslim population is diluted and dispersed among the surrounding Chinese majority (e.g. in the major cities). But in areas where the Muslims constitute the majority (e.g. the Ninghsia Autonomous Region), or a sizable minority (e.g. Kansu, Shensi, and Yünnan), their survival is more assured in the foreseeable future. Should the government take a more liberal view toward minorities, Muslim voices are likely to be heard asking for more freedom of contact with the Muslim world. Furthermore, should instability or widespread unrest plague China again, the Muslims are likely to renew their demands for either secession or at least a more meaningful autonomy.

Bibliography. M. Broomhall, *Islam in China: A Neglected Problem* (1910); R. Israeli, *Muslims in China: A Study of Cultural Confrontation* (1978).
R. ISRAELI

ISLAM IN SOUTH ASIA. 1. Demography and expansion. Islam is the second largest religion of the Asian subcontinent. According to recent census figures it claims in Pakistan, 63 million out of a total population of 65 million; in Bangladesh, 64 million out of 77 million; and in India, 72 million out of 595 million, for a total of 199 million out of 737 million people. Islam is thus the dominant religion in Pakistan and Bangladesh, while constituting a significant minority in India.

Islam would seem to have scored a major success in the subcontinent. Moreover, among the worldwide Muslim community, South Asian Muslims constitute more than one third of its total membership (550 million), placing them well ahead of all other geographic areas where Muslims predominate—the Middle East, Central Asia, and Southeast Asia. (*See* ISLAM IN SOUTHEAST ASIA.)

From a Muslim perspective, however, it can be argued that Islam has failed in the Asian subcontinent. Because it is a universalist, confessional religion that, by definition, supersedes and replaces all prior religious allegiances, Islam ascribes maximum importance to CONVERSION. Historically it became the majority religion in all the areas (except Spain) to which it spread within a century after the death of MUHAMMAD in A.D. 632. When Muslim merchants and itinerant SUFIS reached the Asian archipelago, Islam also became the principal religion for Malaysians and Indonesians. In South Asia, however, it never escaped the status of a minority religion—a strong and influential minority but still a minority.

The reasons for Islam's "failure" in India are evident. The indigenous religious traditions of the subcontinent, often lumped together as HINDUISM, are resistant to change, having accommodated themselves to three major invasions (Aryan, Muslim, and British) and one minor incursion (Greek) without changing their basic identity. Also, the distinctive social structure of the subcontinent, the CASTE system, provided a cohesion among the Indian elites that no foreign group has been able to subvert or destroy. Islam's record must be measured against that of other minority groups in the area. BUDDHISM, which has flourished outside India, has only 3 million adherents in India itself; JAINISM numbers only 2½ million. Among newcomers, two have fared slightly better. CHRISTIANITY has established itself principally in the coastal regions of South India since its introduction in the second century A.D. and claims 15 million members (*see* MAR THOMA CHURCH). SIKHISM, closely linked to Northwest India, has perhaps 6 million adherents.

Islam initially penetrated the region by military conquest. Incessant raiding, leading to invasions, followed by conquest was the typical pattern which Arabs pursued as they moved into Sind in the seventh century and which Central Asian peoples later adopted in order to gain access to the Indus River basin and eventually to the North Indian Plain. There were no large-scale Muslim victories that signaled a collapse of the indigenous Buddhist and Hindu rulers. Rather, there was a twelve-hundred-year period of conflict, from the middle of the seventh century through the middle of the nineteenth century. The earliest major Islamic dynasty in South Asia, the Turco-Afghan Ghaznavids (998-1186), ruled over an area that never extended beyond present-day Pakistan and a small part of North India. It was not until 1192 that Muhammad of Ghur, another Turkish military commander, established a tactical base of operations in the North Indian Plain by his conquest of Delhi. This then made possible the rapid territorial gains achieved by the Ilbaris, Khaljis, and Tughluqs during the thirteenth and fourteenth centuries. In 1355 a Turco-Afghan ruler, Muhammad ibn Tughluq, could claim political control over most of the subcontinent, from the Indus River in the west to the mouth of the Ganges in the east, from Kashmir in the north to all but the tip of Southern India.

Political control over South Asia was not, however, tantamount to Islamization, as had been true for areas previously conquered by Muslim commanders. In the Northwest, present-day Afghanistan as well as Pakistan and Kashmir did become almost completely Muslim, while in the Northeast the vast majority of the inhabitants of East Bengal, present-day Bangladesh, also joined Islam. Elsewhere Islam remained a minority religion.

Neither forced conversions nor large-scale immigrations (often caused by external events, such as the Mongol invasions of the thirteenth century and the Safavid persecution of non-SHI'ITE Muslims in the seventeenth) can explain the dramatic rise in the Islamic sector of South Asian society. A much debated hypothesis ascribes phenomenal success to the efforts of nonaggressive Sufi preachers, and because many present-day South Asian Muslim families trace their own Islamic identity to the conversion of ancestors by these same SHAIKHS, the thesis cannot be dismissed.

2. **Pre-Mogul period** (seventh–early sixteenth centuries). Islam in South Asia made itself visible through public monuments built by Muslim rulers: MOSQUES for community prayer, MADRASAS for educating scholars in Islamic law, halls of justice for administering the law, palaces for housing the rich, and tombs to bury the noble dead. Moreover, Indo-Muslim rulers established an elaborate network of patronage, financing not only the construction of distinctive architectural forms but also employing skilled professionals—dancers, musicians, artists, calligraphers, historians, and poets—to serve in their courts. Conspicuous consumption coupled with lavish expenditure had been characteristic of indigenous Buddhist and Hindu rulers in the pre-Muslim era, and the rivalry between the two civilizations now focused on the public achievements of their respective royalty, maximizing rather than reducing the role of kings in every aspect of Indian society. Rivalry was also reflected in the quality of religious life; neither the BRAHMINS, spokesmen for Hindu orthodoxy, nor their Muslim counterparts, the 'ULAMĀ', were as much acclaimed during the pre-Mogul period as the more liberal representatives of each tradition: the BHAKTI poet-saints and the Sufi shaikhs. Both the latter groups advocated a love mysticism that stretched the boundaries of accepted religious practice and yet effectively gave new meaning to the symbols of Hinduism and Islam.

At no point during the centuries that preceded the Mogul period, however, did any of the Indo-Islamic ruling elite—the military commanders (including the king), the trained scholars (*'ulamā'*), and the anti-establishment Sufi shaikhs—allow the tensions that existed among them to overshadow their common bond as members of the Muslim minority. These elite were immigrants from other parts of the Islamic world rather than indigenous converts. They clustered in urban trade centers, where capital as well as goods accumulated, forts could be built, and Muslim monuments defended against outsiders, whether Hindu or rival Muslim factions. Though Turkish in origin, some of them knew ARABIC, the canonical tongue of Islam, but most used PERSIAN as the language of communication, both for running the court bureaucracies and for poetry, music, and mystical pursuits. Hindūstānī, the language of daily discourse, was seldom used in manuscript writing or inscriptions, the only literary artifacts that remain from this period.

Sufism determined the mood of Indian Islam during this period, chiefly through exemplar representatives of the Chishtī and Suhrawardī orders. The contradictions which generally characterized Indian Islam were telescoped in the lives of these saints. The most famous Chishtī shaikh, for instance, was Niẓām-al-Dīn Awliyā (d. A.D. 1325). Descended from a SAYYID family of Bukhara, he gave up the career of a scholar to become the disciple of Farid-al-Dīn, a fiercely ascetic Chishtī saint from the Punjab. Niẓam al-Dīn lived most of his life in Delhi, despite the fact that it was the seat of government and that his Chishtī predecessors viewed contact with military-political rulers and the secular *'ulamā'* as contaminating. By the time of his death, he had trained a large cadre of disciples whom he commissioned to spread the Chishtī teaching to urban pockets throughout the portion of South Asia under Muslim rule. The celebration of the anniversary of his death ('URS) continues to be attended by devotees from all segments of Indo-Muslim society, including government officials and *'ulamā'*.

Beyond Delhi and Northwest India, in other South Asian cities such as Bijapur in the Deccan and Sonargaon in Bengal, the Sufi masters were also hailed as charismatic spokesmen for Islam. Sometimes they functioned as warrior shaikhs and their tombs became objects of veneration because they were said to have died as martyrs (SHAHĪD) for the Islamic faith. Most often, however, they were reformers and literati, though descendants of the major shaikhs often degenerated into landed elite lacking the spiritual charisma of their forefathers.

3. **Mogul period** (sixteenth-eighteenth centuries). From the thirteenth to the sixteenth century authority had been dispersed locally among various groups of the Turco-Afghan ruling elite, and regionally among various elite groups. Even before Tamerlane's invasion of North India at the end of the fourteenth century, independent Muslim dynasties had arisen in the Deccan and Bengal. After that invasion Delhi ceased to be the principal center of Muslim military and political power, and, during the subsequent Sayyid and Lōdī period, regional dynasties flourished throughout South Asia.

Babur (1483-1530), the first Mogul ruler, was descended from Tamerlane through his father and Ghengis Khan through his mother. He was a multilingual, aesthetically refined warrior with ambitions to reclaim his ancestral homeland in

Central Asia. Thwarted by a superior Uzbekī rival, he turned to Kabul in Afghanistan and eventually to Delhi in North India. Using Kabul as a base of support, Babur engaged the last of the Lōdī sultans, Ibrāhīm, in the battle of Panipat in 1526, and his victory there inaugurated the period of Mogul rule over the Asian subcontinent.

Mogul India has been fantasized as an era of cultural syncretism and artistic creativity. In part it was, but in part it was also a continuation of the struggle, already begun during the Delhi sultanate, to maintain and extend Muslim rule in a country whose inhabitants remained doggedly non-Muslim.

Babur did not succeed in reversing the dissipation of centralized power that had occurred after Tamerlane's invasion. His own reign was cut short by his early death. His son and successor, Humāyūn, had to engage in warfare against fellow Muslims in the Northeast and the Northwest of the new empire, and in 1540, upon losing a decisive battle, he fled to the Safavid capital of Iran, where he was befriended by the redoubtable Shi'ite monarch Shah Ṭahmasp (d. 1576). For fifteen years Humāyūn remained in exile in Iran, until he maneuvered the Safavid court to help him regain the throne of Delhi, principally on the expectation that he, together with his family and the leading families of his realm, would convert to Shi'ism. Like his father, Humāyūn first succeeded in controlling the region of Kabul, and in 1555 he retook both Lahore and Delhi. He had hardly begun to enjoy the fruits of his long-awaited victory when he died in 1556.

Mogul India would never have become an empire equal to its northern neighbors, the Ottomans and Safavids, without the work of Humāyūn's son and successor, AKBAR. Though only thirteen years old when he ascended the throne, he was aided by a skilled and loyal regent, Bayram Khan, who guided him through the early years of his reign. By the age of nineteen Akbar had begun to demonstrate the independence and genius that were to characterize his tenure as sovereign master of Hindustan. He was a brilliant military commander, a far-sighted administrator, and a sensitive, generous patron of the arts and religion. His reign witnessed the recentralization of Muslim rule throughout the subcontinent, established on a firmer basis, with a higher yield, than had been possible in the fourteenth century under Sultan Muhammad ibn Tughluq. Akbar, like his father, did not become a professing Shi'ite, but he did recruit such indigenous Shi'ites as the Sayyids of Barh as well as the non-Muslim elite, particularly Rajputs, into the Mogul bureaucracy. Also, Akbar assumed a more direct control of religious affairs than any previous Mogul or pre-Mogul monarch. By 1579 he had dismissed and sent into exile his own appointee as chief of the *'ulamā'*. In the same year he read the Friday congregational sermon in his own name, having extracted from the leading *'ulamā'* a pledge that he outranked them as a qualified interpreter (MUJTAHID) of the SHARIA, the Muslim law. He went still further in formulating his own personal beliefs into an eclectic monotheism of quasi-Sufi inspiration called *Dīn Īlahī,* "The Divine Religion."

The religious policies of Akbar were not pursued by any of his successors, except perhaps by the intended successor to Shāh Jahān, his eldest son, Dārā Shīkoh, whose spiritual eclecticism surpassed his military prowess; he was defeated and killed by AURANGZĪB in 1657. The later Moguls, including the puritanical Aurangzīb, frequently depicted as a fanatic, were imbued with the ambiance of Sufism. All of them were loyal to particular shaikhs, and often, as Akbar also had done, pledged the income of designated lands or villages to support the descendants and maintain the tomb complex of a notable Sufi. Nor was it by chance that the premier Indian mystical poet in the Persian language, 'ABD-AL-QĀDIR BEDIL (d. 1721), lived in Delhi during the reign of Aurangzīb and was befriended by the Emperor's son, Prince Agẓam. Yet Jahāngīr and Shāh Jahān as well as Aurangzīb were committed to SUNNI Islam and supported not only the *'ulamā'* but also pan-Islamic Sufi orders, such as the Qādiris and Naqshbandis.

Aurangzīb's attitude toward Hindus has sparked the most controversy. His destruction of Hindu temples and imposition of discriminatory taxes against Hindus in part reflected his determination to preserve the status of the Muslim ruling elite by using more forceful tactics than any earlier Mogul emperor had needed. The emergence of Sikhs (*see* SIKHISM), Jats, and Marathas as indigenous groups who challenged Mogul supremacy during the reign of Aurangzīb gave a foretaste of the uncertain future awaiting his successors. In addition, a new Muslim elite assumed power in neighboring Persia and Afghanistan and plundered the provinces and the major cities of North India during the first half of the eighteenth century. The most devastating raid came in 1739, when Nādir Shah looted the Mogul treasury and also removed the famed Peacock Throne from Delhi.

4. **British.** During the reigns of the great Moguls, Europeans had come to India to explore the mysterious East, to engage in proselytizing efforts, or to pursue options for trade. Increasingly the last interest outstripped the others as the British cowed their rivals, the Portuguese, Dutch, and French, in securing the trade route to India and establishing a commercial empire in South Asia that matched the splendor—and also the conspicuous consumption—of its Mogul predecessor.

The British were the first group of foreigners to invade India by sea. They built military cantonments in port cities such as Calcutta, Madras, and Bombay, connecting them with one another and with such interior cities as Delhi, Lahore, and Hyderabad, through extensive telegraph and railway systems. Though their hegemony in Bengal was assured after they defeated the Mogul governor and his forces in the Battle of Plassey (1757), they did not extend formal control over most of the subcontinent till the Revolt of 1857 forced them to depose and exile the last Mogul Emperor, Bahādur Shāh Ẓafar, and establish direct home rule from Parliament.

The British presence affected all major groups in South Asia—the Hindu elite, Marathas, Sikhs, and Afghans as well as Moguls, but the latter were the most visible and therefore the most vulnerable. The rivalry between the Moguls and the British was intensified by the tacit linkage of Western technological superiority to Christian truth claims. Whatever their difficulties with indigenous groups, the Moguls, though representing a minority religion, had at least ruled Hindustan. The British undercut and then terminated their right to rule, while at the same time challenging the twin bases of their religion: the prophethood of MUHAMMAD and the sanctity of the QUR'ĀN. One response was an accommodation to Western values, along with the retention of the kernel of Islamic faith, an approach typified by the modernist reformer and educator Sir Sayyid Ahmad Khan (d. 1898). Another trend was to reject all association with the West and to retreat into a fundamentalist posture in relation to both the West and indigenous Indian traditions. This became the avowed goal of the Deoband *madrasa*, which produced many of the future leaders of Pakistan. Still another reaction was to crystallize Islam into a new millenarian creed articulated by a charismatic leader who himself would usher in the millennium. Such was the path of the AHMADIYYA, under the direction of Ghulām Aḥmad of Qadiyan in Northwest India.

The political expression of Muslim unrest took shape in the Muslim League, founded in 1906, after the British had partitioned Bengal into two sectors (East and West). In 1928, despite an interlude of Hindu-Muslim cooperation against British rule, the National Muslim Party came into being, and with the escalation of events leading up to and following the Second World War, British negotiators yielded to Muḥammad 'Alī Jinnah and created Pakistan (an acronym coined by the poet-philosopher, Muḥammad Iqbāl [d. 1939]), at the same time that they conferred independence upon India in 1947. The emergence of Bangladesh, formerly East Pakistan, in 1971 was a recognition of the difficulty of welding together two geographically, ethnically, and linguistically disparate parts of the Asian subcontinent on the common ground of religion.

Bibliography. General. M. Mujeeb, *The Indian Muslims* (1967); A. B. M. Habibullah, *Foundation of Muslim Rule in India* (1945); K. S. Lal, *Growth of Muslim Population in Medieval India* (1973); B. Lawrence, "Early Indo-Muslim Saints and the Conversion Problem," in R. Israeli, ed., *Islam in Asia* (1980); J. Richards, "Islamic Expansion into South Asia," *South Asia*, III (1973), 94-98.

Pre-Mogul Period. K. A. Nizami, *Some Aspects of Religion and Politics in India during the Thirteenth Century* (1961); R. Eaton, *The Sufis of Bijapur* (1978); B. Lawrence, *Notes From a Distant Flute: Sufi Literature in Pre-Mughal India* (1978).

Mogul Period. S. R. Sharma, *The Religious Policy of the Mughal Emperors* (1940); A. Ahmad, *Studies in Islamic Culture in the Indian Environment* (1964); J. F. Richards, "The Formulation of Imperial Authority under Akbar and Jahangir," in J. R. Richards, ed., *Kingship and Authority in South Asia* (1978), pp. 252-85.

British Period. A. Ahmad, *Islamic Modernism in India and Pakistan, 1857-1964* (1967); S. T. Lokhandwalla, ed., *India and Contemporary Islam* (1971); S. A. Husain, *Destiny of Indian Muslims* (1965); M. R. A. Baig, *The Muslim Dilemma in India* (1974); K. Cragg, *The House of Islam* (1969); M. G. S. Hodgson, *The Venture of Islam*, Vols. II, III (1974).

B. LAWRENCE

ISLAM IN SOUTHEAST ASIA. Islam in Southeast Asia stretches east and south from Southern Thailand through Malaysia, Singapore, and the island chain of Indonesia, then to the north as far as the Southern Philippines. It predominates only in Malaysia and Indonesia, which together form a population of perhaps 150 million, the majority of whom are at least nominally Muslim. It is to this Malaysian-Indonesian Muslim population that the following statements apply.

1. History. *a) Origins.* Islam was imported into Southeast Asia during the spread of Arab and Indian merchants and teachers into the region beginning in the twelfth century A.D. The merchants first traded for riches of the tropics, then stayed to marry the local

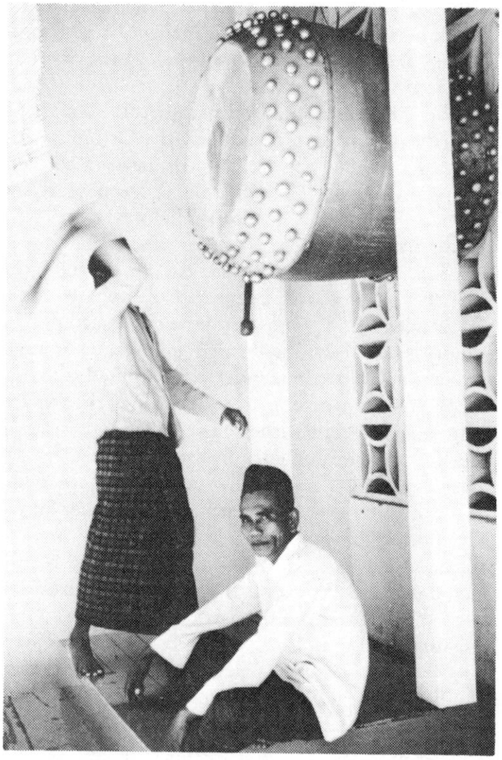

F. M. Denny

Beating the prayer drum at the mosque-tomb complex of Sunan, Ampel, Surabaya, Java

women. The teachers brought with them a mixture of Islamic doctrine, SUFI mysticism, and foreign magic that attracted local rulers. Because the rulers converted to Islam, Islamic merchants found these foreign ports increasingly appealing, and thus conversion and trade encouraged each other.

The first great Muslim port in Southeast Asia was Malacca, on the southern coast of Malaya. It was founded *ca.* 1400 by a local ruler, Parameswara, who converted to Islam and then came to be called Muhammad Iskandar Shah. Said to rival the great ports of Europe in its activity, Malacca was conquered by the Portuguese in 1511, and the impetus in both trade and religion passed to Indonesian ports. Again in Sumatra, Java, and Borneo a typical sequence was repeated: rulers were converted, merchants came to trade, and Islamic teachers settled to teach. Eventually the Islamic tidal wave moved eastward to the outer islands—Ternate, Makassar in Southern Celebes, Banjermassin in Southern Borneo and into the Sulu islands of the Philippines, where the Muslim "Moros" remain a rebellious minority to this day.

b) Growth and change. Beginning in the sixteenth century, the teachers traveled inland and established Islamic schools, known as *pesantren* in Java and *pondok* in Malaya. The strict, rural schools taught the QUR'ĀN, classical commentaries, and mystical exercises to adolescent boys. These schools were the major centers of Islam in Southeast Asia.

Soon after the Arabs and Indians, the Europeans came in search of the same tropical riches. The Portuguese and Spanish established markets in the sixteenth century, followed by the British and Dutch in the seventeenth; the British eventually controlled what is now Malaysia, and the Dutch what is now Indonesia. The new Christian European colonialism and Islam were bound to come to blows, but the confrontations differed according to the particular historical development of Islam in the indigenous society.

In Java, prior to Islam, there had existed a highly developed Hinduized civilization, epitomized in great empires which flourished from the eighth to fifteenth century A.D. A conflict between the Hindu and Islamic forces in Java resulted in the creation in the sixteenth century of the great syncretic empire of Southeast Asia—Mataram. Remnants of the capital of that empire can be found in Jogjakarta and Surakarta on Java.

During the early 1800s a prince of Mataram, Diponegara, was attracted to the purist type of Islam centered around the independent rural schools, the *pesantren*, and he became a kind of prophet, wearing black Arab-styled clothes and meditating in the wilderness. Angered because the Dutch built a road on his ancestral land, Diponegara launched a rebellion which became known as the Java War and was to consume much Dutch energy from 1825-30. In this conflict the anti-Dutch forces led by Prince Diponegara were largely of the purist Muslim contingent, while the Hindu aristocracy sided with the Dutch.

In Malaya and Sumatra, unlike Java, the elite did not become Hinduized. The local rulers of Malaya converted to Islam, and they came to control an indigenous Islamic bureaucracy—a sultanate—which was supported by the colonial government. In Sumatra the local chiefs remained to a degree upholders of indigenous values *(adat)* against Islamic encroachment, but these chiefs had less power than the great courts of Java and were not a significant political factor. In the Acheh war, fought in Northern Sumatra, Muslims held off the Dutch from 1873 to the end of the century.

c) Attempts at reform. With the opening of the Suez Canal and the beginning of steamship travel between Southeast Asia and Mecca around 1870, the number of Southeast Asian Muslims making the pilgrimage to Mecca multiplied. By 1895 there were 11,000 Indonesians annually making the pilgrimage, and by 1911, 29,000—constituting as much as a third of the foreign pilgrims at Mecca.

A few of the more serious pilgrims stayed to study in Mecca and other Middle Eastern centers of Islamic learning such as Cairo, whose al-AẒHĀR University boasted several hundred Malay and Indonesian students through the late nineteenth and early twentieth centuries. Some of these students came under the influence of the Islamic modernists, such as Cairo's MUHAMMAD 'ABDŪH, and from this exposure was launched the most significant twentieth century development in Southeast Asian Islam: reformism.

The two essential tenets of reformism are scripturalism and purification. Scripturalism is manifested in the concept of *ijtihād*—that one must seek truth through one's own rational analysis of the scripture rather than from some source such as a teacher mediating between ALLAH and man. Purification proclaims that Islamic practice must be cleansed of all *adat*—indigenous customs that have, in syncretism, come to be mixed with the practices of the true faith. By steadfastly practicing these two tenets, the reformist expects to return to the true and pure Islam of MUHAMMAD and the holy Qur'ān. He also believes that this original and perfect faith contains the essential knowledge for coping with modern life, and thus the reformist within the Islamic framework justifies such modern practices as science and democracy.

Because Singapore was the port of embarkation and disembarkation for pilgrims, it was the first center for Southeast Asian Muslim reformism. A journal, schools, and associations were begun in Singapore, then spread outward to Malaysia and Indonesia. In Malaysia reformism was blocked by the traditionalist religious bureaucracies of the sultanate that ruled each state. Reformism was also opposed in Indonesia, with traditionalist forces (Kaum Tua) against reformist (Kaum Muda), but the opponents were village teachers and traditionalist merchants rather than an organized royal bureaucracy.

The most successful of the reformers' organizations was the Muhammadijah, founded in 1912 in Jogjakarta by K. H. A. Dahlan. It has since grown to some six million members and six hundred branches throughout Indonesia. In 1926 the traditionalists founded their own organization, Nadatul Ulama ("the Awakening of the 'ULAMĀ' "), which dominates such areas as rural east Java, particularly in the famous school Tebu Ireng, and continues to be a political force in Indonesia.

d) The rise of nationalism. Simultaneous with the founding of Muhammadijah, the first of the Indonesian nationalist parties was established. This nationalistic-Communist-Hinduist mixture opposed Dutch colonialism and has provided the opposite pole to Indonesian Islam. In 1941, Dutch colonialism was ended by the Japanese occupation. Despite the subsequent four years of suffering and disorganization, Indonesia's reformist and conservative Muslim parties were strengthened, and they emerged into the era of independence in 1945 as major elements in the new party system. Masjumi (a coalition of Muhammadijah, Nadatul Ulama and others) was the strongest party in many areas until it was banned by the Sukarno regime in 1960. The Muslims helped weaken that regime during the so-called Gestapu massacres of 1965-66. The government has still not permitted the Masjumi to reorganize, but Nadatul Ulama has remained powerful, and Muhammadijah has created a reformist party (Partai Muslimin), which, however, is not a major political force.

Malaysia in the twentieth century has experienced fewer dramatic changes than Indonesia. The sultanate-states have remained the major outposts of Islam, supported first by the British, then the Japanese, and finally the indigenous government of Malaysia. Two major political parties of Islamic cast have been formed—the Pan-Malayan Islamic Party (PMIP) and the United Malays National Organization (UMNO); the first is more radically Islamic and opposed to the non-Muslim, Chinese power; the second a more moderate coalition between Muslims, Chinese, and others. In Singapore, which separated from Malaysia in 1965, the Muslim party of the Malay minority, Party of United Malays (PKM), has gained relatively little power.

2. Beliefs, creed, and scripture. Devout Southeast Asian Muslims adhere to the basic beliefs of Muslims everywhere. (*See* ISLAM.)

The less purist or reformist and the more syncretic their attitude, the more the Southeast Asian Muslims combine their own indigenous beliefs with those of Islam; in extreme cases, the indigenous overshadows the Islamic. Among the several hundred tribes, societies, and regional and linguistic groups that constitute the Southeast Asian Muslims, the indigenous beliefs vary enormously, and only the broadest general pattern can be sketched here.

The basic pattern is the belief that spiritual power inheres in elements other than Allah. Such elements may vary from the god-king of the Hinduist Javanese to magical daggers and spirits of tree, rock, and field. The self may be seen as the source of ultimate power, as in the mystical cults of Hinduist cast in Java and Sufism in Sumatra and Malaya. The full-blown syncretist mixes all of these with worship of Allah, so that these powers (and usually others besides, including Christ, BUDDHA, and gods of the South Seas) are all supplicated.

Aside from these animistic and mystic beliefs the syncretist will hold, along with belief in heaven and hell, notions of reincarnation or of indigenous afterlives, or of no afterlife. Told together with the biography of Muhammad are legends of indigenous heroes, such as Sunan Kalijaga who, after meditating inside an ox carcass, is believed to have brought Islam together with the Shadow Play (the *wayang kulit,* which portrays Hindu myths by projecting shadows of puppets) and the percussion orchestra (the *gamelan,* which weaves complex melodies on xylophone-like instruments) to form a syncretic culture.

3. Institutions. Southeast Asian Muslim society revolves around three institutions: MOSQUE, school, and court. These focus on the private sphere of life, and it is this sphere, more than any other, which makes for the importance of Islam in Southeast Asia.

The mosque is the place for daily prayer and Friday sermon. It is staffed by an official preacher *(chatib),* a caller-to-prayer *(bilal),* and somtimes other religious officials. It is supplemented by small local prayer houses in villages and neighborhoods.

There are two principal types of Muslim school: the *pesantren* or *pondok* and the MADRASA. The *pesantren/pondok* in its traditional form offers only instruction in reading the Qur'ān and Arabic language commentaries. The *madrasa,* introduced by the reformists, offers a combination of religious and secular education, and its religious education includes more theological and ethical and less textual focus than in the *pesantren.* Additional sources of religious training exist in various forms, such as the afternoon Islamic school in Singapore that supplements the secular government education and the Islamic courses in Indonesian schools, which are secular in other respects.

The *sjariah* (*see* SHARIA)—Islamic law—is elaborated in a court system that supplements the civil court system. The Islamic court focuses largely on questions of inheritance, marriage, and divorce—on all of which Islam supplements civil law.

Malaysia's system of school, mosque, and court differs from the general pattern, for these domains are coordinated by the bureaucracy of the sultanate which controls each state. In Singapore, Islam is only slightly represented in the state government: an Islamic Council and a general advisor (MUFTI). In Indonesia, coordination is provided nationally by the Ministry of Religion.

4. Ethics, ritual, and customs. The devout Muslim should fast during the fast month, abstain from pork and alcohol at all times, do the daily five prayers, tithe, and, if physically and financially able, make the pilgrimage (HAJJ). These "PILLARS," as they are called, constitute the central ritual requirements.

Considerable emphasis is placed on proper relations between male and female. There is no true PURDAH as found in the Middle East, but devout women should cover the head (never the face), and certain avoidances are urged if not always practiced: for example, separate seating of men from women at public gatherings and the handling of a corpse only by members of its own sex.

Most of the virtues preached by Southeast Asian Muslims are common to other traditions—honesty, kindness, charity, diligence. Some of their emphases are especially noteworthy, however. For example, by comparison to at least certain Christian sects, less emphasis is placed on love and on self-abnegation in favor of others (as in "turning the other cheek"). Instead, one is expected to stand up for one's belief, if necessary to the extent of practicing JIHĀD or "holy war." Also, carefully following the law is generally more important than having passionate faith. Last, a stoic dedication *(ichlas)* is more likely to be encountered than the guilt-ridden overachievement associated with the Protestant ethic.

5. **Major festivals.** The major "festival" of the year is the fast month (RAMADAN) which is observed faithfully by the devout. During this period many men worship in evenings in the mosque with special prayers known as *terarih*. At the end of the fast, the day is spent in visiting with parents and others to ask their forgiveness for wrongs of the past year.

Other festivals include a day to celebrate the embarkation of pilgrims to Mecca, a day to give food to the poor, and celebrations of the birth of Muhammad. Traditionalists practice a more elaborate set of rituals than do reformists, and in syncretic settings localized festivals have cropped up also. An example is the Sekaten fair in Jogjakarta, where syncretists march in a parade from mosque to palace to symbolize their unity.

6. **Reflection of religious life in art and architecture.** The mosque is the most obvious Muslim contribution to Southeast Asian architecture. Generally, the large mosque in purist centers follows the architectural pattern of the Middle Eastern homeland, although local variations do occur, particularly in syncretic domains. Thus, in Jogjakarta the royal mosque has a rather flat tile roof, after the style of the palace, instead of minarets. In Ternate the traditional mosques have an orchestra pit for the percussion orchestra *(gamelan)*.

Verbal rather than visual, musical, or dramatic art is the strong suit of Southeast Asian Islam. The first true biographies and histories in the region originated in Muslim circles. The biographies were about Muhammad, but subsequent ones took up other Muslim figures, including local personages. The earliest histories depicted the kingdoms of Northern Java and of Malaya. Though filled with mythical themes and marvelous happenings, these stories also chronicled real lives and events.

Islamic verbal arts in Southeast Asia resemble the forms known in other Muslim areas, such as chanting of the Qur'ān, but the region's enormously rich repertoire of dance, drama, and music contains more Hinduist and indigenous influence than Islamic. These forms are stronger in areas where Islam is weakest, as in Bali, and such examples as do exist in Islamized areas are less well developed. One finds, for example, that the Shadow Play *(wayang kulit)* is more elaborate when performed in Bali than it is in Kelantan, Malaya.

7. **Issues and trends.** The major issue confronting Southeast Asian Islam now is that which it has faced since the beginning of the twentieth century: modernization. Can a religion in its second millennium still serve society? The answer of the pious Muslim has to be yes, for the truths of Islam are regarded as eternal. Yet among these Muslims, different attitudes to modernity can be identified: traditionalist, reformist, and secularist. Traditionalists, exemplified by Nadatul Ulama and certain members of the religious bureaucracies of the Malaysian sultanates, hold out against all reform—preserving the traditional (somewhat syncretic) mysticism, textual focus, and *pesantren*-type schools. Reformists, exemplified by Muhammadijah, have consciously tried to rationalize much of modern life—bureaucratic organization, co-education, government-style schools—within an Islamic framework.

The third group, secularists, hold that Islam is not suited to certain features of modern life, and should be restricted to spheres of private worship and domestic ethics, while the secular state should dominate in other spheres. Such a point of view is regarded by both reformists and traditionalists as a threat, for it disavows the notion that a total society of pure Islam can someday be constructed.

In both Malaysia and Indonesia, owing to the extent of ethnic and religious pluralism, Islam contains a bare majority of the devout believers. The Chinese Buddhist, Batak Christian, Hinduized Balinese and Javanese, and smaller minorities have maintained their own beliefs strongly for generations and seem unlikely to convert without Draconian measures by an Islamic state.

Bibliography. C. Geertz, *Religion of Java* (1960); D. Noer, *The Modernist Muslim Movement in Indonesia 1900-1942* (1973); J. Peacock, *Muslim Puritans: Reformist Psychology in Southeast Asian Islam* (1978); W. Roff, "Southeast Asian Islam in the Nineteenth Century," *Cambridge History of Islam* (1970).

J. L. PEACOCK

ISMĀ'ĪL ĭs mä ēl′ (I). The Arabic form of the biblical name Ishmael, the son of ABRAHAM (Arab. *Ibrāhīm)*, and according to various popular genealogies the ancestor of the North Arabian tribes. In the QUR'ĀN, Ismā'īl is mentioned as having been inspired by ALLAH, as a prophet (Sura 19:54; 21:85; 38:49), and as having assisted his father in the construction of the KA'BA (Sura 2:125-32).

Post-Qur'ānic commentaries and "Stories of the Prophets" elaborate on these references, assigning to Ismā'īl the role of digging the well ZAMZAM when brought to MECCA with his mother, Hagar, after being expelled from Ibrāhīm's household. They also make him, rather than Isaac, the intended sacrificial victim in the test of Abraham (Gen. 22:1-19). Those sources regard Ismā'īl as the ancestor of only the North Arabs, in partial agreement with Gen. 25:12-18. Following the Qur'ān, he is given precedence over his brother Isaac.

Bibliography. Y. Moubarac, *Abraham dans le Coran* (1958); I. Goldziher, *Richtungen der islamischischen Koranauslegung* (1920), pp. 79 ff.; G. Weill, *Biblische Legenden der Musselmänner* (1845), pp. 82-96; aṭ-Ṭabarī, *Ta'rīkh* and *Tafsīr*, esp. Abraham's test, Sura 37:102-112; D. Sidersky, *Les origines des légendes musulmanes* (1933), pp. 50-53.

G. D. NEWBY

ISMĀ'ĪLIYYA ĭs mä ēl´ ē yä (I—Arab.). A branch of the SHI'A with numerous subdivisions, which began to be differentiated from the IMĀMIYYA at the time of the great Shi'ite IMAM Ja'far al-Ṣādiq (d. A.D. 765). They traced the imamate through one of al-Ṣādiq's sons, Ismā'īl, from whom they took their name. Ismā'īl had been designated by al-Ṣādiq to succeed him, but he died while his father was still living. Some Shi'ites maintained that he had not died but would reappear as the MAHDI and would redress the wrongs committed against the family of MUHAMMAD, that is, the murders of ALI and his sons.

Al-Ṣādiq, imam at the time of the 'ABBĀSID victory (A.D. 750), formulated the early doctrine of the office of imam and provided Shi'ism with a sectarian ideology. His prestigious and widely recognized imamate gained ultimate recognition for the line of imams descended from al-ḤUSAYN.

Among al-Ṣādiq's followers were extremist Shi'ites who had aspired to overthrow the existing regime and establish an ideal social order under the descendants of Ali. The early Ismailis, in all probability, grew out of this group which expected their imam to play a messianic role and emphasized the *bāṭin* (esoteric meaning) of all religious words and formulations, meaning known only to Ali and the imams descended from him. Although the Ismailis ascribed tremendous significance to the inspired imam, they also recognized the binding force of the SHARIA, and this was reinforced and even intensified by their elevation of Ali and his descendants as sole custodians of esoteric truth. Muhammad, from whom Ali, as executor, had inherited the secret lore, came to be regarded as the prime figure in the Ismaili hierarchical structure. Ali was the Prophet's sole representative through the process of *naṣṣ* (designation). A succession was formed through delegation of this authority to Ali's descendants until the line reached Ismā'īl's son and successor, Muhammad ibn Ismā'īl, who, according to Ismaili reckoning, was the seventh imam. Ismailis are thus known as "Seveners" (SAB'IYYA). This seventh imam was expected to return as the Mahdi, in whom the missions of all the great prophets were to culminate. He was believed to be in concealment, and during his absence the Ismailis recognized a system of twelve *ḥujjas* (competent religious authorities), each with his own territory, as representatives of the imam. Below the *ḥujjas* in rank were the *dā'īs* (summoners to the Ismaili message) and subordinate *dā'īs*, in a hierarchy down to the ordinary believers. The structure was to facilitate the mission of calling believers to acknowledge the imamate of Ismā'īl's descendants.

In the tenth century A.D. the Ismaili message culminated in the appearance in North Africa of a certain 'Ubaydullah, who claimed to be the Mahdi and the legitimate ruler of all Muslims by virtue of being a descendant of FĀṬIMA through Muhammad ibn Ismā'īl. He established the FATIMID caliphate in Egypt, which marked the beginning of an era of social, economic, intellectual, and religious revolution and united the Ismailis under Fatimid rule. By the eleventh century some prominent *dā'īs* undertook to refine and perfect the doctrine, and by their moderation in esoteric interpretation they ended various doctrinal disputes.

But in the same century Fatimid power underwent an internal crisis. In 1094 after the death of the imam al-Mustanṣir, the main schism in the Ismaili community occurred, and it has continued to the present. Al-Mustanṣir's, two sons, Nizār and al-Must'alī, headed rival factions. Those who upheld the imamate of Nizār started a movement under the leadership of Ḥasan-i Sabbāḥ, a Persian. This movement developed into the radical sect of ASSASSINS at Alamut in Iran. They constituted a constant challenge to the authority of the SUNNITE rulers of Iran, until the execution of their last imam by the Mongols in 1256. After this period little is known about the Nizārīs, and the later lists of their imams differ widely. However, the list which ends with the present AGHA KHAN as their forty-ninth imam came to be generally accepted in the nineteenth century (*see* KHŌJĀS). The Nizārīs are widely dispersed in Syria, Iran, India, and east Africa, and have developed varying understandings of their Alamut heritage.

The imamate of al-Must'alī was recognized by most Ismailis in Egypt and Syria, by the whole Ismaili community in Yemen, and in India. A new subdivision developed among the Must'alians after the assassination of al-Āmir in 1129. Those in Yemen supported the claims made for his infant son al-Ṭayyib, and came to be known as Ṭayyibiyya. In Egypt, al-Āmir's cousin was proclaimed imam and caliph with the title al-Ḥāfiẓ. The Ḥāfiẓiyya, after the overthrow of the Fatimids in 1171, gradually disintegrated, but the Ṭayyibiyya survived in their traditional stronghold in Yemen, where from time to time they were persecuted by Shi'ites belonging to the ZAYDIYYA sect. In India they remained mostly undisturbed, although there too a split occurred in the succession of leaders, which led to another permanent schism, between the Dā'udī and Sulaymānī factions. (*See* BOHORĀS; QARMATIANS.)

Bibliography. M. G. S. Hodgson, *The Order of Assassins* (1955); W. Madelung, "Isma'iliyya," in *EI*.

A. A. SACHEDINA

ISNĀD īs näd´ (I). *See* ḤADĪTH.

ISRAEL BEN ELIEZER īs rä ēl´ bēn ēl ē ā´ zər (Ju). *See* BAAL SHEM TOV.

ISRĀFĪL īs rä fīl´ (I). *See* MALĀ'IKA.

IṢṬA-DEVATĀ īsh´ tū dā vū´ tä (H—Skt.; lit. "chosen god"). Deity chosen for special devotion, based on family or regional tradition or personal preference. The special attention shown to the *iṣṭa-devatā* complements, rather than supplants, devotion to other gods. (*See* ŚAIVISM; VAIṢṆAVISM.)

J. BARE

ĪŚVARA ēsh´ vä rū (H—Skt.; lit. "master, lord, husband, Supreme Being" [*īś*—"to command, rule, reign"]). A common expression for the notion of a personal god or supreme personal being in Indian religion. The term is especially prevalent in devotional contexts such as the BHAKTI sections of the BHAGAVAD GĪTĀ, the various sectarian PURĀṆAS, and the texts of the ŚAIVA and VAIṢṆAVA traditions. In the Indian philosophical traditions (DARŚANAS) Īśvara is variously conceived and accepted or rejected. VEDĀNTA, Nyāya (and probably Vaiśeṣika) as well as YOGA all accept the existence of Īśvara, while MĪMĀṂSĀ and SĀṂKHYA deny it. Vedānta interprets Īśvara as a secondary manifestation *(saguṇa)* of the qualityless *(nirguṇa)* BRAHMAN or Absolute. A personal god, in other words, is ultimately a manifestation of MĀYĀ or "illusion," albeit a useful manifestation. Nyāya accepts Īśvara as a creator god who rules creation and dispenses grace to suffering souls. The pluralistic and atomistic realism of NYĀYA-VAIŚEṢIKA philosophically requires such a notion of god in order to explain how a universe (of plural components) can come together and be sustained. Yoga accepts the existence of Īśvara but denies that god is a creator or in any way active in creation. Īśvara is described simply as a particular "freed" or "isolated" PURUṢA ("consciousness" or "soul") in which the "afflictions" of nondiscrimination do not occur. As such, Īśvara can serve only as a model or symbol, a useful meditative device for the practicing YOGIN.

G. J. LARSON

IZANAGI AND IZANAMI ē zä nä´ gē, ē zä nä´ mē (Sh—Jap.). The most important divine couple in written Japanese mythology, responsible for much of the process of creation. Izanagi is roughly "Male-who-invites," and Izanami is "Female-who-invites."

Japanese mythology is recorded in two eighth century works, KOJIKI and NIHON SHOKI, which are the main sources for the understanding of these two divinities. After heaven and earth were formed and some heavenly deities appeared, there arose what is called the seven generations of the age of the gods; Izanagi and Izanami are the seventh generation, and much more important than the previous generations. The earlier deities order Izanagi and Izanami to begin creation, which they carry out by standing on the floating bridge of heaven and thrusting a jeweled spear into the brine below them. Stirring the water causes it to thicken, and when they withdraw the spear, the drops falling off it create an island, Onogoro, to which the pair descend. The "couples" of the seven generations seem to be brother and sister, but as is the case in many mythological accounts their union plays a crucial role in the initial creative process. Izanagi and Izanami as a brother-sister couple erect a central pillar on the island and circle it as part of a marriage ceremony, becoming the first wedded couple.

They create more islands, after which Izanami gives birth to mountains, seas, plants, animals, and humans. She also gives birth to more divinities, but the birth of the god of fire burns her so severely that she dies and proceeds to the dark land of the dead (Yomi). Izanagi is saddened and decides to visit her, not knowing that she has already decayed and cannot return to the land of the living, since she has already eaten the food of Yomi. She orders him not to look at her, but he lights a torch and sees her decaying body. In a prolonged chase the angered sister and other deities of Yomi try to catch Izanagi, apparently to keep him from returning to the land of light and the living. Through various tricks he escapes and blocks the entrance to Yomi. There is then an angry exchange of threats. Izanami threatens to kill a thousand beings every day in the land of light, in response to which Izanagi declares he will bring about fifteen hundred births every day. His contact with death has polluted him, and when he purifies himself in running water three deities are born, one of whom is the Sun Goddess AMATERASU, from whom the imperial line is descended, and another, Susa-no-wo, who plays a prominent part in subsequent mythology.

Especially because of the episode of flight from Yomi, Westerners have often compared this tale to the Greek account of Orpheus and Eurydice. Less well known are counterparts of other aspects of the tale, such as Pacific area tales of a primordial marriage around a central pillar. In terms of mythology Izanagi and Izanami provide a partial account of the creative process and are responsible indirectly for the origin of death. These two mythological figures are well known by all Japanese, but with the exception of a few shrines dedicated to them, there is no significant cult worshiping them.

H. B. EARHART

J

JACOB BEN MEIR TAM yä kōb′ bĕn mə ēr′ täm (Ju; 1100-1171). Foremost authority on the TALMUD and dominant social leader of the Jewish community in northern France. His writings include religious poetry (PIYYUTIM), biblical commentaries, Hebrew grammars, glosses on the Talmud *(tosafoth),* and numerous legal RESPONSA. K. P. BLAND

JACOBITE CHURCH (Ch). MONOPHYSITE church of Syria, named "Jacobite" by the opponents of Jacob Baradeus (500-578), who traveled widely in support of the Monophysites and was recognized as the spiritual leader of the church in Syria.

With the Arab conquest (*ca.* 640) the Jacobites came under Muslim domination, and with the NESTORIANS and the Orthodox were regarded as a single nation. They were able to expand their missionary activities, spreading into Mesopotamia and Persia. Jacob of Edessa (*ca.* 640-708), known as "the Jerome of Syria," was the church's most outstanding biblical and liturgical scholar.

The Jacobites continued the tradition of Syrian MONASTICISM. In addition to forming religious communities, hermits also practiced ascetic feats such as living on top of a pillar. They were known as stylites (*stylos*—pillar).

Today the head of the church is the PATRIARCH "of the Apostolic See of Antioch," but his seat is in Iraq. Jacobites use the Julian calendar and the pre-Chalcedonian liturgy of St. James. Their liturgical languages are Syriac and Arabic. They are in agreement with the COPTIC Christians in faith and sacraments, but make little use of ICONS.

In the last century schools have been attached to the few remaining monasteries. The purpose of education is to arrest religious decline and to resist missionaries from the West. There are about 100,000 Jacobites today.

Bibliography. A. S. Atiya, *A History of Eastern Christianity* (1968), pp. 167-237. V. KESICH

JAGANNĀTHA jŭg ŭ nä′ tä (H—Skt.; lit. "Lord of the World"). A god worshiped primarily in Orissa as a form of KRISHNA. The Jagganātha temple in Purī is one of the largest Hindu temples in India and the center of this deity's worship. A blend of indigenous tribal and Hindu Purāṇic conceptions, Jagannātha is the focus of a major festival which takes place in the month of Āshāḍha (June-July). The huge temple cart or "chariot" used to carry the temple image during the festival is 45 feet high and has wooden wheels 7 feet in diameter. The inexorable motion of this large vehicle has led to disciples being crushed under its wheels and to the English loan word "juggernaut." L. D. SHINN

BST Photos

Scene from the Jagganātha Festival

JAHANNAM jä hä′ nəm (I). Islamic name for hell, the place of punishment of the unrighteous, frequently contrasted with JANNA, paradise, in the QUR'ĀN. The Islamic term is derived from the biblical Gehenna or Hinnom, a valley near Jerusalem believed to be the entrance to the underworld.

The location of *jahannam* is not clear, but its main features are vividly portrayed. It is a place of fire and great heat. Thus Sura 38:59 reads: "They shall roast in the Fire." Again, Sura 78:21 ff. reads: "Behold, Gehenna has become an ambush, for the insolent a resort, therein to tarry for ages, tasting therein neither coolness nor any drink save boiling water and pus for a suitable recompense." Several verses refer to the Tree of Zaqqūm (Sura 44:45; 56:61) of whose bitter fruit the condemned will eat.

The general picture of *jahannam* in the Qur'ān is of a great pit into which the condemned are thrown. At the same time it is said to have gates. Sura 15:44 refers to the seven gates through which the unrighteous enter. In post-Qur'ānic times the conception of seven levels of hell appeared, likely in parallel to the idea of seven heavens. Moreover, a detailed schematization was developed in which distinctions were made among the condemned so as to have them enter through the appropriate gate, occupy the appropriate level, and undergo the appropriate form of punishment according to the nature of their particular transgressions. It seems likely that DANTE'S *Inferno* was influenced by the Muslim scheme and scenario of punishment.

It is not clear from the Qur'ān whether punishment in *jahannam* is necessarily eternal. Sura 23:106, for example, reads: "In Gehenna dwelling forever," but other verses (e.g., Sura 11:108-9) and some traditions attributed to MUHAMMAD have been interpreted as affirming the possibility of divine pardon of inhabitants of *jahannam*.

See also HEAVEN AND HELL. H. B. PARTIN

JAINISM jân′ ĭsm or jīn′ ĭsm (Skt., from *jaina;* lit. "follower of a jina" [*jina*—"conqueror, victor"]). A system of radical ASCETICISM, founded at least as early as the sixth century B.C. Jina is an honorific title given to the great teachers and ascetics of the movement, particularly to a series of twenty-four great teachers known as TĪRTHAṄKARAS. Jainism's doctrine and history are permeated by religious convictions related to the notion of conquest, and its goal is absolute triumph over all material existence.

1. Teachings and practice
2. History and setting
3. The laity: religious and social life
4. Literature
   Bibliography

1. Teachings and practice. Each living being consists of a sentient "soul," the JĪVA, which has become bound up in material existence, and the goal of a Jaina ascetic is to free the *jīva* from that bondage. (The Jainas categorize the several components of material existence, including matter itself, under the heading *ajīva*, "that which is not *jīva*.") The *jīva's* basic nature is one of perfect knowledge and self-contained bliss; but entanglement in *ajīva* has clouded the *jīva's* natural capacities, and it is destined for endless rebirths (according to the general Hindu notion of SAMSARA) unless it is freed from material bondage.

Each *jīva* is conceived to be a discrete entity, identical in nature to other *jīvas* but eternally separate from them. The *jīvas* do not emanate from a common source; nor will they ever merge into a larger state of consciousness or bliss; nor is there any overarching deity or primary *jīva*. The existence of the *jīva* is known from its activity as the "knower," i.e., the agent of perception and self-knowledge, in living things.

The *jīva's* bondage is held to be the result of KARMA, which Jainas conceive to be a subtle form of matter that clings to the *jīva*. The *jīva* itself is thought to be capable of various states in which it collects more or less karma; thus the more ignorant and agitated the *jīva*, the more likely it is to accumulate karma. Thus "activity" (which is the root meaning of *karma*), both physical and in the form of inner agitation, is seen by Jainas as having actual material consequences. In gross terms, the human body (or the material component of any living thing) may be seen as an accumulation of karma on the immaterial, imperceptible *jīva*.

This being so, the only way to free the *jīva* is to reduce inner and outer activity to a bare minimum and finally stop it altogether. Inactivity will stop further accumulation of karma, but the karma already present must decay before freedom is attained. Ascetic penance can hasten this decay, and the final step to freedom for the *jīva* can be undertaken by destroying the body through inactivity. Translated into practical terms, this means death by self-starvation is permitted or encouraged (an ascetic feat that Jainas still occasionally undertake, but which is permitted only to those at the most advanced level of ascetic practice). Once freed, the *jīva* is held to rise to the upper reaches of the universe, where it abides forever in its innate perfection.

This, then, is a path of solitary conquest whose hallmark is renunciation of virtually all activity that might lead karma to accumulate on the *jīva*. The Jainas hold that only one life-style can lead to freedom, a life of austere MONASTICISM. This has from the beginning taken the form of wandering mendicancy. The Jaina monk or nun is expected to give up home, household, and property; to beg all sustenance; to vigorously avoid doing harm to any other living thing; and to spend the greater part of his or her life wandering on foot from place to place, alone or in small groups.

The basic requirements of this ascetic life-style are shared by all Jainas, although there are differences in detail. The Jainas have devoted much discussion to systematizing and detailing the requirements of ascetic practice. At base, the vows required of monks and nuns resemble those of India's ascetic movements in general: noninjury, truthfulness, not taking anything not given, renunciation of possessions, and celibacy. At the same time, one of these vows has virtually become a hallmark of Jainism, the vow of AHIṂSĀ (noninjury). The Jaina ascetic is obliged to take extraordinary pains to avoid injuring any living being, so much so that the carrying of a small broom or brush with which to sweep tiny creatures out of harm's way is a characteristic Jaina practice.

2. **History and setting.** The Jainas hold a cyclical view of time and the cosmos and view the truths of their tradition as having existed eternally. Within the present cycle of cosmic history, however, they look back to a series of twenty-four great teachers, the Tīrthaṅkaras, or "crossing-makers," who have shown humankind the way to freedom from material bondage. The first Tīrthaṅkara, Ṛṣabha (or ĀDINĀTHA), and twenty-one of his successors are placed in the prehistory of the world. However, the most recent figure in this succession, Vardhamāna Jnāṭṛputra (commonly known as MAHĀVĪRA, "the great hero"), was a contemporary of SIDDHĀRTHA GAUTAMA, the BUDDHA (sixth century B.C.), and for his immediate predecessor in the series, Pārśva, there is some evidence of historicity.

The Jainas place Pārśva *ca.* 850 B.C., and there are indications, both in Jaina and Buddhist texts, that Mahāvīra's later work was built around a core of teachings and practitioners who reached back to Pārśva. Buddhist texts in particular testify that at the time of Mahāvīra's early mission there already existed numerous "unattached ones" (Skt.: *nirgranthas;* Pali: *nigaṇṭhas*) who followed a path known as the "fourfold restraint" *(cātuyāma-saṃvara)*, which is associated with Pārśva. Mahāvīra apparently adopted this path and then modified it in his own teachings.

While it seems likely, then, that Jaina ascetic practices and groups of Jaina monks predate Mahāvīra, it is nonetheless the case that Jainism as a vigorous and coherent movement begins with Mahāvīra. Born in 599 B.C. (trad.), in Northeastern India near the modern city of Patna, Mahāvīra followed a career similar to that of the Buddha. Born into a warrior (KSATRIYA) clan, he abandoned his household at age thirty and spent twelve and a half years in severe ascetic penances, wandering, begging, detaching himself from all worldly desires, and meditating.

At age forty-two he attained complete knowledge (KAIVALYA), and within a few months he had collected eleven followers who assisted him in spreading his teachings. According to Jaina tradition, Mahāvīra's following had swelled to 14,000 monks, 36,000 nuns, and 377,000 lay people by the time of his death.

In 527 B.C. (trad.) Mahāvīra died, in a town now known as Pāvāpurī, near Patna, not far from his birthplace. Leadership of the movement then passed to the survivors from among the eleven original disciples (known in the Jaina tradition as the *gaṇadharas*, "leaders of the assembly"), in particular to one named Sudharman. Under a series of leaders the movement began to spread to South Central and Northwest India. This growth accelerated in the time of the MAURYAN DYNASTY (third century B.C.) as the Jainas profited along with the Buddhists from the Mauryan emperors' disposition to favor ascetic movements and their ideals.

The growth and geographical dispersion of the movement did, however, lead to a division over whether or not a monk is allowed to wear any clothing. Ascetic nudity was practiced by various monastic groups in Mahāvīra's time, and Mahāvīra himself apparently also practiced it during some of his career. One segment of the Jaina community held that any concession whatsoever to the sensibilities and comforts of ordinary life was to be avoided. Monks who adopted this view insisted, therefore, that a monk should be completely naked at all times, giving his karma-body no respite from heat, cold, rough surfaces, etc., and denying any validity to the feelings of shame or arousal that the naked body normally incites.

Another segment of the community did not actually dispute these claims, but rather held that the practice of Jainism's founder was equivocal on the matter of nudity, so that it should not be an absolute requirement for monastic life. The latter group argued that the possession and wearing of only a single white garment was a sufficient renunciation of worldly practices, provided that no inward attachment to the body remained.

The attitudes of these groups toward clothing led to the former being called DIGAMBARAS (lit., "clad [only] in the four directions," i.e., naked) and the latter ŚVETĀMBARAS (lit., "clad in white"). Since the first century A.D., the vast majority of Jainas have identified themselves with one or the other of these submovements.

This split is a problem for historians, since each group has to some extent maintained its own version of the early history of Jainism, and each has its own version of the Jaina scriptures. The split also reveals the deadly seriousness with which radical renunciation is taken in Jainism. Digambaras and Śvetāmbaras do not, by and large, disagree on fundamental points of religious philosophy. Their differences arose over religious practices, specifically the matter of clothing, which led to certain related disagreements, e.g., over the details of monastic rules for begging, etc.

A related point of disagreement is the status of women in monastic orders. The Śvetāmbaras accept orders of nuns, who keep to themselves and follow rigorous monastic rules. The Digambaras do not accept the idea of women in orders. This has led to some rather technical philosophical argument over whether women are capable of attaining release, the Digambaras holding that the karma-bondage which holds a *jīva* in a woman's body cannot be undone until the *jīva* is born into material existence as a male. The Śvetāmbaras hold that there is no difference between the sexes in terms of capacity for attaining release.

In the centuries after the Śvetāmbara-Digambara division, the Śvetāmbaras were predominant in the West and Northwest (modern-day Maharashtra, Gujarat, and Rajasthan), while the Digambaras dominated the movement in Central and Southern India. In both cases the Jainas often enjoyed royal patronage, and were major contributors to the literature, arts, and architecture of the various regions. The period from the Mauryan Dynasty to the twelfth century A.D. was the period of Jainism's greatest growth and influence. Thereafter the Jainas in the South and Central regions lost ground in the face of rising Hindu devotional movements. Jainism retreated to the West and Northwest, which have remained its stronghold to the present.

Unlike Buddhism, Jainism has never seriously spread beyond India; but also unlike Buddhism, it has survived and retained a distinct identity within an Indian context which is predominantly Hindu. The movement is not large, numbering at present fewer than four million; but its practices and teachings have remained strong, and its influence on many dimensions of Hindu culture has been significant.

3. **The laity: religious and social life.** The Jaina community apparently included lay persons from the time of Mahāvīra, and Jainism is noted for the strength of its lay following. Jainism developed a strong relationship between monks, nuns, and lay people, a relationship that has enabled the lay Jaina to identify with the tradition and support it.

The traditional view that the Jaina community has four segments—monks, nuns, laymen, and laywomen—did not come into vogue until a number of centuries after Mahāvīra's death, and the precise nature of the relationship between ascetic and lay person in Jainism's early centuries is not clear. One factor that apparently kept the relationship strong is that Jaina ascetics for the most part kept themselves in close contact with the laity, rather than congregating in monastic centers (as Buddhist monks appear to have done).

Eventually the intellectual leaders of Jainism undertook to develop a series of lesser vows and specific religious practices that would give the lay person an identifiable religious career. More than forty texts were eventually composed to explain and detail the lay person's religious duties as involving eleven stages of increasingly rigorous ascetic restraint, including in the early stages the observance of brief fasts, increasingly restrictive diet, periodic sexual continence, and the like. In the later stages lay persons are to renounce virtually all ordinary activities, so that by the eleventh stage they are ready to undertake full monastic vows.

This series of stages, to which any lay person may aspire, is a means of assuring that the lay community will feel continuity with the ascetic branches of Jainism. But beyond that, every lay person is expected to undertake at least the first stage, which involves a formal statement of allegiance to the Jinas and to the ideals of Jainism. It is held that one who has not undertaken this step is not a practicing Jaina, even to the point that Jaina children who have not done so are regarded as Jainas in name only.

Jainas have also provided for socio-religious ritual activities that place them more or less within the mainstream of Hindu social structure. They generally observe the CASTE system, and follow a set of life-cycle rites that are modified versions of the Hindu "perfections" *(saṃskāras)*, rituals for birth, death, marriage, and the like. The integration of the Jaina lay community and Hindu social patterns was by all accounts a gradual process; but it received its normative form and justification by the late ninth century A.D., when Jinasena composed the *Āipurāṇa*, a Jaina version of the history of the cosmos (on the model of the Hindu PURĀṆAS), in which the first Tīrthaṅkaras are credited with establishing the social order for various pragmatic and political reasons.

The Jainas also maintain a religious cult, including temple rituals, which in many ways resemble Hindu devotional PŪJĀ, consisting of offerings of flowers and fruits before images of the Tīrthaṅkaras. Such practices may date from the centuries immediately after Mahāvīra's death. At the same time, the Jainas stoutly maintain that veneration of the Tīrthaṅkaras does not impute to them the status of divinities, but rather serves only to strengthen the ideal of monastic detachment in the lay person. Even lay Jainism, then, remains doctrinally atheistic.

4. **Literature.** The Jainas have maintained a reverence for learning that is somewhat paradoxical in a radically ascetic tradition. In addition to doctrinal and philosophical texts, Jaina authors have produced important works in a variety of literary modes. For example, Mallinātha, the great commentator on the SANSKRIT poetry of KĀLIDĀSA, was a Jaina, one of many accomplished Jaina authors of secular literature. Jaina monk-scholars are also noted for their formative influence in making regional vernacular languages, especially in South and Central India, into literary vehicles.

The religious and philosophical literature of Jainism falls into two large categories. The Śvetāmbara and Digambara movements preserve separate versions of the Jaina scriptures. The Śvetāmbara canon of scripture, which was not given definitive form until nearly A.D. 500, consists of approximately forty-five texts, in six groups. The oldest and most important of these is a group of eleven texts called *aṅgas* ("limbs"), in which the sermons and dialogues of Mahāvīra himself are collected. The bulk of the forty-five texts are in a language called Ardha-Māgadhi, a vernacular language from the region of Mahāvīra's birth and death.

The Digambaras do not preserve a similar set of texts. They regard as normative a series of writings, the oldest of which date to the early centuries A.D. and were composed by leaders of the movement. The Digambaras hold that the original teachings of Mahāvīra and his disciples have been lost, but that the Digambara texts preserve accurately the substance of Mahāvīra's message. While differently organized, the Digambara texts do duplicate the contents of the Śvetāmbara canon, and this disagreement over the scriptures has not led to fundamental doctrinal differences between the two movements.

Both the Digambaras and Śvetāmbaras have produced a considerable series of works in religious philosophy, principally in Sanskrit, discussing, analyzing, and expanding the original teachings of the tradition. One of their most interesting achievements is the development of a multivalent system of logic, called the *nayavāda,* which seeks to establish seven modes of truth-statement.

This vigorous intellectual and literary tradition is itself one of the factors in the persistence of the Jainas as an ascetic minority in India. It should be noted, however, that the Jainas have also played an important role in conserving, in their libraries, the writings of non-Jaina Hindu authors.

Bibliography. P. S. Jaini, *The Jaina Path of Purification* (1979); R. Williams, *Jaina Yoga* (1963); Mrs. S. Stevenson, *The Heart of Jainism* (1915). K. W. FOLKERT

JALĀL ad-DĪN RŪMĪ. *See* RUMĪ, JALĀL AL-DĪN.

JAMĀL al-DĪN AFGHĀNĪ. *See* AFGHĀNĪ, JAMĀL AL-DĪN.

JAMNIA jăm′ nē ə (Ju). A Palestinian town situated on the coastal plain south of Jaffa, Jamnia (or Yavneh) was captured by the MACCABEES. By the reign of Alexander Jannaeus (103-76 B.C.) the city's population was entirely Jewish. It was there that JOHANAN BEN ZAKKAI reestablished the SANHEDRIN after the fall of JERUSALEM. Johanan's leadership and the legislation he put forward here constitute a watershed in Jewish history which enabled the PHARISEES to take root and prosper.

Of inestimable importance was the decision taken *ca.* A.D. 90 to fix and limit the canon of Hebrew Scripture. (*See* BIBLE.) Prior to this time, while the Pentateuch and Prophets had adhered to a more or less fixed form, the Writings or Hagiographa had remained open and fluid. Recently scholars have argued that the Babylonian text of the Hebrew Bible was also selected there over the more popular and more controversial Palestinian and Egyptian versions. Both the canon and text chosen at Jamnia constitute the authoritative basis for the Hebrew text promulgated by the later MASORETES and known as the Masoretic Text. E. M. MEYERS

JANNA jä′ nə (I—Arab.; lit. "garden"). The Muslim heaven or paradise to which the righteous are consigned after judgment.

Janna is described in several passages in the QUR'ĀN, some comparatively early. For example, Sura 47:16—"This is the similitude of Paradise which the godfearing have been promised; therein are rivers of water unstaling, rivers of milk unchanging in flavour, and rivers of wine—a delight to the drinkers, rivers, too, of honey purified; and therein for them is every fruit, and forgiveness from their Lord." In general, the garden is a place of plenty, pleasure, and repose, much like a luxuriant oasis. Through it flow rivers offering diverse refreshments and in it are trees and fruits of many kinds as well as beautiful, modest maidens (houris, Sura 56:10-25; *see* ESCHATOLOGY §3). There believers will experience the rewards of their obedience and good works. The images are such as would be understood by a desert people.

In paradise are books in which human deeds are recorded, to be presented at the time of the final judgment. Such a conception would not have seemed foreign to Meccan merchants and traders accustomed to keeping ledgers. The Qur'ān also refers (Sura 13:39) to "the Essence" or "the Mother of the Book," an archetype of the Qur'ān and other scriptures. Further, there appeared in post-Qur'ānic times the idea and image of a paradisal KA'BA, archetype of the earthly, Meccan Ka'ba.

The question whether believers will see God in paradise was much debated, especially during the eighth and ninth centuries A.D. when the Mu'tazilites (*see* MU'TAZILA) interpreted seeing God metaphorically. Muslim orthodoxy as well as popular belief insisted on the beatific vision of ALLAH without, however, specifying the manner of the vision.

See also HEAVEN AND HELL. H. B. PARTIN

JANSENISM (Ch). Theological system associated with Cornelius Jansen (1585-1638). It was prominent in France, the Netherlands, and Tuscany in the seventeenth and eighteenth centuries but condemned repeatedly by the PAPACY. It stressed that in the absence of divine grace no person can perform a meritorious action, but that once grace is given, it cannot be resisted. F. OAKLEY

JAPANESE RELIGION. Japanese religion includes practices that have originated in Japan, some as early as prehistoric times, and practices that were imported from other cultures in historic times and have developed along distinctively Japanese lines. At times these traditions have vied with one another and emphasized their differences, but for the most part they have interacted, and usually people have participated in more than one tradition simultaneously.

1. **General features.** Japanese religion includes a number of easily identifiable philosophical and religious traditions. Out of a rich prehistoric religious tradition arose SHINTŌ, Japan's unique blending of veneration of the sacredness of nature and reverence for social ties and national heritage. It was formally organized in the sixth century, under the impact of BUDDHISM. Buddhism was first appreciated for its magnificent art and rituals and was utilized for its magical powers, but later its elaborate philosophical systems were studied. The two specifically Chinese

traditions, CONFUCIANISM and TAOISM, contributed significantly to the Japanese world view, but more as diffuse philosophical and religious influences than as organized religions. Confucianism, and later Neo-Confucianism, served to provide the rationale of loyalty to the state and FILIAL PIETY toward parents, thus constituting an important basis for ethical principles and social relations. Taoism entered Japan in the form of the many practices of cosmology, DIVINATION, and rituals usually known as "religious Taoism" (*see* TAOISM, RELIGIOUS); it briefly formed a Bureau of Divination in the government, after the Chinese pattern, but thereafter was mainly an influence upon Buddhism and Shintō rather than an independent tradition. CHRISTIANITY did not arrive in Japan until FRANCIS XAVIER'S mission in 1549. It flourished for a brief "Christian century" before being banned, and some "hidden Christians" maintained their faith secretly for two centuries. Christianity in Japan today (Catholic, Protestant, and Orthodox) dates from its reintroduction in the second half of the nineteenth century. Although usually perceived as a foreign tradition and claiming less than one percent of the population as members, Christianity has made wider contributions in terms of Bible reading, education, and social reform. Since the early nineteenth century many so-called new religions have arisen and become an increasingly conspicuous force on the religious scene. (*See* KONKŌ-KYŌ; TENRI-KYŌ.)

Much of the character and dynamic of Japanese religion is found outside of, or between, these organized religions. For example, Shintō is much more than the mythological tradition of the country's beginning and the numerous Shintō shrines; Shintō refers also to the pervasive Japanese notion that human and "natural" forms may directly participate in or even become KAMI (sacred or "gods"). The same kind of pervasive influence flows from Buddhism, whose major religious purpose is caring for souls of family dead who have become BUDDHAS (which is almost the same as becoming kami). Aspects of the organized religions were taken over by the people and transmitted as popular religion, apart from ecclesiastical institutions. Also, folk religion has been a prominent force within Japanese religion. Some folk religious traditions, such as the practices of SHAMANISM and rituals for transplanting of rice, may trace their beginning to the prehistoric era. These aspects of formal and informal religion have been inseparably related to the economic, social, and political life of Japan. (*See below* § 3f, g.)

2. The formation. In the prehistoric period Japan consisted of a number of local cultures with diverse backgrounds. The major line of continuity of prehistoric Japanese culture with that of later Japan (and with much of East Asian culture generally) is in the setting of rice agriculture, which entered Japan about the middle of the first millennium B.C. The production of rice made sedentary village life more stable, in turn leading to emphasis on extended families and village cooperation. In the realm of religion, rites focused on seasonal celebrations for fertility and thanksgiving related to agriculture and for veneration of ancestral spirits, who were considered directly responsible for fertility (*see* ANCESTOR VENERATION). From about 500 B.C. to A.D. 500 the area of southwest Japan was developing into a centralized kingdom headed by an imperial family, and toward the latter part of this time span was receiving influence from the Asian mainland. About A.D. 500 the high culture of China entered Japan and immediately became a major influence on elite culture, since Japan at the time had no written language or highly organized systems of government, philosophy, or religion. Japan freely accepted these Chinese imports but just as freely modified them to its own satisfaction, to create a distinctively Japanese culture.

From about the eighth century on, local myths and traditions were more highly unified around one account of creation and the descent of the emperor from the kami, as told in the KOJIKI and NIHON SHOKI, the two earliest Japanese historical chronicles. Partly in reaction to the introduction of the highly organized Buddhist religion, the long tradition of loosely organized Japanese rituals and practice came to be organized as Shintō, the "way of the kami." The major lines of Japanese religion thus took shape, with Buddhism and Shintō the two main organized religions, and Taoism and Confucianism diffuse influences. Some Shintō shrines that apparently began as family shrines changed into territorial shrines and developed branch shrines in other territories. Buddhist institutions were first established in each province by the state, but temples for the common people gradually arose, especially for memorial services.

From about A.D. 800 to 1400 various Buddhist sects and Shintō schools developed. In the premodern period of 1600 to 1867 Buddhist temples became closely allied with the power of the state; families were required to belong to Buddhist temples and have Buddhist memorial services performed for the family dead; at the same time Neo-Confucian thought provided the major rationale for the state (*see* CONFUCIANISM §3.) With the MEIJI Restoration of 1868

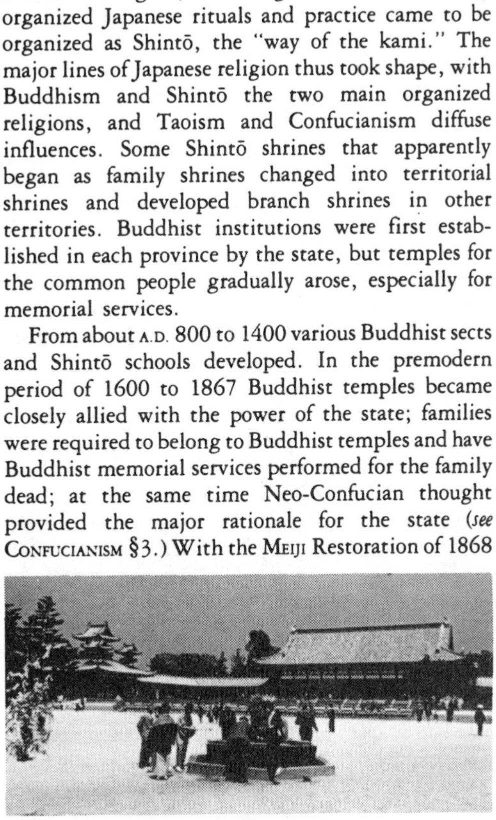

Visual Education Service, Charles A. Kennedy

Courtyard, Heian Shrine, Kyoto, built 1895. In the center is a fountain for purification. Small trees are turned white with hanging fortune papers.

Shintō became prominent in justifying and maintaining the new nation-state, and was influential even in education. From 1868 to 1945 considerable social change occurred, with major innovation in such areas as education and religion, but only since 1945 have all religions been free to organize and compete, as well as cooperate, according to their own principles.

3. **Major themes of traditional Japanese religion.** *a) The interaction among the various traditions.* When Buddhism was accepted, it did not mean that the native tradition of Shintō was rejected. Rather, the foreign Buddhist divinities and native kami were seen to be complementary forces, both of which blessed personal and national life. A person might be married in a Shintō shrine, live his life according to Confucian social teachings, hold some Taoistic beliefs about "lucky" and "unlucky," participate in folk festivals, and have his funeral conducted by a Buddhist temple. Only Christianity has been little influenced by this interaction.

b) The intimate relationship between humans and kami and the sacredness of nature. Natural phenomena such as mountains, streams, and trees are seen as expressing extraordinary power and considered as sacred or kami. Emperors too, as descendants of the kami, were considered forms of kami; and even human beings who acquired special religious power have been considered kami. The spirits of family dead, as ancestors, are considered either as "Buddhas" *(hotoke)* or kami. In short, in Japanese religion kami and Buddhas are not conceived as being in another world so much as they are thought to be within the world of nature and in the lives of human beings

c) The religious significance of the family and family ancestors. From ancient times family lineage has been important, and this was reinforced both by Confucian notions of filial piety and Buddhist rituals for memorializing the dead. The family is a religious institution in its own right, in recent times often featuring both a Shintō-style altar (KAMIDANA) and Buddhist altar (BUTSUDAN). The Buddhist altar is especially important because it enshrines the spirits of family ancestors, regularly memorialized on the anniversary of their deaths. In this fashion the family includes all the hallmarks of a religious institution: divinities (the family ancestors), religious leadership (the head of the household), ceremonies (regular memorial rites for family ancestors), and membership (family as a whole).

d) Purification as a basic principle of religious life. Generally the Japanese people have not experienced "sin" as violation of divine commandments, but they have had a clear sense of impurity or defilement that separated them from their fellows and especially from the kami. Such impurities as sickness and death were most important, and there were both semi-annual and special purification ceremonies to drive out the impurity. The same pattern is reflected in the Shintō custom of ceremonially rinsing the hands and mouth before entering a Shintō shrine. These "outer" purifications, of course, reflect "inner" motivations, and generally in Japan ritual purity has meant trying to live in harmony with the kami (or the sacred).

e) Festivals as the major means of religious celebration. In traditional Japan the pattern of religious activities was determined by the special festival days of each religious institution and annual festivals celebrated by families and the nation as a whole. Especially important have been spring and fall festivals, roughly coinciding with the transplanting and harvesting of rice. The time surrounding New Year's is a long festival period marked by large crowds visiting both Shintō shrines and Buddhist temples. *Bon,* the festival for returning spirits of the dead in late summer, is observed in most homes throughout the nation. *(See* Plate VIa.)

f) The penetration of religious activities into daily life. Religion in traditional Japan was closely related to every aspect of economic and social life. Best known is the way in which every stage of growing rice was accompanied by religious rituals, but there were also rituals and festivals for other occupations. Fishing villages staged harbor festivals, and there were special rites for large catches of fish and safety on the sea. Even guilds for artisans, such as carpenters, had their special patron saints. Socially there were rituals following a person throughout life, from birth to marriage to death. Aesthetic pursuits such as the TEA CEREMONY and flower arranging blend into the religious veneration of the forces of nature and the attainment of a personal harmony with cosmic forces.

James Kirk

Rice transplantation festival, held in June. Here a priest places small flags at each water gate of the paddy to appease the kami related to the flooding of the field.

g) The close relationship between religion and state. In Japan the general rule has been for religious authority to be subservient to political power. From the ancient period of Japanese history, myth sanctioned the "unity of ritual government" *(saisei itchi)* through the notion that the kami created the Japanese islands as a sacred land to be ruled by the emperor, who was a descendant of the Sun Goddess (AMATERASU Ōmikami). Confucian and even Taoist influence helped organize and rationalize the state, and throughout Japanese history the tendency has been for religion to be subservient to the needs and governance of the state. NICHIREN, the exceptional figure who challenged state authority, did so because he had a more radical notion of the unity of state and religion (in this case Buddhism). This support of state by religion has continued until recent times; before and during World War II most religious groups, including Christianity, supported the state in its war efforts.

4. **Religion in modern Japan.** Throughout all of Japanese history religion has undergone gradual and significant change, but from the late nineteenth century change became more rapid and radical. There is no absolute borderline between "traditional" and "modern" Japan, since many aspects of earlier Japan live on today. But the years from the momentous Meiji Restoration of 1868—which marked the formation of a modern nation-state—and the equally important post-World War II period—which marked the enactment of complete religious freedom—are so qualitatively different that they should be considered separately from the pre-1868 period.

Shintō had formed part of the rationale for the Meiji Restoration, when the emperor was "restored" to central importance, symbolically if not in terms of actual power. And although attempts to make Shintō the center of the stage lost out to plans for developing a nation-state along modified Western lines, Shintō did provide a rationale for emphasizing national unity. Partly due to foreign pressure, the ban against Christianity was lifted in 1873; later, in an attempt to further strengthen national unity, most Shintō shrines were declared "nonreligious" extensions of the state, and school visits to Shintō shrines were considered part of civic duty. In this fashion Shintō as "State Shintō" was prominent in the development of national unity prior to 1945.

Buddhism had held favored status during the Tokugawa period (1600-1867), but in the Meiji Restoration it lost its special status to Shintō. However, the time-honored custom of Buddhist memorials for family ancestors did not disappear with the withdrawal of state requirements for these memorials, and to this day such memorials are the major concern of Buddhist temples and priests in Japan. From the Meiji period Japanese Buddhist scholars traveled to Western countries and developed remarkable historical and philological studies of all aspects of Buddhism; nevertheless, these studies have not drastically altered the life of the local Buddhist temple.

Even in the early nineteenth century popular movements formed around pilgrimage associations and charismatic leaders, often expanding into so-called "new religions" (*shinkō shukyō*). Some of these movements were closely related to Shintō, and as part of the government's move to declare Shintō shrines "nonreligious" these more actively evangelistic movements were given the special title of Sect Shintō, thirteen of which were recognized by 1908 (*see* KONKŌ-KYŌ; TENRI-KYŌ). Actually most of these members of Sect Shintō should be considered members of new religions, but until 1945 the government controlled religion closely and did not allow such movements to organize freely; other new religious movements arose and prospered in spite of state interference and occasional persecution, and after 1945 became one of the most active religious forces. (*See* SŌKA GAKKAI; RISSHŌ KŌSEIKAI.)

Christianity reentered Japan just before the Meiji Restoration, but did not become prominent until after the ban was lifted in 1873 and Western influence became more widespread. In the confused social conditions some, especially intellectuals, chose Christianity as the key to forging their identity in the modern world. PROTESTANTISM quickly developed self-supporting and distinctive Japanese institutions. ROMAN CATHOLICISM is respected for its long heritage in Japan, and shares with Protestantism the praise for having contributed to private education.

With the end of World War II in 1945, severe governmental restrictions on religion were lifted and complete religious freedom guaranteed. This meant that former State Shintō was denied any special state privileges, but could exist as a religious institution with the same status as all other religious bodies. It was now possible for all religious groups to organize freely and register with the government to be exempt from taxes. The immediate postwar period saw a proliferation of hundreds of new religious movements, and even the denominational ties of Buddhism and associations of Shintō shrines saw many schisms of independent institutions. Some policies of the Allied Occupation from 1945 to 1952, such as land reform, took away the economic support of some temples and shrines; this has forced these religious institutions and their clergy to seek other means of economic support, such as using buildings for educational purposes and even secular employment by clergy.

Some of the changes in modern Japanese religion have been more gradual and subtle—e.g., the effect of the shift from a rural life style to a more industrial and urban life style. People divorced from the rhythm of nature may feel less affinity for Shintō agricultural rituals; with weakening of family ties traditional Buddhist memorial rites may languish. But the same forces may also stimulate religious practice. There are no longer special festival days for beasts of burden, but there is a lively practice of blessing new cars and providing amulets for "traffic safety"; traditional family memorial services give way to new memorial practices, and the social structure of new religions can be compared to fictive families, with founding figures sometimes seen as divine parents.

Some of the changes in modern Japanese religion have been more sudden and drastic, such as the end of State Shintō in 1945 and the sharp existential

D. K. Swearer

Priest blesses a repair truck with a *haraiguchi*, a wooden pole with strips of white paper fastened at the end and shaken like a mop.

questioning of the meaning of life in the face of incredible human suffering climaxed by two atomic bombings. The past few decades have been a severe test for Japanese religion in its various forms, and secularism and religious indifference are widespread today. Yet balancing this disinterest in religion are the surprising results of numerous surveys which show that even though many people do not "belong" to a religion, a high percentage of the population feels that religion is necessary and beneficial to human life. This may help explain why the new religions have been able to attract so many followers.

Bibliography. H. B. Earhart, *Japanese Religion: Unity and Diversity*. 2rd ed. (1974); I. Hori, ed., *Japanese Religion* (1972); J. M. Kitagawa, *Religion in Japanese History* (1966), and "The Religion of Japan," in *A Reader's Guide to the Great Religions*, C.J. Adams, ed., 2nd ed. (1977).

H. B. EARHART

JAPJI jäp´ jē (S; lit. "recitation"). The morning prayer composed by the founder of SIKHISM, Guru NĀNAK, and the opening piece of the ĀDI GRANTH, the Sikh scripture. Sikh theologians regard it as the quintessence of Nānak's teaching. There is no evidence to establish the date of its composition, but most scholars are of the opinion that it was composed during the last years of the guru's life.

1. **Introduction.** According to the Janam Sākhīs ("birth stories") the opening lines known as the *Mūl Mantra* (root belief) were uttered by Nānak in the presence of God when he was first called upon to undertake his mission at about the age of thirty. These were:

There is one God
He is the Supreme Truth
He, the Creator is without fear and without hate . . .
He, the Omnipresent,
Pervades the Universe.
He is not born,
Nor does He die to be born again.
By His Grace shalt thou worship.

2. **Body.** The five stanzas which follow develop the theme of the nature of the Godhead: (1) God is beyond description or comprehension by reason; and (2) he is unapproachable except by treading the righteous path and by divine grace. The meditation of the GURU and hearing words in praise of the Creator are recommended as means of achieving godliness (stanzas 6 to 11). This is followed by descriptions of the bliss achieved by the believer (stanzas 12 to 17) and denunciation of fools, frauds, and fanatics who are blind to the truth that is God (stanzas 18 and 19). Nānak lauds the power of prayer to purge the soul of accumulated filth and extols the power of the name of the Lord over pilgrimage, austerity, mercy, and giving of alms, because contemplation of the word is an "inner pilgrimage" (stanza 21). He repeats the inability of teachers, meditators, and scholars to know the truth about creation, of the "numerous worlds" in regions beyond the skies (stanzas 22, 23). The next three stanzas (24, 25, 26) are in praise of God's infinite goodness and bounty, and are followed by the *Sodar* ("which gate?"), a kind of TE DEUM describing God's mansion. In slightly different form the *Sodar* appears in other compositions and is also a part of the Sikh's evening prayer *(rahrās)*. The subsequent four stanzas (28 to 31) are in praise of different facets of God's being, culminating in a powerful affirmation (stanza 32) of the unity of the Godhead.

Stanza 33 emphasizes the utter helplessness of mortals to do anything without divine ordinance and is a prelude to the five stages *(khand)* through which humans progress toward realization of God. Starting with *dharm khand* (the "realm of righteousness") he proceeds in stages to *gyān khand* ("realm of knowledge"), *saram khand* ("realm of endeavor"), *karam khand* ("realm of action"), to *sach khand* ("realm of truth where God himself dwells"). The last stanza summarizes some of the points made in the earlier stanzas exhorting mortals to look upon life on earth as a mint to produce pure gold coins with continence, patience, knowledge, reason, fear of God, prayer, love, and the name of the Lord.

3. **Epilogue.** Most scholars attribute authorship of the epilogue to Guru Angad. It is recited at the end of most Sikh rituals.

Bibliography. *See* bibliog. for ĀDI GRANTH.

K. SINGH

JĀTAKA jä´ tŭ kŭ (B—Skt. & Pali; lit. "having to do with birth" [*jā*—"to be born"]). A general term for "birth" or "existence" usually used in the special sense of a story of one of the former lives of the BUDDHA, in which he was a BODHISATTVA, or Buddha to be.

One of the psychic powers possessed by a fully enlightened being, a Buddha, is the ability to remember previous lives. The Buddha for this era, GAUTAMA, is thought to have mentioned his previous births from time to time as illustrations of various doctrinal points. Such "birth stories" (Jātaka) were referred to by early Buddhists as one of the nine types of sacred (oral) teachings, and when the canonical writings were established, a collection of Jātaka stories was included.

The Jātaka collection of the THERAVĀDA school contains 547 stories, and other early schools of Buddhism had similar collections. Later, smaller collections were sometimes made, with an emphasis upon those Jātakas that especially illustrated Buddhist virtues. The most important of these smaller collections is the Jātakamālā, "Garland of Jātaka," written in elegant style—mixed prose and poetry—by Āryasūrā in perhaps the second century A.D., and containing thirty-four Jātakas illustrating the bodhisattva's outstanding self-sacrificing, generosity, etc.

The stylized introduction to each Jātaka localizes the story by stating the country (region of the Indian subcontinent), the name of the ruling king, and the family or class. For example, "Once upon a time the bodhisattva was born into a certain Brahmin family during the reign of King Brahmadatta of Banāras."

The prose story that follows the introduction may be about humans, animals, or both. Some stories are Buddhist versions of FABLES also found in the other Indian collections and in Aesop's Greek collection. Other Jātakas are long narratives of humans who exemplify admirable or loathsome moral behavior. The bodhisattva is typically identified as the noblest person or animal in the story. The Jātaka typically concludes with a summarizing verse and a comment identifying the main characters with peers of the Buddha—sometimes assuming that people play out similar roles in life after life.

The most popular Jātaka among Theravāda Buddhists is the longest and last of the Pali collection, the story of the bodhisattva's birth as Prince Vessantara, a magnanimous prince who gave away anything requested. He was exiled for being too generous, and later gave away even his children and wife to Brahmins who begged for them. In the end, his family and kingdom were restored and he ruled with greater generosity than ever.

From early times Buddhists have filled their temple or STŪPA walls with illustrations of the Jātakas, and the laity often know many of the stories by heart. The stories put such teachings as rebirth, generosity, wisdom, nonattachment, and self-control into dramatic form. However, goodwill (KARUṆĀ) and compassion (METTĀ) as exemplified by the Buddha are the most frequent story themes.

Bibliography. E. B. Cowell, ed., *The Jātaka; or Stories of the Buddha's Former Births* (1973); T. W. Rhys Davids, *Buddhist Birth Stories* (1880).

R. C. AMORE

JĀTI jä′ tē (H). *See* CASTE.

JAYADEVA jī yŭ dā′ vŭ (H—Skt.). The name given to the author of the poem GĪTĀ GOVINDA, as well as a name of that poem's hero, KRISHNA. Legends about his life are many, but very little is known. It is said that he renounced his life as a SANSKRIT scholar and became a religious mendicant; that phase ended when he married a dancing girl at the temple of JAGANNĀTHA in Purī, Orissa. His birthplace is claimed by various villages in Bengal, Orissa, and Mithila. The time of his writing is also speculative, but some evidence points to his association with the court of the king Lakṣmaṇa Sena, who ruled in Bengal during the latter half of the twelfth century A.D.

E. C. DIMOCK, JR.

JEHOVAH jĕ hō′ vä (Ju & Ch). Not found in the text of the Hebrew Bible, "Jehovah" results from an early Jewish custom which, in order to avoid pronouncing the divine name, marked down under the original consonants *Yhwh* (YAHWEH) the vowels of *adonai,* "the Lord," which was to be reverently substituted for the divine name when reading aloud. Later ignorance united the consonants of the original word and the vowels of the substitute into an incorrect hybrid.

D. IRVIN

JEHOVAH'S WITNESSES (Ch). A denomination which emphasizes biblical literalism, aggressive evangelism, and APOCALYPTIC expectations. They have attracted attention by their conspicuous door-to-door and streetcorner missionary work centering on distribution of the magazines *The Watchtower* and *Awake!*; by their derivation of highly distinctive beliefs from the Scriptures; by their refusal to salute the flag, celebrate Christmas as Christ's birthday, or accept blood transfusions; and by their conflicts with various governments around the world.

1. **History.** The organizer of the movement, the American Charles Taze Russell (1852–1916), had been influenced as a young man by Millerite Adventism (*see* SEVENTH-DAY ADVENTISM) and possibly also by the CHRISTADELPHIANS. Like them, Russell passionately rejected eternal punishment. In 1879 he started the *Watchtower*, and in 1881 the Zion's Watch Tower Tract Society. During this period he traveled widely on preaching tours, his sermons were published in numerous newspapers, and his informal following probably numbered millions. Russell preferred organizing only tract societies, with a small army of colporteurs to distribute his literature, and it was only gradually that a denomination emerged. From the beginning Russell kept a firm hand on his multifarious works, and his rigor shaped the denomination's authoritarian character. The International Bible Students Association, founded in London in 1914, has been particularly influential outside the U.S. For many years "Russellites" were simply called Bible Students in many parts of the world.

Russell's successor, Joseph F. Rutherford (1869–1942), was a lawyer, and, like Russell, a prolific writer and authoritarian administrator. The name Jehovah's Witnesses was chosen for the movement, probably at his suggestion, by convention in 1931. Rutherford then took strong measures to centralize the movement, replacing the elected leadership of local congregations with elders appointed by headquarters.

During the Second World War Witnesses in America and Britain suffered public opprobrium and official harassment for their refusal to participate in military service or salute the flag. In the case of West Virginia State Board of Education v. Barnette (1943), the U.S. Supreme Court ruled that persons could not be compelled to perform such actions as saluting the flag contrary to their religious beliefs. In Nazi Germany and Eastern Europe large numbers of Witnesses disappeared into concentration camps.

Under the leadership of the third president, Nathan H. Knorr (1905-77), there was steady growth, and in the 1970s they claimed some 300,000 U.S. members, and over a million worldwide.

2. **Doctrine.** The convictions of Jehovah's Witnesses center on absolute belief in God as the ruler who demands unconditional obedience. The teachings to which he expects submission are clear, exact, and concrete. The infallible source of truth is the BIBLE, which Witnesses accept as literally true in every detail.

Jesus was not God, but the son of God, his first creation, and responsible for all the rest of God's creation. On earth, he was wholly a man. He died as a man, but then was raised by God and restored to a place second only to his Father, Jehovah.

LUCIFER was Jehovah's younger son, put particularly in charge of human beings, a responsibility to which he proved unequal. The primal paradise of Adam and Eve, replete with the joys of innocent sex, is described in glowing, idyllic terms in Witness literature, which also vociferously rejects the concept of evolution. Lucifer, or Satan, destroyed that paradise with his temptation of the first parents, a deed requiring the intervention of his elder brother.

The fulfillment of God's kingdom will occur dramatically, through the battle of Armageddon, the appearance of the Lord in the air, the millennial rule of Christ on earth (all during which resurrection and judgment take place), the unbelievably wondrous "Ages to Come." The process has already begun with the "establishment of the kingdom" in 1914; the consummation will be very soon. Rutherford made the famous statement, "Millions now living will never die." Indeed, the movement has from time to time been embarrassed when premature dates were implied in the literature, but many have made the necessary adjustments and recruited more believers to an imminent but future hope.

Not everyone will participate in that hope. No one but God, Witnesses believe, has immortality by right; for others, death is simply annihilation. But God can restore to life those whom he wishes. The righteous will be resurrected to participate in the millennial kingdom on earth. In addition, a special remnant of 144,000 is even now being raised to the greater privilege of eternal life in heaven.

3. **Worship** takes places in plain edifices called Kingdom Halls. It is heavily instructional, sober and didactic in character. The frequent meetings are chiefly for study. Baptism is by immersion, and mass baptisms take place in celebrative mood, especially at large conventions. The Lord's Supper is a memorial meal held only on the eve of PASSOVER.

4. **Organization** is from the top down, with local leadership appointed by district leaders, who are appointed by the headquarters of the ruling Watchtower Bible and Tract Societies of New York and Pennsylvania or the International Bible Students Association of England. The president has considerable personal power. Members are expected to give primary loyalty to the movement, and to take no part in politics or other activities of the present age. *See* MILLENARIAN MOVEMENTS

Bibliography. J. A. Beckford, *The Trumpet of Prophecy: A Sociological Study of Jehovah's Witnesses* (1975); E. R. Pike, *Jehovah's Witnesses* (1954); C. W. Sterling, *The Witnesses* (1975); H. H. Stroup, *Jehovah's Witnesses* (1945).

R. S. ELLWOOD

JEN rŭn (Con—Chin.). The characteristic virtue of a truly good person. Often translated as "humane," or "human-hearted." It includes bravery, courtesy, loyalty, and diligence in public life. CONFUCIUS regarded it as so transcendent that he was unwilling to say any of his contemporaries had achieved it.

K. CRIM

JEROME (Ch; 331-420). The most accomplished linguist and translator of Christian antiquity. Although he was earlier credited with the translation of the entire BIBLE into LATIN (the Vulgate), his actual translating seems to have been confined to the OT (from the original HEBREW) and the four GOSPELS.

While he was born into a Latin-speaking Christian family, his extensive knowledge of Greek has preserved numerous Eastern Christian writings now extent only, or primarily, in his translations, such as a number of ORIGEN'S homilies and Eusebius' *Onomasticon.*

After extensive study and habitation in a number of places, Jerome, a devoted ascetic, settled permanently in his own monastery in BETHLEHEM (after 386), whence he pursued his biblical studies and a voluminous correspondence with famous contemporaries, vigorously defended virginity, and waged a number of controversies with contemporaries.

Although known as the most famous scholar of his own day, he was quick to take offense when contradicted or criticized, and he frequently used his linguistic gifts and mastery of satire to demolish both living and dead opponents. He also publicly disavowed and attacked former "teachers" and friends —e.g., the classics (in a famous dream represented frequently in art), Origen and Rufinus (his defender and translator), and Ambrose of Milan. Yet he maintained a lifelong friendship with his ascetic women friends.

Bibliography. E. A. Clark, *Jerome, Chrysostom, and Friends* (1979), pp. 35-106; J. N. D. Kelly, *Jerome* (1975).

D. E. GROH

JERUSALEM jĭ rōō´ sə ləm. The ancient capital of Israel; holy city of Jews, Christians, and Muslims. Jerusalem is located at 31° N latitude and 35° E longitude, 750 m. above sea level on the central plateau which runs north to south.

Although habitation in the area of the southeast hill on which the city is located can be traced back to the fourth millennium B.C., Jerusalem became important only when King David captured it from the Jebusites, *ca.* 1000 B.C. and made it his capital. His son Solomon built there the first of the two great temples to YAHWEH which were to be so important in the life of Israel for a thousand years.

After Israel was divided in 922 B.C., Jerusalem remained the spiritual capital of the country and the political capital of the southern kingdom. In 587 B.C. the Neo-Babylonian empire destroyed the city and the Temple and took a great number of the people into captivity. In 538 B.C. Cyrus of Persia permitted some of the captives to return, and about twenty years later they completed a smaller, less opulent temple.

From the sixth century onward, Jerusalem was under foreign rule. After the Persians came Alexander the Great, the Ptolemies of Egypt and the Seleucids of Syria. This last dynasty was dominated by the infamous ANTIOCHUS EPIPHANES, under whom there was a concerted effort to impose Greek customs and thought upon the unwilling people of Jerusalem. Resistance to this effort was made under the leadership of the MACCABEES in 168 B.C. After three years the Temple was retaken and rededicated. The Jews again won a short-lived period of independence in 142 B.C., but the city came to be torn between rival factions until 63 B.C. when Rome established direct control and a long occupation began. The treasures of the Temple were taken by Crassus in 54 B.C.; Herod the Great began his rule as puppet king in 39 B.C., sponsoring a second rebuilding of the Temple. After Herod, Jerusalem was governed by Roman procurators. Under one such procurator, Pontius Pilate, JESUS was accused of treason, tried, and crucified *ca.* A.D. 33.

The inhabitants of the city became increasingly restive under Roman rule, and revolted in A.D. 66. Four years later the Temple was destroyed except for its western foundation wall, often referred to as the Wailing Wall, and the city was leveled. In A.D. 132-35 the city was again in Jewish hands, but the Emperor Hadrian ended this brief period of freedom. The name of the city was changed to Aelia Capitolina, and Jews were now forbidden to live in the city. Hadrian even erected a temple to Jupiter on the former Temple site.

Jews gradually returned to Jerusalem during the third century A.D., and around 325, when Christianity was made the religion of the empire, the Church of the HOLY SEPULCHRE was erected. At the close of the fourth century Jerusalem became part of the Byzantine Empire. (For later periods, *see* AL-QUDS.)

In this city much that is central to three religions took place: David reigned and was buried (I Kings 2:10); Solomon erected the Temple (I Kings 6,7) and surrounded the city with a wall (I Kings 3:1; 9:15); Isaiah was called (Isa. 6:1-5); Josiah discovered the scroll that led to the Deuteronomic reformation; Jeremiah taught there (I Kings 17 and 19); Ezra read the Law and Nehemiah refurbished the walls; the Maccabees overthrew the Hellenizing Seleucids (I Macc. 13:41-53); the vision came to Zechariah (Luke 1:5-23); Jesus taught in the Temple (2:41-51) and spent his last days there; he appeared to the disciples there (Luke 24:33-40); he ascended from the Mount of Olives (Acts 1:12); the death of the first Christian MARTYR, Stephen, took place (Acts 7:58); James, "the brother of the Lord," was killed and PETER imprisoned (12:1-5). In A.D. 691 the Muslims built the DOME OF THE ROCK over the place from which MUHAMMAD ascended to heaven.

Bibliography. B. Mazar, *The Excavations in the Old City of Jerusalem* (1971); Y. Yadin, ed., *Jerusalem Revealed* (1975); K. M. Kenyon, *Jerusalem: Excavating 3000 Years of History* (1969); John Gray, *A History of Jerusalem* (1969).

D. W. O'CONNOR

JESUITS jĕzh´ ə wətz (Ch). Members of the Society of Jesus (SJ), a Roman Catholic RELIGIOUS ORDER founded (1540) by St. IGNATIUS OF LOYOLA. Neither monks nor mendicants, Jesuits replace choral office and habit with disciplined personal formation based mainly on Ignatius' *Spiritual Exercises*. They are noted for highly centralized governance, strong ties to the papacy, and practical zeal shown in missions, schools, study of theology, science, humanities, and retreat work. Their rapid growth and quality made them leaders in the CATHOLIC REFORMATION and, afterward, a strong but sometimes criticized influence. Dissolved in 1773 owing to pressures from monarchs, and reestablished in 1814, the Society is now the largest Roman Catholic religious order of men.

W. H. PRINCIPE

JESUS (Ch; 6 B.C.—A.D. 29?). Palestinian preacher and RABBI, regarded by many Jews as a great teacher, by Muslims as a prophet, by Hindus as an AVATAR, and by Christians (at least traditionally) as the unrepeatable incarnation of the Son of God.

1. **Name.** "Jesus Christ" combines a personal name and a title of office ("christ," from Gr. *Christos* = Heb. *Meshiah*, anointed). "Jesus" represents Greek *Iesous*, the equivalent of Hebrew Joshua (Yehoshua). The combination "Jesus Christ" or "Christ Jesus" is a Christian expression which makes a claim about Jesus' religious significance.

2. **Sources of information.** Knowledge of Jesus depends almost totally on the GOSPELS. Ancient Jewish literature virtually ignores Jesus; the scattered references in the TALMUD mention only a few details and contain no independent traditions about him. The first century Jewish historian Josephus mentions him only twice, *Antiq.* 18.3.3 and 20.9.1, the former of which is almost certainly a Christian addition to the text. Roman historians mention Jesus only as part of fleeting references to Christians. From the second century onward, some Christian writers refer to official reports which the Roman procurator Pontius Pilate sent to Rome about Jesus' trial. This may reflect pious legend; no such reports exist today.

Although apocryphal gospels may contain occasional data which historians can use to reconstruct the life of Jesus, it is to the four Gospels in the NT that historians look, and of these the first three (Matthew, Mark, Luke) provide the most reliable information. Some scholars, however, prefer John's report of the final days of Jesus because it does not have the trial occur on PASSOVER itself. According to the prevailing view, Matthew and Luke depend on Mark; consequently we have only one outline of Jesus' career (Mark). Furthermore, twentieth century research has shown that religious and theological considerations determined the sequence in which Mark placed the short stories and sayings. Consequently, it is impossible to write a critical biography of Jesus.

Furthermore, the entire Christian tradition about Jesus' words, deeds, and death was transmitted from the standpoint of the conviction that Jesus is the Christ. No neutral reports about Jesus exist, or ever existed. In the transmitting process, oral as well as written, Christians modified the sayings of Jesus to make them more useful for Christian communities. Indeed, some sayings appear to have been coined by Christian prophets whose utterances were accepted as the voice of the living Lord (i.e., the resurrected Jesus) and so were mixed with the memories of what Jesus had said during his own lifetime. Since the late eighteenth century scholars have sought criteria for determining precisely what can be regarded as genuinely from Jesus. Few universally accepted criteria have been produced, except for one—Christians are unlikely to have invented something about Jesus which they have to explain away because it was embarrassing. By this criterion, the most solid fact about Jesus is his execution by crucifixion—the most disgraceful form of the death penalty inflicted by Roman authorities.

3. **Dates.** Despite doubts expressed earlier in the present century, today no scholar doubts that Jesus actually existed. It appears that he was born 6-4 B.C., and was executed during Passover season around A.D. 27-30. The duration of his public activity is not known; it was probably longer than the six weeks which Albert Schweitzer suggested and shorter than the traditional three years. Of Jesus' life prior to his public career virtually nothing is known.

4. **Jesus the Jew.** Although Jesus was deeply rooted in the JUDAISM of his time scholars continue to debate how he was related to the various forms of Judaism. The suggestion that Jesus had spent part of his early years at Qumran (where the Dead Sea Scrolls were produced) is modern fantasy. From time to time it has been suggested that Jesus was sympathetic to the Zealots (or their predecessors), an insurrectionist group which later led the revolt against Rome in A.D. 66-70. This claim too falls short of sufficient evidence. For one thing, the Gospels report that Jesus associated repeatedly with *publicans,* Jews who collected taxes for the Romans and so were despised by Jewish patriots. Jesus appears not to have associated with Hellenized Jews either. According to the Gospels, he was repeatedly at odds with the PHARISEES, the predecessors of the rabbis. However, the Gospels do not give a balanced view, because they record only those aspects of the Jesus tradition which were of use to the CHURCH in its own controversies with the SYNAGOGUE. The Gospels had no interest in reporting accurately how much Jesus shared with the Pharisees, to whom he was probably closer than now appears in the texts. The one Jewish group to which Jesus was closest was the followers of JOHN THE BAPTIST, a preacher who called for repentance (unreserved turning to God) in order to be ready for the impending judgment, associated with the End of all things and the rejuvenation of the cosmos. Jesus was baptized by John, and hence accepted his message; after John was beheaded Jesus struck out on his own, though he never repudiated John. Although Jesus was not an apocalyptist (in the sense of one who predicts the time of the End and portrays its character in graphic detail), his message was deeply influenced by fundamental motifs in APOCALYPTIC Judaism, such as the Judgment, the sense of the imminence of the End, the need for unalloyed response to the coming of the KINGDOM OF GOD.

5. **Career.** Jesus' public mission was characterized by five features. (a) He had the audacity to speak for God without recourse to the oral tradition being developed by the Pharisees; instead, he appealed directly to God's will, sometimes appealing to Scripture, as when he forbade divorce even though the TORAH permitted it. Yet he repeatedly affirmed the Torah and never regarded it as a burden to be shed. (b) Jesus was a traveling teacher and preacher, whose central theme was the coming of the kingdom of God. His wanderings did not take him outside his native Palestine, except for one trip to Phoenicia. (c) Jesus' teaching was not characterized by extensive discourses, but by short, pithy statements and by

parables. Jesus' teaching has no system of theology or ethics; it appears to have been rather *ad hoc*. Although the Gospels report that occasionally he taught in synagogues, most of his teaching occurred in informal settings—wherever people gathered or questioned him. The parables are commonly regarded as the most authentic part of the tradition. The discourses which the Gospels report, such as the SERMON ON THE MOUNT, are compilations of sayings delivered on various occasions. (d) Healing and exorcism appear to have been part of Jesus' career, as they were for most holy men and teachers of the era. Jesus regarded the expulsion of DEMONS as a sign that the kingdom of God is so near as to be at work through him. Yet Jesus apparently preferred teaching to healing or exorcism. (e) Jesus gathered around him a group of disciples. Whether there was a clearly defined group of twelve during Jesus' lifetime is disputed. Although other teachers, including the Pharisees, also had pupils around them, Jesus' disciples appear not to have expected to become "masters" someday; rather, the superior status of Jesus over them was permanent. Scholars also debate whether Jesus "founded" the church when he invited persons to become his followers. He did not intend to start his own sect (as his refusal to baptize shows), even less to begin a new religion. In retrospect, however, Christians regarded Jesus' relation with his disciples as the genesis of the church. Some of those who responded to Jesus were marginal to that society; he evidently gained a reputation for eating with tax collectors and "sinners."

6. **Execution.** It remains uncertain whether Jesus foresaw his death, although there is no reason to deny him a sense of foreboding as he went to JERUSALEM. Sayings which predict his fate in detail may well be Christian formulations after the fact. It is also disputed whether Jesus understood his impending death as a sacrifice for human sin. For one thing, even if he had regarded himself as MESSIAH (which many scholars doubt), there was no precedent in Judaism for the idea that the death of the Messiah would save people from sin. Scholars do not take seriously the proposal that Jesus actually manipulated the situation so that he would be killed. It is possible, however, that Jesus believed that his death was part of the "messianic woes" which some Jews expected would precede the Kingdom's arrival.

Since the Gospel accounts of Jesus' arrest, trial, and execution are permeated with Christian theology and apologetic, it is virtually impossible for a historian to reconstruct what happened. Besides, the Gospels themselves report that none of the disciples saw what went on, having fled when Jesus was arrested. The Gospels also have a tendency to exonerate Pilate and to blame the Jewish leaders for Jesus' fate. This pattern reflects the later Christian belief that the fall of Jerusalem in A.D. 70 was divine retribution for the refusal to acknowledge Jesus as the Messiah and the desire to show the Roman authorities that Christianity was not the outgrowth of an insurrectionist plot. One thing is certain: crucifixion was a Roman means of execution. The Romans evidently took Jesus to be an insurrectionist, for they nailed to the cross the charge against him: "King of the Jews." (*See* ANTI-SEMITISM §2.)

Once Jesus' disciples became convinced that God had vindicated Jesus by resurrecting him (*see* RESURRECTION), they tried to persuade fellow Jews, and later Gentiles, of the truth of this conviction, and to explain its religious significance as well—through Jesus' life and death, God had acted decisively to usher in the era of salvation. That conviction was the matrix in which the Jesus tradition was formed, repeated, collected, and written into Gospels. Consequently "the quest of the historical Jesus"—the critical effort to distinguish "Jesus as he really was" from the Christian interpretation of him—continues to be a difficult enterprise. Opinion varies considerably over the amount of solid historical information about Jesus which can be recovered, and over what Christian faith does and does not have at stake in the effort. (For Muslim views of Jesus *see* PEOPLE OF THE BOOK; NABI.)

Bibliography. A. Schweitzer, *The Quest of the Historical Jesus* (1910); M. Goguel, *The Life of Jesus* (1933); G. Bornkamm, *Jesus of Nazareth* (1960); R. Bultmann, *Jesus and the Word* (1939); J. Klausner, *Jesus of Nazareth* (1928); N. Perrin, *Rediscovering the Teaching of Jesus* (1967); X. Leon-Dufour, *The Gospels and the Jesus of History* (1971); J. Jeremias, *New Testament Theology*, Vol. I: *The Proclamation of Jesus* (1971).

L. E. KECK

JESUS PRAYER. *See* MYSTICISM, CHRISTIAN §1; ORTHODOX CHURCHES §5; HESYCHASM.

JEWISH THOUGHT, MODERN. *See* JUDAISM §6.

JHĀNA jä´ nŭ (B). *See* DHYĀNA.

JIHĀD jĭ häd´ (I—Arab.; lit. "striving, exertion" for or against something). The duty of Muslims to exert themselves strenuously "in the cause of God" against both personal ungodliness and the enemies of ISLAM. *Jihād* can mean "holy war," but the struggle for uprightness of life and the propagation of the faith prefers peaceful means such as persuasion and example. "O ye who believe! Shall I show you a commerce that will save you from a painful doom? Ye should believe in ALLAH and His messenger, and should *strive* [*tujāhidūna*, i.e. by *jihād*] for the cause of Allah with your wealth and with your lives. . . . He will forgive you your sins and bring you into Gardens underneath which rivers flow, and pleasant dwellings in Gardens of Eden. That is the supreme triumph." (Qur'ān, Sura 61:10-12, trans. Pickthall.)

Muslims consider themselves as comprising the *Dār al-Islām*, "the Household of Submission," and the rest of the world's peoples as the *Dār al-Ḥarb*, "the Household of Warfare." It is the duty of Muslims to extend the *Dār al-Islām* by means of missionary activities and in some cases even by military *jihād,* if necessary, toward the ultimate goal of a worldwide Islamic community embracing all. However, the QUR'ĀN explicitly admonishes that there shall be "no compulsion in religion" (Sura 2:256). Even so, *jihād* in all of its forms has been a powerful means of persuasion down through the centuries. It is the only form of armed conflict sanctioned by the religion, and those who fall "in the cause of Allah" are martyrs who will immediately taste the joys of salvation (Sura 2:154; 3:169, 195).

Muslims distinguish between the "greater *jihād,*" which is the constant struggle of the individual believer against his own evil tendencies, and the "lesser *jihād,*" which is actual armed conflict in defense of the faith or for its propagation. This duty is sometimes considered to be a sixth PILLAR OF ISLAM.

Bibliography. Qur'ān: 2:128; 8:72; 9:88; 22:78; 25:52; 61:11 and *passim;* M. M. Ali, trans., *A Manual of Hadīth* (1944), pp. 252-65; M. M. Ali, *The Religion of Islam* (1936), pp. 545-99; M. Khadduri, *War and Peace in the Law of Islam* (1955), the standard work in English.

F. M. DENNY

JIKAKU DAISHI jē kä´ koo dī´ shē (B—Jap., 792-862; lit. "great master of boundless compassion"). Posthumous name bestowed by an emperor on the Buddhist priest Ennin. After studying at the TENDAI headquarters on Mt. Hiei, he went to China in 838, where he studied Buddhism for almost ten years before returning to Japan; later he became chief priest of Tendai. He is especially remembered in the West for his diary of his experiences in China.

Bibliography. E. O. Reischauer, *Ennin's Travels in T'ang China* (1955).

H. B. EARHART

JIMMU TENNŌ jĭm´ moo tĕn´ nō (Sh—Jap.; lit. "Emperor Jimmu"). According to the oldest written Japanese chronicles, the first emperor of Japan, assuming the throne about 660 B.C. The eighth century KOJIKI and NIHON SHOKI take Jimmu Tennō as the first human emperor and chronicle the successive emperors and empresses from that time. His name before being titled emperor is Kamu-Yamato-Ihare-Hiko-no-Mikoto. He is considered to have been a direct descendant of the divine pair IZANAGI AND IZANAMI through the Sun Goddess AMATERASU, and is credited with founding the Japanese empire in a move from Kyūshū to the Yamato region (around the old capital of Nara, on the island of Honshū). Beginning in the MEIJI era (1868-1912) great emphasis was placed upon Jimmu Tennō in order to create patriotic fervor for building up Japan as a modern state, but after 1945 this story has been viewed by historians more as a mythological tale than a verifiable historical record.

H. B. EARHART

JINN jĭn (I—Arab.; lit. "demons"). A group of beings created from smokeless fire, according to some, who can change size and shape, can help or harm people, and are capable of receiving SALVATION or damnation, since the QUR'ĀN was sent to them as well as to humans (Sura 114). In pre-Islamic Arabia they were thought to be a class of minor deities related in some way to ALLAH (Sura 37:158) and to assist him (Sura 6:101). Muslims generally have accepted the existence of jinn. Legal scholars have debated their status under religious law, and early Muslim scientists speculated about the physics of their nature. Iblīs (*see* SATAN) is reckoned one of the jinn (Sura 18:51) but also as an angel (Sura 2:34), which has led some commentators to make jinn a "tribe" of angels. The jinn would listen to what was said in heaven but were fended off by meteors (Sura 72:8ff.); they worked for Solomon (Sura 34:12ff.). Post-Qur'ānic commentaries join these ideas with elements of folklore, and stories about jinn and their relations with humans abound throughout the Islamic world. Most familiar to the West are the stories found in the *Thousand and One Nights.* The word *jinn* has been adopted in most languages where Islam predominates and has replaced the names for evil spirits. Jinn were evidently thought to be able to possess a person, making him *majnūn* (Arab.; lit. "crazy, possessed by a jinn"). MUHAMMAD was so accused by his detractors. *See* DEMONS; ESCHATOLOGY §3.

Bibliography. E. Lane, *Lexicon* (1865), pp. 462 ff., and *Manners and Customs* (1966); aṭ-Ṭabarī, *Tafsīr;* D. B. Macdonald, "Djinn," *EI,* with bibliog.

G. D. NEWBY

JĪVA jē´ vä (Ja—Skt.; lit. "life, life-principle" [*jīv*—"to live, to be alive"]). The Jaina term for the immaterial "soul" of each sentient being; one of two basic categories into which the Jainas place all existing things, the other being *ajīva,* that which is existent but not sentient (conscious).

1. ***Jīva* as a category.** Jaina metaphysics divides all existent things into *jīva* (living) and *ajīva* (nonliving). That which is *ajīva* is divided into matter *(pudgala)* and nonmaterial existents, namely, time *(kāla),* space *(ākāśa),* and two entities the Jainas regard as media of motion and rest, *dharma* and *adharma.* (This use of *dharma* and *adharma* is particular to this part of Jaina metaphysics, and should not be confused with the broader Hindu understanding of DHARMA and *adharma.*)

This division into categories reveals a fundamental aspect of *jīva: jīva's* primary meaning is "living," not "being," since both *jīva* and *ajīva* are categories of things that have "being." Therefore, *jīva* is different from *esse* or essence in Western thought. In addition, Jainas regard both *jīva* and *ajīva* as eternal, and there is, therefore, no notion that they are different in strictly ontological terms.

As a category, then, *jīva* is that which is "animated"; it distinguishes "living" things from "existing" things; i.e., *jīva* is alive while matter, space, time, etc., only exist.

2. *Jīva* **as the "soul."** The category or class of *jīva* is made up of an infinite number of individual *jīvas*, which may be understood analogously as the "souls" of all living beings. As noted above, these *jīvas* are eternal and each is a discrete entity (separate from all other *jīvas* and yet like all others). The individual *jīvas* do not emanate from any one source, nor will they ever return to, or merge into, any one all-encompassing *jīva*. Nor is there any hierarchy of *jīvas* since all of them are eternal and alike in basic nature.

This basic nature has two principal components: consciousness *(caitanya)* and bliss *(sukha)*. The first of these is the most important for understanding the notion of *jīva*. The Jainas claim that, as the "animating principle" of living things, the *jīva* demonstrates its own existence in that living things are conscious, i.e., are capable of perception and self-knowledge. The term "sentient" is thus commonly used in Jaina circles to characterize living things.

The other chief component, "bliss," is understood to be self-knowledge that is self-contained, i.e., pure knowledge of the soul by the soul. It is these two kinds of "knowing"—perception and self-knowledge—that distinguish living things from other existent things, and this distinction is due to the presence of the *jīva*.

3. **The** ***jīva*** **in ordinary existence.** The Jainas regard ordinary human existence as the result of the *jīva* becoming associated with, or bound up in, *ajīva*, particularly matter. This bondage occurs by means of KARMA, which the Jainas interpret as a special, subtle form of matter which "clings," as it were, to the *jīva*. The accumulated karma causes the *jīva* to be limited to a particular physical incarnation. Moreover, the *jīva's* innate knowledge and bliss are obscured by the karma that clings to it, resulting in imperfect knowledge, and a desire, not for self-knowledge, but for sensual enjoyment and material acquisition. In short, the *jīva's* capacity to "know" is crippled and perverted by the accumulated karma, and this results in the accumulation of still more karma.

A karma-bound life leads to an endless progression through successive lives of various sorts, depending on the type of karma that is accumulated on the *jīva*. The Jainas commonly divide all living things into broad classes according to the number of sense-faculties they possess, from single-sensed organisms of microscopic size (having only the sense of touch) up to living beings (such as humans) that have five senses. Thus the range of living beings, and of possible forms for successive lives, is immense in Jainism and is explained as the *jīva's* ability to "know" being obscured by karma (the single-sensed creatures having the least capacity to "know" and so on up the scale). In this way, the Jainas share the general Hindu notion of SAMSARA, the endless cycle of rebirth, but they give its actual working a unique explanation.

4. **The** ***jīva*** **in liberation.** The *jīva* in physical bondage, as described above, can only be liberated by intense ascetic practice. The Jainas hold that only one life-style, the monastic life, is appropriate for such practice. The lay person must await a future existence before he or she can attain release.

The actual process of freeing the *jīva* occurs in two stages. First, the generation of karma which clings to and binds the *jīva* must be stopped so far as is possible. In order to accomplish this, the Jaina monk assumes a life-style which involves radical renunciation of as much worldly activity as possible. (Note: in addition to their particular interpretation of karma as a subtle form of matter, the Jainas also understand karma in the broader Hindu sense of "deed" or "action"; therefore, a life of nonaction leads to nonaccumulation of karmic matter.) Second, once the accumulation of new karma has been reduced to a minimum, the previously accumulated karma must decay or exhaust its binding power. Jaina asceticism prescribes certain austerities (TAPAS) that can hasten this decay of karma.

When both these stages have been accomplished, the *jīva* is at last freed of karma's crippling effects. It regains its original nature, i.e., pure consciousness and complete self-knowledge. This state of perfection, called KAIVALYA, involves both a complete separation of the *jīva* from all karmic matter and a complete, pure enjoyment of its innate capacities. The liberated *jīva*, also known as a *siddha* ("one who has accomplished [liberation]"), rises to the upper reaches of the universe and abides there forever in perfection.

5. **The** ***jīva*** **and related concepts.** The Jaina treatment of the *jīva* is in a number of respects similar to the SĀMKHYA (and YOGA) concept of the PURUṢA. In both systems there is a plurality of "souls" which are essentially alike and eternally distinct from one another. In addition, both systems ascribe real existence and eternality to matter (PRAKṚTI in Sāṃkhya).

These similarities must not, however, obscure important differences. Sāṃkhya's understanding of the basic character of the *puruṣa* is quite different from the Jaina concept of the *jīva* as "knower"; and the relationship between the *jīva* and karmic matter is very different from the relationship between *puruṣa* and *prakṛti* in Sāṃkhya. These differences are reflected in different visions of the path to release in the two systems (asceticism vs. meditation or mental discipline).

Beyond such points of difference, though, it should be noted that the Jaina concept of the *jīva* and the Sāṃkhya concept of the *puruṣa* together represent a significant effort toward developing a concept of the "soul" that is neither monistic (ADVAITA) nor unwilling to grant real existence to the material world.

Bibliography. H. von Glasenapp, *The Doctrine of Karma in Jaina Philosophy*, tr. G. B. Gifford (1942); *see* JAINISM bibliog.

K. W. FOLKERT

JIZŌ jē zô´ (B). *See* KSHITIGARBA.

JÑĀNA jə nä´ nŭ (H). *See* VIDYĀ.

JOAN OF ARC (Ch; 1412-1431). Jeanne la Pucelle, the national patroness of France, the "Maid of

Orleans," heroine and martyr of the Hundred Years War whose defense of Orleans and crowning of the dauphin helped France to escape English domination in the fifteenth century. An illiterate peasant girl from Domrémy-la-Pucelle in Champagne, Joan began to hear "voices" and to experience "supernatural visitations" at age thirteen. Later she identified the voices, accompanied by flashes of light, as those of particular saints—Michael, Catherine, Margaret, and others. Her "voices" commanded her to deliver France from English control. Following the treaty of Troyes (1420) the English monarchy had assumed control of France. The legitimate heir, the dauphin, the future Charles VII, was in refuge beyond the Loire. Joan inspired Charles to reassemble the army, and clad in armor Joan herself led a force against English troops gathered at Orleans. The eight-month siege ended, and Joan soon won another astonishing victory at Patay. She persuaded Charles to receive the crown at Reims. The coronation of a French king coupled with her inspiring leadership roused the French people to resist further English assaults. In the attempt to relieve besieged Compiègne (1430) Joan was captured and sold to the English. The bishop of Beauvais placed her on trial. Her visions were declared "false and diabolical," and after having been condemned as a heretic, she was burned at the stake in the marketplace of Rouen in 1431. In 1456 Pope Calixtus III reversed the verdict and declared her sentence unjust. Hailed a saint even during her lifetime, she was canonized in 1920.

Bibliography. R. Pernoud, *The Retrial of Joan of Arc* (1955); H. Guillemin, *Joan, Maid of Orleans* (1973).

H. L. Bond

JŌDO jō´ dô (B). *See* Pure Land Sects.

JOHANAN BEN ZAKKAI yō hä´ nän bĕn zä kī´ (Ju; *ca.* A.D. 1-80). The Rabbi most responsible for reconstructing Judaism after the first Jewish war against Rome (A.D. 66-73), which he had opposed. Legendary accounts mention his being smuggled out of Jerusalem in a coffin to win permission from Vespasian to establish the rabbinic academy at Jamnia (Yavneh).

There he embarked upon a program which stressed Torah study, fulfilling God's commandments, and performing acts of charity, which replaced the Temple service. A nonmessianist, Johanan was content to concentrate on pragmatic matters, ensuring that Judaism would meet successfully the challenges which arose after A.D. 70.

Bibliography. J. Neusner, *Life of Yohanan ben Zakkai* (2nd ed., 1970), and *Development of a Legend* (1970).

E. M. Meyers

JOHN XXIII (Ch; 1881-1963). Born Angelo Giuseppe Roncalli at Sotto il Monte (Bergamo), Italy. Archbishop and papal diplomat in Bulgaria, Turkey, Greece, and France, 1925-1953; Cardinal and Patriarch of Venice, 1953-1958; elected pope in 1958. Called Vatican Council II to renew life and structure of the church and promote Christian unity. Internationalized college of Cardinals, brought Roman Catholic church into the Ecumenical Movement, wrote eight encyclical letters, two of them on social action, *Mater et Magistra* (1961) and *Pacem in Terris* (1963). *See* Aggiornamento; Papacy.

J. Hennesey

JOHN THE BAPTIST (Ch & I). Prophetic forerunner of Jesus, identified in the NT as the Elijah figure of Jewish eschatology. In the Gospels he issues a call to repentance, in preparation for the coming Kingdom of God, and performs Baptism as a sign of repentance. Jesus begins his ministry after his baptism by John. An association of John with the Essene community of Qumran is thought possible by some scholars.

Islam knows John as one of the righteous prophets preceding Muhammad, and the Mandeans trace their origin to John and his disciples.

R. Bullard

JOHN OF THE CROSS (Ch; 1542-91). Mystic and reformer. Born in humble circumstances, he entered the Carmelite Order in 1563 and attended the University of Salamanca. In 1567 he met Teresa of Avila and in 1568 helped found the first house for men in the Reformed Carmelite Order then being organized by Teresa. The reform progressed but met opposition from the unreformed branch of the Carmelites, resulting in difficulties for Teresa and prison for John. After escaping from prison, John traveled widely, wrote important treatises and poems relating to the mystical life, and was spiritual adviser to nuns. Near the end of his life he was savagely attacked by opponents in the Reformed Carmelites. His poems are acknowledged to be among the greatest in the Spanish language. John's way is one of giving up everything for the mystic quest, driven by a burning flame of love which purifies and transforms the mystic until he or she is united with God in a union which John describes in the nuptial imagery of the Song of Songs. His teaching on the two "dark nights" is especially notable: the first is of the senses—loss of images, discursive thought, and feelings; the second is of the spirit—seeming alienation from God, preceding the stage of union with him. *See* Mysticism, Christian.

Bibliography. E. A. Peers, trans., *Works* (1934-5); G. Brenan, *St John of the Cross: His Life and Poetry* (1973), with a new trans. of the poetry, by L. Nicholson; E. A. Peers, *Studies of the Spanish Mystics,* 2nd ed. (1949), I, 183-234.

G. A. Zinn

JŌJITSU jō´ jĭt sə. *See* Nara Buddhism §3b.

JUDAH HA-LEVI jo͞o´ də hä lē´ vē (Ju; 1075-1141). Philosopher, Hebrew poet, and physician; he left Spain toward the end of a life already marked by many travels and embarked on a journey to Eretz Israel, where he apparently arrived only by dint of legend. His many poems, religious and secular, are powerful expressions of a truly astonishing, creative, and sensitive genius. Ha-Levi also composed the highly original and influential Kuzari. *See* Judaism §3e.
K. P. Bland

JUDAH HA-NASI jo͞o´ də hä nä sē´ (Ju). Patriarch of Judea during the late second and early third centuries A.D., Judah "the Prince" is best known for his role as redactor of the Mishnah (*ca.* 200), the first major Jewish corpus of jurisprudence. Son of Rabban Simeon ben Gamaliel, Rabbi Judah greatly enhanced the prestige of the office of patriarch by winning the favor of several Roman emperors, probably Septimius Severus and Caracalla. His astute political sense did much to unify the Palestinian community several generations after the Bar Kochba war; his legal rulings helped ease the economic situation within Eretz Israel and to cement relations with the Diaspora.

At Beth She'arim and at Sepphoris, the major cities of his activity, Judah labored hard to elevate the Hebrew Language to a position of dominance among the sages. His lordly style and independent wealth, however, did not spare him the criticism of his peers.

His role in the redaction of the Mishnah is not clear, except that many rulings became extraneous and noncanonical by virtue of their exclusion from his compilation. The fact that the Mishnah became the standard collection for succeeding generations and the basis for talmudic discussions, Gemara, is ample testimony to his paramount importance. It should be noted that the Mishnah he promulgated was not published in written form, but was committed to memory by authoritative sages and transmitted orally.

Bibliography. S. Lieberman, *Hellenism in Jewish Palestine* (1962), pp.83-99.
E. M. Meyers

JUDAISM. The religion of the Jewish people, including legal and ethical norms, rituals, and beliefs. It is also the history of a socio-ethnic community, extending over several millennia and expressed in mystical and philosophical trends, in folk culture and high literary culture, in ritual actions as well as the rationalizations of those actions. Although almost every religious possibility has been produced within or integrated into its culture and history, there is a clearly recognizable core structure.

1. Biblical Judaism
2. Classical Judaism
3. Medieval trends and thoughts
4. Torah and tradition
5. Liturgy and calendar
6. Modernity and modern thought
Bibliography

American Jewish Archives, Hebrew Union College—Jewish Institute of Religion

A member of a synagogue congregation reads the day's text. The rabbi holds a special pointer and another member holds the Torah scroll.

1. Biblical Judaism. Jews have always read the Hebrew Bible and believe it to be the foundation of their life in community.

Four Covenants structure the Hebrew Bible and point to the overarching theological triad of creation-revelation-redemption. The first covenant occurs in connection with the act of creation. From its beginning the world was an ordered harmony of the animate and the inanimate, created by a Being transcendent to it in will and nature. This world was given to humans, but they rebelled and punishments soon followed. After a cataclysmic flood (Gen. 6–9), God promised a stable universe (Gen. 9:12-17).

The universal focus of the primeval tales narrows to God's unilateral covenant with the Hebrew patriarchs (Gen. 17:9-14). The sign of this covenant is Circumcision, borne by males to remind God of his promise of genealogical continuity. Other promises include inheritance of a special land. The community of faith is thus a natural order (descendants of Abraham) whose meaning and destiny are shaped by divine revelations.

Fulfillment of the patriarchal promises came to include the redemption of Israel from Egyptian bondage. This event and the subsequent covenant at Sinai (Exod. 20–24) transform the people from a natural to a national community. The new covenant is bilateral, initiated by a transcendent God of whom nothing can be known or presupposed except the experienced expressions of his revealed will. Absolute obedience to the covenant is demanded as the precondition for all divine-human relationship and for settled life in the sacred land. Disobedience brings the threat of spiritual and physical exile from God.

The tension of reward-punishment sets up the recurrent biblical polarities of spatial settlement, historical well-being, and servitude to God *vs.* spatial dislocation, historical disaster, and servitude to the nations. Thus a second theological triad is evident: God, Israel (as people and place), TORAH (as covenant and divine will).

The fourth covenant is between God and David, establishing the monarchy and the messianic ideal: an era of historical peace, national independence, and well-being in the homeland (II Sam. 7). The primary context of this ideal is Israel's particular historical reality and relationship with God. The other nations largely serve divine ends (e.g., punishment of Israel). The universal reintegration of mankind is a future ideal linked to Israel's redemption.

Biblical theology thus values a covenantal solidarity expressed by actions. Israel is given a body of commandments and is to "heed," "obey," and "remember" them and depart from idolatry (i.e., all nonsanctioned acts). Love and fear of God are expressed by conformity to the divine will; righteousness is achieved by being faithful to the covenant. Through covenantal allegiance Israel will become a holy people, will be separated from idolators, and will receive spiritual and physical rewards.

The relationship between God and Israel remains open through divine messengers who instruct, warn, denounce, or offer hope. Warnings of imminent doom, appeals to repent, and words of comfort and hope in restoration are inseparable from covenantal obedience. Indeed the mystery of suffering is repeatedly rationalized by the categories of reward and punishment for covenantal obedience.

There is no hesitation to portray God anthropomorphically. His immanence is expressed by attributes of mercy and justice; providential concern is expressed by revelations. Divine transcendence is simultaneously affirmed by the revealing of his name ("I am that I am"; Exod. 3:14; *see* YAHWEH), by polemics against idols, and by recognition of the limitation of shrines to "contain" him or SACRIFICE to "satisfy" him. And yet divine-human reconciliation is not solely a matter of repentant return to covenantal requirements; it requires the agency of sacrifices. Some of these were for guilt and transgressions, but others were made in thanksgiving, or to honor God, or in celebration. The old agrarian-nomadic festivals were transformed by being related to events in the nation's history, but they continued to be celebrated in appropriate cultic form. The concrete role of the Temple in JERUSALEM for individual and national atonement mirrors its centrality as font of God's bounty to Israel and foreshadows its future function in the just reconciliation of humanity.

2. Classical Judaism. The destruction of the Jerusalem Temple (587/6 B.C.) and the subsequent exile from Judea was of major consequence. Independent religious centers emerged in Palestine, Egypt, and Babylonia, generating separate traditions. Decentralization and DIASPORA became facts of national existence, producing theologies of exile and yearnings for a return to ZION. The absence of the Temple required new forms and institutions. An emphatic feature of exilic prophecy is thus spiritual reconciliation with God through human repentance or unilateral divine grace. The postexilic return to Israel established continuity with the past by restoration of the Temple and its service, and by an intensified study of the covenantal laws. But the necessary adjustments of the Torah with ongoing life generated multiple responses among the diverse groups, for whom proper interpretation of scripture was decisive The groups also differed in their leadership, attitudes toward the Temple and sanctity, and assessments of the meaning and duration of history. The written Torah was shared by all Israel; at issue was its true meaning and application.

a) Beginnings of rabbinic Judaism. The destruction of the Herodian Temple by the Romans in A.D. 70 had even greater consequences than the earlier destruction. Most notable was the emerging dominance of the PHARISEES and the consolidation of rabbinical Judaism out of the many Judaisms which had previously existed. In the reconstruction of religious life without a Temple, Pharisaism sponsored a new nonaristocratic and nonpriestly leadership, as well as new religious ideals and actions. The "wise student" and RABBI who replaced the priest based their authority on knowledge and, increasingly, on consensus. SYNAGOGUE prayer, which had been aligned with the Temple service, became increasingly independent, and synagogal liturgies and institutions developed. Private, spontaneous PRAYER was fostered, as was individual and collective repentance for sins. Stress on the power of private acts of spirituality was the consequence of the absence of the Temple and the validation of divine-human reconciliation which cultic atonement provided. Yearnings for the renewal of the old cultic forms resurfaced and underwent necessary reinterpretation.

Among the most important acts of piety was Torah study. Indeed, it was often considered a virtual sacrament capable of ensuring individual atonement or beatitude in the present or hereafter. The need to adapt the Torah of Sinai to the demands of ongoing life produced an intensification of exegesis and the formalization of its techniques. The radical innovation of Pharisaism was the idealization of the "oral Torah" (the sum of traditional and exegetical supplements to the Sinaitic law) and the claim that it had been given by God at the same time as the written Torah of Sinai. It was said that whatever a student might exegetically deduce from the Torah (including inevitable contradictions) was merely the progressive actualization of the Sinaitic oral Torah. The scholars developed systems of deduction and induction to extend, restrict, or simply elucidate the law. There emerged diverse modes of making correlations and validations between different texts, and upon the slightest scriptural hints were founded rabbinic norms (*see* HALAKAH) to make the divine law livable and protect it against infraction.

b) The sanctification of life. The purpose of this theoretical and practical codification was the sanctification of all life. This was the radical religious response of Judaism to the loss of the Temple. All life was sacramentalized, so that even priestly traditions were applied to lay religious life. Thus the family table was likened to an altar, and prohibitions of priestly Temple labor on the SABBATH were reinterpreted and extended to the entire community. Judaism became a priesthood of all believers and observers of the law. Through study and exegesis, Sinai was an ever recurring spiritual moment; God continued to speak and teach through rabbis and students of Torah.

Of all goals, then, study of Torah was the most prized. It led to divine obedience, and so garnered present and future rewards. Through the exegetical extension of the law to all life, every action was considered a MITZVAH, a ritual observance. The end of this scrupulous piety was righteousness in and by the law, and was available to every Jew. Indeed, daily obedience was nothing less than the acknowledgment and celebration of divine Lordship. With the loss of political dominion in the centuries after the destruction of the Temple Israel sought the KINGDOM OF GOD in Palestine and the diaspora by blessing the King of the Universe and obeying his will in all things. So seen, the messianic age would be only an extension of the kingdom of God into every historical and political nook and cranny.

c) Knowledge of God. The sages said that one who would know the will of God should study halakah (in MIDRASH, MISHNAH, and TALMUD); whereas the knowledge and love of God is fostered by AGGADAH (the homiletical, ethical, or theological reflections on the Torah). For it is in the aggadic dicta (the earliest collections of which date from the fourth century A.D.) that one senses the capacity of Torah to reveal its "seventy faces." Diverse theologies coexist in these nonsystematic and nondiscursive compendia: the love and fear of God, his nearness and distance, dynamically intersect. God's transcendence is expressed by many circumlocutions (e.g., The Holy, Blessed One; The Place; Master of the Universe), by the numinous otherness of the *trisagion* ("Holy, holy, holy," Isa. 6:3) and other mystical prayers, and by the emphatic distinction made between Creator and creature. Divine immanence is formulated by hypostases of God's indwelling nature *(Shekhina),* by the glorification of his humble presence in the lowly and ordinary (e.g., the thornbush, Exod. 3:2–4), or by anthropomorphic images of a God who studies, prays, or dons phylacteries (TEFILLIN). The angelic beings which populate the intermediate realm between the world above and that below serve many functions, but they are ultimately dependent upon divine authority alone.

The unity of God as supreme Lord and his active presence as Creator, Revealer, and Redeemer is rehearsed and celebrated throughout aggadic and liturgical formulations. God is portrayed as the one and ever-present Creator, who daily renews and sustains the world. He is the ancient and ever-present Revealer of his will through the Torah studies of scholars, and he is the memorialized Redeemer of Israel, whose former deeds eternally inspire hope for the redemption of the world. The Holy, Blessed One chose Israel in love and gave it his teachings, and Israel's ideal response is that of loving bride and witness to this divine love. The convergence of love given and received (between God and Israel, and between persons) will consummate in redemption.

d) Belief in future rewards. The overwhelming testimony of the early rabbinic literature is that the created universe is good, a hospitable context in which a Jew might lead a life of study and fulfillment of the commandments. As this world is principally the context of God's dominion, it was believed that here one may encounter God and be reconciled with him through obedience. However, the reality of personal and social evil often resulted in the theological deferral of ultimate reconciliation and reward to a world beyond death. Speculations on these "final things" vary considerably. APOCALYPTIC anticipations predicted final battles and sufferings under the leadership of an Ephraimite MESSIAH (ben Joseph); justification of the righteous and damnation of the sinners; the inauguration of the reign of the Davidic Messiah; and such matters as the ingathering of the exiles, the restoration of the Temple, beatific visions of the divine throne, and eternal joy under the protective wings of the *Shekhina.* Roman persecutions, especially those of the second century A.D., were the cause of much suffering and despair. Older traditions of the atoning power of death were joined to a martyrology which saw in the mystery of suffering opportunities for spiritual purification and the consummate expression of the selfless love of God.

Contradictory beliefs existed concerning the state of humans after death. One tradition emphasized bodily resurrection; another taught eternality of the soul. The former view, of Pharisaic origin, is the more faithful to the biblical notion that man is a unity of spirit and body, integrated in life and thereafter. The idea of an eternal soul is of Hellenistic derivation, but the two views generally mingled without complication. Moreover, whatever the otherworldly estate of man, it was a reward for a "life of Torah," the fruit of freely chosen human endeavors. (*See* DEATH §4.) Judaism unremittingly stressed that a person had free choice and so was responsible for which of the two contradictory impulses—good or evil—was ascendant. But the "evil impulse" could provide the sublimated energy for good deeds and creative action.

e) The moral life. The Torah was the acknowledged antidote against the evil impulse. Jews were further guided toward moral action through the imitation of divine attributes derived from scripture. As God clothed the naked, fed the hungry, buried the dead or was charitable to the needy, so Jews were bidden to emulate his ways. Other ideals include reverence for teachers and parents, support of the community, and acts of lovingkindness. While no dogmatic formulation or hierarchy of ideals occurs in early Judaism, some attempts were made to reflect on fundamentals. One pointed to the catalogue of virtues in Psalm 15; another stressed love of neighbor; still another noted that the righteous shall live on faith alone. A negative formulation was that the three great prohibitions were bloodshed, idolatry, and illicit sex. As a whole, spiritual integrity was to know God in all one's ways, and to place oneself in God's presence at all times.

3. **Medieval trends and thoughts.** The worldwide diffusion of Jews continued in late antiquity and the early medieval period. Vibrant Jewish communities were established in Alexandria, Babylonia, Rome, and up the trade routes into the lands of the Franks. The diaspora became an established fact, but the people continued to regard exile as life on the periphery of the national center in Zion. As theologies of exile developed, Jews saw themselves as suffering witnesses to God among the nations. The highest value was attributed to group maintenance through halakhic observance and the responsibility of all Jews for the spiritual and physical welfare of one another.

a) The Talmuds. Though the economic and social development of Jewish settlements varied with local conditions, their legal structure remained resiliently that of Talmudic jurisprudence. The two Talmuds (fourth century Palestinian, fifth century Babylonian) reflect the two principal foci of early Judaism. The Palestinian center was a cradle of early aggadah and homiletical-poetic genres (PIYYUT). Palestine's prestige made it a focal point for Babylonian scholars. Nevertheless, the Babylonian rulings often rivaled those of Palestinian sages, with the latter often deferring to them. Tensions developed over such questions as the calendar, which affected the standardization of Jewish liturgical practice. (*See* CALENDAR, JEWISH.)

b) Sephardi and Ashkenazi. In addition to those differences between Palestine and Babylonia, significant religio-cultural differences developed between the ASHKENAZIC communities of France and Germany and the SEPHARDIC ones of the Near East, North Africa, and Iberia. The Ashkenazic community was shaped by its contacts with Christendom and was characterized by devoted Talmudic scholarship. A spirit of religious literalism often marked these Jews, whose simple piety is testified to by the repeated acts of communal martyrdom at the hands of the CRUSADERS. Despite the martyrdom (KIDDUSH HA-SHEM) Ashkenazic Jews were not prone to messianic-eschatological fervor, as were the Sephardic Jews in Persia, Yemen, and Iberia, and later in Turkey and Palestine. With the decline of the Babylonian academies (*ca.* 1000), the Jews of Spain grew in significance and coördinated their moderate halakhic emphasis with other concerns. Shaped by their ISLAMIC surroundings for several centuries, Sephardic Jews studied philosophy, produced secular and religious poetry, and developed philological methods and applied them to biblical exegesis from the ninth century on. The remarkable riches of this interaction enshrined it in national memory as a Golden Age.

c) Contacts with society. Relations with the surrounding Gentile society affected developments in the socio-economic, spiritual and intellectual realms. Broadly speaking, Jews were part of the corporate structure of medieval feudalism and were granted internal administrative and juridical authority within the framework of well-defined obligations to the host government. The Jews cultivated their way of life and found modes of economic and intellectual interaction with Christians and Muslims. As Arabic philology stimulated Jewish Bible scholarship, so the exchanges between SOLOMON BEN ISAAC (Rashi) and Nicholas of Lyra in France influenced LUTHER centuries later.

d) Forms of literature. Tendencies toward halakhic conformity resulted in legal compendia, exegetical *novellae* on the Talmud, and RESPONSA to questions that required an authoritative decision. In spiritual and intellectual matters a diverse literature arose which variously sought to reconcile Jewish religious commandments and obligations with non-Jewish philosophical and spiritual systems of thought, or, just as often, to disclose the universal truths believed embodied in the halakah. The diverse and often daring speculations explaining the commandments were restrained by the force of halakhic observance. Nowhere is this tension better exemplified than in the multifaceted activities of some of Jewry's greatest figures. SAADIAH BEN JOSEPH and MOSES BEN MAIMON were both philosophers and halakhists of acuity; MOSES BEN NAḤMAN and JOSEPH CARO were at once mystics and halakhists of reknown. No medieval Jew ever imagined that either reason or faith was independent or self-sufficient. Judaism was rather considered a religious system bound by halakhic observances derived from divine revelation and ongoing exegesis.

e) Philosophers. The encounter with Hellenism in ancient Alexandria gave initial expression to Jewish philosophical endeavors. PHILO (first century A.D.) is an example of the attempts to reconcile Stoic philosophy and piety with the Torah. The result was a new spiritual apprehension of the revealed law, now considered an expression of cosmic wisdom. The patriarchal narratives were reinterpreted as allegories of moral and intellectual virtues, and the ancient sacrifices and ceremonies were read as allegories of spiritual growth. Such exegesis permitted Jews to see in their national literature the structures of universal reason. So reconciled, the revealed Torah did not alienate the Jew from citizenship in the universal city of the mind; instead it enabled those who knew the underlying, true sense of the text to enjoy such citizenship. But, Philo stressed, the philosophical spiritualization of Torah is one thing; observance, another. The allegorization of texts and rites must not undermine communal (i.e. halakhic) piety. Whether a response to criticism or not, this emphasis anticipates the response of many other philosophical and mystical spiritualizers of the written Torah to the zealous challenges of their literalistic antagonists.

Moses ben Maimon was the greatest Jewish philosopher of the Middle Ages. He systematized halakhic observance and, in his *Guide for the Perplexed,* achieved a magisterial philosophical reconciliation between Aristotelian rationalism and the revealed Torah. No less than Philo, Maimonides produced an elaborate reinterpretation of Torah into a new intellectual world. Reason and revelation were not contradictory systems for him. As an expression of divine wisdom, the Torah has two levels of meaning. The outer level is in the plain, literal sense of the text which simple piety has always acknowledged and which leads to moral excellence, social harmony, and fear of God. It is educational and motivational, and utilizes the anthropomorphic imagery of common speech. This is both deliberate and necessary, for even philosophy is dependent on metaphor. The philosopher, an adept of the inner meaning of the Torah, knows this and knows how to reconcile the anthropomorphisms with a philosophical God who is the unconditioned first cause, beyond all human knowledge and description. Correctly read, the Torah is a guide to philosophical wisdom and happiness. Divine revelation thus constitutes an independent path to the goal to which philosophers aspire. The Torah and its derived halakhic system support Jews in their intellectual love of God and their yearning for spiritual and rational development and intellectual devotion to the Godhead. Reciprocally, obedience to the commandments makes everyone, in his own degree, a philosopher and adept of truth.

JUDAH HA-LEVI wrote his philosophical treatise KUZARI a half-century earlier than Maimonides' *Guide,* and typifies a counter position to those Jews who sought a systematic harmonization between reason and revelation, between Greek philosophy and Hebrew Scriptures. Ha-Levi radically distinguished between the god of the philosophers and the living God of faith. For him, Judaism is not based on reason or systematic proofs of God's existence, but on personal and national experience. Abraham encountered God; so did all Israel at Sinai. The constitutive events of Israel's past record historical encounters with the living God of Israel. Mindful of the rational philosophical attempts to negate anthropomorphisms by attributing them to the human experience of God's active presence, ha-Levi acknowledged their truth value for the acquisition of faith. Filled with a yearning love for the living God who chose Israel in love, ha-Levi's philosophical prose and poetry glorified the uniqueness of his people, its language, and its land.

f) Mysticism. While the philosophical theologies of Maimonides and ha-Levi convey a mystical ardor, an esoteric tradition of mystical theology had long envigorated Judaism. Mystical traditions go back to old apocalyptic accounts of ecstatic ascents to heaven, to a literature from the third and fourth centuries describing beatific visions of the transcendent throne of divine Glory, and to a daring exegetical tradition which disclosed the secret form and figure of God.

Under the impact of Neoplatonic and GNOSTIC thought patterns, there were by the thirteenth century books reflecting an esoteric doctrine of deity, creation, revelation, sin, and redemption. *The Book of Splendor* (ZOHAR), attributed to Moses de León, was such a book for the mystical elite, and swiftly attained for them the status of holy writ. Like philosophical theology, mysticism was confronted by the authority and ambiguities of scripture. If philosophy spoke of creation out of nothing, mysticism spoke of the emanation of a *deus absconditus* out of his own nothingness. The flow of potencies from a hidden center by this now revealed God constitutes the structure of the Godhead and the ground of all created existence. Man is seen as the microcosmic image of the divine, both a fact of creative revelation and a respondent to it. Due to mysteries variously described as involving the Godhead and man, the original harmony was ruptured and the brokenness of things (humanly expressed by sin) has thrown the world and so God himself out of equilibrium. The religious task is to restore the original state of affairs by a devoted adherence to God through halakhic observance and disciplined contemplation. (*See* KABBALA.)

A profound reinterpretation of this doctrine was made in the sixteenth century by ISAAC LURIA, after the Jews were expelled from Spain. The historical exile of Israel was mystically reflected in a primordial self-exile, or self-contraction of the Godhead, so as to make room for an emanationist creation. Once again the harmonious flow of supernal light was sundered by disruptive processes and splintered throughout matter. The holy and redemptive task of Jews was no less than the restoration of divine unity. Building on the *Zohar,* a complex mythological and erotic symbolism continued to develop to convey the processes of cosmic creation, de-creation, and re-creation. Indeed, the lowest of the potencies was given reality as a feminine dimension within God, which suffered Israel's exile and whose mystical union with its masculine counterpart was part of the process of cosmic restoration. (*See* SEFER BAHIR.)

g) Messianism. The inner contraction of Jews that resulted from historical pain and fragmentation was thus projected onto processes within God, so that the historical life and actions of Jewry were cosmically pivotal. The messianic tensions contained in these dynamics were expressed in sixteenth century Palestine and in the widespread fervor elicited in the next century by the messianic pretensions of SABBATAI ZVI. For many, this cataclysm helped destroy the old rabbinic universe, but there were also many reinterpretations of the Kabbala. The popular pietistic movement called HASIDISM constituted, from the eighteenth century on, such a series of reinterpretations, giving particular emphasis to the integrity of words and deeds, to ecstatic feelings and meditative practices, and to a holy simplicity in the devoted service of God through obeying his commandments. Never did Jewish mysticism seek to undermine the halakhic basis of life except in the antinomian inversions of Sabbatai Zvi's theology.

4. **Torah and tradition.** The designation of Torah in the book of Deuteronomy, where it embraces law and history, is a substantial transformation of older priestly notions of specific "torahs," or instructions, on assorted subjects. As the notion of a comprehensive Sinaitic revelation developed and coordinated older traditions, it was also necessary to align the older Torah teachings to new situations. This was achieved by incorporating later traditions into the revealed content, or attributing revealed status to the traditions. Old laws were thereby reinterpreted, as were narratives, homilies, and prophetic oracles. This dialectic of growth and transformation continued into the rabbinic period. It was the Pharisees who, as noted above, gave a dogmatic, divine authority to customary and exegetical traditions by demonstrating their unbroken link to an oral Torah given to MOSES at Sinai.

Human interpretations were a perpetual unfolding of the original revelation in every area of life. Paradoxically, the Torah depended on exegetical tradition for its ongoing vitality. But if Torah was amenable to so much exegetical interpretation, it was self-evident to the religious mind that, befitting its divine character, "all was in it"—legal minutiae, homiletical eloquence, theological subtlety, Stoic and Aristotelian world views, and the innermost mystical secrets. It was said that the Torah has seventy faces, or four levels of meaning (literal, allegorical, legal-homiletical, mystical), or, more daringly, that Torah has 600,000 possible meanings, corresponding to the number of Israelites who stood at Sinai. The one immutable Torah was thus an illimitable thesaurus of possibilities realized through tradition. In medieval times "tradition" also served to designate the totality of Judaism's achievements. With fitting paradox, the term "Torah" was another such designation.

A remarkable transformation occurs in the mystical tradition, where the revealed Torah is only the outer, material garment of an inner, supernal Torah. The mystical task, guided by exegesis, is to ascend through the exoteric Torah to the divine Source of All, the true Torah. As this supernal Torah is unwritten and beyond language, it is an oral Torah, ceaselessly spoken by God. The written Sinaitic Torah is only an expression of it, as is human oral tradition. The early Hasidic masters continued Kabbalistic traditions of mystical-meditative exegesis. In some circles, moreover, their homilies were called Torah, and the term was often applied even to their doctrines and styles of piety.

5. **Liturgy and calendar.** For Judaism, as for world religions generally, the liturgical calendar establishes the primary life rhythms, and fosters group cohesiveness. Disputes over religious diversity and authority were often marked by calendrical deviations: in ancient Israel, in early Judaism, in the break with CHRISTIANITY, in Judaism's controversy with the KARAITES, in intrarabbinate debates over intercalation.

a) Spring festivals. The roots of Jewish seasonal festivals are biblical and organized around agricultural rhythms, beginning in the spring. Despite this, the festivals of PASSOVER (in origin also semi-nomadic), SHAVOUT, and SUKKOT were already given historical explanations in the Bible. Passover became the historical festival of redemption *par excellence;* Sukkot, the festival of tabernacles, anachronistically signified the providential desert abodes of the newly redeemed slaves. Judaism extended these historical associations: Shavuot came to be associated with the revelation at Sinai, and Passover served not only as a remembrance of redemption but as an anticipation of it for Israel and all mankind. The Passover celebration was filled with messianic longing for release from the bondage of historical exile, and its agricultural symbols, and those of the other festivals, were repeatedly spiritualized.

b) Autumn festivals. Together with this vernal cycle, an autumnal rhythm beginning in the seventh month is found in the old biblical calendars. It marks a period of renewal, culminating in the purification and atonement of the people and its Temple. Judaism now marks this ten-day period as its New Year (ROSH HA-SHANAH) and Day of Atonement (YOM KIPPUR), a time of holiness celebrating the creation of the world and the renewal of Jews through an intensification of prayer, repentance, and good deeds. Ascetic emphasis on penitence and repentance begins one month earlier and extends beyond the fast day of atonement into Sukkot. This time is thus paradigmatic for the acts of repentance before God and man that are always incumbent on Jews. New moon feasts were mystically interpreted as minor Days of Atonement, and the weekly rhythm culminating in the SABBATH was often understood within a framework of piety and renewal.

c) Sabbath. The Sabbath has always been the focus of Jewish piety. It is a time of sanctity, study, and rest from worldliness. Its liturgical content celebrates creation at evening, revelation through Torah recitation at the morning service, and redemption at the closing service. On the Sabbath Jews give special acknowledgment to God's Lordship and await the fullness of his Kingdom. The Sabbath is God's gift to his beloved, Israel; both Israel and the Sabbath are the bride of God to which he turns in covenantal union.

d) Other festivals. Other fast and feast days mark the Jewish year, reminiscent of various biblical and early Jewish times of divine deliverance (PURIM; HANUKKAH) or national tragedies (like the two destructions of the Temple). These feast days have a marked familial aspect, and form part of the many occasions when festivals and life-cycle events have a home context, e.g., circumcision, mourning, Sabbath and festival sanctifications, and the Passover SEDER.

e) Prayer. Following the destruction of the Temple, prayer, "the service of the heart," became predominant. Communal prayer is particularly valued. Private petitions have their place in this and other contexts; personal BENEDICTIONS for every earthly act of God know no bounds. There are three synagogue services daily, with special services on the Sabbath, festivals, and fasts. The order of these services varies within a traditional structure and language. This order includes initial benedictions and study passages; a psalm anthology; a call to prayer and acknowledgment of the one God as Creator, Revealer, and Redeemer; an order of praises and petitions; and avowals of messianic hope. On the Sabbath weekly Torah lectionaries culminate with pertinent selections from the biblical prophets. Special lections are set for special days. The entire Torah is now read yearly, providing yet another rhythm to Jewish life and underscoring the communal and theological centrality of this Torah and its halakhic offshoots (*see* SIDDUR).

6. Modernity and modern thought. The onset and impact of modernity has varied according to geographic locale. In Western Europe processes of social revolution from medieval forms gradually offered Jews the opportunity to enter a neutral society with more or less equal rights. The insularity of traditional life broke down. Because of enthusiasm over new possibilities of thought and social interaction, any hint of dual national loyalty was rejected. Jews became vigorous participants in their European national cultures. Religion took on a marginal and frequently a merely creedal character. One self-definition reflecting these processes was "Germans of the Mosaic persuasion."

a) Moses Mendelssohn. The desire to join the larger society gave an other-directed character even to internal Jewish developments. The activities of the eighteenth century German Jewish philosopher MOSES MENDELSSOHN are paradigmatic. Seeking to argue that Judaism was not particularistic, he contended that while the revealed commandments (which obligate Jews only) give shape to the uniqueness of Jewish destiny, the principles of Judaism are grounded in reason, and so share a common human applicability. Mendelssohn worked successfully for equal rights, but found that the "neutral" society was a Christian one. He was publicly pressured to respond to the conversion of Jews to Christianity. A similar pattern was prevalent in France, where the hidden agenda of civil libertarians was conversion.

b) Moves toward social acceptance. In nineteenth century Germany the movement for the "Scientific Study of Judaism" emerged. For the first time Jews studied their sources not as a guide to piety but as a historical record and as a means to present Judaism's role in universal culture and thereby help achieve social acceptance. The religious reformers of the period removed all hints of particularism from their liturgy and ideology and sought to renovate ceremonies in the light of contemporary tastes. The more traditional camp rejected the radical changes and stressed the eternal validity of Torah and tradition. But even S. R. HIRSCH, its eloquent spokesman, emphasized that Judaism constituted a testimony to a truth that was relevant to all humanity, and that nontraditional studies were allowed. A moderating position held that traditional Judaism was not an eternal verity but an evolving historical phenomenon, so that change should develop from Judaism's own inner principles.

c) The rise of Zionism. In Eastern Europe and Russia change came later and in different forms. Despite inner upheavals the traditional authorities of both pietistic and rational persuasions rebuffed the infiltration of the "enlighteners." But the threat can be measured by tendencies to curtail all change. When new forms finally emerged, nationalistic self-determination took pride of place. The rise of ZIONISM reflects a secularization of messianic dreams, recognizing assimilation as both illusory and anathema, and urging a renovation of Jewish national life as a post-traditional option and necessity. The disillusion with political-social integration in Christian Europe, together with the rise of nineteenth century ANTI-SEMITISM, made survival in a national homeland an urgent task. THEODOR HERZL advocated physical preservation as a first priority and Ahad Ha-Am emphasized the spiritual renewal of Jewry. Zionism was to be the means whereby Jews could assume an active role in their historical destiny, a movement of the spiritual and ethical elite, renewed through contact with nature and invigorated by social ideals and traditional sources.

d) Jewish philosophers. In Europe Jews continued to participate in the social and philosophical ideals of the majority culture. HERMANN COHEN envisioned the messianism of Jewish ethical monotheism as a philosophical socialism; God, who is One and loves the stranger, would preserve his creation for the just reconciliation of all humanity and its needs. Like Cohen, FRANZ ROSENZWEIG regarded nationalism as unnecessary for the fulfillment of Jewish destiny, but he rejected philosophical idealism. A post-traditionalist, Rosenzweig emphasized the encounter between God and dependent, mortal mankind. In this meeting God expresses his love, and this love evokes a human response and creates a sense of responsibility for one's fellow creatures. The religious tradition and its forms bear witness to such encounters and remain potential spiritual vehicles. The liturgical year celebrates the fact of creation, the renewal of revelation, and the future of the divine Kingdom. MARTIN BUBER shared this concern with a personal life of ever-renewed encounter with the Creator. For him, God is the eternal Thou, one who demands perpetual spiritual attentiveness, but cannot be found in symbols or traditional forms. Because these forms bear witness to past encounters with a living divine Spirit, Buber preserved literary traditions of spiritual piety. Through them, he hoped to challenge modern Jews with the ever-present demands of the Spirit, and so renew them spiritually and nationally, in the diaspora and especially in Zion.

e) The Holocaust. But any hope in a symbiosis between a Zionist homeland and the European diaspora was shattered with the murder of six million Jews (*see* HOLOCAUST). Concern with physical survival became the only goal, and the need intensified to create a homeland to preserve Jewish lives and spiritual destiny. This was realized in 1948, with the establishment of the State of Israel. But the resources of renewal were often polarized between modernists who wanted a secular social democracy and traditionalists who wanted a theocracy through the renovation and politicization of halakah. Harmonious visions, such as those of Chief Rabbi Kook, were in the minority. The recurrent question, "Who is a Jew?" reflects the turmoil of a modernized ancient people uncertain whether self-definition lies in secular or traditional categories.

f) American Jewish life. In America different patterns of Jewish life developed: liberal REFORM; traditional ORTHODOX; moderate CONSERVATIVE. Each group tried to accommodate itself to America's social realities and responded variously with liturgical and/or ideological change. While their theological programs supported the common values of God, Torah, and Israel, their emphases differed. Reform emphasized God, Orthodoxy stressed Torah, and Conservatives were primarily concerned with peoplehood.

Theologically the impact of secularism and scientific naturalism elicited the RECONSTRUCTIONIST movement of MORDECAI KAPLAN, which emphasized the evolving civilization of Judaism with its diverse cultural forms and pragmatic adaptations. Kaplan stressed the communal base of Judaism and endorsed traditional forms, while he spoke of God untraditionally as an impersonal force in nature. Such reinterpretations were avoided by ABRAHAM HESCHEL, who, with tireless spiritual vigor, sought to renew for modern Jews a sensibility toward the living reality of religion and a personal God. While noted for his emphasis on the loneliness and anguish of mortal man before God, Joseph Soloveitchik has reformulated for traditionalists the ideals of the halakhic way and its circumscription within the borders of an intense, value-sharing, liturgical community of faith.

Today, however, over the old goals and newer ones —such as the development of informal prayer-study fellowships and concern for the status of women—falls the shadow of the Holocaust, with its shock to traditional Jewish views of God, providence, and theodicy. The philosopher Emil Fackenheim and the novelist Elie Wiesel have given eloquent and passionate counsels of hope to many in their anguish and confusion.

Bibliography. *The Babylonian Talmud*, ed. I. Epstein, 34 vols. (1935-52); *The Midrash*, ed. H. Freedman, 10 vols (1939); *The Zohar* tran. H. Sperling and M. Simon, 5 vols (1949); M. Buber, *Tales of the Hasidim* (1947-49); *The Authorized Daily Prayer Book*. ed. J. Hertz (1957); *Encyclopedia Judaica*, 16 vols. (1971); L. Finkelstein, *The Jews: Their History, Culture, and Religion*, 2 vols. (1950); S. Baron, *A Social and Religious History of the Jews*, 16 vols. (1952-73); J. Guttman, *Philosophies of Judaism* (1964); G. Scholem, *Major Trends in Jewish Mysticism* (1956); G F. Moore, *Judaism in the First Centuries of the Christian Era*, 3 vols. (1927-30); A. Heschel, *God in Search of Man: A Philosophy of Judaism* (1955); N. N. Glatzer, ed., *In Time and Eternity; A Jewish Reader* (1961).

M. FISHBANE

JUDAS MACCABEE (Ju). *See* MACCABEES.

JUDGMENT DAY IN ISLAM. *See* ESCHATOLOGY §3.

JUNAYD, ABU'L-QĀSIM joo nīd′ ä bool′ kä′sēm (I; d. A.D. 910). Distinguished Persian SUFI of Baghdad. Educated in ḤADĪTH and jurisprudence (FIQH), he pursued the mystical path under the direction of his uncle. Like other Sufi masters, he spoke of love, striving, annihilation, and union, but unlike BISTĀMĪ and his own disciple, AL-ḤALLĀJ, Junayd stressed the value of "sobriety" rather than "intoxication" in his numerous elliptical references to knowledge of God.

Occasional reference has been made to a school founded by him (the Junaydīya). Organizers of the earliest major Sufi orders (*see* ṬARĪQA) traced their spiritual affiliation to MUHAMMAD through Junayd and his disciples.

Bibliography. 'Ali Hassan 'Abd el-Qādir, *The Life, Personality and Writings of al-Junayd* (1962).

B. LAWRENCE

JUSTIFICATION BY FAITH (Ch). Justification is a technical expression, appropriated from the OT and JUDAISM, which appears at decisive junctures in PAUL'S letters (Rom. 1:7; 3:21-26; 10:3; Phil. 3:9; II Cor. 5:21). In the symbolism of an eschatological judgment scene God justifies (acquits) his creation. This acquittal, accomplished through the crucified and resurrected Lord, is mediated through the GOSPEL (Rom. 1:16-17). In accordance with the character of this acquittal as grace, the gift is appropriated in the structure of obedience; i.e., God's gift is bestowed as the expression of his lordship. PROTESTANTISM—with occasional exceptions—has pointed to this doctrine as the focus of Paul's thought, indeed of the NT as a whole.

The history of Christian thought contains recurring variations on the meaning of this expression. Does justification (righteousness) refer to a divine attribute which constitutes the norm of judgment? Or, does the term describe God's saving activity for his fallen creatures? In any case, what is the prerequisite for acceptance? Is salvation based on ethical achievement (faith) measured by the norm of God's character, or is acceptance grounded solely in the divine prerogative? These options have been reflected in major theological movements in Christian history.

Bibliography. P. Stuhlmacher, *Gerechtigkeit Gottes bei Paulus* (1965); R. Bultmann, *Theology of the New Testament*, I (1951), 270-329; E. Käsemann, "The Righteousness of God in Paul," *New Testament Questions of Today*, (1969), pp. 168-82.

R. C. BRIGGS

K

KA'BA kä´ bä (I—Arab.; lit. "cube"). The House of Allah, the central shrine of Islam; a cube-like building about forty feet long, thirty-three feet wide, and fifty feet high, constructed of blocks of Meccan granite. The Ka'ba stands at the center of the great open-air Mosque of Mecca, the *masjid al-harām.* It constitutes the Qiblah, the specific point which Muslims face when performing the daily ritual prayers.

The Ka'ba is the center of the world for Muslims. It is "the navel of the earth," the first creation of Allah and the beginning point of all creation. Muslim cosmology locates it on the same axis with seven Ka'bas directly above it in the seven heavens. These Ka'bas, earthly and celestial, are directly below the throne of Allah, which is circumambulated by the angels (Malā'ika) even as the Meccan Ka'ba is circumambulated by humans.

1. **The black stone.** The most sacred object at the Ka'ba is the black stone embedded in the southeastern corner of the building, about five feet above the pavement. It is referred to as the "cornerstone" or "foundation" of the house and as "the right hand of God on earth." The black stone is pre-Islamic, and while its origin is unknown, myths affirm that it fell from heaven. Muslims kiss or touch it on occasion, as, for example, in the performance of the pilgrimage (Hajj), but they insist that it is not an idol and that prayers are addressed to Allah, not to the black stone. In A.D. 930 Qarmaṭians stole the black stone, and some twenty years passed before they returned it.

2. **Description of the Ka'ba.** The Ka'ba has only one door, located in the northeastern wall about seven feet above the pavement. Mobile stairs provide access on the infrequent occasions when the Ka'ba is opened. The interior is furnished only with gold and silver lamps suspended from the ceiling. Unlike many religious buildings the sacrality of the Ka'ba resides more in its exterior than its interior, as is indicated not only by the black stone but by the *multazam,* a six-foot section of the exterior wall between the black stone and the door where worshipers press their bodies in order to receive the *baraka* ("blessing, power") immanent in the holy house.

The Ka'ba is usually covered by the *kiswa* ("robe") of thick black material embroidered with wide bands of Arabic verses from the Qur'ān.

Surrounding the Ka'ba is a broad pavement of polished granite called the *matāf,* the place of circumambulation. Opposite the corner containing the black stone is the building housing the sacred well of Zamzam, and in front of the northeastern wall (the "face" of the Ka'ba) is situated the *maqām Ibrāhīm* ("station of Abraham"), a stone said to preserve the footprint of Abraham, reputed builder of the house; here prayers are offered to Allah.

3. **The pre-Islamic Ka'ba.** As there are no historical records of the origin of the Ka'ba, its age is unknown, but it is thought to predate the birth of Muhammad (*ca.* A.D. 570) by several centuries. At the time of Muhammad the Ka'ba was the principal religious shrine of central Arabia and was visited seasonally by both neighboring and distant tribes for the performance of religious rites of offering, sacrifice, and divination. It appears also to have served as a pantheon. In general, the Ka'ba possessed the traditional characteristics of a Semitic sanctuary. Thus it was located at the center of a sacred territory *(haram),* entry into which imposed restrictions and offered refuge.

4. **Muhammad and the Ka'ba.** The Qur'ān indicates that from the beginning of his prophetic career (about A.D. 610) Muhammad considered the Ka'ba to be the House of Allah.

Two events during the Medinan period prior to the conquest of Mecca especially evidence Muhammad's attitude toward the Ka'ba. The first was the instruction given Muslims in the Qur'ān (Sura 2:142-45) in A.D. 624 henceforth to face the Ka'ba rather than Jerusalem when praying. The second was his effort to visit the Ka'ba from Medina in A.D. 628, which he succeeded in doing the following year.

After the conquest of Mecca by Muslim forces in A.D. 630 Muhammad "cleansed" the Ka'ba, destroying the idols and other evidences of paganism and restoring it to its proper function as the house of the one God. The Qur'ān (Sura 3: 90-92) enjoined on all Muslims the duty of making pilgrimage to the Ka'ba.

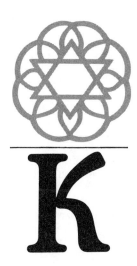

The building standing in Mecca at present is not the original Ka'ba but the most recent of several successive buildings. The Ka'ba has been badly damaged by fire, flood, and attack several times during the Islamic period and subsequently repaired or reconstructed. The present building, using stones from earlier buildings, dates from the seventeenth century. *See* illustration for HAJJ.

H. B. PARTIN

KABBALA kä bä lä´ (Ju—Heb.; lit. "tradition" [*kbl*—"to receive"]). Traditional term for the many forms of Jewish MYSTICISM. The first esoteric doctrines and ecstatic techniques in Judaism originated in Palestine during the Greco-Roman era. All subsequent elaborations and innovations in doctrine and practice are products of the diverse geographical, cultural, and political environments that shaped postbiblical Jewish history. Judaism grew as the religion of a people living with the chronic trauma of the DIASPORA, and Kabbala is one of its responses, perhaps its most profound, to the adversity and crisis-ridden experience of exile.

More specifically Kabbala refers to the dominant trend in Jewish mysticism which may be traced from its beginnings in Jewish life and thought in twelfth century Provence and Spain, through developments in sixteenth century Safed in Galilee, from where it spread throughout Europe and the entire Jewish world. The conceptual components of this tradition derive from three sources: rabbinic Judaism, Jewish GNOSTICISM, and Jewish Neoplatonic, Neoaristotelian philosophy. Rabbinic Judaism supplied a fully developed theology, a sacred and authoritative body of literature based on the BIBLE and the TALMUD, and a vigorous, all-encompassing system of ritual and civil law. Jewish Gnosticism provided a mythical understanding of the dynamics of God's inner life as symbolically reflected in all aspects of reality. The philosophic tradition contributed the doctrines of emanation, the monistic hierarchy of being, mankind as a microcosm, moral purity as a precondition for

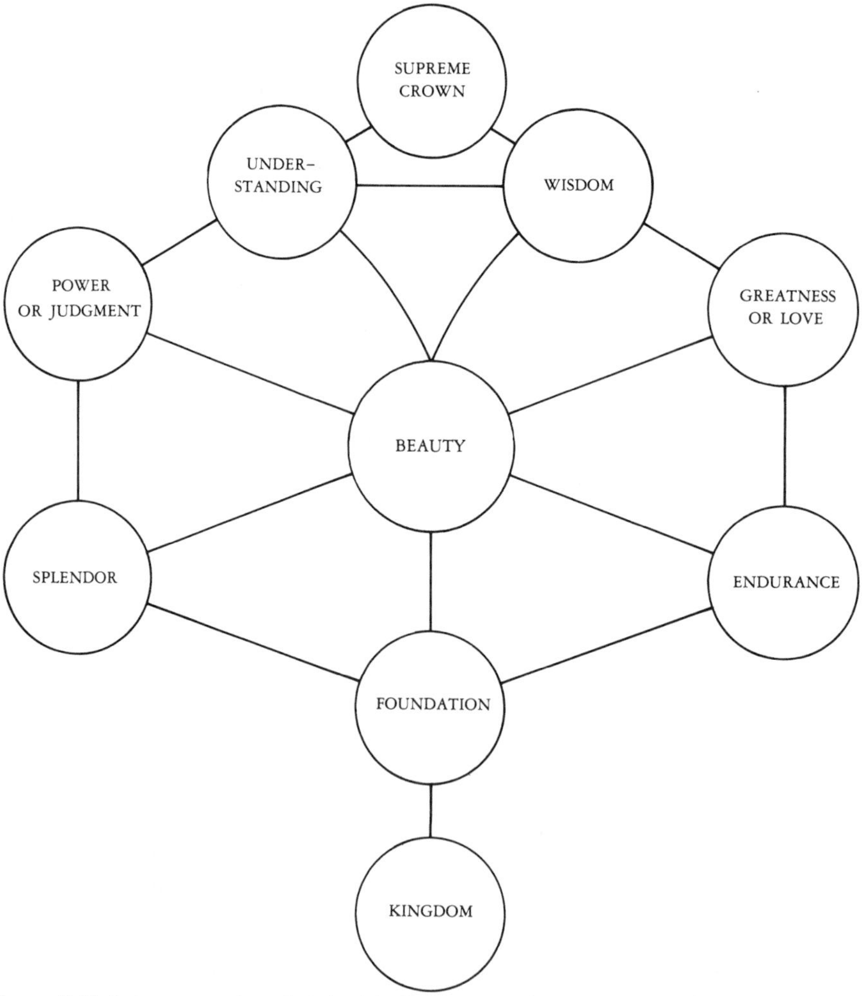

The sefirot, a Kabbalistic representation of relationships between the infinite aspect of deity and the revealed aspects

spiritual enlightenment, and the ultimate return of all reality to its metaphysical roots in the supernal, divine world of the One.

1. **Inwardness.** The agent of this transforming reinterpretation of rabbinic Judaism is the human capacity or appetite for locating the sacred, the real, or the divine in the inward depth of all things. By using a wide variety of ascetic or contemplative techniques that alter ordinary modes of perception, the Jewish mystic claims to pierce reality and thereby to gain insight into, and various degrees of attachment to, the ultimately unified and harmonious source of all being. Except for the radically transcendental conceptions of God's realm elaborated in the first stage of Jewish mysticism, the perspective of Kabbala is inward.

2. **Cosmic effect.** Kabbala also resonates with magical practice and theurgy. From biblical and rabbinic Judaism it absorbed the acknowledgment of, and grateful allegiance to, God's KINGDOM as the goal of religious life. With the rationalistic, scientifically inspired tradition of medieval religious philosophy Kabbala shares the claim that an understanding of the structures and processes of God's kingdom represents the highest form of religious experience, i.e., the psychological and intellectual perfection of human nature. The Kabbala, however, differs from all other varieties of Judaism when it teaches that intuitive contact with the divine carries with it the power and responsibility for creating, as well as sustaining, harmony within the dynamics of God's inner life and unity between God and his creation. It insists that the well-being of God and the destiny of the universe directly depend upon the infinite aspirations and appropriately cosmic deeds of the Jewish mystic.

3. **Before 1492.** The expulsion of the Jews from Spain and Portugal in 1492 divides the eight hundred years of Kabbala into two phases. Before 1492 mysticism remained the aristocratic, esoteric domain of small circles of religious virtuosi. It was dominated by the various themes and emphases characteristic of the ZOHAR, in which human experience and sacred literature become a vast sea of symbolic structures embodying the secrets of God's inner life as it pulses in the interaction of his ten sefirot, the creative facets of God's personality, whose outward expressions comprise the corporeal reality of the universe and whose ebb and flow create the ongoing processes of life. (*See* SEFER BAHIR § 1.) Whatever happens "here" in our universe is happening "there" within God, for justice and mercy, male and female, good and evil, six days of creation and SABBATH, and all other constituents of reality are also the various names of God, pointing to the infinite modalities of his being. The world is created and God is revealed in the progressive unfolding of God out of himself. The various currents in this phase of Kabbala all share this basic perception of the relationship between God and himself and between God and his worlds. To perceive these inner workings of God's life and reciprocally to influence them are the twin goals of the individual mystic.

4. **Later stages.** After 1492 ISAAC LURIA and his disciples reshaped the entire mystical tradition. Judaism's messianic and apocalyptic traditions and its notions of a collective redemption of the Jewish people were fused with the theosophical perspective of the *Zohar*. Earlier Kabbala tended toward panentheism and pantheism; Luria turned to theism and to dualistic separation between God and the universe. For him, evil forces and demonic realms permeate reality on all levels (including the divine) where the harmony of God's being is ruptured. This is symbolically reflected in the ruins of JERUSALEM and in the sorrowful facts of Jewish history and human life. Luria taught that evil, "the other side," could be conquered, and reality saved, through mystically informed, redemptive acts *(tikkun)*. The inward life of all things is still the divine presence, but now it too is a captive to the bondage of life as it is. Restoration becomes the goal of religious life.

Unlike the earlier Kabbala and its more appreciative view of reality, the ascetic mysticism of Luria's cosmic myth of exile and redemption was widely disseminated and captured the imagination of Jewish masses everywhere. It gave rise in the seventeenth century to the antinomian messianism of the Sabbatean movement (*see* SABBATAI ZVI), and in the eighteenth century to the pietistic revivalism of HASIDISM.

Bibliography. G. Scholem, *Major Trends in Jewish Mysticism* (3rd ed., 1954), *On the Kabbalah and Its Symbolism* (1965), and *Kabbalah* (1974).

K. P. BLAND

KABĪR kä bēr′ (H & I; 1440-1518?). Indian saint. Over the centuries so many stories have been attached to the name of Kabīr that even the dates of his life are uncertain. He has become more than a historical figure; he is a symbol of religious tolerance, an example of the possibility of synthesis between ISLAM and HINDUISM.

Kabīr was the son of a Muslim weaver and his wife in North India. Later Hindu writers sought to remove this stigma of low birth by claiming Kabīr was an AVATAR, or a miracle child conceived by the word of God, or, in the manner of MOSES, a baby found floating on a lotus leaf in a pond. As a youth, in the sacred Hindu city of Banāras (*see* HINDU SACRED CITIES) Kabīr was much influenced by Hinduism, so much so that he became fond of chanting the divine name of RĀMA. This practice not only infuriated the Muslims, who were firmly opposed to polytheism, but it also irritated the Hindus, who considered such chanting on the part of a non-Hindu a grave blasphemy.

Kabīr rejected all outward forms of religion—scriptures, CASTE, idolatry, elaborate rituals—and preached a simple love of God. It is obvious that he was influenced by the SUFI sect of Islam, although he avoided religious labels of any kind. Kabīr's beliefs were expressed more in his actions than in any detailed theology. For instance, legend has it that his chosen GURU, Swami Rāmānand, once sent Kabīr to fetch cow's milk to be offered to the ancestors. The disciple disappeared for some time and was finally discovered seated by a dead cow to which he had been trying to feed a handful of grass. The startled Rāmānand asked Kabīr the meaning of his odd behavior. Surely he must know a dead cow cannot eat grass or give milk. Kabīr replied, "If a recently deceased cow cannot eat, how can your long-dead ancestors drink the milk you intend to offer them?"

Kabīr's beliefs are incorporated into his poems. His choice of vocabulary borrows freely from both SANSKRIT and PERSIAN, just as his religion combined the best of Hinduism and Islam. His simple philosophy is summed up in the following verses:

> I do not ring the temple bell:
> I do not set the idol on its throne:
> I do not worship the image with flowers.
> It is not the austerities that mortify the flesh which are pleasing to the Lord,
> When you leave off your clothes and kill your senses, you do not please the Lord:
> The man who is kind and who practises righteousness, who remains passive amidst the affairs of the world, who considers all creatures on earth as his own self,
> He attains the Immortal Being, the true God is ever with him. (*Songs of Kabir* [1915], pp. 108-9)

During his lifetime a religious community of monks and nuns (the Kabīr Panth) was organized to preserve Kabīr's teachings on tolerance and perfect love of God.

Bibliography. C. Vaudeville, trans., *Kabīr*, Vol. I (1974).

P. L. BASU

KADDISH kä′ dĭsh (Ju—Heb.; lit. "sanctification"). A brief ARAMAIC prayer, among the best known in the Jewish liturgy. As an ancient Jewish vernacular, Aramaic was employed so that all might understand this devotion which is frequently recited in the course of a service. Contrary to popular opinion, it is not a prayer for the dead. Its central theme is the glorification of God, with secondary exhortations for a speedy redemption, his acceptance of prayer, and eternal peace. Traditionally one line, "May his great name be forever blessed," is read responsively.

The traditional service includes four variations, recited for different purposes: 1) The complete Kaddish is read by the CANTOR to signify the end of a service. Thus it is chanted just prior to the completion of the SHOFAR blowing on ROSH HA-SHANAH. 2) The half Kaddish, so called because it omits two paragraphs, serves to divide portions of the service and is recited after the TORAH reading. 3) The RABBI's Kaddish apparently developed as a concluding prayer for a rabbinic discourse, publicly delivered; it also follows portions of the service in which specific laws are studied. It differs from the others in that it contains a call for peace to the teachers of Israel. SABBATH candle-lighting laws are traditionally recited on Friday evening, followed by a rabbi's Kaddish. 4) The mourner's Kaddish appears to have developed in the thirteenth century, with the purpose of reaffirming God's greatness by those who have suffered a loss and may question his judgment. The prayer has no added text referring to death and should be viewed by the mourner as an expression of the acceptance of the divine will.

The earliest references to the Kaddish are TALMUDIC (*ca.* sixth century A.D.), and it appears to have been incorporated in the prayer services shortly thereafter, with the provision that it only be recited while standing, in the presence of a MINYAN (a quorum of ten adults). These restrictions continue in effect today.

Local variations of text exist among different communities and SYNAGOGUES. For example, the Yemenite rite emphasizes that God is beyond all praise, the Jerusalem and Safed texts add the word "holy" to signify the sanctity of those cities, and the SEPHARDIC reading includes an additional reference to redemption, the restoration of JERUSALEM, and the revival of the dead.

It is also customary to recite the Kaddish on the YAHRZEIT (anniversary of the death of a close relative), a practice which probably originated in the aftermath of the CRUSADES, when communal memorials were necessary because of the large numbers who were massacred. Collective gave way to individual commemoration and the Kaddish assumed central importance as a means of recalling the memory of a loved one. (*See* DEATH; PRAYER, JEWISH; YIZKOR; KOL NIDRE.)

Bibliography. P. Birnbaum, *The Daily Prayer Book* (1969); D. de S. Pool, *The Traditional Prayer Book* (1960).

D. J. SCHNALL and S. BAYME

MOURNER'S KADDISH

Magnified and sanctified be the name of God throughout the world which He hath created according to His will. May He establish His kingdom during the days of your life and during the life of all the house of Israel, speedily, yea, soon; and say ye, Amen.

Congregation and Mourners

May his great name be blessed for ever and ever.

Mourners

Exalted and honored be the name of the Holy One, blessed be He, whose glory transcends, yea, is beyond all praises, hymns and blessings that man can render unto Him; and say ye, Amen.

May there be abundant peace from heaven, and life for us and for all Israel; and say ye, Amen.

May He who establisheth peace in the heavens, grant peace unto us and unto all Israel: and say ye, Amen.

Sabbath and Festival Prayer Book (1946)

KAGAWA, TOYOHIKO kä′ gä wä tō yō′ hī kō (Ch; 1888–1960). Japanese author, evangelist, social worker, and minister. Baptized in 1902 by H. W. Myers, a Presbyterian missionary, he began his ministry in a Kobe slum in 1909. Leading a strike against a Kobe shipbuilding industry in 1921, he pioneered Japan's labor movement. Christ's redemptive love is the central theme in his writings.

K. Koyama

KAILĀSA kī lä′ sū (H—Skt.). The Himalayan mountain that is the home of the Hindu god Shiva. Often identified with an actual Himalayan peak north of Lake Mānasa (an important center of pilgrimage for worshipers of Shiva), it is symbolically located in the landscape of the heart. From the time of the Vedas, Shiva has been associated with the wild, dangerous, uncivilized aspect of the mountains. As Lord of Kailāsa (Kailāsapati), Shiva sometimes withdraws and meditates in solitude until the gods seek his aid; at other times he is accompanied on Kailāsa by one of his mountain-born consorts, Pārvatī ("daughter of the mountain"), but not by the other, Kālī Vindhyavāsinī ("the dark goddess dwelling in the Vindhya mountains"). In South India another mountain, Aruṇācalam ("red mountain"), replaces Kailāsa as Shiva's home and the paradise that his devotees attain.

W. D. O'Flaherty

KAIVALYA kī väl′ yū (Ja & H—Skt.; lit. "isolation, detachment" [*kevala*—"unconnected, solitary, uncompounded"]). The state of the soul/self in final liberation (cf. Moksa).

In Jainism, *kaivalya* refers to two aspects of the Jīva ("life-principle"/soul) in liberation: (a) the *jīva* is "detached" from all karma (which the Jainas view as a kind of subtle matter that clings to the *jīva*); (b) the liberated *jīva* regains its original condition, which is one of "uncompounded" *(kevala)* knowledge and bliss, i.e., omniscience and perfect self-knowledge. Jainas refer to one who has attained liberation as a *kevalin*, "one who is characterized by uncompounded isolation."

Within Sāmkhya and Patañjali's Yoga, *kaivalya* points to a similar condition in final liberation for the Purusa ("person"/soul). However, the notions of omniscience and bliss are absent, and the "detachment" is more properly a realization of the actual relationship between the Purusa and Prakṛti (the realm of matter and ordinary existence). Here *puruṣa* and *prakṛti* are seen as being fundamentally separate, not actually involved with each other (as the Jainas view the *jīva* and karma). The individual's goal, therefore, is to realize the separation of soul and matter, while in Jainism it is, in one sense, to create that separation.

K. W. Folkert

KALĀM kə läm′ (I—Arab.; lit. "speech, discussion"). Dogmatic theology in Islam, also known as *'ilm al-tawḥīd*, "the science of [the Divine] Unity." One who does *kalām* is a *mutakallim*. While Islam has known considerable and varied theological activity, the formal enterprise has never enjoyed a dominant position among the religious sciences. Legal and ritual issues have been the major foci, to the extent that Sunnite Islam, as Smith suggests, should be characterized as "orthoprax" rather than the conventional "orthodox"—correct practice being more basic than correct doctrine, especially if the latter is understood primarily intellectually.

The Qur'ān is itself a work of religious inspiration, not a theological treatise. *Kalām* arose in the early Umayyad period over certain important issues which were susceptible of varying interpretations in their Qur'ānic formulations. One of the most fateful was free will and predestination, both of which can be scripturally supported (e.g. Suras 17:84; 18:24-31; 39:52-59; 41:17, 18; 76:2, 3). Another was the political question of who should rule the Muslim community and what his qualifications should be, centering in the dissensions among the Shi'ites, Khārijites, and pro-Umayyad peoples (who would eventually dominate as the Sunnis).

There were two tendencies which were particularly significant in laying the foundations of *kalām:* the *Qadariyya*, "free-willers," who held that man as well as God possesses *qadar*, the "capacity to act"; and the *Jabriyya*, "predestinarians," who insisted that God controls everything through his *jabr*, "compulsion." Both these ways of thinking were indigenous to Islam. Other theological and philosophical models, while not without influence, were never determinative in the development of *kalām*. The *Qadariyya* were generally opposed to the Umayyads, whom they regarded as usurpers, while the *Jabriyya* provided theological buttressing for them as a regime willed by God. *Kalām* would thenceforth always have a political and social as well as religious reference, embodying the ancient maxim that Islam is both *dīn wa dawla*, "religion and state." Even the vexed issue of the status of the believer who has committed a grave sin was treated in a manner which led the Khārijites to execute such a person, so he would not contaminate the community, while others postponed (thus their name of Murji'ites—"postponers") the matter until God's final judgment, meanwhile regarding the offender as still a believer, but one who needed to repent.

Legend has it that the greatest school of early *kalām* grew out of this dispute. This was the Mu'tazila, those who "stand aloof" in a neutral position. They became the dominant school of *kalām* in the 'Abbāsid court of al-Ma'mūn (A.D. 813-33) and for some time after. Calling themselves "the People of [the Divine] Justice and Unity," they embraced reason as well as revelation, emphasized human free will for the sake of divine justice, insisted that the Qur'ān was created in time (otherwise it would compromise God's unity), and utterly rejected literal anthropomorphic characterizations of God. Although they have often been admired as "freethinkers" in Western discussions, the Mu'tazilites were earnest, sometimes arrogant intellectuals solidly rooted in their conception of Islam as a total system which, knowing the divine nature by means of reason, deemed itself empowered to act as God's agent in "enjoining the good and forbidding the evil" (Sura 3:104). God, they argued, is constrained by his own nature always to do what is good for his creatures. Here we see Greek philosophical influence: the good is not so because God has willed it; rather, God wills what is good. This is necessity, a notion that was to be extirpated in the *kalām* which eventually triumphed. It holds that whatever God decrees is right because of his inscrutable command (*'amr*), not because of some abstract principle by which his acts can be gauged.

The person who did more than any other to topple Mu'tazilism from its position of intellectual prestige—it had earlier lost its political power to a popular, broad-based movement of pious legists (Hanbalites; *see* IBN ḤANBAL)—was a former adherent, ASH'ARĪ (d. 935), whose followers have down to the present constituted the closest thing to an official school of Sunni *kalām*. The fundamental principle of Ash'arism is that God is absolutely one, sovereign, and beyond rational comprehension. He creates all human acts, which are then acquired by man as his own. The Qur'ān is eternal, uncreated, and all that it contains is literally true, including the many anthropomorphic passages, which must be accepted in all their ambiguity *bilā kayf*, "without asking how." But Mu'tazilism had a salutary effect on Ash'arism in the method of employing logical argument in defense of Islam. This legacy came to be bitterly condemned by the fundamentalist Hanbalites, who wanted no truck with formal rational techniques, regarding them as intrinsically un-Islamic, however appealing they might appear to be. Ash'arī's contemporary, AL-MĀTURĪDĪ (d. 944), founded a school of *kalām* with similar, though slightly more liberal, principles. The Shi'ites have different approaches to *kalām* and have continued to cultivate Mu'tazilite doctrines.

Among the leading Ash'arites were Fakhr al-Dīn al-Rāzī (d. 1209) and al-Shahrastānī (d. 1153), who were influenced toward a philosophical theology by AL-GHAZZĀLĪ (d. 1111), who had grave reservations about the ordinary believer's access to *kalām*, likening it to a dangerous medicine which should be taken only under the strictest expert supervision. IBN TAYMĪYYA (d. 1328), an uncompromising, "orthoprax" Sunni of the Hanbalite school, was nevertheless a perceptive and astute critic of philosophy and Ash'arite *kalām*, championing human free will under a God who remains nevertheless essentially unknowable except as he reveals himself. The WAHHĀBĪYA still keep Ibn Taymīyya's positions alive. A modern type of *kalām* having significant influence is that of the Egyptian MUHAMMAD 'ABDUH (d. 1905), who combined Ash'arite, Māturīdite, and even Mu'tazilite methods and insights into a cautiously eclectic, irenic vision. There have also been new departures in *kalām* in Turkey and on the Indian subcontinent.

Bibliography. L. Gardet, "*'Ilm al-kalām*," *EI;* R. J. McCarthy, *The Theology of al-Ash'arī* (1953), texts in translation; W. C. Smith, *Islam in Modern History* (1957); W. M. Watt, *The Formative Period of Islamic Thought* (1973), and *Islamic Philosophy and Theology* (1962), an elementary survey; A. J. Wensinck, *The Muslim Creed* (1932); H. A. Wolfson, *The Philosophy of the Kalam* (1976). F. M. DENNY

KĀLĪ kä′ lē (H—Skt.; lit. "the black one"). A bloodthirsty goddess of terrible appearance and fearsome habits. Traditionally a consort of SHIVA, Kālī is widely worshiped to this day in Bengal as the supreme mother. *See* GODDESS (INDIA) §3.

Bibliography. D. Kinsley, *The Sword and the Flute—Kālī and Kṛṣṇa* (1975), pt. 2. D. R. KINSLEY

KALI YUGA kä′ lē yōō′ gü (H—Skt.; lit. "age of strife"). Kali is the name of the losing die marked with one spot and, in its religious usage, the name of the final and most degenerate of the four ages (YUGA) which make up the cycle of human time (SAMSARA). The first three ages are likewise named after dice, hence, Kṛta yuga ("Fourth or Perfect Age"), Tretā yuga ("Third Age"), and Dvāpara yuga ("Second Age"). Humanity has already endured the Kali yuga for five thousand years (it began 3012 B.C.), and it will not end for another half-million years, at which time the world will be destroyed by flood and fire and a new cycle *(mahāyuga)* will begin. J. BARE

KĀLIDĀSA kä lī dä′ sü (H—Skt.; lit. "servant of Kālī [the goddess]). The greatest of SANSKRIT poets and dramatists, best known for his drama *Śakuntalā;* probably flourished during the GUPTA DYNASTY.

Little is known of Kālidāsa's life, and estimates of his date range from the second century B.C. to the fifth century A.D., the latter being more generally accepted. The seven works attributed to him have won universal acclaim both abroad and in India. Three of these works are plays, the most famous of which is *Śakuntalā*. Two others—*Kumārasambhava* ("Birth of the War-God") and *Raghuvaṃśa* ("The Dynasty of Raghu")—are epic poems. The remaining two—*Meghadūta* ("The Cloud Messenger") and *Ṛtusaṃhāra* ("The Cycle of Seasons"), the latter of doubtful authenticity—are lyrics.

Kālidāsa drew from a wide variety of sources. The basic story of *Śakuntalā* occurs in the first book of the MAHĀBHĀRATA, though completely recast by the author. The two epics include materials from the PURĀNAS and the RĀMĀYAṆA. The classical systems of Hindu philosophy make their appearance, as do narratives from the VEDAS. Gods, AVATARS, celestial nymphs, demons, hermits, and irascible sages mingle with kings and queens. The HINDU AIMS OF LIFE are implicit, and the concept of KARMA plays an important role. Most characteristic is the fusing of sensual and aesthetic with religious and spiritual values, so marked a feature of much Hindu religious literature.

Bibliography. K. Krishnamoorthy, *Kālidāsa* (1972).

C. R. KING

KĀMA kä´ mŭ (H—Skt.; lit. "desire, pleasure, sexual love" [*kam*—"to love, to have sexual intercourse with"]). Kāma is an important concept in Indian thought paralleling in meaning the Greek word *eros*. At its most general level Kāma means wish or desire, and as such kāma is sometimes condemned in Hindu (and Buddhist) soteriological systems which view desire as the chain that keeps persons bound to SAMSARA, the cycle of birth and death. Kāma, however, also means pleasure, particularly the pleasure experienced in sexual love, and the pursuit of kāma in this sense is legitimized by its inclusion in the four HINDU AIMS OF LIFE and emphasized in the text called the KĀMA SŪTRA.

Kāma is also the name of the Hindu god of love, a Cupid-like figure who incites passion in gods and humans by shooting them with his flower arrows. The most famous incident involving Kāma in Hindu Purāṇic mythology centers on the role he played in helping to bring about the birth of Skanda, SHIVA's son. Once, when the gods were being harassed by the demon Tāraka, it became known that only a son of Shiva could save the gods' cause. Shiva, however, was sunk in deep meditation, and so the gods enlisted Kāma to arouse his passion. When Shiva's meditative trance was broken and the great god discovered that Kāma was to blame for his arousal, Shiva burned up the love god's body with a devastating glance from his third eye. Though in some versions Kāma eventually regains a body, one of his common names is Anaṅga, "the limbless one." G. E. YOCUM

KĀMA SŪTRAS kä´ mŭ sōōt´ räs (H—Skt.; lit. "aphorisms on sexual love"). A class of didactic literature giving instruction on erotic love-making.

KĀMA ("pleasure, sexual love") is one of the four HINDU AIMS OF LIFE and thus was the subject of an extensive literature in ancient and medieval India. By far the best known of these works is the Kāma Sūtra by Vātsyāyana, who probably lived around the beginning of the fourth century A.D. in northern India. Vātsyāyana quotes or refers to a number of previous authorities on erotics whose works are now lost. In addition to several commentaries on the Kāma Sūtra, the most important surviving Hindu books on erotics after the time of Vātsyāyana are the *Rati-Rahasya* ("The Secrets of Passion") by Kokkola (twelfth century) and the *Anaṅga-Raṅga* ("The Theater of Anaṅga, the God of Love") of Kalyāṇamalla (fifteenth century). Numerous other, less refined manuals on erotics, both in Sanskrit and in the Indian vernaculars, were also produced by Hindu authors.

Vātsyāyana's Kāma Sūtra reveals the penchant of Indian technical literature for minute classification. Hence, among the many items listed are the sixty-four female arts, the twenty-four types of men who are successful with women, the twenty-eight means for a woman to get rid of a lover, the sixteen types of kiss, and the various positions of sexual intercourse and their variations. The value of love quarrels, of biting, and of marking the partner's body with the nails is discussed. The characteristics of women from different regions of India are described. Advice is also given about how to acquire and keep a wife, about the art of seduction and the use of go-betweens, about the behavior of courtesans, and about the use of charms and aphrodisiacs.

Bibliography. *The Kama Sutra of Vatsyayana,* trans. Richard Burton (1962). G. E. YOCUM

KAMAKURA kä´ mä kû´ rə (B & Sh—Jap.) 1. A city about thirty miles south of Tokyo, the site of a number of important Shintō shrines and Buddhist temples. It is known widely for the Kamakura DAIBUTSU, a bronze statue of AMIDA cast in 1252, which at 42 feet 6 inches is the second largest in Japan and is highly prized as an art object.

2. A period of Japanese history (1185-1333), marked by a shift of the capital from Kyoto to the city of Kamakura and the establishment of a military dictatorship. It signaled a decline of court life and the aristocracy and of patronage of the Buddhist sects TENDAI and SHINGON. During this period the popular movements of the PURE LAND, ZEN, and NICHIREN sects were organized and became powerful.

H. B. EARHART

KAMI kä´mē (Sh—Jap.; etymology uncertain). An object of worship in SHINTŌ; may be translated as "god," "goddess," "gods," "deity," or "spirit." More broadly, the term connotes the sacred quality of human existence and of the universe.

Since ancient times, phenomena that possess some awe-inspiring, extraordinary quality have been designated kami: thunder, lightning, rocks, mountains, plants, trees, fish, animals, as well as such human beings as a family ancestor, a great warrior, or an emperor. Kami are the central entities in the KOJIKI and the NIHON SHOKI, the earliest extant Japanese writings. A male kami, IZANAGI, and a female kami, IZANAMI, are the instruments for bringing into existence the islands of Japan; through their daughter, the sun kami AMATERASU, they are the progenitors of the unbroken line of imperial rulers of Japan.

Following the introduction of Chinese civilization in the sixth century A.D., the indigenous religious tradition was designated Shintō ("way of kami") in

Visual Education Service, Charles A. Kennedy

The second most popular shrine in Japan, Omononushi-no-Mikoto, Kotohira, Shikoku Island, built in 1878 on a mountainside near the Inland Sea. It is dedicated to the kami who protect seafarers.

distinction to the "way of Buddha" and the "way of Confucius." Kami have been viewed as protectors of the BUDDHAS and BODHISATTVAS and enshrined in the compounds of Buddhist temples, and Buddhist images have also been housed in the precincts of Shintō shrines. This syncretic tendency finds theoretical formulation as *honji suijaku,* whereby kami are understood to be "manifest traces" (*suijaku*) of the buddhas and bodhisattvas, the "original entities" (*honji*). In the Kamakura period (1185-1333), kami were identified with *hotoke* (buddhas) in popular piety, despite resistance to such accommodation on the part of the new Buddhist movements, PURE LAND and ZEN.

Motoori Norinaga (1730-1801), on the basis of his studies of the Kojiki and other ancient Japanese texts, for the first time formulated explicitly the "way of kami" and sought to free it from an accumulation of Buddhist and Confucian interpretations. He saw the relationship between kami and man as intimate and continuous, in that every human being is descended from Izanagi and Izanami with no distinct boundary between the age of kami and human history. Norinaga's "definition" of kami has provided a foundation for all subsequent studies.

Since about 1868, the term kami is weighed increasingly in the context of religious symbols representing a plurality of traditions. The Christian NT term *theos* (God) is most commonly translated kami. For Japanese scholars in religious studies, the concept kami offers a bridge to the work of Western philosophers, theologians, and social scientists.

Bibliography. See entry "kami" in *Shūkyōgaku jiten* [Dictionary of religious studies] (1973), pp. 100-105. Ichiro Hori, *Folk Religion in Japan: Continuity and Change* (1968); Shigeru Matsumoto, *Motoori Norinaga 1730-1801* (1970); Sokyo Ono, *Shinto: The Kami Way* (1962); Tsunetsugu Muraoka, *Studies in Shinto Thought* (1964).

M. L. ROGERS

KAMI NO MICHI kä´ mē nō mē´ chē (Sh—Jap.; lit. "way of kami"). Term with the same meaning as SHINTŌ, formed from the same two Chinese ideograms. In Japanese, the two ideograms are read in combination as *shin-dō* or Shintō; separately, as KAMI and *michi.* Both terms came into use in Japan after the introduction of Chinese civilization in the sixth century A.D.

M. L. ROGERS

KAMIDANA kä mē dä´ nä (Sh—Jap.; lit. "kami shelf"). A miniature SHINTŌ shrine on a high shelf in a place of honor in a traditional Japanese household. Rice, water, or fruit may be offered there daily to various KAMI. At the center of the shrine is usually an inscribed wooden tablet from the main shrine at ISÉ. *See* BUTSUDAN. M. L. ROGERS

KAMMA käm´ mŭ (H, Ja & B). *See* KARMA.

KAMSA kän´ sä (H—Skt.). In the BHĀGAVATA PURĀNA, the demonic king whose reign of terror necessitated VISHNU's descent to earth in the human form of KRISHNA. Most mythic traditions claim that Kaṃsa was the brother of Devikī, the mother of Krishna, a fact which led to his early attempts to kill Krishna while not harming his sister. This situation necessitated miraculous escapes by Krishna from one threat against his life after another by male and female demons sent by Kaṃsa. L. D. SHINN

KĀÑCĪ kän´ chē. *See* HINDU SACRED CITIES.

KANNON kän´ nôn (B). *See* AVALOKITEŚVARA.

KĀPĀLIKA kä pä lĭ´ kŭ (H—Skt.; lit. "skull-wearers"). The Kāpālikas were a sect of ŚAIVISM found throughout India but especially in the South between the eighth and the thirteenth centuries. Widely criticized by other Śaivites for their controversial practices, the Kāpālikas worshiped Shiva in his aspect as Bhairava, the destructive ascetic.

Kāpālika ritual included indulgence in the five tantric (*see* TANTRISM) rites centering upon wine, meat, fish, grain, and sex. The first four rites enabled the ascetic to identify with the deity, while the mixing of wine and meat and the practice of sex were designed to re-enact the primal integration of cosmic and divine polarities. An important feature of the Kāpālika cultus was animal and human sacrifice, especially the sacrifice of a BRAHMIN or nobleman. This was followed by the "great vow" of extreme penance in which the Kāpālika lived the life of an ascetic for twelve years, carrying the deceased's skull. The sacrifice was thought to re-enact Shiva's severing of one of BRAHMĀ's five heads and the subsequent asceticism was thought to interiorize the deity's ascetic power.

Bibliography. D. Lorenzen, *The Kāpālikas and Kālāmukhas* (1972). F. W. CLOTHEY

KAPILAVASTU kŭ pĭ lŭ vŭs´ tŭ (B—Skt.) **KAPILAVATTHU** kŭ pĭ lŭ vŭt´ hŭ (B—Pali). The birthplace of Siddhārtha Gautama, who became the BUDDHA. Kapilavastu, a town of modest size, was the capital of the small aristocratic republic of the Śākyas, which lay in a rich irrigated plain between the foothills of modern Nepal and the Rapti River. GAUTAMA's father, SUDDHODANA, ruled the district as RĀJA. After the Buddha's death Kapilavastu was identified as one of four primary places for pilgrimage. R. H. DRUMMOND

KAPLAN, MORDECAI (Ju; 1881-). Founder of RECONSTRUCTIONIST JUDAISM. In *Judaism as a Civilization* (1934) he describes Jewish religion as an aspect of a creative and evolving civilization. Other works include *Judaism Without Supernaturalism* (1958) and the editing of two prayerbooks. *See* JUDAISM §6f. L. FAGEN

KARAITES kär´ ītz (Ju—Heb.; *karāim*—"scripturalists"). A Jewish sect that arose in Babylonia in the second half of the eighth century A.D. and exerted wide influence over the next several centuries. Holding that the RABBIS had misinterpreted the BIBLE, they rejected the TALMUD and taught that each Jew was to study the Bible and interpret it for himself. K. CRIM

KARBALA kär´ bə lə. A city in Iraq, some ninety-five km. SSW of Baghdad; one of the holiest places of SHI'ITE pilgrimage (ZIYĀRA). Here AL-ḤUSAYN and his supporters were killed on October 10, A.D. 680.

Karbala, with its sanctuary (MASHHAD) of al-Ḥusayn, attained great importance in Shi'ite piety as early as 684, when Sulaymān ibn Surad and his followers visited al-Ḥusayn's tomb. Several traditions supported by the authority of the sixth IMAM, Ja'far al-Ṣādiq, affirm the virtue of the pilgrimage to Karbala as compared with the HAJJ, and al-Ṣādiq encouraged Shi'ites to pay such visits. By the ninth century the practice seems to have been common. In 850 the 'ABBĀSID al-Mutawakkil destroyed the tomb and prohibited visits to the holy places under threat of heavy penalities. This prohibition clearly shows the concern of SUNNITES, especially the CALIPHS, over the growing sanctity of the spot. At Karbala is also located the grave of al-'Abbās ibn 'Alī, al-Ḥusayn's half-brother, whose shrine is famous for its miraculous power to cure the sick.

Bibliography. M. Ayoub, *Redemptive Suffering in Islam: A Study of Devotional Aspects of 'Āshūrā' in Twelver Shī'īsm* (1978); A. Noldeke, *Das Heiligtum al-Husains zu Kerbelā* (1909).
A. A. SACHEDINA

KARMA kär´ mŭ (H, Ja, & B—Skt.; lit. "action, deed, work" [*kr*—"to act, to do"]) **KAMMA** käm´ mŭ (B—Pali). A person's acts and their ethical or physical consequences. Human actions are held to generate the power behind the round of rebirths and deaths which must be endured by the individual until liberation is attained. Thus, in this or in some future existence the individual becomes heir to the consequence (karma) of her or his own deeds. This is a basic doctrine for Hindus, Buddhists, and Jainas, though they differ as to its nature and process.

1. The Hindu view. In the hymns of the RIG VEDA (*ca.* 1200 B.C.) the word "karma" frequently is used in its common meaning of "act or work," often the mighty works of the deities. It is also often used in the more limited sense of *religious acts* such as sacrifice and oblation. There is little evidence in the Vedic hymns for its later sense as deeds which fix one's lot in future existence. Equally lacking in this period is any clear reference to SAMSARA or rebirth, which came to be closely connected with the later understanding of karma.

In the BRĀHMAṆAS, however, the fear of repeated death in the world to come appears as an important new motif. Those who do not perform ritual works are said to become the food of death time after time. Memorial sacrifices to the spirits of the deceased may originally have been intended to prevent their recurring death. Perhaps from such ceremonies arose the practice of merit transfer and, indirectly, the idea that the processes of life and death can be directly influenced by the deeds of the living.

In any case, by the time of the UPANIṢADS (*ca.* eighth and seventh centuries B.C.) belief in karma is unambiguous and begins to replace the eschatology of the earlier Vedic hymns. The Bṛhadāraṇyaka Upaniṣad (IV.4.3-5) says, for example:

> Now as a caterpillar, when it has come to the end of a blade of grass, in taking the next step draws itself together towards it, just so this soul in taking the next step strikes down this body, dispels its ignorance, and draws itself together [for making the transition] . . . . According as one acts, according as one conducts himself, so does he become. The doer of good becomes good. The doer of evil becomes evil . . . . But people say 'A person is made [not of acts, but] of desires only.' [In reply to this I say:] As is his desire, such is his resolve; as is his resolve, such the action he performs; what action (karma) he performs, into that does he become changed. (Hume, p. 140.)

In classical Hinduism differences in social status, health, fortune, lifespan, and the like were all explained as due to past karma. The result is a sense of universal justice and a partial solution to the problem of evil. Karma is generally thought to be impersonal in its operation and inevitable in its consequences. In theistic Hinduism, however, karma is thought to be under the divinity's control, and devotion to him or her is believed to bring release. In other Hindu systems works, knowledge, and meditative discipline are considered effective ways to purification and release.

2. The Buddhist view. A frequently repeated Buddhist formula states that "beings are inferior, exalted, beautiful, ugly, well-faring, ill-faring according to [the consequences of] their kamma." (M I.183 = A I.164, etc.; author's trans.). But whereas Hinduism explains the operation of karma in terms of the repeated rebirth of an eternal and unchanging soul (ATMAN), Buddhism speaks of rebirth while denying the existence of an eternal soul or self. The Buddha spoke of the individual as composed of an everchanging aggregation of five bodily and mental factors (SKANDHA). When an individual dies, a new aggregation arises as a result of past deeds. There is a causal connection between the two lives, but no ultimately real "self" (ANATTA) is carried over from one life to the next. This concept was one of the most difficult for the Buddhists to explain and to maintain.

There is a distinctively psychological emphasis to the Buddhist interpretation of karma. Mental acts are considered of potency equal to or greater than that of bodily and vocal acts. Moreover, one canonical text, the Points of Controversy, insists that the result or fruit of kamma is a matter of subjective experience, that material effects *per se* do not arise directly because of human action.

In the second half of the twentieth century some Buddhist writers have tried to relate the doctrine of karma to Western science. The psychological experience of *déja vu* is taken as evidence of rebirth, and Newton's third law of motion—"To every action there is always opposed an equal reaction"—is taken as a more general statement of karma—every action receives its just reward or punishment.

3. The Jaina view. So fundamental is the theory of karma to the Jaina world view that certain writings of the Buddhist PALI CANON go to great lengths to refute it. The Jainas possess a large number of detailed texts dealing with the problem of karma. Their analysis of karma includes its influx, bondage, duration, and fruition.

The major distinction of the Jaina concept of karma is their claim that karma is material. Accordingly, karma is a subtle form of matter that attaches to the individual soul (JĪVA) which becomes receptive to it as a result of worldly attachments. The embodied state of the soul is the result of the buildup of such karmic matter. All action causes some karmic matter to accumulate, though evil deeds produce a grosser type of karma which is harder to eradicate. The unliberated soul has been bound by karma through eternity. And all passion and action serve only to perpetuate the predicament. Liberation comes about only through the abandonment of action coupled with penance (TAPAS). The former prevents the buildup of further karmic matter, while the latter serves to burn off the karma already accumulated.

Bibliography. R. E. Hume, *The Thirteen Principal Upanishads* (2nd ed., 1931); W. L. King, *In the Hope of Nibbana* (1964), pp. 35-68; M. Spiro, *Buddhism and Society* (1970), pp. 114-59; N. Tatia, *Studies in Jaina Philosophy* (1951), pp. 220-60; H. von Glasenapp, *The Doctrine of Karman in Jain Philosophy* (1942); P. Yevtič, *Karma and Reincarnation* (1927).

J. P. MCDERMOTT

KARMA-YOGA kär´ mŭ yō´ gŭ (H—Skt.; lit. "the yoga of action"). One of the chief forms of YOGA, whereby salvation is gained through meritorious works. Such "works" could include sacrifice, extreme asceticism, moral deeds, or merely the fulfillment of one's given role in society. J. BARE

KARṆA kär´ nŭ (H—Skt.). In the MAHĀBHĀRATA, Karṇa is the son of SŪRYA the sun god, born with golden mail and earrings when his mother Kuntī first tests the MANTRA that enables her to invoke deities to sire children. Being unwed, Kuntī hides him by setting him afloat down a river. A mixed-caste couple raises him. He learns weaponry and impresses DURYODHANA as a match for ARJUNA, so Duryodhana accords him royal status and secures his alliance. Karṇa thus opposes his half-brothers, the PĀṆḌAVAS, Kuntī's legitimate sons.

Karṇa's friendship and generosity are proverbial: he loyally supports Duryodhana and gives away his protective armor and earrings. But he resents Kuntī and despises DRAUPADĪ. As firstborn of the Kaurava and Pāṇḍava cousins, he is technically the rightful king. But he keeps this secret with Kuntī and KRISHNA.

Karṇa marshals the Kaurava army for two days toward the war's end, but when his chariot wheel gets caught in the earth, Arjuna kills him. YUDHIṢṬHIRA had urged Karṇa's charioteer to destroy Karṇa's energy in this duel, this being one of several instances where Yudhiṣṭhira uses questionable means for victory. A. HILTEBEITEL

KĀRTTIKEYA kär tī kā´ yū (H—Skt.; lit. "son of the Kṛttikās"). One of the names associated with the second son of SHIVA, also known as Ṣaṇmukha ("Lord of Six Faces"), SKANDA, Subrahmaṇya, Guha, Kumāra, and in South India, MURUKAṈ. The name derives from the mythical events which immediately follow the god's birth, when he is said to have suckled the breasts of the six Kṛttikā maidens. Kārttikeya eventually appoints the maidens to be the constellation Pleiades (Mbh. III, 231), and the conjunction of stars called Kṛttikai is said to be the "birth day" of the god.

Kārttikeya is the name by which the god is commonly known today in North India, where he is generally understood to be a BRAHMACĀRIN or celibate. Iconographically, he is generally depicted with six faces and six (or sometimes ten) arms. He stands beside his vehicle (VĀHANA), the peacock, and holds in his hands the *śakti* (lance), the *vajra* (lightning bolt), the noose, and the wheel, while the two remaining hands are in the poses (MUDRĀS) of *abhayā* (benediction) and *varada* (granting of boon).

Bibliography. F. W. Clothey, *The Many Faces of Murukaṉ: The History and Meaning of a South Indian God* (1978).

F. W. CLOTHEY

KARUṆĀ kŭ roo nä´ (B—Skt. & Pali; lit. "compassion"). One of the four divine attitudes or blessed dispositions (BRAHMAVIHĀRAS) to be cultivated in BUDDHISM. It is the feeling of compassion one shows for all other living beings. The person possessed of *karuṇā* does not distinguish between his own suffering and that of others. However, *karuṇā* is not vicarious agony over the pains of the world, nor a sentimentalized sympathy, nor a mere sense of pity. It is a compassion devoid of sorrow which leads to positive action in behalf of one's fellow sufferers. It was through the Buddha's great compassion that he warned all beings of harm and exhorted them to good.

Whereas THERAVĀDA Buddhism has frequently subordinated the ideal of compassion to that of wisdom (PRAJÑĀ), MAHĀYĀNA Buddhism gives these two ideals equal importance.

Mahāyāna especially uses the term *karuṇā* to refer to the divine grace of the BUDDHAS and BODHISATTVAS whose thoughts and deeds are governed by compassion. The *Śikṣāsamuccaya* says: "The Bodhisattva . . . need not train himself in too many virtues [DHARMA]. To one virtue . . . [however] the Bodhisattva has to devote himself, . . . Great Compassion" (tran. in Schumann). In Mahāyāna compassion is personified as the bodhisattva AVALOKITEŚVARA.

Bibliography. H. W. Schumann, *Buddhism: An Outline of Its Teachings and Schools* (1973), p. 130.

J. P. McDERMOTT

KASHRUT käsh root´ (Ju). *See* KOSHER.

KĀŚĪ kä´ shē. Ancient name for Banāras. *See* HINDU SARED CITIES.

KAŚYAPA kŭsh´ yŭ pŭ (H & B—Skt.). 1. A Vedic progenitor sage, and one of the seven great RISHIS of Hindu mythology. Kaśyapa figures in many creation legends, the details of which are often inconsistent. The Epics (MAHĀBHĀRATA and RĀMĀYAṆA) identify him as the son of Marīci and as the father of Vivasvat and grandfather of MANU. Through Aditi and her twelve sisters, he is said to have fathered an astounding number and variety of offspring, including the Ādityas, the GANDHARVAS, the ASURAS, the YAKṢAS and rākṣasas, the Piśācas, the NĀGAS, the Rudras, and many, many others.

2. Also known as **KASSAPA** kŭs´ sŭ pŭ (B—Pali). One of the early disciples of the BUDDHA, sometimes called Mahākassapa (Kassapa the Great). As head of the SANGHA at the time of the Buddha's death, he called for the first Great Council to be held at RĀJAGṚHA, in order to determine the authoritative version of the Buddha's teachings. *See* BUDDHIST COUNCILS. J. BARE

KATHAK kŭ´ tŭk (H & I—Skt.; lit. "narrator of the Purāṇas" [*kath*—"to tell, relate"]). A dance form of North India, in its present form a product of Hindu-Islamic synthesis, accompanied by voice and musical instruments, and including both pure dance and interpretative dance based on devotional, heroic, and love songs and lyrics.

Kathak, like other major dance forms of India, traces many of its elements to the Nāṭya Śāstra (*ca.* 100 B.C.–A.D. 100), a comprehensive work on dramaturgy by the legendary sage Bharata Muni. Originally used for the dramatic exposition of religious themes in temples, and heavily influenced by the devotional literature of the KRISHNA BHAKTI movement, Kathak lost much of its Hindu content under Muslim influence from the sixteenth century and came to place heavy emphasis on pure dance techniques, especially rhythm and time. Its traditional patronage came from the courts of Hindu and Muslim rulers alike; its two chief centers are Lucknow in Uttar Pradesh and Jaipur in Rajasthan. The accompanying music falls within the classical North Indian system.

Traditional Kathak performances involve a solo dancer, male or female, or at most two or three soloists. In the pure dance sections of the performance there must be an exact correspondence between the chanted rhythmic syllables of the singer, the strokes of the drummer, and the steps of the dancer. In the interpretative sections the dancer uses movements, facial expressions, and hand gestures (MUDRĀS) to interpret sung texts from both Hindu and Muslim sources. *See* BHARATA-NĀṬYAM; KATHĀKALI.

Bibliography. C. R. Jones, "India's Dance and Dance-Drama," *Chapters in Indian Civilization* (1970).

C. R. KING

KATHĀKALI kŭ tä kŭ´ lē (H—Skt. & Malayalam; lit. "story-play" [*kath*—"to tell, relate"; *kaḷi*—"play"]). A religious dance-drama of Kerala, South India, accompanied by singing and musical instruments and based on Hindu scriptures.

Kathākali, like other major dance forms of India, traces many of its elements to the Nāṭya Śāstra (*ca.* 100 B.C.–A.D. 100), a comprehensive work on dramaturgy by the legendary sage Bharata Muni. It assumed its present form around the latter half of the seventeenth century, drawing other elements from traditional dances, dramatic spectacles, and dance-dramas. Its patronage came from royalty and aristocrats rather than from temples. Episodes from the MAHĀBHĀRATA, the RĀMĀYAṆA, and the PURĀṆAS written into plays in a highly Sanskritized Malayalam are recited by singers accompanied by a small orchestra and continuous drumming, and acted out by elaborately costumed dancers with highly stylized movements, hand gestures (MUDRĀS), and facial expressions.

The high-caste Hindu dancers, almost exclusively male, undergo an arduous training of several years beginning between the ages of ten and twelve. Performances take place at night, on a square ground-level stage lit by a single giant bronze oil-fed lamp, and continue till dawn. Characters of different types are easily identified by their distinctive and different-colored costumes and make-up. The dancing is marked by extraordinary vigor and religious symbolism pervades the entire performance. *See* BHARATA-NĀṬYAM; KATHAK.

Bibliography. K. B. Iyer, *Kathakali* (1955).

C. R. KING

KAUṬILYA kô ṭĭl´ yŭ (H—Skt.; lit. "crookedness"). The reputed author of the ARTHAŚĀSTRA; often identified with Cāṇakya, the BRAHMIN minister of Chandragupta, founder of the MAURYAN DYNASTY (*ca.* 322-298 B.C.).

C. R. KING

KAWATE BUNJIRO kä wä´ tē boon´ jē rō **KONKŌ DAIJIN** kōn kō dī jĭn (Sh—Jap.; 1814-1883; lit. "the great kami Konko"). A peasant whose religious experience, practice, and teaching resulted in the formation of KONKŌ-KYŌ. Born Kantori Genshichi in the village of Urami, near Okayama, he was adopted at age twelve into the Kawate family in the nearby village of Otani and his name was changed to Kawate Bunjiro. Pious and industrious, though luckless, Kawate experienced recurrent illness and other personal and family misfortunes. Though at first he supposed that the irascible KAMI Konjin was his tormentor, he began in 1855 to perceive instead the presence of a benevolent deity whom he called by a new name, TENCHI KANE NO KAMI. On October 21, 1859, Kawate felt himself directed by this deity to a full-time ministry of mediation (TORITSUGI), which he continued almost daily for the remainder of his life. In 1867, to lessen misunderstanding of his activities, he registered as a Shintō priest. In 1868 he adopted the name Konkō Daijin, thus establishing Konkō as the family name by which his successors are known.

Bibliography. See KONKŌ-KYŌ.

H. N. MCFARLAND

KEGON kā gôn´. *See* NARA BUDDHISM §3.

KETHUBIM kē too vēm´ (Ju—Heb. "writings"). Those books of the Hebrew Bible (or TANAK) which, united only by their diversity, constitute a third grouping after the Law (TORAH) and the Prophets (NEBI'IM). They are Psalms, Proverbs, Ruth, Song of Solomon, Job, Ecclesiastes, Esther, Lamentations, Daniel, Ezra, Nehemiah, and I and II Chronicles.

D. IRVIN

KHADĪJA kə dē´ jə (I). First wife of MUHAMMAD; a wealthy widow when she met Muhammad, she took him into her service and later proposed marriage. She is said to have been older than he by some years, but she bore him three sons, who died in infancy, and four daughters, Ruqayya, Zaynab, 'Umm Kulthūm, and FĀTIMA. The marriage provided Muhammad with material and spiritual comfort. She is honored as the first believer and the first convert to Islam, and is represented in tradition as Muhammad's greatest support in the troubled early years of his mission. Her death, just three years before the HIJRA, is seen by most of Muhammad's biographers as a major blow. As a result of her early death, there are no traditions (ḤADĪTH) from her describing the years with Muhammad.

Bibliography. W. M. Watt, *Muhammad at Mecca* (1953), pp. 38-39; Ibn Sa'd, *aṭ-Ṭabaqāt al-Kabīr*, VIII, 7-11; Ibn Isḥāq, *Life of Muhammad*, A. Guillaume, trans. (1955); G. Stern, *Marriage in Early Islam* (1939); W. Robertson Smith, *Kinship and Marriage in Early Arabia* (1903), pp. 273 ff.

G. D. NEWBY

KHAJURĀHO kä jĕr ä´ hō (H & Ja). Cluster of eighty-five temples, dedicated to HINDU and JAINA figures, in Madhya Pradesh, India; built *ca.* 850-1150. The Khajurāho temples, which are divided into three groups covering approximately eight square miles, abound with thousands of images of the major Hindu gods and goddesses, Jaina saints, human devotees, and animals, so that the impression on the visitor is of a sprawling, dancing, vibrating miniature universe in stone. The most intriguing of the Khajurāho figures, those responsible for turning the temples into tourist attractions, are the *maithuna* images which depict sexual coupling in unbelievable variety. Explanations for the explicit sexual imagery of the Khajurāho and KONĀRAK temples have usually fallen into one of the following categories:

1. **Instructional.** In an age when marriages were arranged and couples had little knowledge of sexual matters before the wedding, the temple sculptures were a graphic marriage manual. Such a theory is problematic because many of the positions depicted are impossibly acrobatic and some are even orgiastic (the latter examples being a blatant contradiction of Hindu marriage vows).

2. **Spiritual test.** The abundance of copulating couples on the outside temple walls are there as a test for the devotee. If he can walk by them and feel no lust in his heart, he is ready to progress spiritually. The difficulty with this interpretation is that erotic imagery also appears elsewhere in Hindu art and literature, not just on the outside of temples, and if a test of some sort were necessary, why not on all temples, rather than just a few?

3. **Expressions of transcendence in immanence.** To understand this theme, one must first examine the facial expressions of the figures. The faces exhibit contentment, a kind of dreamy pleasure, not lust or passion. They indicate the theme of transcendence in immanence since they express a pure enjoyment of experience, in an almost detached manner. In Indian religious thought, the idea is expressed in the equation, "*Bhoga* is yoga," or "Delight is the path to the divine." This interpretation is bolstered by the TANTRIC poses which may encourage copulation with "retention of seed."

4. **Unity of opposites.** Perhaps the most reasonable explanation rests on the ideal of unity of opposites: PURUSA and PRAKṚTI, spirit and matter, male and female, divine and human. In unity there is the joy of completion, and the closest approximation of such unity on the human level is to be found in sexual intercourse, which thus becomes a metaphor of the ultimate spiritual goal. As Alan Watts has noted, sexual intercourse is one of the primary ways in which a person comes into conscious union with something outside his or her self. As such, it can be broadly interpreted as a "religious" experience of unity." *See* KĀMA; LINGA; ŚAKTI; TANTRISM; YONI.

Bibliography. H. Zimmer, *Myths and Symbols in Indian Art and Civilization*, J. Campbell, ed. (1962); U. Agarwal, *Khajurāho Sculptures and Their Significance* (1964); A. Watts, *Erotic Spirituality*, with photos by E. Elisofon (1974).

P. L. BASU

KHĀLID IBN al-WALĪD khä līd´ ĭb´ ən äl wä lēd´ (I; d. 642). General in the Battle of Uḥud (624), where his brilliant tactical maneuvers led to the first military defeat of the nascent Muslim community and inspired the consoling revelation of QUR'ĀN 3:147-49. Later Khālid converted to ISLAM and, as the chief general of the Caliph ABŪ BAKR, was responsible for the stunning conquests of Byzantine territory that laid the foundation for a rapidly expanding Islamic empire. *See* ISLAM §3.

B. LAWRENCE

KHĀLSĀ käl´ sä (S; lit. "the pure"). A militant fraternity started by GOBIND SINGH, the tenth and last GURU of the Sikhs, at Anandpur on the Hindu New Year's day, April, 1699.

The first baptism of the sword, *khande ka pahul* ("baptism of the double-edged dagger"), was administered to five selected followers who had offered to lay down their lives at the guru's command. These five, known as *Panj Piyare* ("the five beloved"), belonged to different CASTES. They were made to drink sugared water *amṛta* ("nectar") out of the same bowl and given new names with a shared family name *Singh* ("lion") to signify a new birth. Five emblems were made obligatory for the Khālsā: unshorn hair and beards *(kés)*, a comb *(kangā)* stuck under the turban, a steel bracelet *(kadā)*, knee-length breeches *(kachh)*, and a sabre *(kirpān)*. Since all emblems begin with the letter K, they are known as the *panj* (five) *kakkar*. After baptizing the chosen five, the guru had himself baptized by them, and thus Gobind Rai became Gobind Singh. At the end of the ceremony, the guru hailed the converts with a new form of greeting customary with the Khālsā to this day:

> *Wāhi gurū jī kā Khālsā.*
> *Wāhi gurū jī kī fateh.*
> (The *Khalsa* are the chosen of God.
> Victory be to our God.)

K. SINGH

KHANDHA kän´ dŭ (B). *See* SKANDHA; ANATTA.

KHĀRIJITES kä rə jīts´ (I). The "seceders" who in A.D. 659 left ALI's army at Harūrā, near Kūfa, to form their own military force. They accused Ali of compromising with the supporters of wrongdoers in ceasing to fight against Mu'awiya, the first CALIPH of the UMAYYADS. Most of the early seceders were wiped out by Ali's forces, but their movement was spread by a handful of survivors, one of whom assassinated Ali in 661. The Khārijites were the first sect in Islam to raise issues concerning the qualifications for leadership of the Muslim community (UMMA) and the relationship between faith and works. Their significance lies in their insistence on the possibility of a righteous *umma* based on the QUR'ĀN.

A. A. SACHEDINA

KHIḌR (ELIJAH?) kĭ′ dər (I). A legendary figure popular in Islamic folklore and mystical literature, often identified with the mysterious servant who in the QUR'ĀN (Sura 18:60-82) accompanied MOSES on the journey to "the conjunction of the two oceans." His superiority to Moses in this passage has been explained by orthodox commentators as reference to the testing through trials and tribulations common to all prophetic figures, and by mystical commentators as evidence of the superiority of sainthood to prophecy (*see* NABI; WALĪ; SUFISM), for did not the greatest biblical prophet, Moses, lack the intuitive insight given to "God's servant," as Khiḍr is called in the Qur'ān?

Since "the conjunction of the two oceans" may symbolize the meeting of all opposites (East and West, heaven and earth, intuition and law, immortality and death), Khiḍr figures in numerous legends. In the Alexander Romance cycle he becomes linked to Alexander the Great. In India he is worshiped as a green river-God. In Muslim folklore he has been grouped with JESUS, ELIJAH and IDRĪS to form a quartet of prophets who never tasted death.

Khiḍr is also adept at performing miracles. He can appear anywhere at any time and often in any form. The vision of him is viewed as a singular blessing by Muslims (*see* DREAMS AND VISIONS IN ISLAM). IBN 'ARABĪ claimed direct initiation into Sufism through Khiḍr, bypassing affiliation with a human master in one of the ṬARĪQAS.

Khiḍr has also had his detractors. Not only did orthodox commentators object to the excessive stress on an unnamed figure who appears only once in the Qur'ān, but Sufis themselves often viewed Khiḍr as blameworthy because he prized life over love. Since love transcends immortality, in their view, Khiḍr may become an obstacle rather than a guide to truth.

Bibliography. A. J. Wensinck, "al-Khaḍir (al-Khiḍr), *EI,* IV, 902-5; J. A. Subhan, *Sufism: Its Saints and Shrines* (1960), pp. 116-18; P. Jackson, trans., Sharafuddin Maneri, *The Hundred Letters* (1980), pp. 30, 71.

B. LAWRENCE

KHŌJĀS kō′ jäs (I—Pers.; lit. "lord"). An Indian Muslim CASTE, converted from HINDUISM in the fourteenth century by a Persian missionary of ISMĀ'ĪLIYYA. Since Ismailis were persecuted by the Muslim rulers of India, many Khōjās pretended to be SUNNITES or IMĀMIYYA, and some of them eventually turned to these sects permanently. For this reason there are at present three varieties of Khōjās: 1) the majority, who are Nizārī Ismailis and follow the AGHA KHAN; 2) Sunni Khōjās; and 3) Imamite Khōjās. Most Khōjās are found in western India and east Africa.

A. A. SACHEDINA

KHUṬBA koot′ bə (I—Arab.; lit. "oration"). The sermon delivered at the Friday MOSQUE service, at the time of the two annual festivals, and on critical occasions (such as eclipses). The institution goes back to MUHAMMAD, but has undergone later developments.

The *khuṭba* is the chief feature of the Friday noon congregational worship service (*see* PRAYER IN ISLAM), which it immediately precedes. It is delivered right after the call to prayer (ADHĀN) by a special leader, called the *imām khaṭīb,* who stands on the pulpit facing the worshipers. The sermon is in two parts, between which the *khaṭīb* sits quietly for a brief period of general private prayer. The first *khuṭba* is highly standardized, and must contain praise to God, eulogies of the Prophet, and recitation of the QUR'ĀN. Traditionally there has also been some mention of the ruler (a very important element in classical Islam). The second *khuṭba* is generally hortatory and topical, and provides an opportunity for skilled oratory.

Bibliography. Al-Baghawī, *Mishkāt al-Maṣābīḥ,* ET J. Robson (1960-65), I, 293-95; E. W. Lane, *An Account of the Manners and Customs of the Modern Egyptians* (1860; repr. 1954) has two excellent examples of sermons in translation, pp. 87-92; Muslim, *Ṣaḥīḥ,* ET A. H. Ṣiddīqī (1971-75), II, 407-14.

F. M. DENNY

KIDDUSH kĭ dōōsh′ (Ju—Heb.; "sanctification"). Ceremony, dating from the period of the TALMUD, whereby the holiness of the SABBATH or a festival is proclaimed in the home. It is performed over a cup of wine at the beginning of the meal on the eve of the Sabbath or festival, and consists of two BENEDICTIONS generally chanted by the head of the household—one for the wine and one for the holy day.

B. MARTIN

KIDDUSH HA-SHEM kĭ dōōsh′ hä shām′ (Ju—Heb.; "sanctification of the name" [of God]). Any worthy or pious deed performed by a Jew which leads non-Jews to esteem JUDAISM and thereby sanctifies (or glorifies) the name of Israel's God. In its narrower sense it referred specifically to martyrdom, because the sacrifice of one's life for the sake of God was considered the ultimate and supreme sanctification of his name. An evil or ugly deed is referred to as a *hillul ha-Shem,* a "desecration of God's name."

B. MARTIN

KIERKEGAARD, SØREN kĭr′ kə gôr (Ch; 1813-1855). Danish philosopher and precursor of existentialism who rejected speculative systems, saw truth as subjectivity and believed that Christian doctrines are beyond rational explanation. He influenced neo-orthodox theology. *See* THEOLOGY, CONTEMPORARY CHRISTIAN §3. D. F. OTTATI

KILĒSA kĭ lā´ sū (B—Pali) **KLEŚA** klā´ shū (B—Skt.; lit. "stain, impurity" [*kliś*—"to be distressed"]). Attitudes or dispositions that are obstacles to spiritual perfection. *Kilēsas* or "defilements" are unspecified in the early Suttas of the PALI CANON, but two later ABHIDHAMMA texts list ten defilements, and in subsequent Buddhist thought the defilements have a prominent place. The list of ten *kilēsas* begins with the three evil root causes of mental impurity, namely, greed, hatred, and delusion. The remaining seven are conceit, speculative views, (unproductive) doubt, mental sloth, restlessness, shamelessness, and lack of conscience.

Taken together the ten *kilēsas* represent the spiritually counter productive side of human nature. The path toward mental purity may be seen as a struggle to overcome these defilements, and the saint is one who has done so. In the ordinary person, the defilements bring about evil actions which, leaving behind bad KARMA, ensure future rebirth and suffering. (*See also* SINS, SEVEN DEADLY.)

Bibliography. *Buddhist Psychological Ethics* (1974), a trans. of the Dhammasaṅgaṇī, which lists the ten kilēsas.

R. C. AMORE

KIMBANGUISM kĭm băn´ gōō ĭsm (Ch). The Church of Jesus Christ on Earth by the Prophet Simon Kimbangu. In the span of sixty years it has mushroomed from a persecuted mass movement to become the most influential Independent Church on the continent of Africa, with a membership of over four million in Zaire and several neighboring countries.

One night during the 1918 influenza epidemic in lower Zaire, Simon Kimbangu, a Baptist catechist, heard a voice calling him: "I am Christ, my servants are unfaithful. I have chosen you to bear witness before your brethren and to convert them. Tend my flock." For three years Kimbangu spurned the voice in spite of repeated calls. Finally, on April 6, 1921, he answered the call, entered the house of a sick woman and healed her. Other healings followed in rapid succession as Kimbangu's fame spread throughout the lower Congo.

The Belgian colonial authorities, fearing that a revolutionary political movement had arisen, ordered Kimbangu arrested. For three months he eluded them. In mid-September, after another vision in which he was instructed to return home and be arrested, Kimbangu surrendered.

The prophet was convicted of sedition and hostility toward whites and sentenced to flogging and death. The Belgian king commuted his sentence to life imprisonment, and Kimbangu was incarcerated in Elizabethville, where he lived in solitary confinement until his death in 1951. The parallels between his own life and that of JESUS have a special religious meaning for his followers.

By applying Christianity to local needs and especially the need for healing, Kimbangu ignited a spark that no colonial authority could extinguish. In spite of, and perhaps because of, his imprisonment his followers multiplied. At the time of his sentencing, just five months after his appearance as a prophet, the colonial government also banished 244 heads of families. During the next thirty-six years over 37,000 families were banished to thirty centers throughout the country, but instead of snuffing out the new movement the government was merely paying the travel expenses of a new generation of local missionaries. Banishment served to expand the movement and make it national rather than merely tribal.

In 1969 the church was admitted into membership in the World Council of Churches. This church is widely regarded as having made one of the most creative adaptations of Christianity to African culture. Just as followers of LUTHER, CALVIN, and WESLEY trace their origins to certain creative leaders, so the Kimbanguists believe that the Holy Spirit has come to them in a special way through the life of this twentieth century Zairean prophet.

Bibliography. E. Andersson, *Messianic Popular Movements in the Lower Congo* (1958); "The Essence of Kimbanguist Theology," *WCC Exchange,* July 1978; M.-L. Martin, *Kimbangu: An African Prophet and His Church* (1976).

W. T. DAVIS, JR.

KIMḤI, DAVID kĭm´ hē (Ju; 1160-1235). Biblical exegete and grammarian. His grammatical work *Mikhlol* (lit. "encyclopedia") is a systematic, sometimes original presentation of the scientific, philological study of Hebrew as it had developed up to his day, including the work of his father, Joseph (1105-1170). In his biblical commentaries Kimḥi supplements his understanding of the plain meaning (historical and philological) with excurses that popularize Maimonides' philosophy and his father's anti-Christological readings of scripture. K. P. BLAND

KING, MARTIN LUTHER, JR. (Ch; 1929-1968). National leader in the civil rights movement of the 1950s and 1960s, who rose to prominence with the Montgomery Bus Boycott. He espoused nonviolent civil disobedience and was murdered in Memphis, Tennessee. *See* BLACK RELIGIONS IN THE U.S. §2; AHIṂSĀ.

Bibliography. A. Bishop, *The Days of Martin Luther King, Jr.* (1971).

J. W. WATERS

KINGDOM OF GOD (Ju & Ch). A metaphor for the divine sovereignty over the created order, especially over human affairs. The motif of divine rule is more common in the Bible than the actual phrase "kingdom of God." In the NT "kingdom of heaven" is a synonym, since "heaven" was a common circumlocution for God.

The actual phrase does not occur in the OT, though the idea that YAHWEH is king is common (see, e.g., I Sam. 8; Ps. 47). The so-called "Enthronement Psalms" (e.g., Pss. 93, 97, 99) have the acclamation, "Yahweh reigns!" It is disputed whether or not these psalms were created for liturgies in which the king represented God at an annual festival which included ritual combat with chaos in order to establish the divine order over the cosmos for the coming year—analogous to ancient Mesopotamian ceremonies. Still, the motif of God as a kingly warrior who acts decisively on behalf of his people, Israel, pervades these psalms and other OT materials. In Jewish APOCALYPTIC literature, the coming reign of God was associated with the expected divine intervention at the end of history. Although the rabbis too spoke of the kingdom as future, they also regarded the kingdom as a present reality which could be experienced by those who obeyed the TORAH. Thus converts to JUDAISM were said to take upon themselves "the yoke of the kingdom."

In the NT the phrase is found chiefly in the GOSPELS and was a central motif of JESUS' teaching, especially of his parables. There is, however, no agreement on the exact meaning of the phrase on his lips. Liberal Protestants, from the nineteenth century on, have understood it as both a spiritual sovereignty of God in the human heart and as a moral task (hence they coined the phrase, "build the kingdom of God"). This interpretation, however, was undermined by J. Weiss and A. SCHWEITZER, who argued that Jesus understood the kingdom in an apocalyptic way—God alone would bring it as an alternative to human striving, and would do so soon. Jesus' radical demands were emergency measures for the interval yet remaining (hence Schweitzer's phrase, "interim ethics"). This interpretation, in turn, was opposed by C. H. Dodd, who insisted that for Jesus the kingdom was not near but here—in his own mission. Today most scholars see a tension in Jesus' view—the kingdom is both present in Jesus' activity and impending, both immanent and imminent. Jesus never defined the kingdom, but pointed to aspects of God's rule.

Christian theology, like Jewish piety, has often used "kingdom of God" as a symbol of that state of affairs which accords with God's will, irrespective of the time of its coming. In this vein, for example, H. R. Niebuhr traced the motif in American culture.

Bibliography. J. Weiss, *Jesus' Proclamation of the Kingdom of God* (1971); A. Schweitzer, *The Mystery of the Kingdom of God* (1914); C.H. Dodd, *The Parables of the Kingdom* (1935); H. R. Niebuhr, *The Kingdom of God in America* (1937); R. Schnackenburg, *God's Rule and Kingdom* (1968); G. Klein, "The Biblical Understanding of 'The Kingdom of God,' " *Interpretation,* XXVI (1972), 387-418. L. E. KECK

KĪRTANA kĭr tŭn´ ŭ (H—Skt.; lit. "praise"). A form of religious activity prominent among the VAIṢṆAVAS of Bengal. It consists of the singing of the names and praises of KRISHNA, whom the Bengali Vaiṣṇavas regard as the high god, and is sometimes accompanied by ecstatic dancing. The activity is usually carried on in a private home or in a temple of Krishna, though it sometimes takes the form of a street processional, being then called *nagara-kīrtana* or "city *kīrtana*." The singing is usually accompanied by the playing of *khol,* a long, cylindrical, two-toned drum, and small cymbals.

The daily *kīrtana* is often no more than the chanting of the names of Krishna. But on special festival days songs called *padas* are sung. These *padas,* often beautiful poetry, are arranged in a cycle which tells the story of the love affair between Krishna and RĀDHĀ, the special GOPĪ who comes in later tradition to represent the human soul in love with God. The poems are fourteen or sixteen lines in length, arranged in couplets. The leader of the congregation, called *kīrtanīya* because of his knowledge of the corpus of songs and the quality of his voice, sings the opening couplet, which is repeated by the assembly; the kīrtanīyā then sings the first and second couplets together, followed by the congregation, and so on. The repetition, the rhythm of the drums, and the religious emotion with which the atmosphere is charged sometimes bring on a kind of trance, and one or more of the participants will dance with upraised arms. A full *kīrtana* such as this may last for many hours, and each section of the cycle (e.g., the awakening of love between Rādhā and Krishna, the union of the two, the departure of Krishna from VṚNDĀVANA) will be preceded by a *Gauracandrikā,* a hymn to CAITANYA, who was thought to be an incarnation of Krishna.

In the Bengali Vaiṣṇava system, sixty-four types of devotional activity are thought to be most efficacious, of which *kīrtana* is one of the five most important, because the name of God is thought to incorporate the power and presence of God. Association with other Vaiṣṇavas is also among the most important five; this accounts for the emphasis on congregational worship, rare in Hinduism. So powerful is the name of God that it transforms those who hear and repeat it. A famous story in the Vaiṣṇava tradition is of a Muslim official who, upon hearing a *nagara-kīrtana*, became converted.

Bibliography. E. C. Dimock, Jr., and D. Levertov, *In Praise of Krishna* (1967). E. C. DIMOCK, JR.

KISS OF PEACE (Ch). A mutual salutation of participants in the EUCHARIST, exchanged as a sign of fellowship, and consisting of a kiss or light embrace, hand-clasp, or bow. Referred to in modern usage as the "sign of peace," this liturgical gesture is of apostolic origin (Rom. 16:16; I Cor. 16:20; I Pet.

5:14), and is probably based on Christ's command to make peace before bringing one's gift to the altar (Matt. 5:23-24). C. WADDELL

KNOWLEDGE, HINDU CONCEPT. *See* VIDYĀ.

KNOX, JOHN (Ch; 1514?-1572). Protestant Reformer born near the town of Haddington. Through his leadership CALVINISM, rather than ANGLICANISM, replaced ROMAN CATHOLICISM in Scotland.

Probably educated for the priesthood at St. Andrews, he was briefly associated with George Wishart, who confirmed him in his Protestant views which he had already heard from Protestant preachers Gwilliam and Rough. Captured by the French at the fall of St. Andrews Castle, Knox spent nineteen months as a galley slave in French boats. He was released in 1549 through the efforts of the English and became a leader in the PURITAN wing of the English REFORMATION. When Mary Tudor came to the throne (1553), Knox fled to the continent, going first to Frankfurt and then to Geneva.

When events led to a crisis in Scotland in 1559, Knox returned for good. The Scottish Parliament abolished the Roman Catholic Church in Scotland in 1560, adopting the Scots Confession of Faith of which Knox was a principal author. Knox's proposals for the reorganization of the church were presented in the *First Book of Discipline*. Parliament refused to adopt the *Book*, which would have allowed the Reformed church to continue to control the wealth of the church. Knox wanted to use this for repair of church buildings, the relief of the poor, and an elaborate scheme of universal education.

Knox was involved in continual struggles with Mary Stuart, the Catholic Queen, and with the various factions in church and state. His power inhered in his ability as a preacher and in his personal influence. He contributed significantly to the development of the liberal political tradition in his insistence on the responsibility of the individual to resist evil rulers. J. H. LEITH

KŌAN kō´ än (B—Jap.) **KUNG-AN** (B—Chin.; lit. "public record"). ZEN Buddhist technical term for problem exercises intended to bring students to enlightenment (SATORI) or to test and deepen that experience.

1. **Origin and development.** The kōan came into being in the creative experiments of T'ang dynasty masters (A.D. 618-906) seeking ways of transmitting "the lamp of enlightenment" to their students. Shouts, slaps, questions, and parabolic acts occurred during labor in the fields, formal lectures, private interviews, or chance meetings. The relationship that developed between the teaching and its setting in everyday tasks became an essential ingredient in the development of a unique method for conveying the truth that enlightenment and ordinary mind are not separate. Answering a student's theoretical questions with a simple gesture or reference to the task at hand of hoeing weeds or washing bowls encouraged spontaneous discovery of Buddha-mind (*see* DHARMAKĀYA) in the simplest experiences of the present moment, and hence in all things.

By the close of the T'ang dynasty, Chinese masters were repeating questions and situations that had brought enlightenment to earlier students and were perhaps calling these devices *kung-an,* private teachings now made "public records." When Nan-yüan Hui-yung and other third generation disciples of Lin-chi (d. 867) began using his sayings to test their students, the kōan method was established.

Both in Sung dynasty China and among the heirs of Sung Zen in Japan, disputes arose as the Ts'ao-tung (Sōtō) school identified seated meditation with enlightenment and used kōan sparingly, while the Lin-chi (Rinzai) school emphasized seated meditation as a tool for kōan exercise, and pointed out the danger of laziness in Sōtō's "just sitting." After a period of creativity in KAMAKURA Japan (1185-1333), Rinzai Zen declined until the reforms instituted by HAKUIN EKAKU in the early eighteenth century. Hakuin's systematizing of kōan study set the basic pattern for the use of the kōan to this day.

2. **Examples of kōan.** A *Dharmakāya* kōan is intended to bring students to a first enlightenment. "Ummon was asked, 'What is the pure Dharmakāya?' He replied, 'The blossoming hedge around the privy.' "

The *Kikan* kōan carries the student further, through the "realm of differentiation." "A monk asked Joshu, 'What is the meaning of BODHIDHARMA's coming from the West?' Joshu replied, 'The cypress tree in the garden.' "

Hekiganroku, "Blue Cliff Record," is a collection based on 100 kōan compiled by Setchō (980-1052), to which Engo (1063-1135) added commentary. *Mumonkan,* "Gateless Barrier," was compiled in 1228 by Mumon Ekai. These two Sung dynasty works are the most famous of the kōan collections, classics in the literature of Zen. Many Zen students begin with the first case in *Mumonkan,* the famous *Mu* kōan. "A monk asked Joshu, 'Has a dog Buddha nature?' Joshu answered, *Mu* (nothing)." When the master is satisifed that *Mu* has been solved, the student is allowed to proceed through the cases of *Mumonkan,* followed by the cases of *Hekiganroku.*

3. **The kōan in Zen training.** Life in a Rinzai monastery is a strictly regulated schedule of ZAZEN ("seated meditation"), daily labor, begging, sūtra chanting, and kōan-exercise, all under the direction of an abbot-master. A new monk is assigned a beginner's kōan during a private interview called *dokusan.* Weeks of intensive meditation (*sesshin*), numerous formal appearances before the master (*sanzen*), and lectures on classic kōan (*teisho*) are all aimed at aiding both monks and invited laymen in their kōan exercise.

Although a master may encourage students to apply every intellectual effort toward solving a kōan, the final intent is to frustrate intellectualizing and to bring an experiential crisis called "Great Doubt." Concentrating on the kōan during several hours of zazen each day, one is to live with the kōan day and night until identification of self and kōan takes place, until a breakthrough to enlightenment is certified by the master in *dokusan.* It is not unusual for a monk to labor three years with the *Mu* kōan and another fifteen years with a series of kōan intended to deepen and broaden enlightenment.

Bibliography. I. Miura and R. Sasaki, *The Zen Koan* (1965); A. Shibayama, *Zen Comments on the Mumonkan* (1974); D. T. Suzuki, *Essays in Zen Buddhism,* 2nd series (1953).

C. W. Edwards

KŌBŌ DAISHI kō bō dī shē (B; 773-835 [lit. "great teacher Kōbō"]). Posthumus title of Kūkai, Japanese Buddhist monk and scholar who studied esoteric Buddhism (Shingon) in China and established the Shingon school in Japan. K. Crim

KOJIKI kō jē´ kē (Sh—Jap.; lit. "Record of Ancient Matters"). The oldest extant written record in Japanese, compiled in A.D. 712 under the direction of the imperial court. Using myth, legend, poetry, and historical narrative, it tells the story of the sacred origins of the Japanese archipelago and of the imperial ancestors, and gives an account of the imperial court until the seventh century. English trans. by Donald L. Philippi (1968). M. L. Rogers

KOL NIDRE kōl nīd rē´ (Ju—Heb.; lit. "all vows"). The prayer opening the Yom Kippur service. Among the most popular in Jewish liturgy, the chant is recited three times so that those who arrive late will not miss it. It must begin before sunset and continue beyond.

Kol Nidre is a disavowal of oaths made during the past year (in its Babylonian version) or for the coming year (in its European version). Medieval Christians used this as evidence of Jewish dishonesty and duplicity, though Jewish law severely restricts the efficacy of the Kol Nidre formula, limiting it to vows made between man and God in unadvised haste and thoughtlessness. Thus Kol Nidre reflects the seriousness with which words must be considered.

The origin of the chant is obscure. Some date it to post-Talmudic Palestine (*ca.* A.D. 650), but others claim it is of Babylonian origin and is intended to break the hold of evil forces and magic powers active when vows are abrogated. That early Babylonian religious leaders opposed its recitation is taken as support for the latter theory. A more recent intepretation views Kol Nidre as a communal release for those forced to accept Christian sacraments though remaining loyal Jews. Perhaps the most popular aspect of Kol Nidre is its distinctive melody, often cited as a model for High Holy Day liturgy and for Jewish music. *See* Music in Judaism; Rosh ha-Shanah.

Bibliography. *See* Yom Kippur. D. J. Schnall

KŌMEITŌ kō mā´ tō (B—Jap.; lit. "Clean Government Party"). Begun in 1955 as the political arm of Sōka Gakkai and registered as a political party in 1964. In 1970 it was announced that official connections between Kōmeitō and Sōka Gakkai had been severed. Today it is the second strongest opposition party in the National Diet and local assemblies. The party views itself as middle-of-the-road and has taken leadership in exposing corruption and instigating social reforms and peace negotiations.

N. S. Brannen

KONĀRAK kō nä´ rŭk (H). Temple of the sun god, Sūrya, in Orissa, India. Konārak, or the "Black Pagoda," was constructed in the thirteenth century A.D. and reportedly took twelve years and twelve hundred workmen to complete. It originally consisted of two principal parts: a high tower and a great hall. The tower has long since collapsed, but the great hall, which is one hundred feet long and one hundred feet high, remains as a powerful representation of the sun god's chariot, with six massive twelve foot high stone wheels on each side. The chariot, drawn by seven horses (most of which have been destroyed), appears headed at break-neck speed toward the Bay of Bengal.

The Konārak temple is famous not only because of its size and antiquity, but because of its intricate and often erotic sculptural details. The divine couples cavort joyously in varied postures over the surface of the temple, interspersed with images of dancers, musicians, and heavenly attendants. The explicit nature of the sculptures has been an embarrassment to modern Hindu sensibilities and a puzzlement to Westerners unused to such a blatant juxtaposition of the sensual and the spiritual.

For interpretations of the erotic imagery, *see* Khajurāho. *See also* Linga; Kāma; Śakti; Tantrism; Yoni.

Bibliography. P. Rawson, *Erotic Art of the East* (1968).

P. L. Basu

KONKŌ-KYŌ kōn kō´ kyō (Sh—Jap.; lit. "the religion [teaching] of golden light"). One of the "new religions" with Shintōistic associations but with also a distinctive monotheistic tendency. Arising in a rural setting during the mid-nineteenth century, it began to penetrate urban centers early in the Meiji period (1868-1912). In the twentieth century it has spread throughout Japan and among Japanese communities abroad. Its most characteristic emphasis is divine-human interaction made possible through mediation (Toritsugi) effected by a minister. The faith thus inspired and nurtured is seen as dynamic, open, and relevant to the demands and opportunities of the rapidly changing modern world.

1. **History.** Konkō-kyō developed from the experience and ministry of KAWATE BUNJIRO (1814-83) in a farming community in Okayama prefecture. Within the movement the officially designated date of the founding is October 21, 1859, the day on which Kawate is believed to have been commissioned by the deity TENCHI KANE NO KAMI to a full-time ministry of divine-human mediation. During the remaining twenty-four years of his life this activity was his almost daily occupation. From rural areas near his residence a steadily increasing flow of petitioners came for his assistance. As his reputation grew, some of the rising class of businessmen began to come out from Osaka to explore the pertinence of this peasant's faith to their new, ill-defined socio-economic roles.

2. **Scripture.** Kawate's followers recorded his sayings and collated them after his death under the title *Konkō-kyō Kyōten* (lit. "Konkō-kyō scripture"; ET in Schneider). This includes the oracles calling the founder and his family to their special ministries and numerous aphorisms detailing in simple language the founder's understanding of his experience and faith and his instructions to his followers.

3. **Organization.** In 1885, two years after the death of the founder, Konkō-kyō was organized in a structure less complex, centralized, and authoritarian than that of most other new religious movements in Japan. Three purposes are implicit in the structure: (1) to maintain the centrality of toritsugi as it was developed in the ministry of the founder; (2) to make a clear provision for the succession of spiritual leadership; and (3) to develop a headquarters to coordinate the activities of Konkō-kyō churches and missions and to provide centralized services for their direction and support.

The headquarters of Konkō-kyō are located in the founder's hometown, formerly called Otani but subsequently renamed Konkō to reflect the eminence of its best-known son. Here the two principal officers reside. The chief official is the *Kyōshu* (patriarch), who according to the constitution must be a descendant, either male or female, of the founder. Though responsible for the overall administration of the movement, the *Kyōshu* is principally its spiritual head. The second-ranking official, known as the *Kyōkan*, has managerial oversight of the movement and such agencies as institutes for ministerial training and doctrinal research, a school system, a library, and an agency for propagation through literature.

4. **Relation to Shintō.** For expediency, the founder registered as a Shintō priest, and from 1900 to 1946 Konkō-kyō was registered with the government as one of thirteen officially tolerated sects, designated *kyōha shintō* (Sectarian Shintō). Such registration was the condition of legitimate existence and, at times, of any existence at all. In many externals—the garb of the clergy, the altar furnishings, the forms of worship, the architecture of its churches—Konkō-kyō manifests an obvious affinity to Shintō. In one particular aspect, however, the two are distinguishable: Tenchi Kane no Kami, the deity worshiped in Konkō-kyō, is not one of the KAMI of traditional Shintō.

5. **Doctrine.** As in Japanese religions generally, experience is more important than doctrine, but in this instance the theological implications of experience provide the basis for a genuinely distinctive doctrinal development. The deity who revealed himself to the founder is the "Parent God of the Universe," not a local kami or just one of the myriads of kami in Shintō. The divine nature thus revealed is essential benevolence, in distinction to the capricious, demonic qualities which the founder and his contemporaries had often associated with the other kami. The relationship with deity, made possible through toritsugi, is one of mutual fulfillment. Underlying the divine-human relationship is a concept of mutually contingent being: solely because of the devotee, deity is manifest; solely because of deity, the devotee has being.

6. **Ethics and social outreach.** The traditional Shintō parish is a relatively small community of people united in a common dependence upon a local patron deity. By expanding this concept to its ultimate limit, Konkō-kyō teaches that all people are members of the family of Tenchi Kane no Kami and ought, therefore, to be concerned for one another. This concern is expressed in assistance to needy people, in activities for children, young people and women, and in the promotion of world peace. Women constitute a majority of the membership, and there are more female ministers in this movement than in any other Japanese religion.

7. **Worship.** In most Konkō-kyō churches one or more congregational worship services are held daily. These characteristically include liturgical prayers (some chanted by the congregation) and a sermon.

8. **Major festivals.** Two principal festivals are observed annually at the headquarters and in local churches. The first is held in the spring, on or about April 25, and is dedicated to Tenchi Kane no Kami. The second takes place in the fall, on or about October 25, and honors the memory of the founder. Ceremonies on these and other special occasions characteristically include food offerings made to the deity in a manner closely resembling traditional Shintō rites.

Bibliography. H.N. McFarland, *The Rush Hour of the Gods* (1967); D. B. Schneider, *Konkokyo* (1962).

H. N. McFARLAND

KORAN kə rän′ (I). *See* QUR'ĀN.

KOREAN RELIGION. Lying between China and Japan, Korea was strongly influenced by Chinese culture and served as a major channel for transmitting that culture to Japan. Elements of SHAMANISM have mingled with CONFUCIANISM and BUDDHISM through the centuries in a distinctive manner. Although Taoist writings were studied, RELIGIOUS TAOISM never took root in Korea. The coming of ROMAN CATHOLICISM at the end of the eighteenth century provoked an anti-Western reaction, but in the following century both PROTESTANTISM and Catholicism took root. The period of Japanese domination, 1905-45, produced many stresses that helped determine the religious ferment of the period after liberation.

1. **Earliest period.** The Korean peninsula was inhabited by a variety of northeast Asian peoples from Paleolithic times onward. Dolmens and megaliths are found at a number of sites. The most significant origin myth tells how a deity named Hwanung descended to the summit of Paektu-san on the border between Korea and Manchuria. In response to the request of a she-bear and a tiger he provided them the means for becoming human. Only the bear persevered and completed the change. Hwanung married her, and she bore a son, whom she named Tangun, honored as the founder of Korean society. His birth is dated to 2333 B.C., the fiftieth year of the reign of Yao, legendary emperor of China. Tangun worshiped Hananim, god of heaven, and built an altar to him on Mari-san, Kangwha Island on the coast west of Seoul. *Hananim* (or *Hanŭnim*) became the Korean term for the one high God and was early adapted by Protestants for the Christian God. Today it is the term in most general use throughout Korea.

2. **Shamanism.** A persistent feature of everyday religious life is the role of the *mudang*, or female shaman. Some come from families of *mudangs*, others have experienced a call by some spirit, and still others apparently are attracted by the considerable financial rewards of the profession. Male shamans, often blind, are known as *paksu*; they are much less numerous than are the *mudang*. The major function of a shaman is performing a *kut*, an exorcism of an evil spirit thought to be causing sickness or other misfortune. At a shrine, perhaps a tree or a rock inhabited by a local spirit, the exorcist dances ecstatically, beats a drum, and chants to drive the evil spirit away. Many a spirit has taken on a particular identity and name. Collectively they are known as *kuisin* (Chin. *kuei-shen*).

Prominent old trees, major features of the landscape such as a mountain pass, a hill, or a stream, and places where a violent death has taken place are commonly believed to be inhabited by dangerous spirits. One method of propitiating them is to add a small stone to the pile of stones built up over the years by passersby.

Graves are generally located on a hill or mountain at a site chosen by geomancy (*see* FENG-SHUI) so that evil spirits will stay away and good spirits will bless the survivors. At the autumn festival, *ch'usŏk*, the full moon of the eighth lunar month (late September or early October), offerings of food are made at the graves and prayers are said. These customs, without the benefit of national organizations or government support, continue to be practiced widely.

3. **A thousand years of Buddhist preeminence.** After a period of colonization by the Chinese, three kingdoms arose in Korea: Koguryŏ in the north, around A.D. 100; Paekche in the southwest, around A.D. 316; and Silla in the southeast, around A.D. 326.

In 372 Sunto, a Buddhist monk from northern China, came to Koguryŏ bringing books, images, and relics. The king welcomed him, had two temples built, and entrusted the education of his son to him. Paekche sent to the capital of the Eastern Chin in south China for Buddhist missionaries, including an Indian named Marananda. In 545 the king of Paekche began to send missionaries to Japan, and in 577 sent over the first nun. Silla, slower to accept the new faith, eventually became its stronghold. In 525 the king issued a law prohibiting the killing of animals for food. He was canonized under the name Pŏphŭng, "ascendancy of the DHARMA."

During the following centuries various relics, including a bone from the BUDDHA's head, were enshrined in Korea. Monks began to make pilgrimages to China and to India itself. This was the classic age for the building of temples and monasteries, and the proliferation of MAHĀYĀNA sects from China. The outstanding monks of this period have continued to be revered. Especially eminent among them was Wŏnhyo (617-686), who did much to popularize Buddhist thought. He broke his vow of CELIBACY by marrying a princess, who bore him a son, Sŏl Chong, the outstanding early Korean exponent of Confucianism.

The country was united by Silla, but it was under the following Koryŏ dynasty (935-1392) that Korean Buddhism enjoyed its golden age. In each of the years 1032, 1049, 1053, 1087, 1090, and 1117 the king gave a vegetarian feast at the palace for some ten to thirty thousand monks at one time. Two kings took vows of semi-priesthood, Buddhist festivals became national holidays, and immense libraries were collected. In 958 Buddhist competitive examinations, patterned on China's Confucian examinations, were set up for applicants to government service.

Buddhist scriptures were not only imported; they were printed in Korea from wooden blocks. As an act of faith to protect the nation from barbarian invasions in the eleventh century, the entire known Buddhist canon was carved on blocks, but these were destroyed by the Mongols in 1232. After sixteen years of effort the canon was completed again in 1251 on 81,137 wood blocks, which are preserved today at the Haein-sa monastery near the city of Taegu.

The worship of AMIDA and AVALOKITEŚVARA (Kor. *Kwan-ŭm*) has predominated, but other BODHISATTVAS have been popular. MAITREYA (Kor. *Mi-rŭk*) is represented by many monumental statues. (*See* ART AND ARCHITECTURE, BUDDHIST §§2c, 3).

Temples were usually located in remote and scenic mountain areas, such as the Diamond Mountains in

North Korea. In the southeast the Pulguk-sa near the ancient Silla capital of Kyŏng-ju covers a large area on the lower slopes of a small mountain. Recently much new construction has been done, but down to the end of the Korean war the surviving buildings and stonework were only a reminder of its early greatness. Since all temple buildings were of wood, fire was a constant threat, and through the centuries they had to be rebuilt from time to time. Temple buildings were arranged around and in an open courtyard. As elsewhere, the largest contains the major image of Buddha. At Pulguk-sa two STŪPAS from the age of Silla are prized as national treasures. (*See* illustration, PAGODA.) Government archaeologists studied them in the 1960s and found Buddhist scriptures printed in the eighth century from wood blocks, utensils used in worship, and vessels containing *sari*, calcified stones collected from the cremated remains of monks and considered to be evidence of holiness.

At the crest of the mountain at Pulguk-sa is the celebrated Sŏkkul-am, a cave containing a seated Buddha eleven feet high. The rays of the rising sun shine on the face of the image a few minutes each morning. Around the walls are bas-relief figures of LOHANS, larger than life size. In recent years, because of the great increase in the number of visitors, excess humidity has posed a danger to the carvings, and a replica of the cave was constructed nearby for tourists.

Clark gives a comprehensive discussion of Buddhism through the centuries and its practice in the 1920s.

K. Crim

Buddhist *stūpa* at Pulguk-sa, Korea

4. **The dominance of Neo-Confucianism.** A military adventurer, Yi Sŏng-gye, overthrew the last Koryŏ king and founded the Yi Dynasty (1392-1910). Blaming Buddhism for the decay of the previous dynasty, the new ruler instituted an anti-Buddhist policy that was generally continued by his successors. In 1397 the king confiscated the property of many monasteries and gave it to his followers. In 1405 the thirteen Buddhist sects were forced to merge into seven, and in 1422 the number was further reduced to two: a meditative sect, the *Sun* (Ch'an or ZEN), and a "practical" sect known as *Kyo*. These two continued to be the major organized forms of Buddhism until the twentieth century. Buddhism never recovered from these and other measures, despite the efforts of some kings and dowager queens to encourage the faith.

Confucianism had been widely accepted by the mid-sixth century, but its greatest success came after 1392. Through national temples, examinations for government service, and the wide dissemination of literature, the teachings of CHU HSI came to dominate the intellectual and political life of the nation. (*See* CONFUCIANISM §3.) Sacrifices of unblemished cattle, sheep, pigs, and chickens were offered to Heaven and Earth at the great Sajik shrine in Seoul. On three special occasions a white horse was sacrificed.

In spite of the devastating Japanese invasion of 1592 and the Mongol conquest in 1637, the Yi Dynasty was a time of great cultural achievement in poetry, Confucian literature, architecture, and painting. Confucian philosophy was cultivated, but the philosophers became divided into mutually antagonistic factions. The most revered scholars were Yi T'oegye (1501-70) and Yi Yulgok (1536-84), who differed on the metaphysical basis of human morality (*see* Vos).

5. **Catholicism and the Tonghak.** Catholicism had been active in China since the days of FRANCIS XAVIER (1506-52), but did not reach Korea until more than two centuries later. The first Korean converts were attracted to Christianity by contacts during diplomatic missions to Peking in the 1770s. When a Chinese priest entered Korea secretly in 1794, he found some four thousand Catholics who had never seen a priest. Despite periodic persecution by the government, the church continued to grow. A group of seventy-nine martyrs from the 1839 persecution were beatified in 1925. From 1866 to 1869 some ten thousand Catholics were put to death. The first Korean priest, the Blessed Andrew Kim, was ordained in China and returned to Korea in 1849. The oldest Catholic church in Korea is the Immaculate Conception Cathedral in Seoul, begun in 1888. Paul Ro, the first Korean bishop, became Bishop of Seoul in 1944. After liberation from Japan in 1945 growth was rapid, and by the end of the 1970s there were over a million Catholics in South Korea.

K. Crim

Monumental statue of Maitreya, Nonsan, Korea

Catholicism was popularly known as *Sŏhak,* "Western learning," and to many Koreans was a symbol of European imperialism. In opposition to it, an indigenous movement calling itself *Tonghak* ("Eastern learning") was founded by Ch'oe Che-u (1824-66). In 1860, while sick, he had a vision of a spirit who identified himself as *Sangche* (Chin. *Shang-ti,* a classic name for God) and gave Ch'oe a prayer charm containing twenty-one Chinese characters. Dissolved in water, the charm cured his illness, and this led to the conversion of his family. The government regarded him as a Catholic, brought him to trial, and put him in jail. After a few months he was taken to Taegu, capital of his home province, and beheaded.

The Tonghak movement, officially known as Ch'ŏndo-kyo (Chin. *T'ien-tao chiao,* lit. "sect of the way of Heaven"), continued to grow and in 1893 felt strong enough to petition the king to grant them legal status. When no action was taken, members organized a popular crusade to rid the nation of foreigners. It soon became an outlet for all the pent-up frustrations of the people and posed a threat to Seoul itself. When the court called for China to send an army to put down the revolt, the Japanese sent an army to oppose the Chinese, precipitating the Sino-Japanese war.

In the years that followed, Ch'ŏndo-kyo became a rallying point for opposition to Japan, and about half the signers of the ill-fated anti-Japanese declaration of independence on March 1, 1919 were members. Most of the remainder were Protestants.

The basic statement of belief affirms that "man is God." Man and the universe are one, no idols should be worshiped, no humans are above others, but all should strive to make this earth a heaven. Buildings for public worship and the worship itself have generally been based on Christian models. In 1978 there were 1,700 clergy and over 800,000 members in South Korea.

6. **Protestantism.** Aside from scattered contacts, the first Protestants in Korea were Methodists and Presbyterians, who arrived in 1884-85. A comity agreement kept Protestant groups from competing for converts, and early policy promoted independence from foreign domination by insisting that all churches be self-governing, self-propagating, and self-supporting.

After slow initial growth church membership increased steadily in the early years of the twentieth century. As a result of a Bible study class in Pyongyang, North Korea, a revival broke out in 1907 and spread across the nation. Even after the Japanese annexation of Korea in 1910 baptized membership continued to grow. The Japanese exerted pressure in the 1930s to compel all Koreans to worship at SHINTŌ shrines as an expression of loyalty. Most Protestants opposed this as idolatry, and in reprisal the government closed church-operated schools. After 1945 all Shintō shrines in Korea were dismantled, and the religion ceased to exist there.

Protestantism entered a period of rapid growth after the war of 1950-53. Churches, schools, hospitals, and colleges sprang up everywhere. According to 1978 government figures there are over five million Protestants in South Korea. Internal tensions over doctrine, the ECUMENICAL MOVEMENT, and personality clashes brought about numerous church splits from 1953 on.

7. **Wŏn Buddhism.** In 1916 Pak Chungbin (1891-1943) became enlightened and founded in

southwest Korea a new movement based on the completeness of the DHARMAKĀYA and on Buddha as the ABSOLUTE. It is called Wŏn (complete) Buddhism. Stressing a correct understanding of grace, activity in spreading Buddhist teaching, and selfless service to others, the movement is perhaps the most lively form of Buddhism in South Korea today, with 800,000 members.

8. Other groups. At Sindo-an village in the foothills of Keiryong Mountain near Taejon, a number of indigenous sects have their center. This is popularly regarded as the site of the future capital of the country, under a leader of the Chŏng family, as foretold in a sixteenth century messianic text, the Chŏnggam-nok.

The veneration of Tangun (§1 *above*) as center of a national cult was promoted by Na Ch'ŏl (1864-1916), but it could not operate freely in the Japanese era. After 1945 it was revived and regional centers of worship were built, but the religion lacked popular appeal.

About 1900 a Confucian scholar named Kang Il-sun (1871-1910) claimed to be in touch with the spirits of the universe and to have magical powers. He founded a movement called Chingsan-kyo, from his pen name Chingsan (lit. "Kettle Mountain"). It was largely united around his unusual personality, and after his death it split into a bewildering variety of sects. One centered around the mediumistic powers of Chingsan's concubine, and another was led by his wife. Several of the splinter groups acclaimed him as Maitreya, the coming Buddha.

A number of groups have arisen under Protestant influence. The best known outside Korea is the UNIFICATION CHURCH. In Korea itself more attention has been attracted by an indigenous form of PRESBYTERIANISM under the leadership of Pak T'aesŏn (b. 1915). Pak started holding mass outdoor revival meetings in Seoul in the 1950s. He claimed to be various biblical figures, most notably the "Olive Trees" of Rev. 11:4. By establishing model communities known as "Christian Towns" he sought to build an industrial base for the kingdom of God.

After normalization of relations with Japan in the 1960s, some Japanese movements entered Korea, notably TENRI-KYŌ and SŌKA GAKKAI.

Bibliography. W. Bernatzki, L. Im, A. Min, *Korean Catholicism in the 1970s* (1975); C. A. Clark, *Religions of Old Korea* (1932; rpr. 1961); P. H. Lee, trans., *Lives of Eminent Korean Monks* (1969); S. Palmer, ed., *The New Religions of Korea* (Transactions of the Korea Branch, Royal Asiatic Society), XLIII (1967); S. Palmer, *Korea and Christianity* (1967); F. Vos, *Die Religionen Koreas* (1977), with an extensive bibliog. of works in Asian and European languages. K. CRIM

KOSHER kō´ shĕr (Ju—Heb.; lit. "proper"). The corpus of Jewish dietary laws which govern the choice, preparation, and consumption of food and drink. Complex and detailed, these serve as the basis for numerous TALMUDIC and rabbinic volumes and the core of traditional ordination studies.

Although some types of hybridization are forbidden, dietary laws do not relate to vegetation, all of which is permissible. A variety of restrictions exist upon the consumption of fish, fowl, and animals, however. Some species are considered impure and forbidden under any circumstances. Generally, animals must have both cloven hooves and dual digestive tracts to be permissible (Lev. 11:3; Deut. 14:6), while fish must have fins and scales (Lev. 11:9-12). No such detailed restrictions are offered for fowl, though scripture notes some two dozen forbidden species (Lev. 11:13-19; Deut. 14:12-18), which led sages to deduce that birds of prey and those lacking a crop, gizzard, and talon are forbidden. Some insect forms were permitted (Lev. 11:21-22), but this has largely fallen into disuse.

Fish which meet necessary specifications may be eaten when caught. Animals and fowl, however, undergo stringent caution in their slaughter, so they will not be rendered *treyfah* or torn, and therefore unfit (Exod. 22:30; Deut. 14:21). The details of kosher slaughter being so complex, it is left to a *shoḥet*, or one ritually trained, who will also inspect the carcass. Should some debilitating defect be discovered—e.g. a perforation in the lung—the animal would be declared *treyfah* despite its preparation.

Once the animal is slaughtered, every effort must be made to remove the blood before any meat may be eaten (Lev. 7:26-27; 17:10-14). Coarse salts are generally used in a soaking process popularly known as "koshering," which lasts roughly one hour, after which the meat is washed in cold water. Alternatively, the flesh may be roasted, a process required for liver, which normally holds more blood than other organs.

Aside from the species, the slaughter, and the preparation of meat, restrictions also exist on certain parts of the animal. The sciatic nerve is forbidden and must be removed before the hindquarters can be utilized (Gen. 32:33). Because this process is difficult and costly, such kosher cuts are generally not available in the United States. Similarly, abdominal and intestinal fat is prohibited (Lev. 3:17; 7:23-25) and must be carefully removed before these organs can be used.

Further, no mixture of meat and dairy products may be consumed, prepared, or used for benefit by a Jew (Exod. 23:19; 34:26; Deut. 14:21). Those adhering strictly will generally have separate dishes, utensils, linens, etc. for each food type. Traditionally an extended period of time—from one to six hours, depending on custom—must be observed prior to consuming dairy products after a meat meal. No such restriction exists on meat after eating most dairy products, though a similar practice is common after taking hard cheese. It should be noted that the above proscriptions extend to derivatives of restricted foods—e.g. preservatives, flavorings, etc.—and to any utensils or implements with which they were prepared, rendering kosher food preparation a complex art. As with most other Jewish practices, however, transgression is encouraged when critical questions of health are involved.

Dietary practice has been a mainstay of Jewish ritual, and for it some have been martyred. Nevertheless, it cannot be fully explained from scripture and it is generally categorized among those practices which are to be accepted blindly. However, some Jewish thinkers offer insights. Among these are *purity*—i.e., discipline in food consumption leads to a disciplined and holy life; *morality*—i.e., refraining from the use of blood or the consumption of birds of prey leads to an abhorrence of bloodshed and violence; human *stewardship*—i.e., since man in his natural state was vegetarian, consumption of flesh is a concession to his mortality which may be satisfied only through channels ordained by the Deity.

Mystics argue that the profanation of the soul as well as the body results from forbidden foods and admixtures. Rationalists claim an inherent health value in biblical restrictions, presenting relative Jewish immunity to some medieval diseases as evidence. Historians note that many foods forbidden were those used in pagan rites during the scriptural period. The simplest view of all is that these restrictions are designed to separate the Jewish community in values and practices from the Gentile world.

See also Food, Religious Attitudes Toward; Food Proscriptions, Muslim.

Bibliography. S. Dresner, *The Jewish Dietary Laws* (1966); S. Rubenstein, *The Book of Kashrus* (1967).

D. J. Schnall

KRISHNA, KṚṢṆA krĭsh′ nŭ (H—Skt.; lit. "black, dark"). Along with Rāma, one of the two most famous Avatars of Vishnu. Whether as a lively, blue-skinned baby prankster or as a young, flute-playing lover of the cow-maidens, Krishna is perhaps the most widely worshiped deity in India. Extensive literature, art, and devotional practice center on the Lord of Vṛndāvana whose dance (Līlā) sustains the world.

1. **History and sources.** Attempts to reconstruct the complex history of Krishna as a historical and divine figure expose not one but several "Krishnas" in texts ranging from the early Upaniṣads to the late Purāṇas. Two essentially distinct and dynamic story-traditions can be discerned: (1) a Brahminical Vāsudeva-Krishna who is the son of Devakī and Vāsudeva (Chāndogya Upaniṣad), is a warrior prince of Dvārakā and the Yādava tribe, assists the Pāṇḍava brothers in their war with their cousins (early Mbh.), is a divine sage identical in power and wisdom to Vishnu himself, and teaches the syncretistic path of devotion (Bhakti) in the Bhagavad Gītā; and (2) an

L. D. Shinn

Krishna defeating the serpent Kāliya

indigenous cowherd (Gopāla) Krishna associated with the Ābhīra tribes who is raised by the village step-parents Yaśodā and Nanda (Vishnu Purāṇa and Harivaṃśa), who as a child frolics in the fields and homes of Vṛndāvana, disposing of death-dealing demons, stealing butter or the clothes of the cow maidens (Gopīs), and playing his irresistible flute to entice the *gopīs* to amorous dalliances (Bhāgavata Purāṇa), and then selecting one *gopī,* Rādhā, to know the full range of love's emotions (Gītā Govinda). The traditions, complicated by literary and cultic attempts to interweave Vāsudeva-Krishna with Krishna Gopāla, are viewed by most scholars as a manifold history of several Krishnas. Nonetheless, as witnessed in the Bhāgavata Purāṇa in the ninth century and the Gītā Govinda in the twelfth, devotees have viewed the Krishna stories as an integrated whole as they dote on the prankish baby Krishna and dance with the *gopīs* to the call of the young Krishna's eternal flute.

2. **Myths and symbols.** The Bhāgavata Purāṇa's tenth book blends together the two basic Krishna traditions: Krishna is miraculously placed in the womb of Devakī as a "full descent" *(pūrṇa avatāra)* of the god Vishnu to rid the earth of evil King Kaṃsa and is switched with the baby of a cowherd maiden (Yaśodā) in the village of Gokul (later moving to

Vṛndāvana). As an unusually mischievous young boy, Krishna tricks his mother and other villagers out of their freshly churned butter, steals the *gopīs'* clothes while they bathe in the Yamuna River, and prods his elder brother and friends into forbidden adventures. Krishna is provoked by a buffalo demon and a poison-breasted demoness (Pūtanā) as well as by affronted Vedic gods AGNI and INDRA and the creator god BRAHMĀ into displays of his superior might and divine status. After one last dance *(rāsa līlā)* with the *gopī* girls, Krishna then leaves Vṛndāvana to perform his divine mission of killing King Kaṃsa and restoring righteousness (DHARMA) to the earth before joining the Pāṇḍava brothers in their battle to regain their rightful throne and building his own princely city of Dvārakā.

Of the many episodes in the cowherd Krishna's life, one stands out as a model of Krishna's relationship with the world. While he was playing with his friends one day, a friend called out to Yaśodā, "Krishna is eating dirt!" When questioned by his mother, Krishna invites her to look in his mouth, whereupon Yaśodā sees the whole universe, manifest and latent, spread out before her unsuspecting eyes. For one brief instant, Yaśodā realizes that the whole universe is but a part of Krishna-Vishnu and his play *(līlā),* a drama which reveals and then conceals Krishna's sporting involvement yet ultimate transcendence.

Religious artifacts in stone, wood, or metal often depict famous exploits of Krishna such as his nursing the very life out of the demoness Pūtanā, dancing into submission the hundred-headed serpent Kāliya, or holding Mount Govardhana over his villagers' heads to shield them from the torrential rain caused by the angry god Indra. Paintings, dramas, temple art, and classical dances all likewise depict these and other episodes from the life of Krishna. While usually known as an avatar or form of Vishnu, by the twelfth century Krishna is acclaimed by many devotees as the supreme Lord himself.

3. The impact of Krishna bhakti. Cutting across caste, sectarian, sexual, and elite/popular boundaries and reaching all parts of India in the regional vernaculars, Krishna Gopāla has become a truly pan-Indian deity. The lovable cowherd is extolled in the devotional hymns of the TAMIL-speaking ĀLVĀRS, is the divine lover of Rādhā in the SANSKRIT poem called the Gītā Govinda, and is the object of CAITANYA's Bengali revival with its KĪRTANAS and ecstatic devotionalism. From NIMBĀRKA, a twelfth-century Telegu BRAHMIN, to NĀMDEV, a fourteenth-century low caste tailor-ascetic who wrote works in Marāthī and HINDĪ in praise of Viṭhobā (Krishna), to the sixteenth-century Rajput Princess named MĪRĀBĀĪ who was denounced by her family for her complete devotion to Krishna, the Krishna story has engendered widespread acceptance and adaptation. One striking example of Krishna's emergence in regional syntheses is his residence in Purī as Lord JAGANNĀTHA ("Lord of the World"). Though the image of Jagannātha is Orissian in background, the yearly car festival attracts Vishnu-Krishna pilgrims from all over India. It is such an adaptable Krishna whose praise is now sung around the world by the HARE KRISHNAS.

Bibliography. The basic source for Krishna's life is the tenth book of the Bhāgavata Purāṇa, an abridgement of which is translated by C. Dimmitt and J. A. B. van Buitenen, *Classical Hindu Mythology* (1978), pp. 100-146; T. J. Hopkins, *The Hindu Religious Tradition* (1971), pp. 88-126; D. R. Kinsley, *The Sword and the Flute* (1975), pp. 9-78; M. Singer, ed., *Krishna: Myths, Rites, and Attitudes* (1966).

L. D. SHINN

KRISHNA CONSCIOUSNESS, INTERNATIONAL SOCIETY FOR (H). *See* HARE KRISHNA.

KRISHNAMURTI krĭsh´ nä mûr´ tē (H; 1895-). Born into a South Indian BRAHMIN family, Jiddu Krishnamurti was reared and educated from the age of twelve by C. W. Leadbeater, Annie Besant, and other THEOSOPHISTS at Adyar, outside Madras, and in England and California to prepare him to become the next World Teacher. As time went on his theosophical mentors became more and more convinced of his suitability for that role.

A fever of excitement built up in the 1920s as the Theosophical Society geared itself for the expected manifestation of the Lord MAITREYA through Krishnamurti. But the period of preparation culminated in a series of shattering psychic and physical experiences for Krishnamurti that led him to reject all religions, philosophies, and preconceptions about enlightenment. In 1929 he parted company with the Theosophical Society and began teaching through a kind of therapeutic dialectic demonstrated before large audiences. Lecturing in his magnetic manner in America, Europe, and India, he has since then circled the earth for fifty years like a tireless modern-day Buddha. Indeed his doctrine of a total awareness beyond mental process is similar to that of THERAVĀDA and ZEN. Although he has written relatively little, his countless talks have been recorded, transcribed, and published. In recent years Krishnajī, as he is called by his followers, has founded schools in America, Canada, England, and India to teach his way.

Bibliography. M. Lutyens, *The Years of Awakening* (1975).

C. S. J. WHITE

KṚṢṆA krĭsh´ nŭ (H). *See* KRISHNA.

KṢATRA kshä´ trŭ (H—Skt.; lit. "ruling power, lordly power" [*kṣi*—"to possess, to have power over, to rule"]). In Vedic literature, that vital and universal power present with holy power (BRAHMAN) in the Agni-Soma sacrifice: e.g., "AGNI is Brahman; SOMA is *kṣatra*. By presenting Agni and Soma on the fast day, [by presenting] Brahman and *kṣatra,* the sacrificer's evil is erased" (Kauṣīkatibrāhmaṇa, IX. 5). Although the interdependence of *kṣatra* and Brahman is recognized by virtually all the major sacerdotal traditions of Vedic India, their relationship is controversial and polyvalent—ranging, in the earliest texts, from their virtual identity (e.g. Taitt. Brāh. V.1.10) to their blatant opposition (e.g., Kauṣ. Brāh. VII. 22).

In the Śatapathabrāhmaṇa of the White YAJUR-VEDIC school, a cosmological role is assigned to *kṣatra*. Brahman (holy power) is identified with those deities most central to the Vedic sacrifice (Agni, Bṛhaspati, Prajāpati, *et al.*) and is represented in the human realm by the priesthood. *Kṣatra* is hypostatized as Indra, Soma, Varuṇa and Yama; and is represented in society by the nobility. Hence, *kṣatra* or "lordly power" is always complementary to Brahman or "holy power" in the VEDIC tradition (as reflected in its history and literature); and this complementarity (however resolved) is reflected in Vedic cosmology, society, cult and speculation.

J. S. HELFER

KṢATRIYA kshä´ trī yä (H—Skt.). A generic term for members of the second highest division of Hindu society (*see* CASTE). Though in ritual status inferior to BRAHMINS, Kṣatriyas were traditionally rulers and warriors. Even those Kṣatriyas who today engage in agriculture pride themselves on their warrior tradition. Though TWICE BORN, Kṣatriyas differ from Brahmins and VAIŚYAS by their habit of consuming meat and alcoholic drinks.

C. VON FÜRER-HAIMENDORF

KSHITIGARBA kshī tī gär´ bə (B—Skt.; lit., "earth-womb") **JIZŌ** jī zō (B—Jap.). BODHISATTVA not mentioned in early Buddhist sources, but who has come to hold considerable importance, especially in Japan. In later Buddhist texts he is listed as one of eight or sixteen bodhisattvas. By the third or fourth century A. D. he was known in China, as Ti-t'sang.

Kshitigarba can be interpreted as the bodhisattva who has vowed to save all who live "in the meantime," as the tradition has remembered it, between the BUDDHA'S entry into NIRVANA and the coming of MAITREYA. This includes a ministry not only to all who suffer in the world but also to those who have departed earthly existence and are living in another realm of life. Since about the fifth century A. D., Kshitigarba has been regarded as having power over the hells.

During the development of the Buddhist tradition in China an assimilation of YAMA and Kshitigarba seems to have occurred. Yama also became associated with a Taoist deity, T'ai-shan-fu-chün, who presided over ten kings who judged the dead. (*See* TAOISM, RELIGIOUS.) Both in China and Japan, Kshitigarba has been found in affiliation with these ten kings as a savior.

Among Japanese Buddhists, Kshitigarba (Jizō) is noted for giving aid to those who stand in greatest need—children, women in labor, and the wicked.

Courtesy of the Smithsonian Institution, Freer Gallery of Art, Washington, D. C.

Wooden statue of Kshitigarba (Jizō) from the Kamakura period (Japanese, late 13th century)

In the PURE LAND tradition (Jōdo-shu), Kshitigarba has played a role in receiving and welcoming the faithful upon their death and receiving rites of repentance offered by the faithful.

Usually depicted in an image of a monk, Kshitigarba is often seen holding in his right hand a staff with six rings, suggestive of his efficacious activity in the six dimensions of existence in the realm of desire (*kāmaloka* or *kāmadhātu*), and in the left hand an orb or pearl, of uncertain significance. Occasionally temples will have a room or separate building set apart for Kshitigarba. More regularly, his statue, in stone, will be placed outside at an aesthetically pleasing location in the temple complex. For both the dead and the living, Kshitigarba shows the way. He protects travelers, and small shrines in his honor are erected along the roadside.

On the twenty-fourth of each month it is customary for many in Japan to express their devotion to Kshitigarba (Jizō) in a devotional practice known as *Jizō Ennichi*.

Bibliography. *See* BODHISATTVA. J. R. CARTER

KUAN-YIN kwän´ yĭn (B). *See* AVALOKITEŚVARA.

KUBERA kōō bä´ rū (H & B—Skt.; lit. "ugly body"). The god of the North, riches, and happiness who is also king of the YAKṢAS. He was the object of a small cult as one of the *lokapalas,* "guardians of the world," but appears as a ubiquitous figure in Indian mythology and a devotee of other gods. He is also known as Vaiśravana, "son of Viśravas," Yakṣapati, "lord of *yakṣas,*" and Guhyahapati, "lord of earth spirits."

Kubera was probably a folk deity worshiped by the indigenous people when the ARYANS entered India. He was apparently lord of oceans, streams, and rivers. He is first mentioned in the ATHARVA VEDA as the king of the *yakṣas,* a group of minor benevolent spirits who populate the woodlands and are believed to be guardians of riches hidden in the roots of trees.

In Buddhist literature and art Kubera serves as an attendant and devotee of the Buddha as well as the great king of the North. In Epic literature, however, stories about him are multiplied and he replaces AGNI as the guardian of the North and, rarely, as the guardian of the East. His heavenly position, along with immortality, lordship of wealth, and equality with the gods, was received as a boon from the god BRAHMĀ because of his austerities. Classically he guards the North; YAMA, the god of death, the South; VARUṆA, the West; and Agni or INDRA, the East. This list is later expanded to eight *lokapalas.*

As lord of wealth he set the norm for royal luxury. He is pictured as living in a great mountain palace studded with jewels where he sits as king with his female attendants *(yakṣīs)* and a court. He is accompanied by two wives—Ṛiddhi, "prosperity," and Yakshī, the female *yakṣa* par excellence, and is half brother of a number of demons. In the MAHĀBHĀRATA he is said to have comforted the PĀṆDAVA heroes during their long exile in the forest.

The PURĀṆAS elaborate on this mythology. The goddess MĪNĀKṢĪ is said to have been his daughter. In the Bhāgavata Purāṇa, Kubera is described as living in Lanka, a magnificent city on Mt. MERU, the tall mountain at the center of the earth. Later he is driven out by the demon Rāvaṇa and the city is blown into the sea by the wind god Vāyu. The Padma Purāṇa relates the account of Kubera's receipt of kingship of the *yakṣas* but credits SHIVA with the boon.

The Agni Purāṇa prescribes that his image be installed in temples, seated on a goat with a club in his hand. Most often he is represented as a pot-bellied male with eight deformed teeth, three legs, and a badly deformed body covered with ornaments. He is at times three-headed with four arms and is often shown riding a man or a lamb as his vehicle (VĀHANA). He holds a club or mace *(gada)* in one hand and a bag of treasure or a mongoose vomiting jewels in another. His images are usually carved on the exterior faces of shrines as a guardian.

Bibliography. A. K. Coomaraswamy, *Yakshas,* 2 vols. (1928, 1931). R. N. MINOR

K'UEI-CHI kwā´ ē jē (B—Chin.; 632-82). Pupil of HSÜAN-TSANG, assisted in the translation of Indian MAHĀYĀNA texts, responsible for the sixty chapters of the *Ch'eng-wei-shih lun shu-chi* ("Notes on the Treatise on the Establishment of the Doctrine of Consciousness-Only") which aids in interpreting the work of Hsüan-tsang and the doctrine of the FA-HSIANG school of Buddhism. C. W. EDWARDS

KUFR koo´ fər (I—Arab.; lit. "covering, concealing" [God's blessings]). Unbelief, unfaithfulness. An infidel is a *kāfir. Kufr* and its synonyms are very frequently encountered in the QUR'ĀN, where "ingratitude" is sometimes the basic meaning (e.g., 16:55; 30:33). The *kāfir* will go to JAHANNAM (hell; 3:10).

In the ḤADĪTH MUHAMMAD is reported to have said: "When one commits fornication he is not a believer, when one steals he is not a believer, when one drinks wine he is not a believer, when one takes plunder on account of which men raise their eyes at him he is not a believer, and when one of you defrauds he is not a believer; so beware, beware!" (*Mishkāt,* I, 17).

In early Islam there was much controversy over what made one a *kāfir.* Muhammad declared that even charging a fellow Muslim with *kufr* brings the same sin down on one's own head if the accusation proves unfounded (Muslim 1, 41). It is common nonetheless to encounter denunciations of fellow Muslims as *kāfirs* in the literature of theological dispute. The lawbooks consider the *kāfir* to be unclean, but Jews and Christians are generally regarded less harshly in this respect, being PEOPLE OF THE BOOK. (*See* SHIRK.)

Bibliography. Al-Baghawī, *Mishkāt al-Maṣābīḥ,* ET J. Robson (1960-65), I, 17; Muslim, *Ṣaḥīḥ,* ET A. H. Siddīqī (1971-75), I, 41. F. M. DENNY

KUMĀRAJĪVA kū mä rä jī´ vä (B—Skt.; 350-413). Indo-Iranian Buddhist scholar responsible for the translation of many texts, mostly Mahāyāna, into Chinese at the beginning of the fifth century A.D.

Born in Kuchā in Central Asia of devout Buddhist parents, Kumārajīva studied Sarvāstivādin (*see* BUDDHIST SECTARIANISM) beliefs in his earliest years but was converted to Mahāyāna Buddhism because of its striking doctrine of emptiness (*see* ŚŪNYATĀ). He was ordained a monk at age twenty and studied and taught Buddhist scriptures in Central Asia until, in 383, a Chinese expeditionary force overran Kuchā and took Kumārajīva captive. After nearly two decades at the Liang court, he was brought (in 401) to the Chinese capital of Ch'ang-an. Detained there under rather splendid house arrest, he supervised the Chinese translation of many Buddhist texts over the next decade.

Translation activities. In Ch'ang-an Kumārajīva presided over a state-sponsored translation bureau with a large staff of monks and secretaries. This bureau improved and helped to standardize the transcription of names and translations of Buddhist terminology. Among the important editorial assistants on his staff were SENG-CHAO and Seng-jui. Kumārajīva and his staff provided clearer and more concise editions of, among others, the LOTUS SŪTRA, the Heart and Diamond sūtras, and the Vimalakīrtinirdeśa sūtra (*see* VIMALAKĪRTI). The greatest contribution of Kumārajīva was his translation and editing of NĀGĀRJUNA's MĀDHYAMIKA writings. These texts, especially the Middle Stanzas (*Mādhyamaka-kārikās*), introduced the Chinese to a systematic Buddhist philosophy of emptiness. The translations that Kumārajīva oversaw contributed, both by their extent and their accuracy, to a critical understanding of Buddhism in its new cultural context. The centuries following these translations would see Buddhism becoming an independent and powerful religious force in China. His extensive correspondence with the famous monk Hui-yüan provides insight into the Buddhist concerns of the day and especially the considerable difference between the practical, piety-oriented Buddhism of the South (Hui-yüan) and the more philosophically oriented Buddhism of the North.

Bibliography: *Biographies des moines éminents de Houei-Kiao,* (Kao seng chuan), trans. by Robert Shih (1968), II.1 Kumārajīva, pp. 60-81; R. H. Robinson, *Early Mādhyamika in India and China* (1967); E. Zürcher, *The Buddhist Conquest of China* (1959). J. D. WHITEHEAD

KUṆḌALINĪ kūn′ dū lĭn′ ē (H & B —Skt.; lit. "the coiled one"). The term used in TANTRIC forms of Indian meditation to connote the latent power awakened in the meditation process. As such, it is part of the "subtle body" *liṅga-śarīra. Kuṇḍalinī* rests as dormant power at the base of three ducts visualized as coordinate with the spine, the left duct (*iḍā*) terminating in the left nostril, and the right one (*piṅgalā*) in the right nostril. The central duct "the sleeping one" (*suṣumnā*) is closed. Awakened by yoga, *kuṇḍalinī* opens the *suṣumnā* and moves upward, gradually piercing the "circles" or centers (*cakra*) enumerated as four in Buddhism, as six in Hinduism. From the lowest *cakra* situated between the genitals and the anus, *kuṇḍalinī* moves upward "like a serpent" or "like lightning" until it unites with the "thousand-petalled center" (*sahasrāra cakra*) in the region of the brain, causing SAMĀDHI, the state of complete absorption which ushers in liberation (*see* MOKṢA), the aim of all Indian meditation. The ascent of *kuṇḍalinī* generates occult powers (*see* SIDDHI) which the earnest YOGI must ignore, because they impede the achievement of redemption. Since partial arousal of *kuṇḍalinī* is dangerous, *kuṇḍalinī* yoga must not be undertaken without the guidance of a qualified GURU.
A. BHARATI

KÜNG, HANS kyūng (Ch; 1928-). Swiss Roman Catholic theologian committed to a confrontation between Christian faith and the contemporary world and to the ecumenical reform of the CHURCH. He believes his method expresses the substantial agreement among churches today about BIBLE and tradition, grace and justification, and church and SACRAMENTS. For these views he was censured by his church on December 18, 1979. *See* THEOLOGY, CONTEMPORARY CHRISTIAN §4c. D. F. OTTATI

KURUKṢETRA koo′ rōō kshā′ trū (H—Skt.; lit. "field of the Kurus"). A narrow plain located near modern Delhi, which has served as a natural battlefield throughout India's history. Perhaps most importantly, it is identified as the site of the great eighteen-day battle between the Kauravas and the PĀṆḌAVAS, the epic event around which the MAHĀBHĀRATA was composed. J. BARE

KUSHA koo′ shə. *See* NARA BUDDHISM §3a.

KUSINĀRA koo sĭ nä′ rū (B—Pali) **KUŚINAGARA** koo shĭ nū gä′ rū (B—Skt.). A city of northeastern India located near Kasia, about thirty-five miles east of Gorakhpur. The city is noted especially as the last stopping place in the BUDDHA's final missionary journey and the place where he died. It may be, however, the last place which in his physical weakness he was able to reach in an attempt to return to KAPILAVASTU, the capital of the Śākyas and his birthplace.

Kusināra was the home of a tribal group known as the Mallas. They evidenced great grief when told of the imminent death of the Buddha and requested the privilege of visiting him in his last hours. ĀNANDA, the beloved disciple of the early monastic community and cousin of the Buddha, made this possible by presenting the people in family groups. The Mallas also did special honor to the Buddha through their elaborate and extended funeral rites (Dīgha Nikāya II, 129-67). R. H. DRUMMOND

KUZARI koo zä′ rē (Ju—Arab.). A book by the Spanish Jewish philosopher and poet JUDAH HA-LEVI, subtitled "The Book of Argument and Proof in Defense of the Despised Faith." Written over a long period of time, it reflects ha-Levi's growing dissatisfaction with philosophic speculation and the progressive deepening of his appreciation for history and the fullness of human experience. The purpose of the book was to defend rabbinic Judaism against sectarians like the KARAITES, against other religions, and against the newly emerging Neoaristotelian philosophy. K. P. BLAND

KYRIE ELEISON kē′ rē ĕ ĕ lā′ ē sôn (Ch—Gr.; "Lord, have mercy"). Originally the people's response to the petitions of a LITANY. Such a litany was inserted into the Latin MASS in the fifth century, but eventually disappeared leaving the response "Kyrie eleison" (and "Christe eleison") as a fixed part of the mass. The Kyrie is also used in the DIVINE OFFICE.
R. A. GREER

L

LADINO lă dē´ nō (Ju—Spanish). The Hebrew-script vernacular of the SEPHARDI Jews. A product of several archaic Spanish dialects and Hebrew vocabulary, Ladino was probably not recognized as a Jewish tongue prior to 1492, when Judeo-Spanish exiles carried it with them to Holland, France, and England, as well as North Africa and the Ottoman Empire. Divorced from Castilian, Ladino gradually assumed many features of local speech, particularly under Ottoman influence.

Between the sixteenth and nineteenth centuries an extensive Ladino literature developed, including religious works, poetry, romances, and translations. Secular forms predominated in the last century as religious study declined in many communities. Ladino often varies between that form which reflects greater Castilian influence (Oriental Ladino) and that of North Spanish or Portuguese origin (Western Ladino). Works of theological or rabbinic nature tend to include far more Hebrew vocabulary than secular works.

As a result of displacements and migrations in the twentieth century, Ladino has suffered a sharp decline. Most of its adherents are now in the Americas and Israel. Even the few who remain fluent (largely in Israel) are only nominally so; the written form is nearly extinct. *See* HEBREW LANGUAGE; YIDDISH.

D. J. SCHNALL

LAKṢMAṆA lŭksh´ mŭn ŭ (H—Skt.). RĀMA's most devoted brother. He followed Rāma to the forest and served as his constant companion. Rāma devotees consider Lakṣmaṇa as the incarnation of the great snake ŚEṢA, the bed of VISHNU. V. N. RAO

LAKṢMĪ lŭk´ shmē (H—Skt.; lit. "wealth, riches"). A Hindu goddess. Identical with Śrī and associated with wealth, prosperity, and kingly might. Usually said to be the wife of the god VISHNU. *See* GODDESS (INDIA) §2.

Bibliography. B. Saraswati, "History of Śrī in North India to *c.* A.D. 550" (Ph.D. diss., Faculty of Arts, University of London, 1971). D. R. KINSLEY

LAMA lä´ mə (B—Tibetan; lit. "superior one" [*bla-ma*]). Term commonly used to designate all monks in TIBETAN BUDDHISM, although strictly speaking it should be used only of those regarded as REINCARNATIONS of a BODHISATTVA. The monastic orders have hierarchies of lamas, each rank representing a particular expression of Buddhahood.

D. G. DAWE

LAO TZU lou´ dzə (T—Chin.; lit. "old master") also called **TAO-TE CHING** (dou də jĭng; lit. "the way and its power"). The foremost classic of Taoism (*see* TAOISM, PHILOSOPHICAL §2). It deals with the Tao (Way) as the source and reality of the world and the application of it in life. It is considered a book of mysticism because of its view that the understanding of the Tao is beyond words or concepts. It is also a philosophical work because it is concerned with cosmology, ontology, and ethics.

Like many other books of the same period, the Lao Tzu was compiled as a manual to instruct kings and rulers in the art of government; it teaches that the state that governs least governs best. This is the political meaning of the principle of WU WEI (no-action). As a political work the Lao Tzu is a failure, because its view that the king should rule by no-action has never been taken seriously by any ruler in Chinese history. As a philosophical work, however, it has been immensely influential, because it provides a way of life which has a great appeal to educated Chinese. It teaches them how to survive individually against the background of the social and political upheavals which have been a regular occurrence in Chinese history. The best way to survive is to stay low, be weak, and to curtail ambition and unnecessary desires. Then the chances of being cut down are comparatively slight.

1. Format of the book. The Lao Tzu is a small book ranging between 5,227 and 5,722 words, depending on the differences in versions or editions. The present standard version, based upon an inscription dated A.D. 708, is divided into two parts: part one, entitled the Classic of Tao, has 37 chapters; part two, entitled the Classic of Te (power), has 44 chapters. Its language is terse and cryptic, and its verses are short. Three-word or four-word sentences are common, and over half the lines are rhymed. These rhymed passages probably constitute the oldest part of the book, transmitted orally for a long time and interpreted orally by those familiar with the tradition of this literary genre. Due to the cryptic character of its language and the fact that many of its words had different meaning for the ancients, passages of the Lao Tzu can be interpreted in various ways. This is one reason why throughout Chinese history there have been so many commentaries on the book and why there are over thirty English translations.

2. **Authorship and date.** The authorship and the date of the Lao Tzu have been debated in both Asia and the West, but no conclusive agreement has been reached. In general, scholars are divided into two groups.

a) Traditionalists hold that the book was composed in the sixth century B.C. and its author was Lao Tzu, a senior contemporary of CONFUCIUS. The chief evidence for this belief is the biography of Lao Tzu in the *Records of the Historian (Shih-chi)* by Ssu-ma Ch'ien (*ca.* 145—*ca.* 89 B.C.). Some scholars in this group accept the date but reject the authorship of Lao Tzu on the grounds that the biography has difficulties in establishing the identity of the man Lao Tzu. Traditionalists accept the biography because they believe that the modernist view is based on insufficient historical evidence.

b) Modernists. On the basis of internal evidence, some scholars hold that the book was composed between 350-275 B.C., the latter part of the Warring States period (403-222 B.C.). A number of works composed in this period contain passages similar to parts of the Lao Tzu, and there are many similarities of style. This indicates that it was in this period that the oral tradition of the Lao Tzu was committed to writing. Moreover, the book reflects the conditions of this time of political turmoil. These scholars also reject Lao Tzu as the author of the work, holding that "Lao Tzu" represents a literary genre of wise sayings, the oldest of which can be traced to the sixth century B.C. or even earlier, but all of which belonged to the school known in the Han dynasty as Taoism. Thus the book is an anthology of sayings collected and edited in its period, and its composite nature explains why it is often repetitive.

3. **Controversial interpretations of Lao Tzu's sayings.** Because of the cryptic character of the book, it is possible to interpret the statements in different ways.

a) Cosmological or ontological nature of the Tao. Some scholars hold that Tao as nonbeing is essentially a cosmological concept referring to the creator of the world (chs. 1, 4, 40, 42, 52). (*See* BEING AND NONBEING.) But others argue that the Tao is essentially an ontological concept which should be viewed as the reality within time rather than the cause beyond time. Thus, for example, the following passage, "The Tao produces one; / one produces two; / two produces three; / three produces the myriad creatures" (ch. 42), is ontological rather than cosmological when interpreted symbolically or figuratively.

b) Cyclical or noncyclical interpretation of the principle of reversal. It is well known that the principle of reversal *(fan)* is basic for understanding Tao. Some scholars understand the reversal to mean that when a thing reaches its extreme it reverts to its opposite. Hence, the reversal is understood in terms of cyclical changes from one pole to the other. For example: "It is upon calamity that happiness leans; it is upon happiness that calamity rests" (ch. 58); "The proper becomes again the improper, and the good becomes again the monstrous" (ch. 58). Others believe that the principle of reversal refers to "valuing the soft" or "abiding by the soft"; it is returning to the root or the origin of things which is the Tao. Anyone who chooses to be lowly will not encounter that which is high. Hence the reversal is not a cyclical concept.

c) Purposive or nonpurposive view of human conduct. Here the controversy does not involve the divergent opinions of scholars but discrepancies in the Lao Tzu in regard to human conduct. We are told that the Tao "never acts, yet nothing is left undone" (ch. 37). Thus by the same token one should act spontaneously and be nonpurposive. This is the way one lives in accord with the Tao. On the other hand, there are many passages in the Lao Tzu which teach that in order to obtain the anticipated results one should scheme deliberately. For example, "If you would have a thing shrink, / you must first stretch it; / if you would have a thing weakened, / you must first strengthen it; / if you would take from a thing / you must first give it" (ch. 36). Although the purposive and the nonpurposive views are logically contradictory, they are both present in the Lao Tzu as the parallel expressions of the Tao.

4. **History of the book.** The book was originally called Lao Tzu. It became a classic *(ching)* and received the title of *Tao-te ching* in the Former Han period (206 B.C.—A.D. 8). Although it was originally composed in two parts, its order was by no means uniform. For example, the two earliest extant versions (discovered in 1973) have the reverse order (part one on Te and part two on Tao). (*See* TAOISM, PHILOSOPHICAL §5.) The book did not have chapter divisions until the Sui (581-618) or T'ang (618-907) dynasty. But the number of chapters varies according to editions (67, 68, 72, 81, or 114 chs.) due to different ways of dividing the material. This is another reason for the problems of interpretation, because the different arrangement of chapters necessarily influences the interpretations of the chapters involved.

The earliest extant commentary on the Lao Tzu is called *Hsiang-erh* (discovered in the Tun-huang cave in 1900), composed in the last part of the second century or the early third century A.D. It is a work of RELIGIOUS TAOISM which teaches a method of breath control and the importance of good conduct in promoting longevity. The commentary by Wang Pi (A.D. 226-249) is the earliest extant philosophical commentary on the Lao Tzu, but it was not much studied until the eighteenth century, when the Ch'ing scholars (1640-1912) began to do critical research on the book. The most popular commentary is by a man called "Ho-shang Kung" (the old man on the bank of the Yellow River), a product of the fourth century A.D. Its popularity is due to its emphasis on religious themes for the common folk: the divinity of Lao Tzu, physical immortality, internal ALCHEMY, morality. At present, there are over 350 Chinese commentaries and annotations on the Lao Tzu, and numerous Japanese commentaries.

See CHUANG TZU.

Bibliography. W. T. Chan, trans., *The Way of Lao Tzu* (1963); E. M. Chen, "Is There a Doctrine of Physical Immortality in the *Tao Te Ching?*" *HR*, XII (1973), 231-49; H. G. Creel, "On Two Aspects in Early Taoism," in *What Is Taoism?* (1970), pp. 37-47; C. W. Fu, "Lao Tzu's Conception of Tao," *Inquiry*, XVI (1973), 367-94: J. N. Girardot, "Myth and Meaning in the *Tao Te Ching:* Chapters 25 and 42," *HR*, XXVI (1977), 294-328; Y. H. Jan, "Problems of Tao and *Tao Te Ching*," *Numen*, XXII (1975), 208-34; D. C. Lau, trans., *Lao Tzu: Tao Te Ching* (1963), and "The Treatment of Opposites in *Lao Tzu*," *Bulletin of Oriental and African Studies*," XXI (1958), 344-60.

D. C. YU

LĀT lät (I). A pre-Islamic solar deity, frequently invoked by tribal poets. Among MUHAMMAD'S tribesmen, the QURAISH, she was so highly esteemed that a divine revelation was needed to affirm that Lāt, together with two other goddesses, 'Uzza and Manāt, were not to be approached as intercessors before ALLAH, the Almighty Creator of the universe (Qur'ān 53:19-21).

B. LAWRENCE

LATIN (Ch). Christian Latin, which only gradually replaced Greek as the common language of Christian communities from the end of the second century onward, had as characteristics its specifically Christian ideology, Greek and Hebrew loanwords, Semitic expressions tributary to early biblical translations, and a reflection of popular usage. Tertullian (d. *ca.* 220) began a trend to combine Christian colloquial style with literary elegance. As the West became progressively latinized, Christian Latin became a more universal language, while at the same time developing its specific theological vocabulary. Standardization of biblical Latin owes much to JEROME (d. 420). Meanwhile, as paganism became less a threat to the church, a solemn hieratic form of liturgical Latin evolved, tributary in part to ancient sacral prayer forms. Centralization of administration led to another specialized form of Latin based on imperial curial usage. Reflecting these developments and scholastic influence, medieval Latin produced another type of language, suited to the expression of precise scientific ideas. Renaissance attempts to classicize church Latin left few permanent traces. Insistence by the Reformers on the vernacular was countered for centuries by Roman insistence on Latin as a sacred, universal, and timeless language. The recent Constitution on the Liturgy (1963), while retaining Latin as the language of the Latin rites, opens the way for extensive use of the vernacular which in practice has almost everywhere replaced Latin.

Bibliography. C. Mohrmann, *Liturgical Latin: Its Origins and Character* (1957); *Études sur le latin des chrétiens*, 4 vols. (1961-75), a collection of monographs.

C. WADDELL

LATTER-DAY SAINTS (Ch). The Church of Jesus Christ of Latter-day Saints or the Mormon Church.

Mormons owe their existence to JOSEPH SMITH, a religious seeker living near Palmyra, New York. The Palmyra area spawned many evangelical, utopian, and MILLENARIAN experiments in the nineteenth century. Smith blended these strands with aspects of his PURITAN heritage and the democratic spirit to fashion the largest indigenous American religious group (around 4,500,000 adherents in 1980).

1. **History.** In a vision in 1822 the angel Moroni told Smith where gold tablets, containing God's revelation, were buried. Smith published a translation of them, the BOOK OF MORMON, in 1830 and soon became "seer, translator, prophet, and apostle" of a group committed to restoring the pure religion of the Book of Mormon.

First calling themselves the Church of Christ, Mormons stressed the coming of Christ's kingdom in America and encouraged others to abandon apostate churches and false practices, such as infant BAPTISM and reliance on a professional CLERGY.

In 1831 the group migrated to Kirtland, Ohio, where evangelical pastor Sidney Rigdon (1793-1876) and his congregation joined their ranks. Another revelation prompted Smith to promulgate the "law of consecration and stewardship," which called for redistribution of surplus wealth and property among the faithful. This introduced communitarian principles (the Order of Enoch) to the Mormons and helped finance missionary efforts of a group which moved to Missouri.

After severe financial problems in 1837 Smith joined the Missouri Mormons. Mormons attracted attention by their stress on the "gathering" of believers into an earthly, American Zion and by their criticism of other Christian groups. Violence ensued in the first "Mormon War" (1838), forcing Smith and his followers to move to Nauvoo, Illinois, on the Mississippi.

There Mormons secured a charter (1840) granting virtual freedom from political authority. Though espousing a democratic structure, Smith exerted autocratic control and became increasingly hostile to antagonists. Nauvoo soon became Illinois's fastest-growing settlement, and the Mormons strong enough to dispatch missionaries to Canada and England, where they met with marked success. Over four thousand migrated from England to Nauvoo, where mandatory tithing replaced the "law of consecration" in 1841.

Smith announced his presidential candidacy in 1844, but his calls for retaliation against "Gentile" oppressors and his destruction of an opposition printing press led to his and his brother's arrest. While Smith was jailed in Carthage, Illinois, a mob attacked the jail and murdered Smith.

Schisms resulted from the ensuing leadership vacuum and apprehension over polygamy. Smith had endorsed plural marriage (the Order of Abraham) after a vision in 1843, but it did not become doctrine until 1852. Probably less than 20 percent of the Mormons ever practiced polygamy.

The only splinter group which lasted is the Reorganized Church of Jesus Christ of Latter-day Saints. Supported by Smith's family, this group migrated to Iowa and then back to Missouri. It has resembled other pietistic Protestant sects more than its parent body.

Most of the Nauvoo community accepted the leadership of Brigham Young (1801-77), a converted Vermont METHODIST who had been Smith's confidante. He spearheaded the movement to the Great Salt Lake area of Utah, Mexican territory until 1850. There, in 1847, Mormons began to erect "Zion in the Wilderness," the provisional state of Deseret. Despite a miraculous transformation of much desert into arable land, opposition mounted after the United States gained control.

In 1862 federal law banned polygamy in Utah, and the law was strengthened in 1882. In 1887 authorities dissolved the church corporation, confiscated much communal property, and imprisoned many offenders. Supplementary revelation in 1890 forbade plural marriage.

Abandonment of plural marriage started the "Americanization" of Mormonism. After Utah became a state, Mormons seemed less distinctive, and "Zion" could not be as precisely identified as before. But Mormons did not suffer the same strains as millennialist groups which pinpointed a date for Christ's return. By locating the millennium in space, America, rather than in time, Mormons have been able to assert the primacy of the United States in the divine scheme and blend their expectations with American manifest destiny. Mormon perfectionism has led to considerable achievement in a capitalistic society. Church agencies own many prosperous corporations and industries, from toothpaste factories to cattle ranches, while individuals have gained power in business and politics.

Mormons have also acquired problems characteristic of American society as a whole, especially that of race. Blacks were among the early converts; some became full members and part of the lay priesthood. But proscriptions in the *Book of Abraham* and the *Book of Moses* consigned blacks to second-class status, and by the mid-twentieth century they were excluded from the priesthood. In 1978 a new revelation gave blacks equal status with whites.

While Mormons are still concentrated in Utah and contiguous states, expansion has been nationwide. International missions have also prospered, especially in Europe, Latin America, and Asia. By 1970 missionaries labored in over sixty-five nations. This growth necessitated redefinition of the sense of community central to Mormonism, as had the introduction of public schools in Utah in the 1920s. The latter signaled the end of church control over public life. The reorientation has brought increased emphasis on the family and church-related activities, along with the establishment of agencies and societies promoting church welfare.

2. Belief and practice. Much Mormon theology mirrors such orthodox Christian ideas as belief in free will, repentance, and a providential view of history, but much is distinctive. Smith argued that God is a self-made, finite deity with a material body. Only matter is eternal. Through repentance and baptism by immersion, anyone may gain entrance into Christ's earthly kingdom. The dead may receive baptism and thus share in the millennial age. Before the kingdom comes, the baptized who have died wait in heaven, with material bodies identical to their earthly ones. Some strands of Mormon thought posit a plurality of deities, giving the religion a polytheistic cast.

Mormonism is male-oriented. Women's religious status derives from that of their husbands, and marriages sealed in the temple endure "for time and eternity." Thus the family unit becomes central to Mormon piety and organization.

Structurally, Mormonism has attempted to balance democracy and authority. Male members in good standing constitute a nonprofessional priesthood and share responsibility for individual congregations. Clear lines of authority exist. The lay priesthood is expected to consent without question to higher leadership.

Groups of congregations form a ward, over which a bishop presides for a term up to ten years in length. Bishops appoint persons to lesser posts, regarding the ward as an extended family. Wards are grouped into stakes (dioceses). Over all are the president, two counselors, and the Council of the Twelve Apostles. Togehter they comprise the church's major policy-making body. The president, as successor to Smith, may still receive revelation.

The temple in Salt Lake City is the main ritual center. Other temples include the one in Washington, D.C., completed in the early 1970s. Only members in good standing may enter sacred places within a temple. In Salt Lake City are housed the genealogical records of the church, the world's premier genealogical archive. The passion for accurate records emerges from the practice of baptism of the dead. Also notable is the Church Welfare Plan, which has provided extensive relief for Mormons in national and international emergencies.

The phenomenal Mormon growth comes largely from a volunteer male missionary force. Usually during their twenties males, unless excused, are expected to devote two years' service to the church at their own expense. Now numbering around 30,000, these volunteers bring in over 80,000 converts yearly.

Mormon worship is nonliturgical. Temple rites bear some resemblance to Masonic ritual (*see* FREEMASONRY). Local congregations hold Sunday morning religious instruction and Sunday evening services with the Lord's Supper (*see* EUCHARIST) and lay preaching. Most branches maintain numerous auxiliary activities.

Bibliography. T. O'Dea, *The Mormons* (1957) remains the best study. On particular topics, see R. Flanders, *Nauvoo: Kingdom on the Mississippi* (1965); M. Hill and J. Allen eds., *Mormonism and American Culture* (1972); S. McMurrin, *Theological Foundations of the Mormon Religion* (1955); S. Taggart, *Mormonism's Negro Policy (1970);* L. J. Arrington and D. Bitton, *The Mormon Experience* (1979); *Dialogue: A Journal of Mormon Thought* (1966-) treats historical and contemporary issues.

C. H. LIPPY

LECTIONARY (Ch). A book containing the prescribed readings from Scripture for the EUCHARIST or, more generally, any table for the reading of Scripture in worship. Christian practice originally derived from the SYNAGOGUE. The readings or lessons are arranged for the church year and may be triennial as well as annual.

For Jewish use of lectionaries *see* JUDAISM §5e.

R. A. GREER

LENT (Ch). The major season of fasting, imitative of the forty-day fast of JESUS (Matt. 4:2, Luke 4:2). While some believe there was such a fast in the third century, Lent has firm attestation only from the fourth century, when it appears as six weeks of fasting before EASTER or before HOLY WEEK. It was adjusted to forty days of actual fasting in most places in the seventh century. Further extensions led to a preparatory "pre-Lent" in the Western church, its Sundays called Septuagesima (seventieth), Sexagesima (sixtieth), and Quinquagesima (fiftieth), all prior to the original Sunday of Quadragesima (fortieth). This preliminary season is now suppressed in most Western churches. *See* CALENDAR, CHRISTIAN; ASH WEDNESDAY.

T. J. TALLEY

LEO I, THE GREAT (Ch; *ca.* 400-461). Pope from 440. Considered one of the four "Fathers of the Church"; the most influential administrator of the early church. Leo helped to establish the universal episcopate of the Roman BISHOP, based on the primacy of PETER and on that of his successors as bishops of ROME. (*See* PAPACY.) He sought to establish a vigorous central government throughout Christendom and to unite Roman law with ecclesiastical procedure under the supervision of the Roman pontiff. He secured from the Emperor Valentinian III the decree of June 6, 445, which formally recognized his jurisdiction over all the western provinces. It said that because of the merits of Peter, the dignity of the city, and the decrees of Nicaea, the rulings of the Roman bishop had the force of law; opposition was tantamount to treason. Leo rebuked the Council of Ephesus (449), which he termed "that Robber Synod," and supported only the doctrinal decisions of the Council of Chalcedon (451), while rejecting its apparent acknowledgment of Byzantine church governance in the East. He demanded liturgical, canonical, and pastoral uniformity and attacked MANICHEISM, PELAGIANISM, and other heresies. The most important document attributed to him is the *Tome to Flavian* (449), also called *Epistola dogmatica.* It precisely and forcefully restated the Christological position of the Latin Church. The Council of Chalcedon accepted it as a standard of orthodoxy.

Bibliography. T. G. Jalland, *The Life and Times of St. Leo the Great* (1941).

H. L. BOND

LEO X (Ch; 1475-1521). Pope from 1513; last of the powerful Renaissance popes and the first of the REFORMATION era. Head of the house of the Medici and patron of humanism and the arts, Leo squandered the church's finances and supported the selling of INDULGENCES to construct ST. PETER'S basilica in ROME, which evoked LUTHER'S protest of 1517. He addressed himself from the start of his PAPACY to three critical problem areas: the joint question of reform and conciliarism; the status of the Papal States; and the need for additional finances. He directed to its conclusion the Fifth Lateran Council (1512-17). The French invasion of Italy under Francis I forced Leo to sign a concordat (1516) which gave the French monarch greater authority over the French church. Leo's troubles subsequently mounted. In 1517 the indulgence controversy erupted. To finance St. Peter's reconstruction, Leo had earlier renewed the indulgence of Julius II and had arranged with Albert of Brandenburg for the preaching of indulgences in the archdioceses of Mainz and Magdeburg. In 1518 Leo ordered Luther silenced and in 1520 condemned him on forty-one counts in the BULL *Exsurge Domine.* The following year he EXCOMMUNICATED Luther and named Henry VIII of England "Defender of the Faith" for his defense of the seven SACRAMENTS.

Bibliography. W. Roscoe, *The Life and Pontificate of Pope Leo X* (1973).

H. L. BOND

LEO XIII (Ch; 1810-1903). Born Gioacchino Vincenzo Pecci at Carpineto (Anagni), Italy. Ordained a PRIEST in 1837; nuncio to Belgium (1843-6), ARCHBISHOP of Perugia (1846-78), and CARDINAL from 1853. Elected pope in 1878 he presided over a period of worldwide ROMAN CATHOLIC growth, writing fifty encyclical letters, including *Rerum Novarum* (1891) on the condition of working classes. He promoted the revival of Thomistic philosophy (*see* THOMAS AQUINAS), opened the Vatican archives to research, and negotiated the end to the conflict between the church and the civil government in Germany, but failed in efforts to persuade French Catholics to support the Third Republic. In the BULL *Apostolicae Curae* (1896) he denied the validity of ANGLICAN priestly orders.

J. HENNESEY

LEWIS, C. S. (Ch; 1898-1963). British literary scholar, teacher, Christian apologist, novelist, and poet. Born in Belfast, Clive Staples Lewis was educated at University College, Oxford. He was lecturer and tutor at Magdalen College, Oxford, from 1925 to 1954, when he accepted the Chair of Medieval and Renaissance English at Cambridge. He held that position until failing health forced his resignation shortly before his death. Among Lewis's religious and ethical works are *The Problem of Pain* (1940); *Miracles* (1947); *Mere Christianity* (1952), a collection of three earlier published essays on the essentials of orthodox Christianity; and *Surprised by Joy: The Shape of My Early Life* (1955), memoirs of his struggle with Christian belief. Lewis's fiction, often embodying Christian allegory in its fantasy, includes a science-fiction trilogy (1938-45); a seven-volume children's story, *The Chronicles of Narnia* (1950-56); *The Great Divorce* (1945), a dream-vision of a trip from Hell to the edge of Heaven; and *The Screwtape Letters* (1942), correspondence between an experienced devil and his "junior tempter" nephew.

Bibliography. R. L. Green and W. Hooper, *C. S. Lewis: A Biography* (1974); P. L. Holmer, *C. S. Lewis: The Shape of His Faith and Thought* (1976); C. S. Kilby, *The Christian World of C. S. Lewis* (1964); W. L. White, *The Image of Man in C. S. Lewis* (1969).

D. J. WHITE

LI lē (Con—Chin.). 1. Ritual, rules of propriety, good form. For CONFUCIUS, the outward expression of goodness (JEN). "A man who is not Good, what can he have to do with ritual?" (Analects III,3). 2. Principle, order; that which governs humans and things and brings order to matter and energy *(ch'i)*. *See* CONFUCIANISM §3.

K. CRIM

LIBERATION THEOLOGY (Ch). International movement most closely associated with Latin America. Proponents interpret Christian faith, especially its political relevance, in light of a Marxist reading of the present social situation. They emphasize God as the Liberator of the oppressed in events such as the Exodus. *See* THEOLOGY, CONTEMPORARY CHRISTIAN §4b.

D. F. OTTATI

LIFE CYCLE RITES. A sequence of ritual complexes by which the successive socially recognized stages in a person's life are terminated and initiated; often called rites of passage, from the title of a seminal book by Van Gennep.

1. **Underlying concepts.** *a) Social status and liminality.* Basic to an understanding of life cycle rites is a grasp of the paired concepts of social status and liminality. A social status is a position in a social system which has well-defined properties, rights, and obligations in relation to others of the same status, to others of different statuses, and to all of reality. As long as a person occupies a given status and properly fills the role associated with it—the expected patterns of belief and action—he or she will be secure through the operation of the *quid pro quo* rules of the system. He or she will also be psychologically secure in the confidence of success in fulfilling the role. But during the passage between statuses—that is, during the time of liminality—persons are both themselves in danger and dangerous to others, since they are "neither fish nor fowl." Many anthropologists have emphasized the uncanniness and the perilousness of entities, including human beings, which do not fit neatly into conventional categories. What this reflects is a view of physiological-social maturation which is superimposed on the gradual natural process in terms of a series of discrete social categories.

b) Types of rites. At each definite transition life cycle observances typically include rites of separation, to ensure proper departure out of the prior status; rites of transition, to ensure safety during the hazardous liminal period; and rites of incorporation, to ensure proper identification with and recognition in the new status. These rites are not always sharply differentiated; they often flow into each other, and simultaneously fulfill two or all three functions at once. But it is crucial that in each case each of the three steps be ritually formalized.

c) Diversity of status inventories. All societies have several different age-linked statuses, and mark passage from one to another; but not all have the same statuses, either in number or in kind. Birth, passage into adulthood, marriage, and DEATH are observed in virtually all societies. But some multiply statuses and mark passages at numerous points in a person's biography: passage from infancy to childhood, from childhood to adolescence, from mature adulthood to elder, and so forth. When the rites are observed separately for each individual, they tend to correspond closely to physiologically marked changes, e.g., in puberty rites. When, on the other hand, they are observed simultaneously for an entire set of persons, there can be considerable discrepancy between the rite marking social passage and the corresponding physical change for many initiates. In some societies persons undergo puberty rituals anywhere from age ten to age twenty, according to the time they were born in relation to the fixed collective time of the ritual.

d) Age grades. Some societies, especially in eastern and central Africa, have developed the life cycle system into a complete structure for society, cutting across the primary kinship system. Thus, all youths born within a certain period of years (often seven, more or less) constitute an age class, and move on up through the successive age grades (corresponding to the socially defined statuses) together. As each age class moves corporately into a given age grade, the class previously occupying that grade moves up a step, until at the top the members of the oldest class move by death into the grade of ancestors. Meanwhile, the next lower class moves up into the grade just vacated, to maintain the complete system. The duties assigned to each grade are complementary, and together form a comprehensive system to meet all the needs of society. The obligations of fellow age-class members to each other transcend all others, even the duties of kinship.

e) Sex differences. Life cycle rites are commonly observed for both males and females, but almost always separately and in different ways. The differences reflect each society's understanding of and ideal for masculinity and femininity, and aim to inculcate these into the persons undergoing the rites. Rites for males are generally more elaborate and more public than those for females, reflecting the common view that male statuses are socially more important than female statuses.

2. **Typical points of passage.** *a) Birth.* Interestingly, there are usually few ritual observances surrounding the process of birth itself; rather, there are often complex rituals during gestation and then in the postnatal period.

i. Prenatal rites. Prenatal rites are usually designed to protect mother and fetus from miscarriage, stillbirth, malformation, and birth complications, the universal fears surrounding the anticipation of birth. These rites are most often TABOOS—on certain foods for mother, father, or both; on sexual intercourse; or on certain other activities thought to be dangerous. There are also not infrequently magical practices of a positive nature designed to protect mother and fetus and to ensure future health and prosperity for the latter. Strangely, even in societies which believe that each child is the REINCARNATION of a specific ancestor, there seem to be few if any rituals overtly relating to the passage from the status of ancestor to the status of infant.

The respective roles of mother and father in prenatal rites usually depend on the society's view of their respective roles in procreation. In matrilineal societies, where the father's biological role may be socially denied, he may be only minimally involved. On the other hand, since even in a patrilineal system the mother's role is unavoidably apparent, she is usually deeply involved in all prenatal rites.

ii. Postnatal rites. Postnatal rites can begin immediately at birth, as with the ceremonial cutting of the umbilical cord (separation from the mother), a ritual bath, or other procedure. Apparently as a psychological defense against the trauma of the frequent death of neonates, many societies postpone the rites of incorporation—naming, CIRCUMCISION, social presentation, christening, etc.—to a time a week or more after birth. The rationale is sometimes made explicit: if the child dies before that time, it was not a real human child, and therefore was not destined to stay; grief is not as profound as if a "real" child had died. If the child "decides to stay," its arrival is officially recognized and it is ritually inducted into family and society in the infant status.

There are also sometimes rituals associated with walking or weaning—the latter often coming at age two or three and representing another point of danger and high mortality.

b) Postchildhood and puberty rites. Though these rites, marking passage from childhood to adolescence and sometimes adulthood, are often called "puberty rites," as we have seen they can occur at a time quite distant from physical puberty for some or most of the initiates. Nevertheless, they are intended to mark the passage to responsible adulthood.

i. Rites of separation. Rites of separation can be, by design, painful and traumatic. They often include genital mutilation (circumcision or subincision for boys, cliteridectomy for girls), scarification or tattooing of the body, chipping or knocking out of teeth, as well as ordeals of various kinds. The rationale is that these trials harden the candidate in preparation for an adult role, and it is usually demanded that there be no outward sign of pain. Anthropologists have discovered an interesting statistical correlation between these painful rites and the following conditions in society: (a) patrilineality, that is, counting descent through the father; (b) polygyny; (c) patrilocality, that is, residence of a couple after marriage near the groom's father's home; (d) prolonged taboo on sexual relations between mother and father after the birth of a child; and (e) having small boys sleep with their mothers. This creates a strong bond between mother and son, and remoteness between father and son; yet the son will have to fulfill his adult role very near his mother. Some scholars have proposed a Freudian explanation: the painful rites in such circumstances are needed to break the emotional bond between mother and son so that the latter can shift his attachment to his father, who then becomes his adult role model.

ii. Rites of transition. Rites of transition often include a period, for the individual or group, of prolonged isolation from family and society. Among some Plains Indian tribes a youth would go into the wilderness on a solitary quest for the spirit vision which defined his identity as an adult. In societies where groups go through the experience together, there are often "bush schools" where distinctive, aberrant patterns of behavior are required, such as a special secret "language." (*See* NATIVE AMERICAN TRIBAL RELIGION §3b.)

iii. Rites of incorporation. Rites of incorporation are often begun during transition days, as when the "bush schools" give extended instruction in society's lore and mores, especially in adult roles. This is often the time when sex education takes place. Incorporation is consummated when the candidates are presented to society in their new status, often complete with new name, new clothes, hairdo, and/or adornment, sometimes new place of residence, and of course new rights and duties. This is typically a time of extensive feasting and celebration.

c) Marriage. Marriage usually takes place some time after the puberty rites, though it may follow immediately. It marks yet another change of status. In many societies there is no status of single adult, so that one passes into full adulthood only by marriage. Rites of separation apply quite differently to the man and the woman, depending on which one is expected to move away from home to the home of the spouse. Rites of transition include the almost universal feasting and dancing. Rites of incorporation include the consummation of the marriage and whatever other ceremonial recognition is accorded the newlyweds. The payment of bridewealth or dowry, when these apply, is involved throughout the process. In some societies the marriage is not considered complete until the birth of the first child.

d) Death rituals. Death is recognized by all societies as the last passage in the normal life cycle, even if there is a belief in reincarnation. The rites may include such things as wailing, a wake (with or without a feast), the funeral, the disposal of the corpse, and mourning. These rites are designed on the one hand to minimize for the dead person the trauma of moving out of the status of the living and to facilitate the passage into the next status—HEAVEN, LIMBO, PURGATORY, ancestorhood, living-dead; and on the other hand to meet the needs of the bereaved. For the dead person there may be propitiation and atoning for his sins, prayers, and the provision of his needs in the next world—food, utensils, money. In some societies, when the dead person was especially important, other persons were sent with him: slaves or servants, wife or wives. (*See* BARDO THODÖL.)

For the bereaved there are rites designed to reconcile them to the loss (comparable to rites of separation) and rites designed to move them by stages back to normal life (comparable to rites of incorporation). The wake and mourning are principally involved here.

In many societies, notably in Africa and Madagascar, rites are prescribed periodically in honor of the dead; these take place, for instance, after one year, two years, five years, and so on. Whatever form they take, their purpose is to maintain for the dead person an active role in the affairs of the family, to keep him happy and to enlist his powers on behalf of the living. (*See* AFRICAN TRADITIONAL RELIGION.) In ROMAN CATHOLICISM the rituals of ALL SOULS DAY fit in here.

3. **Religious transition rites.** Strictly speaking, religious transition rites (e.g. BAPTISM and CONFIRMATION) are not part of this topic. But in a number of societies in which Christianity has been introduced, including the Western world, the strictly Christian initiatory rites have often been assimilated and incorporated into existing life cycle rites or substituted for them. Thus, it became convenient very early to combine pre-Christian postnatal rites with baptism and naming in the christening ritual; then confirmation was added and combined with or substituted for older puberty rites of passage from childhood into responsible pre-adulthood. No doubt the Jewish precedent of CIRCUMCISION and BAR MITZVAH also had their influence. Comparable processes are taking place in the non-Western world. *See also* SAṂSKĀRA.

Bibliography. A. van Gennep, *The Rites of Passage* (1908; ET 1960).

C. R. TABER

LĪLĀ lē´ lä (H—Skt.; lit. "sport," "play"). The idea, stressed by VAIṢṆAVAS, that the creating and controlling of the world by God is like the spontaneous and uncalculating self-expression of a sportsman or an artist. The term first occurs in a refutation of an argument that belief in a personal creator is impossible because persons create only out of a desire for things they do not possess—a desire that cannot exist in God, who lacks nothing (Vedānta Sūtra 2.1.32-33) The SŪTRA replies that creative activity does not always spring from want. Great kings who need nothing engage in sport *(līlā)* solely for the joy of free self-expression. In such spirit the Supreme Person sends forth the worlds, moved by an exuberant creativity inherent in his own nature.

The conception that God acts in sport is paralleled in Vaiṣṇava writings by statements that he intervenes to uphold righteousness or to facilitate the liberation of souls. Between these social understandings and the *līlā* teaching there is tension but not contradiction: *līlā* is not used to suggest that God's acts are frivolous, but that they are disinterested and spontaneous. The *līlā* doctrine continues and extends the ideal of selfless action taught earlier by the BHAGAVAD GĪTĀ.

As an interpretation of the phenomenal world, *līlā* is analogous to MĀYĀ in the ADVAITA system of ŚAṂKARA, but it substitutes a faith that the world is God's self-expression for the view that the world obscures and falsifies the divine nature. The *līlā* cosmology provides a theological ground, not fully exploited by Hindus, for delighting in the world as itself a product of God's delight. A more common contribution of the idea has been assisting believers in accepting loss; all natural processes, dissolution as much as creation, are to be seen as the *līlā* of the Lord, mysterious in nature but not devoid of intelligence and love.

Līlā, "a sport," can refer to any individual act of the deity or his avatars, such as an exploit related in myth. The folk-dramas called *Ramalīlā* and *Kṛṣṇalīlā* are thus named because they reenact the deeds of RĀMA and of KRISHNA. The *līlās* of the AVATARS are the focus of meditations that are especially highly developed in the Krishna cult. Devotees sustain in themselves the ideal sentiment of devotion *(bhakti)* by mental review of Krishna's *līlās*. Such reflections are believed to be pursued most effectively in VṚNDĀVANA, where Krishna performed the greatest of his sports on earth. These earthly sports are called his manifest *(prakaṭa) līlās* because they are open to ordinary human knowledge. But unmanifest *(aprakaṭa) līlās* are being performed by Krishna eternally in the heavenly Vṛndāvana above the earthly place of that name. These celestial *līlās* can be seen with the spiritual eye of inward concentration. Vaiṣṇava books prescribe meditation for each of the eight watches of the day. Their aim is to make the meditator in fact, as well as in imagination, a spectator of the creative sports of the god. In the high wonder and devotion that these visions generate, the goal of BHAKTI HINDUISM is attained.

Bibliography. A. K. Banerjee, "The Philosophy of Divine Leela," *Prabuddha Bharata* XLIX (1944), 275-81, 311-16.

N. HEIN

LILITH lī′ lĭth (Ju—Heb.; lit. "night demon"). In medieval and rabbinic literature, Adam's wife before God created Eve. According to the mystical view of Lilith, she is the queen of all demons; consort of Sammael, the chief demon; strangler of children; and seducer of men, in whose dreams she appears in order to cause the sin of nocturnal pollution. Protective amulets must be used against her.

K. P. BLAND

LIMBO (Ch—Lat. *limbus;* lit. "border, hem of a garment"). In Roman Catholic theology the state and place of the dead who, though excluded from the beatific vision, are not guilty of personal sin. Theologians distinguish between (1) the *limbus patrum* (limbo of the Fathers), in which OT saints remained until the resurrection of Christ; and (2) the *limbus infantium* (limbo of infants), in which persons dying in original sin, but innocent of personal guilt, enjoy full natural happiness.

Bibliography. G. Dyer, *Limbo: Unsettled Question* (1964).

C. WADDELL

LIṄGA lĭng′ŭ (H—Skt.; lit. "sign," more particularly "sign of [the male] sex," most particularly "the phallus of the Hindu god Shiva" or its emblematic representation).

1. Iconic form. In origin, the *liṅga* is a phallic representation; this is clear from one of the earliest stone *liṅgas,* the Guḍimallam *liṅga* (*ca.* second century A.D.), explicitly anthropomorphic. In contemporary worship, however, the *liṅga* is often a smooth oblong with no overt sexual characteristics, and it is definitely not regarded as phallic by many of the devotees who wear it or offer PŪJĀ to it. Many carvings of the *liṅga* depict SHIVA in his anthropomorphic form as well, bursting out of the stone

L. D. Shinn

The Nāga Liṅga is a nonanthropomorphic representation of Shiva.

column. Massive monolithic *liṅgas* in the inner sanctum of many Śaiva temples form a "quality-less" *(nirguṇa)* foil to the baroque detail of the crowd of images in the less holy outer parts of the shrine. "Natural" *liṅgas* (formed of rock or ice, usually in caves) are particularly sacred and often become centers of Śaiva pilgrimage. The *liṅga* is usually surrounded by a base *(pīṭha)* representing the female sexual organ (YONI); it is thus technically an androgynous icon, though it is almost always treated as a purely male symbol, the emblem of the god alone rather than of the god united with his consort.

2. Textual origins. In SANSKRIT texts, the *liṅga* is unequivocally phallic and male. The RIG VEDA seems to refer derisively to "phallic worshipers," a possible slur upon the inhabitants of the INDUS VALLEY CIVILIZATION, where phallic stones as well as ring-stones *(yonis)* have been found. The MAHĀBHĀRATA and PURĀṆAS tell of the first epiphany of the *liṅga:* BRAHMĀ and VISHNU were arguing in the midst of the cosmic ocean, each claiming supremacy, when a pillar of flame appeared between them; Brahmā took the form of a royal goose and flew up, Vishnu the form of a boar and plunged down, but neither could find the beginning or the end of the pillar; then Shiva himself emerged from the *liṅga* and commanded them to worship it. Other myths attribute the origin of *liṅga* worship to the castration of Shiva, either by his own hand in a fit of pique at having been superseded at the time of procreation, or at the hands of a group of sages whose wives he had seduced by dancing with them (*see* NAṬARĀJA §2.).

3. ***Liṅga* worship.** Most devotees of Shiva have small stone or metal emblems of the *liṅga* and *yoni* to which offerings of flowers, coconut, incense, and fruit are made daily; similar offerings are made to *liṅgas* installed in temples or at holy places such as sacred trees or ponds. As the *liṅga* is regarded as a fiery, volatile form of Shiva, water may be poured over it to cool and calm it, or a pot of water with a tiny hole may be arranged so as to drip steadily upon it. Young girls often build *liṅgas* of sand on the banks of a river, in hope of obtaining a fine husband like Shiva. *See* ANDROGYNY.

Bibliography. T. Gopinatha Rao, *Elements of Hindu Iconography* (1914), II, 1, 73-111; *see* O'Flaherty refs. in SHIVA bibliog. W. D. O'FLAHERTY

LIṄGĀYAT lĭng′ ä yät (H—Kannada; lit. "wearer of the liṅga"); also **VĪRAŚAIVA** vī′ rū shī′ vū (H—Skt.; lit. "heroic SHIVA worshiper" [*vīra*—"hero"]). A Hindu Śaiva (*see* ŚAIVISIM) caste-sect of South India. Its four million members wear the LIṄGA from the day of birth, and practice strict vegetarianism. (*See* CASTE; HINDUISM.)

1. **Origin.** Liṅgāyatism was born in the twelfth century A.D. in the Kanarese cultural region of South India. It drew its content informally from local Śaiva, JAINA, and Buddhist schools of thought. Basava (Skt. *vṛishabha,* lit. "bull"), a Śaiva BRAHMIN, is revered as its founding prophet. Metaphorically Basava is related to the bull, which accompanies Shiva in Hindu iconography and temple architecture and which is worshiped in agricultural rituals throughout India. Basava's teachings consisted of short devotional sayings in Kannada known as *vachanas,* which are interpreted by some as illustrating the Hindu *bhakti* attitude of personal service to a high god and to his saintly servants such as Basava. (*See* BHAKTI HINDUISM.) But there persists the original eclecticism of Liṅgāyatism too, e.g., in metaphysics, such as the similarities with Jainism of the Liṅgāyat six-stage philosophy of personal spiritual development, and in behavioral prescriptions, such as the meditative posture common to Buddhism and to Liṅgāyat worship of the personal liṅga. Liṅgāyat, Buddhist, and Jaina traditions are similar also for having drawn adherents mainly from the merchant and farming classes of society, and for having stood historically in symbolic revolt against the religious suzerainty of Brahmin priests.

2. **Scriptures.** The Liṅgāyat canon was limited to the orally preserved *vachanas* of Basava and his contemporaries until the Vijayanagar period of South Indian history (A.D. 1336-1650). In the fifteenth century some Liṅgāyat scholars collected, wrote down, and organized the Kannada *vachanas* into so-called "sermons." Others produced manuals of Liṅgāyat ritual and belief, in Kannada and Sanskrit, including Vedānta-style exegeses (on Brahmanical commentaries on Sanskrit texts) which interpreted the Liṅgāyat religion according to Brahmanical metaphysical systems of qualified or special monism (*see* ADVAITA). Meanwhile, very popular Kannada PURĀṆAS, based on Brahmanical models, narrating the lives and miracles of Liṅgāyat saints, and written in a new vernacular literary style of Kannada, also began to appear. The Liṅgāyat canon has seen another burst of expansion since the nineteenth century, with additional Purāṇas on the lives of nineteenth and twentieth century saints, and a twentieth century revival of interest in collecting and publishing obscure *vachanas,* with or without commentary or English translation.

3. **Social institutions.** The outstanding social institutions are monasteries *(maths* or *maṭhas)* and hereditary family priesthoods *(jangamas).* Traditionally the two have been closely associated, in that each *jangama* priest belongs to a lineage which maintains a liṅga shrine that is thought of as a branch *math* authorized by one of five famous all-India liṅgas. The centers of all-India Hindu pilgrimage for these five liṅgas are considered to be *pithas* ("thrones") for *jagadguru* ("world-master") *jangamas,* whose *maths* bear the title of one of the five legendary GURUS of the *jangamas.* In addition to this social structure of primary and branch *maths* with hereditary priesthood, there are local religious establishments, conceived as being external to society, which are maintained by spiritually meritorious red-robed *virakta* ("passionless") ascetics. These establishments are now also called *maths.* Today the *virakta maths* perform many social service functions, including education at high school and college levels, sponsorship of religious performances and publications, and conduct of human and animal welfare work.

4. **Creed and doctrine.** The Liṅgāyat creed is constituted informally by a six-stage philosophy of personal spiritual development, eight symbols *(aṣṭa-varaṇas)* by which Liṅgāyats differentiate their worship from that of other Śaivas, and the claim for the religious preeminence of Shiva and Basava. Five is a particularly sacred number, being identified with the five legendary founders of the *pitha maths* and the *jangama* lineages. Lacking authoritative doctrine for interpreting their flexible creeds, Liṅgāyats depend on local traditions of their regional culture, on Hindu cultural performances emphasizing the miracles of Shiva and his servants, and on the guidance of their *jangamas.* Interpretation is therefore pliable and can incorporate even Brahminical Epic figures such as the PĀṆḌAVAS, RĀMA, and HANUMĀN in its creedal formulations.

5. **Religious practices.** The life-crisis rituals of birth, naming, menarche, marriage, and death all take place in homes and require the services of the *jangama* family priest, whose feet are worshiped with

water as Hindus do to Shiva. The formal initiation into Liṅgāyatism is performed by an ascetic official at a *math*. Liṅgāyats are buried in a seated meditative posture, and without the common Hindu belief that death pollutes other family members. Virtually all Liṅgāyats observe Hindu calendrical festivals. *Nāga-panchmi* festival ("snake's fifth") appears to be important in establishing the gender identity of prepubertal girls. But most religious fairs and processions emphasize male dancing, athletics, and songs of praise to male gods.

6. **Current trends.** Increasingly large numbers of Liṅgāyats have had Western education. One result is that the social services performed by *viraktas* have made them more the *de facto* religious leaders than the SWAMIS of the *pitha maths*. Another result is that research into the *vachana* component of the Liṅgāyat canon is enjoying a modern revival.

Bibliography. W. C. McCormack, "The Forms of Communication in Vīraśaiva Religion," *Journal of American Folklore*, LXXI (1958); 325-35, and "Lingayats as a Sect," *Journal of the Royal Anthropological Institute*, XCIII, pt. 1 (1963), 59-71; S. C. Nandimaṭh, *A Handbook of Vīraśaivism* (1942); S. C. Nandimath, L. M. A. Menzies, and R. C. Hiremath, eds. and trans., *Śūnyasaṁpādane*, I (1965); A. K. Ramanujan, *Speaking of Siva* (1973). W. C. MCCORMACK

LITANY (Ch). A form of supplication consisting of a series of petitions sung or said by the officiant (traditionally the DEACON) and answered by the people with fixed responses such as "Lord, have mercy," "We beseech thee," "Hear us," and "Deliver us." The form appears to have originated in fourth century Antioch, though it is found about the same time in Jerusalem. From the East it spread rapidly throughout the Christian church. The KYRIE of the Latin MASS is the remnant of a litany introduced into the EUCHARIST at ROME in the fifth century, perhaps the *Deprecatio* of Pope Gelasius I (492-96), the text of which still survives.

Litanies (*ektenai*) remain a prominent part of eucharistic liturgies in the East. They represent the chief way in which the people participate in the LITURGY, much of which takes place hidden from view. In the West litanies were adopted largely for use in processions.

During the time of GREGORY I (d. 604) the Major Litanies were introduced at Rome on St. Mark's Day (April 25) as a substitute for pagan ceremonies observed on that day (the *Robigalia*). They were not connected with the feast, but were supplications for God's blessing on the harvest. They were abolished by the ROMAN CATHOLIC Church in 1969. The Minor Litanies were processions held on the Rogation Days, the three days before the feast of the Ascension. Originally introduced by St. Mamertus of Vienne (*ca.* 470) when his diocese was threatened by volcanic eruptions, they gained currency throughout the West. Used as supplications for deliverance from the barbarians as well as from natural disasters, these litanies were chiefly associated with asking God's blessing upon the crops and were the main feature of the Rogation Days. Though retained by the ANGLICAN CHURCHES, since 1969 the Rogation Days have been replaced in the Roman Catholic Church by devotions which may be used at any time at the discretion of local bishops.

In modern practice several litanies are authorized for use in the Roman Catholic Church, including the Litany of the Saints, the Litany of Loreto (based upon older litanies of the Blessed Virgin), the Litany of the Holy Name, the Litany of the Sacred Heart, and the Litany of St. Joseph. Litanies are widely used in private devotions as well.

Anglican Prayer Books retain the Litany, the original form of which appeared in 1544 for use in processions while England was at war. In composing the Litany Thomas Cranmer drew not only upon the Sarum Rogation Litany, but also upon the Litany of St. John Chrysostom and Luther's Latin Litany of 1529. *See* BOOK OF COMMON PRAYER.

Bibliography. A. Baumstark, *Comparative Liturgy*, 3rd ed. (1958), pp. 74-80; M. H. Shepherd, Jr., *The Oxford American Prayer Book Commentary* (1950). R. A. GREER

LITTLE FLOCK MOVEMENT (Ch). Begun in Foochow, China (1922) as an informal student group for prayer and BIBLE study. Under the influence of WATCHMAN NEE it spread widely, its adherents meeting informally for breaking of bread and in assemblies. It was effectively dissolved after Nee's arrest by the People's Republic. K. KOYAMA

LITURGY, CHRISTIAN (Gr. *leitourgia*—"public work"). During the Roman Empire the upper classes were first expected, and later required, to contribute to municipal life by various "liturgies," which included the display of public games as well as the construction and maintenance of public buildings. In the Septuagint the word is applied to the temple service, and came to be used by Christians to refer to any act of public worship. While that meaning has been retained, the word has a specific reference to the EUCHARIST, for which it is the usual term in the East. More narrowly, "liturgy" can refer to the written text of a eucharistic service. It would appear that "liturgy" is becoming a more common term for the Eucharist in Western Christianity. It is so used in the rubrics for the proposed BOOK OF COMMON PRAYER of the American Episcopal Church, as well as in the title "Proper Liturgies for Special Days," which introduces observances for ASH WEDNESDAY, PALM SUNDAY, MAUNDY THURSDAY, GOOD FRIDAY, Holy Saturday, and the Great Vigil of EASTER, all of which are normally integrated with the Eucharist. Liturgy will be taken here to mean the Eucharist and particularly the way the Eucharist has been celebrated.

1. **Origins.** While our evidence is extremely fragmentary, there is no reason to doubt that a

eucharistic liturgy existed in the church from the beginning. The church felt obliged to "do this in remembrance of " Christ (I Cor. 11:24-5). Whether the Last Supper was a PASSOVER meal, as the Synoptic Gospels suppose, or was before Passover, as John's Gospel argues, it had Paschal associations which carried over into the celebration of the Eucharist and the creation of a Christian Passover celebrating Christ's death and resurrection as a new Exodus and new creation. BAPTISM was central to the Christian Passover, as is evident in I Peter, which presupposes a liturgical ceremony uniting Exodus themes with Christ's death and resurrection. Details are uncertain, but it is reasonably clear that many features of the earliest liturgy reflect the Christianized Passover, including the borrowing of Jewish customs. Melito of Sardis' *On the Pascha* (*ca.* 180) demonstrates the persistence of Passover themes, and in Hippolytus' *Apostolic Tradition* (*ca.* 215) we find them integrated with an Easter liturgy of baptism and the Eucharist.

From another point of view the earliest liturgies were influenced by the church's table fellowship, itself deriving from Jewish customs pertaining both to family meals and to meals including a wider fellowship. Even in NT passages where the Passover theme is prominent, it is not forgotten that the context of the liturgy is a meal. The words of institution (Matt. 26:26-28; Mark 14:22-24; Luke 22:17-20; I Cor. 11:24-26) reflect the view that Jesus' words over the bread and wine (the cup of blessing, I Cor. 10:16) were said at specific points during a Passover meal, and that the cup was the one partaken of after supper. More generally, we find references in Acts 2:42, 46 and 20:7 to "the breaking of bread" as a central act of Christian fellowship. I Cor. 11:17-34 allows us to suppose that the meal of fellowship and the Eucharist were united in the earliest church. Even when abuses such as those Paul describes obliged the church to separate the liturgy from the meal (or agape, "love feast"), the impact of customs attached to the meal itself persisted. Jewish blessings and prayers associated with special meals influenced the earliest liturgical forms, for example, eucharistic prayers in the Didache (*ca.* 100).

A third influence on the earliest liturgy was that of Jewish SYNAGOGUE worship. There is no reason to doubt the evidence of Acts that Christians continued to worship in the synagogues until they were excluded toward the end of the first century. When rabbinic Judaism and Christianity began to go separate ways after the destruction of Jerusalem and the Temple in A.D. 70, the Jewish Christians took with them the practices of the synagogue. Justin Martyr (*ca.* 155) tells us that the liturgy begins with scriptural readings, a homily, and prayers. This "liturgy of the word" was almost certainly adapted from synagogue worship.

2. Early development. We know that early in the second century the liturgy had been disengaged from the common meal. One piece of evidence for this is to be found in Pliny the Younger's letter to Trajan, in which he describes the Christian custom of assembling on a fixed day before dawn to sing hymns to Christ as a god and then meeting in the evening for a meal. It is usually assumed that the first assembly was for the liturgy, now celebrated in the early morning, the time of Christ's resurrection, and that the meal was the community agape. This is certainly the pattern that obtains later, and the agape meals faded in importance until by Augustine's time (d. 430) they were little more than charitable meals.

The following sketch of the liturgy early in the second century emerges. Christians would assemble early Sunday morning, usually in a private home. No special place was necessary, but the house church found at Dura-Europos on the Euphrates (third century) as well as the remnants of house churches in Rome show that houses were adapted to Christian worship. Occasionally we may suppose the owner of the house was a Christian, but more often it must have been a master or mistress kindly disposed toward a Christian slave or freedman in the household. The first part of the liturgy consisted of the "liturgy of the word" described above. The second part must have followed the actions of Jesus at the Last Supper. Bread and wine were taken and offered; thanks was given; the bread was broken; and the assembly partook of the bread and wine. This fundamental double pattern has persisted in all liturgies. As we know from Hippolytus (*ca.* 215), little else was fixed. The celebrant of the Eucharist was free to compose his own thanksgiving, and there was an extempore character to the whole of the liturgy.

3. Hippolytus and the liturgy of the Great Church. By the third century scattered churches with divergent beliefs and practices were forged into a body united under one apostolic faith. Scripture and tradition bore witness to the message of the apostles, and a threefold ministry acted as its guardian. (*See* APOSTOLIC SUCCESSION; CLERGY, CHRISTIAN.) This we learn from Irenaeus (d. *ca.* 200), who emphasizes the liturgy of the church as a source of unity and of constant renewal of the apostolic faith. Because of this emphasis, although liturgical forms together with theology and rules of faith continue to be fluid, a tendency to fix liturgical forms began to develop.

Our knowledge of the eucharistic liturgy rests largely upon the *Apostolic Tradition* (*ca.* 215), preserved as the Egyptian Church Order in Ethiopic, Coptic, and Arabic versions and in Latin fragments, and identified as the lost treatise of Hippolytus by Dom Hugh Connolly (1916) and E. Schwartz (1910). Hippolytus had been forgotten because of his schismatic activity and because he wrote in Greek. A conservative rigorist, he was an opponent of the monarchians and of Popes Zephyrinus (197-217) and Callistus (217-22). He apparently set himself up as a schismatic pope at the election of Callistus in 217. Together with Pope Pontianus he was exiled to Sardinia during the persecution of Christians in 235.

Since his body was brought to Rome for burial by the church, it is likely that he was reconciled to Pontianus before his death.

These details suggest that Hippolytus was concerned to set forth the ancient and traditional liturgy in his *Apostolic Tradition.* The first part of the work describes the consecration of a BISHOP and goes on to give the eucharistic prayer used by him. It begins with the SURSUM CORDA, continues with a narrative of the INCARNATION culminating in the words of institution, and concludes with an invocation of the HOLY SPIRIT. The second part is concerned with the catechumenate and baptism. The Easter baptismal Eucharist is mentioned, and we learn that in addition to the bread and wine the newly baptized received cups of milk and honey and of water, symbolizing their entrance through baptism into the true promised land. All these details are set in the framework sketched above. One surprising feature of Hippolytus' eucharistic prayer is the absence of any reference to the OT and, particularly, the omission of the SANCTUS. It is difficult to believe that such a canon was absent in the church. If Jungmann's reasonable suggestion be followed, we may suppose that three sorts of prayers were used—one Christocentric like the example in Hippolytus, one oriented toward the OT and salvation history, and one employing Hellenistic forms such as those found later in Serapion's canon. This view is consistent with our general knowledge of the period. The tendency toward fixing the liturgical forms is balanced by a variety of forms and some retention of the earlier freedom given the celebrant.

4. **Alexandria and Antioch before Constantine.** The tendency toward fixed forms noted in Hippolytus is visibly stronger a century later. As the church grew, regulation became increasingly necessary, and this was effective only if enforced in regional jurisdictions. The divisions of the imperial church into areas ruled by PATRIARCHS in Alexandria, Antioch, Jerusalem, Constantinople, and Rome provided the means for this enforcement.

The first stage is reflected in an early example of Egyptian liturgies, the *Euchologion* of Serapion, bishop of Thmuis in Egypt from 339. A friend of ATHANASIUS and ANTONY, Serapion apparently designed this work to regularize the liturgy in his diocese. Its important features include use of theological terms, elaborate Greek rhetoric and the mixture of prayers into the narrative sections of the canon.

The Clementine liturgy developed in similar manner. The *Apostolic Constitutions,* traditionally ascribed to Clement I (*ca.* 96), is a late fourth century collection of ecclesiastical rules and orders; Book VIII includes the Clementine liturgy, in reality a version of the liturgy of Antioch from the early fourth century. The emphasis in the liturgy, as in its successor the liturgy of St. John Chrysostom, is on a narrative of the salvation history. A definite epiclesis, or invocation of the Spirit, is included.

5. **The classical ancient liturgies.** In the fourth and fifth centuries the liturgy was for the most part regularized in the patriarchal centers. The Latin MASS was established in ROME. In Alexandria the liturgy of St. Mark predominated; in Antioch, the liturgy of St. James, ascribed traditionally to the brother of the Lord. This liturgy can be connected with Cyril of Jerusalem (d. 386) and the important liturgical developments in Jerusalem at that time. Since it was used in Syriac translation by the MONOPHYSITE JACOBITES after 451, it must be no later than the fifth century. In Constantinople two liturgies came into use. The liturgy of St. Basil as we now know it derives from liturgical reforms made by BASIL THE GREAT (d. 379), whose work underlies the liturgy; the earliest manuscript is ninth century. Somewhat later the liturgy of St. John Chrysostom, of obscure origins, was dominant in Constantinople. To these four Greek liturgies must be added the Syriac liturgy of Addai and Mari, composed *ca.* 200 for the Syriac-speaking Church of Edessa, and adopted in modified form by NESTORIANISM when it took over the Syriac Church in the Persian Empire toward the end of the fifth century. It remains the normal liturgy of Nestorian Christians.

Together with the establishment of the Latin mass and the above liturgies, there went the development of the liturgical year. (*See* CALENDAR, CHRISTIAN.) Seasonal variations and special celebrations dictated the use made of the liturgies. Easter, of course, was the focus of the church year for all of Christendom, in spite of disputes over the date of its observance. The HOLY WEEK liturgies of the fourth century Jerusalem Church spread throughout the church, e. g. the Palm Sunday procession and the veneration of the cross. The period of fasting before Easter was variously observed. Following Easter the ASCENSION and PENTECOST were celebrated as early as the fourth century. CHRISTMAS (December 25) was first observed in the West in the fourth century and only gradually replaced the EPIPHANY (January 6) as the major feast in the East. The East has never given Christmas the importance attached to it by the West; the ARMENIAN Church still celebrates January 6 as the Nativity of Christ.

6. **Later developments.** In the West the Roman mass gradually achieved supremacy over other liturgies despite the survival of some Gallic rites (*see* MASS §1). In the East a similar development attaches to the liturgy of St. John Chrysostom. By the thirteenth century it had supplanted the liturgies of St. Mark and St. James. In Eastern ORTHODOX CHURCHES it is still the usual rite, replaced only on certain occasions by the liturgy of St. Basil and the liturgy of the Presanctified. But the picture in the East is far more complex because of schisms resulting from fifth century Christological controversies. After the councils of Ephesus (431) and Chalcedon (451) the

Nestorians migrated to Persia, where they adopted a modified form of the Syriac liturgy of Addai and Mari. After Chalcedon the Jacobite monophysites adopted a Syriac version of the liturgy of St. James, while the Egyptian monophysites used a Coptic version of the liturgy of St. Mark. The Ethiopic Church still uses the liturgy of St. Mark; the Arabic and Armenian Churches use vernacular versions of the Byzantine or Constantinopolitan liturgy. The rough outline just given conceals a great many complications of detail.

In the West the most radical liturgical development took place at the REFORMATION. The Protestant churches sought to replace the Latin mass with their own liturgies. In part this was a protest against the mass, with its doctrines of sacrifice and TRANSUBSTANTIATION and the practice of withholding the cup from the laity. In part it was an attempt to recover a scriptural and primitive form of the liturgy. LUTHER published his *Deutsche Messe* in 1526. The year before, ZWINGLI had published his *Action or Use of the Lord's Supper* in Zurich. In Strassburg BUCER produced his *Psalter, with Complete Church Practice* in 1539. Calvin's *The Form of Church Prayers* came into use in Geneva in 1542. The First English Prayer Book (*see* BOOK OF COMMON PRAYER) of Edward VI was issued in 1549; the Second, in 1552. Puritan books were issued in the sixteenth and seventeenth centuries in England, the most important of which was the *Westminster Directory* of 1644. This list is far from complete, but points out several of the basic liturgies which influenced later developments, particularly in the LUTHERAN, REFORMED, and ANGLICAN traditions.

In modern times the most significant factor in liturgical change has been the Liturgical Movement. This was essentially a revival in the Roman Catholic Church designed to increase congregational participation in worship and to restore the liturgy as practiced in the Middle Ages. Pope Pius X's pronouncements regarding church music (1903) were important. The movement took hold in BENEDICTINE monasteries, in particular Solemnes in France and Marialaach in Germany. It spread to parish and mission life in the Roman Catholic Church and resulted in the liturgical directions of the Second VATICAN COUNCIL, culminating in the new MISSAL of 1970. The Liturgical Movement had an impact on the Anglican Churches, where it reinforced a ritualist revival that followed the nineteenth century Oxford Movement. And it has influenced liturgical revision in many other Protestant churches, resulting in increased emphasis on the Eucharist and the ancient traditions associated with it, as well as upon the congregational aspect of worship.

Bibliography. A. Baumstark, *Comparative Liturgy,* 3rd ed. (1958); F. E. Brightman, *Liturgies Eastern and Western. I. Eastern Liturgies* (1896); F. Cabrol and H. Leclercq, eds., *Dictionnaire d'archéologie Chrétienne et de liturgie,* 15 vols. (1907-53); J. A. Jungmann, *Missarum Sollemnia,* 2 vols., 4th ed. (1958); J. Quasten, ed., *Monumenta Eucharistica et Liturgica Vetustissima* (1935); B. Thompson, *Liturgies of the Western Church* (1961).

R. A. GREER

LITURGY, JEWISH. *See* JUDAISM §5.

LIVINGSTONE, DAVID (Ch; 1813-1873). Scottish explorer and medical missionary in Africa. His early work as a Christian missionary, interested in and sympathetic to the African peoples, was an inspiration to many in Europe, and was responsible for much of the interest in MISSIONS in Victorian England.

R. BULLARD

LOGOS lô´ gôs (Ch—Gr.). In the NT (John 1:1, 14) translated as "word," but equivalent to no single English term. Its importance lies in its use as a technical term in Greek metaphysical thought from the sixth century B.C. until the third century A.D., and in its appropriation by both Jewish and Christian thinkers.

1. Greek philosophy. According to Heraclitus (540-480 B.C.) the basic clue to the nature of reality is to be found in the phenomenon of change. However, the phenomenological flux that is perceptible in the universe at the level of natural phenomena operates according to a principle that limits and restrains the emergence of chaos as ultimate reality. Heraclitus used the term "logos" (principle of order) to identify this law. He seems to have assumed that the principle is inherent in the process itself.

Heraclitus' hypothesis provided a point of reference for later Greek thinkers. According to leading Stoic thinkers (Zeno, Epictetus, Marcus Aurelius), logos is not only the regulative principle in the process of change, but it is Being itself as logos which orders and regulates phenomenal change. Logos is both universal mind or reason *(endithetos)* and that which comes to expression as word or deed *(prophorikos).* Consequently, human rationality both participates in and reflects this universal logos and human nature constitutes the ground and norm for ethical reflection and action.

2. Judaism and Christianity. PHILO (d. *ca.* A.D. 50), a Jewish Alexandrian philosopher, used logos as the vehicle for communicating Jewish religious ideas to his Hellenistic contemporaries. However, the tension between the rationally conceived logos (Greek) and the Jewish concept of the "word" of God resulted in inconsistencies in Philo's use of the term. At the same time, his work provided a significant heritage for later Christian writers who confronted the task of communicating in Hellenistic terms.

Christian appropriation of the logos tradition is explicit in the prologue to the Fourth Gospel (John 1:1-18). The author identifies JESUS as the divine logos (1:3) who is both creator and revealer (1:3-4, 9). Other NT passages reflect the logos tradition without explicit use of the term itself (Col. 1:15-19; Phil. 2:5-9). During the first four centuries of Christian history the logos motif provided an effective vehicle for expression of Christian thought in contemporary patterns of communication, as well as for formulation of the Christian Christological confession. Even in modern times the logos pattern and structure of thought is often assumed in significant theological systems (P. TILLICH).

Bibliography. H. Kleinknecht, "Lego," *TDNT,* IV, 69-136; W. Kelber, *Die Logoslehre von Heraklit bis Origenes* (1958). R. C. BRIGGS

LOHAN lō hän´ (B—Chin.). In MAHĀYĀNA Buddhism the disciples of ŚAKYAMUNI BUDDHA, popularly regarded as representing the solitary way of a THERAVĀDA monk. The word is derived from the SANSKRIT term ARHANT and was adapted into Chinese as *a-lo-han,* later shortened to *lohan.* In Mahāyāna the *arhants* yielded their position as the ideal followers of Buddhist DHARMA to the BODHISATTVAS, but they remained an important feature of iconography and popular piety.

1. **The devaluing of the *arhant.*** The LOTUS SŪTRA teaches that while it has been thought that there are three ways of salvation—the bodhisattva, who aims at salvation for self and for others; the Pratyeka Buddha who aims at salvation for self by his own efforts (*see* BUDDHA, GENERAL CONCEPTS OF); and the *śrāvaka* (hearer), who aims to achieve salvation by becoming an *arhant*—there is in reality only one way. The latter two must abandon their way for the way of the bodhisattva. The "hearers" think that the state of *arhant* is rest, but it is merely temporary repose.

In Chinese Buddhism this resulted in a tendency to regard Lohans as misguided in their search, selfish, seeking to save only themselves. As a result, many paintings and sculptures of Lohans show them as not merely human but grotesque. The great monk artist Kuan-Hsiu (d. 912) created a masterful series of Lohan portraits on silk, which have survived only in copies and through stone carvings based on his portraits. He showed sixteen Lohans with their features distorted by old age and the loneliness of their quest. Their eyebrows hang down to their knees, only a few teeth remain in their gums, there are strange protuberances on their heads, and their eyes bulge from their sockets, staring blankly ahead. The contrast to the serene beauty of images of AMIDA Buddha and the bodhisattva AVALOKITEŚVARA is complete.

2. **Protectors of the law (dharma).** At the same time another development gave the Lohans a more positive role, that of protectors of the Buddhist law. According to one tradition, four great Lohans postponed their entry into NIRVANA to remain in the world until the advent of MAITREYA, the future Buddha. Two of the four, Piṇḍola and Rāhula, assumed especial prominence. Rāhula was the son of GAUTAMA Buddha himself and patron saint of novices, and Piṇḍola a close follower of Buddha. On one occasion Piṇḍola, in his haste to join a party given by

Courtesy of the Smithsonian Institution, Freer Gallery of Art, Washington, D. C.

Lohans doing their laundry, Chinese hanging scroll by Lin T'ing-Kuei (Sung Dynasty, 12th century)

the Buddha, carelessly flew through the air dragging a mountain behind him. This sight so frightened a pregnant woman that she had a miscarriage. As punishment, Piṇḍola was condemned to stay in the world until Maitreya comes. But popular piety, untroubled by inconsistencies, turned this into something positive. Piṇḍola was one who had seen the Buddha and yet remained in the world, and a cult of Piṇḍola developed in China.

3. **The cult of the Lohans.** During the unsettled times between the fall of the Han dynasty in A.D. 220 and the rise of the T'ang in 618, there were many wandering monks from India and Central Asia. The pilgrim HSÜAN-TSANG tells of Lohans going about in the guise of wandering monks, and these non-Chinese figures may have provided models for the artists. In any case, throughout China, Korea, and Japan Lohans have facial features marking them as having come from South Asia or the Middle East. In many cases they came to be regarded as new forms of local genii or humans who resembled demigods. T'ien T'ai Mountain, origin of the TENDAI sect of Buddhism, became the Mt. Olympus of the cult of Lohans. A twelfth century painting by the monk Chou Chi-ch'ang, now in the Freer Gallery, Washington, D.C., shows the famous rock bridge at Mt. T'ien T'ai. A

humble monk stands timidly before a rock that blocks his path over the bridge to the heavenly realm of the Lohans and their palaces. Legend tells that the monk's faith moved the rock and gained entrance for him.

4. **Iconography.** The cult eventually included five hundred Lohans, depicting all that these guardian saints were to be and to do until Maitreya comes. A painting in the Freer by Lin T'ing-kuei, another twelfth century monk, shows five Lohans doing their own laundry, a mundane sign that the way of the *arhant* did not lead to Nirvana (*see* illustration). All five hundred are depicted in life-size statues in animated, cheerful poses in a temple in Jehol, Manchurian capital of the Ch'ing dynasty (1644-1910). The five hundred are also portrayed on a handscroll in the Cleveland museum. Paintings of Lohans continued to be popular feature of temples. In 1756 the Ch'ien Lung Emperor (reigned 1736-96) studied Kuan-Hsiu's paintings and ordered copies made in stone. At the Horyu-ji temple in Japan there are dry clay statues of Lohans mourning the death of Buddha, and in Korea's Sŭkkul-am, bas-reliefs of Lohans and bodhisattvas line the cave walls around the central image of Buddha. Throughout the Far East images are to be seen that depict the Buddha in the center with a bodhisattva next to him on either side, each flanked by a Lohan. (*See* Art and Architecture, Buddhist.)

Bibliography. S. Hedin, *Jehol, City of Emperors* (1933); L. Hurvitz, trans., *Scripture of the Lotus Blossom of the Fine Dharma* (1976); W. Fong, *The Lohans and a Bridge to Heaven* (1958); S. Levi and E. Chavannes, "Les seize arhat protecteurs de la Loi," *Journal Asiatique* (1916), pp. 5-50, 189-304; G. Pommeranz-Liedtke, ed., *Guan Hsiu: Die Sechzehn Lohans* (1961).

K. Crim

LOISY, ALFRED lwä zē′ (Ch; 1857-1940). French biblical scholar, leader in the Modernist movement. Ordained a Roman Catholic priest in 1879, he taught at the Catholic Institute of Paris until dismissed in 1893 for writings on the development of the OT canon and the historicity of Genesis. Five of his books were placed on the Index in 1903 and he was Excommunicated in 1908. J. Hennesey

LOLLARDS (Ch). Name given to the followers of John Wycliffe (1330-84), and later used for other English nonconformists. By 1420 Lollardy was primarily a lower class phenomenon which virtually disappeared after fifty years of persecution. The Lollards emphasized individual interpretation of the Bible and attacked clerical celibacy, Transubstantiation, and papal power.

Bibliography. K. B. McFarlane, *John Wycliffe and the Beginnings of English Nonconformity* (1952).

R. L. Harrison

LORD'S PRAYER (Ch). The prayer that Christian tradition holds Jesus taught his disciples, found in the NT in the Sermon on the Mount (Matt. 6:9-13) and in Luke 11:2-4. The two versions differ and are probably distinct liturgical uses reflecting Aramaic originals. It is related to traditional Jewish prayers such as the Eighteen Benedictions (*see* Amidah), but also bears the stamp of Jesus' teaching concerning the Kingdom of God. It is usual to divide the prayer into two sections, one concerned with God's glorification and the other with human needs. Matthew's version was the one used liturgically even in the ancient church, and it appears with the traditional concluding doxology as early as the Didache (*ca.* 100). Important from antiquity, it took a regular place in all forms of Christian worship and is a fixed part of all Christian Eucharistic Liturgies.

Bibliography. J. Jeremias, *The Prayers of Jesus* (1967) and *The Lord's Prayer* (1964); E. Lohmeyer, *"Our Father"* (1966).

R. A. Greer

LORD'S PRAYER

Our Father, who art in heaven, hallowed be Thy name; Thy kingdom come; Thy will be done on earth as it is in heaven. Give us this day our daily bread; and forgive us our trespasses as we forgive them that trespass against us. And lead us not into temptation. But deliver us from evil. Amen.

Missal (St. Andrew Daily Missal, 1962)

Our Father, who art in heaven, Hallowed be thy Name. Thy kingdom come. Thy will be done, On earth as it is in heaven. Give us this day our daily bread. And forgive us our trespasses, As we forgive those who trespass against us. And lead us not into temptation, But deliver us from evil. For thine is the kingdom, and the power, and the glory, for ever and ever. Amen.

Book of Common Prayer (1928)

Our Father which art in heaven, Hallowed be thy name. Thy kingdom come. Thy will be done in earth as it is in heaven. Give us this day our daily bread. And forgive us our debts, as we forgive our debtors. And lead us not into temptation, but deliver us from evil: For thine is the kingdom, and the power, and the glory, for ever. Amen.

Matt. 6:9-13, KJV

Our Father which art in heaven, Hallowed be thy name. Thy kingdom come. Thy will be done, as in heaven, so in earth. Give us day by day our daily bread. And forgive us our sins; for we also forgive every one that is indebted to us. And lead us not into temptation; but deliver us from evil.

Luke 11:2-4, KJV

LORD'S SUPPER (Ch). See Eucharist.

LOTUS POSTURE (PADMĀSANA) pŭd′ mä sŭ′ nŭ (H & B—Skt.). Most popular meditative posture of Asia, originating in India; the body is immobilized by sitting with the back erect, feet drawn up on opposite thighs, and hands in a variety of possible Mudrās or gestures, as may be observed in many depictions of Shiva and the Buddha.

C. W. Edwards

LOTUS SŪTRA [SADDHARMAPUṆḌARĪKASUTRA sŭd där′ mŭ pōōn dä rē′ kə sōō′ trə (B—Skt.; lit. "scripture of the white lotus of the true dharma")]. One of the most beloved scriptures of MAHĀYĀNA Buddhism.

1. **History.** The history of the Buddhist canon is one of proliferation. What began with a bare catalogue of prohibitions, aimed at monks, became in the course of time the threefold PALI CANON *(tripiṭaka)*. The early Mahāyāna movement devised its own scriptures, each of them apparently designed to replace the entire canon. However, they too proliferated, smaller ones being frequently appended to larger ones. Like all other Buddhist scriptures, the Lotus Sūtra was transmitted orally for some time before it was committed to writing. By then it consisted of two layers of text, an older one in verse and a later one in prose. The verse passages show evidence of having been adapted into SANSKRIT from an original form in Prākit, a vernacular closely related to Sanskrit. The prose sections regularly precede the verse passages, but probably originated as commentary on the verse. Toward the end of the scripture there are chapters that must originally have existed separately, since they have no obvious connection to the rest of the work.

By the time the Lotus Sūtra made its appearance, salvation was imagined to be of three kinds: that of the disciple *(śrāvaka)* who owes his salvation to the Buddha but who does nothing for anyone else (*see* ARHANT; LOHAN); that of the practitioner (Pratyeka Buddha) who achieves it without help, but who likewise helps no one else; and that of the Buddha, who in this incarnation is no one's pupil but who exerts himself to save the world (*see* BODHISATTVA; BUDDHA, GENERAL CONCEPTS OF). The Lotus Sūtra says that the first two do not, in fact, exist. The Buddha in earlier ages preached their existence merely to make the minds of his listeners more accepting of what was to be his ultimate doctrine. It also says that the Buddha, as commonly regarded among men, is merely a manifestation of the real Buddha (DHARMAKĀYA, though the word is not used in that sense in the scripture itself).

2. **Translations.** The Sanskrit text was translated once into Tibetan and six times into Chinese, the earliest dating from A.D. 225. More recently it has been translated into French by Burnouf and into English by H. Kern, both from the Sanskrit, and several times into English from the best known of the Chinese versions, that of KUMĀRAJĪVA. The Sanskrit text which Kumārajīva translated differed in significant respects from that which exists today. At times he transliterated NIRVANA, and at other times he translated it as "extinction." Hurvitz in his translation follows Kumārajīva's usage.

3. **Contents.** (1) As the scene opens, the Buddha has just entered a state of concentration (SAMĀDHI). He emits from between his brows a ray of light that illuminates the entire universe. The bodhisattva

The Fogg Museum, Kimiko and John Powers Collection; photo by O. E. Nelson

The appearance of the bodhisattva Samantabhadra before a monk reading the Lotus Sūtra

MAÑJUŚRĪ, asked by another bodhisattva, MAITREYA, what is the cause of this, replies that the Buddha is indicating that he is about to preach the Lotus Sūtra.

(2) Emerging from his concentration, the Buddha tells his listeners that there is only one path to salvation, not three, and that every Buddha who makes his appearance in the world does so for the sole purpose of teaching this truth.

(3) The Buddha now prophesies to his disciple Śāriputra (SĀRIPUTTA) the latter's future attainment of Buddhahood. Śāriputra, though encouraged by this prophecy, still wishes to know why, if there are not three paths to salvation, the Buddha has so often preached their existence. The Buddha replies with a parable. A rich man had a large house with only one entrance. One day the house caught fire, and the man's many children, heedless of the fire, continued to play in the house. Their father called to them that the house was afire, and that they would perish in the flames if they did not come out. The children, not knowing the meaning of "fire" or "perish," continued to play. The man called out once more, "Come out, children, and I will give you ox-drawn carriages, goat-drawn carriages, and deer-drawn carriages!" Tempted by the desire for new playthings, the children left the burning house, only to find a single ox-drawn carriage awaiting them. Asked whether the

father can be rightly accused of having deceived his children, Śāriputra says that he cannot, since he was merely employing a device to save their lives. Just so, says the Buddha. The world is a great house afire with the flame of passion. When taught the way to Buddhahood, the beings, not understanding what is meant, remain in the trap of their passions. Then the Buddha, in order to rescue them, devises a scheme: the doctrine of the three paths to salvation. Just as the father cannot be accused of deceiving his children, so the Buddha cannot be accused of deceiving the beings with this doctrine, although, in the ultimate sense, the doctrine is not true.

(4) Upon hearing the Buddha's announcement that Śāriputra shall one day become a Buddha, several other disciples express amazement. One of them, Mahākāśyapa, expresses their feelings in this parable: A father and son parted company while the son was still a very young man. In the course of time the father became very rich, while the son became a beggar. Once, during the course of his wanderings, he happened to come to his father's palatial home. The father, at once recognizing him, had him brought into his presence. This only frightened the poor man, and the father let him go. Then he sent two men to ask the beggar whether he wished to do menial labor on the estate. The beggar consented, and worked in this way for many years. One day the rich man told the beggar that, in view of his many years of conscientious service, he would reward him by placing him in charge of all his possessions. After several more years had passed, the rich man gathered his entire household and clan and told them that the beggar was his son, from whom he had been parted many years before, and that he was now reclaiming him and declaring him heir of all his possessions. When the beggar heard this, he was amazed, thinking that he had received something quite unexpected. Just so, says Mahākāśyapa, is the disciple *(śrāvaka)* who is headed for the goal of becoming an *arhant* when told by the Buddha that Buddhahood also is his goal.

(5) The Buddha explains further that Buddhahood is the only goal of Buddhism, and that Nirvana, if properly understood, is only another name for Buddhahood itself. He further tells his listeners that the ordinary fellow is like a man born blind, the Hīnayāna practitioner like a formerly blind man whose blindness has been cured, the Mahāyāna practitioner like a worldling who has acquired powers out of the ordinary.

(6) The Buddha prophesies future Buddhahood for four other listeners.

(7) The Buddha tells the story of his career in a previous era, concluding with a parable: A guide was leading a group of travelers to a spot where a treasure was buried. On the way the travelers grew weary, and some spoke of turning back. The guide, accordingly, conjured up an apparent city on the way, and successfully urged his companions to rest and refresh themselves there. When they had done so, they went on and reached the treasure. Then the guide told them that the city they had seen had been illusory, and he had conjured it up for the purpose of conquering their discouragement. Just so, says the Buddha, are the beings. They tire quickly of the quest for salvation, and the Buddha conjures up imaginary forms of salvation for them midway.

(8) The Buddha preaches future Buddhahood to more disciples, who relate a parable: A person sewed a jewel into one corner of his friend's garment. The friend, not aware of this, made no attempt to use the jewel even when in various straits. Then the man who had sewed it into the garment pointed it out to him, thus enabling him to get out of his difficulties. Just so, say the disciples, is the Buddha. He offers ultimate salvation to the beings, but they, unaware of it, do not avail themselves of it. The *arhant,* thinking he has attained Nirvana, receives an unexpected favor when the Buddha points out to him the availability of a higher form of salvation.

(9) More prophecies of future Buddhahood.

(10) The Buddha now tells his listeners of the merit that awaits those who show proper veneration to the Lotus Sūtra.

(11) An immense reliquary arises out of the earth, and the Buddha says that it contains the body of a Buddha named Prabhūtaratna, who in a previous age preached the Lotus Sūtra. After entering Nirvana, he vowed to produce his reliquary wherever and whenever the Lotus Sūtra should be preached. Then the reliquary opens up, and Prabhūtaratna, seated within it, offers half his seat to the Buddha. A number of beings salute both Buddhas.

The Buddha says, "In a former age, I was a king. A seer preached the Lotus Sūtra to me, thus enabling me to gain salvation. That seer is now my cousin Devadatta. In time to come, he shall himself be a Buddha, Devarāja by name. Anyone who hears what I have said about Devadatta and believes it shall himself gain salvation." The bodhisattva Prajñākūṭa then asks Mañjuśrī how many beings he has converted, and Mañjuśrī tells him, adding that the most distinguished was the daughter of the Nāga (snake-like demigod) king Sāgara. Prajñākūṭa protests, saying that, as woman's body is filthy, no woman could become a Buddha. The *nāga* king's daughter instantly turned into a man, performed the necessary practices, and attained Buddhahood.

(12) More prophecies of future Buddhahood, and promises on the part of sundry beings to propagate the Lotus Sūtra diligently.

(13) The four *sukhavihāras,* i.e., activities in which the bodhisattva feels perfectly at home.

(14) Countless bodhisattvas come from all over the universe to pay homage to the Buddha and to receive his commission to propagate the Lotus Sūtra. The Buddha explains that the number of bodhisattvas

whom he has so commissioned is incalculable. Maitreya then asks how that could have been possible in the short space of the Buddha's preaching career.

(15) The Buddha replies that the commonly accepted notions about the Buddha's lifespan and teaching career have no ultimate validity, that the Buddha is, in fact, limitless in both time and space, assuming various forms in different ages and under different circumstances, but all for one purpose, the salvation of all beings. He illustrates this with the following parable: A physician who had been away from home a long time returned to find his sons suffering from an ailment. He prescribed an appropriate medicine, which certain of them took but which others, mad from the poison, refused. Those who took it were immediately cured, while the others continued to be ill. The physician went away, circulating the rumor that he had died. This shocked the ailing sons back to their senses, after which they took their father's medicine and were cured. When he heard of this, the father made his appearance again. Just so, says the Buddha, are the beings. When offered salvation, some of them refuse it, inducing the Buddha to stage a docetic Nirvana. This instills in them a sense of urgency, born of the fear that the Buddha will not always be among them.

(16) The Buddha narrates the merit which shall accrue to those who venerate the foregoing chapter of the Lotus Sūtra telling of the unlimited nature of the Buddha's lifespan.

(17) and (18) More on the merit accruing to one who extols the Lotus Sūtra.

(19) More on the same, followed by the Buddha's narration of his own behavior in a previous era, in which, as the bodhisattva Sadāparibhūta, he was the object of much contempt and violence, but requited all actions with love and patience.

(20) All the bodhisattvas promise to propagate the Lotus Sūtra; both Buddhas stretch out their tongues, which extend very far and emit a ray of light that illuminates the entire universe.

(21) More on the merit accruing to the person who extols the Lotus Sūtra, followed by spells pronounced by several persons for the protection of such persons from all ill.

(22) The Buddha narrates an incident from a former incarnation of the bodhisattva Bhaiṣajyarāja.

(23) The bodhisattva Gadgadasvara comes out of his own world to salute both Buddhas, and the Buddha tells his listeners about the deeds of this bodhisattva in a previous incarnation.

(24) The Buddha tells his listeners about the efficacy of invoking the bodhisattva Avalokiteśvara.

(25) More about the deeds of certain bodhisattvas in previous incarnations.

(26) The bodhisattva Samantabhadra vows to be the protector of all who extol the Lotus Sūtra and of all who appeal to him for help. The Buddha then entrusts the Lotus Sūtra to him, once more dwelling on the merit that will accrue to those who extol this scripture and the afflictions that will come upon all who harm such persons.

(27) The Buddha leaves the Lotus Sūtra in the care of his listeners, all of whom then go their several ways.

4. **Influence.** While the Lotus Sūtra is much read throughout the Mahāyāna world, in China the T'ien-t'ai school (*see* Tendai) treated it as its Bible. The school flourished in the latter half of the sixth century and early in the seventh, but then, for political reasons, went into decline. It was exported to Korea and Japan, where it survives to the present day. In the thirteenth century Nichiren established a new movement based on the Lotus Sūtra which flourishes today in the various sects of Nichiren Buddhism.

Bibliography. E. Burnouf, trans., *Le lotus de la bonne loi* (1852); L. Hurvitz, trans., *Scripture of the Lotus Blossom of the Fine Dharma* (1976); H. Kern, trans., *The Saddharma-pundarika* (1884), *The Sacred Books of the East,* vol. xxi.

L. Hurvitz

LOURDES lo͝ord (Ch). Popular Pilgrimage center in SW France (Hautes-Pyrenées), made famous by the eighteen appearances of the Virgin Mary to a fourteen-year-old peasant girl, Bernardette Soubirous, between February 11 and July 16, 1858. Miraculous healings were soon reported at the site of the apparitions in the grotto of Massabielle, near which a spring had suddenly welled up on February 25. An initial period of ecclesiastical opposition ended with authorization of the pilgrimages in 1862; and the feast of Our Lady of Lourdes (February 11), extended to the whole Roman Catholic Church in 1907, has since 1969 been celebrated as an optional memorial. Four million pilgrims a year make the pilgrimage, among them many sick persons. Reported cures are examined by a special medical bureau. Of the thousands thus authenticated, the church accepts only sixty-three (as of 1976) as strictly miraculous. *See* Faith Healing.

Bibliography. R. Cranston, *The Miracle of Lourdes* (1955); R. Laurentin, *Lourdes: Histoire authentique,* 6 vols. (1961-66).

C. Waddell

LUBAVICHER MOVEMENT loo bä′ vĭch ər (Ju). Important and vigorous group in Eastern European Hasidism; the name comes from the Russian town of Lubavich, where Dov Ber, second leader and son of the founder, settled in 1813. The group is also known by the acronym *Ḥabad* (*Ḥokmah*—wisdom; *Binah*—understanding; *Dáath*—knowledge), which represents a theoretical emphasis in the system of its founder, Shneur Zalman (1745-1813). Zalman was a direct disciple of the Maggid of Mezeritz, who entrusted him with the composition of a legal guide for Hasidic life. In addition to being a profound student of the Talmud, Zalman was a mystic. His systematic interpretation of Hasidism, *Tanya,* serves as a canonical text for the movement.

Seven successive ZADDIKIM, or masters, have led the movement. Yaakov Yosef (1880-1950), the sixth zaddik, escaped Poland on the eve of the HOLOCAUST and settled in Brooklyn, New York. He built an extensive educational system and in 1948 helped found a Hasidic settlement, Kfar Habad, in Israel. The seventh zaddik, Menahem Mendel Schneerson (b. 1902), studied math and science at the Sorbonne.

Ḥabad Hasidism is characterized by a deep commitment to the study and perpetuation of Talmudic law, by a rigorous striving for moral purity and service to the Jewish community-at large, and by meditation on the mysteries of God's presence in this world in the spirit of Hasidic KABBALA.

K. P. BLAND

LUCIFER lo͞o′ sə fər (Ch—Lat.; lit. "light bearer"). In JEROME's translation of Isa. 14:12, the equivalent of the Hebrew *hēlēl,* usually given in English as "Day Star," denoting Venus, the morning star. This passage describes the fall from heaven of one who said, "I will make myself like the Most High," and is the biblical basis for the belief that SATAN was an ANGEL who rebelled against God and was cast into hell. John MILTON, in his attacks on CLERGY who were greedy for power, used Lucifer as a symbol of anyone who usurps "over spiritual things beyond his sphere." He also incorporated many of the then current legends about Lucifer into his figure of Satan in *Paradise Lost.*

The Latin Bible uses the term "lucifer" also for the signs of the zodiac (Job. 38:32) and for Jesus himself (II Pet. 1:19; RSV "the morning star").

K. CRIM

LUMBINĪ loom′ bĭ nē. A grove of trees near KAPILAVASTU. Traditional accounts agree that Siddhārtha Gautama, who became the BUDDHA, was born in this park on a date near 560 B.C.

In later traditions, Lumbinī Park is also cited as the location where young Siddhārtha, over a succession of days, met with various persons who caused him to consider the ills of human life and to renounce his princely position.

R. H. DRUMMOND

LURIA, ISAAC lûr′ ē ə ē′ säk (Ju; 1534-1572). Central figure in the KABBALA as it developed in Safed in Galilee. Luria's cosmic myth of exile and redemption revolves around three foci: *ẓimẓum,* God's withdrawal into himself in order to produce out of himself both the space for, and the substance of, creation—thus purging himself of the ultimate roots of evil; *shevirath ha-kelim,* the cosmic catastrophe that caused God's substance to fall and be captured in the recalcitrant vessels of existence; and *tikkun,* the process by which God's being is reunited with itself and returns to harmony and unity, and with it the redemption of all life.

K. P. BLAND

LUTHER, MARTIN (Ch; 1483-1546). Protestant reformer; son of a German peasant who found success in the burgeoning mining industry of late fifteenth century Saxony. Luther studied law, but he was driven by religious scrupulosity to enter a monastery in 1505. Marked by superiors for the priesthood and advanced theological study, he became a professor of Bible at the University of Wittenberg, receiving his doctorate there in 1512. His religious crisis persisted, but under the guidance of his superior, Johann von Stauptiz, and through his study of Scripture, along with the reading of AUGUSTINE OF HIPPO and certain German mystics, he gradually answered the critical questions concerning his relationship with God. Luther came to accept Augustine's understanding of grace during his 1513 lectures on Psalms, and in his lectures on the Epistle to the Romans (1515-16), he abandoned Gabriel Biel's proposition, "God gives grace to him who does what is in him." By 1518 he had reached his understanding of faith as the religious faculty which "throws itself upon God," his distinction of law and GOSPEL, and his concept of the believer as simultaneously completely righteous and sinful. These are the key elements in his understanding of JUSTIFICATION through faith in Christ.

His 95 Theses on INDULGENCES of 1517 spread Luther's reputation throughout Europe and made him a popular figure among the German people. In the Leipzig Debate with the Roman Catholic theologian John Eck (1518), and in four tracts published in 1520, Luther's theological position became clear, resulting in a break with Rome. The Roman legate, Cardinal Cajetan, interviewed Luther in 1518 at Augsburg but failed to persuade him to tame his criticism of the papal party, and in 1520 Pope LEO X excommunicated him. In 1521 his appearance before Emperor Charles V at the imperial diet in Worms resulted in an edict outlawing him and his followers.

In 1525 Luther decisively broke with older humanists in his published exchange with ERASMUS on the bondage of the will. He married a former nun, Katherine von Bora, the same year; the pattern of that marriage and the pastoral care both spouses gave each other and their children contributed much to the Protestant view of marriage. Also in 1525 Luther criticized the tyrannous princes and the rebellious peasants who fought each other in the field; Luther's harsh criticism of the peasant cause did not in fact alienate much of the German peasantry, as some scholars have claimed.

Throughout the rest of his life Luther taught theology at Wittenberg to hundreds who spread his message throughout Germany, Scandinavia, Eastern Europe, and beyond.

Luther's personal experience with his doubts about God's mercy is reflected in his understanding of God's Word as law and gospel, which prescribes pastorally sensitive application of the message of wrath to the arrogant and mercy to the broken sinner. His conviction that God uses certain selected elements of the created order to convey forgiveness shaped his understanding of the INCARNATION of Christ and his concept of Word and SACRAMENTS. His joyful embrace of the blessings of the created order is reflected in his concept of the Christian's vocation, which recognizes all tasks in the created order as assignments for divine service. *See* REFORMATION, PROTESTANT.

Bibliography. P. Althaus, *The Theology of Martin Luther* (1966); R. H. Bainton, *Here I Stand* (1950); A. G. Dickens, *The German Nation and Martin Luther* (1974); G. Ebeling, *Luther, an Introduction to His Thought* (1970). R. KOLB

LUTHERAN CHURCHES (Ch). Protestant churches first organized by sixteenth century German princes who responded to the writings of MARTIN LUTHER and built upon popular enthusiasm for Luther's cause. The AUGSBURG CONFESSION was given legal status in the Holy Roman Empire in 1555 and served as a confessional basis for these churches. In Sweden royal conversion of the church to Lutheranism was also supported by popular sentiment; in Denmark, however, and especially in Norway and Iceland, the royal decree for reformation was less enthusiastically supported by the people. The rulers and their theologians used parish visitations to introduce alterations in organization and piety to the local parish, while employing university-educated pastors, equipped with Luther's CATECHISMS and the reformers' LITURGY, hymnody, and sermon and prayer books, to complete the work of reformation.

In Germany thirty years of disputing over the proper interpretation of Luther's message followed his death (1546). The Formula of Concord of 1577 ended this era and introduced the Orthodox period, marked by its loyalty to the Formula's doctrinal settlement, published with other Lutheran CREEDS in the Book of Concord of 1580. The Formula settlement also ensured that Lutheran churches, like Roman Catholic churches in early modern Spain and France, would be under princely domination, which regulated area churches through consistories. In the twentieth century many European Lutherans have adopted the EPISCOPAL system of governance; American Lutheranism became largely CONGREGATIONAL. Lutherans have, however, generally been less concerned with questions of church governance than have other confessions. An emphasis on Luther's understanding of justification through faith in Jesus Christ, comprehended in his pastorally sensitive distinction of law and gospel, has marked Lutheran theology; Luther's emphases on scriptural authority and on word and sacraments as means of grace have also remained central.

The Orthodox period (1577–early eighteenth century) was marked by monumental doctrinal systems couched in the Aristotelian philosophy which dominated European intellectual activity, and by the piety expressed in Paul Gerhardt's (1607-76) hymns, John Gerhard's *Sacred Meditations,* and John Conrad Dannhauer's (1603-66) *Christian Way of Wisdom.*

In reaction to the apathy and laxity of much of state Lutheranism PIETISM arose under the leadership of Philipp Jakob SPENER (1635-1705).

The Pietist August Hermann Francke (1663-1727) headed an institutional complex at Halle which set a pattern for "inner mission," social service and evangelization at home, and sent missionaries to India and to immigrants in the New World. The result of such missions include native churches in Indonesia, Tanzania, and other African and Asian lands as well as immigrant churches in Australia, Brazil and other South American lands, and the United States. In the U.S. eighteenth century German groups are merged with groups of Swedish, Finnish, and Danish origin in the Lutheran Church of America. Nineteenth century German immigrants, with Norwegian and Danish immigrants, formed groups which now make up the American Lutheran Church, while other German immigrants of the nineteenth century formed the Lutheran Church—Missouri Synod and the Wisconsin Evangelical Lutheran Synod. The first three of these now participate in the Lutheran Council in the United States of America (since 1966), a successor to the National Lutheran Council of 1918. Most Lutheran churches participate in the Lutheran World Federation (organized 1947), successor to the Lutheran World Convention (organized 1923). *See* REFORMATION, PROTESTANT.

Bibliography. C. Bergendoff, *The Church of the Lutheran Reformation* (1967); A. Burgess, ed., *Lutheran Churches in the Third World* (1970); H. Fagerberg, *A New Look at the Lutheran Confessions, 1529-1537* (1972). R. KOLB

M

MACCABEES măk′ ə bēs (Ju—Aram.; lit. "hammerer" [*maqqābâ*—hammer]). Leaders of the Jewish revolt (166-164 B.C.) against Antiochus Epiphanes in defense of religious freedom and against forced Hellenization. Their name is derived from Judah "the hammerer," one of five sons of Mattathias, who began the revolt. The original victory of the Jews is commemorated in the festival of Hanukkah.

The successors of Mattathias and Judah are known as Hasmoneans (from Hashman, their clan name). Their exploits are recounted in Josephus and the books of the Maccabees in the OT Apocrypha. The latter Hasmoneans, especially John Hyrcanus I (135-104 B.C.) and Alexander Jannaeus (103-76 B.C.), fought a series of wars of conquest and forced conversion, alienating large segments of the Jewish population. Antigonus (40-37 B.C.) was the last Hasmonean ruler, though Herod the Great's wife Mariamne was a lineal descendant of the Maccabees.

Bibliography. V. Tcherikover, *Hellenistic Civilization and the Jews* (1959).
E. M. Meyers

MADHVA mŭd′ vŭ (H—Skt.). Founder of the Dvaita school of Vedānta philosophy. Born in 1238 A.D. in Pājakakṣetra near Udipi in the Tulu country of Karṇāṭaka (present-day Mysore state), Madhva is credited with some thirty-seven philosophical works. He is also known by the names Pūrṇaprajña and Ānandatīrtha, names given to him at his initiation and ordination ceremonies respectively. Attracting attention by his prodigious abilities in reciting, interpreting, and criticizing scriptural and exegetical texts, Madhva gathered pupils in his classes at Udipi, and accompanied by many of them made numerous trips throughout India, including at least two visits to Badrinath in the Himalayas. He debated a number of prominent scholars throughout his lifetime.

Madhva established his main temple, consecrated to Krishna, at Udipi, and installed in it the idol of Bāla Krishna secured from Dwarka. This temple flourishes to this day, led by a steady line of successors stemming from Madhva and his disciples, who disseminated the Dvaita system throughout India. Tradition holds that in the year 1317, in the midst of a lecture, Madhva disappeared and invisibly retired to Badrinath for good.

Bibliography. C. M. Padmanabhacharya, *Life and Teachings of Sri Madhvāchārya* (abridged, 1970).
K. H. Potter

MĀDHYAMIKA mäd yä′ mĭ kə (B—Skt.; lit. "middle way"). A Buddhist spiritual exercise leading to enlightened nonattachment. From the second century A.D. it took the form of a philosophical school in India; in China (called *San-lun*) it constituted a school from the fifth century A.D., and in Tibet (called *Dbu-ma-pa*) from the eighth century. Though it died out as an independent school, its influence pervades all Mahāyāna thought through its treatises on basic Buddhist concepts and its commentaries on the Sūtras.

The Mādhyamika school, while developing different subschools, emphasizes that all experienced ideas or concrete forms are empty of inherent nature (*see* Śūnyatā). It stresses three aspects of this "Emptiness-teaching": (1) refutation of erroneous views which assume an inherent nature of existing things, (2) the recognition of "dependent co-origination" *(pratītya-samutpāda)* of all experienced phenomena as a way to perceive the emptiness of all phenomena, and (3) the functional distinction between two kinds of truth, conventional *(vyavahāra)* truth and ultimate *(paramārtha)* truth.

The Indian school of Mādhyamika was founded by Nāgārjuna (*ca.* A.D. 150-250), who claimed that his analysis of the Buddhist Dharma continued the intention of the Middle Way (Skt: *Madhyamā-pratipād*) propounded by the Buddha. This "way" was an avoidance of entanglement in views, theories, naïve perceptions, or emotional experiences. The early Buddhist spiritual masters avoided attachment to imagery of "the self" or "ultimate reality" by analyzing every moment of experience into many constituent factors (dharmas). Thus, all phenomenal forms were declared to be "empty" of any inherent reality.

Nāgārjuna continued the criticism of non-Buddhist views of an eternal reality either in the "self" or in some universal ground of being; he also criticized the scholastic Buddhist formulations of inherent characteristics of dharmas and concepts of causality, time, and personality as found in the ABHIDHAMMA literature. A classic abbreviated formulation of the refutation of erroneous view repeated in Mādhyamika writings throughout the centuries is: Nothing becomes real, nothing becomes nonreal; nothing is eternal, nothing is extinct; nothing is identical, nothing is different; nothing comes, nothing goes. Nāgārjuna and subsequent Mādhyamika masters asserted that only by recognizing "emptiness" (śūnyatā) of all existing forms could one account for practical, everyday action and change, as well as for the attainment of enlightenment. The designation, however, that all phenomena are empty rather than nonempty was true only as a practical effort at conventional communication; the highest truth was itself an empty mode of perception which did not become attached to concepts of "empty" or "nonempty." The radical negation of all assertions and the designation of "emptiness" thus were seen as medicines to correct spiritual blindness; they were not health itself.

Indian Mādhyamika divided into two subschools in the late fifth century A.D. over the function of logical proofs. The Prāsaṅgika (from *prasaṅga*, a logical method of drawing a "necessary consequence" from an opponent's view) limited the function of philosophical analysis to denial of the opponents' positions and claimed that the highest truth transcends all concepts. The Svātantrikas ("independents") admitted that positive valid inferences could be drawn from philosophical analyses which resulted in true (independent) information about the phenomenal world, and that words used without false assumptions can help evoke the highest truth that is beyond the duality of verbal or nonverbal perception. Both these subschools argued against other philosophical positions including the Indian Mahāyāna school Vijñānavāda (conscious-only teaching) or YOGĀCĀRA (spiritual discipline practice).

In the eighth century Śāntarakśita, a Mādhyamika master at the great monastery-university at NĀLANDĀ, traveled to Tibet and established a lasting school there. His disciple Kamalaśīla reinforced the Mādhyamika claim when he was called to Tibet to settle a dispute with Ch'an masters from China. In Tibet both subschools of Mādhyamika (along with Vijñānavāda and earlier Indian schools) influenced TIBETAN BUDDHIST doctrinal discussion, combining with the Tibetan form of Buddhism known as Tantrayana. Abhayākaragupta (d. 1123) was one of the greatest teachers synthesizing Mādhyamika and Tantrayana.

Mādhyamika developed prominence among Chinese monks when KUMĀRAJĪVA translated several Sūnyavāda texts in the early fifth century A.D. The monk SENG-CHAO (fifth century) was a crucial figure in transmitting Mādhyamika, and his essays were formative in the development of the San-lun (Three [Mādhyamika] Treatises) school. In the sixth century Fa-lang attracted a large following among the religious through his Mādhyamika teaching, as did his successor CHI-TSANG (549-623). In the seventh century Chi-tsang's Korean pupil Ekwan traveled to Japan, where he taught San-lun (Jap. Sanron; *see* NARA BUDDHISM). While Sanron never became an institution defined by lineage succession, Mādhyamika dialectics, commentaries, and treatises were studied in the Japanese monasteries.

Bibliography. D. Daye, "Major Schools of the Mahayana: Mādhyamika," in C. S. Prebish, *Buddhism: A Modern Perspective* (1975); H. V. Guenther, *Buddhist Philosophy in Theory and Practice* (1971); R. H. Robinson, *Early Madhyamika in India and China* (1967); F. J. Streng, *Emptiness: A Study in Religious Meaning* (1967); A. K. Warder, *Indian Buddhism* (1970).

F. J. STRENG

MADONNA (Ch—from Old Italian; lit. "My Lady"). Archaic form of respectful address often used to designate the Virgin MARY, but now used chiefly with reference to artistic representations of the Virgin. The equivalent term in modern Catholic usage is "Our Lady." C. WADDELL

MADRASA mä drä′ sə (I). The general name for a school in which Islamic subjects are studied. As a general term *madrasa* encompasses a wide range and variety of Islamic schools both historically and institutionally. Such schools are not necessarily identified or associated with a MOSQUE, although historically Islamic education has often centered in the mosque. This was because study of the QUR'ĀN was the main foundation of Islamic learning.

1. **Children's schools.** *Madrasas* have been important institutions for primary religious education. Here children have learned to recite—and often to memorize—the Qur'ān. In this connection they have often been taught reading and writing and perhaps some elements of grammar as well as some literature (e. g., poems). These schools have also provided minimal educational opportunities for the poor and orphaned.

2. **Schools for adults.** The term *madrasa* also includes schools intended for adults and offering a wider range as well as a higher level of Islamic learning. The development of these *madrasas* was in part due to the growth of the Islamic curriculum. The interest and activity shown in the collection and sifting of ḤADĪTH (Traditions) during the eighth and ninth centuries A.D. soon began to be reflected in the teaching of *ḥadīth* in the *madrasas*. The Islamic subjects came to include, besides Qur'ān and *ḥadīth*, *tafsīr* (Qur'ān interpretation), KALĀM ("theology"), and FIQH (jurisprudence), as well as such auxiliary sciences as logic and linguistics. Moreover, the curricula of some *madrasas* broadened to include mathematics, music, and medicine and other

"Greek" sciences. The "Greek" science of philosophy was often in contention (*see* MU'TAZILA) and was usually studied apart from the mosque.

The most important function of the major *madrasas* was to provide advanced instruction in jurisprudence.

3. **Nizāmiyya and al-Azhar.** The major institutions were usually established through the generosity of wealthy, pious benefactors who endowed professorial "chairs" (the term is of Islamic provenance) and established scholarships. An outstanding example is that of Nizām al-Mulk, who in A.D. 1065 provided funds for the construction of a *madrasa* (Nizāmiyya) in Baghdad for training in Shafi'ite law (*see* AL-SHĀFI'Ī). It was this "college" in which AL-GHAZZĀLĪ held a professorship at the end of the eleventh century.

A major Islamic educational institution which developed in close connection with a mosque is al-AZHAR in Cairo. The mosque of al-Azhar is FATIMID, having opened in A.D. 972. Until modern times al-Azhar followed the typical *madrasa* curriculum, but beginning in 1865 and continuing in 1930 a process of organizational, administrative, and curricular changes issued in the designation *al-jami'a al-azharīya* (the University of al-Azhar). It is today the most prestigious center for Islamic study.

H. B. PARTIN

MAGADHA mäg´ ŭ dŭ (B). *See* RĀJAGṚHA.

MAGEN DAVID mä´ gĕn dä vēd´ (Ju—Heb.; lit. "shield of David"). The six-pointed star formed by two equilateral triangles that have the same center and are placed in opposite directions. The use of the symbol is ancient and widespread. During the period of the Second Temple it was common among both Jews and non-Jews, primarily for decorative purposes. In the synagogue of Capernaum (second or third century A.D.) it is found on a frieze alongside the five-pointed star and the swastika.

The six-pointed star appears in early Byzantine churches and a great many medieval European churches. It is likely that it was in imitation of church usage and not as a specifically Jewish symbol that from the late Middle Ages it was placed on some SYNAGOGUES. Its use as a magical symbol and a protective amulet seems to have first become common in the KABBALA in the early fourteenth century.

The chief motivation for its widespread use as an emblem of identification by Jews beginning in the nineteenth century appears to have been a desire for a sign that would "symbolize" Judaism in the same way that the CROSS symbolized Christianity. This brought about the use of the Magen David on Jewish ceremonial and ritual objects, on seals and letterheads, in synagogue decorations, on coats of arms, and in many other ways.

Bibliography. L. A. Mayer, *Bibliography of Jewish Art* (1967).

B. MARTIN

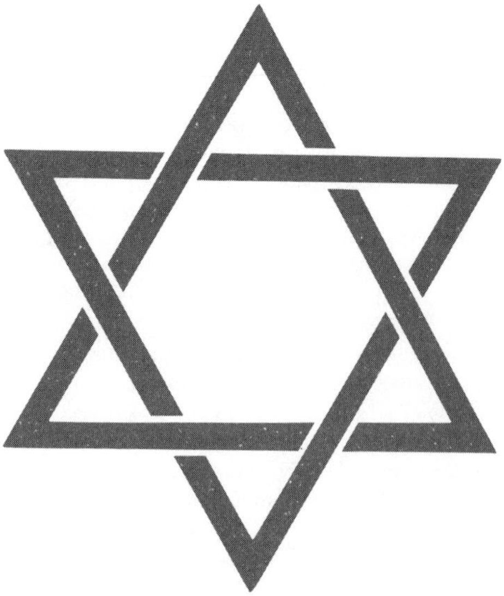

The Magen David

MAGGID mä gēd´ (Ju—Heb.; lit. "one who tells"). 1. A preacher, either itinerant or permanently attached to a SYNAGOGUE. Since premodern RABBIS were not charged with regularly delivering sermons, this function was performed by a specially designated speaker.

2. The voice or figure of revelation from heaven vouchsafed to scholars and saints. This usage flourished between the sixteenth and eighteenth centuries in Jewish MYSTICISM, especially in the school of LURIA.

K. P. BLAND

MAGGID OF MEZERITZ mä gēd´ mĕz´ ə rĭts (Ju; 1710-1772). Dov Baer, a TALMUDIST and renowned preacher, who became the leader of HASIDISM after the death of the BAAL SHEM TOV. He is generally credited with transforming Hasidism into a mass movement and orienting it toward the KABBALA. The Maggid wrote no books of his own, but his disciples compiled an authorized version of his teachings.

K. P. BLAND

MAGIC. The production of effects in the world by means of invisible or supernatural causation. Action based upon belief in the efficacy of symbolic forms.

The practice of magic has been extremely widespread in human societies, particularly in those with well-articulated systems of status and of roles which tend to sensitize their members to symbols and to the efficacy of symbolic behavior. Magic has traditionally concerned itself with relatively limited areas of human experience, such as healing and preventing disease, finding lost or stolen articles, identifying thieves and witches, gaining vengeance, and warding off evil influences. It has generally not evolved elaborate explanatory systems comparable to the systematic theologies of the great religious traditions. The closest comparable magical enterprise would be ASTROLOGY, the study of the "effects" of heavenly bodies primarily upon the world of human activity. However, the connections between astrology and folk magic, especially in the West, have been extremely slender. At most, astrology served to give weight to the notion that all things are connected, that the universe is much like an enormous, integrated organism. While this background of general interconnectedness supported the plausibility of the particular connections assumed by folk magic, it seldom informed the specific content of such magic. Compilations of magical instruction are rather like recipe books which appeal to stories of success for authority.

The academic study of magic is co-extensive with the academic study of religion (*see* RELIGION, STUDY OF) and has focused upon three basic areas: the relation of magic to religion, the function of magic in human societies, and the extent to which the practice of magic is an expression of a distinctive mode of thought, usually indicated by the term "the primitive mind." Woven throughout these problems is the further issue of the extent to which the practitioners of magic actually believe that it works. The most recent scholarship has tended to minimize the distinctions between magic and religion, the primitive and modern minds, and to expand and complicate our notions of the function of magic.

1. **Magic and religion.** One of the earliest accepted distinctions between magic and religion was that of constraint versus supplication. The magician was thought to compel events while the priest humbly begged the indulgence of the gods. The distinction was based upon the assumption that magic worked automatically and mechanically, that effects inevitably followed magical rites, that wishes were instantaneously fulfilled. Magic was regarded as a rather childish attempt to exercise control over the environment in the absence of effective technology. As such, magic appeared entirely anthropocentric, and contrasted with religion, viewed as supplication, it was an exercise in arrogance.

The bulk of the early studies of magic constituted an attempt to account for the belief in its automatic efficacy. Frazer attributed magical beliefs to the faulty reasoning processes of "small minds" which were prone to believe that similar things could influence each other and that things once in contact remained always in contact. Thus water sprinkled over the ground to the accompaniment of thunderlike drums could bring rain, and possession of one's fingernail parings could provide the necessary link to allow a malevolent magician to do one harm. Likeness and contiguity, however, Mauss suggested, were only the paths along which magic flowed and failed to name the very stuff of magic itself. Mauss attempted to discover the sources and nature of magical power, to identify what it was that flowed through the connecting paths. He suggested that it be called "MANA," a Polynesian term which he misinterpreted as a kind of spiritual power to which magic gave one access, residing everywhere in, but not identical with, the world. Mauss' *mana* explanation was later undercut by Malinowski, who argued that the practice of magic did not give evidence of a "universal force residing everywhere," but Mauss did point out the possibility of world views which included hidden forces employable in human enterprises. Malinowski too thought the essence of magic was power, but located it far too narrowly within the individual magician.

A second major distinction between magic and religion was one which associated religion with a "church" or with the central community and relegated magic to the fringes of communal activity or set it outside such activity altogether. A number of related distinctions all emphasize what are taken to be the marginal and limited aspects of magic. In these views magic is characterized as secret instead of open, as private instead of public, as concerned with individual, pragmatic, and empirical matters instead of the broader, communally oriented focus of religion.

These two basic distinctions between magic and religion have failed to withstand the test of ethnography. It is not the case that magic always constrains while religion supplicates, nor that the working of magic is automatic and mechanical. There is no shortage of information on religious rituals which constrain, particularly in the East, and Western religions have sought ways of guaranteeing favorable responses to prayer. On the other hand, magicians more often than not supplicate instead of command, particularly when the magic is carried out by intelligent agents. It is common for magicians to be required to meet strict ritual requirements in order to perform their magic. The magical formulas recorded in Evans-Pritchard's pioneering work among the Azande all take the form of requests. He further demonstrated that instead of being mechanical, magic tends to live in a personal universe which displays intelligence and which can be addressed in the same ways persons are. In the case of the Azande, the medicines which are employed in magic are attributed such a degree of intelligence and moral integrity as to be able to find and punish a witch whose identity is unknown to the magician, and to determine whether they are being properly employed.

The magicality of medieval Christianity undercuts the distinction between magic and religion according to the presence or absence of a church. The medieval church, Thomas has shown, was thoroughly magical, at least at the popular level. The SACRAMENTS were thought to work automatically, mere attendance at MASS was held to be efficacious, and PILGRIMAGE to various shrines provided miraculous cures. Images and even amulets were held to have miraculous efficacy in their abilites to protect people from disease and to cure. Masses which blessed labor, guaranteed safe journeys, and stopped epidemics had the particularistic usage which presumably was a defining characteristic of magic.

Mauss emphasized the ritualistic characteristics of magic which rendered it structurally indistinguishable from religious ritual. Both magic and religion were traditional efficacious rites sanctioned by public opinion. Both were activities taking place at specified times, in specified places, and in specified ways; both involved the use of special apparatus; both displayed a similar ritual structure involving entrance and exit rites as well as a central focus. Magicians, like priests, passed through initiation processes, the transformative power of which is indicated by the fact that name changes were often involved. Recent studies of magic have further emphasized its public status and its intimate connections to the central community and its publicly acknowledged system of beliefs and social obligations. Lévi-Strauss argues that magical healing rituals often function as a kind of group therapy. What occurs on the interpersonal level in such rituals, usually the airing and resolution of suspicion and animosity, is as important as what occurs within the realm of the physical health of the patient. He further argues that magical practices and even accusations of malevolent magic (WITCHCRAFT) have as one of their primary purposes the reinforcement of a society's belief system. In Puritan New England, for example, the reality of magic and witchcraft was defended, although their practice was condemned, as a way of demonstrating the existence of an invisible world and thereby supporting belief in the existence of God, who was the primary inhabitant of that world.

Some recent treatments of magic have sought to do away with the magic/religion distinction altogether. Douglas has proposed equating magic with miracle and sacramentalism. Here the key element becomes sensitivity to condensed symbols and the belief in the efficacy of symbolic forms. In this view magic becomes rather like a style—some religions are magical, others not. The tendency to dismiss ritualistic sacramental religions as magical and hence not truly religious is, Douglas suggests, a mere prejudice which selects the prophetic-Protestant model of inner experience as the paradigm of authentic religiosity. Such an arbitrary determination of what is religious and what is magical fails to take note of the lives of these phenomena in human communities and attributes absolute value to *a priori* definitions.

2. The function of magic. The understanding of magic as an automatically efficacious system of control led directly to Malinowski's well-known psychological interpretation of magic. Malinowski argued correctly that primitive cultures were not entirely magical or mystical, but possessed a solid foundation of empirical knowledge based upon observation and experience. Magic was not employed in those areas in which the primitive's knowledge and technology allowed him to take direct action, but in areas in which knowledge and technology were wanting. Thus magic was viewed as a substitute technology, an attempt to extend control beyond one's areas of technical competence. It thereby reduced the anxiety imposed by the otherwise uncontrollable, the uncanny, or the dangerous by providing at least the appearance of effective action. In attempting to explain how magic functioned within human experience, Malinowski first claimed that religion and magic are really matters of inner experience. This biased equation allowed Malinowski to explain magic away through the vehicle of individual psychology. If magic were an individual phenomenon, Malinowski could argue that the essence of magic was the "spell." The ritual incantations which accompanied or formed part of magical rites here constitute the whole. To explain the belief in magical efficacy, Malinowski suggested that the magician is so carried away by the image of his desired end that he mistakes the release of tension afforded by the vehement expression of his desires for the actual attainment of those desires.

This kind of psychological reductionism has proven unsatisfactory on a number of points. The exclusive focus upon the individual, the absolute centrality of the spell, and the assumption of automatic efficacy have all been contradicted by ethnographic reports. The interpretation of magic as a substitute technology has been dealt a fatal blow by Thomas' significant work, *Religion and the Decline of Magic*. If magic were as Malinowski claimed, then one would expect it to expand into those areas of life where technological competence is lacking. Such was not the case with English magic: the problems to which it was applied as well as its mode of operation were entirely circumscribed by tradition. More importantly, Malinowski's theory clearly implies that magical practices should only cease once there are adequate technological substitutes. Thomas finds that this was not the case in England, for the practice of magic declined severely long before technological developments made it unnecessary in Malinowski's terms. Further, Malinowski's view suggests that magic and "empirical" technologies are rival and mutually exclusive systems of coping. However, the practice of magic, particularly in primitive cultures, evidences no such dichotomy between magical and empirical modes. These two modes operate together, tending to focus on different aspects of the same phenomena. The pressing issue for primitive societies is not the solving of technical problems, but the organization of people into cohesive communities. Magic often functions to achieve such integration.

The psychological analysis of magic has been extended into the social domain and has further explored the notion of the organization of people. Theoreticians such as Douglas and Lévi-Strauss, as well as other field researchers, have begun to suggest that the control of experience is a conscious intention of magical rites. Douglas notes, for example, that the practitioners of rain-magic do not believe that their efforts will produce rain. Consequently, rain-magic is often scheduled to coincide with the onset of the rainy season. The magical rite serves to coordinate human action with "the rhythm of the natural world." The work of magic here is integrative; the moral and natural orders are fused in symbolic forms, experience becomes holistic. Douglas suggests that the function of magic can be fruitfully understood through the concept of "framing." Magic sets off certain experiences and phenomena by providing a focus for attention. In so ordering experience magic thereby alters the quality of experience (one attends to certain aspects and not to others, thus *what* one experiences is altered). This ordering of experience can itself be said to make experience possible; it brings it into being out of chaos. Lévi-Strauss illustrates this process in his essay "The Effectiveness of Symbols." A shaman-priest holds a "sing" to assist a woman with a difficult childbirth. The sing tells of the journey of a SHAMAN and his army, of their difficulties and of their triumph. The place of the journey is a thinly disguised representation of the birth canal—the drama takes place within the woman's body. The sing, Lévi-Strauss suggests, provides a language which allows the woman "to undergo in an ordered and intelligible form a real experience that would otherwise be chaotic and inexpressible."

Magic also often serves as a mechanism of social control. Like religious systems, magic usually attributes misfortune to moral guilt. Consequently magic intended to alleviate misfortune will often focus upon the question of what offense has been committed. The belief that such breaches of social obligations could result in subsequent misfortune is itself a deterrent to aberrant behavior, while the cataloging of one's possible offenses under the impact of misfortune serves as a powerful reminder of one's obligations.

3. **Magic and the issue of primitive mentality.** For the rather self-centered Western imagination, primitive people have often been irrational, confused as to the nature of reality, and poor observers of the world around them. That view was given a definitive yet nonpejorative shape in Levy-Bruhl's now disregarded conception of the primitive mind as entirely "mystical" and fundamentally different from the modern mind. By "mystical" Levy-Bruhl did not mean that primitives were observationally inept, but only that they believed in invisible forces, in causes and connections which could not be perceived by the senses. He argued further that primitives were dominated by "collective representations," socially constructed categories which controlled experience and colored observations. Contemporary sociology of knowledge, however, has demonstrated that the experience of the modern world is also heavily shaped by "collective representations" and therefore, like the primitive, lives within a consensus reality. The importance of this for the study of magic is evident in attempting to understand the persistence of magical beliefs in the face of what would constitute disconfirming evidence for the scientist. Evans-Pritchard noted that an experimental testing of magic would strike the Azande both as inconceivable and as a waste of good medicine.

For recent scholarship, the primitive/modern distinction is seen not as a matter of "minds," but of the degree of social differentiation and of the availability of alternate systems of explanation. Proponents of this view have found that the primitive universe is more unitary than the modern; there are fewer independent social institutions to deal with different aspects of life, and fewer systems of explanation with which to render experience intelligible and orderly. Therefore, evidence which contradicts a belief in magical healing, for example, raises in Horton's words "a horrific threat of chaos." Because the same set of symbolic categories is carried forward to deal with every new aspect of experience, what is threatened by the anomalous is the entire social and belief system. While not all primitive societies practice magic, primitive and magical societies in general can be characterized as employing a language of persons to describe the universe. They do so because persons are for them the paradigm of order and intelligibility. It was, accordingly, in Thomas' estimation, the triumph of the mechanical philosophy, not the development of technology, which constituted the major ingredient in the decline of magic in England. The stripping of the world of the attributes of personality coupled with a growing confidence in human ability rendered magic untenable and unnecessary.

Of course, magic is not absent from the modern world. Astrology has still a widespread if recreational appeal. There have been periodic revivals of interest in the occult and ongoing attempts to provide scientific bases for the magical, as with parapsychology. Many have argued that human beings possess a deep-rooted thirst for "enchantment," rather like a magical *a priori*. While modern Western culture has shown an increasing tendency to distrust ritual or symbolic activity of any kind (hence also magic), it is not unusual for magic to re-enter through the concern for purity. Groups which are intensely focused upon the primacy of inner experience often claim that the attainment of purity will have a beneficent effect upon the world. The most anti-ritualistic Puritan would engage in purification exercises called "days of humiliation" which, by restoring inner purity, could stem the tide of plague or turn the course of battle. To the extent that magic involves invisible or supernatural cause and effect relationships, magical aspects would have to be attributed to such activities. As long as persons make such attempts to claim weight for their own personhood in a larger scheme of things, to link inner self and environment in moral terms, some form of magic is likely to remain extant.

Bibliography. M. Douglas, *Purity and Danger* (1966), pp. 29-111; E. E. Evans-Pritchard, *Witchcraft, Magic and Oracles Among the Azande* (1937), and *Theories of Primitive Religion* (1965); J. G. Frazer, *The Golden Bough* (3rd ed., 1922); R. Horton, "African Traditional Thought and Western Science," *Africa,* XXXVII (1967), 50-71, 155-87; L. Levy-Bruhl, *Primitive Mentality* (1923); C. Lévi-Strauss, *Structural Anthropology* (1963), pp. 167-205; B. Malinowski, *Magic, Science and Religion* (1948), pp. 17-90; M. Mauss, *A General Theory of Magic* (1902); K. Thomas, *Religion and the Decline of Magic* (1971).

D. E. OWEN

MAGNIFICAT mäg nĭ′ fĭ cät *or* män yĭ′ fĭ cät (Ch—Lat.; lit. "my soul magnifies"). MARY's song of praise of God (Luke 1:46-55) who has fulfilled his promises to send the MESSIAH. Psalmlike, it is a possible GOSPEL adaptation of Jewish and early Christian community prayer, accommodated to Mary's motherhood of JESUS. A part of worship at evensong from the sixth century on; often set to music.

E. R. CARROLL

MAHĀBHĀRATA mŭ hä bär′ ŭ tŭ (H—Skt.) The Mahābhārata, by its title, means the "great [story] of the descendants of BHARATA." The term "great" implies an "immensity," and the Epic is said, with only slight exaggeration, to be 100,000 verses long. It is "immense" like the ocean, the soul, and the heavens, and like these it is said, in a famous verse, to contain everything. Much of the Mahābhārata's volume is didactic material, and this led to a debate among late nineteenth century scholars as to whether there was an original narrative core, or whether in its original form the work was already a synthesis of narrative and didactic elements. The issue remains a sensitive one, but it cannot be solved on the basis of any existing text.

The Epic also introduces itself by the name *Jaya,* "victory," a term found in numerous formulas which assert that victory is found where there are truth, DHARMA, and the Lord KRISHNA. It is also called the "Fifth VEDA" and the "Veda of Krishna," the latter being a title of some ambiguity since it can refer either to Lord Krishna or to the reputed author of the poem Kṛṣṇa Dvaipāyana, whose more familiar *nom de plume* is Vyāsa, "the Arranger."

Despite the tradition that Vyāsa was a contemporary of the poem's heroes, it is certain that the main Epic story is much older than the period in which it was compiled as a text. The latter period is commonly thought to have run from about 400 B.C. to A.D. 400. But there is no scholarly consensus on the origins of the story, or whether it is history or myth. Archaeologists have excavated many of the sites mentioned in the Mahābhārata and found that from about 800 to 400 B.C. they shared a common culture identified by a painted gray ware. But the occupants of such sites, probably various ARYAN tribal kingdoms, lived in mud wall huts. If the splendid palaces described in the Epic are works of the imagination, how do such huts enhance the argument that the story preserves some kernel of history? Most probably such Aryan peoples as lived in the painted gray ware area knew some version of the Epic story and passed it on from generation to generation. As we have it now, some of this material—particularly the geography—has been shaped by the settled experiences of these people in this area, the center of which came to be called *Madhyadeśa,* "the middle region." Some of the Epic has also been shaped by theological concerns of *bhakti* ("devotion") which are probably expressed and synthesized into a coherent scheme for the first time, through this narrative, into a "Fifth Veda" (*see* BHAKTI HINDUISM). And other features have their roots in traditional lore of the Aryans that harks back to the Vedic past and the heritage of the Indo-Europeans.

1. The Epic story. The basic heroic story develops from a theme that is recurrent in several of the myths of VISHNU's AVATARS, or divine "descents." The Goddess Earth, oppressed by demons and overpopulation, is in danger of being submerged in the ocean (an image of doomsday: the *pralaya* or "dissolution"). To relieve the earth's burden, the gods descend into human forms. Vishnu heads the list, taking birth as KRISHNA, and Krishna declares the rationale for this appearance in the Epic's theological centerpiece, the BHAGAVAD GĪTĀ, when he tells ARJUNA that he comes into being from YUGA to *yuga* to restore the DHARMA. This intervention involves not only Vishnu, however, but a theologically significant sample of the whole Hindu pantheon.

The main heroic narrative then traces the genealogy of the Lunar (Candra or SOMA) Dynasty back to the origins of the world, and identifies it as the dynasty which rules over the "middle region." The focus narrows to a four generation crisis in the dynasty that culminates in an uncertainty as to who should rule: the sons of Pāṇḍu (PĀṆḌAVAS) or the sons of his blind older brother DHṚTARĀṢTRA (the Kauravas). The Pāṇḍavas' births are part of the divine plan to lift the earth's burden. They are sons of gods, thanks to a MANTRA once obtained by Pāṇḍu's senior wife, Kuntī, which allows her to invoke gods of her choosing to sire sons, and thus compensate for a curse that has rendered Pāṇḍu impotent. With the god Dharma she conceives YUDHIṢṬHIRA, with VĀYU, BHĪMA, and with INDRA, Arjuna; then the junior wife, Mādrī, permitted one utilization of the mantra, calls down the twin AŚVINS and conceives Nakula and Sahadeva. As Wikander and Dumézil have shown, the five gods thus chosen evoke an old Indo-European and Vedic trifunctional pattern which symbolizes an ordered and hierarchical axis within the traditional pantheon: a sovereign principle including a representative of law (dharma); a warrior function with two aspects, one more brutal represented by Vāyu and Bhīma, one more chivalric represented by Indra and Arjuna; and a "third function" concerned among other things with pastoralism and service, traits associated with both the Aśvins and the Pāṇḍava twins. Altogether, the Pāṇḍavas thus represent the principle of dharma, ordered and differentiated hierarchy, over against their cousins, the hundred Kauravas. The latter are incarnate *rākṣasas* (destructive goblins) and represent *adharma*, undifferentiated chaos. They are led by DURYODHANA, incarnation of Kali, "discord," the demon of the KALI YUGA.

As they grow up, all the cousins learn weaponry from DRONA. Arjuna excels at the bow, but soon meets his near match in KARNA. Karṇa is Arjuna's mother Kuntī's oldest son, but this never becomes public until Karṇa's death. Because Karṇa's origins are in doubt, Arjuna refuses to compete with him in a tournament; but Duryodhana champions Karṇa and thus acquires him as his ally. The Pāṇḍavas then join in a polyandric marriage with DRAUPADĪ, incarnation of the goddess Śrī ("prosperity"), and at this important event ally themselves with her brother Dhṛṣṭadyumna, incarnation of AGNI ("fire"), who will marshal their army.

The issue of who should rule is then temporarily resolved by a division of the kingdom, but the Kauravas lead Duryodhana and his counselors to devise a plan to win everything. His maternal uncle Śakuni, a crooked gambler, is backed by Duryodhana against Yudhiṣṭhira in a dice match. Yudhiṣṭhira bets and loses everything, including his brothers and himself, and finally their wife Draupadī. Draupadī is dragged into the gambling hall by Duḥśāsana, Duryodhana's oldest brother, and humiliated. But total shame is avoided when, as Duḥśāsana tries to disrobe her, new saris keep miraculously appearing to cover her. She saves her husbands from servitude and overturns the match's results by asking the moot question of whether Yudhiṣṭhira could legitimately have staked her after betting himself. Yudhiṣṭhira then accepts a rematch of one throw for the stake of thirteen years in exile, to be passed incognito, after which the loser's half of the kingdom will be returned. Yudhiṣṭhira loses and the Pāṇḍavas and Draupadī enter the forest.

The forest years pass, and the disguises assumed by the Pāṇḍavas in the thirteenth and last year enable them to succeed in avoiding detection. But Duryodhana refuses the Pāṇḍavas their half of the kingdom, and both parties seek allies for the inevitable conflict. Krishna agrees to join the Pāṇḍavas as a noncombatant, serving as Arjuna's charioteer. Bhīṣma, Droṇa, and Karṇa side with Duryodhana, the first two honoring their obligations to their royal patron, the third out of friendship and loyalty. Thus the lines are drawn for the great battle. The poets have structured this war carefully.

2. **Recent scholarship.** Two general approaches have emerged which probably reinforce each other. Wikander, Dumézil, Biardeau, and Hiltebeitel have argued that the battle involves a transposition into epic of eschatological myth. Gehrts, Biardeau, and Hiltebeitel have also claimed that the battle involves the narrative dramatization of themes from ritual. As to the first approach, Wikander, Dumézil, and Hiltebeitel have argued that the background myth is Indo-European, with its closest analogues in the "dualistic" eschatologies of ancient Iran and Scandinavia. Biardeau suggests that the eschatological myth which structures the battle is the Hindu myth of the *pralaya* or "cosmic dissolution." As to ritual models, van Buitenen has demonstrated that the Epic's second book, which includes Yudhiṣṭhira's consecration and the dice match, is modeled on the Rājasūya (royal consecration) sacrifice. Gehrts sees the whole Mahābhārata as an extended Rājasūya. His views converge with Hiltebeitel and Biardeau's emphasis that the battle itself is viewed as a sacrifice.

Taken together, these studies arrive at valuable conclusions. The Epic battle is of definitely eschatological proportions. Events are continually compared to the end of the cosmos. Divine and demonic forces mingle and oppose each other, and at the end only theologically significant figures survive: most importantly Krishna and the Pāṇḍavas and, on the Kaurava side, Droṇa's son Aśvatthāman, a "portion" of SHIVA. There seems no hope for the Lunar Dynasty's regeneration since all the Pāṇḍavas' children have been slain. But Arjuna's son Abhimanyu (incarnating the "splendor" of soma—the plant of immortality and the moon of the Lunar Dynasty) has, before he died, left his wife pregnant. The child comes forth stillborn due to a curse by Aśvatthāman (representing the destructive Shiva). But Krishna (the restorative Vishnu) empowers the child with life and thus revives the dynastic line. Biardeau convincingly calls attention to the *pralaya* imagery here (in the *pralaya* myth, after Shiva destroys the three worlds, Vishnu revives them). But Indo-European comparisons have also elucidated aspects of the Epic narrative: particularly the dualistic opposition between Bhīma and Duryodhana (Wikander, Dumézil), certain traits of Krishna (Wikander, Hiltebeitel), and the identification of Abhimanyu with the plant of immortality (Hiltebeitel)

As to the ritual approach, at his birth a voice from heaven predicts that Arjuna will perform three great sacrifices. Two are most likely the Rājasūya and Aśvamedha (horse sacrifice), parts of the story. The third can only be the "sacrifice of battle" or "of weapons," terms used frequently to describe the war. This nullifies Gehrts's argument that the whole Epic is an extended Rājasūya. But both Gehrts and Hiltebeitel have shown that aspects of the battle are modeled on sacrificial themes, most significantly the death of Abhimanyu as a soma sacrifice. And Biardeau has shown that events leading up to the battle also anticipate the battle-as-sacrifice theme, particularly the forest exile as a *dīkṣa* (consecration preparatory to a sacrifice), and the period in disguise, which the Epic calls a return to the womb, as the embryonic rebirth which, in the course of the *dīkṣa*, prepares one to be a sacrificer.

The Epic is of immense popularity in India.

Vernacular versions are known in most Indian languages, and popular variations of the story are widely circulated. Episodes are reenacted in both classical Sanskrit and contemporary village drama, and local place names and legends are frequently Epic-related. A whole cult centers on Draupadī as a South Indian village goddess. It has been said that whereas the RĀMĀYAṆA is the Epic of the Brahmins, the Mahābhārata is the Epic of the masses. Both served as vehicles for the transmission of Indian culture to Southeast Asia and Indonesia, and continue to serve in India as cherished expressions of the ideals of life and the articulation of dharma.

Bibliography. P. C. Roy and K. M. Ganguli, *The Mahabharata* (1884-96; rpr. 1970), 12 vols., most readily available full translation; J. A. B. van Buitenen, *The Mahābhārata* (1973, 1975, 1978), full translation in progress; C. V. Narasimhan, *The Mahābhārata* (1965), best abridgement; M. Biardeau, "Études de mythologie hindoue (IV), II. Bhakti et avatāra," BEFEO, LXIII (1976), 111-263, on the relation of the Mahābhārata to *avatāra* and *pralaya* mythology; G. Dumézil, *Mythe et épopée* (I): *L'idéologie des trois fonctions dans les épopées des peuples indo-européens* (1968; rev. ed. 1974); H. Gehrts, *Mahābhārata: Das Geschehen und seine Bedeutung* (1975); A. Hiltebeitel, *The Ritual of Battle: Krishna in the Mahābhārata* (1976), Krishna's role in relation to Indian and Indo-European myth and ritual; B. B. Lal, "Excavation at Hastināpura and other Explorations in the Upper Gangā and Sutlej Basins, 1950-52," *Ancient India,* X-XI (1954-55), on epic sites in relation to painted gray ware; J. A. B. van Buitenen, "On the Structure of the Sabhāparvan in the Mahābhārata," in *India Maior* (Festschrift Gonda, 1972), pp. 68-84, Rājāsuya sacrifice as model for epic's second book; S. Wikander, "Germanische und Indo-Iranische Eschatologie," *Kairos,* II (1960), 83-88, parallels between Norse and Indian epic; S. Wikander, "Sur le fonds commun indo-iranien des épopées de la Perse et de l'Inde," *La Nouvelle Clio,* I (1950), 310-19.

A. HILTEBEITEL

MAHĀBODHI SOCIETY mŭ´ hä bō´ dē. A Buddhist organization founded in 1891 for the purpose of gaining Buddhist control over the sacred site of Buddha's enlightenment, BODHGAYĀ. Working from Sri Lanka, Hewavitarne (1864-1933) founded the Society with the help of two THEOSOPHISTS. From its base in Calcutta the Society started the *Maha Bodhi Journal* in 1892 (now the oldest Buddhist journal). Control of Bodhgayā was achieved in 1953. With headquarters in Colombo, Sri Lanka, the Society currently publishes *Maha Bodhi,* maintains hospitals and orphanages, and operates centers for worship, study and training in India, Sri Lanka, England, Ghana, Japan, Korea, and the United States. *See* BUDDHISM, LAY §3.

R. C. AMORE

MAHĀ-PARINIBBĀNA SUTTA mŭ hä´ pŭ rĭ nĭb bä´ nŭ so͝ot´ tŭ (B—Pali; lit. "Great Discourse on the Final Decease"). Important canonical discourse describing the final events in the life of the Buddha. Part of the Collection of Long Discourses (DĪGHA NIKĀYA), it exists in Sanskrit and Chinese versions, as well as in the Pali.

It begins with the Buddha's final journey, during which he first becomes ill but suppresses the disease so he can address his followers a final time. He refuses to appoint a successor to lead his movement, noting each individual's responsibility for his or her own destiny. On the road again, he is given tainted food, and becomes deathly ill. In his final instructions to his assembled followers, he reminds them of the impermanence of compound things, and tells them to work out their own salvation diligently. Entering a series of higher states of consciousness, he attains final release (NIRVANA). The text describes his cremation and the development of a cult in his memory. Pilgrimage to sites important in his life is recommended for the laity.

The text is among the latest parts of the PALI CANON, but appears to be enlarged from a much older version, showing signs of editorial change at the hands of THERAVĀDA scholar monks.

Bibliography. Buddhist Publication Society, trans., *Last Days of the Buddha,* Wheel Publication 67-69 (1964).

J. P. MCDERMOTT

MAHARISHI MAHESH YOGI mä hä rē´ shē mä hĕsh´ yō gē (H). *See* TRANSCENDENTAL MEDITATION.

MAHĀSĀṄGHIKAS mŭ hä säng´ hē käs. *See* BUDDHIST SECTARIANISM.

MAHĀSATIPAṬṬHĀNA SUTTA mŭ hä´ sŭ tĭ pŭt´ tän ŭ so͞o´ tŭ. This sutta (SŪTRA) appears twice in the PALI CANON in slightly variant forms: as Dīgha Nikāya (Dialogues of the Buddha) XXII, and as Majjhima Nikāya (Middle Length Sayings) X. It details a method of directing attention ("mindfulness") intensively to one's own body-mind self in order to produce a deep existential awareness of the transitory nature of the self in all its aspects and of its intrinsically painful life situation.

There are four aspects and functions of the self that

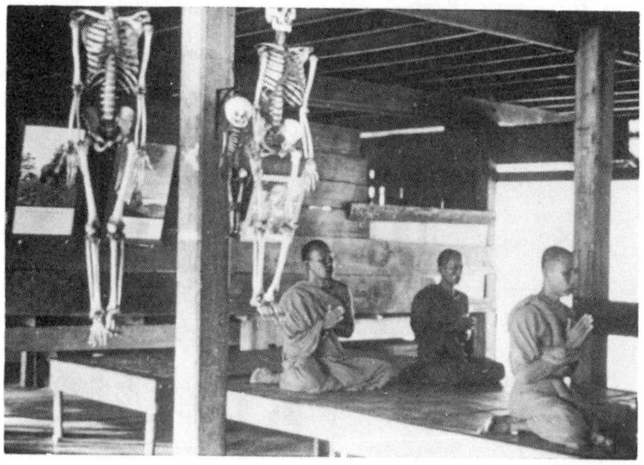

D. K. Swearer

One of the contemplations used in classical Theravāda meditation, exemplified in the Mahāsatipaṭṭhāna Sutta, focuses upon the transitoriness of the body, here represented by a family of skeletons.

are to receive such attention: the physical body in all its parts and activities; feelings and sensations; thought processes; the degree of actual attainment of a Buddhist self-awareness.

The basic technique throughout is to observe the ongoing process which is one's "self" as clearly and objectively as though it were another's. Thus as one walks one thinks, "I walk," or better yet, "walking occurs." The walking process is then observed in progressively smaller segments. And so too with moving an arm, eating, breathing, and so forth. In this way the meditator becomes pervasively aware of his body as process. Or the body may be analyzed into its thirty-one components—hair and down, nails, pus, urine, etc. Or again, one should think of the body in various stages of decay.

After proper body-awareness is achieved, the same technique is to be applied to one's body-feelings, emotions, and mental activities. Like a watchman at a city gate, one's clear, detached, unemotional attention observes the rise, persistence, and disappearance of a feeling or thought. Thus: "Anger rises; it is full-strength; now it is ebbing and is gone." Or, "The perception 'orange' arises, is here, is gone." Increasingly the meditator is detachedly aware in all his actions.

At the fourth level one views his body-mind activities for indications of progress toward full detachment and enlightenment. He observes, for example, whether sense-objects arouse desire in him. He examines "himself" for the presence or absence of fetters, i.e. emotional or intellectual attachments to anything whatever in himself or his experience; and he looks for the growth of the "factors of enlightenment" such as energy, joy, serenity, and equanimity.

Each item is meditated on long enough to attain knowledge and self-collectedness, and then another is taken up. When the meditator has gained a deep, perpetual awareness of himself as a mere process, and, as a result, attachment to self and its world is completely dead, then he grasps for nothing in the world at all. Full success in his efforts will produce the dying out of ill and misery and the attainment of NIRVANA. *See* MEDITATION, BUDDHIST, and bibliog.

W. L. KING

MAHĀTMA mŭ hät′ mŭ (H). *See* GANDHI, MOHANDAS K.

MAHĀVAṂSA mŭ′ hä väm′ sŭ (B—Pali; lit. "Great Chronicle"). A classical history of Buddhism in Sri Lanka (Ceylon). Composed in metrical verse, it is ascribed to the monk Mahānāma, and dates from the late fifth or early sixth century A.D. It covers material similar to the earlier DĪPAVAMSA, but in greater detail and in a more refined literary style. The Mahāvaṃsa was later continued in three stages to give a connected history down to modern times. This continuation is known as the Cūlavaṃsa, or Lesser Chronicle.

Bibliography. W. Geiger, trans., *The Mahāvaṃsa* (1964) and *The Cūlavaṃsa* (1929-30).

J. P. MCDERMOTT

MAHĀVASTU mŭ′ hä väs′ too (B—Skt.; lit. "Great Account"). Buddhist text, perhaps compiled around the beginning of the Christian era. Part of the Monastic Discipline (VINAYA PIṬAKA) of a subsect of the Mahāsāṅghikas, it purports to be an account of the life of the Buddha down to the time of the conversion of his first disciples. It includes much material relating to his previous rebirths (JĀTAKAS). Doctrinally it departs from the THERAVĀDA ideals, showing a trend toward MAHĀYĀNA in establishing a ten-step path for the compassionate saint (BODHISATTVA) to follow, and in its view of the Buddha as a miracle-working hero.

Bibliography. J. J. Jones, trans., *Mahāvastu,* 3 vols. (1949-56).

J. P. MCDERMOTT

MAHĀVĪRA mŭ hä vē′ rä (Ja—Skt.; lit. "great hero" [*mahat*—"great, eminent"; *vīra*—"brave man, hero, chief"]). Honorific title occurring in a variety of early Hindu contexts, eventually coming to be associated with Vardhamāna Jnātṛputra, the sixth century B.C. leader of JAINISM, to the extent that Vardhamāna is commonly named by this title alone (as SIDDHĀRTHA GAUTAMA is called simply "The BUDDHA").

Mahāvīra is regarded by the Jainas as the twenty-fourth and last in a series of enlightened teachers, the TĪRTHAṄKARAS (lit. "crossing-makers"), who have lived in the present cycle of cosmic history. It is to his life and mission that present-day Jainism traces itself. He and the other Tīrthaṅkaras (who are also called "Jinas," "conquerors") are venerated by Jainas, but are not regarded as divine or semi-divine; rather, they are treated as extraordinary persons who attained complete enlightenment as human beings and who then taught others the meaning of enlightenment and the way to attain it.

The dates that Jainas attach to Mahāvīra's life are 599-527 B.C. (Some modern scholars prefer 549-477 B.C.) He was born in Northeastern India, near the modern city of Patna, and died in the town now called Pāvāpūri, in the same region. Thus he lived at nearly the same time, and in much the same area, as Siddhārtha Gautama.

The account of his life that the Jaina tradition preserves also resembles in many ways the life of Gautama. Born into a warrior (KṢATRIYA) clan, Mahāvīra was convinced at age thirty of a need to seek enlightenment and release (MOKṢA) from worldly existence. He then abandoned his household life and went out into the forest alone. There he discarded all of his personal possessions, including all his clothes, pulled out his hair, and set out to live the life of a wandering mendicant.

It appears that Mahāvīra's actions, particularly the discarding of clothing and the pulling out of his hair, were done in conformity to existing ascetic practices. These practices may have been developed by a teacher named Pārśva, whom the Jainas regard as the twenty-third Tīrthaṅkara (Mahāvīra's predecessor in the series), who lived about 850 B.C.

Mahāvīra's ascetic program lasted for twelve and a half years, and was single-mindedly directed toward detachment from physical existence. Wandering on foot, begging all food, wearing little or nothing, he is said to have fasted for long periods of time, to have spoken little, and to have exposed himself to heat and cold (*see* TAPAS). This is consistent with Jaina teachings, which hold that humans (and all living beings) consist of an eternal soul, the JĪVA, which must be freed from entanglement in material existence. The freedom that is attained is not so much a matter of metaphysical insight or enlightenment as it is the detachment of the *jīva* from worldly activity (KARMA) that keeps it in bondage.

At age forty-two Mahāvīra both understood the mechanism of bondage and freedom for the *jīva* and also reached a stage of complete detachment (KAIVALYA) from worldly activity. He began teaching others, and eventually collected a distinctive group of followers. His sermons and dialogues are preserved by the Jainas in that portion of their scriptures known as the *aṅgas,* along with a record of his travels throughout Northeastern India. Among the noteworthy events of his career is a series of encounters with MAKKHALI-GOSĀLA, the leader of ĀJĪVIKAS, whose life is mostly known via Jaina accounts of his dealings with Mahāvīra. *See* FOUNDERS, RELIGIOUS.

Bibliography. P. S. Jaini, *The Jaina Path of Purification* (1979); H. Jacobi, trans., *Jaina Sūtras,* Pt. I (1884).

K. W. FOLKERT

MAHĀYĀNA mä hə yä´ nə (B—Skt.; lit. "great vehicle"). One of the two main branches in BUDDHISM, the other being HĪNAYĀNA or THERAVĀDA. Mahāyāna is sometimes termed the Northern School, since it exists in Tibet, Mongolia, China, Korea, and Japan. This movement, which emphasizes universal salvation, arose as a reaction against the austerity and individualism of early Buddhism.

E. J. COLEMAN

MAHDI mä´ dē (I—Arab.; lit. "the guided one"). Title of the messianic IMAM in SHI'ISM; used in the general Islamic tradition for the awaited descendant of MUHAMMAD who will restore Islamic purity. Human intellect and conscience are guides toward the establishment of a just Islamic order, but in addition God has entrusted to certain individuals the key function of "guidance." In the QUR'ĀN they are termed *muhtadūn* (recipients of guidance) and *hudāt* (guides), and so they attain the status of *hudāt al-muhtadūn* (rightly guided leaders). The title "mahdi," virtually a synonym of this term, seems to have gained importance through its usage in the ḤADĪTH, where it refers to certain individuals in the past and to a future messianic figure. A mahdi is divinely guided in a specific and individual way.

Muslims have the responsibility of establishing the ideal religio-political community, the UMMA, with a worldwide membership of all those who believe in God and his revelation through Muhammad. Muhammad himself planted the seeds of this responsibility, which carry the revolutionary challenge of Islam toward any social order which might hamper its realization. In the persistent aspiration for a more just society these seeds have borne fruit in rebellion throughout Islamic history. Muhammad's message embodied in the Qur'ān provided tremendous spiritual as well as political impetus for the creation of a just society. Consequently, in the years following Muhammad's death, there emerged a group of Muslims who, dissatisfied with the state of affairs under the CALIPHS, looked back to the early period of Islam as the ideal epoch, unadulterated by the corrupt and worldly rulers of the expanding Islamic empire. The idealization of the Prophet himself gave rise to the notion that he was something more than an ordinary man; he must have been divinely chosen and thus was the true leader who could guide his people.

Many began to look forward to the rule of a descendant of Muhammad, the Mahdi, who will also be named Muhammad. He will bear a title similar to that of the Apostle of God and will fill the earth with equity and justice. The growth of such a hope was the inevitable outcome of the consistent stress Islam lays on the realization of the just society under the guidance of divine revelation. With the establishment of various dynasties which failed to promote the Islamic ideal, the desire for a deliverer grew. Those who looked for the appearance of the Mahdi were generally sympathetic to the claims of the Prophet's descendants as heirs to the prophetic mission, and were the early adherents of the Shi'ia. The idea of a messianic imam who would bring an end to corruption and wickedness was especially important in Imamite Shi'ism (*see* IMĀMIYYA) where the firm belief in the return of the twelfth imam as the Mahdi continues to be expressed in the most repeated Shi'ite prayer: "May God hasten release from suffering through his [the Mahdi's] rise."

The title "mahdi" was first used of ALI and AL-ḤUSAYN as a designation of a righteous Islamic ruler. In the messianic sense it seems to have been first used by al-Mukhtār ibn Abī 'Ubayd al-Thaqafī, a man with Shi'ite sympathies, to designate Muhammad ibn al-Ḥanafiyya, a son of Ali by a wife other than FĀṬIMA, in the context of a two-year rebellion against UMAYYAD authority. Ibn al-Ḥanafiyya apparently declined the extravagant claims made for him and died without achieving anything significant. But the result of the movement were far-reaching. Many of its adherents did not accept his death as a reality and declared that he was in hiding and would eventually return. This marked the beginning of the two central beliefs about the Mahdi—his *ghayba* (concealment) and his *raj'a* (return) at the appropriate time. These beliefs helped all Shi'ites to endure under difficult circumstances and to hope for reform pending the coming of the Mahdi. Such expectation did not require that they oppose the establishment actively; rather, lack of information on the exact time when the hidden imam would appear required Shi'ites to be on the alert at all times.

The decades prior to the end of Umayyad rule in A.D. 750 were marked by several Shi'ite revolutions and uprisings headed by adherents of the party of Ali or other members of the HĀSHIMITE clan who demanded a new social order. Although the 'ABBĀSIDS based their revolution on Shi'ite expectations, they abandoned their messianic role after being established as caliphs and adopted SUNNISM. Nevertheless, they persisted in assuming messianic titles in the hope that the caliphate would have some resemblance to the ideals of the Shi'ite imamate and its function of restoring the purity of Islam. Even after this disappointment Shi'ite hopes continued to run high, and it was believed that almost all imams from that time on had not died, but might return as the Mahdi. This was especially true of the followers of the first twelve imams. The twelfth was, however, by no means the last of those who were proclaimed as mahdi, and the title has continued to be bestowed to the present day.

Bibliography. A. A. Sachedina, *Islamic Messianism* (1980).

A. A. SACHEDINA

MAIMONIDES mī môn′ ə dēz (Ju). *See* MOSES BEN MAIMON.

MAITREYA mā trā′ yə (B—Skt.; lit. "friendly one") **METTEYYA** mā tā′ yə (B—Pali). BODHISATTVA who resides in the TUṢITA HEAVEN; the Buddha yet to come.

Mentioned frequently in numerous Buddhist texts, Maitreya represents the oldest notion of a bodhisattva of the present era. (*See* JĀTAKA.) He is known to all Buddhist schools from very early times and in all Buddhist countries, and represents the earliest cult bodhisattva and an old affirmation that the future is finally favorable.

The ideas and aspirations given focus in Maitreya form a foundation for the rise of the bodhisattva doctrine. The early Buddhist tradition spoke of former Buddhas, the Buddha of our era, and Maitreya, who is the future Buddha. The Buddhas have attained final, complete NIRVANA, while Maitreya dwells in Tuṣita Heaven awaiting, as was the case with former Buddhas, the time to leave this realm to enter the realm of humankind. In time, religious aspirations coalesced around this messianic figure, and a belief arose that Maitreya received from Śākyamuni, the Buddha of our era, a prediction that he would attain supreme, perfect enlightenment in the future, and that Śākyamuni gave him a robe and golden thread. (*See* BUDDHA, GENERAL CONCEPTS OF.)

In MAHĀYĀNA, Maitreya is a deity of light, a guide for the departed, a being who consoles the faithful who confess their wrongs, and one who inspires the teaching masters should they become discouraged in moments of doubt. In rapt contemplation these teachers were enabled to attain the Tuṣita Heaven and be in the presence of Maitreya.

The wish to be reborn in the presence of Maitreya, either in the Tuṣita Heaven or when he appears on earth, and then attain salvic insight has been a part of Buddhist hopes in the past, and is so even today among THERAVĀDINS. In Mahāyāna the worship of AMIDA and the hope for salvation in the PURE LAND have become more important than Maitreya.

Bibliography. E. Lamotte, *Histoire du bouddhisme indien* (1958), pp. 775-88.

J. R. CARTER

MAKIGUCHI, TSUNESABURŌ mä kē goo′ chē tsoo nā sä boo′ rō (B—Jap.; 1871-1944). Founder of the movement now known as SŌKA GAKKAI. Born in Niigata Prefecture as the oldest son of Chōmatsu Watanabe and adopted into the Makiguchi family when three years old, he was educated in the Normal School in Sapporo, Hokkaidō, and taught geography there for a brief time. At the age of thirty-one he became principal of Shinbori Elementary School in Tokyo, but his chief interest was his theory concerning human values and the proper method of education in these values. In 1903 he published *Jinsei Chirigaku* (Geography of Life). His writings were collected and published posthumously under the title *Kachiron,* the book which formed the foundation on which the religious organization Sōka Gakkai was built. He joined Nichiren Shō-shū in 1928 and began to relate his own philosophy to the teachings of NICHIREN BUDDHISM. Because Makiguchi and his group would not pay homage to the national SHINTŌ shrine at ISÉ, he and twenty other members were imprisoned in 1943. He died in prison of malnutrition.

N. S. BRANNEN

MAKKHALI-GOSĀLA mūk′ kū lē gō sä′ lū (B—Pali) **MASKARIN GOŚĀLA** mūs kū′ rĭn gō shä′ lū (B—Skt.). One of a frequently cited set of six religious teachers in northeastern India contemporary with Gautama the BUDDHA (*ca.* 560-480 B.C.). Gosāla and his followers were known as ĀJĪVIKAS and apparently were regarded by Buddhists and Jainas alike as the worst of false teachers in both doctrine and life. Criticism of his teaching focused on his denial of any operative cause for moral good or evil in human life. In effect, he denied freedom of the will and ascribed the entire process of rebirth (KARMA and SAMSARA) to fixed fate. Yet he seemed to posit an eschatological end to the pain of rebirth after the "allotted time" for "both fools and wise alike" (Dīgha Nikāya I, 53-54).

Bibliography. See bibliog. for ĀJĪVIKA.

R. H. DRUMMOND

MALĀ'IKA mə lä′ ī kə (I—Arab.; lit. "angels"). In view of its form and the confusion of the root in the singular with the word for king (Arab. *malik*), the word is most likely borrowed into pre-Islamic Arabic from the Northwest Semitic *mal'ak,* "messenger." The plural *malā'ika* occurs frequently in the QUR'ĀN, but the singular only twelve times. In accord with usual Near Eastern views, angels are described as winged, with two, three, or four wings (Sura 35:1), and all angels have defined functions. There is an Angel of Death, unnamed in the Qur'ān (Sura 32:11), and a keeper of Hell, called Mālik, a probable derivative from the common noun. The angels Michael and GABRIEL are messengers (Arab. RASŪL), Gabriel being the most important of all the angels because of his role as bearer of the Qur'ān to Muhammad. The Qur'ān spends little time in descriptions of angels but devotes attention to their role and function. The Qur'ānic attitude assumes a knowledge of and an understanding of angels on the part of the reader, but later commentary expanded on the brief accounts of the angels and added elements derived from Judeo-Christian tradition and from folklore.

Of some concern in the Qur'ān and its commentaries is the status of Iblīs (lit. "the Devil"). In one passage he is termed a JINN (Sura 18:51), but he is also called an angel (Sura 2:34), thus equating the two nonhuman entities in the minds of some commentators. In Sura 2:30 ff. the story of the submission of the angels to the will of ALLAH is given along with the account of the rebellion of Iblīs and his band. In traditions (ḤADĪTH) from 'Ā'ISHA, MUHAMMAD is supposed to have said that angels were created from light and the jinn from fire, the words having the same root in Arabic. The two angels Hārūt and Mārūt (Sura 2:102) and their association with magic have caused the commentators some problems, as have the two angels Munkar and Nakīr, not mentioned in the Qur'ān but only in the commentaries, who have the duty of questioning the dead in the grave to determine whether or not they will be punished or rewarded. Angels are guardians of humankind but also recorders of human deeds (Sura 82:10-12).

The writers of KALĀM sought by combining passages from the Qur'ān, traditions, and ideas derived from philosophy to further define the nature of angels. The Neoplatonists made some of the angels into the animating forces of the spheres, and there was much discussion about whether the angels could be classed as animals.

An angel whose legend has no basis in the Qur'ān or in prophetic tradition, but who is prominent in later eschatological discussion, is Isrāfīl. He is assigned the task of reading the divine decree and of blowing the trumpet to signal the Day of Judgment. *See* ESCHATOLOGY §3; ANGELS.

Bibliography. A. J. Wensinck, *Concordance de la tradition musulmane* (1943); M. M. Pickthall, *Meaning of the Glorious Koran* (1953); W. Eickmann, *Angelologie und Dämonologie des Korans* (1908).

G. D. NEWBY

MALIK IBN ANAS mä′ lĭk ĭb′ən ä′ nəs (I—*ca.* 712-795). Author of the first treatise on jurisprudence in Islam, the *Muwaṭṭa',* and founder of the Malikite school of Islamic law.

Born in MEDINA, where he spent most of his life, Malik became the most prominent jurist of that city. He is often referred to simply as the IMAM of Medina. Little is known of his early life, although many legends abound. He is supposed, for example, to have spent two to three years in his mother's womb and to have been taught FIQH by some nine hundred teachers. He seems to have been in competition for a time with IBN ISḤĀQ, Muhammad's biographer, until Ibn Isḥāq abandoned both *fiqh* and Medina.

Malik's *Muwaṭṭa'* is the earliest work on *fiqh,* written to develop a basis for law by means of a survey of custom (SUNNA) in Medina, but he was writing at a stage when the rules for transmission of ḤADĪTH had not been fully formed and his work was subjected to modification and correction by later scholars. But so rigorous was his criticism of his authorities that his reputation in this area has remained high. Malik did not start from a theoretical position but with the law as it existed, so his work seems somewhat disorganized under the larger topics of contracts, penal law, marriage, etc. But it was so influential that Islamic legal treatises continued this pattern.

While Malik did not start a school, his name came to be used by a branch of Islamic law found in the Maghrib, Africa, and Upper Egypt. A particularly famous adherent of this school was IBN RUSHD (Averroes), who wrote a systematic treatise on the legal system.

Bibliography. See FIQH. G. D. NEWBY

MALIKITES mā′ lə kīts (I). *See* MALIK IBN ANAS.

MANA. An impersonal force or power thought to reside in certain persons, objects, or places, making them dangerous or giving them extraordinary properties. Belief in mana was first described by Codrington and others in connection with the cultures of Melanesia and Polynesia, but it exists in many other places. Its impersonal and mechanical nature distinguishes it from any form of spirit possession or endowment. It is only sometimes sacred and therefore religious; in other cases it evokes the kind of prudential caution displayed by moderns in the presence of high-voltage power lines. Mana resided in Polynesian royalty, making direct contact with them fatal to commoners. It constituted the special abilities of great artists, artisans, orators, and warriors. Objects in which it resided were dangerous. But it could be lost, the person or object thereby becoming once again ordinary.

Bibliography. R. H. Codrington, *The Melanesians* (1891; rpr. 1957).

C. R. TABER

MANĀT mä nät′. Pre-Islamic Arabian goddess. *See* TIME OF IGNORANCE.

MANDALA mŭn′ də lə (H & B—Skt.; lit. "circular, round"). An art form, based upon symmetrically arranged circles within larger concentric circles, which is fundamental to the ritual and meditation of Hindu and Buddhist TANTRISM. Quite possibly the mandala derives from the early Indian form of the STŪPA, a dome-shaped shrine built to house relics of ŚĀKYAMUNI, former Buddhas, or holy men. Placing a relic at the center of the circular *stūpa* created an architectural prototype for the mandala. Again, the ground plan of a *stūpa*, like the skeleton of a mandala, suggested a cosmic axis surrounded by rings. Even ritual at a *stūpa* involved circularity, as the worshiper walked in a circle around the monument in a clockwise direction.

1. **General form.** Typically a mandala presents a central Buddha figure, who is surrounded by a pantheon of subordinate deities, positioned in a geometric composition. This galaxy of supermundane beings is to be interpreted as the manifestation of the Universal Buddha or the BRAHMAN of Hinduism, the primordial One from which the universe emanates and to which it returns. In short, the mandala serves as a cosmoplan, a spiritual blueprint of the universe. As such, it schematically maps the origin, operation, and constitution of the cosmos by disclosing its pattern of spiritual forces. Each mandala depicts both the process by which ultimate reality gives rise to multiplicity and that by which the individual may achieve reabsorption into the One. The proliferation of BUDDHAS, BODHISATTVAS, and attendants in mandalas would have been chaotic if the chief figures had not been thematically emphasized and the hierarchy visually diagrammed. (*See* Plate Ib.)

2. **Parts.** Beginning with the core of a mandala, one finds a fivefold division; a larger Buddha figure is centered among four other Buddhas, which are situated at the cardinal points of the compass. These five Buddha figures are referred to in Nepal as Dhyāni Buddhas, elsewhere as Jinas (conquerors). (*See* BUDDHA, GENERAL CONCEPTS OF.) Their names differ according to the sect that is using the mandala, but the larger figure, whether called Vajrasattva or VAIROCANA, is the primeval Buddha (Ādi-Buddha), which is the personification of the DHARMAKĀYA. Each of the remaining four presides over his own Buddha-field or domain; Akṣobhya rules over the Eastern Paradise, Ratnasambhava the Southern,

Reprinted by special arrangement with Shambhala Publications, Inc., 1123 Spruce St., Boulder CO 80302. From *Tibetan Sacred Art* by Detlef Ingo Lauf. Copyright 1976 by Shambhala Publications, Inc.

Diagram showing the structure of a mandala: (A) outer circle, the Mountain of Fire; (B) second circle, symbols of the Vajra; (C) eight cemeteries, representing the eight forms of consciousness to be overcome; (D) ring of lotus petals; (F) the mandala proper; (G) further circle with Vajra symbols; (H) lotus flower; (I) primal Buddha, center of the mandala

Amitābha (AMIDA) the Western, and Amoghasiddhi the Northern. Usually bodhisattvas or feminine deities are interspersed between the five key figures. At lower levels of awareness the five core Jinas may be equated with an open-ended set of concepts such as the five kinds of perception, the five elements, the five enjoyments (meat, alcohol, fish, a certain grain, and sex), and the five bodily functions. (*See* TANTRISM §5.) But after spiritual progress, one transcends these penultimate interpretations and identifies the five principal emanations with types of wisdom. Thus, the larger figure is associated with enlightened consciousness and the remaining four with subsidiary states of consciousness. Repetitions of the quintuple pattern signify the interpenetration of all things and lead one away from dualistic thinking. One must grasp the cosmic connections that link all creatures as they radiate toward the outermost circle, which represents the periphery of the universe.

3. **Varities.** All mandalas are visual iconographs, but they may be sketched, painted, sculpted, drawn in sand, embroidered on a banner, or even danced. Nonfigurative mandalas exist as well as the figurative, Buddha images sometimes being replaced by Sanskrit symbols. The famous *Śrī* (Auspicious) YANTRA of Hinduism furnishes another sort of nonfigurative example. It is an abstract mandala which features overlapping triangles within concentric circles. Of the nine major interpentrating triangles, five point down, four up; the five downward-pointing triangles symbolize the female principle, the four upward-pointing triangles the male principle. The union and ultimate identity of male and female is dramatized by the dynamic interplay of triangles; their points of intersection, in turn, produce additional triangles which express the movement from duality to multiplicity, the primal activity of differentiation. Thus this *yantra* provides a geometric rendering of the entire universe as reduced to its essentials. Ideally, concentration upon the elements of the *Śrīyantra* results in the discovery of internal counterparts; one finds within oneself the transformations or aspects of the ABSOLUTE which are embodied in the imagery of this mandala.

A somewhat imprecise distinction can be made in terms of relative simplicity or complexity, since some mandalas portray fewer than a dozen deities and others feature well over a hundred. Because the mandala is understood as a microcosm which embodies the various divine powers at work in the universe, the number of deities is limited only by the imagination and industry of the artist. Thus, many mandalas present the viewer with a bewilderingly intricate configuration, a composition which must be carefully "read" and which thereby testifies to the temporal as well as spatial status of pictorial art. Certain mandalas are marked by the prevalence of wrathful figures who exhibit hideous grimaces and enhance their gruesomeness by wielding terrifying weapons. Such beings are a metaphorical reminder that only the most undaunted warrior is fit for battle against the defiling enemies of passion and ignorance. Familiarity with these awesome beings also has the virtue of preparing one for any malevolent deities which he may encounter as forms emerging from his own consciousness. Still another type of mandala arises when a YOGIN simply visualizes the content of a text or painting. In Tantric meditation chanting and contemplation can produce a "mandala world" which is populated by a host of divinities. One then imagines himself to be at the center of his mental mandala, envisions himself in sexual union with a consort, and assimilates all surrounding figures into his own body. In effect, the meditator becomes or realizes his identity with the Universal Buddha. At times a popular Buddha, such as Amida in Japan, becomes the distinguishing centerpiece of a mandala. Given the abundance of spiritual beings portrayed in mandalas, one might naturally raise the question of the ontological status of these creatures. Some practitioners regard them as mere symbols, but others conceive of them as objectively existing entities. Those who subscribe to idealism are able to view all entities as creations of mind and as ontologically equal.

4. **Uses.** Hindu and Buddhist mandalas are basically alike in that both are inspired by the quest to recapture primeval consciousness, that integrity of being which only rapport with the One can restore. On a popular level, however, mandalas commonly function as objects of worship. For example, during the ceremonies which observe the eve of spring, worshipers offer prayers to the deities of the mandala in order to ensure prosperity and protection from adversities. On a magical plane mandalas transcend symbolism and are actually used to conjure up deities. But on a higher level one detects the cosmic deities within himself; finding all gods to be self-contained, one awakens to his divinity and realizes his identity with the Absolute, the Brahman of Hinduism or the void of Buddhism. The passage through the mandala is, then, a movement from particulars to the universal, a journey to the state of equipoise in which SAMSARA and NIRVANA are perceived as identical. To a clouded mind the void has manifestations, but to the unclouded mind there is only the void. In essence, the mandala is an aesthetic instrument for approaching the formless ground of all forms.

Recently Jung has brought the fresh perspective of analytical psychology to bear upon the interpretation of the mandala. According to this theory, the mandala conforms to the microcosmic character of the psyche. Noting that mandalas appeared spontaneously in the dreams of patients who suffered from conditions such as schizophrenia, even though they were unfamiliar with Eastern thought, Jung theorized that these surfacings were instinctual, therapeutic responses to the problem of psychic disintegration. So understood, the mandala becomes a matrix in which the disoriented person may relate and reintegrate seemingly opposed aspects of his self. Jung defined the mandala as "the archetype of wholeness," a universal feature of instinct which is made evident by the basic similarities in mandala forms irrespective of the culture or age in which they originate. Other thinkers, serving to support his account, emphasize that symbols like the cross or swastika are really variations on the mandala theme of a single point from which all else radiates.

Bibliography. G. Tucci, *The Theory of Practice of the Mandala* (1969); J. and M. Arguelles, *Mandala* (1972); C. Jung, *The Archetypes and the Collective Unconscious,* 2nd ed. (1968).

E. J. COLEMAN

MĀNAVA-DHARMAŚĀSTRA mŭn´ ŭ vŭ där´ mŭ shä´ strŭ (H). *See* MANU, LAWS OF.

MANDATE OF HEAVEN (Con—Chin.; *t'ien-ming* tē ēn´ mĭng). The concept that Heaven sanctions the rule of the emperor and his dynasty. Its earliest formulation is found in the *Book of History (Shu Ching),* in proclamations issued by the newly founded Chou dynasty (twelfth century B.C.). The Chou rulers stated that originally the Shang rulers had been given the Mandate (eighteenth century B.C.) after the Hsia dynasty before it had fallen from virtuous ways. They had maintained the Mandate for a number of centuries, but because of recent neglect of the ways of Heaven, the Mandate had been withdrawn, and they had lost their right to rule. The concept represents not only one of the major political theories for the succession of dynastic cycles throughout Chinese history, but in addition a religious commitment of Chinese political culture to bring the order of society into conformity with the ways of Heaven. *See* CONFUCIANISM; MENCIUS. R. L. TAYLOR

MANDEANS măn dē´ ənz. Semitic, GNOSTIC religious group (with adherents today in Iraq and Iran). Though Mandean writings (most notable are the *Ginza* and *Book of John*) were not compiled until *ca.* A.D. 700, some scholars date its origins in the early Christian era and link it with JOHN THE BAPTIST and his followers. Similar in teaching to MANICHEISM, Mandean worship centers in the story of the victory of Manda da Hayye (Knowledge of Life) over demonic forces—a battle promising the triumph and ascent of believers' souls. R. C. GREGG

MANICHEISM măn´ ĭ kē ĭsm. A syncretistic religion inspired by the Babylonian prophet Mani (A.D. 216-277), who incorporated elements of ZOROASTRIANISM, BUDDHISM, GNOSTICISM, and CHRISTIANITY. His elaborate cosmogony involved the fateful captivity of light particles in the realm of darkness and the drama of their liberation by agents (Zoroaster, Buddha, Jesus, Mani) of the Father of Light. Manichee churches won adherents in Mediterranean lands and in Asia and India until the thirteenth century, though frequently outlawed and attacked by orthodox writers. R. C. GREGG

MĀṆIKKAVĀCAKAR män ĭk kŭ vä sŭ gär (H—Tamil; Skt.; lit. "he whose speech is like rubies"). The greatest poet-saint of TAMIL ŚAIVISM, probably having lived in the ninth century. According to hagiographical accounts, Māṇikkavācakar was the chief minister of the king at Madurai before he became a devotee of the god SHIVA. He spent the latter part of his life in the famous South Indian temple town of Chidambaram, where Shiva is worshipped as NATARĀJA. Māṇikkavācakar's greatest work is the *Tiruvācakam* ("sacred utterances"), which is included in the *Tirumurai,* a sacred canon of Tamil Śaivism. Certain aspects of his thought anticipate the later Tamil ŚAIVA SIDDHĀNTA philosophy. G. E. YOCUM

MAÑJUŚRĪ män jū´ shrĭ (B—Skt.; lit. "gentle glory" or "sweet splendor"). BODHISATTVA who personifies insight and wisdom *(prajñā).*

Mañjuśrī is not mentioned in the earliest strata of the Buddhist texts, but by the fourth century A.D. became one of the most popular MAHĀYĀNA bodhisattvas, mentioned prominently in several texts. He appears not to have been a popular subject for artistic representation until about the beginning of the fifth century A.D. In China he became associated with the mountain Wu-t'ai-shan in the Shansi area, which became an object of pilgrimage, especially for the Mongols. There is a tradition that the name Manchuria is derived from Mañjuśrī. In Japan he figures in meditational practices in TENDAI and other schools, but, on the whole, does not play a major role in the life of Japanese Buddhists.

In Buddhist art Mañjuśrī is depicted with a five-pointed coiffure or tiara, holding an ignorance-slaying sword in his right hand and in his left, a book, symbolic of the PRAJÑĀPĀRAMITĀ SŪTRAS.

The origin of Mañjuśrī remains uncertain. Possibly he embodies a cluster of ideas and images associated with Pañcasikha, "Five Locks" or "Five-Crest," a GANDHARVA. Pañcasikha was associated with deities, reporting to the Buddha the activities of the assembly of deities and receiving from the leader of a heavenly realm reports of the good deeds of human beings. Once, when BRAHMĀ Sanaṇkumāra (Brahmā "Forever-Youth") wanted to appear before an assembly of deities, he assumed the form of Pañcasikha. BUDDHAGHOSA records that Pañcasikha, in a previous life-sequence, was a boy wearing his hair in five knots, who set about doing works for public welfare and who died while still young. Regularly Mañjuśrī is called *kumārabhūta,* "one who has become a youth," which means, "one who has become the crown prince."

A bodhisattva of the tenth stage, Mañjuśrī seeks to aid all in their realization of release. He resides in different Buddha-fields, the most prominent of which are those in the east and northeast. (*See* MANDALA.) Mañjuśrī appears to devotees in dreams or meditative visions.

Bibliography. G. P. Malalasekera, *Dictionary of Pāli Proper Names,* (1960), pp. 105-7; W. E. Soothill and L. Hodous, *A Dictionary of Chinese Buddhist Terms* (1937), pp. 153-54; R. H. Robinson and W. L. Johnson, *The Buddhist Religion,* 2nd ed. (1977), pp. 104-6. J. R. CARTER

MANTRA mŭn´ trŭ (H & B—Skt.; lit. "instrument of thought" [*man*—"to think"]). A properly repeated hymn or formula used in ritual worship and meditation as an instrument for evoking the presence of a particular "divinity" *(devatā);* first uttered by an inspired "seer" (Rishi) and transmitted orally from master to disciple in a carefully controlled manner.

Mantra initially referred to the metrical hymns and ritual formulas of the Veda but came to include, especially within the Āgamic or Tantric traditions (*see* Āgama; Tantrism), a wide variety of rhythmically repeated verbal or syllabic compositions that, through the power (Śakti) of their sound-vibrations, are experienced as "mental instruments" for manifesting particular "divinities" within the reciter, i.e., for transforming his or her consciousness into specific forms of psychic power leading to the attainment of various worldly or transcendent ends. Mantra is a complex phenomenon, resisting easy definition and evolving within nearly all Indian religious traditions and beyond India as well. Nevertheless, it is based upon a more or less persistent core.

1. **Common core.** The efficacy of a mantra depends upon its being or containing either a true name (*nāma*) of the "divinity" (e.g., Brahman) or, primarily in Āgamic or Tantric religion, an equivalent esoteric "seed" (*bīja*) syllable (e.g., Oṃ), which is held to be essentially related to the being itself and to embody it when uttered. A mantra is accepted as having been revealed through the "vision" of a "seer" who directly experiences the "divinity" within his or her consciousness and whose mind (*manas*) then formulates a composition (*mantra*) that perfectly captures the name, character, and power of the "divinity." Such a mantra can be used as an instrument for continued evocation of the "divinity" if, and only if, heard (*see* Śruti) from the mouth of a master (Guru) or teacher (Ācārya) who knows how to repeat it correctly, including the proper mental concentration and intention. After initiation into a mantra, the student must undertake a long discipline of repetition (*japa*) of it, audibly or inaudibly, but always and essentially mentally (*manana*), until the rhythm of its sound-vibrations transforms his or her consciousness into the likeness of the "divinity." This identification with the divine power is held to result in various extraordinary "accomplishments" (*see* Siddhi), up to and including final liberation (Mokṣa; Nirvana), depending upon the nature of the particular "divinity" and mantra and the intention of the reciter.

Although the continued, widespread vitality of this phenomenon (*see* Transcendental Meditation) is based primarily upon the *experience* of mantras as effective instruments for shaping and liberating psychic power in the pursuit of specified goals, and although they are employable within various theoretical frameworks, mantras derive their most consistent and plausible rationale from an emanationist metaphysics in which all levels of reality come forth from, and continue to be permeated by, the same source or power. In this scheme sound (*śabda*) has a primary place, usually as the distinctive attribute of space or ether (*ākāśa*), the first physical element manifested and within which all other elements come to exist. Thus, sound and its vibrations (*spanda*) are able to interrelate and interact with all elements and all levels, stimulating resonance or sympathetic vibrations among them. Moreover, every emanation or manifest form, every distinct type or class of reality or being, is produced by and corresponds to a specific configuration of subtle sound-vibration which in turn corresponds to and is expressible by a specific linguistic and cognitive form. This precise correspondence of being, sound, thought, and language is a key assumption underlying this rationale for a mantra's effectiveness.

Also basic is the assumption of a correspondence between each microcosm and the macrocosm. All individuals, having come forth from and continuing to exist within the same sacred power, have the potential to experience, manifest, or become any being or "divinity" by re-forming their psychic power (*cit-śakti*) through the concentrated, intentional repetition of the proper mantra.

2. **Vedic mantras.** The earliest mantras (late second millennium B.C.) were the Sanskrit metrical hymns of the Rig Veda, praising and invoking such divinities as Indra, Agni, Soma, Varuṇa or Sūrya. Tied increasingly to the sacrificial ritual (Yajña), mantras came to be grouped into four collections (Saṃhitās) according to their ritual function: the Rig Veda, the Sāma (primarily Rig Vedic hymns set to music), the Yajur (formulas used with specific ritual actions), and the Atharva (brief incantations or magical spells meant to ward off evil and ensure blessings as well as longer, more speculative hymns concerning Brahman, the creative power released by the mantras and the sacrifice). The term "mantra" came to refer primarily to any portion of these four collections, with certain passages becoming detached from their original loci and functioning in various initiatory, ritual, and meditative contexts, e.g., the Gāyatrī Mantra and the sacred syllable *Oṃ*. In the Upaniṣads, Brahman is also seen as the universal principle of consciousness present in each individual "self" (Atman), thus establishing in elementary form the basic correspondences between being, sound, languages, and thought and between macrocosm and microcosm. (On the Upaniṣadic or Vedāntic metaphysical framework that remains basic for the understanding of all Vedic and Hindu mantras, *see* Brahman.)

3. **Hindu sectarian mantras.** On this Vedic basis but incorporating many non-Vedic elements, the use of mantras has been ramified endlessly within Indian life as various divinities have been evoked in pursuit of the full range of human goals concerning both worldly enjoyment (*bhoga, bhukti*) and liberation (*mokṣa, mukti*). Especially important from the early centuries A.D. on are mantras devoted to the three major Hindu deities, Vishnu, Shiva, and the Goddess (Devī or Śakti), who, in differing hierarchical arrangements, are either identified with Brahman or treated as its highest manifest forms. These mantras

are generally understood as revealed to sages by the deities themselves, recorded in such post-Vedic scriptures as the Purāṇas and Āgamas and handed down by unbroken, authoritative lines of teachers. Sectarian groups, devoted more or less exclusively to one of these deities, are based upon a "root mantra" (*mūla-mantra:* e.g., *nama śivāya,* "homage to Shiva") that is the key element in their initiation ritual and that, along with many other mantras, continues to be recited in the worship of, meditation on, and realization of the chosen deity (Iṣṭa Devatā). In contrast to the Vedic mantras, for which initiation came to be limited to male members of the Twice Born classes, these post-Vedic mantras are generally theoretically open to all members of Hindu society. Moreover, the dominant ritual context switches from the Vedic fire sacrifice to the devotional worship (Pūjā) of images in temples and home shrines (*see* Bhakti Hinduism), bringing about a powerful merging of auditory and visual modes of expressing divine forms.

4. **Hindu Tantric mantras.** It is particularly in the ritually oriented Āgamic or Tantric traditions centered on such temple worship that the theory and practice of mantra is most highly developed and systematically interrelated with other ritual means of manifesting divine presences or forms, including not only divine images but also ritual gestures (Mudrās) and geometric symbols (Yantras; Mandalas), all of which demonstrate the interrelatedness of all levels of existence and are intended to bring them into conformity with a divine form or pattern. The Āgamas or Tantras as ritual texts are often termed *Mantra-śāstras,* "systematic texts dealing with mantras," and give elaborate instructions for reconstructing appropriate mantras for each "divinity," ritual occasion, and purpose. Building upon the Vedic model of the sacred syllable *Oṃ* as a mantra embodying Brahman, each "divinity" as a form of Brahman is identified with a "seed" syllable to be used with or in place of the divinity's proper name. While meaningless in ordinary language, these seed mantras are viewed as having precise esoteric meanings as sound forms corresponding to specific divine forms and are often derived from the first letter of the divinity's name (e.g., *śrīṃ* for Śrī or Lakṣmī, *krīm* for Krishna, *duṃ* for Durgā). Developing alongside of and partly in reaction to these complex and esoteric traditions, other devotional movements have used as more generally accessible mantras either vernacular hymns of praise or the simple divine name, e.g., Rāma or Krishna (*see* Bhakti Hinduism §5; Hare Krishna).

5. **Buddhist mantras.** While based in part upon the emphasis in early Buddhism on the ritualistic and meditative repetition of the words of the Buddha (*buddha-vacana*) and of such formulas as the Three Refuges (Triratna) and the Four Noble Truths, mantras in the strict sense of the word assumed a place of major importance only around the middle of the first millennium A.D. with the emergence of the Tantric form of Mahāyāna termed Mantrayāna ("The Vehicle of the Mantra"), which continues down to the present in its Tibetan form of Vajrayāna and its Japanese form Shingon ("True-Word," the Japanese term for mantra). In this form of Buddhism the universal Buddha nature or Buddha mind (*see* Buddha, General Concepts of), also termed "emptiness" (Śūnyatā), plays a role functionally equivalent to that of Brahman in the Vedic or Hindu systems as the ultimate source or power of which all beings and "divinities" are manifestations and which continues to interrelate them all. The major "divinities" evoked through mantras, *mudrās* and mandalas include the Dhyāni Buddhas, especially the primordial Ādi-Buddha, Vairocana; Bodhisattvas such as Avalokiteśvara and Mañjuśrī; and various feminine forms, such as the Savior Tārā, who are most generally termed "Prajñās" as manifestations of the Buddha's liberating wisdom (Prajñā). As in the Hindu Āgamas or Tantras, each of these divinities has a one-syllable "seed" mantra; and esoteric mantras are constructed for various purposes (*see* Oṃ Maṇipadme Hūṃ). Tantric Buddhists strive, through ritual and meditative means, to experience directly the unity or nonduality of all levels of existence in the Buddha nature or "emptiness." This goal is often expressed as the actualization of the harmony, correspondence, and interpenetration of the "Three Mysteries of the Buddhas"—the mystery of the body realized through ritual gestures (*mudrās),* that of speech through mantras, and that of mind though meditation (Dhyāna; Samādhi). Thus, mantras as sacred speech play the central, pivotal role of revealing and integrating the common, dynamic structures of mind and body.

In nontantric Mahāyāna traditions, especially the devotional Pure Land Sects, the name of the Buddha (Nembutsu) is also often recited as a mantra (*see* Amida).

Bibliography. J. Gonda, "The Indian Mantra," *Oriens,* XVI (1963), 244-97; A. Bharati, *Tantric Tradition* (1965); M. Eliade, *Yoga: Immortality and Freedom* (1958), ch. VI; A. Wayman, *Buddhist Tantras* (1973); S. Beyer, *Cult of Tārā* (1973).

W. G. Neevel

MANTRAYĀNA mŭn trŭ yä′ nə (B—Skt.; lit "mystical syllables vehicle"). Buddhist school of the seventh and eighth centuries which emphasized the magical efficacy of esoteric words or syllables to produce rainfall, repel evil spirits, communicate with a deity, or achieve Buddhahood. *See* Mantra; Tantrism; Shingon.

E. J. Coleman

MANU mŭ′ nōō (H—Skt.; lit. "a thinking being," "man," "mankind" [*man*—"to think, reflect, believe, speculate"]). As a common noun, Manu refers to the thinking, intelligent creature, i.e., a human being, usually male. As a proper name, it is the name of the primal man. Most medieval rulers in India traced their royal lineage back to Manu. Manu is regarded in the RIG VEDA as the original instigator of the sacrifices and ritual observances that form the foundation of orthodox Brahmanic culture. In subsequent strata of Vedic literature, Manu is one of the thirty-one divine beings in the celestial realm and is identified with the creator-god, PRAJĀPATI.

In the myth of the universal deluge recounted in the Śatapatha Brāhmaṇa, Manu, like Noah in the OT and Utnapishtim in the Babylonian creation epic, is chosen to survive the catastrophe. Warned of the imminent disaster by a mythical fish, Manu constructed a boat, tied it to the fish's horn and was carried by the fish to safety. As the sole survivor, Manu poured an oblation of clarified butter (GHEE) and sour milk into the waters. A year later a beautiful maiden arose, and declared herself to be the daughter of Manu. Together they became the ancestors of the new race. In the MAHĀBHĀRATA, the fish is identified with BRAHMĀ, and in the PURĀṆAS with VISHNU as the first of ten incarnations.

Conceived of as a human king, Manu is known as the founder and first king of Ayodhyā (later the capital city of Rāma's kingdom and the modern Oudh) and the father of Ilā, the spouse of Budha, offspring of the moon. Through his son descended the solar race of men and through his daughter, the lunar race.

In later Hindu cosmological speculation, a single great cosmic aeon is designated as the "day of Brahmā" and is divided into fourteen periods called *manvantaras* (Manu cycles), each of which is 306,720,000 years in duration. Each of these periods is created and ruled over by its own Manu (Laws of Manu 1.63). The world is re-created within each subperiod and a new Manu appears to create a new race of men. The current age is the seventh *manvantara*.

The first Manu is called the "Self-existent" by virtue of the fact that he generated himself without the intervention of any other creative agency. He functions as a kind of demiurge to Prajāpati, the chief creator-god in the BRĀHMAṆAS. Manu initiated the cosmogony by creating the ten Prajāpatis or secondary creators. He is also credited with the authorship of the code of laws or moral principles known as the LAWS OF MANU as well as the Kalpa and Gṛhya Sūtras (i.e., manuals of public and domestic rites). Manu is revered throughout India as the supreme authority in all matters pertaining to jurisprudence and religious custom.

Bibliography. H. Bhattacharyya, *The Cultural Heritage of India*, II, pt. 4. (1937, 1962); C. Drekmeier, *Kingship and Community in Early India* (1962); *see* bibliog. for MANU, LAWS OF.

J. B. LONG

MANU, LAWS OF mū´ nōō. A "Treatise on Right Conduct by Manu" known traditionally as *Mānava-dharmaśāstra* or *Manu-smṛti*. This work is a prototypical manual of Hindu jurisprudence, composed of injunctions, prohibitions, and moral pronouncements concerning every important aspect of social and religious life in ancient India. It provides social, ethical, and religious precepts for the governance of corporate life and formulates rules on which the major religious observances in orthodox Brahmanism are established. The VEDAS declare that MANU's words are wholesome, like medicine, and provide an antidote for diseases of every sort.

The breadth and richness of ethical pronouncements is reflected in the diversity of topics treated: cosmogony, duties pertaining to each of the four stages of life (ĀŚRAMAS), the eight forms of marriage, daily rituals and funeral rites, pollution and purification, rules governing the life of women, dietary laws, forms of hospitality, the duties of kings, principles of civil and criminal law, debts, inheritance, the origin and duties of the four CASTES (*varṇas*), gift-giving, sacrifices and, lastly, topics of more metaphysical significance, such as the nature of the soul (ATMAN), the doctrine of KARMA, the path to liberation (MOKṢA), and punishment in hell.

For most peoples on the Indian subcontinent this text, interpreted through its numerous commentaries, especially that of Medhātithi (ninth century), has been invoked as the source of righteousness for all people in all areas of living, as attested by the numerous citations of its teachings in Epic, Purāṇic and other ethical literature. The text consists of 2,694 couplets divided into twelve chapters, and probably took its present shape between the second century B.C. and the second century A.D.

Bibliography. A. S. Altekar, *Sources of Hindu Dharma in its Socio-Religious Aspects* (1952); G. Bühler, *The Laws of Manu*, SBE, XXV, (1866); D. H. H. Ingalls, "Authority and Law in Ancient India," Suppl. to the *JAOS*, XXXI (1911); J. Jolly, *Hindu Law and Custom* (1928); P. V. Kane, *History of Dharmaśāstra* (1930-46).

J. B. LONG

MAPPŌ mäp pō´ (B—Jap.; lit. "end of the DHARMA"). According to MAHĀYĀNA Buddhism there are three periods, or stages, in Buddhism: *Shōhō* (true dharma), which began the year of ŚĀKYAMUNI'S death—949 B.C. (sic; traditional date); *Zōhō* (imaged dharma), beginning one thousand years after Śākyamuni's death and extending for another thousand years—a period of accommodation of the teaching because of human inability to grasp the deep meaning; and *Mappō* (end of the dharma), the period of decadence which NICHIREN claimed to have ushered in (thirteenth century), and which he predicted would last ten thousand years. In the period of Mappō only the truth of the LOTUS SŪTRA is effectual for salvation.

N. S. BRANNEN

MAR THOMA CHURCH (Ch). A church combining Reformation elements with its heritage from the Syrian ORTHODOX CHURCH from which it separated in the nineteenth century. This church claims continuity with the first century church supposedly founded in India by the apostle Thomas. While remaining basically Syrian Orthodox, the vernacular texts (English or Maylayam) and rites have undergone periodic revision and accommodation to Protestant models. Prayer services frequently replace the Sunday EUCHARIST; morning and evening prayer and compline have been retained from the seven traditional canonical hours. The hymn repertory is particularly eclectic. C. WADDELL

MĀRA mä´ rŭ (B & H—Skt.; lit. "killing," or "death"). Known also as Namuci, the Tempter; a demonic figure who appears in early Buddhist texts as the personification of evil, transitory pleasure, and death. As Namuci he appears frequently also in the VEDAS and the later epic poems of Hinduism. The Buddhist scriptures recount in considerable detail Māra's temptation of Siddhārtha Gautama (the BUDDHA) during his struggle for enlightenment, but the oldest materials suggest that this kind of spiritual struggle characterized in some measure the whole of his previous seven-year quest. The story of Gautama's spiritual victory over Māra and his temptations came to play an important role in the faith of the developing Buddhist community. The Buddha ("Enlightened One") was also the Victor (*Jina*). There is evidence, however, that the Buddha continued to meet various temptations throughout his later life.

The essential content of the temptation which Māra presented to Gautama before his enlightenment was to give primary concern to physical health, comfort, and the sensual pleasures of life and to follow the Vedic-Brāhmaṇic way of sacrificial rites. The nature of Gautama's response was in effect to give priority to the higher values of spiritual truth (DHARMA as the "lovely") and ethical goodness, and to commit himself unreservedly to this way (Sutta Nipāta 425-449; Dīgha Nikāya III, 77). After his enlightenment the Buddha was again tempted by Māra to turn back to the ascetic way from his chosen and now tested path of ethical conduct, mental concentration, and spiritual insight, i.e. away from the Middle Way (Saṃyutta Nikāya I, 103-10).

Another temptation overcome at this time, although not specifically presented by Māra, was not to share the truth-reality of his experience with others. However, it is said that the Buddha decided to teach his new path out of compassion (METTĀ) for all living creatures.

Bibliography. *See* bibliog. for BUDDHA, LIFE OF GAUTAMA.
R. H. DRUMMOND

MARCION mär´ sĭ ən (Ch; d. *ca.* 160). Initiator, after moving from Pontus to Rome in mid-second century, of a Christian movement broadly condemned as a GNOSTIC heresy; in the century after his death Marcionite churches spread in the Roman Empire, in some areas vying to become Christianity's dominant expression.

From Paul's juxtaposition of law and gospel Marcion extrapolated two deities (one "just," thus vengeful; the other "good"). Marcion viewed the creator and lawgiver portrayed in Jewish scriptures as inferior and antagonistic to the merciful God unknown until revealed by JESUS (the true Christ, not the MESSIAH of the Jews). Marcion's *Antitheses* contrasted the creator-deity known to Adam, MOSES, etc., with the merciful Father known to none except the Son (Luke 10:22), and the messianic promises of the restoration of Israel with the promise of an eternal, heavenly kingdom by the Christ of the good God. A DOCETIC Christology supported Marcion's idea of salvation as liberation from the created order and its "just" ruler.

Marcion rejected the OT and proposed a list of authoritative holy writings (ten Pauline letters, edited and emended, and an abridged Gospel of Luke). Marcionite churches, noted for ethical rigor, asceticism, and martyr heroism, posed continued challenge to orthodox leaders into the fourth and fifth centuries.

Bibliography. A. von Harnack, *Marcion: Das Evangelium vom fremden Gott,* 2nd ed. (1924); E. C. Blackman, *Marcion and His Influence* (1948); H. Jonas, *The Gnostic Religion,* 2nd ed. (1963).
R. C. GREGG

MĀRGA mär´ gŭ (H & B—Skt.; lit. "path") **MAGGA** mŭg´ gŭ (B—Pali). Used metaphorically in HINDUISM for a course of action or meditation leading to a desired goal, usually spiritual, e.g., BHAKTI-*mārga,* the path of devotion; jñāna-*mārga,* the path of knowledge; KARMA-*mārga,* the path of good works. The concept is used similarly in BUDDHISM, e.g., *aṭṭhangika-magga,* the EIGHTFOLD PATH.
J. BARE

MARIOLOGY (Ch). *See* MARY.

MĀRIYAMMAṈ mä rĭ yŭm mŭn (H—Tamil; lit. "smallpox lady"). A village goddess (*grāmadevatā*) widespread in southern India who both inflicts and wards off smallpox. She is sometimes propitiated with animal sacrifices, particularly goat and chicken. Some myths associate her fearsome nature with a curse pronounced by the gods, while others claim her parents were outcastes (HARIJANS) or relate how she came to have the head of a BRAHMIN and the body of an outcaste. *See* GODDESS [INDIA] §4.
G. E. YOCUM

MARONITE CHURCH mär´ ə nīt (Ch). A community composed of Syrians living primarily in Lebanon; it entered into union with ROMAN CATHOLICISM in the twelfth century.

Although the real founder was Joseph Maron, who lived in the seventh and eighth centuries, the official apostle to the Maronites is St. Maro (A.D. 350-433). A monastery was built on the Orontes River around his shrine. The monks supported CHALCEDONIAN Christology, but under Emperor Heraclius (575-641), who wanted to unite his Syrian subjects against the invading Arabs, the monks accepted non-Chalcedonian doctrine. When the monastery was destroyed (ninth century) the monks and their followers survived in the mountains until the coming of the CRUSADERS, who converted them to Catholicism.

The Maronities, however, continue to preserve some independence. BISHOPS elect their own PATRIARCH, who is confirmed by the pope; some rural clergy are married, and the old Syrian LITURGY is used. But unleavened bread is used in the EUCHARIST, and laity receive only the bread and not the cup in communion.

There are about one million Maronites in the Near East, mainly in Lebanon, and in North and South America. (*See* UNIAT CHURCHES.)

Bibliography. D. Attwater, *Christian Churches of the East* (1961); A. S. Atiya, *History of Eastern Christianity* (1968).

V. KESICH

MARRANOS mä rä´ nōs (Ju). Those Jews who, due to persecution by Roman Catholicism in Spain, beginning in 1391, outwardly adopted CHRISTIANITY while covertly practicing Judaism. Their alleged Judaizing activities led to the establishment of the Spanish INQUISITION, while the influence of unconverted Jews upon the Marranos was the official reason for the expulsion of the Jews from Spain in 1492. Small, isolated communities of Marranos exist today.

M. M. KELLNER

MARRIAGE AND DIVORCE IN ISLAM. 1. Marriage (Nikāḥ nĭ kä´). The Islamic doctrine of marriage and the family has ancient Arabian antecedents, but the new religion raised matters to a higher plane, especially with respect to women's rights. "He created for you helpmeets from yourselves that ye might find rest in them, and He ordained between you love and mercy" (Qur'ān, Sura 30:21). All who are fit should marry early and have children in order to realize full human life and propagate the species. Poverty is no impediment, for God will provide (Sura 24:31). CELIBACY is specifically condemned, except in rare cases.

The QUR'ĀN allows men to have up to four concurrent wives, so long as they are treated equally (Sura 4:3), but monogamy is recommended. The four-wife limitation was an improvement on previous custom and grew out of unusual circumstances in early Islam when many men had been lost in warfare. Polygamy is the exception today, especially in towns and cities.

Marriage may be contracted only between partners who are outside the bounds of legal consanguinity and affinity (Sura 4:23) and are otherwise eligible. Marriage with non-Muslims is forbidden, except that a male Muslim may marry a Christian or Jew (Sura 5:5). Islamic law considers marriage to be a civil contract and not a religious rite. Generally, the prospective groom offers a contract to the intended bride's guardian *(walī),* who may be her father, grandfather, or other near male relation, or even a court appointee. The *walī* declares the bride's consent (the proceedings would not normally reach this stage if a refusal were likely) and negotiates the gift *(mahr)* which the groom must provide her and which remains her property once the marriage is contracted. The actual solemnizing of the contract is accompanied by recitation of the FĀTIḤA, a brief sermon delivered (usually) by the *walī,* and formal witnessing by two competent males.

After the legal ceremony, the festivities ('URS) begin, following traditional but widely varying patterns across the Islamic world. They usually feature a bridal procession and always an elaborate meal symbolizing the new relationship between the two families and providing an appropriate means of public announcement of the marriage. Then there are ceremonies leading up to and celebrating the actual consummation, sometimes including proof of the bride's virginity. Festivities, however strongly recommended and enthusiastically observed, are not legally required, so long as public announcement of the marriage is made, but the FIQH (law) books have a great deal to say about festivities and the kinds of practices which are associated with them.

Another kind of marriage, highly controversial, is *mut'a,* "marriage of enjoyment," which appears to be a pagan Arabian survival. It is forbidden by the SUNNIS but recognized by the SHI'ITES, who contend that the Qur'ān allows it (Sura 4:24) and MUHAMMAD let his soldiers practice it when on campaigns. *Mut'a* is a temporary contract mutually concluded by the man and the woman. As it is so obviously open to abuse, it has generally been strongly condemned since early times.

The husband is responsible for providing his spouse with shelter and maintenance in a manner fitting her status. The wife retains ownership of her own property.

2. Divorce (Ṭalāq tə läk´). Divorce is easier for the male and can be had by the husband's repudiating his wife three times over a prescribed period of intervals. Although the form is simple, the act is very serious, to the point that even a joking *ṭalāq* is legally binding. The Prophet said: "With Allah, the most detestable of all things permitted is divorce." It should always be the last resort, after all attempts at reconciliation have failed (Sura 4:35). The wife may also seek divorce, but only for good reason (e.g., ill treatment or desertion; Sura 4:128). If no just cause exists, a woman may still request divorce, but a saying of the Prophet warns that the "sweet odour of paradise shall be forbidden to her."

There is disagreement as to whether the three repudiations may be said all at once. Generally a first repudiation, uttered by the husband during the wife's "clean" time, is followed by a waiting period *('idda)* of three menstrual cycles *(qurū')*, during which the wife remains in her husband's house, with resumed conjugal relations being permitted if mutually desired. If the woman does not menstruate, the *'idda* is three months; if she is pregnant, it is until delivery. The husband may summarily divorce his spouse after marrying her, if he has not touched her (Sura 33:49), in which case there is no *'idda*. The second repudiation requires a similar waiting period, but the third is irrevocable. The original partners may remarry only after the woman has married another man and has again been divorced or otherwise made eligible. *Ḥalāla*, "being made lawful" again by a brief, contrived intervening marriage, is generally harshly condemned (cf. Deut. 24:3-4).

The bridal gift *(mahr)* is retained by the divorced wife except in case of her adultery, or in the event that she wishes to be freed without any fault being attributed to her husband. If a husband without evidence accuses his wife of adultery and she swears to her innocence, the couple are automatically divorced (Sura 24:6-9), with the *mahr* remaining with the woman. God will judge the truth of the matter. If the husband is missing in action *(mafqūd)*, with no news of him reaching the wife for one year (four years in the Malakite school), divorce is automatic. In some cases the wife desiring divorce can purchase it, but this has often led to injustice against the wife because of extortionate demands. A conditional, automatic divorce clause is often written into marriage contracts for the sake of the wife. The Shi'ite divorce rules are similar to the Sunni's, but formal witnessing is more important.

Bibliography. The Qur'ān (Pickthall trans. used here): marriage; 2:221, 223, 235; 4:3-4, 22 ff.; 24:32-33; 33:50 ff; divorce; 2:226 ff., 230 ff., 241; 4:25; 33:4, 49; 65:1-7; M. M. Ali, *A Manual of Hadith* (1944), chs. 20, 21; J. Schacht, "Nikāḥ" and "Ṭalāq", *SEI*, pp. 447-49, 564-71; W. Heffening, " 'Urs," *SEI*. pp. 606-10 (very full bibliog.); R. Levy, *The Social Structure of Islam* (1957), ch. 2; M. A. Rauf, *The Islamic View of Women and the Family* (1977).

F. M. Denny

MARTYRS, CHRISTIAN. The word "martyr" derives from a Greek term for one who gives witness or testimony. It has both legal and moral connotations of witness to facts, events, personal character, received teaching, or revealed truth. It is so used by pagan, Jewish, and Christian authors generally. Often in the NT it refers to the witness by Jesus' disciples to his life, death, and resurrection (Luke 24:48; Acts 1:8, 22; 3:15; 13:31; 22:15; I Pet. 5:1; II Tim. 2:2).

The special meaning of martyr—one whose testimony for Christ results in death at the hands of unbelievers—is indicated in later NT writings (Acts 22:20, of Stephen; Rev. 2:13, of Antipas of Pergamum; Rev. 17:6, of "blood of saints and martyrs of Jesus"; cf. I Clement 5:4-7, of Peter and Paul). Indeed, Jesus himself, "the faithful witness" (Rev. 1:5; 3:14), was the very model of martyrdom. The imitation of Christ by the martyr and Christ's working in the martyr first become explicit in the *Martyrdom of Polycarp*, bishop of Smyrna, *ca.* 155/56 (1:2, 2:2, 14:2, 17:3, 19:1).

The *Martyrdom of Polycarp* is also the first document to mention annual, anniversary commemoration at the tomb of a martyr (18:3), a custom which became universal in the church in the third century. Each local church kept a list of such dates—called the "birthday" in eternity—and these lists became the basis of early church calendars of fixed feasts. At first these observances consisted of a memorial banquet, customary in Roman funerary rites. By the fourth century they began to be formalized by church authorities into a vigil service followed by celebration of the Eucharist analogous to the Easter rites.

The total number of martyrs prior to Constantine's legalization of Christianity (313) is unknown. Estimates range from 10,000 to 100,000. Certainly large numbers suffered in the general persecutions of the mid-third and early fourth centuries; however, relatively few authentic accounts survive. They consist of two kinds: copies of court proceedings, sentencing, and execution (e.g., Justin in Rome, 165; Cyprian in Carthage, 258), and Christians' eyewitness accounts of their martyrs' ordeals, such as that of Polycarp, or the *Passion of Perpetua and Felicitas* in Carthage (202/3), or Eusebius' *Martyrs of Palestine* (312). An important treatise on the subject is Origen's *Exhortation to Martyrdom* (*ca.* 235).

From Constantine to the present time, Christians in many lands have been martyred for their faith by official execution or by acts of violence. The term "martyr" has also been extended frequently to Christians in many lands who suffered death, not for their faith in Christ, but because of ecclesiastical or theological controversy in the church. *See also* Saints, Veneration of.

Bibliography. On "martyr" and cognate Greek words, H. Strathmann in *Theological Dictionary of the NT*, ed. G. Kittel, IV (1967), 474-514; for early sources, E. C. E. Owen, *Some Authentic Acts of the Early Martyrs* (1927); H. Delehaye, *Les origines du culte des martyrs* (2nd ed., 1933); H. F. von Campenhausen, *Die Idee des Martyriums in der alten Kirche* (2nd ed., 1964); W. H. C. Frend, *Martyrdom and Persecution in the Early Church* (1965).

M. H. Shepherd, Jr.

MARTYRS, ISLAMIC. *See* Mashhad; Shahīd; Ziyāra.

MARTYRS, JEWISH. *See* Anti-Semitism; Holocaust; Kiddush ha-Shem; Yad Vashem.

MARY (Ch). The mother of Jesus. 1. **Biblical material.** Mary is first mentioned in the narratives describing the infancy and childhood of Jesus (Matt. 1:16-2:23; Luke 1:26-56; 2:1-50). These complex narratives are suffused by faith in the risen Lord. Mary appears as Luke's model of the poor people of God awaiting salvation through the Messiah.

The good news, as first proclaimed, began with the public life of Jesus, from his BAPTISM by John to his death and exaltation. In this primitive GOSPEL material only one incident common to the synoptics (Matthew, Mark, Luke) mentions Mary: the coming of his mother and brothers while Jesus is preaching. Luke adds a similar anecdote about the enthusiastic woman who salutes Jesus by praising his mother (Luke 11:27-28). Mark (3:31-35) regards the brothers as antipathetic to Jesus, contrasting them unfavorably with the disciples who are the "true family." If Mark does not clearly include the mother in his negative judgment of Jesus' relatives, neither does he show any special veneration for her. Luke (8:19-21), however, has retailored the incident so that the brothers and especially the mother are counted among believing followers of Jesus, which is true also of Luke's description of them in the upper room before Pentecost (Acts 1:14).

In mentioning Mary during the public ministry, both Matthew and Luke are influenced by the sense of her role as the virgin mother in their infancy narratives. Luke in particular makes a special point of Mary's faithfulness, praised by Elizabeth when Mary comes to visit her (1:39-45). This is also a factor in Mary's reaction when she and Joseph find Jesus in the temple at the age of twelve, and though she does not understand his words she keeps all these things in her heart (2:51).

In John's Gospel Mary appears twice, at Cana (2:1-11) and at GOLGOTHA (19:25-27), the beginning and the end of her son's career. On both occasions her role is totally subordinate to Christ's.

At the crucifixion the words of Jesus, directed to the immediate need of providing for his mother's care, look beyond that need to the church, symbolized by Mary. To Catholic theology Mary is the new Eve, new mother of the living, and it is part of the meaning of Mary's presence at Golgotha that Jesus gives her a spiritual role as mother of the beloved disciple, and the disciple a role as her son.

Not only do Christians differ greatly in their judgments on postbiblical developments in beliefs and pious practices regarding the Virgin Mary, but they also read the NT passages dealing with Mary in light of the particular emphases of their own churches. For example, the acceptance of the belief in the VIRGIN BIRTH of Jesus as meaning literally that Jesus had no human father depends on the tradition of the church that professes this doctrine.

Dependence on a church tradition is even more evident in statements about the mother of Jesus not contained in the Bible, e.g., that Mary remained always a virgin. The Gospels leave undecided the identity of the brothers and sisters; it was only at the end of the fourth century that the conviction of Mary's lifelong virginity became widespread. The leaders of the PROTESTANT REFORMATION held this view, as did JOHN WESLEY; Eastern ORTHODOX CHURCHES and ROMAN CATHOLICS still hold Mary's perpetual virginity, but many other Christians do not.

2. Theological developments. Beyond the NT, Christian reflection about the mother of Jesus grew gradually. One early consideration was that Mary was the obedient "new Eve," bringing life, in contrast to the first Eve, who heard the word of deceit and brought death. Justin (mid-second century) used that comparison, and Irenaeus (d. *ca.* 202) elaborated on it; other writers picked it up so that by JEROME's day (d. 420) it was an axiom to say, "Death through Eve, life through Mary."

The ecumenical Council of Ephesus (A.D. 431) took over the Greek term *theotokos,* lit. "God-bearer," popularly "Mother of God," to protect the truth that the Son of God had indeed become the Son of Mary. At Ephesus, insistence on the title *theotokos* set the seal on the respect for the Virgin Mary that had begun with the Gospels. From the fifth century on, the place of Mary in the liturgy was secure. She was honored in particular feasts in the CHRISTIAN CALENDAR, in the eucharistic prayers, and many other aspects of church life. Early feasts were a celebration of Mary in the CHRISTMAS season and a "memory of Mary" on August 15, a day recalling the Virgin's "passage" *(transitus),* like the birthdays into heaven of the martyrs and other saints. August 15 evolved into the feast of the Dormition ("falling asleep") of the Mother of the Lord, and by the sixth century had become the Assumption, meaning Mary is one with the risen Christ, body as well as soul. Writers began to produce a rich homiletic literature, especially in the East; e.g., in the seventh and eighth centuries, Germanus of Constantinople, John of Damascus, Andrew of Crete. In 1950 Pope Pius XII declared the ASSUMPTION OF MARY to be a Catholic DOGMA.

The NT pictures Mary as a holy woman, favored by God and committed to doing his will. Although some early authors held Mary guilty of at least lesser human failings, e.g., importunity, the prevailing view soon became that Mary was "all-holy," free from personal sin. Unlike the Assumption, which developed relatively smoothly from the time Christians began to celebrate it, Mary's freedom from original sin, known as her IMMACULATE CONCEPTION, has had a tangled history. It took centuries of clarification about the meaning of original sin and the possibility of a "preservative" redemption before Mary's initial holiness found acceptance.

With respect to both the Immaculate Conception and the Assumption there was no uniform opinion among the first Reformers. The attitude of later PROTESTANTISM has been negative, especially on the grounds of lack of scriptural evidence, but also because of a different understanding of two critera of revelation: "consent of the faithful," that is, the present concordant conviction of believers, and the teaching authority of the church. In Eastern churches, both Orthodox and others not in union with Rome, the Assumption has been celebrated liturgically from early times, but these churches see no need to define into dogma the belief in Mary's full union with her son in glory. Although honoring Mary as "all-holy," the same Eastern churches do not hold to the Immaculate Conception, in part because of a different understanding of original sin.

3. **Veneration of Mary.** Veneration of Mary and the SAINTS developed in the first centuries. The MARTYRS were remembered on the dates of their death and their RELICS venerated; the Christians called on them for their prayers in union with the risen Christ, and the custom was extended to other holy people, especially the mother of Jesus and the apostles. By the fifth century the creedal phrase, "communion of saints," comprised the pilgrims on earth, the blessed in heaven, and the dead for whom prayers and MASSES could be offered.

In subsequent centuries a much expanded Marian piety developed, e.g., the prayers and meditations of ANSELM (d. 1109), and the lyrical sermons of BERNARD (d. 1153). The place of Mary was strengthened in the liturgy. From the East the classic feasts spread to the West: Mary's birthday (Sept. 8) and Assumption (Aug. 15); and joint feasts of the Savior and his mother, i.e. Presentation of the Lord, often called the Purification of Mary (the English Candlemas) on Feb. 2, and Annunciation (Mar. 25), the great springtime feast of the INCARNATION. Alcuin of England introduced the custom of dedicating Saturday to Mary at the time of Charlemagne (A.D. 800). The first Reformers continued to venerate Mary even while eliminating practices they condemned as abuses. LUTHER wrote a commentary on the MAGNIFICAT and CALVIN preached on the ANNUNCIATION.

The Reformers forbade invocation of the saints, that is, calling on them in prayer, especially prayers of petition. This was a break with the more than thousand-year-old practice of invocation of Mary and the other saints, a custom that still exists among Catholics, many Anglicans (who prefer "comprecation" to "invocation"), and all Eastern Christians. The Reformation objection was to pre-Reformation abuses in the cult of the saints, with the fear that any concession to invoking even Mary would lead to diminished confidence in Christ the one mediator, setting her mercy against her son's justice.

Leaving aside bizarre extremes which flourish in spite of official disapproval (e.g., recurring claims of appearances of Mary with messages of doom), even authentic forms of Marian piety, liturgical and otherwise, are inevitably interwoven with doctrinal positions. The "communion of saints" is an example of a meeting ground of belief and practice where Christians differ greatly. The role of Mary with respect to the saving work of Christ is another point of doctrinal difference. The terms "mediatrix" and "co-redemptrix" seem to Reformed Christians to imperil the unique mediatorship of Christ. KARL BARTH (d. 1968) protested that Roman Catholic attitudes to the Virgin Mary emphasize human cooperation with God's prevenient grace and convey a concept of church as minister of grace which is alien to the Reformation. The limited use of "mediatrix" by the Second VATICAN COUNCIL and the careful explanation of total dependence on the all-sufficient atoning deed of Jesus open up possibilities of ecumenical dialogue on questions of justification and associated doctrines.

4. **Current ecumenical interest.** In the churches that sprang from the Reformation, the notice given Mary grew less with the passing centuries, while her place grew greater in Roman Catholicism. Yet a veneration of the mother of Jesus often survived in Christian hymns, fulfilling the prophecy of the Magnificat (Luke 1:46-55) that all subsequent generations would call her blessed, because the Almighty had done such great things for her. In recent years an ecumenical reconsideration of the role of Mary has begun, thanks to the activity of Orthodox Churches within the World Council of Churches, through the Faith and Order Conference (1927 onward), and on the Roman Catholic side due to the Second Vatican Council. The Ecumenical Society of the Blessed Virgin Mary was founded in England in 1967, with participation from Anglicans, Methodists, Orthodox, and Roman Catholics, and meets regularly in a number of cities. It has sponsored three international conferences (1971, 1973, and 1975). On similar lines the Ecumenical Society of the Blessed Virgin Mary of the United States began in 1976, and has been meeting twice yearly in the Washington, D.C. area, with membership cutting across denominational lines.

For Mary's role in Islam *see* MARYAM.

Bibliography. R. Brown, *et al.*, eds., *Mary in the New Testament* (1978); W. M. Abbott, S. J., ed., *The Documents of Vatican II* (1966); J. N. D. Kelly, *Early Christian Doctrines* (5th ed., 1978), ch. 18; E. R. Carroll, *Understanding the Mother of Jesus* (1979); J. C. de Satgé, *Down to Earth: The New Protestant Vision of Mary* (1976).

E. R. CARROLL

MARYAM mər yäm′ (I). MARY, the mother of JESUS (Arab. 'Īsā), mentioned frequently in the QUR'ĀN in early as well as late passages. In Sura 19:20 ff., which is named "Mary," the doctrine of VIRGIN BIRTH is mentioned, as also in Sura 66:12 and 3:47. The Qur'ān also knows a version of the IMMACULATE CONCEPTION (Sura 3:36), where Mary and Jesus are kept clean from Satan's touch, giving rise to the Islamic doctrine of impeccability (Arab. *'iṣma*). The Qur'ān also attributes to some a belief that Mary was part of the TRINITY (Sura 5:116), which has led Western scholars to search for Marist sects in pre-Islamic Arabia. Two different genealogies of Mary are known to the commentators, as are numerous stories found in the apocryphal GOSPELS, such as the Palm Tree story, known in England through the Cherry Tree carol.

Bibliography. Ibn Isḥāq, *Life of Muhammad*. A. Guillaume, trans. (1955); J. Robson, *Christ in Islam* (1929); G. Parrinder, *Jesus in the Qur'ān* (1965); S. Zwemer, *The Moslem Christ* (1902); M. M. Pickthall, *Meaning of the Glorious Koran* (1953).

G. D. NEWBY

MASHHAD mä shäd′ (I—Arab.; lit. "a place where a martyr died"). The gravesite of an IMAM of Imamite SHI'ISM, believed to have died as a martyr (SHAHĪD). The QUR'ĀN attests that a martyr is granted special heavenly privileges, and the concept of the sufferings of the imams played an important role in the development of belief in the sanctity of their shrines. The imam as *shahīd* will be called upon to bear witness on the Day of Judgment as to what was revealed to the Prophet and to bear witness to those who acknowledged him and against those who charged him with falsehood. Not only was ALI abandoned and murdered by Muslims; each of the imams after him was persecuted or poisoned by the CALIPHS and their supporters. Thus all are revered as martyrs, and their tombs became sites for annual visitation by Shi'ites, who believed their devotion to the martyred imams, expressed through these pilgrimages, would win forgiveness for their sins and a share in the final victory of the messianic imam al-MAHDI. Pious Shi'ites also look upon the shrines as places where they can share in the imam's sanctity.

Of all the imams it is AL-ḤUSAYN who enjoys the status of the "Chief of the Martyrs," having been betrayed by his own supporters to be tormented with hunger and thirst in the desert and murdered by his enemies at KARBALA in 680. His tomb was probably the first mashhad in Shi'ite piety, and was regarded as holy immediately after his martyrdom. With the concept of mashhad evolved the ritual of ZIYĀRA, salutations offered at the tombs of the imams. Unlike the HAJJ, which has to be performed at a set time, the *ziyāra* can be performed at any time, although some special days are recommended. The concept of mashhad seems to have been well developed by the ninth century, since it was probably the strong emphasis on the pilgrimage *(ziyāra)* to Karbala that led al-Mutawakkil in 850 to destroy the tomb and forbid visits to the site under threat of heavy penalties.

Karbala has maintained its unique place in Shi'ite piety, and the pilgrimage to it came to be accorded a place equal to, if not higher than, pilgrimage to MECCA (hajj). In fact, there have been periods when the pilgrimage to Karbala took the place of the hajj, especially in times of strife between Shi'ite Iran and SUNNITE Turkey.

The shrines of all the imams were richly endowed, and lavish gifts were bestowed by various Muslim rulers, especially those of Shi'ite dynasties. Towns grew up around them, and the sacred areas were adorned with magnificent and costly ornamentation.

A. A. Sachedina

The mashhad of Sayyid Muhammad at Balad, north of Baghdad. Brother of the 11th century Imamite iman, the SAYYID is famous for miraculous healing powers.

All the shrines have some architectural features in common. The tomb lies in a courtyard surrounded by arched halls and cells. Its walls are resplendently decorated with colored tiles. The entrance to the main rectangular building is through a golden outer hall. In the middle of the central golden-domed chamber lies the shrine, surrounded by a silver enclosure. In Iraq two golden MINARETS usually flank the entrance to the shrine.

The shrines are also important centers of Shi'ite learning, and important schools (MADRASAS) grew up around them. Every Shi'ite longs to find a last resting place in the holy precincts of the beloved imams, and this has resulted in the development of extensive cemeteries at all the shrines, especially at Karbala, Najaf, and Mashhad, and in areas near these shrines.

Bibliography. M. Ayoub, *Redemptive Suffering in Islam* (1978); D. M. Donaldson, *The Shī'ite Religion* (1933); A. Nöldeke, *Das Heiligtum al-Husains zu Kerbelā* (1909).

A. A. SACHEDINA

MASORETES mă´ sô rēts (Ju—Heb.; lit. "those who hand on a tradition"). Scholars who fixed and preserved the precise text of the Hebrew BIBLE, adding marginal notations and vocalization of the consonants. Their work, extending from approximately the first to the tenth centuries A.D., resulted in the Masoretic text, the authoritative version of the Bible in JUDAISM. I. CHERNUS

MASS (Ch—Lat. *missa*, the equivalent of *dimissio*, "dismissal"). The common word for the EUCHARIST in ROMAN CATHOLICISM. From the middle of the fifth century it gained currency as the usual name for the Eucharist. The usage depends upon the association of the dismissal with the blessing, and of the blessing with the service as a whole. The Roman mass ends with the words *Ite missa est*, "Go, the mass is ended."

1. **Origins.** Little is known of the beginnings of the Latin mass. Latin was first used in the church in North Africa (*ca.* 200), while Greek remained the chief language of the Roman church into the fourth century. Moreover, the contrast between the Greek LITURGY used in Rome in the early third century and the earliest forms (sixth century) of the Latin Roman mass produces a gap in our knowledge not easily bridged. Nevertheless, it is probable that the canon of the Latin Roman mass existed by the end of the fourth century in a form not radically different from the one that has persisted through the centuries. Such a fixed formulation represents a sharp break with earlier Greek tradition. Our knowledge becomes fuller when we come to the three ancient sacramentaries, which contain the priest's part of the Roman liturgy—the Leonine Sacramentary (*ca.* 540), the Gelasian Sacramentary (sixth century), and the Gregorian Sacramentary (seventh century). What we know of the African Latin mass shows it dependent upon the Roman.

In addition to the Roman mass, Latin liturgies were also found in the Gallic rite, subdivided into the Ambrosian or Milanese (still used in Milan), the Old Spanish or Mozarabic (still used in a chapel of the Cathedral of Toledo), the Celtic (a generic term for liturgies once used by the Irish and the Scots), and the Gallican (used in the early Middle Ages in France). The Gallic liturgies are characterized by an elaboration of forms and by influence from Eastern liturgies which may have entered the West through Milan, imperial headquarters during the fourth century. They are important largely because of their influence on the Roman liturgy; their impact fluctuated with the waxing and waning of the PAPACY and with the empires of Charlemagne and Otto the Great.

2. **Structure.** The structure of the Roman mass in its final form may be represented as follows:

a) *The Entrance Rite:* Preparation, Introit, KYRIE ELEISON, GLORIA IN EXCELSIS, Collect
b) *The Readings:* Epistle, Gradual or Sequence, Gospel, Homily, CREDO, Prayers
c) *The* OFFERTORY
d) *The Canon:* SURSUM CORDA and Preface, SANCTUS and BENEDICTUS QUI VENIT, the Canon itself
e) *The Communion:* LORD'S PRAYER, the Fraction, the Peace, AGNUS DEI, the Communion
f) *The Blessing and Dismissal*

Bibliography. J. A. Jungmann, *The Mass of the Roman Rite* (1959).

R. A. GREER

MATHURĀ mä tû´ rä (H). Ancient commerical center and shrine city on the west bank of the Yamunā River between Delhi and Agra. Revered by Hindus as the place of KRISHNA'S birth and childhood, Mathurā has been a focus of PILGRIMAGE for at least a thousand years. The many scenes of Krishna's deeds were first systematically located in the sixteenth century and connected by a pilgrimage path. A circuit of 120 miles now takes the devout to dozens of sacred spots in Mathurā and in Gokul, Vṛindāban (VṚNDĀVANA), Govardhan, and other outlying towns. Local dramatic troupes reenact the pranks of Krishna in a distinctive mystery play called the *rāslīlā*.

At the dawn of history religion in Mathurā centered upon fertility goddesses, dryads, and NĀGAS (serpents). By the second century B.C. the worship of Krishna was prominent but not predominant; BUDDHISM and JAINISM prospered also, declining only after the seventh century A.D. These faiths were served by a notable indigenous school of sculpture that reached its highest creativity in the first two centuries A.D. when Mathurā was the southern capital of the Kushan Empire. Śaurasenī Prākrit, the earliest vernacular of Mathurā, was esteemed in ancient literature as the most refined of regional languages. The Western Hindī of Mathurā was the standard dialect of Hindī poetry from the sixteenth century until the middle of the nineteenth. It remains the sacred language of the North Indian Krishna cult.

Bibliography. F. S. Growse, *Mathurā: A District Memoir,* 2nd ed. (1880); N. P. Joshi, *Mathurā Sculptures: A Handbook* (1966); N. Hein, *The Miracle Plays of Mathurā* (1972).

N. J. Hein

al-MĀTURĪDĪ äl mä too rē´ dē (I; d. 944). Native of Samarkand and founder of a school of theology comparable to, but less well known than, that of al-Ash'arī. Both lived before Kalām became the dominant theological method of Islam. Al-Māturīdī's views were so closely identified with those of the pivotal Sharia expert, Abū Ḥanīfa (*see* Hanafites), that the latter's name often eclipsed even the memory of the former.

Bibliography. *SEI,* pp. 362-63; W. M. Watts, *Islamic Philosophy and Theology* (1962), p. 78; F. E. Peters, *Allah's Commonwealth* (1973), pp. 463-64.

B. Lawrence

MATZAH, MATZO mä´ tzä (Ju—Heb.; "unleavened bread"). The thin cake baked from unfermented dough which is consumed on the festival of Passover. Consumption of matzah is to remind the celebrant of the hastily baked, unleavened bread of the exodus from Egypt (Exod. 12:39). B. Martin

MAUNDY THURSDAY (Ch). The Thursday before Easter, commemoration of the Last Supper. The term "Maundy" comes from an anthem sung during the ceremony of footwashing, *Mandatum novum* ("A new commandment I give you," John 13:34). This is also the traditional day for the consecration of baptismal oils by Bishops. *See* Holy Week. T. J. Talley

MAURYAN DYNASTY mour´ yŭn. This dynasty, which has been called the first Indian empire (321-185 B.C.), brought significant changes in Indian culture. Its founder, Chandragupta Maurya (321-298 B.C.), not only freed India from Macedonian rule but also united politically a great part of the continent. He established a central administration with the aid of his advisor Kauṭilya, the author of the Arthaśāstra. His imperial system, with the king as the center of power, assisted by a council, decentralized administration, and numerous spies, was maintained and expanded by his son Bindusara (298-273 B.C.) and his grandson, the famous Aśoka (269-232 B.C.).

The empire was strengthened by a decline of the tribes and a growing agrarian economy. With a firm economic basis and the security afforded by political unification, craft guilds, towns, and trade expanded and an urban culture developed.

The Mauryans advocated religious tolerance for all sects, as seen for example in the Twelfth Rock Edict of Aśoka. The Dharma (law) advocated by Aśoka was not exclusively Buddhist but was generally consistent with the moral principles followed by all sects. The dynasty financed the construction of Vihāras (monasteries) and Stūpas. They supported Vedic sacrifices, but the Vedic priesthood felt threatened and did not hold the dynasty in the highest regard. It must also be noted that during this time the Brahmanical system was threatened from within by the emphasis of the Upaniṣads on knowledge, asceticism, and the internalization of various Vedic sacrifices.

The stable situation created by the Mauryan dynasty enabled the Ājīvikas to thrive and Jainism to establish itself among the commercial classes. There is even a legend that Chandragupta became a Jaina monk after abdicating his throne. The schism in the Jaina community over membership, dress, and the limits of scripture took place during this dynasty.

Buddhism spread rapidly during the later Mauryan period, aided by the support of Aśoka. During Aśoka's reign, the Third Buddhist Council was held (*ca.* 250 B.C.) at Pāṭaliputra to establish the Theravādin canon and interpretation as the authoritative preservation of the Buddha's teaching.

During the Mauryan dynasty two devotional sects which were later to achieve prominence were slowly evolving: in the historical account of Megasthenes, the Greek ambassador of Seleucus, and on rock inscriptions of this time, there is mention made of the worship of Shiva and Vāsudeva-Krishna, the deity of the Bhāgavata religion.

After the death of Aśoka a political decline began which resulted in the assassination of Bṛhadratha, the final Mauryan ruler, by his commander in chief Pusyamitra, who founded the Śuṅga dynasty. There is no general agreement as to the reasons for the decline.

Bibliography. D. D. Kosambi, *Ancient India* (1965), pp. 133-65; R. C. Majumdar, ed., *The History and Culture of the Indian People,* vol. II, *The Age of Imperial Unity* (1951); R. Thapar, *A History of India,* I (1966), 70-91.

C. Olson

MAWLID măw´ lĭd **MAWLŪD** măw lōōd´ (I—Arab.; lit. "birthplace," then "birthday"). Term used widely for (1) the birthday or celebration of the birth of Muhammad, traditionally the twelfth of Rabī' I (also his death day); (2) any panegyric poem celebrating the birth of the Prophet (*see* Burdah); or (3) the birthday or birth celebration of any Muslim saint (*see* Walī).

The earliest evidence of Mawlid celebrations for Muhammad is from the eleventh and twelfth centuries. Conservative reformers such as the Wahhābīya have often attacked this custom, as well as birthdays of saints and visiting of saints' tombs, as "innovation" contrary to the Sunna. This has not changed the ubiquitous and immensely significant role of Mawlid observances in Muslim piety throughout the world.

Bibliography. G. E. von Grünebaum, *Muhammadan Festivals* (1951), pp. 67-84; I. Goldziher, *Muh. Studien,* II (1890), 275-378 (ET 1971, pp. 253-341); E. W. Lane, *An Account of the Manners and Customs of the Modern Egyptians* (rpr. 1954), ch. XXIV; Chelebi, *The Meylidi* (ET 1943).

W. A. Graham

MĀYĀ mä´ yä (also Māyādevī). The mother of Siddhārtha Gautama, who became the Buddha. She apparently died a few days after his birth, and the responsibility for raising the boy fell largely on her sister, Mahāprajāpatī Gautamī. Later tradition describes the circumstances of the Buddha's birth as replete with miracles, one account being that of a virgin birth (*Buddhacarita* I, 19-26).

R. H. DRUMMOND

MĀYĀ mä′ yä (H—Skt.) 1. Extraordinary power of an incomprehensible, marvelous, supernatural, or magical sort which enables those who possess it—principally gods and remarkable humans—to produce forms in the realm of phenomena. 2. The phenomenal reality produced in this way.

This concept came to assume crucial significance in certain Hindu attempts to explain the nature of the phenomenal world, particularly those of philosophers within the VEDĀNTA tradition (DARŚANA).

1. ***Māyā* in the Vedas.** In the RIG VEDA *māyā* most commonly denotes the ability of supernatural beings to assume material forms, to change appearance at will, and to produce in the natural world effects over which ordinary humans have no control (e.g., RV 3.53.8; 6.47.18; 10.54.2). It also signifies both the power of these beings to create phenomena in the natural realm and the manifestation of that power and its results, that is, the forms created. For example, in RV 3.61.7 (cf. 5.63.4) the sun's appearance is ascribed to the *māyā* of MITRA and VARUṆA; RV 5.85 attributes the stability of the earth and the constant volume of the ocean, in spite of the influx of rivers, to Varuṇa's *māyā:* and it is due to INDRA'S possession of *māyā* that the firmament does not fall (2.17.5). But it is not the gods or beneficent beings alone who possess *māyā*. Their opponents the ASURAS and *dānavas* also have this special ability at their disposal. Thus *māyā* belongs to Indra as well as to his demonic adversaries Vṛtra (RV 5.30.6) and Śuṣṇa (1.11.7; cf. 1.51.5). More emphatically, in the later ATHARVA VEDA (8.10.2) and Śatapatha Brāhmaṇa (e.g., 2.4.2.5; 7.5.2.20) *māyā* appears as the characteristic power of the *asuras* and is even claimed as their Veda or special knowledge (ŚB 13.4.3.11). Here it is evident that *māyā* connotes power which is rooted in knowledge or wisdom (it is not a "physical" power) and that in itself this power is amoral. As wielded by certain beings under certain circumstances *māyā* benefits human existence; in other situations it clearly is a force antithetical to human welfare.

Instances in which *māyā* is viewed as pernicious power and knowledge reveal a narrower, more specialized meaning, namely, *māyā* as "artifice," "trick," or "deceit." In such cases *māyā* is associated with the kinds of appearances which a magician produces. The gods' ability, especially Indra's, to appear in various guises illustrates this use of *māyā*. The *asuras' māyā* sometimes has this magical, deceptive quality, and *māyā* as legerdemain is also ascribed to sorcerers (RV 7.104.23-24). This meaning also occurs in the later literature when deceptive appearances conjured by gods or demons to serve their own individual ends are explained with reference to *māyā* (e.g., Mbh. 18.3.34; Rām. 3.41.6-7).

Finally, there are those places in the early texts where *māyā* is an attribute of human kings (e.g., AB 8.23.7; ŚB 13.5.4.12). And on occasion the power of the sacrifice is labeled *māyā* (e.g., Taittirīya Brāhmaṇa 3.10.8.2; Āpastambīya Śrauta Sūtra 16.16.1).

2. ***Māyā* in the Śvetāśvatara Upaniṣad and Bhagavad Gītā.** Building upon the early Vedic notion of *māyā*, the Śvetāśvatara Upaniṣad and BHAGAVAD GĪTĀ both recognize *māyā* as the power which enables a supreme being, here envisioned as a personal deity, to create the phenomenal world. As with so many other central Hindu ideas, the understanding of *māyā* evidenced in these two texts forms an important bridge between the early Vedic view and the later applications of this concept in Hindu mythology and philosophy.

Śvet.U 4.9-10 is a key passage for understanding what the later Hindu tradition means by *māyā*. These verses state that the Great Lord *(maheśvara)*, who elsewhere in the text is identified with SHIVA, acting through his *māyā* power, projects the entire phenomenal world into manifestation out of the impersonal monistic substrate of the supreme BRAHMAN. Mentioned as some of the constituents of that *māyā*-produced world are the sacred hymns, sacrifices, ceremonies, and ordinances. Indeed, nature (PRAKṚTI) is identified with *māyā*. Thus *māyā* is both cause and effect. It is the power which brings phenomenal reality into existence and also that reality itself. Moreover, this same *māyā* which produces empirical forms is said to confine the individual soul.

At another point in the Śvet. U (1.10) the claim is made that one can bring about the cessation of *māyā (māyā-nivṛtti)* by meditating upon God, thus achieving union with him and entering into his being. What these passages foreshadow is a position made more explicit in the later tradition, namely, that the world of phenomena is grounded in the mysterious power of the absolute, that the incomprehensible nature of this differentiated world of *māyā* obscures the true identity of the individual souls who move within it, and that by means of spiritual discipline one can penetrate to the true nature of reality and experience an integrating sense of oneness which transcends all appearances of differentiation.

In the Bhagavad Gītā KRISHNA states that it is by means of his *māyā* that he, though in essence unborn and eternal, is able to take form and enter time for purposes of upholding DHARMA (4.6-8). Thus the first clear mention of the important Vaiṣṇava notion of God's AVATARS (incarnations) is associated with *māyā*. Elsewhere the Bh.G (7.14-15) echoes the Śvet.U when *māyā*, as simultaneously the divine power which produces the phenomenal world and that world itself, is said to rob a person of liberating insight *(jñāna)* into the true nature of reality. However, those who put their trust in God can transcend his *māyā* (7.14). Bh.G 7.25 reiterates more strongly the point that *māyā* veils God's essential nature. In summary, *māyā* explains for the author of the Bh.G how God is able to enter the temporal process on behalf of human welfare while he at the same time thereby veils his true unchanging nature.

3. **Māyā in later theistic Hinduism.** The Śvet.U and Bh.G apply the term *māyā* to the two great gods of the later Hindu tradition—Shiva and Vishnu-Krishna. Though the full-blown mythologies of both deities describe a variety of their activities as exemplifying the operation of *māyā,* it is several stories about Vishnu's *māyā* which are most widely known and also of most profound cosmological significance.

One of these myths in a version found in the Matsya Purāṇa relates an experience of the sage Nārada, who, by virtue of his great austerities (Tapas), won a boon from Vishnu. He begged the god to teach him about his *māyā* and Vishnu instructed him to dive into a nearby pond. Nārada emerged from the water as a beautiful young princess who in due course was given in marriage to a neighboring prince. The prince became king and his queen had numerous sons and grandsons. But such happiness and prosperity did not endure. A disastrous war broke out between the queen's father and her husband; and her husband, father, sons, grandsons, and other relatives were all slain in a single battle. When she, as a dutiful wife, threw herself upon the huge blazing funeral pyre which she had ordered constructed for all of her dead relatives, the flames became cool and the pyre became a pond. (*See* Satī §2.) The queen again became Nārada, and Vishnu appeared to lead him from the pond. Such was the manner in which Nārada learned the secret of Vishnu's *māyā.*

What is mythologically depicted in the above story is philosophically postulated in various theistic Hindu doctrinal statements. The phenomenal world, the world of flux and change, is an emanation of divine energy. It is *māyā,* at once attractive, all-consuming, and incomprehensible. Insofar as *māyā* represents the extraordinary ability of God to create forms, to bring material reality into being, it is identified with his feminine, active aspect, his Śakti (energy). Thus certain theistic Hindu systems count *māyā* as a specific aspect of God's feminine energy, and in Śaiva Siddhānta philosophy *māyā-śakti* is even considered to manifest Shiva's beneficent concern for human souls in leading them to release from Samsara. Without his *śakti* God would remain pure, unchanging, passive godhead; the world would never be created; and space and time would cease to exist.

Māyā, like *śakti,* is a feminine noun and achieves personalized expression as Māyā or Mahāmāyā, great goddess and divine creatrix, sometimes cast as a manifestation of Pārvatī-Durgā and hence associated with Shiva, or elsewhere as the consort of Vishnu, whom he impregnates in order to create the world (e.g., Bh.P 3.25). Here it might be mentioned in passing that Māyā is also the name which tradition gives to the mother of the Buddha, playing upon the term's connotations of miraculous creativity and fecundity. In a fundamental sense *māyā* is the universal womb, the matrix out of which forms arise, the source of all life in the world of space and time. However, such forms—indeed life itself—are incomprehensible and unpredictable. *Māyā* symbolizes the fleeting, transitory quality of empirical reality, which, though grounded in the eternal divine essence, is also an inscrutable veil drawn over that essence. To see the world as *māyā* is to see an unpredictable world, almost flimsy in its fleeting quality, a phantasmagoria of forms where life feeds upon death, a world both attractive and repulsive, beauty which is also a snare.

4. **Māyā in Advaita Vedānta.** *Māyā* is sometimes glossed with the English word "illusion," a translation based on a not always accurate interpretation of Advaita Vedānta philosophy, particularly as expounded by the great eighth-century systematizer Śaṃkara. Given Advaita's strict ontological nondualism, an unavoidable philosophical problem arises with regard to the status of the empirical world. How is the world of space, time, and differentiated phenomena related to the supreme, nondual Brahman, which according to Advaita Vedānta is the only true reality? For Advaitins one of the most important ways in which the relationship between Brahman and the world is accounted for is in terms of *māyā.*

If Brahman, the impersonal absolute, is all that really exists, then the perception of duality or plurality is somehow an error. It is this error that is attributed to the operation of *māyā.* Indeed, the experienced world of differentiation is *māyā.* But only from the standpoint of the higher mystical consciousness in which Brahman is experienced and known as the only reality does the phenomenal world lack reality and can be called an "illusion." Ontologically this world which is perceived to be plural is grounded in the absolute and is created by means of the mysterious, inexplicable operation of Brahman's *māyā.* Like a magician, the impersonal Brahman produces appearances which from a higher perspective are seen to be deceptive. Thus, epistemologically *māyā* is conditioned by human ignorance (Avidyā). Failure to recognize the oneness of reality is *māyā.*

All this is not to say that the empirical world does not exist. Śaṃkara, on the basis of men's shared perception of external objects, does not doubt the existence of the world, though that world is not considered to be fully real. That which is truly real *(sat)* is characterized by utter permanence, eternity, and infinitude, viz., Brahman. But neither is the phenomenal world completely devoid of reality; for that which is nonreal *(asat)* could never come into being. The *māyā*-produced world is thus relatively real or, perhaps better said, contingently real. Its existence is derivative and consequently without ultimate significance. In this vein, such modern-day Advaitins as S. RADHAKRISHNAN are careful to avoid facile identification of the phenomenal world of *māyā* with illusion. For Radhakrishnan the phenomenal world is real, but it is a conditioned reality, dependent on the absolute Brahman.

In its understanding of *māyā,* Advaita Vedānta does not mark a radical departure from previous usage. From the Rig Veda onward there is the constant notion of an incomprehensible, marvelous power to create forms in the phenomenal world. Thus, in labeling the phenomenal world *māyā* the later Hindu tradition in its various interpretations advances several important axioms about the nature of that world: *its mystery,* implying that there are definite limits to human comprehension in attempts to grasp the world; *its derivative nature,* implying that material phenomena are not their own creators; and *its fleeting and unsubstantial character,* implying its lack of ultimacy and essential worth as a realm and goal of human endeavor.

Bibliography. E. Deutsch, *Advaita Vedānta* (1969); J. Gonda, *Four Studies in the Language of the Veda* (1959), pp. 119-93, and *Change and Continuity in Indian Religion* (1965), pp. 164-97; T. Goudriaan, *Māyā Divine and Human* (1978); R. Reyna, *The Concept of Māyā* (1962).

G. E. YOCUM

MECCA mĕk′ ə (I). City in west central Arabia (the HEJAZ region); the birthplace of MUHAMMAD, and religious center of the Islamic world. It is the point which Muslims face when praying (QIBLAH) and to which they make pilgrimage (HAJJ). Access is restricted to Muslims, whether residents or visitors.

1. **Pre-Islamic Mecca.** Mecca came into prominence with the emergence of Islam in the seventh century A.D. but it is much older, although its origin and early history are unknown. It seems likely that its importance was related to its possession of a well (ZAMZAM), its favorable location as a station on a trade route for aromatics and spices from the south of the Arabian peninsula and the East, and its religious sanctuary (KA'BA). In other respects Mecca was not well situated. Located in a narrow valley surrounded by rocky hills, it was subject to severe floods from water running off the hills, and has an ovenlike climate during much of the year. Its soil is infertile, making even modest agriculture impossible.

For several centuries before the birth of Muhammad, Mecca was largely populated and dominated by the tribe of the QURAISH. By Muhammad's time they controlled the trade routes and enterprises south and north from Mecca, having supplanted the traders of the Yemen in the south of the Arabian peninsula who dealt in silks, spices, perfumes, and other luxuries from India and China, as well as in the products of the Yemen. Great caravans brought these goods north, especially to Syria, for transshipment to the West. Eventually the Quraish became no ordinary traders but entrepreneurs, brokers, and financiers, gradually acquiring both the capital and the skills to build a prosperous Meccan mercantile economy.

The second source of Mecca's prosperity at the end of the sixth century A.D. was religious. In its Ka'ba Mecca possessed the preeminent religious shrine in central Arabia. Attracting as it did seasonal visitations by tribes of a wide area, it enhanced both the prestige and the purses of its Meccan custodians.

The Quraish were divided into about a dozen clans, each claiming descent from a common ancestor. On the whole, the more powerful clans were those which had gained wealth through the Meccan commercial system. The most influential clans at the time of Muhammad's birth were the 'Abd Shams (or UMAYYAD) and the Makhzūm. The principal leaders of Mecca came from these clans. Muhammad was of the Banū HĀSHIM, one of the weaker clans. Most of the earliest Muslims were either from comparatively weak clans or were junior members of strong clans.

Mecca did not have a strong central government. The *mala'* or senate, composed of heads of clans and other leading men, was essentially a deliberative assembly without executive powers. Its effectiveness in shaping policies and resolving disputes depended on the skills and powers of persuasion of its leading members.

2. **Mecca and Muhammad.** The leading Meccans saw Muhammad's claimed revelations and vocation as a threat to the Meccan system both commercial and religious; they sought to organize opposition to him both before the HIJRA (e. g., by boycotting of his clan) and afterward (militarily).

By the time of Muhammad's conquest of Mecca in A.D. 630 some Meccans were coming to be reconciled to his leadership, in part because Mecca had been weakened in the prolonged conflict and in part in response to positive, reassuring signals, most especially in Muhammad's evident intention to enhance the religious centrality of the Ka'ba. This intention was realized when he became the master of Mecca.

Although Mecca was never the political center of Islam—Muhammad remained there only briefly after the conquest, returning to MEDINA after two or three weeks—it has clearly been the religious center of the Islamic world since A.D. 624. Its religious centrality was reaffirmed when Muhammad journeyed from Medina to Mecca as a pilgrim several months before his death.

3. **Mecca after Muhammad.** With the center of power in Medina under the earliest caliphs and the emigration of important Meccans to Medina, it was principally religion, especially the pilgrimage, which kept Mecca alive. Later caliphs, beginning with Mu'āwiya (d. A.D. 680), founder of the UMAYYAD caliphate, took an interest in Mecca although their capital was now Damascus in Syria. Physical and topographical improvements were instituted, mak-

ing Mecca a somewhat more liveable place. Also under the Umayyads the enlargement and embellishment of the MOSQUE containing the Ka'ba was undertaken. Both the Umayyads and their successors, the 'ABBĀSIDS, expended considerable sums on Mecca, frequently in connection with their own pilgrimages to it. The largess of Hārūn ar-Rashīd (d. A.D. 809) is a splendid example.

Mecca was sacked by the QARMAṬIANS, a heretical Muslim sect, in A.D. 930. They scandalized the Muslim world by carrying off the black stone of the Ka'ba, and some twenty years passed before it was returned.

In A.D. 1517 Mecca was taken by the Ottoman Turks. The sharīf Husayn ibn Ali proclaimed his independence from Turkey in 1924 and established himself as the king of the Hejaz. In 1925 Mecca as well as Medina fell to the sultan of Najd in central Arabia, 'Abd al-'Azīz al-Sa'ūd, thus beginning the current monarchy of Saudi Arabia.

Bibliography. F. Wüstenfeld, ed. and trans., *Die Chroniken der Stadt Mekka,* 4 vols. (1858-61); E. Rutter, *The Holy Cities of Arabia,* 2 vols. (1928); C. S. Hurgronje, *Mekka in the Latter Part of the 19th Century* (1970); E. Esin, *Mecca, The Blessed; Madina, The Radiant* (1963); W. Watt, *Muhammad at Mecca* (1953).

H. B. PARTIN

MEDINA mə dē´ nə (I—Arab.; lit. "the city"). Arabian city about 280 miles north of MECCA to which MUHAMMAD migrated (*see* HIJRA) in A.D. 622, and in which he established the Islamic UMMA ("community").

Medina is the Islamic name for what was known in pre-Islamic times as Yathrib, which consisted of a relatively large, fertile oasis. Both its comparatively moderate climate and its fertility are in contrast to Mecca. At the time of the hijra Medina's population was composed of several Jewish tribes from the north which had probably developed the oasis and of Arab tribes which had emigrated from the south of Arabia. Conflicts between the Arab tribes as well as between the Arabs and Jews were the ostensible reason for the invitation to Muhammad to come to Yathrib in A.D. 622 as an arbiter and peacemaker.

Muhammad promulgated a document known as the "Constitution of Medina," which regulated the relations between the various groups and referred to "a single community" *(umma).* The document represents basic ideas of the Islamic state which emerged in the early formative period of Islam.

During the first year in Medina, Muhammad attempted to win the Jews to Islam. After it was clear that they rejected his prophetic vocation, most of the Jewish population was expelled as untrustworthy. In the meanwhile the Medinans became increasingly involved in armed conflict with the Meccans. Meccan efforts to conquer Medina, climaxed by a siege of Medina (the Battle of the Trench) in A.D. 627, failed. In A.D. 630 the Medinans, joined by other Arabs, captured Mecca.

Several weeks later Muhammad returned to Medina, where he remained the last two years of his life, except for a notable journey to Mecca several months before his death (June 8, A.D. 632) to perform his "farewell pilgrimage." He was buried in Medina and his tomb is located under the green dome of Medina's Mosque of the Prophet. Many pilgrims are drawn to Medina to visit his tomb, often in connection with the pilgrimage to Mecca (HAJJ). Medina also contains the graves of other early Muslim notables, including the caliphs ABŪ BAKR and 'UMAR, other Companions of the Prophet, and members of his family, thus enhancing the significance and sanctity of the city.

The first three caliphs—Abū Bakr, 'Umar, and 'UTHMĀN—made Medina their capital. Medina lost that status, however, never to regain it, when ALI moved the capital to Kūfa in Iraq. Nevertheless, Medina continued to be important as the city where Muhammad had lived the last ten, climactic years of his life. In this connection it became preeminent as a locale for numerous Traditions (ḤADĪTH) as well as a center for the collection of Traditions and the formation of Islamic law (SHARIA), as represented especially by the school of MALIK IBN ANAS (d. A.D. 795).

Medina is usually considered the second holiest city of Islam, ranking after Mecca and before Jerusalem.

Bibliography. E. Rutter, *The Holy Cities of Arabia,* 2 vols. (1928); E. Esin, *Mecca, The Blessed; Madina, The Radiant* (1963); W. Watt, *Muhammad at Medina* (1956).

H. B. PARTIN

MEDITATION, BUDDHIST. Meditation, the inwardly oriented concentration of attention on specified subjects, is the prime spiritual discipline for the attainment of ultimate salvation (NIRVANA) in Buddhism. The religion's name itself derives from the designation of its founder as the BUDDHA ("Enlightened One") after his final meditational experience. It is at this inner experiential depth, analogous to deep devotion and mysticism in other religions, that Buddhist sects are most nearly at one.

1. **The Theravāda model.** *a) Basis and origins.* The actual historical forms of meditation, both in terms and techniques, vary considerably from sect to sect. Nevertheless the basic techniques and main themes of meditation are similar throughout Buddhism. Buddhism seems to have been closely connected in its early years with what later became Hindu YOGA (both its philosophy and system of mind and body training). Some of the marks of that origin still remain in the Buddhist meditational system. It was greatly modified, however, by the differing Buddhist view of salvation as a "going out" of space-time existence into Nirvana, rather than the inward discovery of pure selfhood as in yoga.

The PALI CANON and BUDDHAGHOSA's massive manual, *Path of Purification*—which incorporates a thousand years of tradition and refinement of meditational method—provide us with a basic pattern, even though their claim to embody the exact method of Gautama Buddha cannot be taken literally.

THERAVĀDA meditational practice is the direct application of its world view of the molding of the individual's consciousness of himself and his world. According to this view, all living beings are enmeshed in an eternal round of rebirths (SAMSARA) whose fundamental nature is threefold: impermanence (ANICCA), lack of true reality (MĀYĀ), and dis-ease or suffering (DUKKHA). A living being, whether god, man, animal, or denizen of one of the purgatories, is thrust time after time into another existence by its craving (TAṆHĀ) for continuing life of some sort. Being ignorant of life's true nature, a living being is attracted to renewed existence by the pseudo-pleasures of life. Therefore, ignorance and craving keep rebirth in various forms going on through endless ages. The main function of meditation, therefore, is to lift the veil of ignorance and to cut the cord of that craving. This can be accomplished only at the human level.

b) Basic methods. Finding an isolated place, the meditator assumes the classical physical posture for meditation, the "lotus" position, sitting with legs folded so that each foot rests, sole somewhat upward, in the bend of the opposite knee. In this posture the spine and neck are kept in a straight line, the hands folded together in the lap, and the eyes at least half-closed in a nonfocused gaze. Thus solidly seated, with the lower (abdominal, sexual) centers of feeling stultified, breathing deeply and easily, the meditator can give clear and full attention to the subject of his meditation.

Traditionally, forty subjects were used in meditation (as directed by the meditation master in accordance with the personal character of the meditator). Some subjects may be seen as preparatory for the later intensive efforts: meditation on the Buddha and his virtues, on peace, or on the blessed dispositions of lovingkindness (METTĀ), compassion (KARUṆĀ), joy in others' joy, and equanimity. Other subjects which provide depth of concentration are physical objects such as colors and shapes. A third class embodies the Buddhist themes of impermanence, nonreality, and suffering. Herein one detachedly observes the rise and fall of his breath, visualizes the repulsiveness of the digestive process, thinks of the actual physical components of his body, and objectively views bodies in their stages of decay, as well as the physical and mental elements of his own life-process. (*See* MAHĀSATIPAṬṬHĀNA SUTTA.)

c) Types and results. The experiential results sought by meditation are of two sorts: the *jhānic* states and insight awareness (VIPASSANĀ). The *jhāna* (Skt. *dhyāna* or meditation), variously called musings, absorptions, concentrations, or trances, are eight in number and each is of a successively higher level of internal abstraction. BUDDHAGHOSA's term "peaceful abidings" portrays their basic quality: a trancelike calm in which consciousness of the outside world through the senses is totally cut off. This is achieved by locking the attention on one of the subjects of meditation, such as a color or decaying body state, and gradually refining it until at the highest of the eight levels there is scarcely either sensible object or conscious attention. This type of technique seems to stem from yogic sources, but by itself does not lead to final enlightenment.

The other type of meditation—insight or *vipassanā*—is used either along with the *jhānic* or independently. By it one gains first-hand insight into the true nature of the body-mind self and the everyday world as impermanent, basically unreal, and inherently painful.

This realization is, of course, the essence of the Buddhist world view, and to make it vivid and existentially real to the meditator is the main purpose of meditation. Thus the rise and fall of the abdomen in breathing vividly witnesses to the perpetual flux of the life-cycle from existence to nonexistence. Viewing the repulsiveness of one's own bodily functions, or the stages of bodily decay, gives a direct sense of impermanence and tempers one's love of life. And a clear, detached observation of one's own thoughts and emotions as they are occurring gives a first-hand awareness of oneself as only a fluctuating, impermanent succession of physical-mental states. If used jointly with the *jhānic, vipassanā* awareness provides a realization that not even in those peaceful trances is it possible to escape the life-death changes of existence.

There are two results of this process. On the negative side is the thorough experiencing of the awareness of the transience *(anicca)* and dis-ease *(dukkha)* of embodied existence. This is the absolutely necessary precondition for spiritual progress and final enlightenment. On the positive side there is a foretaste of Nirvana itself. This appears in flashes of an unconditioned, pure awareness that is different in kind from any other awareness. As one advances in *vipassanā* he progressively becomes a "stream-enterer" (SOTĀPANNA) who will never be reborn in less than human estate, a once-returner to human life (SAKADĀGĀMIN), a nonreturner to human life (ANĀGAMIN) and finally an ARHANT who, like the Buddha, will "go out" into final Nirvana upon death.

2. Mahāyāna developments. *a) General character.* MAHĀYĀNA Buddhism, originating in India and spreading through north and east Asia, produced many variations and even radical modifications in the basic meditation pattern. Postures, general techniques, terminology, and final goals remained the same on the surface, but the actual significance and underlying quality of meditation were greatly altered. Mahāyāna also produced several new doctrinal interpretations which had a direct bearing on meditational patterns.

First was the interpretation of the BODHISATTVA, who was now no longer (like the Theravāda bodhisatta) merely a being on the way to the long-ago vowed attainment of Buddhahood and Nirvana in some future age. Instead, the Mahāyāna bodhisattva is pictured as on the verge of attaining Nirvana, but rather than selfishly entering in, deliberately choosing to reincarnate himself endlessly till he shall have brought every other living being to salvation. Thus the bodhisattva came to be the great ideal of human spirituality, almost outshining the presumedly greater Buddhas.

Second, there was the new Mahāyāna doctrine of the innate Buddha-nature within all beings, including grass, trees, and, in some traditions, even stones. Gautama's enlightenment was reinterpreted as consisting in his new-found realization of this truth. (Meditation allows one to acquire this "wisdom" experientially.) The third and capstone doctrine in the Mahāyāna edifice was NĀGĀRJUNA's revolutionary statement that there is not one iota of difference between SAMSARA (life-death existence) and Nirvana.

b) Consequences for meditation. It was inevitable that such developments in doctrine would have a decisive effect on meditational patterns. The ancient language of world alienation, detachment, enlightenment, and final Nirvana was indeed kept, but the new bodhisattva interpretation brought the life of inner spiritual attainment out of the monastery. Now meditation could be and was joined to this-worldly living, using its modes of activity as instruments of spiritual progress. Indeed, in the SŪTRA named after him, the layman VIMALAKĪRTI is pictured as superior in understanding and attainment even to MAÑJUŚRĪ, that great heavenly bodhisattva who stands beside AMIDA Buddha in his PURE LAND. Emotional alienation from the world (a Theravāda goal) is replaced by disinterested activity within it (the Mahāyāna goal).

Another effect of this doctrine and of the teaching about innate Buddhahood was a sense of greater intimacy with the ongoing life-processes. No longer should the meditator single-mindedly concentrate on the impermanence and suffering manifested in his own being. His mind and self, if cured of their egocentricity, are in truth the Buddha mind and self, and enlightenment is the first-hand discovery of this truth.

The belief in the identity of samsara and Nirvana extended and deepened these tendencies. The distinctions between holy and profane, religious and secular, usual and unusual spiritual states are wiped out. Meditation comes to be a discipline in which the innate, natural Buddha-essence of man is made integral to his life in all its dimensions. Spontaneity and integrality of life became the marks of true spiritual attainment. Harmonic interaction with other humans and with nature and the unity-identity of individual mind with universal (Buddha) mind are the goal. Thus, detachment from transitory forms is achieved. The tangible world becomes the manifestation of the formless absolute, and its manifold fullness is the home of emptiness (ŚŪNYATĀ).

c) Varieties of Mahāyāna meditation. It is perhaps in ZEN (Chinese Ch'an) that these Mahāyāna qualities are most clearly and compactly embodied in meditation. As a specifically meditative discipline Zen conceives itself to be a direct, experiential continuation of Gautama's own enlightenment, shorn of the impediments of ritualism, doctrinal forms and statements, and scripturalism. Its use of the well-known KŌAN (puzzle-statement) is designed to break through all intellectual formulations and emotional fixities into the freedom of individual mind that has become Buddha-mind, directly experienced in oneself.

In TIBETAN BUDDHISM, meditation, though in a general sense Mahāyāna, has produced features found nowhere else. Pre-Buddhist BÖN components provide a colorful imagery of demonic forms in which to clothe one's psychosomatic forces. TANTRISM gave rise to extensive sexual symbolisms whose purpose is to unite all elements of the meditator's body-mind internally, and with the creative energy (KUṆḌALINĪ) of the universe. Tantric meditation is noted for its ritual chantings (MANTRA) and psychic-world diagrams (MANDALA) used to produce vivid visualizations.

3. Conclusion. Traditionally only the monastic way of life has been thought capable of sustaining successful meditation. In fact the Buddhist monastic life was constructed to encourage and facilitate a life of meditation. To the layman was left the life of pious good works and accumulation of merit for better rebirths. But through the centuries monks have become more and more involved with lay life—forced, in part, by lay demands into a type of community service. Hence intensive meditation has become the special vocation of a select few monks.

Contemporary meditation patterns throughout the Buddhist world, however, show a general tendency toward adaptation and simplification in order to appeal to a wide variety of people, including lay persons, many of whom are now being taught how to meditate. Noteworthy among such lay-directed types are Theravāda *vipassanā* and several varieties of Zen.

Bibliography. Nyanamoli, trans., *Path of Purification* (1964), difficult, but a classic Theravāda manual of meditation. C. C. Chang, *Teachings of Tibetan Yoga* (1963), knowledgeably sets forth Tibetan meditation techniques; E. Conze, *Buddhist Meditation* (1956), scholarly but not too difficult overview of basic themes and purposes of meditation; Nyanaponika, *The Heart of Buddhist Meditation* (1970), clear, compact introduction to Theravāda meditation, also relevant Pali Canon quotations; D. T. Suzuki, *Zen Buddhism* (1956), history, themes, features of Zen meditation; A. W. Watts, *The Way of Zen* (1957), Western-oriented exposition, clear analysis, suggestive interpretations.

W. L. KING

MEHER BĀBĀ mā´ hər bä´ bä (H; 1894-1969). Born in Poona as Merwan Irani, to parents from Iran and of the ZOROASTRIAN religion, Meher Bābā ("Father of love") had disciples from among India's religious communities, but he received his first initiation from a Muslim woman saint called Hazrat Bābājan. His followers today refer to him as a SUFI master although he is also called AVATAR. Meher Bābā traveled frequently to America and Europe, where his disciples included film stars and titled nobility. He exercised a deep fascination for those with whom he came in contact, although the content of his behavior seemed irrational and erratic on the surface. He took a vow of silence in 1925 and never spoke again until his death. He communicated with his followers by hand signs and by pointing to letters on a letter-board.

As an example of the divine love he taught, he and his disciples cared for insane holy men called *mast*. As he traveled about India, he would seek out such individuals, feed and bathe them, and spend time in their company. But like much else about Meher Bābā the purpose behind this activity remained obscure.

Bibliography. C. B. Purdom, *The God-Man* (1964).

C. S. J. WHITE

MEIJI mā´ ī jē (Sh—Jap.; 1852-1912). Throne name of the emperor who presided over the modernization of Japan after the overthrow of the Tokugawa shogunate (1603-1867). The Meiji Period (1868-1912) was characterized by religious ferment. In 1868 an imperial edict separated BUDDHISM and SHINTŌ, and the "Way of the KAMI" was adopted as the guiding principle of the nation. The cult of the emperor was actively promoted, and a Shintō shrine was erected in the imperial palace to honor the divine ancestors. New religious movements such as TENRI-KYŌ and KONKŌ-KYŌ arose and were accepted as Shintō sects. In 1873 the edict that banned Christianity was set aside, and missionaries, both Catholic and Protestant, had some success in capturing the loyalty of samurai and intellectuals (*see* MISSIONS, CHRISTIAN).

A beautiful and extensive shrine where the emperor Meiji is venerated is located in the center of Toyko. *See* JAPANESE RELIGION.

K. CRIM

MEIR mā ēr´ (Ju). Early second century A.D. RABBI, student of AKIBA, ordained during the great persecutions after the BAR KOCHBA revolt. Forced to flee Israel, he became a central figure at Usha, where the SANHEDRIN was renewed, and had a decisive role in the compilation of the MISHNAH.

E. M. MEYERS

MEKHILTA mē kĭl´ tə (Ju—Aram.; lit. "[Collection of] Rule [s]"). Legal homily *(midrash halakhah)* on Exodus. *Mekhilta de-Rabbi Ishmael* includes teachings of R. Ishmael's school and was compiled not before the end of the fourth century A.D. in Palestine. *Mekhilta de-Rashbi* was compiled no earlier than the fifth century A.D., lost, and reproduced from fragments.

Y. SHAMIR

MELA/MICRONESIAN TRIBAL RELIGIONS. *See* OCEANIC TRIBAL RELIGIONS.

MELANCHTHON, PHILIP mē lăngk´ thŭn (Ch; 1497–1560). One of the early leaders of the PROTESTANT REFORMATION; professor at Wittenberg from 1518 to 1560, where he became an ardent follower of MARTIN LUTHER. As Visitor of Saxon churches and schools, and as director of the reorganization of the universities of Heidelberg, Leipzig, Cologne, and Tübingen, Melanchthon was called "Preceptor of Germany." He was the architect of the AUGSBURG CONFESSION (1530), wrote its Apology (1531), and was instrumental in drafting the Wittenberg Concord (1536). All three documents became foundations of LUTHERAN belief.

Melanchthon's position on the EUCHARIST in the 1540 *Variata* edition of the Augsburg Confession caused "genuine" *(gnesio)* Lutherans to accuse him of crypto-Calvinism. (*See* CALVIN, JOHN.) Melanchthon earned further opprobrium from the "genuine" Lutherans when he helped modify the Augsburg Interim (1547) in the substitute Leipzig Interim (1548), which allowed certain Roman Catholic practices as *adiaphora* or optional. A third controversy arose over Melanchthon's teaching the doctrine of synergism, i.e. that the human will has power to accept or reject the grace offered by God.

Throughout his life Melanchthon engaged in colloquies which failed to solve theological differences: Lutheran-Reformed, Marburg (1529) and Wittenberg (1536); Lutheran–Roman Catholic, Augsburg (1530) and Worms (1557); all three factions, Regensburg (1541).

Bibliography. C. L. Hill, trans., *Melanchthon: Selected Writings* (1962); C. L. Manschreck, *Melanchthon, the Quiet Reformer* (1968).

J. RAITT

MENCIUS mĕn´ shəs; Latinized form of **MENG TZU** mŭng tzə (Con—Chin.; 371-289 B.C.?) 1. Philosopher, second only to CONFUCIUS in importance to the Confucian tradition. 2. The *Mencius,* collected sayings of Mencius.

A native of the state of Ch'i, Mencius studied with a disciple of Confucius' grandson Tzu Ssu. Like Confucius, Mencius traveled from state to state seeking a virtuous ruler capable of practicing the Confucian teachings. The disintegration of the feudal order was even more pronounced than it had been in Confucius' day, and Mencius met with little success.

1. **Mencius as teacher.** Frustrated by repeated failure at the political level, Mencius took up the role of teacher and architect of Confucian thought. He confronted rival schools of philosophy, primarily Mohism and TAOISM, and the *Mencius* records the conversations of Mencius with disciples and rivals alike.

2. **Government by goodness.** Mencius extolled the virtue of "humaneness" or "humanity" (JEN), love for one's fellow man. But he objected strongly to the Mohists, who advocated loving everyone equally without regard to kinship or social structures.

Mencius paired "humanity" with "righteousness" *(i)*, suggesting that the feeling of "humanity" needed to be correlated with the position and specific relationships of the other person. Thus greater "humaneness" should be shown to those closer at hand. Following Confucius' insistence on the need for moral rectification in government, Mencius argued that the ideal ruler must possess the virtues of "humanity" *(jen)* and "righteousness" *(i)*, putting the interests of the people first and his own last. The ruler who neglects the people for himself is not a true ruler. He loses the MANDATE OF HEAVEN, and the people under such circumstances have the right to revolt.

3. **Theory of human nature.** While Confucius left the question of man's true nature ambiguous, Mencius argued that man by nature is good, a position that became the hallmark of the Confucian school. Man's nature possesses the potentiality of goodness just as it is in the nature of water to flow downward (6A2). Water can be made to flow uphill through a series of dams or it can even be splashed above one's head, but in both cases such action is the result of an external force rather than of the nature of the water itself. In the same ways man's nature has the potentiality of goodness even though an external element can force it into bad ways. In his most celebrated passage Mencius suggests that anyone seeing a child about to fall into a well will rescue that child without thinking of any personal gain or loss. This illustrates the beginning of goodness which all humans have by nature (2A6).

4. **The religious dimension.** The Mencian branch of Confucian thought recognizes a continuity between man's nature and the nature of Heaven. Thus the sage *(sheng)* or the gentleman *(chün-tzu)* is the one who has recognized and brought to full manifestation his Heaven-endowed nature and has reached the point of understanding the unity of the ways of Heaven and man.

Bibliography. W. T. Chan, *A Source Book in Chinese Philosophy* (1963), ch.3; W. T. deBary, *Sources of Chinese Tradition* (1960), ch.6; D. C. Lau, trans., *Mencius* (1970); D. Munro, *The Concept of Man in Early China* (1969); A. Verwilghen, *Mencius: The Man and His Ideas* (1967).

R. L. TAYLOR

MENDELSSOHN, MOSES mĕn´ dəl zōn (Ju; 1729-1786). German Jewish philosopher of the Enlightenment. His rationalist reinterpretation of Jewish theology left speculative truth to the realm of reason and redefined Judaism as a system of orthopraxis. His chief work on Jewish thought was *Jerusalem* (1783). *See* JUDAISM §6a.

L. FAGEN

MENDICANT FRIARS (Ch). Religious orders of medieval origin embracing poverty and brotherhood (as *fratres*, thus "friars"). Unlike monks confined to monasteries by vows of stability, friars moved about, preaching and teaching, living by begging (*mendicare*, thus "mendicant"). Principal orders of mendicant friars (now allowed common but not individual property) are FRANCISCANS, DOMINICANS, CARMELITES, and AUGUSTINIANS. (*See* RELIGIOUS ORDERS.)

W. H. PRINCIPE

MENNONITES (Ch). Several Protestant bodies stemming from sixteenth century ANABAPTISTS. When, in 1534-35, revolutionary Anabaptists tried to create by force a "New Jerusalem" in the German city of Münster, they were bloodily suppressed. This debacle triggered the entrance into the movement of Menno Simons (1496?-1561), a Frisian Roman Catholic priest. He had earlier become convinced of the falsity of traditional doctrine and practice but hesitated to break with the church. Taking pity on the desperate and hunted Münsterites, he joined them to bring a balanced leadership. This he accomplished effectively, despite life as an underground itinerant with a price on his head. The movement, grateful for his wise and warm shepherding, took his name. During the latter years of his life Menno established Anabaptist congregations in North Germany. By the late sixteenth century intolerance ebbed in the Netherlands, and Mennonites emerged there as a respected and cultured minority.

Persecution remained severe in Switzerland until the eighteenth century. Many of the Swiss brethren fled or were expelled, but a small number held out in isolated farming valleys. In Southern Germany and Alsace some Mennonites found protection because of their economic contributions as master farmers. Major migration to North America began in 1683. Mennonites spread westward from Pennsylvania, concentrating on locating rural colonies where they perpetuated their faith and German culture.

Prussian Mennonites began migrating to the Ukraine in 1788, where they flourished in large agricultural villages. However, thousands of them left after 1873, when the Tsarist regime began conscripting them. They settled primarily in the midwestern plains of the U.S. and Canada. Many more migrated from Russia to North and South America after World Wars I and II.

In the twentieth century the once-isolated Mennonites experienced a remarkable resurgence of mission activity, resulting in a world church. More than a third of the adult membership of 580,000 are nonwhite. To balance their refusal to perform military service, Mennonites have been eager to show their good will in alleviating human suffering and reducing international tensions.

There are many divisions among Mennonites. The largest groups in the U.S. are the (Old) Mennonite Church, the General Conference Mennonite Church, and the Mennonite Brethren. A small conservative branch, the Old Order AMISH, are widely known because of their resistance to modern technology. A comparable group in faith and dress are the Hutterite

Brethren—founded in 1528—who believe that true Christianity can be practiced only in communal living.

Bibliography. *Mennonite Encyclopedia*, 4 vols. (1954-59); D. F. Durnbaugh, *The Believers' Church* (1968); C. J. Dyck, ed., *Introduction to Mennonite History* (1967); G. H. Williams, *The Radical Reformation* (1962). D. F. Durnbaugh

MENORAH mə nō′ rä (Ju—Heb.; "candelabrum"). (1) The seven-branched candelabrum which was one of the major items in the tabernacle during the Israelites' wanderings in the wilderness and, later, in the Temple in Jerusalem; (2) the eight-branched candelabrum (with an additional socket for the *shammash*, or "server") still used as the chief element in the celebration of the eight-day festival of Hanukkah.

The menorah of the tabernacle is described in two parallel accounts in the Bible (Exod. 25:31-40; 37:17-24). It is suggested (Exod. 25:40) that the pattern for it was shown by God to Moses on Mount Sinai.

The eight-branched Hanukkah menorah is generally modeled after the Temple menorah, although it has also assumed a variety of other forms. According to tradition, one light in it is kindled the first night of the festival and one more added successively on each of the following seven nights.

Bibliography. H. Strauss, "Menorah," *EJ*, XI (1971), 1355-70; S. S. Kayser and G. Schoenberger, eds., *Jewish Ceremonial Art* (2nd ed., 1959). B. Martin

MERIT (B). *See* Puñña.

MERU, MOUNT mā′ rū (B). The early inhabitants of India, looking northward and seeing a mountain range and the north polar star, imagined a mountain, named Meru/Sumeru/Sineru, which they took for the axis of the world and around which they believed the sun and moon circled. They pictured the earth as the lower half of an oval and heaven as the upper half, with earth resting on a sphere of gold, that sphere on one of water, that on one of air, and that on one of space. The earth is divided into four continents, of which India is situated to the south of Meru.

Meru, whose base is submerged in water, is traditionally spoken of as shaped like a top standing on its point, yet at the same time there is mention of winding highways, of four levels, and other features in conflict with that shape. The top is pictured as flower-shaped, with four drooping petals and a high, flat calyx, on the surface of which are thirty-three gods, who, among other things, judge the virtues and vices of all living beings in a palace called "Fair-to-see." Various gods live on other levels. Meru is ringed by seven concentric mountain ranges, the outermost of which is separated from the Himalayas by a series of forests and seas. On Mt. Haima (= Himalaya) is a lake called Anavatapta, "not heated," from which flow the heavenly Ganges, Indus, and Oxus, as well as the river Sītā.

Bibliography. W. W. McGovern, *Manual of Buddhist Philosophy* (1923); L. de la Vallée-Poussin, *l'Abhidharmakośa de Vasubandhu* (1923); W. Kirfel, *Die Kosmographie der Inder* (1920). L. Hurvitz

MERKABAH MYSTICISM mĕr kä′ bə (Ju—Heb.; lit. "chariot"). The earliest phase of Jewish Mysticism, characterized by descriptions of ecstatic ascents to heaven and encounters with the celestial inhabitants of God's supernal realm. The name derives from a literary tradition that associated these celestial revelations with the biblical accounts of angelic figures surrounding the Throne of Glory (Ezek. 1:22-28) and the chariot (I Chr. 28:18) on which it descended.

The movement emerged in Palestine as the outgrowth of the ascetic spirit that first produced much of the Apocalyptic literature of intertestamental Judaism. Its angelic hymnology seems to be a continuation of the sectarian fervor of the Qumran community (*see* Essenes). Its subsequent Palestinian development was shaped by, and directly contributed to, the same cultural and political environment that fostered religious syncretism, hermeticism, Christian Gnosticism, Greek mysteries, and Greco-Roman magic.

Rabbinic Judaism tempered its transcendental image of God with a loving appreciation for God's intimacy and presence (*Shekhina*) and emphasized the study of Torah and its interpretation as the ideal of religious life. Merkabah mysticism, on the other hand, sought religious experiences independent of the study of scripture. It evacuated the divine from this world and located it at the farthest possible remove from ordinary human experience, emphasizing God's awesome grandeur, otherworldly majesty, and numinous quality.

In accordance with this view merkabah mysticism developed a means for bridging the cosmic gap separating humanity from God. To experience God, i.e., to behold him, the mystic must undergo a total transformation induced by ascetic practice and the recitation of hymns declaring the holiness and majesty of God. This transformation, usually described in fiery images, allows the mystic to begin his ascent from earth through the series of seven heavens, celestial palaces and chariots, and angelic realms, each of which resounds with praise of God.

The journey is fraught with danger, since at every level there are hostile angels anxious to expel alien intruders from the divine world. For his protection the mystic must know the precise names of the angels he encounters and the sites he beholds and he must know the proper "seals" or incantations that allow him to continue his journey. At the apex of his ascent he is vouchsafed revelations of the Throne of Glory, of the Divine Garments, and even the statue of God

Himself *(Shiur Qomah)*. Unlike later stages in Jewish mysticism, these descriptions are meant to be taken as actual, not symbolic. There is neither love of God nor a desire to attach oneself to him, but only the ecstatic, albeit passive, vision of God and his realm.

Bibliography. G. Scholem, *Jewish Gnosticism, Merkabah Mysticism, and Talmudic Tradition* (1965).

K. P. BLAND

MESSIAH, JEWISH (Heb.; lit. "the anointed one"). Central eschatological concept in Judaism. Although many references to what may be called messianic phenomena are found in the Hebrew BIBLE, the concept is, strictly speaking, postbiblical. It is the subject of extensive discussions in rabbinic literature.

The Messiah is traditionally considered to be a descendant of King David (whose own descent from Ruth the Moabite emphasizes the generally universalistic character of the messianic idea in Judaism) and thus the legitimate sovereign of Israel. The Messiah, a purely human figure, is expected to redeem the Jews by freeing them from foreign subjugation, by ending the Exile and gathering the Jews together in the land of Israel (*see* ERETZ ISRAEL), and by rebuilding the Temple there. The coming of the Messiah, it is believed, will demonstrate the truth of Judaism to the world and usher in an era of universal peace, harmony, and justice.

The concept of the Messiah (and of the messianic age which the Messiah will introduce) ought not to be confused with the related ideas of the world to come, resurrection of the dead, final judgment day, and human immortality. There is no one single normative account of Jewish eschatology; these terms have been variously defined and their interrelationships variously described. Accounts range from the decidedly supernaturalistic, as in SAADIAH BEN JOSEPH, to the austerely abstract and nonsupernatural, as in MOSES BEN MAIMON.

The messianic hope and expectation is a fundamental motif of the Jewish religion and finds expression in almost all the liturgy and holidays. This is especially the case with the SABBATH and the three pilgrim festivals, PASSOVER, SHAVUOT, and SUKKOT which, in addition to historical and agricultural import, have distinct messianic connotations. The Messiah is an important idea in KABBALA as well. With the exception of HERMANN COHEN, however, almost no Jewish philosopher has paid it systematic attention in a philosophic context.

The fervent hope for the coming of the Messiah on the part of the Jewish people has contributed to the rise of a whole variety of claimants to the role of Messiah in Jewish history (*see* SABBATAI ZVI).

The idea of the personal Messiah was rejected by classical REFORM JUDAISM and replaced with the concept of a "messianic age" characterized by universal justice and peace. Many other Jews (*see* ORTHODOX JUDAISM, CONSERVATIVE JUDAISM) see the creation of the State of Israel as the beginning of the messianic redemption. ZIONISM itself is often understood as a form of secularized messianism.

See also MAHDI.

Bibliography. A. H. Silver, *A History of Messianic Speculation in Israel* (1959); G. Scholem, *The Messianic Idea in Judaism* (1971).

M. M. KELLNER

METHODIST CHURCHES (Ch). Churches or denominations which owe their name and character to the movement led by JOHN WESLEY in the eighteenth century. More than 125 of them are alive today in many countries, having arisen under diverse circumstances and possessing various distinctive features.

While British Methodism was the first and the source of all Methodism, the Methodist Episcopal Church in America was organized in 1784, while Wesley was still alive. Strong missionary programs in the nineteenth century resulted in the planting of churches on all continents. British Methodism inevitably followed the expansion of the British Empire. The missionaries from America founded their churches in India and Africa parallel to the British, but introduced new ones in East Asia, Latin America, and Continental Europe. Most of these churches, bound for decades to the parent organizations in England and America, have in recent years become independent. Their continuing loyalty to John Wesley's evangelical-catholic theology and their use of Charles Wesley's hymns constitute a common tradition.

The largest churches, all having 500,000 members or more, are: the Methodist Church of Great Britain; the Methodist Church of South Africa; and, in the U.S., the African Methodist Episcopal Church, the African Methodist Episcopal Zion Church, and The United Methodist Church. Churches having more than 20,000 members are found in Angola, Congo, Dahomey-Togo, Ghana, Liberia, Nigeria, Zimbabwe, Sierra Leone; India, Malaysia-Singapore, Korea, the Philipppines; Fiji, New Zealand; Germany, Ireland; Jamaica, Mexico, and Brazil. The Christian Methodist Episcopal Church, Free Methodist Church, and Wesleyan Church are groups of similar size in North America.

Unions with other denominations have resulted in the statistical disappearance of some churches as solely Methodist, even though characteristic emphases in theology, worship, and mission continue within the united churches. Thus, in 1925 the United Church of Canada joined together Methodist, Presbyterian, and Congregational churches. The same three in 1977 formed the Uniting Church of Australia. These three in addition to Anglicans formed the Church of South India, 1947, and the Church of North India and of Pakistan, 1971. Methodists in Japan and the Philippines joined larger unions in 1941. However, large numbers of Methodists in North India and the Philippines remain outside the unions. In Belgium,

1978, Methodists united with other Protestants. Currently the small Methodist Church in Italy is uniting with the old WALDENSIAN Church, and several other negotiations for union are in progress. Nearly all these churches belong to the World Methodist Council and the World Council of Churches. *See* CHRISTIANITY IN AFRICA; CHRISTIANITY IN ASIA; BLACK RELIGIONS IN THE UNITED STATES §1b.

Bibliography. *The Encyclopedia of World Methodism* (1974).

J. R. NELSON

METROPOLITAN (Ch—Gr. "mother city"). A BISHOP responsible for ecclesiastical oversight of a region that includes at least one additional bishop; equivalent in ROMAN CATHOLICISM and ANGLICAN CHURCHES to ARCHBISHOP; in the ORTHODOX CHURCHES a rank above archbishop and below PATRIARCH.

K. WATKINS

METTĀ mĕt′ tä (B—Pali; lit. "loving friendship" [*mitta*—"friend"]) **MAITRĪ** mī′ trē (B—Skt.). Lovingkindness, friendliness, or good will. *Mettā* is one of the four sublime moral attitudes (BRAHMAVIHĀRAS) emphasized by the BUDDHA. It has been especially stressed in modern Southeast Asia as a subject for meditation and as the attitudinal base for solving the ills of the world. *Mettā* is love without any element of possessiveness. It does not distinguish between one's own welfare and that of others. It differs from other types of love in being inclusive rather than exclusive. For instance, scriptures tell of an instance when the Buddha calmed a charging elephant merely by radiating *mettā* toward it.

The most famous Buddhist text on lovingkindness is the canonical Mettā Sutta. It says that one who wishes to reach the final goal should meditate: "May all beings come to happiness!/ He should never abuse somebody nor/ despise (in any way) him anywhere;/ from anger and from enmity one must/ not wish for one another (harm or) ill./ Just like a mother at the risk of life/ (tries to) protect her son, her only child,/ just so should he towards all beings make/ his own mind free from (any) boundaries" (trans. in Schumann).

Bibliography. H. W. Schumann, *Buddhism: An Outline of Its Teachings and Schools* (1973), pp. 74-79; W. L. King, *In the Hope of Nibbana* (1964), pp. 150-58.

J. P. MCDERMOTT

MEZUZAH mə zoo′ zä (Ju—Heb.; "doorpost"). The scroll enclosed in a case that is affixed to all the doorposts in a Jewish home in fulfillment of the biblical injunction: "And you shall write them [the words of God] upon the posts [mezuzot] of your house and on your gates" (Deut. 6:9; 11:20). The mezuzah consists of a small piece of parchment, on which several verses are written in Hebrew characters, usually in twenty-two lines. The case containing the mezuzah must have a small aperture so that the word *Shaddai* (meaning "Almighty" but also an acronym for *Shomer Delatot Yisrael,* "Guardian of the doors of Israel") which is inscribed on the back of the scroll is visible through the opening.

B. MARTIN

MIDDLE WAY (B). *See* EIGHTFOLD PATH.

MIDRASH mĭd räsh′ (Ju—Heb.; lit. "inquiry, investigation"). The most common designation for the interpretation of TORAH (divine teaching) in JUDAISM.

1. **Midrash as process.** Traditional Judaism presupposes that divinely revealed truth constitutes a single organic whole: complete, eternally valid, internally consistent, and immutable. But study of Torah inevitably raises problems of lack of clarity, missing information, and apparent internal inconsistencies. In "pure exegesis" the *darshan* (practitioner of midrash) adds explanatory material and tries to reconcile conflicts. The changing circumstances of life demand that Torah be changeable as well, so as to speak more directly to the community. In "applied exegesis" the *darshan* articulates general principles reflected in the historically unique events and words of Torah; these then become suprahistorical paradigms by which new historical situations may be understood. Midrash thus assumes that some part of divine revelation is still implicit in the known Torah and must be revealed through explicit articulation. In this way Torah, while theoretically complete and unchanging, is actually changing constantly, and the *darshan* is participating in the process of revelation. Midrash constitutes an important type of religious experience in Judaism.

While some midrash takes previous midrash as its object, most midrash is based on the written Scripture. It can be divided into "creative historiography," which elaborates on the heroes and events of the Bible by adding concrete details and relating discrete episodes to each other, and "creative philology," which looks for religious meaning in specific letters, words, and sentences of Scripture, often divorced from context. Midrash depends on existing exegetical traditions and the creativity of the individual *darshan* for its sources.

2. **Midrash as substance.** Midrash appears in the Bible itself, as well as in the NT, the Dead Sea Scrolls, the TARGUMS, many types of medieval Jewish literature, and the sermons and interpretive writings of the modern era. However, in Jewish tradition "the Midrash" denotes a specific corpus of texts embodying the midrash of leading rabbis of roughly the first five centuries A.D., as well as many anonymous comments added during the compilation and editing of these texts in the following seven centuries. Throughout these texts there is both "midrash HALAKAH" (interpretation of legal matters) and "midrash AGGADAH" (interpretation of nonlegal matters). Thus midrash as process and substance denotes a method of understanding which is

applicable to any subject matter, rather than a specific content or subject matter in itself.

Bibliography. R. Bloch, "Midrash," *Supplement au dictionnaire de la Bible.* V (1957), cols. 1263-81; I. Heinemann, *Methods of the Aggadah* (2nd ed., 1954) in Heb.; M. D. Herr, "Midrash," *Encyclopaedia Judaica,* XI (1972), 1507-14; M. P. Miller, "Midrash," *IDB Supp.* (1976), 593-97; G. Vermes, "Bible and Midrash," *Cambridge History of the Bible,* I (1970), 199-231; A. Wright, *The Literary Genre Midrash* (1967).

I. CHERNUS

MILINDAPAÑHA mĭ lĭn´ dŭ pän´ yŭ (B—Pali; lit. "Questions of Milinda"). One of the two most authoritative extracanonical texts in THERAVĀDA Buddhism. It was written by a now unknown author in northern India around the first or second century A.D. Originally written in SANSKRIT or Prākrit, it was early translated into Pali, and is no longer extant in the original.

The Milindapañha consists of a series of questions and dilemmas raised by King Milinda (usually identified as the Greco-Indian King Menander), which are then answered by the monk Nāgasena. The stage is set with an account of the past lives of Nāgasena and Milinda. The remainder of the first three books discusses basic doctrinal and ethical issues. These include KARMA, the nature of the individual, the idea of rebirth without transmigration, and the attainment of perfection. This material probably constituted the original work. The remaining four books are lacking in the fourth century A.D. Chinese translation known as the Nāgasena Sūtra, and are likely a later addition. They are concerned with clarifying more technical details of Buddhist thought.

Bibliography. I. B. Horner, trans., *Milinda Questions,* 2 vols. (1963-64); Thich Minh Chau, *Milindapanha and Nagasenabhiksusutra* (1964).

J. P. MCDERMOTT

MILLENARIAN MOVEMENTS. Generally, any religious movement that hopes for a salvation that is a) *collective,* to be enjoyed by all the faithful as a group; b) *terrestrial,* to be realized on this earth; c) *imminent,* to come soon and suddenly; d) *total,* to transform life on earth completely; e) *miraculous,* to be brought about by, or with the help of, supernatural agencies.

The term "millenarian" first appears in the NT book of Revelation (ch. 20) in the context of the final struggle between God and SATAN at the end of history. Millennial expectations are thus strictly speaking one variety of Christian APOCALYPTIC beliefs. However, the term "millenarian" is used by scholars typologically to describe a large number of apocalyptic religious movements in many periods in non-Western as well as Western societies, many of which have had no history of contact with Christianity. Often the term is used interchangeably with "messianism" or "messianic movement," i.e., movements that expect a redeemer who will inaugurate a utopian age (*see* MESSIAH).

1. The persistence of millenarianism. Although the predominant Christian view has been the allegorical interpretations offered by AUGUSTINE in his *City of God* and followed by LUTHER, CALVIN, and the English reformers, an apocalyptic form of millenarianism has had its proponents (*see* MILLENARIANISM).

In Africa, the Caribbean, South America, and Asia there are many millenarian movements whose major symbols reflect contact with Western millenarian ideas reinterpreted by indigenous concerns. Notable examples include the T'ai-p'ing movement in China in the mid-nineteenth century, whose leader Hung Hsiu-Ch'üan believed that he was the younger brother of Christ; the RASTIFARIAN movement in Jamaica, which sought a return to Ethiopia as the black Zion; numerous African movements that regarded their leaders as incarnations of Christ, or as a second Christ; African "Watch Tower" movements directly inspired by missionaries from the JEHOVAH'S WITNESSES; and thousands of ZIONIST movements in Africa that regard biblical prophecy regarding an end to suffering and restoration of Zion for the Jews as applying directly to Africans.

Among the millenarian beliefs and movements that owe nothing to Western traditions are the following: In China, Taoist movements in the first century B.C. and the first and fourth centuries A.D. (*see* TAOISM, RELIGIOUS), and Buddhist-influenced popular millenarian WHITE LOTUS movements from the twelfth through the nineteenth centuries A.D.; in Japan, the *yo-naoshi* movements of the Tokugawa and Meiji periods; in South America, the millennial movements among the Tupi-Guarani in the interior of Eastern Brazil; the "CARGO CULTS" in Melanesia and elsewhere; and in North America, the Ghost Dances that spread through the Plains tribes in the late 1880s, culminating in the defeat of the Sioux Indians at the Battle of Wounded Knee in 1890 (*see* NATIVE AMERICAN TRIBAL RELIGION).

2. Chief characteristics. The history of Western and non-Western millenarianism illustrates the need to distinguish between millenarian beliefs within a tradition or culture and millenarian movements which place a strong emphasis on immediate action. Some of the chief characteristics of the latter include: a) origin in intense revelatory religious experience, b) charismatic leadership, c) missionary zeal, d) emotional commitment, e) promise of a definite, terrestrial blessing, f) moral reform, g) new symbolic forms, h) new voluntaristic organizations with a new sense of community, i) selective but often radical rejection of traditional ways and adoption of new ones, and j) concern for personal and spiritual renewal.

Millenarian movements vary remarkably in the ways in which they conceive of the future paradise, react to traditional moral codes and values, and view their own role in bringing about the new age. These movements also differ in their sense of who will be included in the coming kingdom, as well as in the degree to which hostility toward a powerful group (e.g., colonial powers, whites, Christians) gives direction to their movement. Perhaps most importantly, they vary in their response to the perceived delay in the coming of the millennium that they await so anxiously. Although one would expect that the failure of a prophesied millennium to arrive would create a fatal crisis of credibility, many movements emerge from such crises even stronger than before.

3. **Interpretations.** There are various attempts to understand the origin and functions of millenarian movements.

a) Deprivation theories hold that such movements arise in groups that are experiencing "relative social deprivation," defined as a discrepancy between legitimate expectations and social realities. The coming utopia will correct current injustices.

b) Acculturation theories see millenarian movements as bearers and formulators of responses to the interaction between a literate, technically powerful culture and nonliterate tribal people. In this respect, movements can be described as "nativistic" or "revitalizing" (i.e., seeking to preserve or restore elements of one's own culture) or "adoptive" (introducing elements of a foreign culture).

c) Political theories. It has been argued that millenarian rebellions are politically futile and arise out of the failure of their participants to understand social and political forces which make them deprived. Others argue, however, that millenarian movements are politically fruitful in that they mobilize and unite diverse groups into a single movement.

d) Psychological theories regard millenarian movements as "collective flights from reality" by those who have unresolved and deep frustrations or psychological stress. Others point out that millenarian movements offer structures of meaning that provide solutions to problems of cognitive dissonance.

e) Parsonian identity theories. Critical of deprivation and political theories, Parsonian identity theories stress the way in which millenarian movements offer their followers a transition to a new sacred identity.

f) Liminality theories. Since a chief characteristic of millenarian movements is their orientation toward time, some scholars argue that such movements are a liminal (boundary) community living between present and future.

While all these theoretical approaches are useful, most are reductionistic. It is important to remember that the creativity or destructiveness that millenarian movements display in shaping personalities and in solving religious or cultural problems depends on a great many factors, not all of which are necessarily linked to the structure of the messianic movement or its message as such.

Bibliography. Bibliographical guides: W. La Barre, "Materials for a History of Crisis Cults: A Bibliographical Essay," *Current Anthropology* XII (1971), 3-44; H. Schwartz, "The End of the Beginning: Millenarian Studies, 1969-1975," *Religious Studies Review* II (1976), 1-15. Theoretical approaches: A. Wallace, "Revitalization Movements," *American Anthropologist* LVIII (1956), 264-81; R. Linton, "Nativistic Movements," *American Anthropologist* XLV (1943),230-40; N. Cohn, *The Pursuit of the Millennium,* 3rd ed. (1970); P. Worsley, *The Trumpet Shall Sound* (1957); V. Turner, *The Ritual Process* (1969); D. Aberle, "A Note on Relative Deprivation Theory as Applied to Millenarian and Other Cult Movements," in S. L. Thrupp, ed., *Millennial Dreams in Action* (1970); H. Mol, *The Identity of the Sacred* (1976); J. Zygmunt, "Movements and Motives: Some Unresolved Issues in the Psychology of Social Movements," *Human Relations* XXV (1972), 449-67; Y. Talmon, "Millenarian Movements," *European Journal of Sociology* VII (1966), 159-200.

M. Levering

MILLENARIANISM (Ch). Term commonly used to describe those interpretations of Christian eschatology that stress the Second Coming of Christ in the immediate future, thus preceding the millennium, the peaceful thousand-year reign of the Messiah. Also called premillennialism or chiliasm, millenarianism is frequently contrasted with millennialism and with amillennialism. Millennialism (or post-millennialism) is the belief that the gradual expansion of the Church will bring in the thousand-year reign of peace, after which Christ will return. Amillennialism is the belief that scripture is not clear on questions surrounding the end of time.

Millenarian teachings were widely held in the first two centuries of Christian history by such figures as Justin Martyr (*ca.* 100-165), Irenaeus of Lyons (*ca.* 130–*ca.* 200), and Hippolytus (*ca.* 160-236). However, as the Christian movement matured, millenarianism faded out of mainstream Christian theology, and Eschatology came to concentrate more on the doctrines of Heaven and Hell. Augustine (354-430) put this shift of emphasis into classical form in his *City of God,* saying that the city of God and the city of man exist side by side in history and cannot be distinguished. Thus there are no signs of the coming of the end of time, and the thousand-year reign of Christ is identical with the historical church.

Seventeenth century Puritans revived some elements of the old chiliasm, and taught that such books as Daniel and Revelation should be studied as carefully as the more easily understood portions of the Bible. In part their interest in eschatology was the result of pressure from a hostile government.

During the Enlightenment an optimistic millenarianism expressed itself in an interpretation of biblical prophecy as a prediction of the progress of civilization in overcoming evil. Daniel Whitby of England (1638-1726) and Jonathan Edwards (1703-1758) were leaders in this endeavor. Until the 1870s most American Christians, particularly those in the Revivalist tradition, shared this point of view. It was then that many conservative Protestants became interested in the Dispensationalism of John Nelson Darby and the Plymouth Brethren, later evidenced in the Scofield Reference Bible. The nineteenth century also saw the rise of such millenarian groups as Seventh-

DAY ADVENTISM and the LATTER-DAY SAINTS, while the JEHOVAH'S WITNESSES rose to prominence in the twentieth century. *See* MILLENARIAN MOVEMENTS.

Bibliography. E. R. Sandeen, *Roots of Fundamentalism: British-American Millenarianism 1800-1930* (1970).

G. MILLER

MILTON, JOHN (Ch; 1608-74). British poet and essayist. Milton had intended to prepare for the clergy, but his interests proved to be scholarly and literary. Among his early works are a Christian ode, "On the Morning of Christ's Nativity" (1629); *Comus* (1634), a masque; and *Lycidas* (1637), a pastoral elegy that contains an attack upon corrupt clergy. Milton became an important voice in the Puritan revolution, and in 1641 he wrote the anti-episcopal pamphlet *The Reason of Church Government.* Perhaps because of the desertion of his wife, he published *The Doctrine and Discipline of Divorce* (1643), a justification of divorce. In response to attempts to stop publication of his essays, Milton wrote *Areopagitica* (1644), an attack upon censorship. During the Commonwealth, Milton continued his political writings, yet somehow he escaped execution at the time of the Restoration (1660). Although by 1652 Milton had become almost totally blind, he entered a period of enormous productivity. *Paradise Lost,* his epic poem of the fall of man, was first published in 1667. *Paradise Regained,* Milton's poetic account of Satan's tempting Christ, and *Samson Agonistes,* a poetic drama, were published in 1671. During this time Milton was also at work on his monumental philosophical and theological treatise, *De Doctrina Christiana,* published posthumously.

Bibliography. A. E. Barker, *Milton and the Puritan Dilemma, 1641-1660* (1942); G. N. Conklin, *Biblical Criticism and Heresy in Milton* (1949); W. Empson, *Milton's God* (1961); J. M. Evans, *Paradise Lost and the Genesis Tradition* (1968).

D. J. WHITE

MĪMĀṂSĀ mē män´ sä (H—Skt.). 1. A system of exegesis of the VEDAS.

2. As Pūrvamīmāṃsā, the name of an Indian philosophical system or set of systems. Pūrvamīmāṃsā exegetics emphasizes the injunctive aspects of the Vedic scriptures, viewing Vedic commands as providing the context for all declarations, etc., found there. The philosophical schools founded by Kumārila and Prābhākara (both seventh to eighth century A.D.) maintain that interpretation against the Uttaramīmāṃsā or VEDĀNTA.

The school founded by Kumārila is known as Bhāṭṭa Mīmāṃsā; the one founded by Prābhākara, the Prābhākara Mīmāṃsā. Unlike the classical writers Jaimini, author of the Mīmāṃsāsūtras, and Śabara, the most important commentator on those sūtras, Bhāṭṭa and Prābhākara recognize liberation (MOKṢA) as the highest human aim. They also develop distinctive ontological and epistemological views, and engaged in polemics with rival schools.

The Prābhākara school is noteworthy for its extremely realistic theory of knowledge. It holds that all simple perceptual judgments are straightforward reports of sense experience, hence unquestionably true. False judgments occur only when one judgment is conflated with another. For example, a shell may be mistaken for a piece of silver on the beach; here, the sensory awareness of a silvery thing is combined with one's memory that silver is silvery.

Both schools adopt ontologies which resemble that of NYĀYA-VAIŚEṢIKA, though the Bhāṭṭas modify their metaphysics in the direction of JAINISM, and Prābhākaras in the direction of BUDDHISM.

Bibliography. Ganganatha Jha, *Pūrva-Mīmāṃsā in Its Sources* (1942).

K. H. POTTER

MINĀ mē nä´ (I). *See* HAJJ.

MĪNĀKṢĪ mē näk´ shē (H—Skt.; lit. "she who has fish eyes" [*mīna*—"fish," *akṣa*—"eye"]). Divine queen of Madurai, ancient capital of the TAMIL Pāṇḍyan dynasty, wife of SHIVA "The Beautiful Lord" *(Sundareśvarar)*, and most popular deity in the active Mīnākṣī Sundareśvarar Temple. Her name in Tamil, "She with Beautiful Carp Eyes" *(Aṅkayarkaṇṇi)* is accorded various meanings: her eyes are large like fish eyes; they flash like fish in water; or, like fish eyes they never wink, a theologically important meaning, since as Mother of the Universe she gazes on her children (as a pond carp is said to gaze on its eggs), nurturing them with her power and compassion until their final rebirth out of SAMSARA. In iconography she usually stands alone, gold or green skinned, richly dressed, a parrot perched on a flower in her right hand.

1. **History.** Tamil literature testifies to Shiva's presence in Madurai by A. D. 250 and to a warrior goddess as protector of the city and the Pāṇḍyan rulers by A. D. 450. By the twelfth century Mīnākṣī was Shiva's warrior queen with her own shrine in the temple and a significant place in its myth of origins, the Tamil "PURĀNA of the [Sixty-Four] Sacred Amusements [of Shiva]." The temple was expanded under thirteenth century Pāṇḍyans, damaged by Muslims in the fourteenth, and restored and expanded to its present size by Vijayanagar rulers in the sixteenth and seventeenth. Conceived as the center of a MANDALA with the city walls as outer boundary, its core consists of Shiva's shrine with his LIṄGA and a *kaṭamba* tree, the shrine of Mīnākṣī with her image, and a bathing pond, all in existence according to myth since the earliest of Shiva's self-revelatory "amusements" (*see* LĪLĀ) in a previous era or YUGA. From this center, stone and brick buildings, streets, walls, and towers spread over fourteen acres enclosed by high walls. At the cardinal directions there are majestic gateways covered by thousands of painted images. Three rectangular streets continue the mandala's concentric expansion

which before British rule ended in a rampart and trench surrounding the entire temple-city.

2. **Ritual and myth.** Ritual service of the divine couple is conducted daily by male members of hereditary BRAHMIN families following Śaiva ĀGAMAS. Treated as royalty in their temple-palace, the couple is awakened to hymns at dawn. They bathe, dress, eat, receive praise and worship from servants and subjects, bestow honors and grace, take rest, process, and sleep together in the queen's chamber at night. Among numerous annual festivals the most famous is the twelve-day "Great Cittirai Festival" in April-May involving at times hundreds of thousands of devotees in the coronation of the queen and her marriage to the king as told in the myth of origins: the first Pāṇḍyan of Madurai, without a male heir, sponsored a Vedic sacrifice (*see* YAJÑA) which produced a girl child with three breasts, who was an incarnation of Shiva's consort Umā. As instructed, the Pāṇḍyan nobleman raised her as a prince, trained her in war and crowned her ruler. As "The Invincible" she set out with an all female army to conquer the world, easily doing so until she attacked KAILĀŚA, the abode of Shiva. When Shiva appeared, her third breast disappeared, signaling that she had met her mate. In their wedding at Madurai her brother VISHNU gave her away as bride. The couple ruled the city until a son, Ugra Pāṇḍyan, was born and took charge, whereupon they withdrew into their respective shrines, while the Pāṇḍans ruled on their behalf.

The festival enacting these stories occurs simultaneously with a festival of a Vishnu temple twelve miles northwest during which Vishnu arrives at the river bordering the old city just after the marriage. Though the two festivals are ritually unrelated, the Hindus of the region view them as scenes in one drama: Vishnu travels to his sister's wedding, arrives too late, angrily refuses to enter his brother-in-law's city, and returns home bestowing honors and grace on his own devotees. On the one hand, it would appear that this myth expresses the historical antagonism between high caste urban devotees of Shiva and low caste rural devotees of Vishnu. But on the other, these festivals affirm the religious and social unity these devotees share as traditional Pāṇḍyan subjects with their respective divine lords recognized as members of a single family. In any case, it is Mīnākṣī who unites both gods and men into the order necessary for stability and well-being.

Bibliography. D. Hudson, "Two Citrā Festivals in Madurai," *Interludes: Religious Festivals in South India and Ceylon*, G. R. Welbon and G. E. Yocum, eds. (1978); "Śiva, Mīnākṣī, Viṣṇu—Reflections on a popular Myth in Madurai," *Indian Economic and Social History Review*, XIV (1977), 107-18; film in two parts, "Wedding of the Goddess," by M. R. Binford and M. Camerini (1976).

D. HUDSON

MINARET mĭn ä rĕt′ (I—Arab. *manār*). That part of a MOSQUE from which the muezzin delivers the ADHĀN (call to prayer) five times a day.

Malwiya minaret, Samarra

The architectural device of the minaret did not exist during the time of MUHAMMAD, nor was it incorporated into the earliest mosques. During the early years of ISLAM, the *adhān* was delivered from the roof of the highest house or of the mosque. The minaret developed out of ritualistic and symbolic necessity, utilizing pre-Islamic architectural vocabulary for its definition. Within the immense geographic area that comprised the Muslim world, several types of minarets emerged, based on a variety of architectural prototypes, constructed and embellished with regionally available materials. The minaret in the form of a square tower dominated the early Islamic world in Syria, North Africa, and Spain. It evolved out of the practice of converting Christian churches into mosques and adapting the square bell towers to minarets, as at Damascus. A spiral form of minaret appeared during the 'ABBĀSID Caliphate in Iraq at Samarra and in Cairo, as part of a characteristic North African multilevel minaret. The balconied, cylindrical minaret was the preferred form of the Persians, usually appearing in pairs flanking or above the entrance portal, as at Isfahan. The Seljuks transported the latter to Anatolia, where the Ottomans heightened and slenderized the shape and added a conical spire. Another minaret form is the staircase minaret, comprising a kiosk on the roof of a mosque approached by an external flight of steps. In addition to its ritual function, the minaret in various circumstances took on the symbolism of social and imperial power, as in the Qutb minaret at Delhi.

Bibliography. K. A. C. Creswell, "The Evolution of the Minaret, with Special Reference to Egypt I, II, III," *Burlington Magazine* 48 (1926), 134-40, 252-58, 290-96; E. Diez, "Manara," *Encyclopedia of Islam* III (1936), 227-31; O. Grabar, *The Formation of Islamic Art* (1973).

B. St. L. Lockwood

W. Denny

Qutb minaret, Delhi (13th century)

MINYAN mĭn yän´ (Ju—Heb.; "number"). The minimum of ten adult (over the age of thirteen) males whose presence is required, according to Talmudic law, for the public performance of certain elements of the Synagogue liturgy, such as the repetition by the prayer leader of the Amidah, the recitation of the Kaddish, and the reading of the Torah.

B. Martin

MĪRĀBĀĪ mēr´ ä bī (H; *ca.* 1498-1546). A devotee of Krishna and composer of devotional songs in Hindī. The only daughter of Ratan Singh, a minor aristocrat in Rajasthan, Mīrābāī was deeply religious in her youth, a sentiment heightened by the deaths of her mother, father, and husband within a short time of one another. When she refused to commit Satī (self-immolation on her husband's funeral pyre) her in-laws rejected her.

Mīrābāī lived her later years in an itinerant fashion composing songs in which she identified herself as the wife of Krishna. Like many devotees of Bhakti Hinduism, she rejected ritual and religious artifice in favor of a passionate surrender of the heart to Krishna as the embodiment of universal love and liberation.

Bibliography. S. M. Pandey, "Mīrābāī and Her Contributions to the Bhakti Movement," *History of Religions*, V (1965), 54-73.

P. Courtright

MIRACLES IN ISLAM. Both the Qur'ān and Ḥadīth contain countless episodes that are miraculous in tone and underscore the authority of Muhammad as God's chosen apostle to the Arabs. Qur'ānic miracles are distinguished from pre-Islamic forms of trickery, sorcery, and divination; the Qur'ān itself is honored as God's final miracle. Yet the majority of Muhammad's community has never ceased to expect miracles as proof of the efficacy of their faith. Theologians have acquiesced to popular belief by recognizing two categories of miracles: 1) *mu'jizāt* or prophetic miracles (*see* Nabi) and 2) *karāmāt* or saint-induced wonders (*see* Walī). While the function of miracles varies widely within the Muslim world, common places or agents which facilitate their appearance are Sufi shrines (see, e.g., Aḥmad al-Badawī), Amulets and Charms for warding off Jinn, Dreams and Visions, living Shaikhs, poets, or even charlatan purveyors of magic.

The Wahhābīya and reformist Muslim leaders, such as Muhammad 'Abdūh of Egypt, have derided saint cults and the miracles associated with them. However, millions of Muslims still seek out magicians, wear amulets, invoke charms, and attend the commemorative anniversary ('Urs) of one or more local saints.

Bibliography. G. A. Herklots, trans., *Islam in India* (1921), pp. 192-282; R. J. McCarthy, ed., al-Baqillānī, *Miracle and Magic* (1958), pp. 9-27; J. A. Subhan, *Sufism: Its Saints and Shrines* (1960), pp. 103-12; C. Geertz, *Islam Observed: Religious Development in Morocco and Indonesia* (1968), pp. 25-55; A. Schimmel, *Mystical Dimensions of Islam* (1975), pp. 204-13; P. Jackson, trans., Sharafuddin Maneri, *The Hundred Letters* (1980), pp. 40-51.

B. Lawrence

MI'RĀJ mĭ räj´ (I). The ascension of Muhammad, said to have taken place before his emigration (Hijra) from Mecca to Medina in A.D. 622. It is only hinted at in Qur'ān 17.1, but the biography of Ibn Isḥāq and later prophetic traditions describe both a journey *(isrā')* from Mecca to Jerusalem (*see* al-Quds) and then an ascent *(mi'rāj)* from Jerusalem on the winged steed, Burāq, through seven heavens, stopping at each for converse with appropriate biblical prophets, till at last Muhammad arrived before the empyrean or heavenly throne and conversed with Allah himself. Whether the *mi'rāj* was a vision or a physical event, whether it involved Muhammad's body or only his soul, and to what extent it was embellished through the appropriation of details from Jewish or Christian sources, perhaps with an unconscious parallelism to Shamanistic initiatory rites—all these speculations are finally less important than the enormous subsequent influence of the motif of the *mi'rāj* on Muslim thought and devotion. The giving of the heavenly book and the mandate for believers to pray five times daily were both linked to Muhammad's night journey. For many of the faithful the Prophet's ascent became a foretaste of their own journey to heaven after death. The evening of 27 Rajab in the Muslim calendar is annually set aside for commemorating this sacred event. SUFIS, beginning with Abū Yazīd BISṬĀMĪ, have interpreted the *mi'rāj* as a symbol of their own progress on the path (ṬARĪQA) from the law (SHARIA) to the truth but also back again to the law, just as Muhammad did not dally with the delights of heaven but returned to earth to carry out his awesome prophetic mandate. Nor was the influence of the *mi'rāj* limited to Muslims. The cosmology in DANTE'S *Divine Comedy* may well have had its antecedents in Muhammad's scaling of the heavenly heights.

Bibliography. A. Jeffrey, *A Reader on Islam* (1962), pp. 621-39; G. Widengren, *Muhammad, the Apostle of God, and His Ascension* (1955); J. R. Porter, "Muhammad's Journey to Heaven," *Numen* XXI/1 (1974), 64-80; A. Palacios, *La escatologia musulmana en la divina comedia* (1924); E. Cerulli, ed., *Il "Libro della Scala" e la questione delle fonti arabo-spagnole della Divina Comedia* (1949).

B. LAWRENCE

MISERERE NOBIS mē sĕ rā´ rĕ nō´ bēs (Ch—Lat.; "have mercy on us"). A prayer deriving from the psalms (cf. Ps. 51:1), often used liturgically as the response to a LITANY or to a versicle (short verse said or sung in worship).

R. A. GREER

MISHNAH mĭsh nä´ (Ju—Heb.; lit. "teaching, study" [*shanah*, "to repeat"]). 1. The collection of oral law compiled by Rabbi JUDAH HA-NASI, *ca.* A.D. 200. Also, any paragraph in this collection (called HALAKAH in Palestine). 2. The teaching, or a particular statement, of any rabbinic authority of the first two centuries A.D.; by extension, the teaching of any individual. 3. Oral law in general, to be distinguished from Scripture and legal homily on Scripture (MIDRASH halakah).

Rabbi Judah's Mishnah is a compilation of traditions that arose over a period of more than four centuries, beginning with the "Men of the GREAT SYNAGOGUE" in the late pre-Christian period, who believed they had a legislative function "to make a fence around the Torah." The schools of law developed by HILLEL and SHAMMAI and the academy founded by JOHANAN BEN ZAKKAI all contributed to the growth of the tradition. In the early second century A.D. Rabbi AKIBA (d. *ca.* 135) built on an earlier Mishnah, and he was followed by Rabbi MEIR, who further systematized the material. Finally, by virtue of his learning and authority, Rabbi Judah succeeded in producing the normative text of the Mishnah.

In the Middle Ages Spanish rabbis maintained that even Rabbi Judah's Mishnah was an oral system (written down only in the sixth century A.D.). The French and German rabbis, however, held that R. Judah produced a written text about A.D. 200, and modern scholars agree. The TALMUD already refers to the Mishnah as a text analyzed by the sages.

The Mishnah is divided into six "Orders," which are subdivided into tractates, chapters, and paragraphs: 1. *Zera'im* (seeds), i.e., laws of agriculture, the sabbatical year, etc. (11 tractates, including one on benedictions and prayer); 2. *Mo'ed* (festival), on the sabbath and holidays (12 tractates, dealing also with fast days); 3. *Nashim* (women), marriage, divorce, etc. (7); 4. *Nezikin* (damages), property, inheritance, court procedures, oaths (10, also dealing with pagan practices and the ethics of the sages); 5. *Kodashim* (sacred things), temple, sacrifices, slaughtering, pledges (11); 6. *Ṭorohot* (purities), ritual impurities because of contact with a dead body, leprosy etc. (12).

For early rabbinic teaching not included in the Mishnah *see* BARAITA; TOSEFTA.

Bibliography. H. Danby, trans. & ed., *The Mishnah* (1933), translation and introduction; G. F. Moore, *Judaism in the First Centuries of the Christian Era*, 3 vols. (1927-30), comprehensive, on law and morals; J. Neusner, *From Politics to Piety: the Emergence of Pharisaic Judaism* (1973), on the history of the Pharisees and their teachings. See bibliogs. for HALAKAH; TALMUD.

Y. SHAMIR

MISHNEH TORAH mĭsh nĕh´ tôr´ ə (Ju—Heb.; lit. "repetition of the TORAH"). Traditional term for Deuteronomy; also the code of law written by MOSES BEN MAIMON, integrating philosophic insight and scientific knowledge with the entirety of rabbinic law. It provoked severe criticism for its method and its content, but is still considered authoritative.

K. P. BLAND

MISSAL (Ch). The book in the Western rite (*see* ROMAN CATHOLICISM §5) containing everything sung or said during the MASS, both the propers (i.e. those parts that change by the season) and the ordinary (i.e. those parts that are fixed). Missals were first used instead of separate books in the tenth century.

R. A. GREER

MISSIONS, CHRISTIAN (Lat. *missio,* lit. "a sending"). The systematic effort to extend Christianity to non-Christian peoples by teaching, preaching, and performing social services.

1. **History.** *a) Origin.* The origin of the Christian mission is in the person and work of JESUS Christ. He demanded decision and dedication from his followers: "If any man would come after me, let him deny himself and take up his cross and follow me" (Mark 8:34). Acts 2 tells of the coming of the HOLY SPIRIT upon the disciples, an event which marked the beginning of the missionary church. PETER (Acts 2:36) proclaims the first missionary sermon: "Let all the house of Israel therefore know assuredly that God has made him both Lord and Christ this Jesus whom you crucified." PAUL, a converted PHARISEE, competent in

expressing himself in terms of both Greek and Hebraic culture, engaged in extensive missionary journeys in Asia Minor, Greece, and Palestine (*ca.* A.D. 45–58). His message was centered on the coming of the new humanity through the redemptive event of Jesus Christ, crucified and risen (Acts 17:16-34; I Cor. 1:18-31; Gal. 2:15-3:14).

b) Expansion. In the beginning of the second century Christianity reached Britain in the north and the Persian Gulf in the east. Christianity was considered legal after A.D. 313 (Edict of Milan), and the Roman Empire was Christian from the fifth century on. Stephen Neill speaks of A.D. 100 to 500 as the period of "the Conquest of the Roman World." Christianity reached the Slavic peoples by the ninth century, and the period from the seventh to the twelfth centuries saw the expansion of Christianity into Germany and Scandinavia.

The dissolution of the Roman Empire in the sixth century and the appearance of ISLAM in the seventh century, however, placed Christian expansion in a period of uncertainty. Medieval Christianity felt the pressure of Islam on the east and south. Although eight CRUSADES from the late eleventh century to the latter half of the thirteenth century attempted to stem the Moslem tide, Constantinople fell in 1453, and fifteenth century Europe remained encircled by Islam. Christian expansion then looked toward the openness of the Atlantic ocean. The Spanish reached out to Central and South America, the Portuguese to Brazil, and the English and French to North America. At the same time the Portuguese were arriving in the Far East, setting the stage for the spread of the mission to Asia.

Through the work of the JESUITS Portuguese Goa in India became the center of the Catholic mission in the East, and FRANCIS XAVIER was in Goa in 1542–45 and 1551. Another outstanding Jesuit missionary was Robert de Nobili (in India 1606-56). He experimented with a method of accommodation in the propagation of the gospel and was looked upon as a "Christian BRAHMIN." Such accommodation called for a theological examination, and in 1744 Rome finally decided against any form of accommodation and prescribed total europeanization. Papal dissolution of the Jesuit Order in 1773 was a great blow for the mission in the East. In 1970 the VATICAN approved a liturgy which includes the use of Hindu symbols.

The first Protestant mission in India was sponsored by the king of Denmark. Missionaries Ziegenbalg and Plütschau arrived in Tranquebar in 1706. In 1793 the British BAPTIST William Carey arrived in Bengal. At Serampore he developed a dynamic missionary program in education, Bible translation, and formation of churches. In the nineteenth century missions flourished under British control in India. In the same year (1947) that India and Pakistan declared independence, the Church of South India came into being (a union of ANGLICAN, METHODIST, PRESBYTERIAN, and CONGREGATIONALIST churches). In 1970 the Church of North India was formed by uniting six denominations (the Council of Baptist Churches in Northern India, the Church of the Brethren, the Disciples of Christ, the Church of India, the Methodist Church under the British and Australian Conferences, and the United Church of Northern India). Since 1975 church union conversations are going on among the Church of North India, the Church of South India, and the Mar Thoma Church.

NESTORIAN Christianity reached China in the seventh century, but disappeared after two centuries. The FRANCISCANS arrived in the thirteenth century, and John of Monte Corvino was the first archbishop of Peking. But the Franciscan mission also vanished when the emperor's patronage of Christianity came to an end. In the sixteenth century Jesuit missionaries entered China. The most gifted and creative of them, the Italian MATTEO RICCI, was in China from 1583 to 1610. After eighteen years he finally reached Peking and was granted an imperial audience. His method was to confront the learned elite of China (CONFUCIAN scholars) as their equal in manners, education, and language. The seventeenth and eighteenth centuries were the great centuries of the Jesuit mission, but they were marred by controversy. What should the church's attitude be toward ceremonies in honor of Confucius and the practice of ANCESTOR VENERATION? As in the case of India, Rome decided against accommodation to Asian cultures, and Catholicism declined.

In the early nineteeth century Protestant missionaries arrived in China and made slow but steady progress. In the middle of the century the Tai-Ping Rebellion, which was influenced by the Christian social ideal, ultimately failed in the face of European support of the Ch'ing dynasty. After the proclamation of the People's Republic of China in 1949 the Chinese churches severed their connections with Christian bodies abroad. As their guiding principle they adopted the "Three Self" emphasis developed by the missionary John Nevius in the 1890s (self-supporting, self-governing, and self-propagating).

2. Missiology. Missiology is the theological understanding of the misson of the church as it lives in the concrete context of the historical and cultural situation. Missiological studies explore "the teachings and norms of the Church concerning missionary activity, the roads which the heralds of the gospel have traversed in the course of the centuries, the present condition of the missions, and the methods now considered especially effective" (Vatican II; Decree on the Missionary Activity of the Church, IV. 26).

3. Current Issues. *a) Proclamation or dialogue.* There is much debate as to whether the missionary approach to people of other faiths should be one of proclamation or of dialogue. Some feel that dialogue should replace proclamation. Others are of the opinion that while dialogue gives opportunity for authentic witness it will not replace proclamation, but rather enrich it. This discussion is related to the debate on the relative weight to be given to service (Christian social action) and witness (evangelism).

b) Adaptation or syncretism. A certain amount of adaptation (accommodation) is inevitable when the gospel crosses cultural borders. Whenever adaptation takes place, however, there is a danger of syncretism, the mixing and confusing of the teachings of different religions as if there were no basic difference between them. Adaptation is seen as a creative moment in the life of the church, but syncretism is seen as destructive since it blurs the essential truths of the religions involved.

c) Other issues. The missionary church is confronted by the influence of Marxism in the world today. It also attempts to deal with the problems of the Christian understanding of science and technology, effective methods of combatting racism and militarism, recapturing a sense of the holy in human life, and concern for such basic problems as poverty, hunger, and the denial of human rights. The increasing sense of selfhood of the indigenous leadership of the churches in Asia and Africa is effecting a basic change in the role of the missionary. A significant number of the missionaries working within Asia are now themselves of Asian orgin.

4. Challenge to Christian mission. The two other world religions that have spread widely through missionary activity, BUDDHISM and ISLAM, are active in outreach in the late twentieth century. The AHMADĪYA movement of India has carried its form of Islam to Europe and America, and NICHIREN Shō-shū is an example of a Japanese Buddhist sect that seeks to convert the world. *See* SŌKA GAKKAI.

Bibliography. S. Neill, *A History of Christian Missions* (1964); K. S. Latourette, *A History of the Expansion of Christianity*. 7 vols. (1970 ed.); Lutheran World Ferderation, *Christianity and the New China* (1976); W. M. Abbott, ed., *The Documents of Vatican II* (1966); World Council of Churches, *International Review of Mission*, XLIV (1975), 417-21; N. Goodall, ed., *The Uppsala Report 1968;* D. McGavran, *The Conciliar-Evangelical Debate: The Crucial Documents* (1977); K. Rahner, ed., *Sacramentum Mundi, an Encyclopedia of Theology* (1969), article on "Mission"; J. Blauw, *The Missionary Nature of the Church* (1962), pp. 29-43; D. J. Elwood, ed., *What Asian Christians Are Thinking* (1976); E. P. Nakpil, ed., *The Human and the Holy* (1978). K. KOYAMA

MITRA mĭ′ trŭ (H—Skt.; lit. "friendship" or "contract" personified). A sovereign deity in VEDIC HINDUISM, one of the Ādityas (sons of ADITI), sometimes, as in RIG VEDA 3.59, addressed alone, but usually invoked with his co-ruler, VARUṆA, in the dual compound *mitrāvaruṇa*. An Indo-Iranian background is evident, and the compound *mithra-ahura* in the AVESTA suggests that Ahura functions, here at least, as the counterpart of Vedic Varuṇa. In the later Avesta, Mithra is the most important god after the supreme deity of ZOROASTRIANISM, Ahura Mazda, and still later as Mithras he is the savior god at the center of the Roman mystery cult, Mithraism.

Vedic Mitra's name, "Contract," indicates his mediating role and his ethical and legal functions. He summons men to activity, watches over them with an unblinking eye, and maintains harmony in the social order, just as his cohort, Varuṇa, maintains the cosmic order (ṚTA). While the latter has more to do with the terrible, magical side of sovereignty, Mitra is benign, "friendly," and protective. Associated with them both is a third Āditya, Aryaman, also an Indo-Iranian figure. Vedic Mitra's solar characteristics are not as pronounced as those of Iranian Mithra, but in the texts later than the Rig Veda he is connected with sunrise or the day, with Varuṇa representing the evening or the night.

Bibliography. A. A. Macdonell, *Vedic Mythology* (1897); J. Gonda, *Mitra* (1972). D. M. KNIPE

MITZVAH mĭtz′ vä (Ju—Heb.; "commandment"). (1) A biblical or rabbinic injunction; (2) more generally, any good deed or meritorious act, even though not explicitly commanded in the BIBLE or rabbinic literature.

Traditionally, there are 613 mitzvot (plural) in the TORAH. These are divided into 248 positive commandments and 365 negative commandments, which are said to correspond to the 248 bones and 365 muscles of the human body (or the 365 days of the solar year). Since no count of the laws of the Torah yields exactly 613, various sets of rules have been set forth according to which the commandments are to be counted.

Besides the 613 biblical commandments, there are a large number of mitzvot prescribed by the TALMUD. Many of these—e.g., washing the hands before partaking of food, kindling the SABBATH and festival lights, reading the Scroll of Esther on PURIM—are regarded as sanctioned by the same divine authority as the biblical commandments. Although the rabbis concede that there are differences of importance among the various commandments, they admonish the Jew to "be as careful of a light mitzvah as of a grave one, for you do not know what is the reward for the performance of a mitzvah" (Avot II:1). It was widely believed that the final reward for the performance of the mitzvot would come in the hereafter (Kiddushin 39b).

Liability for the performance of the mitzvot is assumed upon the attainment of religious maturity. (*See* BAR [BAT] MITVAH.) According to Talmudic law, women are exempt from all the positive commandments dependent upon a fixed time or season (Kiddushin 29a); they are, however, required to observe all the negative commandments.

The concept of mitzvah is crucial in Jewish religious thought, reflecting the view that every human act is also an act of obedience to God's will. In practice, Judaism is essentially the observance of the mitzvot.

Bibliography. Maimonides, *The Book of Divine Commandments,* C. B. Chavel, trans. (1940); E. E. Urbach, *Hazal—Pirkei Emunot Ve-De'ot* (1968). B. MARTIN

MODERNISM, CATHOLIC (Ch). Tendencies in European Catholic scholarly circles aimed at adapting the thought, practice, and institutions of ROMAN CATHOLICISM to what was perceived as contemporary philosophical, cultural, scientific, and political reality. No organized movement existed, although there were personal and scholarly links among the French, Italian, and English scholars principally involved. Modernist orientations emerged in the 1890s and died out by 1910 as a result of decisive papal action. Related but not identical developments were "Reform Catholicism" in Germany and "Americanism" in the United States.

The intellectual awakening sparked by Pope LEO XIII and implemented particularly in the several French Catholic "institutes" or universities brought Catholics into contact with developments in philosophy, history, and biblical studies which had been taking place in nineteenth century Germany. Elements in the thought of various Modernists were philosophical subjectivism, emphasis on the immanence rather than transcendence of God, sharp separation of faith and reason, the demand for complete freedom of scholarly research, a call for institutional and educational reform within the church.

Leading figures included ALFRED LOISY, Friedrich von Hügel, George Tyrrell, and Ernesto Buonaiuti. With his encyclical *Pascendi Dominici Gregis* and a list of condemned propositions, *Lamentabili Sane Exitu,* Pius X in 1907 began a vigorous campaign to eliminate Modernist tendencies. An anti-Modernist oath was required of all candidates for orders, church offices, and papal academic degrees.

J. HENNESEY

MOGGALLĀNA mōg gŭl lä´ nŭ (B—Pali) **MAUDGALYĀYANA** moud gŭl yä´ yŭ nŭ (B—Skt.). One of the chief disciples of Gautama the BUDDHA, often associated with the name of another disciple of like standing, SĀRIPUTTA. Moggallāna was a member of the BRAHMIN caste who, together with Sāriputta, left an ascetic religious life with Sañjāya in order to follow the Buddha. It appears that the moderate monastic life-style practiced and taught by the Buddha, in contrast to the harsh and at times repulsive appearance and manners of certain of the religious ascetics of the time, was an important factor in the conversion of these two men. Moggallāna was, along with another chief disciple, Mahākaśyapa (*see* KAŚYAPA), noted for his psychic powers (SIDDHIS). He was used in the work of both teaching and discipline in the early community (SAṄGHA).

Bibliography. R. H. Drummond, *Gautama the Buddha* (1974), pp. 50-53, 67. R. H. DRUMMOND

MOHEL mô hăl´ (Ju—Heb.; "circumciser"). A person authorized and competent to perform the ritual CIRCUMCISION of a male infant.

B. MARTIN

MOHENJO-DARO mō hĕn´ jō dä´ rō. A major site of the INDUS VALLEY CIVILIZATION, possibly one of its capital cities. Located beside the lower Indus River in present-day Pakistan, Mohenjo-daro was an impressive urban settlement covering approximately 240 acres and containing some forty thousand inhabitants. Outstanding among its archaeological remains are the buildings on the "citadel," a high artificial mound, believed to have been the administrative and cultic center of the city. Possibly the city (and the civilization) was ruled from here by a priest-king or a hieratic assembly, although no temples or shrines have been identified for certain.

H. P. SULLIVAN

MOKṢA mōk´ shŭ (H—Skt.; lit. "release, liberation" [*muc*—"to free, to release"]). The most common term for the ultimate goal of various Hindu systems of thought and practice, indicating release of the human self (ATMAN) from the cycle of birth and death (SAMSARA).

The concept of *mokṣa* can only be understood in relation to the Hindu concepts of KARMA and samsara. About the time of the early UPANIṢADS (*ca.* 600 B.C.), the notion that death is followed by birth in another body, which in turn also suffers death, made its first clear appearance in Indian religious literature. Furthermore, the status of an individual's birth was understood to depend upon the kinds of deeds (karma) performed in previous existences. The prospect of virtually endless redeath *(punarmṛtyu)* and rebirth was threatening and led to attempts to find an escape from this perpetual mortality. The solution most commonly recommended in the Upaniṣads is the achieving of liberation through knowledge about the nature of reality, most typically intuitive insight (*jñāna)* into the teaching that the human self is in some sense one with the supreme principle of the universe (BRAHMAN). At this level of insight/consciousness there is no change or decay, and one is utterly free, released from the cycle of transmigration.

Mokṣa also connotes release from bondage to karmic activity and consequently from that which fuels karmic striving, namely, desire. It is thus not surprising that *mokṣa* as the fourth and most important of the HINDU AIMS OF LIFE is in some contexts deemed to be acessible only to one who has renounced the world and devoted full time to asceticism and the pursuit of liberating wisdom (SANNYĀSIN).

The BHAGAVAD GĪTĀ develops further nuances of the concept of *mokṣa*, teaching that liberation can also be achieved by performance of works, especially the duties prescribed by one's social position, so long as such actions are not accompanied by any desire for the result of these works. Moreover, the Gītā recommends loving devotion *(bhakti)* to God as the easiest and best path to release (IX.26-29). By the end of the first millennium A.D. this devotional emphasis came to dominate much of Hindu religious life (*see* BHAKTI HINDUISM). In this theistic context, God may grant his devotees *mokṣa* while destroying their karma and rebirth in an act of divine grace.

Bibliography. W. T. de Bary, ed., *Sources of Indian Tradition* (1958), I, 271-361. G. E. YOCUM

MONASTERIES, BUDDHIST. *See* VIHĀRA.

MONASTICISM, EAST AND WEST (Gr. *monadzein*—"to live alone"). A mode of life secluded from temporal concerns and dedicated exclusively to religious pursuits. All the world's living religions have had some kind of monastic traditions or heritage. In THERAVĀDA BUDDHISM, for instance, the central religious institution has been the monastery, but monasticism has had a peripheral place in JUDAISM (*see* ESSENES), while in CHRISTIANITY monastic institutions are less significant today than during the Middle Ages.

1. **The monastic ideal.** Even when a monastic tradition begins as a response to ecclesiastical laxity, pervasive secularization, or other historical and cultural factors, its adherents see it in relationship to the ideal represented by the religious founder and the founder's teachings. ANTONY OF EGYPT set out into the Egyptian desert in response to Jesus' command, "Sell all you have, give to the poor, and follow me." In HINDUISM, ŚAṂKARA'S Sannyāsi order can be seen as a natural institutional embodiment of his ADVAITA (nondual) world view based on ŚRUTI (revealed truth). In BUDDHISM the monk follows the example of the BUDDHA, who is perceived as the disciplined monk *par excellence*.

Among Western religions Christianity provides obvious and enduring examples of monastic life, as does SUFISM in ISLAM. Forms vary according to ecclesiastical tradition (ROMAN CATHOLICISM, GREEK ORTHODOXY, RUSSIAN ORTHODOXY, the Syrian Church, the COPTIC CHURCH, the ANGLICAN CHURCH), historical period (Medieval Irish, Cluniac, CISTERCIAN), and guiding ideal (desert hermit, BENEDICTINE, TRAPPIST, CARTHUSIAN). All derive authority from the sayings of Jesus, the early Christian community in Jerusalem, and the lives and writings of certain early monks and founders of orders.

Jesus is neither the founder of a monastic order nor the ideal monk, in contrast to the Buddha, who is the model for monastic life. In Christianity monasticism is predicated on the teachings of Jesus that counsel poverty, celibacy, and total dedication to God. It involves isolation from the rest of society, the practice of bodily asceticism (often severe), simple labor (gardening, weaving baskets), prayer, recitation of Scripture, and the quest for perfection in wordless prayer or mystical experience. Amid many changes over the centuries these remain essential constituents of the Christian monastic ideal.

Collections of sayings of and stories about

J. M. Ward

This 11th century cloister reflects the serenity of life in the Monastery of Santo Domingo de Silos, Covarrubias, Spain

renowned DESERT FATHERS set the norm. Cassian's *Conferences* (fifth century) provided a similar summary of the ideal through reports of conversations with venerated leaders. When communal (cenobitic) monasticism emerged, obedience to a rule and to an ABBOT were added to the commitments of poverty and chastity. Cenobitic monks shared all possessions on the model of the early Jerusalem Christians.

Whether living as hermits or in an isolated community, monks sought to acquire the virtue of humility. This meant detachment from worldly desires and possessions, and the loss of an ego-centered world view. Jesus' teachings were fundamental in defining this humility and nonattachment, while the various rules established ways of pursuing the goal.

Asia has many different monastic traditions, including the Hindu mendicants and the JAINA ascetics of India, the THERAVĀDA monastic communities *(bhikkhu-saṅgha)* of Sri Lanka, Burma, Thailand, and Laos, the ZEN monasteries of Korea and Japan, and the TAOIST orders of China still surviving on Taiwan.

The Buddhist monastic community stems from the life of the Buddha himself. According to tradition the Buddha was born into a royal family but upon the recognition that life was fraught with the uncertainties of old age, suffering, and death, he departed from the GRHASTHA life in search of a more lasting truth. This search continued for six years, during which time the Buddha not only studied with some of the famous teachers of his day but practiced various kinds of austerity. Finding extreme ASCETICISM to be inimical to his search for truth, he adopted a middle way between his earlier princely indulgence and his contemporaries' asceticism (*see* EIGHTFOLD PATH). This way focused on the restraint of other-regarding virtues, training the mind through study and meditation (*see* MEDITATION, BUDDHIST), and insight into the true nature of reality. Buddhist monastic life embodies this ideal of the middle way, establishing an environment conducive to these disciplines and goals. While ascetic practices are not unknown, they can legitimately be seen as deviations from the ideal. While contemporary monastic practice includes a variety of public roles, the two standards of Buddhist monastic life have been meditation *(vipaśyanā-dhura)* and study *(gantha-dhura)*.

The Buddhist monastic community (SAṄGHA) embodies the founder's teaching (DHARMA), which is based on the premise that most people live in a state of ignorance and blind attachment to sensory desires. To gain knowledge and overcome attachment it is necessary to change habits of thought and activity. Ideally, the monastic life provides both the break from the ordinary state of things and the context for the realization of the truth. The "three jewels" (TRIRATNA: Buddha, dharma, saṅgha) necessarily intertwine as facets of one ideal.

2. **Historical origins.** Christian monasticism emerged in Egypt in the late third century A.D. and represented a new form of dedicated life. There had been celibate ascetics within local Christian communities for some time, but it was a new thing for persons to move into the desert as hermits and there practice asceticism, live simply, and pray. The fundamental impulse lay in Jesus' message of self-denial and striving for perfection, but examples of non-Christian "holy men," aversion to current society, and increasing laxity in church life may also have been factors.

As more hermits entered the desert, small groups gathered near leading spiritual guides, and loose-knit communities of hermits were formed. Individuals were fairly independent but gathered regularly for liturgy and common discipline. Hermits kept links with society by receiving visitors and weaving baskets for sale in marketplaces.

In the course of the fourth century two communities were founded, one by PACHOMIUS (*ca.* 290-346) in Egypt, and one by BASIL of Caesarea (329-79) in Asia Minor. Pachomius' monks lived in large establishments, shared work, worshiped as a group, and were isolated from society. Basil's monks were less isolated, and their monasteries were centers of charitable service (hospitals, schools, help for poor).

In the Latin West, Cassian and Benedict of Nursia (*ca.* 480—*ca.* 547) defined the monastery as an institution within the church, isolated, dedicated to individual spirituality, yet at the service of the wider church. Prayer always had been the special role of monks. After the ninth century, Benedictine monks were seen as specialists in prayer, interceding for the rest of society.

In the eleventh and twelfth centuries new monastic groups appeared. Some were hermits, others returned to the pure Benedictine Rule (Cistercians), and others began new forms of monastic life (Carthusians). In the later Middle Ages monasticism declined while a new form of religious life, mendicancy (FRANCISCANS, DOMINICANS) ascended. In the sixteenth century PROTESTANTISM rejected monasticism as creating a false caste of especially religious persons. In the past two centuries Christian monastic life has been revived in many quarters.

From the time of the desert hermits there have been female monks (nuns). Most nuns today are in enclosed contemplative orders, isolated from the world. Other female religious orders (sisters) live under vows and a rule but may run hospitals, orphanages, schools, and the like.

At the time of the Buddha (sixth century B.C.) in northern India there had already developed a tradition of religious truth-seekers or homeless wanderers *(parivrājaka)*. Buddhist monasticism is rooted in this tradition. The Buddha, after his enlightenment, traveled about the area of north India known as Magadha teaching the truth he had discovered at his enlightenment. Many were attracted by his teaching and became his disciples and together formed, not a settled, localized group, but a community bound together by common allegiance to a teacher.

The wandering truth-seekers observed a three-month retreat during the monsoon season. Because traveling was difficult, congregations of monks would come together in temporary dwellings, perhaps in caves or residences donated by wealthy landholders. During this time particular forms of collective life gradually emerged, including the recital of a confessional called the PĀTIMOKKHA, reconstructed from the Pali DHAMMAPADA: "Forebearance or patience is the highest kind of penance for he is never a mendicant who hurts or molests others; abstain from all evils, accumulate all that is good, and purify one's own mind—this is the injunction of the Buddha." Other group ceremonies probably included initiation into the order and the presentation of new robes at the conclusion of the retreat. This period also saw the beginnings of an oral tradition in which the teachings of the Buddha were memorized in particular settings and with sufficient mnemonic devices to ensure their retention.

Gradually the communal pattern of the rains retreat extended beyond the three-month period. The temporary dwellings became more and more permanent. This development represents the beginning of what was to become standard practice throughout Buddhist Asia. The settled communal monastery (VIHĀRA) became the backbone of the Buddhist tradition. This institution over time saw the creation of nunneries, was the context for the development of sectarian practice, and at times became a powerful economic institution. Even today in Burma and Thailand there are monastic centers of tens if not hundreds of monks, and in Japan monasteries occupy entire mountainsides.

3. **Ordered life.** As monastic institutions grow in size, regimens become increasingly important. The lives of people dwelling in tightly knit groups like monasteries must be carefully regulated to ensure adherence to the institution's normative ideal and to maintain a harmonious community.

At first, guidance for Christian monks was informal, as elder monks known for their insight advised beginners. With Pachomius and Basil the idea of a *rule* entered monastic tradition. To this day Greek monks generally follow the rules of St. Basil with later customs and additions. In the Latin West, Cassian provided a guide for a monastery in his *Institutes*. A number of rules governed monastic life, from local versions to more general ones like the Irish rule of St. Columban. By the twelfth century the rule of St. Benedict dominated monastic life in western Europe.

Benedict drew upon Basil, Cassian, and others to produce a rule emphasizing individual spiritual practice set in a solid communal structure. The monastery was seen as a large family, independent, isolated and self-supporting in an agricultural setting, with simple needs and a plain but not toilsome life. The abbot, elected by the brothers, had absolute authority. Stability was important: monks were not to wander or to move to another monastery. Monasteries were permanent communities and profession was for life. Three activities were primary: LITURGY (EUCHARIST plus canonical hours), sacred reading *(lectio divina)* for building up spiritual life but not for mere acquisition of knowledge, and manual labor to support the community. At some periods liturgical duties dominated, while individual monasteries or groups have been known for scholarship. Manual labor was often done by non-monks.

The rule gave detailed guidance for various monastic officials, the daily timetable (varied according to season), the liturgy, diet, moral demands, adjudication of quarrels, and numerous other guidelines. Benedict also gave basic spiritual counsel, but referred to Cassian and earlier fathers as further guides. The rule, seventy-three chapters long, was supplemented with local customs providing for differences in location, climate, concerns, and changes over time.

In the ideal sense the early Buddhist monastic order was conceived as a community of saints bent upon the realization of NIRVANA. As the community grew, however, issues of discipline, daily regimen, and monastic routine became more of a preoccupation. S. Dutt observes that the followers of the Buddha developed from a sect bound together by an allegiance to a common teaching into an order bound by a common discipline. The Pātimokkha gradually became a set of rules eventually standardized into 227 in the Theravāda tradition and 250 in the MAHĀYĀNA.

The Pātimokkha, the heart of the monk's discipline, is encased in a body of training rules known as the Vinaya. Most notably in the Vinaya the Buddha is the sole basis of authority for monastic legislation. The monastic rules are divided into seven categories according to the nature of the offense and its penalty. The first category includes the most serious offenses—sexual intercourse, stealing, taking life, false claims to supernatural attainment—for which the punishment is expulsion from the order. Penalties for lesser offenses range from temporary suspension to mere confession of fault.

In general the monastic codes of the three great Buddhist traditions (Theravāda, Mahāyāna, VAJRAYĀNA) are quite similar. Variation occurs in part as a consequence of cultural and historical influences. One difference, however, stems from the doctrinal emphasis in the Mahāyāna tradition on the concept of the compassionate BODHISATTVA. In the Mahāyāna ordination ceremony *(upasampadā)*, in addition to subscribing to the moral precepts fundamental to all Buddhists and the 250 training rules of the monk, the ordainee takes the four bodhisattva vows: to lead all beings to salvation, to make an end of all pain and suffering, to study the works of the great teachers, and to attain to perfect buddhahood.

4. **The monastery as cultural institution.** The monastery is an important cultural center. In particular, it has been school and university, creator and preserver of a literary heritage, and an inspiration for art and architecture.

Almost singlehandedly monks preserved the literary heritage of classical and early Christian times by copying and recopying texts, preserving them when civilization was at a low ebb. Irish and English missionary monks Christianized areas of northern Europe and introduced Latin culture to Germanic peoples. Monks have been poets, historians, annalists, theologians, grammarians, and preachers. They also encouraged and supervised the building of noble structures in Europe and the Middle East. Monks, and especially nuns, brought great artistic skill to the illumination of precious manuscripts. Liturgy was greatly enriched by monks. Great monasteries patronized skilled artisans in all media. Benedictine monks were the schoolmasters of Europe from 700 to 1100, and they still operate colleges and schools today, while monastic workshops, printing presses, and musicians continue ancient traditions and create new ones. Monasteries were also important parts of the economy of their areas—for example, the Cistercians in the medieval English wool trade and German monasteries with their large landholdings.

The significance of the Buddhist monastery as a bearer and transformer of culture can hardly be overemphasized. NĀLANDĀ and the other great Indian monastic universities attracted scholars from various parts of Asia and were important centers of philosophical and literary development. The Buddhist monks of Asia wrote chronicles and doctrinal treatises, commentaries and grammars, poetry and narratives. They sculpted Buddha images and painted murals, designed gardens and made flower arranging an art. Buddhist monks brought Indian cultural and religious traditions to China and Tibet. Monks from Korea and China brought their cultural and religious traditions to Japan. The monastery at times has been a large landholder and an important economic and political force. Indeed, the impact of Buddhism through the medium of the monastery has been so pervasive that it is difficult to imagine what the cultures of southern and eastern Asia would have been like without it. *See also* ZEN §6.

Bibliography. Christian: G. Constable, *Medieval Monasticism: A Select Bibliography* (1976), superb with annotations, and "The Study of Monastic History Today," in *Essays on the Reconstruction of Medieval History*, ed. V. Mudroch *et al.* (1974), excellent; D. Knowles, *Christian Monasticism* (1969), a survey, and *The Monastic Order in England*, 2nd ed. (1963); J. Leclercq, *The Love of Learning and the Desire for God* (1961), on monastic life and culture; G. Zarnecki, *The Monastic Achievement* (1972) on art and architecture. The series Cistercian Studies includes important new books. Buddhist: S. Dutt, *Buddhist Monks and Monasteries of India* (1962), history and culture to A.D. 1200; I. B. Horner, *The Book of Discipline*, S. B. B. X, XI, XIII, XIV, XX, XXV (1913-66), a trans. of the Vinaya Piṭaka of the Theravāda; J. Kennett, *Selling Water by the River* (1972), manual for Sōtō Zen trainees; R. K. N. Losang, *My Life and Lives* (1977), autobiography by Tibetan Gelugpa monk; J. Prip-Moller, *Chinese Buddhist Monasteries*, 2nd ed. (1967), architecture, activities, and rites; S. J. Tambiah, *World Conqueror and World Renouncer* (1976), Thai Buddhism including the *Saṅgha*; H. Welch, *The Practice of Chinese Buddhism 1900-1950* (1967), a major resource. Other: A. Schimmel, *Mystical Dimensions of Islam* (1975), esp. ch. 5 on Sufi orders; D. M. Miller and D. C. Wertz, *Hindu Monastic Life and the Monks and Monasteries of Bhubaneswar* (1976).

D. K. SWEARER and G. A. ZINN

MONISM mōn′ ĭsm (Gr.; lit. "singularism"). Any belief which recognizes oneness or unity as the defining character of reality. In particular, monism can apply to three distinct and logically incompatible metaphysical doctrines. Quantitative monism is the view that there is only one fundamental substance or reality. As expressed by Spinoza, this theory holds that all things should be conceived of as states or manifestations of a single God. Qualitative monism is pluralistic in acknowledging a multitude of substances or real things, but monistic in claiming that all such entities must be understood to be of only one quality, kind, or nature (Leibnitz' virtually indistinguishable monads or Greek atomism). Genetic monism is a cosmological position according to which all phenomena proceed from one basic source. Thus while Pythagoreanism is dualistic in affirming that two principles, the Limit and the Unlimited, produce the universe, Christianity is monistic in describing God as the creator of all things.

E. J. COLEMAN

MONK. *See* MONASTICISM, EAST AND WEST.

MONOPHYSITISM mə năf′ ə sīt ĭsm (Ch). Generally, adherence to a "one-nature" CHRISTOLOGY; specifically, Eastern Christians opposing the Council of Chalcedon's Christology (*see* CHALCEDONIAN DEFINITION) who established ecclesiastical structures separate from those of ORTHODOX CHURCHES. They include the COPTIC, JACOBITE, ARMENIAN, Nubian, and ETHIOPIC communions. D. E. GROH

MONSIGNOR mōn sēn′ yər (Ch). A title of honor conferred upon some high ranking officers in ROMAN CATHOLICISM. K. WATKINS

MONTANISM mōn′ tăn ĭsm (Ch). An ecstatic prophetic movement named after its founder, Montanus (*ca.* A.D. 170). It was known until the fourth century as "the Phrygian heresy" (from its place of origin and greatest support). Montanist prophets claimed direct oracular revelations from God for their teachings on the ecstatic nature of prophesying, on ESCHATOLOGY, and on ASCETICISM. Tertullian of Carthage was their most famous convert (*ca.* 207).

D. E. GROH

MOODY, DWIGHT LYMAN (Ch; 1837-1899). Evangelist and conservative Protestant leader. Following a successful revival in England in 1873-75, Moody became America's leading revivalist and pioneered the techniques of big city REVIVALISM. He devoted the latter part of his career to the establishment of schools. *See* DISPENSATIONALISM.

G. MILLER

MOON, SUN MYUNG mōōn sŭn myŭng (1920-). Founder and prophetic leader of the UNIFICATION CHURCH. Born in northern Korea, Moon was for a time affiliated with the PRESBYTERIAN church. His claim that at the age of sixteen JESUS appeared to him led him to organize his own church after fleeing south during the Korean War.

K. CRIM

MORAVIANS (Ch). A Protestant denomination that traces its origins to JOHN HUSS; known formally as the Unitas Fratrum (Unity of Brethren). In 1458 a band of left-wing Hussites organized a brotherhood at Kunvald, Bohemia. In 1467 they broke with the Catholic Church by ordaining their own ministers.

The movement flourished, numbering 100,000 by 1500, but tensions came with growth. As the learned, wealthy, and noble joined, it was hard to continue the ascetic traditions. The more accommodating faction won out, allowing the Unity to make common cause with the LUTHERAN and REFORMED Churches in several areas (Bohemia, Poland). They expanded as well into East Prussia and Hungary. However, by 1630 the Unity was virtually suppressed through the ferocity of the Counter Reformation. (*See* REFORMATION, CATHOLIC.) Only a few families in Moravia (the "hidden seed") secretly perpetuated the faith. The last great leader, educator-bishop John Amos Comenius (1592-1670), spent much of his life in exile.

Renewal came with Christian David (1690-1751), who brought Moravian families to Eastern Germany. They found protection on the estates of Count von Zinzendorf at Herrnhut, which became a center of PIETISM, but was plagued with internal disputes and arguments with local Lutheran clergy. Zinzendorf stepped into direct leadership, and in 1727 a religious revival resulted in the Renewed Moravian Church.

Under Zinzendorf's energetic, enthusiastic, but occasionally erratic hand, the Moravians became the most aggressive and controversial religious movement in European Protestantism. They built large centers in Germany, the Netherlands, Great Britain, and in North America (principally Salem, North Carolina, and Bethlehem, Pennsylvania). These centers were noted for great creativity in church music, with extensive hymn-composing and high proficiency in performance. This tradition has continued to the present day.

They organized themselves communally, the better to concentrate their energies on outreach. After 1732 this was a far-flung missionary endeavor which sent volunteers to the West Indies, to Africa, and among the North American Indians. Later Moravian missions extended to Latin America, Alaska, Tibet, and North India.

The least understood of the Moravian emphases was their ecumenical vision. Zinzendorf attacked the confessional narrowness of his time and urged all Christians to work together. Contemporaries misunderstood Moravian plans as maneuvers to gain proselytes. Despite setbacks, the Moravian Church has been in the forefront of conciliar and cooperative activities nationally and internationally. Although never attaining large membership, the Moravians have made a substantial impact upon Protestantism in liturgy, music, missions, and ecumenical endeavors.

Bibliography. G. Gollin, *Moravians in Two Worlds* (1967); J. T. Hamilton and K. G. Hamilton, *History of the Moravian Church* (rev. ed. 1967); J. Weinlick, *Count Zinzendorf* (1956).

D. F. DURNBAUGH

MORMONS (Ch). *See* LATTER-DAY SAINTS.

MOSES (Ju, Ch & I; *ca.* 1300 B.C.). Prophet of the god YAHWEH and Hebrew tribal leader of the exodus from Egypt. Moses' Egyptian background seems reflected in his name, perhaps from an Egyptian root "to be born" (cf. Thut-mose). Tracing his birth to the tribe of Levi was apparently intended to establish his priestly role. While exiled from Egypt in Midian, he married the daughter of a Midianite priest. There he encountered Yahweh at the burning bush (Exod. 3) and received his commission to deliver the Hebrew slaves from Egypt, to which he reluctantly agreed. After their escape from Egypt, he led the people for forty years of wandering through the SINAI wilderness, eventually dying without entering the land he sought. He was buried in an unknown grave east of the Jordan River.

Scholarly consensus has it that of the four strands of tradition comprising the Pentateuch, the most reliable information about Moses is found in the Yahwist (J) and Elohist (E) documents. Deuteronomy (D) reflects a later interest in Moses as a prophetic figure, and the Priestly tradition (P) witnesses to the post-exilic significance of the TORAH. Despite the dominant role that Moses plays in the exodus traditions, there is a paradox: Moses is not mentioned in the oldest strata commemorating the event (nor is he in the HAGGADAH for PASSOVER). Only Yahweh is credited with Israel's escape from Egypt.

Noth and von Rad have separated the exodus and wilderness traditions into four major themes: (1) exodus, (2) revelation at Sinai, (3) wilderness wandering, (4) entrance into the Promised Land. The revelation at Sinai (Exod. 19:1–Num. 10:28) seems to be an excursus encompassing a broad range of legal material disrupting the continuity of the other themes. Some (e.g. Smend) see Moses as the central figure holding these originally unrelated themes together. Others (e.g. von Rad) hold that Moses could have been related historically to only one of these themes. Another view (Noth) is that the only authentic Mosaic tradition is that which places his tomb east of the Jordan.

Yet it is as the recipient of the law at Sinai that Moses is chiefly remembered (*see* Ten Commandments; Covenant). With the Exile and the rise of Judaism, the Torah became the nucleus about which every dimension of worship and community life was structured. Accordingly the role of Moses was enhanced, not only as the one to whom Yahweh had revealed his name and who had set into motion the exodus from Egypt, but also as the one most closely connected with the legal material amassed between Exod. 19:1 and Num. 10:28. Thus it is hardly surprising that Moses should be seen as the personification of Jewish legal tradition and as the author of the Pentateuch.

In the NT Moses is compared and contrasted forcefully with Jesus both to enhance the role of the latter (much of Jesus' life and teaching are based on the Mosaic model) and to prepare for the emergence of the new covenant.

In Islam Moses is highly regarded as the prophet of the Jews who was the recipient of Scripture and the Law.

The "horns" of Moses is a description of the prophet that resulted from Jerome's metaphorical rendering of Exod. 34:29 into Latin. Though the expression is generally understood as a radiant or shining face, the meaning of the Hebrew text is uncertain.

Bibliography. M. Noth, *History of Pentateuchal Traditions* (1972); R. Smend, *Das Mosebild von Heinrich Ewald bis Martin Noth* (1959); G. von Rad, *Problem of the Hexateuch and other Essays* (1966).

M. G. Rogers

MOSES BEN MAIMON mō´ zĕz bĕn mī´ môn, **MAIMONIDES** mī môn´ ə dēs (Ju; 1135-1204; with title Rabbi yields acronym "Rambam"). Codifier of Jewish law, rabbinic leader, physician, and philosopher of Judaism, who won the acknowledgment and respect of worldwide Jewry. His burial place in Tiberias is a Pilgrimage site to this day.

Among his legal works are a commentary on the Mishnah, Responsa, and his monumental Mishneh Torah. His philosophic classic is the renowned *Guide for the Perplexed.* He also composed many medical treatises that are extant.

It is misleading to list his achievements in law and philosophy separately, for the interpenetration of these two domains across his entire literary output reflects Maimonides' fundamental perception of Judaism as the philosophically informed society *par excellence.* Even in his own lifetime both the literary method and the ideational content of his integrated presentation of Jewish practice and belief provoked considerable opposition and strife. The subsequent development of medieval Jewish philosophy almost entirely revolves around the views of Maimonides, either for or against. Despite the controversy surrounding his views, Jews universally revered him. *See* Judaism §3e.

Bibliography. S. Baron, *Essays on Maimonides* (1941); I. Twersky, ed., *A Maimonides Reader* (1972).

K. P. Bland

MOSES BEN NAḤMAN mō´ zəz bĕn nä´ män, **NACHMANIDES** näk män´ ə dēs (Ju; 1194-1270; with title Rabbi yields acronym "Ramban"). Talmudist, biblical commentator, mystic, poet, physician, and acknowledged religious authority and central figure of the mid-thirteenth century Spanish Jewish community. His biblical commentary is the first to introduce Kabbalistic ideas by way of guarded allusion. In 1263 he was ordered to defend the Talmud against charges brought by the Dominicans in a trial or inquisitorial hearing in Barcelona. The last years of his life were spent in Palestine.

K. P. Bland

MOSLEM. *See* Muslim.

MOSQUE mŏsk (I; from Arab. *masjīd;* lit. "place of prostration" [*sajada*—"to bow down in worship"]). The mosque is a communal house of Prayer for the performance of the five daily canonical prayers *(ṣalāt)* required of devout Muslims in the Qur'ān (Sura

W. Denny

The Masjid-e Shah, Isfahan; detail of the *qiblah iwān* (Safavid, 17th century)

11:114). Larger mosques may bear the designation *jāmi'* or "congregational mosque."

1. **Origins.** Although the Arabic word *masjīd* originally signified a holy building without specific Islamic meaning, the term has come to mean a hall of prayer. According to Islamic tradition, prayer may be performed in any clean place, but communal prayer under the leadership of an IMAM is preferable, especially for the important noonday prayer on Friday. Various structures for prayer have evolved in Islamic tradition, from the *muṣalla* or *namāzgāh,* an open-air prayer platform, to the major congregational mosques of metropolitan centers. The first Islamic mosque was the house of MUHAMMAD in MEDINA, built as a rectangular courtyard with a shaded portico *(riwāq)* made from the trunks of palm trees on the south side. Under this portico the early Muslims performed the *ṣalāt,* a combination of recited prayers, Qur'ānic passages, and physical prostrations, while facing the south wall which indicated the QIBLAH or direction of the KA'BA in MECCA.

From the Prophet's house in Medina evolved the Arab mosque, a structure incorporating a rectangular courtyard *(ṣāhn)* with *riwāqs* or porticos on all four sides, but with a larger *riwāq,* sometimes composed of many rows of stone columns, on the *qiblah* side.

2. **Functions.** Early mosques served the community as prayer halls and as places of assembly for legislative and judicial functions. These original functions were developed, modified, and amplified throughout Islamic history, and as they became more complex, architectural forms and artistic decoration of the various types of mosque buildings developed to reflect these new functions. The building of mosques in conquered towns and cities was undertaken as an affirmation of Islamic rule, either through the building of a new structure, such as the mosque of 'Amr in Cairo, or through the modification of an existing building, such as the Great Mosque of Damascus. The mosque quickly acquired new functions, serving as a center of administration and as a place for the teaching of the Qur'ān and Islamic traditions. In addition to the major congregational mosques, smaller houses of worship served various sectarian or tribal needs and provided more convenient access for those living in remote surburban quarters. Mosques were also erected as commemorative monuments, serving pilgrims to the tombs of holy personages or sanctifying places associated with important historical events. Mosques were developed as centers of learning; some were eventually surrounded with subsidiary buildings serving various university functions, as typified by the AL-AZHĀR mosque in Cairo, while others combined the functions of mosque and MADRASA in a single architectural setting. Other mosques expropriated the sacred shrines of older religions; the Great Mosque of Isfahan was built on the site of a FIRE TEMPLE, and the mosque al-Aqsa in JERUSALEM was built on the Temple Mount.

W. Denny

The Üc Serefeli Mosque, Edirne (Ottoman, 15th cenury)

Mosques founded by rulers or by dynasties often served a dual purpose, as manifestations of the piety and power of Islamic royalty and nobility in addition to their purely religious functions. The practice of mentioning the ruler's name in the KHUṬBA or sermon after Friday prayers took on enormous political significance as religious confirmation of secular rule, and the mosque was also the place for proclamation of holy war (JIHĀD) and the point of departure for the pilgrimage (HAJJ). In many parts of the Islamic world, but especially in the Ottoman Empire, mosques founded by sultans and their courtiers served as the focal points of complexes of buildings *(külliye)* serving various social and religious needs, such as *madrasas* (colleges), *'imārets* (alms-kitchens), libraries, hospitals, primary schools, hotels and warehouses, bakeries, baths, and cemeteries.

3. **Appurtenances.** Over time various architectural forms and furnishings evolved to serve the diverse functions of the mosque. The most universal of these is the *mihrāb,* a niche or niche-like room usually positioned in the center of the *qiblah* wall, giving architectural distinction to the *qiblah* and providing a decorative focal point for the mosque interior, before which the imam leads congregational

prayers. Two other features evolved in very early Islamic times. The *manāra* or MINARET was a tower or special place on the roof of the mosque from which the muezzin chanted the ADHĀN or call to prayer before the five daily prayers. The form taken by the minaret in various Islamic lands varied widely, with some of the tallest and most elaborate examples clearly placing their visual symbolism ahead of practical function. Another early feature of Islamic congregational mosques was the *maqṣūra*, a special enclosure or screened-off area in the mosque, usually on the *qiblah* wall, reserved for the sovereign. In later times this often took the form of a balcony or high platform raised above the floor.

The dual function of the Friday sermon or *khuṭba*, as a vehicle of religious instruction and as a setting for major political proclamations, aided in the development of the *minbār*, a pulpit usually placed to the right of the *mihrāb*, often raised some height above the floor and given access through a staircase perpendicular to the *qiblah*. Another furnishing found in many mosques was a lectern or *kursi*, a raised desk or large chair adapted to the teaching and recitation of the Qur'ān, which was an important function of the mosque. A third furnishing found generally only in the largest mosques was a *dakka*, a raised platform on which the muezzin sits during the prayer; such platforms were sometimes also built for *hāfiz*, those who had performed the difficult feat of memorizing the entire Qur'ān.

Other features of the mosque evolved as a matter of practicality, taking decorative forms of increasing complexity and symbolic importance over time. Early Islamic puritanism frowned on all embellishment of mosques; when decoration did evolve, it either developed along abstract lines (the arabesque) or it took distinctively religious form as monumental inscriptions. Eventually mosque decorations in many Islamic lands developed a complex "iconography" of inscriptions, usually including the names of God, his Prophet, and the first six imams, together with various prayers and Qur'ānic passages deemed appropriate for certain specific parts of the mosque. The floor was covered with straw mats or with woven carpets, providing the canonical clean place for worship while at the same time adding both beauty to the interior of the mosque and comfort to the knees of worshipers. As the early morning and late evening prayers occurred in times of darkness, lamps of various sorts evolved to light mosque interiors, also symbolizing the presence of divine light (Sura 24:36). The artistic effort expended on monumental calligraphy, carpets, and lamps of various types was often considerable, as was the economic effort; such embellishments for mosques were frequently donated as pious acts and were afforded protection as WAQF endowment.

Two other appurtenances of the mosque deserve mention: the open courtyard or *ṣahn*, usually with porticos or *riwāqs* of graceful arcades on three or more sides, and the presence of water. Despite the evolution of regional mosque types throughout the Islamic world, the feature of the open courtyard, the essential memory of the house of Muhammad in Medina, was preserved in some manner or other, however vestigial, in Muslim houses of prayer from the Pacific to the Atlantic. And since the daily prayers could not take place without prior ritual ablutions (WUḌŪ' or *abdest*), the availability of water was essential. In many mosques, a large ablution fountain known as the *shadirwān* stands in the middle of the *ṣahn*, while others may be found in proximity to the main doors. The sanctity of water in Islam leads to some of the most memorable features of mosques—the pools and channels of running water found in some and the placing of *salsabīls* or playing fountains in others. (*See* PURIFICATION.)

4. Regional variants. The forms taken by mosques in various parts of the Islamic world depended on many factors, among them the local architectural inheritance and materials, factors of climate, and sectarian needs. The primary feature of the traditional Arab mosque was the *ṣahn* or open courtyard and the prayer hall composed of row upon row of columns or piers bearing arcades surmounted by vaults or wooden beams. One of the most famous examples is the great mosque of Qayrawān in Tunisia (*ca.* 836) with its great minaret directly across the *ṣahn* from the *mihrāb* and the *mihrāb* axis emphasized on the exterior by two domes. The *mihrāb* is decorated with lustre tiles, some imported from Mesopotamia and others of local manufacture, while the *maqṣūra*, a latticed screen of turned wooden dowels dating from the eleventh century, is the oldest surviving example. Another columned mosque is that of Cordoba, which was enlarged several times between the eighth and tenth centuries. The characteristic horseshoe arch, with alternating voussoirs of red and cream-colored stone, served as a leitmotif of the building, which was embellished with elaborately carved capitals, inscriptions in carved stone and mosaic, and various vaulted chambers of great complexity.

Other variations on the courtyard mosque, using piers of brick or stone rather than columns, include the mosque of al-Mutawakkil in Samarra, Iraq (*ca.* 848-60) with its circular spiral minaret recalling a Mesopotamian ziggurat, and the great mosque of Aḥmad ibn Tulūn in Cairo (*ca.* 879), whose vast inner courtyard was surrounded by exterior courtyards or *ziyādas* which in former times contained various appurtenances of the building. The Great Mosque of Damascus, founded in 706, was built on the site of a preexisting *temenos* or Greek temple enclosure; its arcades running parallel to the *qiblah* were interrupted by a sort of "nave" perpendicular to the *qiblah*, leading toward the *mihrāb*, surmounted by a dome. The Aqsa mosque in Jerusalem was built with fourteen arcades running perpendicular to the *qiblah*, forming fifteen "naves," the middle one of which was constructed wider than the others. The latter mosque, built within the enclosure or *ḥarām* surrounding the DOME OF THE ROCK in Jerusalem, had no courtyard as such.

In Iran the dominant mosque form from the eleventh century onward was the four-*iwān* mosque-*madrasa*, a large rectangular courtyard surrounded by arcades, with an *iwān*, a large rectangular vaulted structure, in the middle of each side, open to the courtyard. The *miḥrāb*, *minbār*, and other major features of the building were housed in a domical chamber directly behind the *qiblah iwān*. From the earliest examples, such as the Great Mosque of Isfahan, built over many centuries but given its major features in the eleventh century, there evolved an unbroken line of Iranian mosque-*madrasas* all retaining the basic four-*iwān* form. The *iwāns* themselves were decorated by filling up the great arches on the court side with *muqārnas*, that distinctively Islamic faceted architectural decoration composed of three-dimensional geometric arabesques in niche-like form. The Iranian mosques, built of brick, were also decorated with wonderfully complex inscriptions and with colorful glazed brick, mosaic tile, and multicolor or *haftrangī* tiles as the centuries progressed. Among the masterpieces of mosque architecture in Iran must be counted the Congregational Mosque of Varamīn (*ca.* 1322) and the mosque of Shah ʿAbbās I in Isfahan (1612-38).

Anatolia, settled by Turkish invaders from the late eleventh century onward, inherited an architectural tradition from Iran, Central Asia, the Arab lands to the south, and from the indigenous traditions of Asia Minor. The early Anatolian *Ulu Jāmiʿ* or Great Mosques, such as that in Sivas (eleventh century), were large halls with vaulted or wooden ceilings set upon arcades carried by columns or heavy piers, often with only a distant memory of the *ṣāhn* in the form of an open oculus in a central vaulted bay. Decoration in Anatolia consisted of elaborate reliefs in carved stone, as well as ceramic tile, carved wooden mosque furnishings, and carpets. The Ottoman Turks combined traditional features of the Seljuk and Byzantine past with a dazzling sense of interior space and impressive engineering. The open courtyard often remained as a sort of atrium to the Ottoman mosque, which was completely covered by domical forms, buttressed by structural components of remarkable beauty and strength. Great Ottoman mosques such as the Süleymaniye in Istanbul (1559) or the Selimiye in Edirne (1572) had four or more minarets, used to heighten the sense of silhouette which the finest examples always demonstrate. Ottoman mosques were decorated with painted arabesques and calligraphic inscriptions; many examples were also embellished with colorful underglaze-painted tiles from Iznik, in floral, vegetal, and calligraphic designs of great richness.

In India and Central Asia mosque forms owed a great deal to the influence of the Iranian mosque-*madrasa*. The early congregational mosques of India, preeminent among which was the thirteenth century Quwwat al-Islam mosque of Delhi, were often vast in size, consisting in the main of huge open courtyards with large gateways and almost perfunctory enclosing arcades. The seventeenth century Great Mosques of Lahore, Agra, and Delhi have large domical structures on the *qiblah* side to house the major appurtenances of the building, but the proportion of covered to uncovered area in the mosque is very small. The decoration of Indian mosques paralleled that of other architectural genres as Islam strengthened its hold on the subcontinent; the early stone mosques were decorated with carving, sometimes executed by non-Muslim artisans, while the later buildings under the Mogul dynasty often boasted decorations of white marble veneer inlaid with *pietra dura* mosaic work in colored stones. (*See* ISLAM IN SOUTH ASIA.)

Mosques elsewhere in the Islamic world adapted to indigenous traditions, with those in China partaking of various stylistic traits of Chinese temple architecture and those in Indonesia sometimes constructed of palm trunks and thatched roofs. In the twentieth century the new structural potential of steel, glass, and reinforced concrete has led in a variety of directions. In some countries the general trend has been toward the construction of monotonous concrete parodies of traditional buildings, but in other Islamic nations, notably the Arab lands, there have been noteworthy attempts to develop the inherent expressiveness of new materials while preserving a sense of the traditional nature of the mosque. Modern Islamic architecture is still struggling for its own identity; the true test of this identity will be the way its architects come to grips with the building of religious structures such as mosques, whose precedents include so many felicitous combinations of tradition coupled with daring innovation. *See* ART AND ARCHITECTURE, ISLAMIC; illustrations for MINARET.

Bibliography. J. Pederson and E. Diez, "Masdjīd," *EI;* K. A. C. Creswell, *Early Muslim Architecture* (1940); O. Grabar, *The Formation of Islamic Art* (1973); J. Dickie, "Allah and Eternity: Mosques, Madrasas and Tombs" in G. Michell, ed., *Architecture of the Islamic World* (1978).

W. DENNY

MOTT, JOHN RALEIGH (Ch; 1865-1955). American missionary and ecumenical leader, winner of the 1946 Nobel Peace Prize. Mott chaired the Student Volunteer Movement from 1888 to 1920; presided at the World Missionary Conference in Edinburgh (1910); and served as chairman of the International Missionary Council until 1942. He was one of the principal architects of the ECUMENICAL MOVEMENT. G. MILLER

MOUNT OF OLIVES. A hill east of JERUSALEM; site of various Christian sanctuaries: the traditional place where JESUS wept over Jerusalem (Church of Dominus Flevit); taught the LORD'S PRAYER (Basilica of the

Eleona); prayed in the Garden of GETHSEMANE (Church of All Nations or the Russian Church of Magdalene); ascended (Chapel of the ASCENSION), etc.

D. W. O'CONNOR

MUDRĀ mōō´ drä (B, H & Ja—Skt.; lit. "seal," "sign"). A symbolic gesture in dance, ritual, TANTRIC meditation, or iconography, especially gestures of the hand and fingers. In ritual and iconography the symbolic vocabulary is much smaller and more general in meaning; in dance and drama more extensive and specific.

Classical Indian dance requires extensive study in bodily gestures depicting different emotions, attitudes, objects, natural scenery, mythology, and actions. Medieval dance manuals classify hundreds of gestures whose meanings are complex and fully express the content of the text. Standardized gestures of characters, events, and even words make it possible for audiences to follow a story in mime, though different dance or drama traditions often use the same *mudrā* differently or altogether different *mudrās*.

Hindu and Buddhist iconography used stylized gestures to indicate an aspect, function, attribute, or well-known activity of a divinity (e.g., VISHNU), the BUDDHA, a BODHISATTVA, or a personified spiritual power. Ritual *mudrās* can be traced to Vedic times, when they were used to regulate stress, rhythm, and intonation in the chanting of the VEDAS. In current Hindu practice ritual officiants use *mudrās* to make offerings to deities (*see* PŪJĀ). *Mudrās* in tantric Hindu worship are believed to represent deities, to evoke them, to install them, or to repel evil forces. In tantric meditation devotees use *mudrās* to evoke a particular state of spiritual consciousness; by forming the *mudrā* with their own bodies they reinforce spiritual resolve and actualize the presence of divine power or enlightenment in themselves. In Japanese Buddhism the SHINGON school uses *mudrās* extensively. The term *mudrā* in Indian Tantrism has special esoteric meanings. In Hindu Tantra it means parched grain or kidney bean (thought to be an aphrodisiac food); in Buddhist Tantra it refers to the female adept who participates in the ritual meditation. *See* MANTRA.

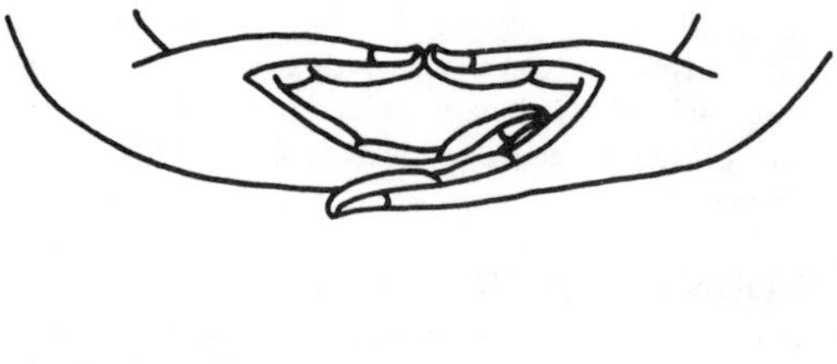

The *dhyāna* (meditation) *mudrā*

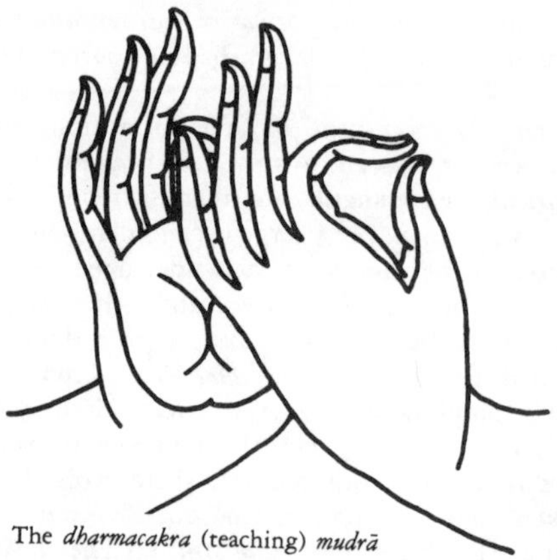

The *dharmacakra* (teaching) *mudrā*

Bibliography. J. Blofeld, *Tantric Mysticism of Tibet* (1970); E. D. Saunders, *Mudra, a Study of Symbolic Gesture* (1960); "Mudra" in B. Walker, *The Hindu World* (1968); K. Vatsyayan, *Classical Indian Dance in Literature and the Arts* (1968).

F. J. STRENG and C. R. KING

MUEZZIN myoo ĕz´ ən (I). *See* ADHĀN.

MUFTI mŭf´ tē (I—Arab.). In SUNNITE Islam a specialist in religious law (SHARIA) whose opinion is sought on interpretations of that law. He issues formal legal opinions on the basis of which a judge may decide a case or an individual may regulate his everyday affairs. The position of the grand mufti among the Sunnis is similar to that of the supreme AYATOLLAH among the SHI'ITES.

A. A. SACHEDINA

MUHAMMAD moo häm´ məd (I; *ca.* 570-632. Arab.; lit. "one praised"). Founder of ISLAM, born in MECCA into an impoverished clan of the dominant tribe, the QURAISH. The record of his life and prophetic activity is found in the QUR'ĀN and in various posthumous traditions, including the ḤADĪTH, which became authoritative for Islamic law. Muhammad's actions and sayings are the paradigm (SUNNA) for proper Muslim behavior. Muhammad is held to be the Seal of the Prophets, the last in the line of prophets which began with Adam. (*See* NABI.) His message, the Qur'ān, is regarded as ALLAH's final revelation to mankind.

1. Birth and early life. Little is known about Muhammad's birth and early life. Traditions place the year of his birth around 570, which is called the Year of the Elephant after the Ethiopian general Abraha's unsuccessful attempt to capture Mecca by an army equipped with a war elephant (Sura 105). In reality, that event must have taken place some time earlier, and it can be shown that the description of it in early Qur'ān commentary and in the first complete biography of Muhammad, the *Sīra* of IBN ISHĀQ, was meant to portray Mecca as the new Jerusalem by paralleling the event with Sennacherib's siege of JERUSALEM. The biographical traditions also depict other miracles at the time of Muhammad's birth, such as an annunciation, but these are late and are not necessary for Muslim belief. What is certain is that Muhammad was orphaned, his father, 'Abdullāh, having died while his mother, Āmina, was pregnant, and his mother shortly after his birth. His uncle, Abū Ṭālib, who is represented favorably in tradition, became his guardian. The *Sīra* reports that Muhammad was put out for fosterage among the bedouin tribe of the abna'a Sa'd ibn Bakr, and a tradition attributed to Muhammad has him claim that he was the most Arab of all because of his descent from the Quraish and his suckling among the abna'a Sa'd ibn Bakr. The story of the opening of Muhammad's breast and the weighing and cleansing of his heart is associated with this tradition and reflects later apologetic interpretations of Sura 94.

Sura 93 summarizes Muhammad's youth and the transition from poverty to prosperity and ease: "Did He not find you as an orphan and give you a home, and find you in error and rightly guide you, and find you impoverished and make you rich?" (Sura 93:6-8). This remembrance is presented in the Qur'ān as the basis for Muhammad's relationship to God and his fellow man, just as Sura 106 enjoins the Quraish to worship God for what he had given them. Part of Muhammad's material success can be attributed to his association at first commercially and then in marriage with the rich widow Khadīja. She was related to the Christian scholar Waraqa ibn Nawfal, but it is not clear whether she or her family provided any religious inspiration or instruction for Muhammad. She did, however, give him social standing and personal support during the initial crises of his religious experiences, and she was the mother of all his children except Ibrāhīm: three sons, who died in infancy (as did Ibrāhīm), and four daughters, Zaynab, Ruqayya, 'Umm Kulthūm, and Fāṭima. It was after his marriage to Khadīja that tradition credits Muhammad with a central role in the rebuilding of the Ka'ba.

Muhammad seems to have followed the customs of his contemporaries, and, if some Western analyses of Qur'ānic passages are to be relied on, he looked first to the religious traditions of his clan and tribe for answers to his spiritual quest. He seems not to have been alone in this search. Traditions tell of at least four other men who broke with polytheism and adopted a form of monotheism. In addition, the presence of a thriving Jewish community along with several Christian denominations actively engaged in missionary efforts in and around Arabia was bound to have an effect on the religious climate.

2. **First revelation and early mission.** Muhammad followed the custom of religious withdrawal and devotion for a month every year. This custom may have been influenced by Christian practices, but it is said to have been the practice of the Quraish before the rise of Islam. It was during one of these devotional retreats on Hira, a mountain near Mecca, that Muhammad had his first religious experience. Opinions differ about which Sura represents the first revelation, a minority giving Sura 74 that position, and the rest holding that Sura 96:1-5 is the first. In any event, the experience came on him suddenly and frightened him. He even contemplated suicide so as not to be thought a *kāhin,* an ecstatic seer, a charge made later by his detractors. But he was dissuaded by a vision of a figure generally identified as the Angel Gabriel, the bearer of God's revelations to Muhammad. The first of these revelations were generally in the form of inspiration (Waḥy) rather than visions. Sometimes Muhammad would wrap himself in a cloak (Sura 74), possibly an inducement for the reception of revelation, but he was not in control or able to predict when revelations would come to him. When they did come, Muhammad would undergo physical changes apparent to those around him, such as shaking and profuse sweating, even on cold days. This led his detractors to charge that he had fits or epilepsy, a charge which persisted among Western writers for many centuries.

The first messages of the Qur'ān emphasize Muhammad's relationship to God, what he received from God, God's goodness, and Muhammad's obligations for that goodness. Then, by extension, these messages were applied to the rest of the Quraish and, ultimately, to all Arabs. There is, however, no agreement about the order of the chapters and sections of the Qur'ān, and many arguments about some aspect of Muhammad's early spiritual life are based on arrangements of the pieces of the Qur'ān to fit the argument. There is general agreement that Muhammad's spiritual awareness began with the realization of his good fortune, partly through his participation in the Meccan trade and partly through his association with Khadīja. Allah is represented as being a good, giving God, who created all people (Sura 96), who controls all the universe (Sura 55), and who provides for all his creation (Sura 80). Human response to these actions of God should ideally be a sense of gratitude and humility, a recognition of the position of being a creature with respect to the creator and benefactor, but humans are usually ungrateful; each is *kāfir,* a term which came to mean "unbeliever" because of the denial of the obligations of Allah's munificence (Sura 96:6 ff.). Humans also have obligations to other people, God's other creatures. One should not oppress the weak, and should be generous with that which God has given (Sura 93:6-11; 92:5-11). Many see Muhammad's early experiences in this social message. There is more than just the responsibility of the individual. God is seen as having given wealth to the tribe of Quraish through their commercial activities, in return for which they are expected to give proper worship (Sura 106). Failure to show gratitude was to invite calamity in this world and the next: "Nay, but verily man is rebellious that he thinketh himself independent! Lo! unto thy Lord is the return" (Sura 96:6-8, Pickthall trans.). This was the return at the Day of Judgment, described in Sura 84 with images of heaven splitting, the earth being spread out, and the sinner being thrown into scorching fire. (*See* ESCHATOLOGY §3.) Muhammad believed he was sent to remind his fellow humans of God's gifts to them and their obligations (Sura 87:9-13).

These themes form the basis of the earliest message of Islam. Muhammad, the warner, is made aware of what he had received from God, and is told of his obligations to God and to his fellow man. These obligations apply to all Arabs who received God's blessing. Failure to heed the warnings would result in dire consequences on the Day of Judgment or even before. While it is not explicitly stated that Muhammad believed his early mission had universal applicability, there is nothing in the early Qur'ānic passages to prevent such an interpretation.

3. **Meccan reaction and Muhammad's response.** A careful reading of the Qur'ān and the traditions indicates that Muhammad enjoyed initial success in persuading people to follow his new message. There is almost universal agreement in the sources that Khadīja was the first to convert to Islam, probably along with her daughters. There is considerable disagreement, however, about who was the first male convert. SHI'ITES claim ALI IBN ABĪ ṬĀLIB. He was about nine and a member of Muhammad's greater household, so it is not an improbable claim. Others claim that the manumitted slave Zayd ibn Hāritha was first, while the standard SUNNITE position holds that ABŪ BAKR, Muhammad's successor, was first. At any rate, the first converts were for the most part not influential in Meccan society, and for a time Muhammad's preaching caused little concern. Possibly the Meccans thought that he was merely another mantic seer who would help them find lost sheep or camels and would settle disputes. As the monotheistic message of Islam became clearer, and Muhammad's stand against the old gods became better understood, the Meccans began to realize that Muhammad and Islam posed a threat to their commercial and religious ascendency in the HEJAZ. The persecutions that resulted were not severe, at least at first, but that seems to be because violent physical harm to Muhammad or his followers, except the poorest of them, would have provoked retaliation that could have erupted into civil war. At this time, for reasons that remain obscure, Muhammad sent a group of his followers to Abyssinia, where it is reported that the Negus, a Christian people, received them warmly. This event, later called a "little *hijra*," may have had economic as well as religious motives, but it seems to have had little impact on problems in Mecca. With the death of his two main supporters—his protector Abū Ṭālib, and his beloved wife Khadīja—Muhammad's position in Meccan society seems to have worsened. The Meccans reportedly attempted an economic boycott of Muhammad's clan, the Hāshimites (*see* HĀSHIM). Though not all the clan followed Muhammad's religion, they remained loyal to the clan ideal and stood by him, except for ABŪ LAHAB, who, along with his wife, is assigned to hell (JAHANNAM) for his actions (Sura 111). While the boycott failed to crush the clan, the situation was critical, for it was clear that Islam could not expand within the hostile Meccan atmosphere. So, Muhammad began to seek other places in Arabia in which to continue his mission.

4. **Muhammad's night journey and ascent to heaven.** Extra-Qur'ānic traditions commenting on Sura 17:1 describe a journey that Muhammad is supposed to have taken from Mecca to Jersualem, and from there through the seven heavens to the throne of God, a journey said to have taken, at most, one night. Early authorities disagree as to whether this was a purely spiritual journey or vision, or whether it was physical, but when it was reported to the new Muslim converts, some turned away in disbelief. Abū Bakr is represented as one of the few true believers, and received the epithet Witnesser of the Truth *(aṣ-Ṣiddīq)*. Later versions of the night journey and ascent stories show elements borrowed from Jewish and Christian tradition. The theme has become a favorite subject for popular stories and legends. (*See* MI'RĀJ.)

5. **The HIJRA.** Muhammad, after several unsuccessful negotiations with towns of the Meccan economic confederation, turned to members of the Arab tribes in the city of MEDINA, ancient Yathrib, who were attracted to him not only for his message but also for his skill as a mediator. During the negotiation period of 621-622, the main outlines of the so-called "Constitution of Medina" were drawn in which Muhammad and his followers became part of the body politic of the city and Muhammad became first among equals as the final arbiter of all disputes. This document assumes the autonomy of at least the two religious communities of the Muslims and the Jews and seems to anticipate later patterns of relationship between Muslims and PEOPLE OF THE BOOK.

By this time, most Meccan converts to Islam had migrated to Medina, a wise precaution in view of growing Meccan hostility. Muhammad and Abū Bakr were the last to leave, pursued by a party of Quraish intent on harming them, since they were then outside the protection of customary law. Muhammad arrived in Medina around September 22, 622, and he and his small band of followers were aided by an even smaller group of Medinans who had converted to Islam before the hijra or shortly thereafter. These and later Medinan converts to Islam were called "helpers" (ANṢĀR), while those who made the migration with Muhammad were the "emigrants" *(muhājirūn)*, a distinction which perpetuated the pre-Islamic North Arab–South Arab rivalry.

Arrayed against him in Medina were tribes of Jews and their Arab allies, who seem to have controlled the major sectors of the local economy. These tribes of Jews, tribes of mixed Jews and Arabs, and some almost exclusively Arab tribes ranged in attitude from actively hostile to generally supportive. All elements of the city had been openly fighting one another for some time, and it was Muhammad's task to weld them into one community.

6. **The establishment of the community at Medina.** To form the community of Islam (*see* UMMA) in Medina, Muhammad had to find a way to support his followers who were living on the charity of the helpers. For this reason and as part of his larger plans in the Hejaz, he adopted the course of raiding a Meccan trade caravan. The first raid took place in one of the months in which there was customary truce on religious grounds. The indignation that this caused even among his followers was allayed in part by the rich booty and finally by the revelation recorded in Sura 2:217. This raid led to the first major Muslim victory at Badr, where the Muslims met a large Meccan armed force rather than the expected rich caravan. A variety of factors, including Muhammad's generalship and Muslim cohesiveness, contributed to the victory, which had the effect of persuading more groups and individuals in the Hejaz to ally themselves with Muhammad and, in some instances, to convert to Islam. Because of the continued Muslim threat to their economic interests, the Meccans mounted an offensive in 624-25. The opposing forces met near a hill called Uḥud, and, in spite of early Muslim success, the Meccans succeeded in slightly wounding Muhammad and forcing the Muslims to flee and regroup on the nearby hill. While this has been termed the first Muslim defeat, the Meccans were unable to follow up their advantage. They made one final attack with an army which included not only those who owed Mecca military service but also a mercenary force of bedouin who were promised an easy victory and rich booty. They besieged the Muslims in Medina (whose exposed flank was fortified by a trench, from which the battle is called the Battle of the Trench), but were unable to prevail and were forced to withdraw. This marks the end of Meccan domination of the Hejaz, confirmed in January, 630, by the Muslim conquest of Mecca.

During this time, Muhammad also dealt directly with the dissident elements in Medina itself. Some groups were openly hostile to Muhammad and had aided the Meccans, while others had only half-heartedly converted to Islam. The main Jewish tribes which had aided Muhammad's enemies were expelled from the city, but a fair number of individual Jews were left. Muhammad's raid against the fortified Jewish city of Khaybar in 628 is significant, because the defeated inhabitants were allowed to remain on their land in payment of a capitulation tax of half their annual crops. This is a continuation of the principles found in the Constitution of Medina and forms, along with other similar incidents, a paradigm for Muslim treatment of subject minorities.

7. **The culmination of Muhammad's career.** By the time of the taking of Mecca in 630 and the cleansing of the Ka'ba of its hundreds of pagan idols, the basic tenets or PILLARS OF ISLAM had been formed. The one institution which had not been set forth was that of the annual pilgrimage (HAJJ), and in March of 632, Muhammad performed the reformed pilgrimage to the cleansed Ka'ba, setting the pattern for this rite for all Muslims. This was his last great act, for, much to the surprise of those who expected him to live until the Day of Judgment, Muhammad, without having provided for a temporal successor, died in early June, 632, in the company of his favorite wife, 'Ā'ISHA, the daughter of Abū Bakr, and was buried in her apartment.

8. **Western views of Muhammad.** Until modern times Western views of Muhammad have, with only rare exceptions, been hostile. The tendencies in the *Sīra* of Ibn Isḥāq which depict Muhammad as an isomorph of various prophets, including JESUS, have been seized upon by Western polemicists to make Muhammad into a deceiver, a heretic Christian priest, and even into the ANTICHRIST. This bias has been so pervasive that it is found in much of the material available in Western languages (see Daniel). Western writers have also criticized Muhammad for the large number of his wives. Recent scholarship is more balanced and appreciative of his life and work. *See also* FOUNDERS, RELIGIOUS.

Bibliography. N. Abbott, *Aishah, the Beloved of Muhammad* (1942); T. Andrae, *Der Ursprung des Islams* (1926) and *Mohammed* (1960); al-Azraqī, *K. Akhbār Makka* (1964); A. Baumstark, "Das Problem eines vorislamischen Christlich-kirchlichen Schrifttums in arabischer Sprache," *Islamica,* IV (1931), 562-75; R. Bell, *Origin of Islam in its Christian Environment* (1926); H. Birkeland, *Legend of the Opening of Muhammad's Breast* (1955); M. M. Bravmann, *Spiritual Background of Early Islam* (1972); N. Daniel, *Islam and the West* (1960); A. Geiger, *Was hat Mohamed aus dem Judenthume aufgenommen?* (1833); M. M. Hamadeh, *Muhammad the Prophet: A Selected Bibliography*, diss., U. Michigan (1965); J. Horovitz, "Earliest Biographies of the Prophet and their Authors," *Islamic Culture,* I (1927), 535-59; M. Ibn Isḥāq, *Life of Muhammad,* A. Guillaume, trans. (1955); A. Jeffrey, "The Quest for the Historical Muhammad," *Muslim World* (1926), 327-48; P. Jensen, "Das Leben Muhammads und die David-Sage," *Islam,* XII (1922), 84-97; R. Paret, *Mohammed und der Koran* (1956); G. Parrinder, *Jesus in the Qur'an* (1965); aṭ-Ṭabarī, *Ta'rīkh* (1879–98); W. M. Watt, *Muhammad at Mecca* (1953) and *Muhammad at Medina* (1956); al-Wāquidī, *K. al-Maghāzī,* M. Jones, ed. (1966); and for references to periodical literature see J. Pearson, *Index Islamicus* (1958-).

G. D. NEWBY

MUHAMMAD 'ABDŪH moo häm′ məd ab dōō (I; 1849-1905). Egyptian advocate of Islamic modernism. He lived all his life in Egypt until banished by the British in 1882 following an unsuccessful revolt against their colonial authority. He traveled, wrote, and taught abroad until allowed to return in 1889.

Muhammad 'Abdūh's early life was dedicated to traditional Qur'ānic studies and MYSTICISM, the impress of which never left him. But during the 1870s he was influenced by JAMĀL al-DĪN AFGHĀNĪ, who was then living in Cairo. While in exile in Paris, he and Jamāl al-Dīn edited a monthly journal. On his return to Cairo, he expressed his views through a monthly journal edited by his disciple, Muhammad Rashīd Riḍā.

The thought of Muhammad 'Abdūh displays a consistent balance. He was concerned not only with the liberation of Muslims from colonial rule but also with the purification of their religious beliefs. Yet he recognized that European rule had introduced healthy changes into Egyptian society, and he wanted to preserve these changes within a system that was at once rational and Islamic. For him, commitment to science and active participation in public life were consistent with Islamic ideals, and he waged an unrelenting battle against secular materialism and Muslim conservatism.

Muhammad 'Abdūh opposed the orthodox religious leaders, the 'ULAMĀ' and *fuqahā,* who in turn were bitterly resentful of his teaching and influence. In their view Islam consisted in adherence to the teachings of the four SUNNI schools of law (*see* SHARIA). Muhammad 'Abdūh argued for a sensitive exercise of individual judgment *(ijtihād)* in matters of law and also a reliance on IJMĀ', or community consensus, in determining legislative policy. Like IBN TAYMĪYYA, he also inveighed against saint worship, opposing the tomb cults which abound in Egypt (*see* WALĪ). Yet by simultaneously stressing the interior, ethical dimension of Muslim duties, he seemed to follow the mystical method of AL-GHAZZĀLĪ.

On balance, Muhammad 'Abdūh's dominant theological outlook was more rational than mystical. The MU'TAZILA, in his view, provided the guidelines by which the superiority of Islam over CHRISTIANITY could be reasserted and the honor of Egypt upheld against the tidal wave of European intellectual colonialism. His goal was to have original and genuine Islam, stripped of its secondary accretions, flourish again—as consistent with the pragmatic demands of Western technology as it had been with the intellectual precepts of Greek philosophy. *See* KALĀM.

Bibliography. "Muḥammad 'Abdūh," *SEI,* pp. 405-7; C. Adams, *Islam and Modernism in Egypt* (1933); J. Jomier, *Le Commentaire coranique du Manār* (1954); N. Safran, *Egypt in Search of Political Community* (1961); A. Hourani, *Arabic Thought in the Liberal Age, 1798-1938* (1962).

B. LAWRENCE

MUHAMMAD, ELIJAH (I; 1897-1975; born Elijah Poole). Leader of the Nation of Islam in the West from 1934, when the founder, W. D. Fard, disappeared, to 1975. Known as "Prophet" and "Messenger of Allah." Under him the movement gained national prominence and international recognition. (*See* BLACK RELIGIONS IN THE UNITED STATES §5.)

J. W. WATERS

MUHAMMAD, WALLACE D. (I). *See* BLACK RELIGIONS IN THE UNITED STATES §5.

MUJTAHID mūj tä hēd′ (I—Arab.). In SHI'ISM a scholar of religious law (SHARIA), who practices *ijtihād,* the issuance of independent rulings on legal or theological questions. These rulings are based on the four sources of sharia: QUR'ĀN, SUNNA, consensus (IJMĀ'), and reason. Any *mujtahid* can attract a following and can attain the title of AYATOLLAH.

A. A. SACHEDINA

MUKYŌKAI moo kyō′ kī (Ch—Jap.; lit. "nonchurch" [*mu* "nothing," *kyōkai* "church"]). A movement initiated by the Japanese independent evangelist Kanzo UCHIMURA (1861–1930). Suggested translations include "nonecclesiastical church movement," "anticlerical church" and "churchless Christianity."

Mukyōkai must be seen in the context of Japanese church history. After the coming of the Jesuits in the sixteenth century there was not time for the church as an organizational and hierarchical organism to develop before the nation was closed and Christianity banned in the early seventeenth century. Nineteenth century Protestant missionaries, mainly from America, did not always share the European heritage of church organization. Japanese Christianity is thus relatively unconcerned about the historic tradition of the ecclesiastical church.

The movement began with the personal Christian experience of its founder. Uchimura first encountered Christianity, not in the church, but at Agricultural College in Sapporo. There he came under the influence of William S. Clark, president of Massachusetts Agricultural College, who was visiting Japan by invitation of the government. From the day he signed the "Covenant of Believers in Jesus" prepared by Clark (1877) he was dedicated to proclaiming the gospel independently of the existing church. He formed prayer and Bible study groups throughout Japan, all of which were disbanded in accordance with his will when he died. Uchimura nurtured a number of influential evangelists in his style, two of whom became president of Tokyo University.

Uchimura described his movement as "a church for those who have no church." The prefix "non" did not mean to "reduce to nothing" or "ignore," but rather represented the movement of Christianity outside the institutional church to reach those who have no money, parents, or home. In his attacks on institutionalism he felt he was in the tradition of LUTHER and KIERKEGAARD.

There is a remarkable balance between faith and social concern in the Mukyōkai tradition. Uchimura himself set the example when he made the first public demonstration of Christian conscience by refusing to bow on receiving the Imperial Rescript on Education in 1891. His outspoken anti-war sentiments were continued by his disciple, Yanaihara, who openly opposed Japan's policy through World War II.

Bibliography. Yoshitaka Kumano, *Nihon Kristokyō Shingaku Shisō Shi* [History of Christian Theological Thought in Japan] (1968), pp. 261–97.

K. KOYAMA

MULLAH mŭl lä´ (I—Arab.). Among the SHI'ITES a scholar of the religious law (SHARIA). He performs minor religious functions, such as leading prayer in the smaller mosques, teaching the QUR'ĀN, preaching the faith, and recounting the *ta'ziya* (stories of the IMAMS). A. A. SACHEDINA

MURUKAN̲ moo roo gŭn (H). TAMIL name for the god known generally throughout Hindu India as SHIVA's son, variously named Subrahmaṇya, SKANDA, or KĀRTTIKEYA. Murukan̲ is first seen, in the Tamil context, in the Caṅkam literature of the first century A.D. Thereafter he persists through several cultural and historical changes until the present, when he remains perhaps the most popular deity of Tamil India, fully embodying ŚAIVISM's vision of divinity.

In early Tamil civilization, Murukan̲ was understood to be the lord of hills, a hunter *par excellence,* possessor of young women, enemy of *cūr* (the malevolent force of the hills), carrier of the lance, and lord of peacock, rooster, and elephant. By the fifth century, as reflected in such texts as the *Paripāṭal* and *Tirumurakārrupaṭai,* the early Southern Murukan̲ had been fused with Skanda, the warrior god of Northern dynasties, and epic mythology was ascribed to him. By the ninth century separate temples such as the one at Laṭankovil had been dedicated to him. By the tenth century and thereafter, his iconography proliferated in the South, depicting him as Ṣaṇmukham ("Lord of Six Faces"), Subrahmaṇya, Brahmaśāstā ("Teacher of Brahmā"), and other manifestations.

After the Chōḻa period (twelfth century) when ŚAIVA SIDDHĀNTA had become systematized as a mature Southern philosophical system, Murukan̲ came to be seen as the full expression of the divine absolute Shiva, even while his concrete manifestations and exploits in Madras State (South India) are celebrated. The poetry of Aruṇakirinātar in the fourteenth or early fifteenth century and of Kumarakurapara in the seventeenth illustrates the resurgent wave of BHAKTI literature addressed to Murukan̲ as the god who combines abstract and concrete, SANSKRIT and Tamil, classical and popular motifs. Tamil literature especially extols his identification with the Tamil country and language.

Since the 1860s worship of Murukan̲ has been increasing steadily in Tamil India, and today his major temples are among the wealthiest in South India. In all, six centers are said to be sacred to him, though over two hundred temples are dedicated to him. The ritual life observed in temples to Murukan̲ is totally Śaivite, though various forms of folk worship—from "possession" to dancing with the *kavaṭi* (arches decked with peacock feathers)—are permitted at his pilgrimage centers. Tamilians worship Murukan̲ in such countries as Sri Lanka and Malaysia, while in Madras State the god remains a symbol of Tamilian self-consciousness, their long cultural history, and the contemporary concern for egalitarianism and unity in diversity.

Bibliography. F. W. Clothey, *The Many Faces of Murukan̲: The History and Meaning of a South Indian God* (1978).
F. W. CLOTHEY

MUSAR MOVEMENT mōō sär´ (Ju). Jewish ethical movement originating in nineteenth century Lithuania as a response to the secularizing effects of the Enlightenment. Its founder, Rabbi Israel Lipkin Salanter (1810-83), initially worked to promote the study of ethical texts among adults. To this end he organized the *Hevrah Musar* (Moral Society) of Vilna and the *Musar Stuebel* (Moral Conventicle) of Kovno. Eventually he directed his efforts to educating the young.

The movement's purpose was to instill a profound sense of ethical responsibility by subverting the students' *yetzer ha-ra* ("evil inclination") in service to God. Through meditation, self-criticism, and self-analysis the student would intimately feel the inherent danger in both immoral activity and immoral impulse. This approach was predicated on the belief that learning consists of two stages, one purely intellectual and the second marked by emotional commitment. In order for thought to be transformed into conviction the student would have to exert continual self-control.

After Salanter's death the movement split into two schools, the now predominant "Slobodka-type" and the more extreme "Nowardak-type." The Musar movement survives in the Talmudic academies in the U.S. and Israel.

Bibliography. L. Ginzberg, *Understanding Rabbinic Judaism* (1974), pp. 355-82.
L. FAGEN

MUSIC, IN CHRISTIANITY. Christianity, like all religions, is not only a way of life but a quest for communion with the supernatural. Therefore music, of all the arts the one nearest the human religious impulse, was admitted early to Christian activity because it provided a language for the deepest expressions of the soul.

In its encounter with the world, Christianity has assimilated the culture of its converts, producing a syncretism which has not only enriched the development of music as art but has enhanced its effectiveness as a valid religious expression. In periods when Christianity was hospitable to the services of creative musicians, music of a high order flourished, because these church musicians, with few exceptions, were conversant with secular music, able to compose and perform it, and capable of adapting it to Christian use.

On the other hand, there has existed within Christianity the suspicion that music is a sensuous art that may abuse its function as an instrument of the faith. This has led to periodic official attempts to curb music and sometimes to reject it altogether. Furthermore, at various times the professional music of Christianity has been bypassed by the common people in favor of simplified folk expression.

1. **The Middle Ages.** *a) Fine art music.* Music as a product of high artistry is illustrated by the elaborate chanting of the psalms which developed in medieval Christianity out of ancient biblical practice (*see* MUSIC, IN JUDAISM). Antiphonal singing produced short refrains which were sung between psalm verses. Not only did these antiphons give wide scope to musical inventiveness, but certain ALLELUIA responses furnished opportunity for vocal improvisation. This embellishment of the LITURGY brought about the development of what is now known as GREGORIAN CHANT. As time went on this repertory was further expanded by musical settings for prose accretions to the liturgy, including those of religious drama. One specialized type of improvisatory accretion connected with the "Alleluia" was the "sequence," a form tremendously popular throughout the Middle Ages (*see* DIES IRAE). Liturgical drama itself, starting as the recitation in dialogue of the biblical stories of EASTER and CHRISTMAS, was also the end product of a long musical development.

The evolution of the official music of Christianity in the West came about through the application of the principle known as troping. Tropes were both literary and musical additions to the established chant literature for the two principal divisions of the Christian liturgy: the MASS and the DIVINE OFFICES. Applied lineally, the troping principle led to the invention of a vast corpus of freely composed texts, sung in unison plainsong.

Applied laterally, troping led to polyphonic music. Polyphony's most primitive type—*organum*—consisted of parallel layers of sound placed below the principal melody at certain theologically sanctioned musical intervals—fourths, fifths, and octaves. These polyphonic settings became more and more intricate as they yielded to the creative energies of church composers. Three, four, and more simultaneous melodies were added above the original chant, each moving with ever greater rhythmic and harmonic freedom. Since this music required considerable skill in performance, it led to the training of specialist groups of clergy musicians.

An early culminating point for this professional style of Christian music came in the elaborate settings of Mass Propers (parts that varied with the feast days) in three and four-part *organum* produced by members of the Parisian School of Notre Dame. The high artistry of its chief representatives, Leonin and Perotin the Great (twelfth century), was continued in colorful motets by anonymous thirteenth century composers. The typical late medieval motet was a vocal composition based on a Gregorian melody to which were added love songs, street cries, and popular hymns in a rhythmically regulated musical structure, thus symbolizing a free and easy mixing of the sacred and secular elements of life.

The medieval motet is a clear example of that syncretism which Christianity often feared and periodically sought to curb. In 1325 Pope John XXII denounced this new secular style and attacked the use of such extreme devices as hocketing—the rapid alternation of two or more voices, one resting while another sounds. But this decree had little effect on the natural course of musical development. Christianity was slowly losing its control over music's progress in the fourteenth century; novel trends *(Ars Nova)* were moving inexorably toward a worldly art which came into full flower with the Renaissance.

b) Folk art music. Alongside aristocratic art music a simpler kind of music existed among the lower classes of medieval society. In the earliest centuries most Christian music had been congregational. But with the legitimizing of the Christian religion and the building of great edifices of worship, emphasis shifted to priestly music *(see above)* rather than the modest singing of the congregations. In the fourth century music was taken completely away from the laity except in places where church control was not absolute.

As a consequence, the common people, denied anything beyond a minimal singing role in worship, created their own religious song outside of church, to a large extent under the inspiration of twelfth century troubadours and minnesingers. Mediated through the influence of FRANCIS OF ASSISI, simple hymns of praise and devotion *(laude)* sprang up among the Italian people. Penitential fraternities invented songs *(Geisslerlieder* in Germany) to be sung during their flagellations and processionals *(see* FLAGELLANTS). In Spain a similar type of song *(cantigas)* gave expression to deep religious emotions, particularly those aroused in venerating the Virgin MARY. Carol singing along with dance arose in England as a joyous expression of faith. And in the East there developed certain semi-religious acclamations used in processionals as well as spiritual folk song and ritual dance in the practice of the ETHIOPIC and COPTIC CHURCHES. In all these instances, Christianity, sooner or later recognizing the potential of such folkish art for indoctrination, infiltrated it with church teachings.

In both art music and folk music a nonapologetic reciprocation of the religious and nonreligious was evident, since a sacred-secular dichotomy was not recognized in the music of Western Christianity until the Council of TRENT.

2. **Renaissance and Reformation.** In the fourteenth century texts for musical settings of the Mass shifted from Proper to Ordinary (the unchangeable parts). Guillaume de Machaut (1300-1377) summarized this transition in his Mass, the first known complete polyphonic treatment of the Ordinary by a single composer. Machaut, however, spent most of his creative energy in the production of courtly *chansons,* and there was little distinction between his ecclesiastical and nonecclesiastical styles.

a) Fine art music. Early in the fifteenth century sacred music in the fields of Mass and motet experienced a resurgence. No longer a microcosm of the cultural life of the time, the motet at the hands of

John Dunstable (*ca.* 1370-1453) and Guillaume Dufay (*ca.* 1400-1474) exhibited a new churchliness. The motet became the vehicle for some of the most advanced musical techniques of the day and the *cantus firmus* Mass began its long line of development. The works of Josquin des Pres (*ca.* 1450-1521) mark an early Renaissance culmination of contrapuntal art. Josquin, also the greatest *chanson* composer of the time, incorporated in his songs motet-like characteristics, such as pervasive imitation. Music in general was still of one style regardless of its intended use.

Building on the creative work of numerous master composers, including Adrian Willaert (*ca.* 1490-1562) and Heinrich Isaac (*ca.* 1450-1517), this aristocractic art music reached its climax with the "golden age" of Roman Catholic religious music in the works of Orlando di Lasso (1532-94) and Pier Luigi Palestrina (*ca.* 1525-94). In brilliant contrast to this exalted *a cappella* style centering in ROME were the magnificent antiphonal works in twelve or more parts with dazzling instrumental accompaniment, produced by Giovanni Gabrieli (*ca.* 1555-1612) for St. Mark's Cathedral in Venice.

In the late sixteenth century there was a concern to purify the official music of Christianity from Renaissance associations that were considered secular and therefore corrupting. This concern guided the pronouncements of the Council of Trent, which criticized poor and irreverent singing in divine service, extravagant use of instruments, and senseless fragmentation of liturgical texts to serve musical ends. The accumulated repertoire of tropes and sequences was largely abolished and music was commissioned according to certain approved principles. Thus the energies of church musicians were harnessed to the ideals and purposes of the CATHOLIC REFORMATION. But this artistically excellent and liturgically controlled music made little provision for the participation of the people.

b) Folk art music. But the people could not be denied, and the pervasive presence of sacred folk song was felt in many regions. In Bohemia, for example, from the fourteenth century onward, sacred song based on Christian chant and secular folk music was at the center of the spontaneous expression of a religious people. In Germany, *Leisen*—hymns of penitence deriving from KYRIE ELEISON—and other carol-like songs were sung by the people at work and worship.

In some respects the PROTESTANT REFORMATION was a surfacing of a great underground movement of popular religious song. LUTHER and CALVIN both sought to magnify the singing of common folk. Luther, building on a lively German singing tradition, gave them their own hymns in the vernacular and encouraged congregational singing. The most common troubadour and minnesinger song form (AAB) of the Middle Ages became the favorite structure of early Lutheran chorales.

The followers of Calvin allowed only the use of scriptural psalms set to plain unaccompanied tunes sung in unison. For generations the singing of English-speaking Christians was dominated by these sturdy metrical psalm tunes, collections of which were the only music books found in many a church and home in seventeenth century England, Scotland, and America (*see* BAY PSALM BOOK).

c) Fine art music (Baroque era). The Reformation also produced distinctive kinds of professional art music. Although Luther's theological break with Rome was complete, he loved its musical legacy. Revolutionary developments in opera, oratorio, and cantata in seventeenth century Italy were readily accepted and assimilated by Protestant composers in Lutheran lands. While Italians like Claudio Monteverdi (1597-1643), Giocomo Carissimi (1605-74), Alessandro Scarlatti (1660-1725), and Antonio Vivaldi (1669-1741) were applying the new recitative and concerted styles developed in the operatic and instrumental fields to the purposes of a revived Roman Christianity, Protestant composers like Heinrich Schütz (1585-1672), Samuel Scheidt (1587-1654), Johann Pachelbel (1653-1706), and Dietrich Buxtehude (1637-1707) were amalgamating these Italianate elements with the older counterpoint and the chorale in choral and instrumental works.

This was also the period of the rise and growth of liturgical organ music. Used originally where there was no choir capable of singing polyphony, the organ came to a position of prominence, especially in Germany, accompanying singing as well as alternating with it and assuming an independent role in partitas, chorale-preludes, toccatas, and fugues.

The culmination of these developments was the consummate work of Johann Sebastian Bach (1685-1750). This master's chorale cantatas and passion oratorios represent the final rapprochement between the dramatic vocal and concertato styles of Italy and the typically Lutheran expression in the chorale. Bach's organ works are the towering achievement in the literature for that instrument.

In England sophisticated art music flourished in the cathedral tradition which attracted the services of the best composers in the Renaissance and Reformation periods. The chief liturgical forms were services and anthems—musical counterparts of the Catholic motets. Major composers in these forms in the Elizabethan Renaissance period were Thomas Tallis (1501-85), William Byrd (1543-1623), and Orlando Gibbons (1583-1625). After a musical interruption during the PURITAN Commonwealth, a high peak of professional musical art was reached in the cantatas, odes, and anthems of England's greatest composer, Henry Purcell (1659-95). This was music with graceful melody and colorful instrumental accompaniment requiring virtuoso techniques in the expression of dramatic values.

After Purcell, the best in sacred, though nonliturgical, music in England is represented in the oratorios of G. F. Handel (1685-1759). Handel's expansive biblical oratorios—sacred counterparts of opera with expressive arias, dramatic recitatives, and grandiose choruses but without staging, costuming, or action—were massive folk dramas of Christian significance expressed in music that summarized with incredible richness all the achievements of the Baroque age.

3. **The modern era.** *a) Fine art music.* The tradition of highly sophisticated religious expression in music continued throughout the nineteenth and twentieth centuries but at a lesser pace. Though Christianity no longer demanded the exclusive service of outstanding composers, occasionally they have applied their best creative efforts to produce isolated masterworks. Among these are Mozart's *Requiem* (1791), Haydn's *The Creation* (1797), Beethoven's *Missa Solemnis* (1823), Mendelssohn's *Elijah* (1846), Horatio Parker's *Hora Novissima* (1893), Elgar's *The Dream of Gerontius* (1900), Honegger's *Le Roi David* (1923), Stravinsky's *Symphony of Psalms* (1930) and *Mass* (1948), Britten's *War Requiem* (1961), and sacred works by America's Charles Ives, Roger Sessions, and Randall Thompson, Britain's Ralph Vaughan Williams, France's Messiaen, and Poland's Kryzystof Penderecki.

These works represent Christianity's affirmation of the art of music—a divine gift allowed to follow its own laws of logical development to achieve its most elaborate means of communication, but that failed to meet the religious and cultural needs of other segments of Christian society.

b) Folk art music. At times of revival, Christians often turned to popular, more or less amateur, music for the expression of exuberant religious feelings. Such was the case in eighteenth century England with the Wesleyan revival (*see* John Wesley), which thrived on the enthusiastic singing of the evangelical hymns of Charles Wesley, set to attractive popular tunes of that day.

In early nineteenth century America, in the white heat of campmeeting revivals (*see* Revivalism), people on the Western frontier used primitive folk hymns and campmeeting spirituals to express their ecstatic feelings. These spontaneous songs, later gathered into Southern collections of both texts and tunes (*see* Sacred Harp), were the chief antecedents of the Gospel Song.

In rural America these easy and catchy gospel songs became the principal musical fare of great masses of people and served as the chief musical vehicle for evangelization. The gospel song was made popular both in the U.S. and Britain through the evangelistic tours of Dwight L. Moody and his musical collaborators. In the present century this popular song, assimilating ragtime and jazz influences, moved into urban revival settings and thus influenced the vogue of contemporary "gospel," "rock," "folk," "country and western," and other varieties of subculture songs of strong appeal.

Wherever Christianity has spread, it has called forth responses of ethnic musical expression. The nineteenth century musical result from the impact of Christianity on American Black culture is the Negro spiritual. (*See* Black Religions in the U.S. §3.) In the Far East hymns and songs have been couched in melodic and rhythmic idioms typical of Oriental cultures, and the same has been true in Africa, Latin America, and other parts of the world.

At one time, musical worship forms and practices in the traditionally missionary-receiving countries tended to reflect the forms and practices of the sending countries. More recently musical traffic has become two-way, and the musical worship of Western Christians is being influenced by elements from basically non-Christian cultures. Examples of this interchange are the experimental use of non-Western instruments and the revival of ritual folk Dance in Western churches.

Bibliography. Works dealing with music generally as a part of thought and culture: P. H. Lang, *Music in Western Civilization* (1941); J. Portnoy, *Music in the Life of Man* (1963). Sources for aspects of music in Christian churches: F. Blume, *Protestant Church Music* (1974); K. G. Fellerer, *The History of Catholic Church Music* (1961); H. T. McElrath, "Music in the History of the Church," *Review and Expositor* LXIX/2 (1972), 141-59; C. Schalk, ed., *Key Words in Church Music* (1978), pp. 87-156.

H. T. McElrath

MUSIC, IN JUDAISM. 1. In the Bible. From Israel's earliest beginnings, music played a significant role in the life of the people. Numerous scriptural examples attest that in biblical times music expressed sadness and happiness, fear and hope, therapy and magic, and praise of God. Up to the reign of Saul (*ca.* 1000 B.C.) music was a folk expression performed by nonprofessionals, especially women. Beginning with David (*ca.* 1000-961 B.C.), professional musicians appeared on the scene.

During the period of the First Temple ("Temple of Solomon," *ca.* 957-587 B.C.) music moved from the realm of folk to art music. Professional musicians, male Levites only, rendered vocal and instrumental music as accompaniment to animal sacrifice. At the reinstitution of the temple service during Hezekiah's reign (715-687), sacrifice was offered to the accompaniment of cymbals, psalteries, harps, trumpets and singing (II Chr. 29: 1, 25-30). The singers in this First Temple were highly skilled and well versed in song. (I Chr. 25:7).

In the time of the Second Temple (*ca.* 516 B.C.–A.D. 70), according to the Mishnah, Levitical singing was important as accompaniment to sacrifice and in chanting the daily psalms. The special training of a Levitical singer took five years, from ages twenty-five to thirty.

2. **In the synagogue.** The eminent position of music in the temple came to an abrupt end with Rome's destruction of Jerusalem in A.D. 70. Instrumental music was banned as a token of mourning. Only the Shofar remained in the New Year liturgy. The Synagogue, already an institution, emerged as the dominant locale for Jewish religious expression.

Prayer and study replaced sacrifice in providing atonement and grace. Lay leadeship replaced priestly and Levitical roles.

a) The ban on instrumental music. Even before the destruction of the temple, the rabbis favored vocal over instrumental music. Each instrument as well as each melody was thought to have its own "ethos," that is, its own inherent quality which might stimulate a corresponding quality in the listener. The apostasy of Elisha ben Abuyah is attributed to his whistling of Greek melodies (Ḥagigah 15b). The ban on instrumental music was relaxed somewhat in later TALMUDIC times for weddings; nevertheless, the ban held firm on SABBATHS and festivals.

b) The vocal tradition. Prayers, the Bible, especially psalms, and study texts comprised the synagogue liturgy. Vocal chant became its primary means of expression. Merely to read scripture without melody was considered a diminution of God (Megillah 32a). Thus developed the cantillation of scripture, one of the primary sources of Jewish musical tradition.

c) The force of tradition. Immediately following the destruction of the Second Temple, the rabbis attempted to preserve the temple ritual, omitting the sacrifical cult. Tradition within the synagogue and the values of Jewish life kept pace with changing environmental conditions. Any tradition generally accepted by the people became binding upon all. R. Jacob Mölin (Maharil), a fifteenth century CANTOR and important authority on HALAKAH, ruled that no local custom, not even a melody, should be changed.

d) The growth and establishment of musical tradition. The binding quality of halakhic authority affected the development of liturgical musical tradition. Thus the *Missinai* tunes, such as KOL NIDRE and *Alenu* of the High Holy Days (ROSH HA-SHANAH, YOM KIPPUR), became permanently identified with the occasions on which they were chanted. As each festival had its unique liturgy, each liturgy had its unique music. As the *Missinai* tunes, so too modal chanting *(Nusaḥ)* identified specific sacred occasions. During this lengthy period (from A.D. 70 to the mid-eighteenth century) prayers and their special chants became fixed within the framework of Jewish tradition.

3. **The modern period.** Three radical changes occurred in the synagogue at opposite ends of the denominational spectrum. In the REFORM synagogue both instrumental music and women's voices were instituted for sabbath and festival worship. Among the HASIDIM the melody assumed a power equal to that of the liturgy itself.

a) Reform. As a direct result of the Enlightenment and the Emancipation, Reform abrogated the halakah. The ban on instrumental music during sabbath and festival worship was lifted. The introduction of the organ necessitated professional musical functionaries, elevated the quality of congregational hymns, and produced a significant literature of art music for the synagogue.

As early as 1810, mixed choirs appeared. Though discouraged by the ORTHODOX synagogue, all Reform and CONSERVATIVE congregations employ mixed choruses today. Recently, Reform has opened the cantorate to women, another first in Jewish history, and agitation within the Conservative movement to move in this direction is occurring. Only the Orthodox, who still maintain separate pews for men and women, continue to exclude women from the pulpit. Among the reasons for this is the Talmudic dictum that "the voice of a woman may lead to licentiousness" (Berakhot 24a).

b) The Hasidic innovation. The Hasidic leaders (zaddikim), who followed in the tradition of the mystics, believed music to be the best medium for attaining SALVATION. The ZADDIK used music to purify the soul, heal the sick, and even perform miracles. It was believed the zaddikim had special access to the heavenly realm, which was more attainable through song than with prayer. Eventually the Hasidim developed a fascinating genre of wordless melodies whose notes alone were sufficient to move God himself.

c) The musical tradition today. Those forces which have secured a place for music within the tradition have also put limitations on that music. The efficacy of the liturgical text and the primacy of the worshiper have remained preeminent. This has limited the development of art music and the role of the professional musician. On those occasions when sophisticated art music did appear in the synagogue, it enjoyed only brief popularity. This was true of the outstanding madrigals of Salomone Rossi, which were published in Venice in 1622, as well as the very high caliber of twentieth century music of such eminent composers as Ernest Bloch, Darius Milhaud, Isadore Freed, and Joseph Achron.

In the Orthodox synagogue traditional chant and congregational melodies dominate sabbath and festival services even where cantors officiate. Only on the High Holy Days is the rendition of the liturgy embellished by the addition of a professional male choir. Likewise, in the Conservative ritual, despite a greater prevalence of cantors, mixed choirs, and organs, congregational participation remains foremost. Even Reform, which continues to remain the predominant exponent of sophisticated liturgical music, is experiencing a revival of congregational participation.

The music of modern Israel has also had a marked influence on all three rituals. The proliferation of popular Israeli melodies set to liturgical texts has penetrated the services of Orthodox, Conservative, and Reform, and has thus added a measure of commonality to Jewish worship that crosses denominational lines.

Bibliography. E. Werner, "Music," *IDB* (1962), *From Generation to Generation* (1962), *The Sacred Bridge* (1959), and *A Voice Still Heard* (1976); A. Z. Idelsohn, *Jewish Music* (1929); H.

Avenary, *The Ashkenazi Tradition of Biblical Chant between 1500 and 1900* (1978); "The Concept of Mode in European Synagogue Chant," *Yuval* II (1971), 11-21; L. Jacobs, *Hasidic Prayer* (1973), pp.67-69; "The Hasidic Dance—Niggun," *Yuval* 1, III (1974), 136-265; H. J. Zimmels, *Ashkenazim and Sephardim* (1958); A. Sendry, *The Music of the Jews in the Diaspora* (1970); "Music," *EJ*, XII (1972). M. ROTH

MUSLIM moos′ lĭm (I—Arab; lit. "one who surrenders"). An adherent of Islam; one who accepts MUHAMMAD as God's prophet and the QUR'ĀN as God's word. Such a believer will pattern all of his or her life on the guidelines elaborated in the SHARIA and upheld by other Muslims. B. LAWRENCE

MUSLIM IBN al-ḤAJJĀJ moos′ lĭm ĭb′ ən äl häj′ jäj (I—Arab.; 817-875). Author of *al-Jāmi'al-Ṣaḥīḥ* ("The Authentic Collection"), which, with the like-named work of BUKHĀRĪ, is renowned in Islam as the most authoritative source of reliable ḤADĪTH. Ranked by some Muslims even over Bukhārī's collection, Muslim's work is in fact superior in its attention to details of *isnād* and careful arrangement of material under the topical headings. Known for knowledge of FIQH as well as *ḥadīth,* Muslim, like Bukhārī, traveled widely in search of learning. W. A. GRAHAM

MU'TAZILA moo ə tĕ′ zĭ lə (I—Arab.; lit. "standing aloof, withdrawal"). The celebrated "rationalist" school of early Islamic theology (KALĀM), whose name may have arisen from a neutral position taken by its antecedents on the question of the status of the Muslim who commits a grave sin. The advocates preferred to call themselves the "People of [the Divine] Justice and Unity." The origins of the movement are obscure, but by the mid-ninth century A.D. its characteristic principles had been worked into a coherent philosophical and political theology which combined Greek logical and metaphysical conceptions with the Qur'ānic revelation, ideally granting them equal status while in practice favoring reason, at least implicitly. Crucial to the Mu'tazilite notion of a just God were human freedom and responsibility. So insistent was the emphasis upon God's unity that even the QUR'ĀN, his Speech, was considered to be created in time so as not to suggest division in the godhead (cf. LOGOS). Far from being "freethinkers," the Mu'tazilites were earnest, at times even puritanical, defenders of Islam from both its external and internal enemies. An inquisition was instituted in Baghdad when the school was for a time in a dominant position under its champion, the 'ABBĀSID CALIPH al-Ma'mūn (A.D. 813-33). But unlike the orthodox SUNNI *kalām* which was destined to replace it, Mu'tazilism also ventured into highly speculative issues with an intellectual rigor—and apparent delight—which would later be condemned as heresy. ASH'ARĪ (d. 935) was influential in stemming the influence in Sunni Islam of this school, although he had originally distinguished himself in it. The SHI'ITES have continued to cultivate Mu'tazilite principles in theological reflection. Al-Zamakhsharī (d. 1144) filled his celebrated Qur'ān commentary with Mu'tazilite interpretations, which Sunni students are warned to resist while absorbing the uniquely valuable philological discussions.

Bibliography. The classic contemporary survey is Ash'arī, *Maqālāt al-Islāmiyyīn;* the most accessible brief treatment is H. S. Nyberg, *SEI,* pp. 421-27; W. M. Watt's *The Formative Period of Islamic Thought* (1973) puts the subject in full perspective; J. R. T. M. Peters' *God's Created Speech* (1976) contains an extensive bibliography. F. M. DENNY

MYSTICISM. Mysticism has been characterized in a variety of ways: an apprehension of an ultimate nonsensuous unity in all things, a direct apperception of deity, the art of union with reality, an immediate contact or union of the self with a larger-than-self. Common characteristics of mystical experience include: (1) a direct, unmediated experience of (2) a reality or dimension of reality not ordinarily perceived, and (3) a cognitive awareness by the experiencer of the profundity of this experience and its consequences for his or her life. Various stages have been ascribed to the mystic's experience, such as the fivefold classification of awakening, purgation, surrender, illumination, and union. Another follows the classical tripartite structure of initiation: preparation, testing/illumination, return. The latter points out that mystical experience does not exhaust the meaning of mysticism. The mystic life in its personal and social dimensions also constitutes an essential aspect of what is meant by mysticism.

Mysticism has been studied by a variety of scholars including philosophers, historians, psychologists, sociologists, and anthropologists. Philosophers analyze mystical language and ontology; historians study the impact of mystics on religious institutions and the development of particular mystical traditions; psychologists explore mystical states of consciousness; sociologists correlate mystical religions with particular kinds of behavior; anthropologists investigate mystical aspects of primitive religions, e.g. SHAMANISM.

Mysticism is commonly associated with religion or religious traditions. Consequently, reference to Christian, Hindu, Jewish, Buddhist or Muslim mystics is meant to distinguish a special class or group of Christians, etc. from others. These groups not infrequently become formally organized within a religious tradition such as the SUFIS in ISLAM, ecstatic devotional sects in HINDUISM, or monastic orders in CHRISTIANITY, like the CARTHUSIANS. Mystics, however, are not confined to either the historic or the primitive religions. For example, many noteworthy modern figures such as Aldous Huxley and Walt Whitman may be considered mystics even though they are not self-consciously identified with a particular religious tradition. Thus, although religion in a formal sense and mysticism are closely related, they are not necessarily to be identified with each other.

1. **Mysticism and religion.** *a) Mysticism as a fundamental criterion to distinguish religious traditions.* Various scholars have claimed that some religious traditions are inherently mystical while others are not, or have used the term in a classificatory manner. Max Weber, for instance, interpreted the BUDDHA'S teachings about NIRVANA and the pursuit of that goal by a celibate monastic order as an "otherworldly mysticism." In general there has been a tendency to distinguish "Eastern religions" as fundamentally mystical and Western religions as basically nonmystical. Stace, for example, finds Buddhism to be inherently mystical because it is based on the enlightenment experience of the Buddha, while in Christianity the emphasis on belief rather than experience tends to deemphasize mysticism. Zaehner takes Hinduism to be more mystical than Christianity or Islam on the grounds that it is not rooted in a belief in a transcendent God and does not have a strong tradition of dogmatic theology. Because of the multivalent nature of all religious traditions, however, the effort to fashion mysticism as a major criterion to distinguish one religion from another seems doomed to the frustration of endless qualification.

b) Types of mysticism within a particular religious tradition. Various types arise from the interaction of the cultural-historical setting, normative religious teachings, and a particular mystical personage. Some students of mysticism have sought to describe different types of Indian religious mysticism, for instance, as sacrificial, UPANIṢADIC, Yogic, Buddhistic, and devotional (BHAKTI). Others have analyzed Islamic mysticism using the categories of ascetics, ecstatics, antinomians, poets, and DERVISHES. The attempt to understand mysticism in its plural forms within different religious traditions provides a more adequate perspective from which to investigate the relationship between religion and mysticism, in particular because it takes historico-cultural dimensions seriously.

c) Mysticism as an individual phenomenon. Although individual religious mystics inherit the values, teachings, and practices of their traditions, they also transform them. In Scholem's analysis, mystics may be classified as conservative, revolutionary, or nihilistic in relation to their traditions. The first rediscover the sources of traditional authority. Their mystical experience reconfirms traditional symbols rather than creating new ones. Revolutionary mystics, on the other hand, represent new developments and transformations of the tradition. Nihilistic mystics are in direct conflict with traditional religious authority, often brought about by historical circumstances, e.g., the attacks on Madame Guyon, MEISTER ECKHART, or the BAAL SHEM TOV. Of whatever type or style, however, mystics play a revitalizing role within their respective traditions. Sometimes their leadership results in the creation or reformation of institutional structures, e.g. St. TERESA OF AVILA's Discalced CARMELITES. On other occasions the intensity of their religious life stimulates a renewal of more experiential and charismatic forms of religious practice, e.g. CAITANYA, or leads to exceptional forms of poetic/theological expression, e.g. JALĀL AD-DĪN RŪMĪ.

2. **Varieties of mysticism.** Is mysticism one or many? Is mystical experience essentially the same among all mystics with variations arising only as a result of historical/contextual differences? Or, do differing descriptions of mystical experiences among Christians, Buddhists, Jews, Hindus and Muslims point to fundamental differences in the nature of the reality which mystics claim to experience? Scholars vary in their opinions. Stace, following the interpretation of Rudolf Otto, distinguishes between extrovertive and introvertive forms of mysticism. Both forms lead to the perception of an ultimate unity with which the perceiver realizes union or in which he loses a sense of personal identity. The extrovertive type sees the unity mirrored in multiplicity; the introvertive type reports a unitary consciousness transcending all multiplicity. In Stace's view the highest or most genuine form of mysticism is the introvertive. Its principles are the same in every age: an elimination of all mental contents, of sensations, images or concepts; a unity in which all distinctions are eliminated.

A major criticism is made of this position because it asserts on the basis of a transubjective unitary experience that there is a unitary universal consciousness. Although this interpretation of a common mystical ontology might be compatible with a religion or a world view fundamentally monistic in nature, it poses problems for monotheistic traditions like Judaism, Christianity, and Islam. Zaehner, for example, argues against such a universal mysticism. While affirming that mysticism is based in a unitive experience, he distinguishes three fundamental types: nature mysticism (all-in-one); isolation of the self or soul from the material world; the return of the soul to God. In the first, typical of pantheism, everything is experienced or seen as an expression of one reality or principle; the second moves beyond all perceived multiplicity as in ŚAṂKARA'S conception of Self (ATMAN) or the notion of pure soul (PURUṢA) differentiated from matter (PRAKṚTI) in the SĀṂKHYA system; in the third, represented by Christian theism, the soul is deified, dwelling in God as an eternal idea. (*See* ORTHODOX CHURCHES.)

Zaehner also conceives these types as stages on the mystic way. Nature mysticism perceives a deeper and more intimate unity to nature than people ordinarily experience. It functions as a preliminary intuition that reality is not confined to ordinary sense experience. The realization of a state of pure soul devoid of all multiplicity represents a purgative stage, the negation of all false and distorted self-images. It functions as a prelude to deification, the direct, unmediated experience of union with God.

The testimonies of those who see their lives from the vantage point of an unmediated, unitive experience do not consistently support the view of a unitary mystical ontology. Variations in such testimony may be explained by distinguishing between descriptions of pure mystical experience on the one hand, and, on the other, interpretations of that experience which inevitably are historically and culturally relative. The testimonies of mystics reflect a transformative journey from darkness to light, from despair to joy, from meaninglessness to fulfillment, or from the unreal to the real. Meister Eckhart (1260-1327), whose thought influenced many fourteenth century German mystics (e.g. Suso, Tauler, Ruysbroeck), speaks of overcoming creatureliness to become lost in God; of being refined by suffering in order to be reborn in the likeness of God *(Book of Divine Comfort).* Teresa of Avila (1515-1582), the great Spanish mystic and Carmelite reformer, describes the life of prayer in four stages leading to union with God in her *Autobiography,* and in *The Interior Castle* she characterizes the soul's relationship with God in terms of seven mansions or stages culminating in an ecstatic intellectual vision likened to a spiritual marriage. She speaks of mystical transformation, using metaphors of the silkworm and butterfly, analogies from nature which illustrate the profound change one undergoes in the experience of divine realities. (*See* MYSTICISM, CHRISTIAN.)

This emphasis holds for the mystics of other religious traditions as well: e.g. Rūmī's poem of the reed flute longing for the day of its return to its place of origin; Farīd al-Dīn Aṭṭar's (d. 1220) allegorical journey of the birds through six valleys—quest, love, understanding, independence and detachment, pure unity, astonishment—culminating in the seventh valley of poverty and nothingness; Śaṃkara's stages of self-realization beginning with restraint of the senses and culminating in BRAHMAN absorption (SAMĀDHI); Mahādevīyakka's journey of devotional ascetism searching for union with SHIVA; the ZEN master's "pathless path" to enlightenment (SATORI); the perfection of the senses of the HASID through the ZADDIK who leads the community to communion with God. The ontology of mysticism varies, forged through the dialectic of the unique relationship between the individual mystics and their contexts. It may be monistic, pantheistic, or theistic; invariably, however, testimonies of mystics fit the pattern of a journey or a way illuminated by a transformative, unmediated, unitive experience with reality, that in whom/which human existence realizes the fullest dimensions of its authenticity.

3. Mystical language. Sources for our understanding of mysticism vary. They include utterances, testimonies, and descriptions of experiences considered mystical; ritual practices, physical/mental disciplines, and the use of consciousness-altering substances; and a variety of interpretations of these experiences. Although some scholars have attempted to distinguish between mystics' first order descriptions of their experiences and second order interpretations of them, the criteria for such a distinction are problematical. A pervasive paradox underlying the study of mystical expressions is the mystics' insistence that their experience transcends ordinary categories of cognizing and, hence, language. If so, what does the mystic's language describe? Or is it meant to be descriptive? Mystical utterances may not be intended primarily to describe either a subjective mode of awareness or an objective reality but to evoke and transform, to act as a catalyst for insight. This suggestion reminds us that mystics are moved to speak as a result of a profound experience, not in order to defend a definition or create a theological system. That their language may seem paradoxical or even illogical suggests not only the noumenal nature of their own experience, but their intention as transformed persons to act as midwives of mystical experience.

The student of mystical literature is struck by its wide variety of genres or forms. Poetry, narratives, aphorisms, even philosophical statements flow from the lips and pens of the mystics. Although such a range of expression defies conclusive categorization, the following fivefold classification will provide a working schematization: ontological, symbolic, poetic, dialectical, narrative.

Most mystics possess an ontology, but some mystical writings are quite explicitly ontological in form. Śaṃkara's *Aparokṣānubhūti,* for example, roughly divides into two parts, the first being the metaphysical of Brahman, the second spelling out a yogic path to Brahman realization. While Meister Eckhart's *Sermons* are certainly not devoid of metaphor and mirror the quality of mystical experience, several are self-consciously philosophical. St. Teresa's *Interior Castle,* on the other hand, is fundamentally mythic-symbolic in form. Her seven mansions provide the reader with a symbolic diagram (MANDALA) of the soul's journey to its true union with God. Similarly the thirteenth century KABBALISTS (e.g. as in the ZOHAR) thought on a mythic/symbolic level. They sought to recapture in symbolic form the reality of the living God who had been attentuated by the rationalistic theology of medieval, rabbinical JUDAISM.

But what can we say of TAGORE'S *Gītāñjali,* the ecstatic devotional poetry of Mahādevīyakka, or the imagistic poetic flights of Jalāl ad-Dīn Rūmī? With image, metaphor, and simile, rhyme and meter, the reader is led to an intuitive awareness of Tagore's encounter with God in sunrise and dew drop, of Devīyakka's spiritual longing for the Lord of White Jasmine (Shiva), and of the fire of Love that ennobles Rūmī's reed flute in the *Mathnawī.* How different in form such poetic expression appears to be in relationship to the enigmatic Zen tale and paradoxical KŌAN or the epigrammatic Sufi sayings, all of which point beyond themselves to a deeper reality, as a finger pointing toward the moon. Finally, there are the narratives, some in autobiographical or biographical form or perhaps episodes from a life story, paradigms of the mystic way.

To a degree these varying genres of mystical literature are descriptive of what the mystics claim to be their experience. Yet they have an even more crucial transformative function. Śaṃkara's ontology provides a cognitive frame for the practice of YOGA and the attainment of *samādhi* knowledge; St. Teresa's castle calls upon readers to open the doors of their own souls to find God; Tagore's metaphors lead to an intuitive sense of a deeper reality beyond the fleeting forms from which they borrow; the Zen paradox jolts the mind from the ruts of the commonplace; the belly laugh response to a Sufi saying negates a stifling self-consciousness; and the life story of the hasid becomes our life story, a transformative, unitive experience of divine reality.

4. **Mystical paths.** Mysticism includes a variety of mystical paths or avenues to mystical experience. Although the direct, unitive experience may seemingly occur in an unplanned and spontaneous manner, religions have either charted paths to achieve it or constructed contexts encouraging its arising. Some of the better known examples include Buddhist meditation, Hindu Yoga, ritual DANCE, and a variety of forms of ritualistic and meditative chant.

Traditionally BUDDHIST MEDITATION has been seen as the heart of Buddhist discipline, especially the life of the monk. Meditation provides the means of transcending blind attachment and, hence, coming to see things as they really are, unmediated by any sort of emotional or conceptual distortion. This state of direct seeing and understanding is one of personal freedom and moral equanimity. Buddhist meditation practices include a focusing or narrowing of the consciousness as preliminary to dynamic process of consciousness expansion. The eight limbs of classical Yoga have both commonalities and differences with early Buddhist meditation. Restraint and focusing of the consciousness figure prominently in both methods; however, the metaphysics of the two systems vary considerably. While early Buddhism posits no absolute such as Brahman or an eternal self or soul like *puruṣa,* the enlightenment experience associated with meditation is aptly characterized by the terms unmediated, unitive and, above all, transformative.

Mystical paths are also embodied in liturgical and ritual forms. Among the best known is Sufi ritual dance. Rūmī, for example, founded the Mawlāwī brotherhood or "whirling dervishes," whose mystical dance *(samā)* was an emulation of the order of the heavenly spheres. Dance as an ecstatic expression of sublime joy and as a means to induce trancelike states was fostered by the great Khurasani Sufi, Abus Sa'īd (d. 1049), the Hindu saint Caitanya, and Hasidic groups, to mention only a few. Of even more universal importance as a mystical path has been the use of chant or the repetition of a verbal formula or MANTRA as a means to focus attention and evoke heightened states of conscious awareness.

Bibliography. S. N. Dasgupta, *Hindu Mysticism* (1959); S. T. Katz, ed., *Mysticism and Philosophical Analysis* (1968); R. Otto, *Mysticism East and West* (1962), Otto's classical comparison of Eckhart and Śaṃkara; G. G. Scholem, *Jewish Mysticism* (1941), the standard survey, and *On the Kabbalah and Its Symbolism* (1969), ch. 1; W. T. Stace, *Mysticism and Philosophy* (1960), a seminal interpretation by a Western philosopher, and *The Teachings of the Mystics* (1960), selections of writings from various traditions chosen to verify Stace's interpretation of mysticism; E. Underhill, *The Mystics of the Church* (1964), a brief historical survey; R. C. Zaehner, *Hindu and Muslim Mysticism* (1969), and *Mysticism Sacred and Profane* (1957), a strongly Christian-oriented interpretation.

D. K. SWEARER

MYSTICISM, CHRISTIAN. The immediate personal awareness of or union with Absolute Reality, i.e. God. Although the experience is inner and individual, writings by mystics in the form of guides, autobiographies, poems, systematic analyses, etc., provide an understanding of the discipline of mind and body leading to mystical experience, the nature of the experience, and its effect upon the mystic's life. Many modern studies (W. R. Inge, W. James, W. T. Stace, R. C. Zaehner) focus on the nature of the experience at the expense of the nature of discipline and the effect upon life.

1. **Discipline.** According to the tradition, mystical experience occurs at the center of the soul, the still point reached when all conscious mental activity has ceased. For much of the Western intellectual tradition, rational thought marks the highest form of consciousness. For mystics, however, rational thought is only another mental activity to be quieted before the really important experiences become possible. Mystics do not reject reason, but they do not regard it as ultimate.

According to the mystics, discipline of mind and body is necessary to reach a state of inner quiet. Consciousness must be detached from concentration on the external world and gradually turned within. The role of discipline is usually understood as purificatory. Although it contains a strong moral element, it is not moralism, but rather a process of detaching the mind and will from delight in the pleasures of sense and reason. Degrees of discipline range from the fierce bodily austerities of the DESERT FATHERS (third to sixth centuries) and FRANCIS OF ASSISI (1182-1226) to the more moderate advice which FRANCIS OF SALES (1567-1622) and Johann Arndt (1555-1621) gave to people living in the world and seeking to follow a mystical path.

Isolation often plays an important role in detachment. It may be as a hermit in the desert (Desert Fathers), in the Italian countryside (Peter Damien, 1007-1072), or on a mountain (MT. ATHOS). Some find isolation in a community dedicated to contemplation (CISTERCIANS; CARMELITE nuns), in a time for daily solitude, or on a retreat. Whatever the form, the effect is to break away from the ordinary relationship of times and places in order to form a new rhythm and center for life.

In the Christian tradition techniques for interiorization and "quieting" have been suggested, but they generally fall short of the detailed teaching of some of the Eastern forms of meditation. Two especially notable examples of specific ways are the Jesus Prayer and the teaching of the *Cloud of Unknowing* (fourteenth century). Attempting to realize a constant state of prayer, Greek, and later Russian, mystics continually repeated the prayer: "Lord Jesus Christ, Son of God, have mercy on me a sinner." This has the functional effect of focusing attention, creating an inner attitude, and initiating transformation.

The author of the *Cloud* commends the repetition of a single word (*God* and *love* are suggested) as a way to focus consciousness and silence the senses and reason. Paintings, sculpture such as crosses, and mental images provided mystics with objects for focusing attention. Certain drawings may also have furnished "maps" of transformation very much on the order of MANDALAS. A drawing described in HUGH OF ST. VICTOR'S (d. 1141) treatises on Noah's Ark was used as both focus and map. In the *Tree of Life* by BONAVENTURE (1221-1274) and the *Spiritual Exercises* of IGNATIUS OF LOYOLA (1491-1556) the technique of vividly imagining scenes from Christ's life is used powerfully for concentration and interiorization. Chanting the liturgy to still the mind is suggested by Richard of St. Victor (d. 1173). In the fourteenth century the hesychast movement in the GREEK ORTHODOX CHURCH introduced techniques of posture and breathing to promote interiorization. (*See* HESYCHASM.)

An important document because of its use over the centuries is the *Conferences* of Cassian (d. *ca.* 433), written after his extensive travels and conversations with leading monks of the eastern Mediterranean world. They provide a rich collection of practical spiritual advice given by great figures of early monasticism.

Among numerous works on discipline, the following additional ones are notable: *The Way to Christ,* by JAKOB BOEHME (1575-1624); *True Christianity,* by Johann Arndt; *The Golden Epistle,* by William of St. Thierry (d. 1148); Sermon 27 on Numbers, by ORIGEN (*ca.* 185-*ca.* 254); the Russian *Philokalia; The Scale of Perfection,* by Walter Hilton (d. 1396); *The Way of a Pilgrim;* and the writings of Thomas Merton (1915-1968).

MEISTER ECKHART (1260-1327) criticized persons who were preoccupied with techniques and their own state of mind. JOHN OF THE CROSS (1542-1591) saw the value of mental techniques and objects when beginning meditation, but felt that such supports must be left behind on the path which leads to the One who is beyond discursive knowing. "In order to arrive at that which thou knowest not [i.e. God], thou must go by a way thou knowest not" (*Ascent of Mount Carmel,* 1.13).

Such criticisms argue that techniques do not produce mystical experience and may indeed impede it. They are only the process by which the mind and body are stilled. In the end, Christian mystics view the experience of divine presence as a gift.

2. Experience. W. James identified four characteristics of this special experience. It is (1) *ineffable,* i.e. beyond the categories of ordinary language, hence the use of highly symbolic language and suggestive metaphors by mystics; (2) *noetic,* i.e. mystics have knowledge, but it differs in nature from usual knowing; (3) *transient,* i.e. limited in duration; and (4) *passive,* i.e. the mystic is the recipient, not the active agent.

Although often considered a single event, the experience may have many stages. Illumination and union are often distinguished, but John of the Cross's inclusion of the "dark night of the soul" between illumination and union reflects the experience of many, for it places a final stage of purification and isolation from God just prior to union. TERESA OF AVILA (1515-1582), Ruysbroeck (1293-1381), and others speak of a "spiritual marriage" in which the experience of union with God, given in a moment in ecstatic mysticism, becomes something of which the mystic is continually aware while carrying out normal activities.

The presence of the image of God *(imago Dei)* in each person is a recurring theme, expressing the conviction that each person has the potential for a direct awareness of God. The image is variously described: a mirror reflecting the blinding brilliance of divine presence (Origen, Gregory of Nyssa, the Victorines, Johann Arndt), a spark (Eckhart), or the ground of the soul (Eckhart, Tauler, Arndt, Boehme). Awareness of the image is "potential," because mystics realize that ordinarily life is alienated from God. The mirror is clouded over, the spark smothered. The moral condition of sin and the mental distraction of attention to the outer world ensure that the image remains unperceived unless discipline is undertaken. Yet "possibility" needs equal stress. The mystic's experience is extraordinary only because it marks the achievement of that which was previously only potential.

Images for the mystic path include ascension (climbing a mountain or ladder), introversion (entering a house, bridal chamber, or temple), and journeying (Hebrews in the wilderness). All denote interiorization and transformation, resulting in a penetration beyond the normal levels of consciousness to a radically different consciousness. Although mystics accept no one ontology or epistemology, most accept three spheres of awareness: the sense world, the inner world of mental reality (including imagination, memory, and abstract thought), and "another" world of spiritual and divine reality. This latter sphere is accessible only through a new awareness and consciousness, associated with the image of God and often described as the intellect or the "eye of the mind." Those mystics who use "intellect" in this way do not mean the kind of rational intellect assumed today, but a totally different mode of apprehending spiritual reality, apart from either sense impressions or rational thought (cf. James' *noetic*).

The language of "sight" is often used to describe this new consciousness. The traditional word for mystical experience—contemplation (Latin: *contemplatio;* Greek: *theoria*)—means "seeing" and "an intense gazing at," thus emphasizing the visual aspect. The contemplative, mystical experience is an interior, spiritual sight of reality, differing from ordinary sight but somehow analogous to it. AUGUSTINE and GREGORY THE GREAT (*ca.* 540-604) speak of contemplation as the partial "seeing" of God, especially understood as "unencompassed Light."(C. Butler, pp. 34-50, 76-92.) Ruysbroeck speaks of being carried beyond things, beyond light, into the Divine Darkness where one receives "the Incomprehensible Light enfolding and penetrating us. And this Light is nothing else but an infinite gazing and seeing" (Underhill, p. 423). The language of "darkness" in mysticism owes much to the writings of PSEUDO-DIONYSIUS THE AREOPAGITE (sixth century). He speaks of God as beyond all knowing and categories, and the mystic experience as one of darkness. But the mystic's darkness is due to the exceeding brilliance of God's light, which "blinds" the human mind.

The symbolic language used to express the nature of mystical union varies greatly, due to personal differences, cultural influences, and the use of biblical themes and images. Passages from the letters of the apostle PAUL and the GOSPEL of John can be cited for motifs of union and ascension. However, one of the most influential and powerful sets of images was first applied by Origen of Alexandria. He used the nuptial imagery of the Song of Songs (yearning of lover and beloved; embrace in the bridal chamber; sharing of mutual love) as symbolic of the mystic quest and its fulfillment in the unitive experience. Later Gregory of Nyssa (*ca.* 330–*ca.* 395) used the same imagery powerfully. In the twelfth century the Cistercians, especially BERNARD OF CLAIRVAUX (1090-1153), employed this nuptial imagery in mystical writings of great insight. Richard of St. Victor (d. 1273), John of the Cross, Johann Arndt, Jakob Boehme, and Ernesto Cardenal (b. 1925) represent only a few of the mystics who have found this language a key for interpreting their experiences and providing guidance for others.

The fourteenth century DOMINICAN Meister Eckhart, who emphasized detachment as the fruit of discipline, describes the mystical experience as the birth of the Eternal Word in the soul. His sermons in German made the riches of his masterful thought available to ordinary Dominican nuns and frairs. His spiritual heirs, the so-called Rhineland mystics, Tauler (*ca.* 1300-1361), Suso (*ca.* 1295-1365), and Ruysbroeck produced magnificent works of interpretation and moving autobiography. The influence of Ruysbroeck can be seen in IMITATION OF CHRIST, a classic of Christian devotion compiled and partly written by Thomas à Kempis (1380-1471).

The FRANCISCAN mystic Bonaventure combined a cosmic vision of the created world as a symbolic manifestation of the creator with a profoundly Christocentric mysticism. Drawing upon the spiritual heritage of Francis of Assisi and earlier mystical writers, Bonaventure expanded the notion of contemplation to include the apprehension of God's presence "in" and "through" the created world and the mind, as well as in the ecstatic mystic experience when senses and reason are quiet.

In the fifteenth and sixteenth centuries emphasis upon the "quiet" mystic increased, stressing the intention of love rather than "knowing" in contemplation. The Spaniard Bernardino de Laredo (1482-1540), whose *Ascent of Mount Sion* brought order and clarity to the previously confused and frustrated mystical quest of Teresa of Avila, is an example.

Teresa and her disciple John of the Cross are often cited as normative for mystical experience and spiritual guidance. John's use of poetic images drawn from the Song of Songs in his own prose and poetry forms one of the great moments in Western mysticism, while Teresa has rarely been equaled in intensity of experience or conviction of expression. John's writings focus on the purifying and unifying effect of the burning flame of love as one ascends Mount Carmel to the summit, which is empty according to human reasoning but full according to divine love and presence. Teresa's straightforward approach transforms everyday images into vehicles of spiritual guidance, always illumined by reference to her experiences. In addition, Dame Julian of Norwich (*ca.* 1342–*ca.* 1413) was a remarkable English solitary, visionary, and mystic who left a unique personal record in her *Showings*. In the twelfth and thirteenth centuries in Germany a notable series of women made their distinctive contributions to explicating mystical experience from the depths of their own experiences: Hildegard of Bingen, Mechthild of Magdeburg, and Elizabeth of Schonau. In the fourteenth and fifteenth centuries Bridget of Sweden, Catherine of Sienna, and Catherine of Genoa stand out as exemplars of ecstatic mysticism, great spiritual guides, and authors of moving narratives of personal mystical and visionary experiences.

Other mystics who contribute to our understanding of the experience include Gregory the Great; Gregory of Palamas, on Greek hesychasm; Blaise Pascal (1623-1662), WILLIAM BLAKE (1757-1827), Lucie-Christine (1844-1908), Pierre TEILHARD DE CHARDIN (1881-1955), GEORGE FOX (1624-1691), and William Law (1686-1761).

Types of Christian mysticism have been placed in certain broad categories. Often mysticism of the intellect is distinguished from that of love. Given the fact that all Christian mysticism is characterized by love, this seems to be an impossible division. More representative of the facts is a distinction based on the nature of the mystic's quest. One group speaks of the world of divine reality as darkness, a desert, an unknowing—empty from a human point but full with divine presence and love. The way to it is a stripping away of consciousness of objects and ideas (e.g., Eckhart, John of the Cross, *Cloud of Unknowing*). The second group speaks of the world of spiritual reality as one of light, as indescribable and enigmatic as the dark, but experienced like the full blaze of a life-giving sun in comparison to which the material and impermanent light of this world is pale and shadowy. The way to this is an increased inner focusing and awareness (e.g., Augustine, the Victorines, Greek Orthodox mystics, Bonaventure). The mystics of the first group may be called *mystics of stripping away or silence.* Those of the second group may be called *mystics of clarification or spiritual vision.*

3. Results. When considering the effects of mysticism upon life, modern interpreters tend to see mystics as fleeing the world, possibly irrationally, and perhaps ignoring the ethical concerns of prophetic religion (e.g., F. Heiler). It is true that many mystics have lived in deprivation and their mental experiences have appeared abnormal when judged by the everyday. Yet their lives have demonstrated that such experiences and even desolation and isolation do not necessarily lead away from concern for others. The experience of God ideally transforms the mystic's person and life so that he or she is conformed to the humility and servantship of Christ (e.g., Richard of St. Victor in *Four Degrees of Violent Charity,* Francis of Assisi), or becomes a spiritual "midwife" (Bernard of Clairvaux, Jacob Boehme, Ignatius of Loyola). Indeed, the mystic experience bears fruit in a new life and relationship to others, and many mystics have been critics and reformers of the church, drawing strength for this vocation from their interior life.

See also MYSTICISM.

Bibliography. Studies: L. Bouyer, *et al., A History of Christian Spirituality*, 3 vols. (1960), an excellent product of modern Catholic scholarship; C. Butler, *Western Mysticism,* 2nd ed. (1926); F. Heiler, *Prayer* (1932); W. R. Inge, *Christian Mysticism* (1899); W. James, *Varieties of Religious Experience* (1902); W. Johnston, *The Still Point* (1970); W. T. Stace, *Mysticism and Philosophy* (1960); E. Underhill, *Mysticism* (1910, rpr. 1955), an old but broad study with good historical survey in appendix; R. C. Zaehner, *Mysticism: Sacred and Profane* (1957). New translations are appearing in two series, "Classics of Western Spirituality" and "Cistercian Fathers." Books of selections with perceptive introductions include W. H. Capps and W. M. Wright, *Silent Fire* (1978); F. C. Happold, *Mysticism* (1963); E. O'Brien, *Varieties of Mystical Experience* (1964); R. C. Petry, *Late Medieval Mysticism* (1957); W. T. Stace, *The Teachings of the Mystics* (1960).

G. A. ZINN

MYSTICISM IN ISLAM. *See* SUFISM.

MYTH, THEORIES OF. The study of myth is at least as old as Plato, who wrote of "myth-telling" ("mythologia" from the Greek μύθος—lit., "a word or story") as an activity akin to poetry but to be distinguished from philosophy. Throughout the ages popular interest in myth-telling has remained strong, and scholarly attempts to understand mythology have attracted much attention, especially in the last century in the West. Myth theories are grouped below according to their claims with regard to the nature and source of myth on the one hand, and the essential use or function of myth on the other.

To ground later theoretical discussions in a common content, the following abridged version of a vision-story by a Oglala Sioux Indian named Black Elk is given (for the full story see Neihardt, pp. 17-39):

While lying sick in his parent's tepee, the nine-year-old Black Elk saw two arrow-like men descend from the sky and heard them call him to his "Grandfathers." Lifted by a little cloud into the sky, Black Elk found himself in the midst of a snow-white plain. His two guides told him to look to the west where twelve black horses pranced, then to the north where twelve white horses stood abreast, then to the east with twelve sorrel horses, and the south with twelve buckskin horses. Black Elk was led by this grand horse procession to a huge cloud, which was transformed into a tepee with a rainbow door. Inside were seated six old men introduced as simply "the Grandfathers" but later recognized as the "Powers" of the four directions, the sky, and the earth. Each of the Grandfathers/Powers gave Black Elk a gift (e.g., a wooden cup with life-giving water, a healing herb, a bow of destruction, and a symbol-laden peace pipe). One gift was a red stick which when thrust into the ground became a living tree and the center of a circle of Sioux tepees. Before returning to earth Black Elk was permitted to view a fierce battle in which his people were routing the hated "Blue-coats" (U.S. cavalry). After learning more sacred wisdom, Black Elk was returned to his parents' tepee with his previous illness cured.

The story later became the basis for a horse dance ritual which dramatized the original vision. Therefore it would appear that what began as a private vision and story later became a shared, corporate narrative of the benevolence and sustained presence of the Grandfathers.

1. Psychological theories of myth. *a) Intellectualist approach.* One basic type of psychological myth theory is that which views myth as a special type of thinking or reasoning.

i. Negative assessment: the mythopoeic. Following in the footsteps of Frederick Max Müller and Ernst Cassier, Henri Frankfort located the source of myth in the mythopoeic thought of primitives. Viewing mythical thinking as emotive and speculative, Frankfort argued that the "primitive" had only one mode of thought—the personal (i.e., I-Thou).

Therefore, all expressions of experiences with natural powers or historical events are colored by a lack of the critical distance used by modern scientific analysts. Frankfort rejected the idea that myths, like fairy tales, are fictional stories told for entertainment and took myths seriously as truthful expressions of the primitive's personalized understanding of the world and its divine causes. For example, in Black Elk's vision the cardinal directions are personified and there is direct communication between animals and humans.

According to Frankfort, myth is the result of the primitive's subjective analysis of concrete phenomena and events. Therefore, the living quality of myths is to be found in the link between myth and ritual. It was not enough for Black Elk to tell of his encounter with the creative powers of the world; his sacred experience needed to be recreated in the horse dance ritual. Thus it is that only the "primitive" mind could produce myths, for modern societies have moved beyond the purely subjective mode of mythical thinking to the "objective" mode of scientific and historical analysis.

ii. Positive assessment: the structuralist. Taking exception to the view that human capacity for thinking has evolved from a prelogical or subjective, "primitive" state to a rational and objective modern one, Claude Lévi-Strauss views the essential process of myth-making as a type of binary thinking which offers a logical model capable of resolving human problems or conflicts.

The Oedipus myth, for example, reveals in its structural *(synchronic)* juxtapositions a message quite different from its narrative message *(diachronic)*. To uncover the latent meaning of this myth, Lévi-Strauss first divides a story into its smallest conceptual units or "mythemes" (e.g., Oedipus kills his father, Oedipus' name means "swollen-foot," and Oedipus marries his mother). Then, by arranging all the separate mythemes into columns of similar meanings or relationships, the underlying oppositional or binary structure is revealed. In the case of the Oedipus myth, Lévi-Strauss posits two columns of opposed themes: (1) "overrating of blood relations" (e.g., loving his mother) versus "underrating blood relations" (e.g. killing his father), and (2) "born from one: the earth" (e.g. the lame Oedipus) versus "born from two: human parents" (e.g. killing the Sphinx). He concludes that the essential message of the Oedipus story is that a conflict in human relationships (with father and with mother) validates a seeming cosmological contradiction regarding the true origin of the human race (i.e., from the earth—an ancient Greek view—or from human reproduction—as known from experience). In other words, the Oedipus myth places human and cosmological contradictions in juxtaposition as a way of validating both conflicts and relieving the anxiety connected with them. Therefore, the underlying, synchronic structure reveals not only the true message of the myth but also the unconscious, binary thought process determinative of the myth itself.

In direct opposition then to assertions that myth arises in emotive, speculative thought, Lévi-Strauss asserts that the binary logic of myth (even though embedded in unconscious processes) is of the same type as that of modern science and is as rigorously applied. The only differences are that what is unconscious process in the primitive mind is conscious in the modern scientist and that the subject matter to which the binary thought process is applied differs. The way Lévi-Strauss might analyze Black Elk's story may be surmised from his lengthy interpretation of another Native American myth, "The Story of Asdiwal." One thing is clear: it would be in the structure, not the narrative, of the myth that Lévi-Strauss would search for the vision's meaning. The far-reaching impact of Lévi-Strauss' structural approach can be seen in its adaptation to ancient Near Eastern mythology by the classicist G. S. Kirk as well as to Indian Śaivite mythology by the historian of religion Wendy O'Flaherty.

b) Psychoanalytic approach. All theories grouped under this rubric share the assumption that the unconscious is the source of mythic symbols and of their need for expression.

i. Negative assessment: the Freudian. The first major proponent of this position was Sigmund Freud, who claimed myths were nothing other than the emergence from the unconscious of psychological needs and wishes played out in the fantastic and symbolic stories of gods and demons. Freud makes the basic assumption that there is an unconscious which is a repository of innate drives (e.g., for immortality) as well as repressed feelings and experiences. Furthermore, one's conscious "controller" (the ego) is usually unaware of the desires and conflicts present in the unconscious. However, dreams, daydreams, and myths are three ways the unconscious drives are disguised and permitted conscious access in varying degrees. Freud calls these symbolically cloaked desires "illusions," and when speaking directly of myth, "the fairy tales of religion." And just as the neurotic patient when healthy can tell the difference between real and imagined happenings, so too will believers in myths dispense with their fairy tales when they come to recognize their real source, the unconscious.

Besides the phallic interpretation that Freud might have made of the red stick which Black Elk thrust into the ground to bring health and happiness back to his people, it is clear that Freud would have reason to suspect wish-projection in the defeat of the Bluecoats, the healing powers given to Black Elk, and the union of all Sioux within the sacred hoop of the nation. Depth psychology calls attention to the complexity of symbols and to the possibility of forgotten or unknown feelings which may emerge through them. Otto Rank's book *The Myth of the Birth of the Hero* is one example of Freudian myth analysis.

ii. Positive assessment: the Jungian. Carl Jung agrees with Freud that myths are original and forceful expressions of the unconscious (also called the "preconscious psyche"). However, Jung moves beyond Freud's definition of unconscious as the innate and repressed feelings and experiences of the individual when he makes a distinction between a "personal unconscious" and what he calls the "collective unconscious" which all persons share regardless of era, culture, or personal experiences. Jung was led by his experiences with dream analysis and, later, myth analysis to the conclusion that similar images or "archetypes" are shared by all humans and, further, that there must be a "collective unconscious" which is the source of these ubiquitously recurring dream and myth images. One universal archetype, the MANDALA, was found by Jung in dreams, myths, and mystic writings and diagrams, where it seemed always to suggest "wholeness" or "perfection." Jung assigned a positive psychological role to this and other integrative symbols which well up from the collective unconscious, because he felt they contributed to the "individuation" or maturation process in persons. Such archetypes as the mandala and the "child-god" were viewed by Jung as life-giving and unifying expressions of the powerful, unconscious psyche. Myths in this context reveal paths to psychological maturity, not simply repressed wishes or guilt.

It should be apparent how Jung would treat the visionary myth of Black Elk, since the Sioux paintings which portray this story reveal its mandala-like design with its four directions, central focus of the tepee, and the movement of the story toward the integration of all social and natural life. The emphasis here would be on the universality of the mandala design, as well as the value which this story and its associated rite offer the Sioux for a personal and collective sense of wholeness and unity. The work of Paul Radin and Joseph Campbell are good examples of Jungian myth analysis.

What all psychological theories of myth have in common is their claim that myths originate in and function essentially as a mental process of human beings. Though the scholars mentioned above may reach diametrically opposed conclusions regarding the character (irrational vs. rational) and location (conscious vs. unconscious) of mythic thinking, they all finally focus on myth as a psychological process and product. Furthermore, myths in this context function to serve existential and psychic needs whether consciously recognized or not.

2. Sociological approaches to myth. It was the sociological functionalism of Bronislaw Malinowski which informed much myth interpretation until the recent burgeoning of Lévi-Strauss' structuralism and the combination approaches of contemporary anthropologists. Malinowski accepted the claim of Emile Durkheim that religion is essentially a social reality and, consequently, that myths express in words the same social truths that rituals express in action. Hence, it is through myths and rituals that a social group renews and reaffirms its unity. Likewise, the individual is strengthened in his or her social identity through the recitation of myths or the performance of rituals. Applying these basic assumptions of Durkheim to his fieldwork among the Trobriand Islanders, Malinowski formulated a coherent sociological theory of myth in his landmark essay "Myth in Primitive Psychology." After briefly confronting some earlier myth theories which treated myths as primitive speculation or fictional fantasies, Malinowski argued that myths are living realities which codify all ritual and social behavior. Further, there is an intimate connection between the sacred tales or myths of a tribe and its practical activities and social organization.

Influenced greatly by Freud, Malinowski did acknowledge that religious beliefs are the products of deep desires and represent both hopes and fears. However, instead of simply agreeing with Freud that myths are cloaked, symbolic expressions of basic human desires or fears, Malinowski said that myths also serve as social "warrants" or codifiers of socially agreed upon needs and beliefs. Myths are intrinsically social in origin and nature and function primarily as sacred narratives which legitimate social institutions. In short, myths are essentially the projection and sacralization of social values and institutions. From this point of view, it would be appropriate to focus on the mythic and ritual codification of the Sioux way of life bound up in the image of the "hoop of the nation," and to stress the desire for unification of all Sioux people which the various symbols of the story represent. But most of all, one would observe the extent to which the values of Sioux society (e.g., unity with nature) were lived out and acted out in retelling Black Elk's vision and in performances of the horse dance and other rituals.

The work of George Dumézil focuses upon social structure and its determinative role in myth-making. In his study of Indo-European and Indian mythology Dumézil concludes that myths are foremost representations of social and cultural realities. For example, tripartite Vedic social structure (priests, warriors, and "producers") gives rise to a threefold Vedic theology and, by extension, threefold mythology. In sum, Vedic myths are Vedic society "writ large in the sky."

The undergirding assumption of most sociological interpretations of myths is that myths are essentially social in origin and function. Whether it is social unity, social institutions, or social mores which are projected and codified in myths, sociological interpretations stress the inherently social nature of myths.

3. Combined approaches. Mircea Eliade is a good example of a "combination" myth theorist. In his book *The Sacred and the Profane,* Eliade directly affirms his theological assumptions, built upon the work of Rudolf Otto. Eliade argues that myths are born out of genuine religious experiences ("hierophanies") and are thus true stories of the encounters between a sacred power and humans. Following Malinowski's emphasis on the pragmatic and living quality of myth, Eliade asserts that myths are paradigms for behavior. Since mythical events occur in sacred time *(in illo tempore),* every myth is in a general sense an expression of a new birth or creation, whether of things, persons, or relationships, which is to be emulated in human acts. Following Jung, though denying final dependence, Eliade uses a comparative approach to find universal or archetypical symbols in myths which arise from what he calls the "transconscious." Eliade would be concerned with the social and psychological implications of the Black Elk myth while comparing the symbols used (e.g., sacred tree) with other such symbols around the world. He would stress the paradigmatic extension of the myth into the behavior of Black Elk and his people, as well as the sense of renewal the story and rite afford.

Many social anthropologists consciously endeavor to consider psychological, sociological, and other variables in their myth analyses. For example, Percy Cohen specifically argues for an eclectic approach to myth interpretation while pointing out the reductionist tendencies of any one method alone. Likewise, Victor Turner's treatment of myth and ritual symbols as "multivalent" leads him to consider both psychological and social factors in his analysis of myths.

4. **Conclusion.** There is no one accepted definition or interpretation of myth. Some scholars view myths as fictional tales born of social necessity (Dumézil), others as thinly veiled expressions of unconscious needs and wishes (Freud), while still others as true depictions of encounters with a sacred reality (Eliade). Shinn offers a twofold definition of myths (as "expressive" or "reflective") which assumes that not all myths have the same source or function. However, even that twofold categorization cannot pretend to encompass everything that is studied as myth. Therefore, while many myth theorists attempt to understand all myths from one or a consistent set of approaches, myths are so varied in their origins and expressions that it is likely that a constantly changing combination of approaches will yield the best results. Furthermore, it is clear from the manifold uses of the term "myth" that characteristics such as truth or falsity and historicity or fiction are not sufficient or necessary criteria in defining and interpreting this universal phenomenon.

Bibliography. J. G. Neihardt, *Black Elk Speaks* (1932, 1972); F. M. Müller, *Contributions to the Science of Mythology,* 2 vols. (1897); E. Cassier, *The Logic of the Humanities* (1961); H. Frankfort, "Myth and Reality," *Before Philosophy* (1949); C. Lévi-Strauss, "The Structural Study of Myth," *Structural Anthropology* (1967), and "The Story of Asdiwal," *The Structural Study of Myth and Totemism* (1967); E. Leach, *Claude Lévi-Strauss* (1970); G. S. Kirk, *Myth* (1970); W. D. O'Flaherty, *Asceticism and Eroticism in the Mythology of Siva* (1973); S. Freud, *The Future of an Illusion* (1927, rev. ed. 1964), and *On Dreams* (1952); O. Rank, *The Myth of the Birth of the Hero* (1952); C. Jung, *Psychology and Religion* (1938), and *The Archetypes and the Collective Unconscious* (1968); P. Radin, *The Trickster* (1956); J. Campbell, *The Hero with a Thousand Faces* (1949); B. Malinowski, "Myth in Primitive Psychology," *Magic, Science and Religion* (1954); E. Durkheim, *Elementary Forms of the Religious life* (1915); G. Dumézil, *L'idéologie tripartie des Indo-Européens* (1958); M. Eliade, *The Sacred and the Profane* (1961), *Patterns in Comparative Religion* (1963), and *Myths, Rites and Symbols,* W. C. Beane and W. G. Doty, eds., I (1975); V. Turner, "Myth and Symbol," *International Encyclopedia for the Social Sciences,* X (1968), 576-82, and *The Forest of Symbols* (1967); P. Cohen, "Theories of Myth," *Man,* IV (1969), 337-53; L. Shinn, *Two Sacred Worlds* (1977). Two collections of essays which include theories of myth not touched upon in this essay (e.g., the myth and ritual school) are T. A. Sebeok, ed., *Myth: A Symposium* (1965); and H. A. Murray, ed., *Myth and Mythmaking* (1960).

L. D. Shinn

N

NABI nä bē´ (I—Arab.; "prophet"; plurals *nabīyūn* and *anbiyā*). Muhammad is regarded as not only the greatest of the prophets, but also as the "seal of the prophets," that is, the last of the prophets, who authenticates the messages of the prophets before him. The term has Hebrew and Aramaic antecedents, as does the exposition of the concept of prophets in the Qur'ān. Islam's relationship to its Semitic, monotheistic predecessors is evident in the prophetology outlined by Muhammad. Sura 6:83-86 of the Qur'ān sets forth what is tantamount to a catechismal listing of the prophets whom Allah guided to the straight path before Muhammad. Most are to be found in the OT and NT, though not always as prophets and often with a different emphasis to the anecdotes for which they have become renowned. First and foremost among them is Abraham, the *ḥanīf* or rightly guided one. He is followed by Isaac and Jacob, Noah, David and Solomon, Job and Joseph, Moses and Aaron, Zachariah and John, Jesus and Elijah, Ishmael (Ismā'īl) and Elisha, Jonah and Lot. (Elsewhere in the Qur'ān Shu'aib and Idrīs are also lauded as prophets.)

The Qur'ānic prophets do not attract equal attention; Moses and Jesus, together with Abraham, are considerably more important than, for instance, Aaron, Elisha, or Lot. Yet all the above are deemed prophets because they appeared among the People of the Book. In this respect they differ from apostles (Rasūl), such as Hūd and Ṣāliḥ, who were sent to the Arabs before the latter were given a book. Often apostles and prophets are bracketed together as related but variant terms. In addition to Muhammad, we find Noah, Lot, Ishmael, Moses, and Jesus depicted as both apostles and prophets for their respective generations. It may be possible to pinpoint a theological distinction between the Qur'ānic usage of apostle and prophet, that every apostle is a prophet but not every prophet is an apostle. Except for Hūd and Ṣāliḥ, that distinction would appear to be valid, but more important, it seems, is to remember that both terms refer to an inspired religious leader, with *nabi* stressing the relationship of the leader to a revealed book *(kitāb)* while *rasūl* underscores his advocacy of truth to a community of people (Umma). Muhammad, therefore, is described in the Qur'ān as God's first apostle to the Arabs (Hūd and Ṣāliḥ notwithstanding) and God's last prophet to mankind, revealing a book without error or contradiction, the Qur'ān.

It is the pivotal role of Muhammad as prophet and apostle which has enlivened Muslim fascination with other prophets, both in and beyond the pages of the Qur'ān. The total number of prophets was said to have reached 124,000, of whom 315 were reportedly apostles. All were endowed with legendary traits, and "proved" their prophetic missions through the performance of extraordinary feats, i.e., miracles (*see* Miracles in Islam). Thus Adam, who is not specifically labeled a prophet in the Qur'ān, becomes a prophet in Islamic tradition by virtue of his encounter with Iblīs (Satan) and his designation as God's successor on earth (Qur'ān 2:29-38). Subsequent stories elaborate Adam's precreation existence, his foreknowledge of world history, and his experiences on Sarandip (Sri Lanka), where he landed following his expulsion from Paradise. Some of the stories have rabbinic, or occasionally Christian, parallels. The stories recounted about Adam and each of the prophets came in time to comprise an independent and widely popular literary genre known as *qiṣaṣ al-anbiyā,* "tales of the prophets." They were exposited in every major Islamic language and dialect. They became integral to the world view of medieval Muslims, adorning Qur'ānic commentaries, works of poetry, moral treatises, and also Sufi speculative writings. An example of the latter is the *Fuṣūṣ al-ḥikam* ("The Wisdom of the Prophets"), written by the renowned Andalusian mystic Muḥyī 'd-Din Ibn 'Arabī. Each chapter describes a major prophet with reference to his distinctive or dominant spiritual quality. Abraham is the epitome of intimacy, Moses of transcendence, and Jesus of prophecy itself. The book, of course, concludes with the wisdom of Muhammad, to underscore the finality of his prophethood and also his summation of all the qualities exemplified by earlier prophets.

Popular piety, and perhaps theological necessity, gradually elevated Muhammad from the role of a mere mortal messenger to the status of a cosmic being equivalent to the perfect man *(al-insān al-kāmil)*. As a result, Muhammad's prophethood, like his humanity, came to acquire an aura of sanctity. The doctrine of sinlessness *('iṣma)*, resembling the doctrine of infallibility accorded their IMAMS by the SHI'ITES, was attached to Muhammad, suggesting that he did not sin as had other men. By analogy, some theologians reasoned, all prophets were to be viewed as sinless; and to emphasize their lofty status, they were categorically compared and contrasted with saints (*see* WALĪ). Prophets never sinned; saints did, though only in minor matters. Prophets had foreknowledge of their ability to do the extraordinary or unexpected, and they performed miracles *(mu'jizāt)* as proofs of their divine mission. Saints, on the other hand, never knew for certain that they could contravene nature's laws and, even if they could, they were advised to restrain themselves. Lacking restraint, they produced only isolated wonders *(karamāt)*.

Despite the numerous ways in which prophets were extolled, the fundamental doctrine at stake, in both dogmatic theology and popular piety, was the finality of Muhammad's prophethood. Saints challenged that doctrine obliquely by asserting that their authority was derivative from, and yet similar to, that of the prophets. Consider the popular tradition, ascribed to Muhammad, that "the SHAIKH among his group is like the prophet among his community *(umma)*." Some mystic leaders went still further, claiming to be renovators *(mujaddidūn)* of the entire Islamic community. Two Indian Muslims, Shaikh Aḥmad Sirhindī (d. 1621) and Ghulām Aḥmad Qādiyānī (d. 1908; *see* AHMADIYYA) for instance, arrogated prophetic functions to themselves, in order, they argued, to restore the law of Muhammad which had been corrupted by intervening generations. Most pious Muslims, including the 'ULAMĀ', have also sensed that corruption has infected and weakened the community of Muhammad's followers, but they have not viewed the redefinition of Muhammad's finality as an acceptable expedient for removing that corruption. Instead, they have found solace in reaffirming the traditional doctrine, as have progressive, modernist Muslims, such as the rationalist-reformer Sayyid Aḥmad Khan (d. 1898).

Bibliography. C. C. Torrey, *The Jewish Foundation of Islam* (rpr. 1967); H. Speyer, *Die biblischen Erzählungen im Qoran* (rpr. 1961); W. M. Thackston, Jr., *Tales of the Prophets*, or *Qiṣṣaṣ al-anbiyā* (1978); Ibn 'Arabī, *The Wisdom of the Prophets*, trans. T. Burckhardt and A. Culme-Seymour (1975).

B. LAWRENCE

NACHMANIDES näk măn′ ĭ dēz (Ju). *See* MOSES BEN NAHMAN.

NAFS näfs (I—Arab.; "self, soul"). In Islamic philosophy SALVATION is viewed as dependent on the soul's release from the bonds of the material world and its return to the eternal realm of spiritual substances from which it originally emanated (*see* RŪḤ). This view is reflected in SUFI depictions of a higher soul, tranquil, purified, contented, and perfected. But most Sufi literature focuses on *nafs* as the lower, carnal, or passionate self, the animal soul with its endless appetites. Control of this lower self becomes the necessary first step on the mystical path. Poverty of the self (*see* FAQĪR) is, therefore, indispensable for repentance, renunciation, and pursuit of the One. Abstention from desirable but harmful objects (food, drink, money, etc.) is seen as not merely an outward observance but an inward state of mind which the seeker must daily cultivate. Numerous stories tell of high-minded Sufis who have held their animal soul in check for a lifetime, only to yield to its instinctual urges on their deathbed and so, by implication, to lose benefits gained from years of abstinence and self-control. *See* JANNA; JAHANNAM; SOUL, SPIRIT.

Bibliography. A. Schimmel, *Mystical Dimensions of Islam* (1975), pp. 112-16.

B. LAWRENCE

NĀGA nä′ gü (H & B—Skt.; etymology uncertain). A group of serpent deities represented as cobras with extended hoods or as part human, part snake. Their worship is ancient, and they appear regularly as minor beings in Indian mythology.

Much scholarly energy has been expended on speculation about the origins of snake-worship. Generally it is agreed that *nāgas* are associated with a Mongolian or Tibeto-Burmese people who occupied Northern India before the entrance of the Aryans. (A preliterate people called the Nagas still exist in Assam today.) The cult is so widespread in India that it must have begun as an aboriginal cult. In many parts of the world the snake is a symbol of immortality because it sheds its skin, seeming eternal. Such an image is found in the BRĀHMAṆAS, though not in the RIG VEDA. In the YAJUR and ATHARVA VEDAS *nāgas* are regularly referred to as *sarpāh*, serpents, a class of semi-divine beings to which hymns are sung to propitiate them and spells are spoken to solicit their protection as well as to control their magic powers or even destroy them (e.g., AV 6.56; 11.9).

Buddhist texts refer to various *nāga* kings and portray the *nāgas* as devotees of the Buddha. In the *Lalitavistara* two *nāga* kings, Nanda and Upananda, appear at the Buddha's birth and shower streams of water over him. In the Mahāvagga, Mucalinda, a serpent king, protects the Buddha from the heavy rains by spreading his hood over the Buddha's head while he sits in trance.

In the Epics an elaborate *nāga* mythology is found. The origin of the *nāgas* is related in the Ādiparvan of the MAHĀBHĀRATA. They are said to live in a world, *nāgaloka*, under the earth. It is later called *kāmaloka*, "world of desire," a beautiful realm offering every imaginable delight. The Epics credit the *nāgas* with vast powers: e.g., the touch of the jewel of their king Vāsuki restored the hero ARJUNA to life.

A number of *nāgas* are famous, and the epithet

nāgarāja ("serpent king") is commonly used. References to Śesa abound in the mythology. In the Bhāgavata Purāṇa the famous *nāga* Kāliya, a multi-headed, fire-breathing demon, who dwelt in the river Yāmuna, terrorized the countryside until defeated by Krishna. However, Vāsuki is most often referred to as the king of *nāgas*. He is the seven-headed serpent who served as a churning rope when the gods churned the primordial ocean to obtain divine nectar *(amṛta)*. Said to be green and a guardian of the North, Vāsuki is worshiped today in the Western Himalayas as Baski Nag.

The queen of the *nāgas,* Manasā, is represented with broken hips and blind in one eye. Her special power counteracts snake venom and protects her devotees from snake-bite during the rainy season. She is worshiped widely in Bengal, where she is called Manasādevī.

Shrines to the *nāgas* are found throughout India. *Nāgakals,* snake-stones, are often erected on South Indian temple grounds or in the shade of an auspicious tree. There women worship to obtain sons or to avert an illness. An annual festival at the beginning of the rainy season, Nāgapañcami, honors the snakes. It is an ancient rite, mentioned as early as the Gṛhya Sūtras (500-200 B.C.), to honor and ward off snakes.

Bibliography. J. P. Vogel, *Indian Serpent Lore* (1926).

R. N. Minor

NAGANUMA, MYŌKŌ nä gä noo´ mä myō kyō´ (B—Jap.; 1889-1957). Co-founder of Risshō Kōseikai. Born in a small village, Shidami-mura, in Saitama Prefecture, Japan, she married early, was divorced, and married a second time when she was thirty-five years old. She was active in the Reiyūkai (a "new religion" of the Nichiren tradition) from 1936 to 1938, where she worked with Nikkyō Niwano. With Niwano, she left the Reiyūkai in 1938 to help establish Risshō Kōseikai, in which she served as vice-president. She was teacher and counselor, applying the teachings of the Lotus Sūtra in every minute area of her life. Mrs. Naganuma was a modern Shaman with a definitie aura of charisma. Having no children of her own, she adopted the second son of her younger brother, Motoyuki Naganuma, who now serves as chairman of the board of directors of Risshō Kōseikai.

N. S. Brannen

NĀGĀRJUNA nä gär´ joo nə (B—Skt.; *ca.* A.D. 150-250?). Indian Buddhist monk recognized as the founder of the Mādhyamika ("Middle Path") school. From the third century onward Buddhists in East Asia and Tibet revered him for his spiritual power and insight and designated him as a Bodhisattva. Eventually several schools acknowledged him as a patriarch.

There are popular accounts in Buddhist literature of a religious adept called Nāgārjuna who lived within five hundred years of this figure and is sometimes identified with him. They probably are different people with the same religious name or in the same spiritual lineage. Scholarly consensus places the Nāgārjuna who is an astute dialectician and author of several philosophical analyses, devotional hymns, and a statement giving ethical advice in the late second century A.D. His style of argumentation and analyses of opponents' positions confirm the earliest biographical accounts that he had classical religious training as a Brahmin, probably in South India. According to the pious biography given by Kumārajīva in the early fifth century, Nāgārjuna was converted to the doctrines and practice of the budding Mahāyāna movement in Buddhism, pursued it to its deepest meaning with the assistance of an extraordinary being, a "Mahanaga bodhisattva," and then taught this truth to other monks, receiving recognition through his success in winning over opponents in philosophical debates.

Nāgārjuna's central teaching was that all existing things are "empty" *(śūnya)* and, therefore, people can actually practice the Buddhist ideal of nonattachment to any idea, emotion, behavior, or physical entity. Through a rigorous dialectical analysis of material form, personal experience, and of an earlier Buddhist classification of the normally invisible momentary constituents of existence (*see* Dharma §5), he sought to aid naïve people, who identified their perceptions and concepts with unconditioned reality, in freeing themselves from their illusion. Often he had to ward off accusations that he was a nihilist or a cryptic idealist. Such accusations, he responded, were made with false implicit and unconscious assumptions that concepts, including "emptiness" (Śūnyatā), "Nirvana," or "me" referred in a one-to-one correspondence to self-existent things *(svabhava).*

The two basic philosophical writings still available in Sanskrit, which are acknowledged by the Buddhist schools and modern scholarship to be substantially Nāgārjuna's composition, are *Mulamadhyamakakarika (Madhyamika Karika,* "Fundamentals of the Middle Way") and *Vigrahavyavartani* ("Averting the Arguments"); seventeen Mādhyamika texts are found in the Tibetan Buddhist canon, and several treatises credited to Nāgārjuna are found only in Chinese.

Bibliography. K. K. Inada, *Nagarjuna: A Translation of His Mulamadhyamakakarika with an Introductory Essay* (1970); K. V. Ramanan, ed., *Nagarjuna's Philosophy as Presented in the Mahā-Prajñāpāramitā-Śāstra* (1966); F. J. Streng, *Emptiness: A Study in Religious Meaning* (1967).

F. J. Streng

NĀGASENA nä gŭ sā´ nŭ (B). *See* Milindapañha.

NAḤMAN OF BRATSLAV nä män brät´ släv (Ju; 1772-1810). Great-grandson of the Baal Shem Tov and founder of a major group in Hasidism. His tales show him to be master of religious narrative and familiar with modern-day struggles between faith and doubt.

K. P. Bland

NAKAYAMA MIKI nä kä yä´ mä mē´ kē (Sh—Jap.; 1798-1887). The founder of TENRI-KYŌ. Born in the historic Yamato area, the first daughter in a farm family with the surname Maekawa, she is said to have been even as a child unusually tender and considerate, qualities that are stressed repeatedly in the chronicles of her life. Her formal education was received at the nearby Jōdo temple (PURE LAND SECT of BUDDHISM), where for three years she received two hours of instruction per day in reading and writing. Otherwise her training was devoted to the acquisition of skills useful to a farm woman. At age thirteen she was married to a prosperous farmer, Nakayama Zembei, ten years her senior. She bore him one son and five daughters, two of whom died in childhood.

H. N. MCFARLAND

NALA nŭ´ lŭ (H). *See* DAMAYANTĪ.

NĀLANDĀ nä´ lŭn dä (B). Best-known of the ancient Buddhist universities, Nālandā was located near modern Rājgir in Bihār. It was active as a seat of learning for over eight hundred years (approximately A.D. 420-1240), and its reputation attracted scholars from as far away as Korea and Java.

The town of Nālandā was said to have been visited by the BUDDHA and was therefore from early times regarded by Buddhists as a holy place. Despite this, it didn't enter into prominence until the fifth century A.D., when a GUPTA king—possibly Kumāragupta I (*ca.* 415-55)—chose to erect a monastery there. After this several other Gupta rulers followed suit by erecting monasteries of their own near the first. Eventually the entire compound was encircled by a wall and the whole became one establishment, called a *mahāvihāra,* "great monastery."

Admission was gained to the university by passing a rigorous entrance examination, and the enrollment of approximately three thousand represented only about one-fifth of the total number of applicants. Once admitted, students pursued studies in grammar, medicine, logic, and other secular subjects in addition to MAHĀYĀNA Buddhism. Lectures were delivered daily from one hundred or so pulpits, arranged according to the different schools of study.

Under the Pāla dynasty (A.D. 760-1142), Nālandā entered into a period of gradual decline. The magnificent manuscript library was destroyed by fire in the tenth century, and by the thirteenth century little remained of its former glory.

Bibliography. S. Dutt, *Buddhist Monks and Monasteries of India* (1962), pp. 328-48.

J. BARE

NĀM näm (S—Skt.; lit. "name"). Used for the various names of God in SIKHISM, which is often described as *Nām Mārga,* the path of the Name as distinct from the ways of action (KARMA), knowledge (VIDYĀ), and devotion (BHAKTI). "I have no miracles except the name of God," wrote Guru NĀNAK, who exhorted his followers to repeat the name of the Lord *(Nām Japo).* He used different names for God: *Pitā* ("Father"), *Prītam* ("Lover"), *Khasam* ("Master" or husband), *dātā* ("Giver"). In the ĀDI GRANTH both Hindu and Muslim names of God appear; however, a common appellation for God in Sikhism is simply *Sat Nām* ("True Name"). The practice of repeating the names of God is based on the belief that such a practice has the potency to overcome evil (*see* MANTRA).

K. SINGH

NĀMDEV näm´ dĕv (H—born *ca.* 1270). A composer of vernacular, devotional songs to the god Viṭhobā, reputed to be a form of KRISHNA, at Paṇḍharpūr in Maharashtra, western India.

Nāmdev was the son of a tailor. According to some authorities, he met and was deeply influnced by the saint Jñāneśvar. He lived most of his life in Paṇḍharpūr composing songs of praise to Viṭhobā and other deities of VAIṢNAVISM. Some of his lyrics from HINDĪ are included in the ĀDI GRANTH of the SIKHS.

Nāmdev's songs were written in direct and inelegant Marāṭhī (the language of Maharashtra) but exhibit a passionate longing for union with Viṭhobā. They have had wide appeal among Marāṭhī-speaking Hindus of all CASTES, especially those who make periodic pilgrimages to Viṭhobā's temple in Paṇḍharpūr. Devotees of Viṭhobā regard Nāmdev as a saint. The following is one of his most revered songs (author's trans.):

Lord, your name is sweeter than nectar,/yet why is my mind not able to receive it?/Lord of Paṇḍharpūr, what can I do?/Why does your form not appear in my meditations?/When I sit listening to songs and stories of praise to you,/I am harassed by sleep and my mind is captured by sensual pleasures./The devotees of Hari (Krishna) loudly extoll the wonders of your name,/but still it does not come to rest in my heart./So says Nāma.

Bibliography. R.D. Ranade, *Pathway to God in Marathi Literature* (1961).

P. COURTRIGHT

NAMMĀḶVĀR nŭm mäl vär (H—Tamil; lit. "our Āḷvār" [*āḷvār*—"one who is immersed (in God)"]). The foremost TAMIL VAIṢNAVA poet-saint; one of the twelve ĀḶVĀRS. He probably lived in the late ninth century in the far south of India. In his poems he sometimes adopts the stance of a cowherd girl (GOPĪ) who is in love with VISHNU-KRISHNA.

G. E. YOCUM

NĀNAK nä´ näk (S; 1469-1539). Founder of the Sikh faith; the second child and only son of Mehta Kalian Das Bedi, a minor official in the revenue department, and his wife Tripta.

1. **Early life.** Most of Nānak's childhood was spent in the village of his birth, Talwandi Rai Bhoe, now named after him Nankana Sahib, about forty miles from Lahore, Pakistan. The family being Bedis

(those who know the VEDAS), a subsect of the KṢATRIYA CASTE, Nānak was taught the rudiments of Hindu religion. He also had a Muslim teacher who taught him something of the QUR'ĀN and the traditions (ḤADĪTH). According to the Janam Sākhīs ("birth stories"), Nānak was a precocious child who took little interest in his studies or his shepherding responsibilities and preferred talking to itinerant Hindu and Muslim holy men.

Nānak was betrothed at the age of twelve to Sulakhni, daughter of Mool Chand Chona of Batala. When he was nineteen Sulakhni came to live with him. She bore him two sons, Sri Chand (b. 1494) and Lakhni Das (b. 1497). Nānak took little interest in family affairs. For some years he worked as an accountant with the viceroy Daulat Khan Lodhi at Sultanpur and stayed with his elder sister, Nanaki, whose husband was also in the service of the viceroy. Under the influence of a Muslim family retainer who could play the rebeck, Nānak began to compose hymns, and the two of them organized community hymn singing. When he was in his thirtieth year, he had his first mystical experience. While bathing in the stream Bein, he disappeared and was assumed to have drowned. According to later hagiographies he was summoned by God and charged with the mission to teach mankind to pray. He emerged from the stream three days later and announced: "There is no Hindu, there is no Mussulman [Muslim]." He gave away whatever he had and decided to become a mendicant.

2. **The four journeys.** The birth stories, whose authenticity has been questioned by scholars, maintain that Nānak undertook four long voyages. The first took him eastward to Hindu holy cities, MATHURĀ, Banāras, and Gayā, through Bengal to Assam. On his return journey he visited the JAGANNĀTHA Temple in Puri as well as the whole of Orissa. Nānak then toured the Punjab, visiting Muslim SUFI establishments, and proceeded to the South of India (TAMIL country and Sri Lanka), returning via the Himalayan mountains as far as Ladakh. The fourth and last odyssey took him westward to MECCA, MEDINA, and Baghdad. On his return journey, while passing through Saidpur, he is said to have been detained in prison by the Mogul invader Babar, who sacked the town. After these journeys he settled down with his family in Kartarpur, a town he had built on the banks of the river Ravi.

The birth stories recount many incidents from these journeys. While at Hardvar on the GANGES he saw bathers throwing water toward the sun as offerings to their dead ancestors. Nānak began throwing water in the opposite direction. When questioned, he replied: "I am throwing water to my fields in the Punjab. If you can throw water to your ancestors in heaven which is millions of miles away, surely I can send it to my fields which are only 250 *kos* from here." The other incident is said to have taken place while Nānak was on his way to Mecca. He fell asleep with his feet toward the KA'BA. When a Muslim woke him and remonstrated angrily for this disrespect to the house of God, Nānak is said to have replied: "Then turn my feet toward some direction where there is no God nor the Ka'ba."

3. **Last years.** Nānak spent the last years of his life at Kartarpur, where he built a *dharmsālā* ("abode of righteousness"), preached, and sang hymns. He appointed a disciple, Lehna, renamed Angad, as his successor in preference to his two sons. The birth stories, obviously borrowing the incident from the life of KABĪR, maintain that both Hindus and Muslims claimed Nānak's body, the former to cremate him, the latter to bury him. The issue was settled by placing flowers on either side of Nānak's body. The side whose flowers remained fresh was to dispose of the body according to its custom. The next morning the mourners found flowers on either side still fresh, but the body had disappeared.

4. **The historical Nānak.** The Janam Sākhīs, on which the traditional account of Nānak's life is based, have been scrutinized by Sikh and foreign scholars and found unreliable as historical evidence. The first was written more than fifty years after Nānak's death, and they contradict each other on material detail (*see* McLeod). Nānak has practically nothing to say of incidents in his life except his presence in Saidpur when it was sacked by Babar in A.D. 1521. Even this does not tally with the sequence of events narrated in the Janam Sākhīs. Later writings of Sikh theologians and historians are equally unenlightening. The only remaining evidence are tablets discovered in Dacca and Chittagong in present-day Bangladesh and one in Baghdad which make oblique references to Nānak's visits there. But none of these tablets can be regarded as conclusive evidence.

Nānak was a poet with uncommon sensitivity to the phenomenon of nature which he employed in his passionate adulation of God. Nine hundred and seventy-four of his compositions are incorporated into the ĀDI GRANTH. *See* JAPJI.

Bibliography. W. H. McLeod, *Guru Nanak and the Sikh Religion* (1968); J. S. Grewal, *Guru Nanak in History* (1969).

K. SINGH

NANDI [also **NANDIN**] nän′ dē (H—Skt.; lit. "the happy one"). Nandi, the mythical bull, is the vehicle (VĀHANA) or mount of the great ascetic/erotic god SHIVA. The bull is often portrayed standing near Shiva in Hindu iconography. He is also portrayed as the mount of both Shiva and his consort PĀRVATĪ as they soar into the atmosphere riding on his back. Nandi can also be found facing the central shrine in most Śaivite temples in India.

The bull associated with a god is an ancient motif in India. INDRA, the famous god of the Vedas, is often described as an all-conquering bull, with the bull as his sacred animal. Indra's bull is replaced by the mythical elephant (Airāvata) in later Hindu myths and legends. It is Indra's elephant that is beheaded by

L. D. Shinn

This large Nandi is located on Chamundi Hill near Mysore, South India.

Nandi and placed upon GAṆEŚA, the elephant-headed son of Shiva. In the famous legend of Shiva's destruction of the "Triple City" of the demons (ASURAS) it is Nandi who leads the initial attack. Nandi is also well known as the doorkeeper, protecting Shiva and Pārvatī from all who would interrupt their sexual pleasures. He is, therefore, more than Shiva's mount. He is also a servant, friend, protector, and at times becomes Shiva himself. This great mythical beast is a striking representation of the impetuous and virile aspect of Shiva's nature.

Bibliography. W. D. O'Flaherty, *Asceticism and Eroticism in the Mythology of Śiva* (1973); *see* bibliog. for VĀHANA.

H. H. PENNER

NANTES, EDICT OF (Ch). *See* EDICT OF NANTES.

NARA BUDDHISM (A.D. 710-784). Introduced to Japan in A.D. 538 and first supported by the Soga clan, Buddhism rose over the objections of the pro-SHINTŌ Mononobe. When in 710 Emperor Shōmu established a new capital at Nara modeled after the capital of China, Buddhism received official support and began to flourish. Internal corruption and growing secularism emerged in the second half of this period. The monk Dōkyo exerted his influence on Empress Shotoku and plotted to ascend the throne. Finally, to curb such clerical interference, Emperor Kammu moved the capital to Heian (Kyoto) in 784.

1. **Buddhism as state religion.** Buddhism enhanced the status of the expanding imperial power and was appreciated primarily for its magico-ritual efficacy—i.e., the protection of the ruler, his estate, and the nation; curing diseases and securing benefits in this world and beyond. The objects of worship were historical Buddhas like ŚĀKYAMUNI, the coming MAITREYA, or benevolent BODHISATTVAS like AVALOKITEŚVARA (Jap.: Kannon) and Bhaiṣaijyaguru (Medicine Master; Jap.: Yakushi). Recognition of the transmundane, savior Buddha, AMIDA, did not emerge until late in Nara. Likewise, the most popular scriptures were not the more philosophical works, but the Survarṇaprabhāsa Sūtra (Sūtra of the Golden Light; Jap.: *Konkōmyōkyō*) and the *Jèn-wang-ching* (Sūtra of the Virtuous King; Jap.: *Ninnōkyō*), both of Chinese origin. Both are "nation-protecting" sūtras, and the former rallied the Four Heavenly Kings to battle against the enemies—at a time when the ruler was pushing north into AINU territories. The first and the last pages of the sūtras were ritually chanted as charms, although Japanese rulers also practiced confessions of sins for the nation. Of the sūtras copied by clerical monks, many were magical and esoteric.

Emperor Shōmu founded temples in all provinces called "Temples of the Golden Light and Four Heavenly Kings Protecting the Nation," and nunneries called "Lotus and Evil Eradicating." The Taika code of law insisted that every household also have a temple, but that meant, at best, every noble clan. Connecting all the provincial temples *(kokubunji)* under one sacred canopy was the East Great Temple, Tōdaiji, at Nara, dedicated to the Sun Buddha VAIROCANA (Jap.: Dainichi Nyōrai). Based on Chinese precedence and the Kegon (*see below*) philosophy of the perfect penetration of the One (Tōdaiji Buddha) into the many (the *kokubunji* Buddhas), Vairocana was supposed to be thus omnipresent, emanating instantaneously into all the local temples. On the eight day of every lunar month, the *Konkōmyōkyō* was chanted in all the official temples for the protection of the king and the welfare of the land. Similar rituals were planned for other festive or crisis occasions. The building of the gigantic Vairocana Buddha statue depleted the coffer; such grandiose piety was hardly the faith of the common folk.

2. **Buddhism and the native tradition.** Buddhas were no longer foreign deities, but generally gained ascendency over native Shintō KAMI. However, at the state level the Sun Buddha was identified with the Sun Goddess, AMATERASU, ancestress to the imperial house, and Tōdaiji had to have the blessing of positive oracles from HACHIMAN, a deity of northern Kyūshū, who miraculously also supplied gold for plating the statue. Hachiman was moved to become the protector of Tōdaiji. Lesser kamis were often considered to be within the cycles of rebirth (SAMSARA), in need of eventual liberation, and so sūtras were chanted on their behalf. In 616, a native oracle gave to Buddhists the function of conducting funerals, a function which Shintō could not handle, and in 700 the first cremation—of a monk trained in China—was reported. Soon afterward emperors and empresses were buried in the Buddhist style in tombs outside the capital, with the fanfare originally reserved for the monks. The securing of bliss for ancestors was a key concern, but the various PURE LANDS were ill-defined in the people's mind. The Pure Land of Amida was indistinguishable from the samsaric heaven or native concepts of paradise.

3. The six Nara Buddhist schools. Six scholarly disciplines were pursued by a small number of monks at designated home temples in Nara. They were extensions of Chinese scholarship.

a) The Kusha (Chin.: *Chü-she;* Skt.: *Abhidharmakośa*) school. A Hīnayāna tradition of the Sarvāstivāda branch committed to a "realist" analysis of phenomena into their component elements *(dharmas).*

b) The Jōjitsu (Chin.: *Ch'eng-shih;* Skt.: *Satyasiddhi)* school. A Hīnayāna tradition of the Sautrāntika branch joining the above "realist" analysis of phenomena to the Mahāyāna doctrine of a pervasive emptiness (Śūnyatā).

c) The Sanron (Chin.: *San-lun,* Three Treatises) school. The Mahāyāna Mādhyamika (Middle Path) philosophy of emptiness committed to a systematic negation of any position by exposing the antinomies innate to "realist" thinking, thereby endorsing the nonduality of samsara and Nirvana as well as other opposites and encouraging a freedom based on nongrasping (of anything as absolute.) *See* Nāgārjuna.

d) The Hossō (Chin.: *Fa-hsiang,* Dharma-characteristics) school. Representing the Buddhist idealism of Yogācāra specifically, the Vijñaptimātratā (Representation Only) philosophy of Dharmapāla and committed to seeing all realities as mere ideations of the mind. *See* Fa-hsiang.

e) The Kegon (Chin.: *Hua-yen*) school. Based on the *Hua-yen* or Avataṁsaka Sūtra (Wreath or Garland Sūtra) and centered on Vairocana as the cosmic Buddha that encompasses all beings—an extravagant grand vision involving the total penetration of the one and the many, the part and the whole, the noumenal and the phenomenal.

f) The Ritsu (Chin.: *Lü;* Skt.: *Vinaya*) School. Dedicated to the study of Hīnayānist monastic precepts or disciplines.

By later standards the six Nara schools were considered narrow, academic, and cloistered traditions, but they provided important intellectual foundations for future developments. Kusha and Jōjitsu were judged Hīnayānist; even Sanron and Hossō were called expedient Mahāyāna; the Ritsu school was superseded later by so-called Mahāyāna precepts; only Kegon, the one school based directly on a Mahāyāna sūtra, could claim the higher, universalistic vision. However, in practice, Kegon's grandiose philosophy catered more to the theocratic vision of Tōdaiji and the rulers. Hossō instead nurtured more social activism. The Ritsu school controlled the right to ordination and would seek to block any unauthorized new schools seeking autonomy either in the Heian period (794-1185) or the Kamakura period (1185-1333). The six schools were overseen by the state. Though displaced by Heian Buddhism, some schools continued through the centuries.

4. Popular Buddhism. Despite the strong alliance of Buddhism with the ruling elite, the universalistic and evangelical spirit of Mahāyāna did spearhead some popular movements. Often popular preaching and social welfare activities mingled with elements of Shamanism. Court intrigues in late Nara might have caused some holy men to retreat to the mountain and further the Yamabushi tradition. By and large, Buddhism supplied to the people anthropomorphic deities and approachable images far more powerful and functionally specialized than the Shintō gods. Above all, as can be inferred from the karmic stories in the *Nihon Ryōiki,* the populace had been taught the doctrines of Karma, samsara, and moral retribution.

Nara Buddhism, like the city of Nara itself, was relatively formal, rigid, and public in character. It carried the stamp of Chinese culture and had to be made indigenous and given independent expression. It had neither the aesthetic sensitivity of the Heian Buddhists toward, for example, the sense of impermanence *(mujō)* or the crisis mentality of Kamakura faiths. The religion was not interiorized and the world was seldom negated. Yet there was strength in its optimism and efficacy in its socio-political functions. W. Lai

NĀRADA nä′ rŭ dŭ (H—Skt.; lit. "water-giver"). Nārada is one of the most colorful sages of classical Indian lore, although he does not fit easily into any of the typical classes of beings. Sometimes he is a Prajāpati (one of the primal beings made by the creator to carry on the creative process), sometimes a Gandharva (heavenly musician) chief; and in sectarian Vaiṣṇavism he is a perpetual Brahmācarin (ascetic) and released soul as an eternal devotee of Vishnu, whose praises he sings. His name seems to connect him with Nārāyaṇa, a name for Vishnu. He travels through all worlds as a lute-carrying musician and eloquent speaker, but where he appears he usually brings as much trouble as pleasure. He is said to delight in conflict, though the dissension he sows is said to be for the welfare of the worlds. For instance, it is Nārada who urges Yudhiṣṭhira to perform the Rājasūya sacrifice that sets in motion the events that build to the Mahābhārata war, and is then on hand at the war's end to neutralize the weapons of doomsday.

A. Hiltebeitel

NĀRĀYAṆA nä rī′ yŭ nŭ (H—Skt.). One of the many names or identities of Vishnu in Bhakti Hinduism; originally a priestly deity identified in late Vedic texts with the Puruṣa (the "Primal Person"). The Mahābhārata further identifies him with both Vishnu and the popular deity Vāsudeva-Krishna, and refers to Arjuna and Krishna, the protagonists of the Bhagavad Gītā, as Nara (man) and Nārāyaṇa (god). Nārāyaṇa most often represents Vishnu in his cosmic aspect, especially in his mythological association with the primordial waters. *See* Śeṣa; Vaikuntha.

T. J. Hopkins

NĀSTIKA näs′ tī kŭ (H—Skt.; lit. "one who says, there is not"). A number of nihilistic schools of thought in ancient India. The *nāstikas* opposed most of the doctrines of orthodox HINDUISM, and were thus atheistic and existentialist in outlook. More generally, this term refers to all religious groups who deny the authority of the VEDAS and, therefore, are deemed unorthodox; that is, "non-Hindu."

J. BARE

NAṬARĀJA nä tä rä′ jŭ (H—Skt.; lit. "king of the dance" [*naṭ*—"to dance," *rājan*—"king"). A form of the Hindu god SHIVA, who appears as Lord of the Dance in texts and icons. The form is particularly prominent in South India, where it almost certainly originated, but has become one of the most popular visual images in India and Hindu Southeast Asia.

1. **Iconographical development.** Naṭarāja first appears on sculptures from the GUPTA period in the fifth century A.D. Shiva appears in this form in bas reliefs at the great temples of ELLORĀ and Elephanta and in numerous bronze sculptures from the Chōḻa empire in South India, dating from the tenth century A.D. Textbooks on dance and theater describe and analyze 108 forms of dance, and textbooks on sculpture provide iconographical details for 108 dances of Shiva, divided into two main groups, gentle and fierce.

2. **Textual development.** Shiva is first depicted as a dancer in the MAHĀBHĀRATA, where he laughs, sings, and dances charmingly, sporting in phallic nakedness with the wives of the sages in a great forest. This erotic dance is described at greater length in the PURĀṆAS, where it results in Shiva's castration by the angry sages and their ultimate worship of his LIṄGA. In South Indian TAMIL texts, however, the castration is replaced by another dance, this time of an aggressive nature: Shiva's dance generates a fiery energy that forms a flame halo about his body and repels the weapons that the sages hurl against him. This destructive dance, called the *tāṇḍava*, is a particular manifestation of the cosmic doomsday dance in which Shiva releases all of his destructive powers to set the universe aflame at the end of the YUGA. Contrasted with the *tāṇḍava* is the *lāsya*, the peaceful erotic dance that Shiva performs in the company of his gentle consort, PĀRVATĪ, or with the wives of the sages. When dancing with his more orgiastic and dominant partner, KĀLĪ, Shiva becomes dangerous again, as she is; when Kālī rages out of control, Shiva engages her in a dance contest and dances her into submission. Bengali texts and icons depict Kālī dancing on the corpse of Shiva, and Tamil texts from the temple of Naṭarāja at Chidambaram in Madras State relate the myth of the dance contest performed in the presence of all the gods and sages.

3. **Interpretations of Naṭarāja.** Many texts have been generated in response to the icon, interpreting the dance of Shiva in terms of BHAKTI theology, particularly ŚAIVA SIDDHĀNTA. In these analyses, Shiva dances to quicken life through his rhythmic activity, releasing the souls of men from the snare of illusion and dancing in the heart of the devotee. Earlier texts, however, emphasize the destructive aspect of the dance: in the Mahābhārata, Shiva produces ashes from his veins to stop the ascetic Maṅkaṇaka from dancing in ecstasy; in the Purāṇas, he performs the dance of death in the burning-grounds. The ascetic dance becomes the doomsday *danse macabre;* the erotic dance creates the universe. In keeping with this ambivalence, the small figure crushed under Shiva's foot in the bronze icons is sometimes said to be a demon of confusion or epilepsy (Apasmāra Puruṣa), but may be a devotee in the most fortunate of situations: under the foot of the lord. *See* ŚAKTI; DANCE, SACRED § 4.

L. D. Shinn

Shiva as Naṭarāja. The drum and fire in his upper hands signify his rhythmic creativity and destructive power; one hand is held in the mudrā of protection.

Bibliography. C. Sivaramamurti, *Naṭarāja in Art, Thought and Literature* (1974); T. A. Gopinatha Rao, *Elements of Hindu Iconography* (1914), II, 1, 221-70.

W. D. O'FLAHERTY

NATION OF ISLAM IN THE WEST. *See* BLACK RELIGIONS IN THE UNITED STATES §5.

NATIONAL COUNCIL OF THE CHURCHES OF CHRIST IN THE U.S.A. A cooperative agency of many ORTHODOX and PROTESTANT churches organized in 1950 from fourteen earlier ecumenical commissions and councils. It is concerned with religious education, home and world mission, humanitarian service, communications, social justice, Christian unity, and world peace. *See* ECUMENICAL MOVEMENT.

J. R. NELSON

NATIVE AMERICAN TRIBAL RELIGION. At the time of European discovery, North America was inhabited by over a million people who spoke a variety of languages and dialects, who were organized into a large number of tribes ranging in size from small bands to confederacies and states of considerable size, and who engaged in diverse forms of environmental adaptation, with hunting and gathering dominating in some areas, agriculture in others. Here also were numerous and diverse systems of thought and action which have been termed religions.

These native peoples were all variants of a basic Mongoloid stock whose ancestors entered the New World by way of a land bridge across the Bering Strait during the last glacial period. These migrants were hunting large game in the plains and the Southwest at least eleven thousand years ago. Over the next ten thousand years various hunting and gathering strategies developed into regional traditions. The exploitation of wild plant resources and small game in the desert West provided the basis for the later development of agriculture in Mexico and neighboring areas, while in the Eastern forests hunting, gathering, and fishing continued as primary means of subsistence.

Archaeological evidence and ethnographic descriptions have provided a much fuller portrait of the past two thousand years. The recognition of the relation between culture and environment led anthropologists during the early years of the twentieth century to formulate the concept of culture areas: geographical regions with generally similar culture patterns. Rejecting environmental determinism, they preferred the notion of culture areas over evolutionary frameworks as a heuristic device in which to consider the diversity of North American

tribal cultures (see map). If the migrants to the New World brought much in common in religion, the vicissitudes of time and space, of migration and adaptation to differing ecological conditions contributed to the differentiation and development of hundreds, perhaps thousands, of tribal religions in native North America. While the culture area concept has proved useful particularly in describing material culture and subsistence strategies, it affords little more than a locational key in considering the myriad symbol systems of kinship and religion.

1. **Methodological issues.** Native American religions have been the subject of a wide range of Euro-American scholarly perspectives. Since none of the peoples here under consideration—except the Maya and the Aztecs—developed writing, nearly all accounts are the products of missionaries, explorers, anthropologists, and historians. All of these descriptions have involved translations into languages, categories, and systems of thought different from those of the native peoples. Some translations have also sought to place these religions in a variety of intellectual frameworks in an effort not only to describe but to understand and explain.

The accounts of missionaries have been noted for their objectivity, from the Jesuit relations of the seventeenth and eighteenth centuries to the work of Father Berard Haile, who recorded vast amounts of Navajo myth and ritual in the twentieth century. Rich descriptions of native American ritual were also produced by a number of explorers, many of whom were associated with the Bureau of American Ethnology (1871-1964). Included here are James Mooney (the Ghost Dance religion), Matilda Coxe Stevenson (the Zuni), Alice C. Fletcher (Pawnee ceremony). Other studies of ritual and religion include John G. Bourke (Apache), Washington Matthews (Navajo), Frank Hamilton Cushing (Zuni), W. J. Hoffman (Ojibway), James Mooney (Cherokee), and J. O Dorsey (Sioux). Although the dominant theoretical orientation in English and American anthropology during the second half of the nineteenth century was evolutionary, almost no effort was made to place native American religions in a cross-cultural framework.

Franz Boas and his students in the American historical school rejected evolutionary theory. They sought to understand historical relationships and emphasized a more inductive approach which came to be called "historical particularism." One of their major concerns was material culture, and they catalogued impressive lists of "culture traits." Nevertheless, Boas (Kwakiutl), A. L. Kroeber (California), Frank Speck (Algonkian groups; Naskapi-Montagnais), Ruth Bunzel (Zuni), Elsie Clews Parsons (Rio Grande and Western Pueblos), Gladys Reichard (Navajo), and Ruth Underhill (Papago), through extensive field work assembled excellent descriptions of native American ritual. Eventually Boas' students produced studies of native American religious ritual in every major culture area, although for the most part their investigations of religion were only part of a wider concern with culture (material and behavioral). During this same period two textbooks appeared—both entitled *Primitive Religion*—which gave considerable attention to native American religions. One was by Robert Lowie, who had done field work among the Crow of Montana, and one by Paul Radin, who had studied the Winnebago and other Eastern woodlands groups.

By the 1930s functionalism and thematic studies were beginning to replace evolutionism and historical studies, and the unit of analysis shifted from "culture traits" to "cultural systems." Ruth Benedict became one of the most popular proponents of the integrationalist (or configurationalist) approach to culture through her book *Patterns of Culture*. This emphasis on cultural systems took many forms. Of these, the structural-functionalism of A. R. Radcliffe-Brown influenced the study of native American religions by placing primary emphasis on kinship and social organization (e.g. F. Eggan). Here and in a variety of psychological studies an effort was made to understand the function of religion in society and in individual personalities.

The impact of Euro-American culture brought about radical culture change in all native American societies. Efforts to describe early religions from documentary evidence, as in William Fenton's ethnohistoric studies of the Iroquois, were one result. In addition, studies of such nativistic and revivalistic movements as Handsome Lake Religion (*see below* §5) and the peyote religion sought the causes of these movements in the experience of relative deprivation.

Since World War II two major approaches have marked a shift in concern from function to meaning. The first, French structuralism, is a cross-cultural methodology which has been applied to a wide range of native American myth and ritual art by Lévi-Strauss. In seeking to delineate the universal laws which regulate the unconscious activities of the human mind, Lévi-Strauss has illuminated not only the logic of systems of classification and myth, but has shown that Amerindian peoples participated in a universe of meaning which extended throughout North and South America.

The second approach, American symbolic anthropology, is concerned with systems of meaning and action and how these are given symbolic expression. Combining ideas from Emile Durkheim and Max Weber, a number of American anthropologists regard cultural or symbolic systems (e.g. kinship, religion and politics) as shaping individual experience and channeling social activities, thereby contributing to both stability and change in individual and social life. These cultural systems provide sets of conceptions of and orientations to the world, embodied in symbols and symbolic forms. Each system consists of "a system of units (or parts) which are defined in certain ways and which are differentiated according to certain criteria. These units define the world or the universe, the way the things in it relate to each other, and what these things should be and do" (Schneider, p. 1). Human beings are conceived of as seekers and creators of meaning, and the primary scholarly concern becomes one of description and interpretation of these activities. This approach involves not only an acceptance of diversity but a sense that it is our ethical responsibility to deal with other people and other conceptual worlds with respect and empathy. Examples of this approach include A. Ortiz's *The Tewa World* (1969) and E. Z. Vogt's *Tortillas for the Gods*.

This brief survey of Euro-American scholarship reveals a number of shifts in interests, approaches and area foci with the negative result that it is not possible to portray the development of native American tribal religions or even—except in a few cases—to provide a full account of one religion at one point in time. Moreover, the concept of religion has been largely Euro-American, and this has shaped the questions asked and the data collected in field studies. In no instance has the thought world of a native American people been so mapped that boundaries might be drawn around a domain one might assuredly call "religion." For example, following E. B. Tylor's definition of religion as involving belief in gods and spirits, many early field workers placed a primary emphasis on determining the presence of spirits, "gods," etc.; the functionalist perspective carried with it an emphasis on ritual and "ceremonialism," and the question of "beliefs" was largely set aside.

2. The religious symbol system. Religion consists, in part, of a set of conceptions of and orientations to the world embodied in symbols and symbolic forms. If we ask how each religious world view is constituted, of what units it is constructed, how these units are defined and given expression, and how the units form a meaningful whole, we will begin to understand the intellectual dimension and perhaps also the emotional dimension of native American symbol systems. The component here termed "world view" includes concepts of space and time, theories as to the origin and destiny of a people, assumptions about the nature of humans and their relations to one another, and their place in the natural order. These notions are given expression in a variety of symbolic media (language, dance, architecture) through the use of color and other visual devices.

a) Space. The cultural construction of space among native American peoples involved systems of two, four, five, and seven units with direction as the primary denotation. Systems with two units were defined by reference to some natural phenomena, e.g., "upstream" and "downstream" among the Yurok of California. Frequently these bipartite conceptions were closely related to categories of person and the organization of the ritual calendar (time), as with the dual organization of the Tewa of New Mexico. Like the Euro-American four-part system of "north," "south," "east," and "west," native American spatial systems consisted of opposed sets of terms, frequently with "up," "down" and a "middle" category added. Also like the Euro-American use of magnetic and polar norths, the directional dimension was linked with culturally significant natural phenomena. The Saulteaux of the central Canadian subarctic made reference to the North star, the movements of the sun, and the "homes" of the four winds. To these were sometimes added "straight up" and "down." However, it was in terms of the four winds that wider aspects of the Saulteaux universe were defined. Among the Chamula, a modern Mayan people in Mexico, the sun is the key symbolic referent. Here the cardinal directions are derived from the relative position of the sun on its east-west path across the heavens: "emergent heat of day" (east), "waning heat of day" (west), "the edge of heaven on the right hand" (north), and "the edge of heaven on the left hand" (south). In the Southwestern culture area, the Zuni directional system was related to wind and temperature changes, and the Hopi system was associated with the position of the sun on the eastern horizon at the summer and winter solstices. This space was bounded, often by mountains but frequently by bodies of water (Hopi, rivers; Zuni, oceans), which were conceived to be continuous with the blue-water above. The world was generally viewed as a flat surface with one or more categories of space above and below. There appears to have been a fairly close correlation between the shape of this world (square or circular) and house form, e.g. nomadic peoples (plains, Navajo) living in circular space, and settled peoples (many Puebloans) occupying square worlds. Many of these systems included a "middle place" (Zuni) and/or a different, sacred "emergence place" (Zuni, Hopi). These central points were related to both horizontal and vertical systems and in the latter case were tied to myths of origin and concepts of lower and upper worlds. For the Navajo, in the first world (black), second (blue), third (yellow), and fourth (white), various plants, animals, and other objects came into being which were associated in this (fifth) world—in an elaborate system of correspondences—with the four directions. For many, "east" was the most auspicious direction, "west" (Hopi) and "north" (Navajo) less often so. While these categories were related as opposed sets or systems, they were frequently related in a sequentially meaningful manner: "east" to "north" in a clockwise movement for the Navajo, "north" to "east" for the Hopi, Zuni, etc. Further, there was sometimes a reciprocal relationship, for example, in which prayer-offerings were made to the four directions and blessings were to come, in turn, to the middle (all Puebloan groups). These logical structures were interrelated with other systems of ideas to form the structure of the world of meaning—the cosmological framework—in which these peoples lived. In this moral topography, different categories of person were associated with or had access to these levels of space, as for the Tewa where various exchanges with the spirits took place at shrines near the point where this world and the world of the spirits intersected.

Perhaps the most elaborate conceptions belonged to the world views of the ancient Maya and Aztecs and their modern descendants. In the state of Chiapas, the modern Tzotzil Indians preserved a spatial image of the universe much like that recorded for the early Maya. For the Tzotzil the earth was a flat, square surface located in the center of the universe. Like the Maya of the ancient codices, these people viewed the sky as a mountain with thirteen steps, six on the eastern side, six on the western, and the thirteenth in the middle forming the summit of the heavens. The underworld was also a pyramidal structure with nine, thirteen, or an indeterminate number of steps. Here spatial and temporal ideas were coordinated, as the sun was conceived to ascend in a cart following a path of flowers, advancing one step per hour until it reached the zenith where it rested for an hour. Resuming its journey it descended toward the western world where it disappeared into the sea, leaving everything in darkness. This passage was then reversed in the lower world, Olontik, the abode of the dead, where the sun descended toward a middle point, midnight, and then began to ascend again. From below, the heavens resembled a dome placed on the surface of the earth with a gigantic ceiba tree rising from the center of the earth toward the heavens. The heavens were the home of benevolent deities: creators and makers of all human, animal, and vegetable life. In the lower world lived evil gods who fought to undo the work of the heavenly gods and tried to win over occupants for the world of the dead. Life was thus a constant struggle between opposing forces of good and evil. As with many other native American peoples, this spatial conception was given architectural expression, as in the *cuauhcalli,* a small stepped pyramid dedicated to the sun, in the great temple of Mexico-Tenochtitlan.

The concepts of "right" and "left" were used throughout native North America as the basis of systems of symbolic classification in terms of which vast amounts of cultural and natural phenomena were ordered. Occasionally, as with the Osage of the southern plains, they constituted the primary symbolic device underlying both world view and ritual practice. As with four-part systems which have the cardinal directions as the primary categories, various associations were made with these two directions. Thus the Osage saw life as deriving from the creative powers of the sky and earth and the continuity of life as dependent on the unity of the two powers. This division was reflected in the social and ritual organization of the Osage, in which the Tsízhu people represented sky and the Hóⁿga, the earth. In tribal ritual these two divisions faced each other in parallel lines extending east and west, with the space in between representing the path traveled by the sun between the sky and the earth. Within this framework, all symbols and symbolic acts were expressed with reference to "left" and "right," with unity of the divisions the ultimate concern.

The units and organization of space were given symbolic expression in a variety of ways, among them color and architectural form. Although direction was defined differently from people to people, color was a primary nonverbal code used to express these significant cultural distinctions. In the chart below, examples from a number of native American groups are given:

	[East]	[South]	[West]	[North]	[Down]	[Up]
Apache	Black	White	Yellow	Blue		
Cherokee	Red	White	Black	Blue		
Cheyenne	Yellow	Black	Red	White		
Creek	White	Blue	Black	Red & Yellow		
Hopi	White	Red	Blue	Yellow	All	Black
Navajo	White	Blue	Yellow	Black		
Sioux	Red	Black	Yellow	Blue		
Zuni	White	Red	Blue	Yellow	Black	All

Architectural form in its most common occurrence—as home or dwelling—is not only adaptational but is meaningful as well. Although many house forms are expressions of significant aspects of kinship and social organization, many are also expressions of significant features of a people's world view. The following statement was made by an Oglala Dakota Sioux near the turn of this century: "The Oglala believe the circle to be sacred because the great spirit caused everything in nature to be round except stone. Stone is the implement of destruction. The sun and the sky, the earth and the moon, are round like a shield, though the sky is deep like a bowl. Everything that breathes is round like the body of a man. Everything that grows from the ground is round like the stem of a plant. Since the great spirit has caused everything to be round, mankind should look upon the circle as sacred, for it is the symbol of all things in nature except stone. It is also the symbol of the circle that marks the edge of the world and therefore of the four winds that travel there. Consequently it is also the symbol of the year. The day, the night, and the moon go in a circle above the sky. Therefore the circle is a symbol of these divisions of time and hence the symbol of all time. For these reasons the Oglala make their tipis circular, their camp-circle circular, and sit in a circle in all ceremonies. The circle is also the symbol of the tipi and of shelter. If one makes a circle for an ornament and it is not divided in any way, it should be understood as the symbol of the world and of time" (Walker, p. 160).

It is not contradictory to hold that architectural form derives its meaning in part from "kinship" and in part from "religion." At times the religious system of meaning may dominate, especially when this space is used for a ritual. A case in point is the Navajo hogan, a conical structure built of wooden poles, laid over with sticks and a thick layer of earth. With each element of the hogan given a symbolic value or attribute, these structures were the proper place for

Navajo ritual as well as their dwelling (*see* B. Haile). In the twentieth century Navajos have adopted the house form of the larger American culture, but the hogan remains, often alongside, as an essential element in the expression and performance of Navajo ritual. In more complex and differentiated societies specialized structures were built for ritual performance, ranging from small shrines to massive earth works and stone pyramids. The concept of space—how it is defined, logically structured, and symbolically expressed—was a fundamental element in the world view of native American peoples and essential to an understanding of ritual performance.

b) Time. Unquestionably the most complex conceptualization of time was that of the ancient Maya who had, in León-Portilla's perspective, an obsessive interest in formulating a science of time with an unending desire for exactitude. The primacy of time in the Maya world view led León-Portilla to propose the concept of "chronotheism" to describe the power and personification involved. The word *kinh*—the semantic complex "sun-day-time"—is the key unit in this system. *Kinh* was not just an abstract concept but a divine being who set forth the rhythmic patterns responsible for creating and governing all existing things. This chronotheism resulted in a concept of a universe in which the passage of time marked the arrival and departure of evil and good divine forces. Hence the Maya had a "chronovision" of the universe: time gave meaning to space and to being. While space seems to have been the more important element in the world view of other native American peoples, here was a "religio-mathematical vision of the universe" with time as the key.

3. **Ritual.** Leach has proposed using the term "ritual" to denote the communicative aspect of behavior. In Leach's words, "All speech is a form of customary behavior, but likewise, all customary behavior is a form of speech, a code of communication. In our dress, in our manners, even in our most trivial gestures we are constantly 'making statements' that others can understand" (p. 523). While all ritual has to do with relationships, what distinguishes religious ritual is that the primary relationship is between humans and spirits, not simply between individuals and/or groups. In part, the paradigmatic elements of world view (the systematic, symbolic expressions of space and time) provide the syntax through which religious ritual communication takes place. However, ritual employs a number of meaning systems besides that of language. Expressive media such as color, dance, masking, percussion, etc. use not only the communicative structure of language but a number of other logical operations: identification, exchange or reciprocity, contrast, inversion, metaphor, inclusion, marking, transformation, transitivity, contiguity, etc. It is important to emphasize that the structure of these nonverbal codes is not identical with language. The number four is frequently used to establish and order space and time, as in the Okipa ritual of the Mandan in which the events of creation are acted out with increasing intensity over four days with four, then eight, twelve, and sixteen appearances of dancers. Metaphor is found throughout Northwest coast ritual and ritual art, as animals and humans are interlocked and coexist by a visual punning which allows feet to become teeth as a human is swallowed by a bear, a cockle's foot to be also a tongue in the shell-face of a rattle, etc. It has further been suggested that many religious rituals attempt to convert meaning into power or to endow power with meaning. It is here, especially, that the subjective, experiential dimensions of native American religion—the joy, laughter, pain, quiet, the moods and motivations—were created and yet were so poorly and infrequently described in ethnographic literature.

a) Calendrical rituals. Rituals may be distinguished as "calendrical" or "critical." Many—perhaps most—native American tribal peoples had annual rituals, some closely tied to lunar and solar observations, others associated with events in the subsistence cycle (hunting, harvesting). For example, following the lengthy and complex midwinter ceremonial, the Iroquois performed a series of rituals: Maple ("they are thankful for the maple"), Sun ("they are thankful for the sun"), Thunder ("they are thankful for the Thunderers"), Seed Planting ("they lay down thanks for the seed"), Strawberry ("they gather berries"), Bean ("they gather beans"), Green Corn ("they gather food"), and Harvest ("the harvest is completed"). For the Pawnee, the several ceremonies of the spring planting and fall harvest formed parallel series of six. The Mandan ritual calendar was associated with the spring, summer, fall, and winter buffalo; ceremonies for warfare and doctoring were held at any time. In addition, rituals relating to agriculture were begun in late winter, when the first water birds appeared, and were held throughout the summer, until the southern flight of these birds had passed.

The logic and complexity of calendrical systems is illustrated by the Hopi of the Southwest whose ceremonial cycle consists of two major periods of masked and unmasked rituals bounded by the summer and winter solstices. Hopi conceptions of time and space were fundamentally bipartite and included an upper world of the living and a lower world of the dead and spirits. The two worlds were related in a number of ways, most clearly expressed in the sun's journey on its daily rounds. The sun had two entrances (lit., houses, homes, *kivas*) located at the extreme ends of its course. In the morning the sun emerged from its eastern house and in the evening descended into its western home. During the night the sun traveled from west to east in order to arrive at its accustomed place the next day. With day and night reversed in the upper and lower worlds, so too were summer and winter and life and death. However, they were not seen as simply opposed but as involved in a system of alternation, continuity, consubstantiality, and reciprocity. This world and the world of the spirits were transformations of each other. At death a cotton mask (a "white cloud mask") was placed on the face of the dead person. The spirits of the dead return to this world as *kachinas* (ancestral spirits), and all *kachinas* were believed to take on cloud form—to be "cloud people." Many Hopi birth and death practices paralleled each other, as death was birth to a new world. It follows then that one half of the Hopi ritual calendar involved "priestly" activities which consisted, in large part, of prayers and prayer offerings to the spirit world, while the other half consisted of activities surrounding the presence of the *kachinas* in this world. The *kachinas*—their masked impersonators—were "messengers of the gods" who came to sit and listen to the petitions of the people and bring them assurances that their prayers had been heard. On these ritual occasions the Hopis "feed" the *kachinas* with prayer offerings, and the masked dancers reciprocate with gifts of food. (*See* Plate VII b.) Thus, these two categories of religious specialist were opposed in space and time and by virtue of the presence or absence of the mask, but were, at the same time, related through the cycle of reciprocity. While one purpose of ritual in this world was to contribute to the well-being of the spirit world, the spirit world was obligated to contribute to the well-being of this world by providing the rain that is essential to crops and, hence, to the health of Hopis and all living things of this world.

b) Critical rituals. In contrast to calendrical rituals which are generally for a social group (e.g., clan, village), critical rituals are almost always directed toward an individual. The girl's puberty ceremony, or *nai'es* ("preparing her"; "getting her ready") of the Cibecue Apache took a young woman symbolically through the four stages of life and emphasized the four major values to which she should aspire: physical strength, an even temperament, prosperity, and a sound, healthy old age. As Basso has noted, "The primary objective of the puberty ceremony is to transform the pubescent girl into the mythological figure . . . Changing Woman. At the request of the presiding medicine man, and 'traveling on his chants,' the power of Changing Woman enters the girl's body and resides there for four days. During this time, the girl acquires all the desirable qualities of Changing Woman herself, and is thereby prepared for a useful and rewarding life as an adult" (p. 64).

Navajo ceremonial practice consisted almost entirely of critical rituals. In the world view of these people everything was related to humans and their activities, including all natural phenomena, which were viewed as either friends or enemies. Earth-Surface-People (humans), the *diyin diné'e* (Holy People), and natural phenomena all possessed the same kinds of souls and all shared the same life-giving forces. However, some natural phenomena and the Holy People shared the quality of being "dangerous" and were capable of causing illness to humans. In nearly all Navajo rituals an actual patient was treated for a real or anticipated ailment. Navajo rituals were of two kinds: (1) "chants" or "sings" *(hatáál)* in which a rattle was used, and (2) all others in which a rattle was not used. Chants had two, five, and nine night forms and were differentiated according to mode of performance as a Holy Way, Ugly Way, or Life Way. A chant was selected according to the perceived origin of the disease of the patient being treated. Holy Way was used if the illness was thought to be caused by the Holy People, Ugly Way if the illness was caused by the ghost of fellow tribesmen or witches, and Life Way for those suffering from injuries attributed to accidents, recent or past. If the cause was not known, DIVINATION was used. The curing "ceremony" was performed by a *hatááli,* a "singer"—so called because singing or chanting accompanied every important act in the ritual performance. In Navajo ritual symbolic objects and actions were used with reference to the patient's body to effect a transformation from a state of "ugly conditions" to a state of "pleasant conditions." Accompanying each chant was a myth which identified the major Holy People symbolized in the chant, aided in interpreting the songs which accompanied the ritual, and explained the origin and significance of objects used during the ritual. The sequential expression of events in time in the myth was transformed into a coincident expression of symbols in the elaborate sand paintings created during the ceremony (*see* Plate VII a). The hogan, the sand paintings, the arrangement of ritual participants all replicated the Navajo conception of their world: the circular horizon, the two sexes, the clockwise movement of the sun, the four directions with their associated colors, jewels, animals, birds, plants, etc. The purpose of a chant is to counteract the "action against" the patient, to remove ugly conditions, to produce immunity by making the patient *diyin* (holy), and thus to create pleasant conditions (health). Here, as elsewhere, communication and exchange are basic elements in the ritual process.

4. **Religious specialists.** In all native American societies, kinship provided symbols which defined and differentiated members of the family and larger social units. These same symbols defined and differentiated the kinds of relationships which these persons should have with each other. Religion also provided sets of symbols which defined and differentiated categories of person and the relationships which existed between humans and members of the spirit world. These human and spirit "persons" constituted a distinctive "religious" system of person categories which were defined and given symbolic expression with distinctive features such as dress and "faces" (masked or painted) and who acted within accepted systems of thought and action.

All native American groups had religious specialists. In some societies the role provided the primary identity for an individual (e.g., the *angakok* of the

Eskimo), while in others an individual might be a religious specialist temporarily, occasionally, and recurrently (e.g., a Hopi male might assume the role of six or more different categories of religious specialist during one year). Some religious specialists operated alone (e.g., the Navajo "singer") while in many other instances they were members of organized groups, "societies" (the plains Crow *bacuśua,* California Chusash *'antap,* and Southwestern Keresan *hictíani* and *cko.yo*). Some religious specialists functioned in reponse to individual life crisis, especially "sickness" (e.g., the Great Basin Paviotso *puhágəm,* and the Mexican Tarahumara *owerúame*) while others performed within the framework of an annual "ritual calendar." Frequently the religious specialist sought to mediate or communicate to the spirits, while in other instances humans represented spirits (e.g., the Puebloan *kachina* and the Navajo *ye'ii* impersonator).

Religious specialists existed and acted in the distinctive temporal and spatial contexts of rituals. In so doing they frequently were significantly attired, and they communicated through ordinary and extraordinary expressive media (e.g., drums, rattles, and other percussion instruments, special languages, dance, smoke, feathers, etc.). In some instances dreams and various hallucinogenically or physically altered states of consciousness provided the source of meaning and power which were experienced and understood in culturally accepted frameworks (e.g., dreams or hallucinations in the Plateau Sanpoil visions quests; use of "torture" in the Mandan Okipa ceremony; use of the drugs *datura* or *toloache* in the rituals of many southern California peoples).

Unquestionably the most common label used to describe native American religious specialists is SHAMAN. As a category of religious specialists "shaman," in Eliade's classic study, denotes a person who undergoes an ecstatic trip to heaven, to the lower world, or to the depths of the ocean. Frequently this voyage is undertaken to cure a sick person or to accompany the souls of the dead to hell. Moreover, in the case of some Siberian peoples it may also take place to present the soul of a sacrificial horse to the Celestial Deity. While in Eliade's view all shamans are healers and conductors of souls, it is the "ecstatic technique" of voyaging which sets the shaman apart from other religious specialists. Throughout ethnographic literature use of the term "shaman" is meant to suggest that the individual possesses or is possessed by powers received in dream, vision, or trance which may be used to cure an individual, usually in the context of an extended family. Unfortunately the term has not been used with care (if it should be used at all)—the Navajo "singer" has been called both a shaman and a priest—and an awareness of the diversity, richness, and complexity of native American religious specialists has been lost or negated.

In many societies a number of religious specialists performed together in complex ritual dramas. The Mandan Okipa ceremony was a four day "dramatization of the creation of the earth, its people, plants, and animals, together with the struggles the Mandan endured to attain their present position" (Bowers, p. 111). While the ritual focuses on the figure of Lone Man, there were other major participants—Speckled Eagle, Giver of the Ceremony or Okipa Maker, and the singers—as well as a number of dancers (in pairs, one from each moiety or tribal division; in fours, representing the cardinal directions), drummers and "fasters" who also participated throughout the ceremony. The third day—"Everything Comes Back Day"—was the time when all the beings who were on earth when the first Lone Man lived among the Mandan appeared. Included in this group is Oxinhede—the Foolish One—who symbolized those who "did not respect sacred things" and whose actions illustrated "the unhappy lot of those who failed to fast or seek supernatural protection through purchase or fasting" (Bowers, p. 144). Throughout the ceremony challenges were sent to the Foolish One to come and match his powers with those of the white-clad Lone Man and his pipe. On this day he appeared on the prairie following a zigzag course to the village. He arrived scantily dressed, painted black, and carrying a long staff. Once in the village he went from house to house seeking valuables, which he regarded as presents to himself and tokens of his good fortune. The Foolish One jumped over any person in his way, and children hid out of fear that he would eat them. Finally, as he approached the circle where the Okipa ceremony was being performed, "the Okipa Maker grasped Lone Man's pipe in both hands and, carrying it before him, advanced toward the Foolish One, challenging that one's right to come among the people to frighten them or bring misfortune or death at the hands of their enemies by breaking up the dances for the buffalos" (Bowers, p. 145). As the tribe's welfare was dependent on the power of Lone Man's pipe overcoming the power of Foolish One's staff, all dancing ceased. The Foolish One was forced to retreat and the people sang victory songs. Accompanied by much laughter the Foolish One then imitated buffalo bulls in breeding season, was rejected by a "sensible" woman but seduces a "foolish" one, etc. After performing during four of the twelve dances he tried to enter the Okipa lodge, and his staff was broken because he tried to enter with the rod crosswise of the door. Women, now losing all fear of him, pelted him with rocks and drove him from the village.

5. Social implications. The religions of native American tribal peoples affirmed the interdependence of humans and spirits in the worlds in which they lived and affirmed those frameworks of meaning and sources of power that give shape and meaning to their lives. Not instrumental or innovative, religion reinforced the solidarity of society by giving expression to its principles and incorporating its units and relationships within the accepted view of the world. While many of these peoples and cultures have largely or totally disappeared, others, especially in the Southwest, have retained much of their native cultural systems, including religion. In other instances, as a response to the radical change brought about by the impact of Euro-American culture, "nativistic" and "revivalistic" movements developed. Handsome Lake Religion—as described by Wallace—is a case in point.

At the middle of the eighteenth century several thousand Senecas lived in the southwestern portion of New York State. Like other Iroquois, the Seneca had a social structure adapted to a situation in which men ranged widely on hunting, war, and diplomatic missions, and women managed the village and agriculture. In this context the stereotypes of "the good hunter," "the brave warrior," and "the forest statesman" were the images of masculine success. However, between 1754, when the French and Indian War began, and the Treaty of Big Tree in 1797, when the Seneca sold their last hunting grounds and became largely confined to eleven tiny, isolated reservations, a series of economic, political, and military disasters made achievement of these ideals virtually impossible. As Wallace portrays it, the good hunter could no longer hunt: game was scarce, and it was dangerous to venture off reservation lands into areas controlled by hostile white men. Without arms and allies, the brave warrior could no longer fight and perceived his women and children to be threatened by the growing military might of the United States. The forest statesman, the third ideal image, was an object of contempt, and in Wallace's perspective this disillusionment was perhaps more shattering than the rest. For nearly a century the Iroquois chiefs had been able to play off British and French, then Americans and British, against each other. From both they had been able to extort "presents" (guns, traps, kettles, axes, food, drink, etc.) and promises of territorial integrity. As a consequence, they had maintained an extensive system of alliances among surrounding tribal groups. Over the course of a few years they were divested of their power. The League of the Iroquois was not long respected. Their political and economic alliances with western native peoples broke down and they were regarded as cowards for having made peace with the Americans. The initial Seneca response to the progress of sociocultural disorganization was—in Wallace's terminology—"quasi-pathological": many became drunkards; witchcraft accusations increased; factionalism made common policy impossible; the household unit became unstable; brawling and fighting were common. But a "revitalization movement" developed in 1799, based on a series of visions reported by one of the disillusioned forest statesmen—a man by the name of Handsome Lake. Handsome Lake preached a code of religious and cultural reform. The Seneca were to give up alcohol; witchcraft was to cease; traditional ceremonies of the annual ritual calendar were to be observed. In time Handsome Lake dealt with two crucial "cultural problems": (1) the role of men in agriculture and (2) the place of the nuclear family in a context of the maternal lineage. Agriculture was to be undertaken by men, and kinship responsibilities were to be focused within the nuclear family rather than in the clan and lineage. Finally, the prophet opposed any further alienation of Seneca land. The "good life" had been redefined. Handsome Lake's code was generally accepted within a few years, and a group of sober, devout, orderly, and technologically up-to-date farming communities replaced what Wallace vividly describes as "demoralized slums in the wilderness." One tribal community had come to grips with its new status in a land now dominated by those who were not native to North America.

Bibliography. A. W. Bowers, *Mandan Social and Ceremonial Organization* (1950); K. H. Basso, *The Cibecue Apache* (1970); M. Eliade, *Shamanism* (1964); F. Eggan, *Social Organization of the Western Pueblos* (1950); G. H. Gossen, "Temporal and Spatial Equivalents in Chamula Ritual Symbolism," in *Reader in Comparative Religion,* W. A. Lessa and E. Z. Vogt, eds. (1972), pp. 135-49, a full description of a world view; B. Haile, "Why the Navaho Hogan?" *Primitive Man,* XV (1942), 39-56; L. Lamphere, "Symbolic Elements in Navajo Ritual," *Southwestern Journal of Anthropology,* XXV (1969), 279-305; E. R. Leach, "Ritual," in *International Encyclopedia of the Social Sciences,* XIII (1968), 520-26; M. León-Portilla, *Time and Reality in the Thought of the Maya* (1973); D. M. Schneider, *American Kinship: A Cultural Account* (1968); W. C. Sturtevant, ed., *Handbook of North American Indians,* 20 vols. (1978-), the authoritative work on all native North American tribal peoples; J. Walker, "The Sun Dance and Other Ceremonies of the Oglala Division of the Dakota," *Anthropological Papers of the American Museum of Natural History,* XVI (1917), 51-221; A. F. C. Wallace, "Origins of the Long House Religion," *Handbook of North American Indians,* XV (1979), 442-48.

L. A. Hieb

NĀYAṈĀR, NĀYAṈMĀR nī yŭ när, nī yŭn mär (H). The collective name given to heroic figures of Śaivism who are traditionally associated with Tamil India (fourth to ninth century A.D.). Tradition claims there were sixty-three such figures, but the number is likely a Śaiva counterpart to an eleventh century listing of sixty-three Jaina saints.

Cuntarār, a ninth century Śaiva poet-saint, speaks of sixty-two individual Nāyaṉārs and nine groups of Nāyaṉārs in his poem *Tiruttoṇṭattokai.* Near the start of the eleventh century Nampi Āṇṭār Nampi in the *Tiruttoṇṭar Tiruvantāti* adds Cuntarār to the list of Nāyaṉārs, making sixty-three.

Of the sixty-three Nāyaṉārs, only eight were known to be poets of repute. Of these, a woman, Kāraikkāl Ammaiyār, who renounced earthly pleasures for devotion to Shiva, is probably the earliest. Another poet, Tirumūlar, is noted for his philosophical treatise *Tirumantiram* (3000 verses devoted to interpreting Sanskrit agamic and tantric material into Tamil). Aiyaṭikaḷ Kāṭavarkōn Nāyaṉār was apparently a Pallavaṉ King (perhaps Simharvarman III,

A.D. 550-575) who renounced his throne to engage in pilgrimage to various shrines; twenty-four of his verses extolling such shrines are extant in the collection known as *Kṣēttirattiruvenpā* ("Poem of the Sacred Places"). Kāri Nāyaṉār of about the eighth century composed Kōvai (a form of Tamil verse), none of which have been preserved.

However, without doubt the best known and most prolific of the Nāyaṉār poets were the three whose poetry comprises the first seven sections of the Tēvāram, a Śaivite canonical collection. Two of these are seventh century figures: Tirunāvukkaracu, better known as "APPAR" or "father," and his younger contemporary, Campantar or Tiruñāṉcampantar, who is generally believed to have been a child prodigy uttering all his poetry before the age of sixteen; the other is the ninth century figure, Cuntarār.

The Nāyaṉārs came from all walks of life and were extolled for various virtues, most commonly, their intense devotion to Shiva or their unstinting hospitality to Shiva's devotees. Tradition maintains that, of the sixty-three Nāyaṉārs, twelve were Vedic BRAHMINS, four were Atiśaiva Brahmins, twelve were kings or chieftains, six were merchants, thirteen were agriculturalists, and ten others including two HARIJANS, were a hunter, fisherman, toddy-tapper, washerman, oil merchant, and shepherd.

The major Nāyaṉārs were the shapers and transmitters of Tamil Śaivism. Using the Epic and PURĀṆIC mythology of Shiva selectively and giving it a locus in Tamil India, those poets sought to make devotional theism the heart of religion. In no small measure motivated by the desire to curb the widespread acceptance of Jainism and Buddhism, the Nāyaṉār poets stressed a number of basic themes: (1) the supremacy, greatness, and terror of Shiva coupled with his grace and personal compassion for his devotees; (2) the concrete and available presence of Shiva in his specific sacred places (hence, the desirability of pilgrimage, festival, and temple ritual); (3) the affirmation of the individual in the experience of BHAKTI or devotion to God and the possibility for all to attain Shiva's grace irrespective of circumstances; (4) the sense of community among Shiva's devotees and the merit in serving and being in the company of such devotees; and (5) the celebration of the experience of Shiva as the highest spiritual attainment.

Each of these themes may have been catalyzed by the presence of Jainism and the desire of the Nāyaṉārs to present Śaivism as the supreme faith of Tamil India. In fact, some aspects of the Śaiva teachings had their Jaina counterparts: e.g., the emphasis on service and hospitality to fellow devotees and the possibility of spiritual attainment irrespective of caste or economic background. Nonetheless, the core of the Śaiva message was quite consciously distinct from that of the Jainas: an unabashed theism; an affirmation of the phenomenal world as God's creation; and the importance and value of the devotional experience for one and all. It was a message which combined the spirit of early Tamil culture with its emphasis on "God-possession" and the celebration of life together with motifs of the ongoing Hindu heritage purveyed through the Epic mythology.

The centerpiece of the Nāyaṉār spirit was the personality of Shiva and his relationship to individual human beings. On the one hand, his awesome and terror-inspiring character is stressed. Specifically, his eight "heroic deeds" mentioned in Purāṇic lore recur in the poetry of the Nāyaṉārs: these acts include the destruction of the three cities which had become a threat to spiritual life; the removal of one of Brahmā's heads (from five to four); and the killing of several different beings representative of malevolent forces (e.g., hedonism, arrogance, and death). Shiva's superiority over BRAHMĀ and VISHNU is also depicted in his becoming a pillar extending further than the other gods could reach. Another story recounts his swallowing of the poison at the time of the churning of the ocean. Even more important, Shiva is depicted as a god who grants his grace to devotees who please him. The devotee, for his part, must learn to attain Shiva's grace. The individuality of the devotee is affirmed in the devotional religious experience in which the relationship with Shiva is compared to that of fragrance to a flower or light to the sun. Common metaphors used by the Nāyaṉārs for this relationship are those of lover and beloved, friend and friend, or parent and child.

The Nāyaṉārs succeeded in establishing Śaivism firmly in Tamil soil, where even today Śaivism remains a viable religious option. In addition, the Nāyaṉārs, together with their VAIṢṆAVA counterparts, the ĀḺVĀRS, were the first to use vernacular language to express their *bhakti* faith, making them pioneers in the resurgence of Hinduism in Tamil India and the harbingers of Hindu devotion throughout the subcontinent.

Bibliography. J. M. Nallaswami Pillai, *Periyapuranam* (1924); M. A. Dorai Rangaswamy, *The Religion and Philosophy of Tēvāram* (1968, 1969); K. Nambiarooran, *Glimpses of Tamil Culture Based on Periyapurāṇam* (1977).

F. W. CLOTHEY

NAZARETH (năz′ ər ĕth). A village 24 km. west of the Sea of Galilee, noted in the NT as the home of MARY and Joseph (Luke 1:26), and the place where JESUS lived as a boy (Luke 2:39, 51). The first mention of a church there was made by Arculf (A.D. 670). Among present-day holy places, only Mary's well may be authentic. D. W. O'CONNOR

NEBI'IM nĕ vē ēm′ (Ju—Heb. "prophets"). A grouping of books of the Hebrew Bible (or TANAK) which includes the "Former Prophets": Joshua, Judges, I and II Samuel, I and II Kings; and the "Latter Prophets": Isaiah, Jeremiah, Ezekiel, Hosea, Joel, Amos, Obadiah, Jonah, Micah, Nahum,

Habakkuk, Zephaniah, Haggai, Zechariah, and Malachi. *See* Torah; Kethubim. D. Irvin

NECROMANCY (Gr. *nekromantia;* lit. "calling up ghosts"). The practice of calling up the spirits of the dead and communing with them in order to maintain fellowship or to predict the future. It is found in many cultures, including ancient Israel, e.g. I Sam. 28:8-19. K. Crim

NEE, WATCHMAN (Ch; 1903–1972). Chinese independent evangelist and writer, founder of the Little Flock Movement. Originally Nee Shu-zu, later called Duo-Sheng, "sound of bells," hence, "Watchman." Converted while a student at Trinity College, Foochow, he was baptized in 1922. Preaching in China and abroad, he reached the height of his influence in 1948. He was arrested in 1952, accused as a capitalist, and released only shortly before his death. K. Koyama

NEMBUTSU nĕm′ boo tsoo (B—Jap.; lit. "thinking on or invoking Buddha"). A practice of the Pure Land school of Buddhism originating in China. It meant at first meditation on the Buddha, and later came to mean invoking the name of the Buddha. In Japan nembutsu usually means reciting the name of Amida with the formula *namu-amida-butsu.* The last two words of the formula identify the Buddha *(butsu)* invoked as Amida, and the first word, *namu* (from the Skt. *names*), is a term of veneration in the Far East, indicating faith or trust in a divine figure. In popular practice this invocation was sometimes shortened to *namaida.*

Some forms of nembutsu practice were known in Japan in the Nara period (710-784) shortly after the introduction of Buddhism, but the Tendai sect and its priests first emphasized this practice in the Heian period (794-1185), and it became a widespread popular practice only with the rise of the Pure Land Sects in the Kamakura period (1185-1333). There was considerable variety in both the earlier and the later forms of practice, but generally the Tendai practices emphasized visualizing inwardly the figure of Amida and the Pure Land of Amida, whereas later practice emphasized recitation of the name of Amida as a means of purifying the person and as an act of faith. There were heated debates as to whether religious merit and salvation were due to the repeated practice (even millions of repetitions, using mechanical means to count the number of recitations) or to the sincere faith of the practitioner.

The exact history of Amida is uncertain, but the Mahāyāna Buddhism that came to China and on to Japan featured belief in Amida as a Buddha that in a former existence had vowed to create his own Buddha-land or Pure Land in the West, where he would bring all sentient beings. Those who invoke Amida's name can be reborn in this Pure Land, which

Visual Education Service, Charles A. Kennedy

Monuments on temple grounds, such as this lantern, were inscribed with the nembutsu as a perpetual recitation of the sacred words.

is practically equivalent to attaining enlightenment or Buddhahood. The practice was so influential that it spread to other sects and was incorporated into their doctrine and ritual; on a popular level it has become one of the most frequently used religious invocations, practiced by many people even if they are not members of a Pure Land sect, and having the general meaning of requesting divine help and protection in time of distress. As a folk practice, nembutsu was sometimes joined with gestures and dance. Because of the promise of rebirth in the Pure Land, the nembutsu often is recited as death draws near. H. B. Earhart

NEO-CONFUCIANISM. *See* Confucianism §3.

NEO-ORTHODOXY (Ch). Theological movement that emerged in the 1920s and dominated Protestant theology until the 1960s. It owed much to the theology of Karl Barth, and emphasized the sovereignty of God, faith and Revelation as divine gifts, and the tragedy, sin, and finitude of human life. *See* Theology, Contemporary Christian §3. D. F. Ottati

NESTORIANISM (Ch). A movement which espoused the "two-natures" Christology of Nestorius (*see* CHRISTOLOGY §3). East Syrian (or Assyrian) Christianity became the carrier of the Nestorian tradition in the fifth century, although they did not officially designate their church as "Nestorian" until the thirteenth century. By the seventh century Nestorians had spread to Persia, Central Asia, and even China. D. E. GROH

NEW TESTAMENT (Ch). The scriptures written by the early Christian church. The list of writings included was made final by the fourth century: four GOSPELS, the Acts of the APOSTLES, twenty-one epistles, and the APOCALYPTIC revelation of John. Together with the OLD TESTAMENT, it constitutes the Christian BIBLE. J. R. CRIM

NICAEA, COUNCIL OF nī cē´ ə (Ch). The first ecumenical council of the church (*see* COUNCILS OF THE CHURCH §3c), which met in the ancient city of Nicaea (modern Iznik, Turkey), beginning on June 19, 325, to settle the dispute over ARIANISM, which had arisen in the Eastern churches, and to resolve liturgical and disciplinary conflicts in various local churches.

The council was summoned by the first Christian emperor, CONSTANTINE, and, concluding its work, joined in the celebration of the twentieth year of his reign (July 25). The exact number of bishops who attended is not known, and no minutes of the proceedings are preserved. However, a highly apologetic letter of Eusebius of Caesarea (in Socrates, *Ecclesiastical History* I.8.35) preserves the earliest text of the creed; and Athanasius of Alexandria (*De Decretis* 19-20) details some of the theological debate which led, for the first time in history, to the insertion of a nonscriptural term into a creed (Gr. HOMOOUSIOS; "of the same substance") to describe the relation of God to Christ. The creed was meant to be a standard for ORTHODOXY and, taken with a series of anathemas adopted, an exclusion of Arianism. (*See* NICENE CREED; CHRISTOLOGY; CREEDS AND CONFESSIONS.)

Among other matters, the "canons," or rules, of Nicaea regularized the date of EASTER, provided conditions for the readmittance of various schismatic and lapsed Christians, and regulated the ORDINATION and jurisdiction of CLERGY.

Bibliography. A. E. Burn, *The Council of Nicaea* (1925); A. Grillmeier, *Christ in Christian Tradition* (ET 1975); J. N. D. Kelly, *Early Christian Creeds,* 3rd ed. (1972).

D. E. GROH

NICENE CREED nī´ sēn (Ch). Formula adopted by the COUNCIL OF NICAEA (325) condemning ARIANISM and affirming the full deity of JESUS Christ as of the "same substance [essence or being] as the Father." *See* CREEDS AND CONFESSIONS §2. J. H. LEITH

NICENE CREED

I believe in one God the Father Almighty, Maker of heaven and earth, And of all things visible and invisible:

And in one Lord Jesus Christ, the only-begotten Son of God; Begotten of his Father before all worlds, God of God, Light of Light, Very God of very God; Begotten, not made; Being of one substance with the Father; By whom all things were made: Who for us men and for our salvation came down from heaven, And was incarnate by the Holy Ghost of the Virgin Mary, And was made man: And was crucified also for us under Pontius Pilate; He suffered and was buried: And the third day he rose again according to the Scriptures: And ascended into heaven, And sitteth on the right hand of the Father: And he shall come again, with glory, to judge both the quick and the dead; Whose kingdom shall have no end.

And I believe in the Holy Ghost, The Lord, and Giver of Life, Who proceedeth from the Father and the Son; Who with the Father and the Son together is worshipped and glorified; Who spake by the Prophets: And I believe one Catholic and Apostolic Church: I acknowledge one Baptism for the remission of sins: And I look for the Resurrection of the dead: And the Life of the world to come. Amen.

Book of Common Prayer (1928)

NICHIREN nē chē rĕn´ (B—Jap.; 1222-1282; lit. "sun lotus," i.e. "sun" standing for Japan and "lotus" for the LOTUS SŪTRA). Japanese Buddhist priest, the founder of NICHIREN BUDDHISM. Nichiren was the son of a fisherman in Kominato village in what is now Chiba Prefecture (NE of Tokyo). His given name was Zennichimaro; commoners had no family name. When he was twelve, his family placed him under the care of Seichōji Temple of the TENDAI sect in his native village. There he earned his priest name, Zenshōbō, at the age of sixteen. For the next ten years he traveled to various temples in search of true Buddhism. At KAMAKURA he studied the teachings of the Jōdo (PURE LAND) sect and ZEN. Later, after a brief return to Seichōji in his home town, he journeyed to Mt. Hiei near Kyoto, where he pursued his studies of the sūtras of the Tendai sect. Driven out of Mt. Hiei because of his radicalism, he moved on to Mt. Kōya (south of Osaka) to study the esoteric sect of SHINGON. It was here that he finally came to the conviction that the only true faith was that taught by DENGYŌ DAISHI, who had introduced Tendai Buddhism to Japan in the eighth century. Dengyō Daishi had taught the ultimate superiority of the LOTUS SŪTRA over all other sūtras. Nichiren, after discovering this truth for himself, returned to his home town to preach to the common people and to announce that enlightenment was available to every person by a simple act of faith in the truth (DHARMA) revealed in the Lotus Sūtra. This simple act of faith which Nichiren called for was the incantation of a prayer of praise (DAIMOKU) to the Lotus Sūtra: "*Namu myō-hō-renge-kyō* (Hail to the wonderful truth of the Lotus Sūtra)."

In February, 1260, Nichiren delivered his famous "memorial," the *Risshō ankoku-ron* (On the Establishment of the Legitimate Teaching for the Security of the Country), in which he denounced the government of the Hōjō regents who ruled from Kamakura, and prophesied that false religions, especially the worship of AMIDA Buddha, would bring disaster to Japan. During the period from 1256 to 1260, Japan had been subjected to a series of calamities: earthquakes, storms, droughts, famine, and epidemics. Nichiren interpreted these calamities as signs of the advent of the final period of the dharma, MAPPŌ. He prophesied that Japan would suffer invasion by a foreign power, a prophecy which was realized in 1268 when an envoy of the Mongol army landed on Kyushu. Japan was saved from an actual invasion by what was called "*kamikaze*" (divine wind).

For his efforts Nichiren bore the wrath of religious and government leaders and was arrested in 1261 and exiled to Izu Peninsula for a period of two years. He was pardoned on February 12, 1264.

Nichiren, however, did not recant. He appeared again in the streets of Kamakura and denounced the government. Regent Saimyōji, Nichiren preached, was in hell, and the current Regent Tokimune was preparing to follow him. This time Nichiren received the death sentence. Tradition has it that the executioner's sword was struck by lightning just at the moment of execution. The execution was stayed, and Nichiren was again sentenced to exile, this time to the remote island of Sado in the Japan Sea.

During the three years of his exile (1271-74) Nichiren wrote his two most important treatises: *Kaimokushō* (On Opening the Eyes) and *Kanjin Honzonshō* (On the Contemplation of the True Worship Object). These two treatises, together with *Risshō ankoku-ron* and two later works, *Senjishō* and *Hōonshō,* form Nichiren's principal writings, and they are preserved today along with some 230 letters of his in the *Gosho* (Holy Writings), which serves as a bible for Nichiren Buddhism. During this exile Nichiren is also believed to have created the original Worship Object *(Gohonzon),* an inscription on wood of the prayer *"Namu myō-hō-renge-kyō."* The Nichiren-shū sect claims it is today enshrined at Mt. Minobu, and Nichiren Shō-shū claims it is enshrined at TAISEKIJI.

Nichiren was pardoned for the second time on March 13, 1274. He still had not recanted but, evidently having decided to leave the more active expressions of his reformism to his younger disciples, he set out to establish the "Vulture Peak," the mythical mountain where ŚĀKYAMUNI is said to have delivered the teaching of the Lotus Sūtra. Nichiren believed that the earthly manifestation of the "Vulture Peak" was to be found in Japan. He selected MT. FUJI as the site and established the temple Kuonji nearby on Mt. Minobu.

Nichiren died at the home of a patron, Uemondayū Munenaka Ikegami, on October 13, 1282. According to Nichiren-shū, Nichiren's remains are now enshrined at Mt. Minobu.

Bibliography. *See* NICHIREN BUDDHISM.

N. S. BRANNEN

NICHIREN BUDDHISM nē chē rĕn′ (B—Jap.; lit. "sun lotus"). A group of Japanese Buddhist sects in the MAHĀYĀNA tradition which trace their origin to the thirteenth century Japanese priest NICHIREN, who sought to restore what he considered to be the orthodox teaching of the historical BUDDHA, ŚAKYAMUNI.

Next to Jōdo Shin-shū (*see* PURE LAND SECTS) Nichiren Buddhism has the largest constituency of all religions in Japan today. There are currently eighteen Nichiren sects registered in the *Shūkyō Nenkan* (Religions Yearbook). Offshoots of Nichiren Buddhism total nineteen, and include such popular "new religions" as REIYŪKAI, RISSHŌ KŌSEIKAI, and Myōchikai Kyōdan. Distinctive of all these branches of Nichiren Buddhism is their common reverence for the LOTUS SŪTRA as the supreme and sufficient Buddhist teaching, and the centrality of the *Gohonzon* (Worship Object), a mandala which inscribes the words of the DAIMOKU "*Namu myō-hō-renge-kyō* (Hail to the wonderful truth of the Lotus Sūtra)."

1. **Central beliefs.** Nichiren believed that DENGYŌ DAISHI, an eighth century Chinese priest, had correctly grasped the meaning of the Buddha's enlightenment with the concept *ichinen sanzen* (lit., "one thought—three thousand"), i.e. that all the DHARMA worlds of Buddhism exist simultaneously in an instantaneous act of meditation. These worlds consist of the ten worlds of hell, hungry ghosts (*see* PRETA), beasts, pandemonium, humans, heavenly beings, those who understand the FOUR NOBLE TRUTHS, the enlightened, the BODHISATTVAS, and the BUDDHAS. Each of these ten worlds exists in each of the others, making a total of one hundred; each of the one hundred has ten aspects, making one thousand; and each of the one thousand has three separate divisions: living beings, the five SKANDHAS, and the space we live in. Because these all exist simultaneously, each person has the potential of becoming enlightened in this present moment.

In addition, all the major sects in this tradition hold the following beliefs: a) Buddha is eternal, without beginning or end; b) Śākyamuni's personal enlightenment guarantees the enlightenment of all; c) the Lotus Sūtra was given by Śākyamuni to supersede and replace all his other teachings; d) Nichiren was the incarnation of Jōgyō, a bodhisattva among the congregation in the sky above Vulture Peak at the time when Śākyamuni delivered the teaching of the Lotus Sūtra; e) Nichiren, identified as Jōgyō, was destined to suffer persecution and untold hardship, but through these sufferings he was able to impart hope to his followers by leaving them the sacred prayer (the Daimoku).

Reynolds Metals Company, Richmond, Va.

Treasury of the Minobusan Kuonji Temple, Minobu-cho, Yamanashi Prefecture, Japan, general headquarters of a sect of Nichiren Buddhism. This contemporary building, built of aluminum, captures the spirit of traditional Japanese Buddhist architecture.

2. Exclusivisim. Nichiren Buddhism has been criticized as belligerent and intolerant in contrast to other forms of Buddhism. This intolerance stems from the founder. Nichiren condemned other sects in the stinging phrase: *"Nembutsu mugen, Zen tenma, Shingon bōkoku, Ritsu kokuzoku* (the NEMBUTSU—AMIDA Buddhism—is hell; ZEN is a devil; SHINGON is the nation's ruin; and RITSU is treason)." The mantle of Nichiren's iconoclasm has fallen most notably on Nichiren Shō-shū followers, and in particlar on SŌKA GAKKAI, a lay organization of Nichiren Shō-shū.

3. Nichiren-shū and Nichiren Shō-shū. From among eighteen disciples Nichiren chose six to carry on the work he had begun and enjoined them to perform the prescribed duties at his grave.

Nichiren Shō-shū possesses two documents, the *Minobu sōjō* and the *Ikegami sōjō,* which it contends prove conclusively that Nichiren selected Nikkō (1246-1333) alone to succeed him. In 1288, Nikkō left Mt. Minobu and in 1290 he established TAISEKIJI, claiming that the other five disciples had repudiated the true teaching of Nichiren and were no longer worthy to perform the duties at his grave. The branch which Nikkō established is known as Nichiren Shō-shū, which means "The Orthodox Faith of Nichiren."

The doctrinal differences between Nichiren-shū and Nichiren Shō-shū may be summarized as follows: In Nichiren-shū, the Buddha is Śākyamuni, the dharma is *Namu myō-hō-renge-kyō,* which stands for the literal meaning of the Lotus Sūtra, and the priest is Nichiren. In Nichiren Shō-shū, the Buddha is Nichiren himself (called Nichiren Dai-Shōnin), the dharma is the *Namu myō-hō-renge-kyō* of the Three Great Hidden Laws, and the priest is Nikkō.

4. The Three Great Hidden Laws (San Dai-hihō). According to Nichiren, the central meaning of Buddhism is expressed in what he referred to as "Three Great Hidden Laws," or "three profound laws." They are the *Gohonzon,* sacred Worship Object, which Nichiren conceived as a MANDALA inscribed with the words *Namu myō-hō-renge-kyō;* the DAIMOKU, literally "title," referring to the name of the Lotus Sūtra but used by Nichiren to mean the incantation *"Namu myō-hō-renge-kyō";* and the *kaidan,* ordination platform, which emphasizes the importance of the priestly succession but is interpreted by Nichiren Shō-shū to mean the establishment of this religion as the national religion of Japan and eventually of the entire world.

5. Nichiren Shō-shū doctrine. Nichiren Shō-shū subscribes to nine "doctrines" found in Nichiren's writings. These may be subdivided into three basic and six derivative doctrines. The three basic doctrines are as follows:

a) "The Five Sets of Comparisons." Nichiren compared religious faiths, showing first that Buddhism is superior to all other religions, that Mahāyāna Buddhism is superior to Hīnayāna, the "true" doctrine of the Lotus Sūtra to the accommodated doctrine of all other sūtras, the last half of the Lotus Sūtra to the first half, and finally that the hidden truth beneath the written letter of the Lotus Sūtra—that is, the truth that the Buddha existed from eternity—is superior to the literal teaching of the sūtra.

b) "The Five Sets of Three Steps." Nichiren classified the sūtras, harmonizing them and resolving obvious contradictions, and concluded that the Lotus Sūtra was not only the most important sūtra (as TENDAI taught) but that it was the only sūtra of relevance to man living in the period of MAPPŌ (End of the Dharma). Finally, the heart of the meaning of the Lotus Sūtra is expressed in the words *Namu myō-hō-renge-kyō,* which Nichiren claimed, if one repeated it as a prayer, was sufficient to bring enlightenment or salvation to anyone.

c) "The Four Fates." Nichiren, in the *Kanjin Honzonshō,* described the "rise and fall," that is, the fate (or career) of all teachings, and shows how Nichiren's own teaching had arisen to surpass all others. Thus (i) Buddhism arises to replace all former alien religions, which fall into disuse; (ii) the doctrine of the Lotus Sūtra then rises and all other Buddhist doctrines fade away; (iii) next, the hidden teaching of the Lotus Sūtra concerning the primordial Buddha arises to displace all other interpretations of the Lotus Sūtra; and (iv) finally, the teaching of Nichiren himself arises as the final, supreme faith.

Bibliography. N. S. Brannen, *Sōka Gakkai, Japan's Militant Buddhists* (1968); K. Murata, *Japan's New Buddhism* (1969); H. N. McFarland, *The Rush Hour of the Gods* (1967).

N. S. BRANNEN

NICHOLAS I (Ch; *ca.* 819/22-867). Pope from 858; the most forceful pope in Carolingian times and one of the founders of the medieval PAPACY. Nicholas made effective in the West the conception of supreme papal authority defined earlier by Gelasius I (d. 496). Maintaining administrative and legal jurisdiction over the other European SEES, he invited appeals to Rome against the decisions of provincial synods and of other METROPOLITANS and BISHOPS. He became the first pope to make use of the False Decretals, a collection of forged documents, falsely attributed to Isidore of Seville (d. 636) but actually compiled in France in the ninth century. Nicholas also extended his claims to the East, and a serious break in relations between eastern ORTHODOX CHURCHES and Western Christianity resulted from his dispute with Photius, the PATRIARCH of Constantinople. At a Roman synod (863) Nicholas declared Photius' appointment illegitimate and EXCOMMUNICATED him. Photius retaliated at a synod in Constantinople (867) by having Nicholas excommunicated. The rupture was made worse by Photius' rejection of the FILIOQUE clause in the NICENE CREED and by Nicholas' efforts to establish Roman dominance in Moravia and Bulgaria. Nicholas' correspondence clearly testifies to his view of full papal authority over the church, whose officers and councils function by his sanction, and over the emperor, a vassal of PETER, whose legitimacy requires papal unction, coronation, and confirmation.

Bibliography. J. Roy, *St. Nicholas I* (1901); F. Dvornik, *The Photian Schism* (1948).

H. L. BOND

NICHOLAS OF CUSA kū´ sä (Ch; 1401-1464). German CARDINAL and BISHOP of Brixen, one of the most original philosophers and theologians of the fifteenth century; he made significant contributions to CANON LAW, political theory, mathematics, and astronomy. Educated at the universities of Heidelberg, Padua, and Cologne, Nicholas became a doctor of canon law in 1432. He developed a program for reform of the church and the empire and supported the supremacy of a church council over the PAPACY. Disillusioned by the failure of the council of Basel, he left the council and supported Pope Eugene IV's claims against it. He sailed to Constantinople (1437-38) to negotiate for reunion of the GREEK ORTHODOX CHURCH with the ROMAN CATHOLIC CHURCH. In 1450 he was sent as papal legate to Austria, Germany, and the Netherlands. He took over his Tyrolean diocese in 1452, but following a bitter dispute with Duke Sigismund of Austria he was forced to leave Brixen for Rome, where he became a leading figure in the CURIA and vicar-general of Rome. Before his death he founded in Kues, his birthplace, the St. Nicholas hospital, which today also houses his extraordinary library. Beginning with his major work, *De docta ignorantia* (1440), his writings drew on the Christian Platonic tradition, rejecting the methods of SCHOLASTICISM and developing two principal themes—"learned ignorance" (we are wise only if we know the limits of the human mind) and the "coincidence of opposites," especially in the infinite God.

Bibliography. P. E. Sigmund, *Nicholas of Cusa and Medieval Political Thought* (1963).

H. L. BOND

NIEBUHR, HELMUT RICHARD nē´ bər (Ch; 1894-1962). Protestant theologian and ethicist. In light of historical revelation he sought a broadly philosophical interpretation of human life in the world. His understanding of moral life required that persons respond to all events as actions of the sovereign God. *See* THEOLOGY, CONTEMPORARY CHRISTIAN §3; ETHICS §1c.

D. F. OTTATI

NIEBUHR, REINHOLD nē´ bər (Ch; 1892-1971). Protestant preacher-theologian who was the prime exponent of NEO-ORTHODOXY in America. His "Christian realism" acknowledged the pernicious effects of sin on individuals and societies. He emphasized justice as the approximation of Christian love in social life. *See* THEOLOGY, CONTEMPORARY CHRISTIAN §3.

D. F. OTTATI

NIHON SHOKI nē´ hôn shô´ kē (Sh—Jap.; lit. "Chronicles of Japan"). Also known as the *Nihongi.* Compiled in A.D. 720 by court officials, it and the KOJIKI (A.D. 712) constitute Japan's oldest extant written records. Modeled on the Chinese dynastic histories it provides a national chronicle from Japan's mythic origins to A.D. 697. English trans. by W. G. Aston (1896).

M. L. ROGERS

NIKĀYAS nĭ kī´ yŭ (B—Pali; lit. "collection"). The five divisions of the SUTTA PIṬAKA, or Discourse Collection, of the PALI CANON. These are: (a) DĪGHA NIKĀYA, or Collection of Long Discourses— consisting mostly of longer independent works dealing with various aspects of Buddhist tradition; (b) Majjhima Nikāya, or Collection of Middle Length Sayings—the best canonical source for the study of Theravāda doctrine; (c) Saṃyutta Nikāya, or Connected Sayings—discourses classified loosely according to topic; (d) Aṅguttara Nikāya, or Gradual Sayings—discourses arranged in graduated order according to the number of items in the categories discussed; and (e) Khuddaka Nikāya, or Minor Anthologies—consisting of fifteen miscellaneous texts of varying date. A later collection than the other Nikāyas, the Khuddaka Nikāya appears to have evolved gradually. Among the most important texts in this fifth Nikāya are the very early Sutta Nipāta, the DHAMMAPADA, and the JĀTAKAS, or birth stories. The Therīgāthā is also notable as a collection of stanzas attributed to about one hundred nuns.

Bibliography. E. J. Thomas, *The Life of Buddha* (1949), pp. 249-75.

J. P. MCDERMOTT

NIMBĀRKA nĭm bär´ kŭ (H—Skt.). A Hindu theologian and sectarian leader, the founding teacher (ĀCĀRYA) of the earliest VAISṆAVA sect devoted to KRISHNA and RĀDHĀ and of the theistic and devotional Dvaita-Advaita ("Duality-Nonduality") school of VEDĀNTA (*see also* ADVAITA; VIŚIṢṬA ADVAITA; DVAITA). Scholarly consensus places him in the thirteenth or fourteenth century A.D., following RĀMĀNUJA and JAYADEVA. Reputedly born a South Indian Telugu BRAHMIN, he settled in the north at VṚNDĀVANA, the major center of Rādhā-Krishna devotion *(bhakti)*. As did Rāmānuja and MADHVA, he fostered the integration of Brahmanical and popular religion by providing Rādhā-Krishna devotion with an authoritative Vedāntic doctrinal basis. He accepted and modified an ancient interpretation of Vedānta termed *Bheda-abheda* ("Difference-Nondifference") in which BRAHMAN as first cause is both distinct from and inseparably related to its effects that are "nondifferent" as parts of the whole. In Nimbārka's system, properly known as "the Teaching of Natural or Essential Nondifference *(a-bheda, a-dvaita)* in the midst of Difference *(bheda, dvaita)*," Brahman is identified with the personal God Krishna; and individual selves are both eternally distinct from him and absolutely dependent upon him for their existence and liberation. Nimbārka paved the way for VALLABHA and CAITANYA in the sixteenth century and for the outpouring of Rādhā-Krishna devotion in the vernacular mystical love songs of such poet-saints as MĪRĀBĀĪ. *See* VAISṆAVISM; BHAKTI HINDUISM.

Bibiography. S. Dasgupta, *History of Indian Philosophy*, Vol. III (1940); R. G. Bhandarkar, *Vaiṣṇavism, Śaivism* (1913).

W. G. NEEVEL

NINTH OF AV (Ju). *See* TISHAH BE'AV.

NIRMĀṆAKĀYA nər mä nə kä´ yä (B—Skt.; lit. "body of transformation"). One of the three aspects which together constitute the Mahāyāna Buddhist conception of TRIPLE BODY (*Trikāya*). As *Nirmāṇakāya,* the eternal Buddha assumes human form and appears on the mundane plane of existence.

E. J. COLEMAN

NIRODHA nĭ rōd´ hŭ (B—Pali & Skt.; lit. "cessation"). Extinction or cessation of something, especially of craving (as a means to NIRVANA) or of consciousness in trance meditation. As the third of the FOUR NOBLE TRUTHS of Buddhism, *nirodha* refers to the goal of extinguishing craving, and with it suffering. *Nirodha* is also one of the eighteen subjects for insight meditation (VIPASSANĀ). In trance meditation there are said to be nine "successive extinctions," which include the eight meditational stages and a ninth stage, "the attainment of extinction" of normal consciousness. *See* MEDITATION, BUDDHIST.

R. C. AMORE

NIRVANA nĭr vä´ nŭ (H, B, & Ja—Skt.; lit. "blowing out, extinguishing" [*vā*—"blow" + *niḥ*—"out, away"]) **NIBBANA** nĭb bä´ nə (B—Pali). The ultimate goal of Buddhism, described in part as a perfectly peaceful and enlightened state of transformed consciousness, in which passions and ignorance are extinguished; also employed by Hindus and Jainas for religious attainment and "release" (MOKṢA).

The Buddhist concept of Nirvana has beckoned and baffled thinkers for centuries, and controversies about the "meaning" of Nirvana are not yet extinguished. Does it signify utter annihilation, as seems to be implied in the Buddhist view that there is no abiding essence (ANATTA)? Is it ecstatic trance? Union with god or an absolute? Some sort of heaven or bliss of paradise? Merely to list the numerous descriptions and definitions of Nirvana in Buddhist literature and in scholarly and polemic texts would not lead very far. Nirvana cannot be understood apart from the complex sets of specific doctrines and practices that define its meaning.

1. **The word "Nirvana."** Difficulties in understanding Nirvana can begin with the word itself. First, Nirvana's form is apparently privative. Before nouns, the prefix *niḥ* often indicates lack or absence of that which the noun signifies. Further, according to Buddhists, Nirvana is the NIRODHA ("cessation") of DUKKHA ("sorrow, suffering"; *see* FOUR NOBLE TRUTHS); and words like *animitta* ("without characteristics") and *amṛta* ("deathless") are frequently employed to describe it. Nevertheless, it would be a mistake to suppose that Nirvana is a "pure negative." Privative expressions often are intended to convey specific,

positive, and dynamic meanings in traditional Indian usage. (*See* e.g., AHIMSĀ.)

The popular metaphor of extinguishing or putting out a fire can also mislead the unwary investigator into thinking that Nirvana is strictly negative. After it has been extinguished (and before it has been kindled), a fire is not visible; but this does not necessarily mean that the fire no longer (or not yet) exists at all. On the contrary, several classical Indian texts (e.g. Śvet.U. I. 13) argue that a fire exists always and only changes its modality. If Nirvana is specifically understood as the extinction of the fires of lust, anger, and delusion, however, then it should be definitive. Such "fires" ought to go out utterly.

Although the etymology seems straightforward enough (and formations from *vā* + *niḥ* are attested in the RIG VEDA), here, too, the situation is more complicated than it first appears. Because Sanskrit vocalic *ṛ* is absent from Middle Indo-Aryan languages like PALI, different roots (like *vā* ["blow"] and *vṛ* ["cover"]) are often associated and confounded. Also, the prefix *ni* ("down, in") may appear for *niḥ* ("out, away"). Therefore, Nirvana's interpreter must contend with a semantic family: a cluster of words including *nivāta/nirvāta, nirvṛta* (Pali; *nibbuta*), *nirvṛti* (Pali, *nibbuti*), and even *nivṛtti* (from *vṛt,* "turn") and a range of meanings extending from "windless, calm, cooled, satisfied, at peace, happy" to "ceased, destroyed, dead." (*See* bibliog.)

2. Nirvana in early Buddhism. The teachings of GAUTAMA BUDDHA and the attitudes of the earliest Buddhist community, insofar as these can be ascertained in the oldest strata of the Pali literature, were intensely practical and profoundly empirical. Speculative implications claimed the attention of later commentators, scholastics, and metaphysicians. Initially, Nirvana was simply, directly, and absolutely the end of the problems of ordinary human existence.

Several insights are at the heart of the Buddha's teachings (DHARMA) in the four noble truths. SAMSARA is marked by three interrelated qualities: *dukkha* ("sorrow, suffering"), ANICCA ("impermanence") and *anatta* ("essencelessness"). Sorrow is caused by ignorant desire (TANHĀ). Nirvana is nothing less than the extinction of desire; hence, the cessation of sorrow. The EIGHTFOLD PATH is the way to Nirvana. So considered, the Buddha's truths are the diagnosis of human afflictions, the assurance that there is a cure, and the prescription. Over against *dukkha,* there is health, i.e., Nirvana, the greatest happiness *(sukha).*

While earliest Buddhist literature contains problematic and apparently contradictory statements about what Nirvana *is,* it is quite clear from those texts what Nirvana *is not:*

a) Nirvana is not death nor is it heaven. Of course, death is known, and heavens *(svarga)* are recognized; but both are involved in samsara. Death is not in itself an ending. It is only an event in a series. Heavens are not permanent abodes (nor are hells). By contrast, Nirvana is permanent and thus is release from samsara.

b) Nirvana is not a postmortem condition or state. It is fully attainable here and now, not merely at death. The Buddha attained it in his lifetime; indeed, he was the Buddha, the TATHĀGATA because he did. His dedicated follower, then and now, aspires to become an ARHANT, one who is "worthy," who has realized Nirvana, in this life.

Some have observed that Buddhist texts apparently acknowledge different "kinds" or degrees of Nirvana, pointing to distinctions between *nirvāṇa* and *parinirvāṇa* and between Nirvana with and without a "remnant of existence." Because of this, it has been suggested that Nirvana "in this life" is not the same as Nirvana after death. The suggestion is in error. *Parinirvāṇa* frequently is translated as "complete Nirvana" because the prefix *pari* is usually completive or perfective and because Buddhist tradition commonly refers to the Buddha's death as his *parinirvāṇa.* However, the "attainment of " Nirvana—as distinct from the "being in" Nirvana—more closely renders the sense of *parinirvāṇa* in the early texts.

Nirvana is an absolute that admits of no degrees or qualifications. It is not partially attained, but the context or circumstances surrounding it may differ. Thus, Nirvana "with *upadhi*"—i.e., with the aggregates (SKANDHA) of phenomenal existence continuing—is not qualitatively different from Nirvana "without *upadhi.*" After realizing Nirvana, there are no more rebirths (*see* KARMA); however, the phenomenal consequences of previous actions will attend Nirvana, without affecting its purity, until the *arhant's* death.

c) Nirvana is not obscure or "mysterious." Through metaphor and figurative expressions and in more literal statements, it is not referred to vaguely. Rather, Nirvana in the early literature is spoken of in clear, vivid, and immediately accessible terms. Nirvana can be "seen," "desired," "known," "approached," "acquired," and "enjoyed." It is real.

d) Nirvana is not annihilation, if by that is meant the utter perishing of the *arhant* at death. One of the Buddha's capital discoveries was that samsaric life is a sequence of interdependent "events" in which no abiding, self-existent entity or ATMAN can be found (or, put another way, no constituent of life-as-process can be identified as or with an Atman). According to Buddhist tradition, the Buddha held that the question of whether or not an *arhant* exists after death was inappropriate and unproductive. Since the *arhant* cannot be localized even in this life, it is impossible to say anything about him after his death. Further, of the three kinds of desire that cause suffering by inspiring acts and infecting them with passion, hatred, and delusion, the thirst for continuing existence and the thirst for complete annihilation are considered to be more detrimental than the craving for pleasure (KĀMA).

The Buddha has been accused of hedging about the *arhant's* destiny. In fact, however, tradition seems to have preserved in these early texts a coherent and positive teaching concerning Nirvana as a religious goal. But while the earliest teachings cohere, they do not constitute a rigorous theory. Subsequently Buddhist schoolmen and others sought to weave consistent systems from the context—specific declarations of the Buddha's teachings.

3. Nirvana and the Buddhist schools. The principal themes of HĪNAYĀNA and MAHĀYĀNA speculations bear directly on Nirvana. Hīnayānists extended and intensified analysis of the constituents and order of existence (dharma) and sought answers to questions of Nirvana's metaphysical status. Mahāyāna schools, radically skeptical about the value of empirical knowledge, avoided *abhidharmic* analysis and categories (*see* ABHIDHAMMA PIṬAKA), exploring rather the most extreme implications of ŚŪNYATĀ, "emptiness," and along the way denying significance to the Buddha's historicity and rejecting the *arhant* ideal. (*See* LOHAN.)

The unity of the primitive Buddhist community (SAṄGHA) was shattered by schism in the second century after the Buddha's death when the "proto-Mahāyāna" Mahāsaṅghikas separated from the traditionalist Sthaviras ("elders") following disputes over the *arhants'* attainments. From the Sthaviras' ranks, other schools and divergent interpretations of Nirvana emerged over a period of time. The Vatsīputrīyas claimed that an indefinable "person" *(pudgala)*—neither identical with the skandhas nor totally distinct from them—persisted in Nirvana. Though their argument was buttressed with references to *Buddhavacana* ("Sayings of the Buddha"), and may well have been in accord with the Buddha's own view, these "personalists" were held to be heretical by the Sthaviras who considered the *pudgala* idea to be at odds with the *anatta* doctrine. The Sarvāstivāda and Vaibhāṣika schools stressed thoroughgoing analysis of specific *dharmas* ("elements of existence") and concluded that Nirvana too was a *dharma,* i.e., an unconditioned *dharma,* a "thing" *(dravya)*. Particular *dharmas* were held to be ultimately unreal, mere phenomena; and Nirvana was the noumenal ground or "substance," the thing-in-itself of which they were appearances. In short, it was Nirvana alone that was real and not those who attained it.

The Sautrāntika school saw matters differently. For its members specifiable *dharmas* were at least nominally real and Nirvana was their extinction, a simple absence or "subsequent nonexistence." The THERAVĀDA Buddhists have consistently maintained that Nirvana is positive, balancing metaphysical discussions of its absoluteness with statements emphasizing its ultimacy as a goal of religious striving. (*See* BUDDHIST SECTARIANISM.)

The Mahāyāna "equation" that "samsara *is* Nirvana" and the BODHISATTVA doctrine added significantly to the complexity of conceptions of Nirvana. NĀGĀRJUNA and the MĀDHYAMIKA school pressed the notion of radical "emptiness" *(śūnyatā)* on all fronts, denying validity to all theoretical constructs and arguments and maintaining that the ultimate truth about samsara and Nirvana was their emptiness. In absolute terms, then, samsara and Nirvana were identical, and wisdom *(prajñā)* simply brings a change in the perspective from which they are viewed. This transvaluation of the phenomenal had important consequences as elaborated in Buddhist TANTRA. Metaphysically, Nirvana is uncharacterizable beyond affirming its "being so" *(tathatā)*. Pursuing further the nature of samsaric "fictions," the YOGĀCĀRINS proposed that samsara was the consequence of mental-ideational projections, empty in themselves, which obscure Nirvana's purity like clouds until they are blown away by the winds of enlightenment.

Through the bodhisattva ideal, the Mahāyānists also reevaluated the true goal of religious life. The *arhant's* aims, in this view, were restricted and selfish, and from death he would not actively help suffering mankind. On the other hand, the bodhisattva vowed to attain enlightenment but to decline its ultimate fruit in favor of helping others to reach it. To the two "kinds" of Nirvana—with and without residue—the Mahāyāna added a third: *apratiṣṭhita* Nirvana, the "not fixed" Nirvana of the bodhisattva who though fully enlightened intentionally reinvolves himself in samsara for the welfare of all. Thus the bodhisattva lives the profound equation of samsara-Nirvana.

4. Nirvana and popular Buddhism. Frustrated and even outraged by subtle discussions of Nirvana in the Buddhist texts and their negative aura, not a few scholars have insisted that no matter what an "intellectual elite" said, the vast majority of Buddhists aspired only to a heaven or a happier rebirth, finding Nirvana as formidable and unappealing as the scholars themselves did. It is not to be doubted that there has been a certain discrepancy between prescription and practice in Buddhism, but it would be misleading to assert that all but a few Buddhists have yearned for some "better life." Rather, Nirvana is an absolute standard by which the improvement of personal, social, and religious circumstances is measured. Nirvana gives meaning and place to heavens and hells for Buddhists, whatever learning they have.

5. Nirvana for Hindus and Jainas. Hindus and Jainas occasionally employ the word "Nirvana" in their texts, usually in the sense of "peace," "calm," or "absence [of distractions and passions]" attending spiritual realization. Nirvana's occurrences in the BHAGAVAD GĪTĀ (II.72; V.24-26; VI.15) have been rendered felicitously as "freedom" in a recent translation (K. W. Bolle [1979]).

Many scholars have been unwilling or unable to see anything in the Buddhist Nirvana but nihilistic implications. As text and practice make clear, however, Nirvana is negative *only* in its negating that which is negative and sorrowful in human experience.

Courtesy Ceylon (Sri Lanka) Tourist Board

Gigantic statues of the Buddha, hewn from rock, Polonnauruva. The recumbent statue represents the Buddha's attainment of Nirvana *(parinirvāṇa)*.

Hence, for Buddhists and for others who have used the term in traditional Southern Asia, Nirvana is supremely and creatively positive.

Bibliography. On the word "Nirvana" ("Nibbana") see *The Pali Text Society's Pali-English Dictionary* (1925). On Nirvana in Buddhist thought, see E. Conze, *Buddhist Thought in India* (1962); M. Eliade, *Yoga: Immortality and Freedom* (1958); R. E. A. Johansson, *The Psychology of Nirvana* (1969); G. C. Pande, *Studies in the Origins of Buddhism* (1957), esp. pp. 397-540; and T. Stcherbatsky, *The Conception of Buddhist Nirvāṇa* (1927). For an anthropologist's perspective, see M. E. Spiro, *Buddhism and Society* (1970); and for scholarship on Nirvana and further bibliog., G. R. Welbon, *The Buddhist Nirvāṇa and its Western Interpreters* (1968).

G. R. Welbon

NIWANO, NIKKYŌ nē wä´ nō nĭk kyō´ (B—Jap.; 1906-). Born Shikazō Niwano in the town of Tōkamachi, Niigata Prefecture, Japan. His drive to discover religious truth led him into many sects that practiced divination. Eventually he joined the Reiyūkai, a "new religion" in the Nichiren tradition, where he was introduced to the Lotus Sūtra and to the group counseling practice called Hōza. From 1935 to 1938 he was an active member of the Reiyūkai, but eventually he became dissatisfied with the attitude of the leader toward the Lotus Sūtra and together with Mrs. Myōkō Naganuma formed a new organization, the present Risshō Kōseikai. Niwano has been active in national and international religious organizations, serving as counselor of the Japan Religious League, Inc., and chairman of the Board of Directors of the Union of New Religious Organizations, Inc.

N. S. Brannen

NIZĀRĪS nĭ zä´ rēz (I). *See* Agha Khan; Assassins.

NON-CHURCH MOVEMENT (Ch). See Mukyōkai.

NONVIOLENCE (H, B & Ja). *See* Ahiṃsā.

NORTH AMERICAN TRIBAL RELIGION. *See* Native American Tribal Religion.

NUN (Ch). A woman who belongs to an organized religious community, ordinarily having subscribed to vows of poverty, chastity, and obedience; usually in Roman Catholicism, but small numbers are also found in Anglican and Orthodox Churches.

K. Watkins

NUNC DIMITTIS noonk dĭ mĭ´ tĭs (Ch—Lat.; "now dismiss thou"). First words of Simeon's song (Luke 2:29-32) in the Vulgate (Latin Bible). Since the fourth century it has been said in the daily office, usually in the evening.

R. A. Greer

NYĀYA-VAIŚEṢIKA nyī´ yŭ vī´ shā shĭ´ kŭ (H—Skt.). A Hindu philosophical system which adopts the standpoint of realism in epistemology and pluralism in metaphysics, originating in two distinct works, the *Vaiśeṣikasūtras* of Kaṇāda (*ca.* A.D. 100?) and the *Nyāyasutras* of Gautama (A.D. 150?). Philosophers of these separate texts realized early that their schools were complementary; Nyāya specializing in logic and epistemology, Vaiśeṣika in metaphysics. Differences between the two are minimal after the seventh century, and their identity is explicitly recognized after the time of Udayana (eleventh century). The development of the system as Navya-Nyāya by Gangeśa (fourteenth century) and his commentators represents a methodological breakthrough in Indian thought analogous to the development of symbolic logic in the Western world, having an impact on a wide spectrum of disciplines.

Classical Vaiśeṣika metaphysics proposes to construe all true statements about the universe as referring to members of precisely seven categories: substances, qualities, motions, universal properties, individuators, inherence, and absences. In Navya-Nyāya times this list was revised—individuators deleted, motion reduced to a quality, and the subclasses of substances and qualities rationalized in line with the new terminology introduced by the new logicians.

Early Nyāya developed elaborate discussions of the theory of inference, the nature of perception, truth and error, and other epistemological topics. Nyāya led the way in analyzing arguments and proposing debate methods. An odd result is that although theism appears not to have been an important part of the thought of Kaṇāda or Gautama, Udayana's treatise on arguments for the existence of God, called *Nyāyakusumāñjali*, is celebrated now as the definitive Indian work on that topic, and is widely studied even today.

Nyāya-Vaiśeṣika's importance should not be underestimated. Controversy between it and the rival Buddhist school of logicians headed by Dignāga and Dharmakīrti dominated philosophizing in the middle of the first millennium A.D., and the influence of Navya-Nyāya one thousand years later is overshadowed only by that of the VEDĀNTA school of ADVAITA.

Bibliography. K. H. Potter, *Indian Metaphysics and Epistemology* (1977); D. H. H. Ingalls, *Materials for the Study of Navya-Nyāya Logic* (1951).

K. H. POTTER

O

OCEANIC TRIBAL RELIGIONS (Australia, Melanesia, Micronesia, Polynesia; *see map*). Today almost all Polynesians, most Melanesians and Micronesians, and many aboriginal Australians are baptized Christians. Still, despite linguistic diversity and the many local variations of the past, it is possible to speak of traditional Australian, Melanesian, and Polynesian *types* of religion. Micronesian religions, though barely explored, included elements of the Melanesian and Polynesian type. Throughout the whole area communities worked in and with stone, shell, bone, obsidian, wood, and vegetable fibers; carved and painted incidents and figures taken from myths which, telling of creation and the local human condition, roughly corresponded with the sacred scriptures of literate societies, and paid their respects in their various ways to guardian and tutelary divinities or powers (gods, ghosts, spirits, ancestors, etc.) associated with places or kin or local groups.

Australians were nomadic hunter-gatherers. The islanders of Melanesia, Micronesia, and Polynesia were horticulturalists who also hunted, fished, and gathered a wild harvest. For all, both religious activity and social mores were integral parts of the economic and political activities. "Religion" is perhaps best appreciated in those dimensions of power which, regarded as divinely as well as humanly derived, guiding yet qualified by local moralities, yielded an appropriate integrity, identity, and high status in relation to what was considered inappropriate or wrong or not moral.

1. **Australian wisdom.** Australian life entailed rhythms of concentration, dispersal, and reaggregation. A band of about thirty or forty persons would spread out to hunt and forage, reassemble in small groups, then disperse again to find food. At regular intervals the whole band or several such bands would converge—as custom and the season decreed—to talk, feast, engage in rituals and ceremonies, trade, and to air and settle disputes. Bands were loosely organized into "tribes" which, sharing a common vernacular, were associated with roughly bounded estates of material and sacred resources. Exploiting environments as diverse as the central deserts, downland, sea coasts, and temperate and tropical forests, all Australians had much the same kinds of integrative organizational forms. Group categories prescribed individual behavior. Clans, families, marriage classes, patrimoieties, matrimoieties, and cult or totem groups were organized on principles of nonexclusiveness. Husband, wife, and children belonged to different marriage classes; clans and totem groups included members of different marriage classes; marriage classes bound together as a patrimoiety were opposed as matrimoieties. The external world of flora, fauna, and topographical features was intimately woven into the fabric of social relationships through personification in myths and rituals which reviewed, enacted, and so revivified the relationships involved.

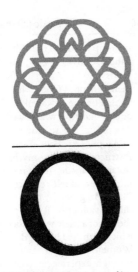

In the beginning was the Dreamtime. Creatures with human, animal, and divine attributes, able to fly, travel vast distances underground or over the land in a trice, encountered each other, quarreled, made it up, transformed themselves into other species, copulated, gave birth to progeny, foraged, made artifacts, hunted, introduced the incest taboo and the forms of marriage, laid out the world, and created the socio-environmental order as it was being reiterated in the present by their descendants and representatives. Sometimes thought to be subject to a power in the sky inherent in thunder and lightning, the activities of the Dreamtime beings were recounted in detail in numerous Myths. Some of these, celebrating the progenitors of a particular totemic group, were the property of the members. Other myths were common property, known to all. Myths were, as they still are, stores of information on seasonal and climatic cycles; the spatial relations of topographical features; how and why these features came to be as they are; the resources to be found there in certain phases of the year; the methods and technologies to be used in processing them; how they should be distributed; what Rituals were appropriate for initiation, the increase of species, rain and prosperity; the problems of raising children; how people could or should behave in given circumstances. Australian myths were geographical guides, technological and socio-economic treatises as well as psychological aids. Incidents from myths were painted and incised on rock faces, cave walls, and bark or wood boards, or on stones called *churinga.* Such treatment justified the myths and were reminders of them. In all, myths and the activities, glosses, songs, and rituals derived from them made up the "Law," the sacred inheritance of the Dreamtime.

Status and prestige were based on a knowledge and effective understanding of the Law and interpreted as intellectual qualities joined to wisdom and experience informed by force of character. Governed by active elders knowledgeable in the Law, Australian communities were in this sense gerontocracies bound to and tied by their Law. On the one hand distinguishing the human from other forms of life, the Law yet brought together the Dreamtime, all creation, and human experience into an integrated semantic whole. Human beings and animals and plants, the stars, thunder, rocky outcrop, desert whirlwind or cooling breeze or stream—all were distinct yet parts of each other, as in the Dreamtime, so now. A human birth was regarded as the reincarnation of a Dreamtime being which, entering the mother through a part of her body, was identified by the place of birth or where the mother first felt the babe kicking in her womb. And these places, associated with the adventures of particular Dreamtime beings, determined the totemic group to which the child should belong, and so the dances, songs, rituals, sacred places, resources, and kinds of inspiration or "dreaming" appropriate to membership. One who knew, understood, and abided by the Law evoked that harmony of inner and outer condition which we ourselves often think of as describing the spiritual.

At puberty boys—but not girls—were formally instructed in the myths of their totem group, isolated, made to undergo ordeals and tests of initiative and self-reliance, then ritually initiated into the totem group by circumcision and, in some places, subincision also. Right through to later middle age the life of a male was punctuated by ritual inductions which signified higher degrees of learning in the Law. Women knew the Law only at second hand and through experience. And because women were not formally instructed in the Law and not held responsible as a man was, many were inclined to be wayward or self-willed. They were sources of trouble certainly, but also provided the dynamic of community life.

Another major source of trouble, challenging the formal harmonies of the Law, was the sorcerer—a man who, knowing the Law, misused it by applying his knowledge not to maintain the Law but to gain his own selfish ends by a demonstration of power over others which flouted the ideal of power within and under the Law. A sorcerer could be a thief or an

adulterer but was primarily a man who caused sickness and death, ultimately to demonstrate his own personal power and contempt of morality. That a sorcerer could be hired underscored the threat to the community and the Law. Dealing successfully with sorcerers, women, and other transgressors of the Law reinforced the authority of the elders and the Law—which integrated the divine, nature, and community.

As Europeans began to settle in Australia, many traditional communities were disrupted. Those who were unable to retreat into areas where no Europeans had settled were denied the shared experience of traditional life that enlivened the Law. The Law withered. Australians became strays in a world where physical survival alone had meaning. Where Europeans were unable to penetrate significantly, Australians held to their Law. The rhythmic clack of boomerangs, the drone of the didgeridoo, songs, dances, rituals, and the dreaming that brought men into vital contact with the Dreamtime ancestors continued. Created once and for all time, man and outer creation yet renewed themselves and were recreated as the Dreamtime beings had and still determined.

2. **Melanesian reciprocity.** While Australians tended to interpret and reinterpret their experience in light of and to accord with their myths, their Law, Melanesians tended to reinterpret their myths so as to justify pragmatic experience. The Law as it came from the Dreamtime embodied both conscience and morality. For Melanesians, however, conscience and morality were achieved through satisfactory reciprocal relationships with others. Among both sets of peoples the sorcerer described and made evident what was evil, wrong, nonmoral, or immoral. But where the Australian Law offered positive goals of achievement both morally and spiritually, its misuse by the sorcerer a constant challenge, Melanesians were much more concerned with avoiding or taking advantage of the varieties of evil or immorality contingently expressed in activities dubbed as sorcery.

Melanesian social life was grounded in the transaction, in the competitive exchange of produce, artifacts, goods, and services within accepted notions of equivalence. Initially determined by categories of kinship and friendship, basically between affines—between men through women ambivalently placed as wife to one and sister to the other—transactions actually engaged could also determine the kinship or friendship categories. Status and prestige depended on the number of transactions entered. A man of high status, a manager, was one whose skills and industry in subsistence activities, joined to self-knowledge, successful risk-taking, and manipulative abilities, enabled him to extend his range of exchanges beyond the normal with a more or less clear conscience.

A Melanesian's knowledge of resources and subsistence techniques was reasonably complete. But Melanesian soils are notoriously variable, root crops are subject to blight and dependent on a rainfall which the Melanesian environment does not always provide. Earthquakes, storms, and floods, which are frequent, might ruin a crop overnight. Animals are often wily, the wild pig dangerous. Catching fish is everywhere a measure of both skill and a mysterious attribute we call "luck." The exchange partner might die or be found wanting in other ways. A disabling sickness, the caprice of a woman standing between man and man, the flare of temper resulting in murder, feud, the activities of a sorcerer—so many things stood between desire and its achievement. Basic skills could be taken for granted within a generally pragmatic address to the world and other people. But succeeding where others failed marked the man of resource and perception able to take advantage of the contingencies of life.

To become such a man of resource, a manager, it was necessary to have some sort of intuitive rapport with the overriding power lying behind the storm, thunder, lightning, flood, and rain. He had to have secret rituals and, most importantly, spells—syllabic jingles thought to exert a control over rain, blight, natural disasters, and the actions of others. These were bequeathed to descendants, or bought, sold, or discarded when obviously not efficacious. The ancestors (usually neutrally benign but potentially troublesome), the clan or lineage guardian spirits, and the spirit guardians of particular localities had to be appeased with sacrifices of produce and pigs which, ceremonially dealt with in feasts, also maintained or enlarged the range of transactions. Being a good father and husband, participating fully in the rituals and other activities of the men's clubhouse, a manager also had to be able to handle the ghost of his dead father or elder brother. Chiding, scolding, giving ambiguous advice regarding his relations with members of the community, such a ghost stood as conscience, to which a man should hearken but not be enslaved.

Ideally a category opposed to the manager, the sorcerer epitomized contempt for the moralities contained in the equivalent transaction. And though sorcerers were often managers and the latter were frequently thought of as sorcerer-like, the difference between them rested on a moral judgment contingently given. The arrogant and self-serving demonstration of power over others described the sorcerer. A manager grounded himself in the morality of reciprocities, knew shame, was a bulwark and asset to community life. Most sorcerers were identified as the residents of other villages, a feature associated with endemic forays and revenge killings that were broken by periods of peace and ceremonial transactions. But since many lingering sicknesses and deaths were diagnosed as due to sorcery, and it was evident from sicknesses and deaths in other villages that sorcerers existed in one's own village, each occurrence was related to moral lesion within the community. Hence sickness and death occasioned examinations of conscience—focused mainly upon instances of trespass and transactional obligations avoided or not fully honored—followed by confession. The discovered wrongdoer should demonstrate shame, the public acknowledgment of the moralities. To this the sorcerer's conscience was thought to be immune.

The village, particularly the cleared space between habitations, was regarded as the place where light, amity, morality, and reciprocity reigned. Here was the men's clubhouse where plans and projects were openly discussed and collectively engaged in, where community rituals were performed, where boys, after a permissive childhood followed by ordeals, instruction and tests and isolation in the bush, were eventually circumcised and initiated into the morality that was proper to manhood. Set apart from the village, a little way into the bush, was the women's menstruation and birth hut, a shaded place where all entered the world. Between the village itself and the bush were the dwellings of those few men and their families who had forfeited proper moral status by opting out of the continuing cycle of competitive transactions. Forest and bush were appropriate to the malign, mysterious, nonreciprocal, and nonmoral; to sorcerers who gathered in gangs to plan their evil deeds and participate in their rituals; to the wild pig or cassowary which might kill a man; to the snake which slithered through the underbrush; the storm and flash flood that overwhelmed the unwary; the mischievous—sometimes malicious—sprites that caused a variety of mishaps such as stubbed toes, barked shins, boils, cuts, tumbles, broken legs and ankles. Nonetheless, though women were generally associated with the qualities of forest and bush in a passive way, a man who did not actively show such qualities failed to provide the village moralities with their creative edge.

The range and variety of Melanesian cultic practices converged in the moralities contained in the equivalent transaction, the hub of peaceful and harmonious relationships as well as of exigencies, emergencies, troubles, disappointment, enmities, and discord. Though the nonreciprocal power inherent in storm and earthquake could not be gainsaid, when manifest in men, as in sorcerers, it should be struck down, made to acknowledge morality or killed. Never slow to take up his weapons to counter or, when deemed necessary, to manifest the nonreciprocal, a Melanesian felt bound to maintain his equivalence, take advantage when another flagged, kill if necessary, or be killed and revenged.

This fierce insistence on a morality of equivalence and reciprocity based on the transaction lies perhaps at the heart of Melanesian Cargo Cults, which are attempts in relation to the consequences of European penetration to create manufactured goods by ritual means. Thinking that European goods were ritually or magically or divinely derived, and since only by having their own access to the goods could they interact with Europeans on a moral basis valid for them, Melanesians have sought the formulas which would provide the goods and yield the basis for an overall moral integrity. In time, viable independence movements have developed from the cults.

3. Polynesian power and taboo. For Polynesians integrity lay in the legitimate exercise of coercive power. They knew the sorcerer—though in relation to so much else in the culture his importance was relatively diminished. They acknowledged the caprice of storms and sprites, the power of thunder, lightning, earthquake and volcanic eruption, and they demanded equivalence in transactions with peers. In their forms of organization, which were hierarchical and authoritarian in contrast to the generally egalitarian Melanesians, they had specific places (Melanesians did not) for the guardian and organizer of cult activities, the priest, as well as for the inspired visionary, the seer. There was a proliferation of ritual procedures, offices, and roles, and transition rites to signal the additional powers and responsibilities which the assumption of an office implied. There were elaborate temples of stone and wood, and rituals involving pig as well as human sacrifice and cannibalism. All ceremonies and rituals were preceded by the very formalized preparation and libation of *kava* (a drink prepared from the root of *piper methisticum*) and reached a climax in the drinking of the *kava*. While Australians measured themselves against an effective and wise understanding of their Law, and Melanesians wrestled with and came to terms with their conscience through transactions, the identity and worth of a Polynesian lay in the services he could demand of others while maintaining the favor of the gods—of whom there were a vast number.

From a somewhat shadowy prime mover associated with the East and the rising sun there proceeded two great divinities: the one male, creative, associated with the sky, Milky Way, birth, first fruits and harvest; the other, female, destructive as well as creative, of the earth, underworld, earthquakes, tidal waves, and volcanic activity. With slightly differing names and attributes from island to island, these three, together with a host of lesser gods or divine powers derived from the mating of sky and earth, as well as many independently derived deities of bush, grove, stream, sea current, eddy and flurry of rock, brooded over Polynesian life. They had to be appeased with feasts, rituals, and sacrifices; their favor bestowed power, and a loss of power signaled their disfavor.

Each differentiated craft, activity, or ability had its divine patrons and enemies upon whose interrelations with men human projects depended. Finding favor in these intricate relationships resulted in *mana,* a demonstrated power of effectiveness which was itself regarded as evidence of divine favor. Whatever the activity, the proven expert had *mana*. The wider the coercive range of this effectiveness, the more important the *mana*. A high chief had the most *mana* because he was born of a chiefly lineage, and because he exercised control over the largest domain and population. Other chiefs, subject to the high chief, had less *mana*. Should a chief become ineffective in exercising political control and exacting obedience, however, it was evident that he had lost the favor of the gods and that his *mana* was diminished. A rival with more *mana, mana* made more manifest, took his place. Alongside the hierarchy of chiefs and lesser chiefs was a hierarchy of priests, men who advised their chiefs and organized rituals and ceremonies. The seer was one who, thought to have animal familiars and susceptible to trances and spirit possession, might be consulted by those who set store by such esoteric insights as he might provide. In times of stress, however, he might exercise a more persuasive power and influence, resulting in a general compliance with the implications of his intuitions.

It is from the Polynesian *tapu* and Captain Cook's account of it that the more commonly known TABOO—present also in Melanesia and Micronesia—is derived. *Tapu* spanned the meanings of "sacred," "holy," "forbidden," and "not done." Though certain places and activities were always *tapu,* chiefs or lesser chiefs down to heads of households could contingently impose a *tapu* within their jurisdictions. A means of *ad hoc* legislation for the chief, imposing a *tapu* was also a test of *mana*. Just as the man who broke a householder's *tapu* on his garden or trees with impunity clearly had more *mana* than the householder, so one who broke a chief's *tapu* challenged the *mana* and the authority of the chief. As the gods exerted power over men, so was power over others the prize of men. Every Polynesian had authority over someone—be it only his wife or child—and every Polynesian was himself subject to others. There was an authoritative chain expressed in *mana* and *tapu,* in certain freedoms and effective control at one end, and in increasing restrictions on initiatives at the other.

Partial resolutions of this authoritative chain occurred in situations described as *noa,* where *tapu* was neutralized and *mana* could be neither gained nor lost; in death; in frequent warfare—killing being the final assertion of absolute power over the killed; and in the Society Islands in the institution known as the *Arioi,* a group of as-though sacred entertainers. To join the *Arioi* a vocation, indicated by trances, visions, and spirit possession, was necessary. Consisting of women as well as men, members of the *Arioi* subjected themselves to the discipline of their calling—the acting and recitation of myths, dancing, singing, acrobatics. Marriage was not permitted, sexual relationships were promiscuous, and females who kept the children they bore were expelled. Excused from subsistence activities, they were fed, housed, and clothed by the chiefs who exacted tribute for this purpose from the households under their control. In time, as induction standards were relaxed and the pleasures of entertaining began to compare favorably with the work of being entertained, this gay band of people moving from island to island—though gaining the admiration of early European travelers—became a severe strain on resources. Ordinary people were ready to break loose from such traditional beliefs and practices.

The quite remarkable conversions to Christianity in the Polynesian islands, and the smashing of temples and statues, cannot wholly be laid at the door of the pitifully few Christian missionaries. Gods, chiefs, priests, and institutions such as the *Arioi* had become an alliance of tyrannies. The surge of popular feeling, helped on by missionaries who could not but take advantage of the situation, was not to be denied. A little later, as Europeans began to settle and their goods began to circulate, there were misgivings. Movements similar to Melanesian cargo cults flourished briefly, then died as generalized Christian ways became the norm.

4. **Micronesian compromise.** While Polynesians were patrilineally organized, and Melanesian communities could be either patrilineal or matrilineal or both, Micronesian peoples were matrilineal. Gods, chiefs, and priests exerted their controls and demanded their rituals and ceremonies—albeit less insistently than in Polynesia. A chief's power over others, his *mana,* was qualified by the fact of matrilineality, by transactional moralities, and by the collectivity of males joined together in a clubhouse. Like the Melanesian manager, a Micronesian chief was vulnerable to sorcery and had to act much more circumspectly than his Polynesian peer. Though prestige was gained through well-managed transactions, yielding *mana,* this was qualified by ranking peers and the threat of sorcery. Gaining *mana* with a conscience well mastered and acceptable to peers and others revealed the man who, knowing himself, others, and the world he lived in, was fulfilling his potential in society as well as in relation to what was considered divine.

While for many persons in a literate and complexly organized civilization the highest religious achievement—spirituality—often goes along with a certain detachment from worldly affairs, this option was not open to the peoples of Oceania. High socio-political status capable of transcending given moralities evinced mastery of the local human condition and values as well as a rapport with, or the favor of, those powers represented as divine. For them—as indeed the greatest religious leaders have insisted—religion was and still remains the most practical of all concerns.

Bibliography. R. M. and C.H. Berndt, *The World of the First Australians* (1964); M. Eliade, *Australian Religions* (1973); A. P. Elkin, *The Australian Aborigines* (1954); U. McConnell, *Myths of the Munkan* (1957); N. D. Munn, *Walbiri Iconography* (1973); T. G. H. Strehlow, *Aranda Traditions* (1947); K. O. Burridge, *Tangu Traditions* (1969); G. Bateson, *Naven* (1936); R. Fortune, *Manus Religion* (1935); P. Lawrence and M. J. Meggitt, eds., *Gods, Ghosts and Men in Melanesia* (1965); J. Layard, *Stone Men of Melekula* (1942); E. Best, *Maori Religion and Mythology* (1924); E. Caillot, *Mythes, legendes et traditions des*

Polynesiens (1914); W. Ellis, *Polynesian Researches* (1829); R. Firth, *The Work of the Gods in Tikopia* (1940); E. S. Handy, *Polynesian Religion* (1927); R. W. Williamson, *Religions and Cosmic Beliefs of Central Polynesia* (1933); F. Steiner, *Taboo* (1956).
K. O. L. Burridge

OFFERTORY (Ch). The part of the Eucharistic Liturgy during which the bread and wine are offered and made ready for consecration. Since the fourth century gifts of Christian charity have been associated with the offertory. In Eastern liturgies it begins the entire service; in the West it is after the liturgy of the Word. *See* Mass.
R. A. Greer

OFFICE, DIVINE (Ch). *See* Divine Office.

OLD BELIEVERS (Ch). Schismatic members of the Russian Orthodox Church. They rejected the liturgical reforms of Patriarch Nikon (seventeenth century), who imposed practices conforming to Greek usage. Old Believers insisted on retaining such older practices as making the sign of the cross with two fingers instead of three.

In the course of time they split into two groups: priestly *(popovtsy)* and priestless *(bespopovtsy).* The latter group produced many smaller groups or sects, which rejected both state and church, depriving themselves of all sacraments except baptism. They lived in apocalyptic expectation of the coming of Antichrist.

Despite severe persecution their numbers continued to grow; by 1917 there were about ten million Old Believers in Russia. Today their numbers are not known. They still preserve the traditions of Moscovite and rural piety, Icons, and church music and are known for their particular steadfastness and loyalty to their faith.
V. Kesich

OLD CATHOLICS (Ch). A group which separated from the Church of Rome out of opposition to Vatican Council I (1870), rejecting its formulation of papal Infallibility. German Catholics, followed by Catholics in Switzerland and Austria, were in the forefront of this struggle. Their bishops were ordained by the Jansenist Church of Utrecht, which had separated from Rome in 1724. In 1897 a "National Polish Church" was formed in the United States.

Old Catholics recognize seven ecumenical councils and the doctrinal teachings of the undivided church before the Great Schism. They have a married clergy, bishops as well as priests. There are about 100,000 Old Catholics.
V. Kesich

OLD TESTAMENT (Ch). Christian name for the collection of writings sacred to both Jews and Christians, consisting of books of holy law, history, prophecy, and poetry. For Judaism, the list of sacred books in the Hebrew Language was fixed by the Synod of Jamnia at the end of the first century A.D. The early church used the Greek translation, which included writings not in the Jewish canon. Jerome doubted the authenticity of these books, but they were only separated from the OT by the Protestant Reformation. Catholics call them "Deuterocanonicals," and Protestants, "Apocrypha."
J. R. Crim

A stylized depiction of the sacred Hindu mantra *Oṃ*, which is made up of three Sanskrit characters representing the three basic phonemes and thought to encompass all possible elements of speech.

OṂ (AUṂ) ōm—with additional protraction of the vowel and weak nasalization (H—Skt.; lit. "yes, so be it"). A Vedic syllable, termed the *Praṇava* ("the Reverberation"), whose properly repeated linguistic sound-form is used as a Mantra for evoking within the reciter the highest form of Brahman. Originally a ritually employed particle of assent, from the Upaniṣads on, *Oṃ* as the supreme syllable *(akṣara)* represents the irreducible form of creative power assumed by Brahman in manifesting both the sacred words of the Veda and the universe as a coherent whole interrelated by linguistically structured sound (*see* Mantra §1). The sound *"Oṃ"* is composed of three phonemes *(a-u-m),* variously identified with and symbolizing the integration of the three worlds, three Vedas, three states of consciousness, etc. In the Māṇḍūkya Upaniṣad the concluding silence is taken as a "fourth," representing the attainment of the highest Self (Atman).

Bibliography. J. van Buitenen, "Akṣara," *JAOS,* 79 (1959), 176 ff.; R. Panikkar, *Vedic Experience* (1977), pp. 766 ff.
W. G. Neevel

OṂ MAṆIPADME HŪM ōm´ mä´ nē päd´ mē hūm´ (B—Skt.). Mantra used extensively in Tibetan Buddhism. Traditionally it is said to be a vocative addressed to Avalokiteśvara hailing the jewel *(maṇi)* in the lotus *(padme),* and thus is a reference to the incarnation of Buddhahood. It came to Tibet in the seventh or eighth century from Indian Tantric Buddhism, retaining its Sanskrit form. The Indian original was probably a vocative to a female deity and symbolized the joining of the male and female principles. While it is universally used by Tibetans, there is no certainty as to its meaning, although esoteric explanations abound. In pious practice emphasis is on frequency of repetition. It is the formula used in Prayer Wheels so that each revolution enunciates the prayer. In yogic practice each sound of the mantra and every stroke of the script used to write it are the objects of meditation. Enunciation of the mantra is said to send forth influences for compassion and good. Oṃ and *hūm* are mystical exclamations that set off what stands between them as of religious significance and function much as do "Hail" and "Amen." *Maṇi* has acquired a special meaning as containing in itself all the doctrine coming from Avalokiteśvara, the guardian saint of Tibet, and his incarnation *Srong bTSansGan Po,* the legendary royal patron of Buddhism. *Padme* embodies the whole of Buddhist practice and morality, while the concluding *hūm* symbolizes their integration as the path to salvation. D. G. Dawe

ŌMOTO ō mō´ tō (Sh—Jap.; lit. "great source"). A religious movement originating in late nineteenth century Japan, based on oracles received through Deguchi Nao and interpreted and expanded by Deguchi Onisaburo. Now a relatively small though stable movement, Ōmoto had upward of two million members in the early 1930s and helped prepare leaders for other movements, notably Taniguchi Masaharu of Seichō no Ie and Okada Mokichi of Sekai Kyūsei-kyō. Its roots are in old Shintō. Traditional arts are stressed.

1. **History.** Officially Ōmoto is said to have originated with Nao's experience in 1892, but as an effective movement it actually began in 1900 when Nao recognized Onisaburo as the promised savior. He became one of Japan's most colorful religious leaders as well as an artist of merit. Scholarly (though largely self-educated), energetic, and outspoken, he interpreted, systematized, and expanded the oracles of Nao and devised an organization and program for their dissemination. Under him Ōmoto expanded remarkably, achieving even international reputation through liaison with other Asian groups and the formation of the Universal Love and Brotherhood Association (ULBA). At the same time, Onisaburo's flamboyance provoked government opposition. In two so-called "Ōmoto Incidents" in 1921 and 1935, he and others were arrested, and in the latter instance all Ōmoto buildings were razed and the movement was disbanded.

Onisaburo began reorganizing in 1946 but died only two years later. Renewal was continued by his wife and daughter, and leadership still remains in the Deguchi family.

2. **Scripture.** The canon consists of two collections: the *Ofudesaki* (not to be confused with the Tenri-kyō scripture of the same name), oracles recorded by Nao on some 200,000 sheets of paper, and the *Reikai Monogatari,* eighty-one volumes produced by Onisaburo.

3. **Headquarters.** Since 1946 most of the buildings have been reconstructed at two sites in Kyoto prefecture: Ayabe is the center of worship and pilgrimage and home of the spiritual leader; Kameoka is the organizational headquarters and training center.

Bibliography. F. Franck, *An Encounter with Omoto* (1975); S. Kobayashi, "Ōmoto, a Religion of Salvation," *Japanese Religions,* II (Apr. 1960), 38-50; H. Thomsen, *The New Religions of Japan* (1963). H. N. McFarland

ONEIDA COMMUNITY (Ch). A perfectionist community founded by J. H. Noyes (1811-86) and existent in Oneida, New York from 1847 to 1880, when it became a joint stock company—Oneida Community, Ltd.—known for its silverware. According to Noyes, Christ's second coming in A. D. 70 made perfect holiness possible. Since selfishness was the heart of sin, true Christian living was communal and involved sharing of both things and persons (requiring the abolition of monogamy). Significant features of the community included the institution of complex marriage, a ritual of mutual criticism, and equality of women.

Bibliography. M. L. Carden, *Oneida* (1969).
M. Endy

ORDERS (Ch). *See* Religious Orders; Bishop; Deacon; Elder; Priest.

ORDINATION 1. (Ch). The ritual commissioning of ministers by prayer and the imposition of hands (Acts 6; 13:1-3). The earliest known text of ordination rites is in the *Apostolic Tradition* of Hippolytus (*ca.* 215), where there are three orders of ministers: Bishops, Presbyters, and Deacons, all ordained by the bishop(s). *See* Clergy, Christian; Sacraments.

2. (Ju). *See* Rabbi. T. J. Talley

ORIGEN ôr´ ĭ jĕn (Ch; *ca.* 185–*ca.* 254). Dominant biblical interpreter and theologian of the patristic period; his exegetical, theological, and apologetic works established him as the most influential and controversial ecclesiastical thinker of the period prior to Nicaea.

Origen headed a school in Alexandria from about 206 to 231, when clashes with the Alexandrian bishop, Demetrius, forced him to move to Palestine. There ordained a presbyter (*see* Clergy), he added regular preaching to his labors as author and traveler. Imprisoned during the Decian persecution (249-251), he died shortly thereafter in Tyre. The chief source for his life is Eusebius' *Ecclesiastical History* VI.

His predominant interest in biblical studies is reflected particularly in the *Hexapla* (an edition of the

OT with the HEBREW text, the Hebrew in Greek letters, and four Greek versions), and in numerous commentaries, sermons, and scholia on books of the Bible. The celebrated treatise *On First Principles* (written *ca.* 229) investigated issues present but not confronted in the apostolic faith. In the course of arguing (against GNOSTIC determinism) the full freedom of individual minds to turn to or from God's Word, Origen constructed an expansive cosmology and daring vision of a restoration of all souls to original purity and the company of God. The apologetic work *Against Celsus* (249) captures the sharp encounter of two redoubtable philosopher-theologians of late antiquity, revealing at the same time much of importance about the state of philosophy and the status of Christianity in the Roman world at the time.

Origen's boldness of thought placed future theologians in his debt, even though certain of his ideas (especially the concept of preexistence of souls) were subject to criticism and were condemned by the Council of Constantinople, 553.

Bibliography. P. Nautin, *Origène, sa vie et son oeuvre* (1977); J. Daniélou, *Origen* (ET 1955). R. C. GREGG

ORIGINAL SIN (Ch). *See* SIN, ORIGINAL.

ORTHODOX CHURCHES (Ch—Gr.; lit. "right belief" [*orthos*—"straight"; *doxa*—"opinion"]). Hierarchical self-governing churches, headed by a PATRIARCH, METROPOLITAN or ARCHBISHOP. They are also called "Eastern," because they stem from countries which shared the Christian heritage of the eastern part of the Roman Empire (Byzantium). Their doctrine, liturgy, and spirituality were shaped in the period of the one undivided church. There is consensus among them in matters of faith, and they are in sacramental communion with one another despite a diversity of geography, cultures, languages, and historical and aesthetic experiences. The patriarchates today are those of Constantinople, Alexandria, Antioch, Jerusalem, Russia, Romania, Bulgaria, Serbia, and Soviet Georgia. There are also Orthodox churches in Greece, Cyprus, Poland, Czechoslovakia, and Finland. Churches outside the traditional Orthodox areas include those in the Americas, western Europe, Japan, and Australia.

1. **History.** From CONSTANTINE on, the church held official status in the empire and became the builder of a new Christian culture. Ecumenical COUNCILS were convoked by the emperor, and their dogmatic formulations and other decisions were imposed as laws on all Christians of the empire. Seven councils were accepted as normative.

After Constantine's conversion, a conflict arose between the secular clergy and the monks. Those who supported a link between church and empire saw in the gathering of bishops with the emperor the image of the messianic banquet. Others perceived dangers here, and wanted to preserve purity of faith and tradition by withdrawing into monastic communities. Eventually these communities succeeded in imposing some of their regulations upon the rest of the church.

With the conversion of the Slavs by Greek missionaries in the eighth century, national churches arose which strove for self-government but considered themselves successors to the universal church.

The most important separations from this church occurred after the Council of CHALCEDON (451), when the MONOPHYSITE churches separated from the Orthodox, and after the eleventh century, when the GREAT SCHISM split the ROMAN CATHOLIC CHURCH from that of the East.

2. **Source of authority.** Orthodox churches recognize the primacy of honor of the Ecumenical Patriarch of Constantinople, but there is no single Orthodox center that has infallible authority (*see* PAPACY; INFALLIBILITY). The ecumenical councils, whose decisions are accepted as infallible, were not organs to which automatic authority was ascribed. The first, NICAEA (325), was accepted only after fifty-six years of bitter controversy.

3. **Tradition.** Tradition is transmitted by the BIBLE, the CREED, doctrinal and canonical decisions and formulations of the Ecumenical Councils, liturgies and hymns, the writings of the fathers, and ICONS. Some parts of this tradition are of permanent value and are unchangeable (e.g., the Bible, the Creed, the DOGMAS of the Ecumenical Councils) while local traditions and customs are not. A major task of Orthodox theologians is to distinguish the essential tradition of the church from various accumulated traditions, practices, and attitudes.

4. **Scripture and tradition.** The Scripture (OT and NT) is not a self-interpreting book for the Orthodox, but is organically linked to the church and its tradition. It is neither subordinate nor superior to tradition, nor can there be any contradictions between them. Therefore they are not regarded as two sources of revelation but one.

The church also recognizes that Scripture contains both human and divine aspects. As the human and divine natures of Christ are inseparable, the gospel of the incarnate Lord is recorded in human words.

5. **Worship and theology.** In the liturgical books we find the best expression of the theology and spirituality of the Orthodox Church. The purpose of worship and theology is mystical union with God. (*See* MYSTICISM.) Theology is not simply expressed in words and image but is sung and lived in the liturgical life. The liturgy is never a private performance by a priest, for he cannot perform the liturgy alone, but an act of clergy and laity working together. The "Jesus prayer," for example, intensified the interest in corporate sacramental life of those participating in the late Byzantine mystical revival known as HESYCHASM.

The language of worship is primarily biblical, with innumerable quotations and allusions from both

Testaments. It is also the language of mystical theology, which is "apophatic" or negative; God is described in the Eucharistic Prayer as "*in*effable, *in*conceivable, *in*visible, *in*comprehensible, ever-existing, and eternally the same." This is the language of prayer, pointing to his majesty and transcendence and at the same time conveying his presence. God is absolutely transcendent in his essence, yet he acts for human salvation: "You have brought us from nonexistence into being, and when we had fallen away you raised us up again and did not cease to do all things until you brought us up to heaven, and endowed us with your kingdom which is to come."

The aim of a Christian life is the acquisition of the HOLY SPIRIT. Both theology and spirituality stress its role and work. The church rejected the Western interpolation of FILIOQUE into the creed, as it implies the subordination of the Holy Spirit to the Father and the Son. Orthodox theologians have pointed out that this doctrine overstressed unity (essence) at the expense of diversity (three persons) of the Godhead. (*See* TRINITY.)

6. **Deification.** God's essence is inaccessible. His uncreated and eternal energies (glory, light, grace, love) permeate the universe and make possible a personal union with man. In its worship the church offers thanksgiving that God has opened the way for man to come to him and has made union with him possible. This is the Orthodox churches' teaching of the deification (*theosis*) of man, a doctrine based on the INCARNATION, which revealed a new perfect humanity. The two separate realities are united forever in Christ, as stated in the formulation of the Council of Chalcedon: unconfusedly, unchangeably, indivisibly, and inseparably. God became man that man might become divine. This union is the goal of prayer and participation in the sacraments; it involves the cooperation of the two wills, divine and human. In this union with God human beings "become partakers of the divine nature" (II Pet. 1:4) without ceasing to be creatures. Other NT writers expressed this union in terms of being or dwelling in Christ. The fathers of the church as well as modern theologians recognize that deification as the goal of Christian life lies at the base of every important theological controversy in the history of the Orthodox churches.

7. **Icons.** ICONS are universally present in Orthodox churches, displayed on the walls and on icon screens. They are not primarily religious pictures, but represent holy men and women who glorified God in their lives and now lead others to his presence. (*See* SAINTS, VENERATION OF.) They make the church on earth and the church in heaven one in the liturgy. The incarnation made the art of the icon possible, and icons are witnesses that God became man. The faithful do not worship icons; they venerate them, as they do the book of the Gospels, which is considered a verbal icon of Christ and which is kept on the altar.

8. **Ecumenical dialogue.** In our time the Orthodox churches are involved in dialogues with other Christian churches but are not in communion with them. From the Orthodox point of view, the main disagreement concerns the nature of the CHURCH and the problem of authority. The Orthodox still maintain the concept of the church held in the first centuries of undivided Christendom, that the local church, gathered around its bishop for celebration of the EUCHARIST, is the Catholic Church. The whole church is not the sum total of local churches but is fully realized in each local eucharistic gathering. These local churches recognize the same faith in other churches, and the unity among them is manifested and realized in the sacrament of unity, the Eucharist. *See* GREEK ORTHODOX CHURCH; RUSSIAN ORTHODOX CHURCH.

Bibliography. T. Ware, *The Orthodox Church* (1963); J. Meyendorff, *Living Tradition* (1978); V. Lossky, *The Mystical Theology of the Eastern Church* (1957).

V. KESICH

ORTHODOX JUDAISM. One of several contemporary interpretations of Judaism (*see* CONSERVATIVE JUDAISM, REFORM JUDAISM, RECONSTRUCTIONIST JUDAISM). Like the other interpretations, Orthodoxy maintains that it best and most faithfully represents the mainstream tradition of Judaism as transmitted from generation to generation. Orthodoxy may be distinguished by its adherence to the belief in the dual revelation at Sinai (*see* TORAH) and by its consequent belief that Jewish Law (*see* HALAKAH) is a divine, not human institution, largely immune to historical forces.

Orthodox Judaism maintains belief in a personal God and takes a generally literalist if not fundamentalist approach to the Hebrew BIBLE. Orthodox Judaism rejects or, more accurately, ignores the findings of biblical criticism. It sees in the study and practice of Torah the highest ideal of human existence and maintains a large number of educational institutions, reflecting the many nuances of Orthodox belief and outlook, dedicated to promoting that end.

Orthodoxy may be distinguished from Reform Judaism by its emphasis on the central place of obedience to Halakah in Jewish life and from Conservative Judaism by its emphasis on the idea that the People of Israel exist primarily by virtue of and in order to keep and serve the Torah, not vice versa. Of the three central ideas of Judaism, it may be said that while Reform and Conservative Judaism emphasize the ideas of God and Israel respectively, Orthodox Judaism emphasizes the idea of Torah.

Contemporary Orthodox Judaism may be roughly divided into left and right wings. This division is by and large one of attitude, not of practice. The left wing of Orthodoxy traces itself to the thought of Rabbi S. R. HIRSCH (Germany, nineteenth century). It is generally appreciative of the value of Western culture and strongly supports ZIONISM and the State of

Israel. This wing of Orthodoxy is closely identified with New York's Yeshiva University, with the Rabbinical Council of America, and with the Union of Orthodox Jewish Congregations of America.

The right wing of Orthodoxy which is today strongly, if not exclusively, identified with HASIDISM traces itself to the thought of Rabbi Moses Sofer (Hungary, nineteenth century). It generally seeks to limit contact with Western culture as much as possible, is very critical of the secular character of the State of Israel, and rejects what it considers to be the pseudo-messianic overtones of Zionism. Closely identified with the *yeshivot* (*see* YESHIVAH) transplanted to North America and Israel from Europe after the HOLOCAUST, right wing Orthodoxy takes its leadership from the deans of these schools.

Bibliography. C. Liebman, *Aspects of the Religious Behavior of American Jews* (1974); E. Rackman, *One Man's Judaism* (1970); D. Rudavsky, *Emancipation and Adjustment* (1967).

M. M. KELLNER

ORTHODOXY AND HERESY (Ch—Gr.; *orthodoxia*—"right opinion"; *hairesis*—"system of thought" or "school"). Terms which function as antonyms in Christian usage, the former designating true doctrine of the CHURCH and the latter describing errant or false teaching which purports to be Christian.

Deriving from a Greek verb meaning "to choose," the word "heresy" initially bore a range of nonpejorative connotations having to do with choice and preference, thus philosophical outlook or school. The term has a decidedly less positive tone in the NT, where it describes a dissident group (Gal. 5:20; I Cor. 11:19), parties within JUDAISM (Acts 5:17; 15:5), and (as characterized by an opponent) the Christians (Acts 24:5). The CHURCH FATHERS continued and elaborated this practice, speaking both of the Jews and pagans as sects or schools not in possession of the truth (Clement of Alexandria, *Stromateis* 7.15) and of false teachers within the Christian community (Ignatius, *Trallians* 6.1; Origen, *Against Celsus* 2.3).

The Christian church has consistently understood orthodox doctrine (regardless of the date of its authoritative articulation in synod or creed) as consistent with and ultimately traceable to the teachings of JESUS, as transmitted to and through the APOSTLES. This view of the source of the truth of Christianity necessarily entails the correlate perception of all heretical doctrine as innovation or deviation from original foundations of belief—the fruit of human presumption and excessive speculation, inspired by SATAN. The declaration that a certain teacher or party is orthodox is, from the historical viewpoint, a retrospective judgment which indicates the emergence of a consensus or a telling victory in doctrinal deliberations which is sustained in subsequent ecclesiastical life. All parties in a dispute claimed to represent the truth of the Christian faith and set about defense of their positions by reference to biblical writings and church traditions. Thus, for example, both Irenaeus (*Against Heresies* 1.2-3) and Ptolemaeus (quoted in Epiphanius, *Heresies* 33.7.9), adversaries in the gnostic controversy, attempt to demonstrate the derivation of their ideas from apostolic tradition.

In his *Epistle* 188, BASIL of Caesarea (*ca.* 330-379) discusses the church's early distinction between heresy and schism. The former involves doctrinal error and blasphemy, thus alienation from the faith, while the latter denotes separation from the church (usually because of dispute over discipline or ecclesiological definition). In his writings against the powerful schismatic church of North Africa, the DONATISTS, AUGUSTINE of Hippo repeatedly challenged them to demonstrate the congruence of their views with those held in other churches throughout the Roman Empire. This test of universality, or catholicity, applied both to church teaching and practice, became (along with the test of apostolicity) a chief criterion of orthodoxy. Vincent of Lerins' statement (in 434) that the Catholic church holds "that which has been believed everywhere, always, by all" (*Commonitory* 2.6) has remained the determinative rule for assessment of Christian truth.

Bibliography. W. Bauer, *Orthodoxy and Heresy in Earliest Christianity* (ET, 1971); S. L. Greenslade, *Schism in the Early Church* (1953).

R. C. GREGG

OUTCASTES (H). *See* HARIJAN.

P

PACHOMIUS pâ kō′ mĭ ŭs (Ch; *ca.* 290-346). Egyptian hermit who decided that the ascetic life could be lived more successfully in community under a moderate rule. He established nine monasteries for men and two for women. The life required total obedience to superiors and common ownership of goods. *See* MONASTICISM. W. O. PAULSELL

PADMA-SAMBHAVA päd′ mə säm bä′ və (B—Skt.; lit. the "Lotus-Born One"). Also called Saroruha, Urgyan, as well as Padmavajra, Padmakara, and other etiological compounds of "Padma." The eighth century A.D. GURU who established TANTRIC Buddhism of the VAJRAYĀNA tradition as the dominant religion of Tibet and was founder of the Nyingmapa sect of TIBETAN BUDDHISM, which venerates him as a second BUDDHA. He is adored as the Guru Rimpoche (Precious Teacher) and is preeminent in sacred texts and iconography as Tibet's teacher of the way of enlightenment.

Knowledge of his life comes from legendary sources into which elements of the accounts of GAUTAMA Buddha and other gurus have been assimilated. He came from Udyana in northwest India, where he was trained by Tantrics and received supernatural powers through an initiation by the Dakinis. In A.D. 747 he was invited by King KHri Srong lDeu bT San to overthrow the DEMONS who had opposed the introduction of Buddhism into Tibet. Buddhist teachers had triumphed over the BÖN shamans in argumentation but were defeated in contests of MAGIC. Padma-Sambhava was able to vanquish his opponents not only in dialectics but supremely in magical deeds. His victory was in part a replacement of Bön by Buddhism and in part a syncretism with Bön SHAMANISM. The traditional stories of his missionary work reflect this in accounts of how he was able to overcome local demons and convert them into protective deities of the Buddhist pantheon. While some sources claim Padma-Sambhava spent as much as fifty years in Tibet, his stay could have been as short as eighteen months. He departed toward the southwest to continue his work of spreading and defending the DHARMA.

Bibliography. H. Hoffman, *The Religions of Tibet* (1961); Y. Tsogyal, *The Life and Liberation of Padmasambhava* (1978).

D. G. Dawe

PAGAN pâ gän. *See* HINDUISM IN SOUTHEAST ASIA §1.

PAGODA pä gō′ dä (B—Portuguese *pagode* or *pagoth,* from Skt. *bhagavat*—"divine" [?] or Sinhalese—*dāgaba* "sacred relic chamber" [?]). Multi-

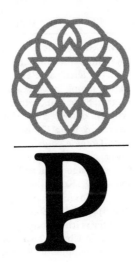

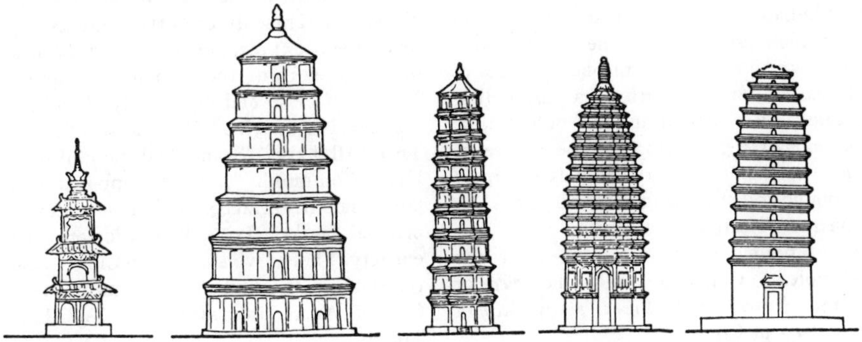

From Michael Sullivan, *The Arts of China*

Types of pagodas

K. Crim

The Śākyamuni *stūpa* at Pulguk-sa, Korea

storied tower of stone, brick, or wood associated with a temple complex or sacred place in Buddhism; Buddhist monument derived from the Indian Stūpa, intended to contain relics of the Buddha, Buddhist saints, or rulers; tiered shrine constructed and visited as acts of devotion, interpreted by some as symbolic of the Buddha's parinirvana, terraces of mythical Mt. Meru, or a sacred representation of the Buddhist cosmos.

1. **Origins.** From earliest times a popular cult of *caityas,* or sacred places, existed in India. These sites may often have included burial mounds. The Buddha was pictured by tradition as reverencing such holy places, and Sūtras report the Buddha advising the raising of monuments to the Buddha as more meritorious than raising memorials to kings. The Buddhists of India adopted the popular *caitya* cult and adapted it to their use. Ashes of the Buddha were divided and placed in *stūpas,* hemispheric domes of brick and plaster crowned with royal umbrellas. Buddhist monks often settled at these holy places, and temple-monasteries developed. The difference between these early *stūpas* and the pagoda is largely semantic, though stylistic changes did occur as *stūpa* construction moved across Asia.

2. **Development.** *Stūpas* multiplied along the merchants' routes to China, becoming the *hpaya* or *sedi* of Burma, the *chö-ten* of Tibet, *phrayachedi* of Thailand, and *t'a* of China.

The precise influences leading to the evolution from *stūpa* mound to the popular multistoried tower of peaked roofs are uncertain. The mast and series of royal umbrellas crowning the *stūpa* may have become the later tiered pagoda tower. The *śikhara* tower of the Indian temple has likewise been cited. The Chinese pilgrim Sung Yün, returning from India in the sixth century, described the thirteen-storied timber *stūpa* erected by King Kaniska, perhaps a major influence upon Chinese pagodas. The Chinese timber watch-tower may also have had great influence on the Chinese pagoda, a style which then spread across Indochina, Korea, and Japan.

3. **Surviving ancient pagodas.** The twelve-sided stone pagoda of Sung-yüeh-ssu in Honan, dating from the sixth century, may be the earliest surviving pagoda in China. Two stone pagodas of the eighth century temple of Pulguk-sa near Kyŏng-ju are among the earliest Buddhist remains in Korea. One of these pagodas, the *Sŏkka-t'ap* ("Śākyamuni *stūpa*"), was made to enshrine a casket containing a crystal bottle with *śarīra* ("relics") of the historic Buddha. The *gojūnotō* ("five-storied-tower") of Horyu-ji at Nara, Japan, is a valuable survivor of the ancient wooden pagodas popular in T'ang China.

4. **From pagodas to *Gohonzon*.** Much of the reverence once directed by Buddhists to the *stūpa* and pagoda gradually was transferred to images of the Buddha and Bodhisattvas, and finally to sūtras or even a small tablet such as the *Gohonzon* (worship object) of Nichiren Buddhism.

Bibliography. *See* bibliog. for Stūpa; Horyu-ji; Art and Architecture, Buddhist.

C. W. Edwards

PALI CANON pä´ lē (B). The most complete and generally regarded as the earliest collection of canonical literature in Buddhism is the Tripitaka first written in the Pali language (Tipiṭaka)—and hence the common designation "Pali Canon"—and belonging to the school of "the Elders" (Theravāda). It is the sacred canon of Buddhists today in Sri Lanka (Ceylon) and the Southeast Asian countries of Burma, Cambodia, Laos, and Thailand. It consists of thirty-one texts written within the first five hundred years after the life of the Buddha.

1. **Versions.** There are in fact several different Tripiṭakas. These differ in the contents of particular texts, the list of texts included, and the arrangement of texts within the canon. Furthermore, the Tripiṭakas of several other early Buddhist schools, e.g. Sarvāstivāda (lit. "The Way of Those Who Hold That 'All Exists' ") and Mahāsāṅghikas (lit. "The Great Community"), were composed in Sanskrit. (*See* Buddhist Sectarianism, Buddhist Councils.) The original Sanskrit Tripiṭakas no longer exist in their entirety. They survive largely in Chinese and Tibetan translations, as well as in fragments uncovered at such Central Asian sites as Gilgit, Tun Huang, and Turfan.

In addition there are vast Tripiṭaka collections in Chinese and Tibetan. These consist primarily of translations of Indian texts and are not limited to the texts of a single school and sect. Other Tripiṭakas such as the Korean and Mongolian canons are derivative from the Chinese and Tibetan collections respectively.

2. Types of literature. According to the testimony of the great fifth century A.D. commentator BUDDHAGHOSA, the texts of the Tripiṭaka can be classified according to their content and literary character into nine genres, known as "limbs." These are (a) prose discourses, (b) discourses in mixed prose and verse, (c) prose analysis, (d) verse texts, (e) exultant utterances, (f) texts beginning with the words "Thus it was said . . . ," (g) tales of previous births of the Buddha, (h) accounts of marvelous events, and (i) discourses in the form of questions which provoke satisfaction or joy. Most of the discourses take the form of a dialogue between the Buddha and another person. The Sanskrit tradition adds three additional genres to this list: (a) introductory material setting the context for a discourse, (b) accounts of exploits, and (c) instructions. From this it can be seen that the Tripiṭaka is a quite diverse corpus of literature.

Stylistically the texts of the Tripiṭaka are often highly repetitious. Apparently this characteristic is a result of their origin as oral literature passed on from teacher to pupil. From an early period professional reciters specialized in specific parts of the canon, their feats of memory being prodigious by modern Western standards. To this day memorization of selected scriptural texts is an important part of Theravāda monastic education.

3. Monastic discipline. The first collection of texts in the Tripiṭaka is the VINAYA PIṬAKA, or "Basket of Monastic Discipline." Composed of five separate works in the Pali version, its core consists of a code of rules governing every aspect of the life of Buddhist monks, together with a similar code for nuns. This code (PĀTIMOKKHA) is the oldest part of the canon. Each rule is set in the context of a story describing the circumstances which led to its legislation, and is accompanied by an early commentary. The Vinaya Piṭaka also outlines the parliamentary procedures governing the communal activities of the monasteries. Together this material provides evidence for a history of the emerging monastic community.

Vinaya collections from five Sanskrit schools also exist. Though based on a common fund of regulations, they treat the material with some liberty, deviating from one another in the number of rules, as well as in overall structure.

4. Discourses. The discourses of the Buddha are to be found in the second "basket," a collection of texts known as the SUTTA PIṬAKA. Here are to be found the basic teachings and ideals of the Buddha illustrated with a wealth of narrative material.

The Pali discourses are further sub-divided into five collections called NIKĀYAS. Four of these have equivalents in the Sanskrit Tripiṭakas where they are referred to as ĀGAMAS. These are collections of longer discourses, middle length discourses, and discourses arranged respectively by topic and according to the numerical progression of their subjects. Again there is some divergence between the Sanskrit and Pali texts, even in the case of discourses which exist in both languages.

Though it is difficult to determine whether any of this material consists of the exact words of the Buddha, it may be assumed that it is largely faithful to the spirit of his personality and teachings. However, some of the material in the discourses does assume developments in the tradition after the time of the Buddha and gives evidence of later editing by monk scholars.

The fifth sub-section of the Pali Sutta Piṭaka is lacking in the Sanskrit versions, though a number of the texts included in it can be found elsewhere in the Sanskrit canons. The fifth Nikāya is a miscellaneous collection of texts, some of them quite important. Not all of these can be strictly classified as discourses. Thus, among the texts of the fifth Nikāya can be found stories of the past lives of the Buddha, many in fable form, a collection of ghost stories encouraging merit making, and a collection of verses by Buddhist monks and nuns.

5. Scholastic analysis. The third canonical collection of texts is known as the "Basket of Higher Subtleties of the Doctrine" (ABHIDHAMMA PIṬAKA). Its works are primarily concerned with the definition of terms, the classification of basic elements of existence, and detailed scholastic analysis of causal relationships. It is exclusively of academic interest. Though both the Pali and the Sanskrit collection of Sarvāstivāda consist of seven works, greater divergence exists between the Pali and Sanskrit versions of the third Piṭaka than is the case with either the monastic disciplines or the discourse collections; and none of the individual texts included are held in common. One text in the Pali Abhidhamma, The Points of Controversy (Kathāvatthu), is concerned exclusively with refuting what it considers to be the heretical views of other Buddhists such as the Mahāsāṅghikas (Great Community).

6. Pali language. Theravāda Buddhists claim that the Buddha spoke Pali, and that they are following the pattern he set in its use for their scriptures. Pali survives today only as a literary language used to express Theravāda religious thought. Though it is ultimately derived from Sanskrit, there has been much scholarly debate as to the actual spoken dialect from which it was developed. Among the proposed sources are the dialects of Magadha, Ujjeni, and Kauśāmbī. The Vināya Piṭaka says that the Buddha allowed his disciples to learn his teachings and spread the message in their own dialects.

It is not clear when Pali came into use as the literary language of Theravāda. There is no indication of knowledge of Pali in the inscriptions of King AŚOKA (*ca.* 274-236 B.C.), who was greatly influenced by Buddhism. Because of this, some scholars (arguing from silence) have concluded that Pali originated after the time of AŚOKA.

7. **Traditional history.** According to Theravāda tradition, the first move toward the compilation of the Tripiṭaka occurred shortly after the death of the Buddha (*ca.* 483 B.C.) at a council of monks held at Rājagṛha. At that time the Vinaya and discourses were supposedly recited. The historicity of this council is generally questioned by modern scholars. *See* BUDDHIST COUNCILS.

A second council was held at Vaiśālī around a century later in response to an effort by some to relax the monastic law. Among the actions of this council was a further recitation of the Vinaya and the arrangement of the oral scriptures into the Piṭakas, Nikāyas, and "limbs."

Theravāda tradition holds that the Tripiṭaka as we now have it, including the Abhidhamma Piṭaka, was fixed at yet a third council in the third century B.C. This was only the finalization of the oral tradition, however. Moreover, Western scholars generally consider the third council a sectarian assembly rather than the universal Buddhist council Theravāda tradition holds it to have been.

One of the ancient chronicles of Sri Lanka completes the account of the canonization process, maintaining that the canon was finally committed to writing in Sri Lanka during the first century B.C.

Bibliography. Most of the Pali Tripiṭaka has been published in English translation as part of the Pali Text Series put out by the Pali Text Society, London. Also consult: R. Webb, *Analysis of the Pali Canon* (1975); B.C. Law, *History of Pali Literature,* 2 vols. (1933); M. Winternitz, *History of Indian Literature,* II (1933); E. Lamotte, *Histoire du Bouddhisme Indien* (1967), pp. 136-283; G. C. Pande, *Studies in the Origins of Buddhism* (1957), pp. 1-247.

J. P. MCDERMOTT

PALM SUNDAY (Ch). The SUNDAY before EASTER, so called because the crowds carried palm branches to welcome JESUS into JERUSALEM (John 12:13). In the fourth century the day was commemorated in Jerusalem by a procession, and this custom was added to the observance of the day as Sunday of the PASSION in the Western church. *See* HOLY WEEK; CALENDAR, CHRISTIAN.

T. J. TALLEY

PAÑCARĀTRA pŭng chŭ răt′ rŭ (H—Skt.; lit. "five" [*pañca*], "night" [*rātri*]). Name of the revelation or scriptures (*see* ĀGAMA) of the earliest Tantric tradition (*see* TANTRISM) of theistic temple ritual and devotion (BHAKTI) dedicated to the worship of VISHNU or NĀRĀYANA, usually in association with the goddess LAKṢMĪ or Śrī; the tradition or system itself is derivatively termed "Pāñcarātra."

The meaning of this name is much disputed. However, in the MAHĀBHĀRATA'S Nārāyaṇīya section, the earliest text (*ca.* third century A.D.) definitely ascribable to this tradition, it can be construed as "night of the five (material elements)," symbolizing the goal attainable by means of the revelation, i.e., MOKṢA or liberation from physical bondage and reunion with Vishnu.

The earliest extant independent Pañcarātra scriptures are placed variously between A.D. 450 and 850. Tradition uses the sacred figure 108 to represent conservatively the number of such ritual texts produced over the centuries to govern Vishnu's worship within many temples and sects throughout India (*see* VAIṢṆAVISM; ŚRĪ VAIṢṆAVA).

Bibliography. F. O. Schrader, *Introduction to the Pāñcarātra* (1916); on the name's meaning as given above, see W. G. Neevel, *Yāmuna's Vedānta and Pāñcarātra* (1977), pp. 8-10.

W. G. NEEVEL

PANCHEN LAMA păn′ chĕn lä′ mə (B—shortened form of Tibetan *pandita chem-po,* "great scholar" and *bla-ma* "superior one," the name given to those believed to be the reincarnation of a BODHISATTVA). Title given to the head of the line of Gelugpa monks of the monastery at Tashilhunpo in Tibet. (*See* BUDDHISM, TIBETAN §3.) He was second in spiritual authority only to the DALAI LAMA. The Panchen Lama is believed to be a physical manifestation of Amitābha (*see* AMIDA).

The first Panchen Lama was bLo-bZang CHos-Kyi-rGyal-mTshan (A.D. 1570-1662), the learned abbot of Tashilhunpo, although his three predecessors are sometimes reckoned as members of this line of succession. He was the tutor of the fifth Dalai Lama, who announced, on the basis of miraculously discovered texts, that the Panchen Lama would be reincarnated as a child. (*See* REINCARNATION.)

There have been seven incarnations in this line. At times the Chinese have sought to promote the influence of the Panchen Lama in the temporal affairs of Tibet as a check on the power of the Dalai Lama. In 1923 the sixth Panchen Lama, Chos-Kyi Nyi-Ma (1883-1937), fled to China after a dispute over taxes with the government of the Dalai Lama. The seventh Panchen Lama, bSKal-bZang Tshe-bRtan, was born in 1938 in the Koko Nor region of Tsinghai Province, China, of Tibetan parents. The Chinese government recognized him as Panchen Lama, although he had not undergone the rigorous tests that determine a true reincarnation. In 1952 he was brought to Tibet by the Chinese Communist forces and installed as abbot of Tashilhunpo. After the 1959 uprising and the flight of the Dalai Lama, the Chinese proclaimed the Panchen Lama leader of "the patriotic element" in Tibet and made him acting chairman of the Preparatory Committee for the Autonomous Region of Tibet. However, the Panchen Lama resisted Chinese pressures to denounce the Dalai Lama as a traitor and was removed from office in 1965.

Bibliography. H. E. Richardson, *A Short History of Tibet* (1962); D. Snellgrove and H. E. Richardson, *A Cultural History of Tibet* (1968).

D. G. DAWE

PĀṆḌAVA pän´dŭ vŭ (H). The name applied to any of the five "sons" of Pāṇḍu, the heroes of the MAHĀBHĀRATA: YUDHISTHIRA, BHĪMA, ARJUNA, Nakula, and Sahadeva. Each Pāṇḍava was supposedly fathered not by Pāṇḍu, but by a god in congress with one of Pāṇḍu's wives. J. BARE

PANNENBERG, WOLFHART pän´ ĕn bûrg (Ch; 1928-). German Protestant, indebted to Hegel and the turn toward ESCHATOLOGY in some biblical studies, for whom a unified account of history is a main task of theology. His work stresses the RESURRECTION OF JESUS as the paradigmatic event in history, the priority of the future in our experience, and Jesus' proclamation of the coming kingdom. *See* THEOLOGY, CONTEMPORARY CHRISTIAN §4a. D. F. OTTATI

PAPACY (Ch). The office and position of the pope, the BISHOP of ROME. In the official list, Pope John Paul II, elected on October 16, 1978, is the 263rd successor of the apostle PETER as bishop of Rome. His title is "bishop of Rome, vicar of JESUS Christ, successor of the prince of the apostles, supreme pontiff of the universal CHURCH, patriarch of the west, primate of Italy, ARCHBISHOP and METROPOLITAN of the Roman province, sovereign of the state of VATICAN CITY, servant of the servants of God."

1. **Primacy and infallibility.** In 1870 VATICAN COUNCIL I declared that the pope has primacy of jurisdiction over the whole church and that under specific conditions he is infallible in proclaiming doctrines of faith and morals. Vatican Council II in 1964 further explained papal INFALLIBILITY and set it in the context of the church and the college of bishops. ROMAN CATHOLIC theological tradition finds biblical warrant for its understanding that Christ conferred supreme teaching and jurisdictional authority on Peter and his successors in Matt. 16:18-19 and John 21:15-17.

2. **Preeminence among bishops.** Emperor Theodosius (380) decreed that all were to hold "that religion which the divine apostle Peter handed on to the Romans." Rome's writ always ran stronger in the West than in the East, where the Eastern patriarchates preferred to acknowledge Roman primacy as one of honor only. Siricius (384-99) was the first Roman bishop to use the title "pope," which GREGORY VII (1073-85) reserved exclusively to the bishop of Rome (although other churches, notably the COPTIC, do not agree).

3. **Civil and ecclesiastical authority.** With the decline of the western Roman empire, popes assumed civil as well as ecclesiastical authority. LEO I (440-61) asserted a high doctrine of monarchical papal power. GREGORY I (590-604) was the father of medieval papacy. The "Donation of Pepin" (754) launched the Papal State, the pope's civil kingdom in central Italy. The first papal coronation was of Nicholas II (1059-61). In the fourteenth century the tiara, or triple crown, became symbolic of the office. Its wearing was abandoned by Paul VI (1963-78), and his two successors, John Paul I (August-September, 1978) and John Paul II (1978-), both refused coronation ceremonies. The papacy of the dark ages was the prey of Roman baronial families, but with Gregory VII began five centuries of struggle with secular rulers, involvement in the CRUSADES, periodic reform movements, and increasing centralization of the church under papal monarchy.

4. **Avignon, Great Schism, and Reformation.** From 1305 to 1377 the popes lived at Avignon in France, and during the GREAT SCHISM (1378-1417) Christendom was divided in allegiance among two and three rival claimants to the papal throne. The Council of Constance in 1415 declared the superiority of an ecumenical council over the pope, a claim rejected by subsequent popes. Earlier popes of the Renaissance and Reformation eras, the notorious Alexander VI (1491-1503) and LEO X (1513-21), were more Renaissance princes than bishops. Only with Paul IV (1555-59) and Pius V (1566-72) did the papacy rally substantially.

5. **Modern papacy.** The rise of the national monarchies and the Enlightenment challenged the seventeenth and eighteenth century papacy, while the French Revolution and Napoleon seemed for a time to threaten its end. Pius VI (1775-99) died the emperor's prisoner, and Pius VII (1800-1823) nearly did so. In the nineteenth century the popes fought against classical and political liberalism and against socialism. Pius IX (1846-78) lost the last of the Papal State with the Italian occupation of Rome in 1870, and in protest he and his successors became until 1929 voluntary "prisoners of the Vatican." LEO XIII (1878-1903) represented a cautious intellectual, political, and social progressivism, a trend reversed by Pius X (1903-14). Europe's political problems preoccupied subsequent popes, among whom Pius XII (1939-58) become known for pronouncements on a wide range of topics. Controversy surrounds his role in World War II. The second VATICAN COUNCIL, under JOHN XXIII (1958-63) and Paul VI, defined the role of the pope in terms of power shared with the bishops.

See AGGIORNAMENTO, ANTIPOPE, APOSTOLIC SUCCESSION, BONIFACE VIII, CURIA, EX CATHEDRA, EXCOMMUNICATION, PRIMATE.

Bibliography. P. Ç. Empie and T. A. Murphy, eds., *Papal Primacy and the Universal Church* (1974).

J. HENNESLEY

PARADISE (I). *See* JANNA.

PARINIRVANA pä´ rŭ nĭr vä´ nŭ (B). *See* MAHĀ-PARINIBBĀNA SUTTA.

PARISH (Ch—Gr. "sojourning, dwelling near"). A geographical region having its own church and minister; the body of persons associated for Christian worship and work in connection with one local church; a congregation. K. WATKINS

PARSIS (Z—Gujarati; "Persians"). Members of the small but influential ZOROASTRIAN community that settled in western India at some point after the Islamic conquest of Iran thirteen centuries ago. The term is often used of Zoroastrians from the Indian subcontinent, who account for three fourths of the world's one hundred thousand Zoroastrians (*see* GABAR).

Strictly speaking, "Parsi" is an ethnic rather than a religious designation in India, where group identity is determined by the father of the family: to be a Parsi, one must be descended from a Parsi male. Within India, therefore, Zoroastrianism has not been open to membership through conversion. Parsis who espouse other religious traditions, or none at all, also remain Parsis ethnically. The definition of Parsi identity in India has legal significance, since access both to FIRE TEMPLES and to certain community housing projects and charities is restricted to Parsis.

Bibliography. E. Kulke, *The Parsees in India* (1974).

W. G. OXTOBY

PĀRVATĪ pär´ vŭ tē (H—Skt.; lit. "daughter of the mountain"). A Hindu goddess. Also known as Umā. Daughter of the Himalaya Mountains (a god personified) and wife of the god SHIVA, whom she wins through severe austerities. Sometimes said to be a reincarnation of the goddess SATĪ. *See* GODDESS (INDIA) §2; KĀRTTIKEYA; GAṆEŚA. D. R. KINSLEY

PASSION (Ch; lit. "suffering" [Lat. *pati*—"to suffer"]). The suffering and death of JESUS on the CROSS. Dramatic reenactments of the final events in the life of Christ are known as passion plays.

K. CRIM

PASSOVER (Ju). One of the three pilgrim festivals (*see* SHAVUOT; SUKKOT) on which Israelites journeyed to Jersualem to attend special Temple rites (Exod. 34:18-20). It begins on the fourteenth day of Nisan (March-April) and is known as the festival of "passing over," the festival of unleavened bread, and the festival of spring.

Each name implies a different aspect of its practice and source. Traditionally the festival is derived from the exodus of the Israelites from Egypt (Exod. 12–15). Scripture tells of ten plagues that God sent on the Egyptians (Exod. 7:14–12:30), the final and most harsh being the slaying of the first-born. Yet the first-born of the Hebrews were spared because the Angel of Death is said to have "passed over" (Heb. *pāsaḥ*) their homes, thus the first name. In addition the ritual offering for this festival is cryptically known as the "paschal" (Heb. *pesaḥ*) lamb. Contemporary scholars have suggested that this may have been the name of a species.

Traditional sources further indicate that in leaving Egypt the Hebrews had no opportunity to leaven their bread. Consequently, they were forced to eat MATZAH, unleavened bread, during their exodus from Egypt.

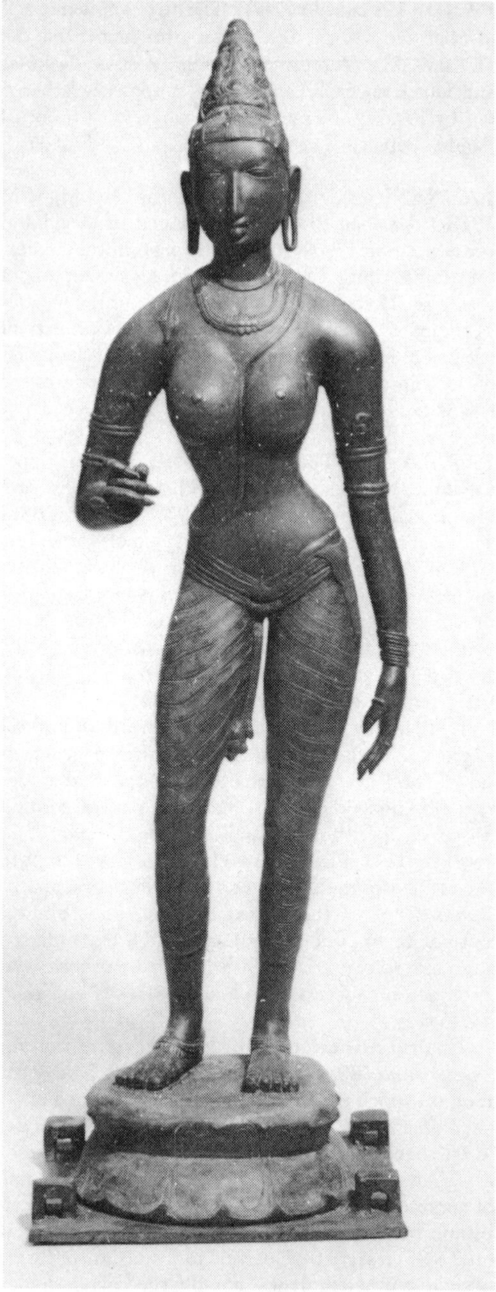

Courtesy of the Smithsonian Institution, Freer Gallery of Art, Washington, D. C.

South Indian bronze statue of Pārvatī (10th century)

Therefore, no leavened or fermented grain product (known collectively as *hametz*) may be found in Jewish possession at any time during the festival. On the first night in Israel and among REFORM Jews elsewhere, and on the first two nights among all others, everyone must eat matzah, the wheat of which has been kept from fermenting.

The third name is derived from the spring season

which is ushered in by this festival. The title has significance in that on the second day of Passover seven weeks of counting are initiated, ending with Shavuot holiday, celebrating the harvest of the first grain. On each of the forty-nine days a measure of barley, the *Omer,* was offered at the Temple.

The disparity in these traditions leads scholars to suggest that contemporary observances are derived from a combination of sources: pastoral, pilgrim, and domestic, each contributing a particular element later combined in the Exodus tradition. Further, with the centralization of ritual under King Josiah (II Kings 23:21-23) many practices observed at home, e.g., the pascal sacrifice, were transferred to the Temple.

Passover is celebrated for seven days in Israel and among Reform Jews elsewhere. The first and last days carry work restrictions similar to those of the SABBATH, while on the intermediate five most labor is permitted. For Jews of ORTHODOX or CONSERVATIVE tradition the festival is celebrated for eight days, and work restrictions are observed on the first and last two days. A special holiday meal and ritual, the SEDER, is observed on the first night or first two nights, when the Exodus story is recounted by word and symbol, based on the Passover HAGGADAH. The celebration of the Passover ritual was considered so important that provision was made for those either ritually impure or at a great distance to perform the rites on the fourteenth of the following month. *See* CALENDAR, JEWISH.

Bibliography. T. Gaster, *Passover, Its History and Tradition* (1949); P. Goodman, *The Passover Anthology* (1961); S. Zevin, *Ha-Moadim be-Halakhah,* 2nd ed. (1947).

D. J. SCHNALL

PAŚUPATI pŭsh´ o͞o pŭ tē (H—Skt.; lit. "Lord of Beasts" [*paśu*—"beast," *pati*—"lord"]). An epithet of the Hindu god SHIVA. As a god of the wilderness, Shiva has been associated with wild animals from the time of his Vedic antecedent, RUDRA, and perhaps even earlier: an INDUS VALLEY image of a horned yogi surrounded by wild animals has been tentatively identified with Shiva. The primary connotation of "paśu," however, is a domestic or sacrificial animal (cf. Latin *pecus*); Shiva is said to have won this title when he forced the gods to give him a share of the sacrifice. In early texts, his mortal worshipers (as well as the gods) are said to be the beasts that Shiva possesses and slaughters. Devotees of this aspect of Shiva are called Pāśupatas; they formed an important sect in ancient and medieval India, taking "animal" vows of a purposely anti-social ("left-hand") nature. This sect was the forerunner of the more blatantly Tantric movements of the KĀPĀLIKAS ("skull-bearers") and Aghoras ("to whom nothing is [too] ghastly"). In the ŚAIVA SIDDHĀNTA interpretation of Paśupati, Shiva is the Lord (Pati) who frees the soul (paśu) from the snare (pāśa)—the bond of illusion and love with which the Lord bound the soul at its creation.

Bibliography. D. H. H. Ingalls, "Cynics and Pāśupatas: The Seeking of Dishonor," *Harvard Theological Review* 55:4 (1962), 282-98; D. N. Lorenzen, *The Kāpālikas and Kālāmukhas: Two Lost Śaivite Sects* (1972); *see* O' Flaherty refs. in SHIVA bibliog.

W. D. O'FLAHERTY

PATAÑJALI pä tän´ jŭ lē (H—Skt.). A famous name in South Asian intellectual history, most probably referring to two distinct, important scholars: (1) a grammarian who lived *ca.* 200 B.C. and composed a treatise entitled *Mahābhāṣya* or "Great Commentary," based on the *Aṣṭādhyāyī* ("Grammar in Eight Parts") of Pāṇini (*ca.* 400 B.C.); (2) the compiler of the classical Yogasūtra, who lived *ca.* A.D. 300-500. *See* YOGA.

G. J. LARSON

PAṬICCASAMUPPĀDA pä tē´ chä săm´ o͞o pä´ dŭ (B—Pali; lit. "dependent origination" [*ud*—"to rise"]) **PRATĪTYASAMUTPĀDA** prä tē tyä´ săm o͞ot´ pä dŭ (B—Skt.). The explanation of the phenomena of the world and the mental and physical conditions of the individual in terms of arising *(samudaya)* and passing away *(nirodha).* This important doctrine, shared by THERAVĀDA and MAHĀYĀNA Buddhism, is claimed as a product of the enlightenment of GAUTAMA BUDDHA. However, the systematic presentation of the "chain of origination" in the formula of the twelve *nidānas* (factors or links) of dependent origination likely arose as the result of later speculation.

1. The twelve *nidānas*. According to tradition, the Buddha pondered over the factors which account for both birth and death in the world with the following results: "1. Dependent on ignorance are volitional activities. 2. Dependent on volitional activities is consciousness. 3. Dependent on consciousness are mental and physical phenomena. 4. Dependent on mental and physical phenomena are the six organs of sense. 5. Dependent on the six organs of sense is contact. 6. Dependent on contact is sensation. 7. Dependent on sensation is desire/craving (TAṆHĀ). 8. Dependent on desire is clinging/grasping. 9. Dependent on clinging is the process of becoming *(bhava).* 10. Dependent on the process of becoming is birth *(jāti).* 11-12. Dependent on birth are old age, death, sorrow, lamentation, misery." (Mahāvagga, I.1,2 author's trans.) Thus in a cause-and-effect manner do Buddhists explain how life comes into being and ultimately results in death and rebirth (*see* SAMSARA; BHAVACAKRA). However, since the Buddhists' concern was to discover the original cause of suffering and the way leading to its cessation, the solution was usually explained in the causation formula in its reverse order; that is, on the complete cessation of ignorance, volitional activities cease; on the cessation of volitional activities, consciousness ceases; on the cessation of consciousness, mental and physical phenomena cease; on the cessation of birth, old age, death, and sorrow cease. It is evident that in both the progressive and reverse order, the origination or cessation of each state of being depends upon its immediate and remote causes. If the contributing factors are absent, the chain of birth will end. This analytical approach to the psychological, physical, and ethical dimensions of an individual's life process has exerted great influence on Buddhism in its many forms.

2. The origin and number of the links. As noticed in the tabulation, there are twelve factors. However, the number of *nidānas* differs greatly from one canonical source to another. The Mahā Nidāna Sutta ("The Great Discourse on Causation") of the Dīgha Nikāya lists only nine links. It does not include 1, 2, and 4 (ignorance, volitional activities, and the six organs of sense). The Mahā Padāna Suttanta ("The Sublime Story") lists only ten of the twelve, omitting 1 and 2. In other instances, the Brahmajāla Suttanta ("The Perfect Net") has omitted the first five links (1-5), and in the Saṃyutta Nikāya (II, 101) only five *nidānas* are listed in the order of 3, 4, 2, 11 and 12. This amazing variety raises questions concerning the original structure of the formula, and leads to the conclusion that the full "chain" developed gradually and only after numerous reworkings culminated in the final form of twelve links.

Still, one verse from the Mahāvagga indicates that concern with causation in a general way likely dates back to the Buddha himself:

> The Buddha hath the cause told
> Of all things spring from a cause;
> And also how things cease to be.
> (Warren, p. 89)

Similarly the popular formula of causation found in the Majjhima Nikāya (II, 32) lends support to the foregoing analysis: "That being thus, this comes to be, from the coming to be of that, this arises. That being absent, this does not happen, from the cessation of that, this ceases" (Rhys Davids, pt. II, 42). This latter text outlines the essential pattern of causation which finds full explication in the Mahāvagga's twelve links. The final form might be dated as late as sometime in the fifth century B.C.

3. The three periods. The twelve *nidānas* are classified into three successive time referents: 1 and 2 belong to the past; 3, 4, 5, 6, 7, 8, 9 and 10 relate to the present; and 11 and 12 are linked with the future. Further, 1, 2, 8, 9 and 10 represent the karmic causes in the past and present; 3, 4, 5, 6, and 7 are the five KARMA results in the present; and 11 and 12 represent the karma results in the future life. Thus the wheel of samsara remains in motion perpetually until one achieves spiritual emancipation through interrupting life's "chain."

The doctrine of dependent origination is also known as the Middle Path. It is the Buddhist answer to the extreme views concerning metaphysical speculation and religious practices during the time of the Buddha. Over the centuries it exerted profound influence on Mahāyāna schools such as the YOGĀCĀRA and MĀDHYAMIKA in India, the T'ien-t'ai (TENDAI) and Hua-yen (Kegon) in China. However, it may be noted that these schools concentrate their interpretations on the metaphysical sphere with great sophistication. They no longer confine themselves to the problem of the arising and the cessation of suffering which was the predicament explained by "chain of existence."

Bibliography. H. C. Warren, trans., *Buddhism in Translation* (1962); T. W. Rhys Davids, trans., *The Dialogues of the Buddha* (1959), pt. I-III; Nyanatiloka, *Fundamentals of Buddhism* (1949), pp. 47-85. W. PACHOW

PĀTIMOKKHA pä´ tĭ mōk´ hŭ (B—Pali; lit. "that which binds" [*muc*—"to bind"]) **PRĀTIMOKṢA** prä´tĭ mōk´ shŭ (B—Skt. [*mokṣ*—"to liberate"]). The Buddhist code of rules governing the monastic life for monks and nuns. Part of the canonical Book of Monastic Discipline (VINAYA PIṬAKA), the Pātimokkha arranges the rules according to the severity of the offense incurred in their violation. The entire Pātimokkha is recited during a ceremony held at the fortnightly assembly (UPOSATHA) of THERAVĀDA monks on the days of the new and the full moons.

1. Versions. Differences exist between the Theravāda Pātimokkha and the Sanskrit Prātimokṣas of other schools of so-called "Southern Buddhism," as well as between the Chinese and Tibetan versions. The number of rules for monks cited in the texts of the various Buddhists schools ranges from 218 to 263. The number for nuns, who were traditionally subordinate to the monks, is higher, ranging from 279 to 380.

2. History of term. Three stages in the use of the term *pātimokkha* can be traced. It was first used to refer to a confession of faith which bound the monastic community together. Shortly after the Buddha's death the term came to refer to the bare monastic legal code which came to replace the old confession as the unifying element. In its earliest form this code may date from 500-450 B.C, thus comprising the earliest stratum of the Vinaya. Eventually, as the monastic order became more highly structured, the Pātimokkha developed into a formal liturgy of monastic confession.

3. Classification of rules. In the PALI CANON the Pātimokkha consists of 227 rules classified under eight categories. (a) The four most serious offenses require permanent expulsion from the order for offenders: incontinence, theft, murder, and making unwarranted claims of spiritual achievement. (b) Thirteen rules entail temporary suspension of the offender and a formal meeting of the order prior to his readmission. These regulations govern the behavior of monks toward the laity, toward women, and among one another. (c) Two rules regulate conversations between a monk and a woman. The severity of the offense in these cases depends on the circumstances. (d) A class of thirty offenses requires forfeiture and expiation. These largely deal with monks who acquire articles not permitted under monastic law. (e) A group of ninety-two offenses requires expiation by the offender. These relate to such matters as false speech, dietary laws, and the use of intoxicants. (f) Some offenses require only public confession by the offender. This class includes four rules relating to a monk who takes food which has not first been formally offered to him. (g) Seventy-five rules govern etiquette. (h) The final section outlines seven methods for settling disputes within the monastic order. *See* SAṄGHA.

Bibliography. T. W. Rhys Davids and H. Oldenberg, trans., "Pāṭimokkha," *Vinaya Texts,* I, SBE, XIII (1968); C. S. Prebish, "The Prātimokṣa Puzzle," *JAOS,* XCIV (1974), 168-83; C. S. Prebish, *Buddhist Monastic Discipline* (1974), trans. and commentary on Prātimokṣa two Skt. texts.

J. P. MCDERMOTT

PATRIARCH pā´ trī ärk (Ch—Gr. "lineage, clan"). One of the major figures in the book of Genesis, especially Abraham, Isaac, and Jacob; BISHOP of one of the five major regions of the ancient church (Constantinople, Alexandria, Antioch, Jerusalem, and Rome), all of which continue, with the exception of Rome, in the ORTHODOX CHURCHES; the head of certain other regions, in Orthodox and ROMAN CATHOLIC CHURCHES; a bishop second only to the pope in rank; a member of the Melchizedek or superior priestly order in the Church of Jesus Christ of LATTER-DAY SAINTS. K. WATKINS

PATRICK (Ch; *ca.* 389–*ca.* 461). "Apostle to the Irish" and patron saint of Ireland. Born in Roman Britain and, as a youth, taken in slavery to Ireland, Patrick returned years later as a missionary BISHOP. He established his own SEE at Armagh and initiated the mass conversion of Ireland. The Patrick legends originate from the seventh century Book of Armagh.

H. L. BOND

PAUL (Ch). First century APOSTLE who played a decisive role in early Christian history. He made three major contributions to the CHURCH. First, as a theologian he made clear the implications of the Christian confession for the life of the Christian community. Second, as a missionary statesman he established churches in the political and cultural centers of the Western world. Third, Pauline theology has served as an instrument of renewal for the life of the church at crucial junctures of its history.

1. **Life.** Paul (called Saul in Acts 7:58, 13:7) was the son of Jewish parents and a native of Tarsus, an important university center in southeastern Asia Minor. The environment in which he learned the content and meaning of his Jewish heritage reflected the perspectives of first century Hellenism.

The details of Paul's life are sketchy. He was born at the beginning of the first century and his CONVERSION to the Christian faith is generally dated prior to A.D. 35. An archaeological discovery at the beginning of this century—the Gallio Inscription—establishes the single concrete date in Paul's life (A.D. 50 in the city of Corinth; *see* Acts 18:12-17). Tradition identifies Rome as the place of his martyrdom, perhaps about the year A.D. 60.

2. **Work.** *a) Writings.* Paul's thought is accessible to us in his letters preserved in the NT. Although as many as fourteen NT works have been attributed to him, contemporary scholarship accepts seven undisputed letters as authentic products of the Apostle's pen (I Thess., I, II Cor., Gal., Phil., Philem., and Rom.). Later apocryphal works written in his name have little direct contact with the Apostle's thought (Acts of Paul, Apocalypse of Paul, Letters of Paul and Seneca, etc.).

b) Missionary work. At the conclusion of Paul's missionary activity (*ca.* A.D. 60) the Christian movement was represented by churches in such distant places as Antioch, Ephesus, Corinth, and ROME. Although the Apostle cannot be given sole credit for this achievement, the author of Acts depicts Paul as the primary agent in the early expansion of the movement.

The details of Paul's activity are obscure, but his letters and Acts (a secondary historical source whose witness must be tested carefully) disclose the general outlines of his twenty-year career. After his conversion he returned to his native land by way of Arabia and Jerusalem (Gal. 1:17-21), and then established churches in Asia Minor (Galatia and Ephesus) and Greece (Philippi, Thessalonica, and Corinth).

Paul's success among the Gentiles led to the first theological crisis in the life of the church (Gal. 2:1-10; Acts 15), a conflict between Jewish and Gentile perspectives. His involvement (Rom. 15:25; II Cor. 8-9; I Cor. 16:1-4) led to his eventual imprisonment (Acts 21:27 ff.) and the end of his missionary activity.

3. **Theology.** Paul's enduring significance for the Christian church arises out of his theological contribution to the self-understanding of the Christian community. The basic contours of his thought were given in the confession of the community which preceded him in the faith (I Cor. 15:3). The constitutive elements of this confession are: a) God inaugurated the eschatological era through the life, death, RESURRECTION and exaltation of JESUS Christ. b) The eschatological character of the time is attested by the presence of the HOLY SPIRIT. c) All persons are now called to repentance in response to this announcement. (*See* JUSTIFICATION BY FAITH.) d) The return of Jesus as judge is imminent. Paul's response to this message constituted his conversion. His letters interpret the implications of this perspective for the historical situations of the first century local Christian communities.

4. **Modern understanding of Paul.** Stimulated by F. C. Baur, nineteenth century scholars investigated the content and interrelationship of Paul's twofold Jewish and Hellenistic heritage. This

research was generally predicated upon the assumption that Paul was an eclectic thinker who attempted to integrate the Christian message into a system derived from some combination of elements from his Jewish-Hellenistic background. This misunderstanding of the character of the Christian proclamation has been corrected in this century, through the impact of KARL BARTH'S call for a return to Pauline theology.

Emphasis on the theological character of Paul's thought raises the issue of the "center" or focus from which Paul's writings are to be understood. Three proposals have dominated the discussion of the subject, namely, justification by faith (LUTHER), eschatology (A. SCHWEITZER), and anthropology (R. BULTMANN).

Bibliography. G. Bornkamm, *Paul* (1971); W. A. Meeks, *The Writings of St. Paul* (1972); K. H. Rengstorf, ed., *Das Paulusbild in der neueren deutschen Forschung* (1964); R. Bultmann, *Theology of the New Testament* I (1951), 190-352; A. Schweitzer, *The Mysticism of Paul the Apostle* (1931); K. Barth, *The Epistle to the Romans* (ET 1935).

R. C. BRIGGS

PELAGIANISM pĕl āj´ ē ən ĭsm (Ch). The doctrine, advanced by British (Irish?) theologian and moralist Pelagius (active in Rome and then in Palestine from 382 to 418), that human nature, as a good creation of God, though susceptible to the example of Adamic sin, retains the possibility of sinlessness, if it is tutored and strengthened by the Mosaic law and by the life and redeeming work of Christ. It was condemned as heterodox in a series of fourth and fifth century church councils. *See* PREDESTINATION; AUGUSTINE OF HIPPO.

R. C. GREGG

PENANCE (Ch). The sacramental reconciliation of sinners. Originally a public exercise, it became a private rite in the early Middle Ages. The penitent makes a confession of particular sins, accepts a penance (penitential exercises to be performed), and receives absolution by the priest. *See* ABSOLUTION; CONFESSION; SACRAMENTS.

T. J. TALLEY

PENN, WILLIAM (Ch; 1644-1718). Theologian, lobbyist for toleration, and traveling preacher in the early SOCIETY OF FRIENDS; founder of their major social experiment, the colony of Pennsylvania; a leading influence in the development of religious toleration in the West.

M. ENDY

PENTECOST (Ju & Ch—Gr.; lit. "fiftieth"). One of three pilgrim feasts in JUDAISM, where it is called SHAVUOT; observed on the fiftieth day after the PASSOVER sabbath. It was the day on which the HOLY SPIRIT descended on JESUS' disciples (Acts 2). For early Christians it marked the end of the fifty-day period of rejoicing begun on Easter. In the fourth century it became a separate feast celebrating both Jesus' ascension and the descent of the Spirit, but later only the latter. Especially in the West it was the most important baptismal day after Easter itself and was favored in the northern climate. There the white garments of the newly baptized gave it the name "Whitsunday."

T. J. TALLEY

PENTECOSTAL CHURCHES (Ch). The Pentecostal movement began in the United States in 1901 in Topeka, Kansas, under the leadership of C. F. Parham, a former Methodist minister. The central teaching of the movement is that the BAPTISM IN THE HOLY SPIRIT is a postconversion experience with the "initial evidence" of GLOSSOLALIA. Most early Pentecostals had been active in a movement in the METHODIST CHURCH emphasizing entire sanctification (*see* PERFECTION, CHRISTIAN). The movement received worldwide attention through the Azusa Street Revival in Los Angeles from 1906 to 1909 under the leadership of a black holiness preacher, W. J. Seymour.

The first Pentecostal denominations were in the southern U. S. and included the Pentecostal Holiness Church, the Church of God (Cleveland, Tennessee), and the Church of God in Christ, which was predominantly black. (*See* BLACK RELIGIONS IN THE UNITED STATES.)

A second group of denominations developed out of the "finished work" teachings of W. H. Durham and included the Assemblies of God, organized in 1914, which soon became the largest Pentecostal denomination in the U. S. Other denominations such as the Pentecostal Church of God and the International Church of the Foursquare Gospel followed Durham's teachings.

A third group appeared after 1916 as the "Jesus Name" or Unitarian Pentecostal Movement. Led by Frank Ewart, they rejected the doctrine of the TRINITY and taught that JESUS Christ was at one and the same time Father, Son, and HOLY SPIRIT. The largest bodies in this group are the United Pentecostal Church and the Pentecostal Assemblies of the World.

Pentecostalism spread rapidly around the world after 1906, due to a vigorous missionary program, and by 1920 it was established in Europe under the leadership of Norwegian Methodist T. B. Barratt; in South America by W. C. Hoover; and in Russia by Ivan Voronaeff. By 1970 the appearance of the CHARISMATIC MOVEMENT in the traditional churches led to the older Pentecostal churches being known as "classical Pentecostals."

The fastest growing Christian movement after World War II, the Pentecostal churches claimed some 35,000,000 adherents in over 120 nations in 1977, with the largest number (9,000,000) in Brazil.

Bibliography. R. M. Anderson, *Vision of the Disinherited* (1979); W. J. Hollenweger, *The Pentecostals: The Charismatic Movement in Their Churches* (1972); V. Synan, *The Holiness-Pentecostal Movement in the United States* (1971).

H. V. SYNAN

PEOPLE OF THE BOOK (I—Arab. *ahl al-kitāb* ähl əl kĭ täb´). A term in the QUR'ĀN designating Jews and Christians and later extended to include Sabaeans (both those mentioned in the Qur'ān and certain star worshipers), and ZOROASTRIANS. Other terms applied to these groups are "People of Protection" and "People of the Covenant." Because of their religions, these groups are entitled to special legal status within the Islamic community. The terms are always used in contrast to the community of ISLAM (UMMA) on the one hand and pagans on the other.

In the Qur'ān the term *ahl al-kitāb* appears alongside specific references to Jews (sometimes called Jews and sometimes called Children of Israel) and Christians. In the Qur'ānic scheme of world history these peoples had received Scriptures from ALLAH which were, at the time of revelation, harmonious with if not identical to the Qur'ān. Later this Scripture, deliberately or by inadvertance, was corrupted, so that the Tawrāt (TORAH), Zabūr (Psalms), and Injīl (GOSPELS) were changed from their original, insofar as they do not agree with the Qur'ān. The Jews fare less well in the Qur'ān than the Christians, who are said to be nearer the Muslims in spiritual qualities (Sura 5:82). The Jews are said to be ungrateful and uncharitable, to violate the very law they so carefully study, and to believe that EZRA is the son of Allah (Sura 9:30). In the Qur'ān "Children of Israel" seems to refer to the biblical Jews, while the "Jews" are the Jews of Arabia in MUHAMMAD'S own time, who, as recent research demonstrates, held heterodox views when compared to our notions of normative JUDAISM.

With regard to Islam's position toward previous Scripture, there is tension between the tendency to accept the Old and New Testaments, particularly as they relate to Qur'ānic topics, and to reject them outright because of faulty transmission. The first attitude prevailed in the first Islamic century, when much Jewish and Christian material was added to the stock of Qur'ānic commentary and lore under the general term *Isrā'īlīyāt*. This gave way to the second attitude during the third and fourth Islamic centuries, when strict separation between Islamic and Judeo-Christian material was recommended to the Muslim community.

The later attitudes of Islamic law toward the People of the Book are determined to a great degree by Muhammad's actions and attitudes toward them and reflect a degree of ambivalence derived from his hopes and disappointments in dealing with the Jews and Christians of Arabia. Added to the so-called "Constitution of Medina" and Muhammad's treatment of the Jews of Khaybar was the "Treaty of 'UMAR" with the Christians of JERUSALEM, a document of doubtful origin but reflecting an early codification of Muslim legal attitudes. When Islam moved out of Arabia, the star worshipers of Harran and certain Zoroastrians claimed refuge under the umbrella of Islamic law by holding that they were People of the Book, identical to the Sabaeans of the Qur'ān.

All religious groups designated as People of the Book had the right, on payment of a special tax, to manage their own affairs, worship freely, maintain property, and hold legal status in Muslim courts. They could not proselytize, build new places of worship, or serve in the military, but they could, and did, hold high places in government and in the private sector. This led non-Muslims in many areas to assist the Muslim conquests in order to rid themselves of more oppressive masters, as in Egypt and the Iberian peninsula. As Muslims came to outnumber non-Muslims in Islamic lands, a process of several centuries, Islamic laws were more rigorously enforced, sometimes to the point of causing great difficulties for the protected minorities, but there were remarkably few cases of actual persecution, the most notable being during the reign of the FATIMID caliph al-Ḥākim (996-1021), whose excesses provided propaganda for the CRUSADES. During prosperous times, the People of the Book were on financial if not social parity with Muslims, but the advantage that the People of the Book, particularly the various Christian groups, had derived from Islam's blindness to any intraconfessional differences became a disadvantage at the time of the Crusades. Islam was equally blind to any difference between Latin Christians and the several Eastern Christian confessions, suspecting them all. The hardened attitudes of the post-Crusade states made life more difficult for non-Muslims, particularly as these states were ruled over by staunchly SUNNITE Turkic peoples who defended their perceptions of Islam by military despotism. Still, the Ottoman empire received many Jews from Spain after they were expelled in 1492 and restored the protected minority status for Jews and Christians in its area of rule under the "millet" system (Turkish from Arab. *milla;* lit. "religious community").

In the present century, with the advent of secular nationalism in Islamic countries and the replacement of the SHARIA by Western-style legal codes, the old concepts of People of the Book are giving way to Western notions of citizenship. In some instances, particularly where national identity and religious confession conflict, the position of the non-Muslim has weakened.

Bibliography. The history of the relations between Muslims and non-Muslims is to be found in most histories of the Islamic world. For Qur'ānic passages, see M. M. Pickthall, *Meaning of the Glorious Koran* (1953), index under "People of the Book, Jews, Children of Israel, and Christians." For Western views see A. S. Tritton, *Caliphs and Their Non-Muslim Subjects* (1930); A. Fattal, *Le statut légal des non-musulmans en pays d'Islam* (1958), both of which need to be supplemented by individual studies. For Jews, see S. D. Goitein, *Jews and Arabs* (1955), and *A Mediterranean Society* (1967-) and *JE* under "Islam." There are no specific monographs dealing with Christians under Islamic rule, but see A. S. Atiya, *History of Eastern Christianity* (1968). For Zoroastrians, see B. Spuler, *Iran in früh-islamischer Zeit* (1952).

G. D. NEWBY

PERFECTION, CHRISTIAN. The belief that persons can so receive God's grace by the working of the HOLY SPIRIT as to experience unblemished love for God and neighbor (Matt. 5:8, 48; I John 4:12).

Equating such perfection with either the vision of God or SALVATION from sin and death, Christians have sought otherworldly escape through monastic ASCETICISM, contemplative MYSTICISM, and moral discipline. The ORTHODOX CHURCHES teach "deification" (Gr. *theosis*) by the sanctifying power of Jesus' resurrection as energized by the Spirit. ROMAN CATHOLICISM has stressed the sacramental, ascetic, and mystical way to the vision of God. PROTESTANTS are divided between those who believe that saved persons remain sinners and those who rejoice in the assurance of full sanctification.

JOHN WESLEY was mainly responsible for the optimistic doctrine of perfection. While never underestimating the power of sin, he believed the gospel promised full liberation from it. Christ, by his sacrificial death, justifies a person, but the Spirit sanctifies by infusing the grace to be wholly constrained by love. Disputes continue over the question of whether perfection comes by sudden regeneration in conversion or is approached gradually after one is "born again." The former is held by Holiness and PENTECOSTAL churches, some of which are derived from METHODISM. Most Methodists today have lost Wesley's belief in perfection, though its appeal persists.

Bibliography. R. N. Flew, *The Christian Idea of Perfection* (1934); J. L. Peters, *Christian Perfection and American Methodism* (1956).

J. R. NELSON

PERSIAN LANGUAGE (I). Though second to ARABIC as a canonical Muslim language, Persian was so widely used, and its conventional images so commonly assumed, that medieval Islamic culture cannot be described without assessing the unique Persian contribution. In poetry the meter and rhyme of Persian were similar to their Arabic counterparts, and a genre important for patronage, the *qasida* (panegyric), was common to both languages. Yet three distinctive genres evolved in Persian: the *ghazal* (lyrical monorhyme), the *rubā'ī* (quatrain), and the *mathnavi* (rhyming couplet). Variation and excellence did not depend on the commonly accepted imagery, but on precision of form and alliterative skill. While prose never attracted Persian authors to the same extent that poetry did, famous writers such as Farid-al-Din 'Attar (d. 1190) and Muslih-al-Din Sa'di (d. 1292) excelled in both poetry and prose or, as in the case of Sa'di's *Gulistan,* deftly combined prose and poetry in an anecdotal framework.

The Persian language has often been linked to the essential and characteristic spirit of SUFISM. ḤĀFIZ SHĪRĀZĪ, the outstanding craftsman of the *ghazal,* may or may not have been a practicing Sufi, but Sufis of every generation have memorized and quoted his verses liberally and written other *ghazals* in imitation of his. Similarly, the quatrain, well known in English through Fitzgerald's rendition of Omar Khayyam's *Rubaiyat,* is a form common to nearly all Sufi poets in Persian, while the *Mathnavi-ye ma'navī* of JALĀL AD-DĪN RŪMĪ popularized the *mathnavi* and epitomized the adaptability of that literary genre. None of these three genres is exclusive to mystically minded Muslim poets, but their relationship to the Sufi movement, both in Iran and in other parts of the Islamic world influenced by Persian culture and language (e.g., Central and Southern Asia), is evident.

Bibliography. J. Rypka, *History of Iranian Literature* (1968); A. Schimmel, *Islamic Literatures of India,* in J. Gonda, ed., *A History of Indian Literature,* Vol. VII/1 (1973).

B. LAWRENCE

PESAḤ pē sä (Ju). *See* PASSOVER.

PETER THE APOSTLE (Ch; died *ca.* A.D. 64). Recognized in the early church as the leader of the disciples, and by the later Roman Catholic Church as the first pope (*see* PAPACY). Information about his life and teachings is limited to the NT. He was married, but only later legendary material alludes to children. His family came from Bethsaida (John 1:44), but he made his home in Capernaum during the period of Jesus' ministry. The Gospels and Acts present Peter's personality and character as vacillating; he could be resolute, but sometimes rash and hasty; at times gentle, but still firm and capable of loyalty and love.

The Gospels agree that Peter was called as a disciple at the beginning of Jesus' ministry, and that he was the spokesman of the disciples and enjoyed some degree of precedence.

There are three problematic, controversial incidents in the NT in which Peter plays a prominent role. The first involves the naming of Peter in Matt. 16:18 ("And I tell you, you are Peter, and on this rock I will build my church"). The basic problem is the reference to the word "rock." The possibilities include Jesus himself, the faith of Peter, or, as most authorities support today, the traditional understanding that the "rock" refers to Peter himself, that the church would be built upon that rock, Peter. The word "church" in Matthew (*ca.* A.D. 85) must be understood as referring to the community of the faithful rather than to a definite ecclesiastical organization.

In the second incident, after Peter had fled when Jesus was arrested, he denied Jesus three times, an act which he later greatly regretted (Mark 14:72). However, this same disciple "turned again" and on the morning of the resurrection ran to the tomb; it was to him that the resurrected Jesus first appeared (I Cor. 15:5).

After Jesus' death Peter emerged as the earliest leader of the church (Acts 1-12). It was he who, through the conversion of Cornelius, introduced

Gentiles into the church, arousing the opposition of the Jewish Christians and others. Probably belatedly and indirectly this action caused his imprisonment and eventual flight to "another place" (Acts 12:17), which O'Connor defines definitely as ROME. There is no satisfactory explanation of why the later ministry of Peter is not dealt with in Acts.

By A.D. 100 it was a firm tradition that Peter had been martyred and buried in Rome, but the tradition of his twenty-five-year episcopate in Rome did not develop until the third century. The claims that Peter founded the church of Rome or served as its first BISHOP (as the word is understood today) rest upon evidence no earlier than the late second century.

That Peter was martyred in Rome under Nero may be inferred from I Clement 5:1–6:4 (A.D. 96) and other later sources. Most authorities accept the VATICAN area as the place of his death, and most believe he was buried there. In the fourth century Constantine built a basilica above the imagined spot, which is marked by a small aedicula. Excavations conducted intermittently between 1939 and 1965 failed to provide conclusive evidence that he was in fact buried there. If a grave of the Apostle did exist in the area at the base of this aedicula, nothing clearly identifiable as that grave remains today.

Five festivals in the calendar of the Roman Catholic Church involve honor paid to Peter, the most important of which is the Festival of Peter and Paul celebrated on June 29.

Bibliography. H. Leclerq, *Dictionnaire d'archéologie chrétienne et de liturgie,* vol. XIV (1948), cols. 2783-2816; J. W. Perkins, *The Shrine of St. Peter* (1957); O. Cullmann, *Peter, Disciple, Apostle, Martyr* (2nd ed. 1962); D. W. O'Connor, *Peter in Rome,* (1970).

D. W. O'CONNOR

PETER LOMBARD (Ch; *ca.* 1100-1160). Medieval theologian. His four *Books of the Sentences* deal with (1) God, (2) creation and fall, (3) incarnation and redemption, and (4) sacraments and the four last things. From the early thirteenth century to the sixteenth, they served as the standard textbook of Catholic theology. *See* SCHOLASTICISM §2.

F. OAKLEY

PHARISEES făr′ ə sēs (Ju). Jewish religious party of the Second Temple period; they adhered to rules of levitical purity and exclusive table fellowship and yet remained in society. Their bonds of fellowship were cemeted in brotherhoods called *havuroth*. Josephus attributes specific religious beliefs to them, including acceptance of the Oral Law as supplementary to TORAH and of the eternity of the soul (*Antiquities* 20.11.2). Their devotion to study, exemplified in HILLEL and JOHANAN BEN ZAKKAI, is also noted by Josephus (*Life* 28).

A more detailed picture of the Pharisees, however, emerges from sources later than A.D. 70, and much controversy today surrounds their characterization during the Second Temple period. The NT references are especially derogatory and do not provide an accurate picture. The MISHNAH, TALMUD, and major TANNAITIC sources constitute the chief repository of their thinking and are testimony to the revitalization of Jewish life in the early centuries of the common era, when classical Pharisaic Judaism took definitive shape.

Bibliography. E. Rivkin, *A Hidden Revolution: The Pharisees' Search for the Kingdom Within* (1978); J. Neusner, *From Politics to Piety: The Emergence of Pharisaic Judaism* (1973).

E. M. MEYERS

PHILO fī′ lō (Ju; *ca.* 25 B.C.—A.D. 50). Jewish philosopher-theologian of Alexandria, Egypt; mediator of Greek thought to both the Jewish and Christian traditions. He successfully met the challenge of Hellenistic culture in a period of great cultural change. Living in the city which dominated the intellectual world of the eastern Roman Empire, Philo was part of the wealthy class of a Jewish community which numbered in the hundreds of thousands.

Writing for both Gentile and Jewish audiences, Philo defended and interpreted the Jewish faith in a new and appealing way. Employing the allegorical method of interpretation he imbued Hebrew Scripture with Platonic ideas and sought to harmonize it with Greek thinking. For the learned Jews he charted a mystical path revealed in allegory; his general exposition of the TORAH appealed to all Jews and was ultimately taken over by the early church fathers. (*See* LOGOS.)

Although some scholars have found traces of rabbinic ideas in his writings, Philo's basic intent seems to have been to show how JUDAISM was a philosophical and mystical religion consistent with Greek ideals in the Platonic tradition. In this way he succeeded in making the Torah intelligible to Jews of the DIASPORA.

Bibliography. E. R. Goodenough, *An Introduction to Philo Judaeus* (1940); H. Wolfson, *Philo* (1947).

E. M. MEYERS

PHYLACTERIES fĭ lăk′ tə rēz (Ju). *See* TEFILLIN.

PIETA pē ā tä′, pyā tä′ (Ch—Italian; lit "pity"). A representation, usually in sculpture, of the Virgin MARY lamenting over the dead body of Christ, first popularized in thirteenth century German devotional art. The most famous example of this type of representation is Michelangelo's famous Pieta in SAINT PETER'S, ROME.

C. WADDELL

PIETISM (Ch). A reform movement in late seventeenth and eighteenth century German Protestantism. It sought to complete Luther's reformation of doctrine with reformation of life, stressing personal regeneration and piety. Pietism reacted against a

Protestant scholasticism which emphasized creeds, participation in sacraments, and rejection of other churches. In its stricter definition Pietism centers around the renewal activities of PHILIPP JAKOB SPENER (1635-1705) and August Hermann Francke (1663-1727), both Lutherans. In its broader sense, Pietism incorporates, first, prior reform currents within the German Reformed; second, links to English Puritanism, Dutch Precisianism, and French Quietism; and third, later contacts with Wesleyanism. (*See* REFORMED CHURCHES; PURITANS; METHODIST CHURCHES.)

Pietist beginnings are often dated from Spener's programmatic *Pia desideria* (1675). Spener called for Bible study, better theological education, lay activity, ethical awakening, and lessened polemics. He developed controversial congregational groups—*collegia pietatis*—in his parish in Frankfurt am Main. Later in responsible church posts in Dresden and Berlin, he extended his influence by recommending Pietists for key pastorates and by extensive writing.

Francke was the organizational genius of Pietism. After moving to Halle, he developed a complex of institutions run along Pietist lines, including an orphanage, several schools, a Bible distribution society, and a mission agency. Combining popular support with patronage from the Brandenburg-Prussian court, Francke and his successors made Halle a center of influence on several continents.

A radical wing of Pietism was separatist. Several distinct movements emerged, especially the Brethren (*see* BRETHREN, CHURCH OF THE) and the Community of True Inspiration (later Amana Society).

More churchly in character was the Renewed Moravian Church (reorganized in 1727), led by Count von Zinzendorf (1700-1760; *see* MORAVIANS). Of the German provincial churches, Württemberg was affected the most deeply and longest by Pietism; a key figure here was J. A. Bengel (1687-1752), famed biblical scholar.

Protestant theology was informed by Pietism through Friedrich Schleiermacher (1768-1834), who called himself a "Moravian of a higher order." In church history Gottfried Arnold (1666-1714) developed a distinctive historiography which highlighted the contributions of earlier dissenters.

Though sharply attacked by Protestant orthodoxy for subjectivism and legalism, Pietism has been one of the predominant shapers of modern Protestantism, particularly in North America. Its concerns for high ethical standards, vital Christian life, warm religious atmosphere, and extensive missionary outreach continue to have broad influence.

Bibliography. D. Brown, *Understanding Pietism* (1978); R. A. Knox, *Enthusiasm* (1950); P. J. Spener, *Pia Desideria*, T. Tappert, trans. (1964); F. E. Stoeffler, *Rise of Evangelical Pietism* (1965) and *German Pietism During the Eighteenth Century* (1973).

D. F. DURNBAUGH

PILGRIM FATHERS (Ch). Name given to the separatist PURITANS who founded the colony of Plymouth, Mass. The group originated at Scrooby, England, and moved to Leyden, Holland, to escape persecution. In November, 1620, they arrived in Massachusetts and in the next few years prospered in spite of many hardships.

G. MILLER

PILGRIMAGE. A form of RITUAL practiced in most of the major religious traditions. In pilgrimage, the religious participant journeys, literally and symbolically, to a sacred center in such a way that the pilgrim is enabled to affirm his or her own identity especially as a member of a specific religious tradition; at the same time, the pilgrim is afforded a new perception of self and context. Pilgrimage is, in microcosm, the acting out of a religious person's life.

1. **The nature of pilgrimage.** Pilgrimage shares many of the general characteristics of ritual in that it often links the pilgrim with an authenticating history and an affirming community, thus acting out the structures that define a person. Pilgrimage is also transformative in that it involves setting out from a *status quo,* undergoing sometimes stressful transition, and inviting an experience of a sacred reality and of new community which often transcends the boundaries with which one started the pilgrimage.

The term pilgrimage is used in at least three senses. There is first the "interior pilgrimage," the "journey of the soul" in a lifetime of growth from spiritual infancy to maturity. There is, second, the literal pilgrimage to some sacred place as a paradigm of the intent of religion itself. This literal journey may be called "extroverted mysticism" (Turner). Finally, every trek to one's local sanctuary is a pilgrimage in miniature insofar as it acts out on a small scale some transition or growth and experience of the sacred and new community which pilgrimage in general affords.

Pilgrimage shares something of the character of all rites of passage (van Gennep) in that it entails separation or setting out at its start and incorporation or the attainment of a new status at its end. The journey itself is, however, the state of being in passage, on the threshold of becoming what one is going to be. Like a number of other rituals, pilgrimage entails ambivalence and polarity. It links the person to society, the local and regional to the universal, the contemporary to the historical, the small group to the transspatial community which gathers at the center.

2. **The motivations for pilgrimage.** Religious persons engage in pilgrimage for many reasons. Not least important is the effort to experience for one's self the historical and sacred power of a place which has definitive meaning for a tradition. Most pilgrimage centers have a mythic or historic significance. The founder of the tradition, a deity, a saint, some historic or mythic figure who helped shape the tradition, is believed to have visited that spot and to have done some significant deed there. To travel to that place is to make the event "happen again" symbolically for oneself and to invoke and interiorize the power of the

sacred believed to have been made manifest there. That is, the pilgrimage to a place like MECCA (HAJJ) or JERUSALEM makes one's religious history come alive and authenticates one's identity with a tradition. A pilgrimage center is sometimes understood to be the foundation of one's spiritual world. Hence, the journey becomes a new beginning, a re-creation or reorienting of one's spiritual cosmos (Eliade). In other terms, a pilgrimage center is a "topocosm" (Gaster) or point of connection where the known, mundane world meets the realm of the sacred and eternal.

There are other reasons, however, for which pilgrimages are made. On some occasions the pilgrimage becomes a ritual of healing or exorcism. Myths and legends abound at the centers of a number of religious traditions (e.g., LOURDES, France or Tiruchendur, South India) which indicate that miraculous healing is believed to have occurred at these places. Pilgrims may go to such centers hopeful that the miracle can happen again in their behalf. In many cases the pilgrimage is a form of penance. Guilt and the desire for expiation from past misdeeds sometimes lead pilgrims to rigorous acts of hardship both en route to and in the pilgrim center. For example, in many Hindu and Buddhist centers (e.g., Kataragama, Sri Lanka), pilgrims can be seen carrying heavy vessels for miles, prostrating themselves again and again, piercing their flesh, dancing until exhausted, or walking on hot coals. Some observers have argued that more than penitence may be involved in such acts, including the desire for enhanced personal status or sacrality, sublimated sexuality, etc. (Obeyesekere). Still another factor which motivates some pilgrims in their journey is gratitude. Not infrequently a vow has been made. Should the deity do a certain favor for the individual, he or she will go to the deity's cult center to express gratitude with an offering. That offering generally expresses a person's economic station and can be given either in cash or in kind.

There are often educative objectives in the pilgrimage. Children as well as adults learn about the history of their tradition by experiencing or re-enacting the historically significant event believed to have occurred at a particular site. Milling with people who share the religious tradition, even though they may have come from geographically or economically diverse backgrounds, serves to broaden one's perspective even as it affirms one's own links with that tradition. Indeed, not a few pilgrimage centers have become major educational centers complete with teaching agencies or formal schools and colleges.

3. Social and spatial aspects of pilgrimage. Beyond these explicitly religious reasons there are other factors evident in pilgrimage. It is apparent, for example, that pilgrimage includes many elements of play as well as work. Fairs, colorful marketplaces, camping, wilderness living—all are features of some pilgrimages which suggest the experience is recreational as well as religious. Pilgrimage also has obvious social dimensions, for pilgrims often travel as a family or clan unit or in "membership groups" from their home towns or regions. The local ties are thereby maintained and strengthened even during the journey. At the same time, the pilgrim center often has an understood linkage with a district, a region, a state, or a nation; in some cases the center even has international ties. Hence, pilgrimage to that center at one time can affirm identities which are local, regional, national, and international. Therefore, the pilgrim can affirm who he is at many geographical levels even in the process of becoming someone more than he was before he left.

Some observers have discerned a stratification of pilgrim centers, ranging from "universal" to local ones, the social function of each stratum tending to differ according to the different kinds of pilgrims which may be attracted to local centers as over against "universal" centers. Bhardwaj, for example, notes that Hindu pilgrimage centers can be stratified at five levels: pan-Hindu; supraregional; regional; subregional (high and low); and local. Generally speaking, shrines at the pan-Hindu level have a "universal" appeal. The enshrined deity tends to be viewed more in philosophical abstractions and is visited by more affluent upper-class Hindus seeking merit in the pilgrimage. The local pilgrimage centers at the other end of the spectrum tend to be more parochial (i.e., more goddesses and local and folk deities tend to be enshrined) and pilgrims tend to be of the lower castes, such as the cultivators and untouchables, seeking specific benefits from the deity at hand. Similarly, Turner has noted that Christian pilgrimage centers can be stratified at four levels: international (Jerusalem, ROME, Lourdes, Guadalupe); national (e.g., San Juan de los Lagos in Mexico or Our Lady of the Pillar in Spain); regional (e.g., Our Lady of Ocatlán for Tlaxcala State in Mexico); and intervillage (as in the various "valley shrines" of Spain).

The most striking characteristic of pilgrimage remains its transformative potential. Pilgrimage is passage from individuality to community; from heterogeneity of background to a new homogeneity of status; from mundane structures to a realm beyond structure; from hierarchies based on affluence or power to a mutuality of simplicity. To be sure, that new state of being may not be experienced by every pilgrim in every pilgrimage. But its ever present possibility is what makes the pilgrimage a quintessentially religious event.

4. The center in pilgrimage. The organizing principle in pilgrimage is the destination—the place where "it" happened and to which the pilgrim goes. The pilgrimage center can be of at least three types: prototypical, syncretistic (Turner), and ecographic. A prototypical center is one which reflects the identifying historic or mythic dimensions of a tradition. It can be where the founder or important personage of a religion is believed to have done important deeds in his life (e.g., Jerusalem, Mecca, SĀRNĀTH). It can be, as in Hinduism, the cultic center of a deity who is believed to have become manifest or to have accomplished miraculous exploits in a specific place (e.g., Tirupati, Palni, or Ramesvaram in South India). It can be a place designated as the cultic center for a religious tradition, as with Amritsar, the site of the GOLDEN TEMPLE of Sikhism. It can be a place associated with saints or prototypical devotees and their lives or deaths.

A syncretistic center, on the other hand, is one in which accretions beyond dimensions of a single religious tradition have been ascribed to a sacred place. These accretions may be of several kinds. (a) Pretraditional dimensions: certain places may have had significance in tribal or local religions before becoming associated with a major historical religion. Such seems to have been the case with such Christian centers as Glastonbury, England, with its persistent Celtic overtones (Turner) and Madurai, South India, a center for the local goddess MĪNĀKṢĪ before she came to be seen as a consort of the Hindu high god SHIVA. It should also be noted that certain prototypical centers (such as Mecca) were in use as religious centers prior to their incorporation into the tradition of a historical religion, but the symbolism or meaning of their earlier religious usage may have been lost. (b) Other traditions: some centers have become associated with the cultic life of more than one religion. This may have occurred in a variety of ways. Personages representing different religions are understood to be related to the main figure of the center. One illustration of this form of center is Sabaramala, Kerala in India. The main shrine there is dedicated to the Hindu deity Ayyappaṉ; nonetheless, a subsidiary shrine is dedicated to the Muslim warrior Vāvar, who is said to have been a friend of Ayyappaṉ. It is also believed that Buddhist mendicants once worshiped at this place. Another type of syncretistic center is one which more than one religion claims to be a place with historic or mythic significance for their respective traditions. This is the case with Jerusalem, important to Jew, Christian, and Muslim, and with Kataragama, Sri Lanka, a sacred spot for Hindus and Buddhists especially, though Christians and Muslims also visit it. (c) Folk, local, or regional accretions: There are centers which have been adopted by some "high religion" but which are ascribed a variety of meanings that reflect folk, local, or regional perceptions. Folk interpretations and local participation in such centers may be based more on the unorthodox or popular significance a place has than on the meanings ascribed to a place by the normative tradition. Such folk and local perceptions greatly increase the popularity of certain centers as at Pandarpur, Maharashtra in India, or Palni, South India.

A third type of center is what might be called ecographic, a center which has assumed significance because of its geographical locus more than for its theological or mythic origins (even though myths purporting to describe the exploits of sacred figures there may have been developed in the course of its use). Such places include Cape Comorin (or Kanyakumāri at the southern tip of India); several spots along the GANGES river, such as Allāhābād at the confluence of the Ganges and Yumnā; parts of the Himalayas which were described by the classical Indian poet KĀLIDĀSA as "divinely ensouled" *(devatātman);* or any number of hills which have been ascribed a specific mythology *ex post facto.*

Some pilgrimage centers, particularly the prototypical ones like Jerusalem or Rome, are of classical antiquity; others are postclassical in origin, yet have been in use since well before the fifteenth century. These include such sites as Canterbury, England; Cologne, Germany (Turner); and probably such Hindu centers as Palni and Tirupati, India. Still other centers are of more recent vintage and are thought to be based on the vision or experience of a nineteenth or twentieth century saint or group of devotees. While these "modern" centers from their inception have made use of the trappings of technological and scientific culture, at the same time they often claim a mythic heritage that links them in some way to an "archaic" tradition.

5. Shrines and sacred objects. At each pilgrimage center there is a replication of sacred shrines, spaces, and objects that multiply the opportunities for access to the sacred and comprise a total "pilgrimage field." Most visible of these are the subshrines which surround and fan out from the central shrine. Typically, subshrines are erected to subsidiary figures related to the main figure revered at the center—ancestral devotees, mediating agencies, or even the major personage in alternative manifestations. Often these subshrines incorporate local or folk traditions which either predate the mainstream tradition or have been linked to it *ex post facto.* Some of these subshrines reflect the social and economic station of certain of the groups who frequent the pilgrim center. For example, Palni, Tamil Nadu, is the second most popular pilgrim center in South India. The main deity of the complex is Subrahmaṇyam, a son of the Hindu high god Shiva. Subrahmaṇyam is enshrined atop a hill at Palni in the guise of an ascetic. However, no fewer than thirty-two major temples are administered by the *devasthanam* or temple office at Palni. Most of these temples are dedicated to Subrahamaṇyam in some other guise or to other major Hindu deities, who are mythically linked to the Subrahmaṇyam cult. Still other subshrines are dedicated to lesser deities. Shrines of the relatively minor deities prove to be particularly popular with low caste pilgrims whose status is consistent with that of the deities worshiped.

In addition to subshrines, "sacred geography" enhances the religious aura of pilgrimage centers. Indeed, the mythology or historical tradition of some centers is shaped by its geography. A river or body of water, for example, can be ascribed significance because the deity performed a miracle there (GANGES), because a prototypical ancestor bathed in it (the beach at Tiruchendur, South India), because it has a supernatural source or curative powers (the Shanmugham river at Palni), or for a combination of mythic and geographic reasons. Similarly, in Hindu pilgrimage, a hill or elevated structure with extensive staircases frequently becomes a replica of "heaven" where the deity resides and where people ascend to be in the deity's presence. Trees, rocks, and other natural entities can assume special significance at these places, particularly if they have contours which suggest some mythic event associated with the sacred personages of the center. Such sacred items are multiple at pilgrimage centers and may have taken on such significance in the total pilgrimage that pilgrims make it a point to include them in their visit. The "map" of a pilgrim's visit—that is, the path followed in his visitations—may, therefore, have a meaningful "shape" as he works his way to the ultimate shrine. For example, a visit may require circumambulations of a hill or town in a concentric or spiraling way (as at Pandarpur, Maharashtra). Such movement enhances the symbolic character of the pilgrimage and makes the pilgrimage field as a whole a microcosm of the pilgrim's sacred world.

As important as ritual space is ritual time. The significance of the pilgrimage is enhanced if one goes not only *where* it happened, but also *when* it happened. Thus, in biblical times it was considered especially beneficial to visit the temple in Jerusalem during the PASSOVER, there to be reminded of God's deliverance of his people. Christian pilgrims try to visit BETHLEHEM at Christmas. Similarly, Muslims, while making their pilgrimage to Mecca, are particularly anxious to visit the Mount of Mercy near Arafat at noon on the ninth day of the twelfth month of the Muslim year *(Dhū'l-Ḥijja),* for it is believed it was in that place on that day centuries ago that the prophet delivered his final sermon. In other contexts festival months at specific centers are marked by the juxtaposition of solar, lunar, and stellar chronometry. Such sacred moments enhance the auspicious aura and power of the pilgrimage and make new beginnings and re-enactments especially possible.

6. Contemporary reflections of pilgrimage. A number of the ventures of contemporary life have assumed the character of crypto-pilgrimage. The nostalgic trip to one's home town to see one's first homestead and meet the "old folks" reflects the pilgrim's concern for reaffirming historical identities. Visits to national shrines and symbols of "civil religion" and national origins, such as Plymouth, Massachusetts, at Thanksgiving, or Washington, D.C. at cherry blossom time, or the tombs of revolutionary figures such as Lenin and Ho Chi Minh, affirm a national or political identity for people who view themselves as part of those larger entities. Retreats to the country, designed to enable one to get away from the pressures of urban life, are often not without tinges of nostalgia for an imagined time when things were pure, natural, or simple. These experiences, like pilgrimage itself, reflect a fundamental human need for remembering and renewal, for self-affirmation and re-creation.

Bibliography. S. H. Bhardwaj, *Hindu Places of Pilgrimage in India* (1973); M. Eliade, *The Sacred and The Profane* (1957); T. H. Gaster, *Thespis* (1956); G. Obeyesekere, "The Fire-Walkers of Kataragama: The Rise of *Bhakti* Religiosity in Buddhist Sri Lanka," in *Religious Continuity and Change in South Asia* (1980); V. Turner, *Dramas, Fields, and Metaphors* (1974); V. and E. Turner, *Image and Pilgrimage in Christian Culture* (1978); A. van Gennep, *The Rites of Passage* (1960).

F. W. CLOTHEY

PILLARS OF ISLAM. The fundamental ritual requirements, known collectively as *'ibādāt* (Arab.; "acts of service, worship"). These number five: 1) SHAHĀDA, the basic creed of Islam, "testifying" that "there is no god but God" and that "Muhammad is the Messenger of God." Uttering this with sincere belief makes one a MUSLIM, upon whom the remaining Pillars are then incumbent. The *shahāda* is recited during the call to prayer (ADHĀN), as well as on many other occasions, both formal and informal. It is technically a topic of dogmatic theology more than of jurisprudence (FIQH), so that most books on jurisprudence begin with the second Pillar, assuming that the first has been fulfilled. The basis for the *shahāda* in the QUR'ĀN is found in Sura 37:35; 47:19; 48:29. 2) *Ṣalāt* or "ritual prayer," which Muslims are required to perform five times daily (at dawn, noon, mid-afternoon, sunset, and evening) as well as on certain other occasions. This is a formal worship service, preferably shared with others (the Friday congregational *ṣalāt* must be communal) with each element minutely regulated, and centering in bowings and prostrations in the direction of the KA'BA in MECCA. (*See* PRAYER IN ISLAM.) 3) ZAKĀT is the legal alms, computed like a tax on certain kinds of property, which Muslims of requisite means are obliged to give at the end of each year to the poor and certain other classes of recipients (Sura 9:60). 4) ṢAWM, or "fasting" during the entire ninth lunar month (RAMADAN), when no food, drink, smoking, or other sensual enjoyment may be had from dawn until the sun has set each day. 5) The HAJJ or pilgrimage to Mecca, which is required once in each Muslim's lifetime, if health and resources allow (Sura 2:196-203; 5:97; 22:27-37). This is performed during the special pilgrimage season in the tenth *(Shawwāl),* eleventh *(Dhū 'l-Qa'da),* and first ten days of the twelfth (*Dhū 'l-Ḥijja*) lunar months, with the central rites being observed from the eighth through tenth of that final month. The hajj is the high point of the Muslim's life, when all that is believed and held dear in the religion comes to a dramatic focus as great multitudes of pilgrims come from all over the world to celebrate their essential unity as Muslim brothers and sisters at Mecca. The pilgrimage is a complex ritual process requiring right intention *(niyya),* purity *(ṭahāra),* and a carefully learned set of instructions ranging from pious utterances at appropriate times and places, circumambulation of the Ka'ba, reenacting certain deeds of ABRAHAM, Ishmael, Hagar, and MUHAMMAD, to offering blood sacrifice (this last being simultaneously shared in throughout the Islamic world on the tenth of *Dhū'l-Ḥijja).* At the very center of the hajj is the "standing ceremony" *(wuqūf)* at Mt. Arafat, where Muhammad delivered his farewell address to the Muslims shortly before his death.

Bibliography. A. Rauf, *Islam: Creed and Worship* (1974), pp. 13-136; see also the specific articles treating each Pillar.

F. M. DENNY

PIRKE ABOTH pēr kā´ ä vōt´ (Ju—Heb.; lit. "chapters of the fathers"). A tractate of the MISHNAH containing wisdom sayings, ethical maxims, and religious injunctions (mainly stressing study of TORAH). Usually translated as "Ethics of the Fathers" or "Sayings of the Fathers." I. CHERNUS

PITṚ pĭ´ trĭ (H—Skt.; lit. "a father"; plural *pitaras,* "the fathers"). In the plural form, *pitaras,* a community of deceased ancestors, the forefathers of a particular individual or the progenitors of humanity in general. In VEDIC HINDUISM an elaborate system of ŚRĀDDHA ceremonies evolved in which sustenance was provided for the deceased by way of regular offerings, particularly balls of rice or barley called *piṇḍas,* cups of water, and sesame. Contemporary Hinduism has reduced the scale, but not the concept, of these vital offerings as obligatory rituals. For their part, now as in ancient India, the *pitaras* look out for the needs of their living descendants, favoring them with wealth, longevity, and progeny. In the early Vedic period a deceased person, subsequent to cremation or burial, was believed to go by the "path" of the Fathers to recover his or her body in a realm of eternal light where, like the gods, he or she might enjoy offerings of SOMA. In the BRĀHMAṆAS a sense of moral judgment in regard to this path becomes explicit. The *pitṛyāna,* "way of the Fathers," in the Upaniṣads is a path distinct from the *devayāna,* "way of the gods": namely, those who after death join the ancestors return to earth to be born again, while those who truly "know" the Self travel a path to final liberation. *See* ANCESTOR VENERATION.

Bibliography. A. A. Macdonell, *Vedic Mythology* (1897).

D. M. KNIPE

PIYYUT pē yōōt´ (Ju—Heb.). A devotional poem. Beginning in Palestine around the fourth century A.D. such poems have been added to the established prayers of the Jewish liturgy for festivals and special SABBATHS.

B. MARTIN

PL KYŌDAN pē ĕl kyō´ dăn (Jap.; lit. "perfect liberty order"). A religious movement organized after World War II. It is conspicuous for its modern accoutrements and symbols and its support of arts and sports. Centered at Tondabayashi near Osaka, it is especially appealing to business-oriented people with its message of health, happiness, and prosperity.

1. **History.** Two prewar movements are antecedent to PL Kyōdan. The first was formed in 1912 by Kanada Tokumitsu (1863-1919). Influenced particularly by the esoteric SHINGON sect of BUDDHISM and a mountain sect, Mitake-kyo, of sectarian SHINTŌ, he formed a movement known as Shintō-Tokumitsu-kyō (the divine way as taught by Tokumitsu) and achieved some prominence as a faith healer.

The second precursor movement was founded by a disciple of Kanada, an Obaku ZEN priest, Miki Chojiro (1871-1938), who with his teenage son, Akisada (b. 1900), came to Kanada in 1916 seeking a new career and relief from recurrent misfortune. Both father and son joined Kanada and received new given names, Tokuharu and Tokuchika, respectively. After Kanada's death in 1919 the movement faded, but in 1924 Miki Tokuharu, believing himself to be the successor and the recipient of new revelation which Kanada had foretold, organized a movement called Jindō-Tokumitsu-kyō (the human way as taught by Tokumitsu). In 1931 the name was changed to Hito no Michi (lit. "the way of man"). This movement flourished, especially among Osaka merchants, during the early 1930s, but by 1936 it had become the object of persecution by the government.

In 1936 Miki Tokuharu passed the leadership of Hito no Michi to his son, Tokuchika, and was subsequently arrested. In 1937 the government ordered the dissolution of the movement, and in 1938 the elder Miki died while free on bail. The younger Miki tried to refute the charges of lèse majesté, but in May of 1945 he too was sent to prison, where he remained until October 9, when his sentence was voided by the Occupation authorities. Shortly after his release Miki Tokuchika began to reconstruct the movement with a remnant of the former members. In recognition and celebration of the new postwar freedom and openness to influences from abroad, he named it Perfect Liberty Kyōdan, more commonly called PL Kyōdan or just PL.

2. **Scripture.** While PL Kyōdan has no official canon, it does have a small collection of writings (trans. R. J. Hammer) which function essentially as scripture. These include prayers used in PL services and, most notably, the Twenty-one Precepts which are the basis of all PL teaching. Additionally the teachings of Miki Tokuchika have the authority of scripture.

3. **Organization.** At the time of the founding of PL Kyōdan in 1946, the headquarters were set up in Kyushu, the southernmost island of Japan. After two other temporary relocations the headquarters (Daihoncho) were established at Tondabayashi, near Osaka. The organization is tightly structured and controlled. At the head is Miki Tokuchika, who is not

only an effective teacher but also a skillful organizer and administrator. In all respects—spiritual, doctrinal, financial—he presides authoritatively over an extensive membership in Japan and abroad by means of a complex network of regional and local agencies.

4. **Doctrine.** The basic summation of PL teaching is the Twenty-one Precepts, but among these the first is by far the most important: "Life is art." It is the PL motto and, in essence, is the gist of the other twenty. This requires each person to see life as art, himself or herself as a potential artist, and the artistic possibilities of every occupation or calling, no matter how exalted or lowly. For one who expresses self as an artist, life is happy and fulfilling. Failure to do so brings suffering in the form of illness or other misfortunes, a warning from God, and calls for an analysis by one of a few spiritually qualified persons, who then will issue a teaching identifying the cause of the problem and prescribing a remedy for it. Beyond this is a special ministry of which only the master teacher is capable—an act of vicarious suffering in which he temporarily assumes the devotee's burden and the responsibility before God for its cause.

5. **Worship.** The PL community is liturgically oriented. Provision is made for observing virtually any special occurrence, ranging from LIFE CYCLE RITES to national holidays. However, two regularly scheduled occasions for worship are most noteworthy: morning worship and thanksgiving service. At 5 A.M. in the summer and at 6 A.M. in the winter a service is held at the headquarters and in most branch churches. It consists of singing, chanting, testimonies of believers, and a sermon, followed by a simple breakfast. Thanksgiving is an evening service, held on the twenty-first day of each month at the headquarters, with similar services taking place simultaneously in all branch churches. This too is an occasion for both ritual and sermon but also for the presentation of monthly thanksgiving offerings. In most acts of PL worship two symbols are conspicuous. One is the official emblem, consisting of a crystal light from which twenty-one rays emanate. This symbol is the visual focal point in PL worship halls. The second is a hand symbol formed by touching thumb to thumb and forefinger to forefinger to describe the circle of the sun while the other fingers are extended to suggest the sun's rays.

6. **Founder's Festival.** One of the most spectacular festivals in Japan is the PL Founder's Festival, held at Tondabayashi each August 1, to commemorate the death of Miki Tokuharu and to renew a prayer for world peace. This festival features a three-hour display of fireworks, synchronized with symphonic music and the dancing waters of illuminated fountains.

7. **Art, architecture, and athletics.** PL Kyōdan has placed major emphasis on art, mostly modern, nontraditional, and frequently avant-garde, and sports, especially golf and baseball, which are emblematic of modern life.

Bibliography. R. S. Ellwood, Jr., *The Eagle and the Rising Sun* (1974); R. J. Hammer, "The Scripture of the 'Perfect Liberty Kyōdan,' " *Japanese Religions*, III (1963), 18-26; H. N. McFarland, *The Rush Hour of the Gods* (1967).

H. N. MCFARLAND

PLYMOUTH BRETHREN (Ch). British evangelical sect which originated in the early nineteenth century. Although the group has remained small, its influence on British and American PROTESTANTISM has been great. John Nelson Darby (1800-1882), one of the early leaders of the group, was the principal architect of DISPENSATIONALISM. Darby appears to have believed that this doctrine should have been a characteristic of the Brethren and that all those who accepted it should join his group, but the doctrine proved attractive to other Christians who remained within their own churches. Today the Brethren are active in missionary work and conduct prophecy conferences in which the dispensational approach to the Bible is advocated.

Bibliography. E. R. Coad, *A History of the Brethren Movement* (1968); T. Veitch, *The Story of the Brethren Movement* (1933).

G. MILLER

POLE, REGINALD CARDINAL (Ch; 1500–1558). Christian humanist educated at Oxford and Padua; in 1530 Pole opposed Henry VIII's divorce and joined leading Italian churchmen seeking reform and Christian unity. Pole helped preside over the first sessions of the COUNCIL OF TRENT. In 1553 he was appointed papal legate to England under Mary Tudor. *See* REFORMATION, CATHOLIC. J. RAITT

POLYNESIAN RELIGION. *See* OCEANIC TRIBAL RELIGIONS.

POOR CLARES (Ch). *See* FRANCISCANS.

POPE (Ch). *See* PAPACY.

PRAJĀPATI prŭ jä′ pŭ tē (H—Skt.; lit. "lord of creatures" [*prajā*—"offspring, creature"; *pati*—"master"]). Creator god in VEDIC HINDUISM, identified with PURUṢA, sometimes with AGNI, and later in the post-Vedic period with BRAHMĀ; he was recognized in the BRĀHMAṆAS as the chief deity and father of the gods. In occasional verses of the RIG VEDA Prajāpati occurs as an epithet, e.g. of Savitṛ (*see* SŪRYA) or SOMA, but in a late speculative hymn (10.121) he emerges as supreme being, god above gods, creator and lord of all that exists, the "golden germ" (HIRAṆYAGARBHA) who evolved in the beginning. Each verse of this influential hymn concludes "What *(ka)* god shall we revere with oblation?" and the final verse replies that it is Prajāpati and no other; the interrogative pronoun *ka* itself becomes a designation of the supreme being.

In the ATHARVA VEDA, Vājasaneyi-saṃhitā and Brāhmaṇas, Prajāpati is supreme among the gods, their father and father of the ASURAS (demons) as well.

For procreation he exercises cosmogonic heat (TAPAS). Significantly, speculation on the sacrifice homologizes creator and creation: Prajāpati is time and space and is mystically identified as the sacrifice (YAJÑA) itself. This gives occasion, e.g. in the ŚB *agnicayana* ritual, for the identification of Prajāpati with both the sacrificial Puruṣa of RV 10.90 and Agni, the sacrificial fire. Prajāpati-Puruṣa-Agni here becomes the cynosure of Vedic mythology and ritual: creation is the projection of the dismembered parts of the Divine Being, every sacrifice is a cosmogonic repetition of the primordial event, and every sacrificer is identified with the Divine Being.

By the time of the early UPANIṢADS, *bráhman* (the sacred word) advances from an aspect of Prajāpati's cosmogonic powers to a transcendent absolute, a universal principle beyond godhead. Simultaneously, theistic propensities develop and promote the god Brahmā, who as a creator perpetuates the role of Prajāpati as a "grandfather" figure in the Epics and PURĀṆAS. There is also in post-Vedic mythology a class of Prajāpatis or primeval creators, all of them the offspring of Brahmā. These are variously ten or seven in number, the latter group identified with the seven ancient sages (RISHIS).

Bibliography. A. A. Macdonell, *Vedic Mythology* (1897); L. Renou, *Vedic India* (ET 1957). D. M. KNIPE

PRAJÑĀ prŭj nyä′ (B—Skt.; lit. "wisdom, intelligence, knowledge, understanding" [*jñā*—"to know"]) **PAÑÑĀ** pŭn′ nyä (B—Pali). Intuitive wisdom; true knowledge of things as they are. *Prajñā* is the specific Buddhist knowledge or wisdom which, as part of the noble EIGHTFOLD PATH, leads to deliverance. As such it is understood to be an experiential knowledge, rather than mere rational knowledge.

Prajñā is the third heading under which the eight divisions of the Buddhist Eightfold Path are traditionally classified, the other two being morality and mental discipline. According to this classification, right thought or intention and right view or understanding constitute wisdom. Spiritually liberating wisdom involves seeing through the delusion that the everyday world and its material comforts are of value and provide happiness. Hence, to be "wise" is to realize the impermanency (ANICCA) and suffering or misery (DUKKHA) life entails, and to "know" there is no permanent self or soul (ANATTA).

Speaking of *paññā* in the Path of Purification XIV.7, Buddhaghosa writes: "What are its characteristic, function, manifestation, and proximate cause? Understanding has the characteristic of penetrating the individual essences of states. Its function is to abolish the darkness of delusion, which conceals the individual essences of states. It is manifested as non-delusion. Because of the words 'One who is concentrated knows and sees correctly' (A V.3) its proximate cause is concentration" (trans. Ñyāṇamoli, p. 481).

The Buddhist scholastic literature lists paññā as one of five mental faculties, one of three kinds of training, and as one of the perfections.

MAHĀYĀNA Buddhism charged THERAVĀDA with overstressing wisdom at the expense of compassion (KARUṆĀ). Such a stress was felt to lead to sterile intellectualism. Although such forms of Mahāyāna as PURE LAND eventually came to stress compassion, Mahāyāna generally regarded the virtues of wisdom and compassion as equally important. Nonetheless an entire genre of Mahāyāna scriptures, the PRAJÑĀPĀRAMITĀ SŪTRAS, has the perfection of wisdom as its central concern, teaching that wisdom consists in the intuitive knowledge of the emptiness (ŚŪNYATĀ) of the basic elements of phenomenal existence (dharmas), and realization of the relativity of ordinary experience.

Bibliography. Buddhaghosa, *The Path of Purification*, Ñyāṇamoli, trans. (2nd ed., 1964), pp. 479-89; F. Streng, *Emptiness: A Study in Religious Meaning* (1967), pp. 82-98.
J. P. MCDERMOTT

PRAJÑĀPĀRAMITĀ SŪTRAS prŭj′ nyä pä rŭ mē′ tä sōō′ trŭs (B—Skt.; lit. "Perfection of Wisdom Scriptures" [*jñā*—to know"; *pāram* + *ita*—"gone to the opposite shore"]). A genre of scriptures important to MAHĀYĀNA BUDDHISM. It consists of a large number of texts written over a period of perhaps more than a thousand years, and preserved in SANSKRIT, Tibetan, and Chinese.

1. **Development.** Four stages have been traced in the history of this literature: (a) The basic texts were composed by unknown authors during the period between 100 B.C. and A.D. 100. The fundamental text from this stage is the Perfection of Wisdom in Eight Thousand Lines. These first-stage texts comprise what is probably the earliest Mahāyāna literature. (b) During the second stage, roughly A.D. 100-300, the basic texts were expanded by means of illustration, elaboration of imagery, and repetition, until versions existed in 25,000 and even 100,000 lines. (c) Between A.D. 300-500 the unwieldy longer versions were greatly condensed into short summaries which provided handy outlines of the basic doctrine. Most influential of these are the highly popular Heart Sūtra and DIAMOND CUTTER Sūtra. (d) Between 500-1200 the process of condensation was carried to its logical extreme under the influence of popular magic and Tantric Buddhism (*see* TANTRISM). The result was a group of MANTRAS considered the epitome of wisdom.

2. **Content.** The basic teaching throughout these scriptures is that so far as their real nature is concerned, the elements (called dharmas) of existence are void or empty. Ultimate reality transcends all existential phenomena and conceptual categories and can only be realized through nondual knowledge; that

is, through intuitive wisdom (PRAJÑĀ), which is none other than the Absolute itself.

Bibliography. E. Conze, *The Prajñāpāramitā Literature* (1960); E. Conze, ed. & trans., *Buddhist Wisdom Books* (1958), and *The Perfection of Wisdom in Eight Thousand Lines and Its Verse Summary* (1973); the four stage chronology is derived from Conze.

J. P. McDERMOTT

PRAKṚTI prä′ krĭ tē (H—Skt.; lit. "making or placing before or at first"). The original or natural form or condition of anything; the principle of "nature" or "materiality" in classical SĀṂKHYA and YOGA philosophy, which is juxtaposed to a second eternal principle, "consciousness" (PURUṢA). *Prākṛti's* manifestations include intellect *(buddhi)*, ego *(ahaṃkāra)*, mind *(manas)*, the five sense capacities, the five action capacities, the five subtle elements, and the five gross elements. G. J. LARSON

PRĀṆĀYĀMA prä nī yä′ mŭ (H—Skt.; lit. "the extending or restraining of breath" [*prāṇa*—"breath, respiration"; *āyāma*—"restraining or extending"]). The fourth "limb" *(aṅga)* of the "eight-limbed" YOGA of PATAÑJALI. The YOGIN seeks to become self-aware of the processes of inhalation, exhalation, and retention or cessation of breathing. *Prāṇayāma* refers primarily to retention or cessation. The time intervals required for respiration are measured in "moments" or "instants" called *mātrās*. The practitioner usually begins by allowing an equal number of *mātrās* for inhalation, exhalation, and retention. Gradually, then, the *mātrās* allowed for retention are extended, and those for inhalation and exhalation are lessened.

G. J. LARSON

PRASĀDA prŭ sä′ dŭ (H—Skt.; lit. "graciousness"). Divine grace, the kindliness and saving power of a god, especially emphasized by devotees of VISHNU and SHIVA. *Prasāda* can be either the direct saving action of the divine or grace mediated through rituals and devotion. In the latter context, *prasāda* has the specific meaning of food which has become sacred by its being offered to the god, usually as an offering in a PŪJĀ ritual, and which thus conveys the god's grace to those who eat it as a gift from him.

T. J. HOPKINS

PRATYEKA BUDDHA prə tyā′ kə bood′ hŭ. *See* BUDDHA, GENERAL CONCEPTS OF §4.

PRAYER, CHRISTIAN. "The ascent of the mind to God," according to John of Damascus; "the soul of religion" (H. E. Fosdick); "the opening of the heart to God" (K. Rahner); "a response to the prior love of God" (D. Steere); "an expression of religious experience" (F. Heiler); a way to know God "face to face" (G. Buttrick). Other popular definitions include the ideas of dialogue and communion with God.

Theologically, the practice of prayer assumes God's presence in human experience and his personal responsiveness to the individual. Motivation for prayer has ranged from a desire for material benefit to a hope for mystical union with the Divine.

1. Biblical background. Primitive Christianity inherited the Jewish tradition of prayer, particularly the psalms and post-exilic synagogue forms. The Gospels of Matthew and Luke present Jesus teaching the LORD'S PRAYER as a model. He promised that prayer in his name is heard and answered, warned against hypocrisy and empty phrases, encouraged prayer in secret, and urged his followers to pray even though God already knew their needs. Paul instructed the Thessalonians to "pray constantly" (I Thess. 5:17) and told the Romans that "we do not know how to pray as we ought, but the Spirit intercedes for us with sighs too deep for words" (Rom. 8:26).

2. Times of prayer. Early Christians continued to observe the Jewish hours of prayer. The Didache suggested praying the Lord's Prayer three times a day. In MONASTICISM the canonical hours of prayer were set at regular intervals in order to sanctify the day. A night office plus seven offices a day of praying the psalms were established on the basis of Ps. 119:62, 164. Praying at stated times became a major element in Christian devotion.

3. Styles. Prayer may be vocal, in which fixed or spontaneous prayers are recited, or mental, in which affections predominate. Contemplative prayer is a simple awareness of the Divine presence devoid of words or concepts. The "prayer of quiet," especially as taught by TERESA OF AVILA, is a passive knowledge of God that sometimes follows a period of spiritual aridity.

4. Forms. These include adoration, thanksgiving, praise, confession, petition, and intercession. The latter two are the most problematic. L. Evely calls that prayer pagan which attempts to change God or call his attention to something of which one feels he is not sufficiently aware, and says that the individual praying, rather than God, is the one changed by prayer. Buttrick, however, affirms that centuries of Christian experience testify, even in the face of skepticism, that prayer does change situations.

5. Popular prayers. The Lord's Prayer is undoubtedly the most frequently used prayer, both individually and corporately. In Eastern Orthodoxy the mystical tradition of HESYCHASM developed around the so-called Jesus prayer ("Lord Jesus Christ, Son of God, have mercy on me a sinner"). The continual recitation of this prayer was believed to produce a mystical awareness of God. It has been popularized in the anonymous Russian *Way of a Pilgrim* and in J. D. Salinger's *Franny and Zooey*. In Roman Catholicism the AVE MARIA, coupled with the meditative use of a ROSARY, has long been a popular form of devotion.

6. Liturgy. The prayer of the church at worship includes the monastic DIVINE OFFICES, prayers associated with the sacraments, and prayers used in corporate worship. There is great variety in the liturgical practices of the churches, but common forms include invocations, collects, pastoral prayers reflecting the concerns of the congregation, prayers for consecrating the elements in the Lord's Supper, and traditional prayers such as the KYRIE ELEISON and the AGNUS DEI.

By the fifth century A.D. liturgical prayers were being standardized and spontaneity was lost. The Roman MASS ultimately became the norm in Western civilization while the liturgy of St. Chrysostom dominated the East. The PROTESTANT REFORMATION produced a host of new liturgies aimed at removing the sacrificial element in the mass. The free church tradition restored spontaneous prayers and rejected fixed forms. The PENTECOSTAL movement has emphasized praying under the influence of the HOLY SPIRIT. Praying in unknown tongues, it teaches, avoids the limitations of language, and some Pentecostals believe that the phenomenon represents the Holy Spirit praying through a person.

7. **Prayer books.** No collection of prayers for private use has survived from ancient Christianity, although some liturgical material was preserved. Judging from the number of commentaries written it appears that the Psalter was widely used for private devotion. Alcuin of York, at the time of Charlemagne, wrote a book on the private use of the psalms for prayer. In the later Middle Ages "Books of Hours" appeared which contained psalms, hymns, prayers, and readings for private use according to the canonical hours. These books were often treasured for their artistic qualities. In modern times many collections of prayers, traditional and contemporary, have appeared, and there has been much experimentation in the use of nontraditional language in prayer.

See AMEN; BAPTISM IN THE HOLY SPIRIT; BREVIARY: DEAD, PRAYERS FOR THE; STATIONS OF THE CROSS.

Bibliography. G. A. Buttrick, *Prayer* (1942); J. Ellul, *Prayer and Modern Man* (1970); L. Evely, *Our Prayer* (1970); H. E. Fosdick, *The Meaning of Prayer* (1915); G. E. Harkness, *Prayer and the Common Life* (1948); F. Heiler, *Prayer: A Study in the History and Psychology of Religion* (1932); T. Merton, *Contemplative Prayer* (1969); D. V. Steere, *Prayer and Worship* (1938). For a selection of prayerbooks using different styles see J. Baillie, *A Diary of Private Prayer* (1949); F. D. LeFevre, *The Prayers of Kierkegaard* (1956); H. Paine and B. Thompson, *Book of Prayers for Church and Home* (1962); W. Rauschenbusch, *Prayers of the Social Awakening* (1910); M. Boyd, *Are You Running with Me Jesus?* (1965). W. O. PAULSELL

PRAYER IN ISLAM (ṢALĀT sə lätʹ—Arab.; lit. "prayer" [*ṣallā* "to pray" in the sense of "to perform the *ṣalāt*"]). *Ṣalāt* is one of the five PILLARS OF ISLAM and the most pervasive and demanding in the life of the believer, as it must be performed five times daily as well as on special occasions. It might be translated as "worship" (Calverly) or as "ritual prayer," for it is the central divine service for Muslims, with all elements strictly prescribed and regulated for both individuals and groups. Another category of prayer is *du'ā'*, which includes supplication, petition, and intercession. It may be either spontaneous or formal, drawing from a rich devotional literature intended for both personal and congregational use. *Du'ā'* may also be a part of the *ṣalāt*. (*see* below § 4). DHIKR, a related term, refers to the "mention" or "remembrance" of God, and figures prominently in SUFI devotional practices.

1. **Times of prayer.** a) "Dawn prayer," from first light until sunrise; b) "noon prayer," from the moment of the sun's zenith until the time when an object's shadow equals its height plus the length of whatever shadow was cast at the zenith; c) "afternoon prayer," anytime between the end of the preceding and sunset; d) "sunset prayer," starting immediately after sunset and ending with darkness; e) "nighttime prayer," from the end of twilight until just before dawn. These are the permissible periods, but actual observance is closely regulated according to schedules for varying locales and latitudes. It is preferable and in fact meritorious to perform the *ṣalāt* at or near the beginning of each period. It is considered a sin to overlap periods. Certain special procedures mitigate this infraction, however.

2. **Prerequisites for *ṣalāt*.** *a) Purification.* On the threshold of prayer is ritual purification, known in general as *ṭahāra* (*see* PURIFICATION). The "lesser ablution" (WUḌŪ'), the minimum requirement, is performed by washing the face and hands to the elbows, rubbing the head with water, and washing the feet up to the ankles. The mouth, nose, and teeth must also be thoroughly cleansed. All this is done according to a set order, with accompanying *du'ā'* prayers, after having first declared the right intention *(niyya)*. For example, after washing the feet, the worshiper prays: "O God! Make firm my feet on the Path on the day when they easily slip on it." Shoes are not worn during the ritual prayer or in a MOSQUE. If water is unavailable, then clean earth (such as sand) may be substituted in a somewhat abbreviated ritual purification exercise, called *tayammum*. Major pollution (as after a seminal emission or menstruation) is removed only by *ghusl*, which is a full bath performed also in a ritualized manner. Once *ṭahāra* is accomplished, the believer is permitted to perform the *ṣalāt* or other ritual practices, such as handling and reciting the QUR'ĀN.

b) Sitr. This is the proper covering of the body. Males at least from the navel to the knees; females the entire body except for the face, hands, and feet.

c) Place and orientation. Ṣalāt need not be performed in a mosque, but the place must be clean and as tranquil and free from distractions as possible. Prayer rugs (SAJJĀDA) are often used but are not absolutely essential. Worshipers must face the QIBLAH (the precise direction of MECCA), which in a mosque is indicated by the prayer niche, known as the *miḥrāb*. Even aboard ship or other conveyance one must so far as possible maintain the correct *qiblah*. The *ṣalāt* may be performed in solitude, but it is much better to

Ewing Galloway, N. Y.

Prayer before the Great Mosque of Delhi

observe it in company with others. The Friday congregational *ṣalāt* may not be performed by an individual.

3. ***Adhān* and *iqāma*.** Before each of the required daily prayers a call to prayer is made, called the ADHĀN. This may be performed by an individual for himself if no muezzin, or crier, is available. A bit later another call, the *iqāma* (lit. "institution, performance"), is made in a more subdued voice but quite rapidly. This initiates the actual prayer service. Thus there is a two-stage passage from profane to sacred time. The *adhān* is delivered to the surrounding community, usually from atop a MINARET, while the *iqāma* is made to the assembled worshipers. The two are almost identical in wording, except that the latter adds "The time to begin the *ṣalāt* is nigh" (repeated once).

4. **The *rak'a*.** Certain elements of each of the daily prayers are obligatory on all occasions. Other elements are either more or less strongly recommended. The main component of each prayer is the *rak'a* (lit. "bending, bowing"), a cycle of bodily postures and movements with accompanying phrases. Each daily ritual prayer has its required number of *rak'as* (two at dawn, four at noon, four in the afternoon, three at sunset, and four at night). Additional *rak'as,* before or after the obligatory ones, may be made according to the practice of different schools or individual needs. More complexity is involved with multiple *rak'as* because of their relationships to each other, and different contexts sometimes require different phrases (such as those on the HAJJ or at the principal festivals). Also, there are slight variations of detail between SUNNIS and SHI'ITES and from one legal school to another. Having fulfilled all the prerequisites, the worshipers stand in straight rows behind the prayer leader (IMAM), who serves as a model by which the worshipers pattern their movements and phrases, following him immediately and never anticipating him. Only the leader's voice should be heard. The imam does not have to be a religious professional; any adult male Muslim of upright life and demonstrated knowledge of the *ṣalāt* may serve. If an individual is performing the prayer

alone, then obviously no imam is required. But if even only two are praying, one must serve as the other's imam, so as to preserve a dignified uniformity in the performance.

In performing the *rak'a* the worshiper assumes a standing posture during which he first declares his formal *niyya,* or "intention," to perform whatever number of cycles he wishes. This ensures sincerity and concentration, and seeks to create a live consciousness free of empty routine. Without this intention the *ṣalāt* is invalid, even though perfectly performed from the technical standpoint. After making the *niyya* the hands are raised with the palms open and facing forward, with the thumbs nearly touching the earlobes and the *niyya* clearly in mind. At this point *Allāhu akbar* (God is most great) is said, and the hands are lowered to the chest or sides. This is called the *takbīr iḥrām* (lit. "the *Allāhu akbar* of entering the state of ritual consecration"), and marks the actual passage into the sacred time and place of *ṣalāt* proper, when no other thoughts are permitted and no interruptions allowed. Then *sūrat al-*FĀTIḤA (the first chapter of the Qur'ān) is recited, followed by *āmīn* (amen). Still standing, the worshiper again raises his hands to the ears, and, repeating another *takbīr,* bends forward at the waist, hands resting on the knees, with head and back forming a straight line, thus forming a right angle with the legs (women keep their hands at their sides). The phrase *subḥāna rabbiyya al-'aẓīm* (Glory belongs to my great Lord!) is repeated three times. Then the standing posture is resumed and, with hands once again raised as before, the worshiper recites *Sami'a allāhu li-man ḥamida, rabbanā la-kum al-ḥamd* (God hears the one who praises him. Our Lord, praise is due to you). Then the worshiper kneels, placing the palms of the hands on the floor, and touching the forehead and tip of the nose to the floor, with hands near the ears and feet resting on curled up toes with soles facing rearward. (Males keep their limbs loosely apart, while females keep theirs together, arms close against the body.) On the descent to full prostration a *takbīr* is recited, during which the whole fluid motion should take place. The worshiper remains prostrate for a period, reciting three times, *Subḥāna rabbīya al-a'lā* (Glory be to my Lord, the Most High!). Next the worshiper assumes a half-sitting, half-kneeling position, every physical feature of which is carefully regulated, from the position of the foot under the body to the placement of the hands on the thighs. A short petition *(du'ā')* for forgiveness of sins is offered in this position. Then there is a final prostration similar to the first, and a final half-sitting position, with a slightly different arrangement of feet and legs. Hands rest on the legs, but the right hand is in a fist, index finger extended and moved from left to right. In this position the worshiper utters a "witness" to the value of good deeds and prayer, praying for peace and blessings on the Prophet, his family, and all of God's righteous servants, and bearing testimony to the oneness of God and the apostlehood of MUHAMMAD. Following this is another short *du'ā'* for forgiveness of past sins and for prosperity and protection in the future. Finally, the worshiper turns his face to the right and says: "Peace be upon you, and the mercy of God and his blessing," which is then repeated immediately with the face turned toward the left. This closing benediction is directed toward one's fellows and thus marks a transition from the "vertical" to the "horizontal," from an exclusive orientation of servant toward God to a broader expression of concern for others and a celebration of God's peace and blessings for his community.

F. M. Denny

Girls at prayer, Jakarta, Indonesia

5. Other obligatory prayers. In addition to the five daily prayers, there are others which are obligatory. The Friday congregational prayer *(ṣalāt al-jumu'a)* is especially important, as it is the one which requires a congregation and features a sermon (*see* KHUṬBA). Friday *ṣalāt* includes within its structure the regular noon prayer, but goes considerably beyond it in both prescribed ritual and etiquette. One should arrive early and listen to the recitation of the Qur'ān and engage in *du'ā'* and meditation. (The former is performed with hands before the chest, palms heavenward.) Before the sermon one should perform individually the four normal *rak'as* of the noon prayer. During the sermon one is required to listen attentively and respectfully, and to abstain from talking or being distracted by extraneous matters. Following the sermon are the two obligatory *rak'as* of the Friday congregational prayer, after which it is recommended to perform four additional ones. Then everyone returns to his normal occupation, Friday not being considered a day of rest (none is prescribed in Islam). Generally, throughout the Islamic world, only men attend Friday congregational prayer. Women pray in mosques at other times in some regions, but generally they pray at home. When they participate in *ṣalāt* in a mosque, they must be at the back, for modesty's sake. A woman never serves as imam, except for an exclusively female congregation.

The funeral *ṣalāt (ṣalāt al-janāza)* does not contain any *rak'as,* but is observed in a standing position throughout. It consists of four *takbīrs,* after each of which a *du'ā'* is offered for the deceased, the whole being concluded with a *salām,* or "peace." The worshiper turns his head to the right and then to the left, saying with each turn, "Peace be upon you and the mercy of God." Additional *ṣalāts* are required at the time of an earthquake, at eclipses of the sun or moon, and on other auspicious natural occasions which are regarded as signs of God's activity.

6. Recommended prayers. Certain other performances of *ṣalāt* are universally observed. Supererogatory *(nawāfil)* prayers are offered in connection with the five daily obligatory ones, on an individual basis. The *'īd* or "festival" *ṣalāt* is performed at each of the two major canonical festivals of the Islamic year: the Feast of Sacrifice (*'īd al-aḍḥā; see* HAJJ) and the Feast of Fast-breaking *('īd al-fiṭr; see* RAMADAN).

Bibliography. The most useful and complete description and analysis is in the semi-official handbook of M. A. Rauf, *Islam: Creed and Worship* (1974), especially pp. 19-102 (many line-drawings of postures and procedures); E. E. Calverley, *Worship in Islam: Being a Translation, with Commentary and Introduction of Al-Ghazzali's Book of the Ihya' on the Worship* (1925); C. E. Padwick's *Muslim Devotions: A Study of Prayer-Manuals in Common Use* (1961); a good sampling of ḤADĪTH on the subject is found in Al-Baghawi, *Mishkat al-Masabih,* ET by J. Robson (1965), I, 114-370.

F. M. DENNY

PRAYER, JEWISH. Prayer in JUDAISM consists of praise, petition, thanksgiving, and confession, and is directed to one God. Petitions are phrased in the plural ("we") rather than the singular, and prayer is considered the effective substitute for the sacrifices specified in the BIBLE (*see* SYNAGOGUE).

1. Ancient beginnings. The Bible recounts many prayers offered by individuals to God. Abraham was effective in prayer because of his prophetic power (Gen. 20:7); Jeremiah has been called in modern times the father of supplication, and Ezekiel the father of the synagogue. To EZRA is attributed the custom of TORAH reading.

Collections of prayers such as the biblical psalms form an intrinsic part of ancient Jewish literature. Outside the Bible there is the Scroll of Thanksgivings from the Dead Sea Scrolls and the pseudepigraphal Psalms of Solomon.

2. Times of prayer. Observance of special times of prayer has been part of Jewish practice since the time of the Temple. In current custom the SHEMA (Deut. 6:4-9; 11:13-21; Num. 15:37-41) is recited when retiring and upon awakening (as well as during services). The AMIDAH is a central feature of the traditional three daily services: *Shaharit* (morning service), *Minhah* (afternoon), and *Ma'ariv* or *'Arvit* (evening). On the SABBATH, festival days, and New Moon days there is an additional service *(Musaf)* after *Shaharit,* and on YOM KIPPUR there is a fifth service *(Ne'ilah)* after *Minhah.* In the KABBALA a midnight service *(Tikkun Hazot)* is observed, lamenting the DIASPORA and praying for the restoration of Israel.

3. Styles of prayer. Certain styles of prayer reflect stages in the history of the Jewish people. The Hosanna (O Save) litanies (*see* SUKKOT) were originally processional prayers, recited responsively by temple priest and people. The confession of sins on the Day of Atonement reflects a law-court pattern, as do approaches to God as judge (beginning "master of the worlds"). Prayer for redemption and Torah blessings ("Blessed be he who gave Torah to his people Israel") are derived from school patterns and study of Torah as well as the sermonic tradition.

In the course of history many prayers became standard, such as *'Alenu* ("It is incumbent upon us to praise the Lord of all . . ."); originally a New Year prayer, it became a daily prayer, and a special version (beginning in the singular) was used in MERKABAH MYSTICISM. For other standard prayers, see SHEMA, KADDISH, AMIDAH, KIDDUSH, KOL NIDRE, PIYYUT, SELIHOT, and HAGGADAH.

With the establishment of routine forms and styles of prayer came the admonition that intention, or devotion, is the soul of prayer. *Kavannah,* or concentration and meditation, became in sixteenth century Kabbala a regulated set of intentions aimed at bringing about a sacred union of the *sefirot* (divine aspects; *see* SEFER BAHIR). In modern HASIDISM cleaving to God, or *devekut,* is the goal of prayer.

4. Liturgical practice and sources. A MINYAN, or quorum of ten male Jews over the age of thirteen, is necessary for public prayer (Babylonian tradition; cf. Mishnah Sanhedrin I.6). Reform minyan may include women. Ritual use of TEFILLIN (phylacteries) and TALLIT (the prayer shawl) are part of the practice of traditional Jewish prayer. Public prayer has long involved the services of a RABBI and a CANTOR.

The centrality of the Jewish homeland is evident in some practices. Traditionally all prayer is said facing Jerusalem, and prayers for rain and dew follow the seasons of the land of Israel. HEBREW, with some ARAMAIC, is the language of prayer. Only in REFORM JUDAISM has a vernacular, first German, then English, come to replace Hebrew in prayer, although Hebrew and Aramaic may still be used for prayers of particular significance, e.g., Kaddish. Reform prayer differs from the Orthodox in that it has no reference to redemption by the MESSIAH and sacrifices. The CONSERVATIVE movement uses both Hebrew and English, as well as additional readings of material, some written by non-Jews (e.g., RABINDRANATH TAGORE).

The first Jewish prayerbook (SIDDUR) is found in a RESPONSUM by Rav Amram Gaon (d. A.D. 875). Different cultural traditions follow different rites in their prayerbooks: e.g., the SEPHARDI, ASHKENAZI, Yemenite, Moroccan, Italian, Austrian. The Hasidim follow *Siddur ha-Ari,* a prayerbook after the custom of Rabbi ISAAC LURIA (1534-72). The prayerbook of R. Schneur Zalman of Liadi (1800) is a result of textual study. Especially important because of its scholarly interpretations is S. Baer's *Avodath Israel* (1968).

Bibliography. I. Elbogen, *Der jüdische Gottesdienst*, 3rd ed. (1931) and A. Z. Idelsohn, *Jewish Liturgy* (1967) are comprehensive studies. On form and style, J. Heinemann, *Ha-Tefillah Be-Tekufat ha-Tanna'im veha-Amora'im,* 2nd ed. (1966). On *devekut* (communion with God), G. G. Scholem, *The Messianic Idea in Judaism* (1971), pp. 203-27. On Liberal and Reform liturgy, J. J. Petuchovski, *Prayerbook Reform in Europe* (1968). *See* bibliog. for BENEDICTIONS.

Y. SHAMIR

PRAYER RUG (I). *See* SAJJĀDA.

PRAYER SHAWL (Ju). *See* TALLIT.

PRAYER WHEEL (B—Tibetan; *Mani CHos AKHor: mani* or "precious" religion wheel, commonly "prayer wheel" or "prayer mill"; perhaps related to Skt. *dharma cakra*). A cylinder inscribed on the outside with a MANTRA, usually OṂ MAṆIPADME HŪṂ, and containing a scroll on which this or other mantras are written; rotation of the cylinder enunciates these prayers and actualizes the forces related to them. The prayer wheel is basic to the piety of TIBETAN BUDDHISM, is found also among the Mongols, who received their Buddhism from Tibet, and is used by devotees of the BÖN religion.

The most common form of the prayer wheel is a cylinder placed on the end of a shaft rotated by the worshiper to offer mantras. Rotation is facilitated by means of a small weight attached by a cord to the side of the cylinder which acts as a fly wheel. Hand operated wheels vary in size from as small as three inches to three feet. Huge prayer wheels, as much as twenty feet in height, are found at shrines, as are rows of wheels to be set in motion by worshipers. Prayer wheels may be turned by wind or water, and Tibetan refugees in America have even built ones turned by electric motors. Gigantic prayer wheels contain whole libraries of sacred texts whose rotation brings merit to those otherwise unable to recite the texts. Although these revolving libraries are also found in Japan, the prayer wheel as such is unique to Tibet.

Two ideas inhere in the piety of the prayer wheel: a deep veneration of sacred texts in their written form, and the efficacy attributed to the process of revolving something or of circling a holy object or place. Piety toward the wheel was so great that wheeled vehicles were not used in Tibet until recently. It was believed to be an impiety to roll a wheel on the ground and to place a burden on it. The direction of rotation of the prayer wheel, like that of circumambulation of holy places, must be clockwise to loose the benevolent powers contained in the mantra written on it. Counter-clockwise rotation is believed to loose malevolent spiritual forces. Followers of the Bön religion, however, rotate prayer wheels counter-clockwise.

Bibliography. W. Simpson, *The Buddhist Praying-Wheel* (1896); R. B. Ekvall, *Religious Observances in Tibet* (1964).

D. G. DAWE

PREDESTINATION (Ch & I—Lat. *praedestinare;* Vulgate trans. of Gr. *proorizō,* "to predetermine"). Broadly, the view that all things are predetermined by God; in particular, God's eternal decree in bringing some people to final SALVATION. To some it also includes the eternal damnation of the nonelect. Some have found consolation in the belief that salvation is dependent on the mercy of an Almighty God rather than uncertain human merit; others have found the doctrine depressing. It has been the source of bitter controversies in both Christianity and Islam. In JUDAISM predestination has not been a major doctrine or given rise to significant controversy.

1. **Christianity.** Though God's election of Israel depicted in the OT is seen to be relevant for this doctrine, most Christian adherents rely heavily on Rom. 8:28-29; 9:6-24; Eph. 1:3-14; and II Tim. 1:9.

Prior to AUGUSTINE (A.D. 354-430) there is insufficient evidence for this doctrine. Augustine seems to have elaborated his position chiefly in opposition to Pelagius, though he claimed to have stated his position prior to the controversy. Pelagius, a British monk who reacted against the determinism of MANICHEISM, did not subscribe to ORIGINAL SIN or humanity's fallen condition but asserted that people could be saved by their own merit without divine assistance (*see* PELAGIANISM). He did maintain, however, that God knows who will be saved through their own efforts. Semi-Pelagians held that except for God's prior grace, SALVATION could not be attained through one's own efforts.

Augustine held that God chooses some to salvation through his infallible, elective grace totally apart from human merit. He did not claim to know why God has withheld his mercy from others, but he emphatically asserted that their fate was just, because everyone is under the condemnation of original sin. Augustine maintained that human freedom is not thereby denied. Because he considered predestination a difficult doctrine, however, he advised that it not be preached to the common folk.

Augustinianism was upheld by the Council of Carthage (418), when Pelagianism was condemned, and again at the Second Council of Orange (529), which repudiated Semi-Pelagianism.

Most medieval theologians, e.g., ANSELM and THOMAS AQUINAS, were essentially Augustinian but also asserted God's universal salvific will. This was in essence affirmed by the Council of TRENT (1545); with subtle variations the Roman Catholic Church has continued to maintain that there is no contradiction between free will and predestination. JANSENISM, which held that divine grace could not be resisted by the elect, was condemned by the pope in 1653.

Although CALVIN has been most prominently associated with the doctrine, both ZWINGLI and LUTHER, as well as the pre-Reformation theologians HUSS and WYCLIFFE, held similar views. Luther's views were almost as strong as Calvin's, but subsequent Lutheran creeds greatly moderated his position.

Calvin's critical logic led him to hold a "double" predestination, both the elect and nonelect being chosen to salvation and damnation respectively. Logically this led him to a limited atonement—Christ died only for those elected to salvation. Roman Catholics have called Calvin's and similar views "predestinarianism." Some followers of Calvin dissented, claiming a "single" election only for the elect. Calvin, like Augustine, saw predestination as a mystery and felt that an attempt to satisfy one's curiosity could only lead to more confusion.

Among Calvinists a controversy developed concerning when God's election occurred. One group called supralapsarians (Lat. *lapsus,* fall) maintained God's choice was made before the fall, since election is not dependent on human merit. Their opponents, infralapsarians, held that God's choice was made subsequent to the fall. The Synod of Dort (1618-19) declared for infralapsarianism. The fullest expression of infralapsarian Calvinism is found in the WESTMINSTER CONFESSION (1647).

The Synod of Dort also ruled against ARMINIUS, a Reformed Church theologian, who objected to the Calvinistic depreciation of free will and his belief in a limited atonement. Arminianism strongly influenced the early METHODISTS, who maintained that each person has the possibility of salvation; it was a source of controversy among early BAPTISTS.

In the twentieth century KARL BARTH revived scholarly interest in predestination, but rejected double predestination as unbiblical. Further, he maintained that only in and through Christ, who is the "elect one and the electing one," can humanity know salvation. Although Barth seemingly maintained that an individual could reject Christ, some of his critics have charged him with universalism. (*See* THEOLOGY, CONTEMPORARY CHRISTIAN §3.)

2. Islam. In the QUR'ĀN and SUNNA there is ample evidence for both human freedom and divine sovereignty (predestination). The issue did not become acute until the UMAYYAD dynasty (A.D. 661-750) when a loosely knit group, the Qadariyya, ironically derived from *qadar* (decree of ALLAH), staunchly defended free will. The MU'TAZILA, often falsely identified in the West as "rationalists," attacked the prevailing Islamic thought on theological rather than political grounds by asserting that God would be unjust if he predestined all human actions, both good and evil. Their views were attacked by al-ASH'ARĪ (A.D. 873-935), who advocated a strict predestination to the extent of divine determinism. His position has been generally accepted as the normative Islamic view.

Bibliography. K. Barth, *Church Dogmatics,* II/2, *The Doctrine of God* (1957); J. Calvin, *Institutes of the Christian Religion,* Book III, Vol. I (1928), 587-838; M. J. Farrelly, *Predestination, Grace, and Free Will* (1964); M. Luther, *The Bondage of the Will* (ET 1957); P. Maury, *Predestination and Other Papers* (1960); H. H. Rowley, *The Biblical Doctrine of Election* (1950); W. M. Watt, *Free Will and Predestination in Early Islam* (1948); A. J. Wensinck, *The Muslim Creed* (1965).

T. O. HALL, JR.

PRELATE (Ch—Lat. "prefer"). A high ranking ecclesiastical official such as BISHOP, ARCHBISHOP, or PATRIARCH. K. WATKINS

PRESBYTER prĕz´ bə tûr (Ch—Gk.; lit. "elder"). In the NT and early Christianity, a member of the governing body of a local church; there is no agreement as to the relationship of presbyter to BISHOP in this period. In many churches, the basic order of ordained CLERGY. In REFORMED CHURCHES, either a clergyman or a member of the laity elected to the office of ELDER. K. CRIM

PRESBYTERIAN CHURCHES (Ch). *See* REFORMED CHURCHES.

PRESBYTERIANISM (Ch—Gr. *presbuteros;* lit. "elder"). Form of church governance in which authority is vested in a presbytery or classis, a regional organization to which the local churches under its jurisdiction send representatives consisting of equal numbers of ministers (*see* CLERGY) and lay elders. Customary in REFORMED CHURCHES. K. CRIM

PRETA prā´ tū (B—Skt.; lit. "a dead person"). One of the states of being. In TENDAI and other MAHĀYĀNA groups, one of the six ordinary states (deity, human, ASURA, *preta,* animal, being in hell) contrasted to the four heavenly realms (BUDDHA, Pratyeka Buddha, BODHISATTVA, *śrāvaka; see* BUDDHA, GENERAL CONCEPTS OF). In China *pretas* came to be called "hungry ghosts" and were thought of as having tiny heads and huge stomachs, so that no amount of food could satisfy them. The *Petavatthu,* an early text in PALI, paints in vivid detail the deformities and frustrations of *pretas.* They were said to reside in hell itself, or one of its anterooms, from which they wander forth at evening in search of food, especially during the seven days ending at the fifteenth day of the seventh lunar month. A special festival, the Ullambana, is held on the fifteenth to relieve their misery by providing them with food and religious instruction, so that in their next birth they may be born in a higher realm.

Bibliography. J. Takakusu, *The Essentials of Buddhist Philosophy* (1956), pp. 131-41; H. Welch, *The Practice of Chinese Buddhism, 1900-1950* (1967), pp. 179-88.

K. CRIM

PRIEST (Gr. derived from presbyter, "elder"). 1. (Ch) An ordained minister in ROMAN CATHOLIC, ANGLICAN, ORTHODOX, and some other churches, authorized to preach, administer the sacraments, and participate in governing the church; a member of the

Aaronic or second order of the Church of Jesus Christ of LATTER-DAY SAINTS.

2. Often used as the translation of terms in various languages that designate personnel who perform similar duties in other religions, e.g. BUDDHISM and SHINTŌ. K. WATKINS

PRIMATE (Ch—Lat. "first"). The BISHOP, ARCHBISHOP, PATRIARCH, or other high ranking ecclesiastical official who holds the place of highest honor among the bishops of a nation or other large area. K. WATKINS

PRIOR (Ch—Lat. "superior"). A high ranking officer in certain organized religious communities; in some orders second in command to the ABBOT, while in others the chief officer; in some cases the officer in charge of a group of houses or local communities of a RELIGIOUS ORDER. K. WATKINS

PROFANATION OF THE HOST (Ju). Accusation that Jews desecrated the wafer (host) used in the Roman Catholic MASS and believed to be changed into the body and blood of Christ. First found in the Middle Ages, the libel is found as late as 1836 in Romania. Jews were said to profane the consecrated host by stabbing and otherwise "tormenting" it. The first such recorded accusation (1243) was followed by many others, particularly in Germany, Belgium, and France. In Spain the accusation was also made against Jews who had been baptized as Christians. *See* ANTI-SEMITISM.

Bibliography. J. Trachtenberg, *The Devil and the Jews* (1943). E. FLEISCHNER

PROPHET IN ISLAM. *See* NABI.

PROTESTANTISM (Ch). That form of Western Christianity which does not accept the authority of the pope of ROMAN CATHOLICISM (*see* PAPACY). It accents biblical authority and highlights the reality of grace in the Christian life.

1. **History: origin, growth, expansion.** The name "Protestant" comes from a statement made by a party of Christians at the Diet of Speyer in Germany (1529). The roots of Protestantism, however, lie well beyond that date in the stirrings of reform that occurred in western Europe almost a century earlier. At that time the Roman Catholic Church was the only Christian body in western Europe, though there had been small breakaway sects throughout the Middle Ages.

In Bohemia, JOHN HUSS became restless over papal authority and concerned about the neglect of the Scriptures and the doctrine of grace, but he was burned as a heretic in 1415. Huss in turn had been inspired by the English reformer JOHN WYCLIFFE (d. 1384). Yet such pioneer critics of Catholic order were not able to sustain a large movement. The permanent Protestant cause began when within a two-decade period MARTIN LUTHER in Germany, JOHN CALVIN and ULRICH ZWINGLI in Switzerland, and a number of reformers in the Netherlands, Scotland, and most of all in England, broke with Roman Catholicism. In the course of the century Protestantism spread throughout northern Europe, which remains its homeland. During this period the Protestant parties also produced documents of faith to define themselves over against Catholicism and each other. (*See* REFORMATION, PROTESTANT; CREEDS AND CONFESSIONS.)

After a creed-writing period in which Protestants solidified their positions and established their boundaries, many felt that spirituality had grown cold. On the continent PIETIST parties thereupon developed to nurture more warmth and the renewal of the established state churches. In England, PURITANISM came as a form of judgment against what it felt was a half-reformed Church of England. It was the Protestantism of this period that English settlers brought to the colonies in the New World.

After the Puritan and Pietist era, many Protestants in Europe and America were influenced by the rationalism of the Enlightenment. This again turned out to be too sterile for most tastes, and an era of revivals, awakenings, and conversions followed. The Wesleyan or METHODIST movement was the largest of these. During this period Protestants also finally were moved to carry on worldwide missionary activity. Numbers of societies for mission were formed in England in the 1790s, and subsequently others sent agents from the United States to join earlier continental missionaries. (*See* MISSIONS, CHRISTIAN.)

The nineteenth century was a period of theological experiment, particularly in Germany. But most Protestants expended their energies on coming to terms with the urban and industrial orders, since they were located where the Industrial Revolution took off most aggressively, and, many said, were among the agents of that Revolution. Twentieth century Protestantism has devoted much energy to overcoming the divisions that dogged the faith since the sixteenth century.

2. **Scripture and teaching.** The early Protestants complained that Catholics had elevated church tradition at the expense of the BIBLE. The Reformation occurred during the expansion of print cultures, and the translation and distribution of Bibles became a passion among Protestants. As Protestants abolished papal authority, they elevated scripture, and some almost idolized it. To this day many Protestants take the Bible literally and have fashioned elaborate doctrines to support claims for its inerrancy and infallibility. (*See* EVANGELICALS; FUNDAMENTALISM.) Others have taken more moderate views, seeing it as the final church authority and hearing in it the Word of God, but recognizing in it many complexities.

No other writings are on par with the Scriptures in Protestantism, though every group tends to revere the creedal documents with which their ancestors defined themselves in the first two Protestant centuries. Protestantism remains a faith devoted to print, however, and disseminates its teachings through written and published sermons, prayers, theology books, and apologies.

Most Protestants have asserted that at the heart of the biblical good news or GOSPEL as they understand it is a witness to the gift of God. This gift takes the form of the divine entrance in history of JESUS Christ, his sacrificing and atoning death on the cross, and the blessing of new and eternal life that comes with his RESURRECTION. In Protestant teaching, no one can merit this gift, and no one can draw the pleasure of God by doing good works. God simply elects to favor humans. (*See* JUSTIFICATION BY FAITH.)

3. **Social institutions.** Protestants took over many of the social forms of western Catholicism and unanimously rejected only the papacy. But while many churches, notably ANGLICANS and some LUTHERANS, kept the office of BISHOP and episcopal patterns, the Protestant tendency has been to disperse power. Local congregations usually have most authority and in some traditions are utterly independent. Protestants also innovated by insisting that laity are on the same status before God as are the CLERGY. In practice, despite this status and the sharing of power, Protestant clergy tend to be honored because the acts of preaching and administering the SACRAMENTS are chiefly theirs.

While Protestants have been especially fertile at inventing denominations, they also pioneered in a shared "errand of mercy." Out of this nineteenth century endeavor came the impulse for voluntary associations to improve human welfare and to spread humanitarian reform. In recent times the tendency in Protestantism of many polities has been to turn bureaucratic, so that even congregationally minded groups like the BAPTISTS link up for many functions.

4. **Ethics and customs.** While Protestants kept alive most features of the Catholic ethic of charity, some modern scholars have ascribed to them a major role in developing the world of production and capitalism. The German sociologist Max Weber, perhaps while neglecting similar motifs among other people, seemed to assign a monopoly to Protestants when he wrote of "the Protestant ethic." In this pattern Protestants felt called of God, and they proved their election by achieving much in the world. They became especially ambitious, zealous to be good stewards. Many of them therefore risked capital, raised their status and social class, became wealthy, and were asked to share their wealth.

While Protestants have included many of the poor of the earth, their chief locations in Europe and North America made it possible for most of them to be moderately well off, and critics have spoken of theirs as a bourgeois ethic. While they have produced their share of fanatics, prophets, MILLENARIANS, and utopians, for the most part the Protestant temperament has been seen as steady, somewhat stern, and moralistic. Protestants have also been supportive of the family, and despite a tradition of restraint among the pleasures of life, have seen themselves as a serene and joyful people.

5. **Rituals and worship activities.** For most Protestants, SUNDAY morning is the time for worship, though many have mid-week and evening gatherings as well. While Catholic Christianity accentuates the MASS or sacred meal, Protestants favor a more verbal kind of service, whose climax usually is the preached word. They like to describe theirs as singing churches, in which the laity participates in the enjoyment of hymns. (*See* MUSIC, IN CHRISTIANITY.) Worship is often informal, but the effort to experience the presence of God lends it solemnity. The Lord's Supper (EUCHARIST) and BAPTISM are the two main rites and the only two regarded as sacraments by Protestants. They follow the calendar which highlights CHRISTMAS, EASTER, and the festival of PENTECOST, but for the most part are less concerned to observe days of SAINTS and MARTYRS than are Catholic and Orthodox Christians. (*See* CALENDAR, CHRISTIAN.)

Protestants appeared on the European scene at a time of decline from high medieval Christian art, when secular themes came to dominate in the Renaissance. But their suspicion of idolatry also led them to minimize images and visual art. There have been exceptions, among them the Dutch master Rembrandt, but most Protestant expression has been in the form of music—one thinks of J. S. Bach or the tradition of English hymnody—and literature. *See* ART AND ARCHITECTURE, CHRISTIAN.

Bibliography. R. McA. Brown, *The Spirit of Protestantism* (1961); J. Dillenberger and C. Welch, *Protestant Christianity Interpreted Through Its Development* (1954); M. E. Marty, *Protestantism* (1972); R. Mehl, *The Sociology of Protestantism* (1970); M. Weber, *The Protestant Ethic and the Spirit of Capitalism* (1930); J. S. Whale, *The Protestant Tradition* (1955).

M. E. MARTY

PROTOCOLS OF THE ELDERS OF ZION (Ju). Late nineteenth century anti-Semitic forgery designed to prove a worldwide Jewish conspiracy to seize financial and political power. Based on medieval legends (*see* ANTI-SEMITISM), the *Protocols* were written in Paris by an unknown author, probably for the Russian secret police of Czar Nicholas II. At first largely ignored, they gained wide acceptance after World War I in many European countries. The theory of a secret Jewish world power was widely used by the Nazis (*see* HOLOCAUST). Since World War II the myth has been dismissed in the West, but persists here and there in Arab countries.

Bibliography. N. Cohn, *Warrant for Genocide* (1967).

E. FLEISCHNER

PṚTHIVĪ prĭ´ tĭ vē (H—Skt.; lit. "earth"). A Hindu goddess personifying the earth. Associated in early texts with the male god Dyaus Pitā, the sky. In later Hinduism she is known as Bhūdevī and becomes the consort of the god VISHNU. *See* GODDESS (INDIA) §1.

D. R. KINSLEY

PSEUDO-DIONYSIUS THE AREOPAGITE sōō´ dō dī ō nĭsh´ ĭ əs ăr´ ē ŏp´ ə jīt (Ch; *ca.* 500). Mystical writer and pseudonymous author of treatises and letters combining Neoplatonic and Christian ideas to establish the pattern of purification, illumination, and union for MYSTICISM. For Dionysius mystic experience is an "unknowing" beyond all thought and a "darkness" produced by absolute divine transcendence *(Mystical Theology)*. The material world is understood as a symbol of invisible divine reality *(Celestial Hierarchies)*. However, true knowledge of God is "negative," reached by defining what God is not *(Letter 5; Divine Names)*. Influential in medieval theology and mysticism, he was accepted until the sixteenth century as the convert of St. PAUL (Acts 17:34). Modern scholarship attributes the works to an unknown Syrian monk of the sixth century.

Bibliography. The English trans. of C. E. Rolt (1920) should be used with care. Excellent French trans. by M. de Gandillac (1943). See *The Cambridge History of Later Greek and Early Medieval Philosophy* (1970), ch. 30.

G. A. ZINN

PŪJĀ pōō´ jä (H—Skt.; lit. "honor, worship"). The ritual offering of various goods, services, and signs of respect to an honored recipient; the most common form of Hindu worship for the past 1,500 years. The most typical form is *deva-pūjā*, the "honoring" of a deity in the form of an image. Like many elements of Hinduism, *deva-pūjā* is a blend of popular religious practices with a ritual form derived from the VEDIC tradition.

Pūjā is first mentioned in the Gṛhya Sūtras, a class of Vedic texts which gives rules for domestic rituals. Among these rules is a set of prescriptions for honoring Brahmins (priests) invited to one's home on the occasion of rites for departed ancestors. The hospitality prescribed is called *pūjā*, and includes many of the ritual actions and MANTRAS (prayers) later used in the worship of deities. It seems clear that *deva-pūjā* began as a special application of these rituals to deities as honored guests in the household, and was then extended to worship of deities elsewhere.

The deities worshiped by *pūjā* are those of the popular devotional theism known as BHAKTI HINDUISM. *Pūjā* in the sense of deity worship is mentioned in an inscription of the second century B.C., but *deva-pūjā* is first described in detail only in special sections added to the PURĀṆAS, the main scriptures of Bhakti Hinduism, from the sixth century A.D. onward. By then, the basic Gṛhya Sūtra ritual had been merged with theistic devotion to produce a ritual used in both home shrines and temples.

The basic form of *pūjā* is most evident in its original setting, the home shrine. Most Hindu households have a special area set aside for performing *pūjā* to family deities in the form of images. The ritual can range from a simple set of worshipful acts to an elaborate procedure. The simplest *pūjā* might be only the offering of water, flowers, or food, burning incense, or reciting a mantra to the deity. More elaborate *pūjā* can involve an extended series of rituals expressing honor and hospitality: invocation and praise, offerings of water for washing and sipping, bathing the image, offering a fresh garment, offering flowers and incense, waving a burning lamp before the deity, offering food and gifts, and bidding the deity farewell.

Many of the same elements appear in *deva-pūjā* performed in temples, but there the context is often altered by the concept of the deity as a king or queen residing in the temple as a palace. The routine of the temple is then modeled after that of a palace, with the temple priests as ministers and staff performing private services and conducting public ceremonies for viewing and worshiping the deity.

Bibliography. P. V. Kane, *History of Dharmaśāstra,* II (1941), 705-40, a detailed history and description of *deva-pūjā;* J. Gonda, *Viṣṇuism and Śivaism* (1970), pp. 75-86, a discussion of the ritual forms and meanings of *deva-pūjā* in Vaiṣṇavite and Śaivite temples.

T. J. HOPKINS

PUÑÑA pûn´ yŭ (B—Pali; "merit") **PUṆYA** pûn´ yŭ (Skt.). The spiritual energy which results from good moral actions (KARMA) and which brings happiness in this or a future life, or rewards in heaven.

1. **Puñña in early Buddhism.** Merit, as the power of good karma, is important in HINDUISM, JAINISM, and especially BUDDHISM. In the VINAYA and the Suttas of the THERAVĀDA canon there are numerous references to *puñña* and *pāpa*, meaning "good karma" and "bad karma." The BUDDHA encouraged lay men and women to lay up treasures of merit so that they could face death without fear. Generous giving is seen as the model of meritorious actions, whereas causing harm is the paradigmatic evil. After death those who are evil and lack merit suffer in hell or in an evil rebirth—such as that of a low animal or a hungry ghost (PRETA)—while meritorious people are reborn in heaven or in a happy earthly life.

The early Buddhists redirected the traditional piety of the laity in an effort to gain support for Buddhism vis-à-vis other sectarian movements and VEDIC Brahmanism by reinterpreting the traditional practices of sacrificing, granting hospitality, making offerings, and venerating holy persons. The new position was reflected in the formula recurrent in the canon confessing that the Buddhist SAṄGHA is "worthy of sacrifice, hospitality, offerings, and veneration—being the unsurpassed merit-field for all the world." The point is that gifts and other support given to Buddhist monks will generate great merit for the giver.

2. **Puñña in popular stories.** The fifth division of the SUTTA PIṬAKA contains several collections of didactic stories that illustrate the effects of *puñña* or *apuñña,* merit and demerit. The underlying belief is that acts of merit bring one a corresponding, multiple reward in heaven, with demerit similarly producing great punishment in hell or as a ghost. For example, in a typical story from the Vimāna-vatthu, "Stories of Heavenly Mansions," we learn that a woman who is now enjoying a heavenly mansion with many lotus ponds earned it by offering lotuses to a Buddha shrine. The fruitfulness of such offering varies with the spirituality (not the need) of the recipient, ranging from a Buddha or ARHANT as the most fertile object of merit down to animals as the least fruitful. Similarly, in some schools of MAHĀYĀNA Buddhism, devotion to Buddhas such as AMIDA is thought to merit rebirth in their respective Buddha-lands.

3. **Means of merit.** As Buddhism developed into a religion that provided spiritual paths to the laity as well as to ordained disciples, acts of "making merit" became more important. Such merit activities are not to be thought of as magical means to heaven, but rather as continuing opportunities for spiritual purification. That is, merit is a spiritual power, not a physical one, so terms such as "treasures in heaven" are metaphorical.

All morally good actions of thought, word, or deed are meritorious, but traditionally ten means of merit are listed: giving, practicing morality, meditating, respecting elders, serving a superior, giving (transferring) the merit obtained, rejoicing at receiving transferred merit, giving instruction in doctrine, listening to preaching and chanting, and correcting one's views. The giving of alms to monks remains the most important means of merit today. Almsgiving is practiced as part of every major festival (often called "merit-making") and daily in those Buddhist countries where monks still go from house to house for alms, as well as on special occasions such as a birthday, anniversary, or memorial, when several monks are invited to a home for "an almsgiving" which includes the meritorious giving of gifts and the transfer or sharing of the merit with others, especially the departed. (*See* DĀNA.) The sharing of merit is itself a meritorious action which does not cause one to forego the merit.

Besides the merit practices oriented to the *Saṅgha,* others center around scripture (translating, copying, reciting, hearing) and the Buddha (veneration of images, the BODHI tree, or a STŪPA).

Merit-making is subordinate to NIRVANA as a goal, and the two are related in theory by saying that progress in merit is at the same time progress in purification, which therefore advances one toward Nirvana. Especially in Theravāda countries the tendency has been for laity and even monks to pursue merit more seriously, assuming sainthood to be beyond reach in this life. This has had the effect of making *puñña* uppermost in popular Buddhism.

Bibliography. R. C. Amore, "The Concept and Practice of Doing Merit in Early Theravada Buddhism" (Columbia Univ. diss., 1970); R. Gombrich, " 'Merit Transference' in Sinhalese Buddhism," *HR,* XI (1971), 203-19; C. von Fürer-Haimendorf, *Morals and Merit* (1967), an anthropological approach.

R. C. AMORE

PURĀṆA pū rän′ ä (H—Skt). Belonging to ancient times, an event of the past, ancient legend; the name of a class of Hindu sacred writings containing ancient stories.

The Purāṇas are collections of Indian myths and legends, and are a major source for understanding Hinduism. They contain cosmologies, legends of the gods, goddesses, demons, ancestors, genealogies, descriptions of pilgrimages, and rituals, and illustrate the importance of CASTE, DHARMA, and BHAKTI. If GANDHI believed the BHAGAVAD GĪTĀ to be a "dictionary for life," then the Purāṇas are the encyclopedia of that dictionary for all of Hinduism.

Written in SANSKRIT, the stories and teachings are told in the form of answers to questions. Because material has been edited, revised, and amplified over a very long period of India's religious history, no Purāṇa has a single author or precise date of composition. Together they comprise an important record of the oral tradition and development of Hinduism as the religion of India.

Although the Purāṇas are numerous, eighteen have been called Mahāpurāṇas ("Great Purāṇas"). Each of the great Purāṇas provides a list of the eighteen which includes its own title. Many of the Purāṇas cite Vyāsa as the original author of the stories, thus making the texts divine, since Vyāsa is also reputed to be the author of the VEDAS. The Mahāpurāṇas agree on the following list: 1) Brahmā, 2) Padma, 3) Vishnu, 4) Shiva, 5) Bhāgavata, 6) Nāradīya (Nārada), 7) Mārkaṇḍeya, 8) Agni, 9) Bhavishya, 10) Brahmavaivarta, 11) Liṅga, 12) Varāha, 13) Skanda, 14) Vāmana, 15) Kūrma, 16) Matsya, 17) Garuḍa, and 18) Brahmāṇḍa Purāṇa. There are also lists of eighteen Upapurāṇas ("Minor Purāṇas").

The stories of the Purāṇas are primarily concerned with the personalities and deeds of BRAHMĀ (the creator), VISHNU (the preserver), and SHIVA (the destroyer), together with each of their consorts; SARASVATĪ (goddess of music and learning), LAKṢMĪ (Vishnu's wife and goddess of fortune), and PĀRVATĪ (Shiva's wife). One of the basic characteristics of the Purāṇas is the "sectarian" message they contain. The Padma Purāṇa, for example, classifies all eighteen Purāṇas as parts of Vishnu's body, while the Shiva, Liṅga, and Skanda Purāṇas are texts which praise the worship of Shiva.

Despite the complexity and diversity of the material we can detect several important topics which the Purāṇas have in common. The first is a description of the "five subjects": 1) creation of the cosmos; 2) destruction and renovation of the cosmos; 3) the genealogy of the gods and sages; 4) a description of the various MANU (father of man) periods of time (*see* MANU, LAWS OF); 5) a history of dynasties which are traced back to ancient, mythical times. The Vishnu Purāṇa follows this description very closely.

The second important topic is the practice of devotion (*see* BHAKTI HINDUISM). The Purāṇas are rich in descriptions of devotional practices such as prayers, recitations of the virtue of a deity, rituals to ancestors, and the importance of pilgrimages to sacred shrines and rivers. In fact, it is claimed that simply reading or hearing the words of a particular Purāṇa provides special advantages in this world or the next. Knowing and practicing the teachings of the Purāṇas breaks the chain of KARMA.

The BHĀGAVATA PURĀṆA, the best example of the Purāṇic stress on devotion and the most famous of all the Purāṇas in India, was the first to be translated into English (1840). It is closely related to the Vishnu Purāṇa in its description of the cosmology and Vishnu's AVATARS (which include the BUDDHA and the life of KRISHNA). Books X and XI remain the most popular of the Bhāgavata's sections because Krishna's legend is given far greater detail here than in either the Vishnu Purāṇa or the Harivaṃśa (the last book of the MAHĀBHĀRATA).

A third important topic is DHARMA, religious and social duty. Given the two major types of salvation in Hinduism, this worldly action (dharma) and other-worldly mysticism (MOKṢA), the Purāṇas clearly demand worldly action in the context of devotion to god. The Purāṇic emphasis on CASTE duties and the first three of the four HINDU AIMS OF LIFE displaces *mokṣa* (release) as the essential path for resolving suffering. The Purāṇas are a crucial correction to the view that Hinduism is primarily a religion of asceticism and otherworldly mysticism.

Bibliography. M. Winternitz, *A History of Indian Literature,* Vol. I (1972); P. V. Kane, *History of Dharmaśāstra,* Vol. I, pt. 1, Vol. V, pt. 2 (2nd. ed., 1962 and after); W. D. O'Flaherty, *Hindu Myths* (1975); C. Dimmitt and J. A. B. van Buitenen, eds., *Classical Hindu Mythology* (1978).

H. H. PENNER

PURDAH pûr′ də (I—Per. *pardah,* Arab. *ḥijāb*; lit. "curtain, screen"). The Islamic institution of secluding women from view of strangers and men and of requiring them to be fully covered and veiled in public. The basis for it is in the QUR'ĀN, Sura 33:53, "And when ye ask of them [the wives of the Prophet] anything, ask it of them from behind a curtain. That is purer for your hearts and for their hearts." Later the separation was extended to include all free Muslim women, especially those of the leisured town classes.

A prominent dimension of *purdah* has been the harem, the private quarters of Muslim homes, closed to outsiders. This institution has exotic associations for Westerners, but in the main it has simply been the domestic menage of women and children. Sura 24:31 lists the categories of persons allowed access to the harem: "And tell the believing women . . . to draw their veils over their bosoms, and not to reveal their adornment save to their own husbands or fathers or husbands' fathers, or their sons or their husbands' sons, or their brothers or their brothers' sons or sisters' sons, or their women, or their slaves, or male attendants who lack vigour, children who know naught of women's nakedness" (Pickthall trans.).

Purdah has largely died out in the modern period, although it persists in more traditional regions like Saudi Arabia and Pakistan. Egyptian women led the way in abandoning the veil around the turn of this century; it was outlawed in Turkey in 1935.

Bibliography. E. W. Lane, *An Account of the Manners and Customs of the Modern Egyptians* (rpr. 1954).

F. M. DENNY

PURE LAND (B—Skt. *sukhāvatī;* Chin. *chi'ng t'u;* Jap. *jōdo*). The "Western Paradise" over which AMIDA Buddha presides. A rich, fertile, and delightful land inhabited by gods and humans, who never meet with or hear of anything unpleasant or painful. The longer version of the Pure Land Sūtra says that rebirth in the Pure Land is the result of good deeds as well as devotion to Amida. The shorter version states that only faith and prayer are necessary.

H. B. EARHART

PURE LAND SECTS (B). Those Buddhist sects of East Asia which emphasize aspects of MAHĀYĀNA Buddhism stressing faith in AMIDA, meditation on and recitation of his name, and the religious goal of being reborn in his "Pure Land," or "Western Paradise." The Pure Land sects are especially important in Japan and Korea.

There was no Pure Land sect as such in India, although Indian Buddhism provided many elements for this later development, including the notion that Amida resides in a kind of paradise or Pure Land (Skt. *Sukhāvatī*) in the West, and that humans may attain Buddhahood through faith in him. This story is contained in several Sanskrit versions and Chinese translations of the Sukhāvatīvyūha Sūtra, which relates how Amida, once a human, received instruction in Buddhism and was able to examine the many Buddha-lands. He was so impressed that he vowed to practice Buddhism until he could create his own Buddha-land and bring all sentient beings to this paradise. After many *kalpas* (cycles of time) and the accumulation of great merit, he attained enlightenment and became Amida Buddha, thereby fulfilling his vow and making it possible for other humans to be reborn in this Pure Land. This is the Indian heritage of the later Pure Land sects, although it is not clear to what extent practices related to the Pure Land were active in India.

Many versions of Buddhism were taken to China, and by the third and fourth centuries A.D. some Buddhists had begun to focus on devotion to the

D. K. Swearer

Pure Land priests demonstrate the mixture of old and new in Japan today.

statue of Amida and to form societies featuring faith in him. Three of the great Chinese Pure Land figures who systematized and spread this faith were T'an-luan (476-542), Tao-cho (562-645), and Shan-tao (613-681). This Chinese development of Pure Land teachings was based on the notion that their time coincided with the last of three declining periods of Buddhism (*see* MAPPŌ), and that in this degenerate age people had to rely on the power of Amida for salvation, rather than their own power as humans. Earlier Buddhism, the "holy path" or difficult manner of practicing Buddhism, was contrasted with this Pure Land path, or easy way of practicing Buddhism. This teaching and its simple practice appealed to the masses and spread quickly, being adopted even by other Buddhist sects, such as ZEN, and spreading to Korea and Japan.

In Japan some aspects of Pure Land teaching were present shortly after the introduction of Buddhism in the sixth century, but little attention was paid to it. It was not until Saichō (DENGYŌ DAISHI) brought back from China practices of meditation centered around Amida that considerable attention was focused on this divinity. Saichō founded the TENDAI sect on Mt. Hiei, which became one of the greatest monastic and scholastic centers in Japan. It was the Tendai sect that preserved the traditions relating to Amida, later rediscovered by founders of Japanese Pure Land sects.

Pure Land devotion had been present since NARA times and practices had spread from the Tendai to other sects, with some figures such as Kūya (903-972) attempting to teach the masses. But Genshin (942-1017) set forth the theoretical basis for preferring the practice of reciting the name of Amida and entering the Pure Land of Amida. This marked a transition from earlier Tendai practices to the simple recitation of Amida's name, *namu-amida-butsu* ("I place my faith in Amida Buddha"), known in Japan as NEMBUTSU. A number of other priests are known for furthering the cause of Pure Land devotion, but the foremost founders in Japan are HŌNEN and SHINRAN, founder of Jōdo Shin-shū (Pure Land True Sect).

Hōnen's intense personal faith and insistence on practicing only the nembutsu made him a powerful leader of the Pure Land sect. He is said to have recited 60,000 or more nembutsu each day, recommending nembutsu as the means of purifying oneself in order to attain enlightenment or to be reborn (*ōjō*) in the Pure Land. In modern times *ōjō* is used euphemistically to refer to a person's death, in the sense of one having gone to paradise.

The Pure Land sects in Japan have split into many different ecclesiastical groups, each with its own doctrinal emphases and religious traditions, but generally three sūtras are authoritative: *Daimuryōju-kyō, Amidakyō, and Kanmuryōjukyō.* The Pure Land groups have more members than any other Japanese Buddhist sects, and Pure Land devotion such as the nembutsu is practiced by many people not formally affiliated with the Pure Land sects.

Bibliography. D. and A. Matsunaga, *Foundation of Japanese Buddhism,* 2 vols. (1974-76). H. B. EARHART

PURGATORY (Ch—Lat. *purgatorius;* lit. "purging"). According to Catholic belief, the state or place of final purification for those who, though they die in God's friendship, have not been freed before death from all traces whatsoever of their sin. Only two points have been defined in Catholic teaching: (1) purgatory exists; (2) prayer for the dead is helpful and appropriate. Agreement between Latins and Greeks on these points was rendered explicit in the Decree of Union at the Council of Florence in 1445; and the same teaching was reaffirmed at the Council of TRENT (Session XXV) without further explication. The notion of purgatory is implicit in the early liturgical and devotional practice of offering prayers and the celebration of the EUCHARIST on behalf of the departed; and early Greek and Latin theologians often speak explicitly about this state of purification after death with reference to II Macc. 12:39-45; Matt. 12:32, 36; I Cor. 3:11-15. Catholic doctrine on purgatory is based chiefly, however, on tradition rooted less in a specific biblical text than in biblical teaching concerning the holiness of God, the nature of sin, the reality of divine judgment, and human destiny to live with God for all eternity. *See* DEAD, PRAYERS FOR THE.

Bibliography. P. Fransen, "The Doctrine of Purgatory," *Eastern Churches Quarterly,* XIII (1959), 99-112; R. Guardini, *The Last Things* (1954).

C. WADDELL

PURIFICATION (I). The QUR'ĀN states: "O ye who believe. When ye rise up for prayer, wash your faces, and your hands up to the elbows, and lightly rub your heads and [wash] your feet up to the ankles. And if ye are unclean, purify yourselves" (5:6). The Qur'ān itself should be handled only by the ritually pure (56:79). According to tradition (ḤADĪTH) MUHAMMAD said: "Purification is half the faith" (MUSLIM IBN AL-ḤAJJĀJ) and "The key to paradise is prayer and the key to prayer is purification" (IBN ḤANBAL).

The law books always begin with religious duties, at the head of which is ritual purity *(Ṭahāra).* There are two types: physical and spiritual, obtained respectively by correct washing and a pious life of service. Physical pollution is of two kinds. (1) *Najāsa* is essentially caused by impure matter touching the body, clothing, or prayer place (e.g. urine, feces, blood, wine and other intoxicants, dogs, pigs, carrion). This is removed by washing with water. (2) *Ḥadath* pertains to the believer's person, and is of two types. *a)* "Minor *ḥadath*" is caused by sleeping; the passing of urine, wind, or feces; loss of consciousness (as in fainting); skin contact between mutually marriageable persons; touching the genitals. It is removed by WUḌŪ', ablution, centering in the acts prescribed in Qur'ān 5.6 (above). When purified in this manner, the believer is permitted to perform the *ṣalāt,* handle the Qur'ān, or enter a MOSQUE. *b)* "Major *ḥadath*" is caused by any seminal emission, any sexual penetration, female orgasm with secretion (these three are also known as *janāba*); menstruation; postpartum bleeding. Purification is by *ghusl,* a thorough bathing of the entire body in a prescribed manner. *Ghusl* is the survivor's first duty toward the corpse of a deceased Muslim, before shrouding and burial. All purification rites must be preceded and accompanied by *niyya,* "right intention," as in performing *ṣalāt.* (*See* PRAYER IN ISLAM.)

There is a considerable etiquette of purity in Islam, in addition to what is mandatory. The lavatory should be entered left foot first and exited with the right (the opposite of entering and leaving a mosque). Only the left hand may be used for cleansing after micturation or evacuation (known as *istinjā',* and performed with paper and/or water and/or stones no fewer than three times). *Ghusl* should be performed before attending Friday *ṣalāt,* after washing a corpse, before entering the state of *iḥrām* of the pilgrimage (see HAJJ), and at other times.

Bibliography. The details often vary between SUNNITES and SHI'ITES and among schools. For a clear overview see M. A. Rauf, *Islam: Creed and Worship* (1974), pp. 21-46; M. M. Pickthall, trans., *The Meaning of the Glorious Koran,* 4:43; 24:21; Al-Baghawī, *Mishkāt al-Maṣābīḥ,* ET J. Robson (1960-65), I, 64-113.

F. M. DENNY

F. M. Denny

Ablutions before prayer, Muhammad Ali Mosque, Cairo

PURIM pŭr ĭm´ (Ju—Heb.; lit. "lots"). A minor festival based on events in the biblical book of Esther, which is read publicly during the festival. A special liturgy is used, but there are no restrictions on work. The story of Esther centers around the attempts of the Persian prime minister, Haman, to kill all Jews throughout the empire on the fourteenth of Adar (February-March), a day chosen by lot *(pur).* Only by the efforts of Mordecai, a Jew living in the capital city, and his cousin Esther was the plot thwarted. Esther had become queen, and she persuaded the king to let the Jews defend themselves. Haman was hanged, and his position was given to Mordecai. The fourteenth of Adar thus became a day of "feasting and gladness" (Esth. 9:22).

Esther was one of the last books admitted to the Hebrew Bible, and the support for the celebration of Purim was from the people rather than from the RABBIS. It is a tradition to eat triangular fruit pies known as *Hamantaschen* (Haman's hats), and contrary to usual Jewish practice heavy drinking is permitted. Food and confections are shared with neighbors, and charity is given to the needy. Special noisemakers are used to drown out the name of Haman each time it occurs as the book is read.

Bibliography. P. Goodman, *The Purim Anthology* (1960).

D. J. SCHNALL

PURITANS (Ch). A name applied to reformist groups discontented with the religious settlement of the Church of England by Queen Elizabeth I (1558-1603). They desired a more thorough reformation according to strict biblical norms by the removal of remnants of Catholic tradition in church government, liturgy, and discipline. Although many conformed to the established church, others separated from it or sought refuge in the American colonies. Puritan ethic and spirituality has been an enduring influence in English and American Protestantism. *See* BAPTISTS; CONGREGATIONALISM; FRIENDS, SOCIETY OF; PILGRIM FATHERS; PIETISM; REFORMED CHURCHES.

Bibliography. W. Haller, *The Rise of Puritanism 1570-1643* (1938); M. M. Knappen, *Tudor Puritanism* (1939); H. Davies, *The Worship of the English Puritans* (1948); A. Simpson, *Puritanism in Old and New England* (1961); P. Collinson, *The Elizabethan Puritan Movement* (1967).

M. H. SHEPHERD, JR.

PURUṢA poo rōō′ shä (H—Skt.; lit. "man, self, person, soul" [possibly from *pṛ*—"to fill with air, to become full of, to become complete"]).

1. In a late RIG VEDA hymn (X.90) Puruṣa is the creator god in the form of a man. With a thousand heads and a thousand eyes this giant offspring of BRAHMĀ "embraced the worlds on all sides" (v.1). As such, Puruṣa is a transcendent and immortal god who becomes partially immanent in his creation (vv. 2-4). From him arose Virāj ("the ruling"), who is usually identified as his feminine counterpart and mate in the creation process (v.5). As a secondary creator born of Brahmā, Puruṣa is often identified with PRAJĀPATI, a Vedic god of creation (cf. ŚB XI.1.6). A second feature of the Puruṣa hymn is the origin of the sacrifice (YAJÑA) in which the divine Puruṣa *is* the offering (vv. 6-10). From the dismembered body of the Puruṣa the four traditional CASTE groupings arise: the BRAHMINS from his mouth, the *rājanya* or KṢATRIYA from his arms, the VAIŚYA from his thighs, and the ŚŪDRAS from his feet (vv. 10-12). Therefore, both the sacrifice as the central ritual of VEDIC HINDUISM and the fourfold grouping of persons according to *varṇa* or birth-class are given scriptural sanction in this celebrated Puruṣa hymn. L. D. SHINN

2. The principle of pure "consciousness" in classical SĀṂKHYA and YOGA philosophy. Consciousness *(puruṣa)* is described as a contentless, transparent, and nonintentional presence, incapable of action of any kind, and totally separate from the transactions and interactions of ordinary awareness (intellect and ego). From an ontological point of view, *puruṣa* is radically distinct from nature (PRAKṚTI), but a fundamental epistemological confusion leads ordinary persons to identify *puruṣa* and *prakṛti*. This failure to discriminate the two principles, usually called nondiscrimination or ignorance (AVIDYĀ), is the basic cause for the suffering that is characteristic of the ordinary human condition. The purpose of Sāṃkhya and Yoga, therefore, is to "isolate" *(kaivalya)* or "discriminate" *(viveka)* the *puruṣa* so that suffering can be overcome.

Sāṃkhya and Yoga affirm a plurality of *puruṣas*. In other words, consciousness is not a cosmic Self or Absolute as it is in the various systems of VEDĀNTA philosophy. G. J. LARSON

Q

QARMAṬIANS kär mā´ shəns (I—Arab.). Derogatory name given to an Ismaili secret revolutionary organization that demanded social reform and justice based on equality (*see* Ismā'īliyya). They were "Seveners" (*see* Sab'iyya), that is, they believed that the seventh and last Imam was Muhammad ibn Ismā'īl, grandson of Ja'far al-Ṣādiq, and that he was to be the Mahdi. They also held to esoteric interpretations of the Qur'ān.

The movement began in southern Arabia in the ninth century A.D., spread by intensive missionary efforts to many regions of the Muslim world, and was of significance until the end of the eleventh century. Under the leadership of Ḥamdān Qarmat, from whom it seems to have taken its name, it prospered in the area of Kūfa, Iraq, from 877 until it was surpressed there about 900. Ḥamdān proclaimed a communal society, admission to which was by initiation. His followers supported the movement by contributions and by a tax of one fifth of all earnings.

The Qarmaṭian "summons to truth" was carried to Yemen, where it developed centers of strength, and as far west as Algeria, where with the support of a Berber tribe it laid the foundation for the Fatimid dynasty (A.D. 909). A second Qarmaṭian movement arose in Bahrein around 900 under one of Ḥamdān's followers, Abū Sa'īd al-Jannābī, who founded a Qarmaṭian state there. This state organized the nomads of eastern Arabia into a powerful military force that conquered the oasis towns of that area and established a prosperous and egalitarian society. Upon the appearance of the Fatimid Mahdi in Algeria, Ḥamdān and his brother-in-law 'Abdān rejected Fatimid claims and withdrew their support, creating a schism in Ismailism. The Ismailis in Bahrein and western Iran also refused to recognize the Fatimid claim to the imamate.

In 930 the Qarmaṭians of Bahrein committed the shocking act of looting the Ka'ba and carrying away the sacred Black Stone, which they did not return until some twenty years later. Subsequently they declined in power but lived on quietly until the end of their independence in 1077.

The Qarmaṭian movement left a deep mark on the intellectual history of Islam, since Qarmaṭian authors, especially members of Ikhwān al-Ṣafā, exerted considerable influence on a variety of Muslim thinkers. Qarmaṭian doctrines were also adopted by other extremist sects, such as the Assassins and the Druzes. The Fatimids retained some Qarmaṭian rituals which had been introduced by the early leaders of the movement in western North Africa. The rapid spread of these doctrines in the Muslim world was seen by Sunnite authors as a threat to the unity of the community, and for that reason they denounced them as contrary to the interests of Islam and sought to trace their origins to pre-Islamic heresies.

Bibliography. B. Lewis, *The Origins of Ismā'īlism* (1940); W. Madelung, "Fāṭimiden und Baḥrainqaramaṭen," *Der Islam,* 34 (1959), 34-88; S. M. Stern "Ismā'īlīs and Qarmaṭians," *Lélaboration de l'Islam* (1961), pp. 99-108.

A. A. Sachedina

QIBLAH kīb´ lə (I). The direction and point which a Muslim faces wherever in the world when performing the daily prayers *(ṣalāt).* The Meccan Ka'ba has been the *qiblah* since about A.D. 624. For the first two years of the Muslim community's existence in Medina, Jerusalem was the *qiblah*. The change to Mecca was commanded by the Qur'ān (Sura 2:142-45) and signaled the reorientation of Islam in terms of an affirmation of its Arabness and its relative independence vis-à-vis Judaism.

Every Mosque is oriented toward Mecca by means of the *mihrāb* (prayer niche) located in one of its walls.

H. B. Partin

QIṢĀS kə säs´ (I—Arab.; lit. "retaliation"). The legal principle of retaliation for either killing or wounding.

In contrast to the practice of the blood feud of pre-Islamic Arabian tribes, the Qur'ān limits the vengeance to which a person is entitled. Sura 5:45-49 recognizes this principle in the Torah, and adds that expiation will result from foregoing it. Sura 2:178-9 prescribes retaliation for the Muslim: "O ye who believe! Retaliation is prescribed for you in the matter of the murdered; the freeman for the freeman, and the slave for the slave, and the female for the female. And for him who is forgiven somewhat by his injured brother, prosecution according to usage and payment to him in kindness. This is an alleviation and a mercy from your Lord. He who transgresseth after this will have a painful doom. And there is life for you in retaliation, O men of understanding, that ye may ward off [evil]" (Pickthall trans.). Several instances in MUHAMMAD'S life indicate that he personally supervised retaliation, and that it can be satisfied by the payment of a fine in certain circumstances.

In SHARIA, both for the SUNNITES and the SHI'ITES, *qiṣāṣ* can only come into play when there is definite proof of guilt; when the person wounded or killed is within the purview of the law; when the guilty party is not otherwise excused, e.g. by insanity, minority, etc.; and when the offended person or his next of kin demands it. Islamic law makes a distinction between accidental and premeditated killing and wounding, and in the case of accident retaliation does not operate, although some schools of law would allow monetary compensation. Then the offended person or his next of kin acts privately, with the state serving only the function of guaranteeing the rights of both parties.

Bibliography. M. M. Pickthall, *Meaning of the Glorious Koran* (1953); A. J. Wensinck, *Concordance de la tradition musulmane* (1965); J. Schacht, *Origins of Muhammadan Jurisprudence* (1959).

G. D. NEWBY

QUAKERS (Ch). *See* FRIENDS, SOCIETY OF.

al-QUDS ăl koods´. The Arabic name for JERUSALEM. The importance of Jerusalem in the Islamic world ranks just behind that of MECCA and MEDINA as a major holy place and PILGRIMAGE focus. This importance dates from the time of MUHAMMAD himself, and stems in part from the efforts of a synchretic Islamic religion to proselytize among Christian and Jewish populations of the HEJAZ. Early Islamic sources record that the first QIBLAH of the house of the Prophet in Medina, which served the early believers as a MOSQUE, was not on the south side toward Mecca but rather on the north toward Jerusalem, a city holy to the Jewish population of Medina. According to tradition, the MI'RĀJ, the miraculous midnight journey of the Prophet, took place from the "further mosque" or the Masjid al-Aqsa, which popular sources associated with the Temple Mount in Jerusalem. And in the later seventh century there was constructed on the Temple Mount the shrine of the DOME OF THE ROCK, which not only marked the purported site of the Prophet's journey but in fact symbolically established the claim of ISLAM to the great city which was holy to the two competing monotheistic religions of the PEOPLE OF THE BOOK. The control of Mecca by a caliphal rival to the UMAYYAD 'Abd al-Malik ibn Marwan prompted the latter to emphasize the Haram al-Sharif, or Noble Enclosure on the Temple Mount, with its legendary Islamic associations, as a center of pilgrimage which for a brief time seems to have rivaled the Meccan HAJJ in Islamic practice.

The history of al-Quds in succeeding centuries was turbulent and complex. Coming under the control of the 'ABBĀSIDS in A.D. 750, it subsequently passed to the Tulunids (A.D. 878) and then to the heterodox FATIMIDS in 966, under whose rule friction between religious groups markedly increased. In 1070 al-Quds came under the rule of the great Seljuks, but a period of violent rebellion against the Seljuks ensued, and in 1096 the city again fell to the Fatimids.

On July 15, 1099, the soldiers of the First CRUSADE captured al-Quds, massacring many inhabitants and carrying off much of the city's treasure. The period of Frankish domination, beginning with the rule of Godefroi de Bouillon, was ended in 1187 under the terms of a treaty with Salah al-din Ayyubi, the famous Saladin, who allowed the Crusaders to leave the city unharmed. Saladin restored the Dome of the Rock and rebuilt the mosque of al-Aqsa, giving it a splendid pulpit which, until its destruction by fire in 1969, was one of the great monuments of Islamic wood carving.

In 1229, in one of the most bizarre episodes in the diplomacy of the Middle East, al-Quds was ceded by Saladin's nephew al-Mu'azzam to the Hohenstaufen emperor Frederick II for a period of ten years. It reverted to Islamic rule shortly thereafter, and in the later thirteenth century came under the rule of the Mamluks, under whom the city was extensively rebuilt and restored, while sinking into relative political obscurity.

Ottoman hegemony in the Middle East resulted in the capture of al-Quds by Selim I in 1517. His son Süleymān I was a great benefactor of the city and restored the Dome of the Rock, adding tile revetments and inscriptions which form a prominent part of its decoration today. The population and geography of al-Quds under the Ottomans have been the subject of intense study, in part for the purpose of formulating political claims to the city in the present century. The nineteenth century history of the city is especially complex in this regard. During World War I the Arabs and General Allenby took al-Quds from the Turks, and Palestine passed under British mandate. In the civil war of 1948 the city was contested by Arab and Jewish forces, and was subsequently divided between Israel and Jordan. (*See* ZIONISM.) In 1967 the Israeli army conquered Arab or East Jerusalem, and the Israeli government undertook a policy of reducing the number of Arabs in the city. Today al-Quds remains an extremely emotional issue in the Arab-Israeli conflict, with each side claiming absolute sovereignty over the city and its holy places.

Bibliography. F. Buhl, "al-Kuds," *EI.*

W. DENNY

QURAISH kūr īsh′ (I). The major tribe in MECCA, into which MUHAMMAD was born. The Quraish seem to have come into Mecca in the pre-Islamic period by force, led by Quṣayy, Muhammad's great-great-great-grandfather. He is recorded as starting the tribe on their life of trade, which eventually made Mecca the major emporium of Arabia as well as a cultic center. The Quraish had possibly been involved in the North-South aromatics trade on the Red Sea before moving inland. The inland move of the trade and the rise of the Quraish reflect the increased military capabilities of the North Arabs through their use of the camel and also the decline of the Sassanian client state of Hira. The fortunes of the Quraish reached their peak just before the rise of Islam, when they were able to control the aromatics trade through both treaty and military might. The decline of the use of incense in the Mediterranean and the rise of Islam contributed to the demise of the Quraish as merchants. After Islam, the tribal identity is subsumed under the term *muhājirūn,* "those who made the HIJRA."

Bibliography. W. Caskel, "Bedouinization of Arabia," *Studies in Islamic Cultural History,* G. E. Von Grunebaum, ed. (1954); R. Bulliet, *Camel and the Wheel* (1957); Ibn Ishāq, *Life of Muhammad,* A. Guillaume, trans. (1955).

G. D. NEWBY

QUR'ĀN kōōr ân′ (I—Arab.; lit. "reciting, recitation, reading" [*Q-R-'*—"to recite, read"]). The collected revelations received by MUHAMMAD, or any single one of them. In this "reciting" in the ARABIC LANGUAGE, Muslims hear God speaking in his own words: it is God's speech *(kalām Allāh)* and self-revelation in much the way that Christ, the Divine LOGOS, is for Christians (an analogy first used by W. C. Smith). The "revealing" (WAḤY) of God's word through Muhammad has been and is the unique, inimitable miracle *(mu'jizah)* for Muslims, providing them with a guide for all aspects of living, a scripture for constant "remembrance" (DHIKR) of God, a shaping determinant of individual and collective thinking, and a comprehensive vision of history and destiny.

1. **External description.** The collected revelations are normally referred to as "The Noble Qur'ān" *(al-Qur'ān al-karīm),* or simply "The Book" *(al-Kitāb),* although the epithets for God's word in the revelations themselves and in Muslim tradition are numerous. The whole is almost the length of the Christian NEW TESTAMENT and consists of 114 main divisions, or suras, which range in length in a common printed text from slightly over two lines (Sura 108) to some 710 (Sura 2). Each sura is made up of short verses (*āyahs,* lit. "signs, wonders"), the exact delineation of which has varied slightly in different copies and editions (Western-language translations follow one of two different systems of versification, which makes it on occasion hard to find a given numerical reference; the variance can be up to seven *āyahs*). The shortest sura, 108, has three brief *āyahs;* the longest, 2, some 286 generally longer ones.

The suras are numbered and arranged in approximate descending order of length, albeit with notable exceptions, the prime being Sura 1, "The Opening" *(al-Fātiḥah),* with only seven *āyahs.* In Muslim usage, each sura is referred to not by number but by name—this usually taken from one of the initial words (e.g., 92, "Night") or some striking passage or phrase (e.g. 2, "The Cow") in the sura. Although very old, the names are evidently not part of the Divine Word, since some suras have more than one name (e.g. 112, "Pure Devotion" or "Unity"). The sura divisions were apparently originally marked by the invocational *basmala* formula ("In the name of God the Merciful, the Compassionate") which begins all but Sura 9—possibly because it belonged originally to Sura 8, which is relatively short for its place (Buhl; but cf. Watt, p. 60). There is no unanimity about the precise chronological order in which the separate revelations came to Muhammad, but texts of the Qur'ān traditionally list every sura as either "Meccan," "Medinan," or a combination of the two, according to whether its contents were sent down during Muhammad's prophetic career in Mecca or Medina. The most influential Muslim ordering is that usually noted in the sura headings of the "standard" SUNNI text (Cairo, 1919), but Iranian, Indian, and other editions give varying ones. Modern non-Muslim scholarship has also attempted historical-critical "chronologization" of the revelations, the three most influential proposals being those of Nöldeke (1860), Bell (1937-39), and Blachère (1947-51). In all schemes, Muslim and non-Muslim, there is general agreement that the preponderance of early (Meccan) material is to be found in the short, dramatic suras and *āyahs* of the final portion of the collected Qur'ān, and most of the later (Medinan) material in the longer, generally less intense passages of the first part of the text.

The contents of the Qur'ān take the form of words from God addressed alternately to all mankind, to the faithful, to the unbelievers, or to Muhammad alone. Passages not in first- or second-person discourse of God are normally preceded by the imperative "Say!" after which follows one or more passages for recitation or proclamation by human lips. The language of the revelations is in prose, but a generally dramatic and poetic, often rhyming, prose that is anything but "prosaic." The power of the language, especially in some of the shorter, more lyrical passages, is overwhelming and all but impossible to capture in translation. The content ranges widely and includes paeans of praise for the One God and his myriad "signs" in the natural world, sharp warnings about the final Day of Resurrection and Judgment, exhortations to piety and good works, reminders of the history of God's dealing with mankind through the long series of previous prophets (*see* NABI) and revelations, commands concerning personal morality and social intercourse, and statements about particular events contemporary with the revelations themselves. Any or all of these and other themes recur repeatedly, often in the same sura, giving the whole a mosaic effect in which the unity of the discrete parts lies not in narrative development so much as stylistic and thematic repetition. The marked repetitiveness of the Qur'ān is indicative of the "recitative" nature of the revelations, a quality underscored by the fact that in daily use the sura divisions of the text take second place to various divisions for purposes of recitation alone: (1) into thirty roughly equal "parts," each of these further halved to yield sixty "portions," and each "portion" subdivided into quarters to give 240 short recitations; (2) into thirds (Suras 1-9, 10-30, 31-114); and (3) into sevenths. While the latter two kinds of division are not normally indicated in printed texts, the 30-60-240 divisions are usually marked for the reader.

2. Revelation and compilation. The early sources recount in some detail how the process of "revealing" *(waḥy, tanzīl)* to Muhammad went on over a long period, perhaps more than twenty years if one dates the first revelation—traditionally the first five *āyahs* of Sura 96—around A.D. 610, as most scholars do. Muslim sources treat in detail the "occasions of revelation," i.e. the historical circumstances in which particular *āyahs* or suras were given the Prophet, and the "modes of revelation," or different ways in which revelations were given—e.g. through the angel Gabriel in waking or in dream, or as an auditory experience. Muhammad seems to have distinguished clearly between what was direct divine word intended for "reciting" *(qur'ān)* and what was inspiration for his own words and acts. The revelations likely received some editing and arrangement in Medina at his hands; certainly some of them were written down, and names of several "scribes of the Revealing" are preserved. Still, at Muhammad's death there was no Qur'ān as a single, codified *book*; still primarily an oral reality for the Muslims, the Arabic "recitations" from the Divine Book in Heaven were not yet a single text "between two boards."

Whether the traditions about early attempts under Abū Bakr and especially 'Umar to collect the "recitations"and organize them are accurate or not, it is clear that under the aegis of the third caliph, 'Uthmān, a largely successful effort was made to compile an "authoritative" text from the variant "readings" *(qirā'āt)* of the best reciters from among the Companions of Muhammad. Carried out by Zayd ibn Thābit (d. 665) and other Companions who "had" the revelations "by heart," the 'Uthmānic recension was an attempt to eliminate divergent arrangements of the Qur'ānic material, to prevent errors and interpolations, and to provide a single text for ritual and educational use in the rapidly expanding Islamic community. Variant readings, such as those of Ibn Mas'ūd (d. 652-53; cf. *EI*), did persist long after 'Uthmān, but these are of relatively minor import and have not been a crucial issue in Muslim life. Recitative variants have even been classified according to seven accepted systems. There has been little discord among Muslims over the integrity of the basic 'Uthmānic text, although some among the Shi'a have made charges of omissions concerning Ali and his descendants. While a few non-Muslim scholars have questioned the antiquity of the received text, these have found little acceptance for their ideas, and the Qur'ān remains of all major scriptures the one with the clearest textual history. This is largely due to the voluminous records and scholarship of the Muslims from early times. They have always recognized (even in some measure when literalist concepts of God's revelation and speech have prevailed) that the faultless preservation and transmission *(tawātur)* of God's Word must be assured by the community (Umma) and its consensus (Ijmā'). The Divine Speech had to be preserved in human hearts, recited on human tongues, and written by human hands. The Muslims themselves, collectively, through every generation, are the bondsmen for the inviolate integrity of the Divine Word; to understand this is to understand in good part the close identification of the *umma* with its scriptural revelation.

3. The Qur'ān as scripture. The religious significance of the Qur'ān is reflected in Muslim attitudes toward and treatment of the Qur'ān, across the centuries and around the globe. In it Muslims find the quintessential expression of God's eternal Word, which is with him on a "preserved tablet," "The Mother of the Book" *(Umm al-Kitāb),* or simply "The Book" *(al-Kitāb).* The Qur'ān sums up, corrects, and completes the revelations given earlier prophets such as Moses and Jesus, and in it Muslims find the basic source for social order, personal ethics, devotion, liturgy, salvation history, eschatology, and the life of faith. Of all Muslim religious sciences, the noblest is the study of God's Word—its meaning, proper reading, and practical application. Qur'ānic interpretation *(tafsīr)* in particular has been prolific and important in every age, normally taking the form of detailed exegesis with historical, grammatical, and theological explanation of every line. Memorization of the entire Qur'ān has been and remains the mark of learning and piety, carrying with it the honored title of Ḥāfiẓ, one who "guards" the Book in the heart. Every performance of Prayer involves recitation from the Qur'ān, and non-Arab Muslims who know no other words of Arabic know enough of it to recite segments in worship. To touch the Qur'ān, one must be ritually pure; to copy it is a sacred task; to give it is to give the finest gift. As proof text *par excellence,* the Qur'ān is "the best saying" (*aḥsan al-ḥadīth:* Sura 39:23). Mystics have chanted and sung, meditated upon, and esoterically interpreted the Qur'ān; grammarians have based rules for Arabic on it; legists and theologians have formulated guidelines for all of life in light of it; artists have embellished almost all

Islamic buildings and artifacts with its words in elaborate calligraphy; conservators of the status quo have claimed it as their authority; reformers have built movements around a return to its preaching; and ordinary people have patterned their lives as well as their speech after its words. The Qur'ān stands at the core of Islamic faith as the active communication of the divine will for humankind.

See also Scriptures, Sacred.

Bibliography. Selected general works: F. Buhl, "Koran," *EI* and "Ḳur'ān," *SEI;* W. C. Smith, "Koran," *Encyclopedia Britannica;* W. M. Watt, *Bell's Introduction to the Qur'ān* (1970); T. Nöldeke, *Geschichte des Qorâns* (1860), rev. by F. Schwally, G. Bergsträsser, O. Pretzl, 3 vols. (1909-35); R. Blachère, *Introduction au Coran* (1947); R. Paret, *Der Koran: Kommentar und Koncordanz* (1971); M. F. 'Abd al-Bāqī, *al-Mu' jam al-mufahras li-alfāẓ al-Qur'ān* [concordance] (1945); al-Suyūṭī (d. 1505), *Itqān al-Qur'ān* (1951 ed.); A. Jeffery, *The Qur'an as Scripture* (1952); I. Goldziher, *Die Richtungen der islamischen Koranauslegung* (1920); P. Nwyia, *Exégèse coranique et langage mystique* (1970); L. as-Said, *The Recited Koran,* B. Weiss *et al.,* trans. (1975). Selected translations: G. Sale, *The Koran* (1734); A. J. Arberry, *The Koran Interpreted,* 2 vols. (1955); R. Bell, *The Qur'ān,* 2 vols. (1937-39); R. Blachère, *Le Coran,* 2 vols. (1949-51); R. Paret, *Der Koran* (1962); A. Yusuf 'Ali, *The Holy Quran* (1934); M. M. Pickthall, *The Meaning of the Glorious Koran* (1953). Selected classical Muslim commentaries: al-Ṭabarī (d. 923), *Tafsīr al-Qur'ān;* al-Zamakhsharī (d. 1144), *al-Kashshāf;* al-Rāzī (d. 1209), *Mafātīḥ al-ghayb;* al-Bayḍāwī (d. *ca.* 1290), *Anwār al-tanzīl.*

W. A. Graham

R

RABBI (Ju—Heb.; "my master"). A sage, i.e., an ordained expounder and interpreter of the Bible and the Oral Law. The term probably originated in Palestine early in the first cenutry A.D. and was bestowed on any person equipped with sufficient learning in rabbinic literature to render decision on matters of Jewish law.

The professional, salaried rabbinate emerged only in the late Middle Ages, when rabbis were appointed as the religious leaders of communities and were expected to devote full time to communal activities, which consisted chiefly in deciding questions in all areas of Jewish law, serving as judges in both civil and criminal cases, conducting a Yeshivah, and supervising various religious institutions, such as ritual slaughtering, the elementary school system, the ritual baths, etc. Until the nineteenth century preaching was not a major activity of the rabbinate. Persons were admitted to rabbinic status only after many years of study of the Talmud and rabbinic codes and after passing examinations by rabbis who were held in great repute for their scholarship and piety. In the nineteenth century rabbinical seminaries and institutions intended specifically for the training of rabbis were established in Western Europe and the United States.

The modern rabbi, who is generally a graduate of a university and a rabbinical seminary, functions quite differently from his pre-nineteenth century counterpart, especially in American Jewry. Except in the case of some Orthodox rabbis, his chief activity is no longer that of legal expert and judge. Nor is he the supervisor of a network of community-wide religious institutions. Instead, he serves as the spiritual leader of a congregation or Synagogue, and much of his time is devoted to the conduct of worship services and preaching, youth and adult education, officiating at weddings and funerals, pastoral work, counseling, interfaith activity, participating in community welfare organizations, etc.

Ordination of rabbis in Orthodox Judaism is conferred by the Yeshivah, or in some cases, by a rabbi who, by virtue of further study, has gained the right to ordain others. In Conservative Judaism it is conferred by the seminary; some Conservative rabbis seek Orthodox ordination as well. In Reform Judaism it is conferred by an accredited theological school. In all branches there are rabbis who have been ordained by theological schools in other countries. Today a number of women serve as rabbis in Reform and Reconstructionist congregations.

Bibliography. "Rabbi," *EJ,* XIII (1971), 1446-58.

B. Martin

RADAK rä däk′ (Ju). *See* Kimhi, David.

RĀDHĀ räd′ hä (H—Skt.; lit. "prosperity, success"). Rādhā is one of the most mysterious figures in all of Indian literature. There is a reference in Bhāgavata Purāṇa (*ca.* tenth century A.D.) Book X to a special Gopī who was "worshiped" or "desired" *(ārādhitā)* by Krishna, and whom he "took to a secret place," and some scholars feel that her name comes from this. The name, however, is linked with that of Krishna in many of the Sanskrit poetic anthologies of the eleventh century in a way that would suggest that the divine pair were familiar figures in the mythology of the time.

In the twelfth-century poem Gītā Govinda she emerges as a full-fledged heroine with characteristics of dignity, strength, and beauty as she carries on a sensual and earthy affair with her divine lover Krishna. In later texts she takes on additional particulars. In the Śrikṛṣṇa-kīrtana, a Bengali text of perhaps the fifteenth century, she has a husband named Āyan Ghoṣ and is clearly described as a young woman between adolescence and maturity whose lineage is within the cowherd clan.

In later poetry and myth Rādhā becomes a metaphor of the soul of the devotee *(bhakta)* in its search for the love of God. In the Vaiṣṇava tradition she also takes on a theological role, becoming the Śakti of Krishna whereby he gives love to and receives love from his devotees. The Bengali saint Caitanya (1486-1533) is thought to have been an incarnation of both Rādhā and Krishna, with the beauty and passion of Rādhā and the divinity of Krishna in a single body.

Bibliography. B. S. Miller, *The Love Song of the Dark Lord* (1977).
E. C. Dimock, Jr.

RĀDHĀ SOĀMĪ SATSANG räd´ hä sō ä´ mē sŭt sŭng´ (S). A sect containing elements of Hinduism and Sikhism; founded by a Hindu banker, Shiv Dayal of Agra (1818-78). He described God as the union of Rādhā symbolizing the soul and Soāmī ("master") symbolizing the creator, hence, Rādhā Soāmī. He emphasized the use of *anhad śabda* ("unstruck music"—divine sounds heard only with the mind) to elevate consciousness from lower to upper spiritual regions. Shiv Dayal paid reverence to the Ādi Granth, and his following consisted of both Hindus and Sikhs. He wrote extensively, and also edited a fortnightly magazine *Prem Putra*.

On his death his followers split. One branch remained at Agra under Rai Saligram Bahadur (1828-98), then under Brahma Sankar Misra (1861-1907) moved to Allāhābād, and finally to Banāras. The Agra branch under Śrī Anand Swarup, who became its head in 1915, set up an industrial estate in the suburb of Dayalbagh, where they also erected a large marble temple.

In 1891 Jaimal Singh (1839-1933) started a Rādhā Soāmī center at Beas, about twenty miles from Amritsar. He was succeeded by Sawan Singh (d. 1948) and Jagat Singh (d. 1951). The present head of the Beas Rādhā Soāmīs is Charan Singh, grandson of Sawan Singh. A sizable township named Dera Baba Jaimal Singh has become the residence of the Guru and headquarters of the movement, which claims a following of over two million, including Hindus, Muslims, Christians, Parsis, and Sikhs.

Orthodox Sikhs do not regard the Rādhā Soāmīs in a favorable light, because the latter believe in a living guru and do not regard the Ādi Granth as their only scripture nor install it in their temples. They also do not subscribe to the Khālsā tradition of baptism.

Bibliography. P. Ashby, *Modern Trends in Hinduism* (1974), pp. 71-90.
K. Singh

RADHAKRISHNAN, SARVEPALLI rä dŭ krīsh´ năn sŭr və pŭl´ lī (H; 1888-1975). Born in Tirutani near Madras, he became not only one of India's leading scholars and educators but distinguished himself as a diplomat and statesman. Educated at various mission schools, he received the M.A. in philosophy from Madras Christian College. He taught philosophy at Calcutta University and at Oxford, and became vice-chancellor of Hindu University in Banāras (1939-48). After independence he served as India's ambassador to the U.S.S.R. (1949-52). From 1952 to 1962 he was vice-president and from 1962 to 1967 president of India. Throughout his life he was an eloquent defender of Advaita Vedānta. He considered it his calling to preach a spiritual revolution as an answer to modern mankind's problems. In numerous works, including *An Idealist View of Life* and *Eastern Religions and Western Thought* he expressed his view that the materialism and skepticism generated by the scientific and technological revolution could only be overcome through a revitalized spirituality, a life of simplicity and asceticism, and a balance between contemplation and activity. A study of the major religions led him to conclude that they had an underlying common core which could be perceived through mystical insight but not discursive reason. At the same time he implied that Advaita Vedānta was superior to other religions because of its more pronounced universality, tolerance, and idealism. Well aware of the fact that Indian religion had been considered deficient in the socio-ethical realm, Radhakrishnan took issue with Albert Schweitzer's view that Hinduism was world-denying and hence unconcerned about ethics. Radhakrishnan argued that the empirical world was not illusory (Māyā) even according to Śaṃkara. He pointed to the fact that Mokṣa depended upon prior moral perfection and that spiritual attainment must result in a life of service and sacrifice. And he pleaded for cooperation, not rivalry, among the world's great religions.

Bibliography. A. McDermott, ed., *Radhakrishnan* (1970); P. A. Schilpp, *The Philosophy of Radhakrishnan* (1952).
A. Lipski

RAHNER, KARL rä´ nər (Ch; 1904-). German priest who may be the premier Roman Catholic theologian today. His thought emerges from a creative reinterpretation of nature and grace in the theology of Thomas Aquinas. For Rahner, human freedom is open to and permeated by the infinite divine mystery. His writings extend from the scholarly to the devotional. *See* Theology, Contemporary Christian §4c. D. F. Ottati

RĀHU rä´ ho͞o (H & B—Skt.; lit. "the seizer" [*rabh*—"to grasp"]). A demon of eclipses who seizes and swallows the sun and the moon. In the Epics and Purāṇas Rāhu disguises himself as a god and drinks some of the elixir of immortality *(amṛta)* attained through the churning of the ocean. Vishnu, informed by the sun and the moon, cuts off Rāhu's head, which, now immortal, remains in the heavens to swallow periodically the tattletale sun and moon. The body or tail of the demon is regarded as Ketu, the "Bright." The sun, moon, Rāhu, and Ketu, plus the five visible interior planets, make up the nine *grahas* ("planets").

Bibliography. E. W. Hopkins, *Epic Mythology* (1915).
D. M. Knipe

RĀJA, RĀJAN rä´ jä (H—Skt.; lit. "sovereign, ruler"). A Sanskrit word for king or ruler, used by

Indian religious traditions to refer to the supreme or paradigmatic religious practice, concept, or person. For example, Patañjali's YOGA system which offers spiritual release is called Rāja Yoga or the "king" of all yogas (disciplines). L. D. SHINN

RĀJA YOGA rä′ jä yō′ gŭ (H). *See* YOGA §3.

RĀJAGṚHA rä jŭ grĭ′ hŭ (B—Skt.) **RĀJAGAHA** rä jŭ gŭ′ hŭ (B—Pali). Capital city (the present Rajgir) of Magadha, primary base of the public ministry of Gautama the BUDDHA and one of the four largest kingdoms of northern India of the time. Rājagṛha, located south of the Ganges River in the modern state of Bihar, was a major economic and cultural center of northeastern India. Its King Bimbisāra was noted for his generous patronage of the Buddha and also of other religious teachers.

R. H. DRUMMOND

RĀKṢASA räk′ shŭ sŭ (H). An ambiguous class of semi-divine or demonic beings in Hindu mythology. *Cf.* ASURA.

RAM MOHAN ROY räm mō′ hăn roi (1772-1833) was born in an orthodox Bengali BRAHMIN family but was educated in English, Persian and Sanskrit, and early showed a rationalistic bent. Studying at a MUSLEM institution in Patna, he became a monotheist. Upon examining the New Testament he declared his admiration for Christian ethics but rejected Christ's divinity. A study of the UPANIṢADS convinced him that they taught monotheism and were free from social abuses. In 1828 he founded the BRĀHMO SAMĀJ for the propagation of his religious and social views. He spent the last part of his life in England. *See* REFORM MOVEMENTS IN INDIA §2.

Bibliography. V. C. Joshi, *Rammohun Roy and the Process of Modernization in India* (1975). A. LIPSKI

RĀMA rä′ mŭ. Hero king of the RĀMĀYAṆA; eldest son of Daśaratha, at whose command he went to the forest leaving his kingdom to his stepbrother Bharata. In VĀLMĪKI's version of the Rāmāyaṇa, Rāma is a human prince, but later devotees treat him as the god VISHNU, who incarnated himself as a human being in order to destroy demons. V. N. RAO

RAMADAN rä′ mə dän (I). The month of the fast throughout the Islamic world; the ninth month of the Islamic (lunar) calendar, traditionally believed to be the month in which the first revelation of the QUR'ĀN was given.

The obligation of fasting (ṢAWM) is the fourth of the PILLARS of ISLAM. It appears that the Muslims adopted the practice of fasting during the early years following the HIJRA (A.D. 622) and that they initially followed Jewish custom as to the time and manner of fasting. After Muhammad's break with the Medinan Jews about A.D. 624 significant changes were introduced by means of Qur'ānic revelation (Sura 2:139-45). The principal changes were (1) to fast during the daylight hours (rather than from sunset to sunset, as was Jewish custom) and (2) to keep the fast for an entire month, Ramadan, one of the sacred months in pre-Islamic times.

Ramadan is a time of personal and communal abstention and religious discipline. Moreover, it is a period of self-examination and forgiveness and thus in some measure parallels the Jewish YOM KIPPUR. Fasting is believed to be effective in cleansing the believer's heart, especially when abstention extends beyond refraining from food and drink and is accompanied by increased religious devotion as shown by reading of the Qur'ān and supererogatory prayers.

The Fast of Ramadan ends with the sighting of the new moon signaling the end of the lunar month. There follows immediately the *'īd al-saghīr* (Little Festival) or *'īd al-fitr* (Festival of Breaking Fast), which lasts several days. It is marked by feasting and the exchange of gifts. In many places it is a more popular festival than the Great Festival which marks the conclusion of the annual pilgrimage (HAJJ).

Bibliography. G. von Grunebaum, *Muhammadan Festivals* (1951). H. B. PARTIN

RĀMAKRISHNA rä′ mŭ krĭsh′ nŭ (H; 1834-86). Acknowledged as one of the great religious geniuses of the modern period, Rāmakrishna also stands at the beginning of the Hindu Renaissance as an archetypal figure. Trained in the classical traditions of Hindu mysticism, he went far beyond the ordinary boundaries of Hindu spiritual practice by experiencing "enlightenment" in Śaiva (ŚAIVISM) and Vaiṣṇava (VAIṢṆAVISM) as well as nondualist and dualist modes. Though married, he led a completely "renounced" life; his wife, Śāradā, "the Holy Mother," came also to be recognized as a fully realized saint. Add to these facts Rāmakrishna's abandonment of traditional priestly food taboos, his sense of identification with JESUS Christ and ALLAH, his selection of extraordinary disciples like VIVEKĀNANDA and Brahmānanda, and his uniqueness grows more discernible.

Born in 1836 in the Bengali village of Kamarpukur, he went to Calcutta as a young man. There the greater part of his life was passed as a priest in the KĀLĪ temple at Dakshineswar. It was while serving as priest that he underwent the intensive training *(sādhanā)* in the Indian spiritual traditions.

In his childhood he had already had unusual experiences. The most famous of these happened one evening as he walked through the countryside and saw a flight of snow-white cranes against a dark cloud. The beauty of the scene pierced him so deeply that he went into trance, lost normal consciousness, and had to be carried home by some villagers who found him lying on the road. These SAMĀDHI states in his later life were witnessed by many persons. Rāmakrishna would go in and out of normal consciousness, and cry, sing, and dance as he experienced ecstasy.

Beginning his *sādhanā* at Dakshineswar, he was obsessed with the desire to see the goddess Kālī face to face. In a state bordering on madness, he offered her idol daily worship. Once in frustration he seized the sword in the image's hand and thought of killing himself. At that very moment Kālī appeared in a vision—the first of many such apparitions of the Divine Mother to him. As he progressed, he assumed the role of HANUMĀN, the monkey devotee of RĀMA, attained NIRVANA in the TANTRA mode through the guidance of a woman guru, experienced the ADVAITAN (nondualist) union of ATMAN with BRAHMAN, and identified so completely with RĀDHĀ, the divine consort of KRISHNA, that he wore woman's dress, expressing the preciousness of feminine spirituality. These are only a few examples.

People began to call him *Paramahaṃsa,* "The Supreme Swan," the title of greatest dignity in the Hindu ascetic tradition. A group of young disciples gathered around him toward the end of his life, and they formed the nucleus of the Ramakrishna Mission which has become worldwide in its operations through the work of Swami Vivekānanda. *See* HINDUISM IN AMERICA §1.

Bibliography. Swāmī Nikhilānanda, *The Gospel of Śrī Rāmakrishna* (1947); J. Yale, *A Yankee and the Swamis* (1961); C. Isherwood, *Ramakrishna and his Disciples* (1965).

C. S. J. WHITE

RAMAKRISHNA MISSION. *See* HINDUISM IN AMERICA §1.

RAMAṆA MAHARSHI rä mŭ´ nŭ mŭ här´ shē (H; 1879-1951). Called Venkataramaṇa in his childhood, he is regarded by many as the greatest Hindu saint of the twentieth century. After an uneventful childhood, he experienced in his later teens a succession of inner transformations that forever destroyed his attachment to body-consciousness. Thereafter he dwelt, it is said, in the transcendent and eternal Self (ATMAN). At age twenty, he settled down on the "hill" of Aruṇācalam at Tiruvannamalai near Madras, where he remained until his death. A spontaneous recognition by others of his spiritual attainment rapidly earned him the status of GURU.

Technically speaking, Ramaṇa was an ADVAITA sage who experienced the identity of the atman and BRAHMAN. Such a saint knows himself as "divine" and "deathless," not because he is a special manifestation of the god VISHNU (*see* AVATAR) but because of his immersion in the universal Spirit. In his last year of life he suffered an extremely painful sarcoma of the left arm but never lost the blissful composure of the *jñānī* ("truly wise").

Bibliography. A. Osborne, *Ramana Maharshi and the Path of Self-Knowledge* (1954).

C. S. J. WHITE

RĀMĀNUJA rä mä´ noo jŭ (H—Skt.). A Hindu philosopher, theologian, and sectarian leader of the eleventh and twelfth centuries A.D.; the classical exponent of the theistically and devotionally oriented VIŚIṢṬA ADVAITA school (*see* VEDĀNTA) and a major ĀCĀRYA or Teacher of the widely influential ŚRĪ VAIṢṆAVA sect dedicated to VISHNU and his consort Śrī or LAKṢMĪ and based in the TAMIL-speaking area of South India.

While his traditional dates are A.D. 1017-1137, evidence suggests that he may have died some twenty or more years later (*ca.* 1157-61). The traditional dates were probably formulated to conform with the story that as a young man he received the coveted teacher's blessing from YĀMUNA, the figure whose works provided his intellectual inspiration, but who died *ca.* A.D. 1038. The Śrī Vaiṣṇava accounts of the lives of their Teachers are dramatized as a search for a scholar who could defend the sect's VEDIC and BRAHMANIC orthodoxy, a status called into question by its deep involvement with such largely non-Vedic and non-Brahmanic movements as the PĀÑCARĀTRA temple tradition and the ecstatic hymns of the Tamil-speaking devotees of Vishnu, the ĀḺVĀRS. Following on Yāmuna's only partially successful efforts, Rāmānuja is presented as a BRAHMIN of such profound Vedic scholarship and such devotion *(bhakti)* to Vishnu and his devotees, no matter what their social status, that he was able to defend the movement successfully and establish it upon firm Vedic intellectual groundings.

The Śrī Vaiṣṇavas accept what is termed the "Dual Vedānta," in which not only the SANSKRIT UPANISADS but also the Tamil hymns of the Āḻvārs are held to contain the "end" *(-anta)* or essence of the Veda or Truth. While Rāmānuja is reputed to have received and given oral instruction in this Tamil "Vedānta," his distinctive achievement was in the formulation of a Sanskritic Vedāntic system based strictly upon Vedic sources but compatible with a theistic mode of popular religion that centered on temple worship and was expressed through devotional hymns. In its essentials, his magisterial system has remained the primary theoretical basis for BHAKTI HINDUISM up to the present day.

1. **Life.** Rāmānuja was born during the reign of the powerful Tamil Chōḻa dynasty and into a Brahmin family with a tradition of Vedic learning and generally Vaiṣṇava leanings. Studying Vedānta at the major intellectual center of Kāñcīpuram, he attracted the attention of Yāmuna's disciples at Śrīrangam, the most important South Indian Vishnu temple. Eventually Yāmuna's disciples initiated him into the Śrī Vaiṣṇava sect and brought him to Śrīrangam as Teacher. From this position of authority his influence spread to other major Vaiṣṇava centers. During several tours of South India and one of North India as well, he debated opponents (especially followers of ŚAMKARA'S ADVAITA Vedānta and worshipers of SHIVA), attempted to reform Vaiṣṇava temple practices, and gathered materials for his own Vedāntic writings. His

strict adherence to Vishnu led him into conflict with a Chōḻa king who was a worshiper of Shiva; and late in his life he had to flee from Śrīrangam to avoid persecution, spending twelve years in exile under the protection of a friendly Hoyśāḻa king in the Mysore region. The best evidence suggests that the Chōḻa king was Kulottunga II (A.D. 1133-50) and that Rāmānuja returned to Śrīrangam in 1150, where he completed his work on his great Vedāntic commentary, the *Śrībhāṣya,* in 1155-56, a few years before his death.

2. **Works.** Rāmānuja's three major and most influential works are the *Śrībhāṣya,* his full commentary on the BRAHMA SŪTRAS; the *Gītābhāṣya,* a commentary on the BHAGAVAD GĪTĀ; and the *Vedārthasaṃgraha,* an independent work presenting his interpretation of the Upaniṣads. Also ascribed to him by tradition are a number of shorter works including two additional brief commentaries on the Brahma Sūtras, a ritual manual, and three prose devotional hymns. The authenticity of these shorter works has been questioned but in most cases the objections seem not to justify denying the traditional ascriptions.

Bibliography. J. B. Carman, *The Theology of Rāmānuja* (1974), the most comprehensive and critical study of Rāmānuja's life, works, and thought; J. A. B. van Buitenen, ed. and trans., *Rāmānuja's Vedārthasaṃgraha* (1956); A. Govindacharya, *The Life of Rāmānujāchārya* (1906); on the date of Rāmānuja's death see T. N. Subramanian, "A Note on the Date of Rāmānuja," *South Indian Temple Inscriptions,* Vol. III, pt. 2, Madras Government Oriental Series no. 157 (1957), 147-60.

W. G. NEEVEL

RĀMĀYAṆA rä mī´ yŭ nŭ (H—Skt.; lit. "the exploits of Rāma"). One of the two major Epics of India, the Rāmāyaṇa is popularly ascribed to the sage-poet, VĀLMĪKI, who is believed to be the "creator of poetry." The SANSKRIT text consists of six books which relate the main story, with a seventh book, the Uttara Rāmāyaṇa ("The Later Story of Rāma") as a sequel.

1. **The Story.** King Daśaratha of Ayodhyā had three wives who gave birth to four sons. RĀMA was the son of the eldest queen, Kausalyā; LAKṢMAṆA and Śatrughna were the sons of the second queen, Sumitrā; and Bharata was the son of the third and youngest queen, Kaikeyī, whom Daśaratha loved most.

In the nearby kingdom of Videha, King Janaka found a girl in a furrow of the earth which he was tilling in preparation for a ritual. He named her SĪTĀ (lit. "furrow of the earth") and raised her. When she came of age, he declared that he would give her in marriage to whoever had the strength to string the heavy bow of SHIVA which was in his possession. Many kings and warriors failed in the test, but Rāma strung the bow and won the bride.

King Daśaratha decided to make Rāma the heir of the kingdom and designated a day for the ritual to declare him crown prince. The evening before the special day Kaikeyī, on the advice of her maidservant Mantharā, demanded of Daśaratha that her son Bharata should be named crown prince instead, and also insisted that Rāma be exiled to the forest for fourteen years. Previously the old king had promised his young wife two boons, so bound by his word, he reluctantly agreed. Accordingly, Rāma went into the forest accompanied by his wife Sītā and devoted brother Lakṣmaṇa. They built a hut in the forest and lived there.

Śūrpaṇakhā, a demon woman of the area, fell in love with Rāma and asked him to marry her. Rāma indicated that because he already had a wife, she should approach Lakṣmaṇa instead. But Lakṣmaṇa rejected her, saying that she had loved Rāma first and not him. Śūrpaṇakhā then attempted to devour Sītā because she thought that her presence was an obstacle to her marrying Rāma. Lakṣmaṇa punished her for this deed by cutting off her nose and ears.

Śūrpaṇakhā was the sister of RĀVAṆA, the ten-headed titan who ruled in Sri Lanka. She reported the incident to her brother, further informing him that Rāma's wife Sītā was the most beautiful woman in the world. Rāvaṇa was outraged by the violence done to his sister, but more than that he was allured by the description of Sītā, and planned to bring her to Sri Lanka and make her his wife. He sent the evil sage Mārīca, disguised as a golden deer, to the vicinity of the hut where Sītā lived. Sītā was entranced by the deer and asked her husband to bring it to her. Leaving Lakṣmaṇa to guard Sītā, Rāma went to catch the deer. Mārīca skillfully led Rāma away into the forest. When Rāma realized that it was futile to try to catch the deer alive, he shot it with an arrow. The dying Mārīca cried, "O Sītā, O Lakṣmaṇa," feigning Rāma's voice. Sītā heard the voice, and thinking her husband was in trouble, sent Lakṣmaṇa to rescue him. Lakṣmaṇa's departure gave Rāvaṇa the opportunity to abduct Sītā. He went to her in the garb of a mendicant, grabbed her, and took her away in his chariot to Sri Lanka.

Rāma grieved for his beloved wife and went in search of her. He secured the aid of the monkey king Sugrīva (see BĀLI) and his monkey armies. Sugrīva's minister HANUMĀN crossed the ocean to Sri Lanka and found Sītā. Rāma then besieged Sri Lanka, defeated Rāvaṇa's armies, and finally killed the titan and brought Sītā back. At the end of the fourteen years Rāma, Sītā, and Lakṣmaṇa returned to Ayodhyā, where Rāma regained his kingdom from his brother Bharata.

In the sequel, "The Later Story of Rāma," Rāma banished his wife under the pressure of public opinion. The inhabitants of Ayodhyā doubted the purity of Sītā's character because she had lived in another man's house. Sītā, pregnant at the time of her banishment, gave birth in the hermitage of Vālmīki to twin sons, Lava and Kuśa. Vālmīki composed the Rāmāyaṇa and taught the boys to sing the story.

In Ayodhyā, Rāma began the horse sacrifice as a means of purification. Vālmīki was invited to the sacrifice; he brought Lava and Kuśa with him and asked them to sing the Rāmāyaṇa for Rāma. Listening to his own story, Rāma discovered that the boys were his own sons and that Sītā was alive and well. Vālmīki declared before the honored guests that Sītā was pure and her character beyond reproach. Sītā appeared before the assembled guests and prayed for mother earth to receive her as a proof of her purity. The earth broke open and received Sītā on a golden throne. Rāma, sad to lose his wife once again, gave the kingdom to his sons and returned to the world of the gods.

2. The nature and role of the Rāmāyaṇa. Compared with the MAHĀBHĀRATA, which is an Epic story incorporating a number of legends and myths, the Rāmāyaṇa is the straightforward story of one hero. Despite a number of discrepancies in the narrative, it is still possible that it is the product of one author. The style of the story indicates that it was composed orally and was probably sung for a long time before being set down in writing. Indian literary tradition identifies the Rāmāyaṇa as poetry *(kāvya)* and considers Vālmīki to be the first poet.

The story of the Rāmāyaṇa has been variously retold by hundreds of poets in all languages and dialects of India. Over its long history the Rāma story eventually became prominent as a vehicle for devotional or BHAKTI HINDUISM. Whereas the Rāma of Vālmīki is a human prince, the Rāma of later Rāmāyaṇas becomes an incarnation (AVATAR) of the god himself. This trend is shown to a certain extent in the first book of Vālmīki's version as well as in parts of his seventh book. For this reason some critics consider the first and seventh books of the Vālmīki version to be later additions. The *bhakti* trend has found its supreme expression in the Tamil *Kamba Rāmāyaṇa*, the Telugu *Raṅganātha Rāmāyaṇa*, and the Hindī RĀMCARITMĀNAS of TULSĪ DĀS.

In these *bhakti* Rāmāyaṇas, as well as in hundreds of praise songs and short poems addressed to Rāma, Rāma is the supreme god VISHNU who incarnated himself to liberate his devotees. Even Rāvaṇa is a devotee of Rāma disguised as his enemy, since according to the *bhakti* tradition even intense enmity toward a god is a form of devotion to him. All the characters of the story participate in devotion to Rāma as their highest goal in life. In this tradition the singing of Rāma's name becomes the chief mode of religious expression. Hanumān, the servant of Rāma, is his greatest devotee and sets the ideal for devotion through total surrender to the will of the god.

Bhakti, however, is only one of the themes that has found expression through the Rāma story. The story has been retold for countless purposes, both sacred and profane, ranging from philosophy to grammar and from politics to humor. But almost all the literary versions of the Rāmāyaṇa pay homage to Vālmīki as the original author, and despite their deviations insist that they have faithfully followed him.

Bibliography. W. D. P. Hill, trans., *The Holy Lake of the Acts of Rāma* (1952), a translation of *Rāmcaritmānas* of Tulsī Dās; H. P. Shastri, trans., *The Rāmāyaṇa of Vālmīki* (1959).

V. N. RAO

RAMBAM räm bäm′ (Ju). *See* MOSES BEN MAIMON.

RAMBAN räm bän′ (Ju). *See* MOSES BEN NAḤMAN.

RĀMCARITMĀNAS räm′ chär ĭt män′ ŭs (H—Hindī; lit. "the mind-pool of Rāma's deeds"). Title of a very popular Rāmāyana in the Avadhī dialect of Hindī, composed about A.D. 1574 by TULSĪ DĀS. Although the Rāmcaritmānas follows the narrative of the RĀMĀYAṆA of VĀLMĪKI and uses the materials of the Adhyātmarāmāyaṇa and other medieval works, it is a new literary creation of about ten thousand verses. In seven books like those of Vālmīki the Rāmcaritmānas relates in turn the childhood of RĀMA, his exile, the abduction of SĪTĀ, Rāma's alliance with the monkeys, the scouting of Laṅka by HANUMĀN, the successful assault on the demons, and the triumphal return of Rāma and Sītā to Ayodhyā. The first and last books contain also many myths of other deities as well as hortatory material. The Rāmcaritmānas ardently urges devotion to Rāma as God of the universe and as gracious personal Lord to be worshiped in the relation of servant to Master *(dāsyabhāva)*. Tulsī Dās presents the heroes of his epic as models of the Hindu virtues. His Rāmcaritmānas offered to its time, in its tolerant and permissive Rāma theology and its only moderately reformist social ideals, a consensual HINDUISM that facilitated unification and revival in the face of ISLAM, and provided a new understanding of the nature of orthodoxy that was popular for three centuries thereafter.

Bibliography. C. Vaudeville, *Étude sur les sources et la composition du Rāmāyaṇa de Tulsī Dās* (1955); W. D. P. Hill, trans., *The Holy Lake of the Acts of Rama* (1952).

N. J. HEIN

RĀMEŚVARAM. räm′ ēsh vŭ rŭm. *See* HINDU SACRED CITIES.

RAPTURE (Ch; derived from the LATIN Bible [I Thess. 4:17] *simul rapiemur,* "we shall be caught up together"). In MILLENARIANISM a belief that either before, during, or immediately after a period of tribulation all true members of the CHURCH—both living and dead—will be "caught up" into the air with Christ, receiving at that time bodies like the body Christ had after his RESURRECTION.

T. O. HALL, JR.

RĀSA-LĪLĀ rä′ sə lē′ lä (H). *See* KRISHNA.

RASHI rä′ shē (Ju). *See* SOLOMON BEN ISAAC.

RASTAFARI MOVEMENT räs tä fä′ rē. A messianic, MILLENARIAN MOVEMENT that originated in

Jamaica in 1930, as a religious response to the coronation of Crown Prince Ras Tafari, as Emperor Haile Selassie of Ethiopia. His biblical titles, "King of Kings" and "Conquering Lion of the Tribe of Judah," seemed to many Jamaicans the fulfillment of an original prophecy of the Jamaican mass leader Marcus Garvey, who, in 1916 on his departure to the United States, told his followers to "look to Africa where a Black King would be crowned, he shall be your Redeemer." The crowning of Ras Tafari and the coincidence of his titles in Rev. 19:16 inspired three men—Leonard Howell, Joseph Hibbert, and Archibald Dunkley—in the belief that the emperor was God. Howell became the most ardent proponent of the new faith.

Rastafarian theology is based on six points: 1) Haile Selassie is the living God. 2) The black man is the reincarnation of Israel. 3) The white man is inferior to the black man. 4) Jamaica is hell, Ethiopia is heaven. 5) Haile Selassie has arranged black repatriation to Ethiopia. 6) The black man shall in the future rule the world.

In 1933 Howell was arrested by the Jamaican government for preaching a revolutionary doctrine. He was charged with treason and his movement was banned. In 1936 he reorganized the movement at Pinnacle, St. Catharine, not far from the capital city of Kingston. In this jungle atmosphere the movement developed its beliefs and practices. Two practices common to the movement are its unique hairdo, called dreadlocks—the growing of the hair to resemble the mane of a lion—and the religious use of *Cannabis sativa,* known in Jamaica as "ganja."

The Rastafarian movement is believed to number from ten to seventy thousand followers. There are two divisions, the old school and the new. The former holds to the belief of an imminent repatriation to Ethiopia, while the latter accepts as its mission involvement in Jamaica as a catalyst for social reform. The new school has contributed much to the island in religious art and music, including the music commonly known as the "reggae."

The movement has branches in England, the United States, and Canada, and on other Caribbean islands.

Bibliography. L. E. Barrett, *The Rastafarian Movement: Sounds of Cultural Dissonance* (1977); J. Owens, *Dread: The Rastafarians of Jamaica* (1976). L. E. Barrett

RASŪL rə sōōl′ (I—Arab.; lit. "one sent"). Messenger, envoy, Apostle; someone sent from Allah to a religious community with a message and, usually, sent to head that community.

In the Qur'ān, Muhammad is called both a *rasūl* and a Nabi (prophet), but the Qur'ānic usage indicates that *rasūl* is a subset of the class of prophets. God sends only one *rasūl* to a religious community (Sura 10:48); Muhammad was sent to his people to whom no *rasūl* had previously been sent (Sura 32:3). Noah, Lot, Ismā'īl, Moses, Shu'aib, Hūd, Ṣaliḥ and Jesus are called *rasūl* in the Qur'ān, but Adam, Abraham, Isaac, Jacob, Aaron, David, Solomon, Job, and others are prophets. Both the *rasūl* and the *nabi* bring scripture from God and warn their communities, but only the *rasūl* acts as the head of the community.

In post-Qur'ānic tradition the distinction between *rasūl* and *nabi* is blurred. The messengers and the prophets are regarded by many as free from sin and error, although authorities differ on the particulars of the applicability. Tradition also increases the number of messengers to over three hundred, without, however, naming them.

It is an article of faith that Muhammad is the *rasūl* of God (*see* Shahāda).

Bibliography. A. J. Wensinck, *Concordance de la tradition musulmane* (1965); *Muslim Creed* (1932), pp. 203-4; J. Horovitz, *Koranische Untersuchungen* (1926), and "Israelitische Propheten im Koran," *ZRG,* XVI (1964), 42-57; Y. Moubarac, *Abraham dans le Coran* (1958), and *Moise dans le Coran* (1954).

G. D. Newby

RĀVAṆA rä′ vŭn ŭ (H—Skt.). Antagonist of the Rāmāyaṇa. He is the titan chief of the kingdom of Sri Lanka, which is inhabited by *rākṣasas* (*see* Asura), a clan of people usually conceived of as demons in mythology. Rāvaṇa is the son of Viśravas by his wife Kesini. Since the couple met at an inauspicious time, all of their progeny had fierce qualities. Rāvaṇa is described as having ten heads and twenty hands. Through his severe austerities (Tapas) he obtained a boon from Brahmā rendering him immune to death at the hands of gods and all other divine beings. Out of his pride, he did not include men or lower animals in the terms of the boon. When he grew too strong and was causing pain to the gods, Vishnu took the form of a human prince, Rāma, and the other gods were born as monkeys for the purpose of killing him. The Jaina Rāmāyaṇas describe Rāvaṇa as a king of noble qualities. V. N. Rao

REBBE rĕb′ bĕ (Ju—Heb.; lit. "master" [*rabbi*—teacher]). A synonym for Zaddik or Hasidic master, sometimes used to refer to an unofficially ordained Rabbi. *See* Hasidism. K. P. Bland

REBIRTH (B, H & Ja). *See* Samsara.

RECONSTRUCTIONIST JUDAISM. An ideology and movement owing its original existence and definition to Mordecai Kaplan, who was influenced by E. Durkheim and J. Dewey. Developed in the context of Conservative Judaism as an articulation of left-wing rationalism, it achieved institutional status with the founding of the Society for the Advancement of Judaism in 1922, and in 1935 began disseminating its ideas in *The Reconstructionist.* With the establishment of the Reconstructionist Rabbinical College in

Philadelphia in 1968, the movement obtained an independent position in Jewish life in the U.S.

Kaplan's *Judaism as a Civilization* (1934) attempts to recast Judaism in a modern scientific framework. He defines the "God-idea" as a function of ever-developing human awareness and experience. Since Judaism possesses, in addition to religious elements, a unique history, literature, language, and social structure, it should be defined as an "evolving religious civilization." Ritual and doctrine express those ideals which the religious group collectively holds sacred.

Kaplan envisioned "the organic community," which would integrate all aspects of Jewish life into a single institution. In turn, individual organic communities would derive inspiration from Israel, as the focus of world Jewry. L. FAGEN

REDEMPTION (Ju & Ch). In Judaism redemption has many meanings, e.g., national deliverance, prominent in Roman times and modern ZIONISM; deliverance from human finitude (not SIN), endowing the righteous with eternal happiness; worldly "self-development"; social reformation; and cosmic victory of good over evil. In Christianity it denotes the act of God in CHRIST whereby through faith man is delivered from sin. *See* ATONEMENT; SALVATION.

T. O. HALL, JR.

REFORM JUDAISM (Liberal or Progressive Judaism). One of several contemporary interpretations of Judaism (*see* ORTHODOX JUDAISM, CONSERVATIVE JUDAISM, RECONSTRUCTIONIST JUDAISM). Growing out of the Enlightenment and claiming to follow MOSES MENDELSSOHN, early Reform Judaism sought to make Judaism in general, and Jewish religious services in particular, more in keeping with "the spirit of the times" and thus stem the contemporary tide of defections from Judaism to the recently opened gates of Western culture. The first avowedly Reform "temple" was founded in Hamburg in 1818. In rabbinical conclaves in Germany, 1844-46, the movement made important strides toward self-definition. In the Pittsburgh Platform of 1875 it adopted a statement of principles, subsequently modified in the Columbus Platform (1937) and in the Centenary Perspective (1976).

Reform Judaism today, centered mostly but not exclusively in North America, stresses an internally pluralistic approach to theology and practice. "Classic" (early) Reform Judaism, however, in its attempt to make Judaism conform to nineteenth century standards and in its revolt against the authority of the past, did indeed have a kind of "orthodoxy" of its own, especially as expressed in the Pittsburgh Platform. It saw revelation as progressive, teaching anew the "essence of Judaism"—ethical monotheism or prophetic Judaism—in every generation. HALAKAH was rejected, since it had outlived its purpose, the preservation of pure Jewish monotheism in a heathen world. Judaism was seen as simply a religious denomination with no ethnic component, thus negating ZIONISM. Classic Reform also rejected the concept of a personal MESSIAH and replaced it with the idea of a messianic age to be achieved through human progress. The continued separate existence of the Jewish people was justified on the basis of its "special genius" for religion and on the "mission" of the Jews to bring the message of ethical monotheism to the world at large.

Such twentieth century developments as continued ANTI-SEMITISM in the West, the HOLOCAUST, the founding of the nation of Israel, and the influx of ceremonially oriented Eastern European Jews into Reform temples forced Reform Judaism to change markedly, an evolution clearly seen in the Columbus Platform and the Centenary Perspective. Reform Judaism today is staunchly Zionist, it is nondoctrinaire in its theology, and it accepts the value and significance of many traditional Jewish customs and ceremonies.

Reform Judaism in the United States maintains a seminary, the Hebrew Union College—Jewish Institute of Religion (Cincinnati); a rabbinical organization, the Central Conference of American Rabbis (CCAR); and a confederation of synagogues, the Union of American Hebrew Congregations (UAHC). This latter organization has been at the forefront of many campaigns for social justice.

Bibliography. E. Borowitz, *Reform Judaism Today* (1978); D. Rudavsky, *Emancipation and Adjustment* (1967).

M. M. KELLNER

REFORM MOVEMENTS IN INDIA. Mostly as a response to challenges from the West, represented by Christianity, rationalism, utilitarianism, and modern science, Hinduism was aroused from centuries of stagnancy to a defense as well as rethinking of its central social and religious norms and teachings. While initially on the defensive against Western criticism, Hindus soon regained confidence in their religious tradition, interpreting it in modern, Western terms. Hinduism not only rebounded but even dispatched missionaries of its own to the West.

1. **Historical background.** It is generally agreed that at the beginning of the nineteenth century, when the British had consolidated their hold on India, Hinduism had reached a nadir. No significant religious movements had occurred since the fifteenth century. Social abuses, such as infant marriage, widow burning, infanticide and polygamy, were denounced by many Westerners. The missionaries—predominantly Protestants—were shocked by what they viewed as Hindu polytheism and idolatry. Not surprisingly the first reaction to Western criticism occurred in Bengal, where Calcutta, the capital of British India from 1780 to 1912, was situated, and where British presence was most conspicuous.

2. **Brāhmo Samāj.** One Indian to respond to Christian missionary criticism was RAM MOHAN ROY. In 1828 he founded the BRĀHMO SAMĀJ in Calcutta. The basic tenets of this reform movement included emphasis on the UPANIṢADS as the source of all wisdom and a claim that these texts teach a monotheistic doctrine of God. Weekly services included readings from the Upaniṣads, hymn singing and sermons on the Christian model. Following the death of Roy in 1833, the Brāhmo Samāj languished until 1843, when Debendranath Tagore (1817–1905) assumed leadership. In contrast to the cosmopolitan, rationalistically inclined Roy, Tagore was an Indian nationalist and a mystic. He deliberately diminished the Christian element in Brāhmo services. After a thorough investigation of the Upaniṣads, he composed, on the basis of reason and mystical insight, a Brāhmo creed, the *Brāhmo Dharma*. It rejected image veneration, reincarnation, AVATARS and Śaṃkara's ADVAITA philosophy, while emphasizing the importance of ethical obligations, charity, and the need for a modern, scientific education. Essentially a conservative, Tagore favored gradual social reforms and, consequently, soon came into conflict with younger, more radical Brāhmos. In 1865 a schism occurred when Tagore's erstwhile disciple, Keshab Chandra Sen (1838-84), seceded in protest against officiating Brāhmo priests continuing to wear the sacred thread, the distinguishing Brahmin caste mark. Sen's group, known as the Brāhmo Samāj of India, in distinction to the *Adi* (original) Brāhmo Samāj of Tagore, embarked upon further reforms, including widow remarriage, caste intermarriage, and education for women. An ardent missionary, Sen was instrumental in disseminating Brāhmo teachings outside Bengal, leading to the establishment of sister organizations in Bombay and Madras. Through Sen's intense personal devotion to Christ, the Christian element in the Brāhmo Samāj was reemphasized. Soon Brāhmos became known for their puritanical conduct and their accent on morality. An eclectic, Sen combined devotion for Christ with enthusiasm for CAITANYA, a devotional Hindu sage. Through Sen's initiative, KĪRTANA (devotional music and chanting) was introduced into Brāhmo services. This was resented by the more rationalistically inclined Brāhmos. Once again the more reform-oriented Brāhmos split off, forming the *Sadhâran* (general) Brāhmo Samāj which concentrated on social service and deemphasized spiritual activity. All three Brāhmo groups continue to exist but, greatly weakened by the two schisms, they have steadily declined in the wake of Hindu revivalism. They had served their intended function by preventing large-scale defection of educated Hindus to Christianity.

3. **Ārya Samāj.** More in tune with the rise of national consciousness was the ĀRYA SAMĀJ. In contrast to the Brāhmo Samāj it attracted some grass-root support, primarily in the Punjab and the United Provinces (Uttar Pradesh). From the start the Ārya Samāj, headed by the pugnacious Swami DAYĀNANDA, was militant. While it too was dedicated to fighting social abuses and championed nonidolatrous monotheism, it accepted reincarnation, defended cow protection, and retained such traditional Hindu rituals as the fire sacrifice. Most importantly, the Vedas were reinstated as the authoritative source of all knowledge, spiritual and pragmatic. Swami Dayānanda instituted the rite of *Suddhi* (purification) and used it to readmit to the Hindu fold those who had converted to Islam and Christianity. In 1892 the Ārya Samāj split into conservative and progressive groups. While retaining a substantial membership in Northern India, the Ārya Samāj shared with the Brāhmo Samāj a fatal weakness: it rejected image veneration, avatars and yogic (*see* YOGA) meditation, all of which form an essential part of mainstream Hinduism.

4. **Ramakrishna Mission.** Chiefly responsible for the renewed confidence in traditional Hinduism was the God-intoxicated Hindu sage, RĀMAKRISHNA Paramahansa (1834-1886). Hitherto Westerners had admired the past greatness of India, but the life of Rāmakrishna was a testimony to the fact that modern India too could produced spiritual giants. An illiterate devotee of the goddess KĀLĪ, Rāmakrishna attracted disciples from all levels of Indian society and was considered an avatar. His ecstatic utterances impressed even sophisticated intellectuals. After successfully testing various Hindu *sādhanās* (spiritual disciplines), Rāmakrishna practiced Christianity and Islam and concluded that they too led to the One. Thus, he concluded, all religions were true. Above all, he rehabilitated image veneration, explaining that it was legitimate to use form to reach the formless. He did make allowance for social service, provided it did not interfere with God-realization. The social service ideal was carried out in a greater way by his foremost disciple, Swami VIVEKĀNANDA, who disseminated Rāmakrishna's teachings in the West. Upon Rāmakrishna's death Swami Vivekānanda founded the Ramakrishna Mission of monks and nuns who combined yogic meditation with social activity. The Ramakrishna Mission gained renown as the major exponent of the VEDĀNTA in East and West. At the same time it was responsible for the establishment of numerous hospitals, orphanages, schools, and lending libraries in India. (*See* HINDUISM IN AMERICA.)

5. **Śrī Aurobindo** (1872-1950) was another product of the interaction between India and the West. He had spent his formative years (1879-93) in England and had to undergo "indianization" upon his return to India at the age of twenty-one. His major intellectual contribution was an evolutionary view of life which ran counter to the traditional, cyclical Hindu view. He further contradicted traditional Hindu cosmology by stating that the aim of evolution was the divinization of the material universe, thus striking a blow at Hindu "otherworldliness." His

evolutionary scheme called for the spiritualization of man's body and mind and the consequent creation of a "superman," a gnostic being, through the process of "integral yoga." Since 1968 an international community at AUROVILLE (South India) has been engaged in implementing his teachings with a view to hastening the evolutionary process and ushering in a new era of gnostic beings (*see* AUROBINDO).

6. Gandhi. Probably the greatest influence on modern Hinduism has been exerted by Mahatma GANDHI. While proudly considering himself a follower of the *Sanātana Dharma* (eternal dharma), he rejected any part of scripture not compatible with reason and morality. Living the life of a karmayogin (a follower of karma as a goal of life), he fought against caste prejudice and for the uplifting of the untouchables whom he named HARIJANS (children of God). In fighting against untouchability and for India's independence he made use of traditional methods and symbols. Through fasting he overcame Brahmin resistance to the opening of Hindu temples to the untouchables. *Satyāgraha* ("truth-force") became his form of civil disobedience, which in turn he based on AHIMSĀ ("non-injury") and *brahmācārya* ("self-suffering"). By proclaiming his indebtedness to Tolstoy, Thoreau, and Ruskin, and expressing reverence for the New Testament, he too symbolizes the merger of East and West.

7. Tagore. Bengal's poet laureate, RABINDRANATH TAGORE (1861-1941), the fourteenth son of Debendranath Tagore, tried to synthesize Western humanism and the perennial wisdom of the Upaniṣads. For the purpose of combining the best of East and West he established an educational institution in Shantiniketan (West Bengal), where modern sciences were taught together with art, music, and literature of orient and occident, all in the natural setting in imitation of the ancient Indian forest academies.

Bibliography. J. N. Farquhar, *Modern Religious Movements in India* (1912); H. v. Glasenapp, *Religiöse Reformbewegungen im heutigen Indien* (1928); Jan Gonda, *Die Religionen Indiens: Der jüngere Hinduismus* (1963); V. S. Naravane, *Modern Indian Thought* (1964); D. S. Sarma, *Studies in the Renaissance of Hinduism* (1944).

A. LIPSKI

REFORMATION, CATHOLIC (Ch). A long process, stretching from the early sixteenth to the mid-seventeenth century, whereby the ROMAN CATHOLIC Church, shaken by the attacks of the Protestant Reformers, achieved spiritual renewal, disciplinary reform, and administrative reorganization. As a result it was able to react with vigor and a considerable measure of success to the new challenges confronting it. Three interrelated strands in the Catholic Reformation are Catholic renewal, Catholic restoration, and Counter Reformation. (*See* REFORMATION, PROTESTANT.)

1. Catholic renewal. Forces of renewal were at work in the church long before MARTIN LUTHER challenged the spiritual and ecclesiastical order. Many of the disciplinary reforms enacted finally at the Council of TRENT (1545-63) had been proposed much earlier at general COUNCILS assembled at Vienne (1311-12), Constance (1414-18), and Basel (1431-49), and again, on the eve of the Reformation, at the Fifth Lateran Council (1512-17). Although little had come of those proposals for churchwide reform, renewal had been achieved piecemeal at the local level in Germany, in France, and above all in Spain. There Cardinel Ximénez de Cisneros (1436-1517), during the period of his ascendancy as ARCHIBISHOP of Toledo and chief minister to the queen (1495 onward), was able to pursue with vigor the reform not only of his own FRANCISCAN Order but also of the diocesan clergy. He persuaded the Catholic monarchs to use their power to appoint as BISHOPS men worthy of bearing spiritual responsibility, and used improved education and spiritual formation to restore the dignity and renew the pastoral ministry of the diocesan priesthood. With the income of his own archbishopric he endowed the new university of Alcalá, which, with its emphasis on scriptural and patristic studies in the original languages, became a distinguished center of biblical studies and produced the great Complutensian Polyglot Bible. Ximénez died in 1517, the year in which Luther issued his ninety-five theses, but the reform he had pursued did not die with him. It is not surprising, then, that the Spanish church was later to make so marked a contribution to the efforts to contain the spread of PROTESTANTISM.

Like so many other late medieval reformers, including Luther himself, Ximénez was a product of the monastic renewal that had generated in the older established orders a drive toward the strict observance of the original rule. It had led to such authentic new departures as the Brothers and Sisters of the Common Life (*ca.* 1384 onward) in northern Europe, the Jesuates (1360 onward) in the south, and the Oratory of the Divine Love (early sixteenth century). All of them had their beginnings in lay confraternities seeking to carve out a middle ground between the forms of life endorsed by the traditional monastic and mendicant orders and the less formal modes of communal life pursued in the thirteenth and fourteenth centuries by the Beghard and Beguine communities. The Oratory, in turn, helped spawn a new religious order, the Theatines (1524), which, along with other new monastic or quasi-monastic groupings such as the Sommaschi (1528), the CAPUCHINS (1528), the Barnabites (1530), and, above all, the JESUITS (1540), were to play an important role in the spread of the Catholic Reformation. (*See* RELIGIOUS ORDERS.)

2. Catholic restoration. Whether or not, in the absence of the Protestant challenge, this renewal could have produced the thoroughgoing renovation that actually occurred remains a matter of dispute. It did, however, nurture among moderate Catholic theologians, even as late as the early sessions of the Council of Trent, a degree of sympathy with the religious aspirations (if not necessarily the theological formulations) of the Protestant Reformers. Thus among those who sympathized with the views of Cardinal CONTARINI (patron of the early Jesuits and in the decade prior to the convocation of Trent perhaps the leading figure in Catholic reforming circles) the attitude toward the Protestants was remarkably conciliatory, even on doctrinal matters. Indeed, the decrees of the Council of Trent on justification and on scripture and tradition, however unsatisfactory in Protestant eyes, allowed leeway for diversity of opinion, and this fact may itself reflect the lingering effects of this conciliatory phase in Catholic reform.

With Contarini's failure, however, to reach a viable doctrinal accommodation with MELANCHTHON and BUCER, themselves the most moderate of the German Protestant theologians, the conservative forces began to come to the fore, and the possibility of reconciliation with the Protestants was dismissed. The church set out to restore a purified medieval past, to bolster hierarchical authority, to achieve a more precise definition of the Catholic faith, and to be implacable in its defense and unremitting in its propagation. Most representative of this school of thought was Cardinal Caraffa, who engineered the foundation of the Roman INQUISITION and who himself became pope in 1555, as Paul IV. With his election Catholic reform at last found decisive papal leadership. Vigorous steps were taken to improve the moral climate at Rome; nonresident bishops living there were driven back to their dioceses; reforming measures were enforced at the papal CURIA; the first INDEX of Prohibited Books was issued; and Italy became a hunting ground for heretics, imagined as well as real.

It was reform of a certain type, at once both defensive and aggressive. A total impasse having been reached with deputations of German Protestants at the Council of Trent during its second phase (1551-52), the driving commitment now was to purify the old Catholic order without in any way dismantling it and then, at all costs, to defend it. With the end of the council in 1563 a series of capable and energetic popes set out to implement the program of reforms that was decreed in its final sessions. Despite persistent difficulties over the jurisdictional claims of the national monarchies, they did this with vigor and dedication, seeking especially, through the institution of diocesan seminaries, to restore clerical efficiency and morale.

In all these endeavors they drew valuable support from the new or reformed monastic orders, and particularly from the Jesuits. IGNATIUS OF LOYOLA'S earliest ambition had been the conversion of the pagans, and his Society's impact on the missionary field was felt in regions as far distant from one another as North America and Japan, India and Peru. But once they became involved in education, especially the teaching of the faith in European universities, the Jesuits were drawn into direct controversy with Protestantism. They ended, above all in Germany, by leading the resistance to Protestant theologians and the spread of Protestant ideas. Because of the success of their educational methods, they also became the schoolmasters of kings, princes, and aristocrats. Just as defense of the old religious order readily passed over into attacks on the new, so too their reliance upon spiritual and ecclesiastical weaponry passed over easily enough into reliance on political influence and strength. This shift of tactic coincided with the revival of the Catholic powers in Europe and the willingness of popes like Pius V to indulge the hope that in some parts of Europe—notably England and the Netherlands—Catholicism might be restored by resort to force. This is the strand in the Catholic reformation to which the expression "Counter Reformation" is most properly applied.

3. Counter Reformation. During the early part of the sixteenth century France had found in the Lutheran princes of Germany useful allies in its ongoing struggle with Hapsburg power in Italy, the Netherlands, and Spain. With the conclusion, however, of peace with Spain in 1559, and with the withdrawal of France into almost half a century of civil war and internal religious strife, the balance of power swung against the Protestant states. For roughly half a century the Hapsburg powers pursued aggressive anti-Protestant foreign policies. The popes of the Counter Reformation and their Jesuit servants were not averse to attempting to cash in on the opportunity which this situation afforded. As a result Pius V was in 1570 willing to declare Queen Elizabeth of England excommunicate and deposed, to declare her subjects released from their allegiance to her, and to lend his support to an uprising in the Catholic north on behalf of the claim of Mary Stuart to the English throne. Thus too Gregory XIII's willingness to support the emperor's struggle with the Protestant estates in Germany, his incitement of revolts in Ireland against the rule of the English queen, his support of the military plans that Philip II of Spain was determined to pursue against the Protestants, and his encouragement of the Catholic Guise faction in France in its struggle against the HUGUENOTS. He unwisely gave a public welcome in 1572 to the news of the massacre of the Huguenot leadership in Paris on St. Bartholomew's Day. As they served their papal masters, the international reputation of the Jesuits gave way to a growing notoriety as purveyors of treachery and as agents, real or imagined, of religious dissension and political subversion.

When, after a period of growing tension, the Protestant nobility of Bohemia revolted in 1618 against the Catholic emperor Ferdinand and offered the throne to a Protestant prince, the Counter Reformation entered its final phase. The whole balance of power was now threatened, the emperor had little choice but to fight back, and the Thirty Years' War began. At its inception, then, it was a religious war, and potentially the greatest and most critical of all the religious wars that punctuated the history of Europe during the century following Luther's breach with Rome. But it was a religious war only until about the year 1635, when Catholic France entered the conflict in alliance with Sweden and several of the Protestant states of Germany. The war ended in 1648 with the peace of Westphalia, which successfully fixed for the future the religious lines of the European states.

Bibliography. P. Jannelle, *The Catholic Reformation* (1949); H. Jedin, *A History of the Council of Trent,* 2 vols. (1957-61); *The New Cambridge Modern History,* Vols. I, II (1957-70); H. O. Evennett, *The Spirit of the Counter-Reformation* (1968).

F. OAKLEY

REFORMATION, PROTESTANT. A movement in the Christian church in western Europe during the sixteenth century which stressed doctrinal reform, centering around the concept of the JUSTIFICATION of sinners by grace through faith in JESUS Christ. It also called for a reform of morals and of the institutions of the church. It may be divided into four major movements, the LUTHERAN, the REFORMED, the ANGLICAN, and the Radical Reformation. All are indebted to the writings of MARTIN LUTHER (1483-1546).

1. Luther and the Lutherans. Luther caught the attention of all Europe in the years following publication of his 95 Theses on indulgences in 1517. His views grew out of his study of the BIBLE, on which he lectured at the University of Wittenberg, and his personal spiritual crisis. His answers to that crisis struck a responsive chord with many late medieval Christians who were dissatisfied with the spiritual and pastoral guidance provided by the church of that day. Especially in Germany, religiosity and piety reached new heights at the eve of the Reformation, but could not satisfy the scrupulosity of sensitive believers like Luther or provide a feeling of personal worth and self-confidence for the average lay person.

Students from the classrooms of Luther and his associate since 1518, the leading humanist PHILIP MELANCHTHON, spread the Lutheran message quickly throughout Germany and beyond. Older humanists such as ERASMUS initially welcomed Luther's reform but parted company with him as he fell under the ban of both pope and emperor in 1520 and 1521. Younger humanists like Melanchthon supported Luther's cause and joined with others in persuading town and countryside of the validity of Luther's message. From enthusiasm for his opposition to Rome, the common people grew to embrace his emphasis on God's free gift of forgiveness through faith in Christ. In 1524 city governments in Nuremberg and Magdeburg adopted the Lutheran pattern of reform, and more than three decades of German princely reform along Lutheran lines, based almost without exception on popular support, began under the leadership of Elector John of Saxony (1525) and Landgrave Philip of Hesse (1526). They, with other princes and representatives of two imperial cities, presented the AUGSBURG CONFESSION, an expression of Lutheran teaching composed by Melanchthon, to Emperor Charles V at the imperial diet at Augsburg in 1530. In the Religious Peace of Augsburg in 1555 it was given official status as the basic legal definition of the Lutheran faith.

Particularly important in the spread of Luther's message were hymns, many of them composed by the reformer himself; his liturgies, issued in Latin (1523) and then in German (1526); his sermon books, which provided his theology in preachable form for parish priests; and his Small and Large CATECHISMS (1529), which offered the basis of religious instruction and a pattern of piety for Luther's followers to the present day.

The Augsburg Confession and its Apology, also by Melanchthon, and Luther's writings, e.g. the Catechisms and his Smalcald Articles (1537), were all claimed as binding confessional definitions for their theology by Lutheran churches during the sixteenth century. They emphasize Luther's Christocentric understanding of SALVATION: God's mercy is comprehended in Christ's death and resurrection for sinners and delivers sinners from guilt and condemnation through faith in Christ, which is produced by the HOLY SPIRIT. Other Protestant reformers echoed this understanding, although not all grasped his pastoral understanding of the dynamic application of God's Word as law and GOSPEL. Luther and other Protestants agreed that the teaching of the church springs only from the Bible and must be criticized in its light. However, the other major Protestant traditions did not fully share Luther's belief that God uses selected elements of the created order to convey grace; the most important disagreements arose among Protestants over Luther's belief that Christ's body and blood are truly sacramentally present in the bread and wine of the EUCHARIST. Attempts to reconcile him with leaders of the Swiss Reformation, above all ULRICH ZWINGLI (1484-1531), at the Marburg Colloquy (1529) failed, although a settlement between other South Germans and the Wittenbergers was reached in the Wittenberg Concord (1536), reached after strenuous efforts at reconciliation by the reformer of Strassburg, MARTIN BUCER (1491-1551).

2. The Reformed tradition. Zwingli, trained by humanist instructors at Vienna and Basel, shared their zeal for reform and from 1519 led the city council of Zurich and others in Switzerland into reformation, often by challenging local Catholic clergy in disputations. Zwingli worked closely with local magistrates in organizing the newly reformed church. He was killed in a battle between Protestant and Catholic cantons (1531) and was succeeded by Heinrich Bullinger (1504-75) as Zurich's chief pastor and theological leader of the Swiss Reformed churches. Bullinger helped prepare the Zurich

Consensus of 1549 and the Second Helvetic Confession of 1566, key definitions of the Reformed position. His writings influenced the thought of English and continental churches.

JOHN CALVIN (1509-64), the single most influential shaper of Reformed thought, became associated with French humanist reformers at the University of Paris in the early 1530s. Sharing the reforming goals of the French humanist pioneer, Jacques Lefevre d'Etaples (*ca.* 1450-*ca.* 1537), these reformers ran afoul of King Francis I and were scattered. In 1536 Calvin arrived in Geneva, where the French humanist William Farel had introduced reform. Except for a brief exile (1539-41), Calvin spent the rest of his life there, making its church a model for Reformed congregations in piety and polity. Though not, as often suggested, a "theocracy," Geneva did respond politically to Calvin's spiritual direction; his concept of the Christian life eventually set the tone for the city. The PRESBYTERIANISM of the Genevan church, with its consistory governing doctrine and morals for the community, and with its four offices of pastor, teacher, elder, and deacon, was incorporated into Reformed churches throughout the world. Calvin's theology, presented in systematic form in his *Institutes of the Christian Religion* (first ed. 1536), in biblical commentaries, and in occasional tracts, such as his polemic against the Roman Catholic cardinal Jacopo Sadoleto, influenced the thought of reformers throughout much of Europe. Many of them were trained in the Genevan Academy, directed by THEODORE BEZA (1519-1605), which sent out graduates to churches in France, the Netherlands, the British Isles, and elsewhere. As theologian and churchman, Beza profoundly influenced the developing Reformed churches; classical Reformed theology was shaped by him and others, including Peter Martyr Vermigli (1500-62) and Jerome Zanchi (1516-90), both educated in Thomist Aristotelianism before they fled Italy and assumed teaching positions in Switzerland and England and in Germany respectively.

Calvinism gained support in France, particularly among nobles and townsmen, and it won legal status after a series of religious wars, in which armies raised by Calvinist congregations and nobles fought the forces of a strong Roman Catholic party which attempted to use the crown during the successive reigns of the three sons of Henry II and Catherine de Medici. These wars, begun in 1562 and climaxing with the massacre of Protestants on St. Bartholomew's Day, 1572, finally resulted in toleration under the Edict of Nantes (1598), issued by the formerly Protestant king Henry IV. Calvinism was accepted in Scotland under the leadership of JOHN KNOX (*ca.* 1505-72), parts of Eastern Europe and Germany, and in the Netherlands, where it linked with a movement for independence from Spain. Within the Dutch Calvinist church a dispute over PREDESTINATION and the synergism of JACOB ARMINIUS (1560-1609) led to the Synod of Dort (1618-19), which set forth a fundamental definition of Reformed theology.

3. The Anglican Reformation. Reformed theology influenced the English Reformation, the stage for which was set by Henry VIII's desire for a male heir who could ensure the peace and prosperity which England had lacked during the fifteenth century. That desire led to his divorce from his first wife, Catherine of Aragon, and to the proclamation of the king as head of the church of England. Although Henry himself remained committed to medieval doctrine, his revolt against papal control of the church and the efforts of certain advisors, e. g. Thomas Cranmer (1489-1556), archbishop of Canterbury from 1532, and Thomas Cromwell, formed the basis for the official introduction of Protestant doctrine under Cranmer's leadership when Edward VI came to the throne in 1547. Already under Henry VIII reformers had issued English translations of the Bible and had begun distribution of Cranmer's *Book of Homilies,* both of which strengthened a popular desire for reform based upon the work of the fifteenth century LOLLARDS, Protestant ideas from Europe, and the reform sentiments of Erasmus' English disciples. In 1548 Cranmer composed the BOOK OF COMMON PRAYER, revised in 1552; it set the tone for English piety and liturgy and served as a powerful instrument for bringing the Protestant faith to the people. In 1552 Cranmer also composed the "Forty-Two Articles," a Protestant doctrinal statement, for the English church. Mary Tudor succeeded Edward VI in 1553 and attempted during her five-year reign to restore Roman Catholicism; her efforts failed for lack of time and adequate personnel. Elizabeth I's reign (1558-1603) marked the firm establishment of English Protestantism, typified by the Book of Common Prayer, the THIRTY-NINE ARTICLES of 1563, and John Foxe's *Book of Martyrs,* particularly treating those executed during Mary Tudor's reign. Under Elizabeth, Puritans sought further purification of the church from medieval practices, stricter piety, and a measure of autonomy for churchmen.

4. The Radical Reformation. The so-called Radical Reformation, a term of modern scholarship, encompasses a number of movements more important because they foreshadow subsequent Western Christian developments than because they commanded the allegiance of many in the sixteenth century. Among the Radicals are those labeled ANABAPTISTS, Spiritualists, and Evangelical Rationalists. Particularly the Anabaptists continued a tradition of criticism against the mainstream of Western Christendom from the high Middle Ages; these critics, individuals and small groups, espoused biblicism, moralism, anti-clericalism, anti-sacramentalism, and millennialism in varying combinations (*see* MILLENARIAN MOVEMENTS). The Swiss–South German Schleitheim Confession (1527) set forth basic Anabaptist principles, including believer's BAPTISM and rejection of participation by believers in governmental activities, especially the use of the sword (although revolutionary Anabaptists attempted to set up a millennial kingdom at Münster in 1535). Persecuted by other Protestants and by Roman Catholics, Anabaptists became a movement of some size chiefly in the Netherlands, under the leadership of Menno Simons (*ca.* 1492/6-*ca.* 1559/61; *see* MENNONITES), and in Moravia, where Jakob Hutter (*d.* 1536) organized Anabaptist communities. Leading sixteenth century Spiritualists included Thomas Müntzer (*ca.* 1489-1525), Sebastian Franck (*ca.* 1499-*ca.* 1543), and Caspar von Schwenckfeld (*ca.* 1489-1561). Among the Evangelical Rationalists the anti-Trinitarian (*see* TRINITY) systems of Michael Servetus (1511-53) and Lelio (1525-62) and Fausto (1539-1604) Sozzini were of particular importance. Fausto Sozzini organized followers in Poland; their beliefs are summarized in the Racovian Catechism of 1605. *See* REFORMATION, CATHOLIC; SOCINIANISM.

Bibliography. H. J. Grimm, *The Reformation Era, 1500-1650* (1965); H. J. Hillerbrand *The World of the Reformation* (1973); H. G. Koenigsberger and G. L. Mosse, *Europe in the Sixteenth Century* (1968); F. Lau and E. Bizer, *A History of the Reformation in Germany to 1555* (1969); J. Lortz, *The Reformation in Germany,* 2 vols. (1968); L. W. Spitz, *The Renaissance and Reformation Movements* (1971).

R. KOLB

REFORMED CHURCHES. The type of PROTESTANTISM that originated in the context of Christian humanism, under the leadership of Ulrich ZWINGLI in Zurich, Martin BUCER in Strasbourg, William Farel and JOHN CALVIN in France and Geneva. Reformed churches of British origin are called PRESBYTERIAN or CONGREGATIONAL to designate their polity.

Both Zwingli and Calvin owed a debt to the German reformer Martin LUTHER. However, the REFORMATION in Switzerland, more radical than the Lutheran, always maintained a distinctive character. According to Luther, reformation should consist of eliminating from church life what Scripture condemns. In contrast, the Swiss reformers insisted that all significant practices of the church must have a positive warrant in Scripture.

Reformed churches reaffirmed the doctrines of the TRINITY and of the person of JESUS Christ from the ancient catholic church, and they shared the classic Protestant doctrines of JUSTIFICATION BY FAITH alone, the priesthood of all believers, the supreme authority of the HOLY SPIRIT speaking through the BIBLE, the sanctity of the common life, and an emphasis upon the necessity of the personal response of faith in the SACRAMENTS. Reformed theology is characterized by an emphasis on the lordship and majesty of God, who is conceived not primarily as truth or beauty but as intention, purpose, energy, and will. The human counterpart of this emphasis is the understanding of the Christian life as the embodiment of the purposes of God and the working out of these purposes in individual life and in history. Thus Reformed church members have been activists, converters, and shapers of culture and history.

The Reformed limited sacraments to BAPTISM and the Lord's Supper (*see* EUCHARIST), which they believed to have been instituted by Jesus Christ and which they insisted should be observed in the context of the worshiping congregation. Reformed worship may best be described as the faithful hearing of the Word of God. Calvin modeled his worship on the reformation of the German MASS at Strasbourg. The worship services devised by William Farel and Zwingli were primarily preaching services with occasional celebrations of the Lord's Supper. Psalm singing was characteristic of Calvinistic worship. The PURITAN movement and the particular experiences of churches, as for example the Reformed church on the American frontier, have also been factors in shaping Reformed worship.

Reformed churches have been dominant in the Reformed cantons of Switzerland, the Netherlands, and Scotland. They were strong minority movements in France, Germany, Hungary, Czechoslovakia, and Poland. Immigration established Reformed churches in the U.S., Northern Ireland, Canada, Australia, New Zealand, and South Africa. Missionary activity planted churches in Africa, Indonesia, Korea, Japan, and Latin America.

Most Reformed churches belong to the World Alliance of Reformed Churches with headquarters in Geneva and with a total membership of more than fifty-five million.

Bibliography. J. H. Leith, *Introduction to the Reformed Tradition* (1977); J. T. McNeill, *The History and Character of Calvinism* (1954).

J. H. LEITH

REINCARNATION. The process by which, in certain belief systems, the soul of a dead person enters another body in order to continue its existence.

Reincarnation depends upon a belief in a soul which is ontologically distinct from the body and which can therefore exist independently from the body, or at least from any particular body. It may or may not correlate with a belief in the absolute IMMORTALITY of the soul. (*See* SOUL, SPIRIT; ANIMISM.)

1. **Hinduism.** In HINDUISM reincarnation is a doctrine oriented to the SALVATION of the individual. Entrapment in a body—any body—is the central problem of the human predicament, and escape from the body into ATMAN ("All-Soul") is salvation. But the achievement of salvation is much too difficult and complex to take place in one lifetime. Therefore, the individual is given countless other chances, in other incarnations. All living things, including human beings, are arranged in a comprehensive hierarchical system. A human being in any one existence is assigned by birth to a given CASTE or noncaste, in which he or she will live out that existence. There is no upward mobility within that lifetime. But how well he or she accepts and lives out the entire complex

of social-religious duties associated with that station in life (*see* Dharma) determines at what level he or she will be reincarnated. The process of evaluation is an automatic, inexorable process of reward-retribution (*see* Karma). Those who have fulfilled their destiny worthily are promoted to a higher rank. Those who have done badly are demoted. Those who have performed in a mediocre way are returned to an equivalent station.

Since all living forms are included in the hierarchy, all life is sacred. This accounts for the refusal of Hindus or Jainas to eat any kind of meat or to kill any living thing, even a fly or a mosquito. Certain animals are in fact exceptionally sacred, including cattle, cobras, and monkeys.

At the very top of the system are the Twice Born castes, culminating in the Brahmin caste. The chief end of a devout Brahmin is to take the final step upward out of the wheel of reincarnation into Atman. His preoccupation, therefore, is to maintain and enhance his ritual purity, which requires a strict segregation in all possible relations from persons of lower caste.

Especially at the top, the duties necessary to achieve perfection are purely individual and oriented to asceticism (*see* Tapas). This is why holy men, struggling to take the final step, are often isolated from society and practice severe forms of self-discipline, self-denial, and self-flagellation. Various formalized disciplines are designed to assist in this process (*see* Yoga). But there is little in the system to function as a social ethic. (*See also* Jainism.)

2. **Buddhism.** Early Buddhism rejected the concept of caste and taught that there is no soul (Anatta) and that the self is impermanent (Anicca). At death, the self is resolved into the five Skandhas of which it is composed. But karma determines one's destiny, and anyone who has not achieved enlightenment will be reborn as a god, a human, an animal, a ghost (Preta), or a denizen of hell. (*See* Samsara.) The question of what then it is that is reborn was answered by analogies drawn from the lighting of one candle by another or the impress of a seal on wax. (*See* Milindapañha.)

In Tibetan Buddhism the dead person is believed to spend up to forty-nine days in an intermediate state known as *bardo* before being reborn. (*See* Bardo Thodöl §3.)

3. **Ancestor-oriented reincarnation.** In some nonliterate societies, whose cultic activities are oriented chiefly to the ancestors in order to maintain and enhance the continuity and prosperity of the kinship group, there is also a belief in reincarnation. But here it is believed that each child is born as the reincarnation of a specific ancestor. Which ancestor is involved is, in some societies, believed to be determined by structured kinship relationships; that is, the ancestor stands in a specific kin relationship to the child in whom he returns. In other cases parents and other relatives watch the infant closely, and discern by means of physical and psychological traits which ancestor has returned. This belief goes much further than the common expression used by Westerners in speaking about a baby, that "he's his grandfather all over again." It is believed quite literally that the ancestor has returned in the child. The ancestor's name is given to the child.

It is necessary in such a society to know which ancestor has returned. Not to know defeats the purpose of the belief, which is to ensure the functional survival of ancestors. In contrast, in ancestor-oriented societies which do not believe in reincarnation, there is often a gradual loss of significance of any particular ancestor, as people who retained distinctive memories of that person die one by one. (*See* Ancestor Veneration.)

4. **Australian aboriginal beliefs.** In a number of Australian aboriginal societies it is believed that each child is the reincarnation of some dead person, though it is not necessary to know which one. Rather, there is a whole world of souls of dead persons who are waiting for any chance to return. This they do by entering into the womb of any woman of childbearing age. These societies believe that the father plays no active procreative role; a child is born at the whim of a soul requiring a new body. But a father is sociologically crucial for the well-being of a child. Therefore, since a woman can become pregnant at any moment, and every child must have a father, it is essential that no woman of childbearing age ever be unmarried, even for a brief interval. Girls are therefore married off, for safety's sake, as soon as they show signs of approaching puberty, and a widow is remarried at her late husband's graveside. Once she is married, of course, any children born to a woman have her current husband for a father, and all is well.

5. **Random reincarnation.** There seems to be a belief among some people in the West, apparently without any systemic religious foundation, in what may be called random reincarnation. This is a part of the widespread emphasis on the occult and the uncanny. There is talk about persons having memories which cannot be explained without recourse to the notion that they are remembering some previous existence. This prior life may have taken place in fairly recent history, or it may go back to antiquity or even to prehistory. But there does not seem to be any organized philosophy behind this belief.

See also Gilgul.

Bibliography. C. J. Ducasse, *A Critical Examination of the Belief in a Life after Death* (1961); J. Head, comp., *Reincarnation in World Thought* (1967). C. R. Taber

REIYŪKAI rā yoo kī´ (B—Jap.; lit. "friends of the spirit association"). A movement within Nichiren Buddhism, founded in Tokyo in 1925 by Kubo Kakutaro (1890-1944), assisted by his sister-in-law Kotani Kimi (1901-71). It was perhaps the most successful new religion prior to and during World War II, when, unlike most other movements, it was free from interference by the government. However, being schism prone, it has been weakened by frequent defections. Especially notable for the long-range effect is the secession in 1938 of NIWANO NIKKYŌ and NAGANUMA MYŌKŌ, who formed RISSHŌ KŌSEIKAI.

After Kubo's death, leadership passed to the high-strung, often hysterical, Kotani Kimi. Her involvement in well-publicized financial scandals in 1949 and 1953 and her continued ineptness in administration resulted in further defections and general decline. Even so, a distinctive program of social service was continued throughout her tenure.

Under the presidency of the founder's son, Kubo Tsuginari, a graduate of Tokyo University, Reiyūkai has been modernized and regenerated, with an influx of young people. A training center has been built on the Izu Peninsula. A sophisticated periodical, *Inner Trip,* attracts a wide readership. The headquarters are in Tokyo.

Bibliography. H. Thomsen, *The New Religions of Japan* (1963). H. N. MCFARLAND

RELICS (Ch—Lat. *reliquiae;* lit. "remains, residue"). The remains of the body of a MARTYR or other saints and, in a wider sense, objects that have had contact with Christ or his saints. First-class (or real) relics include skin, bone, clothing, instruments connected with the martyr's death; second-class (or representative) relics are objects brought into contact with the saint's body or grave. OT references to such projects (Exod. 13:19; II Kings 2:14; 13:21) are less significant than Jewish fear of idolatrous practices and human representations; and NT texts such as Acts 19:12 (cures wrought through handkerchiefs touched to Paul's body) concern new converts from paganism. The earliest clear evidence for the veneration of relics is the account of Polycarp's martyrdom (156 or 157). With the spread of persecution, veneration for the martyrs became linked with their tombs, over which the EUCHARIST was celebrated and churches were built. Theological justification for the veneration (*doulia*) of relics as opposed to worship (*latria*) was found chiefly in the consideration that the bodies of the saints had been members of Christ, temples of the Holy Spirit, and were destined for resurrection in glory. At the REFORMATION, Protestants rejected both the cult of the saints and the veneration of relics. *See* SAINTS, VENERATION OF. C. WADDELL

RELIGION, THE STUDY OF. We know more about the religions of the world than our intellectual ancestors did, but we cannot escape their influence when we think about religion because they set the theoretical framework in which we function. The modern cultural or social scientific study of religion can be divided into five basic types of approach: 1) historical, 2) psychological, 3) sociological, 4) phenomenological, and 5) structural. Philosophical and theological studies of religion have not been included in this present study, although many contemporary works in philosophy or theology of religion are heavily indebted to one or more social scientific approaches. Moreover, there are many varieties within each type of approach, and they often overlap or are combined in the work of a single author or discipline in the study of religion.

1. **The historical approach.** Most studies of religion presuppose some knowledge of history. The historical approach to the study of religion is not unique in its concern for accuracy or the history of a religion. It is unique because of the basic assumption that if you want to understand or explain religion, you must know the history of its origins. Therefore, the meaning of religion is to be found in its history and the major task in this approach is to trace a religious tradition back to its origin. The quest for the origin of religion reached its zenith with the rise of anthropology and evolutionary theory found in the works of scholars such as Tylor, Müller, Frazer, and Schmidt, and the study of religion became identical with the study of the evolution of humanity. For Tylor the history of religion is the record of the development of rationality. Religion could be traced back to a first stage called ANIMISM, the first attempt to explain a particular experience (especially dreams). Tylor traced the history of religion through several distinct stages, from animism to naturism, polytheism, monotheism, and metaphysics. Each successive stage was more rational and more abstract, and the final stage culminated in Western science and ethics. Such grand explanations of religion are no longer taken seriously, because they cannot be confirmed. But the power of such speculations can be recognized by the use of the designation "primitive religion" in our contemporary vocabulary.

The historical approach, however, does not necessarily entail evolutionary stages of religion. What it does assume is that once we have traced the history of a religion we have explained it. The basic problem with this approach is that an explanation of a living religion can never be complete. There is always a tomorrow which may bring change, and the attempt to trace a religion back to its historical origins will always remain conjectural.

The historical approach has also been used to explain the myths and beliefs of major religions. The myths of JESUS, MOSES, and BUDDHA, for example, are analyzed with regard to their historical content. It is assumed that the myths refer to actual historical persons or events, since without some basis in history the stories would be fictions or deceptions. Nevertheless, the investigator is still confronted with the difficult task of explaining why these persons or events were chosen for special treatment in myth and religious belief. (*See* MYTH; FOUNDERS, RELIGIOUS.)

2. **The psychological approach.** Most psychological theories proceed from the premise that

religion is a projection of deep-seated or unconscious conflicts. Freud's explanation of religion remains the classical and most influential expression of this approach. After developing his theory of the Oedipus complex as an aspect of individual development, Freud was struck by the similarities between the consequences of the Oedipal complex and religion. This model for explaining religion, therefore, follows the analysis of the psychological perceptions of infantile projections of parents. Parents are perceived as omnipotent, providential, and all-knowing. The Oedipal complex arises because of the conflict between a boy's natural sexual desire for his mother and the powerful rival he sees in his father. Since what each of us strives for is the satisfaction of pleasure and the avoidance of pain, the boy avoids both the hostility of the father as well as the loss of his love by repressing his feelings. Once this is done, the complex is not resolved but remains in the unconscious. According to Freudian theory this unconscious, unresolved conflict is projected as an external object; i.e., God, the father, omnipotent, and omnipresent, is a symbolic projection of a real father.

Psychological explanations of religion usually trace religious beliefs and practices to their origins in childhood. The similarity between the behavior of neurotics and believers in religion led Freud and his followers to the conclusion that the cause of both could be explained by the mechanism of repression in early childhood. For Freud religion was "the universal obsessional neurosis of mankind." It is, therefore, something negative. Or, to put it in other terms, freedom from neurosis also entails freedom from religion. The problem, of course, is that even if we accept the Freudian theory of neurosis, there is no real evidence that unbelievers are any less neurotic in their behavior than religious believers. The fact that there may be a correlation between intense psychological conflict and religious fervor does not allow us to conclude that one is the cause of the other. Most modern psychologies of religion are aware of this. As a result, the study of religion has become for psychologists an analysis of the function of religion as fulfilling certain psychological needs, often viewed as a positive value for the growth and stability of personality and culture. For example, C. G. Jung's hypothesis of a *collective unconscious* which is symbolized in universal archetypes which can assist persons in their maturation ("individuation") process remains a viable position for many scholars. William James, the American pragmatist, developed a psychological theory regarding religious experience and belief which provides us with a third alternative; namely, religious experience and belief can be studied as pragmatic hypotheses about the world.

3. **The sociological approach.** The difference between psychological and sociological approaches to religion is to be found in their assumptions regarding the referent of the religious life. As we have seen, many psychological studies of religion emphasize the function of religion as a symbolic projection of unconscious psychic conflict or stress. From a sociological point of view religion is a symbolic representation of social life. The classic formulation of the approach is to be found in the work of Durkheim.

We must remember that all approaches we are considering arose out of the collapse of theology and metaphysics as "objective" disciplines. The basic premise which is taken as self-evident by most historicists, psychologists, and sociologists is the positivist notion that nonempirical or unobservable entities are meaningless because they have no referent by which we can understand them. The language of religion, therefore, is basically nonsensical unless its referent can be determined. The study of religion for at least the past two centuries can be viewed as a quest for the objective referent of religion. A referent moreover that is "natural," confirmable by the evidence.

Durkheim simply could not believe that the history of religion was a history of nonsense, deceptions, and delusions. Starting from the premise that society is a reality *sui generis* and is incapable of being reduced to individual experiences, he concluded that religion is a symbolic representation of society. There are such things as real social facts, and religion is to be counted as one of them.

Now if religion is a symbolic representation of what Durkheim called "the collective consciousness," it follows that religion cannot be studied apart from the collective life. One of the major premises of a sociological study of religion is that since religion is basically a social phenomenon, the study of religion is in fact a study of society. A sociological study of religion does not simply explain religion, but rather explains social life by reference to religion as one important variable. The sacred is a representation of society. Gods, demons, totems, and ancestors are symbols which objectify or externalize the reality of the collective life to individuals who participate in it. A sociological approach to religion, therefore, attempts to explain the consequences of religion for the maintenance, stability, and integration of social life.

Although Durkheim's views about Totemism, the collective consciousness, and religion have been revised or rejected, his description of the function of religion remains a cornerstone for modern sociologies of religion.

For Weber, no explanation of a society is complete without serious study of religion as a crucial variable. It is Weber who brought "charismatic leader," "the Protestant ethic," and "this worldly" vs. "other worldly" types of solutions to the problem of theodicy into common usage. His work is also an excellent example of the combination of two approaches, the historical and sociological, for the study of religion.

Scholarship in the psychology, sociology, and anthropology of religion throughout the twentieth century can be summarized as "the age of functionalism." The notion that religion functions to fulfill certain needs in the individual and in society has become a commonsense, self-evident truth. And the power of functional studies of religion is derived from the claim that functionalism can explain why religion exists and persists by means of causal analysis. Functional explanations as a type of causal analysis, however, have encountered several critiques which demonstrate that they are at best a heuristic approach to religion rather than a well-formed theory for explaining religion. It has been pointed out, for example, that the logic of functional explanations is often invalid, or leads to conclusions which are tautologous or trivial. Furthermore, the notion of *needs* is much too ambiguous a concept for use in an explanation of religion. Concepts which in themselves are resistant to explanation are unsuitable for explaining anything at all.

4. **The phenomenological approach.** There are many phenomenologies of religion. In this instance, the term "phenomenology" means "description" and should not be confused with the philosophical phenomenologies of such scholars as Husserl, Merleau-Ponty, or Schutz.

One way of understanding phenomenology of religion is to view it as a reaction to approaches which are historical, psychological, or sociological. Most phenomenologists of religion regard such approaches as "reductionistic." Instead of providing us with proper understanding of religion, they reduce religion to social, psychological, or historical facts. Thus instead of explaining religion, they explain it away.

Phenomenologists of religion turn Durkheim upside down. It is not society but religion that is *sui generis,* i.e., an irreducible phenomenon. What separates phenomenologies of religion from other studies is the assumption that religion is a symbolic expression of "the sacred." The task, therefore, is to describe, integrate, or construct typologies from the data provided by the world's religions as symbols of the sacred. The *sacred,* according to phenomenologies of religion, is a metaphysical, transcendent reality. It is often described as "wholly other," "ultimate reality," "absolute," beyond time and history.

Otto, van der Leeuw, Eliade, and Kristensen exemplify the scope of this approach in the various typologies they offer for studying religion as a manifestation of the sacred. They also exemplify the resistance of the phenomenology of religion to the "reduction" of religion to historical, psychological, or sociological explanations.

Once again it is important to notice that the meaning of religion is dependent upon its referent; here what it refers to is the sacred. The basic problem with this approach is that the referent, the sacred, is not an object, but a transcendent reality. Critics of the phenomenology of religion have pointed out that the claim that the essence of religion is the sacred can neither be confirmed nor disproved.

5. **The structuralist approach.** Structural analysis, a late development in the study of religion, is founded on modern linguistics and is often identified as a branch of "semiology," the study of signs.

Structural analysis is systems analysis. The emphasis is placed on an analysis of the relation between terms or units in a religious system. And just as our competence in speaking a language is basically unconscious, the structural study of religion seeks to describe and explain the unconscious infrastructure which is presupposed in the performance of religion. The questions, then, is not where does religion come from historically, or what do individual symbols represent in society, or what is the essential nature of the sacred. The question is whether we can discover the system which constitutes the rules governing the relation of the symbols to each other and their meaning. From this point of view the history of a religion is a history of different transformations of a structure.

If we wanted to study the great god SHIVA for example, we would first of all analyze the relation of this god with other elements in Hindu mythology. It is the relations and the transformation of these relations that generate, define, and give meaning to the god. The relations in structural analysis are usually sets of oppositions. If, to use another example, we want to explicate CASTE as a religious system, we must explicate the basic set "pure/impure" as the ritual opposition which governs the system.

Since structural analysis is a recent development in the study of religion, one of its weaknesses is its lack of a well-formed set of methodological principles which can be put to use by anyone who wants to test it. The general premises which have been taken from modern linguistics are clear; the concrete application of the principles remains controversial.

Lévi-Strauss remains the basic resource for this approach. Dumont and Tambiah are good examples of the application of structuralism to the study of religion.

6. **Conclusion.** Anyone interested in the study of religion will soon encounter the controversy about whether religion is rational or nonrational, cognitive or expressive, whether religious belief is more like science or music and art. None of the above approaches has settled this issue. In fact, functional analyses of religion can take either side; Durkheim and Malinowski remain classic examples. Wilson, Trigg, and Horton represent the recent debate on this complex problem. The solution may well be found in modern developments in semantic theory. The problems of truth, sense, meaning, and reference are basic issues in semantics, and Lyons provides a useful introduction to this subject. Developments in semantics could lead us to a sixth approach for the study of religion.

Bibliography. H. H. Penner and E. Yonan, "Is a Science of Religion Possible?" *Journal of Religion,* LII (1972), 107-33; J.

Waardenburg, *Classical Aproaches to the Study of Religion,* I (1973); E. B. Tylor, *Primitive Culture* (1871); W. Schimdt, *The Origin and Growth of Religion* (1931); J. G. Frazer, *The Golden Bough* (1890-1936); M. Muller, *Introduction to the Science of Religion,* (1873); *S. Freud, The Future of an Illusion* (1928), and *Totem and Taboo* (1913); C. G. Jung, *Psychology and Religion* (1938); C. G. Jung and C. Kerenyi, *Essays on a Science of Mythology,* (1963); W. James, *The Varieties of Religious Experience* (1902); E. Fromm, *Psychoanalysis and Religion* (1950); G. Allport, *The Individual and His Religion* (1950); E. Durkheim, *The Elementary Forms of the Religious Life* (1915); M. Weber, *The Sociology of Religion* (1963); G. E. Swanson, *The Birth of the Gods* (1961); J. M. Yinger, *The Scientific Study of Religion* (1970); K. Marx and F. Engels, *On Religion* (1957); B. Malinowski, *Magic, Science and Religion* (1954); I. C. Jarvie, *Functionalism* (1973); R. Otto, *The Idea of the Holy* (1923); G. Van der Leeuw, *Religion in Essence and Manifestation* (1963); W. B. Kristensen, *The Meaning of Religion* (1960); M. Eliade, *The Sacred and The Profane* (1959), and *The Quest* (1959); P. Pettit, *The Concept of Structuralism* (1975); David Robey, ed., *Structuralism: An Introduction* (1973); C. Lévi-Strauss, *The Raw and The Cooked* (1969), and *Totemism* (1963); L. Dumont, *Religion, Politics and History in India* (1970); S. J. Tambiah, *Buddhism and the Spirit Cults in North-East Thailand* (1970); B. Wilson, ed., *Rationality* (1970); R. Trigg, *Reason and Commitment* (1973); R. Horton and R. Finnegan, eds., *Modes of Thought* (1973); J. Lyons, *Semantics,* 2 vols. (1977).

H. H. Penner

RELIGIOUS EXPERIENCE. An encounter with what is seen as transcendent reality; varies among major religious traditions; can be theistic or nontheistic, individual or group, passive or active, novel or recurring, intense or mild, transitory or enduring, tradition-centered or not, initiatory or developmental, expected or spontaneous; types may include ascetic, mystical, or prophetic, either reviving, affirming or converting, either confirming, responsive, ecstatic, or revelational.

1. The object of religious experience. Although similar to all other human events, religious experience is, nevertheless, a claim of an encounter with a novel object, i.e. the divine. This accounts for its uniqueness in comparison to all other types of experience. Jesus' experience at his baptism by John and Buddha's enlightenment while sitting in meditation are illustrative of this prime characteristic. Their experience was of God or of transcendent truth. Wach expresses this understanding by describing religious experience as a response to what one experiences as ultimate reality. This is the experience of the "wholly other," as Otto termed it. It results in an atypical sense of the "numinous" which is unlike any other human perception. Some writers (e.g. Clark, James) have used words like "the nonrational" or "the unconscious" to depict this dimension. These terms pertain to the supernatural quality of the event in the perception of the experience.

2. Characteristics. Not only is religious experience unique in terms of its object (i.e. the divine) but it includes three other characteristics according to Wach: first, it is a total response of the total being; second, it is the most intense experience of which humans are capable; and third, it involves an imperative to act. These are considered universal essentials in all religious traditions. They typify the experience of Augustine in Christianity as well as that of Muhammad in Islam.

Augustine described his conversion as the rising of a "mighty storm" which brought a "mighty shower of tears." While he was weeping he heard a child's voice chanting "take and read." He opened the Bible and read from Romans. His life was totally altered, and from then on he gave it in service for the Christian church.

Muhammad had a custom of retreating from Mecca to nearby Mount Hira for meditation and prayer. One night he had an overwhelming religious experience in which a luminous being grasped him by the throat and forced him to say the sacred words. It was the Angel Gabriel, who told him to convey a message to the people and to preach the oneness of God.

Both Augustine and Muhammad evidenced responses that were emotional, volitional, and cognitive, i.e. the response was of the total self. Further, the intensity of the event was unequaled in their previous experience. Finally, there were practical results in the life of each.

Nevertheless there is some warrant for suggesting that Wach's essentials of total response, hyperintensity, and practical outcome may not be universals. Several alternative models have been proposed.

3. Levels of intensity. For example, intensity does not seem to be the same for all religious experiences. Some times one feels more engrossed, grasped, or involved than at others. Stark suggests there are four levels of intensity as a function of the sense of "intimacy with divine power" in these events. In "confirming" religious experiences a person merely senses the existence of the divine. Examples would be the sense of God's presence at a marriage ceremony, of Tao in the presence of a sunset, or of Allah when one enters a mosque. These are the perceptions of a divine presence that validate faith.

In "responsive" religious experience there is the additional perception that the divine has also responded or acknowledged the presence of the believer. Examples are in Conversion when one feels accepted by God or born again or saved from sin. Another illustration is the often reported pilgrimage experience in Hinduism where a devotee is said to receive a "favorable glance" from the chosen deity. Miraculous healings would fit here too.

In "ecstatic" religious experience the intensity of the contact goes one step further. An affectionate friendship-type relationship between the person and the divine occurs. The reports of the Christian mystics about being embraced by and being kissed by Jesus exemplify this process. The report of Rāmakrishna's possession by Kālī indicates this level of intensity. Ecstatic experience is sometimes compared to electric currents, trance phenomena, and a sense of being engulfed with strong sensations exemplified by speaking in tongues, or Glossolalia.

"Revelational" experiences are those in which the divine takes the worshiper into his/her confidence and a message is given. The prophets of the Old Testament evidence this type of experience with God. The insights of the Buddha are also indicative. Visions and voices come with great clarity. God's plan is often revealed, as, for example, to Muhammad. Francis of Assisi's sense that he was called to serve the poor is another example. Joseph Smith's being given the golden plates from which to dictate the Book of Mormon is also an illustration of revelational religious experience.

As can be seen, Stark's scheme proposes that intimacy varies from simple acknowledgment to deep, mutual sharing, according to the intensity of the experience.

4. Other dimensions. Additional dimensions of religious experiences have been suggested by Malony. They are the emphasis, the locale, the frequency, the import, the duration, the direction, and the age at which the experience occurs. These parameters are defined as follows: emphasis—whether the experience is primarily emotional or intellectual or a combination of both; locale—whether the experience occurs alone or in a group; frequency—the extent to which one has had a similar experience before; import—the relative impact a given experience has on the life of the believer; duration—whether the experience lasts for a moment, an hour, or a day; direction—whether the impact of the experience is to confirm present faith, to revive the old, or to convert to a new one; and the age at which the event occurs. Any religious experience can be understood along these descriptive continuums.

5. Social referent. A factor not covered by the above discussion is the social dimension of religious experience. Religious experiences differ in the degree to which they involve forceful action upon, acceptance of, or retreat from society. This was the gist of the typology proposed by the sociologist Max Weber, who suggested religious experiences could be denoted as ascetic, mystical, or prophetic. An ascetic experience includes a formal withdrawal from the world and often involves renunciation of family, possessions, political action, pleasures, and mundane vocations. Theravāda Buddhist monks exemplify this type of religious experience. A mystical experience emphasizes the acceptance of the world as it is and includes humble survival, resignation to what is, contemplation leading to illumination, self-abandonment, and, sometimes, unselfish service to others. The distinction between the ascetic and the mystical experience is often difficult to draw in practice, but the difference is important. For example, there is a clear distinction between St. Francis (the mystic) and St. John of the Cross (the ascetic). The final type is the prophetic. It emphasizes criticism and revision of the social order and involves the call for radical change in human relationships in the name of transcendent ideals. The prophet Amos in the Old Testament typifies this experience.

Milton Yinger amplifies Weber's basic distinctions into subtypes lying along continua between asceticism, mysticism, and prophecy. His categories better describe variations in experience among religious persons than do ideal types. *See* Figure 1.

Figure 1

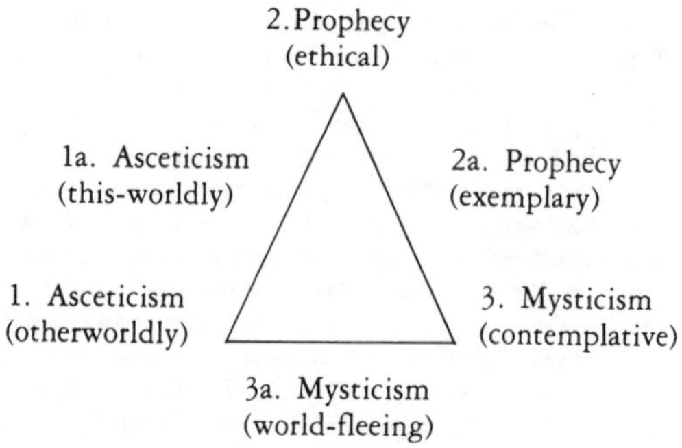

Religious experience as types of responses to "the world"

This-worldly asceticism (1a) is a type of experience exemplified by the rules of St. Benedict, which provide a system for life in the world designed to overcome natural impulses. This is distinctly different from the extreme withdrawal advocated by the Hindu holy man (Sādhu) who secludes himself at a Himalayan mountain retreat.

Exemplary prophecy (2a) is somewhere between prophecy and mysticism. It is no accident that Gautama Buddha is often seen as a prophet while at other times he is labeled a mystic. He was both. He exemplified what he taught in the same manner that the OT prophet Hosea did. Both are to be distinguished from ethical prophets such as Jeremiah and contemplative mystics such as Trappist monks.

World-fleeing mysticism (3a) depicts a religious experience characteristic of the last Āśrama or "life-stage" through which the devout Hindu seeks to escape from the endless cycle of birth and death. This attempt to transcend this world is somewhat different from the Buddha's attempt to provide a path between worldliness and asceticism (i.e. contemplative mysticism).

6. Conversion experiences. Conversion, as contrasted with other recurring events, is usually a one-time experience wherein the individual goes through "a process, gradual or sudden, by which the self hitherto divided, and consciously wrong, inferior, and unhappy, becomes unified and consciously right, superior, and happy" (James, p. 160). This is a psychological description of a fairly typical, almost normative, kind of experience in Protestant Christianity from the late 1700s through the first part of the twentieth century. It was the procedure through which many persons "accepted Christ," "got religion," or "were saved from sin."

a) Types. James identified two types of conversion experiences, the sudden and the gradual. In the sudden type, the self seemed to be quickly and profoundly changed in an almost instantaneous manner. Sinful habits, such as alcoholism, sexual indulgence, and thievery seemed to end, according to the investigations of Starbuck, Coe, Hall, and others in the early years of this century. John WESLEY reported in 1751 that all 652 members of the METHODIST society he queried reported their "deliverance from sin was instantaneous; that the change was wrought in a moment."

James conjectured that sudden conversions occurred in "sick souls" who were unable to tolerate prolonged inner stress or conflict. To achieve serenity they must be radically changed; thus James' term "twice born." In contrast to these converts James described others whom he called the "once born." Those were persons who were "healthy minded" in the sense that they were optimists who feel good can conquer evil. Conversion for them was a slow growth process, and the change was conscious and voluntary. They did not change overnight as in sudden converts. James gave Dr. E. E. Hale, a Unitarian preacher, as an example of this type of religious experience.

A further distinction has been made between "inner" and "outer" conversion. Inner conversion is the experience of gaining unity, peace, meaning, and purpose, while outer conversion is the event of changing to a new faith or the joining of a religious tradition. The former, sometimes called "psychological conversion," was exemplified in the book *Born Again* in which Charles Colson, former aide to President Nixon, experienced a transformation of his life. It did not necessarily include outer (sometimes called "structural") conversion, i.e. the joining of a new church.

It is crucial to note, however, that conversion is normally thought of as an overt shift in allegiance either from *no* faith to *a* faith or from an *old* faith to a *new* faith. Faith is usually defined herein in the traditional manner, i.e. Christian, Hindu, Muslim, etc. Thus, conversion typically has an outer or a structural dimension in that it most often involves an adopting of an explicit religion and the joining of a social group.

b) Social determinants. While James emphasized the personality traits underlying the different types of conversion experiences, others have noted situational and social concomitants which also underlie these phenomena. Lofland studied those who were and were not converted to a cult which felt the end of the world was near. He suggested that for conversion to occur it was necessary that a person "(1) experience enduring, acutely felt tensions; (2) within a religious, problem-solving perspective; (3) which lead to defining himself as a religious seeker; (4) encountering the cult at a turning point in his life; (5) wherein an affective bond to adherents is formed (or pre-exists); (6) where extracult attachments are low or neutralized; (7) and where to become a 'deployable agent' exposure to intensive interaction is accomplished" (Yinger, p. 153). Thus, conversion is both a social opportunity as well as a psychological tendency. It occurs where a combination of psychological stress and social situations coincide, but not when they are absent.

c) Process. Recognition of social factors has led numerous authors to suggest that there is no such phenomenon as instantaneous or sudden conversion which is not part of a process where prior steps can be traced. For example, the conversion experiences of St. Francis of Assisi, MARTIN LUTHER, Muhammad, or the Buddha are all understandable as outgrowths of prior turmoil and situational opportunity. They have their roots in preceding events and do not happen "out of the blue." This does not detract in the least from the sense in the individual that God suddenly appears. Nor does such understanding reduce the divine to human projections. Malony has suggested that this dilemma can be understood by stating that "God is the necessary cause, but we human beings are the sufficient causes for faith, that is, our needs dictate whether we experience faith or not" (p. 37).

The process of conversion has been explained by Tippett as including both periods *of* time and points *in* time. *See* Figure 2.

Figure 2
Process of Religious Experience

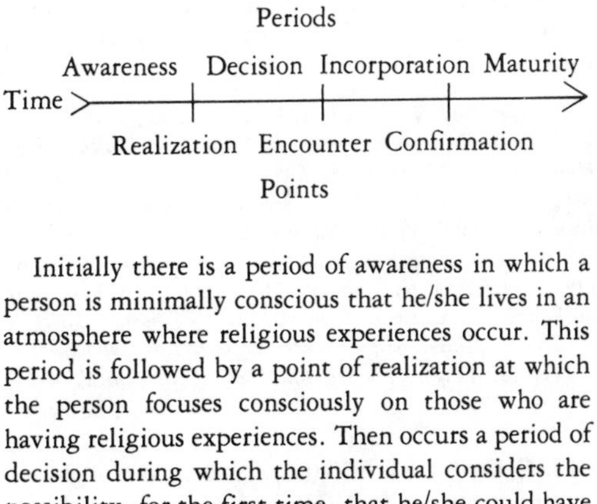

Initially there is a period of awareness in which a person is minimally conscious that he/she lives in an atmosphere where religious experiences occur. This period is followed by a point of realization at which the person focuses consciously on those who are having religious experiences. Then occurs a period of decision during which the individual considers the possibility, for the first time, that he/she could have such an experience. This results in a point of encounter, at which time the person responds in faith and experiences conversion. It can thus be seen that the event "conversion" may be part of a longitudinal process which has been germinating, consciously or subconsciously, for some time.

Tippett's final periods pertain to religious experiences which occur after conversion. First there is the period of incorporation during which the person joins with others in a fellowship of teaching, training, and discipline. This is typically followed by a point of confirmation, at which time the new convert undergoes a "rite of passage" which signifies that he/she is now a full-fledged member of the religious body and can experience religion in its depths. Finally, there is the period of maturity during which the person grows and develops in the life of the religious community. At this time religious experience increasingly takes on a stylized, ritualistic and traditional character.

7. **Church experiences.** This leads to a delineation of religious experiences which are characteristic of this period of maturity. Goodenough has termed these the "church" experiences. "Church" is used here in a generic manner to stand for all those ritualistic activities prescribed by religious bodies in varying traditions around the world. By ritual is meant approved and appropriate religious behavior through which the members are expected to experience the divine and deepen their faiths. These can range from attendance at the MASS, to praying at the WESTERN WALL, to washing in the GANGES River, to the feeding of Buddhist monks when they knock at the door, to SUFI dancing, to a pilgrimage to MECCA, to eating the PASSOVER meal, to taking the EUCHARIST.

These are the religious experiences of the masses as opposed to that of the "reborn" few. It is "secondhand" religion, as James liked to term it. He was biased in favor of the mystical, noninstitutional forms of religious experience and felt that church-type experiences were, by definition, less valid. However, this judgment would not be confirmed by the millions of the faithful who experience their religion through these means. For them, they are valid, intense, and predictable.

Bibliography. W. H. Clark, H. N. Malony, J. Daane, A. R. Tippett, *Religious Experience: Its Nature and Function in the Human Psyche* (1973); E. R. Goodenough, *The Psychology of Religious Experience* (1965); W. James, *The Varieties of Religious Experience* (1908); H. N. Malony, *Understanding Your Faith* (1978); S. Norborg, *Varieties of Christian Experience* (1937); R. Otto, *The Idea of the Holy* (1917); R. Stark, "A Taxonomy of Religious Experience," *Journal for the Scientific Study of Religion,* V (1965), 99; J. Wach, *Types of Religious Experience* (1951); M. Yinger, *The Scientific Study of Religion* (1970).

H. N. MALONY

RELIGIOUS ORDERS (Ch). Associations of groups leading religious life. "Religious," broadly speaking, are persons professing to seek union with God or Christian PERFECTION through faith, hope, and love fostered by common life according to a rule, by vows or promises—usually poverty, chastity (i.e., consecrated CELIBACY), and obedience—by PRAYER and ASCETICISM, by charitable service within and often outside the community. The life of early Christians described in Acts 4:32-35 has frequently served as ideal and model to be adapted to changing times and needs.

1. **Early and Eastern.** Groups of widows and virgins in the apostolic age, and ascetic movements in the second and third centuries, were the forerunners of later developments. In Syria and Egypt many lived as desert solitaries (eremitic or anchoritic MONASTICISM), meeting occasionally with a master like ANTONY (d. 356) for instruction. In Egypt, PACHOMIUS (d. *ca.* 346) fostered the cenobitic type of monasticism, i.e., life in common in a monastery; in Asia Minor, BASIL (d. 379) guided developing brotherhoods by advice and rules but began no order; many Oriental monks, however, view him as their founder.

Since the ORTHODOX CHURCHES' monasteries are usually independent, they do not constitute religious *orders.* The twenty largest monasteries on MT. ATHOS are indeed subject to some decisions of the Holy Community, a central governing body, but they remain autonomous in their own territory, some with other cenobitic groups subject to them.

In modern Greece there are two brotherhoods of theologians, *Zoē* and *Sotir,* composed of priests and laymen who promise poverty, chastity, and obedience, and who do apostolic work. Among Eastern-rite Catholics (UNIATS) some monasteries united in the sixteenth and seventeenth centuries into several Basilian and Maronite Orders, some of which became more active and less monastic. Orders of Basilian nuns likewise grew out of monastic forebears. Some Latin-rite Catholic orders or congregations have Eastern-rite provinces.

2. **Roman Catholic.** The terms "religious order" and "religious" are often used broadly of all types of associations of religious groups and of persons in them. But the CANON LAW of ROMAN CATHOLICISM limits "religious order" to those whose members publicly profess *solemn vows;* those publicly professing *simple vows* belong to "religious congregations." Solemn vows are perpetual, simple vows either perpetual or temporary. Those in solemn vows can neither own nor acquire property, while those in simple vows can own and acquire property but not use it while under vows. The term "religious" is restricted by canon law to those taking *public vows,* whether solemn or simple. Those making *promises* or *private vows* belong to "societies"; they may own, acquire, and use property. Some of these elements may be modified by a new code of canon law being prepared.

In the West various classes of associated religious groups have arisen. Among men these are religious orders (in the strict sense) of canons regular, of monastic associations, of mendicants, and of clerics regular, as well as congregations or societies of clerical religious and of lay religious (brothers). Among women are found orders of monastic nuns and mendicant nuns ("nun" applies strictly to women publicly professing solemn vows) and congregations of sisters who take public simple vows. Recently formed secular institutes have a rule but no public vows nor life or apostolate in common, the members living and working in secular society.

Canons regular arose when priests or canons serving a diocese adopted a *regula* or rule of common life and

ROMAN CATHOLIC RELIGIOUS ORDERS AND CONGREGATIONS

A.A.: Augustinianus Assumptionis: Augustinians of the Assumption (Assumptionists)
C.F.A.: Congregatio Fratrum Cellitarum seu Alexianorum: Alexian Brothers
C.F.X.: Congregatio Fratrum S. Francisci Xaverii: Xaverian Brothers
C.I.C.M.: Congregatio Immaculati Cordis Mariae: Congregation of the Immaculate Heart of Mary (Scheut Fathers)
C.J.: Congregatio Josephitarum Gerardimontensium Josephite Fathers (of Belgium)
C.J.M.: Congregation of Jesus and Mary (Eudists)
C.M.: Congregation of the Mission (Vincentians or Lazarists)
C.M.F.: Cordis Mariae Filius: Missionary Sons of the Immaculate Heart of Mary
C.M.M.: Congregatio Missionariorum de Mariannhill: Missionaries of Mariannhill
C.O.: Congregatio Oratorii: Oratorian Fathers
C.P.M.: Congregatio Presbyterorum a Misericordia: Congregation of the Fathers of Mercy
C.PP.S.: Congregatio Missionariorum Pretiosissimi Sanguinis: Society of the Precious Blood
C.R.: Congregation of the Resurrection
C.R.S.P,.: Clerics Regular of St. Paul (Barnabite Fathers)
C.S.: Missionaries of St. Charles
C.S.B.: Congregation of St. Basil (Basilians)
C.S.C.: Congregatio Sanctae Crucis: Congregation of Holy Cross
C.S.P.: Paulist Fathers
C.S.S.: Congregation of the Sacred Stigmata (Stigmatine Fathers and Brothers)
C.SS.R.: Congregatio Sanctissimi Redemptoris: Congregation of the Most Holy Redeemer (Redemptorists)
C.S.Sp.: Congregatio Sancti Spiritus: Congregation of the Holy Ghost
C.S.V.: Clerks of St. Viator (Viatorians)
Er. Cam.: Congregatio Monachorum Eremitarum Camaldulensium: Monk Hermits of Camaldoli
F.D.P.: Filii Divini Providentiae: Sons of Divine Providence
F.M.S.: Fratris Maristarum a Scholis: Marist Brothers
F.M.S.I.: Filii Mariae Salutis Infirmorum: Sons of Mary, Health of the Sick
F.S.C.: Fratres Scholarum Christianorum: Brothers of the Christian Schools (Christian Brothers)
F.S.C.J.: Congregatio Filiorum S. Cordis Jesu: Sons of the Sacred Heart (Verona Fathers)
I.C.: Institute of Charity (Rosminians)
I.M.C.: Institutum Missionum a Consolata: Consolata Society for Foreign Missions
M.H.M.: Mill Hill Missionaries
M.I.C.: Congregatio Clericorum Regularium Marianorum sub titulo Immaculatae Conceptionis Beatae Mariae Virginis: Marian Fathers
M.S.: Missionaries of Our Lady of La Salette
M.S.C.: Missionaries of the Sacred Heart
M.S.F.: Congregatio Missionarorum a Sancta Familia: Missionaries of the Holy Family
O.A.R.: Order of Augustinian Recollects
O.Carm.: Ordo Carmelitarum: Order of Calced Carmelites (Carmelites)
O.Cart.: Ordo Cartusiensis: Carthusian Order
O.C.D.: Ordo Carmelitarum Discalceatorum: Order of Discalced Carmelites
O.C.S.O.: Order of Cistercians of the Strict Observance (Trappists). Other Cistercisians are of the Common Observance.
O. de M.: Ordo B. Mariae de Merced: Order of Mercy (Mercedarians)
O.F.M.: Order of Frairs Minor (Franciscans)
O.F.M.Cap.: Order of Friars Minor Capuchin (Capuchins)
O.F.M.Conv.: Order of Friars Minor Conventual (Conventuals)
O.H.: Ordo Hospitalarius S. Joannis de Deo: Hospitaller Order of St. John of God
O.M.I.: Oblates of Mary Immaculate
O.P.: Order of Preachers (Dominicans)
O.Praem: Order of Premonstratensians (Norbertines)
O.S.A.: Order of Hermits of St. Augustine (Augustinians)
O.S.B.: Order of St. Benedict (Benedictines)
O.S.B.M.: Ordo Sancti Basilii Magni: Order of St. Basil the Great
O.S.C.: Ordo S. Crucis: Order of the Holy Cross (Crosier Fathers)
O.S.Cam: Order of St. Camillus (Camillians)
O.S.F.: Order of St. Francis: Franciscan Brothers: also various congregations of Franciscan Sisters
O.S.F.S.: Oblates of St. Francis de Sales
O.S.J.: Oblates of St. Joseph
O.S.M.: Order of Servants of Mary (Servites)
O.S.P.: Order of St. Paul the First Hermit (Pauline Fathers)
O.SS.T.: Ordo Sanctissimae Trinitatis Redemptionis Captivorum: Order of the Most Holy Trinity (Trinitarians)
S.A.: Societas Adunationis: Franciscan Friars of the Atonement
S.A.C.: Societatis Apostolatus Catholici: Society of the Catholic Apostolate (Pallottines)
Sch.P. or S.P.: Ordo Clericorum Regularum Pauperum Matris Dei Scholarum Piarum: Piarist Fathers
S.C.J.: Congregatio Sacerdotum a Corde Jesu: Congregation of Priests of the Sacred Heart
S.D.B.: Salesians of Don Bosco
S.D.S.: Society of the Divine Savior (Salvatorians)
S.D.V.: Society of Divine Vocations
S.F.: Congregatio Filiorum Sacrae Familiae: Sons of the Holy Family
S.J.: Society of Jesus (Jesuits)
S.M.: Society of Mary (Marists); Society of Mary (Marianists)
S.M.A.: Societas Missionum ad Afros: Society of African Missions
S.M.B.: Societas Missionaria de Bethlehem: Society of Bethlehem Missionaries
S.M.M.: Societas Mariae Montfortana; Company of Mary (Montfort Fathers)
S.O.Cist: Sacer Ordo Cisterciensis: Cistercians of the Common Observance
S.P.: Piarist Fathers; Servants of the Holy Paraclete
S.S.: Society of St. Sulpice (Sulpicians)
SS.CC.: Congregatio Sacrorum Cordium: Fathers of the Sacred Hearts
S.S.E.: Society of St. Edmund
S.S.J.: Societas Sancti Joseph SSmi Cordis: St. Joseph's Society of the Sacred Heart (Josephites)
S.S.P.: Society of St. Paul
S.X.: Xaverian Missionary Fathers
T.O.R.: Third Order Regular of St. Francis
T.O.S.F.: Tertiary of Third Order of St. Francis

From the 1977 Catholic Almanac

promised sharing of goods, obedience, and celibacy. AUGUSTINE'S example at Hippo remained influential in later periods, and from the eleventh to the thirteenth century the impact of the Gregorian reform led to many groups of canons regular serving churches, hospitals, hospices, or living in semi-monastic solitude. Communities of canonesses were also reorganized under rules at this time.

Among *monks* in the West the rule of Benedict gained predominance so that most monks are BENEDICTINES living in autonomous abbeys or in priories founded from abbeys and subject to them. From the tenth to the twelfth century the Abbey of Cluny exercised great reforming influence over some 1,450 abbeys and priories loosely linked to it. Other reform movements gave rise to new monastic orders, such as the CISTERCIANS, following Benedict's rule interpreted specially. From the fifteenth century Benedictine monasteries began to unite in "congregations" (different from those mentioned above): twenty-one in number today, they form an even looser confederation, the Order of St. Benedict. Monasteries of Benedictine nuns also follow the same ideal. A distinctive, partly eremitical group of monks are the CARTHUSIANS.

Zeal for living the gospel and preaching it in growing towns and cities or in neglected rural areas led to the rise of MENDICANT FRIARS in the thirteenth century; they were also often influential in the new universities. Of seventeen such orders today the largest are FRANCISCANS, DOMINICANS, AUGUSTINIANS, and CARMELITES. Second orders of cloistered nuns, such as the Poor Clares, Dominicans, and Carmelites, share their ideals, receive their guidance, and support their first orders by prayer and penance.

New needs during the CATHOLIC REFORMATION gave rise to orders of *clerics regular,* eight in number today, including the influential JESUITS. Taking solemn vows (although some Jesuits take simple vows), they live in community but have no choral office or religious habit, and devote their time within a flexible regimen to all forms of teaching, missions, preaching, etc. Similar in character, but taking simple vows, are congregations of *clerical religious* and of *lay religious* (brothers), most of which began in the last three centuries for foreign missionary work or to meet local needs.

In the seventeenth century the influence of Mary Ward (founder of the Institute of the Blessed Virgin Mary) and of VINCENT DE PAUL with Louise de Marillac, founders of the Filles de la Charité, freed women from cloistered life to do teaching, nursing, and social work. This change resulted in a great number of congregations of *sisters,* of which about twelve hundred are at present directly linked to the Holy See. In the United States some prominent active congregations of women religious are third orders of Benedictines, Franciscans, Dominicans, and Carmelites, as well as URSULINES, Sisters of St. Joseph, Sisters of Mercy, Sisters of Charity, and others; each name embraces at least several independent congregations, some with thousands of members. Their work has been the core of Catholic schools, hospitals, and social work in recent centuries; today declining numbers and increased lay participation are altering the picture.

3. **Anglican and Protestant.** Where the PROTESTANT REFORMATION held sway, it suppressed most religious orders, but in the nineteenth century a revival of religious life occurred among ANGLICANS. A considerable number of active sisterhoods were formed, and several communities of enclosed nuns also arose. Among men there are also societies of active religious, as well as several Benedictine monasteries. Anglican communities of men and of women, more numerous in England and the United States, also exist in Canada, Africa, Australia, New Zealand, India, Japan, Melanesia, and the Philippines.

In this century the LUTHERAN and REFORMED CHURCHES of Europe have produced more than thirty orders, brotherhoods, or communities, some but not all of which are celibate. Lutheran and Reformed communities are more numerous in Germany, but Lutheran groups also exist in Denmark and Sweden. The French monastery of TAIZÉ is an influential example of religious life in Reformed Protestantism. Even more numerous are European and American societies, usually not celibate, grouping clergy and laity in different ways for shared spiritual renewal and for apostolic activity.

Bibliography. *New Catholic Encyclopedia* (1967): "Monasticism," "Religious, Canon Law of," "Religious Life," "Religious Orders (Communities), Protestant," "Religious Profession, Canon Law of"; M. Rinvolucri, *Anatomy of a Church: Greek Orthodoxy Today* (1966), ch. 4. W. H. PRINCIPE

REPENTANCE (Ju & Ch—Heb. *nāḥam,* "to feel sorry," or *shūb,* "to return"; Gr. *metanoia,* "change of mind"). A change of mind, accompanied by contrition, in which sin is renounced and the repentant turns to God. In Judaism its validity is proved by refusal to commit the same sin when similar opportunity is afforded. In the NT it is described both as an individual's responsibility and a gift of God. T. O. HALL, JR.

REQUIEM rĕ´ kwē ĕm (Ch—Lat.; "rest"). First word of the introit for masses for the dead in the Latin MASS. Hence, a mass for the dead, including the ALL SOULS DAY mass (November 2), funeral masses, and masses on the anniversary of death. Such masses are found as early as the eighth century. *See* DIES IRAE.

R. A. GREER

RESPONSA rĕs pŏn´ sə (Ju—Lat.; lit. "answers of the learned," i.e., *responsa prudentium*). In Hebrew: *she'elot u-teshuvot* (abbreviated as acronym *Shot;* lit. "questions and answers"). Written queries on legal, textual, or exegetic matters and rabbinic replies or decisions of eminent authorities.

Hundreds of thousands of responsa, of the period beginning with the third century A.D., constitute a treasury of historical data preserved in the queries that depict new situations that could not be solved by application of existing law. The replies constitute a special branch of HALAKAH, i.e., precedents or case law, and are a mine of textual interpretation.

The Babylonian TALMUD depicts a correspondence between R. Johanan of Palestine and Rav Samuel in Babylonia on Halakah; and Rav Pappa said, "If it were not for the fact that Rav Avin had spoken of . . . in the letter that he sent, I would not know the law" (Baba Bathra 139a).

The heads of the Babylonian academies (Gaonim) used to receive inquiries from all over the Jewish world with gifts of support for the academies. The letters were discussed by the scholars in open meetings of the academies, and the answers helped establish the authority of the Babylonian Talmud. The Gaonim regulated worship *(Siddur Rav Amram Gaon),* and their instruction reached as far as Spain. Cairo and other stations along the responsa routes became centers, where depositories of copied responsa made it possible to answer repetitious inquiries and to study methods and materials.

Rabbi SOLOMON BEN ISAAC (1040-1105) and his grandson, Rabbenu Tam (1100-1171), are renowned responsists from France and Germany; Rabbi Isaac Alfasi (Rif, 1013-1103) and Maimonides (MOSES BEN MAIMON, 1135-1204) are from North Africa and Spain. In addition to ARAMAIC and HEBREW, Arabic too became a language of responsa.

The responsa of Solomon ben Adret (1235-1310) shed light on self-government among Spanish Jews. Isaac bar Sheshet Perfet (1326-1408) reflects the adoption of Berber customs among Jews (the *Sadaq,* marriage writ, which a wife could cash while living with her husband, unlike the Jewish *Ketubah,* e.g., resp. no. 148). Later responsa came from Italy, the Ottoman Empire, Germany, Poland. Two of the famous responsists are JOSEPH CARO (1488-1575) and Ezekiel Landau (1713-1793).

Modern responsa come from Europe, America, and Israel. The debate on the REFORM movement is reflected in responsa, as well as issues raised by modern inventions, discoveries, and medical advancement (use of electricity on the SABBATH, artificial insemination). Tragic issues related to the HOLOCAUST and definitions of Jewishness related to the Law of Return (citizenship to Jewish emigrants to Israel) are other subjects of modern responsa.

The Institute for Research in Jewish Law, attached to the Hebrew University at Jerusalem, indexes the responsa literature.

Bibliography. S. B. Freehof, *The Responsa Literature and A Treasury of Responsa* (1973), a historic survey and an anthology.

Y. SHAMIR

RESURRECTION (Ju & Ch). A mode of transition to a transformed life after death, involving some sort of body. Resurrection is neither resuscitation (restoration to *status quo ante*), nor release of an inherently immortal soul from the body (though Christian theology combined resurrection with IMMORTALITY), nor REINCARNATION, but the transformation of the whole self. Although belief in resurrection is rooted in the Hebrew BIBLE, only in Christian theology has it been central (e.g., in the APOSTLES' CREED). In Greco-Roman culture many stories circulated about holy men who raised persons from the dead, and similar stories were told also about JESUS and the APOSTLES. In general, however, Christians regarded such events as resuscitations (e.g., Lazarus in John 11:38-44), not as resurrection itself.

The oldest unambiguous statement of resurrection first appears in the latest book of the Hebrew Bible, Daniel (Dan. 12:2); here it is God's recompense for martyrs. Thereafter, resurrection became a common item of belief among the PHARISEES and in Jewish APOCALYPTIC, although there was no standard view. Jews who became early Christians believed in resurrection before they believed that Jesus was resurrected.

The resurrection of Jesus has been central to Christianity from the start. (1) Although the NT never actually describes Jesus' resurrection, there are three types of resurrection materials: confessional assertions that God raised him from the dead (e.g., Rom. 10:9), reports of appearances of the resurrected Jesus (1 Cor. 15:5-8), and stories of the discovery of the empty tomb (the GOSPELS). The oldest description of Jesus' resurrection is in the early second century Gospel of Peter. (2) From the beginning, Jesus' resurrection came to be interpreted in various ways—e.g., as vindication, or as heavenly enthronement. (3) In Christian theology resurrection is not a miracle (a wondrous event in history) but an eschatological event which marks the transition to the New Age destined to replace history. Thus Jesus' resurrection is a prototype of expected general resurrection at the End. (4) Resurrection is therefore not a historical event in the ordinary sense, but a matter of faith. By definition, historical analysis can neither demonstrate nor deny that Jesus' resurrection occurred; it can deal only with belief in resurrection and its consequences for believers. (5) A number of Christian theologians today regard resurrection as a metaphor which expresses the conviction that the whole self has a future beyond death, but others reaffirm the importance of the traditional belief that Jesus' body was raised from death.

Bibliography. R. H. Fuller, *The Formation of the Resurrection Narratives* (1971); L. E. Keck, "New Testament Views of Death," *Perspectives on Death,* L. O. Mills, ed. (1969), pp. 33-98; L. Silberman, "Death in the Hebrew Bible and Apocalyptic Literature," *ibid.,* pp. 13-32; W. Marxsen, *The Resurrection of Jesus of Nazareth* (1970); C. F. D. Moule, ed., *The Significance of the Message of the Resurrection for Faith in Jesus Christ*

(1968), important articles showing major issues; K. Stendahl, ed., *Immortality and Resurrection* (1965), four important essays on the theme in Western culture. L. E. Keck

REVELATION AND MANIFESTATION. Two overlapping concepts which denote the communication and presentation of God, ultimate truth, or the Absolute to humans. "Revelation" and "manifestation" are sometimes used synonymously; at other times revelation is identified with God's self-disclosure or communication, and manifestation is reserved for the form taken by such a communication, as in the case of a vision, materialization, Avatar, or Incarnation. A further complication arises in Christianity from the fact that the incarnation of Christ is often designated as the supreme revelation.

1. **Revelation in Christianity.** Faith is the corollary notion which describes man's free reception of revelation. Neither can exist without the other; in fact, faith can be conceived of as the human response that completes the exchange of activities which constitutes revelation itself. Making room for faith, Thomas Aquinas sharply contrasted natural theology with revealed theology; the first is concerned with God-related truths which can be rationally demonstrated to any intelligent person; the second is concerned with those religious truths which must be accepted on faith, because they are incapable of being understood by human reason. Protestantism has been somewhat suspicious of the efficacy of rationality for the founding of theology. And even Roman Catholicism acknowledges the penultimate status of any natural theology; it can only make men culpable for not accepting revelation, the only means of conveying the will of God and the message of salvation. Thus natural theology necessarily points beyond itself and strives to awaken a yearning for revelation, i.e., the setting forth of God's full glory and design for humankind.

Traditional Catholicism has endorsed a propositional theory of revelation according to which what God reveals is a set of true propositions. Protestantism, however, has been disposed toward a personal interpretation of revelation according to which what God reveals is his own self, his very being, rather than theories or truths about himself. Such thinkers as Karl Barth and Emil Brunner have underlined the existential, "I-Thou" character of revelation in which God makes himself available for relationship with humans. More recently, Catholic thought has proclaimed that a personal encounter is at the heart of revelation. Chapter one of *Dei Verbum* from the Second Vatican Council says, "God chose to reveal himself and to make known to us the hidden purpose of his will, by which, through Christ, the Word made flesh, man has access to the Father in the Holy Spirit."

Emphasizing an affectivistic concept of revelation, Schleiermacher wrote, "What is revelation? Every new and original communication of the Universe to man; and every elemental feeling to me is inspiration." For him, revelation is the direct contact between the soul and God which is evidenced by a feeling of absolute dependence. Christians have understandably attacked Schleiermacher's theology of revelation for according no unique place to the special revelation of Christ. Special revelation has customarily been distinguished from general revelation, which affirms the self-manifestation of God in his act of creation and in his supreme governance of the total world process. In Book 1, chapter 2 of Calvin's *Institutes of the Christian Religion* the two types of revelation are differentiated: "Therefore, since God is first manifested, both in the structure of the world and in the general tenor of Scripture, simply as the Creator, and afterwards reveals himself in the person of Christ as redeemer, hence arises a two-fold knowledge of him." But even the coming of Christ is considered prefatory to his Second Coming, for only then will the triumphant revelation be fully manifest, decisive, and final. While awaiting this unqualified disclosure, each theologian must evaluate the prospect of tentatively confirming revelation through reason. A number of Protestants have joined Catholics in arguing that even if revelation has supremacy over reason, the former must be judged by the latter, or else no one will be able to decide among conflicting revelations. Ultimately, the Christian must ask himself if the NT revelation expresses the fundamental significance of human existence in a more compelling way than do alternative revelations.

2. **Non-Christian traditions.** Liberal Christians, who understand revelation and religious experience as co-extensive, reason that since other religions have religious experience, they also have revelations. More conservative Christians qualify their recognition of non-Christian revelation; thus, Brunner remarked that all religions have "some traces of revelation," but quickly added that other revelations lack the universal validity of the Christian disclosure. Revelation is most readily discerned in Judaism and Islam, which share the prophetic nature of Christianity. Both these religions recognize the chain linking God, intermediate spokesman, and human receivership. Believing that Jesus was not the Messiah, Jews remain in waiting for a revelation which Christians have affirmed as already given. As Brunner puts it, Christians and Jews are in accord on the provisional nature of the OT revelation, but the Christian asserts that the fulfillment of the OT promise has taken place in the NT. In Islam, revelation of the true word is equated with the Qur'ān; therefore, it has been claimed that for Islam, the Word of God is a book; whereas, for Christianity, Christ is the Word of God. As the "seal of the prophets," Muhammad is the receptacle of revelations from Allah, not the Christlike revelation itself. (*See* Wahy.)

Locating a revelatory dimension in the nonprophetic Eastern religions is somewhat problematic. Original Buddhism, for instance, is more accurately characterized as anthropocentric than as theocentric. It is clear that ŚĀKYAMUNI'S enlightenment experience was a self-achieved illumination and not the product of divine intervention. Only in later Buddhism's TRIPLE BODY doctrine can Śākyamuni be perceived as revelatory of a higher reality. In this theory the earthly manifestation of the Buddha is an illusory body which is conjured up by the DHARMAKĀYA that is the real Buddha, the cosmic spiritual body, absolute reality, or TATHATĀ. From this it follows that Śākyamuni was a revelatory instrument to lead the ignorant toward the unadulterated reality of the transcendent Dharmakāya. Given that revelation is definable as an uncovering of the unknown or obscure, Śākyamuni can, of course, also be regarded as a revealer in that he lifted the veil of ignorance from men's eyes.

Strictly speaking, the MONISM of Buddhism and HINDUISM would appear to leave no room for revelation in the sense of a transmission from the divine to man. But Easterners such as RĀMAKRISHNA suggest that the single reality of the BRAHMAN reveals itself in the form of avatars, or manifestations of the divine. Chapters 10 and 11 of the BHAGAVAD GĪTĀ present KRISHNA, the avatar of VISHNU, as the highest spiritual being; thus Christians frequently recognize Krishna as the closest counterpart to Christ. They do, however, observe that Krishna's death was not marked by a resurrection and that Hindu avatars or incarnations are not unique, unrepeatable manifestations as in the case of Christ, who offered himself once for all mankind. Instead, Hinduism embraces a rich plurality of avatars which includes avatars of avatars, animal avatars, and even the Buddha who is appropriated as one more avatar. Fearing that the avatar may be mistakenly equated with the Christ who became man, F. F. Farmer prefers to speak of the "inhistorization" of God in Christ and to restrict "incarnation" to the avatar as the appearance of the divine in a human envelope. Buddhism teaches that Śākyamuni will be succeeded by the buddha MAITREYA, Hinduism identifies Kalkī as the post-Krishna avatar which is yet to come, and SHI'ITE Islam waits for the MAHDI who will follow Muhammad. Christianity, however, announces the return or second coming of Christ. This has led some Christians to posit that the uniqueness of Christ's second coming may point to the uniqueness of his first coming.

In classical TAOISM the metaphysical reality of Tao is revealed through the manifold forms of nature which reflect their formless source. Meditation upon natural objects, processes, or manifestations effects rapport and identity with one's cosmological roots. CONFUCIANISM accommodates revelation by accepting divination, as in the I CHING, and by deferring to the wise pronouncements of ancient sages. CONFUCIUS called himself a transmitter, not an originator (ANALECTS, VII, 1), for he sought to convey the *T'ien Ming* (Will of Heaven) as set forth in the Six Classics. In the end, any theology of revelation asserts that without a profound disclosure of reality, humans remain in darkness and bondage. Thus, revelation is always, and at once, an illumination and a liberation by which humans are delivered from their unsatisfactory spiritual condition.

Bibliography. E. Brunner, *Revelation and Reason* (1946); G. Parrinder, *Avatar and Incarnation* (1970).

E. J. COLEMAN

REVELATION IN ISLAM. *See* WAHY.

REVIVALISM (Ch). PROTESTANT movement concerned with the CONVERSION and SALVATION of the individual; the attempt to appeal to the mass of the population.

1. Origins. Revivalism began in English Puritanism and European PIETISM. Some PURITANS taught that the individual needed the conversion experience to become a full member of the church. William Perkins (1558-1602) and William Ames (1576-1633) examined the conversion experience in detail, and the Puritan could use these descriptions as a standard by which to judge one's own faith.

In contrast to the Puritan emphasis on the JUSTIFICATION of the sinner, European pietists preferred the metaphor of the New Birth. New Birth imagery combined elements of an older tradition of MYSTICISM with the Reformation emphasis on salvation by God's grace and emphasized the need for continual growth in the Christian life.

2. Colonial America. In America, Puritan and pietist influences were present in the colonial period. The New England colonies were founded by Puritans who insisted on conversion as necessary for church membership. Similar views were held in the middle colonies by BAPTISTS, many of the German sects, some members of the SOCIETY OF FRIENDS, and pietists among the Dutch REFORMED.

From 1720 to 1750 the English colonies in North America experienced a GREAT AWAKENING, a revival which did not have any one origin or style. In Massachusetts, Solomon Stoddard (1643-1729), pastor at Northampton, had several seasons of renewal in which large numbers were converted. His grandson and successor, JONATHAN EDWARDS (1703-58), led a revival in the Connecticut Valley in the 1730s. He published an enthusiastic account of this revival in *A Faithful Narrative of the Surprising Work of God* (1737), a work that exerted a major influence on later revivalism.

In the middle colonies the revival was sparked by the preaching of Theodore Frelinghuysen (1691-1748), a Dutch pietist, who conducted revivals in New Jersey. His work inspired PRESBYTERIANS to undertake revival work and had particular impact on the graduates of the Log College, established by William Tennent (1673-1755) to train frontier ministers. Although the revival centered in the New Brunswick Presbytery, members of the New York

Presbytery, many of whom were influenced by Puritanism, supported it.

George Whitefield (1714-70), an itinerant English evangelist, served as the link between the different revivals. Whitefield toured the colonies, preached in the major cities, and established communication between the various leaders. On his most successful tour he is reported to have preached to 25,000 people on Boston Commons.

The Awakening was highly controversial. The evangelists broke established church rules, such as one requiring permission to preach in another minister's parish, and they often ignored theological traditions in the name of practical Christianity. James Davenport (1716-57), a fiery preacher from Long Island, symbolized many of these problems to his contemporaries. His preaching rang with denunciations of the revival's opponents, and he once gathered a crowd in New London to burn luxury items and books written by his enemies.

As a result of such controversies, the Presbyterian Church divided into Old and New Sides, and the CONGREGATIONALISTS spawned many independent churches, called Separates, which refused to join the regular Congregational order. Although the Presbyterians reunited in 1759, most of the Separates became Baptists.

3. John Wesley. After his failure as a missionary to Georgia, JOHN WESLEY (1703-91), an English high churchman, turned to pietism and experienced the New Birth. Although Wesley was a successful evangelist, his primary contribution to revivalism was as an organizer. He gathered his converts into classes and societies that imposed strict discipline. Further, he appointed a number of lay assistants to travel circuits and win new members while strengthening the work already begun.

As a theologian, Wesley departed from the Calvinism (*see* CALVIN, JOHN) of most earlier revivalists by stressing man's ability to cooperate with God in his rebirth. METHODISTS, as Wesley's followers were called, could either move toward PERFECTION or backslide.

After the American Revolution the Methodists became one of the strongest advocates of revivalism in America.

4. Nineteenth century revivalism. In Tennessee and Kentucky the camp meeting type of revivalism became prominent in the early nineteenth century. These meetings originated in Presbyterian sacramental meetings in which small churches came together for the Lord's Supper (EUCHARIST) and several days of preaching. Such frontier preachers as James McGready (1758-1817) won large numbers of converts at these gatherings, and the custom of long evangelistic meetings in which the people camped on the grounds spread to other denominations.

Frontier revivals were exciting events. Individuals fell down as if dead, ran around the meeting praising God, and manifested other signs of emotional release. The Methodists were able to tame the camp meetings, however, and make of them a respectable evangelistic technique.

In New England early nineteenth century revivalism was a calm affair. Converts experienced a change in the direction of their lives which was manifest in a willingness to support benevolent societies concerned with such issues as temperance, foreign missions, and slavery. (*See* MISSIONS, CHRISTIAN.)

CHARLES FINNEY (1792-1875), an upstate New York Presbyterian, brought his "new measures" into revivalism. These included the "anxious bench," the use of evangelistic teams, and prayer for particular persons during services. In his *Lectures on Revivals* (1835) Finney argued that revivals were as much the work of men as of the HOLY SPIRIT, and claimed that a minister could ensure a revival by following the proper means. Professional revivalists, who became common in America at this time, usually based their work on Finney's lectures or an imitation of them.

5. Big city revivalism. Although Finney was a perfectionist who believed that Christians should be involved in social issues, many of the professional revivalists who followed him were largely concerned with individual issues. DWIGHT L. MOODY (1837-99), the first revivalist to develop techniques for reaching urban areas, was a premillennialist (*see* MILLENARIANISM) who believed that it was his mission to save a few from the coming judgment. His preaching, reinforced by his popular song leader, Ira Sankey, tended to be sentimental and folksy.

William "Billy" Sunday (1862-1935) carried the big city style of evangelism to its logical conclusion. His preaching was often as much entertainment as it was proclamation; he deliberately used bad grammar to hold the attention of the crowds.

Outside of the South and parts of the West, revivalism went into dramatic decline after World War I. It tended to become identified with conservative Protestantism and was often influenced by DISPENSATIONALISM.

BILLY GRAHAM was a product of this conservative heritage, and in the 1950s and 1960s was its leading representative in the United States.

The steady growth of conservative churches in the 1970s indicates that the revivalist tradition is still strong in America. Those who have been "born again" (John 3:3) are active participants in programs of evangelism and missions in both conservative and mainline American Protestantism, and the prospects for the tradition's continuation and growth seem bright.

Bibliography. E. Stouffer, *The Rise of Evangelical Pietism* (1965); W. Haller, *The Rise of Puritanism* (1938); W. McLoughlin, *Modern Revivalism* (1959); W. Sweet, *Revivalism in America* (1944); T. Smith, *Revivalism and Social Reform* (1957); A. Heimert, *Religion and the American Mind* (1957).

G. MILLER

RICCI, MATTEO rī´ chī mä tä´ ō (Ch; 1552–1610). Italian JESUIT missionary, mathematician, scientist, and linguist. Reached Goa in 1578 and China in 1583. Possessing the highest religious and scientific qualifications of his day, he encountered the Chinese educated class as their equal and sought to convert the emperor and the entire nation. *See* MISSIONS, CHRISTIAN. K. KOYAMA

RIG (ṚG) VEDA rĭg vā´ dŭ (H—Skt.; lit. "knowledge of the verses" [*ṛc*—"verse of praise" + *veda*—"knowledge"]). The oldest and most important text of VEDIC HINDUISM, a collection (SAṂHITĀ) of 1,028 hymns in ten books, composed in an oral tradition *ca.* 1400-1200 B.C. in northwest India. The verses, in Vedic language (ancient Indic), complex and often esoteric, are in praise of Vedic deities. *See* VEDA. D. M. KNIPE

RINZAI rĭn zī (B). *See* ZEN §5.

RISHI, ṚṢI rĭ´ shē (H—Skt.; lit. "one who has knowledge or sees—a seer"). The singular for "authors" of the earliest RIG VEDA hymns which are the core of the SAṂHITĀ. The names of the Rishis appear in the PURĀṆIC writings with mythological embellishment. Some are regarded as demigods, others are revered "human" beings who in the primordial age heard the cosmos itself utter the sounds that create the basic hymns of the ARYAN people. Thus, the Rishis are the legendary spiritual founders of HINDUISM, who communicated the fundamental beliefs and mystical insights of the faith that were elaborated in subsequent ages. C. S. J. WHITE

RISSHŌ KŌSEIKAI rī shō´ kō sā´ kī (B—Jap.). Religious organization, founded by Nikkyō NIWANO on March 5, 1938, and registered with the Japan Ministry of Education as a *shinkō shūkyō* (i.e. a popular religious sect). The name is officially translated by the organization as "society for the establishment of righteousness and security of the country as preached by Saint NICHIREN; interaction and harmony to completion." The relation of this name to Nichiren's treatise *Risshō ankoku-ron* (On the Establishment of the Legitimate Teaching for the Security of the Country), written in 1260, is apparent. Other similarities to sects of NICHIREN BUDDHISM are its doctrinal basis in the Lotus Sūtra and its use of the DAIMOKU *"Namu myō-hō-renge-kyō."* However, Risshō Kōseikai does not exalt Nichiren to the status of BODHISATTVA (as in Nichiren-shū) or BUDDHA (as in Nichiren Shō-shū), but worships, instead, the historical Buddha, ŚĀKYAMUNI.

1. **History.** In its formative period Risshō Kōseikai was characterized by doctrinal eclecticism, SHAMANISTIC practices which included faith healing, group counseling (HŌZA), and an insistence that members trace their family ancestry and know their individual clan deity. The founder, Niwano, had a background in divination and faith-healing cults, and Mrs. Myōkō NAGANUMA, co-founder and vice-president until her death in 1957, combined some elements of shamanism with spiritual charisma. The first period, 1938-57, consequently was characterized by accommodation to popular folk beliefs and superstitions and appealed to the demand for immediate release from suffering as well as the need to discover individual identity and establish a sense of belonging. Perhaps these characteristics explain why Risshō Kōseikai was the fastest growing "new religion" from the end of World War II until 1950. Membership in 1975 was 4,848,476.

Since Mrs. Naganuma's death, shamanistic elements in Risshō Kōseikai have been de-emphasized, and the original Buddhist orientation has become clearer. Its central teaching, based on the LOTUS SŪTRA, emphasizes: a) the bodhisattva ideal, or compassion for others and zeal to lead others to an experience of salvation; b) messianism, related to the belief that the present age is the period of the deterioration of the DHARMA (MAPPŌ) and that a savior has arisen to deliver all people; and c) the promise of SALVATION, in the form of present happiness and blessings. The doctrinal foundation and teachings of Risshō Kōseikai may be compared with those of SŌKA GAKKAI, its chief rival in the religious world of Japan today.

2. **Beliefs.** Though Risshō Kōseikai is in the Nichiren tradition, it is eclectic. Its doctrine draws not only from Nichiren (and the MĀHAYĀNA School), but also from HĪNAYĀNA Buddhism. The central doctrine may be presented in the framework of the Hīnayāna doctrine of the FOUR NOBLE TRUTHS:

a) The truth of suffering. Human suffering includes spiritual, physical and financial suffering. As in primitive Buddhism, the way to obtain release from suffering is the way of knowledge: one must understand the reason for all suffering in order to exist within the self.

b) The truth of cause. The law of cause and effect is basic to all of life. The believer must seek to understand the cause or there is no way to break the wheel of KARMA, or the twelve-linked chain of origination.

c) The truth of extinction. One must come to understand the concept of "nothingness" (ŚŪNYATĀ), which is fundamental to Buddhism; i.e., all things change, nothing exists except for the moment and in relation to all other existing things, and the ultimate state is the state of NIRVANA—nothingness, or complete bliss.

d) The truth of the path. As Śākyamuni taught when he delivered the teaching of the four noble truths, the final truth is the discovery of the "way out" of our sufferings. Two formulas, in the teachings of Risshō Kōseikai, are offered to the believer: (i) The EIGHTFOLD PATH. In order to break the wheel of karma one must act in the right way. (ii) The six perfections. It is not enough for one to seek salvation for himself; he must also seek salvation for others. This is the way of the bodhisattva, the way of charity, obedience, patience, assiduity, meditation, and wisdom.

3. **Group counseling.** Though other religious groups have systems for counseling, the Hōza practice (inherited from an earlier movement, Reiyūkai) is a distinctive feature of Risshō Kōseikai. It is in the tradition of the Saṅgha, religious community, of primitive Buddhism. These hōza groups (membership of which is determined by various criteria including residence and genealogy) meet at the Great Sacred Hall every morning and afternoon, or at local churches. About a dozen persons constitute a hōza circle, often called "circle of harmony," sitting on the floor in Japanese fashion, knee-to-knee. Group leaders get the discussion started, but members may present any problem and advice is offered, sometimes by the leader and sometimes by other members of the circle.

4. **The search for peace.** The president of Risshō Kōseikai, Nikkyō Niwano, is noted for his involvement in the world peace movement and his efforts to create dialogue among various religious faiths. The International Institute for the Study of Religions, an independent organization with no sectarian ties, is located on the grounds of Risshō Kōseikai headquarters in Tokyo. In September, 1965, President Niwano, after an audience with Pope Paul VI, reported: "I clearly felt that there is little difference between God's love as taught by Christ or the love of humanity and the idea of compassion as advocated by Buddha."

The headquarters of Risshō Kōseikai are located in Nakano Ward, Tokyo, where a number of pink buildings surround the Great Sacred Hall (completed in March, 1964), and facilities include school buildings from kindergarten through high school and a well-equipped modern hospital.

Bibliography. K. J. Dale, *Circle of Harmony* (1975); H. N. McFarland, *The Rush Hour of the Gods* (1967).

N. S. Brannen

RITSU rĭt´ sŭ (B—Jap.; lit. "discipline"; translation of the Skt. *vinaya*). One of the schools of Nara Buddhism. A Reformed Ritsu School was founded by Eison (1201-1290) on the basis that one can informally vow to live by the Buddhist discipline.

K. Crim

RITUAL, NATURE AND THEORIES. Ritual is one of the oldest, most complex, and persistent symbolic activities associated with religion. Ritual is a paradigm and dramatization of the intent of religion itself; it marshals visual and aural symbols along with intellectual and sensual images into a process that provides a participant with both a certain identity and a sense of transformation into a new mode of being. In what is seen, said, and done, ritual expresses the psychic, social, and religious world of its participants even while inviting reflection on the cosmic significance of those known and ordered structures of existence.

1. **Identity and transformation.** Studies of the ritual process in many societies have noted the existence of polar tensions. One of the most basic of these is ritual's way of affirming the participant's identity at the same time that it makes transformation of that identity possible.

a) Social identity. On one side of this tension is ritual's role in affirming who the participant is socially. This function of ritual might be termed "ceremony" (Grimes). Individuals in ritual acts tend to dramatize the social patterns or kinship systems of which they are a part. Social anthropologists from the time of Weber and Durkheim have observed the social setting of ritual acts in various societies. Studies of ritual action in Hindu India, for example, have demonstrated how ritual is often useful in defining social boundaries or managing personal tensions (Opler); how it demonstrates certain socio-political networks (e.g., Cohn and Mariott or Bharathi); or how it serves to resolve social and political conflict, factionalism, or rebellion (Hanchett; Barnett). Rituals often serve to put the participants in touch with their social context, to enable them to affirm that they are a part of a particular community or clan, as if by means of socio-drama they can work out the conflicts that their various social alliances may imply.

b) Psychological and intellectual identity. Ritual also affords identity of a psychological and intellectual kind insofar as it can make the participant aware of values, beliefs, and needs, as well as tensions with the larger social and political order. This dimension of ritual has been observed in various ways. Turner has shown that ritual symbols demonstrate ideological values (i.e., dimensions of the intellectual, moral, and social order), as well as sensory ones (i.e., aspects of one's feelings and desires). Spiro has argued that rituals which address "ghosts" and "spirits" in such societies as Buddhist Burma enable people not only to affirm their belief systems but also to resolve psychological tensions with parents or political authorities which cannot be resolved in the accepted patterns of social exchange. In light of these considerations, it is no wonder that Eliade has remarked that symbols, including those used in rituals, are self-revelatory.

c) Historical identity. Another less noticed way in which ritual affirms one's identity is in its evocation of "history." Ritual is often believed to be handed down by the "fathers"; one takes one's place in a spiritual lineage when the ritual of that lineage is performed. Myths which describe how the ritual or the sacred community—or even the world itself—began are often recited during the ritual. The ritual thus enables the participant to remember or re-enact those authenticating moments. Not infrequently, the sacred fathers or mythical ancestors are invoked and invited into the presence of the worshiping community. Almost always, the ritual experiences of the major religious traditions follow procedures prescribed in classical texts (e.g., PASSOVER in the TORAH). At the least, this invocation of "history" gives to the ritual participant, and to the ritual, a sense of historical identity.

d) Transformation. Yet there is a paradox in the ritual process. Beyond the affirmation of an established identity, ritual may "transform" the participant and provide a new identity. Through acts of confession and rites that resolve conflict or symbolize the process of transition, the participant passes into a new mode of being. In genuine ritual activity, not only does one experience a new sense of community which often transcends the social boundaries brought into the ritual; one is also ushered into the presence of a transcending "other," i.e., experiences a timeless cosmic reality that gives meaning, context, and perspective to all the mundane realities of which one is a part. This transformative effect of ritual has been variously described as *communitas* ("community") by Turner and as "anti-structure" by Ramanujan (that is, the experiencing of a transcending relationship, as with God, that supersedes all other relationships). In this sense, ritual becomes a technique for altering the experience of everyday social reality.

2. The done, the said, and the seen. The symbols and language of ritual speak on many different levels and through many media, and engage and appeal to all the senses. The sense of taste is evoked in the use of bread, wine, salt, or SOMA; the sense of smell in the aromas of burning incense, camphor, or candles, and in the fragrance of flowers and cooked foods; the sense of touch in the laying on or shaking of hands, anointings, and various other gestures; the sense of hearing by the sounds of bells, gongs, and uttered chants. Yet ritual symbolism has been most commonly examined and interpreted in terms of three components; what is done, what is said, and what is seen.

a) What is done. One part of the symbolic intent of ritual is expressed in a sequence of performed acts. These acts taken together often constitute a process which implies transition from one stage of being to another. This process has been described in various terms. One characterization is that the ritual process is a movement from the "raw" to the "cooked" or from nature to culture (Lévi-Strauss) and thus is paradigmatic of the work of persons in the world. From this perspective, ritual is designed to reflect the process of growth and maturation whether it is of a social order, of culture, or of religious awareness. More fundamentally, in the structuralism of Lévi-Strauss, ritual is seen in terms of the paradoxes it enacts and reconciles: illness-health; guilt-atonement; pollution-purity; etc.

Another characterization of ritual understands the ritual process as a cosmogony, the creation of a sacred world or of a replica of a meaningful universe (Eliade; Berger). From this perspective, ritual re-enacts a creative process and intends to establish a sacred world of time, space, and community as opposed to a profane or meaningless one. While this perspective tends to see ritual as a return to the beginning, in fact, ritual also moves one forward toward a meaningful end. Thus, in the ritual process TIME is suspended and the participant can move backward and forward at once as if in an *eternal now.*

Again, ritual has been characterized as a drama which serves as a paradigm of the social process. The ritual becomes at times a form of crisis resolution which is depicted in four stages: breach (violation of social, cosmic laws); crisis (resultant tensions, guilt, threat of extinction, etc.); redressive action (surrogate sacrifices, purgations, etc.); and resolution of the crisis, often expressed in symbolisms of reconciliation, peace, or jubilation (Turner).

Still another way of expressing the intent of ritual actions—and a way commonly voiced in ritual texts and by participants—is the "pleasing of God" or the expressing or attaining of a special relationship (e.g., gratitude, reconciliation) with the Sacred. Kierkegaard described this dimension in Christian ritual by suggesting that ritual was like a drama in which the actors were the congregation; the clergy or priesthood were the "prompters"; and the audience was God.

b) The "said." As important as what is done in ritual is what is said. Utterances during the ritual process can be doxological propositions of faith (e.g., "God is in this place; let us bow down before him"); confessions of wrong-doing made explicitly or implicitly; the use of sacred language (e.g., LATIN, SANSKRIT, HEBREW) or of sonority which enhances awareness of the numinous; the utterance of sounds, chants, MANTRAS, or prayers which are believed to have cosmic or redemptive effect; and the recitation of myths or sacred history which tell participants how and why things are as they are.

As with ritual actions, ritual sounds can embody (or catalyze) the entire ritual process or any single stage in the process. Often such an utterance is intended to do more than one thing. Sound can bring the numinous from peripheral to central awareness. Sound can articulate explicitly or implicitly the mind-set, world view, or stated concerns of ritual participants. Sound can be liminal or transformative, communicating visions of what one can be and carrying persons to those new dimensions as on wings of song. Sound can be cosmogonic insofar as it is thought to be primordial or an agent in the creative process, as in ancient Vedic ritual when the priestly chant reproduced the sound of which and by which the world was believed to be created. What is said and heard, in sum, enhances the power and intention of the ritual process.

c) The "seen." The visible paraphernalia of ritual convey their own meanings which reinforce and supplement the symbolisms of action and sound. The visual symbols of ritual can be interpreted at many levels. Turner, for example, has suggested three levels at which ritual symbols can be interpreted: i) the exegetical—the meanings of which participants in the rituals are themselves consciously aware and which they can articulate; ii) the operational—the meanings of the symbols as expressed in the way they are used in the ritual and in the affective responses they engender in participants; iii) the positional—the meanings which are expressed through the relationship a symbol has to other symbols in the ritual process and also to the total context of a culture or belief system. For example, the positional meaning of a symbol like bread in the Christian EUCHARIST is enhanced by its relationship and contradistinction to wine and also by the ways "bread" reflects the belief system and/or life-style of Christian communicants.

The visual symbols used in ritual are abundant. They include symbols of color (e.g., red, white, green, black, purple); numbers (e.g., one, two, three, four, five, seven, ten, twelve, one hundred eight); shapes (circle, square, triangle); animals (sheep, horse, cattle, snake); vessels (plates, pots, chalices, cups); vestments (headdresses, robes, masks); food stuffs (rice cakes, wafers, bread, fruit); and hosts of other combinations. On occasion the symbol's meaning is divulged in classical religious texts; more commonly, the meanings are implicit and variously perceived by participants. But almost always, the symbol has many levels of meaning even in a single context. "Red," for example, in certain Ndembu rituals represents blood, clay, power, life, potential for evil or for good (Turner).

3. The context of ritual: symbolic time and space. The meaning, significance, and effectiveness of ritual is enhanced by its context. As we have observed, that context includes the social system of which it is a reflection and the belief system which it dramatizes. Beyond that, the special context of ritual is the space and time in which it occurs (Eliade).

a) Ritual space. Certain places take on specific importance in the ritual experience. Cities like MECCA, JERUSALEM, ROME, or Banāras, for example, are *holy steads* which can assume special significance in ritual PILGRIMAGE for persons whose religious identity is delineated by such sites. More commonly, the sacred place of ritual is a building or site especially consecrated and symbolically enhanced for the ritual experience (temple, church, wooded glen). Such places become microcosms where the whole universe is symbolically represented or where the sacred is believed especially available to human beings. Such places often assume suggestive shapes (cross, concentricity, triangle) and include in their environs symbols of mediation between the sacred and the mundane realms (poles, domes, centers, altars, tables, pulpits). In addition to traditional ritual spaces any number of places can be ritually sacralized (a house, a cavern, a riverbank, the foot of a tree, a hilltop) and these become meaningful contexts for ritual events.

b) Ritual time. In the same way, when specific moments of chronologically measured time open into the sacred realm beyond time, they become *tempocosms* or occasions for ritual beginnings, maturations, or breakthroughs. The solar year with its new year, its solstices (e.g., CHRISTMAS), and its equinoxes (e.g., EASTER, PASSOVER) is a part of the chronometry by which festivals are marked. Similarly, the lunar cycle, especially at new and full moon, includes tempocosms when the ritual participant can sense a connection between measured time and cosmic time. Each day has such junctures, as at dawn, noon, dusk, and midnight, which are frequently marked by rituals. Other measures of time which have special significance are astronomical or astrological measurement (as in the ascent of certain constellations), the agricultural year with its seasons of planting, monsoon, and harvest; and junctures of communal or personal life (birth, initiation, marriage, death, inauguration of new buildings or institutions).

4. Types of ritual. That there is a great variety of rituals is clear. In fact, to identify distinctive types of ritual is difficult because there is overlap in intent and meaning between the types. Nonetheless, some helpful distinctions have been made.

a) Corporate, domestic, personal rituals. Rituals have been categorized in terms of whether they are corporate, domestic, or personal. A corporate ritual is one which is community based and serves as a means of creating or affirming the community at large. Communal rituals are performed publicly, according to oral or written SCRIPTURES, usually in specially designated places and at communally understood times, and led by specially designated ritual technicians who serve as mediators between the community and the sacred. Rituals which fall into this category range from the corporate *(śrauta)* rituals of VEDIC HINDUISM to the Catholic MASS.

In domestic rituals the home (or a sacralized place in it) is understood to be sacred cosmos and the parent (or a private functionary) becomes the ritual technician. The intent of domestic rituals includes the education and/or involvement of children in the tradition which gives the family its religious identity. Domestic rituals range from household *(gṛhya)* rituals of Hinduism to the SEDER of the Jewish tradition.

Personal rituals are done in solitude or at least without a structured social context. Such rituals tend to be in places and times that have meaning in one's personal history and express the identity and needs of the religious person as an individual. Not infrequently, in private ritual (as in YOGA) the body or its immediate environs becomes a symbolic cosmos and a medium of access to the sacred. In personal ritual one is often one's own "priest" and appropriates such techniques as meditation, prayer, dream or vision, ecstatic trance, and ascetic self-discipline.

b) Rituals of healing or exorcism. Rituals designed to bring about wholeness in the human and cosmic realms represent yet another type. They are specifically intended to restore health or purity and exorcise evil influences from body, mind, or place. The technicians for these rituals often have specific skills, formulas, or symbol systems (e.g., witch-doctors, ĀYURVEDIC specialists, exorcists). Rituals of healing and exorcism incorporate a variety of techniques: use of surrogate objects to redirect the powers of evil; sacrifice; invocation of sacred forces believed to be especially potent in such instances; evocation of the sense of touch (the "laying on of hands" and the anointing with oil); passing through stages designed to purify or heal; and special powers of the ritual technicians (access to sacred force, firmness, patience, etc.). While such rituals may be used in behalf of specific persons or to redress specific grievances, they are often also thought to have general value for the community or world at large.

c) Festivals. Among the most complex and colorful forms of ritual is the festival. Festivals are celebrated in virtually every society at appropriate junctures of the year in such a way as to make those junctures meaningful. As with virtually all ritual, festivals express the polarities in cosmic and human life: there is fasting and feasting, mourning and rejoicing, penitence and renewal; there is the ushering out of the old, the welcoming of the new. One might make a distinction between two kinds of festival—the *ecofest* and the *theofest*. An *ecofest* (a festival of ecological significance) is a festival which celebrates an astronomical or seasonal event to make it an occasion for remembrance, renewal, or "breakthrough" to the cosmic significance of that event. The South Indian festival Poṅkal, in mid-January, is such an ecofest inasmuch as it celebrates the harvest and the sun's entrance into its "northern" journey after the winter solstice. A *theofest* (a festival of theological significance), on the other hand, is a festival primarily designed to celebrate some event in the life of a deity or sacred being. Easter and the birthday of the BUDDHA are examples. However, many festivals tend to combine the characteristics of both. For example, Christmas celebrates not only the birth of Christ but the winter solstice and the promised return of light. Often festivals are observed at the auspicious coming together of more than one chronometric unit (e.g., solar year, lunar cycle, ascent of a "star" or constellation). The festival is often a paradigm of the life of the sacred figure commemorated and can re-enact a special event or relationship in a community's dealings with the sacred. It is also a reproduction, in miniature, of the cosmic process or world view operative for that society. That is, the festival often acts out a "philosophy of history." Gaster has observed that the Harvest–New Year festivals of the ancient Middle East tended to be acted out in four stages: mortification, purgation, recreation, jubilation. These stages expressed the pattern not only of penitence, forgiveness, and restoration for collective human guilt but also of the agricultural cycle of barrenness, planting, harvest. In the South Indian context the festival often acts out a cyclical pattern to the cosmos, made congruent to the career of the god, in which creation, maturation, destruction of evil-dispensing energies suggest a cosmic process of waxing and waning (Clothey).

d) Rites of passage. Another type of ritual commonly studied, especially since the work of Arnold van Gennep, is the rite of passage (*see* LIFE CYCLE RITES). These rituals are designed to enhance the significance and psychic safety of periods of change in one's lifetime. Some traditional societies have observed up to forty such rites, but in general they are gathered around five periods of the lifetime: i) prenatal (e.g., rituals for the affirmation of pregnancy, for the determination of sex, for fetal growth, and safe delivery); ii) infancy and childhood (e.g., rituals for affirmation of lineage and personhood, naming, first solid food, etc.); iii) initiation and entrance into adulthood (e.g., "adult" baptism, confirmation, BAR MITZVAH, etc.); iv) marriage, including rituals for betrothal, first intercourse and others; v) funeral.

Van Gennep suggested that rites of passage were characterized by three stages of ritual: separation, liminality, and incorporation. That is, each rite includes ritual acts and symbols which depict the separation from an earlier stage of existence, the passage itself, and the incorporation into each new situation.

The funeral, for example, may include rites of separating the corpse from its previous status (e.g., removal from the house, cleansing, etc.); rites of transition (e.g., procession and use of "liminal" symbols which depict the in-between status of the deceased, such as caskets [tomb and womb] and nakedness [birth, death]); and rites of incorporation into a new status (e.g., burial in a grave or commitment to a fire). In one sense, virtually all ritual can be characterized as rite of passage insofar as it permits social and personal passage from one mode of being to another. (*See* PILGRIMAGE; SACRIFICE.)

5. **Ritual and life.** Many of life's experiences have ritual overtones, either because these experiences are vestiges of ritual or because they share its structure or intent. Play, for example, is related to ritual in several respects (Jensen). Both intend to be re-creation, and many aspects of play are re-enactments of "mythic" perceptions, as in the boy who "drives" his toy car like his father. Still other forms of play are vestiges of actions once done ritually, including such diverse games as stilt-walking and play combat. Drama, music, and dance are arts which, in many societies, had their start in religious contexts and are often used even now as part of ritual. Drama in both classical Greek and Indian contexts, for example, often acted out the role of mythical beings or the response of humans to those beings. We have seen that ritual itself is symbolic drama. Music has often been used as rhythmic accompaniment to ritual. In India music started from the ritual chants of Vedic hymnists and eventually served to homologize the inner "spirit" or "emotion" *(rasa)* of the human participant with the

rhythm of the cosmos. Similarly, dance gave the body cosmic dimensions and used it as a medium for expressing the specific mythical deeds of the gods as well as more general eternal truths. Ethics and ritual have both been ways to respond to the eternal and to create new worlds where the paradisal vision of reconciliation, new community, and conflict resolution can be a reality. In a similar way, life is filled with vestiges of rituals and with quasi- and crypto-rituals. INITIATIONS are to be found in countless fraternal orders and in the academic system's use of examinations and graduation. Patterns of greeting, communicating, and relating socially often assume a ritual character. Demonstrations calling for a new order are often symbols of liminality which express the in-between state of "no-longer—not yet." Athletic contests, public entertainment, and mass media have ritual overtones insofar as they reflect a people's values or mores and provide an occasion for access to another "world"—be it the world of "winning" or of timelessness.

Bibliography. S. Barnett, "Approaches to Changes in Caste Ideology in South India," *Essays on South India*, B. Stein, ed. (1975), pp. 149-80; P. Berger, *The Sacred Canopy* (1967); A. Bharathi, "Pilgrimage in the Indian Tradition," *HR*, III (1963), 135-67; F. W. Clothey, "Skanda-Ṣaṣṭi: A Festival in Tamil India," *HR*, VIII (1969), 236-59; B. Cohn and M. Mariott, "Networks and Centers in the Integration of Indian Civilization," *Journal of Social Research* (1958), 1:1-9; M. Eliade, *The Sacred and the Profane* (1957) and *The Two and the One* (1965); T. H. Gaster, *Thespis* (1956); R. Grimes, "Ritual Studies: Two Models," *Religious Studies Review*, II (1976), 13-25; S. Hanchett, "Festivals and Social Relations in a Mysore Village: Mechanics of Two Processions," *Economic and Political Weekly*, VII (1972), 31-33, 1517-22; A. Jensen, *Myth and Cult Among Primitive People* (1963); S. Kierkegaard, *Purity of Heart Is to Will One Thing* (1938); C. Lévi-Strauss, *The Raw and the Cooked* (1969); N. E. Opler, "Family, Anxiety, and Religion in a Community of North India," *Culture and Mental Health, Cross Cultural Studies*, K. Opler, ed. (1959), pp. 273-89; A. K. Ramanujan, *Speaking of Śiva* (1973); M. Spiro, *Burmese Supernaturalism* (1967); V. Turner, *The Forest of Symbols: Aspects of Ndembu Ritual* (1967), *The Ritual Process* (1969), and *Dramas, Fields, and Metaphors: Symbolic Action in Human Society* (1974); A. van Gennep, *The Rites of Passage* (1960).

F. W. CLOTHEY

ROMAN CATHOLICISM (Ch) **1. History.** The adjective "catholic" was applied to the universal Christian church *ca* A.D. 107 by Ignatius of Antioch. For AUGUSTINE (354-430), "catholic" meant geographically universal, uninterrupted in continuity with the Christian past, transcending language, race, and nation. The test of catholicity was communion with the universal church and with the SEE of ROME. After East and West divided, "catholic" was more commonly applied to the Latin western church, although not abandoned in the East. Since the sixteenth century "Roman Catholic" has meant the religious body which acknowledges the pope as head of the universal church and the see of Rome as the center of ecclesiastical unity.

The First VATICAN COUNCIL (1869-1870) called the church "the holy Catholic apostolic Roman Church." It has (1980), some 700,000,000 members in over 2,000 DIOCESES throughout the world. After the PROTESTANT REFORMATION Roman Catholic strength was concentrated in southern Europe, with northern outposts in Lithuania, Poland, and Ireland. Theology and spirituality took on a more Latin cast under the influence of reform movements originating in Spain and Italy. The Council of TRENT (1545-1563) countered the Reformers with doctrinal decrees on BIBLE and tradition, JUSTIFICATION and MASS and SACRAMENTS, and disciplinary decrees on sacraments, seminary training, preaching, indulgences, and reform of clerical life. Liturgical observance and catechetics were standardized. The CATHOLIC REFORMATION placed emphasis on the structured, visible, hierarchical nature of the Christian community. For the JESUIT controversialist Robert Bellarmine (1542-1621) the church was "the congregation of those bound by profession of the same Christian faith and by communion in the same sacraments under the rule of lawful pastors and especially of the only vicar of Christ on earth, the Roman Pontiff." After 1648 the authority of the PAPACY was increasingly challenged by church nationalism (Gallicanism, Josephinism, Febronianism, etc.). Nineteenth century German romanticism emphasized the church as community and as the mystical body of Christ. The church became increasingly centralized on Rome, and in 1870 the dogmas of papal jurisdictional primacy and INFALLIBILITY were proclaimed. Active membership declined after 1850 in European industrial areas, but in the United States a largely urban Catholic community grew rapidly in the same period. Intellectual and social renewal began under Pope LEO XIII (1878-1903), but slowed under Pius X (1903-14), whose emphasis was on spirituality and liturgical reform (*see* MODERNISM, CATHOLIC). Cautious developments in theology and biblical studies resumed, but were overshadowed by debates over the role of the church, of Pius XII (1939-58), and of individual church members during World War II. Under JOHN XXIII and Paul VI the Second VATICAN COUNCIL (1962-65) signaled a new openness to other Christians, to other religions, and to the secular world. In 1978 Polish Cardinal Karol Wojtyla was elected pope, taking the name John Paul II. He is the first non-Italian to hold the papacy since the Dutch Pope Adrian VI (1522-23).

2. Scripture and tradition. In Roman Catholic teaching, revelation is summed up in Christ the Lord, who commanded his APOSTLES to preach the gospel. This they did by preaching and example, by the institutions they established, and by spreading the teachings of the NT, written under the inspiration of the Holy Spirit. To preserve the full and living gospel, the apostles left BISHOPS as their successors. Tradition is reverenced and, together with Scripture, is considered to make up a single sacred deposit of the

Word of God entrusted to the church. Authentic interpretation of the Word of God, whether in written form or in the form of tradition, belongs to the living teaching office *(magisterium)* of the church alone.

3. **Social institutions.** Church government is based on the doctrine of APOSTOLIC SUCCESSION. The bishops with the pope form an episcopal college, and individual bishops share collegial responsibility for the entire church as well as for their own dioceses. The pope has primacy of jurisdiction and, under specified conditions, both he and the body of bishops together with him, when they exercise the supreme teaching office, enjoy the gift of INFALLIBILITY. Roman Catholic congregations are formed in (usually territorial) parishes, and parishes are grouped in dioceses, headed by a bishop who may have auxiliary or coadjutor bishops. Intermediate groups of parishes such as vicariates, regions, or deaneries sometimes exist in dioceses. There are national bishops' conferences and periodic representative international synods of bishops at Rome. Formal church assemblies include diocesan synods, councils on the provincial and national level, and worldwide ("ecumenical") COUNCILS, of which Roman Catholics count twenty-one. In addition to churches, hospitals, and other charitable and welfare works, the church in many countries maintains schools from elementary to university level. Its ordained CLERGY (deacons, priests, bishops) must be male and, except in eastern churches in union with Rome and in the case of married deacons in the Latin rite, celibate (*see* §5). Cooperating with the bishops, but under their own superiors, are the religious orders and congregations of men and women who take vows of poverty, chastity, and obedience.

4. **Beliefs and formulations.** Roman Catholics profess the traditional Christian CREEDS. They believe in the triune God (*see* TRINITY) and in the divinity of CHRIST. ORIGINAL SIN is seen as alienating man from God but not totally corrupting him. Grace truly makes a sinner just. Man cooperates in his salvation. Roman Catholicism has a strong incarnational orientation. The EUCHARIST is the center of the church's life. The MASS is understood as paschal meal (*see* PASSOVER) and as the unbloody repetition of the sacrifice of Calvary. Christ is believed to be really present (*see* TRANSUBSTANTIATION) under the appearances of bread and wine. The seven SACRAMENTS signify and confer grace. There is strong emphasis on the COMMUNION OF SAINTS, with prayer for both living and dead (*see* DEAD, PRAYERS FOR THE) and belief in the intercessory power of the SAINTS in heaven. Catholics specially venerate MARY (*see* IMMACULATE CONCEPTION; ASSUMPTION OF MARY).

5. **Rites.** Most Roman Catholics belong to the Western, or Latin, rite, the LITURGY of which has been revised and simplified in a series of steps since promulgation of Vatican II's Constitution on the Sacred Liturgy (1963). The official liturgical language remains LATIN, but modern languages are widely used. The vestigial Mozarabic rite is preserved in Toledo, Spain, as is the Ambrosian rite in Milan, Italy. In addition to the Latin rite there are Catholics in union with Rome in twenty-one churches which use, in whole or part, the Byzantine, Alexandrian, Antiochene, Armenian, and Chaldean rites. Six of these churches have their own patriarchs.

6. **Ethics.** Roman Catholic ethical teaching relies on revelation, the natural law, and the teaching authority of the church. Particularly influential has been the natural law tradition developed by medieval theologians like THOMAS AQUINAS (*ca.* 1225-74). Increasing use of the sacrament of penance led in modern times to the development of casuistry (the application of general moral principles to individual cases), a science best represented by Alphonsus Liguori (1696-1787). An older insistence on the objective nature of law is now coupled with greater appreciation of subjective, personalist factors. Catholic opposition to abortion is absolute. Considerable debate exists on artificial birth control, the indissolubility of Christian marriage (strongly upheld in official teaching), the possibility of a just war, use of nuclear weapons, and capital punishment. During World War II Catholic moralists condemned saturation bombing. Paul VI reiterated official opposition to artificial birth control in his 1968 encyclical letter *Humanae Vitae*. Beginning with LEO XIII's letter *Rerum Novarum* (1891), successive popes have expressed their concern for social justice. In Latin America, home of 40 percent of the world's Roman Catholics, the church has increasingly sided with proponents of social change.

7. **Major festivals.** CHRISTMAS, EASTER, and PENTECOST are the three great festivals in the church CALENDAR. Four special seasons are kept: ADVENT, Christmas, LENT, Easter. Other feasts are celebrated throughout the year, but the liturgy has been revised to place greater emphasis on the mysteries of redemption, rather than on the saints. ASH WEDNESDAY and GOOD FRIDAY are fast days and the other Fridays of Lent are days of abstinence from meat.

Bibliography. J. L. McKenzie, *The Roman Catholic Church* (1969); L. J. Rogier, ed., *The Christian Centuries: A New History of the Catholic Church* (1964-). J. HENNESEY

ROME (Ch). The capital of modern Italy and one of the most important political and religious centers of the ancient world.

According to legend, Rome was founded by twin brothers in 753 B.C., but archaeological evidence reveals settlements going back to at least the tenth century B.C. Under Pompey and Caesar, in the first century B.C., Rome's power in the Near East was extended and regularized, and by the opening of the Christian era the settled areas of the Roman Empire were governed by senate-appointed officials and procurators responsible to the emperor.

There was little known contact between Israel and

Rome until the period of the MACCABEES, *ca.* 160 B.C., and it was not until 63 B.C. that Palestine came under direct Roman control.

The circumstances of the founding of the Christian church in Rome are unclear, but it is certain that when PAUL wrote Romans (*ca.* A.D. 58) there was an active community in existence there. When PETER arrived and how long he remained is not known. However there are very early (A.D. 96) references to the martyrdom of these two apostles in Rome under Nero in either 64 or 67. ST. PETER'S BASILICA stands on the traditional site of Peter's burial.

The Christian community developed under the emperors Vespasian (69-79) and Titus (79-81), but was severely persecuted under Domitian (81-96), a persecution reflected in the NT books of I Peter and Revelation. By the middle of the second century, a larger organized community is to be found in Rome as well as a school of philosophy conducted by Justin Martyr (*ca.* 100-160). Intermittent persecutions continued from the time of Hadrian (117-38) to Diocletian (284-305), but ended with the Peace of the Church (A.D. 313) and the coming of CONSTANTINE.

Excavations beneath a number of modern churches in Rome reveal remains of early basilica-type churches built during the second, third and fourth centuries. Over forty CATACOMB areas have also been located along the main roads leading from the city. Because of the many holy places in Rome pilgrims have flocked there through the centuries.

Christian asceticism flourished in Rome from the period of Pope Damasus (366-84) and JEROME (*ca.* 360), and from the mid fourth century on the authority of the bishop of Rome developed (*see* PAPACY). This development is chartered in the utterances of Emperor Theodosius I (379-95) and Popes Innocent I (401-17) and LEO I (440-61).

In the Renaissance, Rome was the center for great painters, architects, and artisans of all types. The papal court encouraged these artists, but it also fell victim to pomp and various abuses of power. The desire to reform the church from within culminated in the Council of TRENT (1545-63). Pope Julius II (1503-13) did much to modernize Rome by reordering the streets and completely renovating the Vatican, where the government of the Catholic Church is centered. (*See* VATICAN CITY.)

Today the city remains the center of ROMAN CATHOLICISM and custodian of many ancient sacred monuments. D. W. O'CONNOR

ROSARY (Ch). A method of prayer combining repetition of familiar prayers with meditation on fifteen mysteries or events in the life of Christ and his Mother. Divided into fifteen decades (groups of ten), each decade consists of the LORD'S PRAYER, ten "Hail Marys" (*see* AVE MARIA), and the DOXOLOGY. As a memory aid the prayers are often counted on a string of beads. Usually only a third part of the rosary is prayed at a given time: the joyful mysteries (annunciation, visitation, nativity, presentation, finding in the Temple); the sorrowful mysteries (agony in the garden, scourging, crown of thorns, carrying of the cross, crucifixion); or the glorious mysteries (RESURRECTION, ASCENSION, descent of the HOLY SPIRIT, ASSUMPTION OF MARY, coronation of MARY). The present form of the rosary, dating from the sixteenth century, was preceded by earlier forms popularized by monastic and mendicant orders. In the Roman Catholic Church the memorial of Our Lady of the Rosary, first instituted in 1573 in connection with the victory over ISLAM at Lepanto, is celebrated on October 7; and throughout the entire month, prominence is given to this devotion.

See also TASBĪH. C. WADDELL

ROSENZWEIG, FRANZ rō´ zĕn tsvĭg (Ju; 1886-1929). German Jewish theologian. He reinterpreted Judaism around six focal points: the historical events of creation; revelation; redemption; and the relational components of God, individuals, and world. He collaborated with MARTIN BUBER on a German translation of the BIBLE. *See* JUDAISM §6d.

L. FAGEN

ROSH HA-SHANAH rōsh hă shă năh´ (Ju—Heb.; lit. "head of the year"). The Jewish New Year. In traditional Judaism it is celebrated on the first two days of Tishri (September-October); Reform Judaism observes one day only. Scripturally it is designated as a day of memorial and the blowing of trumpets (Lev. 23:24; Num. 29:1); its designation as the beginning of the year is TALMUDIC and stems from its ascription as the universal birthdate. Unlike some new year celebrations, Rosh ha-Shanah is a day of solemnity on which each person is subject to review and judgment for the coming year. The divine ledgers are said to be open and the fate of the individual is recorded there. Decisions are unsealed, however, so that everyone may still repent, and themes of individual responsibility and divine mercy serve as a liturgical context for the holiday, continuing through YOM KIPPUR, a period known as the "Ten Days of Penitence."

Central to the service is the sounding of the SHOFAR, a ram's horn. Aside from biblical reference, the practice is symbolically linked to the "binding of Isaac" (when a ram replaced him on the altar; Gen. 22:13), the coronation of God, the giving of the TORAH, and the age of the MESSIAH. Most popularly, the notes of the shofar serve to awaken the assembled and call them to penitence. To that end, these notes are designed to imitate weeping and sighs of grief. In response to a debate regarding the nature of the blasts, a variety of sequences is repeated, in some congregations numbering one hundred blasts.

Prayers include three sections of biblical quotations, describing the Lord's kingship, his concern for the troubled, and the blowing of the shofar. Biblical selections describing Isaac's birth (Gen. 21:1-7) and his binding (Gen. 22:9-12) are also read. In Orthodox Judaism it is common to wear white in the SYNAGOGUE as a symbol of purity.

Modern scholars compare Rosh ha-Shanah to the practices of cognate cultures that reckoned the new year by the autumnal harvest. Some suggest that Rosh ha-Shanah had priestly significance during the Temple period, while SUKKOT was the popular harvest festival and new year. Interestingly, the Talmud denotes four new year dates dispersed through the calendar, each with some social and agricultural significance.

It is customary to greet neighbors with "May you be inscribed for a good year." Fruit or bread is often dipped in honey at the meal, symbolizing the hope for a sweet year. Fish, considered a symbol of fortune, are eaten in some communities, while nuts are avoided because their Hebrew numerical value equals that of sin (*see* GAMATRIA). Though the source is obscure, traditional Judaism on the first afternoon of Rosh ha-Shannah has the practice of visiting a body of running water that contains fish. There, prayers and psalms of penitence are recited while crumbs are tossed into the depths, symbolic of sins being cast away. This is known as *tashlīḥ*. *See* CALENDAR, JEWISH.

Bibliography. P. Goodman, *The Rosh Hashannah Anthology* (1971); S. Y. Agnon, *Days of Awe* (1965); S. Zevin, *Ha-Moadim be-Halakhah*, 2nd ed. (1947). D. J. SCHNALL

ROSHI rō´ shē (B—Jap.; lit. "venerable teacher). A term of respect used for the head of a monastery, the chief priest in a temple, or an older lay teacher. In ZEN, a teacher possessing spiritual insight, whose life exhibits his awareness of emptiness (ŚŪNYATĀ) and impermanence (ANICCA), and who takes responsibility for instructing disciples in the practice of Zen.

K. CRIM

ROSICRUCIANS. The earliest verifiable use of the term Rosicrucian, "rosy cross," is an anonymous text, *Fama Fraternitatis* ("Account of the Brotherhood"), which created a brief sensation in Germany upon its publication in 1614. It purports to recount the life of a medieval knight, Christian Rosenkreuz, who traveled to Morocco and the Near East to acquire secret wisdom and an elixir of life. The teachings, employing the symbols of ASTROLOGY and ALCHEMY, and influenced by Kabbalism (*see* KABBALA) were basically in the Neoplatonist tradition typical of Renaissance occultism. The *Fama* was followed by another tract stating that initation into the Rosicrucian Order was now being offered those prepared to join the fraternity of hidden adepts. The documents are now generally considered hoaxes or allegories; Rosenkreuz probably never existed, although he may have been based on the Swiss alchemist and physician Paracelsus.

Rosicrucian teaching and mystique influenced such later developments as SWEDENBORGIANISM, THEOSOPHY, and the late nineteenth century Order of the Golden Dawn. Modern groups using the name and heritage of Rosicrucianism have appeared; the best known is the Ancient and Mystical Order Rosae Crucis (AMORC) founded in 1915 by the American H. Spencer Lewis, with headquarters in California; it advertises its courses widely.

Bibliography. A. G. Debus, *The English Paracelsians* (1966); N. MacKenzie, ed., *Secret Societies* (1971); A. E. Waite, *The Real History of the Rosicrucians* (1887); F. A. Yates, *The Rosicrucian Enlightenment* (1972). R. S. ELLWOOD

ṚṢI rĭ´ shē (H). *See* RISHI.

ṚTA rĭ´ tŭ (H—Skt.; lit. "right, true"). Cosmic order, divine law, truth, righteousness, a concept basic to VEDIC HINDUISM. It was replaced later in Hinduism by the Sanskrit word DHARMA. The constant solar, lunar, and seasonal rhythms were believed to be the result of a universal order and truth. Similarly, the regular course of the Vedic sacrificial system, from the simplest to the most elaborate ritual operation, participated in and contributed to cosmic orderliness and exactitude. And so too the individual, in personal ritual life and in social ethical life, was intimately connected to the natural and moral structure of the universe. It is significant that Vedic tradition understood *ṛta* as an order guarded by various deities, yet not directly dependent upon them. The cosmogonic hymn, RIG VEDA 10.190, relates how *ṛta* was born from primordial heat (TAPAS), before time and space were manifest. While AGNI, the sacrificial fire, protects *ṛta* in the ritual system, it is the sovereign pair of deities, MITRA and VARUṆA (and particularly the latter), who guard *ṛta* in the sense of moral order. The transgressor of *ṛta,* unless relevant expiations were performed, necessarily faced the punishments of Varuṇa. Contrary behavior, *anṛta* ("non-*ṛta*"), could be against the natural order, the ritual system (e.g., omission or error), or the social-ethical norms. This sense of cosmic surveillance of and retribution for all forms of individual behavior is recognized as one important aspect in the development of the late-Vedic doctrine of KARMA.

Bibliography. P. V. Kane, *History of Dharmaśāstra*, Vol. IV (1953), ch. 1. D. M. KNIPE

RUDRA rōō´ drŭ (H—Skt.; lit. "the howler" [probably from *rud*—"to cry, howl, wail"; or *rud, rudh*—"to be red"]). A god in VEDIC HINDUISM, fierce, unpredictable, antisocial, associated with the wilderness and raw natural forces, euphemistically called *śiva* ("auspicious") in a late UPANISAD; the major Hindu deity SHIVA is his successor in post-Vedic traditions. Rudra is father and ruler of the Maruts, storm gods who are also called the Rudras. Although only three hymns of the RIG VEDA are addressed to him, Rudra's character is sharply delineated. He inspires fear in men with his lightning bolt and other weapons, above all as Śarva with his bow and arrows (an Indo-Iranian background is demonstrated by the correspondence of Śarva with the ancient Iranian archer Saurva). He is an outsider among the gods, receiving only the remnants (e.g. entrails) of the sacrifice. The sinister, wrathful, malevolent side of Rudra is complemented by a beneficent side, for he is honored also as a healer and physician, one who has a thousand cooling remedies. This ambivalent power extends to the later Shiva, as do many of the epithets of Rudra such as Paśupati (lord of domestic animals), Mahādeva (great god), Tryambaka (having three mothers), Hara (destroyer), Śaṃkara (beneficent); like the later Shiva he is a mountain dweller, clothed in animal skins, blue-necked, a bull, and one associated with fire (AGNI), the dead, and asceticism. Rudra's sons are the Maruts, a group of young men who direct the storms, sometimes identified as the Rudras or Rudriyas. Variously eight, eleven, or thirty-three in number they are less malevolent than their father and aid INDRA in his heroic deeds. Their names are a litany of the forms of Shiva.

Bibliography. A. A. Macdonell, *Vedic Mythology* (1897); E. Arbman, *Rudra* (1922). D. M. KNIPE

RŪḤ rōōh (I—Arab.; lit. "spirit"). According to many early Islamic theorists, *rūḥ* was identical with NAFS; both terms were thought to refer to a single spiritual substance, with refined material form, light in weight, mobile, and capable of penetrating all parts of the human body. Though created, it was everlasting and at death went to heaven for a preliminary judgment before returning to the grave to await the final Day of Resurrection. Only the spirits of prophets (NABI) and martyrs (SHAHĪD) went straight to heaven at death.

SUFIS, however, distinguish between *rūḥ* and *nafs* in terms of function. According to Suhrawardi, "The spirit is the mine of good and the soul is the mine of evil" (Milson, p. 44.). Hujwiri sees man as composed of spirit, soul, and body, with spirit and soul combatting each other for control of the body and the ultimate destiny of man. *See* JANNA; JAHANNAM; SOUL, SPIRIT.

Bibliography. 'Ali Hujwiri, *Kashf al-Mahjub*, R. A. Nicholson, trans. (1911), pp. 196-210; D. B. MacDonald, "The Development of the Idea of Spirit in Islam", *Acta Orientalia* (1931), 307-51; M. Milson, trans., *A Sufi Rule for Novices* (1975). B. LAWRENCE

RŪMĪ, JALĀL ad-DĪN rōō' mē jə läl' əd dēn' (I; 1207-1273). Paramount mystical poet of Islam in the PERSIAN LANGUAGE. Born at Balkh in Central Asia, he was forced to journey to distant places with his banished father, Bahā ad-Dīn Walad, when the latter became a victim of court intrigue *ca.* 1217. Not until 1227 did Bahā ad-Dīn obtain a professorship in theology at Konya in Rum (Eastern Anatolia; thus the name Rumi, i.e. "[Byzantine] Roman"). Jalāl ad-Dīn, who had been partially trained in mystical and traditional scholarship by his father, succeeded Bahā ad-Dīn and remained at Konya, except for one brief journey, until his own death.

The life of Jalāl ad-Dīn turns on a dramatic meeting in 1244 with the itinerant DERVISH Shams ad-Dīn Tabrīzī. Shams moved into Rūmī's home and so dominated his life and thought that many of his writings, including a vast collection of poems, were dedicated to Shams and written under the pen-name Shams. Shams disappeared from Rūmī's life as mysteriously as he had entered it, but Rūmī had begun an irreversible spiritual odyssey. He was inspired by another SUFI, Ḥusām ad-Dīn Celebī, to write his most famous poem, the *Mathnavī*. Comprising six books, it sets forth loosely connected themes, often narrated as parables or ancedotes in picturesque, highly alliterative verse. Among mystically minded Muslims it is known as "the Qur'ān in Persian." Commentaries on it, imitations of it, works relating to it or inspired by it abound in various languages throughout the Muslim world.

Rūmī also inspired an independent Sufi order (ṬARĪQA), the Mawlāwīya, named after the respectful title *mawlānā* (lit., "our master") accorded the SHAIKH by his disciples. The order was later publicized among European travelers as the "Whirling Dervishes," a name that reflects the prominent role of ritual DANCE in the Mawlāwīs' weekly observance of *samā'* (congregational music).

Bibliography. Jalāl ad-dīn Rūmī, *Mathnawī-i Ma'nawī*, ed. and tr. by R. A. Nicholson, 8 vols. (1925-40); P. Chelkowski, ed., *The Scholar and the Saint* (1975), pp. 169-306; A. Schimmel, *The Triumphal Sun: A Study of the Works of Jalaloddin Rumi* (1979). B. LAWRENCE

RŪPA rōō'pŭ (H & B—Skt.; lit. "form"). One of the five *tanmātras*, or subtle elements; in Hindu philosophy, *rūpa* is the "essence" of form or, sometimes, of color. One of the subtlest aspects of actual matter, *rūpa* is without magnitude and is perceived only through the medium of particular objects. Sometimes the term is used to refer merely to the external form of objects, in which case another term, *svarūpa*, is used for "essential form." *Rūpa* is commonly used, especially in Buddhist philosophy, in still another way—to denote corporeality in the distinction between mind and body *(nāma-rūpa)*.

J. BARE

RUSSIAN ORTHODOX CHURCH (Ch). Until 1918 the national church of Russia; now the predominant religious body in the USSR (*see* ORTHODOX CHURCHES.)

1. **History.** Greek missionaries were active in Kiev in the ninth century, and Grand Prince Vladimir of Kiev was baptized in 988. The following year the whole city was baptized. At first the church was headed by a Greek METROPOLITAN with his seat in Kiev, under the jurisdiction of the Ecumenical

PATRIARCH in Constantinople. Following the Mongol conquest of Russia (1237-1448) the seat of the metropolitan was moved to Moscow. The Russian church became independent of Constantinople when it installed its native metropolitan in 1448. The Ecumenical Patriarch participated in the consecration of the first Russian patriarch in 1589. With the fall of Constantinople, the "Second Rome," in 1453, Moscow became "the Third Rome," the most important center of Eastern Christianity.

Patriarch Nikon (1652-58) reformed the ritual of the Russian church in accordance with liturgical norms prevailing in the Eastern patriarchates, but he forced these reforms on the church in an autocratic manner. This alienated large numbers of believers and clergy, and caused the schism of the OLD BELIEVERS. This schism weakened the church and prepared the ground for Peter the Great (1682-1725), who abolished the patriarchate in 1721 and appointed a lay procurator as his spokesman in the deliberations of the Holy Synod. The patriarch was restored in 1917 with the election of Tikhon, only to lapse after his death in 1925. During the Soviet period churches were closed and believers and churchmen were persecuted on a large scale. In 1943 the Soviet government allowed the church to elect a new patriarch, and since then it has experienced a modest revival under firm political control.

2. **Spirituality.** At first spiritual life evolved in the Monastery of the Caves in Kiev. Its founder, St. Theodosius, stressed humility and concern for the poor and emphasized the place of suffering in Christian life. Under the Mongols the center shifted to the Monastery of the Holy TRINITY (now Zagorsk), founded by St. Sergius (d. 1392), Russia's most popular national saint. Sergius, the first Russian mystic and the inspirer of national opposition to the Mongols, influenced the next two hundred years, a golden age of Russian spirituality, ICON-painting, and architecture. During the Synodal period (1721-1917), despite influences from western Europe upon theology, art, and music, the church continued its spiritual growth, represented by St. Tikhon of Zadonsk (1724-83) and Seraphim of Sarov (1759-1833). The nineteenth century saw the revival of the institution of spiritual elders *(starets),* and the hermitage of Optino (1829-1923) became the main spiritual center.

3. **In the United States.** There are about one million Russian Orthodox in America, in separate jurisdictions. The largest, the Orthodox Church in America, was granted independent status by the Patriarch of Moscow in 1970. The Russian Church Outside Russia or Synodal Church, with its center in New York, has no link with the official church in the USSR.

Bibliography. N. Zernov, *The Russians and Their Church* (1945). V. KESICH

RYŌBU SHINTŌ ryō´ boo shĭn´ tō (S—Jap.; lit. "dual Shintō"). In medieval Japan a syncretistic coordination of Buddhist divinities with the KAMI of JAPANESE RELIGION. For example, the Sun Goddess AMATERASU was equated with the Sun Buddha VAIROCANA, and the inner and outer shrines at ISÉ came to be regarded as representing the two MANDALAS of SHINGON. K. CRIM

S

SAADIAH BEN JOSEPH sä ă dyä´ bĕn yō sāf´ (Ju; 881-942). Chief of the Talmudic academy in Sura, Babylonia; champion of rabbinic Judaism in its struggle with the KARAITES; translator of the Jewish BIBLE into Arabic; author of countless works in poetry, liturgy, rabbinics, HEBREW grammar, and polemics; and rationalist philosopher-theologian, author of a Jewish adaptation of Islamic theology, *The Book of Beliefs and Opinions.* K. P. BLAND

ŚABAD shŭ´ bäd (S—Skt.; lit. "the word"). A term used almost entirely for words from the holy scriptures *(Śabad Bāni),* and thus including the meaning "divine word." In actual practice *śabad* also refers to singing hymns in the Sikh temples. Such singing may be performed by anyone, male or female, but is usually done by professional groups of singers to the accompaniment of harmoniums and tabla drums.
K. SINGH

SABBATAI ZVI săb ə tī´ zə vē´ (Ju; 1626-1676). Jewish mystic whose claim to be the MESSIAH gave rise to a worldwide Jewish messianic fervor; central figure in an antinomian messianic movement whose vitality did not wane until the eighteenth century. Sabbatai was born in Smyrna, where he received a thorough education in the TALMUD. As an adolescent he immersed himself in KABBALA and followed a strict ascetic regimen. Throughout his life he was afflicted with alternating states of depression and elated euphoria. In his exalted states he trespassed Jewish law and committed outrageous deeds. In 1648 he publicly announced that he was the Messiah. After wandering throughout Greece and Turkey, he returned to Smyrna and eventually settled in JERUSALEM and Cairo.

In 1665 word reached Sabbatai of a young Kabbalist, Nathan of Gaza, who was reputed to cure afflicted souls. Nathan was convinced, and succeeded in convincing Sabbatai, that his psychological states were proof of his messianic destiny. Throughout 1665 Nathan, the ideological architect of the movement, spread the news of Sabbatai's identity as the Messiah. Nathan's letters ignited an explosive and enthusiastic response throughout the entire Jewish world. Eventually Sabbatai traveled to Constantinople, where he planned to convert the Sultan to Judaism. After a complicated series of events, Sabbatai, perhaps under the threat of execution, became a Muslim. When news of his apostasy spread, the high-pitched excitement of hope for redemption died away. Sabbatai lived for ten more years surrounded by his devoted believers, who interpreted his paradoxical behavior as one more phase in the tormented life and necessary sufferings of the Messiah.

Sabbatai's apostasy marked not the end, but the true beginning of the Sabbatian movement, which was energized by a passion for revolution. The advent of the Messiah meant release from the oppressive status quo and the creation of a new world and new norms for behavior. If the historical facts proved the contrary, then pure faith in Sabbatai's messianic soul would itself create the state of mind that brings redemption.

The Sabbatian emphasis on the redemptive personality of the leader and its identification of psychological states with divine processes helped prepare the way for the HASIDIC movement.

Bibliography. G. Scholem, *Sabbatai Sevi: the Mystical Messiah* (1973). K. P. BLAND

SABBATH (Ju—Heb. *Shabat*). The Jewish day of rest, identified as the seventh day of the week and observed for twenty-five hours beginning each Friday at sundown. Tradition requires abstention from labor for Jews, their servants and animals, with exceptions made where health is threatened. PRAYER and study are encouraged. It is forbidden to make direct requests of non-Jews.

In the BIBLE, Sabbath is associated with the creation (Exod. 20:8-11), as with the commemoration of divine mercy in the Exodus (Deut. 5:12-15). Modern scholars attribute this divergence to variant authorship, while tradition argues that they are complementary rather than conflicting. Fragmented allusions to the holiness and significance of the Sabbath and detailed instructions regarding Temple sacrifice are numerous in scripture (cf. Gen. 2:1-3; Exod. 23:12; 34:21; Lev. 19:3, 30; Num. 28:3-10). Prophetic references attribute suffering and destruction to the desecration of the Sabbath (cf. Jer. 17:19-27; Ezek. 20:12 ff.; Isa. 56:2-7).

The juxtaposition of one such reference with the account of building the tabernacle (Exod. 35:1 ff.) serves as the Talmudic basis for defining forbidden labor as anything analogous to tasks performed in constructing the tabernacle, e.g. hewing or grinding. Thirty-nine such forms are enumerated, with others inferred. Modern technology has complicated the matter, however, with serious differences emerging over the permissibility of electricity, internal combustion, etc. Even the most traditional have introduced accommodations, such as timing devices for electrical appliances, or an *eruv,* a legal fiction permitting carrying in public places. Unlike other festivals, Sabbath restrictions extend also to food preparation, so that the noon meal must be either cold or indirectly warmed throughout the day.

Liturgically the Sabbath is distinguished from weekdays. TEFILLIN are not worn. *Musaf*—an additional service—is recited, and psalms and chants added, which welcome the Sabbath as an honored guest. Selections from the TORAH are read publicly as part of an annual cycle, completed on SIMHAT TORAH, with a brief reading at the afternoon service as well.

In the home two candles are lit (though some homes light as many as there are family members) and songs welcoming the day are sung. Three meals are taken, and KIDDUSH, a prayer consecrating the day over a cup of wine, is recited at the evening and noon meals. Two loaves, known as *ḥallot,* are served as symbols of the double portion of manna which fell on Friday to compensate for its absence on the Sabbath (Exod. 16:22 ff.). Sabbath meals, utensils, and clothing must be special to mark its distinctiveness. At day's end, *Havdalah* is performed, a brief ceremony with wine, candle, and spices, literally "separating" Sabbath from the days to come. To extend its stay, some add a fourth meal as part of the festivities.

Bibliography. S. Goldman, *Guide to the Sabbath* (1961); A. J. Heschel, *The Sabbath* (1951).

D. J. SCHNALL

SAB'IYYA säb ē´ yä (I—Arab; lit. "sevener"). A name applied to the ISMĀ'ĪLIYYA (especially the QARMAṬIANS), who restricted the IMAMS to seven, the seventh being Muhammad ibn Ismā'īl, grandson of Ja'far al-Ṣādiq, who was expected to be the MAHDI.

The term *sab'iyya* was in all probability first used to signify the Ismaili doctrine that history is divided into seven eras, each inaugurated by a *nāṭiq* (speaking) prophet, who brings a revealed message. Ismailis believed in seven silent imams, one of whom followed each of the seven prophets and disclosed the esoteric aspects of the revelation. The seventh imam in each era becomes the *nāṭiq* of the following era, abrogating the law (SHARIA) of the previous *nāṭiq* and instituting a new one. In the sixth of these eras, MUHAMMAD was the *nāṭiq,* ALI was the silent imam, and, counting from his son al-ḤASAN, the seventh imam was Muhammad ibn Ismā'īl, who was to become the seventh *nāṭiq,* the Mahdi, thus ushering in the seventh era and abrogating the sharia instituted by Muhammad. He would take power as soon as the organization of his loyal adherents was complete.

Ja'far al-Ṣādiq had designated his son Ismā'īl to succeed him as imam, and since such a designation was regarded as divine providence, a controversy arose when Ismā'īl died before his father, and another son, Mūsā al-Kāẓim, succeeded to the office. Al-Kāẓim is regarded as the seventh in the series of twelve imams of the IMĀMIYYA.

The Qarmaṭians were probably an offshoot of a group called Mubārakiyya, who regarded Ismā'īl's son Muhammad as successor to his grandfather al-Ṣādiq. They rejected the claims of the surviving sons of al-Ṣādiq on the grounds that the imamate could not again be vested in two brothers after al-Ḥasan and al-ḤUSAYN, the sons of Ali, and that the imamate must continue among the offspring of the deceased imam. The Qarmaṭians differed from the Mubārakiyya in maintaining that prophecy ended with Muhammad, and that there would be seven imams after him, ending with Muhammad ibn Ismā'īl, who, they asserted, was alive as the Mahdi and would not die until he had conquered the world. In support of this they cited traditions that the seventh among the imams would be the Mahdi.

Also important were the beliefs of the Khaṭṭābiyya, followers of Abū al-Khaṭṭāb Muhammad ibn Abī Zaynab al-Asadī al-Kūfī, who seems to have shaped the Qarmaṭian doctrines of the esoteric interpretation of the QUR'ĀN and of the transference of spiritual authority. Abū al-Khaṭṭāb, who was al-Ṣādiq's disciple in Kūfa, had asserted that the latter had transferred his authority to him by designating him to be his deputy and executor of his will and entrusting to him the "Greatest Name," which was supposed to empower its possessor with extraordinary ability in comprehending hidden matters. This authority was then transferred to Muhammad ibn Ismā'īl after Abū al-Khaṭṭāb's disappearance.

The belief that the seventh imam, whoever he was, was the Mahdi, seems to have been widespread, because after the death of al-Ṣādiq many SHI'ITE groups restricted the number of their imams to seven. The adherents of Mūsā al-Kāẓim refused to acknowledge his death, maintaining that he was alive and would return as the Madhi. These are known as *wāqifiyya,* meaning "those who stopped," i.e. with the imamate of al-Kāẓim. The term implies uncertainty about the imam's death, in contrast to those who affirmed that al-Kāẓim had died, and that the line of imams continued. Al-Shahrastānī used the term also for those Ismailis who expected the return of Ismā'īl. The *wāqifiyya* are thus those who held that the seventh imam, whether Ismāʿīl or al-Kāẓim, was the Mahdi.

Several other Shiʿite factions could be classified as Sabʿiyya. In all cases, the seventh imam was proclaimed as the hidden imam, and in his absence the leadership of these factions rested in the hands of the prominent disciples of the imams. Dissemination of the Sabʿiyya doctrines in different parts of the Muslim world resulted in the appearance of the revolutionary governments of the Qarmaṭians, FATIMIDS, ASSASSINS, and other Ismaili groups. The DRUZES also can be traced back to the early Sabʿiyya. The considerable importance which the Sabʿiyya movement attained is indicated in the religious as well as the political success of these groups. However, the early beliefs of the Sabʿiyya were essentially transformed, and its revolutionary aims gradually gave way to the esoteric and hence quietistic posture of the present day Nizārī (*see* AGHA KHAN) and of the Mustʿali Ismailis. A. A. SACHEDINA

SACRAMENTS (Ch). Effectual signs of grace, ritual acts which both express and bring about a spiritual reality. Just as in the incarnation the eternal Word of God was united with human nature in JESUS Christ, so in the sacraments spiritual gifts are communicated through tangible realities. Beyond that broad concept, however, the term has been variously used by Christian theologians.

1. **Patristic sacramental theology.** The Latin word *sacramentum* entered Christian theological use in the writings of Tertullian (*ca.* 160—*ca.* 225). As early as 197 he was employing the term in its classical meaning, "oath," especially in reference to its military significance and, through that, to its use in connection with initiation into the mystery religions. In early Latin theology it thus was equivalent to the Greek *mysterion,* and was often so used in the Latin NT. Writers of the fourth and fifth centuries used the term for all sorts of liturgical phenomena. AUGUSTINE defined sacrament as sacred sign, applying the term not only to such rites as BAPTISM, but also to the CREED, the LORD'S PRAYER, and EASTER. LEO I used *sacramentum* to mean "mystery" (that which is hidden), "figure" (that which signifies), and "sacrament" in something nearer our modern sense, an efficacious rite. In a statement which seems to include all these, Leo says (Sermon 74), "All that was visible of the Redeemer has passed over into the sacraments." Something of this same broad meaning characterized the term *mysterion* in such Greek fathers as Gregory of Nyssa and John Chrysostom, and was still true for Isidore of Seville in the West in the sixth century. In his *Etymologies* Isidore derives *sacramentum* from "secret," thus making it again the exact equivalent of the Greek *mysterion.* Building on his interpretation, Western writers of the ninth century applied the term not only to such rites as the EUCHARIST, but also to such mysteries of faith as the INCARNATION, which Paschasius Radbertus called "a great sacrament."

2. **Sacraments in scholastic and Protestant theologies.** From the eleventh century a narrowing of the understanding of sacrament can be traced in the Western church as theologians developed more precise definitions. The first major treatise on the sacraments was produced by HUGH OF ST. VICTOR (d. 1141). Although he recognized as many as thirty sacraments, he was nonetheless concerned to distinguish sacraments from other sacred signs. PETER LOMBARD later in the twelfth century formulated the list of seven sacraments which was accepted by most SCHOLASTIC theologians and was canonized for ROMAN CATHOLICISM by the Council of Florence in 1439. These seven are: BAPTISM, CONFIRMATION, PENANCE, EUCHARIST, marriage, holy orders (ORDINATION), and anointing of the sick (UNCTION). In each of these, according to THOMAS AQUINAS and other scholastics, an external rite consisting of a material element (matter) and a verbal formula (form) confers a spiritual benefit objectively when performed with due intention by a competent minister. In point of fact, each element of such a definition is or has been subject to either dispute or variation in practice with regard to one or more of the sacraments. Particularly disputed in the REFORMATION period was the role to be assigned to the subjective disposition in faith of the recipient, a role which most of the reformers wished to expand in contrast to the scholastic emphasis on objectivity.

A further narrowing of the understanding of sacraments appeared in consequence of the scholastic assertion that Christ himself had instituted each of the sacraments. This view was confirmed by the Council of TRENT, but most reformers accepted only baptism and eucharist as having been instituted by Christ (although Lutheran confessions added penance). This marked a further step in the narrowing of the definition of the term which had been under way since the twelfth century. Some reform movements such as the BAPTISTS disallow the concept of sacrament altogether, preferring to call baptism and eucharist "ordinances," commands of Christ to be obeyed but not effective of grace in themselves. Still other movements such as the Quakers (*see* FRIENDS, SOCIETY OF) and the SALVATION ARMY do not observe the rites at all.

3. **Recent sacramental theology.** In the twentieth century the Liturgical Movement, aided by advances in scriptural studies, has tended to reverse this narrowing of the meaning of sacrament and has focused attention once again on the broader liturgical context of the sacraments and their relation to the life of the church. The Dogmatic Constitution on the Church (*Lumen Gentium*) issued by the Second VATICAN COUNCIL says that the CHURCH itself is in the nature of a sacrament, "a sign and instrument, that is, of communion with God and of unity among all men." Such an assertion sees the traditional sacraments less as gifts of grace mediated by the church to individual recipients and more as ritual structures in the life of the church, itself the primordial sacrament. In such perspective baptism appears as the ritual process of initiation into the community which is constituted by

the eucharistic meal through which believers celebrate the unity of the church with Christ. As vital signs of the life of the church, the sacraments can be discussed in that wider liturgical and ecclesiological setting in which earlier patristic theology saw them, and the effect of this development is to expand the concept of sacrament itself to something of its earlier breadth. In whatever number and however understood, however, it seems likely that sacraments will continue to be distinguished from such other sacred signs as ICONS, altars, or vessels, and from such other ritual phenomena as the consecration of churches or monastic profession. The point of such distinction, however, will probably for the immediate future be less the peculiar mode of efficacy of the sacraments than the universality of their presence in the life of the Mystical Body of Christ, who is (in Schillebeeckx's phrase) "the sacrament of the human encounter with God."

Bibliography. P. T. Forsyth, *The Church and the Sacraments* (1917); O. C. Quick, *The Christian Sacraments* (1932); K. Rahner, *The Church and the Sacraments* (1963); E. Schillebeeckx, *Christ, the Sacrament of the Encounter with God* (1963).

T. J. TALLEY

SACRED HARP, THE (Ch). Short title for the most famous of all the nineteenth century shaped-note collections of folk hymns; published in 1844 by Benjamin F. White (Spartanburg, S. C.). The term now refers to the entire tradition that uses differently shaped symbols for the notes of the scale. This notation is used particularly in the rural South and Southwest of the U.S. H. MCELRATH

SACRED HEART, DEVOTION TO THE (Ch). A Roman Catholic devotion based on the symbolism of the physical heart of Jesus as the emblem of love and self-sacrifice. Remotely prefigured in John 19:34, this devotion found clear expression in thirteenth century religious literature, but became generalized only beginning with the sixteenth century. St. John Eudes (d. 1680) was the first to provide a detailed theological basis for the devotion; his efforts met with success, thanks largely to the famous visions (1673-75) of the Visitandine nun, St. Margaret Mary Alacoque. Admitted into the Universal CALENDAR only in 1856, the feast is now observed on the third Friday after PENTECOST.

Bibliography. J. Stierli, ed., *Heart of the Savior* (1957).

C. WADDELL

SACRED THREAD (H—Skt.; *yajñopavīta*, lit. "sacrificial cord"). A ritual cord given to the TWICE BORN of high caste Hindus during their initiation, being worn over the left shoulder and under the right arm. According to early texts its composition and color reflect one's CASTE. Ideally it made a sacrificer prosperous (TĀ 2.1) and was the spiritual bond uniting the universe and all beings (ŚB 7.3.2.13). It remains a mark of high religious and social status in India. C. OLSON

SACRIFICE (from Latin *sacrificium,* the action of making sacred [*sacer*—"holy" + *facere*—"to make"]). A ritual offering in the form of a presentation to, or an exchange with, divine beings, sacred powers, or ancestors. The intention is to establish communication, an orderly relationship, and certain benefits on behalf of an individual, a particular community, or an entire society. The material of sacrifice and the performer of the sacrifice are both understood to be transformed in some crucial way during the course of the ritual. Some form of sacrifice is significant in almost every religion, preliterate or historic, and in some traditions it is considered to be the paramount religious expression. This universality, as well as the great diversity of types, methods, materials, performers, and recipients of sacrifice and the variety of declared intentions for the performance, has led to a number of competing theories concerning the nature and function of sacrifice. General explanations or theories of sacrifice appeared in antiquity in Egyptian religion (e.g. in the Book of the Dead for the cult of Osiris), VEDIC HINDUISM (particularly among the authors of the BRĀHMAṆAS), Iranian speculation (e.g. on the *Yasna* ceremony), Confucian ritual texts (e.g. *Li Ching*), Greek philosophy (e.g. Plato, Philochorus), and Hebrew religion (e.g. the Pentateuch, Ezekiel, Deutero-Isaiah).

In the West it is especially since the nineteenth century that historians, anthropologists, historians of religion, and psychologists have directed attention to sacrifice in their regional, general, or methodological studies. Until the most recent generations theorists were limited by 1) a lack of reliable comparative historical and ethnographical data, 2) evolutionist, rationalist, and theological biases, 3) the quest for the "origins" of sacrifice, often taken to be definitive for the origins of "religion" as well, and 4) selective distancing of certain forms of sacrifice (e.g. EUCHARIST or PASSOVER) from all other such phenomena. Contemporary literature, with biases yet unlabeled, is less concerned with isolating "the most primitive form" and more inclined to recognize the complex and multifaceted character of sacrifice and the need for interpretations based upon competent, well-diversified textual and field studies. From an analysis of current publications, however, it is apparent that the point of departure for theories of sacrifice is still either preliterate societies, particularly African, or the ancient Mediterranean, with Greece and Israel supplying the favored data. Relatively few studies consider Islam or the historic religions of South Asia, Iran, East Asia, Southeast Asia, or Mesoamerica as elements of comparison and theory.

1. **The nature of sacrifice.** Essentially sacrifice involves the voluntary giving or giving up of a valued substance or mode of being to a sacred power or a being of higher status. Often the giving up is

understood to be a destruction of the life or essence of the offering, or in personal terms a death, necessarily involving the sacrificer in the ambiguities of a killing, an act of violence, and a valued transmutation, perhaps even a liberation, of both the offering and the offerer. Frequently too the sacrifice takes the form of a sacramental meal. A discussion of sacrifice must be broad enough, however, to include its disparate forms, and a survey of the materials of sacrifice reveals a wide range of media, both physical and abstract.

a) Materials, victims, and substitutes. Perhaps the most remarkable offering is the god himself. The Puruṣa Sūkta of the VEDAS portrays the paradigmatic act, the god PURUṢA as self-sacrifice, an oblation systematically dismembered to create all cosmic elements. In the NEW TESTAMENT and early church theology it is CHRIST, the son of God, who becomes divine victim, the lamb immolated as an oblation and ATONEMENT for humanity. In ROMAN CATHOLICISM the MASS is a continuous reenactment of Christ's sacrifice. Human sacrifice, a powerful religious statement among the early cultivators in particular, survived into many of the great historic civilizations. The most extreme instance occurred at the height of the Aztec empire when tens of thousands of victims provided hearts and blood on the altars of Huitzilopochtli and other gods. Blood offerings are obtainable from animals as well, and every kind of domestic animal has served as victim, the bull or horse favored by the Proto-Indo-Europeans, the calf, lamb, or kid in the Passover of ancient Judaism, and the pig or fowl in numerous agrarian societies. The Vedic horse sacrifice *(aśvamedha)* was a zoological marvel, with 609 animals assembled at 21 poles; the 297 wild creatures, including everything from gnats and bees to crocodiles and elephants, were "offered" by release, while the featured horse and selected goats, bulls, ewes, rams and others were immolated.

The association of blood with the seat of life and blood offerings to chthonic, often feminine powers is part of a widespread Neolithic pattern. The earliest evidence of animal sacrifice, however, comes from Paleolithic hunters who preceded Neolithic cultivators by tens of thousands of years. For many of them, apparently, the bones and not the blood were the seat of life, and their sacrificial arrangements of skulls and long bones of the hunted animal (e.g. the prehistoric cave bear in the Drachenloch caves) is strikingly paralleled by the rites of the surviving circumpolar hunters, fishers,and even some herders, who sacrifice bears, deer, whales, and reindeer (formerly hunted) by mounting skulls and long bones to face the animal guardian who receives them. Another sacrifice documented from the archaic reindeer hunters was the submergence in lakes of two-year-old does with stones in the thoracic cavities, perhaps as a first-kill offering at the start of the summer season.

In addition to deities, humans, hunted or domestic animals, birds and fish, sacrifices were offered of innumerable fruits, vegetables, flowers, and beverages (milk, water, fermented drinks). Cooked cereal foods are particularly prominent in sacrifices to the dead. An archaic example of vegetation sacrifice survives in the respective SOMA and *haoma* cults of Vedic Hinduism and ZOROASTRIANISM: a divine plant, ritually beaten and killed, then pressed to obtain its essential juices, is consumed sacramentally by the priests. Other frequently sacrificed materials include clothing, tools, weapons, jewelry, toys, even models of dwellings.

The range of materials is not complete without mention of the human or divine parts, essences, instincts, and activities that frequently become the "offering." Australian tribals regularly open their veins to make blood sacrifices, North American Indians offered their fingers, and in ancient Scandinavian mythology Odin sacrifices his eye, Tyr his hand. The Hindu goddess KĀLĪ is worshiped with self-decapitations. Understood symbolically, sacrificial offerings may be made of breath (the YOGIN), sexuality (the monk), society (the anchorite), speech (the TRAPPIST), food and mobility (the Jaina in *sallekhanā*). The Hindu SANNYĀSIN ceases to sacrifice because he has renounced all; he *is* the sacrifice.

Substitutes and surrogates are everywhere in evidence, a part for a whole, an animal for a human, a fruit or a dough image for an animal, and so on. The Vedic sacrificers discussed substitutes for soma *ca.* 800 B.C. The flesh that is circumcised (*see* CIRCUMCISION) or subincised in what are still among the more enigmatic rituals has been frequently interpreted as a substitute for human sacrifice. The Nuer sacrifice an ox to the Spirit, the ox being the ritual surrogate for a man; when oxen are scarce a wild cucumber represents the ox, and it is so immolated.

b) Performers and recipients. The performer of a sacrifice may be an individual lay sacrificer (alone with his offering), or a specialist (an intermediary such as a priest), or even an entire staff of priests, who perform the ritual on behalf of the sacrificer or patron. In any case it is the sacrificer who is transformed, who must therefore be consecrated in order to enter into the sacred time and sacred space of the ritual drama. The sacrificer may be a householder offering on behalf of his family, or an elder, a chief, a king, or a universal emperor (e.g. the *cakravartin*) benefiting his tribe, his nation, or the world itself. The ancient high cultures of Egypt, the Near East, India, China, Japan, and Mesoamerica all provide examples of sacred kingship in which the ruler was a special intermediary in the sacrificial system.

The recipients—gods, goddesses, animal guardians, ancestors, spirits—either remain in their otherworldly realms to receive offerings conveyed to them by fire, smoke, air, or water, or they journey to the altar or site to take their portions directly. Ancestors, for example, in the enormously important mortuary cults of India, China, and Japan, must be sustained by constant sacrifices (*see* ANCESTOR VENERATION; ŚRĀDDHA). In certain cases the recipient may arrive to take part in a sacramental meal, or may even be identified with the victim consumed by his devotees.

2. **The interpretation of sacrifice.** We cannot separate history and theory: the description, whether textual analysis or anthropological report, is inevitably shaped by the perspective of the describer. But we can discuss the declared intentions of the tradition apart from the theories generated by outside observers.

a) Declared intentions. An Aztec myth understands the dismemberment of the earth goddess as providing the material of creation. The MYTH served the Aztecs as a paradigm for every human sacrifice. This worldwide practice of human sacrifice, to take this one example, has been explained by myths and traditions in dozens of ways. The victim is a messenger to the gods or the other world, a securer of fertility, a hostage to gain safe passage, a construction or foundation bearer, a prophylactic against disease, drought, famine, death, or demons, a thank offering for victory in war or successful crops or the birth of a royal son, a scapegoat to remove collective sins, a propitiation of divine wrath, a servant for the privileged dead, and so forth. A single sacrifice may reveal multiform, perhaps even contradictory intentions, and thus like the myth that supports it be the more expressive of the mysteries and ambiguities of creaturely existence.

b) External interpretation and theory. The Latin formula *do ut des* ("I give so that you will give") survived from antiquity into nineteenth century interpretations of ritual offerings. The anthropologist E. B. Tylor, in the fashion of his era, posited a three-stage evolution. Originally sacrifice was a gift to supernatural beings in propitiation or the hope of material reward. Later it took the form of homage with the more sophisticated expectation of divine favor. Finally, in religion's highest stage, sacrifice became abnegation and renunciation. Tylor's schema thus accounted for a continuum from the gifts or bribes of "primitives" to self-sacrifice in the "high" religions. Two other nineteenth century anthropologists proposed widely influential theories. W. Robertson-Smith, intrigued by the concept of TOTEMISM, interpreted sacrifice as communion, a covenantal meal in which the devotees and their deity are assimilated by means of the flesh and blood of the totemic animal or "theanthropic victim." Smith suggested that later forms of sacrifice such as the mystical, expiatory, piacular (propitiatory), or honorary (gift-giving) were, despite their variations, also intended to secure a covenant, following the model of the more ancient blood-sacrifice kinship bond. Smith's friend and colleague at Cambridge, J. G. Frazer, made sacrifice a central theme of *The Golden Bough*. Sacred kingship, the immolation of the priest or king as a means of rejuvenating the dying god, the later substitution of animal and then agricultural for human offerings (with the sacrifice of vegetation spirits a parallel to that of the totemic animal), and the expiation of sin (scapegoat) were all components of a theory that prefixed an age of magic to an age of religion.

At the turn of the century two sociologists, H. Hubert and M. Mauss, produced a study of sacrifice based upon historic rather than preliterate societies. Concentrating on Vedic and ancient Hebrew rituals, they analyzed structurally the sacrificial drama in which a victim mediates between the worlds of the sacred and the profane. Attention was drawn to the significant modifications of religious and moral state undergone by the sacrificer as concomitants of the consecration and immolation of that victim. The sacrificer, they said, both gains and loses from contact with the victim prior to its immolation: life and power are transferred *from* the intermediary while sin, pollution, and death are passed on *to* it. The redemptive character of killing was also noted: when "religious forces . . . reach a certain level of intensity, they cannot be concentrated in a profane object without destroying it."

Focus on ritual killing, totemism, and surrogate victims was also primary in the psychological theories of Freud, who declared in his final study that sacrifice is the origin of religion. In his analysis of the patricide that resolves the paradigmatic oedipal situation Freud understood the animal victim as simultaneously tribal totem and ritual surrogate for the slain father. Culture, instituted by this primordial murder, is then the "body of death." Although his insistence on the historical rather than mythical validity of his thesis found little support, Freud's efforts helped to clarify, from the perspective of depth psychology, the myth-ritual problem of the killing of a deity or culture hero as a primordial event to be celebrated in "history" as the drama of sacrifice.

A. E. Jensen, an ethnologist following the *Kulturkreislehre* of Frobenius, Graebner, and Schmidt, investigated ritual killing (as distinct from sacrifice) among 1) archaic root-crop cultivators, 2) the younger cereal grain cultivators, and 3) emergent high cultures. His discussion of ritual killing was based upon reports from Ceram (Moluccas) on the *Dema,* primordial beings taking human, animal, or plant form, who murder a *Dema*-deity. That unmotivated and definitive event ended primal time and initiated root-crop cultivation (the *Dema* becoming mortals, the victim their food), labor, sexuality, death, and cultural institutions. Jensen traced this mythologem to the archaic tuber planters, all of whose cultic activities (puberty and death rites, human and animal immolation, head-hunting, cannibalism) comprise re-presentations of this primordial murder. Sacrifice, being an offering to a god, is thus a later development among the high cultures, according to Jensen. Eliade has discussed in wider contexts this relationship between the paradigmatic event of mythic time and the ritual reenactment in human time, with particularly detailed discussions of cosmogony, initiatory symbolism, human sacrifice, and construction sacrifice.

R. Firth, an anthropologist, has contributed another perspective, directing attention to economic as well as spiritual factors and noting that the character, types, and frequency of sacrifice may be linked to the control of available resources. For example, the material sacrificed may be completely destroyed or reserved for consumption by the worshipers, or the choice of surrogate victim may vary according to economic necessities. Recent studies adding to the methodological discussion of sacrifice have appeared from E. E. Evans-Pritchard on African societies (particularly the substitution sacrifice of the Nuer), W. Burkert on the continuities between Paleolithic hunting sacrifices and the rituals of ancient Greece (the tripod-cauldron of the Delphic priestess, new year festivals, the Anthesteria, Eleusinian mysteries), and R. Girard on the violent destruction of the scapegoat or *pharmakos*.

Bibliography. H. Hubert and M. Mauss, *Sacrifice: Its Nature and Function* (1898, ET 1964); E. O. James, *Sacrifice and Sacrament* (1962); A. E. Jensen, *Myth and Cult Among Primitive Peoples* (1951, ET 1963); J. Maringer, *The Gods of Prehistoric Man* (1956, ET 1960); R. K. Yerkes, *Sacrifice in Greek and Roman Religions and Early Judaism* (1952); E. B. Tylor, *Primitive Culture,* 2 vols. (1871), esp. Vol. II, ch. 18; W. Robertson-Smith, *Lectures on the Religion of the Semites* (1889, 3rd ed. 1927); S. Freud, *Totem and Taboo* (1913, ET 1918), and *Moses and Monotheism* (1939, ET 1960); M. Eliade, *Zalmoxis, the Vanishing God* (1972), and *A History of Religious Ideas,* Vol. I (1978); R. Firth, "Offering and Sacrifice: Problems of Organization," in *Reader in Comparative Religion,* W. A. Lessa and E. Z. Vogt, eds. (3rd ed. 1972); E. E. Evans-Pritchard, *Nuer Religion* (1956); W. Burkert, *Homo Necans: Interpretationen altgriechischer Opferriten und Mythen* (1972); R. Girard, *Violence and the Sacred* (1977).

D. M. KNIPE

SADDHARMA PUṆḌARĪKA SŪTRA səd där´ mŭ poon də rē´ kə so͞o´ trə (B). *See* LOTUS SŪTRA.

SADDUCEES sä´ dū sēs (Ju). Deriving their name from King David's priest Zadok, this Jewish sect differs on several crucial issues with the PHARISEES. By rejecting the Oral Law they accepted only what Scripture expressly enjoins. They also rejected the Pharisaic belief in eternity of the soul. Unfortunately, except for Josephus we have no documents which can be attributed to them. They disappeared in A.D. 70 with the destruction of the Temple.

Probably attached to the upper classes, the landed gentry, and merchants, and mostly constituted of priests, the Sadducees represented a conservative aristocracy whose best interests were served by maintaining the *status quo.* So long as the Temple stood their importance was assured.

E. M. MEYERS

SĀDHU säd´ ho͞o (H—Skt.; lit. "holy man, saint, or sage"). Applied to ascetics without reference to sectarian affiliation. In common usage refers to a wide variety of individuals who have the external appearance of renunciation. However, *sādhu* rightly fits only serious spiritual aspirants—generally those living a wandering, ascetic life.

C. S. J. WHITE

L. D. Shinn

An itinerant Vaiṣṇava *sādhu* at the Jagannātha Temple, Purī, India. His body marks signify complete submission to Vishnu in all his many names and forms.

ṢAḤĀBA sä hä´ bä (I—Arab.; lit. "companions"). The Companions of the Prophet MUHAMMAD. Since the time of the second CALIPH, 'UMAR (r. 634-44), and in large part due to his register *(dīvān),* they have occupied the position of highest prestige among SUNNI Muslims. They were the first Meccans to accept Muhammad's ecstatic utterances as divine revelation and to become members of his community (UMMA). To them are attributed most of the ḤADĪTH used to gauge the Prophet's exemplary behavior (SUNNA). Ten of them, including the first four caliphs, were promised admission into Paradise (JANNA) by Muhammad himself.

Resenting ALI's exclusion from the caliphate, Shi'ites curse rather than praise all the *ṣaḥāba* except, of course, Ali. They therefore reject the six Sunni collections of *ḥadīth* as deliberate distortions of the Prophet's conduct and discourse; they rely instead on *ḥadīth* that omit mention of the *ṣaḥāba* and are traceable to Ali, his immediate family, and his most prominent descendants, the IMAMS. *See* ISLAM §3.

Bibliography. "*Ṣaḥāba,*" *SEI,* p. 488; A. Guillaume, trans., M. ibn Ishaq, *The Life of Muhammad* (1955).

B. LAWRENCE

SAINT PETER'S BASILICA (Ch). The largest church in Christendom (length, 619 feet), built on the traditional site of PETER'S crucifixion and burial on the Vatican Hill, ROME. The present sixteenth century structure, to which Bramante, Raphael, and Michelangelo contributed, replaced the earlier basilica built by CONSTANTINE (d. 337).

C. WADDELL

SAINTS, VENERATION OF (Ch). In NT terminology "saint" is virtually interchangeable with "Christian": the person who lives in Christ as a member of the household of the faith (Eph. 2:19-22). In a more restricted sense, "saint" refers to one who, having practiced the Christian virtues to a heroic degree, and having passed through death into fullness of life with God, can be officially proposed by the church as a model of Christian living and as an intercessor for the faithful on earth and in PURGATORY.

An OT adumbration of this concept is found in II Macc. 15:12-16, where Judas Maccabeus relates "a dream, a sort of vision," of the high priest Onias and the prophet Jeremiah. Onias prays "with outstretched hands for the whole body of the Jews" (v. 12), and Jeremiah is described as "a man who loves the brethren and prays much for the people and the holy city" (v. 14).

That certain persons have a privileged place or function in the life to come is suggested in the NT by texts such as Matt. 19:28 (the Lord's faithful disciples "will also sit on twelve thrones, judging the twelve tribes of Israel"), Heb. 12:1 (the cloud of witnesses), Rev. 6:9-11 (souls of the martyrs beneath God's altar) or 7:13-17 (they who have come out of the great tribulation and are clothed in white robes). But the ultimate theological foundation for the veneration of those who are closest to God lies rather in NT teaching concerning the COMMUNION OF THE SAINTS, the mystical body of Christ, and the nature of the CHURCH.

In the post-apostolic church, the clearest early reference to the commemoration of a saint is found in the account of the martyrdom of Polycarp, Bishop of Smyrna (156 or 157), whose followers decide to hold an annual celebration of his martyrdom. Closely linked in its origins with the veneration of MARTYRS, devotion to the saints was expressed less by liturgical commemorations than by praise and imitation. By the end of the third century the saints were already being invoked as intercessors; and the cult of martyrs was gradually extended to include those whose life of virtue could be considered as a witness equivalent to that of martyrdom: virgins, ascetics, confessors. This last category originally comprised those who suffered for the faith but were not martyred. Later it was applied more generally to people of evidently holy life.

Devotion to the saints found various forms of expression: veneration of their ICONS (chiefly in the East) or veneration of their RELICS (chiefly in the West); dedication of places of worship or of altars under their patronage; written accounts of the lives of individuals saints, for the purpose of devotional reading or of use in the LITURGY; MASS and DIVINE OFFICE formularies, as well as prayer texts of a more personal sort; PILGRIMAGES, which became increasingly popular during the Middle Ages.

With the spread of devotion to the saints came the need to develop a vocabulary clearly distinguishing between the worship given God alone (*latria*, an act of the virtue of religion) and the veneration given the servants of God (*doulia*, an act of the virtue of reverence).

As a means of ensuring the faithful against possible deception, the official recognition of claims to sainthood became increasingly institutionalized in the form of CANONIZATION processes reserved to papal authority (first recorded instance, St. Ulrich of Augsburg, in 993). The dogmatic constitution *Lumen Gentium* (Second VATICAN COUNCIL, 1964) situates the practice of devotion to the saints within the context of the total mystery of Christ and his church, and gives as a pastoral norm: "Let the faithful be taught . . . that the authentic cult of the saints consists not so much in the multiplying of external acts, but rather in the intensity of our active love. By such love, for our own greater good and that of the church, we seek from the saints *example* in their way of life, *fellowship* in their communion, and *aid* by their intercession."

Bibliography. J. Douillet, *What Is a Saint?* (1958); W. M. Abbot and J. Gallagher, eds., *The Documents of Vatican II* (1966), p. 84.

C. WADDELL

ŚAIVA SIDDHĀNTA shī′ vū sĭd dän′ tū (H—Skt.; lit. "the Tenets of the Devotees of Shiva). An influential medieval school of Hinduism, concentrated primarily in south India (especially in Madras State) and represented primarily through the medium of TAMIL language and literature. This is one of the four Śaiva sects which follow either the VEDAS or the Sanskrit and Tamil ĀGAMAS ("traditional" texts) or both. (*See* ŚAIVISM.)

1. **Sources.** Śaiva Siddhānta is a sect which follows a Sanskrit canon composed of Āgamas and another 150 sub-Āgamas. The Āgamas of this tradition are dedicated entirely to SHIVA as the All-god and are composed of instructions for the construction and consecration of temples, shrines, and altars and for the performance of important Śaiva rites and festivals. Another portion of the Āgamic literature is constituted of hymns composed by the sixty-three Śaiva singer-saints (NĀYANĀRS), addressed to local forms of Shiva and filled with expressions of intense devotional sentiments. These texts date from *ca.* A.D. 800. The hymns were collected by Nambi (*ca.* A.D. 1000) in a volume called *Tirumuṟai*. Another Śaiva work worthy of mention is the *Śivajñānabodha* ("Understanding the Knowledge of Śiva") by Meykaṇṭatēvar (thirteenth century). In the vast corpus of Tamil hymnic literature, the moving religious lyric, *Tiruvācakam* of MĀNIKKAVĀCAKAR (ninth century), stands out as a masterful blending of

profound devotionalism and a highly abstract metaphysics.

2. **Doctrines.** The doctrines of this religion revolve around three basic topics: God (Shiva or *Pati,* Lord, who is Absolute Being, Unconditioned Wisdom and Perfect Bliss); the Soul *(paśu)*; and the noose or bond of ignorance *(pāśa).* The world is created by God (efficient cause), by means of his conscious volition (instrumental power), and *māyā* or creative energy (material cause). Because the world is a product of divine creativity, it is no illusion (contrary to the teachings of ŚAṂKARA), but rather is a real and value-filled (though transitory) cosmos. Liberation from bondage to ignorance and rebirth requires the grace (Skt., *prasāda,* Tamil, *arul)* of Shiva. Śaivas believe that the integrity and distinctness of the human soul (ATMAN) is maintained even in the state of emancipation (MOKṢA). The world is not the product of God's playfulness but is expressive of his ultimate purpose in liberating the eternal souls, which are imagined after the fashion of cattle *(paśu),* bound by the noose of impurity *(mala)* or spiritual ignorance which compels them to produce KARMA. Once the soul has reached a sufficiently high level of spiritual development that it can search for the highest insights, God offers his grace in the form of the teachings of a spiritual mentor (GURU) and thereby brings the purified soul to a true knowledge of the divine nature, and thence to spiritual liberation and perfect peace. An important offshoot of this sect is the LIṄGĀYAT school founded by Basava ca. 1150.

Bibliography. S. N. Dasgupta, *History of Indian Philosophy,* V (1955); V. A. Devasenapathi, *Śaiva Siddhānta as expounded in the Śiva-jñāna-siddhiyar and its 6 Commentaries* (1960); M. Dhavamony, *Love of God in Śaiva Siddhānta* (1971).

J. B. LONG

ŚAIVISM shī′ vĭsm (H—Skt. deriv.: "the cult of Shiva"). The English designation for a number of distinct but related communities in India who worship SHIVA (Śiva) in his many forms as the chief among the gods or as the Supreme Deity. Since the word refers to a loosely allied network of cults and not to a single religious community, there is no equivalent term in any Indian language.

Śaivism is predominant in south India, particularly in Madras State. Generally this sect is more closely identified with the austere practices of ASCETICISM (e.g., fasting, meditation, mortification of the body) than is VAIṢṆAVISM. The goal of such practices is to liberate the mind or soul from its binding attachment to the body and the physical world. Among the many tangible features which distinguish Śaivas in general and YOGIS in particular are: covering the body with ashes; three horizontal ash marks across the forehead; going about naked or with a loin cloth; wearing the hair long, matted, and plaited to form ropes and piled up on the head in a cowrie-shell configuration and wearing a necklace or rosary of *rudrāksha* berries representing the "austerities." In addition, Śaiva practices include such self-mortifying vows as inserting needles through parts of the body, lying on beds of nails, and walking on beds of live coals.

Devotees of Shiva revere him either in one or another of his many anthropomorphic forms or in his phallic manifestations (LIṄGA). The latter form represents Shiva as the impartite and absolute ground of existence of the universe and all its creatures. Worshipers attempt to "cool" the *liṅga* by anointing it with various ritual substances (e.g., milk, water, curds, honey, GHEE) while reciting invocations of praise and petition to him.

The most important scriptures of the Śaiva tradition are the Śvetāśvatara Upaniṣad (often thought of as the BHAGAVAD GĪTĀ of Śaivism), a litany entitled *Śatarudrīya* ("Hymn to the Hundred Rudras"), the *Śiva-gītā,* the *Śiva- saṃhitā* (a text of Tantric implications), the Śiva Purāṇas (which include the myths of Shiva and ritual and ethical instruction), manifold collections of devotional hymns in the vernacular languages (e.g., Māṇikkavācakar's *Tiruvācakam* in TAMIL), and the collection of ritual manuals called *Śivāgamas,* mostly in Tamil.

While the lists of the main schools or sects of Śaivism in the PURĀṆAS and stone inscriptions diverge somewhat, the most important schools seem to be the following: (1) Pāśupata, mentioned in the MAHĀBHĀRATA as one of five extant cults, probably to be identified as the Śiva-bhāgavatas in Pāṇini and popularized by Lakulīśa (*ca.* second century B.C.). (2) KĀPĀLIKA or *Kālāmukha,* "those who carry a skull (as an alms bowl)," who worship Shiva in his horrific form as "Bhairava," wear necklaces of skulls and elevate the mind by drinking wine and other intoxicating substances. (3) *Trika* or Kashmir Śaivism, composed of two branches: *Spandaśāstra,* "Treatise on Quivering," established by Vasugupta and his pupil Kallaṭa, and *Pratyabhijñanaśāstra,* "Treatise on the Philosophy of Recognition," founded by Śivadṛṣṭi, systematized by Udayākara and Abhinavagupta, which adhered to a radically nondualist form of VEDĀNTA. (4) *Vīraśaiva* or LIṄGĀYAT, the foundation of which is attributed to Basava (*ca.* twelfth century A.D.) in Kārnataka (Mysore), whose adherents reject caste, worship the GURU as an incarnation of Shiva, and identify themselves with a miniature *liṅga* worn around the neck. (5) *Smārta* (or the cult of the Pentad), whose members appeal to the SMṚTI literature as their final authority, worship five gods daily in compliance with scriptural injunctions (i.e., the Sun, ŚAKTI or the mother goddess, GAṆEŚA, VISHNU, and Shiva). Some traditional texts have claimed that the Smārta tradition was popularized by the ADVAITA teacher ŚAṂKARA, but this claim rests on dubious evidence. (6) *Śaiva* (or ŚAIVA SIDDHĀNTA), systematically articulated by Meykaṇṭatēvar in the work *Śivajñānabodha* in the thirteenth century as the basis of Tamil Śaivism. According to Meykaṇṭatēvar, there are three fundamental entities in the universe—God *(pati),* bondage *(pāśa),* and soul *(paśu).* The soul is created essentially free by Shiva, but it becomes bound through ignorance of its true nature. The bonds of ignorance are broken and the individual soul is liberated by achieving right knowledge of the primal relationship between God and man through selfless devotion to the creator.

The popular religious values of Tamil culture are expressed in eleven collections of devotional hymns composed from the ninth and tenth centuries onward by the sixty-three NĀYAṆĀRS or Śaiva singer-saints. These collections of hymns, combined with the *Periyapurāṇam,* form the basis of Tamil Śaivism. The devotional hymns dedicated to Shiva reveal a deeply moving sense of a personal relationship between devotee and God, combined with an awareness of human dependence upon God's grace for both life and salvation.

Bibliography. R. G. Bhandarkar, *Vaiṣṇavism, Śaivism and Minor Religious Systems* (1913, 1965); C. V. N. Iyer, *The Origin and Early History of Śaivism in South India* (1923); D. Lorenzen, *The Kāpālikas and Kālāmukhas: Two Lost Śaivite Sects* (1972); W. D. O'Flaherty, *Ascetisim and Eroticism in the Mythology of Śiva* (1973); V. S. Pathak, *Śaiva Cults in Northern India* (1960); A. K. Ramanujan, *Speaking of Śiva* (1973).

J. B. LONG

SAJJĀDA səj jä′ də (I—Arab.; from *sajada,* "to bow down, prostrate oneself" in worship). The prayer rug used by Muslims in the *ṣalāt* (*see* PRAYER IN ISLAM). The term is not known in the QUR'ĀN or ḤADĪTH, but some sort of prayer mat is said to have been used by MUHAMMAD. Muslims of humble means worship on the bare ground, but most try to use some sort of ground cover, ranging from richly woven rugs with a pattern at one end indicating the direction (QIBLAH) one faces while praying, through reed mats, skins, newspapers, to something as basic as a pocket handkerchief for the forehead alone.

F. M. DENNY

SAKADĀGĀMIN sä kŭ dä′ gä mĭn (B—Pali; lit. "once-returner") **SAKṚDĀGĀMIN** säk rĭ dä′ gä mĭn (B—Skt.). The second of the four fruitions in THERAVĀDA sanctity. When a disciple diminishes lust, hatred, and illusion, and destroys the three fetters (*see* SOTĀPANNA), he returns to this world once only and will put an end to rebirth (*see* ANĀGĀMIN; ARHANT).

W. PACHOW

SAKKA säk kä′ (B—Pali; lit. "the Able One" [*sak*—to be able"]) **ŚAKRA** shäk′ rä (Skt.). INDRA, the important war and rain god of the Indo-ARYANS, appears in Buddhism as Sakka, Lord (Indra) of the Gods. The name Śakra, meaning "mighty, capable," is one of Indra's epithets in the VEDAS. Consistent with Indian mythology, the Buddhists conceived of Sakka as seated on a marble throne, presiding over the heaven of the thirty-three gods, atop MT. MERU, the mythical king of mountains.

In Buddhism, Sakka is a former human, promoted to lordship because of great virtue, who rules as a god of peace and morality, not as a war god. Once Sakka came with a ferocious black hound to frighten people into being moral, but since the coming of GAUTAMA BUDDHA, he is content to be a protector of Buddhist teaching. As such, Sakka helped Buddha resist the tempter MĀRA, encouraged Buddha to teach, praised Buddha, etc.

Many JĀTAKA stories tell of Sakka coming from heaven to discern whose great virtue had caused his marble throne to overheat (a sign that someone more meritorious might take his place).

Parallel with the decline of Indra in Hinduism, Sakka became less important to Indian Buddhists, and beyond India his role as protector has been usurped by local deities.

Bibliography. "The Sakka Suttas," *The Book of the Kindred Sayings* (1971), I. 279-307.

R. C. AMORE

ŚAKTI shŭk′ tē (H—Skt.; lit. "power, might"). The creative power of the divine or the ABSOLUTE. Creation in Hinduism is often described as the process whereby a deity releases his or her power, which animates the world or creates the world. *Śakti* is that generative power and is usually depicted as the feminine pole within the divine. The other pole is the passive, inactive aspect of the divine usually associated with the masculine or a deity without qualities. In mythology and iconography the active pole, *śakti,* is usually personified as a goddess, and the consorts of Hindu gods are often called their *śaktis.* The term came to be so typically applied to goddesses in Hinduism that worshipers of the divine feminine are known as Śāktas (those who revere *śakti*). As the creative, active aspect of the divine, *śakti* is said to be similar to MĀYĀ, which is usually understood in the context of VEDĀNTA philosophy as appearance grounded in ignorance. In many myths, however, *māyā* is spoken of as the magical ability of the gods to create, and it is in this sense that various goddesses as *śakti* are referred to as *māyā. See* GODDESS (INDIA).

D. R. KINSLEY

ŚAKUNTALĀ shŭ koon′ tŭ lä (H). *See* KĀLIDĀSA.

ŚĀKYAMUNI shäk′ yŭ mōō′ nē (B—Skt.). A term frequently used to denote GAUTAMA the BUDDHA. It appears only rarely, however, in the earliest strata of texts. The original meaning is apparently "the holy one, or sage, of the Śākyas." The Buddha's disciples were at times called the followers of the Śākyan.

R. H. DRUMMOND

ṢALĀT sä lät′. *See* PRAYER IN ISLAM.

SALVATION (Lat. *salvatio*; Gr. *sōteria*). Salvation may be understood as the state of being safe from destructive forces, natural or supernatural, and as the act of deliverance from destruction, pain, loss, death, sin, curse, punishment, or suffering. The Latin *salus* and French *salut*—"whole," "healthy"—imply the notion of salvation as healing, a metaphor found in many religious traditions. The human predicament of sin, death, ignorance, and impurity is an "illness" from which salvation brings "healing." This meaning also is evident in the German *Heil*—healing or salvation—and *heilig*—the holy or sacred—which is the source of salvation. Salvation implies such concepts as whole, healthy, strong, vigorous, enjoying well-being and bliss. The concept of salvation, in this sense, points back to a period in which no distinction was drawn between bodily healing or deliverance from this-worldly needs and the bliss hoped for ultimately in the heavenly realms. In fact, it was the worldly deliverances that were primary to human religiousness and provided the metaphors and imagery of absolute salvation that emerged in CHRISTIANITY, JUDAISM, ISLAM, ZOROASTRIANISM, HINDUISM, and BUDDHISM.

1. Salvation as a category of religion. In its earliest English literary usage "salvation" had only a Christian meaning as the deliverance from sin and death and admission to eternal bliss brought to humankind by the ATONEMENT of JESUS. In modern English usage the word has a broad range of meanings in both secular and religious discourse as a characterization of human deliverance and fulfillment. However, it has only been since the rise of the modern historical study of religions that the term has been used in a comparativist sense as a characterization of various religions. For much Christian theology, in both its traditional and Barthian forms (*see* BARTH, KARL), salvation is not a comparativist category because it was held that there was nothing outside of Christian faith that could be characterized as salvation. However, Catholic theologies have long recognized the legitimacy of "natural theology" and "natural religion" as providing a possible source of salvation. In liberal Protestantism there is openness toward the presence of salvation in other religions, in social, political movements of liberation, and in psychotherapy.

The phenomenological analysis of religion by Van der Leeuw, Eliade, and others has shown that salvation is a universal concern of religion. Religion is directed toward salvation, never toward life as it is given. In this respect, all religions are religions of salvation because they give promise of some form of deliverance. In its most general form, salvation is power, natural or supernatural, experienced as good. The experience of deliverance from the woes and limitations of human existence is the foundation from which religious traditions emerge, not vice versa.

2. The structure of salvation. *a) Structural elements.* Early in religious history, salvation was not a clearly defined concept. The coming of the rain, the growth of crops, safety from wild beasts, the birth of children were all called salvation, because in them is encountered the power that transforms the gloom of life into joy. Yet even in these most basic experiences there emerges a structure characteristic of salvation, containing three elements: a notion of the human predicament, some vision of the goal or fulfillment of human beings, and a characterization of the means for going from the former to the latter.

Awareness of the human plight stems from the human capacity for self-transcendence as expressed in the awareness of an existence that goes beyond the limitations of life here and now. Teachings on salvation characterize the sources of these limitations that afflict humankind in a variety of ways as SIN, impurity, ignorance, DEATH, attachment, fate, KARMA, or control by malevolent beings. Salvation embraces a conception of released humankind. The movement from lostness to fulfillment is seen as the work of a savior figure, either human or divine, or in the actualization of some human capacity currently hidden from awareness but available to those knowing the means of salvation. Faith in sacred teachings, moral obedience, ritual acts, sacramental participation, meditation, ascetic practices, and personal trust in a savior are means by which salvation is reached.

b) Other-help and self-help. The means by which the transition from lostness to fulfillment is made fall into two categories. In some traditions emphasis is upon human impotence and the divine initiative in salvation by the bestowal of a savior and the enabling power or grace. Other traditions stress the actualization of human powers of will, reason, affection, meditation, or moral action. Formal doctrinal reflection stresses the distinction between reliance on oneself and reliance on an Other with great clarity, while in popular piety they are frequently blended. In Christianity the theologies of AUGUSTINE, LUTHER, and CALVIN have stressed human impotence in turning from sin and the sole sufficiency of grace, while Pelagius, Arminius, Catholic SCHOLASTICISM, and Protestant PIETISM have stressed acts of personal decision, good works, and ASCETICISM. In the Jōdo Shin-shū Buddhism of SHINRAN, salvation is by pure grace from the compassionate redeemer AMIDA Buddha and is not dependent on human action, while ZEN Buddhism finds salvation in the actualization of human powers by a disciplined life. The legal traditions of Hinduism teach that salvation comes only with the expiation of evil deeds through many REINCARNATIONS, while worshipers of SHIVA may speak eloquently of grace and faith against all works, as in *The Tiruvācakam* of the TAMIL poet Māṇikkavācakar.

3. Salvation as limited or absolute. In its limited sense salvation refers to deliverance from illness, danger, or want, and is characterized by such words as "healing," "victory," "driving out of the demons," or the receiving of "gracious gifts." In contemporary humanistic religious traditions this salvation is described in psychological terms as acceptance, forgiveness, or hope. But these acts of salvation are, by their very nature, temporary and incomplete. The healed may become sick again, the enemies return, and despair again threaten to overwhelm the psyche. No matter how dramatically miraculous this salvation may be, there is a need for further salvation. By contrast, salvation in the absolute sense is the passing beyond all impediments, limitations, and contradictions that characterize the human situation. It is final and needs no repetition. It is entrance into the KINGDOM OF GOD, in which the victory over sin and death is complete. It is the liberation (MOKSA) in which escape is made from the circle of reincarnations (SAMSARA). It is the passing beyond all attachments into NIRVANA that comes from freedom of desire and the realization of voidness (ŚŪNYATĀ). It is entering paradise after the last judgment by ALLAH to the life of bliss.

Salvation in the limited and the absolute sense plays a part in all religious traditions, although the relationship and relative importance of the two vary greatly. The experience of partial salvation may be seen as intimations or foretastes (NT Gr. *arrabōn, aparchē*) of the ultimate salvation. Yet there is also the warning against preoccupation with limited salvation as a distraction from absolute salvation. Jesus warned, "Nevertheless do not rejoice in this, that the spirits are subject to you; but rejoice that your names are written in heaven" (Luke 10:20), as did HASIDIC and SUFI teachers. In the Buddhist and Hindu traditions too much concern with the limited salvation of being miraculously extricated from danger, freed from demons, or healed of illness holds the danger of keeping one chained to samsara.

In TAOISM and CONFUCIANISM, by contrast, emphasis is on the limited salvation granted by moral obedience and conformity with the forces that determine a particular time and place. Absolute salvation that frees one from the determining forces of the cosmos is only a peripheral possibility. Similarly in SHAMANISM and ANIMISM salvation is found in the ability of the shaman, "person of power," to control the divine and the demonic forces that affect all life. Deliverances brought by the rainmaker, healer, exorcist, or magician are the main concern, while ultimate salvation is only a distant concern. The creator or the "high" god is disinterested in or disconnected from the world. Salvation is sought amidst the immanent supernatural forces that control human destiny and is inevitably limited.

In contemporary existentialist interpretations of Christianity and Judaism salvation is the overcoming of psychic conflict and the resolution of the search for meaning. Salvation is the regaining of wholeness. There is little concern for an absolute salvation beyond the limits of historical existence. The symbols of absolute salvation in scriptures and traditions are reinterpreted as MYTHS expressing the unconditioned character and healing power of Being itself. By contrast, Christian APOCALYPTICISM has emphasized the absolute salvation of the kingdom of God, relegating what limited deliverances are found "in this present evil age" to signs of the coming kingdom. GNOSTICISM and MANICHEISM viewed the world as so contaminated as to render deliverances within it impossible. Their focus was on gaining the saving knowledge needed to escape the cosmos.

The distinction between limited and absolute salvation is not to be confused with salvation before and after death. There is the possibility of ultimate salvation for some while still in history, the *jivan-mukta* in Hinduism or the BODHISATTVA, and there is limited salvation in after-death states, such as on the *bardo* plane of TIBETAN BUDDHISM. (*See* BARDO THODÖL.) In Hindu tradition entrance into a paradisiacal state after death or into a higher form of reincarnation is a limited salvation and not final liberation. In Christianity the departure of the souls of the blessed dead to heaven is not absolute salvation. The soul in heaven awaits reunion with the body at the resurrection of the end times, when the faithful enter the kingdom.

4. Two types of absolute salvation. Continuing historical and philosophical reflection raises the question of how various conceptions of salvation relate to one another. Hick argues that the notion of an absolute salvation implies that there are not many different final states of human fulfillment but only one. He claims that the bewildering variety of teachings on salvation exist only in what he calls the "pareschatologies" of the different religions, i.e., in their teachings on the ways to salvation, while their teachings on "eschatology," absolute salvation, converge. Such an announcement of convergence is premature. A typological analysis of absolute salvation reveals at least two major sets of options: salvation as the transformation-fulfillment of the self, the world, and history, or salvation as liberation of the self by its merging into some greater whole.

When absolute salvation is conceived as transformation-fulfillment, the metaphors of salvation are personalistic with an emphasis upon new communities of transformed persons—messianic kingdom, city of God, paradise. Salvation is in the fullness of being (Gr. *plērōma*) in which the structures of nature and personhood are not destroyed but brought to fulfillment. In these traditions time is crucial, with absolute salvation coming only at the end of time, as in Christianity and Judaism with their teachings on a messianic age, or Islam in the notion of entrance into paradise after the final judgment.

By contrast, absolute salvation may be seen as liberation of the self from the conditions of historical existence and personhood. Absolute salvation, in this sense, is in freeing the self from all attachments to conditioned existence, including attachment to the empirical self. Its basic metaphors are those of absorption—the drop of water falling into the sea, or the light of the candle merging into the sun. The self fulfills its destiny by losing the parameters of its particularity in the voidness of the unconditioned (Skt. *śūnyatā*, BRAHMAN *nirguṇa;* Ger., *Urgrund, Ungrund).* The traditions of Hinduism, Buddhism, Sufism, as well as Neoplatonism and Christian MYSTICISM represent this understanding of salvation.

Here time is not crucial in salvation. The worlds of history and nature are seen as shadowy images of the real, or even as illusion (MĀYĀ). They do not enter into the absolute salvation. The cosmos and history are an eternal circle that is not to be transformed but escaped. By contrast, in the transformation-fulfillment vision of salvation, nature, history, and personal existence are good, although currently flawed, and will be redeemed.

Bibliography. E. J. Sharpe and J. R. Hinnells, eds., *Man and His Salvation* (1973); G. van der Leeuw, *Religion in Essence and Manifestation* (1948); S. J. Samartha, ed., *Living Faiths and Ultimate Goals* (1974); M. Eliade, *Cosmos and History* (1954); G. H. Anderson, ed., *The Theology of the Christian Mission* (1961); J. Hick, *Death and Eternal Life* (1976).

D. G. DAWE

SALVATION ARMY (Ch). Worldwide missionary movement. As defined by WILLIAM BOOTH, the founder, "an organization existing to effect a radical revolution in the spiritual condition of the enormous majority of the people of all lands." More recently it has defined itself as "an international religious and charitable movement, organized and operated on a military pattern, a branch of the Christian faith." Born in poverty, Booth was ordained a minister by the Methodist New Connection in 1858, but broke with this tradition three years later in order to do itinerant evangelism. In 1865 he founded a group in the slums of London, known as the Christian Mission; in 1878 the name was changed to Salvation Army. William became its first general and wrote the *Orders and Regulations* for all the officers who owed him, as their general, unquestioning obedience. From the first the Army was marked by military government and discipline. William and his wife, Catherine, became tireless forces in its expansion around the world. Prior to his death in 1912 he appointed his son, William Bramwell Booth, as his successor. However, upon Bramwell's resignation due to illness, the High Council of the Army's territorial leaders met in London to elect a successor. This established a procedure of election which has been retained.

The Army is generally described as ultra-conservative Protestant. Its conditions of membership include conversion, acceptance of its doctrines, abstinence from alcohol, and a pledge to support energetically the Army's principles and work. Membership is divided into commissioned officers (ordained ministers, male and female) and soldiers (the laity). No sacraments are celebrated but emphasis is placed on public testimony and militant evangelism.

The "social scheme" came as a result of Booth's important volume, *In Darkest England and the Way Out* (1890). The book's purpose was to bring unemployed persons into "self-helping and self-sustaining communities." Booth thus sought to rescue the "submerged tenth" of the population—the unemployed, homeless, vicious, criminal, and their many children. Conversion remained his main objective, but in this volume he altered his strategy to include social reform. With its motto "a man may be down, but he is never out," the Army sought to make conversion possible by rescuing people from social and personal problems. The "social scheme" has resulted through the years in hundreds of rescue homes, hospitals, children's homes, maternity homes, and food and shelter stations scattered around the world. Over one hundred weekly or monthly periodicals are published in more than thirty languages. Among the best known of these are *The War Cry, The Young Soldier,* and *All the World.*

Bibliography. R. Sandall, *History of the Salvation Army,* 3 vols (1947); H. Wisbey, *Soldiers Without Swords* (1956).

G. H. SHRIVER

SĀMA VEDA sä´ mŭ vā´ dŭ (H—Skt.; lit. "knowledge of the melodies" [*sāman*—"melody, song, chant" + *veda*—"knowledge"]). One of the four primary texts of VEDIC HINDUISM, a collection (SAṂHITĀ) of verses from the RIG VEDA rearranged according to a musical tradition utilizing seven notes. Composed in the late second or early first millennium B.C., it was transmitted orally in three recensions. It served as an index to melodies for the SOMA sacrifices. *See* VEDA.

D. M. KNIPE

SAMĀDHI sŭ mä´ dĭ (H, B & Ja—Skt./Pali; lit. "putting together, composing, concentrating" [*sam-ā,* "together," and *dhā,* "put"]). Intense mental concentration as a controlled psychic exercise; the particular trance-like condition attending or issuing from it; popularly, the tomb or site of burial of any YOGI or saint believed to have attained liberation.

1. Classical Hindu Yoga. YOGA, understood broadly as any ascetic and more or less systematic technique (or combination of techniques) for restraining, harnessing, and concentrating psycho-physical faculties to the end of going beyond the ordinary human condition, is of uncalculated antiquity in India and is characteristic of ongoing, traditional Indian religious practice. *Samādhi* is inseparable from Yoga and is sometimes regarded as its core. In the Yogasūtra of PATAÑJALI (extant text possibly from the third or fourth century A.D.), the goal of Yoga is described as the "stopping of the activity of thought." Considered both analytically and prescriptively, Patañjali's Yoga has eight interrelated constituents or steps, of which the highest is *samādhi.*

The first six stages of "eight-part Yoga" concern moral and physical restraints. Stages one and two articulate principles of the morality that is the foundation of the spiritual quest. Physical control is the focus of stages three, four, and five. The sixth stage is "mental concentration" (*dhāraṇā*). If Patañjali's Yoga is the practical reflex of understanding the human predicament as the consequence of an incomprehensible interaction of spirit and matter, *dhāraṇā* might seem to be its goal. Some teachers suggest that it is. Certainly *dhāraṇā* is a refined "fixing" of the mind on a single object with such intensity that thought is stilled and the subject is freed from such distinctions as that between knower and the known. Still, *dhāraṇā* is only a threshold to Yoga's final two transcendent stages, DHYĀNA and *samādhi*.

In *dhyāna*, meditation continues without the support or occasion that characterizes *dhāraṇā* (at least at the beginning). Meditation deepens and *samādhi*, the true and absolute independence of spirit (PURUṢA) from the material (PRAKṚTI) is attained. As a transcendental state of perfect interiorization or inward return to being (an "enstasis"), *samādhi* is to be sharply distinguished from an "ecstatic" going forth.

Though *samādhi* lies outside the furthest reach of ordinary thought and discourse, it does not elude two curious qualifications. First, it may be either "impure" or "pure." Impure *samādhi* is said to be accompanied by some trace of "consciousness" or "knowledge" and, hence, carries the "seed" of possible rebirth. Pure *samādhi* is not adulterated in any way. Second, despite the fact that it is arguable that the yogin who has attained *samādhi* "ought" to die (or at least to disappear), *samādhi* is not necessarily "permanent" or "definitive" in that sense. Adepts may "return" from it to life in the world; and, according to tradition, those who do are called *jīvanmukta*, "liberated but alive." The nature of such living contradictions is no more easily fathomed than *samādhi* itself. But for the religious, they are teacher-saints, essential testimony to the truth of Yoga, and their burial sites are named *samādhi*.

2. *Samādhi* in Buddhism. The term is employed by Buddhists in two discrete but related senses. Used in a broad, encompassing way, it signifies mental cultivation (*bhāvanā*) or meditation in general as one of the three divisions of the EIGHTFOLD PATH. In more narrow, technical usage *samādhi* is refined mental concentration and a perfect "one-pointedness" of mind. As such, it closely resembles the *dhāraṇā-dhyāna-samādhi* triad in Yoga, with one crucial difference: from the Buddhist perspective *samādhi* is not itself the goal. Rather, it is a product of the mind, hence conditioned and composite and, at best, only a preliminary exercise helping to prepare the way to enlightenment. Its significance consists in its being part of a process of discovery. Alone and isolated from that process, it is incomplete and potentially dangerous because it can delude the aspirant into mistaking a mind-produced state for ultimate truth. The traditional (THERAVĀDA) biography of the Buddha emphasizes this point by asserting that the Buddha studied Yoga under masters and reached the highest levels of control and concentration only to reject them as not yielding complete insight.

Most Buddhists, however they estimate *samādhi*, see it as means and not as goal. Therefore the issue revolves finally around the relationship and respective importance of the two distinctive kinds of meditation denoted by *sati* and *samādhi*. The former is an "ecstatic" operation of perfectly attentive, probing insight. The latter, on the other hand, is "enstatic"—a progressively enhanced concentration and withdrawal resulting in ever-deepening "transic" conditions. Both are prescribed, and they can be seen as moments in a unitary discipline. But there is a manifest tension between them that has inspired diverse evaluative responses which have added to the richness and complexity of Buddhist thought over time. *See* SATORI.

3. Jainism and *samādhi*. *Dhyāna* (Prākrit *jhāṇa*) or *bhāvanā* is the generic term for meditation favored by the JAINAS, and *samādhi* is commonly used as a simple equivalent. Jainas seek to destroy all accumulated KARMA and to prevent the formation of new. To this end, a rigorously austere physical and mental discipline called TAPAS is enjoined. Meditation (*dhyāna*, or, less frequently, *samādhi*) is its most important internal or mental aspect. The aspirant is to proceed through increasingly refined stages of meditation until the climax of ascetic endeavor is reached and he is released.

The entire internal and external disciplinary program for Jainas may be deduced from AHIṂSĀ (noninjury) and its implications. Hence, concentrated meditation aims particularly at perfecting *samatva*, a condition in which all beings are regarded equal (therefore ruling out the possibility of exploitation or injury). Attaining this pure state prevents new karmic formations. But definitive release requires extinction of old karma, and theoretically *samatva* could be achieved without (or before) the aspirant's being truly liberated. Consequently severe physical asceticism is a visible index of inner, spiritual progress, and *samatva* properly entails complete physical immobilization and death. For the Jainas, then, to be liberated *and* alive (*jīvanmukta*) is either self-contradictory or a merely anticipatory state. In fact, duly regarding context, *samādhi* could be translated in all three Indian religious traditions as "religious death."

Bibliography M. Eliade, *Yoga: Immortality and Freedom* (1958); J. Varenne, *Yoga and the Hindu Tradition* (1976); J. H. Woods, trans., *The Yoga System of Patañjali* (1972).

G. R. WELBON

SAMARITANS sə mār′ ĭ tənz. Descendants of the original inhabitants of biblical Samaria, destroyed in 722 B.C., who claim to be the remnant of the northern tribes of Israel. More than half of the few hundred survivors of this group live in the city of Nablus, close to their sacred mountain, Gerizim, on the West Bank of the Jordan. The most widely known feature of their worship is the sacrifice of the traditional lambs at Mt. Gerizim during their PASSOVER festival.

Their Pentateuch is preserved in important manuscripts which diverge from the more standard versions, and their sectarian views have made them a perennial subject of concern to biblical historians. Their opposition to EZRA and Nehemiah illustrates their rivalry with the Jews in the Persian period; the erection of their own temple at Mt. Gerizim in the late fourth century B.C. indicates their desire to have their own cultic center. The Hasmonean king John Hyrcanus (*see* MACCABEES) destroyed that temple in 128 B.C., an action which led to further separation of the Samaritans from the Jews. Samaritan writings and beliefs have come to play an increasingly important role in evaluating sectarian views of the Second Temple period, especially those in the Pseudepigrapha and Dead Sea Scrolls. A number of scholars have asserted that Samaritan influence can be found in the NT and the early church.

Bibliography. T. H. Gaster, "Samaritans," *IDB*, pp. 190-197; J. D. Purvis, *The Samaritan Pentateuch and Origin of the Samaritan Sect* (1968).
E. M. MEYERS

SAMBHOGAKĀYA säm bō gə kä´ yə (B—Skt.; lit. "body of bliss"). One of the three aspects which together constitute the Mahāyāna Buddhist conception of TRIPLE BODY (*Trikāya*). As *Sambhogakāya,* the eternal Buddha appears in the form of a heavenly figure. E. J. COLEMAN

SAṂHITĀ sŭm hē´ tä (H—Skt.; lit. "joined, connected, compiled"). Originally *saṃhitā* referred to the connected or continuous style of recitation of the words and verses of the VEDAS. Therefore it is often used to distinguish the four earliest Vedic hymn collections from later commentaries or collections of scriptures (e.g., UPANIṢADS) which are also called "Vedas" by some authors. L. D. SHINN

ŚAṂKARA shän´ kä rä (H—Skt.). The most important and best known of classical Hindu philosophers. Usually thought of as the founder of ADVAITA VEDĀNTA, Śaṃkara established the Daśanāmi order of SANNYĀSINS.

Scholarly debate is still going on about the exact dates for Śaṃkara's life. The best current thinking suggests the end of the seventh, beginning of the eighth century A.D. although he is still commonly cited as living from 788-820 on the basis of the respected opinion of several scholars.

Most of the traditional accounts agree that Śaṃkara was born in Kalādi, a small village in modern Kerala. One famous story concerns the early taking of vows of *sannyāsa*, or renunciation, by the child of eight years or so who assured his despairing mother that he would return to give her the last rites even though this is not required—and possibly not even allowed—for a *sannyāsin*. There is also a story, regarded by some as infamous, that Śaṃkara tricked his mother into consenting to his taking ascetic vows by pretending a crocodile was about to swallow him in the river and would not release him except to a religious life.

After leaving home the young Śaṃkara is said to have met his GURU, Govinda, on the banks of the Narmadā river, but he soon resumed his travels, beginning his teaching in Kāśī (modern Vārāṇasī or Banāras). There he attracted disciples, initially Padmapāda, with whom he went on pilgrimage to Bādrināth, the headwaters of the Ganges. Remaining there for four years, he wrote his major works before the age of sixteen, according to one account, and then returned to Kāśī for more teaching and converting. After several more years he was off to Prayāga (Allāhābād), where he met the elderly Kumārila (*see* MĪMĀṂSĀ), who sent him on to see Maṇḍana Miśra (*see* VEDĀNTA §2). Debating with Maṇḍana with the understanding that the loser would become the winner's pupil, he defeated this Mīmāṃsā philosopher, but Maṇḍana's wife Bhāratī challenged him to further debate, and temporarily embarrassed Śaṃkara by pointing out that he was woefully inexperienced in worldly ways, specifically first-hand knowledge of sex. Śaṃkara is supposed to have asked for a temporary leave of absence from the debate to gain the necessary experience, which he accomplished by entering the body of a powerful and amorous king for a few months. Returning, he defeated Bhāratī and both she and her husband became disciples of Śaṃkara, Maṇḍana taking the name of Sureśvara.

After returning to his birthplace to attend to his mother's funeral as he had promised, Śaṃkara set out on an extensive tour, during which he established the four great monasteries of Advaita in the four corners of India—at Sṛṅgeri in the south, Dwarkā in the west, Bādrināth in the north, and Purī in the east. A powerful tradition also claims a fifth at Kāñchi, i.e., Conjeeveram. One of his favorite disciples was appointed pontiff at each of these centers. Another story tells of his meeting with the Śaiva (*see* ŚAIVISM) philosopher Abhinavagupta during this tour, who cursed Śaṃkara with a nasty disease, but Padmapāda caused the curse to rebound to Abhinavagupta himself, who died of it.

Śaṃkara's life is agreed by all to have been very short, though remarkable in productivity. According to most sources he died at the age of thirty-two in the Himalayas.

Bibliography. A. Kuppuswami, *Śrī Bhagavatpāda Śaṅkarācārya* (1972). On Śaṃkara's date, consult A. W. Thrasher, "The dates of Maṇdana Miśra and Śaṃkara," *Wiener Zeitschrift Für die Kunde Südasien* (1979).
K. H. POTTER

SĀṂKHYA säng´ kyä (H—Skt.; lit. "enumeration, calculation" [*khyā* with prefix *sam*—"to count up, sum up, enumerate, calculate"]). An orthodox system of Hindu philosophy (DARŚANA) that emphasizes a fundamental dualism of two abiding and pervasive principles: (i) nature or materiality (PRAKṚTI); and (ii) consciousnes or soul (PURUṢA).

1. **Nature's manifestations.** Nature in and for itself is not manifest and is made up of three inherent constitutents (GUṆAS): *sattva* (intelligibility or

brightness); *rajas* (activity or passion); and *tamas* (dullness or inertia) in perfect balance or equilibrium. Because of the presence of consciousness, however, nature is continually undergoing a series of transformations and combinations, or, to put the matter another way, the inherent constituents of matter do not maintain their balance or equilibrium but successively dominate and activate one another. These transformations and combinations generate our awareness of a manifest world (objectivity) and generate the manifestation of awareness itself (subjectivity). Twenty-three such manifestations of nature *(prakṛti)* are of crucial significance for understanding how we apprehend the world, both subjectively and objectively: (i) intellect or will *(buddhi),* the first manifestation of nature; its essential function is "ascertainment" or "discrimination," and together with an organism's predispositions it serves as the basis for ordinary subjectivity; (ii) ego (AHAMKĀRA), a second manifestation of nature, derived from intellect *(buddhi);* its essential function is providing an awareness of personal identity within a manifest world; (iii) mind *(manas),* a manifestation of nature derived from ego; its essential function is ordinary cognition (i.e., thinking, imagining, remembering, etc.) or what might be called simply "common sense"; it is both subjective and objective; (iv) the five sense capacities *(buddhīndriyas),* manifestations of nature, derived from ego; their functions are hearing, touching, seeing, tasting, and smelling; these too are both subjective and objective; (v) the five action capacities *(karmendriyas),* manifestions of nature, derived from ego; their functions are speaking, walking, grasping, defecating, and orgasm; they also are both subjective and objective; (vi) the five subtle elements *(tanmātras),* manifestations of nature, derived from ego; their function is to provide the subtle forms of the perceptions of hearing, touch, sight, taste, and smell; these elements are largely objective but involve some subjectivity; and (vii) the five gross elements *(mahābhūtas),* manifestations of nature, but derived from the subtle elements; their function is to provide the gross sensations of space, air, fire, water, and earth; these are largely objective. The above twenty-three manifestations of nature, together with the two abiding and pervasive principles of *prakṛti* and *puruṣa,* make up the total of the twenty-five basic principles of classical Sāṃkhya.

2. The human predicament. In the classical Sāṃkhya analysis, nature *(prakṛti),* together with its twenty-three subsidiary manifestations, functions as a closed causal system apart from consciousness *(puruṣa).* Intellect, ego, mind, perception, and sensation are all epiphenomena of the *guṇas.* Analytically, all of the manifestations of nature relate to nature itself as "parts" to the "whole." Synthetically, they relate to nature itself as "effects" to the ultimate material "cause." Within nature there is never anything new. Each "part" is a function of the total "whole." Every "effect" is simply a manifestation of the primary material "cause." In other words, classical Sāṃkhya is not a dualism of mind and body, or thought and extention, all of which are within the closed causal system. The dualism of Sāṃkhya, rather, is the dualism of *prakṛti* on the one hand, and contentless consciousness *(puruṣa),* on the other.

Sāṃkhya, therefore (like the classical YOGA of PATAÑJALI), makes a clear distinction between "ordinary awareness" (namely *buddhi, ahaṃkāra, manas,* etc.) and "consciousness" *(puruṣa).* Ordinary awareness is intentional, reflective, and directed, while consciousness (in this Indian sense) is a nonintentional medium through which ordinary awareness shows itself. Consciousness, in other words, is a foundation for freedom, completely separate from the intentional involvements of ordinary, reflective thought. Everyday awareness (as, for example, in intellect, ego, and mind) is a manifestation of the *sattva-guṇa* of nature *(prakṛti),* but nonintentional consciousness *(puruṣa)* is completely separate from the *guṇas.*

The problem, however, is that ordinary persons make the mistake of identifying awareness and consciousness and thereby suffer under the misapprehension that they are caught up in the closed causal system of materialism. The purpose of Sāṃkhya (and Yoga), therefore, is to discover and clarify the distinction between awareness and consciousness so that suffering can finally be eradicated. The practitioner comes to realize that suffering is a product of the mistaken identification of the intellect and ego (ordinary awareness) with the unchanging self (consciousness), and that when discrimination *(jñāna)* occurs, the practitioner is able to disentangle the apprehension of *buddhi* from *puruṣa,* and the suffering that is caused by repeated births and deaths then ceases. In other words, suffering is an epistemological problem generated by the fundamental ontological dualism of *prakṛti* and *puruṣa.*

3. The solution. The Sāṃkhya system accepts three reliable means of knowledge as a basis for constructing its analysis, namely, perception, inference, and the reliable instruction of accomplished teachers and sacred texts. The Sāṃkhya analysis begins with the ordinary experiences of pleasure, pain, and delusion. Pleasure or the feeling of quiet fulfillment or certitude is the empirical counterpart of intelligibility *(sattva).* Pain or the feeling of discomfort, together with the urge to be free from it, is the empirical counterpart of activity *(rajas).* Delusion or the feeling of alienation is the empirical counterpart of dullness *(tamas).* Serious reflection always begins with the experience of pain or discomfort, for it is in that experience that one begins to wonder about the possibility of attaining a condition that is totally free from suffering. The Sāṃkhya adherent then proceeds by introspection and philosophical inference to analyze the structures of ordinary subjective and objective awareness in the conviction that a foundation for freedom may be found that is apart from the closed causal system of *prakṛti.* When the practitioner finally discerns the contentless, transparent, and nonintentional principle of consciousness *(puruṣa),* he attains "isolation" *(kaivalya),* the apprehension that there is such a foundation.

Classical Sāṃkhya was first articulated around the middle of the fourth century A.D. in a text called Sāṃkhyakārikā ("Verses on the Sāṃkhya") by Īśvarakṛṣṇa. Numerous commentaries were composed in subsequent centuries, the most notable being the Bhāṣya ("Commentary") of Gauḍapāda (*ca.* seventh or eighth century); the Tattvakaumudī ("Moonlight on the Principles of Sāṃkhya") of Vācaspatimiśra (*ca.* ninth or tenth century); and the Yuktidīpikā ("Clarification of the Arguments of Sāṃkhya," date unknown). A late collection of aphorisms or SŪTRAS is also extant, entitled Sāṃkhyapravacanasūtra ("Aphorisms on the Exposition of Sāṃkhya"), together with the commentaries of Aniruddha, Mahādeva and Vijñānabhikṣu (*ca.* A.D. 1400-1600). For a discussion of the history of Sāṃkhya, *see* YOGA 1b, c.

Bibliography. K. C. Bhattacharya, *Studies in Philosophy* (1956) I, 129-211; M. Eliade, *Yoga: Immortality and Freedom* (1958); E. H. Johnston, *Early Sāṃkhya* (1937); A. B. Keith, *The Sāṃkhya System* (1949); G. J. Larson, *Classical Sāṃkhya: An Interpretation of Its History and Meaning* (2nd edition, 1979); T. G. Mainkar, trans., *The Sāṃkhyakārikā of Īśvarakṛṣṇa* (1964); S. S. Suryanarayana Sastri, trans., *The Sāṅkhyakārikā of Īśvara Kṛṣṇa* (1948).

G. J. LARSON

SAMSARA sŭm sä′ rŭ, sŭng sä′ rŭ (H, B & Ja—Skt./Pali/Prākrit; lit. "going through, wandering" [*sam*—"together"; *sṛ*—"go, run, flow"]). Transmigration or rebirth; passing or cycling through successive lives as a consequence of moral and physical acts (KARMA); everyday life in the world.

Samsara is a result or state of affairs whose cause and explanation is karma, and it cannot be understood apart from individual formulations of that "doctrine of action." If acts entail consequences, a single lifetime may not be long enough for any given act to fructify. Samsara expresses a distinctive understanding of the human condition: to live is to act, and to act is to live, to die, to be reborn. The sequence could be without end. In general, therefore, the goal of Indian soteriologies is to break out of this vicious cycle.

1. Origins. Early texts of the VEDAS do not mention samsara. The idea first appears as "redeath" (*punarmṛtyu*) rather than "rebirth," thus stressing its negative aspects. Because of its relatively late occurrence in the Vedas some scholars have suggested that samsara has non-Vedic origins. The matter cannot be definitively resolved, but if Vedic speculation on the efficacy of ritual action—karma in its fundamental meaning—is not the source of the idea of samsara it certainly contributed significantly to its elaboration. Properly executed ritual was thought to bring about specific, desired results, and flawed ritual action had undesirable results. In one sense samsara represents this ritual view of karma generalized to a social and cosmic process.

A further observation regarding origins is that early Aryan texts link samsara to observed rhythms and cycles in nature. According to the Chāndogya Upaniṣad, humans travel along one of two paths after death. Those who have led austere, contemplative lives in the forest go the "way of the gods," passing through temporal units (day, fortnight, etc.) and ultimately transcending time and samsara. "They do not return; indeed they do not return." However, those who were householders (GṚHASTHA) and performed sacrifice and other duties (DHARMA) follow the "way of the ancestors." They cannot reach the "year" (time's master unit), let alone go beyond it. They return. Successively becoming sky, air, smoke, mist, and cloud, they fall to earth as rain to become seeds and plants. Eaten by men, they enter the semen. There follows impregnation, conception, and the cycle's renewal.

2. Traditional views. Samsara is the impetus and *raison d'être* for various quests for "release" (MOKṢA). It has positive and even reassuring this-worldly aspects as well. It is a theodicy by which otherwise puzzling situations are rendered explicable. Signifying order and affirming justice, it bears testimony to dharma. Moreover, while it confirms an individual's place in the cosmos, it stresses individual responsibility. "Wandering" from life to life is not a destiny or fate imposed from without. It is the result of individual acts, and a person must accept responsibility for his or her personal circumstances. Further, the responsibility implies freedom.

"Transmigration" or "reincarnation" is not always an apt translation of samsara, but it accords with the view dominant among Hindus and JAINAS. Here, an essential self (ATMAN; JĪVA) properly may be said to "migrate," inhabiting and vivifying body after body. From this perspective samsara can be seen as a kind of prison in which the "real" self is locked in successive prison cells (i.e., bodies). Ignorance (variously conceived) is the root cause. To break free is to attain right knowledge, whereupon the self either soars beyond samsara or comes to understand that bondage is an illusion (MĀYĀ).

3. Adaptations. India's religious devotees have a different attitude. (*See* BHAKTI HINDUISM.) For them, samsara is a problem to the extent that it involves failing to perceive and to acknowledge the omnipotent deity's presence in its created order (i.e., the world). Release (*mokṣa*) would be intolerable for the devotee if it were to mean merely isolation (*kevala*) or "union." The devotee seeks release only from the distractions and temptations of ordinary life so that he may praise and meditate upon his god or goddess without interruption. Samsara is not to be transcended; rather, devotees are to master themselves and approach god within it.

Some Buddhists have yet another view of samsara, for they deny any abiding self that could transmigrate. "Births-and-deaths-in-sequence" or simply "rebirth" would be an admissible translation. Samsara for Buddhists is the unenlightened life characterized by suffering (DUKKHA). They subject such a life to close analysis with distinctive results. Life is seen to be a process, a series consisting of an uncountable number of instants, each caused and conditioned—in short, a birth. What is ordinarily seen as a single life is many. Nothing "material" (however subtle) moves from instant to instant. Instead, one moment gives rise to the next, which "is" as a result of what preceded it and will cause that which follows (*see* PAṬICCASAMUPPĀDA).

In a sense, samsara is more vividly conceived as a problem by Buddhists than by other Indian traditions, though apparent physical death is trivialized as an event when considered to be no more than one of a countless number of "deaths." Through the centuries the various Buddhist schools have reached different solutions. Some have stressed the need to transcend samsara and to achieve a release (NIRVANA) that is uncaused and undying. Others have emphasized that the correct understanding of exactly "how things are" reveals the truth and yields the realization that samsara itself is the truth and the goal, for life is nothing other than how it is.

Bibliography. W. N. Brown, *Man in the Universe* (1966), pp. 68-87. G. R. WELBON

SAṂSKĀRA sŭm skär´ ŭ (H—Skt.; lit. "to put together, to make perfect" [*kṛ*—"to make, to do" + *sam*—"together"]). Perhaps best translated by the English word "sacrament," *saṃskāras* are the LIFE CYCLE RITES of traditional Hinduism. Given canonical status by the Gṛhya Sūtras (the ritual manuals of the householder), the *saṃskāras* number variously from twelve to more than forty, though all lists include a birth ceremony *(jātakarman),* an initiation ritual *(upanayana; see* TWICE BORN), and a marriage ceremony *(vivāha).* Perhaps because the *saṃskāra* rituals affirm and attempt to enhance life on earth, the funeral rite (*see* ŚRĀDDHA) is not usually included among the Hindu *saṃskāras.* L. D SHINN

SANCTUS sänk´ toos (Ch— Lat.; "holy"). First word of the hymn sung or said as the conclusion of the preface to the EUCHARISTIC prayer in most LITURGIES. It is based upon the cry of the cherubim in Isa. 6:3, reflects Jewish liturgical practice, and despite its omission by Hippolytus (*ca.* 215) was in ancient use in the church. *See* MASS. R. A. GREER

SAṄGHA säng´ hŭ (B—Pali) **SAṂGHA** säng´ hŭ (B—Skt.; lit. "community, assembly"). The BUDDHA, the DHARMA, and the *Saṅgha* comprise the traditional "Three Jewels" (TRIRATNA) in which Buddhists seek refuge from DUKKHA, the unsatisfactoriness of worldly existence. From its origins the *Saṅgha* or assembly of Buddhist monks has sought to preserve and expound the teachings of its founder. Originally, the *Saṅgha* was perceived to be a unified brotherhood of faith and mission, the "*Saṅgha* of the Four Quarters." While this ideal has never been abandoned entirely, not long after the Buddha's death independent communities or *Saṅghas* grew up and monks began to reside in self-sufficient monasteries (VIHĀRAS). These were built and supported by the laity who earned spiritual merit through their donations and who benefited from the good example, the preaching, and the instruction provided by the monks.

1. **Origins.** Before the time of the Buddha there had existed in India a diverse community of religious mendicants—wandering almsmen (BHIKKUS and *parivrājakas*), world renouncers (SANNYĀSINS), and ascetic recluses (ŚRAMAṆAS). These persons had cast off the bonds which tied them to the world, seeking instead the path of salvation, either independently or at the feet of a teacher or master *(Satthā)* whose salvific message or dharma (Pali *dhamma*) had attracted them. The primitive *Saṅgha* can be viewed as one among numerous sects in India's wandering community; in this case, its members were joined by allegiance to their teacher, the Buddha, and pursued the dhamma taught by him. Despite its similarities with other mendicant communities, however, the Buddhist *Saṅgha* was conceived by its founder to be a universal assembly of monks, i.e., the "*Saṅgha* of the Four Quarters," transcending the narrow limits of a sect and dedicated to the service of the many. "Go ye now, O Bhikkhus, and wander, for the gain of the many, for the welfare of the many, out of compassion for the world, for the good, for the gain, for the welfare of gods and men" (Mahāvagga, I, 11, 1). Although the Order continued to evolve in sectarian directions, the *Saṅgha* of the Four Quarters remained the ideal.

2. **The rain retreat.** One long-standing tradition in the community of wanderers was the annual rain retreat (Pali *vassa*), made necessary by the monsoons of India. For the duration of the rainy season between July and October mendicants were forced to abandon their wandering and to seek suitable shelter. So ancient was this custom in the wanderers' communities that it had acquired the characteristics of a religious observance and was enjoined by the canonical rules governing each sect. The primitive Buddhist *Saṅgha* spent the rain retreat in two types of loosely connected settlements: ĀVĀSAS in the country and *ārāmas* near towns and cities. Although these settlements were not permanent and although the residents at each dwelling place met there by coincidence, the yearly rain retreat had a lasting effect upon the *bhikkhus'* sense of community. Out of this experience gradually emerged their institutional life and practices.

Among the institutions which developed during the rain retreat was the fortnightly recitation of the PĀTIMOKKHA, a confession of faith symbolizing and furthering the bond which held together the primitive *Saṅgha*. The ceremonial occasion in which this ritualistic recital occurred was termed the UPOSATHA. As the *Saṅgha* matured from one sect within the wanderers' community into a monastic order, the Pātimokkha became a code of offenses against the collective life, with punishment for each offense stipulated. The evolving Pātimokkha was not primarily an assertion of faith in the dhamma but the acceptance of a normative discipline. Other rites instituted by the primitive *Saṅgha,* such as the ceremony marking the conclusion of the rain retreat *(pavāraṇā)* and the distribution of robes *(kaṭhina),* reveal a departure from the simple life of wandering almsmen toward the settled existence of a monastic community.

In the process, it became customary for monks to return to the same *āvāsa* or *ārāma* for each rain retreat, so that it was possible to distinguish those who dwelt at one location from those of another. As early as the fourth century B.C. the practice of leaving the *āvāsa* or *ārāma* at the end of the rainy season was abandoned, even though the ideal of the wandering life never disappeared completely. A new unit within the *Saṅgha* was thus recognized: a single monk-fraternity residing at a permanent settlement or monastery *(vihāra).* Each *saṅgha's* unity or completeness was preserved through the institution of "Rules of the Order" *(saṅghakamma),* which in its mature form was a set of procedures governing nearly all transactions of the *saṅgha.* By affirming the unitary nature of each *saṅgha,* the *saṅghakamma* enabled each monastic community to function as an autonomous entity. In order for a *saṅghakamma* to be authoritative the entirety or completeness *(samagattā)* of the *saṅgha* was required, exclusive of nuns, male or female novices, or others disqualified for various reasons. With the monks assembled, the issue in question was read aloud, discussed, and then voted upon. Monks signified acceptance of a proposal by listening in silence as the proposal was read three times. If no agreeable solution could be reached, the dispute was referred to a committee or to the elders of a nearby monastery. In either case, the *saṅghakamma* process fostered the unity and collective action of a *saṅgha.*

3. The monastic code. Coinciding with the institutionalization of the ideal *Saṅgha* of the Four Quarters into independent monk-fraternities was the development of the Vinaya or monastic code of the Order, the most complete collection of which is the VINAYA PIṬAKA of the PALI CANON. The Vinaya, which exists virtually unchanged in Buddhist monasteries today, contains numerous rules encased in legends about the Buddha and the early community. Serving as a charter of organization for the primitive *Saṅgha,* the Vinaya evolved into a system of regulations through which each assembly governed itself. Through the process of *saṅghakamma* the Vinaya was designed to further the independence and autonomy of each community as well as the unity of the *Saṅgha* at large.

The democratic principles evident in the proceedings of the *saṅghakamma* are in keeping with the anti-authoritarian sentiment of early Buddhism. At the Buddha's last rain retreat in Beluva, when he was close to death, his disciple ĀNANDA urged him "to leave instructions as touching the order" (Mahā-Parinibbāna Sutta, II, 31), presumably hoping that the Buddha would name a successor or leave a constitution for the *Saṅgha.* But the Buddha replied that the Order must not pledge allegiance to any person but rather must take refuge in the dhamma. "The truths and rules of the order *(dhamma-vinaya)* which I have set forth and laid down for you all, let them, after I am gone, be the Teacher to you" (*ibid.,* VI, 1). Ostensibly the Buddha was impressed with the tribal councils found among the clans of northern India, in which tradition he himself was purported to have been raised. The practice of conducting affairs in an assembly form of government was thereby translated into the monastic practice of *saṅghakamma.*

4. Development of a hierarchy. In spite of this practice, however, the continued growth and increasing material acquisitions of the monasteries made the development of a hierarchical order within the *Saṅgha* inevitable. Epigraphic evidence and the accounts of Chinese pilgrims reveal that abbots or chief monks began to emerge in Indian monasteries, contrary to Vinaya stipulation. In Ceylon, prior to the ninth century A.D., each monastery appointed a resident chief monk, whose responsibility included the order and discipline of the community. Nonetheless, even with the *Saṅgha's* growing administrative complexity, it retained its mistrust for authority and continued to function in a collective manner. In Ceylon, for example, administrative action involving the monastery's labor force was undertaken with the consent of the full community. And in China important decisions were brought before the entire assembly of monks by their elected abbot.

5. Monasteries. As the monasteries grew in size and complexity, their traditional monk-oriented outlook was modified and they became great centers of secular as well as religious scholarship and culture. These "great monasteries" *(mahāvihāras)* or universities were the fruit of a long educational tradition within the *Saṅgha.* In the community's early days each monk underwent a ten-year probationary period of dependence upon a teacher, during which he was instructed in canonical doctrine and philosophy. The aim of this monastic education was to produce a monk well schooled in the dhamma. Gradually, however, monastic education was liberalized until, during the latter part of the GUPTA DYNASTY (A.D. 320-540), the curriculum in the *mahāvihāras* included languages, grammar, history, logic, medicine, and other secular subjects, as well as the traditional studies in canonical literature. As centers of learning and culture in India, the *mahāvihāras* such as NĀLANDĀ and Vikramaśilā attracted students and pilgrims from China and Tibet and sent out missionaries to all of Asia.

The extensive *mahāvihāras* which arose in India during the Gupta age and elsewhere throughout Asia in later centuries were built and maintained by donations from the laity. Although the *Saṅgha* often received support from the state and royalty (especially in lands where Buddhism was the officially recognized religion of state, such as Ceylon), donations to the Order were principally from wealthy merchants and landowners. Their generosity was inspired by pious devotion to the Order (as one of the religion's Three Jewels) and by the desire to earn spiritual merit for the life to come. As the monasteries increased in size and expense, it became necessary to develop permanent sources of income. In Ceylon, for instance, several types of endowment were specified: lands, fields, and villages; water tanks and canals; wet-field and dry-field lands; funds held in trust for the monastery; and income generated through the levying of taxes and the collection of fines. Although slaves were prohibited by the Buddha, they too represented a source of income for the monasteries. Donations were given both to maintain slaves at the monasteries and to free them from slavery. In fact, the practice developed in Ceylon for wealthy lay Buddhists to offer slaves to the monastery and then to ransom them, thereby gaining "double merit" for the donor. The laity were also employed as laborers and servants by the monastery, an arrangement beneficial both to the monastery, which required large numbers of workers for its maintenance, and to the lay workers, who were able to earn a living with the help of the monks. (*See* BUDDHISM, LAY §5.)

6. **Relationship to the state.** From its inception, the *Saṅgha* has been a vital element in every aspect of Buddhist life and society. As an independent, self-governing organization, the Order has often been directly involved in affairs of the state. At various times and places the *Saṅgha* has either enjoyed governmental support and patronage or it has suffered political persecution and abuse. It has served as both a legitimizer of the ruling power and its severest critic, in the modern era as in former times. The great size and wealth of Buddhist monasteries, as well as the self-governing nature of the *Saṅgha,* has brought about varied interactions between the Order and the state. Early in its history the *Saṅgha* in India enjoyed a protected status as a self-regulating corporate body due to the ancient Indian political practice of *samaya* (lit. "agreement or contract"), according to which the ruler was constitutionally bound to defend the *Saṅgha* from internal or external disruption and to ensure that its Vinaya codes were properly enforced. Emperor AŚOKA was applying the principles of *samaya* when he intervened in the internal affairs of the Order to evict schismatics, and his reign became normative for later Buddhist views on how the state and the *Saṅgha* should interact. While the Aśokan example of an ideal monarch did not prevent sectarian divisions within the Order or injustice in society, it served to involve later monarchs in stimulating monastic reforms and became the standard by which political authority itself was judged by Buddhists. (*See* BUDDHIST SECTARIANISM.)

In most THERAVĀDA countries, Buddhism has been either heavily subsidized or, in fact, the officially recognized religion of the state. In turn, the *Saṅgha* has often been intimately involved in governmental affairs. In ancient Ceylon, a monk was named to the position equivalent to that of Chief Justice of the State; in Thailand, the king, as all laymen, was expected to spend some time in a monastery. In China, however, the relationship of the Order to the government has varied considerably. At times Buddhism has been persecuted as a foreign influence, with attempts made to exert political control over the *Saṅgha* through the state examination system and through the selling of ordination certificates. At other times, as during parts of the T'ang dynasty (A.D. 618-907), Buddhism was highly favored and a special Commissioner of Religion was appointed to earn merit for the state by holding frequent vegetarian banquets for the monks as well as by erecting Buddhist temples, statues, and monasteries. In Japan, since the introduction of Buddhism in the mid-sixth century A.D., there has been a continuing dialectical relationship between political authorities on various levels and several sects within Japanese Buddhism. As in India vis-à-vis forms of the Brahmanic tradition and the BHAKTI sects, and as in China in relationship to both CONFUCIAN and TAOIST supporters, so in Japan the Buddhist involvement in worldly affairs was often rendered more complex because of the indigenous tradition of SHINTŌ. One particularly important development for the *Saṅgha* in Japan was the emergence in the thirteenth century of married priests, started by SHINRAN, who founded the Jōdo Shin-shū (PURE LAND True Sect). Over the centuries this came to mean that traditional monastic life was complemented by temple life, in which priests served directly amongst the laity.

As Buddhism began to spread to the West in the mid-twentieth century, as a form of practice and not simply as a tradition to be studied, the concept of a *Saṅgha* has become even more complex and the laity are often seen as full members under the leadership of either a priest or a monk, underscoring in a new way the meaning and role of the *savakasaṅgha,* the wider congregation of the Buddha's disciples. *See* BUDDHISM IN AMERICA; MONASTICISM, EAST AND WEST.

Bibliography. K. Ch'en, *Buddhism in China* (1964); G. De, *Democracy in Early Buddhist Sangha* (1955); S. Dutt, *Buddhist Monks and Monasteries of India* (1962), *Early Buddhist Monarchism* (1960), and *The Buddha and Five After-Centuries* (1957); N. Dutt, *Early Monastic Buddhism* (1960); R. A. L. H. Gunawardana, *Robe and Plough: Monasticism and Economic Interest in Early Medieval Sri Lanka* (1979); E. M. Mendelson, *Sangha and State in Burma: A Study of Monastic Sectarianism and Leadership* (1975); W. Rahula, *History of Buddhism in Ceylon* (1966); E. O. Reischauer, trans., *Ennin's Diary: The Record of a Pilgrimage to T'ang in Search of the Law* (1955); E. O. Reischauer, *Ennin's Travels in T'ang China* (1955); S. J. Tambiah, *World Conqueror and World Renouncer* (1976).

B. L. SMITH

SANHEDRIN săn hē´ drĭn (Ju). The supreme legal, political, and religious organization of the Jewish people in Roman Palestine. Rabbinic sources conflict with Jewish Greek sources and the GOSPELS in portraying it as primarily concerned with religious matters, but it functioned occasionally as a court also.

Prior to the first Jewish war against Rome, A.D. 66-73, the seat of the Sanhedrin was in JERUSALEM. After the war the Sanhedrin was reconvened at JAMNIA, where it became the main political and religious authority for Jews throughout the Roman Empire. After the BAR KOCHBA war it moved to Galilee.

Bibliography. H. Mantel, *Studies in the History of the Sanhedrin* (1961). E. M. MEYERS

SAN-LUN sän loon´ (Chin.). *See* NARA BUDDHISM §3c.

SANNYĀSIN, SAṂNYĀSIN sŭn yä´ sĭn (H—Skt.; lit. "one who gives up or lays aside"). Renouncer; the last of the four stages of life (ĀŚRAMA). When a Hindu male has reached a point of disgust with desire for the world, he should enter this stage. Giving up all possessions except some cast-off garments and a begging bowl, renouncing his name, CASTE, and previous associations, he should wander in the world free from all attachments and desires, seeking only final liberation (MOKSA).
P. COURTRIGHT

SANRON sän rôn´ (Jap.). *See* NARA BUDDHISM §3c.

SANSKRIT, LANGUAGE AND LITERATURE săn´ skrĭt (H & B). Sanskrit derives its name from *samskṛta,* "perfected, cultured," as contrasted with *prākṛta,* "natural, uncultured," and is referred to as *dēvavāni,* the language of the gods. The VEDAS represent the earliest use of the language, which since then has had a continuous literary history. Sanskrit is divided into two dialects, *vaidika* and *laukika,* representing, respectively, the language as used in the Vedas and in later texts.

In the modern period it has retained its sacred status and literary superiority. It remains the ritual language of Hinduism, and its literature continues to be regarded with respect, even though modern Hindus use the vernacular for literary expression and intellectual communication.

1. **History and status.** Belonging to the Indo-European family of languages, Sanskrit, or an early dialect of it, was the language of the ARYAN tribes who entered India in the second millennium B.C. The Vedic Aryans believed that the power of language, as uttered in chants (MANTRAS), controlled the world around them. A Vedic aphorism states that even one word well learned and correctly pronounced fulfills every desire, like the divine cow in heaven. Precise learning and accurate pronunciation were important in the study of the Vedas. A calamity could result from incorrect pronunciation of a Vedic text.

Their obsession with the accuracy, pronunciation, and power of the word led the Vedic BRAHMINS to the study of grammar at a very early date. To each grammar text were appended sections related to proper pronunciation of language sounds. In these sections, called *prātiśākhyas,* the phonology of the language was decribed with reference to the place and manner of articulation.

The early association of the concept of sacred power with the correct use of the spoken word endowed studies of grammar with religious purity. Pāṇini (fifth century B.C.), Vararuci (300 B.C.), and PATAÑJALI (*ca.* 200-150 B.C.), the great ancient grammarians of Sanskrit, were revered as sages, *munis,* who had access to superior knowledge. A legend relates that Pāṇini heard the sounds of the drum (*ḍamaru*) played by Lord SHIVA fourteen times at the end of his cosmic dance. The sounds of the drum formed the fourteen SŪTRAS known as Śiva Sūtras which were the basis for the highly complex algebraic rules written by Pāṇini in his grammar *Aṣṭādhyāyī.* Vararuci updated Pāṇini's grammar by including a number of classical usages which Pāṇini had not covered. Patañjali, believed to be an incarnation of the divine grammarian, the great snake ŚEṢA, wrote the *Mahābhāṣya,* a commentary explaining Pāṇini's rules. Pāṇini was considered to be the great legislator of language; as a result, the language developed within the structural confines established by his grammar, regarded as infallible.

The language retained its sacred status because Brahmins imputed both a sacred and a prestigious value to erudition in grammar. The texts of Pāṇini and Patañjali were treated as sacred texts, just like the Vedas, and were taught only to the Brahmin CASTE. Traditionally the student of *Mahābhāṣya* has begun his lesson with a ritual prayer to the sage-grammarians and has received instruction while in a special state of purity.

Sanskrit ceased to exist as a spoken language long before the Christian era, but it continued to be venerated and was used for ritual, intellectual, and literary purposes.

2. **Hindu Sanskrit literature.** This body of literature is traditionally divided into the following categories: Vedas, ŚĀSTRAS, PURĀṆAS, and Kāvyas.

a) Vedas. "The Vedas" is a collective name applied to the body of literature which includes the main text of the four Vedas and their ancillary material. This literature is categorized as ŚRUTI, "heard texts," the gods' words as heard by the sages through revelation.

b) Śāstras. The Śāstras include codes of conduct and policy related to the four goals of life in this world: DHARMA (law), ARTHA (profit), KĀMA (pleasure), and MOKSA (liberation). It is believed that the Śāstras uphold the Vedas, and therefore they are classified as SMṚTI, "texts built on remembered knowledge." Each goal in life has its own Śāstra. Dharmaśāstra literature includes not only the LAWS OF MANU, YĀJÑAVALKYA, and other authorities but also scores of related commentaries. The best known work in the category of Arthaśāstra literature is the code of KAUṬILYA, also known as Cāṇakya. Vātsyāyana's KĀMA SŪTRA and other works on the science of erotics belong to KĀMAŚĀSTRA literature. A body of literature called *darśanas* (lit., "that which is seen," hence, interpretive and speculative texts) is included in the category of Mokṣaśāstra ("liberation teaching"). These texts are accepted or rejected on the basis of adherence to or divergence from the Vedas. *Darśanas* which do not uphold the Vedas as the standard of reality are rejected as unorthodox. The acceptability of the orthodox *darśanas* has varied over time, depending upon the popularity of the philosophical schools (DARŚANAS) they represent.

The authority of a Śāstra is determined by the reputation of the author to whom it is ascribed. As with the grammarians, the purported authors of Śāstras are famed as sages. By definition they were superhuman in wisdom and thus infallible. Although a scholar may comment on a Śāstra and interpret it correctly, he may not write his own Śāstra.

c) Purāṇas. Purāṇas are primarily texts of mythological history. Reputedly composed by the sage Vyāsa, who edited the Vedas and composed the MAHĀBHĀRATA and the BHĀGAVATA PURĀṆA, the important Purāṇas total eighteen. They describe the myths of creation and destruction and the eternal battle between the demonic and divine forces of the universe, and include stories of the gods and of the AVATARS (incarnations) of VISHNU.

The date of composition of the Purāṇas is difficult to determine since they were composed and transmitted orally. Some of them may be as early as the first century A.D., but the final canon of eighteen was not crystallized before *ca.* A.D. 900. In fact, Skanda Purāṇa, perhaps the most flexible of all the Purāṇas, had new sections added up until the mid-sixteenth century. A story or ritual could gain authenticity just by being inserted into the Purāṇas; e.g., new temples and new deities acquired legitimacy through a Sanskrit composition in the appropriate meter which claimed to be part of the Skanda Purāṇa.

In contrast to the Vedas, which were chanted mainly for the power of their sounds and were not understood by many reciters, Purāṇas were recited for their meanings. Their mythology and the code of conduct they incorporated were popularized through public recitations. Purāṇas thus served as the popular form for the content of the Śāstras, which were available only to the expert.

Related in style to the Purāṇas were the Epics (*itihāsa:* lit. "so it was"), the Mahābhārata and the RĀMĀYAṆA. Although not classified as Purāṇas, they played a popular role analogous to that of the Purāṇas. The authors of both these influential works were sages. The Mahābhārata was attributed to Vyāsa and the Rāmāyaṇa to VĀLMĪKI. In all likelihood the Epics were collections of popular local legends which had been adapted to Brahminical purposes. The Mahābhārata and the Rāmāyaṇa are stories which were generated by the tensions of joint family relationships and disputed inheritance of paternal property. They contain a powerful heroic element which is intermingled with extensive didactic passages. The authenticity of the text of the Mahābhārata is suggested by its status as the fifth Veda. The BHAGAVAD GĪTĀ, which acquired scriptural status, is a part of the Mahābhārata. Along with the BRAHMA SŪTRAS and UPANIṢADS, the Bhagavad Gītā is considered a key text for Hindus. Almost every leader of a new school in Hinduism writes a commentary on the Bhagavad Gītā.

d) Kāvya. Kāvya (poetry), in contrast to Vedas, Śāstras, and Purāṇas, is composed by ordinary humans. KĀLIDĀSA, Bhavabhūti, and the other great poets of Sanskrit literature were not sages. Despite the efforts of medieval literary criticism to elevate the status of poet to that of a seer—an aphorism states that no one who is not a seer can be a poet—and despite the identification of the sage Vālmīki as the first poet, the classical tradition did not treat Kāvya as sacred. There was, in fact, some hesitation to permit spiritual students to read Kāvyas.

In an effort to acquire religious respectability the literary tradition identified a similarity between aesthetic experience (*rasānanda*) and religious experience (*brahmānanda*). As a result a meeting point between poetry and sacred texts was established. It was claimed that Vedas, Purāṇas, and Kāvyas teach the same dharma. The difference between them is only in the manner of their teaching. Vedas speak like a king, Purāṇas teach like a colleague, and Kāvyas advise like a girlfriend. Nevertheless, poetry was still ranked at a lower level than the sacred texts composed by the sages.

3. Sanskritization. The very high status afforded the Sanskrit language made it desirable for new movements within Hinduism and non-Hindu religions within India to employ Sanskrit rather than one of the vernacular languages for their texts and rituals.

a) Bhakti cults. An important development in the history of religious literature and the Sanskrit language took place with the advent of the *bhakti* (devotion) sects (sixth to seventeenth centuries). In contrast to classical Brahminism, the origins of which were embedded in Sanskrit, the literature of the *bhakti* cults originated in the regional languages. Later, *bhakti* cults were absorbed into the structure of Hinduism, and an important feature of this absorption was the use of Sanskrit as a ritual language (*see* BHAKTI HINDUISM). The composition of the Bhāgavata Purāṇa (*ca.* tenth century) is representative of this process.

As Sanskrit gained acceptability as a ritual language, a number of respected texts were composed incorporating the rituals of Vishnu and Shiva temples. These ĀGAMA texts were treated with the same respect that had been shown to the Vedic ritual texts during the classical period.

The influence of *bhakti* was most evident in poetry. Because *bhakti* was considered to be one of the nine *rasas* (sentiments), aesthetic experience became equated with religious experience. Books such as the GĪTĀ GOVINDA, which describes the love play of

KRISHNA, became sacred works since their authors were recognized devotees of the god.

A related body of *bhakti* literature was *stotras* ("praise songs"). They were sung both in temples and homes and were elevated to sacred status.

b) Non-Hindu literature. Sanskritization also affected Buddhism, Jainism, and the lesser known heterodox religions of India.

The earliest Buddhist literature was composed in Prākrit languages (Middle Indic vernaculars closely related to Sanskrit), but by the first century B.C. some Buddhists began partially to Sanskritize their writings. The resulting "mixed Sanskrit" or "Buddhist Hybrid Sanskrit" is the language of numerous important texts, such as the *Mahāvastu* and the *Lalitavistara,* two long biographies of the Buddha. Later, Buddhists also wrote in pure Sanskrit.

The earliest Jaina literature is also in Prākrit, but by the eighth century the Sanskritization movement had encompassed Jainism as well. For example, the *Tattvārthādhigamasūtra,* by Umāsvāti, is a highly regarded philosophical treatise written in Sanskrit.

Buddhists and Jainas also wrote Sanskrit poetry, Purāṇas, and treatises on logic.

Bibliography. T. Burrow, *The Sanskrit Language* (1973); J. Gonda, *Medieval Religious Literature in Sanskrit: A History of Indian Literature,* Vol. II, fasc. 1 (1977); J. F. Staal, ed., *A Reader on the Sanskrit Grammarians* (1972); M. Winternitz, *A History of Indian Literature,* 3 vols. (rev. ET 1929 ff.).

V. N. RAO

SARASVATĪ sär ŭ svä´ tē (H). A Hindu goddess, associated in Vedic texts with a river in Northwest India. In later Hinduism she becomes the wife of the god BRAHMĀ and is associated with wisdom and learning. *See* GODDESS (INDIA) §1.

D. R. KINSLEY

SĀRIPUTTA sä rĭ po͞ot´ tŭ (B—Pali) **ŚĀRIPUTRA** shä rĭ po͞o´ trä (B—Skt.). One of the chief disciples of Gautama the BUDDHA, often linked with the name of another disciple of like standing, MOGGALLĀNA. Both men were of the BRAHMIN CASTE and had been religious ascetics under a teacher named Sañjāya. According to the PALI CANON, after meeting the Buddha and hearing his teaching, both were converted to the way of the Buddha and brought with them all of the other 250 disciples of Sañjāya. Like his friend, Sāriputta was given a leadership role in the SAṄGHA, which included both teaching and dispensing discipline. In a notable conversation with a monk named Yamaka, Sāriputta is recorded as rejecting the doctrine impute by Yamaka to the Buddha that upon death the ARHANT (one who has attained the goal) in fact perishes. Sāriputta termed this teaching an evil heresy. He affirmed continuity of the self as distinguished from the body or any of the elements of existence (Saṃyutta Nikāya III, 109-16). Sāriputta is also recorded as having expressed a singularly high faith in the person of the Buddha shortly before the latter's death. He was gently reproved by the Buddha for making statements beyond his personal knowledge (Dīgha Nikāya II, 82). The Buddha, however, evidently thought highly of him for his character and wisdom.

Bibliography. R. H. Drummond, *Gautama the Buddha* (1974), pp. 50-53.

R. H. DRUMMOND

SĀRNĀTH sär´ nät (B & Ja). The Buddha, shortly after his enlightenment at BODHGAYĀ, traveled northwest to Sārnāth, a deer park at the outskirts of the city of Vārāṇasī (Banāras). There he found five ascetics, his former associates, and preached to them of the middle path and the FOUR NOBLE TRUTHS, thus "setting the wheel of dharma in motion." Consequently, from the time of AŚOKA to the Muslim period, Sārnāth flourished as one of the four great pilgrimage sites. Archaeological remains and the accounts of two Chinese pilgrims indicate that once Sārnāth contained a university plus numerous STŪPAS, shrines, and monasteries that accommodated perhaps fifteen hundred monks and nuns.

Most of the ancient structures are now in ruins, but a few still stand. These include the Dhamekh *stūpa,* a brick and stone cylindrical structure that rises nearly 150 feet above the ground, and the stump of the commemorative pillar erected by the emperor Aśoka. A modern temple built and operated by the MAHĀBODHI SOCIETY enshrines objects from Taxila, another ancient Buddhist center of worship and study. The tradition of JAINISM reveres Sārnāth as the area where the eleventh TĪRTHAṄKARA, Śrī Amsanatha, practiced asceticism and later died. A modern Jaina temple there is dedicated to him.

R. C. AMORE

SARVĀSTIVĀDINS. sär väs tĭ vä´ dĭns. *See* BUDDHIST SECTARIANISM.

SARVODAYA sär vō´ dä yä (H—Skt.; lit. "universal uplift"). A fundamental principle of GANDHI'S ideology, which states that the physical, economic, and spiritual resources of a society should be used for the "uplift" of its members. The concept had its roots in HINDU and JAINA philosophy, but was elaborated by Gandhi into a full-blown theory of applied economics and politics.

J. BARE

ŚĀSTRA shä´ strŭ (H—Skt.; lit. "teaching, command"). A class of religious teachings or compilations of such teachings; thus a synonym for "religious or moral treatise," applied to a wide variety of Hindu writings on law (e.g., DHARMAŚĀSTRA), theology/philosophy (e.g., Vedāntaśāstras), etc.

L. D. SHINN

SAT, SATYA sŭt´ yŭ (H, B & Ja—Skt.; lit. "truth" [*sat*—"being, existence, essence, morally right"]).

Since *sat* denotes the root of all existence, one must not just *speak* the truth but should also *be* truthful. Both *sat* and *satya* are mentioned in the VEDAS in the context of metaphysics and cosmology. Cosmologically *satya* stands for the ultimate region or the ground of six *bhuvanas* or regions called Bhuh, Bhuvah, Svah, Mahah, Janah, and Tapah (*see* TAPAS).

It is in this sense that PRAJĀPATI (Lord of creation) has been mentioned as the central invisible reality and referred to as "truth of truths" *(satyasya satyam)*.

Divinity (both as supreme person and BRAHMAN) has been defined as the embodiment of *sat* (existence), *cit* (consciousness), and *ānanda* (bliss). According to the BHAGAVAD GĪTĀ, VISHNU as the supreme lord is designated by three epithets: Oṃ (logos), *tat* (reality) and *sat* (being).

Ethically *sat* is synonymous with righteousness and *satya* refers to the practice of truth through body, mind, and speech. One can attain self-realization or God-realization through the acceptance and practice of truth. HINDUISM, JAINISM, BUDDHISM, and SIKHISM all accept truth as the highest virtue. Two outstanding practitioners of truth in India are the legendary King Harishchandra, who sacrificed everything including his own life for the sake of truth, and Mahātma GANDHI in our own time, who made of truth a combined spiritual and political path (SATYĀGRAHA). Gandhi identified nonviolence (AHIMSĀ) with truth, and truth with the all-pervasive, nonsectarian "God."

Bibliography. I. C. Sharma, *Ethical Philosophies of India* (1965), chs. III, XV. I. C. SHARMA

SATAN (Ju, Ch & I—Heb. *satan* [accuser]; Gr. *daibolos* [slanderer]; Arab. *shaiṭān*). The ruler of superhuman beings or personified powers, usually conceived as malevolent. The awareness of the ominous element in human experience is expressed in terms of hostile numinous beings who threaten human well-being, either in this life or beyond. In this context, the human situation is thought to reflect a transcendent conflict between opposing powers of good and evil. The literature of ZOROASTRIANISM, JUDAISM, and CHRISTIANITY reflects an extended process of development of the concept of Satan's person and role.

1. **Old Testament and Judaism.** The OT contains only three explicit references to Satan as a distinct personality (I Chr. 21:1; Zech. 3:1-2; Job 1-2). In these references Satan is the agent who in obedience to God tests or accuses the righteous, and not the responsible source of evil. God is sometimes understood in this latter role in the Old Testament (Isa. 45:7; I Sam. 16:14, etc.).

Satan emerged as a prominent figure in extracanonical Jewish literature during the four centuries prior to the Christian era. In these writings Satan directs his subordinate agents (fallen angels) in opposition to God (Jubilees 10:1-10). He bears other names, such as Mastemah (Hos. 9:7) and Belial (Testament of Levi 3:3). As God's adversary he seduces the righteous to sin (Testament of Naphtali 3:1), perverts God's plan (Jubilees 48:2), and accuses the righteous before God (Ethiopic Enoch 48:7). However, the righteous have God's promise of help in the choice between good and evil. Rabbinic literature emphasizes this promise but sublimates Satan's role in the drama.

The Dead Sea Scrolls present a distinctive portrait of Satan (Belial). Created by God, he is predestined to lead his hosts in a final assault againt the righteous (War Scroll). The conflict is to be consummated by God's decisive intervention in the establishment of his kingdom. (*See* KINGDOM OF GOD.)

2. **Christianity.** The NT does not contain a unitary concept of Satan's person and role, but rather reflects first century Jewish understanding. Satan is the supreme superhuman spirit of evil who stands in unalterable opposition to God. Satan is designated by names which refer to his activity: "tester" (I Thess. 3:5); "accuser" (Rev. 12:10); "ruler of the powers of the air" (Eph. 3:2). Jesus' miracles are said to have imposed definitive limits upon his power (Luke 12:10). God's judgment will bring his rule to an end (Rev. 12:10).

The art and literature of the medieval church reflect the mentality of the era. Satan is depicted as a horrible monster who presides over the subterranean furnace to which the damned have been consigned for eternity (cf. MILTON, *Paradise Lost;* DANTE, *The Divine Comedy; see* LUCIFER). Contemporary interest in the numinous sometimes expresses itself in the occult worship of Satan. *See* SATANISM; DEMONS, DEMONOLOGY.

Bibliography. W. Foerster, "Satanas," *TDNT*, VII, 151-65, and "Diabolos," *TDNT*, II, 71-81; G. Menshing, *et al.*, "Teufel," *Die Religion in Geschichte und Gegenwart*, VI, 704-12. R. C. BRIGGS

3. **In Islam,** as in Judaism and Christianity, Satan (Shaiṭan) is the personification of evil, the fallen angel who tempts Adam to err and is banished from heaven for his disobedience of the divine command (Qur'ān Sura 2:34-38). Yet the QUR'ĀN also identifies him as one of the JINN (Sura 18:51). A creature of fire, he opposes the angels (MALĀ'IKA), who are creatures of light, and as the chief of the jinn, he will preside over hell till Judgment Day (Sura 7:11-18, 15:30-44). Yet the Qur'ān implies that even in hell he will continue to be God's servant and may ultimately be redeemed (e.g., Sura 15:38).

The paradox of Satan's role in the divine economy has inspired the imagination of SUFI adepts, leading some to laud him as a tragic anti-hero, but among most Muslims he is feared as the ultimate tempter, eager to make believers go astray and join the ranks of idolaters and polytheists in hell. *See* SIN, MUSLIM CONCEPT OF; ESCHATOLOGY §3.

Bibliography. "Iblīs," *SEI*, pp. 145-46; "Shaiṭān," *SEI*, pp. 523-24; A. Schimmel, *Mystical Dimensions of Islam* (1975), pp. 193-96; P. Jackson, trans., Sharafuddin Maneri, *The Hundred Letters* (1980), pp. 69-72. B. LAWRENCE

SATANISM. The worship of the power which Judaism and Christianity regard as the origin of evil.

Although the ancient Gnostics and Manicheans (*see* Manicheism) and the medieval Albigenses were certainly not Satanists, roots of the modern movement may lie in their belief that the God of the OT is really a fraud whose promises are unreliable and whose morality is of dubious worth.

The Satanism of the nineteenth and twentieth centuries is a product of the occultism and "decadence" of late romanticism and shares its mood, vividly portrayed in its Satanist aspects in J. K. Huysmans' novel *Là-Bas* ("Down There"). The theatrical 1890s French Satanist cult represented there has been more or less duplicated in a number of modern European and American groups. Headed by a high priest who may dress so as to represent the devil, worship culminates in an emotionally intense evocation and praise of Satan. Perhaps the traditional Black Mass, which parodies the Roman Catholic mass, will be the centerpiece; perhaps some contemporary variation of it is used. In any case, the worship will have strong overtones of corporate ventilation of anger and frustration directed toward the Judeo-Christian God. In the Church of Satan founded in 1966 by Anton LaVey in San Francisco, the practice of "cursing" of "enemies" by individual members in a group setting perhaps approaches the therapeutic value of psychodrama. But other Satanist groups cater more to the fantasies of persons of unbalanced, often sadomasochistic, tendency. The number of real Satanists is miniscule.

Ideologically, Satanists seem to be divided into three groups. Some modern Satanists regard the Judeo-Christian devil as actually the true deity of this world, synonymous with the life force and the "healthy" natural impulses, and God as a sinister being who piously urges an unwholesome repression of nature and the flesh. For the most "liberal" wing of Satanism, represented by LaVey, the whole Satanist symbol system is little more than a myth and ritual to help people accept their carnal and materialist sides without guilt. For others Satan is indeed the prince of evil whom they embrace for his own sake, and in hope of reward after death in his dark domain. *See* Demons, Demonology.

Bibliography. R. Bellah and C. Glock, eds., *The New Religious Consciousness* (1976); R. Cavendish, *The Black Arts* (1967); R. Ellwood, *Religious and Spiritual Groups in Modern America* (1973); A. Lyons, *The Second Coming: Satanism in America* (1970); H. T. Rhodes, *The Satanic Mass* (1955).

R. S. Ellwood

SATGURU, SADGURU săt gōō´ rōō (S & H —Skt.; lit. "true teacher"). An honorific title added to most Sikh and some Hindu Gurus. Belief in the divine intervention of the guru, which is one of the pillars of Sikhism as well as Bhakti Hinduism, is based on the conviction that knowledge of essential truths cannot be acquired through the study of books, penance, or contemplation, but only transmitted by one who has attained enlightenment, i.e., a guru.

Rules of succession of gurus vary in India, but usually it is the guru who chooses his successor from among his disciples. Among the Sikhs the eight gurus were descendants of the same family. It is usually assumed that the spirit of the founder passes to the bodies of the successors "as one lamp lights another."

K. Singh

SATĪ sŭt´ tē (H—Skt.; lit. "faithful wife"). Refers both to a Hindu goddess and to the practice of widow suicide.

1. The goddess Satī is said to have attracted Shiva by her rigorous austerities and to have married him for the welfare of the world. A particular demon was harassing the gods and had been given the boon that he could only be killed by a son of Shiva. Satī was appointed by the gods to lure Shiva into marriage and so bring about a son who would defeat the demon. However, the divine plan was thwarted when the sage Dakṣa sponsored a great sacrifice but failed to invite Shiva because of Shiva's anti-social behavior. Shiva was not insulted by this, but Satī was, and in a fit of pique she committed suicide. Enraged at his wife's death, Shiva then destroyed Dakṣa's sacrifice and began to wander the world carrying Satī's corpse. In order to distract Shiva from his dead wife, Vishnu followed him and began to cut pieces from her body until nothing remained. Wherever a piece of Satī's body fell, there a place sacred to the goddess was instituted, and today throughout India as many as 108 *pīṭhas,* or seats, of the goddess are known, each one being associated with a particular part of Satī's body. Many texts claim that Pārvatī is a reincarnation of Satī.

2. Satī (Eng. "suttee") also refers to a faithful wife, and particularly to the ritual practiced in Hinduism until the twentieth century of widows committing suicide by burning themselves on their husband's funeral pyre. Hindu law books (*see* Manu, Laws of) often emphasize that a wife should serve her husband as a god and in this way realize her spiritual fulfillment. The practice of suttee, which is actually not enjoined in most law books, represents the culminating act in such a life of devotion to one's husband. In the nineteenth century the British authorities and some Hindu reformers, such as Ram Mohan Roy, were critical of the practice and eventually succeeded in outlawing it. Critics of the practice pointed to cases of suttee in which the widow's death did not appear voluntary but took place at the provocation of greedy relatives. The extent to which the name of this practice is associated with the goddess Satī is not clear. Although Satī killed herself because her husband was insulted, and thus performed a faithful act, Shiva himself was severely pained by the act. *See* Goddess (India).

D. R. Kinsley

SATORI sä tō´ rē (B—Jap.) **BODHI** bō´ dē (B—Skt.) **WU** wōō (B—Chin.). The experience of enlightenment; the realization of Buddha-mind; that which GAUTAMA experienced under the Bō (BODHI) tree, and hence the goal of Buddha's followers.

1. **Gautama's enlightenment.** The nature and content of satori are sought in the enlightenment experience of Gautama under the Bō tree. The various schools of Buddhism, therefore, have placed differing emphasis upon Gautama's experience in accord with their understanding of the nature of enlightenment and the path leading to it.

Emphasis is sometimes given to Gautama's long process of trial and error, choice of a middle path between asceticism and indulgence, and the realization that all things in the world are impermanent (ANICCA), unsatisfactory (DUKKHA), and nonsubstantial (ANATTA). When one is liberated from ignorance, both craving (TAṆHĀ) and grasping (*upādāna*) cease and enlightenment is achieved.

Others have emphasized enlightenment as the result of Gautama's meditative practice, the attainment of SAMĀDHI and the four DHYĀNA (meditation) states. PURE LAND SECTS have focused upon the role of the grace of AMIDA, while TENDAI has detailed fifty-two stages on the road to perfect enlightenment.

2. **Satori in Zen.** The Japanese term for enlightenment, "satori," is given special meaning and viewed as the single aim of ZEN. Whereas Indian Buddhism often emphasized stages on an ascending path to enlightenment, Chinese and Japanese Buddhists gave Zen its emphasis upon the sudden experience of awakening to one's true nature, to Buddha-mind. A unique discipline involving ZAZEN (seated meditation), *sanzen* (interviews with the master), and KŌAN (problem exercises) was devised to drive the disciple in unremitting concentration toward "great doubt" followed by a "great death" in which "body and mind are cast off." On penetrating to one's "original enlightenment," the Buddha-nature within, an ineffable joy and peace follow.

A first enlightenment experience is often designated *kensho,* "seeing into one's own nature," and may be followed by many experiences of "small satori" and "great satori" in the course of the cultivation and maturing of the Zen life. The essence of satori remains the same in each experience, but cultivating profundity is viewed as a lifetime discipline.

Rinzai Zen emphasizes a program of kōan exercises breaking through to deepening satori experiences, while Sōtō Zen identifies the practice of zazen itself with enlightenment. For both Rinzai and Sōtō, satori is PRAJÑĀ (unitive wisdom) which is ŚŪNYATĀ (emptiness) which is NIRVANA.

D. T. SUZUKI, Carl Jung, and Alan Watts pointed out close resemblance between satori and liberation of the "unconscious" in Western psychotherapy, and Suzuki also borrowed from Western descriptions of mystical experience, as in his eight characteristics of satori: irrationality, intuitive insight, authoritativeness, affirmation, sense of beyond, impersonal tone, feeling of exaltation, and momentariness.

Bibliography. D. T. Suzuki, *Essays in Zen Buddhism* (1953), and *The Field of Zen* (1969); P. Kapleau, *The Three Pillars of Zen* (1965). C. W. EDWARDS

SATYA SAI BĀBĀ süt´ yŭ sī bä´ bä (H; 1926-). More than through his teaching, Satya Sai Bābā is famous because of his miracles. Among these, the spontaneous creation of sacred ash, *vibhuti* (sometimes in large quantities), from his apparently empty hand remains a mystery. He also "materializes" food, jewelry, and various kinds of souvenir objects which he gives to his devotees. Moreover, some followers report such feats by him as healing, mind reading, precognition, and bilocation. Skeptics and critics have challenged his powers, but no substantial refutation has occurred in the nearly forty years of his public life.

He was born November 23, 1926 in the village of Putaparti in Andhrapradesh State in South India. On May 23, 1940 he proclaimed himself Sai Bābā reincarnated and began to perform miracles publicly. His special powers linked him with the nearly as well-known miracle-worker Sai Bābā of Shirdi, Maharashtra, who died in 1918.

According to his biographers, Satya Sai Bābā's family was at first unwilling to surrender him to the life of an AVATAR but had finally to admit his extraordinary capacities. The hagiographies of Indian saints bear certain resemblances, partly because of the developmental character of human lives in general. Nevertheless, a significant difference in Satya Sai Bābā's life story was the very early age at which he filled the role of avatar and GURU, a fact explained on the basis of arduous spiritual discipine in previous births as well as by the working of the "grace" of God who wills to appear in human form in an unexpected time, place, or person. Thus, Satya Sai Bābā contrasts with other HINDU HOLY PERSONS, such as RAMAṆA MAHARSHI, who clearly underwent a critical period of inner transformation prior to full self-realization.

In recent years Satya Sai Bābā has turned his attention to the problems of Indian society as a whole, with special emphasis upon education of the young. Like many of India's contemporary leaders, he urges preservation of indigenous cultural forms in the face of pressure to westernize. At the same time, he has an international following—including Westerners—for many of whom he resembles the Christian Savior. These followers seem drawn as much by his dynamic yet attractive personality as by the uncanny happenings which occur around him.

The cults of the most famous contemporary Hindu saints arrogate to themselves diverse aspects of the Hindu mythical and ritual traditions. It would appear that for his followers Satya Sai Bābā assumes the combined role of deity, guru, and saint not bound by the Hindu tradition alone. Worship focused upon his portrait or idol is the practice of Satya Sai Bābā groups scattered around the world.

Bibliography. H. Murphet, *Sai Baba Man of Miracles* (1975); C. S. J. White, "The Sai Bābā Movement: Approaches to the Study of Indian Saints," *JAS*. XXXI 4 (1972).

C. S. J. WHITE

SATYĀGRAHA sät yä grä´ hŭ (H—Skt.; lit. "truth force"). A key concept in the political and religious thought of GANDHI. Drawing upon the Indian association of truth *(satya)* with true "being" *(sat)*, Gandhi developed a set of political techniques based on nonviolence (AHIṂSĀ) and self-sacrifice (TAPAS) which he called *Satyāgraha*. Thus *Satyāgraha* is often equated with other kinds of nonviolent political resistance. L. D. SHINN

SAUTRĀNTIKA sou trän´ tĭ kə. *See* BUDDHIST SECTARIANISM.

SĀVITRĪ sä´ vĭ trē (H—Skt.) The name of both a Hindu goddess and of her earthly counterpart (whose story of conjugal devotion is recorded in the MAHĀBHĀRATA). Because of her refusal to abandon her husband, even in the face of death, Sāvitrī has become a symbol of love and faithfulness throughout later Indian literary traditions.

Sāvitrī's story, which serves even today as a model and inspiration for the women of India, is a classic human drama of life and love confronting death. Aśvapati, a pious and generous king, was grieved because he had not been blessed with children. In order to remedy this intolerable situation, he subjected himself to eighteen years of religious devotion to the goddess Sāvitrī. The goddess was so moved by his moral purity, his self-denial, and his daily prayers that she appeared before him and promised to give him a daughter. The child, named Sāvitrī, grew into a woman of such virtue and beauty that when the time for her to marry arrived, no man had the moral courage to ask for her hand. Being dutifully alarmed at the thought of her unhappiness and the prospect of his loss of progeny, her father sent her in search of a suitable husband. The faithful daughter visited all the royal courts of the neighboring kingdoms but could find no man worthy of her. Returning home in despair, she accidentally met Prince Satyavan, who was living in the forest with his deposed father. Sāvitrī loved him immediately and chose him for her husband. Since no man could match Satyavan in piety, virtue, and courage, everyone rejoiced with the happy couple except the sage Nārada, who foresaw that fate had decreed that the prince would die in one year. Aśvapati was shaken by this prediction and implored Sāvitrī to abandon her plan to marry Satyavan. But Sāvitrī would not be so easily deterred from achieving her heart's desire. She announced that she had made her choice of husband and would not recant.

Because of the steadfastness of her love, Sāvitrī and Satyavan were married and lived together in conjugal bliss. But after the fateful year had passed, YAMA, the god of death, came to take Satyavan. But even Yama could not separate Sāvitrī from her husband; she followed the god of death as he carried the soul of her prince away and disputed vigorously with him. So moved was the god by her love, her virtue, and her wisdom, that he granted her several wishes, including her desire to have children. When Sāvitrī told the god that she could love only Satyavan and therefore could not have children unless Satyavan were revived, the god realized that he had been trapped by his own promises and agreed to return Satyavan to life and to Sāvitrī. The prince awakened in his beloved's arms as if from a dream, and the two lived happily together with many children.

In the minds of Indians today, especially women, Sāvitrī is the symbol of beauty and grace, of purity and marital faithfulness, and of the power of a noble life. She, unlike the women in many Indian stories, was not passive, submissive, or totally dependent. She knew her own mind, was faithful only to her own heart, and by the power of her inner strength was able to overcome man's most persistent enemy, death itself.

It is this image of inner strength that led the contemporary yogin-poet, AUROBINDO, to choose the story of Sāvitrī as a vehicle for the literary expression of his personal pilgrimage. In a narrative poem of over 24,000 lines, Aurobindo has expanded the story of Sāvitrī's struggle with love and death into a saga of spiritual adventure which describes not only the yogin's personal experience, but also the evolution of consciousness of the entire race.

Bibliography. P. C. Ray, trans., *The Mahābhārata* II, 865-88; P. Nandakumar, *A Study of Sāvitrī* (1962).

J. COLLINS

SAVITṚ sŭ´ vĭ trĭ (H). *See* SŪRYA.

SAVONAROLA, GIROLAMO sä vō nä rō´ lä, jē rō lä´ mō (Ch; 1452-98). A friar of the DOMINICAN ORDER, Savonarola began preaching in 1490 against the secularism and gross immorality that were prevalent in Florence and throughout the church. His sermons, filled with apocalyptic and prophetic utterances, attracted large crowds. Calling upon the city to repent of its sins, he proclaimed that the church and the city would suffer judgment and punishment, followed by renewal. In 1494, with the army of French King Charles VIII approaching the city, Savonarola claimed that his prophecies were about to be fulfilled. The French victory overthrew the Medici government, and Savonarola was instrumental in the establishment of a Florentine republic. His influence was such, however, that Florence took on the appearance of a theocracy. Legislation regulating public life came from his visions of a godly city destined to serve as a model for the rest of Italy.

Savonarola's pro-French political stance put him at odds with the territorial goals of Pope Alexander VI. When the pontiff attempted to silence his criticisms, the friar turned his preaching against the licentiousness of Alexander's court. As long as the people of Florence supported him, Savonarola was safe. But in 1498 the populace rejected his moral strictures, and with the participation of papal emissaries, Savonarola was tortured, condemned, and executed. Almost immediately, he was seen as a victim of corruption in the church and thus helped set the stage for the Reformation. *See* REFORMATION, CATHOLIC; REFORMATION, PROTESTANT.

Bibliography. D. Weinstein, *Savonarola and Florence* (1970).

R. L. HARRISON

ṢAWM sôm (I—Arab.; "fasting"). A rigorous ritual observance of fasting enjoined on Muslims in the QUR'ĀN as one of the five PILLARS OF ISLAM; a month-long practice coinciding with RAMADAN, the ninth month in the Muslim lunar calendar. Until recent times it has been strictly observed in most Islamic countries: all non-traveling Muslim adults who are sane and in good health are expected to forego food, drink, and other bodily delights from dawn till sunset. Usually a full meal is consumed before dawn, a light snack after sunset and then another full meal after the early evening PRAYER. The period of fasting ends when the new moon, signaling the start of the tenth month, Shawwal, has been sighted. A major feast also marks the occasion.

All nights during Ramadan are holy, but none more so than Lailat al-Qadr, "the Evening of Power," which is extolled in the Qur'ān (Sura 97) as the time chosen by God for his first revelatory disclosure to Muhammad.

SUFIS attach great importance to voluntary fasting as a supererogatory means of redirecting natural energies; many SHAIKHS have practiced "the fast of David," eating one day and fasting the next, for much of their adult life.

Publicly the majority of Islamic countries still adhere to the canonical fast of Ramadan, and social pressure to uphold its strictures also continues to influence even those who would privately like to abandon, or at least modify, them.

Bibliography. "Ṣawm," *SEI*, pp. 504-7; S. H. Nasr, *Ideals and Realities of Islam* (1966), pp. 115-16; A. Schimmel, *Mystical Dimensions of Islam* (1975), pp. 114-17.

B. LAWRENCE

SAYYID sä' yĭd (I—Arab.). A term applied generally to those who possess some authority in their own sphere as a master, a husband, a tribal chief, an owner, etc.; in a stricter sense it is confined to the individual members of the *ahl al-bayt*, "people of the house," that is, MUHAMMAD'S immediate family, which included ALI. The title has come to be restricted to the descendants of al-ḤASAN and al-ḤUSAYN, although at the popular level holy persons, SUFI masters, and some prominent theologians have been addressed as sayyid.

Sayyids or *mīr* (Per.) wear green turbans to distinguish them as being descendants of the Prophet. This use of green as a mark of the sayyids seems to have originated with the Alid IMAMS, because when al-Ma'mūn, the 'ABBĀSID caliph, designated Ali al-Riḍā, the eighth Imamite imam, as his successor in 816, he gave up the traditional 'Abbāsid black for green. Among the SHI'A, men of learning (sayyids) wear black turbans in contrast to the white ones worn by the nonsayyid.

In addition sayyids are forbidden to receive *ṣadaqa*, charitable gifts. According to some jurists this prohibition was applied specifically only to members of the Hāshimite clan (*see* HĀSHIM), and thus only to those who could be considered close enough kin of the Prophet to qualify for the share given his family in the distribution of the special tax, *al-khums* ("the fifth"). Imams descending from FĀTIMA also had the privilege of being addressed as *ibn rasūl allāh* (son of the Prophet), and early FATIMIDS, the Idrīsids of Morocco, and Alid rulers of Tabaristan, used the title of sayyid as the token of their descent from Muhammad's family. The sayyids were recognized by the Arabs, Turks, and Persians as being among the *ahl al-bayt* and were sometimes addressed as al-SHARIF, as in the case of the sharifs of MECCA, who were descendants of al-Ḥasan.

Devotion to the sayyids is an integral part of Shi'ite piety, deriving from the verse of the QUR'ĀN which says: "Say (O Muhammad), I do not ask of you any reward for it but love for my near relatives" (42:23). The "near relatives" are Fāṭima's descendants, on whom blessings are to be conferred in ritual prayers (*ṣalāt*) and at other times. This devotion (*walaya*) will save believers on the Day of Judgment.

A. A. SACHEDINA

SCHECHTER, SOLOMON shĕk' tər (Ju; 1850-1915). The founder of CONSERVATIVE JUDAISM in the United States. He emphasized the community of Israel, which he called "catholic Israel," as the source of religious authority. His scholarly reputation rests on his *Studies in Judaism* (1896-1924) and *Some Aspects of Rabbinic Theology* (1909), and on his discovery of the Cairo Geniza.

L. FAGEN

SCHILLEBEECKX, EDWARD shĭl' ə bēks (Chr; 1914-). Belgian Roman Catholic especially concerned with the legitimate interpretation of the religious tradition. He identifies two sources for theology: the biblical message and our present world of experience. The task of theology is to interpret Christian faith in a way that is true to the gospel and adequate in the modern world. *See* THEOLOGY, CONTEMPORARY CHRISTIAN §4.

D. F. OTTATI

SCHOLASTICISM (Ch). Though frequently used (often with derogatory overtones) to denote a particular set of doctrinal positions allegedly dominant throughout the Middle Ages, scholasticism is in fact a looser and broader term. It may more appropriately be taken to denote a movement of thought characteristic especially (though not exclusively) of medieval schools and universities from the twelfth to the early sixteenth centuries and distinctive both in its method and content: in its method by a marked emphasis on systematizing knowledge, and a rigorous use of logic to find acceptable ground amid the clash of competing authorities; in its content by a persistent attempt to apply the philosophic reason not only to logic, epistemology, ethics, natural science, and metaphysics, but also to those fundamental Christian beliefs grounded not in reason but in scriptural revelation.

1. **Foundations of medieval scholasticism.** Three thinkers of late Roman antiquity laid the foundations of scholasticism. AUGUSTINE of Hippo (354-430) provided the motive; Cassiodorus (*ca.* 485–*ca.* 580) identified the institutional means; Boethius (*ca.* 480–*ca.* 525) mediated the materials that made the method possible. It was important for the future of European intellectual life that Augustine shared with his pagan predecessors a high estimate of the value of a general education in the liberal arts. In his influential work, *De Doctrina Christiana,* he urged Christian scholars to retain what amounted to the old Roman curriculum in the liberal arts as necessary preparation for the more important and higher studies in Christian philosophy and theology. Given the turbulent political conditions of the early medieval period, the disappearance of the traditional educational institutions, and the concomitant decline of learning, it is even more important that educated monks like Cassiodorus—or JEROME (*ca.* 331–420)—should have succeeded in making the study of the liberal arts an integral part of monastic life.

It had become customary to regard the liberal arts as seven in number and to divide them into two groups: the *trivium* (grammar, rhetoric, and logic) and the *quadrivium* (theory of music, astronomy, arithmetic, and geometry). In the early Middle Ages far more attention was devoted to the subjects of the *trivium* than to those of the *quadrivium,* with special emphasis on grammar and rhetoric, at least until the second half of the twelfth century. While this represents a less restricted curriculum than the names themselves might suggest, its limitations are readily obvious. Indeed, its dominance is explicable only if one recalls that the knowledge of Greek had long since been lost in the West and that direct contact with the Greek philosophical and scientific tradition was limited for centuries to a handful of translated fragments. However Platonic the sympathies of many medieval thinkers, especially those of the twelfth century, they were largely dependent for their Platonism upon what they learned from such authors as Cicero, Augustine, and the Neoplatonists. Before the mid-twelfth century Aristotle was even less well known, and the masters of logic were forced to rely on the merely introductory treatises to Aristotle's logic that were available in the Latin translations made by Boethius.

Thin though it may have been, it was enough to enable ANSELM of Canterbury in the late eleventh century to move boldly in the direction of applying philosophic reason to the task of eliciting the meaning of revealed truths. In so doing he evoked once more the maxim of Augustine: "Understand in order that you may believe; believe in order that you may understand," and the signal he gave, amplified in the twelfth century in the school of Anselm of Laon (d. 1117) and of his brother Ralph (d. 1133), came to set the tone for the flourishing cathedral schools of the day and for the universities that began to appear at the end of the century.

2. **Scholasticism in the high and later Middle Ages.** During the course of the twelfth century two critical developments occurred which together determined the final shape of medieval scholasticism. The first was the finalization of the scholastic method; the second, the beginning of the reception of Aristotle's writings, an event that was to determine the content of scholastic thinking.

In the school of Anselm of Laon we encounter the first systematic organization of theological questions, with divergent passages from the Scriptures and from the church fathers arranged in collections of "Sentences." So far as its distinctive method is concerned, scholasticism arose out of the attempt to resolve by criticism and by subtle logical distinctions the problems inevitably generated by the discrepancies in the viewpoints of the authorities cited. The method was hammered out in the course of the twelfth century and it was not only logicians and theologians like PETER ABELARD or PETER LOMBARD who contributed to its formation. Abelard, it is true, applied the dialectical method to theology without reservation, and his *Sic et non* proved highly influential. Again, the *Sentences* of Peter Lombard, in which the scholastic method was fully achieved, was to become the major textbook of the medieval theologians. But one should not overlook the contributions of lawyers like Gratian (d. *ca.* 1159), in whose *Decretum* conflicting legal authorities are balanced against each other and a systematic attempt is made to harmonize them. Indeed, the full title of that great work, the *Concord of Discordant Canons,* suggests at once the intellectual dilemma that gave rise to the scholastic method and the nature of the method itself.

The renewal of direct contact with the philosophical writings of Greek antiquity did much, however, to sharpen that dilemma. During the late twelfth and early thirteenth centuries, via translations made from the Greek itself and from Arabic translations of the Greek, the Latin world gradually came into contact for the first time not just with Aristotle's logic in its totality but with the whole body of his writings and with an extensive array of Arabic commentaries on those writings, especially those of the great Muslim philosopher Averroes (IBN RUSHD, 1126-98).

The effect of this reception of Aristotle was dramatic. The gradual recovery of his logic had pushed grammar and rhetoric to one side within the *trivium*, and now it was the fate of logic to be put in its place as simply one part of the first philosophic and scientific system Western thinkers had encountered. Despite initial footdragging on the part of the ecclesiastical authorities, by 1255 the curriculum of the faculty of arts at the University of Paris included the whole corpus of Aristotle's writings. It was in his categories that budding philosophers and professional theologians increasingly were trained to think, and with his scheme of things that they had to struggle to harmonize their Christian beliefs.

That proved to be no easy task. Aristotle's world view was much harder to reconcile with the biblical vision of God, man, and the universe than was the Platonic and Neoplatonic viewpoint with which such scholars as Augustine or Anselm of Canterbury had succeeded in coming to terms. The difficulties involved, moreover, were exacerbated by the fact that the crucial portions of Aristotle first arrived in Arabic, interwoven with the paraphrases and commentaries of Avicenna (IBN SĪNĀ, 980-1037) and Averroes to such a degree that for some time Latin thinkers were unable to determine which ideas were actually Aristotle's and which those of his commentators, whose thinking, after all, was by no means purely Aristotelian in inspiration.

Thus the modified Aristotle with whom the scholastics first had to cope appeared to teach not only the eternity of the world but its necessity. That is to say, his world was not a created world presupposing a free decision of the omnipotent divine will, but a world that necessarily and eternally flowed from the divine principle, on the analogy of a stream flowing ceaselessly from its source. As such it was a determined world in which everything had to be what it was and in which there was no room for either the providence of God or the free will of man. To the extent, moreover, that the Aristotle encountered was that of Averroes, he was also an Aristotle who denied to man any form of individual immortality.

The scholastics of the mid-thirteenth century faced up to this Aristotle in three broadly differing ways. (i) Teachers of philosophy in the university faculties of arts, such as Siger of Brabant (d. *ca.* 1284) and Boethius of Dacia (d. late thirteenth century) at Paris, made their peace with Aristotle by digging in along the lines of professional departmentalism and separating what they taught as philosophers, or as commentators on "*the* philosopher" (i.e. Aristotle), from what they believed (or claimed to believe) as Christians. This course, however, left them open to the charge of espousing the so-called Latin Averroist doctrine of the "double truth."

For theologians, however, no such option existed. Either they had to turn their backs on Aristotle's metaphysics and natural philosophy, and by so doing cut themselves off from the more advanced intellectual currents of their day, or they had somehow to make him acceptable. (ii) One group, composed largely though not exclusively of FRANCISCANS, while making use in greater and lesser degree of Aristotelian terminology and absorbing some of his ideas, drew the line at the point at which such ideas appeared to conflict with the teaching of Augustine. This group, which includes such figures as Alexander of Hales (d. 1245), BONAVENTURE, Matthew of Aquasparta (d. 1302), Richard Fishacre (d. 1248), Robert Kilwardby (d. 1279), and John Peckham (d. 1292), is frequently labeled "Augustinian." (iii) Another group, to which the DOMINICAN friar ALBERTUS MAGNUS belonged, responded with greater openness to Aristotle. They sought first to penetrate the veil of commentary and to ascertain how much of the troublesome material must with certainty be ascribed to Aristotle himself. It was out of such attempts to isolate the authentic teaching of Aristotle and to reconcile it with Christian belief that there emerged the synthesis that is by common consent regarded as the greatest of medieval philosophico-theological achievements, the system that THOMAS AQUINAS elaborated and that found its most impressive statement in his *Summa Theologica*. Being convinced that it was Aristotle who had most profoundly explored the rational intelligibility of the world, he sought, while blending Augustinian and Aristotelian ideas, to base his own understanding of that world upon a remarkably thoroughgoing assimilation of Aristotelian rationalism. But this was at the price of being regarded by many contemporaries as having assimilated Aristotelian rationalism somewhat more successfully than any Christian should.

Nowhere is the price more evident than in his assuming the primacy of reason over will, not only in man but also in God. When in late thirteenth century academic circles a theological reaction set in, it sought to vindicate the freedom and omnipotence of God at the expense, if need be, of the ultimate intelligibility of the world. Thus many subsequent theologians, especially the Franciscans, tended to take divine omnipotence as their fundamental principle, to set God over against the world he had created, and to regard the order of that world as deriving not from any sort of participation in the divine reason, but rather from the peremptory mandate of an autonomous divine will. This tendency was manifest in the primacy that DUNS SCOTUS accorded to the divine will over the divine intellect. It became dominant in the thinking of such philosophers and theologians as Robert Holcot (d. 1349), Pierre d'Ailly (d. 1420), Gabriel Biel (d. 1495), and Bartholomaeus von Usingen (LUTHER'S teacher at

Erfurt, d. 1532) who aligned themselves with the "nominalist" school, which owed its fundamental inspiration to William of Occam. That school taught that general concepts or terms, such as "mankind" or "the church," have no objective existence, in contrast to the "realist" school, which asserted that they do. Realism grew in influence in the later Middle Ages, but never triumphed over its rivals.

3. **Postmedieval scholasticism.** Although scholasticism fell into disrepute during the era of Renaissance and Reformation, it never wholly lost its vitality. Three phases in its postmedieval career may be singled out as important manifestations of that vitality.

First was the Catholic scholasticism of the Counter-Reformation era which, from the mid-sixteenth to the mid-seventeenth centuries, was espoused especially by teachers of the Dominican, Jesuit, and Franciscan orders. While it betrayed no doctrinal uniformity and was nourished by Catholic universities across Europe and in the New World, it drew its greatest support from Spain and its most profound inspiration from Thomas Aquinas, whose *Summa Theologica* now replaced Lombard's *Sentences* as the standard textbook in theology. It was in Spain that the Dominicans Francisco de Vitoria (d. 1546) and Domingo de Soto (d. 1560) shared with the Jesuits Luis de Molina (d. 1600) and Francisco Suarez (d. 1617) the distinction of developing on Thomistic foundations a body of legal and political theory that contributed greatly to the elaboration of the natural-law theory of the state (see esp. Suarez, *Tractatus de Legibus,* 1612).

Second was the Protestant scholasticism that developed under Melanchthon's inspiration (despite Luther's antipathy toward the schoolmen) and by the early seventeenth century in Germany, the Low Countries, and England was producing works that can properly be designated as scholastic—e.g., the *Opus Metaphysicum* of Christoph Scheibler (d. 1659)—and that were destined to make their influence felt even in the colonies of the New World.

Third was the revival of scholasticism that took place in Roman Catholic universities and seminaries, notably at Rome and Louvain, during the course of the nineteenth and twentieth centuries. Primarily an attempt to recover the authentic teaching of Aquinas and to bring his insights to bear on the problems and dilemmas of the modern world and modern intellectual life, it owed much to papal sponsorship, notably that of Pope Leo XIII (1810-1903). In the wake of the Second Vatican Council (1962-65), however, although historical studies of medieval scholasticism continue to flourish, Thomism itself has come to exercise a diminished influence over Roman Catholic theology.

Bibliography. E. Gilson, *History of Christian Philosophy in the Middle Ages* (1955); D. Knowles, *The Evolution of Medieval Thought* (1962); F. Copleston, *History of Philosophy* (1946-75), vols. 2, 3, 4, and 6; B. Hamilton, *Political Thought in Sixteenth Century Spain* (1963); J. L. Perrier, *The Revival of Scholastic Philosophy in the Nineteenth Century* (1909); *New Catholic Encyclopedia,* XII, "Scholastic Method," "Scholastic Philosophy," "Scholastic Terms and Axioms," "Scholastic Theology," "Scholasticism."

F. Oakley

SCHWEITZER, ALBERT shvīt´ zər (Ch; 1875-1965). Alsatian musician, theologian, missionary. After gaining fame as an interpreter of Bach, and making signal contributions to the study of Jesus and Paul, he won a medical degree and founded in 1913 a hospital at Lambaréné, Gabon, where, except for occasional visits to Europe and the United States, he worked until his death. He propounded an ethic based on reverence for life, including the nonhuman.

R. Bullard

SCIENTOLOGY. A religious movement founded in 1952 by L. Ron Hubbard, U.S. science fiction writer and author of the best-selling book *Dianetics* (1950), which launched a popular self-enhancement movement out of which Scientology emerged. The basic postulate of dianetics is that experience, in this or previous lives, is recorded in the brain as "engrams," later restimulated by similar but not identical situations to cause inappropriate and self-defeating behavior. Through processed exposure of the engrams one can erase them, "go clear," and be "at cause" of one's behavior.

Scientology accepts the dianetic teaching and provides "processing" for going clear. But it also imparts other concepts later taught by Hubbard, especially those regarding the "thetan" or soul. The thetan is not only entrapped by its own engrams, but is also caught in MEST (matter, energy, space, time) itself, and must be liberated through further teachings offered through the movement to become an OT, "Operating Thetan."

Scientology has ministers who perform some religious rites and sacraments, and who have also often been involved in social work. But their most time-consuming function is generally individual counseling, for which a financial contribution is expected.

Scientology is tightly organized from the top down, with a close-knit inner circle and many highly committed adherents. It has been the topic of considerable controversy and several encounters with government agencies in the U.S. and the British Commonwealth. In the 1970s it had several hundred thousand followers, at least, and impressive property holdings.

Bibliography. R. Ellwood, *Religious and Spiritual Groups in Modern America* (1973); G. Malko, *Scientology: The Now Religion* (1970); R. Wallis, *The Road to Total Freedom: A Sociological Analysis of Scientology* (1976).

R. S. Ellwood

SCOFIELD, CYRUS INGERSON (Ch; 1843-1921). Fundamentalist leader and editor of the *Scofield*

Reference Bible (1909), which presents DISPENSATIONALIST eschatology in notes and study aids alongside the text of the King James Version. It became the standard reference Bible of conservatives. A revision, *The New Scofield Reference Bible,* was published in 1967. G. MILLER

SCRIPTURES, SACRED. Sacred scriptures are oral and/or written traditions which tend to be concerned with (1) the expression and transmission of spoken and written sounds and words as holy or sacred power; (2) the meaning, value, ideals, cohesiveness, and self-identity of a people in their environment together with the standards of normal and ideal behavior for individuals; (3) orienting and relating the people toward reality, the transcendent, or the divine; (4) diagnosing and resolving human concerns, hopes, and anxieties by transforming human existence into desired practical and ideal forms; and (5) depicting and exhorting a holy way or path authenticated, revealed, or discovered through a holy person or religious community.

1. Scriptural contents and their usage. *a) Sacred sounds and holy words.* Until recent times holy traditions were orally transmitted for extended periods of time before being committed to written form. Except in oral cultures (such as VEDIC HINDUISM) where special memorization techniques were utilized, oral memory is generally thematic rather than verbatim, so that incident and narrative structure were preserved, but speeches were rendered typically rather than exactly (except for short passages that were regarded as particularly important). Since oral cultures have memory but no written records, the past is present in speech and social institutions. The repetition of tradition kept knowledge available. The holy word was, and to a great extent remains, a sound event spoken aloud and heard by living persons.

The word is in part effective due to the information it communicates. The tradition names the gods and goddesses and tells their myths and the stories of their actions so that the worshiper, knowing who they are, may invoke their presence and power. Because they reveal the divine, sacred words are powerful. The ancient hymn singers and priests of the Hindu Vedas recited the creative speech of the divinity Vac, which eventually developed into the BRAHMAN, the holy power of the great rituals that symbolizes Ultimate Reality. In the Hebrew BIBLE God creates through divine speech. In the Gospel of John, divine speech is the eternal "Word of God" incarnate in the man JESUS.

The power of sacred words frequently concerns the shape and structure of the sounds as much as it depends upon the cognitive meaning. Especially in the religious traditions derived from Indian roots, the sciences of melody, meter, breathing patterns, chant, and MANTRA become keys to sacred power and are incorporated into the sacred tradition. Tradition brings holy power to bear also by manipulating syllables and word stems, by associative etymologies, and by acrostic arrangements of lines. The mystery of the sacred word is suggested by its being whispered.

When oral traditions are written down, they become holy objects to be treated with awe and veneration, sometimes to be accorded divine honors (e.g. the ĀDI GRANTH Sahib in the SIKH tradition). Sacred language tends to be archaic, and translation, at least for cultic use, is often resisted, requiring those who preserve the tradition to learn the original language of the text (e.g., Arabic QUR'ĀN, Sanskrit VEDAS, and Hebrew Bible). Written scriptures are worn as amulets, serve as vouchers for oaths, vows, blessings, and curses, are applied to exorcise unwelcome spirits, and are utilized as devices for divination. Those who hear, memorize, or copy sacred tradition are blessed (e.g., BHAGAVAD GĪTĀ 18. 70-71; Rev. 1:3).

b) Sacred scriptures and the people of the faith. Sacred tradition, oral and written, belongs to a specific people with whom it has an interdependent living relationship. The sacred sounds express and celebrate holy tradition through holy, authoritative persons for a people who belong to the tradition and who consent to its authority. The authority of the tradition stems in part from its claims for presenting an ancient truth or wisdom. CONFUCIUS claimed to be recovering the ways of Yao and Shun, Chinese mythical sage-kings. The DHARMA or teaching perceived by GAUTAMA the BUDDHA was taught by previous Buddhas. The Qur'ān reveals the eternal truth previously revealed in other "books." Priests as mediators of the tradition are typically conservative transmitters of the past. Prophets speak to the needs of particular occasions within the parameters of the tradition, often with the voice of the god(s). The authority of other mediators is vouched for by their special relation to ultimate reality or the divine. JAINA and Buddhist scriptures consist in large measure of words of the Master (MAHĀVĪRA, Gautama Buddha). AVATARS and the INCARNATION embody the transcendent, and their words and acts become scriptures. ZOROASTER received Asha, the truth, in visions of Ahura Mazda expressed in his *Gāthās* (hymns).

Sacred scriptures express and provide identity, authorization, and ideals for the people of the tradition. The narrative of the people of the faith tells how various institutions were authorized, how agreements and covenants were ratified, the history of government and dynasties, and the relationship of authority and power. The NIHON SHOKI and the KOJIKI tell of the birth of the world, the stories of the gods and goddesses, the formation of the Japanese islands, and the divine institution of the office of the emperor. The narratives of the Hindu Epics and PURĀṆAS (lit. "stories of ancient things"), like the narratives of many scriptures, tell as well how the land was acquired, the actions of the gods at various places (particularly those of cultic significance), list important peoples and families, trace genealogies, and in the process provide a charter for and theories of human history and human society. The recitation of the story is celebration and renewal as communal event with reenactment of the paradigmatic events of the social ethos in ritual plays, dances, and games that both express social structure and mitigate and compensate for its inequities.

Scriptural models for proper behavior tend to spread over the entire range of cultural life, including the delineation of public and domestic law, customs, the standards of morality and proper intention, regulations concerning purity and pollution, rewards for right conduct, punishments for infractions or derelictions of duty, and compensations and expiations.

Most of the important forms of oral expression of the culture eventually find their place in the written tradition. Sacred scriptures readily assimilate oral tradition and literature that concentrates upon the typical, such as folk wisdom, folktales, legends, and fabulous tales that often circulate from one culture to another. Cross-cultural folk influence is especially noticeable in stories of the lives of religious founders.

c) Relations with the divine. The self-sustaining character of sacred truth that is eternally true is characteristic of all sacred scriptures to some extent, but it is especially emphasized in scriptural traditions that center around an impersonal ultimate reality and a fixed, dependable order for the concrete, phenomenal world. Jaina scriptures, early TAOIST scriptures, and the Hindu Vedas derive their authority from their self-luminosity, their self-evident eternal truth, rather than from gods.

Accounts of active relationships with the divine are prominent in sacred scriptures in general, including perhaps the majority of later Hindu scriptures. The character of the gods is spelled out in their names or attributes, their acts in the past, their promises, decisions, and revelations, and where appropriate, in cosmogonic myths. The divine appears in dreams, trance, auditions, inspiration, visions, and during ordinary consciousness. Much of sacred scripture purports to be the speech of gods (especially the Qur'ān, also sections of the Hebrew Bible), a narrative of the acts of gods in relation to their people, or the words of the Master in whom the divine transcendent is present in unique fashion (especially THERAVĀDA Buddhist Suttas, the BHAGAVAD GĪTĀ and the NEW TESTAMENT Gospels). The divine/transcendent is the focus of group worship, private devotion, and much of the ritual. Worship and devotion both address the divine and use the divine words in sacred scripture to empower, to address, and to hear. Sacred scripture makes the gods known through their names, attributes, and actions so that their presence may be invoked. By recalling their commandments, covenants, and promises, scripture makes worship possible. The worshipers sing hymns of praise and voice prayers of thanksgiving and petition to gods, offer sacrifices and donations, and confess their faith and trust.

d) Transformations of human existence. Religion is a way of life, with stages through which one passes, crises to be met, problems to be solved, and ideals toward which one aspires. Religious rituals linked to life cycles are generally intended to effect changes in individuals and groups from one social stage to another (e.g., from biological individual to member of society, to adulthood, to marriage, to eldership, to life after death); to sanctify and secure the rhythms of time and the sequence of seasons; and to lay out and renew sacred spaces and sacred institutions. Transformations of crisis deal with unforeseen, irregular threats to both group and individual welfare such as human or animal illness, problems with the environment, factionalism or threat from other groups, wrongdoing that requires adjudication and expiation, and crises of leadership.

Sacred scriptures give expression in woes and laments to the serious evils with which humans must live and die; in confessions for the sinfulness, frailty, or ignorance of human nature; and in sober descriptive declarations of the finitude, contingency, and insignificance of human life. To these problems the sacred scriptures bring a context of meaning and hope for eventual resolution. Resolution sometimes leads to expectations of a new saving power that has intervened but not yet come to fruition through avatars, culture heroes, incarnations, or new prophets. Intervention is sometimes expected in a future that inaugurates a new age, or sets things right in individual afterlife or at the end of the world in a universal judgment.

Transformations to an ideal status highlight the transcendent aspirations of sacred traditions. The Hindu holy man's (SANNYĀSIN) initiation is marked by his funeral (i.e., the death of his worldly life). The Buddhist monk withdraws from society into a new community, the SAṄGHA, where his career is both for his own liberation and for the ideal good of the society. Beyond the official status of holy man or monk that may be conferred in an extraordinary rite of passage is the inner spiritual transformation that occurs between individuals and the divine/transcendent/ultimate reality. This transformation may be for individuals in any status (laymen and laywomen) particularly when it is bestowed by a god as grace in relation to their faith, trust, and obedience. For some persons the quest for transformation becomes their vocation—a total transformation of the human condition in union with ultimate reality or with god, saved or liberated from all anxiety and dread. Ideal transformation is a turning around of the self, a rebirth or awakening. Sacred scriptures guard against misunderstanding by using forms of communication that for many readers appear to be deliberately obscure. The truth is sometimes presented in puzzles, mazes, riddles, paradoxes, and parables; in exaggerations, contradictions, negations, jokes, secret language, and absurdities. Sacred language becomes a vehicle that communicates only when it *moves* the hearer toward the ideal.

2. **Written texts, canons, and interpretation.** Tradition, the community of faith, religious authority, and the general context are interdependent. A living religious tradition both reinterprets itself as these factors change and does so in a fashion that preserves the continuity and authority of the truth of the past. With the exception of the Hindu tradition, in which oral transmission has remained the norm until the twentieth century, most sacred traditions were committed at least in part to writing at fairly early dates. Primary scriptures become relatively fixed when there is general consensus among the people of the faith, when there is an authoritative institution that can determine the limits of scripture, when it is believed that incorrect religious belief is socially and politically divisive, and when a competitive situation obtains in which the people feel that the "true faith" and "true revelation" need to be limited to protect against misuse and misappropriation.

Canons ("norm," "measure") of scripture and levels of scriptural authority have been "officially" proclaimed in most of the religious traditions with a Semitic heritage. Jewish tradition ranks the three sections of Hebrew scripture (comprehensively referred to as "Tanak") as follows: TORAH (Books of Moses), Nebi'im (Prophets), and Kethubim (Writings). A rough order of importance for many Christian traditions would be Gospels, Epistles, and OLD TESTAMENT. In the Islamic tradition the sources of the SHARIA (pathway) are ranked: The Qur'ān, the SUNNA (customary usage of the Prophet) collected in ḤADĪTH, IJMĀ' (consensus of the community), and *qiyās* (analogical reasoning). As the Islamic case makes clear, tradition and text interact in interpretation. There are favorite scriptural passages which serve as "keys" by which the whole of the scripture is interpreted. Different levels of meaning for scriptural passages are also distinguished in different communities, with the "spiritual" meaning extremely variable.

Canons of sacred scripture exist in Asian religious traditions, although with less rigidity. Hindu tradition distinguishes ŚRUTI ("what is heard") from SMṚTI ("what is remembered"). But only a few Hindu communities use these limitations with any strictness. The Ādi Granth Sahib is primary scripture for the Sikh tradition. Some Hindu theistic sects have favorite primary texts, but no two agree on the list of texts considered authoritative. Theravāda Buddhists have a relatively fixed collection called the TRIPIṬAKA (*see* PALI CANON), but this is the canon only of Theravāda Buddhism. MAHĀYĀNA Buddhist scriptures are vast. The Tibetan translations called Kanjur (translation of the ordinances) run over a hundred volumes, while the Tanjur (translation of the doctrine) runs some 225 volumes. The Japanese translation of the Mahāyāna texts is over 6,000 volumes.

Written scriptural texts are not necessarily fixed. A scripture can be changed by editorial glosses, rearrangement, and by translation into new languages. New texts can be added to the old tradition by archaicization, especially by discovering "lost" texts that are then published under the name of authoritative figures from the distant past. New sets of scriptures are frequently validated in relation to previous scripture by use of the theory that previous scriptures were accommodated to spiritual immaturity, and that the disclosure of the truth is successive (New Testament in relation to the Old Testament; the Qur'ān in relation to both the Hebrew Bible and the New Testament; Mahāyāna Buddhist scriptures in relation to HĪNAYĀNA [small vehicle] scriptures). The claim that the present age is spiritually degenerate and needs a new dispensation authorizes many religious scriptures (Hindu Purāṇas, Sikh Granth, Buddhist LOTUS SŪTRA).

Sacred oral tradition precedes and overlaps sacred scripture. As long as the tradition is alive, it retains an oral form in its recitation in individual and communal worship. The control exercised by religious authorities in oral-aural cultures through their choice of parts of the tradition to recite and through their accompanying interpretation continues after the tradition is written by hand. With few written copies available and with illiteracy general, sacred scriptures continue to be available primarily in cultic celebration accompanied by their authoritative interpretation. With the introduction of printed scriptures and general literacy, sacred scriptures in the modern period became publicly available documents for individuals to read and interpret as they are able, separated from the community and the continuing oral tradition of interpretation of religious authorities.

Bibliography. G. Lanczkowski, *Sacred Writings: A Guide to the Literature of Religions* (1966); F. F. Bruce and E. G. Rupp, *Holy Book and Holy Tradition* (1968); M. Pye and R. Morgan, *The Cardinal Meaning: Essays in Comparative Hermeneutics* (1973); F. Heiler, *Erscheinungsformen und Wesen der Religion* (1961), pp. 266-364; J. Leipoldt, *Heilige Schriften: Betrachtungen zur Religionsgeschichte der antiken Mittelmeerwelt* (1953); W. O'Flaherty, *The Critical Study of Sacred Texts* (1979).

J. Y. FENTON

SECOND COMING (Ch). The belief that CHRIST will physically return to earth at the end of the present age. The Greek term for the event is *parousia* (lit. "presence," though sometimes denoting "coming" or "arriving"); most scholars agree that the NT writers viewed it as imminent. The phrase "second coming" was not employed until *ca.* A.D. 150. *See* ESCHATOLOGY.

T. O. HALL, JR.

Drawing by Wm. Kurelek. American Jewish Archives, Hebrew Union College—Jewish Institute of Religion

Boy searching for the *afikomen* in the Seder ceremony

SEDER sē´ dĕr (Ju—Heb.; lit. "order"). The dinner meal on the first night or first two nights of PASSOVER. The ritual recalls the bondage in Egypt and the Exodus and its attending miracles. Among the foods eaten are MATZAH (unleavened bread), bitter herbs, roasted meat, and greens. Children are encouraged to participate in various parts of the ceremony, including the search for a hidden matzah (*afikomen*). *See* HAGGADAH. D. J. SCHNALL

SEE (Ch—Lat. "seat"). The ecclesiastical authority of a BISHOP in some churches; the area governed, and the center or city from which that oversight is administered; most commonly used to refer to the POPE'S jurisdiction (Apostolic or Holy See). K. WATKINS

SEFER BAHIR sā´ fĕr bä hĕr´ (Ju—Heb.; lit. "book of brilliance"). Fundamental text of Jewish MYSTICISM that appeared in southern France at the end of the twelfth century. Some of its terminology and the general character of its doctrines show a marked affiliation with the various GNOSTIC systems of the Hellenistic era.

1. **Sefirot.** The heart of its teaching is the doctrine of *sefirot,* the constituent elements of God's emergent, inner life. Since the *Bahir* represents the stage of KABBALA just prior to its adaptation of Neoplatonic philosophy, it lacks both the emanationist scheme and the concept of EN SOF (the transcendent, totally hidden reality of God himself) so characteristic of later developments in Jewish mysticism. God does not *have* these sefirot, he *is* these sefirot; they are the "potencies" of his creative being corresponding to, and concretized everywhere in, the language of scripture, the workings of the universe, and the forms of Jewish ritual and prayer. Reinterpreting an older source, the *Sefer Yeẓirah* (Book of Creation), which spoke of ten primal cosmological numbers (sefirot) created by God, the *Bahir* fixes the number of these divine potencies or qualities at ten. While they are usually discussed as a whole in the symbolic language of ten kings, lights, or utterances by which the world was created, there is a basic division between the upper or first three and the lower seven, a division universally accepted in later Kabbalistic literature. The first is usually termed Thought or "Supernal Crown," and is symbolically associated with the letter *aleph,* the human ear, and the Holy Palace. The second is Wisdom or Primal Torah, and the third is Understanding, Knowledge, articulate Torah, or the Mother of the World. The lower seven are variously associated with the symbolism of seven children of the King, seven Holy Forms, seven Praises of God, or the seven Days of Creation. *See* illustration for KABBALA.

2. **Femininity.** The treatment of the tenth sefirah is of particular significance in the *Bahir* and

throughout the Kabbala, in that the symbols associated with it are unmistakably feminine. Here the older rabbinic notions of *Shekhina,* God's immanence, and *Knesset Israel,* the covenantal community of earthly Israel, are combined with philosophic notions of God's created glory *(kavod)* and then transformed into one of the potencies of God himself. The *Bahir* abounds in parables and homilies concerning queens, brides, princesses, seas, vessels, daughters, and precious stones, all of which allude to androgynous or quasi-biological processes within God. K. P. Bland

SEFIROT sə fē rōt′ (Ju). *See* Sefer Bahir §1; Kabbala §3.

SEICHŌ NO IE sā chō′ nō ē′ ē (Jap.; lit. "house of growth"). A syncretistic religious movement purporting to teach the truth that is common to all religions as understood and reformulated by Taniguchi Masaharu. The emphasis is on health, happiness, and prosperity, made possible through the power of mind free of all negativism.

1. **History.** The story of Seichō no Ie is largely the story of its founder, Taniguchi Masaharu. An intelligent, sensitive, articulate person, Taniguchi experienced much hardship and frustration as a child, youth, and young adult, partly as a result of untoward circumstances, partly as a result of his own poor judgment. At age nineteen he entered the literature department of Waseda University in Tokyo. Though he remained for only one year, his exposure to the works of such American and European writers as Poe, Tolstoy, Wilde, Baudelaire, and Schopenhauer produced in him an intoxication with new ideas. The interplay of these and other Western ideas with those derived from Japanese classics became a hallmark of Taniguchi's intellect. To this he added experimentation with psychic phenomena—hypnotism and spiritualism—and participation, for four years, in Ōmoto. What gradually emerged from the crucible of his trouble-plagued life was the conviction that suffering is unreal—that the material is only the shadow of the mind, and that therefore the escape from suffering begins with one's own wish and is effected through the power of one's own mind. This is the gist of an essay which he wrote and published in 1921, the quick and profitable sale of which proved that there was a market for his message. However, it was not until 1928 that he discovered the key that really opened up his career. In a bookstall in Kobe he found a copy of *The Law of Mind in Action* by Fenwicke Holmes of the New Thought movement in the U.S. Here he found his own basic thesis compellingly stated and saw the means by which to synthesize Buddhist pantheism and Christian theism.

Seichō no Ie had its official beginning in 1930 when Taniguchi began to publish a magazine bearing this name. The initial subscribers became the charter members of the new movement. From its first headquarters in Kobe it was moved to Tokyo in 1934 and has remained centered there.

The decade of the 1930s, a time of impressive growth for Seichō no Ie, saw also the rapid escalation of Japanese militarism and imperialism. During a period when many religious movements were being harassed or even disbanded by the government, Seichō no Ie enjoyed a favored status. Taniguchi personally endorsed the principles and activities of the government and, through the publications and activities of Seichō no Ie, sought to enhance the morale and effectiveness of the fighting men and the factory workers. Because of apparent implication in the war effort Taniguchi and some of his staff were purged in 1945 by the Occupation officials. Though Seichō no Ie suffered some decline in the immediate postwar period, Taniguchi was able to hold his organization together and when the Occupation ended in 1952 was fully ready to resume his publishing activities. Since then the movement has grown remarkably, with a special appeal to middle- and upper-middle-class Japanese, including a notable number of intellectuals. During this period Seichō no Ie also has achieved prominence for its espousal of and leadership in numerous ultra-conservative or right-wing causes.

2. **Scripture.** Taniguchi is a prodigious writer, and certain of his writings comprise the scripture of Seichō no Ie. The basic canon of teachings is a compilation entitled *Seimei no Jissō* (lit. "the reality [truth] of life"). It began with the collecting in a single volume of the first issues of *Seichō no Ie* magazine and has since been so substantially augmented by an autobiography of Taniguchi and other of his writings that it now includes more than forty volumes.

A part of the canon is a notable text entitled *The Holy Sūtra of Seichō no Ie: Nectarean Shower of Holy Doctrines,* purportedly revealed by an angel to Taniguchi in 1931 while he sat in meditation. This is a precise, unequivocal statement of each basic tenet in language reminiscent of Apocalyptic literature.

3. **Organization.** In an impressive headquarters building in Tokyo the world organization of Seichō no Ie is centered. From there the lines of authority flow downward to regional, prefectural and local agencies and outward directly to overseas installations. The organizaton exists principally for disseminating the teachings of Taniguchi, the movement's charismatic medium of revelation and power. In this effort local agencies play an effective role through the distribution of literature and the sponsorship of lectures and retreats.

4. **Doctrine.** The fundamental doctrine of Seichō no Ie is that human beings are children of God (Buddha) and therefore, sharing the perfection that characterizes all divine creation, are naturally happy and healthy. Sin and guilt are unreal, that is, not a part of creation; but a misguided sense of their reality can produce afflictions that also are experienced and perceived as real, though they are not. Deliverance

comes from knowing that one is a child of God, hence perfect, and from reconciliation through gratitude with all persons and things.

5. **Worship.** The principal act of worship is the practice of meditation *(shinsōkan)* involving a special technique in which believers are carefully instructed. When practiced correctly and regularly it results in divine empowerment.

6. **Current issues and trends.** A major concern of Seichō no Ie is the quality of patriotism and morality in Japanese society. This concern is manifested in a variety of ways—from campaigns to reduce the number of deaths in traffic accidents and to limit the practice of abortion to efforts to restore the national flag and anthem to the status of respected symbols of the nation's life and purpose. *See also* Konkō-kyō; PL Kyōdan; Tenri-kyō.

Bibliography. R.S. Ellwood, Jr., *The Eagle and the Rising Sun* (1974); H. N. McFarland, *The Rush Hour of the Gods (1967); Taniguchi, Divine Education and Spiritual Training of Mankind* (1956).

H. N. McFarland

SEKAI KYŪSEI-KYŌ sĕ kī´ kyoo sā kyō´ **SEKAI MESHIA-KYŌ** sĕ kī´ mĕ shē ä kyō´ (Jap.). A religious movement founded by Okada Mokichi (1882-1955), who was known as the *Meishu-sama* ("spiritual leader"). It heralded the creation of an ideal world—a paradise on earth characterized by peace, health, prosperity, and beauty—through the purifying power of divine light. The official English name is "The Church of World Messianity." A nationwide movement in Japan, it has spread to Japanese communities, notably in Hawaii, California, and Brazil, where it has also attracted a significant number of non-Japanese devotees.

1. **History.** World Messianity evolved from the personal struggles and spiritual experiences of Okada Mokichi. Born to a poor family in Tokyo, he was subject in his early life to a variety of chronic illnesses. As a young adult he engaged in several business enterprises, some of which succeeded temporarily, but overall his life was a story of recurrent frustration, climaxed by almost total ruin in the great Kanto earthquake of 1923. Since 1920 he had been a somewhat casual devotee of Ōmoto, and following the earthquake he became intensely involved in that religion, which by its communications from the spiritual world promised a new age.

In 1926 Okada had the first of two experiences pivotal to his eventual career. A divine spirit, identified at the time as that of Kannon (Avalokiteś-vara), the Bodhisattva of mercy, entered him, commissioned him to a ministry of salvation, and shed upon him the divine light which was to be dispensed through him. The second experience occurred in 1931 when Okada climbed a mountain and there was inspired to recite a prayer, called *Amatsu Norito,* which he identified as the most powerful of all prayers, the recitation of which was to become the central act of worship in World Messianity.

Motivated by these experiences, Okada became a prominent teacher and healer in Ōmoto, but receiving recurrent signs that he was being prepared for a special ministry, he left Ōmoto in 1934 and in the following year formed his own organization, Dai Nihon Kannon Kai (lit. "Great Japan Kannon Association"). Focusing his attention on healing, he developed the practice of *jōrei,* a manual technique for channeling divine light. Though he prospered for a time, he soon incurred the hostility of the wartime government and was forced to curtail his activities for the duration of World War II.

In the new freedom of postwar Japan, Okada resumed his work with great success. In 1950 he adopted a new name for his flourishing movement, Sekai Kyūsei-kyō or Sekai Meshiya-kyō, indicating thereby his intention to work within a context of internationalism and religious pluralism.

Okada was succeeded in 1955 by his widow, called *Nidai-sama* ("second generation"). At her death in 1962 she was succeeded by her married daughter Fujieda Itsuki, called *Sandai-sama* ("third generation") or *Kyōshū-sama* ("spiritual leader").

2. **Organization.** As a symbol and foretaste of the new age, the World Messianity Church has built two mini-paradises in Hakone and Atami, both beautiful resort areas. The tombs of the founder and his wife and an excellent art museum are located at Hakone. Administrative offices, as well as a great sanctuary and a second art museum, are at Atami. A training center and school have been established in Kyoto. The organization is tightly centralized and is administered by a corps of officials responsible directly to Kyōshū-sama.

3. **Doctrine.** The basic belief is that God revealed to Okada his intention to purify and reconstruct the world by releasing his divine light through Okada's ministry. The result will be a world free of disease, poverty, and conflict. The present time with all its strife and suffering is a necessary transition from the old age to the new.

4. **Activities.** World Messianity's program to prepare the way for paradise on earth has three principal components: *jōrei,* natural farming, and the creation and appreciation of beauty. *Jōrei* is a manual technique for channeling divine light to the body of a person or to other objects to cleanse them of inhibiting spiritual accretions called "clouds," "toxins," or "negative vibrations." Natural farming is an agricultural method rejecting artificial fertilizers and insecticides in order to preserve the natural purity of the soil, which then can be permeated by spiritual energy that God supplies. The creation and appreciation of beauty is also a means of spiritual purification, enhanced by the establishment of models of exemplary beauty which then can be emulated elsewhere in an infinite succession.

Bibliography. R. S. Ellwood, Jr., *The Eagle and the Rising Sun* (1974); H. Thomsen, *The New Religions of Japan* (1963).

H. N. McFarland

SELF-REALIZATION FELLOWSHIP. *See* Hinduism in America §3a.

SELIHOT sĕ lē hōt′ (Ju—Heb; lit. "forgiveness"). Liturgical poetry, prayers for pardon, recited on the Ten Days of Penitence, Rosh ha-Shanah, Yom Kippur, and public fasts, calling on the Lord to respond as he did to scriptural heroes. The earliest known order of selihot is found in the ninth century prayer book of Rabbi Amram.

D. J. Schnall

SENG-CHAO sĕng′ jou (B—Chin.; A.D. 374 or 384–414). Disciple of Kumārajīva, outstanding Chinese master of the Mādhyamika or San-lun School of Mahāyāna Buddhism, author of the treatises in the *Chao Lun* ("Essays of Chao").

Seng-chao had studied Lao Tzu and Chuang Tzu prior to his reading the Vimalakīrti and converting to Buddhism. His treatises "The Immutability of Things," "The Emptiness of the Unreal," and "Prajñā is not Knowledge" synthesized the thought of Taoism and Buddhism. He viewed Prajñā as "sage-knowledge," an identification with *wu* ("nonbeing"), which is Nirvana.

C. W. Edwards

SEPHARDIM sĕ fär dĭm′ (Ju—Heb.; lit. "Spaniards"). Jews of Spanish or North African ancestry, distinct from those of East or Central Europe, the Ashkenazim. In the Bible (Obad. 1:20) Sepharad refers to Asia Minor, but it was associated with Spain in the Middle Ages. The term has popularly come to include Jews of the Muslim world as well.

Sephardi is primarily a cultural or linguistic designation, referring to distinctive religious practice and law. The Shulhan Aruch, a law code compiled by Joseph Caro and binding on Sephardim, is often more liberal than Ashkenazic counterparts and reflects differences in ritual and dietary rules. A unique vernacular, Ladino, was also developed. Sephardic heroes include the giants of Jewish philosophy, e.g. Moses ben Maimon, Saadiah, and Judah ha-Levi, while boasting a "Golden Age" in Spain (*ca.* 950-1150) when culture flourished in every creative realm.

Openness to secular influence marked the Sephardim, who regarded it as an asset, but since it was contrary to Ashkenazic sensibilities, it led to serious rifts and disputes. Indeed it may be that secularism led naturally to a skeptical unwillingness to find anything transmundane in religion. Consequently, in facing persecution most Sephardim chose Baptism rather than death and led a Marrano or hidden Jewish existence thereafter. While most were lost to Judaism as a result, some sustained their religious identity over generations.

Expulsion by the Inquisition and new forms of economic activity resulted in emigration to Holland, Britain, the Ottoman Empire, and, later, the New World. Sephardic communities developed distinctive institutions—e.g., the *Ḥaham Baḥshi,* or chief rabbi, presiding over the Jews of the Ottoman Empire who comprised a "millet" or autonomous minority under Ottoman rule. In Britain as well, Sephardim retained their distinctive religious leadership and the *Ḥaham* was both independent from and equal to the Ashkenazic chief rabbi. Further, Synagogue officials were more than religious functionaries, holding actual communal leadership as well.

Sephardim of Western Europe prospered. Unlike Ashkenazim, they regarded emancipation as unnecessary, for they already had attained social and economic integration. Yet poverty was not unknown. Beneath the affluence of the grandees were many Sephardim who struggled to eke out a living in small business.

Sephardim have persisted as a dwindling but prosperous and recognizable minority among Western Jews. Those of Arab lands, however, suffered from the cultural and economic decline of their locale and, after 1948, from growing Arab hostility to the State of Israel. Anticipating little future in the Muslim world, masses of these Jews emigrated to Israel. The preponderant majority were absorbed, though integration efforts have resulted in tensions difficult to alleviate because of Israel's beleagered status. Some measure of success has been lately attained, yet disparities between Western and Oriental Jews remain one of Israel's pressing problems.

Bibliography. A. Angel, "The Sephardim of the United States: An Exploratory Study," *American Jewish Year Book* (1973), pp. 77-138; R. Patai, *Israel Between East and West* (1953); H. Zimmels, *Ashkenazim and Sephardim* (1958).

D. J. Schnall and S. Bayme

SERMON ON THE MOUNT (Ch). The traditional designation for Jesus' programmatic discourse in Matt. 5–7. Given the similarity to Luke 6:20-49 ("the Sermon on the Plain"), it appears that both Gospels draw on an older discourse, itself a compilation of individual sayings, doubtless spoken on various occasions. Matthew expanded this older compilation and made it the first of five discourses (Matt. 5–7; 10; 13; 18; 23–25).

The sermon begins with Beatitudes and ends with the parable of the two houses—as does the Sermon on the Plain. Whether Matthew omitted the "woes" (Luke 6:24-26) or Luke added them is not clear. In Matthew there follow the "antitheses"—six statements which contrast the tradition ("You have heard . . .") with Jesus' own statement of God's will ("but I say to you. . ."). The introduction to the "antitheses" makes clear Jesus' devotion to the Torah (Matt. 5:17-20). Matt. 6:1-18 organizes sayings according to the traditional Jewish triad of piety: alms, prayer (expanded to include the Lord's Prayer and related material), and fasting. Matt. 6:19-34 concerns freedom from concern for material wealth. Matt. 7 has no clear organization.

For Matthew the sermon is an announcement of the way "righteousness" is inherent in Jesus' message of the KINGDOM OF GOD. Jesus' own teaching is to be discerned in the sermon's individual sayings which can be judged to be reasonably authentic.

The sermon has played a prominent role in Christian theology and ethics, and has been interpreted in a variety of ways, such as the "new law" binding on the believer, the pure will of God, or "interim ethics" (emergency measures for the brief time remaining before the kingdom comes). Jewish scholars have rightly pointed to the numerous parallel teachings in rabbinic literature.

Bibliography. W. D. Davies, *The Setting of the Sermon on the Mount* (1964), deals with historical and literary matters in Matthew; M. Dibelius, *The Sermon on the Mount* (1940); H. McArthur, *Understanding the Sermon on the Mount* (1960), good survey of types of interpretation; H. Windisch, *The Meaning of the Sermon on the Mount* (1951); G. Friedlander, *The Jewish Sources of the Sermon on the Mount* (1911; rpr. 1969); G. Bornkamm, "Der Aufbau der Bergpredigt," *New Testament Studies* 24 (1978), 419-32.

L. E. KECK

ŚEṢA, SHESA, shā´ shū (H—Skt.; "residue"). A mythological serpent (NĀGA) associated with the god VISHNU as his protective couch and foundation for the earth. Identified, at times, with Ananta, "endless."

The worship of snakes in India is ancient, but Śeṣa is not mentioned until the Epic period (400 B.C.). In the MAHĀBHĀRATA (Ādiparvan 12, 356-64), Śeṣa practices extreme austerities and the god BRAHMĀ grants him any reward. He chooses that he might rejoice forever in righteousness, peace, and asceticism. Pleased with such piety, Brahmā grants him the privilege of bearing the earth. From then it is said that he carries the earth on his head and encircles the earth with his coils, an idea that is probably early. (Cf. the mythological Norse snake Midgardsormr.)

BALARĀMA, KRISHNA'S elder brother, is believed to be an incarnation of Śeṣa. At his death a white snake was seen issuing from his mouth and rushing to the ocean. And though he is usually associated with the god Vishnu, in the Mahābhārata Śeṣa is said to have been born of Shiva and to have served as the axle of his divine vehicle.

Śeṣa is most well known from the PURĀNAS and Indian art as the thousand-headed serpent on whom Vishnu reclines, shaded by his hood, during the night before creation. Śeṣa is also said to destroy the creation at the end of the age by fire from his mouth. He was created from remnants after the creation of the three worlds. Hence his name, "Residue."

R. N. MINOR

SEVENTH-DAY ADVENTISM (Ch). Religious movement native to the U.S. but worldwide in scope, with numerous institutions ranging from nursing and medical schools to Bible schools. Its roots are in the movement begun by William Miller (1782-1849) in the 1840s, but Miller himself did not become a member. A diligent student of the Bible, he calculated from the prophecies of Daniel that the world would end between March 21, 1843 and March 21, 1844. Samuel Snow, a Millerite leader, recalculated and named October 22, 1844 as the date of the end. After the "great disappointment," as the day was called, a small number continued to cling to the adventist belief, and several groups finally converged to form Seventh-Day Adventism. Hiram Edson, Joseph Bates, and Ellen White (1827-1915) were the central figures in this evolutionary process. The doctrine that in 1844 Christ entered the heavenly sanctuary to judge the sins of those living and dead, the observance of the seventh day as the sabbath, and the belief that Ellen White was a true prophet, whose words and visions were to be held sacred, formed the basis for the birth of the new church.

By 1855 headquarters for the group had been established in Battle Creek, Michigan, and in 1860 the name Seventh-Day Adventist was officially adopted. In 1863 the first national meeting of the new denomination was held. In 1903 the General Conference Headquarters and the Review and Herald Publishing Association were moved to Takoma Park, Maryland, a suburb of Washington, D.C.

The source of authority for belief is the Bible, but the writings of Ellen White are held in such high esteem that for all practical purposes it is the Bible as interpreted by Ellen White. The church is evangelical and conservative, with a major interest in the last judgment and the end of the world. Adventists believe that these are the last days, and that the end of the world is near. Holding that an eternal hell for the wicked is not in keeping with the concept of a "loving Father," they believe in annihilation for the wicked and eternal bliss for the saved. After a thousand-year reign of the saints with Christ in heaven, the wicked will be raised and then, along with Satan, annihilated. Out of the chaos of the old earth there will emerge a new earth which the redeemed will claim as their everlasting home. This is the basis for their theology of hope.

The doctrine of the "investigative judgment" carried out by Christ in the heavenly sanctuary has led to strict moral requirements for membership, including abstention from alcohol and tobacco. The Fourth Commandment, "Remember the sabbath day, to keep it holy," is the great test of loyalty. The church practices believer's baptism by immersion and the Lord's Supper preceded by the ordinance of footwashing. *See* MILLENARIAN MOVEMENTS.

Bibliography. G. Schwartz, *Sect Ideologies and Social Status* (1970), and *Seventh-Day Adventists Answer Questions on Doctrine* (1957).

G. H. SHRIVER

SHABBAT shä bät´ (Ju). *See* SABBATH.

SHAFĀ'A shä fä' ä (I—Arab.; lit. "petition, intercession"). Intercession before God in someone's behalf, especially on the Day of Judgment. Intercession is treated in over twenty-five places in the QUR'ĀN, most commonly as being of no avail to evildoers (e.g. 40:18; 2:48, 123, 254), especially idolaters who believe that their false gods can intercede for them (cf. 6:94; 30:13; 36:23; 39:43). This warning is twice directed to the Children of Israel (2:48, 123), apparently chiding their faith in angelic intercession—something the Qur'ān affirms to be possible, but only when God so wills (40:7; 53:26; 21:28).

In the ḤADĪTH and later Muslim thought, *shafā'a* is elaborated and specified at length. Both angels and (as in Jewish tradition) also human beings—most often the prophets, but also the 'ULAMĀ', martyrs (*see* SHAHĪD), saints (*see* WALĪ), Shi'ite IMAMS, and the righteous generally—are said to be capable of intercession on behalf of the less perfect among the faithful. Even the funerary prayers *(janā' iz)* are intercessory in nature. Most important, however, has been MUHAMMAD'S special role as intercessor *par excellence* for his UMMA. Qur'ānic support for his intercession has been found traditionally in the "praised place" (17:79) and "reward" (93:5) promised to him by God. The *ḥadīth* has extensive and graphic descriptions of how Muhammad will be first among the prophets in intercession on the Last Day, and how, when given a choice of favors from God, he chose the right to intercede for his people at judgment.

Bibliography. A. J. Wensinck, *SEI,* pp. 511-12; T. Andrae, *Mohammed, The Man and His Faith* (1917 [ET 1936]).

W. A. GRAHAM

al-SHĀFI'Ī äl shä' fə ē (I; 767-820). Abū 'Abdullāh ibn Idrīs al-Shāfi'ī, founder of the Shāfi'ite school of law, most famous for his exposition of the "roots of jurisprudence," which forms the basis for most Islamic legal considerations.

Al-Shāfi'ī was so highly regarded from such an early date that his biographical notices tend to be more hagiographic than accurate. A QURAISH of the clan of HĀSHIM, and therefore distantly related to MUHAMMAD, he was raised in MECCA and received both an Arab and a Muslim education. He studied with MALIK IBN ANAS in MEDINA, had Shi'ite involvements in the Yemen, spent time in Baghdad and Mecca, and died in Egypt.

In the area of substantive commentary on legal practice, al-Shāfi'ī, because of his eclectic and broad education, was able to make penetrating analyses of practices current in his time, but he is more famous for his *Rasāla,* written in the last years of his life, which expounds his theoretical positions on the foundations of law. According to his system, the four roots are QUR'ĀN, the SUNNA of Muhammad, consensus (IJMĀ'), and analogic reasoning *(qiyās).* While these elements had been present before his time, al-Shāfi'ī remade the Islamic legal system by redefining these terms. There was no dispute about the Qur'ān's role in law, but there was controversey about its interpretation. Starting with the Qur'ānic injunction to obey both Allah and Muhammad (Sura 4:69), he raised the position of Muhammad's *sunna* above that of only first among equals, making Muhammad's actions the interpreter of the Qur'ān. By the use of the notion of consensus, he legitimized the then current practice of the Muslim community as it was seen in retrospect to conform to the historical perceptions of the age of Muhammad and the Companions (ṢAḤĀBA). Finally, the limitation of human reasoning to analogic reasoning removed much of the individual idiosyncrasy from legal practice. His theory can be seen as a compromise between the strict Traditionists and the so-called Rationalists.

The Shāfi'ite school has had its greatest influence in East Africa, South Arabia, and Southeast Asia, although al-Shāfi'ī's personal influence is felt in all schools. The Shāfi'ites stand with the Hanbalites (*see* IBN ḤANBAL) in opposing admission of judicial or public interest in legal consideration, and are most consistent in applying rules of analogy throughout their system, preferring judicial reasoning to weak traditions. They opposed legal strategems in their early stages of development but admitted some in later periods. The Shāfi'ite school was generally adopted by the ASH'ARITE speculative theologians after the tenth century.

Bibliography. *See* FIQH.

G. D. NEWBY

SHĀF'ITES shä' fīts (I). *See* AL-SHĀFI'Ī.

SHAHĀDA shă hä' dă (I—Arab.; lit. "profession [of faith]"). The first and indispensable pillar of the five PILLARS OF ISLAM. It has two parts: 1) *lā ilāha illā 'llāh* "there is no god but God"; and 2) *wa-Muḥammadan rasūlu 'llāh* "and Muhammad is the apostle of God." A person, by making this statement *in Arabic* with sincere intent to become a Muslim, does become a Muslim, though full participation in the Islamic community (UMMA) entails numerous other obligations, including the frequent restatement of the *shahāda* in ritual PRAYER *(ṣalāt). See* ALLAH; TAWḤĪD.

B. LAWRENCE

SHAHĪD shä hēd' (I—Arab.; lit. "witness"). One who has witnessed to Islam under duress, i.e., a martyr. The QUR'ĀN frequently uses the word in its primary sense, but it early came to refer to those who died on the battlefield fighting for Islam. As martyrs, they were assured automatic, immediate entrance into paradise (JANNA), and according to later Muslim traditions they were also able to intercede on behalf of others.

Martyrs are especially esteemed among the SHI'A and among SUFI loyalists (for whom the first martyr was al-Ḥallāj). Their tombs continue to be places of veneration and pilgrimage, just as their example continues to inspire present-day Muslims. *See* Mashhad; Ziyāra. B. Lawrence

SHAIKH shāk (I—Arab., lit., "old man"). (1) As *Shaikh al-Islām,* the chief Muslim religious functionary of a particular city or province. (2) As *Shaikh al-balad,* the headman of a town or village. (3) But the principal literary and popular reference of shaikh is to a spiritual master in the Sufi tradition. Usually someone becomes a Sufi shaikh (also known as *pīr* [Per.; lit., "old man"] or *murshid* [Arab.; lit., "one who directs"]) only by submitting to the discipline of another shaikh. There is an alternative route of initiation, however: Khidr, who in the Qur'ān instructed Moses, can also confer the cloak of investiture on Muslims possessed of signal spiritual prowess. The most famous example of such an initiation is *Shaikh al-Akbar,* "the greatest Shaikh," a title given to the Andalusian mystic Muḥyī 'd-dīn Ibn 'Arabī. Even while allowing for the possibility of self-initiates, however, Sufis reaffirm the exceptionality of this deviation from the path (Ṭarīqa); a popular tradition, ascribed to Muhammad, bluntly warns: "When somone has no shaikh, then Satan becomes his shaikh."

For Sufis there are few limits to the authority vested in the shaikh. Like a king among his courtiers or a general at the head of his troops, the shaikh has absolute power over initiates in the Sufi path who bind themselves to him by an oath of allegiance. The disciple, according to one Sufi dictum, is analogous to a corpse in the hands of a washerman. He moves wherever he is moved; he is dead to himself. The granting of such awesome power to the shaikh was not limited to this life; it extended to the life beyond, which was thought populated by deceased shaikhs, ranked hierarchically according to their cosmological powers, with the *quṭb* or pole at the top (*see* Walī/Wilāyat). Shaikhs, therefore, were inevitably compared with prophets (Nabi), and for the disciples of a *pīr* or *murshid* the theological space separating their master from the Prophet was perilously narrow. In the modern decline in influence of organized Sufism it has been suggested that veneration of the shaikh has often surpassed veneration of the Prophet.

Bibliography. A. Schimmel, *Mystical Dimensions of Islam* (1975), pp. 101-6, 234-38. B. Lawrence

SHAKERS (Ch). A celibate communistic sect founded by Ann Lee (1736-84). Converted in 1758 in England to the Shaking Quakers (so called for their ritualistic dancing), Lee received revelations indicating that she was Christ in female form, that sexual activity was the cause of sin, and that she was to take her small group to the New World to establish the millennial church. Shaker communities came into existence in 1787 at New Lebanon and Watervliet, New York. Among those affected by Revivalism the movement spread to much of New England and then to Kentucky, Ohio, and Indiana. The Shakers reached their apogee between 1830 and 1850, with roughly six thousand members in twenty communities, and have since declined to the point of virtual extinction, with communities remaining only in Canterbury, New Hampshire and Sabbathday Lake, Maine.

The defining practices are celibacy, communal ownership of property, separation from the world, and communal confession of sin, with emphasis on its sexual origins. Shaker agricultural communities are known for their inventions, architecture, and furniture design. Worship is based on silent group meditation and distinctive dances and songs. Shakers believe that God and all human beings are both male and female; that Christ was incarnate in both Jesus and Ann Lee; that it is possible to communicate with the spiritual world and to receive revelations, physical healing, and sinlessness; and that salvation will be universal.

Bibliography. E. D. Andrews, *The People Called Shakers* (1953). M. Endy

SHALOM shä lōm´ (Ju—Heb.; lit. "peace"). A common greeting wishing peace, used upon meeting or departing. It is often joined with *alekhem,* meaning "peace upon you." The wish for peace, among the most exalted in Judaism, is attached to festival greetings or landmarks and identified in rabbinic literature as a divine appellation.

D. J. Schnall

SHAMANISM. Commonly used to refer to the ideas, practices and beliefs associated with individuals (referred to as shamans) who show evidence of magical or spiritual powers. The word "shaman" is derived through Russian from the Siberian Tungusic *šaman,* and, although its ultimate root may not be Siberian, there are in the languages of many of the peoples indigenous to Siberia and Central Asia cognate words denoting specific magico-religious practices in which malignant powers were overcome with the aid of helping spirits. In a technical sense shamanism is a specific form of religious practice confined to this geographic area. An enormous amount of study has been directed to these practices, primarily by Russian ethnologists and philologists who have tended to associate them primarily with spiritual healing. In Western scholarship, particularly that concerned with the study of religion, Eliade's definition of shamanism as "techniques of ecstasy" has become broadly accepted. He claims that a definitive feature of the shaman is the capability of entering into a state of ecstasy in order to participate directly in the spiritual dimensions of reality, as healer, diviner, clairvoyant, and psychopomp (escort of the soul of the deceased to the domain of the dead). While this is a limiting definition, it permits the term "shamanism" to refer to certain magico-religious elements found in the religions of many nonliterate peoples and in world religions that arose in both the East and the West.

1. **Shamanism in religion and society.** Shamanism is itself not a religion, but a set of techniques and an ideology attached to a religion which has its own history and system of beliefs. Therefore, shamanism must always be considered in the context of the religion and society in which it is found. Shamanism or shamanic elements may be found in religions all over the world and from Paleolithic times. It takes many forms and serves a variety of roles. This is true even in the most narrow use of the term. Still, if we consider the shaman minimally as one who specializes in techniques of entering into a trance during which his soul is believed to leave his body and ascend to the sky or descend to the underworld, certain forms of cosmology, religion, and society usually correspond to such belief.

a) Cosmology. The shamanic flight of the disembodied soul is dependent upon various forms of the classic three-storied cosmology—the earth surrounded by a sky world above with an underworld below. These may be further segmented into complex cosmological ideograms. Since it is the vocation of the shaman to break through these planes in order to establish communication between cosmic zones, various forms of symbolic structures may be used to indicate the path or channel of communication. Common and worldwide in distribution are symbols of the center of the world, the world axis, which not only support the cosmic structure but provide the means for communication between levels. This central axis may be represented as a tree, a mountain, or a pillar, and these symbols are given ritual representation in shamanic rites. For example, the Siberian shaman climbs a tree erected in the *yurt* (tent) in which he is performing, symbolizing the ascent of his soul to the sky world. This type of cosmology, however, is not the product of shamanism nor is it restricted to contexts which include shamanic activity.

b) Religion. Among the theological and religious ideas essential to shamanism is the assumption that in the multileveled cosmology, spirits and deities existing at the upper and lower levels have the power to affect the lives of human beings in the earth world. This is seen clearly in the theories of disease which are associated with shamanism. Illness may be caused by the loss of the soul or principle of vitality, either by theft or enticement of spirits or offended deities. Illness may also be caused by the projection of harmful objects or substances into the body by entities from these other worlds. The shaman, whose speciality is to communicate with the other worlds in order to rescue one's vitality, etc., is unique only in the situation which presupposes that communication between worlds is not ordinarily possible. Therefore, it is common to find shamanism in cultures whose religion is based on the worship of a high god who has receded or become inactive, and whose role has been filled by the rise of numerous ancestor spirits and spirits of nature. The mythology associated with shamanism depicts the loss of communication between humans and spirits at the close of the primal era, a loss that need not necessarily be interpreted as a "fall" but corresponds with this kind of experience. Shamanism is linked to the individual's capabilities to communicate with spirits, and since this is a trait closely associated with hunter-gatherer peoples, it may account for shamanism's probable great antiquity and near universality.

c) Society. In many cultures there are distinct categories of shamans, such as divisions between "white" (benevolent) and "black" (malevolent). Still, it is clear that a shaman at any level is a shaman because of his or her unique abilities, and is no ordinary person. It is common to find shamans highly respected and revered but also feared and isolated from the rest of society. While the shaman is a powerful person upon whom society depends for the services he can render, his powers often make him suspect when harm or disaster comes to a community.

Scholars have debated the psychology of the shaman. A common position advanced by Russian scholars is that the shaman suffers certain nervous disorders, especially a kind of hysteria linked to the experience of the severe Arctic environment. Others have rooted the shaman's skills in epilepsy. This position is countered by the argument that while the shaman often enters his vocation as a result of illness or epileptoid attack, his initiation and training amount to a cure. In any case, the distinctive character of the shaman is his ability to control ecstasy and to enter trance at will. Shamans also require great mastery of their physical and psychological dimensions in order to perform their often difficult acts.

2. **The career of the shaman.** *a) Selection and initiation.* Generally, a shaman may come to his vocation either by inheriting it or by responding, often unwillingly, to a call. These may not be mutually exclusive. Where heredity is a factor, potential shamans are often elected at an early age and observed and taught until the time when they undergo proper initiation and assume their career. Spontaneous vocation commonly corresponds with the arrival of sexual maturity and frequently coincides with an illness.

Much of the distinctive character of shamanism is reflected in the initiatory experiences of the shaman, which usually include an ecstatic or vision experience often linked with extended rituals or an illness. The imagery of these experiences is remarkably similar wherever shamanism is found. In the vision or ritual the shaman commonly observes himself undergoing morbid experiences such as death accompanied by dismemberment, reduction to a skeleton, having his body cooked. This destruction is succeeded by the reconstitution of the shaman's body with more powerful organs or parts. The initiatory experience commonly includes a journey to the sky worlds or the underworlds and the acquisition of helping spirits upon whom the shaman may call in the future. The symbolism of shamanic initiation centers upon death, portraying the acquisition of the powers and techniques characteristic of the shaman. The shaman-elect becomes like a dead man, like a spirit. He transcends ordinary human limitations and gains the power to enter the domain of gods and spirits. The initiation amounts to a transformation of the individual from an ordinary person into a shaman. In many cases the shaman may have undergone training prior to this initiatory experience, but training is commonly a part of the extended initiatory process. A common sign of the shaman's vocation is the acquisition of a special language with which to communicate with the spirits. It may be an animal language, for helping spirits are most commonly in the form of animals.

b) Relationship with spirits. In order for a shaman to break the plane of ordinary experience, he must have the aid of helping spirits, with whom he maintains a familiar relationship. It is well known that throughout the world ordinary individuals have frequently developed familiar relationships with guardian spirits, often in animal form, whom they have held as guides and sources of power. The shamanic relationship with spirits must be seen in light of this larger phenomenon and differs only in the shaman's capacity for voluntary ecstatic experience. While the ordinary individual may be protected and directed by a guardian spirit, he does not have the capacity to enter states of ecstasy at will in order to intervene on a wide scale in the affairs of the spirit world. For the individual with a guardian spirit it is a more or less private affair, while for the shaman it is a vocation.

All shamans have tutelary and helping spirits, but they control only a limited number of these spirits. In shamanic performances, the shaman will become the animal spirit or god with whom he is familiar, and often the actions and voice of the shaman in trance are those of his animal familiar spirit. But it is notable that the shaman is not thought to be possessed by the spirit, but rather transformed into the spirit, because it is the shamanic techniques which control the situation. In light of the shamanic mythology which reports a time when humans could speak to the gods and animals, the shaman's powers may be understood as an overcoming of the intervening separation, and a return to that primal era.

c) Functions and techniques. The shaman is indispensable in any situation that concerns the experiences of the human soul, for the soul or life essence is subject to the actions of agents in the worlds of the spirits, deities, sorcerers, demons, and ghosts (*see* DEMONS, DEMONOLOGY).

Perhaps the function most commonly associated with shamanism is that of the doctor or healer. This function is linked to the perception of illness as related to the status of the human soul. A number of circumstances may be involved, though it is usually assumed that the soul has the capability and inclination to leave the body. It may be beckoned by a ghost or some malevolent spirit or power. The soul may be stolen by demons or sorcerers and imprisoned in the lower worlds. Or the soul may be impaired by the intrusion of objects of malevolence or WITCHCRAFT projected into the body. Only the shaman has the power to rectify this situation. Commonly the shamanic approach has two phases, the first to diagnose or "see" the relevant condition, and the second to rectify the situation. If the soul has departed from the body, the shaman must use his powers to "see" where it has gone and what obstacles must be overcome to restore it to the body of the one suffering; then he must use his powers to enact the restoration. In the case of an intruding malevolent object, the shaman's powers are first focused upon locating the object in the body of the ailing person, then upon the removal of the object, usually by a technique of sucking. The shaman's powers to heal are dependent upon the techniques through which he enters a state of ecstasy, during which his soul is free to penetrate the underworld and the sky world.

A related function of the shaman is that of the psychopomp, an escort of the soul of the dead to the domain of the dead. This most dangerous of tasks requires that he symbolically undergo death. The dangers of these journeys into the underworld as either doctor or psychopomp are often depicted in such images as the crossing of a sea on a bridge only a hair in width.

As escort to other worlds the shaman is also associated with sacrifical rites and is responsible for delivering the spirit of the sacrificial animal to its intended place. While sacrifice is perhaps unexpected in the context of shamanism, this role demonstrates the extent to which the vocation of the shaman may serve many religious contexts and purposes.

Likewise, other minor functions of the shaman are divination and clairvoyance. These may be used in conjunction with healing, but they are commonly used to find lost persons, to recover lost objects, to control the weather, and to perform related tasks of value to the shaman's community.

While it is more the role of the sorcerer than the shaman, it is not unknown for a shaman to use his powers to harm his enemies or those of some client. In some areas it is common for shamans to engage in battles with each other while in the form of their animal spirits.

Shamanic techniques often include magical acts or miracles, giving the shaman a place in the history of MAGIC. They often handle or swallow red hot coals, plunge their arms in boiling water, cut open their stomachs, which are instantly healed, magically release themselves from bonds, exercise kinesis, and so on. These acts correspond with the shaman's surpassing of ordinary human limitations and are visible signs of the invisible flight of his soul into other realms.

d) Costume. While a special costume is not a universal feature, it is sufficiently important to merit brief discussion. Shamans' costumes in Siberia and Central Asia are well known and reflect the definitive characteristics of shamanism. In each shamanic performance the shaman is, in effect, reenacting his initiatory experience. The costume often incorporates the symbolism of that experience, including such things as skeleton symbolism and symbols of the helping spirits of the shaman. Shamanic masks do not serve to disguise the shaman, but rather to announce the incarnation of a mythical personage. Of special importance is the drum which is widely a part of the shaman's equipment. It bears immense symbolism, representing in itself a microcosmic structure. The drum comes from the sacred tree which stands at the center of the world and supports the various levels of the cosmos. It is upon or within this tree that the shaman makes his ascent to the sky worlds. The drum which is constantly beaten during shamanic performances creates a kind of musical magic through which the shaman may enter into a trance and be transported on his mystical itinerary. The costumes, masks, drums, rattles, and equipment of shamans vary throughout the world, and their symbolism cannot be understood apart from the specific cosmology and initiatory experiences of the shaman and his culture.

3. **History and incidence.** Perhaps the greatest amount of controversy related to the study of shamanism has centered on its origin and history. When by narrow definition shamanism is restricted to Asia, scholarly concern has been focused upon its origin. Philologists have speculated that the Tungusic word *šaman* may have derived from the Pali *samana* through the Chinese *sha-men,* which would suggest that shamanism in Siberia may have derived from origins in south Asia and India. This was discounted for a while, but recent research has revived this possibility. Other evidence suggests that some of the symbolism of Tungus shamanism has been influenced by Buddhism, such as the drum, shamanic music, and the use of mirrors as part of the costume. Russian scholars have tended to see shamanism as a form through which religion evolves. From this perspective they have placed it in an evolutionary development of healing practices from antiquity, based on utilization of elements within nature which developed a spiritual aspect at a later stage. Since in this view shamanism is distinctive of an early stage in the development of religion and culture, it is by implication inferior to later developments.

In terms of the broader definition of shamanism which does not restrict it to Asia, other striking factors must be considered. The most significant is that shamanic ideologies and techniques are documented among nonliterate peoples all over the world. For example, there are remarkable similarities in certain elements of the shamanic mythologies and techniques of the peoples of Australia, Siberia, South America, and many other areas which have had no likelihood of contact for millennia. Study of evidence of the religion of Paleolithic hunters suggests distinct shamanic elements. The antiquity of the cosmology, as well as the general religious types which are associated with shamanism, is well documented. When shamanism is placed in the context of the history of the religious motivation to regain communication with gods and spirits lost at the time of the creation of man (the return to origins, the nostalgia for paradise), its religious dimensions become obvious. It is notable that from this perspective shamanism need not be correlated with any particular stage of human or religious development, but is rather fundamental to the character of religion. *See* SOUTH AMERICAN TRIBAL RELIGIONS §1a.

Bibliography. M. Eliade, *Shamanism: Archaic Techniques of Ecstasy* (1964), contains an extensive bibliography of both English and foreign works on shamanism. For Russian works on Siberian shamanism consult the writings of S. M. Shirokogoroff (Shirokogorov), especially *Psychomental Complex of the Tungus* (1935). For recent collections of papers on shamanism see C. M. Edsman, ed., *Studies in Shamanism: Symposium on Shamanism, Finland* (1967), and *Artscanada,* vol. 30, nos. 184-187 (1973-1974).

S. D. GILL

SHAMMAI shăm mī´ (Ju; *ca.* 50 B.C.—A.D. 30). Contemporary of HILLEL, who served as vice-president of the SANHEDRIN with him. Although he was thought to be more stringent and conservative than Hillel, many of his rulings do not lend themselves to such a view. His method of biblical interpretation, however, does tend to be more literal. Little is known of his life and only twenty of his rulings survive. The best known saying attributed to him is: "Make your study of the Torah a matter of established regularity, say little and do much, and receive all men with a friendly countenance" (*Avoth* 1.15).

E. M. MEYERS

SHARIA shă rē´ ă (I—Arab.; lit. "watering place," then "a way or path to water" [*sh-r-*'—"to (make) enter and drink water," "to direct toward, ordain," "to make clear, plain"]). Comprehensive term used to designate the proper mode and norm of life in ISLAM, the moral "path" or "way" that God has willed and ordained, "marked out" and "made clear," for human beings to move along. As both W. C. Smith and F. Rahman have pointed out, the term "sharia" was not much used in early Islam and has been widely used only in very recent times. This is apparently because at least until the speculative thought of the ninth century A.D., the term had not yet received its common later sense of "the religious (i.e., revealed) law" as opposed to theological (i.e., reasoned) speculation, let alone its most recent usage of "traditional Muslim law" as opposed to modern "secular law" derived from European models. This latter usage encourages a confusion of sharia with FIQH, at least insofar as it stresses its formal, systematic, and institutional or jurisprudential aspect at the expense of its personal, normative, and moral or religious aspect. Properly, sharia is the inclusive term in Muslim eyes for the right, i.e., divinely ordained and revealed, "way" to live; as such, it encompasses law *(fiqh),* moral and religious action *(dīn),* rational speculation (KALĀM), mystical thought *(taṣawwuf),* and personal piety *(taqwah, 'ibāda).* The most common use of *sharī'a* and its plural, *sharā'i'* in older texts is simply as the "way(s)" or "path(s)" that a particular group follows. Thus those who wrote about Islamic heresies described the *sharā'i',* or "mores," of this or that religious community, and SUFI writers speak of "the SUNNA and sharia of the saints *(awliyā',* plural of WALĪ)," referring to their customary practices.

Sharia must thus be carefully distinguished from *fiqh.* It is properly the ideal, God-given path that humans ought to follow. *Fiqh* (jurisprudence) is one among the "religious sciences" *('ulūm shar'īyah),* i.e., those scholarly disciplines that seek to understand and elucidate God's will for humankind. These include scriptural interpretation *(tafsīr),* ḤADĪTH studies *('ulūm al-ḥadīth),* and theological inquiry *(kalām, 'ilm al-tawḥīd),* along with *fiqh.* Even in modern Muslim faculties of law, which in many universities are called "colleges of sharia," the curriculum includes not only jurisprudence but also systematic studies in QUR'ĀN and *ḥadīth,* without which the sharia is unintelligible and unapproachable. In the final analysis, sharia as a concept is better rendered by "morality" or even "religion" than by "law." As Rahman points out, "all legal and social transactions as well as all personal behaviour, is [*sic*] subsumed under the Sharī'a as the comprehensive principle of the *total way of life."*

For the Muslim, God ordains *(shara'a)* the "total way of life." His ordaining *(shar')* is made known to humans in prophetic revelation and, especially for the SHI'A, in post-prophetic revelatory guidance. The overarching standard or normative practice that results is sharia.

Bibliography. That the concept sharia needs much further serious study is clearly indicated by the brilliant analysis of W. C. Smith in "The Concept of *Sharī'a* among some *Mutakallimūn," Arabic and Islamic Studies in Honor of Hamilton A. R. Gibb,* G. Makdisi, ed. (1965), pp. 581-602. The most thoughtful introduction to sharia is that of F. Rahman, in his *Islam* (1966), which agrees with Smith's ideas. On the specifically legal dimension of sharia, see J. Schacht, *SEI,* and N. J. Coulson, *A History of Islamic Law* (1964), both of which include further bibliography.

W. A. GRAHAM

SHARIF shä rēf′ (I—Arab.; lit. "noble, honored"). A freeman descended from respectable ancestors who is spiritually or materially preeminent; a head of a prominent family responsible for tribal affairs, and regarded as aristocratic. Arabs, Turks, and Persians use the term as a title of honor for any descendant of MUHAMMAD, although such distinction does not accord with Muslim egalitarianism. Unlike the Persians, Arabs traditionally gave such titles as *sharif* or SAYYID to those who had earned rather than inherited them. Yet in spite of the tendency to level class differences, the belief persisted that illustrious qualities are transmitted to one's descendants. Kinship with the Prophet was thus an important claim to nobility *(sharaf),* and gradually Muhammad's whole clan, the Hāshimites (*see* HĀSHIM), were so designated. SHI'ITES, however, have restricted the title *sharif* to descendants of AL-ḤASAN and AL-ḤUSAYN.

A. A. SACHEDINA

SHAVUOT shă vū ōt′ (Ju—Heb.; lit. "weeks"). One of the three pilgrim festivals (*see* PASSOVER; SUKKOT) on which it was required in biblical times that all males visit JERUSALEM (Deut. 16:1-17). It is celebrated on the sixth of Sivan (May-June) in Israel and among REFORM Jews elsewhere, while others extend the holiday to include the seventh. Variously referred to as the festival of harvest and the festival of first fruit, Shavuot is also known as PENTECOST since it falls fifty days after Passover.

There are two diverse themes in the observance of this holiday. One is agricultural, as witnessed by its biblical link to the first fruit to ripen or to the harvest. In ancient Israel the first grain harvested was brought to the Temple with joy and celebration, and a recitation was made uniting the bringer to the founders of the faith. In addition, a measure of barley (the *Omer*) was offered on each of the forty-nine days between Passover and Shavuot. The tradition of "counting the *Omer,*" i.e. designating each of these forty-nine days with a blessing, is still practiced.

A second theme is based on the TALMUDIC reference to this festival as the anniversary of Israel's receiving the TORAH. By biblical account (Exod. 19:1) the Hebrews reached Mount SINAI "in the third month" after their Exodus and received the revelation three days later, on the sixth of Sivan. It is traditional, therefore, to spend the first night of the holiday immersed in study. A liturgy, composed of selections from a variety of classical texts, has been compiled for recitation on that night. It is appropriate to read the biblical description of the giving of the Torah (Exod. 19:1–20:26), in a special melody, with the congregation standing. The book of Ruth is also read, since its story takes place during the harvest season and King David (whose ancestry is traced through Ruth) is said to have died on Shavuot. In many traditions it is the practice to read the medieval poem *Akdamut,* an alphabetical acrostic describing the glory of God, his Torah, and Israel's faithfulness to it.

On Shavuot the SYNAGOGUE is decorated with flowers and greens to welcome the summer season and an early harvest. In addition, the Talmud refers to this festival as the judgment day for the fruit of the tree. It is also popular to eat dairy dishes, particularly blintzes (cheese crepes) and kreplach (triangular, dough-filled cheese pies) symbolic of the Torah, which is said to be as essential as milk to an infant. *See* CALENDAR, JEWISH.

Bibliography. P. Goodman, *Shavuot Anthology* (1975); S. Zevin, *Ha-Moadim be-Halathah,* 2nd ed. (1947).

D. J. SCHNALL

SHEMA shə mä′ (Ju—Heb.; "hear"; the first word of Deut. 6:4: "Hear, O Israel, the Lord is our God, the Lord is One"). A statement central to the Jewish liturgy and which, because of its emphasis on the unity of God, has come to be regarded as the Jewish "confession of faith." Although it is often employed to refer only to the single verse Deut. 6:4, the Shema, from a liturgical point of view, consists of three biblical passages (Deut. 6:4-9; 11:13-21; Num. 15:37-41) which are to be read every morning and evening.

According to the MISHNAH (*Tamid* v: 1), the practice of *Keriat Shema,* "the reading of the Shema," was included in the daily service of the Temple and adopted by the SYNAGOGUE. Regulations governing the reading of the Shema are given in the first three chapters of the Mishnaic tractate *Berakhot* ("Benedictions").

In addition to the traditional recitation of the Shema twice each day, in the morning and evening service, the first of its three passages is also recited by the individual as a night prayer before going to sleep (*Berakhot* 4b). Its first verse, Deut. 6:4, is chanted in the synagogue when the scrolls of the TORAH are taken out of the ARK. From the Middle Ages on it has been customary to conclude the Day of Atonement (YOM KIPPUR) service with the solemn recital of this verse. It is also spoken by or on behalf of a dying Jew as his final confession of faith, and throughout the centuries Jewish martyrs have gone to their deaths proclaiming its words.

Bibliography. I. Abrahams, *A Companion to the Authorized Daily Prayerbook,* rev. ed. (1922); A. Z. Idelsohn, *Jewish Liturgy and its Development* (1932).

B. MARTIN

SHEMA

Shə mä′ yēs rä ĕl′ ä dō noi′
ĕ lō hä′ nōō
ä dō noi′ ĕ hōd′.

Hear, O Israel: the Lord our God, the Lord is One.

SHEMONEH-ESREH shə mō nā′ ĕs rā′ (Ju). *See* AMIDAH.

SHEOL shĕ ōl′ (Ju—Heb.; etymology unknown). The underworld, or place of abode after death. Envisioned as lying deep beneath the earth (Num. 16:30-34; Job 11:8; Amos 9:2), it may have gates (Isa. 38:10), or be approached by a descending road (Prov. 5:5; 7:27). Seen as a power from which God can rescue (Pss. 18:5-6, 116:3-4, Isa. 28:15-18), or punishment of evil persons (Ps. 9:17; Job 24:19; Isa. 5:14), or the fate of all (Ps. 89:48).

D. IRVIN

SHI'A shē′ ä **SHI'ITE** shē′ īt (I—Arab.; lit. "separate or distinct party"). The branch of Islam composed of those sects that are followers of ALI and upholders of his direct succession to the office of IMAM after MUHAMMAD. They refuse to accept the imamate of ABŪ BAKR, 'UMAR, and 'UTHMĀN, who preceded Ali in the office of CALIPH.

1. **Origins.** The origins of the Shi'a are difficult to reconstruct, because of unfair presentation of their views by SUNNI authors and biased reporting by later Shi'ites. A consistent picture of the early Islamic community and its attitude toward the question of leadership *(imāma)* is indispensable for understanding the Shi'ite movement. Muhammad's message, as embodied in the QUR'ĀN, provided tremendous spiritual as well as socio-political impetus for the establishment of the ideal community (UMMA) of

SHI'A

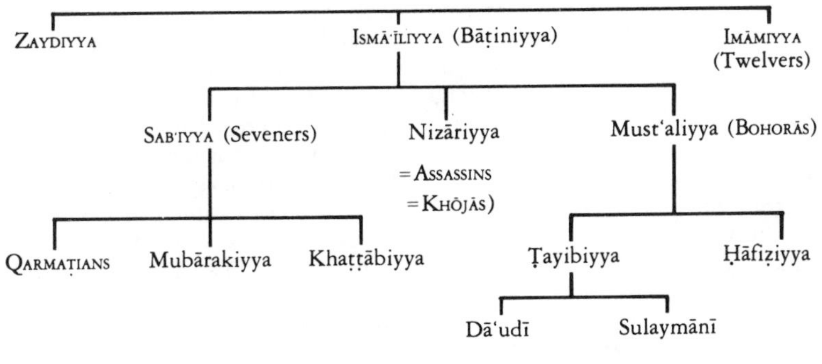

Islam. Muhammad himself was not only the founder of a new religion but also the guardian of a new social order. Consequently the question of leadership was the crucial issue which divided Muslims into various factions in the decades after his death. The early years of Islam were characterized by constant victories of the Muslim armies under the first three caliphs. But as this period came to an end and civil war broke out in A.D. 656, discussion arose over the necessity of a qualified leadership to assume the office of imam. Most of these early discussions on the imamate dealt with political issues, but eventually they took on religious implications as well. The rise of several imams and the sympathetic, even enthusiastic, following that they attracted clearly shows a desire to order Muslim society so as to fulfill its historic responsibility—the formation of a just society with an appropriate political organization.

2. **The concept of the imamate.** The Shiʿa, from the early days of the civil war in 656, thought of the imamate in both religious and political terms. They maintained that Muhammad was a charismatic leader who held both spiritual and temporal power. His spiritual authority included the power to interpret the message in the Qurʾān without corrupting the revelation. Islam, in order to continue its function of directing the faithful toward a more just social order, was in need of a leader who could perform the Prophet's role authoritatively. The exaltation of the Prophet and his rightful successor gave rise to the concept of an imam from among the descendants of the Prophet who could create an ideal Islamic community. The entire spiritual edifice of the Shiʿa was built on the *walaya* (love and devotion) to Ali, who became the first Shiʿite imam. In fact, *walaya* to Ali became the sole criterion for judging true faith.

The Shiʿite concept of the imamate was bound to meet with strong resistance, since it not only demanded the recognition of Ali and his descendants as the succession of rightful imams, but also was a challenge to the rule of the UMAYYAD caliphate and a rallying point for all who felt discriminated against or maltreated by the ruling house. The early Shiʿa were united in their recognition of Ali and in their aspiration for a just order. Consequently, from its inception Shiʿism was an opposition party.

Several protest movements arose under a wide range of leaders from among Ali's descendants who were able to arouse in their followers a genuine religious urge to achieve political goals. However, Shiʿite attempts at direct political action met with strong resistance from the ruling dynasty, and very early their efforts met with failure. The resultant frustration produced further Shiʿite factions. The radical Shiʿites insisted on armed resistance to the oppressive rule of the caliphate. These were known as *ghulat* (extremists) because of the extravagant claims they made for their imams. Moderate Shiʿites, having seen the futility of direct political action, were prepared to postpone indefinitely the establishment of true Islamic rule.

It was probably the murder of AL-ḤUSAYN by Umayyad troops at KARBALA in 680 and later the failure of the revolt of Zayd (739), al-Ḥusayn's grandson, which marked the turn toward a quietist attitude by the Shiʿa, who until then had been willing to fight for their ideals. But they continued to lack a specific ideology as late as the ʿABBĀSID victory in 750. It was then that the great imam, Jaʿfar al-Ṣādiq, who had been largely responsible for the moderation and discipline of the radical elements, provided Shiʿism with a sectarian ideology. Moderate Shiʿites continued to uphold the imamate of the descendants of al-Ḥusayn through Jaʿfar al-Ṣādiq until the line reached the twelfth imam, who was believed to be the MAHDI and the "hidden imam," and whose return they awaited. These were the IMĀMIYYA or "Twelvers."

3. **Political struggles.** The radical Shiʿites had become so strong by the mid-eighth century that one of their sects was able to help organize the revolution which established the ʿAbbāsid caliphate. These rulers, however, disappointed their Shiʿite followers by abandoning the messianic role and embracing Sunnism. It was at this time that the idea arose of a divinely guided savior imam, the Mahdi, who was believed to be endowed with divine knowledge like that of the Prophet himself. This idea stirred the imaginations of all who had been deprived of their rights under the existing regimes. Ambitious men found that they could manipulate the genuine religious devotion of ordinary people in the name of the descendants of Ali. But the failure of these individuals to establish the rule of justice gave rise to the two central beliefs in the idea of the Imam Mahdi, the concealment *(ghayba)* and return *(rajʿa)* of the Messianic Imam at the appropriate time. These beliefs helped the Shiʿites endure under difficult circumstances. Lack of information on the exact time when the hidden imam would appear required them to be alert at all times.

In the political turmoil of the period al-Ṣādiq had the opportunity to propagate Shiʿite viewpoints without inhibition and to modify the radical tone of early Shiʿism into a more sober and tolerant school of Islamic thought. Al-Ṣādiq was accepted by all Shiʿites as their imam, including those of radical bent who attempted to establish the political power of Ali's descendants. He was also accepted as an authentic transmitter of the ḤADĪTH in the Sunnite compilation. This indicates that it was almost certainly under his leadership that moderate Shiʿism, with its veneration of the Prophet's family, came to be accepted by the Sunnite majority as a permissible interpretation of Islamic piety. His attitude toward politics became the cornerstone of the imamite political theory, which, in the absence of political guidance from the hidden imam, did not teach its followers to overthrow tyrannical rulers and replace them by the imam. Instead, the leadership of the community was divided into temporal and spiritual spheres. The former was vested in the ruling dynasty, which in theory required designation *(naṣṣ)* by the Prophet, but was acceptable as long as its sphere of action was limited to the execution of the law. The spiritual sphere also required a clear designation by the Prophet, passed on through his descendants, since the holder of spiritual authority was empowered to elaborate and interpret the Prophet's message without committing error. It was believed that from the day Muhammad died, spiritual authority resided in Ali, duly designated by the Prophet. This leadership was handed on through a line of imams, each of whom was designated by his predecessor. When the Messianic Imam appears, temporal and spiritual authority will merge in his person, and he, like the Prophet, will uniquely unite the two spheres of ideal Islamic rule. Thus the idea of imamate by designation among Ali's descendants, continuing through all political circumstances, was complemented by that of an imamate based not primarily on political claims, but on the special privilege of possessing prophetic knowledge. *See* ASSASSINS; KHĀRIJITES; MASHHAD; QARMAṬIANS; SAB'IYYA; SAYYID; SHARIF; ZAYDIYYA; ZIYĀRA.

Bibliography. M. G. S. Hodgson, "How Did the Early Shī'a Become Sectarian?" *JAOS* 75(1955); al-Bābu 'l-Hādī 'Ashar, *A Treatise on the Principles of Shi'ite Theology* (1928); Muḥammad b. 'Alī b. Mūsā b. Bābūya, *A Shi'ite Creed* (1942); R. Strothmann, *Die Zwölfer Schī'a* (1926); D. M. Donaldson, *The Shī'ite Religion* (1933).

A. A. SACHEDINA

SHIELD OF DAVID (Ju.) *See* MAGEN DAVID.

SHIN shĭn (B). *See* PURE LAND SECTS.

SHINGAKU shĭn′ gä koo (Jap.; lit. "heart [mind] learning"). A religious and ethical movement begun by Ishida Baigan (1685-1744) in 1729 and continuing until about the time of the MEIJI Restoration in 1868. Its principal appeal was to merchants living in cities, initially in Kyoto and Osaka, later in Tokyo and other major cities throughout Japan; but it also affected the peasantry and samurai and left a residue of influence in the ethics textbooks of the new public school system developed by the Meiji government.

Born to a farm family, Ishida was introduced in his youth to merchant life in Kyoto. Choosing to follow a way of self-improvement rather than material profit, he spent twenty years in self-directed study and five years in study under an older teacher, exploring the teachings of SHINTŌ, BUDDHISM, CONFUCIANISM, and TAOISM. At about age forty he was rewarded by an experience of enlightenment and soon thereafter began to give occasional lectures. In 1729 he opened a lecture hall and for the remainder of his life lectured there regularly—eventually to large audiences. He developed three basic teaching methods which were used in Shingaku throughout its history: the lecture, the question and answer session, and the practice of meditation.

Though Ishida's teaching was syncretic, he was influenced most directly by the Chinese sage MENCIUS. His basic admonition was "know the heart," that is, know the heart of heaven and earth and the unity of one's own heart with it and then live out the ethical implications of such mystical knowledge. This involved the practice of loyalty, FILIAL PIETY, and brotherliness within the obligations and opportunities associated with one's own occupation. In applying his teaching more precisely, he saw each class in the Tokugawa feudal society (samurai, farmers, artisans, merchants) as playing essential and respectable roles, the appropriate performance of which would lead to a prosperous, well-ordered society. His defense of the new and often despised merchant class was especially noteworthy.

While Ishida was Shingaku's founder and tone-setter, the movement owed much of its effectiveness and longevity to the organizational skill of one of his pupils, Teshima Toan (1718-1786). Himself a famous preacher and able writer, Teshima aided the movement most by giving it structure. The result was a controlled extension of Shingaku throughout much of Japan, with dozens of able preachers and writers reaching thousands of Japanese citizens with a message that seemed both timely and challenging.

By the middle of the nineteenth century Shingaku began to lose its cohesiveness through the splitting off of independent regional centers. Finally the policies of the Meiji government, favoring Shintō and calling for the establishment of a public school system, caused the demise of the fragmented movement. The consequence of its existence, however, can be traced in a multitude of longer-range influences.

Bibliography. R. N. Bellah, *Tokugawa Religion* (1957).

H. N. MCFARLAND

SHINGON shĭn gôn′ (B—Jap.; lit. "true or mystical word," translation of Skt. MANTRA). The Japanese sect of esoteric Buddhism founded and organized by Kūkai (KŌBŌ DAISHI), based on his interpretation of the esoteric Buddhist tradition he brought back to Japan from China. Shingon emphasizes doctrine, art, and especially ritual of an esoteric character, that enables humans to attain enlightenment or Buddhahood within the physical body of ordinary existence. The esoteric tradition was so popular that it spread to other sects and became an important influence on culture and popular beliefs.

The origins of Shingon go back to the Buddhist version of TANTRISM in India, which developed a number of traditions focusing on the religious power of incantations and iconography. There was no school in India directly corresponding to Shingon, but the bulk of esoteric Buddhist writings and rituals arrived in China about the eighth century A.D., where they were translated and organized in a preliminary fashion; however, no full-scale esoteric Buddhist sect developed in China. Kūkai traveled to China in 804 as a government emissary and spent thirty months mainly studying and practicing the esoteric Buddhist tradition. The rituals, ritual tools, and esoteric teachings he brought back to Japan constituted the basis for his formulation of the Shingon sect.

Kūkai preferred practice to theory, as is seen both in his selection of esoteric practices during his study in China and in his organization of the Shingon sect. Just as "shingon" means a kind of mystical word for invocation, the esoteric Buddhist tradition generally assumed that Buddhist teachings were divided into the secret or mystical teachings and the public or revealed teachings. Kūkai followed the precedent of esoteric Buddhism in preferring the secret teachings to the public teachings, and developed his sect along the lines of practice that incorporated these secret teachings. Although the historical Buddha Śākyamuni expressed public teachings, they are inferior to the deeper, mystical truths expounded by Mahāvairocana, the Great Sun Buddha and source of all esoteric truth, known in Japan as Dainichi. (*See* Vairocana.)

One of the most important esoteric writings authoritative for Shingon is the Mahāvairocana Sūtra (Jap. Dainichikyō). This text is the basis for one of the two Mandalas or iconographic representations of the esoteric pantheon and its doctrine; it also teaches that the esoteric truth should be incorporated into a person's body, speech, and mind (three important categories of Shingon doctrine). The other major Shingon textual authority is the writing known in Japanese as Kongōchōkyō, the basis for the counterpart mandala. These two mandalas, which individually symbolize the dualities of all life, conceived together represent the higher unity beyond all dualities. Although these mandalas contain hundreds of Buddhist divinities, one of the principles behind them is the notion that humans have inherent Buddha nature within themselves; by meditating on the mandala a person is able to realize this inherent Buddhahood (or seen differently, realize the person's identity within the Buddha). In this case, of course, the Buddha is the Sun Buddha, the source of all truth.

These teachings are acted out through colorful rituals, such as the fire ritual known as *goma* (Skt. *homa*), and a kind of ordination rite (known as *kanjō*) of sprinkling water on a person. Mystical formulas (known in Japan as *darani*) and their shortened versions, Mantras, were practiced within Shingon but soon came to be adopted by other sects and used by the people as magical utterances.

Kūkai was a contemporary of Saichō (Dengyō Daishi), founder of Tendai. Both had some connections with the court, but in their lifetimes Saichō was more influential than Kūkai, and Saichō's more inclusive sect was an important watershed of later sect developments, notably Pure Land and Nichiren. By contrast, Kūkai's later influence was more indirect in terms of providing the esoteric coloring of Japanese Buddhism and folk faith, and as an important figure for Japanese literature. Ironically, popular faith in Kūkai is more extensive than that in Saichō, and the title of *daishi* is associated with him perhaps more than any other Buddhist figure, even though Kūkai received the title Kōbō Daishi later than Saichō received that of Dengyō Daishi. Many folk tales abound about Kōbō Daishi, and the term *daishikō* (lit. "great master association") refers to devotional groups organized around the veneration of Kōbō Daishi.

Bibliography. M. Kiyota, *Shingon Buddhism: Theory and Practice* (1978).

H. B. Earhart

SHINRAN shĭn răn´ (B; 1173-1262). Japanese Buddhist priest and scholar; founder of Jōdo Shin-shū (Pure Land True Sect). He studied Tendai Buddhism at Mt. Hiei, but left to work with Hōnen, whom he followed in emphasizing the sole practice of Nembutsu. Shinran came to favor the aspect of faith behind the recitation rather than the number of recitations. He stressed the inability of man to attain salvation, therefore insisting on the necessity of absolute faith in Amida (rather than one's own work of recitation). Shinran is famous for marrying, and for advocating the open marriage of monks, since he wanted to minimize the distance between clergy and laity. He continues to be respected and studied for his deep insight into human nature.

H. B. Earhart

SHINTŌ shĭn´ tō (Jap.; "way of the kami or gods"). Japanese religious tradition that emerged out of prehistoric religious practices and such influences as Buddhism and Chinese religions, and developed distinctive beliefs and practices. The world view found in Shintō is central to Japanese culture and has often been closely related to the national identity.

1. **Formation.** In the middle of the first millennium B.C. Japan's hunting-gathering culture gave way to a combination of agriculture (particularly rice) and fishing as the basis of a sedentary village life. This culture featured a strong sense of family lineage and social cooperation, with religious emphasis on rites of fertility and Ancestor Veneration. Possibly under the influence of subsequent migration from the Asian continent, a leading family came to be the center of an imperial line in southwestern Honshu. Families and villages carried out their own religious observances according to rather diverse local customs, while the imperial line began to assume ritual leadership for the country as a whole.

Until the coming of Chinese culture, bringing the highly organized religion of Buddhism about A.D. 500, the native tradition apparently had no name, but to distinguish it from Buddhism (called *Butsudō,* "the way of the Buddha") the native tradition was given the name Shintō (the way of the Kami); the *tō* of Shintō and the *dō* of Butsudō are variant pronunciations of the same Sino-Japanese character (Chin. *tao*) meaning the "way." (Shintō can also be pronounced in the Japanese fashion, *kami no michi.*) The Kojiki (712) and

James Whitehurst

Festival at a small Shintō shrine commemorating its founding. Procession of priests and attendants carry representations of the kami, accompanied by flutes and drums

the NIHON SHOKI (720) begin with an account of creation, expressed in the Chinese terms of YIN AND YANG, and then record the role of the gods (kami) in creating the Japanese islands and the imperial line. The divine pair IZANAGI AND IZANAMI were responsible for bringing forth the Sun Goddess (AMATERASU Ōmikami), the divine antecedent of the emperor. These mythological accounts gathered together the rather diverse local traditions and unified them into one national heritage.

2. **Major features.** A characteristic feature of Shintō is the notion of kami, which pervades all of Japanese culture. Mythological accounts give a picture of the kami as dwelling in heaven or inhabiting the earth as the sacred forces within nature. The notion of kami as sacred power is broad and flexible; the emperor is formally considered a "manifest kami" because of his direct descent from the Sun Goddess, and in popular practice living humans with extraordinary spiritual powers as well as family ancestors are considered to be kami.

The so-called "ritual prayers" *(norito)* were included in the documents concerning Shintō in the A.D. 927 compilation called *Engi-shiki*. These prayers—sometimes more akin to magical formulas and incantations—seek to maximize agricultural harvests and blessings on social units or territories, while avoiding destruction and ill fortune. Especially worthy of mention is the rite of exorcism and purification *(harai)* performed at the middle and end of the year, to drive out all impurities or "pollution." On the popular level the most important meeting between people and the kami was in seasonal festivals *(matsuri)*, when the presence of the kami was invoked and people came into more direct contact with them.

The earliest shrines may have been natural objects, such as boulders, trees, and waterfalls, which were the dwelling place of the kami. Even today the sacred character of these special boulders and trees is indicated by surrounding them with straw ropes. However, from prehistoric times a special type of raised wooden shrine developed; it may hark back to stilted structures from the South Pacific, and may have been the earliest form of palace. The classic form of this shrine is still seen in the ISÉ SHRINE today, with its massive unpainted wooden pillars and thatched roof, widely hailed as one of the world's architectural treasures. As different shrine traditions emerged, variations of the Shintō shrine developed. Some are too small for humans to enter, and some are quite large. Entrance to the precincts of a shrine is marked by an archway called TORII; water is provided for the worshiper to rinse hands and mouth as symbolic purification before coming into contact with the kami. A basic division in many shrine buildings is between the larger *haiden* (oratory or hall of worship) and the smaller *honden* (the inner sanctuary or main shrine) behind it. In contrast to Buddhist temples, Shintō shrines usually do not feature statues; rather, ancient relics such as mirrors and swords are sometimes considered the dwelling place of the kami. Offerings such as fish and vegetables are presented to the kami and later eaten. Offerings to the kami were made in the home in ancient times, and in more recent times a form of Shintō altar (KAMIDANA) was located in most homes.

Shintō priests in ancient times were members of special hereditary "clans" or ritual families which served the court. Later these families became the nucleus of medieval schools of Shintō thought and practice which incorporated Buddhist and Confucian notions. Large shrines still utilize full-time priests, but many small shrines are served by part-time priests. In the countryside there was often a rotating priesthood, which was passed among the heads of the local households. Generally the role of Shintō priests has been to present offerings and formally mediate between the kami and the local populace. In ancient times priestesses called *miko* played an important part in Shintō, and this practice survived later in the tradition of imperial princesses serving at the Isé Shrine. In recent history *miko* are only helpers of priests.

Traditionally each shrine observed the New Year's festival, spring and fall festivals, and special festivals honoring the local shrine—all of which helped form the religious year for the local people. In fact, many local customs linked the people as parishioners to the shrine in whose territory they lived. For example, the first time a newborn child left the home was for a visit to the local shrine to be blessed as a "child" of the local kami. Individuals also visit their local shrine (or distant larger shrines) for petitioning the kami in time of personal crisis. Except for some of the medieval schools, Shintō has shunned formal theological systems, favoring instead a sincere reverencing of the kami and respect for ritual purity.

3. **Shintō in modern Japan.** Two junctures have been of exceptional importance for Shintō in modern Japan: the MEIJI Restoration of 1868 and the end of World War II in 1945. The Meiji Restoration marked an end to the Tokugawa period (1600-1867) and its favoritism of Buddhism and Neo-Confucianism (*see* CONFUCIANISM §3), restoring the emperor to symbolic importance in the government and sharply separating Shintō from Buddhism; the intention was to make Shintō the religious basis of the government. This did not work out, but Shintō was used by the government to justify loyalty to the emperor as a symbol for unifying the new nation-state, and Shintō mythology was transformed into an ideology used by the educational system to inculcate loyalty to the state. During the Meiji period (1868-1911) Shintō was declared "nonreligious" in the attempt to maintain freedom of religious belief while requiring Shintō teachings in the public schools; this development is usually called State Shintō. (Some active Shintō groups were recognized as "Sect Shintō" and operated as organized religions; *see* KONKŌ-KYŌ; TENRI-KYŌ.)

Visual Education Service, Charles A. Kennedy

Basic costume of the Shintō priest dates to the Heian period (9th-11th century A.D.). The wooden blade held in the hand or tucked in the sash was originally an emblem of rank.

After 1945 drastic changes occurred within Shintō, as in all of Japanese culture. Partly due to efforts of the Allied Occupation, Shintō was "disestablished," meaning that it was once more recognized as a religion free to exist the same as any other religion, but without state support or special privilege. The intimate association between Shintō and the war effort dampened enthusiasm for participation in Shintō, but more damaging were the gradual changes in life-style, as Japan moved from an agricultural way of life toward an urban, industrial society. Moreover, after World War II the land reform took away land from many shrines, forcing them to use their buildings for such purposes as kindergartens or to have their priests seek part-time employment. The postwar period has been a difficult time for Shintō, and in modern homes the Shintō altar has been given up more frequently than the Buddhist altar (BUTSUDAN).

But some feel that the postwar changes present Shintō with the challenge it needs to form a new and vital tradition. Obligatory financing and participation in local shrines is no longer possible, and new forms of organizing local people along the lines of voluntary organizations are being tried. Shintō has long defined a distinctively Japanese spiritual tradition, and will continue to do so, both in Japanese culture generally as well as in its influence upon other religions, notably Buddhism and the new religions. *See* JAPANESE RELIGION.

Bibliography. W. H. M. Creemers, *Shrine Shinto After World War II* (1968); D. C. Holtom, *The National Faith of Japan: A Study in Modern Shinto* (1938); T. Muraoka, *Studies in Shinto Thought* (1964). H. B. EARHART

SHIRK shĭrk (I—Arab.; lit. "partnership, association"). Idolatry, polytheism, the worship of anything other than (or alongside) God, singled out in the QUR'ĀN as the one unforgivable sin (Sura 4:48, 116). One who commits *shirk* is a *mushrik*. An important synonym for *shirk* is KUFR, although they are not always to be equated.

Sometimes the PEOPLE OF THE BOOK, i.e. Jews and Christians, are included among the *mushriks* (e.g., Sura 98:1, 6), but most often the literal idolatry of Arabian paganism is meant (e.g., Sura 6:137; 29:41; 43:15, 16). The opposite of *shirk* is TAWḤĪD, the affirmation of the divine unity in word and deed, regarding nothing to be worthy of comparison to God.

No movement has been more sedulous in rooting out *shirk* than the Wahhābīs (*see* WAHHĀBĪYA), who have aimed their condemnations most especially at popular saints' cults and the visitation of tombs and other holy places. (*See* ZIYĀRA.) The theorists of this sect also view belief in intercession (except for that of the Prophet on Judgment Day), superstitious practices, swearing by anyone but God, divination, and indeed any behavior which does not center in obedience to God as one, as *shirk*.

Bibliography. *The Meaning of the Glorious Koran,* M. M. Pickthall, trans., index, under "idolators"; Muslim, *Ṣaḥīḥ,* ET A. H. Ṣiddīqī (1971-75), I, 50 ff. F. M. DENNY

SHIVA, ŚIVA shĭ′ vŭ (H—Skt.). Shiva is, with Vishnu, one of the two great gods of Hinduism. His worship can be traced back to the shadowy figure of RUDRA in the RIG VEDA (*ca.* 1200 B.C.) and extends to every part of India and Hindu Southeast Asia. Though he is often casually referred to as the Destroyer (by Hindus as well as by Western scholars), his true nature includes orgiastic and philosophical traits, though destruction is indeed his forte.

1. **History.** Many strands make up the long thread of Shiva's history in India. There is a striking resemblance between the medieval image of Shiva and a steatite seal unearthed from the ruins of the INDUS VALLEY CIVILIZATION (*ca.* 2200 B.C.); this seal depicts an ithyphallic male seated in a yogic posture, with horns on his head and wild animals around him. Because Shiva in his aspect of Lord of Beasts (PAŚUPATI) is often represented in this way, it is tempting to identify the two figures, though this tenuous connection would span two millennia. Far more reliable is the tradition that traces Shiva back to Rudra in the Rig Veda, a sinister god who haunts the mountains and the wilderness and is worshiped at crossroads, away from all the other gods. Rudra is a killer of men and cattle, a god of the untamed storm; he brings disease, but he is also a healer and master of drugs.

To this Vedic base were added aspects of Shiva borrowed from other Vedic gods (phallic worship associated with INDRA, incestuous and androgynous creation associated with PRAJĀPATI, fiery eroticism associated with AGNI) as well as orgiastic traits that may have originated with hill tribes. By the time of the UPANISADS, Shiva was the object of fervent devotion and the special god of YOGIS. His name appears on Kuṣāṇa coins and inscriptions from the first century B.C., evidence that by then he was God to many important Hindus.

2. **Texts.** After the Vedic hymns to Rudra, the Śvetāśvatara Upaniṣad is the first great text devoted to the worship of Shiva, who is there regarded as the seat of godhead and the controller of KARMA and SAMSARA. In the Epics Shiva is recognized as God in several late passages, despite the greater attention paid to VISHNU (as KRISHNA and as RĀMA). Shiva is ominously present in the MAHĀBHĀRATA at several points when disaster comes to fruition, but he is also praised in hymns celebrating his 1,008 names. He appears to ARJUNA in the form of an outcaste hunter, subjects him to a violent combat, and gives him magic weapons.

The principal myths of Shiva are known to the RĀMĀYAṆA and to the earliest PURĀṆAS, dating from the fourth century A.D. (Vāyu, Brahmāṇḍa and Varāha Purāṇas), but he is the central object of worship only in Purāṇas composed several centuries later (Kūrma, Vāmana, and Matsya). Roughly contemporaneous with the second group of Purāṇas are the TAMIL Śaiva texts composed by the NĀYAṆĀRS and the SANSKRIT Śaiva texts composed in Kashmir; during this period, too, the Śaiva philosopher ŚAMKARA is said to have written his hymns of devotion to Śiva.

Between the tenth and twelfth centuries the South Indian Vīraśaivas composed their highly individualistic poems to Śiva in Kannada, and by this time the great Śaiva Tantras were in use. The South Indian Śaivas of this period also composed, in Sanskrit and Tamil, the bulk of the ĀGAMAS as well as the documents of the ŚAIVA SIDDHĀNTA. But by far the richest source of texts dealing with the myth and ritual of Shiva is the group of later Purāṇas (Śiva, Liṅga, and Skanda Purāṇas).

3. **Sects.** Most worshipers of Shiva are members of no particular sect, who merely observe daily worship (PŪJĀ) of Shiva either in the form of a LIṄGA or as an anthropomorphic image, in a private shrine in the

corner of a house or at a temple devoted to Shiva (where Purāṇic texts are recited). But several groups of wandering ascetics base their activity upon an *imitatio dei* as described in the mythology of the Sanskrit Purāṇas or in local vernacular texts. Foremost among these are the Pāśupatas, of whom there are several subgroups; probably the oldest is the Lakulīśa sect, followers of the "Lord with the Club," an ancient sage regarded as an incarnation of Shiva, usually depicted as ithyphallic as well as holding a reiteratively erect club. Later offshoots of the Pāśupatas included the Kālamukhas ("Black-faces," a possible reference to black streaks painted on the face), KĀPĀLIKAS ("Skull-bearers"), and the Nāthas ("Masters," of whom the Gorakhnāthīs of the Punjab are the most numerous).

4. Sites. Mount KAILĀSA is Shiva's lofty abode, a mountain in the Himalayas; South India regards its own sacred mountain, Aruṇācalam, as Shiva's favorite home. Besides these natural sites that are places of pilgrimage, the great temples and shrines dedicated to Shiva include the caves at Elephanta near Bombay, the cluster of mushroom-topped temples at Bhubaneshwar in Orissa, many of the erotic temples at KHAJURĀHO, the immense temple complex at Chidambaram, the rock-hewn Kailāsa at Elephanta, and the entire city of Banāras. Many myths describe Shiva's passionate attachment to Banāras: it is said that when Shiva had beheaded BRAHMĀ, the skull stuck to his hand while he wandered all over India until he came to Banāras, where the skull fell from his hand at the spot known since then as Kapālamocana, "Skull-releasing." Later, in order to make Banāras his home, Shiva corrupted a virtuous king (and devoted Śaiva) who had made the city his own; he then drove the king away and refused to leave the city, which is therefore known as Avimukta, "The Nonabandoned." *See* HINDU SACRED CITIES §3.

5. Myths and symbols. In addition to his general qualities of supreme God for those who worship him, Shiva symbolizes particular aspects of life for all Hindus, Śaivas and non-Śaivas alike. These aspects tend to become polarized into clusters of myths and symbols dealing with procreation or renunciation, or both.

As the god of the *liṅga,* Shiva is worshiped by women who wish to become pregnant, and he is celebrated in myths telling of his various marriages (to SATĪ, the daughter of Dakṣa; to PĀRVATĪ, daughter of the mountain Himalaya; to the river GANGES; and to many local goddesses throughout India) and of the birth of his two sons, SKANDA and GAṆEŚA. As the god of renunciation, Shiva is said to set in motion the fire and flood of doomsday, and he is visualized as an outcaste yogi who lives in the cremation grounds among the corpses and withdraws into deep meditation for centuries on end. These apparent polarities are constantly resolved and restated; on the cosmic level doomsday leads to the rebirth of the universe, and on the anthropomorphic level Shiva vacillates between periods of asceticism and periods of orgiastic union with Pārvatī, in which his sexual powers are heightened by his YOGA. His ability to transcend these and other opposites is often expressed in the image of the androgyne, half-man half-woman (Ardhanārīśvara), or in its derivative variant, Vishnu-Shiva (Hari-Hara). (*See* ANDROGYNY.)

His destructiveness has both cosmic and local dimensions. Shiva is said to have destroyed with a single arrow the three cities of the demons on earth, in heaven, and in the atmosphere; this act is a metaphor for the destruction of the three worlds themselves at doomsday. He is also said to have destroyed the sacrifice of King Dakṣa in revenge for not having been invited to it, beheading Dakṣa and thus in effect performing the sacrifice himself, using Dakṣa as the sacrificial animal and even replacing the head with that of the sacrificial goat. At the end of this episode Shiva was given a share of the sacrifice; the myth thus explains the assimilation of this unsavory outsider into orthodox Hinduism, where he has become, ironically, the Brahmins' god *par excellence*. *See* ŚAIVISM.

Bibliography. Primary Texts: *Liṅga Purāṇa,* J. L. Shastri, trans. (1973); *Śiva Purāṇa,* J. L. Shastri, trans. (1970). Secondary Texts: R. G. Bhandarkar, *Vaiṣṇavism, Śaivism, and Minor Religious Systems* (1913); S. Chattopadhyāya, *The Evolution of Theistic Sects in Ancient India* (1962); S. Dasgupta, *A History of Indian Philosophy,* V: *Southern Scholars of Śaivism* (1962); T. A. G. Rao, *Elements of Hindu Iconography* (1916), II, 1; S. Bhattacharji, *The Indian Theogony* (1970), pp. 23-210; W. D. O'Flaherty, *Asceticism and Eroticism in the Mythology of Śiva* (1973), *Hindu Myths* (1975), pp. 116-174, and *The Origins of Evil in Hindu Mythology* (1976), pp. 272-320.

W. D. O'FLAHERTY

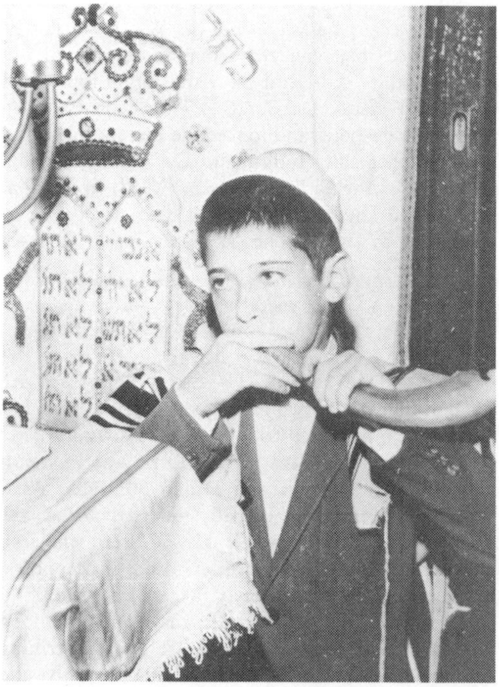

American Jewish Archives, Hebrew Union College—Jewish Institute of Religion

Here the shofar is blown by a young student

SHOFAR shō´ fär (Ju—Heb.). The ram's horn sounded in the SYNAGOGUE during the Hebrew month of Elul preceding the High Holy Days and especially during the services of ROSH HA-SHANAH (New Year) and once at the concluding service of YOM KIPPUR.
B. MARTIN

SHOGHI EFFENDI shō ghē´ ĕf fĕn´ dē (Ba; 1898-1957). The oldest grandson of 'ABDUL-BAHĀ, designated by his grandfather as "Guardian of the Cause" or leader of the Bahā'ī community. He was the principal translator of BAHĀ' ULLĀH'S writings and is responsible for the central organization of the community. *See* BAHĀ'Ī §1.
C. J. ADAMS

SHŌTOKU shō´ tō koo (B; 573-621). Prince regent of Japan during the reign of his aunt, the Empress Suiko, from 593 until his death. He was perhaps the person most responsible for the early flourishing of BUDDHISM in Japan. The prince had a strong personal faith in the Buddhist teachings and saw Buddhism as a great cultural force. Indifferent to sectarian divisions, he placed his trust in the universalism of the LOTUS SŪTRA. A great admirer of Chinese culture, Shōtoku tried to establish a balance of SHINTŌ, CONFUCIANISM, and Buddhism. He sent many young scholars, officials, and Buddhist priests to China for training. For the welfare of his father's soul he founded the HORYU-JI temple near his own palace. Soon after his death he came to be regarded as an earthly manifestation of AVALOKITEŚVARA. He is credited with having promulgated in 604 Japan's first constitution.
K. CRIM

SHROUD OF TURIN (Ch). A burial cloth of ancient linen preserved since 1578 in the Royal Chapel of the Cathedral of Saint John the Baptist, Turin, Italy, and held by an increasing number of specialists to be the cloth in which Christ was buried. Measuring approximately fourteen feet three inches by three feet seven inches, and woven chiefly in a three-to-one twill from linen containing minute traces of cotton fibers, this fabric bears the negative frontal and dorsal image of a man laid out in death and covered with wounds. Scientific study of this shroud began only in 1898, when glass negatives developed by the photographer Secondo Pia reversed the negative images and revealed the photographic positive likeness of a bearded man approximately five feet eleven inches tall, thirty to forty-five years old. Anatomical analyses of the image, which is outlined not by pigmentation but by delicate cloth-stains, point to severe buffeting of the face, flagellation (thongs with twin pellets of bone or metal), "crowning" with a spiked circlet, crucifixion (nails through chief wrist folds and between metatarsal bones of feet), and piercing of the right side between fifth and sixth ribs—details which conform to scriptural accounts of the death of Jesus. Increasingly sophisticated testing has tended to confirm the authenticity of the shroud, though in some instances results have been simply inconclusive (though not negative).

Bibliography. I. Wilson, *The Shroud of Turin* (1978), with copious bibliography.
C. WADDELL

SHULHAN ARUCH shûl hän´ ä rook´ (Ju—Heb.; lit. "prepared table"). A sixteenth century legal code, composed by JOSEPH CARO, considered the most definitive, authoritative text in Jewish rabbinic law. It consists of four main volumes: *Oraḥ Ḥayyim,* which deals with daily life, the SABBATH, and the cycle of festivals; *Yoreh De'ah,* which deals with dietary laws, ritual purity, and mourning; *Even Ha-Ezer,* which deals with family law; and *Ḥoshen Mishpat,* which deals with civil and criminal law. Its language is rabbinic HEBREW.

The *Shulhan Aruch* was prepared by Caro as a digest of his encyclopedic commentary on the legal code known as the "Four Rows," written by Jacob ben Asher. Unlike his larger work, the *Shulhan Aruch* states only the law itself without discussion of sources or precedents or rationale.
K. P. BLAND

SIDDHĀRTHA sĭd dhär´ tŭ (B—Skt.) **SIDDHATTHA** sĭd hŭt´ tŭ (B—Pali). The personal name of Gautama the BUDDHA, Siddhārtha means "one who attains the goal." This name does not appear in the earliest texts, but since no other personal name has been attributed to the Buddha, there is no positive reason to discount the later tradition.
R. H. DRUMMOND

SIDDHI sĭd´ dē (H—Skt.; lit. "accomplishment, performance, fulfillment, complete attainment, success, perfection" [*sidh*—"to be accomplished, be successful, succeed"]). Paranormal psychic powers that the YOGIN attains while practicing *saṃyama* (or the "complete retraining" characteristic of the higher stages of practicing YOGA). Productive attitudes of awareness that are conducive to the attainment of "isolation" or "freedom" *(kaivalya)* for the follower of SĀṂKHYA. The *siddhis* are said to be eight in number, but the listings differ in varying texts. In the literature of Yoga two listings are common. The Yogatattva Upaniṣad (vss. 73-75) lists the eight *siddhis* as follows: (i) clairaudience; (ii) clairvoyance; (iii) moving through long distances quickly; (iv) paranormal vocal power; (v) assuming whatever form the yogin desires; (vi) vanishing from sight at will; (vii) deriving gold from iron by smearing the excrement and urine of the yogin on iron; (viii) moving through ethereal space. Vyāsa's *Bhāṣya* on Yogasūtra III.45, however, lists the eight as follows: (i) becoming small as an atom; (ii) becoming exceedingly light; (iii) becoming large; (iv) attaining the paranormal ability to touch the moon; (v) irresistible will; (vi) control over all physical things;

(vii) mastery over all appearances; and (viii) the ability to place anything wherever the yogin wills it. In the classical Sāṃkhya texts, moreover, the eight *siddhis* are taken to be productive attitudes of awareness rather than paranormal attainments. In Sāṃkhya-kārikā 51 they are listed as follows: (i) the use of reasoning; (ii) careful study; (iii) oral instruction from a teacher; (iv) discussion with knowledgeable persons; (v) purity or generosity; (vi) detachment from psychological suffering; (vii) detachment from interpersonal suffering; and (viii) detachment from the suffering caused by fate. G. J. LARSON

SIDDUR sĭ dŏŏr′ (Ju—Heb.; lit. "order, organization" [of prayers]). The prayerbook of JUDAISM.

The oldest Jewish prayerbook preserved was compiled by Rav Amram Gaon for ninth century Spanish Jews. Prayerbooks include daily, Sabbath, and festival services, liturgy and blessings, the Psalms, Song of Songs, Chapters of the Fathers. Different local usages and liturgies are presented in SEPHARDI, ASHKENAZI, Yemenite, and other versions.

Mystic "intentions" (*kavvanot*) were introduced into prayerbooks by Lurianic KABBALA in the sixteenth century. R. Shneur Zalman of Ladi established a classical HASIDIC prayerbook (1816). Isaac Seligman Baer indicated the prayers' sources in his *Avodat Yisrael* (1868).

REFORM JUDAISM introduced shorter services and prayers in the vernacular, eliminated requests for the restoration of the sacrifices and the coming of the MESSIAH, and modfied the idea of the choice of Israel. Prayerbooks of CONSERVATIVE JUDAISM use Hebrew and the vernacular side by side and introduce supplemental readings. RECONSTRUCTIONIST prayerbooks delete the anthropomorphic and supernatural. Modern prayers commemorate the victims of the HOLOCAUST and ask for the welfare of Israel. Some Israeli prayerbooks include prayers to be uttered before the WESTERN WALL. Ashkenazi Jews assigned the term *Mahzor* to festival prayerbooks, which they came to distinguish from prayerbooks of the daily services.

See HAGGADAH; SELIHOT; PRAYER, JEWISH.

Bibliography. Orthodox: P. Birnbaum, ed., *Daily Prayer Book* (1949); *High Holyday Prayerbook* (1951). Conservative: The Rabbinical Assembly of America and the United Synagogue of America, *Sabbath and Festival Prayer Book* (1946); *Weekday Prayer Book* (1961). Reform: Central Conference of American Rabbis, *Shaarey Tefillah, Gates of Prayer* (1975).

Y. SHAMIR

SIGN OF THE CROSS (Ch). A liturgical and devotional gesture consisting of the tracing of a cross as a reminder of the grace that comes from the death of Christ. Three chief forms: (1) the small sign traced with right thumb on brow (as early as second century), and later also on lips and breast (as at the gospel in the Roman Catholic MASS); (2) the large sign traced by right hand from forehead to center of chest, then from shoulder to shoulder (left to right in West, right to left in East); (3) the sign of blessing made on persons or things with open right hand, and often accompanied by a spoken blessing.

C. WADDELL

SIKHISM sēk′ ĭsm (Skt. [*śiṣya*—"disciple"]). The Sikh Gurdwārās Act of 1925 defines a Sikh as "one who believes in the Ten Gurus and the Granth Sahib." The line of GURUS began with NĀNAK (b. A.D. 1469) and ended with GOBIND SINGH (d. 1708). The Granth Sahib (*see* ĀDI GRANTH) is the scriptures of the Sikhs, compiled by the fifth guru, Arjun, in A.D. 1604 and regarded by the Sikhs as the "living" embodiment of their ten gurus.

1. **Background influences.** Sikhism is an eclectic faith combining the teachings of BHAKTI HINDUISM and the Muslim SUFIS. Since all the Sikhs' ten gurus and the vast majority of those who accepted their teachings were Hindus, the influence of Hinduism on the development of Sikhism was preponderant; that of Islam is evident largely in the emphasis on monotheism and the rejection of idol worship and the CASTE system.

Scholars trace the resurgence of the *bhakti* cult to the ĀLVĀR and NĀYAṆĀR saints of South India and the stress on a single sacred reality to ŚAMKARA (eighth century A.D.), the expounder of ADVAITA—pure monism. Śaṃkara's monism rejected worship of idols, the caste system, and many practices of the BRAHMINS. A theistic adaptation of Śaṃkara's teachings was argued by RĀMĀNUJA (A.D. 1017-1137), a worshiper of VISHNU, who advocated the path of *bhakti* or devotion over knowledge (VIDYĀ) or action (KARMA) as the way to achieving salvation. Rāmānuja's teachings were propagated by his disciple Rāmānanda (1360-1470), who went a step further by accepting Muslims as well as Hindus of lower castes as his disciples. The most distinguished of Rāmānanda's disciples was KABĪR (*ca.* 1440-1518), who spread the message of *bhakti* across the North Indian Plain.

The impact of ISLAM on Indian religious thought was largely due to the influence of Sufi mystics. By the time of Nānak's birth there were over a dozen orders of Sufis in India, of which the Chishtiyā was the most important. The Islam of the Sufis was close to the Bhakti Hinduism preached by Kabīr. They believed in mystic union with God through ascetic discipline and chanting of litanies (DHIKR) under the guidance of a teacher, *pīr*. They also welcomed non-Muslims to their hospices.

2. **Guru Nānak.** At the time of Guru Nānak's birth (A.D. 1469) the Lodhi Afghans were ruling Northern India. The invasion of Timur in A.D. 1398 dealt the ruling dynasty a crippling blow from which it never recovered. Most of Nānak's life was spent in these uncertain times when there was little law or order in the countryside. He was in his late fifties when the Mogul Babar invaded India, defeated the Lodhi and a combination of Hindu RĀJAS, and set up a dynasty of his own. Nānak described it as the dark

night of falsehood in which the moon of truth could not be seen.

Nānak was thirty when at Sultanpur he proclaimed his mission to preach. His Janam Sākhīs (birth stories) describe it in detail. One morning, as was his custom, he had gone to bathe in a nearby stream. He disappeared in the water and was considered drowned. According to the biographers, he was summoned to the presence of God, who charged him with a mission in the following words: "Nānak . . . I am with thee. Through thee will my name be magnified. . . . Go in the world to pray and teach mankind how to pray. Be not sullied by the ways of the world. Let your life be one of praise of the word (Nām), charity *(dān),* ablution *(ishnān),* service *(sevā),* and prayer *(simran)."*

Nānak is reported to have been missing for three days and three nights. He reappeared on the fourth. The opening pronouncement of his mission was: "There is no Hindu; there is no Mussulman [Muslim]."

According to Sikh tradition (though questioned by some scholars), Nānak undertook four long voyages which took him all over India and finally to Mecca, Medina, and Baghdad. He spent the last years of his life preaching and singing hymns. He also built a temple (*dharmsālā*—"abode of righteousness"). He died in September, 1539, at the age of sixty-nine.

3. **Succession of Sikh gurus.** It is not certain whether Nānak intended to reform Hinduism, to bring the Hindus and Muslims close to each other, or to start a religious movement of his own. However, the impact of his personality on his following, which consisted of both Hindus and Muslims, was such that they began to describe themselves as *Nānakprasthas* (followers of Nānak's path), or his disciples—Sikhs. Before he died he appointed a disciple, Angad, to carry on his mission.

Guru Angad (1504-52) adopted a script current in Northern India into a new form, Gurmukhi ("from the mouth of the guru"), and compiled a hymnal of Guru Nānak's compositions, to which he added his own. He also formed the "the guru's *langar*" (kitchen), where disciples broke bread together, into a regular institution. Angad was succeeded by another disciple, Amar Das (1479-1574), as the third guru. Amar Das organized the Sikhs into twenty-two *manjīs* or bishoprics for the purpose of propagating Nānak's teachings and collecting a ten percent tax, the *dasvandh,* to defray the expenses of the guru's establishments. Amar Das nominated his son-in-law Ram Das Sodhi as the fourth guru. Thereafter guruship remained in the Sodhi family. Ram Das set up a new town and had a large pond dug in its middle. He nominated his son Arjun (1503-1606) as the fifth guru. Guru Arjun compiled the sacred scripture of the Sikhs, the Granth Sahib (Ādi Granth), consisting of the hymns of the first four gurus, his own compositions, and writings of Hindu and Muslim saints of Northern India. He also built the Harimandir (Temple of God) in the middle of the pond dug by his father. During Arjun's tenure the township started by his father became an important trading center and place of Pilgrimage. It came to be known thereafter as Amritsar—the pool of immortality (*see* Golden Temple).

During Arjun's time the Sikhs acquired a distinct religious identity of their own. He wrote:

I do not keep the Hindu fast, nor the Muslim Ramadan.
I serve Him alone who is my refuge.
I serve the one Master, who is also Allah.
I have broken with the Hindu and the Muslim,
I will not worship with the Hindu, nor like the Muslim go to Mecca,
I shall serve Him and no other.
I will not pray to idols nor heed the Muslims' *azan.*
I shall put my heart at the feet of the one Supreme Being
For we are neither Hindus nor Mussulmans.

Arjun also began trade with Afghanistan, Persia, and Turkey and became a merchant prince of considerable importance. He held court, received emissaries, and came to be addressed as the *Sachā Pādshāh*—"the true emperor." Even Emperor Jehangir's son, who had revolted against his father, came to Arjun for help.

Guru Arjun's involvement in Muslim politics brought the wrath of the emperor on his head. He was arrested and after being severely tortured was allowed to drown in the river Ravi. His martyrdom created a gulf between the Sikhs and Muslims and ended the pacifist phase of Sikhism. Before his incarceration, Arjun had nominated his son Hargobind as the sixth guru and girded him with two swords symbolizing spiritual and temporal power: "Let him sit armed upon the throne and maintain an army to the best of his ability" was the order.

Guru Hargobind raised a group of horse and foot soldiers. Emperor Jehangir had him detained in the fort of Gwalior for several years, but no sooner was he released than he regrouped his armed followers and fought against the Moguls.

Hargobind was succeeded by his grandson Har Rai (1630-64) and Har Rai by his son Harikrishan (1656-64) as the seventh and eighth gurus. Harikrishan having died a child, Emperor Aurangzīb tried to nominate a successor. This intervention by the Mogul court was frustrated by the Sikhs acclaiming Hargobind's surviving son, Tegh Bahadur (A.D. 1621-75), as their ninth guru. Tegh Bahadur spent the earlier part of his ministry in comparative inactivity at Anandpur in the foothills of the Himalayas. After some years he emerged from retirement and traveled through the Punjab and Uttar Pradesh with his wife and chosen band of followers. He left his pregnant wife at Patna (where his only son Gobind Rai was born) and went as far as Sylhet, Chittagong, and Sondip. On his return journey he again visited many towns in the Punjab. His popularity and preaching did not please the Mogul court. He was arrested, brought to Delhi, and beheaded on November 11, 1675.

The Mogul empire began to decay rapidly, as the bigotry of Aurangzīb and the ruling class antagonized a large section of the Hindus. The Marathas rose in opposition, and even Rajput princes who had supported the Moguls became indifferent. But the Punjab, which was predominantly Muslim, remained loyal.

Gobind Rai (1666-1708) spent his childhood and youth in the serenity of the Sivalik hills, where he trained in martial arts and composed poems. These are found in the anthology called Dasam Granth (the book of the tenth guru). He built a chain of fortresses and raised a militia. On the Punjabi New Year's Day in A.D. 1699 he baptized the KHĀLSĀ (a military fraternity), gave them and himself a new common family name, "Singh" (lion), and made it obligatory for them to wear their hair and beards unshorn and always carry a sabre *(kirpān)*. He also prescribed rules of conduct.

Gobind Singh is said to have explained these innovations to the assemblage: "I wish you all to embrace one creed and follow one path, obliterating all differences of religion. Let the four Hindu castes, who have different rules laid down for them in the Śāstras, abandon them altogether and, adopting the way of cooperation, mix freely with one another. Let no one deem himself superior to another. Do not follow the old scriptures. Let none pay heed to the GANGES and other places of pilgrimage which are considered holy in the Hindu religion, or adore the Hindu deities, such as RĀMA, KRISHNA, BRAHMĀ, and DURGĀ, but all should believe in Guru Nānak and his successors. Let men of the four castes receive baptism, eat out of the same vessel, and feel no disgust or contempt for one another."

Sikhs who did not accept baptism into the Khālsā fraternity came to be known as *Sahajdhāri* (those who take time to adopt). But those once baptized who later cut their hair or beards were rejected as *patits* (renegades).

Gobind Singh fought several successful engagements against the Hindu princely states of the Sivalik hills, but he was not able to withstand the might of the Moguls. He lost all his four sons; the two elder boys were killed fighting, and the two younger were taken prisoner and executed. Gobind himself was killed by two hired assassins at Nanded in the Deccan on October 7, 1708. According to Sikh tradition, before his death Gobind proclaimed that the line of gurus was at an end and thereafter the Sikhs were to regard the Ādi Granth as the living symbol of the ten gurus.

There are no reliable estimates of the numbers of the Khālsā or the Sahajdhāri Sikhs at the time of the death of Guru Gobind Singh. But it can be assumed that the total could not have been significant. It was in the seventeenth and the eighteenth centuries, when the Khālsā became a military and political power between the Indus and the Yamunā rivers, and particularly during the forty years' rule of Maharajah Ranjit Singh (A.D. 1799-1839) that large numbers of Hindu peasants converted to the Khālsā. The Sikhs continued to increase in numbers during British rule, largely because of the special favors accorded to the Khālsā in the army and the civil services, as well as due to the efforts of the Singh Sabha movement at the start of the twentieth century. In the census of 1951 the number of Sikhs (both Sahajdhāri and Khālsā) was recorded as 6,219,134. In the census of 1971 the figure stood at 10,378,797, or less than two percent of the population of India.

4. **Nānak's teachings.** Nānak, having been born a Hindu, was brought up on the sacred texts of the Hindus. His compositions show familiarity with the VEDAS and the UPANIṢADS. He was also exposed to the all-pervasive influence of the *bhakti* cult, notably the hymns of Kabīr, and his travels in the Punjab brought him into contact with various orders of Sufis. In addition to these positive influences were Nānak's negative reactions to Hindu ascetics, particularly the *Kānphatō* (pierced ear) YOGIS who practiced severe austerities enjoined by HAṬHA YOGA.

The opening lines of the JAPJI (morning prayer) are regarded by Sikhs as their *Mul Mantra* ("root belief"). Nānak spelled out his concept of God as one, supreme, uncreated creator of all things, beyond birth, death, and rebirth, omnipresent, and the supreme truth.

Nānak believed that God was *sat* (meaning both truth and reality), as opposed to *asat* (falsehood) and MĀYĀ (illusion). Nānak based his principles of social behavior on his concept of God. If God is truth, to speak an untruth is to be ungodly. Untruthful conduct not only hurts one's neighbors, it is also irreligious.

Nānak's God was beyond description, because he was *nirānkār*—formless. The best one could do is to admit the inability to define him.

> Thou hast a million eyes, yet no eye hast Thou.
> Thou hast a million forms, yet no form hast Thou.
> Thou hast a million feet, yet no feet hast Thou.
> Thou are without odor, yet millions of odors emanate from Thee.
> With such charms, O Lord, hast Thou bewitched me.
> Thy light pervades everywhere.

But the fact that God cannot be defined or proved by reasoning should not inhibit us from learning about truth and reality. This we can do by treading the path of righteousness.

Nānak used the terminology of both Hinduism and Islam to denote God. He was the Father *(Pitā)*, the Lover *(Prītam)*, the Master *(Khasam, Mālik* or *Sāhib)*, the Great Giver *(Dātā)*. He was *Rab, Rahīm, Rām, Govinda, Murāri* and *Harī*. Nānak, although he started by calling him *Aumkāra* ("Lord of Sound"), familiar to readers of the Vedas and the Upaniṣads, later called him *Sat Kartār* (the "True Creator") or *Sat Nām* (the "True Name").

The Sikh word for God is *Wāhi Guru*. It is not certain when the term came into vogue. *Wāhi Guru* ("Hail guru") is an exclamation of praise like the Muslim's *Subhān Allah*—("Allah be praised"). It has come to be the personification of God. Just as the Suras of the QUR'ĀN begin, "In the name of Allah the Beneficent, the Merciful," the chapters of the Ādi Granth begin with "The One God—by the grace of Guru, worship." There were other aspects of God that Guru Nānak took from the Vedas. Before creation God was *nirguṇa* ("qualityless") and in a state of profound meditation. After creation he became the repository of all qualities *(saguṇa)*. Likewise the symbolic representation of God as the mystic syllable OṂ in some of the Upaniṣads, as containing all that is past, present, and future, is echoed in the guru's *Dakhni Onkar*—as the creator of Brahmā, consciousness, time and space, the Vedas, the emancipator, the essence of the three worlds.

In equating God with the abstract principle of truth or reality, Nānak avoided the difficulty encountered by religious teachers who describe God only as the Creator or the Father: If God created the world, who created God? If he is the Father, who was his father? But Nānak's system has its own problems. If God is truth, what is the truth? Nānak's answer was that in situations when you cannot decide for yourself, let the guru be your guide.

Nānak made the institution of guru the keystone of his religious system. Without the guru as a guide, insisted Nānak, no one can attain MOKṢA (release). The guru keeps you on the straight and narrow path of truth; he is the goadstick which keeps man, who is like a rogue elephant, from running amok; he applies the salve of knowledge to your eyes so you can see the truth that is God; he is the divine ferryman who ferries us across the fearful ocean of life. The guru or the satguru (the true guru), was just a shade below God.

> The guru's word has the sage's wisdom,
> The guru's word is full of learning,
> For though it be the guru's word
> God Himself speaks therein.

However, Nānak did not equate the guru with God. The guru was to be consulted, respected, cherished, but not to be worshiped. He was a teacher, not a reincarnation of God, not an AVATAR nor a MESSIAH. Nānak constantly referred to himself as the bard *(dhādi)*, slave, and servant of God.

Nānak describes the qualities one should look for in the guru: "Take him as guru who shows the path of truth, who tells you of the One of whom nothing is known, who tells you of the divine word."

Nānak rejected ASCETICISM, penance, and torturing the flesh as steps toward enlightenment. "Be in the world but not worldly," he said.

When questioned by a group of yogis how a man could attain release from worldly attachments, he replied:

> The lotus in the water is not wet
> Nor the water-fowl in the stream.
> If a man would live, but by the world untouched,
> Meditate and repeat the name of the Lord Supreme.

Although Nānak left his family when he first launched on his spiritual quest and was often away on his travels, he always came back to them. He propagated the religion of the householder (GṚHASTHA). He advocated the company of holy men as an essential requisite of righteous living. And though he equated truth with God, he put righteous behavior even above truth.

Nānak denounced the caste system because it vitiated the relationship between man and man and contravened the ordinances of God, who created all men as equal. He was equally critical of concepts of purity and impurity that sprang out of notions of higher and lower categories of human beings.

Human birth, said Nānak, is a priceless gift. It is the opportunity that God gives us to escape the cycle of birth, death, and rebirth (SAMSARA). The aim of life should be union with God. Salvation lies in blending our light with the light eternal. The BHAGAVAD GĪTĀ advocated three alternative paths to salvation; that of action *(karma-mārga)*, of knowledge *(jñāna-mārga)*, and of devotion *(bhakti-mārga)*. Guru Nānak accepted the path of *bhakti*, laying emphasis on the worship of the Name *(nāma-marga)*. "I have no miracles except the name of God," he said.

Nānak believed that by repetition of the *nām* ("name") one conquered the greatest of all evils, the ego (*haumain*—literally, "I am"). So great did Nānak estimate the power of the ego that he described those who conquered it as having attained salvation while still alive *(jivanmuktas)*. Nānak believed that the ego carried in it the seed of salvation which could be nurtured to fullness by *nām*. Once the power of the ego is properly channeled, the conquest of the other five sins—lust, anger, greed, attachment, and pride—follows as a matter of course. The wanderings of the restless mind are stilled and it attains a state of bliss. It is in that state of superconscious stillness that the tenth gate, the *dasam duār* (the body having only nine natural orifices), is opened and one receives a vision of God and merges one's light with the light eternal.

Nām japō—"Worship the name of the Lord"—exhorted Nānak. But this meant more than a parrot-like repetition of *Rāma, Rāma, Rāma*. To Nānak, *Rām* implied prayer, an understanding of the words of the prayer, and their translation into a code of living. The path of the recitation of God's name *(nāma-marga)* requires three things: realization of the truth within the heart, its expression in prayer, and detachment from worldly things. He believed that a person's real battle in life is fought with his or her self. Nānak exhorted, "Overcome the base desires and battle with the mind. . . . Use knowledge as a double-edged dagger. . . . Then will base desires subside within the mind." For such a one who conquers himself the cycle of birth, death, and rebirth is ended and he attains salvation.

Nānak believed in the triumph of human will over fate and predestination. He believed that all human beings have a basic fund of goodness which, like the pearl in the oyster, only awaits the opening of the shell to emerge and enrich them. Just as the deer wanders about in the woods to fall in the snares of poachers or become a victim of the hunter's darts, so persons fall in the snares of *māyā* (illusion). The chief task of the guru is to make persons aware of the treasure within themselves and then help them to unlock the jewel box.

A method advocated by Nānak was the gentle one of *sahaj.* Just as a vegetable cooked on a gentle fire tastes best because its own juice gives it the proper flavor, so a gradual training of the body and mind will bring out the goodness that is inherent in all human beings. There is no general rule applicable to everyone; each person should discipline himself or herself according to physical capacity and temperament. Ascetic austerity, penances, and celibacy had no place in Nānak's religion. In addition to self-imposed discipline of the mind, he advocated listening to hymn singing. He advised his followers to rise well before dawn and listen to the soft strains of music under the light of the stars. He believed that in the stillness of the ambrosial hours one was best able to have communion with God.

Nānak did not believe in PILGRIMAGES to holy places or rivers or in the use of priests to recite prayers or perform rituals for others. Every Sikh was to be his or her own priest.

5. Social institutions: Sikh temples and priesthood. The *dharmsālās* ("abodes of righteousness") stated by Nānak evolved features distinct from the Hindu temple, the most unique being the guru's *langar,* lit. "kitchen," a communal meal where people could break bread without distinction of religion or caste. The kitchen was maintained from offerings of food-grains, GHEE, vegetables, and money. The *dharmsālās* also became rest-houses for travelers. Some time later the *dharmsālā* came to be known as the *gurdwārā* ("gateway to the guru"). Those that were connected with incidents in the lives of the gurus went by different names, e.g. birthplaces of Nānak at Talwandi and Gobind Rai at Patna, and the *gurdwārā* in Delhi marking the site of the execution of Tegh Bahadur. Four *gurdwārās* have specially elevated status; from them encyclicals binding on the community can be issued. Called *akāl takht* ("Throne of the Timeless God"), they are at Amritsar, Anandpur, Patna, and Nanded.

Although the gurus did not designate any priestly caste and empowered all Sikhs to perform rituals connected with births, marriages, and deaths, during the period of Muslim repression a priestly class known as *mahant* belonging to the Udāsī sect, who could pass as Hindus, were allowed to take charge of many of the most important *gurdwārās,* including the birthplace of Nānak and the Harimandir in Amritsar. The Udāsī *mahants* introduced many Hindu rituals and began to treat *gurdwārās* under their control as their hereditary property. A passive resistance movement in the 1920s succeeded in dispossessing the *mahants.* In 1925, the Sikh Gurdwārās Act was passed transferring control of all Sikh *gurdwārās* to an elected body known as Shiromani Gurdwārā Prabandhak Committee (S.G.P.C.).

The Sikh *gurdwārās* in India have an annual income of over Rs.5 crores (625 million U.S. dollars), which is dispersed by the S.G.P.C. to maintain schools, colleges, hospitals, orphanages, and also to run the *gurdwārā* kitchens. Currently a commission has been appointed by the Punjab government to advise on changes in the Sikh Gurdwārās Act of 1925.

Although Sikhism recognizes no priestly caste, many people today make a living as *granthī* (scripture reader) and *rāgī* (hymn singer).

6. Rituals and festivals. Sikhs are expected to rise before dawn, bathe, and recite the Japji. During the day four other prayers are recited. Sikh baptism *(pahul)* is performed in front of the Ādi Granth, but recitations include writings of Guru Gobind Singh as well. Sikh marriages are performed by the couple going round the Ādi Granth four times to the recitation of selected hymns.

Sikhs observe all Hindu festivals of Northern India as well as the birthdays of their gurus, the martyrdoms of Gurus Arjun and Tegh Bahadur, and the birth anniversary of the Khālsā, at which time they take out the Ādi Granth in procession.

7. Sikh sects and orders. *a) Udāsī.* There are several religious orders of Sikhs based either on disputes over the succession of gurus or points of ritual and tradition. Thus followers of Sri Chand, the ascetic elder son of Guru Nānak, described themselves as Udāsī ("detached"). And though they continued to be in the mainstream of Sikhism, they did not convert to the Khālsā started by Guru Gobind Singh. During the period of Sikh persecution by the Muslim rulers, the Udāsī took over the management of several Sikh shrines. Their introduction of Hindu idols and ritual in Sikh temples met with the disapproval of orthodox Sikhs, and they were divested of their control in the 1920s. Most Udāsī today observe Hindu customs and pay nominal homage to the Ādi Granth.

b) Nirmalā ("unsullied") were a class of theologians started by Guru Gobind Singh. He sent a group of scholars to Banāras to study Sanskrit and the Vedas to be better equipped to interpret the writings of the gurus, which make frequent allusions to Hindu mythology and sacred texts. Nirmalā wear white clothes and are vegetarians.

c) Nihangī are an order of militant Khālsā started during the time of Guru Gobind to act as shock troops. The word *nihang* derives from the Persian for "crocodile." They wear blue clothes and always carry arms on their person. They are subdivided into two groups, the *buddha dal* (veterans army) and the *taruna dal* (youthful army). Today they live largely on alms and are notorious for their addiction to hashish.

d) Namdhārī. A subsect of the Sikhs founded by Balak Singh (1797-1862) at Hazro in the Northwest Frontier Province. Balak Singh criticized the rich life-style of the Sikh aristocracy, preached the virtues of poverty, and exhorted the Sikhs to practice no ritual except repeating God's name, therefore *namdhārī* (adopters of the name). The Namdhārī continue their tradition of simple living. They dress in white handspun cloth, abstain from liquor, and are vegetarians. Their *gurdwārās* are unostentatious, and their wedding ceremonies performed in austere simplicity.

e) Other sects. Besides the above orders, there are sects who believe in the succession of gurus continuing after Guru Gobind Singh and pay homage to a living guru. The most important of these are the Nirānkāri, who include persons of all religions without requiring conversion to Sikhism.

8. Current issues. The most important issue facing the Sikhs is the growing incidence of Khālsā Sikhs cutting off their long hair and beards and gradually relapsing into Hinduism. The majority of young Sikhs living abroad are clean-shaven. The same is increasingly true of the Westernized, affluent classes of Sikhs in India. The many attempts to revive the Khālsā tradition have had limited success.

Bibliography. K. Singh, *A History of the Sikhs,* 2 vols. (1963-66); S. Singh, *Philosophy of Sikhism* (1966); W. M. McLeod, *Guru Nanak and the Sikh Religion* (1968); C. H. Locklin, *The Sikhs and their Scriptures (1958); The Sacred Writings of the Sikhs,* UNESCO sponsored (1960); M. A. Macaliffe, *The Sikh Religion* (1909); J. D. Cunningham, *The Religion of The Sikhs* (2nd ed. 1853). K. SINGH

SĪLA sē´ lü (B—Pali; "character, conduct") **ŚĪLA** shē´ lü (Skt.). Morality; conduct, either good or bad; conduct, especially with regard to the precepts undertaken by lay and ordained Buddhists. *Sīla* is the first of the three categories of Buddhist instruction. It is said that the disciple must follow basic morality before going on to master the second and third instructions, concentration and wisdom. Thus *sīla* is the foundation of the Buddhist path.

The bases of good morality are the five precepts, recited during worship by lay Buddhists as voluntarily binding upon their lives and not as divine commandments: "I undertake to observe the precept to abstain from killing living beings; to abstain from taking what is not given; to abstain from sexual misconduct; to abstain from false speech; to abstain from intoxicating drinks and drugs that cause moral carelessness."

Many lay Buddhists take upon themselves eight *sīlas* during Buddhist holy days, such as the new moon and full moon days. The eight include the five just quoted, except that the person abstains "from all sexuality" rather than merely from sexual misconduct, plus abstentions "from eating after midday" (no. 6), "from viewing entertainment shows and wearing adornments" (no. 7), and "from sleeping on high, luxurious beds" (no. 8). A few Buddhists, especially pious, elder ones, undertake to keep the eight precepts every day. The lay Buddhist who keeps the eight precepts is in effect observing all but one of the first ten rules binding on ordained Buddhist monks (BHIKKHUS). In the list of ten monastic rules, number seven in the list just given counts as two, and the tenth vow, abstinence from handling gold and silver, is not taken by the laity.

Bibliography. The best canonical source on *sīla* is the Sigalovada Suttanta of the Dīgha Nikāya, as trans. in T. W. Rhys Davids, *Dialogues of the Buddha,* III; or in Narada Thera, *Everyman's Ethics,* Wheel Publication no. 14.

R. C. AMORE

SIMEON STYLITES sĭm´ ē ən stī´ lī tēz (Ch; *ca.* 390-459). Syrian saint who lived chained atop a sixty-foot-high pillar for thirty-seven years, offering spiritual advice to those gathered below. Many disciples followed his example. He defended the CHALCEDONIAN Christological formula.

W. O. PAULSELL

SIMEON BAR YOHAI sĭm´ ē ən bär yō hī´ (Ju). A rabbinic authority and disciple of Rabbi AKIBA, who was active in Palestine during the mid-second century A.D. Tradition teaches that he and his son spent twelve years secluded in a cave, where they miraculously survived the failed revolt led by BAR KOCHBA. Later mystical traditions mistakenly identified him as the author of the ZOHAR. He is buried in present-day Meron in Israel, an important PILGRIMAGE site.

K. P. BLAND

SIMHAT TORAH sĭm hät´ tôr´ ə (Ju—Heb; lit. "rejoicing of the Law"). The festival immediately following SUKKOT. In Israel and among REFORM Jews it falls on the twenty-second of Tishri (September-October), and its celebration is joined with the rituals and practices of the preceding day. It is independently observed on the twenty-third of Tishri among all other Jews.

The holiday celebrates the completion of the public reading of the TORAH, which traditionally follows a one-year cycle. As symbol of the joy taken in its completion and the subsequent renewal of Torah study, all the scrolls are carried about with much singing and dancing. The procession circles the SYNAGOGUE seven times while prayers are offered. The final verses of Deuteronomy (33:1-29) are read as often as necessary, so that each male may be called to read the Torah. The practice is carried out on the eve and morning of the festival and is the only occasion at which the Torah is read publicly at night.

Subsequently, the first verses of Genesis (1:1–2:3) are read. Special significance is attributed to being called to read the last verses of Deuteronomy and the first of Genesis; these men are known as "the groom of the Torah" and "the groom of Genesis" respectively in traditional Judaism. It is customary for those so honored to offer contributions or a repast for those assembled.

Bibliography. A. Yaari, *Toledot Hag Simhat Torah* (1964).

D. J. SCHNALL

SIN, CHRISTIAN AND JEWISH CONCEPT. Anything, including attitudes, actions, or omissions, which separates a person from God. It is a theological or religious term in distinction to crime, a legal concept. Most conventional definitions such as "disobedience" or "rebellion against God" are too limited in scope.

1. **Biblical terminology for sin.** A great variety of words in both OT and NT are translated "sin." In the OT there are over twenty such words. In the NT *hamartia* is the most frequent word for sin. In some classical Greek usages it denoted "missing the mark of excellence through some human weakness or lack," but in the NT it means moral evil and has three general usages; i.e., the sinful act, human animosity to God, and the personification of evil.

2. **Origin of sin.** Genesis 3 is an attempt to explain that which the writer already knew to be a universal human experience by which humans are in need of God's redemptive activity. Sin is here ascribed to human culpability and not divine authorship. Historically Christian theology has held a belief in ORIGINAL SIN, a term which has often been interpreted to mean inherited sin and guilt. Jewish theology has not generally subscribed to this concept.

3. **Source of sin.** In Christianity, at least since AUGUSTINE, sin has been seen as due to human pride and has not been generally identified as the absence of good or as some other negation, nor found in human weakness, imperfection, or ignorance. People seek security and meaning for life in self rather than God, and the human overestimation of oneself is a universal attitude. Temptation is the appeal of evil under the guise of some good.

4. **Mortal and venal sins.** The OT distinguishes between deliberate sins and those committed through ignorance, weakness, or where the sinner was not totally responsible. This latter category could be propitiated by sacrifice, but the former only by throwing oneself on God's mercy. The RABBIS continued this distinction and defined idolatry, adultery, and murder as the deadliest of sins, with idolatry being the worst. The distinction in ROMAN CATHOLICISM between mortal and venal sins should be understood against that background. A mortal sin is one of such proportion as to render the sinner liable to eternal punishment and can "be forgiven only by the sacrament of penance," whereas venal sins are more easily forgiven. Mortal sins are to be distinguished from the unpardonable (unforgivable) sin which some have interpreted as final rejection of Christ. (*See* SIN, UNFORGIVABLE.)

Some denominations have taught that humans are "totally depraved," that is, as bad as possible or unable to discriminate between good and evil; or depravity may indicate that sin is pervasive in its influence on the entire human personality.

5. **Forgiveness of sin.** REPENTANCE is the means by which humans attain forgiveness and their alienation from God is ended, although this does not obviate all the results of sinful actions. Judaism has emphasized, where appropriate, the necessity of retribution to those harmed by sin. *See* SINS, SEVEN DEADLY.

Bibliography. L. Berkhof, *Systematic Theology* (1941), pp. 219-61; E. Brunner, *Man in Revolt* (1939), pp. 114-211; R. Niebuhr, *The Nature and Destiny of Man* (1943); H. W. Robinson, *The Christian Doctrine of Man* (1926).

T. O. HALL, JR.

SIN, MUSLIM CONCEPT. According to the QUR'ĀN, humanity has erred by straying from the straight path (Sura 1:5), and God has sent successive prophets to different peoples in different epochs to provide guideposts leading back to the straight path. For Muslims the framework of faith is not sin and salvation but error and guidance (*see* ISLAM §1).

Evil, therefore, is tantamount to distraction. For Muslims everywhere the invisible world is populated with two opposite kinds of spirits: 1) JINN, powerful and evil, who appeal to man's lower soul (NAFS) and whom SATAN (Shaiṭān), their leader, urges to either disguise reality or actually harm people; and 2) MALĀ'IKA, angelic creatures who incite persons to be aware of their higher souls (RŪḤ), to repent and to return to the Lord.

Except for prophets (*see* NABI), whom God has protected from sinning, all human beings are potentially negligent and, in that sense, sinful. For SHI'ITES the IMAMS are infallible and consequently as sinless as the prophets. Saints, despite their special power *(baraka),* still sin, albeit in minor matters *(see* WALĪ).

Bibliography. S. H. Nasr, *Ideal and Realities of Islam* (1972), pp. 138-42; P. Jackson, trans., Sharafuddin Maneri, *The Hundred Letters* (1980), pp. 15-25, 85-89, 312-15, 360-66.

B. LAWRENCE

SIN, ORIGINAL (Ch). Inherited sin and guilt or a universal human inclination to commit sin; called "original" because it is thought to come from the primeval parents, Adam and Eve.

This doctrine does not appear in the OT, but some see similarities in the Jewish *yetzer ha-ra,* "evil inclination." In Jewish theology, however, it is not evil *per se* and is balanced by *yetzer ha-tov,* "good intention." Major NT support is found in Rom. 5:12-19, especially in vs. 12.

It was AUGUSTINE (d. 430) who first explicitly stated that all persons inherit Adam's sin and guilt by natural generation. He also held that all humans were present in Adam and thus participated in his sin and fall. He formulated this position in controversy with the British monk Pelagius, who, while not denying Adam's historicity or his sin, maintained that all persons were born free of sin. Each individual, however, is influenced by the bad examples of Adam and his descendants. The Council of Carthage (A.D. 418) condemned PELAGIANISM as heretical.

Most medieval theologians followed Augustine, though some were semi-Pelagian. THOMAS AQUINAS, the Council of TRENT, and the Reformers, especially LUTHER and CALVIN, were essentially Augustinian, as are many twentieth century conservative Protestants. Grotius (d. 1645), a noted Dutch jurist, held that Adam did not act just as an individual but as the "federal" head or representative of the whole human race, and thus all persons represented by him are considered sinners.

The official Roman Catholic view has not changed since the Council of Trent, but some discern a change of emphasis in the second VATICAN COUNCIL'S relatively brief statements on the subject. Some Catholic scholars are currently reassessing the doctrine; e.g., the New Dutch Catechism defined original sin as "the sin of mankind as a whole (including myself) insofar as it affects every man."

Nineteenth century liberal Protestants, following the findings of biblical scholarship, denied the historicity of Adam and Eve as primeval progenitors of the human race, and many, under the impact of evolutionary views, saw man as becoming better and better. Historical views of original sin were discounted. Twentieth century NEO-ORTHODOXY, while not holding Adam to be a historical individual, has taken the idea of original sin seriously. Adam has been interpreted as "Everyman" and original sin as a universal inclination to improper self-interest, which has resulted in the universal corruption of mankind.

Bibliography. M. Halverson and A. Cohen, eds., *A Handbook of Christian Theology*, (1958), pp. 348 ff; P. Jewett, "Original Sin and the Fall of Man," *Southwestern Journal of Theology*, XIX (1976), 18-30; B. McDermott, "The Theology of Original Sin: Recent Developments," *Theological Studies*, XXXVIII (1977), 478-512; L. Sabourin, "Original Sin Reappraised," *Biblical Theology Bulletin*, III (1973), 51-81.

T. O. HALL, JR.

SIN, UNFORGIVABLE (Ch). Blasphemy against the HOLY SPIRIT, after which repentance is impossible. The early church held that this consisted in accrediting the works of JESUS to SATAN; some held it could be committed only during Jesus' earthly career. AUGUSTINE and others interpreted it as final rejection of Christ. Still others believe that only believers can commit this sin (Heb. 6). T. O. HALL, JR.

SINAI sī′ nī, sī′ nī ī (etymology uncertain). A mountain where God revealed his law to MOSES and entered into a COVENANT with the people of Israel. Its traditional location is Jebel Musa (Mountain of Moses), near the southern end of the peninsula of Sinai.

The peninsula, 60,000 square kilometers in area, is triangular in shape and lies between the continents of Asia and Africa, with the Gulf of Suez to the west, the Gulf of Aqaba to the east, and the Red Sea to the south. The rugged land contains little water and is reminiscent of the surface of the moon. Little vegetation is found except in oases. The high mountains of the south are composed of crystalline rocks; farther north are Nubian sandstone, igneous rocks, and marine strata. The northern plain has a cover of gravel or wandering sand dunes.

In the literary strata of the Pentateuch which modern scholars designate as Yahwist (J) and Priestly (P), the mountain is known as Sinai (e.g. Exod. 19-24), while in the so-called Elohist (E) and Deuteronomic (D) literature, it is called Mt. Horeb (Deut. 1; 4:10 etc.; I Kings 19:8). From this mountain God let his presence be known through lightning, thunder, and fire (Exod. 19:16,18). Since there is no volcanic evidence at the traditional location at Jebel Musa, a few scholars prefer a site in northwest Arabia, while others believe it may have been located southwest of the Dead Sea, in the vicinity of Kadesh-barnea.

At the base of Jebel Musa lies the Monastery of Saint Catherine, named for a Christian martyr of Alexandria. Helena, mother of the Emperor CONSTANTINE, built a chapel there (A.D. 325), and the Emperor Justinian built a church (A.D. 527). The monastery is the repository of many of the most ancient manuscripts and icons.

Bibliography. G. E. Wright, "Sinai," *IDB*, IV (1962), 376-78.

D. W. O'CONNOR

SINS, SEVEN DEADLY (Ch). Character traits which can produce specific, though not necessarily mortal, SINS. Although the list of deadly sins is not of Christian origin, the sins all appear in the NT. The earliest Christian list—eightfold—dates from the fourth century. GREGORY I (d. A.D. 604) named seven. Further changes produced a roster which now includes pride, covetousness, lust, anger, gluttony, envy, and sloth. T. O. HALL, JR.

SISTER (Ch). A female member of a religious order; a mode of address in many Protestant churches, used of ministers and laity. K. WATKINS

SĪTĀ sē′ tä (H—Skt.). Heroine of the RĀMĀYAṆA, daughter of King Janaka of Videha. Janaka found her in a casket when he was tilling the ground in preparation for a ritual to obtain children. He named her Sītā (lit. "furrow of the earth"). She is also called

Vaidehī and Maithilī, names derived from the country (Videha) and the city (Mithila) of her birth. In the RIG VEDA, Sītā is the deity of fertility. According to a Buddhist JĀTAKA tale, she was the daughter of Daśaratha and was married to her own brother RĀMA. In the JAINA Rāmāyaṇas of Jinasena and Guṇabhadra, as also in some folk versions of the Rāma story, Sītā was the daughter of RĀVAṆA (demon antagonist), and was abandoned immediately after her birth because of predictions that she would bring ruin upon her father's kingdom. In the *bhakti* ("devotional") Rāmāyaṇas, Sītā is elevated to the status of the goddess LAKṢMĪ. Sītā is also popularly viewed as the ideal wife and supreme model of Hindu womanhood. V. N. RAO

ŚIVA shī´ vŭ (H). *See* SHIVA.

SKANDA skän´ dŭ (H—Skt.; lit. "seed" [*skandṛ*—"to spill out or ooze"]). God who rises to prominence in Epic India between the second century B.C. and the fifth century A.D. Known as the son of SHIVA, he was patronized by various rulers, including those of the GUPTA DYNASTY, and eventually became especially popular in Tamil India when he was amalgamated with the South Indian god MURUKAṈ.

There are two basic mythological themes associated with Skanda as "seed": on the one hand, he is generated of AGNI, in dalliance with Svāhā. As such, he represents the sacrificial system; i.e., born of sacrifice amidst *śara* thickets in a golden environment. On the other hand, he is generated of RUDRA-Shiva, who though in ascetic withdrawal (TAPAS) on Mt. Meru provides the semen *(retas)*—in earlier accounts (e.g., Mbh. III, 223-32) in the company of Umā (PĀRVATĪ), and in later accounts (e.g., the Skanda PURĀṆA) issuing six sparks *(tejas)* from his forehead.

Skanda is conceived on the new moon day; he is suckled by the six Kṛttikā maidens; on the sixth day he grows to manhood; he is crowned general of the divine army, is given the weaponry of the gods, then goes out to defeat the troublesome ASURAS. He is given in marriage to Devasenā ("divine army"); he is said to have six faces, hence his name Ṣaṇmukha. By virtue of his being the son of Agni and Shiva he assumes their power and authority; he also replaces INDRA as the divine warrior; indirectly he is the son of several "mothers"—Umā or Pārvatī, Svāhā, Gaṅgā, Dharā (or earth), and the six Kṛttikās (KĀRTTIKEYA).

Epic myth-makers ascribe to him primordiality and eternal youth (Kumāra), wisdom (as expressed in the name Subrahmaṇya) and the healing powers associated with sacrifice and the ĀYURVEDIC system. In medieval South India after Skanda had merged with the Tamil Murukaṉ, the god is understood as the fullness of divinity in the ŚAIVA SIDDHĀNTA tradition, he who teaches his own father the mysteries of existence, and the inspiration and source of TAMIL literature.

Bibliography. F. W. Clothey, *The Many Faces of Murukaṉ: The History and Meaning of a South Indian God* (1978).

F. W. CLOTHEY

SKANDHAS skän´ dŭs (B—Skt.; lit. "heaps"). One classification of dharmas (*see* DHARMA §5c) employed throughout Buddhism, according to which a "self" or "person" is merely an empty convention, a label whose true referent is not a unified thing but rather five "heaps" or *skandhas: rūpa* ("form," the physical factors), *vedanā* ("feelings"), *saṃjñā* ("perceptions"), *saṃskāras* (roughly "volitions"), and *vijñāna* ("consciousness"). Analysis reveals not an intrinsic self but a set of aggregates of conditioned dharmas.

G. R. WELBON

SMĀRTAS smär´ tŭs (H—Skt.; lit. "relating to the smṛti" [*smṛ*—"to remember"]). 1. Scriptures dealing with religious ritual and based on the SMṚTI. The Smārtas include the Gṛhya Sūtras, which cover domestic rites and rites of passage (e.g., birth, marriage, death), and the Dharma Sūtras, which set forth rules governing all sorts of social interaction.

2. BRAHMINS who composed the Smārta texts as well as those who blended theistic devotion with Brahmanical orthodoxy. This latter group has used popular devotional texts (PURĀṆAS, Epics, etc.) to convey its Brahmanical defense of theism in the context of ritual duty. J. BARE

SMITH, JOSEPH (Ch; 1805-1844). Founder of LATTER-DAY SAINTS. Smith moved to New York in 1816 where he later had the vision which generated Mormonism. He led followers westward in 1831. Smith was murdered in an Illinois prison in 1844.

C. H. LIPPY

SMṚTI smrĭ´ tē (H—Skt.; lit. "that which is remembered" [*smṛ*—"to remember"]). A whole body of Hindu religious and legal literature composed after the Vedic period, which was "remembered" and handed down by oral transmission. The term is used in contradistinction to ŚRUTI, the name applied to the divinely revealed texts of the VEDA and VEDĀNTA. Taken in its widest sense, *smṛti* literature includes the Epics (MAHĀBHĀRATA and RĀMĀYAṆA), the Vedāṅgas (explanatory Vedic texts written in sūtra form), the SŪTRAS, the DHARMAŚĀSTRAS or legal texts, and the Nīti Śāstras or ethical texts. J. BARE

SNAKE HANDLING (Ch). The practice of snake handling first appeared in America in 1909 under the ministry of George Hensley of Grasshopper, Tennessee. A member of the Tennessee-based Church of God, Hensley took his teaching from a literal interpretation of Mark 16:17-18, where "taking up serpents" was listed as one of the "signs following" the believer. Hensley taught that a full restoration of NT Christianity would necessarily include the handling of snakes as a sign of the anointing of the HOLY SPIRIT.

For a time the Church of God defended the practice, but by 1922 it disavowed snake handling, and Hensley organized his followers into the "Church of God With Signs Following." All other major Pentecostal bodies branded the practice as "fanaticism" and forbade it.

Snake handlers insist on using venomous serpents. Practitioners are often bitten and some occasionally die as a result. This is looked on as desirable in order to prove to skeptics that dangerous serpents are actually used. Since Mark 16:18 also declares that "if they drink any deadly thing, it shall not hurt them," some snake handlers also drink poison in their services as further confirmation of their devotion.

The practice of snake handling persists in several dozen rural churches in the Appalachian highlands from Kentucky to Georgia. The American Civil Liberties Union has defended the religious freedom of snake handlers against attempts to outlaw the practice.

Bibliography. W. La Barre, *They Shall Take Up Serpents* (1962); A. Robertson, *That Old-Time Religion* (1950).

H. V. Synan

SOCIAL GOSPEL (Ch). An international movement that reinterpreted moral norms, found primarily in the teaching of Jesus and the OT prophets, and applied them to the issues that emerged with industrialization and the working classes ("the social question"). Although the movement was strongest from 1890 to 1920, it continues to exert an influence. *See* Theology, Contemporary Christian §2.

D. F. Ottati

SOCIETY OF JESUS (Ch). *See* Jesuits.

SOCINIANISM (Ch). A sixteenth century form of the Radical Reformation, stemming from the Sienese rationalists Laelius and Faustus Socinus (Sozzini). Laelius (1525-62) forged a Unitarian creed which was developed by his nephew, Faustus (1539-1604), who, after studying and publishing in Basle settled in Poland. There he exerted a decisive influence on the already anti-Trinitarian Minor Reformed Church, which for a time bid for religious dominance in Poland. Through an academy, a press, and a communitarian settlement, Socinianism spread.

Public awareness of Socinian heresy brought reprisals—mob violence in Faustus' final years, suppression of academy and press and flight of ministers in 1638, and the death penalty for Socinians in 1658. Exile communities were established in Transylvania, Germany, the Netherlands, and England. In England, Socinianism developed significant local rootage and in the eighteenth century a Unitarian denomination emerged.

Although known for repudiation of the Trinity, the divinity of Christ, and the Atonement, Socinianism was, at heart, a biblical rationalism. Scripture was taken as revelation. Human reason was used to interpret it, and its content was held to accord with reason (though containing things above reason). Jesus was mortal but still the revelation of God and his only-begotten Son. Final victory over evil and individual resurrection for those who imitate Christ attest the lovingkindness of the one God.

Bibliography. E. M. Wilbur, *A History of Unitarianism*, 2 vols. (1945, 1952); G. H. Williams, *The Radical Reformation* (1962).

R. E. Richey

SŌKA GAKKAI sō´ kä gäk´ kī (B—Jap.; lit. "value creation society"). Lay organization of Nichiren Shō-shū (*see* Nichiren Buddhism); incorporated in 1952, but dating from 1937 when Tsunesaburō Makiguchi founded it under the name Sōka Kyōiku Gakkai (Society for Education in the Creation of Value). Sharing certain characteristics in common with Japan's postwar new religions, Sōka Gakkai has experienced phenomenal growth, especially in the 1950s, until today it has a membership of 16,480,060 family units. Sōka Gakkai, however, does not consider itself to be a "new religion" but rather a lay auxiliary of Nichiren Shō-shū, the "orthodox" faith expounded by the thirteenth century priest Nichiren. International branches of this group do not call themselves Sōka Gakkai but Nichiren Shō-shū, as, for example, the NSA, Nichiren Shō-shū of America.

1. **History.** *a) Formulation and persecution* (1937-45). Makiguchi regarded his views as an alternative to the government's regimentation of thought concerning values and the government came to consider the movement disloyal. In 1943 Makiguchi and twenty other leaders were arrested on the charge of lèse majesté and imprisoned. The organization was banned, and Makiguchi died in prison.

b) Organization and growth (1945-60). Jōsei Toda, the second president of Sōka Gakkai, revived the organization upon his release from prison in 1945 and set out to vindicate the work of Makiguchi. Toda, in addition to his charisma and dynamism, was a serious student of Buddhist philosophy, a pragmatist, and a genius at organization. He formally organized Sōka Gakkai, as it is known today, on May 3, 1951, and set as his goal the winning of 750,000 family units before his death. When he died on April 2, 1958 at the age of fifty-eight, the goal had been reached. This period is marked by frenzied conversion activity (called *shakubuku*), the use of coercion and threats to enlist members. He also promoted Shamanistic practices such as faith healing, built a solid organization pyramid, inaugurated a thoroughgoing indoctrination program for converts, encouraged the destruction of Buddhist altars, Shintō god-shelves, Bibles, and family name-tablets in homes of members of other branches of Buddhism, founded numerous publications, established fundamental doctrines and encouraged their teaching, and had physical facilities of many types constructed.

c) Establishment and world mission (1960-79). The

third leader, Daisaku IKEDA, who resigned in 1979, was a gifted organizer. This period was characterized by the soft-pedaling of aggressive conversion tactics and growing acceptance of the organization by society. The movement has formulated its doctrine, trained leaders, set up educational institutions including Sōka University, and become involved in politics through Sōka Gakkai's political arm, KŌMEITŌ. The *kaidan* (altar) was considered established by the dedication of the Grand Worship Hall, Shōhondō in 1972 as the center of the faith which members believe will sweep the world (*see* NICHIREN BUDDHISM §4). An international organization was set up in 1978.

2. **Teachings.** Though all members of Sōka Gakkai are also members of Nichiren Shō-shū (and vice-versa today), the formulation of the teachings has been carried out by laymen—beginning with Makiguchi and his utilitarian philosophy, but notably through the writings and teaching of Jōsei Toda, who wrote many commentaries on the meaning of the LOTUS SŪTRA and the nature of the Nichiren Shō-shū faith. The heart of Sōka Gakkai teachings may be expressed in the statement "Any person can achieve happiness now."

a) Any person. No person is lost. According to the Lotus Sūtra, as interpreted by Nichiren, everyone can attain buddhahood. This is the truth written "beneath the letter" of the Lotus Sūtra.

b) Achievement of happiness as a human possibility is a central teaching which was best explained by the founder, Makiguchi, in the *Kachiron*. He defined what he considered to be the three basic values: the good, the beautiful, and the beneficial. Truth is rejected as a value, because there is nothing a person can do about it. But an individual can arrange his environment in such a way as to create what is good, beautiful, and beneficial. Happiness is the highest value.

c) Happiness is the key word. The cause of unhappiness is false belief (the keynote of Nichiren's preaching), either on the part of the individual in his present existence or through the cause-effect relationship inherited from some previous existence (in which it is seen that Sōka Gakkai believers follow the traditional doctrine of KARMA). To break the evil curse, one simple incantation of the DAIMOKU *"Nam myō-hō-renge-kyō"* is sufficient. (Sōka Gakkai has shortened the first word from *namu* to *nam.*) Successive repetitions bring successive release, cumulative merit, and happiness.

d) Now is the time of salvation (Buddhist enlightenment for all people). The period of MAPPŌ (end of the DHARMA) was initiated with Nichiren's birth (1222). The savior, Nichiren, appeared and through belief in what he revealed all people can be saved.

Bibliography. *See* NICHIREN BUDDHISM.

N. S. BRANNEN

SOLOMON IBN GABIROL sôl′ ə mən ĭb′ ən gä bē rôl′, **AVICEBRON** ä vē′ cə brôn (Ju; 1020-1057). Neoplatonic philosopher and poet who spent his life in Spain. He is known to Latin SCHOLASTICISM as Avicebron, the author of a profound metaphysical treatise entitled *Fons Vitae* ("Source of Life"). Its original Arabic text was lost, and except for some fragmentary translations into Hebrew, scholars have had to rely on the Latin version. Gabirol's Hebrew poetry is still used today in the Jewish liturgy.

K. P. BLAND

SOLOMON BEN ISAAC sôl′ ə mən bĕn yē′ säk (Ju; 1040-1105; with the title RABBI yields acronym "Rashi"). Commentator *par excellence* on the TALMUD and BIBLE; originator of the northern French style in scholarship and founder of an important academy at Worms. The style of his commentaries on the Bible is concise and combines traditional MIDRASHIC interpretations with an emphasis on the plain meaning of scripture as it is revealed through careful examination of grammar, syntax, and philological detail. His Talmudic commentary, the greatest of his literary achievements, is a model of pedagogical genius and mastery of the elliptical dialectics of the often perplexing Talmudic style. K. P. BLAND

SOMA sō′ mū (H—Skt.; lit. "pressed" juice or plant [*su*—"to press"]). A plant or its juice, probably hallucinogenic, prominent in the mythology and ritual of VEDIC HINDUISM in ancient India, deified and praised in 120 hymns of the RIG VEDA. After INDRA and AGNI the god Soma has the most recognition; the entire ninth book of the Rig Veda is devoted to him. Proto-Indo-European religion may have promoted the cult of a divine plant or elixir bestowing immortality and wisdom. An Indo-Iranian background is clearly attested by numerous similarities in language, mythology, and ritual between the AVESTAN *haoma* and Vedic *soma.*

According to the Vedic poets, Soma, the lord of plants, had mountainous or celestial origins; in RV 4.26 and 27 the theft of soma from the highest heaven was accomplished by an eagle. The reddish-brown, tawny-yellow stalks or "fingers" of the plant were pressed or pounded between stones on the sacrificial area. Priests then purified the juice by filtering it through sheep's wool, collected it in tubs, offered portions to the gods, and together with the sacrificer drank the remainder from special cups. Soma was variously mixed with water, milk, curds, clarified butter (GHEE), barley, and possibly honey. Three pressings occurred each day during soma sacrifices.

The exhilarating effects of soma drinking were linked to poetic insight and immortality (soma is *amṛta,* "not mortal"), the fertility of the land, animals, and people, healing powers, light giving and wealth attaining, and not least, Indra's drunken invincibility in battle. In the late Rig Veda and subsequent texts soma was identified with the moon, the lunar phases being the result of gods and PITṚS drinking soma. Already in the BRĀHMANAS, *ca.* 800

B.C., substitutes for the early Vedic plant were admitted, including various creepers, grasses, and flowers. Indian writers and, since the eighteenth century, European scholars have labored to identify the "original" plant. One recent hypothesis proposes the hallucinogenic *Amanita muscaria* or fly-agaric mushroom.

Bibliography. A. A. Macdonell and A. B. Keith, *Vedic Index of Names and Subjects*, II (1912), 474-79; R. G. Wasson and W. D. O'Flaherty, *Soma* (1968). D. M. KNIPE

SOTĀPANNA sō tä´ pän nä (B—Pali; lit. "stream-entrant") **ŚROTĀPANNA** shrō tä´ pän nä (B—Skt.). The first of the four fruitions in THERAVĀDA sanctity. When a disciple destroys the three fetters (belief in a permanent entity, belief in rituals, and doubt), he becomes a "stream-entrant" of the holy path and will not be reborn in any state of woe. *See* SAKADĀGĀMIN; ANĀGĀMIN; ARHANT.

W. PACHOW

SŌTŌ sō tō´ (B). *See* ZEN §5.

SOUL, SPIRIT. That which gives life to any animate thing; or the inner, essential, or noncorporeal part or dimension of any animate thing; or a noncorporeal but animate substance or entity; or a noncorporeal but individuated personal being.

Defining and describing the domain of "soul" and "spirit" is complicated by two kinds of problems. In the first place, there is confusion in the use of the English words which goes far beyond the normal problems of polysemy and which in fact rests on profound differences in the belief systems held by speakers of English. In the second place, the confusion is compounded when the English words are used, in either popular or scholarly discourse, to translate words from other languages which often reflect beliefs quite unlike those usually attached to the English terms. Variant beliefs are held about the very existence of soul-spirit; about its relation to matter; about whether it is universally one or many; about what kinds and categories of spirits there are; about how human soul-spirit relates to the body and to psychological states and processes; about the origin and destiny of the human soul-spirit, including questions of its pre-existence and immortality.

1. **Dimensions of the domain.** *a) Existence or nonexistence.* Though belief in the existence of some kind of noncorporeal substance or entity has been almost universal for as long as we have any knowledge of the question, skepticism also has a long history, especially among Western intellectual elite groups, at least ever since the later Greek philosophers. Unbelief has usually taken the form of materialism in its various guises, and appears to have gained ground in intellectual circles in the West since the eighteenth century.

b) Relation to matter. Most animists, as well as most of the ancient Greek thinkers, ancient Hebrew thinkers, and others, consider soul-spirit to be a form or kind of matter, or at least see no sharp ontological discontinuity. HINDUISM and BUDDHISM stand at the opposite pole in insisting that matter is an illusion and that soul-spirit is real reality. Apparently under the influence of such Asian ideas, mediated through Neoplatonism, mystery religions, and GNOSTICISM, medieval Christian thought postulated a strong dualism reinforced by ethical dualism. It is in reaction against this dualism that modern Western empiricists and logical positivists argue in their derision of the "ghost in the machine" theory.

c) One or many. The most fully monistic answer is no doubt given by Hinduism, which asserts that all reality is ultimately included within BRAHMAN (Ultimate Reality) and that salvation consists in losing individual existence through absorption in ATMAN ("All-Soul"). A different kind of monism is found in pantheism, and yet another in some versions of ANIMISM, in which soul is equated with life as such and is not involved in the distinctive individual personality. Most other traditions, including the Western ones, have affirmed the real individuality of spirits and souls.

d) Human souls-spirits. i. Simple or composite. In Western Christian tradition the usual debate centered around whether soul and spirit were distinct entities within the human being, coordinate with the body (the trichotomous view), or whether they were identical (the dichotomous view). Extensions and elaborations of the discussion involved relations of the soul or spirit respectively to body parts and psychological processes, as well as their respective relations to God and the nature of their survival after death. In some versions of animism the human being is very complex indeed, involving as distinct substances or entities life, breath, blood, name, shadow, individual personality, and so on. In addition, human beings are subject to invasion by extraneous nonhuman spirits, often but not always with deleterious results.

ii. Relation to the body. A common belief in animism is that the soul is a kind of inner double which pervades the body. Alternate views hold that it is localized in the nostrils, throat, or neck (especially when it is equated with the breath); in the heart or other internal organs; in the head; or elsewhere. It may also be identified with the shadow (or even, when photography is introduced, with a photographic image). When the soul-spirit is composite, different parts of it may be differently located in the body.

iii. Relation to psychological states and processes. There are many views of how soul or spirit may relate to psychological states and processes, such as perception, consciousness and altered states of consciousness, conscience, rationality, memory, intuition, imagination, emotional states, attitudes, temperament, and personality. If it is composite, different parts of it may be assigned different psychological functions; the assignment may closely parallel the bodily location of the various parts.

iv. Pre-existence and immortality. The question of when the soul-spirit originates and when it ends has received all possible answers. Systems which deny that it can exist apart from the body say it begins at some specific point (conception, some moment during gestation, birth, or some moment after birth) in the life of the body and ends at death. Systems which affirm that it can exist separately also usually hold that it begins at some time chronologically related to conception or birth; but they sometimes teach that soul-spirit has a prior, independent origin, or even that it pre-existed eternally. This last position can correlate with either ontological monism (the individual soul-spirit is a momentarily "broken-off bit" of All-Soul), or with ontological individuation. As for the postdeath destiny of soul-spirit, possibly the least common belief is that it ends completely and finally at death. Much more common are beliefs in some qualified or absolute survival. Options include: survival in an afterlife, with or without retribution and segregation for lifetime conduct; semi-survival in a quasi-afterlife, with or without ultimate extinction; survival for a time near the grave, with or without visible manifestations to the living in the form of a ghost; survival for as long as persons live who remember the dead individual, with subsequent gradual extinction; REINCARNATION; and so on. (*See* IMMORTALITY.)

v. Communication with the dead. In spiritism a medium is needed to establish links between the living and the dead; the communication is usually initiated by the living, though it can be done by the dead. In ANCESTOR VENERATION communication may be initiated either by the living or by the dead, and in either case the spirits of ancestors can and do take an active role in the lives of their surviving kin, guiding them, protecting them, enforcing tradition, and so on. Ancestors are cared and provided for, placated through libations and offerings, consulted before important decisions, and in other ways centrally included in the life of the ongoing community. Only rarely is a medium needed; kinship with the dead is much more important than mediumistic abilities. In societies that practice ancestor cult, it is accorded the highest social approval. Spiritism, however, even when it is believed in, may or may not be generally approved. (*See* SPIRITUALISM.)

e) Nonhuman spirits. i. Nature spirits. The commonest type of nonhuman spirits, especially in animism, are nature spirits. These are intimately associated with some nonhuman aspect of the world: an object such as a mountain, a river, the sun, the moon, etc.; or a process or property of nature such as thunder and lightning, fertility, etc. All of nature is, in fact, inhabited or possessed by spirit(s). The relationship is said to be completely analogous to the way a soul-spirit inhabits or possesses or animates a human being; that is, the spirit inheres in the object or process and endows it with its essential nature and properties. These spirits are assigned different degrees and kinds of power, usually dependent on the perceived power of the natural phenomenon in question, and different dispositions toward human beings (benevolent, malevolent, indifferent, capricious), usually dependent on the perceived effects of the phenomenon. The interplay or struggle between these spirits goes a long way to explain the incomprehensible randomness of human experience.

ii. Ethically defined spirits. Some spirits are not primarily known in terms of connection with natural phenomena, but in terms of their intrinsic moral character: there are good spirits (ANGELS, good fairies, etc.) and bad spirits (DEMONS, devils, etc.). In general, good spirits are seen as benevolently related to human beings, so that they can be enlisted to help human beings, by means of good conduct and/or appropriate ritual. Evil spirits, on the other hand, must be placated or warded off with the help of good spirits or magic. The realm of these spirits can become highly elaborated as their number multiplies; they can exist in complex hierarchies with diverse properties, functions, and manifestations (cf. the "principalities and powers" of Col. 1:16). They may be headed by sovereign spirits, either of opposite disposition and equal powers (ethical dualism) or of unequal powers, as in late Hebrew and traditional Christian thought. A common belief is that an evil spirit can invade or possess a human being, causing abnormal behavior which is deleterious or dangerous to the possessed person or others. Manifestations of such possession may include (the symptoms of) dementia, catatonia, epilepsy, witchcraft, the evil eye, and many more.

iii. Divine spirits. At some point difficult to specify, one crosses the line between ancestor spirits, nature spirits, or ethically defined spirits, on the one hand, and truly divine spirits, on the other. That there is a distinction can be seen from the ancient Greek differentiation between the gods and goddesses on the one hand, and the nymphs and satyrs on the other. But that the distinction is not always clear can be seen from the debate about the translation of *elohim* (in its plural sense) or *benai elohim* in some OT passages: should these be rendered "gods," or "divine beings," or even "angels"? (Cf. Ps. 8:5 and Heb 2:7.) It seems likely from critical study of the myths as well as from *apriori* considerations adduced by Tylor among others that the nature spirits represent the oldest stratum of belief, and that ethically defined spirits and divine beings represent later stages. It is possible that at least some divine spirits may represent "promoted" versions of earlier nature or ancestor spirits. In personality and character gods often seem surprisingly human, subject to temptation, changeableness, and fault. It may be in this more fully rounded personality as well as in their more exalted status that gods differ most from nature spirits.

iv. God as spirit, the Spirit of God. see below §2 c, e.

2. Representative belief systems. *a) In preliterate societies. See* Animism §1.

b) Hinduism and Buddhism. Hinduism affirms that reality is fundamentally spiritual, while matter is Māyā, illusion. And all reality is one, so that individual existence is an illusion. Salvation consists in being freed from these illusions by absorption into Atman. Buddhism also stresses the search for liberation, but its doctrine of Anatta denies that there is a soul or self that transmigrates.

c) Ancient Hebrew beliefs. The earliest Hebrew thought held that the *ruach* of a human being was the breath, given by God; the presence of *ruach* constituted a living being *(nephesh),* and its loss was death (Gen. 2:7). The *ruach* was in the nostrils, but the *nephesh,* when localized, was in the blood (Gen. 9:4; Lev. 17:11), the head, the face, the heart, or the viscera. Neither was an immaterial principle in the strict sense. Later the *ruach* became the seat of most psychological processes. By Intertestamental and NT times, at least among the Pharisees, Jewish views of human nature reflected the influence of the Greek distinction between *psychē* and *sarx.* Simultaneously there developed in the same tradition belief in the immortality of the soul and in the Resurrection of the dead. Philo in the first century A.D. went furthest in syncretizing Jewish and Neoplatonic thought.

Nature spirits and ancestor spirits played no role in official Hebrew religion, though nature spirits show up in the officially condemned involvement in Canaanite cults.

As for the *ruach elohim,* it seems to have begun as the Spirit of God (powerful wind); seeming ambiguity in Gen. 1:2 may be an artifact of a later distinction not made by the earliest Hebrews. This was in any case a power principle, effecting divine purposes both in the nonhuman universe and in human experience: ecstasy, prophecy, and even special skills are attributed to *ruach elohim* (I Sam. 19:23, 24; Exod. 31:3). It was this Spirit which enabled and drove the charismatic leaders of Israel's prekingdom history, and later the prophets. Still later the *ruach elohim* began to be personalized, a process which was completed in the NT.

d) Ancient Greek beliefs. The Homeric literature reflects earlier animism, except that the pantheon has been elaborated. In human beings *psychē* was a vital force or breath which left at death through the mouth or through a wound. It could then appear as a ghost, but after burial went to a shadowy, depersonalized underworld. It bore no relation to mental functions. The Pythagoreans, and later Plato, developed this simple idea, splitting *psychē* and *sarx* and assigning mental functions to *psychē.* Plato also added the concept of *pneuma* (etymologically "wind"), which at the macrocosmic level was the "breath of the universe" and at the microcosmic level was identical with the *psychē* of a human being. Both Socrates and Plato also spoke of a kind of inspiration which came from the universal *pneuma* and produced poetry and ecstasy. The Stoics and Epicureans rematerialized *psychē* and *pneuma* by conceiving of them as composed of very small atoms.

e) New Testament beliefs. Surprisingly, the NT does not develop an extensive understanding of our topic. The writers reflect their basically late Jewish thought world, with some Hellenistic influence. On the whole, Greek *psychē* is simply identified with Hebrew *nephesh,* and *pneuma* with *ruach,* as in the Septuagint. This is especially true in the realms of human nature and angels and demons.

However, the NT develops much further than either the OT or the Pharisees the concept of the *pneuma theou,* the Spirit of God (Holy Spirit). Both the *ruach elohim* of the OT and the quasi-divine spirit of Plato are transcended in a quite extensive and original way, as the Holy Spirit is hypostasized and the foundations for a later full-blown pneumatology are laid.

f) Traditional Christian beliefs. Christian tradition for many centuries rested on a synthesis: OT and NT ideas were read through Hellenistic spectacles. To this was added an Oriental influence (especially in the depreciation of the body). The norm, as far as human nature was concerned, was either dichotomism or trichotomism; soul-spirit was good, immortal, involved in salvation; body was evil, mortal, not involved in salvation. To satisfy concern about the destiny of various categories of human souls after death, doctrines of Limbo and Purgatory were developed. The existence of angels, demons, and Satan were affirmed, and their nature and powers widely discussed, as well as means of coping with them. Exorcism was prominent. Traditional orthodoxy defined rigorously the place of the Holy Spirit in the Trinity and distinguished between proper manifestations of divine gifts and manifestations of demonic and satanic power.

g) Modern views. Today, in the Western world, many continue to hold to traditional Christian orthodoxy in this area. At the opposite extreme are the materialists of various sorts who deny the existence of soul-spirit. In between are Christians who try to make an accommodation between the essentials of their faith and a world view which makes angels, demons, and Satan less than convincing. Efforts to reconcile traditional vocabulary with modern psychological theories are rife, but there is no consensus. Meanwhile, among less sophisticated persons there persists a wide variety of unformed but widely held beliefs which can be called animistic; spiritism, Astrology, belief in gremlins, as well as Satanism and Witchcraft, are thriving. There is also an influence of Asian ideas.

Outside the West, traditional religions, Christianity in diverse forms, and secular Western influences are competing and creating a great deal of confusion and even anomie, especially among persons exposed to modern education.

Bibliography. E. Durkheim, *The Elementary Forms of the Religious Life* (1915); E. E. Evans-Pritchard, *Theories of Primitive Religion* (1965); P. Radin, *Primitive Religion* (1937); *IDB*, articles "Soul" and "Spirit" (1962); *IDBS*, article "Spirit," (1976); *TWNT* articles "pneuma," Vol. 6 (1969), and "psuchē," Vol. 9 (1974); *The New Schaff-Hertzog Encyclopedia of Religious Knowledge*, article "Soul and spirit, Biblical conceptions of" (1911); E. B. Tylor, *Primitive Culture* (1871).

C. R. Taber

SOUTH AMERICAN TRIBAL RELIGIONS. The result of development from Shamanism introduced to the New World by peoples who migrated from Siberia at least 35,000 years ago, and of sixteenth century Catholicism introduced by Europeans, South American religions reflect the diffusion of ideas over vast areas as well as social and technological adaptation to local environments. Everywhere, religion is functionally related to other social institutions and constitutes the core of cultural values and morality.

1. **History: origin, growth, diffusion.** Humans reached Tierra del Fuego no later than ten thousand years ago. They were hunters and gatherers, with no knowledge of plant cultivation or the domestication of animals, who had moved along the river systems, the coasts, and the basins of the Andean chain. All evidence points to their belief in a host of animistic spirits and their reliance on shamanism to cope with

Location of South American tribes

the supernatural world. They had no high gods, no priests, no temples; in short, they had none of the paraphernalia characteristic of the more complex agricultural societies which took millennia to develop and which reached their culmination in the Inca Empire.

As peoples came into contact with one another, ideas were exchanged and concepts of the supernatural became enriched and varied. Besides the basic common attributes of shamanistic practices and beliefs noted in both North and South America, there are myth themes found on both continents which also indicate the continuities of the diffusion of ideas. In South America the fundamental assumptions about the supernatural and shamanistic engagement with spirits differed only slightly from one society to the next and were conditioned by the chance diffusion of ideas and the manner in which they were worked into local conditions of living.

a) The shamanistic pattern. The most general characteristic of shamanism is that the shaman deals personally with the supernatural and has its power. This distinguishes him from the priest or other ritual leader who does not grapple with the supernatural and has no personal power, but is, rather, an intermediary between the people and the spirits and gods. The main function of the shaman is to cure supernaturally induced illness. This is done on an individual basis, although in some societies the shaman may work for the good of the entire community, in hunting, fishing, and other activities.

There are two principal ways of curing illness. One is by extracting supernatural intrusions from the body of the patient; the other is by recapturing the sick person's soul. The most widespread curing techniques involve sucking the affected part of the body, massage with medicinal and magical herbs, and blowing smoke or pouring holy water over the body. In cases of extreme illness, shamans may enter a state of trance, very often after taking drugs, and use ventriloquism to represent voices of the spirits before an assemblage of onlookers. A drug-induced trance is not entered into lightly. It is a very dangerous condition for a shaman, because at this time he communes with his familiar spirits and directly contests the forces of evil. Although variations in practices and corresponding beliefs exist, there is a common pattern to shamanism wherever it is found in South America. The durability and consistency of shamanic practice are seen in the appearance of a classic Siberian form of shamanism among the Mapuche Indians of Chile.

b) Three types of social evolution. Changes in religious belief went together with changes in social development. In hunting and gathering societies and among tropical forest cultivators (who also depended heavily on hunting, fishing, and gathering), the shaman continued to be the most important religious functionary. As some societies became more complex, as a result of agricultural and technological advances, the role of shaman was complemented by that of the ritual priest. The shaman's main duties were confined to curing, and the priesthood came to be responsible for most public ceremonies. This development reached its culmination in the central Andes, where the shaman functioned at the level of folk society while a hereditary priesthood operated at an imperial level and was closely associated with military and political institutions. Thus, there came to be a correlation between the type and complexity of social groups and the kinds of religious institutions attached to them.

i. Hunting bands and tropical forest villagers. Although hunters and gatherers and tropical forest horticulturalists had important differences, they shared many social features. Social units were relatively small and structured by age, sex, and kinship. Political organization was weak, the head man having little or no coercive power. Individual behavior was sanctioned by tribal custom in the area of kinship and morality, exclusive of overriding state institutions. Many of the tribes lived in marginal areas, which had limited resources, and used simple survival techniques—both of which kept population low and affected group composition. Social institutions were adapted to subsistence needs. Public ceremonial was limited to LIFE CYCLE RITES, and concepts of the supernatural, magic, and shamanism were quite similar in their outlines. In many instances the shaman was the only specialist in the community and, even so, had to participate in productive work to support himself. These societies were socially and culturally homogeneous, having little status differentiation among the population. The principal distinction between them was that the tropical forest villagers practiced horticulture and had a more reliable food source which, in ideal circumstances, supported a denser population than that of hunting and gathering peoples.

ii. Circum-Caribbean and sub-Andean chiefdoms. Although similar in technology and material culture to the villagers of the tropical forests, peoples of the circum-Caribbean and sub-Andean regions lived in richer environments which supported, through more intensive cultivation and exploitation of abundant river and ocean resources, much larger and more permanent settlements, many of which were fortified against attack. Villages were composed of multi-kin groups organized on the basis of status as well as on age, sex, and kinship. Warfare and religion were closely related, insofar as captives were sacrificed to the gods. Warriors were able to attain higher social rank through valorous acts. Captive enemies formed a class of drudge laborers in some societies. There were powerful chiefs who had military and economic control over large populations, sometimes federations of villages. There was a priesthood and a warrior class which enjoyed special privilege and were freed from day-to-day subsistence activities. Religion centered on a priest-temple-idol complex, with shamanism relegated to curing individual illness. In less well-developed societies, however, shamans did serve priestly functions in certain public rites.

iii. Central Andean civilization. Kingdoms and empires of the central Andes had the most highly developed agriculture, based on intricate irrigation systems, the densest population, the most efficient transportation—the combination of which permitted the growth of urban centers and resulted in political and religious controls over masses of people. Patterns implicit in the chiefdoms were fully developed in these civilizations. Indeed, the cultural developments of the central Andes diffused widely over South America, beginning about 1000 B.C. At this time there was a steady cultural exchange between Mexico and Peru which affected numerous peoples in the geographically intermediate regions. Even hundreds of years before the rise of the Inca Empire there were kingdoms in the central Andes in which there existed hereditary class systems, war for conquest of territory and population, temple cults with hereditary priests who attended a hierarchy of state gods, public ceremonies which formed a ritual cycle connected to agriculture, and the regimentation of commoners, who were conscripted into the armies, were forced to build and maintain vast irrigation networks, roads, monuments, and huge temples and fortresses.

2. The heritage of European conquest. In discussing the living religions of South American peoples, we must consider not only their evolutionary background but the wrenching force exerted between the fifteenth and sixteenth centuries by European conquerers, missionaries, and settlers. Some societies were wiped out during the first generations of exploration and have left no trace of their religious beliefs and institutions. Others have been able to maintain traditional social and religious organization. A third category has retained relatively few social institutions, although some traces of traditional belief have become mixed with rural Catholicism.

The Spaniards overran the Taino Arawak chiefdom on Hispaniola and other similar societies in the circum-Caribbean area early in the conquest period. Even the Inca were defeated in the first half of the sixteenth century. Around this time the Portuguese invaded Brazil and the Spaniards made inroads beyond the mouth of the Rio de la Plata in Argentina. The Portuguese overwhelmed the chiefdom of the Tupinambá and the Spanish quickly defeated the Querandí and Charrua, yet upon entering the Gran Chaco had to fight for years with the fierce Abipón, Mocoví, and other Guaycuruan-speaking peoples. These tribes eventually succumbed to missionization and disease, and were socially extinct by the eighteenth century. Some of their folk beliefs, however, have filtered down into today's rural Catholicism.

Farther south, in the pampas and Patagonia, the takeover of the Puelche and Tehuelche took longer, for it was effected through the establishment of large cattle ranches. On Tierra del Fuego, the Ona clashed with settlers in the early nineteenth century and are now extinct. Their western neighbors, the Yahgan, were assimilated as mestizos ("mixed bloods"), a fate shared by the nearby Alacalúf and Chono.

Although there is a correlation between population size and density, technology and resources, and overall social and religious complexity, it is not a mechanical one and, in itself, is no measure of a society's ability to survive and maintain its values in the face of unexpected onslaught. Some of the societies which rapidly succumbed to European invasion were very complex and populous, such as the sub-Andean Chibcha and the Taino Arawak. Inca society tumbled at the state level of organization and Catholic missionaries made every effort to stamp out traditional religion. But the masses of Quechua-speaking Indians survived. Quechua is still the hearth language of over five million highland Indians and exerts a conservative force on religion and social life, such that the stamp of the Inca is quite visible in contemporary Peru.

At the other end of the scale, peoples such as the Yahgan and Ona, although incomparably simpler and less populous, held out much longer, mainly because they lived in a dispersed pattern in a part of South America which the Spaniards did not settle in force.

a) Southern hunters and gatherers. Although there were significant cultural differences among the Ona, Yahgan, Alacalúf, and Chono, there was also a good measure of social similarity associated with hunting life. The Yahgan, who numbered about five thousand and who survived until recently, may well serve as an example of those tribes sharing simple social and religious institutions and beliefs.

The Yahgan had no traditional tribal organization, priesthood, government institutions, and the like which could be diminished by contact with Europeans; rather, they had always lived in small nomadic family groups. They have been described, along with the Alacalúf, as "aquatic nomads" who spent most of their lives in dugout canoes exploiting the shellfish beds of the innumerable small islands in their territory, each family going its own way. Large gatherings of people occurred only rarely when a major source of food, such as a stranded whale or a sizeable pack of seals, was found. It was on these chance occasions that an organized religious life among the Yahgan became most apparent. Families congregated in great numbers and staged elaborate initiation rites for boys and girls. These ceremonies were conducted by elders of the society, not by shamans. Evident too was the Yahgan belief in an otiose Supreme Being, who presided over these initiation rites but who did not otherwise play a role in the life of the people. The rest of the time, individuals turned to shamans for curing and for hunting and fishing success.

b) Tropical forest villagers. Even though tropical forest villagers live a more sedentary life made possible by horticulture, their populations are relatively small and widely dispersed. However, there is a similarity of beliefs throughout the tropical forests which knows no linguistic or regional boundaries, due, in great part, to earlier migrations of peoples throughout the area. The Guaraní, for example, migrated from the Atlantic coast to what is now Paraguay. The Tupian Chiriguano migrated to the foothills of the Andes in search of a promised land. The Chocó are still migrating from Colombia into Panama. The cosmogony and shamanistic beliefs of the tropical forest region are cut from the same cloth, and the borrowing and mixture of ideas was a continous process. The grandfather of the migrating Tupians was a sky god and the cult centering on this belief hoped to reach the Land of the Grandfather, where they would have a better life in the afterworld. Almost everywhere there is found a Creator, a Father, an old man and his wife who are for the most part otiose deities and culture heros, who have bestowed upon the people all necessary knowledge. This belief gained new impetus after the Indians had begun to suffer from their relations with whites.

The Tupian-speaking Mundurucú of the Matto Grosso are an intermediate example between those Indians whose religion has become extinct and those who have been able to maintain at least a semblance of their traditional beliefs and practices. Their subsistance base is the tropical forest. Each village has a chief, whose power is limited, and a shaman, who also takes part in special village-wide ceremonies which propitiate patrilineal ancestors. (*See* ANCESTOR VENERATION.)

In the early twentieth century the Mundurucú became involved in the Brazilian rubber economy, and many hundreds of them abandoned village life, settling on the Cururú and Tapajós rivers in individual family households, where they tapped latex for a living. A Catholic mission and a Brazilian Indian agency were established among them, and traditional life soon disappeared. There remain, however, seven villages away from the riverine area and in the rolling savannah, where an effort is made to maintain traditional life. Despite the many social changes among the Mundurucú, shamanism preserves its role in curing as well as in hunting, fishing, and agricultural endeavors. The long-term prognosis, however, is not good.

Just north and east of the Mundurucú region, there is a large area occupied by Gê-speaking peoples, the Apinayé, Canela, Sherente, Cayapó, and, to the southeast, the Caingang, Carajá, and Bororo. The Gê peoples share similar beliefs about celestial beings, animism, and shamanism, although there may be different emphases on particulars from one society to another. All have creation myths in common. The Apinayé, for example, receive their moiety (division into two parts) organization from the sun; the Canela pray to celestial deities for rain, good harvests, and successful hunting. The Caingang believe that wild animals which they hunt are controlled by a master spirit who governs their increase. Ceremonies are staged by segments of the total population of each village, such as moieties, clans, and men's associations, although there are community-wide rites on certain occasions. These ceremonies are complex and varied but have in common such similar features as singing, dancing, relay racing, clowning, and mock combat.

To indicate the widespread similarity over thousands of miles of the tropical forest area, it need only be pointed out that the Witoto, who live in western Amazonia and speak a language different from Tupian or Gê, also believe in a beneficent father god, who lives above; have an ancestor cult which is celebrated by masked dancers and trumpet players; and have shamanistic practices which are identical to those found elsewhere. Again, the Cashinawa, in the foothills of the southern Peruvian Andes, believe in a Great Ancestor, who is culture hero and creator of the people. He cares for souls of the dead, who go to live with him and his wife in a pleasant afterworld. The Jívaro of the Peruvian and Ecuadorian *montaña* have a supreme otiose deity and an ancestor cult but also have beliefs which differ from those just described. For example, they have a concept of a supernatural essence which gives power to both objects and things. They also believe in a rain god and an anaconda god who have this essence, as do the shrunken heads of their enemies.

c) Residue of chiefdoms. Circum-Caribbean chiefdoms no longer exist. There are surviving societies, however, such as the Cágaba of northern Colombia and the Warrau of the Orinoco delta, which represent certain characteristic elements of former chiefdoms and which have undergone different forms of deculturation. They have managed to survive by moving into undesirable areas and have adjusted to life in the tropical forest, which, of course, does not support the complex sort of social organization they had in the sixteenth century. The Cágaba have retained a priesthood which conducts public rituals celebrating the several stages in the life cycle on a village-wide basis. Their society may be classified as a theocracy run by priests, who are instructed in a ten-year training period, during which they learn sacred songs and secret knowledge, in order to propitiate the Mother of all things. Among the Cágaba priests also double as curers, thus blurring the line between priest and shaman. The Warrau, who fled into the marshes of the Orinoco delta and maintain a tropical forest level of social organization, have retained, nevertheless, vestiges of a priest-temple-idol complex and certain social ranks reminiscent of former times. Each large settlement has a special temple containing a wood, bone, or clay idol, which represents Our Grandfather. A special, often hereditary, priest cares for each of these shrines and is distinguished from a shaman. The Warrau supreme deity is a creator god, but he also causes disease, flood, and other natural disasters, and is propitiated by the priesthood in public ceremony to alleviate suffering.

d) The Inca-Quechua continuum. An examination of Inca religion reveals that some aspects have survived almost unchanged in contemporary highland Peru, despite intensive efforts by missionaries to eradicate them. The Inca emphasized ritual behavior rather than mysticism and spirituality. The hereditary priesthood served the need of society and concerned itself with the food supply and the maintenance of state institutions among several million Quechua-speaking people. Religion was geared to major economic, political, and military activities, and sacrifices (especially of llamas) took place at major religious ceremonies. Immorality and purification were chief concerns of the state religion. A large number of supernatural beings of varying importance were worshiped. A supreme being, Viracocha, was the focus of belief and practice. There were nature gods, such as Thunder or Weather, and celestial beings ranked below the sun, moon, stars, earth, and sea. Other supernatural powers worshiped by the Inca were places and objects of only regional or local importance called *huacas*. Mummified remains of Inca leaders were paraded around the central plaza of Cuzco on state occasions.

Priests wielded great authority in everyday life and controlled the temples which were repositories for images of gods and residences of the priests and the virgins of the sun (chosen women of the Empire). They also ran the great public ceremonies which were geared to the agricultural cycle. At the folk level, shamans cured individuals and dealt with evil spirits.

Quechua religion today retains a good deal of Inca influence, though essentially it is a special form of Catholicism. It is not difficult to see how the overlay of Catholic beliefs and ritual syncretized with traditional Quechua ideas. Religion is important in the daily life of any highland community and ceremonialism is allied to the most practical and serious objectives of the community. Public ceremonies are high points in the life of the people, and magic and curing rites are central to all human relationships.

The Quechua classify their supernatural beings into dichotomous entities, such as good and bad spirits, terrestrial and celestial beings, deities in contrast to spirits, a Catholic pantheon of saints and a traditional assembly of spirits. The lower deities can be manipulated by shamans. Ceremonies on Catholic saints' days are permeated with pre-Spanish beliefs and include fertility rites which invoke memories of Inca times. In the countryside shamans *(curanderos)* handle illness with a blend of folk beliefs and Catholicism.

e) The Mapuche. The Indians of southern central Chile are unique in South America as an example of how a very large, though not especially complex society withstood Spanish conquest and held out against Chileans until defeated in 1882. They had experienced tremendous population decline but, thanks to peaceful reservation life, now number around one-half million (close to the aboriginal estimate). They were horticulturalists, but, unlike the central Andean peoples, had no irrigation systems, no centralized government, no priesthood, and no large-scale ceremonies.

Localization of their increasing population on patrilineally organized reservations resulted in significant changes in social and religious organization while, at the same time, age-old beliefs crystallized around an increasingly complex set of social institutions. The reservation chief is also elder of the patrilineal descent group and ritual leader imbued with traditional lore. Ceremonies are staged for crop and animal increase, at which sheep are sacrificed at an altar on a sacred field. Several thousand people may attend. Since souls of dead chiefs "walk with the sons of the gods," there is a direct connection along patrilineal lines between the living and the pantheon. The dead live in a tranquil, pleasant world. *Nenechen* is the ruler of the Mapuche and lives in the sky with his wife, Old Woman—as do all the other deities, such as Sun, Moon, Volcano, Southwind, and Abundance.

Shamanism is of great importance and is in the Siberian pattern, which includes drum-beating, use of sleigh bells, sacred pole ladder, trance, ventriloquism, blowing smoke and water, sucking affected parts of patients, and DIVINATION. Most shamans are women, and curing is their main occupation.

The Mapuche have resisted missionary efforts since the sixteenth century and have incorporated only a few, insignificant Catholic elements into their religion. They believe that the whites have their own distinctive god and the Mapuche theirs.

3. Current status and prospect. Several very different and complex evolutionary developments have taken place in the religions of native South America, often boosted by European influence. It is likely that the smaller tribal societies will become absorbed into the mestizo element of their nations and that their traditional religions will eventually disappear, although shamanism will probably survive in diminished importance as part of folk Catholicism. The diffusion of native religious ideas is very likely no longer taking place. So we are left with a contest between Christianity and whatever viable Indian religions remain.

Educated South Americans rely on a long educational program to incorporate Indians into the national culture, which means conversion to Catholicism and fluency in the national language. But what will be the effects of the recent decree that Quechua take its place with Spanish as an official language of Peru? Indian religious traditionalism may well be fostered, since language is a conservative channel for ideas—and Quechua-speakers constitute almost one half of the population and almost one hundred percent of the highland peoples. While the Quechua are in no danger of being forced from their highland bastion, the half million Mapuche, surrounded by white Chileans, recently suffered military atrocities at the hands of national troops and could conceivably be subjected to intense political and economic pressures which could disperse them geographically and end their way of life.

Bibliography. L. C. Faron, *Hawks of the Sun: Mapuche Morality and its Ritual Attributes* (1964), the only structural-functional study of a living native South American religion; M. J. Harner, *The Jivaro* (1973); D. Maybury-Lewis, *Akwe-Shavante Society* (1974); R. F. Murphy, *Headhunters' Heritage: Social and Economic Change Among the Mundurucu Indians* (1960); J. H. Steward, ed., *Handbook of South American Indians* (1946-1959), I-VII; J. H. Steward and L. C. Faron, *Native Peoples of South America* (1959), contains summaries of past and contemporary native religions in a complete ethnographic framework; J. Wilbert, *Survivors of Eldorado* (1972).

L. C. FARON

SOUTH ASIAN TRIBAL RELIGIONS. In South Asia old and new cultural forms persist side by side. This is only partly due to the geographical conditions which have caused many regions to remain relatively inaccessible. More important has been the ideology of HINDUISM (*see* CASTE). The Hindu world view, which accepted the innate and immutable differences between the various caste groups, saw nothing incongruous in the persistence of archaic and "primitive" cultures at no great distance from centers of sophisticated historical civilization.

Though some of the least developed Indian tribes have been reduced to fewer than a thousand members, the total strength of tribal populations in India is close to 40 million. The conventional grouping of the tribes is based on linguistic criteria. Speakers of Dravidian languages are found mainly in South India and include primitive hunters and food-gatherers such as Chenchus and Kadars, as well as relatively advanced farming peoples such as Gonds and Oraons. Tribes speaking Munda languages and extending over parts of Madhya Pradesh, Bihar, and Orissa include the Santal, Ho, Gadaba, Bondo, and Saora. Very different from all these tribes of peninsular India are the Tibeto-Burman tribes of Northeast India, who inhabit such hill regions as Nagaland as well as the territory bordering on Tibet. There is no absolute correspondence between linguistic and cultural groupings, since tribal religions contain a great variety of disparate elements which occur in various combinations even within one linguistic region.

No tribal society in South Asia is without a belief in supernatural beings. Most tribes are convinced of the possibility of establishing contact between humans and invisible beings of divine or demonic nature conceived of in anthropomorphic terms.

1. **Cosmology and creation.** Among most of the food-gatherers and some of the primitive shifting cultivators there is no idea of a world divided into several basically different spheres. Men, gods, and spirits dwell within the same sphere, even though the seat of certain gods may normally not be accessible to human beings. The greater number of tribes, however, have a clear idea of an underworld inhabited by deities and spirits as well as the dead. Others think of the land of the dead either as a region situated in the extreme east or west of the world of men, or in some cases as a kind of heaven in the clouds. Some of the tribes of Northeast India view the world as a series of tiered spheres.

Many Indian tribes have no precise idea regarding the creation of the world, and where creation myths are known, they usually bear traces of Hindu influence. The origin of the human race, on the other hand, is the subject of a rich mythology, and it is not unusual for several conflicting beliefs about the first humans to be current within the same tribal society.

2. **The nature of gods.** All religious concepts encountered among tribal populations involve a belief in invisible forces that affect the fortunes of humans. Such forces are thought of as personal and capable of reacting to the approaches of men, whatever forms these approaches may take. The idea that the gods are of a nature essentially different from that of humans and that they possess powers superior to human force does not necessarily mean that they are considered immaterial; rather, most tribesmen believe that under certain circumstances deities and spirits can be seen, heard, and felt.

Although supernatural powers are attributed to gods, one rarely encounters the belief in deities with limitless power. Many of the gods are dependent on regular offerings and sacrifices and get angry if their cult is neglected. The relationship between humans and gods is reciprocal, but this reciprocity can operate at different levels. At the most primitive level the gods render their worshipers certain services in exchange for sacrificial animals and food offerings. In this barter relationship there is little emotion involved, and no striving for a spiritual union with divine figures. Indeed, some of the gods, such as the bloodthirsty disease goddesses (e.g. Śītalā), are of so forbidding a character that no man or woman can desire any contact with them other than that prescribed by the ritual to ward off their unwelcome attention. Such rituals are not performed inside a settlement but at the border of the village land with the idea of sending the goddess off as speedily as possible.

On the other hand, there are deities considered basically benevolent and concerned not so much about the offerings given them as about the veneration rendered by their worshipers. One of these benign deities is the earth goddess revered by many agricultural tribes. The earth mother is not in need of the offerings given by her "children," but it is believed that prayers accompanied by such offerings as the blood of fowls and pigs are likely to increase the abundance of her gifts. Similarly the clan deities of such tribes as the Gonds stand to the clan members in a close and intimate relationship, and myths and legends relate how in the heroic age, and even today, the clan ancestors have been led and protected by their deities. Failure to worship these deities may, according to mythology, cause a god to appear to the clan priest in his dreams and remind him of his duties. The belief in the protective presence of the deities is reinforced by the way in which during feasts and rituals a god may possess one of the worshipers. The frequency of states of trance (when the gods speak through the mouth of a seer) are to the members of the tribe irrefutable proof of divine presence and interest in human affairs. Elaborate seasonal rituals are based on the assumption that powerful divine beings can influence the course of nature, and that good fortune depends largely on their favor.

Though the manner in which various deities are worshiped may differ widely, there is the underlying belief that all gods desire to be venerated and that they have the power, if not always the will, to grant their devotees' requests.

The concept of a supreme deity is found among many, though by no means all, tribal societies. Although perceived by some tribes as an otiose deity, this supreme being is credited by others with both the power and the will to intervene decisively in human affairs. Many tribes refer to this supreme god as BHAGAVĀN, a term of SANSKRIT origin and likely reflective of the influence of Hinduism. Among the Gonds, for instance, Bhagavān, who presides over the court of immortals, is equated with SHIVA, and in some myths he figures as the husband of the goddess PĀRVATĪ. Though Gonds consider him superior to all other gods, they do not accord him as much worship as they do to many lesser deities. Unlike the priests of the clan gods and other earth-bound deities the devotees of Bhagavān never fall into trance, and it is considered unimaginable that the supreme being should ever manifest himself by speaking through the mouth of an oracle priest.

Nearly all the tribes associate the supreme deity in one way or another with the sky or the sun. The Konyak Nagas of Northeast India refer to the supreme being as Gawang, which means literally "sky-earth," and think of him in anthropomorphic terms. Gawang is believed to be able to see and hear everything human beings do and to be angered by certain breaches of the moral order.

However exalted such figures as Bhagavān and Gawang may be, they are never considered to have a claim to anyone's exclusive worship or to be in opposition to a being representing the forces of evil. Unlike many primitive populations in other parts of the world, Indian tribal peoples lack any idea of a god or demon who opposes the benevolent supreme being or stands from the beginning in a position of hostility to humanity.

3. Religion and morality. In most Indian societies the link between religious ideas and moral concepts is extremely tenuous. Many tribes believe that the gods and spirits are indifferent to the moral conduct of their devotees, and will grant them protection and assistance as long as the customary offerings are given. Rarely do tribal gods appear in the role of law-givers, and the Konyak high god Gawang is exceptional in his concern about human moral lapses. There is a widespread belief that the breaking of a TABOO may bring about misfortune, but the idea prevalent among many tribes that actions capable of attracting supernatural sanctions may be committed unknowingly shows that the completed deed, not the intention, is thought to bring such retribution. The belief in supernatural sanctions, moreover, does not necessarily presuppose a sense of "sin." Most of the preliterate tribal languages have no word for sin, but loan words, such as the Hindī *pap* ("evil," "bad"), are widely used without, however, conveying the concept of a voluntary breach of a divine command. Gods and spirits may be feared by men whose actions are thought to have aroused their anger, but this sense of fear is different from the feeling of guilt aroused in other societies by willful disobedience of divine commands. Many tribal gods and spirits are cruel, jealous, and grasping, and it is hardly surprising that actions objectionable to such self-seeking immortals are not necessarily considered morally reprehensible.

Nowhere in tribal India are there priests whose function is supervising and influencing the moral conduct of their fellow villagers or tribesmen. Their task is the maintenance of harmonious relations between humans and supernatural powers and not the laying down of moral rules. They are employed to discover the causes of disease or ill luck, and if a god or spirit is found responsible for such an occurrence they try to avert his wrath. Thus they help their community in the struggle against illness and misfortune, but in this struggle moral values are rarely involved.

4. Concepts of the soul and the afterlife. Some Indian tribal populations have only vague notions of an afterlife, but others have definite ideas about different elements in the make-up of the human personality and speculate in great detail about the conditions of these elements after a person's death.

The Hill Reddis of Andhra Pradesh and some other tribes have no concept of a soul as an entity different from the body. Deceased relatives to whom food is given at the time of certain ceremonies are referred to as "the elders" or simply "the departed," but never as the "souls of the departed" or the "ancestral spirits." In contrast, the Gonds, another tribe of the Deccan, distinguish between two elements in the human personality, respectively known as *jiv* and *sanal*. The *jiv* is the life force without which no human being can exist. It is sent by Bhagavān, the supreme god, into a child while it is still in the mother's womb, and it remains with the individual until the moment of death, when it returns to Bhagavān and joins a pool of *jiv* until it is reincarnated in another human being. Yet an individual's personality is not believed to adhere to the *jiv*, and no one ever remembers an earlier life. The element in which the personality survives is the *sanal* (lit. "the one who has gone"), and this comes into being as a separate entity in the moment of death. The *sanal* follows the corpse-bearers from the village to the burial or cremation ground, and after the funeral enters the land of the dead, where it joins its clan deity and the company of its deceased kinsmen. The dead, however, are not far removed from the world of the living. They come to the habitations of their kinsmen, and at the time of the ritual eating of the first fruits, offerings for the departed are placed on the roofs. Far from dreading contact with the dead, the Gonds believe in the beneficial influence of friendly *sanal*. Other tribes too are conscious of a mutual dependence between the living and the dead. The living have to care for the departed by giving them offerings of food and performing rituals for their benefit, and the departed are believed to aid the growth of crops and the fertility of humans and animals.

The Apa Tanis of Northeast India have a particularly clear idea of the netherworld, and their SHAMANS and priests claim to visit in their dreams the regions inhabited by gods, spirits, and departed human beings. Anyone who died a natural death is thought to go to Neli, a place below the earth which looks very much like the Apa Tani valley. On the way to Neli the dead come to the house of Nelkiri, the guardian of the underworld, and there they meet their kinsmen and friends who preceded them in death. In Neli a man who was rich on earth will again be rich, a slave will serve his master, and a woman will return to her first husband. The dead cultivate their land, and ultimately they die once more and go to a land of the dead which lies below Neli. Though Neli is a real underworld, it has no gloomy associations but is thought to be a good and happy place. Those who died an unnatural or violent death are believed to go to a land in the sky.

The Apa Tanis believe that during sleep a man's soul may leave his body and stray into Neli, and that there it may be waylaid and detained by a spirit. The man deprived of his soul will fall sick and will ultimately die unless a shaman capable of entering the underworld ransoms the captured soul by promising the spirit sacrifices of fowl, pigs, or cattle. This traffic between the world of the living and Neli gives the Apa Tanis a knowledge of the underworld unrivaled in the eschatological beliefs of most other Indian tribesmen.

5. Tribal beliefs and historic religions. In view of the longstanding contacts between many tribal populations and Hindu society it is hardly surprising that many Hindu ideas have infiltrated the thinking of tribal communities. Such influences are particularly noticeable among tribes of Middle India whose original Dravidian or Munda languages have given way to Aryan ones. Only in the remote regions of Northeast India, and particularly in Arunachal Pradesh, are there tribal groups that have had little or no contact with Hindu populations, and it is there that the tribal religions of Tibeto-Burman–speaking peoples have persisted in their pristine form. TIBETAN BUDDHISM has affected only a limited number of tribal groups in the Himalayan highlands, and where it has, it has led to a merging of the two systems of thought rather than to a wholesale displacement of tribal beliefs. Conversion to CHRISTIANITY, on the other hand, has resulted in a total abandonment of tribal faiths in such regions as Nagaland, where foreign missionaries had been active since the end of the nineteenth century.

Bibliography V. Elwin, *The Religion of an Indian Tribe* (1955); C. von Fürer-Haimendorf, "The After-Life in Indian Tribal Belief," *Journal of the Royal Anthrop. Institute*, 83 (1953), 37-49, *Morals and Merit* (1967), and *The Gonds of Andhra Pradesh* (1979).
C. VON FÜRER-HAIMENDORF

SOUTHEAST ASIAN TRIBAL RELIGIONS. In Southeast Asia, a region which includes the countries of Burma, Thailand, Laos, Cambodia, Vietnam, Malaysia, Singapore, Indonesia, the Philippines, and the British dependency of Brunei, there are several million people who adhere to religions which are communicated through an oral rather than a written tradition. These religions are followed by tribal peoples who live mainly on the peripheries of the dominant societies; that is, by peoples who live in the mountainous regions of the larger islands and of the mainland of Southeast Asia or on the small isolated islands of the eastern archipelago. A few tribal peoples—totaling perhaps not more than ten thousand—live in nomadic bands and support themselves through hunting and gathering in the forests of the region. While their numbers are small, the religions of such groups as the Negrito Semang on the Malay Peninsula, the Punan-Penan of Borneo, the elusive Mrabri or Yumbri (the "spirits of the yellow leaves") of northern Thailand, and the recently "discovered" Tasaday of Mindanao in the Philippines hold especial interest because they reflect, at least in part, an adaptation to a hunting-and-gathering mode of existence.

The vast majority of tribal religions are found among peoples who are agriculturalists or horticulturalists. For the most part these tribal peoples live in village-based societies, but a few groups—e.g., the Tai of northern Laos and northern Vietnam—have been organized, at least until quite recently, into chiefdoms. There are well over a hundred different tribal groups on the mainland of Southeast Asia and their members speak languages belonging to a number of quite distinct language families (Austroasiatic or Mon-Khmer, Tibeto-Burman, Austronesian or Malayo-Polynesian, Tai, Maio-Yao, Karen, and Viet-Muong). While all the tribal peoples of the insular part of the region speak languages belonging to the same language family (Austronesian or

Malayo-Polynesian), there are still over sixty distinct groups.

While each tribal religion in Southeast Asia has unique characteristics which reflect adaptation and development in different contexts, these religions also share certain patterns. Some similarities can be explained as being a consequence of historical contact whereby some pattern or form has been diffused from one society to another or carried by peoples who have migrated from one place to another. Other similarities can be interpreted as reflecting the ordering of similar experiences (e.g., birth, illness, death, or, less universally, concerns regarding crops by those who are agriculturalists or horticulturalists) with reference to similar modes of thought.

1. Cosmology and beliefs in supernatural powers. Available evidence on tribal religions indicates that, except where conversions to one of the major historic religions have taken place, the underlying structure of reality for tribal peoples of this area is dualistic. However they may be expressed, the two fundamental cosmic principles of tribal religious thought are complementary as well as opposed; they cannot, thus, be equated with good and evil or with God and the Devil in the Christian tradition. A fundamental contrast between tribal religions and historic religions is to be found in the fact that the latter nearly all posit an ultimate transcendence of the oscillation between order and chaos, fertility and barrenness, life and death, whereas tribal religions do not.

The fundamental structure of reality is expressed in tribal religions, not in an analytical theology, but through the medium of MYTH. In some cases, as among the Tetum of Timor, the dualism of the cosmos is quite explicit in the mythology. Tetum myths tell of the division between "the earth," the world of humans where males are dominant, and "the world inside," symbolized as a huge womb, where women dominate. The world inside is both the source of life and the receptacle of death, the place in which the soul is reintegrated following the cessation of physical life. Among the Karen of Burma and Thailand, the fundamental opposition is between the creator god, Y'wa, and the basically female divinity which inflicts suffering and death upon humans while at the same time providing them with the gift of culture. The dualism of Karen thought is further manifest in their ideas about the afterworld; rather than being a place apart from the ordinary mundane world, it is the mirror image, the inversion of that world.

The cosmology of the Toradjas of Sulawesi in Indonesia has been elaborated on a basic dualistic structure: the world of men is contrasted with both an upper world and a lower world and with an abode in the southwest where the forefathers live and an abode in the northeast where the deified ancestors (known by the SANSKRIT-derived word *deata*) live. The Ifugaos of the highlands of Luzon have similar ideas: they posit the existence of five realms, the known world of humans being contrasted with a skyworld and an underworld and with a region downstream and one upstream.

While there may be a basic similarity in structure of cosmologies of Southeast Asian tribal religions, there are marked variations in the beliefs regarding the forms in which the power or force of the cosmological principles manifest themselves. That these manifestations take the form of varieties of supernatural beings has led to the classification of tribal religions as ANIMISTIC. The Negrito Semang, a hunting-and-gathering people of Malaya, believe, for example, that the most important supernatural powers are the *chinoi,* humanoid yet invisible creatures who are equated in Semang thought with birds, flowers, and other natural phenomena, with human fetuses, and with the fertility of wild plants. Access to the power of this highly generalized class of beings is gained by the actions of SHAMANS, called *halak,* who in trance-states become *chinoi*. The *chinoi* mediate, according to Semang belief, between humans and the ultimate powers, the *orang hidup*. The only significant beings among the *orang hidup* are Tak ("Grandfather") Pedn; his son, brother or alter ego, Karei; and Yak ("Grandmother") Manoi, wife of Karei.

In marked contrast to this limited pantheon among the Semang, the Ifugaos, a horticultural people living in the mountains of Luzon, recognize some forty classes of different types of divinities. Perhaps as many as fifteen hundred different named supernatural beings have been identified for the Ifugaos, although not all beings are recognized in a single Ifugao community.

In many tribal religions ANCESTOR VENERATION is widely practiced, and in some, several types of ancestral spirits are distinguished. The Toradja of central Sulawesi, for example, make a distinction between the *anitu,* hero-ancestors who have the power to provide generalized protection to others besides their own descendants, the *angga ntau tu'a,* revered ancestors for whom elaborate secondary death rituals have been performed, and ordinary *angga,* the recently dead. Ancestor worship is particularly pronounced in societies in which important social and economic functions are carried out by groups made up of members who recognize that they share descent from the same forebears. The Tetum of Timor, for example, a people who organize themselves according to a principle of patrilineal descent, propitiate remote as well as more recent ancestors, although the most remote ancestor is believed to have lived only seven generations back. Among the Karen of Burma and Thailand, a people who do not have kin groups larger than the household, the only ancestors worshiped are those associated with the household, beings whose precise relationships to members of the household or to other ancestors is not a matter of concern.

Most tribal peoples in Southeast Asia believe that serious afflictions and death can be caused not only by malevolent spirits but also by human beings who have become sorcerers or witches. Typically, as among the Mnong Gar of southern Vietnam, shamans called in to perform cures may seek to determine whether an illness has been caused by a spirit or a sorcerer and, if the latter, to determine who is the sorcerer. In some societies, as among the Semang, shamans may also be sorcerers or witches. While in some groups sorcery or witchcraft is not often evoked as an explanation for illness or death, other groups, such as the Tetum of Timor, believe that nearly every death has been caused by the ill will of such humans.

2. **Beliefs in anima and the afterlife.** Most, if not all, tribal peoples in Southeast Asia hold that spirits and witches cause afflictions and death by attacking the anima or vital essence of the person. Although the term "soul" is often used to translate such concepts as the *k'la* of the Sgaw Karen of Burma, the *amirue* of the Ma'anyan Dayak of Borneo, the *tondi* of the Batak of Sumatra, the *kaduduwa* of the Apayao or Isneg of the Philippines, or the *hêeng* of the Mnong Gar of southern Vietnam, and so on, this term carries a connotation of insubstantiality and immortality which is not necessarily implied by the Southeast Asian concepts. For each of these peoples, as well as for many other Southeast Asian tribal peoples, the vital essence has a tenuous attachment to the corporeal body, and it is believed that certain stressful events—e.g., the death of a close relative, a shift in residence, a change in social status, or just being awakened abruptly—may cause the essence to take fright and leave the body or may render it vulnerable to attack by spirits or sorcerers. Some peoples believe that the vital essence is compounded of many elements or that there are several different types of essences associated with each individual. The Mnong Gar of southern Vietnam, for example, believe that each person has a quartz-*hêeng,* located behind the forehead, which serves to orient the body; a spider-*hêeng,* located in the head, which can flee the body and must, thus, be returned periodically; and a buffalo-*hêeng,* which exists in the sky where it is cared for by spirits and which will die when the person dies.

All tribal peoples believe that death is marked by an irrevocable separation between the body and the anima, following which the anima undergoes a marked transformation of state. Among some groups—notably the Dayaks of Borneo and the Toradjas of Sulawesi—final death rites do not take place until several years after death. During the transitional period the anima enters a liminal state during which it poses a danger to the living. Only after the final rites—which are quite spectacular in some Dayak and Toradjan societies—can the anima be further transformed into a spirit and join other ancestors. However, this state too may not be the final one. For example, among the Ma'anyan Dayaks the *amirue,* after passing through a transitional state during which it is called *adiau,* becomes, at the final mass cremation of many corpses which have been stored up for several months to several years, an *amirue* once again. These final rites mark the passage of the *amirue* into the land of the dead, Datu Tunjung. It does not, however, remain forever in this state, but will eventually (in most cases) be reborn into the world of humans.

Reincarnation beliefs, although different from those of the Ma'anyan Dayak, are found in many tribal religions. Even where they are lacking, there is no conception of a heaven as a state which is infinitely better and preferable to the one experienced while alive. Typically, as among the Semang of Malaya or the Batak of Sumatra, the netherworld is a shadowy place about which little interest is shown. Concern is shown primarily for those anima which have become ghosts, following an unnatural death (e.g., the death of a woman while giving birth, death in battle after which the head has been taken, death following from some unexpected calamity, suicide, and so on), or which are still in a liminal state between the world of the living and the world of the dead, or which have become ancestral spirits.

3. **Religious practices and practitioners.** Sacrifices of domesticated animals, and in some cases in the past even of humans, are a conspicuous feature of most Southeast Asian tribal religions. Only a few groups do not practice sacrifices, and most of these, like the Kédang of Lembata in eastern Indonesia, are groups in which large numbers have been converted to Christianity or Islam. The hunting-and-gathering Semang, who lack domesticated animals, are exceptional, but they also carry out a form of self-sacrifice by offering the deities their own blood produced by making a cut near the shin bone. The most typical sacrifice in Southeast Asian tribal religions involves the immolation of a chicken as an offering to the spirit or group of spirits from whom a boon or cessation of affliction is sought. Some groups, such as those found in southern Vietnam, also sacrifice other small domesticated animals such as ducks and dogs. In many groups it is believed that for some favors to be gained it is necessary to offer a large animal. Thus, for example, the Sgaw Karen offer a pig at annual rituals held by households to ward off the wrath of ancestral spirits. A rich Hmong (Meo) family may sacrifice several pigs as well as chickens in its efforts to satisfy the beings who are believed to be causing a serious illness of one of its members.

Many peoples in Southeast Asia also sacrifice even larger animals, typically water buffaloes (also known as carabao). While buffalos may be sacrificed in order to gain release from an affliction, they are also often sacrificed as a means of enhancing the social and ritual status of a man rich enough to sponsor such a sacrifice. Buffalo sacrifices associated with "feasts of merit," while best known from accounts about groups living in northern Burma and in areas adjacent to India (e.g., among Nagas, Chins, and Kachins), have also been reported for many other groups throughout the region, from northern Burma to southern Vietnam, and from Sulawesi to northern Luzon.

For some groups in the past, the supreme sacrifice was the offering of a human head. Among the Toradja of Sulawesi, for example, mourning for an important person was supposed to be brought to an end with the offering of a head obtained through a raid on a neighboring people. The Wa of northern Burma took heads which they placed on gates entering their villages. The ghosts of those whose heads were taken were believed to serve as guardians of the community, protecting it against forces which endangered the health of villagers or the productivity of crops. The Wa particularly favored the heads of strangers, including those of Burmese, Chinese, or Westerners. Although there was a brief resurgence of headhunting, particularly in Borneo, during World War II, it is now a practice of the past in Southeast Asia.

In many tribal religions the most important religious practitioner is a person who is able to enter into a shamanistic trance and to make contact with the world of spirits, ghosts, and witches. In some societies the role of shaman is hereditary, but more typically shamans learn their practice from other shamans who may or may not be relatives. However recruited, a shaman must be able to enter a trance state during which it is believed that he has journeyed to the world of spirits and/or the world of the dead. In some societies, such as the Semang, shamans are always males, but in a number of other tribal groups women as well as men become shamans. Among the Ma'anyan Dayak, for example, six of the seven types of shamanic roles *(wadian)* are performed by women.

Some tribal groups, notably those which are organized beyond the village level, have other types of religious practitioners as well as shamans. For example, among the Black Tai of Laos and northern Vietnam there is a hereditary priesthood *(mo)* from which the chief priests are drawn; these priests perform the rituals for the dominant spirits of the land. Some tribal peoples also have become followers of prophets or charismatic leaders. Among the Karen of Burma, traditional prophets *(wi)* acquired reputations for curing and DIVINATION which extended beyond a few villages. During the last century Karen charismatics, like comparable figures elsewhere, have often become the foci of MILLENARIAN MOVEMENTS; in many cases these movements have drawn on beliefs from Christianity or other historic religions for their messages. The proliferation of such religious movements, found among groups as widely separated as the Chin of northern Burma and the Igorot of northern Luzon, reflects the rapid changes that have been occurring in tribal societies.

4. Decline of tribal religions. For centuries tribal peoples in Southeast Asia have been steadily, if slowly, assimilated into neighboring Buddhist, Islamic, Sinitic, and Christian civilizations. The pace of change greatly accelerated from about the middle of the nineteenth century on, when the impact of the world economy and of colonial governments (except in Thailand, where indigenous rulers played much the same role) also began to be felt in previously remote areas. Christian missionaries have, where political conditions permitted, been very assiduous over the past century in taking their message to tribal peoples, and the changing political and economic situation has often made these peoples quite receptive to the Christian message. (*See* MISSIONS, CHRISTIAN.)

During the American period in the Philippines, Protestant missionaries began to compete with Catholics in the effort to convert the remaining "pagans." In Indonesia during the Dutch period, large segments of the previously tribal populations of Sumatra, Borneo, and the Moluccas were converted to Christianity. In Burma, Christian missionaries had great success among the Karen and also among the Chin, Kachin, and other tribal groups. Missionary activity among tribal peoples in Laos, Cambodia, and Vietnam intensified after World War II, and in the turmoil of the wars in Indochina, Christian missionaries again found many who were willing to accept their teaching.

The wars in Indochina also brought other changes in the lives of tribal peoples in this area. The new Communist governments are committed to eliminating "superstitions" while still respecting the integrity of tribal ethnic identities.

Although tribal religions are not under such direct attack elsewhere in the region, the decline of these religions still continues. Despite a few efforts to rationalize tribal religions—as, for example, among some Bornean groups who have sought to create a tribal religious organization which can compete on equal ground with Islam and Christianity—and despite the periodic resurgence of tribal beliefs in new millenarian guises, tribal religions in Southeast Asia remain truly vital only in those few areas which are still relatively isolated from the inexorable forces of contact and change.

Bibliography. The following list contains references to only a very small part of the ethnographic literature on tribal religions in Southeast Asia. More extensive bibliographical guides can be found in the reference works which are also included here. R. F. Barton, *The Religion of the Ifugaos* (1946); I. Carey, *Orang Asli: The Aboriginal Tribes of Peninsular Malaysia* (1976), contains good summary accounts of the religions of the Negrito Semang, the Senoi, and the proto-Malays; includes bibliography; G. Condominas, *We Have Eaten the Forest* (1977), excellent account of the religion of the Mnong Gar of southern Vietnam; includes bibliography; R. E. Downs, *The Religion of the Bare'e-speaking Toradja of Central Celebes* (1956); F. Eggan and A. Pacyaya, "The Sapilada Religion: Reformation and Accommodation among the Igorots of Northern Luzon," *Southwestern Journal of Anthropology,* XVIII (1962), 95-113; D. Hicks, *Tetum Ghosts and Kin* (1976), concerning the Tetum who live on the island of Timor; A. B. Hudson, "Death Ceremonies of the Ma'anyan Dayaks," *Sarawak Museum Journal,* XIII (1966), 341-417; K. G. Izikowitz, "Fastening the Soul, Some Religious Traits among the Lamet (French Indochina),"

Götesborgs Högskolas Arsskrifft, XLVII (1941), 1-32, and *Lamet: Hill Peasants in French Indochina* (1951); H. E. Kauffmann, "Some Social and Religious Institutions of the Lawa (Northwestern Thailand)," *Journal of the Siam Society*, LXI (1972), 235-306; LXV (1977), 181-226; C. F. Keyes, *The Golden Peninsula: Culture and Adaptation in Mainland Southeast Asia* (1977), ch. 1 provides an interpretative overview together with analyses of the religions of the Semang, Chin and Karen; A. T. Kirsch, *Feasting and Social Oscillation: Religion and Society in Upland Southeast Asia* (1973), an interpretative analysis of the Naga, Chin, Kachin, and Lamet religious systems; E. R. Leach, *Political Systems of Highland Burma* (1954), concerns the Kachin of northern Burma and also provides an influential interpretation of tribal religion in Southeast Asia; F. M. LeBar, ed. and comp., *Ethnic Groups of Insular Southeast Asia*, 2 vols. (1972, 1975), includes summary accounts of tribal religions and provides bibliographical guides to the relevant literature for Indonesia, the Philippines, and Malaysian Borneo; F. M. LeBar, G. C. Hickey, and J. K. Musgrave, *Ethnic Groups of Mainland Asia* (1964), comparable volume for mainland Southeast Asia; H. I. Marshall, *The Karen People of Burma* (1922); N. Chindarsi, *The Religion of the Hmong Njua* (1976), concerns Hmong of northern Thailand; H. Schärer, *Ngjaju Religion: The Conception of God among a South Borneo People* (1963); P. Schebesta, *Among the Forest Dwarfs of Malaya* (1927), concerning the Negrito Semang; J. L. Schrock, *et al.*, *Minority Groups in the Republic of Vietnam* (1966); *Minority Groups in North Vietnam* (1972), handbooks prepared for the U.S. Army containing summary accounts of the religious systems of tribal peoples of Vietnam together with relevant bibliographies; T. Stern, "*Ariya* and the Golden Book: A Millenarian Buddhist Sect among the Karen," *JAS*, XXVII (1968), 297-328; J. H. Telford, "Animism in Kentung State," *Journal of the Burma Research Society*, XXVII (1937), 86-378, concerning religion of tribal groups in Burma; P. O. L. Tobing, *The Structure of the Toba-Batak Belief in the High God* (1956), concerning the Batak of Sumatra; A. R. Walker, ed., *Farmers in the Hills: Ethnographic Notes on the Upland Peoples of North Thailand*, good bibliographical guide to and summary of the ethnographic literature, particularly for the Lahu.

C. F. KEYES

SPENER, PHILIPP JAKOB (Ch; 1635-1705). Leader of German Lutheran PIETISM. Of Alsatian birth, the well-educated and gentle reformer held important church posts in Frankfurt am Main, Dresden, and Berlin. His best-known publication, the tract *Pia desideria* (1675), set off a storm of controversy among Lutheran orthodoxy.

D. F. DURNBAUGH

SPIRIT. *See* SOUL, SPIRIT.

SPIRITUALISM, SPIRITISM. A mode of thinking based on the belief that the spirits of the dead, or other spirit beings, communicate with the living. Such communication normally takes place through a medium, a person who has a contact among the spirits.

Spiritualists with some justice claim that theirs is the "oldest religion in the world," for it has roots in ANIMISM and SHAMANISM. The modern movement dates from 1848, when two teen-age sisters, Margaretta and Katie Fox, of Hydesville, New York, reported "rappings" in their home, which they interpreted as messages from a peddler who had died in the house. A Spiritualist enthusiasm sparked by these revelations swept the country and spread to Europe and Latin America. The ground had been well prepared for it by the teachings of SWEDENBORGIANISM, popularized in America by John Chapman ("Johnny Appleseed") and A. J. Davis, by interest in Native American shamanism, and by spirit phenomena among the SHAKERS.

After rapid growth in the 1850s Spiritualism declined, but small Spiritualist churches have continued to exist, and Spiritualist ideas have had an influence greater than the number of committed Spiritualists would suggest. In Brazil, Spiritualism, often mingled with African and quasi-Catholic influences, has been a major religious force. The movement has attracted such prominent proponents as Sir Arthur Conan Doyle and Sir Oliver Lodge. The celebrated magician Houdini devoted much effort to exposing Spiritualism.

Apart from the place given "spirit readings," "spirit healings," and the role of the medium, Spiritualist meetings have many similarities to PROTESTANT worship services with BIBLE reading, PRAYER, and SACRAMENTS. Women have long held a high proportion of leadership positions. JESUS is regarded as having been a medium, and his RESURRECTION as an example of how spirits live on after death.

Most churches are independent, centering around the charisma of particular mediums and ministers, but various associations exist. The National Spiritualist Alliance of the U.S.A. (founded in 1913) has headquarters in Lake Pleasant, Massachusetts, and the International General Assembly of Spiritualists (founded 1936) is based in Norfolk, Virginia.

Bibliography. S. Brown, *The Heyday of Spiritualism* (1970); R. S. Ellwood, *Alternative Altars* (1979); J. S. Judah, *History and Philosophy of the Metaphysical Movements in America* (1967); G. K. Nelson, *Spiritualism and Society* (1969).

R. S. ELLWOOD

ŚRĀDDHA shräd′ hä (H—Skt.; lit. "application of faith" [*śraddhā*—"faith"]). A system of offerings for deceased ancestors, based upon the VEDAS. It is perhaps the strongest feature of VEDIC HINDUISM to have survived into the modern period.

Important throughout the history of Hinduism has been the concept that each person owes three "debts": to the sages (RISHIS), gods (DEVAS), and ancestors (PITṚS). The last debt is removed by continuing one's lineage with a son. On the day of a death it is the eldest living son who serves as sacrificer in the cremation rites, the "final offering," i.e. of the body. At that time the immediate ritual task is to provide the PRETA, the disembodied spirit of the deceased, with a temporary ritual body, an invisible medium that enables the deceased to join the company of his or her ancestors (*pitṛs*). Without these ceremonies the

D. M. Knipe

Śrāddha offering in Banāras

preta is liable to become a troublesome ghost *(bhūta)*. With proper performance, however, the ritual body is constructed part by part in ten days (parallel to ten lunar months of gestation). After special *śrāddhas* on the eleventh day a dramatic climax occurs on the twelfth day when a *piṇḍa,* a ball of food (usually cooked rice), representing the deceased, is cut into three pieces. The pieces are mixed with three *piṇḍas* representing the deceased's father, grandfather, and great-grandfather, who are located respectively in earth, midspace, and heaven. Ancestors beyond three generations belong to those remote regions from which eventual rebirth takes place; they are less in need of the *piṇḍas,* water, and sesame seed offered to the closest three levels of the paternal and maternal lines. A widow may be ritually assumed into either her husband's or her father's lineage. In antiquity this twelfth-day rite, *sapiṇḍīkaraṇa,* was on the anniversary of death, but in contemporary practice the sacrificer (eldest living son) may perform offerings in a few hours that suffice for an entire year.

In addition to these *śrāddhas* linked to a specific death any householder may perform other *śrāddhas* at regular occasions. In fact, one of the five daily YAJÑAS (sacrifices), the *mahāyajñas* of Hinduism, is to the ancestors. More elaborate are the *śrāddhas* conducted on the new-moon day of each month, when the ancestors, sometimes represented by special BRAHMIN surrogates, are fed *piṇḍas,* water, and sesame. In some parts of India the *piṇḍas* are set out for crows to eat. Every year, particularly during the special *pitṛ*-half of a certain lunar month, a "dark" fortnight in September-October, tens of thousands of pilgrims journey to sacred centers such as Banāras, Gayā, or Nāsik to have *śrāddhas* performed on the river bank for their deceased parents or other ancestors. All these *śrāddhas* reinforce a symbiotic relationship: offerings sustain and promote the dead, and the dead, with the benefits of celestial residence, look out for the needs of their living descendants. The basic texts concerning the *śrāddhas* are the Gṛhya Sūtras. They were composed late in the first millennium B.C., but their structure goes back centuries earlier to the SAṂHITĀS and BRĀHMAṆAS, particularly in connection with the cult of SOMA. *See* ANCESTOR VENERATION.

Bibliography. P. V. Kane, *History of Dharmaśāstra,* IV (1953), 334-551; D. M. Knipe, "Sapiṇḍīkaraṇa," in F. E. Reynolds and E. H. Waugh, eds., *Religious Encounters with Death* (1977), pp. 111-24. D. M. KNIPE

ŚRAMAṆA shrŭ´ mŭn ŭ (Ja & B—Skt.; lit. "one who exerts great effort" [*śrama*—"effort, endeavor"]) **SAMANA** sŭ´ mŭn ŭ (Ja—Prākrit). An ascetic monk or nun who strives to attain liberation.

In SANSKRIT three designations are used interchangeably: *śramaṇa, samana,* and *śamana. Śrama* means being engaged in spiritual disciplines without any desire for the fruit; thus, a *śramaṇa* is one who attempts to achieve salvation with nonattached effort. *Samana* is from *sama* (equality), hence, a *samana* is one who regards all living beings as equal. *Śamana* is derived from *śamana* (control of sensations and emotions), therefore, the *śamana* is one who controls his or her sensual urges with a view to attaining enlightenment.

Because all three aspects of *śramaṇa* have been accepted in Jainism and Buddhism, their monks and nuns are called *śramaṇas.* They are often contrasted with the Hindus who follow the BRĀHMAṆAS, or the Brahmanic way, according to which the lives of individuals are regulated by CASTE duties *(varṇāśrama dharmas). Śramaṇas* do not accept caste or its religious consequences, but advocate equality of opportunity for every individual to attain NIRVANA without any social or spiritual differentiation. Nonetheless the distinction between the ascetics and the laypersons common in Hinduism has been accepted in the *śramaṇic* traditions. *Śramaṇas* are usually divided into monks (SĀDHUS) and nuns *(sāhvis),* while the laity is further divided into *śrāvakas* (male followers) and *śrāvikās* (female followers). *Śramaṇas* encourage abrupt and complete renunciation, whereas Brahmanic Hinduism espouses a graduated path which requires complete renunciation only as the final life stage (ĀŚRAMA).

A *śramaṇa* must maintain mental equilibrium and undergo penance or self-discipline for the attainment of Nirvana. Both Jaina and Buddhist *śramaṇas* emphasize the discipine of nonviolence (AHIṂSĀ) and truth (SAT). The tradition exemplifies an extreme form of humanistic self-reliance, without external aid from any divine source, rejecting any personal god or grace (with the exception of MAHĀYĀNA Buddhism, which accepts grace). The BUDDHA himself seems not to have postulated God or advocated grace as a mode of salvation. In Jainism the final stage of a *śramaṇa* is called *snataka* (graduate), a stage equivalent to that of the BODHISATTVA (enlightened one) of Buddhism.

As opposed to the Brahmanic literary tradition of the VEDAS, the UPANIṢADS, etc. the *śramaṇas* have their own canonical literature; Jainas have the ĀGAMAS based on the preachings of MAHĀVĪRA and Buddhists the TRIPIṬAKA based on the teachings of the Buddha.

The Vedic and Brahmanic rituals rejected by the *śramaṇas* as the way to perfection were also rejected or reinterpreted by Hindus who advocated YOGA as a path for the attainment of MOKṢA. Hence, the attainment of liberation or Nirvana *(jivanmukti)* in the *śramaṇic* tradition is not basically different from the Upaniṣadic concept of *mokṣa*. Furthermore, both Brahmanic and *śramaṇic* traditions accept the notions of KARMA and SAMSARA, and both agree that Nirvana or *mokṣa* means freedom from reincarnation. Consequently, the ultimate aims of both traditions are similar, though the means differ. Both traditions have been strengthened by the spiritual achievements of great personalities and sages. Both accept spiritual discipline, including penance in some form or the other, as the means to the attainment of perfection or enlightenment. Still, the authority of the Vedas for all Hindus and the reliance on divine grace in BHAKTI HINDUISM continue to provide essential barriers between the *śramaṇic* traditions of asceticism and the various strands of the Hindu tradition.

I. C. SHARMA

ŚRĪ shrē (H—Skt.; lit. "fortune, prosperity"). 1. An honorific prefix used before the names of gods, noble men, and revered scriptures. 2. An epithet of the goddess LAKṢMĪ.

J. BARE

ŚRĪ VAIṢṆAVA shrē vīsh´ nŭ vŭ (H—Skt.). A South Indian theistic sect of worshipers of VISHNU and the goddess ŚRĪ or LAKṢMĪ (*see* BHAKTI HINDUISM); widely known for its leading Teacher RĀMĀNUJA and as the first movement led by BRAHMINS to integrate fully a popular, largely non-Brahmanical devotional movement employing a vernacular language, i.e., the ecstatic *bhakti* of the TAMIL hymns of the ĀḺVĀRS.

1. **Popular and Brahmanical elements.** This sect's synthesis of popular and Brahmanical elements provided a model for other movements that employ vernacular languages. In addition to the Āḻvārs' hymns, the major elements which informed this sect included the Pāñcarātra tradition of temple worship (*see* PŪJĀ), BHĀGAVATA devotion to KRISHNA as an AVATAR of Vishnu, and Rāmānuja's theistic VEDĀNTA. In a radical enlargement of the Hindu scriptural base, both the post-Vedic PAÑCARĀTRA scriptures (ĀGAMA) and the Tamil hymns were declared equal to the VEDAS in authority and made the basis for a new ritual and devotional path of liberation open to all persons irrespective of CASTE. To symbolize this openness, the major Āḻvār, a ŚŪDRA named NAMMĀḺVĀR (*ca.* late ninth century A.D.) was placed at the head of the "preceptorial succession" as the primary human intermediary between Vishnu and his devotees.

The Bhāgavatas, a popular movement with a longer tradition of support by Brahmins, provided the sect's intellectual leadership. Its ĀCĀRYAS or Teachers were drawn primarily from among Bhāgavata Brahmins with strong traditions of Vedic and Vedāntic scholarship. The first two majors Ācāryas, Nāthamuni (*ca.* tenth century) and his grandson YĀMUNA (eleventh century), initiated the successful defense of Pāñcarātra and the Āḻvārs. Rāmānuja (eleventh-twelfth centuries) provided the final essential element in the synthesis, a theistic system of Vedānta based strictly upon Vedic sources but compatible with temple worship and the Āḻvārs' *bhakti*. (*See* VIŚIṢṬA ADVAITA). Rāmānuja won for popular theistic devotion a secure place within the Vedic tradition that has not since been effectively challenged.

2. **Divisions.** While all Śrī Vaiṣṇavas revere both their Vedic and their Tamil heritages, there has been a continuing tension between these two sides. In the fourteenth and fifteenth centuries this tension hardened into a sectarian division between the "Southern" (TEṄGALAI) and the "Northern" (VAḌAGALAI) schools, with the former emphasizing the Tamil heritage and making a larger place for non-Brahmin groups while the latter stresses the Sanskritic or Vedic and has in practice little involvement with non-Brahmins. *See* VEDĀNTA §3.

Bibliography. J. B. Carman, *The Theology of Rāmānuja* (1974); W. G. Neevel, *Yāmuna's Vedānta and Pāñcarātra* (1977); K. Rangachari, *The Sri Vaishnava Brahmans* (1931); J. S. M. Hooper, trans., *Hymns of the Āḻvārs* (1927).

W. G. NEEVEL

ŚRUTI shrōō´ tē (H—Skt.; lit. "that which is heard" [*śru*—"to hear"]). That body of Hindu scriptures considered to have been directly revealed by the gods through the ancient sages. The term is used in contradistinction to SMṚTI, the name applied to later canonical literature of human authorship. Included as *śruti* are not only the hymns of the VEDAS, but also the auxiliary BRĀHMAṆAS and the UPANIṢADS. Most sacred of Hindu religious literature, the *śruti* is regarded as the highest possible authority in all matters.

J. BARE

STAGES OF LIFE (H). *See* ĀŚRAMA.

STAR OF DAVID (Ju). *See* MAGEN DAVID.

STATIONS OF THE CROSS (Ch). A popular devotion in ROMAN CATHOLIC and many ANGLICAN churches, consisting of a prayer and brief meditation before each of the series of fourteen representations of Christ in his last journey from praetorium to tomb. The number of representations, generally ranged at intervals around the walls of the church, was fixed at fourteen by Clement XII in 1731. Of the events commemorated, nine are based on GOSPEL narratives, and five (3,4,6,7,9) are from early popular tradition: (1) Jesus is sentenced; (2) he receives the cross; (3) he falls a first time; (4) he meets his mother; (5) Simon of Cyrene helps carry the cross; (6) Veronica wipes the face of Jesus; (7) Jesus falls a second time; (8) he addresses the women of Jerusalem; (9) he falls the third time; (10) he is stripped of his garments and (11) nailed to the cross; (12) Jesus dies; (13) his body is taken down from the cross, and (14) laid in the tomb.

C. Waddell

STEINER, RUDOLF (Ch; 1861-1925). German scholar and religionist. Drawing on Theosophy and traditional Christianity, he developed a movement which he called Anthroposophy and propagated it through books and lectures and through programs to reform education, health, and agriculture.

K. Crim

STIGMATA stĭg mät′ ə, stĭg′ mət ə (Ch—plural of Gr. *stigma;* lit. "mark, brand"). Bodily wounds or pains considered, in the Christian context, as a visible sign of participation in Christ's passion. Though the scriptural point of reference usually given is Gal. 6:17 ("I bear on my body the marks of Jesus"), St. Francis of Assisi (d. 1226) is the first recorded stigmatic. Since then cases of stigmatization have been frequently verified even into modern times, though no reliable catalog of such stigmatics exists. Because there is no intrinsic connection between holiness and stigmatization, this phenomenon has never been considered a reliable sign of personal sanctity, and Catholic scholars tend to consider it as attributable to natural causes until the contrary is proved. Agreement is general that stigmatization, when it occurs, is a concomitant of ecstasy; and since ecstasy, though often supernatural in cause, is in itself a psychophysiological state, stigmatization as such does not belong to the order of the miraculous. Cases are known of Muslim stigmatics with wounds corresponding to those received by Muhammad in battle.

Bibliography. R. Biot, *The Enigma of the Stigmata* (1962).

C. Waddell

STŪPA stōō′ pŭ (B—Skt.; Pali *thūpa;* Sinhalese *dāgäba*). A commemorative monument and reliquary which traces its beginnings back to pre-Buddhist burial mounds known originally in India as *caitya.* According to tradition, the Buddha himself specified in the Mahā-Parinibbāna Sutta that his body was to be cremated and buried beneath a *stūpa,* which was to be the only devotional focus and reminder of his life, death, and enlightenment. Buddhists adopted this form, therefore, as an architectural symbol of the Buddha's death, transforming it into a symbol of his enlightenment. In this process, the emphasis shifted from the relic within the *stūpa* to the form and transcendent meaning of the *stūpa* itself, and the *stūpa* became the most important monument in the Theravāda tradition.

This change did not mean that the role of the *stūpa* as a reliquary was lost. Instead, relics were categorized into three broader types: (1) relics consisting of physical remains of the Buddha or any other person regarded as worthy of veneration; (2) objects used by the Buddha, but later expanded to include objects

L. D. Shinn

The famous Sāñcī Stūpa in central India, attributed to the patronage of King Aśoka (3rd century B.C.)

used by his disciples or by Buddhist saints; and (3) symbolic objects associated with Buddhism, such as Sūtras and instruments used in ceremonial practices. Though these relics are no longer the main focus of the *stūpa,* they still play an important role in sanctifying the *stūpa* and in linking its symbolism to the historical Buddha.

1. **Form.** Under Emperor Aśoka (*ca.* 273-232 B.C.) of the Mauryan Dynasty Buddhism received state sanction and numerous *stūpas* were erected throughout India. The earliest forms were simple earthen mounds with a receptacle for a relic in the center and a wooden parasol-like addition at the top. Under the Śuṅgas (185-73 B.C.) and the Śātavāhanas (*ca.* 100 B.C.—A.D. 200) these monuments were enlarged, and the brick and wood construction was changed into stone.

Stūpa I at Sāñchī, which was expanded during this period, represents the early shape of the *stūpa* and serves as the prototype for later works. It consists of a hemispherical dome (*aṇḍa,* egg; or *garbha,* womb) resting on a high circular base (*medhi*). Around this base is a path for circumambulation (*pradakṣina*) on the ground level, encircled by a railing or fence (*vedikā*) demarcating the sacred enclosure. The railing consists of a series of pillars (*stambhas*) connected by three horizontal beams (*sūci*) crowned by a continuous coping (*uṣṇiṣa*). This railing is broken by four entrances marked by elaborately carved gateways (*toraṇas*), which are made up of two tall pillars supporting three architraves in a manner reminiscent of earlier gateways constructed in wood. Above the hemispherical dome is a square terrace (*harmikā*) with railing, supporting a pole or mast (*yaṣṭi*) crowned by three disks or umbrellas (*chatra*). Within the circumambulation path (*pradakṣiṇāpatha*) on the ground level is a double stairway (*sopāna*) leading to a second circumambulation path on a higher level.

Of the above elements the circumambulation path, the base, the dome, the mast, and the disks or tiered umbrellas are found in almost all South Asian *stūpas*. Though most *stūpas* are surrounded by a type of railing that sets them off from the outer world, this is not an invariable feature. Also, while the *stūpa* as a freestanding monument is the most important and prevalent form, there are at least two other basic types. One is the votive *stūpa,* small and simple in form, erected at sacred sites by pilgrims for the attainment of merit. Another type is that seen in rock-cut temples or *caitya* halls as at Kārlī and Ajaṇṭā. The earlier monastic caves at such places have a freestanding *stūpa* within an apse. Often it can be circumambulated, an evidence of the ritualistic importance of the *stūpa* as a symbol of the Buddha and his enlightenment. In later cave temples the *stūpa* was replaced by stone figures of the Buddha as the principal object of veneration.

2. **Symbolism.** Over the centuries the Buddhist *stūpa* has acquired complex symbolic connotations.

James Ware

Castle Peak Monastery, Hong Kong: small *stūpa* built for a local priest whose photograph appears in the niche.

One prominent feature of its symbolism is its representation of the universe, in which the dome (*aṇḍa*) becomes the dome of the sky and the square terrace (*harmikā*) is viewed as a sanctuary beyond this world. The *yaṣṭi* or pole, piercing through both the dome and the terrace and supporting the planes of heaven (*chatras*), represents the Buddha who has transcended all. On another level the *stūpa* stands for the Buddhist path to enlightenment. The dome (as the egg or womb) represents the forces of life and death which must be transcended in order to experience enlightenment. The terrace, interpreted as a sacrificial altar, becomes the symbol of spiritual death and rebirth, the point which connects this world and the absolute.

The *stūpa's* symbolic features also reflect the assimilation of forms and concepts from various religious and folk cults. The elaborate carvings on the gateways at Sāñchī, for instance, depict Indian mythic figures of several sorts as well as specifically Buddhist themes. The dome of the *stūpa* can be seen as Mt. Meru, the ancient Indian symbol of the center of the universe; the mast with its disks form a cosmic tree, representing both beneficence and wisdom. The yogic idea of achieving enlightenment by developing one's consciousness through the five centers of psychic force (*cakras*) within the human body is portrayed by the mast and its disks, each disk representing one *cakra*. Enlightenment is therefore attainment of the highest level, symbolized by the uppermost point on the *stūpa*.

The development of MAHĀYĀNA Buddhism also influenced the form and function of *stūpas*. Its conception of the Buddha as a savior leading others to freedom came to be represented by the vertical elements of the *stūpa*, which were elaborated as the doctrine of grace evolved and as the practice of devotion to the Buddha was increasingly seen as a central feature of the path toward salvation. In spite of the increased emphasis upon verticality in later monuments, however, the *stūpa* retained a balance between its horizontal and vertical elements, both symbolically and aesthetically. In other words, the dome or horizontal element symbolizing inner concentration was balanced by the vertical mast which represents devotion and enlightenment through grace. In this respect, the two major streams of Buddhism, the HĪNAYĀNA and Mahāyāna traditions, were fused.

3. Worship. Paying homage to a *stūpa* consists of pilgrimage to the site, presentation of offerings, the chanting of Sūtras, and circumambulation. In the latter, the physical treading of the path is transformed into an enactment of the spiritual path to enlightenment. Such a synthesis of the physical and the spiritual is illustrated in its most developed form at Borobudur in Java, built between 750-850 A.D. (*See* BUDDHISM IN SOUTHEAST ASIA §1.) This elaborate monument consists of three circular terraces of diminishing size placed above five square terraces. The overall form of the structure preserves the shape of a flattened hemisphere crowned by a large bell-shaped *stūpa*. The effect is that of one *stūpa* superimposed on another larger one. Each of the nine levels (five square, three circular, and the crowning *stūpa*) contains an area for circumambulation, the different levels being connected by stairways. The square terraces are surrounded by high walls which isolate each level from the others. These walls serve as galleries with extensive relief carvings which form a continuous narrative, moving from a depiction of life's miseries (on the lowest level) to the Buddha's teachings about salvation to scenes of a monk's path toward enlightenment (on the highest levels). (*See* FOUR NOBLE TRUTHS; EIGHTFOLD PATH.) The transition from the mundane to the transcendent in subject matter is accompanied by a change in artistic representation which progresses from natural to schematic forms. The transition from square terraces to circular ones is abrupt, for the latter are without walls. The schematic forms developed in the relief carvings are replaced by seventy-two small *stūpas* containing meditating Buddha figures, partially exposed through open lattice work. The circle as a symbol of the absolute combines with the timeless quality of the meditating figures in furthering the theme of transcendence. This theme culminates in the solid and austere form of the central *stūpa*, whose abstractness carries the idea of schematization to its conclusion. Here the path completes its progression from the transient to the eternal and from fragmentation to oneness.

4. Development. In general, the spread of Buddhism across Asia took two different routes. One moved south, from India to Sri Lanka and to Southeast Asia; the other went through Central Asia to China, Korea, and Japan. With this spread, Buddhist doctrine and art were modified through encounters with various religions, cultures, and artistic traditions. One noteworthy change was the practice of concentrating *stūpas* in capital cities. This may be illustrated in Sri Lanka, where the ancient capitals of Anurādhapura (*ca.* third century B.C.—tenth century A.D.) and Polonnaruva (tenth-thirteenth centuries A.D.) contained many *stūpas (dāgäbas)*, marking the growth of Buddhism's impact upon society in comparison to its less influential political role within India, where one finds *stūpas* in more isolated and remote sites.

In South and Southeast Asia, the Indian *stūpa* (as exemplified at Sāñchī) served as a model, though it is difficult to trace the line of stylistic development because, owing to their sanctity, *stūpas* once consecrated were rarely demolished. Instead, in later ages larger and more elaborate forms were often built over earlier ones. To do so was, in fact, regarded as an act of considerable merit.

In Sri Lanka, Burma, and Thailand the distinction between different parts of the *stūpa* became less abrupt than those found in India, and a smooth bell-shape with increased verticality evolved. The mast and disks merged into a cone shape, carrying the curved surface of the dome gradually to a single point. Along with the emphases on elongation and verticality there was also a trend toward further complexity and elaboration. In Sri Lanka, for example, platforms were added at the four cardinal points, supporting sculptured figures of the Buddha. In Burma the base *(medhi)* became much higher and was divided into numerous terraces. Tibetan *stūpas (chorten)*, also very elaborate and exact in form, reflected the complex ritual and systematic doctrine of TIBETAN BUDDHISM. Another basic alteration in form appeared in Burma, where the *stūpa* became a part of temple architecture; the interior of the large terraced base was opened to form a chamber for the cella or *stūpa*, a cosmic mountain within the cosmic womb *(garbha)* or cave.

As the Buddhist doctrine traveled east, the *stūpa* took on a very different form to become the PAGODA. The square multistoried structure of the pagoda is said to have been inspired by the *stūpa* of King Kaniṣka at Peshawar (*ca.* second century A.D.). As described by a Chinese pilgrim, this *stūpa* was a tower constructed in wood and topped by an iron mast, with a striking similarity in form to that of Oriental pagodas. The question remains as to how this style evolved from those located at Sāñchī and Bhārhūt, but clearly the pagoda has much in common with the multistoried watch towers of the Han dynasty (206 B.C.—A.D. 220) in China, especially in its square or octagonal form and in its prominent roofs which project at each level. On the other hand, the existence of a tower as a reliquary monument in East Asia stems from the influence of Buddhism. The parallels with Indian forms are obvious in the use of a mast which runs the entire length of the pagoda, culminating in a series of disks at the top. Furthermore, the pagoda itself may be viewed as an elaboration and development of the *yaṣṭi*, or mast, and *chatras*, or umbrellas, from early Indian *stūpas*. Regardless of form and development, the pagoda of East Asia never assumed the importance the *stūpa* had in Theravāda Buddhism. This is principally due to the fact that in the Mahāyāna tradition figures of the Buddha and of BODHISATTVAS replaced the *stūpa* as the focal point in worship.

Bibliography. S. Bandaranayake, *Sinhalese Monastic Architecture* (1974); T. Bhattacharyya, *The Canons of Indian Art* (1963); S. Dutt, *The Buddha and Five After-Centuries* (1957); J. Fergusson, *History of Indian and Eastern Architecture,* Vol I (1967); Lama Anagarika Govinda, *Psycho-cosmic Symbolism of the Buddhist Stūpa* (1976); E. B. Havell, *The Art Heritage of India* (1964); J. Kidder, *Early Buddhist Japan* (1972); G. H. Luce, *Old Burma—Early Pagān,* 3 vols. (1969-70); J. Marshall and A. Foucher, *The Monuments of Sāñchī,* 3 vols. (1938); D. Mitra, *Buddhist Monuments* (1971); S. Paranavitana, *The Stūpa in Ceylon* (1946); D. Seckel, *The Art of Buddhism* (1964); A. Soper, *The Evolution of Buddhist Architecture in Japan* (1942); N. Wu, *Chinese and Indian Architecture* (1963); H. Zimmer, *The Art of Indian Asia,* 2 vols. (1955). See also several volumes of the *Encyclopedia of World Art.*

B. L. SMITH

SUBUD sōō′ bood. Movement started in Indonesia after World War I by Muhammad Subuh (b. 1901). Power is communicated by personal contact between a "helper" and a probationer in a gathering (*latihan*) marked by ecstasy, shouting, leaping, GLOSSOLALIA, etc.

K. CRIM

SUCHNESS (B). *See* TATHATĀ.

SUDDHODANA sŭd hō′ dŭ nŭ (B—Pali; lit. "pure rice"). Personal name of the father of Siddhārtha Gautama, who became the BUDDHA. Suddhodana was evidently RĀJA of the land of the Śākyas, a small aristocratic state whose capital city was KAPILAVASTU. His rule, however, was under a measure of suzerainty of the king of Kośala, one of the four largest kingdoms of northern India. The term "rule," moreover, may signify no more than the work of the elected president of the assembly of nobles. Later tradition suggests that Suddhodana anticipated his son's renunciation of family, worldly power, and pleasure by doing everything he could to prevent this. When Siddhārtha's mother MĀYĀ died shortly after his birth, Suddhodana evidently married her sister Mahāprajāpatī Gautamī, who is said to have later become the first Buddhist nun.

Bibliography. R. H. Drummond, *Gautama the Buddha* (1974), pp. 27-30.

R. H. DRUMMOND

ŚŪDRA shoo′ drä (H—Skt.). A generic term for members of the lowest rank of the traditional fourfold Hindu social structure (*see* CASTE). Most of the agricultural and artisan castes (*jāti*) are of Śūdra status, and though ritually inferior to the TWICE BORN castes, Śūdras seldom suffer from any social discrimination and often enjoy great political power.

C. VON FÜRER-HAIMENDORF

SUFISM sōōf′ ĭsm **TAṢAWWŪF** tä sou wōōf′ (I—Arab. [*ṣūf*—"wool"; *ṣūfī*—"wool-clad"]). The name most often applied to Islamic MYSTICISM consisting of three overlapping but distinct historical periods: classical, medieval, and modern.

1. **Classical Sufism.** The origins of the Sufi movement are obscure. Some hold that Sufism was intrinsic to primitive Islam, that MUHAMMAD himself was a Sufi, as were his companions and the first four CALIPHS (Lings, pp. 100-104). There is no doubt that certain Sufi concepts, e.g., *faqr* ("pious poverty"; *see* FAQĪR) and *tawakkul* (total reliance on God), as well as characteristic practices, e.g., DHIKR (constant repetition of the divine name) and *samā'* (listening to poetry or music), had antecedents dating back to the first century of Islam. More difficult is the task of discerning the complex undercurrents of political and religious ideology that characterized late UMAYYAD and early 'ABBĀSID Islam. Some members of ascetic protest movements may have been influenced by contact with ZOROASTRIANS, BUDDHISTS, HINDUS, and also MONOPHYSITE Christians. Christian ascetics, for instance, were known to have worn woolen garments not dissimilar from those which the early Sufis wore and by which they came to be known. Whatever the point of original inspiration, *taṣawwūf* in its formative period must have reflected attitudes and activities, rituals and rigors, intrinsic to the geographic locale where the ninth and tenth century masters lived and taught. Thus Fuḍayl ibn 'Iyāḍ of parched Khurasan became renowned for his renunciation of family life, DHU'L-NŪN MIṢRĪ of temperate Egypt for his lilting summation of ontological polarities, Abū Yazīd BISṬĀMĪ of mountainous Bistam for his profusion of mind-staggering aphorisms, and JUNAYD of cosmopolitan Baghdad (though born in Persia) for his adherence to social norms while engaging in a ceaseless, inner struggle. Later Sufi theorists, such as Ali Hujwīrī (d. 1702), found it convenient to ascribe ascetic, antinomian tendencies to Khurasanian masters and moderate, accommodative teachings to their Iraqi counterparts. Yet we know too little about the actual lives of early Sufis to venture more than tentative speculations about the impact of environment on their spiritual formation. Even major figures such as Bisṭāmī and Junayd represented not so much a place as a disposition that came to be esteemed among Sufis of a later generation and was then retrospectively

associated with a ninth or tenth century master, usually through anecdotes or dicta (Bisṭāmī) and occasionally through treatises or letters (Junayd). Sufi exemplars from the classical period were remembered as stereotypes of piety rather than historical figures. Only Ḥusayn ibn Manṣūr AL-ḤALLĀJ, the dissident disciple of Junayd, was a partial exception. Thanks to the efforts of the French orientalist Massignon, we now have enough data to sketch part of the actual life of Ḥallāj, yet Massignon's studies, like later Sufi references to Ḥallāj, principally focus on the significance of poetic symbols, ḤADĪTH citations, legendary dicta, and anecdotal synopses that uniquely characterized this joyous martyr to love. In short, Ḥallāj is finally important in the Sufi tradition not for who he was but for what he came to represent: the model of the mystic lover.

By the late tenth century theorists attempted to consolidate and synthesize the elements of Sufi teaching. The handbooks they produced abound in correlations—between desirable virtues and exemplary individuals, between technical terms and schools of thought. The formative period of *taṣawwūf* is reduced to a maze of obscure proper names and recondite Arabic key words. Ali Hujwīrī typifies this approach. His *Kashf al-maḥjūb,* hailed as the oldest Persian treatise on Sufism, reviews the entire classical phase of Islamic mysticism in one lengthy chapter (ch. 14), linking each famous master to a particular doctrine and then reviewing variant interpretations of the same doctrine. Struggle with the lower self (NAFS), for instance, is set forth as the preeminent legacy of the Sahlīs (followers of the ninth century Shaikh Sahl ibn 'Abdallāh Tustarī), but its complement, RŪḤ or spirit, is scarcely mentioned; the full assessment of *rūḥ* occurs much later in the chapter when Hujwīrī exposes the heresy of the Ḥulūlīs or incarnationists.

2. **The medieval period** is demarcated by a new kind of doctrinal systematization among Sufi theorists and by the popularization of Sufi teaching through the establishment of mystical orders. After Hujwīrī there were numerous other efforts to consolidate and systematize Sufi thought. Two of the most successful came from the pens of intellectual giants who, unlike Hujwīrī, approached *taṣawwūf* in a holistic framework, relating it to other major fields of philosophical or theological enquiry explored by the cosmopolitan elite of medieval Islam. The first synthesizer, Abū Ḥāmid (often known as Imam) AL-GHAZZĀLĪ (d. 1111), had been a professor at the major center of traditional learning in Baghdad, the Niẓamiyya MADRASA (college), before resigning his post in 1091 to become a Sufi. His *magnum opus,* the *Iḥyā 'ulūm ad-dīn* ("The Bringing to Life of the Religious Sciences"), examined every approach to knowledge before affirming that only the inner truth sought by Sufis could satisfy the comprehensive, painstaking demands of the Islamic faith. Abū Ḥāmid, in the opinion of many, was a lesser mystic

F. M. Denny

Sufi procession, Mawlid of Aḥmad al-Badawī, Tanta, Egypt. The old man in the middle is the shaikh; men in the lower right corner hold up hands for blessing.

than his brother, Aḥmad (whose pithy verse is still prized among Sufi devotees), but he performed a valuable service in wedding *taṣawwūf* to SUNNI Islam without slighting the authority of either. The second catalytic genius of the medieval period was Muḥyī 'd-dīn IBN 'ARABĪ (d. 1240). A Spanish mystic, familiar with Christian as well as Islamic philosophical categories, he probed the deepest levels of meaning in Muslim scripture and described the central concept of TAWḤĪD (oneness of God) with originality that both captivated and antagonized his fellow Muslims.

Subsequent expositions of theoretical or theosophical Sufism invariably dealt with concepts such as the perfect man *(al-insān al-kāmil)* and the pole *(quṭb)* [*see* WALĪ, WILĀYAT], and touched upon the metaphysical dimensions of light and love, precisely because the prolific, influential writings of Ghazzālī and Ibn 'Arabī made it impossible to avoid them. Yet, in a sense, the mood of medieval Sufism was determined as much by mystical poetry as by systematic or speculative theology. Ibn 'Arabī had written Arabic verse, some of which cryptically extolled the beautiful Persian woman whom he had once met on the HAJJ, but his fame rested on his prose treatises. Quite different was the éclat of Mawlānā JALĀL AD-DĪN RŪMĪ. A brilliant theologian, tireless raconteur, and inventive poet, he channeled his spiritual vision into verse which captivated the imagination of Persian-speaking Muslims everywhere. There were numerous mystical poets who wrote in the PERISAN LANGUAGE before Rūmī. Sa'dī of Shiraz (d. 1293), moreover, was Rūmī's contemporary, and he, together with a later Shirazi lyricist, ḤĀFIZ (d. 1390), had an enormous impact on mystically minded Muslims. Yet Rūmī's ecstatic verse, as it poured forth in mammoth collections like the *Mathnavī* and *Dīvān-i Shams-i Tabrīzī*, epitomized a quality of medieval Sufism: its devotees plunged into the quest for love, forsaking home, reason, and even life to find their Beloved. The alliterative, unsystematic, anecdotal versifications of Rūmī came closer to the mood of that quest than the refined, comprehensive tomes of Ghazzālī or the deft, dialectical soundings of Ibn 'Arabī.

Rūmī also inspired the formation of a Sufi order (*see* ṬARĪQA) popularly known as the Whirling DERVISHES. The establishment of mystical orders signaled the development of popular Sufism on an unprecedented scale. Prior to the eleventh century there appear to have been loosely defined communities of Sufis, gathering together for companionship. There were rules but no rigid lines of authority or precedence among the members. By the end of the eleventh century and throughout the rest of the medieval period, however, the SHAIKH emerged as the locus of attention and activity within Sufi communities. He was distinguished from other men by his daily discipline and charismatic blessing. Usually such a person was born into a wealthy or at least respected family, educated in traditional scholarship, exposed to numerous people and places through extensive travel, converted to *taṣawwūf* through a divine vision or unusual human encounter, and then given credentials by an already acknowledged master to be his successor. Founders of most of the major pan-Islamic orders conform to this pattern. In fact, many of them are spiritually interdependent. Thus 'ABD-AL-QĀDIR JĪLĀNĪ (d. 1166), the eponymous founder of the Qādirī order, was himself a teacher of Abū Hafs 'Umar Suhrawardī, the pivotal organizer of the Suhrawardī order. Major shaikhs were not only related in the same generation, but they also traced their common affiliation back to early Sufis—in the case of the Suhrawardīs and their twelfth and thirteenth century contemporaries, to the tenth century saint Junayd. Another major pan-Islamic order, the Naqshbandiyya, traced their lineage back to Junayd's spiritual opposite, the northwest Iranian shaikh Abū Yazīd Bisṭāmī. Other regionally based orders, such as the Badawiyya, named after the Egyptian saint AHMAD AL-BADAWĪ (d. 1276), were not as conscious of their classical roots, though they too maintained genealogies that linked them to the first generation of Muslims and even to the Prophet Muhammad. It is, in part, because of their shared sense of spiritual interdependency that the orders, despite intense loyalty to their own shaikhs, minimized conflict with one another, and during the later medieval period some masters sought—and frequently obtained—simultaneous membership in two or more orders.

The social role of the orders is reflected in their buildings and organization. A residential center or hospice was maintained for disciples, family, and visitors; often it was situated near a tomb and was linked to other similar convent-tomb complexes in adjacent regions. Death marked an important transition in the function of these complexes, for at the death of a shaikh his successor *(khalīfa)* had to be chosen. The principle for selection varied from order to order. The will or last testament of the shaikh was determinative; usually it excluded women but, unlike Muslim inheritance laws, it did not invariably conform to primogeniture. The date of the master's death subsequently became the occasion for an annual feast ('URS), celebrating both his union with God and continuous intercession on behalf of his followers.

Other intensive devotional gatherings, including DHIKR exercises and lengthy musical performances *(maḥāfil-e samā')*, characterized most medieval Sufi communities. Such gatherings provoked antagonism with the 'ULAMĀ', learned functionaries who were custodians of ritual PRAYER *(ṣalāt)*. Especially in regions of the world where Islamization had barely begun, the Sufi shaikhs, with their charisma, their devoted followers, and their convivial public ceremonies, attracted greater attention, sympathy, and support than the sincere but dull, educated but aloof *'ulamā'*. Since Islam, with few exceptions (e.g., India and Spain), was a state religion and public prayer an expression of political control, Sufis could, and often did, provoke not only the *'ulamā'* but also governmental authorities. In some cases, the shaikhs chose to cooperate with devout Muslim rulers; in other cases they refused to participate in court life.

Doctrinal disputes hounded the great shaikhs and their followers throughout the medieval period. The extreme veneration accorded the master in his group made it necessary to distinguish him from the Prophet Muhammad, who, by the intrinsic nature of Islam, had to be venerated at a still higher level than even the greatest shaikh. Primitive Islam had forbidden worship of Muhammad or any other man. And yet Sufis, in their love of the Prophet, did pray to him, as they did also to deceased saints. Orthodox Muslims objected to such excesses, and the controversy gave rise to more and more refined efforts to distinguish sainthood from prophethood, to elevate one without diminishing the other and somehow to preserve the authority and integrity of each. For SHI'ITE Muslims the controversy took another form. Always respectful of Muhammad because of their special attachment to his family, they weighed their intercessory prayers and devotional life toward ALI and Ali's successors, the IMAMS. In their eyes excessive veneration of Muhammad and invocation of the saints detracted from the preeminence of the hidden imam (whether he was seventh or twelfth in line from Ali), and thus was objectionable. Because most Sufi masters also tended to support the belief structure and ritual pattern of Sunni Islam, whatever their differences with particular *'ulamā'* or rulers, the evolution of a Shi'ite brand of Sufism was always a minor phenomenon, and after the establishment of the aggressively pro-Shi'ite, anti-Sufi Safavid empire in sixteenth century Iran, it became even less noticeable.

It is also important to note that Islamic mysticism persisted outside the established orders *(ṭarīqa)*. In addition to the magisterial shaikhs, their select disciples, and numerous lay followers, *taṣawwuf* encompassed "holy fools," spiritual ecstatics who were also social eccentrics, openly flaunting the norms of acceptable behavior. Known as *malāmatī* or *qalandar,* these were the itinerant dervishes whom European travelers later dubbed *faqirs*. Their rejection of conventional mores led them to mock even the patterned life that pertained in the convent-tomb complexes of the famous shaikhs. They were a throwback to the earliest Sufis, whose ascetic behavior had contrasted with the worldly piety of ninth century Baghdad, and it is probably for this reason, i.e., to gain a perspective on themselves, that Sufis of the medieval period usually accepted even the vilest abuse hurled at them by anonymous *qalandar*.

3. **Modern Sufism.** The time of greatest influence for the Sufi orders coincided with the regional hegemony of the Ottoman and Mogul empires, spanning approximately three centuries, 1500-1800. The number of Muslims affiliated with Sufi brotherhoods during this period was certainly not less than half the population and may have been as high as 80 percent.

One reason for the swelled ranks of Sufi orders was their catalytic role in the expansion of Islam. Pan-Islamic brotherhoods like the Qādiriyya and the Rifā'iyya were instrumental in winning to Islam geographic areas as disparate as Anatolia and West Africa, while regional orders, such as the Badawiyya and Shādhiliyaa (both derived from the Rifā'iya) helped to intensify Islamic loyalties in Egypt and the Magrib. From the thirteenth century on, North India was populated with the convent-tomb complexes of the Chishtiyya and the Suhrawardiyya. Distant Southeast Asia withstood any wide-scale Islamization until the late sixteenth century. But it was Qādirī and Shaṭṭārī masters who succeeded in penetrating the complex Hindu-Javanese belief system of the archipelago. In fact, the belated ascendancy of mystical Islam in Indonesia aptly illustrates the flexibility of the shaikhs as agents in the spread of Islam. Affiliated with urban-based craft guilds and trade corporations, many of them with headquarters in the Arabian heartland of Islam, Sufi masters traveled to the archipelago by ship with Muslim traders. They were well received by kings in the major port cities, occasionally marrying princesses, and in other ways too gaining influence in the courts. As they increasingly moved inland after 1600, the shaikhs converted the inhabitants of Hindu-Buddhist hermitages to Islam and transformed the indigneous structures into hospices and *madrasas*. (*See* ISLAM IN SOUTH ASIA; ISLAM IN SOUTHEAST ASIA.)

What happened to Sufism subsequently, especially during the period of European colonial expansion into all parts of the Muslim world, is still not well understood. Two interconnected developments account for the largely negative assessment of the latter-day role of the brotherhoods: (1) WAHHĀBĪYA, an eighteenth century puritanical-revivalist movement emanating from Arabia, condemned Sufism along with all other accretions to the pristine creed declaimed by Muhammad in seventh century HEJAZ. Wahhābī polemic echoed the fourteenth century diatribes of IBN TAYMĪYYA, but with a difference. Sufi brotherhoods were excoriated not only as syncretistic dilutions of pure Islam but also as contributing causes to the political-military weakness of Muslim ruling groups vis-à-vis resurgent Europe. (2) Western scholars confirmed the judgment of the Wahhābīs by extolling the formative period of theoretical Sufism and debunking what followed it. Though the emergence of orders might have led to a reification of Sufi subtleties or a calcification of Sufi energies, the opposite, in fact, seems to have been the case. Eighteenth century India, for instance, produced two of the foremost geniuses of Islamic history, both intimately related to organizational as well as theoretical *taṣawwūf:* Mīrzā 'ABD-AL-QĀDIR BEDIL (d. 1721) and Shāh Walī Allāh Dihlawī (d. 1762). During the turbulent nineteenth century, moreover, organized Sufism proved itself a unique vehicle for both reviving Islamic consciousness and mobilizing Islamic resistance to European colonialists. It was because they represented kinship groups, classes, professions and lineages integrated vertically under the authority of an all-powerful shaikh that the brotherhoods could and did assume political roles. Nor were they an isolated phenomenon of nineteenth century Islamic society: the Mahdist (*see* MAHDI) and pro-CALIPHATE movements also emerged during this period, sometimes among overlapping constituencies of like-minded Muslims. Their common redirection to a nonmystical sphere of activity, viz., JIHĀD or holy war against infidels, was prompted by the same perceived threat that motivated the Wahhābīs: European encroachment on Islamic soil. Thus, Wahhābīs and Sufi activitists, despite their differences, shared enough of the same ideology that the *mujāhidīn* ("holy warriors"), an influential group of nineteenth century North Indian Muslims, have been alternately described as neo-Sufis or neo-Wahhābīs. The *mujāhidīn* were, in fact, both. They espoused political and scripturalist aims similar to the Wahhābīs, at the same time that they affirmed their links to reformist Naqshbandi shaikhs. Devotion to Sufism and militant anti-colonialism also characterized several nineteenth century African revivalists, from Usmān dan Fodio of the traditional Qādiriyya to al-Ḥajj 'Umar Tal of the neo-Sufi Tijaniyya. Even African orders which deemphasized military confrontation and confined themselves to traditional pursuits could not avoid being drawn into the escalating conflict between Christian and Muslim, European and African, foreigner and native. The pro-Ottoman but politically quiescent Sanūsiyya, for example, were victimized by the manipulation of French and Italian forces, first having to curtail and then later redirect their activities prior to the outbreak of World War I.

During the twentieth century other Sufi orders have shared the fate of the Sanūsiyya. Nowhere in the Muslim world today does organized Sufism have political leverage comparable to that which it exercised for much of the last century. On the one hand, there are isolated manifestations of the traditional forms of authority and teaching in some orders: Aḥmad al-'Alawī of the North African Darqawiyya, for instance, has influenced many Europeans, including the British orientalist M. Lings, while other neo-Sufi shaikhs, such as Idries Shah, Pir Vilayet Khan, and Sam Lewis, have tried to introduce Sufism to Westerners unacquainted with Islam.

Bibliography. C. Geertz, *Islam Observed* (1968); N. R. Keddie, ed., *Scholars, Saints and Sufis* (1972); M. Lings, *What is Sufism?* (1975); B. G. Martin, *Muslim Brotherhoods in Nineteenth-Century Africa* (1977); F. Meier, "The Mystic Path," in B. Lewis, ed., *The World of Islam* (1976), pp. 117-40; L. Massignon, *Receuil de textes inedites concernant l'histoire de la mystique en pays d'Islam* (1929); M. Molé, *Les mystiques musulmans* (1965); R. A. Nicholson, ed., *The Kashf al-mahjub* (1936); A. Schimmel, *Mystical Dimensions of Islam* (1975); J. S. Trimingham, *The Sufi Orders in Islam* (1971).

B. Lawrence

SUKKOT sŭ kōt′ (Ju—Heb.; lit. "booths"). One of the three pilgrim festivals (*see* Passover; Shavuot), so named because of the practice of living in temporary shelters for its duration (Exod. 34:18-26). Beginning on the fourteenth of Tishri (September-October) the holiday extends for seven days. Traditional restrictions on work apply for the first day in Israel and among Reform Jews elsewhere, while others observe such restrictions for the first two days. Depending on place and tradition, the holiday is followed by one or two days of festival known as *Shemini Aẓeret* and Simhat Torah.

The practice of dwelling in a booth *(sukkah),* reduced in modern times largely to taking meals there, is symbolic of those tabernacles in which the Israelites are said to have lived during their Exodus (Lev. 23:39-43). These "tabernacles" are covered with straw or greens but not so fully as to obstruct starlight. There must be at least three walls, and the *sukkah* may not be constructed beneath a tree or other covering. It is customary to decorate the *sukkah* with flowers and fruits as well as symbols of the preceding High Holy Days. A *sukkah* will generally be built adjacent to the synagogue for communal use by those without one of their own.

Though linked to the Exodus, Sukkot is also pastoral in its theme. It celebrates the yield of wheatfield and vineyard and is called the "feast of the ingathering" (Exod. 23:16; Deut. 16:13). Further, the Bible instructs (Lev. 23:40) the worshiper to take four species of produce, traditionally the citron, myrtle, palm branch, and willow, to be blessed on each day of the festival, waved in every direction, and then carried in procession around the Synagogue.

The seventh day of the festival is known as *Hoshana Rabba* (many hosannas) after its liturgy, which includes the recitation of lengthy responsive readings whose refrain is "hosanna" during a procession seven times around the synagogue. In Orthodox Judaism it ends with the beating of five willow branches. Originally linked to Temple rites and the harvest, the day has become a finale for the Lord's judgment, ordained on Yom Kippur. It is also the practice to read the book of Ecclesiastes on Sukkot, because its somber theme is said to be appropriate to the autumn season.

Modern scholars have identified Sukkot with either New Year or confirmation feasts common in the ancient Near East. Ostensibly the purpose was to confirm cultic identification with God and renew his covenant with Israel. The practice of living in booths is said to be based on nomadic observances which were much later identified with the Exodus and made to parallel other pilgrim festivals. (*See* Calendar, Jewish.)

Bibliography. J. Farbrikant, *A Guide to Sukkot* (1958); P. Goodman, *The Sukkot and Simhat Torah Anthology* (1973); S. Zevin, *Ha-Moadim be-Halakhah* (1947).

D. J. Schnall

American Jewish Archives, Hebrew Union College—Jewish Institute of Religion

Modern Sukkot booth at a Cincinnati home

SUNDAY (Ch). The first day of the week, the day on which Jesus rose from the dead, and the principal day of worship in Christian tradition (I Cor. 16:1-3; Acts 20:7-12).

1. **Sunday and the week.** Sunday cannot be understood apart from the SABBATH and the week it delineates. Established as a day of rest for man and beast, sabbath was not a subdivision of any other time cycle, but marked every seventh day, uninterrupted by the turning of months or years. So fundamental was it, indeed, that the Genesis account of the creation of the world relates as well the creation of the week. The early Christian observance of the first day of the week was not a substitution for the sabbath, but assertion of a new age inaugurated by the RESURRECTION. Such second century sources as the Epistle of Barnabas speak of this day as the "eighth day," the day beyond the sabbath of the old dispensation, the day beyond this age. Sunday is the eschatological "Lord's Day" in Rev. 1:10.

2. **The planetary week.** The assignment of planetary names to the days of the week in paganism probably began with the assignment of the sabbath to Saturn, but all the days of the week were probably assigned to planets by the beginning of the Christian era. Justin Martyr (*ca.* A.D. 150) speaks of Christian assemblies on "the day of the sun," and some have seen this as a reflection of the popularity of the sun cult on the language of Christian apology, if not on Christian practice. Whatever is to be said of the influence of the sun cult in the second century, there is less doubt of its influence in the fourth. By fairly general agreement, the Emperor CONSTANTINE'S edicts limiting work on Sunday (A.D. 321) reflected his devotion to the sun as divinity as much as, if not more than, his devotion to the risen Christ. From that time, in any case, Sunday did become a Christian surrogate for the sabbath rest, whereas it had previously been only the day for Christian assembly.

3. **Sabbatarianism.** There was still, however, no overt confusion with the sabbath as such, and *sabbato* continued to designate Saturday in liturgical books. Fasting was enjoined on some sabbaths at Rome, but in the East the sabbath was a liturgical day (apart from HOLY WEEK) and fasting was prohibited on it as it had been in JUDAISM. Later Western legislation strengthened the prohibitions on work and enjoined attendance at mass on Sunday. Overt sabbatarian understanding of Sunday can be dated from 1595, when N. Bound published *The True Meaning of the Sabbath.* This was countered by King James I's *Book of Sports* (1618) which, while forbidding work, encouraged lawful recreation on Sunday. PURITAN reaction during the Commonwealth forbade all recreation, even going for a walk. Such strict legislation was peculiar to England and Scotland and was unknown on the continent.

4. **The twentieth century.** While to one degree or another Sunday closing laws continue in force in many areas of the world, the present century has seen much more lenient attitudes regarding Sunday observance. For example, since 1964 ROMAN CATHOLICISM has allowed the liturgical obligation of Sunday to be fulfilled on Saturday evening.

Bibliography. W. Rordorf, *Sunday* (1968); S. Bacchiocchi, *From Sabbath to Sunday* (1977).

T. J. TALLEY

SUNDAY SCHOOLS (Ch). It is not known when the practice of using Sundays for special instruction began. In the eighteenth century such schools could be found among a few English and American METHODISTS and some German PIETIST groups, but Robert Raikes (1735-1811) is justly called the "father of the Sunday school." This British publisher established schools for the poor which were designed not only to teach faith and morals, but to provide the basic skills needed to survive in an emerging industrial economy, especially reading and simple mathematics. By 1787 such schools had enlisted one quarter of a million students in Great Britain.

The American Sunday school was originally modeled after the English, but American conditions and attitudes began early to transform the institution. Both rich and poor were taught together, and since public education was widely available, especially in the North, the Sunday school was able to concentrate on religious education. Both men and women were enlisted as teachers.

The Sunday school was a major component in the Protestant plan to evangelize the West. The American Sunday Union was established in Philadelphia in 1824 by EVANGELICALS who were also promoting other types of Christian institutions. The Sunday school thus became part of a larger program that included revivals, church colleges, and seminaries. Traveling agents selling religious literature became common figures on the frontier. Stephen Paxton, one of the best known of these colporteurs, established over 1,200 schools in twenty years of ministry. Wherever possible, Sunday school libraries were established.

The Sunday school was sensitive to changes in thought among nineteenth century evangelicals. In the early part of the century Sunday school literature reflected the popular emphasis on death and redemption, but by 1860 the child was seen as a holy innocent who could be shaped by the school into a Christian adult.

The second half-century of Sunday school work was marked by both consolidation and expansion. National Sunday School Conventions, led by such men as B. F. Jacobs, John H. Vincent, and DWIGHT L. MOODY, enlisted workers and began the highly successful Uniform Lesson Plan, consisting of biblical passages that would be studied in all schools on the same Sunday. These lessons attracted adults as well as children.

In the twentieth century some Sunday schools moved toward paid directors and, occasionally, even paid teachers. New curricula were designed to meet the needs and abilities of the students, and social issues received attention along with traditional biblical instruction.

Bibliography. R. Lynn and E. Wright, *The Big Little School: Sunday Child of American Protestantism* (1976); A. A. Brown, *A History of Religious Education in Recent Times* (1923).

G. Miller

ŚUṄGA shoong′ gü (H). Name of a North Indian dynasty which held power from 185-73 B.C., having its capital at Pāṭaliputra and later at Vidisā. Direct successors to the Buddhist Mauryas, the Śuṅgas were Brahmin reactionaries who instigated a campaign of persecution against the Buddhists. Externally, the dynasty found its main enemy in the Bactrian Greeks, prolonged contact with whom seems to have significantly influenced the art of the period. Plagued by wars with the Greeks and by internal dissolution, the dynasty gave way in 73 B.C. to that of the Kāṇvas.

J. Bare

SUNNA soo′nə (I—Arab.; lit. "way, course, manner of acting"). Customary practice as a paradigm for future behavior. As a result of its use in Islamic law, *sunna* came to mean the deeds, sayings, and attitudes of Muhammad, and then the interpretation of these by the various schools of Islamic law.

In pre-Islamic Arabia, the deeds of a prominent member of society were often regarded as precedents, at least for his family group. A custom was ascribed to some specific individual, thought to be responsible for all future actions based on the original deed. The community preserved these deeds by actually doing them and by reporting them in prose and poetry.

In the Qur'ān, the term *sunna* is used to refer to the established decree of Allah through past prophets (Sura 17:77; 33:38,62 *et passim*), but the concept of precedent-setting behavior shows up in the Cain-Abel story (Sura 5:32): "For that cause We decreed for the Children of Israel that whosoever killeth a human being for other than manslaughter or corruption on the earth, it shall be as if he had killed all mankind, and whoso saveth the life of one, it shall be as if he had saved the life of all mankind," a concept found in Judaism as well (*Mishnah,* Sanhedrin 4).

A *sunna* of Muhammad existed from an early date, but during the Umayyad caliphate, Muhammad did not take precedence over the *sunnas* of Abū Bakr, 'Umar, 'Uthmān, or Ali, and others, although there was a clear preference for acting in the same manner as the Prophet. With the rise of the 'Abbāsids and the development of jurisprudential methodology, Muhammad's position was raised from merely the first among equals to that of the chief source for Muslim behavior. The various schools of Islamic law interpreted the actions of Muhammad in slightly different ways, and in time *sunna* came to designate the doctrines of the schools. Within the Islamic community Traditionists (*ahl al-ḥadīth*) advocated strict and sometimes literal adherence to the *sunna* of Muhammad, and others allowed for freer interpretation in juristic reasoning *(ahl ar-ra'y)*. The term Sunnite (*ahl as-sunna wa-l-jama'a,* lit. "People of Sunna and Community") came to mean catholic, universal Islam as opposed to the party of Ali, the Shi'ites. *See* Fiqh; Sharia; Ḥadīth.

Bibliography. M. M. Bravmann, *Spiritual Background of Early Islam* (1972); N. J. Coulson, *History of Islamic Law* (1964); J. Schacht, *Origins of Muhammadan Jurisprudence* (1955); I. Goldziher, *Muslim Studies,* II, S. Stern, trans. (1971), 17–37.

G. D. Newby

SUNNI, SUNNITE soon′ ē, soon′ īt (I—Arab.). The designation of the major division of Islam. In situations where the Qur'ān does not provide a solution to a problem of correct behavior, Sunnis appeal to the Sunna (behavior or practice) of Muhammad in Medina, or to the Ḥadīth. In contrast to the Shi'a, which believes in a line of inspired Imams, Sunnis accept the validity of the historical line of Caliphs.

K. Crim

ŚŪNYATĀ shōōn yä′ tä (B—Skt.; lit. "emptiness," "openness"). The nonsubstantial and undependable quality of habitual experience which, at the same time—when seen through the spiritual exercise of wisdom—is total freedom. The Buddhist tradition has sometimes stressed freedom from the phenomenal world (Nirvana), and at other times freedom to experience completely the concrete richness of life. In either case śūnyatā functions less as an attribute of ultimate reality than as a practical religious designation of the real possibility for ultimate fulfillment. Nevertheless, according to Buddhist teaching, perfect enlightenment requires a person to see "the way things are."

The terms śūnyatā and *śūnyam* (empty) have been used variously and sometimes in highly specialized and technical ways. The range of meanings is indicated by five overlapping usages: (1) the relative character of all forms in existence, (2) the nonsubstantial character of all universal elements and mental categories by which the arising and dissipation of existence is explained, (3) the unconditioned freedom from pain and deceptive thought construction, (4) the pure base or source of deepest insight and unrestricted, creative Mind, and (5) the actualized all-inclusive emptiness that inheres in the realization that there is no distinction between total freedom and concrete conditioned experience.

In early Buddhism as found in the Pali Nikāyas, emptiness referred primarily to worldly experience; the changing flux of existence was said to be empty of lasting value and self-established being. It was important to know that apparent pleasures, overwhelming physical or social power, or apparently substantial sense-based objects (e.g. earth, plants, or animals) were empty of self-existence and therefore unworthy of one's ultimate commitment. By recognizing the emptiness of all forms, a person could escape attachment to seductive, but illusory, emotional and mental supports. Even "the self" had no independent existence; it was a composite of physical, psychological, and mental factors. To recognize that all phenomenal entities were empty, and thus relative, required more than intellectual comprehension; it required meditation (DHYĀNA) in which one emptied the mind of all ideas and emotions. (*See* MEDITATION, BUDDHIST.)

About 200-100 B.C. some Indian Buddhists stressed the emptiness of all experience to the point where they were called *Śūnyavādins* ("spokesmen for emptiness"). They claimed that not only were conventional notions and sense objects empty of ultimate reality, but also empty were such religious concepts as Buddha or Nirvana and the explanations of the Buddhist scholars (the ABHIDHAMMA masters) when they defined the underlying factors (dhammas) of existence. (*See* DHARMA §5.) The *Śūnyavādins* criticised non-Buddhists and fellow Buddhists who claimed that there were any particular things or any universal ideas or processes which existed by their own self-substantiated nature. This criticism was systematized in the MĀDHYAMIKA school, founded by NĀGĀRJUNA in the late second century A.D.

The followers of Mādhyamika used a dialectic critique of all philosophical viewpoints to avoid emotional and intellectual entanglements. They recognized that ideas, imagery, and structures of language, which habitually provide people with meaning, have a subtle implicit power to bind people to their own constructions of imagery and abstractions without perceiving the nature of life. When people can let go of their ideas and perceptions of themselves and of things in the recognition that all experienced forms originate in mutual dependence on one another *(pratītya-samutpāda),* then they realize the emptiness (*śūnyatā,* or "openness") of life's processes, and they can be free.

By the fifth century A.D. some Indian Buddhists, while recognizing the empty character of all phenomena that is most profoundly known when the processes for knowing are themselves experienced as empty, wanted a more positive formulation of the nature of experience. (*See* YOGĀCĀRA.) They affirmed "Mind-in-itself" as the source of all true perception as well as the power for creating all forms. While the ordinary mind that people habitually use entangles them in fictions and appearances, Mind-in-itself is without such entanglements; it is without (ordinary) mind, like empty space. This Mind-in-itself is also called the Buddha-mind, or the "original true Mind"; the major spiritual exercise was "to know your own mind" which included emptying oneself of everything that is not the "original true Mind."

In the continuing MAHĀYANA effort to probe the depth of emptying oneself there was the recognition that there were different levels of knowing, some more free, others more entangled with illusion. At the deepest level of freedom there was no longer attachment to a discriminating mentality, which meant that any notion or act was empty of inherent good or bad, and its spiritual value had to be judged according to its capacity to manifest wisdom and compassion in a relative context of experience. The emptiness, then, that is beyond both inherent essences and external phenomena, but inclusive of both, is a total openness to all possibilities while at the same time the purest possible manifestation of the actuality of a particular thing. "All-inclusive emptiness" is not rejection of particular actualities or notions of universal essences, but the recognition that they originated in mutual interdependence and, therefore, they disappear. To perceive everything as empty is to realize that existence depends on both BEING AND NONBEING, and that both knowing and disentanglement from knowing can function on the path of enlightenment.

Bibliography. E. Conze, *Buddhist Thought In India* (1962); S. Hisamatsu, "The Characteristics of Oriental Nothingness," *Philosophical Studies of Japan,* Vol. II (1960); K. Nishitani, "The Standpoint of Sunyata," *Eastern Buddhist,* Vol. VI, nos. 1 & 2 (1973); R. H. Robinson, *Early Mādhyamika in India and China* (1967); F. J. Streng, *Emptiness: A Study in Religious Meaning* (1967).

F. J. STRENG

SURA sōōr´ rə (I—Arab.; etymology unknown). The name given to the 114 divisions of the QUR'ĀN; in the Qur'ān itself it can refer to the separate portions of the Scripture revealed to MUHAMMAD, as in Sura 2:23; 10:38; 11:13; 24;1. G. D. NEWBY

SŪRDĀS sōōr´ däs (H; *ca.* 1483-1563). One of the greatest of the medieval Hindī poets; known chiefly for his devotional lyrics addressed to the god KRISHNA. He also adapted and translated into Hindī several well-known classical works. J. BARE

SURSUM CORDA soor´ soom kôr´dä (Ch—Lat.; "lift up your hearts"). Introduction to the dialogue between celebrant and people that immediately precedes the preface and SANCTUS in the MASS; found as early as Hippolytus (*ca.* 215) and thereafter in almost every Christian LITURGY.

R. A. GREER

SŪRYA sōōr´ yŭ (H—Skt.; lit. the "sun" and the "sun-god" [*svar*—"to shine"]). One of two names for both the sun and the sun deity in VEDIC HINDUISM, the other being Savitṛ. Ten hymns of the RIG VEDA praise Sūrya, who crosses the sky in a chariot drawn by a single horse or by seven mares. Sometimes the poets depict him as a bird or a wheel. He is all-seeing or, variously, he himself is the eye of MITRA and VARUṆA. Like them he is an Āditya, one of the sons of the goddess ADITI. Dyaus, the sky, is his father, and Uṣas, the Dawn, his wife (or sometimes his mother). Sūryā, also called Saṃjñā, is variously the wife or daughter of Sūrya. Savitṛ (from *su*—"to stimulate"), a golden deity celebrated in eleven Rig Vedic hymns, is the inciter or impeller who arouses men to life each day; the famous dawn prayer and initiatory verse of Hinduism, the GĀYATRĪ MANTRA (RV 3.62.10), is addressed to him. In many Vedic ritual texts the first morning oblation is directed to Sūrya while addressing this verse to Savitṛ. In post-Vedic mythology the identity of Sūrya and Savitṛ is further advanced, and such names as Vivasvat and Āditya are also used.

Bibliography. A. A. Macdonell, *Vedic Mythology* (1897); J. Gonda, *Die Religionen Indiens,* Vols. I-II (1960-63).

D. M. KNIPE

SŪTRA so͞o´ trŭ (H & B—Skt.; lit. "thread" [*siv*—"to sew"]) **SUTTA** so͞ot´ tŭ (B—Pali). A short, pithy verse or aphorism, or a collection of such verses. This was the predominant mode for the expression and transmission of rules in grammar, philosophy, law, ritual, meter, and so on. Sūtras were composed with an eye to economy of expression and mnemonic ease, and were often couched in technical language; as such they are frequently difficult to comprehend without the aid of a commentary.

"The Sūtras" generally indicates those connected with the VEDAS. The great treatises of MAHĀYĀNA Buddhism are also called Sūtras or Suttas, but their style is much more expansive than that of their Hindu counterparts. J. BARE

SUTTA PIṬAKA so͞ot´ tŭ pĭ´ tŭ kŭ (B—Pali; lit. "Basket of Discourses") **SŪTRA PIṬAKA** (B—Skt.). The second of three collections of texts making up the Tipiṭaka, or PALI CANON of Buddhism. It is a major source of Buddhist doctrine and ethics and contains the discourses of the Buddha as well as much narrative material. It also includes accounts of numerous episodes from the Buddha's life, but no complete biography.

1. **Divisions.** Schools which used Sanskrit as their scriptural language arranged the discourses in four subcollections known as ĀGAMAS. These correspond in the Pali tradition of THERAVĀDA to subcollections known as NIKĀYAS. These are: (a) Collection of Long Discourses, (b) Collection of Middle Length Sayings, (c) Connected Sayings, and (d) Gradual Sayings. In addition the Pali Sutta Piṭaka adds a fifth subcollection of Miscellaneous Anthologies.

From the existence in early Buddhism of specialists in the recitation of the Long Discourses and Middle Length Sayings respectively, we can conclude that these were the first of the subcollections actually to exist as such. They present the Buddha's teachings, illustrating them with examples from everyday life. The emphasis is on moral conduct, insight, and mental discipline. The discourses show little concern with metaphysics and ritual, rejecting, for example, the Hindu emphasis on sacrifice. Speculations concerning original creation are also avoided.

Among the most important discourses in these two Nikāyas are: (a) The Discourse on the Great Decease (MAHĀ-PARINIBBĀNA SUTTA), which gives a connected account of the last days of the Buddha; (b) Satipaṭṭhāna (Discourse on the Foundations of Mindfulness), the scriptural foundation of awareness meditation as practiced in Southeast Asia today (*see* MEDITATION, BUDDHIST); and (c) The Discourse on the Turning of the Wheel of Doctrine, which sets forth the truths of suffering, its roots in ignorance and craving, and its end in the eightfold path to release. The collections of Connected Sayings and Gradual Sayings in large part rearrange the material of the two earlier collections.

2. **The Fifth Nikāya.** The Miscellaneous Anthologies vary greatly from one to another. The Sutta Nipāta is perhaps the oldest text in the canon. Particularly famous is its Discourse on Loving-kindness. The DHAMMAPADA (lit. "Path of Truth") is an authoritative treatise on Buddhist virtues, while the JĀTAKAS, or birth stories, contain more than five hundred stories—many in fable form—purporting to be accounts of incidents from the previous lives of the Buddha.

3. **Form and style.** With the exception of certain texts from the Miscellaneous Anthologies, the discourses are largely in prose with a scattering of verses. The texts are often repetitious to aid memorization. In the classic form each of the Buddha's discourses begins with the phrase: "Thus have I heard . . ." This is followed by a description of the setting, and then the discourse itself, concluding with an expression of approval by the listeners.

Bibliography. B. C. Law, *History of Pali Literature,* 2 vols. (1933); R. Webb, *Analysis of the Pali Canon* (1975); H. C. Warren, *Buddhism in Translations* (1962).

J. P. McDERMOTT

SUTTEE sə tē´ (H). *See* SATĪ §2.

SUZUKI, DAISETZ TEITARO sū zū´ kē dī´ sĕtz tā tä´ rō (B—Jap.; 1870-1966). Buddhist scholar largely responsible for the popularity of Buddhism, particularly Rinzai ZEN, in the West.

Suzuki was born in North Japan to a family of samurai rank with limited means. Upon leaving Ishikawa High School, he became a village English instructor. As a disciple to Zen masters at Engakuji Monastery in Kamakura, he received the name "Daisetz" ("great humility") as a mark of enlightenment. Writing and lecturing in the United States, Europe, and Japan, Suzuki produced over twenty works in English and a comparable number in Japanese. He emphasized an experiential approach to Buddhist studies and utilized Western psychological and Christian mystical concepts in explaining Zen to Westerners.

Bibliography. D. T. Suzuki, *Essays in Zen Buddhism* (1949, 1953), and *Zen and Japanese Culture* (1959).

C. W. EDWARDS

SVAYAṂVARA svŭ yŭm vär′ ŭ (H—Skt.; lit. "self-selection, free choice" [*svayam*—"self, free," *vara*—"to choose, to select"]). The selection of a husband by a young woman. It is one of the eight legally approved types of Hindu marriage, prevalent till the eleventh century A.D.

Normally, the celebration of a *svayaṃvara* ceremony was widely publicized, and suitors were invited from far and wide without any restriction of caste, creed, or status. The young woman would observe all of the assembled suitors and put the *jaimālā* (the garland of victory) around the neck of the man of her choice. Sometimes the choice depended on the fulfillment of a special condition involving a test of the skill or prowess of the suitor. For example, in the well-known *svayaṃvara* of Princess SĪTĀ, the condition to be fulfilled was the breaking of the huge ancient bow of SHIVA. RĀMA, the young prince of Ayodhyā, fulfilled this condition.

Another example is that of ARJUNA, who won DRAUPADĪ as his wife by exhibiting extraordinary skill in archery and successfully hitting the eye of a fish which he could see only in a reflection.

Even in the present practice of arranged marriage in India there is a covert choice on the part of the bride, disguised in the custom of getting the verbal consent of the girl before the final scriptural rite of marriage.

Bibliography. S. Radhakrishnan, *Religion and Society* (1946).

I. C. SHARMA

ŚVETĀMBARA shvā′ täm bä rä (Ja—Skt.; lit. "white-clad"). One of the two major monastic traditions in JAINISM. The name refers to the requirement that monks and nuns renounce all possessions and wear only simple white cotton garments. This practice stands in contrast to the ascetic nakedness practiced by the DIGAMBARAS.

K. W. FOLKERT

SWAMI swä′ mē (H—Skt.; lit. "one who possesses, a lord"). An honorific title in India used synonymously with "lord," "teacher," or "master." The title is often given to religious or political leaders as a sign of their high position (though not necessarily implying spiritual leadership, as GURU does).

L. D. SHINN

SWEDENBORGIANISM (Ch). The name commonly given the Church of the New Jerusalem, often called the "New Church," and its teachings, which are based on the writings of the Swedish scientist, seer, and mystical philosopher Emmanuel Swedenborg (1688-1772). Basic teachings include belief in progress in spirit worlds after death (but a rejection of mediumistic SPIRITUALISM), in "correspondences" or affirmation of direct causes in the spiritual world for terrestrial events, in an elaborate allegorical method of interpreting scripture, and an unusual doctrine of the TRINITY which holds that Jesus Christ is himself the one and only God, Father (as divine essence), Son, and Holy Spirit being embodied in him.

The Swedenborgian church has never been large, though it has attracted some persons of excellent intellect. In the 1970s the two Swedenborgian denominations in America reported a total of about eight thousand members. Swedenborgianism has had, however, an influence on American spiritual life out of proportion to its numbers. New England transcendentalism, spiritualism, THEOSOPHY, and "new thought" (the "science of mind" and "positive thinking" tradition) have all, in various ways, been deeply affected by the wisdom of the Swedish philosopher.

Worship is simple but dignified, employing certain liturgical forms. Swedenborgians believe that the Bible, expressing the divine mind, in some sense *is* God; a gesture is made toward the open scriptures on the altar at certain points in the service when the name of God is mentioned.

Bibliography. S. Toksvig, *Emmanuel Swedenborg, Scientist and Mystic* (1948); M. B. Block, *The New Church in the New World* (1932).

R. S. ELLWOOD

SYNAGOGUE (Ju—Gr.; lit. "assembly"). A house of worship in JUDAISM.

1. **Origin.** When the Palestinian community was uprooted in the Babylonian Exile (after 587 B.C.), and the JERUSALEM Temple was destroyed, the need for communal worship become increasingly urgent. Most scholars, therefore, see the "house of assembly" as a creation of the DIASPORA. In fact, the earliest known remains of ancient synagogues are in Egypt, and there is evidence of synagogues in Greece as early as the first century B.C. Evidence of Palestinian synagogues before A.D. 70 is sparse, but those at Masada, Herodium, Tarichaeae (Magdala), and Gamla are worthy of mention.

The existence of these synagogues as well as the attested remains of Jewish sectarian temples in Egypt, Transjordan, and Palestine indicate that the second Jewish Temple (515 B.C.—A.D. 70) did not function as the exclusive place of Jewish worship.

2. **Function.** The synagogue's main function has been community prayer *(beth tefillah*—Heb.; lit. "house of worship"), although it was associated with private prayer. Some scholars connect private prayer with the emergence of the PHARISEES, a popular movement within late Second Temple Judaism. (*See* PRAYER, JEWISH.)

The synagogue is also associated with study and as such is called *beth midrash,* or "house of study." It is not clear whether the "house of study" was part of the main sanctuary in antiquity or was adjacent to it, as is the practice today. Both the prayer and the study functions of the synagogue may be related to the centrality of scripture and its proper interpretation. The *bema,* the platform from which the TORAH is read, is further indication of the importance of scripture.

Such platforms are found as early as the third century A.D., and are customary in medieval and modern synagogues. In antiquity the *bema* was always situated on the wall facing Jerusalem. In medieval and modern times it is often found in the center of the sanctuary before the Holy ARK, which is on the wall of orientation, facing Jerusalem.

The synagogue was also intended as a place of assembly, *beth knesset,* a place where town meetings were held and where business was conducted. From the first century A.D. to the present, the synagogue was also constructed in such a way as to function as a hospice, *beth orhim.*

3. **Design and decoration.** The ancient synagogue has often been considered an adaptation of the Roman basilica, but recent discoveries suggest that it might represent an adaption of older Palestinian temple types. Among the known architectural types are basilicas, broadhouses, apsidal structures, and even combinations of these types. While Jews in the diaspora often imitated features of the Jerusalem Temple, the TALMUD (Menahot 28b) commanded that a synagogue should not be constructed after the pattern of the Temple.

Despite prohibitions against figural art in the TEN COMMANDMENTS, both Palestinian and diasporan synagogues depict a wide variety of animal and human motifs on their frescoes, mosaics, and sculpture from as early as the mid-third century A.D. The basic repertoire of symbols consists of the ark (doubled-door chest), the MENORAH, felines, eagles, signs of the zodiac, etc. Palestinian art in particular is characterized by the orientalizing feature of showing figures frontally, indicative of the struggle between Judaism and the more universal language of Hellenism in Roman and Byzantine times.

In the art and architecture of the synagogue, therefore, Jews adapted to life outside the Temple, and assimilated to the dominant aesthetics of their time. This represents a shift from the collective religion of earlier times to the more individualized religion of the synagogue which could be exported to all lands and communities. (*See* ART AND ARCHITECTURE, JEWISH.)

4. **Modern times.** Until modern times the synagogue remained the heart of the Jewish experience. With the liberalizing tendencies of eighteenth and nineteenth century thought, various innovations came to characterize the synagogue of REFORM and CONSERVATIVE Jews. It was German Reform which introduced the organ and music into synagogue worship, taken over to some extent in twentieth century conservative synagogues (*see* MUSIC IN JUDAISM). The adoption of sermons, clerical garb, the vernacular language, and a general acceptance of secular education along with religious education provided the essentials for the development of the modern synagogue. The participation of women in worship, first in the Reform community and later in many other liberal congregations, has emerged as a major issue even in ORTHODOX circles.

Thus as the synagogue emerged from the GHETTO community of medieval times, modernity influenced it more than any other factor in history. In antiquity and in the Middle Ages the synagogue was the carrier of all Jewish values as well as the focus for most communal activities. Today such secular causes as philanthropy and ZIONISM provide other outlets. The tenacity of the synagogue as an abiding feature of Jewish civilization, however, suggests a continuing context for those mythic elements of tradition that transcend historical time.

Bibliography. E. R. Goodenough, *Jewish Symbols of the Greco-Roman Period,* I (1953), 178-268; J. Gutmann, ed., *The Synagogue: Studies in Origins, Archaeology and Architecture* (1975); E. M. Meyers, "Synagogue Architecture," *IDBS*.

E. M. MEYERS

T

TABERNACLES, FEAST OF (Ju). *See* Sukkot.

TABOO. A strong prohibition backed by sanctions, often of a sacred or supernatural nature. Taboos may attach to persons (e.g. lepers in the OT), to objects, to places, to activities, or to words and expressions. They may apply to everyone at all times; or only to some (e.g. taboos imposed on women and children with respect to male prerogatives); or only on some occasions (e.g. the widespread taboo on sex before battle or before religious ritual). Violations are variously thought to be punished by (a) direct intervention of the sacred, (b) immanent or automatic sanctions, or (c) humans acting on behalf of the sacred. Two kinds of rationale underlie many taboos: fear of being overwhelmed by the intrinsic positive power of the object (cf. the deadly holiness of Yahweh on Mt. Sinai, Exod. 19); or fear of being defiled or devitalized by the draining negative power of the object (cf. the taboo on corpses in the OT). Dietary taboos sometimes serve (as in Judaism) as a pervasive sign of the separateness between one people and other peoples (*see* Kosher; Food Proscriptions); or they may signal a special mystic relationship between the people and the taboo object (*see* Totem). Finally, the incest taboo is universal, but it takes many forms not readily reducible to a single functional explanation.

C. R. Taber

TAGORE, RABINDRANATH tä gôr´ rō bĭn´ drä nät (H; 1861-1941). Bengali writer, artist, and educator; first Asian to win the Nobel Prize for literature. Rabindranath was the fourteenth and last child of Debendranath Tagore, a leader of the Brāhmo Samāj. The Tagores were a wealthy and distinguished family, so from earliest childhood Rabindranath was exposed to the best of Western and Indian culture and education and to the excitement of a growing nationalism. He wrote his first poem at age eight, and by the time of his death had produced a vast body of literature including poems (many of which he set to music himself), short stories, novels, dramas, books and essays on religion and education, and letters written to friends and family on his many trips abroad. In 1912 he undertook the translation into English of some of his mystical poems in a collection entitled *Gītāñjali* ("Song Offerings"). A friend presented a copy to the English poet William Butler Yeats, whose enthusiasm generated much interest in the previously unknown Indian writer. In 1913 Tagore, largely on the basis of these poems, was awarded the Nobel Prize.

Gītāñjali centers around the theme of the search for God, whose presence Tagore found in nature and in the spirit and daily life of his fellowmen. He was a Hindu, but not in a narrow, sectarian sense. Tagore saw religion as a quest and a process rather than a dogma and a ritual, and for this reason his poems have a universal appeal. He was particularly influenced by the Bāuls, the wandering minstrels of Bengal who worship through music and who, paradoxically, yearn for union with a God who is ever out of reach, yet so close to humanity that he is called the "Man of my heart."

An equally strong theme in Tagore's poems is his love of country, an expression of an almost spiritualized nationalism which envisioned the political unity of his fellow Indians as symbolic of a deeper unity of spirit and purpose which would one day include all humanity. Ezra Pound once said that "Tagore has sung Bengal into a nation," but the power of his poetic expression extended well beyond Bengal. Tagore composed the song which became the Indian national anthem, *Jana Gaṅa Mana* ("The Mind of the Multitude of the People"), which expresses the essential unity of all the peoples of India. Another of his compositions, *Āmār Śonār Bāṅgla* ("My Golden Bengal"), based on a Bāul tune, is the national anthem of the Muslim nation of Bangladesh.

Bibliography. K. Kripalani, *Tagore: A Biography* (1962); A. Chakravarty, ed., *A Tagore Reader* (1971).

P. L. Basu

T'AI-CHI tī jē (T & Con—Chin.; lit. "great ultimate"). The One through which the Tao manifests itself and then differentiates into two forces

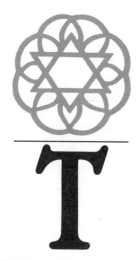

(Yin and Yang) that interact to produce the world of phenomena. *See* Taoism, Religious §3.

M. Levering

TAISEKIJI tī sā´ kē jē (B—Jap.; lit. "Great Rock Temple"). Head temple of Nichiren Shō-shū, located near Fujinomiya in Shizuoka Prefecture, with Mt. Fuji in the background. The temple was founded in 1290 by Nikkō, an immediate disciple of Nichiren. Some thirty-five buildings, including modern lodgings for pilgrims, are overshadowed by the main worship hall (completed in 1972). *See* Nichiren Buddhism; Sōka Gakkai.

N. S. Brannen

TAIZÉ tä zā´ (Ch). An interdenominational and international monastic community founded at Taizé (SE France) in 1940 by its present prior, Roger Schutz (b. 1915). Originally founded as a form of Monasticism within Protestantism, the community of more than seventy men with vows of Celibacy, submission to authority, and common property is engaged chiefly in promoting Christian unity. Close ties are maintained with the World Council of Churches, Constantinople, and Rome. Small groups of brothers work at many different tasks in Latin America and Africa.

Bibliography, J. Heijke, *An Ecumenical Light on the Renewal of Religious Community Life: Taizé* (1967); P. C. Moore, *Tomorrow Is Too Late: Taizé, an Experiment in Christian Community* (1970).

C. Waddell

TĀJ MAHAL täj mŭ häl´ (I—Per.; lit. "crown palace"). A monument in the city of Agra (Uttar Pradesh, India), regarded as the finest architectural achievement of the Mogul period. Conceived under the supervision of the Emperor Shah Jahan (1592-1666) as a mausoleum for his favorite wife, Mumtaz Mahal, and built between 1632 and 1647, the Tāj is a superbly integrated monument. It is composed of an octagonal central structure crowned with a dome some 250 feet in total height which is executed principally in white marble. A pair of matched buildings in sandstone stand one on each side of the central tomb. The building to the northwest of the plan is a *masjid* or Mosque; its counterpart is a rest house. The total rectangular walled complex is 1,000 by 1,860 feet in dimension. It contains a four-quartered garden divided by water courses; the analogical symbolism refers to the four divine rivers and the gardens of paradise. Functionally the Tāj is a royal mausoleum of a great ruler and his consort. Symbolically it is a replica of the throne of God in paradise (*see* Allah). The careful selection of complementary Suras from the Holy Qur'ān, significantly placed at particular points in the architectural decor, supports this concept. The overall plan and spiritual ethos of this masterpiece are based upon ideas developed within Islamic thought by the Sufi mystics. *See* Islam in South Asia.

Bibliography. W. E. Begley, "The Myth of the Taj Mahal and a New Theory of its Symbolic Meaning," *The Art Bulletin*, XLI (1979), 7-27.

C. R. Jones

L. D. Shinn

The Tāj Mahal viewed from its garden

TAJWĪD təj wēd´ (I—Arab.; lit. "embellishment, adornment"). The art of Qur'ān recitation, embracing correct pronunciation and performance and the ritual attitudes and acts required in the practice. Qur'ān recitation is of fundamental importance for Muslims, and in some respects is akin to a sacrament in that it is a participation in God's speech, which the believers are commanded to repeat often.

1. The terminology of recitation. The word *qur'ān* itself means "recitation." From the same root (q-r-') are *qirā'a*, which means recitation both in the sense of what is recited (the text) and actual performance; *qāri'*, "reciter, reader"; and *muqri'*, a master qualified to teach recitation as performance as well as the highly technical and difficult subject of "readings" (acceptable textual variants). All *muqri's* are *qāri's*, but the reverse is not the case. Another term for recitation is the Qur'ānic *tilāwa* (Sura 2:121), which contains also the sense of "following" the message as an obedient believer. The term *tajwīd* is absent from the Qur'ān and extremely rare in the Ḥadīth, having come to prominence as a technical term only in about the third Muslim century.

2. Types of *tajwīd*. *a) tartīl*—slow, deliberate, nonmusical chanting for pondering the meaning (cf. Sura 73:4, "And chant the Qur'ān very distinctly (*tartīlan*)"); *b) ḥadr*—rapid recitation, so as to cover a lot of the text (e.g., for merit); and *c) tadwīr*—in between the other two. In addition to its generic meaning, *tajwīd* can mean a specific type of performance: slow, highly embellished chanting in a dramatic and quasi-musical style. This is very popular, and some performers have a vast and devoted following. The question of the place of melodies in recitation is complex and controversial.

3. **The technical side of *tajwīd*.** The details cannot be grasped without a knowledge of Arabic and the Qur'ānic text (and indeed the history of the text). Much of the subject concerns the precise pronunciation of individual letters and words, which vary with their relative positions to each other. The proper "stops" *(waqf)* and "starts" *(ibtidā')* are also regulated in minute detail, for they govern syntax. The layperson can glimpse something of all this in Ibn al-Jazarī's (d. A.D. 1429) gloss: "*Tajwīd* is not slurring of the tongue, nor hollowing of the mouth [so as to deepen the tone], nor twisting of the jaw, nor quavering of the voice, nor lengthening of the doubled consonants, nor cutting short the lengthened vowels, nor buzzing the nasals, nor scamping the r's. Recitation *(qirā'a)* shuns these practices, and the hearts and ears reject them. On the contrary, gentle, sweet, pleasant, fluent recitation is what we point to and present as of the greatest importance in what we say: with no inaccuracy, nor affectation, nor manneredness, nor extravagance, and no straying from the natural hallmarks of the Arabs, and the speech of the truly eloquent and pure in the 'Readings' and accepted performance standards" (*Al-Nashr*, II, 213). *Tajwīd* is properly learned from a living master who received his training through an authoritative chain extending back through the Companions and the Prophet MUHAMMAD to GABRIEL. There are many small handbooks on *tajwīd* which cover only the minimum required for correct oral recitation by the average Muslim.

Bibliography. Qur'ān 25:32; 17:110; 73:4; 75:16-19; 2:121; 87:6, 8, 9. *Ḥadīth:* Al-Baghawī, *Mishkāt al-Maṣābīḥ*, ET J. Robson (1960-65), II, 446-70, a rich sampling of various dimensions of the subject; treatments of the subject in English are rare, the most accessible and comprehensive being Labib as-Said, *The Recited Koran* (1975), an abridged translation of the Arabic by B. Weiss, M. A. Rauf, and M. Berger. The standard medieval treatise is Ibn al-Jazarī's *Al-Nashr fī 'l-Qirā'āt al-'Ashr*, in two volumes (1926), which deals extensively with textual matters. F. M. DENNY

TALLIT tä lēt´ (Ju—Heb.). The rectangular prayer shawl in which adult male Jews wrap themselves during the morning service throughout the year. Formerly the tallit was worn only by married men, but in modern times it has become customary for boys to begin wearing it following their BAR MITZVAH. The tallit is to be made either of wool or silk, in white, with stripes at its ends. The most important requirement is that it have at each of its four corners *tzitzit* (fringes), the wearing of which is prescribed in the BIBLE (Num. 15:38-39). B. MARTIN

TALMUD täl´məd (Ju—Heb.; lit. "learning," "study," "teaching"). The Jewish library of oral law and tradition consisting of MISHNAH and GEMARA. Two such compilations exist, reflecting eight hundred years of discourse in the academies of Jewish law: the Jerusalem Talmud (edited *ca.* A.D. 450) and the Babylonian Talmud (*ca.* A.D. 500), sacred to ORTHODOX JEWS and second only to the BIBLE in authority.

1. **History.** *a) Mishnah.* Oral law (HALAKAH) and custom existed in biblical times and responded to changing conditions under Persian, Hellenistic, and Roman rule. The Mishnah, the written text of the oral law, was produced by JUDAH HA-NASI (*ca.* A.D. 200), and is a compilation of the rabbinic opinions of the preceding centuries. It includes six sections or "orders" that deal with laws of agriculture, the Sabbath and holidays, family relations, property and court procedures, the Temple cult, and ritual impurity. The Talmuds are the compilations of rabbinic opinions since the Mishnah, and use the Mishnah text, portion by portion, as the point of departure for discussion

b) The Jerusalem Talmud. Johanan ben Nappaha (A.D. 199-279), head of the academy of Tiberias, was the most outstanding teacher whose opinions are found in Gemara of the Jerusalem Talmud. The text of this Gemara covers only the four orders of the Mishnah dealing with agriculture, festivals, family life, and property problems. Byzantine persecution gave impetus to the editing of this work, which stopped *ca.* A.D. 450 and was never finished.

c) The Babylonian Talmud. At an academy established in Sura (A.D. 219), and another in Nehardea, later to move to Pumbedita, the traditions of Babylonian Jewish scholarship developed, including critical analysis of traditions. The Babylonian Talmud has no Gemara on agricultural laws of the Mishnah (which related to Palestine), but in addition to the other orders covered by the Jerusalem Talmud has Gemara on the orders dealing with sacrifices and impurities. The Iranian magi, and especially the government of Piruz (A.D. 458-485) in Babylonia, produced pressures leading to the compiling of the Babylonian Talmud. After A.D. 500, editorial work was continued, with versions of the Gemara being checked for at least a century. The Babylonian Talmud came to be the authoritative text of the oral law, and is usually meant when the word "Talmud" is used alone.

2. **Major religious beliefs.** *a) God.* Common values are reflected in the statements of the sages and are hidden among their pragmatic opinions. God is depicted in anthropomorphic language (he wears phylacteries, Berakhot 6a), perhaps to emphasize his closeness and the need to imitate him ("He clothed the naked, so do you," Sota 14a). "The Holy One, blessed be He, is in partnership with the father and mother of a person, as He gives man his soul" (Nidda 31a). He sustains the whole world and judges it every

day, yet as he deals with it, he tempers justice with mercy (Abodah Zarah 3b). "Everything is in the hands of Heaven except the fear of Heaven" (Berakhot 33b).

b) Ethics. The Golden Rule of HILLEL is "What is hateful to yourself, do not do to your fellowman. That is the whole Torah and the remainder is but commentary. Go, learn it" (Shabbat 31a). God's choice of Sinai rather than a tall mountain for revelation teaches humility (Sota 5a). Charity, honesty, and lovingkindness are tools of human social and moral coexistence: "We must support the poor of the Gentiles with the poor of Israel, visit the sick of the Gentiles with the sick of Israel . . . because of the ways of peace" (Gittin 61a). A famous saying summarizes human obligations: "The day is short, and the work is great, and the laborers are sluggish, and the reward is much, and the Master is urging" (PIRKE ABOTH II, 20).

3. ***Forms.*** Talmudic law regulates all aspects of life. It is based on the work of the AMORAIM, the results of argument (Babylonian Talmud, Baba Bathra 142b) and majority rulings (Berakhot 9a). Not all legal problems are solved, and there is no difference between religious and civil law. The Gemara's analysis of the Mishnah attempts to achieve precision and ensure practical results.

Everything in the Talmud that is not Halakah is AGGADAH, which includes legends aimed at ethical development, interpretation of dreams, medical practices, and astromony. The Garden of Eden and Gehenna (*see* HEAVEN AND HELL; JAHANNAM), the messianic idea, the resurrection of the dead and the day of judgment are all discussed. Best known are certain sayings. "Say a little and do much" (Pirke Aboth I, 15). "Prepare yourself in the ante-chamber so you may enter the Hall" (*ibid.* IV, 21). "Everyone who adds diminishes" (Sanhedrin 29a).

4. ***Interpretation.*** *a) Polemic.* In the Middle Ages the Jewish KARAITE sect argued that the Bible is revelation but the Talmud is the work of human minds. Medieval Christians denounced the Talmud as a blasphemous work of folly (Paris, 1240); this was followed by a burning of books. Later the view developed that the Talmudic Aggadah proves Christian truth (Barcelona, 1263).

b) Commentaries, responsa, and codes. Treatises were added to the Talmud in the Gaonic period (such as Aboth de-Rabbi Nathan). Novellae were added through the centuries. Rashi (SOLOMON BEN ISAAC, 1040–1105) is the most prominent commentator on the Talmud, but during the twelfth and thirteenth centuries the Tosafists ("men of additions") added notes opposing him on many passages. Other interpretations can be found in RESPONSA, continuing to the present day. Various codes of Jewish law such as the SHULHAN ARUCH of JOSEPH CARO reflect Talmudic teachings.

5. **Manuscripts, versions, and publications.** R. N. Rabinovicz edited in *Dikdukei Soferim* variant versions of the Talmud. The first printed Talmud was issued by the Christian Daniel Bomberg in Venice (1520-23). The best known modern edition is the *Vilna Shas*. Since 1965 El Am has published the Talmud with English translation and commentary. Beginning in 1967 Adin Steinsaltz edited a critical Talmud edition with vowels and illustrations.

Bibliography. A. Cohen, *Everyman's Talmud* (1949), on the Talmud's philosophy; A. Steinsaltz, *The Essential Talmud* (1976); H. L. Strack, *Introduction to the Talmud and Midrash* (1931).

Y. SHAMIR

TAMIL tă′ məl. A language of the DRAVIDIAN family, whose presence in the Indian subcontinent evidently predates the arrival of the ARYANS. Spoken since the earliest historical times in the southernmost portion of India, Tamil is the oldest historically attested language of this family (third-second century B.C. cave inscriptions) and has a literary tradition older than that of any other language of India except Sanskrit and perhaps Pali. Unlike these, however, it continues in use to this day as the mother tongue of over forty million people. The main importance of Tamil as a religious language is its role in the development of Hindu devotionalism, which since the seventh or eighth century has been the major orientation of religious thought in south India, eventually spreading to much of the rest of India (*see* BHAKTI HINDUISM). Tamil texts are also relevant to the history of JAINISM and BUDDHISM, important rivals to Hinduism in south India until the revivalism of the *bhakti* movement. In recent centuries ISLAMIC and CHRISTIAN texts have been composed in Tamil and the Tamil language is the central symbol in the current revival of Tamil cultural nationalism.

1. **The classical period.** The earliest surviving Tamil literature (*ca.* first-third century A.D.) is a highly sophisticated bardic poetry on the twin themes of love and war, seen as the central issues of subjective, private experience and objective, public experience, respectively. Though fundamentally secular in concern, these poems refer to various deities (e.g., MURUKAṈ) and religious practices (e.g., trance dancing) that presumably reflect Dravidian traditions prior to the cultural Aryanization so evident later and of which there is already some evidence in these poems. Collections of didactic poems and aphorisms on the conduct and meaning of life appear later (fourth-sixth centuries), reflecting the apparent influence of Jaina and Buddhist thought. Most celebrated of these is the *Tirukkuṟaḷ*, whose nonsectarianism has made it currently popular as a kind of "scripture" for Tamil cultural nationalism. The first long narrative poem or "epic" in Tamil, *Cilappatikāram* (fifth century), is attributed to a Jaina, but its story of the faithful wife who becomes the goddess of chastity and fidelity is more importantly the classic expression of the concept of noble womanhood central to Tamil cultural values.

2. **The *bhakti* turning point.** Elements of devotionalism or *bhakti* can be traced in the Tamil poetry of earlier periods as well as in SANSKRIT texts such as the BHAGAVAD GĪTĀ, but it was in the seventh to ninth centuries that the notion of a personal dimension possible in human approach to the supreme godhead led in the Tamil region to the resurgence of the worship of Hindu deities and the decline of the nontheistic philosophies (including ŚAṂKARA'S ADVAITA nondualism). Devotees of SHIVA (*see* NĀYAṈĀR) and of VISHNU (*see* ĀḺVĀR) traveled about debating religious opponents and composing intensely emotional hymns addressed to the particular manifestation of the deity in each temple. In later centuries these hymns were collected into sectarian canons, introduced into the respective temple liturgies, and eventually revered as revealed literature on a par with the VEDAS. The theology implicit in the attitudes of love toward God is the basis on which later tradition elaborated the faiths which are to this day the most influential systematizations of Hinduism in south India (*see* ŚAIVA SIDDHĀNTA; ŚRĪ VAIṢṆAVISM).

3. **Hindu consolidation.** Although poetry in the didactic and *bhakti* genres continued, and Jainas and Buddhists also remained active for some time as scholars and poets, the tenth century and beyond is primarily characterized by the literary elaboration of Hindu religious culture, chiefly the composition of Tamil epics and PURĀṆAS in emulation of Sanskrit originals. The greatest of these is the Rāmāyaṇa by Kampaṉ (twelfth century). A purely original Tamil work in this genre is the *Periyapurāṇam* (twelfth century), an account of the lives of the Śaivite *bhakti* saints which is itself included in the Śaivite canon of sacred poetry. Beyond mainstream Hinduism, Tamil has been the medium of the anti-orthodox radicalism of the Siddha poet-YOGIS, the erudition of grammars and commentaries on literary classics, the wisdom and wit of oral folk tradition, and much else which illustrate the richness of the total context in which the predominantly Hindu character of Tamil as a religious language should be seen.

Bibliography. K. A. Nilakanta Sastri, *A History of South India* (1966); K. V. Zvelebil, *The Smile of Murugan: On Tamil Literature of South India* (1973).

J. LINDHOLM and V. NARAYANAN

TANAK tä näk´ (Ju). A word formed by uniting the initial letters of the three groupings of books in the Hebrew BIBLE; T (TORAH, "law"), N (NEBI'IM, "prophets") and K (KETHUBIM, "writings") with the addition of two vowels for the sake of pronunciation. Equivalent to the Hebrew Bible or Protestant OT.

D. IRVIN

TAṆHĀ tän´ hä (B—Pali; lit. "thirst") **TṚṢṆA** trĭsh´ nü (Skt. [*tṛṣ*—"be thirsty"]). The craving or desire that is a primary motivation in human behavior, but which must be eliminated if spiritual perfection is to be achieved. The second of the FOUR NOBLE TRUTHS is that craving (*taṇhā)* is the cause of suffering. Craving also is said to be one of the twelve spokes of the wheel of dependent origination; that is, craving is one of the psychological forces that keeps most humans bound up in the cycle of rebirth (SAMSARA).

Taṇhā is often associated with passion and greed, for the most dramatic forms of craving are the sexual and egotistic ones, but *taṇhā* also includes all the psychological drives that lead people to seek pleasure and avoid pain. Thus, *taṇhā* involves all six sense organs (eyes, ears, nose, mouth, skin, and mind), as manifest in craving for pleasant sights, sounds, smells, tastes, feelings, and mental images.

Buddhists distinguish craving 1) for sensual pleasures, 2) for existence (which leads to rebirth), and 3) for self-annihilation. Buddhists also classify kinds of *taṇhā* according to which of the three worlds (sensual, heavenly, or immaterial) one craves. An early text says the Buddha taught, "Dig up the root of craving," for the extinction of craving is Nirvana (Dhammapada 337).

R. C. AMORE

TANIGUCHI MASAHARU tä nē goo´ chē mä sä hä´ roo (Jap.; 1893-). Founder of SEICHŌ NO IE and author of numerous works on divine healing and Japanese ethics and national temperament. After a traumatic youth, he gradually came to the conviction that was to govern his life, namely, that sickness and other misfortunes are the product of mind and are therefore controllable by mind.

As a supporter of imperialism before and during World War II, Taniguchi was among those purged by the Allied Occupation (1945-52). Little affected, he continued to speak and write and thereby attracted from among middle- and upper-middle-class Japanese a substantial following devoted to him as spiritual leader and as spokesman for ultra-rightest causes. He is also accorded respectful recognition among divine science movements in the U.S.

Bibliography. *See* SEICHŌ NO IE.

H. N. MCFARLAND

TANNAIM tä nä ēm´ (Ju). Palestinian sages and teachers of the MISHNAH or BARAITA beginning with the disciples of HILLEL and SHAMMAI (*ca.* A.D. 10), up to the generation of JUDAH HA-NASI (*ca.* A.D. 220). Reciters of the Mishnah in later academies of the Talmudic period were also called tannaim.

Y. SHAMIR

TANTRISM tän´ trĭsm (H, B & Ja—Skt.; lit. "that which extends, spreads"). 1. In a general sense, a non-Vedic practice (*see* VEDAS), including rites open to women and persons not of the BRAHMIN caste. It also includes the worship of deities for the purpose of specific religious merit or worldly gain. 2. In a narrower but more popular sense, an esoteric, radical way to achieve Mokṣa (emancipation from rebirth and suffering). It includes a large body of scriptural and oral lore, parallel, and in Hinduism and Jainism, marginal to official scriptures. While orthodox Hindus view occult powers (*see* Siddhi) as impediments to the quest for *mokṣa,* tantrics court them as proofs of progress. The orthodox view a temperate life-style as essential to the pursuit of Yoga, but tantrics cultivate the sensuous elements in their psychic makeup.

1. **Types of tantrism.** First is the clandestine, often eroticized version of yoga. In Tibetan Buddhism it is synonymous with the "diamond vehicle" (*see* Vajrayāna) and is part of mainstream doctrine and practice. In Hinduism, however, it is peripheral and antagonistic to orthodoxy and orthopraxis. Second, tantrism on the Indian subcontinent is largely identified with shamanistic behavior, with sorcery and witchcraft. A tantric is a person who commands extrahuman forces for his own benefit or that of his clients. Third, a learned convention among Hindu scholars calls all non-Vedic practice tantric (*see* Vedic Hinduism), particularly domestic and women's rites. Practicing tantrics pay less attention to scripture than to personal transmission from their Guru and to psycho-experimental manipulations.

2. **Tantric literature.** Hindu tantrics are at pains to show that their texts are truly Vedic. Their apologetic centers almost entirely on asserting Vedic respectability, because mainstream Hindus kept attributing clandestine and nefarious actions to them. Since Buddhist tantric teachings were absorbed into the Vajrayāna canon, Tibetan tantrics never felt such need for legitimation. Hindu tantric texts are a distinct, less respected, and often censured corpus, having canonical status only for the rather small audience of learned tantrics, few of whom are Brahmins. In fact, tantrism is overtly anti-brahmanical (though not anti-Vedic) and can be seen as a rebellion against Brahmin sacerdotalism.

3. **History of tantrism.** Although the roots of this tradition are very ancient, the material was reduced to writing only later. The first tantric works were Buddhist, e.g. the *Mañjuśrīmūlakalpa* "radical institutions of Mañjuśrī" and the *Guhyasamājatantra* "tantra of secret association," both compiled between A.D. 300 and 600. The first authentic and extant Hindu tantric texts are the *Mahānirvaṇatantra* "tantra of the great liberation" of the eleventh century and the *Kaulāvalinirṇaya* "description of the garland of adepts" of approximately the fourteenth century. These texts derive much of their raw material from folk sources which may reach back into pre-Vedic times. The manipulation of chthonic powers, the psychodynamic experimentation underlying tantrism, is much closer in form and content to what many scholars now perceive as *Indian* contrasting with *Aryan* on the subcontinent. The robust, extrovert, philosophically naïve tenor of the Vedas, the books of the Aryans, differs sharply from tantric style and lore, tantric apologetic notwithstanding. Tantrism became strong in areas of late or weak Aryan, Brahmanical penetration.

There is some support for the notion that the earliest era (*see* Indus Valley Civilization) contained proto-tantric elements like ithyphallic representations of a fertility god. If there is a connection, the origins of tantrism could indeed be placed as far back as 2500 B.C. The early portions of the Vedas indicate strong opposition to phallic worship. In later sections, however, phallic ritual was accepted and established (*see* Linga). By about 1000 B.C., phallic lore was apparently well established.

Since the tantric style originated with non-Aryan segments of the population, it remained identified with low-caste ritual. Tantrics courted, trained, and revered teachers of low-caste background who were barred from Vedic ceremony. This included women and non-Hinduized tribal groups.

In Buddhist tantrism being female or of low caste was a positive qualification. In theory at least, Brahmins were disqualified from tantric apprenticeship, but most of the later commentators on tantric codes were Brahmins, particularly from Bengal, a region where even Brahmins are largely nonvegetarian and often given to the worship of mother-goddesses.

After the destruction of two main centers of Buddhist learning by a Muslim chieftain in the eleventh century, tantric Buddhism retained ecclesiastic status only in Tibet. A few pockets of Vajrayāna institutions probably survived into the fourteenth century in northeastern and southwestern India, after which time it was defunct in India.

Organized Hindu tantrism peaked between the ninth and the fourteenth centuries under feudal and royal patronage. The decline of sophisticated, scriptural tantrism coincided with and was accelerated by new rural cults of monotheistic devotionalism (*see* Bhakti Hinduism), which shared an anti-erotic, puritanical ideology. To the teachers and followers of these cults, tantrism epitomized all that was reprehensible, to be shunned and rejected primarily because of its sensuous overtones, and secondarily due to its being tied in the popular mind to magical practices.

4. **Tantric teachings.** The theologies of tantrism are not fundamentally different from those of mainline Hinduism, Buddhism, and Jainism; it was tantric practice which roused the ire of the orthodox.

a) *Hindu tantrism* theologically largely overlaps with the monistic school (*see* Advaita), which postulates a single existent, Brahman (neuter), defined as "being-consciousness-ecstasy," *saccidānanda.* Multiplicity is a delusion (*see* Māyā) and the intuitive, irreversible realization of numerical oneness with Brahman implies liberation. The tantric seeker, however, conceptualizes Brahman as the union of the male and female principles; namely, Shiva (benign) and ŚAKTI (energy). In this initial polarity the male stands for the quiescent, for cognition, and for wisdom. The female represents action, conation, and the energetic élan. While Shiva and *Śakti* belong to the general pantheon, they are here transmuted into the cosmic principles of cognition and action. "The universe arises through the copulation of Shiva and *Śakti*." The process is reversed in the experience of the individual adept who by applying the proper techniques realizes that even that cosmic duality is illusion and that the ultimate reality is the nondual Brahman. This knowledge dissolves the adept's ego and the impersonal Absolute shines forth. The successful practitioner, while identifying with Shiva if he is male and with *Śakti* if female, eventually transcends this partial, albeit divine duality to *be* the Absolute.

b) Buddhist tantrism (*see* VAJRAYĀNA) postulates the exactly obverse polarity. Here the male principle is Buddhahood, active, outgoing, energetic. It is the means (Skt. *upāya*) of emancipation and compassion (Skt. *karuṇā*) as instantiated by the numerous Buddhas and BODHISATTVAS (*see* BUDDHISM) and visualized in sexual embrace with their female counterparts, which represent the quiescent, static, wisdom principle (Skt. *prajñā*). The two poles are symbolically juxtaposed as the "diamond" (Skt. *vajra*, hence Vajrayāna), conjoined with the "bell" (Skt. *ghaṇṭā*) representing the womb. The intuitive knowledge of their underlying oneness propels the aspirant from the experimentally fertile yet ephemeral *karuṇā-prajñā* model into the liberating, incontrovertible knowledge of momentariness and voidness (Skt. *śūnyatā*), again in line with mainstream Mahāyāna doctrines. The one who interiorizes this knowledge realizes that both worldly being (SAMSARA) *and* salvation (NIRVANA) have no essence, and that Nirvana and samsara are identical.

c) Jaina tantric teachings differ in no way from the atomistic doctrines of the official texts (*see* JAINISM). The distinction between orthodox and tantric Jainism lies entirely in the tantrics' emphasis on meditations using MANTRAS, particularly those pertaining to the goddess Padmavatī, the tutelary deity of Jaina tantrics.

5. **Practice and meditation** are ranked far above scriptural and all other theological knowledge in all tantric schools. The basic difference between orthopractical yoga (*see* PATAÑJALI) and other mainstream Hindu, Buddhist, and Jaina meditation on the one side, and tantric practice on the other, lies in what makes tantrism suspect to the orthodox: its full harnessing rather than the renunciation and rejection of the senses and its maximizing of the sensuous personality in contrast to the ascetic style of the official traditions.

Hindu tantrism of the "right hand" (*dakṣiṇācāra*) is coextensive with all nonbrahmanical ritualistic performance (*see* §1, above). The critical break with mainstream Hinduism occurs in the "left way" (*vāma-mārga*) practices. The aspirant must first master the usual techniques of physical control (*see* HAṬHA YOGA) before proceeding to the more esoteric meditations. "Haṭha Yoga is to tantric yoga what a B.A. is to a Ph.D. degree," a modern tantric explained. Next, the aspirant learns to raise the "dormant power" (*see* KUṆḌALINĪ) within himself or herself. It is here that the discipline diverges from orthodox yogic practice, which is a solitary procedure. The neophyte is initiated into a "circle" (*cakra*) of fellow aspirants consisting of an equal number of male and female disciples, guided by a male adept (*cakreśvara*) and his adept female consort (*cakreśvarī*). All male participants are designated as Shiva, all female ones as *Śakti*. The latter sit to the left of their male counterparts—hence "lefthanded" tantra. The convening of a *cakra* is controlled by complex astrological and ritualistic preparations. The ritual commences with prolonged chanting of Vedic and tantric texts. Each participant then silently meditates on the special formula (*see* MANTRA) given to her or him by the guru, who may or may not be the *cakreśvara*, while the latter keeps chanting the requisite hymns. At this stage, the participants imbibe impressive quantities of "victory" *vijayā*, a *sandhā*-term for *cannabis sativa* (i.e., marijuana) blended with sherbet and sweet milk. This introduces the core segment of the exercise, namely the seriatim use of the "five Ms" (*pañca-makāra*), which stand for the initial letters of the Sanskrit words for the main "ingredients" (i.e., fish [*matsya*], meat [*māṃsa*], parched grain or kidney bean believed to be aphrodisiacs [*mudrā*], liquor [*mada*], and finally sexual union [*maithuna*]). All these are highly stylized events with little leeway for innovation. During the last phase, the *Śaktis* place themselves astride their Shivas and initiate copulatory movement, in line with the doctrinal notion of woman as energy and man as quiescent. Since "Shiva without *Śakti* is (like a) corpse," no tantric male can achieve emancipation without being thus aided by a *Śakti*.

The key technique within this ritual is retention of semen during *maithuna*. It is in effect a ritualized *coitus reservatus* for the avowed purpose of achieving simultaneous control of mind, breath, and semen. This technique is seen as a shortcut, albeit a dangerous one, to *mokṣa*. Tantrics aver that this successfully controlled *maithuna* rushes the *kuṇḍalinī* upward into the "thousand-petalled lotus" atop the subtle body, merging the Shiva and *Śakti* principles. This explains, in part at least, the importance and the ubiquity of the phallic shape of the Shiva icon (*see* LIṄGA) as joined to the *pīṭha* "seat, vulva." Shiva must not be formally worshiped in any anthropomorphic form like other deities; the *liṅga-pīṭha* icon is mandatory (*see* YONI). Shiva is the tutelary god of all ascetics, the "vanquisher of Cupid." The contradiction is only apparent: the ithyphallic representation is nonpriapic. It implies complete control as retention of semen at the point of orgasm. The nonejaculatory union of the tantric adepts thus reenacts the cosmic resorptive union, just as regular coitus culminating in ejaculation replicates the priapic, procreative aspect of Shiva and *Śakti.*

6. **Buddhist tantric practice** (*see* VAJRAYĀNA) is based on similar psycho-experimental principles, but the actual copulation between the practitioners is less formalized. In Vajrayāna practice today the preliminary exercises take up a much larger portion than sexual congress; in fact, the latter element is now often eliminated. Meditation consists in increasingly complex visualizations of and gradual identification with divinities of the Vajrayāna pantheon. (*See* MANDALA.) The advanced practitioners interiorize the "honorable father and honorable mother" (Tibetan *yab yum*) imagery of the deities in sexual embrace. Where there is actual copulation, retention of semen is axiomatic: "having brought down the *vajra* into the lotus, let him not eject the knowledge mind." Such use of code or "intentional language" is a feature shared by Hindu and Buddhist tantrism. It serves as key terminology for the initiates and as a means to screen the teachings from outsiders. "Knowledge-mind" *(bodhicitta),* for example, is a code term for semen.

Not part of the formal ritual, consumption of alcohol is accepted and even recommended by some meditation masters preceding the practice of visualization and interiorization.

7. **Places and calendars.** Neither Buddhist nor Hindu tantrics adhere to a specific calendar of festivals and celebrations—there are no tantric festivals *per se.* However, certain regional festivals connected with the worship of female deities are regarded as auspicious occasions for tantric practice. There is a very large number of such shrines on the subcontinent, but the majority of pilgrims are hardly aware of the site's tantric significance.

8. **Tantric art** is a term of recent Western origin. Yet it is safe to assume that most of the erotic imagery on Hindu shrines, especially in southern and southeastern India, is due to tantric inspiration. Muslim chiefs destroyed a large number of shrines in northern India, which accounts for the virtual absence of erotic sculpture in that area. Such representations were and are abominations to Muslims, Christian missionaries, and modern puritanical Hindus. Nepalese Hindu temples display an abundance of such imagery. The best known and most readily accessible shrines are KHAJURĀHO in central India, KONĀRAK, Purī, and Bhuvaneshvar in the eastern State of Orissa, and hundreds of shrines in the south.

Tibetan and Nepalese Vajrayāna has generated and continues to produce tantric artifacts in quantity, and some of exquisite craftsmanship as well. Painted silk and paper scrolls (*thanka*), *yab yum* bronzes particularly from Nepal, and *vajra-ghaṇṭā* bell metal representations have entered the international market in quantity after the Chinese occupation of Tibet.

9. **Current trends** indicate a steady decline of Hindu tantrism and a strong revival of Buddhist tantra in the diaspora in North America and Western Europe. India's official culture being puritanical and its threshold of tolerance low, tantrism is virtually blacklisted by administrators. In the late 1950s there were sporadic police actions against tantric centers like that of Pagli Baba, an eminent tantric in Orissa. Śrī Rajneesh, a psychology lecturer turned tantric guru, attracts large Indian and foreign audiences in Bombay. He concocted his own version of tantrism, incorporating enough general urban Hinduism to make it tolerated in spite of some protest. Yogi Bhajan, a Sikh customs officer turned guru in California, teaches a blend of hardline SIKHISM and *kuṇḍalinī* yoga. He distinguishes between "white" (acceptable) and "red" (wicked) tantrism, terms entirely of his own invention. Ananda Marg, whose leader was aquitted of a charge of murder of some renegade disciples, has a large, monastically garbed following in India and chapters on many North American college campuses and represents itself as tantrism. (*See* HINDUISM IN AMERICA §2.)

On the popular level, tantric practice has been observed and reported over the past three decades, and there is no reason to believe that its occurrences have significantly increased or decreased. Groups of male tantrics gather in remote forest areas and meet with women who seek the same powers or who have been persuaded to participate "for pleasure." The women divest themselves of their blouses (hence "way of the blouse" for this ritual), which they place on one heap. The men then approach, each of them picking one blouse. Each man then enters into a one-night liaison with the owner of the blouse. This guarantees randomness, which is part of the tantric notion that the "other woman" (*parā-strī,* i.e. either not the practitioner's wife, or another man's wife) is *parā-śakti* (the highest power), the prefix *parā* meaning both "other" and "highest." There is little chanting, except for some preparatory invocations in the vernacular language, interspersed with some Sanskrit mantras. There is no insistence on retention of semen during the act. The target of the rite is not liberation, but occult powers. Modern Hindus who hear about these events condemn them as "dirty" and "superstitious," and as things Hinduism must reject if it is to survive in this age of science.

The energetic missionary work of a number of learned Tibetan lamas in the West has, by contrast, created nuclei of serious Vajrayāna practice in Europe and America. The number of expatriate Tibetan monks is on the increase, adding leadership and direction to Occidentals who seek this experience, a thing which was totally impossible before Buddhism's forced exit from Tibet. No tantrics are left in Chinese-occupied Tibet, and the Tibetan refugees settled in India are bound to assume the prevailing Indian mores which frown upon esoteric practice.

Bibliography. A. Bharati, *The Tantric Tradition* (1975). Hindu and general tantrism: H. V. Guenther, *The Tantric View of Life* (1975). Buddhist: Ph. Rawson, *Tantric Art* (1973). Mainly Hindu: D. I. Lauf, *Tibetan Sacred Art: The Heritage of Tantra* (1976).

A. Bharati

TAO-SHENG dou′ shēng (B—Chin.; *ca.* A.D. 360-434). One of Kumārajīva's most famous disciples, teacher of the Prajñā sūtras and Nirvana sūtra at Lu-shan; an eloquent Chinese Buddhist monk whose revolutionary theories involved him in controversy, banishment, and fame.

Tao-sheng argued that Śūnyatā and the Buddha-nature are identical and indivisible, that enlightenment must therefore be sudden and complete, and that there need be no Pure Land, for the Buddha-nature is within every sentient being. His bold theories contributed to later developments in Ch'an (Zen). *See* Buddha, General Concepts of.

C. W. Edwards

TAO-TE CHING dou də jǐng′ (T). See Lao Tzu.

TAOISM, PHILOSOPHICAL dou′ ĭsm (Chin. [*tao*—"way"]). A system of Chinese thought which views Tao ("the Way") as the source and reality of man and nature, possessing the characteristics of change, spontaneity, nonpurposiveness, and reversion to the origin. Comprehension of these characteristics and their incorporation into the life of the individual and into society are the principal concerns of Taoism. Philosophical Taoism views man as a creature of nature and teaches that instincts, feelings, imagination, fantasy, and idiosyncrasies should be allowed to have free exercise, in contrast to Confucianism, which views man as a rational and moral creature who owes obligations to society and the state. Philosophical Taoism also believes that the natural world and the Tao are essentially one, in contrast to Chinese Buddhism, which views the natural world as only the manifestation of the metaphysical entity called "emptiness" (Śūnyatā).

1. **Philosophical and religious Taoism.** Prior to 1950 the majority of the Sinologists believed that philosophical and religious Taoism are incompatible. Their main argument is that philosophical Taoism accepts death because it is a natural occurrence and an occasion to return to the Tao, whereas religious Taoism resists death by practicing Alchemy in order to achieve physical immortality. There is also a difference in substance: philosophical Taoism is rational, contemplative, and nonsectarian; whereas religious Taoism is magical, cultic, esoteric, and sectarian. *See* Taoism, Religious.

Since 1950, chiefly due to the work of French scholars Marcel Granet and Henri Maspero and their students, many Sinologists have come to the realization that these two groups may be viewed as belonging to a common tradition. Recent research on the books of Lao Tzu and Chuang Tzu have shown that they contain allusions which reflect a nostalgic longing for the myths and rituals of archaic China. These myths and rituals include the wish for some form of physical immortality, the development of a magical body impervious to harm or injury, and the motif of flight in the sky. Recent research on the Taoist canon has also shown that the religious Taoists began to utilize the Lao Tzu and Chuang Tzu as early as the philosophical Taoists did. Thus both groups can claim that they are the heirs of these scriptures.

2. **Formative period** (700-100 B.C.). The rise of Taoism in the Warring States period (402-222 B.C.) was probably a reaction to Confucianism's preoccupation with the acquisition of knowledge and the ordering of a civilized state. Because Taoists believed that humans should imitate nature, they wanted to go back to the primitive tradition of China prior to the existence of kings and ministers, in the hope of finding enduring values and principles. This is the period of the earliest extant Taoist classics: Lao Tzu (300-250 B.C.), Chuang Tzu (300 B.C.), and Huai Nan Tzu (works of Prince Huai Nan, 122 B.C.), a period when Confucianism was already prominent. What these books have in common is the recollection of the primordial conditions of China where the tranquility of pastoral and village life prevailed and where people lived in a nearly natural state.

a) Tao as the source, beginning, essence of the cosmos. Tao is the "creator" *(tsao-wu chu),* though it is impersonal and inseparable from the creation. As the source or potentiality of creation, it is called nonbeing (*wu,* lit. "nothing") and as creation (whether physical or conceptual) it is called being (*yu,* lit. "to exit"). (*See* Being and Nonbeing.) As the creator, Tao is undifferentiated and has no forms or images; thus it is called nonbeing. But as creation, Tao has myriad forms or images and is therefore called being. These two aspects are really inseparable, for nonbeing depends upon being for the attainment of definitive forms and being depends upon nonbeing for its source and potentiality.

Tao is the philosophical equivalent of chaos *(hun-tun)* in the archaic creation myth in which chaos is depicted as Emperor Hun-tun, who is faceless and without heart or other organs. The later myth of creation from the corpse of P'an-ku, who emerged from the egg-like lump, appears to be a derivation of the myth of chaos. Thus, cosmologically speaking, chaos, nonbeing, and Tao are synonymous.

In the Huai Nan Tzu, chaos is viewed as the ether or material force (Ch'i, lit. breath, vapor, or air); it contains the union of Yin and Yang forces. When these forces were divided, creation began. This means that creation begins when there is motion or when each divided force is united with its opposite to create a new synthesis.

b) Tao as the principle of reversion in nature, society, and the individual. The movement of Tao from one pole to its opposite is called "reversal" *(fan).* This characteristic is manifested in the cycles of day and night, heat and cold, and life and death in nature; infancy and aging, fortune and misfortune, joy and sorrow in human life; and wealth and poverty, war and peace, and order and chaos in society. Although the cyclical movements require that there be two poles, the poles are not equal. Taoism, particularly Lao Tzu, prefers the low poles with their attributes of darkness, ignorance, poverty, softness, weakness, withdrawal. Whereas the high pole inevitably reverts to its opposite, the low pole will enable the Taoist to remain where he is. This does not mean that he is able to transcend the principle of the reversal, for he still sees and is affected by it in nature and in society. But insofar as he is able to manage his own life, he rejects the high pole in order to stay close to the Tao, which in its abyss is quiescent, tranquil, and nonpurposive.

c) Tao as the transformation of things. While Lao Tzu believed that the cyclical movements are the expression of the Tao, Chuang Tzu took a step further because of his greater interest in logic and epistemology. He believed that all opposites presuppose a given perspective. To say that X is large presupposes a perspective about space. But another person with a different perspective may say that X is small. Hence X is both large and small. Chuang Tzu takes the position that all propositions referring to things or classes of things are relative. Because this is so, they contradict one another when seen from different points of view, and consequently the opposites are equal (X is both large and small). Thus debates and disputations cannot lead to absolute truth. This is the philosophical reason behind Chuang Tzu's doctrine of the "equalization of things" *(ch'i-wu).* Names (words) are relative and are conditioned by the users' perspectives, but because Tao is absolute and does not rest on a particular stance, it cannot be known through the conventional use of words. The only way to understand the Tao is through intuition *(tzu-jan* or WU WEI), the attitude that does not discriminate or make distinctions about things but responds immediately or spontaneously.

Thus for Chuang Tzu the Tao refers to changes that take place spontaneously in nature, society, and individuals. Human destiny is to submit to natural changes, so that humans too are continuously transformed. In this way, they and the world are one.

d) Ethic of noncontrivance. Taoists believed that human contrivance should be avoided because it is counter-productive and contrary to the spontaneity of the Tao. Warfare and strife could be avoided if the leaders practiced the ethic of noncontrivance *(wu wei).* This ethic means that human conduct should follow intuition or should be as natural as water flowing downward and fire rising upward. It is conduct unmediated by thought or deliberation and is akin to reflex actions. This doctrine is a specific example of the general concept of spontaneity *(tzu-jan),* according to which the Tao is nonpurposive, nondeliberate, and continuously transforming. It is in this context that the Taoists criticized Confucianism and Mohism (followers of Mo Ti, flourished 479-438 B.C.). Confucianism's alleged moral nature of man and its moral concept of the cosmos have distorted both man and nature. And Mohism's emphasis upon the doctrine of universal love by self-sacrifice is an extreme example of human contrivance.

e) Human creativity. The Taoist doctrine of "no knowledge" or "ignorance" is predicated on the conviction that accumulation of knowledge can make a person inflexible or subject to a false sense of security that refuses to come to terms with new realities. Thus knowledge can be a hindrance to freedom, to becoming one with the cosmos, or being continuously transformed. For this reason Taoism advocates the gradual "elimination of knowledge" in order to gain true wisdom or intuition. For example, a butcher has to become unconscious of the knowledge of his trade in order to be a master of his art—one who can intuit where and how to cut. Creativity is possible only when the knower is no longer concerned about his accumulated knowledge.

Following the same line of argument, Taoism believes that individuals, society, or the state should keep in close touch with the primitive, simple, and undifferentiated source of creativity, which is like the "uncarved block" that can be made into an instrument, like water that can nourish, or like a woman who can give birth.

f) Affinity between Taoism and Legalism. In this formative period one of the many rival schools was Legalism *(fa-chia),* whose philosophy reflects a curious affinity with Taoism, although they were wide apart in their views of the state and the individual. Both held a naturalistic world view, and both believed that the Tao is impersonal, nonpurposeful, and nonmoral. For this reason both schools criticized the moralism of Confucianism, and both advocated noncontrivance as the norm for the ruler. However, the Legalists believed that the state must first of all strictly administer rewards and punishments in order to induce the people to work hard and to obey the state. Only after the law (state machinery) has come to function automatically does the ruler follow the principle of noncontrivance in his relation with the people. Thus noncontrivance in Legalism presupposes a totalitarian state. The ruler foregoes favoritism, but it is not his business to be concerned with morality.

Taoists were opposed to equating morality with the Tao, but they held that when people live close to nature, they possess a moral intuition which can dictate how they should act in a given situation.

3. **Mature period** (100 B.C.—A.D. 600). The maturation of Taoism corresponds roughly to the Han empire (206 B.C.—A.D. 220) and the period of the Political Disunion (southern and northern dynasties, 265-589). In the Han dynasty China became a great empire and Confucianism was transformed into a metaphysical or semi-religious system befitting its

role as the spokesman of the state. Taoism was forced to play a secondary role in philosophy and to make certain compromises with Confucianism. For example, it made Confucius a great Taoist sage and accepted Confucian morality as having relative value. But for several centuries after the fall of the Han dynasty, Taoism played a far more important role as the leading philosophy of China. The North was ruled by a succession of non-Chinese rulers of Turkish and Tibetan origins, and the South was under a succession of Chinese dynasties. Han Confucianism lost its appeal because as a metaphysical system for the defense of an empire it was no longer applicable; there was no Chinese empire. The non-Chinese rulers feared Confucianism as a threat to their own political power and therefore turned to Buddhism to find ideological justification of their right to rule. In the South members of the ruling class and the intellectuals, many of whom were refugees from the North, resorted to Taoism as a philosophical and spiritual release from their political and social frustrations, and Taoism became the leading philosophy there.

a) School of "dark learning." This school, which attempted to reinterpret the thought of earlier Taoism, is referred to as "dark learning" *(hsüan-hsüeh)* because its interpretation of nonbeing is beyond conceptual analysis and therefore conveys a sense of mystery. In the West it is called Neo-Taoism. Its leading figures were Wang Pi (226-249), author of a commentary on the Lao Tzu, and Kuo Hsiang (d. 312), author of a commentary on the Chuang Tzu.

i) Nonbeing as an ontological state. In earlier Taoism nonbeing preceded being in the process of creation; hence it is the creator of the world. But for the Neo-Taoists, nonbeing is not the antecedent of being; it refers to the self-transcendence of being when it is stripped of all the names to describe or define it. Thus nonbeing is an ontological concept of the oneness of all things without reference to their distinction or differences. Although it is not the creator, it is nevertheless a supreme, though indescribable, state that can be attained by the individual. Realization of that state is called freedom *(hsiao-yao)*.

ii) Self-creation and interdependence. Because the Tao does not create, everything is self-created *(tu-hua)*. Creation is a continuous process. A thing arises because of the convergence of certain conditions, but they are not its cause. It creates itself through its becoming. Although things are not causally dependent on one another, they are, however, naturally interdependent. Thus, for example, the teeth depend on the lips to keep warm and the lips on the teeth to stay firm. Self-creation and interdependence are both natural. If everything follows its natural endowment, it is at the same time also expressing the interdependence of things.

iii) Meaning of wu wei. In earlier Taoism, *wu wei* meant essentially noncontrivance; but in Neo-Taoism contrivance is admitted as long as it is not against one's natural capacity, and *wu wei* means following one's natural capacity.

iv) Equalization of things. In earlier Taoism the doctrine of equalization of things was applied in order to avoid assertion in the world; if opposites are really equal, it is useless to side with either one. But in Neo-Taoism anyone can be active in whatever position he occupies as long as his performance is not against his natural capacity. Thus if a person of meager capacity has a position which fits him, it is neither low nor high. By following his natural capacity he has transcended the polarity of low or high with respect to his position. No one, however, in following his natural capacity should become ensnared by his own performance; that is, he should be emotionally free from attachment to his own work.

b) Influence on Buddhism. While there is no evidence that Buddhism influenced the development of Neo-Taoism, Neo-Taoism clearly influenced Buddhism in its first phase of development in China. In this period Neo-Taoists and Chinese Buddhist monks belonged to the same elite scholarly class, and their common background enabled them to develop a sense of camaraderie. Moreover, the first renowned Chinese scholarly monks had all been Neo-Taoists before they became Buddhists, and they used Taoist language to explain Buddhist terms. Thus, for example, the concept of emptiness (śūnyatā) was equated with the Taoist term of "nothing" *(wu)*. This method was called *ke-yi* (lit. "analogy").

c) School of primitive anarchism. Both the founder of the Wei dynasty (220-265) and that of the Chin dynasty (265-402) usurped the throne from kings whom they had served. The instability of the dynasties and the low morality of the rulers were the social reason for the rise of anarchistic thought in this period. Among the Taoists, Juan Chi (210-263) and Pao Ching-yen (*ca.* 274-*ca.* 334) affirmed anarchism and advocated a return to primitive society. Pao Ching-yen advocated two significant ideas. 1) Kingship is not really based on the Mandate of Heaven, but is the result of the strong oppressing the weak and of the educated deceiving the uneducated. The Mandate of Heaven is simply an attempt to justify this social phenomenon. 2) Kingship is contrary to the simple naturalism of primitive society. In archaic China people lived in equality and contentment, following the rhythms of nature for their model and having no ambition or worldly desires. It was only after the establishment of kingship that primitive tranquility was disrupted and evils began to multiply.

d) School of pastoral hermits. Due to low morale in government and to rigid bureaucratization, the scholar-officials either resorted to the practice of "pure conversations" *(ch'ing-t'an)* among their fraternal groups as a means of compensating for their political frustrations or retired to their home villages as "hermit-farmers." The best known among the latter group is Tao Yuan-ming (365-427), a retired official, poet, and gentleman-farmer. Many of his pastoral poems convey the idea that the simple rustic life of the farmer is the ideal expression of the cycles of nature, and to that extent he and nature are one.

e) Taoist syncretism. The book *Lieh Tzu,* composed around A.D. 300, depicts the legendary life of a Taoist of the same name. It represents the syncretic tendency characteristic of Taoism in its subsequent development. The book recounts a large number of myths and marvelous tales about ancient China and its neighbors which seem to reflect the author's conviction that people need to stretch their imagination beyond the rational and moral categories that were the special concern of Confucianism. Perhaps the author believed that through these tales the readers might recover the sense of wonder and curiosity so important for genuine living. It also depicts Lieh Tzu and other mythological characters flying in the sky as their regular means of travel. This motif of "magical flight" goes back to an archaic ritual of Chinese SHAMANISM vividly described in the *Songs of the South (Ch'u-tz'u).* Although the author of the *Lieh Tzu* might have used the "flight" only in the allegorical sense, his frequent reiteration of it may be construed as a subconscious reenactment of an ancient ritual. The book several times refers to the cult of physical immortality (*see* TAOISM, RELIGIOUS §§5, 6) in a negative sense. But on one occasion when the author refers to the progressive spiritual discipline of the Yellow Emperor who finally "rose into the sky" (i.e., became an immortal), he does not comment negatively. Thus his attitude toward this cult is ambivalent. It also gives explicit approval to the practice of alchemy by Lieh Tzu's teacher. The author assumes that it is important for the Taoist to pursue some sort of breathing exercise, apparently a reference to the internal alchemy of religious Taoism.

4. **Influences on Buddhism and Neo-Confucianism.** Even in later stages when Buddhism recognized the ways it differed from Taoism, it continued to be influenced by the latter. The rise and development of ZEN (Ch'an) Buddhism, during the Sung (960-1279) and Ming (1368-1644) dynasties, was due to the fusion of Buddhism and Taoism. Chinese MAHĀYĀNA Buddhism was speculative and metaphysical in approach, as shown by the Hua-yen and T'ien T'ai (TENDAI) schools, both of which emphasized philosophical studies and the discipline of meditation. Taoism, by emphasizing spontaneity, intuitional understanding, and the acceptance of the natural world as it is, was able to bring Buddhism closer to the matrix of Chinese thought.

The Confucianism of the Sung and Ming periods is called Neo-Confucianism due to the influences of Taoism and Buddhism. (*See* CONFUCIANISM §3.) The pioneer of Neo-Confucianism, Chou Tun-i (1017-73), constructed his cosmology in terms of the Taoist concept of the Nonultimate *(wu-chi)* which is the creative source of the world process. The Neo-Confucian understanding of enlightenment was also influenced by Taoism. It is said that when one is enlightened *(hsing-wu),* he has "no-mind" or "no-feeling," meaning that in encountering an object he can identify the mind or feeling of the object as his own mind or feeling. By not having a particular thought or feeling he is able to identify himself completely with the object encountered. This is nothing other than an application of the Taoist principle of spontaneity or nonpurposiveness.

5. **Taoist studies in contemporary China.** In late 1973, a group of silk manuscripts were discovered in a Han dynasty tomb in central China. The most important of these are closely related to Taoism, including two versions of the Lao Tzu. Version A was recorded prior to 206 B.C. and version B was made during 206-195 B.C. These are the oldest known copies of the Lao Tzu. Neither version is divided by chapters, in contrast to the present text. They are, however, divided into two sections: section 1 is entitled *te* (power) and section 2 is entitled *tao.* This is the reverse order of the present Tao-Te Ching, which begins with the section on *tao* (chs. 1-37) and is followed by the section on *te* (chs. 38-81). We know that the earliest commentary on the Lao Tzu, *Chieh Lao* (exposition of Lao Tzu) by Han Fei-tzu, an outstanding Legalist, follows the same reverse order. This indicates that these two copies of the Lao Tzu probably originated in circles sympathetic to Legalist positions on political and social matters.

Manuscripts found lying on top of version B of the Lao Tzu contain four texts: (1) *Ching-fa* (Tao as law), (2) *Shih-ta ching* (ten great chapters), (3) *Ch'eng* (balance), and (4) *Tao-yüan* (Tao the origin), totaling over eleven thousand words. According to scholars in the People's Republic of China, these four texts are the long lost *Huang-ti szu-ching* (The four scriptures of the Yellow Emperor), works of the Yellow Emperor sect, a Taoist school with strong interest in government and law which was active in the Han dynasty. These texts, except number 4, which is a philosophical description of the Tao, reflect a great interest in political and social matters under the concept of law. However, the ultimate source of law is the Tao. Thus, in contrast to Legalism, the Yellow Emperor sect believed that law has a cosmological origin. This sect disappeared during the period of the Political Disunion when the Chinese intellectuals lost their interest in political affairs. But the discovery of these four texts in the tomb built around 168 B.C. indicates the influence of the sect in this period.

Another interesting discovery is a piece of silk inscribed with figures and notes of explanation. It is called *Tao-yin t'u* (illustration on the induction of breathing exercise) and illustrates how to breathe like such animals or birds as the bear, hawk, and ape. The notes refer to abstinence from eating grains and the nourishment of the self by feeding on the purified breath which one has generated. All these are well known ancient Taoist practices.

The four texts of the Yellow Emperor sect fill a gap in the history of this sect and clarify its relation with Legalism in the Han dynasty, and the illustrations strengthen the belief that there was a close relationship between philosophy and religion in early Taoism.

Bibliography. W. T. Chan, *A Source Book in Chinese Philosophy* (1963); H. G. Creel, *What Is Taoism?* (1970); C. W. Fu, "Creative Hermeneutics: Taoist Metaphysics and Heidegger," *Journal of Chinese Philosophy*, III (1976), 115-43; A. C. Graham, trans., *The Book of Lieh-tzu* (1960); Y. L. Fung, *A History of Chinese Philosophy* (1952-53), I, 170-91, 395-99, II 168-236; Y. H. Jan, "The Silk Manuscripts of Taoism," *T'oung Pao*, LXIII (1978), 65-84; M. Kaltenmark, *Lao Tzu and Taoism*, (1969); R. B. Mather, "The Controversy Over Conformity and Naturalness During the Six Dynasties," *HR*, IX (1967-70), 160-80; J. Needham, *Science and Civilisation in China*, II (1956), 33-164; H. Welch, *Taoism* (1957). D. C. YU

TAOISM, RELIGIOUS dou´ ĭsm, **TAO-CHIAO** dou jē ou´ (Chin.; lit. "the teaching of the way"). One of the four major religious traditions in China (with CONFUCIANISM, BUDDHISM and CHINESE POPULAR RELIGION); a series of organized religious movements that worship the Tao ("the Way") and its emanations and observe magical, physical, alchemical, and meditative practices aiming at immortality.

1. **Characteristics of Taoist religious movements.** Organized Taoist movements have been a continuous and significant part of the religious life of China since the second century A.D. They are typically communal, i.e., they invoke sacred power and recreate cosmic harmony for the sake of blessings to both communities and individuals. They are esoteric, for their full traditions are transmitted only to an initiated priesthood. They are characteristically messianic or eschatological, envisioning an immanent or accomplished end to the old order and the coming of a new age of the rule of Tao. (*See* MILLENARIAN MOVEMENTS.) Their messianism is sometimes "this-worldly," seeking political or military achievement; at other times messianic goals are sought in another world. They are ethical, teaching in simple precepts the demand of Tao for moral self-restraint, humility, and unselfishness. They teach that transgressions are punished, that penitence and confession are efficacious, and that there are terrible consequences of moral depravity that seeks to profit at the expense of others.

Taoist movements generally possess and transmit revealed scriptures and covenants, whose content is concerned as much with ritual and practice as with doctrine. The possibility of revelation is not limited to one episode or historical period, and the movements claim frequent direct communication with the divine powers and have repeatedly announced powerful new revelations that rival, incorporate, or supersede previous ones, creating new scriptures, liturgies, and practices.

2. **Religious Taoism and philosophical Taoism.** *See* TAOISM, PHILOSOPHICAL.

3. **Cosmology.** The first concern of the Taoist religious movements has been the Tao that is the origin of all things. The supreme Tao in its unmanifest state, itself permanent and unchanging, is seen as the first in a series of generating causes. In a typical formulation the Tao unmanifest gives birth to a "breath" (CH'I) in a state of a primordial chaos (*hun-tun* or T'AI-CHI). This in turn gives rise by movement to the active principle yang, and by stillness to the principle of rest, yin (*see* YIN AND YANG). The interaction of these two principles engenders the phenomenal world, which unlike the permanent Tao is relative and changing. The Tao through yin and yang is constantly creating the phenomena of existence, but is not identical with them. Yin and yang act through five fundamental agents—wood, fire, earth, metal, and water (WU-HSING), which in turn interact with each other to produce the ever-changing universe of things. When the original *ch'i* of the primordial chaos is divided into yin and yang, dissolution and death are introduced. The interaction of yin and yang (or, from another point of view, the five agents) can be seen in the progress of the seasons through the cycle of the year. Yin, inactivity (also coldness, wetness, dormancy, darkness), is dominant in the winter months; gradually yang reasserts itself until the flourishing vegetation and heat of spring and summer reflect yang's fullest dominance over yin. As the ripe fruit must fall to the earth, so yang at its extreme must soon give place to yin again. Yet while the seasons move cyclically, the seasons of human life lead only to death.

In the unmanifest world *(hsien-t'ien)* the Tao is in perfect creative harmony; in the manifest world *(hou-t'ien)* the balance is disturbed, and in the microcosm of the human body there are forces (often personified as demons or worms) that tempt one away from integration in the Tao and the full continuance of vitality. But the death-dealing forces in the human microcosm can be reversed, and the sequence of progression from life to death, yang to yin, can move back from death to life, yin to yang, so that humans can reach the eternal state of potentiality which characterizes the newborn child. Thus immortality, not endless preservation of this body, but rather a state of new, transcendent being called the *chen-jen* ("true human"), has been an important goal for many.

The cosmos is populated by a vast array of forces, hierarchically conceived. Highest of course is the unmanifest Tao itself. Next is the primordial chaos, then the Three Officials *(San Kuan)*, or Three Heavenly Worthies *(San-ts'un* or *T'ien-ts'un)*. Below them is a vast bureaucracy of gods, who inhabit nine heavens, followed by demons, humans, animals, ghosts, etc. The same energies of yin and yang and the five agents are at work on all the levels. In some sense the levels correspond and resonate with one another;

each level reiterates the structure and dynamics of the macrocosm, the human being itself being one such microcosm. Just as Three Officials in the macrocosm display the harmony, creativity, and order of the unmanifest Tao, so the Three Officials in the human body can be brought through ritual, meditation, and control of desires to restore harmony among the forces within the body, enabling the human person to encounter and embody the Supreme One (primordial chaotic simplicity) and the unmanifest Tao itself. When this happens, a new immortal being is created and nourished within the human body.

To keep the cosmos in order, the divine emanations of the Tao in the upper levels of the hierarchy rule after the manner of earthly emperors, with ministers, armies, and local bureaucratic functionaries, a bureaucracy modeled originally after the Han Dynasty (206 B.C.—A.D. 220) imperial government.

4. **Functions of the priesthood.** To be ordained to Taoist priesthood is on one level to be taught the arts that lead to personal immortality; on another level it is to take up the duties and powers of a local official in the divine government, communicating the needs and the gratitude of earthly communities to the higher divine officials, expelling and controlling evil spirits, and on occasion summoning other divine officials and armies to aid in the fight. Since the same macrocosmic gods also inhabit the body, the summoning of gods to assist or attend is sometimes conceived of as calling upon external gods; at other times as projecting out into the external world the gods from within oneself.

The same forces that can be conceptualized anthropomorphically as gods can also be considered energies to be refined, harmonized, and combined; no tension is felt in the simultaneous use of political/bureaucratic and physical/alchemical metaphors for the interaction of fundamental cosmic forces. Thus the priest may send "memorials" (government petitions) to the personified Three Officials of the universe as the local bureaucratic representative of divine rule, and, in the same ritual, seek to "refine, purify, and unite" in the center of his bodily microcosm these same three fundamental powers, now conceived of as the life-giving substances of breath, "spirit," and seminal essence. No contradiction is seen between asking the chief cosmic bureaucrats of the Tao to protect individuals and respond to the needs of the community, and at the same time bringing about microcosmic harmony in the body through meditative practice and causing it to radiate out and restore the harmony of the community as macrocosm.

5. **Immortality: the goal.** Texts that predate the earliest organized Taoist movements of the second century A.D. testify to a belief in immortal beings *(hsien)*, often portrayed as birdlike creatures, who can fly long distances and who live on holy mountains or islands for centuries without growing old, sustained only by dew or marvelous fruits. In the third and second centuries B.C. emperors climbed holy mountains to perform sacrifices in the hope of receiving from immortals the elixir of longevity; expeditions were also sent in search of the legendary isles of P'eng-lai, believed to be the immortals' blessed abode. Later many believed that immortals frequently appeared disguised among men to transmit their immortality formulas and magical powers to worthy humans. The idea that humans could become immortals was stoutly defended in the early fourth century A.D. by the aristocrat Ko Hung, whose work *Pao-p'u-tzu* is an encyclopedic collection of paths to immortality in his time. An adept who had succeeded in restoring to the body the pure energies it possessed at its birth or in transmitting it into a purer, lighter substance could "ascend to heaven in broad daylight," perhaps taking with him his entire household, including his dogs and chickens. Women have not been excluded from immortality; HSI WANG MU, prominent in Taoist mythology and folklore, is a queen of the immortals; further, the famous set of EIGHT IMMORTALS includes a woman.

6. **Immortality: the means.** Because Taoists do not conceive of spirit and matter as discontinuous, they have not conceived of immortality as attained by liberating spirit from matter, but rather as conserving, harmonizing, and transforming the body-mind's own energies. The correspondence between the human microcosm and the macrocosm is at the basis of all techniques to "nourish the vital force." Many of the following techniques arose apart from or prior to communal Taoist movements, and continued to be practiced outside these movements as well.

a) Hygienic and dietary disciplines. Taoists believe that the five major organs of the body (lungs, heart, spleen, liver, kidneys) correspond to and partake of the five agents (*see* §3). One means to immortality has been to eat foods and medicinal herbs that contain the energies corresponding in quality to each of the agents. Alternatively, one might abstain from grains, for they feed the "three worms" within the body. Desires are seen as leading to the loss of vital forces; the sense organs (which are orifices through which vital forces may depart) must be closely controlled. Gymnastic exercises assist the circulation of energies through the body and eliminate internal obstructions which can cause disease.

b) Respiratory techniques. Breath *(ch'i),* one of the fundamental energies of life, can be made more nourishing to the body by deep and controlled respiration. The Taoist breathes not only air but also emanations from the five directions, the sun, moon, and stars, and certain times of the day and year. Here again the aim is to bring the microcosm into its true relationship with the macrocosmic forces.

c) Circulation of inner breath. Ordinary respiration came to be replaced for many by the circulation of an "inner breath," a vital energy no longer associated with the air of the atmosphere. Immortality or longevity can be achieved by purifying and refining the "inner breath" and perfecting its circulation.

d) Sexual techniques. Immortality can be sought by nourishing the yang, the force of growth, so as to assure its triumph over the decaying energy of yin. One way for a man to nourish the yang within himself is to retain the seminal essence normally ejaculated in sexual intercourse, and to cause it to rise through the body to "repair the brain." A woman can achieve the same end by the suppression of orgasm. Immortals are often shown with a huge, domed skull, the repository of their yang energies. Others seek to mix the seminal essence with breath *(ch'i)* and spirit in the alchemical furnace of the body to produce the immortal embryo.

e) Alchemical techniques. See ALCHEMY §1.

f) Moral actions and attitudes. Good deeds, humility, impartiality, and control over the passions have all been seen as conserving vitality and restoring personal harmony with the Tao, whose activities display these qualities in the macrocosm.

7. **Organized communal Taoist movements.** The tradition of fully developed Taoist religious movements began in the second century A.D. with the Way of the Great Peace (T'ai-p'ing Tao) and the Way of the Celestial Masters (T'ien-shih Tao), also known as the "Teaching of the Five Pecks of Rice" *(*Wu-Tou Chiao) after a famous tax levied by the organization on its members. Both movements were politically messianic, believing that a new rule of Tao had begun. The T'ai-p'ing Tao (known also as "the Yellow Turbans") led a rebellion against the Han, and at one point controlled eight provinces. The Way of the Celestial Masters organized twenty-four parishes in West China, where they apparently offered political as well as spiritual government. The T'ai-p'ing movement was destroyed when their bid to found a new order was suppressed militarily. The Celestial Master sect, on the other hand, went on to become an established religion; abandoning its exclusive political claims, it was recognized as a legitimate religious movement by the government in A.D. 215.

a) The Celestial Master sect. The Celestial Master sect was founded on a revelation from LAO TZU to one Chang Tao-Ling of the beginning of a new age. According to this revelation, the universe was henceforth to be ruled by the Three Officials. Like the Han imperial officials, they were to be the protectors of justice and order; bad deeds by mortals were to be punished by illness and shortening of life. Confession and repentance would bring about suspended or shortened sentences, with restoration of health. Members received the protection of heavenly generals with "demon armies"; in return they swore allegiance and abided by a number of commandments (seven-year-old children had 5 commandments, married adult couples 72, "teachers" [the first nonlay rank] 180). The Tao-Te Ching, interpreted esoterically, was a central revealed text, and dietetic, respiratory and meditative regimens were practiced, along with sexual rites, with immortality as the goal. The earliest "Yellow Court Canon," a meditative text teaching the visual invocation of gods within the body, is attributed to this sect. "Masters" and "officials" married and lived among the people.

James Ware

This small Taoist temple in Hong Kong features the image of Lao Tzu on a side altar.

b) Mao-shan. During the fourth and fifth centuries two further series of revelations transformed the Taoist movement. The first is known as the Mao-shan revelations, given in visionary visitations to three southern aristocrats by perfected immortals (chief among whom was a woman). The immortals announced that they belonged to a heaven higher in perfection and authority than any previously known; they further predicted a cataclysmic end to the present age and the dawn of a new era; the recipients of the revelations would be spared to become officials in the new divine government. In the meantime the recipients should strive for immortality by practicing the methods also newly revealed. The authentic texts of these revelations were dictated in inspired ecstatic poetry of great literary beauty, and were written in a beautiful handwriting only an immortal could have produced. The liturgies of the Celestial Masters sect were for the most part to continue in the new age, but some of its practices were to be superseded; foremost among these were the sexual rites which had brought Taoists a bad reputation. Possession of a secret text ritually transmitted assured one a place in the new order.

c) Ling-pao. Whereas the mediumistic revelations of Mao-shan were chiefly concerned with eschatology and meditation, the new revelations contained in the Ling-pao literature contributed a new and lasting liturgical tradition, which now overlies and supersedes many of the simpler rites of the Celestial Master sect. The first *Ling-pao Ching* ("Canon of the Sacred Jewel"), believed to have been revealed early in the third century, was written down beginning *ca.* A.D. 397. The Tao is personified in a series of Heavenly Worthies *(T'ien-ts'un),* each representing a different aspect of the Tao and worshiped in a separate liturgy. The rites were called *chai* ("retreat"), from the abstinence with which they began. They lasted a day and a night, or for three, five, or seven days. Rites of the Yellow Register *(Huang-lu),* originally for the benefit of the state, now are primarily directed toward the salvation of the dead, while rites of the Golden Register *(Chin-lu)* benefit the living.

d) Taoism and Buddhism. The Taoists' chief rivals for religious authority were the Buddhists. Although they attacked many Buddhist beliefs and practices, they adopted celibacy, MONASTICISM, and the ideas of rebirth and KARMA.

e) Later developments. Between 1100 and 1400 three developments occurred that have helped shape modern Taoism. The first, the revival of the Celestial Master tradition (also known as the Cheng-i [Orthodox One] tradition), based at Lung-hu Shan in Kiangsi Province, began to establish that sect's present position as the leading arbiter of orthodoxy in Taoism. The second was the rise of a new sect called Shen-hsiao ("Divine Empyrean"), after the new higher heavenly realm and the new age of divine rule that it revealed. The rituals which Shen-hsiao introduced remain among the most popular traditions today. A third group of three new sects that arose in the twelfth century has been compared in purpose and effect within the Taoist movement to the PROTESTANT REFORMATION in European Christianity. They rejected many magical elements—charms, talismans, techniques for achieving immortality—and taught a return to personal cultivation. As Lao Tzu and other early "philosophical Taoists" had done, they stressed humility, altruism, and the renunciation of desires, seeing these as both the means to and the signs of spiritual immortality. The Ch'uan-chen sect, the only one of this group surviving today, has maintained a tradition of personal cultivation (including practices that resemble BUDDHIST MEDITATION) and relatively strict celibate monasticism guided by, among other works, the Tao-Te Ching (*see* LAO TZU).

8. **Taoist scriptures.** The concept of a canon of all Taoist scriptures (Tao Tsang) goes back to the Taoist ritualist and reformer Lu Hsiu-ching (A.D. 406-477). He mentioned 1,228 scriptures, of which 1,090 were known to the world and 138 were "still in heaven," that is, not yet revealed. He divided them into three *tung,* a term whose root meaning is "cave." (Mysterious mountain caves where one could communicate with immortals and await the coming of the new age were important in many Taoist traditions, especially in Mao-shan.) The Mao-shan scriptures were to comprise the first "cave," entitled "Perfection," with Ling-pao scriptures following in the second, entitled "Sublimity." The last apparently was to contain the scriptures of a tradition closely related to the Mao-shan and Ling-pao. About a century later four new sections were added as appendices; these included for the first time the Tao-Te Ching, the T'ai-p'ing Ching (*see* §7), and the texts of the Celestial Master school. The present edition of the canon, which retains traces of this original plan, dates from 1444 with a supplement from 1607, and contains 1,476 titles. Of these only a small number are important in liturgy and self-cultivation today. The canon contains histories, biographies, charms, registers of gods with precise descriptions, alchemical texts, and many other kinds of literature.

9. **Taoism today.** Little is known about the fate of the Taoist tradition in the People's Republic of China. The White Cloud Monastery in Peking housed Taoist monks until the mid-1960s, and the government announced in 1958 that 30,000 Taoist priests were still active. Elsewhere Taoist traditions are alive wherever traditional Chinese culture survives (e.g., Taiwan, Singapore, Indonesia, Thailand, Hong Kong, Hawaii). The strongest Taoist tradition is found in Taiwan, where priests receive ordination from the sixty-fourth Celestial Master, Chang Yüan-hsien, allegedly a descendant of Chang Tao-ling. Taoist priests *(Tao-shih)* today, like the "libationers" of the earliest Celestial Master sect, are married and pass their esoteric knowledge and ordination to one of their sons. Taoist monastic institutions, which were important on the mainland of China until 1949 (due in part to the tax-exempt status given only to celibate religious communities), have never become established in Taiwan.

Taoist priests in Taiwan perform a vast array of ceremonies. Among these are rituals of exorcism and healing for individuals, and great community sacrifices for thanksgiving, for petition for general blessings, for averting calamities, inauguration of temples, ordination of priests, anniversaries (birthdays) of deities, etc. These rituals reflect the influence of all the historical developments mentioned above. In addition to bringing specific blessings, such rituals renew the unity and vitality of the communities and enable priests to attain immortality through the meditations of inner alchemy at their core.

Bibliography. M. Kaltenmark, *Lao tseu et le taoisme* (1965; ET 1969); H. Welch, *Taoism: The Parting of the Way,* rev. ed. (1965); H. Maspero, *le Taoisme et les religions chinoises,* rev. ed. (1971); J. Ware, *Alchemy, Medicine and Religion in the China of A. D. 320: The Nei P'ien of Ko Hung* (1966); M. Saso and D. W. Chappell, eds., *Buddhist and Taoist Studies,* I (1977); M. Saso, *The Teachings of Taoist Master Chuang* (1978) and *Taoism and the Rite of Cosmic Renewal* (1972); M. Porkert, *The Theoretical Foundations of Chinese Medicine* (1974); N. Sivin, "On the Word

'Taoist' as a Source of Perplexity," *HR*, XVII (1978), 303-30; K. M. Schipper, "The Written Memorial in Taoist Ceremonies," in Arthur P. Wolf, ed., *Religion and Ritual in Chinese Society* (1974), and "The Taoist Body," *HR*, XVII (1978), 355-86; M. Strickmann, "The Longest Taoist Scripture," *HR*, XVII (1978), 331-51; M. Stickmann, "The Mao Shan Revelations," *T'oung Pao*, LXIII (1977), 1-64; Anna K. Seidel, *La divinisation de Lao tseu dans le Taoisme des Han* (1969).

M. LEVERING

TAPAS tŭp´ ŭs (H, B & Ja—Skt.; lit. "heat or warmth" [*tap*—"to be heated"]). Penance or physical and mental austerity.

1. Vedic concepts *Tapas* has a metaphysical and cosmological origin according to the VEDAS, where it encompasses the concept of "creative heat." As such, *tapas* is more general than fire and, homologous to the qualities of sound (*see* MANTRA), serves as a link between the physical and spiritual aspects of sacrifice (YAJÑA). In effect, *tapas* ritually duplicates for the ascetic seeker the AGNIHOTRA or daily fire sacrifice performed by the householder. The RIG VEDA mentions *tapas* as a creative force impelling even the creation of the one universal Being (RV 10.127.1.4). It is the essential element in the universe at the cosmic, solar, planetary, and human levels. AGNI, cosmic heat, and Vaiśvānara, the heat in the human heart, are representations of Vedic *tapas*. Just as the gods (e.g., SHIVA) resort to *tapas* or ascetic denial as an aid to creative power and activity, the ascetic seeker likewise utilizes the world-altering heat which penance produces. *Tapas* as the creative and liberating heat of the daily ritual sacrifice and the ascetic's self-mortification was recognized by all the classical systems of Indian philosophy and religion except the materialistic CĀRVĀKAS as an essential aid to the attainment of liberation (MOKṢA).

2. Epic and Purāṇic applications. *Tapas* has been classified in the BHAGAVAD GĪTĀ as (1) virtuous (*sāttva*), (2) ambitious (*rājas*), or (3) perverted (*tāmas*). The first is performed with nonattachment to the act performed (to its good or bad results), the second for personal gain and the attainment of SIDDHIS (extraordinary powers), and the third for acquiring worldly power or gain. There are numerous stories in the PURĀṆAS exemplifying all three types.

King Śivi of Kāśī was tested for his truthfulness and charity by Lord VISHNU and INDRA, who assumed the forms of a dove and a hawk. Śivi had given refuge to the dove, and the hawk demanded the dove's weight of flesh from Śivi's body as ransom for it. The dove became so heavy in the scale that all the flesh cut from the body of Śivi could not balance the scale, and finally Śivi's skeleton jumped onto the scale. At this point, by the power of Lord Vishnu, Śivi was restored to normal health and wholeness. The king's willingness to suffer in order to do his kingly duty (protection) was untainted by self-interest—a mark of virtuous (*sāttva*) *tapas*.

The sage Viśvāmitra wished to attain the status of a Brahmarishi ("priestly sage") in emulation of the Brahmarishi Vasiṣtha, who always addressed him as Rājarishi ("kingly sage"). Viśvāmitra performed extreme penances (*tapas*) and acquired extraordinary powers with which he killed the sons of Vasiṣtha. He came to the house of Vasiṣtha and hid in the dark, ready to smash Vasiṣtha with a huge stone. At that very moment, Vasiṣtha asked his wife to go to Viśvāmitra's house to borrow some salt. His surprised wife asked him how he could urge her to go to the house of his sworn enemy. The sage remarked, "He is not my enemy. Ours is a difference of principles. I call him Rājarishi and he wants me to call him Brahmarishi. I cannot do so, because I feel that he has yet to attain that status." On hearing this, the hiding Viśvāmitra threw away the stone and fell at the feet of Vasiṣtha, who, lifting and embracing him, said, "How are you, Brahmarishi?" Viśvāmitra said, "Why did you not designate me as such before and save the lives of your sons?" Vasiṣtha replied, "At that time you were only Rājarishi and now you have become Brahmarishi." The austerities Viśvāmitra performed due to his desire to be a priest are an example of ambitious (*rājas*) *tapas*.

Stories of the practice of *tāmas* or perverted *tapas* tell of persons of demonic nature like HIRAṆYAKAŚIPU, RĀVAṆA, and KAṂSA who resort to extreme self-mortification only for worldly rule, revenge on an enemy, or wealth. In these cases *tapas* operates as a divine economy of energy wherein austerities produce such "heat" (*tapas*) that a boon or benefit of equal value must be granted (usually by Indra, Shiva, or a god of equal status) regardless of the evil or misguided end sought.

3. *Tapas* in other Indian traditions. *Tapas* as self-discipline is an aid to enlightment for HINDUISM, BUDDHISM, and JAINISM, though each tradition varies in its acceptance of the degree of austerities encouraged. One end of the spectrum is Buddhism's rejection of all extreme penances but encouragement of an austere life-style (one meal a day, sleeping on the ground, etc.). At the other end of the spectrum Jainism gave *tapas* a central place in its theory and practice. Jaina philosophy argues that KARMA is a "material" which attaches itself to the soul (JĪVA) and can be eliminated only by rigorous penance which "burns" it off. Many sects of the sixth century, like the ĀJĪVIKAS, used self-mortification as a primary means of release (*mokṣa*) and set an example the Jainas emulated.

Regardless of the excessiveness or moderation of the ascetic practices permitted or required by all of India's major religious traditions, *tapas* has remained in all of them a primary mark of spiritual attainment.

Bibliography. F. Holck, "Some Observations on the Motives and Purposes of Asceticism in Ancient India," *Études Asiatiques*, XXIII (1969), 45-57; H. Jacobi, *Jaina Sūtras* (1968), pp. 320-24; T. Hopkins, *The Hindu Religious Tradition* (1971), pp. 25-27 and *passim*.

J. C. SHARMA

TARGUM tär´ gŭm (Ju—Heb. & Aram.; lit. "translation, interpretation"). An ARAMAIC interpretive translation of a part of the Hebrew BIBLE. In the last pre-Christian centuries Aramaic was the vernacular of many Jews. In order to make the Hebrew Bible comprehensible when read in the SYNAGOGUE, interpretive translations were offered orally after each line of the Pentateuch and each three lines of the Prophets. (Some find in Neh. 8:8 the biblical paradigm for this.) A wide variety of renderings must have existed, some quite literal and some employing much interpretive MIDRASH, but gradually several relatively fixed traditions seem to have crystallized. The targums thus reflect the ways in which the Bible was understood by the ordinary Jew of early rabbinic times. An interesting theological feature of the targums is their use of circumlocutions such as *shekinah* (presence) and *memra* (word) for the names of God in the Bible; this may reflect a desire to avoid using the name of God and to avoid anthropomorphism in speaking of God.

Four targums to the Pentateuch are extant today. The Targum Onkelos, though probably originating in Palestine, received an "official" redaction in Babylonia and was commonly used in the synagogue service of medieval and modern times. The other three seem to be versions of the Palestinian tradition: Pseudo-Jonathan (falsely ascribed to Jonathan ben Uzziel), Neofiti I (not discovered until 1956), and a "Fragmentary Targum" covering 850 verses of the Pentateuch. These contain much more explicit midrash than Onkelos. The Targum Jonathan on the Prophets holds a middle line between literal translation and interpretation; the targums on the Writings (third section of the Hebrew Bible) show varying degrees of literalness.

A crucial unresolved problem is the dating of the targums. The discovery of targum fragments among the Dead Sea Scrolls proves that written targums did exist in pre-Christian times. Some scholars assert that the Palestinian tradition in particular preserves the targum tradition substantially as it existed in the first century A.D., thus throwing invaluable light on both the language and the religion of earliest CHRISTIANITY (and perhaps JESUS himself) as well as contemporary Judaism. Others point out that the extant targums result from a process of re-editing not completed until the fifth or even the seventh century; thus there is no way to know with certainty which parts of the extant targums do in fact preserve authentic early material. The many parallels between the targums and rabbinic midrash may be used to argue the priority of either source or the existence of an unknown source in the oral tradition upon which both drew.

Bibliography. J. Bowker, *The Targums and Rabbinic Literature* (1969); A. Diez-Macho, *Neophyti I* (1968-74) with English trans.; M. McNamara, *The NT and the Palestinian Targum to the Pentateuch* (1966); *Targum and Testament* (1972); G. Vermes, *Scripture and Tradition in Judaism* (2nd ed., 1973); B. Grossfeld, *A Bibliography of Targumic Literature* (1972; see later supplements). I. CHERNUS

ṬARĪQA tär ē´ kä (I—Arab.; lit. "path, way"). A widely used technical term referring to true Islam, to the SUFI tradition, and to individual Sufi brotherhoods. In the first sense, *ṭarīqa* is equivalent to the phrase "the straight path" in the opening chapter (Sūrat al-FĀTIHA) of the QUR'ĀN. Just as unbelief (KUFR) and polytheism (SHIRK) characterize infidels, i.e., deviants from the straight path, so faith in God and total reliance on his will characterize the traveler on the straight path, i.e., the true Muslim. In handbooks of Sufi theorists, increasingly popular from the eleventh century on, *ṭarīqa* acquired a second, more specific denotation of an intermediate stage leading from observance of the law (SHARIA) to realization of the truth. Much of the controversy surrounding Sufism concerns the relationship of the path to the law. Itinerant, antinomian Muslims, such as the *qalandar,* dispensed with the law; strict 'ULAMĀ' (the learned functionaries of Islam) denied the validity of the way. Moderate Sufis try to adhere to the requirements of both. Many medieval theorists stressed the complementarity of the outer (law) and the inner (truth), assuming the path as an implicit link between them. The fourteenth century master Sharaf-al-Manerī wrote, "The Law is like the body, Truth like the soul. Just as a man cannot live without either body or soul, so he cannot believe unless he adheres to both the Law and the Truth." Others have grafted truth to law by extending the mystic path into a multidirectional quest. The journey *to* God is followed by a journey *into* God, which, however, then leads to a journey *from* God back to the phenomenal world. The paradigm for this spiritual ascent and descent is the MI'RĀJ or ascension of the Prophet MUHAMMAD, whom Sufis extol not only as the founder of Islam but also as the model Sufi.

By the twelfth and thirteenth centuries the way became channeled into organized brotherhoods, each with hierarchical lines of authority emanating from a single, all-powerful SHAIKH. These brotherhoods or *ṭarīqas* (also *silsilas*) exhibited enormous variety. Some were pan-Islamic in scope and activity; others were solely regional. Some were politically influential; others were distrustful of any governmental connection. Collectively, the brotherhoods helped to extend the perimeters of the Muslim world. Without them Sufism would have been limited to literary artifacts and ecstatic personalities of the early medieval period.

Bibliography. J. A. Subhan, *Sufism: Its Saints and Shrines* (1960), pp. 67-102; A. Schimmel, *Mystical Dimensions of Islam* (1975), pp. 98-186. B. LAWRENCE

TASBĪḤ täs bē´ (I—Arab.; lit. "praising or glorifying [God]"). The specific act of praising God (*see* ALLAH) through use of a ROSARY. No QUR'ĀNIC verse or prophetic dictum (*see* ḤADĪTH) legitimates the use of prayer beads, yet Muslims have relied on the *tasbīḥ* since the ninth century, either to recollect the "beautiful names of God" *(al-asmā' al-ḥusnā)* or to count invocatory phrases repeated time and again in ceremonial remembrance (Dhikr). Since true remembrance is said to go beyond counting, however, some have argued that recourse to the *tasbīḥ* ought to be interpreted as spiritual immaturity. So common has their use become among both Shi'ite and Sunni Muslims that the beads almost seem to function as an Islamic variant of worry beads.

Bibliography. C. A. Herklots, *Islam in India* (1921), pp. 149-50; A. Schimmel, *Mystical Dimensions of Islam* (1975), pp. 169-79.

B. Lawrence

TAT TVAM ASI tŭt´ tvŭm´ ŭ sē´ (H—Skt.; lit. "that thou art"). First appeared in the Chāndogya Upaniṣad. One of the best-known maxims of Hindu scripture, it reminds the speaker that "thou," the individual soul or Atman, and "that," the Universal Soul or Brahman, are one and the same.

J. Bare

TATHĀGATA tŭ tä´ gŭ tŭ (B—Skt.; probable meaning "thus gone," that is, one who has traversed the road to enlightenment). A term which Gautama the Buddha evidently preferred above all others to refer to himself. In the earliest *gāthās* (psalms), however, the word is not used of the Buddha. A possible translation according to the usage of the Pali texts is "truth-finder," or "one who leads others by the truth." "One who has attained wisdom," and "true or perfect human being," may be the meaning in certain cases. The term is also used as an adjective applied to each of the Three Jewels (Triratna) of the Buddhist religious life: the Buddha, Dharma, Saṅgha. Here the meaning is evidently that of "perfect," even though the texts of early Buddhism do not ascribe moral perfection to members of the monastic order, and there is some evidence that the Buddha himself was not regarded by his disciples as completely without fault (Dīgha Nikāya II, 139).

If the Buddha actually used the term in referring to himself, he probably intended to indicate his having attained knowledge of and relationship with ultimate Reality (Tathatā, or suchness). In the earlier texts the Buddha consistently manifests a distinct reserve with reference to the meaning and role of his own person (Saṃyutta Nikāya III, 121). He apparently had, however, no doubts regarding the truth of the reality which he had experienced and taught (Dīgha Nikāya I, 12-46).

The term "Tathāgata" was also used to denote the state of "being" that is otherwise described as Nirvana. By implication, such a condition has a continuity which transcends physical death. The texts affirm that terminology derived from the transitory phenomena of life in this world is not adequate to denote the nature of a Tathāgata's life after physical dissolution. But this fact was not intended to indicate annihilation of the higher self; that was termed an "evil heresy" (Saṃyutta Nikāya III, 109-116).

Bibliography. Hajime Nakamura, *Shin Bukkyō Jiten* (1962), pp. 412-13; Vinaya-Piṭaka, Mahāvagga I, 22-24.

R. H. Drummond

TATHATĀ tŭt´ ŭ tä (B—Skt.; lit. "in-that-way-ness," "suchness," "thusness") **CHEN-JU** jŭn rū (B—Chin.) **SHINNYO** shĭn´ yō (B—Jap.). The Mahāyāna doctrine of truth or reality as experienced without attachment or duality by the enlightened mind; knowing the thing as it is through the intuitive wisdom (Prajñā) of Buddha-mind; Śūnyatā ("emptiness") as viewed from the positive perspective; the absolute in the relative, perfect enlightenment in ordinary daily activities.

1. Related terms. The Buddha is often referred to as the Tathāgata, a title employing *tathā* ("such") and the verb "to come" or "to go." The Diamond Sūtra affirms that "Tathāgata is synonymous with *tathatā*," and Tathāgata has been interpreted as "one who has arrived at suchness."

Tathatā sometimes occurs with the prefix *bhuta,* giving the emphatic sense "true suchness." The term *Tathāgatagarba* ("womb of the thus-come") can be a synonym for Ālayavijñāna ("storehouse consciousness") of Yogācāra, and both can be synonyms for suchness. As a fundamental term for the absolute, the underlying oneness of the Mahāyāna quest, suchness can serve as a synonym for Dharmakāya, Dharmadhātu, śūnyatā, Satori, and Nirvana.

2. Mahāyānist texts. The Prajñāpāramitā Sūtras emphasize the wisdom of śūnyatā and identify this emptiness with suchness. Suchness is emptiness, emptiness is suchness. The Laṅkāvatāra Sūtra, in its teaching of eight consciousnesses, describes the eighth as *ālayavijñāna* ("storehouse consciousness"), synonymous with *Tathāgatagarba* ("womb of the thus-come"). Activity of these consciousnesses results in five dharmas (knowledge-states), the fifth of which is suchness, transcending the categories of being and nonbeing. "The Awakening of Faith in the Mahāyāna" contains an extended discussion of "The Greatness of the Attributes of Suchness." It is suchness that permeates into ignorance, causing beings to aspire to Nirvana. Suchness is beyond analysis, as it has no parts, is "of one flavor." Buddhas and all sentient beings are "identical in suchness."

3. Suchness and śūnyatā. Suchness and śūnyatā ("emptiness") are two perspectives on the same truth, but śūnyatā has been by far the more popular expression in the Mahāyāna. Suchness, as the more positive expression, may have been viewed as too susceptible to interpretation in terms of ego and substantiality, while emptiness better suggested absence of all graspable attributes.

4. Fundamental to Zen. Suchness, as the more positive statement of the truth of śūnyatā, finally came to play a fundamental role in Zen. Transmitted through the Prajñāparamitā Sūtras and the Laṅkāvatāra Sūtra, suchness became the affirmation of "everyday-mindedness" that revealed the identity of samsara and Nirvana, Buddha-mind and ordinary-mind. Suchness expressed Zen's discovery of sudden and perfect enlightenment in the simplest acts of daily living, as in Layman P'ang's famous verse:

My supernatural power and miraculous acts—
Drawing water and carrying firewood.

Bibliography. D. T. Suzuki, *Essays in Zen Buddhism,* Third Series (1953); Y. Hakeda, trans., *The Awakening of Faith* (1967).

C. W. EDWARDS

TAWHĪD tou hēd′ (I—Arab.; lit. "union"). A technical term equivalent to *īmān,* "faith," frequently contrasted with KUFR, "disbelief." It underscores Muslim belief in the absolute, unqualified oneness of God. (*See* ALLAH.) The creedal *locus classicus* for *tawhīd* is the first half of the SHAHĀDA or Muslim profession of faith: "There is no god but God." From the time of JUNAYD, SUFIS have maintained that there are three levels at which Muslims understand and apply *tawhīd:* 1) the common people are content to utter the words of the *shahāda* and fulfill the external demands of faith; 2) the elite, whose numbers include an occasional scholar, along with all Sufi initiates, recognize the imperative to internalize *tawhīd* and to eliminate every action, thought, or feeling that detracts from God; 3) the elite of the elite, who are Sufi SHAIKHS, actually experience annihilation *(fanā')* of everything but God from their minds and bodies, from their unconscious as well as their conscious states. What remains for them is permanence *(baqā'),* though there has been extensive controversy over whether there is a human (and therefore finite) residue in their experience of *baqā',* and also an obligation to adhere to the norms of Muslim law (SHARIA). How to define *tawhīd* is the central issue in the debate over unity of being versus unity of witness, stemming from the writings of Muhyī 'd-dīn IBN 'ARABĪ.

Bibliography. T. Burckhardt, *An Introduction to Sufi Doctrine* (1959), pp. 57-63; M. N. Siddiqi, "*Tawhīd:* The Concept and the Process," in K. Ahmad and Z. I. Ansari, eds., *Islamic Perspectives* (1979), pp. 17-33.

B. LAWRENCE

TAYLOR, JEREMY (Ch; 1613-1667). English theologian, moralist, and spiritual writer, appointed Bishop of Down and Connor in 1661. His best known works are *Liberty of Prophesying,* a plea for tolerance; *Ductor dubitantium,* a manual for confessors; and *Holy Living* and *Holy Dying,* devotions of lasting influence.

M. H. SHEPHERD, JR.

TE DEUM tā dē′ oom (Ch—Lat.; "Thee, O God"). First words of an ancient hymn to the TRINITY traditionally ascribed to Ambrose (and AUGUSTINE). From the sixth century it has been used in the Western morning office, and commonly used on festal occasions as a hymn of thanksgiving.

R. A. GREER

TEA CEREMONY. The ceremonial art of preparing and drinking tea, which in Japan was practiced as an aesthetic and religious discipline. Japanese terms for this ceremony are *cha no yū* (lit. "hot water for tea) or *chadō* (lit. "tea-way"). It became so highly formalized that in Western languages it is sometimes referred to as the "tea cult" or as "teaism."

The cultivation and drinking of tea began in ancient China, where it was prepared in various forms and often used for medicinal purposes. It became popular as a beverage for social meetings, and as early as the eighth century A.D. was extolled by Lu Yü in his *Classic of Tea* (Chin. *Ch'a Ching),* which details the utensils, brewing, and drinking of tea as a social art form. Later, Buddhist priests of the ZEN school drank tea as a means of staying awake during meditation.

Tea was imported to Japan and used especially at the court from the eighth century A.D. onward, but Japanese importation of tea seeds and cultivation of the plant is usually attributed to Eisai (1141-1215), a Japanese Buddhist priest and founder of the Rinzai branch of Zen Buddhism in Japan; Eisai is also credited with writing the first Japanese treatise on tea, *Drink Tea and Prolong Life (Kissa yōjō ki).* Zen influence on the tea ceremony is noticeable, especially in Zen's emphasis on meditation in order to achieve personal peace and oneness with nature; but these features are found throughout much of Japanese culture, especially in the artistic disciplines or "ways."

From the KAMAKURA period (1185-1333) the Chinese technique of preparing this beverage from powdered tea leaves became the basis for the distinctively Japanese tea ceremony. Through the ages the refinement of the ceremony resulted in a prizing of simplicity both in the performance of the ceremony and in the hearts of the participants. However, this simplicity exists within a highly refined setting—often in a special tea hut of rustic design, within a carefully laid out garden. The various utensils, especially the wide bowls in which the tea is served, are themselves exquisite works of art, as are the one or two other art objects displayed—a wall hanging or a flower arrangement. The few guests in the small hut listen to the boiling of the tea water in an iron kettle over a charcoal brazier, while the tea master carefully lays out the utensils and gracefully follows the steps of whipping the powdered tea and hot water into the beverage.

Performing the ceremony and drinking the tea are only the externals of a complex spiritual process which has as its goal communing with nature and achieving inner peace. Sen Rikyū (1522-91) is one of the great masters who codified the tea ceremony, which is handed down from master to pupil in several traditions or "schools."

H. B. EARHART

TEFILLIN tə fē lēn′ (Ju—Aram.; commonly translated as "phylacteries," from the Greek word for "amulet"). The pair of black leather cases containing scriptural passages bound on the head and left arm by adult (thirteen and over) Jewish men during the morning service on all days of the year except the SABBATH and the biblically prescribed holy days. The commandment to wear the tefillin is based on four biblical passages (Exod. 13:1-10, 11-16; Deut. 6:4-9; 11:13-21), within each of which there is a reference to having the words of the TORAH as "a sign upon your hand and as a memorial between your eyes." This was taken literally in postbiblical times as an actual commandment, and the portions of the Torah selected for its fulfillment were these four passages.

The religious significance of wearing the tefillin is summarized by Maimonides: "The holiness of tefillin is great, for as long as the tefillin are on the head and arm of a man, he is humble and Godfearing, avoids levity and idle talk, and does not conceive evil thoughts, but turns his heart only to words of truth and justice" (*Hilkhot Tefillin,* 4).

Bibliography. A. Cowen, *Tefillin* (1960); Maimonides, *Seven Minor Treatises,* M. Higger, ed. and trans. (1930), pp. 24-30.

B. MARTIN

TEILHARD DE CHARDIN, PIERRE tā´ yâr də shâr dăn´ (Ch; 1881-1955). French priest who interpreted the universe as an evolutionary process in which the divine unfolds. His vision influences religious humanists, the rediscovery of nature among Protestants, and the reinterpretation of natural law among Roman Catholics. D. F. OTTATI

TEMPLARS (Ch). The Poor Knights of Christ and the Temple of Solomon; a military RELIGIOUS ORDER, originally housed near Solomon's Temple, founded in 1119 by Hugh de Payens, who vowed to protect pilgrims en route from the coast to JERUSALEM. The order received vast holdings and established banking centers to support its enlarged purpose of defending the Holy Land. *See* PILGRIMAGE; CRUSADES.

H. L. BOND

TEN COMMANDMENTS (Ju & Ch). The ten "words" which, according to Exod. 34:28 (cf. Deut. 4:13; 10:4), MOSES was commanded to write on two stone tablets. Deut. 5:22 indicates the ten words are found in Deut. 5:7-21. Tradition also identifies Exod. 20:3-17 as the source, and this text is the usual form in which the commandments are known.

The significance of the Ten Commandments for the biblical tradition and Western culture in general can scarcely be exaggerated. These words embody ethical and social injunctions which subsequent legislation has sought to implement.

The commandments are numbered according to two traditions. The ROMAN CATHOLIC and LUTHERAN CHURCHES, following Clement of Alexandria, Origen, and AUGUSTINE, combine the commandment prohibiting the worship of other gods with that forbidding the making of images, but treat the coveting of the neighbor's wife and his house as two. The TALMUD, PHILO, the Eastern ORTHODOX, and REFORMED CHURCHES treat the injunction on coveting as one commandment, while separating the worship of other gods from the making of images.

The commandments dealing with relations to God prohibit (1) worshiping any god other than YAHWEH, (2) making, worshiping or serving images of any kind, (3) dishonoring the name of Yahweh, and (4) labor on the SABBATH. Those involving human relations begin by emphasizing children's obligations to parents. This is followed by prohibitions against killing, adultery, stealing, bearing false witness, and coveting a neighbor's wife and house.

Bibliography. E. Nielsen, *The Ten Commandments in New Perspective* (1968); J.J. Stamm and M.E. Andrews, *The Ten Commandments in Recent Research* (1967).

M. G. ROGERS

TENCHI KANE NO KAMI tĕn chē kä´ nē nō kä´ mē (Sh—Jap.). The name given by KAWATE BUNJIRO, founder of KONKŌ-KYŌ, to the deity who commissioned him. The name is rendered officially as "The Parent God of the Universe." There is an evident historical association between this deity and the demonic Shintō KAMI Konjin, but the benevolence and universality of Tenchi Kane no Kami represent both the transcending and the repudiation of that association. H. N. MCFARLAND

TENDAI tĕn dī (B—Jap.) **T'IEN-T'AI** tyĕn tī (B—Chin.). An academic school of Buddhism organized in sixth century China by CHIH-I on T'ien-t'ai Shan ("Heavenly Terrace Mountain") and carried to Mount Hiei in Japan by the Japanese monk Saichō in the early ninth century.

1. **Nature of Tendai.** Sometimes called the Lotus School, Tendai developed as a distinctly Chinese approach to the enormous variety of Indian Buddhist SŪTRAS available in Chinese translation by the sixth century. Chih-i sought a comprehensive synthesis of the diverse teachings by arranging them chronologically into five periods of the Buddha's ministry, four methods of teaching, and four modes of doctrine. Though eclectic in approach, Chih-i placed the LOTUS SŪTRA at the apex of the Buddha's teaching, emphasized a synthesis of phenomenon and noumenon in his exposition of "threefold truth," and elaborated a doctrine of interdependence in "three thousand realms in an instant of consciousness." All this was included in a comprehensive approach which united the practice of meditation and intellectual insight as "the two wings of a bird." These emphases were to influence PURE LAND SECTS and ZEN on the one hand, and Hua-yen (Kegon; *see* NARA BUDDHISM §3) and Neo-Confucianism on the other (*see* CONFUCIANISM §3).

2. **Background.** From the time of An Shih-kao in the second century to KUMĀRAJĪVA in the fifth, large numbers of HĪNAYĀNA and MAHĀYĀNA sūtras represent-

ing conflicting teachings were translated into Chinese. Taking these sūtras as literal sermons of the earthly BUDDHA, Chinese scholars sought to make sense of the inconsistencies through *p'an chiao,* "dividing the teachings" into categories according to some principle.

3. **Founding.** The founding and organization of Tendai are generally attributed to Chih-i (538-597), though his teacher Hui-ssŭ (515-577) is sometimes designated founder, and Hui-ssŭ's teacher, Hui-wen (active *ca.* 550), has been credited with certain of its doctrines. Little is known of Hui-wen, though he may be responsible for the formulation of the "threefold truth" based on his study of the *Treatise on the Middle Doctrine* of the Three-Treatise School. His disciple, Hui-ssŭ, is said to have been a meditation master in north China, to have obtained the Dharma-Lotus SAMĀDHI through concentration on the Lotus Sūtra, and to have received guidance through a vision of MAITREYA.

While Hui-ssŭ was preaching in south China, Chih-i (or Chih-k'ai), the "Great Master of Tendai," became his disciple and attained *samādhi* while studying the Lotus Sūtra. After eight years at the Ch'en dynasty capital, Chih-i withdrew to Mount T'ien-t'ai, gathered disciples, was honored by Ch'en and Sui emperors, and received the title "Man of Wisdom" *(chih-che).* His disciple Kuan-ting (561-632) recorded his lectures, and from these derive the "Three Great Works" of Tendai: *Profound Meaning of the Lotus Sūtra, Commentary on the Lotus Sūtra,* and *Great Concentration and Insight.*

4. **Five periods and eight teachings.** Chih-i was a brilliant scholar with a phenomenal grasp of the Buddhist canon. Utilizing the scriptural affirmation that the Buddha suited his message to his hearer's capacity through "skillful means," Chih-i arranged the sūtras into five chronological periods. The first period was the preaching of the Avataṁsaka Sūtra during the three weeks immediately following enlightenment. Realizing that few understood this profound teaching, the Buddha utilized a second period of twelve years, preaching the elementary doctrines of the ĀGAMAS, or Hīnayāna scriptures, the "period of the inducement." The third period, lasting eight years, compared the Mahāyāna doctrine with the Hīnayāna in order to destroy the pride of those satisfied with the Hīnayāna ideal, and hence the name "period of rebuke." The fourth period, the final eight years of the Buddha's life, was devoted to the mature teachings, the Lotus Sūtra, harmonizing all previous approaches in one vehicle of universal Buddhahood.

But Chih-i realized that the Buddha's audiences were mixed, and therefore more than one method of teaching and mode of doctrine could have been used at the same time. These he called the "eight teachings," including sudden, gradual, secret, and indeterminate methods, and four doctrines, including the Hīnayāna, that common to Hīnayāna and Mahāyāna, that special to BODHISATTVAS, and the round or perfect doctrine of the Lotus Sūtra's middle path.

5. **The threefold truth.** Central to Tendai doctrine is the "perfectly harmonious threefold truth" of the Empty, the Temporary, and the Middle. The first truth is that all things (*dharmas*) are empty of self-nature, for they depend on causes. The second truth is that all things are produced by causes, and so do have temporary existence. The third truth is that all things are thereby both empty and temporary, the truth of the Middle. This threefold truth is in reality one, affirming that emptiness (ŚŪNYATĀ) and this phenomenal world, universality and particularity, are identical. Buddha-nature must therefore be in all beings, leading us to the Tendai doctrine of universal salvation.

6. **Three thousand realms in an instant.** Threefold truth leads to the further affirmation that all levels of existence so interpenetrate that they are immanent in every instant of thought. Tendai counts three thousand realms of existence in this universe, for there are the ten realms consisting of Buddha, bodhisattva, Pratyeka Buddha (*see* BUDDHA, GENERAL CONCEPTS OF), śrāvaka, DEVA, demon, humans, hungry ghosts (*see* PRETA), beasts, and the depraved, and each of these contains the other nine, thus giving one hundred realms. Each of the one hundred realms has the ten features of thusness (*see* TATHATĀ), including form, nature, substance, energy, activity, condition, effect, reward, cause, and ultimate state, yielding one thousand realms. Each of these one thousand is divided into living beings, the five aggregates (SKANDHAS), and space, totaling three thousand realms. In the phrase *i-nien-san-ch'ien* ("three thousand realms in an instant of thought") Tendai affirms that all phenomena interpenetrate, and each and every thing in the universe manifests Buddha-mind in its totality.

7. **Concentration and insight.** Tendai's impressive harmonization of Buddhist doctrines and approaches includes a synthesis of the southern Chinese emphasis upon scholarship and the northern Chinese focus upon Buddhist practice. Hui-ssŭ has been credited with the work *The Method of Concentration and Insight,* and one of the "Three Great Works" based on Chih-i's lectures was entitled *Great Concentration and Insight.* Concentration *(chih)* brings realization of the emptiness of all things. Insight *(kuan)* brings awareness that all things are not only empty but also have temporary existence. Cultivation of mind through meditative practice became an important part of the Mount T'ien-t'ai discipline, an emphasis that continued on Mount Hiei in Japan and blossomed in the later meditative schools of Buddhism.

8. **Tendai in Japan.** Japan received Buddhism through Korea by the end of the sixth century, Chinese Buddhist sects were imported throughout the seventh century, and powerful sectarian temples influenced the government at Nara during the eighth

century (*See* NARA BUDDHISM). In 794, in part to escape such influence, the capital was moved to Heian (Kyoto), and it is then that Tendai became a major religious factor in Japan.

In 788 a young monk named Saichō (DENGYŌ DAISHI; 766-822) had established a small temple northeast of Kyoto on Mount Hiei. When the capital was moved to Kyoto, Emperor Kammu commissioned Saichō to study in China and return with a form of Buddhism suitable to the new location. Saichō studied Tendai in China during the year 804 and, upon returning to Japan, introduced it at his temple, Enryakuji, on Mount Hiei. With the emperor's support, he ordained a hundred disciples in 807. Maintaining a strict discipline on Hiei, his monks lived in seclusion for twelve years of study and meditation. The nature of Tendai remained a broad synthesis, and Saichō himself introduced elements of the popular esoteric Buddhism, SHINGON, which was taught by his contemporary Kūkai on Mount Kōya. Later, such esoteric practices came to dominate Tendai. Further synthesis occurred when attempts were made, under the name *ichijitsu Shintō* ("SHINTŌ of one truth"), to include Shintō beliefs and practices in Tendai.

Following Saichō, Tendai esoteric practices multiplied. Under Ennin (794-864) the study of MANDALA, the performance of *kanjō* (anointing ceremonies), and NEMBUTSU, calling upon AMIDA Buddha, were instituted. In the tenth century, succession disputes between Tendai monks of the line of Ennin and Enchin (814-891) led to opposing Tendai centers at Mount Hiei, the *sammon* ("Mountain Order") and at Miidera, the *jimon* ("Church Order"). Warrior monks (*sōhei*) were employed in such disputes, and Tendai leaders began to hire mercenary armies who threatened rivals and even marched on the capital to enforce monastic demands. Centuries later, in 1571, Shōgun Nobunaga ended this Buddhist militancy by burning the temples on Mount Hiei and destroying the monastic communities.

Great changes in Japanese society, particularly from the KAMAKURA period (1185-1333), led to the origin within Tendai of popularizing movements which contributed a variety of vital new sects to Japanese Buddhism. Tendai's synthesis had grown so broad that any attempt to master the whole had become virtually impossible. Attempts were therefore made to isolate one focal emphasis. Further, the growing power of the provinces, small landowners, and the samurai led to the search for pious practices within the competence of all believers.

HŌNEN (1133-1212), founder of the Jōdo-shū (Pure Land sect), preached Amidism within Tendai until driven into exile by more conservative monks. SHINRAN (1173-1262) likewise studied Tendai at Hiei before founding Jōdo Shin-shū (Pure Land True sect), and NICHIREN (1222-82) studied at Hiei, where he focused upon Chih-i's affirmation of the Lotus Sūtra as apex of the Buddha's teaching. In quite another direction it is noteworthy that both Eisai (1141-1215), founder of Japanese Rinzai Zen, and DŌGEN (1200-1253), founder of Japanese Sōtō Zen, were trained in Tendai on Mount Hiei.

9. The contemporary scene. Buddhism in modern China has been largely eclectic, and so Tendai has continued to play a role, often in concert with Ch'an (Zen) practices. T'en-hsü, who founded several monasteries from 1921 to 1932, belonged to the Tendai sect by Dharma lineage, and Ch'an by tonsure. The situation of Tendai, as of Buddhism generally under the communist government, is problematic, though visiting Japanese Buddhists have gone on pilgrimage in recent years to do homage to the mummified body of Chih-i on Mount T'ien-t'ai and have been impressed by the care given the site.

In modern Japan the "new religions," Jōdo, Jōdo Shin-shū, Nichiren sects, and Zen sects far outnumber Tendai in adherents, though mergers of Tendai groups have occurred with hope for future revivals (*see* JAPANESE RELIGION §4). In both China and Japan the chief contribution of Tendai has been its impressive synthesis of Buddhist doctrines and its ability to provide the impetus for new and vital sects and movements.

Bibliography. K. Chen, *Buddhism in China* (1964); E. D. Saunders, *Buddhism in Japan* (1964); H. Dumoulin, ed. *Buddhism in the Modern World* (1976).

C. W. EDWARDS

TEṄGALAI tĕn gŭ lā (H—Tamil & Skt.; lit. "southern or Tamil literature and culture" [Tamil *teṉ*, "southern"; Skt. *kalā*, "art, culture, learning"]). The "Southern School," a ŚRĪ VAIṢṆAVA subsect stressing the TAMIL hymns of the ĀḺVĀRS and holding "surrender" (*prapatti*) and absolute dependence upon VISHNU's grace to be the only efficacious means of liberation (*see* VAḌAGALAI; VEDĀNTA §3).

W. G. NEEVEL

TENRI-KYŌ tĕn rē kyō´ (Sh—Jap.; lit. "the religion [teaching] of heavenly wisdom [reason]"). An independent religion with SHINTŌ associations. Arising as a faith-healing cult in a rural setting during the mid-nineteenth century, it has become a stable religion, influential throughout Japan and among Japanese communities abroad. It is in certain respects the prototype of the "new religions" of modern Japan. (*See* KONKŌ-KYŌ; PL KYŌDAN; SEICHŌ NO IE.)

1. History. Tenri-kyō had its beginning in the early nineteenth century, when conditions in rural Japan were extremely oppressive, provoking numerous peasant uprisings. In part Tenri-kyō was a religious alternative to riot, providing a vision of a happy life on earth through religious faith and practice. The movement was begun by a peasant woman, NAKAYAMA MIKI (1798-1887), who herself experienced much deprivation and suffering.

In 1838, when Miki was forty-one, she was asked to serve as a medium assisting an exorcist in his efforts to cure her ailing family members. During the ritual, she slipped into a trance and a deity (KAMI) began to speak through her lips. Identifying himself as "the true and original God," he announced his intention to take Miki's body and mind as his shrine and to save the world through her. Though the family at first demurred, after three days (during which Miki remained in a trance) they acceded to the deity's demands; whereupon all were healed of their various ills and Miki was released from her trance. For the next fifteen years Miki's life as the shrine of a great deity (identified as Tenri-O-no-Mikoto) was erratic and puzzling. She gave away most of her family's possessions. Many thought her to be demented. Gradually, however, a few devotees attached themselves to her. She acquired a widespread reputation as a healer, especially adept in curing smallpox and assuring painless childbirth. She devised and taught an ingenious, symbolic dance, which was to become the basis of Tenri-kyō ritual. By 1863 a movement had formed, and in that year a small shrine was built. In that year also Miki was joined by Iburi Izo, a carpenter whose wife had been miraculously healed. Known subsequently as Master Iburi, he was to become Miki's successor and the author of a substantial body of canonical writings.

During most of the remaining twenty-four years of Miki's life the movement which she headed grew rapidly, but under the new political regime of the MEIJI period (1868-1912) its status was for years indeterminate and it encountered considerable opposition and persecution. Though in 1867 the movement had been approved under Shintō auspices, Miki subsequently had to face both Shintō and Buddhist inquisitors, and she was frequently arrested and jailed for her activities.

2. **Scriptures.** The Tenri-kyō canon is composed of three writings: (1) the *Mikagura Uta* (lit. "sacred dance songs"), composed by Miki between 1866 and 1875 to be sung or chanted in association with the sacred dance; (2) the *Ofudesaki* (lit. "tip of the writing brush"), written by Miki between 1869 and 1882 to record the divine revelations concerning the basic aspects of Tenri-kyō doctrine, worship, and life; and (3) the *Osashizu* (lit. "directions," "instructions"), a voluminous work written by Master Iburi between 1887 and 1907, recording responses to specific issues which had been brought to Miki and himself. Reflecting the limited formal education of both authors, each of these works was written in a simple phonetic script *(hiragana)* and includes no Chinese characters.

3. **Organization.** Near the old capital Nara, on the Nakayama family land, the headquarters of Tenri-kyō have been built, and around them has grown a city called Tenri. It is a most impressive installation, including a great worship hall, a sanctuary of the founder, and numerous other buildings housing offices, a school system, a university, a library, an ethnological museum, dormitories, a modern hospital, and other facilities. Much of the work of construction and maintenance is supplied by volunteer laborers.

At the head is the *Shimbashira* (patriarch; lit. "main pillar"), the first of whom was Miki's grandson. He has been succeeded by others in the Nakayama family line.

4. **Relation to Shintō.** As a religion sprung from the folk faith of rural Japan, Tenri-kyō manifests some of the characteristics of Shintō, such as certain altar furnishings, food offerings, vestments, and architectural details. For a short time during the life of the founder the movement had official Shintō sanction, and for some years prior to the end of World War II in 1945 it was registered arbitrarily as one of the thirteen Shintō sects recognized as legitimate by the government. Since 1945, however, Tenri-kyō has disavowed its identity as a sect of Shintō.

5. **Doctrine.** Having been in existence for well over a century, Tenri-kyō has developed some comprehensive doctrinal statements; however, the basic elements of belief can be succinctly stated. The deity worshiped in Tenri-kyō has the name Tenri-O-no-Mikoto but is most often referred to as *Oyagami* (lit. "God the parent"). He is the creator and sustainer of all things. Human beings receive from him on loan their bodies and all other "possessions." Failure to understand this indebtedness and their dependence on God results in the accumulation of dust *(hokori)* on their souls. Only as this dust is swept away through the faith and practice revealed through Miki can salvation be achieved, that is, joyous life *(yokigurashi)* on earth.

6. **Worship.** Worship is central in Tenri-kyō both in the local churches and in the main sanctuary at Tenri. In the latter, services are performed twice a day, at sunrise and at sunset. Each service is led by the Shimbashira and includes as its central act a dance of creation performed by five men and five women in a recessed area below floor level and at the point believed to be the center of the universe. On the twenty-sixth day of each month a special service is held, and three times during the year there are grand festivals: the Ascension of the Founder on January 26; the Birthday of the Founder on April 18; the Founding of Tenri-kyō on October 26.

Bibliography. R. S. Ellwood, Jr., *The Eagle and the Rising Sun* (1974); C. B. Offner and H. Van Straelen, *Modern Japanese Religions* (1963); H. Thomsen, *The New Religions of Japan* (1963). H. N. MCFARLAND

TERESA OF AVILA (Ch; 1515-1582). CARMELITE mystic and reformer. A woman of rare spiritual power and insight, Teresa overcame severe physical illnesses, a long period of spiritual confusion, misleading spiritual guidance, and hostility from the leadership of her order to become one of the great figures in the history of MYSTICISM. In 1535 she entered a Carmelite convent in Avila, Spain. At age thirty-nine, after eighteen years of troubled spiritual life, she underwent a spiritual transformation and began to have visions and mystical experiences. In 1560 she formed a group to return to the severe original Carmelite rule and after overcoming ecclesiastical and lay opposition founded convents of Reformed or Discalced Carmelites. In 1568 several men, including JOHN OF THE CROSS, founded, at her urging, a reformed house for men.

Her spiritual teaching is the result of her own experiences, expressed in untechnical, ordinary, but powerful language. Her works are some of the most important in the history of mysticism, both for her experiences and for her analysis of stages in the mystical quest. (*See* autobiography; *Way of Perfection: Interior Castle.*) She distinguishes discursive meditation, prayer of the heart, prayer of union, and spiritual marriage. Teresa herself experienced ecstatic contemplation with loss of external consciousness and of the use of her limbs.

Bibliography. E. A. Peers, trans., *Works* (1946) and *Letters* (1951); M. Auclair, *Saint Teresa of Avila* (1953); E. A. Peers, *Studies of the Spanish Mystics*, I (1949), 107-82.

G. A. ZINN

THEOLOGIA GERMANICA (Ch). An anonymous mystical classic of the fourteeth century. Generally regarded as a product of the Friends of God, an informal association of Christian mystics who shared a desire for mystical union with God, it presented instruction for achieving that end.

MARTIN LUTHER said that next to the Bible and AUGUSTINE, the *Theologia Germanica* taught him more of God than any other book. He had it printed in 1516 and again in 1518.

The book admonishes the Christian to renounce self-will as an obstacle to union with God, seeking instead poverty of spirit. As one becomes more aware of the Divine, there is a greater sensitivity to sin and an increase in suffering, which are signs of spiritual progress.

W. O. PAULSELL

THEOLOGY, CONTEMPORARY CHRISTIAN.

1. **Background.** The scientific revolution, the Enlightenment, the industrial revolution, and the various social and intellectual movements of the century that ended with World War I radically changed intellectual and cultural history, resulting in a new attitude toward all established authorities. Change was increasingly accepted as the normal state of life. The scientific revolution beginning with Copernicus and continuing through Darwin and Einstein radically altered not only the human perception of the world but also the place of human beings in the world.

No nineteenth century development created more distress for the church than the application of critical, historical methodology to the study of the BIBLE. A new historical consciousness also made people more aware of the historical relativity of their judgments and of the way their history had shaped their convictions. Karl Marx (1818-83) compounded the problem by pointing to the ideological character of faith—the way in which religion is shaped by and used to promote the believer's own interests. Sigmund Freud (1856-1939) declared that as modern knowledge has taken away the status of man's location in the universe (Copernicus) and the uniqueness of human origins (Darwin), he would take away the dignity of freedom.

The church was also increasingly aware of other religions, raising the question of their significance for Christian faith.

2. **The nineteenth century (1776-1918).** Theology in the nineteenth century can be broadly typed in terms of its response to these developments. The most influential theologians, generally designated liberal, sought to incorporate as much of the new knowledge as possible into Christian faith and life. Others sought either to ignore or to defy new developments. A third group was primarily concerned with the relationship of Christian faith to the new social situation and was known as the SOCIAL GOSPEL movement.

Friedrich Schleiermacher (1768-1834) was the first major constructive theologian to take the new intellectual and cultural situation seriously. Facing the question of the possibility of theology, he proposed to develop theological statements as the implications of religious experience. By regarding doctrines as religious affections set forth in speech, he freed theology from much of the Enlightenment criticism of the Bible and gave theology its own independent basis in the indubitable fact of Christian experience. This also gave Schleiermacher a critical principle limiting theological statements to those which were rooted in the immediate content of religious self-consciousness and eliminating such doctrines as the VIRGIN BIRTH. On the other hand Schleiermacher insisted that Christian faith is distinguished from other faiths by the fact that "in it everything is related to the redemption accomplished by JESUS Christ." Religious authority can never be imposed from without, but arises out of the experience of the Christian community itself.

G. W. F. Hegel (1770-1831), a German idealist, approached the same problem in a different way, stressing the rationality of reality and Christianity as the final philosophy, making use of the doctrines of the TRINITY and the person of Jesus Christ as means of expressing the interdependence of God and the world, of the unity of God and man, and of the way God comes to full realization through the consciousness of the "spiritual community." Christian faith was thus protected from the new historical and rational criticisms by its translation into philosophy. Karl Marx was among a number of left-wing disciples of Hegel who became critics of Christian faith.

Albrecht Ritschl (1822-89) agreed with Schleiermacher that Christian theology has its roots in Christian experience, but differed from Schleiermacher in his understanding of the nature of that experience. The proper object of theology is the historical revelation that constitutes the GOSPEL in the NT. This knowledge can only be appropriated by faith in the form of value judgments. Our knowledge of Jesus Christ is never simply a judgment of fact but a judgment of worth or value. The gospel elicits a trust in God's providence that delivers believers from bondage to the impersonal forces of nature. Ritschl also emphasized the KINGDOM OF GOD, as the "organization of humanity through action inspired by love."

Ritschl's famous student Adolf Harnack (1851-1930) wrote the best known popular statement of liberalism, *What is Christianity?* defining the heart of the faith as "the kingdom of God and its coming. Secondly God the Father and the infinite value of the human soul. Thirdly, the higher righteousness and the commandment of love."

Ritschl exercised great influence on liberal theology in America. Horace Bushnell (1802-76) had prepared Americans for the new theology especially with his studies of the person and work of Christ (*God in Christ,* 1849) and his major theological work, *Nature and the Supernatural* (1858). Evangelical liberals such as William Adams Brown (1865-1943) and Henry P. Van Dusen (1897-1978) had wide influence. This theology owed four characteristics to its nineteenth century heritage: (1) devotion to truth, (2) tentativeness, (3) emphasis on the principle of continuity, (4) liberal spirit. To its evangelical background it owed (1) authority of Christian experience, (2) loyalty to the historic faith, and (3) missionary compassion.

In the Church of England (*see* ANGLICAN CHURCHES) the attempt to accommodate Christian faith to contemporary thought found expression in three sets of essays: (1) *Essays and Reviews* (1860) written during the evolution controversy and facing the problems of biblical criticism, (2) *Lux Mundi* (1889), and (3) *Essays Catholic and Critical* (1926), whose authors believed that "catholic" and "critical" were not in necessary contradiction.

The new currents of theology did not have the freedom to develop in Roman Catholicism. *The Syllabus of Errors* (1864) rejected most nineteenth century developments, and when a movement parallel to the theological developments in Protestantism emerged in the 1890s with Louis Duchesne (1843-1922), ALFRED LOISY (1857-1940), and George Tyrell (1861-1909), it was condemned in two papal pronouncements of 1907.

Alongside theologians struggling to discover ways of affirming the possibility of Christian theology there were conservatives such as Charles Hodge (1797-1878) at Princeton and F. A. G. Tholuck (1797-1877) in Germany, who restated the traditional faith without taking new developments as seriously. By the end of the nineteenth century this kind of conservatism was no longer possible; it took the form of FUNDAMENTALISM, which represented the congealing of a particular conservative and defiant reaction to cultural developments.

3. The revival of classical traditions (1918-55). Theology entered a new period with the close of World War I. Karl Holl's essay on LUTHER'S understanding of religion (1917) ushered in a renewal of Reformation studies. The developing ECUMENICAL MOVEMENT encouraged theologians to share across denominational lines. The decisive event, however, that signaled the new theological era was the second edition of KARL BARTH'S commentary on Romans (1922; ET 1935).

Barth was the most influential spokesman of what was variously known as New Reformation theology, neo-orthodoxy, crisis theology, or theology of the word. It took its cue from the Protestant Reformers and AUGUSTINE, emphasizing revelation and the crisis character of human existence. Neither a liberal nor a fundamentalist, Barth accepted the nineteenth century and the Enlightenment, but he reaffirmed classical Christianity. Liberalism had emphasized the continuity between Christianity and the world; Barth emphasized the discontinuity between creator and creature, between the revelation in Jesus Christ and God's general revelation in the world, between the church and the human community. God in his freedom speaks when and where he chooses, and the responsibility of the creature is to hear the word. Theology for Barth is the self-test that the church makes of its message. The word of God in preaching must be tested by the word of God in Jesus Christ as attested in scripture. The fundamental problem is heresy, not paganism.

Emil Brunner (1889-1965) shared many of Barth's emphases but was more concerned than Barth to affirm the general revelation of God in creation and the apologetic task of proclaiming the message in such a way as to meet contemporary needs. LUTHERAN theology experienced a similar revival under the leadership of the Swedish theologians Gustaf Aulén (1879-1977) and Anders Nygren (1890-1978).

PAUL TILLICH (1886-1965) worked out a position known as "belief-ful realism." While affirming the kerygmatic nature of theology, he insisted that all theology must be apologetic. His method of correlation used philosophy in the analysis of the human situation to raise the questions which the gospel elicited and answered.

RUDOLF BULTMANN (1884-1976) focused on the question of how the gospel can be proclaimed in a post-Enlightenment age. His program of demythologization proposed to free the Christian message from the mythological language which enclosed the existential truth about the human situation. In this way Bultmann reaffirmed the classical Lutheran doctrine of JUSTIFICATION BY FAITH alone.

The new era in theology came to America with the publication of *Moral Man and Immoral Society,* by REINHOLD NIEBUHR (1892-1971), in 1932. Niebuhr had been trained in liberalism and in the social gospel tradition, and was influenced by the American philosophical tradition that ran through Pierce, Royce, James, and Dewey. The decisive theological influences were Augustine, the Reformers, and KIERKEGAARD. *Moral Man and Immoral Society* challenged the expectations of both secular and religious liberalism. Niebuhr was influenced in this period by the Marxist analysis of the social situation which underlined the role of interests in human affairs. The self which reasons and the self which prays may use either reason or religion to advance its own interests. Niebuhr recognized that both reason and religion are resources for social justice, but that they may be used as instruments of oppression. He believed that force would continue to be a factor in human affairs, because man is not only a creature of instinct and impulse but is also corrupted by self-interests. Niebuhr's theology can best be described as a Christian realism which denies neither human dignity nor human sin. It emphasizes the freedom of the human spirit, opening indeterminate possibilities for good and for evil. It rejects despair, cynicism, and skepticism on the one hand, and utopianism and fanaticism on the other. Niebuhr put together the Protestant doctrines of justification and sanctification in a way that acknowledged the sins of good as well as of bad people and at the same time enlarged the Reformed doctrine of sanctification by the more creative insights of the Renaissance. Niebuhr's apologetic method was to uncover the inadequacy of secular categories, especially in political science, for understanding the human situation and to demonstrate the greater adequacy of Christian categories, including the doctrine of sin, for understanding human experience.

H. RICHARD NIEBUHR (1894-1962) wrestled with the problem posed by Troeltsch, who emphasized the relative and historical character of every human enterprise. He reaffirmed the Christian doctrine of revelation without minimizing that relativity. He also affirmed the radical monotheism of the Judeo-Christian tradition against every effort to control or to enclose God within the finite. He worked to revive ANSELM'S theological program of "faith seeking understanding." Revelation reconstructs and transforms culture without denying its integrity or its positive worth. He also proposed an ethic of response to the activity of God.

William Temple (1881-1944), whose theological roots were overwhelmingly Augustinian, sought to unite theology and philosophy in his *Nature, Man and God* (1934).

Roman Catholic and some Anglican theologians found their clue in THOMAS AQUINAS. Most notable was Jacques Maritain (1882-1973) in *True Humanism,* (1936; ET 1938) and Étienne Gilson (1884-1978), a historian of medieval thought whose *Spirit of Medieval Philosophy* (1934; ET 1936) was one of the classics of the period.

4. Since 1955. With the waning of Barth's influence in Europe and Niebuhr's in America and with the emergence of a new historical situation, a new period of theology began emerging about 1955. Characterized by the absence of any single overpowering theologian, and by the lack of any theological consensus, it is unified by an awareness that the theology of the post–World War I era had answered the questions of the nineteenth century too easily and prematurely. These questions were now reopened. It also contended that theology needed to affirm in a more positive way the values of the created order and that theologians had to assume greater responsibility for the course of human affairs.

a) Problems of theological method. i. The problem of history. In 1953 Ernst Käsemann published an essay "The Problem of the Historical Jesus," opening anew the question of what could be known by a historian about Jesus. James Robinson *(A New Quest of the Historical Jesus,* 1959) believed new understandings of history enhanced the possibilities of historical knowledge of Jesus. Van Harvey in *The Historian and the Believer* (1960) dealt with the problem from the general perspective of historical method. WOLFHART PANNENBERG (*Revelation as History,* 1968) attacked the existentialist theology, seeking a vindication of God in history.

ii. The problem of "God talk." Questions raised about the use of language and the nature of theological statements were taken seriously in *New Essays in Philosophical Theology* (1955). Its contribution was largely critical in showing the nature and limits of language.

iii. Death of God theologies were closely related to the discussion of language, one of the premises being that the word "God" had lost all meaning.

iv. The new hermeneutic excited interest in the 50s and early 60s, focusing on the hermeneutical task of moving from the NT to the modern world. Utilizing the resources of the new understandings of history and of existentialism generally, a group of biblical interpreters influenced by Bultmann sought to make the gospel speak in terms of the existential condition of people today, the event that became the text thus becoming by the new hermeneutic an event again today.

v. Theology as story likewise concentrated on the hermeneutical problem, as in Hans Frei's *The Eclipse of Biblical Narrative* (1974).

Concern for theological method in a more general sense, but with the specific intention of establishing the intellectual validity of the enterprise as well as its integrity, was the intent of Langdon Gilkey *(Naming the Whirlwind,* 1969); David Tracy (*Blessed Rage for Order,* 1975); Gordon Kaufman *(An Essay on Theological Method,* 1975); Albert Outler and Shubert

Ogden in *Perkins School of Theology Journal* (Winter, 1973).

b) Thematic. Particular themes tended to become organizing principles of theology.

i. The theology of the secular began with a renewal of interest in the writing of Dietrich Bonhoeffer in the late fifties, affirming the goodness of creation and of the world as the arena of faith. See *New Man* (1956), by Ronald Gregor Smith; *The Secular City* (1965), by Harvey Cox.

ii. The Christian-Marxist dialogue was a source of theological activity, especially in Europe, as detailed by Roger Garaudy in *A Christian-Communist Dialogue* (1968) and Jan Lochman's *Encountering Marx* (1976).

iii. A theology of hope was in part a reaction against the New Reformation theology of the decades following World War I, which had been pessimistic about the possibilities of human history. Jürgen Moltmann, drawing on the work of the Jewish Marxist philosopher Ernst Bloch as well as the theological resources of the Bible and the Christian tradition, organized his theology around the theme of hope in his influential *Theology of Hope* (1967).

Political theology, closely associated with the theology of hope, may be defined as a protest against the "privatization" of Christian faith and the use of the application of the Christian message to contemporary society as the norm or focus of all theological work.

iv. The *black experience* and the concern to state Christian faith in this context in America produced a large literature, of which James Cone's *Black Theology and Black Power* (1969) was one of the most influential.

v. Theologies of celebration and play include Harvey Cox's *Feast of Fools* (1970) and Jürgen Moltmann's *Theology of Play* (1972).

vi. Liberation theology, with a strong base in Latin America, became one of the most influential of the theological movements. It focused on the liberation of human beings from the various bondages of race, sex, class, and economic oppression and concentrated on theology as critical reflection on "praxis," as in Gustavo Gutierrez, *A Theology of Liberation* (1979).

c) Restatements of older traditions. Theologians who used the philosophical ideas and concepts of Alfred North Whitehead to restate the Christian message were among the most influential and constructive of the period. This work had begun much earlier, especially with the work of Charles Hartshorne *(The Divine Relativity,* 1948). Its influence greatly expanded in this period through the work of Daniel D. Williams, *The Spirit and Forms of Love* (1968); Schubert Ogden, *The Reality of God* (1966); John Cobb, *A Christian Natural Theology* (1965).

Roman Catholic theology received new life after the negative impact of the encyclical *Humani Generis* in 1950, with the papacy of JOHN XXIII and the Second VATICAN COUNCIL (1962-65), which brought a new freedom for theological activity. KARL RAHNER *(Foundations of Christian Faith,* 1976), Bernard Lonergan *(Method in Theology,* 1972), and HANS KÜNG *(On Being a Christian,* 1976) among others explored a wide range of theological topics. In addition, Roman Catholic scholars contributed to the study of the Protestant Reformers and of the Bible in an ecumenical context.

The theologians who carried on the work of the New Reformation theology (1920-50), as well as older traditions, produced works that can be described as modern or critical orthodoxy. In this category are Albert C. Outler *(Who Trusts in God,* 1968), Gordon Kaufman *(Systematic Theology, A Historicist Perspective,* 1968), and *The Common Catechism* (1975), prepared by Protestant and Roman Catholic scholars in Europe.

Alongside critical orthodoxy, conservative theology continued to have vigor while making mild revisions in the light of the cultural challenges.

Theology from the perspective of Eastern ORTHODOX CHURCHES found expression in the earlier period in the work of Sergius Bulgakov *(The Orthodox Church,* 1955), and Nikolai Berdyaev *(The Destiny of Man,* 1937). This theological tradition is traced by John Meyendorff in *Byzantine Theology: Historical Trends and Doctrinal Themes* (1975).

d) Theology in non-Western cultures. One of the most significant developments in the post–World War II period was the emergence of indigenous theologies expressed in the language and concepts of cultures in Africa and the Far East. Among influential non-Western theologians were John S. Mbiti *(Concepts of God in Africa,* 1970), D. T. Niles *(Buddhism and the Claims of Christ,* 1967), and Kazoh Kitamori *(Theology of the Pain of God,* 1965).

Bibliography. J. C. Livingstone, *Modern Christian Thought* (1971); C. Welch, *Protestant Thought in the Nineteenth Century,* Vol. I (1972); K. Barth, *Protestant Theology in the Nineteenth Century* (1973); H.P. Van Dusen, *The Vindication of Liberal Theology* (1963).

J. H. LEITH

THEOSOPHY thē äs′ ə fē (Gr. *theos,* "god"; *sophia,* "wisdom"). Generally, a strain of mystical thought found in Western philosophy from Pythagoras on, and best known in the work of JAKOB BOEHME; specifically, the teachings of the Theosophical Society, founded in New York City in 1875 by Helena Petrovna Blavatsky (1831-1891) and Henry Olcott (1832-1907). In 1878 the founders moved to India, and the international headquarters for the movement is today at Adyar. Annie Wood Besant (1847-1933) led the movement after Olcott's death. Theosophy is monistic, and seeks to learn about reality through mystical experience and by finding esoteric meanings in sacred writings. The Theosophical Society is important historically for its popularization of Indian religious philosophy. *See* Hinduism in America.

Bibliography. J. Boehme, *Six Theosophic Points*; H. Blavatsky, *The Secret Doctrine* (1888); C.W. Braden, *These also Believe* (1949).

J. R. Crim

THERAVĀDA tĕr ŭ vä′ dŭ (B—Pali; lit. "way of the elders"). The sole remaining active member of the group of schools collectively referred to (by Mahāyānists) as Hīnayāna. It flourishes today in Sri Lanka, Burma, Thailand, Laos, and Cambodia, and is the most widely researched of all the early schools of Buddhism.

1. **History.** By the reign of King Aśoka, Buddhism had splintered into three primary sectarian groups: the Sthaviras, Mahāsāṅghikas, and Pudgalavādins. (*See* Buddhist Sectarianism.) Of the three, the Sthaviras were most active in Aśoka's capital city of Pāṭaliputra. Aśoka, however, believed that heretical notions were becoming prevalent in the Sthavira Buddhist community and sought to purge the order by holding a council (*See* Buddhist Councils.) As a result of the council, the heretical group was driven from the area, migrating to the northwest of India, and later developing into the well-known Sarvāstivādin school. The orthodox group took on the name Vibhajyavādins or "distinctionists."

Aśoka, the most missionary minded of all the early Indian kings, spread this form of Buddhism through his missionaries. His son Mahinda led a mission to Sri Lanka, where he helped to establish it as a state religion. By the middle of the second century B.C., this form of Buddhism became known as Theravāda or "the way of the elders."

King Duṭṭhagāmiṃī consolidated Theravāda Buddhism during the first century and his successor, King Vaṭṭagāmaṇī, sponsored the writing down of the voluminous Pali Canon, i.e., the scriptures of Theravāda, marking the first time that any Buddhist canon had been committed to writing.

From Sri Lanka Theravāda spread to South and Southeast Asia, where it continues to flourish to this day. An unfortunate philological twist, however, has given rise to much sectarian politics involving the Theravāda school. One of the original Indian Buddhist schools, at the time of the first schism in the Buddhist community, referred to itself as the Sthaviravāda. Now Theravāda is the exact Pali counterpart of the Sanskrit word Sthaviravāda. Consequently, the Theravāda school refers to itself as the "original" Buddhist group preserving in pristine purity the teachings of Buddha. Bareau has conclusively shown that such a claim is historically unfounded, and that the Indian Sthaviravādins and the Theravādins in Sri Lanka are *not* identical groups.

2. **Literature.** The scriptures of the Theravāda school, known collectively as the Pali Canon, constitute perhaps the most complete set of sacred texts of any Buddhist school. They are organized into three major parts: the Vinaya Piṭaka or "basket of disciplinary regulations," the Sutta Piṭaka or "basket of discourses," and the Abhidhamma Piṭaka or "basket of higher philosophy."

3. **Doctrine.** While accepting those doctrines common to all early Buddhists (i.e., Four Noble Truths, three marks of existence, five Skandhas, and dependent origination), the Theravādins are perhaps the most doctrinally conservative of all Buddhist schools. Unlike some other so-called Hīnayāna sects (i.e., the Mahāsāṅghikas) or the Mahāyānists, the Theravāda school stresses the humanity of Gautama Buddha, devoid of any supramundane speculations. (*See* Buddha, Life of Gautama.) Equally, for the Theravādins, there is only one Bodhisattva, namely Gautama. In contrast to the Sarvāstivādins, the Theravādins assert that past and future do not exist, and in reaction to the Mahāsāṅghikas, assert that Arhants are perfect in all respects. There is no intermediate existence between rebirths, as posited by some other Buddhist schools, and although Nirvana is open to all Buddhists, it is virtually impossible for the nonmonastic to attain enlightenment. Thus, we can note that the Theravāda school has strongly resisted doctrinal change and innovation, and approaches the modern world in quite the same fashion as its ancestors.

Bibliography. H. Bechert, *Buddhismus, Staat und Gesellschaft in den Ländern Theravāda Buddhismus,* 2 vols. (1966-67); R. Lester, *Theravāda Buddhism in Southeast Asia* (1973); A. Bareau *Les sectes bouddhiques du petit véhicule* (1955).

C. S. Prebish

THIRTY-NINE ARTICLES (Ch). Creedal formulation (1563) of the Anglican Churches. A revision of the Forty-Two Articles of 1553, they are firmly rooted in the English Reformation. As a part of the Elizabethan settlement (1563) they sought to provide a minimal basis for a comprehensive national church which intended to preserve both Protestant and Catholic traditions in England. *See* Creeds and Confessions §5.

J. H. Leith

THOMAS AQUINAS ə kwī′ nəs (Ch; *ca.* 1225-1274). Dominican friar; by common consent the greatest of Christian philosophers and theologians in the Middle Ages; Canonized in 1323.

Educated at the universities of Naples and Paris and at the Dominican school at Cologne, where he was a student of Albertus Magnus, he taught theology from 1252-72 at Paris, at several Dominican houses in the vicinity of Rome, and at the University of Naples. During those years of intense work he produced the enormous body of writings to which he owes his enduring reputation. These include commentaries on some of the books of the Bible, commentaries on the *De Trinitate* of Boethius and on no fewer than twelve works of Aristotle (including the *Metaphysics*, the *Physics*, the *Ethics*, and the *Politics*).

They also include a large number of short tracts, hymns, sermons, letters, and disputations on philosophical and theological matters, as well as the three works for which he is best known: his *Commentary on the Sentences of Peter Lombard* (*ca.* 1253), reflecting the formative stage in his thinking, the *Summa Contra Gentiles* (1259-64), an apologetic work seeking to explain the Christian faith by means of a masterful synthesis of theology with Aristotelian philosophy, and the *Summa Theologica,* intended as a synthesis of his whole work, begun in 1266 but still incomplete at the time of his death.

Although his thinking bore the clear imprint of AUGUSTINE'S theology and showed Stoic and Neoplatonic influences, it was Aquinas' central endeavor to meet the threat posed to Christian orthodoxy by the flood of Aristotelian or purported Aristotelian writings that, by the mid-thirteenth century, had made their way into the intellectual mainstream of Christian Europe. First, he addressed the problem posed by the fact that the crucial portions of Aristotle had first arrived interwoven with the paraphrases and commentaries of the Muslim philosophers IBN SĪNĀ (980-1037) and IBN RUSHD (1126-98), and incorporating some views (such as the denial that the world was a created one) that were clearly heterodox. Secondly, having ascertained what material was to be ascribed to Aristotle himself, he attempted the difficult task of reconciling it with the tenets of the Christian faith. Aquinas was committed to the notion that "grace does not destroy nature but perfects it," and that revelation, therefore, does not abrogate the achievements of human reason but simply completes them. This led him to produce a synthesis that has come to be recognized as the greatest of medieval theological achievements. But not even his philosophical and theological diplomacy were enough to counter the worries of his more conservative contemporaries. While they recognized his genius, they treated his conclusions with some reserve. His influence increased in the sixteenth century, but it was only in the nineteenth that he gained the reputation as the medieval Catholic thinker *par excellence*. *See* SCHOLASTICISM §2.

Bibliography. F. C. Copleston, *Aquinas* (1955); E. Gilson, *The Christian Philosophy of St. Thomas Aquinas* (1956), includes a "Catalogue of St. Thomas's Works" by I. T. Eschmann. Translation of the *Summa theologica* by the English Dominican Fathers, *The Summa Theologica* (22 vols., 1912-36); and of the *Summa contra gentiles* by A. C. Pegis, J. F. Anderson, V. J. Bourke and C. J. O'Neil, *On the Truth of the Catholic Faith,* 5 vols. (1955-57).
F. OAKLEY

THOMAS À KEMPIS (Ch). *See* IMITATION OF CHRIST.

THREE JEWELS, THREE REFUGES (B). *See* TRIRATNA.

THUG (H—Hindī *ṭhag,* from Skt. [*sthag*—"to conceal"]). A member of a secret hereditary cult devoted to human sacrifice, which flourished in Northern and Central India from ancient times until the late nineteenth century. The thugs were devotees of the goddess Bhavānī, a form of KĀLĪ, and favored robbing and strangulation of carefully selected victims as the means by which they could honor her. Their name was borrowed by the British to express the meaning "gangster" or "robber." J. BARE

T'IEN-T'AI tyĕn tī (B). Chinese name for TENDAI.

TILLICH, PAUL tĭl′ lĭk (Ch; 1886-1965). Lutheran theologian whose politics earned expulsion from Nazi Germany. His correlation of theological answers with basic questions that culture raises about human life attracted wide attention in America. *See* THEOLOGY, CONTEMPORARY CHRISTIAN §3.
D. F. OTTATI

TIME. The conceptualization and abstraction of something called time is not common to all human beings, but it is distinctive of humankind to utilize a temporal dimension to express one's orientation within reality. It is at once the gift and the burden of humanity that life is perceived as an affair in and of time. While the nature of time may at first seem commonplace and obvious, it nonetheless raises issues as profound as those of the nature of life itself. Whatever the approach, any discussion of the nature of time is bound to encounter frustrations similar to those expressed by AUGUSTINE centuries ago when he wrote in his *Confessions,* "What then is time? If no one asks me, I know; if I want to explain it to a questioner, I do not know."

1. **The modern experience of time.** The rise of modern science and the development of technology correlate with the increasing accuracy of measuring and keeping time. Principles of modern physics are based in temporal categories, and accurate measuring and keeping of time is essential to the development of technology and the coordination, scheduling, and maintenance of activities among large groups of people. As a result of the global explosion of communication capabilities, we experience an incredible condensation of activities within every moment of time. With advances in information retrieval and methods of forecasting, often linked to computer technology, the past and the future are more available to us. With the acceptance of the observations of astronomy and the idea of evolution, we find ourselves holding as commonplace a timescape of natural and human history which would have been incomprehensible to our ancestors. Our timescape has not only expanded outward, it has also expanded inward with the growing understanding of biological rhythms, aging processes, and subatomic physics.

So drenched are we with our own uniquely modern sense of time that we may find other views of time almost beyond our comprehension. For those not a part of our cult of punctuality, for those who do not perceive time in endless expanses, for those with no word for time, we have little sympathy and may find their views untenable.

2. **Time and religion.** As a fundamental means of orientation for all human beings, time is basic to world view and religious thought. Temporal orientations are not commonly made explicit as concepts, but they are implicit in one's way of life, in language, and in religious practices. This requires our exposition and translation of what we can observe of time in culture. Temporal perspectives are revealed in time reckoning related to ecological and occupational concerns as well as the conventions of social structure. Time perspectives are revealed in the way history is recounted and in mythology and ritual.

a) Time in nonliterate cultures. The historian of religion Mircea Eliade has done perhaps more than any other recent scholar to reveal the religious character of certain conceptions of time. In *Cosmos and History,* he examines a broad spectrum of religious phenomena, primarily in contemporary and archaic nonliterate cultures, to illustrate a view of time which he sees as especially religious in character. This view is based on the belief that repetition of sacred events which took place in the beginning of time is fundamental to human orientation. There is a regular, periodic return to and repetition of this first time. Time is renewed annually, as is the whole of creation. This renewal is usually celebrated and effected in a rite of the new year which first brings the cosmos into a state of dissolution symbolized by reversals and periods of saturnalia. From this return to a state of precreation chaos, the world takes shape anew through the reenactment of the cosmogonic acts. In Eliade's view it is the repetition of acts of the gods or ancestors who first created the world and established the way of life that gives time its meaning. He stresses that since time embodies the eternal repetition of sacred acts it is fundamentally religious in character. This view denies the nonrepetitive and irreversible aspect of time, and time may then be renewed through reversal and return. Eliade sets this view in contrast to the historical views of time which characterize Western civilizations. He feels that when history itself is held to be sacred, difficulties arise because of the accumulation of events in history. This amounts to what Eliade calls the "terror of history," for there is no relief from the accumulation of the succession of catastrophies (both personal and cultural), the pressure of progress, and the presence of evil. Eliade sees little possibility for redemption when the process of history which enfolds and engenders these things is itself held to be sacred. This view runs counter to those of JUDAISM, CHRISTIANITY, and ISLAM.

While this view is illustrated by reference to myth-centered and nonliterate peoples, it is not restricted to them. Nor is it in any way an adequate representation of nonliterate cultures, where views of time are as complex, sophisticated, and varied as among the great civilizations.

b) Jewish view. As set forth in the BIBLE, God's act of creation brought the cosmos into being and ordered time by giving history its beginning. God continues his work in history through a COVENANT with his people. With regard to time, God is at once transcendent (the creator of history and the cosmos) and immanent (an active part of history through his relationship with his people). In this biblical view time is not stagnating, for not only is there a beginning from which time proceeds, but there is an end toward which history is directed. History is not a simple unfolding of God's plan followed willingly by his people, for when God created free beings, he introduced into history the element of uncertainty. The character of history is consequently perceived more in terms of dissonance than harmony, and more in terms of uncertainty than sublimity. The longed-for end of time is envisioned as the *parousia,* the time when all the apparent failures and mistakes of history will be repaired or overcome by the MESSIAH.

After the beginning of the era common to Judaism and Christianity, Jewish RABBIS reinterpreted this messianic view of time in a manner which reflects the character of Judaism from that time to the nineteenth century. Without rejecting the messianic vision, the rabbis shifted away from orienting life so fully toward the expectations of the end of time. They saw history as something to be lived in and attended to, even in its most ordinary aspects of maintaining a home and a family. History was still the medium of reality, but an imminent end was not such a major concern, and as a consequence, as Neusner has shown, history for classical Judaism was more like a timeless present, a kind of eternity.

c) Christian view. Christianity has a view of time which is a modification or transformation of the biblically based Jewish view. Time is seen as a continuous succession of moments in which the events of human life are bent toward the future in order to meet their fulfillment. Christian history is given its meaning in its future expectation or potentiality. Yet the most distinctive aspect of the Christian view of time is that it is centered on CHRIST, as is reflected in the practice of dating the events of history from his birth. This was the ultimate example of God's intervention in history. The events of Christ's life were directed toward his death and RESURRECTION, which fulfilled his purpose. History, both that which preceded and that which was to follow, was given an axis, a point about which meaning and direction could be defined. All history before the advent of Christ is significant in terms of its preparing the way for him. All history after Christ is measured against the example he set.

The Christian view of time, like the Jewish view, looks toward the *parousia,* in this case Christ's SECOND COMING. But in the Christian view, the Christ who is to come has already come. This identification of the end of time with its center point is the most distinctive characteristic of Christian history. It is a history bound in the tension of having the era or kingdom of Christ revealed (indeed, in some interpretations already begun), yet without realizing its final consummation. Through the resurrection of Christ, his followers are given the opportunity to live by the model of Christ, whom they see as the center of all history.

d) Indian views. The concept of time common to the religious traditions arising in India, notably HINDUISM and BUDDHISM, is in marked contrast to the Jewish and Christian views. Early Indian literature presents time as the infinite evolution and dissolution of the entire cosmos, a cyclic process involving the succession of ages of very long duration (*see* YUGA). Life in Indian cultures is viewed as a continuous series of transmigrations of the soul from life form to life form (SAMSARA) governed by the law of KARMA, which determines one's destiny on the basis of performance in past lives. The consequence of infinite cycles of time and endless REINCARNATION has commonly been interpreted as the base for a world-negating emphasis in Hinduism and Buddhism.

Because the life cycles in Indian religions are always bent upon dissolution, there is absolutely no hope for fulfillment within time itself. Thus all soteriological systems in India are based upon a means of gaining deliverance from the cosmic illusion, that is, from the illusion that events which take place in time are real (*see* MĀYĀ). Any thing or event placed against the background of the doctrine of cosmic cycles is reduced to insignificance; it is emptied of its reality. Thus the only possibility for fulfillment is to escape from time, and this is equivalent to the abolition of the human condition, the cessation of becoming. In India religious goals are most commonly stated in terms of temporal categories which have been overcome. The BUDDHA, for example, described himself after his enlightenment as one who had transcended the aeons, as a man not of the times.

Negative views of time and history are always countered in Indian religious thought by the importance granted to human activity in the world. Humans are encouraged to act according to their stations and phases of life (DHARMA). Few are the opportunities to totally forsake one's historical conditions in order to strive as an ascetic for an immediate union with universal being. Only by following one's duty is there hope of attaining such an opportunity in some future lifetime. For most the path taken must be the fulfillment of vocation in time, but without the idolization of history.

The Indian doctrine of cosmic cycles thus teaches the unreality of the universe and of time itself, but in doing so encourages the use of time as a vehicle to deliverance.

e) Chinese views. The popular but erroneous notion that the Orient is characterized by a mystical timelessness in contrast to the strongly historical character of Western civilizations has been corrected by Needham, who showed that a dedication to history was firmly entrenched in Chinese civilization at a much earlier time than in Western civilizations. The evidence for this ranges from the meticulous dating of objects and inscriptions to the continuous writing of histories of dynasties from the Chou Dynasty (1111-249 B.C.) on. The development of astronomical and mechanical time measurements preceded similar developments in the West by centuries.

TAOISM, however, had from ancient times a deep appreciation for cyclic changes, especially as illustrated by analogy with life cycles in the world of nature. Chinese Buddhism retained the doctrine of cosmic cycles, but the T'ien T'ai (TENDAI) school believed that the world is imminent in one moment of thought, and the belief in a succession of ages culminating in an age of MAPPŌ, or "extinction of dharma," became central to NICHIREN BUDDHISM in Japan.

CONFUCIANISM steadfastly held to the reality of history, and CONFUCIUS believed that the future could be foretold on the basis of a knowledge of the past. A strong orientation to family and to society reinforced the view that history is the arena of meaningful human conduct and the way to fulfillment. ANCESTOR VENERATION and FILIAL PIETY not only had religious importance, but served the processes of government and society. While the elders and past generations were highly valued, progressive theories argued that each generation surpassed the earlier in knowledge and wisdom.

3. Geometric metaphors for time. The language we use to describe and interpret various concepts of time is limited. In Western languages words related to time are usually nouns, and time is spoken of as a thing. We have few words which refer directly to the experience of time and have to resort to spatial imageries to refer to the most characteristic aspect of our experience of time, that is, its motion. We speak of time as long or short, as the distance between two events, as a numbered value on a scale spatially conceived. Our typological distinctions between concepts and experiences of time have taken geometrical form, predominantly in the static figures of the straight line and the circle.

These simple geometric patterns are used as metaphors for time, and it is commonly believed to be sufficient to identify which basic pattern is applicable in order to determine the character of a view of time. From the examples above, we might rather quickly associate nonliterate and Indian views with the circle (cyclical) and Jewish, Christian, and Confucian views with the straight line (linear). Such interpretations are commonly, but erroneously, read from the geometric shapes alone. The straight line is open, progressive, oriented to the reality of both past and future, while the circle is closed, repetitive, and denies the reality of past and future.

But it can be readily seen that these geometrical metaphors are not only simplistic, they are misleading and inaccurate. First of all, there is nothing inherently geometic about the nature of time. And more importantly, any geometric correspondence to concepts and experiences of time does not tell much about the character of time. In the examples given above, there are clearly differences between the Jewish and Christian views of time on the order of the differences between the two religious traditions. Even the linear aspect is interpreted very differently. The rectilinear view of time in the West is often cited as a major cause for the rise of modern science and technology, but the notion of a similar shape of time in China embedded, if anything, more deeply led in a different way. The eternal return to the era of the gods and ancestors which Eliade has shown to characterize many religious traditions is a cyclic process, but its role in human orientation to reality is very different from that which in India results in belief in the doctrine of cosmic cycles. The cyclic aspect of the one view gives assurance that life is being fulfilled, while in the other it is the assurance that life cannot be fulfilled in any time.

No cyclic view actually prescribes exact repetition; there is always some aspect which gives time a direction. Likewise, in views which appear to be rectilinear there are commonly cycles. For example, the liturgical calendars of Judaism and Christianity have a decidedly repetitive character in weekly and annual cycles. The ongoing historical orientation is paralleled and complemented by the cyclic repetition of ritual. (*See* CALENDAR, CHRISTIAN; CALENDAR, JEWISH.)

More important to the understanding of any concept of time than what geometric shape it approximates is whether time is open or closed, how the past relates to the present, whether the present is empty or full of content, how the future guides or restricts human action. Such questions must be used to evaluate how temporal categories are drawn on to speak of reality and to provide orientation in order to accomplish the fulfillment of human life.

Bibliography. J. T. Fraser has promoted the interdisciplinary study of time, an effort which has resulted in the publication of several collections of essays on a wide range of areas accompanied by extensive bibliographies. J. T. Fraser, *Voices of Time* (1966), Fraser, F. C. Haber, and G. H. Müller, *The Study of Time,* Vol. I, and Fraser and N. Lawrence, Vol. II (1972). Other valuable collections are L. Gardet, *et al., Cultures and Time* (1976) and J. Campbell, *Man and Time* (1957). *See also* M. Eliade, *Cosmos and History: The Myth of the Eternal Return* (1954); J. Needham, *Time and Eastern Man* (1964); and J. Neusner, *Between Time and Eternity: The Essentials of Judaism* (1975).

S. D. GILL

TIME OF IGNORANCE, JĀHILIYYA jä hə lē´yə (I—Arab.; lit. "rashness, barbarism, ignorance"). The period or condition in Arabia before the advent of ISLAM or, sometimes, the period of paganism in other lands before the arrival of Islam. It expresses the conviction that the arrival of the prophet MUHAMMAD was the pivotal event in history. By means of the QUR'AN and the paradigmatic actions of Muhammad (SUNNA), a new moral order was introduced to replace the pagan ideal of knightly martial honor, with its excesses of drinking, boasting, and fighting. Islam retained the best of the old order (forebearance, generosity, honor) and added social responsibility and individual response, based on a higher order than instinctural passions. The term *jāhiliyya* occurs in Sura 3:154; 5:50; 33:33; and 48:26. On the basis of Sura 33:33 some commentators distinguish more than one period of *jāhiliyya* because of the occurrence of the phrase "the first *jāhiliyya.*"

Bibliography. I. Goldziher, *Muslim Studies,* I (1966), 201-8; E. W. Lane, *Arabic-English Lexicon,* II (1872), 477-78; M. M. Bravmann, *Spiritual Background of Early Islam* (1972), pp. 1-63; A. J. Wensinck, *Corcordance de la tradition musulmane,* I (1936), 392-94; aṭ-Ṭabarī, *Tafsīr,* XXII (1954), 4-5.

G. D. NEWBY

TĪRTHA tĭr´ tŭ (H—Skt.; lit. "a passageway, a ford" [*tṝ*—"to cross over"]). A temple, ghat, shrine, tree, or sacred place of pilgrimage that is imbued with divine power. These holy "crossings," or "passageways" to the divine, are usually associated with a god or goddess but also may include the burial site of notable holy persons. *See* HINDU HOLY CITIES; HINDU HOLY PERSONS; TĪRTHAṄKARA. L. D. SHINN

TĪRTHAṄKARA tĭr tän´ kä rŭ (Ja & H—Skt.; lit. "crossing maker" [*tīrtha*—"passage, crossing, ford"; *kṛ*—"to make, to do"]). One who enables others, by example and teaching, to attain liberation. As an honorific title in JAINISM it denotes twenty-four great ascetic teachers in a line reaching back into the prehistory of the present world. The most recent Tīrthaṅkara in Jainism was MAHĀVĪRA (traditionally 599-527 B.C.).

The term is related to a rich variety of images within the Jaina and Hindu traditions. For the Jainas, it suggests that their FOUNDERS or great teachers are chiefly important because of their role in showing others the way to "cross over" ordinary life (samsara) and reach liberation. Hence the Tīrthaṅkaras are not doctrinally treated as divinities, and the actual "crossing" is the task of each individual.

Within the Hindu tradition as a whole, the term TĪRTHA refers to a variety of places and methods which assist in transcending ordinary existence, including HINDU SACRED CITIES such as Banāras, ascetic orders, and various sacred objects. Its general meaning is that of an "opening to the sacred." Tīrthaṅkaras are those who create such openings, or show others how to traverse them.

K. W. FOLKERT

TISHAH BE'AV tĭ shä´ bə äv´ (Ju—Heb.; lit. "the ninth of [the month] Av"). Jewish day of fast, mourning the destruction of the Jerusalem Temple.

Nebuchadnezzar of Babylon destroyed Solomon's Temple (586 B.C.), according to the Bible, on either the tenth (Jer. 52:12-13) or the seventh of Av (II Kings 25:8-9). Titus the Roman destroyed the Second Temple (A.D. 70) on the tenth (Josephus, *The Jewish War,* 6: 249-50), the day observed by the KARAITES. The MISHNAH (Ta'anit IV: 6) and TALMUD (Ta'anit 29a) preserved a tradition that the beginning of the destruction of the Temple was on the ninth of Av; Bethar, stronghold of the BAR KOCHBA Revolt, was crushed on that day (A.D. 135); a year later, the Emperor Hadrian razed Jerusalem. Even the expulsion of the Jews from Spain is alleged to have occurred on this day.

In the Bible the day is known as "the fast of the fifth [month]" (Zech. 8:19). With the Second Temple erected, some questioned the need for the fast. The fast closes a three-week period of mourning, which includes a more intensive nine-day period. If the date falls on the SABBATH, the fast is delayed until Sunday. The book of Lamentations and dirges are read in synagogues, and customs of mourning for kin are observed. Baths, leather footwear, and even enjoyable study are prohibited. Some visit the WESTERN WALL.

Bibliography. H. Schauss, *Jewish Festivals* (1938), pp. 96-105, exposition of history and customs.

Y. SHAMIR

TORAH tôr´ ə (Ju—Heb.; lit. "instruction, teaching"). Regularly used in the first four books of the BIBLE to indicate some particular instruction or teaching. In Deuteronomy it becomes a proper noun, referring to the Pentateuch itself (first five books of the Bible). Thus Lev. 26:46 has "These are the statutes, laws, and *torahs,*" but a parallel section of admonitions in Deut. 28:58 has ". . . all the words of this Torah, written in this scroll" (author's trans.). The Deuteronomic usage, begun in apparent anticipation of the Pentateuch's completion, remained dominant as the Hebrew Bible developed, and was at times amplified as "the Torah scroll" or "the Torah of God" or "the Torah of MOSES." In poetic contexts and in Proverbs the connotations are unclear. Further, II Chr. 35:26 reads, "The remaining history of Josiah is as written in God's Torah." The Josiah events of II Kings 22-23 must be intended, indicating an expanded Torah, now encompassing also the prophetic books (NEBI'IM).

Expanding the definition in a different direction, the MISHNAH and the TALMUD dwell on an Oral Torah that accompanies the Written Torah, their combined study being life's ultimate, mystical quest. The MIDRASH elaborates a personified, wisdomlike Torah that reigned at creation. The Qumran sect's Habakkuk commentator likewise had oral tradition in mind when he termed the supporters of the Righteous Teacher "observers of the Torah," whereas the Man of Lies "desecrates the Torah for all to see." In medieval texts, MOSES BEN MAIMON named his code MISHNEH TORAH ("Review, or Replica, of Torah"), which treats primarily the legal traditions and unfolding HALAKAH. This usage continued in rabbinic literature, giving rise to a definition of Torah as embracing the whole body of Jewish religious knowledge and its observance.

It became the *summum bonum* in YIDDISH culture, with a popular lullaby wishing baby "raisins, almonds, and knowledge of Torah." In Israel a group of observant librarians and Judaica bibliographers form a "Torah library association." The international Agudath Israel named its efforts on behalf of Russian Jews the Torah Action Program; rabbis wielding strong moral influence are "Torah leaders," with political overtones for secular factions. During 1978 the Anglo-Jewish press publicized a panel on "Judea and Samaria, Occupied or Liberated? A Torah View." Yet the Jewish Publication Society's recent Pentateuch translation is entitled *The Torah* (Philadelphia 1962), showing that the original identification persists as well. The illogic of such concurrent usage is mitigated by a tendency that seeks to ascribe to the Mosaic books the full tradition and, conversely, to view all Jewish lore as immanent in scripture. This dynamic is a likely factor in the shift of meaning in the history of the literature. Another factor is the continued use in the Bible of its meaning as instruction or teaching, permitting a degree of elasticity after Torah became a proper noun. In academic circles "Torah" is used to signify doctrine, hypothesis, or discipline. RSV translates Torah as "law," under the influence of the Greek versions of the Bible.

A. LICHTENSTEIN

TORII tô´ rē ē (Sh—Jap.; lit. "bird-perch"). A simple open gateway signaling the presence of KAMI and marking off the sacred precincts of a SHINTŌ shrine from the ordinary world. Constructed of wood, stone, or sometimes metal, the torii consists of two columns supporting two crossbeams arranged one above the other.

M. L. ROGERS

A typical torii

TORITSUGI tō rē tsoo′ gē (Sh—Jap.; lit. "agency," "intermediation"). Term used in KONKŌ-KYŌ to designate the ministry of mediation, bringing a devotee into communion with the deity TENCHI KANE NO KAMI. Toritsugi was initially practiced by the founder KAWATE BUNJIRO and is continued through his successors and the other ministers of Konkō-kyō.

H. N. MCFARLAND

TOSEFTA tō sĕf′ tə (Ju—Aram.; lit. "addition [to the Mishnah]"). Collection of supplements to and interpretations of the MISHNAH, following its order. Though sometimes attributed to R. Hiyya (*ca.* A.D. 200) or to other TANNAIM, the Tosefta was compiled anonymously in the decades before A.D. 450.

Y. SHAMIR

TOTEM. An object, often an animal, which is conceived to have a mystical or symbolic relationship to a group of people. The complex of beliefs and practices involved is called totemism. Totemism is widespread among societies that practice ANCESTOR VENERATION, but it has been especially studied in relation to Australian aborigines. (*See* OCEANIC TRIBAL RELIGIONS; NATIVE AMERICAN TRIBAL RELIGION.)

1. **Early theories.** Totemism came to the knowledge of Western scholars in the nineteenth century, and several theories were advanced to explain it. Smith argued, on the basis of virtually no evidence, that the ancient Semites were organized into matrilineal clans which were related to diverse species of animals, each species the totem of a clan. Killing and eating the totem animal was an act of communion with the god who was represented by the totem. All communion in the Judeo-Christian tradition rested on this base.

Freud borrowed some ideas from Smith, but went much further in constructing a fanasty of the primordial past. He imagined a scenario at the dawn of humanity in which the father of the band monopolized the females. The sons, in their rage and lust, killed the father and ate him to gain access to the females (including their mothers, thus explaining the Oedipus complex). Then, in remorse, they instituted a taboo on eating the totem animal, which they identified with their father. This father also turns out in Freud's thinking to be God.

Durkheim held that society or the social group itself was its own god, at least implicitly. The totem was an objectification of the divinity; the worship of the totem focused the attention of society on itself and so provided the essential glue to hold society together. This was the earliest form of religion in Durkheim's scheme, and it pertained to the most "primitive" societies, notably the Australians.

2. **Contemporary ideas.** Modern scholars recognize that there is a great diversity of customs which are lumped under this label, and that it may be unwise to try to explain all the manifestations of totemism with a single theory. In some cases the totem (which may be a plant or inanimate object as well as an animal, though it is most often an animal) is identified with the primordial ancestor; all contemporary exponents of the totem species are therefore mystically related to the descendants of the ancestor. This in some cases does lead to the practice of ritual killing and eating of the totem. In other cases it leads rather to a TABOO on killing and eating the totem; or, if it is a matter of survival, the animal may be killed, but with appropriate rites of propitiation and atonement.

Lévi-Strauss, the most widely followed modern student of totemism, holds that totemism represents a link between two worlds, the natural and the social. Each world is divided into parallel species, which are mystically related one-to-one across the divide, thus powerfully uniting the universe. *See* ANIMISM; FOOD, RELIGIOUS ATTITUDES TOWARD.

Bibliography. E. Durkheim, *The Elementary Forms of the Religious Life* (1915); E. E. Evans-Pritchard, *Theories of Primitive Religion* (1965); S. Freud, *Totem and Taboo* (1918); C. Lévi-Strauss, *Totemism* (1962); W. R. Smith, *The Religion of the Semites* (1889).

C. R. TABER

TOWERS OF SILENCE (Z). Cylindrical walled structures, open to the sky, which serve for the disposal of the bodies of the dead in traditional ZOROASTRIAN communities in Asia. In the towers, situated at a distance from the older towns, the Zoroastrian corpses are exposed to the air, so that the flesh is consumed by vultures and the bones bleached by the sun. Zoroastrians have advocated this practice from a conception of purity, in which the putrefying corpse is prevented from polluting the traditional elements: earth or water in the case of burial, and air or fire in the case of cremation. They have also advocated the practice as democratic: the corpses of rich and poor, alike in death, are covered only with a sheet, which is removed inside the tower. The institution has been questioned in modern Indian settings such as Bombay, where the majority of Indian PARSIS live, since the city's growth long ago surrounded the towers and has threatened the vulture population in the adjacent park area. In the past century new Zoroastrian settlements in urban centers both in India and overseas have established cemeteries, not towers, though in Colombo, Sri Lanka, the graves are enclosed by a circular wall resembling a tower. In Iran, use of the towers was discontinued by government order, and cemeteries established, in the early 1970s. Shifts in usage have taken place in the past as well: the ancient Persian kings were buried in tombs, not exposed; and the traditional Persian term for a tower, *dakhma,* most likely comes from a root *(dhṃbh)* which implies burial rather than cremation or exposure.

W. G. OXTOBY

TRADITION IN ISLAM. *See* ḤADĪTH; SUNNA.

TRANSCENDENTAL MEDITATION (TM) (H). An international Hindu movement found primarily in North America. The founder, Maharishi Mahesh Yogi (born as Mahesh Prasad Varma) was trained as a physicist, but in 1959 he began a ten-year series of tours to the West, teaching an elementary form of VEDĀNTA and YOGA practices called TM (transcendental meditation). Since the emphasis of the training is so firmly on meditation techniques rather than philosophical or religious beliefs, even the followers of the movement are undecided about whether it should be considered religious. Although the Maharishi maintained his original center in the Indian holy city Rishikesh, in Uttar Pradesh, the TM movement was never as popular in India as it became abroad. He eventually established the movement's international headquarters in Switzerland, and Maharishi International University was created at the former site of Parsons College in Iowa. TM is the most accessible form of Hindu practice available in America, and especially after the Maharishi's highly publicized friendship in the 1960s with the musical group the Beatles, it likely has had a direct influence on more Americans than any other single Hindu movement or teacher. *See* HINDUISM IN AMERICA.

M. JUERGENSMEYER

TRANSMIGRATION (B, H & Ja). *See* SAMSARA.

TRANSUBSTANTIATION (Ch). The doctrine of the total conversion at consecration of the bread and wine of the EUCHARIST into the substance of CHRIST'S body and blood. Its classical statement by THOMAS AQUINAS depends on Aristotelian concepts whose adequacy has been questioned by such modern theologians as E. Schillebeeckx. *See* CONSUBSTANTIATION.

T. J. TALLEY

TRAPPISTS trăp′ ĭsts (Ch). Monks of one branch of the CISTERCIANS. This popular name derives from La Trappe, a monastery whose abbot, A. de Rancé (d. 1700), began one of several reform movements later united to form the Cistercians of the Stricter Observance (OCSO). Trappists seek contemplative union with God by a very austere life of PRAYER, silence, and manual labor. *See* RELIGIOUS ORDERS.

W. H. PRINCIPE

TRICKSTER. A term apparently coined by Daniel Brinton in 1868 and commonly used thereafter by anthropologists, folklorists, and historians of religions to designate a figure, almost invariably male, found in the oral traditions of preliterate peoples the world over; he is characterized by a complex of traits, chief of which is "trickiness" or deceitfulness. Although seldom worshiped, the trickster is widely regarded as a sacred personage in that he belongs to the time of origins and his deeds have the effect of establishing conditions for all times. Occasionally this figure is the principal creator in a tribe's mythology, but more often he stands in some kind of parallel relationship, either complementary or antagonistic, to the Supreme Being/Creator, frequently being the latter's brother or son.

While some writers regard all features of the trickster's make-up other than trickery or buffoonery as secondary accretions, most authorities consider the character to be a complex consisting of the following: primordiality, inordinate pride and egocentricity, physical weakness or deformity, amorality and a contemptuousness for propriety, unlimited ambition, a paradoxical combination of cleverness and stupidity, and a perennial optimism and good humor. Usually the trickster is grossly erotic, insatiably hungry, and eternally adventurous.

Although several minor characters in a tribe's mythology may be tricksters, often one trickster will stand out as the most popular figure in the entire oral tradition of the tribe. Ordinarily in such instances he will be both trickster and "culture hero," i.e. the principal author of a people's culture; and his stories, or a part of them, will be an integral part of the most sacred traditions. The more humorous tales, often ribald, may however be relegated to a lesser, "profane" category of narratives.

Trickster stories appear to belong to the most archaic levels of culture and oral literature. Frequently the trickster is theriomorphic (animal-like in form) and lives in a world of "animal-people," though both he and they behave anthropomorphically most of the time. Hunters, rather than agriculturalists, are more likely to feature a trickster as their leading MYTH-figure, perhaps because trickery is so integral to the technique of hunting. Tricksters tend to decline in importance as more "exalted" characters, divine or heroic, come to the fore in mythology. Yet a well-defined trickster is difficult to extirpate from the affections of a people, as is attested by the persistence of a Hermes or Pan among the cultured Greeks or a KRISHNA in India.

The trickster is a being who "lives" in his narratives, and the ritual of storytelling constitutes his only cult in NATIVE AMERICAN TRIBAL RELIGION. Certain African tribes give offerings to their tricksters as demigods, and still other tribes (such as the Pueblos) have trickster-like clowns in their sacred ceremonials. The most distinctive feature of West African tricksters is their connection with DIVINATION, the device by which they mediate the will of the gods but also enable men to subvert it.

Tricksters are most prominent in oral traditions of North America, West Africa, the South Pacific, and eastern Siberia. The Iroquois are the only group of Amerindians who lack a major trickster. The lecherous, foolish, voracious, yet creative Coyote appears all over the western U.S.; Hare or Rabbit is the major trickster in the Southeast and northern states; Raven plays the role on the Northwest Coast and in eastern Siberia. While the same or similar tales are told across the continent, each tribe has its distinctive traditions; the Hare of the Southeast is not the same as the Hare of the Great Lakes area, nor are the Siberian and American Raven tricksters the same. Some tribes, such as the Oglala, have degraded the trickster to the role of an evil being, but in most tribes he is the popular culture hero and fool.

Among the Polynesians, Maui is the trickster–culture hero. He has been described as a "defier of precedent, a remodeler of the world and its society, and a mischievous, adolescent trickster" (Luomala, p. 28). Throughout Africa the most popular oral narratives concern tricksters. Special studies have been made of Ture, the Zande Spider-man; Ananse, the Akan Spider; Ogo-Yurugu, the Dogon Jackal or "Pale Fox"; Eshu-Elegba, the anthropomorphic divine trickster of the Yoruba, and his counterpart, Legba, of the Fon of Dahomey. The West African tricksters are living deities who mediate between gods and men via divination.

Pettazzoni believed the trickster was a degraded high god, while Radin saw him as a figure in the process of evolution upward, from self-centered cheat to noble culture hero. Jung equates the trickster with the Shadow archetype, while Lévi-Strauss regards him as a mediator between oppositions. For Mararius the trickster is the mythical magician who breaks taboos and suffers for doing so, thus embodying and mediating between ambivalences in society. Campbell equates the trickster with the shaman, who also lives by trickery; but Ricketts maintains that the trickster is the opposite of the shaman, incarnating a view of man and his place in the cosmos that is basically anti-god and "humanistic," rather than submissive and visionary. According to Pelton, the trickster enables people to integrate the anomalous and the ambiguous into a sacred whole, and so to experience transcendence over the world.

Thus, while a consensus has not been reached, there is increasing agreement that the trickster is an important religious myth symbol expressing a profound apprehension of mankind's place in the universe.

Bibliography. P. Radin, *The Trickster* (1956); R. Pettazzoni, *The All-Knowing God* (1956); E. Evans-Prichard, *The Zande Trickster* (1967); G. Dieterlen, *Le Renard Pâle* (1963); J. Campbell, *The Masks of God: Primitive Mythology* (1959); K. Luomala, *Maui-of-a-Thousand-Tricks* (1949); N. O. Brown, *Hermes the Thief* (1969); M. Ricketts, "The North American Indian Trickster," *HR*, V, (1966); R. Pelton, *The Web of Purpose, the Dance of Delight; Four West African Tricksters* (Ph.D. Diss., U. of Chicago, 1974); L. Mararius, "Le mythe du 'trickster,' " *Revue de l'histoire des religions*, 175 (1969); B. Babcock-Abrahams, " 'A Tolerated Margin of Mess': The Trickster and his Tales Reconsidered," *Journal of the Folklore Institute*, XI (1975); B. H. Lopez, *Giving Birth to Thunder* (1977).

M. L. RICKETTS

TRIMŪRTI trī mûr′ tē (H—Skt.; lit. "the trimorphic god," "the One with three forms" [*tri*—three; *mūrti*—form]). A mythic and iconographic motif representing one god in three aspects (i.e., BRAHMĀ the creator, VISHNU the preserver, and SHIVA the destroyer). The earliest expression of the idea is found in the RIG VEDA, exemplified in the triadic manifestation of fire: AGNI (terrestrial fire on the domestic hearth), Vidyut (aerial embodiment in lightning), and SŪRYA (celestial form in the sun).

L. D. Shinn

The *Trimūrti*, Brahmā, Vishnu, and Shiva, are depicted on their vāhanas on a temple gateway in Madras, South India

In the Rig Veda there was a custom of delineating into triadic patterns various individual gods (e.g., Angi, INDRA, and Sūrya), divine agencies (fire, air, and sun), or classes of deities (Vasus, Rudras, and Ādityas), correspondent to the three levels of the universe. A more advanced form of this procedure is to be noted in the BHAGAVAD GĪTĀ (10.23) where Krishna, the All-god, declares that his own eternal essence is manifested in the various celestial bodies and divine beings. In the UPANIṢADS (Maitrāyaṇīya 4.5) the One is discovered in a meditative state to be embodied in a series of triadic entities and persons (Fire, Air, and Sun; Time, Breath, and Food; Brahmā, Rudra, and Vishnu). The custom of conceptualizing the gods Brahmā, Vishnu, and Shiva as many modes of the one God plays no significant role in the religious ideology of the two Indian Epics, being recognized only in one late passage in the MAHĀBHĀRATA. Even in an appendix to this work (10660 ff.), after introducing the notion of *Trimūrti,* Brahmā is ignored in favor of a single bipolar deity of an androgynous nature, composed of Vishnu and Shiva. Shiva is identified with Fire (Agni) and Vishnu with the Moon (SOMA), with these two divine powers constituting the entire universe. Thereby the triad is reduced to a duad and addressed as *Hari-Hara* (Vishnu-Shiva), as the "two highest" divinities who are in essence one, as creator, preserver, and absorber.

It is only in the PURĀṆAS that the *Trimūrti* concept becomes a standard and pervasive doctrine. But at no time has this concept of divinity been worshiped.

Two other permutations of this motif deserve notice. First, Shiva himself often manifests the three aspects of the godhead. He is depicted in myth and iconography as possessing three heads, three eyes, and three forms (time, masculine spirit, and Brahman). An impressive representation of this image of Shiva is located in the main sanctuary of the Elephanta Caves, situated on an island off the coast of Bombay City. A similar adaptation also occurs in Vishnu sectarianism. Second, according to the beliefs of the thoroughgoing *Śaktas* or goddess worshipers, the ŚAKTĪ or Divine Mother is the only creator, preserver, and destroyer of the universe and is herself the matrix from which the triad of deities composing the *Trimūrti* spring into being, these masculine deities being nothing more than aspects of her nature. It is instructive to observe that Ellamma, a major mother goddess of Indian folk-religion, becomes the mother of the *Trimūrti*, hatching out the gods as a hen does.

Bibliography. J. Gonda, "The Hindu Trinity," *Anthropos* 63 (1968), 212-26 (rpr. in *Selected Studies*, Vol. IV, 1975); H. S. Joshi, *Origin and Development of Dattātreya Worship in India* (1964); N. Söderblom, "Holy Triads," *Transactions of the IIIrd International Congress of the History of Religions* (1908).

J. B. LONG

TRINITY (Ch). The DOGMA, formulated authoritatively in fourth century church COUNCILS, that Christians worship one God in three *persons* (Father, Son, HOLY SPIRIT) and one *substance*.

The diversity of early Christian thought about God is only partially revealed in the NT, which understands the being designated as "God" and "Father" to be the Holy One of Israel, the creator and lord of history. Important references to JESUS consider him God's "MESSIAH" (John 1:41), "son" (Luke 1:35), "image" (Col. 1:15), and as a being who existed, with God, before his earthly life (Phil. 2:5-8; John 1:1-5). He is himself worthy of the appellation "God" (I John 5:20). OT understandings of the Spirit of God are extended in describing the Holy Spirit's descent at Jesus' baptism, the appearance of "another Counselor" after Jesus' departure to the Father (John 14:15-17), and the events of PENTECOST (Acts 2). No schematic conception of God as triune being is found in the NT, though the threefold Pauline doxologies (e.g., II Cor. 13:14) and Matt. 28:19, which urges BAPTISM "in the name of the Father and of the Son and of the Holy Spirit," served as bases for further doctrinal treatment of the church's experience of God.

In response to GNOSTICISM, existing tripartite baptismal affirmations (Hippolytus, *Apostolic Tradition* 21-22) were transformed into definitive declarations of orthodox truth (Tertullian, *Prescription of Heretics* 13; Irenaeus, *Against Heresies* 1.2-3). The resulting "rule of faith" (variously phrased by second and third century theologians) taught: 1) the identity of the Christian God with the creator, the God of Jewish scriptures; 2) the true humanity, actual death, and resurrection of Jesus, Son of God (anti-docetic claims crucial to orthodox definitions of SALVATION and future hope; and 3) the reality of the Holy Spirit, who foretold Jesus' advent through the prophets and continues to guide believers.

Under pressure to explain to a hostile Roman world how Christians counted themselves monotheists, Christian apologists (notably Justin Martyr, d. 165) combined Johannine and Stoic-Platonic understandings of the term LOGOS ("Reason," or "Word") in order to maintain that the Son was both God's own self-expression and a being distinct from him. Destined to assume central position in Trinitarian and Christological doctrine, this Logos theology had to survive the challenge of two groups which considered it ditheistic and sought (in very different ways) to protect the oneness of God: *modalist monarchians* (also called Sabellians, Patripassians) understood God as a single being whose names described successive modes of his activity (Father: creation; Son: salvation; Spirit: SANCTIFICATION); *dynamic monarchians* (adoptionists, Psilanthropists) insisted that Jesus, a mere man, received (through the Spirit's visitation) the power of God, becoming God's Son through adoption. The former view was denounced for disallowing a distinction between the three persons, and the latter for failing to differentiate between Jesus and other inspired holy men, thereby throwing into question the status of the Christ to whom Christians addressed their prayers.

Though wary of adoptionism, the major Trinitarian theologians prior to NICAEA (325) assumed that the Son and Spirit were lesser in rank than God the Father. In speaking of God as one divine substance and three persons, Tertullian (*Against Praxeas* 2-9) notes that the three are in different grades or degrees, and ORIGEN, while teaching the commonality of essence linking Son and Spirit to God the Father, envisions in his Trinitarian scheme (as in his cosmology) a hierarchical arrangement which positions the Son as a "second God" (*Against Celsus* 5:39) and limits the Spirit's sway to the CHURCH (*On First Principles* 1.3).

In the course of the protracted and bitter ARIAN controversy (318-381) the view of the divine Triad that gained dominance stressed the common essence or nature of the three persons, as well as their co-eternity and co-equality. Against the claims of Arius and his followers that 1) the divine Son is a creature related to the Father by will, not by nature, and 2) the persons of the Trinity are dissimilar in essence, the creed of Nicaea insisted that the Son is "begotten, not made" and "consubstantial with the Father" (*see* HOMOOUSION). In following decades a troubled Christendom debated the dangers of monarchianism and tritheism, sought ways of defining the Son's relationship to the Father, and wrestled with questions about the status of the Son and of the Holy Spirit (thought to be an ANGEL by the Pneumatomachians). Forceful in the deliberations were the Cappadocian churchmen, BASIL of Caesarea, Gregory of Nazianzus, and Gregory of Nyssa, whose defenses of the full deity of the Holy Spirit (Basil, *On the Holy Spirit*) and arguments for God as one essence or substance *(ousia)* in three persons *(hypostases)* inform the orthodox creedal formula which triumphed (supported by the Emperor Theodosius) in the Council of Constantinople in 381. The Trinitarian confession of Constantinople upholds the co-eternity and co-equality of the Father, Son, and Holy Spirit, one God, but avoids the controversial *homoousion* in reference to the Spirit, who is termed "Lord" and "is worshiped and glorified together with the Father and the Son." Neither the operations of God nor distinctions of origin within the Godhead (the Father is unbegotten, the Son begotten, the Spirit proceeding from the Father through the Son) reveal, the Cappadocians argued (against the Arian Eunomius), the essence of God, which remains mystery.

Trinitarian thought in Western Christendom consistently stressed the distinct persons less than the unifying substance, the unity of God. AUGUSTINE'S treatise *On the Trinity* (written from 399 to 419) is expressive of this perspective in that it finds intrapersonal analogies (e.g., self-knowledge and self-love) most appropriate for explication of the life of the triune God.

Later Trinitarian thought in ROMAN CATHOLICISM, in ORTHODOX CHURCHES and in PROTESTANTISM follows in its basic lines the fundamental insights of the Cappadocian Fathers and Augustine of Hippo. The Orthodox Churches, however, reject the insertion of FILIOQUE into the NICENE CREED.

Bibliography. G. L. Prestige, *God in Patristic Thought*, 2nd ed. (1952); J. N. D. Kelly, *Early Christian Creeds*, 2nd ed. (1960) and *Early Christian Doctrines*, 2nd ed. (1960); G. C. Stead, *The Divine Substance* (1977); A. von Harnack, *History of Dogma*, Vols. II-V (ET 1902 ff.). R. C. GREGG

TRINITY SUNDAY (Ch). A feast in honor of the Holy TRINITY kept locally in France on the Sunday after PENTECOST from the late tenth century. Resisted at ROME, it achieved universal observance only in 1334. Liturgical books in England and northern Europe numbered summer Sundays after Trinity, not after Pentecost as was customary elsewhere.

T. J. TALLEY

TRENT, COUNCIL OF (Ch). The nineteenth ecumenical council of the ROMAN CATHOLIC Church. As the enunciator and embodiment of the ideals of the CATHOLIC REFORMATION, this council represented the realization of widespread hopes for a reforming council, hopes that had been repeatedly dashed by the foot dragging of the popes and the diplomatic rivalries of the European monarchs since the start of the PROTESTANT REFORMATION. Called by Pope Paul III, the council finally assembled on December 13, 1545 after several delays. Twenty-five sessions later, on December 4, 1563, it was finally dissolved by Pius IV.

Its work fell into three phases. During the first two (1545-48 and 1551-52), although the council had decided to address concurrently controversial questions of DOGMA and matters of ecclesiastical discipline, discussion focused largely on doctrine: the authoritative text of the BIBLE, the relation between scripture and church tradition, ORIGINAL SIN, JUSTIFICATION, the seven SACRAMENTS in general and the EUCHARIST in particular. During the last phase (1562-63) the doctrinal discussions of the second phase were completed, but the central focus was on ecclesiastical discipline—above all, on a BISHOP'S duty to reside in his diocese and on the education and spiritual formation of the diocesan CLERGY.

The central doctrinal affirmations of Trent, clearly distant from Protestant formulations, ended whatever hopes the emperor and the moderate Catholic theologians may have had for a reconciliation with PROTESTANTISM, although they were framed in such a way as to permit a greater diversity of opinion than was apparent at the time to their Protestant critics. Similarly, although the council's disciplinary reforms did not go as far as many Catholic reformers had hoped, they did succeed in creating a firm foundation for the restoration of ecclesiastical discipline and the creation of a properly educated diocesan clergy. Doctrinal affirmations and disciplinary reforms together served to restore confidence and to promote a renewal of spiritual life in a church increasingly caught up in the bitter struggle with Protestantism. *See* COUNCILS OF THE CHURCH.

Bibliography. P. Janelle, *The Catholic Reformation* (1949); H. Jedin, *A History of the Council of Trent*, 2 vols. (1957-61).

F. OAKLEY

TRIBAL RELIGIONS. *See* AFRICAN TRADITIONAL; NATIVE AMERICAN; OCEANIC; SOUTH AMERICAN; SOUTH ASIAN; SOUTHEAST ASIAN.

TRIPIṬAKA trĭ pĭ´ tŭ kŭ (B—Skt.; lit. "three baskets" [*piṭ*—"to assemble"]) **TIPIṬAKA** (B—Pali). The corpus of sacred texts in Buddhism, first composed in Pali and so called because it is made up of three "baskets" or collections of texts. These consist of the monastic discipline, discourses of the Buddha, and scholastic analysis. *See* PALI CANON.

J. P. MCDERMOTT

TRIPLE BODY (*Trikāya*; B—Skt.). MAHĀYĀNA Buddhist concept according to which the BUDDHA has three distinct modes of existence, the DHARMAKĀYA or Body of Dharma, the NIRMĀṆAKĀYA or Body of Transformation, and the SAMBHOGAKĀYA or Body of Bliss.

While THERAVĀDA Buddhism perceived the historical Buddha, Gautama, as the supreme teacher among men, Mahāyāna favored elevating him to the status of a deity. In fact, deification of the Buddha became one of the hallmarks of Mahāyāna thought. Many disciples found it unthinkable that a being of Gautama's moral excellence and perfect wisdom could utterly cease to exist after a mere eighty years on this earth. Tendencies toward the apotheosis of the Buddha eventually culminated in the Triple Body doctrine. In addition, the need to bring coherence to the bewildering plurality of Buddhas and BODHISATTVAS, which came to be recognized in Mahāyāna literature, contributed to the articulation of the *Trikāya*.

1. **Dharmakāya.** Just as all three bodies can be seen as aspects of one Buddha, the *Nirmāṇakāya* and *Sambhogakāya* can be viewed as aspects of the *Dharmakāya*. Through it, the Buddha discloses his true character as suchness or absolute existence; the other two bodies are provisional or derivative in their existence, owing their being to the Dharma Body. This essential body is undifferentiated, that is, devoid of any particularity, for to be particular or specific is to be limited, and the *Dharmakāya* is absolutely unlimited in nature. Being free of all determinations or boundaries, it is formless, like space itself, as opposed to the other two bodies, which have determinate form. Our universe is a particular expression or evolution from the universal *Dharmakāya,* which is the unifying source of all particularities. Therefore, the real body of the Buddha was not his physical one but his spiritual or Dharma Body.

Ethics is implicit in the concept of *Dharmakāya*. A person should love his neighbor, because all beings are one as manifestations of the same *Dharmakāya*. The truth of the *Dharmakāya* is realized only when the mind is emptied of illusions and biases to leave room for enlightenment.

On the macrocosmic level *Dharmakāya* is the creative unity behind all plurality; on the microcosmic level, it is the Buddha nature inherent in all sentient beings. This immanence means that all beings are potential Buddhas and thus lends support to the Mahāyāna ideal of universal salvation. Through the omnipresence of the *Dharmakāya* all sentient creatures are one, but this is evident only after enlightenment eliminates all dualism of self versus others. The *Dharmakāya* is sometimes interpreted as a personal being rather than as a totally abstract reality. When so understood, it is said to have infinite compassion, omniscience, and omnipotence, since it lovingly regards all beings as children, intelligently directs the way of the universe, and freely operates without external determination. As a living soul, the *Dharmakāya* expresses itself in nature as the *Nirmāṇakāya* and in thought as the *Sambhogakāya*. These manifestations are intended to assist sentient beings in their achievement of Nirvana.

In the end, the *Dharmakāya* can only be reached through a mystical experience. Since it is beyond the grasp of most minds, the *Nirmāṇakāya* and *Sambhogakāya* provide more accessible expressions.

2. **Nirmāṇakāya.** The *Nirmāṇakāya* is the incarnation of the eternal Buddha on the mundane plane. For the ignorant masses, the *Dharmakāya* must assume the physical form of a distinct historical personality. The appearance of the *Dharmakāya* in the human form of Gautama is only one of an infinite number of *Nirmāṇakāyas*. In fact, Mahāyāna acknowledges Christ, Socrates, Confucius, and any number of other historical figures as *Nirmāṇakāyas*. Finding it unthinkable that there would be only one earthly manifestation of the Absolute or *Dharmakāya* in all of human history, Mahāyāna holds that *Nirmāṇakāyas* are universal, appearing everywhere and in all eras. In the Buddhist tradition, numerous *Nirmāṇakāyas* or earthly Buddhas preceded Gautama, and MAITREYA is spoken of as the *Nirmāṇakāya* of the future. The *Dharmakāya* adapts itself to the spiritual needs of the least cultured human beings by manifesting itself in devils, animal gods, and ancestral spirits.

3. **Sambhogakāya.** In the same way as the *Nirmāṇakāya* is accessible to ordinary human beings, the *Sambhogakāya* appears to above average bodhisattvas. As *Sambhogakāya,* the eternal Buddha or *Dharmakāya* takes on a celestial form, complete with radiant halo, for the vision of bodhisattvas alone. Unlike the *Nirmāṇakāya,* which is short-lived, the *Sambhogakāya* is conceived of as eternal; the *Nirmāṇakāya* can be understood as a transitory, earthly manifestation of the heavenly *Sambhogakāya*. In effect, the *Sambhogakāya* is an intermediate body; when an individual is no longer content with the limited *Nirmāṇakāya* expression of the Buddha and is not yet able to comprehend the Buddha as Absolute Being or *Dharmakāya,* the *Sambhogakāya* serves as a sort of transition. Of course, the *Sambhogakāya,* like the *Nirmāṇakāya,* is only a manifestation of the primordial *Dharmakāya*. Enlightenment takes place when the individual's concept of the *Sambhogakāya* is superseded by an intuition of the *Dharmakāya*. Actually there are numerous *Sambhogakāyas* in order to suit the temperament and spiritual level of individual bodhisattvas.

The *Sambhogakāya* can be described as a subjective projection or creation of the bodhisattva himself in that he has conjured up the *Sambhogakāya* as an idealized expression of the *Nirmāṇakāya*. Such a *Sambhogakāya* partakes of qualities from both other bodies. On the one hand, it is thought of as eternal like the *Dharmakāya;* on the other hand, like the *Nirmāṇakāya,* it is perceived to have a definite form.

Bibliography. B. L. Suzuki, *Mahayana Buddhism* (1963), pp. 52-63; D. T. Suzuki, *Outlines of Mahayana Buddhism* (1963), pp. 217-76. E. J. COLEMAN

TRIRATNA trē rät′ nŭ (B—Skt.). The "Three Jewels" or "treasures" of the Buddhist tradition most broadly are the BUDDHA, the Dhamma (Skt. DHARMA), and the SAṄGHA. In a devotional sense these are referred to as the "Three Refuges" (Pali *Tisaraṇa*), as each devotee seeks refuge in these along the path to enlightenment. The chanting of this affirmation is the most pervasive and basic ingredient within Buddhist devotional practice. It has its roots within the earliest Buddhist communities and remains normative in the present day.

On one level the threefold affirmation is a simple act of piety; on other levels it is the nucleus of exceedingly complex theories and practices with respect to the various ways in which these fundamental elements have been construed by the Buddhist tradition, in both HĪNAYĀNA and MAHĀYĀNA forms. The nature of the Buddha, for instance, came to be perceived in innumerable legendary guises soon after the passing of the historical GAUTAMA, highlighted both by the JĀTAKA tales and by the accounts of his earthly existence. This process was given further doctrinal form by the Mahāyāna concept of the Three Bodies of the Buddha (*see* TRIPLE BODY), as part of the Great Vehicle's distinction between form and formlessness. So too with the understanding of dhamma (dharma), about which, at the most rudimentary level, there were distinctions between the dhamma as the Buddha's teaching about NIRVANA and the eight stages of the path *and* dhamma as a world-ordering principle. Ultimately, Buddhist tradition asserts the primacy of dhamma, with warrant from the earliest texts, with the Buddha seen to be not only its expositor but its embodiment. Finally, one may see within the tradition's understanding of the *Saṅgha* from the beginning a threefold differentiation between the spiritual elite *(ārya-saṅgha),* the monastic community per se *(bhikkhu-saṅgha),* and the wider congregation of disciples (Pali *sāvakasaṅgha).* The Buddhist tradition agrees, for the most part, that in order to attain the highest levels each must take refuge in these three treasures within oneself.

Bibliography. B. Sangharakshita, *The Three Jewels* (1970); E. J. Thomas, *The Life of Buddha as Legend and History* (1949); *see* bibliogs. for SAṄGHA and UPOSATHA. B. L. SMITH

TRUTH (H, B & Ja). *See* SAT, SATYA.

TULSĪ DĀS tōōl′ sē däs (H; 1532(?)-1623). The monastic and pen name of a HINDĪ poet and RĀMA devotee. A cast-off urchin, he was adopted by ascetic followers of the teacher Rāmānanda and became a successful public reciter on Rāmaite themes. In early life he lived in Ayodhyā, and later in Banāras. His masterpiece, the RĀMACARITMĀNAS. is unmatched among Hindu sacred writings in present popularity. (*See* RĀMĀYAṆA.) His *Kṛṣṇagitavali* indicates his acceptance of the legitimacy of the worship of the AVATAR KRISHNA.

Bibliography. R. Allchin, *Tulsi Das, Kavitavali* (1964), and "The Place of Tulsi Das in North Indian Devotional Tradition," *JRAS* (1966), 123-40. N. J. HEIN

TURBAN (I; Persian *dulband*). Cloth headgear worn by men in Islamic lands. The Arabic term is *'imāma,* specifically the length of cloth wound round any sort of cap. MUHAMMAD is said to have worn an *'imāma,* but there is no mention of the article in the QUR'ĀN. It never became a binding duty for Muslims to wear the turban, and in modern times there has been considerable debate between liberals and conservatives over its status.

There are distinctions of style, color, and size according to sect, family, occupation, and status. Only a descendant of Muhammad (SAYYID) may wear a green turban and garments. Among Shi'ites a Sayyid wears a black turban. Large turbans are worn by religious scholars, for whom it is not considered ostentatious. Most Muslims wear white turbans.

Considerable etiquette is connected with the turban: it should not be worn before the beard has begun to grow, the first wearing of a new turban should be on a Friday, and at saints' tombs in Egypt and other countries a turban rests on a special stand on or near the sarcophagus. Traditionally, the length of cloth which makes a turban should be long enough to serve as its owner's shroud.

Bibliography. E. W. Lane, *An Account of the Manners and Customs of the Modern Egyptians* (1836, rpr. 1954), pp. 34-36; W. Björkman, "Turban," in *SEI* (1953), 596-99, with extensive bibliography. F. M. DENNY

TUṢITA HEAVEN tōō′ shē tə (B). One of the planes of form (RŪPA); a heaven attained by the merit of good works. It is here that GAUTAMA Buddha dwelt as a BODHISATTVA, prior to his last birth, and where MAITREYA now awaits his last birth.

K. CRIM

TWELVERS (I). *See* IMĀMIYYA.

TWICE BORN (*Dvija;* H—Skt.). A designation of Hindus of the BRAHMIN caste; it also is applied to the KSATRIYA and VAIŚYA castes. Referring to these castes as twice born announces the purity of their ARYAN blood as well as their religious status as those who may receive initiation into VEDIC study.

In contrast, the ŚŪDRAS and others outside the traditional caste bounds cannot receive sacramental rebirth and are called "once born" (*eka-jati*). By being excluded from the rite of initiation and study of the sacred Vedic texts they are prohibited from using the Vedic MANTRAS and practicing the Vedic rituals which can lead to salvation (MOKSA).

It seems that originally the initiation rite was primarily for educational purposes, opening for the child the sacred lore of Vedic society. For example, the term initiation is used in the Atharva Veda

D. M. Knipe

Twice born initiation ceremony *(upanayana)*

(11.5.3) in the sense of a preceptor taking charge of a student. This is also true in some Brāhmaṇical ritual texts (ŚB 11.5.4).

The idea of a sacramental rebirth belongs to the later Vedic period. Here a young man is said to receive his initial birth from his mother and his second, spiritual, birth from his initiation (AV 11.5.3). The student's rebirth is symbolized in terms of the teacher changing the boy into an embryo and keeping him in his belly for three nights. In later texts, the climax of the rite occurs with the reciting of the sacred GĀYATRĪ MANTRA (RV 3.62.10) to the student by his preceptor. The teaching of the sacred mantra indicates the second birth of the child. From this time forward the teacher is regarded as the father and the Gāyatrī Mantra as the mother of the initiate (Laws of Manu 2.170). By the sixth century B.C. the initiation rite had become fully established and was assumed to be universally incumbent on the upper three castes.

Only by performing the initiation rite can one become twice born. The student has been spiritually transformed. His body has been sanctified and he has been purified from all previous and future evil deeds and their consequences (Laws of Manu 2.26). The student is now fit for union with BRAHMAN (Laws of Manu 2.28).

Ideally, the young man who has been initiated has passed from his former state of ignorance, impurity, and irresponsibility into a sacred social position of wisdom, purity, and responsibility. Not only could the twice born expect to participate in the social benefits of their new status, but they could also expect to assume major responsibility for the well-being of society.

Bibliography. P. V. Kane, *History of Dharmaśāstra,* vol. II, Part 1, ch. 7; Carl Olson, "The Existential, Social, and Cosmic Significance of the Upanayana Rite," *Numen,* vol. XXIV, fasc. 2 (1977), 152-60; R. B. Pandey, *Hindu Samskaras* (2nd rev. ed. 1969), pp. 111-52.

C. OLSON

TYNDALE, WILLIAM (Ch; 1494?-1536). An early English Protestant, whose translation of the NT (1525) and much of the OT into English provided the basis for the King James Version of the Bible. Foreshadowing teachings of the PURITANS, Tyndale late in his life placed emphasis on the role of law in salvation. *See* REFORMATION, PROTESTANT.

R. L. HARRISON

U

UCHIMURA, KANZO oo chĭ mo͞o´ rä kän´ zō (Ch; 1861–1930). Independent evangelist, thinker, writer, critic, and founder of Mukyōkai (nonchurch) movement in Japan. He combined cultural sensitivity for Japanese history with study of the Bible. He published the periodical *Seisho no Kenkyu* (Study of the Bible), 1900–1930. K. Koyama

UDRAKA RĀMAPUTRA oo drŭ´ kŭ rä mä po͞o´ trŭ (B—Skt.). A religious teacher of Magadha, one of the four major kingdoms of northern India and the geographical base of the itinerant ministry of Gautama the Buddha. Shortly after Gautama left his family on his religious quest, he traveled in a southeasterly direction toward the major culture centers of the Ganges river basin. Of the teachers whom he met at this time two names are cited in particular, Ārāḍa Kālāma of Vaiśālī and Udraka Rāmaputra of Magadha. Both these teachers made use of a threefold structure which came to be characteristic of monastic Buddhism: teaching (Dharma), discipline (Vinaya), and order (Saṅgha). Gautama evidently practiced meditation for some time under the leadership, in turn, of Kālāma and Rāmaputra. According to what may be a later scholastic interpretation, the methodology of Kālāma led to the sixth stage of mental awareness and that of Rāmaputra to the seventh. Thus neither reached the eighth stage of a later Buddhist meditation formula. Whatever the truth of this interpretation, Gautama was not satisfied with the teaching and practice of these men and continued his quest independently (Majjhima Nikāya I, 163-66).

R. H. Drummond

'ULAMĀ' o͞o lă mä´ (I—Arab.; plural of *'ālim,* "one who knows, an expert, a scholar"). Collective designation for Muslim religious scholars, "those who possess [right] knowledge *('ilm)*" and thus are authorities for all aspects of Islamic life. Apparently from the beginning of Islam, Muslims looked for direction to those men and women noted for their competence in the quadrivium of Islamic learning: Arabic Language (grammar and lexicology), Qur'ān and Qur'ānic studies, Ḥadīth and *ḥadīth* studies, and Fiqh (religious law). Often the foci of pious opposition to political authority perceived as unjust, the *'ulamā'* were also those to whom rulers and administrators turned for guidance and for legitimation. What began, however, as the informal and consensual role of the most learned—as custodians of the Sunna and critics of its neglect—gradually became institutionalized, so that the *'ulamā'* became a recognized professional class. So uniform did their role throughout Islam become that a fourteenth century *'ālim* could move from Andalusia to Egypt or even India and be accepted and employed at once. In many areas they formed an aristocratic and sometimes endogamous social class.

There were two major factors in this transformation to a professional role. (1) The crystallization of religious law *(fiqh),* through which *'ilm* became less a personal quality and more a mastery of particular data and methods. The *'ulamā'* became the arbiters of the now authoritative Ijmā' as well as conservators of the tradition of Qur'ān and *ḥadīth* interpretation and perpetuators of *taqlīd*—the system of binding legal precedent. (2) The increasingly important role of the *'ulamā'* in society. Particularly after the tenth century decline of stable central government, the *'ulamā'* came to be powerful both as representatives of the universally acknowledged Sharia and as mediators of lawsuits, administrators of inheritances and endowments (*see* Waqf), large property-holders, teachers, preachers, and judges. The elaboration of the Madrasa system of education consolidated their position and standardized their training.

It is not then surprising that the renascent central authorities of the Ottomans, Safavids, and Moguls (from *ca.* 1500) attempted to control or suppress the *'ulamā'*. The Ottomans, for example, organized them into a regimented hierarchy. Those who wanted official position were promoted through standard grades and, in the *madrasas,* ranked by status. All *'ulamā'* came under direction of the Shaikh al-Islām, the supreme judiciary authority of the empire, who had power to judge the legitimacy of civil law by recourse to the broader and higher standards of the sharia.

Despite governmental efforts to control them, the *'ulamā'* remain today a kind of fulcrum between the people and their rulers. This is most evident in SHI'ITE Iran, where the *'ulamā'* are uniquely powerful. The events there during the 1970s present the classical model of the *'ulamā'* uniting a demoralized people to repudiate an oppressive civil authority in the name of Islamic ideals.

Bibliography. M. Hodgson, *The Venture of Islam,* Vol. II (1974); J. Berque, *Egypt: Imperialism and Revolution* (1972); T. Naff and R. Owen, eds., *Studies in Eighteenth Century Islamic History* (1977), pts. I, II; R. Bulliet, *The Patricians of Nishapur* (1972); N. Keddie, ed., *Scholars, Saints, and Sufis* (1972).

W. A. GRAHAM and A. K. REINHART

UMĀ oo′ mä (H). *See* PĀRVATĪ; GODDESS (INDIA).

'UMAR IBN al-KHAṬṬĀB oo mär′ ĭb′ən ăl kăt tăb′ (I; *ca.* 581-644). Second CALIPH of Islam, devoted companion of MUHAMMAD, and initiator of the administrative mechanisms which made the Islamic empire possible.

Islamic traditions represent 'Umar as having converted around the age of twenty-six, four years before the HIJRA, after violently opposing Islam. His personality and will were extremely forceful. Throughout Muhammad's Medinan career, 'Umar seems to have been in complete harmony with the policies of both the Prophet and ABŪ BAKR, the first caliph, with whom he shared the honor of being father-in-law of Muhammad. No military exploits were credited to him, but he was involved in the revelation of portions of the QUR'ĀN (Sura 2:125; 33:53; and 66:6). At the death of Abū Bakr, there seems to have been no formal designation of 'Umar as successor, but his rule received almost unanimous acceptance, the only opposition deriving from supporters of ALI. Once in office, he assumed the title Commander of the Faithful, and dared to dismiss Khālid ibn al-Walīd, early Islam's most spectacular general, who had challenged his authority. 'Umar instituted a system of checks on provincial administrators by dividing the authority between the military and civil commander and the fiscal officer. He established the pension register and the office of judge, regulated worship in the MOSQUES, and established a number of military centers, which later developed into famous Islamic cities. 'Umar was assassinated by a disgruntled slave before providing for a successor. Despite rumors, there is no indication of a conspiracy to kill him, but the histories are unanimous that he was more feared than liked, particularly because he expected all to adhere to his own severe ascetic standards.

Bibliography. M. A. Shaban, *Islamic History A.D. 600-750* (1971), pp. 28-61; A. J. Wensinck, *Handbook of Early Muhammadan Tradition* (1927).

G. D. NEWBY

UMAYYADS o͞o mī′ yăds (I). The first dynastic ruling house in ISLAM (661-750), self-declared heirs to the orthodox or patriarchal CALIPHATE (632-661). From their capital in Damascus they extended the borders of the Islamic empire to India in the east and to Spain in the west. The early Umayyad caliphs were adept military tacticians and effective bureaucrats; they also left a rich legacy in poetry, Greek to Arabic translations, and architectural monuments. But they never solved the problem of how to deal with non-Arab converts to Islam *(mawālī);* these, together with Arab discontents looking for a return to pristine Islam, supported the 'ABBĀSID forces, who defeated the Umayyads in 750. A lone Umayyad dynast escaped to Spain and established there a regional dynasty that lasted until 1031.

Bibliography. C. Cahen, "The Patriarchal and Umayyad Caliphates," in P. M. Holt, *et al., The Cambridge History of Islam,* I (1970), 74-103; F. E. Peters, *Allah's Commonwealth* (1973), pp. 94-136.

B. LAWRENCE

UMMA oom′ mä (I—Arab., lit., "people" or "community"). The worldwide community of Muslims. Though the Arabic *jamā'a* is nearly synonymous with *umma,* the former is now associated almost exclusively with the SUNNI branch of Islam, as in the expression *ahl al-sunna wa-l-jamā'a,* "people of the custom and the community [of Muhammad]," while *umma,* both in meaning and in usage, encompasses the entire Muslim community, SHI'ITE as well as Sunni.

Umma is both a scriptural and theological concept and a descriptive historical reality. In both senses it has far-reaching importance.

1. **History.** The earliest Islamic usage of *umma* occurs in the QUR'ĀN, where it is integral to MUHAMMAD'S revelatory *dicta* on prophecy. Each community is defined by the presence in its midst of a prophetic or apostolic figure (*see* NABI), whose function is to declare the divine intent for the community to which he has been sent (Sura 6:42, 10:48, etc.). While many of the prophets, including Muhammad, were not accepted without resistance, hostility, and often violent opposition to their teaching, it is they alone who provide the standard by which their respective communities will ultimately be judged on the Day of Reckoning (*see* ESCHATOLOGY §3).

The Qur'ān extolls Muhammad as God's chosen apostle to the Arabs; at the same time, it alludes to the intrinsic unity of all humanity as a single community (see, e.g., Sura 10:19, 11:118). The potential recovery of unitary identity is possible through common adherence to a revealed book *(kitāb).* All PEOPLE OF THE BOOK *(ahl al-kitāb),* therefore, are esteemed because of their book, however much they may have reviled their respective prophets or distorted the true content of prophetic discourse. Muhammad is viewed as the final prophet, to whom was revealed a book without error or contradiction, the Qur'ān. His book surpassed other books, even as his prophecy was the culmination of all prophecy. Yet the subsequent evolution of protected peoples in the expanding Muslim world partially derives from the Qur'ānic appeal to the original social unity of mankind. (*See* ISLAM §1.)

The notion of *umma* or community was variously interpreted by the Muslim rulers who succeeded Muhammad and tried to apply his revelatory utterances to changing circumstances. The decisive norm was established under the second CALIPH, 'UMAR (r. 634-44). At his direction a *dīvān* or register was compiled. Excluding Jews and Christians, it ranked members of Muhammad's community by a strict chronological standard: the date of their profession of loyalty *(bai'at)* to the Prophet. Highest on the list were the Meccans who had been senior companions of Muhammad (*see* SAḤĀBA). Next were the loyal helper families of MEDINA (*see* ANṢĀR), followed by later Meccan converts to Islam, and then Arab tribes, according to the date of their leaders' profession of Islam. The Prophet's wives and family were also accorded a special albeit imprecise place of respect (*see* SAYYID).

'Umar's *dīvān* was never abrogated, but it was challenged by some and ignored by others. Shi'ite Muslims, who recognize no legitimate successor to Muhammad before ALI, the fourth caliph (r. 656-661), claim for themselves a relationship of supreme intimacy to Muhammad through Ali, the Prophet's closest male relative among the *ṣaḥāba*. Shi'ites reject 'Umar's *dīvān,* along with 'Umar. By contrast, the *mawālī,* or clients to the Arabs in lands conquered beyond the peninsula, at first paired their own social ranking to an Arab tribe under the UMAYYADS (661-750), but then gradually came to seek an independent, regional identity under the 'ABBĀSIDS (750-1258) and subsequent dynasties (*see* ISLAM §3c).

The proliferation of regional ruling groups under the later 'Abbāsids, the emergence of three major, often competing medieval Islamic empires, and finally the development of a series of Muslim nation-states in the present century—all seem to undermine the validity of *umma* as a workable concern vital to the world view of Muslim peoples. Yet the ideal persists; its tenacity should not be minimized or disregarded because of historical circumstances, many of them beyond the control of Muslim leaders. The pan-Islamic movement of the late nineteenth and early twentieth centuries (*see* JAMĀL al-DĪN AFGHĀNĪ) and the current widespread revival of Islamic loyalties indicate that *umma* as a vision of religious solidarity continues to inspire Muslims when they react to threats—whether perceived as Western, colonialist, secular, modernist, or communist—against the traditional norms and values of Islam. (*See* ISLAM §§4, 5.)

2. The present *umma*. At the present time the demographic profile of Islam is more non-Arab than Arab, more Asian and African than Middle Eastern. The total number of Muslims worldwide is not less than 650 million and perhaps as high as 1 billion. There are few authoritative sources on demographic statistics, in large part because few Muslim countries conduct a periodic census with the persistent attention to detail that characterizes the census process in Western Europe and the United States. One respected source is the 1975 Report of the Center for Integrative Studies, University of Houston. Of the 675 million people it cites as Muslim, 127 million reside in Southeast Asia (principally in Indonesia, the largest Muslim country in the world; *see* ISLAM IN SOUTHEAST ASIA). Another 198 million are spread throughout the three major states of South Asia: Pakistan, India, and Bangladesh (*see* ISLAM IN SOUTH ASIA), while Africa, excluding Egypt, contains approximately 140 million Muslim inhabitants. The entire Middle East, including Iran and Turkey, does boast more than 150 million Muslims, but if one focuses only on the *Arab* Middle East (and, therefore, discounts most of the population of Iran and Turkey, which is non-Arab), the maximum number of Middle Eastern Muslim Arabs dwindles to 80 million or less than one eighth of the total worldwide population of Muhammad's community.

Thus it is necessary to discard the common assumption that Islam is an ethnically Arab, regionally Middle Eastern religion. Muslims do face an Arabian city, MECCA, when they pray daily (*see* QIBLAH); they do believe in an Arabian prophet of the QURAISH tribe, MUHAMMAD; and they do accord a unique role to ARABIC as the language of the Qur'ān and ritual PRAYER. But Islam itself is a transregional, multilinguistic, polyethnic, culturally varied community. Muslims bow to Mecca from many directions of the planet Earth.

Not only the size but the condition of the Muslim community in certain countries is especially difficult to assess. The above mentioned study from the University of Houston, for instance, includes figures for the U.S.S.R.; its Muslim inhabitants are said to number 23 million. Yet Alexandre Bennigsen, the foremost authority on Islam in the Soviet Union, citing the latest (1979) census estimates that the Muslim population which is concentrated in the southern reaches of the Soviet state exceeds 43 million. If his figures are correct, then the Soviet Union is at present the fifth largest Muslim country, ranking after Indonesia, Pakistan, India, and Bangladesh but ahead of Nigeria, Turkey, and Iran as well as all the Arab Muslim countries. Even more important than its current size is the projected growth rate of the Soviet Muslim community. If it continues to expand at the current rate of 50 percent per decade, Soviet Muslims, most of whom are Sunni Turks still pursuing ancestral customs and resisting efforts at assimilation, will number 80 to 100 million by the turn of the century. What role such a sizable religious minority can or will play in an atheistic communist state is uncertain, but their size suggests that they must exert a degree of influence on both the domestic and foreign policies.

Bibliography. *SEI*, pp. 603-4; L. Gardet, "*Djamā'a*," *EI*, II, 411-12; B. Lewis, ed., *Islam and the Arab World* (1976), pp. 345-47; A. Bennigsen, "Islam in the Soviet Union," unpublished paper delivered at Duke University, Apr. 10, 1980. B. LAWRENCE

'UMRA oom´ rä (I). The ensemble of rites performed by Muslim pilgrims at the KA'BA in MECCA (*see* HAJJ). The *'umra* may be performed separately or as part of the pilgrimage. It is sometimes called the "little pilgrimage." H. B. PARTIN

UNCTION (Ch). The SACRAMENT of anointing the sick with oil and praying for healing and forgiveness (Jas. 5:14-15). In the medieval West the forgiveness was emphasized and the rite was limited to those at the point of death (extreme unction). Today, it is treated as a sacrament of total healing, both physical and spiritual. T. J. TALLEY

UNIAT CHURCHES (Ch; Polish—*unia*, from Lat. *unio*). Eastern churches that profess doctrinal teachings (including FILIOQUE) of the ROMAN CATHOLIC Church, accept papal primacy, and are in communion with Rome. These churches retain their own liturgies and languages and follow their canon law. They have a married clergy.

The official Roman Catholic term for Uniats is "Ruthenian" (Lat.—"Russian"). At Brest, Poland, in 1596 Michael Ragoza, Metropolitan of Kiev, and several other bishops in southwest Russia, then under Polish rule, accepted union with Rome on the terms of the Council of Florence (1439), separating from the ORTHODOX CHURCH and forming the Uniat Church in the Ukraine. The majority of the Orthodox in this area refused the *unia*, and with changing political fortunes many Uniats returned to the Orthodox Church. Byzantine-rite Uniats are also found in Polish Galicia, Czechoslovakia, and Hungary.

There are other Uniat churches. In the period of the Crusades (1198-1291) Armenians of Cilicia joined Rome. Due to Roman Catholic missionary activities, a group of NESTORIANS, called Chaldeans, became Uniats in 1551. Subsequently other groups of Eastern Christians formed Uniat churches, separating from Orthodox, MONOPHYSITE, or Nestorian churches. Only the Syrian MARONITES of Lebanon, who joined Rome in 1182, have no counterpart Eastern church.

Worldwide there are over ten million Uniats.

Bibliography. D. Attwater, *Christian Churches of the East* (1961). V. KESICH

UNIFICATION CHURCH. A MILLENARIAN MOVEMENT founded in Korea in 1954 under the leadership

Rev. and Mrs. Sun Myung Moon at the first graduation ceremony of the Unification Theological Seminary, 1977

of the Rev. SUN MYUNG MOON; its official name is the Holy Spirit Association for the Unification of World Christianity. Members are dubbed "Moonies," after the name of their leader.

1. **History.** Moon's early years were idealized as his influence grew. He tells how JESUS appeared to him on EASTER morning, 1936, and asked him to take responsibility for establishing the KINGDOM OF GOD on earth. In experiences reflecting Korean SHAMANISM, Moon communicated with MOSES, Jesus, BUDDHA, and others, and he has continued through the years to "travel in the spirit world."

After the end of World War II in 1945, Moon began to gather followers in Pyongyang, northern Korea. Opposition from the communist authorities led to his arrest and two years' imprisonment. Freed by UN forces in 1950, he moved to Pusan in the south and laid the foundations for his church. The church spread to Japan and Western Europe, and as early as 1959 began its growth in the United States. World mission headquarters are located in mid-town Manhattan, and many activities are centered on an estate at Tarrytown, N. Y. and a seminary at Barrytown, N. Y. Opposition to communism led Moon to concentrate his efforts in the U. S. as the leading nation of the free world. During the bicentennial of American independence in 1976 he placed particular stress on America's world role, and held a rally in Yankee Stadium and another at the Washington Monument.

2. **Beliefs.** *Divine Principle*, based on Moon's lectures about the revelations he has received, has

gone through several revisions. The Korean text was revised in 1972 as *Wŏn-li Kang Non* ("Lectures on Principle," cf. Li [2]) and the English, which differs slightly, in 1973. Beginning with creation, the work sets forth a view of history characterized by human sin and God's efforts to establish his kingdom on earth. Humanity is to be restored to its original perfect state by a principle of indemnity, by which all sin and wrong in the world must be put right at the proper time. Adam and Eve, the first parents, sinned, so a second Adam and a second Eve were to pay the indemnity. Jesus came to earth as the second Adam; he was not God himself, but was related to God "as body is related to mind" *(Divine Principle,* p. 211). All Jesus' contemporaries failed to support him, and he did not marry, so he could complete only a spiritual restoration through the Holy Spirit, who played the role of the second Eve. The material world remained under the power of Satan.

Through an elaborate system of parallels between periods of biblical time and periods since Jesus, Moon teaches that the time is near when a new Messiah, the Lord of the Second Coming, will arise in Korea, complete the indemnity, marry the new Eve, found a sinless humanity, and establish God's kingdom. While not openly claiming to be the messiah, Moon and his present wife (his first marriage ended in divorce in the 1950s) are carrying out their roles in accordance with his prophecies about the messiah. As spiritual parents of church members the Moons take responsibility for arranging marriages between members and unite hundreds of couples in matrimony in mass ceremonies. Since sex is believed to have been the original sin of Eve, sexual mores are puritanical and are strictly enforced.

The strong element of messianism found in Korean Religion was borrowed by Moon, who cites the *Chŭng Kam Nok,* a cult text from the fifteenth or sixteenth century, to support the claim that the messiah will come from Korea. Moreover, Moon's suffering at the hands of Korean communists has produced a consistent opposition to all communist movements. Korea, divided at the 38th Parallel, is the front line where the free world and the communist world confront each other, and thus the suitable home for the victor from the East (Isa. 41:2).

3. Theological education. In 1977 Unification Theological Seminary graduated the first fifty students from a two-year program in religious education. Students have been drawn from Japan, the U. S., and several European countries. There is no ordination for graduates. Most work in regional centers of the church, but a significant number pursue graduate degrees at leading schools of religion. Despite energetic efforts by the church, the N. Y. State Board of Regents has declined to accredit the seminary.

4. Opposition. There has been criticism of recruitment practices and economic activities. Charging that the church has "brainwashed" its converts, parents have hired professional "deprogrammers" to abduct their children out of the church and reorient their thinking. The American Civil Liberties Union has consistently opposed such deprogramming.

Other critics attack the church's financial policies. In keeping with the goal of establishing the kingdom of God, the church engages in various economic enterprises and sends members out to sell flowers or to gather contributions on the street. Proceeds go to central headquarters. Critics cite a preoccupation with material goods and a high standard of living for church leaders as evidences of worldliness.

In 1975 the Unification Church applied for membership in the Council of Churches of New York City. The National Council of Churches then conducted a theological analysis of Unification doctrine and concluded, "The claims of the Unification Church to Christian identity cannot be recognized."

Bibliography. S. Choi, "Korea's Tong-il Movement," *Transactions of the Korea Branch, Royal Asiatic Society* (1967); I. L. Horowitz, *Science, Sin, and Scholarship* (1978), a collection of essays by supporters and opponents of the movement; Y. O. Kim, *Unification Theology and Christian Thought* (1975), by a theologian of the church; F. Sontag, *Sun Myung Moon* (1977).

K. Crim

UNITARIAN UNIVERSALIST ASSOCIATION

(Ch). A congregationally governed denomination created in 1961 by the merger of the American Unitarian Association and the Universalist Church of America with the purpose "to cherish and spread the universal truths taught by the great prophets and teachers of humanity in every age and tradition, immemorially summarized in the Judeo-Christian heritage as love to God and love to man." The new denomination, active in liberal causes, continues its predecessors' commitment to live in the tension between humanistic liberalism and Christianity. Outside its native New England its membership tends to consist of well-educated, upper-middle-class converts.

1. American Unitarianism. A defining feature of Unitarianism is the rejection of the orthodox doctrine of the Trinity. In denying the deity of Jesus and affirming the unity of God, American Unitarianism claims the heritage of the ancient Arians, the Socinians of the Reformation, and the English Unitarian movement of the Enlightenment. Early institutionalizations in America reflect English influence. However, the major impetus toward Unitarianism came, ironically, from New England Puritanism, within which cosmopolitan elements became receptive to Enlightenment ideas. With the preaching of William Ellery Channing and his *Unitarian Christianity* (1819), the movement acquired name, definition, theology, and leadership. Committed to Scripture interpreted by reason, Channing preached the unity of God, a unified Jesus

ction of
, and a
manity.
terature
ntalism
nomina-
hristian
tuitive,
nted by
German

distin-
ne quip:
n them
d to be
was an
nt with
sted on
dence in
(1803),
dogma:
ealed in

...Lord Jesus Christ, by one Holy Spirit
of Grace, who will finally restore the whole family of mankind to holiness and happiness." Under popular, circuit-rider leadership the movement spread, particularly in New England, until by the 1850s there were some 800,000 members in congregations loosely knit in associations and a General Convention. By 1900 Universalism was the sixth largest denomination; thereafter it declined. Its theological development and reaction to cultural movements paralleled that of the Unitarians, making possible the merger of 1961.

Bibliography. E. Cassara, ed., *Universalism in America: A Documentary History* (1970); E. A. Robinson, *American Universalism* (1970); E. M. Wilbur, *A History of Unitarianism*, 2 vols. (1945, 1952); C. Wright, *A Stream of Light* (1975).

R. E. RICHEY

UNITED CHURCH OF CHRIST. A Protestant denomination, dating in America from the arrival of the PILGRIMS in 1620. The Congregational Church merged with the Christian denomination in 1931 to form the Congregational Christian churches. In 1961 these merged with the Evangelical and Reformed to form the United Church of Christ. There are approximately 6,500 churches in the U.S. with 1,800,000 members, served by 9,500 clergy.

The denomination does not require acceptance of a particular creed, nor does it recognize the authority of the APOSTOLIC SUCCESSION. Authority emanates from the individual members of the local church. The church recognizes the two biblical SACRAMENTS of BAPTISM and the Lord's Supper (EUCHARIST) and accepts the TRINITY. The majority do not believe in the VIRGIN BIRTH, holding that what JESUS taught and how he lived, rather than the manner of his birth, is of prime significance. The denomination applies scientific method to the study of the BIBLE and regards it as revealing the will of God. While believing that death is not the end of life, members do not regard HEAVEN AND HELL as places, but conditions of either eternal presence with or separation from God. Sin is indifference or direct opposition to the expressed will of God as revealed by Jesus Christ.

The denomination is dedicated to the preservation of human dignity, the elimination of intolerance, the equality of men and women, ecumenical cooperation, and the responsibility of all to "work and pray for the transformation of the world into the Kingdom of God."

Bibliography. D. Horton, *The United Church of Christ* (1962).

D. W. O'CONNOR

UNTOUCHABLES (H). *See* HARIJAN.

UPANIṢAD o͞o pŭn´ ĭ shŭd (H—Skt.; lit. "to sit down near to" [*upa*—"near"; *ni*—"down"; *sad*—"to sit"]). (1) secret; (2) mystical doctrine or teaching; (3) independent treatises or portions of BRĀHMAṆAS and ĀRAṆYAKAS containing the culmination of VEDIC wisdom.

1. Nature and meaning. In the Brāhmaṇas and Āraṇyakas, *upaniṣad* is a generic term referring in one sense or another to a secret, an esoteric word, phrase, or oral teaching, or, rarely, to an injunction of religious action. As "that which is hidden or secret," it can refer to sacred as well as profane ideas (*see* CU VIII.8.5; TU I.11.6; II.9.1; III.10.6; Śvet. U V.6). Only rarely, until the early medieval period, did *upaniṣad* refer to a complete text or to a body of texts. (*See* BĀU IV.1.2 and Mait. U II.3.)

Not until the eighth century A.D. does *upaniṣad* come to denote the corpus of late Vedic texts now known as "the classical Upaniṣads." Since that time Upaniṣad has referred to one of the texts identified by ŚAMKARA as an authoritative source of *vedāntavijñāna* ("the end-of-the-Veda wisdom"). Virtually all modern scholars include the following among the ancient or classical Upaniṣads: Īśa, Kena, Kaṭha, Maitrī, Praśna, Muṇḍaka, Aitareya, Māṇḍūkya, Kauṣītaki, Chāndogya, Taittirīya, Śvetāśvatara and Bṛhadāraṇyaka. These, with the Vedānta Sūtras (See BRAHMA SŪTRAS), constitute the authoritative sources of the Vedānta "schools" of thought (DARŚANA).

2. Diversity. The content and symbolism of each Upaniṣad is as disparate as the history, traditions, and texts of the Vedic schools from which they came. Thus the symbolism of the Yajur Vedic Upaniṣads reflects the function of the *adhvaryu* priests who were responsible for the physical aspects of the sacrifice (e.g., the use of the altar as symbol of the universe in TU II.1-5; the horse sacrifice as symbol of the cosmogony in BĀU I.1-2). Likewise, the Sāma Vedic Upaniṣads reflect the *udgātṛ* priest's role as a singer of meters (cf. CU I-II). Even in those instances in which the focus of a particular passage is on one or another of the dominant speculative issues of the Upaniṣads, the disparity of their origins is clear. For example, the dominant speculative issue in the Upaniṣads of the Yajur Vedic tradition (particularly when YĀJÑAVALKYA is involved) revolves about the ATMAN.

The orthogenetic relation of each Upaniṣad to its tradition is only one of the factors which mitigate the contention that the classical Upaniṣads contain a common body of doctrine expressing the identity of all with BRAHMAN, the supreme spirit. Such consistency in content and meaning as has been gained has resulted either from dogmatic efforts (e.g., those of Śaṃkara or RĀMĀNUJA) to erase the real differences among the Upaniṣads or from ideologically motivated translations, sometimes from the original, which attempt to minimize those differences. The Upaniṣads resist such attempts not only because of their diverse origins, but also because they incorporate the developing speculation of the various Vedic schools (*śākhas*) prior to the close of the Vedic canon. Of course, in the case of many of these texts, the problem of attempting to ignore their specific origins is most difficult since they are merely portions of Brāhmaṇas or Āraṇyakas (e.g., Bṛhadāraṇyaka, Chāndogya, and Taittirīya).

The classical Upaniṣads reflect the social, political, and spiritual interests, the moral and aesthetic values, and, occasionally, the geographical area of the Vedic *śākhas*. In short, the disparity in content and focus of the Upaniṣads remains because they were never intended to be a separate, systematized collection.

3. Contents. Generally the Upaniṣads agree on certain vague notions regarding the problems of the human condition and the solutions. They tend to agree on the superiority of the spiritual to the physical, that knowledge is preferable to ignorance, that a disciplined life is requisite to the attainment of one's spiritual goals, that (even for the spiritual elite) certain rites are mandatory, that the manifest universe is the act of one divine agency, that works (KARMA) and knowledge (VIDYĀ) are both necessary for release from SAMSARA, that ignorant action is the cause of rebirth, and that knowledge of one's innermost spiritual being is crucial. If the classical Upaniṣads are approached with a critical eye, however, it becomes clear that any explication of their teaching must recognize their diversity.

For example, although the classical Upaniṣads generally agree that the manifest universe resulted from the creative act of a single divine agency, they present a bewildering and contradictory array of cosmogonies, both among different Upaniṣads and within a single text. Taking into account only those cosmogonies containing the term *agra* ("in the beginning"), one notes that the Bṛhadāraṇyaka alone has five different scenarios of the creation, four of them in the same book (I.2.1, I.4.1, I.4.10, I.4.11, and V.5.1).

Thus, in one Upaniṣad, there are four different creative powers (death, PURUṢA, Brahman, and water) creating five different entities (mind, an androgynous being, mundane power, all this, and Brahman). To complicate matters further, the creative principle in two of the cosmogonies, Brahman, is itself created in the last. If only the creative agencies differed, one might argue that they were merely different names for the same entity; but the clear difference in both means of creation and its effect forces one to recognize the disparity. In other classical Upaniṣads what occurred "in the beginning" is expressed still differently.

Analogous problems exist in attempting to arrive at a consistent rendering of either Brahman or Atman. Brahman is variously identified as: "the space outside a person" (CU III.12.7); "he who moves about in a dream" (CU VIII.10.1); as that which shines when a sacrificial fire burns and dies when the fire does not burn (KB II.12); "this whole world" (CU II.14.1); as that power which "sustains all works" (BĀU I.6.3); as "the formed and the formless, the non-existent (*asat*) and the existent (*sat*)" (Mait. U VI.3).

The ambiguity surrounding Atman is similar. Atman is variously "the undying, immortal, fearless Brahman" (BĀU IV. 4.25); that of which food is "the highest form" (Mait. U VI.11); "the Atman of the person that consists of the essence of food" (TU II.1.1); "the Atman of the Brahman" (TU I.6.2); and "that from which all works arise" (BĀU I.63).

Together with the cosmogonic variations cited above, the varying views of Brahman and Atman demonstrate and represent the different kinds of speculative and philosophical acumen developed over a period of at least four hundred years in different priestly schools (*śākhas*) often geographically removed from each other. Many of the problems of interpretation can be clarified by interpreting the Upaniṣads within their original contexts, but complete consistency cannot be expected from one text to another or within a given text.

However, the fact that the classical Upaniṣads are filled with ambiguity, paradox, and outright contradiction does not negate the herculean labors of theologians such as Śaṃkara or Rāmānuja. Indeed, the contrary is the case. Had the Upaniṣads been a unified corpus of doctrine at the close of the Vedic period, had they been consistent, and had they possessed the undisputed authority of the Vedānta, there would have been no occasion for the brilliant edifice erected by Śaṃkara. In their ambiguity lay their virtue, and in their disparate collections Śaṃkara discovered the key to an original and radical vision of human spirituality.

Bibliography. R. Hume, *Thirteen Principal Upanishads* (1971); P. Deussen, *Philosophy of the Upanishads* (rpr. 1966).

J. HELFER

UPOSATHA ōō pō´ sä tä (B—Skt.). The fortnightly observance (full-moon and new-moon days) which became an occasion for the reciting of the code of monastic law (PĀTIMOKKHA) which binds each monk and nun to one another and to the community. The

Pātimokkha has been part of the larger effort, represented by the VINAYA PITAKA and its commentary literature, to foster unity, cohesiveness, and discipline within the monastic Buddhist tradition. (*See* SANGHA.)

As the keeping of *uposatha* became institutionalized, the days of the moon's first and last quarters were added to the new- and full-moon days, and the four days together became the pervasive Buddhist weekly observance for laity as well as monks. *Uposatha* services began to include repetition of the precepts, paying homage (PŪJĀ) to the image of the BUDDHA, recitation of portions of the PALI CANON, and sermons by the monks. For the more devout laity, the five traditional Buddhist precepts against killing, stealing, lying, committing sexual offenses, and taking intoxicants were expanded to eight, with primary emphasis on avoiding luxury. While the keeping of *uposatha* has been common to both the THERAVĀDA and MAHĀYĀNA traditions, with widely varying practices in different contexts, it is currently observed more regularly in Sri Lanka and portions of mainland Southeast Asia.

Bibliography. S. Dutt, *Buddhist Monks and Monasteries of India (1962);* E. Frauwallner, *The Earliest Vinaya and the Beginnings of Buddhist Literature* (1956); C. Prebish, *Buddhist Monastic Discipline* (1975); *see* bibliog. for PĀTIMOKKHA.

B. L. SMITH

'URS oors (I). 1. A wedding celebration, for Muslims an indispensable, lavish part of every lawful union between man and woman. While the QUR'ĀN makes minimal provision for such ceremonies, the ḤADĪTH contains ample references to the etiquette which should be observed prior to and during the *'urs*, as well as afterward in the bridal chamber. Wedding customs vary from region to region, and often practices that were locally prevalent have been incorporated into Muslim ceremonies. (*See* MARRIAGE AND DIVORCE IN ISLAM.)

2. The anniversary of the death of an important SUFI SHAIKH. Numerous pilgrims, not all of them initiates into the order (ṬARĪQA) of the deceased saint and, in some places, even non-Muslims, come to the tomb of the shaikh, hoping to obtain the blessing *(baraka)* which he is thought to convey more powerfully on that occasion than at any other time.

B. LAWRENCE

URSULINES ûr′ sə lĭnz (Ch). To instruct girls at Brescia, St. Angela Merici in 1535 founded the Company of St. Ursula (a popular patron of education). From Angela's beginnings arose different religious communities called Ursulines. Many Ursuline communities in North America are independent of each other and vary in organization, way of life, and apostolate. *See* RELIGIOUS ORDERS.

W. H. PRINCIPE

'UTHMĀN IBN 'AFFĀN oot′ män ĭb′ ən äf fän′ (I). Third CALIPH (A.D. 644-56) of ISLAM. 'Uthmān was an early, pre-HIJRA convert to Islam, although he was a member of the UMAYYAD clan which took a leading role in opposing Muhammad. After the death of the second caliph, 'UMAR, in A.D. 644, he was chosen caliph by the council named by 'Umar on his deathbed. Since he was an Umayyad, his appointment may be seen as a victory of the old Meccan oligarchy.

His caliphate was a troubled one, leading to a series of civil wars which fragmented the Islamic community. 'Uthmān was charged by his critics, especially in the provinces, with nepotism in that he favored Umayyads in appointments—for example, the appointment of his kinsman Mu'āwiya (later the founder of the Umayyad Dynasty, A.D. 661-750) as governor of Syria. The traditional portrait of 'Uthmān among Islamic historians is of a weak, indecisive caliph dominated by his family.

Opposition to 'Uthmān's caliphate formed in Medina, especially among members of the family of the Prophet and other Meccans, and more overtly in Iraq and Egypt. In June, A.D. 656, a group of Egyptian army rebels with grievances invaded Medina and mortally wounded the caliph, thus establishing what proved to be a terrible precedent.

The outstanding achievement of 'Uthmān's caliphate was his establishment of the definitive text of the QUR'ĀN shortly after A.D. 650. H. B. PARTIN

al-'UZZA əl oo′ zə. Pre-Islamic Arabian goddess. *See* TIME OF IGNORANCE.

V

VADAGALAI väd ä gū lā (H—Tamil & Skt.; lit. "northern or Sanskrit literature and culture" [Tamil *vata*, "northern"; Skt. *kalā*, "art, culture, learning]). The "Northern School," a Śrī Vaisnava subsect stressing its Sanskritic, Vedic, or Brahmanical heritage relatively more than its "Southern" or Tamil elements. In contrast to the Tengalai or "Southern School," it holds that both divine grace and human initiative are necessary for liberation (*see* Vedānta §3).

W. G. Neevel

VĀHANA vä´ hŭ nŭ (H—Skt.; lit. "drawing, bearing, carrying" [*vah*—"to transport, to use"]). Any vehicle or animal used for transporting, carrying, or riding.

One of the most fascinating aspects of Hindu iconography is the association of various animals and birds with gods, goddesses, and other mythical beings. Deities are often depicted riding on the back of an animal or bird, or the *vāhana* can be found alongside or underneath the deity.

Hindu gods and goddesses can be easily identified once we know their specific *vāhana*. For example, the gander (Hamsa), is the mount of Brahmā and his consort Sarasvatī. The eagle (Garuda) is the well-known support for Vishnu, and Laksmī (also Śrī, Vishnu's consort) has an owl for her mount. Shiva's vehicle is Nandi, the famous mythical bull, and a lion is the mount for Pārvatī, Shiva's wife. Shiva's son, the elephant-headed Ganeśa, has a mouse (or rat) for his vehicle. Skanda, Shiva's second son, rides on a peacock. Yama, the god of death, is carried by a buffalo. Agni, the famous god of the Vedas, has a ram (or goat) and Indra in Hinduism rides his famous elephant Airāvata. Kubera, lord of the genii (Yaksas) is known as "he whose *vāhana* is a man."

Bibliography. W. D. O'Flaherty, *Hindu Myths* (1975); J. Gonda, *Change and Continuity in Indian Religion*, Ch. 3 (1965); J. Gonda, *Visnuism and Śivaism* (1970); H. Zimmer, *Myths and Symbols in Indian Art and Civilization* (1962), and *The Art of Indian Asia*, 2 vols. (1955).

H. H. Penner

VAIKUNTHA vī koon´ tū (H—Skt.). The name given to the sacred abode of Vishnu, said by some texts to be located on the slopes of Mt. Meru or in the Northern Ocean. The Ganges flows through this paradise, which is described as a place of pools and lotuses, gold and precious jewels. However, in other texts Vaikuṇṭha is simply called Vishnu's "own abode" *(sva lokam)* which is beyond space, time, and the effects of good and evil. Vaikuṇṭha's residents reflect their chosen Lord and are sky-blue in color, have four arms (a sign of nonhuman status), and are brilliantly adorned with fine jewels and pearls (Bh.P II.9.9-22). Vishnu is often pictured either seated upon a throne or lying upon his celestial couch, the serpent Śesa (Bh.P X.89.52-57). Unlike the heavens controlled by the process of Samsara, Vaikuṇṭha is an eternal abode. Since Vaikuṇṭha can be experienced also in the devotee's heart, it sometimes is equated with Vishnu himself.

J. Bare

VAIROCANA vī rō´ chə nə (B—Skt.; lit. "shining forth"). Originally regarded as an attribute of the earthly yet illumined Śākyamuni, Vairocana eventually came to be identified with a particular celestial Buddha (*see* Buddha, General Concepts of). The Japanese sun goddess Amaterasu has been understood as a manifestation of this celestial figure, probably because the etymology of Vairocana suggests the radiation of light. But it is in Tibetan Buddhism that Vairocana has received its fullest expression. Tibetans conceived of this celestial being as one of the five Dhyāni Buddhas, the other four which surround him being Amitābha (*see* Amida) in the west, Akṣobhya in the east, Amoghasiddhi in the north, and Ratnasambhava in the south. Dhyāni Buddhas are so named because they are depicted in a posture of meditation *(dhyāna)*: located in the heavens, these beings represent the ontological transition point between earth and Nirvana. Unlike a Bodhisattva, a Dhyāni Buddha has attained full Buddhahood; but unlike Śākyamuni he has achieved his Buddhahood in a nonhuman form.

In the seventh century Vairocana was popularized through his central placement in the art form of the

MANDALA; as the effulgent centerpiece of this art work, he took on a preeminence which was not enjoyed by the remaining four Dhyāni Buddhas. While some Tibetans interpreted all five Dhyāni Buddhas as offspring or outpourings from the Absolute, the Primordial or Ādi-Buddha, other Tibetans, like members of the Japanese SHINGON sect of Buddhism, identified Vairocana as the Ādi-Buddha. Thus, Vairocana became the chief object of devotion or meditation for the Shingon school and some adherents of Tibetan Buddhism. So conceived as the supreme reality, Vairocana became the originative principle which gives rise to all other Buddhas and bodhisattvas. In short, Vairocana was equated with the DHARMAKĀYA which produces and underlies all things. Śākyamuni and Amitābha are, respectively, an earthly expression and a celestial manifestation of the ultimate, cosmic reality which is known as the Dharmakāya. Ten billion beings, including Śākyamuni, were regarded as lesser Buddhas, because their ignorance could only be eliminated through the instruction of major or Dhyāni Buddhas. These, in turn, are taught by Vairocana, who is omnipresent and radiates the most intense light.

Vairocana, then, is a complex notion, for it has been used to describe realities on three distinct levels. On the mundane level it was interpreted as the NIRMĀṆAKĀYA (earthly Buddha) or Śākyamuni; on the celestial level it pertained to the SAMBHOGAKĀYA (heavenly Buddha) or Dhyāni Buddha; and on the transcendental level it was treated as synonymous with the Dharmakāya (ultimate Buddha) or True Buddha. To further complicate matters, in the eighth century the Kegon (Hua-yen) sect (*see* NARA BUDDHISM) gave a political dimension to the concept by equating the Japanese emperor with Vairocana and the balance of society with his phenomenal emanations. Perhaps the most imposing artistic rendering of Vairocana is the seated image, at the Tōdaiji temple in Nara, which was erected in A.D. 752 and which towers some fifty feet.

E. J. COLEMAN

VAIŚĀLĪ vī′ shä lē (B—Skt.) **VESĀLĪ** vā′ sä lē (B—Pali). Capital city of the district of Videha, of which the Licchavis were the major ethnic group at the time of Gautama the BUDDHA. Vaiśālī, located north of the Ganges River, was a prosperous cultural center noted for its religious teachers. One of these was ĀRĀḌA KĀLĀMA, under whose guidance Gautama carried on religious practices for a short time. The city was evidently an important center of the Buddha's ministry and was later chosen as the location of the so-called second general BUDDHIST COUNCIL. The Licchavis came to be among the Buddha's most devoted followers (Aṅguttara Nikāya IV, 1979-88).

R. H. DRUMMOND

VAIṢṆAVISM vīsh′ nä vī süm (H—Skt.; *Vaiṣṇava* [from the name of the Hindu high god VISHNU, an ancient VEDIC deity and one of the members of the TRIMŪRTI]). Religious groups and theologies having as deity one or another of Vishnu's AVATARS (a term usually translated as "incarnations," but more literally meaning "descents"). These groups may be found in all parts of India.

Of the fourteen avatars recognized by most texts and traditions, RĀMA and KRISHNA are the two major deities of Vaiṣṇavism, usually but not always exclusive of one another. It is to these two avatars of Vishnu that most Vaiṣṇava votaries are related in the religious attitude of *bhakti* (*see* BHAKTI HINDUISM).

1. **The Rāma sect.** Their primary text is the Epic RĀMĀYAṆA, first composed in Sanskrit by VĀLMĪKI sometime around the beginning of the Christian era. The Epic was later redone in a variety of regional languages and in a more specifically devotional mode by various writers, e.g., Kamban (twelfth century) in Tamil, TULSĪ DĀS (fifteenth-sixteenth centuries) in Hindī, and Krittivās (mid-fifteenth century) in Bengali. The story is basically that of the conquest of the evil forces of the universe by the good, the latter personified by Rāma and his allies, the army of the monkey king, but in the course of the Epic various ideals of Indian social behavior are established which include Rāma as the righteous king and his wife SĪTĀ the epitome of female chastity.

2. **The Krishna sect.** Here the texts and traditions are more various. Krishna the great warrior and king is extolled in the Harivaṃśa ("The lineage of Hari," Hari being another name for Krishna), an appendix to the great SANSKRIT Epic MAHĀBHĀRATA, and in fact throughout that Epic. Perhaps the most famous textual reference to Krishna is in the BHAGAVAD GĪTĀ, a philosophical and moral homily embedded in the Epic. But the Epic Krishna represents the high and transcendant God, and it is not such a God who is the object of popular Vaiṣṇavism, but rather Krishna the child or Krishna the lover of the GOPĪS. The best known text which deals with these aspects is the BHĀGAVATA PURĀṆA, a relatively late (*ca.* tenth century A.D.) work, probably from South India. In particular, the tenth book of this PURĀṆA deals with the love between the *gopīs* and Krishna, which became in the theology of devotion the allegory of the love between the worshiper and his god.

There are many schools of Krishna-centered Vaiṣṇavism across the subcontinent, all of them characterized by poetry and song as expressions of religious devotion. Some of them, such as that represented by the poet SŪRDĀS (1483-1563) in North India, have the child Krishna as their deity. Most others, such as that of the ĀḺVĀRS (sixth-tenth centuries) of the Tamil-speaking country and that of CAITANYA in Bengal, are devoted to Krishna the youth in his LĪLĀ with the *gopīs*. They all have much in common, however, and insight into them can be gained by looking at a single one, the Caitanya movement of Bengal. This movement is of interest too because it is on it that the Krishna Consciousness movement (i.e., the "HARE KRISHNAS") is based.

3. Doctrine. The doctrine basic to all Vaiṣṇava schools is that of *bhakti,* single-minded devotion to a personal god. This devotional relationship may take any of five forms, depending upon the individual worshiper's makeup. Krishna seen as the transcendent god and the worshiper as insignificant (the least preferred mode, as it is the least personal); Krishna as the master and the worshiper as servant; Krishna as child and the worshiper as parent; Krishna as friend and the worshiper as friend; and Krishna as lover and the worshiper as beloved, i.e., *gopī.* If worship is sufficiently intense, the worshiper is transformed, and one of these five becomes the state of loving relationship which he knows for eternity as well as in this life.

4. Poetry and song. The essential expressions of Vaiṣṇava devotion are poetry and song and are recorded most often in the regional languages (i.e., Hindī, Bengali, Marathi, Tamil, etc.) rather than in Sanskrit. A second feature of this regionalization of Vaiṣṇavism is the assumption that the individual is in direct relationship with God, and does not need a priest as intermediary, as he does in the Sanskritic Brahmanical tradition. The hymns are hortatory and also the results of devotion. Vaiṣṇavism is thus not only iconoclastic vis-à-vis the Brahmanical tradition, but also developed new ideas about the relationship between aesthetic and religious truth; namely, that true religious expression is also perfect poetry because both are the result of "salvation."

5. Social aspects. It is difficult to say where the movement gained its strength. In most parts of the subcontinent, followers usually gave up names which indicated caste or family and took on religious titles (*dās* means, for example, "servant"). This was symbolic also of the religiously egalitarian stance of the movement. Furthermore, in South India and in Bengal, at least, many important members of the movement, important poets also, are known to have been women; this too is unusual in the context of Brahminical society. It would be a mistake, however, in this context to equate social and religious egalitarianism.

Although the initial wide-ranging enthusiasm which surrounded early Vaiṣṇavism has died out in most parts of India over the centuries, Vaiṣṇavism remains one of the most powerful forces in the religious and intellectual life of that part of the world.

Bibliography. S. K. De, *Early History of the Vaiṣṇava Faith and Movement* (1961); E. C. Dimock, Jr. *et al, The Literatures of India: An Introduction* (1976); J. Gonda, *Aspects of Early Viṣṇuism* (1969), and *Viṣṇuism and Śivaism* (1970).

E. C. Dimock

VAIŚYA vīsh´ yä (H—Skt.). A generic term for members of the third division of traditional Hindu society (*see* Caste). Initially Vaiśyas were traders and husbandmen, but today most do not engage in agricultural work, though they may own land or be involved in commerce and banking. Like Brahmins and Kṣatriyas, the Vaiśyas are among the Twice Born castes, and they tend to be strict in the observance of caste rules and dietary prescriptions. Hence, vegetarianism is a hallmark of the majority of Vaiśyas.

C. von Fürer-Haimendorf

VAJRAYĀNA vŭj´ rŭ yä´ nə (H & B—Skt.; lit. "thunderbolt or diamond vehicle"). A label for a North Indian school of Tantrism of the sixth century A.D. and for one form of Tibetan Buddhism that arose in the seventh century. These esoteric movements emphasized meditation, employed Tantras, Mandalas, Mantras, and Mudrās. Tantrayāna and Mantrayāna are alternative names for Vajrayāna. Vajra, in the sense of a thunderbolt, calls to mind the sudden dawning of enlightenment. Vajra, in the sense of a diamond, suggests the impenetrable, ultimate reality which can destroy all other things but is itself indestructible. The secrecy of Tantric doctrines was preserved by expressing them in a secret language intelligible only to the initiated. Mandalas depicted an elaborate cosmology with the five Dhyāni Buddhas (*see* Buddha, General Concepts of) and their female partners at the center; encircling them are five Bodhisattvas and their female counterparts; surrounding them were any number of other figures. All such beings were interpreted as emanations from the Ādi-Buddha, the invisible Absolute. Once a Yogin had internalized a painted mandala, he was to reproduce it imaginatively, conjure up the Ādi-Buddha, and identify with this primordial reality. Rituals were also to be enacted mentally rather than physically. Ultimately one should arrive at the conclusion that only consciousness exists. (*See* Yogācāra.) Again, for the fully awakened person, there is no fundamental difference between Nirvana and Samsara or any other apparent opposites. Enlightenment itself is a realization of the unity of all polarities such as self-other, sacred-profane, and male-female.

Because sexual union is a paradigm for grasping the nondual character of reality, numerous art works vividly portrayed men and women joined in sexual intercourse. Moreover, Tibetan Buddhists actually advocated various acts of sexual intercourse as important ingredients in their religious rituals. Such acts were justified on the controversial grounds that the way to overcome the passions is through the passions. This claim can be interpreted in two ways. First, it may imply that by fully indulging in a given passion, one reaches a point of revulsion. Second, the assertion may mean that only one who can rise above a passion in the very heat of that passion has fully conquered it. A variety of sexual practices, including incest, were characteristic of Vajrayāna for a time, but gradually more conservative exponents of this school prevailed. Perhaps influenced by the philosophy of subjective idealism, they argued that the sexual relations which were encouraged in the Tantras were to be mentally acted out rather than physically executed. Misinterpreting the ontological tenet that all dualisms are unreal, some individuals reasoned that violating conventional morality could be justified on the grounds that all dichotomies, including that of good and evil, are to be repudiated. In response, reformers argued that if a person is really one with all other human beings, then he will do to them only what he would have done to himself.

Bibliography. H. Hoffman, *The Religions of Tibet* (1961); H. V. Guenther, *The Origin and Spirit of Vajrayana* (1959).

E. J. Coleman

VALLABHA vŭl′ lŭ bŭ (H—Skt.; *ca.* A.D. 1479-1531). A Hindu theologian and sectarian leader, founding teacher (Ācārya) of a Vaiṣṇava sect devoted to the deity Krishna and of the theistic Śuddha Advaita ("Pure Nonduality") school of Vedānta. With his contemporary, Caitanya, a major factor in the flowering of Krishna devotion in North India, he may also have been contemporary with the Hindī poet Sūrdās, whose devotional hymns were drawn upon to enhance the movement's popular appeal (*see* Bhakti Hinduism §5). Reputedly a precocious child, born near Banāras to South Indian Telugu Brahmin parents, by eleven he had mastered the Vedic scriptures and begun a pilgrimage around India. Settling at Vṛndāvana, he claimed a direct revelation from Krishna establishing a "new dispensation" of "nourishing grace" *(puṣṭi,* hence *Puṣṭi-Mārga* or "Path of Grace") to be entered into through a special initiation called *Brahma–sambandha* ("Relationship with the Divine, Brahman") in which one surrenders all he is and has to Krishna, receiving in return an abundant life of "play" (Līlā), bliss (Ānanda), love *(prema)* and "divine service" *(seva).* An extremely "world-and-life-affirming" system, Śuddha Advaita is a "nondualism" or panentheism that stresses the "purity," goodness, and reality of the world and the self as parts of the whole, Krishna, in explicit opposition to Śaṃkara's acosmic and nontheistic "absolute nondualism" *(kevala-*Advaita), which rejects the world and relationships as ultimately "impure" Māyā or "illusion."

Bibliography. B. M. C. Parekh, *Sri Vallabhacharya* (1943); M. I. Marfatia, *Philosophy of Vallabhācārya* (1967).

W. G. Neevel

VĀLMĪKI väl mē′ kē (H—Skt.). Legendary author of the Rāmāyaṇa. A folk etymology of his name indicates that he was born out of a *valmīka* (anthill) which grew around him as he was meditating. According to a folk legend, he was initially a bandit, but some sages took pity on him and taught him to chant the Mantra "marā, marā, marā." As he chanted, the syllables became inverted and produced the name "Rāma," by the power of which his bad Karma was burned away. The first book of the Rāmāyaṇa has a story about the invention of poetry by Vālmīki. One day in the forest he saw a hunter kill the male of a mating pair of krauñca birds. At the sight of the female bird crying at the loss of her mate Vālmīki was so moved that he cursed the hunter. The spontaneous curse happened to take the form of a verse. Brahmā, the god of creation, appeared before Vālmīki and told him that what he had just said was poetry, and that he should compose the story of Rāma in the new form. Indian literary tradition thus considers Vālmīki to be the first poet.

Vālmīki is also a character in the Rāmāyaṇa and in one version he shelters the abandoned Sītā, teaches her twin sons the Rāma story which he had composed, and eventually plays the role of reconciler between Rāma and Sītā.

V. N. Rao

VĀNAPRASTHA vä nŭ prŭs′ tŭ (H—Skt.; lit. "one who dwells in the forest"). Forest-dweller; the third of the four stages of life (Āśrama). When a Hindu male saw the birth of his first grandchild, he was to abandon the householder stage of life and enter a period of study, meditation, and gradual renunciation. Ideally he should move into the forest and live in poverty and simplicity. He should continue to keep the sacred fires, and his wife could accompany him, although they should remain chaste.

P. Courtright

VĀRĀṆASĪ vär än ä′ sē. Contemporary name for Banāras. *See* Hindu Sacred Cities.

VARṆA vär′ nä (H). *See* Caste.

VARUṆA vŭ′ rōō nŭ (H & B—Skt.; meaning and etymology uncertain; perhaps from *var*—"to bind" or "to envelop"). Sovereign deity in early Vedic Hinduism, maintainer of the cosmic order (Ṛta) and foremost of the Ādityas, the sons of Aditi. Often he is invoked in a dual compound, *mitrāvaruṇa,* with another sovereign god, Mitra. Although the name Varuṇa does not survive in ancient Iran, his functional correspondence to the supreme deity of the Avesta, Ahura Mazda, suggests an Indo-Iranian background. A third Āditya, Aryaman, associated with both Varuṇa and Mitra, was also known in Iran. While Mitra represents the human, contractual side of Vedic sovereignty, Varuṇa is the magical, terrible, cosmic sovereign, one who is all-seeing and all-knowing as he guards the universe he has created. He changes forms with his occult power (Māyā), and snares and binds with his noose *(pāśa)* those whose acts are counter to *ṛta.* Numerous hymns in the Rig Veda beg his forgiveness for sins committed, or seek release from diseases by which he has punished transgressions. Few anthropomorphisms are used in depictions of Varuṇa; he is universal monarch *(samrāj)* by virtue of his transcendent character, and he is associated with the sky and the celestial waters.

Already in the Rig Veda Indra emerges as a rival sovereign, and he eventually eclipses Varuṇa's kingship, just as Varuṇa appears to have usurped the functions of Dyaus at the primordial level of Vedic mythology. In post-Vedic mythology Varuṇa is a minor figure, regent of the western quarter and lord of the waters.

Bibliography. A. A. Macdonell, *Vedic Mythology* (1897); H. Lüders, *Varuṇa,* 2 vols. (1951-59). D. M. KNIPE

VASUBANDHU vəs û bən′ dŭ (B; *ca.* fourth-fifth century A.D.). Indian philosopher whose *Viṃśatikā* (*The Treatise in Twenty Stanzas on Consciousness-Only*) helped establish the YOGĀCĀRA (Mind-Only) school of Mahāyāna BUDDHISM. After his brother, Asaṅga, converted him from HĪNAYĀNA to MAHĀYĀNA, Vasubandhu greatly contributed to the development and defense of the Yogācāra movement. According to this school, the mind, which is constituted by a flow of various ideas, is the sole reality. Physical objects which seem to be external—our body and all other material objects—are simply ideas or projections of mind. Such a theory is called subjective idealism, since it regards all seemingly objective entities as subjective ideas. Vasubandhu and his followers offered various grounds in support of their thesis. It was suggested that consciousness or perception of external objects was analogous to consciousness of dream objects. Just as one interprets the objects of a dream as existing exclusively in consciousness, so also one should interpret all perceptual objects as ideas existing only within the mind. To see that external objects are lacking in objectivity is to awaken, much as one awakens from a dream and realizes that dream objects are objectively unreal. The fact that dreams can produce images no less vivid than those of perception lends weight to the analogy.

Yogācārins also argued that it is superfluous to explain perceptions by positing the existence of external objects as their cause, since perceptions may be no more than one variety of the diverse types of ideas of which the mind itself consists. Another consideration in favor of idealism grew out of the observation that consciousness and the objects of consciousness are constantly conjoined in one's experience. In effect, the Yogācārin shifted the burden to the materialist by asking him to demonstrate that any object exists apart from consciousness. *See* MONISM. E. J. COLEMAN

VATICAN CITY (Ch). The smallest independent state in the world (109 acres), created by the Lateran Pacts of 1929 and located in ROME on the right bank of the Tiber. Sovereignty is vested in the pope as head of the ROMAN CATHOLIC Church, though the actual administration is carried out by the Papal Commission for Vatican City (three cardinals and a secretary) and a governor who is assisted by a central council composed of the heads of the central offices (secretariat; monuments, museums, galleries; technical services). Vatican City has its own courts of justice. Internal security and public order are ensured by four corps: the Noble Guard and the Palatine Guard (with chiefly ceremonial functions), the Swiss Guards (133 members) and the Gendarmerie (184 policemen). The official language is Italian, though the city has its own flag, stamps, currency, and extensive system of communications. Permanent diplomatic relations are maintained with more than fifty countries, but in a manner compatible with a policy of absolute political neutrality. Though the State of Vatican City is formally distinct from the Holy See (the religious office of the pope), both are united in the person of the pope, who is both ruler of the state and head of the church (*see* PAPACY). The temporal sovereignty of the state is primarily to ensure for the Holy See total independence in the exercise of its spiritual mission.

Bibliography. J. Neuvecelle, *The Vatican: Its Organization, Customs, and Way of Life,* (1955); R. Neville, *The World of the Vatican* (1962). C. WADDELL

VATICAN COUNCILS (Ch). Two councils of the ROMAN CATHOLIC Church. The first met in 1869-70 and the second 1962-65. Nearly eight hundred BISHOPS and other prelates attended Vatican I. The council issued two final constitutions, *Dei Filius,* on the interrelationship of faith and reason, and *Pastor Aeternus,* on the pope's primacy of jurisdiction and INFALLIBILITY. About three thousand bishops and others attended Vatican II, in which delegates from other Christian churches and communities participated as observers. The council's most important documents were the three constitutions on Divine Revelation, the Church, and the Church in the Modern World. Decrees on Religious Freedom, Ecumenism, and Non-Christian Religions heralded new Catholic openness. The council chose as its principal biblical metaphor for the CHURCH that of the People of God. While maintaining the basically hierarchical nature of church government, with the pope at its head, it emphasized the collegial role which all bishops have in that government and stressed that the function of all church authority is one of service to the ecclesial community. Vatican II was the first council in Christian history to issue no condemnations. *See* JOHN XXIII.

Bibliography. C. Butler, *The Vatican Council, 1869-1870* (1962); J. Hennesey, *The First Council of the Vatican: The American Experience* (1963); G. MacGregor, *The Vatican Revolution* (1958); W. M. Abbott, ed., *The Documents of Vatican II* (1966); H. Vorgimler, ed., *Commentary on the Documents of Vatican II,* 5 vols (1967-1969). J. HENNESEY

VĀYU vä′ yo͞o (H & B—Skt.; lit. the "wind" [*vā*—"to blow"]). A god of wind and warfare whose cult was of considerable significance in the archaic Indo-Iranian religion. In the AVESTA, Vayu, the mighty wind, armored as a warrior in his golden chariot, was patron of the warrior class and was a god of death and fate. In the RIG VEDA of ancient India, Vāyu was born from the breath of PURUṢA, was a close associate of the warrior deity INDRA, and was the first to drink the SOMA. A macro-microcosmic correspondence of universal wind and vital breath *(prāṇa)* perpetuated his role in the UPANIṢADS. In the MAHĀBHĀRATA Vāyu was the father of the warrior hero BHĪMA. *See* VEDIC HINDUISM.

Bibliography. A. A. Macdonell, *Vedic Mythology* (1897).

D. M. KNIPE

VEDA vā´ dŭ (H—Skt.; lit. "knowledge"). Sacred knowledge, revelation, that which has been "heard" (ŚRUTI), according to the Hindu religious tradition. First in an oral tradition only, then much later in a written tradition as well, the Vedas transmit the ancient revelations in a series of hymns, ritual texts, and speculations composed over a period of a millennium beginning *ca.* 1400 B.C. The plural, "the Vedas," refers to this entire corpus of literature extending from the RIG VEDA to the UPANIṢADS and including also, in the broadest of definitions, later works such as the SŪTRAS that serve as ritual manuals for each of the Vedic schools, and Vedāṅgas, exegetical "limbs of the Veda" that provided auxiliary religious sciences such as grammar and astronomy. There is, however, a sense of "the Vedas" restricted to the primary "collections" (SAṂHITĀS) of the Rig Veda, the YAJUR VEDA, and the SĀMA VEDA, or these three plus the ATHARVA VEDA. Thus "the Vedas" in Indian tradition may refer to three texts, four texts, or a great library of sixty to eighty texts. In any case, traditional India has always understood "the Vedas" to be unitary and eternal, produced neither by god nor man, yet nonetheless "heard" (*śruti,* as distinct from all subsequent religious tradition, SMṚTI, which is of inspired human authorship), and also "seen" or intuited by the ancient seers, the RISHIS, who transmitted them to humankind. The Vedas constitute BRAHMAN, the sacred word, and the oral tradition that preserved this word over numerous centuries prior to the introduction of writing is still the preferred medium when the Vedas are utilized liturgically.

1. Saṃhitās. The basis of the Vedas, and of VEDIC HINDUISM, is the set of four *saṃhitās* composed in ancient Indic (archaic Sanskrit) during the early centuries of migrations by Indo-Aryan speakers into northwest and north central India. The Rig Veda, or Veda of the *ṛcaḥ,* "verses," is the oldest, a collection of verses in various meters arranged in 1,028 hymns to INDRA, AGNI, SOMA, the AŚVINS, VARUṆA, MITRA, PURUṢA, RUDRA, and dozens of other deities. Composed *ca.* 1400-1200 B.C., the ten books *(maṇḍalas,* "cycles") of the Rig Veda include six "family books" (books 2-7) of hymns collected and transmitted by specific families of seers and four probably later cycles, including books 1 and 8, a ninth book devoted entirely to Soma, and the final addition, book 10, with its numerous esoteric and philosophical speculations. The focus of all the *saṃhitās,* and of the Vedic tradition itself, is the liturgical use of MANTRAS, sacred formulas. These verses or parts of verses taken from all sections of the Rig Veda are the proclamation of *bráhman* and are loudly and forcefully chanted by the *hotṛ,* the chief priest in the ritual system. Mantras are pieced together according to the dictates of a specific YAJÑA (sacrifice) or other ceremony, with no regard for "story line" or continuity in its parent hymn. The hymns may, in fact, postdate many essential mantras.

Second to the Rig Veda in importance are additional *saṃhitās* that borrowed mantras from the Rig Veda and applied them to specific ritual situations. The Yajur Veda is the collection of mantras and explanatory materials assigned to the *adhvaryu,* the executive priest, and his assistants, a group that performs the major operations of the sacrifice. The Sāma Veda similarly uses mantras from the Rig Veda, adapting them to a musical tradition, probably the oldest one in continuous existence. The *sāmans* ("melodies"), primarily intended for the Soma sacrifices, are sung in a seven-note scale by the *udgātṛ* and his assistants. The fourth *saṃhitā,* the Atharva Veda, stands somewhat apart in its inclusion (in addition to Rig Vedic and official cult verses) of spells and incantations of a folk religious or medical character. Nevertheless it, too, has been assigned to a major priest (the *brahmán; see* BRAHMIN) and his assistants, thus rounding out a full sacrificial staff of sixteen—four major priests, each with three attendants, each responsible for a *saṃhitā.*

The organization as well as the content of the three later *saṃhitās* initiated an elaborate speculative as well as liturgical symbol system and this was perpetuated by a variety of schools (*śākhās,* lit. "branches"). These schools declared responsibility for a specific textual recension of one of the *saṃhitās,* committing the mantras and other materials to memory in a variety of complicated recitation patterns *(pāṭhas).* Traditional texts speak of more than a thousand such *śākhās,* but there are fewer than a dozen different schools surviving in India today, and some of them may have only a single locale.

2. Other Vedic texts. The ritual and theological speculation begun in the *saṃhitās* was continued in a system of commentaries known as BRĀHMAṆAS, India's earliest prose works, dating from the tenth to the seventh centuries B.C., probably the same period in which the *saṃhitās* were undergoing final redaction. Most *śākhās* generated such discourses: e.g., the Aitareya school of the Rig Veda produced an Aitareya Brāhmaṇa, and the Taittirīya school of the Yajur Veda, a Taittirīya Brāhmaṇa, always with the sacrificial system and the explanation of mystical homologies at the center of discussion. Generally later than the Brāhmaṇas are the "forest texts" or ĀRAṆYAKAS, esoteric collections of mantras, priestly commentaries, and verses for specific rituals. The Upaniṣads, the earliest of which date from the sixth or fifth century B.C., are often closely linked with the Āraṇyakas, and sometimes the Brāhmaṇas as well. For example, there is a separate Aitareya Āraṇyaka and Upaniṣad, and a separate Taittirīya Āraṇyaka and Upaniṣad. However, one of the Yajur Veda schools, the Vājasaneya or White Yajur Veda, has amalgamated its later interpretive appendices to its *saṃhitā* so that the last portion of its Brāhmaṇa, the Śatapatha, is an Āraṇyaka concluded by an Upaniṣad (the famous Bṛhadāraṇyaka Upaniṣad).

The *śākhās* did not confine their literary production to the period from the Rig Veda to the Upaniṣads—technically, the extent of the Vedas. Rather, they continued to develop lengthy texts known as SŪTRAS, such as Śrauta Sūtras, Gṛhya Sūtras, and DHARMA Sūtras, manuals for each school's version of the public cult, the domestic rites, and the religious law, respectively. Since these important Sūtras cite the mantras from their proper traditions, and often contain explanatory matter not found in earlier texts, they serve as valuable guides to the Vedic tradition.

Bibliography. J. Gonda, *Vedic Literature* (1975); L. Renou, *Vedic India* (ET 1957); A. B. Keith, *Religion and Philosophy of the Veda and Upanishads* (1925, rpr. 1969); M. Winternitz, *A History of Indian Literature*, I (ET 1927).

D. M. KNIPE

VEDĀNTA vä dän´ tü (H—Skt.; lit. "end of the Veda"). 1. The UPANIṢADS. 2. Those philosophical systems which claim to take their inspiration from the Upaniṣads.

The Upaniṣads are the concluding sections of the VEDAS and represent a collection of diverse speculations relating to liberation, metaphysics, and epistemology. Although Hindus refer to Vedānta in the singular as if there were one system which represented the thought expounded in the Upaniṣads, it is apparent that the several Vedānta systems which developed after the middle of the first millennium A.D. interpret the Upaniṣads in widely divergent fashion, and it is to those various systems that the term "Vedānta" most often refers when the context is classical Indian philosophy. In recent times, however, "Vedānta" has come to designate an amorphous world view frequently thought of as the essential philosophical core of Hinduism; this view is sometimes also referred to as "neo-Vedānta."

1. **Early history.** Although the earliest Upaniṣads probably date back to the beginning of the first millennium B. C., the only systematic summary of Vedānta tenets before A.D. 600 extant today is the BRAHMĀ SŪTRAS (or *Vedāntasūtras*) attributed to Bādarāyaṇa. These aphorisms or SŪTRAS present a laconic exegesis of various Upaniṣadic passages and their brevity permits disparate interpretations, which they received at the hands of the major thinkers discussed below.

Bādarāyaṇa's sūtras are traditionally contrasted with the *Mīmāṃsāsūtras* of Jaimini, which may have been written at about the same time (perhaps in the first or second century B.C.). Jaimini views the entire corpus of Vedic scripture as essentially composed of injunctions to perform ritual actions, while Bādarāyaṇa distinguishes a portion of scripture, largely to be found in the Upaniṣads, whose function is to convey information about liberation and the way to it. Since both Jaimini and Bādarāyaṇa are engaged in scriptural exegesis (MĪMĀṂSĀ) their two approaches are frequently termed "early (*pūrva*)" and "later (*uttara*)" Mīmāṃsā respectively. Pūrva Mīmāṃsā emphasizes those parts of scripture (the *karmakāṇḍa*, basically found in the earlier sections of the Vedas, e.g., the BRĀHMAṆAS) which have to do with action (KARMA), while Uttara Mīmāṃsā, i.e., Vedānta, emphasizes those parts (the *jñānakāṇḍa*, found in the Upaniṣads) which relate to knowledge (*jñāna*).

Although the Brahma Sūtras are the only extant text from this early period, references in later writings confirm the existence of other Vedāntic texts, mostly commentaries on Upaniṣads, which have been lost. In some cases name of authors are provided, among which are found Upavarṣa, Bodhāyana, Sundara Pāṇḍya, Bhartṛprapañca, Brahmadatta, Bhartṛmitra, Ṭaṅka and Draviḍācārya. Sometimes authors are merely referred to as commentators (*vṛttikāra*).

2. **Advaita Vedānta.** The most widely known of classical Vedānta systems is called ADVAITA, "non-dualism," since it argues that all distinctions are unreal and that the only reality, BRAHMAN, is unique, partless, and unrelated to any other reality. The earliest extant text expounding this point of view is attributed to Gauḍapāda (*ca.* A.D. 600); a set of stanzas (*kārikā*) commenting on the Māṇḍūkya Upaniṣad, and a text which seems to owe some of its inspiration to Buddhism, although the significance of this is disputed by scholars.

Advaita is, however, usually closely associated with the eighth century philosopher ŚAṂKARA or Śaṃkarācārya. Little hard evidence is available about him, though traditions abound. Modern scholarship tends to accept his authorship of half a dozen works, though traditional ascriptions make him responsible for several hundred. Among those agreed by all to be authentic, the *Brahmasūtrabhāṣya*, a commentary on Bādarāyaṇa's sūtras, is the most important; indeed, it is probably the most widely studied text of classical philosophy in India today, and it is the author of this work who is often called "the greatest Indian philosopher." The same hand appears to have written commentaries on the Bṛhadāraṇyaka, Chāndogya, Taittirīya, and Aitareya Upaniṣads, and very possibly most of the other Upaniṣads in the oldest group. He is also the author of a treatise titled *Upadeśasāhasrī*, or at least large portions of it. Tradition makes him the author of a commentary on the BHAGAVAD GĪTĀ, but on this—as with other works—scholars are not unanimous.

Advaita thought was also pioneered by Maṇḍana Miśra (probably a contemporary of Śaṃkara), author of *Brahmasiddhi*, a difficult but influential work. Śaṃkara's pupils Padmapāda and Sureśvara, commenting on their teacher's writings, developed Advaita thought, and subsequent generations of Advaita philosophers proliferated. Differences of emphasis arose: Maṇḍana's brand of thought was reflected in Vācaspati Miśra's tenth-century *Bhāmatī*, and a school of post-Śaṃkara Advaita is known as the Bhāmatī school; the readings of Padmapāda and perhaps Sureśvara reported in Prakāśātman's (tenth-century) *Vivaraṇa* on Padmapāda's *Pañcapādikā* led to references to the Vivaraṇa school of post-Śaṃkara Advaita. Hundreds of works were written through the following centuries, prominent among which may be counted Śrīharṣa's *Khaṇḍanakhaṇḍakhādya*, an Advaitic critique of NYĀYA-VAIŚEṢIKA logic; Vidyāranya's *Pañcadaśī*, a popular exposition in terms available to the layman; Citsukha's *Citsukhī* and Madhusūdana Sarasvatī's *Advaitasiddhi*, lengthy works notable for the intricacy of their analysis and arguments; Sadānanda's *Vedāntasāra* and Dharmarāja's *Vedāntaparibhāṣā*, handbooks for students beginning study of the system.

The purpose of any Indian philosophy (except CĀRVĀKA) is to point the way to liberation from the bondage of rebirth (SAMSARA). Bondage is a product of ignorance (AVIDYĀ, sometimes also termed MĀYĀ). The true Self, that is, Brahman, is not bound, does not transmigrate, is eternally liberated. But bondage is beginningless and operates with mechanical regularity as long as ignorance is not removed.

Since liberation results from the removal of ignorance, it follows that it is knowledge, not action, which liberates, for only correct knowledge (*vidyā*) can replace ignorance. Thus the *karmakāṇḍa* or action-section of scripture can at best lead one to heaven, but it cannot produce final liberation from rebirth, since KARMA will continue to operate as long as ignorance remains. Karma means actions and their results, and a person's ability to act depends on his seeing differences between agents, actions, and their results; this appearance of distinctions is the product of ignorance, and will continue until ignorance is removed. Especially difficult to remove is the distinction between the knower and the objects known. Yet, the liberating knowledge is pure immediate consciousness without any subject or object distinguished, and it is this pure consciousness which is in fact the only real thing, the Self or Brahman. Since we are constantly conscious, it follows that we are always liberated, but we do not know it because ignorance veils our true Self, superimposing upon it varied qualities and relations.

How can ignorance be removed? Since all distinctions are the product of ignorance, any positive account of a path to liberation, since it will involve distinctions, must ultimately be false. However, some false views are less misleading than others. By criticizing worse views one arrives by stages at better ones. For example, the view that effects are different from their causes (*asatkāryavāda*) is worse than the view that the effect is essentially identical with its cause (*satkāryavāda*); within the latter, the view that the cause transforms itself into its effect (*pariṇāmavāda*) is worse than the view that it manifests its appearance as effect without itself changing in so doing (*vivartavāda*); still, all views which take causation seriously are inferior to those which espouse non-origination (*ajātivāda*), since causal relations involve difference and are thus tinged with ignorance.

Again, the view that one needs a distinct judgment to verify or justify true knowledge (*paratahprāmāṇya*) is worse than the view that true knowledge justifies itself (*svatahprāmāṇya*); however, both these views are ultimately inferior to the view that truth is not to be found in judgments, that one cannot attain ultimate understanding through the instruments of knowledge (*pramāṇa*).

Thus in a dialectical fashion one may move closer to true understanding by criticizing inadequate views. In the end, though, all positive views are inadequate because they predicate properties of that Self or Brahman which is really without properties. According to Śaṃkara as interpreted especially by Sureśvara, reasoning, study, and meditation when properly practiced can get one to a stage where he is ready to be liberated by hearing one of the "great sentences" (*mahāvākya*) of scripture such as "That (Brahman) are Thou, Śvetaketu" (Chāndogya Upaniṣad VI. 8.7). Hearing this, one immediately becomes enlightened with Self-knowledge. Śaṃkara regularly equates such a liberated person with the highest of the four stages of life, renunciation or *sannyāsa*. A SANNYĀSIN cannot truly act, since he knows that there are no distinctions and thus is provided no scope for activity. We who perceive the *sannyāsin* moving about in the world are still conditioned by ignorance, and so we attribute actions to him; in reality he does not act, nor do we.

Śaṃkara is held to have established an order of *sannyāsins*, the Daśanāmis or "ten-named ones," by traveling throughout India establishing monasteries, of which the principal ones are located at Bādarināth, Dwarkā, Purī, Śṛṅgeri and Conjeeveram. Properly ordained *sannyāsins* of this order are known as *svāmin* (SWAMI). They take one of the following ten names: Giri, Puri, Bhāratī, Sarasvatī, Tīrtha, Āśrama, Vana, Āraṇya, Parvata, Sāgara.

The original philosophy of Advaita as Śaṃkara and Maṇḍana taught it appears to have preceded the development of the devotional period of Hinduism (*see* BHAKTI HINDUISM). Śaṃkara saw God and Brahman as essentially identical, but not entirely so; Advaita celebrates a distinction between Brahman without qualities, *nirguṇa* Brahman, and God, *saguṇa* Brahman, which is Brahman endowed with creative powers by which he manipulates ignorance to produce a plurality of selves (JĪVA) and a world of objects of awareness. It follows that in this philosophy God is himself tinged with ignorance, since he involves distinctions which are the products of ignorance. The problems of understanding the relationships among these various categories—Brahman, God, selves, world, ignorance—involve post-Śaṃkara thinkers in myriad philosophical complexities.

3. **Viśiṣṭa Advaita Vedānta.** An interpretation of the Upaniṣads which stresses theism and devotion was developed by philosophers of the ŚRĪ VAIṢṆAVA sect, a popular movement of South India stemming from the teaching of the ĀḶVĀR mystics of the first millennium A.D. Among teachers of this school Nāthamuni (tenth century) is frequently viewed as the first; his grandson Yāmunācārya or Āḷavandār expounded its philosophy in several important treatises. RĀMĀNUJA (1017-1137?) is renowned as the most important representative of the school, as he wrote several influential independent treatises as well as commentaries on the Brahma Sūtras and the Bhagavad Gītā, and anchored the system in a manner parallel to that in which Śaṃkara anchored Advaita by attracting disciples and establishing *maṭhas* (schools or retreats, sometimes associated with temples). After Rāmānuja the school divided into two important sects, that of the TEṄGALAIS, led by Piḷḷai Lokācārya (1264-1327?), and that of the VAḌAGALAIS, led by Vedānta Deśika or Veṅkaṭanātha (1268-1369?). Numerous later writers carried on their traditions.

The supreme principle recognized by Upaniṣadic authorities is Brahman, and Vedānta schools part company most noticeably over their conception of it. Rāmānuja takes Śaṃkara severely to task over the conception of *nirguṇa* Brahman and the related thesis that all differences are merely projections of ignorance or *māyā*. For Viśiṣṭa Advaita there is only one Brahman and that is God, *saguṇa* or "with qualities," specifically the qualities spoken of in the Upaniṣads as truth (*satya*), awareness (*jñāna*), and endlessness (*ananta*). Whereas these qualities, like all distinctions, are interpreted by Advaita as ultimately unreal, Viśiṣṭa Advaita takes them literally. Brahman is truth or reality as substance with modes, the basic modes being conscious selves (*jīva* or *cit*) and unconscious matter (*acit*). Brahman is awareness (not objectless pure consciousness, as in Advaita, a notion that Rāmānuja rejects as logically untenable). Brahman is the self-aware Self (ATMAN), seat of all consciousness. Brahman is endless in that it is the inexpressible synthesis of all limitations due to thought infected by ignorance, which in Viśiṣṭa Advaita connotes incomplete understanding. Brahman is the unconditioned.

This same Brahman is God (ĪŚVARA), the inner controller (*niyantā* or *antaryāmin*) of each individual self, as well as the ruler and redeemer whose creation provides the stage for the individual selves' quest for realization through karmic activity. He is the single Self (*śeṣin*) immanent in each individual self and pervading them all. The aim of the Vedāntin then is to achieve the perfection of this all-Self by giving oneself to God which is that Self.

By practice of desireless action (*karma-yoga*), achievement of direct awareness of Brahman (*jñāna-yoga*), leading to devotion (*bhakti yoga*) the seeker strives for a state of release from the cycle of rebirth, an identity with God in a blissful perfection. Viśiṣṭa Advaitans tend to exalt devotion or *bhakti* among the classical "paths" to liberation, although the emphasis here differs among members and sects.

Especially as developed after Rāmānuja, Śrī Vaiṣṇavism developed a unique emphasis on devotional philosophy, in which the isolation (*kaivalya*) or lordliness of the liberated self is viewed as a penultimate step toward the ultimate end of man, which is selfless service to God (*kaiṅkārya*). Indeed, the route to this end through the combination of *karma*, *jñāna*, and *bhakti yoga* comes to be a far harder one to follow than direct adoption of *prapatti* or "self-surrender" to God's grace, by which the seeker at once loses all attachment and warrants the saving grace of Śrī (the female aspect of the God VISHNU), who destroys all the seeker's karmic residues including those whose operation has already begun.

The most important of the eighteen points of difference between the Teṅgalai and Vaḍagalai schools of Viśiṣṭa Advaita concern their respective views of grace, volition, and redemption. The Vaḍagalais, emphasizing the necessity of human freedom, hold that the soul seeks refuge by clinging to God as the young monkey clings to its mother for protection. The Teṅgalais, on the other hand, view grace as independent of human decision; according to them, a person is saved through God's gift, just as the kitten is saved from danger by its mother picking it up in her mouth and carrying it away. Other differences between the sects turn on points of theology and the moral standards expected of God's servants.

4. **Dvaita Vedānta.** Founded by MADHVA or Ānandatīrtha (1238-1317), this Vedāntic system called "dualistic" in fact emphasizes (in direct contrast to Advaita) the distinctions between God, self, and the various things in the world. Madhva wrote over thirty works, including commentaries on the older Upaniṣads, on the Brahma Sūtras and the Bhagavad Gītā, as well as ten philosophical treatises independently developing the ideas of the system. The center of Dvaita thought is at Udipi in south Kannara, near Madhva's birthplace, at a temple founded by Madhva and dedicated to KRISHNA.

The Dvaita literature is especially impressive in its logical analyses and dialectical polemics against Advaita. Among numerous writers in addition to Madhva one may point to Jayatīrtha (1365-88), a prolific commentator on Madhva's works, and Vyāsarāya or Vyāsatīrtha (1478-1589), author of *Nyāyāmṛta, Tarkatāṇḍava* and other intricately argumentative treatises.

Madhva views the plurality of worldly things and selves as compatible with Upaniṣadic statements about the supremacy of Brahman. Brahman, God, is independent *(svatantra)*, while all else is dependent.

Madhva's Brahman is that principle which controls the evolution into various forms of material nature, which by obscuring the natural luminosity of each self constitutes that self's bondage.

Since creation is solely God's, it follows also that liberation is entirely in God's hands, and is due to his grace. The path to release consists of thinking and meditating on scriptural statements so as to achieve direct awareness of God, a path of knowledge which is indistinguishable from one of devotion. However, the final step can only be accomplished by God's grace. Furthermore, as with Viśiṣṭa Advaita the achievement of liberation involves realization of one's subservience to God. A peculiarity of Dvaita thinking about release is the recognition of gradations in it. Since each individual self is a distinct entity with its own nature, in release each self realizes that nature, and it is natural therefore that the bliss experienced by each self in release will differ from that of others.

5. **Other Vedānta systems.** Several other Vedānta schools developed distinctive philosophical views, mostly emphasizing the devotionalism which we have seen coming to the fore in Viśiṣṭa Advaita and Dvaita, while harking to Advaita where possible in their insistence on self-realizational intuition. Notable among them are the Dvaita-Advaita system of NIMBĀRKA. Another important variety is the Śuddha Advaita of VALLABHA, which with CAITANYA's Bengal Vaiṣṇavism provided the philosophical background for the flowering of the Krishna cult in North India.

Bibliography. On Advaita *see* E. Deutsch, *Advaita Vedānta* (1969); E. Deutsch and J.A.B. van Buitenen, eds., *A Source Book of Advaita Vedānta* (1971); for Viśiṣṭa Advaita *see* P. N. Srinivasachari, *The Philosophy of Viśiṣṭādvaita* (1943); for Dvaita, *see* B. N. K. Sharma, *A History of the Dvaita School of Vedanta* (2 vols., 1960, 1961); M. I. Marfatia, *The Philosophy of Vallabhācārya* (1967); U. Mishra, *Nimbārka School of Vedānta* (1966).

K. H. POTTER

VEDANTA SOCIETY. *See* HINDUISM IN AMERICA §1.

VEDIC HINDUISM vā´ dĭc. The earliest level of HINDUISM; it developed among the Indo-Aryan–speaking communities of northwest and north central India in the last half of the second millennium B.C. and flourished in large areas of the entire subcontinent during the first millennium B.C. In a broader sense Vedic Hinduism may also refer to those forms of classical, medieval, and modern Hinduism that remain faithful to one or more of the textual, ritual, or theological traditions of this ancient Vedic period. The focus of Vedic Hinduism was and is the VEDAS, a great collection of traditions on the sacrifices, esoteric speculations, and mythologies of ancient India, composed in Vedic (ancient Indic), the archaic precursor of the SANSKRIT language, and transmitted, as they are still today, by small communities of BRAHMIN specialists. These late-second-millennium and early-first-millennium B.C. texts, beginning with the RIG VEDA, were composed as an oral tradition by various poet-philosophers and ritual specialists, then compiled and redacted in a system of schools (*śākhās*, "branches"), each of them preserving one or more of the SAMHITĀS, BRĀHMANAS, ĀRANYAKAS, UPANISADS, and (later) ritual SŪTRAS. The extraordinary productivity of these nine or ten centuries of poetic-ritualistic collaboration resulted in a uniform religious system that is known as the Vedic religion, a religion that did not survive the ancient period but left more or less of an imprint upon all the subsequent religious traditions of India. It contributed most significantly to the ritual, mythological, philosophical, and social structures of classical, medieval, and modern Hinduism. Textually speaking, then, Vedic Hinduism designates those individuals or communities whose religious authority is ŚRUTI (the Vedas as a coherent revelation).

Throughout its long history Hindu India has persistently spoken of "the Vedas" as authoritative, if not precisely canonical, declaring them to be the "bedrock" of civilization, the wellspring of religion, philosophy, and literature. But in fact for the last twenty centuries or so the majority of Hindus have based their religious beliefs and practices on SMRTI. The fundamental textual bases of Hinduism (the Epics, PURĀNAS, Tantras, Śāstras, ĀGAMAS, YOGA Sūtras, etc.) are all *post*-Vedic, regarded at best as *smṛti*, that is, of human "traditional" origin, by contrast with the Vedas, *śruti*, or that which is "heard" as a mystical revelation from the sacred realm. This means that Hindus today, with the exception of pandits and scholars, hold the Vedas in vague spiritual regard, but are scarcely aware of their nature and contents or of the particular dimensions of contemporary Hinduism that derive from the Vedic heritage.

1. **Tradition.** From the standpoint of Vedic tradition the most important declaration about the Vedas is that *śruti* is eternal, and therefore of nonhuman origin (*apauruṣeya*). Although mysteriously intuited by the ancient sages (RISHIS, "seers"), the Vedas have neither divine nor human genesis, no source in time, no connection with "history." Secondly, the Vedas are understood still today, despite their reduction to writing in recent centuries, as essentially an oral tradition. The sacred verbal power that is BRAHMAN resides in the recitations, particularly of MANTRAS, the verse-prayers of the Rig Veda that are employed throughout the Vedic liturgy. For some twenty-five to thirty centuries a variety of complicated recitation patterns have been employed by the ritualists to assure the preservation of every mantra and of every accompanying directive and exegetical note. The liturgical calendar of the public cult has not survived, but almost any village or hamlet in India today provides the opportunity, particularly in higher caste domestic rituals such as weddings or ancestral offerings, to hear the immense power in the recitation of mantras, those sacred sounds whose meaning is usually unknown to

the families involved, but whose vigorous efficacy is assured by the ancient meters and accents.

Thirdly, there are the Brahmins themselves, the class (*brāhmaṇa varṇa*) that became an elite repository of the Vedic tradition, uppermost in the hierarchy of classes, godlike in its access to and transmission of the Vedas, responsible not only for the preservation of the mantras and their application in the ritual system, but also responsible as living human models of the truth and exactitude that *śruti* itself displays. Bolder than the gods themselves, they intended no less than the personification of *bráhman*, the sacred verbal power. For a long time confined to Twice Born males and kept beyond the hearing of women and Śūdras, the mantras and the tradition of *śruti* gradually found their elitist enclave penetrated by a process of "Sanskritization," and today it is not unknown for women to read and meditate upon Vedic texts, or for lower castes to borrow certain domestic Vedic rites.

Finally, it should be mentioned that Vedic Hinduism became the touchstone of religious orthodoxy for India in the *āstika/nāstika* distinction, all *āstika* traditions "affirming" belief in the Vedas and, rather vaguely, the Vedic world view in general, all *nāstika* traditions, such as anti-Vedic Jainism and Buddhism, "rejecting" the same. As is often pointed out, however, Vedic Hinduism itself has always been far more preoccupied with orthopraxy, correct practice, than orthodoxy, right belief.

2. Ritual. Later Hindu tradition (*see,* e.g., Mīmāṃsā) considered the texts of its Vedic antecedents divisible into two departments (*kaṇḍas*), one concerned with rituals (*karma*), the other devoted to speculation (Vidyā, "knowledge"). There is no doubt that the ritual system was the dominant concern, probably from the beginning of the Vedic age. The sacrifice, Yajña, soon regarded as a mystical entity in itself, became the basis for one of the most complex ceremonial codifications known to the history of religions. Vedic rituals fall into one of two categories: *śrauta* (from *śruti*), rituals performed in the official or public cult by as many as seventeen priests using three fires; and *gṛhya* (from *gṛha,* "house"), the domestic ceremonies performed on one fire by the householder himself or by one or more priests employed on his behalf. Manuals for these rituals were generated by the various Vedic schools, the Śrauta Sūtras being compiled in roughly the same period as the Brāhmaṇas, Āraṇyakas, and Upaniṣads, and the Gṛhya Sūtras in the period of the Upaniṣads.

a) Śrauta rites. Employing from one to seventeen Brahmins, *śrauta* rites were conducted on elaborate sacrificial compounds, continued for a single day or as much as two years, and concluded with the destruction or casting away of the compound and all its equipment. They centered on offering into the altar fires oblations (*homas*) of milk, butter, honey, grain, fruit, domestic animals, water, *sūra* (an intoxicant), and the all-important Soma juice, pressed from the plant for the rites of greatest consequence. All these oblations were accompanied by mantras chanted or sung according to their various traditions by the major priests (*hotṛ, adhvaryu, udgātṛ, brahman*) and their assistants. The sacrificer (*yajamāna*), for whom the rite was performed, underwent an initiatory, ontological transformation in the course of the event; it was his bodily measurements that determined the sacrifice field, his household fires that became the three sacred fires and the three levels of a newly created world. *See* Sacrifice.

The fundamental *śrauta* ceremony, once obligatory every morning and evening for Twice Born householders, was the milk offering to Agni known as the Agnihotra. Other rites celebrated the installation of the new fire, each new-moon and each full-moon day, each of the four-month seasons (Spring, Rains, Autumn), the firstfruits of rice, barley, millet, and bamboo crops, and the *paśubandha* (animal sacrifice, normally a goat). The soma sacrifices were of seven types, the basic one being the annual *agniṣṭoma,* "in praise of Agni." Among the great soma *yajñas* were the consecration of a king (*rājusūya*), the horse sacrifice (*aśvamedha*), the *mahāvrata,* a solstice rite, and the *pravargya,* a milk-and-butter oblation into the *mahāvīra* ("great hero") pot. In recent years two of the great soma rituals have been reenacted: the *vājapeya* ("drink of strength") for three days near Poona, Maharashtra, in 1956, and the *agnicayana* ("building of the fire altar") for twelve days in Panjal, Kerala, in 1975, the former a collaborative effort on the part of pandits and ritualists from various parts of India, the latter primarily accomplished by the Nambudiri Brahmins of Kerala. Only minor changes were introduced (e.g. the substitution of vegetable for animal victims) and the scenes might well have been from the year 1000 B.C.

b) Gṛhya rites. The domestic ceremonies, conducted by one or more priests at the invitation of the householder, or quite properly by the householder himself, take place at a single offering fire. The usual offerings are grains and clarified butter, occasionally (in ancient times) an animal. Some of the concerns of the *śrauta* system, such as recognition of new- and full-moon days, are duplicated at the *gṛhya* level. The fivefold *mahāyajñas* ("great sacrifices") are also listed in the Gṛhya Sūtras: *brahma, pitṛ, deva, bhūta,* and *manuṣya-yajña,* respectively to *brahman* (i.e. Vedic recitation), the ancestors (*see* Pitṛ; Śrāddha), the gods (Devas), "the beings" (i.e. spirits, including animals, birds, and the dead, who receive *bali* offerings), and humans (i.e. guests or beggars).

The Life Cycle Rites (Saṃskāras) are the core of the domestic ceremonies. A traditional set of some twelve to sixteen rites of passage, more concerned with the consecration of an individual in transition than with material sacrifice, include conception (as a conclusion to the marriage rite), the generation of a male, safe delivery, birth (*jātakarma*), name-giving, first feeding, first tonsure, initiation (*upanayana,* an "introduction" to the Guru for the first hearing of the

GĀYATRĪ MANTRA and investiture with the SACRED THREAD), marriage *(vivāha)*, and cremation *(antyeṣṭi*, the "final offering"). *Saṃskāras* require the sacred fire, *homa* offerings, mantras, and the presence of Brahmins, who are fed in the closing stage of each rite, but it is the father, or father-to-be, who may be the actual performer.

c) Contemporary rites. Unlike the *śrauta* system, which apparently diminished in importance after the GUPTA period (*ca.* fifth century A.D.), the *gṛhya* series provides strong continuities between certain domestic rites of ancient and modern India. Devotions with mantras at the *saṃdhyas*, the "joints" of day and night (dawn and dusk), are the latter-day successors of the morning and evening *agnihotras* of the Vedic householder. The *mahāyajñas* (great sacrifices) and various *homas* (oblations) survive, but above all it is the *saṃskāras* and the *śrāddhas*, the rites of passage and the schedule of ancestral offerings, that display the strongest link to the Vedic age. Regardless of language, sect, or subculture, all areas of India contribute to a remarkable homogeneity in the performance of childhood rites, initiations (now more often a symbolic prefix to marriage), marriages, funerals, and offerings to deceased ancestors. Local customs have been interpolated in the *prayogas* and *paddhatis* (ritual manuals); a goddess pot might have been substituted for the *mahāvīra* pot, and some lower castes may perform without Vedic mantras, but the ritual outline is essentially Vedic.

Most contemporary ritual life, however, reflects long centuries of departure from Vedic norms. The Āgamas and other ritual materials have replaced the Vedic texts, just as the Epics and Purāṇas superseded in popular affection the core of Vedic mythology. Great temples of stone replaced the disposable compounds of the Vedic sacrifice, the single or triple fire system atrophied, and attendance upon the images of deities resident in the homes, shrines, and temples (PŪJĀ) preempted the *yajña* itself. (It has been estimated that during the last hundred years there have been in India approximately six hundred *āhitāgnis*, establishers and maintainers of the *yajña* fire, with more than half of them in the more conservative south—Andhra, Tamil State, and Kerala). From the time of the Upaniṣads on, more attention was given to the interiorization of sacrifice than to the material dramas themselves. The great cycle of sacrifices was restructured as a festival and pilgrimage calendar with numerous regional and local innovations and a general skeleton of post-Vedic mythological referents. Often Vedic antecedents go unrecognized—as, for example, in the Vedic *sarpabali* background to the all-India serpent's festival, Nāgapañcamī, or the goat sacrifices *(paśubandhas)* at lunar-solar conjunctions that underlie the semi-annual goddess rites of Durgāpūjā. Through all the transformations many Vedic structural features remain. Traditional performance of rites is still declared by intention: some rites are obligatory *(nitya)* and normative, such as daily temple or household *pūjās;* others are also indispensable for those concerned with correct practice, but are special or occasional *(naimittika)*, such as the marriage ceremony; still others are optional *(kāmya)* and

D. M. Knipe

Brahmins bathing in the Ganges on the ceremonial day of changing the sacred thread

purposive, such as an offering or vow with a personal end in view.

3. **Speculation.** The source of speculation in ancient India was a ceaseless curiosity about the nature and function of sacrifice. The ritual operation (*karma*) being the primary cosmic act, it was the task of man to probe its innermost secrets and explain its mysteries. The later *saṃhitās* and particularly the Brāhmaṇas were directed to the "one who knows" the correspondences (*bandhus* or *nidānas*), those mystical homologies between all the entities of phenomenal reality. In these speculations, closely linked to the *śrauta* rituals, there was simultaneously the search for an irreducible life principle to define and unlock the entire macro/microcosmic code (*brahman*, "word"; *prāṇa*, "breath"; TAPAS, "heat"; etc.), a reduction of godhead to a participating rather than controlling level of cosmic circularity, and an assumption on the part of Vedic man of responsibility for the maintenance of cosmic forms. Just as in the ritual truth and exactitude in performance automatically accomplish all desired ends, so too the direct realization of mystical correlations securely establishes the "knower" in the cosmic order (ṚTA): one who intuits ultimate cosmic relationships is ultimately cosmically related. This direction in ritual-magical speculation eventually led to the esoteric teachings of the Upaniṣads ("correspondences"), where the ultimate identity, the highest knowledge, was declared to be revealed in the ATMAN-BRAHMAN homology. Woven through this speculation, and connecting the philosophical hymns of Rig Veda 10 to the Upaniṣads composed a millennium later, is a remarkable tension between mystery and availability. Knowledge, truth, immortality, light are concealed, cryptic (*parokṣa*, "out of sight") and filled with mystery (*guhya*); at the same time they are available to some—the rishis, the *yajamāna* who performs the sacrifice, and eventually, according to the Upaniṣads, the realizer of Atman-Brahman.

One of the most enduring themes of Vedic speculation, and of Indian thought generally, proceeded from the Puruṣa Sūkta (Rig Veda 10.90), the most important of Vedic cosmogonies. Creation is the result of a sacrifice, the self-immolation and dismemberment of the god PURUṢA. In the Brāhmaṇas it is PRAJĀPATI, "Lord of Creatures," who is the link between Puruṣa and *brahman*, simultaneously the sacrifice, all of time and space, and the transcendent. And it is the sacrificer, identified with Puruṣa-Prajāpati, who can reverse the ritual manifestation process, reintegrate himself and attain the unmanifest, precreative state. Coupled with the *śrāddha* cult and the late-Vedic process of interiorizing the sacrifice, this speculation was of the utmost importance for the developing concepts of transmigration and rebirth (*see* KARMA; SAMSARA), as well as for new doctrines of salvation that regarded ritual activity as inadequate (*see* MOKṢA). A reemergence of theism in the later Upaniṣads prefigured the classical Hindu devotional and sectarian tendencies (*see* BHAKTI HINDUISM). And finally, this late-Vedic period also produced the notion of *varṇāśramadharma*, "the cosmic law of class and stage of life" (*see* DHARMA; CASTE; ĀŚRAMA).

4. **Mythology.** It is in the hymns of the Rig Veda that we find the strongest display of mythological detail, prior to a dismantling of verses and motifs into mantras for liturgical needs. Correspondence between the myths and the *yajña* system is not clearly presented in the Rig Veda recension, but subsequently, in the period of the other *saṃhitās* and the Brāhmaṇas, the rituals that are the central preoccupation of Vedic religion take clear precedence, mythologies are abstracted to stock references, and even the gods are reduced to participatory roles, being invited to and dismissed from the great cosmic dramas of sacrifice produced by man. The foremost gods of the Rig Veda, many of them revealing Indo-Iranian or Proto-Indo-European ancestries, are INDRA, AGNI, Soma, the AŚVINS, and VARUṆA. Others of importance are MITRA, VISHNU, RUDRA, SŪRYA, VĀYU, YAMA, BṚHASPATI, VIŚVAKARMAN, Puruṣa, Prajāpati, Tvaṣṭṛ, Pūṣan, Dyaus, and Vivasvat. Although there are numerous individual and collective feminine powers in Vedic mythology, goddesses do not have prominent roles in the pantheon. Those most frequently mentioned are Uṣas, ADITI, SARASVATĪ, Vāc, and PṚTHIVĪ. Among the central Vedic themes that live on in Epic and Purāṇic mythology are the great battle between the gods (*devas*) and the demons (ASURAS), the winning of cosmogonic waters in the victory of Indra over the demon Vṛtra, the theft of soma from heaven, the dismemberment of Puruṣa-Prajāpati, the concealment and collection of Agni, and the three strides of Vishnu.

It is a striking fact that none of the half-dozen central characters of Rig Veda mythology maintained genuine prominence in classical Hindu myths. Sectarian Hinduism centers upon Vishnu, Rudra-Shiva, and the various forms of the goddess, each of them, and most apparently Vishnu, being in some ways a pantheon melding both Vedic and non-Vedic motifs, functions, and iconographies. Vishnu, for example, perpetuates in classical mythology his many connections with the sacrifice and divine-human mediation, and his various AVATARS elaborate on the three steps of the Rig Veda (dwarf avatar) as well as the flood (fish) and earth-diver (boar) motifs of the Śatapatha Brāhmaṇa. Rudra's wild, unpredictable nature, his connections with Agni and fire symbols, and his ambivalent ascetic tendencies live on in the Shiva myths of the MAHĀBHĀRATA and Purāṇas. Both VAIṢṆAVA and ŚAIVA mythology, ritual, and iconography consciously replicate the Puruṣa Sūkta theology and symbolism.

Other Vedic deities survived in minor Hindu (and Buddhist and Jaina) mythological roles—for example, as the *lokapalas*, world protectors at the eight compass points, all but KUBERA being major Vedic gods.

Bibliography. J. Gonda, *Die Religionen Indiens*. 2 vols. (1960-63) and *Vedic Literature* (1975); L. Renou, *Vedic India* (ET 1957); P. V. Kane, *History of Dharmaśāstra*. 5 vols. (1930-62), esp. vols. II and IV on rituals; A. A. Macdonell, *Vedic Mythology* (1897); A. B. Keith, *The Religion and Philosophy of the Veda and Upanishads*. 2 vols. (1925). D. M. KNIPE

VEHICLE (B). Means or way by which one achieves enlightenment in Buddhism. THERAVĀDA Buddhism was described as HĪNAYĀNA (lesser vehicle) by later Buddhists who sought reform and referred to their path as MAHĀYĀNA (greater vehicle). MANTRAYĀNA (sacred sound vehicle) Buddhism advocated reciting mystical sounds as the way to salvation. For Hindu use of the term *see* VĀHANA.

E. J. COLEMAN

VESĀLĪ vē´ sä lē (B). *See* VAIŚĀLĪ.

VICAR vĭc´ ər (Ch—Lat. "substitute"). In ANGLICAN CHURCHES a person assigned responsibility in a designated place to perform ministerial functions as the deputy or representative of another ordained minister; in some other churches a person preparing for ordination who is assigned to a PARISH and authorized under the pastor's supervision to preach and teach; in ROMAN CATHOLICISM used of the pope as Christ's representative on earth.

K. WATKINS

VIDYĀ vīd´ yä (H—Skt.; lit. "knowledge" [*vid*—"to know"]). Equivalent to *jñāna* ("knowledge") in the ancient and medieval texts of Hinduism; knowledge based upon the *pramāṇas* (perception, inference, etc.), as well as knowledge which results from the authority of the revealed texts or from mystical (yogic) experience.

1. **Vedic period.** The earliest concept of *vidyā* did not distinguish between spiritual and secular knowledge. *Vidyā* referred to knowledge of the three VEDAS and the prescribed sacrifices as well as to all other modes of knowledge—ranging from knowledge of "worms, flies, and ants" to that of "the true and the false" (CU VII.2.2). For BRAHMINS, knowledge of the hymns and prayers (MANTRAS and BRĀHMAṆAS) of the revealed texts was of particular significance, enabling them to revitalize and renew the Vedic cosmos by means of ritual and sacrifice. For those of other CASTES *vidyā* was necessary to the social, political, and religious stability of the society as well as a primary means to the fulfillment of one's DHARMA and the attainment of immortality in heaven (*see* VEDIC HINDUISM).

2. **Upaniṣadic period.** A skeptical attitude toward *vidyā* began to emerge in the late Vedic period with challenges to the value of sacerdotal knowledge from within the priestly class itself and from outside it. The view evolved that mere knowledge of what must be done to attain release could not bring release, but could only lead to rebirth. Moreover, in itself *vidyā* was equivalent to ignorance or AVIDYĀ (BĀU IV.4.10).

The tendency of the heterodox schools (DARŚANAS) was to deny the relevance of *vidyā* or to view it as an impediment to release, although initially the orthodox *darśanas* viewed *vidyā* as an essential correlate to action (KARMA), either sacrificial or meditative. For example, one of the later and more philosophical Upaniṣads concludes, "Those who perform the rites, who are learned in scriptures, . . . who offer oblations . . . with faith, to them alone one may declare this knowledge of Brahman, to them alone by whom the rite has been performed. . . . Let none who has not performed the rite read this" (MU III.2.10-11).

Opposing the critical realism of MĪMĀṂSĀ was the skepticism of VEDĀNTA which distinguished between knowledge which is appropriate to truth and ultimate reality *(parāvidyā)* and that which is appropriate to the world of change, relationality, and SAMSARA *(aparāvidyā)*. The primary authority for this view was found in the Upaniṣads; for example, "Two kinds of *vidyā* are to be known, . . . the higher as well as the lower. Of these, the lower is the Rig Veda, the Yajur Veda, the Sāma Veda, the Atharva Veda . . . And the higher is that by which the Undecaying is apprehended" (MU I.1.5).

As the conclusion of the Muṇḍaka Upaniṣad indicates, however, Upaniṣadic distinctions between higher and lower forms of knowledge also affirmed the latter and its relation to action. *Aparāvidyā* and karma were viewed as necessary correlates and as requisite preparation for *parāvidyā* and MOKṢA ("liberation"). (Cf. MU I.2.12 and TU I.3.3.)

3. ADVAITA **Vedānta.** As opposed to other exponents of Vedānta, ŚAṂKARA argued that true knowledge and action were unrelated, i.e., that *parāvidyā* annihilated *all* prior knowledge and that knowledge of anything but the undifferentiated BRAHMAN was equivalent to *avidyā* or ignorance. For Śaṃkara, *avidyā* was the "presupposition on which are based all the practical distinctions—those made in ordinary life as well as those laid down by the Vedas—between means of knowledge, objects of knowledge, and all scriptural texts. . . . Hence perception and all other means of right knowledge and the Vedic texts, have as their object that which is dependent on *avidyā* or Nescience" (Vedānta Sūtras, V.I, p. 6). In short, only *parāvidyā*, the intuitive or nonrelation "experience" of the total identity of knower and known (*see* TAT TVAM ASI), could fulfill human desire for release from samsara.

The Advaita view, never dominant in Indian spirituality, has tended to be the focus of Western and Indian scholarship since the nineteenth century. A more balanced and historically accurate presentation of the role of *vidyā* in Indian spirituality would also emphasize the significance of views similar to those of RĀMĀNUJA and his VIŚIṢṬA ADVAITA.

Bibliography. G. Thibaut, *Vedānta Sūtras*, SBE vols., 34, 38, (rpr. 1962). J. HELFER

VIHĀRA vī här′ ū (B—Pali & Skt.; lit. "dwelling place" [*vihārati*—"to dwell"]). A dwelling place for monks. An organized monastery, but in earliest use a temporary monk's hut constructed within the boundaries of a rains retreat *(vassa)* settlement, either made by the monks themselves (ĀVĀSA) or donated by a patron *(ārāma)*. Later, *vihāra* denoted one of five kinds of *leṇa*, a monastery proper, although a fifth century A.D. source stipulates only two types, *vihāra* and *guhā* (cave). These terms apparently became normative designations for organized monasteries in northern and southwestern India respectively, the *vihāra* being a free-standing building and *guhā* either a natural or constructed cave.

In addition to its generalized signification, *vihāra* also has more restricted meanings, e.g. a meeting hall for monks or a place for congregational meetings including both monks and lay persons. In northern Thailand, for example, the *vihāra* refers to a building used for daily morning and evening monastic chanting ceremonies, lunar sabbath services, and novitiate ordinations. On monastery compounds the *vihāra* is distinguished from the higher ordination (UPOSATHA) hall, monastic dwellings *(kuṭi)*, reliquaries *(caitya)*, and schools for monks and novices *(vidyālaya)*.

The development of the Buddhist monastery reflects the growth of the order from a small group of mendicants to an extensive monastic population situated in permanent establishments. Cultural influences also conditioned the structure of monastic institutions and the pattern of monastic life. Simple cave dwellings of Sri Lanka, the huge monastic complex in Lhasa, Tibet, and the great Zen monasteries of Kyoto, Japan, offer contrasting models of monastic structures. These differences reflect, in part, the evolution of Buddhist monasticism from the mendicant ideal of early Indian Buddhism, when monks dwelt temporarily in caves and other natural shelters, to the state-supported monasteries of China and Japan with massive landholdings. The early simplicity of the monastic life grew to an opulence surpassed only by royal courts. Even today in countries like Burma and Thailand the village monastery will be materially better off than the farmers who support it. Although monastic institutions inevitably became more complex with increased size and more wealthy with generous support from the laity, the ideal of simplicity has remained an important symbol. The early wandering (eremetic) style of monastic life persists alongside settled (cenobitic) monastic establishments. Furthermore, particular aspects of monastic life in large *vihāras* still reflect the ancient mendicant ideal. (*See* SAṄGHA; MONASTICISM EAST AND WEST.)

The most famous Indian monastic dwellings were the caves occupied from the third century B.C. through the tenth century A.D. Located in the Western Ghat region of what is today Mahārashtra, the sites of AJAṆṬĀ, ELLORĀ, Kārlī, Bhājā, Pitalkhorā, and Nāsik help unfold the history of the development of the Buddhist monastery in India. The oldest caves are mere hermit cells with rockhewn beds and niches for lamps and the few possessions owned by their occupants. Gradually they were improved, and courtyards and verandahs were added. The living room became more spacious until it was converted into an oblong, pillared hall *(maṇḍapa)* with a rear sanctuary enshrining a relic *(caitya)* or a Buddha image. During the GUPTA period extensive rock carving and wall murals enhanced the cave monasteries' aesthetic beauty, viz. Ajaṇṭā. Kārlī is considered by many to be the most magnificent example of the Indian cave monastery. With a *caitya* hall over 125 feet long and 45 feet wide, lined on each side with fifteen monolithic pillars, the structure bears a striking resemblance to an early Christian church with nave and side aisles terminating in an apse. Cave monasteries of various types are found throughout Buddhist Asia, most notably those at Tun-huang and Lungmen in China, which date from the fourth century A.D.

Throughout India *vihāras* constructed of brick date from the beginning of the second century B.C. or even earlier. Progressively they developed from relatively small and simple to larger and more elaborate structures. In particular, as the needs of the laity were served the monastery developed a dual structure, one to accommodate monastic life and the other lay, devotional activities. At the ancient site of Taxila (West Punjab and Pakistan), where Buddhism appears to have flourished from the first century B.C. to about the sixth century A.D., devotional shrines or chapels are found adjoining monasteries. In Nāgārjunakoṇḍa on the east coast of India, where Buddhism flourished in the third and fourth centuries A.D., apsidal shrines were actually built within monastic residential areas. These structures reflect changes in Buddhist thought and the increasingly significant role of the laity. This dual style of structure spread throughout the rest of Buddhist Asia. In THERAVĀDA countries today monastic lodgings, schools, and ordination halls (part of the *saṅghavāsa)* are formally distinguished from that part of the monastery (known as the *Buddhavāsa*) which is dominated by lay devotional practice focusing on the reliquary and image hall.

Throughout the history of Buddhism the size and significance of monasteries have been contingent on the degree of lay support (*see* BUDDHISM, LAY). Monastic lands in fifth century China were so significant that the Buddhist monastery became a crucial factor in the agro-economy of North China. In Tibet, the Potala palace completed at the end of the seventeenth century was the center of government from which Tibet was ruled as a theocratic state under the sway of the DALAI LAMA. In Japan during the period of NARA BUDDHISM monasteries ringing the city became so influential politically and economically that the capital was moved to Kyoto. Kyoto itself still has many impressive monastery compounds. Myōshin-ji, the largest Rinzai ZEN school, is an agglomeration of 3,500 temples and 15 monasteries with a large monastery-temple complex in the northwestern section of the city. Second in size only to the old Imperial Palace, the Myōshin-ji compound follows the classical pattern of Chinese Zen temples. *See* HORYU-JI; ART AND ARCHITECTURE, BUDDHIST.

Bibliography. S. Dutt, *Buddhist Monks and Monasteries of India* (1962), pp. 58, 126-50. D. K. SWEARER

VIJÑĀNAVĀDA vĭj nyä nū vä´ dū (B—Skt.; lit. "consciousness doctrine"). The designation which VASUBANDHU preferred for YOGĀCĀRA.

VIMALAKĪRTI vĭ mä lä kĭr´ tĭ (B—Skt.; lit. "famous for [being] stainless" [*vi-mala*—stainless; *kirti*—famous for]) **CH'ING-MING** (B—Chin.). Lay bodhisattva, hero of the Mahāyāna Buddhist scripture, The Teaching of Vimalakīrti (Vimalakīrtinirdeśa Sūtra).

Vimalakīrti was a BODHISATTVA and layman who appeared in the north Indian town of Vaiśālī, using a variety of skillful means *(upāya)* to teach that enlightenment can be realized in the midst of this world if one empties oneself of all clinging and illusions. In the sūtra which bears his name and which was probably written during the first century A.D. (the original Sanskrit has been lost, the text surviving in its Chinese and Tibetan translations), Vimalakīrti appears as a person paradoxically involved in social life—married, with children, frequenting a range of business and recreational establishments—and yet not ensnared by the attachments of the world and, in fact, fully enlightened. He feigns a serious illness, drawing others to his sickroom in order to teach them, with attractive imagery and compelling miracles, about emptiness and enlightenment. The bareness of his sickroom symbolizes the emptiness of all apparent reality, as his assumed illness illustrates the compassion of a bodhisattva for all living things.

1. **Emptiness.** The doctrine of emptiness (*see* ŚŪNYATĀ) as taught by Vimalakīrti denies ultimate reality and religious efficacy to everything that appears to exist. This includes not only the human body, but also Buddhist practices such as meditation, begging, and even becoming a monk. Vimalakīrti further argues that even emptiness is to be emptied, so that his followers will not cling to this doctrine and insight. Vimalakīrti's eloquent testimony to the nonduality and emptiness of all reality reaches its climax in his response to his followers' request for his interpretation of such ultimate nonduality: he remains silent! Perfect enlightenment is attendant on the practical realization of this radical emptiness, complemented by a compassion for all living things.

2. **Popularity in China.** The religious orientation and life-style of Vimalakīrti made him very popular in China. Being a layman, he illustrated that becoming a monk, with its implied celibacy and childlessness, was not essential for the attainment of enlightenment. His emphasis on religious emptiness recalled Taoist notions of emptiness and detachment. (*See* TAOISM, PHILOSOPHICAL §2.) Even the style of Vimalakīrti's verbal repartee with his followers was reminiscent of the mode of salon debate fashionable in China in the third and fourth centuries A.D. Both his teaching and his personal demeanor illustrated to the Chinese that Buddhist beliefs and holiness were compatible with their own cultural convictions and heritage. This sūtra did not become the exclusive property of any one sect, but enjoyed a broad and continuous influence in Chinese and Japanese Buddhism.

Bibliography. R. Thurman, *The Holy Teaching of Vimalakirti* (1976); R. B. Mather, "Vimalakīrti and Gentry Buddhism," *HR,* VIII (1968-69), 60-73; J. D. Whitehead, "The Sinicization of the Vimalakīrtinirdeśa sutra," *Bulletin of the Society for the Study of Chinese Religions*, V (1978), 3-51.

J. D. WHITEHEAD

VINAYA PIṬAKA vĭn´ ä yū pĭ´ tū kū (B—Pali & Skt.; lit. "Basket of the Discipline"). The first of the three collections of writings in the Buddhist PALI CANON. It is chiefly concerned with the rules to be observed by the SAṄGHA, or monastic order. The rules are traditionally attributed to the Buddha, though a number assume a more fully developed polity than existed in his day. Indeed, some of the Vinaya material seems to come from as late as the first century B.C. Prior to his death the Buddha is said to have relieved the monastic community of the duty to adhere to the minor precepts. However, due to either its unwillingness or inability to distinguish between significant and minor rules, the full body of regulations was maintained. Though the various schools of Buddhism have their own versions of the Vinaya, the general outline of the contents is largely the same from school to school. The diversity which does exist appears to be the result of later development of the original core of regulations stemming from local needs and emphases.

The core of the Monastic Discipline consists of a basic code known as the PĀTIMOKKHA, containing separate rules for monks and nuns. It is generally agreed that these constitute the original Vinaya. The Pali Vinaya as we have it today consists of the Sutta Vibhaṅga, or Classification of Discourses; Khandakā, or Divisions; and Parivāra, that is, Accessory Materials, or Appendix.

1. **Sutta Vibhaṅga.** This corresponds to the Vinaya Vibhaṅga, or Exposition of Discipline, in the Sanskrit Versions. In it the Pātimokkha rules are accompanied by an ancient word by word commentary. For each rule there is a story describing the events which led the Buddha to formulate that particular regulation. These stories contain a wealth of information concerning the nature of society at the

time. For some of the rules later legal discussions concerning exceptions and complicated applications are also included.

2. Khandakā. Equivalent to the Vinaya Vastu, or Subjects Concerning Discipline, in the Sanskrit versions, it is subdivided into a Greater Section (Mahāvagga) and a Lesser Section (Cūlavagga). It begins with a fragmentary biography of the Buddha covering the period from his enlightenment to the conversion of Sāriputta, an important disciple. It also contains rules governing admission to the order, the fortnightly assembly (UPOSATHA), and rainy season retreats, as well as regulations pertaining to the daily life of monks and nuns. Other major concerns are parliamentary procedure and methods of dealing with schism. Here too the circumstances surrounding the formulation of the rules are described. The Cūlavagga concludes with accounts of the first two Councils (*see* BUDDHIST COUNCILS).

3. Parivāra. It recapitulates the contents of the other Vinaya texts in catechetical form. A later work by a Sinhalese monk, its influence is apparently confined to Theravāda.

Bibliography. E. Frauwallner, *Earliest Vinaya and the Beginnings of Buddhist Literature* (1956); C. Prebish, "Theories concerning the Skandhaka," *JAS*, XXXII (1973), 669-78; I. B. Horner, *Book of Discipline*, 5 vols. (1938-52); E. Lamotte, *Histoire du Bouddhisme Indien* (1967), pp. 181-97.

J. P. MCDERMOTT

VINCENT DE PAUL (Ch; 1581-1660). French ROMAN CATHOLIC priest, evangelist, and advocate of the poor; founder of the Vincentian Fathers and of the Daughters of Charity; CANONIZED in 1737. He worked for the improvement of the conditions of prisoners and the rural poor. F. OAKLEY

VIPASSANĀ vĭ päs´ sŭ nŭ (B—Pali; lit. "see, discern" [*vis*—"see"]). Insight, especially spiritual insight as gained through Buddhist MEDITATION. A distinction is made between insight gained after practicing concentration and "bare insight" or "dry insight" gained without such practice.

The three characteristics of existence—impermanence (ANICCA), suffering (DUKKHA), and no-self (ANATTA)—are the most important subjects of insight meditation. The emphasis is upon seeing all realities, especially one's own mental and physical faculties, as they really are. This purifies the mind by eliminating mental conflicts.

Bibliography. Buddhaghosa, *The Path of Purity*, P. M. Tin, trans. (1970), ch. 22; L. Sayadaw, *Manual of Insight* (Wheel Publication 31/32, 1961). R. C. AMORE

VIRGIN BIRTH (Ch). The ordinary English phrase for the virginal conception of JESUS; it refers not to his actual birth but to his being conceived of the Virgin MARY without a human father. The infancy narratives of the GOSPELS say the Virgin conceived Jesus by the power of the HOLY SPIRIT. Matthew's account (1:18-24) is from the viewpoint of Joseph, who was informed in a dream that Mary would bear a son. Luke (1:26-38) follows the account of the ANNUNCIATION to Mary. Both give genealogies that exclude Joseph as the father of Mary's child.

The tone of the Gospel narratives has nothing in common with stories from ancient mythology. In the biblical narratives God in his power supersedes the ordinary pattern of human procreation to bring about the conception of Jesus the Savior. The virgin birth is not an antecedent argument that Jesus is truly Son of God, as if having a human father would have to exclude divine sonship. It is a question rather of accepting the historical virgin birth as revelation and then investigating its value, as a sign for Jesus' identity.

The NT affirmation of the virgin birth is repeated by subsequent early authors and enshrined in the creeds, e.g., "conceived by the Holy Spirit, born of the Virgin Mary" (APOSTLES' CREED). LUTHER, CALVIN, and other leaders of the PROTESTANT REFORMATION as well as John WESLEY in the eighteenth century, all affirmed the virgin birth as biblical truth and included it in formularies of faith. With the rise of challenges to Gospel miracles in the eighteenth century, and the radical biblical criticism of the nineteenth, the literal reading of the virgin birth came under attack. KARL BARTH was an outstanding defender of the factual truth of the virgin birth, which he held to be a striking sign of God's intervention to bring about the new creation independently of human means. ROMAN CATHOLICISM, ORTHODOX CHURCHES, and non-Chalcedonian churches of the East, as well as a great many Protestants and ANGLICANS, hold a literal virgin birth as Christian faith, not primarily for the sake of the Virgin but as God's deed in her Son.

One opinion of modern scholars is that the virgin birth is a theological symbol, signifying that Jesus was Son of God from his conception, although he had both human mother and human father. Such an interpretation has its own difficulties: where did the early Christians and the writers of the Gospels derive such a notion? Given normal Jewish insistence on family inheritance from the father, why would Christians invent a virgin birth story that suited so awkwardly their conviction that Jesus was "son of David"? Following the canons of historical criticism, it may be concluded that Matthew and Luke do not prove a literal virginal conception, although many Christians hold a literal interpretation of the doctrine. Acceptance of the virgin birth as historical fact rests on the faith of the individuals and the traditions of the church bodies concerned.

Bibliography. R. E. Brown, *The Virginal Conception and Bodily Resurrection of Jesus* (1973); J. McHugh, *The Mother of Jesus in the New Testament* (1975); J. Ratzinger, *Introduction to Christianity* (1970), ch. on "Conceived by the Holy Spirit, born of the Virgin Mary." E. R. CARROLL

VIRTUES, SEVEN (Ch; from Gr. *aretē*—achievement of excellence, or highest function or purpose). A Christian combination of the four natural or cardinal virtues of Greek and Roman philosophy—wisdom (prudence), fortitude (courage), temperance, and justice—with the three NT virtues—faith, hope, and love.

T. O. HALL, JR.

VISHNU, VIṢṆU vĭsh′ nōō (H—Skt.). One of the great Hindu gods, rivaled in importance only by SHIVA. Like Shiva, he is the central figure in one of the complex religious systems which make up the Hindu tradition, and is a major unifying factor in the development of BHAKTI HINDUISM. In nonsectarian Hinduism, Vishnu is honored as the protector and maintainer of world order. In sectarian VAIṢṆAVISM, where he is worshiped as the supreme deity, he is considered to be the source and prime agent of the universal process as creator, preserver, and destroyer alike.

1. **History.** Vishnu was a relatively minor god in the early VEDIC period, but he had qualities which supported his later rise to prominence. His foremost distinction was the three strides by which he traversed earth, atmosphere, and heaven. Established in "the highest place," his special heaven, Vishnu is said to enter the three worlds as the pervader of the universe. World-winning and all-pervasive, he eventually was identified with the all-powerful Vedic sacrifice itself in the BRĀHMAṆAS, the later Vedic ritual texts, where he is several times referred to as the highest of the gods.

Vishnu's identification as the sacrifice indicates his status by the end of the Vedic period. His importance in Bhakti Hinduism, however, came only after he had been merged with the popular god Vāsudeva-Krishna, whose main support came from a non-Vedic theistic movement dating back to at least the second century B.C. It was the devotees of this movement, the BHĀGAVATAS, who produced the BHAGAVAD GĪTĀ, the text which laid the foundation for Vishnu's later rise to prominence.

The Gītā presents the Bhāgavatas' case for devotion to Vāsudeva-Krishna as a valid means of salvation. In the course of this argument, it introduces two concepts essential to the further development of Vishnu: the concept of AVATARS or "descents" of the Lord into the world, and the concept of the transcendent Lord as the Supreme Person, the Puruṣottama, who has brought forth the phenomenal world from his own nature. When the Vedic Vishnu was merged with Vāsudeva-Krishna in the later portions of the MAHĀBHĀRATA, these concepts became the organizing principles for the expanding Vaiṣṇavite religious system.

2. **The avatars of Vishnu.** Beginning with the imperial GUPTAS in the fourth century A.D., Vaiṣṇavism benefited greatly from the support of Hindu rulers who saw in Vishnu the prototype for their own role as world protectors. Many of these rulers chose for their personal deities various incarnations of Vishnu which emphasized his protective aspects, and thus gave official support to the avatar concept. New theistic texts such as the Vishnu Purāṇa developed the concept of avatars into a theory of periodic incarnations of Vishnu to rescue the world from distress. Guided by this doctrine, a great variety of world-protecting deities came to be associated with Vishnu as avatars.

L. D. Shinn

These symbols of Vishnu—war conch and discus weapon—protect the entrance to the Aligarh (Vishnu) Temple near Madurai, South India

KRISHNA was viewed in the PURĀṆAS as the foremost human avatar of Vishnu. RĀMA, the righteous hero-king of the RĀMĀYAṆA, was less important in the Purāṇas than in the Epics, but he also had a place in the growing list of avatars. Nonhuman incarnations were included as well, most notably the boar avatar who raised the earth from the primordial waters, the man-lion avatar who rescued the devotee Prahlāda from his demon-king father, and the fish who rescued MANU from the flood. The number of avatars was eventually standardized at ten, although the various Purāṇic lists do not agree on the ten to be included. The great strength of the avatar doctrine was in fact its open-endedness, since potentially any savior figure could be included. (*See* Plate IVc.)

3. **Vishnu's cosmic forms.** The avatars are primarily concerned with the tasks of protection and salvation in this world. Vishnu himself, by contrast, was raised to cosmic status as the creator and overseer of the entire universal process. Vishnu is portrayed mythologically as floating on the cosmic ocean on the coils of the great serpent Ananta or ŚEṢA, periodically awakening from his sleep to bring forth the creator god BRAHMĀ to create the material world and its beings. (*See* Plate IVa.) This created world exists through many cycles in which Vishnu is active in his avatar forms to relieve distress, but finally, at the end of the series of cycles, Vishnu in his RUDRA form destroys the world and dissolves it back into its primal potentiality. Even this is not the ultimate state, however, for the cosmic form of Vishnu and the cosmic waters are only aspects of the Supreme Person (also called "The Lord," BHAGAVĀN) who transcends all form. It is he who has brought forth all the stages of

manifestation as part of his eternal LĪLĀ or "sport," and it is he—the eternal Vishnu—who will ultimately resolve all form back into the state of unity from which it has emerged.

Bibliography. Primary texts: *The Bhagavad Gītā,* trans. E. Deutsch (1968); *The Viṣṇu Purāṇa,* trans. H. H. Wilson (1969). Secondary sources: S. Bhattacharji, *The Indian Theogony* (1970); J. Gonda, *Viṣṇuism and Śivaism* (1970); J. M. McKnight, Jr., "Kingship and Religion in India's Gupta Age," *JAAR,* XLV 2 Supplement (1977), 677-701; W. D. O'Flaherty, *Hindu Myths* (1975); *see* bibliog. for BHAKTI HINDUISM.

T. J. HOPKINS

VIŚIṢṬA ADVAITA vĭ shĭsh´ tŭ ŭd vī´ tŭ (H—Skt.; lit. "nonduality of that which is distinguished [by qualities]" [*vi-śiṣ*—"to distinguish"; *dvi*—"two"]). A theistic system of VEDĀNTA based upon the works of RĀMĀNUJA. Often rendered ambiguously as "Qualified Nondualism," the term refers to the nature of the godhead and of its relationship to individual selves and the physical universe. BRAHMAN, termed "without a second" in the UPANIṢADS, is in this theological system a personal god characterized by "an ocean of auspicious qualities" and worshiped with loving devotion (*see* BHAKTI HINDUISM). Selves and the universe, while distinguishable from Brahman, are not a "second," separate category of reality but are also "qualities" or attributes possessed by and inseparably related to him. The "organismic" nature of this nondual relationship is indicated by the body-self analogy in which Brahman as the supreme self indwells and controls individual selves and the universe, his "body." (Cf. ADVAITA; DVAITA.)

Bibliography. P. N. Srinivasachari, *The Philosophy of Viśiṣṭādvaita* (1946).

W. G. NEEVEL

VISUDDHIMAGGA vĭ sood´ hĭ mŭg´ gŭ (B—Pali; lit. "Path of Purification"). A classic compendium of Buddhist doctrine and standard guide to THERAVĀDA meditation. One of the most authoritative noncanonical texts, it was written in the fifth century A.D. by BUDDHAGHOSA, the greatest of the Theravāda exegetes. The contents are structured into three main divisions, covering in turn: (1) virtue (SĪLA)—chs. 1 and 2; (2) concentration (SAMĀDHI)—chs. 3-13; and (3) intuitive wisdom (PRAJÑĀ)—chs. 14-23.

Chs. 3-11 are a detailed analysis of the process of concentration and how to achieve it, along with a discussion of the forty classical subjects of meditation. This is followed in chs. 12 and 13 by a description of the rewards of concentration. Next comes a theoretical analysis of true understanding and the nature of experience (chs. 14-17), including commentary on the FOUR NOBLE TRUTHS and the Buddhist concepts of conditionality (PAṬICCASAMUPPĀDA) and release (NIRVANA). Chs. 18-21 provide practical instructions for applying this theory to personal experience. Ch. 22 outlines the successive stages of spiritual realization, while the work concludes in ch. 23 with an analysis of the benefits of understanding.

Bibliography. Ñyāṇamoli, trans., *The Path of Purification* (1964).

J. P. MCDERMOTT

VIŚVAKARMAN vĭsh´ vŭ kär´ mŭn (H & B—Skt.; lit. "all-maker" [*viśva*—"all" + *karman*—"action, creation"]). Divine architect in VEDIC HINDUISM and later mythology. Two hymns of the RIG VEDA (10.81 and 82) depict him as all-seeing, all-creating, with eyes, faces, arms, and feet in all directions (compare the later BRAHMĀ); creation is at once a sacrifice by and the craft of this divine carpenter or smith, who is here envisioned as lord of sacred speech and the primordial embryo. In subsequent Vedic texts this monotheistic tendency in favor of Viśvakarman is reduced and the name is applied to the lord of beings, PRAJĀPATI. In post-Vedic mythology Viśvakarman carries the roles of divine artisan, maker of weapons (VISHNU'S discus, bows for RĀMA, Vishnu, SHIVA), chariots for ARJUNA and Shiva, SKANDA'S golden wreath, the houses of various deities and sages, even the city of Lanka. Architecture is traditionally attributed to Viśvakarman. Many of the functions of Viśvakarman are shared by another artisan-creator deity, Tvaṣṭṛ.

Bibliography. A. A. Macdonell, *Vedic Mythology* (1897).

D. M. KNIPE

VIVEKĀNANDA, SWAMI vĭ´ vē kä nŭn´ dŭ (H; 1863-1902), whose original name was Narendranath Datta, was born in a Western-educated, middle-class family in Calcutta. While attending Calcutta University he was greatly attracted to the views of Mills, Hume, and Spencer. Although initially a skeptic, he had a spiritual yearning which came to the fore at his meeting with the great sage RĀMAKRISHNA in 1881. He set aside plans for a legal career, became a SANNYĀSIN and eventually the spiritual heir of Rāmakrishna. Following Rāmakrishna's death Vivekānanda embarked upon a pilgrimage across India which made him aware of the abject poverty and apathy of the Indian masses. He became convinced that India could be regenerated through a reinterpretation of the VEDĀNTA. Speaking all over India he emphasized that man was potentially divine and that he must manifest his divinity through selfless, dynamic activity. Practicing Vedānta need not mean contempt for this world but rather vigorous involvement in this world, thus reflecting the divine immanence. India could only regain its dignity by cultivating self-confidence, overcoming caste rigidity, and accepting Western science and technology. Vivekānanda prophesied that the age of the common man, the ŚŪDRA, was at hand. And he insisted that the liberation of India required the emancipation of women. Attending the Parliament of Religions in Chicago in 1893, he proposed the exchange of Indian spiritual wisdom for Western material accomplishments. For this purpose he founded the Ramakrishna

Mission centers dedicated to meditation and social and educational service all over India, and Vedānta meditation centers in the United States and Europe. He enlisted Western disciples, such as Margaret Noble (Sister Nivedita), to aid him in his work in India. Compressing an intense activity into a few years, Vivekānanda overexerted himself, and died at the age of thirty-nine.

Bibliography. R. C. Majumdar, ed., *Swami Vivekananda Centenary Memorial Volume* (1963). A. Lipski

VOID (B). *See* Śūnyatā.

VOODOO vōō dōō (Dahoman *voduns,* "lesser deities, spirits, sacred objects"). A syncretistic religion of African origin practiced by autonomous cult groups.

Voodoo is one of a number of Afro-American religions which have preserved African religious traditions within a Western setting. The religion developed largely from Dahoman sources, incorporating elements from other West African traditions, as well as elements of Catholicism. The major centers of Voodoo practice have been located in Haiti, where the religion played a significant role in the war for independence (1791-1804), before spreading via emigration to Cuba and finally New Orleans. Similar religious systems can be found in other areas which had West African slave populations, particularly Brazil.

The central religious activity of Voodoo cults involves possession by a number of deities of African origin called *loas* in Haiti. In ceremonies led by a *hungan* or *mambo* (male and female priests), each possessed individual (called a "mounted horse") enacts a highly specific ritual performance involving dance, song, and speech appropriate to the particular possessing deity. While in the Dahoman context the gods "mounted their horses" for pleasure, in the context of slavery and its aftermath possession became directed toward serious ends: healing, warding off evil, bringing good or evil fortune. Marriage to a deity provided devotees with an ongoing protective relationship, as well as ritual responsibilities.

Voodoo appears highly syncretistic in its borrowing from Catholicism, but this process has taken place rather selectively. The Voodoo ritual calendar follows that of Catholicism, and African Voodoo deities are associated (though not equated) with various Christian saints. Since slavery disrupted the African rhythms of time, Catholic ritual provided Voodoo with patterns for reorientation. Additionally the Catholic hierarchical cosmology, replete with figures both divine and human, proved comfortably familiar to persons with West African backgrounds who had similarly structured cosmologies. Borrowing from Catholicism also served the pragmatic function of disguising Voodoo ritual from hostile political and ecclesiastical authorities. Practitioners of Voodoo appear to have maintained a great deal of separation between traditional African and borrowed Christian motifs. While the characteristics of traditional gods have been substantially altered over time, the gods have not taken on characteristics of their associated saints. Further, the saints do not possess devotees. Voodoo has provided its adherents with a powerful tradition of religious experience; its practice of animal sacrifice has allowed persons to contribute to the life of the cosmos; but perhaps most importantly, it has provided for a collective memory embodied in ritual performance which has allowed the maintenance of a sense of cultural integrity despite the forces of slavery and discrimination. *See* African Traditional Religions.

Bibliography. R. Bastide, *The African Religions of Brazil* (1960); M. Herskovits, *The Myth of the Negro Past* (1941); A. Metraux, *Voodoo in Haiti* (1959). D. E. Owen

VṚNDĀVANA vrĭn dä′ vä nŭ (H—Skt.; lit. "grove of a multitude"). A grove or garden associated with the earthly play of the Hindu god Krishna and his cowherd friends. The Vṛndāvana which is situated in Mathurā district is said in the later Purāṇas to be only an earthly reflection of the heavenly Vṛndāvana, where dancing, playing, and frolicking of Krishna with the Gopīs (female cowherds) continually takes place. During the life of Krishna on earth, Vṛndāvana was the site of the famous *rāsa līlā* dance (where Krishna and the *gopīs* danced in a circle with Krishna the partner of each) which inaugurated Krishna's mission on earth. *See* Līlā L. D. Shinn

W

WAHHĀBĪYA wə hä′ bē yə (I). A highly conservative reform movement founded in eighteenth century Arabia by Muhammad Ibn 'Abd al-Wahhāb (1703-92). The name, given by opponents, later became conventional. Adherents, however, have preferred to call themselves "Unitarians" *(muwaḥḥidūn),* because of their fervid emphasis on the divine unity and their corresponding diligence in uncovering and rooting out all attitudes and acts which could be regarded as idolatry (SHIRK).

1. Historical background. Muhammad Ibn 'Abd al-Wahhāb was born near Riyadh of a branch of the Tamīm tribe and received a sound Islamic education. He traveled widely in search of learning and became expert in SUFI doctrine as well as in the more orthodox Islamic sciences. Gradually his leanings became thoroughly Hanbalite (*see* IBN ḤANBAL). Though he was often at the center of controversy, his uncompromisingly strict religious views were accepted by the tribal chief Muhammad Ibn Sa'ūd of nearby Dar'iya. Religious authority was assumed by Ibn 'Abd al-Wahhāb, political and military power by Ibn Sa'ūd. This venture determined the future of the movement, which has continued to the present day as a powerful religio-political combination in Arabia, where the Sa'ūdī dynasty and Wahhābī fundamentalism dominate absolutely.

Dar'iya soon became a theocratic state and the center of an increasingly vast territory. Ibn Sa'ūd's able son, 'Abd al-'Azīz, continued military conquests, with Ibn 'Abd al-Wahhāb as religious guide. After the reformer's death the fortunes of the Sa'ūdī dynasty continued to advance. Its territorial dominion eventually included all of the HEJAZ and Najd, and much of the rest of the Arabian Peninsula from the Red Sea to the Persian Gulf. The Wahhābīs even went beyond Arabia in attacks on Damascus in Syria and Najaf in Iraq. Later there was a significant branch of the movement in India.

The nineteenth century brought reversals to the Sa'ūdī dynasty, and Ottoman punitive expeditions, under Egyptian command, finally overthrew the first Wahhābī empire in 1818. But early in the present century the Sa'ūdīs regained their old position under the great 'Abd al-'Azīz II, who was crowned king of Hejaz and Najd in 1930. His descendants continue to rule the modern kingdom of Saudi Arabia.

2. Doctrines. Wahhābī reforms were aimed at excising all beliefs and behavior not soundly rooted in the pristine period of Islam, roughly the first three centuries. Thus the QUR'ĀN, the SUNNA, and the four orthodox Sunni law schools (FIQH) were regarded as the normative sources for faith and order. All else was viewed as *bid'a,* heresy (lit. "innovation"). Two classical figures had an especially forceful influence on the formation of Wahhābī doctrine: Aḥmad Ibn Ḥanbal (d. 855), the founder of the most conservative law school, and IBN TAYMĪYYA (d. 1328), the activist Hanbalite jurist, who wrote scathing denunciations of the veneration of saints.

The central issue around which the Wahhābī reforms revolved was the popular cult of saints (*see* WALĪ). The building of mausoleums, especially of the MOSQUE-tomb type, and visiting them for veneration and blessings were declared to be *shirk.* Early Wahhābīs ruthlessly destroyed many shrines and stamped out all activities associated with them. They scrutinized all aspects of their fellow believers' behavior, to judge it as deviant or pure. In this they were reminiscent of the KHĀRIJITES of early Islam. They were particularly hostile toward Sufism in all forms, although ironically they resembled a Sufi order in the way in which they organized into cooperatives for work and, when necessary, holy warfare (JIHĀD).

Centering all in absolute devotion to the one, transcendent, sovereign God, the Wahhābīs declared that it is *shirk* to seek intercession of any creature with God (except MUHAMMAD on the Last Day), or to utter any other than God's name in PRAYER. It is unbelief to deny divine predestination in all things, to interpret the Qur'ān allegorically, or to claim knowledge of religion based on anything other than Qur'ān, Sunna, or the consensus (IJMĀ') of the early orthodox legists. Further, the rosary (*subḥa; see* TASBĪH) was forbidden in the meditation on the Divine Names (although the fingers could be used to keep count, as the Prophet is reported to have done). Mosques were to be utterly simple and functional, with neither MINARETS nor decorations. Even celebration of the Prophet's birthday (MAWLID) was forbidden.

3. **Legacy.** While the Wahhābīs were relentless and at times cruel in their punishment of heresy—and by their standards a very wide range of otherwise innocuous and commonplace attitudes and activities could be construed as such—at bottom they were animated by an intense moral fervor which sought in all things to purify the total environment for the proper service of God. Arabian Islam had sunk to a low level, and both private and public behavior in the sacred pilgimage centers of MECCA and MEDINA was frequently corrupt and unrestrained. The Wahhābī movement is significant also because it was a thoroughly indigenous, premodern reform within the bosom of Islam and not a reaction to Western ideas and incursions, as was the case with later movements across the Muslim world.

In spite of its fanatical puritanism and early excesses, Wahhābīsm did inspire later reformers in widely dispersed regions to overcome the stagnating effects of blind conformity to outmoded views and to make new efforts in applying the Qur'ān and Sunna to changing times. In a sense, Wahhābīsm can be characterized as an imposing Muslim expression of TILLICH'S idea of the "Protestant principle," which is the "guardian against the attempts of the finite and conditional to usurp the place of the unconditional in thinking and acting."

Bibliography. There is as yet no full-scale treatment of the movement in English. For a detailed survey of the military and political facts, see H. St. J. B. Philby, *Arabia* (1930). A concise but informative discussion of the movement and its literature is the article "Wahhābīya," by D. S. Margoliouth, in *SEI* (1953). An important modernist Muslim appreciation is F. Rahman, *Islam* (1966), pp. 240-47. F. M. DENNY

WAḤY wäh′ yə (I—Arab.; lit. "inspiration, revelation"). Before the rise of Islam the term was applied to mantic poets and was so used once in the QUR'ĀN (Sura 91:8), but thereafter it is applied primarily to prophets (NABI) and messengers (RASŪL) who receive inspiration from ALLAH, either directly or by means of such messengers as the angel Gabriel (*see* MALĀ'IKA). It is also distinguished from *tanzīl*, which denotes more the content of that which is sent down or inspired rather than the process, which is *waḥy*.

In Qur'ānic usage *waḥy* applies to revelation or inspiration from Allah to his creatures. This includes angels (Sura 8:12) and humans, who are usually but not necessarily prophets. In Sura 28:7 MOSES' mother is inspired by Allah's instructions. In Sura 6:113 adversaries of prophets "inspire," but these "devils of humankind and JINN" apparently do so with Allah's permission.

In the Islamic conception of history the Qur'ān was revealed to MUHAMMAD from the heavenly prototype, that is, a *tanzīl,* and represents the culmination of a series of revelations. It is not then surprising to find the term *waḥy* applied to previous messengers, such as Noah (Sura 23:27), Joseph (Sura 12:15), Isaac and Jacob (Sura 21:73), and indeed all the prophets (Sura 21:7). But it is clearly understood that the chief recipient of *waḥy* is Muhammad: "Lo! We have revealed it, a lecture in Arabic, that ye may understand. We narrate unto thee [Muhammad] the best of narratives in that We have inspired in thee this Qur'ān" (Sura 12:2-3). It is a revelation to be said aloud as a warning (Sura 6:19), in plain language. A person once inspired is compelled by that inspiration to act (thus Isaac and Jacob to do good deeds in Sura 21:73 and Muhammad to warn in Sura 6:19).

By tradition, the first portion of the Qur'ān revealed to Muhammad was Sura 96:1-5. This event is said to have taken place while Muhammad was on a retreat on MT. HIRA near MECCA. The angel Gabriel appeared to him and, showing him a piece of brocade on which were these verses and pressing them against Muhammad, commanded him to recite. This is not the only pattern found in Islamic literature for *waḥy,* however. Sometimes an angel would appear to Muhammad in the form of a man; sometimes there would be bells or a buzzing like bees, or the sound of forged metal. Often there would be pain, and Muhammad would shake, move his lips, and perspire heavily, even on cold days. He would often fall into a trance, turn red in the face, and cover his head. In an early experience he asked his wife, KHADĪJA, to wrap him in a cloak. When these traditions became known outside Islam, instead of regarding them as genuine marks of experience with the divine, polemicists descibed his experience as fits. Revelation was not always constant. Tradition holds that there was a pause in the process of revelation which ended with the coming down of Sura 74 or Sura 93, and another time, when Muhammad was questioned, he said that he would give an answer the next day. Revelation was withheld from him for fifteen days, however, finally to be answered by Sura 18, particularly verses 24-5: "And say not of anything: Lo! I shall do that tomorrow, except if Allah will. And remember thy Lord when thou forgettest." These events took place early in Muhammad's career, and one can see that revelations came more regularly in the Medinan period, but nowhere is it indicated that Muhammad was able to "control" the onset of *waḥy.* In the scandal about 'Ā'ISHA, Muhammad is portrayed as genuinely distressed during the interval between the accusations and the resolution of the affair with Sura 24:6-20, which enjoins four eyewitnesses to prove adultery.

Circumstances or occasions for revelations are found in Muslim tradition for some, but certainly not all, of the passages of the Qur'ān. Those that come from the Medinan period often refer to specific questions about practice and procedure, the answers to which are sometimes the verses of the Qur'ān. But more often the answers to procedural and religious questions are found in ḤADĪTH. When Muhammad's sayings and actions, supplementing Qur'ānic legislation, became the paradigm for Muslim behavor (SUNNA) and one of the foundations of the law, the doctrine was employed that Muhammad had been both inspired in all his actions and free from error from at least the time of his prophetic call. *Waḥy* would, under that understanding, be a constant state of affairs, with *tanzīl* the bringing down of the specific revelation of the Qur'ān. This would be in keeping with the impression from the literature that there was no specific time, place, or attitude more favorable than another in which Muhammad would receive revelation, since he was inspired while he was eating, having his head washed, holding a bone in his hand, preaching, etc. Attempts were made by some commentators to understand the Night Journey as spiritual and a form of *waḥy* rather than a physical journey. (*See* MI'RAJ.)

Those religious groups who have claimed to be Muslim and who have also claimed that their leaders have received revelation are not considered part of the Muslim community by the majority of the world's Muslims. (*See* BAHĀ'Ī.)

Bibliography. Ibn Isḥāq, *Life of Muhammad,* A. Guillaume, trans. (1955), pp. 109 ff.; aṭ-Ṭabarī, *Ta'rīkh,* I, 1146 ff.; T. Andrae, *Mohammed* (1955); W. M. Watt, *Muhammad at Mecca* (1953) and *Muhammad at Medina* (1956); T. Nöldeke, *Geschichte des Korans,* F. Schwally, ed. (1909); A. J. Wensinck, *Concordance de la tradition musulmane* (1969); N. Daniel, *Islam and the West* (1960), for a discussion of Western attitudes toward Islamic revelation and Muhammad as a prophet.

G. D. NEWBY

WAILING WALL (Ju). *See* WESTERN WALL.

WALDENSES [also **VAUDOIS** vou dwä'] (Ch). Reform movement originating in twelfth-century France, presumably founded by Peter Waldo or Valdes. According to tradition, in response to Matt. 19:21 ("If you would be perfect, go, sell what you possess and give to the poor") Waldo gave away his considerable wealth and began preaching poverty and simplicity as the appropriate way to follow Christ. His attitude toward the wealth and worldliness of the church aroused opposition, and in 1184 he was excommunicated by the Council of Verona.

Once rejected by the church, Waldo and his followers organized themselves, ordaining their own priests. They rejected purgatory and some of the sacraments, celebrated the Lord's Supper only once a year, and denied the propriety of holy days and prayers for the dead. They followed a morally rigorous mode of life and spread rapidly by preaching, carrying their message throughout southern France, northern Italy, Spain, and central Europe, including Bohemia, where Waldo died in 1217.

Pope INNOCENT III proclaimed a crusade against the movement in 1209 and persecution became widespread and severe, forcing many into Alpine valleys, where they were able to survive. Cordial contacts with Swiss Protestants led to a 1532 synod at which the Waldenses became essentially an extension of the REFORMED CHURCHES. Persecution continued sporadically until 1848, when full religious freedom was granted to those Waldenses still in northern Italy. *See* REFORMATION, PROTESTANT.

Bibliography. K Selge, *Die Ersten Waldenser,* 2 vols. (1967).

R. L. HARRISON

WALĪ, WILĀYAT wä lē´, wī lä´ yət (I—Arab.; lit. "saint" and "sainthood"). How the terms first came to be applied to SUFIS is not known, but from an early date it was explained that the Qur'ānic verse: "He loves them and they love Him" (Sura 5:59, tr. A. J. Arberry) meant: God is their friend *(walī),* and they are his friends. The QUR'ĀN also contains repeated reference to "the friends of God" *(awliyā' Allāhi).*

Saints are thought to constitute an invisible hierarchy, with a discrete cosmological ranking. In all there are perhaps forty thousand "friends of God," including three hundred chosen *(akhyār),* forty deputies *(abdāl),* seven pious *(abrār),* four pillars *(awtād),* three substitutes *(nuqabā'),* and one pole or nourisher *(quṭb, ghawth).* The numbers in some categories vary, but the importance of this cosmological scheme for Sufi devotion cannot be overstated. The *quṭb* saint, in particular, is posited as the ontic pole or axis around which the entire universe revolves. He is "the perfect man" *(al-insān al-kāmil),* for the sake of whose perfection all the elements of nature, and even all other humans, have been brought into existence. MUHAMMAD was the perfect man in his time, but since the world would cease to function without a *quṭb* saint, others have come after Muhammad, though they lacked his prophetic mandate.

Sainthood and prophethood (*see* NABI), therefore, overlapped as authoritative categories for mystically minded Muslims. The differentiation was as essential as it was problematic. On the one hand, the *quṭb* saint was differentiated from the hidden IMAM of SHI'ITES (though they shared a common theological mold as salvific mediators); at the same time, he was distinguished from the Prophet Muhammad—usually on a temporal basis, implying that the *quṭb* was doing the work of the Prophet in his generation. For some Sufi theorists, moreover, the distance of sainthood from prophethood was as slight as a single vowel: *walāyat* meaning "lordship" was reserved for prophets, while *wilāyat* or "friendship" was reserved for saints.

Wilāyat also had a practical connotation. It defined the geographical area within which a particular saint was recognized as the preeminent spiritual leader for his generation. In populous urban centers or remote regions of Asia where more than one Sufi order had been introduced, conflicting *wilāyat* claims were inevitable, but they were less frequent and less intense than might be expected. The WAHHĀBĪYA movement has been uncompromisingly opposed to the veneration of saints and has destroyed many shrines where they were venerated. (*See* Ṭarīqa; Shaikh.)

Bibliography. ʿAlī Hujwīrī, *Kashf al-mahjūb,* tr. R. A. Nicholson (1911), pp. 210-41; Nizam ad-Din Yemeni, *Laṭā'if-i Ashrafī* [the Discourses of Sayyid Ashraf Jahāngīr Simnānī] (1878), pp. 36-70; M. Molé, *Les mystiques musulmans* (1965), pp. 78-83; M. Hodgson, *The Venture of Islam,* II (1974), 227-30. B. Lawrence

WANDERING JEW. A folkloristic, Christian legend of a Jew who, as a consequence of repudiating Jesus, is condemned never to die but always to wander homeless in the world until the Second Coming of Jesus. Many poets, dramatists, and artists over the centuries have used this motif in their work. *See* Anti-Semitism. K. P. Bland

WANG YANG-MING wäng yäng mĭng (Con—Chin; 1472-1520) **ŌYŌMEI** ō yō mā (Con—Jap.). Neo-Confucian philosopher of the Ming dynasty (1368-1644). He rejected Chu Hsi's orthodox interpretation of the Confucian classics in favor of the School of Mind *(Hsin-hsüeh),* which sought through innate knowledge the unity of human mind and principle *(li). See* Confucianism §3

R. L. Taylor

WAQF wäkf (I—Arab.; lit. "stoppage [of money]"). A pious endowment or charitable trust. From the eleventh century on, with the ascendancy of Turkish rule in central Islamic lands, property was set aside to support religious schools (Madrasas), Mosques, hospitals and other institutions. *Waqf* bequests were also made for members of a wealthy Muslim's immediate family, though they were not strictly heritable. All landholdings characterized as *waqf* had the dual benefit of being exempt from both taxation and government seizure. The rents yielded by them were increasingly a source of income for urban religious functionaries ('Ulamā'), displacing the Zakāt or charitable tax, which it was the right and duty of every Muslim ruler to collect. In modern times family *waqf* have been reformed, centralized, or liquidated, while those serving the public welfare have survived.

Bibliography. *SEI,* pp. 624-28; M. G. S. Hodgson, *The Venture of Islam,* II (1974), 51, 124-25.

B. Lawrence

WEEKS, FEAST OF (Ju). *See* Shavout.

WENCESLAS wĕn′ səs lôs (Ch; *ca.* 907-929). Duke of Bohemia and patron saint of Czechoslovakia, Wenceslas attempted to convert the Czechs and to resist opposition from his brother Boleslav I, who had him murdered. Venerated as a Martyr, he became a symbol of Czech Christianity and nationalism—and the subject of the fanciful nineteenth century English carol "Good King Wenceslas." H. L. Bond

WESLEY, JOHN (Ch; 1703-1791). Founder of the Methodist movement. An Anglican priest, he was a prodigious evangelical preacher, writer, organizer, and folk-theologian. While a student at Oxford, he and his brother Charles led the Holy Club of devout students, called "Methodists" by scoffers.

Beginning in 1735 the brothers spent two frustrating years in the American colony of Georgia. Feeling his Christian belief was cold and sterile, John returned to London. On May 24, 1738, in a meeting in Aldersgate Street, he felt his "heart strangely warmed" by the sense of assurance of forgiveness and the sufficiency of God's grace. As preacher in houses, halls, and open fields he called thousands to believe and repent. On horseback he traversed Great Britain and Ireland, organizing small societies.

Wesley's teaching combined traditional Christology with the Reformation's emphasis on Justification by Faith alone. He saw the depth of sin matched by the height of the sanctification to which the Holy Spirit leads persons of faith. Rejecting Calvin's inexorable Predestination, he affirmed the freedom of human will as prompted by grace. He disavowed intent to form a new church but, though he remained an Anglican, Methodism eventually became another church body. *See* Perfection, Christian.

Bibliography. A. C. Outler, ed., *John Wesley* (1964), a documented interpretation of his theology; M. Schmidt, *John Wesley, a Theological Biography,* 3 vols. (1962-66).

J. R. Nelson

WESTERN WALL (Ju). Remnant of the ancient wall around the Temple Court in Jerusalem; the holiest site in Judaism.

About 57 m. long x 20 m. high, the wall contains large stones from Herod's Temple, and underground perhaps some from Solomon's Temple. Legend holds that since the destruction of the Temple by the Romans (A.D. 70) the *Shekhina* (Divine Presence) has not left the wall.

Pilgrims say special prayers before the wall—a Synagogue without a roof—and requests are placed on notes in its crevices. Non-Jews call it "the Wailing Wall."

Bibliography. Z. Vilnay, *Legends of Jerusalem* (1973); M. C. Klein and H. A. Klein, *Temple Beyond Time* (1970); B. Mazar, *The Mountain of the Lord* (1975). Y. Shamir

WESTMINSTER ABBEY (Ch). A royal church and national shrine of the English people, in the city of Westminster, London. Founded by Edward the Confessor and dedicated to St. Peter (1065), it has witnessed the coronation of English sovereigns since William the Conqueror. The attached Benedictine monastery was dissolved by Henry VIII (1540) and was reconstituted by Elizabeth I (1561) as a collegiate church with dean and chapter. The present church building was begun by Henry III in 1245, but was not completed until *ca.* 1500. Henry VII founded the present east-end chapel in 1502. The west towers were finished in 1745. *See* ART AND ARCHITECTURE, CHRISTIAN; Plate V*a*.

Bibliography. E. Carpenter, ed., *A House of Kings, The Official History of Westminster Abbey* (1966); J. Perkins, *Westminster Abbey, Its Worship and Ornaments,* 3 vols. (1938-52).

M. H. SHEPHERD, JR.

WESTMINSTER CONFESSION (Ch). The work of the Westminster Assembly, London, 1647; the most influential statement of REFORMED theology among English-speaking PRESBYTERIANS and CONGREGATIONALISTS, drawing upon the native Augustinianism of Britain and the PURITAN theology as well as the more classical Reformed sources. Composed by an assembly of Puritan theologians along with commissioners from the Church of Scotland, it is distinguished by its precision in definition and logical coherence in statement. *See* CREEDS AND CONFESSIONS §5.

J. H. LEITH

WHEEL OF LIFE (B). *See* BHAVACAKRA.

WHITE LOTUS SOCIETY (Chin.; *Pai-lien chiao*). Chinese religious sect which developed out of PURE LAND Buddhist lay associations in the southern Sung dynasty (A.D. 1127-1279), but which departed from its orthodox antecedents by instituting married clergy and full-time vegetarianism. By the late thirteenth century this movement had developed its own rituals and temples, and had incorporated a variety of folk practices and beliefs from TAOISM.

In the early fourteenth century, reforming monks succeeded in keeping some White Lotus members in the orthodox Pure Land tradition. At the same time, however, heterodox sect leaders were writing their own scriptures and borrowing MILLENARIAN ideas from MANICHEISM and the cult of MAITREYA, the future Buddha. These ideas included the division of time into three periods or stages, and the promise of paradise on earth in the third stage through the coming of a savior. In the mid-fourteenth century several White Lotus groups rebelled against Mongol rule in the name of both Maitreya and the Manichean King of Light.

In the sixteenth century popular sects of the White Lotus type developed a new form of scripture texts called *pao-chüan* ("precious books"), which were based on the myth of a mother goddess who created mankind and sought to save all by bringing them back to her paradise. These groups were also characterized by charismatic leadership, hierarchical organization, membership rituals, and congregational worship. Some of them organized eschatological uprisings against the government, the most famous of which took place between 1796-1805, the so-called "White Lotus rebellion." Similar sects still flourish in Taiwan. *See* CHINESE POPULAR RELIGION.

Bibliography. D. L. Overmyer, *Folk Buddhist Religion: Dissenting Sects in Late Traditional China* (1976).

D. L. OVERMYER

WILLIAM OF OCKHAM (Ch; *ca.* 1280-1347 or 1349). English FRANCISCAN philosopher, theologian, and controversialist; author of the principle of economy of thought known as Ockham's razor, which asserts that "what can be done with fewer [assumptions] is done in vain with more." (*See* SCHOLASTICISM §2.)

F. OAKLEY

WILLIAMS, ROGER (Ch; 1603-1683). PURITAN leader and founder of Rhode Island. After graduation from Cambridge, Williams went to Massachusetts in 1631. Almost immediately he attracted attention by his arguments that the churches of the colony were corrupt in their imperfect separation from the Church of England, that the colony ought to pay the Indians for the lands which it had taken, and that complete religious liberty should be given to all residents. In 1635, shortly after his election as pastor of the Salem Church, he was tried by the General Court and ordered to leave the colony. The following January he went to the head of Narragansett Bay, where he established Providence Plantations on lands purchased from the Indians. He was instrumental in persuading other religious dissenters in the area to accept a common government. While in Rhode Island, Williams tentatively accepted BAPTIST principles and was baptized, but he was not content with the teachings of any group.

Unlike other Puritans, he held that the government had no authority over human conscience and that all religious positions had an equal claim to the protection of the law. In 1644 he published a full defense of his position in *The Bloody Tenet of Persecution.*

Bibliography. P. Miller, *Roger Williams* (1953); J. Garrett, *Roger Williams* (1970).

G. MILLER

WIRD wĭrd (I—Arab.; lit. "invocatory prayer"; pl. *awrād*). The litanies sometimes recited by Muslims at the end of canonical PRAYERS (*ṣalāt*) but more often recited as part of private devotional or free prayer *(du'ā')*. To the SUFI orders, *awrād* have a twofold significance: 1) they are efficacious in obtaining certain wishes because the SHAIKH has imparted a special power *(baraka)* to his wording of these invocations; 2) they link members of one generation of Sufi devotees to their predecessors in earlier generations through an *isnād,* or chain of bona fide transmitters, that is recited along with the *awrād.* The conclusions of Sufi corporate gatherings, whether for remembrance (DHIKR) or musical recital *(samā'),* is also marked by the intoning of *awrād.*

B. LAWRENCE

WISE, ISAAC MAYER (Ju; 1819-1900). Founder of American REFORM JUDAISM. He emphasized the need for a union of congregations, a college to train RABBIS, and a reform of Jewish ritual. His own version of contemporary American Jewish ritual, *Minhag America,* was published in 1856. L. FAGEN

WITCHCRAFT (Old English: *wicce,* "female magician," *wicca,* "male magician," rel. to *wiccian,* "practice of magical arts"). The performance of MAGIC for evil ends.

1. **The figure of the witch.** Numerous societies have attributed to human beings the power to inflict misfortune upon others through supernatural means. Witchcraft has been held responsible for a wide variety of misfortune: preventing butter from churning, causing accidents and injuries of all kinds, destroying the fertility of the earth, animals and human beings, and even causing death. Contemporary research on psychosomatic illness clearly indicates that witchcraft beliefs can indeed cause serious illness and that counter-magic consequently can also be somatically effective. The power by which such malevolence is accomplished is invariably preternatural although its specific source can vary greatly. It is sometimes hereditary, indwelling in the witch quite apart from intentionality; it is often generally available from the storehouse of magical powers which can be employed for good or ill; and it is also supplied by various supernatural beings such as demons or evil spirits with whom witches are believed to make compacts. Whatever the particular source of their power, witches are thought to be in league with cosmic forces of evil. It is therefore understandable that the imagined figure of the witch is usually the opposite of what is considered normal for human beings. Thus witches skulk about at night, fly or walk on their hands, worship devils and even have sexual relations with them, and sacrifice or devour children; the more heinous the conduct, the more believable. The figure of the witch, sometimes called the "nightmare witch," embodies what a society considers inhuman, and in so doing provides a model of what people ought not to be like.

2. **The function of witchcraft beliefs.** Witchcraft has often been thought to provide societies with explanations for what are taken to be undeserved misfortunes, those which otherwise would be attributable only to chance. If one is struck by a falling branch, witchcraft does not explain the resulting wound, but does explain why that particular branch happened to fall just as one was passing underneath. Other functional approaches have suggested that witchcraft accusations serve as a socially legitimated expression of hostility. Kluckhohn's work on Navajo witchcraft claims that witchcraft accusations are instances of displaced aggression in a society which condoned few expressions of hostility. In African tribal societies, witchcraft accusations have been seen as providing legitimate grounds for otherwise disallowed lineage fission and division of villages which have grown too large, cumbersome, and fraught with conflict. Witch doctors whose function it is to identify witches usually proceed by ferreting out the patterns of animosity within a village, particularly those of the afflicted person, in an attempt to discern likely suspects. Such a procedure is often capable of uncovering animosity, of making it explicit, and occasionally of providing at least a temporary resolution. Studies of witchcraft in England also connect accusations with conflict. Quarrels often resulted in witchcraft accusations, particularly when they were followed by inexplicable illnesses or similar misfortunes. It was often the unneighborly person, specifically the abrasive beggar, who was designated a witch, possibly as a way of alleviating one's guilt at having turned him or her away empty-handed.

While these examples suggest that witchcraft may play a socially useful role, functional interpretations must always be aware that witchcraft accusations and explanations are often terrifying and dysfunctional. The plausibility of the functional view depends upon the claim that cultures cannot tolerate chaos, that any explanation, even a terrifying one, is better than no explanation at all. Certainly the attribution of illness to witchcraft at least allows one to take some counter action (anti-witchcraft magic, making restitution to the witch or even killing him or her).

3. **The witchcraft society.** A common social experience runs through all instances of witchcraft accusations. In each case the social structure itself places persons in ambiguous relations with each other and fails to provide them with mechanisms through which the resulting conflict can be expressed and resolved. The Englishman turning beggars away was constrained by a "Poor Law" which simultaneously forbade begging and yet required parishes to be responsible for the poor. An African tribesman might face a social system which at once encouraged affectionate cooperation *and* the contradictory responsibility of each man to seek to become chief.

A second common characteristic of witchcraft societies is that they are marked by a strong sense of group identity and strong pressure to conform to group norms. Their dualistic cosmologies divide the world into warring forces of good and evil. Individuals in such societies are placed in anxiety-producing situations, for the pressure to conform to and to achieve one's identity in terms of the group is constantly undercut by the disarray of the system of relationships and their governing classifications. Douglas has suggested that the figure of the witch gives symbolic expression to such a social experience. Persons accused of witchcraft are normal in outward appearance, yet are believed to harbor within themselves the powers of cosmic evil.

A functional analysis would suggest that witchcraft accusations allow the resolution of such conflict. However, it is seldom the case that the conflict is permanently resolved, for the social structure which generated accusations is either left unaffected or made even more problematic. Douglas' revision of the functionalistic approach sees witchcraft accusations as an expression of social malaise instead of simply as an attempted cure. It is invariably the case that those accused of witchcraft do in fact present to their accusers a real threat. Accused witches are just barely normal. They are often in league with external powers—social, economic, and political—which actually pose a threat to the community making the accusations. Additionally, the threat is always a subtle one; accused witches are seldom grossly deviant; if they were, the society would have other means of dealing with them. It is the ambivalence of suspected witches as well as of the social system which is the key. Witchcraft accusations are generally an attempt to strip away the guise of normality and expose the danger which lurks on the inside. This is accomplished on two levels: the evil power residing within the body of the witch is exposed, and at the same time the evils lying within the social body are identified and expelled. Witchcraft accusations consequently often accompany revitalization and MILLENARIAN MOVEMENTS which seek to eliminate alien evils and restore the purity and wholeness of the social body. Far from being an eruption of the irrational into public life, witchcraft accusations point to underlying social tensions and conflicts and give them an often appropriate symbolic form.

Bibliography. P. Boyer and S. Nissenbaum, *Salem Possessed* (1974); M. Douglas, *Natural Symbols* (1973), and *Witchcraft Confessions and Accusations* (1970); L. Mair, *Witchcraft* (1969); M. Marwick, ed., *Witchcraft and Sorcery* (1970); C. Kluckhohn, *Navaho Witchcraft* (1967).

D. E. OWEN

WOMEN: STATUS AND ROLE IN WORLD RELIGIONS. The difference between men and women has been a source of fascination for many of the world's religious traditions. On the one hand, the simultaneous opposition, yet complementarity of the sexes has been taken as a model and symbol for a whole series of other pairings: for example, matter and spirit, instinct and intellect, chaos and order, change and permanence. On the other hand, the biological roles of the sexes have, for many religious traditions, evidenced different modes of creative power operating in the world. Thus religions have recognized male and female divinities, who give and take life and order in ways distinctive to their sex (*see* FEMININE DIMENSIONS OF THE SACRED). But men and women themselves have also been experienced as reservoirs of creative, and sometimes threatening, sacral forces. All of these perceptions have carried implications for women's status vis-à-vis men, and they have also helped shape the roles that women have been able to, or encouraged to, develop.

But here we come to a puzzling problem. Many tribal religions, and apparently also many of ancient times, have drawn upon women's sacred and symbolic values to weave rich fabrics of cosmic and ritual balance. In such traditions women often assume roles as significant ritual functionaries, shamans, and seers. The world's largest and most successful religions, however, have often used the same values to exclude women from many important arenas of religious life and to justify their practical subordination to men. The reasons for this apparent reversal are complex, but the facts are indisputable. As a normal rule, in the great religious traditions of the world, women have been expected to play a role, religious and social, second to that of men.

Until very recent times, however, such considerations have only rarely discouraged women from active participation in the religious arenas allotted to them, such as the women's orders of CHRISTIANITY, BUDDHISM, and JAINISM, as well as corresponding lay communities. Women have furthermore generated their own rites and cults, as in the so-called "calendrical" rites of HINDUISM and in the "vows" undertaken by women in ISLAM. Women have also risen to prominence as saints, prophets, and scholars; while in some traditions vestiges of older patterns remain in the activities of female mediums and diviners (*see* WITCHCRAFT).

1. **Judaism.** JUDAISM, oldest of the West's major living religions, draws on an ancient patriarchal heritage shaped in part by responses to competing ancient Near Eastern traditions in which women played conspicuous cultic roles. In the ancient Hebrew laws women were viewed as potential sources of pollution, through the menstrual flow and the impurities of childbirth. But as mother, a woman was also essential for both the biological and cultural continuity of the chosen people. In a tradition that continues to place great emphasis on the family unit as matrix of most religious life, the domestic role has remained the Jewish woman's central opportunity for religious service. As wife and household manager, a woman frees her husband and sons for prayer and study of the TORAH—while Jewish law has exempted her from these same central duties. She administers the dietary laws and lights the candles that usher in the SABBATH. As mother she bears children to perpetuate the Jewish community and is responsible for instilling in her sons the desire to study Torah.

In traditional rabbinic Judaism women had no formal role in public life or in the life of the synagogue. Despite all influences to the contrary, rare women achieved fame for their scholarship (cf. Bruria, wife of Rabbi Meir). More ancient Hebrew records preserve the memory of a few women prophets, such as Miriam the sister of MOSES, the "judge" Deborah, and the prophetess Huldah. In much more recent times women won unusual prominence in HASIDISM, with a number achieving the role of *rebbe,* or spiritual leader.

2. **Christianity.** "In CHRIST," says the apostle PAUL, "there is neither male nor female" (Gal. 3:28). But Christ's church has furthered discrimination between the sexes ever since the same apostle told women to keep their hair covered and their mouths closed in church.

Much of the traditional Christian attitude toward women can be traced to the dualism, inherited from the Greek world, that has shaped Christian thought since the tradition's earliest centuries. Spirit and matter, soul and body, are separate and in conflict. Woman is more "carnal"; hence, like other things of the flesh, she should be kept subordinate. This same dualistic thinking led, in ROMAN CATHOLIC Christianity, to a significant denigration of married women—i.e., those most directly implicated in carnal life—as opposed to virgins—i.e., those who denied the claims of their bodies for the sake of spiritual development.

Christian custom continued menstrual and childbirth taboos inherited in part from its Jewish parent (*see* CHURCHING OF WOMEN); these were once an important contributing factor to the Catholic tradition's long-standing refusal to ordain women to the priesthood. However, nonclerical orders for women have existed since very early Christian times and have pursued a broad range of vocations, from service to secluded contemplation (*see* NUN; FRANCISCANS; CARMELITES).

Within their allotted "places" women have made massive contributions to Christianity. Women were very prominent in the early church, and have remained important as laywomen until the present day. Christian women became martyrs, and later famous saints and mystics (*see* TERESA OF AVILA). At times, women's orders have had twice the membership of their male counterparts.

3. Islam. The revelation to MUHAMMAD that gave rise to Islam called for a massive restructuring of the social order. In Islam's early years this effectively improved the status of women, placing new restraints on divorce and polygamy and requiring husbands to support their wives, as well as bringing women the right to inherit and retain control of their dowries (*see* MARRIAGE AND DIVORCE, ISLAM). The QUR'ĀN still taught, nonetheless, that "men are in charge of women, because Allah hath made the one of them to excel the other" (Sura 4:34; trans. M. M. Pickthall). To temper the dangers of sexual attraction and also to protect woman followers of the faith from insult, the Qur'ān called for modesty in the form of covering one's inner dress and ornaments in public. In time, however, and under pressure of local custom, such teachings were cited to justify demands that women be veiled from head to foot in public. In some regions, and especially among the upper social classes, women were totally secluded in the home *(purdah)*. Muslim popular culture also preserved strict menstrual taboos; among other prohibitions, these excluded from the mosques both menstruating women and those who had recently given birth. Menstrual taboos also closed to women some religious offices, such as that of IMAM, or prayer leader.

As in Christianity and in many other new religions that challenge repressive establishments, women were very prominent in the early Muslim community (*see* KHADĪJA; 'Ā'ISHA); in later centuries some once again became prominent scholars. Women such as the mystic poetess Rabia were important to the SUFI orders; a number of these had women's branches and convents from very early times. Even though largely restricted to the home, many women of traditional Muslim countries have elaborated their own religious networks and practices, transmitting religious instruction and holding gatherings in their homes.

4. Hinduism. Considerations of status and role for any group in Hindu society are largely determined by the ancient conception of DHARMA. This conception communicates simultaneously the image of a sacred, all-embracing, and organic cosmic order and the belief that any individual's preeminent duty is to fulfill the "place" that one inherits within it. Dharma precepts identified a woman's place as wife and mother; traditionally a woman was out of place, anomalous, unless this role was achieved. The dharma teachings further stipulated that a woman should always be subordinated to some male: in childhood, to her father; in maturity, to her husband; and in old age, to her sons. A married woman was instructed to take her husband as her god. She also observed numerous menstrual taboos to shield him and her family from her pollution. Woman's dharma excluded her from virtually all public roles, including the priesthood practiced by the BRAHMIN CASTE; for many centuries women could not learn or recite Hinduism's sacred language, SANSKRIT.

At the same time, a woman who fulfilled perfectly the discipline of her "place" was thought to win considerable, even superhuman, power. As in Judaism, motherhood acquired an exaggerated honor. From very ancient times a married Hindu woman has been considered a ritual unit with her husband. Thus she shares with him responsibility for many observances performed in the home as well as the merit of his religious accomplishments. An extensive cycle of domestic rituals concerned with the family's well-being has become almost exclusively women's religious province.

If a woman's "place" was lost, through her husband's death or his decision to enter an ascetic life, she again became anomalous. A widow was extremely inauspicious and was expected, in effect, to become invisible. An ascetic's wife enjoyed a theoretically higher status; but practically her position remained ambiguous. As with men, any woman whose domestic responsibilities have been completed is allowed to take up the ascetic life. Some women have exercised this option; but for the most part they have enjoyed less honor than male ascetics. In contrast, a few women have been very important in Hindu devotional movements which claim that all castes and both sexes have equal access to their chosen deity and to salvation (*see* MĪRĀBĀĪ; BHAKTI HINDUISM).

5. Buddhism shares with Christianity the somewhat paradoxical position of assuming an equal potential for spiritual development of men and women, while affirming inequity between the sexes at the beginning of the spiritual path. The Buddhist position, however, is not based on the saving grace of deity, but rather on the workings of KARMA, or cosmic justice, which traces all inequities of birth to the effects of deeds in previous lives. This position has required that women be given equal opportunity with men to follow Buddhism's path of renunciation; this was institutionalized in early Buddhist days by the founding of parallel orders for monks and nuns. At the same time, the initial sexual inequity has justified a practical subordination of women to men; this, too, has found institutional expression both in Buddhist norms for domestic life and in the men's and women's monastic rules: the most notorious example is the stipulation that monks must always be treated as senior to nuns.

For a variety of reasons not yet well known, the order of Buddhist nuns did not fare equally well in all regions where Buddhism became established. In India, after several prosperous centuries, it faded into obscurity; in Sri Lanka the succession of THERAVĀDA ordination for nuns apparently died out before it could be transmitted to Southeast Asia. However, the order became quite powerful in China and remained a significant force in Chinese Buddhism until the Maoist revolution; it continues to be important in the Taiwanese exile community.

Surprisingly, after the founding years, Buddhist nuns in India left little impression as communal leaders and scholars. In China, Buddhist laywomen attached to the courts achieved distinction for their scholarship. Laywoman-donors have been prominent throughout the Buddhist tradition, with the first, much-cited example set by the celebrated merchant's daughter Visākhā.

6. **East Asia.** The history of woman's fate in the interlocking traditions of East Asia is at the same time the most intriguing and the most problematic. All evidence suggests that women were once a very significant part of religious life in East Asia. The early importance of powerful medium-priestesses called *miko* is well documented in Japan; vestiges still remain in the female priesthood of the imperial shrine at ISÉ and in the role of female mediums and ascetics in popular SHINTŌ practice. Woman shaman-seers remain active in other popular traditions throughout East Asia, and there is reason to believe that they, too, once enjoyed more prestigious positions (*see* SHAMANISM). Early Taoist teachings, therefore, may have continued an ancient tradition when they proclaimed ideals of cosmic balance (YIN AND YANG) and of "becoming female" to the Tao. But real women were also important to the Taoist Heavenly Masters sect, achieving the rank of priestess and consequent deification. (*See* TAOISM, RELIGIOUS.)

CONFUCIANISM, which came to dominate both Chinese and other East Asian social theory, moved firmly in the opposite direction. In its grand cosmic hierarchy, earth's subordination to heaven became the model for woman's subordination to man. Marriage was the normative state for a woman, and submission to husband the appropriate expression of cosmic piety for a wife. In various times and regions the Confucian norm was interpreted with varying degrees of severity. But by the nineteenth century it was cited to condone the severe oppression of Chinese women that moved various reformers to call for their liberation.

As in most other traditions taboos surrounding menstruation and childbirth additionally shaped the lives of East Asian women. Japan still preserves remnants of menstrual taboos and exclusions. But the folk tradition in China has, perhaps, carried its unease with women's generative processes to the greatest extreme; unless a woman's offspring performed a special rite to redeem her, the mother could expect to be immersed for a time in a pool of blood in hell when she died. A menstruating woman could not participate in any family rites; furthermore, a woman retained enough residual pollution to prevent her from officiating at the rites of major family gods during other times as well.

7. **The contemporary scene.** The twentieth century has, of course, seen numerous changes in women's status and role, both within and beyond the confines of organized religion. In large part such changes are attributable to the twin forces of secular ideology, which often calls into question traditional religious norms and values, and the political and social revolution which has often been its by-product.

In the Christian and Jewish traditions an important phenomenon has been the emergence and growing influence of a feminist critique. While some feminists are increasingly alienated from traditional religions that they regard as male-centered and male-dominated, others have worked within the traditions for reform of offending imagery and institutional strictures. One by-product has been women's increasing access to roles that were formerly closed. Thus, REFORM JUDAISM now ordains woman rabbis, ANGLICAN women have won ordination to the priesthood, and women are entering various branches of the Protestant ministry in increasing numbers.

Traditional Islamic restrictions on women have also been subjected to searching critique, often influenced by Western secular values. In many modern Islamic nations women have put aside the veil and gained access to education, as well as positions of leadership in secular, and especially professional, life. Sometimes, however, changes emerging too quickly have provoked a religious backlash.

The liberation of women in the People's Republic of China was a secular development, brought about by a revolution that overturned most traditional religious norms. But a striking phenomenon in other regions of South and East Asia has been new prominence for women in roles of religious leadership. Woman GURUS, as well as women's associations and/or orders, have been important in several Hindu movements of the twentieth century. In Japan, woman founders of so-called "New Religions" such as

TENRI-KYŌ and RISSHŌ KŌSEIKAI have renewed the charismatic vocations and style of the old shamanic tradition. Women have also been newly active in Buddhism. Thus the order of Taiwanese Mahāyāna nuns has extended a branch to the United States, while women in Thailand have reestablished the ordination of nuns in their own Theravāda tradition.

Bibliography. Materials on this topic are sparse for some traditions and times, and scattered throughout many sources. For cross-cultural approaches, see N. Falk and R. Gross, eds., *Unspoken Worlds: Women's Religious Lives in Non-Western Cultures* (1980) and D. L. Carmody, *Women and World Religions* (1979). Valuable information on individual traditions can be found in the following: for Christianity and Judaism, R. R. Ruether, ed., *Religion and Sexism* (1974); for Islam, E. W. Fernea and B. Q. Bezirgan, eds., *Middle Eastern Muslim Women Speak* (1977); for the period of Buddhist origins, as recorded in Pali literature, I. B. Horner, *Women under Primitive Buddhism* (1930); for Sanskrit and Chinese Buddhist sources, D. Paul, *Women in Buddhism* (1980). For women under Hindu dharma the best starting point is still two older and somewhat ponderous works: J. J. Meyer, *Sexual Life in Ancient India* (1930) and S. R. Sastri, *Women in the Sacred Laws* (1953). For Japan, see H. Okano, *Die Stellung der Frau im Shinto* (1976); also for excellent accounts of contemporary women shamans, C. Blacker, *The Catalpa Bow* (1975). China presents the most difficult problem, for resources in Western languages are still very fragmentary; but see R. H. van Gulik, *Sexual Life in Ancient China* (1961); also, E. Ahern, "The Power and Pollution of Chinese Women," in M. Wolf and R. Witke, eds., *Women in Chinese Society* (1975), pp. 19-24.

N. E. A. FALK

WORLD COMMUNITY OF ISLAM. *See* UMMA; BLACK RELIGIONS IN THE UNITED STATES §5.

WORLD COUNCIL OF CHURCHES (Ch). *See* ECUMENICAL MOVEMENT §2.

WU-HSING wo͞o shĭng (T—Chin.; lit. "five movements"). The five agents (sometimes translated "elements") that in different mixtures compose all things: wood, fire, earth, metal, and water. (*See* TAOISM, RELIGIOUS; TAOISM, PHILOSOPHICAL.)

M. LEVERING

WU WEI wo͞o wā (T—Chin.; lit. "inaction"). The basic attitude taught by LAO TZU; the avoidance of aggressiveness; doing only that which is natural and spontaneous. By showing compassion and humility and by returning good for evil, one will be able to influence the actions of others. K. CRIM

WUDŪ' woo do͞o′ (I). The Islamic rite of "minor" ablution for PURIFICATION and sacralization preceding the performance of PRAYER (*ṣalāt*). It is prescribed by the QUR'ĀN (Sura 5:7; 4:43) and detailed by Traditions (ḤADĪTH). Specifically, the face, head, hands, and feet (that is, the parts of the body normally exposed to the world) are washed. If water is not available, sand or dust may be used. MOSQUES and other places of prayer are usually provided with running water for the performance of *wuḍū'*.

Ghusl, a washing of the entire body, is the "major" ablution and is performed in cases of gross ritual impurity. H. B. PARTIN

WYCLIFFE, JOHN (Ch; 1330-1384). English church reformer. Wycliffe argued against nominalism and the power of the papacy, emphasizing the concept that believers are responsible directly to God, and the importance of vernacular scriptures; his own translation of the Bible into English was completed by his followers, the LOLLARDS.

R. L. HARRISON

Y

YAD VASHEM yäd vä shām´ (Ju). The world's largest memorial to the six million Jews murdered in the Holocaust, located in Jerusalem. Its extensive archives serve as a worldwide research center. It publishes its own studies and periodicals, e.g., *Yad Washem Studies,* Jerusalem, P.O. Box 7044.

E. Fleischner

YAHRZEIT yär´ tzīt (Ju—Yiddish; lit. "time of year"). The popular term for the anniversary of a death, usually that of a close relative, but it may also commemorate a national or religious figure. In traditional Judaism the observance includes the mourner's being called to read the Torah, recite the Kaddish, and lead the service. It is also customary to light a twenty-four hour memorial candle. *See* Death; Yizkor.

D. J. Schnall

YAHWEH yä´ wĕ (Ju & Ch—Heb.; etymology unknown). The sacred name of God in the Hebrew Bible. Since Hebrew was written without vowels, the four consonants YHWH (the "tetragrammaton") offer no clue to the original pronunciation. Based in part on Theodoret of Cyrrhus' memory of the Samaritan pronunciation, the name is generally rendered "Yahweh."

The Masoretes consistently marked the name with vowel signs indicating that the divine name *Adonai* ("Lord"), or at times *Elohim* ("God"), was to be substituted for it when the Bible was read. Confusion about this custom led to misreading the name as Jehovah. In most English versions of the Bible it is translated "Lord."

Although the name Yahweh was first revealed to Moses in Exod. 3:14, it occurs in the creation story (Gen. 2) and is said to have been used from the time of Seth and Enosh (Gen. 4:26).

M. G. Rogers

YAJÑA yŭj´ nyŭ (H—Skt.; lit. "worship, honor" [*yāj*—"to worship"]). Sacrifice, the primary religious activity throughout the Vedic period of ancient India. The sacrifice brings about a transformation in the sacrificer, who declares either general or specific purposes for his offerings. *Yajñas* were divided into relatively simple domestic *(gṛha)* rites, performed usually on one fire by the householder, with offerings of butter and grain cakes, and great public *(śrauta)* rites requiring three fires, sixteen or seventeen priests, offerings of animals and Soma, and as much as two years of activity. The great public rites are rarely performed in modern times, but some orthodox Hindus observe *yajñas* such as the five daily offerings to the gods, beings, ancestors, the seers, and men (guests, beggars). *See* Vedic Hinduism; Śrāddha.

Bibliography. P. V. Kane, *History of Dharmaśāstra,* Vol. II (1941), Pt. I, chs. 17-18; Pt. II, chs. 19-35.

D. M. Knipe

YĀJÑAVALKYA yŭj´ nŭ vŭlk´ yŭ (H—Skt.; lit. "a speaker of things related to sacrifice" [*yaj*—"to sacrifice"; *valk*—"to speak"]). Promulgator and reputed founder of the White Yajur Vedic school of adhvaryu priests (*see* Vedic Hinduism). Traditionally credited with rearranging the text of the Black Yajur Veda to separate the Mantras (revealed formulas) from the Brāhmaṇas (exegetical commentaries). He is repeatedly named in the Upaniṣads of the Atharva Veda as a renowned teacher of yoga and advocate of mendicancy, and regarded in the Mahābhārata as a primary source of the yoga doctrine and, together with Vyāsa and Paila, as a canonical authority on the Vedic sacrifice.

In the Śatapatha Brāhmaṇa, Yājñavalkya is usually considered the principal authority on ritual procedure and interpretation and a paradigm of adhvaryu and mīmāṃsist (*see* Mīmāṃsā) attitudes in his emphasis on sacrificial works and action as opposed to the metaphysical speculation favoured by representatives of the Rig Veda and Sāma Vedas. E.g., in the Bṛhad Āraṇyaka Upaniṣad he successfully championed the interpretations of the adhvaryu priests against representatives of the Rig Veda and Sāma Veda schools in the court of Janaka of Videha by using common sense and by showing the limits of argumentation and speculation—responding with,

"No, no" (*neti, neti*) when his adversaries urged a conclusion that exceeded the limits of human knowing (BĀU III. 6. 1). J. S. Helfer

YAJUR VEDA yŭ´ joor vā´ dŭ (H—Skt.; lit. "knowledge of the sacrificial formulas" [*yajus*—"sacrifice, prayer" + *veda*—"knowledge"]). One of the four primary texts of Vedic Hinduism, a collection (Saṃhitā) of ritual materials and directions for the sacrifices and for invocations of deities, composed at the close of the second or early in the first millennium B.C. Four schools have preserved texts of the Black Yajur Veda in mixed verse and prose, and two schools have transmitted the White Yajur Veda in verse only. *See* Veda. D. M. Knipe

YAKṢA yŭk´ shŭ (H). A class of demigods who serve Kubera, the lord of wealth, and aid him in guarding his treasures. They range in disposition from benevolent to mischievous and in size from dwarf to giant, and are generally regarded as *puṇya-jana*, "auspicious beings." J. Bare

YAMA yä´ mŭ (H—Skt.; lit. "restrainer," "punisher," or "twin" [*yam*—"to restrain," "to subdue"]). Closely related to Bṛhaspati and Agni as conductor of the departed souls to the underworld. Indian counterpart to the Greek gods Pluto and Minos, as patron deity of the spirits of the deceased; mythical primal man and patriarchal ruler of mankind; first creature to die and to discover the path of the ancestors to the world beyond. As one of the eight World-protectors, he is assigned sovereignity over the southern direction, considered in India to be the abode of spirits and, hence, highly inauspicious.

In early Vedas, Yama was a king, then a minor deity who was apotheosized for his discovery of the secret of immortality. In the Mahābhārata he rose to full rank of divinity after a struggle with the gods. In later literature he is often depicted as the deputy of Shiva (who is also conceived of as the Lord of the Dead) as well as Shiva's archenemy who, as the dispenser of immortality, destroys death.

His countenance, especially in later literature, is ominous and terrifying, striking even the most courageous soul with dread. He is green in color, attired in red garb, and rides a buffalo. His messages of death are often carried by a pigeon or an owl. He bears in either hand a club and a noose with which he captures human souls at "the appointed time." He is accompanied by two brindled dogs with four eyes each. Their task is to seek out those who are to die, guard the path leading to Yama's realm and, perhaps, exclude those who belong elsewhere. As overlord of the souls of the deceased, Yama rules over the twenty-one or twenty-eight hells in which the souls whose deeds were wicked in the last lifetime are cast. The region called Tamisra ("dark pit") is a place of total darkness where sinners are tortured by Yama's servants, with fire, diseases, boils, scorpions and unquenchable thirst. On leaving the body the soul repairs to this region where the Recorder, named Citragupta, reads from the "Register of Human Deeds" concerning the actions of the deceased, weighs those deeds on a balance, and passes the appropriate sentence.

Yama's devotees approach him in supplication for boons of happiness, longevity, and even immortality. His power to bring or withhold death is depicted in two famous stories: (1) his dialogue with the student Nacitekas, who persuades him to reveal the mysteries of death (Kath. U. 1. 1.); (2) his struggle with Sāvitrī over the fate of her husband (Mbh. 3. 281-3).

In the Epics and Purāṇas, Yama appears as a fully developed lord of the deceased, psychopomp, and ruler over the realm of the dead. A few of his epithets are: Kāla, "time"; Antaka, "ender"; Mṛtyu, "death"; Pitṛi-pati, "Lord of the Ancestors"; and Dharma-rāja, "King of Righteousness." Most importantly, he is Dharmendra (Lord of Justice), who judges the deeds of the departed and conducts the righteous ones to heaven and the wicked to one of the many hells (*nārakās*) presided over by his emissaries.

Bibliography. W. D. O'Flaherty, *The Origins of Evil in Hindu Mythology* (1976); U. Schneider, "Yama und Yamī," *Indo-Iranian Journal*, X (1967), 1-32; A. Wayman, "Studies in Yama and Māra," *ibid.*, III (1959), 44-73, 112-31.

J. B. Long

YAMABUSHI yä mä´ boo shē (B & Sh—Jap.; lit. "lying down in the mountains"). The Japanese religious ascetics who practiced austerities on sacred mountains to acquire religious power, and then used this power to serve the religious needs of the people through rites such as exorcism and prayer. At first they operated as wandering ascetics and exorcists, but later they developed into a nationwide phenomenon with many local centers. Generally the movement traces its origins to a legendary figure, En no Gyōja, of the seventh century, but its historical development is obscure before the twelfth century. Known generally as *Shugendō* ("the way of acquiring extraordinary power"), this movement blended Japanese notions of sacred mountains with other traditions such as Taoism and Shintō, and especially Tendai and Shingon Buddhism. Eventually the *yamabushi* became organized into complex ecclesiastical organizations centered on numerous sacred mountains and competed actively with one another for adherents and spheres of influence.

Due in part to the government policy of separating Shintō and Buddhism after the Meiji Restoration of 1868, *Shugendō* was officially disbanded in 1872, when its priests and buildings tended to assume Shintō and Buddhist forms. After 1945, with complete religious freedom, some groups have reclaimed the *Shugendō* name and revived the practice of *yamabushi* rituals. H. B. Earhart

YĀMUNA yä´ moo nū (H—Skt.). A theistic philosopher and devotional poet, "Teacher's Teacher" of RĀMĀNUJA, and first exponent of the ŚRĪ VAIṢṆAVA school of VIŚIṢṬA ADVAITA VEDĀNTA whose works are extant. Flourishing *ca.* A.D. 1022-38 at Śrīrangam, the major South Indian VISHṆU temple, he was the pivotal figure between his grandfather Nāthamuni (*ca.* tenth century), the first in this line of Teachers (ĀCĀRYAS), and Rāmānuja (eleventh-twelfth centuries). Nāthamuni and Yāmuna are remembered as learned Bhāgavata BRAHMINS who were specially beloved of KRISHNA and who used their Vedic training and dialectical skills to defend and promote the post-Vedic PAÑCARĀTRA scriptures and the TAMIL hymns of the ĀḺVĀRS. Yāmuna in his *Āgama-prāmāṇya* ("The Authoritativeness of the [Pañcarātra] Revelation") represents a tradition of theistic Vedānta that views Pāñcarātra temple worship (PŪJĀ) as an equally valid and indeed superior alternative to the ancient Vedic ritual. His Sanskrit hymn, *Stotra-ratna*, reflects the Āḻvārs' ecstatic devotion (BHAKTI) and is reputedly the work that first attracted Rāmānuja. Verses of the *Stotra-ratna* are recited daily by Śrī Vaiṣṇavas and other Hindus, while his other hymn, *Catuś-ślokī*, is a classic of devotion to the goddess Śrī or LAKṢMĪ. Rāmānuja's major Vedāntic works were inspired by Yāmuna's *Siddhi-traya* and his *Gītā-artha-saṃgraha*, a verse summary of the BHAGAVAD GĪTĀ.

Bibliography. M. Narasimhachari, *Contribution of Yāmuna* (1971); W. G. Neevel, *Yāmuna's Vedānta and Pāñcarātra* (1977); J. A. B. van Buitenen, trans., *Yāmuna's Āgama Prāmāṇya* (1971).

W. G. NEEVEL

YANTRA yŭn´ trŭ (H & B—Skt.; lit. "machine, engine" [*yam*—"to hold, sustain"]). MANDALAS or icons used in TANTRISM and YOGA as the focus of meditation or worship. *Yantras* often employ sexual symbolism to represent the continuing act of creation. The *Śrīyantra*, with its complexity of color and design, is regarded as the most potent.

J. BARE

YARMULKA yär´ mool kə (Ju—Yiddish). The skull cap worn in observance of the traditional Jewish custom of covering the head. Strictly ORTHODOX Jews wear the yarmulka (or *kippah*, as it is called in Hebrew) continuously during their waking hours, and traditionalist Jews cover their heads with it when reciting prayers or studying sacred texts.

B. MARTIN

YESHIVAH yə shē´ vä (Ju—Heb.). A school in which the TALMUD and rabbinic literature are the chief subjects of study. It had its prototype in the academies of Palestine and Babylonia during the Talmudic age. The traditional yeshivah is not intended only for those aspiring to become RABBIS but for all Jews who wish to acquire higher Jewish learning.

B. MARTIN

The *Śrīyantra*

YIDDISH yĭd´ ĭsh (Ju). The vernacular of ASHKENAZI Jews, a combination of several languages written in HEBREW script. Its syntax is primarily German, with vocabulary reflecting the venue of the speaker. Although it was long prominent, migration, repression, and the HOLOCAUST have reduced Yiddish to secondary status in most communities, a recent surge of scholarly interest notwithstanding.

Yiddish usage and dialect differ by geography and sociology. Rabbinic Yiddish includes TALMUDIC Hebrew and ARAMAIC, while merchants incorporated peasant vernacular in their speech. Western, Eastern, and Southern Europeans differed in vocabulary and dialect, and subregional variances were common.

Yiddish history is divided into four periods. Prior to 1250 French and Italian Jews, speaking a vernacular known as Laaz, came into contact with early German, adapting it and Hebrew to their needs. In the following era (through 1500) this Yiddish confronted Slavic influences of East European Jews. The trend continued as Jewish life expanded eastward (*ca.* 1500-1700), and generations of Yiddish speakers who had little contact with German accommodated to patterns heard about them. In the modern period Yiddish was attacked by Western Jews as an impediment to their integration. Sholom Aleichem (1859-1916) used the language as an effective literary medium, and in 1978 the Yiddish writer Isaac Bashevis Singer won the Nobel Prize for literature. It is the major language of older European immigrants to America and some HASIDIM.

Bibliography. J. A. Fishman, *Yiddish in America* (1965); M. Weinreich, *History of the Yiddish Language* (1979).

D. J. SCHNALL

YIN AND YANG yĭn, yäng (Con & T—Chin.). A cosmological theory expressing the interdependence of opposite movements in nature, society, and man.

The words "yin" and "yang" originally meant the dark side and the bright side of the mountains, and were probably symbols of a fertility cult. The Yin Yang school of thought was founded by Tsou Yen (*ca.* 305—*ca.* 240 B.C.). It combined the concept of yin yang with the theory of the five agents *(wu hsing)*—wood, fire, earth, metal, water—and made them into a cosmology of cyclical movements. In the Han dynasty (206 B.C.—A.D. 220) this school was incorporated into both Confucianism and Taoism and since then has been the basis of cosmological speculation in Chinese thought. The idea of yin yang was also pervasive in CHINESE POPULAR RELIGION.

1. Yin yang in Confucianism. Confucius himself probably did not teach the idea of yin yang, as the ANALECTS does not mention it. It was the I CHING, the Confucianism of Tung Chung-shu (*ca.* 179—*ca.* 104 B.C.), and Neo-Confucianism that emphasized the yin yang theory (*see* CONFUCIANISM §§2, 3.) The yang refers to the active, male, hard, or expansive pole; and the yin to the passive, female, soft, or contracting pole. The reciprocity between these two poles constitutes a cycle of movements, which is the meaning of change, time, or causality in Confucianism. The theory of the five agents is a more elaborate explanation of the reciprocity between yin and yang. Wood and fire belong to yang, and metal and water to yin. Earth assists the other four agents, and thus belongs to both yin and yang. In Neo-Confucianism the idea of yin yang was used to explain the creation of the cosmos, and the theory of the five agents was applied to explain the creation of the myriad things. Both the idea of yin yang and the theory of the five agents are an explanation of the opposite poles of the cycle, and there is no implication of good and evil in the yin yang concept.

2. Yin yang in PHILOSOPHICAL TAOISM. Taoism too uses the theory of yin yang to explain the rhythm of the ebb and flow in nature and man, but also to explain the relation between BEING AND NONBEING. The former is an expression of yang and the latter of yin. Ontologically speaking, nonbeing is higher than being because it is the source of being. This also means that ontologically yin is more valued than yang.

3. Yin yang in RELIGIOUS TAOISM. The yin yang idea and the concept of the five agents correspond symbolically to the different forces and centers in the human body for the explanation of the circuits of breathing in internal ALCHEMY. In essence, the human body is viewed as a miniature cosmos. Thus the adept follows his internal circuits of breathing in the same way as the cosmos follows the cycles of yin yang movements.

4. Yin yang in popular religion. *See* CHINESE POPULAR RELIGION; FENG-SHUI.

See illustration for I CHING.

Bibliography. W. T. Chan, *A Source Book in Chinese Philosophy* (1963), pp. 244-50; Y. L. Fung, *A History of Chinese Philosophy*, D. Bodde, trans., II (1953), 7-87 (Tung Chung-shu); J. Needham, *Science and Civilisation in China*, II (1956), 232-91 (school of yin yang, Tung Chung-shu).

D. C. YU

YIZKOR yĭts kōr′ (Ju—Heb.; lit. "remember"). First word of the memorial prayer recited on the last day of each pilgrim festival and YOM KIPPUR. It calls upon the Lord to remember the soul of a parent, spouse, child, brother, or sister and in Orthodox and Conservative Judaism is normally accompanied by pledges of charity in their memory. *See* KADDISH; YAHRZEIT.

D. J. SCHNALL

YMCA (YOUNG MEN'S CHRISTIAN ASSOCIATION). A society for young men founded in England by George Williams in 1844. Its original purpose was to provide for the spiritual development of young working men, and in its early years it reflected the various emphases of nineteenth century EVANGELICALS. Today it is less explicitly evangelical and provides a wide variety of services to young men.

G. MILLER

YOGA yō′ gŭ (H—Skt.; lit. "discipline" [*yuj*—"to yoke, harness, use, set to work, concentrate the mind"]). A set of psychosomatic theories and techniques for doing meditation, unique in South Asia from ancient times to the present. The theories and techniques of Yoga encompass a wide range of religious phenomena, including (a) a sophisticated theoretical method for transforming human awareness (namely, the classical Yoga of PATAÑJALI, often called Rāja Yoga); (b) difficult physical postures and breathing exercises for attaining control of the body as well as unusual psychological states (namely, the Yoga of Exertion or HATHA YOGA); (c) elaborate visual and auditory systems of symbolization, involving the imagery of sexuality and intricate ritual activites, for achieving paranormal and/or magical "perfections" (SIDDHI), namely, tantric Yoga (*see* TANTRISM) with its subvarieties and related techniques of the Yoga of Audition or MANTRA YOGA, the Yoga of Dissolution or Laya Yoga, and the Yoga of Serpent Power or KUNDALINĪ Yoga. Although the word "Yoga" can also be used for Buddhist and JAINA meditation (*see* MEDITATION, BUDDHIST), it is most often used in Hindu contexts to refer to the traditions enumerated above.

1. History and literature. A precise account of the origin and history of Yoga is impossible, but there are four important periods for which literary and historical materials provide clues as to the manner in which the traditions of Yoga took shape.

a) Ancient sources (3000-800 B.C.). Various archaic traditions of ascetic spirituality undoubtedly provided the cultural context from which the later Yoga traditions developed. One such tradition is SHAMANISM with its ecstatic spiritual "virtuosi," its techniques of trance, and its religious symbolism of ascent and descent. Some have even suggested that the Central

Asian word "shaman" is related to the Sanskrit terms Śramaṇa and *śamana* (meaning "wandering" and "quieting" respectively). However, the "ecstatic" spirituality of shamanism differs phenomenologically from the largely "enstatic" spirituality of the later Yoga traditions.

Another possible source is the Indus Valley Civilization (2500-1500 B.C.). Among the archaeological evidence (in the form of steatite seals and terra cotta figurines), one seal in particular pictures what appears to be a deity or a holy man seated in a posture characteristic of later Yoga. With the coming of the Aryans toward the middle of the second millennium (*ca.* 1500 B.C.), however, stronger evidence is available for documenting the presence of an ascetic spirituality in South Asia. Rig Veda X.136 describes a long-haired ascetic *(muni)* who has attained paranormal capacities. Similarly, Book XV of the Atharva Veda describes a peripheral Aryan group, called *Vrātya,* who practice austerities, engage in strange breath exercises, and assume unusual bodily postures. Also the early Upaniṣads mention the "interiorization" or meditative, introspective appropriation of the old Vedic fire sacrifice in terms of Tapas or "internal burning." Thus, although the term "Yoga" does not appear, it is clear enough that environments such as these provided the context out of which Yoga traditions would emerge.

b) Proto-Yoga (800 B.C.—A.D. 200). In this second period there is direct evidence for the emergence of what can be called "proto-Yoga" tradition(s). Buddhist and Jaina traditions of meditation arose along with various traditions of *śramaṇa* or *yati* ("wandering ascetics"). In the "verse" Upaniṣads (namely, Kaṭha, Śvetāśvatara, Maitrī, etc.) the word *yoga* or "discipline" was used for the first time. This is also where the first clear references to Sāṃkhya philosophy is found, and subsequently the traditions of Sāṃkhya and Yoga appear to have been closely allied. In these Upaniṣads technical yogic terminology appeared—e.g., Āsana or "posture," Prāṇāyāma or "restraint of breathing." Moreover, toward the end of this period, in such texts as the *Mokṣadharma* portion of the Mahābhārata and the Bhagavad Gītā Yoga as a method of disciplined praxis is clearly emerging as a distinct method for attaining Mokṣa or release. This Yoga is contrasted with Sāṃkhya or "disciplined knowing," which is described as an alternate method for achieving *mokṣa.* Some historians of South Asian religion have argued that Patañjali himself lived in this second period (*ca.* 200 B.C.) and that, therefore, the Yogasūtra, which describes the classical, philosophical system of Yoga, was already extant. This argument is unconvincing, however, for it assumes that the ancient grammarian, Patañjali (*ca.* 200 B.C.), is the same as the Patañjali who is the author of the Yogasūtra. The philosophical views of the two texts, however, are so divergent that it is highly unlikely that they were composed by the same author. Much more likely is that the Patañjali of the Yogasūtra is a product of the third or "classical" period of Indian intellectual history and that a plurality of Yoga traditions characterize this "proto-Yoga" period.

c) Classical Yoga or Patañjali Yoga (A.D. 300-900). In the opening centuries of this period North India reached a notable level of political stability under the Gupta Dynasty (A.D. 320-540), and Hindu poetry, drama, art, religion, philosophy, and law attained "classical" expression. The various systems of orthodox Hindu thought were systematically formulated for the first time (in collections of aphorisms or Sūtras together with elaborate commentaries). Much of the material came from earlier centuries, but the systematic consolidation achieved in this third period provided a broader perspective for serious reflection than the earlier centuries had allowed. The old Sāṃkhya traditions appear to have been particularly vigorous, and were consolidated in the fourth century in classical expressions such as Īśvarakṛṣṇa's Sāṃkhyakārikā ("Verses on the Sāṃkhya"). Shortly thereafter (and possibly in response to the Sāṃkhya consolidation) Patañjali appears to have compiled the older and disparate Yoga traditions into what we now know as the classical Yogasūtra, and after another century Vyāsa had composed his important commentary entitled *Yogasūtrabhāṣya* ("Commentary on the Aphorisms of Yoga"). This latter work's laconic style led to the writing of various subcommentaries, the most notable of which is the great treatise of Vācaspatimiśra entitled *Tattvavaiśāradī* ("An Unerring Interpretation of the Principles of Yoga," *ca.* 850-950). These texts of Patañjali, Vyāsa, and Vācaspatimiśra (together with the various subcommentaries) represent the normative core of classical Yoga, both as theoretical systems of reflection and as practical manuals for authoritative practice.

d) Medieval and later Yoga (A.D. 900-1600). Following the classical period there emerged yet one more important treatise on classical or Patañjali Yoga, the *Yogavārttika* ("A Supplementary Commentary on Yoga") of Vijñānabhikṣu (*ca.* 1550). A quite different set of Yoga traditions also began to emerge. These were frequently allied with Śaivite (see Śaivism) and other sectarian traditions and are associated with the names of Matsyendranath, Gorakhnath, and the so-called "eighty-four *siddhas*" or "perfected ones." The principal texts of these later traditions are the *Haṭhayogapradīpikā* ("A Short Commentary on the Discipline of Exertion"), the *Gheraṇḍa-saṃhitā* ("Gheraṇḍa's Collection") and the *Śiva-saṃhitā* ("Śiva's Collection"). Based to some extent on the classical tradition, they are mainly syncretistic conflations of tantric ritual, archaic auditory and visual techniques for attaining paranormal states, catalogs of unusual body postures, and speculative discussions of human spiritual physiology (*see* Tantrism). These later traditions very likely represent a regression to the older, preclassical pluralism of archaic yogic spiritualities which Eliade has aptly characterized as that "protean Yoga" that

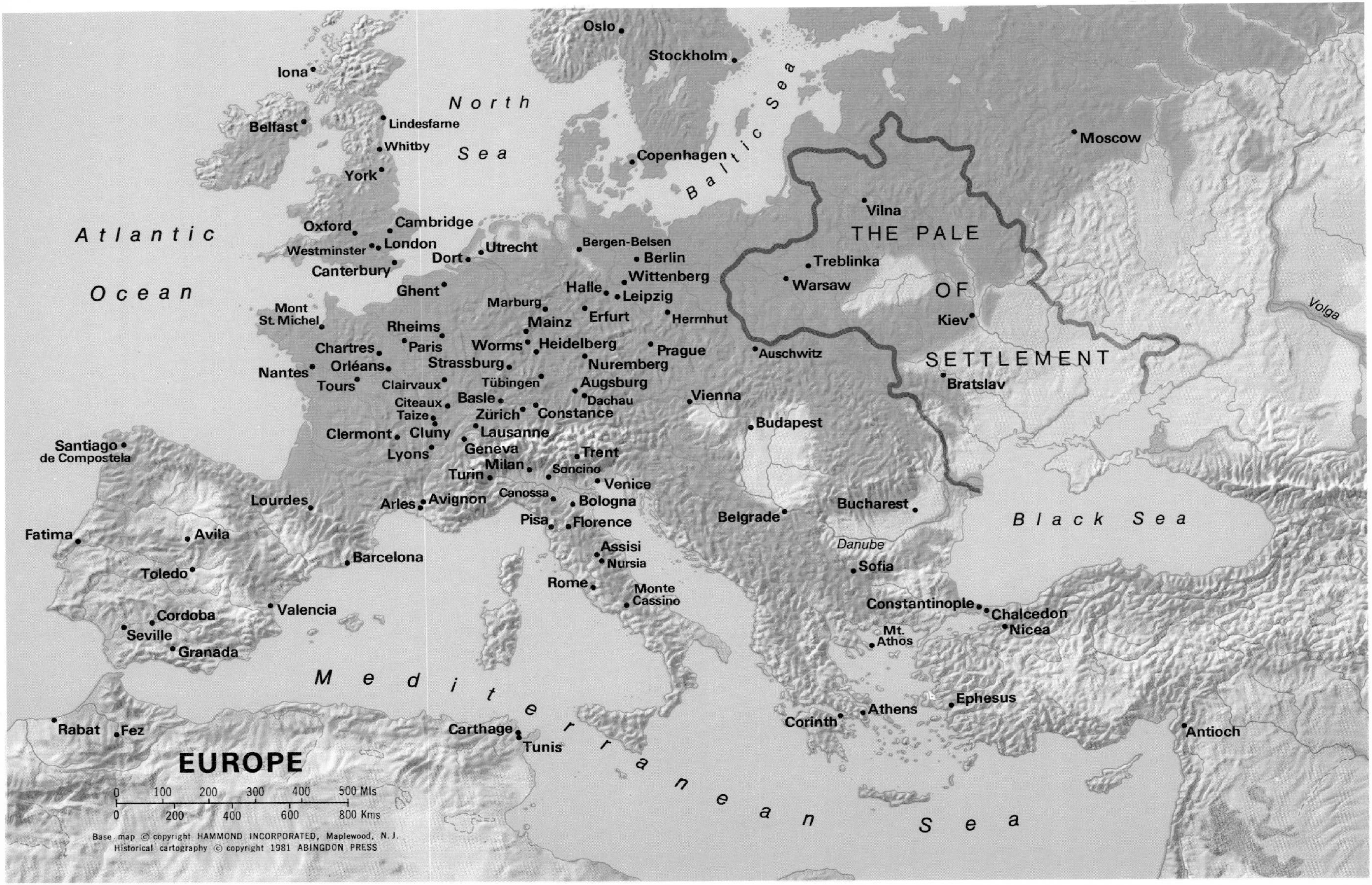
EUROPE
Atlantic Ocean
North Sea
Baltic Sea
Black Sea
Mediterranean Sea
THE PALE OF SETTLEMENT
Volga
Danube
Oslo
Stockholm
Iona
Belfast
Lindesfarne
Whitby
York
Copenhagen
Moscow
Vilna
Oxford
Cambridge
Westminster
London
Canterbury
Dort
Utrecht
Bergen-Belsen
Berlin
Wittenberg
Halle
Leipzig
Treblinka
Warsaw
Ghent
Mont St. Michel
Marburg
Mainz
Erfurt
Herrnhut
Kiev
Rheims
Paris
Worms
Heidelberg
Prague
Auschwitz
Chartres
Orléans
Nantes
Tours
Strassburg
Nuremberg
Clairvaux
Tübingen
Augsburg
Dachau
Bratslav
Citeaux
Taize
Basle
Zürich
Constance
Vienna
Budapest
Clermont
Cluny
Lausanne
Geneva
Lyons
Santiago de Compostela
Trent
Milan
Turin
Soncino
Venice
Lourdes
Arles
Avignon
Canossa
Bologna
Pisa
Florence
Belgrade
Bucharest
Fatima
Avila
Barcelona
Assisi
Nursia
Sofia
Toledo
Rome
Monte Cassino
Constantinople
Chalcedon
Nicea
Valencia
Cordoba
Seville
Granada
Mt. Athos
Ephesus
Athens
Corinth
Antioch
Rabat
Fez
Carthage
Tunis
0 100 200 300 400 500 Mls
0 200 400 600 800 Kms
Base map © copyright HAMMOND INCORPORATED, Maplewood, N.J.
Historical cartography © copyright 1981 ABINGDON PRESS

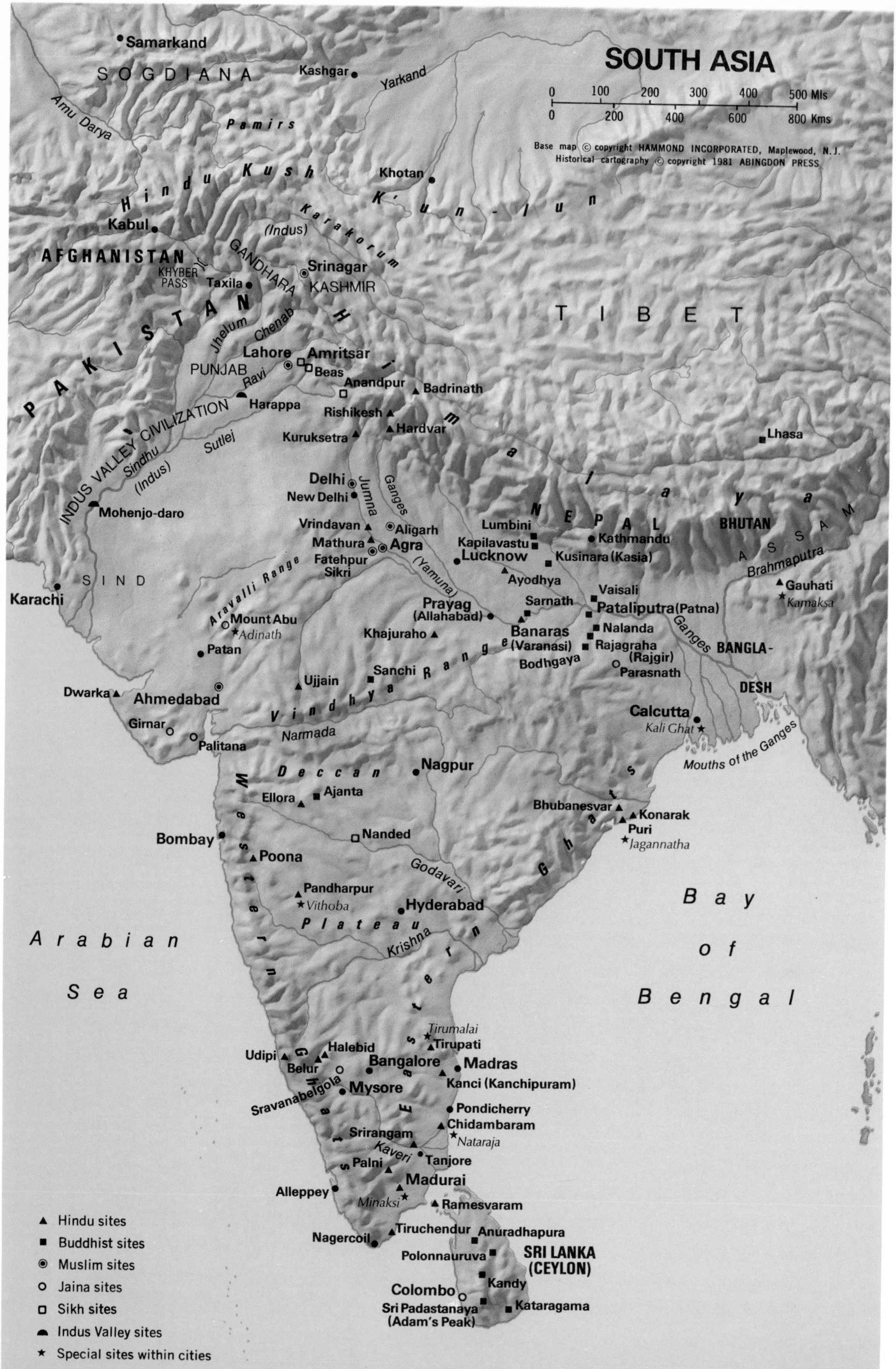
SOUTH ASIA
0 100 200 300 400 500 Mls
0 200 400 600 800 Kms
Base map © copyright HAMMOND INCORPORATED, Maplewood, N.J.
Historical cartography © copyright 1981 ABINGDON PRESS
Samarkand
SOGDIANA
Kashgar
Yarkand
Amu Darya
Pamirs
Hindu Kush
Khotan
K'un-lun
Karakorum
(Indus)
Kabul
AFGHANISTAN
KHYBER PASS
GANDHARA
Srinagar
KASHMIR
Taxila
PAKISTAN
Himalaya
TIBET
Jhelum
Chenab
Lahore
Amritsar
PUNJAB
Beas
Ravi
Anandpur
Badrinath
Harappa
INDUS VALLEY CIVILIZATION
Rishikesh
Hardvar
Kuruksetra
Sutlej
Lhasa
Sindhu
(Indus)
Delhi
New Delhi
Jumna
Ganges
Mohenjo-daro
NEPAL
Lumbini
Kathmandu
BHUTAN
ASSAM
Vrindavan
Aligarh
Mathura
Agra
Kapilavastu
Kusinara (Kasia)
Fatehpur Sikri
Lucknow
Brahmaputra
SIND
Aravalli Range
(Yamuna)
Ayodhya
Vaisali
Gauhati
Kamaksa
Karachi
Sarnath
Pataliputra (Patna)
Prayag (Allahabad)
Mount Abu
Adinath
Nalanda
Khajuraho
Banaras (Varanasi)
Rajagraha (Rajgir)
Ganges
BANGLA-DESH
Patan
Bodhgaya
Parasnath
Sanchi
Vindhya Range
Ujjain
Dwarka
Ahmedabad
Calcutta
Kali Ghat
Girnar
Palitana
Narmada
Mouths of the Ganges
Deccan
Nagpur
Ellora
Ajanta
Bhubanesvar
Konarak
Puri
Jagannatha
Bombay
Nanded
Poona
Godavari
Western Ghats
Eastern Ghats
Pandharpur
Vithoba
Hyderabad
Plateau
Bay of Bengal
Arabian Sea
Krishna
Tirumalai
Tirupati
Halebid
Udipi
Belur
Bangalore
Madras
Kanci (Kanchipuram)
Mysore
Sravanabelgola
Pondicherry
Chidambaram
Nataraja
Srirangam
Kaveri
Tanjore
Palni
Madurai
Alleppey
Minaksi
Rameswaram
Tiruchendur
Anuradhapura
Nagercoil
Polonnauruva
SRI LANKA (CEYLON)
Kandy
Colombo
Kataragama
Sri Padastanaya (Adam's Peak)
▲ Hindu sites
■ Buddhist sites
◉ Muslim sites
○ Jaina sites
□ Sikh sites
◓ Indus Valley sites
★ Special sites within cities

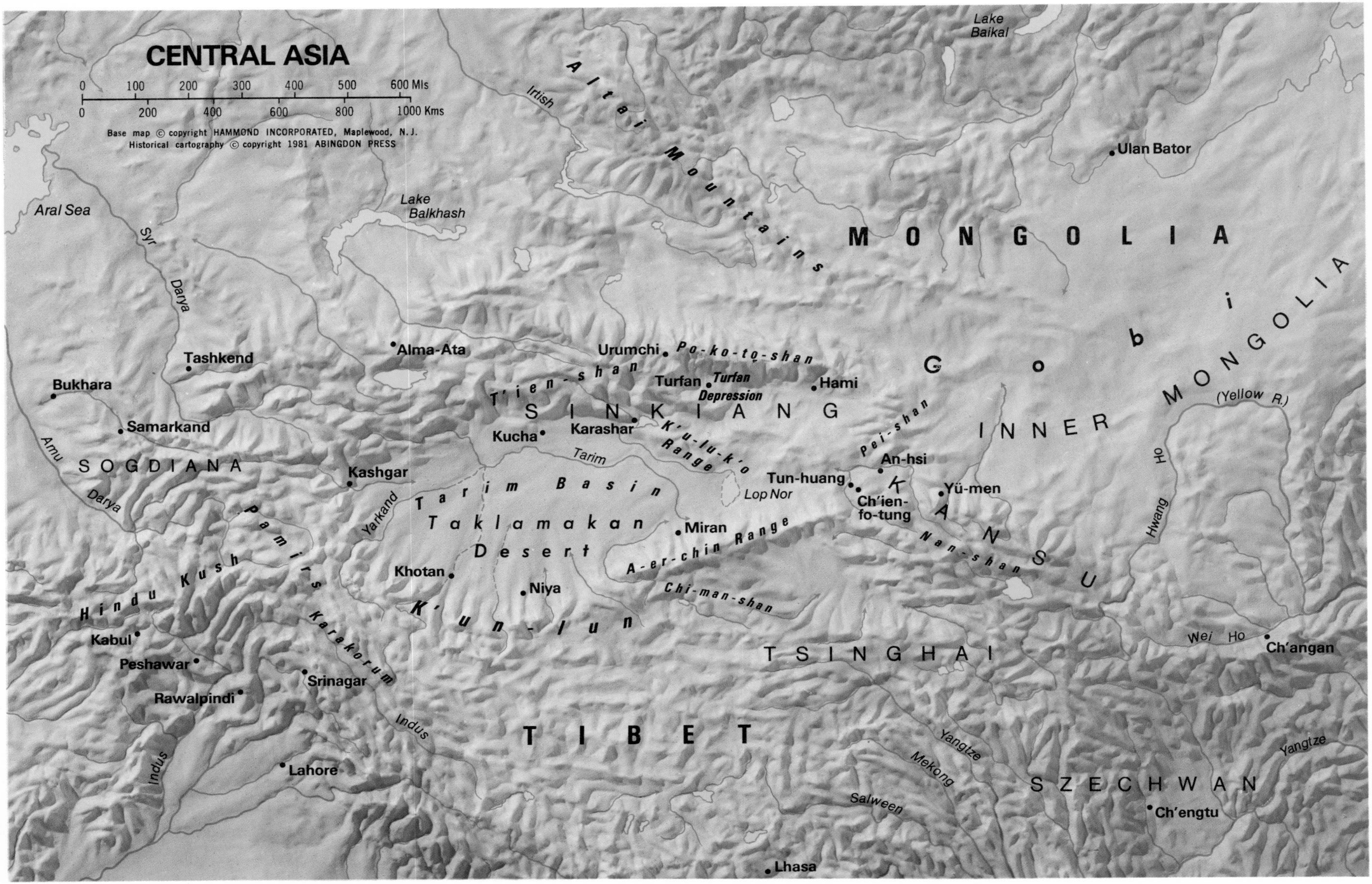
CENTRAL ASIA
0 100 200 300 400 500 600 Mls
0 200 400 600 800 1000 Kms
Base map © copyright HAMMOND INCORPORATED, Maplewood, N.J.
Historical cartography © copyright 1981 ABINGDON PRESS
Lake Baikal
Ulan Bator
Altai Mountains
Irtish
Lake Balkhash
Aral Sea
Syr Darya
MONGOLIA
Gobi
INNER MONGOLIA
(Yellow R.)
Hwang Ho
Alma-Ata
Tashkend
Bukhara
Samarkand
Amu Darya
SOGDIANA
Urumchi
Po-ko-to-shan
T'ien-shan
Turfan
Turfan Depression
Hami
SINKIANG
Kucha
Karashar
K'u-lu-k'o Range
Tarim
Pei-shan
An-hsi
Tun-huang
Ch'ien-fo-tung
Yü-men
KANSU
Lop Nor
Kashgar
Yarkand
Tarim Basin
Taklamakan Desert
Miran
A-er-chin Range
Nan-shan
Chi-man-shan
Khotan
Niya
K'un-lun
Pamirs
Hindu Kush
Karakorum
Kabul
Peshawar
Srinagar
Rawalpindi
Indus
Lahore
TIBET
TSINGHAI
Wei Ho
Ch'angan
Yangtze
Mekong
Salween
SZECHWAN
Ch'engtu
Lhasa

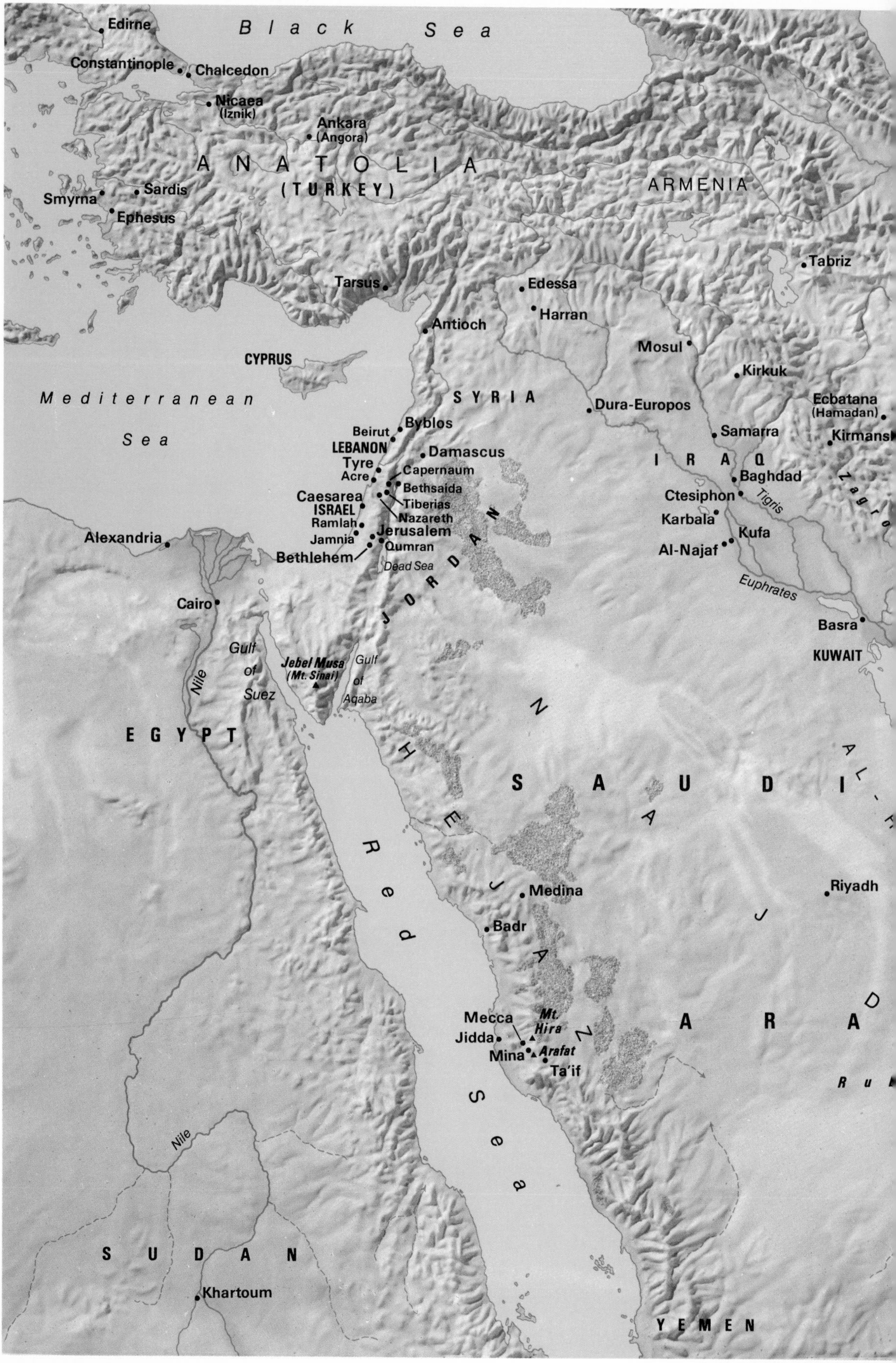
Black Sea
Edirne
Constantinople
Chalcedon
Nicaea
(Iznik)
Ankara
(Angora)
ANATOLIA
(TURKEY)
ARMENIA
Smyrna
Sardis
Ephesus
Tabriz
Tarsus
Edessa
Harran
Antioch
Mosul
CYPRUS
Kirkuk
Mediterranean Sea
SYRIA
Dura-Europos
Ecbatana
(Hamadan)
Beirut
Byblos
Samarra
LEBANON
Damascus
Tyre
Acre
Capernaum
Bethsaida
Tiberias
Nazareth
IRAQ
Baghdad
Ctesiphon
Tigris
Caesarea
ISRAEL
Ramlah
Jamnia
Jerusalem
Qumran
Bethlehem
Dead Sea
JORDAN
Karbala
Kufa
Al-Najaf
Alexandria
Euphrates
Cairo
Basra
KUWAIT
Gulf of Suez
Jebel Musa
(Mt. Sinai)
Gulf of Aqaba
Nile
EGYPT
HEJAZ
NAJD
SAUDI ARABIA
Red Sea
Medina
Riyadh
Badr
Mecca
Mt. Hira
Jidda
Mina
Arafat
Ta'if
Nile
SUDAN
Khartoum
YEMEN

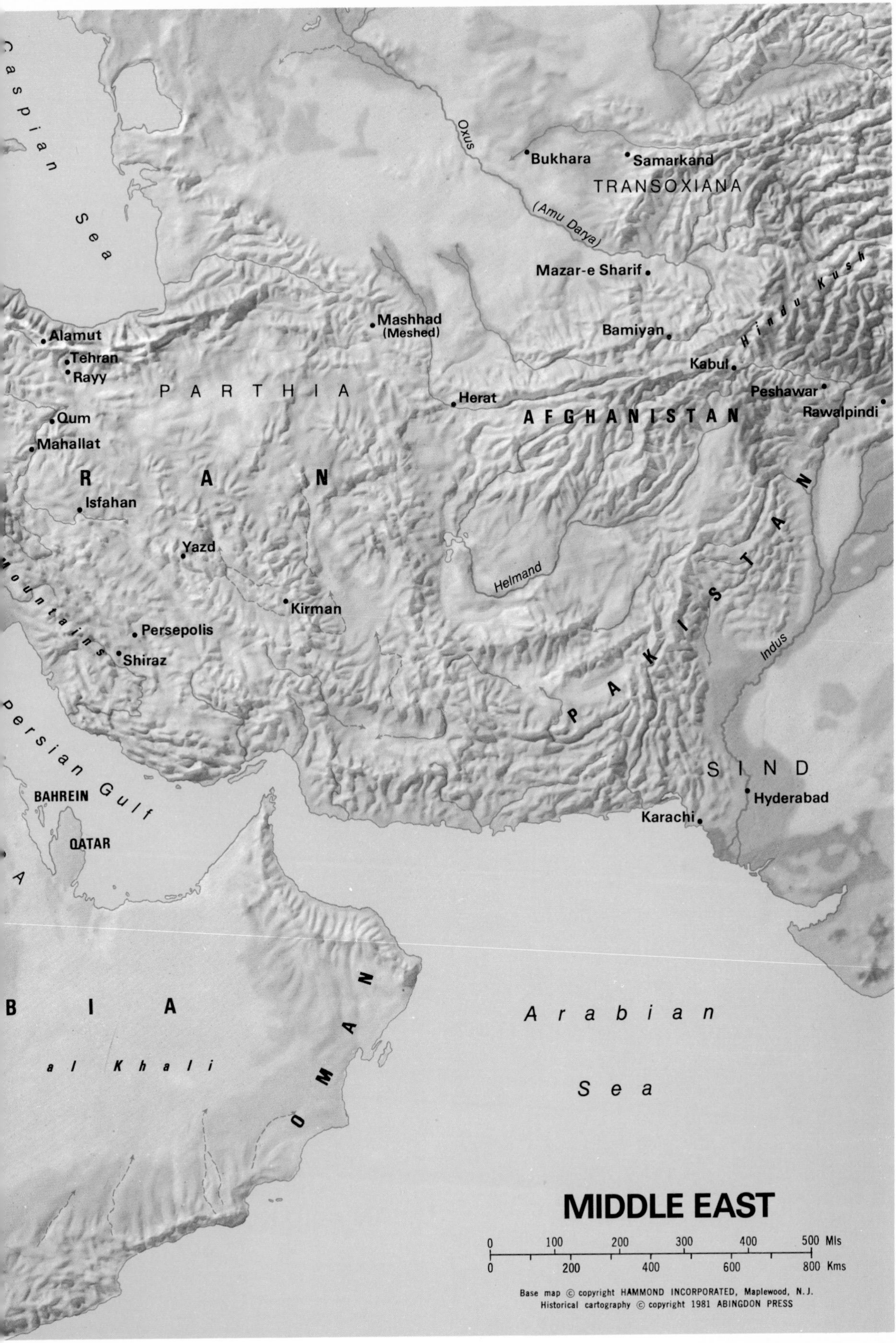

Caspian Sea

Oxus

• Bukhara   • Samarkand

TRANSOXIANA

(Amu Darya)

Mazar-e Sharif •

Hindu Kush

• Alamut   • Mashhad   Bamiyan •
• Tehran   (Meshed)
• Rayy   Kabul •   Peshawar
                                                          • Rawalpindi

P A R T H I A   • Herat   A F G H A N I S T A N

• Qum
• Mahallat

I   R   A   N

• Isfahan   P
                                                                       A
          • Yazd   K
                                                                       I
                    • Kirman   Helmand   S
                                                                       T
• Persepolis   A
M   N
o • Shiraz
u
n   Indus
t
a
i
n
s
                                                                       S I N D
P e r s i a n   G u l f
                                                              • Hyderabad
BAHREIN
                                              Karachi •
A   QATAR

B   I   A   O
                               M
                               A
                               N   A r a b i a n
   a l   K h a l i

                                                   S e a

MIDDLE EAST

0   100   200   300   400   500 Mls
0   200   400   600   800 Kms

Base map © copyright HAMMOND INCORPORATED, Maplewood, N.J.
Historical cartography © copyright 1981 ABINGDON PRESS

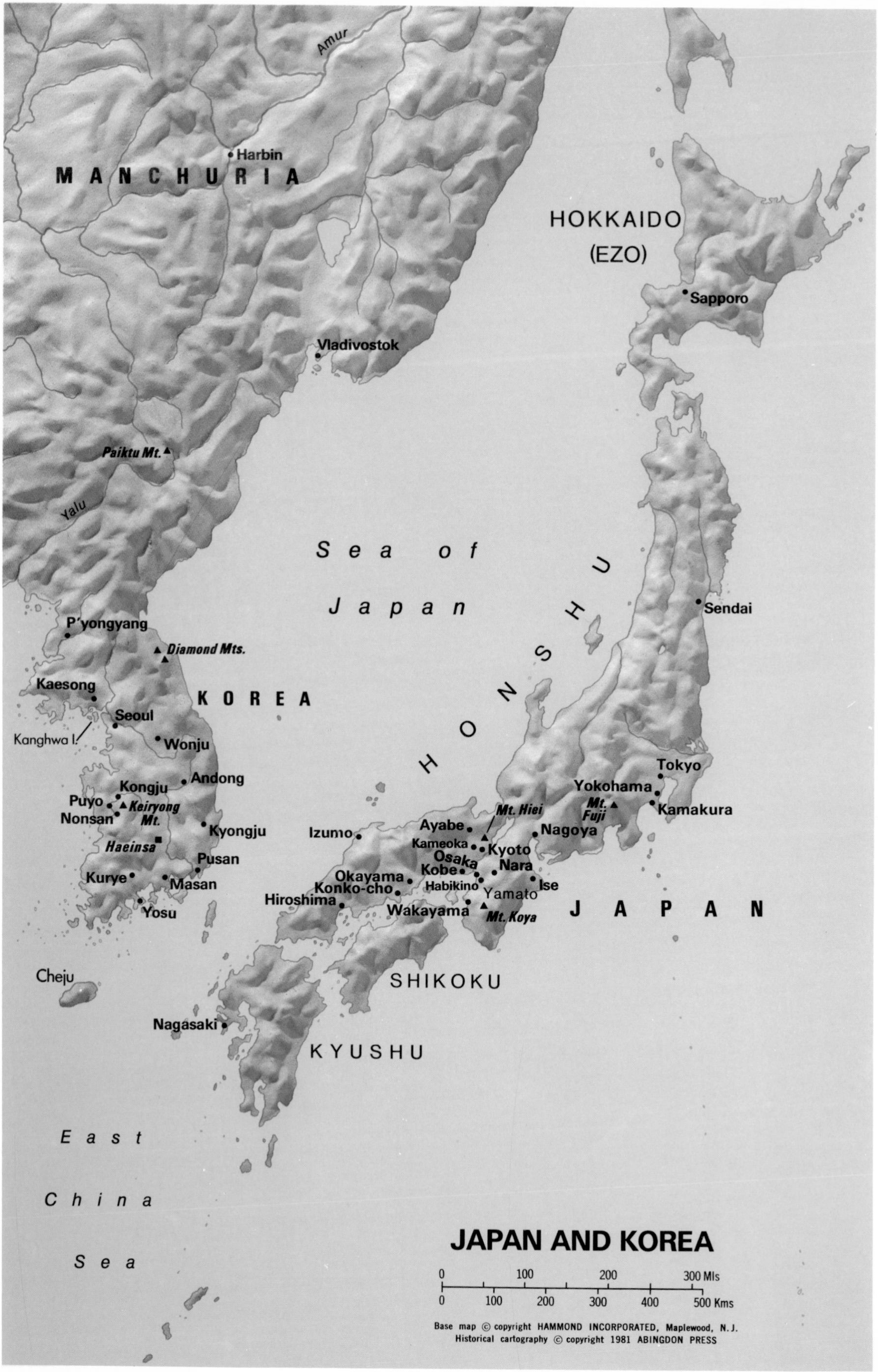
Amur
Harbin
MANCHURIA
Vladivostok
HOKKAIDO
(EZO)
Sapporo
Paiktu Mt.
Yalu
Sea of Japan
HONSHU
Sendai
P'yongyang
Diamond Mts.
Kaesong
KOREA
Seoul
Kanghwa I.
Wonju
Tokyo
Andong
Kongju
Yokohama
Puyo
Keiryong Mt.
Mt. Fuji
Nonsan
Mt. Hiei
Kamakura
Ayabe
Kyongju
Izumo
Nagoya
Haeinsa
Kameoka
Kyoto
Osaka
Pusan
Nara
Kobe
Okayama
Kurye
Masan
Ise
Habikino
Konko-cho
Yamato
Hiroshima
Yosu
Wakayama
Mt. Koya
JAPAN
SHIKOKU
Cheju
Nagasaki
KYUSHU
East China Sea
0 100 200 300 Mls
0 100 200 300 400 500 Kms

JAPAN AND KOREA

Base map © copyright HAMMOND INCORPORATED, Maplewood, N.J.
Historical cartography © copyright 1981 ABINGDON PRESS

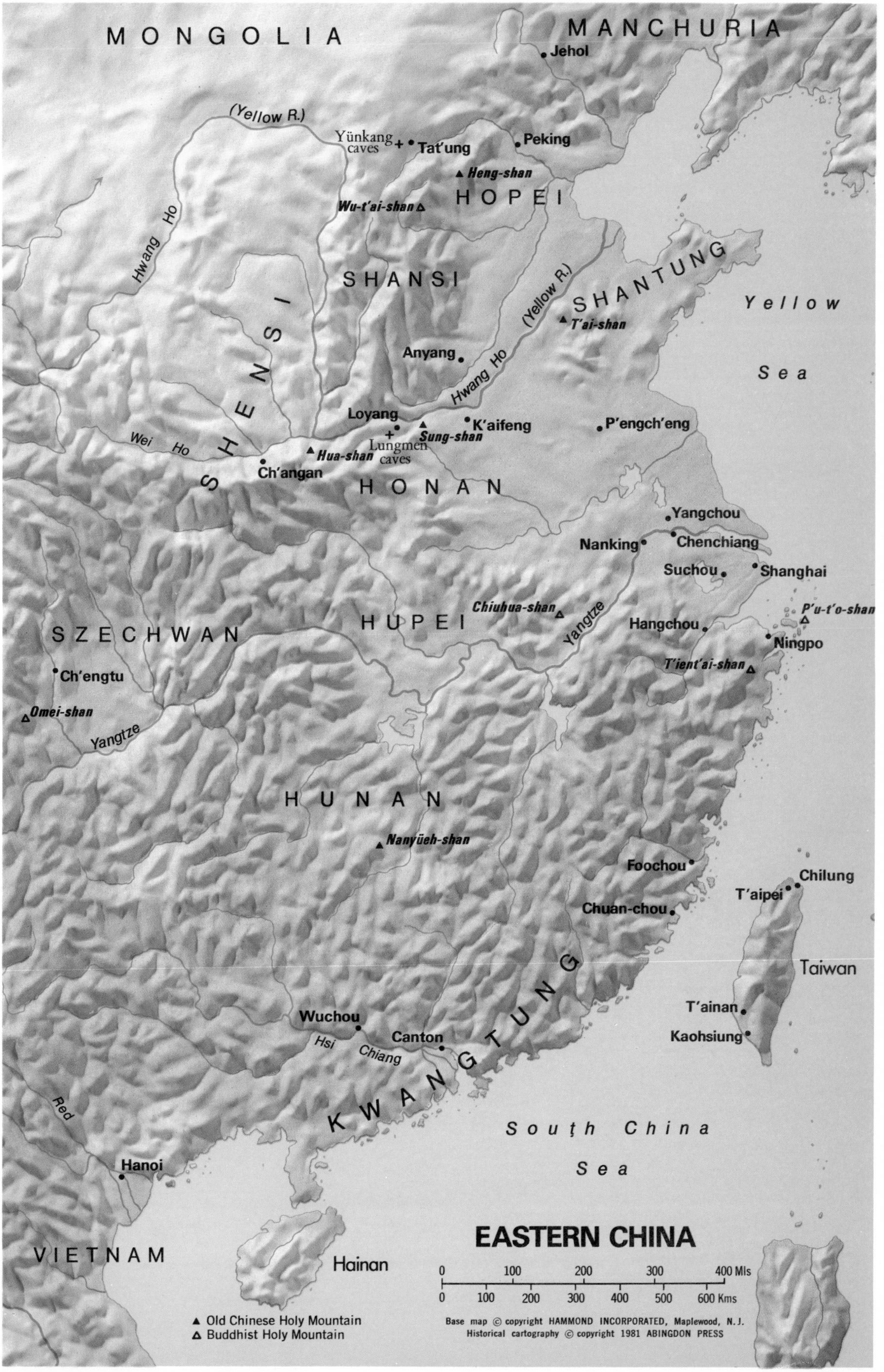
MONGOLIA
MANCHURIA
Jehol
(Yellow R.)
Yünkang caves
Tat'ung
Peking
Heng-shan
HOPEI
Wu-t'ai-shan
Hwang Ho
SHANSI
SHANTUNG
(Yellow R.)
Yellow Sea
T'ai-shan
SHENSI
Anyang
Hwang Ho
Loyang
K'aifeng
P'engch'eng
Sung-shan
Wei Ho
Hua-shan
Lungmen caves
Ch'angan
HONAN
Yangchou
Nanking
Chenchiang
Suchou
Shanghai
Chiuhua-shan
P'u-t'o-shan
HUPEI
Hangchou
SZECHWAN
Yangtze
Ningpo
T'ient'ai-shan
Ch'engtu
Omei-shan
Yangtze
HUNAN
Nanyüeh-shan
Foochou
Chilung
T'aipei
Chuan-chou
Taiwan
KWANGTUNG
T'ainan
Wuchou
Kaohsiung
Canton
Hsi Chiang
Red
South China Sea
Hanoi
VIETNAM
Hainan
EASTERN CHINA
0 100 200 300 400 Mls
0 100 200 300 400 500 600 Kms
▲ Old Chinese Holy Mountain
△ Buddhist Holy Mountain
Base map © copyright HAMMOND INCORPORATED, Maplewood, N.J.
Historical cartography © copyright 1981 ABINGDON PRESS

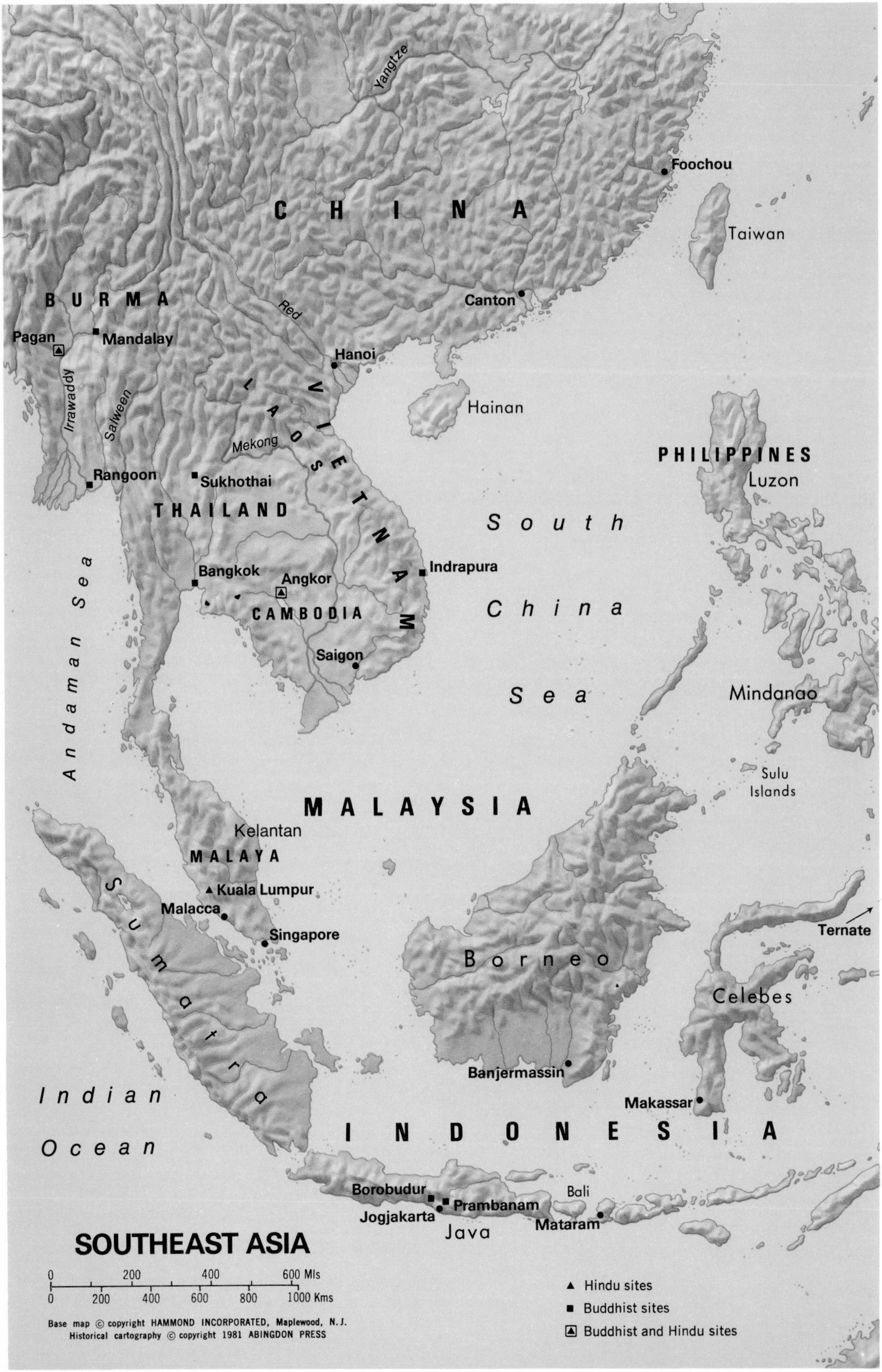

CHINA
Yangtze
Foochou
Taiwan
Canton
BURMA
Red
Pagan
Mandalay
Hanoi
Irrawaddy
Salween
LAOS
VIETNAM
Hainan
Mekong
PHILIPPINES
Luzon
Rangoon
Sukhothai
THAILAND
South China Sea
Bangkok
Angkor
Indrapura
CAMBODIA
Andaman Sea
Saigon
Mindanao
Sulu Islands
MALAYSIA
Kelantan
MALAYA
Kuala Lumpur
Malacca
Singapore
Ternate
Sumatra
Borneo
Celebes
Banjermassin
Indian Ocean
Makassar
INDONESIA
Borobudur
Prambanam
Bali
Jogjakarta
Mataram
Java
SOUTHEAST ASIA
0 200 400 600 Mls
0 200 400 600 800 1000 Kms
Hindu sites
Buddhist sites
Buddhist and Hindu sites
Base map © copyright HAMMOND INCORPORATED, Maplewood, N.J.
Historical cartography © copyright 1981 ABINGDON PRESS

appears to have pervaded all of South Asian culture from ancient times.

2. **Types of Yoga.** Although the rich and multivalent traditions of Yoga cannot be easily categorized, the Indian tradition itself has attempted this task, and it is instructive to note two important indigenous typologies. One comes from the Bhagavad Gītā, which describes three distinct types of Yoga (see §§ a, b, c below), and the other from the Yogatattva Upaniṣad, which describes four distinct types (see §§ d, e, f, g below). Both are widely accepted in Indian intellectual history and are cited even today as the standard "types" of Yoga in South Asia.

a) Discipline of knowledge (Jñāna Yoga). The essential features of this discipline are outlined in Bhagavad Gītā II.11-39. The method is one of reflective meditation by means of which the yogin seeks to discriminate the difference between the unchanging self or consciousness (PURUṢA), on the one hand, and the changing patterns and transformations of ordinary awareness in one's embodied condition, on the other. The Gītā (II.39) refers to this type of discipline as *sāṃkhya*. but the reference is not to the technical school of philosophy (DARŚANA) of that name but, rather, to the method of attaining "release" by means of reflective introspection.

b) Discipline of action (KARMA Yoga). As contrasted with reflective introspection, this second type of Yoga (described in Ch. III of the Gītā) focuses on the manner in which a yogin should comport himself vis-à-vis action (karma) in the embodied condition. One cannot avoid some kinds of action, but one can avoid becoming attached to the fruits of one's action *(karma-phala)*. Discipline of action, therefore, is performing those actions that must be done but not allowing oneself to become attached to the fruits of the action.

c) Discipline of devotion (BHAKTI Yoga). Finally, the Gītā (primarily in Ch. XII) describes a third type of discipline. This is by far the easiest method (XII.6-8) and requires continuing faith in Lord KRISHNA (XIII.20) along with devoting all of one's actions to the Lord. The one so acting performs the discipline of devotion (bhakti-Yoga), transcends the embodied condition (with the help of the compassionate power of the Lord), and attains "release" (Gītā XIV.26).

d) Discipline of audition (MANTRA Yoga). The repetition of allegedly sacred sounds or utterances (mantras), derived from the letters of the Sanskrit alphabet and practiced for a period of twelve years under the guidance of a GURU, will culminate in the attainment of discriminative knowledge together with paranormal capacities (SIDDHIS). Yogatattva Upaniṣad (vss. 21-22) prescribes such a discipline of audition (mantra Yoga) for persons of only average or below average intelligence.

e) Discipline of dissolution (Laya Yoga). The practice of dissolution *(laya)* means becoming totally absorbed in the various manifestations of primal materiality (*see* PRAKṚTI; SĀṂKHYA) and the transformations of ordinary awareness *(citta-vṛtti)*, and is described in Yogatattva Upaniṣad, vs. 23. Whether walking, standing, sleeping, or eating, the yogin should meditate on the Lord (ĪŚVARA) as a symbol of undifferentiated dissolution *(citta-laya)*.

f) Discipline of exertion (HAṬHA YOGA) The Yogatattva Upaniṣad (vss. 24-128) describes this type of Yoga as a rigorous program of bodily discipline, respiratory exercise, and digestive constraint that a yogin should practice in preparation for Rāja Yoga (see below). Some eighty bodily postures (ĀSANA) are referred to, four of which are specifically designated, namely *siddha*, *padma*, *siṃha* and *bhadra*. Complicated breath exercises are also prescribed with an emphasis on measuring the length of inhalation, exhalation, and retention. The diet is also rigorously controlled. These difficult practices purify the veins or channels of the body and make available new sources of energy (ŚAKTI) in the various bodily centers *(cakra)*.

g) Discipline of the classical way (Rāja Yoga). This is the normative discipline (both in theory and practice) as set forth by Patañjali in the Yogasūtra, and will be discussed further below. In the Yogatattva Upaniṣad the discipline of the classical way is referred to in vss. 129 ff.

3. **Discipline of the classical way (Rāja Yoga or Patañjali Yoga).** The Yogasūtra is divided into four sections: (1) "Concentration" (SAMĀDHI), (2) "Practice" *(sādhana)*, (3) "Paranormal Power" *(vibhūti)*, and (4) "Isolation" (KAIVALYA). The ontology and epistemology of Patañjali's Yoga are derived largely from classical Sāṃkhya philosophy. Unlike the Sāṃkhya, however, which is nontheistic, classical Yoga accepts the existence of a lord (ĪŚVARA), although the lord in classical Yoga is neither a creative nor a gracious deity. The lord, rather, is a kind of model or symbol for meditation, and thus has only heuristic rather than philosophical significance within the system. The following exposition is based largely on the Yogasūtra (YS) and the *Yogasūtrabhāṣya* of Vyāsa.

a) "Consciousness" and "awareness." A crucial distinction in classical Yoga (and for that matter in Indian philosophy generally) has to do with the problematic intuition that there is a fundamental difference between "consciousness" *(puruṣa)* on the one hand, and "ordinary awareness" *(citta)*, on the other. Whereas "ordinary awareness" is always an awareness *of* something and thus is reflective, intentional, and directed vis-à-vis that complex network of "entities" (both objective and subjective) of our commonsense, everyday world, "consciousness" is, by contrast, a precognitive, prereflective "presence" or "medium" in which or through which "ordinary awareness" shows itself. "Consciousness" in this Indian sense is a transparent witness or, perhaps better, a kind of reflecting mirror that shows the intentionality of "ordinary awareness" but is not itself intentional. The basic problem of the human condition, however, is that this fundamental distinction between consciousness and ordinary awareness is apparent only to those who have engaged in intensive meditative introspection. For most persons the distinction between consciousness and ordinary awareness is blurred, and suffering results. People mistakenly identify themselves with ordinary, intentional awareness and thereby become victims (in their own apprehensions of themselves) of the vicissitudes of conventional, everyday existence. The possibility of a realization of radical freedom (from transient self and the world of rebirth) is always available if one could intuit the "presence" of the transparent, prereflective, pure consciousness. The purpose of classical Yoga, therefore, is first of all to provide an analysis of human experience which makes clear the difference between consciousness *(puruṣa)* and ordinary awareness *(citta)*, and, secondly, to provide a practical method for the isolation *(kaivalya)* of the essential self *(puruṣa)*.

The goal of Yoga, then, is to disentangle *puruṣa* from *citta*, so that *puruṣa* (or pure consciousness) can show itself as a foundation of freedom that is apart from ordinary experience. This can only be accomplished by quieting down and, ultimately, eliminating the "transformations of ordinary awareness." Hence, in YS I.2 Yoga is defined as the "cessation of the transformations of ordinary awareness."

b) The "transformations of awareness" and the "afflictions." "Transformations" *(vṛtti)* of "awareness" *(citta)* include (i) correct but conventional, everyday knowing; (ii) doubt, uncertainty, and mistaken knowing; (iii) varieties of verbalization or, in other words, linguistic symbolizations; (iv) memories; and (v) even the awareness characteristic of dreaming and sleep (YS I.5-11). Furthermore, in bringing about the "cessation of the transformations of ordinary awareness" the yogin must counteract those typical mind-sets that "afflict" ordinary experience, including (i) the chronic tendency to blur the difference between consciousness and ordinary awareness; (ii) the inclination to identify oneself only with one's ego or intentional individuality; (iii) the inclination to become attached to pleasant experiences; (iv) the inclination to avoid painful experiences; and (v) the instinctive inclination to fear death (YS II.2-9).

c) The means for overcoming afflictions and the "eight-limbed Yoga." Under the guidance of a guru the yogin utilizes various techniques for bringing about the cessation of the transformations of ordinary awareness. These include (i) disciplined and repeated practice on both a theoretical and practical level; (ii) renunciation of worldly attachments of all kinds; (iii) meditation and devotion to selected deities that serve as useful foci for concentration; and (iv) such corollary techniques as continuing faith *(śraddhā)*, increasing bodily strength and control, improving one's memory and general awareness, practicing concentration and trance (SAMĀDHI), and cultivating one's intuitive skills (PRAJÑĀ) [YS I.20]. The yogin also practices moderate ascetic exercises (TAPAS) and studies and recites appropriate sacred texts (YS II.1). These practices are all systematized by what the Yogasūtra (II. 28ff.) calls the "eight-limbed discipline" *(aṣṭāṅgayoga)*, which includes: (i) interpersonal restraint, including noninjury, nonfalsehood, etc. *(yama)*; (ii) internal restraint, including personal cleanliness, moral purity, etc. *(niyama)*; (iii) appropriate bodily postures that are comfortable and conducive to long-term meditation (ĀSANA); (iv) cultivation of an awareness of the respiratory processes and voluntary control over them (PRĀṆĀYĀMA); (v) detachment of one's sense capacities (seeing, etc.) from their objects *(pratyāhāra)*; (vi) attaining one-pointed concentration on an object of meditation *(dhāraṇā* and *ekāgratā)*; (vii) attaining an even flow of awareness vis-à-vis the object of concentration (DHYĀNA); and (viii) attaining a trancelike or "enstatic" awareness in meditation wherein the experience of "subject" and "object" disappears and one realizes the inherent nature of awareness itself *(samādhi)* [YS II.28-III.4].

The first five of these "limbs" are referred to as "external" or preparatory (YS III.8), and the last three are referred to as "internal" or crucial (YS III.7). The last three are also characterized as *saṃyama*, or "complete restraining," for they bring the yogin to the threshold of his goal, namely to the discrimination of the difference between consciousness and ordinary awareness.

d) Concentration (samādhi) and final cessation. The eighth "limb," *samādhi*, carries with it various important discriminations or "coalescences," namely (i) the complete apprehension of the nature of gross, physical existence; (ii) the complete apprehension of the nature of subtle, mental existence; (iii) the complete apprehension of the nature of the functioning of the sense capacities; and (iv) the complete apprehension of the nature of ordinary awareness or *citta* itself (YS I.17).

These four enable the yogin to discriminate everything in "ordinary awareness" including ordinary awareness itself *(citta)*. All such discriminations, of course, still presuppose some sort of "support" (namely, awareness itself), and thus the four are characterized as *samādhi* "with support" (YS I.17).

The final attainment, however, is to move beyond all support or, in other words to get beyond awareness to pure "consciousness" *(puruṣa)*, the foundation of freedom. Such, however, is to move beyond all discriminations, even though discrimination has been the vehicle by means of which the yogin has moved to this level. When the yogin takes this final "step," he passes into *samādhi* "without support," which is "cessation" *(nirodha)* together with "isolation" and "freedom" *(kaivalya)* from all ordinary awareness (YS I.2). As the yogin passes into the higher levels of discrimination, he naturally attains various paranormal experiences. Patañjali describes these attainments *(siddhi)* in Book III of the Yogasūtra but cautions that they may become serious obstacles to the realization of the authentic goal of Yoga, namely the liberating discrimination of the difference between "consciousness" *(puruṣa)* and "ordinary awareness" *(citta)*.

Bibliography. K. C. Bhattacharya, *Studies in Philosophy* (1956), I, 221-326; M. Eliade, *Yoga: Immortality and Freedom* (1970); H. Aranya, *Yoga Philosophy of Patañjali* (1963); G. J. Larson, *Classical Sāṃkhya: An Interpretation of its History and Meaning* (2nd ed., 1979); P. A. M. Sastri, ed., *The Yoga Upaniṣads* (1968); J. H. Woods, trans., *The Yoga-System of Patañjali* (1927). G. J. LARSON

YOGĀCĀRA yō´ gə chär´ ə (B—Skt.; lit. "practice of YOGA or mental discipline"). A major school of MAHĀYĀNA Buddhism according to which consciousness alone is real. This doctrine of subjective idealism was expounded upon by Asaṅga and VASUBANDHU in the fourth century A.D. Dreams, in which internal states appear as external objects, furnish the Yogācārins with an analogy in support of their thesis. *See* ĀLAYAVIJÑĀNA. E. J. COLEMAN

YOGANANDA, PARAMAHANSA yō gü nän´ dä pär´ ŭ mä hän´ sŭ. *See* HINDUISM IN AMERICA §3a.

YOGI yō´ gē, **YOGIN** yō´ gĭn (H—Skt.; lit. "one who is joined" [*yuj*—"to join"]). A follower of one of the many schools of YOGA; or, less strictly, any Hindu ascetic. J. BARE

YOM KIPPUR yōm kĭ po͞or´ (Ju—Heb.; lit. "Day of Atonement"). A day of solemn penitence observed on the tenth of Tishri (September-October). It is the last of the Ten Days of Repentance that begin with ROSH HA-SHANAH and open the Jewish Calendar year. Following the biblical injunction "You shall afflict yourselves" (Lev. 16:29; 23:27-29; Num. 29:7), it is forbidden to eat, drink, wash, wear leather, or have sexual relations. In addition, prohibitions on labor similar to those on the SABBATH are in force.

The liturgy of the day is extensive, and it is common for worshipers to spend the entire day at the SYNAGOGUE. Yom Kippur is ushered in by the KOL NIDRE prayer, voiding all vows made in haste or thoughtlessness. The YIZKOR, commemorating the death of loved ones, is read, as are SELIHOT, liturgical poems whose theme is forgiveness. *Viduy,* an admission of guilt for a variety of sins, is incorporated throughout the liturgy.

On Yom Kippur an elaborate priestly service at the Temple was alluded to in the BIBLE (Lev. 16:2-34) and expanded in the TALMUD. On this day the high priest was permitted to enter the Holy of Holies and utter the divine ineffable name, the Tetragrammaton. Various animal sacrifices were offered and a purgation rite performed, in which two goats were used. One was offered on the altar to purify the Temple from the sins of Israel, while the second was sent to the wilderness after these same sins had been transferred to it. This vicarious atonement, however, would be efficacious only were it accompanied by the personal remorse of the congregation.

The closing prayer, *Ne'ila* or *Ne'ilat Shearim* (lit. "the closing of the gates"), is so named as it represents the final few moments before the gates of divine mercy, opened wide in anticipation of Israel's repentance, will be shut. Rosh ha-Shanah is considered the day on which one's fate is determined for the coming year, but on Yom Kippur it is said to be sealed, and *Ne'ila* ends that process. Though God is always merciful and prepared to accept the penitent even at the point of death, these moments are especially conducive to divine grace. Rabbinic sources indicate that for those unable to repent on Yom Kippur this period may be extended to *Hoshana Rabbah,* the last day of the SUKKOT festival, which immediately follows.

The eve of Yom Kippur is considered a semi-festival on which rituals are performed in preparation for the holy day. Some visit ritual baths, purifying themselves through ablutions. It is traditional to ask forgiveness of those to whom injustice may have been done and to absolve oneself of foolhardy commitments before an *ad hoc* tribunal of three. A major meal is eaten just prior to the commencement of the fast at sundown. *See* CALENDAR, JEWISH.

Bibliography. P. Goodman, *The Yom Kippur Anthology* (1971); S. Zevin, *Ha-Moadim be-Halakhah* 2nd ed. (1947); P. Birnbaum, *The High Holyday Prayer Book* (1951).

D. J. SCHNALL

YONI yō´ nē (H—Skt.; lit. "womb," more particularly the womb of the Goddess). The *yoni* of the Goddess is worshiped, often unconsciously, by many Hindus who worship the LIṄGA. But in ancient times the Goddess was revered in her own rite, and the *yoni* was a sacred symbol depicted both in abstract form (ring-stones) and as a part of the Goddess who crouched with thighs spread and *yoni* exposed in the act of childbirth (the Uttānapada figure). TANTRIC icons and texts emphasized the erotic rather than the fertile qualities of the Goddess and told a myth to explain the origin of the shrines of the *yonis* (*Śākta-pīṭhas*): when SATĪ died, SHIVA carried her corpse and danced, disturbing the world, until VISHNU cut the corpse apart limb by limb; at the place where each limb fell, a shrine arose, and Shiva became present there in the form of the *liṅga.* The *yoni* fell in Assam (Kāmarūpa), a center of tantric worship.

Bibliography. D. C. Sircar, "The Śākta Pīṭhas," *Journal of the Royal Asiatic Society, Letters,* 14:1 (1948), 1-108.

W. D. O'FLAHERTY

YUDHIṢṬHIRA yo͞od hĭst´ hĭ rü (H—Skt.). In the MAHĀBHĀRATA, Yudhiṣṭhira is the oldest PĀṆḌAVA brother, born when Pāṇḍu asks Kuntī to invoke the god Dharma to sire a virtuous son. Though inclined toward renunciation, it is his DHARMA ("duty") to rule. Helped by KRISHNA and his brothers, he is consecrated emperor; but he loses everything at the dice match to Duryodhana, the final terms being the Pāṇḍavas' exile. He is seen as an addicted, uncompassionate gambler who would even bet his wife, yet also as one who knowingly conforms to fate and is his brothers' and wife's Guru. In the battle he and Krishna play decisive roles in causing the deaths of the Kaurava army's marshals (Bhīṣma, Droṇa, Karṇa, and Śalya). Then he laments the sins that have produced the Pāṇḍava victory and rules reluctantly. At the end, only he ascends to heaven in his own body, refusing out of compassion to abandon his dog which turns out to be the god Dharma in disguise.

Through Yudhiṣṭhira numerous issues concerning dharma are articulated. It seems that it is his dharma to inaugurate the Kali Yuga. Possibly the god Dharma whom Yudhiṣṭhira incarnates is the Vedic god Mitra, but it seems more likely he impersonates the Dharma-rāja Yama, god of the dead. Like Yama he metes out death dispassionately, even inclining toward renunciation, and leads others (his brothers and wife) into the nether world. Dharma's disguise as a dog also points to Yama's dogs at the entrance to the nether world. A. Hiltebeitel

YOUNG, BRIGHAM (Ch). *See* Latter-day Saints.

YUGA yōō´ gä (H—Skt.; lit. "yoke" [*yuj*—"to yoke, to join"]). An age, or period of time, part of an elaborate mythological system of four great ages *(yugas)* found principally in Sanskrit Purāṇas, Epics, and writings of astronomers *ca.* 200 B.C.–A.D. 500. *Yuga* implies a period of time determined either by human generations or, more commonly, by the conjunction of astral bodies (sun, moon, and/or planets). The term is found most often in a series of four *yugas* named Kṛta or Tiṣya, Tretā, Dvāpara, and Kali. Together the aggregate is called a *caturyuga* ("four ages") or a *mahāyuga* ("great age").

1. Vedic tradition (*ca.* 1000-600 B.C.). The names of the four *yugas,* with some variations, occur in certain Vedic Saṃhitās, Brāhmaṇas and Upaniṣads, in two contexts: (a) *Dice*—Kṛta means "well-done" or "best," and the names Tretā, Dvāpara and Kali can be related to the numbers 3, 2, and 1, respectively; the series of four played some role in a game of dice whose nature is unknown (*see* RV I.41; X.34; X.43; AV VII.52, 114; ŚB V.4.4; XIII.3.2; etc.). (b) *Moon*—The four names are associated with phases of the moon (ŚB IV.5.6, etc.). Used alone, *yuga* refers either to some indefinite length of time or to a period of five years, the basis of the lunisolar calendar used in connection with the Vedic sacrifice (e.g., Jyotiṣavedāṅga I.6).

2. Purāṇas and Epics (*ca.* 200 B.C. – A.D. 500). It is in the Purāṇas and the Mahābhārata that the four *yugas* take significant shape as part of a complex and composite mythological system of time (e.g., Bh.P III.11; XII.2, 3 and Mbh. III.148; XII.70, 224). First, the four *yugas* form part of a calendar that organizes time from the *nimeṣa,* "eye-blink," to the lifespan of the god Brahmā, an almost incalculable period; its central metaphor is the symmetrical division of periods of time into equal halves that are light and dark, evidently modeled on a day-and-night oppositional sequence. Second, the *yugas* are connected variously with the deities Brahmā and Vishnu. And third, they are related to a progressive and gradual decline in Dharma, "law," or "virtue." It is probable that this complex calendrical, theological, and ethical system was built up gradually during several centuries of accretion from simpler origins, but virtually no trace of those origins is to be found in extant literature. Three phases of expansion can be discerned in the calendar as it appears in Vishnu Purāṇa I.3, as follows:

a) One human year

15 *nimeṣas* =	1 *kaṣṭha*	12 *kṣaṇas* =	1 *muhūrta*
30 *kaṣṭhas* =	1 *kāla*	30 *muhūrtas* =	1 *ahorātra*
30 *kālas* =	1 *kṣaṇa*	360 *ahorātras* =	1 human year

b) One year of the Devas (lesser gods)

1 human year	= 1 day of the *devas*
360 days of the *devas*	= 1 year of the *devas*
1 *mahāyuga* or *caturyuga*	= an aggregate of four *yugas* plus a morning and evening twilight for each *yuga*

Kṛta Yuga	= 4000	
morning twilight	= 400	
evening twilight	= 400	
	4800 *deva* years	= 1,728,000 human years
Tretā Yuga	= 3000	
morning twilight	= 300	
evening twilight	= 300	
	3600 *deva* years	= 1,296,000 human years
Dvāpara Yuga	= 2000	
morning twilight	= 200	
evening twilight	= 200	
	2400 *deva* years	= 864,000 human years
Kali Yuga	= 1000	
morning twilight	= 100	
evening twilight	= 100	
	1200 *deva* years	= 432,000 human years.
Mahāyuga	= 12,000 *deva* years	= 4,320,000 human years

c) Lifetime of Brahmā

1 day of Brahmā = 1000 *mahāyugas* = 4,320,000,000 human years

1 year of Brahmā = 360 Brahmā days = 1,555,200,000,000 human years

1 lifetime of Brahmā = 100 Brahmā years = 155,520,000,000,000 human years

Note that one day of Brahmā is also called a *kalpa* and is equivalent to fourteen *manvantaras;* these are apparently two other measures of time superimposed on the *yuga* system.

3. **Astronomy.** Whereas the Jyotiṣavedāṅga mentions only a lunisolar *yuga* of five years, the later astronomers Āryabhaṭa (A.D. 499), Varāha Mihira (A.D. 505), and Brahmagupta (A.D. 628) all describe a 4,320,000 *mahāyuga* comformable to the Purāṇic sources and three principal others: a sixty-year cycle that includes the circuits of sun, moon, and the planet Jupiter, or Bṛhaspati; the *Saptarṣi* cycle of 2700 or 2800 years that relates the annual equinoctial appearance of the moon to the twenty-seven or twenty-eight ecliptic constellations; and, in Āryabhaṭa, a *caturyuga* of 4000 years in which each *yuga* lasts 1000 years. The astronomers used the concept of *yuga* to signify a Great Year whose beginning and end were identified by a particular conjunction of planets, sun, and moon; their purpose was to establish a vast calendar of cosmic time.

4. **Functions.** The myth of the four *yugas* in the Purāṇas and Epics serves several simultaneous functions. (a) *Calendar.* First, as a calendar it stands in the middle of a complex system of time reckoning that unites both linear and cyclical time frames. It begins with a fairly literal linear model of the human year, from an eye-blink to 360 nights and days, and ends with the unthinkable lifespan of the god Brahmā, after which period the universe dissolves into potentiality only to re-emerge again for a similar period of time, recycling in this way forever. The purpose of this cosmic calendar is to delineate a virtually incalculable period of time within which the created world devolves each time it emerges into existence, and also to locate the present era more or less in the middle of this calendar. Several Purāṇas and the Mahābhārata identify the present historical period as the last Kali Yuga in the first day of the second half of Brahmā's life, which, by astronomical calculation is said to have begun at the end of the Mahābhārata war in 3102 B.C. (b) *Theology.* Two deities in the Hindu pantheon are particularly related to the *yugas:* Brahmā, agent of creation, whose lifespan is equated with the length of created time, and Vishnu, agent of the preservation of the world, who is said to descend in AVATARS, periodically taking animal or human form in order to restore the balance of good and evil on earth. In the Purāṇas and Epics these descents are numerous and unsystematized for the most part, being identified with the four *yugas* in a variety of ways; in medieval VAIṢṆAVA theology, ten classic descents are identified and distributed among the four *yugas* in a roughly evolutionary scheme which is still a popular Hindu belief. (c) *Dharma.* As the number of years in each of the four *yugas* decreases each time the series recurs, so do the status of DHARMA ("law," or "virtue") and the lengths of people's lives. And each *yuga* recognizes a correspondingly different virtue among human beings appropriate to this decline: in Kṛta, self-discipline; in Tretā, wisdom; in Dvāpara, sacrifice; in Kali, generosity. Or, dharma is likened to a cow who stands on four feet in Kṛta, but on three, two and one successively in each succeeding *yuga,* as virtue wanes. The last, or Kali Yuga, identified with the present era, is the most wicked of all, noted for the neglect of dharma, mixing of CASTES, greed, and political disorder. The Mānava Dharmaśāstra (*see* MANU, LAWS OF) uses this theme to introduce the necessity of its laws to regulate human society; it is because in the Kali Yuga humankind is too morally weak to attend to virtue without benefit of civil law.

5. **Other traditions.** Similar systematic myths of time that include four ages, or multiples of four, can be found in Buddhist, Jaina, Greek, and Iranian sources, but whether or not they all share a common origin is still undetermined.

Bibliography. J. F. Fleet, "The Kaliyuga of B.C. 3102," *JRAS* (1911); W. Kirfel, *Das Purāṇa Pañcalakṣaṇa* (1927); F. E. Pargiter, *Ancient Indian Historical Tradition* (1922); H. H. Wilson, trans., *Vishnu Purāṇa* (1840); H. Zimmer, "The Hindu View of World History According to the Purāṇas," *The Review of Religion,* VI.3 (1942). C. DIMMITT

YŪPA yōō´ pū (H—Skt.; lit. "post" [probably from *yup*—"to obstruct"]). The sacrificial post in rituals in VEDIC HINDUISM, selected from one of a dozen special trees (e.g. Khadira for SOMA rites) and ritually "planted" on the border of the sacrificial field. In animal sacrifices, victims must be tied to *yūpas,* usually numbering eleven, but twenty-one for the horse sacrifice. The *yūpa* also represents fertility powers, serves as a link with celestial regions, and is often identified with the thunderbolt *(vajra).*

D. M. KNIPE

YWCA (YOUNG WOMEN'S CHRISTIAN ASSOCIATION). A society for women founded in England in 1855. The association had parallel interests with those of the YMCA and has developed in a similar fashion. Today it has a broad-based program concerned with all areas of the development of young women. G. MILLER

Z

ZADDIK tsäd dēk´ (Ju—Heb.; lit. "righteous"). A righteous, saintly, faithful, or God-loving person; in medieval Jewish ethics, the morally perfected human being; in Eastern European Hasidism, a charismatic master or leader. His disciples usually attributed supernatural powers to the zaddik and granted him almost absolute authority over their lives.

K. P. Bland

ZAKĀT zə kät´ (I—Arab.; lit. "purity, integrity"). One of the Pillars of Islam; the obligatory alms which the faithful give at the close of each year, according to their means. More than a "poor-tax," it is a fundamental of the faith and an act of worship. The recipients are (Qur'ān, Sura 9:60) the poor, the actual collectors of alms, those to be reconciled (originally the recalcitrant pagans of Mecca), slaves to be freed, debtors, those defending Islam, and travelers. In addition to benefiting others, *zakāt* purifies that which remains to the giver and serves further to increase God's bounty, because it is compared to a loan to God which he will repay double (Sura 57:18). *Zakāt* is not to be equated with charity *(ṣadaqah),* which although not obligatory is strongly recommended at all times and highly meritorious.

Zakāt is compulsory on monetary wealth, trade goods, livestock, farm produce, and certain other kinds of property, provided a certain minimum quantity is owned. Specific amounts are sometimes a complex matter, but to give an idea, both money and merchandise which have been owned for a full year are taxed at the rate of 2½ percent. Produce of tilled land is computed at either 5 or 10 percent, depending on irrigation costs. Livestock is taxed in separate categories according to number of head. *Zakāt al-Fiṭr,* the cost of one day's food, is given at the end of Ramadan, the month of fasting.

Bibliography. M. A. Rauf, *Islam: Creed and Worship* (1974); for sayings of the Prophet Muhammad on the subject see M. M. Ali, *A Manual of Hadith* (1944), pp. 208-21.

F. M. Denny

ZAMZAM zäm zäm´ (I). The sacred well located beside the Ka'ba in Mecca. It is pre-Islamic in origin and probably the reason for the establishment of human habitation in the valley of Mecca.

Zamzam was incorporated into Islam through a myth of its origin and the example of its veneration by Muhammad. It is said to have appeared miraculously to provide water for Hagar and her son Ishmael, whom Abraham abandoned in this place at the command of Allah.

Muslim pilgrims drink of its sacred water, especially after circumambulation of the Ka'ba, and carry it away in bottles. It is popularly regarded as health-giving.

H. B. Partin

ZARATHUSTRA zär â thōōs´ trâ. *See* Zoroastrians.

ZAYDIYYA zä ē dē´ yä (I). A Shi'ite group who supported the revolt of Zayd ibn Ali, al-Ḥusayn's grandson, in Kūfa in A.D. 739. Zayd was the next Alid to be killed after the martyrs of Karbala, and as such is revered by the Zaydiyya. (*See* Shahīd; Mashhad.) The Zaydiyya are distinguished from all the other Shi'ite groups in that they did not recognize the necessity of an Imam, nor did they accept the principles of *naṣṣ al-jalī* (clear designation) and *'iṣma* (infallibility) as prerequisites in a person assuming the imamate (*see* Imāmiyya). *Naṣṣ* implied recognition of a hereditary line of imams from the descendants of Fāṭima, but the Zaydites accorded the office of imam to any Fatimid who openly fought against an oppressive ruler. From the beginning the Zaydiyya seem to have been divided into two main factions: the compromisers (Batriyya) and the revolutionaries (Jārūdiyya). Both subdivisions maintained the superiority of Ali over all Companions of the Prophet (*see* Ṣaḥāba). But the former, in contrast to all other Shi'ite groups, held the doctrine of the "imamate of the inferior," according to which, although Ali was best fitted to be the imam, it was right to acknowledge the imamate of Abū Bakr and 'Umar, since Ali had let them hold the position. They were thus trying to work out a compromise between the Shi'a and the Sunni by acknowledging the Caliphates of Abū Bakr and

'Umar, while admitting their inferiority to Ali.

The revolutionary Zaydites asserted that MUHAMMAD had designated Ali as imam, not by name, but by describing his person, and that those who did not recognize his imamate became unbelievers. Following Ali, his two sons, al-ḤASAN and al-Ḥusayn, were imams. Thereafter any new imam had to be appointed by a small council from among the descendants of either al-Ḥasan or al-Ḥusayn. The new imam should issue his call to allegiance by rising in rebellion. Unlike the Batriyya, the Jārūdiyya held the radical views of the early Shi'a and rejected any attempt to compromise on the question of acknowledging the first three caliphs. From the ninth century onward the Jārūdiyya view of the imamate came to prevail among the Zaydiyya, particularly after the establishment of the Zaydī state in Yemen.

Zaydiyya doctrines were formulated by the theologian al-Qāsim al-Rassī, who based his teaching on MU'TAZILITE principles, though with some fundamental differences. His demand that the imam be qualified in Islamic law and doctrine, with sufficient political initiative to carry out armed rebellion against usurpers, excluded many Alid pretenders and rulers, who were sometimes, in the absence of truly qualified imams, termed "restricted imams." The list of Zaydī imams varies, because there was always uncertainty regarding the recognition of a "restricted" or "full" imam, though there was consensus on many. The last Zaydī imam to rule Yemen was Muhammad al-Badr, whose policies ushered Yemen into the twentieth century. The constitution of the Yemen Arab Republic abolished the Zaydī imamate in 1971, declaring Yemen an Islamic state in accord with the "principles of Muslim social justice."

Bibliography. R. Strothmann, *Das Staatsrecht der Zaiditen* (1912); W. Madelung, "Imāma," *EI,* and *Der Imam al-Qāsim ibn Ibrāhim und die Glaubenslehre der Zaiditen* (1965); 'Alī b. Ismā'īl al-Ash'arī, *Maqalat al-islāmiyyīn* (1969); al-Ḥasan b. Mūsā al-Nawbakhtī, *Firaq al-shi'a* (1931).

A. A. SACHEDINA

ZAZEN zä´ zĕn (B—Jap.; lit. "sitting cross-legged in meditation"). The basic discipline of ZEN in which the body is immobilized in the traditional LOTUS POSTURE, breathing is regulated, and the mind is unified in a profound concentration. By extension, zazen may designate any activity performed in total awareness, or the Zen experience itself.

C. W. EDWARDS

ZEALOTS zĕl´ əts (Ju). Usually identified with the Jewish freedom fighters who led the first war against ROME in A.D. 67-68. While they shared many common beliefs with the PHARISEES, and no doubt emerged from their ranks, they are best characterized as a grouping within society before the outbreak of open warfare with Rome. In addition to being ultranationalistic, the Zealots saw the Temple as the symbol of victory over the Romans and therefore did all they could to purify it of Gentiles and those who cooperated with Rome. The Zealots more or less disappeared with the fall of Jerusalem (A.D. 70) and Masada (A.D. 73), only to reappear in the messianic followers of BAR KOCHBA in A.D. 132-35.

Bibliography. D. M. Rhoads, *Israel in Revolution* (1976), pp. 97-110; M. Simon, *Jewish Sects at the Time of Jesus* (1967), pp. 43-46; M. Stern, "Sicarii and Zealots," in *The World History of the Jewish People, VIII* (1977), 263-301.

E. M. MEYERS

ZEN zĕn (B—Jap.; lit. "meditation"). Japanese pronunication of the Chinese *Ch'an,* an abbreviation of *Chan-na,* Chinese rendering of the Sanskrit DHYĀNA ("meditation"); a discipline whose aim is enlightenment; the art of transmitting Buddha-mind; a unique tradition within MAHĀYĀNA BUDDHISM resulting from the meeting of India's *dhyāna* tradition and doctrines of ŚŪNYATĀ (emptiness) and bodhi (enlightenment) with China's practicality and Taoist tradition, systematized and brought to high artistic expression in the culture of Japan. (*See* TAOISM, PHILOSOPHICAL; TAOISM, RELIGIOUS.)

1. The nature of Zen. Zen has only one essential: the direct experience of enlightenment (SATORI). Encouraging, deepening, and expressing that experience in all of life is its sole purpose. Contrary to some popular views, Zen is not against philosophical understanding, study of SŪTRAS, or development of liturgy, but is quick to reject these concerns once they threaten to become objects of desire and hence obstacles to the one essential. Enlightenment is the unfolding of the inner mind experienced without attachment as universal Buddha-mind.

Zen may be viewed as both an art and an established school of Mahāyāna Buddhism. Focused upon direct experience and cognizant of the variety of human types and capacities, Zen developed as the art of fashioning teaching to individual needs to bring students to direct enlightenment. Masters devised ingenious teaching techniques in their avoidance of "speaking too plainly" so that disciples would not cling to concepts and miss the essential discovery realized only in direct experience.

As a Mahāyāna school, Zen has shared traditions, sūtras, rules, and rituals with other Mahāyānists. It has participated in Mahāyāna's vitalist religious thrust, salvationist focus, and democratizing tendencies, but has sought to protect against an aristocratic scholasticism and retreat from everyday life to which some Mahāyānist groups were prey. Under Chinese influence, Zen identified *dhyāna* (meditation) with PRAJÑĀ (intuitive wisdom), and located both in the ordinary tasks of the present moment. In this spirit, Layman P'ang affirmed: "My supernatural power and marvelous deeds—drawing water and carrying firewood."

Courtesy the Cleveland Museum of Art

Priest sewing under morning sun; Japanese hanging scroll (14th century)

2. Formative influences. Religious developments in India from the time of the Upaniṣads emphasized *dhyāna* and the master-disciple relationship. Buddhist *dhyāna* teachers followed the trade routes to China, where they were afforded friendly reception among Chinese already attracted to the meditative practices of Taoism. *Dhyāna* (Zen) Buddhism became heir to this line of development.

MĀDHYAMIKA and YOGĀCĀRA schools became especially popular for a time in China, and one might view Zen as a Chinese synthesis and adaptation of these two schools. Its bringing together of the Mādhyamika's way of negation and intuitive enlightenment with the Yogācāra's meditational discipline in the presence of native Taoist traditions may explain Zen's growth in popularity and the demise of the Mādhyamika and Yogācāra schools in China. Zen's anti-scholasticism and reinterpretation of meditation as everyday activity may also have drawn upon a Chinese rediscovery of elements present in the original teachings of the Buddha.

In spite of its anti-scholasticism, Zen was influenced by a number of sūtras: tradition affirmed that BODHIDHARMA delivered the Lankāvatāra-sūtra to his disciples; the PRAJÑĀPĀRAMITĀS were often in evidence; and the "silence of VIMALAKĪRTI" in the sūtra bearing his name has been called "pure Zen."

The Indian teacher KUMĀRAJĪVA and meditation master Buddhabhadra were at work in China by the beginning of the fifth century A.D., and, together with their disciples and collaborators, did much to prepare the way for Zen. Among Kumārajīva's disciples, SENG-CHAO, who brought together Mādhyamika and Taoist texts, and TAO-SHENG, who advocated a doctrine of sudden enlightenment, are preeminent. Tao-sheng has, in fact, been credited by some as the "actual founder of Zen."

3. Origin and early history. Such traditional Zen sources as *Record of the Transmission of the Lamp* (A.D. 1004) wove legend and history together so tightly that it is often impossible to separate them. From the eighth century in China the southern sect of Zen appears to have collected miraculous tales and patriarchal biographies to legitimate its lineage, and that effort likely provided much of the existing material on the beginnings of Zen.

Traditional accounts locate the origin of Zen in an esoteric teaching of the Buddha. Standing on Vulture Peak, Buddha held a lotus before his disciples, smiled, and remained silent. One disciple, Mahākāsyapa, received the wordless sermon and smiled in recognition. The Buddha announced, "I have this treasure of unmistakable teachings, wonderful mind of NIRVANA, and have given it to Mahākāsyapa." Zen tradition names twenty-eight Indian patriarchs, each delivering this "lamp of enlightenment" to his carefully chosen successor. The twenty-eighth patriarch, BODHIDHARMA, carried the "lamp" to China, becoming the first patriarch and founder of the Ch'an (Zen) tradition.

We know little of the patriarchs immediately following Bodhidharma. Hui-k'ê was followed by Seng-ts'an, who is credited with writing the famous *Seal of the Believing Mind.* Tao-hsin, the fourth patriarch, established a sizable monastic community. Tradition described the fifth patriarch, Hung-jen, as gathering able disciples at the Yellow Plum Monastery where he lectured on the Diamond Sūtra.

A controversy regarding the legitimate heir to Hung-jen led to a schism and became critical in the development of Zen. The earliest line of transmission apparently named Shen-hsiu, a respected disciple of Hung-jen, as sixth patriarch. But a monk in the southern provinces, Shen-hui, attacked the legitimacy of Shen-hsiu, asserting that his own teacher, HUI-NENG, an illiterate kitchen laborer in Hung-jen's monastery, had secretly been given the patriarchal robe and bowl by Hung-jen and sent south across the Yangtze for fear of the jealousy of the more learned monks.

Much of the legend regarding Hui-neng, including details in the famous T'an Ching (Platform Sūtra) credited to him, was likely the work of Shen-hui, who sought to replace the urban scholasticism of Shen-hsiu and northern Ch'an with a more rustic, experiential southern style. When masters of the T'ang dynasty (618-906) decided in favor of Hui-neng's legitimacy, a revolutionary new Ch'an was born, preaching "sudden enlightenment" and a radical iconoclasm that rejected sūtra study, ritual, and veneration of images. T'ang heirs to these emphases could burn sūtras and Buddha images, and affirm, as did I-hsüan, founder of the Lin-chi sect, "If you meet the Buddha, kill him."

4. Ch'an masters of T'ang China. During the two centuries from Bodhidharma to Hui-neng, there was little evidence of the shouts, slaps, and seemingly bizarre riddles many have come to associate with Zen. It was the great Ch'an masters of China's T'ang dynasty who pioneered these new methods.

One of Hui-neng's disciples, Huai-jang, had as his disciple a famous innovator, Ma-tsu (d. 788), and another of Hui-neng's disciples, Hsing-ssu, had an equally famous disciple, Shih-t'ou (d. 790). The disciples of Ma-tsu and Shih-t'ou were responsible for the founding of the five Ch'an sects, the "Five Houses": Lin-chi, Ts'ao-tung, Wei-yang, Yün-men, and Fa-yen. The Lin-chi founded by I-hsüan and the Ts'aotung founded by Liang-chieh and Pen-chi gradually incorporated the others and flourish to this day as the Rinzai (Lin-chi) and Sōtō (Ts'ao-tung) sects of Japan.

Pai-chang (d. 814) developed a monastic rule suited to Zen communal life and enforced the new precept, "a day without work, a day without eating." Within these work-meditation communities the T'ang masters extended the enlightenment opportunities of formal seated meditation (ZAZEN) and formal interviews (sanzen) to every aspect of daily life. "Sudden enlightenment" meant that the idea of acquiring merits or progressing by stages was rejected. Masters now utilized shouts, slaps, questions, and parabolic acts to trigger enlightenment. The relationship that developed between the teaching and its setting in everyday tasks became an essential ingredient for conveying the truth that enlightenment and ordinary mind are not separate. Anecdotes recalling the vivid life-teachings of the T'ang masters would later become the *kung-an* (KŌAN) used by Sung dynasty masters and their Japanese heirs to teach their own students, and so the kōan would take its place with zazen and sanzen in the basic curriculum of Zen.

5. The Sōtō and Rinzai sects in Japan. According to tradition, Buddhism was introduced to Japan from Korea in A.D. 552. Under the vigorous patronage of Prince SHŌTOKU (d. 621) Buddhist studies and art flourished, and a variety of Buddhist sects were transplanted directly from China. From the seventh century, some secs in Japan included Zen practices, but it was during the KAMAKURA period (1185-1333) that the Zen of Sung dynasty China was established in Japan through the efforts of two Japanese monks, Eisai and DŌGEN.

Visual Education Service, Charles A. Kennedy

Zen pebble and rock garden

Eisai (d. 1215) traveled to China and trained with Lin-chi masters, bringing the Lin-chi (Rinzai) sect to Japan in 1191, though elements of the Tendai and Shingon sects were included in his practice. Under Eisai's influence Zen found friendly reception with the Shoguns and initiated its lasting alliance with the samurai and patriotic concerns.

Dōgen (d. 1253), credited with founding the Sōtō sect, established the first independent Zen temple of Japan in 1236.

Civil wars, followed by strict government control of religion, led to loss of zeal and discipline in the Zen monasteries of Japan. Hakuin Ekaku (d. 1768), a Rinzai priest, is known as "reviver of Zen" for his reorganizing of Zen discipline and training based upon a vigorous course of kōan exercise.

The Rinzai and Sōtō sects are among the most influential forms of Buddhism in Japan today, claiming about 2½ million and 7 million adherents respectively. Rinzai has been called *kanna* Zen, "kōan-introspecting Zen," emphasizing seated meditation as a tool for kōan exercise resulting in a first enlightenment, or *kenshō*. Sōtō has been called *mokushō* Zen, "silent illumination Zen," utilizing the kōan sparingly and identifying zazen itself with enlightenment. A third Zen sect, the Ōbaku, was brought to Japan from China in 1654 by the monk Ingen. Sometimes called "Nembutsu-Zen," it combines Zen and Pure Land practices.

6. **Life in the Zen monastery.** Though Zen is relevant to all circumstances, the monastic life has continued at the heart of Zen discipline and practice. Walled gardens with ancient wooden gateways, a Buddha hall *(butsuden)*, Dharma hall *(hattō)*, meditation hall *(zendō)*, tea-hut, and small service buildings are to be found on the outskirts of many Japanese cities, providing a simple environment for the training of from two to thirty or more monks. The Rinzai sect, for example, maintains about forty such monasteries in Japan today, several of which have subtemples attracting laymen for zazen training and tourists for viewing the gardens and art treasures.

A day in the monastery combines simplicity with discipline, focusing upon seated meditation (zazen), instruction from the *roshi*, or master (sanzen), manual labor *(samu)*, religious mendicancy *(takuhatsu)*, and recitation of the sūtras.

Ordinarily the monks rise at three A.M., wash, recite sūtras, have a private sanzen called *dokusan*, and breakfast together. Zazen, housecleaning, and either a lecture *(teishō)* or hike through town or countryside begging donations for the monastery and its charities bring the monks to the mid-day meal by ten or eleven A.M. Zazen until one P.M. and manual labor in the vegetable gardens or at other chores until four P.M. are followed by the evening meal and sūtra recitation. Zazen begins again at dusk under the watchful eye of a supervisor appointed to strike any dozing monks with a bamboo rod *(keisaku)* to awaken and encourage them. Another visit to the *roshi* is allowed, and the day ends by eight or nine P.M. when the monks lie down under quilts *(futon)* on the *zendō* floor for sleep. Each monk is assigned one *tatami* mat (a 3½ by 7 ft. pallet covered with woven straw). This serves as his place of meditation, his meal table, and his bed.

James Kirk

Zen calligraphy is a highly polished art form.

7. **Zen and the arts.** The one essential of Zen, the direct experience of enlightenment, is believed to show itself in all life. *Zen-ki*, "Zen activity," is the expression of universal Buddha-mind in the tiniest details of nature, the ordinary activities of daily life, and the arts and crafts of the enlightened.

The anecdotes from the lives of T'ang dynasty masters collected in the *Mumonkan* and *Hekiganroku* witness to the Sung dynasty's appreciation that simple gestures, sights, and sounds are all capable of displaying Zen artistry. Enlightenment verses, the spontaneous lines of monochrome ink, paintings, and the free broad strokes of T'ang masters' calligraphy were among the earliest examples of Zen art in China. Painting in the irregular "broken ink" or "splashed ink" styles reached its height from the late T'ang, through the Sung, and into the Yüan dynasties, with such Sung artists as Liang K'ai, Mu-chi, and Yü-chien excelling. While artists of other Buddhist schools painted transcendent Buddhas in golden paradises, the Zen artists painted a flesh and blood Śākyamuni (*see* BUDDHA, LIFE OF GAUTAMA), the determined face of an earthly Bodhidharma, and Buddha-mind as displayed in persimmons, chestnuts, monkeys at play, rocks, and streams.

T'ang and Sung dynasty Zen art found high appreciation in Japan. Inspired by these Chinese exemplars, Japanese Zen ink painting *(sumi)* and calligraphy flourished in Kamakura during the thirteenth and fourteenth centuries and in Kyoto from the fifteenth through the seventeenth centuries, with Mokuan, Kaō, Sesshū, and many other eminent artists emerging. The Zen arts established the aesthetic norms for the court, the samurai, the early merchants, and even the peasants. The Zen style dominated *kyūdo, kendo, aikido,* and other martial arts, the Way of Tea, the HAIKU form in poetry, ikebana, the temple rock garden, and the Nō drama.

Resonating with the native Japanese aesthetic focused on nature's spontaneous irregularity within a seasonal pattern, a Japanese Zen aesthetic emerged. Leaving behind the quest for *miyabi* (courtly refinement) and *okashi* (the charmingly amusing), it discovered the profundity of *aware* (melancholy sensitivity) in a haiku by Bashō, *sabi* (the faded and lonely) in a TEA CEREMONY in a thatched hut, *wabi* (poverty) in the earth-tones of a Korean tea bowl, and *yūgen* (mystery) in the subtle gestures of a Nō performer.

8. Zen and the modern world. Zen shares features which characterize Buddhism's entry into the modern world in general. Buddhism in recent decades has displayed a self-conscious effort at renewal and relevance, often presenting itself as the religion most compatible with the scientific age. Renewal has emphasized lay movements, Pan-Buddhist ecumenical organizations, and an extension to Western nations. The tendency toward synthesis with non-Buddhist religious elements, characteristic of Buddhism in previous centuries, has continued in popular synthesizing religious movements since World War II, especially in Vietnam, Korea, and Japan, and suppression of monastic life and rapid secularization of clergy has marked Buddhism's existence under communist regimes in China, North Korea, and Vietnam.

Of special note in China were the 1950-52 land reforms which led to confiscation of monastery landholdings and the disrobing of monks. The Cultural Revolution of 1966 apparently closed all temples, though the policy was eased in 1972, and the government placed emphasis upon Buddhism as China's cultural heritage. While most Chinese monasteries were of Ch'an heritage, Ch'an, Pure Land, and other forms of Buddhism had deeply interpenetrated, and all felt the effects of change.

In Vietnam the Buddhism practiced in the local pagodas was a synthesis between Thien (Zen) and Tinh-do (Pure Land), while a few large pure Thien monasteries acted as spiritual centers for training local leadership. Movement toward Buddhist unification and an active Buddhist peace movement during the Vietnam conflict found support in Vietnamese Thien, though its present situation is problematic.

In Korea all forms of Buddhism except Zen were forced to unite in the fifteenth century, though Zen meditation continued to play an important role alongside AMIDA worship and esoteric practices in monasteries. Many monasteries were burned during the war with the communists (1950-53), though the south emerged with a strong lay movement, university-centered Buddhist scholarship, and vigorous training programs in Zen meditation at such centers as the Haein-sa monastery. An emergent popular religion, "Wŏn Buddhism," has fostered meditation through service called "Zen without time or place." (*See* KOREAN RELIGION §7.)

Japanese Zen suffered some destruction during World War II, went through a period of depression following the war, and more recently has experienced a noticeable revival. The work of D. T. SUZUKI and new appeal for Japanese youth impressed by the positive reception of Zen in the West have marked recent years.

Zen's impact on the West, especially the United States, is a significant aspect of Zen today. Zen master Soyen Shaku's appearance at the World Parliament of Religions at the Chicago World's Fair of 1893, several decades of work by D. T. Suzuki, and the influence of Zen centers in Hawaii and California have all had an impact. Reputable scholars, Japanese and American *roshis,* and Zen institutes and monasteries are increasingly visible and active.

In Europe scholarship in Buddhist texts has generally overshadowed interest in Zen practice, though Rudolph Otto and Eugen Herrigel in Germany and more recently the work of Christmas Humphreys in England have done much to popularize Zen meditative practice. Zen has found especially friendly reception in the West among psychotherapists, poets, and artists.

Bibliography. G. C. Chang, *The Practice of Zen* (1959); H. Dumoulin, *A History of Zen Buddhism* (1963); P. Kapleau, *The Three Pillars of Zen* (1965); D. T. Suzuki, *Zen and Japanese Culture* (1959); E. Nishimura, *Unsui: A Diary of Zen Monastic Life* (1973).

C. W. EDWARDS

ZION zī´ ən (Ju & Ch). Canaanite fortress on the eastern hill of JERUSALEM, conquered by David *ca.* 996 B.C.; probably expanded and called City of David. Later identified with the Temple area, Jerusalem, the people of Jerusalem, the Jewish nation, the CHURCH, and the Heavenly Jerusalem. Currently a symbol of Jewish desire for a nation in Israel. *See* ZIONISM.

T. O. HALL, JR.

ZIONISM (Ju). The Jewish yearning to return to ERETZ ISRAEL. While ZION is a biblical term related to JERUSALEM (Ps. 126:1), Nathan Birnbaum coined the term "Zionism" in 1885 for political efforts to restore the Jews to Israel. The longing to return appears in much of Jewish literature over the centuries. The twelfth century philosopher JUDAH HA-LEVI lamented that he was in Spain physically but his heart was in "the East." Pilgrims journeyed to Palestine, expressing an ongoing connection with that land in which some Jews had always continued to live.

Modern Zionism grew from the failure of Jewish emancipation and the resurgence of ANTI-SEMITISM in nineteenth century Europe. Confronted with Russian pogroms and the Dreyfus trial, Leon Pinsker and THEODOR HERZL independently concluded that exile was an abnormal condition and the Gentile world had failed to protect Jews. A homeland was required in which Jews might become like all other nations, acquiring their own land and language.

Neither Herzl nor Pinsker insisted that Palestine be that land. Any territory able to absorb numbers of refugees would do. They differed, however, in their assessment of Gentiles. Herzl assumed that the world powers would assist in his mission while Pinsker despaired of Gentile aid, urging Jews to solve their problems via "auto-emancipation." These and other differences were argued at the first Zionist Congress in Basel, Switzerland, 1897, which attracted activists of a variety of shadings, whose goal was the creation of an international charter to secure a Jewish homeland. A bank and colonizing company were later organized to provide a sound financial structure for the movement.

Despite Herzl's efforts to maintain cohesion, Zionism often became a controversial element in Jewish life. Among the ORTHODOX, some RABBIS opposed it as a forbidden attempt to bring about the Messianic era, as did early REFORM Jews who viewed it as a nationalist formulation conflicting with their perceptions of Judaism as purely a religious denomination. Within the Zionist camp, Asher Ginsburg denounced Herzl's program as lacking in cultural identity and insisted that practical efforts to develop Palestine precede efforts to obtain international support.

After Herzl's death in 1904 leadership of the movement fell to such "practicalists," notably Chaim Weizmann. An immigrant chemist living in Britain, he was instrumental in obtaining the BALFOUR DECLARATION, a 1917 statement promising British support for a Jewish homeland in Palestine. In 1923 the League of Nations granted Britain a mandate over Palestine for the purpose of preparing the population for independence. Ironically, similar promises of independence had also been made to the Arab population.

Parallel to these developments, a steady stream of Jewish immigrants went to Palestine. Known as *aliyot* and divided by historical period, these migrations helped to people the agricultural settlements, reclaim the land, and establish the political and social institutions of the period. Beginning in the late nineteenth century the immigrations assumed a socialist tinge.

Unfortunately, the reality of competing nationalist claims to Palestine was never clearly confronted. In 1939 under Arab pressure, Britain promulgated a White Paper annulling the Balfour Declaration and limiting Jewish immigration to Palestine, an act of particular significance considering the rise of Nazism. The HOLOCAUST, however, turned public opinion toward the need for a Jewish state, and in 1947 the United Nations voted to partition Palestine into Jewish and Arab states, an act rejected by the Arab League, which waged war on the fledgling Jewish state. By 1949 the State of Israel concluded armistice agreements with its adversaries and had taken in battle considerably more than had been promised by the UN plan. Israel defended its existence in three more wars during the ensuing twenty-five years.

Contemporary Zionist organizations in the DIASPORA reflect the political shadings of their early leaders and include socialist, religious, and revisionist groupings generally divided among male, female, and youth divisions united under national federations. These, in turn, relate to Israel via the Jewish Agency, a quasi-governmental unit representing Israel to Jewish communities elsewhere. Zionist ideology came under much diplomatic pressure, culminating in the 1975 UN resolution linking it to racism. While the resolution passed, it also drew many who had been at the periphery of Zionist support into an active commitment.

Bibliography. A. Hertzberg, *The Zionist Idea* (1959); W. Laqueur, *History of Zionism* (1972); H. Sachar, *History of Israel* (1976).

D. J. SCHNALL and S. BAYME

ZIYĀRA zē yä´ rä (I—Arab.; lit. "visit"). The ritual of devotion which SHI'ITES offer at the tombs (MASHHAD) of the IMAMS, whom they regard as martyrs (SHAHĪD) and as still living, because a martyr never really dies. Unlike the HAJJ, which is performed at a set time, the *ziyāra* may be performed any time, although some special days are recommended. It is regarded as an act of covenant renewal between an imam and his people.

A. A. SACHEDINA

ZOHAR zō´ här (Ju—Heb.; lit. "splendor"). The classic text in Jewish MYSTICISM, whose influence and authority almost rank with that of the BIBLE and the TALMUD. Historical and literary analysis reveal that its ARAMAIC language and Galilean setting are a fiction, and that the homilies and conversations of its

TANNAITIC speakers are pseudepigraphic. The bulk of the various strata and minor treatises comprising the *Zohar* was written by Moses de Léon (d. 1305) and published in Spain around the year 1285. Other writings by a different author on related themes were added sometime around 1300.

1. **Cosmic unity.** In such phrases as "see how precisely balanced are the upper and lower worlds" or "it is likewise in the upper world," the *Zohar* again and again expresses its fundamental faith in unity. "The whole world, upper and lower, is organized on this principle, from the primary mystic center to the very outermost of all the layers. All are coverings, the one to the other, brain within brain, spirit inside spirit, shell within shell." Whether dealing with the TORAH or man's soul, the *Zohar* delights in uncovering how all things belong to, and symbolically recapitulate, the layered structure of God's being. The upper world or the realm of EN SOF and *sefirot* (*see* SEFER BAHIR §1) corresponds to, and resides within, the lower world or the realm of the physical universe and human culture.

2. **Reciprocal influence.** To see multiplicity instead of this unity or to mistake outer appearance for inner reality is to cause a separation in the unity of all being. Such separations partake of the primal sin. Repeatedly the *Zohar* asserts that "the lower world and the upper sustain each other" and that "from below must come the impulse to move the power above." The transitive effect of proper sexual joy between husband and wife or the correct observance of Jewish ritual is to unify God. Improprieties in such principal areas of human behavior cause a corresponding defect in God's being.

Unlike Abraham Abulafia's (b. 1240) mysticism of ecstatic, prophetic KABBALA and its YOGA-like set of meditative techniques, the *Zohar* is devoted to the cultivation of a mode of consciousness that perceives all reality, especially the Torah, as symbolic allusion to God's inner life and to the notion that the Jewish mystic maintains the peace of the universe.

Bibliography. J. H. Sperling and M. Simon, trans., *Zohar* (1933).

K. P. BLAND

ZOROASTRIANS zōr ə ăs´ trē əns. Followers of the religious tradition which bears the name of its prophet, Zoroaster. Heirs of a tradition that goes back to the dawn of recorded history in Iran, and that was at times Iran's official religion, the Zoroastrians today number scarcely more than a hundred thousand worldwide, chiefly in India and Iran (*see* PARSIS; GABAR). Those who have clung to the ancient faith have been a small, sometimes persecuted remnant during the thirteen centuries since the spread of Islam. Nonetheless many Zoroastrians today, though members of a minority that numbers less than one in a thousand in the population of Iran and only about one in ten thousand in India, are highly educated and enjoy an influence out of all proportion to their numbers. Historically, too, the Zoroastrian faith has played an important role in the drama of Middle Eastern religious history as a close relative of the monotheistic traditions of Judaism, Christianity, and Islam.

1. **Zoroastrian history.** The Zoroastrian experience relates to two culture areas—the Middle East and India—and any adequate view of the broad sweep of Zoroastrian tradition must relate that tradition to both. Indian materials provide the principal context prior to about 600 B.C., Middle Eastern for the following twelve centuries to the time of Muhammad, and the Indian context then tends to dominate again during the thirteen centuries from Muhammad to the present.

Two migrations from central Asia, one into Iran and one into India, appear to have taken place before the end of the second millennium B.C. They were related, as we can conclude from vocabulary and grammatical forms in the languages of the region. In India the VEDAS, the oldest SANSKRIT literature of the Hindus, comprise the hymns of a population known as the ARYANS, who invaded the Indian subcontinent and subjugated it. Meanwhile, the Avestan texts contain the hymns of people who named their land Iran—literally, "the land of the Aryans." The religion of the Indo-Iranian ancestors of both Hindus and Zoroastrians likely included a polytheistic pantheon of nature deities and a sacrificial cultus attended by a priestly class.

It must have been in such a context that the Iranian prophet Zarathustra—or Zoroaster, as his name comes to us through ancient Greek writers—preached his message. Since the Gāthās, certain hymnic passages in the AVESTA, are our only evidence for him, it is not certain precisely where or when he lived. On grounds of their apparently archaic linguistic form it is tempting to date the Gāthās well before 1000 B.C., and many Zoroastrians date the prophet several thousand years earlier still and claim him as mankind's first prophet. Yet certain ancient historical traditions date him within a century of the establishment of the Achaemenid dynasty, around 600 B.C.; the ethical character of his teaching, moreover, matches that of the Hebrew prophets of roughly the same date. All that we can say with certainty is that Zoroaster lived somewhere in Iran sometime before the Achaemenids.

The Middle Eastern phase of Zoroastrian history opens with the Achaemenid dynasty (559-331 B.C.), best known in the West as the Persian opponents of the ancient Greeks. The question to what extent the Achaemenids were Zoroastrian is problematical; they acknowledged the same chief deity, Ahura Mazda, as did Zoroaster, but their inscriptions and records make no mention of the prophet. It is clear, however, that their priesthood and ritual were consistent with much of what is preserved in the Avesta. The priests were known as magi, and fire was a central symbol of the cult.

A century after Alexander's conquest of Iran, a new dynasty reasserted local control: the Parthians (247 B.C.—A.D. 226). The principal cult of the Parthians was that of Mithra, a deity in the old Indo-Iranian pantheon who has an honored place in Zoroastrianism as well. The cult of Mithra spread and developed also in the Roman Empire after Roman armies fought the Parthians, Rome's principal rivals in the East.

Zoroastrianism in its classic form emerged under the Sasanian empire (A.D. 226-651). Late in the third century, through the efforts of a high priest named Kartīr, the Zoroastrian tradition was made the state religion. Fire temples were expanded, the Avestan scriptures collected, and an extensive theological as well as secular literature written in Pahlavi, the Iranian language of the time. To this day the Zoroastrian religious calendar reckons from A.D. 632, the year of accession of the last reigning Sasanian king, Yezdegird.

2. **Parsis.** Three fourths of the world's Zoroastrians today live in India, not Iran, and are called PARSIS. Their residence in India is the result of migration following the Islamic conquest of Iran. The circumstances of the migration are probably more diverse and complex than the traditional narrative, but according to a seventeenth century poem in Persian, the *Kisseh-e Sanjan* ("Story of Sanjan"), Zoroastrian refugees from Iran made their way by sea to the west coast of India where the local sovereign accepted them as a distinct and tolerated minority.

Whatever the circumstances of the migration, the Parsis were established in villages and cities in Gujarat, using the Gujarati language, by the time of European contact from the fourteenth century onward. Known for their trustworthiness and enterprise, they flourished as middle level managers, particularly in the British textile trade with Gujarat, and in the nineteenth century became pioneers of industry and commercial enterprise, particularly in Bombay. Still influential today, they are now a largely urban minority facing attrition of numbers through the small size of educated families, emigration, and marriage with other communities.

Emigration has taken Parsis to centers of commercial opportunity throughout the English-speaking world in recent times. Families of Parsis settled in port cities from South and East Africa to Ceylon, Burma, Singapore, and Hong Kong. Three thousand now live in Britain, especially London, and there have been recent migrations to Australia. In the United States and Canada the principal Parsi destination in recent decades has been Toronto, where over a thousand now live.

Meanwhile, in Iran, other Zoroastrians maintained the faith under Muslim rule despite hardships, in remote villages near Yazd and Kirman (*see* GABAR). Since the relaxation of persecution by Reza Shah in the 1920s, Iran's Zoroastrians have been able to participate in the urban development of the country and many have moved to Tehran. Iran's shift to an Islamic republic in 1979 introduced uncertainties for the Zoroastrians again, whose formal status is that of a tolerated minority.

3. **Zoroastrian teachings.** Central to Zoroastrianism is faith in God, known by the Avestan name Ahura Mazda ("the Wise Lord"), later shortened in Pahlavi to Ohrmazd. He is the supreme lord of creation, and for practical and devotional purposes the only one. Zoroastrian tradition does, however, associate with Ahura Mazda in a subordinate way a number of other divine figures from the old Indo-European pantheon, such as Mithra. There is also a group of seven divine attributes manifested as the Amesha Spentas ("Holy Immortals"): Good Mind, Order, Dominion, Devotion, Wholeness, Immortality, and the Holy Spirit; somewhat like the Christian doctrine of the TRINITY, these seem to be theological personifications of qualities named in various contexts in the Gāthās but not systematically listed there.

In addition to the hosts of good entities and spirits, Zoroastrianism supposes corresponding evil spirits. From the creation through the present age to the final judgment and reordering of the universe, the events of this world are seen as a contest between the powers of good and evil. It is incumbent on the faithful to choose the right, not only so that individually they may achieve the reward of the righteous beyond death, but so that good may triumph in the world. Upon death, according to Zoroastrian belief, the soul of the deceased crosses a bridge, the Chinvat Bridge ("Bridge of the Separator"), which widens to permit easy passage of the righteous but shrinks to a knife-edge for the wicked so that they fall into the abyss of torment below.

Zoroastrian attention to the role of an evil spirit, named Angra Mainyu in Avestan and shortened to Ahriman in Pahlavi, has led to characterization of the religion as dualistic. Indeed, the classical Zoroastrianism of the Sasanian and post-Sasanian era voiced dualistic doctrines in which Ahura Mazda and Angra Mainyu were virtual equals. As narrated in the Pahlavi book the *Bundahishn* ("Original Creation"), though, God enjoys a certain advantage over his foe from the beginning so that the ultimate victory of the good is ensured. In any event, Zoroastrians in modern times have been emphatic in stressing the supreme lordship of Ahura Mazda and the monotheistic character of their faith. (*See* DUALISM.)

Zoroastrian ethical teachings place great stress on personal honesty and on striving for the harmony of all creatures both in the world of nature and in human society. The world, as such, is seen as good and to be enjoyed; ASCETICISM finds little place in Zoroastrian tradition. At the same time there is the danger of physical pollution within the world, so that elaborate steps are taken in Zoroastrian ritual and practice to maintain purity.

4. **Zoroastrian practices.** The ceremonial obligations of the Zoroastrian tradition are carried out in

large measure by the priests. The prayers are always said in Avestan rather than in modern vernaculars, since Zoroastrians have traditionally held that the proper pronunciation of the specific Avestan sounds has a MANTRA-like or charm-like power to make the prayer efficacious. Moreover, the prayers are said on behalf of an individual by the priest, whether or not that individual is present at the temple. As a result, a Zoroastrian fire temple is not characteristically a place for congregational worship at stated times but more like a shrine which the individual layperson may approach at any time.

Only males may be priests. Eligibility for priesthood is hereditary, as priests may marry and raise families. To become a priest, a boy learns the Avestan prayers and services, generally by rote; he may also be instructed in their meaning, but the education can hardly be termed theological. Practicing priests wear only white, symbolic of purity. There are three grades of priests: in ascending order, *mobed, ervad,* and *dastūr*. Priests among the Parsis of India have often been employed on a piecework rather than a salary basis: that is, they receive fees from individuals for saying particular prayers on their behalf and for their relatives. Amid the secularity and the economic pressures of modern times, it is clear that many persons trained and even practicing part-time as priests have turned to other lines of work to support themselves, especially in Zoroastrian communities outside India.

Central to Zoroastrian worship is the maintenance of a fire as the sign of divine power, presence, and purity. In FIRE TEMPLES such a fire will burn constantly. In other prayer halls and in private homes a fire may be kindled for special services performed outside the temple, particularly the *jashan,* a type of thanksgiving service.

Every Zoroastrian child is initiated into the duties of the religion before puberty in a ceremony called the *navjote* ("new birth"). Boys and girls receive two items which they are then to wear constantly under their clothing for the remainder of their life, except when bathing: a white undershirt called the *sudreh* and a hollow woven wool cord called the *kusti,* which is long enough to be tied three times aound the waist. Several times a day, including after washing, the Zoroastrian is to retie the *kusti,* saying certain fixed prayers. Tying is also a feature of the Zoroastrian marriage service, when the priest symbolically wraps the couple together with a long cord as they sit beside each other.

Zoroastrian funeral practices include the ceremonial washing of the corpse, putting the *sudreh* and *kusti* and a white sheet on it, and the filing by of relatives and friends for last respects. It is then consigned to the TOWER OF SILENCE *(dakhma)* for disposal. On the third and fourth days after death, prayers are offered for the safe passage of the soul across the Chinvat Bridge, to face judgment of the actions done during life on earth.

The annual cycle of Zoroastrian observance follows a calendar of twelve months of thirty days each, plus five extra days at the end of the year. Though there is no rhythm of weekly observance and no regular congregational worship, there is a recurring pattern of devotion on a monthly cycle as certain days are sacred to fire, to water, to particular Amesha Spentas, and so on. Principal ceremonial activity comes at the end of the year, when for a number of days prayers are said for the spirits of the departed. Because of discrepancies in separated communities over the past thousand years, there are now three Zoroastrian calendars and three New Year seasons: two in late summer and one, reflecting a return to the festival's Iranian origins, at the spring equinox.

5. Zoroastrianism and other religions. The fascination which Zoroastrianism has for students in the modern West has included not only the problem of piecing together the internal development of the tradition from scanty and often conflicting evidence, but also the tantalizing question of its historical interaction with other religions.

Since the middle of the nineteenth century students of ancient JUDAISM have viewed Iran as a source of possible influences on the religion of Israel. The notion of Satan as God's rival, the notion of life after death, and the notions of a sequence of world ages and a final judgment and redemption are some instances of teachings which can be argued to have been elaborated in Israel's faith only after the advent of Achaemenid Persian rule in the eastern Mediterranean. Yet apart from a few suggestive words such as "paradise" from the Iranian *pairidaēza,* "pleasure garden," few specific details of transmission reward the investigator, and the general concepts are susceptible of explanation as developments from other sources internal and external to Israel. The evidence remains almost as fragmentary and as circumstantial, but still as suggestive, as it was a century ago.

Zoroastrianism has also borrowed from other traditions, and again in circumstances which are often elusive for the historian to specify. Prayer in the fire temple five times a day looks like the PRAYER pattern in ISLAM (*ṣalāt*, for example; or did Islam derive the custom from Zoroastrians?). The *kusti* is reminiscent of the SACRED THREAD worn by upper-caste Hindus, and may well go back to a common Indo-Iranian source. Other similarities in custom between Parsis and Hindus, particularly when not shared by Iranian Zoroastrians, likely reflect the situation of Parsi life in Gujarat. The tradition has shown itself adaptable to changing environments in past ages, and can be expected to continue to develop in the future.

Bibliography. M. Boyce, "Zoroastrianism," and J. Duchesne-Guillemin, "The Religion of Ancient Iran," in C. J. Bleeker and G. Widengren, eds., *Historia Religionum* (1969-71); R. P. Masani, *The Religion of the Good Life, Zoroastrianism* (1938); J. J. Modi, *The Religious Ceremonies and Customs of the Parsees* (1922).
W. G. OXTOBY

ZWINGLI, ULRICH tsvĭng´ lē (Ch; 1484-1531). Swiss Protestant reformer. Between 1516 and 1519

Zwingli developed characteristically Protestant positions apparently without significant Lutheran influence. His beliefs arose out of his humanistic background which was critical of clerical abuses and emphasized study of the Bible. Zwingli accepted the Bible as the sole authority for Christian belief and affirmed justification by faith alone as the means by which salvation comes. He also urged Swiss independence from outside powers, both secular and ecclesiastical. The combination of humanism and patriotism provided the matrix for Zwingli's Reformation ideas.

He was appointed preacher in the main church in Zurich in December, 1518. His powerful sermons led to a series of debates during 1523-25 that resulted in the reformation of Zurich. Some of his followers, urging more thorough reform, became ANABAPTISTS.

Zwingli understood the Lord's Supper to be a symbolic observance, rejecting completely the real presence (*see* EUCHARIST). Despite a meeting with Luther in 1529, the two were unable to reconcile their positions, and this became the primary point at issue in the division between Lutherans and Zwinglians. Zwingli's attempts to spread the Reformation in Switzerland led to conflict with Roman Catholic cantons, resulting in the Second Cappel War in which Zwingli was killed. His approach to the Reformation provided the basis of what was to become the REFORMED CHURCHES. *See* REFORMATION, PROTESTANT; LUTHER, MARTIN.

Bibliography. G. R. Potter, *Zwingli* (1977).

R. L. HARRISON